Eighteenth EDITION

SCHROEDER'S
ANTIQUES
PRICE GUIDE

Edited by Sharon & Bob Huxford

COLLECTOR BOOKS

A Division of Schroeder Publishing Co., Inc.

Searching For A Publisher?

We are always looking for knowledgeable people considered experts within their fields. If you feel that there is a real need for a book on your collectible subject and have a large comprehensive collection, please contact Collector Books.

COLLECTOR BOOKS
P.O. Box 3009
Paducah, Kentucky 42002-3009

Introduction

As the editors and staff of *Schroeder's*, our goal is to compile the most useful, comprehensive, and accurate background and pricing information possible. Our guide encompasses nearly five hundred categories, many of which you will not find in other price guides. Our sources are varied; we use auction results and dealer lists, and we consult with national collectors' clubs, recognized authorities, researchers, and appraisers. We have by far the largest Advisory Board of any similar publication on the market. Each year we add several new advisors and now have over 450 who cover almost all our categories. They go over our computer print-outs line by line, deleting listings that are misleading or too vague to be of merit; they often send background information and photos. We appreciate their assistance very much. Only through their expertise and experience in their special fields are we able to offer with confidence what we feel are useful, accurate evaluations that provide a sound understanding of the dealings in the market place today. Correspondence with so large an advisory panel adds months of extra work to an already monumental task, but we feel that to a very large extent this is the foundation that makes *Schroeder's* the success that it has become.

Our Directory, which you will find in the back of the book, lists each contributor by state. These are people who have allowed us to photograph various examples of merchandise from their show booths, sent us pricing information, or in any way have contributed to this year's book. If you happen to be traveling, consult the Directory for shops along your way. We also list clubs who have worked with us and auction houses who have agreed to permit us the use of photographs or data from their catalogs.

Our Advisory Board lists only names and home states, so check the Directory for addresses and telephone numbers should you want to correspond with one of our experts. Remember, when you do, **always** enclose a self-addressed, stamped envelope (SASE). Thousands of people buy our guide, and hundreds contact our advisors. The only agreement we have with our advisors is that they edit their categories. They are in no way obligated to answer mail. Some are dealers who do many shows a month. The time they spend at home may be very limited, and they may not be open to contacts. There's no doubt that the reason behind the success of our book is their assistance. We regret seeing them becoming more and more burdened by phone and mail inquiries. We have lost some of our good advisors for this reason, and when we do, the book suffers and consequently, so do our readers. Many of our listed reference sources report that they constantly receive long distance calls (at all hours) that are really valuation requests. If they are registered appraisers, they make their living at providing such information and expect a fee for their service and expertise.

If you find you need more information than *Schroeder's* provides, there are other sources available to you. Go to your local library; check their section on reference books. Museums are public facilities that are willing and able help you establish the origin and possibly even the value of your particular treasure. Check the yellow pages of your phone book. Other cities' phone books are available from either your library or from the telephone company office. Look under the heading *Antique Dealers*. Those who are qualified appraisers will mention this credit in their advertisement. But remember that if you sell to a dealer, he will expect to buy your merchandise at a price low enough that he will be able to make an appreciable profit when he sells it. Once you decide to contact one of these appraisers, unless you intend to see them directly, you'll need to take photographs. Don't send photos that are under or over exposed, out of focus, or shot against a background that detracts from important details you want to emphasize. It is almost impossible for them to give you a value judgement on items they've not seen when your photos are of poor quality. Shoot the front, top, and the bottom; describe any marks and numbers (or send a pencil rubbing), explain how and when you acquired the article, and give accurate measurements and any further background information that may be helpful.

The auction houses listed in the Directory nearly all have a staff of appraisal experts. If the item you're attempting to research is of the caliber of material they deal with, they can offer extremely accurate evaluations. Of course, most have a fee. Be sure to send them only professional-quality photographs. Tell them if you expect to consign your item to their auction. If you disagree with the value they suggest, you are under no obligation to do so.

Nearly 500 categories are included in our book. We have organized our topics alphabetically, following the most simple logic, usually either by manufacturer or by type of product. If you have difficulty in locating your subject, consult the index. Our guide is unique in that much more space has been allotted to background information than in any other publication of this type. Our readers tell us that these are features they enjoy. To be able to do this, we have adopted a format of one-line listings wherein we describe the items to the fullest extent possible by using several common-sense abbreviations; they will be easy to read and understand if you will first take the time to quickly scan through them.

The Editors

Editorial Staff

Editors
Sharon and Bob Huxford

Research and Editorial Assistants
Michael Drollinger, Nancy Drollinger, Donna Newnum, Loretta Woodrow

Layout
Beth Ray, Terri Hunter, Donna Ballard

Cover
Beth Summers

On the cover: mahogany dresser, $1,815.00; McCoy, Two Kittens in a Basket, 1950s, $600.00; Fruits 3½" juice tumbler, Federal Glass Co., $60.00; Hull Iris ewer, 13½", $675.00; Paramount movie poster, *Now and Forever*, 1934, 40"x60", linen backed, $2,500.00 – 3,500.00; R.S. Prussia footed teapot, 6½", $285.00.

Listing of Standard Abbreviations

The following is a list of abbreviations that have been used throughout this book in order to provide you with the most detailed descriptions possible in the limited space available. No periods are used after initials or abbreviations. When two dimensions are given, height is noted first. If only one dimension is listed, it will be height, except in the case of bowls, dishes, plates, or platters, when it will be diameter. The standard two-letter state abbreviations apply.

For glassware, if no color is noted, the glass is clear. Hyphenated colors, for example blue-green, olive-amber, etc., describe a single color tone; colors divided by a slash mark indicate two or more colors, i.e. blue/white. Teapots, sugar bowls, and butter dishes are assumed to be 'with cover.' Condition is extremely important in determining market value. Common sense suggests that art pottery, china, and glassware values would be given for examples in pristine, mint condition, while suggested prices for utility wares such as Redware, Mocha, and Blue and White Stoneware, for example, reflect the probability that since such items were subjected to everyday use in the home they may show minor wear (which is acceptable) but no notable damage. Values for other categories reflect the best average condition in which the particular collectible is apt to be offered for sale without the dealer feeling it necessary to mention wear or damage. For instance, advertising items are assumed to be in excellent condition since mint items are scarce enough that when one is offered for sale the dealer will most likely make mention of that fact. The same holds true for Toys, Banks, Coin-Operated Machines, and the like. A basic rule of thumb is that an item listed as VG (very good) will bring 40% to 60% of its mint price — a first-hand, personal evaluation will enable you to make the final judgement; EX (excellent) is a condition midway between mint and very good, and values would correspond.

Am............American	dvtl............dovetail	litho............lithograph	re............regarding
appl............applied	emb............embossed, embossing	lt............light	rfn............refinished
att............attributed to	embr............embroidered	M............mint	rnd............round
bbl............barrel	Emp............Empire	mahog............mahogany	rpl............replaced
bk............back	eng............engraved, engraving	mc............multicolor	rpr............repaired
bl............blue	EPNS...electroplated nickel silver	MIB............mint in box	rpt............repainted
blk............black	EX............excellent	MIG............Made in Germany	rstr............restored
brn............brown	Fed............Federal	MIP............mint in package	rtcl............reticulated
bulb............bulbous	fr............frame, framed	mk............mark	rvpt............reverse painted
bsk............bisque	Fr............French	MOC............mint on card	s&p............salt and pepper
b3m............blown 3-mold	ft, ftd............foot, feet, footed	MOP............mother-of-pearl	sgn............signed
C............century	G............good	mt, mtd............mount, mounted	SP............silverplated
c............copyright	gr............green	NE............New England	sq............square
ca............circa	grad............graduated	NM............near mint	std............standard
cb............cardboard	grpt............grain painted	NP............nickel plated	str............straight
Chpndl............Chippendale	H............high, height	NRFB....never removed from box	sz............size
CI............cast iron	Hplwht............Hepplewhite	opal............opalescent	trn............turned, turning
compo............composition	hdl, hdld............handle, handled	orig............original	turq............turquoise
cr/sug............creamer and sugar	HP............hand painted	o/l............overlay	uphl............upholstered
c/s............cup and saucer	illus......illustration, illustrated by	o/w............otherwise	VG............very good
cvd............carved	imp............impressed	Pat............patented	Vict............Victorian
cvg............carving	ind............individual	pc............piece	W............width
dbl............double	int............interior	ped............pedestal	wht............white
decor............decoration	Invt T'print..Inverted Thumbprint	pk............pink	w/............with
dk............dark	irid............iridescent	pnt............paint	w/o............without
Dmn Quilt........Diamond Quilted	L............length, long	porc............porcelain	X, Xd............cross, crossed
drw............drawer	lav............lavender	prof............professional	yel............yellow
dtd............dated	ldgl............leaded glass	QA............Queen Anne	(+)............has been reproduced

A B C Plates

Children's plates featuring the alphabet as part of the design were popular from as early as 1820 until after the turn of the century. The earliest English creamware plates were decorated with embossed letters and prim moralistic verses, but the later Staffordshire products were conducive to a more relaxed mealtime atmosphere, often depicting playful animals and riddles or scenes of pleasant leisure-time activities. They were made around the turn of the century by American potters as well. All featured transfer prints, but color was sometimes brushed on by hand to add interest to the design.

Be sure to inspect these plates carefully for damage, since condition is a key price-assessing factor, and aside from obvious chips and hairlines, even wear can substantially reduce their values.

For further information we recommend *A B C Plates & Mugs, Identification and Value Guide,* by Irene and Ralph Lindsay (Collector Books). Our advisor for this category is Dr. Joan George; she is listed in the Directory under New Jersey.

Ceramic

Abraham Lincoln, blk transfer, 7½" 600.00
Aesop's Fables, Lion & Mouse, mc transfer, Staffordshire, 7" 175.00
At the Seaside, blk transfer, HC Edmiston, 7¼" 140.00
B Is for Bobby's, bl transfer, unmk, 7" 140.00
Baby, blk transfer, emb ABC rim, Powell & Bishop, 7" 140.00
Behold Him Rising, Christ scene, mc transfer, J&G Meakin, 5¼" ...165.00
Blind Girl, mc transfer, unmk, 5¼" 135.00
Blood Relations, puppies in basket, brn transfer, 7" 115.00
Cat & mouse, blk transfer w/mc, Elsmore & Son, 7" 195.00
Children under umbrella w/doll, red transfer, unmk, 7½" 130.00
Children w/scale & net, bl transfer, emb ABC rim, umk, 8½" ...120.00
Crane & toad, mc transfer, ABCs across plate, unmk, 7¼" 140.00
Cruel boy, brn transfer, emb ABC rim, unmk, 6½" 120.00
Crusoe Making a Boat, bl transfer, BP Co, 6" 135.00
Family harvesting wheat, mc transfer, emb ABC rim, unmk, 5" .135.00
Ferret, blk transfer, emb ABC rim, Wm Adams & Co, 7" 135.00
Fishing Elephant, blk transfer, CA & Sons, 1890-1912, 7" 135.00
Flowers & leaves, mc transfer, umk, 7" 145.00
Franklin's Proverbs, Experience Keeps..., mc transfer, unmk, 5" ..150.00
Franklin's Proverbs, For Age & Want..., blk transfer, unmk, 8¼" .130.00
Frolics of Youth, Now I'm Grandmother, blk transfer w/mc, 8" ..140.00
Girls (2) & pony, mc transfer, emb ABC rim, unmk, 7¼" 120.00
Highland Dance, mc transfer, emb rim, unmk, 5½" 140.00
Horse portrait, mc transfer, W Adams & Co, 7¼" 140.00
House, pk lustre, emb ABC rim, unmk, 6½" 120.00
House Sparrow, mc transfer, emb ABC rim, Edge Malkin, 6" 140.00
L'Hama Hammock, blk transfer, JF Wileman, 5¾" 125.00
Little Bo Peep, blk transfer, Manufactured for HC Edmiston, 6" .125.00
London Dog Seller, blk transfer, Powell & Bishop, 7" 135.00
Men plowing, mc transfer, Staffordshire, 4½" 110.00
Mug, C & D, child & devotion, mc transfer, unmk, 2½" 145.00
Mug, D for Donkey, Dove & Daisy, mc transfer, 2½" 135.00
Mug, DEF, shuttlecock scene, red transfer, Staffordshire, 2¾" 165.00
Mug, E Is for Elephant, mc transfer, unmk, 2½" 175.00
Mug, EF, Biblical illustrations, blk transfer w/mc, 2¼" 135.00
My Face Is My Fortune, bulldog, blk transfer, CA & Son..., 7½" .130.00
Nursery Rhymes, Goosey Goosey Gander, mc transfer, unmk, 8½" .190.00
Oh Here Is Old Robert..., mc transfer, unmk, 8" 140.00
Old Mother Hubbard, mc transfer, Rd No 75,500, 7¼" 220.00
P Is for Peter, blk transfer, unmk, 7¼" 120.00
Playground, mc transfer, unmk, 6" 140.00
Polar bear w/cubs, mc transfer, BPCo, 7½" 225.00

Pray Tell Us Ladies..., blk transfer, unmk, 6" 130.00
Rider Rents Horse, blk transfer, CA & Sons, 7½" 115.00
Rupert & Spot, mc transfer, BP&Co, 7¼" 135.00
Spelling Bee, mc transfer, emb ABC rim, unmk, 5¾" 130.00
William Penn, brn transfer, unmk, 6½" 250.00
Young Artist, brn transfer, blk ABC rim, unmk, 6½" 130.00
Young Charioteer, mc transfer, emb rim, unmk, 5½" 140.00

Glass

Bo Peep w/Bears 55.00
Cane center, 6" 30.00
Christmas Eve, Santa w/tree & toys, ABCs on stippled rim, 6⅛" .90.00
Clock, Thousand Eye, amber, ABC rim 90.00
Clock & days, vaseline, 7" 75.00
Duck, ABC rim, 6" 60.00
Elephant w/howdah on bk, ABC rim, Ripley & Co, 6" 90.00
Flower bouquet, ABCs on stippled ground, frosted flowers, 6" ...75.00
Flying stork & #s, marigold carnival 65.00
Garfield, ABC rim 75.00
Old Independence Hall, stippled ABCs, scalloped, 7" 100.00
Quilted center, ABCs & #s on stippled ground 105.00
Rooster, hen & chicks, ABC rim 65.00
Thousand Eye, clock center, apple gr, 6" 60.00
Thousand Eye, clock center, vaseline, 6" 55.00

Tin

Monkey on a barrel, 'Lava' tin, 6⅛", $165.00.

Photo courtesy
Phil Helley

Cup, emb ABC rim, unmk, 1⅝" 165.00
General Tom Thumb, emb ABC rim, mc pnt, unmk, 3" 250.00
Her Majesty Queen Victoria, unmk, 8" 350.00
Hi Diddle Diddle..., unmk, 8¾" 90.00
Jack & Jill, gr/blk litho, Lava, 6" 100.00
Kittens litho, Ohio Art, 6¼" 110.00
Lion, emb ABC rim, unmk, 2⅞" 300.00
Mary Had a Little Lamb, unmk, 7¾" 145.00
Peter Rabbit, mc litho, unmk, 7¾" 350.00
Plain center, emb ABC rim, unmk, 6¼" 60.00
Victoria & Albert, emb ABC rim, unmk, 5⅞" 165.00
Washington bust & stars, emb ABC rim, unmk, 6" 185.00

Abingdon

From 1934 until 1950, the Abingdon Pottery Co. of Abingdon, Ill., made a line of art pottery with a white vitrified body decorated with various types of glazes in many lovely colors. Novelties, cookie jars, utility ware, and lamps were made in addition to several lines of simple yet striking art ware. Fern Leaf, introduced in 1937, featured molded vertical feathering. La Fleur, in 1939, consisted of flowerpots and flower-arranger bowls with rows of vertical ribbing. Classic, 1939 – 40, was a line of vases, many with evidence of Chinese influence. Several marks were used, most of which employed the company name. In 1950 the company reverted to the manufacture of sanitary ware that had been their mainstay before the art ware division was formed.

Highly decorated examples and those with black, bronze, or red glaze usually command at least 25% higher prices.

For further information we recommend *Abingdon Pottery Artware 1934 – 1950, Stepchild of the Great Depression*, by Joe Paradis (Schiffer).

#098, figurine, upright goose, 1934-50, 3½"	40.00
#116, vase, Classic, 10", from $20 to	25.00
#117, vase, Classic, gr, 10"	35.00
#118, vase, hdls, powder bl, 10"	25.00
#120, planter w/bow, bl	20.00
#151, flowerpot, 6"	22.00
#152, vase, yel, 8¾"	22.00
#305, bookends, sea gull, 9¼", pr	80.00
#321, bookends, Cossack/Russian, blk, 6½" or 8½", pr	85.00
#324, vase, bottle form, yel w/wht int, 3¾"	110.00
#370, bookends, Cactus, 6", pr	70.00
#374, planter/bookends, Cactus, lt gr, 7", pr	100.00
#377, wall pockets, Morning Glory, ivory, 9x6¼", pr	87.00
#388, figurine, pouter pigeon, 4½"	40.00
#392, vase, Morning Glory, 5½"	35.00
#393, bowl, Morning Glory, 7"	35.00
#400, tea tile, geisha, sq, 5"	50.00
#408, bowl, leaf, beige, 1937, 6½"	40.00
#412, vase, Volute, wht, 1937-40, 15½"	125.00
#416, figurine, peacock, 7"	95.00
#422, vase, Fern Leaf, wht, 10"	30.00
#428, bookend, Fern Leaf, 5½"	45.00
#429, vase/candle holder, Fern Leaf, 8"	25.00
#435, wall pocket, Tri-Fern, 9", from $135 to	150.00
#444, bookend/planter, dolphin, decor, 5¾", pr	50.00
#450, bowl, Asters, flared rim, oval, 11½" L	45.00
#452, bowl, Asters, 9x14½"	45.00
#453, vase, Asters, 8"	25.00
#460, bowl, Panel, 8"	25.00
#463, vase, Star, 7"	18.00
#469/#470, figurines, Dutch boy & girl, 1939-40, 8", pr	50.00
#474, cornucopia, yel, 5½"	18.00
#476, window box, 10½" H	20.00
#482, dbl cornucopia, peach, 11"	50.00
#484, fan vase w/bow, bl, 8¼"	35.00
#486, vase, Acanthus, silver o/l birds on peach, 11"	150.00
#487, floor vase, Egret, 14"	150.00
#497, figurine, Blackamoor, w/decor, 7½"	95.00
#501, bowl, Shell, pk, sm	20.00
#505, candle holder, Shell, dbl, 4"	20.00
#507, vase, Shell, oval, wht, 7½"	25.00
#509, ashtray, elephant, 5½"	50.00
#510, ashtray, donkey, 5½"	50.00
#512, vase, Swirl, gr, 9"	20.00
#513, vase, Swirl, 9", from $15 to	25.00
#514, vase, Swirl, chartreuse, 11", from $25 to	35.00
#515, vase, gold rim & hdls, 6¾"	45.00
#520, vase, gr, 9"	25.00
#522, vase, Barre, 9"	35.00
#528, bowl, Hibiscus, bl, 15"	40.00
#532, bowl, console; gold trim, 14½" L, from $25 to	30.00
#532 & #575, console set, bl, 3-pc	25.00
#533, bowl, Shell, yel, 12"	22.00
#536, bowl, Regency, gr, 7x9x5"	40.00

#552, vase, squatty, 13"	40.00
#557, vase, draped design, pk, 11"	40.00
#563, urn, coral w/wht decor, 9"	33.00
#564, bowl, Scallop, pk, 11"	18.00
#568, mint compote, pk, ftd, 1942-47, 6" dia	28.00
#569D, cornucopia, bl w/decor, 10" L	27.50
#571, figurine, goose, blk, 5"	40.00
#572, figurine, pelican, gr, 5"	55.00
#573, figurine, penguin, decor, 5½"	40.00
#576, window box, gr, 12¼" L	25.00
#581, vase, dbl cornucopia; bl, 8½"	40.00
#593, vase, bow knot, bl, 9"	35.00
#596, vase, sea horse	65.00

#601, butterfly wall pocket, 1934 – 50, 8½", from $85.00 to $95.00.

Photo courtesy Betty and Bill Newbound

#610, bowl, Shell, 9"	25.00
#616D, vase, Cactus, w/sleeping Mexican man, 6½"	35.00
#620, vase, anemones, daisies & tulip, bl w/gold	30.00
#629, vase, Poppy, 6½"	30.00
#640, wall pocket, Triad, 5½"	40.00
#652, planter, puppy, decor, 6¾"	25.00
#654, vase, Tulip, 6½"	20.00
#659, vase, Hackney, 8½"	30.00
#667, planter, gourd, 5½"	20.00
#675D, wall pocket, match box form, 5½"	50.00
#676D, wall pocket, book form, 6½"	48.00
#681/#682, sugar bowl & creamer, Daisy	30.00
#699, wall pocket, apron, 6"	50.00
#711, wall vase, carriage lamp, 10"	25.00
#714, candle holders, Star, 4¼", pr	30.00
#3906, figurine, shepherdess & faun, blk, 11½"	250.00
Cookie jar, #471, Old Lady, plain, 1942	210.00
Cookie jar, #471, Old Lady, rare gr	195.00
Cookie jar, #495, Fat Boy	250.00
Cookie jar, #549, Hippo, decor, 1942	225.00
Cookie jar, #561, Baby, Blk decor	300.00
Cookie jar, #588, Money Bag, 1947	70.00
Cookie jar, #602, Hobby Horse	185.00
Cookie jar, #611, Jack-in-Box	275.00
Cookie jar, #622, Miss Muffet	205.00
Cookie jar, #651, Choo Choo (Locomotive)	150.00
Cookie jar, #653, Clock, 1949	100.00
Cookie jar, #663, Humpty Dumpty, decor	250.00
Cookie jar, #664, Pineapple	95.00
Cookie jar, #665, Wigwam, minimum value	250.00
Cookie jar, #674, Pumpkin, 1949	250.00
Cookie jar, #677, Daisy, 1949	45.00
Cookie jar, #678, Windmill, from $185 to	225.00
Cookie jar, #692, Witch, minimum value	350.00
Cookie jar, #693, Little Girl	60.00
Cookie jar, #694, Bo Peep	240.00
Cookie jar, #695, Mother Goose, from $295 to	350.00
Cookie jar, #696, Three Bears	90.00

Adams

Wm. Adams, whose potting skills were developed under the tutelage of Josiah Wedgwood, founded the Greengates Pottery at Tunstall, England, in 1769. Many types of wares including basalt, ironstone, parian, and jasper were produced; and various impressed or printed marks were employed. Until 1800 'Adams Co.' or 'Adams' impressed in block letters identified the company's earthenwares and a fine type of jasper similar in color and decoration to Wedgwood's. The latter mark was used again from 1845 to 1864 on parian figures. Most examples of their product found on today's market are transfer-printed dinnerwares with ornate backstamps which often include the pattern name and the initials 'W.A. & S.' This type of product was made from 1820 until about 1920. After 1890 the word 'England'; was included in the mark; 'Tunstall' was added after 1896. From 1914 through 1940, a printed crown with 'Adams, Estbd 1657, England,' identified their products. From 1900 to 1965, they produced souvenir plates with transfers of American scenes, many of which were marketed in this country by Roth Importers of Peoria, Illinois. In 1965 the company affiliated with Wedgwood. Although there were other Adams potteries in Staffordshire, their marks incorporate either the first name initial or a partner's name and so are easily distinguished from those of this company. See also Spatter; Staffordshire; Adams Rose.

Bowl, covered vegetable; foreign courtyard, brn transfer, 13" 300.00
Cup & saucer, scenic view, dk bl transfer, 2⅜x3⅝", 5¾" 160.00
Cup & saucer, Sower, pk transfer, scalloped 75.00
Pitcher, floral, bl underglaze w/mc, cobalt hdl, unmk, 8" 300.00
Plate, Sea, pk transfer, 9½", set of 4 (1 w/hairline) 200.00
Plate, Seasons, pk transfer, 9½" 75.00
Plate, unidentified scenic view, dk bl, scalloped, 6¾", EX 110.00
Platter, Sea, red transfer, 15" 375.00
Teapot, Oriental scenic view, dk bl transfer, 7¼" 380.00
Teapot, Sower, pk transfer, rectangular, 7⅝", EX 150.00

Adams, Matthew

In the 1950s a trading post located in Alaska contacted Sascha Brastoff to design a line of porcelain with scenes of Eskimos, Alaskan motifs, and animals indigenous to that country. These items were to be sold in Alaska to the tourist trade.

Brastoff selected Matthew Adams to design the Alaska series. Pieces from the line he produced have the Sascha B mark on the front; some have a pattern number on the reverse. They did not have the rooster backstamp. (See the Sascha Brastoff category for information on this mark.)

After the Alaska series was introduced and proved to be successful, Matthew Adams left the employment of Sascha Brastoff and opened his own studio. Pieces made in his studio are signed Matthew Adams in script and may have the word Alaska on the front. Where his studio (or studios) was is unknown at the present time, but a 'Made in Alaska' paper label has been found, suggesting that he may have worked from that location. Our advisor for this category is Marty Webster; he is listed in the Directory under Michigan. Feel free to contact Mr. Webster if you have any further information.

Ashtray, Eskimo (full), hollow star shape, 13" 75.00
Ashtray, Eskimo family, 8½" 40.00
Ashtray, walrus, star shape, 10x12" 95.00
Ashtray, walrus on gr, 6" dia 25.00
Bowl, console; glacier on bl, 12x20" 165.00
Bowl, Eskimo on blk, 9" 45.00

Bowl, grizzly bear on brn, free-form, 6½" L 55.00
Bowl, polar bear on gr, free-form, 7½" L 50.00
Bowl, ram on gr, free-form, 7" 55.00
Bowl, seal, oval, 9" 50.00
Bowl, seal on blk, free-form, w/lid, #145, 7½" L 75.00
Bowl, walrus, yel, w/lid, 7" 75.00
Bowl, walrus & glacier on brn, free-form, 8" 65.00
Bowl, walrus on blk, free-form, #104, 6½" L 50.00
Box, glacier on bl, w/lid, 7" 75.00
Charger, caribou on dk bl, 18" 150.00
Charger, walrus, dk bl, 17" 150.00
Coffeepot, ram on gr, 11½", +6 4½" mugs 180.00
Compote, grizzly bear on brn, tall, 8½" dia 70.00
Cookie jar, mother & child on brn 75.00
Cracker jar, Eskimo mother & child on brn, 7" 80.00
Cup & saucer, sled on bl 25.00
Dish, Eskimo lady on gr, elbow shape, 12" 50.00
Humidor, seal on gr, #025, 5¾" 85.00
Jar, Eskimo on Ice Blue, 6" 30.00
Jar, Eskimo woman on brn, w/lid, 7½" 50.00
Jar, polar bear on gr, w/lid, 7" 65.00
Jar, walrus on lt bl, w/lid, #1492, 7½" 50.00

Lighters, seal or walrus decoration, $115.00 each.

Lighter, glacier, 6" 40.00
Pitcher, Eskimo, 13" 90.00
Pitcher, Eskimo mother & child, 13", +6 5½" mugs 195.00
Pitcher, grizzly bear, 11", +6 4" tumblers 200.00
Pitcher, Husky dog, wht on teal, bulbous, 5" 65.00
Plate, Eskimo girl, #162, 7½" 30.00
Platter, house, 12" 45.00
Pot, walrus, w/lid, 12" 55.00
Shakers, rams on gr, 4", pr 40.00
Tankard, man on brn, 19", +6 mugs 250.00
Tankard, polar bear on blk, w/lid, 13" 200.00
Teapot, walrus on Ice Blue, 6½" 75.00
Tile, mountains & glacier on blk, 10x8½" 75.00
Tile, walrus on bl, 10x8½" 75.00
Tumbler, cabin 20.00
Vase, glacier on gray, #143, 5½" 50.00
Vase, house on yel, 11½" 100.00
Vase, iceberg on gray, 7" 40.00
Vase, mother & child on teal, cylindrical, 17" 165.00
Vase, mountain & glacier on blk, #114, 12" 80.00
Vase, polar bear on gr, 10" 140.00
Vase, reindeer, 4½" 45.00
Vase, sea lion, 6½" 85.00
Vase, sea lion & seaweed, oval, #128, 8" 95.00
Vase, seal & glacier on brn, free-form, #911, 11" 155.00
Vase, walrus on ice on bl, 10" 110.00

Adams Rose, Early and Late

In the second quarter of the 19th century, the Adams and Son Pottery produced a line of hand-painted dinnerware decorated in large, red brush-stroke roses with green leaves on whiteware, which collectors call Adams Rose. Later, G. Jones and Son (and possibly others) made a similar ware with less brilliant colors on a gray-white surface.

Unless otherwise noted, our values are for items in mint condition or nearly so; be sure to discount prices for damage.

Wash bowl, late, footed, hairlines, 13½" diameter; Pitcher, late, baluster form with pulled spout and scrolled handle on flared foot, 14¼", $425.00 for the set.

Bowl, early, rare sz, 9"	825.00
Bowl, late, England, 2⅞x6⅛"	65.00
Bowl, late, mk Imperiale Royale, Belgium, 3x5½"	38.50
Coffeepot, early, scroll hdl, dome lid, mk Adams, rpr, 12", EX	630.00
Creamer, early, arched paneled sides, scroll hdl, rpr, 5"	150.00
Creamer, early, 3", EX	165.00
Creamer, late, scalloped rim, England/#d, 5½"	200.00
Pitcher, early, scalloped rim w/emb scrolls, mk Adams, 8", EX	450.00
Pitcher, late, 6¾"	300.00
Pitcher, milk; late, emb shell on spout, mk England, 8", EX	275.00
Pitcher, milk; late, oval, plain rim, no mk, 8½"	110.00
Plate, early, 9"	235.00
Plate, late, England, 9"	90.00
Plate, late, mk Adams, 9½"	90.00
Plate, toddy; early, Adams, 5"	350.00
Plate, toddy; early, plain rim, mk Adams, 5", VG	135.00
Platter, late, 12", EX	135.00
Soup plate, early, scalloped rim, Adams, 10¾"	240.00
Sugar bowl, late, England, rpr, 6", EX	220.00
Tea bowl & saucer, early	330.00
Tea bowl & saucer, late	130.00
Wash bowl, late, emb floral vine at rim, 14½"	175.00

Advertising

The advertising world has always been a fiercely competitive field. In an effort to present their product to the customer, every imaginable gimmick was put into play. Colorful and artfully decorated signs and posters, thermometers, tape measures, fans, hand mirrors, and attractive tin containers (all with catchy slogans, familiar logos, and often-bogus claims) are only a few of the many examples of early advertising memorabilia that are of interest to today's collectors.

Porcelain signs were made as early as 1890 and are highly prized for their artistic portrayal of life as it was then . . . often allowing amusing insights into the tastes, humor, and way of life of a bygone era. As a general rule, older signs are made from a heavier gauge metal. Those with three or more fired-on colors are especially desirable.

Tin containers were used to package consumer goods ranging from crackers and coffee to tobacco and talcum. After 1880 can companies began to decorate their containers by the method of lithography. Though colors were still subdued, intricate designs were used to attract the eye of the consumer. False labeling and unfounded claims were curtailed by the Pure Food and Drug Administration in 1906, and the name of the manufacturer as well as the brand name of the product had to be printed on the label. By 1910 color was rampant with more than a dozen hues printed on the tin or on paper labels. The tins themselves were often designed with a second use in mind, such as canisters, lunch boxes, even toy trains. As a general rule, tobacco-related tins are the most desirable, though personal preference may direct the interest of the collector to peanut butter pails with illustrations of children, or talcum tins with irresistible babies or beautiful ladies. Coffee tins are popular, as are those made to contain a particularly successful or well-known product.

Perhaps the most visual of the early advertising gimmicks were the character logos, the Fairbank Company's Gold Dust Twins, the goose trademark of the Red Goose Shoe Company, Nabisco's ZuZu Clown and Uneeda Kid, the Campbell Kids, the RCA dog Nipper, and Mr. Peanut, to name only a few. Many early examples of these bring high prices on the market today.

Our listings are alphabetized by product name or, in lieu of that information, by word content or other pertinent description. When no condition is indicated, the items listed below are assumed to be in excellent condition, except glass and ceramic items, which are assumed mint. Remember that condition greatly affects value (especially true for tin items). For instance, a sign in excellent or mint condition may bring twice as much as the same one in only very good condition, sometimes even more. On today's market, items in good to very good condition are slow to sell, unless they are extremely rare. Mint (or near-mint) examples are high.

We have several advertising advisors; see specific subheadings. For further information we recommend *Zany Characters of the Ad World* by Mary Jane Lamphier, *Advertising Character Collectibles* by Warren Dotz, *Value Guide to Advertising Memorabilia, Second Edition*, by B.J. Summers, *The World of Beer Memorabilia* by Herb and Helen Haydock, *Encyclopedia of Advertising Tins, Vol. II*, by David Zimmerman, and *Huxford's Collectible Advertising* by Sharon and Bob Huxford. All of these books are available at your local bookstore or from Collector Books. See also Advertising Dolls; Advertising Cards; Automobilia; Coca-Cola; Banks; Calendars; Cookbooks; Paperweights; Posters; Sewing Items.

Key:
cb — cardboard	ps — porcelain sign
cl — celluloid	sf — self-framed
lcs — litho on canvas sign	tc — tin container
pp — pre-prohibition	ts — tin sign

A&P Coffee, jigsaw puzzle, A&P Coffee Experts, 1932, 9x10", EX	60.00
AC Spark Plugs, thermometer, metal, Sparky in tub, bl, 21", G	150.00
Adkin's Nut Brn Tobacco, store bin, tin, In Packets Only, VG	100.00
Alka-Seltzer, neon sign on rvpt case, bl, 7x27x6", EX+	400.00
Allis-Chalmers, eng image of earth mover, EX	100.00
Alta Coffee, jar/kerosene lamp, promotional, unused, NM	220.00
Anheuser-Busch, display figure, waiter, chalkware, 20", EX	190.00
Anheuser-Busch, print, Westward Ho, fr, EX	200.00
Apache Beer, plaque sign, chalk relief, bar scene, 14x9", NM	485.00
Arden, diecut figure, Ardie w/products, 36x21", EX+	925.00
Aunt Jemima Wheat Bran, cloth sack, Quaker Oats Co, 23x18"	145.00
Ayer's Hair Vigor, paper sign, Restores..., brunette, 13x10", VG	400.00
Baker's Chocolate, poster, Chocolate Girl w/tray, 36x26", NM	300.00
Banquet Tea, teapot dispenser, ceramic, w/metal stand, 11", EX	450.00
Bartels Brewing Co, tray, lancer w/mug, 1900, 12" dia, NM+	150.00

Beacon Blankets, cb stand-up, Brrrr!, man in bed, 41x40", EX ...**130.00**
Beehive Overalls, pocket mirror, girl in overalls, oval, NM **300.00**
Ben-Hur 5¢ Cigars, ts, chariot on wood-tone ground, 19x27", EX ...**650.00**
Bevo, tip tray, The All-Year-Round Soft Drink, rectangular, EX+ ..**300.00**
Bireley's, wall lamps, bottle shaped, w/brackets, 12", pr **800.00**
Blatz Beer, display figure, keg man holding mug, EX **100.00**
Blony Gum, display, cb truck w/wooden wheels, 8x14", EX **350.00**
Borden's, cookie cutter, yel plastic head of Beulah, 2¼", EX **50.00**
Borden's, needle book, Elsie, 1950s, 5", EX **55.00**
Borden's, place mat, paper, Elsie, For Over 125 Yrs..., 11x17", M .**25.00**
Bowl of Roses Pipe Mixture, pocket tin, vertical, short, EX **135.00**
Bowl of Roses Pipe Mixture, pocket tin, vertical, tall, NM **280.00**
Bud Light, display figure, Bud Man, 17½", EX **145.00**
Bud Light, display figure, Spuds McKenzie, vinyl, light-up, NM ...**150.00**
Budweiser, sign, neon, A-&-Eagle logo, 1930s-40s, 10x27", VG+ ..**200.00**
Bull Durham, cb sign, My! It Sure Am..., Blk couple, 30x21", EX ...**1,500.00**
Burma Shave, ts, Grandpa Knows..., 6-pc, 1930s, NM **700.00**

Buster Brown

Buster Brown was the creation of cartoonist Richard Felton; his comic strip first appeared in the *New York Herald* on May 4, 1902. Since then Buster and his dog Tige (short for Tiger) have adorned sundry commercial products but are probably best known as the trademark for the Brown Shoe Company established early in this century. Today hundreds of Buster Brown premiums, store articles, and advertising items bring substantial prices from many serious collectors.

Sign, embossed tin, Golden Sheaf Bakery, Buster Brown and Tige, 1915 – 20, 20x28" in frame, G+, $300.00.

Photo courtesy Gary Metz

Book, Blue Ribbon Book of Jokes & Jingles #2, 1905, EX **950.00**
Clock, tin body w/glass face, electric, lights up, 15" dia, VG **475.00**
Comic book, 1959, EX **25.00**
Container, BB Mustard, cb w/tin top & bottom, red, 2-oz, EX **95.00**
Display, tin diecut, BB in shoe pulled by Tige, 2-pc, 24", VG .**4,000.00**
Display, tin diecut, BB w/cracker, Tige jumping, 2-pc, 40", G ..**2,000.00**
Match holder, tin, party scene w/BB serving bread, 7x2", rare, NM .**1,400.00**
Pin-bk button, Resolved That the Best Bread..., 1½" dia, EX **35.00**
Roaster, aluminum, rnd w/lid, giveaway, rare **98.00**
Rug, BB & Tige, yel w/bl border, 5 yel stars, 47" dia, VG **375.00**
Shoe rack, tin diecut, BB beside Tige holding up rack, 12", EX **1,200.00**
Sign, cb hanger, BB Bread, BB writing on chalkboard, 11x8", EX ...**200.00**
Sign, flange, Get Them Here, diecut image of BB, 24x16", G .**1,800.00**
Sign, wood, BB Quality...Since 1904, BB/Tige, 2-sided, 23", VG ...**125.00**
Watch fob, BB Shoes, cello, 1930s, NM **125.00**

Canada Dry, clock, Enjoy..., glass front, PAM, 1962, 15" dia, EX ..**500.00**
Canada Dry, sign, light-up, frosted glass box, 1930s, 7x14", NM ..**400.00**
Carnation Milk, cb sign, Here It Is Muvvie!, toddler, 22x36", EX+ ...**375.00**
Carter's Overalls, ps, Union Made, train, red/wht/bl, 6x15", EX+ ..**1,350.00**
Ceresota Flour, jigsaw puzzle, The Flower of..., 1900, 7x9", EX ..**125.00**
Chicklets Gum, trolley sign, woman on gr, 11x21", VG+ **120.00**

Clarke's Pure Rye Whiskey, rvpt sign, boy, 1900, 12x12", VG ..**2,000.00**
Cleo Cola, thermometer, wood, Drink.../Rich in Flavor, 15", VG ...**125.00**
Colgate's Cashmere Bouquet, magazine ad, baby, 1919, 21x17", NM+ **60.00**
Consolidated Biscuit Co, cb box, toy house, 1932, 9x9x5", EX+ ..**85.00**
Coors Beer, neon sign, red/wht/blk, mountain graphic, NM **100.00**
Corona Larks, humidor, tin w/hinged glass lid & marque, 10", EX+ ..**75.00**
Crawford Cooking Ranges, yardstick, VG **65.00**
Dan Patch Cut Plug, tc, rectangular, blk/red/yel, NM **185.00**
Decoret, string holder, tin, 19x13", EX **2,035.00**
DeLaval, broom holder, tin, 1911, 3" dia, NM (orig envelope) ..**475.00**
DeLaval, thimble, 1910, EX **475.00**
Dentyne Chewing Gum, toothbrush holder, figural boy, 1930s, NM+ ..**275.00**
Deutsch Tailoring Co, tape measure, cl/metal, 1½" dia, EX **80.00**
Diamond Dyes, cabinet, wood, tin front, court jester, 27", EX+ ...**1,250.00**
Dill's Best, tray, phrase/graphics on wood-grain, 12" dia, EX **180.00**
Doan's Pills, thermometer, wood diecut, man w/sore bk, 21", VG .**250.00**
Donald Duck Coffee, tc, sample, pry lid, yel, 3" dia, EX **475.00**
Double Cola, menu board, tin blkboard, red/wht/bl, 28x20", NM+ ...**75.00**

Dr. Pepper

A young pharmacist, Charles C. Alderton, was hired by W.B. Morrison, owner of Morrison's Old Corner Drug Store in Waco, Texas, around 1884. Alderton, an observant sort, noticed that the drugstore's patrons could never quite make up their minds as to which flavor of extract to order. He concocted a formula that combined many flavors, and Dr. Pepper was born. The name was chosen by Morrison in honor of a beautiful young girl with whom he had once been in love. The girl's father, a Virginia doctor by the name of Pepper, had discouraged the relationship due to their youth, but Morrison had never forgotten her. On December 1, 1885, a U.S. patent was issued to the creators of Dr. Pepper. Our advisors for Dr. Pepper are Craig and Donna Stifter; they are listed in the Directory under Illinois.

Art plate, girl looking right, rare, EX **850.00**
Bottle topper, Cindy Garner, EX+ **165.00**
Calendar, 1947, complete, NM **350.00**
Calendar, 1951, complete, NM **225.00**
Clock, Art Deco style, rvpt, red/gold/blk/wht, 1930s, NM **3,700.00**
Clock, bottle cap, light-up, plastic w/metal back, 12" dia, EX **70.00**
Decal, Please Pay When Served, 1930s-40s, 8x9", unused, EX+ .**200.00**
Door plate, tin, In Case of Emergency..., 1930s-40s, 8", EX+ **200.00**
Drinking glass, flared, etched logo, 1910s, NM **1,200.00**
Fan, cb w/wooden hdl, pretty girl, Earl Morgan art, EX **75.00**
Fan pull, cb, beach girl w/umbrella, G **80.00**
Menu board, tin blkboard, ...When Hungry Thirsty..., 1940s, VG+ ...**250.00**
Opener, metal, diecut lion's head, etched letters/design, 3", EX ...**85.00**
Opener, slide type w/enamel logo, G **80.00**
Postcard, Free! 6 Bottles of..., arrow points to 6-pack, NM **15.00**

Sign, aluminum with black and red enameling, 1930s, 10" diameter, NM, $375.00.

Photo courtesy
Craig and Donna Stifter

Sign, cb, Join Me!, girl in car, 1940s, 32x40", NM **575.00**
Sign, cb, Smart Lift, snow girl w/dog, walnut fr, '40s, 19x40", EX **450.00**

Sign, flange, bottle cap atop Sold Here, 1950s-60s, 18x22", NM ..**1,000.00**
Sign, flange, Fountain/Drink..., yel/red/wht, 1961, 15x22", NM ...**750.00**
Sign, paper, Try Frosty..., bottle/sodas, 1950s, 17x22", EX+ **65.00**
Sign, porc, Drink..., red oval/gold V emblem on wht, 8x22", EX+ ..**175.00**
Sign, porc, Drink..., wht center band/numbers, 1950s, 10" dia, EX ..**375.00**
Thermometer, tin, Drink a Bite..., bottle, 1936, 13", EX **975.00**
Thermometer, tin, Drink DP/Good for Life, bottle graphic, 17", EX ..**675.00**

Dr Shoop's Lax-ets, match holder, tin, Only 5¢ Per Box, EX **165.00**
Dr Swett's Root Beer, thermometer, tin, cap logo, 17", NM **200.00**
Dunham's Concentrated Cocoanut, store bin, tin, 12x10x10", VG ..**350.00**
Dutch Java Coffee, pocket mirror, Secret of Happiness, 2" dia, EX+ **50.00**
Eblings Extra, display goblet, etched, frosted rim, 11x7" dia, NM .**60.00**
Empire Pilsner Style Beer, coaster, paper, 2-sided, 4½" dia, VG+ .**85.00**
Entenmann's, bank, chef figure w/tray of donuts, ceramic, 10", M **75.00**
Esterbrook Pens, dispenser, tin, rnd w/marque, rotates, 14", EX+ **400.00**
Fairbank's Gold Dust...Powder, trolley sign, twins, 11x26", EX ...**1,200.00**
Fairbank's Washing Soap, drawing/pnt book, ...Work & Play, EX ..**110.00**
Fairmont Creamery Co, pot scraper, red/gold/cream/blk, 3x2", EX .**140.00**
Federal Cartridge Co, sf cb sign, hunting dogs, '37, 17x19", VG+ ..**55.00**
Ferris Waists, sf ts, lady combs girl's hair, oval, 23x17", EX+ ...**2,300.00**
Fisk Tires, display figure, Fisk Boy, compo, 32", EX **800.00**
Fleischmann's Yeast, door plate, bl/wht, 4", NM+ **250.00**
Four Roses Whiskey, display figure, bulldog, plaster, 11", VG+ ...**85.00**
Fred Krug Brewing, charger, tin, girl, Beach litho, 24" dia, G **550.00**
Friend's Oats, bowl, china, girl in center, 1900, 6" dia, NM **160.00**
Frostie Root Beer, clock, bottle cap shape, 18" dia, VG **100.00**
Furnald's Hair Brushes, paper sign, bedroom scene, 10x13", G+ ...**475.00**
Gem Damaskeene Razor, clock, wood case/pendulum, 27", EX .**1,150.00**
Goodrich, print, A Midsummer Hallucination, fr, 26x32", G **500.00**
Gotham Watches, display, automated hand w/watch, 1955, 16x16x6", EX ..**300.00**
Grape Nuts Cereal, string holder, tin, 1910s, 12", VG **160.00**
Green River Whiskey, charger, tin, She Was Bred in Old KY, VG .**500.00**
Green Spot, cb sign, Thirsty?, girl at cooler, 33x23", NM+ **185.00**
Gulf, thread container/thimble, metal, cylindrical, 2", EX **300.00**
Hall's Ice Cream, cb diecut stand-up, boy w/ice cream, 36x24", EX ..**385.00**
Hamm's Beer, display, light-up slant-top building, VG **150.00**
Happy Hour Coffee, can, sample, screw lid, red, 2" dia, EX+ **350.00**
Harvard Jumbo Peanuts, tc, rnd, pry lid, 10-lb, G **100.00**
Hercules Powder Co, paper sign, pheasant, 1915, 25x15", G ..**1,000.00**
Hershey's Choclatier, tc, mc on yel, knob on lid, 1950s, 6", EX ...**75.00**
Hiawatha, display bust, chalkware, 19", EX **140.00**
Hickory Children's Garters, wood diecut sign, boy/girl, 18x11", VG ..**350.00**

Hires

Charles E. Hires, a drugstore owner in Philadelphia, became interested in natural teas. He began experimenting with roots and herbs and
soon developed his own special formula. Hires introduced his product to
his own patrons and began selling concentrated syrup to other soda
fountains and grocery stores. Samples of his 'root beer' were offered for
the public's approval at the 1876 Philadelphia Centennial. Today's collectors are often able to date their advertising items by observing the
Hires boy on the logo. From 1891 to 1906, he wore a dress. From 1906
until 1914, he was shown in a bathrobe; and from 1915 until 1926, he
was depicted in a dinner jacket. The apostrophe may or may not appear
in the Hires name; this seems to have no bearing on dating an item.
Our advisors for Hires are Craig and Donna Stifter; they are listed in
the Directory under Illinois.

Ad, Nat'l Temperance, 1897, Drink It & World..., boy/bottle, EX .**40.00**
Bottle carrier, wood, Quarter Case, VG+ **30.00**
Bottle topper/bottle, diecut cb, 10¢ Off/Try a Real Blk Cow, EX .**12.00**

Clock, light-up, ...w/Roots Bark Herbs, red/wht/bl, 15" dia, EX .**385.00**
Dispenser, hourglass shape, w/spigot & pump, 13", EX **1,550.00**
Drinking glass, curved top, etched, Enjoy Hires..., NM+ **160.00**
Menu board, tin, Drink...Bottles, blkboard w/bl & wht stripes, NM .**125.00**
Mug, ceramic, tapered, Join Health..., Hires Boy in tux, 5", NM ..**325.00**
Mug, hourglass shape, Hires boy, wht ceramic, 4", EX **175.00**

Poster, cardboard, 1930s-style
lady with glass, framed, 38¾x24",
EX, $600.00 at auction.

Recipe book, EX **65.00**
Sign, cb, diecut, Hires Boy pointing, EX+ **85.00**
Sign, cb, For Finer Flavor, lady w/food tray, rnd, 12", NM **160.00**
Sign, cb stand-up, Hires to You!..., party, 1940s, 16x12", EX **85.00**
Sign, flange, Made w/..., check-mk logo, red/wht/bl, 12x14", EX **325.00**
Sign, paper, So Good w/Food/R-J logo, hostess/food, 34x54", NM ..**400.00**
Sign, rvpt, Drink...For Thirst & Cheer, 33x25", VG **6,500.00**
Sign, tin, ...It Hits the Spot, Josh Slinger, 1915, 9x18", EX **650.00**
Sign, tin, Ask for Hires in Bottles, wht on bl, 10x28", VG+ **135.00**
Sign, tin, diecut bottle, 1950s, 22x6", M **250.00**
Sign, tin, R-J logo on bl, 7x12", EX **70.00**
Sign, tin, Toast to Good Taste..., R-J logo, 11x35", NM **275.00**
Syrup bottle, rvpt 8-sided label, emb knob lid, 13", EX+ **875.00**
Thermometer, tin, Drink..., bottle on bl & wht stripes, 27", EX+ ..**325.00**
Thermometer, tin bottle shape, Since 1876 label, 29", NM **250.00**
Trade card, bust image of lady, Haskell Coffin art, 1917, NM+ **60.00**
Tray, Just What the Doctor Ordered..., 1914, rnd, 13", G **350.00**

Holly Brand Chocolates, tray, lady, 1910, 19" dia, VG **500.00**
Holsum Bread, push bar, pnt tin, red diecut loaf on bl bar, NM .**200.00**
Holsum Bread, string holder, tin, bl/blk/wht, 16", EX **400.00**
Hunting Smoking Tobacco, cloth pouch, paper label, 2-oz, EX .**285.00**
Imperial Egg Food, paper sign, Blks loading train, 26x17", EX **700.00**
Indianapolis Glove Co, thermometer, wood, keyhole shape, 11", VG **100.00**
IW Harper Whiskey, Vitrolite sign, dog/cabin, 1909, fr, 28x22", NM .**1,850.00**
Jacob Ruppert's Rose Bud, tray, roses/logo on yel, oval, 17", EX .**340.00**
John J Clark's Spool Cotton, oak cabinet, 2-drw pop-up desk, VG ...**600.00**
Johnson's Peacemaker Coffee, bin, tin cabin shape, 25x24x18", EX .**1,100.00**
Jolly Time Hulless Pop Corn, pail, red, boy/girl, 1-lb, VG+ **45.00**
Jumbo Brand Peanut Butter, measuring cup, tin, 12-oz, VG+ .**1,100.00**
Jumbo Brand Peanut Butter, pail, gold, elephant, 1-lb, VG **600.00**
Just Suits Cut Plug, lunch box, red, EX+ **75.00**
Ken-L Ration, thermometer, tin, For Best Results!..., 27", EX+ .**120.00**
Kendall Motor Oil, thermometer, dial type, wht, 12" dia, EX **160.00**
Kessler Whiskey, compo display figure, football, 46", VG **900.00**
Kibbee Bros Cough Drops, tc, sample, gr, EX+ **150.00**
King Midas Flour, string holder, tin, 1908, 20x14", EX+ **1,400.00**
Kis-Me Gum, jar, sq w/beveled edges, rnd fluted rim, emb, 11", VG ..**150.00**
Kool Cigarettes, door plate, Pull...So Refreshing, NM+ **60.00**
La Teresa Cigars, tc, rnd, slip lid, EX+ **120.00**

Lee Riders, display, cb diecut, boy rocks on horse, 22", EX+ **480.00**
Lemp St Louis/Falstaff Beer, charger, House of Falstaff, 24", VG+ .**275.00**
Liberty Beer/Am Brew Co, tip tray, Indian/peace pipes, 4" dia, NM ..**300.00**
Lid Kandy, pail, Jackie Coogan, EX+ **230.00**
Life Savers, display box, tin, 3-tiered, 1920s, 14x10x15", EX+ ...**825.00**
Lion Collars, display rack, wood, holds 6 collars, 29", VG **200.00**

Log Cabin Syrup

Log Cabin Syrup tins have been made since the 1890s in variations of design that can be attributed to specific years of production. Until about 1914, they were made with paper labels. These are quite rare and highly prized by today's collectors. Tins with colored lithographed designs were made after 1914. When General Foods purchased the Towle Company in 1927, the letters 'GF' were added.

A Cartoon series, illustrated with a mother flipping pancakes in the cabin window and various children and animals declaring their appreciation of the syrup in voice balloons, was introduced in the 1930s. A Frontier Village series followed in the late 1940s. A schoolhouse, jail, trading post, doctor's office, blacksmith shop, inn, and private homes were also available. Examples of either series today often command prices of $75.00 to $200.00 and up.

Can opener, metal, Towle's **15.00**
Spoon, SP, log cabin on end of tree-trunk hdl, ca 1910, NM **65.00**
Syrup glass, product name on red panel, 2-spout, 2x1¾", EX **60.00**
Syrup tin, animal skin on door, w/label, 1909-1914, ½-gal, EX+ ...**180.00**
Syrup tin, bear in doorway, 1930 series, 4", EX+ **300.00**
Syrup tin, bear in doorway, 1930s series, 5", VG+ **200.00**
Syrup tin, boy in doorway, w/label, 1918 series, sample sz, EX **350.00**
Syrup tin, boy in doorway, w/label, 1918 series, 1-gal, EX **275.00**
Syrup tin, boy in doorway, 1918 series, 4", EX+ **200.00**
Syrup tin, boy in doorway, 1930s series, 5", EX+ **140.00**
Syrup tin, Dr RU Well, 1940s, 4", EX+ **360.00**
Syrup tin, Express Office, 1940s, 5", EX+ **170.00**

Syrup tin, Frontier Inn, cowboys and horse, five-pound, NM, from $200.00 to $225.00.

Syrup tin, Frontier Jail, 1940s, 4", EX+ **225.00**
Syrup tin, girl in doorway, 1930s series, 4", EX+ **150.00**
Syrup tin, girl in doorway, 1930s series, 5", EX+ **150.00**
Syrup tin, name on sign nailed to wall, 1950s series, 58-oz, EX+ ...**135.00**
Syrup tin, paper label, 1897-1909, 1-gal, VG **70.00**
Syrup tin, sq w/grip hdl, sm screw lid, w/label, 1895-1900, VG+ ..**1,820.00**
Syrup tin, Trading Post, 1940s, 6", EX+ **200.00**

Lowney's Breakfast Cocoa, tc, sample, filigreed image of lady, EX ...**145.00**
Lucky Strike, pocket tin, vertical, gr, 4", EX+ **100.00**
Lucky Strike, pocket tin, vertical, wht, full, NM **725.00**
Luzianne Coffee & Chicory, pail, red or wht, 3-lb, EX **60.00**
Mail Pouch Tobacco, string holder, tin, Pat 1908, 20", G **2,350.00**
Mandeville & King Flowers, paper sign, pansies, 1908, 27x17", EX ..**250.00**
Marathon, tin thermometer, red/wht/bl, 16", EX **90.00**

Master Big Loaf, pc, Really Big!/Really Good!, dk bl, 22x41", NM+ ...**325.00**
Mayo's Tobacco, lunch box, collapsible, bl, EX+ **250.00**
Maytag, compo display figure, Maytag man by washer, 10", EX **70.00**
Metz Jubilee Beer, radio, plastic bottle shape, 24", VG **225.00**
Miller High Life, motion lamp, plastic bottle in ice bucket, EX .**250.00**
Mobil Oil Co, weather vane, porc winged horse, red/wht, 32x27", EX+ .**1,500.00**
Mountain Dew, pin-bk button, hillbilly, 1964, 4" dia, rare, EX **25.00**

Moxie

Ashtray, ceramic, rnd w/3 rests, Moxie man in center, EX+ **70.00**
Bottle carrier, cb box, Drink Moxie, EX **25.00**
Bottle carrier, wood crate, Drink Moxie, EX **25.00**
Bottle topper/bottle, cb, Moxie man, You Need Moxie..., EX **135.00**
Clock, Baird, figure-8, 31", rstr **1,500.00**
Clock, plastic, Since 1884/Old Fashion Moxie, gold fr, 16x16", EX ...**200.00**
Dispenser, glass jug inverted on milk glass base, EX+ **425.00**
Display, cb diecut stand-up, Moxie man w/case, 16x6", EX+ **320.00**
Fan, celluloid, blades held by ribbon, 1910-20s, EX, from $45 to ..**75.00**
Fan, Eileen Percy, 1918, NM **75.00**
Fan, Muriel Ostriche/Moxie man, 1915, EX+, from $30 to **50.00**
Fan, rocking horse/Moxie man, 1922, from $75 to **150.00**
Sign, cb diecut stand-up, Wake Up!, lady/Moxie man, 37x23", G+ .**500.00**
Sign, cd diecut, Muriel Ostriche behind bottle crate, 24x20", VG **135.00**
Sign, cl, 1¢ Sale/Family Size.../3 for 36¢..., 36x49", EX **200.00**
Sign, diecut, keyhole, Drink..., red/wht/bl, 10x8", NM+ **100.00**
Sign, flange, tin, 8-sided, Drink...100%, red/gr/wht, 8x8", VG+ .**325.00**
Sign, tin, belt-buckle shape w/gold name, 1910s, 5x6", NM+ **500.00**
Sign, tin, Drink Moxie, wht on red, yel border, 19x27", EX **200.00**
Sign, tin, Drink Moxie/horsemobile, 27x39", rare, G **2,100.00**
Syrup jug, glass, paper label, EX **100.00**
Thermometer, tin, It's Always a Pleasure..., 1950s, 25", EX **350.00**
Tip tray, I Just Love Moxie Don't You?, Moxie girl, 6", VG **75.00**
Tray, Moxie man, hdls, 10" dia, VG **650.00**

National Brewing Co, tray, brewery/bottle logo, rectangular, EX ..**365.00**
Niagara Punch, ts, Drink..., bottle, red/bl/yel, '20s, 9x20", NM ..**150.00**
Nic Nac Chewing Tobacco, store tin, 5¢ Packets, yel, G **350.00**
NuGrape, blotter, bottle image, EX+ **30.00**
NuGrape, clock, light-up, tilted bottle, Telechron, 15" dia, EX .**275.00**
Ohio Match Co, paperweight/mirror, rnd, EX+ **90.00**
Oilzum, clock, light-up, Choice of Champions, PAM, 15" dia, NM ..**525.00**
Old Gold Cigarettes, tin door plate, Push/Pull, pack w/legs, NM ..**170.00**
Old Timbrook, tray, Daddy of Them All, oval, 16", EX **175.00**

Old Crow

Old Crow whiskey items have become popular with collectors primarily because of the dapper crow dressed in a tuxedo, top hat, etc., that was used by the company for promotional purposes during the 1940s and throughout the 1960s. However, there is a vast variety of Old Crow collectibles, some of which carry only the whiskey's name. In the 1970s ceramic decanters shaped like chess pieces were available; these carried nothing more than a paper label and a presentation box to identify them. In 1985, the 150th anniversary of Old Crow, the realistic crow that had been extensively used prior to 1950 re-emerged.

Very little Old Crow memorabilia has been issued since National Distillers Products Corporations, the parent company since 1933, was purchased by Jim Beam Brands in 1987. No reproductions have surfaced, although a few fantasies have been found where the character crow was borrowed for private use. Our advisors for Old Crow collectibles are Judith and Robert Walthall; they are listed in the Directory under Alabama.

Ad, magazine; full pg, 1940s-60s, ea, from $1 to 5.00
Bank, wooden bbl, 1985, 6" 15.00
Bar pc, holds napkins & stirrers 45.00
Booklet, Drinking Magic, drink recipes, etc 10.00
Bottle, 5th, w/labels, 1950s 10.00
Bottle opener, metal, bottle shape, 2⅝" 30.00
Cuff links, gold-tone metal, crow statuette, 1⅛", MIB 65.00
Figure, plastic, blk-banded wht base, 1960s, 10", from $25 to 45.00
Figure, soft plastic, rnd base, ca 1970, 10", from $18 to 25.00
Flask, emb realistic crow, w/labels, 1-pt 10.00
Highball glass, blk-screened design 5.00
Phone dialer, plastic, flat crow figure 10.00
Pin-bk button, Love Bird, 1970, 3" dia 5.00
Pitcher, ceramic, Broken Leg decor 35.00
Pitcher, clear glass, blk screened design 25.00
Plaque, ceramic plate w/appl 4¾" crow, 8", NM 125.00
Pourer, soft plastic, blk full-figure crow, from $5 to 10.00
Roly poly, plastic, 9" 95.00
Shot glass, blk screened Old Crow, from $4 to 8.00
Sign, wood w/mirror w/blk realistic crow, 1985 ....25.00
Standee, cardboard, 8" 30.00
Stirrer, plastic, fancy, flat crow in center, from $2 to 3.00
Stirrer, plastic, full-figure crow on end, from $1 to 3.00

Orange-Crush, cardboard sign, 1940s, 20x36", EX, $180.00.

Oliver Chilled Plows, sf ts, 2 men outside storefront, 32x23", EX ..7,000.00
Orange Crush, menu board, glass case w/menu slots, NM+ 500.00
Orange Julep, tray, beach girl w/parasol, 13x11", EX 275.00
Orange Kist, cb diecut stand-up, R Armstrong girl, 12x9", VG ..245.00
Ox-Heart Brand Peanut Butter, porc door plate, We Sell..., 7x4", NM ..700.00
Pabst BR Beer, display figure, boxer in ring, pot metal, VG+ 100.00
Pal Ade, thermometer, tin, yel, 1950, 24", NM 400.00
Par Buster, cigar box, golfer, 5¢ on corner band, 1934, EX 85.00
Parrot/Monkey Baking Powder, tc, paper label, 3", full, EX 375.00
Paw-Nee Olde Style Oats, cb container, yel w/red, 2-lb 10-oz, EX ..120.00
PCW Cough Drops, tc, sq, yel on gr, Somers Bros litho, pre-1901, EX ..60.00
Peerless Fruit Chewing Gum, vendor, wood w/porc front, 31", VG+ ..4,180.00
Penn's No 1, pocket tin, vertical, EX+ 3,350.00

Pepsi-Cola

Pepsi-Cola was first served in the early 1890s to customers of Caleb D. Bradham, a young pharmacist who touted his concoction to be medicinal as well as delicious. It was first called 'Brad's Drink' but was renamed Pepsi-Cola in 1898. Various logos have been registered over the years. The familiar oval was first used in the early 1940s. At about the same time, the two 'dots' (indicated in our listings by '=') between the words Pepsi and Cola became one, though more recent items may carry the double-dot logo as well, especially when they're designed to be reminiscent of the old ones. The bottle cap logo came along in 1943 and with variations was used through the early '60s. Our advisors for Pepsi are Craig and Donna Stifter; they are listed in the Directory under Illinois.

Ashtray, ceramic, bottle w/lamp shade center, Bill's Novelties, EX+ ..275.00
Ashtray, chrome bowl w/pnt bottle cap, P-C Montreal, 1956, EX+ 75.00
Blotter, To Think Better Drink P-C 5¢..., 1905, G 80.00
Bottle, miniature; paper P=C label, 4½", EX+ 25.00
Bottle, miniature; pnt P=C label, 3½", VG 18.00
Bottle carrier, cb, bl/wht stripes, w/6 full 12-oz bottles, NM 50.00
Bottle carrier, wood, Bigger Better, w/6 12-oz bottles, EX+ 180.00
Bottle opener, bottle shape, mc tin litho, 1930s, 4", EX 40.00
Bottle topper, Pepsi & Pete, I Make Sure..., 1930s, 14x12", EX+ ..625.00
Calendar, 1941, Hits the Spot, complete, EX+ 325.00
Calendar, 1943, Am Art Series, complete, EX+ 85.00
Change purse, leather/metal, The World's Best Drink, EX 275.00
Charm, gold tone, P=C on shamrock w/horseshoe on chain, NM ...60.00
Clock, Be Sociable/Have..., sm bottle cap, 1955, 15" dia, NM ...875.00
Clock, mantel, turning ballerina, musical, Germany, 1920s, 6", EX+ .575.00
Clock, Say Pepsi Please, light-up, 1970s, 22x16", EX+ 30.00
Clock, Say Pepsi Please, #s on gold perforated fr, 16" sq, EX 100.00
Clock, Time for P=C, Sessions, 1930s, 14" sq, EX+ 250.00
Cooler, metal, center-hinged lid, 4-legged stand, 1930s, 24", G+ .1,400.00
Dispenser, metal streamline style, P-C Ice Cold, red/wht/bl, NM 600.00
Door handle, tin, Enjoy P=C/Bigger Better, 1940s, EX+ 225.00
Door plate, Drink P=C/5¢ bottle, yel, 1930s, 14x4", NM 1,100.00
Door plate, Enjoy.../P-C bottle caps, yel/wht, 1954, 14x4", EX ..230.00
Drinking glasses, Pepsi & Pete Safedge Tumblers, 6 in box, EX+ ..775.00
Fan, cb, wood hdl, Drink P=C 12 oz...5¢/Pepsi Cops, 1940, NM+ .120.00
Lighter, can shape, silver-bl w/wht diagonal stripes, 1960s, EX+ ..50.00
Lighter, Super Automatic..., bottle cap logo, Japan, 1¾", EX+ 75.00
Matchbook cover, Pepsi Cop drinking from bottle, NM 35.00
Matchbox w/stick matches, Now It's Pepsi!, bottle cap, M 20.00

Menu board, tin litho, red and black border around blue, 1939, 30x19½", EX, $200.00.

Menu board, tin, Enjoy..., yel w/blkboard bottom, 27x19", EX+ ...165.00
Menu board, wood, 2 rows of slots, P=C/ribbon, '40s, 20x25", EX ..750.00
Money clip, brass/chrome dollar sign, 1950s, 2", NM+ 65.00
Napkin holder, trapezoidal w/cap logo, wht w/bl ends, 1940s, EX ..350.00
Pocket mirror, rectangular, P=C/The Light Refreshment, EX+ ..100.00
Push bar, porc, Enjoy...Iced, red on wht, yel tabs, 3x32", EX 150.00
Push bar, porc, Have a.../P-C bottle caps, yel, '50s, 3x32", NM ..220.00
Rack, wire, 3-tiered, diecut cap logo, 1940s, 42x22", VG 175.00
Radio, bottle form, Bakelite, ftd base, 24", EX 550.00
Shakers, early bottles w/P=C oval labels, EXIB, pr 165.00
Sign, cb, Be Sociable..., lady in fur hat, 2-sided, 26x37", VG 170.00
Sign, cb, The Am Beverage, girl w/glass, 1907-08, 27x21", rare, G+ ..4,000.00
Sign, cb diecut stand-up, Santa in long johns, 20x16", EX 55.00
Sign, cb standee, grocer in wht apron, 1930s, 68", VG+ 875.00
Sign, glass light-up, Enjoy/P-C/Hits the Spot, musical notes, EX+ .600.00
Sign, plastic light-up, Have A...Lt Refreshment, 1950s, EX 500.00

Sign, porc, bottle cap shape, P-C logo, 1940s-50s, 18" dia, EX+ .**875.00**
Sign, tin, bottle on bl, bl raised border, 49x16", NM **1,750.00**
Sign, tin, bottle on wht, wht raised border, 1950s, 48x18", NM .**925.00**
Sign, tin, Ice Cold Drinks, bear/starry sky, 1960s-70s, 23x23", EX+ ...**475.00**
Sign, tin, P=C 12 oz 5¢/bottle on wht, beveled, 1930s, 13x5", EX .**1,100.00**
Sign, trolley; Something To Hoe.../3 garden girls, '40s, 11x28", EX ..**650.00**
Thermometer, tin, Buy P=C Big Big Bottle, red/wht/bl, 27", VG+ ...**300.00**
Tip tray, 1910, EX+ **1,400.00**
Tray, 1909, Gibson Girl, oval, 14x11", G **450.00**
Tray, 1940, Bigger & Better, stylized flowers, 11x14", EX **50.00**
Vendor, ballpark; wood, wht/bl stripes, w/strap, 1950s, 6x19", NM .**325.00**

Peter Pan Fresh Bread, broom holder, stenciled tin, EX+ **350.00**
Peter Rabbit Peanut Butter, pail, VG **225.00**
Peters Loaded Shells, cb diecut sign, dog/product box, 25x22", VG **700.00**
Peters Shoes, ps, name in script, red/wht/bl, rnd ends, 8x39", EX+ **200.00**
Pick Wick Club, cigar box, holds 50, 1917 tax stamp, unopened, EX .**100.00**
Pickwick Coffee, mask, cb, Mr Pickwick face, 1930s, NM+ **65.00**
Piel's Beer, display figure, pot metal, elf w/glass by stump, VG+ .**150.00**
Pizza Hut, bank, Pizza Hut Pete, plastic, 1969, 7½", NM **55.00**

Planters Peanuts

The Planters Peanut Co. was founded in 1906. Mr. Peanut, the dashing peanut man with top hat, spats, monocle, and cane, has represented Planters since 1916. He took on his modern-day appearance after the company was purchased by Standard Brands in November 1960. He remains perhaps the most highly recognized logo of any company in the world. Mr. Peanut has promoted the company's products by appearing in ads; on product packaging; on or as store displays, novelties, and premiums; and even in character at promotional events (thanks to a special Mr. Peanut costume).

Among the favorite items of collectors today are the glass display jars which were sent to retailers nationwide to stimulate 'point-of-sale' trade. They come in a variety of shapes and styles. The first, distributed in the early 1920s, was a large universal candy jar (round covered bowl on a pedestal) with only a narrow paper label affixed at the neck to identify it as 'Planters.' In 1924 an octagonal jar was produced, all eight sides embossed, with Mr. Peanut on the narrow corner panels. On a second octagon jar, only seven sides were embossed, leaving one of the large panels blank to accommodate a paper label.

In late 1929 a fishbowl jar was introduced, and in 1932 a beautiful jar with a blown-out peanut on each of the four corners was issued. The football shape was also made in the 1930s, as were the square jar, the large barrel jar, and the hexagon jar with yellow fired-on designs alternating on each of the six sides. All of these early jars had glass lids which after 1930 had peanut finials.

In 1937 jars with lithographed tin lids were introduced. The first of these was the slant-front streamline jar, which is also found with screened yellow lettering. Next was a squat version, the clipper jar, then the upright rectangular 1940 leap year jar, and last, another upright rectangular jar with a screened, fired-on design similar to the red, white, and blue design on the cellophane 5¢ bags of peanuts of the period. This last jar was issued again after WWII with a plain red tin lid.

In 1959 Planters first used a stock Anchor Hocking one-gallon round jar with a 'customer-special' decoration in red. As the design was not plainly evident when the jar was full, the decoration was modified with a white under-panel. The two jars we've just described are perhaps the rarest of them all due to their limited production. After Standard Brands purchased Planters, they changed the red-on-white panel to show their more modern Mr. Peanut and in 1963 introduced this most plentiful, thus very common, Planters jar. In 1966 the last counter display jar was distributed: the Anchor Hocking jar with a fired-on large

four-color design such as those that appeared on peanut bags of the period. Prior to this, a plain jar with a transfer decal in an almost identical but smaller design was used.

Some Planters jars have been reproduced: the octagon jar (with only six of the sides embossed), a small version of the barrel jar, and the four peanut corner jar. Some of the first were made in clear glass with 'Made in Italy' embossed on the bottom, but most have been made in Asia, many in various colors of glass (a dead giveaway) as well as clear, and carrying only small paper stickers, easily removed, identifying the country of origin. At least two reproductions of the Anchor Hocking jar with four-color designs have been made, one circa 1978, the other in 1989. Both, using the stock jar, are difficult to detect, but there are small differences between them and the original that will enable you to make an accurate identification. With the exception of several of the earliest and the Anchor Hocking, all authentic Planters jars have 'Made in USA' embossed on the bottom, and all, without exception, are clear glass. Unfortunately, several paper labels have also been reproduced, no doubt due to the fact that an original label or decal will greatly increase the value of an original jar. Jar prices continue to remain stable in today's market.

In the late 1920s, the first premiums were introduced in the form of story and paint books. Late in the 1930s, the tin nut set (which was still available into the 1960s) was distributed. A wood-jointed doll was available from Planters Peanuts Stores at that time. Many post-WWII items were made of plastic: banks, salt and pepper shakers, cups, cookie cutters, small cars and trucks, charms, whistles, various pens and mechanical pencils, and almost any other item imaginable. In recent years the company, now a division of Nabisco, has continued to distribute a wide variety of novelties.

Note that there are many unauthorized Planters/Mr. Peanut items. Although several are reproductions or 'copycats,' most are fantasies and fakes. Our advisors for Planters Planters are Judith and Robert Walthall; they are in the Directory under Alabama.

Key:
al — aluminum
cc — common colors
  (green, light blue, red, tan)
MrP — Mr. Peanut
okl — octagon knob lid
pfl — peanut finial lid
pl — plastic
pm — papier-mache
pnut — peanut

Ceramic ashtray, 4" Mr. Peanut (green pants) behind 3½" shell-shaped dish with green rim, two peanuts at back, no holes for cane, $400.00; Bisque ashtray with 4" Mr. Peanut (black pants) behind 3" shell-shaped dish, three peanuts at back, wire cane, $75.00.

Badge, employee, metal, Planters in red, EX **300.00**
Bank, pl MrP figure, dk bl, 9", EX **150.00**
Booklet, Helping the Veteran Help Himself, 1944, 5x7¼", EX **45.00**
Booklet, How To Figure Your Income Tax, 1943, 5x7¼", EX **45.00**
Booklet, Our Fighting Forces, 1943, 10x13", EX, from $35 to **45.00**

Booklet, Planters Presents Our Fighting Forces, premium, 1943, EX .45.00
Clock, alarm; MrP on face, 1966-70, MIB 85.00
Clock, red pl, Lifesavers/MrP logo, wall type, 12½" dia 85.00
Clock, wall, MrP & Lifesavers logo, red case, 1991, 12½" dia ..125.00
Clock, wall, orange, yel & bl, 1980, 13x17", EX 40.00
Container, pm pnut, 1-lb, w/box: Biggest Pnut in World, EX 95.00
Cookie cutter, pl MrP bowing & tipping hat, red or bl, EX 15.00
Costume, MrP, cloth body w/pl mask, 1970s, unused, NMIB 75.00
Dish, pressed glass, rnd w/octagon base, MrP center, 5½", M (+) .20.00
Fork & spoon set, salad; wood w/ceramic MrP tops, MIB 115.00
Jar, Barrel, pfl, paper label, 1935, 12¼", EX 250.00
Jar, Clipper, orig tin lid, 1938, EX 100.00
Jar, Fishbowl, okl, no label, 1929, 12½", EX 75.00
Jar, Fishbowl, Planters emb on base, orig label, 11", VG, $150 to .175.00
Jar, Football, pfl, 1931, 8½", EX 225.00
Jar, Four Peanut Corner, pfl, 1932, 14" (+) 225.00
Jar, Octagon, 6 sides emb, pfl, clear & colors, repro 35.00
Jar, Octagon, 7 sides emb, okl, no label, 12", EX (+) 85.00
Jar, Octagon, 8 sides emb, okl, 1924, 12", EX (+) 250.00
Mug, pl MrP head, cc, M, from $5 to 10.00
Nodder, MrP, compo, 6½", MIB 140.00
Oven mitt, MrP figure, MIP 10.00
Peanut butter spreader, MrP, yel pl 4.00
Punch board, MrP, M (+) 125.00
Puppet, hand; MrP figure, rubber, 1950s, 6", EX 600.00
Shakers, MrP figure, HP china w/rhinestone, 4½", M, pr 125.00
Sign, cb diecut stand-up figure of MrP, 1980s, 12", M 10.00
Sign, paper, ...MrP Sale/Stock Up..., MrP/girl, 1960s, 15x36", EX .65.00
Spoon, nut server, cc, pl, MrP hdl, from $3 to 5.00
Statue, pot metal, MrP on beveled base, 7½", EX 600.00
Stein, MrP figure, #d, promotional item, 1994, MIB 100.00
Straw, pl, MrP on top 6.00
Thermometer, Deep Fry w/Planters Pnut Oil, MrP as chef, MIB ...175.00
Tote bag, Planters Pnuts/MrP on bl cloth, 1980s, 18x12", M 10.00
Toy, walking MrP, pl wind-up, cc, blk/tan, 1950s, 8½", EX 275.00
Tray, Planters Pnut Co/Fresh Roasted..., MrP, oval, 1980s, 14" 30.00
Umbrella, 2-color w/single image of MrP, 1980s, M 40.00

Polar Bear Ginger, container, cb, red/wht on bl, 1½-oz, NM 50.00
Popper's Ace Cigars, display case, plane on marque, 11x10x8", VG ...850.00
Pratt's Foods, jigsaw puzzle, Uncle Sam, 1910, 6½x9", EX 65.00
Pure Beer Brewing Co, tray, men playing cards, oval, 16", EX 515.00
Putnam Dyes, fan, cb w/wood hdl, peacock, 1930s, NM 25.00
Quaker Oats Quisp Cereal, beanie, MIB 400.00
Quick Meal Ranges, tip tray, Ask Your Dealer, chicks, oval, NM+ 230.00

RCA Victor

Nipper, the RCA Victor trademark, was the creation of Francis Barraud, an English artist. His pet's intense fascination with the music of the phonograph seemed to him a worthy subject for his canvas. Although he failed to find a publishing house who would buy his work, the Gramophone Co. in England saw its potential and adopted Nipper to advertise their product. The painting was later acquired and trademarked in the United States by the Victor Talking Machine Co., which was purchased by RCA in 1929. The trademark is owned today by EMI in England and by General Electric in the U.S. Nipper's image appeared on packages, accessories, ads, brochures, and in three-dimensional form. You may find a life-size statue of him, but all are not old. They have been manufactured for the owner throughout RCA history and are marketed currently by licensees, BMG Inc. and Thomson Consumer Electronics (dba RCA). Except for the years between 1968 and 1976, Nipper has seen active duty, and with his image spruced up only a bit

for the present day, the ageless symbol for RCA still listens intently to 'His Master's Voice.' Our advisor for RCA Victor is Roger R. Scott; he is listed in the Directory under Oklahoma.

Radiotrons man, Cameo Doll Co., jointed wood, 1920s, 15", M, $900.00.

Photo courtesy Dunbar Gallery

Bank, Nipper, felt over pot metal, mk Radio Corp of Am, 6", NM ..125.00
Buckle, His Master's Voice, brass, Nash Tiffany London 25.00
Chair, NP-pipe fr w/armrest, plastic bk/seat, logo on bk, M 100.00
Curtains, RCA 40.00
Figure, Nipper, chalk, Victor, 4" 40.00
Figure, Nipper, crystal, Fenton, 4" 50.00
Figure, Nipper, molded plastic, 36", EX 235.00
Figure, Nipper, papier-mache, 14" or 18", from $200 to 400.00
Figure, Nipper, papier-mache, 36" 600.00
Figure, Nipper, plaster, 14½x7½x5", VG 200.00
Necktie, Nipper, M 20.00
Needle tin, Nipper, 3-color, NM, from $25 to 50.00
Pin-bk button, I Support Nipper, 1930s, ½", EX 45.00
Plate, Nipper, collector's edition 50.00
Puzzle record, Victor, MIP 100.00
Record brush, Lucite hdl, in faux leather snap case 30.00
Record display, dog & phonograph, chalk 150.00
Shakers, dog & RCA, phonograph, plastic, pr 45.00
Shakers, Nipper, Lenox, 3", pr 55.00
Shakers, Radio Corp of Am, 1940s, pr 40.00
Sign, plastic/metal, light-up, 1940s, 15x37", EX 200.00
Sign, porc, Authorized Dealer..., 1940s, 18x24", EX 165.00
Sign, porc, record shape w/trademark image on red label, 24", VG .300.00
Sign, tin, Nipper Listening, fr, 13½x19", G 500.00
Sign, tin, Victor Talking Machines, dog & Victrola, 13½x9", VG ..500.00
Watch fob, EX 30.00
Water glass, etched Nipper, set of 6 ....100.00

Red Goose Shoes

Realizing that his last name was difficult to pronounce, Herman Giesecke, a shoe company owner resolved to give the public a modified, shortened version that would be better suited to the business world. The results suggested the use of the goose trademark with the last two letters, 'ke,' represented by the key that this early goose held in his mouth. Upon observing an employee casually coloring in the goose trademark with a red pencil, Giesecke saw new advertising potential and renamed the company Red Goose Shoes. Although the company has changed hands down through the years, the Red Goose emblem has remained. Collectors of this desirable fowl increase in number yearly, as do prices. Beware of reproductions; new chalkware figures are prevalent.

Clock, rnd, light-up, glass front, metal fr, Telechron, 1930s-40s, NM .400.00
Dispenser, Golden Egg, cb & papier-mache goose, w/sign, EX ...325.00

Figure, red-painted plaster of Paris goose, 12", NM, $400.00.

Figure, plaster goose, premium, 4", NM+ 40.00
Rug, Half the Fun of Having Feet, gold on gray, 27x59", rare, EX 325.00
Sign, goose shape, wht & yel neon, 1930s-40s, 24x12", NM+ ..1,900.00
Sign, porc, red goose on yel ground, red border, 17x12", EX 250.00
Sign, tin, For Boys & Girls, yel, red border, 13x19", VG 110.00
String holder, CI goose figure, 11x17", VG 1,900.00

Red Raven, charger, tin, Dear Old Red Raven, 24" dia, VG 450.00
Red Seal Battery, ts, flange, battery shape, 1915-25, 25", EX+ ...875.00
Red Seal Peanut Butter, pail, marching musicians, VG 90.00
Red Seal Peanut Butter, pail, nursery rhymes, EX+ 175.00
Reddy Kilowatt, apron, She Loves Me, Reddy pulling petals, M ...40.00
Reddy Kilowatt, figure, lg head, blk outlet base, EX-, minimum .100.00
Reddy Kilowatt, figure, red plastic, RK on base, sm head, EX 200.00
Reddy Kilowatt, measuring glass, RK holding logo, 1930s, 5", M .42.00
Reddy Kilowatt, pin-bk button, RK by wall plug/name, 1" dia, EX 55.00
Reddy Kilowatt, sign, diecut hardboard figure, red/wht, 10x9", VG .115.00
Reed's Gilt Edge Tonic, mantel clock, grandfather style, 18", VG ...700.00
Remington UMC, paper sign, snowy hunt scene, Collins, 26x18", VG ...675.00
Rexall Baby Talcum, tc, Comfort for the Little One, EX+ 120.00
Richardson's Wash Silks, cabinet, wood w/rvpt front, 36", EX ...675.00
Rising Sun Stove Polish, paper sign, Donaldson Bros, 28x18", EX ..675.00
Rockford Watches, tip tray, oval, EX+ 220.00
Rockford Watches, tip tray, rectangular, G+ 60.00

Roly Poly

The Roly Poly tobacco tins were patented on November 5, 1912, by Washington Tuttle and produced by Tindeco of Baltimore, Maryland. There were six characters in all: Satisfied Customer, Storekeeper, Mammy, Dutchman, Singing Waiter, and Inspector. Four brands of tobacco were packaged in selected characters; some tins carry a printed tobacco box on the back to identify their contents. Mayo and Dixie Queen Tobacco were packed in all six; Red Indian and U.S. Marine Tobacco in only Mammy, Singing Waiter, and Storekeeper. Of the set, the Inspector is considered the rarest and in near-mint condition may fetch more than $1,000.00 on today's market.

Detective, Mayo, VG/EX 500.00
Dutchman, Dixie Queen, EX 400.00
Dutchman, Mayo, VG/EX, from $300 to 550.00
Inspector, Mayo, EX 675.00
Mammy, Mayo, EX+, from $600 to 850.00
Mammy, Red Indian, EX+ 750.00
Satisfied Customer, Dixie Queen, NM+ 900.00
Satisfied Customer, Mayo, VG/EX, from $425 to 625.00
Scotland Yard, Mayo, G 550.00

Singing Waiter, US Marine, VG/EX, from $400 to 600.00
Storekeeper, Mayo, EX 500.00

Round Oak Stoves, print, cb, Doe-Wah-Jack standing, 25x9", EX+ ..750.00
Royal Crown Cola, clock, rnd neon, rainbow marque, 36x32", EX .1,300.00
Royal Crown Cola, thermometer, tin, bottle by gauge, 14", EX .100.00
Ruhstaller's, tip tray, California Invites the World, VG+ 100.00
Sarony Cigarettes, roulette game, EX 30.00
Sauer's Flavoring..., thermometer, wood, None Better, 1910, VG ..250.00
Sauer's Pure Vanilla, thermometer, wooden box, 1920, 22", VG+ .250.00
Schlitz, paperweight, glass, encased brewery scene, VG 100.00
Schlitz, tray, globe logo w/train, rnd, deep rim, VG 75.00
Seal of NC Tobacco, broadside, Currier & Ives, 1883, 15x19", EX .330.00
Sears, Roebuck & Co Roasted Coffee, tc, hinged lid, 25-lb, EX ...80.00
Sears, Roebuck & Co Tea, pail, striped, 5-lb, EX+ 130.00
Sharples, match holder, tin, The Pet of the Dairy, NM 745.00
Sharples, pin-bk button, Different From the Others..., EX+ 50.00
Sharples, pot scraper, The 1909 Tubulars Are Better..., EX 235.00
Sierra Ice Cream, tray, sundaes/mtn logo, oval, deep rim, NM ...235.00
Singer Sewing Machines, thermometer, porc, modern logo, 35", NM ..2,600.00
Sir Walter Raleigh Cigarettes, change receiver, brass/wood/glass, VG ..50.00
Slinky, display, cb, automated boy w/Slinky, ca 1956, 17x17x8", EX ..750.00
Smith Bros Cough Drops, blotter, For That Cough, 7x12", M 20.00
Smith Bros Cough Drops, paperweight, CI drop shape, 2x1", EX .135.00
Squeeze, ts, Drink...All Flavors, kids on bench, 10x28", NM 200.00
Squirt, chalk figure, Squirt boy/bottle, 1947, 13", EX 650.00
Squirt, cuff links, enameled metal Squirt boy, M, pr 30.00
Star Naphtha Washing Powder, ts, 5¢..., mc, 26x20", M 385.00
Sunbeam Bread, cookie tin, Miss Sunbeam/...Greetings, 8", EX ...25.00
Sunbeam Bread, ts, loaf shape, Enriched Bread, 1957, 28x60", EX+ .1,500.00
Swans Down Cake Flour, mirror/paperweight, cl, 4" dia, VG 200.00
Sweet Orr Work Clothes, cb standee, man in overalls w/sign, 60", NM .800.00
Tinkertoy, display, automated paddle wheel, 1940, 19", EX 450.00
Tip-Top Tobacco, pail, orange, G 230.00
Tom's Toasted Peanuts, thermometer, tin, 16", NM+ 160.00
Tutt's Liver Pills, cigar cutter, CI figural ship's wheel, 6", VG 550.00
Uncle John's Syrup, display, cb cutout, John/child, 5-pc, 24", NM+ .600.00
Uncle Tom's Mint Chewing Gum, cb, display box, 2x9x4", EX+ ...300.00
Uneeda Biscuits, cb standee, boy in yel slicker w/box, 51", EX ...775.00
Union Leader Cut Plug, lunch box, basketweave, EX 50.00
Union Leader Cut Plug, milk can, red, 9", EX 235.00
Universal Blend Coffee, pail, Uncle Sam w/flag, red/wht/bl, EX+ ..700.00
Vanity Coffee, tc, key-wind, peacock on red circle, 1-lb, EX 220.00
Vernor's Ginger Ale, thermometer, dial type, gr/yel, 12", NM ...300.00
Victor Talking Machines, magazine ad, Nat'l Geographic, 1903, NM .90.00
Victoria Tea/Montgomery Ward, tc, sq, yel, ca 1900, 2-lb, EX+ ...135.00
Wagner's Ice Cream, ts, Eat Wagner's...It's Good/graphics, 14x20", VG .275.00
Walker's King of Soaps, string holder, 5", G 225.00
Walla-Walla Pepsin Gum, glass jar, sq w/t'print lid, emb, 13", EX .465.00
Wendy's, paperweight, Wendy's Decade II, metal, rnd, EX 40.00
Westinghouse Mazda Lamps, cb masks, Toonerville folks, EX, 4 for .100.00
Whistle Soda, coat rack, wooden panel w/advertising, 8x36", EX+ ..275.00
Whistle Soda, pocket mirror, rectangular, 1940s, NM 150.00

Willys Jeep, double-sided shield-shaped sign, red, white, and blue, 26x24", NM, $400.00.

White Clover Peanut Butter, pail, red/yel/bl shield, 1-lb, EX+ ...**550.00**
White Manor Manor Pipe Mixture, pocket tin, vertical, 3", NM ...**230.00**
White Oak Coffee, store bin, tin, 18x18x14", G **100.00**
Wiedemann's Fine Beer, sign, mc spinner light-up, '50s, 16" dia, NM .**350.00**
Wild Root, shaving mug, ceramic, cojoined cups, 1927, EX **110.00**
Will's Star Cigarettes, pc, name/pack, yel/wht/brn, 24x13", VG ..**150.00**
Winchester, paper sign, Sioux, Ferra art, 1976, 21x12", NM+ **85.00**
Winchester After Shave Talc, tc, red, EX+ **200.00**
Wishing Well Orange, thermometer, tin, yel, 1961, 41", M **200.00**
Wonder Bread, ts, receding loaf shape, 1950s, 25x36", NM+ **475.00**
Wrigley's, calendar holder, tin/cb, 1920s, 17x9", G **500.00**
Wrigley's Spearmint Gum, trolley sign, Dr Googles..., 11x21", EX ..**90.00**
Xtra Brau, tap knob, ball shape, blk/wht, VG+ **150.00**
Yago Sangria, radio, bottle form, NMIB **65.00**
Yale Coffee, tc, sample, metallic bl, VG+ **75.00**
Yellow Bonnet Coffee, tc, sample, pry lid, EX **500.00**
Yellow Cab, calendar pad holder, 1950s, 11x7", EX+ **50.00**
Zig Zag Confections, match safe, VG+ **150.00**
Zuane La Parot Talc, tc, oval, gold/red on blk, 6", EX **240.00**

7-Up

The Howdy Company of St. Louis, Missouri, was founded in 1920 by Charles L. Grigg. His first creation was an orange drink called Howdy. In the late 1920s Howdy's popularity began to wane, so in 1929 Grigg invented a lemon-lime soda called Seven-Up as an alternative to colas. Grigg's Seven-Up became a widely accepted favorite. Our advisors for this category are Craig and Donna Stifter; they are listed in the Directory under Illinois.

Ashtray, cb, sq w/scalloped corners, Put Your Ashes.../logo, EX+ .**35.00**
Ashtray, glass, sq w/rnd corners, logo w/decorative border, G **15.00**
Bill hook, cl button, I'd Hang for a Chilled 7-Up, EX+ **35.00**
Bottle topper/bottle, cb, Easter bunny atop egg next to girl, NM ..**32.00**
Bottle topper/bottle, Fresh Up for St Pat's, logo/shamrocks, EX ...**22.00**
Broom stand, sign on 2-legged rack, wht on red, 1940s, 28x20", EX+ **600.00**
Calendar, 1953, complete, EX+ **65.00**
Clock, rectangular, First Against Thirst, vertical, bowed sides, VG ..**60.00**
Clock, rnd, You Like It/It Likes You, gr/wht, 1950s, M **600.00**
Cuff links, pnt logo, M, pr **30.00**
Door plate, aluminum, Come In/oval bubble logo/Likes You, wht, EX+ ..**85.00**
Drinking glass, aluminum, 7-Up logo, 5", EX+ **45.00**
Drinking glass, red/wht appl label w/girls, M **165.00**
Matchbook, 7-Up/The Uncola, M **8.00**
Menu board, wood-tone tin w/menu slots, red oval logo, 23x9", EX+ ..**225.00**
Music box, can shape, plays theme to Love Story, NM **50.00**
Push bar, porc, Fresh Up w/Seven-Up!, logos ea end, 3x32", NM+ .**220.00**
Sign, cb, Enjoy Seven-Up Float, w/graphics, fr, 20x33", NM **100.00**
Sign, flange, ...Likes You, gr w/wht line & scrolls, 10x13", NM .**200.00**
Sign, paper, Fresh Up! w/ 7-Up Float, gr, 4x18", NM+ **15.00**
Sign, porc, 7-Up/bubbles logo, wht/blk on red, 1951, 20x17", NM+ ..**425.00**
Sign, school crossing, diecut cartoon cop w/sign, 1950s, 60", G .**800.00**
Sign, sf cb, All-Family Drink!, bowling scene, 1952, 13x23", NM+ ..**150.00**
Sign, tin, Anti-Acid/Lithiated Lemon Soda, 1920s, 20x9", G **250.00**
Sign, tin, Real 7-Up Sold Here, w/bubbles, 14" dia, G **230.00**
Sign, tin bottle shape, wet-look, 2-sided, 44x13", EX **275.00**
Thermometer, dial type, 7-Up Likes You, 10" or 12", NM **200.00**
Thermometer, porc, The Fresh Up Family Drink, wht, 15", EX .**130.00**
Tie clip, enameled logo on bar, EX **15.00**
Toy truck, tin, friction, driver in plastic dome, 1950s, 9", EX+ ..**335.00**

Advertising Cards

Advertising trade cards enjoyed great popularity during the last

quarter of the 19th century when the chromolithography printing process was refined and put into common use. The purpose of the trade card was to acquaint the public with a business, product, service, or event. Most trade cards range in size from 2" x 3" to 4" x 6"; however, many are found in both smaller and larger sizes.

There are two classifications of trade cards: 'private design' and 'stock.' Private design cards were used by a single company or individual; the images on the cards were designed for only that company. Stock cards were generics that any individual or company could purchase from a printer's inventory. These cards usually had a blank space on the front for the company to overprint with their own name and product information.

Four categories of particular interest to collectors are:

Mechanical — a card which achieves movement through the use of a pull tab, fold-out side, or movable part.

Hold-to-light — a card that reveals its design only when viewed before a strong light.

Diecut — a card in the form of something like a box, a piece of clothing, etc.

Metamorphic — a card that by folding down a flap shows a transformed image, such as a white beard turning black after use of a product.

For a more thorough study of the subject, we recommend *Reflections 1* and *Reflections 2* by Kit Barry; his address can be found in the Directory under Vermont.

Values are given for cards in near-mint condition.

Gold Dust Washing Powder, diecut, $40.00.

Adam's Yellow Kid Gum, Yellow Kid in sleigh w/Duchess **50.00**
Ager's Dry Hop Yeast, man, woman, boy by stone wall **6.00**
American Eagle Tobacco Co, National league, baseball pitcher ..**350.00**
Amorilas Water Perfume, bottle diecut **35.00**
Andrews Hardware, anthropomorphic tools & stove **50.00**
Babbit & Chapin Clothier, JS Prince bicyclist **35.00**
Babbitt Soap, artist w/palette facing easel **6.00**
Babbitt Soap, boy & girl holding toy w/dog **7.00**
Bon Ami Soap, 2 chicks in coconut shell **10.00**
Bon Ami Soap, 5 chicks in straw hat **10.00**
Bosch Co 1902 Wallpaper, 2 elves & woman **20.00**
Bovril, product bottle **12.00**
Brunswick & Balke Pool Table, 5 frogs at table **100.00**
Clark's ONT Thread, baby w/rattle **6.00**
Clark's ONT Thread, boy playing drum **5.00**
Clark's ONT Thread, Brooklyn Bridge scene **15.00**
Clark's ONT Thread, cowboy roping steer **7.00**
Clark's ONT Thread, diecut spool, mother w/baby **8.00**
Clark's ONT Thread, girl on bench playing w/cat **8.00**
Clark's ONT Thread, mtn scene, Mt Hood OR **8.00**
Clark's ONT Thread, Seal Rocks... ....**8.00**
Clark's ONT Thread, Spring, woman seated outside **8.00**
Clark's ONT Thread, Summer, woman w/binoculars **8.00**
Clark's ONT Thread, 2 boys w/kite **6.00**

Constable Hook, play w/Grace Cartland 7.00
Continental Champagne, fancy building 35.00
Coup's Circus, camels pulling circus wagon 35.00
Curtis Davis Soap, man tipping hat to girl in garden 5.00
David Brown Soap, man on globe 45.00
Dobbins Electric Soap, woman & roses, child in bk 8.00
Domestic Sewing Machine, Black couple in wagon, boy 8.00
Domestic Sewing Machine, Prize Brown Leghorns 7.00
Domestic Sewing Machine, Rochester by Aberdeen 7.00
Domestic Sewing Machine, woman holding bird 6.00
Enterprise Baking Powder, girl w/5 toys 6.00
Farnicum Medicine, bottle & crowd 15.00
Fearless Stoves, Rathbone Co, 2 women & Black 25.00
Frank Miller's Crown Dressing, girl pushing doll in carriage 9.00
Franklin Printing Co, Benjamin Franklin bust 150.00
Frash & Co Champagne, pavillion 35.00
Gilman, Tuttle Co Furniture, Boston, girl w/fan 25.00
Gloss Soap, girl, butterfly on hand, flowers on arm 5.00
Hale's Honey Horehound & Tar, 2 kids & beehive 20.00
Henkel Baking Powder, girl w/ABCs, book & doll 6.00
Herder & Sons Scissors, bl & wht shears 20.00
Ivorine Soap, girl washing clothes in washtub outside 9.00
Ivorine Soap, girl washing dishes in kitchen 7.00
Jollities, theatre play, crying baby 4.00
JP Coats Thread, boy w/blkboard 6.00
JP Coats Thread, girl holding dog 6.00
JP Coats Thread, girl w/daisies in hair 6.00
Judge Magazine, political cartoon 35.00
Kimball Cigarette, formal woman w/folding fan 40.00
Kimball Cigarette, man & woman in library 40.00
Lavine Cleaner, actress Maude Granger 5.00
Lavine Cleaner, baby girl on swan w/product 6.00
Lavine Cleaner, diecut paint palette & monkey 6.00
Lavine Cleaner, diecut paint palette & owl 6.00
Leader Sewing Machine, girl losing balloon 6.00
Levi Strauss, closed front & open front jumper jackets 225.00
Levi Strauss, engineer's coat & combination coat 225.00
Levi Strauss, man w/cigar, spring bottom pants 225.00
Levi Strauss, miner w/shovel & pick, blouse, overall 225.00
Magnolia Ham, Alpine mountain scene w/climbers 10.00
Maxwell's Prepared Gypsum Paint, Black painter w/brush 30.00
Mayflower Baking Powder, sick bird, boy on hat 8.00
Merchant's Gargling Oil, monkey & Darwin rhyme 20.00
Merchant's Worm Tablets, woman & 2 children 20.00
Mrs Pott's Sad Iron, 3 Black angels 40.00
National Yeast, girl hugging tree 6.00
New Home Sewing Machine, girl w/basket of roses 6.00
New Home Sewing Machine, lion family w/machine 7.00
Niagara Corn Starch, girl w/cat 6.00
Niagara Fire Insurance, water falls scene 35.00
Otis Bros Haymaker Mowing Machine, bl & wht 35.00
Payson's Ink, 2 boys w/oversz ink package 35.00
Plimpton Hoes, bl & wht hoe w/partial hdl 20.00
Poor Man's Torches, bl & wht, 2 kids & 3 wolves 15.00
Price's Baking Powder, 2 water nymphs, red flower 9.00
Quaker Ranges, woman playing golf 25.00
Sea Foam Yeast, saluting boy soldier 6.00
Sedgwick Fence & Gate, horse & wagon going by fence 35.00
Singer Sewing Machine, native-costumed women, 1903 ......8.00
Soapine Soap, man on telephone pole 6.00
Sporting Life Publishing Co, boy & old man reading 35.00
Sporting Life Publishing Co, newsboy selling paper 35.00
Spotted Fawn Tobacco, Gem City Tobacco Works, fawn 40.00
Standard Sewing Machine, boy w/girl in wheelbarrow 7.00

The Ensign, theatre production, Trent affair, 2 ships 35.00
Trymby & Rehn Furniture, living room 20.00
Tufts' Arctic Soda, bear family drinking soda 45.00
White Sewing Machine, boy & girl w/broken sled 7.00
Wilson Packing Corned Beef, tree cutter w/girl 9.00

Advertising Dolls and Figures

Whether your interest in ad dolls is fueled by nostalgia or strictly because of their amusing, often clever advertising impact, there are several points that should be considered before making your purchases. Condition is of utmost importance; never pay book price for dolls in poor condition, whether they are cloth or of another material. Restoring fabric dolls is usually unsatisfactory and involves a good deal of work. Seams must be opened, stuffing removed, the doll washed and dried, and then reassembled. Washing old fabrics may prove to be disastrous. Colors may fade or run, and most stains are totally resistant to washing. It's usually best to leave the fabric doll as it is.

Watch for new dolls as they become available. Save related advertising literature, extra coupons, etc., and keep these along with the doll to further enhance your collection. Old dolls with no marks are sometimes challenging to identify. While some products may use the same familiar trademark figures for a number of years (the Jolly Green Giant, Pillsbury's Poppin' Fresh, and the Keebler Elf, for example) others appear on the market for a short time only and may be difficult to trace. Most libraries have reference books with trademarks and logos that might provide a clue in tracking down your doll's identity. Children see advertising figures on Saturday morning cartoons that are often unfamiliar to adults, or other ad doll collectors may have the information you seek.

Some advertising dolls are still easy to find and relatively inexpensive, ranging in cost from $1.00 to $100.00. The hard plastic and early composition dolls are bringing the higher prices. Advertising dolls are popular with children as well as adults. For a more thorough study of the subject, we recommend *Advertising Dolls with Values* by Myra Yellin Outwater (Schiffer). Our advisor for this category is Jim Rash; he is listed in the Directory under New Jersey. Values are for dolls in near mint condition; be sure to discount prices for soil, missing parts, wear, or damage of any type.

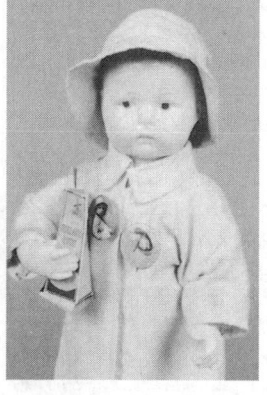

Uneeda Biscuits, boy with composition head and limbs, cloth body, original clothes, molded-on black boots, holds original box and Golden Anniversary pin (1948), 15", EX, $300.00.

A&W Great Root Bear, brn plush, 1975, 13", from $20 to 35.00
Adams Black Jack, rabbit, cloth litho, ca 1930, 11" 75.00
Alka Seltzer, Speedy, vinyl bank, 5½" 300.00
Am Federal Savings & Loan, Uncle Sam, cloth litho, 1976, 14" 8.00
Am Rice & Food Mfg, Cook's Teddy Bear, cloth litho, 1927, uncut .65.00
Archie Comics, Archie, cloth litho, early 1970s, 18" 10.00
Arkadelphia Milling Co, Dolly Dimple, cloth litho, 17" 55.00
Aunt Jemima Pancake Flour, Aunt Jemima, cloth litho, 1910, 15" .150.00

Aunt Jemima Pancake Flour, Diana, cloth litho, Davis Milling, 1910 .125.00
Bear Brand Hosiery, Papa Bear, cloth litho, 1930s, 9" 50.00
Beaver Enterprises, beaver, plush, 1959, 12" 10.00
Betty Crocker Products, Betty Crocker, cloth litho, 13" 28.00
Big Boy, plastic, 1974-78, 10" 10.00
Bird's Eye Frozen Foods, Mike, cloth litho, 1953, 11" 15.00
Borden, Elsie, vinyl & aqua plush, 1950s, 15" 90.00
Campbell Soup Co, boy, vinyl, Bicentennial premium, 10" 50.00
Campbell Soup Co, boy & girl, vinyl, 1970s, 9", MIB, pr 200.00
Chiquita Brand, Chiquita Banana, cloth litho, 1944, 10" 20.00
Close-Up Toothpaste, Dumbo, plastic, Disney/Dakin, 8" 20.00
Country Kitchen Restaurants, Country Boy, cloth litho, 1975, 24" ..12.00
Cream of Wheat, Chef, cloth litho, 1-pc legs, 1930, 20" 125.00
Diaparene/Sterling Drug Co, Diaparene Baby, vinyl, 1980, 5" 75.00
Domino Sugar, Domino Bear, plush, 1975, 15" 7.00
Dutch Boy Paint, Dutch Boy, cloth w/mask face, 1953, 15" 20.00
Eskimo Pie Corp, boy, cloth litho, 1975, 15" 25.00
Franklin Life Ins, Uncle Ben, cloth litho, 1970s, 12" 12.00
General Mills, Trix Playmate rabbit, vinyl, 1977, 9" 35.00
Gerber Products, Gerber Baby, Sun Rubber, 1954, 12" 100.00
Green Giant, Giant, gr vinyl, Product People, 9½" 75.00
Herald Press, old-fashioned girl, cloth litho, 1971, 16" 9.00
Hood Dairies, Harry Hood, vinyl, 1981, NM+ 75.00
Humble Oil (now Exxon), tiger pillow, cloth litho, 1960s, 11x11" ...6.00
IGA Stores, Tablerite Kid, cloth litho, 12" 9.00
Jack Frost Sugar, Jack Frost, cloth litho, 1975, 15" 35.00
Junior Mints, Fonz, cloth litho, Henry Winkler face, 1976, 16" ..15.00
Kellogg's, Goldilocks, cloth litho, 1925, 14" 45.00
Kellogg's, Tony the Tiger, plush fabric, 16" 35.00
Kelly Services, Kelly Girl, cloth litho, yarn hair, 1978 ....15.00
Lee Uniforms, Buddy Lee, cowboy outfit, hard plastic 450.00
Libby, Libby doll, cloth litho, Mattel, 1974, 14" 35.00
Long John Silver's, Long John Silver, cloth litho, 1972, 17" 7.00
Maxwell House Coffee, bear, brn plush w/shirt & night cap, 1971 ...10.00
McDonald Corp, Hamburgler, cloth litho, mk, 1972, 15" 10.00
McDonald Corp, Ronald McDonald, cloth litho, 1971, mk 8.00
Mr Bubble, bath soap container, pk plastic, 10" 40.00
Nabisco, Master ZuZu clown, compo/cloth, w/cookie box, 1915 ...375.00
Nabisco Chips Ahoy, girl in bl dress/hat, vinyl, 4½", NM+ 20.00
Orange Plus, orange plush toy, rnd figure w/plastic eyes & hat 15.00
Pacific Power & Light, Col Watt, cloth litho, 1973, 15" 15.00
Peter Pan Ice Cream, Peter Pan, cloth litho, 1972, 8" 20.00
Pillsbury, Pillsbury Doughboy, cloth litho, 1972, 11" 35.00
Pine Sol, bear, fur fabric, sitting, 1978, 15x15" 25.00
Play Doh, boy doll, cloth litho, Rainbow Craft Inc, 1969 ....20.00
Quaker Oats, Cap'n Crunch, hard plastic bank, 7½" 75.00
Shakey's Pizza, Shakey Chef, fabric litho, 18" 30.00
Squirt, Squirt Boy, squeeze vinyl, 1961, 6", very rare, M 450.00
Star-Kist, Charlie the Tuna, plush, premium, 1983, NM 40.00
Star-Kist, Charlie the Tuna w/arms up, squeeze vinyl, 1973, 8", MIB ..175.00
Tango Orange Drink, Tango VooDoo, vinyl, MIB 55.00
Tastykake Bakeries, baker, cloth litho, 13" 15.00
Travelodge, Sleepy Bear, squeeze vinyl, 1970s, 5½", M 45.00
Vigortone, pig, cloth litho, 17" 15.00

African Art

African art does not consist of a single class of objects. Rather, these often powerful images and objects are carved by many varying African tribes and groups across the central continent; each item represents specific cultural and spiritual functions and meanings. Many kinds of materials are used including wood, metal, fiber, ivory, and bone. Large numbers of these items are now being produced and sold to the tourist trade, but 'authentic' African art is generally considered to consist of objects which were used in cultural and/or religious activities. The items listed here are authentic, in good condition, without provenance, and considered to be of average aesthetic quality. Scott Nelson, a collector of African art, is our advisor; his address is listed in the Directory under Washington, D.C.

Basket, Nigeria, open, fiber w/cowrie shells, 8x10" 125.00
Beads, trade, ceramic, string of 20 ....100.00
Bracelet, Ashanti, bronze, knobs 30.00
Cloth, Kuba, geometric design, 18" sq 175.00
Comb, Ashanti, bird's head surmount, 4" 200.00
Container, Luba, gourd, wooden figural stopper 260.00
Container, Warega, ivory tusk, 15" 500.00
Divination board, Yoruba, animals, 20" dia 475.00
Doll, Ewe, pnt figure, 5" 175.00
Doll, Mossi, abstract human figure 275.00
Door, Dogon, granary, human figures, 26" 1,500.00
Drum, Hemba, geometric designs, 22" 275.00
Figure, Baule, standing female, 14" 250.00
Figure, Dogon, crouched male, 10" 650.00
Figure, Yoruba, pnt Colonial, 12" 175.00
Goldweight, Ashanti, bronze turtle 125.00
Hat, Kuba, fiber, blk pnt 175.00

Headdress, Bamana, Tchiwara (antelope), horizontal, $475.00.

Photo courtesy Scott Nelson

Headrest, Luba, supporting human figure, 5" 375.00
Heddle pulley, Senufo, bird surmount, 5" 275.00
Ibejis, Yoruba, 9", pr 375.00
Knife, Kuba throwing, str blade, 14" 125.00
Lock, Bamana, door, 2 figural surmounts, 14" 575.00
Mask, Bamana, N'Tomo, 14" 275.00
Mask, Dan, human face, 15" 375.00
Mask, Dogon, Kanaga, 26" 800.00
Mask, Karumba, polychrome, antelope, 21" 475.00
Mask, Pende, helmet, female initiation, 12" 675.00
Maske, Pende, human face, 8" 275.00
Pendant, Yoruba, ivory human figure, 4" 800.00
Pipe, Cameroons, elephant, brass, 14" 275.00
Ring, Dogon, bronze, horse & rider 275.00
Slingshot, Baule, animal head, 5" 85.00
Stool, Lega, human figural supports, 13" 475.00
Whisk, Yoruba, human figure, wood & horsehair, 12" 275.00

Agata

Agata is New England peachblow (the factory called it 'Wild Rose') with an applied metallic stain which produces gold tracery and dark blue mottling. The stain is subject to wear, and the amount of remaining stain greatly affects the value. It is especially valuable (and rare) on satin-finish items when found on peachblow of intense color. Caution! Be sure to use only gentle cleaning methods.

Currently rare types of art glass have been realizing erratic prices at auction; until they stabilize, we can only suggest an average range of values. In the listings that follow, examples are glossy unless noted otherwise. A condition rating of 'EX' indicates that the stain shows a slight amount of wear. Our advisors for this category are Betty and Clarence Maier; they are listed in the Directory under Pennsylvania. See also Green Opaque.

Bowl/lady's spittoon, flared scalloped neck, EX mottling, 5½" ...**600.00**
Celery vase, sqd/scalloped rim, M mottling, 6½" **950.00**
Cruet, NM mottling **2,000.00**
Pitcher, sq rim, sparce mottling, 6¼" **725.00**
Pitcher, water; sqd spout, allover mottle, 7", from $3,100 to ...**3,700.00**
Toothpick holder, 3-corner rim, 2" **625.00**

Tumbler, EX color and mottling, 3¾", from $600.00 to $750.00.

Photo courtesy Betty
and Clarence Maier

Tumbler, whiskey; EX mottling, 2½" **175.00**
Tumbler, scattered bl spots, 3¾" **400.00**
Vase, lily; EX color & mottling, 7" **950.00**
Vase, lily; subtle decor, 7" **345.00**
Vase, scalloped top, M mottling, 6½x3½" **1,200.00**
Vase, waisted tricon rim, M mottling, 3½" **1,600.00**

Agate Ware

Clays of various natural or artificially dyed colors combined to produce agate ware, a procedure similar to the methods used by Niloak in potting their Mission Ware. It was made by many Staffordshire potteries from about 1740 until about 1825.

Bowl, brn stained w/bl, ca 1750, sm rim chips, 5¼" **1,380.00**
Bowl, brn w/bl to cream, sm rprs, 1750s, 4" dia **575.00**
Bowl, cream, brn & rust, scalloped rim, ca 1750, 5¾", NM **1,600.00**
Jug, cream; mask & paw ft, foo lion finial, rpr lid, 1750s, 6⅝" .**1,600.00**
Jug, cream; pear shape, 3 mask & claw ft, minor rstr, 3¼" **2,185.00**
Mug, rust & cream, ca 1750, 3" **1,100.00**
Spoon tray, shaped rim, flared sides, ca 1750, 5½" **635.00**

Akro Agate

The Akro Agate Co., founded in 1914 primarily as a marble maker, operated in Clarksburg, West Virginia, until 1951. Their popular wares included children's dishes, powder jars, flowerpots, and novelty items along with the famous 'Akro Aggies.' Much of their glass was produced in the distinctive marbleized colors they called Red Onyx, Blue Onyx, etc.; solid opaque and transparent colors were also produced. Most of the wares are marked with their trademark, a crow flying through the letter 'A' holding an Aggie in its beak and one in each claw. Other marks include 'J.P.' on children's pieces, 'J.V. Co., Inc.,' 'Braun & Corwin,' 'N.Y.C. Vogue Merc Co. U.S.A.,' 'Hamilton Match Co.,' and 'Mexicali Pickwick Cosmetic Corp.' on novelty items. In

1936 Akro obtained the molds from the Balmer-Westite Co. of Weston, West Virginia. Westite produced a similar line of products for several years. Their ware is drab in color when compared to Akro and is generally unmarked. The embossed Westite logo does appear occasionally on the bottoms of some pieces. Westite is commonly accepted as a companion collectible of Akro.

For more information we recommend *The Collector's Encyclopedia of Children's Dishes* by Margaret and Kenn Whitmyer, available at your local bookstore. Our advisor for miscellaneous Akro Agate is Albert Morin; he is listed in the Directory under Massachusetts.

Chiquita

Cup, baked-on colors, 1½" **7.50**
Cup, gr opaque, 1½" **6.00**
Saucer, baked-on colors, 3⅛" **3.00**
Set, cobalt transparent, 12-pc, MIB **125.00**
Set, cobalt transparent, 16-pc, MIB **150.00**
Sugar bowl, gr opaque, 1½" **7.00**
Sugar bowl, opaque colors other than gr, 1½" **18.00**
Teapot, gr opaque, w/lid, 3" **18.00**

Concentric Rib

Creamer, sm, gr or wht opaque, 1¼" **8.00**
Set, sm, gr or wht opaque, 10-pc, MIB **60.00**
Set, sm, gr or wht opaque, 8-pc, MIB **45.00**
Sugar bowl, sm, gr or wht opaque, 1¼" **10.00**
Teapot, sm, opaque colors other than gr or wht, 3⅜" **35.00**

Concentric Ring

Cereal, lg, any opaque color, 3⅜" **22.00**
Cup, lg, any opaque color, 1¼" **30.00**
Plate, sm, any opaque color, 3¼" **8.00**
Plate, sm, bl marbleized, 3¼" **22.00**
Saucer, sm, any opaque color, 2¾" **3.50**
Set, sm, solid opaque colors, 16-pc, MIB **175.00**
Sugar bowl, lg, any opaque color, w/lid, 1⅜" **35.00**
Teapot, sm, cobalt transparent, 3⅜" **50.00**

Interior Panel, Stippled Interior Panel

Cereal, lg, azure bl, 3⅜" **30.00**
Creamer, lg, topaz transparent, 1⅜" **22.00**
Creamer, sm, azure bl, 1¼" **32.00**
Cup, sm, bl & wht, 1¼" **28.00**
Cup, sm, gr lustre, 1¼" **14.00**
Cup, sm, pk lustre, 1¼" **12.00**
Cup, sm, pumpkin, 1¼" **20.00**
Plate, lg, yel opaque, 4¼" **10.00**
Plate, sm, pk lustre, 3¾" **6.00**
Plate, sm, red & wht, 3¼" **12.00**
Plate, sm, yel opaque, 3¾" **9.00**
Set, lg, bl & wht, 21-pc, MIB **500.00**
Set, lg, topaz transparent, 21-pc, MIB **225.00**
Set, sm, pk lustre, 16-pc, MIB **175.00**
Sugar bowl, lg, yel opaque, w/lid, 1⅞" **50.00**
Sugar bowl, sm, azure bl, 1¼" **35.00**
Sugar bowl, sm, pk lustre, 1¼" **27.00**
Sugar bowl, sm, topaz, 1¼" **20.00**
Teapot, lg, lemonade & oxblood, w/lid, 3¾" **85.00**
Teapot, lg, topaz transparent, w/lid, 3¾" **40.00**
Teapot, sm, topaz transparent, w/lid, 3⅜" **25.00**

J.P. (Made for J. Pressman Company)

J.P. (Made for J. Pressman Company), Little Mother Pastry Set, MIB, $250.00.

Photo courtesy Margaret and Kenn Whitmyer

Creamer, lg, lt bl transparent or crystal, 1½" 32.00
Cup, lg, lt bl transparent, 1½" 25.00
Plate, lg, gr transparent, 4¼" 15.00
Set, lg, baked-on color, 17-pc, MIB 125.00
Set, lg, gr or brn transparent, 16-pc, MIB 350.00
Sugar bowl, lg, lt bl transparent or crystal, 1½" 32.00
Teapot, lg, lt bl or crystal, w/lid, 2¾" 50.00

Miss America

Creamer, forest gr, 1¼" 65.00
Cup, wht w/decal, 1⅝" 50.00
Plate, decal or forest gr, 4½" 45.00
Saucer, forest gr, 3⅝" 15.00
Saucer, wht 15.00
Set, wht w/decal, 17-pc, MIB 650.00
Sugar bowl, forest gr, w/lid 80.00
Teapot, wht, w/lid 85.00
Teapot, wht w/decal, w/lid, 3¼" 140.00

Octagonal

Cereal, lg, beige or pumpkin, 3⅜" 20.00
Creamer, lg, dk bl, closed hdls, 1½" 12.00
Creamer, sm, any opaque color, open hdl, 1¼" 16.00
Cup, lg, lemonade & oxblood, closed hdl, 1½" 25.00
Cup, lg, pumpkin, closed hdl, 1½" 20.00
Plate, sm, lime gr, 3⅜" 8.00
Plate, sm, yel, 3⅜" 8.00
Set, lg, dk bl, 21-pc, MIB 160.00
Set, lg, gr or wht, 21-pc, MIB 160.00
Set, lg, lemonade & oxblood, 21-pc, MIB 450.00
Sugar bowl, lg, beige & pumpkin, closed hdl, w/lid, 1½" 18.00
Tumbler, sm, any opaque color, 2" 12.00

Raised Daisy

Creamer, sm, yel, 1¼" 50.00
Plate, sm, bl, 3" 14.00
Saucer, sm, yel, 2½" 10.00
Teapot, sm, gr, no lid, 2⅜" 35.00
Teapot, sm, yel, no lid, 2⅜" 45.00
Tumbler, sm, yel, 2" 27.00

Stacked Disc

Creamer, sm, gr or wht, 1¼" 12.00
Cup, sm, any opaque color other than gr or wht, 1¼" 14.00

Cup, sm, wht, 1¼" 6.00
Plate, sm, any opaque color other than gr or wht, 3¼" 5.00
Saucer, sm, gr or wht, 2¾" 3.00
Set, sm, gr opaque, 21-pc, MIB 145.00
Tumbler, sm, any opaque color other than gr or wht, 2" 14.00

Stacked Disc and Interior Panel

Cereal, lg, any solid color, 3⅜" 25.00
Creamer, lg, cobalt transparent, 1⅜" 32.00
Creamer, sm, bl marbleized, 1¼" 40.00
Cup, lg, cobalt transparent, 1⅜" 27.50
Cup, sm, gr transparent, 1¼" 22.00
Plate, lg, any solid color, 4¾" 12.00
Plate, lg, cobalt transparent, 4¾" 15.00
Plate, sm, gr transparent, 3¼" 8.00
Set, lg, any solid color, 21-pc set, MIB 370.00
Set, sm, bl marbleized, 8-pc, MIB 275.00
Set, sm, cobalt transparent, 16-pc, MIB 290.00
Sugar bowl, sm, bl marbleized, 1¼" 45.00
Teapot, lg, cobalt transparent, w/lid, 3¾" 75.00
Teapot, lg, gr transparent, w/lid, 3¾" 55.00
Tumbler, sm, gr transparent, 2" 14.00

Stippled Band

Creamer, lg, azure transparent, 1½" 35.00
Creamer, sm, amber transparent, 1¼" 30.00
Cup, sm, gr transparent, 1¼" 8.00
Cup, sm, topaz transparent, 1¼" 7.00
Plate, lg, gr transparent, 4¼" 6.00
Plate, sm, amber transparent, 3¼" 6.00
Saucer, sm, amber transparent, 2¾" 2.50
Set, lg, gr transparent, 17-pc, MIB 165.00
Set, sm, amber transparent, 16-pc, MIB 145.00
Sugar bowl, lg, azure transparent, w/lid, 1½" 55.00
Sugar bowl, lg, gr transparent, w/lid, 1½" 35.00
Teapot, lg, amber transparent, w/lid, 3¾" 40.00
Teapot, sm, amber transparent, w/lid, 3⅜" 22.00

Miscellaneous

Photo courtesy Albert Morin

Flowerpots, Plain Band, any color, #298, $12.00 each.

Ashtray, Hotel Edison, orange 125.00
Ashtray, Hotel Lincoln, gr 95.00
Ashtray, leaf, gr/wht 12.00
Ashtray, lg & heavy, any color 95.00
Ashtray, oxblood, hexagonal 65.00
Ashtray, oxblood, sq 28.00
Ashtray, rectangular, no tab, any color 185.00
Ashtray, Rotary, blk 45.00
Ashtray, Victory Star, rare 300.00
Basket, bl/wht, 1-hdl, rare 450.00

Basket, bl/wht, 2-hdl 45.00
Bell, bl 75.00
Bell, yel, rare 400.00
Bowl, gr, ftd, lg 425.00
Bowl, Graduated Dart, blk, #320 ....200.00
Bowl, orange, tab-hdld, #321 ....65.00
Candlesticks, orange, 3¼", pr 400.00
Cornucopia, bl/wht, #765 ....18.00
Flowerpot, gr, #1308 ....200.00
Flowerpot, ivory, #1307 ....450.00
Flowerpot, orange, #1310 ....225.00
Flowerpot, Ribs & Flutes, marbleized, #307 ....48.00
Flowerpot, Ribs & Flutes, orange, #296 ....30.00
Flowerpot, Thumbpot, bl, #290 ....35.00
J Vivaudou, apothecary, pk, #329 ....145.00
J Vivaudou, mortar & pestle, blk 35.00
J Vivaudou, puff box, pk, rare 250.00
Jardiniere, Graduated Dart, orange, #306 ....80.00
Jardiniere, Narrow Ledge, gr, #314 ....45.00
Jardiniere, Ribs & Flutes, bl, #306CF 75.00
Knife, grid style, pk transparent, #739 ....95.00
Lamp, bl, 3-pc 150.00
Lamp, marbleized, 5-pc 95.00
Marble box, Popeye #116, yel box 1,250.00
Marble box, tin, #150 ....350.00
Marble box, 100 #00 glassies 200.00
Planter, factory decor, #654 ....45.00
Planter, Japanese, orange 450.00
Planter, Lily, #658 ....24.00
Powder jar, Apple, gr 375.00
Powder jar, Mexicali, bl/wht 75.00
Powder jar, Ribbed, blk 65.00
Vase, Graduated Dart, gr, tab hdls, #317 ....85.00
Vase, Graduated Dart, wht, #312 ....145.00
Vase, Ribs & Flutes, yel, #311 ....195.00
Westite, ashtray, blk, hexagonal 75.00
Westite, bud vase, marbleized, #310 ....275.00
Westite, flowerpot, marbleized, #301 ....65.00
Westite, Japanese planter, gr/wht 250.00

Alexandrite

Alexandrite is a type of art glass introduced around the turn of the century by Thomas Webb and Sons of England. It is recognized by its characteristic shading, pale yellow to rose and blue at the edge of the item. Although other companies (Moser, for example) produced glass they called alexandrite, only examples made by Webb possess all the described characteristics and command premium prices. Amount and intensity of blue determines value. Our advisors for this category are Betty and Clarence Maier; they are listed in the Directory under Pennsylvania.

Wine, blue to purple rim (intense colors), amber body, stem, and base, 4½x2½", $2,500.00.

Photo courtesy Betty and Clarence Maier

Finger bowl, Honeycomb, crimped/ruffled, 3¾", +underplate .2,200.00
Punch cup, 2¾x2¼" 600.00
Toothpick holder, Honeycomb, bulbous w/hexagonal rim, 2½" ..2,200.00
Tumbler, juice; 6-panel bowl, wafer base, EX color, 3" 985.00
Vase, Honeycomb, waisted crimp top, flanged rim, 4¼" 900.00
Vase, mushroom shape w/wide flange, EX color, 2½x4½" 1,600.00
Vase, Optic Honeycomb, ovoid w/flared ruffled rim, 4¼" 1,250.00
Wine, purple rim (average color), amber body, stem, base, 4½" ..1,100.00

Almanacs

The earliest evidence indicates that almanacs were used as long ago as ancient Egypt. Throughout the Dark Ages they were circulated in great volume and were referred to by more people than any other book except the Bible. *The Old Farmer's Almanac* first appeared in 1793 and has been issued annually since that time. Usually more of a pamphlet than a book (only a few have hard covers), the almanac provided planting and harvesting information to farmers, weather forecasts for seamen, medical advice, household hints, mathematical tutoring, postal rates, railroad schedules, weights and measures, 'receipts,' and jokes. Before 1800 the information was unscientific and based entirely on astrology and folklore. The first almanac in America was printed in 1639 by William Pierce Mariner; it contained data of this nature. One of the best-known editions, Ben Franklin's *Poor Richard's Almanac,* was introduced in 1732 and continued to be printed for twenty-five years.

By the 19th century, merchants saw the advertising potential in a publication so widely distributed, and the advertising almanac evolved. These were distributed free of charge by drug stores and mercantiles and were usually somewhat lacking in information, containing simply a calendar, a few jokes, and a variety of ads for quick remedies and quack cures.

Today their concept and informative, often amusing, text make almanacs popular collectibles that may usually be had at reasonable prices. Because they were printed in such large numbers and often saved from year to year, their prices are still low. Most fall within a range of $4.00 to $15.00. Very common examples may be virtually worthless; those printed before 1860 are especially collectible. Quite rare and highly prized are the Kate Greenaway 'Almanacks,' printed in London from 1883 to 1897. These are illustrated with her drawings of children, one for each calendar month. See also Greenaway, Kate.

1861, Benjamin Franklin, EX 20.00
1871, AL Scovill & Co Farmers' & Mechanics', 5x8", EX 15.00
1872, Family Christian, 60-pg, 4¾x7¾", EX 10.00
1872, Vinegar Bitters, 48-pg, 5½x8", VG 12.00
1874, Family, 32-pg, 4½x7½", VG 8.00
1878, Centaur, EX 25.00
1879, Maine Farmer's, EX 15.00
1884, Shaker, mc cover, 32-pg, NM 48.00
1889, Washington Life Ins Co, 49-pg, 6x8" 22.50
1894, Agricultural..., Lancaster PA, EX+ 20.00
1898, Old Farmer's, 48-pg, 5x7½" 7.50
1910, Bucklens, 33-pg, 7x9", VG 10.00
1913, Park & Pollard Co Year Book, 48-pg, 5x7" 8.00
1915, Marshall's, 48-pg, 3¼x5", EX 10.00
1917, Metropolitan Life Ins, 32-pg, 5½x7¾", VG 5.00
1919, Ayers American, EX 12.50
1927, Swamp Root, 33-pg, 6x8½", EX 15.00
1932, Crusader's, 64-pg, 6x9", G 5.00
1933, Dr Miles, 32-pg, 6x9½", EX 8.00
1936, Telephone, AT&T, 32-pg, 7x10", MM 50.00
1937, Dr Miles, EX 30.00
1938, Uncle Sam's, 60-pg, 6x9", EX 10.00
1941, Dr Miles, 32-pg, 6x9½", EX 5.00

1950, Journal Bulletin, 310-pg, 5x7", EX 9.00
1956, Trail Blazers' Almanac & Pioneer Guidebook, NM 20.00

Aluminum

Aluminum, though being the most abundant metal in the earth's crust, always occurs in combination with other elements. Before a practical method for its refinement was developed in the late 19th century, articles made of aluminum were very expensive. After the process for commercial smelting was perfected in 1916, it became profitable to adapt the ductile, nontarnishing material to many uses.

By the late '30s, novelties, trays, pitchers, and many other tableware items were being produced. They were often handcrafted with elaborate decoration. Russel Wright designed a line of lovely pieces such as lamps, vases, and desk accessories that are becoming very collectible. Many who crafted the ware marked it with their company logo, and these signed pieces are attracting the most interest. Wendell August Forge (Grove City, PA) is a mark to watch for; this firm produced some particularly nice examples and upwardly mobile market values reflect their popularity with today's collectors. In general, 'spun' aluminum is from the '30s or early '40s, and 'hammered' aluminum is from the '50s.

For further information, refer to *Hammered Aluminum, Hand Wrought Collectibles*, by our advisor for this category, Dannie Woodard (listed in the Directory under Texas), and *Collectible Aluminum, An Identification and Value Guide* (1997 updated values), by Everett Grist.

Ashtray, sailboat on water, W August Forge, 4½" sq 20.00
Basket, ship, fluted/serrated rim, sq-knot hdl, Federal Silver, 9" ...25.00
Basket, tomato, tray w/serrated rim, sq-knot hdl, Everlast, 11" 10.00
Beverage set, hammered, 8 tumblers w/ 13" L hdld tray, unmk 35.00
Bookends, leaping bass w/water spray, Bruce Fox, 3x7" 185.00
Bowl, anodized, geometric, fluted/serrated rim, Kraftware, 2x11" .10.00
Bowl, bittersweet, notched rim, W August Forge, 1x5" 20.00
Bowl, dogwood, fluted/crimped rim, W August Forge, 2x7" 20.00
Bowl, plain spun (no pattern), flared rim, Kensington, 3½x11" 5.00
Buffet server, hammered, ribbon hdls/ft, tulip finial, R Kent 35.00
Buffet server/bun warmer, tulip legs, II Farberware, 8x9" 20.00
Butter dish, bamboo, bamboo finial, Everlast, 4x4x7" 10.00
Cake stand, shields band/serrated rim/ped ft, Wilson Metal, 8x12" .15.00
Candlesticks, beaded S-shape tulip form, II Farberware, 8", pr 45.00
Candy dish, bird-&-grapes side hdl on oval, M Bowman, 13" 15.00
Candy dish, 2 serrated leaves, twisted-loop hdl, Buenilum, 6x5" .10.00
Casserole, bamboo, bamboo finial on lid, no hdls, Everlast, 4x7" .10.00
Casserole, dogwood/butterflies, ring finial, w/insert, Armour, 10" ...50.00
Casserole, tulips, open floral/ribbon hdls, low ped, unmk, 6x8" ...10.00
Chocolate pot, mums, petal finial, Continental, 10" 85.00
Cigarette box, bittersweet, hinged lid, W August Forge, 1½x3x5" ..75.00
Compote, hammered, deep bowl w/rolled lip, ped ft, unmk, 5x6" .10.00
Crumb brush & tray, flowers w/ribbons on hammered ground, unmk .25.00
Dresser set, 2 glass dishes, tulip-&-ribbon lids/tray, R Kent 45.00
Hurricane lamp, 2 glass chimneys w/twisted hdl, Buenilum, 10x9" ...30.00
Ice bucket, acorn/leaves, cane-shaped hdls, Continental, 3x7" 15.00
Ice bucket, hammered w/fluted rim, barbell hdls, Everlast, 5x10" .15.00
Lazy Susan, glass inserts, Continental #1021 ....35.00
Lazy Susan, ivy, upturned rim, appl leaf hdls, low ped ft, unmk, 13" 10.00
Matchbox cover, shotgun/flying ducks/clouds, W August Forge ...75.00
Napkin holder, flowers/ribbon on fan shape w/4-leaf ft, unmk, 3½x6" ...15.00
Napkin holder, thistle, crimped edge, unmk, 4x2x6" 10.00
Nut bowl, flowers/leaves, ruffled/serrated rim, ped ft, Wilson, 7" ..10.00
Pitcher, bamboo, ice lip, rolled rim, Everlast, 8" 25.00
Pitcher, tulips, hammered, Rodney Kent, 10" 30.00
Plate, dogwood, W August Forge, 9" 30.00

Popcorn popper, ducks, W August Forge, 9" 75.00
Tidbit, mums, crimped edges, 2-tier, Continental, 9¼" 85.00
Tidbit, tulip spray, 2-tier, unmk, 10" 15.00
Tray, berry/leaf, Victorian ladies on china insert, Cromwell, 16" dia .45.00
Tray, bittersweet, notched rim, appl hdls, unmk, 12x21" 30.00
Tray, duck hunting scene, fluted rim, LA Hand Forge, 18" dia 85.00
Tray, goldfish, hammered rim w/beaded edge, unmk, 10x14" 45.00
Tray, hammered peach design, 16" dia 30.00
Tray, sandwich; crane/bamboo/hammered, appl hdls, Hand Forge, 9" ...30.00
Tray, sandwich; ducks in flight/hammered, oval, Everlast, 10x12" ..15.00
Tray, sandwich; tennis player, Hyman Blum, 10x16" 45.00
Umbrella stand, larkspur, W August Forge, 22" 285.00

AMACO, American Art Clay Co.

AMACO is the logo of the American Art Clay Co. Inc., founded in Indianapolis, Indiana, in 1919, by Ted O. Philpot. They produced a line of art pottery from 1931 through 1938. The company is still in business but now produces only supplies, implements, and tools for the ceramic trade.

Values for AMACO have risen sharply, especially those for figurals, items with Art Deco styling, and pieces with uncommon shapes. Our advisor for this category is Virginia Heiss; she is listed in the Directory under Indiana.

Bowl, bl gloss, oval w/sea horses, #127, 5½x10" 135.00
Bowl, bl gloss, rnd w/scroll hdls, #170, 2½x7" 150.00
Figurine, Chihuahua dog, bl gloss, #209, 2½x5" 175.00
Figurine, dancer (male), wht gloss, #208, 9½" 275.00
Figurine, penguin, wht matt, 7" 150.00

Vase, green, bulbous with stylized handles, #18, early mark, 9x9", $350.00.

Vase, bl matt, hdls, #4, 4¾" 50.00
Vase, blk matt w/buttresses, #27, 6" 150.00
Vase, cream w/bl & gr, stick form, #74, 8" 135.00
Vase, dk gr matt, kneeling nude hdls, #90, 8x10½" 750.00
Vase, gr & silver, #S-2, 3½" 40.00
Vase, lt gr matt, trumpet form, #164, 11x3" 140.00
Vase, med bl glossy mottle, rnd w/low sq relief panels, #98, 6" ...150.00

Amberina

Amberina, one of the earliest types of art glass, was developed in 1883 by Joseph Locke of the New England Glass Company. The trademark was registered by W.L. Libbey, who often signed his name in script within the pontil.

Amberina was made by adding gold powder to the batch, which produced glass in the basic amber hue. Part of the item, usually the top, was simply reheated to develop the characteristic deep red or fuchsia shading. Early amberina was mold-blown, but cut and pressed amberina was also produced. The rarest type is plated amberina, made by New

England for a short time after 1886. It has been estimated that less than 2,000 pieces were ever produced. Other companies, among them Hobbs and Brockunier, Mt. Washington Glass Company, and Sowerby's Ellison Glassworks of England, made their own versions, being careful to change the name of their product to avoid infringing on Libbey's patent. Prices realized at auction seem to be erratic, to say the least, and dealers appear to be 'testing the waters' with prices that start out very high only to be reduced later if the item does not sell at the original asking price. A lot of amberina glassware is of a more recent vintage — look for evidence of an early production, since the later wares are worth much less than glassware that can be attributed to the older makers. Generic amberina with hand-painted flowers will bring lower prices as well. Our values are taken from auction results and dealer lists, omitting the extremely high and low ends of the range. Our advisor is Debby Maggard; she is listed in the Directory under Ohio. See also Libbey.

Basket, amber ft & hdls, HP florals, New England, 9x4" 475.00
Basket, melon ribbed, thorn hdl w/star & berry prunts, 7x6" 325.00
Berry set, Daisy & Button, 7-pc, NM 500.00
Bottle, Swirl, amber cut/faceted stopper, 9½x3" 175.00
Bowl, Daisy & Button, sq, Hobbs, 2x7" 500.00
Bowl, Invt T'print, 3 amber scroll ft, squat/incurvate, 3½" 300.00
Bowl, Swirl, bl swirl bands, Mt WA, 2¾x4½" 300.00
Bowl, Venetian Dmn, appl amber rim, Mt WA, 3¾x9½" 950.00
Bowl, Venetian Dmn, EX color, 3-corner, 2¼x4½" 325.00
Celery vase, Flattened Hobnail, scalloped top, Mt WA, 6¾" 850.00
Cracker jar, Invt T'print, glass lid, bbl shape, att Hobbs, 8" 795.00
Cruet, Invt T'print, amber hdl & stopper, 5½" 650.00
Cruet, Invt T'print, invt goblet form, trifold rim, NE, 6¾" 850.00
Cruet, Swirl, invt goblet body, trilobe rim, 6" 535.00
Custard cup, Dmn Quilt, amber reeded hdl, EX color, 2¾" 200.00
Goblet, water; lt ribbing, lt red to amber, 6" 300.00
Mug, bbl shape on wafer ft, rope hdl, 4¾" 75.00
Nut dish, Daisy & Button, boat shape, Gillinder, 6" L 295.00
Pitcher, Daisy & Button, str sides, heavy, Hobbs Brockunier, 5" ...425.00
Pitcher, Invt T'print, amber reeded hdl, sq mouth, 7¾x7" 450.00
Pitcher, Invt T'print, low angular width, heavy, 8x8½" 485.00
Pitcher, Invt T'print, reverse color, crystal hdl, 7¾" 350.00
Pitcher, Invt T'Print, sq top, amber reed hdl, 4½" 325.00
Pitcher, milk; Invt T'print, amber reed hdl, sq mouth, NE, 6" 450.00
Pitcher, tankard; paneled, amber hdl, 4½" 400.00
Pitcher, tankard; paneled, amber reeded hdl, 6¾" 600.00
Punch cup, Dmn Quilt, amber reeded hdl, 2½" 130.00
Punch cup, fuchsia coloring, amber reeded hdl 120.00
Punch cup, pear shape, clear hdl, ribbed panel, 3¼" 95.00
Shakers, Invt T'print, cylindrical, 3½", pr 225.00
Spooner, Dmn T'print, bulb w/lg flared scalloped rim, Mt WA, 4" ..695.00
Sugar bowl, Invt T'print, sq mouth, amber reeded hdls, 4½" 450.00
Toothpick holder, Dmn Quilt, sq top, NE 475.00
Toothpick holder, Dmn Quilt, tricorner, NE, 2¼" 475.00
Tray, Daisy & Button, Hobbs Brockunier, 14" L 750.00
Tumbler, cut w/Russian pattern on sides & bottom, 3¾" 1,150.00
Tumbler, Dmn Quilt, NE, 3¾" 175.00
Tumbler, lt ribbing, amber reeded hdl, NE, 3¾" 375.00
Tumbler, Swirl, EX color, 3⅞" 150.00
Tumbler, Venetian Dmn, EX color, Mt WA, 4" 135.00
Vase, bottle form, 8" 125.00
Vase, Dmn Quilt, appl rigaree, dimpled sides, ruffled, NE, 5½" ...1,000.00
Vase, Hobnail, radiating amber ft, flattened sides, 8½x7" 225.00
Vase, Invt T'print, fuchsia rim & shoulder, 3x2" 350.00
Vase, lily; appl wafer base, EX color, 6¾" 700.00
Vase, lily; EX color, 10" 675.00
Vase, lily; flint, ca 1880s, 15" 800.00
Vase, lily; lt ribbing, NE, 8" 500.00

Vase, Swirl, trumpet shape, folded rim w/amber edge, 20" 750.00

Plated Amberina

Creamer, 3x4½" 5,000.00

Cruet, amber cut stopper, 7x3½", $5,000.00.

Mug, amber hdl 2,300.00
Pitcher, bulbous w/tricorn rim, dk amber hdl, 6¼" 10,000.00
Pitcher, tankard; amber hdl, 7" 12,000.00
Plate, ruffled, 6⅜" 1,300.00
Punch cup, EX color, 2¾" 2,450.00
Shade, for hanging lamp 10,700.00
Sugar bowl, amber loop hdls, 2" 5,500.00
Tumbler, lemonade; w/hdl, 4¾" 4,000.00
Tumbler, 4" 2,450.00
Vase, lav to red to yel, NE Glass, 3½" 3,200.00
Vase, slight swirl at 3-fold rim, 9½", from $4,000 to 5,000.00

American Bisque

The American Bisque Pottery operated in Williamstown, West Virginia, from 1919 to 1982. The company was begun by Mr. B.E. Allen and remained an Allen family business until its sale in 1982. Figural pottery was produced from approximately 1937 until about the time the pottery closed.

American Bisque pottery is often identified by the 'wedges' or dry-footed cleats on the bottom of the ware. Many cookie jar designs are unique to the American Bisque Company, such as cookie jars with blackboards and magnets, cookie jars with lids that doubled as serving trays, and cookie jars with 'action pieces' which show movement. American Bisque pieces are very collectible and are available in a broad variety of color schemes; some items are decorated with 22 – 24k gold. Many items are modeled after highly popular copyrighted characters.

For further information, we recommend *American Bisque, Collector's Guide With Prices*, by our advisor Mary Jane Giacomini; she is listed in the Directory under California.

Photo courtesy Ermagene Westfall

Cookie jars: Wilma Flintstone, marked USA, from $750.00 to $1,000.00; Fred Flintstone, marked USA, from $700.00 to $950.00. Both have been reproduced, Buyer Beware!

Ashtray, Marietta Modern, free-form, mk 715-A 20.00
Ashtray, State of Ohio shape, 5" 20.00
Bank, Attitude Papa, wht w/bl on top, unmk, 8½" 75.00
Bank, Chicken Feed, yel sack w/blk writing, unmk, 4½" 25.00
Bank, Cinderella, mk, 1950, 6½" 165.00
Bank, Cowboy Donald Duck, unmk, 7" 160.00
Bank, Dumbo, cream w/gold trim, yel belly, mk Walt Disney, 6¼" ...115.00
Bank, Figaro, gray, lt bl suspenders, unmk, 6¾" 75.00
Bank, Mr Pig, cream w/gr suspenders, Made by APCO, unmk, 6" ..30.00
Bank, Popeye, center stopper, full outline ft, unmk, 7" 450.00
Bank, Rainy Day Pig, unmk, 6¼x7½" 75.00
Bank, Roy Rogers & Trigger, unmk, 7½" 160.00
Bank, Sweet Pea, yel pajamas & bl hat w/blk bill, unmk, 8¼" 500.00
Cookie jar, Baby Bear, unmk 60.00
Cookie jar, Baby Elephant w/sailor cap, mk USA, 10¼" 115.00
Cookie jar, Bear & Beehive, Corner Cookie Jar #804 USA 425.00
Cookie jar, Blackboard Clown, #901, emb/stamped mk, 13¾" ...300.00
Cookie jar, Boots, USA #742 ....110.00
Cookie jar, Boy Pig, unmk 90.00
Cookie jar, Carousel, USA 175.00
Cookie jar, Cat, w/indented dots, mk USA 131A, 12¼" 85.00
Cookie jar, Churn Boy, mk USA, 11¾" 225.00
Cookie jar, Clown Bust (Pinkie Lee), incised USA, 10½" 375.00
Cookie jar, Cookie Barrel, USA 20.00
Cookie jar, Cookie Truck, USA 75.00
Cookie jar, Cow & Moon, #806 USA, rare 950.00
Cookie jar, Cowboy Boots, mk USA 742, 12½" 200.00
Cookie jar, cylinder w/bluebirds, unmk 35.00
Cookie jar, Dancing Elephant, unmk 150.00
Cookie jar, Davy Crockett in the Bushes, unmk, 11" 750.00
Cookie jar, Feed Sack, red cold pnt, mk USA, 9½" 85.00
Cookie jar, Gift Box, USA 225.00
Cookie jar, Girl/Boy Bear, turnabout, mk, 12½" 75.00
Cookie jar, Goofy Rabbit, USA 275.00
Cookie jar, Granny, mk USA, 12¾" 165.00
Cookie jar, Ice Cream Freezer, airbrushed, mk USA, 9¾" 250.00
Cookie jar, Jack-in-Box, USA 150.00
Cookie jar, Joe Carioca, mk, 12¾" 425.00
Cookie jar, Kitten, on quilted base, USA 135.00
Cookie jar, Kitten & Beehive, USA 60.00
Cookie jar, Little Mo (Mohawk Indian), unmk, 12", minimum ..3,000.00
Cookie jar, Magic Bunny, USA 125.00
Cookie jar, Majorette, unmk, 11¼" 250.00
Cookie jar, Milk Wagon, USA #740 ....125.00
Cookie jar, Moon Rocket, USA 325.00
Cookie jar, Pig w/Straw hat, USA 140.00
Cookie jar, Puppy, USA 70.00
Cookie jar, Recipe Jar, incised USA, 9½" 100.00
Cookie jar, Rubble's House (Flintstones), mk USA, 10" 750.00
Cookie jar, Sack of Cookies, USA 55.00
Cookie jar, Schoolhouse w/bell in lid, USA #741 ....70.00
Cookie jar, Seal on Igloo, USA 295.00
Cookie jar, Sentry, #743 USA 95.00
Cookie jar, Spool of Thread, thimble finial, USA 175.00
Cookie jar, Stern-wheeler w/bell in lid, USA 275.00
Cookie jar, Sweethearts (Umbrella Kids), USA #739 ....325.00
Cookie jar, Yarn Doll, unmk 150.00
Cookie/candy jar, Casper w/Lollipops, mk USA, 11¾", minimum ..1,500.00
Gravy boat, 22-24k gold, Genoe's lamp style, APCO, 5" 60.00
Grease jar, Churn, brn w/cold-pnt flower petals, unmk, 6½" 20.00
Lamp, Davy Crockett, w/orig paper shade, unmk, 7½" 225.00
Lamp, nursery; Happy Face Clock, unmk, 7¼" 55.00
Lamp, Thumper, mk, 6½" 150.00
Night light, Davy Crockett hunting a bear, 4½" 45.00

Night light, The Shoe, cream w/yel roof, Apco, unmk, 6" 45.00
Pitcher, apple form, mk USA, 6" 75.00
Pitcher, Santa Claus, unmk, 9¾" 350.00
Planter, Dalmatians, unmk, 5½" 32.00
Planter, Davy Crockett Powder Horn, unmk, 8" 60.00
Planter, Figaro, airbrushed, unmk, 6" 50.00
Planter, Happy Fish, mc, mk, 4¾" 25.00
Planter, Mare & Foal, unmk, 5¾" 32.00
Planter, rabbit in log, mc, unmk, 5¾" 24.00
Planter, Sailfish, unmk, 8x10½" 50.00
Planter, Southern Belle, unmk, 7½" 26.00
Planter, Thumper, mk Thumper, Walt Disney Productions, 6½" .65.00
Planter, Winter Couple, unmk, 7½" 30.00
Plate, Christmas tree, red cold pnt, 22-24k gold, unmk, 14½" 75.00
Shakers, Clowns, mk c APCO, 3½", pr 18.00
Shakers, Mickey & Minnie, unmk, 3½", pr 40.00
Teapot, lattice pattern, wedge-shaped ft, APCO, 7¼" 30.00
Vase, thistle motif w/gold trim, 2-hdl, circular ft, APCO, 5" 20.00
Wall pocket, Pluto w/Cart, mk c Pluto WDP, 6¾" 120.00

American Encaustic Tiling Co.

A.E. Tile was organized in 1879 in Zanesville, Ohio. Until its closing in 1935, they produced beautiful ornamental and architectural tile equal to the best European imports. They also made vases, figurines, and novelty items with exceptionally fine modeling and glazes. See also tiles.

Bookends, putti play w/rabbit, matt blk & silver, mk 325.00
Bowl, eagle on rock w/wings out at side, gr, high glaze, mk............285.00
Box, Oriental landscape, burnt orange, 2¼x7½x4¾", NM 300.00
Figurine, elephant, gunmetal on blk drip, 5½" 110.00
Inkwell, matt blk & silver, dbl, w/logo 255.00
Plaque, HP, pastel scene, 9x6", orig fr 325.00
Trivet, AETCo logo in center, 8-sided, mc, 6" dia 125.00
Vase, gr & brn gloss, 7", NM 100.00
Vase, red-brn semigloss, mk, sm flakes at base, 8" 325.00

American Indian Art

That time when the American Indian was free to practice the crafts and culture that was his heritage has always held a fascination for many. They were a people who appreciated beauty of design and colorful decoration in their furnishings and clothing; and because instruction in their crafts was a routine part of their rearing, they were well accomplished. Several tribes developed areas in which they excelled. The Navajo were weavers and silversmiths, the Zuni, lapidaries. Examples of their craftsmanship are very valuable. Today even the work of contemporary Indian artists — weavers, silversmiths, carvers, and others — is highly collectible. Unless otherwise noted, values are for items with no obvious damage or excessive wear (EX/NM). For a more thorough study we recommend *Arrowheads and Projectile Points*, *Indian Axes*, *Indian Artifacts of the Midwest*, and *Collector's Guide to Indian Pipes, Identification and Values*. All four have been written by our advisor, Lar Hothem; you will find his address in the Directory under Ohio.

Key:
bw — beadwork
dmn — diamond
E — Eastern
NE — Northeastern
p-h — prehistoric

S — Southern
s-s — sinew sewn
W — Western
x — cross

Apparel and Accessories

Before the white traders brought the Indian women cloth from which to sew their garments and beads to use for decorating them, clothing was made from skins sewn together with sinew, usually made of animal tendon. Porcupine quills were dyed bright colors and woven into bags and armbands and used to decorate clothing and moccasins. Examples of early quillwork are scarce today and highly collectible.

Early in the 19th century, beads were being transported via pony pack trains. These 'pony' beads were irregular shapes of opaque glass imported from Venice. Nearly always blue or white, they were twice as large as the later 'seed' beads. By 1870 translucent beads in many sizes and colors had been made available, and Indian beadwork had become commercialized. Each tribe developed its own distinctive methods and preferred decorations, making it possible for collectors today to determine the origin of many items. Soon after the turn of the century, the craft of beadworking began to diminish.

Bandolier, Blackfoot child's, tube w/mc bw, 1890s, 30x8" **200.00**
Belt, Athabascan, wht buckskin w/embr bluebird/floral, 1920s **50.00**
Belt, Crow, bw panel w/#16 cut beads, 1880s, 42" **150.00**
Belt, Flathead, full bw w/drop #16 cut beads, 1890s, 32x2½" **750.00**
Blouse, Navajo, velvet w/silver-button trim, sleeves, '30s, 50" **125.00**
Coat, Crow, wht buckskin w/bw & fringe, 1870s-80s, 38" L, EX ..**9,000.00**
Dress, Hopi, handwoven manta, blk w/yarn & 6 silver conchos, 40" ...**250.00**
Dress, Plateau child's, antelope hide w/bw & fringe, 1920s, 34" .**800.00**
Dress, Shoshone, tanned elk hide, fringed/floral bw, 38" **300.00**
Dress/manta, Hopi, blk w/dmn twill ends, good weave, 1920s, 54" ..**500.00**
Gauntlets, Plateau, mc floral bw on hide, 1930s, 14x6", EX **100.00**
Gauntlets, Shoshone, floral bw/fringe on buckskin, 13x7" **150.00**

Hat, Crow, reservation, beaded band, ca 1940, 7¼", NM, $400.00.

Jacket, Cree, floral bw front & bk, fringed, 1930s, EX **350.00**
Jacket, Ojibway, tanned buckskin w/bw & fringe, 1940s, med sz .**150.00**
Jacket, Shoshone, tanned buckskin, fringe/floral bw, 1950s, 62" .**275.00**
Leggings, Nez Perce lady's, full geometric bw, 1940s, 13x7" **100.00**
Leggings, Sioux, bw strip on tanned hide, fringe, 1920s, 30x10" ..**700.00**
Moccasins, Arapaho, s-s w/bw, mineral pnt, hard sole, 1870s, 10" ..**500.00**
Moccasins, Blackfoot, hide w/full bw toes, resoled, 1940s, 10" ...**100.00**
Moccasins, Cheyenne, bw at sole & toe on tanned hide, 1930s, 10" ..**150.00**
Moccasins, Cheyenne, bw on commercial leather, 1950s, 11" **150.00**
Moccasins, Cheyenne, lazy-stitched bw on hide, ca 1900, 9", VG .**250.00**
Moccasins, Cheyenne, mc bw on toe, parfleche soles, 1900s, 11" ...**550.00**
Moccasins, Cree, tanned buckskin w/floral bw toes, 1940, 11" ...**100.00**
Moccasins, Plains, full maple-leaf bw, mc on wht, 1950s, 9" **175.00**
Moccasins, Plateau, bw floral on hide, 1950s, 9" **125.00**
Moccasins, Plateau, high-tops w/floral/star bw, parfleche soles ...**150.00**
Moccasins, Sioux, full bw s-s rawhide soles, 1900s, 11" **550.00**
Moccasins, Sioux, full geometric bw on s-s buckskin, 1940, 10" .**200.00**
Moccasins, Sioux, lazy-stich mc bw on s-s hide, 1890s, 10" **1,050.00**
Moccasins, Sioux, mc geometric bw on hide, ca 1930, 11" **300.00**
Moccasins, Sioux, pine tree bw uppers, 1880s, 8" **550.00**
Moccasins, Sioux, quilled w/bw edging, coned tongues, 1890s, 10" .**1,400.00**
Moccasins, Sioux baby's, much bw, 1890s, 3" **175.00**
Moccasins, Woodlands, floral bw on smoke-tanned moose, 1920s, 9" .**100.00**

Rain sash, Hopi, wht w/tassels & fringe, 1960s, 114x8" **75.00**
Shirt, Crow medicine warrior's, w/medicine balls/ermine/etc, 1990s ..**1,000.00**
Shirt, Crow war; made for museum display, 20th C, lg **1,300.00**
Shirt, Sioux war; hide w/ochre stain, fringe/bw/hair drops, 20th C ..**750.00**
Vest, Apache, stylized star bw trim on hide, cloth lined, 1940s .**125.00**
Vest, Blackfoot, bw geometrics on buffalo hide, 1890s, 21x19" .**3,400.00**
Vest, Ojibway, ornate bw floral on blk trade cloth, 1900s, 22" ...**275.00**
Vest, Sioux child's, mc floral/bird bw on hide, 16x16", NM **2,000.00**
Vest, Sioux child's, teepee/star bw front & bk, 1985, 12x15" **375.00**

Arts and Crafts

Carving, Seri, big-horn sheep, ironwood, 1960s, 18x14x6" **50.00**
Cloth, Navajo, sand-painting memory, HP, 1940s, 27x40" **250.00**
Painting, Navajo, Appaloosa & Paint foals running, H Begay, 1970 ..**200.00**
Painting, Navajo, boy w/horse, dog, rainbow Yei, Begay, 13x17" .**300.00**
Painting, Navajo, dancers w/fire dance wands, Begay, 20x17" **650.00**
Painting, Navajo, 2 dancers w/Yei, Chee, 1970, 14x20" **200.00**
Sand painting, Navajo, Sweat House, 4 Yeis, 1960, fr, 24x24" **90.00**
Sculpture, Pueblo, lady w/long hair, ca 1950s, 16x9" **100.00**
Textile, Chimayo, dmn center, 3-color on wht, 1940s, 80x50" ...**115.00**
Watercolor, Hopi, kachina face & corn in bowl, Sumatzkuku, 7x9" ..**50.00**
Watercolor, Hopi, Qoqolo kachina, matted/fr, 1940s, 10x7" **55.00**

Bags and Cases

The Indians used bags for many purposes, and most display excellent form and workmanship. Of the types listed below, many collectors consider the pipe bag to be the most desirable form. Pipe bags were long, narrow, leather and bead or quillwork creations made to hold tobacco in a compartment at the bottom and the pipe, with the bowl removed from the stem, in the top. Long buckskin fringe was used as trim and complemented the quilled and beaded design to make the bag a masterpiece of Indian art.

Apache, bw w/whirling logs/heart/arrow on hide, 1900s, 12x6" .**250.00**
Apache, medicine, buckskin w/pnt decor & fringe, 1900 ....**125.00**
Apache, strike-a-lite, lightning decor, tin cones, 1870s, 5½" **625.00**
Arapaho, strike-a-lite, bw buckskin w/tin cones, 4x4½" **125.00**
Arapaho, strike-a-lite, geometric bw & tin cones, 1890s, 6x3" ...**500.00**
Arikira, medicine, buffalo scrotum w/bw & ochre, 1870s, 4x6" ..**200.00**
Blackfoot, medicine, hide w/red ochre & geometric bw, 1900, 6x4" .**225.00**

Cheyenne, hide 'strike-a-lite' bag with geometric designs and tin cone suspensions, ca 1890, 7x4", $700.00.

Cheyenne, hide w/full bw & tin cone dangles, 1900s, 8x4" **325.00**
Cheyenne, tobacco, bw on hide, fringe, 1900s, 21x3" **750.00**
Cree, flat type, full floral bw, 1920s, 5x4¾" **200.00**
Crow, belt pouch, contour bw w/#16 cut beads, 1890s, 6x6½" .**1,000.00**

Crow, parfleche, pnt geometrics, rectangular, 1910s, 7x11" 225.00
Flathead, floral bw on moose hide, drawstring, 1940s, 10x7" 200.00
Nez Perce, corn husk w/pictorial butterflies, 1880s, 21x16", NM ..2,200.00
Nez Perce, full bw V shape w/mc floral & fringe, 1920s, 5x7" 200.00
Ojibwa, loom beaded bandolier, 1890s, 6x14" 800.00
Plains, parfleche, buffalo hide w/pnt decor, 20th C, 14x13" 300.00
Plains, pouch, 4-point mc bw on tanned hide w/tin cones, 6" dia .90.00
Plateau, full contour bw w/old-time florals, 1910s, 9x7" 200.00
Plateau, parfleche, folded rawhide w/pnt geometrics, 1910s, 27x15" .200.00
Sioux, knife, full geometric bw on s-s hide, 1910s, 11x3" 400.00
Sioux, knife, traditional bw on parfleche, tin drops, 12" 100.00
Sioux, parfleche, geometrics, 20th C, 28x13", pr 1,000.00
Sioux, pipe, antelope hide, bw/quills/fringe, 1890s, 40x5" 2,250.00
Sioux, pipe, quillwork/drops/dangles/fringe, s-s hide, 1890s, 35" .1,050.00
Sioux, saddle, bw on elk hide w/fringe, s-s, 1880s, 14x85", NM 7,950.00
Sioux, Tipi bag, bw & quills, horsehair pendants, 1890s, 19x10" .1,500.00
Ute, strike-a-lite, geometric bw, s-s on buffalo, 1890s, 4x2" 375.00

Baskets

In the following listings, examples are basket form and coiled unless noted otherwise.

Apache, olla, blackened devil's claw on golden willow, 19½", minor stitch damage, $900.00.

Apache, mc stars, 1920s, 6x14" 175.00
Apache, San Carlos mc 4-point stars, half-dmns at rim, 1920s, 2x7" ..575.00
Apache, 4-point star/dmns/checkerboard half-dmns, 1930s, 2½x10" ..900.00
Apache, 5-point stars w/half-dmns at rim, 1940s, 2x6½" 200.00
Hopi, tray, Crow Mother 3-color design, 15" dia 300.00
Hopi, wicker, checkered design, unfaded, 1930s, 5x15" 300.00
Hopi, 3rd Mesa, bright geometrics, 1960s, 1½x10" 100.00
Klamath, burden, stair design in V shape, 1910, 13x15" 550.00
Klamath, dbl band, brn on tan, 1900s, 5x7" 85.00
Klamath, dbl serrated bands, w/weaver's photo (Bath), 1900s, 4x6" ..250.00
Mescalero Apache, water bottle, horsehair hdls, pitch covered, 7" 120.00
Mission, bowl, 2 rattlesnakes (1 brn/1 blk), ca 1900, 10x19" ..2,850.00
Mission, 5 human figures/geometrics, 1920s, 4x14" 650.00
Mono, serrated/alternating blocks, 1920s, 3½x8" 600.00
Paiute, bowl, concentric bands, dbl rim, 1900s, 2x12" 60.00
Panimint, radiating stair steps, rim ticking, 1930s, 5x10" 1,300.00
Papago, bowl, 6 human figures & cacti, 1930s, 4x15" 325.00
Papago, connecting whirling logs, w/lid, 1930s, 4x5" 150.00
Papago, duck figure, 1950s, lt damage to beak, 8x18" 50.00
Papago, olla, S geometrics, w/lid, ca 1950, 10x9" 130.00
Papago, skip stitch, hdls, w/lid, 1960s, 8x8" 25.00
Papago, storage, half-dmns, 1950s, 10x17" 125.00
Pima, boat shape, coyote tracks/chickens decor, 1930s, 8" L 185.00
Pima, bowl, spiral stair steps, willow/devil's claw, 1920s, 3x14" ..325.00
Pima, bowl, stair steps, 3x4" 60.00
Pima, grain storage, ca 1900, 23x26" 300.00
Pima, tight weave, flared sides, fret design, 1920, 4x5" 250.00
Pima, traditional maze decor in devil's claw, 1930s, 10x15", M .1,150.00

Pima, tray, fret pattern, EX patina, 1920s, 3x8" 650.00
Pima/Papago, Kaiha burden, wood/woven fibers, mini, 12" 750.00
Pit River, bowl, fine twined, stair steps on V design, 1900s, 9x11" .800.00
Pit River, redbud geometric motif, 1910s, 8x15" 1,350.00
Pomo, 3-point star, floating horseshoe design, 1900s, 1½x4" 525.00
San Carlos Apache, bowl, V design, mini, 2x3" 125.00
Tlingit, oblong w/openwork & triangular mc designs, 1910s, 3x7" .350.00
Tsimshan, sq root type w/horizontal Vs, w/lid, 1920s, 4x7" 350.00
Ute, wedding pattern w/12 faded points, 1940s, 13" dia 80.00
Washo, banded design, single rod, skip stitches, w/lid, mini 40.00
Washo, lg butterflies (rare), ca 1910, 10x30" 2,000.00
Washo, red swastikas, 1930s, 3x7" 200.00
Yavapai, star w/in star w/eagles/deer/tracks, 1940s, 3½x16" 3,750.00

Blades and Points

Relics of this type usually display characteristics of a general area, time period, or a particular location. With study, those made by the Plains Indians are easily discerned from those of the West Coast. Because modern man has imitated the art of the Indian by reproducing these artifacts through modern means, use caution before investing your money in 'too good to be authentic' specimens.

Adena, cream & tan flintridge, Robbins variety, Woodland, 4⅞" ..250.00
Benton, dull wht speckled chert, Archaic, KY, 5⅛x1⅝" 325.00
Clovis, wht Burlington chert, well fluted, MO, 2x¾" 150.00
Corner-notch, wht flint, serrated edge, Archaic, MO, 3⅛" 550.00
Dalton, wht Burlington chert, resharpened, Paleo, MO, 2⅝x1" .175.00
Hardin, gray flint w/dk swirls, Archaic, IL, 5x1⅛x⅜" 400.00
Hardin, tan chert, barbed, early Archaic, IL, 2¾" 110.00
Holland, lt tan flint w/specks, Late Paleo, MO, 3⅝x1¼" 350.00
Hopewell, wht & gold Flintridge, Mid-Woodland, 3½" 165.00
Jakie, orange chert, stemmed, Mid-Archaic, MO, 2⅛x1⅛" 50.00
Lanceolate, gray flint, stemmed shoulder type, Paleo, 4¼" 325.00
Lost Lake, banded hornstone, well made, Early Archaic, OH, 3" ..350.00
Snyders, orange & pk chert, Mid-Woodland, 2⅞" 185.00
Snyders, red chert, Mid-Woodland, 4x2½" 275.00
Stanfield, bl-gray flint w/purple spots, Archaic, KY, 4x2" 300.00
Turkey-tail, dk hornstone, early Woodland, IN, 6¼" 1,200.00

Ceremonial Items

Club, dance; Sioux, conical stonehead, wood/sinew hdl, 1890s, 19" .500.00
Collar, dance; Sioux, otter fur w/trade mirrors, 1900s, 64" 150.00
Dance stick, buffalo rib w/bw & badger ft, 20th C, 14x3" 50.00
Dance stick, sheep horn w/bw & fringed hdl, 20th C, 28x9" 235.00
Dress, dance; Apache, bl trade cloth w/tin-cone/wht cloth fringe ..100.00
Drum, Pawnee Lightning Society, ca 1900, 11" 600.00
Drum, Pueblo, wood w/pnt designs on hide covering, 1930s, 8x7" .150.00
Drum, Sioux, hide covered, sq hand type, 1920s, 15x14" 50.00
Drum, powwow; Sioux pnt head, ca 1900, 34" 250.00
Drum, Taos, cottonwood log w//hide-covered beads, hide top, 19x17" .110.00
Fetish, buffalo effigy, for hunting ceremony, 1930, 3x4" 150.00
Fetish, turtle umbilical cord type w/full bw, 20th C, 6x5" 225.00
Headdress, buffalo fur w/horns, pnt parfleche band, 20th C, 17x9" ..60.00
Headdress, Cheyenne, dyed turkey feathers, ermine drops, recent ..100.00
Kilt, dance; Santa Domingo, pnt canvas, hide trim, cone drops .900.00
Ladle, Plains, mtn sheep horn, for feasts, 1870s, 20x8" 600.00
Love flute, Cheyenne, cvd animal tone adjuster, pnt decor, 1940s 70.00
Mask, dance; Northwest Coast, cvd cedar, pnt features, 1960s, 10" ...350.00
Mask, dance; Northwest Coast, cvd/pnt wood, horsehair, 1950s, 11" .225.00
Moccasins, dance; Pueblo, bl w/brn trim, wht soles, cutouts, 10" ..55.00
Rattle, dance; Hopi, pnt mc swirls, 1960s, 11x5" 70.00
Rattle, dance; Sioux, turtle shell, bw/wrapped hdl, 20th C, 17" 50.00

Rattle, medicine; Crow, hide w/human face & horsehair, 1880s, 12" .700.00
Rattle, Navajo, pnt hide head, hdl w/horsehair drop, 1950s, 8" 75.00
Rattle, Navajo/Pueblo, gourd head, natural, cvd hdl, 1930s, 8" 55.00
Rattle, Sioux, turtle shell w/beaded hdl, ca 1985, 15x4" 30.00
Shield, pnt rawhide w/hanging feathers, 20th C, 18" dia 60.00

Dolls

Plains, hide bodies, wooden heads and hands, hide clothing with beadwork, braided hair, ca 1900, 10½", 11¼", $4,600.00 for the pair.

Apache, buckskin female, bw costume, human hair, 1930, 18x6" .600.00
Crow, hide body, trade cloth dress, drop earrings, 1870s, 8½" .1,600.00
Flathead, full bw buckskin outfit, beaded face, 1935, 8x5" 160.00
Hopi, Kachina, Antelope, cvd/pnt, Ramos, 1983, 22x9" 600.00
Hopi, Kachina, Corn Maiden, cvd/pnt wood, Numkena, 20" 125.00
Hopi, Kachina, cottonwood & mineral pnts, ca 1936, 8" 1,100.00
Hopi, Kachina, fur costume, ca 1930, 10x5", EX 350.00
Hopi, Kachina, Hemis, cvd/pnt, unsgn, 1983, 33x9" 85.00
Hopi, Kachina, Hoole w/bow & rattle, Espinoza, 1970, 17" 75.00
Hopi, Kachina, Morning style, bell in hand, on base, 1940s, 15x8" .125.00
Hopi, Kachina, Owl, traditional kilt, turtle rattle on leg, 10" 75.00
Hopi, Kachina, w/pine branch & rattle, ca 1970, 11" 95.00
Makah, basketry figural w/braids & bead earrings, 1950s, 7" 100.00
Navajo, traditional dress/jewelry, velvet blouse, 1950s, 22" 100.00
Pueblo, traditional hand-spun clothes, hide face, 1920s, 6", VG ..50.00
Shoshone, buckskin w/full bw, ca 1920, 8", EX 175.00
Storyteller, Acoma, female w/6 babies, mc, W Aragon, 1960s, 5½" ..200.00
Storyteller, Acoma, 4 babies, blk-on-red fish & bird decor, 6x6" ..65.00
Storyteller, Cochiti, singer style, 4 babies, M&L Trujillo, 9x6x4" ..250.00
Storyteller, Cochiti, 6 babies, Martha Arquero, 5x5" 150.00

Domestics

Blanket, camp; geometric design, fringe, 1920s, 66x64" 125.00
Blanket, dbl saddle; mc w/sawtooth border, 1920s, 50x32" 70.00
Blanket, Navajo, transitional butterfly design, 1910s, 57x79" 600.00
Blanket, Sunday saddle; commercial yarn, 1940s, 30x42" 100.00
Canteen, tobacco; Navajo, handwrought silver, 1900s, 2½" 100.00
Cradle, Apache, bw xs on yel hide, w/sun visor, mini, w/doll 350.00
Cradle, Apache, willow w/yel ochre buckskin cover, 1910s, 34x12" 450.00
Cradle, Athabascan, bw belt holds baby on mother's bk, 1900, 49x5" .800.00
Cradle, Wasco, hide-covered brd w/full bw, 1890s, mini, 6x3" 400.00
Cradle, willow w/yel-ochred canvas cover, 1930s, 31x12" 150.00
Cradleboard, Hupa, woven basketry, ca 1900, 26x10x4", VG 100.00
Mug, plainware, dog-head hdl, p-h, 4x2½" 95.00
Mug, Tularosa, trilobe, doe-head hdl, p-h, rstr, rare, 4x5" 475.00
Pillow, Iroquois, bw floral on velvet (lg beads), 1900s, 6x7" 75.00
Spoon, Plains, bent horn w/bird effigy bw hdl, 20th C, 11x4" 95.00
Spoon, Plains, buffalo horn, bird effigy bw hdl, 20th C, 9x3" 250.00

Jewelry and Adornments

As early as 500 A.D., Indians in the Southwest drilled turquoise nuggets and strung them on cords made of sinew or braided hair. The Spanish introduced them to coral, and it became a popular item of jewelry; abalone and clam shells were favored by the Coastal Indians. Not until the last half of the 19th century did the Indians learn to work with silver. Each tribe developed its own distinctive style and preferred design, which until about 1920 made it possible to determine tribal origin with some degree of accuracy. Since that time, because of modern means of communication and travel, motifs have become less distinct.

Quality Indian silver jewelry may be antique or contemporary. Age, though certainly to be considered, is not as important a factor as fine workmanship and good stones. Pre-1910 silver will show evidence of hammer marks, and designs are usually simple. Beads have sometimes been shaped from coins. Stones tend to be small; when silver wire was used, it is usually square. To insure your investment, choose a reputable dealer.

Belt, Navajo, wrought silver/coral conchos, 20th C, 42" 280.00
Belt, Navajo, 8 3" oval conchos, 9 silver butterflies, oval buckle ...400.00
Belt, silver conchos (16 pre-1900 US silver dollars), 1935, 40" ..250.00
Bolo, Navajo, cvd turq face set in coral/silver, 1970s, 4" 130.00
Bracelet, Navajo, early-style pawn pc w/gr turq, 1940s, 2½x1½" ...200.00
Bracelet, Navajo, oval turq & silver, 1975, child sz, 5x2" 110.00
Bracelet, Navajo, petrified wood cabochon in silver, 3-wire shank ..75.00
Bracelet, Navajo, silver w/lg free-form turq stone, 1970, 7½x4" ..150.00
Bracelet, Navajo, stamped silver w/gr turq cabochon, 1950s 90.00
Bracelet, Navajo, 9 gr turq cabochons w/stamped silver dots, 1940s .150.00
Bracelet, watch; Navajo, silver w/14 King Mine nuggets, 1960 .....75.00
Bracelet, Zuni, silver w/inlaid Kachina dancer, 1975, 6x2" 180.00
Bracelet, Zuni, turq & silver needlepoint type, 1980s, 6x3" 100.00
Breast plate, Crow, hairpipe w/new leather/beads, 20th C, 25x9" 200.00
Breast plate, Sioux, bone w/beads/coin suspensions, 1920s, 42" ...1,050.00
Breast plate, Sioux, fully quilled w/sm quilled band, 1940, 14x12" ...360.00
Buckle, Navajo, silver filled design w/turq, 1950s, 4x2½" 150.00
Buckle, Navajo, silver w/bl gem turq stone, 1975, 7x2" 75.00
Buckle, Zuni, turq & silver cluster, ca 1975, 3x2½" 80.00
Hair pc, Blackfoot, bw strip w/plaited hair, 1910s, 9" 600.00
Hair pc, Caddo, bow w/ribbon drapes, metal spot decor, 1900, 5x10" ..550.00
Hat band, 12 oval conchos made from quarters, ca 1960, 24" 80.00
Necklace, Navajo, bl Padre beads, silver/turq pendant 50.00
Necklace, Paiute, tube beads, loom bw pendant w/turkey design ..50.00
Necklace, Pueblo, spider web turq nuggets, 1-strand, 1980s 70.00
Necklace, Pueblo, turq nuggets, silver cross pendant 55.00
Necklace, Pueblo, 3 strands red branch coral, silver clasp, 1960s ..50.00
Necklace, Pueblo, 7 strands malachite heishi w/silver cone ends ..55.00
Necklace, Pueblo, 7-strand shell beads, p-h, 30" 275.00
Necklace, Santa Domingo, thunderbird pendant w/inlay on twine .175.00
Necklace, Santa Domingo, 1-strand graduated wht shell heishi, 1940s ..60.00
Necklace, squash blossom, silver dime beads/dollar appendages, 1935 .300.00
Necklace, squash blossom w/lg natural turq stones, 1940, 32" 180.00
Necklace, squash blossom w/single turq in Naja, 1935, 20" 375.00
Necklace, Zuni, 3-strand, turq fetishes on red heishi 100.00
Pendant/pin, Navaho, Old Pawn turq/silver cluster, 1940, 4¾" dia .175.00
Pendant/pin, Old Pawn, Bl Gem turq stone, 1940s, 5x2½" 95.00
Pin, Navajo, silver human head shape w/7 turq stones, 3x2½" 85.00
Roach, head pc of deer & porcupine hair, ca 1930, 13x7" 175.00
Squash, Navajo, 8-stone naja, 5 turq stones in blossom ea side ..225.00

Pipes

Pipe bowls were usually carved from soft stone, such as catlinite or red pipestone, an argilaceous sedimentary rock composed mainly of clay. Steatite was also used. Some ceremonial pipes were simply styled, while others were intricately designed naturalistic figurals, sometimes in bird or frog forms called effigies. Their stems, made of wood and often covered with leather, were sometimes nearly a yard in length.

Catlinite elbow bowl w/cvd bear effigy stem, 19th C, 19½" **1,000.00**
Glacial Kame, gr hardstone, tube type, IL, late Archaic **200.00**
Hupa, tubular, steatite & wood, ca 1900, ⅞" dia, 4¼" L **800.00**
Iroquois, human effigy, lt brn pottery, 1600-1700, 2½x3½" **850.00**
Mic-Mac, catlinite w/dot decor, 1650-1750, 2", from $500 to **700.00**
Midwest, banded stone, recumbent buffalo form, 20th C, 5x10" ..**85.00**
Pipe tomahawk, brass head, tacked wooden stem, 20th C, 23x8" ...**350.00**
Plains, catlinite L bowl w/EX patina, 1890s, 4x3" (bowl alone) ...**100.00**
Plains, catlinite T bowl w/bw on tacked wooden stem, 20th C, 14" .**110.00**
Plains, catlinite/pewter inlaid stone w/puzzle stem, 20th C, 31" **100.00**
Sioux, blk steatite T bowl w/cvd 3-pc steatite stem, 1985, 16" ...**225.00**
Sioux, catlinite L bowl, wood stem w/cvd animals, 1920s, 24x2x4" ...**325.00**
Sioux, catlinite T bowl w/fine twisted wooden stem, 1930s, 24" ...**175.00**
Sioux, cvd wood/catlinite, turtles/elk heads, 19th C, 28½" **3,800.00**
Sioux, hand-cvd catlinite w/twisted mc stem, 1870s, 37" **1,850.00**
Sioux, inlaid blk T bowl, quilled wooden stem, 1880s, 22x3½" .**1,500.00**
Sioux, T-bowl style w/lead inlay, rnd wood stem w/quill drop **75.00**

Pottery

Indian pottery is nearly always decorated in such a manner as to indicate the tribe that produced it or the pueblo in which it was made. For instance, the designs of Cochiti potters were usually scattered forms from nature or sacred symbols. The Zuni preferred an ornate repetitive decoration of a closer configuration. They often used stylized deer and bird forms, sometimes in dimensional applications.

Acoma, canteen, stylized water bird, 20th C, 10" **450.00**
Acoma, olla, mc decor, sgn, ca 1930, 10" dia **500.00**

Acoma, pot, stylized parrot decoration, 10" diameter, $350.00.

Acoma, seed jar, mc parrot, Jessie Garcia, 6½x10" **500.00**
Anasazi, bowl, blk on wht geometrics/lines, p-h, 6x11" **450.00**
Anasazi, bowl, Roosevelt blk lineation on wht, p-h, 3x7" **250.00**
Anasazi, effigy jar, dog-head hdl, minor rstr, p-h, 6½x7" **375.00**
Anasazi, olla, pnt geometrics, brn/yel, p-h, 10x12" **500.00**
Anasazi, pitcher, blk & wht curvilinear decor, p-h, 7x6" **200.00**
Anasazi, vessel, bird effigy, redware, p-h, no rstr, 4x5x3" **300.00**
Cahuilla, olla/jar, fire-clouded redware, hemispherical, 11x11" ..**275.00**
Chaco, duck pot, geometrics, blk on wht, rstr, p-h, 5x4½" **175.00**
Conchiti, effigy pot, 1900s, orig unrstr, 9x10" **800.00**
Hopi, bear paws, faded pnt, Nampeyo Daisy Hoover, 1950s, 8x8" ..**200.00**
Hopi, bowl, blk feathered arches on creamy orange slip, 7" dia ..**115.00**
Hopi, bowl, stylized design, Feather Woman, 1875, 4x8" **400.00**
Hopi, vase, stylized parrot, mc, T Burton, ca 1960, 6½x5" **50.00**
Mesa Verde, bowl, blk on wht bands, vegetal pnt, p-h, rpr, 3x6" ..**225.00**
Miracopa, jar, blk decor on red, 7" dia **150.00**
San Juan, bowl, red, no decor, ca 1910, 4x10" **60.00**
San Juan, bowl, tan & ivory decor on redware, 4½" dia **65.00**

Santa Clara, ashtray, pnt on polished blk, T Naranjo, 1940s, 2x8" ...**90.00**
Santa Clara, basket, blkware, rain clouds, F Naranjo, 1960, 7x5" .**70.00**
Santa Clara, bowl, blkware w/deep-cvd designs, Rose, 4¼" **120.00**
Santa Clara, box, blkware, geometrics, Reysita, 1950s, 2½x5" **150.00**
Santa Clara, cup & saucer, blkware, 1930s **75.00**
Santa Clara, jar, redware, mc decor, pencil sgn, 3½" **150.00**
Santa Clara, jar, wedding; blkware, dbl-spout, invt rainbow, 9½" ..**200.00**
Santa Clara, turtle, cvd, blkware, Guitierrez, ca 1975, 2x7" **100.00**
Santa Clara, wedding vase, blkware, ca 1900, 10x7½", EX **120.00**
Santa Domingo, pitcher, floral decor, dbl spout, ca 1920, 11" **150.00**
Tularosa, mug, blk-on-wht dog's head, no rstr, 1200s, 5x5" **400.00**
Zia, olla, bird & rainbow, blk/red on cream, Medina, 1980, 10x10" ..**300.00**
Zuni, pot, frog effigy, 4 frogs in relief, no rstr, 19th C, 6x6" **400.00**

Pottery, San Ildefonso

The pottery of the San Ildefonso pueblo is especially sought after by collectors today. Under the leadership of Maria Martinez and her husband Julian, experiments began about 1918 which led to the development of the 'black-on-black' design achieved through exacting methods of firing the ware. They discovered that by smothering the fire at a specified temperature, the carbon in the smoke that ensued caused the pottery to blacken. Maria signed her work (often 'Marie') from the late teens to the 1960s; she died in 1980. Today a piece with her signature may bring prices in the $500.00 to $4,500.00 range.

Bottle, blkware, w/stopper, Carmelita Dunlap, 1974, 11" **500.00**
Jar, blkware, feathers, Maric & Julian, 1925, 5x6" **1,600.00**
Olla, mc design (pre-blkware), ca 1920, 10x10" **200.00**
Plate, blkware, rain clouds, oblong, sgn Rose, 1950s, 5" L **100.00**
Plate, blkware, serpent, Marie & Santana, 1950-60, 15", EX ..**1,000.00**
Vase, wedding; blkware, serpent design, twin spouts, 1940s, 10x6" ..**150.00**

Rugs, Navajo

Central lozenge, Ganado Red, 1960s, 36x52" **250.00**
Central lozenge, soft weave, ca 1930, 46x74" **850.00**
Crystal (early) w/natural fishhook motif, 1935, 117x77" **2,000.00**
Geometric stepped terraces, 3-color on gray, 22x45" **125.00**
Geometrics in blk/wht/gray, fine weave, 1935, 36x47" **325.00**
Geometrics w/floating dmns, 4-color, 1930-40, 76x50" **550.00**
Natural wool w/connecting parallelograms, 1930s, 40x93" **385.00**
Serrated dmn w/floating half dmns, red/blk/wht, 1930s, 60x42" .**200.00**
Serrated zigzags w/floating dmns, 1940s, 66x38" **350.00**
Swallow tail border w/fishhooks & dmns, 5-color, 1970, 62x39" .**525.00**
Terraced geometrics, mc vegetal dye, 30x66" **250.00**
Vallejo stars in panel, multiple borders, 7-color, 51x84" **1,760.00**
Yei (4 figures) w/cornstalk, 1930s, 45x64" **200.00**
2 Grey Hills, geometrics, natural/vegetal dyes, 1970s, 48x26" **225.00**
2 Grey Hills, stair step border, natural/vegetal dyes, 60x39" **300.00**

Shaped Stone Artifacts

Bannerstone, bottle type, quartzite, Archaic, MO, 2¼x2" **1,100.00**
Bannerstone, butterfly type, banded slate, 6" W **2,000.00**
Bannerstone, hardstone, ridged-edge triangle, IN, 2½x1¾" **800.00**
Bannerstone, striped slate, tubular, IN, 2x4" **400.00**
Birdstone, banded slate, Late Archaic, 3¼x5" **3,000.00**
Boatstone, red quartzite, polished, Woodland, 4¼" **800.00**
Discoidal, Midwest, polished, concave dish ea side, 2x4" **125.00**
Gorget, banded slate, coffin shaped, Late Archaic, 5½" **500.00**
Gorget, hematite, Archaic, MO, 2½x1¾" **200.00**
Grinding stone, close-grained sandstone, basin: 11x16x3½" **85.00**
Pendant, blk hardstone, 21 tally mks at edges, 2⅛x1¼" **150.00**

Plummet, gr diorite, Archaic, MO, 1¾" **100.00**

Stoneware

Bowl, Diegueno, coastal stone, La Jollan type, p-h, 2½x7" **55.00**
Bowl, pecked coastal stone, La Jollan type, p-h, 2½x7" **35.00**
Pestle, Diegueno, knob-head pecked stone, p-h, 11" **65.00**

Tools

Adz, hardstone, grooved & polished, Archaic, IL, 3x8½" **495.00**
Adz, wht chert, Archaic, 2⅝x6½" **450.00**
Axe, gray-gr granite, ¾-groove, Archaic, 3¾x2¾" **135.00**
Axe, Hohokam, ¾-groove, pioneer-phase style, p-h, 11x3½" **550.00**
Axe, Hohokam, ¾-groove, pointed bit, p-h, 3x5" **80.00**
Axe, Midwest, ¾-groove, p-h, 4x7x2½" **100.00**
Axe, streaky hardstone, ¾-groove, 4¼" H **300.00**
Celt, gr slate, Archaic, IL, 2x4⅛x1⅛" **25.00**
Celt, Hopewell, speckled hardstone, IL, 2⅜x4⅜" **100.00**
Drill, lt gray flint, Archaic, IL, 3x1" **50.00**
Drill, tan chert, Archaic, IN, 3⅜" **125.00**
Drill/reamer, Thebes, lt gray flint, EX balance, IN, 3" **135.00**
Maul, blk hardstone w/overall polish, ¾-groove, 2¾x3¾" **100.00**
Maul, granite-like hardstone, full groove, Archaic, 5x3⅛" **100.00**
Pestle, polished stone, Archaic, minor damage, 5½x2¾" **150.00**

Weapons

Bow, Apache, pnt wood, museum quality, 1880s, 32x¾" **350.00**
Bow, cvd/pnt, from Klamath River, 1850, 52x3" **400.00**
Club, Eastern Sioux, ball head, hardwood w/EX patina, 1880s, 25" **500.00**
Club, Penobscot, root wood w/cvd heads/eagle heads, 1910s, 22" **250.00**
Club, Plains, egg-shaped stone w/hide-wrapped/bw hdl, 20th C, 25" **90.00**
Club, Plains, flop knob w/bw buckskin cover & hdl, 20th C, 36x2" **70.00**
Club, Plains, stone w/hide-wrapped hdl, Indian Wars era, 20x7" .**250.00**
Club, Plains, wooden gunstock club w/brass tacks, 20th C, 30x9" ..**125.00**
Club, stone w/bw on wood hdl, 1985, 22x4" **50.00**
Club, war; Iroquois, twisted wood, glossy patina, 1850s, 26" **225.00**
Club, war; Plains, horsehair wrapped wooden hdl, 1890s, 23x8" ..**50.00**
Mace, banded gr slate, unknown age, 10x4" **60.00**

American Painted Porcelain

The American china-painting movement can be traced back to an extracurricular class attended by art students at the McMicken School of Design in Cincinnati. These students, who were the wives and daughters of the city's financial elite, managed to successfully paint numerous porcelains for display in the Woman's Pavilion of the 1876 United States Centennial Exposition held in Philadelphia — an amazing feat considering the high technical skill required for proficiency, as well as the length of time and multiple firings necessary to finish the ware. From then until 1917 when the United States entered World War I, china painting was a profession as well as a popular amateur pursuit for many people, particularly women. In fact, over 25,000 people were involved in this art form at the turn of the 20th century.

Collectors and antique dealers have only recently 'discovered' American hand-painted porcelain, and they are just becoming aware of its history, beauty, and potential value. Until now, there was no all-inclusive source to turn to for information on this subject. *American Painted Porcelain: Collector's Identification & Value Guide* and *Antique Trader's Comprehensive Guide to American Painted Porcelain* by Dorothy Kamm are the culmination of a decade of research; we recommend them highly for further study.

Though American pieces are of high quality and commensurate with their European counterparts, they are much less costly today. Generally, you will pay as little as $10.00 for a 6" plate and less than $50.00 for many other items. Values are based on aesthetic appeal, quality of the workmanship, size, rarity of the piece and of the subject matter, and condition. Age is the least important factor, because most American painted porcelains are not dated. (Factory backstamps are helpful in establishing the approximate time period an item was decorated, but they aren't totally reliable.) See Clubs and Newsletters for information regarding *Dorothy's Kamm's Porcelain Collector's Companion,* each issue of which contains comprehensive material expounding on artists, patterns, dating, and functions of china.

Our advisor for this category is Dorothy Kamm; she is listed in the Directory under Florida.

Photo courtesy Dorothy Kamm

Whiskey set, ears of corn, signed, Surquist, ca 1903 – 1917, eight-piece, from $300.00 to $400.00.

Bonbon bowl, from $18 to **85.00**
Bowl, fruit; from $60 to **80.00**
Box, 4¾" dia, from $50 to **75.00**
Cake plate, from $35 to **65.00**
Candlestick, from $45 to **100.00**
Celery tray, from $35 to **75.00**
Creamer & sugar bowl, from $30 to **40.00**
Cruet, from $60 to **80.00**
Cup & saucer, bouillon; from $35 to **45.00**
Cup & saucer, from $25 to **35.00**
Ewer (depends on sz), from $100 to **150.00**
Gravy boat, from $55 to **75.00**
Hatpin holder, from $88 to **98.00**
Jam jar, from $30 to **50.00**
Jardiniere (depends on sz), from $65 to **375.00**
Mug, from $30 to **75.00**
Napkin ring, from $10 to **25.00**
Pin tray, from $30 to **50.00**
Pitcher, lemonade; from $175 to **225.00**
Plate, 6", from $10 to **35.00**
Plate, 8", from $35 to **65.00**
Salt cellar, from $20 to **40.00**
Shakers, pr, from $20 to **30.00**
Stein, from $75 to **95.00**
Tea or coffee set, ea set, from $175 to **250.00**
Vase, 6-7", ea, from $45 to **65.00**

Amethyst Glass

The term amethyst simply describes the rich color of this glassware, made by many companies both here and abroad since the 19th century.

Bottle, scent; Argus, 3 appl rings on neck/lip, no stopper, 6" **300.00**

Bowl, free-blown, slight kick-up base w/pontil, 3x9" 2,750.00
Candlestick, joined by wafer to base, B/K 4028, 8¼" 475.00
Decanter, 3-sided w/mc Deco enamel, spearhead stopper, 13⅝" ...175.00
Salt cellar, blown, appl ft, 2⅜" 275.00
Sugar bowl, blown, appl ft, galleried rim & lid, 8¼" 275.00
Tumbler, paneled, flint, 3½" 170.00
Vase, blown, urn shape, clear appl ft (worn), 13" 275.00
Vase, hex base, 3-printie bowl w/wafer, minor flakes, 10⅜" 2,975.00
Vase, hex waterfall base, panel & arch bowl w/ruffle, 11½" 1,500.00
Vase, Hobnail, bulbous, unmk, 8x19" 125.00
Vase, HP florals, wht w/gold, ped base, 13¼" 85.00
Vase, mc florals w/butterfly in flight, 10¾x4½" 225.00
Vase, mc florals w/sanded gold leaves, 4⅜x3¼" 88.00
Vase, sq base, 8-sided baluster stem, Bigler bowl w/ruffle, 11" .1,650.00
Vase, tulip; paneled, 8-sided bowl/petal rim, early, 9⅞" 1,300.00

Amphora

The Amphora Porcelain Works in the Teplitz-Turn area of Bohemia produced Art Nouveau-styled vases and figurines during the latter part of the 1800s through the first few decades of the 20th century. They marked their wares with various stamps, some incorporating the name and location of the pottery with a crown or a shield. Because Bohemia was part of the Austro-Hungarian empire prior to WWI, some examples are marked Austria; items marked with the Czechoslovakia designation were made after the war. All decoration described in the listings that follow is hand painted unless otherwise indicated. Our advisor for this category is Jack Gunsaulus; he is listed in the Directory under Michigan.

Ewer, emb gr leaves on irid body, unmk, 5½" 95.00
Ewer, forest scene, mc w/gold, dragon hdl, slim, mk, 9½" 450.00
Jar, duck reserves, fox finial, ftd ball form, 10½" 600.00
Jardiniere, vintage on mottled tan, cobalt trim, low hdls, 6½" ...250.00
Lamp, World on ball form base, rpl shade, 8½" 400.00
Mug, geometrics w/foxes on cobalt, sgn, 5¾" 500.00
Pitcher, owl on limb, yel, bl & tan, 10" 600.00
Pitcher, Scottish Rose, mc on ivory mottle, mks, 11½x8" 400.00
Planter, Deco style w/portrait reserve, 3 low hdls, 7" 500.00
Planter, ram's head hdl, 4-ftd, Deco decor, 3¾" dia 450.00

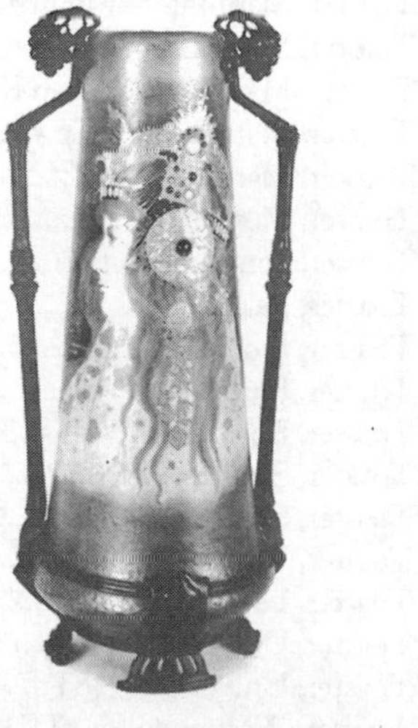

Vase, Art Nouveau lady with jeweled headdress, multicolor jewels and much gold on blue mottle with a large gold sun, bronze holder with berries and leaves, 23½x11", $3,500.00.

Vase, blk berries appl at rim & as ft on irid gold, sqd, 15" 1,500.00
Vase, cell clusters/'agate' cabochons on gilt, 4-lobe rim, 6" 1,200.00
Vase, Deco floral on tan w/bl rim, 6⅞" 200.00
Vase, Egyptian reserve, brn/tan/wht, bottle form, 13⅝" 450.00
Vase, Egyptian sgraffito w/pebbled turq, mk, 13" 500.00
Vase, floral on tan, 5½" 250.00
Vase, floral relief, peach on cobalt, open hdls, 4-ftd, 12" 350.00
Vase, floral reserves, mc on bl w/gold, 18", pr 220.00
Vase, lady (flowers in hair) reserve among trees, 14½" 1,400.00
Vase, lg flowers w/'agate' centers on ribbed gold, 12x14" 2,500.00
Vase, mc Deco-style goemetrics w/cobalt, sm hdls, 13½" 1,000.00
Vase, pate-sur-pate florals, twisted top, 7" 225.00
Vase, trees & gold birds encircle top, 10" 650.00
Vase, 3-D/emb children at shoulder, violet w/gilt, 10" 1,300.00

Animal Dishes With Covers

Covered animal dishes have been produced for nearly two centuries and are as varied as their manufacturers. They were made in many types of glass (slag, colored, clear, and milk glass) as well as china and pottery. On bases of nests and baskets, you will find animals and birds of every sort. The most common was the hen.

Some of the smaller versions made by McKee, Indiana Tumbler and Goblet Company, and Westmoreland Specialty Glass of Pittsburgh, Pennsylvania, were sold to food-processing companies who filled them with prepared mustard, baking powder, etc. Occasionally one will be found with the paper label identifying the product and processing company still intact.

Many of the glass versions produced during the latter part of the 19th century have been recently reproduced. In the 1960s, the Kemple Glass Company made the rooster, fox, lion, cat, lamb, hen, horse, turkey, duck, dove, and rabbit on split-ribbed or basketweave bases. They were made in amethyst, blue, amber, and milk glass, as well as a variegated slag. Kanawha, L.G. Wright, and Imperial made several as well. It is sometimes necessary to compare items in question to verified examples of older glass in order to recognize reproductions. Reproduction is continued today.

For more information, we recommend *Covered Animal Dishes* by our advisor, Everett Grist, whose address is in the Directory under Tennessee. In the listings below, when only one dimension is given, it is the greater one, usually length. See also Greentown.

Atterbury Duck, milk glass, mk Patent Apld For, 11" 245.00
Atterbury Hen on lacy base, milk glass w/amethyst head 295.00

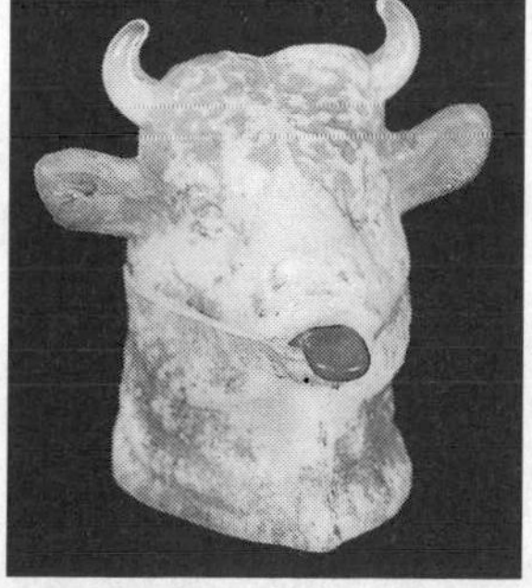

Bull's head, painted milk glass, tongue ladle, Atterbury, Pat July 17 1888, $250.00.

Chick in vertical egg, milk glass, 3¾" 125.00
Chicks on oblong basket, milk glass w/pnt details, 2¼x4¼" 325.00
Dog (Pekingese) on base, milk glass, att Sandwich, 4¾" 800.00
Dolphin, Sawtooth; milk glass, repro by Kemple or St Clair 75.00
Dolphin on sauce dish, milk glass, att Westmoreland, 7¼" 100.00
Donkey, pk, powder jar, att Jeannette 20.00
Duck, Pintail; on dmn basketweave base, Westmoreland, 5½" 55.00
Duck on cattail base, milk glass, unmk, 5½" 120.00
Duck soap dish, clear, pnt bill 15.00

Elephant w/rider, milk glass, Vallerysthal, 7" **350.00**
Fish, Entwined; milk glass, Aug 6 1889 in lid, 6" dia **170.00**
Fish on collared base, clear frosted, unmk **150.00**
Fox (ribbed) on lacy base, milk glass, dtd Aug 6 1889 in lid **175.00**
Hand & Dove, milk glass, rectangular, mk WG on base **110.00**
Hen, amberina, LE Smith, 5½" **45.00**
Hen, Str Head; clear w/HP details, unmk Imperial, sm **15.00**
Hen on basketweave base, milk glass, Vallerysthal, 2" **35.00**
Hen w/chicks, milk glass, pnt comb, ea pc mk McKee, 5½" **450.00**
Hen w/chicks, milk glass, unmk McKee, 5½" **200.00**
Lamb on picket fence, milk glass w/bl opaque head, Westmoreland ...**125.00**
Lion, British; milk glass, emb base, unmk, 6¼" **95.00**
Quail on scroll base, milk glass, unmk, 5½" **85.00**
Rabbit, Atterbury; bl opaque, glass eyes, dtd base, 6" **425.00**
Rabbit on wheat base, milk glass **350.00**
Robin on ped base, any color, mk WG **60.00**
Robin on ped base, bl opaque, unmk Westmoreland late repro **45.00**
Rooster, goofus on milk glass base, att Westmoreland, 5½" **65.00**
Rooster on wide-rib base, bl opaque, Westmoreland, 5¼" **85.00**
Setter on sq base, bl opaque, att Vallerysthal **210.00**
Swan, Block; clear frosted, Challinor Taylor, 7" **245.00**
Swan, Block; milk glass, Challinor Taylor, 7" **300.00**
Swan, clear frosted, Vallerysthal, 5½" **65.00**
Swan, milk glass, ea pc mk McKee, 5½" **450.00**
Swan, Raised Wing; milk glass, molded eyes, Westmoreland **150.00**
Turtle, amber transparent, lg **100.00**
Turtle, dk amber, knobby bk, LG Wright repro **45.00**

Appliances, Electric

Antique electric appliances represent a diverse field and are always being sought after by collectors. There were over one hundred different companies manufacturing electric appliances in the first half of the 20th century; some were making over ten different models under several different names at any given time in all fields: coffeepots, toasters, waffle irons, etc., while others were making only one or two models for extended periods of time. Today collectors and decorators alike are seeking those items to add to a collection or to use as accent pieces in a period kitchen. If you're especially interested in vintage fans, we recommend *The Collector's Guide to Electric Fans* by John Witt (Collector Books).

Always check the cord before using and make sure the appliance is in good condition, free of rust and pitting. The prices below are for appliances in good to excellent condition. Prices may vary around the country.

If you have any questions regarding antique appliances, feel free to contact our advisor, Jim Barker; he is listed in the Directory under Pennsylvania.

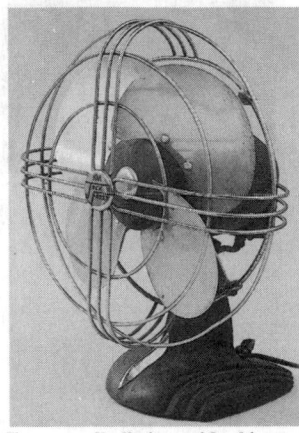

Fan, Jack Frost, oscillating, Art Deco styling, EX, from $25.00 to $35.00.

Photo courtesy Ken Hutchison and Greg Johnson

Blender, Knapp-Monarch Liquidizer, Deco style, 1940s, EX **55.00**
Blender, Waring, chrome base, heavy glass, EX **45.00**
Bottle warmer, Sunbeam, chrome w/plastic knobs, 1950s, 13" ...**95.00**
Coffee set, Krome Kraft, gold Bakelite hdls **140.00**
Coffee set, Royal Rochester #17152, EX **75.00**
Coffee set, Universal, #E817604, EX **95.00**
Coffee urn, Manning-Bowman, chrome & yel Bakelite, 14x11", VG .**70.00**
Fan, Century, #S-3, 12" blade, 1918, EX **150.00**
Fan, Emerson, #PI 241, 12" blade, 1899-1900, EX **350.00**
Fan, Emerson, #1510, 12" blade, 1906-09, EX **200.00**
Fan, Emerson, #21646, 12" blade, stamped steel hub, 1914-16, EX ..**75.00**
Fan, Emerson, #27666, 16" blade, 1919-22, EX **150.00**
Fan, General Electric, #265731, 12" blade, 1906, EX **175.00**
Fan, General Electric, #272036-1 Coin-op, 12" blade, 1915, EX ...**200.00**
Fan, General Electric, #342864, 12" blade, 1908, EX **175.00**
Fan, General Electric, #78X593, 12" blade, 1946, EX **55.00**
Fan, Gilbert, A-54, EX **95.00**
Fan, R&M, #1401, 12" blade, 1910, EX **150.00**
Fan, Singer 'Ribbon,' Bakelite, paper label, 10x6", M **175.00**
Fan, Westinghouse, #165366, EX **100.00**
Foot massager, Dr Scholl's, enamel & metal, chrome base **40.00**
Hot plate/stove, Wilwear, NP body coil-spring element, 1900s, 3" ..**20.00**
Mixer, Dormeyer, chrome, 1950s **85.00**
Mixer, General Electric, #49X390 ....**65.00**
Mixer, Hamilton Beach Model G, EX **50.00**
Mixer, Sear's Powermaster DeLuxe, cast-metal base, 1930s, EX ...**55.00**
Percolator, Hotpoint, #114517 ....**85.00**
Percolator, Keystoneware, chrome, rnd body on ped base, 12" ...**125.00**
Percolator, Manning-Bowman, NP w/Bakelite hdls, 12", EX **150.00**
Percolator, Universal, ftd, 12-cup **35.00**
Refrigerator, General Electric, coil top **300.00**
Toaster, AEG **85.00**
Toaster, Bee Vac #12, EX **165.00**
Toaster, Calkins Breadfaster **55.00**
Toaster, Edicraft **350.00**
Toaster, El Toasto, EX **150.00**
Toaster, Electrex **90.00**
Toaster, Fitzgerald Extra Fast **85.00**
Toaster, Hot Point #129T31 ....**175.00**
Toaster, Inventum **95.00**
Toaster, K&M Telematic **95.00**
Toaster, L&H Electrics #204 ....**75.00**
Toaster, Manning Bowman #1220 ....**85.00**
Toaster, Manning Bowman #1226 ....**150.00**
Toaster, Manning Bowman K-64 ....**45.00**
Toaster, Marion Flip Flop #66, M **85.00**
Toaster, Marshall Field **75.00**
Toaster, Mesco **650.00**
Toaster, Paragon Electric **300.00**
Toaster, Pelouze **250.00**
Toaster, Proctor #1405 ....**75.00**
Toaster, Proctor #1461 ....**45.00**
Toaster, Royal Rochester #13530, EX **75.00**
Toaster, Simplex #215 ....**95.00**
Toaster, Sunbeam T-9 ....**75.00**
Toaster, Toast-A-Lator **150.00**
Toaster, Universal E9410 ....**500.00**
Toaster, Universal E942 ....**65.00**
Toaster, Universal E948T **85.00**
Toaster, Westinghouse #TK14 ....**75.00**
Toaster, Westinghouse #TT-72 ....**40.00**
Toaster, Westinghouse #TT23 ....**65.00**
Waffle iron, Bersted, #212 ....**35.00**
Waffle iron, chrome w/Bakelite hdls, Deco styling, 1930s, EX **45.00**

Waffle iron, Electra Hot, #705 ....**55.00**
Waffle iron, Lady Hibbard on ceramic insert, Bakelite hdls **135.00**
Waffle iron, Thermax, #3931 ....**35.00**
Waffle iron, Westinghouse, #284186 ....**65.00**
Waffle iron, White Cross, #255 ....**40.00**

Arc-En-Ciel

The Arc-En-Ciel Pottery Company operated in Zanesville, Ohio, from 1903 until 1907. Artware was produced only until 1905, typically finished in a high lustre gold glaze. Though not always marked, those pieces that are carry the half-circle rainbow logo containing the company name.

Vase, gold lustre, emb stylized irises, 10", pr **150.00**
Vase, gold lustre, mk, 12" **220.00**
Vase, oak leaves at rim, stems form swirls, lt gr-bl, 6½" **330.00**
Vase, rose & gold irid, flared neck & base, #549, 6" **85.00**

Arequipa

The Arequipa Pottery operated from 1911 until 1918 at a sanitorium near Fairfax, California. Its purpose was two-fold: therapy for the patients and financial support for the institution. Frederick H. Rhead was the originator and director. The ware, made from local clays, was often hand thrown, simply styled and decorated. Marks were varied but always incorporated the name of the pottery and the state. A circular arrangement encompassing the negative image of a vase beside a tree is most common.

Examples are evaluated according to quality of artwork; size and shape are less important. Those done by Rhead himself are most desirable.

Vase, bl matt, cvd mermaid/fishes/plants, 4x6" dia **800.00**
Vase, floral, cvd/incised on gr & brn matt, sgn, EM, 8½" **225.00**
Vase, gr matt (suspended), bulbous bottom, #1051, 8" **750.00**
Vase, gr mottled matt, #1049, 3¾x3¾" **375.00**
Vase, hand-cut bell flowers under clear brn, 11x6¼" **700.00**

Argy-Rousseau, G.

Gabriel Argy-Rousseau produced both fine art glass and quality commercial ware in Paris, France, in 1918. He favored Art Nouveau as well as Art Deco and in the '20s produced a line of vases in the Egyptian manner, made popular by the discovery of King Tut's tomb. One of the most important types of glass he made was pate-de-verre. Most of his work is signed.

Items listed below are pate-de-verre unless noted otherwise.

Night light, 3 triangular panels w/flowers, iron base, 8" **7,000.00**
Nut bowl, vines/berries form irregular rim, 1½x3½" **1,550.00**
Plaque, 2 tigers amid rayed panels, 7x6" **5,750.00**
Vase, spiders/brambles, spherical, 4¾", EX **3,000.00**
Vase, thistle blossoms/leaves, rose on gray frost, 6" **3,400.00**

Art Deco

To the uninformed observer, 'Art Deco' evokes images of chrome and glass, streamlined curves and aerodynamic shapes, mirrored prints of pink flamingos, and statues of slender nudes and greyhound dogs. Though the Deco movement began in 1925 at the Paris International

Exposition and lasted to some extent into the 1950s, within that period of time the evolution of fashion and taste continued as it always has, resulting in subtle variations.

The French Deco look was one of opulence — exotic inlaid woods, rich material, lush fur and leather. Lines tended toward symmetrical curves. American designers adapted the concept to cover every aspect of fashion and home furnishings from small inexpensive picture frames, cigarette lighters, and costume jewelry to high-fashion designer clothing and exquisite massive furniture with squared or circular lines. Vinyl was a popular covering, and chrome-plated brass was used for chairs, cocktail shakers, lamps, and tables. Dinnerware, glassware, theaters, and train stations were designed to reflect the new 'Modernism.'

The Deco movement made itself apparent into the '50s in wrought iron lamps with stepped pink plastic shades and Venetian blinds. The sheer volume of production during those twenty-five years provides collectors today with fine examples of the period that can be bought for as little as $10.00 or $20.00 up to the thousands. Chrome items signed 'Chase' are prized by collectors, and blue glass radios and tables with blue glass tops are high on the list of desirability in many areas.

Those interested in learning more about this subject will want to read *Collector's Guide to Art Deco* by Mary Frank Gaston and *Affordable Art Deco, Identification & Value Guide,* by Hutchison & Johnson. See also Bronzes; Chase; Frankart; Jewelry; Lalique; Radios; etc.

Armoire, rosewood veneer, curved edge, lg rnd mirror, 75x67" ..**900.00**
Ashtray, ceramic, cobalt bl, Snufferette...Executive **45.00**
Ashtray, nude stands before sphere tray, gr-pnt metal, British, 11" ..**300.00**
Barometer, gr/yel Bakelite housing, rnd dial, 5x4" **120.00**
Bedroom suite, walnut veneer, leather drw fronts, Sikes, 5 pcs ..**1,000.00**
Book rest, yel Lucite, folding style for train travel, Pat 1938 ....**150.00**

Boudoir lamp, green-painted pot-metal seated figure beside amber crackle glass globe, marked Kelly Creations, 8x8½", $500.00 to $600.00.

Photo Courtesy Mary Frank Gaston

Box, ebonized walnut w/foil roundel & red-pnt plaques, 15" **450.00**
Box, jewelry; red/blk/wht geometrics on brass, 8x5" **75.00**
Box, powder; frosted seminude figural, unmk, 8½" **100.00**
Cabinet, drop front w/3 drw, 4 ebonized legs form U-base, 36" ..**400.00**
Clock, octagonal on ped, metal nude on platform ea side, 13" ...**200.00**
Coffee urn, chrome sphere w/yel Bakelite trim, Manning-Bowman, 16" ..**255.00**
Compote, brass, abstract dancers support bowl, 1930s, 9½" **350.00**
Desk, walnut, triangular w/kneehole, Fletcher Aviation, rfn ...**2,100.00**
Fan, ceiling; airplane engine & propeller form, chrome **1,400.00**
Figurine, girl w/fan-shaped skirt, chrome on marble base, Am, 4½" ..**145.00**
Figurine, nude w/arms around knees, chrome, onyx base, '20s, 4" **150.00**
Figurine, seminude female w/bowl, gr ceramic, Kent Art Ware, 11" .**175.00**
Figurine, Spanish woman, pot metal & ivorene on marble base, 10" ..**325.00**
Incense burner, Egyptian female w/arms out, Ronson, 1924 ....**425.00**
Incense burner, Egyptian lady figural, ceramic, Lisne, 6½" **400.00**
Incense burner, nude w/turban kneels by burner, Art Metal Works ..**350.00**
Lamp, draped nude w/tambourine, pnt wht metal/marble, Fayral, 21" .**2,200.00**
Lamp, nude (cast metal) sits on rock by glass ball, 7x9" **190.00**

Panel, Reubenstine & Nijinsky, inlaid woods/MOP, Barbier, 42x36" .1,150.00
Perfume vial, whippet figural, clear glass w/pnt details, 1920s, sm .125.00
Plaque, woman w/head on shoulder, chrome on bl glass, pr 75.00
Sconce, 5 mirror panels w/stencil rays in iron mts, 26", pr 2,100.00
Sculpture, after Le Verrlon, gr-patina nude holds onyx ball, 13" ...190.00
Table, coffee; veneer cube on blk plinth, sq glass top, VG 500.00
Table, zebra-grain exotic wood veneer, maple, Wenge (att), 58" L .2,200.00
Torchere, spun aluminum shade, blk columns, R Wright, VG, pr 425.00
Vanity, 3-drw, brass pulls, lg rnd mirror behind 250.00
Vase, bronze w/sterling flowers, cylindrical, Heintz, 13" 375.00
Vase, bud; bronze w/sterling leaves, Heintz, 12" 275.00
Vase, chrome urn form w/ribbed body, unmk, 9", pr 55.00

Art Glass Baskets

Popular novelty and gift items during the Victorian era, these one-of-a-kind works of art were produced in just about any type of art glass in use at that time. They were never marked. Many were not true production pieces but 'whimsies' made by glassworkers to relieve the tedium of the long work day. Some were made as special gifts. The more decorative and imaginative the design, the more valuable the basket. Our advisor for this category is Deborah Maggard; she is listed in the Directory under Ohio.

White opaque with pale blue crimped rim, pink twisted handle, Venetian, 6¼", $115.00.

Apricot w/gold mica stripes, dk pk int, str sq rim, hdl, 7x6" 325.00
Bl opal o/l w/2 rows Hobnail, melon ribs, ruffled, 11x11" 375.00
Bl satin, crimped rim, camphor thorn branch hdl, 6" 95.00
Cranberry, squat w/ruffled edge, clear hdl, 7x5" 250.00
Dk red to cherry to lt yel, wht int, pie-crust edge, 8x8" 265.00
Dmn Quilt, vaseline opal to pk, petal edge, twist hdl, 7x8" 275.00
Emerald w/clear petal top, lt swirling, clear twist hdl, 6¾" 110.00
Gr overshot to clear, emb pineapple melon ribs, sqd hdl, 7x5" ...285.00
Hobnail, pk opal w/vaseline twisted hdl, ruffled/4-lobed, 6x9" ...325.00
Hobnail, rose w/pk o/l, bl hdl/ft/rim, 12½x11½" 300.00
Hobnail, wht w/sky-bl int, 4-lobe amber ruffle/hdl, 7" 265.00
Pk o/l w/HP flowers, fold-down crimped rim, looped thorn hdl ..150.00
Pk w/wht ext, mc spatter/mica in bottom, shaped/crimped rim, 11" ...345.00
Spangle, apricot w/wht int, 2-lobe crimped rim, 7x6" 250.00
Spangle, bl o/l w/clear briar hdl, 9x5¾" 325.00
Spangle, med bl w/mica lines, crimped rim, twist hdl, 8x5" 185.00
Spangle, pk/yel/brn/gr w/silver, ruffled, twist hdl, 10x10x9" 325.00
Spangle, tan w/gold ext, cranberry int, amber ft/hdl, 7x4" 175.00
Spatter, bl/wht, ruffled, clear hdl, 5¼x4½" 80.00
Spatter, brn/gr on wht, clear thorn hdl, star rim, 7½x7" 275.00
Spatter, pk/yel on wht, clear loop hdl, 3-lobe ruffle, 8x5" 225.00
Spatter, royal bl/tan/opal, heart shape, crimped rim, 8x8½" 225.00
Spatter, wht (surface appl) on gr, trn-down brim, clear ft/hdl, 6½" 100.00
Spatter, wht in sapphire, bl thorn hdl, star-shape rim, 6x6" 225.00
Tomato, ribbed, crimped/ruffled, clear hdl, Sandwich, 6x7½" 250.00

Wht w/bl int, lobed body, 8-point crimped rim, loop hdl, 7x6" ..185.00

Art Nouveau

From the famous 'L'Art Nouveau' shop in the Rue de Provence in Paris, 'New Art' spread across the continent and belatedly arrived in America in time to add its curvilinear elements and asymmetrical ornamentations to the ostentatious remains of the Rococo revival of the 1800s. Nouveau manifested itself in every facet of decorative art. In glassware Tiffany turned the concept into a commercial success that lasted well into the second decade of this century and created a style that inspired other American glassmakers for decades. Furniture, lamps, bronzes, jewelry, and automobiles were designed within the realm of its dictates. Today's market abounds with lovely examples of Art Nouveau, allowing the collector to choose one or several areas that hold a special interest. Our advisor for this category is Steven Whysel; he is listed in the Directory under Florida. See also Bronzes; Galle; Jewelry; Loetz; Tiffany; Silver; specific manufacturers.

Brush, silver repousse foliage & figures, mk, set of 3 ....200.00
Buckle, silver w/lady's portrait & repousse floral, 2¼x1¾" 230.00
Buckle brooch, Nouveau repousse sterling front, 2¼x1½" 60.00
Candelabrum, bronze, 4-lily, organic base, Jessie Preston, 17" .3,500.00
Coal scuttle, floral-emb copper, brass shovel, English, VG 250.00
Curio, 2-door, EX mahog, leaded glass, marquetry, eng floral ..3,500.00
Firescreen, copper w/wrought iron, floral design, EX 550.00
Frame, cast bronze w/flower & lady's head, 12x8" 150.00
Jardiniere & ped, eng water lilies, EX 1,200.00
Jug, claret; periwinkle bl glass w/hinged pewter top/hdl, 13" 225.00
Lamp, cast metal, caramel slag shade w/acorn finial, 23x18⅜" ...425.00
Light, figural bronze bat over Loetz irid ball shade, 21" W 5,750.00
Tray, pewter, bees & berries, openwork, mk, 1½x9x7" 260.00
Vase, bud; metal circle of nudes support vaseline glass vase 200.00

Arts and Crafts

The Arts and Crafts movement began in England during the last quarter of the 19th century, and its influence was soon felt in this country. Among its proponents in America were Elbert Hubbard (see Roycroft) and Gustav Stickley (see Stickley). They rebelled against the mechanized mass production of the Industrial Revolution and against the cumulative influence of hundreds of years of man's changing taste. They subscribed to a theory of purification of the styles: that designs be geared strictly to necessity. At the same time they sought to elevate these basic ideals to the level of accepted 'art.' Simplicity was their virtue; to their critics it was a fault.

The type of furniture they promoted was squarely built, usually of heavy oak, and so simple was its appearance that as a result many began to copy the style which became known as 'Mission.' Soon factories had geared production toward making cheap copies of their designs. In 1915 Stickley's own operation failed, a victim of changing styles and tastes. Hubbard lost his life that same year on the ill-fated *Lusitania*. By the end of the decade the style had lost its popularity.

Metalware was produced by numerous crafts people, from experts such as Dirk van Erp and Albert Berry to unknown novices. Prices for Arts and Crafts accessories rose dramatically in 1988, but by the beginning of 1991 leveled off and (in some cases) dropped. Metal items or hardware should not be scrubbed or scoured; to do so could remove or damage the rich, dark patina typical of this period. Our advisor for this category is Bruce Austin; he is listed in the Directory under New York. See also Roycroft; Silver; Stickley; specific manufacturers.

Key: h/cp — hammered copper

Armchair, Limbert, English style, cut-out at top, caned seat/bk .1,200.00
Armchair, McKinley, Prairie School, caned bk, shaped supports .250.00
Ashtray, Kipp, h/cp, 4½" dia 100.00
Ashtray, van Erp, h/cp, w/copper liner, EX hammering, 8" dia ...200.00
Ashtray, van Erp, h/cp, 4" dia 75.00
Bookcase, Limbert #341, 3 mullioned doors, copper hdw, 46x48" ...4,250.00
Bookcase, Limbert #358, 2-door, overhang/bksplash, long corbels ..3,500.00
Bookcase, 2 glazed do w/intersecting dbl mullions, 54x42" 1,300.00
Bookends, Sorensen, acid-etched copper emb w/landscape, 5x3½" .475.00
Bookends, van Erp, h/cp, sm appl 'C,' 6x6" 400.00
Bookrack, Carence Crafters, copper w/English roses, '02, 12" 50.00
Bookrack, Limbert, shaped slab sides, 2 slats hold books, 12" 450.00
Bowl, Shreve, hammered silver w/riveted rim band, 1¼x8" 275.00
Bowl, van Erp, h/cp, partial cleaning, 3x8" 550.00
Bowl, Weiner Werkstatte, ceramic, stylized 4-color petals, 4x7" ...950.00
Bowl, WMF, hammered SP, petal top, 3 ball ft, 11" 150.00
Box, gesso finish w/mc moth on brn & gold, EX quality, 12½" L .300.00
Box, Old Mission Kopperkraft, h/cp, detailed design at top, 5", VG .250.00
Box, van Erp, copper w/3 attached coins, 1½x11x3½" 350.00
Cabinet, strong Oriental influence, 2 base drw, 56x61" 1,700.00
Candelabra, wrought iron, 5-light, tripod base, 60", pr 2,300.00
Candlesticks, brass, elaborately cut out, 3-light, 15x11", pr 400.00
Candlesticks, Pairpoint, SP, X-base w/emb leaves, 6", pr 250.00
Candlesticks, Tudric #0871, hammered pewter, lip flange, 7", pr ..400.00
Candlesticks, Zimmerman, h/cp, petal base/bobeche, 12x5", pr ..2,500.00
Chair, hall; shaped plank bk w/floral inlay, 43x19" 700.00
Chair, Morris; Limbert #517, slanted arms curve at bk, rstr ..2,600.00
Chair, rocking; Limbert #8036, 4-slat bk, shaped arms, VG 250.00
Chair, rocking; mahog, 7-spindle bk, thru-tenons, corbels 300.00
Chair, side; Crocker Co, 3-slat bk w/cutout ea corner, VG 100.00
Chair set, Limbert #1711, 2-slat bk w/arched top, 6 for 3,250.00
Chest, Limbert, oak, 2 sm drw:4, thru-tenons, rfn, 43x34" 1,600.00
China cabinet, Limbert #1365, arched doors, 1 mullion ea, 60x42" .4,750.00
China cabinet, Limbert #452, shelf/long corbel ea side, 58x44" .6,500.00
China cabinet, Prairie School, 2 doors w/slatted o/l, 62x45" ...1,200.00
Coat rack, oak, trestle base, 5 brass hooks, 70x45x20" 250.00
Compote, hammered pewter, 3-strap ped w/shallow bowl, 11" ...100.00
Cup, child's; Kalo, rabbit emb, inscribed/1916, 2x3¾" 500.00
Curtains, peach flowers/stems on tan linen, 3 66x33" panels, VG ...450.00
Daybed, Limbert #651, slanted headrest, cut-out sides, 74" 1,000.00
Desk, Limbert #701, ash, drop-front w/wood-burnt portrait, 44" .1,000.00
Dresser, Limbert, 2 sm drw over 2, thru-tenons, rfn, 36x40" 850.00
Easel, oak, dentil molding, geometric cutouts, flush tenons 1,200.00
File cabinet, Chas Rohlfs, ornate cvg, pull-out tray, 38x18" .11,500.00
Firescreen, walnut shield-form w/repousse copper panel, 34", VG .1,100.00
Footstool, Lakeside Craft Shop, leather top, drw, 11x20x13" 700.00
Jardiniere, ceramic, 4 panels ea w/mission scene, gr irid, 7" 300.00
Jardiniere, Turchin, h/cp, emb scalloped shoulder, 8½x12" 1,400.00
Lamp, amber glass & oak, pyramidal shade w/spindle border, 24" ..650.00
Lamp, Heintz, bronze, appl silver lilies; cut-out shade, 10x9" ...1,700.00
Lamp, Heintz, bronze w/dancers o/l; silk-lined cut-out shade, 12" ..700.00
Lamp, van Erp, h/cp w/rivets; mica/copper 18" shade, no mk ..5,000.00
Lamp, 16" molded shade pnt w/stylized floral; floral-emb std 800.00
Letter opener, van Erp, h/cp, flat/tapered w/wider hdl, 11½" 250.00
Light fixture, h/cp ceiling mt & 4 lanterns, all w/wht shades ..1,600.00
Light fixture, oak 14" pyramid fr w/cutouts & tan glass, +mts 240.00
Light fixture, 4 lanterns, glass in brass-wash fr/mts 1,000.00
Magazine stand, Limbert #304, arched apron, overcoat, 64x16" .1,200.00
Night stand, Lifetime #1203, 1-drw, shelf, rfn, 30x20x15" 600.00
Pedestal, Limbert Ebon-Oak, inset cane panels, rfn/rpl, 34" 950.00
Picture fr, linen w/Jugenstil design, 4-color, 7x7" 300.00
Plant stand, Limbert, 12" dia top, flaring legs, 33" 900.00
Plant stand, Limbert #269, 4 long corbels/X-base, 36", VG 1,200.00
Punch bowl, hammered SP, ftd, scalloped top, 10x18" 300.00

Rose bowl, Liberty, pewter, roses/stems/inscription, hdls, 10" 475.00
Sconce, Mackmurdo (att), brass w/emb flowers, 2-arm, 13x9½" ...200.00
Secretary, mullioned door, 3-drw w/mirror & desk, 57" 750.00
Settee, Limbert, 2-seat, open arms, narrow bk splats, 46" 1,300.00
Settle, Limbert, drop arms w/corbels, reuphl bk/seat, 68", VG ...1,200.00
Sideboard, Limbert #1366, 2-drw, plate rail, 40" 4,000.00
Sideboard, Limbert #362, mirror, 3-drw/4-door, 52x51" 3,000.00
Sideboard, Prairie School, 2 o/l doors+sm drw+2 doors, mirror ..800.00
Sofa, Lifetime, low bk/drop arms w/slats, leather pads, 83" 4,500.00
Stand, 3 slab sides w/keyed-through tenons, 27x15", G 100.00
Table, dining; Limbert #1459, 48" dia top, sq ped, extended ft ..1,600.00
Table, dining; Limbert #1494-B54, 4-post ped, 54" dia, +6 leaves .4,750.00
Table, lamp; Limbert #190, 22" dia top, X-stretchers 1,300.00

Table lamp, Limbert #376, reticulated mica shade, three wrought copper arms on hammered copper base, riveted pulls, 20x16", $3,500.00.

Table, library; Limbert, cut-out panels over side shelves 1,500.00
Table, library; Limbert #1129, drw, arched apron, shelf, 48" 950.00
Table, library; Limbert #1141, 2-drw, corbels, rfn top, 48" 1,400.00
Table, Limbert, clip-corner 15" top, cut-out plank sides, rfn ...2,700.00
Table runner, velvet, pine-cone emb leather ends, fringe, 29" ...1,000.00
Tablecloth, allover Persian mc embr on linen, 42x93" 3,000.00
Tablecloth, fleur-de-lis, 3-color embr on natural, 20x33", EX 125.00
Tea set, Lebolt, hammered silver, faceted, pot: 8x11", 3-pc 900.00
Tile, daffodil w/whiplash leaves, 3-color, 6", in oak fr 375.00
Tile, incised path/house, 4-color, mk, 3½x6" 325.00
Tray, Dixon (att), h/cp w/2-color enamel/etched designs, 10" 475.00
Tray, Jarvie, h/brass, sculpted edge, hdl cutouts, 18x11", VG 450.00
Umbrella stand, Lakeside Crafts Shop, 8-sided, leather straps, VG ...350.00
Umbrella stand, mahog, 4 sq uprights w/pyramid finials, 28x10" ..220.00
Vase, Dixon, h/cp, bulbous w/rolled rim, 6x6" 250.00
Vase, Dixon (att), h/cp, heavy, swollen cylinder, 5" 260.00
Vase, h/cp, ovoid, minor wear, 4½x3" 425.00
Vase, Heinrichs, h/cp w/NP trim, 10-sided cylinder, 7" 150.00
Vase, Heintz, bronze w/appl silver cornflower, slim tube, 12" 350.00
Vase, Heintz, bronze w/appl sterling roses, 11x4¾" 700.00
Vase, Heintz, sterling floral on bronze, gr/brn bkground, 10" 450.00
Vase, Jarvie, h/cp, bulbous body, 5", VG 325.00
Vase, Kipp, brass can/pewter base, tooled geometrics, 3½" 200.00
Vase, Kipp, h/cp, cylinder w/emb quatrefoils, 4x1¾", NM 1,500.00
Vase, van Erp, h/cp, 7x5", VG 1,300.00
Wall hanging, peacock feathers embr on lined silk, 55x48", EX .600.00
Woodblock, Bertha Lum, arched passageway/foliage, 5½x4", +fr ...325.00
Woodblock, Bertha Lum, trees/sailboats/birds, 1913, 9x13", +fr .1,200.00
Woodblock, Chase, trees/mtns: Summer Land, 13x9", +fr & matt .2,200.00
Woodblock, Pedro Lemus, Driftwood, men/riverbank, 9", in fr ..1,000.00

Austrian Glass

Many examples of fine art glass were produced in Austria during the times of Loetz and Moser that cannot be attributed to any glasshouse in particular, though much of it bears striking similarities to the products of both artists.

Centerpc, gr irid, HP florals, gilt/silvered metal fr, 15½" **460.00**
Goblet, floral enamel, gr/pk w/gold outlines, 9" **250.00**
Vase, bright gr, 4 appl shells w/long trails, 8" **175.00**
Vase, dk amber w/4 spotted irid pulled motifs, dimpled, 7" **635.00**
Vase, fish form, amber irid & violet w/burgundy threads, 5⅜" ..**1,035.00**
Vase, gold w/silver o/l leaves, dimpled sides, 4-lobe rim, 4½" **545.00**
Vase, oil spots, gold on clear, 4-leg, hdls, 4-lobe rim, 4½ **575.00**
Vase, purple w/silver stripes & spots, 4-lobe rim, 10" **635.00**

Austrian Ware

From the late 1800s until the beginning of WWI, several companies were located in the area known at the turn of the century as Bohemia. They produced hard-paste porcelain dinnerware and decorative items primarily for the American trade. Today examples bearing the marks of these firms are usually referred to by collectors as Austrian ware, indicating simply the country of their origin. Of those various companies, these marks are best known: M.Z. Austria; Victoria, Carlsbad, Austria (Schmidt and Company); and O. & E.G. (Royal) Austria. Of these three companies, Victoria, Carlsbad, Austria, is the most highly valued.

Though most of the decorations were transfer designs which were sometimes signed by the original artist, pieces marked Royal Austria were often hand painted and so indicated alongside the backstamp.

Collectors should note that in our listings transfer decorations showing 'signatures' (sgn) such as 'Wagner,' 'Kauffmann,' 'LeBrun,' etc., were not actually painted by those artists but were merely based on their original paintings. Our advisor for this category is Mary Frank Gaston.

Ewer, wild roses w/gold, Rococo gold scroll hdl, 11¾x6" **125.00**
Humidor, 3 Grecian men & lady inspect wall, Victoria, 7" **275.00**
Mug, 2 women w/sheep, HP, 5" **135.00**
Oyster plate, tiny pk flowers, Limoges style **120.00**
Pitcher, tankard; lady in lav dress on gr w/gold, Imperial, 12" **135.00**
Plaque, Rhine river castle tapestry scene, beehive mk, 13" **175.00**
Vase, Nouveau style, pierced/looped base & rim, Dressler, 12½" ..**325.00**
Vase, roses, wht/lav on lav-gray, sgn Simon, cylinder, MZ, 15" ..**225.00**

Autographs

Autograph collecting, also known as 'philography' or 'love of writing,' used to be a hobby shared by a few thousand dedicated collectors. But in recent years, autograph collecting has become a serious pursuit for more than 2,000,000 collectors worldwide. And in the past decade, more investors are adding rare and valuable autograph portfolios to their traditional investments. One reason for this sudden interest in autograph investing relates to the simple economic law of supply and demand. Rare autographs have a 'fixed' supply, meaning that unlike diamonds, gold, silver, stock certificates, etc., no more are being produced. There are only so many Abraham Lincoln, Marilyn Monroe, and Charles Lindbergh autographs available. In the meantime, it's estimated that more than 20,000 new collectors enter the market each year, thus creating an ever-increasing demand. Hence, the rare autographs generally rise steadily in value each year. Because of this scarcity, a serious collector will pay over $10,000.00 for a photograph signed by both Wilbur and Orville Wright, or as much as $25,000.00 for a handwritten letter of George Washington.

But by far, the majority of autograph collectors in the country do it for the love of the hobby. A polite letter and self-addressed, stamped envelope sent to a famous person will often bring the desired result. And occasionally one receives not only an autograph but a nice handwritten letter thanking the fan as well!

In terms of value, there are five general types of autographs: 1) mere signatures on an album page or card; 2) signed photographs; 3) signed documents; 4) typed letters signed; and 5) handwritten letters. The signatures are the least valuable, and handwritten letters the most valuable. The reasoning here is simple: with a handwritten letter, not only do you get an autograph but the handwritten message of the person as well. And this content can sometimes increase the value many times over. A handwritten letter of Babe Ruth's thanking a fan for a gift might fetch a few thousand dollars. But if the letter were to mention Ruth's feelings on the day he retired, it could easily sell for $10,000.00 or more.

Today the Internet has become a popular way to buy and sell autographs. A word of warning: be very careful when buying over the Internet. It is an easy way for unscrupulous forgers to sell their fakes and disappear. Teenagers need to be especially aware that many of the photos 'signed' on the Internet of Sarah Michelle Gellar, Brad Pitt, Katie Holmes, Leonardo DeCaprio, Kate Winsett, and many others are either signed by secretaries or are outright forgeries. Make sure the Internet dealer offers a full money-back guarantee of authenticity and belongs to one of the major autograph organizations. Ask how long the dealer has been in business and for personal references if possible. Remember the old Latin warning, 'caveat emptor,' let the buyer beware.

There are several major autograph collector organizations where members can exchange celebrity addresses or buy, sell, and trade their autographed wares. Philography can be a fun and rewarding hobby. And who knows! In ten or twenty years, those autographs you got for free could be worth a small fortune!

In the listings below, photos are assumed black and white unless noted color. Our advisor for autographs is Tim Anderson; he is listed in the Directory under Utah.

Key:
ADS — handwritten document signed
ALS — handwritten letter signed
ANS — handwritten note signed
AQS — autograph quotation signed
CS — counter signed
DS — document signed
ins — inscription
ISP — inscribed signed photo
LH — letterhead
LS — signed letter, typed or written by someone else
PLH — personal letterhead
sig — signature
SP — signed photo

Greta Garbo, handwritten note on 3x4" paper, dated 1930, signed Garbo, matted with photo portrait, $990.00.

Aaron, Hank; sig on batting helmet **150.00**
Aikman, Troy; sig on Wilson football **150.00**
Ali, Muhammed; sig on boxing gloves, pr **200.00**

Allen, Marcus; sig on authentic Russel Athletic replica jersey ...300.00
Allman Bros, SP, color, 8x10" 75.00
Alma-Tadema, Sir; ALS, laid down, Dec 23, 1892, 4x3" card, VG .30.00
Anderson, Loni; SP, in swimsuit, color, 8x10" 20.00
Arliss, George; ANS, 2-17-29, 2x8", VG 25.00
Baer, Max; sig on card, 2x3" 100.00
Banks, Ernie; sig on baseball 35.00
Barrymore, Drew; SP (nude), 8x10" 125.00
Barrymore, John; SP, 11x14" 1,500.00
Barrymore, Lionel & Ethyl; sig, 1 above the other, 2x8", VG 100.00
Beatty, Warren; SP, color, 8x10" 85.00
Beecher, Henry Ward; ANS, August 1885, 5x3", EX 75.00
Benny, Jack; LS, 1-pg of personal stationery, July 7, 1965, EX 150.00
Bird, Larry; sig on golf ball 25.00
Bow, Clara; SP, 8x10" 500.00
Burns, William J; sig, 5-1-22, 2x8", VG 25.00
Burroughs, Edgar Rice; sig, 3½x2" card, VG 175.00
Busey, Gary; SP, color, 8x10" 22.00
Bush, George; sig on baseball 150.00
Cagney, James; SP, 10x13" 150.00
Carrey, Jim; SP, color, 8x10" 50.00
Carson, Johnny; SP, color, 8x10" 25.00
Cher, SP, color, 8x10" 65.00
Churchhill, Winston; sig, 3x2", laid down, VG 600.00
Clapton, Eric; sig on guitar 750.00
Clemens, Samuel; sig below printed quote, 4x2", VG 850.00
Connery, Sean; SP, Red October still, 8x10" 100.00
Coolidge, Calvin; sig, 9-29-30, 2x8", VG 95.00
Costello, Elvis; sig on Trust album 125.00
Crawford, Cindy; SP, swimsuit, color, 8x10" 35.00
Crosby, Bing; sig on card, 4x2½" 50.00
Curtis, Jamie Lee; SP, color, 8x10" 35.00
Davis, Bette; ISP, 8x10" 125.00
DeNiro, Robert; SP, color, 8x10" 150.00
Dickens, Charles; ALS to lawyers, 2 pg, 5x6", EX 1,800.00
Dillon, Matt; SP, color, 8x10" 45.00
DiMaggio, Joe; sig on baseball cap 225.00
Dream Team I, team sig on leather basketball 850.00
Earnhardt, Dale; SP, color, 8x10" 25.00
Eastman, George; sig on 3½x2" card, VG 100.00
Eastwood, Clint; SP, Dirty Harry, 8x10" 45.00
Einstein, Albert; LS (German), 1-pg stationery, 1952, VG 2,250.00
Eisenhower, Dwight D; LS, 1-pg, June 21, 1955, 6x9" 500.00
Fairbanks, Douglas; SP, 11x14" 1,500.00
Farmer, Frances; SP, 11x14" 2,500.00
Fontaine, Joan; SP, 11x14" 300.00
Ford, Gerald; sig on baseball bat 300.00
Ford, Gerald; SP, color, 8x10" 40.00
Ford, Harrison; SP, color, 8x10" 100.00
Garland, Judy; SP, 8x10" 1,000.00
Gibson, Mel; SP, head shot, 8x10" 100.00
Goddard, Paulette; SP, 11x14" 500.00
Goodman, Benny; sig on sheet music, Big Apple, 1937, EX 175.00
Gretzky, Wayne; sig on hockey puck 55.00
Grey, Zane; sig on card, 3½x2" 45.00
Harrison, George; sig on Musician magazine, Nov 1987 ....200.00
Hauer, Rutger; SP, color, 8x10" 60.00
Jolson, Al; SP, 5x7" 175.00
Jordon, Michael; SP, color, 8x10" 125.00
Keitel, Harvey; SP, color, 8x10" 35.00
Lee, Robert E; sig on Confederate news article, 1⅛x2½" 2,200.00
Leigh, Janet; SP, 11x14" 125.00
Maddux, Greg; sig on baseball cap 65.00
Moore, Demi; SP from Striptease, 8x10" 90.00

Mother Teresa, sig on prayer card, 3¼x6½" 250.00
Navarro, Ramon; SP, 11x14" 750.00
Nicholson, Jack; SP, color, 8x10" 75.00
Nickalaus, Jack; sig on golf ball 50.00
O'Neal, Shaq; sig on basketball 200.00
Orbinson, Roy; SP, gold wooden fr, 15x17½" overall 135.00
Pesci, Joe; SP, color, 8x10" 26.00
Pitt, Brad; SP, color, 8x10" 100.00
Ripken Jr, Cal; sig on jersey 450.00
Rose, Pete; sig on baseball cap 40.00
Russell, Kurt; SP, color, 8x10" 50.00
Russell, Rosalind; SP, 11x14" 500.00
Seagal, Steven; SP from Under Siege, 8x10" 60.00
Shearer, Norma; SP, 11x14" 750.00
Stanwyck, Barbara; SP, 11x14" 500.00
Stewart, James; sig on contract 150.00
Stewart, James; SP, 4x5" 40.00
Sting, sig on Dream of the Big Turtles album 100.00
Stone, Sharon; sig on contract for The Tonight Show 200.00
Taylor, Lawrence; SP, color, 11x14" 65.00
Temple, Shirley; SP, 11x14" 1,500.00
Tracy, Spencer; LS, 1938, EX 500.00
Turner, Kathleen; SP, color, 8x10" 24.00
Tyson, Mike; sig on boxing gloves, pr 150.00
Wayne, John; SP from True Grit 500.00
West, Adam; SP as Batman, 8x10" 60.00
Who, The; sig on guitar 775.00
Willis, Bruce; SP from Pulp Fiction, color, 8x10" 50.00
Wilson, Woodrow; LS, eng Wht House LH, thank-you, 1918 ....250.00

Automobilia

While some automobilia buffs are primarily concerned with restoring vintage cars, others concentrate on only one area of collecting. For instance, hood ornaments were often quite spectacular. Made of chrome or nickel plate on brass or bronze, they were designed to represent the 'winged maiden' Victory, flying bats, sleek greyhounds, soaring eagles, and a host of other creatures. Today they often bring prices in the $75.00 to $200.00 range. R. Lalique glass ornaments go much higher!

Horns, radios, clocks, gear shift knobs, and key chains with company emblems are other areas of interest. Generally, items pertaining to the classics of the '30s are most in demand. Paper advertising material, manuals, and catalogs in excellent condition are also collectible.

License plate collectors search for the early porcelain-on-cast-iron examples. First year plates (e.g., Massachusetts, 1903; Wisconsin, 1905; Indiana, 1913) are especially valuable. The last of the states to issue regulation plates were South Carolina and Texas in 1917, and Florida in 1918. While many northeastern states had registered hundreds of thousands of vehicles by the 1920s making these plates relatively common, those from the southern and western states of that period are considered rare. Naturally, condition is important. While a pair in mint condition might sell for as much as $100.00 to $125.00, a pair with chipped or otherwise damaged porcelain may sometimes be had for as little as $25.00 to $30.00.

For more information we recommend *American Automobilia: An Illustrated History and Price Guide* by Jim and Nancy Schaut. See also Gas Globes and Panels.

Badge, employee; Chevrolet 45.00
Belt buckle, 1981 Car Craft Street Machine Nationals 20.00
Blotter, Buick touring car in landscape/logo, 1924, 4x9", NM 28.00
Blotter, Dodge Brothers Trucks, 1929, 4x9", EX 85.00

Book, Am Automobile Racing, Bochroch, spiral bound, EX 25.00
Book, Andretti, Bill Libby, Tempo paperbk, 1970, EX 10.00
Book of oil change tags, Kendall, 1950s, unused 15.00
Booklet, 1935 Ford 12.50
Bracelet, Goodyear blimp on gold-tone charm, w/chain, EX 10.00
Brochure, Oldsmobile sales, 1936, M 65.00
Brochure, Packard, Luxurious Motoring, 1925, 11x6", EX 150.00
Cable set, ignition; Bendelac, ca 1932, 10½x7x2", in box 70.00
Folder, 1965 Qualifying Indy 500, GC Murphy Special #67, w/ad ..10.00
Folder, 1985 Dodge Challenger, Dunkel-Davis, 4-pg, 8x10", EX ..10.00
Gauge, tire pressure; Schrader, for balloon tires, EX 15.00
Glass, Indy 500 logo front, winners thru 1967 reverse, EX 15.00
Handy-oiler, Phillips 66 Fine Parts, complimentary, M 20.00
Hatpin, Garlit's Kendall Rear Engine Dragster, EX 15.00

Hood ornament, Superman, plated white metal, LW Lee Mfg. Co, Natl Comic Pub, extremely rare, 6¾x10", EX, $1,050.00.

Hood ornament, flying horse, diecast chrome w/SP, 6x6", EX 250.00
Hood ornament, Goddess of Speed, zinc w/chrome plate, '30s ...350.00
Hood ornament, 1940 Plymouth, VG 50.00
Hood ornament, 1947 Chevrolet, VG 55.00
Hood ornament, 1949 Mercury, VG 40.00
License plate, Cadillac 1914, porc, wht on red, EX 1,100.00
License plate, IL, Amateur Radio, 1961, VG, pr 25.00
License plate, MA, 1910, porc, VG 90.00
License plate, ME, 1909, porc, VG 65.00
License plate, PA, 1913, porc, 6x14", VG 160.00
License plate attachment, Chrysler, tin, top hat/gloves, 6x9", VG+ .275.00
License plate attachment, Hudson 6, tin, sleek bird, 4x14", EX+ 110.00
License plate attachment, Mobiloil Pegasus horse, tin, EX 175.00
License tag, Seminole Indian, Florida, bl/wht, 1963, rare, VG+ .275.00
Manual, owner's; 1949 Hudson 8 ....35.00
Media guide, driver biographies, stats, car info, etc, 1958, EX 35.00
Mug, clear glass, 1957 red Corvette hardtop, EX 10.00
Mug, Esso, wht w/tiger, Fire-King, EX 10.00
Mug, Jimmy Bryan w/1958 Belond AP Special, EX 35.00
Mug, thermal; Snap-On, dragster w/flames, EX 15.00
Pamphlet, Harley-Davidson Motorcycles ..., 1923, 12-pg, EX 75.00
Penknife, silver metal, D-A Lubricant emb letters, USA, 30s, EX .35.00
Pennant, Auburn car, ca 1939, NM 195.00
Pennant, 1915 Buick, wht on bl felt, M 150.00
Pennant, 1915 Paige-6, felt, $1385 auto & name, red on wht, 37", EX .165.00
Photo, Knox's Super Trix '66-7 Nova at Englewood 7/71, EX 5.00
Photo, Prosperity Train, 190 Buicks on train, 1915, 14x24", EX ...700.00
Pin, Cadillac Craftsman, gold w/logo, 1947, EX 35.00
Pin, manager's; Texaco, Bakelite Scottie, MOC 100.00
Pin, Packard Master Serviceman Mechanic, bl/red/wht, 2x½", VG .100.00
Pin, Soap Box Derby, pewter, car & Chevy emblem, 1969, EX 25.00
Plate, Ford, 300-500 club award, WM Rogers SP, 1962, 6" 10.00
Pocketwatch, Harley-Davidson, 1920s, EX 725.00
Postcard, color photo of Eddie Sachs in #2 Autolite Special, EX 15.00
Postcard, Indy 500, cars at start, Cord pace car, EX 5.00
Press release, Don Garlits career record, 4 pgs, 1980, EX 5.00

Program, Motordome Speedway, 1992, EX 3.00
Program, Sports Car Club of Am, Southern AZ, Wilcox, May 1956 ..10.00
Program, Watkins Glen, 7/22-23/72, EX 10.00
Program, Winston Western 500, Riverside, 1981, EX 5.00
Promotional car, 1953 Corvette, 40th Anniversary, 1993, MIB ...50.00
Promotional car, 1968 Old's Toronado 85.00
Radiator cap, Nash 30.00
Radiator cap, Winged, w/Am La France motometer, NP brass ...250.00
Radiator emblem, Hudson Super 6, triangular, cloisonne, 3", EX .75.00
Radiator shield, Pegasus on waxed cb, 1930s, VG+ 135.00
Record book, Nascar 1952, cover art of step-down Hudsons 35.00
Rule book, Englewood Speedway, 1970, Super Stocks & Figure 8s, EX .10.00
Ticket, 1963 Indy 500, w/'62 winner Roger Ward & car, w/rain check .25.00
Tin, Lastik King Sz Dust Cloth, w/cloth, M 10.00
Visor, Harley-Davidson, leather, M 30.00
Weather vane, Pontiac, metal diecut logo, 42x53", NM 250.00
Whetstone, Stewart Trucks, oval, blk/red on wht, 2x3", VG 440.00
Yearbook, IMCA, 1960 ....15.00

Autumn Leaf

In 1933 the Hall China Company designed a line of dinnerware for the Jewel Tea Company, who offered it to their customers as premiums. Although you may hear the ware referred to as 'Jewel Tea,' it was officially named 'Autumn Leaf' in the 1940s. In addition to the dinnerware, frosted Libbey glass tumblers, stemware, and a melmac service with the orange and gold bittersweet pod were available over the years, as were tablecloths, plastic covers for bowls and mixers, and metal items such as cake safes, hot pads, coasters, wastebaskets, and canisters. Even shelf paper and playing cards were made to coordinate. In 1958 the International Silver Company designed silverplated flatware in a pattern called 'Autumn' which was to be used with dishes in the Autumn Leaf pattern. A year later, a line of stainless flatware was introduced. These accessory lines are prized by collectors today.

One of the most fascinating aspects of collecting the Autumn Leaf pattern has been the wonderful discoveries of previously unlisted pieces. Among these items are two different bud-ray lid one-pound butter dishes; most recently a one-pound butter dish in the 'Zephyr' or 'Bingo' style; a miniature set of the 'Casper' salt and pepper shakers; coffee, tea, and sugar canisters; a pair of candlesticks; an experimental condiment jar; and a covered candy dish. All of these china pieces are attributed to the Hall China Company. Other unusual items have turned up in the accessory lines as well and include a Libbey frosted tumbler in a pilsner shape, a wooden serving bowl, and an apron made from the oilcloth (plastic) material that was used in the 1950s tablecloth. These latter items appear to be professionally done, and we can only speculate as to their origin. Collectors believe that the Hall items were sample pieces that were never meant to be distributed.

Hall discontinued the Autumn Leaf line in 1978. At that time the date was added to the backstamp to mark ware still in stock in the Hall warehouse. A special promotion by Jewel saw the reintroduction of basic dinnerware and serving pieces with the 1978 backstamp. These pieces have made their way into many collections. Additionally, in 1979 Jewel released a line of enamel-clad cookware and a Vellux blanket made by Martex which were decorated with the Autumn Leaf pattern. They continued to offer these items for a few years only, then all distribution of Autumn Leaf items was discontinued.

It should be noted that the Hall China Company has produced several limited edition items for the National Autumn Leaf Collectors Club (NALCC): a New York-style teapot (1984); an Edgewater vase (1987, different than the original shape); candlesticks (1988); a Philadelphia-style teapot, creamer, and sugar set (1990); a tea-for-two set and a Solo tea set (1991), a donut jug, and a large oval casserole.

New items for the NALCC: small ball jug, one-cup French teapot, and a set of four chocolate mugs. The NALCC has also given their club members special items over the past few years made for them by Hall China: a sugar packet holder, a chamberstick, and an oyster cocktail. Other items are scheduled for production. All of these are plainly marked as having been made for the NALCC and are appropriately dated. A few other pieces have been made by Hall as limited editions for an Ohio company, but these are easily identified: the Airflow teapot and the Norris refrigerator pitcher (neither of which was previously decorated with the Autumn Leaf decal), a square-handled beverage mug, and the new-style Irish mug. A production problem with the square-handled mugs halted their production. The company then issued a regular conic-style mug with a round handle. Additional items available now are a covered onion soup, tall bud vase, china kitchen memo board, and egg drop-style salt and pepper shakers with a mustard pot. They have also issued a deck of playing cards and Libbey tumblers. See *The Garage Sale & Flea Market Annual* (Collector Books) for suggested values for club pieces. Our advisor for this category is Gwynne Harrison; she is listed in the Directory under California.

Teapot, Birdcage, Club piece, 8", $145.00.

Baker, French; 2-pt, from $150 to	175.00
Baker, French, 3-pt	20.00
Baker, oval, Fort Pitt, 12-oz ind	225.00
Baker/souffle, 4½"	50.00
Baker/souffle, 4⅛"	12.00
Bean pot, 1-hdl	1,000.00
Bean pot, 2-hdl, 2¼-qt	250.00
Bowl, cereal; 6½"	12.00
Bowl, cream soup; 2-hdl	35.00
Bowl, flat soup; 8½"	20.00
Bowl, fruit; 5½"	6.00
Bowl, mixing; set of 3: 6¼", 7½", 9"	65.00
Bowl, refrigerator; metal w/plastic lids, 3 for	275.00
Bowl, Royal Glas-Bake, set of 4	200.00
Bowl, salad; 9"	20.00
Bowl, vegetable; divided, 10½", from $90 to	125.00
Bowl, vegetable; oval, w/lid, 10"	75.00
Bowl, vegetable; oval, 10½"	25.00
Bowl, vegetable; rnd, 9"	150.00
Bowl cover set, plastic, 8-pc: 7 assorted covers in pouch	90.00
Bread box, metal	400.00
Butter dish, 1-lb, regular, ruffled top	450.00
Butter dish, ¼-lb, regular, ruffled top	175.00
Butter dish, ¼-lb, Square Top, rare	1,200.00
Butter dish, ¼-lb, Wings	1,800.00
Cake plate, 9½"	28.00
Cake safe, metal, motif on top & sides, 5"	50.00
Cake safe, metal, side decor only, 4½x10½", from $35 to	45.00
Cake stand, metal base, orig box, from $150 to	225.00
Candy dish, metal base, from $450 to	500.00
Canister, metal, rnd, w/coppertone lid, set of 4, from $200 to	500.00

Canister, metal, rnd, w/ivory plastic lid	10.00
Canister, metal, rnd, w/matching lids, set of 3, from $200 to	300.00
Canister, metal, sq, set of 4, from $250 to	350.00
Casserole, Royal Glas-Bake, rnd, w/clear glass lid	90.00
Casserole, Tootsie-hdl, w/lid	22.00
Cleanser can, metal, sq, 6", M	1,400.00
Coaster, metal, 3⅛"	8.00
Coffee dispenser/canister, metal, wall type, 10½x19" dia	400.00
Coffee maker, 9-cup, w/metal dripper, 8"	45.00
Coffee percolator, Douglas, w/warmer base, MIB	300.00
Coffee percolator, electric, all china, 4-pc	350.00
Cookie jar, Zeisel	300.00
Creamer, New Style	25.00
Creamer, Old Style, 4¼"	45.00
Cup & saucer, regular	10.00
Cup & saucer, St Denis	30.00
Custard cup	10.00
Drip jar, w/lid	20.00
Flatware, silverplate, ea	35.00
Flatware, stainless, ea	30.00
Fruit cake tin, metal	10.00
Gravy boat, w/underplate (pickle dish)	55.00
Hot pad, metal, red or gr felt-like backing, rnd	20.00
Hot pad, oval, 10¾", from $12 to	15.00
Hurricane lamp, Douglas, w/metal base, pr	600.00
Marmalade jar, 3-pc	100.00
Mug, beverage	60.00
Mug, Irish coffee	125.00
Mustard jar, 3½", 3-pc	100.00
Napkin, ecru muslin, 16" sq	50.00
Pickle dish or gravy liner, oval, 9"	25.00
Picnic thermos, metal	375.00
Pie baker, 9½"	35.00
Pie plate, Heatflow, clear glass, Mary Dunbar	70.00
Pitcher, utility; 2½-pt, 6"	25.00
Place mat, paper, scalloped, from $35 to	40.00
Place mat, set of 8, MIP	325.00
Plate, 10"	18.00
Plate, 6"	8.00
Plate, 7¼"	10.00
Plate, 8"	18.00
Plate, 9"	12.00
Platter, 11½"	28.00
Platter, 13½", from $25 to	28.00
Playing cards, regular or Pinochle, dbl deck, from $150 to	200.00
Sauce dish, serving; Douglas, Bakelite hdl, w/warmer base	600.00
Shakers, Casper, regular, pr	30.00
Shakers, range, hdl, pr	30.00
Sugar bowl, New Style	30.00
Sugar bowl, Old Style, 3½"	40.00
Tablecloth, cotton sailcloth w/gold stripe, 54x54", from $100 to	150.00
Tablecloth, cotton sailcloth w/gold stripe, 54x72", from $125 to	150.00
Tablecloth, ecru muslin, 56x81"	300.00
Tablecloth, plastic	150.00
Teakettle, metal enamelware	250.00
Teapot, Aladdin	70.00
Teapot, long spout, 1935-42	70.00
Teapot, Newport, dtd 1978, from $175 to	200.00
Teapot, Newport, from $175 to	200.00
Toaster cover, plastic, fits 2-slice toaster	50.00
Towel, dish; pattern & clock motif	60.00
Towel, tea; cotton, 16x33"	60.00
Trash can, metal, red	400.00
Tray, glass, wood hdl, 19½x11¼", from $100 to	130.00

Tray, metal, oval 100.00
Tray, tidbit; 3-tier 100.00
Tumbler, Brockway, 13-oz 45.00
Tumbler, Brockway, 16-oz 45.00
Tumbler, Brockway, 9-oz 45.00
Tumbler, frosted, 14-oz, 5½" 20.00
Tumbler, frosted, 9-oz, 3¾" 32.00
Tumbler, gold frost etched, flat, 10-oz 65.00
Tumbler, gold frost etched, flat, 15-oz 65.00
Tumbler, gold frost etched, ftd, 10-oz 65.00
Tumbler, gold frost etched, ftd, 6½-oz 65.00
Vase, bud; sm or regular decal, 6" 225.00
Warmer base, oval 200.00
Warmer base, rnd 160.00

Aviation

Aviation buffs are interested in any phase of flying, from early developments with gliders, balloons, airships, and flying machines to more modern innovations. Books, catalogs, photos, patents, lithographs, ad cards, and posters are among the paper ephemera they treasure alongside models of unlikely flying contraptions, propellers and rudders, insignia and equipment from WWI and WWII, and memorabilia from the flights of the Wright Brothers, Lindbergh, Earhart, and the Zeppelins. See also Militaria. Our advisor for this category is John R. Joiner; he is listed in the Directory under Georgia.

Demitasse cup and saucer, Pan American, Presidential pattern by Noritake, 1960s, $35.00.

Photo courtesy Dick Wallin

Banner, Welcome Lindbergh, printed cloth, 1927, 14x10", EX 38.00
Book, Of Flight & Life, Lindbergh, 1948, w/dust jacket 32.00
Cachet, Golden Anniversary US Air Mail Washington DC, 1968 .3.50
Desk model, DC-9 McDonnel Douglas, Ozark Airlines, EX 650.00
Engine, prop, working model, 14" L 450.00
Hand towel, Air France, wht w/bl woven stripe, 1970 ....10.00
Mail bag, Midway Airlines, yel & blk, lg 98.00
Model, Electra, Lockheed, metal, Am Air Lines, 28" 1,700.00
Model plane, Caledonian Airlines, 10" wingspan, 11" L 45.00
Photo, Betty Lou Coupe, 9-yr-old aviator, 1927, 6½x9½" 40.00
Photo, Lindbergh as mail pilot, loading mail into plane, 1926 ......22.00
Photo, Spirit of St Louis, sepia, 1927, 5x7", EX 10.00
Plate, Lindbergh sepia photographic portrait, fr, 1927, M 150.00
Playing cards, Air India, 1992, EXIB 10.00
Playing cards, Gillies Aviation, seaplane bks, 1930s, NMIB 40.00
Playing cards, Pan Am Scenic, photo bks, VG+, broken box 20.00
Postcard, Delta, 3 lg jets, 1981, 5x8" 1.50
Poster, Internat'l Air Races, St Louis, 1923, for pole, in fr 750.00
Print, Air Racing w/Rosco Turner, Hubbel, 1940s, 12½x17" 100.00
Print, Atomic Warfare Is Born, Enola Gay in flight, 8x10" 300.00
Print, TWA, for Thompson Products by Charles Hubbell, 12x14" ...98.00
Shot glasses, Southern Air Lines, #1 through #30, complete set .1,300.00
Sign, Continental, Seat Occupied, plastic, early, 4x12" 3.00
Sign, United Air Lines, porc, sm shield 550.00
Swizzle stick, Am Airlines, bl plastic w/flag 1.00

Timetable, Northwest Orient, 1958, 4x8" 10.00

Baccarat

The Baccarat Glass company was founded in 1765 near Luneville, France, and continues to this day to produce quality crystal tableware, vases, perfume bottles, and figurines. The firm became famous for the high-quality millefiori and caned paperweights produced there from 1845 until about 1860. Examples of these range from $300.00 to as much as several thousand. Since 1953 they have resumed the production of paperweights on a limited edition basis. Our advisors for this category are Randall Monsen and Rod Baer; their address is listed in the Directory under Virginia. See also Bottles, Commercial Perfume; Paperweights.

Bottle, doves/flowers, flask form, Chevalier, mk, 1920s, 5⅜" ..1,430.00
Bottle, scent; clear w/bl arches & gold, flower-type stopper, 7" ..700.00
Bottle, scent; gr, emb ovals in squat base, flaring neck, 8" 450.00
Bottle, scent; Rose Tiente Swirl, w/Pinwheel stopper, 5" 90.00
Bottle, scent; Rose Tiente Swirl, w/stopper, 7⅛x2⅞" 88.00
Bucket, champagne; #894061, gilt hdls, lg 679.00
Butter dish, notch-cut band on dome lid w/knob, 6¼x6⅝" 130.00
Compote, cut border, finely crafted stem, rnd ft, 10⅜x10⅜" 475.00
Compote, Rose Tiente Swirl, gold trim, 3½x7", pr 150.00
Compote, turned-down t'print cut edge, 8-sided ft, 4¼x5½" 120.00
Decanter, Rose Tiente Swirl, w/6 cordials 500.00
Figurine, panther, mk, 6½" 150.00
Pitcher & wash basin, Rose Tiente Swirl 800.00
Tazza, Rose Tiente, scalloped, turned-up rim, 3¼x5" 110.00
Tumble-up pitcher & glass, Rose Tiente Swirl 350.00

Badges

The breast badge came into general usage in this country about 1840. Since most are not marked and styles have changed very little to the present day, they are often difficult to date. The most reliable clue is the pin and catch. One of the earliest types, used primarily before the turn of the century, involved a 't-pin' and a 'shell' catch. In a second style, the pin was hinged with a small square of sheet metal, and the clasp was cylindrical. From the late 1800s until about 1940, the pin and clasp were made from one continuous piece of thin metal wire. The same type, with the addition of a flat back plate, was used a little later. There are exceptions to these findings, and other types of clasps were also used. Hallmarks and inscriptions may also help pinpoint an approximate age.

Badges have been made from a variety of materials, usually brass or nickel silver; but even solid silver and gold were used for special orders. They are found in many basic shapes and variations — stars with five to seven points, shields, disks, ovals, and octagonals being most often encountered. Of prime importance to collectors, however, is that the title and/or location appear on the badge. Those with designations of positions no longer existing (City Constable, for example) and names of early western states and towns are most valuable.

Badges are among the most commonly reproduced (and faked) types of antiques on the market. At any flea market, ten fakes can be found for every authentic example. Genuine law badges start at $30.00 to $40.00 for recent examples (1950 – 1970); earlier pieces (1910 – 1930) usually bring $50.00 to $90.00. Pre-1900 badges often sell for more than $100.00. Authentic gold badges are usually priced at a minimum of scrap value (karat, weight, spot price for gold); fine gold badges from before 1900 can sell for $400.00 to $800.00, and a few will bring even more. A fire badge is usually valued at about half the price of a law badge of the same time and material. Our advisor for this category is Gene Matzke; he is listed in the Directory under Wisconsin.

Detroit Metropolitan Police, #932, silver metal cap badge, $35.00.

Appleton Police, NP star w/copper 73, hallmk, 1940s, EX **70.00**
Bensenville Police, NP star w/copper #, state crest, 1940s **72.50**
Deputy Sheriff, NP shield w/eagle & NJ state crest, 1950s **45.00**
Driver's, Official...Presidential 1977 Inaugural, #d, M **75.00**
MD Division of Corrections, state seal on gilt metal, 1970s **65.00**
Military aide, blk metal w/blk & gold, seal on left, 1977, 2x4" **60.00**
NY City Police, NY City crest, silver, dtd 1859, EX **675.00**
Police in blk letters on 8-sided NP star, ca 1920s **75.00**
Police on silver shield w/eng star, blk enameling, ca 1900 ....**150.00**
Private Detective, pierced NP shield w/center star, 1920s **40.00**
Secret Service Police, MI state crest on NP shield, EX **150.00**
Sterling (MI) Police w/Detroit seal on NP 6-pointed star, 1930s ..**75.00**
US Immigration Chief Inspector, bl enamel on gilt metal, 1980s .**65.00**
Wheeling Steel Corp #319, Steubenville Works **30.00**

Banks

As always true, the continuing impact of auctions shows in the listings. Again, condition, condition, condition is what is driving the market. The spread between a bank in good condition and an excellent or original condition example continues to widen. It is imperative that you realize the importance of paint and the completeness of a bank. Also some banks have a wide margin of value based on color variations. It becomes more and more important that you attend as many shows and auctions as possible. Direct contact with collectors and knowledgeable dealers is the only way you can get a feel for prices and the desirability of banks, both mechanical and still. Banks continue to hold their value. However, it is becoming extremely important for collectors to understand the market.

Let's take a look at the price variations possible on an Uncle Sam mechanical bank. If you find one with considerable paint missing but with some good color showing, the price would be around $1,000.00. If it has repairs or restoration, the value would drop to something like $800.00 or less. If you had another example, and it had two thirds of its original paint and no repairs, it would be priced around $1,800.00. One with minor nicks and 90% of the original paint could go as high as $3,500.00. Or if you find one that is in near-original paint and has no repairs, $5,000.00 would not be out of line. This should help you see what causes price variations. After considering all of these factors, remember the final price is always determined by what a willing buyer and seller agree on for a specific bank.

The category of mechanical banks is unique. Along with cast-iron toys, they are among the most outstanding products of the Industrial Revolution and are recognized as some of the most successful of the mass-produced products of the 19th century. The earliest mechanicals were made of wood or lead, but when John Hall introduced Hall's Excelsior, a cast-iron mechanical bank, it was an immediate success. J. & E. Stevens produced the bank for Hall and soon began to make their own designs. Several companies followed suit, most of which were already in the hardware business. They used newly developed iron-molding techniques to produce these novelty savings devices for the emerging toy market. Mechanical banks reflect the social and political attitudes of the times, racial prejudices, the excitement of the circus, and humorous everyday events. Their designers made the most of simple mechanics to produce banks with captivating actions that served not only to amuse but to promote the concept of thrift to the children. The quality of detail in the castings is truly remarkable. The most collectible examples were made during the period of 1870 to 1900; however, they continued to be made until the early days of World War II. J. & E. Stevens, Shepard Hardware, and Kyser and Rex are some of the more well-known manufacturers; most made still banks as well.

Still banks are widely collected, and you can literally choose from thousands of banks. No one knows exactly how many different banks were made, but at least three thousand have been identified in the various books published on the subject. Cast-iron examples still dominate the market, but the lead banks from Europe are growing in value. Tin and early pottery banks are drawing more interest as well. American pottery banks which were primarily collected by Americana collectors are becoming more important in the still bank field. This market has not been as volatile as the mechanical banks, but the number of collectors is growing. The auction market on still banks is not as extensive as with the mechanicals, but some nice examples do turn up. Collectors and dealers are still the best source.

Book of Knowledge Banks were produced by John Wright (Pennsylvania) from circa 1950 until 1975. Of the thirty models they made during those years, a few continued to be made in very limited numbers until the late 1980s; these they referred to as the 'Medallion' series. (Today the Medallion banks command the same prices as the earlier Book of Knowledge series.) Each bank was a handcrafted, hand-painted duplicate of an original as was found in the collection of The Book of Knowledge, the first children's encyclopedia in this country. Because the antique banks are often priced out of the range of many of today's collectors, these banks are being sought out as affordable substitutes for their very expensive counterparts.

As both value and interest continue on the increase, it becomes even more important to educate one's self to the fullest extent possible. We recommend these books for your library: *The Dictionary of Still Banks* by Long and Pitman, *The Penny Bank Book* by Moore, *Penny Banks Around the World* by Don Duer, and *The Bank Book* by Norman. If you are primarily interested in mechanicals, *Penny Lane*, a book by Davidson, is considered the most complete reference available. It contains a cross-reference listing of numbers from all other publications on mechanical banks.

In the listings that follow, banks are identified by M for Moore and N for Norman.

Our advisor for mechanicals is Diane Patalano, listed in the Directory under New Jersey; Dan Iannotti (for Book of Knowledge) is listed under Michigan; and our still bank advisor is Larry Egelhoff, who is listed in the Directory under Indiana.

Key:
CI — cast iron   NPCI — nickel-plated cast iron
EPCI — electroplated cast iron

Advertising

Calumet Baking Powder, N-1660, tin litho & paper, sm, EX **190.00**
Chevrolet, tin globe, The Symbol of Savings..., Chein, 5", EX+ ..**60.00**
Chrysler, Mr Fleet, vinyl, 1970s, NM **350.00**
Colonel Sanders **40.00**
Del Monte clown **25.00**
Dodge, barrel shape, metal, Switch to Dodge & Save Money, 3", EX .**50.00**
EnArCo Wht Rose Gasoline, sq tin can form, 4½x3x3", EX **230.00**
Esso Happy Bank, plastic, 7x3" dia, NM **90.00**

GE Refrigerator, M-1330, CI, worn pnt, 3¾" 80.00
Green Giant, musical 45.00
Magic Chef stove, M-1339, wht metal, EX pnt, 3½" 105.00
Marathon carnival pig 35.00
McDonald's, wastebasket form 20.00
Oscar Mayer Weinermobile 25.00
Shakey's Pizza 25.00
Sinclair Dinosaur, M-777, wht metal, 8½" 145.00
Skelly Motor Oil, tin can form, 2½x2" dia, EX 50.00
Trenton Trust, 75th Anniversary, pnt CI, EX 675.00

Book of Knowledge Banks

Always Did 'Spise a Mule (Jockey), NM 285.00
Artillery Bank, NM 345.00
Boy on Trapeze, NM 595.00
Cabin Bank, NM 285.00
Cat & Mouse, M 425.00
Dentist Bank, NM 275.00
Eagle & Eaglets, M 425.00
Humpty Dumpty, MIB 400.00
Indian & Bear, M 475.00
Leaping Frog, MIB 395.00
Magician, NM 425.00
Milking Cow, NM 345.00
Owl (turns head), M 300.00
Paddy & the Pig, M 385.00
Punch & Judy, M 375.00
Tammany, NMIB 365.00
Teddy & the Bear, NM 335.00
Trick Pony, NMIB 365.00
Uncle Remus, MIB 425.00
Uncle Sam, M 350.00
World's Fair, scarce bronze version, NM 375.00

Mechanical

Bulldog Bank, painted cast iron, brown version, J. and E. Stevens, Pat. 1880, NM, $2,200.00.

Photo courtesy Dunbar Gallery

Afghanistan, N-1020, pnt CI, Mechanical Novelty Works, 1885, G ..1,540.00
Always Did 'Spise a Mule, Jockey; N-2950, CI, poor pnt 550.00
Bad Accident, N-1150, pnt CI, EX 1,100.00
Bad Accident, N-1150-A, pnt CI, J&E Stevens, ca 1891, EX .2,400.00
Bill E Grin, N-1230 (similar), pnt aluminum, EX 260.00
Bird on Roof, N-1270, pnt CI, EX 2,300.00
Boy on Trapeze, N-1350, pnt CI, VG 2,600.00
Boy Robbing Bird's Nest, rpt CI, J&E Stevens 1,540.00
Boy Scout Camp, N-1370, pnt CI, EX 1,700.00
Butting Ram, N-1590, pnt CI, EX 5,600.00
Chief Big Moon, N-1740, CI, worn pnt 1,025.00
Circus, pnt CI, pony & clown in ring, Shepard Hdw, 1887, EX 15,000.00
Columbian Magic Savings, N-1950, CI, worn pnt 380.00

Creedmore, N-2000-B, pnt CI, VG 645.00
Dapper Dan, N-2070, tin litho, EX 240.00
Dinah, N-2150-A, pnt CI, EX 1,100.00
Dog on Turntable, N-2170, pnt CI, VG/EX 550.00
Dog on Turntable, N-2170-A, pnt CI, Judd Mfg, 1870s, M 1,425.00
Eagle & Eaglets, N-2230-B, pnt CI, J&E Stevens, NM 1,800.00
Fortune Teller, N-2460-B, pnt CI, fortune in window, G 145.00
Frog on Round Base, N-2530, CI, VG 800.00
Girl in Victorian Chair, N-2630-A, pnt CI, Reed, EX 12,000.00
Hall's Excelsior, N-2710-C, pnt CI, J&E Stevens, 1869, M 2,200.00
Hall's Lilliput (Yel & Red), pnt CI, J&E Stevens, Pat 1877, EX ..1,200.00
Hall's Lilliput, N-2740, pnt CI, VG 550.00
Hen & Chick, N-2790, pnt CI, EX- 3,200.00
Humpty Dumpty, N-2900, CI, mc pnt w/touchup, 7¾", VG ...1,000.00
Humpty Dumpty, N-2900, CI, worn pnt, G 650.00
Indian & Bear, N-2980-A, pnt CI, J&E Stevens, ca 1900, EX .2,800.00
Indian Shooting Bear, N-2980, pnt CI, EX- 2,600.00
Initiating Bank, 2nd Degree; N-3010, pnt CI, EX 1,500.00
Jolly N, Starkies, N-3270, pnt aluminum, EX 130.00
Jolly N Figure, aluminum, bright mc pnt, Austrian (?), M 3,850.00
Jolly N w/High Hat, N-3130, pnt CI, VG 675.00
Lion & Monkeys, N-3650, 1 peanut, pnt CI, Kyser & Rex, 1883, EX ..2,200.00
Mason, N-3800, pnt CI, Shepard Hdw, 1887, EX 4,000.00
Merry-Go-Round, M-1514, CI, worn pnt, 4⅝" 400.00
Monkey & Coconut, N-3940, CI, pnt traces, G- 700.00
Monkey & Coconut, N-3940, pnt CI, J&E Stevens, 1886, VG .2,650.00
Mosque, N-4010, pnt CI, EX 2,150.00
Motor Bank, N-4020, CI, worn pnt 3,300.00
Novelty, N-4260, pnt CI, J&E Stevens, 1873, EX 1,200.00
Organ Bank, N-4310, boy & girl, pnt CI, Kyser & Rex, 1882, NM ...3,400.00
Owl Turns Head, N-4380-A, pnt CI, J&E Stevens, 1880, VG ...415.00
Pay Phone, N-4470-A, NP CI, J&E Stevens, G 715.00
Picture Gallery, N-4560, pnt CI, Shepard Hdw, ca 1885, VG ..13,750.00
Pig in Highchair, N-4570, CI, worn pnt, G 675.00
Professor Pug Frog, N-4690-A, pnt CI, J&E Stevens, 1886, EX .6,800.00
Punch & Judy, N-4740-C, Shepard Hdw, EX 4,000.00
Rabbit in Cabbage, N-4790-A, pnt CI, Kilgore, ca 1925, G- 275.00
Sambo, N-4990, pnt CI, VG 550.00
Santa Claus, N-5010, CI, worn mc pnt, 5⅞", VG 1,100.00
Speaking Dog, N-5170, pnt CI, EX 2,500.00
Stump Speaker, N-5370, CI, G 800.00
Stump Speaker (Gr Jacket), pnt CI, Shepard Hdw, VG 2,300.00
Tammany, N-5420-B, pnt CI, J&E Stevens, 1873, M 2,000.00
Trick Buffalo, M-558, pnt CI, 5½", EX 875.00
Trick Dog (Yel & Brn Base), pnt CI, Hubley, EX 900.00
Uncle Tom w/Star, pnt CI, Kyser & Rex, Pat 1882, EX 525.00
US & Spain, pnt CI, N-5800, EX 550.00
World's Fair, N-6040, pnt CI, EX 1,200.00

Registering

Dime Coin Barrel, M-921, pnt CI, 4", EX 160.00
Jackie Robinson, dime register, tin litho, 2½" 500.00
Popeye, 10¢ register, metal, EX/NM 65.00
Registering Dime Savings, N-4870, pnt CI, EX 975.00
Superman, dime register, tin litho, 3", EX, from $225 to 250.00
Thrifty Elf, dime register, tin itho, 2½" sq 170.00
Uncle Sam, dime register, tin litho, 2½" sq 270.00

Still

Andy Gump, M-217, CI, worn pnt, 4⅜", G, from $450 to 900.00
Apple, M-1621, pnt CI, 3", EX 750.00
Baby in Cradle, M-51, pnt CI, 3¼", EX+ 1,550.00

Banque, M-1148 (similar), brass, EX pnt, 5¼" 320.00
Baseball on 3 Bats, M-1608, pnt CI, 5¼", EX 1,800.00
Baseball Player, M-18, CI, worn mc pnt, 5¾", G 260.00
Baseball Player, M-19, pnt CI, lt wear, 5¾", EX 350.00
Baseball Player, M-20, pnt CI, 5¾", EX 315.00
Basset Hound, M-380, CI, worn pnt, 3⅛" 290.00
Bear on Hind Legs, M-710, CI, worn pnt, 6⅛" 125.00
Bird Cage, M-925, CI/tin, worn, 3⅞" 100.00
Boston Bull Terrior, M-421, pnt CI, 5¼", EX 300.00
Boy w/Lg Football, M-10, CI, worn pnt, 5⅛" 1,550.00
Cadet, M-8, pnt CI, 5¾", EX 520.00
Capitalist, M-5, pnt CI, 5", EX 1,800.00
Captain Kidd, M-38, CI, worn pnt, 5⅝" 300.00
Castle w/2 Towers, M-1114, pnt CI, 7", EX 1,200.00
Cat, Seated; M-370 (similar), pnt lead, glass eyes, 5¼", EX 1,400.00
Cat on Tub, M-358, CI, worn pnt, 4⅛" 150.00
Century of Progress (1934), M-1064, pnt CI, 4½", EX 1,350.00
Circus Elephant, M-462, pnt CI, 3⅞", NM 350.00
City Bank, M-1111, pnt CI, 4⅛", EX 250.00
Colonial Gentleman, M-317, ceramic, 2¼" 200.00
Colonial House, M-992, pnt CI, 4", VG 220.00
Columbia, M-1077, pnt CI, 7", EX 650.00
Columbia Tower, M-1118, pnt CI, 6⅞", EX 560.00
Crown Bank, M-1226, pnt CI, 3⅝", EX 110.00
Crown Bank on Legs, M-1150, pnt CI, 4⅝", EX 1,150.00
Dog on Tub, M-359, pnt CI, 4", EX 240.00
Dolphin, M-33, pnt CI, 4½", EX 675.00
Donkey w/Hinged Saddle, M-498, lead, worn pnt, 3⅝" 65.00
Double Door, M-1125, pnt CI, 5½", EX 250.00
Duck, M-615, CI, worn pnt, 4⅞" 250.00
Eagle w/Shield, M-676, pnt CI, 3⅞", EX 600.00
Egyptian Tomb, M-1113, pnt CI, 6¼", EX 360.00
Eiffel Tower, M-1074, pnt CI, 8¾", EX 775.00
Elephant, Deco; M-449, CI, worn pnt, 4⅜", G 95.00
Fort Mt Hope, M-1189, pnt CI, 2⅞", EX 600.00
Foxy Grandpa, M-320, CI, worn pnt, 5½", VG 330.00
Fruit Basket, M-919, pnt CI, 2¾" 600.00
Give Me a Penny, M-167, pnt CI, 5⅝", EX 425.00
Globe on Arc, M-789, CI, worn pnt, 5¼", G 210.00
Globe Savings Fund, M-1199, pnt CI, 7⅛", EX 2,300.00
Goose, M-614, pnt CI, 3¾" 240.00
Hall's Excelsior, N-2710, pnt CI, EX 500.00
Hen, M-549, CI, worn pnt, 6" 825.00
High Rise, M-1220, CI, worn pnt, 3¼" 210.00
Hippo, M-718, pnt CI, 2", NM 5,400.00
Home Bank w/Dormers, M-1232 variant, pnt CI, 5¼", EX 675.00
Home Savings Bank, M-1237, pnt CI, dog's head finial, 5¾", EX 320.00
Horse, M-513, prancing on oval base, CI, worn pnt, 5⅛" 130.00
Huskey, M-411, pnt CI, 5", EX 570.00
I Hear a Call, M-438, CI, worn pnt, 5⅜" 165.00
Independence Hall, M-1211, pnt CI, 3-in-1, 6⅜", EX 3,000.00
Independence Hall, M-1242, pnt CI, 10", EX 3,000.00
Independence Hall, M-1244, pnt CI, 8⅞", EX 1,800.00
Independence Hall Tower, M-1202, pnt CI, 9½", EX 2,500.00
Indiana Silo, M-1247, EX 1,600.00
Iron Master's Cabin, M-1020, CI, worn pnt, 4½", G 1,500.00
King Midas, M-13, pnt CI, 4½", EX 1,050.00
Liberty Bell (Harper), M-780, pnt CI, 3¾", NM 450.00
Lion, M-759, open mouth, CI, worn pnt, 3½" 60.00
Lion, M-765, tail left, CI, worn pnt, 4", G 160.00
Lion on Tub, M-753, CI, worn pnt, 5⅜" 80.00
Mammy w/Spoon, M-168, CI, worn pnt, 5⅞", G 110.00
Marietta Silo, M-1246, pnt CI, 5½", EX 700.00
Mary & Lamb, M-164, CI, poor pnt, 4⅜" 425.00
Mascot, M-3, pnt CI, 5¾", EX 1,200.00
Middy, M-36, CI, poor pnt, 5¼", G 70.00
Minuteman, M-44, pnt CI, 6", EX 460.00
Model-T Ford, M-1483, pnt CI, 4", EX 300.00
Monkey w/Hat, M-740, pnt CI, 3⅞", EX 1,025.00
Monkeys, M-743, pnt CI, 3¼", EX 250.00
Mulligan, M-177, CI, gold pnt, 5¾", EX 650.00
Multiplying Bank, M-1184, pnt CI, 6½", EX 1,900.00
New Heatrola Bank, M-1354, CI/tin, 4½", EX, from $100 to 145.00
Noah's Ark, M-1465, compo, 2⅝", EX 130.00
Norman Stove, M-1344 (similar), pnt CI, 2⅜", EX 160.00
North Pole Freezer, M-1371, pnt CI, 4¼", EX 625.00
Old Beggerman, M-55, pnt lead, 7½", EX 270.00
Parlor Stove, M-1357, pnt CI, 6⅞", EX 240.00
Pavillion, M-1104, pnt CI, 3⅛", EX 460.00
Pearl Street Building, M-1096, pnt CI, 4¼", EX 600.00
Penthouse, M-1235, pnt CI, 5⅞", EX 725.00
Pig, I Made Chicago Famous, M-631 variant, pnt CI, 2⅝", EX 850.00
Polish Rooster, M-541, pnt CI, 5½", EX 1,750.00
Poor Weary Willie, M-90, pnt tin, 4¾", EX 170.00
Porky Pig, M-264, pnt CI, lt wear, 6", EX 180.00
Rabbit Lying Down, M-565, CI, worn pnt, 2⅛", VG+ 550.00
Radio, M-830, CI/tin, EX pnt (red, bl or gr), 3½", from $375 to 450.00
Reliable Parlor Stove, M-1356, pnt CI, 6¼", EX 440.00
Roof Bank, M-1122 variant, lead, VG pnt, 5½" 325.00
Rooster, M-547, pnt CI, 4⅝", EX 260.00
Rooster, M-548, CI, worn pnt, 4¾", G 190.00
Rooster, M-548 variant, brass, 4⅝" 180.00

Photo courtesy Larry Egelhoff

Safe Deposit (left and center), M: $600.00, EX: $275.00, average: $200.00; Property of the Savings Fund, M: $650.00.

Santa Claus, M-59, CI, worn pnt, 5⅞", VG 190.00
Santa Claus on Base, M-56 variant, pnt aluminum, 7⅛", EX 190.00
Santa w/Tree, M-61, pnt CI, 5⅞", EX 355.00
Seated Cat w/Bow, M-364, CI, worn pnt, 4⅜" 300.00
Share Cropper, M-173, CI, poor pnt, 5½" 150.00
Spaniel, Begging; M-361, pnt lead, 4⅜", EX 300.00
State Bank, M-1078, pnt CI, 8", EX 580.00
State Bank, M-1079, pnt CI, 6¾", EX 400.00
State Bank, M-1633, pnt CI, 5½", EX 260.00
Stop Sign, M-1479, CI, worn pnt, 4½" 450.00
Trolley, M-1472, pnt CI, 3", EX 625.00
US Air Mail, M-848, pnt CI, 6⅜", EX 330.00
US Mailbox on Victorian Base, M-861, pnt CI, 7½", EX 1,025.00
Washington Bust, M-153 (similar), brass, 8" 1,450.00
Westminster Abbey, M-973, CI, worn pnt, 6¼", VG 325.00
Woolworth Building, M-1041, CI, worn pnt, 5¾" 75.00
York Stove, M-1351, pnt CI, 4", EX 410.00
Young N, M-170, CI, worn pnt, 4½" 140.00

Barber Shop Collectibles

Even for the stranger in town, the local barber shop was easy to find, its location vividly marked with the traditional red and white striped barber pole that for centuries identified such establishments. As far back as the 12th century, the barber has had a place in recorded history. At one time he not only groomed the beards and cut the hair of his gentlemen clients but was known as the 'blood-letter' as well, hence the red stripe for blood and the white for the bandages. Many early barbers even pulled teeth! Later, laws were enacted that divided the practices of barbering and surgery.

The Victorian barber shop reflected the charm of that era with fancy barber chairs upholstered in rich wine-colored velvet; rows of bottles made from colored art glass held hair tonics and shaving lotion. Backbars of richly carved oak with beveled mirrors lined the wall behind the barber's station. During the late 19th century, the barber pole with a blue stripe added to the standard red and white as a patriotic gesture came into vogue.

Today the barber shop has all but disappeared from the American scene, replaced by modern unisex salons. Collectors search for the barber poles, the fancy chairs, and the tonic bottles of an era gone but not forgotten. See also Bottles; Razors; Shaving Mugs.

Box, sterilizer, plastic/metal/porc/glass, Nu-Vita, 5x8½x6½" **60.00**
Cabinet, shaving mug; wood w/3 glass doors, 46x25½" **450.00**
Case, counter-top display; Gillette, wood/glass, 2x18x14" **65.00**
Chair, horse figural, wood/metal/porc, glass eyes, 48x20x36", VG ..**2,500.00**
Chair, horse figural, wood/porc, Koken, 45x22x42", VG **2,200.00**
Chair, walnut & oak w/cvd gargoyle heads, rstr **900.00**
Globe, glass w/CI wall-mt base, 12½x9¼x9¼" **2,100.00**
Jar, antiseptic; frosted glass, metal lid, 10x3¾", EX **55.00**
Jar, Sanek Cellucotton, decal on glass, aluminum lid, 9½" **85.00**
Jar, Sanek Neck Strips, decal on glass, aluminum lid, 9½" **150.00**
Pole, cast aluminum w/glass cylinder, w/clock, 41x13x11" **150.00**
Pole, glass w/porc ends, metal wall mt, lights up, 23x5½" **150.00**
Pole, metal, red/wht/bl w/glass cover, porc ends, 37", VG **400.00**
Pole, milk glass cylinder w/red/bl pnt, metal fr, lights up, 24" **150.00**
Pole, milk glass globe & cylinder, metal fr, 30" **500.00**
Pole, milk glass panels, metal fr, porc top/bottom, 35" **800.00**
Pole, milk glass panels, metal fr, porc top/bottom, 44" **1,000.00**
Pole, porc, mts to building, ca 1900, minor chips, 42" **575.00**
Pole, porc & glass w/orig insert, metal base, free-standing, 73" ...**900.00**
Sign, Hair Bobbing, 2-sided porc flange, 12x24", EX **200.00**
Sign, Haircutting, rvpt in wood fr, 36x18", EX **555.00**
Sign, porc, curved to fit around pole, 49x8", EX **275.00**
Sign, 2-sided paper w/glass front, lights up, metal fr, 15x29x5" ..**100.00**
Sign, 2-sided porc, decorative iron hanger, 38x30" **500.00**
Sign, 2-sided porc flange, lt rust, 12x24" **80.00**
Sterilizer, chrome, for razors, Sterilizer Corp of Am, 9½x7x5" ...**175.00**
Sterilizer, glass w/metal fr, 2 wire racks, 10x7x11" **155.00**
Sterilizer, metal w/CI base, Ideal Metal Works NY, 59x18", VG ..**850.00**
Sterilizer, wood & metal w/glass front/sides, Paidar...NY, 20x14x12" ...**235.00**
Sterilizer, wood/metal/glass, Erie City Mfg, 11x13x9", VG **200.00**

Barometers

Barometers are instruments designed to measure the weight or pressure of the atmosphere in order to anticipate approaching weather changes. They have a glorious history. Some of the foremost thinkers of the 17th century developed the mercury barometer, as the discovery of the natural laws of the universe progressed. Working in 1644 from experiments by Galileo, Evangelista Torrecelli used a glass tube and a jar of mercury to create a vacuum and therefore prove that air has weight. Four years later, Rene Descartes added a paper scale to the top of Torrecelli's mercury tube and created the basic barometer. Blaise Pascal, working with Descartes, used it to determine the heights of moun-

tains; indeed, only later was the correlation between changes in air pressure and changes in the weather observed and the term 'weather-glass' applied. Robert Boyle introduced it to England, and Robert Hook modified the form and designed the wheel barometer.

The most common type of barometer is the wheel or banjo type. Second is the stick type. Modifications of the plain stick would be the marine gimballed type, followed by the laboratory or Kew or Fortin type. Others are the Admiral Fitzroys of which there are twelve or more types. The above all have mercury contained in either glass tubing or wood-box cisterns.

Another type of barometer is the aneroid, working on atmospheric pressure changes. They come in all sizes ranging from 1" in diameter to 12" or larger. They may be in metal or wood cases. There is a Barograph which records on a graph that rotates around a drum powered by a seven-day clock mechanism. Pocket barometers (altimeters) vary in sizes from 1" diameter up to 6" diameter. One final type of barometer is the symphisometer, a modification of the stick barometer used for a limited time and not as accurate as a conventional marine barometer. Our advisor for this category is Bob Elsner; he is listed in the Directory under Florida.

American

Barograph reading barometer, mahogany, Negretti & Zambra, $950.00.

Photo courtesy Bob Elsner

B Pike & Sons, NY, silvered scale, 14" thermometer, 1880s **2,450.00**
DE Lent, Rochester NY **950.00**
FD McKay Jr, Elmira NY, dbl-trn wood columns **3,100.00**
Simmons & Sons, Fulton NY **950.00**
Storm King model by EC Spooner Boston, 42" stick, EX **1,000.00**
Taylor Instruments, NY, 1927, 28" stick **300.00**

English

Admiral Fitzroy, oak w/mercury tube, 41", VG, from $500 to .**2,500.00**
Angle barometer, right, John Whiteburst, ca 1790, from $12,000 to **15,000.00**
Ballard Cranbrook, wheel type, broken tube, rstr cornice, 38" **775.00**
L Casella, London, rosewood, stick **1,450.00**
Marine gimballed, A Walker, wood w/brass mts, VG, from $3,200 to **4,000.00**
Marine gimballed, Frodsham-Keen Liverpool, wood/brass, VG ...**1,500.00**
Spelzini, London, wheel type, MOP, 10" **1,250.00**
Stanley, Petersborough, wheel type, silvered scale/thermometer, 6" **1,450.00**

Other Barometer Types

Aneroid, w/½-rnd thermometer **250.00**
Aneroid, 4-6" dia, brass case **150.00**
Barograph reading barometer, mahog, Negretti & Zambra **950.00**
Pocket barometer (altimeter), w/case, from $200 to **300.00**

Barware

Back in the thirties when social soirees were very elegant affairs thanks to the influence of Hollywood in all its glamour and mystique, cocktails were often served up in shakers styled as miniature airplanes, zeppelins, skyscrapers, lady's legs, penguins, roosters, bowling pins, etc. Some were by top designers such as Norman Bel Geddes and Russel Wright. They were made of silverplate, glass, and chrome, often trimmed with colorful Bakelite handles. Today these are hot collectibles, and even the more common Deco-styled chrome cylinders are often priced at $25.00 and up. Ice buckets, trays, and other bar accessories are also included in this area of collecting.

For further information we recommend *Vintage Bar Ware Identification & Value Guide* by Stephen Visakay, our advisor for this category; he is listed in the Directory under New Jersey.

Glass cocktail shaker, chrome top, flashed green and cut, unknown American maker, ca 1935, $100.00.

Photo courtesy Stephen Visakay

Canape tray, satin chromium over brass, 1935, ½x4⅝x6¾"	10.00
Cigarette dispenser, brass & Bakelite bartender, Art Metal, 8"	550.00
Cocktail cup, Catalin w/chrome stem, mk Nudawn USA, 1930s	10.00
Cocktail cup, glass insert, mk Farber Bros, Pat, 4¼"	11.00
Cocktail cup, rooster, glass, 1930s-40s, 3½x3¼" bowl	22.50
Cocktail dish, bar scene w/drink names, 1930s, 8"	90.00
Cocktail glass, rooster scenes, ftd, 1930s, 3½x3¼"	8.00
Drink stirrer, female form, plastic, 1930s, 7"	5.00
Ice chopper, cobalt glass w/silk-screened recipes, 1930s, 11½"	65.00
Ice chopper, Ice-O-Mat, metal & plastic, 1940s, 9"	35.00
Ice tongs, NP, ca 1928, 1x7½"	40.00
Martini spike/Vermouth dispenser, syringe shape, 1950s, 6½"	25.00
Mixer, outboard motor shape, battery operated, Swank, 6"	50.00
Serving set, hammered NP, shaker/tray/10 stemmed cups, 1927	175.00
Shaker, artillery shell, 3-pc brass, inscribed ...Panama '04	200.00
Shaker, Boston Lighthouse, Silver City, 48-oz, 21"	1,700.00
Shaker, Catalin, SP recipe dial top, English, mk, 1930s	265.00
Shaker, cylindrical, SP, mk Italy, 11½"	115.00
Shaker, glass, pnt yel w/rooster motif, SP top, mk, 1930s, 10"	210.00
Shaker, glass w/pnt duck, SP top, cobalt-ft base, ca 1927, 9¼"	90.00
Shaker, gr w/crystal hdl, chrome fittings, Cambridge, 1930s, 11"	105.00
Shaker, Krome Kraft w/orange Catalin trim, 1940s-60s, mk, 12¾"	50.00
Shaker, lantern form, cranberry glass, SP, English, mk, 1930s	400.00
Shaker, leather on wood, pnt/lacquer, Fr, 1930s, 11¾x3⅛"	275.00
Shaker, martini; ruby glass, appl sterling trim, 9⅜"	150.00
Shaker, mk Gorham GA13825, Sterling, cojoined sqs, 12"	4,000.00
Shaker, onyx, silk-screened recipes, 1930s, party sz, 1"	175.00
Shaker, pressed glass, cranberry flashed, SP top, 1930s, 11"	135.00
Shaker, ribbed glass, pnt blk bands, Czech, 1930s	100.00
Shaker, rooster's head & breast in SP on brass, 1920, 10⅞"	625.00
Shaker, ruby glass w/fighting cocks in appl sterling, 1930, 12"	275.00
Shaker, skyscraper, chrome plate w/blk enamel cap & base, 12¼"	60.00
Shaker, SP, rooster finial, cork stopper, 1920s, stamped, 14"	115.00
Shaker, SP w/grape leaf design, unmk, 1920s, 12½"	75.00
Shaker, standing dumbbell, chrome w/plastic cap, 1930s, 12"	110.00
Shaker, Town Crier's bell, chrome, walnut hdl, 1937, 10⅜"	60.00

Shot jigger, graduated, Napier, stemmed, 4"	85.00
Snack tin, triangular, gold w/blk dots, martini pictured, 1930s	12.00
Soda siphon, chrome w/enameled top, Bel Geddes, mk, Pat, 10"	160.00
Soda siphon, etched Shipstones Nottingham w/star, 12¾"	40.00
Swizzle sticks, glass, tuxedoed men, 1930s, 7¼", ea	15.00
Traveling bar, chrome-plated plane, ca 1928, German, 18-pc, 12"	4,000.00
Traveling bar, shaker form, NP, 9-pc, mk Germany, ca 1928, 8"	85.00
Tumbler, glass, dice sealed in bottom, 4"	6.00

Baskets

Basket weaving is a craft as old as ancient history. Baskets have been used to harvest crops, for domestic chores, and to contain the catch of fishermen. Materials at hand were utilized, and baskets from a specific region are often distinguishable simply by analyzing the natural fibers used in their construction. Early Indian baskets were made of corn husks or woven grasses. Willow splint, straw, rope, and paper were also used. Until the invention of the veneering machine in the late 1800s, splint was made by water-soaking a split log until the fibers were softened and flexible. Long strips were pulled out by hand and, while still wet and pliable, woven into baskets in either a cross-hatch or hexagonal weave.

Most handcrafted baskets on the market today were made between 1860 and the early 1900s. Factory baskets with a thick, wide splint cut by machine are of little interest to collectors. The more popular baskets are those designed for a specific purpose, rather than the more commonly found utility baskets that had multiple uses. Among the most costly forms are the Nantucket Lighthouse baskets, which were basically copied from those made there for centuries by aboriginal Indians. They were designed in the style of whale-oil barrels and named for the South Shoal Nantucket Lightship where many were made during the last half of the 19th century. Cheese baskets (used to separate curds from whey), herb gathering baskets, and finely woven Shaker miniatures are other highly-prized examples of the basket-weaver's art.

In the listings that follow, assume that each has a center bentwood handle (unless handles of another type are noted) that is not included in the height. Unless another type of material is indicated, assume that each is made of splint. Conditions described as 'EX,' 'VG,' or 'G' indicates some measure of damage.

For further information we recommend *Collector's Guide to Country Baskets* by Don and Carol Raycraft, available from Collector Books. See also American Indian; Eskimo; Sewing; Shaker.

Apple, wood bottom, bail hdl, 12" dia	125.00
Bread, rye straw, flat bottom, flared rim, 4⅜x10½"	25.00
Buttocks, 20-rib, thick bl pnt, 2¼x5x4¼"	575.00
Buttocks, 22-rib, bl & blk stripes, some age, 8½x17x14"	140.00
Buttocks, 26-rib, natural w/faded red & gr, 4¼x7¼x7¼"	220.00
Buttocks, 28-rib, dk gr pnt, wear/holes, 6½x11x13"	175.00
Buttocks, 30-rib, pnt mc floral, minor damage, 5x10½x10"	440.00
Buttocks, 38-rib, natural patina, 4x7½x7"	200.00
Buttocks, 40-rib, old grayish pnt, 7x14x13½"	350.00
Buttocks, 56-rib, well made, med patina, 4¾x8x7"	300.00
Buttocks, 58-rib, orange varnish, twist-detail hdl, 7x13x13"	375.00
Cheese, 2 cvd wood hdls, 7x24", EX	400.00
Domed lid, circular conforming base, gr pnt, 19th C, 15x15"	485.00
Gathering, melon shape, stationary hdl, 1800s, 2x4x3½"	450.00
Gathering, rectangular, flat bottom, 19th C, 5⅝x14⅝x8½"	150.00
Market, sides taper in slightly, 8x19x12½"	95.00
Market, wicker, wrapped hdl, 19th C, 8¼x14½", EX	50.00
Melon, blk pnt, 19th C, minor breaks, 9x9½"	550.00
Melon, gr & salmon pnt decor, 19th C, minor breaks, 12x11¾"	450.00
Melon, 14-rib, red stain, 3¼x6x6"	165.00

Mini, rectangular, dbl-hinged, 19th C, 5x8¼x4½" 345.00
Mini, 8 melon ribs w/mc stripes, 1⅜x2¼" 200.00
Mini egg (1), old brn patina, 3x3½" 100.00
Nantucket, tight weave, fine patina, 7"+hdl 2,300.00
Nantucket, trn wood base, woven cane/splint, Mitchell Ray, 9x8½" ...800.00
Nantucket, trn wooden bottom, 4½x6½", EX 450.00
Nantucket, trn wooden bottom w/ivory inset, Boyer, 4x6½x6" ..745.00
Nantucket, vertical ribs, wooden bottom, 4¼x9¾" 850.00
Nantucket, vertical ribs, wooden bottom, 5¾x8½", G 275.00
Nantucket, wooden bottom, 6¾x14" 1,200.00
Potato print designs in red/bl/gr, 5½x14½x11¼" 500.00
Rectangular, cvd D-shape hdl, EX patina, sm break, 10x16x8" ..100.00
Rectangular, EX patina, minor damage, 7¼x12½" 275.00
Rectangular, gray weathered finish, rim hdls, lt damage, 11x17" ...175.00
Rectangular, old gray-gr pnt, wrapped rim, fixed hdls,, 10x22x16" ...2,000.00
Rectangular, red stain, flat bottom, 4 arched hdl mts, 9x14x7" ...250.00
Rectangular, pnt pk & blk, 2-hdld, Am, 19th C, 5x15x10" 490.00
Rectangular, wrapped rim, pierced hdls, 1890s, 9x27x22", EX ...400.00
Rectangular, yel & bl stripes, lined w/1848 newspaper, 14½x17½" 600.00
Rice straw, mc floral decor, Oriental export, 7" L 50.00
Rye straw, domed lid, missing hdls, 24" dia 200.00
Rye straw, oval, minor wear, 4½x10¾x8½" 50.00
Winnowing, splint bottom, 3" bentwood rim, 21" dia 300.00

Batchelder

Ernest A. Batchelder was a leading exponent of the Arts and Crafts movement in the United States. His influential book, *Design in Theory and Practice*, was originally published in 1910. He is best known, however, for his artistic tiles which he first produced in Pasadena, California, from 1909 to 1916. In 1916 the business was relocated to Los Angeles where it continued until 1932, closing because of the Depression.

In 1938 Batchelder resumed production in Pasadena under the name of 'Kinneola Kiln.' Output of the new pottery consisted of delicately cast bowls and vases in an Oriental style. This business closed in 1951. Tiles carry a die-stamped mark; vases and bowls are hand incised. Our advisor for this category is Jack Chipman, author of *Collector's Encyclopedia of California Pottery, Second Edition;* he is listed in the Directory under California.

Ashtray, lt bl matt, hexagonal w/emb advertising, 4½", EX 275.00
Bowl, decagonal, chartreuse w/maroon overglaze, 13" 175.00
Bowl, dk teal, rose int, Pasadena mk, 2x7" 85.00
Tile, cherub in tree, bl semi-matt, 5¾x2½" 225.00

Tile, Dutch boy with windmill beyond, brown with blue wash, 4", $225.00.

Tile, Evangelist series, bl engobe, 9"sq, set of 6, M 5,700.00
Tile, feathery bird, bl patina, thick, 4" sq 200.00
Tile, La Mayan, terra cotta, 3½" 150.00
Tile, medieval man w/guitar, 15x9" 1,000.00
Tile, peacock, 5¾", NM 325.00

Tile, peacocks, pk & yel, 3" sq 125.00
Vase, caramel/brn gloss w/bl & gray highlights, 4" 250.00
Vase, teal over brn gloss, 5" 300.00
Vase, yel, flared rim, 6" 200.00
Vase, yel, 7" sq 175.00

Battersea

Battersea is a term that refers to enameling on copper or other metal. Though originally produced at Battersea, England, in the mid-18th century, the craft was later practiced throughout the Staffordshire district. Boxes are the most common examples. Some are figurals, and many bear an inscription. Values are given for examples with only minimal damage, which is normal. Our advisor for this category is John Harrigan; he is listed in the Directory under Minnesota.

Bonbonniere, European scene on underside, 1½x2¾", EX 625.00
Box, bluebird on foliage, hinged lid, 1½" 285.00
Box, florals on bl, wht lid w/couple in landscape, oval, 2⅝" 195.00
Box, grisaille classical scene w/gold, 3½" dia 500.00
Box, lady's torso form, head forms lid, 3" 1,600.00
Box, Remember Her Who Gives This Triffle on turq, 1x1¾", EX ..200.00
Box, snuff; French/English naval battle, 2" L 750.00
Box, 2 boxers/10 spectators on lid, cobalt base, ¾x2x1½" 375.00

Candlesticks, Georgian in the Rococo taste, cobalt reserves on white with floral sprigs and gold, late 1700s, 9¾", $1,500.00 for the pair.

Mirror knob, castle landscape, brass mt, late 1700s, 1½x2", pr ...325.00
Mirror knob, lady's portrait, late 1700s, 1⅜", pr, EX 350.00
Mirror knob, putti artists, late 1700s, 1⅞" dia, pr, G 375.00
Needle case, floral & insects on yel, rstr, 4¾" L 550.00
Opera glasses, children hunting & fishing, 4" W, in case 425.00

Bauer

Originally founded in Paducah, Kentucky, in 1885, the J.A. Bauer Company moved to Los Angeles where it was re-established in 1910. Until the 1920s their major products were terra-cotta gardenware, flowerpots, and stoneware and yellow ware bowls. During prohibition they produced crocks for home use. A more artful form of product began to develop with the addition of designer Louis Ipsen to the staff circa 1915. Some of his work, a line of molded vases, flowerpots, bowls, etc., was awarded a bronze medal at the Pacific International Exposition in 1916.

In 1930 the first of many dinnerware lines was tested on the market. Their initial pattern, Plain Ware, was well accepted and led the way to the introduction of the most popular dinnerware in their history and with today's collectors, Ring Ware. It was produced from 1932 into the early 1960s in solid colors of jade green, royal blue, dusty burgundy, ivory, Chinese yellow, Delph blue, orange-red, and (in very limited quantities) black or white. Its simple pattern was a design of closely-spaced concentric ribs, either convex or concave. Over the years, more than one hundred shapes were available. Some were made in limited quantities, resulting in rare items to whet the appetites of Bauer buffs today. Other patterns were La Linda, produced during the 1940s and 1950s, and Monterey Moderne, introduced in 1948 and remaining popular into the 1950s (made in pink, black, gray, brown, and green).

After WWII a flood of foreign imports and loss of key employees drastically curtailed their sales, and the pottery began a steady decline that ended in failure in 1962. Prices listed below reflect the California market. For more information we recommend *Collector's Encyclopedia of Bauer Pottery: Identification & Values* (Collector Books) and *The Collector's Encyclopedia of California Pottery, Second Edition*, both by Jack Chipman, our advisor for this category. Mr. Chipman's address may be found in the Directory under California.

In the lines of Ring and Plain ware, pricing depends to some extent on color. Use the low end of our range of values for light brown, Chinese yellow, orange-red, jade green, red-brown, olive green, light blue, turquoise, and gray; the high-end colors are delph blue, ivory, dusty burgundy, cobalt, chartreuse, papaya, and burgundy. Black is 50% higher than the high end; to evaluate white, double the high side. Use the low end of the range to evaluate Monterey items in all colors but Monterey blue, burgundy, and white — those are high-end colors. You'll need to double the high end for black in this line as well as Monterey Moderne. An in-depth study of colors may be found in the books referenced above.

Art Pottery

Flower bowl, cobalt matt, low, rare, 12", minimum value	950.00
Flower holder, gr matt w/dk specks, 2x4½"	85.00
Jardiniere, mossy gr, 6"	250.00
Rose jar, mossy gr, 6"	250.00
Vase, dk gr overdrip, rare, 8", minimum value	950.00

Brusche Al Fresco and Contempo

Photo courtesy Jack Chipman

Lazy Susan, speckled yellow, 14", $65.00.

Casserole, Fr; Al Fresco, Dubonnet, 2-qt	50.00
Creamer, Al Fresco, Dubonnet, jumbo	25.00
Mug, Contempo, Pumpkin, 8-oz	12.00
Pitcher, Al Fresco, Misty Gray, 2-pt	40.00
Plate, bread & butter; Contempo, pk, 6"	6.00
Shakers, Al Fresco, Coffee brn, jumbo, pr	24.00

Cal-Art Pottery

Figurine, hippo, matt cream, mini, rare, minimum value	300.00
Pitcher, vase; matt yel, 10"	150.00
Vase, matt pk, tab hdls, 10"	100.00
Wall pocket, matt wht, early, very rare, 6½"	300.00

Matt Carlton

Ashtray, Mexican hat, Delph bl, 3", minimum value	250.00

Basket, orange-red, hdld, 8", minimum value	1,500.00
Bowl, orange-red, sq, 2½x6"	85.00
Candle holder, blk, hdld, 2x3¾", minimum value	250.00
Match holder, orange-red, 2"	150.00
Vase, fan; blk, grooved, hdld, 10", minimum value	1,800.00
Vase, jade gr, flattened, ribbed, 8½", minimum value	375.00
Vase, jade gr, ribbed, pinched twist hdls, 8¾", minimum	800.00
Vase, orange-red, Hybrid Rebekah, twist hdls, 8¼", minimum	800.00
Vase, royal bl, ribbed, flared rim, 5¼", minimum value	450.00

Florist and Garden Pottery

Bowl, Indian; blk, 6", minimum value	300.00
Cactus jar, gr, handmade, 8-cup, 6x12", minimum value	350.00
Flowerpot, orange-red, Deco-style, 5", minimum value	200.00
Jardiniere, Biltmore, Delph bl, 12"	250.00
Jardiniere, blk, ruffled rim, 8", minimum value	375.00
Pot, pinnacle; chartreuse, 8"	75.00
Pot saucer, jade gr, 5"	25.00
Sand jar, wht speckled glaze, 20"	350.00
Strawberry pot, burgundy, 8-cup, 9"	200.00
Swirl pot, burgundy, 6"	60.00

Hi-Fire Pottery

Cat feeder, turq, 5", minimum value	300.00
Flower bowl, wht, mk, fluted, 3½x11", minimum value	250.00
Rose bowl, Monterey bl, 7"	85.00
Vase, garden; orange-red, hand-thrown, 2-hdl, 15", minimum	800.00
Vase, wht, 'ring' cylinder, 10"	175.00

La Linda

Bowl, cereal; burgundy, 6"	25.00
Butter dish, matt pk	65.00
Creamer, burgundy	15.00
Cup, gray (late period color), jumbo, scarce, minimum value	50.00
Gravy boat, gr	25.00
Plate, salad; brn, 7½"	8.50
Platter, burgundy, oval, 12"	30.00
Saucer, matt yel	6.00
Shaker, brn	6.00
Tumbler, matt ivory, w/clip-on metal hdl	20.00

Monterey

Ashtray, Monterey bl, rare, minimum value	200.00
Bowl, fruit; ftd, 12"	100.00
Bowl, serving; blk, rare, 9", minimum value	250.00
Centerpc, Monterey bl, 2 detachable candle holders, minimum	375.00
Coffee server, w/lid	65.00
Cup	20.00
Plate, bread & butter; 6"	10.00
Plate, dinner; 9"	18.00
Platter, oval, 10"	40.00
Relish plate, 3-section, 10"	85.00
Teapot, old style, 6-cup	100.00
Tumbler	15.00

Monterey Moderne and Related Kitchenware

Batter bowl, yel, angle hdl, 2-qt	65.00
Bowl, mixing; burgundy, #36	15.00
Bowl, serving; brn, 13"	85.00

Bowl, soup; blk, 5¼"	45.00
Bowl, vegetable; brn, divided, 8½"	50.00
Casserole, olive gr, brass finished metal fr, 1½-qt	55.00
Coffeepot, pk, angle hdl, w/lid, 6-cup, minimum value	175.00
Creamer, pk	12.50
Mug, burgundy, no hdl, 8-oz	20.00
Pitcher, beater; bl speckled, 1-qt	35.00
Pitcher, burgundy, angle hdl, 2-qt	80.00
Plate, bread & butter; Mission Modern, chartreuse/brn, 6"	12.50
Plate, dinner; burgundy, 9½"	20.00
Plate, dinner; Epiphyllum Spray decal, 10½"	30.00
Plate, grill; Mission Modern, rnd, 3-section, 10½"	25.00
Plate, salad; gray, 7½"	10.00
Platter, brn, 10"	22.00
Ramekin, yel	12.00
Sugar bowl, chartreuse, 2-hdl, w/lid	22.00
Teapot, wht speckled, 4-cup	50.00
Teapot, yel, normal hdl, 6-cup	85.00
Tumbler, gray, metal hdl	25.00
Vase, pillow; Barnyard Scene decal	50.00

Plain Ware

Bean pot, ind	85.00
Bowl, mixing; #1, 3½-gal, minimum value	750.00
Bowl, pudding; #6, 10¼"	100.00
Bowl, salad; 10½"	125.00
Coffee cup	125.00
Creamer	40.00
Goblet, minimum value	150.00
Lamp base, 4½", minimum value	400.00
Mug, beer	175.00
Mug, 4", minimum value	75.00
Pitcher, Dutch; 12", minimum value	475.00
Plate, bread & butter; 6½"	15.00
Plate, butter; blk, 4½", minimum value	135.00
Ramekin, blk	30.00
Sherbet	175.00

Red, White, and Yellow Ware

Ant trap, dk gr, Pat mk, 5"	65.00
Butter jar, whtware, hand decor, mk, w/lid, 1-lb	45.00
Condiment pot, redware, open, mk, 3¼"	30.00
Fumigator, brn, 2-gal	85.00
Milk crock, whtware, 1-gal, 10½x4½"	50.00
Olla, redware, w/faucet, 3-gal, 12¾"	100.00
Pin tray/ashtray, raised old west scene, yelware, minimum	350.00
Pot, lion; redware, 14"	200.00

Ring Ware

Bottle, water; open	175.00
Bowl, batter; 1-qt	150.00
Bowl, mixing; #18	65.00
Bowl, mixing; #30	55.00
Bowl, punch; 14"	500.00
Bowl, salad; low, 12"	150.00
Bowl, salad; low, 9"	120.00
Butter dish, oblong, w/lid, ¼-lb	275.00
Butter dish, rnd	250.00
Candle holder, 2½"	85.00
Cigarette jar, w/lid	450.00
Coffee server, wooden hdl, w/lid, 8-cup	125.00

Cookie jar, minimum	600.00
Drip coffeepot, minimum	500.00
Egg cup, minimum	300.00
Goblet, blk, minimum value	250.00
Gravy bowl	175.00
Honey jar, w/1 or 2 bees on lid, minimum value	2,000.00
Mug, bbl shape	200.00
Nappy, #9	100.00
Pitcher, beer; minimum	600.00
Pitcher, cream/syrup	125.00
Pitcher, ice water; jade gr, #58	350.00
Plate, bread & butter; 5"	50.00
Plate, dinner; 10½"	100.00
Plate, relish; 5-compartment	150.00
Plate, salad; 7½"	45.00
Plate, soup; 7½"	100.00
Platter, oval, 9"	45.00
Saucer, AD	100.00
Spice jar, #2	250.00
Sugar bowl	65.00
Sugar shaker, minimum	350.00
Teapot, other than blk, 6-cup	175.00
Tumbler, bbl shape w/metal hdl	200.00

Bavaria

Bavaria, Germany, was long the center of that country's pottery industry; in the 1800s, many firms operated in and around the area. Chinaware vases, novelties, and table accessories were decorated with transfer prints as well as by hand by artists who sometimes signed their work. The examples listed here are marked with 'Bavaria' and the logos of some of the various companies which were located there.

Plate, stag portrait, scalloped rim, marked Punch Bavaria, 9½", $65.00.

Bowl, chrysanthemums & roses w/gold, emb scrolls, 3x10½"	45.00
Coffee set, floral w/gold, melon ribs, mk, 9½" pot+cr/sug	95.00
Pickle dish, mc floral w/gold on elongated leaf form, 11x4½"	32.00
Pitcher, cider; crab apples/bk: cherries, Classic, 1920, 5"	80.00
Plate, roses, mc on pastel w/gold, ZS&Co, 12⅜"	70.00
Plate, swans & lily pads, scalloped cobalt border, 12½"	100.00
Tankard, strawberries w/gold, 11"	165.00
Teapot, alternating panels w/gold, +6 c/s	215.00
Vase, gold lustre floral, sgn Sisters of Notre Dame, 11½"	95.00
Vase, pr exotic birds on berry branches, sgn Yark, 15", pr	200.00

Beer Cans

In the early 1930s one of America's largest can-manufacturing companies approached an East Coast brewery with a novel concept —

beer in cans. The brewery decided to take a chance on the idea, and in January 1935, the beer can was born.

The 'church key' style can opener was invented at the same time, and early flat-top cans actually had instructions on how to use it to open a can.

Canned beer soared in popularity, and breweries scrambled to meet the canning challenge. Since many companies did not have a machine to fill a flat-top can, the cone top was invented. Brewery executives believed its shape would be more acceptable to consumers used to buying bottled beer, and it easily passed through existing bottling machinery. The more compact flat-top can dominated sales, and by the 1950s cone tops were obsolete.

About values: Condition is critical when determining the value of a beer can. Prices quoted are for like-new condition cans, free of rust, dents, scratches and other damage. Like any collectible, value drops in direct proportion to condition, and off-grade cans are often worth no more than one-half of retail value. Our advisor for this category is Dan Andrews; he is listed in the Directory under California.

Information in our descriptions is given in this specific order:
1) name of brew;
2) company — may be simply repetetive; and
3) city /state or state.

ABC, Maier, LA, red, wht & bl, flat top 10.00
Ace High, Ace, Chicago, wht w/red face, flat top 35.00
Acme, Acme, San Francisco, blk w/wht face, flat top 10.00
Ballantine Ale, Ballantine, Newark, gold w/gr logo, flat top 20.00
Billy, 4 breweries, aluminum or steel, tab top, ea 50
Budweiser, AB, St Louis, gold w/blk eagle, flat top 20.00
Burgermeister, Burgermeister, SF, wht w/Burgie man, flat top 8.00
Canadian Ace, Canadian Ace, Chicago, brn w/wht face, cone top ..15.00
Coors, Coors, Golden CO, 1990 Long Beach Grand Prix, tab top ..2.00
Country Club Malt Liquor, Pearl, St Jo MO, wht, tab top 1.00
Croft Cream Ale, Croft, Boston, gr w/yel logo, flat top 85.00
Dixie 45, Dixie, New Orleans, gold & wht, flat top 100.00
Drewry's, Drewry's, South Bend IN, wht w/RCMP mountie, flat top ..25.00
E&B, E&B, Detroit, bl background, gold front, cone top 30.00
Eastside, Los Angeles, LA, bl w/eagle logo, flat top 15.00
Falstaff, Falstaff, St Louis, brn w/wht shield, cone top 20.00
Fisher, Fisher, Salt Lake City, wht w/red logo, flat top 7.00
GB, Grace Bros, Santa Rosa CA, yel w/orange letters, flat top ...225.00
Grain Belt, Grain Belt, MN, metallic orange, cone top 30.00
Heritage House, numerous breweries, yel w/red shield, tab top, ea ..1.00
Highland, Missoula, Missoula MT, Scotch check design, flat top .10.00
Iron City, Pittsburg, Pittsburg, 1975 Steelers, tab top 1.00
Jax, Jackson, New Orleans, red, blk & wht, flat top 200.00
JR, Pearl, San Antonio, aluminum, tab top 50
Kol, Silver Springs, Tacoma WA, bl & wht stripes, flat top 4.00
L&M, Maier, Los Angeles, blk w/yel letters, flat top 40.00
Lone Star, Lone Star, San Antonio, wht w/red shield, flat top 15.00
Lucky Lager, Lucky, San Francisco, gold w/red X, flat top 10.00
Mile Hi, Tivoli, Denver, red, wht & bl, flat top 25.00
Miller High Life, Miller, Milwaukee, blk w/wht face, flat top 10.00
Milwaukee's Best, Gettleman, Milwaukee, red, wht & tan, flat top 15.00
Naragansett Ale, Naragansett, Cranston RI, gold, blk & red, flat top ..150.00
Olde Frothingslosh, Pittsburg, Pittsburg, bl, tab top 12.00
Olympia, Olympia, WA, gold, wht & beige, flat top 3.00
Pabst Export, Pabst, Milwaukee, silver, bl & red, flat top 20.00
Pearl, Pearl, San Antonio, TX football schedule, tab top 1.00
Pfeiffer, Pfeiffer, Detroit, yel w/cartoon character, flat top 20.00
Primo, Schlitz, Honolulu HI, gold w/wht face, tab top 2.00
Ranier Ale, Ranier, San Francisco, gr w/orange face, cone top 35.00
Regal Pale, Regal Pale, SF, wht w/bl & gold shield, flat top 6.00
Reingold, Liebmann, NY, 7 different Miss Rheingolds, flat top, ea .300.00

Ruppert Knickerbocker, Ruppert, NY, wht w/man, flat top 25.00
Schlitz, Schlitz, Milwaukee, brn & wht w/globe, flat top 6.00
Schmidt, Heileman, St Paul, 20+ colorful outdoor scenes, tab top, ea .1.00
Tavern Pale, Atlantic, Chicago, gray w/maroon shield, flat top ...25.00
Utica Club, West End, Utica NY, wht w/bl & red letters, flat top ..25.00
Walters, Walters, Pueblo CO, red, blk & gold, flat top 25.00
Whales White Ale, National, Baltimore, blk & wht, tab top 50.00
Wooden Shoe, Wooden Shoe, Minster OH, red, wht & bl, cone top .45.00
Yusey, Pilsen, Chicago, red, wht & bl w/eagle, flat top 20.00
007, National Phoenix, 7 different colors & girls, tab top, ea 300.00

Bellaire, Marc

Marc Bellaire, originally Donald Edmund Fleischman, was born in Toledo, Ohio, in 1925. He studied at the Toledo Museum of Art under Ernest Spring while employed as a designer for the Libbey Glass Company. During World War II while serving in the Navy, he travelled extensively throughout the Pacific, resulting in his enriched sense of design and color.

Marc settled in California in the 1950s where his work attracted the attention of national buyers and agencies who persuaded him to create ceramic lines of his own, employing hand-decorated techniques throughout. This resulted in the building of a studio in Culver City. He produced high-quality ceramics, often decorated with ultramodern figures or geometric patterns and executed with a distinctive flair. His most famous line was Mardi Gras, decorated with slim dancers in spattered and striped colors of black, blue, pink, and white. Other major patterns were Jamaica, Balinese, Beachcomber, Friendly Island, Cave Painting, Hawaiian, Bird Isle, Oriental, Jungle Dancer, and Kashmir. Kashmir usually has the name Ingle on the front and Bellaire on the reverse.

It is to be noted that Marc was employed by Sascha Brastoff during the 1950s. Many believe that he was hired for his creative imagination and style.

During the period of 1951 – 1956, Marc was named one of the top ten artware designers by *Giftwares Magazine*. After 1956 he taught and lectured on art, design, and ceramic decorating techniques from coast to coast. Many pieces were one of a kind, commissioned throughout the United States.

During the 1970s he set up a studio in Marin County, California, and eventually moved to Palm Springs where he opened his final studio/gallery. There he produced large pieces with a Southwestern style. Mr. Bellaire died in 1994. Our advisor for this category is Marty Webster; he is listed in the Directory under Michigan.

Platter, multicolored angels on gray, signed and dated 1958, 14" diameter, $400.00 (believed to be a personal presentation piece).

Photo courtesy Marty Webster

Ashtray, Bird Isle, blk birds on cream, 8" 85.00
Ashtray, Clown, mc on cream, 7" 65.00
Ashtray, Jamaica, musicians on brn, 10x14" 85.00
Ashtray, Mardi Gras, figures on blk, rolled rim, 9" 100.00
Ashtray, Mardi Gras, figures on blk, 14x14" 225.00
Ashtray, Still Life, matt fruits & leaves, 10x15" 100.00

Bowl, Beachcomber, low teardrop shape, 12" L	100.00
Bowl, Cotillian, lady w/bl bird, 13x9"	125.00
Box, Jamaica, man w/guitar, free-form, B46, 8"	135.00
Box, Mardi Gras, w/lid, 10" dia	200.00
Candlestick, Jamaica Man, 10½"	125.00
Compote, Cave Painting, 4-ftd, 6x12"	100.00
Compote, Cotillian, 4-ftd, 8x17"	225.00
Cookie jar, Stick People, wooden lid, 10"	150.00
Ewer, Mardi Gras, figures on blk, hdl, 10"	400.00
Figurine, Mardi Gras, man reclining, very slim, 18"	1,000.00
Figurine, Mardi Gras, man standing, very slim, 24"	1,000.00
Figurine, Polynesian, man standing, 12"	500.00
Lamp, Mardi Gras, long-neck vase on wood base, 28"	450.00
Platter, Friendly Island, 10"	135.00
Platter, Hawaiian, 3 figures on orange, 7x13"	100.00
Platter, Mardi Gras, figures on blk, 12x18"	250.00
Platter, Polynesian Dancer, egg shaped, 11x15"	250.00
Tray, Jungle Dancer, figure on blk/gr, 12" dia	145.00
Vase, Balinese Women, hourglass shape, 8"	100.00
Vase, Black Cats, hourglass shape, 8"	100.00
Vase, Mardi Gras, hourglass shape on 3 ft, 11"	125.00
Vase, Polynesian Woman, 9"	100.00
Vase, Stick People, irregular beak-like opening, 12"	250.00

Belleek, American

From 1883 until 1930, several American potteries located in New Jersey and Ohio manufactured a type of china similar to the famous Irish Belleek soft-paste porcelain. The American manufacturers identified their porcelain by using 'Belleek' or 'Beleek' in their marks. American Belleek is considered the highest achievement of the American porcelain industry. Production centered around artistic cabinet pieces and luxury tablewares. Many examples emulated Irish shapes and decor with marine themes and other naturalistic styles. While all are highly collectible, some companies' products are rarer than others. The best-known manufacturers are Ott and Brewer, Willets, The Ceramic Art Company (CAC), and Lenox. You will find more detailed information in those specific categories. Our advisor for this category is Mary Frank Gaston.

Key:
AAC — American Art China   ABC — American Beleek Works
    Company

Bowl, scalloped border, pk & wht floral decor, AAC, 5" dia	160.00
Bowl, tiny flowers w/in & w/o, gold trim, AAC, 2½x5"	350.00
Creamer, soft pk int, gold trim, AAC, 3½"	260.00
Cup, demitasse; non-factory gold decor on wht porc, 2¼"	110.00
Cup & saucer, morning glories, Morgan	150.00
Mug, Souvenir David's Society...Dinner, Sherry's, 3/1/1899, 4¼"	345.00
Plaque, 2 birds on branches, brn & beige, 14½"	110.00
Shell vase, pk lustre int, ABC, 4x5"	175.00
Vase, swan form, wht w/gold trim, ABC, 4"	115.00

Belleek, Irish

Belleek is a very thin translucent porcelain that takes its name from the village in Ireland where it originated in 1859. The glaze is a creamy ivory color with a pearl-like lustre. The tablewares, baskets, figurines, and vases that have always been made there are being crafted yet today. Shamrock, Tridacna, Echinus, and Thorn are but a few of the many patterns of tableware which have been made during some periods

of the pottery's history. Throughout the years, their most popular pattern has been Shamrock.

It is possible to date an example to within twenty to thirty years of crafting by the mark. Pieces with an early stamp often bring prices nearly triple that of a similar but current item. With some variation, the marks have always incorporated the Irish wolfhound, Celtic round tower, harp, and shamrocks. The first three marks (usually in black) were used from 1863 to 1946. A series of green marks identified the pottery's offerings from 1946 until the seventh mark (in gold/brown) was introduced in 1980 (it was discontinued in 1992). The most current mark, the eighth, is blue. Belleek Collector's International Society limited edition pieces are designated with a special mark in red. In the listings below, numbers designated with the prefix 'D' relate to the book *Belleek, The Complete Collector's Guide and Illustrated Reference, Second Edition,* by Richard K. Degenhardt (published by Wallace-Homestead Book Company, One Chilton Way, Radnor, PA 19098-0230). Our advisor for this category is Liz Stillwell; she is listed in the Directory under California.

Key:
A — plain (glazed only)	I — 1863 – 1890
B — cob lustre	II — 1891 – 1926
C — hand tinted	III — 1926 – 1946
D — hand painted	IV — 1946 – 1955
E — hand-painted shamrocks	V — 1955 – 1965
F — hand gilted	VI — 1965 – 3/31/1980
G — hand tinted and gilted	VII — 4/1/1980 – 12/22/1992
H — hand-painted shamrocks	VIII — 1/4/1993 – current
and gilted	
J — mother-of-pearl	
K — hand painted and gilted	
L — bisque and plain	
M — decalcomania	
N — special hand-painted decoration	
T — transfer design	

Further information concerning periods of crafting (baskets):
1 — 1865 – 1890, BELLEEK (three strand)
2 — 1865 – 1890, BELLEEK CO. FERMANAGH (three strand)
3 — 1891 – 1920, BELLEEK CO. FERMANAGH IRELAND (three strand)
4 — 1921 – 1954, BELLEEK CO. FERMANAGH IRELAND (four strand)
5 — 1955 – 1979, BELLEEK® CO. FERMANAGH IRELAND (four strand)
6 — 1980 – 1985, BELLEEK® IRELAND (four strand)
7 — 1985 – 1989, BELLEEK® IRELAND 'ID NUMBER' (four strand)
8 – 12 — 1990 to present (Refer to *Belleek, The Complete Collector's Guide and Illustrated Reference, 2nd Edition,* Chapter 5)

Round Covered Basket, D124-E, J, small, 7½x7½", $5,000.00.

Acorn Trinket Box, D500-III, B&D	275.00
Belleek Flowerpot, Floral, D211-III, J, 2½"	250.00
Blarney Tea Ware Cream, D570-II, A, sm	350.00
Butterfly Collection Preserve Jar, D1906-VII, F	60.00
Cherub Font, D1110-V, A, lg	125.00
Cherub Trinket Box, D1621-V, L	150.00
Chinese Tea Ware Tray, D487-I, K	2,500.00
Clam Salt, D1517-I, B, 2½"	285.00
Cleary Mug, D218-III, B, 2½"	190.00
Cone Flowerpot, D223-V, mid sz, 4"	75.00
Coral & Shell Wall Bracket, D1518-VI, A, 8¼"	175.00
Diamond Biscuit Jar, D600-I, A	950.00
Diamond Salt, D293-III, B	60.00
Dolphin Spill, D189-VI, J, 6½"	95.00
Dragonfly Vase, D1915-VII, D	90.00
Earthenware Mug, D858-I, T	150.00
Echinus Tea Ware Tea & Saucer, D645-II, B	300.00
Echinus Tea Ware Teapot, D659-I, G, sm	800.00
Enchanted Holly Coffee Mug, D1925-VII, D, 3¾"	60.00
Erne Tea Ware Tea & Saucer, D445-II, C	300.00
Erne Tea Ware Tray, D449-II, A	1,800.00
First Sight of Miss Liberty, D1882-VII, E&M, 1986	100.00
Fish Spill, D184-I, B, 7"	800.00
Flask, D1523-I, K, 6"	1,550.00
Flowered Menu Holder, D275-II, A	500.00
Flowered Salad Bowl, D116-III, J, 8½x8½"	900.00
Flowered Spill, D45-II, J, lg, 5"	375.00
Grass Tea Ware Honey Pot on Stand, D755-I, K	850.00
Greyhound, Single, D1138-VI, L, 6"	325.00
Harebell Vase, D180-VI, K, 8"	70.00
Harp Shamrock Tea Ware Tea & Saucer, D524-III, E	130.00
Harp Shamrock Tea Ware Teapot, D525-V, E	200.00
Indian Corn Spill, D190-I, D, 6"	300.00
Irish Harp, D77-V, E, sm, 5½"	150.00
Irish Pot, Shamrocks, D213-III, E, 3½"	150.00
Irish Wolfhound, D1823-VII, A, Lrd Ed 1978	135.00
Leaf Plate, D632-II, B, sz 5, 6"	200.00
Leprechaun, D1142-IV, D, 5¼"	250.00
Lily Cream & Sugar, D235-II, A	150.00
Marine Vase, D135-IV, B, sm, 7½"	400.00
Mask Hurricane Lamp, D1474-VII, A	125.00
Mask Tea Ware Milk Jug, D1485-VI, A	90.00
Moore Vase, D87-V, B, 6½"	90.00
Neptune Tea Ware Tea & Saucer, D414-III, C	250.00
Neptune Ware Cream & Sugar, D417&16-III, C, sm	250.00
New Shell Tea Ware Cream, D1382-V, B, lg	50.00
New Shell Tea Ware Tea & Saucer, D1385&86-III, B	150.00
Nickel Flowerpot, D209-III, A	200.00
Octagon Flowerpot, D219-VI, B, mid sz, 4"	65.00
Oval Shamrock Box, D604-III, E	300.00
Primrose Butter Plate, D1554-III, B, 5"	110.00
Rathmore Cream, D236-III, B	150.00
Rope Handle Mug, D215-II, B	225.00
Scroll Cream & Sugar, D252-III, B	200.00
Sea Horse Flower Holder, D130-I, A	750.00
Shamrock Ware Sandwich Tray, D1334-III, E	350.00
Shamrock Ware TV Set, D2017-VII, E	85.00
Sheerin Vase, D1781-VII, K, 8¼"	90.00
Single Henshall Spill, Floral, D61-III, J, 6"	275.00
Swan, D255-II, A, sm, 3¼"	225.00
Thistle Top Vase, Floral, D1782-V, D, 5¼"	125.00
Thorn Tea Ware Tea Stand, D2069-I, G, 7" dia	750.00
Toy Shell Cream & Sugar, D250-V, B	90.00
Triple Spill, D145-II, B, sm, 6"	300.00

Bells

Some areas of interest represented in the study of bells are history, religion, and geography. Since Biblical times, bells have announced morning church services, vespers, deaths, christenings, school hours, fires, and community events. Countries have used them en masse to peal out the good news of Christmas, New Year's, and the endings of World Wars I and II. They've been rung in times of great sorrow, such as the death of Abraham Lincoln.

Dorothy Malone Anthony is the author of a series of ten books entitled *World of Bells*. Her address is in the Directory under Kansas. All have over two hundred colored pictures covering many bell categories. See also Nodders; Schoolhouse Collectibles.

Brass, Prince of Wales symbol (three ostrich feathers), heavy, $35.00.

Photo courtesy Dorothy Malone Anthony

Bell metal, old rpl wrought-iron arm, 10½x10" dia	165.00
Bell metal, trn wood hdl w/brass acorn-shaped finial, 12x6¾"	85.00
Brass, Art Deco by Chase, USA, w/jade hdl, 3¾"	42.00
Brass, cherub as stem holds tap bell aloft, 10x3½"	125.00
Brass, Dick Turpin hdl, 5¼"	35.00
Brass, Dutch girl w/umbrella & bag, 4"	65.00
Brass, ebonized wood hdl w/brass finial, 6¾x3⅝"	35.00
Brass, lady w/fan, hat & long gown, figural, 6"	65.00
Brass, Miss Muffet, clapper legs, not old, 2½"	25.00
Brass, Prince of Wales ostrich feathers hdl, 4¾"	35.00
Brass, Queen Elizabeth hdl, 1953 Coronation, 5¼"	35.00
Brass, trn hdl w/line cvg, brass hdl finial, 10½x6"	75.00
Brass, trn wood, nut finial, 9⅝x5⅝"	50.00
Bronze, Chiantel Fondeur, Swiss, mk 1878, 3"	25.00
Bronze, evangelist's, no openwork, 3"	40.00
Bronze, nun figural, 4¼"	75.00
Ceramic, Jim Beam Town Crier of Eatanswil, 4½"	50.00
Ceramic, Renaissance, Lenox, 6½"	45.00
Dinner, MOP & brass on alabaster base, Victorian, 4"	150.00
Glass, amberina satin, Pilgrim, 7½"	50.00
Glass, Bohemian, bird & house, red, 5½"	45.00
Glass, Diamond Daisy, early Am, Pat appl'd, 1800s, 5⅞"	55.00
Glass, pressed, mk Comp of Rubel Furniture Co, 5¼"	50.00
Iron, International Harvester hay baler, 6" dia	55.00
Silver, Gorham, beehive finial, #039, old	45.00
Sleigh, #12 key type	25.00
Sleigh, 13, graduated 1-1⅝", on leather strap, EX	165.00
Sleigh, 19 heavy #1 to #10 key type on orig leather strap	300.00
Sleigh, 2 3½", Swedish-cut, on old strap	35.00
Sleigh, 30 1", brass, on orig leather strap	275.00
Sleigh, 38, NP brass, on orig 72" strap, VG	175.00
Sleigh, 7 grad (lg: 4x4½"), brass, on 39" leather strap	170.00

Wood, Dog, Basenji, from Africa, 5" 25.00

Bennington

Although the term has become a generic one for the mottled brown ware produced there, Bennington is not a type of pottery, but rather a town in Vermont where two important potteries were located. The Norton Company, founded in 1793, produced mainly redware and salt-glazed stoneware; only during a brief partnership with Fenton (1845 – 47) was any Rockingham attempted. The Norton Company endured until 1894, operated by succeeding generations of the Norton family. Fenton organized his own pottery in 1847. There he manufactured not only redware and stoneware, but more artistic types as well — granite-ware, scroddled ware, flint enamel, a fine parian, and vast amounts of their famous Rockingham. Though from an esthetic standpoint his work rated highly among the country's finest ceramic achievements, he was economically unsuccessful. His pottery closed in 1858.

It is estimated that only one in five Fenton pieces were marked; and although it has become a common practice to link any fine piece of Rockingham to this area, careful study is vital in order to be able to dis-tinguish Bennington's from the similar wares of many other American and Staffordshire potteries. Although the practice was without the per-mission of the proprietor, it was nevertheless a common occurrence for a potter to take his molds with him when moving from one pottery to the next, so particularly well-received designs were often reproduced at several locations. Of eight known Fenton marks, four are variations of the '1849' impressed stamp: 'Lyman Fenton Co., Fenton's Enamel Patented 1849, Bennington, Vermont.' These are generally found on examples of Rockingham and flint enamel. A raised, rectangular scroll with 'Fenton's Works, Bennington, Vermont,' was used on early exam-ples of porcelain. From 1852 to 1858, the company operated under the title of the United States Pottery Company. Three marks — the ribbon mark with the initials USP, the oval with a scrollwork border and the name in full, and the plain oval with the name in full — were used dur-ing that period.

Among the more sought-after examples are the bird and animal figurines, novelty pitchers, figural bottles, and all of the more finely modeled items. Recumbent deer, cows, standing lions with one forepaw on a ball, and opposing pairs of poodles with baskets in their mouths and 'coleslaw' fur were made in Rockingham, flint enamel, and occa-sionally in parian. Numbers in the listings below refer to the book Ben-nington Pottery and Porcelain by Barret. Our advisors for Bennington (except for parian and stoneware) are Barbara and Charles Adams; they are listed in the Directory under Massachusetts.

Key: c/s — cobalt on salt glaze

Baker, Rockingham, flared sides, 2⅛x14⅛x10¾" 450.00
Baking dish, flint enamel, 8-sided, 1849 mk, 2x8¾x8¾" 650.00
Bank, flint enamel, ftd ball form w/tall finial, 1850-60 mk, 6½" .750.00
Book flask, Bennington Battle, brn/tan/gr mottle, 5½", EX 700.00
Book flask, Bennington Battle, flint enamel, rstr, 11" 2,500.00
Book flask, Bennington Battle G, flint enamel, rpr, 8" 1,200.00
Book flask, Bennington Battle G, flint enamel, unmk, 8" 1,500.00
Book flask, Bennington Companion G, 1849-58 mk, 8" 1,500.00
Book flask, Departed Spirits, dk brn/yel mustard mottle, 5½" 425.00
Book flask, Hermit's Life & Suffering, flint enamel, 1859-58, 6" .975.00
Book flask, Ladies' Companion, flint enamel, 1849-58 mk, 5½" ..875.00
Book flask, Life of Kossuth, brn/cream/gr mottle, 6", EX 875.00
Bottle, Coachman, Rockingham, Lyman Fenton..., 10⅜", EX 800.00
Bottle, Coachman, Rockingham, 1849 mk, rstr, 11" 800.00
Bottle, shoe form, Rockingham, 6x6½" 175.00
Bottle, Toby, flint enamel, brn/orange on tan, 1849 mk, 10¾" ..1,000.00

Bottle, Toby, Rockingham, no tassels, ft show, 1849 mk, 10½", EX 675.00
Candlestick, flint enamel, brn w/gr traces, 9⅜x4¾" 600.00
Candlestick, Rockingham, brn mottle, 8x4⅛" 600.00
Cuspidor, flint enamel, dk brn on cream w/dk bl, unmk, 4x9" 250.00
Cuspidor, flint enamel, 1849 mk 400.00
Foot warmer, Rockingham, shell & scroll devices, 1847 mk, 9" .300.00
Humidor, Gothic Arches, Rockingham, 8-sided, 8½x6¾x4¾" ..900.00
Inkwell, sleeping youth figural, Rockingham, 4x5½" 300.00
Lion, flint enamel, gr/orange/cream, 1849 mk, rstr, 7½x11" 4,500.00
Paperweight, spaniel figural, 1849-50 mk, 3x4½" 800.00
Pie plate, Rockingham, 1849 mk, 11¼", NM 650.00
Pitcher, flint enamel, Alternate Rib, 1849 mk, 10", EX 900.00
Pitcher, flint enamel, Tulip & Heart, 1849 mk, 6½", EX 775.00
Pitcher, Toby, Ben Franklin, Rockingham, 1849 mk, 6", EX 950.00
Snuff jar, Toby, flint enamel, 1849 mk, rstr, 4¼" 675.00
Spaniel on base, flint enamel, 10½x8¼x5½", EX 600.00
Tile, flint enamel, lattice w/in fr, 1849 mk, 7" sq 600.00
Vase, Tulip, flint enamel, mk DD, 9", NM 800.00
Wash bowl, flint enamel, brn/gr/bl speckles, 1849 mk, 13½" 600.00

Stoneware

Crock, #2/accents, c/s, L Norton, stone ping on bk, 11" 200.00
Crock, #2/flower (simple), c/s, Julius Norton, stain, 10½" 145.00
Crock, #2/flower (triple), Norton & Fenton, prof rstr, 10½" 175.00
Crock, #2/flower basket, c/s, J&E Norton, line, 9½" 990.00
Crock, #3/flower (simple), c/s, Norton & Fenton, flaking, 12½" .155.00
Crock, #3/flower basket, c/s, J Norton & Co, rstr, 10" 800.00
Crock, #3/leaf (dotted), E&LP Norton, rpl ears, 10½" 90.00
Inkwell, lion's head, mid 1800s, att, 2x2⅜", EX 230.00

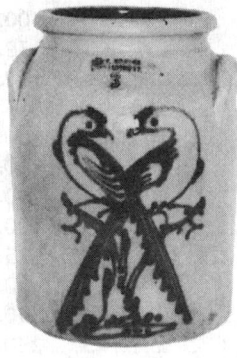

Jar, crossed double peacocks, cobalt on salt glaze, J&E Norton & Co., professional restoration, ca 1855, three-gallon, 13½", $2,850.00.

Jar, #2/flower (triple), c/s, Norton & Fenton, stain/line, 10½" ...210.00
Jar, #3/peacocks in tree, c/s, J&E Norton, prof rstr, 13½" 2,850.00
Jar, #4/peacocks in tree, c/s, J&E Norton, 1855, 14" 5,000.00
Jug, #1/bird on branch, c/s, J Norton & Co, 11" 525.00
Jug, #1/flower (dbl), c/s, Julius Norton, 1840s, stain, 11" 330.00
Jug, #2/bird on branch, c/s, J&E Norton, chip, 13½" 525.00
Jug, #2/floral spray (stylized), c/s, E&LP Norton, 1870s, 14" 280.00
Jug, #2/floral spray (stylized), J&E Norton, sm chips, 14" 175.00
Jug, #2/flower (simple), c/s, Julius Norton, ca 1840, 14" 770.00
Jug, #2/peacock on stump, c/s, J&E Norton, prof rstr, 14" 855.00
Jug, #3/bird on plume, c/s, J Norton & Co, prof rstr, 16" 330.00
Jug, #3/flower (stylized), c/s, J&E Norton, ca 1859, 15½" 525.00

Beswick

In the early 1890s, James Wright Beswick operated a pottery in Longston, England, where he produced fine dinnerware as well as orna-mental ceramics. Today's collectors are most interested in the figurines made since 1936 by a later generation Beswick firm, John Beswick, Ltd. They specialize in reproducing accurately detailed bone-china models of authentic breeds of animals. Their Fireside Series includes dogs, cats, elephants, horses, the Huntsman, and an Indian figure, which measure up to 14" in height. The Connoisseur line is modeled after the likenesses of famous racing horses. Beatrix Potter's characters and some of Walt Disney's are charmingly re-created and appeal to children and adults alike. Other items, such as character Tobys, have also been produced. The Beswick name is stamped on each piece. The firm was absorbed by the Doulton group in 1973. Our advisor for this category is Nicki Budin; she is listed in the Directory under New York.

Figurine, American Quarterhorse, brn glaze, #2186 ....200.00
Figurine, Benjamin Bunny, Beatrix Potter, V2, brn mk 125.00
Figurine, Benjamin Bunny Sat on a Bank, V1, brn mk 75.00
Figurine, Benjamin w/Peter Rabbit, Beatrix Potter, brn mk 135.00
Figurine, Burnham Beauty, draft horse, standing, lg 250.00
Figurine, Cecily Parsley, Beatrix Potter, V2, brn mk 60.00
Figurine, Fox, #1016-A 95.00
Figurine, Guilty Sweethearts, Kitty Macbride 75.00
Figurine, Highland Cow, glossy, #1740, 5¼" 120.00
Figurine, Jemimah Puddleduck, Beatrix Potter, gold mk 200.00
Figurine, Jeremy Digging, Beatrix Potter, brn mk 195.00
Figurine, Johnny Townmouse, Beatrix Potter, gold mk 195.00
Figurine, Just Good Friends, Kitty Macbride 75.00
Figurine, Lady Mouse, Beatrix Potter, brn mk 45.00
Figurine, Little Pig Robinson, Beatrix Potter, 1st gold mk 450.00
Figurine, Miss Moppet, Beatrix Potter, brn mk 35.00
Figurine, Miss Moppet, Beatrix Potter, gold mk 295.00
Figurine, Mr Benjamin & Peter Rabbit, Beatrix Potter, brn mk .100.00
Figurine, Mr Benjamin Bunny, Beatrix Potter, brn mk 35.00
Figurine, Mrs Tittlemouse, Beatrix Potter, gold mk 325.00
Figurine, Old Mr Pricklepin, Beatrix Potter, bk stamp 115.00
Figurine, Old Woman Knitting, Beatrix Potter, brn mk 135.00
Figurine, Owl, #2026 ....75.00
Figurine, Peter Rabbit, Beatrix Potter, gold mk 295.00
Figurine, Pickles, Beatrix Potter, brn mk 450.00
Figurine, Pigling Bland, Beatrix Potter, 1st version, bk stamp 350.00
Figurine, Ribby, Beatrix Potter, gold mk 195.00
Figurine, Samuel Whiskers, Beatrix Potter, gold mk 195.00
Figurine, Timmy Willie, Beatrix Potter, gold mk 325.00
Figurine, Tom Kitten, Beatrix Potter, gold mk 125.00
Figurine, Tom Kitten w/Butterfly, Beatrix Potter, brn mk 225.00
Figurine, Tomasina Tittlemouse, Beatrix Potter, brn mk 95.00
Figurine, Tommy Brock, Beatrix Potter, brn mk 70.00
Teapot, Sairey Gamp 80.00
Toby mug, Barnaby Rudge 70.00

Big Little Books

The first Big Little Book was published in 1933 and copyrighted in 1932 by the Whitman Publishing Company of Racine, Wisconsin. Its hero was Dick Tracy. The concept was so well accepted that others soon followed Whitman's example; and though the 'Big Little Book' phrase became a trademark of the Whitman Company, the formats of his competitors (Saalfield, Goldsmith, Van Wiseman, Lynn, and World Syndicate) were exact copies. Today's Big Little Book buffs collect them all.

These hand-sized sagas of adventure were illustrated with full-page cartoons on the right-hand page and the story narration on the left. Colorful cardboard covers contained hundreds of pages, usually totaling over an inch in thickness. Big Little Books originally sold for 10¢ at the dime store; as late as the mid-1950s when the popularity of

comic books caused sales to decline, signaling an end to production, their price had risen to a mere 20¢. Their appeal was directed toward the pre-teens who bought, traded, and hoarded Big Little Books. Because so many were stored in attics and closets, many have survived. Among the super heroes are G-Men, Flash Gordon, Tarzan, the Lone Ranger, and Red Ryder; in a lighter vein, you'll find such lovable characters as Blondie and Dagwood, Mickey Mouse, Little Orphan Annie, and Felix the Cat.

In the early to mid-'30s, Whitman published several Big Little Books as advertising premiums for the Coco Malt Company, who packed them in boxes of their cereal. These are highly prized by today's collectors, as are Disney stories and super-hero adventures. Our advisor for this category is Ron Donnelly; he is listed in the Directory under Alabama.

Note: At the present time, the market for these books is fairly stable — values for common examples are actually dropping. Only the rare, character-related titles are increasing.

Junior Nebb on the Diamond Bar Ranch, Whitman #1422, 1938, VG, $20.00.

Andy Panda's Vacation, Whitman, #1485, EX 35.00
Big Chief Wahoo & the Magic Lamp, Whitman, #1483, EX 20.00
Black Beauty, Sal, 1934, EX 25.00
Blondie & Dagwood in Hot Water, Whitman, #1410, EX 25.00
Boss of the Chisholm Trail, Saalfield, #1153, 1939, VG- 15.00
Brer Rabbit, Song of the South, Whitman, #1426, NM 75.00
Buck Jones in Ride 'Em Cowboy, Whitman, #1116, EX 40.00
Buck Jones in the Roaring West, Whitman, #1174, NM 65.00
Buck Rogers in the War w/Planet Venus, Whitman, #1437, NM .100.00
Buffalo Bill Plays a Lone Hand, Whitman, #1194, NM 35.00
Captain Easy Behind Enemy Lines, Whitman, #1474, EX 30.00
Captain Midnight vs Terror of the Orient, Whitman, #1458, EX ...60.00
Chester Gump in the Pole to Pole Flight, Whitman, #1402, NM ...45.00
Count of Monte Cristo, Lynn, #1, 1934, EX 40.00
Cowboy Millionaire, Saalfield, #1106, 1935, EX 30.00
Danger Trails in Africa, Whitman, #1151, EX 15.00
Daniel Boone, World Syndicate Publishing, 1934, EX 15.00
Death by Short Wave, Saalfield, #1151, 1938, EX 30.00
Dick Tracy & the Blackmailers, Dell, 1939, EX 75.00
Dick Tracy & the Racketeer Gang, Whitman, #1112, EX 40.00
Dick Tracy on the High Seas, Whitman, #1454, NM 55.00
Dixie Dugan & Cuddles, Saalfield, #1188, 1940, EX 35.00
Don Wilson Navy Intelligence Ace, Whitman, #1418, EX 30.00
Donald Duck Forgets To Duck, Whitman, #1434, EX 45.00
Donald Duck in Volcano Valley, Whitman, #1457, EX 40.00
Erik Noble & the Forty Niners, Whitman, #772, NM 30.00
Felix the Cat, Whitman, #1439, EX 50.00
Fighting President, Engle Van-Wiseman, #6, 1934, EX 20.00
Flash Gordon & the Tournaments of Mongo, Whitman, #1171, NM .110.00
Flint Roper & the Six Gun Showdown, Whitman, #1467, EX 15.00
Freckles & the Lost Diamond Mine, Whitman, #1164, VG- 25.00
G-Man & the Gun Runners, Whitman, #1469, EX 15.00

G-Man vs the Red X, Whitman, #1147, EX 20.00
G-Men on Lightning Island, Dell, 1936, EX 35.00
Gene Autry & the Hawk of the Hills, Whitman, #1493, NM 60.00
Gene Autry in Law of the Range, Whitman, #1483, EX 25.00
Guns in the Roaring West, Whitman, #1426, EX 15.00
Jack London's Call of the Wild, Lynn, #L14, 1935, EX 25.00
Jackie Cooper in Gangster Boy, Whitman, #1402, EX 25.00
Joe Palooka, Heavyweight Champion, Whitman, #1123, EX 40.00
John Carter of Mars, Dell, 1940, EX 140.00
Johnny Forty-Five, Saalfield, #1164, 1938, EX 25.00
Jungle Jim, Whitman, #1138, NM 80.00
Kazan King of the Pack, Whitman, #1471, EX 15.00
Kit Carson, World Syndicate Publishing, 1933, EX 15.00
Last Man Out, Saalfield, #1128, 1937, EX 20.00
Last of the Mohicans, #L30, 1936, EX 30.00
Little Men, Whitman, #1150, NM 35.00
Little Miss Muffet, Whitman, #1120, EX 25.00
Little Orphan Annie & the Haunted Mansion, Whitman, #1482, NM ...55.00
Little Women, Whitman, #757, NM 40.00
Lone Ranger & the Red Renegades, Whitman, #1489, NM 50.00
Lost Patrol, Whitman, #753, EX 30.00
Mandrake the Magician, Whitman, #1167, VG 30.00
Men of the Mounted, Whitman, #755, EX 25.00
Mickey Finn, Saafield, #1170, 1940, EX 20.00
Mickey Mouse & the Sacred Jewel, Whitman, #1187, EX 50.00
Mickey Mouse & the 7 Ghosts, Whitman, #1475, EX 50.00
Mickey Mouse in the World of Tomorrow, Whitman, #1444, NM .75.00
Mickey Mouse on Sky Island, Whitman, 1417, EX 55.00
Mr District Attorney, Whitman, #1408, EX 25.00
Mutt & Jeff, Whitman, #1113, EX 50.00
Nancy & Sluggo, Whitman, #1400, EX 30.00
Nevada Rides the Danger Trail, Saalfield, #1146, 1938, EX 20.00
One Night of Love, Saalfield, #1099, 1935, EX 30.00
Our Gang Adventures, Whitman, #1456, EX 35.00
Pilot Pete Dive Bomber, Whitman, #1466, EX 15.00
Pluto the Pup, Walt Disney's; Whitman, #1467, EX 45.00
Popeye's Ark, Saalfield, #1117, 1936, EX 35.00
Popeye Sees the Seas, Whitman, #1163, EX 45.00
Powder Smoke Range, Whitman, #1176, EX 25.00
Red Barry Ace Detective, Whitman, #1157, EX 20.00
Red Death on the Range, Whitman, #1449, EX 20.00
Robin Hood, Engle Van-Wiseman, #10, 1935, EX 35.00
Robinson Crusoe, Whitman, #719, soft cover, NM 60.00
Scrappy, Whitman, #1122, NM 60.00
Sequoia, Whitman, #1161, EX 20.00
Skippy, Whitman, #761, EX 30.00
Smilin' Jack & the Border Bandits, Dell, 1941, EX 50.00
Smilin' Jack & the Coral Princess, Whitman, #1464, NM 45.00
Smokey Stover the Foo Fighter, Whitman, #1421, EX 40.00
SOS Coast Guard, Whitman, #1191, EX 22.00
Spook Riders on the Overland, Saalfield, #1144, 1938, EX 20.00
Tailspin Tommy & the Hooded Flyer, Whitman, #1423, EX 25.00
Tarzan & the Lost Empire, Whitman, #1442, NM 70.00
Terry & the Pirates, Whitman, #1156, NM 55.00
Three Finger Joe, Saalfield, #1129, 1937, EX 15.00
Three Musketeers, Whitman, #1131, Feature Movie Book, oversz, EX ..40.00
Tiny Tim in the Big, Big World, Whitman, #1472, EX 45.00
Tom Mason on Top, Saalfield, #1102, 1935 ....30.00
Tom Mix & the Hoard of Montezuma, Whitman, #1462, EX 30.00
Treasure Island, Whitman, #1141, EX 40.00
Two-Gun Montana, Whitman, #1104, NM 30.00
Wimpy the Hamburger Eater, Whitman, #1458, EX 30.00
World War in Photographs, Whitman, #779, EX 20.00
Zane Grey's Tex Thorne Comes Out West, Whitman, #1440, VG ..20.00

Bing and Grondahl

In 1853 brothers M.H. and J.H. Bing formed a partnership with Frederick Vilhelm Grondahl in Copenhagen, Denmark. Their early wares were porcelain plaques and figurines designed by the noted sculptor Thorvaldsen of Denmark. Dinnerware production began in 1863, and by 1889 their underglaze color 'Copenhagen Blue' had earned them worldwide acclaim. They are perhaps most famous today for their Christmas plates, the first of which was made in 1895. See also Limited Edition Plates.

Bowl, salad; Sea Gull, sq, 10" 100.00
Christmas ornament, horse-drawn carriage on 2¼" circle, 1986, MOC .25.00
Coasters, Sea Gull, 3¾" dia, set of 8 ....120.00
Coffeepot, Sea Gull, dome lid, dolphin handle, from $150 to 195.00
Compote, Sea Gull, 3-dolphin ft, 5½" 100.00
Cup & saucer, Blue Fluted 28.00
Cup & saucer, Sea Gull, from $25 to 30.00
Figurine, boxer, #2212, 5½x6" 90.00
Figurine, boy & girl, she reaching to kiss his cheek, #1614 ....100.00
Figurine, boy skier, #2358KT 95.00
Figurine, boy w/umbrella under ea arm, 7½" 80.00
Figurine, bulldog, #1676, 3¼x4" 80.00
Figurine, chicken, #2194 ....75.00
Figurine, cocker spaniel, #2095, 6x8½" 180.00
Figurine, dachshund, sitting up, #1603, 7½x2½" 185.00
Figurine, dachshund, standing, #1752, 4x8" 185.00
Figurine, fish, #2174, sm 48.00
Figurine, Fish Lady, #2233 ....300.00
Figurine, fox terrier, #1889, 6x8" 130.00
Figurine, frog, brn tones, #2467, 2¼x3¾" 40.00
Figurine, girl, #2324 ....110.00
Figurine, girl lying on stomach reading, #2304, 7¾" 90.00
Figurine, girl w/kitten, #1779, 7" 75.00
Figurine, Great Dane, seated, #1773, 6x9½" 295.00
Figurine, Great Dane, standing, #2124, 10x12" 325.00
Figurine, lady feeding chickens, #2220 ....400.00
Figurine, little girl w/doll, patterned dress, #1721 JC, 8" 90.00
Figurine, Love Refused, #1614 ....155.00
Figurine, rooster, #2192, 4" 95.00
Figurine, seal, #1733, 7x8" 175.00
Figurine, water baby w/seaweed 85.00
Figurine, Young Love, boy kisses girl on cheek, 7½" 80.00
Plate, Blue Fluted, 9½" 28.00
Plate, Sea Gull, 9½" 30.00
Sauce boat, Sea Gull, dolphin hdls, 9½" L 120.00
Tray, pond lily pad w/3-D girl, med to lt bl, #2378 PU, 7" L 75.00
Tray, Sea Gull, triangular, 9" 65.00
Vase, Blue Fluted, #208/32, 2½x2" 40.00

Binoculars

There are several types of binoculars, and the terminology used to refer to them is not consistent or precise. Generally, 'field glasses' refers to simple Galilean optics, where the lens next to the eye (the ocular) is concave and dished away from the eye. By looking through the large lens (the objective), it is easy to see that the light goes straight through the two lenses. These are lower power, have a very small field of view, and do not work nearly as well as prism binoculars. In a smaller size, they are opera glasses, and their price increases if they are covered with mother-of-pearl (fairly common but very attractive), abalone shell (more colorful), ivory (quite scarce), or other exotic materials. Field glasses are not valuable unless very unusual or by the best makers, such as Zeiss or Leitz. Prism binoculars have the objective lens offset from the eyepiece and give a much better view. This is the standard binocular form, called Porro prisms, and dates from around 1900. Another type of prism binocular is the roof prism, which at first resembles the straight-through field glasses, with two simple cylinders or cones, here containing very small prisms. These can be distinguished by the high quality views they give and by a thin diagonal line that can be seen when looking backwards through the objective. In general, German binoculars are the most desirable, followed by American, English, and finally French, which can be of good quality but are very common unless of unusual configuration. Japanese optics of WWII or before are often of very high quality. 'Made in Occupied Japan' binoculars are very common, but collectors prize those by Nippon Kogaku (Nikon). Some binoculars are center focus (CF), with one central wheel that focuses both sides at once. These are much easier to use but more difficult to seal against dirt and moisture. Individual focus (IF) binoculars are adjusted by rotating each eyepiece and tend to be cleaner inside in older optics. Each type is preferred by different collectors. Very large binoculars are always of great interest. All binoculars are numbered according to their magnifying power and the diameter of the objective in millimeters. 6 x 30 optics magnify six times and have 30 millimeter objectives.

Prisms are easily knocked out of alignment, requiring an expensive and difficult repair. If severe, this misalignment is immediately noticeable on use by the double-image scene. Minor damage can be seen by focusing on a small object and slowly moving the binoculars away from the eye, which will cause the images to appear to separate. Overall cleanliness should be checked by looking backwards (through the objective) at a light or the sky, when any film or dirt on the lenses or prisms can easily be seen. Pristine binoculars are worth far more than when dirty or misaligned, and broken or cracked optics lower the value far more. Cases help keep binoculars clean but do not add materially to the value.

As of 1999, any significant changes in value are due to Internet sales. Some of the prices listed here are lower than would be reached at an on-line auction. Revisions of these values would be inappropriate at this point for these reasons: First, values are fluctuating wildly on the Internet; 'auction fever' is extreme. Second, some common instruments can fetch a high price at an Internet sale, and it is clear that the price will not be supported as more of them are placed at auction. In fact, an overlooked collectible like the binocular will be subject to a great increase in supply as they are retrieved from closets in response to the values people see at an on-line auction. Third, sellers who have access to these Internet auctions can use them for price guides if they wish, but the values in this listing have to reflect what can be obtained at an average large antique show. The following listings assume a very good overall condition, with generally clean and aligned optics.

Our advisor for this category is Peter Abrahams, who studies and collects binoculars and other optics. Please contact, especially to exchange reference material (SASE required with written questions). Mr. Abrahams is listed in the Directory under Oregon.

Field Glasses

Fernglas 08, German WWI, 6x39, military gr, many makers 50.00
Folding, modern, hinged flat case, oculars outside 10.00
Folding or telescoping, no bbls, old 125.00
Ivory covered, various sm szs & makers 180.00
LeMaire, bl leather/brass, various szs & makers 25.00
Metal, emb hunting scene, various sm szs & makers 45.00
Pearl covered, various sm szs & makers 90.00
Porc covered, delicate painting, various szs & makers 175.00
US Naval Gun Factory Optical Shop 6x30 ....75.00
Zeiss 'Galan' 2.5x34, modern design look, early 1920s 100.00

Prism Binoculars (Porro)

Barr & Stroud, 7x50, Porro II prisms, IF, WWII 110.00
Bausch & Lomb, 6x30, IF, WWI, Signal Corps 50.00
Bausch & Lomb, 7x50, IF, WWII, other makers same 80.00
Bausch & Lomb Zephyr, 7x35 & other, CF 150.00
Bausch & Lomb/Zeiss, Pat 1897, 8x17, CF 140.00
Crown Optical, 6x30, IF, WWI, filters 45.00
France, various makers & szs, if not unusual 30.00
German WWII 10x80, eyepcs at 45 degrees, 3-letter code (makers) .450.00
German WWII 6x30, 3-letter code for various makers 60.00
Goertz Trieder Binocle, various szs, unusual adjustment 90.00
Huet, Paris 7x22, other sm szs, unusual shapes 80.00
Leitz 6x30 Dienstglas, IF, good optics 65.00
Leitz 8x30 Binuxit, CF, 1950s 150.00
M19, US military 7x50, ca 1980 ....150.00
Nikon 9x35, 7x35, CF, 1950s 95.00
Nippon Kogaku, 7x50, IF, Made in Occupied Japan 150.00
Ross Stepnada, 7x30, CF, wide angle, 1930s 250.00
Ross 6x30, standard British WWI issue 50.00
Sard, 6x42, IF, very wide angle, WWII 800.00
Toko (Tokyo Opt Co) 7x50, IF, Made in Occupied Japan 45.00
Universal Camera 6x30, IF, WWII, other makers same 50.00
US Naval Gun Factory Optical Shop 6x30, IF, filters, WWI 70.00
US Naval Gun Factory Optical 10x45, IF, WWI 180.00
US Navy, 20x120, various makers, WWII & later 3,000.00
Warner & Swasey (important maker) 8x20, CF, 1902 ....250.00
Wollensak 6x30, ca 1940 ....50.00
Zeiss, Starmorbi 12/23/42x60, turret eyepcs, 1920s 2,000.00
Zeiss Deltrintem 8x30, CF, 1930s 95.00
Zeiss DF 95, 6x18, sq shoulder, very early 150.00
Zeiss Teleater 3x13, CF, bl, leather 100.00
Zeiss 15x60, CF or IF, various models 600.00
Zeiss 8x40 Delactis, CF or IF, 1930s 200.00

Roof Prism Binoculars

Hensoldt, Dialyt, various szs, long tapered bbl, 1930s-80s 110.00
Hensoldt Universal Dialyt, 6x26, 3.5x26, cylindrical, 1920s 80.00
Leitz Trinovid, 7x42 & other, CF, 1960s-80s, EX 375.00
Zeiss Dialyt, 8x30, CF, 1960s 400.00

Bisque

Bisque is a term referring to unglazed earthenware or porcelain that has been fired only once. During the Victorian era, bisque figurines became very popular. Most were highly decorated in pastels and gilt and demonstrated a fine degree of workmanship in the quality of their modeling. Few were marked. See also Heubach; Nodders; Dolls; Piano Babies.

Boy and girl at well, both in 19th-century costumes, finger damage, 1890s, 19", pair, $800.00.

Black man playing accordion, 4" **125.00**
Boy, wht suit w/pastel trim, holds hat beside, 12" **145.00**
Boy & girl w/horn & music book, 1800s attire, 9¾", 10", pr **165.00**
Couple under umbrella, pastels, 6" **135.00**
Girl on swing, pastels, #430, Depose, 10" **100.00**
Man w/flower basket stands before 2 vases, pastels, Fr, 8x5" **135.00**
Shepherdess & 2 suiters, 19th C, rprs, 16" **1,000.00**
Three Graces, Continental, 12½" **110.00**
Vase, woman in gold-beaded gown sits on conch shell, 7½" **110.00**
2 maids support shell, 9½" **135.00**

Black Americana

Black memorabilia is without a doubt a field that encompasses the most widely exploited ethnic group in our history. But within this field there are many levels of interest: arts and achievements such as folk music and literature, caricatures in advertising, souvenirs, toys, fine art, and legitimate research into the days of their enslavement and enduring struggle for equality. The list is endless.

In the listings below are some with a derogatory connotation. Thankfully, these are from a bygone era and represent the mores of a culture that existed nearly a century ago. They are included only to convey the fact that they are a part of this growing area of collecting interest. Black Americana catalogs featuring a wide variety of items for sale are available; see the Directory under Clubs, Newsletters, and Catalogs for more information. We also recommend *Black Collectibles* by P.J. Gibbs; and *Black Dolls, Books I* and *II,* by Myla Perkins, all published by Collector Books. See also Cookie Jars; Postcards; Posters; Sheet Music.

Ad, Aunt Jemima, Lenten Meal w/Real Appeal, full pg, 1952, EX .**18.00**
Ad, Aunt Jemima, Saturday Evening Post pg, 1920 ....**18.00**
Ad, Aunt Jemima Party, full color, full page, 1950s, EX **18.00**
Ashtray, Amos & Andy, chalkware, lt flaking, 7½" **200.00**

Book, Little Black Sambo, Helen Bannerman, animations by Julian Wehr, 1933, G, $40.00.

Book, Booker Washington a Child of Slavery, 1st ed, 1915, VG ..**40.00**
Book, Gigi & Gogo, Liger-Belair, 15-pg, 1943, 8¾x6¼", EX **75.00**
Book, Judge's Library Black Art, 1901, 28-pg, 8¼x22¾", EX **150.00**
Book, Miss Minerva on Old Plantation, ES Sampson, 1923, 301-pg, EX .**75.00**
Book, Uncle Tom's Cabin, Young Folks Edition, Boylan, Whitman, 1947 .**70.00**
Book, Watermelon Pete, E Gordon/C Powers Wilson, 14-pg **80.00**
Booklet, Porgy & Bess, S Goldwyn, Pearl Baily photo inside, 1959 ..**85.00**
Books, Black History Publication Series Vol I-V, 1984, M **50.00**
Box, Fairbanks Gold Dust Washing Powder, giant sz, 1920s, unopened ..**95.00**
Brush, pnt caricature wooden hdl, 1910s-40s, 4½-8", ea, $45 to ...**65.00**
Coin, GW Carver/BT Washington half dollar, 1952, 1¼" dia **40.00**
Condiment set, nude natives & straw hut, Made in Japan, 3x5" ..**250.00**
Cookbook, Aunt Jemima, Pancakes Unlimited, 31-pg, 1958, EX .**65.00**
Cookbook, 10 Separate...Cook Books in 1, Mammy on jacket, 1947 ..**70.00**

Cookie jar, Aunt Jemima, F&F **400.00**
Creamer & sugar bowl, Aunt Jemima & Uncle Mose, F&F **175.00**
Dish towel, mammy printed on wht linen on ea side, 25x16", M .**40.00**
Doll, celluloid, girl w/stationary eyes, jtd limbs, 10" **100.00**
Doll, cloth, Carver Washington, Hallmk, 9", MIB **70.00**
Doll, compo baby, pnt eyes/mouth, molded hair, jtd, 13", EX ..**115.00**
Doll, Golliwog, felt, average condition, 3-4", from $85 to **150.00**
Doll, hand-knit boy (wool yarn), mc embr features, 12" **70.00**
Doll, plastic, bl pnt eyes, mk Tudor Rose, MIE, 4½" **30.00**
Doll, stockinette, mohair, girl w/sewn-on head, stuffed body, 9" ..**175.00**
Doll, Topsy-Turvy, blk/wht compo, all orig/restrung, 7½" **295.00**
Figurine, boy in alligator, pnt bsk, Germany, 1920s, 1¼x3½" **100.00**
Figurine, boy in sunsuit, pnt bsk, Germany, ca 1910, 4⅞x4½" ...**200.00**
Figurine, boy on hippo, pnt bsk, Germany, ca 1920, 2x4" **115.00**
Figurine, girl w/doll, well dressed, pnt bsk, Germany, 8½" **250.00**
Game, Little Black Sambo, w/board/spinner/etc, 1945, EX **125.00**
Hand bill, Hi Henry's Premium Minstrels, full color, 5¼x3" **35.00**
Hot pad mitten, Mammy, c Lagniappe CF NO Ltd, 1975, 8x5½", NM ..**25.00**
Humidor, boy on cotton bale, pnt bsk, brn tones, Germany, 7½" ..**525.00**
Humidor, boy on log, pnt terra cotta, Austria, 1920s, 7½" **900.00**
Lawn sprinkler, Sprinklin' Sambo, flat metal figure, 30x8" **115.00**
Letter opener, sterling w/Sunny South character finial, 5¼" **165.00**
Lithograph, angel, boy & girl w/dog, C Gilbert, 22½x18½" **190.00**
Lithograph, Pore Lil Mose, Ef I Wuz..., 1901, 10½x14" **75.00**
Marionette, Topsy, Hazelle's Popular..., 1940, 14", MIB **375.00**
Match holder, Johnnie Griffin, CI **160.00**
Memo holder, Mammy, resin, 1940, EXIB **55.00**
Music folio, Rag-Tune Folio #2..., Jos W Stern, 1894, 55-pg, EX ..**225.00**
Nodder, boy, early pot metal, EX **125.00**
Nodder, chef w/arms extended **225.00**
Nodder, clown, pnt bsk, Ardalt Japan, #6530A, 6" **225.00**
Noisemaker, tin litho man w/harmonica, spinner type, 4½" **25.00**
Note pad holder, Mammy w/pencil, pnt pressed wood, 1940s, 10½" ..**65.00**
Pamphlet, message on segregation, JC Bishop, 1950s, 5-pg **15.00**
Pancake shaker, Aunt Jemima, bl plastic, late '50s, 8½", EX **85.00**
Paperweight, Mammy figural, pnt CI, 4½" **100.00**
Paperweight, Mammy figural, pnt lead, 2½" **125.00**
Pencil sharpener, man's face w/hat & bow tie, metal, Germany, 1½" ..**150.00**
Photo, minstrel show cast, most in Blk face, 1920s, 10x5¾" **35.00**
Place card, Aunt Jemima ea side, 2½x4½", EX **35.00**
Place mat, Aunt Jemima, story of her kitchen **18.00**
Plate, Coon Chicken Inn, Syracuse, 8" **450.00**
Playing card (Old Maid), Seedy Sambo or Honey Pie, ea **25.00**
Postcard, Amos & Andy, mc, NM **30.00**
Postcard, But Where Is Car I Told You To..., full color, 1930s, NM ..**28.00**
Postcard, Jocular Jinks of Kornelia Kinks, 1907, EX **40.00**
Postcard, leather, mc stamped image/lettering, ca 1900, EX **25.00**
Postcard, Some Elegant Chocolate Screams, 3 babies, ca 1900, M ..**30.00**
Postcard, This Am No Lemon, boy w/watermelon, ca 1900, EX ...**12.50**
Poster, Malcom X 1925-1965, commemorative, 1967, 22x17" ...**450.00**
Poster, Racism Chains Both, mc, Communist Party, 1970, 23x18" ..**120.00**
Pot holder caddy, chef, chalkware, blk skin tones, 1930s, 6" **45.00**
Print, Cup of Fate, Mammy reading tea leaves, H Roseland, 18x20" ..**135.00**
Print, Ignorance Is Bliss, man w/leaking jug, Kemble, 13x9" **55.00**
Program, An Evening w/Ray Charles, 1950s, EX **20.00**
Program, FHS Minstrels & Vaudeville Entertainment, 1897, 8-Pg ..**50.00**
Recipe box, Mammy, yel plastic, Fosta **175.00**
Record & book, Brer Rabbit & Tar Baby **30.00**
Shakers, Aunt Jemima & Uncle Mose, F&F, 3½", pr **65.00**
Shakers, Aunt Jemima & Uncle Mose, red plastic, F&F, 5", pr **75.00**
Shakers, butler & maid, ceramic, brn w/mc, 1930s, 4½", pr **125.00**
Shakers, chefs carving, ceramic, brn w/yel clothes, 3", pr **110.00**
Shakers, piggybk kids, ceramic, brn skin w/mc & gold, 4¾", pr ...**165.00**
Shakers, redcap porter, holds suitcases, Japan, 4½", 3-pc set **250.00**

Shakers, turbaned children, dk brn w/mc clothes, Japan, 3½", pr	.70.00
Sheet music, By Watermelon Vine..., couple cover, 1904, 3-pg, EX	..40.00
Sheet music, Com Moses Pay De Rent, 3-pg, 1904, VG	.35.00
Sheet music, I Wish I Was in Dixie, minstrel cover, 1936, EX	.35.00
Sheet music, Whistling Rufus, caricature cover, 1899, 11x14", EX	..45.00
Spice jar, Aunt Jemima, plastic figural, F&F, from set of 6, ea	.50.00
Spoon/wall plaque, Mammy, Rockingham	.80.00
Stereo view, children in cotton field, Keystone, 1899, EX	.20.00
Syrup, Aunt Jemima, F&F, 5½"	.70.00
Thermometer, Dapper Dan, M	.45.00
Tin, Hy-Beaute Special...Hair Dressing, bl/wht, 1949, 3½" dia	.32.00
Tin, Queen Supreme Hair Dressing, gold/blk/wht, 1930s, 2¼"	.28.00
Tin, Roreen Ointment & Brightener, 1930s, 2" dia, NM	.28.00
Tumbler, Mammy's Shanty (restaurant), enamel on clear glass	.20.00
Tumbler, Stephen Foster Melodies, Ring Ring de Banjo, 6¾"	.30.00
Tumbler, 3 men shooting craps on frosted glass, 7"	.30.00
Valentine, I Sho Is Yo..., dialect poem, blk skin tones, 1930s, EX	.25.00
Vase, Sambo, brn skin, gold shoes, rose lips, 1940s, 7¾"	.95.00

Black Cats

Made in Japan during the '50s, these novelty cats may be found bearing the labels of several different importers, all with their own particular characteristics. The best known and most collectible of these cats are from the Shafford line. Even when unmarked, they are easily identified by their red bows, green eyes, and white whiskers, eyeliners, and eyebrows. Relco/Royal Sealy cats are tall and slender, and their bow ties are gold with red dots. Wales is a wonderful line with yellow eyes and gold detailing; Enesco cats have blue eyes, and there are other lines as well. When evaluating your black cats, be sure to inspect their paint and judge them accordingly. 50% paint should relate to 50% of our suggested values, which are given for cats in mint (or nearly mint) paint. Note: Internet auctions have recently caused prices to soar on the hard to find items. Our values reflect this influence.

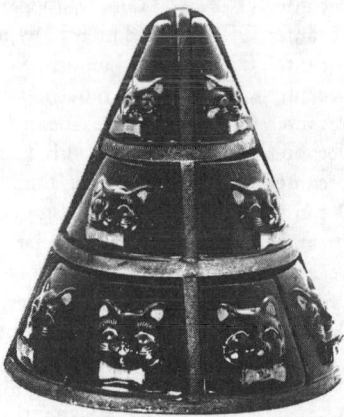

Spice set, eight separate pieces with embossed faces in triangular wooden frame, Shafford, minimum value $450.00.

Ashtray, flat face, Shafford, hard to find sz, 3¾"	.30.00
Ashtray, flat face, Shafford, 4¾"	.18.00
Bank, seated cat w/coin slot in top of head, Shafford, from $175 to	..200.00
Bank, upright cat, Shafford-like features, mk Tommy, 2-part	.165.00
Cigarette lighter, Shafford, 5½", from $150 to	.175.00
Cigarette lighter, sm cat stands on book by table lamp	.65.00
Condiment set, 2 joined heads, J&M bows w/spoons, Shafford, 4"	.75.00
Cookie jar, lg cat head, Shafford, from $90 to	.100.00
Creamer & sugar bowl, Shafford	.45.00
Cruet, upright cat w/yel eyes, open mouth, paw spout	.30.00
Decanter, long cat w/red fish in his mouth as stopper	.60.00
Decanter set, upright cat, yel eyes +6 plain wines	.35.00
Demitasse pot, tail hdl, bow finial, Shafford, 7½"	.110.00
Grease jar, sm cat head, Shafford, scarce, from $75 to	.85.00

Ice bucket, cylindrical w/emb yel-eyed cat face, 2 szs, ea	.75.00
Mug, Shafford, scarce, 4", from $65 to	.75.00
Mug, Shafford, 3½"	.55.00
Pitcher, squatting cat, pour through mouth, Shafford, rare, 5"	.85.00
Planter, cat & kitten in hat, Shafford-like pnt	.30.00
Planter, upright cat, Shafford-like pnt, Napco label, 6"	.20.00
Pot holder caddy, 'teapot' cat, 3 hooks, Shafford, from $170 to	..195.00
Shakers, long crouching cat, shaker in ea end, Shafford, 10"	.165.00
Shakers, rnd-bodied 'teapot' cat, Shafford, pr	.140.00
Spice set, 6 sq shakers in wooden fr, Shafford	.175.00
Spice set, 6 sq shakers in wooden fr, yel eyes	.125.00
Stacking tea set, red collars, gold ball, yel eyes, 3-pc	.75.00
Teapot, bulbous body, head lid, gr eyes, Shafford, med sz	.45.00
Teapot, bulbous body, head lid, gr eyes, Shafford, 4-4½"	.30.00
Teapot, bulbous body, head lid, gr eyes, Shafford, 7"	.75.00
Teapot, cat face w/dbl spout, Shafford, scarce, 5", from $200 to	..250.00
Teapot, panther-like appearance, gold eyes, sm	.20.00
Teapot, yel eyes, 1-cup	.30.00
Toothpick holder, cat on vase atop book, Occupied Japan	.12.00
Tray, flat face, wicker hdl, Shafford, lg	.165.00
Utensil rack, flat-bk cat w/3 slots for utensils, cat only	.125.00
Wall pocket, flat-bk 'teapot' cat, Shafford	.125.00
Wine, emb cat face, gr eyes, Shafford, sm	.75.00

Black Glass

Black glass is a type of colored glass that when held to strong light usually appears deep purple, though since each glasshouse had its own formula, tones may vary. It was sometimes etched or given a satin finish; and occasionally it was decorated with silver, gold, enamel, coralene, or any of these in combination. The decoration was done either by the glasshouse or by firms that specialized in decorating glassware. Crystal, jade, colored glass, or milk glass was sometimes used with the black as an accent. Black glass has been made by many companies since the 17th century. Contemporary glasshouses produced black glass during the Depression, seldom signing their product. It is still being made today.

To learn more about the subject, we recommend *A Collector's Guide to Black Glass, Books I and II*, written by our advisor, Marlena Toohey; she is listed in the Directory under Colorado. Look for her newly updated value guide. See also Tiffin, L.E. Smith, and other specific manufacturers.

Ashtray, fish shape, 3¾x4¾"	.20.00
Ashtray, hat shape w/Dobbs emb on rim, 1920-50, 2½"	.30.00
Ashtray, kettle form, Daisy & Button, ca 1940, 2½" H	.30.00
Atomizer, satinized w/gilt decor, 1920-40, 7"	.65.00
Bonbon w/swan hdl, clear neck & head, Viking	.35.00
Bottle, shoe shape, screw cap, ca 1880-1910, 3½x5¼"	.100.00
Bowl, cupped, ftd, Mt Pleasant #515	.27.50
Bowl, hdls, 2x6½"	.25.00
Bowl, serving; center hdl, LE Smith, 9" sq	.35.00
Bowl, 12-sided, unknown mfg, ca 1924-35, 9"	.35.00
Celery dish, Greensburg's #681, 1930s	.36.00
Creamer, Cloverleaf, Hazel-Atlas, 1930s	.15.00
Cup & saucer, Ovide, floral sterling decor	.18.00
Flower bowl, Hobnail, LE Smith, 6½" dia	.27.50
Pin tray, att Dithridge & Co, 5"	.20.00
Relish, 3-part, deep, 3x7"	.30.00
Saucer, Octagon, ca 1930s	.7.50
Server, dbl hdls, 12"	.30.00
Vase, bud; HC Fry #804, 1929-33	.27.50
Vase, fan; 8-sided ft, LE Smith #1000, 1930s-30s	.45.00
Window box, Snake Dance, LE Smith #404	.35.00

Blown Glass

Blown glass is rather difficult to date; 18th and 19th century examples vary little as to technique or style. It ranges from the primitive to the sophisticated, but the metallic content of very early glass caused tiny imperfections that are obvious upon examination, and these are often indicative of age.

In America, Stiegel introduced the English technique of using a patterned, part-size mold, a practice which was generally followed by many glasshouses after the Revolution. From 1820 to about 1850, glass was blown into full-size three-part molds. In the listings below, glass is assumed clear unless color is mentioned. Numbers refer to a standard reference book, *American Glass*, by Helen and George McKearin. See also Bottles and specific manufacturers. Our advisor for this category is Mark Vuono; he is listed in the Directory under Connecticut.

Bowl, amber, folded rim, 4⅝x6½" 715.00
Bowl, amber, hollow bulbous ft, 3½x4" 415.00
Bowl, lt gr, urn shape, ftd, knop stem, 7½x6¾" 500.00
Candlestick, appl ft & font, Am, 9¼" 180.00
Canister, 2 appl cobalt rings on body/1 on lid, appl hdl, 9" 880.00
Canister, 2 appl cobalt rings on body/1 on lid, 10" 600.00
Celery vase, Pillar mold, wheel-cut decor, appl stem, 9⅜" 220.00
Cheese cover, aqua, folded rim, corseted sides, 8¾x8½" 180.00
Compote, gr, appl ft & hollow stem, 6¾x11¼" 450.00
Compote, swirled violet & amethyst, appl ft & stem, 6½x7½" ...770.00
Compote/punch bowl, plain rim, solid stem, eng initials, 10x13" .325.00
Creamer, 8 slightly swirled ribs, 3⅝", NM 250.00
Cuspidor, chocolate-amber, flared rim, pontil, sm chip, 4⅜" 170.00
Decanter, lt amethyst, Pillar mold, collar mouth, pontil, 11⅜" 90.00
Egg cup, Dmn Point, canary, flint, att Sandwich, 3¾" 450.00
Flowerpot/bowl, yel, appl ft, folded lip, 4⅞" 125.00

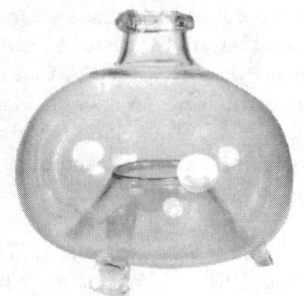

Fly trap, clear with three applied feet, Pat Appd For embossed on applied string lip, American, 1880 – 1910, 6⅞", $325.00.

Fly trap, clear, appl seal: Pieca A Mouche..., appl ft, 7" 160.00
Fly trap, turq (rare) w/overall t'print, open base, 6" 1,200.00
Goblet, gr, appl ft, hollow stem, 13" 95.00
Jar, sapphire bl, Pillar mold, ruffled lip, pontil, 12¼" 275.00
Rolling pin, bright orange-amber, tooled knob hdls, 15⅝" 180.00
Rolling pin, deep root beer-amber, 1 pontiled end, 15½" 140.00
Rolling pin, med sapphire bl, tooled knob hdls, pontil, 14¾" 160.00
Salt cellar, cobalt, 16 vertical ribs, appl ft, pontil, 3⅛" 230.00
Salt cellar, cobalt, 18-dmn, tooled rim, appl ft, pontil, 3⅛" 210.00
Salt cellar, olive-amber, 16 tightly swirled ribs, 2⅛" 140.00
Shot glass, dk grass gr, 6-sided, pontil, 2" 170.00
Shot glass, golden yel, 6-sided, smooth base, 2" 135.00
Shot glass, pk-amethyst, 6-sided, pontil, 2" 90.00
Sugar bowl, appl ft, tooled rim, pontil, w/lid, 6½" 350.00
Taster, dk teal gr, 10-sided, mug base, tooled rim, pontil, 3" 120.00
Taster, orange-amber, pontil, 2⅜" 250.00
Tumbler, deep milky yel-gr, 6-sided, pontil, 3⅜" 700.00

Tumbler, dk emerald gr, tooled lip, smooth base, 2⅞" 325.00
Tumbler, dk peacock bl, 8-sided, pontil, 3¾" 425.00
Tumbler, dk sapphire bl, 6-sided, smooth base, 3¼", NM 110.00
Tumbler, golden yel, 6-sided, pontil, 3¾" 450.00
Tumbler, lt pk-amethyst, 9-sided, pontil, 3½" 175.00
Tumbler, lt sapphire bl, 6-sided, tooled rim, smooth base, 3⅛" ..175.00
Tumbler, pk-amethyst, teardrop, tooled mouth, smooth base, 3⅜" .80.00
Vase, amber, flared lip, appl ft, 8⅛" 600.00
Vase, amethyst, hexagonal, 3 printie bowl, scalloped, 9", NM ...1,100.00
Vase, dk grass gr, hexagonal, t'print & ellipse bowl, 7⅛" 935.00
Vase, 3-Printie, canary, gauffered rim, hex base, 10½" 1,200.00
Wine, clear w/red & cotton twist stem, English, 6½" 250.00

Blown Three-Mold Glass

A popular collectible in the 1920s, '30s, and '40s, blown three-mold glass has again gained the attention of many. Produced from approximately 1815 to 1840 in various New York, New England, and Midwestern glasshouses, it was a cheaper alternative to the expensive imported Irish cut glass.

Distinguishing features of blown three-mold glass are the three distinct mold marks and the concave-convex appearance of the glass. For every indentation on the inner surface of the ware, there will be a corresponding protuberance on the outside. Blown three-mold glass is most often clear with the exception of inkwells and a few known decanters. Any colored three-mold glass commands a premium price.

The numbers in the listings that follow refer to the book *American Glass* by George and Helen McKearin. Our advisor for this category is Mark Vuono; he is listed in the Directory under Connecticut.

Birdcage fountain, GI-12, pontil, 5¼" 50.00
Decanter, GI-29, sapphire bl, smooth base, Sandwich, ½-pt 150.00
Decanter, GI-29 w/H Gin, w/stopper, 8½" 1,150.00
Decanter, GII-18, flared mouth, w/stopper, att Sandwich, 1-pt ..110.00
Decanter, GIII-15, flared mouth, w/stopper, att Keene, 1-qt 120.00
Decanter, GIII-16, flared mouth, pontil, w/stopper, Keene, pt ...230.00
Decanter, GIII-16, yel-olive, sheared mouth, pontil, Keene, 1-pt .375.00
Decanter, GIII-19, flared mouth, pontil, att Keene, 1-qt 550.00
Decanter, GIII-19, w/stopper, stain, 8" 140.00
Decanter, GIII-2 w/Brandy, w/stopper, 8¼" 500.00
Decanter, GIII-2 w/Wine, irregular rim, w/stopper, 8½" 500.00
Decanter, GIII-24, flared mouth/rayed base, w/stopper, 10" 120.00
Decanter, GIII-6, pontil, no stopper, att Sandwich, 1-pt 80.00
Decanter, GIV-5, flared mouth, pontil, w/stopper, 1-pt 180.00
Decanter, GIV-7 w/Rum, tooled mouth, pontil, stopper, 10¾" ..200.00
Decanter, GV-10, Sandwich Star, folded lip, bubbles, 11¼" 500.00
Decanter, GV-8, bar lip, pontil, 7¼" 450.00
Decanter, GV-8, pontil, rpl stopper, 9" 75.00
Decanter, GV-9, flared mouth, pontil, w/stopper, 11½" 185.00
Decanter, unlisted, sapphire bl, flared mouth, Fr, 19th C, 1-qt+ ..350.00
Decanter, unlisted Baroque-type pattern, sapphire bl, Fr, 1-pt 250.00
Flip glass, GII-18, sheared rim, pontil scar, 5⅝" 130.00
Inkwell, GII-18, dk olive-amber, disc mouth, 1⅞" 150.00
Inkwell, GII-18, yel-olive, tooled disc mouth, pontil, 2⅛" 180.00
Inkwell, GII-2, yel olive-amber, tooled mouth, 1¾x2⅛" 180.00
Pitcher, GI-29, appl hdl, 7" 1,045.00
Pitcher, GII-27, aqua, appl hdl, stain, 7" 7,590.00
Pitcher, GIII-12, tooled mouth w/spout, pontil, mini, 2" 150.00
Salt cellar, GIII-25, cobalt, roughness on ft, 1¾x3⅛" 440.00
Tumbler, GIII-14, bbl form, tooled rim, att Keene, 3⅜" 190.00
Tumbler, GIII-18, lt wear/stain, 3½" 165.00
Tumbler, VG-5, fern decor, pontil, Am, 1820-40, 4⅝" 110.00

Blue and White Stoneware

Salt glaze or molded stoneware was most commonly produced in a blue and white coloration, much of which was also decorated with numerous 'in-mold' designs (some 150 plus patterns). It was made by practically every American pottery from the turn of the century until the mid-1930s. Crocks, pitchers, wash sets, rolling pins, and other household wares are only a few of the items that may be found in this type of 'country' pottery, now one of today's popular collectibles.

Logan, Brush-McCoy, Uhl Co., and Burley Winter were among those who produced it; but very few pieces were ever signed. Naturally, condition must be a prime consideration, especially if one is buying for resale; pieces with good, strong color and fully molded patterns bring premium prices. Normal wear and signs of age are to be expected, since this was utility ware and received heavy use in busy households. In the listings that follow, crocks, salts, and butter holders are assumed to be without lids unless noted otherwise. For further information we recommend *Blue and White Stoneware* (1981) by Kathryn McNerny and *Collector's Encyclopedia of Salt Glaze Stoneware* (1997) by Terry Taylor and Terry and Kay Lowrance. See also specific manufacturers.

Bank w/Money Bank stencil, coin slot, break to open, 4x3" 1,000.00
Batter jar, Wildflower, appl wood & wire hdl, 5x7" 275.00
Bean pot, Boston Baked Beans, Swirl, heavy diffused pattern 500.00
Bowl, Daisy on Waffle, 10¾" 95.00
Bowl, mixing; Flying Bird, 4x7½" 325.00
Bowl, Reverse Pyramids w/Reverse Picket Fence, 2½x4½" 95.00
Bowl, Wildflower, 4½x7" 125.00
Bowl (milk crock), Apricot, w/hdl 225.00
Box, powder; Wildflower & Fishscale, w/lid 325.00
Butter crock, Basketweave & Morning Glory, w/lid, 4x7½" 400.00
Butter crock, Butterfly, orig lid & bail, 6½" 225.00
Butter crock, Cows, appl wood & wire hdl, w/lid, 4½x7¼" 500.00
Butter crock, Daisy & Waffle, 4x8", NM 175.00
Butter crock, Draped Windows, 4½x8" 225.00
Butter crock, Eagle, orig lid & bail, M 750.00
Butter crock, Lovebirds, w/lid, 5½x6", M 500.00
Butter crock, Peacock, w/lid, 6x6" 550.00
Butter crock, Wild Flower, w/lid, 6½x7¼" 175.00
Canister, Basketweave, Coffee, orig lid, 7½" 350.00
Canister, Basketweave, Pepper, orig lid, 4½" 200.00
Canister, Basketweave, Put Your Fist In, orig lid, 7½" 750.00
Canister, Basketweave, Sugar, orig lid, 7½" 350.00
Canister, Basketweave, Tobacco, orig lid, 7½" 750.00
Canister, Snowflake, rpl lid, 6½x5¾" 150.00
Chamberpot, Fishscale & Wild Rose, no lid, 5½x9¼" 200.00
Chamberpot, Wildflower, stenciled pattern, 6x11" 135.00
Chamberpot, Wildflower & Fishscale, w/lid 450.00
Coffeepot, Oval, Diffused Bl, bl-tipped knob, str sides, 11x4" .1,500.00
Coffeepot, Peacock, patterned sloped sides, 7x10" 3,300.00
Cookie/biscuit jar, Flying Bird, orig lid, 9x6¾" 1,200.00
Cooler, iced tea;, Blue Band, flat lid, complete, 13x11" 295.00
Cooler, water; Apple Blossom, brass spigot, 17x15" 2,000.00
Cooler, water; Cupid, brass spigot, patterned lid, 15x12" 700.00
Cooler, water; Polar Bear, brass NP spigot, rare, 2-gal, 17x15" .4,000.00
Cooler, water; Polar Bear, Ice Water, no lid, 15¼" 385.00
Crock, Peacock, rstr bail & hand grip, 5½x9" 500.00
Cup, measuring; Spearpoint & Flower Panels, 6x6¾" 400.00
Cup, Wildflower w/emb ribbon & bow, 4½x2½" 85.00
Cuspidor, Butterfly & Shield, 6x7½" 175.00
Cuspidor, Flower Panels & Arches, 7x7½" 250.00
Custard cup, Fishscale, 5x2½" 125.00
Foot warmer, Diffused Bl, A Warm Friend, 12½x6½" 275.00

Grease jar, Flying Bird, orig lid, 4x4½" 900.00
Ice crock, Barrel Staves, rope/tongs/ice block emb, 4½x6" 225.00
Mug, Basketweave & Flower, 5x3" 150.00
Mug, beer; advertising, Diffused Bl, sqd hdl 150.00
Mug, Cattails 150.00
Mug, plain 65.00
Mug, Windy City (Fannie Flagg), Robinson Clay Products 200.00
Pie plate, Bl Walled Brick-Edge star emb base, 10½" 200.00
Pitcher, American Beauty Rose, 10" 500.00
Pitcher, Apricot, 8" 250.00
Pitcher, Avenue of Trees, allover bl, 9x7" 200.00
Pitcher, Basketweave & Morning Glory, 9" 300.00
Pitcher, Bl Band, plain 150.00
Pitcher, Bl Band Scroll, emb design 300.00
Pitcher, Butterfly, 9x7" 450.00
Pitcher, Castle & Fishscale, 8" 195.00
Pitcher, Cattails, bulbous, 6" 300.00
Pitcher, Cattails, 9½" 275.00
Pitcher, Cherries & Leaves, w/printing, 9½" 385.00
Pitcher, Cherry Cluster, 7½" 650.00
Pitcher, Columns & Arches, 8¾x5" 400.00
Pitcher, Daisy Cluster, 7x7" 700.00
Pitcher, Doe & Fawn, EX color 250.00
Pitcher, Dutch Boy & Girl by Windmill, 9" 175.00
Pitcher, Dutch Landscape, stenciled, Diffused Bl, tall 275.00
Pitcher, Eagle w/Shield & Arrows, rare, 8" 800.00
Pitcher, Flying Bird, 9" 600.00
Pitcher, Garden Rose, 9", NM 500.00
Pitcher, Girl & Dog, regular bl, 9" 675.00
Pitcher, Grape & Shield, 8½x5" 150.00
Pitcher, Grape Cluster on Trellis, allover bl, 7x7" 225.00
Pitcher, Grape w/Rickrack, any sz 250.00
Pitcher, Grazing Cows, bl, 7½" 400.00
Pitcher, Grazing Cows, bl, 8" 250.00
Pitcher, hot water; Wildflower & Fishscale 150.00
Pitcher, Indian Good Luck (Swastika), 8½" 175.00

Pitcher, Indian Head in War Bonnet, pale blue, waffled body, 8¼", chipped base, $225.00.

Pitcher, Indian Head in War Bonnet, dk bl, waffled body, 9" 350.00
Pitcher, Iris, 9" 300.00
Pitcher, Leaping Deer, 8½" 350.00
Pitcher, Leeping Deer in 1 oval, Swan in other (mfg error), 8" ..1,200.00
Pitcher, Lincoln, allover deep bl, 10x7" 600.00
Pitcher, Lincoln, allover deep bl, 6x4" 250.00
Pitcher, Lincoln, allover deep bl, 7x5" 300.00
Pitcher, Lincoln, allover deep bl, 8x6" 350.00
Pitcher, Lovebird, pale color, 8½" 300.00
Pitcher, Monk, dk cobalt 350.00
Pitcher, Peacock, EX color & mold, 7¾x6½", M 1,000.00
Pitcher, Poinsettia, 6½" 385.00
Pitcher, Rose on Trellis, 8x5½" 225.00
Pitcher, Scroll & Leaf, advertising, 8" 450.00

Pitcher, Stag & Pine Trees, 9" 375.00
Pitcher, Swan, in oval, deep color, 8½", EX 400.00
Pitcher, Swan, lt bl, 8½" 300.00
Pitcher, Wild Rose, solid bl, 9x6" 450.00
Pitcher, Wild Rose, sponged bands, 9" 450.00
Pitcher, Wildflower, stenciled 200.00
Pitcher, Windmills, 7¼", EX 195.00
Pitcher, Windy City (Fannie Flagg), Robinson Clay, 8½" 450.00
Roaster, Diffused Bl, appl hdls, flat finial, 9x19" 225.00
Rolling pin, Bl Band, advertising, Andka, NE, 14x4" 900.00
Rolling pin, Bl Band, no advertising, 14x4" 400.00
Rolling pin, Swirl, baker's sz, 16" 1,200.00
Rolling pin, Wild Flower, advertising, Analomink PA, dtd 1905 .900.00
Rolling pin, Wildflower, plain 350.00
Rolling pin, Wildflower, w/IL advertising, 15x4½" 550.00
Salt crock, Butterfly, orig lid 250.00
Salt crock, Daisy on Snowflakes, orig lid, 6½x6" 250.00
Salt crock, Eagle, w/lid 575.00
Salt crock, Lovebirds, orig lid, 9" 450.00
Salt crock, Peacock, w/lid 550.00
Soap dish, Beaded Rose 150.00
Soap dish, Indian in War Bonnet 250.00
Soap dish, Wildflower & Fishscale 150.00
Spice set, Basketweave, 6-pc 1,750.00
Toothbrush holder, Bow Tie, stenciled flower 50.00
Toothbrush holder, Wildflower & Fishscale 150.00
Vase, Swirl, cone shape 250.00
Vinegar cruet, 4½x3" 300.00
Wash bowl & pitcher, Rose on Trellis 300.00
Wash bowl & pitcher, Wildflower & Fishscale 500.00
Wash set, Wildflower & Fishscale, complete, 7-pc 1,775.00
Whipped cream jar, 4¾x6¾" 475.00

Blue Ridge

Blue Ridge dinnerware was produced by Southern Potteries of Erwin, Tennessee, from the late 1930s until 1956 in twelve basic styles and two thousand different patterns, all of which were hand decorated under the glaze. Vivid colors lit up floral arrangements of seemingly endless variation, fruit of every sort from simple clusters to lush assortments, barnyard fowl, peasant figures, and unpretentious textured patterns. Although it is these dinnerware lines for which they are best known, collectors prize the artist-signed plates from the '40s and the limited line of character jugs made during the '50s most highly. Examples of the French Peasant pattern are valued at double the prices listed below; very simple patterns will bring 25% to 50% less.

Our advisors, Betty and Bill Newbound, have compiled three lovely books, *Blue Ridge Dinnerware, Revised Third Edition,* and *The Collector's Encyclopedia of Blue Ridge, Volumes I* and *II,* all with beautiful color illustrations and current market values. They are listed in the Directory under North Carolina. For information concerning the National Blue Ridge Newsletter, see the Clubs, Newsletters, and Catalogs section of the Directory.

Ashtray, advertising, rnd 60.00
Ashtray, Mallard, box shape, 3½x2½" 40.00
Basket, aluminum edge, 7" 25.00
Bonbon, flat shell, Pixie 125.00
Bowl, cereal/soup; 6" 15.00
Bowl, fruit; 5" 8.00
Bowl, salad; 10½" 75.00
Bowl, vegetable; rnd, 8" 25.00
Box, candy; rnd w/lid, rare 160.00

Box, Dancing Nudes, rare 850.00
Box, powder; rnd 180.00
Box, Seaside 175.00
Butter dish, Woodcrest 60.00
Celery, Skyline 40.00
Child's feeding dish 150.00
Child's plate 125.00
Chocolate pot 250.00
Creamer, Colonial shape, no hdls 18.00
Creamer, demitasse 75.00
Cup & saucer, demitasse; china 45.00
Cup & saucer, Holiday 65.00
Deviled egg dish 60.00
Dish, baking; 13x8", w/metal stand 45.00
Gravy tray 29.00
Jug, batter; w/lid 90.00
Lamp, china 250.00
Lazy susan, complete 750.00
Pitcher, Abbey, china 180.00
Pitcher, Betsy, china 190.00

Pitcher, Sculptured Fruit, black handle, 7½", $95.00.

Pitcher, Spiral, 7" 75.00
Pitcher, Watuga 400.00
Plate, divided, heavy 35.00
Plate, salad; Bird, 8½" 75.00
Plate, sq, 8" 20.00
Plate, Square Dance, 14" 250.00
Platter, regular pattern, 15" 40.00
Platter, Turkey w/Acorns, 15" 90.00
Relish, Charm House 160.00
Relish, loop handle, china 85.00
Relish, shell shape, deep, china 85.00
Relish, T-hdl 75.00
Sconce 85.00
Shakers, Apple, 2¼", pr 40.00
Shakers, chickens, pr 150.00
Shakers, ftd, china, tall, pr 85.00
Shakers, Palisades, pr 30.00
Shakers, Skyline, pr 25.00
Sugar bowl, Colonial, eared, open 25.00
Sugar bowl, ped ft, open 65.00
Sugar bowl, Woodcrest, w/lid 25.00
Teapot, Charm House 300.00
Teapot, Mini Ball 200.00
Teapot, Piecrust 125.00
Teapot, Skyline 95.00
Toast, French Peasant, w/lid 300.00
Tray, snack; Martha 160.00
Tray, Waffle Set, 9½x13½" 110.00
Vase, bud 160.00
Vase, ruffled top, 9½" 125.00

Vase, Tapered 110.00

Blue Willow

Blue Willow, inspired no doubt by the numerous patterns of the blue and white Nanking imports, has been popular since the late 18th century and has been made in as many variations as there were manufacturers. English transfer wares by such notable firms as Allerton and Ridgway are the most sought after and the most expensive. Japanese potters have been producing Willow-patterned dinnerware since the late 1800s, and American manufacturers have followed suit. Although blue is the color most commonly used, mauve, and black lines have also been made. For further study we recommend the book *Blue Willow*, with full-color photos and current prices, by Mary Frank Gaston, our advisor for this category. In the following listings, if no manufacturer is noted, the ware is unmarked. See also Buffalo.

Bowl, batter; inside decal..75.00
Bowl, berry; Japan, sm 5.00
Bowl, cereal; Royal, 6¼" 12.00
Bowl, England, 5½" 6.00
Bowl, English, ped ft, 5x9¼" 150.00
Bowl, flat soup; Homer Laughlin, 8" 15.00
Bowl, Homer Laughlin, 5" 6.00
Bowl, rectangular, Globe Pottery, 9x7" 48.00
Bowl, soup; flat, England 18.00
Bowl, soup; Ridgway 20.00
Bowl, 5¼" 4.00
Bowl English, rtcl sides, hdls, 10" L 900.00
Bowl, vegetable; Brown & Steventon, w/lid, 9" 155.00
Bowl, vegetable; w/lid, child sz, 5⅜" 40.00
Bowl, vegetable; w/lid, Royal 65.00
Butter dish, Royal, ¼-lb 35.00
Cake plate, hdls, 10½" 20.00
Casserole, Homer Laughlin, w/lid 45.00
Cheese dish, Mason 200.00
Creamer, rnd, Japan, sm 15.00
Creamer, Staffordshire, cow form, Kent, M 1,250.00
Cruets, oil & vinegar; Japan, tall 90.00
Cup, stacking; USA 6.00
Cup & saucer, inside decal, Japan 10.00
Gravy boat, Royal 15.00
Kerosene lamp w/reflector, Japan 50.00
Lamp, oil; patterned top & base, Japan 65.00
Measuring cups, hanging, set of 4+ceramic holder 265.00
Mug, Japan 15.00
Pie plate/shallow bowl 40.00
Pitcher, Allerton, 8¼" 250.00
Pitcher, milk; gold trim, Myott England, 5¼" 120.00
Pitcher & bowl, Wedgwood 1,450.00
Plate, Allerton, 9" 9.00
Plate, dinner; Japan, from $10 to 15.00
Plate, dinner; unmk Royal 6.00
Plate, England, 6¼" 5.00
Plate, grill/dinner; Japan 20.00
Plate, Japan, 6" 5.00
Plate, Maastricht, 6" 10.00
Plate, salad; England 13.00
Platter, English, pearlware, ca 1830, 24¾" 600.00
Platter, Homer Laughlin, 11" 20.00
Platter, Ridgeways, 13½x11" 125.00
Platter, Stone Ware, 16x12½" 115.00
Shakers, Royal, pr 18.00

Snack set, Royal, 8-pc, MIB 145.00
Spice jars, book style, set of 6 in 2-drw wood rack 200.00
Steak knives, set of 6 in orig box 25.00
Sugar bowl, open hdls, w/lid, lg 40.00
Tea set, Japan, serves 4, 20-pc 220.00
Tea set, Occupied Japan, child sz, 18-pc 525.00
Teacup, Homer Laughlin 10.00
Teapot, Allerton 175.00
Teapot, child sz, 3¾x5¼" 30.00
Teapot, Homer Laughlin 60.00
Teapot, Royal..65.00
Teapot, unusual shape, Allerton 165.00
Thermos, modern 25.00
Tumbler, water; glass 18.00
Tureen, sauce; inside pattern, w/lid & ladle 225.00
Tureen, scalloped, ftd base, w/lid, unmk Japan, 10x6" ...150.00
Wall rack, 2 wooden-hdld utensils, Japan 165.00

Bluebird China

Made from 1910 to 1934, Bluebird China is lovely ware most often decorated with bluebirds flying among pink flowering branches. Another style depicts larger, more slender bluebirds in flight. The latter variety was made by Knowles, Taylor, Knowles; W.S. George (Derwood); French Co.; Sterling Colonial; and Pope Gosser. All of it was inexpensive dinnerware and reached the height of its popularity in the second decade of this century. Many potteries produced it, and shapes differ from one manufacturer to another. Besides the companies we've already mentioned, you'll find the trademarks of Cleveland; Carrolton; Homer Laughlin (today the most expensive, most collected, and most available of all the lines); Limoges China of Sebring, Ohio; Salem; Taylor, Smith, Taylor; and there are others.

Our advisor for this category is Kenna Rosen; she is listed in the Directory under Texas.

Bowl, berry; Cleveland, ind 12.50
Bowl, deep, Derwood, WS George, 4¾" 25.00
Bowl, deep, Homer Laughlin, 5½" 35.00
Bowl, gravy; w/saucer, Hopewell China 50.00
Bowl, sauce; SP Co, 4½" 12.50
Bowl, soup; PMC Co, 8" 30.00
Bowl, vegetable; Cleveland, 9¾" 45.00
Butter dish, 4½" holder w/in 7" dish, Steubenville 85.00
Butter pat, unmk 15.00
Casserole, Homer Laughlin Empress, rnd, w/lid, 8½" ...100.00
Casserole, Ostro China, 10½" dia 95.00
Casserole, Pope Gosser, w/lid, 10½x10½" 100.00
Casserole, Royal China Internat'l, 7x11½" 125.00
Casserole, Taylor Smith & Taylor, w/lid, 11x7½" 130.00

Chocolate cup, footed, 3½", $35.00.

Coffeepot, Sterling Colonial 150.00
Creamer, Derwood, WS George 30.00
Creamer & sugar bowl, Knowles Taylor Knowles 75.00
Creamer & sugar bowl, SPCo, w/lid 85.00
Creamer & sugar bowl, w/lid, Homer Laughlin 100.00
Cup, coffee; unmk 3½" 25.00
Cup, tea; unmk 15.00
Cup & saucer, SPCo 25.00
Dish, oval, Hudson, Homer Laughlin, 1x5¼x4" 20.00
Gravy w/underplate, Homer Laughlin, 4x9¾" 75.00
Ladle, sauce; gold scrolling 40.00
Pitcher, water; Salem China, 10" 125.00
Plate, baby's, ELP Co China, 7½x7½" 150.00
Plate, dessert; Limoges, 6" 8.00
Plate, dinner; Cleveland China, 9" 25.00
Plate, dinner; Knowles Taylor Knowles, 9¾" 22.50
Plate, dinner; Wilmer Ware 20.00
Plate, Homer Laughlin, 8½" 35.00
Plate, National China, 8" 22.50
Plate, rtcl, sq, unmk, 9" 35.00
Plate, scalloped, Homer Laughlin, 7¼" 35.00
Plate, Steubenville China, 9" 22.50
Platter, Edwin M Knowles, 14½x11" 75.00
Platter, Hopewell China, 13x10" 75.00
Platter, Hopewell China, 17½x13" 100.00
Platter, sqd oval, Carrollton, 17¾x12¾" 95.00
Platter, Thompson Glenwood, 13x10" 75.00
Platter, unmk, 9x7" 45.00
Platter, West End Pottery Co, 15½x11" 100.00
Saucer, Homer Laughlin 5.00
Sugar bowl, Illinois China Co, w/lid, 7x6" 50.00
Syrup, unmk, 4" 35.00
Teapot, Carrollton 250.00
Teapot, ELP Co, 8½x8½" 250.00
Teapot, Homer Laughlin 400.00

Boch Freres

Founded in the early 1840s in La Louviere, Boch Freres Keramis became the foremost producer of art pottery in Belgium. Though primarily they served a localized market, in 1844 they earned worldwide recognition for some of their sculptural works on display at the International Exposition in Paris.

In 1907 Charles Catteau of France was appointed head of the art department. Before that time, the firm had concentrated on developing glazes and perfecting elegant forms. The style they pursued was traditional, favoring the re-creation of established 18th-century ceramics. Catteau brought with him to Boch Freres the New Wave (or Art Nouveau) influence in form and decoration. His designs won him international acclaim at the Exhibition d'Art Decoratif in Paris in 1925, and it is for his work that Boch Freres is so highly regarded today. He occasionally signed his work as well as that of others who under his direct supervision carried out his preconceived designs. He was associated with the company until 1950 and lived the remainder of his life in Nice, France, where he died in 1966. The Boch Freres Keramis factory continues to operate today, producing bathroom fixtures and other utilitarian wares. A variety of marks have been used, most incorporating some combination of 'Boch Freres,' 'Keramis,' 'BFK,' or 'Ch Catteau.' A shield topped by a crown and flanked by a 'B' and an 'F' was used as well.

Bowl, geometrics, bl/cobalt on wht crackle, #10L9/#1187, 10" ...**435.00**
Box, jewelry; mc Deco florals on wht crackle, rectangular, sm **325.00**

Box, solid/floral rays, blk/gr/mc, 3x5" 300.00

Vase, polar bears in five panels, waves and spots on base and neck, green-gray on amber and brown, Ch. Catteau, B.F.K., #1020 B Gres, 16", $6,900.00.

Vase, animals, mc w/gold, stamp mk, 7x6" 460.00
Vase, birds, 3-color on wht crackle, Keramis, 2x6" 900.00
Vase, Deco flowers on creamy wht, mk, 12" 425.00
Vase, floral, cream & brn on blk band on brn mottle, 10½" 490.00
Vase, Oriental bl crackle, #900 ....225.00

Boehm

Boehm sculptures were the creation of Edward Marshall Boehm, a ceramic artist who coupled his love of the art with his love of nature to produce figurines of birds, animals, and flowers in lovely background settings accurate to the smallest detail. Sculptures of historical figures and those representing the fine arts were also made and along with many of the bird figurines, have established secondary-market values many times their original prices. His first pieces were made in the very early 1950s in Trenton, New Jersey, under the name of Osso Ceramics. Mr. Boehm died in 1969, and the firm has since been managed by his wife. Today known as Edward Marshall Boehm, Inc., the private family-held corporation produces not only porcelain sculptures but collector plates as well. Both limited and non-limited editions of their works have been issued. Examples are marked with various backstamps, all of which have incorporated the Boehm name since 1951. 'Osso Ceramics' in upper case lettering was used in 1950 and 1951. Our advisor for this category is Leon Reimert; he is listed in the Directory under Pennsylvania.

Alec's Red Rose, ltd ed, 6¾x4½", from $350 to 425.00
Arizona Queen of Night Cactus, 1976, 10" 600.00
Baby Blue Jay, #436 ....135.00
Baby Bluebird, #442 ....135.00
Baby Chickadee, #461 ....135.00
Baby Crested Fly Catcher, #458 ....148.00
Baby Robin, #437, from $150 to 175.00
Baby Woodthrush, #448 ....180.00
Blue Nile Rose, #30080, 8x5", from $400 to 435.00
Fledgling Blackburnian Warbler, #478 ....180.00
Fledgling Kingfisher #449 ....200.00
Hummingbird approaching cactus flower, #440, 8¼" ...350.00
Louisiana Whooping Crain w/Cattails, ltd ed, #888, 1984, 18x22" .900.00
Madonna, bsk, mk Boehm USA, 6" 56.00
Marsh Harrier w/Water Lilies, porc & bronze, 25" ...1,150.00
Mockingbirds, ltd ed, 10¼" 1,095.00
Panda w/Cub, ltd ed, 16x10x8" 3,750.00
Pascali Rose w/Freesia, ltd ed, 1978, 10" 500.00
Peace Rose, F345, 6x4" 355.00
Scissor-tailed Flycatcher, 1977, 13½" 1,400.00
Supreme Orchid Cactus w/Horned Toad, ltd ed, 1976, 6½" 400.00
Tree Sparrow, #468 ....245.00

Tropicana Rose, ltd ed, 1978, 4" **220.00**
Yellow-throated Warbler, #431, 9½" **300.00**
Yellowhammers (2 w/babies at nest), 10¾" **1,200.00**

Bohemian Glass

The term 'Bohemian glass' has come to refer to a type of glass developed in Bohemia in the late 16th century at the Imperial Court of Rudolf II, the Hapsburg Emperor. The popular artistic pursuit of the day was stone carving, and it naturally followed to transfer familiar procedures to the glassmaking industry. During the next century, a formula was discovered that produced a glass with a fine crystal appearance which lent itself well to deep, intricate engraving, and the art was further advanced.

Although many other kinds of art glass were made there, collectors today use the term 'Bohemian glass' to most often indicate clear glass overlaid or stained with color through which a design is cut or etched. (Unless otherwise described, the items in the listing that follows are of this type.) Red or yellow on clear glass is common, but other colors may also be found. Another type of Bohemian glass involves cutting through and exposing two layers of color in patterns that are often very intricate. Items such as these are sometimes further decorated with enamel and/or gilt work.

Basket, red, eng deer & trees, 5⅜" **125.00**
Beaker, amber, eng Reinstein castle scene on fluted body, 5" **250.00**
Beaker, cobalt, cut facets, ca 1850-60, 4¾", NM **265.00**
Beaker, cobalt, gold couple, ca 1860, 6½" **250.00**
Beaker, cobalt on wht on clear, eng spa scenes w/gold, 1860s, 5¾" ..**500.00**
Beaker, pk on wht on clear, cut facets, 1850-60, 5¾" **275.00**
Beaker, red, eng spa scenes on circular facets, 1860s, 4¼", EX **200.00**
Beaker, wht on gr, gold floral, oval facets, ca 1930, 5½" **125.00**
Bowl, red, eng naturalistic scenes, 5x6" **150.00**
Bread plate, bl, eng deer & pine tree, 13x8" **175.00**
Compote, red, eng stag in wooded landscape, 1930s, 11½" **375.00**
Decanter, red, eng vine/floral panels, bull's eye, t'print, 13" **125.00**
Decanter, red, eng vintage, 9¼", NM **85.00**
Flask, uranium yel-gr, eng stag scene, silver cap, 1850-60, 6½" ..**600.00**
Goblet, bl, gold lady, ca 1900, 6" **115.00**
Goblet, cobalt w/clear stem, gold floral, ca 1900, 6½" **125.00**
Goblet, red, eng view of Battle Monument Baltimore, 7" **600.00**
Goblet, red, gold decor, wht snake around stem, 1860s, 6", NM ..**175.00**
Lamp, oil; red on wht on clear, pnt maiden, 1880s, 18" **900.00**
Pitcher, amber, HP 24k gold leaf, 1950s, 15½", +4 tumblers **250.00**
Pokal, cranberry, eng Gothic design, ca 1860, 15½", NM **835.00**
Pokal, red, eng floral, 15¾" **250.00**
Powder dish, red, eng bird in branches w/gold **85.00**
Stein, red, eng dog in forest, pewter mts, 5½x3¼" **375.00**
Vase, amber, eng floral, 1920s, 11" **150.00**
Vase, gr, HP floral, ca 1890, 14" **100.00**

Bookends

Though a few were produced before 1880, bookends became a necessary library accessory and a popular commodity after the printing industry was revolutionized by Mergenthaler's invention, the linotype. Books became abundantly available at such affordable prices that almost every home suddenly had need for bookends. They were carved from wood, cast in iron, bronze, or brass, or cut from stone. A few were made of chalkware or glass. Today's collectors may find such designs as ships, animals, flowers, and children. Patriotic themes, art reproductions, and those with Art Nouveau and Art Deco styling provide a basis for a diverse and interesting collection.

Currently, figural cast-iron pieces are in demand, especially examples with good original polychrome paint. This has driven the value of painted cast-iron bookends up considerably.

For further information we recommend *Collector's Guide to Bookends, Identification and Values*, by Louis Kuritzky, our advisor for this category; he is listed in the Directory under Florida. See also Arts and Crafts; Bradley and Hubbard.

Asian Warriors, gray metal with celluloid faces, polished stone base, JB Hirsch (after Bruno Zach), ca 1930, 7¼", $225.00.

Photo courtesy Louis Kuritzky

Angelus Call to Prayer, gray metal, K&O, ca 1925, 4" **125.00**
Bazaar Scene, gray metal, Austria, ca 1920, 6¼" **325.00**
Bronco Rider, gray metal, Dodge, ca 1947, 5" **75.00**
Caricature Pony, gray metal, K&O, ca 1935, 5½" **150.00**
Celeste, gray metal, Ronson, ca 1925, 5" **225.00**
Cocker Spaniel, gray metal, Frankart, ca 1934, 6¼" **150.00**
Cougars, bronze clad, Armour Bronze, ca 1925, 5½" **175.00**
Covered Wagon, CI, WH Howell, #14, ca 1926, 4½" **65.00**
Cupid & Psyche, gray metal, #501, ca 1928, 4½" **135.00**
Deco Bust, gray metal, Abbot Schy 47, 1947, 7¼" **150.00**
Elephant Heads, gray metal, Jennings Bros #1531, 1928, 7" **185.00**
Elephant on Library, gray metal, Ronson, ca 1918, 4" **110.00**
Elks, CI, Judd, ca 1920, 5¼" **115.00**
Flowered Bird, CI, #1269, ca 1925, 6½" **275.00**
Foo Dogs, CI, ca 1920, 5" **175.00**
Full Sails, CI, Connecticut Foundry, 1930, 4½" **20.00**
Girl Posing, gray metal, Dodge, company tag, ca 1947, 7" **170.00**
Gladiators, bronze on marble base, ca 1932, 7¾" **600.00**
In the Clouds, CI, #73, ca 1925, 6" **150.00**
Indian Archer, bronze, WB, ca 1925, 5½" **125.00**
Indian Scout, gray metal, Jennings Bros, ca 1927, 5" **170.00**
Lady Godiva, glass, Haley, ca 1940, 6" **135.00**
Leaping Greyhounds, gray metal, Ronson #12314, 1930, 5½" **195.00**
Library Monk, gray metal, Ronson, 1920 ....**125.00**
Lincoln (seated), gray metal, Nuart, 1924, 6½" **110.00**
Lindbergh Propeller, CI, NS #650, ca 1928, 6½" **170.00**
Lion figural, patinated bronze, 5x7x3" **1,300.00**
Looney Tunes, chalk, Disney, 1994, 7" **85.00**
Not Quite Bookish, gray metal, K&O, ca 1930, 8" **225.00**
Oak Leaf, gray metal, PM Craftsman, ca 1965, 6½" **45.00**
Pirate w/Chest, CI, Littco, ca 1928, 5¼" **80.00**
Prancers, gray metal, K&O, ca 1932, 10" **125.00**
Sailfish, gray metal, PM Craftsman, ca 1965, 8" **65.00**
Setters, CI, Littco, ca 1925, 5" **115.00**
Ski Queen, gray metal, K&O, ca 1932, 6½" **175.00**
Speedboat, gray metal, Jennings Bros, ca 1934, 3½" **200.00**
Stars & Stripes, brass, ca 1935, 4" **110.00**
Ten Commandments, gray metal, Ronson, 1922, 3¾" **175.00**
The Mill, CI, Verona, ca 1925, 6¾" **60.00**
Tip Toes, bronze clad, Pompeian Bronze, ca 1925, 10" **325.00**
Toadstool & Frog, gray metal, McCelland Barclay, 1922, 4¼" **195.00**
Town Crier, gray metal, PM Craftsman, ca 1965, 7¼" **50.00**
Warbler, gray metal, Nuart, ca 1930 ....**225.00**
Washington Crossing Delaware, bronze finish, K&O, '32, 6¾" **125.00**

Weather-beaten Mariner, gray metal, Ronson, ca 1930, 6" **150.00**
Wedding Children, gray metal, Nuart, ca 1934, 5½" **90.00**
4-H, brass, ca 1930, 5" **65.00**

Bootjacks and Bootscrapers

Bootjacks were made from metal or wood. Some were fancy figural shapes, others strictly business! Their purpose was to facilitate the otherwise awkward process of removing one's boots. Bootscrapers were handy gadgets that provided an effective way to clean the soles of mud and such. Our advisor for this category is Louis Picek; he is listed in the Directory under Iowa.

Bootjacks

Am Bull Dog, CI pistol shape, folding, blk pnt **90.00**
Beetle-shaped jaws, CI, no pnt, ca 1880 ....**50.00**
Boss emb on shaft, lacy CI, 15" L **150.00**
Fish (stylized), cvd wood, worn finish, 22" L **135.00**
Heart figural, CI, scalloped sides, 13" L **145.00**
Lever action, wood & CI, EX **150.00**
Naughty Nellie, CI, worn copper pnt, 10½x4½x4½" **135.00**
Pine w/sq nails, lg, early **80.00**
Try Me, CI, openwork, no pnt, 1890s, 12x4" **75.00**

Bootscrapers

Figure sits on arch above two-tiered scraper, painted cast iron, much wear, 13", $170.00.

Aunt Jemima figure atop, CI, rpt, 14½" **285.00**
Baroque scrollwork, CI, set in marble block, 14" **95.00**
CI, base pushes into ground, Holcroft & Sons label, 19" **60.00**
Dachshund, CI, old gr pnt, 21" **275.00**
Eagle relief & classical lady in oval, CI, Portland Foundry **300.00**
Griffins, CI, EX cast detail, oval dish base, 10x14x9½" **220.00**
Lyre, brass on CI pan, 12x15" **300.00**
Pig silhouette, cut-out eye, CI, 8½x12" **215.00**
Ram's horn scrolls, wrought iron, in marble block **150.00**
2 quail ea end, CI, rectangular pan, pnt traces, 7x16" **295.00**

Boru, Sorcha

Sorcha Boru was the professional name used by California ceramist Claire Stewart. She was a founding member of the Allied Arts Guild of Menlo Park (California) where she maintained a studio from 1932 to 1938. From 1938 until 1955, she operated Sorcha Boru Ceramics, a production studio in San Carlos. Her highly acclaimed output consisted of colorful, slip-decorated figurines, salt and pepper shakers, vases, wall pockets, and flower bowls. Most production work was incised 'S.B.C.' by hand.

Bowl, appl lilies at ruffled rim, 6½" **85.00**
Bowl, maroon, appl peony on lid, 6" **85.00**
Cup, 3 dinosaur hdls **75.00**
Figurine, bl jays, mc, male: 5¼x11", female: 6½x9¼", pr **350.00**
Figurine, Penelope, fawn, 6" **85.00**
Figurine, shepherdess **155.00**
Pitcher, pk lustre florals w/gold centers, beading, 6½" **80.00**
Shakers, bride & groom, pr **175.00**
Shakers, elephants, pr **95.00**
Shakers, man & woman fox hunters, pr **165.00**
Shakers, sailor boy & girl, pr **125.00**
Sugar shaker, lady figural, 6" **110.00**
Vase, appl florals & leaves, 8" **75.00**

Bossons Artware

Bossons are the world renowned Character Wall Masks and other cherished artware products from Congleton, Cheshire, England. Bossons closed their operations in December 1996. There are no plans to resume production. Collectors have been assured that the Bossons family will not sell their name or any of their molds. (Rumors regarding a fire and pilfering of molds at the Bossons factory are unfounded, and remaining molds are safely stored and held by the Bossons family.)

In 1944 the late William Henry Bossons, a retired pottery manufacturer/chemist, began making Christmas figures out of metal and plaster as a hobby. Mr. Bossons, assisted by a few employees who remained with the company until retirement, sold those door to door. Then in 1946 he founded the Bossons design and manufacturing company and remained at the helm until his death in 1951. His son, W. Ray Bossons, took over as chairman and managing director until the factory closed in 1996. The company was always entirely owned and managed by the Bossons family. It was a British company with its entire output manufactured in England. During the past few years of operation, all of the molds and patterns for several popular Bossons were destroyed as 'obsolete models.' These molds were destroyed in '92: Bretonne Lady, Rumanian, Sardinian, Cheyenne, Pancho, Old Timer, and all 8" Scenic Plaques including: Village 'Pub', Old Watermill, Village Shop, Shakespeare's Birthplace, Ann Hathaway's Cottage, Old Irish Cottage, Robert Burn's Birthplace, Waiting for the Tide, and Unloading the Boats. In 1994, these were destroyed: Mozart, King Henry VIII, Catherine of Aragon, Anne Boleyn, Punjabi, and Fijian.

Market Trends: All Bossons are now categorized as discontinued. As stock holdings are depleted, Bossons are appreciating in value at a very fast rate. Still, Bossons collecting involves a very volatile and unpredictable market, but one for serious investors to consider. It is known that Bossons did not keep detailed production records. Though interest is spreading worldwide due to the influence of the Internet, many of the major collectors are located in the United States. Many items originally sold for under $5.00 (U.S.). A few popular models were distributed in military post exchanges through the 1960s into the '80s; but after 1948, much of the company's production went overseas, and this continued to be the case through the years. In 1968 a publication by Ray Bossons entitled 'Who's Who and What's What? Bossons Artware...' was regularly exported to nearly forty countries around the globe. No wonder, then, that there are so many hidden 'jewels' still to be discovered all over the world.

Brief historical sketches about production and history can be found in previous editions of this guide (1995 – 99). New discoveries, especially unusual prototypes that were never released, are often detailed in the quarterly newsletter 'Bossons Briefs,' published by the International Bossons Collector's Society. A detailed and pictorial history and a listing of nearly every Bossons ever produced can be found in the two authorized volumes by Dr. Robert E. Davis entitled *The Imagical World of Bossons*, Vol. 1, 1946 – 82, and Vol. II, 1982 – 1994. (Contact the International Bossons Collectors Society, 1787 Morgan Valley Road, Rockmart, GA 30153 or our advisor for information.)

Please note that Bossons was never a line-production effort — each was a hand-painted work of art. This limited the numbers produced and was planned by Bossons, though they also wanted their products to be obtainable at reasonable prices to be used in home decoration.

Major points to remember about Bossons: 1) not all will have the name incised under the collar (e.g., Syrian, Smuggler, Tibetan, and Tyrolean); 2) not all character studies are Bossons — Legends and Naturecraft products are not Bossons; 3) most carry the incised copyright: 'Made in Congleton, England,' on the back and in most cases under the collars; 4) Fraser-Art products are Bossons, so are products marked Briar Rose and Ivorex; 5) a signature is not a critical consideration when determining value, though they can be used for authentication. Sculptor/modeler initials include FW (Fred Wright), AB and AWB (Alice Brindley), and WRB (W Ray Bossons). Other initials are merely those of production paintresses; 6) watch for fakes and look-alikes (there are many) — know your dealer.

Suggestions for determining Bossons values based on rarity and condition: A. Obtain the copyright date from under the collar (or on the back) of the wall mask. B. Reference *Imagical World of Bossons* to learn how many years the model was produced. Length of production helps determine rarity; price them accordingly. With few exceptions, the earlier (1958 – 63) and the latest (1986 – 96) are found in fewer numbers. Examples in rare color combinations may be valued at 200% to 300% of retail. C. Condition is a major factor in determining value — if mint and in typical colors, a Bossons is worth 100% of its retail value.

In the listings that follow, we give premium prices for pristine, mint-condition examples, either factory 'mint' or perfectly returned to their original structural and coloring beauty by a professional restoration artist recommended by Bossons. Our groupings (subcategories) have been suggested by Ray Bossons.

Our advisor for this category is Dr. Don Hardisty; since 1984 he has been recommended by Bossons to restore their products. He is listed in the Directory under New Mexico.

Key:
AWB — Alice W. Brindley	OEC — older edition, common
FW — Fred Wright	RE — recent edition
MU — modeler unknown	REBR — recent edition becoming
OEBR — older edition	rare
becoming rare	WRB — W. Ray Bossons

The Americans

Harry: View a — rare coloring (yellow and white striped shirt), from $1,200.00 to $1,500.00; View b — typical coloring, from $600.00 to $900.00.

Photo courtesy Dr. Don Hardisty

Cheyenne, red jacket, #68, 1970-92, c 1967, FW/OEC, 11", $150 to **215.00**

York, 1st ed, #153, 1986-88, no copyright, AWB/REBR, 6½", $185 to **225.00**
York, 2nd design/coonskin cap, #153, 1988-96, AWB/RE, 6½", $125 to ...**145.00**

Birds of Prey Wall Figures

Bossons Eagle (gypsum plaster), #54, 1964-69, FW/OEBR, 12", $150 to ...**185.00**
Fraser-Art Eagle, Stonite, 1966-94, WRB/OEBR, 18" wingspan, $175 to .**225.00**

Cats of Character and Dogs of Distinction

Persian Cat, bl, #172, 1989-92, AWB/REBR, 3¾", from $65 to ...**85.00**
Persian Cat, blk, #169, 1989-92, AWB/REBR, 3¾", from $65 to .**85.00**
Poodle, blk, #100, 1969-90, MU, OEC, 5", from $45 to **65.00**
Poodle, wht, #101, 1969-90, MU, OEC, 5", from $45 to **65.00**

The Dickensian Collection

Mr Pickwick, #21, 1964-96, FW, OEC, 4¼", from $85 to **125.00**
Scrooge, #94, 1981-96, AWB, RE, 5½", from $85 to **145.00**

The Europeans

Sardinian, bl hat, #34, 1962-69, c 1961, MU, OEC, 5½", $145 to .**165.00**
Sardinian, gr hat, #162, '89-92, c '88, MU/REBR, 5½", $125 to ...**145.00**
Tyrolean, #83, 1972-96, MU, OEC, 6", from $85 to **130.00**

High-Relief Floral Plaques

Four Seasons, #s 163-166, 1990-94, AWB, REBR, 6", ea, from $85 to ..**125.00**
Spring Flowers, 1st ed, 1958-?, MU, RE, 14", from $85 to **150.00**
Spring Flowers, 2nd ed, #117, 1982-96, FW, OEC, 14", $125 to ...**165.00**

High-Relief Scenic Plaques

Anne Hathaway's Cottage, 1956-?, MU, OEBR, 14", from $100 to ...**125.00**
Old Watermill, #174, 1988-92, AWB, REBR, 8", from $85 to ...**145.00**
Village Pub, #175, 1988-92, AWB, REBR, 8", from $85 to **145.00**
Village Shop, #176, 1988-92, AWB, REBR, 8", from $85 to **145.00**

Men of the Desert, Mountains and Sea

Desert Hawks, #65, 1962-96, FW, OEC, 7", from $125 to **165.00**
Kurd, #41, 1964-95, MU, OEC, 5¼", from $65 to **85.00**

Regal and Traditional

Beefeater, #142, 1966-96, FW, OEBR, 8", from $100 to **150.00**
King Henry VIII, #150, 1986-94, c 1985, AWB, REBR, 7", $150 to **225.00**

The Seafarers

Bargee, #168, 1988-96, AWB, REBR, 5¼", from $100 to **165.00**
Buccaneer, #61, 1966-96, c 1964, FW, OEC, 7½", $125 to **145.00**
Old Salt, #80, 1969-96, c 1971, MU, OEBR, 5", from $85 to **135.00**

The Victorians

Sherlock Holmes, #146, 1984-96, AWB, RE, 6½", from $125 to **150.00**
Victorian Fireman, #157, 1989-94, AWB, RE, 6¾", from $115 to ..**145.00**

Wildlife Wall Figures

Owlets & Squirrel, #223, 1993-96, AWB, REBR, 9", $215 to **250.00**
Raccoon, #55, 1964-96, Amuchastegui (modeler), OEC, 12½", $95 to .**135.00**

Bottle Openers

Around the turn of the century, manufacturers began to seal bottles with a metal cap that required a new type of bottle opener. Now the screw cap and the flip top have made bottle openers nearly obsolete. There are many variations, some in combination with other tools. Many openers were used as means of advertising a product. Various materials were used, including silver and brass.

A figural bottle opener is defined as a figure designed for the sole purpose of lifting a bottle cap. The actual opener must be an integral part of the figure itself. A base-plate opener is one where the lifter is a separate metal piece attached to the underside of the figure. The major producers of iron figurals were Wilton Products, John Wright Inc., Gadzik Sales, and L & L Favors. Openers may be free-standing and three-dimensional, wall hung, or flat. They can be made of cast iron (often painted), brass, bronze, or aluminum.

Numbers within the listings refer to a reference book printed by the FBOC (Figural Bottle Opener Collectors) organization. Those seeking additional information are encouraged to contact FBOC, whose address can be found in the Directory under Clubs, Newsletters, and Catalogs. The items below are all in excellent original condition unless noted otherwise.

Alligator, wht metal, F-139 ....25.00
Auto Jack, chrome, F-211 ....32.00
Bear head, CI, F-426, 3¾" 130.00
Clown head, brass, F-417 ....55.00
Cowboy w/guitar, aluminum, F-27a 15.00
Donkey, brass, F-60, 3⅝" 15.00
Donkey, CI, F-61 ....50.00
Elephant, brass, F-48a, 3⅜" 15.00
Elephant, CI, F-46 ....35.00
Fish, abalone, F-162 ....20.00
Goat, CI, F-71, tall 70.00
Hanging Drunk, CI, wall mt, F-415 ....80.00
Lamppost Drunk, mtd on ashtray, F-1 ....20.00
Lamppost Drunk, pot metal, F-1c 10.00

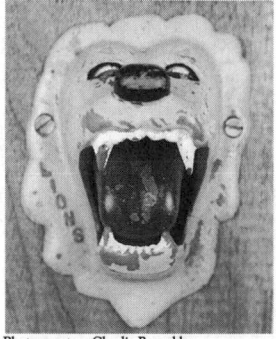

Lion, painted cast iron, mechanical, wall mount, F-433, EX, $3,500.00.

Photo courtesy Charlie Reynolds

Lobster, CI, F-168 ....30.00
Miss 4-Eyes, CI, F-408 ....85.00
Monkey, aluminum, F-89b, 2⅝" 15.00
Negro, brass, wall mt, F-402 ....35.00
Negro, CI, wall mt, rpt, F-402 ....65.00
Nude w/wreath, pot metal w/copper finish, F-173, 5¾" 20.00
Parrot, CI, F-108, lg 50.00
Pelican, CI, F-129, from $65 to 75.00
Pretzel, CI, F-232 ....45.00
Rooster, brass, F-97b, 3" 15.00
Sea gull, CI, F-123 ....60.00

Shoe, aluminum, F-209, 3¾" 140.00
Shovel, brass, F-221 ....20.00
Sign Post Drunk, CI, F-11 ....15.00
Squirrel, brass, F-93, 2⅝" 15.00
Straw Hat Sign Post Drunk, CI, F-13 ....45.00
Trout, CI, F-159 ....120.00
4-Eyed Lady, CI, wall mt, F-407 ....100.00
4-Eyed Man, CI, wall mt, F-413 ....60.00

Bottles and Flasks

As far back as the 1st century B.C., the Romans preferred blown glass containers for their pills and potions. Though you're not apt to find many of those, you will find bottles of every size, shape, and color made to hold perfume, ink, medicine, soda, spirits, vinegar, and many other liquids. American business firms preferred glass bottles in which to package their commercial products and used them extensively from the late 18th century on. Bitters bottles contained 'medicine' (actually herb-flavored alcohol), and judging from the number of these found today, their contents found favor with many! Because of a heavy tax imposed on the sale of liquor in 17th-century England by King George, who hoped to curtail alcohol abuse among his subjects, bottlers simply added 'curative' herbs to their brew and thus avoided taxation. Since gin was taxed in America as well, the practice continued in this country. Scores of brands were sold; among the most popular were Dr. H.S. Flint & Co. Quaker Bitters, Dr. Kaufman's Anti-Cholera Bitters, and Dr. J. Hostetter's Stomach Bitters. Most bitters bottles were made in shades of amber, brown, and aquamarine. Clear glass was used to a lesser extent, as were green tones. Blue, amethyst, red-brown, and milk glass examples are rare. (Please note that color is a strong factor when pricing bottles. For example, an amber Hostetter's bitters sells for $25.00 or less, but a green variant can bring hundreds of dollars. An aqua scroll flask may bring $50.00, but a cobalt blue variation will command over $1,000.00.)

Perfume or scent bottles were produced abroad by companies all over Europe from the late 16th century on. Perfume making became such a prolific trade that as a result beautifully decorated bottles were fashionable. In America they were produced in great quantities by Stiegel in 1770 and by Boston and Sandwich in the early 19th century. Cologne bottles were first made in about 1830 and toilet-water bottles in the 1880s. Rene Lalique produced fine scent bottles from as early as the turn of the century. The first were one-of-a-kind creations done in the cire perdue method. He later designed bottles for the Coty Perfume Company with a different style for each Coty fragrance.

Spirit flasks from the 19th century were blown in specially designed molds with varied motifs including political subjects, railroad trains, and symbolic devices. The most commonly used colors were amber, dark brown, and green.

From the 20th century, early pop and beer bottles are very collectible as is nearly every extinct commercial container. Dairy bottles are a relatively new area of interest; look for round bottles in good condition with both city and state as well as a nice graphic relating to the farm or the dairy.

Bottles may be dated by the methods used in their production. For instance, a rough pontil indicates a date before 1845. After the bottle was blown, a pontil rod was attached to the bottom, a glob of molten glass acting as the 'glue.' This allowed the glassblower to continue to manipulate the extremely hot bottle until it was finished. From about 1845 until approximately 1860, the molten glass 'glue' was omitted. The rod was simply heated to a temperature high enough to cause it to afix itself to the bottle. When the rod was snapped off, a metallic residue was left on the base of the bottle; this is called an 'iron pontil.' (The presence of a pontil scar thus indicates early manufacture and increases the value of a bottle.) A seam that reaches from base to lip marks a machine-made bottle from after 1903, while an applied or hand-finished lip points to an early mold-blown bottle. The Industrial Revolution saw keen competition between manufacturers, and as a result, scores of patents were issued. Many concentrated on various types of closures; the crown bottle cap, for instance, was patented in 1892. If a manufacturer's name is present, consulting a book on marks may help you date your bottle.

Among our advisors for this category are Madeleine France (see the Directory under Florida), Mark Vuono (Connecticut), Steve Ketcham (Minnesota), Monsen and Baer (Virginia), and John Tutton (Virginia). In the listings that follow (most of which have been taken from auction catalogs), glass is assumed to be clear unless color is indicated. Numbers refer to a standard reference book, *American Glass*, by George and Helen McKearin. See also Advertising, various companies; Avon; Barber Shop Collectibles; Blown Glass; Blown Three-Mold Glass; California Perfume Company; Czechoslovakia; De Vilbiss; Fire Fighting; Lalique; Medical Collectibles; Sandwich Glass; Steuben; Zanesville Glass.

Key:

am — applied mouth	grd — ground pontil
bbl — barrel	GW — Glass Works
bt — blob top	ip — iron pontil
b3m — blown 3-mold	ps — pontil scar
cm — collared mouth	rm — rolled mouth
fl — filigree	sb — smooth base
fm — flared mouth	sl — sloping
gm — ground mouth	sm — sheared mouth
gp — graphite pontil	tm — tooled mouth

Barber Bottles

Frosted purple amethyst, rib pattern with white and gold Art Nouveau floral decor, pontil scar, metal stopper, 7⅞", $240.00; Emerald green with white and gold Art Nouveau decor, pontil scar, metal stopper, 7⅞", $220.00.

Bird on branch, gold on cobalt, sb, sm, 8⅜" 350.00
Checkerberry wheel-cut on clear, sb, rm, 6⅝" 70.00
Dk amethyst w/orange/wht decor, ps, sm, 7⅝" 90.00
Eiffel Tower form, sb, tm, 7½" 120.00
Hobnail, clambroth opal w/hint of pk, tm, pontil, 6⅝" 150.00
Hobnail, turq bl opal w/bl wht hobnails, rm, pontil, 7" 150.00
Hobnail, yel w/amber tone, sb, rm, 7⅜" 70.00
Jos Doan Tonic, milk glass w/mc floral/bird, pewter top, 9½" 375.00
Mary Gregory boy on purple amethyst, ribbed, ps, rm, 8⅛", NM ..190.00
Mary Gregory girl tennis player on cobalt, ps, flake, 8⅛" 325.00
Powder bl opaque, panel reserve for label, sb, tm, 10¼" 95.00
Ribbed, clear to cobalt at base, sb, gm, 7½" 200.00
Ribbed, cobalt w/mc decor, corset waist, ps, rm, 7¾" 140.00
Ribbed, cobalt w/mc elaborate Nouveau floral, ps, rm, 7⅝" 250.00
Ribbed, cobalt w/pk & wht decor, bell form, ps, sm, 7⅞" 75.00
Ribbed, cranberry w/mc decor, ps, sm, 7⅜" 300.00
Ribbed, dk amethyst w/orange/wht decor, bell form, ps, sm, 8" ..100.00

Ribbed, grass gr w/wht & gold decor, ps, tm, 7⅜" 400.00
Ribbed, med pk amethyst w/mc decor, ps, rm, 7" 275.00
Ribbed, turq w/red/wht/gold decor, bell form, ps, sm, 8" 170.00
Ribbed, yel-gr w/mc elaborate floral, bbl form, ps, sm, 7⅝" 250.00
Silver o/l on clear, pewter rabbit stopper, tm, monogram, 6¼" ...200.00
Spatter, mc on clear, sb, tm, 9¼" 300.00
Striped, cranberry opal w/wht swirl, sb, rm, 8⅛" 625.00
Striped, cranberry opal w/wht vertical, sb, rm, 7¼" 375.00
Striped, turq bl opal w/wht swirl, pontil, rm, 6⅞" 475.00
Thumbprint, turq w/mc decor, ps, rm, 8¼" 190.00
Toilet Water, Koken Barbers... & mc floral on milk glass, 7¾" 90.00
Toilet Water, ruby to clear, ps, rm, flake, 7" 160.00
Witch Hazel, floral, mc on milk glass, sb, rm, 9" 80.00

Bitters Bottles

Baker's Orange Grove, med amber, sb, sl cm, EX+ label, 9½" 375.00
Big Bill Best, med amber, sb, tm, EX label, 1900-10, 12" 130.00
Bourbon Whiskey, strawberry puce, sb, am, bbl, 9¼", NM 375.00
Brown's Celebrated Indian...1867, dk chocolate-amber, queen, 12" .4,800.00
Bryant's Stomach, olive gr, 8-sided lady's leg, 12" 6,750.00
Doctor Fisch's...WH Ware...1866, amber, sb, fish, 11½" 300.00
Dr AS Hopkins Union Stomach, golden yel-amber, sb, cm, 9½", NM 75.00
Dr Campbell's Scotch, golden yel-amber, strap side, ½-pt, 6¼" .475.00
Dr Frank's Laxative Tonic, golden yel-amber, stain, 6⅝" 210.00
Dr J Hostetter's Stomach, deep olive gr, sb, sl cm, 9⅞", NM 190.00
Dr Lamot's Botanic, golden yel-amber, sb, cm, 8⅝", NM 110.00
E Long's Indian Herb, med amber to yel-amber, queen, 12" ..11,500.00
Ferro Quina Stomach...USA & Canada, red-amber, sb, tm, 9" 65.00
Great Universal...Geo J Byrne..., amber, sb, dbl cm, 10¾" 1,350.00
Greeley's Bourbon Whiskey/Greeley's, lt bl-aqua, bbl, 9⅜" 2,850.00
Hall's...EE Hall New Haven...1842, med amber, sb, bbl, 9⅛" 180.00
Hartwig/Kantorowicz, med yel-olive gr, sb, am, 1880s, 9¼" 75.00
Holtzermann's Pat Stomach..., med amber, 4-roof cabin, 9⅞" 275.00
Kelly's Old Cabin...1863, dk chocolate-amber, log cabin, 9⅜" .2,350.00
McKeever's Army, med amber, drum & cannonballs, 10½" 1,450.00
National Bitters, yel, Pat 1867 on sb, ear of corn, 12⅝" 925.00
Poor Man's Family, aqua, sb, tm, NM orig label, 6⅜" 95.00
Reed's, amber, sb, dbl cm, lady's leg, stain, 12⅜" 120.00
Royal Italian...Gianella Genova, pk-amethyst, sq cm, 13⅝" 675.00
Russ St Domingo...NY, yel-topaz, sb, appl sl cm, bubbles, 10" 375.00
Simon's Centennial...Trade Mark, aqua, Washington bust, 9⅞" .650.00
Sol Frank's Panacea...NY, med amber, sb, lighthouse, 10⅛" 190.00
St Drakes 1860 Plant'n...1862, med amber, w/label, 10⅜" 100.00
Texas Blood Purifier & Tonic..., golden amber, 10" 1,250.00
The Fish Bitters/WH Ware/1866, amber, fish, 11½" 220.00
1834 John Root...1834 Buffalo NY, med bl-gr, semi-cabin, 10", NM .725.00

Black Glass Bottles

Many early European and American bottles are deep, dark green, or amber in color. Collectors refer to such coloring as black glass. Before held to light, the glass is so dark it appears to be black.

Blacking, dk sapphire bl, 8-sided, ps, am, 4¼" 425.00
Demijohn, dk root beer-amber, ps, sl cm, sm stain, 16½" 120.00
Demijohn, med olive gr, sb, am, crude, bladder shape, 16½" 325.00
Demijohn, yel-olive, tri-pontil base, cm, flattened ovoid, 19½" .200.00
Demijohn, yel-olive gr, ps, appl sl cm, swirls/bubbles, 17⅝" 195.00
Mallet, dk olive-amber, ps, am, 12½" 700.00
Onion, dk olive gr, ps, appl string lip, flakes, 10¾" 300.00
Onion, dk olive-amber, ps, appl string lip, sm stain, 12¾" 1,050.00
Seal: (coat of arms) 1785, dk olive gr, ps, am, squat, 9½" 1,500.00
Seal: Jas Oakes Bury 1783, dk olive gr, ps, am, 10⅝", NM 825.00

Utility, olive-amber, sb, appl dbl cm, lt stain, 6⅞" 110.00
Wine, med olive-amber, ps on deep kick-up, am, 10⅝", NM 825.00

Blown Glass Bottles and Flasks

Chestnut flask, 10-dmm, bl-aqua, ps, sm, 4⅝" 575.00
Chestnut flask, 10-dmn, dk tobacco-amber, ps, sm, 5¾" 925.00
Chestnut flask, 10-dmn, med yel-amber, ps, sm, 4⅞" 775.00
Chestnut flask, 10-dmn, yel w/olive tone, ps, sm, 5½" 2,900.00
Flask, 15-dmn, dk bl-aqua, ps, sm, 9½" 550.00
Flattened club, 30 right-swirl ribs, ps, sl cm, 10¼" 110.00
Ludlow, gr, am, sm stain, 8½" 200.00
Nurser, 12-dmn, dk gr-aqua, ps, fm, 6½" 150.00
Nurser, 14-dmn, dk bl-aqua, ps, fm, 7⅜" 150.00
Pitkin flask, lt gr, 30 broken left-swirl ribs, ps, 5⅞" 250.00
Pitkin flask, med emerald gr, 16 broken right-swirl ribs, ps, 6" ...400.00
Pitkin flask, smoky clear, 22 broken right-swirl ribs, 5⅝" 220.00

Cologne, Perfume, and Toilet Water Bottles

Bellows form, med amber, emb crown & fleur-de-lis, ps, 3¼" 140.00
Bunker Hill Monument, cobalt, sb, tm, sm chip, 11⅞" 400.00
Dmn form, aquamarine, full-figured Indians on 2 sides, 4⅞" 80.00
Elephant w/rich trappings figural, pontil, 4¾" 500.00
Gothic Arch, sapphire, bl, knight in 1 panel, pontil, 4⅛" 850.00
Harrison's Columbian Perfumery, sb, fm, 5⅛", EX 35.00
HE Swan, horn-o'-plenty body, fluted neck, sb, 6" 30.00
Pillar mold, grass gr, scalloped rim, cut pillars, 7" 350.00
Powder bl opaque opal, ps, fm, orig blown stopper, 5¼" 55.00
Ring & Star, canary, 8-sided stopper, 7" 375.00
Sandwich type, amethyst, Argus, fm, appl ring, pontil, 6" 1,300.00
Sandwich type, cobalt, polygonal, sb, rm, 4¾" 425.00
Sapphire bl, palmette/scrolled acanthus/X-hatch, corseted, 5½" ..1,800.00
Shield form, sapphire bl, 12-ray sunburst, sm, ps, 2¾" 325.00
Spatter w/appl rigaree, mc, orig stopper, 7⅜" 550.00
Sunburst, cobalt, ps, tm, Am, 1850-60, 2¾" 375.00
Sunburst, dk emerald gr (rare color) ps, tm, chip, 3" 650.00
Sunburst, ps, tm, Am, 1855-65, 3", NM 75.00
Teardrop, citron, 19 vertical ribs, pontil, lt haze, 2⅞" 230.00
Teardrop, dk amethyst, 24 swirled ribs, sm, ps, 2⅞" 110.00
Teardrop, robin's-egg bl w/gray-amethyst streaks, ps, 3" 375.00
Teardrop, sapphire bl, 20 swirled ribs, ps, 3⅜" 110.00
12-sided, amethyst, s/rm, sb, 7¾" 200.00
12-sided, cobalt, sb, partially fm, 5⅛" 120.00
12-sided, cobalt, sb, tm, 7⅝" 120.00
12-sided, cobalt, sl shoulders, sb, rm, 4¾" 100.00
12-sided, emerald gr, sheared rm, sb, 4¼" 180.00
12-sided, lt electric bl, sl shoulders, sb, rm, haze, 6⅛" 80.00
12-sided, lt to med cobalt, sb, tm, 1860-80, 5¾" 110.00
12-sided, med bl-gr, sl shoulders, sb, rm, haze, 4¾" 90.00
12-sided, med pk-amethyst, sb, fm, 6½" 190.00
12-sided, med smoky pk-amethyst, ps, fm, 7⅝" 300.00
12-sided, smoky steel bl, ps, fm, seed bubbles, 7⅜" 875.00
12-sided, teal, flared, s/rm, sb, 5½", NM 195.00
15 vertical ribs, purple amethyst, ps, rm, tam stopper, 4" 875.00
8-sided, amethyst, waisted, s/rm, sb, 4¾" 425.00

Commercial Perfume Bottles

One of the most popular and growing areas of perfume bottle collecting is what are called 'commercial' perfume bottles. They are called commercial because they were sold with perfume in them — in a sense one pays for the perfume and the bottle is free. Collectors especially value bottles that retain their original label and box, called a perfume

presentation. If the bottle is unopened, so much the better. Rare fragrances and those from the 1920s are highly prized. 'Tis a sweet, sweet hobby. Our advisors are Randy Monsen and Rod Baer; they are listed in the Directory under Virginia.

Photo courtesy Monsen and Baer

Subtilite, Houbigant, crystal Buddha figural, stopper fitted with brass ring, Baccarat emblem on bottom, 3¼", $255.00.

A de Markoff, Tiara, frosted flask, M in coral moire box 77.00
Babs Creations, Forever Yours, clear heart, brass cap, 3", +dome ..145.00
Baccarat, Liu, blk crystal w/gold/blk label, #679, 1929, 3½" 467.50
Baccarat/D'orsay, Milord, portrait on clear, #793, 1944, 2¼" 55.00
Bienaime, Vermeil, clear butterfly-like shape, ca 1936, MIB 45.00
Brisson, Quatier Latin, envelope shape, late 1940s, MIB 155.00
C Dior, Miss Dior, urn shape w/molded rings, 3¾", MIB 66.00
Cara Nome, White Mink, triangular form, 2", MIB 330.00
Caron, Le Babac Blond, gold label on clear, 3¼", MIB 110.00
Caron, Tabac Blond, clear flat oval, molded stopper, 3¼", MIB .110.00
Caron, Voeu de Noel, emb floral on wht opal, bar stopper, 3½" ...357.50
Cheramy, Cappi, flask shape, paper label, frosted top, 2½" 99.00
Ciro, Surrender, faceted gemstone shape, labels, 4", MIB 100.00
Corday, Quand?, blk w/gold lettering, ca 1935, 3⅜" 285.00
Coty, Muse, gold label, frosted overcap, 4", MIB 275.00
Cruselias, Besame, blk, triangular, 3⅜", MIB 198.00
De Valois, Chypre, vertical ribs, amber stopper, 4", MIB 66.00
Deroc, Gai Monmartre, red windmill w/metal blades, 1925, 5½" ..880.00
Drialis, Gardenia, blk flattened teardrop, 4¾", MIB 155.00
Duvelle, Le Gui, gr teardrop w/metallic labels, 3¼", MIB 165.00
Elesbre-Rochambeau, Chypre, butterfly w/fabric wings, 2¾", MIB ..990.00
Eroy, Adoree, frosted nude (stopper) kneels on cushion, 4¼" 285.00
F Denney, Night Life, stage & curtains shape, 1940s, 3½", MIB ...357.50
Grenoville, Byzance, blk flask, 1930s, 2¼", M, +tasseled box 165.00
Guerlain, Apres L'Ondee, rnded ribs, pine cone stopper, 4½", MIB .230.00
Guerlain, Violette a Deux Sous, flask form, ca 1910, 5¼" 285.00
Guerlain, Vol de Nuit, dk olive gr, brass cap, 2¾", MIB 77.00
Henri Defrance, Apres 5 Heures, oval facets, 2", MIB 55.00
Houbigant, Presence, vertical pleats intersect, 1930s, 4", MIB ...185.00
Jovoy, Allez...Hop!, puppy w/lg paws, ca 1924, 4¼", NM 1,200.00
L Lelong, Impromptu, clear/frosted tower, no label, 6½" 145.00
L Lelong, Jabot, frosted bow shape, 2⅜", M, +hatbox box 1,200.00
L Lelong, Orgueil, gold-encased curvaceous shape, 4¾", MIB 525.00
Lansell, Coucou, clear w/feather bird, frosted top, 7", MIB 4,125.00
Lazell, Bocadia, blk enamel, gold label, 1920s, 4", MIB 77.00
Lentheric, Dark Brilliance, clear & frosted w/gold, 3", MIB 100.00
Lola Beer, Demona, baluster, frosted top, 4⅜", MIB 297.00
Mademoiselle, Chanel 31, red & wht label, C stopper, 4" 660.00
Mury, Caresse d'Amour, clear w/frosted stopper, 1917, MIB 330.00
Penelope, Diamant Noir, blk dmn form, sealed, 3¼", MIB 300.00
Pinaude, Scarlett, gold/wht lady figural, ca 1937, 7" 120.00
R Hudnut, La Reverie, clear invt cone w/gold enamel, 2¾" 175.00
R Hudnut, Le Debut Noir, blk octagon, molded stopper, 2½" 357.50
R Hudnut, Sweet Orchid, frosted rectangle, 3", MIB 175.00
Tappan, Clean Sweep, metal whisk broom w/frosted   , 3¼" ...440.00

Dairy Bottles

Anderson Bros, Drink Milk..., bl pyro, 10-oz 10.00
Beltz Dairy, Palmerton PA, red pryo, rnd, qt 15.00
Borden's, Elsie portrait, red pyro, sq, lg cap, ½-pt 7.50
Borden's, Gail Borden signature/profile, wht pyro on amber, qt 25.00
Cloverdale Farms, plastic snap cap, red pyro, sq, qt 18.00
Cloverleaf, cream top, red pyro, rnd, qt 25.00
Cloverleaf, modern top, red pyro, qt 28.00
Cooper Dairy Half Pint Liquid, baby face, sb, cap seat, ½-pt 110.00
Cop the Cream Glenside...It Whips, baby face, sb, 1-pt 85.00
Cream Top, Party Tonight?..., gr/orange pyro, sq, qt 17.50
Ethan Allen, wht pyro on amber, sq, qt, NM 10.00
Fisher Dairy...MI, lady, blk pyro, rnd, qt 15.00
Hi Acre...Farms, Heidi (cow) portrait, orange pyro, rnd, qt 10.00
KY Acres...Buy War Bonds..., orange pyro, sb, 1-qt 110.00
Maine Milk, cow & lighthouse, maroon pyro, qt 8.00
Mission Milk, mission roof in circle, orange pyro, qt 15.00
Morningside Farm...CA, barn & sunburst, orange pyro, rnd, qt 15.00
O'Donnell's Milk...CT, dairy barn scene, orange pyro, rnd, qt 15.00
Plain's Dairy, A Augusto & 4 cows, red pyro, rnd, pt 10.00
Sunnyhurst, Hoppy's Favorite Milk, qt 75.00
Superior...Millville NJ, baby face, sb, cap seat, 1-qt 95.00
Tecroney Dairy, Clymer NY, baby reaching, maroon pyro, rnd, qt ...15.00
Vermont Country Egg Nog, cow w/holly sprig, maroon pyro, qt ...10.00
Wyman's...Rehoboth MA, children, orange pyro, rnd, qt 15.00

Figural Bottles

Clown figural, frosted turquoise blue, marked Depose, smooth base, 13⅝", $300.00.

Auto, clear w/frosted satin mouth, sb, 1910s, 6½x7¼" 250.00
Baby's bottle, milk glass w/red & yel, sb, screw cap, 11½" 110.00
Bear, dense amethyst, tm, sb, Russia, 1860-80, 11¼" 350.00
Czar Nicholas II, milk glass, ps, gm, head stopper, 10" 500.00
Fish, turq bl, sb, sm, 10⅞" 75.00
Fountain, cranberry flashed on clear, Depose on ps base, 11" 400.00
Gnl Boulanger, orig mc pnt, Depose on sb, no stopper, 15" 70.00
Japanese man standing, JGP on forehead, golden amber, sb, 6½" ...250.00
Joan of Arc, Jeanne D'Apc Bonbons..., milk glass, 16½" 275.00
John Bull, bright orange-amber, tm, sb, ca 1900, 11¾" 200.00
Jules Grevy, D&D Depose, sb, tm, 11½" 70.00
Lady w/book, DD Alsace Depose, powder bl, sb, fm, 13⅜" 575.00
Locomotive, clear w/pale yel tint, cm, sb, ca 1880s, 12" 275.00
Madame Depose, cobalt, ps, partially fm, orig stopper, 13⅜" ...1,050.00
Man in the Moon, decanter, topaz carnival w/mc pnt, 11⅛" 325.00
Moses, Poland Water H Ricker..., aqua, sb, am, 11¼" 75.00
Owl, clear, Pat Apd For on sb, tm, 1890-1910, 5" 100.00
Pineapple, med amber, sb, dbl cm, Am, 1865-75, 9", NM 135.00
Pineapple, med golden amber, sb, appl dbl cm, Am, 1865-75, 9⅛" ...145.00
Policeman, Liqueur Raspail Paris..., cobalt w/orig pnt, sb, 14½" ...75.00
Russian General bust, amethystine & satin frost, tm, sb, 11" 425.00
Santa Claus, MC Husted, sb, tm, 12¼" 75.00
Shoe, blk amethyst, sb, gm, orig metal cap, pnt toe, 3⅝" 110.00
St Joseph Bonbon, Bonbons John Tavernier, NM pnt, 16" 100.00
Uncle Sam, Pat Apl'd For on sb, gm, metal high cap, 9½" 75.00
Victorian lady, yel honey-amber, tm, ps, Depose, 1890s, 13⅜" .1,000.00

Flasks

Cornucopia/Urn, GIII-13, dk teal gr, ps, sm, ½-pt 575.00
Cornucopia/Urn, GIII-15, med bl-gr, ps, sm, ½-pt 475.00
Cornucopia/Urn, GIII-17, bl-aqua, ps, dbl cm, 1-pt 170.00
Eagle w/Banner/Clasped Hands, GXII-2, yel w/olive tone, sq cm, 1-qt ..1,100.00
Eagle w/Banner/plain, GII-143, bright yel-gr, ip, cm, calabash ...170.00
Eagle/Cluster of Grapes, GII-55, dk bl-aqua, ps, sm, 1-qt 140.00
Eagle/Coffin & Hay, GII-48, lt smoky-gr, ps, sm, 1-qt 260.00
Eagle/Eagle, GII-105, med emerald gr, sb, am, crude, pt 500.00
Eagle/Eagle, GII-24, lt emerald gr, ps, sm, pt 450.00
Eagle/Eagle, GII-24, lt yel-gr, ps, sm, pt 400.00
Eagle/Eagle, GII-24, med sapphire bl, ps, sm, pt, NM 2,600.00
Eagle/Eagle, GII-26, aqua 'clambroth,' ps, sm, qt 275.00
Eagle/Eagle, GII-26, dk bl-gr, ps, sm, crude/bubbles, qt 1,300.00
Eagle/Eagle, GII-26, dk yel-amber w/olive tone, ps, qt, NM 1,950.00
Eagle/Furled Flag, GII-52, aqua, sm, ps, 1-pt, 6¾" 210.00
Eagle/Glass Works, GII-35, bl-aqua, vertical ribs, 1-qt 170.00
Eagle/Lyre, GII-22, dk bl-aqua, ps, sm, pt 775.00
Eagle/Masonic Arch, GIV-32, dk bl-aqua, ps, sm, 1-pt 325.00
Eagle/Masonic Arch, GIV-32, yel-amber to red-amber, rm, ps, 1-pt .1,650.00
Eagle/Masonic Arch, GIV-32, yel-olive, ps, sm, crude, 1-pt 2,600.00
Eagle/Morning Glory, GII-19, dk bl-aqua, dbl cm, 1-pt 525.00
Hunter/Fisherman, GXIII-4, dk gr-aqua, ps, sl cm, calabash 90.00
Jenny Lind/Glasshouse, GI-99, dk yel-olive, calabash, 10½" ...2,350.00
Jenny Lind/Lyre, dk bl-aqua, ps, sm, qt, NM 725.00
Lafayette/Clinton, GI-81, med yel-olive, ps, sm, ½-pt 525.00
Murdock & Cassel/Zanesville OH, GX-14, dk gr-aqua, ps, 1-pt, NM .1,650.00
Scroll, GIX-10c, med teal bl, open p, sm, 1-pt 1,500.00
Scroll, GIX-11, moonstone w/pk tint, ps, sm, 1-pt 1,400.00
Scroll, GIX-16, yel olive-amber, open p, sm, 1-pt 450.00
Scroll, GIX-20, med yel-gr (rare), ps, sm, 1-pt 1,300.00
Scroll, GIX-6, dk bl-aqua, ip, sm, shallow chip, 1-qt 110.00
Scroll (PB&B), GIX-39, ps, sm, ½-pt 825.00
Success to RR/Horse Pulling Cart, GV-4, med yel-olive, 1-pt, NM ..450.00
Sunburst, GVIII-3, med yel-olive w/amber tone, ps, pt 475.00
Union/Clasped Hands/Cannon, GXII-42, bl-aqua, ip, sm, ½-pt .400.00
Washington/Taylor, GI-38, lt sapphire bl, sb, sm, 1-pt 650.00
Washington/Taylor, GI-40, med yel olive-amber, ps, bubbles, pt ..800.00
Washington/Taylor, GI-40c, med bl-gr, ps, sm, crude, pt 500.00

Food Bottles and Jars

MB Espy Philada, aqua, ip, rm, whittled, 11⅝" 425.00
Mustard, Victoria (coat of arms), milk glass, figural lid, 8⅛" 130.00
Peppersauce, dk aqua, roped corners, ps, sl cm, 11" 200.00
Peppersauce, med bl-gr, cathedral, ps, dbl cm, 8¾" 450.00
Peppersauce, smoky clear, cathedral, ps, am, haze, 20" 210.00
Pickle, aquamarine, cathedral arches, ip, rm, 9" 325.00
Pickle, aquamarine, protruding irregular panels, ip, tm, 11¾" 170.00
Pickle, dk bl-gr, fluted shoulders & base, ip, 12¼" 550.00
Pickle, gr-aqua, 3 fancy cathedral designs, sq, sb, rm, 11½" 140.00
Pickle, lt apple gr (citron), cathedral, sb, am, 13½" 350.00
Pickle, lt bl-gr, cathedral, sb, rm, whittled, 11¾" 400.00
Pickle, lt gr, petals at shoulder & base, 8-sided center, 11" 325.00
Pickle, lt yel-gr, sq w/fancy cathedral arches, sb, cm, 11¾" 200.00

Pickle, med bl-gr, cathedral, sb, rm, 12¼" 475.00
Pickle, med to dk bl-gr, cathedral, sb, am, 11½" 500.00
Pickle, R&F Atmore, bl-aqua, cathedral, sb, rm, 11⅜" 230.00
Pickle, red-amber, cloverleaf shape, sb, cm, 8⅛" 475.00
Pickle, WDS NY, lt gr-aqua, ip, rm, 7¾" 180.00
Pickle, Wm Underwood...Boston, aquamarine, cathedral, ps, 8¾" 325.00
Wells Miller & Provost, dk aqua, ps, crude, 12" 525.00
Wide mouth, dk tobacco-amber, ps, appl string lip, 10¾" 400.00
Wide mouth, med olive gr, ps, 2½" W mouth, scarce sz, 9" 210.00
Wide mouth, yel-olive gr, ps, sm, 13¾" 110.00
William Underwood & Co Boston, 64-oz, bl-aqua, ip, 12⅝" 190.00
WK Lewis & Co Boston, bl-aqua, ip, am, 10½" 325.00
WK Lewis & Co Boston, dk bl-aqua, ip, am, flake, 10½" 275.00

Ink Bottles

Barrel, WE Bonney, aqua, sb, am w/spout, 5⅛", NM 150.00
Barrel, WE Bonney, lt bl-aqua, sb, partially rm, EX label, 2⅝" 85.00
Building, bl-aquamarine, tooled cm, sb, 2⅝" 550.00
Feline (reclining), NA Depose, brass cap, sb, 2⅛x4⅝" 375.00
Free-blown, dk bl aqua, ps, sheared/tm, 3⅜" 425.00
Harrison's Columbian, aqua, 8-sided, ps, rm, 1¾" 80.00
Harrison's Columbian, cobalt, ps, rm, 2" 175.00
Harrison's Columbian (reversed N), aqua, 8-sided, am, 3⅞" 120.00
Lion (recumbent), cobalt, sb, gm, flake, 2⅜" 1,950.00
Log cabin, sb, sq cm, 2⅜", NM 200.00
Monkey, clear, sb, sm, rare, 2¼" 400.00
Snail, sb, 1⅞", EX 150.00
Teakettle, cobalt, gm, sb, shallow chip, 2" 190.00
Teakettle, dk sapphire bust of Ben Franklin, sb, 2⅞", NM 1,900.00
Teakettle, milk glass, sb, gm, sterling neck band/lid, 1⅝" 300.00
Turtle, David's, med teal, sb, tm, 1¾" 375.00
Turtle, J&IEM, med sapphire bl, sb, tm, 1⅝", NM 1,400.00
Turtle, J&IEM, med yel-olive, sb, tm, 1⅝" 675.00
Umbrella, Hover Phila, med emerald gr, 8-sided, ps, rm, 2⅜", NM 185.00

Medicine Bottles

Warner's bottles listed below are not American versions, and so are valued higher than those from Rochester, New York.

G.S. Thuber - Arnold's Vital Fluid - Boston Mass, aqua, rectangular, open pontil, collared mouth, 7", $120.00; Dr. H.H. Higbee - Remedy For - Pulmonary - Diseases, aqua, round, open pontil, flared lip, 5¾", NM, $275.00. (Most druggist bottles are in the $5.00 to $10.00 range; these are rare. The pontil scar adds a great deal to value as well.)

ABL Meyers AM Rock Rose New Haven, dk emerald bl-gr, ip, 9½" 1,500.00
Alexanders Simaleau, sapphire bl, ps, am, 6¼" 650.00
Allan's Anti-Fat Botanic..., dk sapphire bl, sb, sl cm, 7⅝", NM .300.00
Anker (anchor) Anchor Sarsaparillian..., gr-aqua, sb, tm, 9" 135.00
Bolton Drug Co Improved Magnesia..., cobalt, sb, tm, 6¾" 150.00
C Brinckerhoff's Health Restorative..., med olive gr, ps, 7¼" 950.00
DR GW Phillips Cough Syrup..., ice bl-aqua, ps, sl cm, 7½", NM ...160.00
Dr HB Skinner Boston, med bl-gr, ps, am, whittled, 6" 650.00
Dr Kennedy's...Discovery, dk bl-aqua, ps, sl cm, 8¾" 120.00
Dr Perkins Syrup.., dk bl-gr, ip, sl cm, seed bubbles, 9⅜" 2,400.00
GW Merchant Chemist Lockport NY, dk gr, sb, 7⅛" 135.00
Hampton's V Tincture...Balto, yel olive-amber, ps, 6¼" 1,100.00
I Covert's Balm of Life, olive gr, ps, sl cm, 6" 1,100.00
Negative Electric Fluid, NW Seet (S bkward), aqua, rm, 3⅜" 95.00
Rang's Syrup of Tar, bl-aqua, sb, teardrop flask, 5½" 375.00
Rohrer's Expectoral Wild Cherry..., med amber, sb, cm, 10⅝" ...210.00
Sims Tonic Elixer Pyrosphate..., med amber, sb, 7¼", MIB 110.00
Terp-Heroin Foster's, med amber, Pat Dec 11 1894 on sb, 8⅝" ..160.00
Tippecanoe HH Warner & Co, amber, dtd base, log, label, 9" ...200.00
Tippecanoe HH Warner & Co, amber, dtd base, log, no label, 9" ...75.00
USA Hosp Dept, med yel-olive gr, sb, dbl cm, seed bubbles, 9½" .600.00
USA Hosp Dept, med yel-olive gr to dk, sb, dbl cm, 9½" 475.00
USA Hosp Dept, straw yel w/olive tone, sb, dbl cm, 9½" 1,150.00
USA Hosp Dept, yel olive-amber, sb, appl dbl cm, 9" 500.00
Warner's Safe Cure (safe) Pressburg, blood red, sb, 9½" 600.00
Warner's Safe Cure (safe)...Frankfurt..., med amber, sb, 9¼" 175.00
Wood's Great Pepper Mint Cure..., med cobalt, sb, 5½" 450.00

Mineral Water and Soda Bottles

A Dearborn & Co NY...Never Sold, cobalt, ip, sl cm, 7¼", NM ..80.00
Adirondack Spring Whitehall NY, dk emerald gr, sb, dbl cm, 1-pt 210.00
Beitz & Bro Easton PA Premium..., cobalt, 8-sided, ip, bt, 7⅝" ..230.00
Boston & Co From London, dk olive-amber, 10-pin, 6⅝", NM .575.00
C Lomax Chicago Congress Water, cobalt, ip, am, flake, 7¼" ...185.00
Caladonia Spring Wheelock VT, med yel-amber, sb, dbl cm, 9½", NM 175.00
CB Owens Root Beer Cincinnati, cobalt, sb, am, 12-sided, 8⅜" ..1,350.00
Clarke & Co New York, dk olive gr, ip, sl dbl cm, 1-qt 275.00
Congress & Empire Spring...NY, yel w/olive tone, sb, 1-qt 300.00
H Nash & Co Root Beer Cincinnati, cobalt, ip, am, 12-sided, 8¾" ..950.00
Heiss Phila H Union Glass Works..., dk sapphire bl, ip, 7⅜" 80.00
Hennessey & Nolan Albany NY Hoxsie, dk red-amber, sb, am, 6¾" ...75.00
Hopkins' Chalybeate Baltimore, dk yel-olive gr, ip, dbl cm, 7½" ..325.00
I Sutton Cincinnati, cobalt, ip, bt, 7⅜" 170.00
J Price's Improved, lt bl-gr, 10-pin, ps, rm, potstone, 7¾" 140.00
JT Brown Chemist Boston Dbl..., teal bl-gr, torpedo, 9⅛" 210.00
P Babb Balto, med bl-gr, ip, sl dbl cm, 8¼" 450.00
P Conway...Union GW, cobalt, mug base, ip, sl cm, 7½" 300.00
Patent (on shoulder) Phoenix GW Phila, emerald gr, ip, 7½", NM ..300.00
Poland...(banner) PMSW (monogram)..., aqua, Moses figural, 11" 70.00
WP Knicker Bocker...NY 1848, sapphire bl, 10-sided, ip, 7¾" ...135.00

Poison Bottles

Durfee Embalming Fluid..., sb, tm, label, 8⅝" 130.00
Label under glass, Acidum Tannic, wht/blk/gold on turq, 10¼" .130.00
Label under glass, Ferri Subcarb, blk/gold on cobalt, 11⅛" 220.00
Label under glass, Silver Nitrate 5%, blk/wht/gold on amber, 4⅝" ..40.00
Label under glass, Syr: Aurant, red/blk on cobalt, ps, 8" 95.00
Lattice & Dmn, cobalt, sb, tm, orig Poison stopper, label, 4¾" 90.00
Lattice & Dmn, cobalt, sb, tm, orig Poison stopper, 11¼" 550.00
Lattice & Dmn, cobalt, sb, tm, orig Poison stopper, 7⅛" 185.00
Lattice & Dmn, cobalt, USPHS on sb, tm, 1-gal, 13¼" 1,600.00
Not To Be Taken/Rd No 461701, lt sapphire bl, sb, tm, 3½" 80.00
Poison, amber, UDCo/WCW on sb, rm, label, 3⅛" 400.00
Poison, yel-amber, sb, tm, label, 4⅞" 170.00
Poison (skull & X bones) DP Poison, cobalt, sb, coffin, 3" 600.00
Poison (skull & X bones) Poison, cobalt, sb, tm, label, 2" 210.00
Poison Not To Be Taken, cobalt w/mc pnt label, sb, rm, 6" 135.00
Poison/Pat Appl'd For, cobalt, sb, tm, skull, prof rpr, 4" 650.00
Poison/Pat Appl'd For, cobalt, skull, prof rpr, 3⅝" 300.00
Poison/Poison, cobalt, CLG Co/Pat Appl'd For on sb, tm, 4" 200.00

Poison/Poison, cobalt, UDCo/WGW on sb, label, 8⅛", NM 250.00
Poison/Poison, dk red-amber, sb, tm, orig cork, 10¼" 130.00
Poison/Poison, med amber, Norwich on sb, coffin, 4⅞" 850.00

Sarsaparilla Bottles

Dr Townsend's...Albany NY, bright yel-gr, sb, tm, 9⅝" 130.00
Dr Townsend's...Albany NY, dk bl-gr, M on sb, sl cm, 9½" 100.00
Dr Townsend's...Albany NY, dk emerald gr, ip, sl cm, 9⅝" 300.00
Dr Townsend's...Albany NY, dk olive gr, sb, sl cm, 9¼" 75.00
Dr Townsend's...Albany NY, dk olive-amber, ps, sl cm, crude, 9⅛" ..120.00
Dr Townsend's...Albany NY, dk yel olive-amber, ps, sl cm, 9¾" ...180.00
Dr Townsend's...Albany NY, med bl-gr, ip, sl cm, dull, 9⅞" 80.00
Dr Townsend's...Albany NY, med emerald gr, sb, cm, 9⅛" 120.00
Old Dr Townsend's...Albany NY, dk tobacco-amber, ip, sl cm, 9½" 1,000.00
Old Dr Townsend's...NY, med cornflower bl, ip, sl cm, 9½" 800.00
Turner's....Buffalo NY, dk aqua, sb, cm, 12¼" 400.00

Spirits Bottles

Bininger's (clock face) Regulator..., amber, ps, am, 6" 400.00
Cylinder, dk forest gr w/mc Brandy & decor, ip, cm, 11¼" 85.00
Distilled in 1848 Old KY...Bininger..., med amber, ps, cm, 8" 175.00
Distilled in 1848...Am Bininger...NY, golden yel-amber, bbl, 9⅜" 130.00
Duffy Crescent Saloon...KY, amethystine tint, pig, sb, 7⅝" 675.00
Duffy Crescent Saloon...KY, aqua, sb, pig, 7⅝" 1,200.00
EG Booz's Old...Philadelphia, GVII-4, med amber, cabin, 7¾" ..210.00
Geo C Hubbel & Co, aqua, sb, sl dbl cm, semicabin, 10⅛" 110.00
Good Old Bourbon in a Hog's (arrow), golden amber, pig, 6¾" .250.00
HB Kirk & Co Wine Merchant NY...1853, bl-aqua, sb, tm, label, 8" 200.00
Hesperidina MS Bagley Un Barril, yel-olive, sb, dbl cm, bbl, 9" .160.00
Hopatkong...JC Hess & Co Phila, cobalt, sb, am, 10⅜", EX 400.00
London Jockey Clubhouse Gin (jockey/horse), dk olive-amber, 9¼" 625.00
PJ Mullaine 35th St...NY, amber, sb, tm, label, strap side ½-pt 55.00
RB Cutter Pure Bourbon, dk red-puce amber, ps, 8½" 200.00
Smokine Imported...Winnepeg Man Smokine, red-amber, cabin, 6⅝" 175.00
Turner Brothers NY, dk red-amber, sb, am, bbl, 9⅞" 325.00
Vertical ribbed pattern, amber, ps, appl hdl/mouth, 8½" 375.00
Young & Holmes Cincinnati O, root beer-amber, sb, semicabin, 9½" .350.00

Miscellaneous

Lavender Salts, Goetting & Co, See California Perfume Co.

Boxes

Boxes have been used by civilized man since ancient Egypt and Rome. Down through the centuries, specifically designed containers have been made from every conceivable material. Precious metals, papier-mache, Battersea, Oriental lacquer, and wood have held riches from the treasuries of kings, snuff for the fashionable set of the last century, China tea, and countless other commodities. In the following descriptions, when only one dimension is given, it is length. See also Toleware; specific manufacturers.

Alms, Orphans Fund/Widows Fund pnt on dvtl wood, 19th C, 6", pr .6,325.00
Apple, pine w/old red pnt, conical ft, 4x10x9¾" 300.00
Bentwood band, floral paper, newspaper lined, 19¾" 175.00
Bentwood w/folk-art peafowl on branch among trees, 19th C, 9½" ..325.00
Bible, oak English w/cvg, wrought-iron hinges, 23¼" 440.00
Bride's, bentwood w/HP 18th-C couple, German verse, 7x18x12" ...2,300.00
Candle, red-pnt pine, slide top, Am, ca 1800, 6⅜x22x10" 400.00
Cheese, bl-pnt pine, Am, 19th C, 6½x12⅛" dia, EX 175.00
Coal, cvd English mahog w/brass mts, 19th C, 18x14x14" 300.00
Comb, softwood, sm shelves, cvd front, nailed, 12⅜x9x4" 100.00
Document, dvtl, hinged lid, vinegar decor, gr/brn on mustard, 12" ...575.00
Document, dvtl maple, nails, red grpt, 5x10x5⅜" 375.00
Dome top, dvtl pine w/old bl, wrought-iron lock, 19½" 635.00
Glass, amber w/intricate HP/gilt, ormolu ft w/cherubs, 5x4½" ...275.00
Glass, cobalt, florals, ormolu ft/hdls, 5x4¾" dia 275.00
Glass, cobalt, wht fleur-de-lys/lg gold Xs, 5x5" dia 295.00
Glass, gr, lady w/horn & flowers in ivory, hinged, 4½" dia 165.00
Glass, lime gr, silver leaves/wht flowers, ormolu ft, 4x4" dia 175.00
Glass, lime gr w/gold, hinged lid, ormolu ft, 4⅝x4" dia 185.00
Glass, pk o/l w/gold & mc flowers, clear knob finial, 4x3" 110.00
Glass, ruby w/wht & gold floral, hinged, 2¾x5½" dia 175.00
Glass, sanded w/ivory scrolls & gilt, egg shape, brass ft, 4¾" 165.00
Knife, mahog veneer Hplwht, pnt florals & inlay, 14½", pr 3,750.00
Mini, elaborate HP/sponging, 1800s, 3¾x3¾x6½" 800.00
Pantry, bentwood, iron tacks, early gr pnt, 3x6½x5", EX 275.00
Pantry, bentwood w/gr pnt, overlapped/copper tacks, 9¾" dia 260.00
Pine w/orig brn & yel grpt, machine dvtl, wire nails, 16" 195.00
Pipe, cherry, 1-drw, scrolled top w/crest, 18" 6,600.00
Pipe, maple, 1-drw, heart cutout, ca 1800, 20x5⅜x4⅜" 1,035.00
Poplar w/orig red sponging on gr-yel, wrought-iron hdl, 29" 495.00
Silver w/repousse children at play, Germany 800, 3" 165.00
Silver w/repousse classical figures, pierced lid, 1902, 2¾" 360.00
Spice, bentwood, Spices stenciled in blk, ca 1900, 3½x9⅜" 300.00
Spice, bentwood, tin bands, w/8 containers, EX 400.00

Storage box, red-painted pine with carved geometric designs, mid-18th century, cracks and minor losses, worn paint, 8¾x17x10¼", $2,185.00.

Storage, brn & tan sponging on dvtl wood, bail hdls, 10x24x12" ...100.00
Storage, slant-lift lid, compartments, dvtl pine, 18x26x17" 5,175.00
Trinket, bentwood, wooden pegs, early bl pnt, 1⅝x4⅜x4" 825.00
Wooden, str-lap construction, mc floral decor, oval, 5x17x13" ...1,800.00
Writing, curly walnut veneer, cherry fitted int, 8¾x13" 165.00
Writing, walnut, hinged lid, fitted int, 8x16x11" 85.00

Boyd Crystal Art Glass

This small but productive glasshouse has more than 300 molds and has produced more than 350 colors. They are very collector oriented and alter their mark every five years. In 1978 they used a simple B in a diamond. Today, with four changes behind them, the original mark is now encompassed by four additional lines. Vaseline collectors have increased in number, and many of Boyd's Vaseline pieces (variations include Firefly and Citron) are increasing in value rapidly. Many of Boyd's colors — Golden Delight, Peridot, Pippin Green, and others — fluoresce under black light, and are now highly sought after.

In the near future, watch for price increases for Joey the Horse, as the mold has recently been converted to a carousel horse, preventing further production. Li'l Joe the Horse has met the same fate and is now very limited. As always, satins and hand-painted pieces are commanding 10 – 50% more than the same items in the regular finish.

Internet exposure and the heightened awareness of Boyd collectibles that resulted have caused an increase in prices of from 5% to 85% in some cases. We will wait to see where they level off before endorsing what may be erratic values. Our advisor for this category is Joyce Pringle; she is listed in the Directory under Texas.

Key: R — retired

Airplane, Banana Cream	17.50
Airplane, Vanilla Coral	18.00
Airplane, Vaseline	32.50
Angel, Green Bouquet	20.00
Artie the Penguin, Banana Cream (R)	8.00
Artie the Penguin, Classic Black	8.25
Artie the Penguin, Vaseline (R)	22.00
Bird Salt, Cardinal Red	12.50
Bow Slipper, Rubina	18.00
Brian Bunny, Cashmire Pink (R)	15.00
Bunny Salt, Alpine Blue	7.00
Bunny Salt, Sky Top Blue	40.00
Cat Slipper, Nile Green	9.50
Cat Slipper, Rubina	23.50
Chick Salt, Mirage	7.00
Chick Salt, Ruby Gold	140.00
Christmas Willie the Mouse, 1992	20.00
Elizabeth Doll, Crown Tuscan Carnival (R)	10.00
Elizabeth Doll, Lime Green Carnival (R)	42.50
Hand Dish, Chocolate Carnival	6.50
JB Scotty, Cashmire Pink (R)	28.50
JB Scotty, Daffodil (R)	35.00
JB Scotty, Ebony	65.00
JB Scotty, Mint Green (R)	30.00
JB Scotty, Mirage (R)	12.00
Jeremy Frog, Nile Green	9.50
Joey the Horse, Cashmire Pink (R)	22.00
Joey the Horse, Delphinium	20.00
Joey the Horse, Persimmon (R)	24.00
Kewpie, Cobalt	8.00
Kitten on a Pillow, Golden Delight (R)	24.00
Li'l Joe, Country Red (R)	18.50
Li'l Joe, Milk White (R)	19.00
Li'l Joe, Pistachio (R)	20.00
Li'l Luck, Ritz Blue (R)	25.00
Louise Doll, Ice Blue (R)	65.00
Louise Doll, Mother's Day, 1996, HP	25.00
Lucky the Unicorn, Classic Black Slag	20.00
Owl, Katydid	22.50
Owl Bell, Lavender	10.00
Owl Bell, Pocono	15.00
Patrick the Bear, Country Red (R)	15.00
Sammy the Squirrel, Alexandrite (R)	20.00
Sammy the Squirrel, Teal (R)	12.00
Taffy Carousel Horse, Purple Frost	16.00
Teddy the Tugboat, Daffodil	15.00
Train Set, Alpine Blue	54.00
Turkey Salt, Sunkist Carnival	11.00
Zak the Elephant, Alice Blue	30.00
Zak the Elephant, Oxford Gray (R)	20.00

Bradley and Hubbard

The Bradley and Hubbard Mfg. Company was a firm which produced metal accessories for the home. They operated from about 1860 until the early part of this century, and their products reflected both the Arts and Crafts and Art Nouveau influence. Their logo was a device with a triangular arrangement of the company name containing a smaller triangle and an Aladdin lamp.

Lamps

Banquet, HP globe w/flowers, cast base, sgn, 37"	450.00
Base, bronzed metal & faux marble dolphin, 2-socket, att, 20"	460.00
Desk, roof-shape 7½x7½" shade w/metal flower-&-urn o/l, 10"	400.00
Gone-w/the-Wind, chrysanthemums on pk, mk, 1890s, 27½", $250 to	350.00
Metal o/l 7" oak leaf shade; 3-owl std, 11", VG	900.00
Rvpt 22" 8-panel tulip shallow dome shade; 3-leg stand	950.00
Slag-glass 15" 8-sided shade w/metal floral fr; columnar std	575.00
Slag-glass 18" shade w/brass-washed metal o/l, 22"	600.00
Slag-glass 6-sided 'brick' shade; 3-owl std, 12", VG/EX	690.00

Miscellaneous

Andirons, brass, dmn-shaped motif, att, 22"	275.00
Andirons, brass wash, block tops, emb geometrics, 22", pr	250.00
Andirons, CI, sunburst, 16½x18", pr, from $700 to	1,000.00

Andirons, cast brass and iron with sunburst finials, #9510, Pat'd Aug 24 1886, 16½", from $700.00 to $1,000.00 for the pair.

Bookends, Field & Riley, CI, mk, ca 1925, 5½"	95.00
Bookends, Gnome in Library, CI, ca 1924, 5"	195.00
Bookends, John Alden & Priscilla, CI, mk, ca 1925, 5¾"	150.00
Bookends, Pilgrim Landing, CI, mk, ca 1925, 5½"	175.00
Bookends, Tom & Huck, CI, mk, ca 1925, 7"	300.00
Candlesticks, copper w/faceted glass jewels, ornate hdl, 12", pr	1,200.00
Clock, lion blinker, Pat Appl For 1858, minor rstr, 8"	1,600.00
Doorstop, woman in ruffled dress, bl w/blk bows, #7798, 13x6¾"	600.00
Fireplace tools, iron w/brass wash, 3-pc, in stand, 31"	600.00
Letter holder, brass, oval sides, 3½" H	100.00
Match safe, scarab, cold pnt, rare	750.00
Pen & ink stand, brass, 2 wells, w/drw, angular base, 10"	220.00

Brass

Brass is an alloy consisting essentially of copper and zinc in variable proportions. It is a medium that has been used for both utilitarian items and objects of artistic merit. Today, with the inflated price of copper and the popular use of plastics, almost anything made of brass is collectible, though right now, at least, there is little interest in items made after 1950. Our advisor, Mary Frank Gaston, has compiled a lovely book, *Antique Brass and Copper*, with full-color photos. See also Candlesticks.

Bucket, hammered, old rpr to base, 19th C, 16x20" dia 150.00
Clock jack, w/CI spit wheel, Geo Salter, working, 17" 440.00
Doorknob, profile of lady, RE Mfg Metal Comp Cast Co 65.00
Humidor, bell shape, dk patina, w/lid, 130s, 7" 75.00
Jamb hooks, urn top, England or Am, ca 1800s, 2¾", pr 515.00
Kettle, hinged wrought-iron arched hdl, Pats 1851...1970, 7x11" .75.00
Kettle, rolled rim, arched iron hdl, 13" dia, +wrought tripod 110.00
Kettle shelf, rtcl top & apron, English, 14x12½" 250.00
Ladle, skimmer; flattened hook hdl, ca 1800, 2" dia, 9" L 475.00
Ladle, tasting; wrought-iron hdl w/hook, 1¾" dia, 6½" hdl 400.00
Muffin pan, wrought-iron hdl, England, 19th C, 12¼" dia 60.00
Taper jack, rnd base w/pierced heart, arched finger hdl, 5⅝" 425.00
Tray, desk; emb decor, ftd, w/2 inkwells & letter rack 550.00
Warming pan, chased tulips & fruit, 19th C, 42" L 300.00

Brastoff, Sascha

The son of immigrant parents, Sascha Brastoff was encouraged to develop his artistic talents to the fullest, encouragement that was well taken, as his achievements aptly attest. Though at various times he was a dancer, sculptor, Hollywood costume designer, jeweler, and painter, it is his ceramics that are today becoming highly regarded collectibles.

Sascha began his career in the United States in the late 1940s. In a beautiful studio built for him by his friend and mentor, Winthrop Rockefeller, he designed innovative wares that even then were among the most expensive on the market. All designing was done personally by Brastoff; he also supervised the staff which at the height of production numbered approximately 150. Wares signed with his full signature (not merely backstamped 'Sascha Brastoff') were personally crafted by him and are valued much more highly than those signed 'Sascha B.,' indicating work done under his supervision. Until his death in 1993, he continued his work in Los Angeles, in his latter years producing 'Sascha Holograms,' which were distributed by the Hummelwerk Company.

Though the resin animals signed 'Sascha B.' were neither made nor designed by Brastoff, collectors of these pieces value them highly. According to the book cited in the above paragraph, after he left the factory in the 1960s, the company retained the use of the name to be used on reissues of earlier pieces or merchandise purchased at trade shows.

In the listings that follow, items are ceramic and signed 'Sascha B.' unless 'full signature' or another medium is indicated.

For further information we recommend *The Collector's Encyclopedia of Sascha Brastoff* by Steve Conti, A. DeWayne Bethany, and Bill Seay; available from Collector Books or your local book store. Our advisor for this category is Jack Chipman, author of *Collector's Encyclopedia of California Pottery, Second Edition*, another source of valuable information for Brastoff collectors. Mr. Chipman is listed in the Directory under California.

Ashtray, abstract, free-form, unmk, 10" 75.00
Ashtray, abstract design, 6" 40.00
Ashtray, amoebic design, chartreuse w/bl & yel, rnd 60.00
Ashtray, bl flowers on olive gr, metal enamelware, 6½" 30.00
Ashtray, Chi Chi Birds, #07, 10" 80.00
Ashtray, Roof Tops, free-form, 7" 50.00
Ashtray, tulips, 17" 150.00
Ashtray, Vanity Fair, #05, 5x9" 55.00
Ashtray/incense burner, fireplace w/chimney, bronze/gold, 7" 75.00
Bowl, abstract gr design, ftd, 8" 50.00
Bowl, Rooster, enamel on copper w/gold, 8¼" dia 150.00
Bowl, silver-gray & wht w/gold, ftd, 2½x5" 40.00
Bowl, Star Steed, 3-ftd, 10" 150.00
Bowl, Surf Ballet, bl & platinum, gold mk, 2½x5" 20.00
Box, Ballet, 7x5½" 125.00
Box, cigarette; Star Steed 100.00

Box, Roof Tops, 7x5½" 125.00
Bust, Moderne Woman, wht matt, 14½x7" 225.00
Candle holders, gr/bl resin, 6", pr 50.00
Coffeepot, floral, 15" 100.00
Coffeepot, Vanity Fair, 15" 100.00
Cup & saucer, Smoke Tree 15.00
Cup & saucer, Surf Ballet, pk & gold, lg, from $20 to 40.00
Dish, Jewel Bird, #F40, 10" 65.00
Dish, Roof Tops, 3-ftd, 8¼x8¼" 95.00
Dish, Vanity Fair, ovoid, 7" 75.00
Ewer, Star Steed, metallic 95.00
Figurine, Foo Dog, ceramic, 21", NM, pr 510.00
Figurine, musk ox, resin, gold 350.00
Figurine, owl, gr resin, 14" 350.00
Figurine, Peek-a-Boo Bears, bl resin, pr 600.00
Figurine, prancing horse, blk & gold, 10½" 350.00
Figurine, seal, marigold resin, 9" L 300.00
Figurine, woodpecker, dk gr resin, 6" 275.00
Flowerpot, Jewel Bird, #046B, 6" 65.00
Humidor, pipe shape, underside of lid is ashtray 92.00
Lighter, gold circles/crosses/lines, 4½" dia 25.00
Luncheon set, Surf Ballet, pk/gold/wht, 31-pc 450.00
Mug, stylized horse 40.00
Pitcher, abstract ballet scene on blk, early 1st factory mk 295.00
Planter, blk & gold pipe, lg 40.00

Plate, stylized leaves, teal, maroon, and gold, 12", $100.00; Matching 5" vase, $75.00.

Plate, African dancer, full signature, 12" 575.00
Plate, chop; abstract design, #053, 17" 210.00
Plate, floral, gr on copper enamel, 11¾" 65.00
Plate, fruit; 11" dia 65.00
Plate, Merbaby, 9" 85.00
Plate, Misty Blue, 1960 commemorative pc, free-form, 10½x9½" ...40.00
Plate, Roof Tops, enamel on copper, 15" 125.00
Platter, Jewel Bird, gold on yel & gr, 17" dia 200.00
Smoking set, gr floral, enameled on copper, 5-pc 250.00
Tile, mc rooster, 7¼x9¼" in fr 125.00
Tray, Chi Chi Birds, #052, 15" 150.00
Tray, horse, grays & whts on bl-gray, mk, free-form, 9x8" 55.00
Tray, iris on gr w/gold, 15" dia 100.00
Vase, fruit on brn, rectangular, 9⅜" 120.00
Vase, horse pnt under glaze, full sgn, 8½" 450.00
Vase, Log Cabin, ovoid, 12" 195.00
Vase, stylized lion in ochre over bl, swooping rim, 8x6" 135.00
Vase, WWII army tank pnt under glaze, 3-ftd 250.00

Brayton Laguna

Durlin E. Brayton made handcrafted vases, lamps, and dinnerware in a small kiln at his Laguna Beach, California, home in 1927. He soon married, and with his wife, Ellen Webster Grieve, as his partner, the small business became a successful commercial venture. They are most famous for their amusing, well-detailed figurines, some of which were commissioned by Walt Disney Studios. Though very successful even through the Depression years, with the influx of imported novelties that deluged the country after WWII, business began to decline. By 1968 the pottery was closed. For more information on this as well as many other potteries in the state, we recommend *The Collector's Encyclopedia of California Pottery, Second Edition,* by Jack Chipman; he is listed in the Directory under California.

Bowl, burgundy, wavy lip, handmade, 4"	65.00
Box, Fr peasant, rnd	45.00
Candlestick, purple, hdl, early, pr	400.00
Candlesticks, Blackamoors seated, mc w/gold, 5"	150.00
Chess pc, Bishop, maroon & gold, 13"	165.00
Chess pc, Queen, 12"	150.00
Cookie jar, Christina (Swedish Maiden)	425.00
Cookie jar, Gingerbread House	250.00
Cookie jar, Mammy, burgundy base, turq bandana (+)	1,300.00
Cookie jar, Matilda	475.00
Cookie jar, Provincial Lady, yel scarf & apron	375.00
Cookie jar, Wedding Ring Granny (Grandma) (+)	500.00
Creamer & sugar bowl, early Laguna colors	150.00
Figural group, jazz singer, piano & piano player, 3-pc	1,500.00
Figurine, abstract cat, reclining, blk, 18" L	145.00
Figurine, bird, orange matt, 7½"	75.00

Figurine, Blackamoor man, kneeling, pastel jewels, 14½", $300.00.

Photo courtesy
Pat and Kris Secor

Figurine, Blackamoor w/bowl, gold & jewels, 8"	75.00
Figurine, bride & groom from Matrimony series, 8"	120.00
Figurine, calf, cow & bull family, purple, from $350 to	450.00
Figurine, Chinese man, gr & violet, rare, #535, 17"	375.00
Figurine, circus horse & ringmaster, pr	155.00
Figurine, Dopey, Disney copyright	375.00
Figurine, Ellen, Childhood series	125.00
Figurine, Fifi & Zizi (cats), pr, 9"	200.00
Figurine, fox, red, #H-57	100.00
Figurine, Gay Nineties, bartender trio	150.00
Figurine, gazelle, gold trim on woodtone	120.00
Figurine, Goose Girl, bl & wht	95.00
Figurine, horse, stylized, blk, H28, 9½x10"	250.00
Figurine, horses, fighting, yel & gr, Carol Safholm, pr	275.00
Figurine, Italian man & push cart	100.00
Figurine, Jamacian dancers, fruit hat/drum, 12", 11½", pr	1,000.00
Figurine, Miranda, bl plaid, Childhood series	100.00
Figurine, Olga, red & blk, Childhood series	130.00
Figurine, owl, woodtone & crackle, 6"	55.00
Figurine, panther, blk, jeweled collar, pacing, 20", NM	225.00
Figurine, peasant lady, K-29B	80.00
Figurine, penguin, aqua, 7"	85.00
Figurine, Petunia & Sambo, Childhood series, 6¼", 8", pr	500.00

Figurine, Pluto, sniffing, 3⅛"	125.00
Figurine, quail, bl/blk, #B-40 & #B-41, pr	200.00
Figurine, rooster, olive gr/drab gold, 17x12"	145.00
Figurine, spotted fawn, from Disney's 'Snow White,' no mk, 9"	75.00
Figurine, Voodoo dancers, C Safholm, rare, 16", pr, minimum	1,500.00
Flower holder, girl in pk w/2 wolfhounds, 10½"	95.00
Flower holder, Sally	50.00
Pitcher, men in cityscape, bl & grays, B2 Laguna Beach, 8¼"	195.00
Pitcher, owl form, mk, dtd 1941	80.00
Planter, baby w/pillow, pk, 4"	65.00
Planter, Frances, bl & wht	75.00
Planter, silver, 10x5", w/pr of candlesticks	100.00
Shakers, Calico Cat & Gingham Dog, pr	85.00
Shakers, circus clown & dog, pr	175.00
Shakers, Mammy & Chef, 6", 6¾", pr	175.00
Shakers, Provincial peasant couple, pr	75.00
Sugar bowl, Gingham Dog	80.00
Teapot, Provincial, brn w/tulip stand	125.00
Toothbrush holder, Gingham Dog	150.00
Vase, Dutch man leaning on basket (vase), 9½"	125.00
Vase, Victorian boot, 4"	30.00
Wall hanger w/flowerpot, caballero, maroon & wht	95.00

Bread Plates and Trays

Bread plates and trays have been produced not only in many types of glass but in metal and pottery as well. Those considered most collectible were made during the last quarter of the 19th century from pressed glass with well-detailed embossed designs, many of them portraying a particularly significant historical event. A great number of these plates were sold at the 1876 Philadelphia Centennial Exposition by various glass manufacturers who exhibited their wares on the grounds. Among the themes depicted are the Declaration of Independence, the Constitution, McKinley's memorial 'It Is God's Way,' Remembrance of Three Presidents, the Purchase of Alaska, and various presidential campaigns, to mention only a few.

'L' numbers correspond with a reference book by Lindsey; 'B' refers to a book by Belknap. Our advisor for this category is Darlene Yohe; she is listed in the Directory under Arkansas.

American Flag, 38 stars, L-51, 11x8"	235.00
Banner Baking Powder	85.00
Bible	50.00
Black Builders of Bicentennial, 1776-1976	35.00
Cleveland/Thurman, clear/frosted, L-325, 9½x8½"	215.00
Columbus, milk glass, B-5A, 9½"	45.00
Constitution	60.00
Continental Hall, hand hdls, 12¾"	85.00
Cupid & Venus, 10½" dia	55.00
Eagle, Constitution, motto, oval	60.00
Egyptian, Cleopatra center, 13" L	55.00
Fleur de Lis w/Pan American (Buffalo) Exposition center	17.50
Frosted Lion, Give Us This Day, 12½x9"	175.00
Garden of Eden, Give Us This Day, 12½x9"	35.00
Garfield Drape, We Mourn, L-303, 11½"	55.00
Garfield Memorial, L-302, 10" L	40.00
Gladstone, 9"	45.00
Grant, Let Us Have Peace	65.00
Grant, Let Us Have Peace, amber	85.00
Heroes of Bunker Hill	70.00
Independence Hall	125.00
It Is Pleasant To Labor, grapes & leaf center, 12¾" dia	55.00
Knights of Labor, amber, oval, L-512, 12"	145.00

Liberty Bell, Signers 95.00
Memorial Hall 65.00
Merry Christmas, bells in center, shallow bowl shape 75.00
Mormon Tabernacle, stippled border, rare 425.00
Moses Montifiore, L-239 ....75.00
Nelly Bly, L-136, 12" 200.00
Niagara Falls, clear/frosted, L-489, 16" L 135.00
Pope Leo XIII, 10" 35.00
Prescott Stark 60.00
Ruth the Gleaner, Gillinder 145.00
Santa Maria Variant 15.00
Sheridan Memorial 40.00
Three Presidents, In Remembrance, 12½x10" 95.00
Warrior 80.00
Washington & 13 Stars, milk glass, B-1 ....50.00
Wildflower, sq 28.00
101, farm implement center 65.00

Bride's Baskets and Bowls

Victorian brides were showered with gifts, as brides have always been; one of the most popular gift items was the bride's basket. Art glass inserts from both European and American glasshouses, some in lovely transparent hues with dainty enameled florals, others of Peachblow, Vasa Murrhina, satin or cased glass, were cradled in complementary silverplated holders. While many of these holders were simply engraved or delicately embossed, others (such as those from Pairpoint and Wilcox) were wonderfully ornate, often with figurals of cherubs or animals. The bride's basket was no longer in fashion after the turn of the century.

Watch for 'marriages' of bowls and frames. To warrant the best price, the two pieces should be the original pairing. If you can't be certain of this, at least check to see that the bowl fits snugly into the frame. Beware of later-made bowls (such as Fenton's) in Victorian holders and frames that are being made in Taiwan.

Our advisor for this category is Deborah Maggard; she is listed in the Directory under Ohio. In the listings that follow, if no frame is described, the price is for a bowl only.

Amber w/wht int, gold decor, sq w/scalloped rim, 12" 565.00
Apricot to yel w/bl liner, gold-traced mums, ruffled, 5x11" 210.00
Bl satin o/l w/florals, ruffled, 14"; on 13½" SP stand 1,000.00
Blk amethyst satin; gilt-bronze fr w/stallions, 10½x12" 300.00
Brn to cream o/l satin w/gold/silver floral, 3¾x11⅛" 250.00
Burmese, ribbed/crimped/ruffled, Mt WA, 5x9"; Tufts fr, 12" 500.00
Burmese, wht fluted rim, 8"; 5" deer/leaves appl to fr 965.00
Cranberry w/swirled ribs, fluted wht rim; ornate SP fr, 13" 250.00
Gr o/l satin w/emb lattice at rim, 3⅝x11½" 195.00
Gr satin to wht w/HP florals; SP Meriden fr w/angels, 12" 250.00
Maroon to cream o/l, emb decor, HP florals, att Wheeling, 11⅜" .195.00
Peach & wht spatter, HP florals; ormolu ped ft, 4½x11½" 225.00
Peach o/l w/HP floral, scalloped rim, 2½x10" 195.00
Peachblow, ribbed, crimped/ruffled rim, New Martinsville, 11" .200.00
Peachblow o/l w/mums & fall flowers, 4x8"; Wilcox fr, 12" 450.00
Peachblow w/floral, crimped rim, Webb, 3x9"; lidld fr 275.00
Peachblow w/orange flowers, crimped rim, 2x9" 100.00
Pk MOP Herringbone w/mums & gilt, lime int, ruffled, 10½" 900.00
Pk o/l w/clear & opaque ribbon edge, florals, 2¾x9¾" 225.00
Pk o/l w/gold floral enameling, 2⅝x10⅜" 295.00
Pk satin w/emb decor, 10x12"; rstr SP ftd fr 300.00
Pk w/wht ext, crimped amber rim, 8"; on ornate silver std, 11" ..180.00
Purple o/l w/mc orchids, ruffled, 3¼x10" 265.00
Purple to wht w/florals, scalloped rim, 3½x10¾" 225.00
Vaseline w/V-bar pattern; ornate rstr SP ftd fr w/bail hdl 250.00

Bristol Glass

Bristol is a type of semi-opaque opaline glass whose name was derived from the area in England where it was first produced. Similar glass was made in France, Germany, and Italy. In this country, it was made by the New England Glass Company and to a lesser extent by its contemporaries. During the 18th and 19th centuries, Bristol glass was imported in large amounts and sold cheaply, thereby contributing to the demise of the earlier glasshouses here in America. It is very difficult to distinguish the English Bristol from other opaline types. Style, design, and decoration serve as clues to its origin; but often only those well versed in the field can spot these subtle variations.

Vase, pink with gold painted decor, stick neck, 10", $95.00.

Bottle, scent; bl opaque w/HP floral, tulip stopper, 10½", pr 175.00
Cracker jar, bl, daisies/foliage, SP mts, 6½x4¾" 175.00
Ewer vase, pk, intricate gold pattern/neck ring/hdl, 6½" 125.00
Pitcher, wht, fall leaves edged in yel coralene, wht hdl, 8" 125.00
Rose bowl, wht, duck on snowy bank, 4" 150.00
Sweetmeat, bl w/floral, SP mts, 5½" 145.00
Sweetmeat, lt gr w/egret & bush, SP mts, 4⅜" 125.00
Teapot, cream w/birds/scenes, appl spout, 5¼x4½" 275.00
Vase, aqua, ruffled/swirled, wht floral relief, 9½" 125.00
Vase, jack-in-pulpit; gray-gr w/lt bl int, floral, 8½" 58.00
Vase, lt bl, 3 cherubs in clouds, 8x3⅝" at base 70.00
Vase, pale custard, water scene, stick neck, 14¼" 150.00
Vase, wht, coach & horses, w/gold, bl rim & ft, 14" 100.00
Vase, wht opal w/mc floral & gold, 8⅞" 65.00
Vase, wht w/mc flowers, bulbous, mk PK, 17½" 175.00

British Royalty Commemoratives

Royalty commemoratives have been issued for royal events since Edward VI's 1547 coronation through modern-day occasions, so it's possible to start collecting at any period of history. Many collectors begin with Queen Victoria's reign, collecting examples for each succeeding monarch and continuing through modern events.

Some collectors identify with a particular royal personage and limit their collecting to that era, ie., Queen Elizabeth's life and reign. Other collectors look to the future, expanding their collection to include the heirs apparent Prince Charles and his first-born son, Prince William.

Royalty commemorative collecting is often further refined around a particular type of collectible. Nearly any item with room for a portrait and a description has been manufactured as a souvenir. Thus royalty commemoratives are available in glass, ceramic, metal, fabric, plastic, and paper. This wide variety of material lends itself to any pocketbook. The range covers expensive limited edition ceramics to inexpensive souvenir key chains, puzzles, matchbooks, etc.

Many recent royalty headline events have been commemorated in a variety of souvenirs. Buying some of these modern commemoratives at the moderate issue prices could be a good investment. After all, today's events are tomorrow's history.

For further study we recommend *British Royal Commemoratives* by our advisor for this category, Audrey Zeder; she is listed in the Directory under Washington.

Key:
anniv — anniversary
bd — birthday
chr — christening
com — commemorative
cor — coronation
EPNS — electro-plated nickel
    silver

inscr — inscribed
jub — jubilee
LE — limited edition
mem — memorial
Pr — Prince
Prs — Princess
wed — wedding

Plate Queen Victoria 1897 Jubilee, worn gold, 1¾x8¾", $95.00.

Album, Royal Family 1983 3-ring binder, 200 pictures 85.00
Bank, Prs Elizabeth/Margaret 1937, gold portrait/mc bkground, tin .95.00
Beaker, Charles/Diana betrothal, mc portrait/decor, Caverswall ..155.00
Beaker, Edward VII 1902, enameled mc portrait w/decor, 3½" ...125.00
Beaker, George VI cor, sepia portrait, mc decor, 3⅝" 35.00
Beaker, Victoria 1897 jub, pk emb portrait w/decor, 4" 175.00
Bell, Charles/Diana 1982 wedding, mc portrait, Royal Albert, pr ...110.00
Book, Elizabeth II cor, Her Majesty Queen..., child's book 25.00
Book, George V 1935 jub, GVR the King's Book, Raphael Tuck .25.00
Book, Queen Alexandra's Christmas Gift Book, hardbk, 1908 .....35.00
Book, Victoria 1898 jub, 50 Years a Queen, hardbk, Maxwell 75.00
Booklet, His Royal Highness Prince of Wales, Pitkins, 1958 ....25.00
Booklet, Princess Margaret's Betrothal, Pitkins, 1960 ....20.00
Bookmark, Elizabeth II 1977 jub, blk leather, mc decor, 9" 20.00
Bottle, beer; Charles/Diana 1981 wed, empty, Ind Cooper of Wales .40.00
Bottle, beer; Elizabeth II 1977 jub, George Gale & Co, empty 25.00
Bowl, Edward VIII 1937, mc portrait w/crown, Grindley, 1x5" 55.00
Bowl, Elizabeth II 1935 opening of St Lawrence Seaway, Tuscan .45.00
Bowl, George VI 1937 cor, sepia portrait, ⅝x2¾" 45.00
Bowl, Victoria 1887 jub, brn portrait w/mc decor, 1x8⅛" 175.00
Bust, Edward VIII 1937, cream soapstone, 5½" 125.00
Bust, Elizabeth II cor, bsk w/rose gown, Foley, 6" 125.00
Calendar, Edward VIII, sepia portrait/previous monarchs, 1937 ...45.00
Child's dish, George V 1911 cor, mc portrait/decor, 1½x8" 145.00
Child's dish, George VI 1937 cor, mc portrait/decor, 1½x7" 125.00
Child's toy dish, Prs Elizabeth, sepia portrait, 1937, 4½" 60.00
Compact, Elizabeth II cor, mc portrait, unused in orig folder 55.00
Compact, George V jub, mc king/queen & decor, 2¼" 79.00
Cup & saucer, Charles/Diana '81 wed, mc portrait, Canada 65.00
Cup & saucer, Edward VII 1902 cor, peach w/portrait & decor ..195.00
Doll, Prs Diana, vinyl, gr satin dress, Peggy Nisbet, 8" 250.00
Doll, Victoria, plastic, blk dress, modern mfg, 7½" 25.00
Egg cup, Elizabeth II cor, royal cypher, mc decor, ftd 25.00
Egg cup, George V & Queen Mary cor, mc portrait, ftd, pr 55.00

Egg cup, George VI cor, shaded portrait, ftd, gold rim 35.00
Ephemera, Duchess of Windsor, unused letter paper/envelope 65.00
Ephemera, Edward VIII 1936 proclamation, souvenir announcement 50.00
Ephemera, George V 1911 opening of parliament, paper napkin ..35.00
Ephemera, George VI, cor sheet music, Coronation Song 25.00
Ephemera, George VI 1946, victory message to school children ...25.00
Figure, Elizabeth II/Pr Philip jub, mc formal wear, 5", pr 60.00
Framed picture, Elizabeth II jub, needlepoint textile, 15x10" 60.00
Glass, Charles/Diana 1981 wed, covered jar, blk portrait on clear ...65.00
Glass, Edward VIII 1937, beaker, frosted wht portrait, 4½" 30.00
Glass, George VI 1937 cor, basket, clear w/emb portrait/decor 95.00
Glass, George VI 1937 cor bowl, pressed/cut crystal, 2x9" 125.00
Glass, Prs Diana 30 bd dish, gr w/emb portrait/decor, 3½" 30.00
Glass, Victoria 1887 jub dish, amber w/emb portrait/decor, 10" .165.00
Horse brass, Elizabeth II jub, brass w/emb crown 20.00
Loving cup, Elizabeth II 1977 jub, gold decor, 6x3" 40.00
Loving cup, Pr William '82 birth, Bunnykins decor, Doulton 60.00
Loving cup, Prs Diana 1997 mem, mc portrait, Chown, LE 400 .125.00
Magazine, Country Life Royal Wedding Number, November 28, 1947 .35.00
Magazine, Sphere, Funeral of King George V, February 1, 1936 ...45.00
Matchbook, Elizabeth II cor cover, mc portrait/decor, Eddy 10.00
Matchbook, George V 1935 jub, Bryant & Mays, unused 25.00
Medallion, Duke of York 1827 mem, brass w/emb portrait, 1" 55.00
Medallion, Edward VII cor, emb king/queen, Cocoa premium, 1" .45.00
Medallion, Victoria 1887 jub, brass w/emb portrait, 1½" 50.00
Miniature, Charles/Diana 1983 Australia/New Zealand, tankard, 1" .50.00
Miniature, Pr of Wales 1900 brass box, emb decor, ⅝" 60.00
Mug, Charles/Diana '81 wed, blk portrait on tan, stoneware 55.00
Mug, Charles/Diana 1996 divorce, mc portrait, china, Coronet .125.00
Mug, Edward VII cor, lithophane bottom, mc decor, 3x3¼" 125.00
Mug, Edward VIII 1937, mc portrait/decor, molded crown hdl 60.00
Mug, Edward VIII 1937, mc protrait/decor, official design 50.00
Mug, Elizabeth II 50th wed anniv, blk w/mc, Chown, LE 100 ....125.00
Mug, George V cor, brn portrait, mc decor, Late Foley/Shelly 75.00
Mug, George VI cor, blk portrait on yel, Booths Ltd 50.00
Mug, George VI proclamation of Royal Exchange, mc decor 50.00
Mug, Pr William 1st bd, mc portrait, bone china, Coronet 55.00
Mug, Pr William 1997 confirmation, mc portrait, ltd ed 80 ....125.00
Mug, Victoria 1897, bl/gray portrait & decor, JC&N, 3¼" 195.00
Mug, Victoria 1897, sepia/enamel portrait, era event pictures 225.00
New Testament, Edward VII cor com by Religious Tract Society .70.00
Newspaper, Edward VII, Fort Dodge Messenger, June 2, 1937 ......30.00
Newspaper, Edward VIII cor, NY Herald, August 10, 1902 ....50.00
Newspaper, Victoria 1838 cor, Globe, June 28, 1838 ....175.00
Newspaper, Victoria 1887 jub, Times, June 22, 1887 ....60.00
Novelty, Charles/Diana wed, clock, mc portrait, gold fr, battery ..95.00
Novelty, Edward VII 1937, purse mirror, mc portrait/design, 3" dia ...50.00
Novelty, Elizabeth II 1977 jub, soap dish, plastic, mc decor 25.00
Novelty, Victoria 1872, button, brass w/emb portrait, ¾" 59.00
Paperweight, Elizabeth II jub, sterling on marble, Asprey 85.00
Paperweight, Prs Diana 1997 mem, rnd dome, etch portrait/decor ..55.00
Photograph, Duke & Duchess Windsor 1940 at Bermuda, blk/wht 45.00
Pitcher, George VI 1939 Canada visit, blk/wht king/2 Prs, Meakin ...75.00
Pitcher, Prs Royal/Pr Prussia 1858 wed, flow bl w/lustre 875.00
Pitcher, Victoria 1840 wed, blk glaze, emb figures, 7" 250.00
Pitcher, Victoria 1897, cobalt glaze, emb portrait, Doulton 600.00
Plaque, Edward VII cor, bronze w/emb decor, Schwathe, 6x9" ...650.00
Plaque, Victoria 1897, terra cotta w/emb portrait/decor, 3" 115.00
Plate, Charles/Diana '81 wed, cobalt w/gold, Bing & Grondahl, 10" .225.00
Plate, Charles/Diana '81 wed, ornate bl/gold decor, Minton, LE 325.00
Plate, Charles/Diana '81 wed, sepia portrait w/mc, Hammersley, 9" .55.00
Plate, Charles/Diana '81 wed, 24k gold portrait, Prinknash, 6½" .65.00
Plate, Charles/Diana '87 650 anniv Duchy Cornwall, Panorama .185.00
Plate, Edward VII cor, mc portrait/decor, pierced rim, 7½" 150.00

Plate, Edward VIII 1937, mc portrait in cor robe, hdl, Aynsley ..**110.00**
Plate, Edward VIII 1937, mc portrait in cor robe, Royal Winton, 9" ..**90.00**
Plate, Elizabeth II cor, brn translucent w/emb portrait, 6" **35.00**
Plate, George V cor, mc portrait/decor, Royal Doulton, 6" **95.00**
Plate, George VI 1938 visit Empire Exhibit, Paragon, 5" **45.00**
Plate, Pr William 1983, mc portrait w/parents, Caverswall, 8½" ...**150.00**
Plate, Prs Diana 1984, name 'Royal Prs' ship, Royal Doulton **195.00**
Plate, Victoria 1897 jub, mc portrait/decor, scalloped, 10" **150.00**
Postcard, George VI 1939 visit NY World's Fair, mc, unused **20.00**
Postcard, Prs Diana '97 mem, mc portrait, Enterprise, set of 6 ......**25.00**
Postcard, Victoria mem, blk portrait & border, unused **25.00**
Pot lid, Pr Consort 1860s mem, mc portrait/decor, Pratt **295.00**
Pot lid, Victoria 1850, mc queen on balcony fr, Mayer print **350.00**
Puzzle, Elizabeth II cor, mc queen, 180-pc, unopened box **60.00**
Spoon, Edward VI cor, emb portrait, ornate decor, SP, 4¼" **75.00**
Spoon, Elizabeth II cor, emb profile portrait/decor, SP **25.00**
Spoon, Prs Elizabeth 1930s, emb portrait/decor, EPNS **45.00**
Teapot, Charles/Diana wed, bl/wht portrait, Broadhurst, 4-cup .**185.00**
Teapot, George VI 1939 Canada visit, yel w/mc portrait, Winton .**125.00**
Textile, Edward VII, tablecloth, bl portrait w/mc, 44x46" **50.00**
Textile, George VI cor, embr sampler, 16x20" **155.00**
Textile, Prs Diana tapestry pillow, mc portrait, 12x12" **50.00**
Thimble, Elizabeth II 40th Anniv accession, sepia/brn, Caverswall .**35.00**
Tin, Elizabeth II 1952 Trooping of Colours, mc portrait on horse ...**55.00**
Tin, Pr Wales 12930s, mc uniformed portrait on red, Thorne **75.00**
Tin, Pr Wales 1929 NE Coast Exhibition, mc decor, Wilkin **75.00**
Tin, Victoria 1897, mc portrait/decor, Parkinson, 1x8x3½" **175.00**
Toby mug, George VI cor, mc uniform, Royal Winton, 3¾" **150.00**
Trinket box, Elizabeth II 1977 jub, dk bl heart shape, Wedgwood .**75.00**

Bronzes

Thomas Ball, George Dessell, and Leonard Volk were some of the earliest American sculptors who produced figures in bronze for home decor during the 1840s. Pieces of historical significance were the most popular, but by the 1880s a more fanciful type of artwork took hold. Some of the fine sculptors of the day were Daniel Chester French, Augustus St. Gaudens, and John Quincy Adams Ward. Bronzes reached the height of their popularity at the turn of the century. The American West was portrayed to its fullest by Remington, Russell, James Frazier, Hermon MacNeil, and Solon Borglum. Animals of every species were modeled by A.P. Proctor, Paul Bartlett, and Albert Laellele, to name but a few.

Art Nouveau and Art Deco influenced the medium during the '20s, evidenced by the works of Allen Clark, Harriet Frismuth, E.F. Sanford, and Bessie P. Vonnoh.

Be aware that recasts abound. While often esthetically satisfactory, they are not original and should be priced accordingly. In much the same manner as prints are evaluated, the original castings made under the direction of the artist are the most valuable. Later castings from the original mold are worth less. A recast is not made from the original mold. Instead, a rubber-like substance is applied to the bronze, peeled away, and filled with wax. Then, using the same 'lost wax' procedure as the artist uses on completion of his original wax model, a clay-like substance is formed around the wax figure and the whole fired to vitrify the clay. The wax, of course, melts away, hence the term 'lost wax.' Recast bronzes lose detail and are somewhat smaller than the original due to the shrinkage of the clay mold.

Bayre, Lion (Qui Marche), rubbed gr patina, 1850-70, 9x15½" ..**2,530.00**
Bayre, lion pouncing on hare, brn patina, ca 1890, 9x22" **1,550.00**
Bayre, Panther of India, dk gr/blk patina, 5¼x11" **990.00**
Brodauf, nude woman, Deco style, brn-blk patina, 25¼x14" **715.00**

Chiparus, lady stands between 2 Borzois, gilt, onyx base, 16" ..**13,500.00**
Chiparus, seated girl in short tunic wraps paw of Afghan, 9" ...**1,495.00**
Clessinger, Taureau-Romain (bull), brn patina, 1857, 6⅜x8" .**1,980.00**
Demanet, nude male archer seated, gr-brn patina, 23½" **1,600.00**
Dubois, pheasant boy w/kettle, tattered clothes, 1 shoe, 16" **925.00**
Focht, javelin thrower in action on rocky outcrop, 20" **4,600.00**
Gaudez, AE; Mozart, dk brn patina, 19" **880.00**
Gladenbetk, AG; nude warrior, marble plinth, late 19th C, 5½" ..**500.00**
Gomerth, G; Franco-Prussian soldiers, ivory inlay, 14x8¼" **770.00**
Krapt, Distant Prey: cougar on rocky base, 1980 ....**350.00**
Lavergne, AJ; boy w/cane pole baits hook, wears brim hat, 7" **375.00**
Lorenzetti, Diana & running gazelle, rnd base, 22½" **950.00**
Mignez, Boar Hunt, brn patina w/gilt traces, 12¾x22" **3,300.00**
Moreau, Fleurs Printemps, table lamp, 44½x21" **2,300.00**
Moreau, Muse des Fleurs, winged lady w/lyre, 27" **465.00**
Nanning, R; Hussar on horsebk, ca 1900, 15¾x14¼" **800.00**
Riche, lion & lioness, brn patina, ca 1900, 15x16" **3,080.00**
Rousau, lion on rocky outcrop, gr patina, 10½" **900.00**
Sala, E; kneeling nude, sqd base, blk plateau, 17½" **800.00**
Samson, bust of cavalier, dk red-brn patina, 22" **880.00**
Schmitt, Balanced Dancer, ivory balls in hands, ca 1925, 21" .**3,000.00**
Shaffert, draped nude w/sword, blk marble base, 13" **495.00**
Sudre/Paris, Bust of Mars, verde antico base, 9¼x4¾x12½" **1,100.00**
Thill, G; bust of satyr, verdigris, marble base, 20th C, 11½" **330.00**
Unsgn, discus thrower on marble plinth, 19th C, 5¾x4x14¼" ...**850.00**
Unsgn, nude warrior thrusting dagger, late 19th C, 5⅞x3x9" **500.00**
Unsgn, Sphinx, blk marble base, late 1800s, 10¼x6x4½" **385.00**
Unsgn, winged youth clutching goose, late 19th C, 5" **55.00**
Van Der Straten (after), lady, hair up, behind lg fan, 19" **1,350.00**
Wilson, GA; Blk boy by hydrant in formal dress w/banjo, 25" ...**1,125.00**
Wyk, Femme Avec Taureau, brn patina, '98, 19x22x12¾" **1,100.00**

Brouwer

Theophilis A. Brouwer, an accomplished artist even before his interests turned to the medium of pottery, started a small one-man operation in 1894 in East Hampton, New York. Two years later he relocated in Westhampton, where he perfected the technique of fire-painting, learning to control the effects of the kiln to produce the best possible results. In 1925 he founded the Ceramic Flame Company in New York, but it is for his earlier work that he is best known. Brouwer died in 1932.

Vase, Sea-Grass flame-pnt gr/brn mottle, sphere w/sm neck, 5" .**1,500.00**
Vase, yel/amber irid flame pnt, whalebone mk, 3x4½" **850.00**

Brownies by Palmer Cox

Created by Palmer Cox in 1883, the Brownies charmed children through the pages of books and magazines, as dolls, on their dinnerware, in advertising material, and on souvenirs. Each had his own personality, among them The Bellhop, The London Bobby, The Chairman, and Uncle Sam. But the oversized, triangular face with the startled expression, the protruding tummy, and the spindle legs were characteristics of them all. They were inspired by the Scottish legends related to Cox as a child by his parents, who were of English descent. His introduction of the Brownies to the world was accomplished by a poem called *The Brownies Ride*. Books followed in rapid succession, thirteen in the series, all written as well as illustrated by Palmer Cox.

By the late 1890s, the Brownies were active in advertising. They promoted such products as games, coffee, toys, patent medicines, and rubber boots. 'Greenies' were the Brownies' first cousins, created by Cox to charm and to woo through the pages of the advertising almanacs of the G.G. Green Company of New Jersey. Perhaps the best-known endorsement in the Brownies' career was for the Kodak Brownie, which became so popular and sold in such volume that their name became synonymous with this type of camera. Our advisor for this category is Anne Kier; she is listed in the Directory under Ohio.

Plate, five Brownies wrapped in tattered American flag, 12 Brownies along rim, china, 7½", $80.00.

From the collection of Anne Kier

Almanac, G Green Woodbury, Cox illus, 1890	25.00
Ashtray, Brownie scene, RS Germany 1913	80.00
Basket, SP, Brownies w/chocolate advertising, Tufts	155.00
Book, Another Brownie Book, Appleton Century, 1941, 30th print, EX	45.00
Book, Another Brownie Book, NY, 1890, 1st ed, VG	150.00
Book, Brownie Clown of Brownietown, Century, 1908, EX	200.00
Book, Brownies & Prince Florimel, Century, 1918, VG	110.00
Book, Brownies at Home, Cox illus, Century, 1893, EX	150.00
Book, Brownies at Home, 1942, w/dust jacket, VG	35.00
Book, Little Goody Two Shoes, 1903, EX	40.00
Book, Queerie Queers, color plates, EX	125.00
Bottle, soda; emb Brownies, M	30.00
Candlestick, Bobby, majolica, 7½"	295.00
Candy dish, 15 Brownies, Tufts SP, ball ft, 7x5½"	210.00
Cloth, 6 printed dolls to stuff, uncut, NM	450.00
Comic sheet, 1907, lg, EX	35.00
Crate label, 1930s, 10x12", NM	15.00
Creamer, Scotsman head, majolica, 3¼"	75.00
Dish, 2 Brownies w/golf clubs, 4"	100.00
Doll, Brownie, Palmer Cox, orig clothes & top hat, 37", EX	300.00
Figures, papier-mache w/stick legs, jtd arms, 1900s, 5", EX, 4 for	1,200.00
Game, Brownie Horseshoes, early, complete in box	85.00
Game, 9-Pins, 1883, G	1,495.00
Ice cream bag, Cox illus, 5¢ orig value, 1930s, M	20.00
Knife, silver, deeply molded hdl	85.00
Magazine page, Ladies' Home Journal, Cox illus, ca 1890	25.00
Napkin ring, SP, Brownie climbs up side	175.00
Nodder, compo figure, wooden legs, Germany, ca 1900, 7⅝", EX	275.00
Package of needles, Policeman, 1893 Columbian Expo	50.00
Pencil box, rolling pin shape, 15 Brownies in boat	100.00
Pitcher, Brownies playing golf on tan, china, 6"	155.00
Plate, SP, Brownies on rim, 8½"	65.00

Plate, 10 action Brownies on rim, china, 10"	80.00
Sheet music, Dance of the Brownies	30.00
Sign, emb Brownies on tin, Howell's Root Beer, EX	185.00
Spoon, SP	60.00
Table set, brass, emb Brownies, 3-pc (knife/fork/spoon), no box	45.00
Whiskey taster, German head, majolica, 3¼"	85.00

Brush-McCoy, Brush

George Brush began his career in the pottery industry in 1901 working for the J.B. Owens Pottery Co. in Zanesville, Ohio. He left the company in 1907 to go into business for himself, only to have fire completely destroy his pottery less than one year after it was founded. In 1909 he became associated with J.W. McCoy, who had operated a pottery of his own in Roseville, Ohio, since 1899. The two men formed the Brush-McCoy Pottery in 1911, locating their headquarters in Zanesville. After the merger, the company expanded and produced not only staple commercial wares but also fine artware. Lines of the highest quality such as Navarre, Venetian, Oriental, and Sylvan were equal to that of their larger competitors. Because very little of the ware was marked, it is often mistaken for Weller, Roseville, or Peters and Reed.

In 1918 after a fire in Zanesville had destroyed the manufacturing portion of that plant, all production was contained in their Roseville (Ohio) plant #2. A stoneware type of clay was used there, and as a result the artware lines of Jewel, Zuniart, King Tut, Florastone, Jetwood, Krakle-Kraft, and Panelart are so distinctive that they are more easily recognizable. Examples of these lines are unique and very beautiful, also quite rare and highly prized!

After McCoy died, the family withdrew their interests, and in 1925 the name of the firm was changed to The Brush Pottery. The era of hand-decorated art pottery production had passed for the most part, having been almost completely replaced by commercial lines. The Brush-Barnett family retained their interest in the pottery until 1981 when it was purchased by the Dearborn Company.

For more information we recommend *The Collector's Encyclopedia of Brush-McCoy Pottery* by Sharon and Bob Huxford, and *Sanford's Guide to Brush-McCoy Pottery, Books I and II,* written by Martha and Steve Sanford and edited by David P. Sanford, our advisors for this category. They are listed in the Directory under California.

Of all the wares bearing the later Brush script mark, their figural cookie jars are the most collectible, and several have been reproduced. Information on Brush cookie jars (as well as confusing reproductions) can be found in *The Encyclopedia of Cookie Jars* by Joyce and Fred Roerig; they are listed in the Directory under South Carolina.

Cookie Jars

Raggedy Ann, W 16 USA, from $475.00; Boy with Balloons, unmarked, from $850.00.

Antique Touring Car, minimum value	700.00

Chick in Nest (+)	400.00
Cinderella Pumpkin, #W32	200.00
Circus Horse, gr (+)	950.00
Clown, yel pants	250.00
Clown Bust, #W49, minimum value	325.00
Cookie House, #W31	125.00
Covered Wagon, dog finial, #W30, minimum value (+)	550.00
Cow w/Cat on Bk, brn, #W10 (+)	125.00
Cow w/Cat on Bk, purple, minimum value (+)	1,000.00
Davy Crockett, no gold, mk USA (+)	300.00
Dog & Basket	250.00
Donkey w/Cart, ears up, #W33, minimum value	800.00
Donkey w/Cart, gray, ears down, #W33	400.00
Elephant w/Ice Cream Cone (+)	500.00
Elephant w/Monkey on Bk, minimum value	5,000.00
Fish, #W52 (+)	500.00
Formal Pig, gr hat & coat (+)	300.00
Gas Lamp, #K1	75.00
Granny, pk apron, bl dots on skirt	325.00
Granny, plain skirt, minimum value (+)	400.00
Happy Bunny, wht, #W25	225.00
Hen on Basket, unmk	125.00
Hillbilly Frog, minimum value (+)	4,500.00
Humpty Dumpty, w/beany & bow tie (+)	275.00
Humpty Dumpty, w/peaked brn hat & shoes	250.00
Laughing Hippo, #W27 (+)	750.00
Little Angel (+)	800.00
Little Boy Blue, #K24 Brush USA, lg (+)	800.00
Little Boy Blue, gold trim, #K25, sm	700.00
Little Girl, #017 (+)	550.00
Little Red Riding Hood, gold trim, mk, lg, minimum value (+)	850.00
Little Red Riding Hood, no gold, #K24 USA, sm	550.00
Night Owl	125.00
Old Clock, #W10	165.00
Old Shoe, #W23 (+)	125.00
Panda, #W21 (+)	250.00
Peter, Peter Pumpkin Eater, #W24	300.00
Peter Pan, gold trim, lg (+)	800.00
Peter Pan, sm	550.00
Puppy Police (+)	585.00
Sitting Pig (+)	400.00
Smiling Bear, #W46 (+)	350.00
Squirrel on Log, #W26	100.00
Squirrel w/Top Hat, blk coat & hat	275.00
Squirrel w/Top Hat, gr coat	250.00
Stylized Owl	350.00
Stylized Siamese, #W41	400.00
Teddy Bear, ft apart	250.00
Teddy Bear, ft together	200.00
Treasure Chest, #W28	150.00

Miscellaneous

Birdbath ornament, 2 frogs on base, no decor, 1920s-30s, 7½"	275.00
Bookends, Venetian, Indian chief, Ivotint, 1929, 5x5½", pr	300.00
Bowl, Jetwood, incurvate rim, type 1, #01, 2½x7½"	600.00
Bowl, Pastel Ware, Amaryllis shape, #011, 2x6", from $45 to	60.00
Candlestick, Vogue, blk geometrics on wht, 12"	325.00
Candlestick, Zuniart, Indian-style decor, #032, 1923, 10", pr	1,100.00
Candlesticks, Amaryllis KolorKraft, #026, 9", pr	250.00
Cuspidor, emb frog & lily pads on brn, 1910, 5½"	195.00
Figurine, Horace Falcon, blk, 7"	160.00
Flowerpot, Rockcraft, gray/pk/cream, 3½x9"	75.00
Hanging pot, Floradora, 5x7", from $65 to	100.00

Hanging pot, Stardust Flying Saucer	100.00
Jar, Ali Baba; yel, 2-hdl, 16½", from $200 to	300.00
Jardiniere, Blue Birds, 1915, 7½"	350.00
Jardiniere, Egyptian, bl, 1923, 5½"	200.00
Jardiniere, Jewell, geometrics on tan, 1923, 7½"	700.00
Jardiniere, Pastel Ware, emb grapes, shape #244, 6", from $85 to	120.00
Jardiniere, Rockcraft finish, 7½", from $85 to	140.00
Jardiniere, Stonecraft, #241, 1923, 6"	150.00
Jardiniere & pedestal, Athenian, 1928, 39" overall	1,300.00
Jewelry caddy, mermaid	150.00
Lamp, Wise Bird, 9", from $195 to	225.00
Lamp base, globe form, red w/brn base, 5½", from $50 to	85.00
Lamp base, Wise Bird (owl) figural, 1927, 9"	225.00
Lawn ornament, squirrel, wht w/brn highlights, 10", from $150 to	200.00
Match holder, Kolorkraft, gr, 6", from $40 to	65.00
Oil jar, bl to brn drip, 25½", from $400 to	650.00
Oil lamp, Ivotint, 8x4", from $450 to	600.00
Ornament, birdbath, wht, 2 frogs, 1 standing, 1 sitting, 7½"	200.00
Ornament, frog, on hind ft, 7½", from $65 to	85.00
Ornament, frog figural, 1967, 11½"	250.00
Planter, ostrich, mk Brush 109	40.00
Planter, swan, mk Brush USA 629	50.00
Planter, yel bird w/brn highlights by pk flower, mk USA 246	25.00
Planter, yel cat w/head trn	60.00
Porch urn, wht stoneware, 8½", from $75 to	115.00
Radio bug, 1927, 9½x3", from $500 to	950.00
Sand jar, Athenian, removable saucer, 18", from $400 to	800.00
Umbrella stand, Athenian, shape #75, 17", from $400 to	600.00
Vase, Bittersweet, 10"	95.00
Vase, Bronze Line, palette mk USA 720, 8"	40.00
Vase, Glo-Art, shape #767, 6"	95.00
Vase, King Tut, scarab, 12"	2,200.00
Vase, King Tut, walking figures, 12"	3,500.00
Vase, Majolica, Amaryllis shape, 6½", from $75 to	125.00
Vase, Onyx (bl), #1050, 6½"	75.00
Vase, Onyx (bl), swan hdls, #747, 5"	65.00
Vase, Onyx (brn), hdls, #22, 9"	85.00
Vase, Onyx (brn), shouldered, 4"	45.00
Vase, Zuniart, geometrics in matt & gloss, #049, unmk, 7"	750.00
Wall plaques, African masks, mk USA, 10½", pr	300.00
Wall pocket, doghouse, brn house, wht dog w/blk spots	100.00
Wall pocket, duck in flight	95.00

Buffalo Pottery

The founding of the Buffalo Pottery in Buffalo, New York, in 1901, was a direct result of the success achieved by John Larkin through his innovative methods of marketing 'Sweet Home Soap.' Choosing to omit 'middle-man' profits, Larkin preferred to deal directly with the consumer and offered premiums as an enticement for sales. The pottery soon proved a success in its own right and began producing advertising and commemorative items for other companies, as well as commercial tableware. In 1905 they introduced their Blue Willow line after extensive experimentation resulted in the development of the first successful underglaze cobalt achieved by an American company. Between 1905 and 1909, a line of pitchers and jugs were hand decorated in historical, literary, floral, and outdoor themes. Twenty-nine styles are known to have been made. These have been found in a wide array of color variations.

Their most famous line was Deldare Ware, the bulk of which was made from 1908 to 1909. It was hand decorated after illustrations by Cecil Aldin. Views of English life were portrayed in detail through unusual use of color against the natural olive green cast of the body. Today the 'Fallowfield Hunt' scenes are more difficult to locate than

'Scenes of Village Life in Ye Olden Days.' A Deldare calendar plate was made in 1910. These are very rare and are highly valued by collectors. The line was revived in 1923 and dropped again in 1925. Every piece was marked 'Made at Ye Buffalo Pottery, Deldare Ware Underglaze.' Most are dated, though date has no bearing on the value. Emerald Deldare, made with the same olive body and on standard Deldare Ware shapes, featured historical scenes and Art Nouveau decorations. Most pieces are found with a 1911 date stamp. Production was very limited due to the intricate, time-consuming detail. Needless to say, it is very rare and extremely desirable.

Abino Ware, most of which was made in 1912, also used standard Deldare shapes, but its colors were earthy and the decorations more delicately applied. Sailboats, windmills, and country scenes were favored motifs. These designs were achieved by overpainting transfer prints and were often signed by the artist. The ware is marked 'Abino' in hand-printed block letters. Production was limited; and as a result, examples of this line are scarce today. Prices only slightly trail those of Emerald Deldare Ware.

Our advisors for this category are Fred and Lila Shrader; they are listed in the Directory under California.

Key:
BS — bottom stamp
BW — Blue Willow
C — commercial ware marked
   Buffalo China
RW — Rouge Ware
T&P — Trylon & Perisphere
TL — top logo
TM — top mark

Abino

Ashtray/matchbox holder, 6" dia	825.00
Creamer, sailing vessels underway, choppy water	470.00
Cup & saucer, sailboats	675.00
Mug, coastal scene w/distant lighthouse, 4½"	525.00
Plaque, pastoral scene at dusk w/path leading to far cottage, 13"	1,550.00
Plate, sailing vessels underway, choppy water, 6¼"	300.00
Powder jar, shoreline scene w/windmills in bkground, w/lid, 4½"	765.00
Teapot, shoreline scene w/sailboats in distance, 5½"	885.00
Toothpick holder, shoreline scene, 2¼"	385.00
Tray, dresser; lake & mtn scene w/boats in foreground, 9x12"	1,100.00
Vase, tall-masted ship & colorful clouded sky, corset shape, 12"	1,025.00

Deldare

Tankard, Fallowfield Hunt — The Hunt Supper, 1908, 12¼", $1,600.00; Tankard, Emerald, Dr. Syntax Setting Out to the Lakes..., 1911, 9x8", $1,700.00.

Bowl, Emerald, Art Nouveau decor, 5½"	325.00
Bowl, flat rim soup; Fallowfield Hunt, 9"	450.00
Bowl, fruit; Fallowfield Hunt, 9"	680.00
Bowl, sauce; Fallowfield Hunt, 5"	185.00

Candle holder, shield-bk; Village scene, 6¾"	1,400.00
Candlestick, Fallowfield Hunt, 9"	630.00
Candlestick holder w/finger ring, Village scene, 5" dia	650.00
Chocolate pot, Ye Village scene, 10"	695.00
Creamer, Fallowfield Hunt scene, 3"	635.00
Cup, punch; Fallowfield Hunt decor, 2¼"	250.00
Cup & saucer, chocolate; Emerald, Dr Syntax	400.00
Cup & saucer, Emerald, Dr Syntax	445.00
Cup & Saucer, Fallowfield Hunt scene	285.00
Egg cup, untitled, Fallowfield Hunt decor, 3¾"	1,200.00
Hair receiver, Ye Village Street, 4½" dia	435.00
Humidor, Fallowfield Hunt, 6¼"	1,250.00
Humidor, Ye Lion Inn, 7"	1,000.00
Jardiniere, Ye Village Street, 9x8½"	1,600.00
Mug, Emerald, Art Nouveau decor, 2½"	1,050.00
Mug, Emerald, Dr Syntax, 4½"	645.00
Mug, Fallowfield Hunt scene, 4¼"	450.00
Mug, Village Life, finger rest on hdl, child sz, 2½"	1,400.00
Mug, Ye Lion Inn, 4¼"	225.00
Pitcher, Fallowfield Hunt scene, 6"	600.00
Pitcher, Fallowfield Hunt scene, 9"	900.00
Pitcher, Village Scene: Their Manner of Telling Stories..., 6½"	290.00
Plaque, Fallowfield Hunt, Breakfast at Three Pigeons, 12"	675.00
Plate, At Ye Lion Inn, 6¼"	115.00
Plate, cake; Ye Village Gossips, open fancy hdls, 10½"	485.00
Plate, calendar; Emerald, 1910, 9½"	1,685.00
Plate, chop; An Evening at Ye Lion Inn, 14" dia	650.00
Plate, Emerald, Dr Syntax, 8¼", from $500 to	590.00
Plate, Emerald, Dr Syntax, 9¼", from $1,000 to	1,300.00
Plate, Fallowfield Hunt, 8½"	185.00
Plate, Ye Town Crier, 8½"	87.00
Plate, Ye Village Gossips, 9½"	145.00
Platter, Ye Village Gossips, 8½x6½"	490.00
Powder jar, Emerald, Art Nouveau decor, 4¾"	1,100.00
Powder jar, Ye Village Street, 5" dia	600.00
Sugar bowl, Fallowfield Hunt scene, w/lid, 4"	650.00
Sugar bowl, Scenes of Village Life, open, 2¾"	565.00
Tankard, Emerald, Dr Syntax, 12"	2,000.00
Tea tile, Fallowfield Hunt, 6" dia	585.00
Tea tile, Traveling in Ye Olden Days, 6¾" dia	240.00
Teapot, Emerald, Dr Syntax, 5½"	680.00
Teapot, Fallowfield Hunt, 4½"	750.00
Teapot, Village Life in Ye Olden Days, 5¾"	535.00
Tray, calling card; Fallowfield Hunt, 7½"	375.00
Tray, calling card; Ye Lion Inn, tab hdls, 7½"	310.00
Tray, dresser; Dancing Ye Minuet, 9x12"	575.00
Tray, pin; Emerald, Dr Syntax, 6¼x3½"	1,100.00
Vase, Emerald, Art Nouveau decor, baluster shape, 8½"	1,090.00

Miscellaneous

Ashtray, Multifleure, cowboy hat shape, C, 5¾" dia	85.00
Ashtray w/matchbox holder, Tahoe Tavern, C, 5¾" dia	65.00
Bowl, fruit; Gaudy Willow, 5½"	65.00
Bowl, salad; Natural Wood decor, HP, C, 5½" dia	35.00
Bowl, vegetable; BW, 9" sq	235.00
Butter pat, BW, 3¼" dia	45.00
Butter pat, CCC intertwined, C	15.00
Butter pat, copper teakettle, Dayton, C, 3½"	35.00
Butter pat, Davenports in script, C	35.00
Butter pat, Gaudy Willow, 3¼" dia	175.00
Butter pat, Park Lane, C, 3¼" dia	28.00
Butter pat, pk roses w/gold trim, 3" dia	19.00
Butter pat, red geometric border w/blk pinstripe, Mco, C	25.00

Butter pat, Vienna, dk bl w/rich gold trim, 3¼" dia 45.00
Butterpat, Bluebird, 3¼" 45.00
Candle holder, Hotel Baltimore, w/finger ring 88.00
Canister, Pepper, wht w/gold trim, 3" 48.00
Chamber pot, Chrysanthemum, w/lid 165.00
Chamber pot, sm pk roses w/gold, no lid 85.00
Child's feeding dish, Campbell Kids scene w/o ABC rim, 7½" 85.00
Child's feeding dish (hot water), Bluebird, 7¾" 135.00
Creamer, Boos Bros, yel flowers w/brn stripe hdl, C, 3¼" 48.00
Creamer, BW, hdl, ind, C, 3¼" 50.00
Creamer, BW, no hdl, ind, C, 2¾" 40.00
Creamer, BW, 5" 145.00
Creamer, Forget-Me-Not, rich gold trim 65.00
Creamer, Roycroft Inn, no hdl, ind, C, 3" 175.00
Cup & saucer, Beverly, rich gold trim 55.00
Cup & saucer, Bonrea, teal w/rich gold trim 55.00
Cup & saucer, bouillon; Gaudy Willow, rich gold trim 175.00
Cup & saucer, demitasse; BW 95.00
Cup & saucer, demitasse; BW, C 35.00
Cup & saucer, demitasse; Mandalay, C 35.00
Cup & saucer, Hotel Churchill, C 35.00
Cup & saucer, Multifleure Lamelle or Natural Wood, C 45.00
Cup & saucer, USFS, C 65.00
Egg cup, BW, C, 2¾" 45.00
Fish set, rich gold trim, 15x11" platter +6 9" plates 495.00
Jug, BW, w/flat lid, 5" 195.00
Jug, Geranium, bl & wht, 6½" 475.00
Jug, Geranium, teal & wht, 6½" 275.00
Jug, Hounds & Stag, mc, 6½" 645.00
Mug, Bing & Nathan (adv) w/a Friar on reverse, 4½" 165.00
Mug, BW, 3½" 150.00
Mug, Celebration, Fascination, Vacation, etc, 4½", ea 79.00
Mug, Friar, mc, w/finger rest 85.00
Mug, Roosevelt Bears, child sz, 3½" 245.00
Mug, Sunbonnet, Campbell Kids, various scenes, child sz, 3½" 65.00
Pitcher, BW, C, 10" 75.00
Pitcher, BW, rich gold trim, cobalt hdl & spout, 8" 550.00
Pitcher, Chrysanthemum, 7" (hot water jug for bath set) 100.00
Pitcher, George Washington, rich gold trim, 7" 620.00
Pitcher, Robin Hood, wht bkground, 8" 625.00
Pitcher, Roosevelt Bears, 8" 2,200.00
Pitcher, Sailor (lighthouse on reverse), 9¼" 685.00
Pitcher, Whirl of the Town, 7" 1,000.00
Pitcher & bowl, sm pk & yel roses, 11½" & 13½" dia 385.00
Plate, Ahwahnee Hotel, rust & blk geometric designs, C, 7½" 39.00
Plate, Bangor, cobalt, brn & gr transfer on ivory w/gold, 10" 85.00
Plate, BW, reverse: First Old Willow Ware Mfg'd in America, 9" .185.00
Plate, Christmas, 1962, rich gold trim 235.00
Plate, commemorative; Independence Hall..., teal & wht, 10½" ..60.00
Plate, commemorative; New Bedford, Mass, bl & wht, 10½" 100.00
Plate, commemorative; Niagara Falls, teal, 7½" 65.00
Plate, commemorative; Theodore Roosevelt, rich gold trim, 8" .265.00
Plate, Delft-like, bl & wht, reverse side: Aonia Ware, 10" 490.00
Plate, fishes (swimming along edge), bl on Blue Lune ware, C, 10" .55.00
Plate, Geranium, mc on teal, 10" 145.00
Plate, World's Fair, 1939, T&P w/colorful border, C, 10" 255.00
Platter, Buffalo Hunt, teal w/rich gold trim, 14x11" 310.00
Platter, USBF, C, 4½x7" 39.00
Punch bowl, Tom & Jerry in blk on Colorido ware, 11¼" dia 195.00
Sauce boat, fishes swimming, blk on Blue Lune ware, C 55.00
Sherbet, Roycroft, ped ft, 2¾x3¾" 125.00
Teapot, Ahwahnee Hotel, rust & blk geometric decor, C, ind 90.00
Teapot, Bluebird, 5½" to top of finial 185.00
Toothbrush holder, Leighton Hotel, cylindrical, 5x2½" dia 35.00

Toothpick holder, Natural Wood decor, C, 1¾" 55.00
Vase, floral w/gold, HP, angular hdls at shoulders, urn-like 300.00
Vase, Geranium, bl & wht, 4" 225.00

Buggy Steps

The recent increased interest in western collectibles has stimulated a renewed awareness in all horse-drawn memorabilia. A good example of this is the buggy step. This device allowed the passenger to enter or exit the vehicle without the driver's assistance. Steps may be hinged, pivoted, adjustable, folding, and spring loaded. The elaborate handwork of the blacksmiths who created them was equal to that of the finest wheelwrights, carpenters, and leather workers involved in the manufacture of early wheeled vehicles (1865 – 1910). For listings of no-name steps with multiple designs, see previous editions of this book. Prices suggested here are for steps in mint to good condition. Rust, breaks, and pitting reduce their value. Our advisor for this category is John Waddell; he is listed in the Directory under Texas.

Abbott Buggy Co, sq, bolt-on, 3x3" 45.00
ABC Co, sq, tee-mt, 3x3" 55.00
Cole, oval, slot-mt, 3½x2¼" 45.00
Columbia Carriage, egg shape, tee-mt, 5¼x3½" 70.00
CW Co, sq shield, bolt-on, 3½x3½" 38.00
Dean Co, oval, tee-mt, 3½x2¼" 65.00
Deere, (brass insert) rectangle, tri-fork mt, 4½x3" 75.00
Eckhart, oval, tri-fork mt, 5x3½" 55.00
Emerson, oval, tee-mt, 5x3½" 65.00
Frazier Co, sq, bolt-on, 3½x3½" 45.00
Freeport, oval, tri-fork mt, 4½x3½" 50.00
Harper, oval, trifork mt, 5x3½" 65.00
Henney, oval, tri-fork mt, 5x3½" 65.00
Maple Leaf in oval, tri-fork mt, 4½x3½" 50.00
Moon Bro's, oval, tri-fork mt, 4½x3½" 65.00
NWS Co, open initial, bolt-on, 5x2½" 45.00
Peru, rnd, tee-mt, 4½" 65.00
Spaulding, oval, tri-mt, 3½x2½" 65.00
Staver, oval, tri-fork mt, 4½x3½" 65.00
Studebaker, rectangle, tri-fork mt, 5x3¼" 65.00

Burmese

Burmese glass was patented in 1885 by the Mount Washington Glass Co. It is typically shaded from canary yellow to a rosy salmon color. The yellow is produced by the addition of uranium oxide to the mix. The salmon color comes from the addition of gold salts and is achieved by reheating the object (partially) in the furnace. It is thus called 'heat sensitive' glass. Thomas Webb of England was licensed to produce Burmese and often added more gold, giving an almost fuchsia tinge to the salmon in some cases. They called their glass 'Queen's Burmese,' and this is sometimes etched on the base of the object. This is not to be confused with Mount Washington's 'Queen's Design,' which refers to the design painted on the object. Both companies added decoration to many pieces. Mount Washington-Pairpoint produced some Burmese in the late 1920s and Gundersen and Bryden in the '50s and '70s, but the color and shapes are different. Our advisors for this category are Dolli and Wilfred Cohen; they are listed in the Directory under California. In the listings that follow, examples are assumed to have the satin finish unless noted 'shiny.' See also Lamps, Fairy.

Bonbon, Mt WA, swollen optic rib sides, turned-in edge, 5" L ...350.00
Bowl, berry; Mt WA, pie-crust rim, 2¾x9" 950.00
Bowl, Mt WA, Dmn Quilt, 1x6¼" 225.00

Bowl, Mt WA, rectangular rim, 2x5x4½" 425.00
Bowl, Mt WA, ruffled/pulled rim, 3 shell ft, 6x7¼" 1,500.00
Bowl, Webb, crimped star-form rim, Queen's, 2¼x4" 375.00
Compote, Gundersen, ruffled, baluster stem, 4¾x7¾", pr 325.00

Candelabra, Webb, green and brown ivy and leaf decor, 13¾", $2,100.00.

Condiment set, mums, ribbed, cruet & pr s&p in Pairpoint fr .2,500.00
Creamer, Mt WA, bulbous, 4" 400.00
Cruet, Mt WA, shiny, melon ribs, mushroom stopper, 7" 1,250.00
Cup & saucer, Mt WA, tapered 2" cup, 4¾" saucer, w/label 400.00
Custard cup, shiny, 2⅞" 385.00
Epergne, 5 lily vases & fairy lamp on ped in 8" bowl, 12" 3,800.00
Epergne, 7 dome shades on ped base in 8" crimped bowl, 11" .3,500.00
Ginger jar, Mt WA, asters/gold berries, 5" 1,595.00
Goblet, Mt WA, shiny, 6½" 950.00
Lamp, evening; shiny, jack-in-pulpit 4¾" crimped shade, 7½" ...575.00
Pitcher, bulbous w/sqd hdl, 7x9", +4 4" tumblers 1,850.00
Pitcher, Mt WA, yel hdl, 7x6½" 1,000.00
Plate, Gundersen, EX color, 9" 495.00
Potpourri jar, ovoid w/dome lid, metal screen, 4¾" 475.00
Rose bowl, Mt WA, 8-crimp rim, 2½x2½" 335.00
Rose bowl, Webb, flower, lav/bl on satin, 2¼" 225.00
Rose bowl, Webb, flowers/fall foliage, crimped, sm 275.00
Shakers, Mt WA, ribbed pillar, 4", pr 400.00
Sherbet, Mt WA, thin walled, 2½" 450.00
Sugar bowl, Mt WA, wishbone ft, berry prunt over pontil, 3½" .650.00
Sweetmeat, Webb, flowers/gilt branches/butterfly, 2½x4½" 800.00
Syrup pitcher, Mt WA, florals/mums, sqd hdl, SP lid, 6½" 2,750.00
Toothpick holder, Mt WA, mums, bulbous, sq rim, 3" 675.00
Toothpick holder, Mt WA, mums w/gold, bulbous, sq rim, 2⅝" 695.00
Toothpick holder, Mt WA, pine cones/needles, sq top, 3" 675.00
Toothpick holder, Mt WA, 3-corner rim, 2¼" 425.00
Toothpick holder, Webb, ivy/berries, 6-sided rim, 2¾" 695.00
Tumbler, Mt WA, EX color, thin walls 285.00
Tumbler, Mt WA, ivy, 3¾" 395.00
Tumbler, Mt WA, Queen's pattern: daisies, 3¾" 850.00
Tumbler, Mt WA, shiny, 3¾" 275.00
Tumbler, Mt WA, 3¾" 275.00
Tumbler, whiskey; Mt WA, sq rim, 2½" 175.00
Tumbler, whiskey; Webb, thin walls, 2⅞" 325.00
Vase, bird in flight/gold moons, 4½" 575.00
Vase, bud; in SP holder w/seated Oriental mk Pairpoint, 8½" 445.00
Vase, jack-in-the-pulpit; Mt WA, crimped rolled rim, 11" 475.00
Vase, jack-in-the-pulpit; Mt WA, tightly crimped, 10" 750.00
Vase, jack-in-the-pulpit; Mt WA, tightly crimped, 15½" 950.00
Vase, jack-in-the-pulpit; Pairpoint, shiny, wide flange, 5¼x6¾" .575.00
Vase, lily; Gundersen, 9½" 375.00
Vase, lily; Mt WA, EX color, 12¼" 750.00
Vase, lily; Mt WA, 15" 950.00
Vase, lily; Mt WA, 6½" 395.00

Vase, Mt WA, asters, bulbous, scroll hdls, pencil neck, 12½" .1,975.00
Vase, Mt WA, bamboo, gourd shape, 11½x6½" 1,875.00
Vase, Mt WA, daisies, squat/bulbous, 3x3½" 850.00
Vase, Mt WA, gold ferns/florals allover, tricon rim, 12" ..4,000.00
Vase, Mt WA, gourd form, incurvate rim, 12x6½" 825.00
Vase, Mt WA, gourd form, thin walls, 8x4" 650.00
Vase, Mt WA, ivy sprig, bottle form w/long neck, 9½" .750.00
Vase, Mt WA, outstanding color, 12¼" 875.00
Vase, Mt WA, pansy sprays, stick neck, 10" 650.00
Vase, Mt WA, prunus blossoms, beaded rim, elongated gourd, 9" .850.00
Vase, Mt WA, Queen's pattern, gourd shape, 8x5" 3,500.00
Vase, Mt WA, Queen's pattern, stick neck, 12x6¾" 3,950.00
Vase, Mt WA, shiny, bulbous, 5½" 550.00
Vase, Mt WA, yel rigaree collar w/button & tassels, 5" 1,900.00
Vase, Webb, clematis vines, ovoid, 8" 1,400.00
Vase, Webb, cylindrical w/short collar rim, 6" 275.00
Vase, Webb, floral, ruffled, bulbous/squat, wide throat, 3¾" 475.00
Vase, Webb, ivy, petaled flared rim, Queen's, 3" 290.00
Vase, Webb, ivy, 8½x4½" 1,275.00
Vase, Webb, leaves/berries, crimped flange, 3" 350.00

Butter Molds and Stamps

The art of decorating butter began in Europe during the reign of Charles II. This practice was continued in America by the farmer's wife who sold her homemade butter at the weekly market to earn extra money during hard times. A mold or stamp with a special design, hand carved either by her husband or a local craftsman, not only made her product more attractive but also helped identify it as hers. The pattern became the trademark of Mrs. Smith, and all who saw it knew that this was her butter. It was usually the rule that no two farms used the same mold within a certain area, thus the many variations and patterns available to the collector today. The most valuable are those which have animals, birds, or odd shapes. The most sought-after motifs are the eagle, cow, fish, and rooster. These works of early folk art are quickly disappearing from the market.

Molds

Wheat pattern, EX patina, small crack, 4¾" diameter, $65.00.

Acorn, 1 in ea of 2 sqs, trn hdl, 4x7" 100.00
Acorn & 2 oak leaves, 3½" dia 110.00
Acorn/sheaf of wheat/thistle/nut, brass hooks, 2x6x5½" 75.00
Berry (lg) & leaves, 4" dia, EX 165.00
Cherries (3) on twig, rpr hinge, 4¼x8½" L 60.00
Cow, EX cvg, ca 1820, w/plunger, 5" dia 375.00
Flower in serrated circle, circles in center, 1800s, 8½" L 115.00
Lamb & foliage, 3⅜" dia, EX 400.00
Sheaf of wheat w/rosettes & foliage, EX cvg, 5" dia 150.00
Swan, EX cvg, maple, ca 1830, 4" dia 210.00

Thistle, 3⅝" dia 125.00

Stamps

Acorn w/cap & chip-cvg, notch-cvd border, 4" dia 150.00
Compass star flower, scrubbed, smooth bk, 5" dia 110.00
Cow & keg, 1-pc w/trn hdl, age cracks, 3¼" dia 110.00
Cow facing right, leaf below head, notched-cvd edge, 5¼x3" 65.00
Dbl-sided, geometric star flowers, chips, 3" dia 110.00
Dbl-sided, leaves/radial design, 2" dia 400.00
Dbl-sided, radial design ea side, paddle shape, 4⅛" dia 850.00
Dbl-sided, 6 lobes w/herringbone design/simple tulip, 4" dia 200.00
Eagle w/branch & star, old patina, self-trn hdl, 4¼" dia 225.00
Eagle w/wings wide (crudely cvd), plain rim, 1-pc w/hdl, 3¾" 200.00
Flower & star, cvd maple, 4⅜" dia 175.00
Flower & 4 birds, primitive, 1-pc, flat hdl, 4¾" dia, EX 250.00
Flower w/stem & petals, notch-cvd finger grips on bk, 4" dia 175.00
Hearts (2) & radial design, 5⅛x2½" 225.00
Leafy cluster & 5-pointed star, walnut, 5x3" 140.00
Leaves (3) on stem, leafy border, 1-pc w/hdl, 4¼" dia 150.00
Radial design, cvd softwood, sawtooth rim, 4¼" dia 95.00
Sheaf of wheat, stars at top, leaves at bottom, oval, 5" W 100.00
Sunburst w/monogram, 1-pc w/flat bk, 3¾" dia 200.00
Thistle, inserted wooden hdl, 5" dia 125.00
Tulip, leaves & heart, old dk varnish, missing hdl, 4" dia 110.00
Tulip & geometrics w/stars, 4¼" dia 210.00
Tulip & leaf, cvd softwood, flat bk, 4" dia 150.00
Tulip & stars, 1-pc trn hdl, old dk finish, 5" dia 125.00

Buttonhooks

The earliest known written reference to buttonhooks (shoe hooks, glove hooks, or collar buttoners) is dated 1611. They became a necessary implement in the 1850s when tight-fitting high-button shoes became fashionable. Later in the 19th century, ladies' button gloves and men's button-on collars and cuffs dictated specific types of buttoners, some with a closed wire loop instead of a hook end. Both shoes and gloves used as many as twenty-four buttons each. Usage began to wane in the late 1920s following a fashion change to low-cut laced shoes and the invention of the zipper. There was a brief resurgence of use following the 1948 movie 'High Button Shoes.' For a simple, needed utilitarian device, buttonhook handles were made from a surprising variety of materials: natural wood, bone, ivory, agate, and mother-of-pearl to plain steel, celluloid, aluminum, iron, lead and pewter, artistic copper, brass, silver, gold, and many other materials, in lengths that varied from under 2" to over 20". Many designs folded or retracted, and buttonhooks were often combined with shoehorns and other useful implements. Stamped steel buttonhooks often came free with the purchase of shoes, gloves, or collars. Material, design, workmanship, condition, and relative scarcity are the primary market value factors. Prices range from $1.00 to over $200.00, with most being in the $10.00 to $75.00 range. Buttonhooks are fairly easy to find, and they are interesting to display. Our advisor for this category is Richard Mathes; he is listed in the Directory under Ohio. See also 'The Buttonhook Society' listing in the Directory under Clubs, Newsletters, and Catalogs.

Buttonhook/penknife, ivory side plates, man's 50.00
Collar buttoner, stamped steel, advertising, closed end, 3" 20.00
Glove hook, gold-plated, retractable, 3" 90.00
Glove hook, loop end, agate hdl, 2½" 60.00
Shoe hook, colored celluloid hdl, 8" 15.00
Shoe hook, lathe-trn hardwood hdl, dk finish, 8" 15.00
Shoe hook, SP w/blade, repousse hdl, Pat Jan 5 1892, 5" 40.00

Shoe hook, stamped steel, advertising, 5" 8.00
Shoe hook, sterling, floral & geometrics, 8" 55.00
Shoe hook, sterling, Nouveau lady's face, 6½" 75.00
Shoe hook, sterling, W w/arrow, hammered Florentine decor, mk .55.00
Shoe hook/shoehorn combination, steel & celluloid, 9" 35.00

Bybee

The Bybee Pottery was founded in 1809 in the small town of Bybee, Kentucky. Their earliest wares were primarily stoneware churns and jars. Today the work is carried on by sixth-generation Cornelison potters who still use the same facilities and production methods to make a more diversified line of pottery. From a fine white clay mined only a few miles from the potting shed itself, the shop produces vases, jugs, dinnerware, and banks in a variety of colors, some of which are shipped to the larger cities to be sold in department stores and specialty shops. The bulk of their wares, however, is sold to the thousands of tourists who are attracted to the pottery each year.

Garlic roaster, mauve, 6x6" 20.00
Pitcher, feldspathic brn-cream, conical finial, 1950s, 11½" 70.00
Pitcher, lt bl, Cornelison Bybee mk, 4½" 40.00
Strawberry planter, deep rose, mk, 1950s, 3¼" 20.00
Tea set, gr, Cornelison Bybee mk, 3-pc set, NM 45.00
Tray, bl spongeware, 2½x12x6½" 25.00
Vase, emb grass-like pattern, 5¾x4⅜" 200.00
Vase, gr feldspathic variant, stoneware, waisted, 1930s, 8½" 350.00
Vase, lt gr, mk, 5x3½" 150.00
Vase, rose & lav mottle, trumpet neck, #d, mk, 6" 120.00
Vase/flower arranger, cobalt, hdls, #540, 6x6" 105.00

Cabat

From beginning experimentation with pottery in New York City around 1940, through several different types of clay, designs, and glazes, and relocation to Arizona, the Rose Cabat 'Feelie,' so named because 'it feels so good,' evolved into present forms and glazes in the late 1950s. Rose was aided and encouraged through the years by her late husband Erni. Their small 'weed pots' are readily recognizable by their light weight, tiny thin necks, and soft glazes. Pieces are marked with a hand-incised 'Cabat' on the bottom.

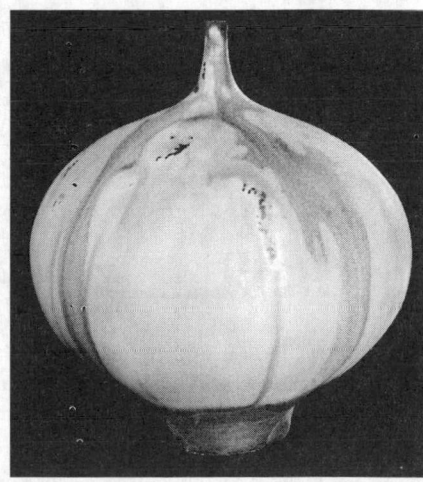

Vase, blue with streaks of turquoise, 2", from $150.00 to $200.00.

Vase, bl matt w/yel highlights, 3x4" 250.00
Vase, dk/lt brn lg-mottle matt, 3x2" 210.00

Calendar Plates

Calendar plates were advertising giveaways most popular from about 1906 until the late twenties. They were decorated with colorful underglaze decals of lovely ladies, flowers, animals, birds and, of course, the twelve months of the year of their issue. During the 1950s they came into vogue again but never to the extent they were originally. Those with exceptional detailing, or those with scenes of a particular activity are most desirable, so are any from before 1906.

1907, Christmas scenes, 9" 60.00
1908, lady dressed in red driving car 45.00
1909, cat lapping up cream 35.00
1909, Christmas, holly & berries 50.00
1909, flowers & fruit, 7" 35.00
1909, Gibson Girl 42.00
1909, monks drinking wine, 9" 55.00
1909, strawberries 35.00
1909, William Jennings Bryan 55.00
1910, Fly Fishing 50.00
1910, Old Rose Distilling, Chicago 35.00
1910, scene at swimming hole 32.50
1911, cherries, pear & apple 28.00
1912, Lincoln, Garfield & McKinley 75.00
1913, Gibson Girl fishing 42.50
1915, George Washington 32.00
1915, man canoeing 28.00
1918, Allied flags, 8" 37.50
1919, Am flag, 8" 30.00
1921, bluebirds & various fruits 28.00
1921, Marc MacDermott portrait 32.00
1929, valentine & flowers 27.50

Calendars

Calendars are collected for their colorful prints, often attributed to a well-recognized artist of the period. Advertising calendars from the turn of the century often have a double appeal when representing a company whose tins, signs, store displays, etc., are also collectible. See also Parrish, Maxfield.

1910, girl on telephone diecut, with pad, 10x14", EX in frame, $80.00; 1900, girl in ruffled bonnet diecut, full pad, 8x9" plus mount and frame, $215.00.

1886, Grit Newspaper, cb, boy sells papers in snow, 11x8", EX ..125.00
1888, Farmers Fire Insurance, girl/harvesters by river, 10x7", NM ..280.00
1889, Quincy Mutual Fire Insurance Co, cb, 3 rats/cat, 10x7", EX .375.00
1889, Singer Manufacturing, emb paper, girl/pansies, 12x9", EX+ ..85.00

1892, Singer Sewing Machines, paper, girl w/straw hat, 9x6", EX .135.00
1892, Walter A Wood, cb, 3 girls, 2-sided, 7x6", NM+ 50.00
1895, Hood's Sarsaparilla, cb heart shape, 2 girls, NM+ 95.00
1896, Walter Wood Mowing & Reaping..., cb, children, 9x8", EX .140.00
1899, Am Seal Pnt, Uncle Sam/Spanish-Am War heroes, 21x13", NM .335.00
1899, Grit Newspaper, cb, girl waving flag at mirror, 12x9", EX ...125.00
1900, Babcock & Teague Druggists, diecut, girl/violets, 12x8", NM+ ...150.00
1900, Excelsior Bottling Co, Season's Greetings..., 23", VG 625.00
1900, Fairbanks Fairy Calendar, cb, girl in uniform, 13x10", NM+ 210.00
1901, Swift & Co, diecut cb, Am Girl, 32x15", VG 70.00
1901, Youth's Champion, trifold diecut, lady/roses, vertical, EX+ 45.00
1902, G Engel Hardware, diecut, girls/rabbits/chicken, 13x11", EX ...35.00
1902, Good Store, boy/girl in wheelbarrow/rabbit, 11x7", EX+ ..145.00
1902, Hood's Sarsaparilla, 4 regional girls, vertical, EX+ 65.00
1903, Bel-Cap-Sic Plaster, cb diecut, girl/dog at beach, 10x13", EX+ ...50.00
1903, Hanson Drug Co, cb diecut, lady's head in hat, 13x7", NM+ ...75.00
1903, Lambertville Rubber Co Snag-Proof Boots, 10x7", EX+ ...110.00
1904, Great Atlantic & Pacific Tea Co, girl, McEntee art, 16x12", G 75.00
1905, A Bauder, cb diecut, 2 children in wagon, 14x11", EX 150.00
1905, German Fire Insurance, cb, patriotic scene, 14x11", EX+ ...45.00
1905, Plano Harvesting Machines, Indian brave, 19x13", EX+ ...165.00
1906, Frank Mogle Liquor Dealer, paper, 2 dogs, 15x11", NM ...100.00
1907, DuPont, paper, hunt scene, Osthaus art, 29x15", EX+ 635.00
1907, Ed Wilkins, cb diecut, cartoon pilgrim, 12x8", NM 25.00
1907, Kellogg Iron Works, cb stand-up, 4 caricatures, 8x12", NM+ ...130.00
1907, Kreger's Bakery & Ice Cream..., kids/donkey, 20x15", VG+ ..40.00
1909, AF Movitt Druggist, cb diecut, girl/roses, 17x12", EX+ 180.00
1909, Independent Tea Co, cb diecut, girl/lilacs, 20x15", NM+ .225.00
1909, Peters, paper, hunt scene, G Muss Arnolt art, 27x14", VG ..165.00
1909, Wichita Construction Co, Indian maiden, vertical, NM+ ..465.00
1910, AO Fisher...Cigar Boxes, At the Opera, 20x15", VG 450.00
1910, Evans & Price, cb diecut, boy/girl on path, 8x6", EX 125.00
1910, Harrington & Richardson Arms, hunting, Arnold, 27x14", VG 990.00
1910, Kelly's Famous Flour, paper, boy/girl at table, 26x21", EX 375.00
1911, HC Sattler, Horses & Mules Bought..., boy/girl, 15x10", EX ...275.00
1912, Champion Harvesting..., farmer/horse/child, 20x13", EX+ 170.00
1913, DeLaval, complete, EX 2,500.00
1914, GF Carls, diecut, cherub/mill/flowers/birds, 15x11", EX 65.00
1915, H Favart Boots/Springfield IL, cb diecut, girl, 7x4", EX+ 30.00
1917, Peters Cartridge Co, 2 dogs in harvested field, 29x16", G .300.00
1918, Weaver's, mother w/baby, full pad, 20x15", VG+ 40.00
1919, Peters Cartridges, linen, dogs & pups on hunt, 24x14", EX .550.00
1919, Uncle Sam Stock Medicine, Uncle Sam/NY Harbor, 20x15", NM 225.00
1921, Southern Fertilizing Co, girl w/dog, full pad, 20x12", VG+ ...50.00
1922, Dutch Boy Paints, complete, 16x9", NM 50.00
1922, Sunshine Biscuits, Sunshine Girl, Earl Christy, 18x8", EX .50.00
1923, DeLaval, paper, boy husking corn, 24x12", EX 100.00
1925, Remington, Let 'Er Rain, 29x15", EX+ 560.00
1926, Hupmobile, cars/sailboats/people, 31x14", EX+ 160.00
1927, DeLaval, complete, EX 550.00
1927, Nehi, girl on beached boat, 21x11", EX 200.00
1927, Round Oak Stoves, 22x12", M 150.00
1927, Union Grain Co, children w/chicks, full pad, 18x10", VG+ ...25.00
1929, D Agostini Confectionery, patriotic theme, 22x16", EX+ 55.00
1929, Lee Wizzit Overalls, children in overalls, 10x14", NM 495.00
1929, Somerset Dairy, sunset scene, full pad, 22x8", NM 30.00
1932, Goodrick Silvertown, man w/cane, boy fishing, 17x11", NM ..50.00
1932, Squire's/Arlington Pork Products, 29x15", EX 175.00
1935, Goodyear, bear/fisherman, Hintermeister art, 21x12", NM .25.00
1936, Duplex Bread, Duplex Is Good Bread, toddler, 17x9", EX ..32.00
1937, Jewel Tea Co Inc, Going to Town, 13x8", EX+ 30.00
1939, Bergoff Beer, paper, baseball game w/rows of players, VG+ .55.00
1940, Dionne Quints, 5 sm girls, full pad, 12x10", NM 50.00
1940, Keen Kutter, winter cabin by stream in scissors fr, NM 50.00

1941, Trailways, 24", NM 20.00
1942, Clicquot Club Ginger Ale, complete, 24x12", NM 100.00
1943, Maas & Steffen Furs, otter in snow, no pad, 30x21", EX ...200.00
1944, John Deere, 2 children at storefront, 16x11", NM 125.00
1944, Maas & Steffen Furs, otter on snow bank, 24x17", VG 160.00
1945, Squirt, 24x16", complete, NM+ 65.00
1946, Great Northern Railway, Julia-Wades-In-Water, 34x16", EX+ .130.00
1946, Kist, Get Kist for a Nichel (sic), garden girl, 26x14", NM+ ...165.00
1946, Maas & Steffen Furs, hunter/dogs/polar bear, 47x26", NM ...700.00
1947, Jewel Tea Co Inc, Coffee & Grocery Specialists, 13x8", EX ..25.00
1948, Clicquot Club Beverages, complete, EX+ 150.00
1948, Squirt, 4 different girls, 22x16", EX 100.00
1949, Fisk Tires, Fisk Boy, 33x19", complete, NM 225.00
1951, Great Northern Railway, Angry Bull, 34x16", NM+ 100.00
1952, OshKosh Tools, pinup girl on ladder, 32x16", NM+ 100.00
1953, Mission Beverages, 25x14", NM 100.00
1955, Great Northern Railway, Many Guns, 34x16", EX+ 100.00
1957, Hoover Bearings, 1912 Indy race scenes, M 98.00
1957, North Shore Foundry Co, DiMaggio/boy batting, 33x16", EX .55.00
1968, Mid-State Co, beautiful lady, Elvgrens art, 33x16", EX+ ..100.00
1976, Winchester, Sioux, Ferrara art, 21x12", NM+ 125.00

Caliente

Caliente was a line of colored dinnerware made by the Paden City Pottery Company in Paden City, West Virginia. It was produced during the 1930s and 1940s in tangerine, yellow, blue, green, and cobalt blue.

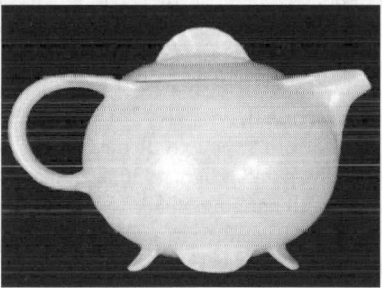

Teapot, $45.00.

Bowl, salad; 10" 25.00
Bowl, 5½" 10.00
Bowl, 9" 20.00
Candle holder 15.00
Creamer 14.00
Cup & saucer 15.00
Plate, dinner; 10" 17.50
Plate, 6" 5.00
Plate, 9½" 10.00
Platter, 12" 20.00
Platter, 14" 25.00
Sugar bowl, w/lid 18.00

California Faience

California Faience was the trade name used by William V. Bragdon and Chauncy R. Thomas on vases, bowls, and other artware produced at their pottery known as 'The Tile Shop' in Berkeley, California, from 1920 to 1930. Faience tile was the principal product of the business during these years and is the favorite with today's collectors. Items in a glossy glaze are rare and therefore more valuable. Tiles were marked 'California Faience' with a die stamp.

Lamp base, ochre/gr speckled matt, porc, 8¾x7½" 450.00
Trivet, floral, bl on wht, bl band, 5" 250.00
Vase, raspberry gloss, 3½x2¾" 200.00
Vase, robin's egg bl speckled matt, 2¼x4½" 375.00
Vase, yel semimatt, bulbous, 5x5¼" 225.00

California Perfume Company

D.H. McConnell, Sr., founded the California Perfume Company (C.P. Company; C.P.C.) in 1886 in New York City. He had previously been a salesman for a book company, which he later purchased. His door-to-door sales usually involved the lady of the house, to whom he presented a complimentary bottle of inexpensive perfume. Upon determining his perfume to be more popular than his books, he decided that the manufacture of perfume might be more lucrative. He bottled toiletries under the name 'California Perfume Company' and a line of household products called 'Perfection.' In 1928 the name 'Avon' appeared on the label, and in 1939 the C.P.C. name was entirely removed from the product. The success of the company is attributed to the door-to-door sales approach and 'money back' guarantee offered by his first 'Depot Agent,' Mrs. P.F.E. Albee, known today as the 'Avon Lady.'

The company's containers are quite collectible today, especially the older, hard-to-find items. Advanced collectors seek 'go with' items labeled Goetting & Co., New York; Goetting's; or Savoi Et Cie, Paris. Such examples date from 1871 to 1896. The Goetting Company was purchased by D.H. McConnell; Savoi Et Cie was a line which they imported to sell through department stores. Also of special interest are packaging and advertising with the Ambrosia or Hinze Ambrosia Company label. This was a subsidiary company whose objective seems to have been to produce a line of face creams, etc., for sale through drugstores and other such commercial outlets. They operated in New York from about 1875 until 1954. Because very little is known about these companies and since only a few examples of their product containers and advertising material have been found, market values for such items have not yet been established. Other items sought by the collector include products marked Gertrude Recordon, Marvel Electric Silver Cleaner, Easy Day Automatic Clothes Washer, pre-1915 catalogs, and California Perfume Company 1909 and 1910 calendars.

There are hundreds of local Avon Collector Clubs throughout the world that also have C.P.C. collectors in their membership. If you are interested in joining, locating, or starting a new club, contact the National Association of Avon Collectors, Inc., listed in the Directory under Clubs, Newsletters, and Catalogs. Those wanting a national newsletter or price guides may contact Avon Times, listed in the same section. Inquiries concerning California Perfume Company items and the companies or items mentioned in the previous paragraphs should be directed toward our advisor, Dick Pardini, whose address is given under California. (Please send a large SASE and be sure to request clearly the information you are seeking; not interested in Avons, 'Perfection' marked C.P.C.'s, or Anniversary Keepsakes.)

Note: Our values are for items in mint condition. A very rare item or one in super mint condition might go for 10% more. Damage, wear, missing parts, etc., must be considered; items judged to be in only good to very good condition should be priced at up to 50% of listed values, with fair to good at 25% and excellent at 75%. Parts (labels, stoppers, caps, etc.) might be evaluated at 10% of these prices.

Am Ideal Talcum, tin, left profile of lady, 1911, M 110.00
Baby Powder, tin, CP trademk, 1905, M 120.00
Baby Powder, tin, Eureka trademk, 1898, M 130.00
Bandoline, 1908, 2-oz 100.00
Bay Rum, glass stopper, 126 Chambers St NY, 1898, 16-oz 210.00
Cut Glass Perfume, stopper, ribbon, 7-sided rnd label, 1915 ....230.00

Daphne perfume, emb glass, flat glass stopper, 1- & 2-oz, 1925 ..**140.00**
Dermol Massage Cream, milk glass, 1923, 1-lb **110.00**
Face Lotion, CP trademk, 1908 ....**115.00**
French Perfumes, 1900s, ¼-oz to 2-oz, ea **125.00**
Lait Virginal, 1900, 2-oz **150.00**
Lavender Salts, gr w/metal top, glass stopper, 1890s **250.00**
Massage Cream, stoopper, 1896 ....**160.00**
Mission Garden Talc set, 2 tins in silk-lined box, 1923, M **230.00**
Natoma Rolling Massage Cream, 1916 ....**150.00**
Natoma Rose Perfume, 1-oz w/atomizer, free sample label, '14, M ...**180.00**
Pyrox Tooth Powder, bl tin, M **80.00**
Shampoo Cream, man's face on lid, 1896, 4-oz, M **135.00**
Toothwash, brass stopper, 1921, 2-oz **100.00**
Trailing Arbutus Cream, tubes, 1925, M **40.00**
Traveler's Perfume, metal cover, glass stopper, 1900 ....**135.00**
Vernafleur Compact, SP, single & dbl, 1928, M **40.00**
Vernafleur Toilet Soap set, 3 bars in box, 1925, M **115.00**
Violet water, glass stopper, Eureka trademk, 1908, 8-oz **200.00**
Witch Hazel, 1896, 8-oz **115.00**

Calling Cards, Cases, and Receivers

The practice of announcing one's arrival with a calling card borne by the maid to the mistress of the house was a social grace of the Victorian era. Different messages (condolences, a personal visit, or a goodbye) were related by turning down one corner or another. The custom was forgotten by WWI. Fashionable ladies and gents carried their personally engraved cards in elaborate cases made of such materials as embossed silver, mother-of-pearl with intricate inlay, tortoise shell, and ivory. Card receivers held cards left by visitors who called while the mistress was out or 'not receiving.' Calling cards with fringe, die-cut flaps that cover the name, or an unusual decoration are worth about $3.00 to $4.00, while plain cards usually sell for around $1.00.

Cases

Silverplate with cathedral in relief, 3¼x2½", $95.00.

Abalone & pearl w/cameo, 4" **85.00**
Ivory, cvd birds & flowers, Oriental, 3¾" L **195.00**
Silver, floral eng, Gorham **185.00**
Sterling, Victorian w/eng, place for coins/powder/mirror **295.00**
Sterling silver, Japonesque taste, SJ Child Clyde NY, MIB **140.00**
Tortoise shell w/detailed emb florals, 4" **92.50**

Receivers

Brass, Nouveau nude on shell, Lo-Mar Works **70.00**
Bronze, ornate w/low ped, Victorian, Oudry, 12½" **360.00**
Pewter-like metal, lady w/flowing hair, 4½x7" **90.00**
Porc, bust of armoured knight, Derby, 3¾x5" **95.00**
SP, cherub figure supports holder overhead, Pairpoint, 6⅝" **200.00**
SP, child w/croquet mallet on base, gold washed, 10" **250.00**

SP, fluted edge, ornate ft & fretwork, 6x7" **75.00**
SP, tiny leaves on earth-like surface, Wilcox, 7" **40.00**

Camark

The Camden Art and Tile Company (commonly known as Camark) of Camden, Arkansas, was organized in the fall of 1926 by Samuel J. 'Jack' Carnes. Using clays from Arkansas, John Lessell, who had been hired as art director by Carnes, produced the initial lustre and iridescent Lessell wares for Camark ('CAM'den, 'ARK'ansas) before his death in December 1926. Before the plant opened in the spring of 1927, Carnes brought John's wife, Jeanne, and stepdaughter Billie to oversee the art department's manufacture of Le-Camark. Production by the Lessell family included variations of J.B. Owens' Soudanese and Opalesce and Weller's Marengo and Lamar. Camark's version of Marengo was called Old English. They also made wares identical to Weller's LaSa. Pieces made by John Lessell back in Ohio were signed 'Lessell,' while those made by Jeanne and Billie in Arkansas during 1927 were signed 'Le-Camark.' By 1928 Camark's production centered on traditional glazes. Drip glazes similar to Muncie Pottery were produced, in particular the green drip over pink. In the 1930s commercial castware with simple glossy and matt finishes became the primary focus and would continue so until Camark closed in the early 1960s. Between the 1960s and 1980s the company operated mainly as a retail store selling existing inventory, but some limited production occurred. In 1986 the company was purchased by the Ashcraft family of Camden, but no pottery has yet been made at the factory.

For further information we recommend *Collector's Encyclopedia of Camark Pottery, Volume I*, by David Edwin Gifford. Our advisor for this category is Tony Freyaldenhoven; he is listed under Arkansas.

Ashtray, frosted gr, leaf shape, 1st block letter, 7¼" **25.00**
Candlesticks, rose design, HP, 2-light, #269D, 5", pr **85.00**
Charger, bl & wht stipple, ruffled edge, 1st block letter, 13¼" ...**225.00**
Cup & saucer, petal design, #436, 2½" dia **25.00**
Figural cat, wall hanging, #058, 15" L **85.00**
Fishbowl holder, wistful cat, #900, 8½" **35.00**
Flower frog, dbl swan, #318, 8" **35.00**
Humidor, mirror blk, 1st block letter, brn sticker, 5½" **130.00**
Lamp base, brn stipple, brn sticker, 6" **170.00**
Pitcher, bird in hdl, #842, 8¾" **60.00**
Pitcher, brn stipple, ink stamp, 6¼" **225.00**
Pitcher, Morning Glory, HP, #800MG, 14" **275.00**
Pitcher, orange gr overflow, emb floral, unmk, 11" **130.00**
Planter, rose gr overflow, unmk, 13½x5¼x8½" **325.00**
Vase, Aztec red mottle, shouldered, sticker, 6" **190.00**
Vase, bulb bottom, fluted top, #974, 6½" **25.00**
Vase, gold crackle, stick neck w/flared base, unmk, 8½" **350.00**
Vase, iris (HP/bas-relief), dbl hdls, #803R, 7" **125.00**
Vase, Lessell, palm tree scenic, gold sticker, 7" **600.00**
Vase, mulberry, lt overflow, ring hdls, block letter mk, 6" **170.00**
Vase, Old English Rose, river & trees scenic, LeCamark, 8" **900.00**
Vase, olive gr overflow, brn sticker, 4½" **90.00**
Vase, swirl pattern, hdls, #783, 3½" **15.00**
Vase, yel crackle, bottle neck, sticker, 16¼" **1,200.00**
Vase, yel to gr to bl, shouldered, sticker, 8½" **225.00**
Vase, yel top w/runs over bl below, bulbous, unmk **100.00**
Vase, Delphinium Blue, stick neck, unmk, 5" **15.00**

Cambridge Glass

The Cambridge Glass Company began operations in 1901 in Cambridge, Ohio. Primarily they made crystal dinnerware and well-designed accessory pieces until the 1920s when they introduced the concept of color that was to become so popular on the American dinnerware market. Always maintaining high standards of quality and elegance, they produced many lines that became bestsellers; through the '20s and '30s they were recognized as the largest manufacturer of this type of glassware in the world.

Of the various marks the company used, the 'C in triangle' is the most familiar. Production stopped in 1958. For a more thorough study of the subject, we recommend *Colors in Cambridge Glass* by the National Cambridge Collectors, Inc.; their address may be found in the Directory under Clubs. *Glass Animals and Figural Flower Frogs of the Depression Era* by Lee Garmon and Dick Spencer is a wonderful source for an in-depth view of their particular aspect of glass collecting. They are both listed in the Directory under Illinois. See also Carnival Glass; Glass Animals. In the listings below items are crystal unless noted otherwise. Note: Internet sales have driven prices of nude stems downward; our values reflect this influence.

Apple Blossom, crystal, bowl, flat, 12" 35.00
Apple Blossom, crystal, butter dish, w/lid, 5½" 125.00
Apple Blossom, crystal, tray, sandwich; center hdl, 11" 25.00
Apple Blossom, pk or gr, bowl, pickle; 9" 40.00
Apple Blossom, pk or gr, mayonnaise, 4-ftd, w/ladle & liner 70.00
Apple Blossom, pk or gr, stem, cordial; #3130, 1-oz 145.00
Apple Blossom, pk or gr, vase, 2 styles, 8", ea 125.00
Apple Blossom, yel or amber, cup, AD 50.00
Apple Blossom, yel or amber, pitcher, 76-oz 250.00
Apple Blossom, yel or amber, plate, dinner; sq 65.00
Apple Blossom, yel or amber, stem, parfait; #1066 ....100.00

Candlelight, pitcher, #3400/141, $325.00.

Photo courtesy
Gene Florence

Candlelight, butter dish, #3400/52, 5" 150.00
Candlelight, creamer, #3900/41 ....20.00
Candlelight, decanter, #1321, ftd, 28-oz 175.00
Candlelight, shakers, #3900/1177, pr 95.00
Candlelight, stem, water; #3776, 9-oz 35.00
Candlelight, stem, wine; #3776, 3½-oz 55.00
Candlelight, vase, #6004, ftd, 8" 55.00
Caprice, bl or pk, ashtray, #216, 5" 25.00
Caprice, bl or pk, bowl, #49, 4-ftd, 8" 115.00
Caprice, bl or pk, bowl, salad; #80, cupped, 13" 175.00
Caprice, bl or pk, candlestick, #74, 3-light 125.00
Caprice, bl or pk, creamer, #41, lg 30.00
Caprice, bl or pk, plate, salad; #23, 7½" 27.50
Caprice, bl or pk, stem, water; #1, 10-oz 47.50
Caprice, bl or pk, tray, celery or relish; #124, 3-part, 8½" 45.00
Caprice, bl or pk, tumbler, #14, str sides, 9-oz 105.00
Caprice, bl or pk, vase, #252, blown, 4½" 160.00
Caprice, crystal, bottle, bitters; #186, 7-oz 175.00
Caprice, crystal, bowl, pickle; #102, 9" 25.00

Caprice, crystal, butter dish, #52, ¼-lb 295.00
Caprice, crystal, candlestick, #1577, 5-light 125.00
Caprice, crystal, coaster, #13, 3½" 15.00
Caprice, crystal, cruet, oil; #100, w/stopper, 5-oz 70.00
Caprice, crystal, plate, #30, 16" 50.00
Caprice, crystal, vase, #243, 8½" 110.00
Caprice, crystal, vase, #249, 3½" 70.00
Chantilly, bonbon, 2-hdld, ftd, 7" 17.50
Chantilly, bowl, tab hdld, 11" 35.00
Chantilly, butter dish, ¼-lb 225.00
Chantilly, candy box, w/lid, ftd 145.00
Chantilly, hat, sm 175.00
Chantilly, mustard jar, w/lid 75.00
Chantilly, plate, service; 4-ftd, 12" 30.00
Chantilly, stem, cocktail; #3625, 3-oz 27.50
Chantilly, stem, cordial; #3779, 1-oz 62.50
Chantilly, stem, wine; #3600, 2½" 32.00
Chantilly, stem, wine; #3775, 2½" 32.00
Chantilly, tumbler, tea; #3625, ftd, 12-oz 24.00
Chantilly, vase, globular, 5" 35.00
Cleo, bl, bowl, fruit; 5½" 30.00
Cleo, bl, bowl, vegetable; oval, Decagon shape, 9½" 100.00
Cleo, bl, platter, 12" 160.00
Cleo, bl, stem, wine; #3077, 3½-oz 95.00
Cleo, colors other than bl, candlestick, 3-light 70.00
Cleo, colors other than bl, compote, 4-ftd, 6" 35.00
Cleo, colors other than bl, decanter, w/stopper 235.00
Cleo, colors other than bl, pitcher, #3077, w/lid, 63-oz 275.00
Cleo, colors other than bl, server, center hdl, 12" 35.00
Cleo, colors other than bl, tray, serving; hdld, 12" 155.00
Cleo, colors other than bl, vase, 5½" 75.00
Cleo, colors other than bl, wafer tray 225.00
Crown Tuscan, basket, novelty; #1506/1, 4" 70.00
Crown Tuscan, cigarette holder, #1337, ebony ashtray ft 225.00
Crown Tuscan, epergne vase, #2355 ....90.00
Crown Tuscan, figurine, mannequin head, 18" 3,500.00
Crown Tuscan, flower block, #2899, 3" 80.00
Crown Tuscan, jug, Doulton shape, #3400/152, 76-oz 1,000.00
Crown Tuscan, vase, #1253, paper label, 12" 320.00
Crown Tuscan, vase, #1283, ebony ft 180.00
Decagon, pastel colors, bowl, berry; 10" 15.00
Decagon, pastel colors, bowl, cranberry; belled, 3½" 17.50
Decagon, pastel colors, bowl, vegetable; rnd, 9" 20.00
Decagon, pastel colors, compote, 5¾" 15.00
Decagon, pastel colors, cup 6.00
Decagon, pastel colors, plate, grill; 10" 12.00
Decagon, pastel colors, plate, 7½" 4.00
Decagon, pastel colors, stem, water; 9-oz 17.00
Decagon, pastel colors, tray, celery; 11" 12.00
Decagon, pastel colors, tumbler, ftd, 12-oz 20.00
Decagon, red or bl, bowl, cereal; flat rim, 6" 25.00
Decagon, red or bl, bowl, cream soup; w/liner 30.00
Decagon, red or bl, ice bucket 60.00
Decagon, red or bl, mayonnaise, w/liner & ladle 50.00
Decagon, red or bl, relish tray, 6 inserts 125.00
Decagon, red or bl, saucer 3.00
Decagon, red or bl, tray, service; oval, 12" 30.00
Diane, bonbon, 2-hdl, 5¼" 20.00
Diane, bowl, celery or relish; 3-part, 9" 25.00
Diane, bowl, finger; #3106, w/liner 37.50
Diane, bowl, flared, ftd, 12" 42.00
Diane, cabinet flask 250.00
Diane, cocktail shaker, glass top 150.00
Diane, pitcher, ball shape 150.00

Diane, plate, bonbon; 2-hdl, ftd, 8" 11.00
Diane, plate, torte; 14" 45.00
Diane, stem, cocktail; #1066, 3-oz 16.00
Diane, stem, cocktail; #3122, 3-oz 14.00
Diane, stem, water; #1066, 11-oz 25.00
Diane, sugar bowl, scroll hdl, #3400 ....14.00
Diane, tumbler, #1066, 3-oz 22.00
Diane, tumbler, #3122, 2½-oz 30.00
Diane, tumbler, juice; ftd, 5-oz 30.00
Diane, tumbler, tea; #1066, 12-oz 22.00
Diane, tumbler, 13-oz 32.00
Diane, vase, flower; 11" 65.00
Diane, vase, flower; 13" 110.00
Diane, vase, globe shape, 5" 35.00
Elaine, bowl, celery/relish; 3-part, 9" 35.00
Elaine, bowl, celery/relish; 5-part, 12" 37.50
Elaine, bowl, nut; 4-ftd, ind, 3" 50.00
Elaine, cocktail icer, 2-pc 60.00
Elaine, hat, 9" 295.00
Elaine, plate, dinner; 10½" 65.00
Elaine, stem, cordial; #1402, 1-oz 60.00
Elaine, stem, cordial; #3104, 1-oz 150.00
Elaine, stem, cordial; #3500, 1-oz 60.00
Elaine, stem, goblet; #3104, 9-oz 125.00
Elaine, tumbler, tea; #1402, 12-oz 24.00
Elaine, vase, ftd, 8" 55.00
Gloria, crystal, bowl, cereal; rnd, 6" 24.00
Gloria, crystal, bowl, oval, 4-ftd, 12" 35.00
Gloria, crystal, creamer, ftd 12.00
Gloria, crystal, pitcher, ball shape, 80-oz 160.00
Gloria, crystal, plate, dinner; sq 60.00
Gloria, crystal, stem, claret; #3035, 4½-oz 30.00
Gloria, crystal, stem, cordial; #3120, 1-oz 135.00
Gloria, crystal, stem, wine; #3130, 2½-oz 20.00
Gloria, crystal, sugar shaker, w/glass top 295.00
Gloria, crystal, tumbler, #3120, ftd, 10-oz 12.00
Gloria, crystal, vase, neck indent, 11" 75.00
Gloria, gr, pk or yel, bowl, nut; 4-ftd, ind, 3" 70.00
Gloria, gr, pk or yel, bowl, vegetable; 2-hdl, 9½" 90.00
Gloria, gr, pk or yel, butter dish, w/lid, 2-hdl 295.00

Gloria, pink, creamer, tall, footed, $25.00.

Gloria, gr, pk or yel, icer, w/inserts 90.00
Gloria, gr, pk or yel, plate, bread & butter; 6" 9.00
Gloria, gr, pk or yel, saucer, sq 3.00
Gloria, gr, pk or yel, vase, sqd top, 12" 130.00
Imperial Hunt Scene, colors, bowl, 3-part, 8½" 65.00
Imperial Hunt Scene, colors, decanter 235.00
Imperial Hunt Scene, colors, pitcher, #3085, w/lid, 63-oz 295.00
Imperial Hunt Scene, colors, stem, cordial; #3085, 1-oz 175.00
Imperial Hunt Scene, colors, stem, sherbet; #3085, low, 6-oz 22.50
Imperial Hunt Scene, colors, tumbler, #3085, ftd, 12-oz, 5⅜" 40.00
Imperial Hunt Scene, crystal, creamer, ftd 15.00

Imperial Hunt Scene, crystal, stem, #1402, 18-oz 60.00
Imperial Hunt Scene, crystal, stem, tomato; #1402, 6-oz 40.00
Imperial Hunt Scene, crystal, tumbler, #1402, flat, 5-oz 20.00
Mt Vernon, amber or crystal, ashtray, #71, oval, 6x4½" 12.00
Mt Vernon, amber or crystal, bottle, toilet; #18, sq, 7-oz 65.00
Mt Vernon, amber or crystal, bowl, #121, flared, 12½" 35.00
Mt Vernon, amber or crystal, bowl, #136, oval, 4-ftd, 11" 27.50
Mt Vernon, amber or crystal, butter tub, #73, w/lid 65.00
Mt Vernon, amber or crystal, candlestick, #35, 8" 25.00
Mt Vernon, amber or crystal, cigarette holder, #66 ....15.00
Mt Vernon, amber or crystal, compote, #96, belled, 6½" 22.50
Mt Vernon, amber or crystal, decanter, #52, w/stopper, 40-oz 70.00
Mt Vernon, amber or crystal, honey jar, #74, w/lid 32.00
Mt Vernon, amber or crystal, pitcher, #13, 66-oz 85.00
Mt Vernon, amber or crystal, plate, dinner; #40, 10½" 30.00
Mt Vernon, amber or crystal, relish, #80, 2-part, 12" 30.00
Mt Vernon, amber or crystal, stein, #84, 14-oz 30.00
Mt Vernon, amber or crystal, stem, water; #1, 10-oz 15.00
Mt Vernon, amber or crystal, tumbler, #59, tall, 14-oz 22.00
Mt Vernon, amber or crystal, vase, #54, ftd, 7" 35.00
Mt Vernon, amber or crystal, whiskey tumbler, #55, 2-oz 10.00
Nude stem, amber, bud vase 800.00
Nude stem, amber, wine 300.00
Nude stem, amethyst, brandy 90.00
Nude stem, amethyst, mint dish 900.00
Nude stem, carmen, champagne 195.00
Nude stem, carmen, cigarette box, tall 650.00
Nude stem, carmen, claret 225.00
Nude stem, carmen, comport, short 495.00
Nude stem, carmen, comport, tall 595.00
Nude stem, carmen, cordial 500.00
Nude stem, carmen, goblet, banquet 600.00
Nude stem, carmen, goblet, table 250.00
Nude stem, cobalt, ashtray 550.00
Nude stem, cobalt, bud vase 1,250.00
Nude stem, cobalt, cordial 950.00
Nude stem, cobalt, ivy ball 550.00
Nude stem, cobalt, sauterne 700.00
Nude stem, cobalt, tulip cocktail 650.00
Nude stem, cobalt, V cocktail 650.00
Nude stem, cobalt, wine 325.00
Nude stem, crystal, cigarette holder w/ashtray ft 550.00
Nude stem, crystal, cordial 350.00
Nude stem, crystal, mint dish 800.00
Nude stem, crystal/amber, cocktail 145.00
Nude stem, crystal/blk, cocktail 125.00
Nude stem, dk gr, ashtray 225.00
Nude stem, Heatherbloom, champagne 650.00
Nude stem, Moonstone, candlestick, w/bobeche 900.00
Nude stem, Moonstone, comport, tall 400.00
Nude stem, pk, ashtray 750.00
Nude stem, pk, brandy 180.00
Nude stem, pk, champagne 500.00
Nude stem, pk, comport, short 700.00
Nude stem, pk, ivy ball 500.00
Nude stem, royal bl, goblet, banquet 500.00
Nude stem, smoke, cocktail, tall 560.00
Nude stem, smoke/crackle, goblet, table 750.00
Nude stem, yel, brandy 90.00
Nude stem, yel, hoch 600.00
Portia, basket, 1-hdl, 7" 225.00
Portia, bowl, celery or relish; 5-part, 12" 37.50
Portia, bowl, flared, 4-ftd, 10" 40.00
Portia, candlestick, 5" 22.00

Portia, cocktail shaker, w/stopper **95.00**
Portia, stem, brandy; #3126, low ft, 4-oz **40.00**
Portia, stem, claret; #3121, 4½-oz **60.00**
Portia, stem, cordial; #3121, 1-oz **60.00**
Portia, stem, cordial; #3130, 1-oz **60.00**
Portia, stem, wine; #3124, 3-oz **30.00**
Rosalie, amber, bowl, Decagon shape, 12" **80.00**
Rosalie, amber, bowl, 3-part, w/lid, 3⅝" **40.00**
Rosalie, amber, bowl, 3-part, w/lid, 8½" **40.00**
Rosalie, amber, creamer, ftd **12.00**
Rosalie, amber, marmalade **85.00**
Rosalie, amber, plate, dinner; 9½" **35.00**
Rosalie, amber, stem, cordial; #3077, 1-oz **60.00**
Rosalie, amber, tumbler, #3077, ftd, 2½-oz **25.00**
Rosalie, amber, wafer tray **75.00**
Rosalie, bl, pk or gr, bowl, basket; 2-hdl, 7" **30.00**
Rosalie, bl, pk or gr, bowl, finger; w/liner **40.00**
Rosalie, bl, pk or gr, bowl, flanged, oval, 15" **95.00**
Rosalie, bl, pk or gr, bowl, 11" **45.00**
Rosalie, bl, pk or gr, compote, 2-hdl, 5½" **80.00**
Rosalie, bl, pk or gr, ice bucket or pail **95.00**
Rosalie, bl, pk or gr, pitcher, #955, 62-oz **225.00**
Rosalie, bl, pk or gr, relish, 2-part, 11" **35.00**
Rosalie, bl, pk or gr, stem, goblet; #801, 10-oz **30.00**
Rosalie, bl, pk or gr, tumbler, #3077, ftd, 12-oz **35.00**
Rose Point, ashtray, #3500/129, sq, 3¼" **55.00**
Rose Point, ashtray, #3500/131, oval, 4½" **65.00**
Rose Point, bell, dinner; #3121 ....**150.00**
Rose Point, bowl, #1398, 13" **115.00**
Rose Point, bowl, #3500/28, 2-hdl, 10" **77.50**
Rose Point, bowl, #500/16, ftd, 11" **110.00**
Rose Point, bowl, cereal; #3400/10, 6" **85.00**
Rose Point, bowl, fruit; #1534, blown, 5" **80.00**
Rose Point, bowl, rimmed soup; #361, 8½" **250.00**
Rose Point, bowl, salad; Pristine #427, 10" **145.00**
Rose Point, butter dish, w/lid, rnd, #506 ....**185.00**
Rose Point, candelabrum, #3500/94, 2-light **100.00**
Rose Point, candlestick, #3121, 7" **75.00**
Rose Point, candlestick, #3500/74, ram's head, 4" **110.00**
Rose Point, candlestick, #3900/72, 2-light, 6" **45.00**
Rose Point, candlestick, Pristine #500 ....**135.00**
Rose Point, candy box, #3400/9, w/lid, 7" **145.00**
Rose Point, cocktail shaker, #97, metal top, 12-oz **310.00**
Rose Point, compote, #3500/36, 6" **125.00**
Rose Point, creamer, #3900/41, ftd **20.00**
Rose Point, decanter, #1320, ftd, 14-oz **425.00**
Rose Point, hat, #1701, 9" **595.00**
Rose Point, ice bucket, #1402/52 ....**210.00**
Rose Point, marmalade, #147, 8-oz **155.00**
Rose Point, pitcher, #3900/116, ball shape, 80-oz **225.00**
Rose Point, pitcher, #70, w/ice lip, 20-oz **235.00**
Rose Point, plate, dinner; #3900/24, 10½" **140.00**
Rose Point, plate, salad; #3900/22, 8" **20.00**
Rose Point, plate, torte; #3400/65, 14" **130.00**
Rose Point, saucer, AD; #3400/69 ....**55.00**
Rose Point, stem, claret; #3121, 4½-oz **90.00**
Rose Point, stem, cordial; #7966, plain ft, 1-oz **135.00**
Rose Point, stem, sherry; #3106, 2-oz **45.00**
Rose Point, sugar bowl, #3400/16, ftd **35.00**
Rose Point, tray, #3500/67, rnd, 12" **165.00**
Rose Point, tray, celery/relish; #3900/120, 5-part, 12" **70.00**
Rose Point, tray, relish; #3500/113, hdld, 4-part, 15" **195.00**
Rose Point, tray, relish; #3500/85, 2-hdl, 10" **70.00**
Rose Point, tumbler, #3000, cone shape, ftd, 3½-oz **95.00**

Rose Point, tumbler, #3400/92, 2½-oz **110.00**
Rose Point, tumbler, #3900/117, 5-oz **50.00**
Rose Point, vase, #1301, ftd, 10" **75.00**
Rose Point, vase, #1309, 5" **70.00**
Rose Point, vase, #1336, 18" **2,000.00**
Rose Point, vase, #3500/44, ftd, 8" **125.00**

Tally Ho, mug, ruby, $40.00.

Valencia, ashtray, #3500/124, 4½" dia **18.00**
Valencia, bowl, #1402/88, 2-hdl, divided, 6" **20.00**
Valencia, bowl, finger; #1402/100, w/liner **35.00**
Valencia, creamer, #3500/14 ....**17.00**
Valencia, honey dish, #3500/139, w/lid **140.00**
Valencia, ice pail, #1402/52 ....**75.00**
Valencia, plate, breakfast; #3500/5, 8½" **12.00**
Valencia, stem, claret; #1402 ....**45.00**
Valencia, stem, claret; #3500, 4½-oz **45.00**
Valencia, sugar basket, #3500/13 ....**95.00**
Valencia, tray, relish; #3500/67, 6-pc, 12" **125.00**
Valencia, tumbler, #3500, ftd, 10-oz **16.00**
Wildflower, bowl, celery/relish; 5-part, 12" **35.00**
Wildflower, bowl, relish; #3900/123, 7" **18.00**
Wildflower, compote, #3900/136, 5½" **35.00**
Wildflower, hat, #1703, 6" **225.00**
Wildflower, plate, #3400/176, 7½" **10.00**
Wildflower, plate, torte; #3900/167, 14" **45.00**
Wildflower, stem, cordial; #3121, 1-oz **57.50**
Wildflower, stem, parfait; #3121, low, 5-oz **35.00**
Wildflower, tumbler, water; #3121, 10-oz **22.00**
Wildflower, vase, flower; #278, ftd, 11" **60.00**

Cameo

    The technique of glass carving was perfected 2,000 years ago in ancient Rome and Greece. The most famous ancient example of cameo glass is the Portland Vase, made in Rome around 100 A.D. After glass blowing was developed, glassmakers devised a method of casing several layers of colored glass together, often with a light color over a darker base, to enhance the design. Skilled carvers meticulously worked the fragile glass to produce incredibly detailed classic scenes. In the 18th and 19th centuries Oriental and Near-Eastern artisans used the technique more extensively. European glassmakers revived the art during the last quarter of the 19th century. In France, Galle and Daum produced some of the finest examples of modern times, using as many as five layers of glass to develop their designs, usually scenics or subjects from nature. Hand carving was supplemented by the use of a copper engraving wheel, and acid was used to cut away the layers more quickly.

    In England, Thomas Webb and Sons used modern machinery and technology to eliminate many of the problems that plagued early glass carvers. One of Webb's best-known carvers, George Woodall, is credited with producing over four hundred pieces. Woodall was trained in the art by John Northwood, famous for reproducing the Portland Vase in

1876. Cameo glass became very popular during the late 1800s, resulting in a market that demanded more than could be produced, due to the tedious procedures involved. In an effort to produce greater volume, less elaborate pieces with simple floral or geometric designs were made, often entirely acid etched with little or no hand carving. While very little cameo glass was made in this country, a few pieces were produced by James Gillinder, Tiffany, and the Libbey Glass Company. Though some continued to be made on a limited scale into the 1900s (and until about 1920 in France), for the most part, inferior products caused a marked reduction in its manufacture by the turn of the century. Beware of new 'French' cameo glass from Romania and Taiwan. Some of it is very good and may be signed with 'old' signatures. Watch for stencil-cut designs that are 'disconnected' and segmented. Know your dealer! Our advisor for this category is Don Williams; he is listed in the Directory under Missouri. See also specific manufactures.

English

Bowl, roses, rainbow on wht, angle body, ruffled rim, 6x8" 1,295.00
Perfume, lay-down; floral/bee, wht on med bl, silver cap, 4" ...2,150.00
Perfume, lay-down; floral/bk: vine, wht on olive, 2½" 2,500.00
Perfume, scent; seashells/ferns, wht on med aqua, 3½x3½" 1,450.00
Vase, bamboo stalks/fern fronds, wht on citron, 5½" 1,250.00
Vase, berries/bk: butterfly, wht on citron, stick neck, 9½" 700.00
Vase, campanula blossoms/bk: violet, wht on citron, 4½" 725.00
Vase, floral/bk: butterfly, wht on pk, ovoid w/can neck, 8" 1,650.00
Vase, fuchsias/buds, bk: butterfly, wht on red, 6" 2,100.00
Vase, ivy vines, wht on citron, stick neck, 3½" 1,000.00
Vase, leafy branch w/2 flowers & buds, wht on red, 6½" 2,000.00
Vase, morning glories, wheel-cvd detail, wht on citron, 9" 2,000.00
Vase, trumpet flowers, decorative rim, wht on citron, 3¾" 400.00
Vase, 2 acorns on leafy branch, wht on citron, 5½" 700.00
Vase, 4 birds/florals, wht on red, classic shape, 5" 3,500.00

French

Bowl, tropical island, gr/rose w/frost sky, Arsall, 6x5" 700.00
Cruet, florals/netting, ruby on frost w/gold, St Louis, 9" 400.00
Lamp, floral on 12" shade/base, dk gr on citron, Lamartine 2,500.00
Perfume warmer, floral, wine on orange, Degue, 5½" 600.00
Sconce, persimmons/leaves, pk on clear frost, 6x12" 600.00
Shade, floral sprays, lime/brn on peach, dome shape, 4x7" 450.00

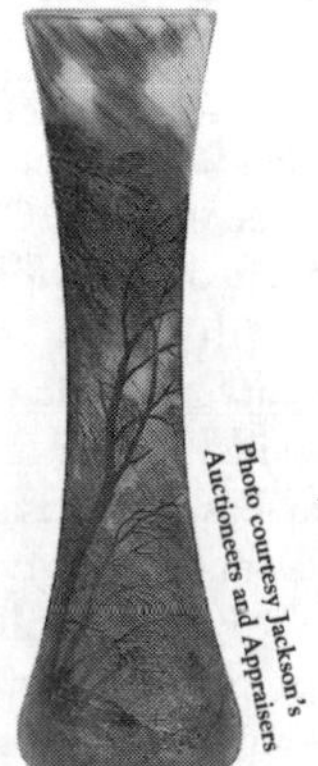

Photo courtesy Jackson's Auctioneers and Appraisers

Vase, rain scene, dark brown and rust on yellow, Michel, 12", $1,100.00.

Vase, bearded iris, orange on pk, Arsall, 16x7" 1,200.00
Vase, boats/island/hills, olive on citron, Michel, ftd, 7" 450.00
Vase, exotic flowers, maroon on pk, Andre Delatte, 8x7" 690.00
Vase, floral, orange on frost, wide ftd base, Croismare, 4¾" 325.00
Vase, floral/vines, bl/rust, ormolu garlands etc, Abel Combe, 9" ..250.00
Vase, fuchsia/s, burgundy on citron, Arsall, 12x5" 750.00
Vase, grapes, amber on opal/amber, fire polished, stick neck, 9" .250.00
Vase, hops/foiliage, med gr on citron, stick neck, Roger, 11" 450.00
Vase, irises, ruby on citron, Cristallerie de Pantin, 8" 1,250.00
Vase, lav/deep bl irid w/floral, dimpled dbl gourd, 5½x6" 1,100.00
Vase, leaves/florals, lt bl on frost, Pantin, 3¾x6½" 1,250.00
Vase, morning glories, D Christian Meistnthal/Lothringen, 6" .2,750.00
Vase, raspberries, gr on opal mottle, 3-fold rim, Kralik, 11" 650.00
Vase, sailboats, maroon on yel, Michel, 7½x4½" 950.00
Vase, sailboats/branches, blk on gr, Michel, 6x3" 575.00
Vase, trumpet flowers, dk bl on gr, ftd, Roger, 9" 775.00
Vase, violets on frost, Cristallerie de Pantin, 3x6½" 350.00

Candle Holders

The earliest type of candlestick, called a pricket, was constructed with a sharp point on which the candle was impaled. The socket type, first used in the 16th century, consisted of the socket and a short stem with a wide drip pan and base. These were made from sheets of silver or other metal; not until late in the 17th century were candlesticks made by casting. By the 1700s, styles began to vary from the traditional fluted column or baluster form and became more elaborate. A Rococo style with scrolls, shellwork, and naturalistic leaves and flowers came into vogue that afforded the individual silversmith the opportunity to exhibit his skill and artistry. The last half of the 18th century brought a return to fluted columns with neoclassic motifs. Because they were made of thin sheet silver, weighted bases were used to add stability. The Rococo styles of the Regency period were heavily encrusted with applied figures and flowers. Candelabra with six to nine branches became popular. By the Victorian era when lamps came into general use, there was less innovation and more adaptation of the earlier styles. See also Silver; Tinware; specific manufacturers.

Key: QA — Queen Anne

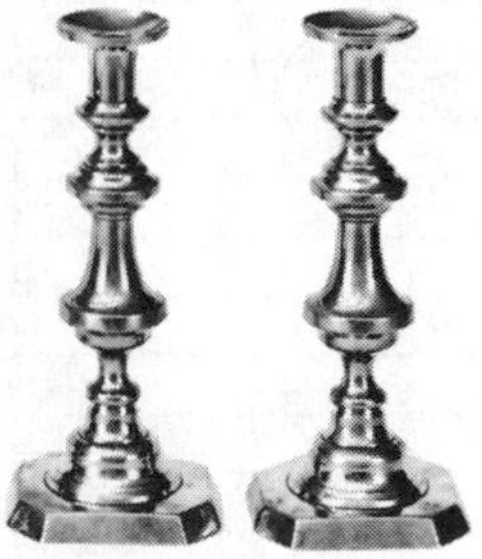

Brass, English, ca 1820 – 40, 10", outstanding condition, $275.00 for the pair.

Brass, Beehive & Dmn, sq base, w/ejector, 10¾", pr 140.00
Brass, Capstan, rnd base, wide drip pan, 5⅜x4⅜" 150.00
Brass, QA, conforming shaped bobeche, 1740, rpr, 8", pr 1,035.00
Brass, QA, English, 1750s, 9" 345.00
Brass, QA, old solder rprs, 7½", pr 275.00
Brass, QA, scalloped ft, rpr, 8¼" 165.00
Brass, QA w/petal base, stamped Joseph Wood, 7⅜", pr 3,750.00
Brass, QA w/petal base & pushup, 7⅝" 900.00
Brass, 3 paw ft, lg pan & spike, 12½", pr 115.00
Bronze, Fr Regency, cast cups, marble columns, 1840s, 12", pr ...465.00
Bronze, QA, scalloped detail, 8¼", pr 300.00
Bronze d'ore, fluted urn, putti masks & drape decor, 17", pr 1,500.00
Candelabra, Fr Emp gilt & patinated bronze, 3-light, 21", pr ..6,000.00
Candelabrum, Louis XV bronze d'ore, 6-light, 1850s, 36x15" .2,100.00
Glass, apple gr opaque, hexagonal w/wafer, early, 9" 2,000.00

Glass, clambroth dolphin base/bl opaque petal socket, 9½", pr ..**2,200.00**
Glass, clambroth w/bl opaque socket, acanthus, 11" **1,045.00**
Glass, clambroth w/bl opaque socket, hexagonal, 9½", pr, NM **1,265.00**
Glass, dk bl opaque, dolphin/dome base, att Bakewell Pears, 6", pr ..**900.00**
Glass, lav & clambroth, columnar w/petal socket, 9¼" **550.00**
Hogscraper, brass/sheet iron, w/mechanism mk Shaw, 7½x4" **500.00**
Hogscraper, sheet iron, ejector mechanism sgn Bill, 18½", pr .**2,200.00**
Hogscraper, sheet iron, w/ejector/drip catcher, 5¾", pr **160.00**
Wrought iron, loom light, w/candle socket & trammel, 18" **415.00**
Wrought iron, sticking tommy, 12½" **275.00**

Candlewick

Candlewick crystal was made by the Imperial Glass Corporation, a division of Lenox Inc., Bellaire, Ohio. It was introduced in 1936, and though never marked except for paper labels, it is easily recognized by the beaded crystal rims, stems, and handles inspired by the tufted needlework called candlewicking, practiced by our pioneer women. During its production, more than 741 items were designed and produced. In September 1982 when Imperial closed its doors, thirty-four pieces were still being made.

Identification numbers and mold numbers used by the company help collectors recognize the various styles and shapes. Most of the pieces are from the #400 series, though other series numbers were also used. Stemware was made in eight styles — five from the #400 series made from 1941 to 1962, one from #3400 series made in 1937, another from #3800 series made in 1941, and the eighth style from the #4000 series made in 1947. In the listings that follow, some #400 items lack the mold number because that information was not found in the company files.

A few pieces have been made in color or with a gold wash. At least two lines, Valley Lily and Floral, utilized Candlewick with floral patterns cut into the crystal. These are scarce today. Other rare items include gifts such as the desk calendar made by the company for its employees and customers; the dresser set comprised of a mirror, clock, puff jar, and cologne; and the chip and dip set.

Ashtray, #400/133, rnd, 5" **8.00**
Ashtray, #400/134/1, oblong, 4½" **6.00**
Ashtray, #400/172, heart shape, 4½" **10.00**
Ashtray, #400/174, heart shape, 6½" **15.00**
Ashtray, #400/650, 3-pc nesting set, sq **110.00**
Ashtray, #400/653, sq, 5¾" **40.00**

Basket, beaded rim, rare, 6½", $275.00.

Photo courtesy
Gene Florence

Basket, #400/40/0, hdl, 6½" **30.00**
Bell, #400/108, 5" **75.00**
Bowl, #400/106B, belled, 12" **90.00**
Bowl, #400/113A, hdls, deep, 10" **115.00**
Bowl, #400/125A, oval, w/partition, 11" **265.00**

Bowl, #400/128B, punch base, belled, 10" **70.00**
Bowl, #400/13F, 10" **45.00**
Bowl, #400/17F, shallow, 12" **47.50**
Bowl, #400/181, hdls, 6½" **30.00**
Bowl, #400/183, 3-ftd, 6" **60.00**
Bowl, #400/42B, 2-hdl, 4¾" dia **12.00**
Bowl, #400/49H, heart shape, w/hdl, 5" **20.00**
Bowl, #400/63B, belled, 10½" **60.00**
Bowl, #400/72B, 2-hdl, 8½" **22.00**
Bowl, #400/74SC, fancy crimped edge, 4-ftd, sq, 9" **70.00**
Bowl, centerpiece; #400/13B, flared, 11" **55.00**
Bowl, cottage cheese; #400/85, 6" **25.00**
Bowl, finger; #3400, ftd **30.00**
Bowl, float; #400/101, 1½x13" **65.00**
Bowl, fruit; #400/103F, bead stem, 10" **175.00**
Bowl, jelly; #400/59, w/lid, 5½" **60.00**
Bowl, mint; #400/51F, w/hdl, 6" **20.00**
Bowl, pickle/celery; #400/57, 7½" **27.50**
Bowl, relish; #400/208, 3-ftd, 3-part, 10" **90.00**
Bowl, relish; #400/234, divided, sq, 7" **125.00**
Bowl, relish; #400/268, 2-part, 8" **20.00**
Bowl, relish; #400/55, 4-part, 8½" **22.00**
Bowl, relish; #400/60, 7" **25.00**
Bowl, salad; #400/75B, 10½" **40.00**
Butter dish, #400/276, w/lid, no beads, California **125.00**
Cake stand, #400/67D, low ft, 10" **52.50**
Candle holder, #400/115, 3-way, beaded base **110.00**
Candle holder, #400/175, 3-bead stem, tall, 6½" **95.00**
Candle holder, #400/224, 2-bead stem, 5½" **90.00**
Candle holder, #400/66C, petaled rim, 2-bead base, 4½" **60.00**
Candle holder, #400/79R, rolled edge, 3½" **12.00**
Candle holder, #400/86, mushroom shape **35.00**
Candy box, #400/140, beaded, ftd, w/lid **250.00**
Candy box, #400/245, sq w/rnd lid, 6½" **195.00**
Coaster, #400/78, 4" **7.00**
Compote, #400/220, 3-bead stem, 5" **70.00**
Compote, fruit; #400/103C, crimped, ftd, 10" **150.00**
Creamer, #400/30, bead hdl, 6-oz **8.00**
Cruet, oil; #400/164, 4-oz **55.00**
Cruet, oil; #400/279, bulbous bottom, 6-oz **80.00**
Cup, AD; #400/77 ....**17.50**
Decanter, cordial; #400/82/2, w/stopper, 15-oz **295.00**
Hurricane lamp, #400/76, candle base, 2-pc, w/hdl **150.00**
Icer, seafood/fruit cocktail; #400/53/3, 2-pc **95.00**
Knife, butter; #4000 ....**295.00**
Mirror, standing, rnd, 4½" **110.00**
Nappy, #400/74B, 4-ftd, 8½" **65.00**
Pitcher, #400/19, low ft, 16-oz **210.00**
Pitcher, #400/419, plain, 40-oz **40.00**
Plate, #400/145D, hdls, 12" **27.50**
Plate, #400/42D, hdls, 5½" **10.00**
Plate, #400/52C, crimped, hdls, 6¾" **25.00**
Plate, #400/72E, sides upturned, hdls, 10" **22.50**
Plate, salad; #400/5D, 8½" **10.00**
Plate, service; #400/92D, 14" **30.00**
Plate, serving; #400/92V, cupped edge, 13½" **40.00**
Punch ladle, #400/91 ....**30.00**
Sauce boat liner, #400/169 ....**40.00**
Saucer, AD; #400/77AD **5.00**
Shakers, #400/190, beaded base, ftd, pr **47.50**
Stem, brandy; #3800 ....**27.50**
Stem, claret; #3800 ....**30.00**
Stem, cordial; #3400, 1-oz **37.50**
Stem, goblet; #4000, 11-oz **30.00**

Stem, sherbet; #3400, low, 5-oz	**10.00**
Stem, sherbet; #400/190, tall, 5-oz	**15.00**
Sugar bowl, #400/31, plain ft	**6.50**
Tray, lemon; #400/221, center hdl, 5½"	**30.00**
Tray, party; #400/68D, center hdl, 11½"	**30.00**
Tumbler, juice; #3400, ftd, 5-oz	**17.50**
Tumbler, juice; #400/18, 5-oz	**37.50**
Tumbler, old-fashion; #400/19, 7-oz	**32.50**
Tumbler, tea; #400/18, 12-oz	**47.50**
Tumbler, water; #3800, 9-oz	**25.00**
Vase, #400/143C, crimped rim, flat, 8"	**70.00**
Vase, #400/193, ftd, 10"	**165.00**
Vase, #400/87R, rolled rim w/beaded hdl	**35.00**
Vase, bud; #400/107, beaded ft, 5¾"	**55.00**
Vase, fan; #400/287F, 6"	**30.00**

Candy Containers

Figural glass candy containers were first created in 1876 when ingenious candy manufacturers began to use them to package their products. Two of the first containers, the Liberty Bell and Independence Hall, were distributed for our country's centennial celebration. Children found these toys appealing, and an industry was launched that lasted into the mid-1960s.

Figural candy containers include animals, comic characters, guns, telephones, transportation vehicles, household appliances, and many other intriguing designs. The oldest (those made prior to 1920) were usually hand painted and often contained extra metal parts in addition to the metal strip or screw closures. During the 1950s these metal parts were replaced with plastic, a practice that continued until candy containers met their demise in the 1960s. While predominately clear, they are found in nearly all colors of glass including milk glass, green, amber, pink, emerald, cobalt, ruby flashed, and light blue. Usually the color was intentional, but leftover glass was used as well and resulted in unplanned colors. Various examples are found in light or ice blue, and new finds are always being discovered. Production of the glass portion of candy containers was centered around the western Pennsylvania city of Jeannette. Major producers include Westmoreland Glass, West Bros., Victory Glass, J.H. Millstein, J.C. Crosetti, L.E. Smith, Jack Stough, and T.H. Stough. While 90% of all glass candies were made in the Jeannette area, other companies such as Eagle Glass, Play Toy, and Geo. Borgfeldt Co. have a few to their credit as well.

Buyer beware! Many candy containers have been reproduced. Some, including the Camera and the Rabbit Pushing Wheelbarrow, come already painted from distributors. Others may have a slick or oily feel to the touch. The following list may also alert you to possible reproductions:

Amber Pistol, L #144 (first sold full in the 1970s, not listed in E&A)

Auto, D&P #173/E&A #33/L #377

Auto, D&P #163/E&A #60/L #356

Black and White Taxi, D&P #182/L #353 (A number of metal roofs have appeared. They are different from originals because the white section is more silvery in color than the original cream. These closures are put on original bases and often priced for hundreds of dollars.)

Camera, D&P #419/E&A #121/L #238 (original says 'Pat Apld For' on bottom, reproduction says 'B. Shakman' or is ground off)

Carpet Sweeper, D&P 296/E&A #133/L #243 (currently being sold with no metal parts)

Carpet Sweeper, E&A #132/L #242 (currently being sold with no metal parts)

Charlie Chaplin, D&P 195/E&A #137/L #83 (original has 'Geo. Borgfeldt' on base; reproduction comes in pink and blue)

Chicken on Nest, D&P #10/E&A #149/L #12

Display Case, D&P #422/E&A #177/L #246 (original should be painted silver and brown)

Dog, D&P #21/E&A #180/L #24 (clear and cobalt)

Drum Mug, D&P #431/E&A #543/L #255

Happifats on Drum, D&P #199/E&A #208/L #89 (no notches on repro for closure to hook into)

Fire Engine, D&P 258/E&A #213/L #386 (repros in green and blue glass)

Independence Hall, D&P #130/E&A #342/L #76 (original is rectangular; repro has offset base with red felt-lined closure)

Jackie Coogan, D&P #202/E&A #345/L #90 (marked inside 'B')

Kewpie, D&P #204/E&A #349/L #91 (must have Geo. Borgfeldt on base to be original)

Mailbox, D&P #216/E&A #521/L #254 (repro marked Taiwan)

Mantel Clock, D&P #483/E&A #162/L #114 (originally in ruby flashed, milk glass, clear and frosted only)

Mule and Waterwagon, D&P #51/E&A #539/L #38 (original marked Jeannette, PA)

Naked Child, E&A 546/L #94

Owl, D&P #52/E&A #566/L #37, (original in clear only, often painted; repro found in clear, blue, green, and pink with a higher threaded base and less detail)

Peter Rabbit, D&P #60/E&A #618/L #55

Piano, D&P #460/E&A #577/L #289 (original in only clear and milk glass, both painted)

Rabbit Pushing Wheelbarrow, D&P #72/E&A #601/L #47 (eggs are speckled on the repro; solid on the original)

Rocking Horse, D&P #46/E&A #651/L #58 (original in clear only)

Safe, D&P #311/E&A #661/L #268 (original in clear, ruby flashed, and milk glass only)

Santa, D&P 284/E&A #674/L #103 (original has plastic head; repro is all glass and opens at bottom)

Santa's Boot, D&P #273/E&A #111/L #233

Scottie Dog, D&P #35/E&A #184/L #17 (repro has a ice-like color and is often slick and oily)

Station Wagon, D&P #178/E&A #56/L #378

Stough Rabbit, D&P #53/E&A #617/L #54

Uncle Sam's Hat, D&P #428/E&A #303/L #168

Others are possible. If in doubt, do not buy without a guarantee from the dealer and return privilege in writing.

The prices in this column have taken into consideration auctions, dealer lists, and show prices, and represent an average of all. Values are given for undamaged examples with original paint and metal parts when applicable or unless noted otherwise. Repaired pieces (often repainted) are worth only a small fraction of one that is perfect.

Our advisor for glass containers is Jeff Bradfield; he is listed in the Directory under Virginia. You may contact him with questions, if you will include an SASE. See Clubs, Newsletters, and Catalogs for the address of the Candy Container Collectors of America. A bimonthly newsletter offers insight into new finds, reproductions, updates, and articles from over four hundred collectors and members, including all authors of books on candy containers. Dues are $18.00 yearly. The club holds an annual convention in June in Reading, Pennsylvania, for collectors of candy containers.

'L' numbers used in this guide refer to a standard reference series, *An Album of Candy Containers*, Vols 1 and 2, by Jennie Long. 'E&A' numbers correlate with *The Compleat American Glass Candy Containers Handbook* by Eikelberner and Agadjanian, revised by Adele Bowden. D&P numbers refer to *The Collector's Guide to Candy Containers* by Doug Dezso and Leon and Rose Poirier, recently published by Collector Books.

Airplane, P-38 Lightning; Victory Glass, D&P 82/E&A 12/L 326	**.250.00**
Airplane, Spirit of St Louis; tin & glass, D&P 85/E&A 9/L 321	**.600.00**
Amos & Andy, in car, Victory Glass, E&A 21/L 77	**550.00**
Apothecary Jar, Old Fashion #2, Stough, D&P 116/L 558	**15.00**
Barney Google on Pedestal, D&P 189/E&A 72/L 79	**250.00**
Battleship, Victory Glass, orig closure, E&A 97/L 338	**30.00**

Bulldog w/Oblong Base, Stough, orig closure, E&A 186/L 16 ....**50.00**
Bus, Chicago; greyhound on side, Victory, E&A 118/L 343 ....**450.00**
Bus, Rapid Transit; Victory Glass, D&P 155/E&A 116/L 345 ....**600.00**
Candy Pump, looks like a gas pump, gr, Millstein, E&A 595/L 240 ....**150.00**
Cannon, cobalt, orig tin, D&P 385/E&A 122/L 534 ....**550.00**
Cannon, Muzzle Loader; metal carriage, E&A 130/L 452 ....**1,000.00**
Cannon, US Defense Field Gun; Stough, E&A 128/L 142 ....**350.00**
Cannon on Truck, unmk, E&A 126/L 141 ....**2,500.00**

Car (small flat top hearse), tin snap-on closure, found in several glass and paint colors, from $450.00 to $525.00.

Car, Air Flow; Victory Glass, G pnt, E&A 61/L 369 ....**450.00**
Car, Electric Coupe; Vail Bros, D&P 162/E&A 48/L 355 ....**85.00**
Car, Four Door; West Bros, D&P 168/E&A 41/L 348 ....**900.00**
Car, Miniature Streamlined; Victory Glass, D&P 173/E&A 33/L 377 ....**30.00**
Car, Reo; Victory Glass, E&A 62/L 368 ....**550.00**
Car, Station Wagon; Millstein, D&P 178/E&A 56/L 378 ....**50.00**
Car, West Limousines; Westmoreland, E&A 45/L 351 ....**175.00**
Car, Yellow Taxi; Westmoreland, D&P 184/E&A 43 ....**1,000.00**
Cat, Winking, Stretched Neck; Victory, orig pnt, D&P 6/L 5 ...**4,000.00**
Chick on Sagging Basket, E&A 148/L 8 ....**75.00**
Clock, Alarm; D&P 477/E&A 161/L 118 ....**300.00**
Clock, Mantel; w/ or w/o coin slot, D&P 482/E&A 164/L 116 ..**225.00**
Condiment Set, Rainbow Candy; milk glass, egg shaped, E&A 175/L 503 ...**60.00**
Die, Brandle & Smith, D&P 421/E&A 175-1/L 268 ....**30.00**
Dime Safe, CD Kenny, D&P 312/E&A 661B **120.00**
Dolly's Bathtub, Victory, orig pnt, D&P 292/E&A 82/L 226 ..**3,500.00**
Dolly's Milk Bottle, Avor/VG Co, D&P 109/E&A 527/L 66 ....**50.00**
Elephant, Genteel; in suit jacket, Cambridge, D&P 42/E&A 207/L 33 .**350.00**
Felix by Barrel, Pat Sullivan, D&P 200/E&A 211/L 86 ....**700.00**
Fire Engine, Fire Dept No 99; Victory, D&P 252/E&A 214/L 385 .**100.00**
Fire Engine, Ladder Truck, Victory, D&P 264/E&A 216/L 384 .**275.00**
Fire Engine, No 11, Stough, orig closure, D&P 259/E&A 212/L 388 ....**45.00**
Flossie Fisher's Bed, Geo Borgfeldt, D&P 299/E&A 234/L 127, EX **4,000.00**
Flossie Fisher's China Cabinet, Borgfeldt, D&P 301/E&A 235/L 129 .**1,500.00**
Foxy Doctor's Playkit, Empire Products, 4 bottles, D&P 463/L 657 ....**150.00**
Goblin Head, lg loop finial, D&P 263/E&A 242/L 162 ....**650.00**
Gun, Beaded Border Grip; blown, D&P 390/E&A 246 ....**25.00**
Gun, Diamond in Grip Revolver; blown, D&P 391/E&A 264C ..**25.00**
Gun, Grooved Barrel; dmn cross on grip, D&P 392 ....**35.00**
Gun, Revolver; Victory Glass, D&P 404/E&A 255/L 149 ....**35.00**
Gun, Three Dot; Stough, D&P 401/E&A 250B/L 155 ....**25.00**
Helicopter, Stough, D&P 91/E&A 306/L 329 ....**200.00**
Horn, Clarinet; JC Crosetti, D&P 448/L 285 ....**35.00**
Horn, Musical Clarinet; Stough, D&P 451/L 616 ....**35.00**
Hot Doggie, bl & amber, Widmer, D&P 24/E&A 320/L 14 ....**800.00**
Hound w/Sm Glass Hat, Stough, D&P 28/E&A181/L 21 ....**20.00**
Independence Hall, coin slot in roof, D&P 130/E&A 342/L 74 .**400.00**
Jack O'Lantern, Big Str Eyes; EX pnt, D&P 264/E&A 347/L 160 ..**300.00**
Jeep, Millstein, orig closure, D&P 410/E&A 350/L 390 ....**35.00**

Kaleidoscope, D&P 429/E&A 353/L 250, rare, minimum value ..**8,000.00**
Kiddie Kar, Victory Glass, D&P 430/E&A 360/L 253 ....**275.00**
Koala, mk San Diego Zoo, D&P 49/L 467 ....**20.00**
Lamp, Candlestick Base; Stough, D&P 322/E&A 370/L 559 ....**350.00**
Lamp, Hobnail; Stough, D&P 329/E&A 365/L 209 ....**350.00**
Lamp, Hurricane; JC Crosetti, D&P 330/E&A 366/L 211 ....**350.00**
Lamp, Mini Kerosene; AM Products, Hong Kong, D&P 336/L 561 ....**15.00**
Lamp, Monkey; Stough, D&P 338/E&A 533/L 214 ....**425.00**
Lamppost, glass globe, pewter stand, D&P 341/L 553 ....**150.00**
Lantern, Barn Type #1; D&P 345/E&A 426/L179 ....**85.00**
Lantern, Barn Type #2, Westmoreland, D&P 346/E&A 427/L 178 ....**100.00**
Lantern, Diamond Glass, wire bail, D&P 353/E&A 441-1/L 183 .**40.00**
Lantern, Stough's #79; D&P 365/E&A 447-1/L 196 ....**30.00**
Lantern on Stand, 6 panels, wire stand, D&P 358/L 571 ....**55.00**
Lanterns, Twins on Anchor; Vanstyle Specialty, D&P 370/E&A 385/L 186 .**30.00**
Liberty Bell w/Hanger, wire bail, Westmoreland, D&P 95/E&A85/L 229 ..**60.00**
Locomotive, Am Type #23; clear or bl glass, D&P 489/E&A 480/L 417 .**175.00**
Locomotive, Dbl Window #888; Victory Glass, D&P 491/E&A 483 ...**30.00**
Locomotive, Man in Window #888; Cambridge, D&P 497/E&A 486/L 419 .**400.00**
Locomotive, Sm Plain Friction Closure; D&P 501/E&A 493-1/L 410 ..**175.00**
Locomotive, Stough's #8; D&P 507/E&A 477 ....**35.00**
Luggage, Trunk w/Rnd Top; Westmoreland, D&P 378/E&A 789/L 219 ..**150.00**
Mail Box, Westmoreland, orig pnt, D&P 216/E&A 521/L 254 ..**300.00**
Man on Motorcycle, Victory Glass, D&P 446/E&A 522/L 392 ..**600.00**
Nurser, Baby Dear; rubber nipple, Victory, D&P 117/E&A 555/L 64 ...**40.00**
Nurser, Waisted; JC Crosetti, D&P 125/E&A 548/L 71 ....**30.00**
Piano, coin slot, ruby flashed/milk glass, D&P 460/E&A 577/L 289 .**425.00**
Powder Horn, blown, D&P 411/E&A 589/L 265 ....**95.00**
Pumpkin Head Policeman, unmk, orig pnt, D&P 270/E&A 592/L 163 .**1,900.00**
Rabbit, Crouching; ears tucked, unmk, D&P 54/E&A 615/L 41 ...**125.00**
Rabbit Eating Carrot, Stough, D&P 55/E&A 609/L 53 ....**40.00**
Rabbit on Dome, VG Co, D&P 65/E&A 607/L 46 ....**525.00**
Rabbit Running on Log, gilt on clear, Avor, D&P 62/E&A 603/L 42 .**300.00**
Racer, Pointed Front; orig tin parts, D&P 471/E&A 638/L 431 ..**2,500.00**
Radio, Tune In; D&P 219/E&A 643/L 290 ....**175.00**
Rolling Pin, Victory Glass, D&P 310/E&A 660/L 267 ....**300.00**
Safety First on Pedestal, orig pnt, D&P 205/L 465 ....**2,000.00**
Santa by Sq Chimney, threaded chimney top, D&P 275/E&A 672G/L 100 ..**1,200.00**
Santa Claus, Shackman, D&P 284/L 524 ....**20.00**
Santa Claus, Victory Glass, 6", D&P 285 ....**5,000.00**
Santa Claus in Long Coat, English, D&P 279 ....**350.00**
Santa Claus Leaving Chimney, Victory, D&P 281/E&A 673/L 102 ..**150.00**
Scottish Terrier, 1 paw forward, head turned, D&P 34 ....**60.00**
Soda Fountain, Par Beverage, D&P 440/L P-34 ....**125.00**
Soldier by Tent, G orig pnt, D&P 208/E&A 688/L 108 ....**3,500.00**
Submarine, Geo Borgfeldt, D&P 104/E&A 101/L 337 ....**600.00**
Suitcase, D&P 377/E&A 707/L 216 ....**50.00**
Swan Boat, rabbit & chick riders, Victory, D&P 74/E&A 713/L 60 .**900.00**
Tank, Man in Turret; Victory Glass, D&P 412/E&A 722/L 437 ..**40.00**
Tank, WWI; D&P 415/E&A 721/L 434 ....**175.00**
Telephone, Desk Type; JC Crosetti, D&P 221/E&A 731/L 312 ...**35.00**
Telephone, Flat Top Hinge; VG Co, D&P 225/E&A 737/L 300 ..**50.00**
Telephone, Lynne, Raised Dial; Stough, D&P 231/E&A 740/L 307 .**50.00**
Telephone, Pewter Top #2; bl tinted glass, D&P 237 ....**250.00**
Telephone, Redlich's Screw Top #2; Redlich, D&P 242/E&A 742-1 ..**450.00**
Telephone, Tall Musical Toy; Stough, D&P 248/L 586-C **45.00**
Train, Parlor Car; D&P 516/E&A 169/L 403 ....**325.00**
Truck, Delivery; D&P 526A/E&A 782/L 605 ....**1,000.00**
Uncle Sam Hat, no label or closure, D&P 428/E&A 303/L 168 ...**40.00**
Uncle Sam Hat, political label, slotted closure, D&P 428/E&A 303/L 168 ..**175.00**
Village Church, glass cross, coin slot, D&P 135/E&A 809/L 513 .**500.00**
Village Princess Theatre, w/insert, D&P 141/E&A 813/L 76 ......**150.00**
Village Railroad Station, w/insert, D&P 142/E&A 802/L 514 ....**350.00**
Village Tudor House, w/insert, D&P 145/E&A 806/L 76 ....**450.00**

Wagon, US Express; Westmoreland, D&P 530/E&A 821/L 440 ..**750.00**
Wheelbarrow, Victory Glass, orig closure, D&P 531/E&A 832/L 273 .**100.00**
Windmill, Dutch; Play Toy, no blades, D&P 534/E&A 843/L 448 ....**30.00**
Windmill, Dutch; Play Toy, orig blades, D&P 534/E&A 843/L 448 ....**100.00**
World Globe, pewter stand, D&P 445/E&A 860/L 276 ....**525.00**
Ye Olde Oaken Bucket, w/ or w/o divider, D&P 293/E&A 831/L 237 .**95.00**

Papier-Mache, Composition

These types of candy containers are generally figural. Many are holiday related. Our advisor for this category is Jenny Tarrant; she is listed in the Directory under Missouri. See also Christmas; Halloween.

Apple, cb, red & yel, sm stem, opens around middle, 2" **70.00**
Beer keg, papier-mache, cloth bat on top, 3½", from $75 to **100.00**
Black cat, papier-mache, mohair covered, glass eyes, 7½", EX **535.00**
Cabbage head, papier-mache vegetable man, 6", VG **1,265.00**
Devil on boot, cb boot, compo-headed devil, Germany, 6", EX .**355.00**
Dog w/pointed cap & eggshell pants, papier-mache, 5½", VG ...**425.00**
Duck emerging from egg, papier-mache, glass eyes, mc, 4", EX ...**275.00**
Duck w/jtd neck, papier-mache & wood, lead ft, 6", VG **65.00**
Elephant, limbs/etc are vegetables, papier-mache, 5½" L, EX **600.00**
Football, cb, opens at middle, 1¾" to 8", from $60 to **80.00**
Geo Washington on candy box, compo, Germany, 4-5", ea **225.00**
Melon head, molded cb w/insert in bk, 6½", EX **250.00**
Melon head on spring legs, pressed cb, Germany, 6", VG **220.00**
Melon head w/bow tie, pressed cb, 4", EX **440.00**
Parasol, cb w/fabric/lace trim, wood hdl, 2½", from $150 to **175.00**
Peanut, emb cb, realistic, 2½" to 4¼", ea, from $45 to **75.00**
Pear head, papier-mache vegetable man, 6½", VG **1,100.00**
Pear w/bulging eyes, movable ball nose, papier-mache, 2¾", EX .**450.00**
Potato, cb w/emb eyes, rich brn, 2½", from $45 to **55.00**
Rabbit, papier-mache, bobbing head, glass eyes, W Germany, 7", VG ...**95.00**
Rabbit, pnt clothes, bunnies under arms, papier-mache, Germany, 6½" .**350.00**
Rooster, papier-mache & feathers, glass eyes, Germany, 7", EX .**100.00**
Sewing basket, cb, resembles wicker, 3", from $175 to **200.00**
Turkey, compo, Japan, 4" to 5", ea **65.00**
Turkey, compo, Japan, 6" to 7", ea **88.00**
Turkey, compo, Japan, 8" to 9", ea **150.00**
Turkey, compo, lead ft, Germany, 4" **65.00**
Turkey, compo, lead ft, Germany, 5" **75.00**
Turkey, compo, lead ft, Germany, 6" **95.00**
Turkey, compo, lead ft, Germany, 7" **150.00**
Turkey, compo, lead ft, Germany, 8" **200.00**
Turkey, compo, lead ft, Germany, 9" **300.00**
Turkey, papier-mache, Japan, 5½" **65.00**
Turkey hen, compo, lead ft, Germany, 4" **125.00**
Turkey hen, compo, lead ft, Germany, 5" **185.00**
Turkey hen, compo, lead ft, Germany, 6" **250.00**
Wall clock, cb, pnt face, pendulum/weights/hands, 3" **135.00**

Canes

Fancy canes and walking sticks were once the mark of a gentleman. Hand-carved examples are collected and admired as folk art from the past. The glass canes that never could have been practical are unique whimseys of the glass-blower's profession. Gadget and container sticks, which were produced in a wide variety, are highly desirable. Character, political, and novelty types are also sought after as are those with handles made of precious metals.

For more information we recommend *American Folk Art Canes, Personal Sculpture*, by George H. Meyer, Sandringham Press, 100 West Long

Lake Rd., Suite 100, Bloomfield Hills, MI 48304. Other possible references are *Canes in the United States* by Catherine Dike and *Canes From the 17th – 20th Century* by Jeffrey Snyder. Our advisor for this category is Bruce Thalberg.

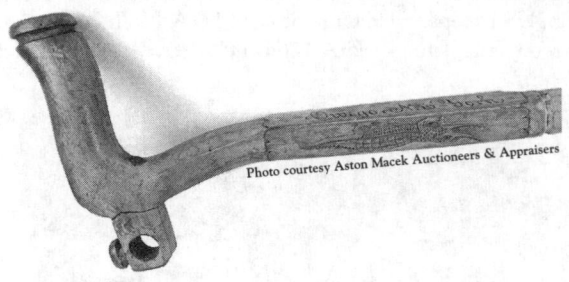

Photo courtesy Aston Macek Auctioneers & Appraisers

Memorial, chip-carved wood, dated 1874, attributed to Dean family of Woego, NY, with provenance, $2,000.00.

Bakelite, lady's mirror/comb in vanity hdl, wood shaft, 1920s **750.00**
Bone/metal, fishing rod telescopes in metal shaft, 1880s **1,100.00**
Boxwood, pug-on-ped hdl, gilt collar, hardwood shaft, 1880s ..**1,100.00**
Cloisonne floral ball-top hdl, partridgewood shaft, 1900s **900.00**
Day's Pat percussion gun, underhammer mechanism, English, 1840s .**750.00**
Glass, clear w/gr & opal appl threading, 47½", EX **400.00**
Glass, core swirl of red, wht & bl, 39" **125.00**
Hickory stanhope, Lookout Mtn TN (4 views), ca 1890 ....**450.00**
Ivory, cvd hdl opens for tiddly winks, ebonized shaft, 1870s **900.00**
Ivory, dragon hdl w/inlay MOP butterfly top, ebony hdl, 1890s ..**1,000.00**
Ivory, mtn lion on stump, stepped partridgewood shaft, 1870s ...**1,100.00**
Ivory, seminude lady, silver collar, hardwood shaft, 1890s **1,050.00**
Ivory, spaniel, glass eyes, 2-tone lignum vitae shaft, 1870s **750.00**
Ivory, 1000 faces ball hdl, silver collar/horn ferrule, 1890s **400.00**
Ivory cvd top opens for pen/ink pot/stanhope/seal, ebony shaft .**1,400.00**
Japanese, mixed metal knob, bugs/insects/flowers, sgn, 1890s **300.00**
Meissen porc floral knob hdl, mahog shaft, 1900s **800.00**
Paperweight knob w/mc blossoms, copper ferrule/ebony shaft, 1900s .**800.00**
Pewter, Republican elephant hdl, dk bamboo shaft, 1890s **350.00**
Porc, cobalt pistol hdl w/HP, silver collar, ebony shaft, 1870s **475.00**
Porc, HP lady/cherub knob, Fr, 1880s **250.00**
Purfume bottle in ivory hdl, glass dauber, wood shaft, 1900s **950.00**
Silver, horse-head hdl w/glass eyes, ebony shaft, 1860s **550.00**
Silver & ivory, skull hdl, horn ferrule, ebony shaft, 1890s **750.00**
Sweet grass over wooden form w/velvet strips, Am Indian, 1900s .**225.00**
Tortoise shell, gold sunburst decor hdl w/inlay, rosewood shaft .**1,200.00**
Vegetal ivory, cvd Black man's head, glass eyes, 1870s **650.00**
Whale ivory, hand clutches snake w/coral inlay, bone shaft, 1850s .**2,300.00**
Wood, Am Indian, life-sz cvd rattlesnake, opal eyes, 1870s **1,800.00**
Wood, claw-&-ball hdl, overall folk cvgs, silver band, 1903 ....**475.00**
Wood, cvd bust of Civil War soldier, glass eyes, malacca shaft ...**575.00**
Wood, cvd terrier's head, movable mouth glove holder, 1920s ...**350.00**
Wood, frog-w/glass-eyes hdl, sterling collar/horn ferrule, 1889 ...**650.00**
Wood, lg folk-art bird hdl w/mc details, vine-cvd shaft, 1890s ...**600.00**
Wood, Turk automaton, eyes change from clear to red, 1880s .**1,200.00**
Wood, whippet-head hdl, silver collar, hardwood shaft, 1890s ...**650.00**
Wood, winking walrus hdl w/2 ivory tusks, malacca shaft, 1890s .**750.00**
Wood, 1939 NY World's Fair, Trylon & perisphere hdl, bl/orange ..**250.00**
Wood & silver wolf, glass eyes, crook hdl, hardwood shaft, 1880s ..**850.00**

Canton

Canton is a blue and white porcelain that was first exported in the

1790s by clipper ships from China to the United States, a practice that continued into the 1920s. Canton became very popular along the east coast where the major ports were located. Its popularity was due to several factors: it was readily available, inexpensive, and (due to the fact that it came in many different forms) appealing to the housewife.

The porcelain's blue and white color and simple motif (teahouse, trees, bridge, and a rain-cloud border) have made it a favorite of people who collect early American furniture and accessories. Buyers of Canton should shop at large outdoor shows and up-scale antique shows. Collections are regularly sold at auction. Collectors usually prefer a rich, deep tone rather than a lighter blue. Cracks, large chips, and major repairs will substantially affect values. Prices of Canton have escalated sharply over the last twenty years, and rare forms are highly sought after by advanced collectors. Our advisor for this category is Hobart D. Van Deusen; he is listed in the Directory under Connecticut.

Basket, fruit; rtcl rim, 9¼"	500.00
Basket, fruit; rtcl rim, 9⅝", w/mismatched undertray	750.00
Bidet, 19th C, 24"	800.00
Bowl, lobed, gilt rim, 19th C, 9¾"	865.00
Bowl, rctl, w/8¾" undertray, 19th C	500.00
Bowl, salad; 19th C, 9¾", NM	800.00
Bowl, scalloped rim, 8¼", NM	400.00
Bowl, vegetable; w/lid, 9x8", VG	400.00
Bowl, vegetable; w/shaped lid & bl finial, 11½"	300.00
Coffeepot, mismatched lid, 19th C, 7¼"	500.00
Creamer, U-shaped spout, 3¼"	130.00
Ginger jar, w/lid, 7"	125.00
Jug, cider; staple rpr, 11½"	1,000.00
Plate, hot water; std form, 11", pr	400.00
Platter, canted corners, early 1800s, 20", NM	1,000.00
Platter, pierced drip tray, 19th C, 17½"	900.00
Platter, well & tree, rain cloud border, ftd, 14½x11"	700.00
Platter, well & tree, 19th C, 16", NM	800.00
Platter, 19th C, 17", NM	525.00
Punch bowl, river scene, rain cloud border, 4x11½"	1,300.00
Tea caddy, w/lid, 6½", EX+	990.00
Teapot, rain cloud border	450.00
Tray, quatrefoil, 10¾x8", VG	300.00
Tureen, mismatched lid, 19th C, 8½"	550.00
Tureen, w/lid, 10¾"	800.00
Tureen, w/lid, 19th C, 12" L	900.00

Capodimonte

The relief style, highly colored and defined porcelain pieces in this listing are commonly called and identified in our current market place as Capodimonte. It was King Ferdinand IV, son of King Charles, who opened a factory in Naples in 1771, and began to use the mark of the blue crown N (BCN). When the factory closed in 1834, the Ginori family at Doccia near Florence, Italy, acquired what was left of the factory and continued using its mark. The factory continued until 1896 when it was then combined with Societa Ceramica Richard of Milan which continues today to manufacture fine porcelain pieces marked with a crest and wreaths under a blue crown with R. Capodimonte.

Boxes and steins are highly sought after as they are cross collectibles. Figurines, figure groupings, flowery vases, urns, and the like are also highly collectible, but most items on the market today are of recent manufacture. In the past several years, Europeans have been attending U.S. antique shows and auctions in order to purchase Capodimonte items to take back home, since many pieces were destroyed during the two world wars. This has driven up prices of the

older ware. Our advisor for this category is James Highfield; he is listed in the Directory under Indiana.

Bottle, perfume; drunkards & revelers surround, BCN, 6"	165.00
Box, angels & pnt flowers, BCN France, 2x2x1½"	295.00
Box, baby grand piano, R Capodimonte mk	75.00
Box, Biblical scenes, Meissen mk, 11½x6½x7½"	10,350.00
Box, garden scene w/fire pot, B Altman mk, 8x6x3¼"	200.00
Candlesticks, sq base, Keramos mk, 10½", pr	120.00
Casket, playful putti & mask hdls, BCN, 14½x8x7½"	800.00
Cup & saucer, demitasse; BCN, 2x4½"	118.00
Ewer, 4 jaguar heads at base, Pan figural hdl, BCN, 17"	1,100.00
Mug, putti surround, winged female nude hdl, BCN, 8"	313.00
Plaque, nativity scene, octagonal, BCN, ca 1800, 13¾x12"	1,300.00
Plate, Christmas 1973, ltd ed (of 1000), 7½"	13.00
Plate, horse & soldier, Occupied Japan, 6¼"	20.00
Stein, cherub finial, jaguar hdl, BCN France, 15½"	1,750.00
Stein, goat & cherub finial, screaming mask hdl, BCN, 9"	650.00
Stein, revelry scene (continuous), lion finial, BCN, 9"	805.00
Tea set, R Capodimonte mk, 15-pc	425.00
Urn, sea god & nymphs, lion finial, BCN, 16½", pr	2,300.00
Vase, classical figures, acanthus borders, BCN, 29"	2,900.00
Vase, fluted shape, gold crown & N	415.00
Vase, monkey hdls, BCN France for Ovington, NY, 10¼"	400.00

Carlton Ware

Carlton Ware was the product of Wiltshaw and Robinson, who operated in the Staffordshire district of England from about 1890. During the 1920s, they produced ornamental ware with enameled and gilded decorations such as flowers and birds, often on a black background. In 1958 the firm was renamed Carlton Ware Ltd. Their trademark was a crown over a circular stamp with 'W & R, Stoke on Trent,' surrounding a swallow. 'Carlton Ware' was sometimes added by hand.

Bowl, Deco tree on cream, orange mottle lustre trim, 12¼" L	350.00
Bowl, Foxglove, oblong, 9½"	40.00
Bowl, fruit; emb grapes, 4½"	36.00
Bowl, Rouge Royale, simple gold trim, 6½x10"	65.00
Bowl, salad; emb tomatoes, oblong, 9"	60.00
Bowl, Verte Royale, exotic birds/trees, w/gold, 10" L	195.00

Condiment set, three monks on tray, 1950s, $60.00.

Jar, Oriental couple w/fans in landscape w/gold, w/lid, 9x4½"	450.00
Jar, Oriental village scene on bl w/much gold, w/lid, 9"	450.00
Lamp, fantasy bird, no fittings, 12"	550.00
Plate, swallow flies against lg fantasy star, gold/lav, 5¾"	85.00
Toast rack, yel w/orange knob, 4-slice	75.00
Vase, exotic landscape & bird on bl lustre, 5⅞x3½"	450.00
Vase, exotic landscape & birds on deep bl w/much gold, 7x4"	450.00
Vase, Oriental scenes on dk bl w/gold, MOP lustre int, 11x4"	395.00
Vase, Oriental temples & houses on blk w/orange band & gold, 4⅜"	110.00

Vase, Oriental village/birds, mc/gold on orange/blk, 6x3½" **145.00**
Vase, Persian, mc on bl w/gold, flaring cylinder, 6" **250.00**
Vase, Persian scene, mc/gold on deep bl, 10½x4¾" **395.00**
Vase, Persian scene on bl lustre, w/lid, 6½" **295.00**
Vase, Persian scene w/gold, MOP lustre int, gold band, 6x3⅝" ..**250.00**

Carnival Collectibles

Carnival items from the early part of this century represent the lighter side of an America that was alternately prospering and sophisticated or devastated by war and domestic conflict. But whatever the country's condition, the carnival's thrilling rides and shooting galleries were a sure way of letting it all go by — at least for an evening.

For further information on chalkware figures, we recommend *The Carnival Chalk Prize* by our advisor, Thomas G. Morris, who is listed in the Directory under Oregon.

In the shooting gallery target listings below, items are rated for availability from 1 (commonly found) to 10 (rarely found) and all are made of cast iron. Our advisors for shooting gallery targets are Richard and Valerie Tucker; their address is listed in the Directory under Texas.

Chalkware Figures

Sailor Boy, Remember Pearl Harbor, JY Jenkins, 1942, $175.00.

Photo courtesy Tom Morris

Alice the Goon, from Popeye, 1930-40, 10" **150.00**
Bathing Beauty, HP, 1928, sgn on bottom, 16" **155.00**
Boy, w/top hat, tux, cane & spats, 1930s, 8" **45.00**
Boy & Dog, mk Pals, 1935-45, 10x9" **45.00**
Bulldog, sitting, 1925-35, 10¼" **65.00**
Cat, flat bk, 1940-50, 6" **10.00**
Charlie McCarthy, sitting down, 9½" **60.00**
Cowboy, ashtray, 1930-40, 8¼" **45.00**
Dancing Girl, fan dancer, ashtray, 1940s, 10½" **95.00**
Donald Duck, head bank, Disney, 1940-50, 10½" **80.00**
Indian, lamp, 1940, 7½" **95.00**
Jackie Coogan, thumbs in overalls, mk My Boy, pk chalk, rare, 17" ..**250.00**
Kewpie, jointed arms, mohair wig, 1920s, 12½" **165.00**
Little Lady, HP, jointed arms, mohair wig, 1920-30, 12" **165.00**
Mae West, w/lg hat & parasol, 1930-40, 14" **125.00**
Nude, w/feathers, 1930-40, 12" **125.00**
Nude bust, lamp, Art Deco style, 1930-40, 8½" **135.00**
Posing Lady, lying on side, HP, 1920s, 3½x7" **135.00**
Sitting lady, pk chalk, HP, ca 1920, 6½" **65.00**
Three Little Pigs, flat bk, 5x5½" **30.00**

Shooting Gallery Targets

Battleship, worn wht pnt, Mangels, 5, 6¼x11⅜", $200 to **300.00**
Birds (8) on bar, worn pnt, Mangels, 9, 3½x41½", $700 to **800.00**
Bull's eye w/pop-up duck, old pnt, Quackenbush, 5, 12" dia, $300 to .**400.00**

Cat w/bull's eye, worn pnt, Wurfflein, 10, 14¼x19", minimum .**1,000.00**
Dbl star spinner, worn mc pnt, Mangels, 3, 8x2¾", $100 to **200.00**
Dog running, worn wht pnt, Smith or Evans, 5, 6x11", $100 to .**200.00**
Duck, detailed feathers, old pnt, Parker, 4, 3¾x5½", $100 to **200.00**
Duck, detailed feathers, worn pnt, Evans, 4, 5½x8½", $100 to ...**200.00**
Eagle w/wings wide, mc pnt, Smith or Evans, 5, 14¾", $500 to ..**600.00**
Greyhound, bull's eye, old patina, Parker, 8, 26" W, minimum ...**1,000.00**
Harlequin w/bull's eye, worn pnt, Hoffman, 9, 20½", minimum .**1,000.00**
Monkey, standing, worn rpt, 10, 9¾x8½", $300 to **400.00**
Owl, bull's eye, wht traces, Evans, 6, 10¾x5⅛", $400 to **500.00**
Pipe, old patina, Smith, 1, 5⅝x1¾", value less than **50.00**
Rabbit running, bull's eye, old patina, Parker, 8, 12x25", minimum **1,000.00**
Rabbit standing, worn pnt, Smith or Mueller, 9, 18x10", $900 to **1,000.00**
Reindeer (elk), worn rpt over wht, 5, 10x9", $300 to **400.00**
Saber-tooth tiger, old patina, Mangels, 10, 7¾x13", $500 to **600.00**
Soldier w/rifle, pnt traces/old patina, Mueller, 5, 9x5", $100 to ..**200.00**
Squirrel running, old patina, Smith, 4, 5⅛x9¼", $100 to **200.00**
Swan, worn wht pnt, Mueller, 7, 5¾x5", $200 to **300.00**

Carnival Glass

Carnival glass is pressed glass that has been coated with a sodium solution and fired to give it an exterior lustre. First made in America in 1905, it was produced until the late 1920s and had great popularity in the average American household, for unlike the costly art glass produced by Tiffany, carnival glass could be mass produced at a small cost. Colors most often found are marigold, green, blue, and purple; but others exist in lesser quantities and include white, clear, red, aqua opalescent, peach opalescent, ice blue, ice green, amber, lavender, and smoke.

Companies mainly responsible for its production in America include the Fenton Art Glass Company, Williamstown, West Virginia; the Northwood Glass Company, Wheeling, West Virginia; the Imperial Glass Company, Bellaire, Ohio; the Millersburg Glass Company, Millersburg, Ohio; and the Dugan Glass Company (Diamond Glass), Indiana, Pennsylvania. In addition to these major manufacturers, lesser producers included the U.S. Glass Company, the Cambridge Glass Company, the Westmoreland Glass Company, and the McKee Glass Company.

Carnival glass has been highly collectible since the 1950s and has been reproduced for the last twenty-five years. Several national and state collectors' organizations exist, and many fine books are available on old carnival glass, including *The Standard Encyclopedia of Carnival Glass* by Bill Edwards and Mike Carwile and *Dugan & Diamond Carnival Glass, 1909 – 1931* by Carl O. Burns.

Acanthus (Imperial), plate, marigold, 10" **275.00**
Acorn (Fenton), bowl, gr, 6¼-7½", ea **250.00**
Acorn Burrs (Northwood), butter dish, marigold, w/lid **90.00**
Acorn Burrs (Northwood), tumbler, amethyst **200.00**
Amaryllis (Northwood), compote, wht, sm **450.00**
American (Fostoria), tumbler, marigold, rare **100.00**
Apple Blossom Twigs (Dugan), bowl, gr, 7" **170.00**
Apple Blossoms (Dugan), plate, amethyst **275.00**
Apple Tree (Fenton), tumbler, bl **65.00**
Arcadia Basket, plate, marigold, 8" **50.00**
Arcs (Imperial), compote, amethyst **90.00**
Asters, bowl, marigold **60.00**
Australian Diamond (Crystal), creamer, amethyst **80.00**
Australian Panels (Crystal), creamer, marigold **50.00**
Autumn Acorns (Fenton), bowl, bl, 8½" **150.00**
Balloons (Imperial), compote, smoke **90.00**
Banded Diamonds (Crystal), bowl, amethyst, 5" **75.00**
Banded Diamonds & Bars (Finland), tumbler, marigold, 3¼" **550.00**
Banded Drape (Fenton), tumbler, gr **75.00**

Banded Panels (Crystal), sugar bowl, amethyst, open 60.00
Banded Portland (US Glass), toothpick holder, marigold 150.00
Barbella (Northwood), tumbler, vaseline 225.00
Basket of Roses (Northwood), bonbon, marigold, scarce 300.00
Basketweave (Northwood), compote, bl 120.00
Beaded Block, pitcher, milk; clambroth 75.00
Beaded Bull's Eye (Imperial), vase, amethyst, 8-14", ea 225.00
Beaded Mirrors (Jain), tumbler, marigold, rare 200.00
Beaded Shell (Dugan), bowl, amethyst, ftd, 5" 40.00
Beaded Shell (Dugan), mug, bl 200.00
Beaded Swirl (English), compote, bl 60.00
Beads & Bars (US Glass), spooner, marigold 125.00
Bellaire Souvenir (Imperial), bowl, marigold, scarce 185.00
Bells & Beads (Dugan), bowl, gr, 7½" 115.00
Belted Rib, vase, marigold, 8" 95.00
Big Basketweave (Dugan), vase, peach opal, 6-14", ea 175.00
Big Fish (Millersburg), bowl, marigold, 8½" 525.00
Bird of Paradise (Northwood), bowl, advertising; amethyst 400.00
Birds & Cherries (Fenton), compote, bl 60.00
Blackberry (Fenton), vase whimsey, wht, rare 800.00
Blackberry (Northwood), compote, bl 80.00
Blackberry Spray (Fenton), bonbon, marigold 35.00
Blackberry Wreath (Millersburg), bowl, ice cream; gr, 10" 650.00
Blocks & Arches (Crystal), pitcher, marigold, rare 100.00
Blossomtime (Northwood), compote, gr 650.00
Boggy Bayou (Fenton), vase, amethyst, 12-15", ea 150.00
Booker, cider pitcher, marigold 600.00
Border Plants (Dugan), bowl, amethyst, ftd, 8½" 600.00
Bouquet (Fenton), tumbler, marigold 30.00
Boutoniere (Millersburg), compote, gr 270.00
Bow & Knot, perfume bottle, marigold 45.00
Britt, tumbler, bl, rare 1,000.00
Broken Arches (Imperial), punch bowl, marigold, w/base 365.00
Brooklyn, bottle, amethyst, w/stopper 95.00
Bubble Waves, compote, peach opal, rare 600.00
Bull's Eye & Diamond, mug, marigold 150.00
Bull's Eye & Loop (Millersburg), vase, gr, rare, 7-11", ea 500.00
Bulldog, paperweight, marigold 1,250.00
Bumblebee, hatpin, amethyst 70.00
Bunny, bank, marigold 35.00
Butterflies (Fenton), bonbon, gr 75.00
Butterfly, oil lamp, marigold 1,500.00
Butterfly (Jeannette), pin tray, marigold 15.00
Butterfly & Berry (Fenton), creamer, marigold, w/lid 100.00
Butterfly & Berry (Fenton), tumbler, amethyst 70.00
Butterfly & Fern (Fenton), tumbler, gr 85.00
Buttermilk Plain (Imperial), goblet, red 125.00
Buzz Saw (Cambridge), cruet, marigold, rare, 6" 550.00
Cambridge 2351, punch cup, amethyst, scarce 65.00
Cane (Imperial), pickle dish, pastel 45.00
Cane & Scroll (Sea Thistle) (English), rose bowl, marigold 125.00
Cane Panels, tumbler, marigold 250.00
Capitol (Westmoreland), bowl, amethyst, ftd, sm 70.00
Captive Rose (Fenton), compote, gr 100.00
Carnival Honeycomb (Jeannette), plate, amethyst, 7" 95.00
Cartwheel, #411 (Heisey), goblet, marigold 75.00
Cathedral (Brockwitz), chalice, bl, 7" 190.00
Cathedral (Brockwitz), rose bowl, bl 250.00
Channeled Flute (Northwood), vase, gr, 10-16", ea 125.00
Checkerboard (Westmoreland), goblet, marigold, rare 350.00
Checkers, rose bowl, marigold 85.00
Cherokee, tumbler, bl 65.00
Cherry (Dugan), cruet, wht, rare 650.00
Cherry (Millersburg), butter dish, marigold, w/lid 250.00

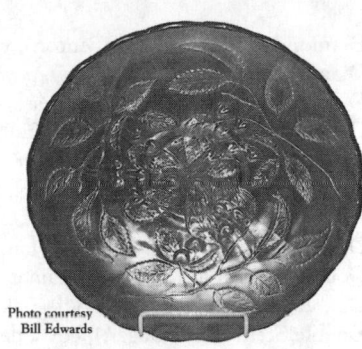

Cherry (Millersburg), bowl, marigold, 9", $90.00.

Photo courtesy
Bill Edwards

Cherry & Cable (Northwood), spooner, marigold, rare 225.00
Cherry Blossoms, tumbler, bl 40.00
Cherry Chain (Fenton), bonbon, amethyst 60.00
Cherry Circles (Fenton), bonbon, amethyst 65.00
Cherry Stippled, tumbler, marigold 110.00
Chesterfield (Imperial), pitcher, marigold, w/lid 150.00
Chippendale Souvenir, creamer, amethyst 85.00
Chrysanthemum (Fenton), bowl, gr, ftd, 10" 310.00
Circle Scroll (Dugan), vase, whimsey; blk amethyst, rare 300.00
Cobblestones (Fenton), bonbon, amethyst 150.00
Cobblestones (Imperial), bowl, gr, 8½" 150.00
Coin Dot (Fenton), plate, marigold, rare, 9" 200.00
Coin Spot (Dugan), compote, gr 70.00
Columbia (Imperial), cake plate, amethyst, scarce 180.00
Concave Diamonds (Northwood), pickle castor, marigold, complete ..475.00
Concave Flute (Westmoreland), vase, gr 65.00
Constellation (Dugan), compote, peach opal 225.00
Coral (Fenton), compote, gr, rare 500.00
Corinth (Dugan), vase, amethyst 50.00
Cornucopia (Jeannette), candlesticks, marigold, pr 80.00
Coronet, tumbler, marigold 30.00
Cosmos (Millersburg), bowl, gr, ruffled, scarce, 6½" 150.00
Cosmos & Cane (US Glass), spooner, marigold 100.00
Country Kitchen (Millersburg), sugar bowl, marigold 400.00
CR (Argentina), ashtray, bl 300.00
Crab Claw (Imperial), bowl, marigold, 10" 50.00
Crackle (Imperial), bowl, gr, 9" 30.00
Crackle (Imperial), shakers, aqua, pr 60.00
Crocus VT, tumbler, amethyst 65.00
Crystal Diamonds (Crystal), bowl, marigold 65.00
Cut Arches (English), banana bowl, marigold 80.00
Cut Arches (Fenton), compote, bl 55.00
Cut Flowers (Jenkins), vase, marigold, 10" 175.00
Cut Sprays, vase, peach opal, 9" 75.00
Dahlia (Dugan), tumbler, amethyst, rare 185.00
Daisy (Fenton), bonbon, marigold, scarce 250.00
Daisy & Cane (Brockwitz), spittoon, bl, rare 1,275.00
Daisy & Drape (Northwood), vase, amethyst 850.00
Daisy & Plume (Northwood & Dugan), compote, peach opal, ftd .160.00
Daisy Block (English), rowboat, amethyst, scarce 275.00
Dandelion (Northwood), mug, marigold 325.00
Davenport, tumbler, lemonade; marigold 35.00
Diagonal Band, tankard, amethyst, scarce 700.00
Diamond & Daisy Cut (US Glass), compote, bl 75.00
Diamond & Rib (Fenton), vase, funeral; gr, 17-22", ea 1,000.00
Diamond & Sunburst (Imperial), wine, gr 60.00
Diamond Band (Crystal), sugar bowl, marigold, open 45.00
Diamond Cut Shields, tumbler, marigold 150.00
Diamond Daisy, plate, marigold, 8" 95.00
Diamond Lace (Imperial), tumbler, marigold 190.00
Diamond Point Columns (Fenton), banana bowl, marigold 80.00

Diamond Point Columns (Fenton), vase, bl 90.00
Diamond Point Columns (Late), powder jar, marigold, w/lid 40.00
Diamond Points (Northwood), vase, gr, 7-14" 100.00
Diamond Ring (Imperial), bowl, fruit; amethyst, 9½" 90.00
Diamonds (Millersburg), pitcher, gr 350.00
Diving Dolphins (English), bowl, bl, ftd, 7" 270.00
Dorothy, perfume, marigold 50.00
Double Dolphins (Fenton), vase, fan; pastel 90.00
Double Loop (Northwood), creamer, gr 170.00
Double Scroll (Imperial), candlesticks, amethyst, pr 80.00
Double Stem Rose (Dugan), bowl, peach opal, dome base, 8½" .210.00
Dragon & Lotus (Fenton), bowl, marigold, ftd, 9" 110.00
Drapery (Northwood), rose bowl, bl 425.00
Duckie, powder jar, marigold, w/lid 20.00
Dugan's Flute, vase, marigold, 7-13", ea 45.00
Dutch Mill, ashtray, marigold 65.00
Eagle Furniture (Imperial), plate, advertising; amethyst 1,500.00
Egg & Dart, candlesticks, marigold, pr 90.00
Elegance, tumbler, marigold, enameled, rare 500.00
Elks (Fenton), bowl, Atlantic City; bl, scarce 1,400.00
Elks (Millersburg), paperweight, amethyst, rare 1,500.00
Embroidered Mums (Northwood), bonbon, wht, stemmed 1,300.00
Emu (Crystal), compote, amethyst, rare 500.00
Enameled Prism Band, tumbler, gr 65.00
English Hob & Button (English), epergne, marigold, metal base .125.00
Engraved Floral (Fenton), tumbler, gr 95.00
Estate, (Westmoreland), sugar bowl, peach opal 90.00
Exchange Bank, plate, advertising; amethyst, 6" 500.00
Famous, puff box, marigold 75.00
Fan-Tail (Fenton), bowl, bl, ftd, 5" 220.00
Fanciful (Dugan), plate, marigold, 9" 300.00
Fancy Flowers (Imperial), compote, gr 175.00
Fashion (Imperial), bride's basket, marigold 125.00
Fashion (Imperial), tumbler, amethyst 300.00
Feather Swirl (US Glass), vase, marigold 65.00
Feathered Serpent (Fenton), bowl, amethyst, 10" 75.00
Fenton's #649, candlesticks, vaseline, pr 160.00
Fenton's Cherries (Fenton), banana boat, marigold, rare 700.00
Fenton Smooth Rays, bowl, gr, tricornered, 6½" 50.00
Fentonia Fruit (Fenton), tumbler, marigold, rare 165.00
Fern (Northwood), compote, amethyst 70.00
Ferris Wheel, hatpin, amethyst 400.00
Field Thistle (US Glass), pitcher, marigold, scarce 200.00
File (Imperial & English), compote, amethyst 50.00
File & Fan, bowl, peach opal, ftd, 6" 160.00
Fine Cut & Roses (Northwood), rose bowl, gr, ftd 350.00
Fine Cut & Star, banana boat, marigold, 5" 150.00
Fine Cut Flowers & VT (Fenton), goblet, gr 125.00
Fine Cut Rings (English), celery tray, marigold 160.00
Fine Cut Rings Vt (English), celery vase, marigold 150.00
Fir Cones (Finland), tumbler, bl 275.00
Fish Net (Dugan), epergne, gr 240.00
Five Hearts (Dugan), rose bowl, marigold, rare 1,600.00
Flannel Flower (Crystal), compote, amethyst, lg 155.00
Flared Wide Panel, atomizer, marigold, 3½" 90.00
Flashing Stars, tumbler, bl, rare 350.00
Flora (English), float bowl, bl 200.00
Floral & Grape (Dugan), pitcher, amethyst 200.00
Floral & Optic (Imperial), rose bowl, marigold, ftd 75.00
Floral & Wheat (Dugan), compote, amethyst 45.00
Flower Medallion (Indiana Glass), tumbler, marigold, rare 500.00
Flowers & Spades (Dugan), bowl, amethyst, 10" 90.00
Fluffy Peacock (Fenton), tumbler, gr 225.00
Flute (Northwood), creamer, amethyst 85.00

Flute (Northwood), sherbet, marigold 35.00
Flute & Cane (Imperial), punch cup, marigold 25.00
Flute #700 (Imperial), butter dish, gr, w/lid 210.00
Flute #700 (Imperial), pitcher, bl 600.00
Folding Fan (Dugan), compote, peach opal 125.00
Footed Rib (Northwood), vase, marigold 50.00
Forget-Me-Not (Fenton), tumbler, gr 50.00
Fostoria #600 (Fostoria), napkin ring, marigold 75.00
Four Flowers (Dugan), plate, gr, 9-10½", ea 350.00
Four Flowers Vt (European), plate, amethyst, rare, 10½" 450.00
French Grape, bowl, marigold, 4" 180.00
Frosted Block (Imperial), pitcher, milk; marigold, rare 90.00
Fruit & Berries (English), bean pot, bl, w/lid, rare 425.00
Fruit Salad (Westmoreland), punch bowl, amethyst, w/base, rare .700.00
Fruits & Flowers (Northwood), fruit bowl, marigold, 10" 125.00
Garden Mums, bowl, gr, 8½-10" 80.00
Garden Path (Dugan), compote, amethyst, rare 375.00
Garden Path Vt (Dugan), rose bowl, marigold, rare 450.00
Garland (Fenton), rose bowl, bl, ftd 110.00
Gay 90s (Millersburg), tumbler, amethyst, rare 1,150.00
God & Home (Dugan), tumbler, bl, rare 275.00
Golden Flowers, vase, marigold, 7½" 95.00
Golden Grapes (Dugan), bowl, gr, 7" 50.00
Golden Pansies, tray, marigold, 5½x10" 350.00
Good Luck (Northwood), plate, gr, 9" 875.00
Gooseberry Spray (US Glass) (Palm Beach exterior), compote, bl ..275.00
Graceful (Northwood), vase, amethyst 100.00
Grape (Imperial), cup & saucer, amethyst 175.00
Grape (Imperial), punch cup, amethyst 45.00
Grape & Cable (Fenton), orange bowl, marigold, ftd 110.00
Grape & Cable (Fenton), spittoon whimsey, marigold, rare 1,200.00
Grape & Cable (Northwood), bowl, berry; gr, 5½" 60.00
Grape & Cable (Northwood), cologne, amethyst, w/stopper 225.00
Grape & Cable (Northwood), decanter, marigold, w/stopper 600.00
Grape & Cable (Northwood), hatpin holder, bl 800.00
Grape & Cable (Northwood), nappy, bl, made from punch cup .100.00
Grape & Cable (Northwood), sherbet, marigold 40.00
Grape & Cable (Northwood), tumbler, amethyst, jumbo 75.00
Grape & Gothic Arches (Northwood), tumbler, marigold 35.00
Grape Arbor (Northwood), tumbler, amethyst 100.00
Grape Leaves (Millersburg), bowl, marigold, rare, 10" 600.00
Grape Leaves (Northwood), bowl, bl, 8½" 90.00
Grape Wreath (Millersburg), bowl, ice cream; gr, 10" 175.00
Grecian Daisy, tumbler, marigold, scarce 60.00
Grecian Urn, perfume, marigold, 6" 50.00
Greek Key (Northwood), tumbler, gr, rare 300.00
Halloween, spittoon, marigold 600.00
Harvest Poppy, compote, marigold 320.00
Hawaiian Lei (Higbee), creamer, marigold 75.00
Headdress, compote, gr 80.00
Heart & Trees (Fenton), bowl, gr, 8¼" 400.00
Heart & Vine (Fenton), plate, amethyst, rare, 9" 475.00
Heart Band Souvenir (McKee), mug, gr, lg 165.00
Hearts & Flowers (Fenton), compote, marigold 350.00
Heavy Diamond (Imperial), sugar bowl, marigold 35.00
Heavy Grape (Imperial), nappy, marigold 45.00
Heavy Grape (Imperial), punch cup, gr 75.00
Heisey #357, water bottle, marigold 190.00
Heisey Colonial, dresser tray, marigold 100.00
Heisey Flute, toothpick holder, marigold 150.00
Heisey Puritan (#341), compote, amethyst 250.00
Hex Base, candlesticks, amethyst, pr 125.00
Hobnail (Crystal), salver, amethyst 190.00
Hobnail (Millersburg), rose bowl, amethyst, rare 400.00

Hobnail (Millersburg), spooner, marigold, rare 275.00
Hobnail Vt (Millersburg), jardiniere, bl, rare 1,200.00
Hobstar & Arches (Imperial), bowl, fruit; amethyst, w/base 300.00
Hobstar & Feather (Millersburg), butter dish, marigold, rare ..1,500.00
Hobstar & Feather (Millersburg), creamer, amethyst, rare 800.00
Hobstar & Feather (Millersburg), punch cup, bl, scarce 350.00
Hobstar & Feather (Millersburg), tumbler, marigold, rare 850.00
Hobstar & Tassels (European), tumbler, marigold 125.00
Hobstar Band, celery dish, gr, scarce 400.00
Hobstar Panels (English), creamer, marigold 45.00
Hobstar Reserved (English), spooner, marigold 45.00
Holly Sprig or Whirl (Millersburg), card tray, gr, hdld 140.00
Honeybee (Jeannette), honey pot, bl, w/lid 180.00
Honeycomb & Clover (Fenton), bonbon, amethyst 50.00
Honeycomb Ornament, hatpin, bl 125.00
Hoops, rose bowl, marigold, low, 6½" 75.00
Horse Radish, jar, marigold, w/lid 55.00
Horse's Head (Fenton)(Horse Medallion), bowl, nut; amethyst, rare .250.00
Hourglass, vase, bud; marigold 30.00
Humpty-Dumpty, mustard jar, marigold 75.00
Imperial #302 (Imperial), cruet, marigold, rare 300.00
Imperial #499 (Imperial), sherbet, gr 30.00
Imperial Jewels (Imperial), plate, amethyst, 7" 75.00
Inca (Czech), bottle, marigold 175.00
Intaglio Daisy (Dugan/Diamond), bowl, amethyst, 4½" 90.00

Photo courtesy
Bill Edwards

Intaglio Daisy (English), bowl, marigold, 7½", $50.00.

Intaglio Ovals (US Glass), plate, pastel, 7½" 100.00
Interior Flute, sugar bowl, marigold 60.00
Interior Swirl, tumbler, marigold 50.00
Inverted Coin Dot (Fenton-Northwood), tumbler, amethyst 95.00
Inverted Feather (Cambridge), creamer, marigold, rare 400.00
Inverted Strawberry (Cambridge), celery dish, amethyst, rare .1,300.00
Inverted Thistle (Cambridge), butter dish, marigold, rare 500.00
Iris (Fenton), goblet, buttermilk; gr 65.00
Jack-in-the-Pulpit (Dugan), vase, bl 80.00
Jackman, whiskey bottle, marigold 50.00
Jacob's Ladder, perfume bottle, marigold 60.00
Jacobean Ranger (Czech & English), tumbler, marigold 195.00
Jasmine & Butterfly (Czech), tumbler, marigold 25.00
Jester's Cap (Northwood), vase, amethyst 100.00
Jeweled Heart (Dugan), pitcher, marigold, rare 900.00
Jewels (Dugan), candlesticks, gr, pr 175.00
Keg, toothpick holder, marigold 20.00
Keystone Colonial (Westmoreland), compote, amethyst, 6¼" ...300.00
King's Crown (US Glass), wine, marigold, stemmed 50.00
Kittens (Fenton), bowl, bl, ruffled, scarce 600.00
Kokomo (English), rose bowl, marigold, ftd 45.00
Lacy Dewdrop (Westmoreland), tumbler, pastel 275.00
Late Enameled Bleeding Hearts, tumbler, marigold 175.00
Late Waterlily, pitcher, marigold 50.00

Lattice & Daisy (Dugan), pitcher, bl 300.00
Lattice & Grape (Fenton), tumbler, peach opal 500.00
Lattice Heart (English), compote, marigold 60.00
LBJ Hat, ashtray, marigold 35.00
Lea & Vt (English), creamer, amethyst, ftd 50.00
Leaf & Beads (Northwood), nut bowl, gr, ftd, scarce 150.00
Leaf Chain (Fenton), bonbon, marigold 45.00
Leaf Tiers (Fenton), sugar bowl, marigold, ftd 90.00
Liberty Bell, cookie jar, marigold, w/lid 40.00
Lily of the Valley (Fenton), tumbler, marigold, rare 700.00
Lion (Fenton), bowl, bl, scarce, 7" 350.00
Little Beads, compote, peach opal, sm 65.00
Little Daisy, bottle, pastel 500.00
Little Stars (Millersburg), bowl, amethyst, scarce, 7" 150.00
Loganberry (Imperial), vase, marigold, scarce 325.00
Long Hobstar (Imperial), punch bowl, marigold, w/base 125.00
Long Thumbprint Vt, compote, marigold 30.00
Lotus & Grape (Fenton), bowl, bl, ftd, 9" 75.00
Lovebirds, bottle, marigold, w/stopper 575.00
Lustre & Clear (Imperial), butter dish, marigold 75.00
Lustre Flute (Northwood), bowl, gr, 8" 65.00
Lustre Rose (Imperial), fernery, gr 60.00
Lustre Rose (Imperial), tumbler, gr 40.00
Mae West (Dugan), candlesticks, bl, pr 95.00
Many Fruits (Dugan), punch cup, gr 40.00
Maple Leaf (Dugan), spooner, bl 70.00
Marilyn (Millersburg), tumbler, marigold, rare 150.00
Martha, compote, marigold, 7½" 300.00
May Basket (English), basket, gr, 7½" 95.00
Melon Rib, candy jar, marigold, w/lid 30.00
Memphis (Northwood), bowl, fruit; gr, w/base 600.00
Mexican Bell, goblet, marigold, flashed 40.00
Mikado (Fenton), compote, bl, lg 450.00
Miniature Blackberry (Fenton), compote, bl, sm 175.00
Minuet, tumbler, marigold 75.00
Mirror & Crossbar (Jain), tumbler, marigold, rare 400.00
Mirrored Lotus (Fenton), rose bowl, bl, rare 500.00
Mitered Diamond & Pleats (English), bowl, bl, 4½" 30.00
Moongleam (Heisey), pitcher, gr, w/lid 400.00
Morning Glory (Imperial), vase, marigold, squat, 4-7", ea 40.00
Morning Glory (Millersburg), tumbler, gr, rare 1,100.00
Multi-Fruits & Flowers (Millersburg), punch cup, bl, rare 3,000.00
My Lady powder jar, marigold, w/lid 150.00
Napolean, bottle, pastel 85.00
Near Cut (Cambridge), decanter, gr, w/stopper, rare 3,500.00
Nesting Swan (Millersburg), bowl, bl, tricornered, rare 3,500.00
Niagara Falls (Jeannette), pitcher, milk; marigold 35.00
Night Stars (Millersburg), card tray, gr, rare 850.00
Nippon (Northwood), plate, bl, scarce, 9" 725.00
Northwood Swirl, tumbler, gr 125.00
Notches, plate, marigold, 8" 50.00
Number 600 (Fostoria), toothpick holder, marigold 50.00
O'Hara (Loop), goblet, marigold 25.00
Octagon (Imperial), bowl, fruit; gr, 10-12", ea 150.00
Octagon (Imperial), wine, marigold 25.00
Oklahoma (Mexican), tumble-up, marigold, complete 200.00
Omnibus, tumbler, gr, rare 795.00
Open Flower (Dugan), bowl, gr, flat or ftd, 7" 50.00
Open Rose (Imperial), plate, amethyst, 9" 325.00
Optic (Imperial), rose bowl, smoke 100.00
Optic & Buttons (Imperial), tumbler, clambroth, 2 shapes, ea 40.00
Optic Flute (Imperial), compote, marigold 50.00
Orange Peel (Westmoreland), punch cup, amethyst 40.00
Orange Tree (Fenton), hatpin holder, bl 275.00

Orange Tree (Fenton), mug, red, 2 szs, ea 650.00
Orange Tree (Fenton), powder jar, gr, w/lid 500.00
Orange Tree Orchard (Fenton), tumbler, gr 55.00
Oriental Poppy (Northwood), tumbler, bl 375.00
Paden City #198, syrup, marigold, w/liner, rare 300.00
Palm Beach (US Glass), banana bowl, amethyst 200.00
Palm Beach (US Glass), sugar bowl, marigold, w/lid 95.00
Panama (US Glass), goblet, marigold, rare 150.00
Paneled Daisy & Cane, basket, marigold, rare 700.00
Paneled Dandelion (Fenton), tumbler, gr 70.00
Paneled Holly (Northwood), bonbon, gr, ftd 75.00
Paneled Palm (US Glass), mug, marigold, rare 100.00
Paneled Smocking, sugar bowl, marigold 50.00
Paneled Twigs, tumbler, marigold 200.00
Pansy (Imperial), dresser tray, gr 65.00
Parlor, ashtray, bl 95.00
Peach (Northwood), butter dish, wht 275.00
Peaches, wine bottle, marigold 45.00
Peacock (Millersburg), bowl, ice cream; bl, 5" 750.00
Peacock & Dahlia (Fenton), bowl, gr, 7½" 150.00
Peacock & Grape (Fenton), nut bowl, bl, ftd, scarce 150.00
Peacock & Urn (Fenton), plate, gr, rare, 9" 900.00
Peacock & Urn (Northwood), plate, amethyst, rare, 6" 600.00
Peacock & Urn & Vts (Millersburg), compote, marigold, lg, rare ..1,400.00
Peacock at the Fountain (Northwood), butter dish, gr 600.00
Peacock at the Fountain (Northwood), punch cup, aqua opal ..1,500.00
Peacock Tail Vt (Millersburg), compote, gr, scarce 200.00
Pearl & Jewels (Fenton), basket, wht, 4" 200.00
Pearly Dots (Westmoreland), rose bowl, amethyst 75.00
Penny (Dugan), match holder, amethyst, rare 500.00
Perfection (Millersburg), tumbler, marigold, rare 600.00
Persian Garden (Dugan), bowl, fruit; peach opal, w/base 700.00
Persian Medallion (Fenton), bonbon, amethyst 110.00
Persian Medallion (Fenton), hair receiver, bl 85.00
Petals (Northwood), compote, gr 200.00
Pickle, paperweight, amethyst, 4½" 75.00
Pillar & Flute (Imperial), celery vase, marigold 60.00
Pinched Swirl (Dugan), spittoon whimsey, peach opal 175.00
Pine Cone (Fenton), plate, bl, 6¼" 300.00

Pineapple (English), bowl, amethyst, 7", $70.00.

Photo courtesy
Bill Edwards

Pineapple (English), compote, bl 60.00
Plain Coin Dot (Fenton), rose bowl, marigold 65.00
Plain Jane (Imperial), bowl, amethyst, 9" 70.00
Plain Rays, compote, gr 60.00
Plazza, hatpin, amethyst 425.00
Plume Panels (Fenton), vase, bl, 7-12", ea 150.00
Poinsettia Interior (Northwood), tumbler, marigold, rare 450.00
Pony (Dugan), bowl, amethyst, 8½" 300.00
Poppy (Millersburg), compote, gr, scarce 725.00
Poppy (Northwood), tray, bl, oval, rare 450.00
Poppy Show (Imperial), vase, gr, old only, 12" 1,000.00

Poppy Vt (Northwood), bowl, bl, 7-8", ea 175.00
Pretty Panels (Northwood), pitcher, gr 150.00
Princely Plumes, candle holder, amethyst 300.00
Prism Band (Fenton), tumbler, bl, decor 55.00
Prisms (Westmoreland), compote, gr, scarce, 5" 100.00
Prisms & Daisy Band (Imperial), compote, marigold 35.00
Puppy, candy holder, marigold, mini 100.00
Puzzle (Dugan), compote, gr 85.00
Question Marks (Dugan), bonbon, amethyst 55.00
Radiance, tumbler, marigold 90.00
Rainbow (Northwood), bowl, marigold, 8" 45.00
Rambler Rose (Dugan), pitcher, bl 300.00
Ranger (European), tumbler, marigold 115.00
Ranger (Imperial), sherbet, marigold, ftd 65.00
Ranger (Mexican), pitcher, milk; marigold 150.00
Raspberry (Northwood), pitcher, milk; gr 400.00
Ray & Ribbons (Millersburg), bowl, gr, tricornered 275.00
Regal Swirl, candlestick, marigold, ea 75.00
Ribbed Holly (Fenton), goblet, bl 70.00
Ribs (Czech), soap dish, marigold 60.00
Rising Sun (US Glass), tumbler, bl, rare 600.00
Rock Crystal (McKee), punch cup, amethyst, rare 75.00
Roll, pitcher, clambroth, rare 300.00
Roly-Roly, jar, marigold, w/lid, 7" 70.00
Rosalind Vt, compote, gr, rare, 6" 550.00
Rose Band (Brockwitz), tumbler, marigold, rare 700.00
Rose Panels (Australian), compote, marigold, lg 150.00
Rose Show (Northwood), plate, bl, 9½" 1,650.00
Rose Spray (Fenton), compote, marigold 175.00
Rosettes (Northwood), bowl, gr, ftd, 7-9", ea 200.00
Round-Up (Dugan), plate, bl, rare, 9" 550.00
Royalty (Imperial), punch cup, marigold 35.00
Rustic (Fenton), vase, bl, 10-14", ea 70.00
S-Repeat (Dugan), tumbler, amethyst 125.00
Sailboats (Fenton), goblet, gr 500.00
Sawtooth Band, tumbler, marigold, rare 400.00
Scottie, powder jar, marigold, w/lid 20.00
Scroll Embossed (Imperial), bowl, red, 8-9", ea 600.00
Scroll Embossed Vt (English), ashtray, amethyst, hdld, 5" 60.00
Seacoast (Millersburg), pin tray, gr, rare 800.00
Seaweed (Millersburg), bowl, ice cream; gr, rare, 10½" 1,200.00
Shasta Daisy, tumbler, marigold 35.00
Shell (Imperial), plate, gr, 8½" 500.00
Shell & Jewel (Westmoreland), creamer, marigold, w/lid 55.00
Sheraton (US Glass), pitcher, pastel 170.00
Shrine (US Glass), toothpick holder, amethyst 650.00
Signature (Jeannette), sherbet, marigold, scarce 25.00
Silver & Gold, tumbler, marigold 50.00
Singing Birds (Northwood), creamer, gr 125.00
Single Flower Framed (Dugan), plate, amethyst 300.00
Six Petals (Dugan), bowl, bl, 8½" 125.00
Six Rings, tumbler, marigold 25.00
Ski-Star (Dugan), bowl, bl, 5" 250.00
Small Blackberry (Northwood), compote, gr 75.00
Small Thumbprint, creamer, marigold 60.00
Smooth Rays (Imperial), champagne, marigold 40.00
Smooth Rays (Northwood), bonbon, gr 55.00
Smooth Rays (Westmoreland), compote, gr 55.00
Snow Fancy (Imperial), creamer, marigold 50.00
Soda Gold (Imperial), tumbler, marigold 50.00
Souvenir Banded, mug, marigold 85.00
Sowerby Flower Block (English), flower frog, marigold 60.00
Spiderweb (Northwood), candy dish, smoke, w/lid 40.00
Spiral (Imperial), candlesticks, gr, pr 195.00

Split Diamond (English), creamer, marigold, sm 40.00
Spring Basket (Imperial), basket, marigold, hdld, 5" 50.00
Springtime (Northwood), butter dish, gr 475.00
Square Daisy & Button (Imperial), toothpick holder, pastel, rare .125.00
Star, goblet, buttermilk; marigold 25.00
Star & Drape (Crystal), pitcher, marigold 165.00
Star & File (Imperial), celery vase, marigold, hdld 50.00
Star & File (Imperial), rose bowl, gr 125.00
Star & Flower, hatpin, bl 1,200.00
Star Cut, tumbler, marigold 25.00

Star Medallion, milk pitcher, green, $80.00.

Photo courtesy Bill Edwards

Star Rosette, tumbler, marigold, scarce 150.00
Starbright, vase, bl, 6½" 50.00
Starburst Lustre (Northwood), compote, gr 80.00
Starflower, pitcher, bl, rare 200.00
Stars & Bars (Cambridge), wine, marigold, rare 150.00
States (US Glass), butter dish, marigold, w/lid, very rare 600.00
Stippled Petals (Dugan), basket, amethyst, hdld 160.00
Stippled Rays (Fenton), compote, bl 40.00
Stippled Rays (Imperial), creamer, gr, stemmed 70.00
Stippled Rays (Northwood), compote, marigold 50.00
Stork & Rushes (Dugan), punch cup, bl 35.00
Strawberry (Fenton), bonbon, amethyst 75.00
Strawberry (Millersburg), compote, marigold, rare 675.00
Strawberry (Northwood), plate, gr, 9" 400.00
Strawberry Scroll (Fenton), tumbler, bl, rare 250.00
Strutting Peacock (Westmoreland), sugar bowl, gr, w/lid 100.00
Style (Crystal), bowl, marigold, 8" 100.00
Sunflower (Millersburg), pin tray, amethyst, rare 500.00
Sunk Daisies, rose bowl, bl, rare 600.00
Sunk Diamond Band (US Glass), tumbler, marigold, rare 50.00
Sunray, compote, amethyst 45.00
Sweetheart (Cambridge), cookie jar, gr, w/lid, rare 1,100.00
Swirl Vt (Imperial), epergne, gr 200.00
Swirled Ribs (Northwood), tumbler, marigold 70.00
Taffeta Lustre (Fostoria), bowl, console; gr, rare, 11" 150.00
Ten Mums (Fenton), tumbler, bl, rare 100.00
Texas, tumbler, bl, giant sz 250.00
Thin Rib & Drape, vase, amethyst, 4-11" 225.00
Thin Ribs (Fenton), candlesticks, marigold, pr 80.00
Thistle (Fenton), bowl, bl, 8-10" 140.00
Thread & Cane (Crystal), salver, marigold 110.00
Threaded Wide Panel, goblet, marigold, 2 szs, ea 50.00
Three Flowers (Imperial), tray, marigold, center hdl, 12" 60.00
Three Roll, tumble-up, marigold, complete 90.00
Three-in-One (Imperial), toothpick holder, gr, rare (Vt) 85.00
Thumbprint & Spears, creamer, gr 60.00
Tiered Panels, cup, marigold, scarce 30.00
Tiers, tumbler, marigold 60.00
Tiger Lily (Imperial), tumbler, bl 350.00
Tiny Berry, tumbler, bl 45.00

Top of the Morning, hatpin, amethyst 100.00
Tracery (Millersburg), bonbon, gr, rare 1,100.00
Tree Bark (Imperial), bowl, console; marigold 35.00
Tree Bark Vt, planter, marigold 60.00
Tree of Life, pitcher, marigold 60.00
Tree Trunk (Northwood), jardiniere whimsey, bl, rare 2,500.00
Triads (Brockwitz), butter dish, marigold 65.00
Triplets (Dugan), bowl, gr, 6-8" 65.00
Tulip (Millersburg), compote, gr, rare, 9" 825.00
Tulip Panels, ginger jar, marigold 125.00
Twins (Imperial), bowl, marigold, 9" 40.00
Twitch (Bartlett-Collins), sherbet, marigold 45.00
Two Fourty Nine, candle holders, red, pr 700.00
Unshod, pitcher, marigold 85.00
Valentine, ring tray, marigold 80.00
Venetian (Cambridge), creamer, marigold, rare 550.00
Vineyard (Dugan), tumbler, amethyst 100.00
Vineyard Harvest (Jain), tumbler, marigold, rare 250.00
Vintage (Dugan), powder jar, bl, w/lid 375.00
Vintage (Fenton), compote, gr 55.00
Vintage (Fenton), plate, bl, ruffled, 11" 295.00
Vintage Leaf (Fenton), bonbon, gr, card tray shape 135.00
Vogue (Fostoria), toothpick holder, marigold, scarce 250.00
Voltec (McKee), butter dish, amethyst, w/lid 150.00
Waffle Block (Imperial), creamer, marigold 60.00
Waffle Block (Imperial), punch cup, marigold 20.00
Waffle Weave, inkwell, marigold 95.00
Water Lily (Fenton), bonbon, gr 55.00
Water Lily & Cattails (Fenton), bonbon, bl 90.00
Water Lily & Cattails (Northwood), pitcher, bl 6,000.00
Western Thistle, pitcher, cider; bl 350.00
Wheat (Northwood), sweetmeat, gr, w/lid, rare 9,500.00
Whirling Star (Imperial), compote, gr 85.00
White Oak, tumbler, marigold, rare 300.00
Wide Panel (Fenton), glass, lemonade; marigold, hdld 30.00
Wide Panel (Fenton), vase, bl, 7-9" 60.00
Wide Panel (Imperial), plate, red, 10-12", ea 500.00
Wide Panel (Northwood), epergne, gr, 4-lily, scarce 1,850.00
Wide Panel Vt (Northwood), pitcher, tankard; marigold 200.00
Wigwam (Heisey), tumbler, marigold, rare 150.00
Wild Fern (Australian), compote, amethyst 250.00
Wild Grape, bowl, marigold, Vt, scarce, 8¾" 100.00
Wild Rose (Millersburg), lamp, gr, rare, sm 1,100.00
Wild Strawberry (Northwood), bowl, gr, 9-10½" 300.00
Wildflower (Dugan), plate, marigold, 9" 175.00
Wildflower (Northwood), compote, bl, plain interior 450.00
Wine & Roses (Fenton), wine, bl 100.00
Wishbone (Imperial), flower arranger, marigold 90.00
Wishbone (Northwood), tumbler, gr, scarce 210.00
Woodpecker (Dugan), wall vase, marigold 70.00

Wreath of Roses, punch bowl, blue, $390.00; Matching punch cups, $40.00 each.

Wreath of Roses (Dugan), bowl, nut; marigold **70.00**
Wreath of Roses (Fenton), compote, gr **50.00**
Wreathed Cherry (Dugan), bowl, bl, oval, 10½" **300.00**
Wreathed Cherry (Dugan), tumbler, wht **150.00**
Zig Zag (Fenton), tumbler, bl, decor **80.00**
Zig Zag (Millersburg), bowl, marigold, tricornered, 10" **575.00**
Zipper Vt (English), sugar bowl, marigold, w/lid **55.00**
Zippered Heart (Imperial), bowl, marigold, 5" **40.00**
474 (Imperial), punch bowl, gr, w/base **850.00**
474 Vt (Sweden), compote, gr, 7" **90.00**
49'er Vt (Inwald), decanter, marigold, scarce **175.00**

Carousel Figures

For generations of Americans, visions of carousel horses revolving majestically around lively band organs rekindle wonderful childhood experiences. These nostalgic memories are the legacy of the creative talent from a dozen carving shops that created America's carousel art. Skilled craftsmen brought their trade from Europe where American carvers took the carousel animal from a folk art creation to a true art form. The 'golden age of carousel art' lasted from 1880 to 1929.

There are two basic types of American carousels. The largest and most impressive is the 'park style' carousel built for permanent installation in major amusement centers. These were created in Philadelphia by Gustav and William Dentzel, Muller Brothers, and E. Joy Morris who became the Philadelphia Toboggan Company in 1902. A more flamboyant group of carousel animals was carved in Coney Island, New York, by Charles Looff, Marcus Illions, Charles Carmel, and Stein & Goldstein's Artistic Carousel Company. These park-style carousels were typically three, four, and even five rows with forty-five to sixty-eight animals on a platform. Collectors often pay a premium for the carvings by these men. The outside row animals are larger and more ornate and command higher prices. The horses on the inside rows are smaller, less decorated, and of lesser value.

The most popular style of carousel art is the 'country fair style.' These carousels were portable affairs created for mobility. The horses are smaller and less ornate with leg and head positions that allow for stacking and easy loading. These were built primarily for North Tonawanda, New York, near Niagara Falls, by Armitage Herschell Company, Herschell Spillman Company, Spillman Engineering Company, and Allen Herschell. Charles W. Parker was also well known for his portable merry-go-rounds. He was based in Leavenworth, Kansas. Parker and Herschell Spillman both created a few large park-style carousels as well, but they are better known for their portable models.

Horses are by far the most common figure found, but there are two dozen other animals that were created for the carousel platform. Carousel animals, unlike most other antiques, are oftentimes worth more in a restored condition. Figures found with original factory paint are extraordinarily rare and bring premium amounts. Typically, carousel horses are found in garish, poorly applied 'park paint' and are often missing legs or ears. Carousel horses are hollow. They were glued up from several blocks for greater strength and lighter weight. Bass and poplar woods were used extensively.

If you have an antique carousel animal you would like to have identified, send a clear photograph and description along with a LSASE to our advisor, William Manns, who is listed in the Directory under New Mexico. Mr. Manns is the author of *Painted Ponies*, containing many full-color photographs, guides, charts, and directories for the collector.

Key:
IR — inside row   OR — outside row
MR — middle row   PTC — Philadelphia Toboggan Company

Coney Island-Style Horses

Carmel, IR jumper, unrstr **4,800.00**
Carmel, MR jumper, unrstr **8,900.00**
Carmel, OR jumper w/cherub, rstr **30,000.00**
Illions, IR jumper, rstr **5,200.00**
Illions, MR stander, rstr **9,200.00**
Looff, IR jumper unrstr **6,200.00**
Looff, OR jumper, unrstr **21,500.00**
Stein & Goldstein, IR jumper, unrstr **5,700.00**
Stein & Goldstein, MR jumper, rstr **9,000.00**
Stein & Goldstein, OR stander w/bells, unrstr **39,000.00**

European Horses

Anderson, English, unrstr **3,500.00**
Bayol, French, unrstr **3,000.00**
Heyn, German, unrstr **3,500.00**
Hubner, Belgian, unrstr **2,800.00**
Savage, English, unrstr **3,500.00**

Menagerie Animals (Non-Horses)

Photo courtesy Dunbar Gallery

Porky Pig, Mexican kiddie carousel figure, flesh body with red jacket, restored, 1950s, 19x29", from $1,200.00 to $1,500.00.

Dentzel, bear, unrstr **28,000.00**
Dentzel, cat, unrstr **37,000.00**
Dentzel, deer, unrstr **13,500.00**
Dentzel, lion, unrstr **45,000.00**
Dentzel, pig, unrstr **9,000.00**
E Joy Morris, deer, unrstr **10,000.00**
Herschell Spillman, cat, unrstr **12,500.00**
Herschell Spillman, chicken, portable, unrstr **7,000.00**
Herschell Spillman, dog, portable, unrstr **6,500.00**
Herschell Spillman, frog, unrstr **24,000.00**
Looff, camel, unrstr **10,000.00**
Looff, goat, rstr **15,000.00**
Muller, tiger, rstr **32,000.00**

Philadelphia-Style Horses

Dentzel, IR 'topknot' jumper, unrstr **6,200.00**
Dentzel, MR jumper, unrstr **12,700.00**
Dentzel, OR stander, female cvg on shoulder, rstr **32,500.00**
Dentzel, prancer, rstr **9,500.00**
Morris, IR prancer, rstr **7,000.00**
Morris, MR stander, unrstr **9,500.00**
Morris, OR stander, rstr **20,000.00**
Muller, IR jumper, rstr **5,700.00**
Muller, MR jumper, rstr **12,000.00**
Muller, OR stander, rstr **42,000.00**

Muller, OR stander w/military trappings **75,000.00**
PTC, chariot (bench-like seat), rstr **8,900.00**
PTC, IR jumper, rstr **4,000.00**
PTC, MR jumper, rstr **12,800.00**
PTC, OR stander, armored, rstr **52,000.00**
PTC, OR stander, unrstr **29,500.00**

Portable Carousel Horses

Allan Herschell, all aluminum, ca 1950 ....**750.00**
Allan Herschell, half & half, wood & aluminum head **1,500.00**
Allan Herschell, IR Indian pony, unrstr **2,500.00**
Allan Herschell, OR, rstr **3,200.00**
Allan Herschell, OR Trojan-style jumper **3,800.00**
Armitage Herschell, track-machine jumper **2,800.00**
Dare, jumper, unrstr **3,000.00**
Herschell Spillman, chariot (bench-like seat) **3,800.00**
Herschell Spillman, IR jumper, unrstr **2,400.00**
Herschell Spillman, MR jumper, unrstr **2,900.00**
Herschell Spillman, OR, eagle decor **4,500.00**
Herschell Spillman, OR, park machine **10,000.00**
Parker, MR jumper, unrstr **4,200.00**
Parker, OR jumper, park machine, unrstr **7,500.00**
Parker, OR jumper, rstr **5,800.00**

Cartoon Art

Collectors of cartoon art are interested in many forms of original art — animation cels, sports, political or editorial cartoons, syndicated comic strip panels, and caricature. To produce even a short animated cartoon strip, hundreds of original drawings are required, each showing the characters in slightly advancing positions. Called 'cels' because those made prior to the 1950s were made from a celluloid material, collectors often pay hundreds of dollars for a frame from a favorite movie. Prices of Disney cels with backgrounds vary widely. Background paintings, model sheets, storyboards, and preliminary sketches are also collectible — so are comic book drawings executed in India ink and signed by the artist. Daily 'funnies' originals, especially the earlier ones portraying super heroes, and Sunday comic strips, the early as well as the later ones, are collected. Cartoon art has become recognized and valued as a novel yet valid form of contemporary art. In the listings below all cels are gouache on celluloid unless noted otherwise.

Key:
ab — airbrushed   WD — Walt Disney
HB — Hanna-Barbera   KFS — King Features Syndicate
WB — Warner Brothers

Animation Cels, Full Color

Alice in Wonderland, WD, Caterpillar w/hookah, 1951, 8x5½" ..**1,600.00**
Deputy Droopy, MGM, w/Slim & glue bottle, 1955, 7½x6", pr ..**1,100.00**
Donald Duck, WD, as Scarlet Pimpernel, 1950s, 8x10", pr **1,000.00**
Flintstones, HB, Pebbles & Bamm-Bamm, 1992 ....**50.00**
Gilligan's Island, HB, Gilligan w/Skipper, in fr **265.00**
Jonny Quest, HB, eating cornflakes, 1964 ....**425.00**
Lady & Tramp, WD, Jock portrait, 1955, 7x7"+fr **865.00**
Lady & Tramp, WD, Lady, full figure, 1955, 4½x3½" **2,000.00**
Little Mermaid, WD, Ariel portrait, sgn Keane, w/seal, 7x11" .**2,150.00**
Mighty Mouse, Terrytoons, full figure, 1960s, 9x19" **1,350.00**
Peter Pan, WD, Hook & Mr Smee, w/label, prof rstr, 1953, 4x4" .**785.00**
Peter Pan, WD, Mr Darling, 8x7" **500.00**
Ren & Stimpy, Nickelodeon, portraits, 1991, 9x12", pr **900.00**

Robin Hood, WD, dressed as gypsy, 6x7" **500.00**
Sniffles, WB, mouse by cheese, 1940s, 8½x9"+fr **4,000.00**
Song of South, WD, Rabbit & Tar Baby, w/seal, 1986, 11x15" .**1,750.00**
Thru the Mirror, WD, Mickey & King of Hearts, 1936, 6x8" .**1,100.00**
Tom Terrific, Paul Terry, w/Mighty Manfred, 1957, 3x3½" **550.00**
Who Framed Roger Rabbit?, w/Eddie & weasels **3,000.00**
Wild Honey, MGM, bear mother & baby, 1942, 9x22" **1,900.00**
Winnie the Pooh, WD, w/Piglet/Christopher Robin, 1980s, 11x14" .**1,350.00**
101 Dalmatians, WD, Pongo, w/label, 1961, 8x10" **1,350.00**

Animation Drawings

Donald Duck, WD, full figure w/riding crop, 5½x4" **275.00**
George Jetson, HB, at desk in uniform, 1960s **150.00**
Gulliver's Travels, 2 kings singing, 7½x5½" **350.00**
Jerky Turkey, Tex Avery, w/pilgrim **250.00**
Jerry the Mouse, production pc from Flirty Birdy, 1945 ....**300.00**
Jetson family, HB, in spacemobile, bl graphite, ...**85.00**
Mickey Mouse, WD, signed Walt Disney, orange crayon **4,000.00**
Peter Pan, WD, John making war hoop, pencil, 5x3½" **275.00**
Pinocchio, WD, as real boy, 1940, 4½x5" **350.00**
Quick Draw McGraw, HB, w/whip, 1959 ....**110.00**
Snow White & 7 Dwarfs, WD, wicked witch, red/gr pencil, 1937, 8x6" ...**1,500.00**
Speed Buggy & gang, HB, graphite & bl pencil, 1973 ....**40.00**
Woody Woodpecker, Lantz, graphite & pencil, 5" image, 1960s .**1,100.00**

Miscellaneous

Sunday page, bottom half, Bringing Up Father, MacManus, 1920s, 9¼x16½", $400.00.

Comic book cover, Phantom #30, Sherwood, February 1969, 12½x19" **400.00**
Model sheet, Superfriends, HB, A Toth, 1973 ....**650.00**
Orig daily strip, Buck Rogers, M Anderson, December 1947 ......**350.00**
Orig daily strip, Dick Tracy, Gould, February 12, 1965 ....**750.00**
Orig daily strip, Hagar the Horrible, Browne, November 14, 1986 ..**225.00**
Orig daily strip, Steve Canyon, Caniff, December 20, 1951 ......**350.00**
Orig Sunday page, Dick Tracy/BO Plenty, March 15, 1953 ....**1,400.00**
Orig Sunday page, Tillie the Toiler, Westover, August 1931 .....**250.00**
Orig Sunday strip, Tarzan, Hobarth, March 8, 1942 ....**4,500.00**
Painting on board, star trails & meteor showings, Dollens **250.00**

Cartoon Books

'Books of cartoons' were printed during the first decade of the 20th century and remained popular until the advent of the modern comic book in the late '30s. Cartoon books, printed in both color and black and white, were merely reprints of current newspaper comic strips. The books, ranging from thirty to seventy pages and in sizes from 3½" x 8" up to 11" x 17", were usually bound with cardboard covers and were often distributed as premiums in exchange for coupons saved from the daily paper. One of the largest of the companies who printed these books was Cupples and Leon, producer of nearly half of the two hundred titles on record. Among the most popular sellers were *Mutt and Jeff, Bringing Up Father,* and *Little Orphan Annie.*

Angelic Angelina, Cupples & Leon, 1909, EX **150.00**
Bringing Up Father, #18, Cupples & Leon, scarce, VG **75.00**
Bringing Up Father, #2, Cupples & Leon, EX **80.00**
Bringing Up Father, #4, Cupples & Leon, EX+ **105.00**
Charlie Chaplin in the Army, Donohue, EX **100.00**
Famous Comics, Captain & Kids, Whitman, 1934, EX **50.00**
Felix the Cat, McLoughlin, 1931, EX **200.00**
Foxy Grandpa & Little Brother, Donohue, EX **150.00**
Little Annie Rooney, McKay, 1943, 48-pg, NM **60.00**
Little Orphan Annie Never Say Die, Cupples & Leon, VG **45.00**
Mutt & Jeff, #5, Cupples & Leon, 1916, VG **80.00**
Mutt & Jeff, #6, Cupples & Leon, 1919, EX **125.00**
Popeye, Saafield, 1934, 40-pg, EX+ **400.00**
Smitty, Cupples & Leon, 1928, VG **35.00**
Tarzan, Grosset & Dunlap, 1929, EX **75.00**
Tillie the Toiler, #4, Cupples & Leon, EX **65.00**
Winnie Winkle, #4, Cupples & Leon, EX **45.00**

Cash Registers

From 1884 until 1916, the National Cash Register Company dominated the field with a massive over-choice of styles and functions. 1,600,000 registers had been built before the termination of the 'antique styles.' An inexpensive, painted-on woodgrain patterned steel cabinet replaced the ornate plates, though the mechanisms remained unchanged. Serial numbers were consecutive, making dating simple. Many registers were chopped up for brass shell casings in the two world wars, and as a result, those that remained became more attractive to collectors. Of the NCRs, scholars speculate that about half of them survive. Add to that the many other existing brands, and it is estimated that there are nearly two million registers to discover.

Register values are fixed by a machine's scarcity and charm, including add-on fixtures such as brass or glass topsigns, clocks, and personalized nameplates. National used eight designs on metal registers and four on inlaid wood machines.

The condition code of registers in this column is quite simple: Good (G), Very Good (VG), and Mint (M), restored by a professional. About 20% variation in prices can be attributed to geography and buyer/seller differences.

Internet Web pages have jumped into the pricing fray, sometimes creating a carnival-like frenzy when prices aren't fixed. *Schroeder's* will provide a standard but also be mindful of permanent changes generated by the Net.

Two excellent books on cash registers are *Antique Cash Registers, 1880 – 1920,* by Bartsch and Sanchez (Mr. Bartsch's address may be found in our Directory under Oregon); and *The Incorruptible Cashier,* Vols. I & II, by John Apple, listed in our Directory under Wisconsin.

Dial, emb brass, emb pattern on drw, 25", EX **6,500.00**
Monitor #1A, wood w/CI Amount of Sale sign, ca 1900, 9x13x14" .**415.00**
NCR #1, Am detail adder, VG **2,650.00**
NCR #2 or #3, inlaid oak or mahog, scarce **2,250.00**
NCR #3, mahog inlay, deep wood drw, ca 1886, VG **4,500.00**
NCR #5, narrow scroll, glass topsign, M **2,750.00**
NCR #7 or #8, detail adder, fleur-de-lis, VG **850.00**
NCR #13 or #14, Ionic CI, 1899, G **750.00**

NCR #30, bronze, total adder, VG **1,400.00**
NCR #33, 1903, VG **900.00**
NCR #47, oak w/mahog inlay, VG **2,250.00**
NCR #50, Renaissance design, orig clock, M **2,500.00**
NCR #52, Renaissance design, orig clock, extended base, VG ..**2,900.00**
NCR #52 or #52¼, Renaissance design, extended base, VG ...**2,900.00**
NCR #64, Bohemian pattern, iron, 25-key, 1901, VG **600.00**
NCR #78, custom built to eliminate bk window, NP, 1902, VG ..**950.00**
NCR #129-130, bronze, VG **950.00**
NCR #130, Art Nouveau cabinet, M **1,600.00**
NCR #135, Art Nouveau pattern, CI, 31-key, 1905, VG **600.00**
NCR #215 or #216, bronze fleur-de-lis, VG **950.00**
NCR #226, rare bilingual topsign, VG **900.00**
NCR #250 or #251, bronze, VG **900.00**
NCR #312, #313, or #317, dolphin pattern, VG **800.00**
NCR #322, #323, or #327, marble 3 sides, extended base, M ..**1,800.00**
NCR #322, #323, or #327, marble 3 sides, extended base, VG .**1,300.00**
NCR #324, VG **700.00**
NCR #332, #333 or #349, orig topsign, M **1,150.00**
NCR #332, #333 or #349, orig topsign, VG **550.00**
NCR #336, brass, M **950.00**
NCR #337, dolphin design, M **950.00**
NCR #338, dogwood pattern, English numerals, CA, 1910-16, VG **475.00**
NCR #360, 37 keys, rings to $60, 1908-09, M **1,500.00**
NCR #441, #442, Empire design w/quartered-oak base, M **1,750.00**
NCR #441, Empire pattern, M **1,750.00**
NCR #441E, electric, VG **950.00**
NCR #442E-L, EX orig **1,400.00**
NCR #452E, electric, M **2,000.00**

NCR #455, brass and marble, oak drawer, EX original, $1,000.00.

NCR #522, 2-drw, electric bar model, 1910-16, M **2,500.00**
NCR #522, 2-drw, electric bar model, 1910-16, VG **1,800.00**
NCR #711-#717, mahog-grain finish on steel, M **275.00**
NCR #1054, glass automatic w/box attachment, 1910-16, M .**1,200.00**

Cast Iron

In the mid-1800s, the cast-iron industry was raging in the United States. It was recognized as a medium extremely adaptable for uses ranging from ornamental architectural filigree to actual building construction. It could be cast from a mold into any conceivable design that could be reproduced over and over at a relatively small cost. It could be painted to give an entirely versatile appearance. Furniture with openwork designs of grapevines and leaves and intricate lacy scrollwork was cast for gardens as well as inside use. Figural doorstops of every sort, bootjacks, trivets, and a host of other useful and decorative items were made before the 'ferromania' had run its course. See also Kitchen, Cast-Iron Bakers and Kettles; and other specific categories.

Cast Iron

Aquarium, shell decor, ped ft, 8-sided w/glass panes, Fiske, 48x37" 3,335.00
Armchair, cornucopia bk, rod seat, old pnt, 30x25x16", pr 1,550.00
Armchair, fern details, worn silver rpt, old rprs, 30" 415.00
Bench, grape clusters & C scrolls, wht pnt, EX 300.00
Coal grate, arched bk, scrolled top, serpents at sides, 18x22x11" .120.00
Cornice, Louis XV Revival style, floral w/C scrolls, 9x42x12" 300.00
Door lock, barn; violin shape, w/key, 19th C, 14" 330.00
Figure, frog, old worn mc pnt, 11" L 250.00
Figure, greyhound, recumbent, bronze-blk patina, 27" L 3,300.00
Figure, greyhound, recumbent, old pnt traces, 49" L, pr 8,250.00
Footstool, button-bk covering, rtcl apron, 19th C, 8x12" 220.00
Garden set, laurel pattern, wht pnt, settee+2 armchairs 3,800.00
Hitching post, jockey, old mc rpt, rpl/rpr, 33" 660.00
Hitching post, jockey, old rpt, Wht Oak Foundry...NJ, 47" 1,757.00
Hitching post, log form, Am, 19th C, 48" 575.00
Hitching post, tree w/vines, old gr & wht pnt, 64" 440.00
Pot on frame, rnd bottom, w/3-legged stand, 20x22" dia 135.00
Seat, scrolling floral design, swivel base, wht pnt, 1850-70 ....750.00
Settee, fern details, James W Carr label, silver rpt, 39" 660.00
Settee, vintage openwork, rpl bk ft, wht rpt, 57" 250.00
Stove plate, Wedding Fable, ca 1768, 24x27½" 800.00
Table, Laurel pattern, cabriole legs, shelf stretcher, 23x29" 250.00
Table, rtcl top & legs, old wht rpt, 26x40" dia 110.00
Teakettle, scrolls on shoulder, base fits into stove, 8x12" 60.00
Urn, campagna, gadrooned rim, lobed body, blk surface, 25", pr ..770.00
Urn, campagna w/egg & dart decor, pnt, 1880s, 32½x17½" 865.00
Urn, Neoclassical, egg & dart rim, old blk pnt, 19th C, 39", pr .4,950.00
Urn, 2 herons & flowers, blk pnt, 20th C, 12x9½" 125.00

Castor Sets

Castor sets became popular during the early years of the 18th century and continued to be used through the late Victorian era. Their purpose was to hold various condiments for table use. The most common type was a circular arrangement with a center handle on a revolving pedestal base that held three, four, five, or six bottles. Some had extras; a few were equipped with a bell for calling the servant. Frames were made of silverplate, glass, or pewter. Though most bottles were of pressed glass, some of the designs were cut, and on rare occasion, colored glass with enameled decorations was used as well. To maintain authenticity and value, castor sets should have matching bottles. Prices listed below are for those with matching bottles and in frames with plating that is in excellent condition (unless noted otherwise). Note: Watch for new frames and bottles in both clear and colored glass; these have recently been appearing on the market. Our advisor for this category is Deborah Maggard; she is listed in the Directory under Ohio.

Key: D&B — Daisy and Button

Five cut and etched bottles, silverplated frame in the Aesthetic taste, angular scrollwork handle, ca 1885, 16½", $300.00.

3-bottle, Am Shield; pewter fr w/eagle, mini, child sz 125.00
3-bottle, D&B; SP fr w/toothpick holder finial 175.00
3-bottle, Gothic Arch, blown, orig stoppers; pewter fr 115.00
4-bottle, Banded Ring; orig pewter fr, child sz 150.00
4-bottle, cranberry, orig stoppers; pressed glass holder 375.00
4-bottle, Log & Star, amber; orig ped-base fr 275.00
4-bottle, pressed, SP tops; orig SP fr w/rnd base, 6½" 65.00
4-bottle, ribbed band; pewter fr, mini 150.00
5-bottle, cut, Honeycomb, amberina; Meriden SP fr, 14" 900.00
5-bottle, Honeycomb; ornate Wilcox fr 295.00
6-bottle, Bellflower, metal lids; 13½" pewter fr mk Gleason 300.00
6-bottle, cut vintage; SP Rogers Smith & Co fr 235.00
6-bottle, D&B, pressed; oversz 18" decor Meriden fr 395.00
6-bottle, D&B; ornate rstr Wilcox fr, revolves 375.00
7-bottle, Chrysanthemum, cut; Gleason ftd fr w/movable doors .1,600.00
7-bottle, cut crystal; gadrooned/shell-border Geo III fr 495.00

Catalina Island

Catalina Island pottery was made on the island of the same name, which is about twenty-six miles off the coast of Los Angeles. The pottery was started in 1927 at Pebble Beach, by Wm. Wrigley, Jr., who was instrumental in developing and using the native clays. Its principal products were brick and tile to be used for construction on the island. Garden pieces were first produced, then vases, bookends, lamps, ashtrays, novelty items, and finally dinnerware. The ware became very popular and was soon being shipped to the mainland as well.

Some of the pottery was hand thrown; some was made in molds. Most pieces are marked Catalina Island or Catalina with a printed incised stamp or handwritten with a pointed tool. Cast items were sometimes marked in the mold, a few have an ink stamp, and a paper label was also used. The most favored colors in tableware and accessories are 1) black (rare), 2) Seafoam and Monterey Brown (uncommon), 3) Toyon Red (orange), 4) other brights, and 5) pastels with a matt finish.

The color of the clay can help to identify approximately when a piece was made: 1927 to 1932, brown to red (Island) clay (very popular with collectors, tends to increase values); 1931 to 1932, an experimental period with various colors; 1932 to 1937, mainly white clay, though tan to brown clays were also used on occasion.

Items marked Catalina Pottery are listed in Gladding McBean. For further information we recommend *The Collector's Encyclopedia of California Pottery, Second Edition*, by our advisor, Jack Chipman; he is listed in the Directory under California.

Dinnerware

Catalina Island, bowl, berry 45.00
Catalina Island, bowl, cereal 75.00
Catalina Island, bowl, fruit; ftd, sq, 13" 180.00
Catalina Island, bowl, vegetable; rnd, 8½" 145.00
Catalina Island, candle holder, low 95.00
Catalina Island, coffee server, slanted opening, w/lid, rare 300.00
Catalina Island, coffeepot, Deco style, rare 325.00
Catalina Island, compote, ftd, lg 225.00
Catalina Island, cup, coffee/tea 55.00
Catalina Island, cup mug, demi 45.00
Catalina Island, custard cup 50.00
Catalina Island, mug, 6" 55.00
Catalina Island, pitcher, squat base, 9" 250.00
Catalina Island, plate, bread & butter; coupe design, 6" 25.00
Catalina Island, plate, chop; #622, 17½" 200.00
Catalina Island, plate, dinner; wide rim, 10½" 75.00
Catalina Island, plate, rolled rim, 12½" 100.00

Catalina Island, plate, salad; 7" **45.00**
Catalina Island, salt cellar **50.00**
Catalina Island, saucer, 6½" **20.00**
Catalina Island, sugar bowl, w/lid **80.00**
Catalina Island, teapot, traditional English style **275.00**
Catalina Island, tumbler, 4" **35.00**
Catalina Island, wine cup, hdld **35.00**
Rope Edge, casserole, w/lid **125.00**
Rope Edge, chop plate, 13½" **95.00**
Rope Edge, creamer **40.00**
Rope Edge, cup & saucer **50.00**
Rope Edge, plate, dinner; 10½" **35.00**
Rope Edge, plate, salad; 8½" **30.00**
Rope Edge, sugar bowl **50.00**
Rope Edge, teapot **225.00**

Miscellaneous

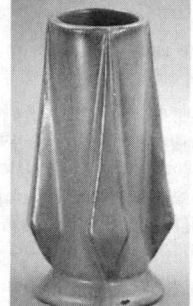

Vase, Desconso Green, thinning at edges of kite-shaped buttresses to expose the red color of the clay, 6", $250.00.

Ashtray, fish form, turq, #551, 5x7" **200.00**
Ashtray, fish form, 4½", from $125 to **175.00**
Ashtray, goat beside tray, bl, 4", minimum value **375.00**
Ashtray, sombrero shape, Toyon Red, 2½x4" **250.00**
Bookend, monk, Descanso Green, ca 1932, 5x4", minimum value .**500.00**
Bowl, console; shell form, turq, 8⅜", +pr 5½" candlesticks **275.00**
Bowl, console; turq, 10¼x12", +pr triple candlesticks **450.00**
Bowl, Starlite, rectangular, low, 15" **150.00**
Bowl, yel/gr, oval, fluted, 17" **175.00**
Candlestick, Catalina Blue, flared ft, mk, 1930s, 3" **65.00**
Carafe, red, early red clay **200.00**
Charger, Dutch lady, sgn Graham, #d, 14" **750.00**
Charger, swordfish, ivory **375.00**
Cigarette box, horse-head finial, sq **200.00**
Coaster, plain, bl, red clay **35.00**
Ewer, bl matt, red clay, 1927-32, 9x6" **300.00**
Match safe, flying fish emblem in relief, rectangular **200.00**
Pipe rest, sleeping Mexican figural, Toyon Red w/cold pnt, 3½x8" .**425.00**
Planter, fish motif, 3½x3½" **175.00**
Plate, Deco-style parrots, 10¼" **800.00**
Plate, HP Mexican scene, mk, ca 1932, 11½", minimum value ..**600.00**
Shakers, cactus, early red clay, 4½", pr **200.00**
Vase, stepped body, angle hdls, Monterey Brown, brn clay, mk ..**375.00**
Vase, Toyon Red, shouldered, 8" **400.00**
Vase, Toyon Red, 8x2½" **350.00**
Vase, wht, red clay, ca 1927-32, 8½x6" **275.00**
Vase, yel, Deco design w/hdls, red clay, 1927-32, 9x5½" **375.00**
Wall pocket, seashell form, turq, mk **250.00**

Catalogs

Catalogs are not only intriguing to collect on their own merit, but

for the collector with a specific interest, they are often the only remaining source of background information available, and as such they offer a wealth of otherwise unrecorded data. The mail-order industry can be traced as far back as the mid-1800s. Even before Aaron Montgomery Ward began his career in 1872, Laacke and Joys of Wisconsin and the Orvis Company of Vermont, both dealers in sporting goods, had been well established for many years. The E.C. Allen Company sold household necessities and novelties by mail on a broad scale in the 1870s. By the end of the Civil War, sewing machines, garden seed, musical instruments, even medicine, were available from catalogs. In the 1880s Macy's of New York issued a 127-page catalog; Sears and Spiegel followed suit in about 1890. Craft and art supply catalogs were first available about 1880 and covered such varied fields as china painting, stenciling, wood burning, brass embossing, hair weaving, and shellcraft. Today some collectors confine their interests not only to craft catalogs in general but often to just one subject. There are several factors besides rarity which make a catalog valuable: age, condition, profuse illustrations, how collectible the field is that it deals with, the amount of color used in its printing, its size (format and number of pages), and whether it is a manufacturer's catalog verses a jobber's catalog (the former being the most desirable).

A Flanagan Co, school furniture & supplies, 1931, 114-pg, G **34.00**
Abbott's Magic Novelty Co, 1947, 832-pg, G- **41.00**
Adriance, Platt & Co, agricultural, 1907, 44-pg, G **54.00**
Alpine Safe & Lock Co, 1906, 43-pg, G **74.00**
American La France, firefighting equipment, 1923, 47-pg, EX **95.00**
American Mask Mfg Co, 1948, 23-pg, VG **28.00**
American Steel & Wire Co, agricultural fences, 1927, 24-pg, G ..**13.00**
Anderson Electric Car Co, 1911, 46-pg, VG **420.00**
Atlas Boat Supply Co, 1948, 172-pg, G **26.00**
B Crystal, women's coats, 1898, 20-pg, VG+ **28.00**
Benjamin Moore & Co, paints, 1928, 10-pg, G+ **19.00**
Beretta Pistols, 3 models, 1956, 20-pg **25.00**
Berger Mfg Co, roofing materials, ca 1929, 19-pg, G+ **44.00**
Blickensderfer Typewriters, 3 models, 10 cases, Pat 1892, 30-pg ...**75.00**
Brewer Bros Co, hardware, ca 1912, 52-pg, G **38.00**
Buchanan Co, photographic materials, 1899, 105-pg, EX **150.00**
Buffalo Mfg Co, kitchen equipment, 1904, 118-pg, G+ **98.00**
Burley & Co, pottery, 1896, 134-pg, VG **135.00**
Butcher & Gibbs, agriculture, 1931, 32-pg, VG **34.00**
C Aultman & Co, harvesting & threshing machines, 1880, 4-pg, G .**30.00**
Carl Fisher Inc, brass musical instruments, 1928, 51-pg, G+ **61.00**
Charles Williams Store, general merchandise, 1926, 312-pg, G ...**31.00**
Chicago Roller Skates, 1936, 32-pg, EX **30.00**
Chicago Writing Machines, typewriters, ca 1900, 12-pg, G **26.00**
CJ Lundstrom Co, furniture, ca 1913, 48-pg, G+ **43.00**
Crouse-Hinds Co, airport lighting, 1929, 12-pg, G **54.00**
CT Telephone & Electric, 1909, 28-pg, G **63.00**
David T Abercrombie Co, camping equipment, 1932, 62-pg, VG+ .**28.00**
Deming Co, well (water) systems, 1934, 40-pg, G+ **23.00**
Eagle Electrical Supply, residential lighting, 1937, 56-pg, G **41.00**
Ed Jones, rotary supplies, ca 1948, 8-pg, G+ **10.00**
Empire Mfg Co, metal wagon wheels, ca 1910, G **12.00**
Fada Radios, 8 models, 1930, 14x12" foldout **30.00**
FAO Schwarz Christmas, many illus, 1939 ....**190.00**
Felton, Sibley & Co, brushes, 1931, 24-pg, VG **17.00**
Francis Bannerman Sons, firearms, 1940, 288-pg, G **47.00**
Galloway Terra-Cotta Co, pottery, ca 1916, 44-pg, G+ **172.00**
GB Weiss & Sons, shoes, 1891, 36-pg, G **32.00**
General Motors Corp, automobiles, 1968, 28-pg, VG **29.00**
Geo A Williams & Sons, heating, 1917, 32-pg, G **28.00**
Geo E Watson Co, painter's supplies, 1932, 144-pg, G **41.00**
Grossman Stamp Co, 1930, 114-pg, G **24.00**

H Hueg & Co, baking needs, 1901, 48-pg, G+ **44.00**
H&A Selmer Inc, musical instruments, 1928, 48-pg, G **46.00**
Halcolite Co, lighting fixtures, 1922, 51-pg, VG **41.00**
Hall Mammoth Co, chicken farming, 1910, 72-pg, G **16.00**
Hawkins Co, traps, 1926, 14-pg, VG+ **44.00**
Herbert J Riley, lantern supplies, 1903, 268-pg, G **94.00**
HG Gastings Co, dog supplies, ca 1930s, 14-pg, VG **16.00**
Hilton Hughes & Co, gifts, ca 1893, 26-pg, VG **31.00**
Hoskins Office Supplies, 1912, 420-pg, 9x12" **150.00**
Imperial Brass Mfg Co, welding, 1918, 36-pg, G **22.00**
J Lynn Co, jewelry, ca 1902, 84-pg, G **23.00**
J Stevens Arms & Tool Co, firearms, 1912, 88-pg, G **67.00**
James B Hayes, shoes, ca 1932, 1-pg, G **5.00**
James W Queen & Co, microscopes & supplies, 1889, 108-pg, G .**152.00**
John H North Co, hats & accessories, 1914, 36-pg, G+ **33.00**
Johnson Smith & Co, novelties, 1940, 600-pg, G **38.00**
Jones Scales Works, pre-1900, 32-pg+, G- **29.00**
JT Johnson, window screens, ca 1928, 6-pg, VG **10.00**
Kalamazoo Stove Co, 1935, 36-pg, G **34.00**
Kent, Woodman & Co, telephones, ca 1894, 5-pg, G **32.00**
Keramic Supply Co, ceramics, ca 1928, 64-pg, VG **22.00**
Keystone Farm Machines, ca 1900, 128-pg, EX **65.00**
Kimball Tire Chase Co, tires, ca 1913, 18-pg, G- **16.00**
King Novelty Co, ca 1929, 48-pg, G **16.00**
Kretchmer Mfg Co, beekeeping, 1912, 80-pg, G **27.00**
Larkin Co, groceries, 1914, 6-pg, G+ **17.00**
Lenox Inc, china, 1936, 16-pg, VG **75.00**
LL Bean Inc, camping equipment, 1941, 66-pg, G+ **36.00**
Marshall Field Christmas, 8 pgs of toys, 1939, 56-pg **30.00**
Marvin Smith Co, horse-powered machinery, 1896, 90-pg, G **44.00**
Maytag Co, Gyrofoam Aluminum Washer, ca 1927, 13-pg, VG+ .**35.00**
Messinger Mfg Co, farm machinery, ca 1920, 16-pg, G **19.00**
Metropolitan Sewing Machine Co, 1910, 100-pg, VG **33.00**
Michigan Steel Boat Co, 1914, 56-pg, G **96.00**
Montgomery Wards & Co, general merchandise, 1932, 68-pg, G .**12.00**
Montgomery Wards & Co, horse-drawn vehicles, 1905, 36-pg, VG ..**83.00**
Morley Bros, bicycles, 1899, 16-pg, VG **77.00**
National Cash Register Co, window advertising, 1925, 32-pg, G .**17.00**
National Plan Service, floor plans, 1954, 16-pg, VG **16.00**
New Jersey Homes, 32 color pgs, 1927, 114-pg, EX **45.00**
Niagara Falls Power Co, electricity, 1901, 38-pg, G+ **23.00**
Ohio Machine Tool Co, ca 1929, 60-pg, G **24.00**
Osborn Bros Supply Co, leathercraft, 1910, 32-pg, G+ **32.00**
Planet Farm, garden tools, 1936, 72-pg, EX **25.00**
Plasticville USA, toys, color, 1957, 12-pg, EX **35.00**
Pope Mfg, juvenile bicycles, 1904, 12-pg, EX **50.00**
Rawlings Farm Machinery, 1900, 80-pg **75.00**
Remington Arms Co Inc, firearms, 1938, 44-pg, VG+ **63.00**
Sears, Roebuck & Co, household goods, 1922, 1176-pg, G+ **98.00**
Sears, Roebuck & Co, mens made-to-order clothes, 1934, 16-pg, G ..**26.00**
Sedgewick Machine Works, dumbwaiters, 1927, 32-pg, G+ **24.00**
St Albans Foundry Co, agricultural, 1898, 32-pg, VG **98.00**
Theodore Bender, beekeeping, no date, early, 12-pg, VG **12.00**
Thurner, Whyland Co, confectionery, pre-1900, 22-pg, VG **26.00**
Union Cutlery Co, ca 1929, 13-pg, G **46.00**
Union Emblem Co, jewelry, ca 1930s, 32-pg, VG **18.00**
United Cork Co, cork tile floors, ca 1932, 8-pg, G **19.00**
Webster Lumber & Supply, interior woodwork, 1930, 80-pg, VG .**34.00**
Weir Stove Co, woood stoves, ca 1923, 4-pg, G+ **15.00**
Westinghouse Electric, appliances, 1936, 28-pg, G **24.00**
Westinghouse Machine Co, steam engines, 1905, 35-pg, G **78.00**
Willys-Overland Co, automobiles, 1915, 22-pg, G **89.00**
WL Blake & Co, plumbing & steam supplies, 1936, 396-pg, VG .**28.00**
Wurlitzer, stringed instruments, 1910s, 48-pg, 9x11½", NM **75.00**

WW Kimball Co, organs, ca 1920s, 36-pg, VG **38.00**
York Silk Mfg Co, 1904, 23-pg, G **19.00**

Caughley Ware

The Caughley Coalport Porcelain Manufactory operated from about 1775 until 1799 in Caughley, near Salop, Shropshire, in England. The owner was Thomas Turner, who gained his potting experience from his association with the Worcester Pottery Company. The wares he manufactured in Caughley are referred to as 'Salopian.' He is most famous for his blue-printed earthenwares, particularly the Blue Willow pattern, designed for him by Thomas Minton. For a more detailed history, see Coalport.

Bowl, floral & butterfly, cottage reserves, blk w/mc, 2⅝x5" **350.00**
Cup & saucer, bird on branch, brn w/mc, 1¾x2⅞", 4⅝" **300.00**
Cup & saucer, Fallow Deer, blk w/mc, 2⅛x2¾", 5", NM **90.00**
Cup & saucer, floral, brn transfer, bl stripe rim, EX **85.00**
Cup & saucer, milkmaid milking, brn w/mc, 2¼", 5½" **325.00**
Cup & saucer, shepherd & sheep, brn transfer w/mc, rpr **100.00**
Pitcher, milk; Oriental scene, brn transfer, hairline, 5½" **300.00**
Plate, boy w/sheep, brn transfer, floral border, bl stripe, 7⅜" **110.00**
Plate, deer & floral border, brn w/mc, 6" **300.00**
Sauce dish, milkmaid & cows, blk w/mc, 4¼", EX **50.00**
Sugar bowl, appl flower finial (prof rpr), mismatched lid, 5½" ...**275.00**
Waste bowl, peony & fence decor, bl & wht, 4¾" **275.00**

Ceramic Art Company

Jonathan Coxon, Sr., and Walter Scott Lenox established the Ceramic Art Company in 1889 in Trenton, New Jersey, where they produced fine belleek porcelain. Both were experienced in its production, having previously worked for Ott and Brewer. They hired artists to hand paint their wares with portraits, scenes, and lovely florals. Today artist-signed examples bring the highest prices. Several marks were used, three of which contain the 'CAC' monogram. A green wreath surrounding the company name in full was used on special-order wares, but these are not often encountered. Coxon eventually left the company, and it was later reorganized under the Lenox name. See also Lenox. Our advisor for this category is Mary Frank Gaston.

Demitasse liner, pastel and gold-paste floral interior and exterior, sterling silver holder, lavender mark, $150.00.

Photo courtesy Mary Frank Gaston

Bell, tulip shape, wht w/silver decor, unmk **160.00**
Bowl, raspberries/florals/shadow leaves, sgn Marsh, '97, 9" **225.00**
Clock, florals & gold, bl bleeding, Ansonia works, mk, 9" **1,000.00**
Jug, pharmacy; Rx silver o/l on brn gloss, 4½" **375.00**
Mug, monk, brn tones, sgn Pyle, 4½" **120.00**
Stein, currants, red on brn, sgn Arten, emb base/hdl, 5½" **150.00**
Stein, monk w/wine glass, copper/sterling lid, ½-litre, NM **450.00**
Table lamp, plain wht w/scalloped base, unmk, 20½" **275.00**

Vase, lg roses, gilt hdls, flared neck, mk, 10" 600.00
Vase, poinsettias on red-tinge wht, ftd w/trumpet neck, 19" 400.00
Vase, poppies, orange on gr to yel, ewer shape, mk, 5x7" 125.00

Ceramic Arts Studio, Madison

The Ceramic Arts Studio Company began operations sometime prior to the 1940s, but it was about then that Betty Harrington started marketing her goods through this company. Betty Harrington was the designer primarily responsible for creating the line of figurines and knickknacks that has become so popular with collectors. There were two others — Ulli Rebus, who not only designed several of the animals and various other pieces but taught Betty the art of mold-making as well; and Ruth Planter, who's work may have been limited to 'Honey.' About 65% of these items are marked, but even unmarked items become easily recognizable after only a brief study of their distinctive styling and glaze colors. At least eight different marks were used, among them the black ink stamp and the incised mark: 'Ceramic Arts Studio, Madison, Wisc.' A paper sticker was used in the early years.

After the 1955 demise of the company in Madison, the owner (Ruben Sand) went to Japan where he continued production under the same name using many of the same molds. After a short time, the old molds were retired, and new and quite different items were produced. Most of the Japan pieces can be found with a Ceramic Arts Studio backstamp. The Japan identification was often on a paper label and can be missing. Japan pieces are never marked Madison, Wisc., but not all Madison pieces are either. Red or blue backstamps are exclusively Japanese.

Another company that also produced figurines operated at about the same time as the Madison studio. It was called Ceramic Art (no 's') Studio; do not confuse the two.

A second and larger building in the C.A.S. complex in Madison was for the exclusive production of metal accessories. The creator and designer of this related line was Zona Liberace, Liberace's stepmother, who was art director for the line of figurines as well. These pieces are rising fast in value and because they weren't marked can sometimes be found at bargain prices. They were so popular that other ceramic companies bought them to complement their own lines, so they may also be found with ceramic figures other than C.A.S.'s.

Our advisor for this category is BA Wellman; his address can be found under Massachusetts. Mr. Wellman encourages collectors to write him with any new information concerning company history and/or production. He sends Jeff, Rosie, and Vera a 'thank you' for helping us with this year's updates. See also Clubs, Newsletters, and Catalogs.

Ashtray, hippo, 3½" 165.00
Bank, Skunky, 4" 195.00
Bell, Winter Bell, 5¼" 95.00
Candle holder, Speak No Evil, Angel on Cloud, 5" 130.00
Candle holder, Triad Girl, center, 5" 150.00
Candle holder, Triad Girl, right or left; from $90 to 110.00
Candle holders, Bedtime Boy & Girl, 4¾", pr 170.00
Figurine, Adonis, 9" 280.00
Figurine, Alice, 4½" 200.00
Figurine, angel w/candle, 5" 80.00
Figurine, Archibald dragon, 8", minimum value 275.00
Figurine, Autumn Andy, 5" 95.00
Figurine, Benny, elephant, 3½" 90.00
Figurine, bird on birdhouse, 4½" 100.00
Figurine, Caddy, mountain goat, 5¼" 200.00
Figurine, camel, young, 5½" 150.00
Figurine, chipmunk, 2" 40.00
Figurine, Cinderella & Prince, bl, 6½", pr, from $175 to 185.00
Figurine, Colonial boy & girl, pr 165.00

Figurine, Cupid, 5", rare, from $250.00 to $300.00.

Figurine, doe, stylized, 3¾" 125.00
Figurine, Dutch boy & girl, 4½", pr 65.00
Figurine, Egyptian man, very rare, 9½" 300.00
Figurine, fawn, from Indian group, 4¼" 50.00
Figurine, flute girl, rare, 4½" 165.00
Figurine, Frisky the colt, 3¾" 125.00
Figurine, gremlin, standing, 4" 300.00
Figurine, Hai, topless, 8" 165.00
Figurine, Hans & Katrinka, yel w/brn trim, 6½", pr 95.00
Figurine, Hansel & Gretel, 1-pc, 3" 100.00
Figurine, Harry & Lillibeth, Gay 90s Couple #1, pr 115.00
Figurine, Inky & Dinky, skunks, 2¼", 2", pr, from $60 to 85.00
Figurine, Japanese kabuki man, rare, 8½" 300.00
Figurine, June, 4½" 45.00
Figurine, kitten w/ball of yarn 45.00
Figurine, lamb, plain 50.00
Figurine, leopards fighting, 8½" L, pr 230.00
Figurine, Lightning the stallion, 5¾" 190.00
Figurine, Little Jack Horner, 4½" 85.00
Figurine, longhorn ox, 3" L 90.00
Figurine, Mary & lamb w/bow, 6¼", 4", pr 80.00
Figurine, Mexican girl, 6½" 85.00
Figurine, Mop-Pi & Smi-Li, pr 125.00
Figurine, Mr Monkey, scratching, 4" 100.00
Figurine, Pansy, 6" 175.00
Figurine, Pekingese, 3" 95.00
Figurine, Pioneer Sam & Pioneer Suzie, 5", pr 95.00
Figurine, pixie on toadstool, 4" 45.00
Figurine, Promenade man & woman, pr 175.00
Figurine, Rhumba dancers, pr 130.00
Figurine, Sambo, 3½" 300.00
Figurine, shepherd, 8½", from $100 to 135.00
Figurine, Spaniel mother & baby, pr 150.00
Figurine, Square Dance boy & girl, pr 175.00
Figurine, St George on charger, 8½" 250.00
Figurine, swan, neck up, 6" 120.00
Figurine, Temple Dance woman, 6½" 250.00
Figurine, Ting-a-ling & Sung-tu, pr 75.00
Figurine, tortoise w/hat, crawling, 2½" L 125.00
Head vase, African man, 8" 325.00
Head vase, Barbie, 7" 150.00
Head vase, Becky, 5¼" 125.00
Head vase, Lotus, 8½" 135.00
Head vase, Sven, 6" 175.00
Lamp, fireman on base, very scarce 500.00
Pitcher, Adam & Eve, 3" 60.00
Pitcher, Aladdin-lamp form, mini, 2" L 80.00
Plaque, Attitude & Arabesque, pr 150.00
Plaque, Goosey Gander, 4½" 100.00
Plaque, Greg & Grace, pr 135.00
Plaque, Hamlet, 8" 225.00
Plaque, striped fish mother, 5" 90.00

Plaque, Zor & Zorina, pr 150.00
Shakers, bear mother & baby, brn, snuggle, pr 90.00
Shakers, Black boy & alligator, pr 275.00
Shakers, boy in chair, snuggle, 2¼", pr 95.00
Shakers, Chinese couple, 4¼", pr 40.00
Shakers, cocks, fighting, pr 70.00
Shakers, dog & doghouse, snuggle, pr 150.00
Shakers, elephants, S&P trunks, pr 80.00
Shakers, fish, up on tails, pr 75.00
Shakers, fox & goose, 3¼", 2¼", pr 150.00
Shakers, frog & toadstool, pr 95.00
Shakers, horse heads, brn or gr, pr 70.00
Shakers, monkey mother & baby, snuggle, pr 100.00
Shakers, mouse & cheese, 2½", pr, from $30 to 40.00
Shakers, Paul Bunyan & tree, pr 200.00
Shakers, penguins, Mr & Mrs, 3½", pr 100.00
Shakers, Sabu (Black boy) & elephant, pr 250.00
Shakers, sea horse & coral, pr 125.00
Shakers, Thai & Thai-Thai, pr 145.00
Shakers, Wee Dutch boy & girl, 3", pr 45.00
Shelf sitter, banjo girl, 4" 100.00
Shelf sitter, boy w/dog & girl w/cat, pr 145.00
Shelf sitter, Budgie & Pudgie parakeets, 5", pr, from $125 to 150.00
Shelf sitter, Collie mother, 5" 65.00
Shelf sitter, cowboy, 4¾" 80.00
Shelf sitter, Dutch boy, 4½" 35.00
Shelf sitter, farm boy (w/pole) & girl, pr, from $100 to 125.00
Shelf sitter, Fluffy & Tuffy cats, 7", pr 185.00
Shelf sitter, Jack & Jill, pr 80.00
Shelf sitter, Maurice & Michelle, 7", pr 165.00
Shelf sitter, Nip & Tuck, 4", 4¼", pr 60.00
Shelf sitter, Pete & Polly, parrots, chartreuse, pr 185.00
Shelf sitter, Pierrot & Pierrette, 6½", pr 185.00
Shelf sitter, Sun-Li & Su-Lin, chubby, 5½", pr 95.00

Metal Accessories

Arched window for Madonna & Child, 14" 80.00
Artist palette w/shelves, left & right, 13" across 95.00
Beanstalk for Jack, rare 95.00
Birdcage w/perch for birds, 14" 65.00
Diamond shadow box, for Attitude & Arabesque, 15½x13¾" 55.00
Frame w/shelf, 22" sq 55.00
Holder for planter 45.00
Musical score, 14x12" 80.00
Pocket step shelf, w/planter, rnd, 8" 75.00
Pyramid shelf 75.00
Sofa, for Maurice & Michelle, 10x3¾" 65.00
Star for an angel, flat blk 80.00
Triple ring shelves 125.00

Chalkware

Chalkware figures were a popular commodity from approximately 1860 until 1890. They were made from gypsum or plaster of Paris formed in a mold and then hand painted in oils or watercolors. Items such as animals and birds, figures, banks, toys, and religious ornaments modeled after more expensive Staffordshire wares were often sold door to door. Their origin is attributed to Italian immigrants. Today regarded as a form of folk art, 19th century American pieces bring prices in the hundreds of dollars. Carnival chalkware from this century is also collectible, especially figures that are personality related. For those, see Carnival Collectibles.

Bull, bank, old worn brn & amber, edge wear, 15¼" L 600.00
Cat, blk & wht w/red & bl ribbon, wear/damage, 12", EX 180.00
Cat, VG pnt, 1800s, 5½" 345.00
Deer, detailed pnt, removable antlers, early 1900s, 18x15x9" 175.00
Figurine, poodle, mc details, minor rstr, 7¾" 190.00
Girl, reading, lt pnt wear, 1800s, 18½" 1,200.00
Lion, worn mc pnt w/gr base, 10" L, VG 130.00

Photo courtesy
Aston Macek Auctioneers
and Appraisers

Poodles, one hollow and one with solid base, original paint, $525.00 for the pair.

Ram, wht w/mc details, floral base, 5⅜x5⅛x2½" 300.00
Sheep w/lamb, VG pnt, minor rpr, 1800s, 7" 500.00
Squirrel, worn red & gr pnt, flakes on base, 5" 250.00
Stag's head, minor abrasions, varnished, 11¾" 300.00

Chase Brass & Copper Company

Americans were shocked in 1923 when an invitation to stage an exhibit at the first major postwar fair, *The 1925 Exposition des Arts Decoratifs et Industriels,* was declined by the American government because the U.S. could not comply with the exposition's requirement that only original work would be exhibited. Even though American industry produced a vast quantity of varied goods, there was very little 'original American' to show, since most design ideas were being brought in from Europe.

This blow to American prestige and the uproar that resulted prompted a dispatch of designers (among them Donald Deskey, Walter Dorwin Teague, and Russel Wright) to the Paris exhibition. They were to determine what steps would be necessary in order for U.S. designs to compete with European standards. They returned championing the new modernist style. By the mid-1930s, products were being designed and marketed that were attractive to the reluctant consumer insistent upon buying a streamline style that was uniquely American. During the decade of the '30s, the Chase Brass & Copper Company offered lamps, smoking acessories, and housewares similar to those Americans were seeing on the Hollywood screen at prices the average buyer could afford. These products are highly valued today, not only because of their superior quality but also because of those who created them. Walter von Nessen, Gerth & Gerth, Rockwell Kent, Russel Wright, Lurelle Guild, and Dr. A. Reimann were some of Chases' well-known designers. Emily Post, who served as a spokesperson for Chase, promoted a trend away from expensive silver and toward chromium serving pieces.

Besides chromium, Chase manufactured many products in brass, copper, nickel plate, or a combination of these metals; all are equally collectible. Some items had glass inserts which collectors also seek. A few items can even be found in silver plate.

Nearly all Chase products were marked, either on the item itself or on a screw or rivet. However, a few authentic pieces were not, for reasons that remain unknown, and because Chase sold screws, rivets, nails, etc., with their own logo, not all items having those Chased-marked components were actually made by them. It should also be noted that during the 1930s, China produced good quality plated-ware copies; so when you're not absolutely positive an item is Chase, buy it if you like it, understanding that its authenticity may be in question. But be cautious. Check unmarked items to make sure they measure up to Chase's standard of quality; lighting fixtures that are unmarked may be compared with pictures of verified examples.

For safety's sake, replace both cords and internal wiring before attempting to use any electrical product. Not only will you be protected against possible loss from fire, but you will enhance the value of your collectible as well.

Prior to 1933, Chase made smoking accessories for the Park Sherman Co. Some are marked 'Park Sherman Co., Chicago, Illinois, Made in Chase Brass.' Others carry a Park Sherman logo. It is believed that the 'heraldic emblem' insignia of Park Sherman was also used during this period. Many items are identical or very similar to Chase-marked pieces. Produced in the 1950s, National Silver Co.'s 'Emerald-Glo' pieces look very much like Chase, but Chase did not make them. (It is very possible that the company purchased Chase Tooling after the Chase Specialties Line was discontinued.)

For more thorough study we recommend *Art Deco Chrome, The Chase Era*, and *Art Deco Chrome, Book 2, A Collector's Guide, Industrial Design in the Chase Era*. Both are authored by Richard J. Kilbride; Mrs. Kilbride is listed in the Directory under Connecticut. Also available are *Chase Complete* and *Chase Lamps — Lighting the Thirties*, by Leslie Piña and Donald-Brian Johnson (Schiffer) and *Chase Catalogs, 1934 and 1935*, with introduction by same authors (also Schiffer). In the listings that follow, examples are polished unless noted satin. For further information contact the Chase Collector's Society, listed in the Directory under Clubs, Newsletters, and Catalogs. Our advisor for this category is Barbara Endter; she is listed in the Directory under New York.

Wine cooler, chromium, child Bacchus in relief, designed by Rockwell Kent, #27015, 1935 – 1937, 9¼", $550.00 to $600.00.

Ashtray, Aristocrat, chromium, #835, 5½" L 45.00
Ashtray, Globe, chromium, #17068, from $50 to 60.00
Band box, chromium, red plastic hdl, 3-compartment, #852, 7⅛" L .85.00
Bar caddy, chromium, jigger/opener/corkscrew/ice breaker, #90141 .15.00
Bell, Ming, chromium, #13007, from $50 to 60.00
Bookends, Davy Jones, wheel, brass/walnut/Bakelite, #90142 ....60.00
Bookends, horse, very stylized, polished brass, #17044, 6" 650.00
Bookends, Moderne, brass/copper w/rivets/panels, #11246, 6½", G .775.00
Box, New Two-Tray, polished chromium or copper, shell knob, #17106 .55.00
Box, Occasional, chromium w/plastic hearts, glass insert, #90144 ...45.00
Butter dish, chromium, #17067, 6" dia, from $100 to 110.00
Cake & sandwich trowel, polished chromium w/wht knob, #17060 ...55.00
Canape plate, #27001, from $15 to 20.00
Candle holders, Bubble, copper on plastic base, #17063, 2½", pr .80.00
Cigarette box, Bacchus, Rockwell Kent, bronze, #847, from $1,000 to .1,200.00
Cigarette holder, Bubble, open chromium sphere on sq, #860, 2¼" ...50.00
Cigarette lighter, Automatic Table, chromium, #825, 3¼", $40 to .50.00
Cocktail ball, chromium, #90071, from $25 to 30.00
Cocktail set, Gaiety, chromium, shaker/4 cups/tray, #90064 ......110.00

Cocktail shakers, Gaiety, chrome w/blk rings #90034, from $40 to ..45.00
Coffee service, Comet, chromium, percolator/cr/sug/tray, #90120 ..275.00
Coffee urn, Coronet, polished chromium/plastic, electric, #17088, 12" .300.00
Crumber set, Tidy, moon shape, chromium, plastic hdls, #90092 .45.00
Dish, Tulip, polished chromium, scroll hdl, #90095, from $45 to .50.00
Flower bowl, Diana, chromium on plastic base, #15005, 10", from $45 to ...75.00
Fork & spoon, chromium w/plastic hdls, #90076, 10⅛", pr, $40 to .50.00
Ice bowl, chromium, w/tongs, #28002, from $65 to 75.00
Ice crusher, polished chromium, #90135, 6", from $40 to 50.00
Ice drink cup, chromium, #90085, 5¼", from $25 to 35.00
Napkin holder, chromium/plastic, ball weight, #90148, 6x4" 50.00
Newspaper rack, English bronze or brass & copper, #27027, $200 to ..250.00
Pancake/corn set, chromium pitcher/s&p/bl glass tray, #28003 ..250.00
Percolator, Comet, chromium, #17084, from $110 to 125.00
Pitcher, syrup; Sparta, chromium, wht plastic hdl, #90056, 4", $40 to ..50.00
Pitcher, water; Sparta, chromium, wht plastic hdl, #9055, 8" 85.00
Pretzel Man, copper, #90038, from $100 to 120.00
Sauce bowl, Lotus, chromium, blk hdl, +tray/ladle, #17045, $40 to .45.00
Server, Four-In-Hand, chromium, plastic hdl, 2 mid-trays swivel ...125.00
Shakers, Blue Moon, chromium w/bl ball top, #90066, 1936, $100 to .125.00
Shakers, Blue Moon, chromium w/ribbed top, #90066, 1937-40, $100 to 125.00
Silent butler, chromium w/plastic hdl, #17111, 11⅜", from $45 to .55.00
Sugar shaker, chromium, #90057, from $50 to 60.00
Teakettle, chromium, similar to Comet, electric, #17083, from $100 to .120.00
Teakettle, chromium, similar to Comet, non-electric, #17082 ...100.00
Tray, cracker & cheese; chromium, w/walnut slicing board, #09016 ..80.00

Chelsea Dinnerware

Made from about 1830 to 1880 in the Staffordshire district of England, this white dinnerware is decorated with lustre embossings in the grape, thistle, sprig, or fruit and cornucopia patterns. The relief designs vary from lavender to blue, and the body of the ware may be porcelain, ironstone, or earthenware. Because it was not produced in Chelsea as the name would suggest, dealers often prefer to call it 'Grandmother's Ware.'

Grape, bowl, 8" 30.00
Grape, coffeepot, stick hdl, 2-cup, 7" 75.00
Grape, creamer 35.00
Grape, cup & saucer 35.00
Grape, egg cup 25.00
Grape, pitcher, milk, 40-oz 60.00
Grape, plate, 6" 12.00
Grape, plate, 7" 18.00
Grape, plate, 8" 20.00
Grape, sugar bowl, w/lid 50.00
Grape, teapot, octagonal, 10" 125.00
Grape, teapot, 2-cup 75.00
Grape, waste bowl 40.00
Sprig, cake plate, 9" 40.00
Sprig, cup & saucer 40.00
Sprig, pitcher, milk 45.00
Sprig, plate, dinner 25.00
Sprig, plate, 7" 18.00
Thistle, butter pat 15.00
Thistle, cup & saucer 35.00
Thistle, plate, 7" 15.00
Thistle, sugar bowl, 8-sided, w/lid, 7½" 45.00

Chelsea Keramic Art Works

The Chelsea Keramic Art Works Robertson and Sons Pottery was established in 1872 in Chelsea, Massachusetts, by several members of the Robertson family, including Hugh C. Robertson who later formed the Dedham Pottery. Though their very early artware utilized a redware body, by the late 1870s it was replaced with yellow or buff burning clay. A line called Bourg-la-Reine (underglazed slip-decorated ware with primarily blue and green backgrounds) was produced, though not to any great extent. Other pieces were designed in imitation of Asian metalware, even to the extent that surfaces were 'hammered' to further enhance the effect. Occasionally live flora was pressed into the damp vessel walls to leave a decorative impression. They also made glazed plaques and tiles. Hugh C. Robertson ran the pottery alone after 1884 and labored to re-create the ancient Ming-era blood-red glaze. Although world acclaim greeted his rediscovery of what he then called 'Robertson's Blood,' his red-glazed vases cost too much to produce and bankruptcy followed in 1889. Supported by wealthy Boston art patrons, Hugh's pottery reopened in 1891 as the Chelsea Pottery U.S., and began using his other 1880s rediscovery, the crackle glaze, producing cobalt blue-decorated dinnerware. When this firm moved to Dedham in 1895 the ware became known as Dedham Pottery. From 1875 to 1880 the pottery was marked Chelsea Keramic Art Works Robertson and Sons in either two or three impressed lines. Earlier pieces were not marked. The impressed mark CKAW in a diamond formation was also used between 1875 and 1889. From 1891 through 1895 the impressed letters CPUS in a cloverleaf was utilized for the new firm. After the move to Dedham, only new Dedham Pottery marks were used. See also Dedham Pottery.

Charger, Love: appl birds on branch, olive-gr, Walker, 11" 750.00
Ewer, sea gr mottle, 10x5½" 750.00

Lamp base, floral branches in relief, glossy blue-green, drilled base, marked, ca 1880, 7¼x4¾", $175.00.

Lamp base, lg 3-D horse chestnuts/leaves, mustard matt, 5x9" ...**950.00**
Leaf dish, steel bl w/speckled cobalt, 3¾" **300.00**
Pilgrim flask, morning glories cvg/bk: bird, gr mottle, 9x7" **750.00**
Pitcher, Greek Key, mahog drip on olive to gr, 1800s, 7¾" **900.00**
Plate, Horse Chestnut, bl on wht, H Robertson, clover mk, 10" ..**300.00**
Plate, Pineapple, bl on wht, cloverleaf mk, 8½" **400.00**
Plate, Rabbit, bl on wht, att Robertson, clover mk, 8½" **225.00**
Vase, bud; gr/brn gloss, leaf hdls, 6x3¼" **350.00**
Vase, bud; steel bl w/brn streaks, trumpet neck, early, 6¼x2½" ..**600.00**
Vase, palm tree under bl, sgn HCR, pillow form, 6½x6¾", NM .**175.00**
Vase, sang-de-boeuf, shouldered, 6x3½" **1,300.00**
Vase, sang-de-boeuf lustre over celadon gloss, 9x4½" **2,200.00**
Vase, volcanic sang-de-boeuf, classic form, 4x2½" **600.00**
Vase, volcanic/curdled sang-de-boeuf, ovoid, 8x4¼" **3,750.00**

Chicago Crucible

For only a few years during the 1920s, the Chicago (Illinois) Crucible Company made a limited amount of decorative pottery in addition to

their regular line of architectural wares. Examples are very scarce today; they carry a variety of marks, all with the company name and location.

Vase, brn matt w/emb vertical leaves, mk, 6½" **350.00**
Vase, gr matt, cylindrical neck, angle hdls, 10½" **600.00**
Vase, gr matt, twisted cylinder, 9", EX **800.00**
Vase, olive & aqua matt, mk, 8" **425.00**
Vase, olive gr over brn w/aqua, 6 vertical leaves, mk, 6¼" **450.00**
Vase, textured bl w/vertical leaves, mk, 6½" **450.00**
Vase, 2-tone gr matt, cvd decor, 4½" **750.00**

Children's Books

Children's books, especially those from the Victorian era, are charming collectibles. Colorful lithographic illustrations that once delighted little boys in long curls and tiny girls in long stockings and lots of ribbons and lace have lost none of their appeal. Some collectors limit themselves to a specific subject, while others may be far more interested in the illustrations. First editions are more valuable than later issues, and condition and rarity are very important factors to consider before making your purchase. For further information we recommend *Collector's Guide to Children's Books, 1850 – 1950, Volume Two*, by Diane McClure Jones and Rosemary Jones; and *Whitman Juvenile Books Reference & Value Guide* by David and Virginia Brown. Both are available from Collector Books or your local bookstore.

A For Angel, Montresor, Knoph, 1969, VG+ **18.50**
Adventures of Holly Hobbie, Delacourte, 1980, 1st ed, EX **20.00**
Alice-All-By-Herself, Coatsworth, 1938, 1st UK ed, EX **60.00**
Anno's Counting Book, Anno, Crowell, 1977, 1st Am ed, EX **28.00**
Annotated Snark, Gardner, Simon & Schuster, 1962, 1st ed, VG+ .**35.00**
Beloved Belindy, Gruelle, ca 1926, EXIB **125.00**
Black Stallion's Filly, Farley, Random House, 1952, 1st ed, VG ...**35.00**
Boy's King Arthur, Lanier, Scribner's, 1922, 321-pg, EX **38.00**
Christmas Miniature, Buck, John Day, 1957, 1st ed, 40-pg, EX **25.00**
Clambake Mutiny, Beatty, Young Scott, 1964, 1st ed, 66-pg, VG ..**20.00**
Clyde Crashcup & Leonardo, Kurtz, Wonder, 1965, VG **8.00**
Come Again, Pelican, Freeman, Viking, 1961, 1st ed, 44-pg, sgn, VG .**60.00**
Crooked Little Path, Burgess, Little Brown, 1946, 1st ed, VG **50.00**
Davenports & Cherry Pie, Dalgliesh, Scribner's, 1949, 1st ed, EX .**40.00**
Fawn, Peck, Little Brown, 1975, 1st ed, 143-pg, VG+ **18.00**
Flaxin Braids, Turngren, Prentice Hall, 1937, sgn, EX **25.00**
Friendly Bear, Bright, Doubleday, 1957, 1st ed, VG **20.00**
Fun O' the Fair, Grahame, Dent, 1929, 30-pg, VG **50.00**
Geoffrey's Window, Marks, Milton Bradley, 1921, 236-pg, EX **40.00**
Halloween Tree, Bradbury, Knoph, 1972, 8th print, 145-pg, sgn, EX .**65.00**
Honey Bear, Willson, Algonquin, 1923, VG **25.00**
Island's Stallion's Fury, Farley, Random House, 1951, 243-pg, VG .**35.00**
Jo's Boys, Alcott, Roberts Bros Boston, 1886, 1st ed, 365-pg, VG ...**35.00**
Joy Toy Man of Joy Toy Town, Davies, ca 1930, EX **75.00**
Lad With a Whistle, Brink, Macmillan, 1941, 1st ed, 235-pg, EX ...**25.00**
Lances of Lynwood, Yonge, Macmillan, 1929, 1st ed, 217-pg, VG ..**35.00**
Letters From Foxy, Ross, Pantheon, 1966, 1st US ed, 103-pg, VG+ ..**18.00**
Magic Maize, Buff, Houghton Mifflin, 1953, 76-pg, VG **30.00**
Magic Meatballs, Yaffe, Dial Press, 1979, 1st ed, VG **15.00**
Mother Goose, Tudor, Oxford University Press, 1944, 87-pg, VG ..**45.00**
Mrs Mallard's Ducklings, Delafield, Shepard, 1946, 1st ed, VG **25.00**
Night Before Christmas, Reckham illus, w/dj **45.00**
Nursery Songs, Gale, Simon & Schuster, 1942, 1st ed, 40-pg, EX .**50.00**
On Green Meadows, Burgess, Little Brown, 1944, 1st ed, 182-pg, VG .**50.00**
Other Crowd, Ashley, Harcourt Brace, 1929, 231-pg, VG **15.00**
Owl & the Pussycat, Lear, Macmillan, 1983, 1st ed, EX **25.00**
Oxford Book of Poetry for Children, Blishen, Watts, 1963, VG ...**27.00**

Penny Fiddle, Graves, Doubleday, 1960, 1st ed, 63-pg, VG 20.00
Peter Pan in Kensington Gardens, Barrie, Scribner's, 1906, EX .100.00
Pig-Tale, Lewis Carrol, Little Brown, 1975, 30-pg, VG 25.00
Piggins, Yolen, Harcourt Brace, Jovanovich, 1st ed, VG 22.00
Restless Robin, Flack, Houghton Mifflin, 1937, VG 25.00
Romance of a Christmas Card, Wiggin, Houghton Mifflin, 1916, VG .25.00
Rumpty-Dudgets Tower, Hawthorne, Stokes, 1924, 72-pg, VG 45.00
Runaway Flea Circus, Lauder, Random House, 1958, 1st ed, VG .30.00
Sarah Somebody, Slobodkin, Vanguard, 1969, 1st ed, 71-pg, VG ..22.00
Secret Door, Newcomb, Dodd Mead, 1946, 1st ed, 162-pg, EX 40.00
Secret Garden, Burbett, Lippincott, 1962, 256-pg, VG 35.00
Skeezix Goes to War, King, Whitman, 1944, 344-pg, VG 15.00
Snow Queen, HC Anderson, Scribner's, 1972, cloth, 95-pg, 9½x7" ..25.00
Team That Stopped Moving, Christopher, Little Brown, 1975, VG .20.00
Teenie Weenie Town, Donahey, Whittlesey House, 1942, 1st ed, VG ...50.00
Thief Island, Coatsworth, Macmillan, 1943, 1st ed, 118-pg, VG ..15.00
Tim & Ginger, Ardizzone, Walck, 1965, EX 30.00
Turkey for Christmas, de Angeli, Westminster, 1949, 1st ed, EX .50.00
West From Home, Ingalls, Harper & Row, 1974, 1st ed, 124-pg, EX .20.00
Wilding Princess, Fox, Volland, 1929, 1st ed, 79-pg, VG 50.00
Winterbound, Bianco, Viking, 1936, 1st ed, 234-pg, EX 45.00

Children's Things

Nearly every item devised for adult furnishings has been reduced to child size — furniture, dishes, sporting goods, even some tools. All are very collectible. During the late 17th and early 18th centuries, miniature china dinnerware sets were made both in China and in England. They were not intended primarily as children's playthings, however, but instead were made to furnish miniature rooms and cabinets that provided a popular diversion for the adults of that period. By the 19th century, the emphasis had shifted, and most of the small-scaled dinnerware and tea sets were made for children's play.

Late in the 19th century and well into the 20th, toy pressed glass dishes were made, many in the same pattern as full-scale glassware. Today these toy dishes often fetch prices in the same range as those for the 'grown-ups'!

Authorities Margaret and Kenn Whitmyer have compiled a lovely book, *The Collector's Encyclopedia of Children's Dishes*, with full-color photos and current market values; you will find their address in the Directory under Ohio. See also A B C Plates; Canary Ware; Clothing; Stickley; Willow Ware; etc.

Key: ds — doll size

China

Bowl, Blue Marble, bl & wht, oval, England, 4½" 45.00
Bowl, soup; Dimity, gr & ivory, England, 4¼" 12.00
Bowl, soup; Humphrey's Clock, bl & wht, Ridgway 35.00
Bowl, soup; Lively Fern & Floral, gr & wht, 1850s, 4¼" 25.00
Bowl, Twin Flower, flow bl, deep, oval, England, 3¾" 100.00
Bowl, vegetable; Gaudy Floral, England, 4" 55.00
Bowl, vegetable; Scenes From England, bl & wht, England, w/lid, 4" .135.00
Cake plate, Blue Willow, Made in Japan, 5¼" 45.00
Casserole, Blue Acorn, mk RSR (England), 5" 35.00
Casserole, Blue Willow, Made in Japan, 4¾" 48.00
Casserole, Blue Willow, oval, ribbed, England, 2" 50.00
Casserole, Floral, Made in Japan, w/lid, 6⅝" 14.00
Casserole, Flow Blue Dogwood, Minton, 4½" 95.00
Creamer, Blue Banded, Dimmock & Co, 2¾" 25.00
Creamer, Brundage Girls, Germany, 4" 32.00
Creamer, Chinaman (figural), Japan, 2⅛" 35.00

Creamer, Dutch Windmill decal, Germany, 3½" 22.00
Creamer, Girl w/Pets, brn & ivory, Charles Allerton & Sons, 3⅛" .20.00
Creamer, Holly, Germany, early 1900s 30.00
Creamer, Mickey Mouse, Made in Japan, 2" 27.00
Creamer, Pink Banded Floral, England, 3½" 12.00
Creamer, Playful Zoo Animals, Edwin M Knowles, 2¾" 15.00
Creamer, Standing Pony/Green Lustre, Germany, 3¼" 20.00
Cup & saucer, Gumdrop Tree, Southern Potteries, 2¼", 4½" 32.00
Cup & saucer, Lady Standing by Urn, 1⅞", 4⅜" 32.00
Cup & saucer, Moss Rose, Made in Japan, 1½", 3½" 7.00
Cup & saucer, Nursery Rhyme, Germany, 1¾", 3¾" 14.00
Cup & saucer, Nursery Rhymes, W&Co, 2", 5" 24.00
Gravy boat, Greek Key, brn & wht, mk RSR (English), 4½" 32.00
Gravy boat, Kite Flyers, bl & wht, England, 3¼" 100.00
Mug, Archery, lady shooting arrow, pk transfer, 2½" 120.00
Mug, Bridesmaid, Germany, 2⅝" 90.00
Mug, Coalport Blue Willow, Made in England, 1⅞" 22.00
Mug, Dr Franklin's Maxims, mc transfer, 2½" 135.00
Mug, Prosper - Freedom, brn transfer eagle & shield, 2½" 135.00
Pitcher & bowl, Pink Lustre, England, 3", 4½" 85.00
Plate, Acorn, brn & wht, Cork, Edge & Malkin, 4⅞" 8.00
Plate, Basket, Salem China, 6¼" 7.00
Plate, Blue Onion, England 12.00
Plate, Calico, brn & ivory, England, 3⅞" 10.00
Plate, Forget-Me-Not, bl & wht, England, 2¾" 20.00
Plate, Maiden-Hair Fern, Ridgway, late 1800s, 4½" 11.00
Plate, Mary Had a Little Lamb, Brentleigh Ware, 3¾" 12.00
Plate, Pagodas, mc on wht (bl dominate), England, 4½" 13.00
Plate, Pembroke, brn on ivory, Bistro England, 4½" 11.00
Plate, Pink Open Rose, Made in England, 4½" 7.00
Platter, Fancy Loop, gr & ivory, England, 5" 22.00
Platter, Fishers, gr & ivory, CE&M, 5" 30.00
Platter, Gold Floral, bl band w/gold floral on wht, England, 5" 25.00
Platter, Spirit of Children, Jack & Jill, England, 5" 25.00
Server, Blue Banded Ironstone, mk Iron Stone, 2x3" 10.00
Sugar bowl, By the Mill, brn & wht, David Methvin & Sons, w/lid ..35.00
Sugar bowl, Merry Christmas/Pink Lustre, Germany, w/lid, 3⅝" ..40.00
Sugar bowl, Playful Cats, pk trim, Germany, w/lid, 2¾" 40.00
Sugar bowl, Punch & Judy, bl & wht, England, w/lid, 4½" 40.00

Tea set, children decals on porcelain, marked Modele u-f France Depose, 1900 – 37, four-place, EX, $150.00.

Tea set, Columbian Star, lt bl transfer, Ridgway, 11-pc set, EX .1,200.00
Tea set, Red & White Rose, Germany, 6-place 215.00
Tea set, wht ironstone, pot+cr/sug+6 plates+6 c/s, EX 100.00
Teapot, Gaudy Ironstone, England, 4½" 160.00
Teapot, Humphrey's Clock, bl & wht, Ridgway, 4½" 85.00
Teapot, May, bl & wht, England, 5" 75.00
Teapot, Snow White, Disney, Made in Japan, ca 1937, 3¼" 70.00

Teapot, Stick Spatter, Staffordshire, 5" 80.00
Teapot, Tan Lustre & Wht, England, 5¼" 50.00
Tureen, Athens, bl & wht, Davenport, 1850s, 3½" 55.00
Tureen, Forget-Me-Not, bl & wht, English, 3⅞" 125.00
Tureen, Rhodesia, floral w/gold, Royal Semi-Porcelain, 4¾" 55.00
Waste bowl, Water Hen, bl & wht, England, 2½" 60.00

Furniture

Examples with no dimensions given are child size unless noted doll size.

Armchair, oak Windsor bow-bk, rpl rail/spindles, rfn, ca 1870s, 23" .150.00
Armchair, Windsor style w/orig yel-gr pnt & flower stencil, 22" .175.00
Armchair, 2-slat ladder-bk w/spindle arms, 23½", pr 200.00
Armchair rocker, 2-spindle bk, stencil on cream, rprs, 28" 450.00
Bed, brass, scrolled head/ft brds, ball finials, 1910, 18x18" 110.00
Bed, CI filigree, ds, 15x8¾", EX 85.00
Bed, Murphy, chestnut, 1930s, 15x10½x6" 475.00
Bed, walnut Vict, trn legs, domed/paneled head/ft brds, 46x49" .300.00
Bureau, pine, 4 dvtl drw, iron lock, skirt, 20x18x8¼" 375.00
Cabinet, Hoosier; gr w/decal, Schoenhut's...USA, 17¼x11¼" ..2,750.00
Chair, arrow-bk, plank seat, saber legs, rosewood grpt, 25" 65.00
Chair, fan-bk Windsor, brn pnt & gold striping, MA, 1800s, 25" ..1,500.00
Chair, Hitchcock, rolled crest, rush seat, blk pnt w/gold, 21" 750.00
Chair, 2-slat ladder-bk w/acorn-finial posts, rush seat, 30½" 200.00
Chairs, worn lt gr w/blk & gold decor, 22", pr 600.00
Chest, dome top, old crackled bl, never had hinges, 11x15x10" .600.00
Chest, mahog Am Late Classical, 3-drw, mirror, 1850s, 22x15x18" ...550.00
Chest, pine Chpndl w/pnt decor, 4-drw, bracket ft, 1790s, 28x24" .2,900.00
Cradle, bentwood, orig pnt w/stencil, wheels, Ford Johnson, 54" ..600.00
Cradle, crusty blk pnt w/wht & mustard decor, 37" 200.00
Cradle, hooded, stained softwood, cutouts, nailed, 1890s, ds 120.00
Cradle, hooded style w/old red pnt, w/mattress/pillow, 22" 300.00
Cradle, sq nails, heart cutouts, 19th C, ds, 11x5½x4½" 125.00
Cradle, walnut w/curly maple brackets, trn finials, PA, 40" 880.00
Cupboard, step-bk, orig red pnt, 19th C, mini 275.00
Desk, Davenport, top lifts to expose drws, 7¼x4¾x12½" 700.00
Desk, Governor Winthrop, bracket ft, ca 1810, 12" 1,000.00
Desk, roll top; oak & chestnut, 15x18x9" 900.00
Dressing screen, stick & ball type, 3-fold, 45" H 450.00
Dry sink, orig buttermilk pnt, 2 doors, 7½x8x3¾" 475.00
Highchair, arrow-bk w/old brn rpt w/yel striping & decor, 33" ...165.00
Highchair, Windsor rod-bk w/old blk pnt & gold spindles, 34" ..975.00
Highchair, Windsor style w/mc pnt & gold stencil, 34" 350.00
Ice box, oak, 3-doors, w/ice compartment/drain/etc, 17x12x6" ..900.00

Rocker, painted and decorated Windsor, shaped crest with floral decor, plank seat, Pennsylvania, 1850s, 18", EX, $3,450.00.

Rocker, ladderbk w/mustard pnt, rush seat, wear, 23" 260.00
Rocker, rabbit w/pnt-on clothing as sides, 1910, wear, 24" 300.00
Secretary, Dutch Marquetry, stepped int, shaped front, 1840s, 33" .8,000.00
Table, baking; red buttermilk pnt, drws, porc knobs, 16x10x20" 2,000.00
Table, mahog turtle-top w/bow-cvd legs, fancy skirt, 5x8x5¼" ...375.00

Table, pine Country, drop-leaf, deep skirt w/drw, 20x21x32" 200.00
Washstand, tiger maple, 3-drw, 6 wooden knobs, gallery, 6" 375.00

Glass

Acorn, butter dish, frosted, 4" 350.00
Acorn, spooner, clear, 3⅛" 110.00
Acorn, sugar bowl, clear, w/lid, 4¾" 200.00
Arched Panel, pitcher, amber, 3¾" 96.00
Arched Panel, tumbler, clear, 2" 8.00
Austrian, butter dish, canary, 2¼" 350.00
Austrian, creamer, chocolate, 3¼" 325.00
Baby Thumbprint, cake stand, clear, 3" 110.00
Baby Thumbprint, compote, clear, w/lid, 4" 175.00
Banded Portland, pitcher, blush 56.00
Bead & Scroll, butter dish, dk gr, bl or amber, 4", ea 300.00
Bead & Scroll, creamer, clear w/gold, 3" 88.00
Bead & Scroll, sugar bowl, clear, w/lid, 4" 125.00
Block, butter dish, amber or bl, ea 185.00
Block, creamer, clear 60.00
Block, sugar bowl, amber or bl, w/lid, 4½", ea 150.00
Braided Belt, spooner, amber or lt gr, 2⅝" 150.00
Bucket (Wooden Pail), butter dish, clear, 2¼" 280.00
Bucket (Wooden Pail), creamer, clear, 2½" 75.00
Button Panel, creamer, clear, 2½" 52.00
Button Panel, spooner, clear w/gold, 2¾" 67.00
Buzz Saw, butter dish, clear, 2⅜" 35.00
Chicks & Pugs, mug, vaseline 75.00
Chimo, butter dish, clear, 2⅜" 125.00
Chimo, punch cup, clear, 1½" 18.00
Clear & Diamond Panel, creamer, clear, 2¾" 22.00
Cloud Band, butter dish, clear, 3¾" 125.00
Cloud Band, sugar bowl, milk glass w/decor, w/lid, 4" 120.00
Colonial Flute, bowl, berry; clear w/gold, 1" 25.00
Colonial Flute, punch bowl, clear, 3⅛" 50.00
Colonial Flute, tumbler, clear, 2" 5.00
Dewdrop, creamer, clear, 2¾" 60.00
Diamond Ridge, butter dish, clear 195.00
Diamond Ridge, sugar bowl, clear, w/lid 150.00
Doyle #500, tray, clear, 6⅝" 35.00
Drum, mug, clear, 2½" 32.00
Drum, sugar bowl, clear, w/lid, 3½" 110.00
Dutch Boudoir, pitcher, milk glass, 2¼" 95.00
Fernland, butter dish, olive or emerald gr, 2⅝", ea 54.00
Fernland, creamer, cobalt, 2⅜" 40.00
Fine Cut Star & Fan, butter dish, clear, 2½" 35.00
Frances Ware, pitcher, bl or vaseline, 4¾", ea 130.00
Frances Ware, tumbler, clear w/amber trim, 2¼" 50.00
Galloway, tumbler, blush, 2" 20.00
Grapevine w/Ovals, creamer, clear, 2" 67.00
Grapevine w/Ovals, mug, clear, 1⅞" 35.00
Hawaiian Lei, cake plate, clear 50.00
Hobnail w/Thumbprint Base, sugar bowl, clear, w/lid, 4" ..68.00
Hobnail w/Thumbprint Base, tray, bl or amber, 7⅜", ea ..60.00
Horizontal Threads, creamer, clear 35.00
Inverted Strawberry, bowl, master berry; clear, 1⅝" 65.00
Inverted Strawberry, punch bowl, clear, 3⅜" 52.00
Kitten, cup, bl carnival, 2⅛" 200.00
Lamb, creamer, clear, 2⅞" 85.00
Lamb, spooner, milk glass 165.00
Liberty Bell, spooner, clear, 2⅜" 150.00
Lion, butter dish, clear w/frosted head, 4¼" 180.00
Lion, cup & saucer, clear, 1¾", 3¼" 60.00
Michigan, creamer, clear, 2⅞" 45.00

Michigan, sugar bowl, clear w/red & gr, w/lid, 4¼"	115.00
Nursery Rhyme, berry set, clear, 7-pc	227.00
Nursery Rhyme, punch bowl, bl opaque, 3¼"	350.00
Oval Star, berry set, clear, 1 lg+6 sm	100.00
Oval Star, creamer, clear	20.00
Oval Star, tumbler, clear, 2¼"	11.00
Pattee Cross, pitcher, clear w/gold, 4½"	80.00
Pattee Cross, punch cup, clear, 1⅛"	22.00
Peacock Feather, cake stand, clear, 3"	95.00
Pennsylvania, butter dish, clear, 3½"	110.00
Pennsylvania, creamer, gr, 2½"	95.00
Pert, spooner, clear, 3"	125.00
Rex (Fancy Cut), pitcher, clear, 3½"	60.00
Rex (Fancy Cut), punch bowl, clear, 4⅜"	125.00
Rooster, butter dish, clear, 2¾"	200.00
Rooster, creamer, clear, 3¼"	130.00
Rose in Snow, mug, bl, In Remembrance	95.00
Sawtooth, creamer, clear, 3½"	32.00
Sawtooth, spooner, clear, 3¼"	40.00
Sawtooth Band, sugar bowl, clear w/ruby stain, w/lid, 4⅛"	150.00
Stippled Diamond, butter dish, clear, 2¼"	90.00
Stippled Diamond, sugar bowl, bl or amber, w/lid, 3⅛", ea	130.00
Sultan, butter dish, gr or gr frosted, 3¾", ea	300.00
Sunbeam, creamer, clear, 2⅞"	65.00
Sunbeam, sugar bowl, clear, w/lid, 3⅛"	115.00
Tappan, sugar bowl, milk glass, w/lid, 4"	30.00
Thumbelina, butter dish, clear, 2¼"	30.00
Thumbelina, creamer, clear, 2¼"	20.00
Tulip & Honeycomb, bowl, clear, oval, 1¾"	65.00
Tulip & Honeycomb, spooner, clear, 2½"	25.00
Two Band, butter dish, clear, 2"	75.00
Wee Branches, cup & saucer, clear, 1⅝", 3"	60.00
Wee Branches, mug, clear, 2"	45.00
Wheat Sheaf, punch bowl, clear, 3½"	32.00
Whirligig, butter dish, crystal, 2½"	27.00
Whirligig, punch bowl, clear, 4¾"	35.00
Wild Rose, butter dish, milk glass, 3½"	75.00
Wild Rose, punch cup, milk glass	22.00
Wild Rose, sugar bowl, milk glass, open, 1¾"	60.00

Miscellaneous

Bottle, nursing; baby's head on front	25.00
Conestoga circus wagon, wood w/metal wheels, doors slide, 22" L	100.00
Kaleidoscope, Lady Liberty mc pnt decor, 19th C, 8"	850.00
Noah's ark, pnt wood (worn), 11 animals & 1 person, 6¼" L	465.00
Rocking horse, dapple gray pnt w/red traces, worn saddle/etc, 45"	495.00
Rocking horse, pine w/worn orig pnt, NP 'button' eyes, 39"	220.00
Sleigh, wood w/mc pnt details, old rpr, 40"	385.00
Snow shoes, metal, pnt red w/yel stripes, 22" L, pr	120.00
Tea set, Little Miss Homemaker, Plastic Art, 15-pc, MIB	35.00
Teakettle, porc, rnd w/flat bottom, S spout, bail hdl, EX	175.00
Telephone, Speed Phone, red metal w/bell, NM	65.00
Typewriter, Smith Corona, 1950s, MIB	40.00
Wagon, wood/wood spoke wheels, Lewis Gear...Mich, 32", EX	450.00

Chintz

'Chintz' is the generic name for English china with an allover floral transfer design. This eye-catching china is reminiscent of chintz dress fabric. It is colorful, bright, and cheery with its many floral designs and reminds one of an English garden in full bloom. It was produced in England during the first half of this century and stands out among other styles of china. Pattern names often found with the manufacturer's name on the bottom of pieces include Florence, Blue Chintz, English Roses, Delphinium, June Roses, Hazel, Eversham, Royalty, Sweet Pea, Summertime, and Welbeck, among others.

The older patterns tend to be composed of larger flowers, while the later, more popular lines can be quite intricate in design. And while the first collectors preferred the earthenware lines, many are now searching for the bone china dinnerware made by such firms as Shelley. Prices are already formidable and rising. You can concentrate on reassembling a favorite pattern, or you can mix two or more designs together for a charming, eclectic look. Another choice may be to limit your collection to teapots (the stacking ones are especially nice), breakfast sets, or cups and saucers. For further information we recommend *Charlton Book of Chintz, I, II, and II*, by Susan Scott. Our advisor is Mary Jane Hastings; she is listed in the Directory under Illinois. See also Shelley.

Anemone, ashtray, sq, sm	80.00
Anemone, candy tray, metal hdl	165.00
Apple Blossom, plate, James Kent, 10"	165.00
Balmoral, bowl, vegetable; Ascot shape, 9¼" sq	255.00
Balmoral, breakfast tray, Royal Winton	150.00
Balmoral, teapot, Albans shape, blk mk, 6-cup, NM	750.00
Bedale, teapot, Elite shape, gr mk, 6-cup, NM	550.00
Beeston, plate, Royal Winton, 6"	95.00
Beeston, teapot, Royal Winton, 4-cup	695.00
Black Beauty, creamer & sugar bowl on tray, Lord Nelson	375.00
Black Beauty, cup & saucer, Lord Nelson	165.00
Black Beauty, tennis set	195.00
Black Pekin, jug, Royal Winton, 8"	150.00
Blue Anemone, sandwich tray, Royal Winton, 10"	175.00
Blue Pekin, tidbit, 2-tier, Royal Winton	135.00
Briar Rose, cake plate, tab hdl, Lord Nelson	180.00
Cheadle, bowl, dk pk, Ascot shape, 8¼" sq	255.00
Cheadle, cruet set (shakers/mustard/tray), Cloverleaf shape	400.00
Chelsea, pitcher, Royal Winton, 5"	495.00
Chelsea, teapot, stacking, Delamere shape, 3-pc, 5½", NM	1,150.00
Clevedon, jam pot w/liner, Royal Winton	350.00
Cotswold, cake plate & server, Royal Winton	350.00
Cottswald, bedside set, pot+5 pcs, Countess shape, NM	1,265.00
Country Lane, milk jug, Lord Nelson, 5"	325.00
Cranstone, basket, Royal Winton	395.00
Cranstone, salad bowl, Rheims shape, SP rim, gr mk, 4¼x8"	515.00
Crocus, candy dish, wht, Gordon shape, w/lid, mk, 8"	715.00
Crocus, coffeepot, wht, Albans shape, gr mk, rpr, 8"	575.00
DuBarry, cheese keeper, James Kent	295.00
Eleanor, coffeepot, Albans shape, blk mk, 8", NM	650.00
English Rose, plate, Royal Winton, 5" sq	125.00
Estelle, basket, Dudley shape, Royal Winton, 4½"	500.00
Estelle, hot water pot, Albans shape, Royal Winton, 7"	600.00
Ester, plate, Royal Winton, 9"	145.00
Evesham, butter dish, Royal Winton	300.00
Evesham, toast rack, 2-slice, blk mk, 2½x4½"	345.00
Fireglow, flower vase, wht, Gem shape, no mesh, mk, 4¾"	300.00
Fireglow, toast rack, wht, 2-slice, Queen shape, gr mk, 2½x4½"	275.00
Floral Feast, bedside set: tray, cup, cr/sug, toast rack, NM	550.00
Floral Feast, Elite shape, gr mk, 4-cup, NM	750.00
Florence, breakfast set, Royal Winton, 6-pc	3,200.00
Florence, cheese keeper, Dane shape, blk mk, 4x6½"	520.00
Florence, vase, bulbous, Winton, 4"	165.00
Florida, candlestick, Crown Ducal, 8½"	545.00
Florita, jam set, James Kent	495.00
Green Tulip, milk jug	700.00

Hazel, butter dish, Ascot shape, 4½x6" sq 200.00
Hazel, creamer & sugar bowl, Royal Winton 175.00
Hazel, cruet set (shakers/mustard/tray), Cloverleaf shape 450.00
Hazel, cup & saucer, Royal Winton 95.00
Hazel, teapot, Royal Winton, 4-cup 650.00
Heather, jug, wht hdl, 5" 285.00
Hydrangea, creamer, breakfast; James Kent 225.00
Ivory Chintz, vase, cylindrical w/bulbous base, Crown Ducal, 10¾" .152.50
Joycelynn, bud vase, Royal Winton 195.00
Julia, creamer & sugar bowl, Royal Winton 195.00
Julia, cup & saucer, Royal Winton 195.00
Julia, relish, 2-part, gr mk, 9x5" 575.00
Julia, tray, for breakfast set, Royal Winton 400.00
Julia, tray, Royal Winton, 10" 350.00
June Festival, shakers, Royal Winton, pr on tray 100.00
June Roses, cake plate, Royal Winton 295.00
Kew, shakers, Royal Winton, pr 175.00
Lorna Doone, pie plate & server, Barker Bros 230.00
Lorna Doone, plate, Midwinter, 7" 70.00
Lorna Doone, plate, Midwinter, 9" 125.00
Majestic, bowl, cereal; Royal Winton 125.00
Majestic, creamer & sugar bowl, Royal Winton 175.00
Majestic, jug, Globe shape, bl mk, 4¼" 430.00
Majestic, mint boat, Era shape, w/underplate, bl mk, 2¼" H 300.00
Marguerite, basket, bl trim, Hampton shape, gr mk, 3½" 172.00
Marguerite, creamer & sugar bowl 165.00
Marguerite, jam jar, SP rim & lid 165.00
Marguerite, pitcher, Royal Winton 110.00
Marguerite, plate, Royal Winton, 5" sq 65.00
Marguerite, salt shaker, metal lid 65.00
Marguerite, teapot, Countess shape, bl trim, 4-cup, NM 230.00
Marguerite, teapot, Royal Winton 475.00
Marigold, candy dish, scalloped, James Kent 175.00
Marina, cheese keeper, 3½x6" 230.00
Marina, plate, 7½" sq, 5 for 275.00
Marina, teapot, Lord Nelson, lg 595.00
Marion, candy box, Candy Box shape, w/lid, blk mk, 5½x4" 240.00
Marion, plate, Royal Winton, 6" 95.00
Marion, plate, Royal Winton, 7" 100.00
May Festival, bud vase, blk bkground, Lune shape, blk mk, 4¾" .100.00
May Festival, candy dish, dk bl ground, Gordon shape, w/lid, 8" .430.00
Mayfair, jam pot, Chelsea shape, w/liner & lid, 4" 275.00
Maytime, vase, Empire, 8½" 220.00
Nantwich, sandwich tray, Ascot shape, gr mk, 12x6½" 300.00
Nantwich, strainer, Royal Winton 225.00
Old Cottage, basket tray, Royal Winton 220.00
Old Cottage, biscuit barrel, blk mk, 5¾" 1,100.00
Old Cottage, bowl, sauce; Royal Winton, 4¾" sq 20.00
Old Cottage, coffeepot, Perth shape, gr mk, 8" 775.00
Old Cottage, cup & saucer, Royal Winton 120.00
Old Cottage, dinner bell 400.00
Old Cottage, jam pot, Royal Winton, w/undertray, metal lid/spoon .225.00
Old Cottage, pitcher, Royal Winton, 3¾" 40.00
Old Cottage, plate, Royal Winton, 6" 90.00
Old Cottage, plate, Royal Winton, 8" 120.00
Old Cottage, relish, 4-part, Royal Winton 245.00
Orient, teapot, stacking, Delamere shape, 3-pc, 5½", NM 335.00
Pansy, creamer & sugar bowl on tray, Lord Nelson 140.00
Pansy, mint boat, w/underplate, Lord Nelson, 2¾x4" ...175.00
Pekin, biscuit barrel, bl, HP decor, Rheims shape, 6½" .375.00
Pekin, plate, blk, 10" dia, 4 for 255.00
Peony, dish, 3-part, Royal Winton 235.00
Peony, sauce boat & underplate, Crown Ducal, 5½" 150.00
Pink Chintz, cup & saucer, Crown Ducal 110.00

Primula, strainer, 3-ftd, Crown Ducal, 3x8" dia 300.00
Priscilla, dish, 3-part, James Kent 265.00
Purple Chintz, cheese keeper, blk hdl, 5x8" 375.00
Queen Anne, biscuit barrel 426.00
Queen Anne, lamp, 11½" 450.00
Queen Anne, relish, canoe shape, gr mk, 10½" 140.00
Queen Anne, relish, 5-part, Marina shape, 12x10½", EX 150.00
Quilt, trivet, Royal Winton 175.00
Richmond, cup & saucer, Royal Winton 110.00
Rosalynde, bedside, James Kent 950.00
Rose of DuBarry, basket, Royal Winton 350.00
Rose of DuBarry, egg cups, bucket shape, set of 4, NM .285.00
Rose of DuBarry, vase, Tunis shape, 12¼", NM 400.00
Rosetime, tea set, wht hdls, 6-cup pot+cr/sug+tray 575.00
Royal Brocade, creamer, Lord Nelson 70.00
Royal Brocade, cup & saucer, farmer's; Lord Nelson ...275.00
Royal Brocade, shakers, Lord Nelson, pr on tray 160.00
Royal Brocade, teapot, stacking, chintz hdls/spout, 6½", NM 350.00
Royalty, butter dish, Ascot shape, 3x6" sq, NM 335.00
Royalty, sugar bowl, Twin Winton 50.00
Rutland, bedside set: tray, cup, cr/sug, toast rack, NM .375.00
Rutland, relish, 3-part, Gem shape, 8" 175.00
Somerset, fife bowl, Royal Winton 375.00
Somerset, nut dish, bl trim, ftd, Bow shape, 3½" 240.00
Somerset, pie plate & server, blk mk, 10" dia 460.00
Somerset, relish, canoe shape, bl trim, 11" L 200.00
Spring, canoe, Royal Winton 200.00
Spring, cup & saucer, Royal Winton 135.00
Spring Blossom, plate, dinner; Crown Ducal, 9" 81.00
Spring Blossom, reamer, hairline, rare 835.00
Stratford, luncheon plate, yel border, Ascot shape, 8¾" .100.00
Summertime, bread tray, Royal Winton, 12x6" 395.00
Summertime, coffeepot, Ascot shape, blk mk, 8½", NM 850.00
Summertime, cup & saucer, Royal Winton 125.00
Summertime, flower vase, gr trim, Gem shape, gr mk, 6" 515.00
Summertime, hot water pot, Countess shape, gr mk, 5½" 660.00
Summertime, plate, Royal Winton, 8" sq 95.00
Summertime, relish, canoe shape, gr mk, 10½" L 300.00
Summertime, shakers, Royal Winton, pr 90.00
Summertime, teapot, Ascot shape, bl mk, 4-cup 800.00
Summertime, teapot, Ascot shape, gr mk, 6-cup 850.00
Summertime, teapot, Elite shape, gr mk, 6-cup 925.00
Summertime, tidbit, 2-tier, Royal Winton 230.00
Sunshine, candy dish, w/lid, blk mk, 2x4x3½" 240.00
Sunshine, creamer & sugar bowl, Royal Winton 265.00
Sunshine, plate, Royal Winton, 9" 95.00
Sunshine, teapot, yel wash, Albans shape, gr mk, 4-cup .775.00
Sweet Pea, bonbon, ftd, bl mk, 2½x7¼" 460.00
Sweet Pea, bud vase, Royal Winton 200.00
Sweet Pea, butter dish, Ascot shape, 3x6" sq 430.00
Sweet Pea, grandfather's cup & saucer, blk mk, rpr 220.00
Sweet Pea, hot water pot, Royal Winton, 6-cup 450.00
Sweet Pea, trivet, Ascot shape, gr mk, 5¾" sq 300.00
Tapestry, dresser tray, James Kent 495.00
Victorian Rose, shakers, Fife shape, 2½", on 6" tray 250.00
Welbeck, bowl, vegetable; Ascot shape, bl mk, 9¼", NM 375.00
Welbeck, breakfast set, Royal Winton, 6-pc 3,000.00
Welbeck, canoe, Royal Winton 375.00
Welbeck, creamer & sugar bowl, Royal Winton 275.00
Welbeck, jam pot, Rheims tall shape, w/liner & lid, 4" .515.00
Welbeck, muffineer, Ascot shape, SP lid, 3½x7" sq 425.00
Welbeck, plate, Royal Winton, 5" sq 100.00
Welbeck, salad bowl, Rheims shape, SP rim, gr mk, 4x8" 515.00
Wildflower, canoe, Royal Winton 300.00

Chocolate Glass

Jacob Rosenthal developed chocolate glass, a rich shaded opaque brown sometimes referred to as caramel slag, in 1900 at the Indiana Tumbler and Goblet Company of Greentown, Indiana. Later, other companies produced similar ware. Only the latter is listed here. See also Greentown. Our advisors for this category are Jerry and Sandi Garrett; they are listed in the Directory under Indiana.

Barber bottle (cologne), Venetian, w/stopper 650.00
Bowl, Aldine, w/lid, oval 1,650.00
Bowl, Beaded Triangle, 4½" 350.00
Bowl, Chrysanthemum Leaf, smooth rim, 4⅜" dia 200.00
Bowl, Shield w/Daisy & Button, 8⅜" dia 1,300.00
Box, Aurora, open, rectangular, 9x5½" 1,500.00
Butter dish, Wild Rose w/Bowknot 550.00
Butter dish, Wild Rose w/Scrolling, child sz 700.00
Carafe, Chrysanthemum Leaf 2,500.00
Celery tray, Jubilee, 10" L 350.00
Compote, Chrysanthemum Leaf, 4½" dia 400.00
Compote, Melrose, 8½" dia 350.00
Creamer, Rose Garland 1,350.00
Creamer, Strigal, tankard style 165.00
Cruet, Geneva, w/stopper 1,250.00
Flowerpot, Russell 1,250.00
Lamp, Cloverleaf 1,000.00
Mug, Serenade, 4¾" 175.00
Nappy, Navarre, hdld 300.00

Pitcher, Geneva, $1,000.00.

Pitcher, File 2,000.00
Pitcher, milk; Feather 1,300.00
Plate, Serenade, 6¼" dia 250.00
Salt dip, master; Honeycomb, rnd, 3½" dia 650.00
Salt shaker, Geneva 350.00
Sauce dish, Melrose, scalloped edge, 3¾" dia 200.00
Sauce dish, Waffle 450.00
Sauce dish, Wild Rose w/Bowknot 125.00
Smoking set, 3-pc 1,000.00
Spooner, Sultan, child sz 300.00
Spooner, Touching Squares 1,000.00
Syrup jug, Geneva, metal lid 600.00
Tray, comb & brush; Venetian, 8x10" 450.00
Tray, ring; 4x5" 400.00
Tumbler, Chrysanthemum Leaf 550.00
Vase, Beaded Triangle, 6¼" 250.00
Vase, Masonic, 6" 475.00

Christmas Collectibles

Christmas past . . . lovely mementos from long ago attest to the ostentatious Victorian celebrations of the season.

St. Nicholas, better known as Santa, has changed much since 300 A.D. when the good Bishop Nicholas showered needy children with gifts and kindnesses. During the early 18th century, Santa was portrayed as the kind gift-giver to well-behaved children and the stern switch-bearing disciplinarian to those who were bad. In 1822 Clement Clark Moore, a New York poet, wrote his famous *Night Before Christmas*, and the Santa he described was jolly and jovial — a lovable old elf who was stern with no one. Early Santas wore robes of yellow, brown, blue, green, red, white, or even purple. But Thomas Nast, who worked as an illustrator for *Harper's Weekly*, was the first to depict Santa in a red suit instead of the traditional robe and to locate him the entire year at the North Pole headquarters.

Today's collectors prize early Santa figures, especially those in robes of fur or mohair or those dressed in an unusual color. Some early examples of Christmas memorabilia are the pre-1870 ornaments from Dresden, Germany. These cardboard figures — angels, gondolas, umbrellas, dirigibles, and countless others — sparkled with gold and silver trim. Late in the 1870s, blown glass ornaments were imported from Germany. There were over 6,000 recorded designs, all painted inside with silvery colors. From 1890 through 1910, blown glass spheres were often decorated with beads, tassels, and tinsel rope.

Christmas lights, made by Sandwich and some of their contemporaries, were either pressed or mold-blown glass shaped into a form similar to a water tumbler. They were filled with water and then hung from the tree by a wire handle; oil floating on the surface of the water served as fuel for the lighted wick.

Kugels are glass ornaments that were made as early as 1820 and as late as 1890. Ball-shaped examples are more common than the fruit and vegetable forms and have been found in sizes ranging from 1" to 14" in diameter. They were made of thick glass with heavy brass caps, in cobalt, green, gold, silver, red, and occasionally in amethyst.

Although experiments involving the use of electric light bulbs for the Christmas tree occurred before 1900, it was 1903 before the first manufactured socket set was marketed. These were very expensive and often proved a safety hazard. In 1921 safety regulations were established, and products were guaranteed safety approved. The early bulbs were smaller replicas of Edison's household bulb. By 1910 G.E. bulbs were rounded with a pointed end, and until 1919 all bulbs were hand blown. The first figural bulbs were made around 1910 in Austria. Japan soon followed, but their product was never of the high quality of the Austrian wares. American manufacturers produced their first machine-made figurals after 1919. Today figural bulbs (especially character-related examples) are very popular collectibles. Bubble lights were popular from about 1945 to 1960 when miniature lights were introduced. These tiny lamps dampened the public's enthusiasm for the bubblers, and manufacturers stopped providing replacement bulbs.

Feather trees were made from 1850 to 1950. All are collectible. Watch for newly manufactured feather trees that have been reintroduced.

For further information concerning Christmas collectibles, we recommend these highly informative books: *Christmas Collectibles* by Margaret and Kenn Whitmyer; and *Christmas Ornaments, Lights, and Decorations, A Collector's Identification and Value Guide, Volumes I through III*, by George Johnson. All are available from Collector Books or your local bookstore.

Note: values are given for bulbs that are in good paint, with no breaks or cracks, and in working order. Examples termed 'mini' measure no more than 1½".

Bulbs

Andy Gump in vest & tie, mc on milk glass, Japan, 1935, 2¾" 45.00

Angel in long robe, mc on clear, Japan, 1925, 2½", from $60 to ..**70.00**
Apple, red celluloid, ca 1915-25, 1¾", from $30 to **40.00**
Apple, red on milk glass, C-7½ base, Japan, 2½", from $10 to **15.00**
Baby in sock, mc on milk glass, Japan, 1920-50s, 1¾", from $15 to ...**25.00**
Bird, mc on clear, exhaust tip, from $25 to **35.00**
Bird in birdhouse, mc on milk glass, Japan, 1935-50, 1½" **20.00**
Bozo Clown, mc on milk glass, Japan, ca 1950, 2½", from $25 to .**35.00**
Bubble light, C-7 base, new, ea, from $1.50 to **2.00**
Bubble light, Paramount Oil, C-6 base, various styles, ea **35.00**
Bubble light, rocket ship, plastic base, from $15 to **30.00**
Canary on long spike, Mazda, ca 1920, 4¼" L, from $150 to **175.00**
Carriage lantern, mc on clear, exhaust tip, 2¼", from $50 to **75.00**
Cat in suit w/glasses, mc on clear, from $150 to **175.00**
Cat sitting w/bow, mc on milk glass, Japan, 2¼", from $30 to **35.00**
Cat w/mandolin, mc on milk glass, Japan, 1925-55, sm, from $10 to .**15.00**
Cats (2) in basket, mc on milk glass, Japan, 2¼", from $55 to **65.00**
Cross on disc, mc on milk glass, Japan, 1¾", from $25 to **35.00**
Doc (dwarf) head, Disney, Japan, ca 1970, 2", from $40 to **50.00**
Dog, brn on clear, exhaust-tip tail, from $115 to **130.00**
Dog in basket, mc on milk glass, Japan, 2¾", from $25 to **35.00**
Dog on rnd basket, mc on clear, mini, from $25 to **30.00**
Donald Duck, Disney, Japan, ca 1970, from $14 to **18.00**
Ear of corn, gr to yel on milk glass, Japan, 4", from $20 to **30.00**
Ear of corn, yel & gr on clear, sm, from $225 to **250.00**
Fish, red celluloid, ca 1915-25, 2½", from $30 to **40.00**

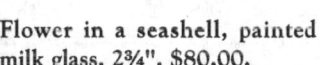

Flower in a seashell, painted milk glass, 2¾", $80.00.

Photo courtesy
Margaret and
Kenn Whitmyer

Frog, gr on clear, Mazda, ca 1925-55, 2¼", from $25 to **35.00**
Hippo girl in dress, mc on milk glass, Japan, 4½", $175 to **200.00**
Indian Chief, mc on clear, mini, from $65 to **75.00**
Kayo (Peewee), mc on milk glass, Japan, 1935, 2¼", from $30 to .**35.00**
Kewpie doll, mc on clear, Japan, 3", from $75 to **100.00**
Kewpie doll, mc on clear, mini, from $20 to **25.00**
Man in moon on star, mc on milk glass, Japan, 2", from $15 to **25.00**
Monkey, mc on clear, Mazda, from $225 to **250.00**
Monkey holding vine, mc on clear, from $25 to **35.00**
Ocean liner, mc on milk glass, Japan, ca 1950, 2¾", from $75 to ..**100.00**
Old King Cole, mc on clear, full figure, 2½", from $100 to **125.00**
Orange, orange on clear, Japan, ca 1930, 1¾", from $10 to **15.00**
Peacock, mc on milk glass, mini, from $40 to **50.00**
Pear, red to yel on clear, lg, from $15 to **25.00**
Pelican, red & bl on milk glass, Japan, ca 1950, 2¼" **30.00**
Pig w/lg head, in suit, mc on milk glass, Japan, 1950s, 2¾" **55.00**
Pineapple, mc on milk glass, Japan, ca 1950, 2", from $70 to **80.00**
Puffed Up Cat, mc on milk glass, Japan, 1950s, 1½", $55 to **65.00**
Rabbit in clothes w/concertina, tan celluloid w/blk pnt, 4¾" **80.00**
Rabbit in suit, mc on clear, mini, from $30 to **35.00**
Rabbit playing banjo, mc on milk glass, mini, from $15 to **25.00**
Sailor holding parrot, tan celluloid w/pnt details, 4" **50.00**
Santa (3-face), mc on milk glass, Japan, 2¼", from $20 to **30.00**
Santa standing w/bag, mc on clear, mini, from $20 to **25.00**

Santa w/hands in sleeves, mc on clear, sm, from $75 to **100.00**
Seashell, pnt milk glass, spiraled shape w/rosettes, Japan, 2" **45.00**
Smitty, mc on milk glass, Japan, ca 1955, 2½", from $30 to **35.00**
Snowman w/stick, mc on clear, exhaust tip, from $45 to **55.00**
Snowman w/stick, mc on milk glass, Japan, 1930-55, 2", from $6 to .**12.00**
Squirrel, mc on milk glass, Japan, ca 1950, 2", from $20 to **25.00**
St Nicholas (fat), mc on clear, exhaust tip, from $100 to **125.00**
St Nicholas in Roses, mc on clear, from $30 to **40.00**
Steamship, celluloid, 1915-25, 5", from $80 to **85.00**
Tadpole, gr on clear, mini, from $90 to **100.00**
Thumbelina on rose, mc on milk glass, Japan, 3¼", $35 to **45.00**
Walnut, brn-gray on clear, ca 1920, 1¾", from $20 to **30.00**

Candy Containers

Bell, cb, scrap decor, US, 1930s, 5½" W, from $25 to **35.00**
Birdcage, Dresden, gold or silver, 3-D, 2", from $250 to **275.00**
Bull head, Dresden, gold or silver, hollow neck, 3-D, 3" **525.00**
Butterfly, Dresden, gold or silver, 3-D, 5½", from $275 to **300.00**
Cornucopia, printed cb, 3½", from $15 to **20.00**
Couger head, Dresden, gold or silver, 3-D, 2½", from $475 to **525.00**
Crown, Dresden, gold or silver, 3-D, 2½", from $200 to **225.00**
Guitar, cb litho, appl strings, bk lifts off, 3½" **75.00**
Heart, Dresden, gold or silver, 3-D, 2-2½", ea **150.00**
Horse head, Dresden, gold, silver or natural, 3-D, 3" **450.00**
Lyre, Dresden, gold or silver, 3-D, 3" or 4", ea, from $190 to **250.00**
Rabbit, Dresden, gold, silver or natural, 3-D, 2", from $275 to ...**300.00**
Ram head, Dresden, gold or silver, 3-D, 3", from $325 to **350.00**
Rooster head, Dresden, natural, 3-D, 3", from $325 to **350.00**
Santa, compo, Germany, 5" **450.00**
Santa, compo, Germany, 6" **550.00**
Santa, compo, Germany, 7" **750.00**
Santa, compo, Germany, 8" **750.00**
Santa, compo, Germany, 9" **850.00**
Santa, papier-mache, USA, 5-7", ea **75.00**
Santa at top of boot, plaster/cb/cotton batting, Japan, 6½" **85.00**
Santa w/sack or chimney, papier-mache, USA, 8-11", ea **135.00**
Snowman, papier-mache, USA, 7" **75.00**
Snowman, spun cotton, hollow tube inside, 4", from $125 to **150.00**
Stork, Dresden, natural, 3-D, 4", from $250 to **275.00**

Ornaments

Acorn, mold-blown, std type, 1-1½", ea, from $3 to **6.00**
Anchor, tin, faceted indents, Germany, 3¼" **110.00**
Angel, cotton batting, silver wings, Germany, 3" **130.00**
Angel, wax, flying, Dresden wings, fabric sash, 5½" **265.00**
Angel in basket, mold-blown, Germany, 3", from $160 to **175.00**
Angel w/harp on cloud, scrap w/tinsel, 6", from $25 to **35.00**
Angel w/open book, scrap only, 4½", from $10 to **15.00**
Baby Jesus, wax, lying on bk, Germany, 6", from $75 to **100.00**
Baby w/bottle, mold-blown, 3½", from $175 to **200.00**
Baby w/bottle, scrap paper doll, Germany, 30", from $250 to **300.00**
Barrel, free-blown, fat, wire-wrapped, 3¼", from $60 to **80.00**
Basket, tin, lg loop hdl, flat, Germany, 3¼", from $45 to **60.00**
Basket of grapes, mold-blown, 3½", from $30 to **40.00**
Bear w/heart, mold-blown, Germany, 3", from $125 to **150.00**
Beetle, mold-blown, well-defined wings, 8 paper legs, 3" **95.00**
Bell, crushed glass on spun cotton, Japan or Germany, 2½" **15.00**
Bird on disc, mold-blown, crude, 3¼", from $15 to **18.00**
Bird w/berry, mold-blown, plaster berry, 4", from $45 to **55.00**
Birdhouse, mold-blown, emb bird, Germany, 3½", from $35 to **45.00**
Boy in flower basket, mold-blown, Germany, 2¼", from $40 to **55.00**
Butterfly frame, tin, wire-wrapped, Germany, 2½" **45.00**

Candle, mold-blown, w/clip, Germany, 4", from $90 to 100.00
Cherub boy, mold-blown, Germany, 3½", from $90 to 100.00
Cherub boy, wax w/molded diaper, Dresden wings, Germany, 3½" 50.00
Cherub on ball, mold- & free-blown, Germany, 4½", from $125 to 150.00
Church, mold-blown, 3 windows ea side, Germany, 3", from $20 to 35.00
Clown, mold-blown, 1-pc suit, Germany, 4¾", from $40 to 50.00
Clown head w/glass eyes, mold-blown, Germany, 3¾", from $150 to ..175.00
Corn w/lg leaves, mold-blown, crude, 3", from $5 to 10.00
Cross, tin, Germany, 3¼", from $60 to 70.00
Cuckoo clock, mold-blown, Germany, 3½", from $50 to 60.00
Dog in dog house, mold-blown, Germany, 3", from $60 to 70.00
Drum, mold-blown, emb ropes, Germany, 2x1½" dia, from $20 to 25.00
Duck in egg, mold-blown, emerging, Germany, 3¼", from $175 to .200.00
Eagle & Liberty Shield, mold-blown, 3½", from $150 to 175.00
Elephant on ball, mold-blown, Austria, 3", from $90 to 110.00
Fan, tin, filigreed w/faux gems, flat, Germany, 3¾", $35 to 45.00
Fish basket, tin, 1-pc 3-D casting, Germany, 2" L, from $40 to 55.00
Frog on leaf, mold-blown, Germany, 2½", from $35 to 50.00
Frog w/violin, mold-blown, 2¾", from $70 to 85.00
Gingerbread house, mold-blown, 3", from $30 to 35.00
Giraffe, free-blown w/annealed limbs/ears/tail, 1920s, 2½" 25.00
Girl in beehive, mold-blown, Germany, 2¼-3", from $70 to 150.00
Goldilocks, mold-blown, Germany, 1970s, 3", from $45 to 60.00
Gramophone, free-blown, morning-glory horn, wire-wrapped, 4¾" ...165.00
Guitar, American; mold-blown, figure-8 shape, 2", from $5 to 10.00
Heart on heart, mold-blown, Germany, 2", from $10 to 18.00
Hummingbird, mold-blown, spun-glass wings, 2½", from $30 to ..40.00
Hummingbird, scrap w/spun-glass wings & tail, 4½", $20 to 30.00
Icicle, free-blown, hollow, 10" & up, ea, from $20 to 30.00
Icicle, free-blown, hollow, 2", from $1 to 5.00
Iris on a heart, mold-blown, 2½", from $15 to 25.00
Lighthouse, mold-blown, 3", from $35 to 45.00
Lion head, mold-blown, EX details, 2¾", from $300 to 375.00
Little Miss Muffet, mold-blown, Germany, 4", from $60 to 100.00
Man in cello, mold-blown, 1980s, 3½-4", ea, from $200 to 225.00
Man in the Moon (frowning), mold-blown, 2¾", from $75 to 85.00
Mushroom w/face, mold-bown, 2¾", from $140 to 175.00
Owl, free-blown, tubular body w/annealed wings/etc, 1920s, 3" 35.00
Owl on ball, mold-blown, Germany, 3¼", from $70 to 85.00
Parachutist, mold-blown, Germany, 1970s, 4¼", from $125 to ...150.00
Pear, mold-blown, unsilvered, 5", from $35 to 45.00
Person, spun cotton, porc face, crepe-paper clothes, 3" 250.00
Person, spun cotton, scrap face, Dresden trim, 3", from $175 to .250.00
Pineapple, mold-blown, unsilvered, Germany, 3", from $60 to 75.00
Pipe w/str stem, free-blown, 10", from $100 to 125.00
Purse w/emb roses, mold-blown, Germany, 1970-80s, 2¼" 45.00
Rooster, mold-blown, wings folded, spun-glass tail, 3", $60 to 75.00
Rose on leaf, mold-blown, Germany, 2¾-3", ea, from $70 to 90.00
Rosebuds, mold-blown, European, 1¼-3", ea, from $10 to 25.00
Rosette, spun glass, sm Santa head scrap ea side, 2" dia 35.00
Santa, cotton batting, cast plaster face, Japan, 8", from $90 to ...110.00
Santa, cotton batting, Japan, 3", from $30 to 45.00
Santa, scrap w/tinsel, Germany, 4½x1¼", from $15 to 25.00
Santa, spun cotton, Dresden trim, Germany, 3", from $175 to ...200.00
Santa at Chimney, mold-blown, Germany, 3", from $150 to 175.00
Santa in airplane, mold-blown, tinsel wire wings, Germany, '50s, 3" .25.00
Santa in holly, scrap w/tinsel, 6¾", from $45 to 55.00
Santa w/bag & toys, mold-blown, 3-3¾", ea, from $30 to 50.00
Shark, mold-blown, no emb scales, spun-glass tail, Germany, 4½" .125.00
Skein of yarn, mold-blown, Germany, 1¾", from $20 to 30.00
Snow angel boy w/tree, scrap w/tinsel, 2½", from $30 to 40.00
Snow girl bust, scrap w/tinsel, Germany, 4½", from $20 to 30.00
Snowflake, silver-colored wire, 6-pointed, Germany, 5", $5 to 10.00
Squirrel, mold-blown, EX details, Austria, 1970s-80s, 3" 45.00

Squirrel, spun cotton, from $280 to 310.00
St Nicholas head, scrap only, 3¾", from $5 to 10.00
Star, foil, emb decor, dbl-sided, ca 1950, 4", from $3 to 5.00
Star, mold-blown, 6-pointed, emb center, 2½", from $10 to 15.00
Steamship, free-blown, spun-glass smoke, 5½", from $140 to 160.00
Sun face on disc, mold-blown, Germany, 1970s, 2", from $6 to 10.00
Swan, free-blown, spun-glass tail, std form, 3" 10.00
Swan w/rider, free-blown w/scrap figure, 4", from $40 to 50.00
Tree, free-blown, wire-wrapped base, 1950s, 5", from $20 to 30.00
Virgin Mary, mold-blown, kneeling, Germany, 4", from $15 to 20.00
Walnut, wax, emb detail, Germany, 2", from $25 to 35.00
Woodpecker, mold-blown, spun-glass wings & tail, Germany, 3½" ..45.00

Miscellaneous

Doll, Santa, plaster, West Germany, 9", from $150 to 170.00
Doll, Santa, straw-stuffed fabric, canvas pnt face, 25" 200.00
Doll, Santa w/lg bag, papier-mache & plaster, 4½", from $125 to ..150.00
Fence, feather, per section, from $25 to 35.00
Fence, wood, per section, from $10 to 15.00
Figure, flat lead; hollow cast, 3-D, Germany, 1-2", ea, from $8 to .18.00
Figure, reindeer, pnt cast lead, Germany, 1¼-4", from $25 to 35.00
Figure, Santa, celluloid, Germany or Japan, 3-6", ea, from $35 to ..150.00
Figure, Santa & sleigh, celluloid, 2 separate reindeer, Japan, 12" ..85.00
House, cb w/cellophane windows, w/hook, Japan, sm 5.00
Lantern, Santa head, milk glass, 2-faced, battery, Amico, 6" 40.00
Light, bust of King Edward, cobalt, smooth base, 4" 300.00
Light, floral, powder bl opaque, pontiled, 3¼" 300.00
Light, tulip, cobalt, smooth base, 3⅝" 130.00
Toy, Santa squeaker, fur beard, 6½", from $375 to 400.00
Tree, bubble light; paper needles, 1950s-early '60s, 12" 125.00
Tree, bubble light; paper needles, 1950s-early '60s, 36" 200.00
Tree, cellophane, gr, ca 1935, from $20 to 35.00
Tree, feather; Germany, Japan or US, 6", ea, from $50 to 75.00
Tree, feather; Germany, Japan or US, 24-30", ea, from $125 to .150.00
Tree, feather; Germany, Japan or US, 48-54", ea, from $300 to .350.00
Tree, feather; Germany, Japan or US, 84-90", ea, from $600 to .800.00
Tree, Visca, gr & wht, ca 1950, 40-60", from $30 to 35.00

Chrysanthemum Sprig, Blue

This is the blue opaque version of Northwood's popular pattern, Chrysanthemum Sprig. It was made at the turn of the century and is today very rare, as its values indicate. Prices are influenced by the amount of gold remaining on the raised designs. Our advisors for this category are Betty and Clarence Maier; they're listed in the Directory under Pennsylvania.

Bowl, master fruit; oval, 5x10½", $600.00.

Bowl, berry; sm 325.00
Butter dish 1,250.00

Celery	600.00
Compote, jelly	600.00
Condiment tray, rare, VG gold	750.00
Creamer	385.00
Cruet, EX gold, from $975 to	1,200.00
Pitcher, water	1,100.00
Shakers, pr	450.00
Spooner, from $300 to	350.00
Sugar bowl, w/lid	600.00
Toothpick holder	450.00
Tumbler	350.00

Clarice Cliff

Between 1928 and 1935 in Burslem, England, as the director and part owner of Wilkinson and Newport Pottery Companies, Clarice Cliff and her 'paintresses' created a body of hand-painted pottery whose influence is felt to the present time.

The name for the oevre was Bizarre Ware, and the predominant sensibility, style, and appearance was Deco. Almost all pieces are signed. There were over 160 patterns and more than 400 shapes, all of which are illustrated in *A Bizarre Affair — The Life and Work of Clarice Cliff*, published by Harry N. Abrams, Inc., written by Len Griffen and Susan and Louis Meisel.

Note: Non-hand-painted work (transfer printed) was produced after World War II and into the 1950s. Some of the most common names are 'Tonquin' and 'Charlotte.' These items, while attractive and enjoyable to own, have little value in the collector market. Our advisors for this category are Wilfred and Dolli Cohen; they are listed in the Directory under California.

Bowl, Bizarre, Fantasque Range, cone shape in X base, 4½x9"	950.00
Bowl, Fantasque Range, cone shape in X base, 4x7½", EX	750.00
Bowl, Rhodanthe, stylized plants, mc on cream, 2⅞x7⅝"	375.00
Cup & saucer, Gay Day, yel/orange/gr, 4 for	635.00
Jam jar, Crocus, mc w/gr stems on brn, B Rigers, 3½x3¼"	450.00
Jug, Coral Firs, mc bands, 11⅝x7¼"	1,350.00
Jug, Lotus; Anemone, floral, mc on cream, 11⅝x7¼"	1,195.00
Jug, Lotus; Autumn, house & landscape, 11¾x8"	1,295.00
Jug, Lotus; Gardenia, mc floral bands, 11⅜x7⅛"	1,265.00
Jug, Rhodanthe, stylized plants, mc on cream, 6⅝x3⅝"	650.00
Plate, Bizarre, magenta w/mc & gilt HP, L Knight, 1934, 10"	695.00
Toast rack, Cabbage Flower, gr/brn/dk orange, 3x5"	350.00
Vase, Bizarre, Delecia, stepped joined cylinders, 7x3"	1,300.00
Vase, Bizarre, trees, blk/gr on orange/yel, stepped cone, 6"	995.00
Vase, Coral Firs, trees & landscape, 8¼x6"	1,295.00
Vase, floral sprays on brn stems, corseted, 9¼x8"	1,295.00
Vase, Inspiration, bl & wht flowers on bl to gr, mk, 7¼x8"	1,495.00
Vase, Inspiration Lily, purple lilies on bl-gr, 7x3"	1,495.00
Vase, pansies, mc on yel w/mc drips, 10½x4½"	995.00
Vase, Windbells, tree bands, mc on gr, 8x6"	1,450.00
Wall pocket, Bizarre, Delecia, bk: 2 offset semi-circles, 10"	1,000.00

Cleminson

A hobby turned to enterprise, Cleminson is one of several California potteries whose clever hand-decorated wares are attracting the attention of today's collectors. The Cleminsons started their business at their El Monte home in 1941 and were so successful that eventually they expanded to a modern plant that employed more than 150 workers. They produced not only dinnerware and kitchen items such as cookie jars, canisters, and accessories, but novelty wall vases, small trays, plaques, etc., as well. Though nearly always marked, Cleminson wares are easy to spot as you become familiar with their distinctive glaze colors. Their grayed-down blue and green, berry red, and dusty pink say 'Cleminson' as clearly as their trademark. Unable to compete with foreign imports, the pottery closed in 1963. Our advisor for this category is Jack Chipman, author of *The Collector's Encyclopedia of California Pottery*; he is listed in the Directory under California.

Ashtray, stylized fruit, 10"	36.00
Button holder, Southern lady	45.00
Canister, Cherry, tea sz	35.00
Cleanser shaker, Katrina, lady figure, 5 holes, 6½"	30.00

Cookie jar, Mother's Best, lovebirds finial, $300.00.

Cookie jar, Carrot Head	165.00
Cookie jar, Cookie Bank	225.00
Cookie jar, Cottage House	225.00
Cookie jar, Gingerbread House	225.00
Cookie jar, King, 10½"	550.00
Cookie jar, Pig	275.00
Cookie jar, Potbellied Stove	200.00
Cookie jar, Way to a Man's Heart	175.00
Cup & saucer, Gramma's	35.00
Darner, lady figural, Darn It, HP decor	30.00
Dinner bell, Fancy Pants maid, bl dress/fancy leggings, w/tag	85.00
Egg cup, lady in apron, early	36.00
Egg cup, man w/blk coat & striped pants	36.00
Egg timer, head figural, 3x2½"	65.00
Hair receiver, girl w/folded hands, 2-pc	45.00
Match holder, Cherry, wall mt	40.00
Mug, Make Mine Stronger, strong man, 3⅜"	35.00
Mug, Morning After, w/lid	35.00
Pancake server, Big Top Circus, juvenile	85.00
Pin holder, Bobbie Guard, 4x2¾"	50.00
Pitcher, Cherry, oil-can shape, 9"	55.00
Plaque, boy & girl profiles, oval, 4x3", pr	45.00
Plaque, man w/scissors, lady w/basket, 4x5", pr	55.00
Plaque, teapot, A Kitchen Bright	40.00
Ring holder, Chef	45.00
Shakers, Cherry, 6", pr	40.00
Shakers, Distlefink, lg, pr	35.00
Shakers, kangaroos, w/orig label, pr	50.00
Spoon rest, floral decor, 3-lobed, 8½"	27.00
Sprinkler, Chinese boy	40.00
Wall pocket, Antoine, chef's head, ink stamp, 7¼"	75.00
Wall pocket, cauldron w/wire hdl, Kitchen Is the Heart...	25.00
Wall pocket, Tea Time	45.00
Wall pocket, teapot, Penny Saved Is a Penny	40.00

Clewell

Charles Walter Clewell was a metal worker who perfected the technique of plating an entire ceramic vessel with a thin layer of copper or bronze treated with an oxidizing agent to produce a natural deterioration of the surface. Through trial and error, he was able to control the degree of patina achieved. In the early stages, the metal darkened and if allowed to develop further formed a natural turquoise-blue or green corrosion. He worked alone in his small Akron, Ohio, studio from about 1906, buying undecorated pottery from several Ohio firms, among them Weller, Owens, and Cambridge. His work is usually marked. Clewell died in 1965, having never revealed his secret process to others.

Prices for Clewell have advanced rapidly during the past few years along with the Arts and Crafts market in general. Right now, good examples are bringing whatever the traffic will bear.

Bowl, #384-25, rust over gr patina, incurvate, stress line, 3x9" ...**200.00**
Candlesticks, #N202, dk patina, sq shafts, pyramid base, 8", pr ..**900.00**
Humidor, rust over gr patina, rivet design on body & finial, 4" ..**350.00**
Mug, #1035, Utopian, gr/gold bronze patina, emb vines **210.00**
Mug, copper clad w/external rivets, mk Clewell Coppers, 4⅛" ...**125.00**
Vase, #191-211, rust over gr patina, minor stress lines, 10" **900.00**
Vase, #288-2-9, copper clad w/verdigris, 9x4" **260.00**
Vase, #321-24, crusty gr on orange-copper, 6¼" **700.00**
Vase, #364-25, copper w/verdigris, 6½" **330.00**
Vase, #366-215, gr/orange patina, 15" **1,000.00**
Vase, #369-2, rust over gr patina, broad shoulders, 5½" **550.00**
Vase, #412-6, bl/gr patina, ftd cone form, 9" **375.00**
Vase, #426-2-6, rust over gr patina, ftd trumpet form, 9" **950.00**
Vase, bud; #354, rust over gr patina, trumpet form, 6½" **260.00**
Vase, Moss Aztec blank, stems/leaves/berries, 8", NM **375.00**
Vase, Owens blank, tiny neck, slip decor shows through, 6" **250.00**

Clews

Brothers Ralph and James Clews were potters who operated in Cobridge in the Staffordshire district from 1817 to 1835. They are best known for their blue and white transfer-printed earthenwares, which included American Views, Moral Maxims, Picturesque Views, and English Views. A series called *Three Tours of Dr. Syntax* contained thirty-one different scenes with each piece bearing a descriptive title. Another popular series was *Pictures of Sir David Wilkie* with seven prints. (Though we once thought that the Don Quixote series was made by Clews, new information seems to indicate that it was made instead by Davenport.) Both printed and impressed marks were used, often incorporating the pattern name as well as the pottery. See also Staffordshire, Historical.

Platter, The Valentine, dark blue transfer, Wilkie, 17", EX, from $900.00 to $1,100.00.

Creamer, Christmas Eve, dk bl transfer, 5½" **265.00**
Cup plate, Christmas Eve, dk bl transfer, no border, 3½" **275.00**
Pitcher, boats before castle w/flag, dk bl transfer, 4", NM **2,500.00**
Pitcher, milk; Basket Vase & Floral, dk bl transfer, 5" **250.00**
Pitcher, Water Girl, 2 dk bl transfers, rstr chips/wear, 4¾" **350.00**
Plate, Beehive, dk bl transfer, 6" **85.00**
Plate, Dr Syntax Taking Possession..., dk bl transfer, 10" **270.00**
Plate, Valentine, dk bl transfer, hairline/rstr, 9" **160.00**
Platter, Advertisement for a Wife, dk bl transfer, 15¼" **1,600.00**
Platter, floral & scroll border, creamware, 16¾", NM **225.00**
Platter, Valentine, dk bl transfer, wear, 17", from $900 to **1,100.00**
Saucer, Christmas Eve, Select Views, dk bl transfer **25.00**
Tureen, sauce; Don Quixote, Repose in wood, dk bl transfer, EX .**725.00**

Clifton

Clifton Art Pottery of Clifton, New Jersey, was organized ca 1903. Until 1911 when they turned to the production of wall and floor tile, they made artware of several varieties. The founders were Fred Tschirner and William A. Long. Long had developed the method for underglaze slip painting that had been used at the Lonhuda Pottery in Steubenville, Ohio, in the 1890s. Crystal Patina, the first artware made by the small company, utilized a fine white body and flowing, blended colors, the earliest a green crystalline. Indian Ware, copied from the pottery of the American Indians, was usually decorated in black geometric designs on red clay. (On the occasions when white was used in addition to the black, the ware was often not as well executed; so even though two-color decoration is very rare, it is normally not as desirable to the collector.) Robin's Egg Blue, pale blue on the white body, and Tirrube, a slip-decorated matt ware, were also produced.

Vase, bl matt w/dk bl & gr drips, 12" **295.00**
Vase, brn/gr crystalline w/gr/tan/cream drip, 1906, 5½x6½" **550.00**
Vase, cream/olive/bl crystalline, stick neck, 1906, 4½" **260.00**
Vase, emb stems/berries, ivory on lt gr matt, 1906, 2x4" **160.00**
Vase, geometrics, brn/tan on reddish matt, 3" **325.00**
Vase, lt yel crystalline w/brn streaks, trumpet neck, 1906, 7" **450.00**
Vase/lamp base, bl & cream gloss, paper label, 15x4¼" **300.00**

Clocks

In the early days of our country's history, clock makers were influenced by styles imported from Europe. They copied the European's cabinets and reconstructed their movements — needed materials were in short supply; modifications had to be made. Of necessity was born mainspring motive power and spring clocks. Wooden movements were made on a mass-production basis as early as 1808. Before the middle of the century, metal movements had been developed.

Today's collectors prefer clocks from the 18th and 19th centuries with pendulum-regulated movements. Bracket clocks made during this period utilized the shorter pendulum improvised in 1658 by Fromentiel, a prominent English clock maker. These smaller square-face clocks usually were made with a dome top fitted with a handle or a decorative finial. The case was usually walnut or ebony and was sometimes decorated with pierced brass mountings. Brackets were often mounted on the wall to accommodate the clock, hence the name. The banjo clock was patented in 1802 by Simon Willard. It derived its descriptive name from its banjo-like shape. A similar but more elaborate style was called the lyre clock.

The first electric novelty clocks were developed in the 1940s. Lux, who was the major producer, had been in business since 1912, making wind-up novelties during the '20s and '30s. Another company, Mastercrafter Novelty Clocks, first obtained a patent to produce these clocks in the late 1940s. Other manufacturers were Keebler, Westclox, and Columbia Time. The cases were made of china, Syroco, wood, and plastic; most were animated and some had pendulettes. Prices vary according to condition and rarity.

Except for the novelty clocks whose values are on the increase, clock prices have been stable for several years. Unless noted otherwise, values are given for eight-day time only clocks in excellent condition. Clocks that have been altered, damaged, or have had parts replaced are worth considerably less.

Our advisor is Bruce A. Austin; he is listed in the Directory under New York. Our novelty clock advisors is Anita Levi (Allegheny Mountain Antiques Gallery); she is listed in the Directory under Pennsylvania.

Key:
br — brass
dl — dial
esc — escapement
mcr — mercury
mvt — movement
OG — ogee
pnd — pendulum
reg — regulator
rswd — rosewood
TS — time & strike
wt — weight
vnr — veneer
2nds — seconds

Calendar Clocks

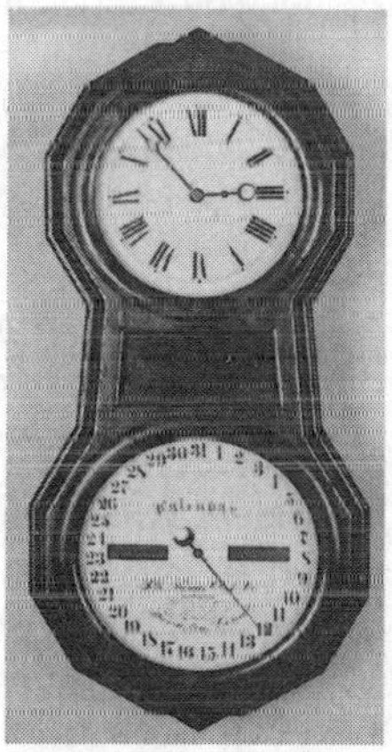

Seth Thomas Office Calendar #1, rosewood veneer, two painted zinc dials, eight-day time only movement, period pendulum, ca 1865, 41", minor restoration, $1,200.00.

Fr, alabaster, 4-yr Julian perpetual calendar, TS, 16" 1,050.00
Ithaca #4 Favorite, TS, 8" dls, walnut, 32", NM 1,885.00
Ithaca #4 Hanging Office, 30-day, walnut, ca 1880, 28" 850.00
Jerome Register, walnut, orig labels/dls, 1880, 28", VG 800.00
LF&WW Carter, mantel, rswd, rectangular, 2-wt, 1864, 33" ..1,100.00
New Haven Referee, oak reg, 1912, cracked bk/losses, 35½" 225.00
S Thomas '12" Drop Octagon,' mahog, 1910, NM orig, 23½" 550.00
S Thomas Office #2, 1865, VG rstr, 43" 675.00
S Thomas Office #3 (Peanut), 1879, M rstr, 23" 3,100.00
Sessions Star Regulator, pressed oak w/stars, 1910, orig, 38" 400.00
Waterbury Rochester, walnut gingerbread (1 pc rpl), 1910, 29" .150.00
Wm L Gilbert Rnd Long Drop, wt drive, mahog vnr, 34" 2,375.00
WS Adams, office, 2nd spring-drive on side, 1870, 17" 600.00

Novelty Clocks

Ballerina, musical, wood & metal w/plastic face, United 160.00
Beer Bbl Drinkers, non-animated, Lux Pendulette, minimum value .350.00
Bird in cage, Mastercrafters 150.00
Boy fishing, metal, United 150.00
Boy Scout, Lux Pendulette, non-animated 400.00
Carousel, Mastercrafters, electric 165.00
Clown w/tie (Happy), eyes & tie move, Lux, 9¼x4" 800.00
Couple swinging, United, fancy case 225.00
Covered wagon, driver's arm moves, NM 60.00
Enchanted Cottage, bird bobs/clock ticks, Lux, '05, 10" 100.00
Fireplace, plastic, Mastercrafters, 1950s 90.00
Frog band, 4 CI frogs around dl, Am, Pat dtd 1883, 11" 360.00
Harmony, Ansonia, M 250.00
Lighthouse w/sailboats, United 250.00
Majorette twirling baton, United, 1950s 150.00
Organ grinder & monkey, rpt/rstr, ca 1860, 17½" 1,750.00
Panda bear, eyes move, Spartus, plastic 80.00
Pickanniny Pendulette #304, Lux, 8¾x4½" 1,000.00
Popeye, Aerolux, glow bulb, w/base 350.00
Sally Rand, Lux, from $800 up to 1,200.00
Sambo, blinking eye, CI w/EX pnt, Am, ca 1860, 16" 1,625.00
Ship's wheel & fish, United, 1950s 135.00
Topsey, blinking eyes, CI, Am, ca 1860, 16½", EX 1,875.00
Waterfall, old style, Mastercrafters 115.00
Windmill, Chronoart, 1930s, rstr 175.00

Shelf Clocks

Ansonia, marble/onyx w/2" dl, column ea side, 1900, 7" 250.00
Ansonia Art & Commerce, dbl statue, TS, gong, 20½" 1,525.00
Ansonia Chippendale, TS, walnut w/gilt/HP, 1883, 20" 620.00
Ansonia Crest, ornate metal w/3-D Cupid, 1901, 12" 260.00
Ansonia Fisher, TS, gong, broken base ornament, 22" 975.00
Ansonia La Manche Royal Bonn, TS, gong, 13¾" 600.00
Ansonia LaNord Royal Bonn, TS, gong, 2-pc dl, 11¾" 750.00
Ansonia LaTosca Royal Bonn, TS, gong, 2-pc dl, 14½" 700.00
Ansonia LaVerdon Royal Bonn, TS, gong, 2-pc dl 800.00
Ansonia Marquise crystal reg, TS, open esc mvt, 15½" 750.00
Ansonia Novelty #44, cast pot metal locomotive, 1900, 8", NM ..925.00
Ansonia Prism reg, TS, open esc mvt, pnd, 10¾" 400.00
Ansonia Shakespeare, 2-pc porc dl, open esc, bronze finish, 15" ...750.00
Ansonia Triumph, silver cherubs, walnut w/mirrors, 24½" 400.00
Ansonia Troubadour, TS, gong, rprs, ca 1895, 16½" 750.00
Atkins, gallery, 30-day, aluminum dl, walnut vnr, 26½" 900.00
Birge Gilbert & Co, triple deck, TS, mahog w/iron gong, 36" 550.00
Birge Peck & Co, TS/wts, rswd column type, 32" 250.00
Bristol, iron front, orig pnt/MOP, full label, 1855, 19" 325.00
Camfret Kuss & Co, cuckoo, dbl fusee mvt, old rprs, 16x12¾" .900.00
Chelsea, mahog w/inlay & bamboo trn, house strike, 1917, 11" .450.00
E Ingraham Atlantic kitchen, TS, oak, 23" 150.00
E Ingraham Industry & Labor, TS, pnd, oak, 23" 350.00
E Ingraham Mt Vernon, TS, alarm, oak, pnd, 23" 450.00
E Ingraham Peace, dove/olive branch finial, oak, pnd, 23" 300.00
EN Welch Good Luck, brass horseshoe novelty, 1-day, 6", VG ..275.00
Eureka Clock Co Ltd London, porc dl, battery, 12¾x7½" 2,250.00
Forestville (JC Brown), OG, wts, geometric tablet, sgn dl, 29" ...250.00
Fr, gilt spelter, 3-D boy & goose atop, gong, 1890, 15" 700.00
G Becker, 400-day/disc pnd, porc dl w/emb rim, 1906, 11" 325.00
Gilbert, 30-hr, OG, orig tablet w/animals, 1870s, 26", VG 130.00
Jahresuhrenfabrik, 400-day/disc pnd, porc dl, 1900, 11" 200.00
John Hunt, 30 hr OG, br works, all orig, 1840, 26" 200.00
Junghans, mahog bracket w/chimes, bevel glass, 1910, 17", EX ..550.00
S Thomas #8028, TS, musician finial/etc, 1876, 18" 550.00
S Thomas Adamantine, Dtd 1897, EX orig, mvt needs cleaned, 11" ..175.00
S Thomas Bona, gilt spelter carriage type, porc dl, 1905, 5¾" 150.00
S Thomas Chime #95, Westminster chime, mahog, 11x7¼" 225.00
S Thomas Emp #18, crystal reg, floral wreath dl, 1910, 12", VG ...250.00
S Thomas Emp #20, crystal reg, gilt bronze, 4 columns, VG orig ..525.00
S Thomas Vixen, jeweled sash, porc dl, 1907, EX orig, 6" 250.00
Sessions, mahog tambour, porc dl, well-made mvt, 10½" H 100.00

Sessions, Mission oak, strikes w/bell on ½ & gong on hr, 17" **100.00**
Silas B Terry...Conn, 30-hr, br mvt, 1840s, mahog vnr, 24" **1,950.00**
Walterhalter & Hoffmeyer, ebony wood, br ft, 11" **300.00**
Waltham, mahog easel-mt boudoir, jeweled lever mvt, 1930, 10½" **250.00**
Waterbury Hillsdale kitchen, TS, oak, 22" **175.00**
Waterbury Vendee crystal reg, mahog columns/base/top, pnd **525.00**

Tall Case Clocks

Aaron Willard, mahog w/figured vnr & inlay, rstr, 92" **16,500.00**
Ansonia Reg #11, burl walnut, br mvt, pnd, 1883, 105x36" ..**10,500.00**
Cherry Hplwht, fluted quarter columns, br works, 19", EX **7,150.00**
Cherry/curly maple Chpndl, br trim, gilt metal face, rfn, 94" .**3,300.00**
Fed mahog w/tiger maple inlay, waist door, Fr ft, 100" **26,450.00**
Jas Harris-Whitney, pnt iron dl, oak w/inlay, 93" **3,175.00**
Mahog English, bracket ft, broken-arch top w/br rosettes, 84" ..**5,000.00**

Wall Clocks

Am Cuckoo, Mission style, wooden fr mvt, 1925, 18" **150.00**
Barnes & Bartholomew, 2-door/3-glass/triple deck, mahog, 36" .**350.00**
Black Forest cvd walnut cuckoo, stag pediment, late 19th C ...**1,100.00**
Black Forest wag-on-wall, wood dl, arched top, Whizzer works, 15" **450.00**
Brewster & Ingraham, dbl steeple, TS, mahog, 20" **1,050.00**
Dutch, 30-hr w/Dutch striking, 1-wt mvt, pnd, walnut, 58" **825.00**
E Ingraham Reflector, figure-8, 1895, EX orig, 29½" **700.00**
F Campos banjo, Perry's Victory tablets, rope cvg, 1980, NM **550.00**
Gustav Becker, enclosed wag, br spandrels, 29" **500.00**
Junghan's Musical, plays on the hour, br pnd, 18½" **350.00**
Junghan's Westminster Chime, strikes on 8 rods, walnut, 39" **800.00**
Lenzkirch #81, spring wall reg, 14-day, 1870, losses, 17½" **525.00**
Lenzkirsch, br/spelter, pnd, hangs from chain, 21" **400.00**
Morbier, 1-hand (no minute hand) 61" pnd, 15" case, rare **1,225.00**
New Haven Willis banjo, 12-day jeweled lever, rvpt ship, 18: **150.00**
New Haven Wilson banjo, 30-day, 1920, lacking sidearm, 41" ..**450.00**
New Haven Wilson banjo, 30-day, 1925, rfn but orig, 40" **475.00**
S Thomas, banjo, orig early mvt, mahog, 29" **800.00**
S Thomas, short drop, TS, walnut, 22" **230.00**
S Thomas '12" Octagon Drop,' vnr, pnd, 1910, 23½", EX **400.00**
S Thomas Lever, oak vnr, dbl wind mvt w/2nds, 1885, 16" dia ..**200.00**
S Thomas Lunar, TS, oak, ca 1909, 41" **1,725.00**
S Thomas Reg (resembles #32), wt, oak, 67" **1,775.00**
S Thomas Reg #2, cherry, 1890, rstr/near orig, 36" **1,600.00**
S Thomas Reg #2, walnut vnr, wt, 1863, 34" **1,300.00**
S Thomas Reg #6, cherry, steeples/drops, M rstr/near orig, 49" ..**2,100.00**
Walnut Vict Gothic Revival, appl ornaments, rpl works, 49" **350.00**
Waltham banjo, Mt Vernon tablets, eagle, 1925, orig, 21" **475.00**
Waltham mini spring banjo, lever mvt, wind through dl, 20" **225.00**
Waterbury Eton, pressed oak, TS, EX labels, 1912, EX rstr, 39" .**575.00**
Waterbury Pelican store reg, oak, 1920, EX orig, 37½" **400.00**
Waterbury Reg #18, ca 1893, oak, 49½" **1,275.00**
Westminster Chime Co, oak, silvered dl, 1910, 31" **225.00**
Yamato, oak, 11" paper dl, 2nds, TS, ca 1900, 16" dia **125.00**

Cloisonne

Cloisonne is a method of decorating metal with enameling. Fine metal wires are soldered onto the metal body following the lines of a predetermined design. The resulting channels are filled in with enamels of various colors, and the item is fired. The final step is a smoothing process that assures even exposure of the wire pattern. The art is predominately Oriental and has been practiced continuously, except during war years, since the 16th century. The most excellent examples date from 1865 until the turn of the century. The early 20th century export variety is usually lightweight and the workmanship inferior. Modern wares are of good quality and are produced in Taiwan as well as China.

Several variations of the basic art include plique-a-jour, achieved by removing the metal body after firing, leaving only the transparent enamel work; foil cloisonne, using transparent or semitranslucent enameling over a layer of embossed silver covering the metal body of the vessel; wireless cloisonne, made by removing the wire dividers prior to firing; and cloisonne executed on ceramic, wood, or lacquer rather than metal.

Ashtray, dragon form, coin silver with cloisonne inlay, central tray mounted with jade, ca 1900 – 1930, China, 2¾x3½", $400.00.

Bowl, flowers & birds panels, Japan, 3⅛x4" **125.00**
Jar, floral, mc on red, 8¼" **175.00**
Jar, flowers & butterflies on bright bl, Japan, 3⅞" **50.00**
Spoon, demi; pique-a-jour, mc flowers in bowl & hdl tip **150.00**
Vase, long-stem spider mums on bl, Japanese, 8½x3" **295.00**
Vase, Persian motifs/bird in flight, goldstone bands, 9x3½" **225.00**
Vase, sparrows/butterflies/flowers on bl, dragon at rim, 13" **600.00**
Vase, wren/cherry tree/shrub on red, 19" **850.00**

Clothing and Accessories

More and more collectors are getting involved in the fascinating field of antique, vintage, and collectible clothing, once considered the realm of museum curators and historical societies. Today's collector is highly discriminating; most specialize in certain types of clothing or certain historical periods. This makes it important to know exactly how old an item is before determining a value. Gone are the days when it was sufficient to broadly categorize a dress as simply 'Victorian' or 'old,' as clothing from certain historical periods has increased in value faster than examples from other eras. A mistake in dating an item can cause a loss of several hundreds of dollars on the collectors' market. For example, prices for special-occasion dresses of the Civil War era have skyrocketed in recent years. Another big jump in market value is being seen in dresses of the late 1870s and early 1880s. Meanwhile, prices of dresses from the 1890s and 1900s have remained fairly stable.

Once the age of an item of clothing is ascertained, three other factors come into play in determining a price. The first is condition, as a noticeable rip or stain will devalue an item just as surely as a crack will devalue a glass vase. The second factor is quality: is it well made or made by a famous designer? Were fabrics and trimmings expensive or elaborate? Generally speaking, the more elaborate the item, the higher the value. The third factor is size. Today a large portion of collectors are searching for items which they can wear, therefore extremely small sizes are somewhat less valuable than larger ones.

For further information, as well as an easy to use guide for dating women's clothing, we recommend *Antique & Vintage Clothing: A Guide to Dating and Valuation of Women's Clothing, 1850 – 1940*, by our advisor, Diane Snyder-Haug, available from Collector Books or your local bookstore. Our values are for items of ladies' clothing in excellent condition unless otherwise described.

Key:

cap/s — cap sleeves	ms — machine sewn
embr — embroidery	n/s — no sleeves
hs — hand sewn	plt — pleated
l/s — long sleeves	s/s — short sleeves

Bathing suit, blk sateen, flower applique, s/s, 1920s, w/cap 75.00
Bed jacket, rayon w/lace trim, 1940s 25.00
Bib overalls, Osh Kosh, vest bk, M 45.00
Bib overalls, Payday, union made, sanforized shrunk, old, NM 90.00
Blouse, cream silk w/pk & bl embr, l/s, collar, 1912 ....65.00
Blouse, lingerie, beaded trim, ca 1920, from $45 to 125.00
Blouse, lingerie or 'pneumonia,' delicate trim, 1910s, $65 to 95.00
Bodice, openwork eyelet (lined), peplum style, s/s, 1880s 60.00
Camisole, ca 1900, from $40 to 65.00
Camisole, tucks & lace inserts, fitted bk, drawstrings, 1900 ....65.00
Cap, leather, Harley-Davidson, 1950s 50.00
Cape, bl feathers, long, 1920s, EX 275.00
Coat, lady's, red wool w/velvet details, 1880s 250.00
Coat, lady's, turq velvet w/silk lining, 1930s, EX 165.00
Coat, lady's, wool w/mink collar, 1960s 30.00
Dress, ballgown, satin, low neckline w/lace, s/s, ca 1863, NM 825.00
Dress, blk & wht wool w/satin trim, train, l/s, 1901 ....250.00
Dress, blk brocade, lace & pleats, l/s, 1890s, 2-pc, G 95.00
Dress, blk taffeta, ostrich feathers at neck/overskirt hem, 1912 ..285.00
Dress, brn & wht silk & lace, skirt has train, pagoda/s, 1903 ......325.00
Dress, brocade, lace collar/sheer front, leg-o'-mutton/s, 1897, NM .425.00
Dress, christening; cambric, handmade, long, ca 1900 ....120.00
Dress, coral silk w/sequins/beads/rhinestones, train, ca 1914 ......330.00
Dress, cotton batiste w/crochet lace, pearl buttons, 1-pc, 1908 ...325.00
Dress, cotton chemise, flounced yoke, ca 1924 ....40.00
Dress, cotton w/velvet cuffs, ruffled neck, kick-up/s, 1890s, G 100.00
Dress, crepe chemise w/asymmetrical hem, lace yoke, s/s, 1927 ....65.00
Dress, day, elegant trim, 1890s, from $125 to 325.00
Dress, day; gr/blk wool, blk jet buttons, pleated waist, l/s, 1868 ..250.00
Dress, day; little or no trim, 1890s, from $95 to 125.00
Dress, day; little trim, ca 1911-18, from $65 to 200.00
Dress, day; muslin print, V-neck, tiered skirt, bell/s, hs, 1853, EX ..200.00
Dress, dk cotton print, gathered waist, l/s, ca 1863 ....165.00
Dress, dk linen, eyelet openwork/embr/tucks, 2-pc, 1890s 150.00
Dress, embr Limerick lace/Duchesse lace/silk ribbon, l/s, 1909, NM ..495.00

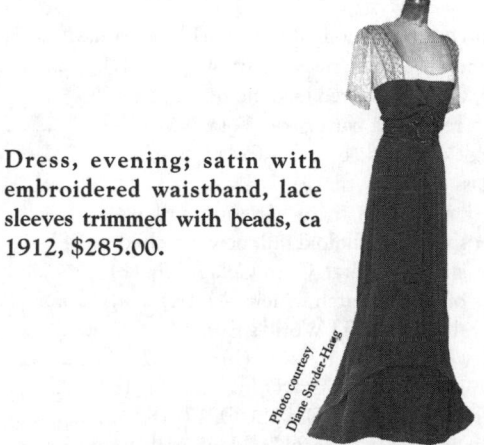

Dress, evening; satin with embroidered waistband, lace sleeves trimmed with beads, ca 1912, $285.00.

Photo courtesy
Diane Snyder-Haug

Dress, evening; bl rhinestones, Egyptian style, long, 1930s 175.00
Dress, evening; cut velvet, backless, cape/s, 1930s 295.00
Dress, evening; heavy satin w/scoop neckline, n/s, ca 1955 ....68.00
Dress, figured silk, lace trim, ruffled hem, l/s, 1890s 275.00

Dress, flapper style w/beading, 1920s, from $125 to 800.00
Dress, gr linen w/lace yoke, l/s, hooks/eyes at bk, 1-pc, 1911 ......125.00
Dress, maternity; lining adjusts, drop shoulders, l/s, 1920s 235.00
Dress, mourning; blk net/lace/ribbon trim, l/s, ca 1900 ....300.00
Dress, mourning; blk w/jet beads, l/s, pleats, 1880s 325.00
Dress, organdy chemise, low waist, s/s, ca 1919 ....45.00
Dress, printed muslin, l/s, high waist, l/s, ca 1865 ....165.00
Dress, rayon w/velvet trim, cloth flower, l/s, ca 1936 ....45.00
Dress, satin & velvet w/tie-bk skirt, johnny collar, l/s, 1870s 425.00
Dress, satin/cotton, bodice/over & underskirts, 3-pc, 1880s 375.00
Dress, sheer muslin, Bertha cape w/cloth flower, s/s, 1860s 235.00
Dress, taffeta, full skirt, short jacket, late 1940s, M 100.00
Dress, traveling; glazed cotton, boned belt, 3-pc, 1906, w/purse .200.00
Dress, traveling; satin, button-up, l/s jacket, 1870s 295.00
Dress, velvet/satin w/fringes, kick-up sleeves, johnny collar, 1887 ....395.00
Dress, visiting; silk w/velvet, includes jacket, ca 1864, NM 525.00
Dress, walking; tweed, ribbon/lace trim, l/s, 1890s 150.00
Dress, wedding; ecru net w/much embr, 1930s 185.00
Dress, wedding; satin, l/s, pearl beads train, cloche veil, 1930s, M .495.00
Dress, wedding; taffeta w/seed pearls, l/s, handmade, 1940s, NM ..350.00
Dress, wedding; wht lawn, l/s, full skirt, petticoat, 1900s 250.00
Dress, wht cotton batiste w/much trim, ca 1900, from $300 to ...800.00
Dress, wht linen tailor-made, bustle, pearl buttons, l/s, 1885 ......225.00
Dust coat, sack style, ca 1915 ....95.00
Fur coat, leopard skin, stroller length, 1955, EX 1,100.00
Fur jacket, sheared raccoon, 1930s, 26" 95.00
Gloves, beaded pk kidskin, opera length, Jouvin, Paris, M 35.00
Gloves, wht kidskin, opera length, mk Kislav, MOC 35.00
Hat, brimmed, 1930s, from $20 to 45.00
Hat, child's, navy velveteen, 1960s, w/drawstring purse 15.00
Hat, cloche style, 1920s, from $25 to 95.00
Hat, lady's, lace w/ostrich feather brim, ca 1909 ....95.00
Hat, lady's, little trim, 1910-20, lg, from $45 to 95.00
Hat, man's, Boater style, 1930s, MIB 85.00
Hat, man's fedora, blk felt, 1940s 20.00
Hat, man's top hat, nutria, 1890s, 6" H, EX 125.00
Hat, straw, blk lace trim, ca 1887, sm 45.00
Hat, toque-style w/applique lace ties/cloth flowers, ca 1893 ....185.00
Hat/bonnet, little trim, ca 1850-1910, from $20 to 125.00
Hat/bonnet, ornate trim, ca 1850-1915, from $95 to 200.00
Jacket, blk lace, peplum, l/s, 1930s 35.00
Jacket, boy's, wool & rayon, Rugby Knitting, 1940s, EX 38.00
Jacket, man's, denim, Lee 101-J, red & gold folded tag, M 275.00
Jacket, man's, denim, Lee 101-LJ, dk bl, M 160.00
Jacket, man's, denim, Levi 1st Edition, lined, EX, from $600 to .700.00
Jacket, man's, denim, Montgomery Wards 101, buckle-bk, M 240.00
Jacket, man's smoking; plaid taffeta w/silk lining, 1940s 80.00
Jacket, man's winter work; cotton w/knit waist band, 1940s 50.00
Jacket, man's work; denim, Lee, sanforized shrunk, dk bl, '70s, M ..75.00
Jeans, denim, Levi, Big E tab on both bk pockets, buckle-bk, M .3,700.00
Jeans, denim, Levi 501, buckle-bk, dk bl, M 1,350.00
Jeans, denim, Levi 501 Redline, single stitch, EX 450.00
Jeans, denim, Levi 501XX, rpr 300.00
Knickers, boy's, wool, full legs w/cuffed bottom, 1920s 45.00
Knickers, cotton tweed, +s/s jacket, 1930s 50.00
Mittens, bl & wht homespun, pr 110.00
Nightgown, wide crochet insert at top, l/s, ca 1905 ....125.00
Pantaloons, eyelet lace hem 75.00
Parasol, embr cotton cover, str wooden hdl, ca 1910 ....85.00
Parasol, muslin cover, wooden hdl, 1870s 100.00
Parasol, printed silk, grained wooden hdl, ca 1880s 125.00
Petticoat, cotton w/tucks & lace, ca 1900 ....125.00
Petticoat, quilted, changeable taffeta, 1850s 90.00
Petticoat, wht linen w/crochet lace, ca 1900 ....145.00

Shawl, Chinese embr on cream, 48" sq+18" fringe 295.00
Shawl, gr & wht wool, fringed, ca 1890s, 64x128", EX 150.00
Shawl, paisley, mc wool, ends fringed, minor damage, 112x62" ..170.00
Shawl, paisley, woven wool, 70x70" 330.00
Shawl, silk w/mc embr, Russia, 74x40"+20" fringe on 3 sides 300.00
Shawl, woven lacy silk, 30x60" +12" fringe 115.00
Shirt, boy's, Fruit of Loom label, 1940s, EX+ 20.00
Shirt, man's, brn silk, collarless, ca 1880 ....65.00
Shirt, man's, Hawaiian, floral, rayon crepe, Iolani, 1940s, EX 125.00
Shirt, man's, Hawaiian, ltweight cotton, palms, plastic buttons ...35.00
Shirt, man's, Hawaiian, printed cotton, pearl buttons, s/s, 1970s .30.00
Shirtwaist, sheer batiste w/embr & lace, 1900s, from $85 to 300.00
Shirtwaist, silk w/delicate lace, ruffle, l/s, 1900s 80.00
Shoes, blk patent, button strap w/fan, ca 1910, pr 60.00
Shoes, blk silk w/strap over instep, 1920s, pr 45.00
Shoes, child's, blk oxfords, Red Goose, 1950s, pr 30.00
Shoes, high-laced, blk, 1890s, pr 65.00
Shoes, high-laced, blk leather w/embr suede upper, ca 1885 ....250.00
Shoes, man's, high-top boots, 1880s, pr, G 40.00
Shoes, man's, Nike high-top sneakers, bl & wht, ca 1980, M 120.00
Shoes, platform style, vinyl uppers, 1960s, pr 25.00
Shoes, sling-bk heels, Lucite w/seashells decor, 1950s, pr 40.00
Skirt, bl w/front lace, long train, 1880s 85.00
Stockings, brn cotton, Anna, NM, pr 7.50
Stockings, sheer silk, seamed, 1940s, pr, MIB 15.00
Suit, man's, herringbone wool, 2-button, wide shoulders, 1930s .150.00
Sunsuit, child's, cotton, 1930s 12.50
Sweater, boy's, dk bl & tan, leather buttons, 1940s, sm 30.00
Sweater, boy's, wht knit, Rugby Sportswear, 1940s 30.00
Sweater, mink collar, l/s, ca 1936 ....45.00
Teddy, rayon, lacy trim, 1940s 45.00
Tie, man's, Confederate flag print, 1940s, MIB 140.00
Trousers, boy's, Tom Sawyer Brand, 1940s, EX 25.00
Vest, man's, brocade, printed cotton lining, 1880s, EX 65.00
Vest, silk, draped bottom, beaded, 1920s 40.00

Cluthra

The name Cluthra is derived from the Scottish word 'clutha,' meaning cloudy. Glassware by this name was first produced by J. Couper and Sons, England. Frederick Carder developed Cluthra while at the Steuben Glass Works, and similar types of glassware were also made by Durand and Kimball. It is found in both solid and shaded colors and is characterized by a spotty appearance resulting from small air pockets trapped between its two layers.

Plate, pk to opal mottle, att Monart, 7" 35.00
Vase, bittersweet/opal, tapered w/clear ft, Kimball, 8½" 300.00
Vase, opal/amethyst mottle, shouldered, att Kimball, 4¾" 250.00
Vase, opal/yel/orange mottle, flared stick neck, Kimball, 14" 500.00
Vase, orange/brn/opal mottle, tapered, Kimball, 12", pr 600.00

Coca-Cola

J.S. Pemberton, creator of Coca-Cola, originated his world-famous drink in 1886. From its inception the Coca-Cola Company began an incredible advertising campaign which has proven to be one of the most successful promotions in history. The quantity and diversity of advertising material put out by Coca-Cola in the last one hundred years is literally mind-boggling. From the beginning, the company has projected an image of wholesomeness and Americana. Beautiful women in Victorian costumes, teenagers and schoolchildren, blue- and white-collar workers,

the men and women of the Armed Forces (even Santa Claus) have appeared in advertisements with a Coke in their hands. Some of the earliest collectibles include trays, syrup dispensers, gum jars, pocket mirrors, and calendars. Many of these items fetch prices in the thousands of dollars. Later examples include radios, signs, lighters, thermometers, playing cards, clocks, and toys — particularly toy trucks.

In 1970 the Coca-Cola Company initialed a multimillion-dollar 'image-refurbishing campaign' which introduced the new 'Dynamic Contour' logo, a twisting white ribbon under the Coca-Cola and Coke trademarks. The new logo often serves as a cut-off point to the purist collector. Newer and very ardent collectors, however, relish the myriad of items marketed since that date, as they often cannot afford the high prices that the vintage pieces command. For more information we recommend *Huxford's Collectible Advertising, Fifth Edition; B.J. Summers' Guide to Coca-Cola, Second Edition;* and *B.J. Summers' Pocket Guide to Coca-Cola;* also *Coca-Cola Commemorative Bottles* by Bob and Debra Henrich. You may wish to call our advisors for this category, Craig and Donna Stifter, at 630-789-5780; they are listed in the Directory under Illinois.

Key:
CC — Coca-Cola   tm — trademark

Reproductions and Fantasies

Beware of reproductions! Prices are given for the genuine original articles, but the symbol (+) at the end of some of the following lines indicate items that have been reproduced. Warning! The 1924, 1925, and 1935 calendars have been reproduced. They are identical in almost every way; only a professional can tell them apart. These are *very* deceiving! Watch for frauds: genuinely old celluloid items ranging from combs, mirrors, knives, and forks to doorknobs that have been recently etched with a new double-lined trademark. Still another area of concern deals with reproduction and fantasy items. A fantasy item is a novelty made to appear authentic with inscriptions such as 'Tiffany Studios,' 'Trans Pan Expo,' 'World's Fair,' etc. In reality, these items never existed as originals. For instance, don't be fooled by a Coca-Cola cash register; no originals are known to exist! Large mirrors for bars are being reproduced and are often selling for $10.00 to $50.00.

Of the hundreds of reproductions (designated 'R' in the following examples) and fantasies (designated 'F') on the market today, these are the most deceiving.

Belt buckle, no originals thought to exist (F), up to 10.00
Bottle, dk amber, w/arrows, heavy, narrow spout (R) 10.00
Bottle carrier, wood, yel w/red logo, holds 6 bottles (R) 10.00
Clock, Gilbert regulator, battery-op, ¾-sz, NM+ (R) 175.00
Cooler, Glascock Jr, made by Coca-Cola USA (R) 350.00
Doorknob, glass etched w/tm (F) 3.00
Knife, bottle shape, 1970s, many variations (F), ea 5.00
Knife, fork, or spoon w/celluloid hdl, newly etched tm (F) 5.00
Letter opener, stamped metal, Coca-Cola for 5¢ (F) 3.00
Pocket watch, often old watch w/new face (R) 10.00
Pocketknife, yel & red, 1933 World's Fair (F) 2.00
Sign, cb, lady w/fur, dtd 1911, 9x11" (F) 3.00
Soda fountain glass holder, word 'Drink' not orig (R) 5.00
Thermometer, bottle form, DONASCO, 17" (R) 10.00
Trade card, copy of 1905 'Bathtub' foldout, emb 1978 (R) 25.00

The following items have been reproduced and are among the most deceptive of all:

Pocket mirrors from 1905, 1906, 1908, 1909, 1910, 1911, 1916, and 1920

Trays from 1899, 1910, 1913, 1914, 1917, 1920, 1923, 1925, 1926, 1934, and 1937

 Tip trays from 1907, 1909, 1910, 1913, 1914, 1917, and 1920

 Knives: many versions of the German brass model

 Cartons: wood versions, yellow with logo

 Calendars: 1924, 1925, and 1935

These items have been marketed:

 Brass thermometer, bottle shape, Taiwan, 24"

 Cast-iron toys (none ever made)

 Cast-iron door pull, bottle shape, made to look old

 Poster, Yes Girl (R)

 Button sign, has 1 round hole while original has 4 slots, most have bottle logo, 12", 16", 20" (R)

 Bullet trash receptacles (old cans with decals)

 Paperweight, rectangular, with Pepsin Gum insert

 1930 Bakelite radio, 24" tall, repro is lighter in weight than the original, of poor quality and cheaply made

 1949 cooler radio (reproduced with tape deck)

 Tin bottle sign, 40"

 Fishtail die-cut tin sign, 20" long

 Straw holders (no originals exist)

 Coca-Cola bicycle with cooler, fantasy item: the piece has been totally made-up, no such original exists

 1914 calendar top, reproduction, 11¼x23¾", printed on smooth-finish heavy ivory paper

 Countless trays — most unauthorized (must read 'American Artworks; Coshocton, OH.')

Centennial Items

 The Coca-Cola Company celebrated its 100th birthday in 1986, and amidst all the fanfare came many new collectible items, all sporting the 100th-anniversary logo. These items are destined to become an important part of the total Coca-Cola collectible spectrum. The following pieces are among the most popular centennial items.

Bottle, gold-dipped, in velvet sleeve, 6½-oz 75.00
Bottle, Hutchinson, amber, Root Co, ½-oz, 3 in case 375.00
Bottle, International, set of 9 in plexiglas case 500.00
Bottle, leaded crystal, 100th logo, 6½-oz, MIB 150.00
Medallion, bronze, 3" dia, w/box 100.00
Pin set, wood fr, 101 pins 300.00
Scarf, silk, 30x30" 40.00
Thermometer, glass cover, 14" dia, M 35.00

Coca-Cola Originals

Bottle carrier, 1950s, aluminum, with six green bottles, NM, $100.00.

Apron, cloth bib type, Pause.../Refresh!, shows bottle, EX 115.00
Art plate, topless girl, gold fr, EX+ 1,250.00
Ashtray, glass, Have a Coke/Drink CC on rim, rnd, M 30.00
Awning, 1950s, canvas, Drink CC..., red & wht, 60", EX 575.00

Blotter, 1920, Drink CC/Delicious & Refreshing, NM 2,500.00
Blotter, 1929, One Little Minute for a Big Rest, man w/bottle, EX 425.00
Blotter, 1935, A Home Run w/Three On, boy on bicycle, NM+ ..200.00
Blotter, 1953, Good!, Sprite Boy w/bottle in snow, Canadian, NM .12.00
Bottle, gr, str sides, Birmingham Bottling Co, wht letters, G ...1,300.00
Bottle, 1910s, clear, CC Bottling Works/Rochester, 4-oz, NM+ ..325.00
Bottle case, 1940s, wood, bent corners, yel/red, G 150.00
Bottle topper, 1929, cb, bathing beauty on emblem, EX 1,500.00
Bottle topper, 1950s, plastic button w/2 gold bottles, 7", NM 825.00
Calendar, 1907, complete, EX+ 17,000.00
Calendar, 1913, incomplete, G 4,000.00
Calendar, 1918, beach scene, complete, rare, EX+ 10,500.00
Calendar, 1921, complete, NM+ 3,500.00
Calendar, 1933, complete, VG+ 350.00
Calendar, 1938, complete, G 260.00
Calendar, 1957, complete, NM+ 175.00
Chair, child's booster w/metal fold-up fr, emb CC on bk, red, VG+ .785.00
Change receiver, 1960s, plastic, Frozen CC mascot behind cup, NM+ .200.00
Cigar band, drinking glass, NM+ 150.00
Clock, 1940s-50s, neon, rocking bottle, Drink..., 20" dia, EX+ ..3,600.00
Cooler, airline; 1950s, red, hinged lid w/grip hdl, opener, NM ...450.00
Cooler, picnic; 1950s, 6-pack, metal, red, grip & swing hdls, NM ..475.00
Dispenser, 1920s-30s, frosted glass on red porc base, 17", NM .6,200.00
Dispenser, 1940s, metal streamline, red, Drink CC Ice Cold..., EX ..425.00
Dispenser, 1950s, wooden barrel, red, ftd, 2 spigots, 28", VG+ ...375.00
Display, 1935, cb, Friends for Life, Rockwell art, 36", VG 2,500.00
Display bottle, 1930s, gr glass, Pat'd Dec 25 1923, 20", NM 275.00
Display bottle, 1980s, gr glass, 20", NM+ 50.00
Display rack, 1960s, wire stand w/fishtail signs, 58x17x16", EX .275.00
Doll, 1950s, Buddy Lee, compo, in uniform & hat, EX+ 875.00
Doll, 1960s, Frozen CC mascot, stuffed striped cloth, NM 150.00
Drinking glass, 1904, flared w/etched CC & syrup line, 4", NM .660.00
Drinking glass, 1936 Anniversary, bell-shaped, gold letters, NM+ ..450.00
Drinking glass holder, 1900s, silver, CC in script, hdld, NM ...2,100.00
Festoon, 1930s, nautical, Drink CC/It's Cooling..., 9-pc, EX+ ...3,385.00
Festoon, 1950s, sporting, Whatever You Do/Wherever..., NM+ ..2,300.00
Festoon, 1950s, square dance, w/orig envelope, 5-pc, NM+ 1,400.00
Game, 1940s-50s, Broadsides, Milton Bradley, EX+ 80.00
Lamp, 1920s, bottle form w/cap on emb metal base, 20", NM+ .7,200.00
Light fixture, 1930s, milk glass globe w/tassel, all orig, NM+ .3,500.00
Lighter, 1960s, flip top, Things Go Better..., leaf design, NM+ 70.00
Magazine ad, 1904, Lillian Nordica, complete w/coupon, 10x7", NM .250.00
Match safe, 1908-12, pocket sz, flip top, Drink a Bottle..., VG+ ...7,200.00
Menu, 1903, Hilda Clark, EX 850.00
Menu board, 1930s, tin, Specials To-Day, blkboard, 27x19", NM ..550.00
Menu board, 1941, tin, Drink CC, silhouette girl, 28x20", EX ...425.00
Needle case, 1925, NM 90.00
Note pad, 1902, 5x2½", NM 950.00
Opener, wht plastic hdl, Serves Hospitality in the Home, M 30.00
Playing cards, 1915, M (sealed box) 3,500.00
Playing cards, 1960, Be Really Refreshed, masquerade party, NMIB .165.00
Pocket mirror, 1910, EX+ 250.00
Postcard, 1910, CC Girl, NM+ 775.00
Push bar, 1930s, porc, Ice Cold CC in Bottles, wht/red, 2x30", NM .550.00
Push bar, 1930s, porc, Refresh Yourself...in Bottles, 26", VG+ ...480.00
Radio, 1960s, vending machine form, Drink CC on wht top panel, VG .65.00
Record, 1966, Let's Go Go Go for Three in a Row, 45 rpm, EX+ ..20.00
Sign, 1905, cb, Lillian Nordica, CC at Fountains 5¢, 42x26", G ...2,175.00
Sign, 1907, trolley, paper, Tired?..., soda jerk, 10x20", VG 2,300.00
Sign, 1914, cb, Betty, orig mat & fr, 39x31", EX 1,000.00
Sign, 1914, tin, Ice Cold...Here, str-sided bottle, 20x28", EX ..1,700.00
Sign, 1920s, cb diecut trifold, lady on aquaplane, EX 6,000.00
Sign, 1920s, porc, Drink CC, wht on red, yel/gr border, 10x30", VG .300.00
Sign, 1920s, tin, Drink CC/Delicious &..., 1923 bottle, 11x35", VG ..525.00

Sign, 1920s, tin, Gas Today/Drink While You Wait, 20x28", VG **750.00**
Sign, 1920s, trolley, paper, Around the Corner..., lady, 11x21", EX ..**2,600.00**
Sign, 1920s, trolley, paper, Fall/Winter/Spring/Summer..., 10x20", NM ..**4,000.00**
Sign, 1930s, cb, Christmas Greetings..., Santa w/letter, NM ...**4,200.00**
Sign, 1930s, cb, Drink CC, beach couple, vertical, EX **1,500.00**
Sign, 1930s, cb, Drink CC, girl/horse against sky, vertical, VG+ .**1,000.00**
Sign, 1930s, cb diecut, Partner..., J Cooper/W Berry, EX+ **1,800.00**
Sign, 1930s, cb diecut, Stop for a Pause..., traffic cop, G **1,050.00**
Sign, 1930s, glass w/chrome, Drink..., Brunoff, rectangle, NM .**3,500.00**
Sign, 1930s, tin, Drink CC Sold Here Ice Cold, bottle, 54x18", EX .**675.00**
Sign, 1930s, tin, Gas To-Day/Drink...Ice Cold/...Here, 54", EX .**1,700.00**
Sign, 1930s, tin, Ice Cold...Sold Here, mc, 20" dia, NM+ **1,250.00**
Sign, 1930s, wood, ...Ice Cold, triangle/arrow, 2-sided, 28", EX + ...**750.00**
Sign, 1940s, cb, Coke Headquarters, girl/serviceman, 26x16", NM .**650.00**
Sign, 1940s, cb, Coke Party, 3 ladies at table, 16x27", EX+ **475.00**
Sign, 1940s, cb, Drink CC..., beach girl in bl, 50x29", EX+ **1,400.00**
Sign, 1940s, cb, Entertain..., girl at microphone, 20x36", EX **700.00**
Sign, 1940s, light-up, Edgebrite hanger, trapezoidal, 12x20", EX+ ..**1,750.00**
Sign, 1940s, masonite, Drink CC, girl w/bottle, mc, 12x34", EX .**250.00**
Sign, 1940s, porc, CC, silhouette carhop/car on wht emblem, 52", NM ...**1,200.00**
Sign, 1940s, tin, bottle shape, 16", VG **65.00**
Sign, 1940s, tin, Take Home a Carton, 6-pack, 60x36", EX **475.00**
Sign, 1940s, trolley, Yes, girl & hand-held bottle, 11x28", EX+ .**750.00**
Sign, 1950s, cb, Coke Time, couples by fire, horizontal, NM **600.00**
Sign, 1950s, cb, Good Taste for All, 27x16", NM **300.00**
Sign, 1950s, cb, Here's...Good, masquerade couple, fr, 27", VG .**350.00**
Sign, 1950s, cb, See Kit Carson TV Show, 16x24", NM **200.00**
Sign, 1950s, celluloid, CC/bottle, red/gold, orig envelope, M **375.00**
Sign, 1950s, light-up, Work Safely/Work Safety-Wise, box fr, 16", VG .**725.00**
Sign, 1950s, porc, bottle shape, 12", VG+ **150.00**
Sign, 1950s, porc, Drink CC, fishtail on wht/gr, 16x44", VG **180.00**
Sign, 1950s, porc, Fountain Service..., red/gr, 12x28", EX **800.00**
Sign, 1950s, porc flange, Iced CC Here, red/yel, 20", NM **550.00**
Sign, 1950s, tin, button, red, CC/bottle, 16" dia, rare, EX+ **1,400.00**
Sign, 1950s, tin, button, Yes!...Sprite Boy/bottle, 16" dia, NM ..**775.00**
Sign, 1950s, tin, button w/arrow, Drink CC/Sign Of..., 16 dia, NM ...**900.00**
Sign, 1950s, tin, CC/Sprite Boy/bottle/button, gold/wht, 12" dia, M .**2,100.00**
Sign, 1950s, tin, Serve CC at Home, 6-pack, 53x17", NM **1,000.00**
Sign, 1950s, tin, 6-pack shape, Delicious & Refreshing, 12x11", EX+ .**725.00**
Sign, 1960s, cb, It's Twice Time..., scooter couple, 32x27", NM+ ...**200.00**
Sign, 1960s, cb, Santa's Helpers, Santa w/bottles, 32x66", VG+ ..**120.00**
Sign, 1960s, cb, Zing/Refreshing..., pool lady, 32x67", NM **150.00**
Sign, 1960s, cb diecut, Free Decorations, Santa, 20x12", EX **85.00**
Sign, 1960s, Pick Up 6 for Home Refreshment, 6-pack, 50x16", EX ..**525.00**
Sign, 1960s, tin, fishtail, CC, wht on red, 12x26", NM **250.00**
Sign, 1980s, neon, CC Classic/The Official..., 28" dia, NM+ .**1,700.00**
String holder, 1930s, Take Home CC in Cartons, 2 tin panels, NM ..**1,200.00**
Syrup barrel, 1910s, wood, 10-gal, rnd paper end labels, EX+ **330.00**
Syrup jug, 1960s, glass w/paper label, paper cup/Coke glass, EX **20.00**
Thermometer, 1905, wood, Drink CC, Delicious & Refreshing, 21", VG+ **475.00**
Thermometer, 1940s, dial, Drink CC, bottle, 12" dia, NM+ **600.00**
Thermometer, 1950s, porc, Drink CC/Coke Refreshes, 36", EX+ .**1,320.00**
Thermometer, 1950s, tin, bottle shape, 17", NMIB **150.00**
Tip tray, 1903, VG **900.00**
Tip tray, 1910, NM+ **1,400.00**
Tip tray, 1916, EX+ **275.00**
Tip tray, 1920, EX+ **250.00**
Toy, 1920s-30s, Robin Hood Bo-Arro (Boys & Girls), unused, NM ...**175.00**
Toy airplane, 1973-74 Albatros, red/wht w/blk trim, EX+ **100.00**
Toy bus, 1950s-60s, ATC/Japan, Gray-Line..., metal, 4x14", VG ..**300.00**
Toy dispenser, #16, w/4 plastic flared glasses, NMIB **135.00**
Toy truck, 1950s, Linemar, squash cab, tin, friction, 3", EX+ **140.00**
Toy truck, 1956, Marx #1088, stake bed/Sprite Boy, tin, yel, NMIB ..**1,150.00**
Toy truck, 1970s, Buddy L #5117, red/wht, contour logo, 9", VG+ ..**40.00**

Trade card, 1907, Drink CC High Ball, waitress, fold, VG+ ..**1,250.00**
Umbrella, 1930s, wht, red/blk lettering, gold bottles, 60", VG ...**900.00**
Watch, 100th Anniversary, gold-tone face w/leather strap, NM ...**120.00**

Trays

Values are given for trays in excellent plus condition (C8+). Those that have been reproduced are marked with a (+). The 1934 Weismuller and O'Sullivan tray has been reproduced at least three times. To be original, it will have a black back and must say 'American Artworks, Coshocton, Ohio.' It was not reproduced by Coca-Cola in the 1950s.

All 10½x13½" original serving trays produced from 1910 to 1942 are marked with a date, Made in USA, and the American Artworks Inc., Coshocton Ohio. All original trays of this format (1910 – 40) had REG TM in the tail of the C.

1941, Ice Skater, 10½x13¼", NM, $400.00.

Photo courtesy Gary Metz

1897, Victorian lady, 9¼" dia, VG	15,000.00
1901, Hilda Clark, 9¾", VG	4,000.00
1903, Hilda Clark, oval, 18½x15", EX	6,000.00
1905, Lillian Russell, glass or bottle, 10½x13¼", EX	3,500.00
1906, Juanita, glass or bottle, oval, 13¼x10½", EX	2,200.00
1907, Relieves Fatigue, 10½x13¼", NM	3,300.00
1907, Relieves Fatigue, 13½x16½", EX	3,600.00
1908, Topless, Wherever Ginger Ale..., 12¼" dia, NM	9,500.00
1909, St Louis Fair, 10½x13¼", EX	1,800.00
1909, St Louis Fair, 13½x16½", NM	3,000.00
1910, Coca-Cola Girl, Hamilton King, 10½x13¼", VG	850.00
1913, Girl in Lg Hat, Hamilton King, oval, 12¼x15¼", EX	650.00
1914, Betty, oval, 12¼x15¼", EX+	575.00
1914, Betty, 10½x13¼", EX	600.00
1916, Elaine, 8½x19", NM	500.00
1920, Garden Girl, oval, 12¼x15¼", EX+	800.00
1921, Autumn Girl, oval, 12¼x15¼", EX+	800.00
1922, Summer Girl, 10½x13¼", NM	950.00
1923, Flapper Girl, 10½x13¼", NM	400.00
1924, Smiling Girl, brn rim, 10½x13¼", EX	650.00
1924, Smiling Girl, maroon rim, 10½x13¼", EX	850.00
1925, Party, 10½x13¼", NM	500.00
1926, Golfers, 10½x13¼", VG	700.00
1927, Curbside Service, 10½x13¼", EX	750.00
1928, Bobbed Hair, 10½x13¼", EX+	650.00
1929, Girl in Swimsuit w/Glass, 10½x13¼", EX+	450.00
1930, Swimmer, 10½x13¼", EX	425.00
1930, Telephone, 10½x13¼", NM	550.00
1931, Boy w/Sandwich & Dog, 10½x13¼", NM	950.00
1932, Girl in Swimsuit on Beach, Hayden, 10½x13¼", EX+	625.00
1933, Francis Dee, 10½x13¼", NM	700.00

1934, Weismuller & O'Sullivan, 10½x13¼", NM 900.00
1935, Madge Evans, 10½x13¼", NM 375.00
1936, Hostess, 10½x13¼", NM 475.00
1937, Running Girl, 10½x13¼", NM 350.00
1938, Girl in the Afternoon, 10½x13¼", NM 300.00
1939, Springboard Girl, 10½x13¼", EX 285.00
1940, Sailor Girl, 10½x13¼", NM 350.00
1942, Roadster, 10½x13¼", NM+ 425.00
1950s, Girl w/Wind in Hair, screen bkground, 10½x13¼", M 100.00
1950s, Girl w/Wind in Hair, solid bkground, 10½x13¼", NM ...175.00
1955, Menu Girl, 10½x13¼", M 65.00
1957, Birdhouse, 10½x13¼", NM 100.00
1957, Rooster, 10½x13¼", NM 175.00
1957, Umbrella Girl, 10½x13¼", M 375.00
1961, Pansy Garden, 10½x13¼", NM 30.00

Machines

Though interest in Coca-Cola machines of the 1949 – 1959 era rose dramatically over the last few years, values currently seem to have leveled off and actually dropped 15% to 20%. The major manufacturers of these curved-top, 5¢ and 10¢ machines were Vendo (V), Vendorlator (VMC), Cavalier (C or CS), and Jacobs. Prices are for machines in excellent or better condition, complete and working. They vary greatly according to geographical location.

Cavalier, model #CS72, EX orig 1,400.00
Cavalier, model #CS72, M rstr 3,200.00
Cavalier, model #C27, M rstr 2,800.00
Cavalier, model #C27, orig 1,200.00
Cavalier, model #C51, EX orig 850.00
Cavalier, model #C51, M rstr 1,800.00
Jacobs, model #26, EX 1,200.00
Jacobs, model #26, M rstr 2,500.00
Vendo, model #23, EX orig 550.00
Vendo, model #39, EX orig 800.00
Vendo, model #39, M, rstr 2,500.00
Vendo, model #44, EX orig 2,500.00
Vendo, model #44, M rstr 3,750.00
Vendo, model #56, EX orig 1,200.00
Vendo, model #56, M rstr 3,200.00
Vendo, model #80, EX orig 500.00
Vendo, model #80, M rstr 1,250.00
Vendo, model #81, EX orig 1,200.00
Vendo, model #81, M rstr 3,200.00
Vendorlator, model #27, EX orig 1,200.00
Vendorlator, model #27, rstr (w/stand) 2,750.00
Vendorlator, model #27A, EX orig 800.00
Vendorlator, model #27A, M rstr 2,000.00
Vendorlator, model #33, EX orig 800.00
Vendorlator, model #33, M rstr 2,250.00
Vendorlator, model #44, EX orig 1,500.00
Vendorlator, model #44, M rstr 3,200.00
Vendorlator, model #72, EX orig 800.00
Vendorlator, model #72, M rstr 1,700.00

Coffee Grinders

The serious collector of kitchenwares and country store items rank coffee mills high on their want lists. A trend is developing toward preferring examples whose manufacturers are easily identifiable. Names to look for include Arcade, Daisy, Elgin National, Enterprise, Sun, Parker, Swift, Landers, Frary and Clark, Simmons Gardware Co., Logan and Strobridge, Bronson-Walton, Russel & Erwin, Wrightsville Hardware Co, and there are others. While some of these are from the 20th century, many are earlier.

Side mills usually have a brass tag located on the tin hopper. If the hopper was cast iron, the name was usually cast into the metal. Some of the less expensive versions had no identification. Paper labels were often used on the front of lap mills and table styles, though sometimes you will find these labels in a drawer or even inside the mill. Because decals and labels are prone to flake off and fade, when they are still legible, they contribute considerably to a mill's value. Canister mills had names and patent dates molded into the cast-iron housing or on the canister itself. Commercial mills used in country and general stores were made of cast iron. Important information such as manufacturer and patent dates were usually cast into the housing, base, or wheels. Such identification helps determine date of manufacture.

To evaluate a coffee mill, remember that it should be complete, with original decals or labels. Missing or broken parts decrease the value considerably as do incorrect replacement parts. Excellent examples of early coffee mills are rapidly becoming difficult to find. Beware of many imported impostors that are on the market today. A high-quality, authentic restoration of a cast-iron or wooden box mill will serve to enhance their values as long as the correct decals and labels are used.

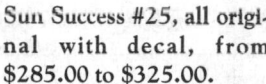

Sun Success #25, all original with decal, from $285.00 to $325.00.

Adams Pat, lap, pewter hopper, wood w/orig knob, EX 155.00
AK & Sons #237707, CI, octagon base, rnd hopper, heavy, EX .325.00
American Duplex No 50, electric, working, VG 85.00
Arcade, Crystal No 44, CI, glass hopper, Arcade lid & cup, EX .225.00
Arcade, Favorite No 30, EX 180.00
Arcade, glass catchers, mk Arcade Freeport Illinois 175.00
Arcade, Imperial, table, closed CI hopper, wood box 110.00
Arcade, Imperial No 999, decal, 1-lb box, EX 155.00
Arcade, Jewel, canister, rectangular glass hopper, w/lid, EX 695.00
Arcade, lap, fancy CI top & hopper, wood box, EX 110.00
Arcade, Our Baby, G label, mini, EX 95.00
Arcade, table, w/decal, orig drw, Pat 6, 5, 1884, 1-lb, NM 155.00
Arcade Crystal No 40, canister, orig lid & catcher, EX 325.00
Arcade No 147, lap, fancy CI closed hopper, wood box, EX 95.00
Arcade No 5, side, CI, Pat June '94, VG 85.00
Belmont, Lightning No 23, canister, tin & CI, EX 225.00
Blacksmith-made, funnel shape, 1-hdl, open hopper, wall mt 345.00
Blacksmith-made, funnel shape, 2-hdl, wall mt to 2x4", VG 375.00
Bronson-Walton, Belmont Coffee, CI & tin, orig 125.00
Bronson-Walton, Monitor, table, tin, w/cup, ca 1909, EX 125.00
Bronson-Walton, Silver Lake, canister, glass hopper, EX 425.00
Chase & Sanborn, coffee bin 175.00
Clark & Clawson No 1, CI, dbl grind, Pat 1886, 6" wheel 525.00
Crescent, CI, Rutland VT, orig pnt, 15" wheels, EX 675.00
Daisy No 867, mini, CI top, wood box & drw, orig decal, EX 95.00
Elgin Nat'l, floor, silver hopper, 24" wheels 1,500.00

Elgin Nat'l No 44, CI, reed, w/eagle & pan, 15" wheels, 24" **775.00**
Elgin Nat'l No 48, CI w/eagle, orig lily decal, 2 wheels **725.00**
Elma, counter, CI, closed hopper, 10" single wheel, 17", EX **175.00**
Elma No 2, CI, single wheel, 12½" **145.00**
Enterprise, Baby No 2, orig pnt & decals, 2 wheels, 7½", EX **995.00**
Enterprise, counter, CI, brass hopper, Pat 1873, 6" wheels, VG .**775.00**
Enterprise, floor, CI, CI hopper, Pat 1898, 39" wheels, 72", VG ...**2,500.00**
Enterprise No 0, CI, wall mt, w/orig catcher **75.00**
Enterprise No 0, table, CI, clamps on, EX **75.00**
Enterprise No 12½, orig pnt/decals, 24¾" wheels **1,200.00**
Enterprise No 2, orig pnt/decal, 2 8¾" wheels **750.00**
Enterprise No 3, counter, CI, wood drw, orig pnt/decals **575.00**
Enterprise No 6, brass hopper, 2 wheels, rstr, NM **895.00**
Fairbanks Morse, floor, CI, brass hopper, 2 wheels, 27", EX **3,100.00**
Grand Union Tea, canister, red, orig writing/pnt, Pat 1910 ....**125.00**
Hobart No 265, electric, covered hopper **375.00**
J Fisher, dvtl mahog, pewter hopper, orig drw, handmade **225.00**
Juvenile, lap, CI top, wood box, orig drw & decal, EX **125.00**
L'il Tot, mini, CI hopper & drw front, wood box, decal **95.00**
Landers, Frary & Clark, canister, CI & tin, Pat 1905, VG **80.00**
Landers, Frary & Clark, Crown #20, counter, 8" wheels **795.00**
Leslir & Krater, table, wood, Pat Oct 5, 1886, rare, NM **625.00**
Levering Coffee Bin, wood, rectangular **125.00**
Mini, canister, boy & girl, 5½x1½" **85.00**
Nat'l, counter, CI works, covered hopper, wood drw, 1-wheel **125.00**
Nat'l Specialty No 0, table, CI, covered hopper, clamps on **125.00**
New Model, lap, CI w/CI drw, bottom opens all 4 sides, EX **95.00**
Olde Thompson, lap, orig drw, EX **65.00**
Parker, side, CI, front grind adjusts, Pat 1876, on orig board **75.00**
Parker Eagle No 50, side, CI, Pat 1860, EX **95.00**
Parker No 2, counter, CI, orig decals, 9" wheels, EX **795.00**
Parker No 260 Columbia, table, side grind, 1-lb, EX **275.00**
Parker No 3000, drw, eagle on top, 11" wheels, orig **725.00**
Parker No 350, side, orig lid, Pat 4/1876, EX **85.00**
Parker No 449, canister, CI, orig lid & catcher, EX **145.00**
Parker No 5000, counter, CI, Pat 1897, 12" wheels, 17", VG **750.00**
Parker No 555, screw cap, label, 1-lb, EX **135.00**
Parker No 700, counter, CI, wood drw, 17" wheels, G **795.00**
Peck, Stow & Wilcox Internat'l #360, lap, unusual **155.00**
PS&W, Vortex No 40, lap, wood box, CI hopper **145.00**
PS&W No 3500, side, CI, britannia hopper, orig lid, EX **95.00**
Richmond, side, CI, Chatham Conn (2 szs made), EX, ea **135.00**
Royal, side, CI w/CI cup, open hopper, Pat Apr 15, 1890, VG **95.00**
Russell & Erwin, lap, CI hopper, wood box, top adjusts **95.00**
Russell & Erwin No 60, britannia hopper, wood box **90.00**
Silvers No 1, CI, dbl-grind, w/cup, EX **485.00**
Simmons Defiance, label, CI fill lid, 1-lb box, EX **125.00**
Star Model A, floor, 34½" wheels, G **700.00**
Star No 12, CI, brass hopper, 2 wheels, rstr, EX **2,500.00**
Sun Mfg No 1080, orig label & drw, 1-lb box, EX/NM **425.00**
Sun Success No 25, cylinder, 2 different szs, EX, ea **225.00**
Thomas Robert & Co, coffee bin **300.00**
W Cross & Sons, lap, CI w/orig CI drw, brass hopper & pull **85.00**
Waddel A9, orig drw & label, box type, EX **125.00**
Wright, John; CI, red or gr, ca 1968, 2 6¾" wheels, NM **350.00**
Wrightsville Hdwe, CI, eagle pnt on lid, 2 wheels, sm **350.00**

Coin-Operated Machines

Coin-operated machines may be the fastest-growing area of collector
interest in today's market. Many machines are bought, restored, and used for
home entertainment. Older examples from the turn of the century and those
with especially elaborate decoration and innovative features are most desirable.

Exhibit 1¢ Personality Indicator,
oak case, cast-iron legs, ca 1925,
78", EX original, $4,000.00.

Arcade Machines

Booze Barometer, ca 1950, NM **295.00**
Buckley Jewel Box Digger, floor model, EX orig **2,000.00**
Caille Cailoscope, ca 1905, EX **2,500.00**
Caille Cupid's Post Office, ca 1905, rstr **3,250.00**
Caille Rubber Neck Lung Tester, ca 1905, EX rstr **7,200.00**
Caille Uncle Sam Grip, ca 1910, EX rstr **4,000.00**
Chicago Coin, Speedway, rstr **1,000.00**
Exhibit Supply Grandfather's Clock, ca 1925, VG orig **2,600.00**
Exhibit Supply Kiss-O-Meter, NM **1,100.00**
Exhibit Supply Streamline Digger, rstr **2,750.00**
Genco Gypsy Fortune Teller, EX+ **3,200.00**
Golden Arm Strength Tester, EX orig **450.00**
Gottlieb Whizz Bang, 1932, EX orig **700.00**
Mills Lion Lung Tester, ca 1905, VG **3,500.00**
Mills World Horoscope, ca 1905, EX **4,500.00**
Mutoscope Indian, ca 1900, EX orig **6,000.00**
Seeburg Chicken Sam, ca 1931, EX orig **1,000.00**

Jukeboxes

Aerion #1200, 1947, EX **2,000.00**
AMI F-120, 1954, EX orig **1,000.00**
Packard Pla-Mor, 1946, EX orig **3,750.00**
Rockola #1426, 1947, EX orig **4,700.00**
Rockola #1434 Rocket, 1950, NM **3,000.00**
Rockola #1448, 1955, EX orig **2,200.00**
Rockola Tempo, 1959, EX orig **2,800.00**
Seeburg #147MA, rstr **3,400.00**
Seeburg #220, 1958, EX rstr **3,500.00**
Seeburg A, plays 45s, 1948, EX orig **2,500.00**
Seeburg C, 1952, 100 selections, EX **4,000.00**
Seeburg M, 1946, EX **900.00**
Seeburg R, 1954, EX orig **2,600.00**
Wurlitzer #61, countertop style, 1938, NM **4,000.00**
Wurlitzer #700, 1940, old rstr **4,500.00**
Wurlitzer #1050, EX **3,700.00**
Wurlitzer #1700, 1954, EX orig **3,000.00**
Wurlitzer #2500, 1960, NM rstr **1,750.00**
Wurlitzer P-30, 1935, NM **2,800.00**

Pinball Machines

Bally Aladdin's Castle #N-12, EX **995.00**
Bally Atlantic City Bingo #D-12, 1952, EX **600.00**
Bally Circus #N-11, electromechanical, 1973, EX **695.00**
Bally Dolly Parton #N-9, 1979, EX **695.00**
Bally Elvira #N-15, 1989, cleaned, rstr rubber, working **1,800.00**

Bally Harlem Globetrotters #N-13, 1979, EX 625.00
Bally Supersonic #N-31, airplane in bk glass, 1979, EX 595.00
Bally Truck Stop #N-14, 1988 ....1,395.00
Bally 6 Million Dollar Man #N-32, 6-player, 1978, EX 675.00
Gottlieb Drop-a-Card #N-12, electromechanical, 1971, EX 475.00
Gottlieb Bank-a-Ball #N-1, 1965, EX 695.00
Gottlieb Humpty Dumpty #N-11, wood rail, 1947, EX 1,600.00
Williams Black Knight 2000 #N-17, clean, rstr rubber, working .1,345.00
Williams Pin Bot #N-7, clean, rubbered, G working 1,245.00

Slot Machines

Bally Double Bell 5¢/25¢, EX orig 3,650.00
Buckley Bones 25¢, countertop, 1936, NM 4,800.00
Caille Big 6 Lone Star Twin 5¢, oak cabinet, VG 27,500.00
Caille Big 6 25¢, rstr 15,500.00
Caille Boomer, EX 1,900.00
Caille Center Pull 5¢, w/vendor, EX orig 4,650.00
Caille New Century Detroit 5¢, upright w/music, EX orig 14,000.00
Caille Roulette 5¢, floor model, 1904, EX 45,000.00

Caille Silver Cup 5¢, nickel-
plated cast iron, rotating dials,
ca 1912, 20½x14", EX original, $8,000.00.

Caille Superior, w/mint vendor, 1927, EX 2,000.00
Caille Venus Twin, ca 1907, NM 60,000.00
Caille Victory Bell, w/mint vendor, EX 4,000.00
Groetchen Columbia Bell 5¢, 1936, NM 1,250.00
Groetchen Turf Flash, VG 1,200.00
Jennings Century, reserve jackpot, mint vendors, 1933, VG ...2,750.00
Jennings Chinese Front, console, EX 2,900.00
Jennings Dixie Bell 5¢, ca 1937, EX 1,350.00
Jennings Governor 10¢, Indian head front, 1964, EX 1,995.00
Jennings Little Duke 1¢, w/side vendor, rstr 2,500.00
Jennings New Victoria 5¢, w/vendor, 1921, EX 1,850.00
Jennings Peacock 5¢, rstr 2,400.00
Jennings Silver Club 25¢, rstr 2,000.00
Jennings Silver Moon Chief Ball 5¢, 1941, NM 1,995.00
Jennings Sportsman 5¢, w/golf-ball vendor, 1932, VG 2,000.00
Jennings Standard Chief 5¢, EX orig 2,100.00
Jennings Sun Chief, NM 2,500.00
Mills Bursting Cherry 1¢, 1937, 26", EX 2,300.00
Mills Diamond Front Chrome 5¢, 1939, VG orig 1,995.00
Mills Dice Machine, EX 3,100.00
Mills Futurity, 1936, EX 3,200.00
Mills Jockey, EX 3,450.00
Mills OK 5¢, w/candy vendor, 1922, EX 2,750.00
Mills Operator Bell 5¢, 1910, EX 5,850.00
Mills QT Diamond Front 1¢, 19", VG 1,250.00

Mills Skyscraper 5¢, rstr 1,950.00
Mills Torch Front Jackpot 5¢, 1928, EX 2,800.00
Mills War Eagle Silent Bell 25¢, 1931, NM 2,900.00
Mills Wolf's Head Silent Gooseneck 5¢, 1931, EX 2,500.00
Pace Chrome Deluxe 5¢, rstr 1,850.00
Pace 8 Star Bell 25¢, EX orig 1,750.00
Watling Blue Seal Gooseneck Jackpot 25¢, 1929, rstr 2,500.00
Watling Rol-A-Top Bird of Paradise, 1938, EX orig 4,250.00
Watling Treasury 5¢, eagle on front, 1936, NM 5,000.00

Trade Stimulators

Caille Fortune, 1¢ ball gum vendor, 1927, EX orig 1,450.00
Caille Good Luck, ca 1902, EX orig 1,400.00
Daval Am Eagle, EX orig 375.00
Daval Buddy, cigarettes, w/gum vendor, ca 1946, EX 495.00
Daval Reel Spot, 1937, EX orig 485.00
Dropisch Star, nickel drop, EX 1,450.00
Fields Blackjack 21, ball flip, 1931, VG 350.00
Gottlieb Indian Dice 1¢, 1937, VG 850.00
Groetchen Mercury, 3-reel, cigarette symbols, 1939, EX 400.00
Groetchen Yankee, ca 1941, NM 400.00
Keeney Steeplechase, marble horse race game, 1935, EX+ 800.00
Mercury Pay Out 1¢, EX orig 325.00
Mills Bell Boy, 3-reel, 1932, VG 1,995.00
Mills New Target Practice, penny drop, 1925, EX 650.00
Pace New Deal, poker game, 1935, EX 650.00
Rockola Hold & Draw, ca 1934, EX orig 1,000.00
Whitney Seven Grand, dice game, ca 1939, EX orig 700.00

Vendors

    Vending machines sold a product or a service. They were already in common usage by 1900 selling gum, cigars, matches, and a host of other commodities. Peanut and gum-ball machines are especially popular today. The most valuable are those with their original finish and decals. Older machines made of cast iron are especially desirable, while those with plastic globes have little or no collector value. When buying unrestored peanut machines, beware of salt damage.

    The coin-operated phonograph of the early 1900s paved the way for the jukeboxes of the '20s. Seeburg was first on the market with an automatic eight-tune phonograph. By the 1930s Wurlitzer was the top name in the industry with dealerships all over the country. As a result of the growing ranks of competitors, the '40s produced the most beautiful machines made. Wurlitzers from this era are probably the most popularly sought-after models on the market today. The model #1015 of 1946 is considered the all-time classic and often brings prices in excess of $7,000.00.

    The http://GameRoomAntiques.com web site and *Antique Amusements, Slot Machine, and Jukebox Gazette* are excellent sources of information for those interested in coin-operated machines; see the Clubs, Newsletters, and Catalogs section of the Directory for publishing information. Jackie and Ken Durham are our advisors; they are listed in the Directory under the District of Columbia.

Northwestern, peanuts, yellow porcelain base, replaced label, 16", EX, $295.00; Columbus Model 41A, 1946, 14½", NM, $600.00; Northwestern Model 33 1¢, metal, green porcelain and glass, 16", EX, $295.00.

Abbey, gum, ca 1935, EX 95.00
Adams Pepsin Tutti-Fruiti Gum, 2-column, EX 3,500.00
Advance Big Mouth #11, peanuts, 1923, rstr 295.00
Atlas Master, gum, NM orig 75.00
Beechnut Gum 1¢, porc, child illus, early 1920s, EX 4,000.00
Climax, gumball, glass globe, 1920, NM 650.00
Columbus A, gum, glass globe, hourglass CI base, 1920s, EX 350.00
Columbus L, gum, 1910, EX orig 3,000.00
Columbus M, hexagonal globe, EX orig 275.00
Columbus Model 18 1¢, lg globe, CI base, 1930s, EX 700.00
E-Z, gumball, aluminum base, 18", EX 775.00
Federal Dispenser Corp...CA, US postage stamps, porc, 20x8x4½" .150.00
Ford Chewing Gum 1¢, gum, faded label, plastic globe 45.00
Griswold Red Star, peanuts, 1919, rstr 2,000.00
Happy Jap 1¢, gum, CI, clockwork, 1902, 15", VG 6,000.00
Lion Vendor, gloves, M 250.00
Manikin Baker Boy, gum, animated, EX orig 4,650.00
Mansfield Automatic Clerk, gum, 1901, VG 995.00
Master Fantail, 1¢/5¢ slits for gum, 1931, NM 1,200.00
Modern Merchandising, Gillette Razor Blades, 19x2½x4½" 85.00
Mutoscope Old Mill, bulk vendor, 1928, NM 1,500.00
National Vending, Wilbur's Chocolate, glass dome, M 600.00
Northwestern #33 Jr, gum, 1933, EX 285.00
Oak Acorn, gum, ca 1950, NM 95.00
Price, collar buttons, ca 1901, EX orig 1,200.00
Pulver Gum, Clown, yel case, 1930s, M (unused) 795.00
Pulver Gum, Duck, sgn Walter Lutz, wrinkle finish, 20", MIB ...1,600.00
Pulver Gum, Yel Kid, animated, 2-panel, 24", EX orig 800.00
Pulver Hot Chew, chrome plated 250.00
Simmons A, gum, porc base, ca 1930, NM 250.00
Smilin' Sam, peanuts, 1921, EX orig (+) 3,500.00
Snoopy Gum, clockwork, man drops gum from scoop, 20", EX ..1,500.00
Star, popcorn, floor model, EX orig 800.00
Triple Columbus, peanuts, w/orig stand, EX 1,500.00
Victor V, gum, 1940, EX 100.00

Cole, A. R.

A second generation North Carolina potter, Arthur Ray Cole opened his own shop in 1926, operating under the name Rainbow Pottery until 1941 when he adopted his own name for the title of his business. He remained active until he died in 1974. He was skilled in modeling the pottery and highly recognized for his fine glazes.

Photo courtesy Southern Folk Pottery Collectors Society

Cups, variegated green, earthenware, marked, 1950s, 3¼", $40.00 for the pair.

Bowl, Chrome Red, earthenware, hdls, att J Kiser, 4¼x12½" 150.00
Bowl, 4-color splotches, looped hdls, mk, 5x9" 150.00
Casserole, forest gr, stick hdl, dome lid, mk, 5½x13½" L 60.00
Vase, yel on mirror blk, hdls, 1920s-30s, sgn/mk, 24", NM 325.00

Compacts

The use of cosmetics before WWI was looked upon with disdain. After the war women became liberated, entered the work force, and started to use makeup. The compact, a portable container for cosmetics, became a necessity. The basic compact contains a mirror and a powder puff.

The vintage compacts were fashioned in a myriad of shapes, styles, materials, and motifs. They were made of precious metals, fabrics, plastics, and in almost any other conceivable medium. Commemorative, premium, patriotic, figural, Art Deco, plastic, and gadgetry compacts are just a few of the most sought-after types available today. Those that are combined with other accessories (music/compact, watch/compact, cane/compact) are also very much in demand. Vintage compacts are an especially desirable collectible since the workmanship, design, techniques, and materials used in their execution would be very expensive and virtually impossible to duplicate today.

Our advisor, Roselyn Gerson, has written four highly informative books: *Ladies' Compacts of the 19th and 20th Centuries*; *Vintage Vanity Bags and Purses*; *Vintage and Contemporary Purse Accessories*; and *Vintage Ladies' Compacts*. She is listed in the Directory under the state of New York. See Clubs and Newsletters for information concerning the compact collectors' club and their periodical publication, *The Powder Puff*.

Cameo, Kigu, gold-tone w/lady's profile, 3⅛" sq 80.00
Carryall, baton, Elgin Am, mock tortoise shell/gold-tone, 8½" ..350.00
Carryall, clutch, Evans, silver-tone, lattice/rhinestones, 5½" 100.00
Carryall, clutch, unmk, wht enamel w/blk polka-dots, 4¼" 300.00
Carryall, clutch, unmk, wht metal, red leather/tassel, 5" 175.00
Carryall, clutch, Zell, dbl access, beveled MOP, 4" 100.00
Carryall, cylinder, La Mode, dbl access, gold-tone, chain, 3½" ...250.00
Carryall, suede ball, Blum's Vogue, gold trim, rope hdl, 3" 275.00
Envelope, unmk, wht enamel top w/King Geo VI stamp, 2½x3" ...175.00
Fan, Henriette, gold-tone w/silver-tone o/l, 4¾x2" 150.00
Hand w/engagement ring, Volupte, gold-tone, 4½x2" 250.00
Heart, Kigu, gold-tone w/gazelles on etched rays, 3x3" 60.00
Heart, Superb, HP horse head on gold-tone, 2⅞" 50.00
Musical, Elgin Am, blk enamel lid w/gold-tone design, 3x2" 125.00
Octagonal, Allwyn, ivory enamel/oval rhinestone decor, 2½" 150.00
Octagonal, Montral, bl champleve enameled lid w/dancers, 2" ..200.00
Octagonal, unmk, petit-point w/blk Bakelite border, 2½" 80.00
Oval, Evans, gold-tone w/floral motif on etched sunrays, 2¾" 80.00
Oval, Yardley, bee/honeycomb/wht-circle motif on gold-tone, 3½" ..50.00
Rectangular, Schick, gold-tone w/MOP star design, 2¾" 65.00
Rnd, Evans, blk enamel w/rhinestone shooting-star decor, 2½" .175.00
Rnd, Jaciel, wht metal, emb butterfly/floral motif, 2" 65.00
Rnd, Marian Bialac, jade chips w/gold-tone fr, 3⅛" 90.00
Rnd, Schildkraut, mc beads/buttons/sequins on blk, 2¾" 90.00
Rnd, Stratton, gold-tone w/HP flamingos on bl irid enamel, 3" .125.00
Rnd, unmk, brn pigskin w/running Scottie dog, 3¼" 80.00
Rnd, unmk, red Bakelite w/marcasite butterfly, gold trim, 3" 115.00
Rnd, Vanstyle, waterbird/reed decor on blk enamel, 4" 100.00
Scalloped, Kigu, gold-tone w/allover stylized design, 3½" 80.00
Shell, Volupte, gold-tone w/sm shell & sunray design, 3" 65.00
Sq, Charles of the Ritz, gold-tone w/6-sided initial disk, 2" 100.00
Sq, Gourielli, gold-tone w/emb bow-tie design, 3" 90.00
Sq, SF Co Fifth Ave, mc shells/faux pearls on gold-tone, 2¾" ...125.00
Sq, unmk, blk Bakelite dome lid w/rnd gilt rococo inlay, 2¼" 80.00
Sq, Volupte, gold-tone w/butterfly in spider web, 3" 125.00
Suitcase, Kigu, bark-like gold-tone, straps/hdl, 2½x3¼" 125.00
Vanity, arrowhead, Woodworth, sunray center/geometric trim, 3" ..125.00
Vanity, book, Mondaine, floral design on tan leather, 3" 80.00
Vanity, clamshell, Elgin Am, encased pearlized effect, 2¾" 125.00
Vanity, cushion, Lupe, gold swirl design on red enamel, 3" 150.00

Vanity, cushion, Tu-Adore, gr Bakelite w/foil country scene, 2" ...**100.00**
Vanity, keystone, unmk, blk silhouette lady on ivory, 3¼" **100.00**
Vanity, oval, Vashe, champleve cattail decor on dome lid, 3" **90.00**
Vanity, pendant w/chain, unmk, gold-tone, Sphinx/pyramids, 2½" ...**200.00**
Vanity, rectangular, Foster, rhinestone floral decor, 2¾" **150.00**
Vanity, rectangular, Lentheric, blk enameled beveled lid, 1¾" ..**125.00**
Vanity, rectangular, R Thornton, gold crest on blk enamel, 3" ..**125.00**
Vanity, rectangular, unmk, initials on banded wood top, 2½" **50.00**
Vanity, rnd, Woodsworth, wht metal, Art Deco lady's profile, 2" ..**250.00**
Vanity, saddlebag, unmk, bl faux guilloche, wht/gold trim, 3" **150.00**
Vanity, shield, Elgin Am, wht metal, Art Deco lady/dog, 2¼" ...**200.00**
Vanity, shield, Lorette, gold-tone/bl enamel side panels, 2½" **80.00**

Computing Devices

Computing, calculating, and adding devices come in many shapes, sizes, and weights. Some are complex machines with many moving parts while others, such as slide rules, are quite simple in construction. These devices were used by scientists, accountants, engineers, and many other professionals when mathematical computations and exactness were required. Examples of devices and machines with early patent dates are usually of greatest interest to collectors. Our advisor for this category is Dale Beeks; he is listed in the Directory under Iowa.

Adder, Addometer, 7 numbered wheels, EX in case **35.00**
Adder, Gem, chain drive, pocket sz, EX **65.00**
Adder, Webb, Pat 1867, wooden base, EX **600.00**
Adder, Webb, Pat 1889, all metal, EX **165.00**
Adder, Webb type, unsgn, all metal, EX **110.00**
Curta, pepper-grinder type, EX in case **750.00**
Machine, Brunsviga midget, wooden cover, EX **200.00**
Machine, Burroughs, push button, glass sides, lg **125.00**
Machine, Comptometer, copper case, push buttons **45.00**
Machine, Comptometer, wooden case, G **900.00**
Machine, Millionaire, metal case, heavy, lg, VG **1,800.00**
Slide rule, beginner's, EX in case **12.00**
Slide rule, circular, Gilson, EX in case **45.00**
Slide rule, demonstration, Picket, 84" L, EX **250.00**
Slide rule, Keuffel & Esser NY, typical, EX **22.00**
Slide rule, Thachers, cylindrical, Pat 1882, EX in case **1,600.00**

Consolidated Lamp and Glass

The Consolidated Lamp and Glass Company of Coraopolis, Pennsylvania, was incorporated in 1894. For many years their primary business was the manufacture of lighting glass such as oil lamps and shades for both gas and electric lighting. The popular 'Cosmos' line of lamps and tableware was produced from 1894 to 1915. (See also Cosmos.) In 1926 Consolidated introduced their Martele line, a type of 'sculptured' ware closely resembling Lalique glassware of France. (Compare Consolidated's 'Lovebirds' vase with the Lalique 'Perruches' vase.) It is this line of vases, lamps, and tableware which is often mistaken for a very similar type of glassware produced by the Phoenix Glass Company, located nearby in Monaca, Pennsylvania. For example, the so-called Phoenix 'Grasshopper' vases are actually Consolidated's 'Katydid' vases.

Items in the Martele line were produced in blue, pink, green, crystal, white, or custard glass decorated with various fired-on color treatments or a satin finish. For the most part, their colors were distinctively different from those used by Phoenix. Although not foolproof, one of the ways of distinguishing Consolidated's wares from those of Phoenix is that most of the time Consolidated applied color to the raised portion of the design, leaving the background plain, while Phoenix usually applied color to the background, leaving the raised surfaces undecorated. This is particularly true of those pieces in white or custard glass.

In 1928 Consolidated introduced their Ruba Rombic line, which was their Art Deco or Art Moderne line of glassware. It was only produced from 1928 to 1932 and is quite scarce. Today it is highly sought after by both Consolidated and Art Deco collectors.

Consolidated closed its doors for good in 1964. Subsequently a few of the molds passed into the hands of other glass companies that later reproduced certain patterns; one such reissue is the 'Chickadee' vase, found in avocado green, satin-finish custard, or milk glass. Our advisor for this category is Jack D. Wilson, author of *Phoenix and Consolidated Art Glass, 1926 – 1980*; he is listed in the Directory under Illinois.

Key: mg — milk glass

Ruba Rombic, jug, Smoky Topaz, 8¼", $2,750.00.

Bird of Paradise, fan vase, gr, 11" **240.00**
Bird of Paradise, fan vase, pk, 6" **100.00**
Bittersweet, vase, bl, gr & orange on satin mg, 9½" **150.00**
Bittersweet, vase, gold on custard, 9¾" **175.00**
Bittersweet, vase, gr cased, 9¾" **225.00**
Blackberry, umbrella vase, orange frosted, 18" **500.00**
Catalonian, bowl, 3-color Rainbow finish (rare color), 3x9½" ..**430.00**
Catalonian, Nasturtium vase, amethyst on clear **200.00**
Catalonian, Sweet Peas vase, 3-color Rainbow finish (rare), 4½" ..**108.00**
Catalonian, vase, tricorner, red, #1101, 10" **200.00**
Catalonian, Violet vase, 3-color Rainbow finish (rare), 4" **155.00**
Chickadee, vase, gr wash on crystal, 7" **110.00**
Chickadee, vase, red (rare), 7" **400.00**
Chrysanthemum, vase, coral & gr on satin mg, 12" **165.00**
Chrysanthemum, vase, glossy gr/pk on bright mg (unusual finish) ...**200.00**
Con-Cora, cookie jar, violets on mg, 6½" **145.00**
Dancing Girls, lamp, red w/gold highlighting **800.00**
Dancing Girls, vase, 2-color bl on satin mg, 12" **400.00**
Dancing Ladies, vase, cranberry flash on crystal, ormolu mt, 11½" ..**1,750.00**
Dancing Nymph, tumbler, ftd, crystal frosted, 6½" **95.00**
Dancing Nymph, tumbler vase, crimped, cranberry flashed, 5¼" ..**400.00**
Dancing Nymph, tumbler vase, crimped, wht frosted, 5¼" **155.00**
Dogwood, lamp, ruby stain on crystal, glass: 10½" **145.00**
Dogwood, vase, lav cased (rare color), 10¾" **565.00**
Dogwood, vase, pk & gr on satin mg, 10½" **250.00**
Dogwood, vase, reverse ruby stain on crystal, ormolu mts, glass: 11" ...**500.00**
Dogwood, vase, tricolor on satin mg, 10½" **223.00**
Dragonfly & Cattails, vase, 3-color on mustard, ormolu mts, rare ..**315.00**
Fish, tray, yel wash **200.00**
Floral, vase, 2-color on custard, 9" **155.00**
Florentine, vase, gr, collared, flat, 12" **290.00**
Florette, cookie jar, pk satin, #3758-9 ....**250.00**
Florette, cracker jar, red, w/lid, 6" **150.00**
Foxglove, vase, reverse cranberry flash on crystal, 10" **160.00**

Hummingbird, vase, violet birds on matt mg, 5½" 130.00
Jonquil, vase, brn on satin mg, 6½" 155.00
Katydid, fan vase, Rueben Blue (rare color), 9x8½" 280.00
Katydid, tumbler vase, honey, 8¼" 145.00
Katydid, tumbler vase, med bl, 8¼" 273.00
Katydid, vase, ovoid, gr, 7x8¼" 200.00
Katydid, vase, ovoid, gr on custard, 7x8¼" 195.00
Katydid, vase, wht frost wash, #212, 8¼" 130.00
Le Fleur, lamp, orange & gr on satin mg, glass: 11" 275.00
Le Fleur, vase, lt bl, ormolu mts, 11" 400.00
Line 700, fan vase, clear bl crystal, 6" 140.00
Line 700, vase, bl w/satin int, 7" 170.00
Line 700, vase, purple opal (rare color), 7" 500.00
Line 700, vase, ruby flash on crystal (rare color), 10" 450.00
Lovebirds, banana boat, bl on custard, 15" L 450.00
Lovebirds, lamp, cinnabar on tan, glass: 10" 350.00
Lovebirds, vase, 3-color on satin custard, 10" 435.00
Nuthatch, planter, oval, brn cased (rare color), 9½x5" 225.00
Nuthatch, planter, oval, purple cased (rare color), 9½x5" 320.00
Nuthatch, planter, oval, 4-color on custard, 9½x5" 185.00
Pine Cone, vase, honey cased (rare color), 7" 180.00
Pine Cone, vase, straw opal, 6½" 190.00
Regent Line, cookie jar (florette), rose/wht opal cased, #758, 6½" ..370.00
Ruba Rombic, almond dish, Jungle Green, rare, 3" 375.00
Ruba Rombic, ashtray, Lilac, 2 nicks, 3½" 830.00
Ruba Rombic, ashtray, wht opal, 3½" 1,100.00
Ruba Rombic, bonbon, Sunshine (extremely rare), 7" 800.00
Ruba Rombic, bottle, smoke, 9¼x7", EX 800.00
Ruba Rombic, bowl, cupped, Silver, rim chips, 8", from $1,000 to ..1,200.00
Ruba Rombic, candlestick, Smoky Topaz, 4½" W 235.00
Ruba Rombic, celery dish, Jungle Green, rare, 12" W 800.00
Ruba Rombic, compote, Jungle Green, rare, 7" 900.00
Ruba Rombic, creamer, Sunshine, 3½" 355.00
Ruba Rombic, creamer & sugar bowl, Jungle Green, chip 500.00
Ruba Rombic, creamer & sugar bowl, Smoky Topaz 357.50
Ruba Rombic, perfume bottle, Lilac, 5" 1,850.00
Ruba Rombic, plate, Jungle Green, flake, 8" 60.00
Ruba Rombic, sundae, Smoky Topaz, chip on base 150.00
Ruba Rombic, toilet bottle, Lilac, 7¾" 1,900.00
Ruba Rombic, tray for whiskey set, Lilac, 11½x10½" 2,000.00
Ruba Rombic, tumbler, flat, Jungle Green, 4" 175.00
Ruba Rombic, tumbler, ftd, Jade, 6" 225.00
Ruba Rombic, vase, Jungle Green, 6½" 900.00
Ruba Rombic, vase, Smoky Topaz, 9½" 1,600.00
Ruba Rombic, whiskey set, Jungle Green, complete, 8-pc 3,750.00
Sea Gulls, lamp, yel cased, glass: 11x10" 450.00
Sea Gulls, vase, gold on custard, chip, 11x10" 225.00
Shade, blown-out grapes/lattice (4 repeats), 8x14" 750.00
Tropical Fish, vase, orange on Seafoam Green, 9" 390.00
Tropical Fish, vase, reverse ruby stain on crystal, 9" 400.00

Cookbooks

Cookbooks from the 19th century, though often hard to find, are a delight to today's collectors both for their quaint formats and printing methods as well as for their outmoded, often humorous views on nutrition. Recipes required a 'pinch' of salt, butter 'the size of an egg' or a 'walnut,' or a 'handful' of flour. Collectors sometimes specialize in cookbooks issued as advertising premiums. Especially desirable are the figurals that were shaped like a jar, a slice of bread, or some other form relative to the product. Others with unique features such as illustrations by well-known artists or references to famous people or places are priced in accordance. Cookbooks written earlier than 1874 are the most valu-

able and when found command prices as high as $200.00; figurals usually sell in the $10.00 to $15.00 range.

As is true with all other books, if the original dust jacket is present and in nice condition, a cookbook's value goes up by at least $5.00. Right now, books on Italian cooking from before circa 1940 are in demand, and bread baking is important this year. For further information we recommend *A Guide to Collecting Cookbooks* by Col. Bob Allen and *Price Guide to Cookbooks and Recipe Leaflets* by Linda Dickinson. Our advisor for this category is Charlotte Safir; she is listed in the Directory under New York.

Key:
BH&G — Better Homes & Gardens   dj — dust jacket
CB — cookbook

Cooking the Modern Way, Planters, 1948, EX, $22.00.

All About Home Baking, General Foods Corp, 1933, G 10.00
All American CB II, Walsworth Pub, 1985, VG 12.00
All-In-One Oven Meals, Ruth Bean, 1952, hardbk w/dj, G 8.00
America's Best Recipes, Oxmoor House, 1989, VG 10.00
American Cookery, James Beard, 1972, hardbk w/dj, VG 38.00
American Family CB, Melanie DeProft, 1974, hardbk w/dj, VG ..15.00
Aunt Jemima's Pancakes Unlimited, 1958, 31-pg, EX 75.00
Aunt Sammy's Radio Recipes Revised, USDA, 1931, softcover, G 12.00
Bakery Cakes & Simple Confectionary, Floris, '68, hardbk w/dj, G 20.00
Betty Crocker's CB, Golden Press, 1970, looseleaf paperbk, VG ..15.00
Betty Crocker's Picture CB, 1st ed/2nd print, 1950, G 50.00
BH&G Barbecue CB, Meredith Press, 1965, G 7.00
BH&G Complete Step-By-Step CB, Meredith, 1978, hardbk w/dj, G 12.00
BH&G Cooking for Two, Meredith Press, 1968, G 3.00
BH&G Encyclopedia of Cooking, Meredith, 1973, set of 20 vol, G ..30.00
BH&G Fast Fixin' Meat Recipes, Meredith, 1988, softcover, VG ..3.50
BH&G The New CB, Meredith, 1968, VG 12.00
Bless This Food: The Anita Bryant Family CB, 1975, hardbk w/dj, VG ...15.00
Book of Hors D'oeuvres, Lucy G Allen, 1941, hardbk w/dj, VG 9.00
Casserole Specialties, Nedda C Anders, 1965, hardbk w/dj, VG ..10.00
CB for Good Nutrition, Carlton Fredericks, 1977, hardbk w/dj, VG ...5.00
Chafing-Dish Specialties, Nedda Casson Anders, 1954, hardbk w/dj, G 7.00
Classic Am Cooking, Pearl Byrd Foster, 1983, hardbk w/dj, G 15.00
Clockwatcher's CB, Ann Dare, 1973, hardbk w/dj, G 9.00
Cook It Quick, Arthur Hawkins, 1971, hardbk w/dj, G 10.00
Cooking & Preserving Vegetables, Am Culinary Society, 1974, VG ...7.00
Cooking the Chinese Way, Nina Froud, 1963, hardbk w/dj, VG 5.00
Cooking w/Fruits & Nuts, M Hodgson, 1st ed, 1973, hardbk w/dj, VG .18.00
Cooking w/Style, Charlotte Adams, 1967, hardbk w/dj, VG 8.00
Cooking w/Wine, Cora, Rose & Bob Brown, 1960, hardbk w/dj, VG .8.00
Creative Cooking Reader's Digest, 1977, VG 10.00
Creative Wok Cooking, Ethel Graham, 1976, hardbk w/dj, EX ...15.00
Culinary Arts Institute's Cooking Magic, G 25.00
Eggs & Cheese CB, Home Cooking Library, 1985, VG 5.00
Elsie's CB, Borden, 1st ed, 1952, 374-pg, EX 32.00
Elsie's Hostess Recipe Book, Borden, 1970s, M 25.00

Esquire Culinary Companion, Charles H Baker, 1959, hardbk w/dj .25.00
Family Circle Favorite Recipes CB, 1977, hardbk w/dj, G 8.00
Family Circle Quick Menu CB, Jean Hewitt, 1978, hardbk w/dj, EX ...10.00
Fish Cookery, James Beard, 1954, 8th print, hardbk w/dj, VG 10.00
Four Seasons CB, Charlotte Adams, 1971, hardbk, 319-pg, EX ...15.00
Galloping Gourmet, Graham Kerr, 1970, hardbk, EX 10.00
Good Housekeeping Institute: Good Meals...Prepare Them, 1929, G ..10.00
Good Housekeeping: Special Diet CB, 1971, softcover, G 7.00
Great Cooks CB, James Beard, 1974, hardbk w/dj, VG 20.00
Herb & Spice Sampler CB, Avanelle Day, 1967, hardbk w/dj 6.00
Italian Desserts & Antipasto, A Catanzaro, 1958, hardbk w/dj, VG ...15.00
Jambalaya CB, Jr League of New Orleans, 1980, spiral, VG 7.00
Let's Cook It Right, Adelle Davis, 1962, hardbk w/dj, G 9.00
Menus for Entertaining, James Beard, 1965, hardbk w/dj, EX 12.00
Midnight CB, Mario Thomas, 1971, hardbk w/dj, EX 5.00
Nancy Drew CB, Carolyn Keene, 1973, EX 20.00
New York Times Large Type CB, Jean Hewitt, 1968, hardbk w/dj, VG 12.00
One-Dish CB, Robert Ackart, 1975, hardbk w/dj, VG 5.00
Pillsbury Kitchen's CB, 1979, loose-leaf paperbk, EX 10.00
Pillsbury's Bake Off Main Dish CB, 1968, G 5.00
Pillsbury's Creative Cooking in Minutes, 1971, VG 3.00
Settlement CB, Simon & Shuster, 3rd ed, 1976, hardbk, EX 10.00
Singles First Menu CB, Charlotte Adams, 1975, hardbk w/dj, G ..12.00
Two in the Kitchen, Joe & Jeanne Anderson, 1974, hardbk w/dj .10.00
Vegetarian Gourmet Cookery, Alan Hooker, 1982, softcover, EX ..8.00
World of Breads, Dolores Casella, 1966, hardbk w/dj, G 15.00
World of Nut Recipes, Morton Gill Clark, EX 8.00

Cookie Cutters

Early hand-fashioned cookie cutters have recently been commanding stiff prices at country auctions, and the ranks of interested collectors are growing steadily. Especially valuable are the figural cutters; and the more complicated the design, the higher the price. A follow-up of the carved wooden cookie boards, the first cutters were probably made by itinerant tinkers from leftover or recycled pieces of tin. Though most of the 18th-century examples are now in museums or collections, it is still possible to find some good cutters from the late 1800s when changes in the manufacture of tin resulted in a thinner, less expensive material. The width of the cutting strip is often a good indicator of age; the wider the strip, the older the cutter. While the very early cutters were 1" to 1½" deep, by the '20s and '30s, many were less than ½" deep. Crude, spotty soldering indicates an older cutter, while a thin line of solder usually tends to suggest a much later manufacture. The shape of the backplate is another clue. Later cutters will have oval, round, or rectangular backs, while on the earlier type the back was cut to follow the lines of the design. Cookie cutters usually vary from 2" to 4" in size, but gingerbread men were often made as tall as 12". Birds, fish, hearts, and tulips are common; simple versions can be purchased for as little as $12.00 to $15.00. The larger figurals, especially those with more imaginative details, often bring $75.00 and up. The cookie cutters listed here are tin and handmade unless noted otherwise.

Amish man and woman, tin (man has replaced brass handle, PA origin, $125.00 for the pair; heart, $20.00.

Photo courtesy Aston Macek Auctioneers & Appraisers

Bird, flat bk, 4¼" **25.00**
Bird in flight, crimped wings & tail, arched hdl, 3" dia **45.00**
Bird in flight, flat bk, 5½" **85.00**
Bird w/puffed breast, flat bk, 3¼" **50.00**
Boot, flat rectangular bk, 4⅞x3¼" **35.00**
Deer (stag), flat bk, 6¾" **85.00**
Deer leaping, flat bk, 4" **50.00**
Dog, flat bk, 6½" **35.00**
Dog w/wagging tail, flat bk, 4¼" **25.00**
Dutch woman, flat bk, 4¼" **25.00**
Dutchman, open bk, 5" **25.00**
Dutchman dancing, flat bk, 9½x6⅝" **100.00**
Eagle, flat bk, 4" **60.00**
Elephant, flat bk, 4⅞" **70.00**
Fish, open bk, 3¼" **25.00**
Flower w/crimped edge, arched hdl, 2⅜x1½" **30.00**
Flower w/scalloped petals, crimped leaf on stem, 4¾x3" **75.00**
Giraffe, flat bk, 5¾" **75.00**
Goat, folded rim, 5½x3¾" **200.00**
Hand (open) flat bk, 3⅝x2¼" **85.00**
Hatchet, flat bk, 5½" **85.00**
Hearts, molded edges, PA, 19th C, nesting set of 5, 2½-8" **500.00**
Horse, arched hdl, 3¾x3¼" **35.00**
Horse, trotting, crimped mane, 3¾x9¾" **70.00**
Horse (primitive), flat bk, 7" L **100.00**
Horse & rider, 6¾" **155.00**
Horse w/bobbed tail & crimped mane, flat bk, 3½x5¼" **35.00**
Lady in long dress & crimped cap, 6¾" **150.00**
Lady in long dress & sm flat-top hat, arched hdl, 4¼x1¾" **75.00**
Leaf, arched hdl, 2x2½" **22.00**
Lion, flat bk, 4¼" **65.00**
Man in the Moon, arched hdl, 2⅝x1⅞" **90.00**
Man in waist-length coat & crimped cap, 6⅛" **150.00**
Man on horsebk, sheet metal, #206 Germany, 9⅞x8" **75.00**
Man wearing hat, arms at sides, 4⅛x2⅝" **65.00**
Man wearing hat, full figure, flat bk, 7¾" **125.00**
Preacher in swallow-tail coat & hat w/brim, flat bk, 6¼x3½" **275.00**
Rooster, flat bk, 5¾" **90.00**
Rooster, folded rim on side, flat bk, 5¾x4¾" **75.00**
Rosette oval, open bk, arched hdl, 1¾x1" **70.00**
Teardrops (6) in rectangular, folded rim, no hdl, 3x3¾" **55.00**
Tulip, oval bk w/arched hdl, 2⅜x1½" **30.00**
Tulip & 3 leaves in oval w/crimped edge, arched hdl, 3½" **40.00**
Whale, flat bk, 3¾" **50.00**

Cookie Jars

The appeal of the cookie jar is universal; folks of all ages, both male and female, love to collect 'em! The early '30s' heavy stoneware jars of a rather nondescript nature quickly gave way to figurals of every type imaginable. Those from the mid to late '30s were often decorated over the glaze with 'cold paint,' but by the early '40s underglaze decorating resulted in cheerful, bright, permanent colors and cookie jars that still have a new look fifty years later.

Stimulated by the high prices commanded by desirable cookie jars, a broad spectrum of 'new' cookie jars are flooding the marketplace in three categories: 1) Manufactures have expanded their lines with exciting new designs specifically geared toward attracting the collector market. 2) Limited editions and artist-designed jars have proliferated. 3) Reproductions, signed and unsigned, have pervaded the market, creating uncertainty among new collectors and inexperienced dealers. One of the most troublesome reproductions is the Little Red Riding Hood jar marked McCoy. Several Brush jars are being reproduced, and because the old molds are being used, these are especially deceptive. In addition to these reproductions, we've also been alerted to watch for cookie jars marked Brush-McCoy made from molds that Brush never used. Remember that none of Brush's cookie jars were marked Brush-McCoy, so any bearing the compound name is fraudulent. For more information on cookie jars and reproductions, we recommend *The Collector's Encyclopedia of Cookie Jars* by Fred and Joyce Roerig; they are listed in the Directory under South Carolina. Another good source is *An Illustrated Guide to Cookie Jars* by Ermagene Westfall. Our advisors for this category are Charlie and Rose Snyder; they are listed in the Directory under Kansas.

The examples listed below were made by companies other than those found elsewhere in this book; see also specific manufacturers.

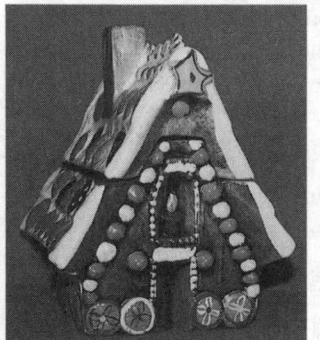

Gingerbread house, California Originals, marked 857 USA, $45.00.

Photo courtesy Ermagene Westfall

Albert Apple, Pitman-Dreitzer & Co, from $125 to	150.00
Alice in Wonderland, Japan	95.00
Balloon Lady, Pottery Guild, unmk	125.00
Barnyard Santa, Clay Art	45.00
Basketball, WH Hirsch Mfg	125.00
Bear, California Originals, #2648	45.00
Bear, Pearl China Co, bl w/hand decorated 22k gold	175.00
Beehive, WH Hirsch, 10½"	175.00
Big Bird, Newcor	45.00
Blushing Chipmunk, Terrace Ceramics, #4254	45.00
Buick Convertible, Appleman	750.00
Bull Dog Police, Japan	30.00
Cadillac, North American Ceramics, unmk	125.00
Car w/Flat Tire, Fitz & Floyd	275.00
Cat on Safe, California Originals, #2630	45.00
Charlie Brown, Benjamin & Medwin Inc	45.00
Chipmunk, Japan, #2863	30.00
Chips Ahoy, unmk, cylinder	45.00
Climbing Bear, Japan	35.00
Clown, Pan American Art	55.00
Clown Head, Enesco, E-5835	150.00
Clown on Elephant, California Originals, #896	55.00
Cocky (Dandee Rooster), DeForest of California, from $200 to	225.00
Cookie Cola, Doranne of California, #CJ67	65.00
Cookie Guard, Enesco Imports	25.00
Cookie Time Mouse, Japan	20.00
Cookieville, Treasure Craft	45.00
Corvette, North American Ceramics, #ACC J9, impressed	150.00
Cow in Overalls, American Pottery Co	75.00
Cow on Moon, yel Doranne of California, #J2	325.00
Crawling Turtle, California Originals, #2738, rabbit lid	35.00
Davy Crockett, Sierra Vista, rare, 10⅞", minimum value	1,500.00
Doctor, Doranne of California, CJ-130	225.00
Dog, California Originals, #458	35.00
Dog on Stump, California Originals, #2620	35.00

Donkey w/Sack of Oats, Doranne of California, #CJ-108	75.00
Dorothy & Toto, Treasure Craft	375.00
Duck Decoy, Treasure Craft, unmk	50.00
Elf School House, California Originals, #2643, unmk	50.00
Elsie, Pottery Guild, unmk	400.00
Ernie, California Originals, Muppets #973	85.00
Ernie, The Keebler Elf, F&F Mold & Die Works	125.00
Fat Cat, Sigma	275.00
Fish, Doranne of California, #J9	45.00
Fishing Hippo, Japan	85.00
Frog w/Bow Tie, California Originals, #2645	45.00
Glass Bowl, Santa, Treasure Craft	195.00
Gnome, Holiday Designs	40.00
Goose, Sigma, #53, paper label	60.00
Grandma's Cookies, Kromex, Frito Lays trademark	35.00
Hi Diddle Diddle, Robinson-Ransbottom, #317, gold trim	375.00
Hollow Tree, Friendship Pottery, mk Keebler Co 1981	95.00
Horse Mechanic, Japan	45.00
Humpty Dumpty, Clay Art, from $100 to	175.00
Hunting Dog, Japan	85.00
Ice Wagon, Treasure Craft	95.00
Indian, Lane, artist signed, rare, 10⅛"	950.00
Juke Box, Vandor	175.00
King, DeForest of California	950.00
King Kong, Treasure Craft	275.00
Little Girl, Pottery Guild, unmk	225.00
Mammy, Maurice Ceramics, WD 40 USA	55.00
Marsh Pig w/Apple, Marsh Ceramics, unmk	95.00
McGruff, Sigma, #239	375.00
Monkey, Treasure Craft	40.00
Mother Goose, Doranne of California, #CJ 16	125.00
Mother-in-the-Kitchen, bl, Enesco, 9½"	495.00
Mother-in-the-Kitchen, pk, Enesco, 9½"	395.00
Mushroom on Stump, California Originals, #2956	30.00
Noah's Ark, Maurice of California	375.00
Oscar the Grouch, California Originals, #972, Muppets	90.00
Paddington Bear, Toscany	525.00
Panda, Fitz & Floyd	125.00
Peasant Woman, Dept 56 Inc	125.00
Peter Porker, DeForest of California	275.00
Pillsbury Best Flour Sack, TPC, Taiwan	65.00
Pirate Bust, Treasure Craft	325.00
Poodle, Deforest of California	75.00
Popcorn Vendor, Sigma, paper label, minimum value	450.00
Rabbit w/Carrot, Doranne of California, #CJ 106	60.00
Raccoon Cookie Can, Japan, unmk	35.00
Rocking Chair Granny, Carol Gifford	275.00
Rooster, Gilner, #G-22	50.00
R2-D2, Roman Ceramics	250.00
Sailor Elephant, Treasure Craft, unmk	45.00
Sailor Monkey, Japan	20.00
Santa w/Toy Bag, Alberta's Molds, Winton Design	95.00
Sheriff Pig, Robinson-Ransbottom, #363, gold trim	275.00
Smiling Pear, Japan, #6-C-30	30.00
Smokey Bear, peppermint stick figural holder	600.00
Spaceship, NAPCO, Japan	900.00
Spice, Treasure Craft, unmk	85.00
Stagecoach, Sierra Vista	225.00
Teddy Bear, Treasure Craft	45.00
Tenderheart Bear (Care Bears), American Greetings	425.00
Train, Sierra Vista	95.00
Wind in the Willows, Sigma	225.00
Windmill, Fredericksburg Art Pottery	50.00
Winged Monkey, Treasure Craft, Wizard of Oz, 13⅝"	375.00

Wonder Woman, California Originals, #847, DC Comics, rare, 14" **1,100.00**
Yellow Cab, California Originals, unmk **275.00**

Cooper, Susie

A 20th-century ceramic designer whose works are now attracting the attention of collectors, Susie Cooper was first affiliated with the A.E. Gray Pottery in Henley, England, in 1922, where she designed in lustres and painted items with her own ideas as well. (Examples of Gray's lustreware are rare and costly.) By 1930 she and her brother-in-law, Jack Beeson, had established a family business. Her pottery soon became a success, and she was subsequently offered space at Crown Works, Burslem. In 1940 she received the honorary title of Royal Designer for Industry, the only such distinction ever awarded by the Royal Society of Arts solely for pottery design. Miss Cooper received the Order of the British Empire in the New Year's Honors List of 1979. She was the chief designer for the Wedgwood group from 1966 until she resigned in 1972. After 1980 she worked on a free-lance basis until her death in July 1995. Our advisor is J. David Ehrhard; he is listed in the Directory under California.

Photo courtesy ,. David Ehrhard

Tulip vase, #S95, $250.00; Cubist jug, #G2, $100.00; Beechwood sugar bowl (part of coffee set), #S-55, hand painted, $30.00; Jazz Age vase, hand painted, #S101, $400.00; Meat dish, #S62, $150.00.

Bowl, cream soup; Gardenias, 1960s 30.00
Bowl, Cubist, Gray's Period, 8" 400.00
Bowl, fruit; washed red bands, earthenware, 1930s, 6" 25.00
Bowl, sgraffito squirrels, 4½" 500.00
Charger, Rooster, 14" 400.00
Chocolate pot, Patricia Rose, pk rose, 7½" 100.00
Coffeepot, Nosegay, bl wash, 7¼" 125.00
Coffeepot, Sea Anemone, 7¾" 180.00
Coffeepot, yel wash w/blk lines, Kestrel shape, 7¾" 225.00
Creamer & sugar bowl, Gardenias, 1960s, w/lid 48.00
Cup & saucer, lily, gold bands, Doric shape 48.00
Cup & saucer, Wedding Ring 70.00
Dinner service, colored rings, serves 8 w/serving pcs, 62-pc 1,265.00
Egg cup, Gray Leaves w/gr wash 35.00
Gravy boat, Gardenias, 1960s 50.00
Jug, Crocus, turq, 6" 250.00
Jug, Paris, Tiger Lily 95.00
Jug, tulips emb on olive gr, 6½" 165.00
Plate, circus clown & lady, gr & blk border, Gray's Period, 10" ..300.00
Plate, Gardenias, 1960s, 8" 20.00
Plate, Pear in Pompadour, gr/blk/red/yel, 6" 40.00
Plate, Swansea Spray, gr wash band, 7" 35.00

Plate, washed red bands, earthenware, 1930s, 10" 28.00
Platter, Dresden Spray, gr-wash border, 14" L 125.00
Platter, Tiger Lily 80.00
Sauce boat, Gray Leaf w/gr wash 50.00
Teapot, Nosegay, 5" 85.00

Coors

The firm that became known as Coors Porcelain Company in 1920 was founded in 1908 by John J. Herold, originally of the Roseville Pottery in Zanesville, Ohio. Though still in business today, they are best known for their artware vases and Rosebud dinnerware produced before 1939.

Coors vases produced before the late '30s were made in a matt finish; by the latter years of the decade, high-gloss glazes were also being used. Nearly fifty shapes were in production, and some of the more common forms were made in three sizes. Typical colors in matt are white, orange, blue, green, yellow, and tan. Yellow, blue, maroon, pink, and green are found in high gloss. All vases are marked with a triangular arrangement of the words 'Coors Colorado Pottery' enclosing the word 'Golden.' You may find vases (usually 6" to 6½") marked with the Colorado State Fair stamp and dated 1939. For such a vase, add $10.00 to the suggested values given below.

For further information we recommend *Collector's Encyclopedia of Colorado Pottery, Identification and Values,* by Carol and Jim Carlton, who provide miscellaneous listings. Our Rosebud advisor is Jo Ellen Winther. All are listed in the Directory under Colorado.

Rosebud

Casserole, with lid, 9½" diameter, $100.00.

Ashtray 175.00
Baker, oval, deep, sm 25.00
Baker, 9¼" 45.00
Bowl, pudding; 7-pt 75.00
Bowls, pudding; 2-pt 35.00
Casserole, str sides, 7" 55.00
Casserole, str sides, 8" 65.00
Cookie jar, deluxe, rope hdls, w/lid 110.00
Creamer 30.00
Cup & saucer 45.00
Custard set, 6 w/wire rack 105.00
Dish, fruit/sauce 15.00
Dish, oatmeal 25.00
Dish, vegetable; deep 35.00
Egg cup 50.00
Jar, utility; w/lid 85.00
Loaf pan 40.00
Pitcher, sm, w/lid 95.00
Plate, dinner; 8" 25.00
Plate, pie 35.00
Plate, used under muffin cover, 6" 35.00

Plate, 7" 12.00
Ramekin, hdld 35.00
Refrigerator set 110.00
Shakers, kitchen, pr 45.00
Shakers, table, pr 35.00
Sugar bowl, w/lid 40.00
Teapot, 2-cup, rare 165.00

Miscellaneous

Cake knife, Hawthorne, decalcomania 75.00
Creamer, Mello-Tone or Rockmount 10.00
Mortar & pestle, cobalt 55.00
Shakers, Coorado, gr, pr 65.00
Teapot, Tulip, decalcomania 110.00
Vase, bud; yel high gloss, 8" 30.00
Vase, Golden, bl matt, integral hdls, 6" 45.00
Vase, Matchless, gr matt, emb ribs, 8" 70.00
Vase, Trinidad, wht matt w/turq int, hdls, 12" 125.00

Copper

Handcrafted copper was made in America from early in the 18th century until about 1850, with the center of its production in Pennsylvania. Examples have been found signed by such notable coppersmiths as Kidd, Buchanan, Babb, Bently, and Harbeson. Of the many utilitarian items made, teakettles are the most desirable. Early examples from the 18th century were made with a dovetailed joint which was hammered and smoothed to a uniform thickness. Pots from the 19th century were seamed. Coffeepots were made in many shapes and sizes and along with mugs, kettles, warming pans, and measures are easiest to find. Stills ranging in sizes of up to fifty-gallon are popular with collectors today. Mary Frank Gaston has compiled a lovely book, *Antique Brass and Copper*, with many full-color photos and current market values.

Apple butter kettle, forged copper, with original three-legged stand, 1870 – 80s, 13½x19¾", dents and stains, $275.00.

Coal scuttle, ped base, tin lined, lacquered, 16" H 250.00
Colander, rolled rim, appl copper mt w/hanging ring, 3x11" 70.00
Funnel, str sides w/folded rim, long brass spout, 12x6½" 30.00
Kettle, hammered, flared rim, wrought copper hdls, 6½x14" 125.00
Kettle, stewing; 5½x8" 150.00
Lantern, porch; cage style, Victorian, 22" 175.00
Loving cup, 2-hdld, 13" 160.00
Pitcher, str sides, rolled rim, lg rnd spout, ribbon hdl, 9" 50.00
Rum warmer, rolled rim, copper hdl w/heart-like attachment, 11" ..95.00
Snuff case, w/brass & silver, 3½x3", w/2" shovel 400.00
Teakettle, brass hdl & finial, 11", EX 100.00
Teakettle, dvtl, swivel hdl stamped 5, soldered rpr, 7½" 85.00

Teakettle, sturdy type, swivel hdl stamped 1840, 8¼" 195.00

Copper Lustre

Copper lustre is a term referring to a type of pottery made in Staffordshire after the turn of the 19th century. It is finished in a metallic rusty-brown glaze resembling true copper. Pitchers are found in abundance, ranging from simple styles with dull bands of color to those with fancy handles and bands of embossed, polychromed flowers. Bowls are common; goblets, mugs, teapots, and sugar bowls much less so. It's easy to find, but not in good condition. Pieces with hand-painted decoration and those with historical transfers are the most valuable.

Figurine, dog, EX molded features, lt wear, 7½" 450.00
Pepper pot, yel band at waist, dome dop w/flat finial, 4½", EX 75.00
Pitcher, classical scenes, Am eagle at spout, 5½", EX 175.00
Pitcher, deer relief & scrolls, 5⅝" 275.00
Pitcher, floral relief sides, mc decor, 4" 75.00
Tumbler, floral decor on wide brn band, 2¾x3" 45.00
Vase, shepherdess w/sheep (purple transfer), hdls, 7" 225.00

Coralene Glass

Coralene is a unique type of art glass easily recognized by the tiny grains of glass that form its decoration. Lacy allover patterns of seaweed, geometrics, and florals were used, as well as solid forms such as fish, plants, and single blossoms. (Seaweed is most commonly found and not as valuable as the other types of decoration.) It was made by several glasshouses both here and abroad. Values are based to a considerable extent on the amount of beading that remains. Our advisors for this category are Betty and Clarence Maier; they are listed in the Directory under Pennsylvania.

Vase, peachblow with yellow seaweed, ruffled rim, white cased, Mt. Washington, 7¼", $550.00.

Photo courtesy
John A. Shumann III

Box, custard w/scattered roses, ormolu hdls/ball ft, 5x5" 425.00
Cracker jar, rose Dmn Quilt w/yel seaweed, silver mts, 7" 800.00
Creamer, tomato red w/gr & clear casing, coralene floral, 4" 150.00
Ewer, bl Herringbone w/yel seaweed, ruffled, camphor hdl, 8" ...300.00
Pitcher, peppermint striped w/yel branches, amber hdl, 6½" 495.00
Rose bowl, pk Snowflake MOP w/yel wheat, 3-ftd, 3¾x5" 695.00
Tumbler, peachblow w/yel seaweed, 3¾" 325.00
Vase, bl Dmn Quilt w/pk flowers & gr leaves, 6¾" 225.00
Vase, peachblow satin, bulbous w/long can neck, 4-lobe rim, 8" ..475.00
Vase, pk Dmn Quilt w/yel fleur-de-lis, 8" 325.00
Vase, pk Herringbone MOP w/allover yel overlapped leaves, 9" ..400.00
Vase, pk w/allover rows of yel swags, shouldered w/can neck, 7" ..395.00

Vase, wht w/yel seaweed, pk crimped ruffle w/camphor edge, 8" ..**140.00**

Cordey

The Cordey China Company was founded in 1942 in Trenton, New Jersey, by Boleslaw Cybis. The operation was small with less than a dozen workers. They produced figurines, vases, lamps, and similar wares, much of which was marketed through gift shops both nationwide and abroad. Though the earlier wares were made of plaster, Cybis soon developed his own formula for a porcelain composition which he called 'Papka.' Cordey figurines and busts were characterized by old-world charm, Rococo scrolls, delicate floral appliques, ruffles, and real lace which was dipped in liquefied clay to add dimension to the work.

Although on rare occasions some items were not numbered or signed, the 'basic' figure was cast both with numbers and the Cordey signature. The molded pieces were then individually decorated and each marked with its own impressed identification number as well as a mark to indicate the artist-decorator. Their numbering system began with 200 and in later years progressed into the 8000s. As can best be established, Cordey continued production until sometime in the mid-1950s. Boleslaw Cybis died in 1957, his wife in 1958. Our advisor for this category is Sharon A. Payne; she is listed in the Directory under Washington.

Key: ff — full figure

#155, lamp, little girl figure **95.00**
#300/#301, man & lady, 16", pr, from $175 to **250.00**
#302/#303, man & lady, burgundy/peach, 16¼", pr, from $175 to ...**250.00**
#303, man, plumed hat, ff, 16" **150.00**
#304/#305, Grape Harvesters, 15", pr, from $175 to **225.00**
#324R, mallard, 1940s, 14" **200.00**
#325, Chinese wood duck, intricate base, EX colors, rare **350.00**
#343, pheasant, vibrant mc, very early, scarce, 17" **325.00**
#504, lady, gray & bl dress, w/basket of grapes, 16" **150.00**
#624, cup & saucer, appl pk roses, leaves on cup **55.00**
#852, wall decoration, nosegay, experimental **110.00**
#909, clock, bird on roses at top, scrolled, 14½", EX **155.00**
#1027, centerpiece planter, swan, lg **200.00**
#2244?, lamp, appl roses, brass base, no shade **60.00**
#3158, lady, gold headband, much lace, 13½" **125.00**
#4004, lamp, bust on metal fr, orig shade, pr **180.00**
#4039, man w/curls & lace, ff, 7½" **75.00**
#4524-25A, lamp, Cupid, bl wings, roses, rare **175.00**
#5002, bust, lady, long curls, 5" **60.00**
#5011, bust, lady w/wide lace collar, 6" **60.00**
#5012, lady **75.00**
#5014, bust, lady **60.00**
#5020, bust, man w/long curls, lace cravat, 6" **60.00**
#5026, bust, lady in open-lace mantilla, Jr Miss Group, 6" **60.00**
#5027, bust, lady w/bow on hat, rose on dress, 7½", NM **60.00**
#5028, bust, lady w/blond curls emerging from pk hat, 6" **90.00**
#5029, lady, Elizabeth, high collar, Raleigh Group, 7½" **85.00**
#5030, bust, Junior Miss series, lg hat, lace shawl **75.00**
#5041, man, ff, gray coat, rose & pk trim, 11½" **125.00**
#5042, man, pk knee britches, powdered wig, 11½" **125.00**
#5045, Neopolitan Boy, w/basket of breadsticks, 9½" **95.00**
#5047, Yorkshire Girl, ff, grapes in dress folds, 10" **95.00**
#5047/#5048, man & lady, 10", pr, NM **200.00**
#5070, lady **100.00**
#5080, lady **100.00**
#5082A, lady w/roses, lace ruffle at hem, 10½", NM **125.00**
#5089, lady, ringlets, lace, lg bustle, 10¾" **125.00**
#6000, box, appl roses on lid, gold trim, 5x7" dia **65.00**

#6004, bluebird on stump, lg **110.00**
#6029, box, appl roses on lid, 5x7x5½" **65.00**

#6037, covered box with applied roses and cherubs, 6x7x10", $225.00.

#6038, box, appl roses, ftd, 3½x5" sq **55.00**
#6046, ashtray **22.00**
#6405, lady, flower-trimmed hat, pk & gray dress, 10½" **110.00**
#7004, tray (or shallow bowl), 13x9" **100.00**
#7028, wall shelf, nude encircling cornucopia bottom, 8x6½" ...**100.00**
#7032, candlesticks, pk roses, 7½", pr **125.00**
#7033, vase, wide mouth, 9" **60.00**
#7094, vase, Orientals in relief, appl flowers, 9x8" **165.00**
#8001/219, box, roses appl to lid, 3¾x3¼" **45.00**
#8002, pin/ashtray, 4" sq **30.00**
#8016, bowl, 3 appl roses, rtcl, gold trim, 5½x5" **45.00**
#8024, pin tray, 7" **25.00**
#8061A, poodle lamp base, pk, 7x10½x5"+base **200.00**

Corkscrews

The history of the corkscrew dates back to the mid-1600s, when wine makers concluded that the best-aged wine was that stored in smaller containers, either stoneware or glass. Since plugs left unsealed were often damaged by rodents, corks were cut off flush with the bottle top and sealed with wax or a metal cover. Removing the cork cleanly with none left to grasp became a problem. The task was found to be relatively simple using the worm on the end of a flintlock gun rod. So the corkscrew evolved. Endless patents have been issued for mechanized models. Handles range from carved wood, ivory, and bone to porcelain and repousse silver. Exotic materials such as agate, mother-of-pearl, and gold plate were also used on occasion. Celluloid lady's legs are popular.

In the following descriptions, values are for examples in excellent condition, unless noted otherwise. Our advisor for this category is Roger Baker; he is listed in the Directory under California.

Abyssinian type w/threaded tube, dbl hdls **78.00**
Carter's Ink, folding, Pat 1894 ....**12.50**
England, champagne tap, screw-in cork, hdls make faucets, ca 1890s .**60.00**
England, ebonized wood hdl, thick disc, 1880s, EX **25.00**
England, Farrow & Jackson LTD..., sq shaft, wire helix, 1885 ......**85.00**
England, polished steel peg & worm, ca 1810, 4½" **130.00**
England, steel w/gold finish, cube-shaped ends, 3" **130.00**
England, 4-finger pull, w/button, ca 1895 ....**27.50**
France, wood dbl hdl, cvd portrait in rnd fr, NM **40.00**
France, wood hdl, metal ends, dimpled shaft, ca 1875, EX **30.00**
Germany, Hercules, wood hdl **40.00**
Germany, spring over shaft, ca 1895, VG **22.50**
Germany, spring-release helix worm, steel cage, 1880s **45.00**

Happy Face, ca 1935, 10" 75.00
Italy, bar man figural, dbl-lever style, 10½" 55.00
Italy, swivel-collar type, NP brass, VG 25.00
Italy, swivel-over collar type, NP brass, VG 25.00
John Watts Sheffield England, NP w/center worm, ca 1909 ....37.50
London Rock, rack & pinion actions, unmk English, 1800s 150.00
Magic Lever Cork Drawer, Pat Appl For, ca 1925, VG 45.00
Old Snifter, Senator Volstead, brass, fixed hat, w/opener 200.00
Perpetual, dbl-threaded shaft, automatic reverse, unmk 75.00
Rosewood hdl, gilted shaft & worm, modern 12.00
Staghorn hdl, mk sterling cap, 7½" 85.00
US, brass band & boar's tooth hdl, 6", EX 85.00
US, H&B Mfg Co, rosewood hdl, w/brush & ivory plug, 1880s 58.00
US, Hollwig 1891 Pat, Pabst Milwaukee advertising, EX 130.00
US, Roundlet, bullet shape, EX 58.00
US, Williamson 1897 Pat Bullet, copper finish, early 80.00
US Clough 1910 Pat, Hennessy advertising on wood sleeve 42.00
Weir's Pat 12804 25, Sept 1884, VG bronze finish 125.00

Cosmos

Cosmos, sometimes called Stemless Daisy, is a patterned glass tableware produced from 1894 through 1915 by Consolidated Lamp and Glass Company. Relief-molded flowers on a finely crosscut background were painted in soft colors of pink, blue, and yellow. Though nearly all were made of milk glass, a few items may be found in clear glass with the designs painted on. In addition to the tableware, lamps were also made.

Butter dish, 6x8", $275.00.

Bottle, cologne; orig stopper, rare 300.00
Creamer 150.00
Lamp, banquet, kerosene, 24" 575.00
Lamp, banquet, slender base, rnd globe, all orig, 16" 525.00
Lamp, mini, 7½", EX 275.00
Lamp, parlour; half-shade on matching base, 8" 375.00
Lamp, 10" 450.00
Pickle castor, mk SP fr 500.00
Pitcher, milk; 5" 250.00
Pitcher, syrup; 6" 300.00
Pitcher, water 350.00
Shakers, tall, orig lids, pr 175.00
Spooner 125.00
Sugar bowl, open 150.00
Sugar bowl, w/lid 185.00
Sugar shaker 400.00
Tumbler, 3¾" 75.00

Cottageware

You'll find a varied assortment of novelty dinnerware items, all styled as cozy little English cottages or huts with cone-shaped roofs;

some may have a waterwheel or a windmill. Marks will vary. English-made Price Brothers or Beswick pieces are valued in the same range as those marked Occupied Japan, while items marked simply Japan are considerably less pricey. Our advisor for this category is Grace Klender; she is listed in the Directory under Ohio. All of the following examples are English unless noted otherwise.

Mugs, Price Brothers, 3⅞", $50.00 each;
Water pitcher, Price Brothers, 8", $150.00.

Bank, dbl slot, Price Bros, 4½x3½x5" 85.00
Bell, Price Bros, minimum value 150.00
Biscuit jar, wicker hdl, Maruhon Ware, Occupied Japan, 6½" 65.00
Bowl, salad; Price Bros 65.00
Butter dish, oval, Burlington Ware, 6" 55.00
Butter dish, Price Bros 60.00
Butter pat, emb cottage, rectangular, Occupied Japan 18.00
Chocolate pot, Price Bros 135.00
Condiment set, mustard, 2½" s&p, on 5" hdld leaf tray 75.00
Condiment set, mustard pot, s&p, row arrangement, 6" 45.00
Condiment set, mustard pot, s&p, tray, row arrangement, 7¾" 45.00
Condiment set, 3-part cottage on shaped tray w/appl bush, 4½" ..75.00
Cookie jar, pk/brn/gr, sq, Japan, 8½x5½" 65.00
Cookie jar/canister, cylindrical, Price Bros 125.00
Cookie or biscuit jar, Occupied Japan 85.00
Creamer, windmill, Occupied Japan, 2⅝" 25.00
Creamer & sugar bowl, Price Bros, 2½", 4½" 45.00
Cup & saucer, chocolate; str-sided cup: 3½x2¾", saucer 5½" 40.00
Cup & saucer, Price Bros, 2½", 4½" 45.00
Demitasse pot, Price Bros 100.00
Dish w/cover, Occupied Japan, sm 35.00
Egg cup set, 4 on 6" sq tray, Price Bros 60.00
Grease jar, Occupied Japan, from $25 to 35.00
Marmalade, Price Bros 40.00
Pin tray, Price Bros, 4" dia 20.00
Pitcher, tankard, rnd, 7⅞" 125.00
Platter, oval, 11¾x7½" 55.00
Sugar box, for cubes, Price Bros, 5¾" L 45.00
Tea set, Japan, child's, serves 4, Japan 150.00
Teapot, Keele Street, +cr/sug 95.00
Teapot, Occupied Japan, 6½" 50.00
Teapot, Price Bros, 6¼" 70.00
Toast rack, 3-slot, Price Bros, 3½" 65.00
Toast rack, 4-slot, 5½" 75.00
Tumbler, Occupied Japan, 3½", set of 6 ....60.00

Coverlets

The Jacquard attachment for hand looms represented a culmination of weaving developments made in France. Introduced to America by the early 1820s, it gave professional weavers the ability to easily create complex patterns with curved lines. Those who could afford the new loom adaptation could now use hole-punched pasteboard cards to weave floral patterns that before could only be achieved with intense labor on a draw-loom.

Before the Jacquard mechanism, most weavers made their coverlets in geometric patterns. Use of indigo-blue and brightly colored wools often livened the twills and overshot patterns available to the small-loom home weaver. Those who had larger multiple-harness looms could produce warm double-woven, twill-block, or summer-and-winter designs.

While the new floral and pictorial patterns had displaced the geometrics in urban areas, the mid-Atlantic, and the Midwest by the 1840s, even factory production of the Jacquard coverlets was disrupted by cotton and wool shortages during the Civil War. A revived production in the 1870s saw a style change to a center-medallion motif, but a new fad for white 'Marseilles' spreads soon halted sales of Jacquard-woven coverlets. Production of Jacquard carpets continued to the turn of the century.

Rural and frontier weavers continued to make geometric-design coverlets through the 19th century, and local craft revivals have continued the tradition through this century. All-cotton overshots were factory produced in Kentucky from the 1940s, and factories and professional weavers made cotton-and-wool overshots during the past decade. Many Jacquard-woven coverlets have dates and names of places and people (often the intended owner — not the weaver) woven into corners or borders. In the listings that follow, examples are blue and white unless noted otherwise. When dates are included, they appear on the coverlet itself as part of the woven design.

Key: mdl — medallion

Jacquard

Capital WA border/bldgs, dove corners, 4-color, 80x82" 500.00
Christian/Heathen border, peacocks, 75x80", EX 550.00
Floral, geometric borders, 3-color, sgn/1858, 78x80", VG 900.00

Floral and star design with trees and birds, natural, dark blue, red, and green, signed and dated 1835, two-piece, 96x82", EX, $875.00.

Floral, star center, single weave, 1-pc, 66x78", VG 275.00
Floral, vintage borders, red/bl/wht, 2-pc, single weave, 68x85" ...440.00
Floral mdls, bird corners, 1847, 2-pc, 76x79" 600.00
Floral mdls, bl/red/gr/wht, 1-pc, worn/holes, 78x90" 185.00
Floral mdls, building borders, 4-color, 1845, 74x99" 1,300.00
Floral mdls, lion border, 2-pc, dbl weave, 86x92" 1,950.00
Floral mdls, red/natural, 2-pc, dbl weave, 72x86" 440.00
Floral mdls, 4-color, 1-pc, Probst & Seip 1847, 76x90" 500.00
Floral mdls, 4-color, 1-pc, single weave, 84x96", G 385.00

Floral mdls/church/etc, OH, 1842, 73x84" 465.00
Floral/stars/leaves/dmn band, 3-color, 2-part, PA, sgn/1841 ....500.00
Geometric floral, rose border, 4-color, 2-pc, 1848, 62x86, VG ..470.00
Lover's Knot variant, pine-tree border, navy/rust, 84x74" 500.00
Peacock & young, Christian/heathen border, 1846, 68x84" 385.00
Rose & star mdls, bird borders, 1844, red/wht, 81x88" 825.00
Rose & star mdls, 4-color, OH, 1858, 2-pc, 65x81" 385.00
Rose mdls & birds, 4-color, single weave, 1842, 70x85", EX 770.00
Rose mdls & stars, 3-color, single weave, 1859, 86x87", NM ..1,300.00
Rose mdls/flowerpots/eagles, bl/red/wht, 2-pc, 72x82" 500.00
Rough & Ready 1847 in corners, dbl weave, 2-pc, 75x82" 4,950.00
Stars/floral mdl/birds, bl/red, 2-pc, dbl weave, 88x71" 500.00

Overshot

Bow ties & dmns, 4-color, 2-pc, lt wear, 93x66" 245.00
Optical pattern, 2-color, 2-pc, 94x76" 250.00
Optical pattern, 3-color, worn, 78x84" 175.00
Optical pattern, 3-color, 2-pc, minor wear, 96x80" 215.00
Twill weave, 3-color, 2-pc, minor wear, 88x81" 155.00

Cowan

Guy Cowan opened a small pottery near Cleveland, Ohio, ca 1909, where he made tile and artware on a small scale from the natural red clay available there. He developed distinctive glazes — necessary, he felt, to cover the dark red body. After the war and a temporary halt in production, Cowan moved his pottery to Rocky River, where he made a commercial line of artware utilizing a highly-fired white porcelain. Although he acquiesced to the necessity of mass-production, every effort was made to insure a product of highest quality. Fine artists, among them Waylande Gregory, Thelma Frazier, and Viktor Schreckengost, designed pieces which were often produced in limited editions, some of which sell today for prices in the thousands. Most of the ware was marked 'Cowan,' except for the 1930 mass-produced line called 'Lakeware.' Falling under the crunch of the Great Depression, the pottery closed in 1931.

The use of an asterisk (*) in the listings below indicates a nonfactory name that is being provided as a suggested name for the convenience of present-day collectors. One example is the glaze *Original Ivory, which is a high-gloss white that resembles undecorated porcelain. It was used on many of Cowan's lady 'flower figures' (Cowan's more graceful term for what some collectors call frogs).

Our advisor for this category is Mark Bassett; he is listed in the Directory under Ohio. With Victoria Naumann, Mark is the author of *Cowan Pottery and the Cleveland School*, a detailed history of Cowan Pottery and of Guy Cowan's students, colleagues, and designers. Prices quoted are for examples in mint condition, unless noted otherwise.

Key: Sp/I — Special Ivory

Bookends, #519, Boy & Girl, Sp/I, Wilcox, 6x4x3½" 350.00
Bookends, #840, elephant (angular), Caramel, Postgate, pr 500.00
Bowl, #729, Pterodactyl, April Green & Sp/I, Blazys, 5½x14½" ..125.00
Bowl, #733-B, turq & Sp/I, 9¼" 75.00
Candlesticks, triple candelabra, Sp/I, #773, 5½x11", pr 200.00
Charger, sea scene, MOP, Frazier, #X-4, 11" 500.00
Comport, #C-1, caramel, tulip shape 30.00
Comport, #809, Sp/I, 3½x6¼" 35.00
Console bowl (B4) w/flamingo (#D-2D), Oriental Red, Gregory ..750.00
Decanter, #X12/X13, King/Queen, Oriental Red, Gregory, 12", pr .1,100.00
Decanter/bookend, King (seated), Sp/I, Gregory, 10x5" 450.00
Flower frog, #F-7, swan, Sp/I, Gregory, 12x6" 1,300.00

Flower frog, #F-9, Pan (on toadstool), Sp/I, Gregory, 10", NM ..**1,300.00**
Flower frog, #680, Heavenward, *Orig Ivory, RGC, 8x4" **425.00**
Flower frog, #687, Loveliness, Sp/I, RGC, 12x5¾" **800.00**
Flower frog, #709, Grace, *Orig Ivory, RGC, unmk, 6½" **500.00**
Flower frog, #720, Swirl Dancer, *Orig Ivory, RGC, 10½" **1,300.00**
Flower frog, #721, Laurel, *Orig Ivory, RGC, 10" **850.00**
Flower frog, #764, Pavlova candelabra, Sp/I, RCG, 9x10½" **750.00**
Flower frog, #805, Tambourine Dancer, Sp/I, Gregory, 10" **2,500.00**
Flower frog, #929, Wildwood Stag, Sp/I, Gregory, rstr, 14" **1,100.00**
Humidor, #X-7, ribbed, Azure, Frazier, 6" **250.00**
Lamp, #L-17, squirrel & flamingo, Shad White, Gregory, 9" **350.00**
Lamp, based on #V-32, maple leaves, Plum, Gregory, 12" **350.00**
Lamp, based on #V-32, maple leaves, Shad White, Gregory, 12" ..**250.00**
Paperweight, #D-3, elephant, Sp/I, Postgate, 3¾x2½" **300.00**
Sculpture, #686, Scarf Dancer, *Orig Ivory, RGC, 7¼" **300.00**

Sculptures: Introspection, by A. Drexler Jacobson, black matt, impressed mark, $2,100.00; Giulia, by A. Drexler Jacobson, black matt, 10", $3,500.00.

Sculpture, Antinea, head on fluted base, blk, Jacobson, 14" ...**5,000.00**
Sculpture, Chinese horse, foliage, RH Cowan, 9½" **1,700.00**
Sculpture, Congo Head, blk/bronze, Gregory, 1931, rstr, 15" ...**3,750.00**
Sculpture, Pierette, ballerina, Primrose, Andersen, 8" **650.00**
Sculpture, Russians, 3 musicians/dancer, Parchment, Plazys **5,250.00**
Vase, #V-4, wide vertical ribs, leaf decor base, Foliage, 10¾" **300.00**
Vase, #V-43, horizontally ribbed, flared lip, Azure, 12" **400.00**
Vase, #V-90, oval, Egypt Blue, blk lid, RGC, 13" **500.00**
Vase, #V-99, globular, scroll hdls, Terra Cotta, Schrekengost, 6" **400.00**
Vase, #508, *Gunmetal over Marigold flambe (great glaze), 7½" ...**400.00**
Vase, #550, Larkspur, 4" **50.00**
Vase, #560, *Gunmetal over Sea Green flambe, 12¾" **600.00**
Vase, #595, bulbous, flared lip, Delphinium, 7½" **125.00**
Vase, #648, Apple Blossom Pink, 5¼" **80.00**
Vase, #756, bottle shape, Egypt Blue, 14" **350.00**
Vase, pillow shape, emb flowers in oval reserve, Larkspur, 8x8" .**400.00**

Cracker Jack

Kids have been buying Cracker Jack since it was first introduced in the 1890s. By 1912 it was packaged with a free toy inside. Before the first kernel was crunched, eager fingers had retrieved the surprise from the depth of the box — actually no easy task, considering the care required to keep the contents so swiftly displaced from spilling over the side! Though a little older, perhaps, many of those same kids still are looking — just as eagerly — for the Cracker Jack prizes. Point of sale, company collectibles, and the prizes as well have over the years reflected America's changing culture. Grocer sales and incentives from around the turn of the century — paper dolls, postcards, and song books —

were often marked Rueckheim Brothers (the inventors of Cracker Jack) or Reliable Confections. Over the years the company made some changes, leaving a trail of clues that often help collectors date their items. The company's name changed in 1922 from Rueckheim Brothers & Eckstein (who had been made a partner for inventing a method for keeping the caramelized kernels from sticking together) to The Cracker Jack Company. Their Brooklyn office was open from 1914 until it closed in 1923 The first time the sailor Jack logo was used on their packaging was in 1919. The sailor image of a Rueckheim child (with red, white, and blue colors) was introduced by these German immigrants in an attempt to show support for the U.S.A. during the time of heightened patriotism after WW I. For packages and 'point of sale' dating, note that the word 'prize' was used from 1912 to 1925, 'novelty' from 1925 to 1932, and 'toy' from 1933 on.

The first loose-packed prizes were toys made of wood, clay, tin, metal, and lithographed paper (the reason some early prizes are stained). Plastic toys were introduced in 1946. Paper wrapped for safety purposes in 1948, subjects echo the 'hype' of the day — yo-yos, tops, whistles, and sports cards in the simple, peaceful days of our country, propaganda and war toys in the '40s, games in the '50s, and space toys in the '60s. Few of the estimated 15 billion prizes were marked. Advertising items from Angelus Marshmallow and Checkers Confections (cousins of the Cracker Jack family) are also collectible. When no condition is indicated, the items listed below are assumed to be in excellent to mint condition. 'CJ' indicates that the item is marked. Note: An often-asked question concerns the tin Toonerville Trolley called 'CJ.' No data has been found in the factory archives to authenticate this item; it is assumed that the 'CJ' merely refers to its small size. For further information see *Cracker Jack Toys, The Complete, Unofficial Guide for Collectors*, by Larry White. Our advisor for this category is Wes Johnson; he is listed in the Directory under Kentucky. Also look for *The Prize Insider* newsletter listed in the Directory under Clubs, Newsletters, and Catalogs.

Dealer Incentives and Premiums

Badge, pin-bk, celluloid, lady w/CJ label reverse, 1905, 1¼" **65.00**
Blotter, CJ question mk box, yel, 7¾x3¾" **185.00**
Book, pocket; jester on cover, CJ Riddles **65.00**
Book, pocket; riddle/sailor boy/dog on cover, RWB, CJ, 1919 ......**55.00**
Book, Uncle Sam Song Book, CJ, 1911, ea **55.00**
Cart w/2 movable wheels, wood dowel tongue, CJ **75.00**
Corkscrew/opener, metal plated, CJ/Angelus, 3" **85.00**
Golf tee set, wood tees in paper 'matchbook' folder, CJ, 1920s ...**725.00**
Harmonica, full scale, emb CJ, early, 5⅛" **365.00**
Jigsaw puzzle, CJ or Checkers, 1 of 4, 7x10", in envelope **35.00**
Mask, Halloween; paper, CJ, series, 10" or 12", ea **28.00**
Match holder, hinged, eng gold-tone case, CJ, 2½x1⅞" **650.00**
Mirror, oval, Angelus (redhead or blond) on box **89.00**
Pen, ink; w/nib, tin litho bbl, CJ **485.00**
Pencil top clip, metal/celluloid, oval boy & dog logo **220.00**
Pencil top clip, metal/celluloid, tube shape w/package **220.00**
Puzzle, metal, CJ/Angelus, 1 of 15, '34, in envelope, ea **14.00**
Riddle card, 2 series of 20, w/package/from factory, CJ, '07, ea **8.00**
Tablet, school; CJ, 1929, 8x10" **195.00**
Truck, steel, wood wheels for CJ package, unmk **85.00**
Wings, air corps type, silver or blk, stud-bk, CJ, '30s, 3", ea **85.00**

Packaging

Box, popcorn; Question Mark box end for CJ 'Toy,' 1923-27 .....**110.00**
Box, popcorn; red scroll border, CJ 'Prize,' 1912-25, ea **115.00**
Box, popcorn; store display, CJ 'Novelty,' 1925-32, ea **90.00**
Canister, tin, CJ Coconut Corn Crisp, 1-lb **55.00**
Canister, tin, CJ Coconut Corn Crisp, 10-oz **65.00**

CJ Commemorative canister, mc scene, 1990s, ea 9.00
Crate, shipping; wood, CJ, Rueckheim Bros Eck, 1902-22, lg 165.00

Prizes, Cast Metal

Badge, 6-point star, mk CJ Police, silver, 1931, 1¼" 55.00
Button, stud bk, Me for Cracker Jack, boy & dog, oval 55.00
Button, stud bk, Xd bats & ball, CJ pitcher/etc series, 1928 ....130.00
Coins, Presidents, 31 series, CJ, 1933, ea 9.00
Dollhouse items: lantern, mug, candlestick, etc; no mk, ea 6.50
Horse & wagon, CJ, 3-D, silver or gold, early, 2½", ea 250.00
Ring, alphabet letter setting (series), unmk, ea 4.00
Rocking horse, no rider, 3-D, inked, early, 1⅛" 25.00
Rocking horse w/boy, 3-D, inked, early, 1½" 32.00
Tootsietoy series: boats, cars, animals; '31, ¾"-1½", ea 7.00

Prizes, Paper

Book, Animals (or Birds), to color, Makatoy, unmk, 1949, mini ..35.00
Book, Bess & Bill on CJ Hill, series of 12, 1937, mini 105.00
Book, Birds We Know, CJ, 1928, mini 105.00
Book, drawing w/tracing paper, CJ, 1920s, mini 110.00
Book, Twigg & Sprigg, CJ, 1930, mini 105.00
Booklet, stickers/wisecracks/riddles, Borden, CJ, 1965 on 3.00
Disguise, ears, red (out of carrier), unmk, 1950, pr 30.00
Disguise, ears, red (still in carrier), CJ, 1950, pr 65.00
Disguise, glasses, hinged, cello lenses, CJ Where Ever..., '33 ....125.00
Disguise, mustache, blk/brn, in carrier, CJ, 1949 ....55.00
Fan, lady's, folding, mc, unmk 45.00
Fortune Teller, boy/dog on film in envelope, CJ, '20s, 1¾x2½" 80.00
Game, Midget Auto Race, wheel spins, CJ, 1949, 3⅜" H 45.00
Game spinner, ...baseball at home, rectangle, CJ, 2¾" W 125.00
Game spinner, ...baseball at home, unmk, 1946, 1½" dia 60.00
Hat, Indian headdress, CJ, 1931, 2½" H 125.00
Hat, Indian headdress, CJ, 1950s, 5⅜" H 275.00
Hat, Me for CJ, early, ea 120.00
Magic game book, erasable slate, CJ, series of 13, 1946, ea 25.00
Movie, boy at blkboard, turn wheel: draws/erases, CJ, '31, 2" 175.00
Movie, Goofy Zoo, turn wheel(s): change animals, unmk, 1939 ...25.00
Movie, pull tab for 2nd picture, yel, early, 3", in envelope 125.00
Sand toy pictures, pours for action, series of 14, 1967, ea 25.00
Top, golf game, wood stick center, CJ, 1933 ....57.00
Transfer, iron-on, sport figure or patriotic, CJ, 1939, ea 22.00
Transfer, iron-on, sport figure or patriotic, unmk, 1939, ea 6.00
Whistle, Blow for More, CJ box/boy/dog, yel, 1931, ea 55.00
Whistle, pressed paper, series of 10, 1948-49, CJ, 1¼x2", ea 34.00
Whistle, Razz Zooka, C Carey Cloud design, CJ, 1949 ....32.00

Prizes, Plastic

Animals, standup, letter on bk, series of 26, Nosco, 1953, ea 4.00
Animals, standup on base, assorted, Nosco or CJ, 1947 on, ea 2.00
Baseball players, 3-D, bl or gray team, 1948, 1½", ea 8.00
Disc, emb comic character, series of 12, 1954, unmk, 1½" 16.00
Disc, emb fish plaque, oval, series of 10, 1956, unmk, ea 14.00
Dog, 3-D, hollow base, series of 10, CJCO, 1954, ea 6.00
Figure, circus; stands on base, 1 of 12, Nosco, 1951-54 ....2.50
Figure on rocking base, semi-flat, 1 of 9, Cloud design, '56 ....4.00
Fob, alphabet letter w/loop on top, 1 of 26, 1954, 1½" 4.00
Magnifying glass, many designs/shapes, from 1961, ea 1.00
Palm puzzle, ball(s) roll into holes, dome or rnd, from 1966 ....6.00
Palm puzzle, ball(s) roll into holes, rectangle, CJ, 1920s, ea 55.00
Palm puzzle, ball(s) roll into holes, sq, CJ, 1920s, ea 45.00
Pinball game, lever shoots ball/score in holes, 1964 to recent 5.00

Ships in a bottle, 6 different, unmk, 1960, ea 6.00
Signs, road; Stop, Caution, etc, yel, series of 10, 1954-60, ea 5.00
Spinner, tops varied colors, 10 designs, from 1948, ea 2.50
Toys, take apart/assemble, variety, from '62, assembled, ea 2.00
Toys, take apart/assemble, variety, from '62, unassembled, ea 5.00
Whistle, tube w/animals on top, CJ, series, 1950-53, 1⅜" 7.00

Prizes, Tin

Badge, boy & dog diecut, complete w/bend-over tab, CJ 150.00
Badge, boy & dog diecut, w/o tab at top, CJ 95.00
Badge, emb/plated CJ officer, 2⅜" or 1⅝", early, ea 110.00
Badge, litho, red/wht/bl, boy/dog, CJ, 1920s, 1¼" dia 150.00
Bank, 3-D book form, red/gr or blk, CJ Bank, early, 2" 120.00
Bookmark, dogs, 4 different, 1941, 3", ea 34.00
Brooch or pin, various designs on card, CJ/logo, early, ea 125.00
Cash register, litho, More You Eat, CJ, early, 1⅞" 275.00
Clicker, 'Noisy CJ Snapper,' pear shape, aluminum, 1949 ....34.00
Clicker, CJ Telegraph, Pat 1897, inked, 1¾" dia, ea 145.00
Doll dishes, tin plated, CJ, '31, 1¾", 1⅞", & 2⅛" dia, ea 35.00
Fortune Wheel, 2-pc litho, CJ, 1939-41, 1¾" 105.00
Helicopter, yel propeller, wood stick, unmk, 1937, 2⅝" 27.00
Horse & wagon, litho diecut, CJ & Angelus, 2⅛" 65.00
Horse & wagon, litho diecut, gray/red mks, CJ, 1914-23, 3⅛" 395.00
Model T Ford, License: NY 1915 #999, blk/wht, CJ, rare, 2" 410.00
Pocket watch, silver of gold, CJ as numerals, 1931, 1½" 55.00
Sled, tin plated, CJ, 1931, 2" L 35.00
Small box shape: Elect Alarm Clock, litho, unmk, 1⅛" 75.00
Small box shape: electric stove litho, unmk, 1⅛" 80.00
Small box shape: garage litho, unmk, 1⅛" 75.00
Small box shape: radio litho, bl, unmk, 1⅛" 80.00
Soldier, litho, die-cut standup, officer/private/etc, unmk, ea 17.00
Spinner, wood stick, Always on Top, red/wht/bl, CJ, 1½" dia 25.00
Spinner, wood stick, Fortune Teller Game, red/wht/bl, CJ, 1½" ...90.00
Spinner, wood stick, Question Mark Box at center, CJ 50.00
Spinner, wood stick, 2 Toppers, red/wht/bl, Angelus/Jack, 1½" 85.00
Stand up, comic character, 1 of 10, CJ, 1936-46, ea 105.00
Stand up, oval Am Flag, series of 4, unmk, 1936-45, ea 35.00
Stand up, rectangle litho, boy & dog, ca 1916, lg or sm, ea 155.00
Tall box shape: Frozen Foods locker freezer, '47, unmk, 1¾" 75.00
Tall box shape: grandfather clock, unmk, 1947, 1¾" 65.00
Tall box shape: radio, Tune in w/CJ, brn/yel, 1939, 1¾" 125.00
Tall box shape: Refrigerator Car, CJ, 1947, 1¾" L 155.00
Train, engine & tender, litho, CJ Line/512 ....125.00
Train, litho coach only, red, unmk, 1941 ....24.00
Train, litho engine only, red, 1941, unmk 20.00
Train, Lone Eagle Flyer cars, unmk 65.00
Train, Lone Eagle Flyer engine, unmk 60.00
Tray, emb, litho w/early package, smaller version 115.00
Tray, emb, litho w/early package, 2¼x1¾" 95.00
Truck, litho, RWB, CJ/Angelus, 1931, ea 65.00
Wagon shape: Caterpillar tractor, unmk, 1931, 1¾" L 35.00
Wagon shape: CJ Shows, yel circus wagon, series of 5, ea 140.00
Wagon shape: Playtime Trailer (auto trailer), unmk, 1947 ....40.00
Wagon shape: tank, orange/red/gr camouflage, unmk 65.00
Wagon shape: Tank Corps No 57, gr & blk, 1941 ....30.00
Wheelbarrow, tin plated, bk leg in place, CJ, 1931, 2½" L 35.00

Miscellaneous

Ad, comic book, CJ, ea 14.00
Ad, Saturday Evening Post, mc, CJ, 1919, 11x14" 18.00
Hat, ball park vendor cap, CJ, 1930s 30.00
Lunch box, tin, 2 hdls, CJ, 1980s, 4½x5x6" 25.00

Lunch box, tin emb, CJ, 1970s, 4x7x9" **30.00**
Medal, CJ salesman award, brass, 1939, scarce **125.00**
Sign, bathing beauty, 5-color cb, CJ, early, 17x22" **460.00**
Sign, boy or girl w/box of CJ, 5-color cb, early, 17x22", ea **460.00**
Sign, Jack & Bingo, die-cut litho, easel standup, CJ, early **450.00**
Sign, Jack & Bingo, standing on early CJ package, mc cb, rare ..**520.00**
Sign, Santa & prizes, mc cb, Angelus, early, lg **220.00**
Sign, Santa & prizes, mc cb, Checkers, early, lg **1,000.00**
Sign, Santa & prizes, mc cb, CJ, early, lg **265.00**

Cranberry Glass

Cranberry glass is named for its resemblance to the color of cranberry juice. It was made by many companies both here and abroad, becoming popular in America soon after the Civil War. It was made in free-blown ware as well as mold-blown. Today cranberry glass is being reproduced, and it is sometimes difficult to distinguish the old from the new. Ask a reputable dealer if you are unsure.

For further information we recommend *American Art Glass* by John A. Shumann III, available from Collector Books or your local bookstore. See also Cruets; Salts; Sugar Shakers; Syrups.

Bowl, Hobnail with applied white opalescent ribbon edge along ruffled rim, 3¼x8¾", $275.00.

Photo courtesy John A. Shumann III

Bottle, scent; allover sm gold stars, bubble stopper, 6" **185.00**
Bottle, scent; gold wave-pattern band, cut stopper, 4½x2" **125.00**
Box, florals, 16 clear shell ft, 7x6" dia **295.00**
Creamer, Optic, fluted top, clear hdl, 5x2¾" **90.00**
Creamer, 3-flute edge, paneled, pontil, EX color, 5" **75.00**
Decanter, leaves/stars eng, music box in base, stick neck, 12" **295.00**
Decanter, wht flowers/gold branches, cut clear stopper, 9½" **195.00**
Liqueur set, gold trim, 9" bottle+6 sm tumblers on 8½" tray **275.00**
Pickle jar, Honeycomb w/bird & floral, worn SP lid, 6" **150.00**
Pitcher, florals, int ribs, crystal loop hdl, 12x9" **275.00**
Pitcher, frosted Hobnail, sqd rim, camphor hdl, 8" **150.00**
Pitcher, Invt T'print, bird/foliage, clear hdl, 8" **575.00**
Pitcher, Invt T'print, mc flowers, bulbous, Mt WA, 9x7½" **475.00**
Pitcher, lg ice bladder, clear hdl, 10x5" **225.00**
Pitcher, Optic, clear reeded hdl, milk sz, 7½x4½" **125.00**
Sugar shaker, 12-panel, cylindrical, sterling top, 6" **335.00**
Sweetmeat dish; rstr SP fr, branch hdl, 5¼x5⅛" **195.00**
Vase, gold/wht/bl floral, mini, 2½" **125.00**
Vase, Swirl, allover gold mottling, 8x3½" **150.00**
Vase, wide floral bands, bulbous w/flared neck, 5¼x4¼" **175.00**

Creamware

Creamware was a type of earthenware developed by Wedgwood in the 1760s and produced by many other Staffordshire potteries, including Leeds. Since it could be potted cheaply and was light in weight, it became popular abroad as well as in England, due to the lower freight charges involved in its export. It was revived at Leeds in the late 19th century, and the type most often reproduced was heavily reticulated or molded in high relief. These later wares are easily distinguished from the originals since they are thicker and tend to craze heavily. See also Leeds; Wedgwood.

Coffeepot, cauliflower florets emb on gr, floret finial, 8" **1,500.00**
Figurine, cat, rust & brn slip, ca 1760, rstr, 4¼" **575.00**
Figurine, deer, recumbent, free-form grassy base, late 1700s, 4" ..**515.00**
Figurine, gentleman, on sq base, late 1700s, rstr, 4½" **200.00**
Fiugurine, cat, brn mottle, rstr ear, ca 1780, 5¾" **1,035.00**
Leaf dish, w/berry branch, bird perched on side, 1780s, rstr, 11" ..**515.00**
Mug, brn slip bands between scroll borders, ca 1800, 2¾" **350.00**
Plaque, Admiral Nelson portrait, self-fr, 1807, 5½x6⅞" **400.00**
Teapot, emb acanthus spout, ribbed hdl, 4¾", NM **385.00**
Teapot, Harlequin & Columbine, ca 1780, rstr, 6¾" **400.00**
Teapot, vines & flowers on globular form, crabstock hdl, 3¼" ...**920.00**
Tureen, grapes-on-leaf form, branch hdl, w/lid & stand, 8" L **500.00**

Crown Ducal

The Crown Ducal mark was first used by the A.G. Richardson & Co. pottery of Tunstall, England, in 1925. The items collectors are taking a particular interest in were decorated by Charlotte Rhead, a contemporary of Suzie Cooper and Clarice Cliff, and a member of the esteemed family of English pottery designers and artists.

Ashtray, King Geo VI coronation, C Rhead, 1937, 5½" **85.00**
Bowl, Bristol, bl, scalloped rim, 8" **35.00**
Bowl, floral decor w/blk int, mk, 4⅜x10¼" **100.00**
Bowl, squeezebag floral on beige, C Rhead 3⅜x10" **250.00**
Candlesticks, birds & butterflies, blk on orange, slim, 10⅜", pr **45.00**
Creamer & sugar bowl, Primula **95.00**
Cup & saucer, Florida **145.00**
Jug, mc leaves on gray w/gr trim, C Rhead, 5¾" **380.00**
Plate, tan/orange/dk brn, C Rhead, #4926, 10½" **430.00**
Vase, fruit & flowers, lustre, C Rhead, Bursley Ware, 8" **440.00**
Vase, Indian Tree, brn/orange on patterned gold, C Rhead, 5" ..**175.00**
Vase, leaf band on mushroom form, mc gloss, 6½x2" **140.00**
Vase, poppies & leaves, orange lustre & gr on blk, 6" **95.00**
Vase, poppies on blk, orange lustre int, 7¾x6⅝" **195.00**

Crown Milano

Crown Milano was a line of decorated milk glass (or opal ware) introduced by the Mt. Washington Glass Co. of New Bedford, Massachussetts, in the early 1890s. It had previously been called Albertine Ware. Some pieces are marked with a 'CM,' and many had paper labels. This ware is usually highly decorated and will most likely have a significant amount of gold painted on it. The shiny pieces were recently discovered to have been called 'Colonial Ware' and have a laurel wreath and a crown. This ware was well received in its day, and outstanding pieces bring high prices on today's market. Advisors for this category are Wilfred and Dolli Cohen; they are listed in the Directory under California.

Atomizer, fall foliage on rose w/tapestry texture, 4" **650.00**
Bottle, scent; nasturtiums, mc on gr to brn, sprinkler top, 5¼" ...**375.00**
Bowl, floral/gold scrolls on yel, 3-corner, 3x9" **1,750.00**
Bowl, pansies on gray/tan lace medallions on almond, 7x10" **550.00**
Cracker jar, bamboo, gr/gold/brn on pnt burmese, SP trim, 6" **900.00**
Cracker jar, lotus/gilt on gr-shadowed hobnail, lid w/butterfly ...**600.00**

Cracker jar, mums/roses, flaring U-form, 5" dia 985.00
Creamer & sugar, floral/gold ribbons, glass lid, #2052/140 ......1,250.00
Creamer & sugar, pansies on yel to wht, #401 ....750.00
Ewer, florals on gold netting at shoulder on ivory, 6x9" 500.00
Flower holder, mushroom shape, dots/oak leaves on wht, 3½x5" 425.00
Letter holder, wild roses on pnt burmese, blown-out florals 875.00
Pitcher, fall holly w/red berries, gold motifs, pulled rim, 8" 750.00
Rose bowl, chintz, pk/yel on wht, spherical, #619, 3½x4" 385.00
Sweetmeat, holly w/ruby berries on tan-shadowed Dmn Quilt, 4" 1,000.00
Sweetmeat, holly/ruby jewel berries on pnt tan spirals, 3" 900.00
Syrup, netting, gold on pk, florals, melon ribs, 6" 1,850.00
Tumbler, gold bows/flower garlands, shiny, 3¾" 400.00

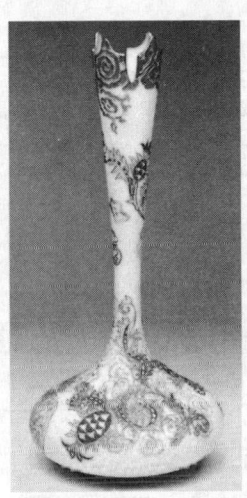

Vase, slit and shaped rim, elongated slim neck on bulbed body, brown swirled design with white enameling, gold leafy outlines, 15", $1,100.00.

Vase, florals on ivory, gold scrolls on apricot at rim, 9x9" 700.00
Vase, florals/gold scrolls on bl-gray shadow floral, 7x8" 775.00
Vase, gold fern fronds on tan shadow leaves, stick neck, 15" 750.00
Vase, gold fern fronds on wht, ball body, stick neck, 9½" 425.00
Vase, gold ferns/scrolls on tan & wht, ball shape w/short neck, 9" .1,200.00
Vase, gold floral on ivory, melon rib, sm 4-lobe rim, 8½" 750.00
Vase, gold laurel wreath w/2 nudes on shiny wht, 10½" 900.00
Vase, gold spider mums on allover brn shadow blossoms, 5x7" ...750.00
Vase, gold wild roses on peach mottle, jeweled, leaf hdls, 5x7" ..1,200.00
Vase, gold-lined gold ferns on tan shadows, swirls, 5x5"" 700.00
Vase, jack-in-the-pulpit; floral on pnt burmese, 9¾" 775.00
Vase, leaves/gold scrolls on blush, twist stick neck, hdls, 12" ..1,900.00
Vase, lion/2-headed eagle in shield, jewels, shell hdls, 9x4" 950.00
Vase, petit-point iris/tan traceries, scalloped, ball shape, 4½" 875.00
Vase, thistles, gold-lined on lt yel, flared sides, 14" 2,250.00
Vase, thistles w/gold on beige, elongated ovoid, 12½" 1,100.00

Cruets

Cruets, containers made to hold oil or vinegar, are usually bulbous with tall, narrow throats and a stopper. During the 19th century and for several years after, they were produced in abundance in virtually every type of glassware available. Those listed below are assumed to be with stopper and mint unless noted otherwise. Our advisor for this category is Elaine Ezell; she is listed in the Directory under Maryland.

Apollo, rose, McKee 95.00
Argonaut Shell, custard w/gold & decor 775.00
Basketweave, bl 90.00
Bead Swag, milk glass, Heisey 225.00
Beaded Medallion, gr 250.00
Beveled Star, gr 175.00

Big Button, amber stain 225.00
Bulging Loops, pk cased 400.00
Caprice, Cambridge 100.00
Carmen, amber stain 225.00
Christmas Pearls, gr opal 395.00
Chrysanthemum Base Swirl, wht satin opal 190.00
Chrysanthemum Sprig, custard, w/gold & decor, 6¾" 395.00
Chrysanthemum Swirl, cranberry opal 795.00
Circled Scroll, bl opal 575.00
Cone, yel satin 275.00
Cranberry, gold flowers, clear bubble stopper, 8x3¼" 165.00
Cranberry w/bl forget-me-nots, 3-petal top, 8" 175.00
Croesus, gr w/gold, 6½" 395.00
Croesus, purple w/gold, 6½" 525.00
Daisy & Fern, Apple Blossom mold, bl opal 295.00
Daisy & Fern, bl opal, Indiana mold, LG Wright 85.00
Delaware, gr w/gold 325.00
Dewey, amber 95.00
Esther, gr w/gold, lg 350.00
Esther, gr w/gold, sm 195.00
Everglades, custard, EX gold & decor 1,200.00
Fern, bl opal 325.00
Geneva, custard, floral decor 475.00
Georgia Gem, custard, w/gold 350.00
Guttate, cranberry 425.00
Herringbone, bl opal 395.00
Hobnail, bl opal, Hobbs 350.00
Hobnail, cranberry opal, Hobbs 395.00
Hobnail, sapphire bl, faceted stopper, 7¼" 385.00
Hobnail, vaseline opal, Hobbs 365.00
Hobnail, wht opal, Hobbs 295.00
Hobstar & Daisy, vaseline 95.00
Intaglio, bl opal 250.00
Intaglio, custard, w/gold & decor 395.00
Invt Fan & Feather, custard, w/gold & decor, scarce, 6½" 1,100.00
Invt T'print, amber, hinged top, 8¼x3¼" 135.00
Invt T'print, amberina, bulbous, tricon rim, amber hdl, 6" 325.00
Invt T'print, rubena verde, petticoat form, faceted stopper, 7" ...295.00
IOU, gr, sm 95.00
Ivy Scroll, gr w/gold 195.00
Kings 500, cobalt w/G gold 895.00
Lattice, wht-ribbed opal 195.00
Leaf Bracket, chocolate 195.00
Leaf Medallion, amethyst w/gold 695.00
Lilac w/yel mums, swirled, bulbous, faceted stopper, 6" 150.00
Majestic, ruby stain 350.00
Mardi Gras (Duncan #42) 80.00
Mary Gregory, girl feeding rooster on cranberry, flat sides 425.00
Minnesota 65.00
National's Eureka, ruby stained 245.00
Nevada, gr, w/decor 195.00
Opal, bl w/lt bl & wht stripes, hollow stopper, amber hdl, 7" 345.00
Paden City's #210, vaseline 100.00
Peloton, bl w/mc strings, swirl mold, faceted ball stopper 7" 500.00
Polka Dot #398, cranberry, Hobbs & Brockunier 325.00
Prize, gr w/gold 265.00
Purple wash on clear, heavy gold decor, twist hdl, 8" 265.00
Ransom, vaseline 265.00
Reverse Swirl, bl opal 375.00
Rib & Beaded Band, amber, Imperial 85.00
Ring Band, custard, w/roses & gold 450.00
Sapphire bl, 8 optic panels, HP bird on branch, #22, 8" 285.00
Scottish Moore, wht opal 295.00
Seaweed, bl opal 395.00

Spangle, cased amber, amber hdl/faceted stopper, bulbous, 7" 200.00
Stars & Stripes, cranberry opal 575.00
Swirl (raised), bl opal, Hobbs 285.00
Swirl Amberina, tricon rim, amber hdl/faceted stopper, 6½" 250.00
Swirled Feather, gr, 8" 125.00
Swirled Feather, red, 6" 145.00
Tacoma, ruby stain 245.00
Tiny Optic, amethyst w/decor 125.00
Utopia Optic, cranberry 350.00
Victoria, satin, Fostoria 90.00
Wide Stripe, bl opal 395.00
Wild Bouquet, bl opal 495.00
Wild Bouquet, custard, no decor, w/clear stopper 995.00
Zipper Dart, gr 195.00

Cup Plates, Glass

Before the middle 1850s, it was socially acceptable to pour hot tea into a deep saucer to cool. The tea was sipped from the saucer rather than the cup, which frequently was handleless and too hot to hold. The cup plate served as a coaster for the cup. It is generally agreed that the first examples of pressed glass cup plates were made about 1826 at the Boston and Sandwich Glass Co. in Sandwich, Cape Cod, Massachusetts. Other glassworks in three major areas (New England, Philadelphia, and the Midwest, especially Pittsburgh) quickly followed suit.

Antique glass cup plates range in size from 2⅝" up to 4¼" in diameter. The earliest plates had simple designs inspired by cut glass patterns, but by 1829 they had become more complex. The span from then until about 1845 is known as the 'Lacy Period,' when cup plate designs and pressing techniques were at their peak. To cover pressing imperfections, the backgrounds of the plates were often covered with fine stippling which endowed them with a glittering brilliance called 'laciness.' They were made in a multitude of designs — some purely decorative, others commemorative. Subjects include the American eagle, hearts, sunbursts, log cabins, ships, George Washington, the political candidates Clay and Harrison, plows, beehives, etc. Of all the patterns, the round George Washington plate is the rarest and most valuable — only four are known to exist today.

Authenticity is most important. Collectors must be aware that contemporary plates which have no antique counterparts and fakes modeled after antique patterns have had wide distribution. Condition is also important, though it is the exceptional plate that does not have some rim roughness. More important considerations are scarcity of design and color.

Our advisor for this category is John Bilane; he is listed in the Directory under New Jersey. The book *American Glass* by George and Helen McKearin has a section on glass cup plates. The definitive book is *American Glass Cup Plates* by Ruth Webb Lee and James H. Rose. Numbers in the listings that follow refer to the latter. When no condition is indicated, the examples listed below are assumed to have only minor rim roughness as is normal. See also Staffordshire; Pairpoint.

R-277, light green, Sandwich, 3¼", EX, $1,200.00; R-455, violet (unrecorded), Sandwich, 3½", VG+, $750.00.

R-100-A, scarce, G 41.00
R-101, VG 51.00
R-103, rare, G 62.00
R-104, VG 35.00
R-124-A, VG 39.00
R-150, G 31.00
R-151-A, G- 28.00
R-158-A, G 39.00
R-159-A, G 39.00
R-162-B, EX- 36.00
R-164-A, EX 40.00
R-165, VG 35.00
R-169-B, EX 40.00
R-172-A, EX 40.00
R-174, EX 45.00
R-176-A, EX 43.00
R-22, EX 32.00
R-23, G+ 26.00
R-236, G 28.00
R-255, VG 20.00
R-257, VG- 32.00
R-258, VG 30.00
R-269, VG 30.00
R-27, VG 30.00
R-271-A, VG 30.00
R-28, VG 30.00
R-291, VG- 26.00
R-30, VG 64.00
R-31, rare, VG+ 74.00
R-311, VG- 20.00
R-313, VG 21.00
R-323, VG- 18.00
R-332-B, G- 12.00
R-334, G+ 17.00
R-334-A, G 15.00
R-339, VG 19.00
R-340, G 15.00
R-343-B, VG, scarce 35.00
R-37, VG 43.00
R-379, VG- 12.00
R-39, VG 30.00
R-390-A, G+ 11.00
R-396, VG 13.00
R-402, VG 14.00
R-41, G+ 38.00
R-465-H, VG 23.00
R-465-N, G 16.00
R-467-A, G 15.00
R-476, G- 13.00
R-48, G- 23.00
R-501, G- 10.00
R-54, G+ 45.00
R-546, G+ 15.00
R-55, VG- 80.00
R-56, VG+ 52.00
R-565-A, G+ 26.00
R-566-A, scarce, G- 33.00
R-57, 546, G+ 15.00
R-593, scarce, G 42.00
R-594, VG- 32.00
R-605-A, scarce, G 105.00
R-610-A, VG 34.00
R-610-C, VG 40.00
R-610-C, VG- 40.00

R-619-A, G	39.00
R-636, VG-	42.00
R-637, very rare, VG-	260.00
R-643, VG	26.00
R-66, VG	76.00
R-661, VG	39.00
R-666, VG	35.00
R-670, VG-	60.00
R-670-A, VG	39.00
R-676-C, G	47.00
R-677, VG	38.00
R-679, VG	34.00
R-693, G+	75.00
R-72, rare, VG+	78.00
R-79, G	32.00
R-88, opal, 3¾", EX	350.00
R-95, VG+	35.00
R-99, VG	70.00

Cups and Saucers

The earliest utensils for drinking were small porcelain and stoneware bowls imported from China by the East Indian Company in the early 17th century. European and English tea bowls and saucers, imitating Chinese and Japanese originals, were produced from the early 18th century and often decorated with Chinese-type motifs. By about 1810, handles were fitted to the bowl to form the now familiar teacup, and this form became almost universal. Coffee in England and on the continent was often served in a can — a straight-sided cylinder with a handle. After 1820 the coffee can gave way to the more fanciful form of the coffee cup.

An infinite variety of cups and saucers are available for both the new and experienced collector, and they can be found in all price ranges. There is probably no better way to thoroughly know and understand the various ceramic manufacturers than to study cups and saucers. Our advisors for this category, Susan and Jim Harran, have written a book, entitled *Collectible Cups and Saucers, Identification and Values,* published by Collector Books. Over 400 full-color photos fill this exciting book which is divided into six collectible categories: early years (1700 – 1875), cabinet cups, 19th and 20th century dinnerware, English bone china, miniatures, and figurals. The Harrans are listed in the Directory under New Jersey.

Teacup, hand-painted scenes and flowers, Dresden, ca 1905, $225.00.

Cafe au lait, pastel flowers w/gold, Haviland, 1920s	95.00
Coffee, Blue Ship, 8-sided, Rookwood, 1923+	125.00
Coffee, mythological scene, pk w/gold, Austria mk, 1890-1918	65.00

Coffee, paneled design, maroon/wht/yel & gold, att Old Paris	80.00
Demi, appl flowers outside, HP w/in, fluted, Dresden, 1880s	275.00
Demi, classical figures in relief, Capodimonte style, 1880-1900	180.00
Demi, copy of 18th C Dr Wall Worcester pattern, Sampson, 1830	400.00
Demi, emb shells w/gold, gold coral hdl, Coalport, 1891-1939	175.00
Demi, pk flower transfer, ribbed cup, Zeb, Scherzer & Co, 1900	40.00
Tea, Cupid & lady, mulberry transfer, London style, unmk, 1850s	90.00
Tea, DuBarry Rose, Tuscan China, 1947-60	40.00
Tea, gold scrolls on wht, can form w/loop hdl, Sevres, ca 1808	325.00
Tea, Henley, loop hdl, Aynsley, ca 1900-30	50.00
Tea, HP flowers & gold scrollwork, str-side cup, Minton #5641	120.00
Tea, HP roosters on bl lustre, Shafford, 1950+	40.00
Tea, Maytime, pk & wht floral w/gold, Crown Staffordshire, 1938	35.00
Tea, mc chinoiserie, unmk Hilditch style, ca 1815-30	100.00
Tea, mc flower panels w/cobalt & gold, Gaudy Welsh, 1860s	120.00
Tea, Prunis, Caneware, Wedgwood, ca 1815	225.00
Tea, See Players..., commemorative portraits, Ceramic Art Co	250.00

Currier & Ives by Royal

During the 1950s dinnerware decorated with transfer-printed scenes taken from prints by Currier and Ives was manufactured by Royal China and given as premiums through A&P stores. Though it was also made in pink and green, the blue is by far the most popular. Pie plates in black and brown can be found, but no china sets in these colors have been reported. Today it is readily available at reasonable prices, and it has become a very popular collectible at malls and flea markets around the country. Included in our listings are pieces from Hostess sets, which should be of great interest to collectors. New pieces which have been added to the price list include the clock, coffee mug with round handle, tall cup, snack plate, spoon rest/wall plaque, second-type gravy and underplate, and third-type sugar bowl with no handles. Also, the 11½" round platter with the 'Rocky Mountains' scene has been added (very rare). Currier and Ives by Royal is one of the fastest growing collectibles on the market today. Our advisors for this category are Treva and Jack Hamlin; they are listed in the Directory under Ohio; e-mail address: trevajo@ezwv.com. See also Clubs and Newsletters.

Ashtray, 5½"	18.00
Bowl, cereal; tab hdl, 6¼"	48.00
Bowl, cereal; 6¼"	15.00
Bowl, dessert; 5½"	5.00
Bowl, soup; 8"	14.00
Bowl, vegetable, 9"	25.00
Bowl, vegetable; deep, 10"	35.00
Butter dish, Fashionable decal	55.00
Butter dish, Road Winter decal	40.00
Casserole, angle hdls	115.00

Casserole, tab handles, $250.00.

Clock, 10" plate, bl #s, 2 decals	150.00

Creamer, angle hdl 8.00
Creamer, rnd hdl, tall 48.00
Cup, angle hdl 4.00
Cup, rnd hdl, tall, 9" 10.00
Gravy boat, pour spout 20.00
Gravy boat, tab hdls 48.00
Ladle, gravy; all wht 50.00
Lamp, candle; w/globe 250.00
Mug, coffee; reg 35.00
Mug, coffee; rnd hdl 35.00
Pie baker, 9 decals, 10" 30.00
Plate, bread; 6½" 5.00
Plate, calendar; 10" 20.00
Plate, chop; Getting Ice, 11½" 45.00
Plate, chop; Rocky Mountains, 11½" 65.00
Plate, chop; 12¼" 35.00
Plate, dinner; 10" 7.00
Plate, luncheon; 9" 25.00
Plate, Rocky Mountains, 11½" 65.00
Plate, salad; 7¼" 15.00
Plate, snack; w/cup well, 9" 50.00
Platter, oval, 13" 35.00
Platter, tab hdls, 10½" dia 30.00
Platter, 13" dia 75.00
Saucer, 6⅛" 2.00
Shakers, pr 40.00
Spoon rest, wall hanging 75.00
Sugar bowl, hdld, w/lid 18.00
Sugar bowl, no hdls, flared top 48.00
Sugar bowl, no hdls, w/lid 35.00
Teapot 150.00
Tidbit tray, 3-tier, orig only 75.00
Tray, gravy boat; like 7" plate 48.00
Tray, gravy boat; regular 20.00
Tumbler, iced tea; 12-oz, 5½" 17.50
Tumbler, old fashioned; 7-oz, 3¼" 17.50
Tumbler, water; 8½-oz, 4¾" 17.50

Hostess Set Pieces

Bowl, candy; 7¾" 25.00
Bowl, dip; 4⅜" 20.00
Pie baker, 11" 45.00
Plate, cake; flat, 10" 45.00
Plate, cake; ftd, 10" 75.00
Plate, serving; 7" 20.00
Tray, deviled egg 150.00

Custard Glass

     As early as the 1880s, custard glass was produced in England. Migrating glassmakers brought the formula for the creamy ivory ware to America. One of them was Harry Northwood, who in 1898 founded his company in Indiana, Pennsylvania, and introduced the glassware to the American market. Soon other companies were producing custard, among them Heisey, Tarentum, Fenton, and McKee. Not only dinnerware patterns but souvenir items were made. Today custard is the most expensive of the colored pressed glassware patterns. The formula for producing the luminous glass contains uranium salts which imparts the cream color to the batch and causes it to glow when it is examined under a black light.

Argonaut Shell, bowl, master berry; gold & decor, 10½" L **275.00**

Argonaut Shell, bowl, sauce; ftd, gold & decor 75.00
Argonaut Shell, butter dish, gold & decor 350.00
Argonaut Shell, compote, jelly; gold & decor, scarce 165.00
Argonaut Shell, creamer, gold & decor 155.00
Argonaut Shell, creamer, no gold 110.00
Argonaut Shell, pitcher, water; gold & decor 475.00
Argonaut Shell, shakers, gold & decor, pr 435.00
Argonaut Shell, spooner, gold & decor 160.00
Argonaut Shell, tumbler, gold & decor 110.00
Bead Swag, bowl, sauce; floral & gold 50.00
Bead Swag, goblet, floral & gold 65.00
Bead Swag, wine, floral & gold 60.00
Beaded Circle, bowl, master berry; floral & gold 275.00
Beaded Circle, butter dish, floral & gold 500.00
Beaded Circle, pitcher, water; floral & gold 750.00
Beaded Circle, shakers, floral & gold, pr 1,000.00
Beaded Circle, spooner, floral & gold 185.00
Beaded Circle, tumbler, floral & gold, very rare 150.00
Cane Insert, berry set, 7-pc 450.00
Cane Insert, table set, 4-pc 450.00
Cherry & Scales, bowl, master berry; nutmeg stain 145.00
Cherry & Scales, creamer, nutmeg stain 125.00
Cherry & Scales, pitcher, water; nutmeg stain, scarce 350.00
Cherry & Scales, sugar bowl, w/lid, nutmeg stain, scarce 150.00
Cherry & Scales, tumbler, nutmeg stain, scarce 75.00

Chrysanthemum Sprig, master berry bowl, no gold, 4½x10½x7¾", $175.00.

Chrysanthemum Sprig, bowl, master berry; gold & decor 300.00
Chrysanthemum Sprig, bowl, sauce; ftd, gold & decor 60.00
Chrysanthemum Sprig, butter dish, gold & decor 375.00
Chrysanthemum Sprig, celery vase, gold & decor, rare 700.00
Chrysanthemum Sprig, compote, jelly; no decor 100.00
Chrysanthemum Sprig, creamer, gold & decor 135.00
Chrysanthemum Sprig, cruet, gold & decor, 6¾" 395.00
Chrysanthemum Sprig, pitcher, water; no decor 350.00
Chrysanthemum Sprig, shakers, gold & decor, pr 300.00
Chrysanthemum Sprig, spooner, gold & decor 135.00
Chrysanthemum Sprig, sugar bowl, gold & decor 250.00
Chrysanthemum Sprig, toothpick holder, EX gold 250.00
Chrysanthemum Sprig, toothpick holder, gold & decor 375.00
Chrysanthemum Sprig, tray, condiment; gold & decor, rare 595.00
Chrysanthemum Sprig, tumbler, gold & decor 80.00
Dandelion, mug, nutmeg stain 175.00
Delaware, creamer, breakfast; pk stain 75.00
Delaware, tray, pin; gr stain 85.00
Delaware, tumbler, pk stain 65.00
Diamond w/Peg, bowl, master berry; roses & gold 225.00
Diamond w/Peg, bowl, sauce; roses & gold 50.00
Diamond w/Peg, butter dish, roses & gold 275.00

Diamond w/Peg, creamer, ind; no decor 35.00
Diamond w/Peg, creamer, roses & gold 85.00
Diamond w/Peg, mug, souvenir 50.00
Diamond w/Peg, napkin ring, roses & gold, rare 175.00
Diamond w/Peg, sugar bowl, w/lid, roses & gold 175.00
Diamond w/Peg, toothpick holder, roses & gold 175.00
Diamond w/Peg, tumbler, roses & gold 75.00
Diamond w/Peg, wine, roses & gold 65.00
Diamond w/Peg, wine, souvenir 55.00
Everglades, bowl, master berry; gold & decor 215.00
Everglades, butter dish, gold & decor 395.00
Everglades, creamer, gold & decor 155.00
Everglades, spooner, gold & decor 160.00
Everglades, sugar bowl, w/lid, gold & decor 235.00
Everglades, tumbler, gold & decor 100.00
Fan, bowl, sauce; good gold 60.00
Fan, butter dish, good gold 345.00
Fan, creamer, good gold 110.00
Fan, pitcher, water; good gold 300.00
Fan, spooner, good gold 100.00
Fan, sugar bowl, w/lid, good gold 175.00
Fan, water set, good gold, 7-pc 725.00
Fine Cut & Roses, rose bowl, fancy int, nutmeg stain 100.00
Fine Cut & Roses, rose bowl, plain int 85.00
Geneva, bowl, master berry; floral decor, rnd, 9" 130.00
Geneva, bowl, sauce; floral decor, oval 50.00
Geneva, bowl, sauce; floral decor, rnd 50.00
Geneva, butter dish, no decor 135.00
Geneva, compote, jelly; floral decor 95.00
Geneva, creamer, floral decor 115.00
Geneva, pitcher, water; floral decor 275.00
Geneva, shakers, floral decor, pr 280.00
Geneva, spooner, floral decor 100.00
Geneva, sugar bowl, w/lid, floral decor 175.00
Geneva, syrup, floral decor 500.00
Geneva, toothpick holder, floral w/M gold 375.00
Georgia Gem, bowl, master berry; good gold 135.00
Georgia Gem, bowl, master berry; gr opaque 115.00
Georgia Gem, butter dish, good gold 200.00
Georgia Gem, creamer, good gold 100.00
Georgia Gem, creamer, no gold 60.00
Georgia Gem, cruet, good gold, from $350 to 395.00
Georgia Gem, powder jar, w/lid, good gold 80.00
Georgia Gem, shakers, good gold, pr 140.00
Georgia Gem, spooner, souvenir 55.00
Grape (& Cable), bottle, scent; orig stopper, nutmeg stain 650.00
Grape (& Cable), bowl, centerpc; ftd, nutmeg stain 450.00
Grape (& Cable), bowl, nutmeg stain, 7½" 60.00
Grape (& Cable), butter dish, nutmeg stain 300.00
Grape (& Cable), compote, jelly; open, nutmeg stain 150.00
Grape (& Cable), compote, nutmeg stain, 4½x8" 300.00
Grape (& Cable), creamer, breakfast; nutmeg stain 80.00
Grape (& Cable), humidor, bl stain, rare 950.00
Grape (& Cable), humidor, nutmeg stain, rare 900.00
Grape (& Cable), pitcher, water; nutmeg stain 550.00
Grape (& Cable), plate, nutmeg stain, 8" 65.00
Grape (& Cable), punch bowl, w/base, nutmeg stain 1,900.00
Grape (& Cable), spooner, nutmeg stain 155.00
Grape (& Cable), sugar bowl, breakfast; open, nutmeg stain 85.00
Grape (& Cable), tray, dresser; nutmeg stain, scarce, lg 375.00
Grape (& Cable), tray, pin; nutmeg stain 150.00
Grape (& Cable), tumbler, nutmeg stain 75.00
Grape & Gothic Arches, bowl, master berry; pearl w/gold 200.00
Grape & Gothic Arches, bowl, sauce; pearl w/gold, rare 80.00

Grape & Gothic Arches, butter dish, pearl w/gold 235.00
Grape & Gothic Arches, favor vase, nutmeg stain 80.00
Grape & Gothic Arches, goblet, pearl w/gold 75.00
Grape & Gothic Arches, pitcher, water; pearl w/gold 300.00
Grape & Gothic Arches, sugar bowl, w/lid, pearl w/gold 135.00
Grape & Gothic Arches, tumbler, pearl w/gold 65.00
Grape Arbor, vase, hat form 90.00
Heart w/T'print, lamp, good pnt, scarce, 8" 450.00
Heart w/T'print, sugar bowl, ind 95.00
Honeycomb, wine 65.00
Intaglio, bowl, master berry; gold & decor, ftd, 9" 250.00
Intaglio, bowl, sauce; gold & decor 50.00
Intaglio, butter dish, gold & decor, scarce 300.00
Intaglio, creamer, gold & decor 125.00
Intaglio, cruet, gold & decor, from $395 to 450.00
Intaglio, pitcher, water; gold & decor 395.00
Intaglio, spooner, gold & decor 135.00
Intaglio, sugar bowl, w/lid, gold & decor 180.00
Intaglio, tumbler, gold & decor 95.00

Inverted Fan and Feather, pitcher, gold trim, 7¼", $700.00.

Inverted Fan & Feather, bowl, sauce; gold & decor 75.00
Inverted Fan & Feather, butter dish, gold & decor 400.00
Inverted Fan & Feather, compote, jelly; gold & decor, rare 500.00
Inverted Fan & Feather, cruet, gold & decor, scarce, 6½" 1,100.00
Inverted Fan & Feather, pitcher, water; gold & decor 700.00
Inverted Fan & Feather, punch cup, gold & decor 250.00
Inverted Fan & Feather, spooner, gold & decor 165.00
Inverted Fan & Feather, sugar bowl, w/lid, gold & decor 250.00
Inverted Fan & Feather, tumbler, gold & decor 115.00
Jackson (Alaska Variant), bowl, sauce; good gold 50.00
Jackson (Alaska Variant), creamer, good gold 85.00
Jackson (Alaska Variant), pitcher, water; good gold 250.00
Jackson (Alaska Variant), shakers, good gold, pr 195.00
Jackson (Alaska Variant), tumbler, good gold 50.00
Louis XV, bowl, master berry; good gold 250.00
Louis XV, butter dish, good gold 250.00
Louis XV, creamer, good gold 85.00
Louis XV, pitcher, water; good gold 250.00
Louis XV, sugar bowl, w/lid, good gold 165.00
Louis XV, tumbler, good gold 65.00
Maple Leaf, bowl, master berry; gold & decor, scarce 350.00
Maple Leaf, butter dish, gold & decor 350.00
Maple Leaf, compote, jelly; gold & decor, rare 475.00
Maple Leaf, creamer, gold & decor 150.00
Maple Leaf, pitcher, water; gold & decor 400.00
Maple Leaf, shakers, gold & decor, very rare, pr 1,000.00
Maple Leaf, spooner, gold & decor 175.00
Maple Leaf, tumbler, gold & decor 100.00
Panelled Poppy, lamp shade, nutmeg stain, scarce 900.00
Peacock & Urn, bowl, ice cream; nutmeg stain, sm 80.00

Punty Band, shakers, pr 175.00
Punty Band, spooner, floral decor 100.00
Punty Band, tumbler, floral decor, souvenir 65.00
Ribbed Drape, butter dish, scalloped, roses & gold 400.00
Ribbed Drape, compote, jelly; roses & gold, rare 200.00
Ribbed Drape, creamer, roses & gold, scarce 180.00
Ribbed Drape, pitcher, water; roses & gold, rare 365.00
Ribbed Drape, shakers, roses & gold, rare, pr 400.00
Ribbed Drape, spooner, roses & gold 195.00
Ribbed Drape, toothpick holder, roses & gold 475.00
Ribbed Drape, tumbler, roses & gold 75.00
Ribbed Thumbprint, wine, floral decor 80.00
Ring Band, bowl, sauce; roses & gold 50.00
Ring Band, butter dish, roses & gold 300.00
Ring Band, compote, jelly; roses & gold, scarce 195.00
Ring Band, cruet, roses & gold, scarce 500.00
Ring Band, pitcher, roses & gold, 7½" 375.00
Ring Band, shakers, roses & gold, pr 155.00
Ring Band, syrup, roses & gold, scarce 475.00
Ring Band, toothpick holder, roses & gold 155.00
Ring Band, tray, condiment; roses & gold 200.00
Tarentum's Victoria, bowl, master berry; gold & decor 200.00
Tarentum's Victoria, butter dish, gold & decor, rare 350.00
Tarentum's Victoria, celery vase, gold & decor, rare 300.00
Tarentum's Victoria, pitcher, water; gold & decor, rare 375.00
Tarentum's Victoria, spooner, gold & decor 135.00
Tarentum's Victoria, sugar bowl, w/lid, gold & decor 175.00
Vermont, butter dish, bl decor 195.00
Vermont, toothpick holder, bl decor 175.00
Vermont, vase, floral decor, jeweled 125.00
Wild Bouquet, butter dish, gold & decor, rare 750.00
Wild Bouquet, creamer, no gold 145.00
Wild Bouquet, cruet, no decor, w/clear stopper 995.00
Wild Bouquet, spooner, gold & decor 175.00
Wild Bouquet, tumbler, no decor 100.00
Winged Scroll, bowl, master berry; gold & decor, 11" L 250.00
Winged Scroll, butter dish, good gold 235.00
Winged Scroll, butter dish, no decor 175.00
Winged Scroll, celery vase, good gold, rare 400.00
Winged Scroll, compote, ruffled, rare, 6¾x10¾" 495.00
Winged Scroll, cruet, good gold, rpl clear stopper 400.00
Winged Scroll, hair receiver, good gold 135.00
Winged Scroll, shakers, bulbous, good gold, rare, pr 400.00
Winged Scroll, shakers, str sides, good gold, pr 300.00
Winged Scroll, sugar bowl, w/lid, good gold 175.00
Winged Scroll, tumbler, good gold 75.00

Cut Glass

The earliest documented evidence of commercial glass cutting in the United States was in 1810; the producers were Bakewell and Page of Pittsburgh. These first efforts resulted in simple patterns with only a moderate amount of cutting. By the middle of the century, glass cutters began experimenting with a thicker glass which enabled them to use deeper cuttings, though patterns remained much the same. This period is usually referred to as Rich Cut. Using three types of wheels — a flat edge, a mitered edge, and a convex edge — facets, miters, and depressions were combined to produce various designs. In the late 1870s, a curved miter was developed which greatly expanded design potential. Patterns became more elaborate, often covering the entire surface. The Brilliant Period of cut glass covered a span from about 1880 until 1915. Because of the pressure necessary to achieve the deeply cut patterns, only glass containing a high grade of metal could withstand the process. For this reason and the amount of

handwork involved, cut glass has always been expensive. Bowls cut with pinwheels may be either foreign or of a newer vintage, beware! Identifiable patterns and signed pieces that are well cut and in excellent condition bring the higher prices on today's market. See also Dorflinger; Hawkes; Libbey; Tuthill; Val St. Lambert; other specific manufacturers.

Key:
dmn — diamond   X-cut — crosscut
strw — strawberry   X-hatch — crosshatch

Humidor, Hobstar and Oval, silver-mounted canister form, matching stopper, 6x9½" diameter, $700.00.

Bonbon, hobstars, cane & fan, star-form rim, 6" 90.00
Bottle, scent; allover hobstars, faceted stopper, 5½" 250.00
Bottle, scent; hobstars, cane & fan, floral-cut stopper, 5" 175.00
Bottle, scent; relief dmns & bars, heart-form lay-down, 4" 240.00
Bowl, Alhambra, Canadian cut, rampant lion mk/R, 8" 450.00
Bowl, amber, cane, 8-scallop, Union Glass Co blank, 5x9" 3,450.00
Bowl, egg nog; pinwheels/cane bands, scalloped hobstar ped, 8x11" ..1,450.00
Bowl, hobstar chain & fans, scalloped & notched, 8" 1,150.00
Bowl, hobstars, strw dmn bands, X-hatch, 5x10" 350.00
Bowl, hobstars (3) among vertical threading, hexagonal, 3x8" ..200.00
Bowl, hobstars & cane, hobstar base, ped ft, hdls, 5½" 175.00
Bowl, hobstars & pinwheels, 8" 100.00
Bowl, Hunt's Royal variant, 9" 250.00
Bowl, Kimberly variant, 24-point hobstar center, 3½x10½" 425.00
Bowl, Orient, flashed pinwheels, notching & fan, ftd, 9" 385.00
Box, cane & hobstars on lid & base, heart shape, 5½" 125.00
Box, dresser; flashed hobstar lid, rayed base w/star center, 5" 225.00
Box, dresser; floral top, Harvard bottom, 7" sq 300.00
Box, hobstar bars fr wheel-cut daisies on lid, 3x7" L 1,100.00
Box, powder; hobstars, notched base, lg hobstar lid, 6" 180.00
Box, sqs w/stars, hobstar circle on top, hinged, 5" sq 250.00
Butter dish, florals w/brilliant centers, faceted knob, 8" 275.00
Butter dish, pinwheels/fans, hobstar tray, 4x7" 300.00
Butter pats, hobstars, flashed hobstars, 2½", set of 10 ....250.00
Carafe, water; hobstars, nailhead & X-hatch, faceted stopper, 8" ..110.00
Celery, hobstars/fans, flared pattern ped, cut rim, 8" 450.00
Compote, floral, 7" 60.00
Compote, hobstars w/star of nailhead bands, petticoat base, 9" ..550.00
Compote, pinwheels/X-hatch, pinwheel base, sgn Maple City, 7" ..175.00
Compote, sm hobstar clusters/decorated ovals alternate, 7x9" 700.00
Cordial, Persian, rayed base, 2¼" 45.00
Cracker barrel, X-cut dmn band, silver mts, oval, 4½" 225.00
Creamer & sugar bowl, decorated hobstars/X-hatch, Hoare, 2½" .75.00
Creamer & sugar bowl, hobstars, dmns, X-hatch sqs, mini 100.00
Cruet, bands of hobstars & notchings alternate, Hoare, 7" 225.00
Cruet, hobstars/X-hatch, hobstar base, petticoat form, 7" 60.00
Decanter, allover dmn point, matching stopper, sq, 13", pr 425.00
Decanter, hobstars w/honeycomb neck, 3-notch hdl, bulbous, 9" ..240.00
Decanter, pinwheels, long neck, faceted stopper, 12" 360.00
Flask, pocket; lg hobstars, X-hatching, sterling cap dtd 1897 ......550.00

Flower center, hobstars, notched prism, step-cut neck, 5x5"	275.00
Goblet, floral & Russian variation, dbl-teardrop stem, 7"	125.00
Humidor, pinwheels, rayed bulbous cover, 9½"	200.00
Ice bucket, allover dmn point, w/drain, 3-ftd, 6x5¾"	110.00
Ice bucket, hobstars, cane & fan, tab hdls, sgn Hoare, 5½"	175.00
Knife rests, faceted knobs, 3¼" L, set of 6	150.00
Ladle, hdl w/hobstars, X-hatch & cane, Pairpoint bowl, 15"	425.00
Ladle, hobstar & fan hdl, 11"	275.00
Lamp, 10 hobstars w/lg central hobstar, honeycomb stem, 23x12"	3,500.00
Lamp 12" dome shade, baluster base/ft, hobstars/cane, 22"	3,700.00
Mayonnaise, hobstars & cane, flared, 5", +6" tray	395.00
Mustard, lg cane & notched prism, faceted knob, 4"	55.00
Mustard, strw dmn & fan, faceted knob, bulbous bottom, 4"	195.00
Pitcher, allover hobstars w/step-cut neck, bulbous, 8"	425.00
Pitcher, hobstars & notching, 9"	175.00
Pitcher, hobstars/notched prism, mk silver collar, 13", +stirrer	1,600.00
Pitcher, milk tankard; pinwheels & fans, notched hdl, 6¼"	140.00
Pitcher, tankard; hobstar bands/cane bands alternate, 12"	275.00
Pitcher, water; Wreath, hobstars w/panels of lg cane, 10"	130.00
Plate, hobstar formed w/bands of cane, hobstar border, 9"	250.00
Punch bowl, floral w/Harvard border, 2-part, 13½x12"	700.00
Punch bowl, Florence hobstar panels, t'prints w/X-hatch, 13x14"	2,100.00
Punch bowl, hobstars & cane, 2-part, 10x10"	500.00
Relish, cut ferns & hobstars, lg fan-cut end tabs, 12" L	150.00
Relish, hobstars & Hunt's Royal variant, oval, 12"	125.00
Relish, 4 feathered vesicas w/hobstars, hobstar ends, Straus, 12"	200.00
Rose bowl, Russian variant (no buttons), spherical, 10x10", NM	575.00
Salt cellar, cane, 1½" dia, set of 12	75.00
Salt cellar, master; hobstars & fans, paperweight base, ped ft	120.00
Spooner, X-hatch dbl bull's eye, waisted w/hdls, 4¾"	125.00
Toothpick, hobstars, rayed base, ped ft, 3¼"	70.00
Tray, hobstar fans w/notching & X-hatch, scalloped, 12" dia	250.00
Tray, ice cream; 8 lg hobstars in deeply scalloped border, 15"	650.00
Tray, poinsettias, 3-ftd, 10" dia	80.00
Tumbler, flutes/dmn band, wheel eng vintage/etc, 3¾"	1,800.00
Tumbler, prism/dmn bands w/wheel-eng dog cart/boy/birds, etc, 4"	1,000.00
Vase, allover Harvard, flared & scalloped, bulb bottom, 16"	600.00
Vase, feathered flowers, hobstars, ped ft, sgn Clark, 12"	475.00
Vase, flowers on long leafy stems, sqd shape, 20"	550.00
Vase, Harvard & hobstars w/step-cut stem, chalice form, 10"	375.00
Vase, hobstars, fan & relief dmns, flared notched rim, 16"	550.00
Vase, hobstars, notching, X-hatch & prism, egg form, 7¾"	375.00
Vase, hobstars & cane, step-cut neck w/hobstar band, 12"	500.00
Vase, lg pinwheels & flashed stars, trumpet shape, 12"	60.00
Wines, hobstars, elongated t'prints, Hindu, sgn Hoare, set of 6	160.00

Cut Overlay Glass

Glassware with one or more overlying colors through which a design has been cut is called 'Cut Overlay.' It was made both here and abroad. Watch for new imitations!

Claret glass, Napoleon (Monarch), green to clear, 4⅝", $135.00.

Photo courtesy
John A. Shumann III

Bottle, scent; wht to bl w/ovals & trefoils, 5½"	150.00
Bottle, scent; wht to clear, dbl gourd w/faceted neck, 7½"	400.00
Bottle, scent; wht to clear, spiral snake, gold stars, 8¾"	500.00
Jug, whiskey; wht to clear, calligraphy eng, star-cut base, 9½"	6,500.00
Window pane, amethyst to clear w/shield design, 7x11"	250.00

Cut Velvet

Cut Velvet glassware was made during the late 1800s. It is characterized by the effect achieved through the execution of relief-molded patterns, often ribbing or diamond quilting, which allows its white inner casing to show through the outer layer.

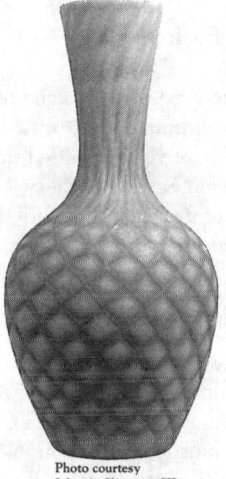

Vase, Diamond Quilted in robin's egg blue, white lining, stick neck, 9", $250.00.

Photo courtesy
John A. Shumann III

Celery vase, Dmn Quilt, bl, box-pleated rim, Mt WA, 6½"	725.00
Lamp, Dmn Quilt, rose to wht, orig ball shade, chimney, 17"	495.00
Pitcher, Invt T'print, pk, pinched sides, 3-lobe rim, 5½"	300.00
Vase, Basketweave, bl to wht, rolled-in pinched rim, 6", pr	850.00
Vase, Dmn Quilt, bl, stick neck, 7", pr	275.00
Vase, Dmn Quilt, bl, 7½x3½"	125.00
Vase, Dmn Quilt, dk purple, dbl gourd w/4-lobe ruffle, Mt WA, 10"	300.00
Vase, Dmn Quilt, pale gold, dbl-gourd shape, Mt WA, 13½x6"	650.00
Vase, Dmn Quilt, rose, bulb w/knob neck, crimped/ruffled, 7"	125.00
Vase, Dmn Quilt, yel, flared/folded rim, Mt WA, 9½x6"	375.00
Vase, Herringbone, bl, fan form w/crimped rim, 6½"	200.00
Vase, Herringbone, deep bl (rare), ruffled, Mt WA, 7½x3½"	450.00
Vase, Honeycomb, pk w/camphor trim, fan-crimped rim, 5½"	200.00

Czechoslovakian Collectibles

Czechoslovakia came into being as a country in 1918. Located in the heart of Europe, it was a land with the natural resources necessary to support a glass industry that dated back to the mid-14th century. The glass that was produced there has captured the attention of today's collectors, and for good reason. There are beautiful vases — cased, ruffled, applied with rigaree or silver overlay — fine enough to rival those of the best glasshouses. Czechoslovakian art glass baskets are quite as attractive as Victorian America's, and the elegant cut glass perfumes made in colors as well as crystal are unrivaled. There are also pressed glass perfumes, molded in lovely Deco shapes, of various types of art glass. Some are overlaid with gold filigree set with 'jewels.' Jewelry, lamps, porcelains, and fine art pottery are also included in the field.

More than seventy marks have been recorded, including those in the mold, ink stamped, acid etched, or on a small metal nameplate. The newer marks are incised, stamped 'Royal Dux Made in Czechoslovakia' (see Royal Dux), or printed on a paper label which reads 'Bohemian Glass Made in Czechoslovakia.' (Communist controlled from 1948, Czechoslovakia once again was made a free country in December 1989. Today it no longer exists; since 1993 it has been divided to form the world's two newest countries, the Czech Republic and the Slovak Republic.) For a more thorough study of the subject, we recommend you refer to the books *Made in Czechoslovakia* and *Made in Czechoslovakia, Book 2*, by our advisor, Ruth A. Forsythe; she is listed in the Directory under Ohio. Another fine book is *Czechoslovakian Glass & Collectibles*, Volumes I and II, by Dale and Diane Barta and Helen M. Rose. We also recommend *Czechoslovakina Perfume Bottles and Boudoir Accessories* by Jacquelyne Y. Jones North. In the listings that follow, when one dimension is given, it refers to height; decoration is enamel unless noted otherwise. See also Amphora; Erphila.

Candy Baskets

Gr varicolored w/red opaque o/l, matching hdl, 8½" 250.00
Mottled autumn colors, ruffled rim, crystal thorn hdl, 6½" 200.00
Mottled bl & yel, yel ruffled rim, jet twisted hdl, 8" 250.00
Mottled red & yel, crystal twisted thorn hdl, 7" 220.00
Pk varicolored, matching hdl, 8" 190.00
Yel w/jet rim, plain crystal arched hdl, 6½" 200.00

Cased Art Glass

Bowl, mc autumn-colored mottle, 4½" 60.00
Bowl, wht, wide ruffled edge w/maroon rim, stemmed ft, 6" 135.00
Pitcher, orange w/cobalt rim & hdl, tricorner top, 5" 85.00
Vase, bl mottled, slim form, 6½" 70.00
Vase, blk/turq/yel mottle, shouldered ftd, 4¼" 75.00
Vase, gr ball shape w/brn linear design, 6" 120.00
Vase, mc autumn-colored mottle, 4 clear ft, slim, 11¾" 80.00
Vase, mc mottle on blk, w/appl bl hdls, 8⅜" 100.00
Vase, solid red w/3 cobalt buttress ft, 6¾" 100.00
Vase, wht mottle on red, blk trim at flared rim, ftd, 7" 80.00

Cut Glass Perfume Bottles

Double-cut stopper with panther on one side and lady with flower garland on the other, highly cut base, 6⅜", $500.00.

Photo courtesy Monsen and Baer

Amber arch shape w/clear figure stopper, 5½" 250.00
Amber shouldered shape w/faceted amber stopper, 6⅛" 145.00
Amethyst arched shape w/jewels, frosted floral stopper, 5⅜" 360.00
Amethyst shouldered shape w/matching fan stopper, 5¼" 225.00
Bl shouldered shape w/clear fan stopper, 4⅝" 125.00
Blk transparent frost, matching stopper, 4⅞" 195.00
Crystal flared shape w/long slim yel prism stopper, 6½" 155.00
Crystal shouldered form w/floral intaglio stopper, 5¾" 75.00
Gr waisted shape w/matching spear-like stopper, 5⅜" 125.00

Pk low-dome shape, frosted floral stopper, 6⅛" 180.00
Red shouldered form w/bottle neck, crystal stopper, 5⅞" 450.00

Lamps

Boudoir, lady figural (Goebel), glass-flower skirt, 10¼" 950.00
Kerosene, pnt milk glass, 12¾" 185.00
Perfume, bl, cut bl shade, 4" 150.00
Perfume, enamel decor, 4" 150.00
Student, metal base, acid-cut shade, 21" 900.00
Table, Art Deco base w/matching conical shade, 9" 900.00
Table, basket form, crystal beads, bl glass flowers, 8½" 950.00
Table, dk bl lustre, rpl shade, 13¼" 200.00
Table, mc mottled satin base & shade, 12½" 450.00
Table, peacock figural, beaded tail, brass body, onyx base, 12¼" .1,200.00
Wall sconce, crystal, 2-light (candle bulbs), prisms, 14½" 250.00

Mold-Blown and Pressed Bottles

Amber arch shape w/jewels, amber stopper, 3½" 110.00
Bl lustre w/enamel, atomizer, 6½" 110.00
Bl w/pnt decor & jewel top, atomizer, 7¼" 175.00
Blk w/gilt-metal band, atomizer, 9½" 170.00
Cranberry opal Hobnail, 5½" 85.00
Crystal frost w/HP daisies, atomizer, 6½" 95.00
Crystal sq w/jewel stopper, 4" 85.00
Crystal w/overall jewels, 2⅜" 145.00
Dk bl enamel w/jewels, scarce, 3" 185.00
Pk w/jewel stopper, 7¼" 65.00
Topaz tinted, jet stopper, 5" 45.00

Opaque, Crystal, Colored Transparent Glass

Candy jar, gr, appl apricot base w/3 buttressed ft, w/lid, 6" 250.00
Decanter, topaz tinted, carriage scene, Borokistol, 10¼" 140.00
Old fashioned, bubbly gr w/HP decor, 3⅜" 55.00
Pitcher, bl w/enameled exotic bird, w/lid, 11¼" 350.00
Vase, bl lustre, ftd chalice form, 5⅞" 750.00
Vase, crystal w/canes & yel stripe decor, bulbous, 5¾" 275.00
Vase, crystal w/red overlay, ftd goblet form, 8¼" 165.00
Vase, mc mottle, stick neck, 8⅛" 85.00
Vase, pk lustre w/lustre threading at top, ftd, 9⅜" 275.00
Vase, pk mottled colors, flared rim, ftd, 9¼" 150.00
Wine, bubbly gr w/HP decor, 4¼" 55.00

Pottery, Porcelain, Semiporcelain

Photo courtesy Guy S. Forsythe

Planter, floral decor on lavender, green interior, handles, Eichwald Majolica, 7", $165.00.

Bowl, Deco HP decor on scarlet, 2½x4" 385.00
Clock, faux marble w/flower basket, German works, 7" 135.00

Creamer, bird figural, 4¾" 45.00
Creamer, duck figural, mc, 3¾" 40.00
Creamer, elk head 50.00
Creamer, pk lustre, 3¼" 20.00
Figurine, elephant, 4½" 50.00
Figurine, lady, Deco-style, wht, 9¾" 250.00
Flower holder, bird on stump, 5⅜" 40.00
Planter, floral on lav, gr int, hdls, Eichwald Majolica, 7" 165.00
Plate, HP yel chicks on wht, 6½" 35.00
Potato server, potato form w/butter pat finial, 5" 30.00
Teapot, rooster on tan, child sz, 5¼" 45.00
Vase, Egyptian chariot decor w/head hdls, 8½" 385.00
Vase, Egyptian figures in band on streaked tan, 8½" 400.00
Wall pocket, woodpecker on tree trunk, mc, 7¾" 95.00

D'Argental

D'Argental cameo glass was produced in France from the 1870s until about 1920 in the Art Nouveau style. Browns and tans were favored colors used to complement floral and scenic designs developed through acid cuttings. Our advisor for this category is Don Williams; he is listed in the Directory under Missouri.

Cameo

Lamp, 8" dome shade/base w/orchids, red on citron, 18" 6,500.00
Vase, castle, red/maroon on opal amber, 10x5" 1,150.00
Vase, lake fr by trees on yel opal/maroon, 13¾" 1,500.00
Vase, palm trees/oasis, red/wine on citron, slender, 12" 1,600.00
Vase, poppies/pods, gray-blk on lt gr frost, 6¾" 400.00
Vase, riverside landscape, amber/red/maroon, bottle form, 12" .1,150.00
Vase, riverside/mtn landscape, amber/burgundy, ovoid, 8" 865.00
Vase, trees/water, wine-brn on amber, slim, 7½" 650.00
Vase, 3 framed landscapes, red/blk on yel/wine, 12x6" 1,150.00

Daum Nancy

Daum was an important producer of French cameo glass, operating from the late 1800s until after the turn of the century. They used various techniques — acid cutting, wheel engraving, and handwork — to create beautiful scenic designs and nature subjects in the Art Nouveau manner. Virtually all examples are signed. Our advisor for this category is Don Williams; he is listed in the Directory under Missouri.

Cameo

Vase, wild flowers, red, silver, white, and green on white frost with yellow tint, applied glass ornamentation, rolled lip, pedestal foot, signed, 8", $9,500.00.

Bowl, floral, cut/pnt on yel/clear, 4-lobe top, 3¼x5½" 1,650.00
Box, birds/snow, blk on orange, 2x3" dia 3,500.00
Ewer, trumpet flowers, emb silver ft/hdl/neck/lid, 12" 4,880.00

Ewer, 2 insects/flowers, gold/bl on lt bl/gr, squatty, 4" 4,000.00
Lamp, 6½" dia shade & base w/raspberries on yel/gr, 15" 7,500.00
Plaque, geese/lake, blk on orange mottle, 7x11", +fr 1,750.00
Shot glass, summer scene silhouette on citron, 2" 1,250.00
Toothpick holder, berries, cut/pnt on yel/clear, 1¾" 950.00
Vase, appl spider on etched web w/grape leaves on mottle, 6" .3,750.00
Vase, berried stalks, gr/yel on opal, pulled/notched rim, 10" ...2,300.00
Vase, berries/leaves, mc on yel/wht, sq, 4½x2" 1,600.00
Vase, berries/vines, red on amber, ovoid, 6⅜" 1,800.00
Vase, bird on snow/forest, blk on wht opal, stick neck, 11" 6,500.00
Vase, bud; thistle stalk, maroon on rainbow texture, 4½" 575.00
Vase, cockscomb stalks/grasses, rust on amber/orange, 13½" ...2,500.00
Vase, cornflowers/webs/bees, gilt neck/base motif, ftd, 7¾" 5,250.00
Vase, cyclamens, maroon pnt on gr/mottled frost, sqd, 4¾" 2,200.00
Vase, Deco floral/geometric panels, amber on frost, 9x11" 800.00
Vase, fall scene, yel/tan on yel mottle, flattened, bun ft, 10" 8,000.00
Vase, fleur-de-lis/crown/sword, cut/gilded, 7½" 1,100.00
Vase, floral, cut/pnt on purple/yel/pk, cylinder, 3½x2½" 1,350.00
Vase, floral, red/wine on yel/gr/clear mottle, sq, 4¾x2" 2,100.00
Vase, floral stalks, red/gr on yel to red/gr, disk ft, 11½" 3,200.00
Vase, floriform; leaves, gr/opal/gold, petal edge, 5x7" 1,250.00
Vase, foxglove stalks, tan/brn on amber, ftd floriform, 21" 4,500.00
Vase, iris, fuchsia/blk-gr on wine/almond, bottle form, 20" 4,500.00
Vase, leaves over bulb bottom, dk gr on martele pk, 12x4" 6,600.00
Vase, leaves/seed pods, dk gr on pk/yel mottle, 19" 2,450.00
Vase, lilacs, naturalistic wht/gr, pillow form, 6¾x7" 3,450.00
Vase, rain scene, cut/pnt on pk/gr, 2¼x1" 1,800.00
Vase, sailboats (11), cut/pnt on yel/orange, 1½x2¼" 1,200.00
Vase, seascape, brn on yel/gr mottle, bun base, 24" 4,300.00
Vase, snowy woodland, mottled sky, dmn-section rim, 7" 2,800.00
Vase, snowy woodland pnt on orange/olive, egg shape, 3¼" 2,900.00
Vase, spring trees on lt bl/opal/lime, ftd, 6" 2,700.00
Vase, spring waterfront, cut/pnt, shouldered cylinder, 9¾" 4,400.00
Vase, star flowers, brn on yel/amber mottle, shouldered, 8" 2,000.00
Vase, summer scene w/village, blk on dk bl/frost, bell form, 4" .2,100.00
Vase, summer woodland/meadow, wine/gr on bl mottle, 10" 6,000.00
Vase, sweet peas, wine/gr on apricot/wht, ftd, 11½x3½" 1,350.00
Vase, thistle blooms/vines, cut/pnt on lt amethyst, 3¾x3" 700.00
Vase, tulips, purple on gr/yel, 2¾" 750.00
Vase, tulips (long-stem), pnt/gilt on opaque gr/amber, hdls, 7" ..2,875.00
Vase, tulips/ferns on yel/orange, 3½x2¾" 900.00
Vase, vines/pods cascade from folded rim, gr on yel opal, 11" ..3,000.00
Vase, wheat stalks, pnt/gilt on purple/wht mottle, 11x3" 5,750.00
Vase, wisteria, cut/pnt on frost/gr-yel, 15x3¾" 2,600.00
Vase, wisteria, pk on lt teal martele, silver base, 16½" 3,300.00

Enameled Glass

Atomizer, landscape scene, gilt metal mts, missing bulb, 7½" .1,200.00
Bowl, mums, mc/gilt on amber, shaped rectangle rim, 3¾x7¾" L 800.00
Creamer, windmill/harbor, bl-blk on opal texture, w/lid, 4¾" .1,750.00
Cup & saucer, windmill/harbor, bl-blk on opal texture, 1¾"; 5" .950.00
Punch cup, harbor scene/peasant, blk on textured opal, 1¾" 750.00
Salt cellar, harbor scene w/cottage, oval, 1⅛" 900.00
Sugar bowl, harbor scene, blk on opal, w/lid, 4¾" 2,200.00
Vase, Dutch scene/sailboats, blk on frost, ftd, 3¼" 850.00
Vase, Post Tenebras Lux, mc shield, wht goose, 5¾" 2,500.00
Vase, thistles, burgundy on yel mottle, 4½" 500.00

Miscellaneous

Bowl, etched sunflowers/vines on citron & gold-brn, 7½x12" .2,500.00
Bowl, yel/wht/dk bl frosted spatter, 2¾x6" 175.00
Box, glossy orange w/blk knob on dome lid, 5" 150.00

Compote, cranberry mottle w/opal & dk bl foil inclusions, 10" ..**600.00**
Decanter, clear w/cut & polished panels w/gold trim, 11x4" **175.00**
Flowerpot, tiny bubbles in clear, flared U-form, 5¾" **345.00**
Lamp, orange/wine w/mica suspended shade; heart-ft C shaft .**2,300.00**
Tumbler, cluthra type w/yel & orange swirl stripes, 4" **150.00**
Tumbler, mistletoe, clear w/gilt & wht berries, dtd 1910, 3½" ...**500.00**
Vase, etched leafy band on clear, fine-rib pillow form, 4" **800.00**
Vase, etched woven 'splint' on gr, ovoid w/long neck, 6¾" **345.00**
Vase, pk/purple/wht spatter, purple base, long slim neck, 22" **500.00**
Vase, topaz w/repeating etched geometric panels, 7¾" **375.00**

De Vez

De Vez was a type of acid-cut French cameo glass produced by Cristallerie de Pantin in Paris around the turn of the century. Our advisor for this category is Don Williams; he is listed in the Directory under Missouri.

Bell, floral, cranberry on gold irid, brass hanger, 8½x6½" **2,100.00**
Bowl, firs/islands/mtns/birds, blk-gr on yel opal, sq rim, 4" **650.00**
Vase, Dutch landscape, purple/pk/orange/yel, cylinder, 7½" **800.00**
Vase, floral, purple-blk on citron, bun ft, shouldered, 7x2½" **650.00**
Vase, maid/goat on mtn, vista behind, dk to lt bl, 8x4" **1,650.00**
Vase, mtn/trees/lake, dk bl on yel/pk, 4x1¾" **650.00**
Vase, ships in harbor, wine on opal/amber, 4" **450.00**
Vase, swans/plants, gray-gr w/apricot tint, stick neck, 10" **800.00**
Vase, trees/cactus/mtns, dk bl on bl-gray/ivory, 9x3" **900.00**
Vase, 3 storks, blk on lt bl, bulbous w/cup rim, 4¾" **650.00**
Vase, 5-petal flowers, frosted/pk, 3¾" **260.00**

De Vilbiss

Perfume bottles, atomizers, and dresser accessories marketed by the De Vilbiss Company are appreciated by collectors today for the various types of lovely glassware used in their manufacture as well as for their pleasing shapes. Various companies provided the glass, while De Vilbiss made only the metal tops. They marketed their merchandise not only here but in Paris, England, Canada, and Havana as well. Their marks were acid stamped, ink stamped, in gold script, molded in, or on paper labels. One is no more significant than another. Our advisor for this category is Randy Monsen; he is listed in the Directory under Virginia.

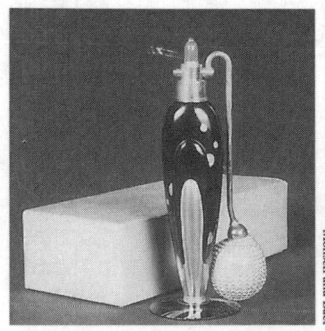

Atomizer, black glass with abstract gold pattern, Bakelite crown top, 6½", with instructions, MIB, $550.00.

Photo courtesy Monsen and Baer

Atomizer, amber w/bl ft, gold mesh bulb, att Steuben, 6½" **440.00**
Atomizer, bl & wht opal w/wheel-cut decor, slim, crochet bag, 8" .**550.00**
Atomizer, blk Deco style w/gold, sq w/faceted shoulders, 3¾" **88.00**
Atomizer, blk disc w/silver swirls, silver attachment, 1¾" **110.00**
Atomizer, cranberry w/gilt metal mts, rpl bulb, 7" **300.00**
Atomizer, frosted floral w/gold metal cap & tassels, mk, 5¼" **175.00**
Atomizer, gold on crystal w/gold draped lady stem, 7¼" **750.00**
Atomizer, gr w/wht swirls, baluster, gold attachment, 7" **120.00**

Atomizer, Imperial, cased peach to bl w/gold & turq stones, 7¼" .**1,350.00**
Atomizer, Lenox White Rabbit, rare **350.00**
Atomizer, orange irid w/metal top, long stem, 5" **185.00**
Atomizer, orange/blk/gold rvpt w/orig ball/net, mk, 7¼" **412.50**
Atomizer, pk, gold caryatid stem, orig bulb, 7¼" **1,250.00**
Atomizer, pk w/gold attachment & ft, Deco lines, mk, 3¾" **135.00**
Atomizer, Steuben Alabaster w/gilt ft **300.00**
Atomizer, wht satin w/gold enamel bird, rpl ball, 7" **715.00**
Bottle, gold & blk on clear, bell shape, flat dropper, 4" **135.00**
Bottle, lt amber, 6 panel w/hex ped ft, dropper, 6¼" **200.00**
Bottle, lt pk w/dk pk enamel & clear stem, flat dropper, 7" **200.00**
Bottle, pk satin w/mc enamel & gold, dropper, 4¾" **200.00**
Box, powder; gold enamel w/mc flowers, acid etched, 5¾" **87.50**
Lamp, perfume; exotic bird on glass insert, sq, 8½" **150.00**
Lamp, perfume; nude figure on glass insert, rnd, 7" **400.00**
Shaker, bath powder; bl opal **125.00**
Vanity set, lt bl & crystal frost, 4-pc, rare **400.00**

Decanters

Ceramic whiskey decanters were brought into prominence in 1955 by the James Beam Distilling Company. Few other companies besides Beam produced these decanters during the next ten years or so; however, other companies did eventually follow suit. At its peak in 1975, at least twenty prominent companies and several on a lesser scale made these decanters. Beam stopped making decanters in mid-1992. Now only a couple of companies are still producing these collectibles.

Liquor dealers have told collectors for years that ceramic decanters are not as valuable, and in some cases worthless, if emptied or if the federal tax stamp has been broken. Nothing is further from the truth. Following are but a few of many reasons you should consider emptying ceramic decanters:

1) If the thin glaze on the inside ever cracks (and it does in a small percentage of decanters), the contents will push through to the outside. It is then referred to as a 'leaker' and worth a fraction of its original value.

2) A large number of decanters left full in one area of your house poses a fire hazard.

3) A burglar, after stealing jewelry and electronics, may make off with some of your decanters just to enjoy the contents. If they are empty, chances are they will not be bothered.

4) It is illegal in most states for collectors to sell a full decanter without a liquor license.

Unlike years ago, few collectors now collect all types of decanters. Most now specialize. For example, they may collect trains, cars, owls, Indians, clowns, or any number of different things that have been depicted on or as a decanter. They are finding exceptional quality available at reasonable prices, especially when compared with many other types of collectibles.

We have tried to list those brands that are the most popular with collectors. Likewise, individual decanters listed are the ones (or representative of the ones) most commonly found. The following listing is but a small fraction of the thousands of decanters that have been produced.

These decanters come from all over the world. While Jim Beam owned its own china factory in the U.S., some of the others have been imported from Mexico, Taiwan, Japan, and elsewhere. They vary in size from miniatures (approximately 2 oz.) to gallons. Values range from a few dollars to more than $3,000.00 per decanter.

Most collectors and dealers define a 'mint' decanter as one with no chips, no cracks, and label intact. A missing federal tax stamp or lack of contents have no bearing on value. All values are given for 'mint' decanters. A 'mini' behind a listing indicates a miniature. All others are fifth or 750 ml unless noted otherwise. Our advisor for this category is Roy Willis; he is listed in the Directory under Kentucky.

Aesthetic Specialties (ASI)

Car, Stanley 1909, blk or gr 65.00
Car, Stanley 1911, blk 75.00
Kentucky Derby 30.00

Ballantine

Fisherman 18.00
Gold Bag 25.00
Knight 10.00

Beam

Casino Series, Barney's Slot Machine 25.00
Casino Series, Binion's Horseshoe 10.00
Casino Series, Harold's Club Pinwheel 30.00
Centennial Series, Civil War, North 29.00
Centennial Series, Civil War, South 45.00
Centennial Series, Edison Light Bulb 20.00
Centennial Series, Reno 6.00
Centennial Series, San Diego 5.00
Executive Series, 1958, Gray Cherub 125.00
Executive Series, 1959, Tavern Scene 40.00
Executive Series, 1973, Phoenician 12.00
Executive Series, 1974, Twin Cherubs 18.00
Executive Series, 1987, Twin Doves 18.00
Executive Series, 1988, Holiday Carolers 50.00
Foreign Series, Australia Hobo (Swagman) 20.00
Foreign Series, Australia Magpies 18.00
Foreign Series, Germany, 1970 ....10.00
Foreign Series, Italy, Boys Town 9.00
Foreign Series, Seoul, Korea 20.00
Foreign Series, Thailand 6.00
Organization Series, Ducks Unlimited #11 ....65.00
Organization Series, Ducks Unlimited #12 ....50.00
Organization Series, Ducks Unlimited #13 ....39.00
Organization Series, Ducks Unlimited #14 ....45.00
Organization Series, Ducks Unlimited #15 ....90.00
Organization Series, Homebuilders 25.00
Organization Series, LVNH Owl 18.00
Organization Series, Marine Devil Dog 40.00
Organization Series, Pearl Harbor, 1976 ....12.00
Organization Series, Shrine, Moila w/Camel 19.00
Organization Series, Shrine, Moila w/Sword 22.00
Organization Series, Telephone #1, Wall 25.00
Organization Series, Telephone #3, French Cradle 22.00
Organization Series, Telephone #5, Pay Phone 50.00
People Series, John Henry 35.00
People Series, King Kamehameha 18.00
People Series, Leprechaun 20.00
Political Series, 1968 Clown, Republican or Democrat 12.00
Political Series, 1972 on Football, Republican or Democrat 15.00
Regal China Series, AC Spark Plug 38.00
Regal China Series, Black Canasta, 1957 ....15.00
Regal China Series, Canteen 20.00
Regal China Series, Coffee Mill 15.00
Regal China Series, Franklin Mint 10.00
Regal China Series, Grand Canyon 8.00
Regal China Series, Jug, 1978, brn or oatmeal 6.00
Regal China Series, King Kong 20.00
Regal China Series, London Bridge 6.00
Regal China Series, New York World's Fair, 1964 ......15.00
Regal China Series, Pony Express 10.00

Regal China Series, Redwood 6.00
Regal China Series, Tombstone 10.00
Regal China Series, Yosemite 5.00

Wheel Series, 1903 Model A Ford, red or black, $50.00.

Wheel Series, Bass Boat 38.00
Wheel Series, Chevy '57 Belair Hot Rod 110.00
Wheel Series, Corvette, 1968, bl 65.00
Wheel Series, Corvette, 1968, maroon 60.00
Wheel Series, Dodge Challenger, 1970 Hot Rod 60.00
Wheel Series, Dump Truck, Gravel 45.00
Wheel Series, Ford, 1913 Model T, gr or blk 50.00
Wheel Series, Ford, 1929 Phaeton 70.00
Wheel Series, Space Shuttle 65.00
Wheel Series, Stutz Bearcat, yel or gray 50.00
Wheel Series, Thomas Flyer, bl or ivory 65.00
Wheel Series, 1934 Fire Chief Car 80.00
Wheel Series, 1956 Thunderbird, blk or gray 100.00

Brooks

Tractor, Fordson, 1971, $20.00.

American Legion, Hawaii 15.00
Bear, Golden 8.00
Bowler 15.00
Cable Car 6.00
Cannon 9.00
Charolais Bull 15.00
Clown w/Accordion 29.00
Dollar, Silver 9.00
Elephant, Big Bertha 20.00
Greensboro Open, 1972 ....28.00
Hog, Razorback, 1969 ....22.00
Jester 10.00
Ontario Racer #10 ....35.00
West Virginia Mountain Lady 22.00
West Virginia Mountain Man 65.00

Double Springs

Cord, 1937 ....35.00

Owl, brn or red 15.00
Peasant, boy or girl 5.00
Tiger on Ball 20.00

Famous Firsts

Hurdy Gurdy 18.00
Phonograph 45.00
Renault Racer #3A 65.00
Riverboat, Robert E Lee 65.00
Telephone, Floral 25.00
Telephone, French 40.00
Telephone, Johnny Reb 35.00

Hoffman

Aesop's Fables, 6 different, ea 25.00
Bird, Turkey, 1980 ....35.00
Dogs, mini, 1978, 6 different, ea 30.00
Dogs, mini, 1981, 6 different, ea 22.00
Generation Gap Pair, mini 15.00
Indy 500 Commemorative, 1972 ....30.00
Indy 500 Commemorative, 1973 ....50.00
Mr Lucky Series, Mr Cobbler 29.00
Mr Lucky Series, Mr Cobbler, mini 15.00
Mr Lucky Series, Mr Doctor 38.00
Mr Lucky Series, Mr Doctor, mini 18.00
Mr Lucky Series, Mr Sandman 25.00
Mr Lucky Series, Mr Sandman, mini 12.00
Russell, CM, Series, Red River Breed 45.00
Russell, CM, Series, Red River Breed, mini 15.00
Wildlife Series, Falcon & Rabbit 65.00
Wildlife Series, Falcon & Rabbit, mini 15.00
Wildlife Series, Owl & Chipmunk 45.00
Wildlife Series, Owl & Chipmunk, mini 15.00

Kontinental

Gandy Dancer 25.00
Homesteader 30.00
Innkeeper 30.00
Medicine Man 50.00
Pharmacist 35.00
Prospector 40.00
Prospector, mini 20.00
Saddle Maker 35.00
Saddle Maker, mini 20.00

Lionstone

Annie Christmas 20.00
Betsy Ross 25.00
Blacksmith 29.00
Buccaneer 25.00
Calamity Jane 25.00
Dancehall Girl 50.00
Engineer, Railroad 29.00
Falcon 25.00
Gambler 20.00
Gambler, mini 15.00
Jesse James 22.00
Lonely Luke 25.00
Lonely Luke, mini 18.00
Lucky Buck 25.00

Lucky Buck, mini 18.00
Molly Brown 20.00
Mountain Man 22.00
Paul Revere 30.00
Quail 25.00
Roadrunner 25.00
Roadrunner, mini 15.00
Sheriff 22.00
Sheriff, mini 15.00
Sodbuster 20.00
Stage Driver 25.00
Tinker 25.00
Vigilante 20.00
Woodhawk 25.00

McCormick

Bicentennial Series, Ben Franklin 25.00
Bicentennial Series, Ben Franklin, mini 18.00
Bicentennial Series, John Hancock 25.00
Bicentennial Series, John Hancock, mini 18.00
Bicentennial Series, Thomas Jefferson 25.00
Bicentennial Series, Thomas Jefferson, mini 18.00
Caio Baby 25.00
Carver, George Washington 30.00
Edison, Thomas 25.00
Elvis, Designer I 150.00
Elvis, Designer II 190.00
Elvis, Designer III 250.00
Elvis, Silver Anniversary 150.00
Ewing, JR 50.00

Gunfighter Series,
Black Bart, $35.00.

Gunfighters, 8 different, ea 35.00
Gunfighters, 8 different, mini, ea 25.00
Houston, Sam 35.00
Lobsterman 30.00
Missouri, China 10.00
Missouri, Glass 7.00
Packard, 1937, blk or cream 50.00
Pocahontas 90.00
Shrine, Midian 12.00
Strowger Telephone 45.00
Thelma Lu 35.00
Thelma Lu, mini 18.00
Twain, Mark 30.00

Old Bardstown

Foster Brooks	20.00
Surface Miner	25.00
Tiger	35.00

Old Commonwealth

Coal Miner #3, w/Lump of Coal	40.00
Coal Miner #3, w/Lump of Coal, mini	20.00
Coal Miner #5, Coal Shooter	30.00
Coal Miner #5, Coal Shooter, mini	20.00
Fireman, Volunteer #5	75.00
Fireman, Volunteer #5, mini	30.00
Fireman, Volunteer #6	75.00
Fireman, Volunteer #6, mini	30.00
Horses of Ireland	30.00
Irish Lore	25.00
Lumberjack	30.00
Oktoberfest	45.00

Old Fitzgerald

Old Ironsides	5.00
Pheasant Rising	7.00
Ram, Bighorn	7.00
Texas 'Hook'em Horns'	20.00
Tree of Life	7.00
Venetian	4.00

Old Mr. Boston

Anthony Wayne	10.00
Molly Pitcher	8.00
Nathan Hale	10.00
Race Car #9, red or yel	48.00

Ski Country

Antelope, Pronghorn	60.00
Basset Hound	55.00
Basset Hound, mini	35.00
Buffalo Stampede	50.00
Buffalo Stampede, mini	20.00
Caveman	28.00
Caveman, mini	18.00
Chicadees	70.00
Chicadees, mini	35.00
Condor	50.00
Condor, mini	30.00
Ducks Unlimited, Bufflehead	58.00
Ducks Unlimited, Bufflehead, mini	35.00
Ducks Unlimited, Oldsquaw	65.00
Ducks Unlimited, Oldsquaw, mini	35.00
Eagle, Easter Seals	60.00
Eagle, Easter Seals, mini	30.00
Falcon, Gyrafalcon	75.00
Falcon, Gyrafalcon, mini	30.00
Falcon, Peregrine	85.00
Falcon, Peregrine, gal	300.00
Falcon, Peregrine, mini	20.00
Fox Family	65.00
Fox Family, mini	40.00
Hawk Eagle	150.00

Hawk Eagle, mini	75.00
Indian, Ceremonial Dancers, #1, Eagle	200.00
Indian, Ceremonial Dancers, #1, Eagle, mini	35.00
Indian, Ceremonial Dancers, #2, Buffalo	180.00
Indian, Ceremonial Dancers, #2, Buffalo, mini	40.00
Kangaroo	35.00
Kangaroo, mini	25.00
Labrador w/Duck	125.00
Labrador w/Duck, mini	40.00
Meadowlark	60.00
Meadowlark, mini	30.00
Owl, Horned	85.00
Owl, Horned, mini	85.00
Peacock	100.00
Peacock, mini	60.00
Penguin Family	60.00
Penguin Family, mini	30.00
Polar Bear	60.00
Polar Bear, mini	30.00
Raccoon	50.00
Raccoon, mini	35.00
Ringmaster	35.00
Ringmaster, mini	25.00
Swan, Black	50.00
Swan, Black, mini	45.00
Woodpecker, Gila	70.00
Woodpecker, Gila, mini	35.00

Wild Turkey

Crystal, Baccarat	225.00
Crystal, Wedgwood	225.00
Flask, silver, plastic-covered	10.00
Flask, stainless steel, leather-covered	20.00
Mack Truck	28.00
Series I, #1	250.00
Series I, #2	150.00
Series I, #3	60.00
Series I, #4	60.00
Series I, #5	30.00
Series I, #6	25.00
Series I, #7	25.00
Series I, #8	45.00
Series II, Lore #1	25.00
Series II, Lore #2	35.00
Series II, Lore #3	45.00
Series II, Lore #4	50.00
Series III, #7, Turkey & Red Fox, mini	50.00

Decoys

American colonists learned the craft of decoy making from the Indians who used them to lure birds out of the sky as an important food source. Early models were carved from wood such as pine, cedar, balsa, etc., and a few were made of canvas or papier-mache. There are two basic types of decoys: water floaters and shorebirds (also called 'stick-ups'). Within each type are many different species, ducks being the most plentiful since they migrated along all four of America's great waterways. Market hunting became big business around 1880, resulting in large-scale commercial production of decoys which continued until about 1910 when such hunting was outlawed by the Migratory Bird Treaty.

Today decoys are one of the most collectible types of American folk art. The most valuable are those carved by such artists as Laing,

Crowell, Ward, and Wheeler, to name only a few. Each area, such as Massachusetts, Connecticut, Maine, the Illinois River, and the Delaware River, produces decoys with distinctive regional characteristics. Examples of commercial decoys produced by well-known factories — among them Mason, Stevens, and Dodge — are also prized by collectors. Though mass-produced, these nevertheless required a certain amount of hand carving and decorating. Well-carved examples, especially those of rare species, are appreciating rapidly, and those with original paint are more desirable. Writer Carl F. Luckey compiled a fully illustrated identification and value guide, *Collecting Antique Bird Decoys*. In the listings that follow, all decoys are solid-bodied unless noted hollow.

Key:
CG — Challenge Grade	PG — Premier Grade
MDF — Mason's Decoy Factory	RP — repaint
OP — original paint	SG — Standard Grade
ORP — old repaint	WDF — Wildfowler Decoy Factory
OWP — original working paint	WOP — worn original paint

Black Duck, Callie O'Neal, thin crack on bottom, minor WOP ...**600.00**
Black Duck, Huff, hollow, dry OP, EX feathering, 1900-20 .....**1,000.00**
Bluebill drake, Gus Moak, hollow cvd, rpt, prof rpr, 1920s **400.00**
Bluebill drake, Keyes Chadwick, OWP w/some rpt **300.00**
Bluebill drake, MDF, SG, glass eyes, ORP, VG+ **200.00**
Bluebill hen, WDF, stamped underside, 'JD' under bill, EX OP ..**150.00**
Brant, Cooper Pedmore, doweled body halves, cracked neck, OWP .**200.00**
Brant, Joseph Lincoln, prof rpt to bill, wear to OP **3,750.00**

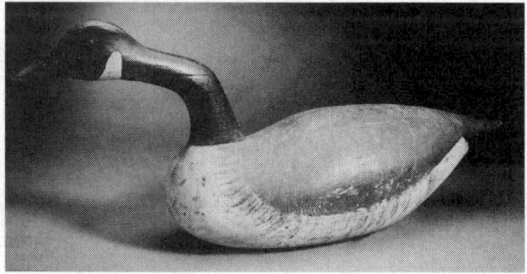

Canada goose, carved and painted, attributed to Joe Lincoln, age cracks, 12½x30", $9,775.00.

Canada Goose, Bradford Salmon, OWP, G **700.00**
Canada Goose, WDF, branded COE, EX OP **250.00**
Canvasback drake, Duncan Ducharme, rpt, sm cracks **170.00**
Canvasback drake, glass eyes, sm cracks & shot mks, EX OP **70.00**
Canvasback drake, Hiram Hotze, lead keel removed, RP, EX **375.00**
Canvasback drake, Ralph Malpage, detailed feathering, NM OP, EX ...**150.00**
Common Loon, Charles Birdsall, WDF stamp, sgn & dtd 1970, NM .**1,000.00**
Coot, Ben Schmidt, reglued bill, underside crack, EX+ OP **475.00**
Dove, Haertel, trn head, branded HH, NM OP **2,700.00**
Dowitcher, John Dilley, relief wing cvg, NM OP **7,500.00**
English Wood Pigeon, iron bill, movable wings, VG+ OP **450.00**
Golden Plover, Wm Folger, shoe-button eyes, ca 1860s, EX OP .**9,000.00**
Goldeneye drake, branded SF, sm dents, wear to OP **125.00**
Greenwing Teal, Charles Reeves, branded COE, EX OP **500.00**
Greenwing Teal drake, Lashbrook, stamped & sgn, NM OP, EX .**850.00**
Greenwing Teal drake, MDF, NM OP, rare **850.00**
Heron, Grayson Chesser, bill reglued, 1970s, WOP **350.00**
Hooded Merganser drake, Tuffield King, sm dents, NM OP **250.00**
Mallard drake, Holmes, sm dents, WOP, early **1,000.00**
Mallard drake, Otto Garren, crack in neck, OWP **160.00**
Mallard drake, Schoenhieders, dents, OWP **500.00**

Mallard hen, Animal Trap Decoy Co, orig tag, NM OP **100.00**
Mallard hen, Carl Koch, sm dents, EX OP **50.00**
Mallard hen, Judge Cameron, branded, OP on head & bill, o/w rpt ..**300.00**
Mallard hen, Kessler, sm crack in neck, EX OP **310.00**
Mallard hen, MDF, PG, NM OP, never rigged **2,400.00**
Merganser hen, Christie Bros, tight age line, EX OP, VG **4,000.00**
Old Squaw, Bob White, hollow, mk lead keel w/logo, M, pr **700.00**
Pied-Billed Grebe, Haertel, hollow cvd, sgn & dtd 1970, M ...**1,200.00**
Pintail drake, Dodge Factory, EX OP, rare, ca 1880 ....**675.00**
Pintail drake, Doug Jester, sm dents, EX OP **800.00**
Pintail drake, Richard Sheppard, bill reglued, VG WOP **175.00**
Pintail drake, Whittington, sgn & dtd 1970, NMOP, EX **500.00**
Pintail drake, Wilcoxen, hollow, neck crack, old overpnt gone .**200.00**
Pintail hen, MDF, SG, rstr pnt w/traces of OP **150.00**
Redhead drake, Chris Smith, hollow, OWP **200.00**
Ruddy Duck, Francis Collins, detailed feathering, NM OP **125.00**
Ruddy Turnstone, Townsend, rpl bill, 1870-80, EX OP **1,900.00**
Snow Goose, Robert Manning, hollow cvd, NM OP, VG **150.00**
Stilt Sandpiper, Haertel, wooden base sgn, 1985, M **1,900.00**
Teal hen, Paul Wieberg, glass eyes, reglued bill, EX OP **150.00**
Virginia-style Curlew, McIntyre, sgn, NM OP, EX **450.00**
White Wing Scoter, Gus Wilson, relief wing cvg, VG WOP **900.00**
Widgeon drake, MDF, CG, G OP **700.00**

Dedham Pottery

Originally founded in Chelsea, Massachusetts, as the Chelsea Keramic Works, the name was changed to Dedham Pottery in 1895 after the firm relocated in Dedham, near Boston, Massachusetts. The ware utilized a gray stoneware body with a crackle glaze and simple cobalt border designs of flowers, birds, and animals. Decorations were brushed on by hand using an ancient Chinese method which suspended the cobalt within the overall glaze. There were thirteen standard patterns, among them Magnolia, Iris, Butterfly, Duck, Polar Bear, and Rabbit, the latter of which was chosen to represent the company on their logo. On the very early pieces, the rabbits face left; decorators soon found the reverse position easier to paint, and the rabbits were turned to the right. (Earlier examples are worth from 10% to 20% more than identical pieces manufactured in later years.) In addition to the standard patterns, other designs were produced for special orders. These and artist-signed pieces are highly valued by collectors today.

Though their primary product was the blue-printed, crackle-glazed dinnerware, two types of artware were also produced: crackle glaze and flambe. Their notable volcanic ware was a type of the latter. The mark is incised and often accompanies the cipher of Hugh Robertson. The firm was operated by succeeding generations of the Robertson family until it closed in 1943. Our advisor for this category is Dale MacLean; he is listed in the Directory under Massachusetts. See also Chelsea Keramic Art Works.

Dinnerware

Ashtray, Rabbit, stamped/registered/1931, 3¾" **325.00**
Bacon rasher, Grape, stamped, 1½x9¾" **425.00**
Bacon rasher, Rabbit, stamped, 1½x9¾" **375.00**
Bonbon, Rabbit, stamped/registered, 3½x4½" **500.00**
Bowl, Azalea, stamped/registered, 3⅛x7¼" **250.00**
Bowl, Polar Bear, stamped/registered, 2x5⅛" **575.00**
Bowl, Rabbit, hand sgn, 3x6" **500.00**
Bowl, Rabbit, stamped/registered/1931, 2x5" **200.00**
Bowl, rice; Butterfly, stamped, mini, 2x3½" **425.00**
Bowl, rice; Rabbit, stamped, mini, 2x3" **250.00**
Bowl, soup; Rabbit, stamped, 1¾x9" **300.00**
Bowl, Standing Rabbits, stamped/registered, 2½x5" **1,400.00**

Bowl, whipped cream; Rabbit, hand sgn/stamped, 2¾x7¼" 425.00
Candle snuffer, Rabbit, triangular, unmk, 2x1¼" 500.00
Charger, Rabbit, stamped (twice)/imp (twice), 12", NM 700.00
Compote, Rabbit, imp, 1¾x7¼" 850.00
Creamer, Chick, stamped, mini, 3x3¼" 2,200.00
Cup & saucer, Rabbit, registered, 4½", 7" 450.00
Cup & saucer, tea; Rabbit, 1931 bl mk, 2", 6" 225.00
Cup & saucer, tea; Swan, stamped/registered, 2", 6" 400.00
Cup & saucer, Turkey, stamped/registered, 3¼" 400.00
Cup plate, Rabbit, stamped, 4½" 300.00
Egg cup, dbl; Rabbit, stamped, 3x3" 300.00
Figurine, Rabbit, stamped/registered, 3" 600.00
Finger bowl, Magnolia, hand sgn, 2½x4⅜" 275.00
Flower holder, turtle figural, stamped, 3½" 600.00
Goblet, Rabbit, unmk, 4¾x3", NM 350.00
Marmalade jar, Rabbit, registered, 4½x4½" 650.00
Mug, child's, Elephant & Baby, stamped/registered, 3½x4¼" .1,500.00
Mug, child's, Rabbit, stamped, 3½x4¼" 450.00
Mustard jar, Azalea, stamped, 3¼x3" 300.00
Olive dish, Rabbit, stamped/registered/1931, 1¾x8" 450.00
Pickle dish, Swan, stamped, 1¾x10" 600.00
Pitcher, Azalea, stamped, 5x6" 550.00
Pitcher, Night & Day, Rooster & Owl, stamped, 5x5" 550.00
Pitcher, Oak Block, trunk w/branch hdl, stamped/registered, 5¾" .600.00
Pitcher, Rabbit, #7, stamped/registered, 5⅛x4½" 425.00
Pitcher, water; Rabbit, stamped/imp, 7x7½" 1,000.00
Plate, Azalea, stamped/imp, 10" 575.00
Plate, Bird in the Potted Orange Tree, imp, 10" 600.00
Plate, Butterfly, stamped/registered/imp (twice), 6⅛" 450.00
Plate, Chick, stamped/registered/imp (twice)/R2, 6" 2,500.00
Plate, Day Lily, stamped, rstr, 6⅛" 800.00
Plate, Dolphin, imp, 6½" 550.00
Plate, Dolphin, stamped/imp/B, 6½" 550.00
Plate, Double Turtle, stamped, 6⅛" 700.00
Plate, Elephant & Baby, registered/imp (twice), 9¾" 850.00
Plate, Elephant & Baby, stamped/imp (twice), 6" 600.00
Plate, Grape, stamped/imp, 8½", EX 300.00
Plate, Horse Chestnut, imp, 8½", NM 300.00
Plate, Horse Chestnut, stamped/registered/imp, 6" 225.00
Plate, Iris, Davenport rebus, stamped, 10" 425.00
Plate, Iris, registered/imp (twice), 8½" 300.00
Plate, Iris, resembles Davenport art, stamped, 10" 350.00
Plate, Lion Tapestry, stamped/imp, 8¾" 1,500.00
Plate, Lobster, stamped/registered/imp, 6" 600.00
Plate, Luna Moth, stamped/imp, 8½" 800.00
Plate, Magnolia, Davenport rebus, stamped/imp, 10" 425.00
Plate, Magnolia, stamped/imp, 8¼" 300.00
Plate, Magnolia, stamped/registered/imp, 6¼" 225.00
Plate, Mushroom, Davenport rebus, stamped, 8½" 800.00
Plate, Mushroom, stamped/imp, prof rstr, 10" 400.00
Plate, Pineapple, imp, 10" 800.00
Plate, Polar Bear, stamped/registered/imp (twice), 7¾" 650.00
Plate, Poppy, stamped/imp, 8½" 850.00
Plate, Rabbit, Davenport rebus, stamped, 8½" 325.00
Plate, Rabbit, stamped/imp, 10" 300.00
Plate, Rabbit, stamped/imp, 8¼", 4 for 950.00
Plate, Rabbit, stamped/registered/imp, 6" 225.00
Plate, Rabbit, stamped/registered/1931, 7¾", 4 for 900.00
Plate, Single-Ear Rabbit, stamped/imp, 8¼" 350.00
Plate, Snowtree, stamped/imp, 8¼" 300.00
Plate, Snowtree, stamped/registered/imp, 6" 275.00
Plate, Swan, imp, 10" 600.00
Plate, Swan, stamped, 6½" 400.00
Plate, Tufted Duck, imp, 8¾" 475.00

Plate, Turkey, imp, 8½", NM 350.00
Plate, Turkey, stamped/imp, 10" 425.00
Plate, Turkey, stamped/registered, Centenary mk, 6" 325.00
Plate, Water Lily, Davenport rebus, stamped/imp, 6" 225.00
Platter, Rabbit, stamped/imp, 7¾x13", NM 1,000.00
Shakers, Rabbit, registered, 3¾x2¼", pr 400.00
Stein, Rabbit, Devanport rebus, stamped/hand sgn, 4¾x5" 700.00
Sugar bowl, Rabbit, dome lid, hand sgn, 4¾x4½" 375.00

Sugar bowl, Rabbit (two-eared), blue bands at rim and lid, marked Registered, 4", $325.00.

Tea stand, Owl, stamped/imp, 7¾" 1,450.00
Teapot, Rabbit, resembles Davenport, stamped, 7⅛x8" 850.00
Tile, Rabbit, stamped/registered, 5½" 375.00
Tray, Rabbit, rolled edge, stamped, 14" 1,000.00
Tureen, Rabbit, domed lid, stamped, 3x9½", NM 750.00
Tureen, Rabbit, domed lid, stamped/registered, 3x7½" 500.00

Miscellaneous

Vase, apple gr w/silver-gray streaks, hand mk, 8¼x4¼" 550.00
Vase, bl/cafe-au-lait flambe lustre, 7½" 750.00
Vase, dripping/glossy brn/umber, HR, 8" 550.00
Vase, frothy bl/clear gr flambe, 10x8", NM 800.00
Vase, garnet to gr lustre flambe, 6½x5" 1,200.00
Vase, gr drip on red flambe, 9x5" 800.00
Vase, mirror blk/brn crystalline, Robertson, 10x6" 1,000.00
Vase, oxblood/gunmetal lustre drip, 9x4½" 1,300.00
Vase, plume, bl on wht crackleware, #38, 5x4½" 1,600.00
Vase, red/dk brn textured flambe (EX glaze), Robertson, 8x6" ...2,700.00
Vase, thick curdled volcanic moss/brn, bulbous, can neck, 11" .2,300.00
Vase, volcanic, dripping flesh-tone, BW/HR, 10x5½" 650.00
Vase, volcanic brn/gr curdled drip, 8½x5" 1,100.00

Degenhart

The Crystal Art Glass factory in Cambridge, Ohio, opened in 1947 under the private ownership of John and Elizabeth Degenhart. John had previously worked for the Cambridge Glass Company and was well known for his superior paperweights. After his death in 1964, Elizabeth took over management of the factory, hiring several workers from the defunct Cambridge Company, including Zack Boyd. Boyd was responsible for many unique colors, some of which were named for him. From 1964 to 1974, more than twenty-seven different moulds were created, most of them resulting from Elizabeth Degenhart's work and creativity, and over 145 official colors were developed. Elizabeth died in 1978, requesting that the ten moulds she had built while operating the factory were to be turned over to the Degenhart Museum. The remaining moulds were to be held by the Island Mould and Machine Company, who (complying with her request) removed the familiar 'D in heart' trademark. The factory was eventually bought by Zack's son, Bernard Boyd. He also acquired the remaining Degenhart moulds, to which he added his own logo.

In general, slags and opaques should be valued 15% to 20% higher than crystals in color.

Baby Shoe (Hobo Boot) Toothpick Holder, Dark Slag, unmk 35.00
Baby Shoe (Hobo Boot) Toothpick Holder, Opalescent 12.00
Baby Shoe (Hobo Boot) Toothpick Holder, Red 20.00
Baby Shoe (Hobo Boot) Toothpick Holder, Toffee 15.00
Basket Toothpick Holder, Milk Blue 15.00
Basket Toothpick Holder, Sparrow Slag 20.00
Beaded Oval Toothpick Holder, Fog 20.00
Beaded Oval Toothpick Holder, Heather 20.00
Beaded Oval Toothpick Holder, Mulberry 20.00
Beaded Oval Toothpick Holder, Royal Violet 25.00
Beaded Oval Toothpick Holder, Rubina 60.00
Bell, Bluebell 12.00
Bell, Charcoal 12.00
Bell, Frosty Jade 20.00
Bell, Milk Blue 12.00
Bell, Sea Foam 12.00
Bird Salt & Pepper, Antique Blue, pr 35.00
Bird Salt & Pepper, Emerald Green, pr 30.00
Bird Salt w/Cherry, Autumn 20.00
Bird Salt w/Cherry, Blue & White 25.00
Bird Salt w/Cherry, Canary 20.00
Bird Salt w/Cherry, Champagne 20.00
Bird Salt w/Cherry, Dichromatic 20.00
Bird Salt w/Cherry, Fog 15.00
Bird Salt w/Cherry, Jade 25.00
Bird Salt w/Cherry, Mint 25.00
Bird Toothpick Holder, Bernard Boyd's Ebony 35.00
Bird Toothpick Holder, Ivory 25.00
Bird Toothpick Holder, Pink 20.00
Bow Slipper, Blue Green 20.00
Bow Slipper, Canary 15.00
Bow Slipper, Custard 20.00
Bow Slipper, Old Lavender 15.00
Bow Slipper, Pigeon Blood 25.00
Bow Slipper, Sunset 15.00
Buzz Saw Wine, Bloody Mary 65.00
Buzz Saw Wine, Buttercup 30.00
Buzz Saw Wine, Desert Sun 35.00
Buzz Saw Wine, Ice Blue Carnival 40.00
Buzz Saw Wine, Lemon Custard 40.00
Buzz Saw Wine, Peach Blo 25.00
Buzz Saw Wine, Vaseline 20.00
Chick Salt Covered Dish, Blue Green, 2" 20.00
Chick Salt Covered Dish, Emerald Green, 2" 20.00
Chick Salt Covered Dish, Pine Green, 2" 20.00
Coaster, Crystal 8.00
Coaster, Red 15.00
Coaster, Vaseline 8.00
Colonial Drape Toothpick Holder, Cobalt 20.00
Colonial Drape Toothpick Holder, Milk Blue 15.00
Daisy & Button Creamer & Sugar, Cobalt 90.00
Daisy & Button Hat, Frosty Jade 15.00
Daisy & Button Hat, Persimmon 15.00
Daisy & Button Hat, Rose Marie 15.00
Daisy & Button Salt, Dark Amber 12.00
Daisy & Button Salt, Lime Ice 15.00
Daisy & Button Toothpick Holder, Dishromatic 25.00
Daisy & Button Toothpick Holder, Mint Green 20.00
Daisy & Button Wine, Crystal 15.00
Daisy & Button Wine, Sapphire 15.00
Elephant Head Toothpick Holder, Caramel 60.00

Elephant Head Toothpick Holder, Honey Amber 27.00
Elephant Head Toothpick Holder, Jade 65.00
Elephant Head Toothpick Holder, Milk Blue 40.00
Forget-Me-Not Toothpick Holder, Angel Blue 15.00
Forget-Me-Not Toothpick Holder, Apple Green 20.00
Forget-Me-Not Toothpick Holder, Blue Green 20.00
Forget-Me-Not Toothpick Holder, Buttercup 20.00
Forget-Me-Not Toothpick Holder, Chartreuse 20.00
Forget-Me-Not Toothpick Holder, Dogwood 40.00
Forget-Me-Not Toothpick Holder, Grape 20.00
Forget-Me-Not Toothpick Holder, Misty Green 22.00
Forget-Me-Not Toothpick Holder, Orchid 20.00
Forget-Me-Not Toothpick Holder, Periwinkle 15.00
Forget-Me-Not Toothpick Holder, Shamrock 15.00
Forget-Me-Not Toothpick Holder, Sparrow 18.00
Forget-Me-Not Toothpick Holder, Twilight Blue 20.00
Gypsy Pot Toothpick Holder, Blue Green Marble 25.00
Gypsy Pot Toothpick Holder, Ivory 25.00
Gypsy Pot Toothpick Holder, Maverick 45.00
Gypsy Pot Toothpick Holder, Tomato 50.00
Hand, Blue Fire 15.00
Hand, Desert Sun 12.00
Hand, Ivorene 15.00
Hand, Twilight Blue 15.00

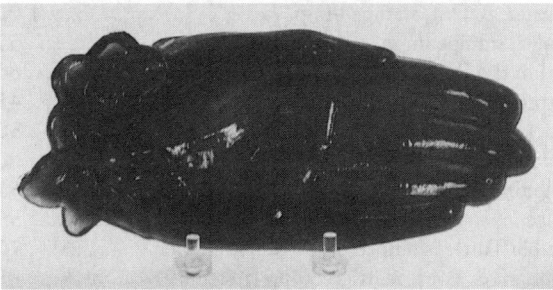

Hand, Tomato, 5", $25.00.

Heart & Lyre Cup Plate, Brown 8.00
Heart & Lyre Cup Plate, Gold 8.00
Heart & Lyre Cup Plate, Mint Green 10.00
Heart Jewel Box, Blue Jay 25.00
Heart Jewel Box, Crown Tuscan 30.00
Heart Jewel Box, Gun Metal 30.00
Heart Jewel Box, Teal 20.00
Heart Toothpick Holder, Bernard Boyd's Ebony 35.00
Heart Toothpick Holder, Blue Slag 30.00
Heart Toothpick Holder, Buttercup Slag 25.00
Heart Toothpick Holder, Dark Slag, unmk 35.00
Heart Toothpick Holder, Gray Tomato 25.00
Heart Toothpick Holder, Pink Lady 20.00
Heart Toothpick Holder, Sea Foam 20.00
Hen Covered Dish, Baby Green, 3" 30.00
Hen Covered Dish, Bloody Mary, 5" 100.00
Hen Covered Dish, Caramel, 3" 50.00
Hen Covered Dish, Green, 3" 20.00
Hen Covered Dish, Honey Amber, 5" 50.00
Hen Covered Dish, Nile Green, 3" 25.00
Hen Covered Dish, Rubina, 5" 225.00
Hen Covered Dish, Taffeta, 3" 30.00
High Boot, Pine Green 30.00
High Boot, Willow Green 25.00
Kat Slipper (Puss & Boots), Autumn 20.00
Kat Slipper (Puss & Boots), Bloody Mary 50.00

Kat Slipper (Puss & Boots), Holly Green	20.00	Stork & Peacock Child's Mug, Gold	20.00
Kat Slipper (Puss & Boots), Pine Green	35.00	Stork & Peacock Child's Mug, Pine Green	25.00
Kat Slipper (Puss & Boots), Tiger	40.00	Texas Boot, Chocolate	25.00
Lamb Covered Dish, Amberina, 5"	75.00	Texas Boot, White	15.00
Lamb Covered Dish, Crystal, 5"	30.00	Texas Creamer & Sugar, Amberina	100.00
Lamb Covered Dish, Lemon Custard, 5"	70.00	Texas Creamer & Sugar, Cambridge Pink	50.00
Lamb Covered Dish, Rose Marie, 5"	45.00	Texas Creamer & Sugar, Crown Tuscan	100.00
Mini Pitcher, Fawn	20.00	Texas Creamer & Sugar, Milk Blue	100.00
Mini Pitcher, Jade	25.00	Texas Creamer & Sugar, Peach Blo	50.00
Mini Slipper w/o Sole, Aqua	25.00	Tomahawk (Hatchet), Crown Tuscan, unmk	50.00
Mini Slipper w/o Sole, Emerald Green	15.00	Turkey Covered Dish, Bittersweet, 5"	75.00
Mini Slipper w/Sole, Champagne	35.00	Turkey Covered Dish, Forest Green, 5"	50.00
Mini Slipper w/Sole, Persimmon	35.00	Turkey Covered Dish, Sapphire, 5"	40.00
Owl, Angel Blue	35.00	Wildflower Candle Holders, Amethyst, pr	50.00
Owl, Blue Slag	75.00	Wildflower Candle Holders, Ruby, pr	150.00
Owl, Bluebird #1	50.00	Wildflower Candy Dish, Bluebell	25.00
Owl, Chad's Blue	50.00	Wildflower Candy Dish, Custard	35.00
Owl, Concord Grape	50.00	Wildflower Candy Dish, Shamrock	25.00
Owl, Delft Blue	50.00		
Owl, Dickie Bird	150.00		
Owl, Ebony	65.00		
Owl, Gray Slag	45.00		
Owl, Indigo	100.00		
Owl, Jabe's Amber	65.00		
Owl, Light Caramel	90.00		
Owl, Lime Sherbet	35.00		
Owl, Mission	45.00		
Owl, Orchid	35.00		
Owl, Rose Marie	25.00		
Owl, Sahara Sand	50.00		
Owl, Spice Brown Slag	50.00		
Owl, Unique Blue	150.00		
Owl, Wonder Blue	45.00		
Pooch, April Green	15.00		
Pooch, Blue Gray	20.00		
Pooch, Blue Marble	20.00		
Pooch, Brownie	15.00		
Pooch, Dapple Gray	15.00		
Pooch, Fantastic	50.00		
Pooch, Gray Tomato	35.00		
Pooch, Heatherbloom	35.00		
Pooch, January Blizzard	100.00		
Pooch, Odd Ball	35.00		
Pooch, Powder Blue Slag	45.00		
Pooch, Sapphire	15.00		
Portrait Plate, Cobalt	45.00		
Pottie Salt, Milk White	12.00		
Pottie Salt, Sapphire	6.00		
Priscilla, End of Day	200.00		
Priscilla, Periwinkle	95.00		
Robin Covered Dish, Amethyst, 5"	50.00		
Robin Covered Dish, Bloody Mary, 5"	100.00		
Robin Covered Dish, Custard, 5"	60.00		
Robin Covered Dish, Lavender Blue, 5"	90.00		
Robin Covered Dish, Tangerine, 5"	175.00		
Roller Skate (Skate Shoe), Custard Slag	75.00		
Seal of Ohio Cup Plate, Champagne	10.00		
Seal of Ohio Cup Plate, Milk White	20.00		
Seal of Ohio Cup Plate, Sunset	12.00		
Star & Dew Drop Salt, Henry's Blue	25.00		
Star & Dew Drop Salt, Lemon Custard	25.00		
Star & Dew Drop Salt, Topaz	20.00		
Stork & Peacock Child's Mug, Aqua	25.00		
Stork & Peacock Child's Mug, Chocolate	20.00		

Delatte

Delatte was a manufacturer of French cameo glass. Founded in 1921, their style reflected the influence of the Art Deco era with strong color contrasts and bold design. Our advisor for this category is Don Williams; he is listed in the Directory under Missouri.

Key: fp — fire polished

Cameo

Bowl, morning glories, bl to purple, 3x5½"	275.00
Vase, azaleas, pk on pk/gr, classic form on bun ft, 13x5"	900.00
Vase, exotic floral, gr on citron mottle, fp, stick neck, 18"	1,000.00
Vase, iris, amethyst on wht mottle, 10"	660.00

Miscellaneous

Vase, floral, blk/bl/gr pnt on bright bl, 3½x1¾"	100.00
Vase, snowy woodland pnt on aqua, stick neck, 7¾"	300.00

Delft

Old Delftware, made as early as the 16th century, was originally a low-fired earthenware coated in a thin opaque tin glaze with painted-on blue or polychrome designs. It was not until the last half of the 19th century, however, that the ware became commonly referred to as Delft, acquiring the name from the Dutch village that had become the major center of its production. English, German, and French potters also produced Delft, though with noticeable differences both in shape and decorative theme.

In the early part of the 18th century, the German potter, Bottger, developed a formula for porcelain; in England, Wedgwood began producing creamware — both of which were much more durable. Unable to compete, one by one the Delft potteries failed. Soon only one remained. In 1876 De Porcelyne Fles reintroduced Delftware on a hard white body with blue and white decorative themes reflecting the Dutch countryside, windmills by the sea, and Dutch children. This manufacturer is the most well known of several operating today. Their products are now produced under the Royal Delft label.

For further information we recommend *Discovering Dutch Delftware, Modern Delft and Makkum Pottery*, by Stephen J. Van

Hook (Glen Park Press, Alexandria, Virginia). Examples listed here are blue on white unless noted otherwise. See also specific manufacturers. Our advisor is Ralph Jaarsma; he is listed in the Directory under Iowa.

Bottle, Lambeth, floral, chipped lid, 8¾" 385.00
Bowl, Dutch, landscape & floral, molded rim, 8¼", NM 300.00
Bowl, Dutch, landscape w/figure, shallow, 12" 550.00
Bowl, English, floral, fluted, oval, 12⅜" 440.00
Bowl, punch; Bristol, landscape scenes, 1750s, 11½", EX 1,850.00
Charger, Dutch, bowl of flowers, blk & yel trim, 12⅝", NM 825.00
Charger, Dutch, floral decor w/tree, 14", EX 550.00
Charger, Dutch, floral w/mc trim, 13¼", NM 880.00
Charger, Dutch, landscape, floral rim, 12", EX 195.00
Charger, Dutch, scene of building w/floral, 13", EX 600.00
Charger, English, floral Fazackerley pattern w/mc, 13¼" 825.00

Humidors/tobacco storage jars, Holland, exotic scene with figure and sailing ship, late 18th century, imperfections, lids missing, 10", $2,100.00 for the pair.

Inkwell, Dutch, floral, heart shape, 4½", EX 495.00
Plate, Dutch, floral, bl w/mc, 8¾", EX 195.00
Plate, Dutch, floral, inscription front & bk, 9", EX 195.00
Plate, Dutch, flowers in pots w/insects, 8½", 5 for 825.00
Plate, Dutch, Oriental bridge scene, acanthus leaf border, 9" 275.00
Plate, England, floral, ca 1760, 8⅞", EX 485.00
Plate, English, Fazackerley design w/mc, rpr, 9" 165.00
Sauce boat, Dutch, Oriental design, scroll hdls, 8¼" L, EX 450.00
Strainer, Dutch, floral, 3 short ft, 9⅛" 525.00
Tea caddy, Dutch, scalloped edge, cork closure, 6", EX 550.00
Trinket pot, English, floral, 2-hdl, 5¼", EX 495.00
Vase, Dutch, figures & foliage, baluster, 18th C, 3⅛", EX 400.00
Wall pocket, English, cornucopia w/cherub head, 7¾", NM ...1,100.00

Denver

The Denver China and Pottery Company began production in 1901 in Denver, Colorado. The founder, William A. Long, used materials native to Colorado to produce underglaze-decorated brownware as well as other artware lines. Several marks were used: an impressed 'Denver' (often with the Lonhuda Faience cipher inside a shield), an imprinted 'Denaura,' and an arrow mark.

Mug, gray matt w/pnt blkberries, shield mk, att Leffler, 4" 150.00
Napkin ring, blk & brn, 2x2" 95.00
Vase, appl berries, bsk w/high gloss int, 3-ftd, 5x4½" 225.00
Vase, appl sculpted daffodils, att Eugene Roberts, minimum 650.00
Vase, columbine HP on bsk, sgn Leffler, minimum value 650.00
Vase, floral tulip decor, Lonhuda, 6x9" 650.00
Vase, tulips cvd on smooth gr matt, ovoid w/sm rim, Denaura, 9" .2,400.00

Denver Terra Cotta Pottery

While on his honeymoon in Colorado, a young chemist by the name of George Frackt became aware of the natural clay deposits there. As an employee of the St. Louis Terra Cotta Company in Missouri, he was impressed with the samples he had analyzed and decided to establish his own terra cotta plant in Denver.

Within a short time, he opened a two-story plant with twelve employees, where he made finished products in high-gloss colors. The company consolidated with Northwestern Terra Cotta Company in 1924. Artificial stone or concrete came into production in 1925 and continued into the late 1920s. The exact date of closing is unknown. Look for pieces of great weight with high-gloss colors and stamped marks.

Ashtray, gargoyle, gr, blk or red high gloss, minimum value 95.00
Bookends, charging elephants on sq base, 7x8", pr 500.00
Bookends, owls on sq base, gray, 7x5", minimum value 225.00
Planter, open-mouthed frog, gr, stamped, 4x5", minimum value ...125.00
Vase, buttressed, clear glaze over yel clay, stamped, 6x7" 125.00

Denver White

In 1894 Frederick and Frank White settled in Denver, Colorado, and formed the F.J. White & Son Pottery Company. They located at 1434 Logan Street. After the death of Frederick in 1919, Frank moved the pottery to 1560 South Logan, where he remained until the company closed. He had a kiln set up at home and worked each day on the pottery, often selling his products in his front yard. On many occasions he was commissioned to produce specialty items for customers.

Each piece is hand thrown and many are dated. They are usually incised with the name Denver and the letter 'W' inside the capital 'D.' Many items are decorated with Colorado scenery. Though most pieces are matt glazed with a glossy interior, some later examples were completely glossy. The Whites would also add a small band to some of the ware, similar to what you see on Wedgwood pottery today. They created a line with swirled colors as well. On March 6, 1960, Frank White died at the age of 91.

Our advisors for this category are Jim and Carol Carlton, authors of *Collector's Encyclopedia of Colorado Pottery;* they are listed in the Directory under Colorado.

Bowl, gray, 6x8" 150.00
Cookie jar, pine-cone decor, squirrel finial, inscription, 8x6" 300.00
Creamer, pine-cone decor, minimum value 55.00
Cup & saucer, bl high glaze 35.00
Ginger jar, brn & gr, w/lid, minimum value 175.00

Vase, pine cones on white, artist signed, 3¾", from $150.00 to $175.00.

Vase, bl, crimped edge, 6" 95.00
Vase, bl & wht swirl, 4", minimum value 150.00

Vase, gray w/gr glaze int, dtd 1917, 5", minimum value 195.00
Vase, matt bl w/appl reeding, 5", minimum value 175.00
Vase, matt dk gr, 3-hdl, dtd 1917, 5½" 350.00
Vase, mc swirl glaze, 6" 150.00
Vase, mountain & deer scenery, sgn Skiff, 10" 500.00

Depression Glass

    Depression glass is defined by Gene Florence, author of several bestselling books on the subject, as 'the inexpensive glassware made primarily during the Depression era in the colors of amber, green, pink, blue, red, yellow, white, and crystal.' This glass was mass produced, sold through five-and-dime stores and mail-order catalogs, and given away as premiums with gas and food products.

    The listings in this book are far from being complete. If you want a more thorough presentation of this fascinating glassware, we recommend *The Collector's Encyclopedia of Depression Glass*, *The Pocket Guide to Depression Glass*, *Elegant Glassware of the Depression Era*, and *Very Rare Glassware of the Depression Years*, all by Gene Florence, whose address is listed in the Directory under Kentucky. See also McKee; New Martinsville.

Key:
AOP — allover pattern   PAT — pattern at top

Adam, bowl, dessert; pk, 4¾" 20.00
Adam, bowl, pk, oval, 10" 30.00
Adam, candy jar, gr, w/lid, 2½" 100.00
Adam, plate, cake; pk, ftd, 10" 25.00
Adam, plate, dinner; gr, 9" sq 30.00
Adam, plate, sherbet; pk, 6" 9.00
Adam, shakers, gr, 4", pr 110.00
Adam, sugar bowl, pk 17.50
Adam, tumbler, gr, 4½" 27.50
Am Pioneer, coaster, gr, 3½" 30.00
Am Pioneer, goblet, water; gr, 8-oz, 6" 50.00
Am Pioneer, mayonnaise, gr, 4¼" 90.00
Am Pioneer, tumbler, crystal, 8-oz, 4" 30.00
Am Sweetheart, bowl, cereal; Cremax, 6" 10.00
Am Sweetheart, bowl, soup; smoke & other trims, 9½" 125.00
Am Sweetheart, plate, salad; bl, 8" 97.50
Am Sweetheart, saucer, bl 25.00

Aunt Polly, sugar bowl, blue, $30.00.

Photo courtesy Gene Florence

Am Sweetheart, tidbit, red, 2-tier, 8" & 10" 225.00
Aunt Polly, bowl, gr, 2x4¾" 15.00
Aunt Polly, creamer, irid 30.00
Aunt Polly, plate, luncheon; bl, 8" 20.00
Aunt Polly, tumbler, bl, 8-oz, 3⅝" 30.00
Aunt Polly, vase, irid, ftd, 6½" 50.00
Aurora, bowl, pk, deep, 4½" 55.00
Aurora, plate, pk, 6½" 12.00
Avocado, bowl, relish; pk, ftd, 6" 25.00

Avocado, creamer, crystal, ftd 22.00
Avocado, plate, luncheon; gr, 8¼" 20.00
Avocado, sugar bowl, crystal, ftd 12.00
Beaded Block, bowl, jelly; pk, hdls, 5" 10.00
Beaded Block, jelly, stemmed; other than amber, 4½" 27.00
Beaded Block, plate, gr, rnd, 8¾" 22.00
Block Optic, bowl, cereal; gr, 5¼" 15.00
Block Optic, candy jar, yel, w/lid, 2¼" 65.00
Block Optic, comport, mayonnaise; gr 35.00
Block Optic, goblet, wine; pk, 4½" 37.00
Block Optic, mug, gr 33.00
Block Optic, plate, grill; pk, 9" 30.00
Block Optic, plate, luncheon; yel, 8" 5.00
Block Optic, sherbet, pk, 5½-oz, 3¼" 7.50
Block Optic, tumbler, gr, flat, 12-oz, 4⅞" 25.00
Bowknot, bowl, cereal; gr, 5½" 22.50
Bowknot, tumbler, gr, ftd, 10-oz, 5" 22.50
Cameo, bowl, salad; gr, 7¼" 57.50
Cameo, bowl, sauce; crystal, 4¼" 6.00
Cameo, creamer, gr, 4¼" 28.00
Cameo, goblet, water; gr, 6" 50.00
Cameo, pitcher, juice; gr, 36-oz, 6" 60.00
Cameo, plate, dinner; yel, 9½" 9.00
Cameo, platter, yel, closed hdls, 12" 40.00
Cameo, tumbler, juice; gr, 5-oz, 3¾" 30.00
Cherry Blossom, bowl, cereal; pk, 5¾" 45.00
Cherry Blossom, bowl, pk, hdls, 9" 45.00
Cherry Blossom, coaster, gr 13.00
Cherry Blossom, gr, PAT, ftd, 36-oz, 8" 55.00
Cherry Blossom, plate, cake; gr, 3-leg, 10¼" 35.00
Cherry Blossom, plate, dinner; Delphite, 9" 20.00
Cherry Blossom, platter, pk, oval, 11" 40.00
Cherry Blossom, saucer, Delphite 45.00
Cherry Blossom, tray, sandwich; pk, 10½" 30.00
Cherryberry, bowl, berry; gr, 4" 8.50
Cherryberry, creamer, irid, sm 12.00
Cherryberry, pitcher, gr, 7¾" 175.00
Cherryberry, tumbler, crystal, 9-oz, 3⅝" 20.00
Chinex Classic, bowl, cereal; castle decal, 5¾" 15.00
Chinex Classic, bowl, soup; w/decal, 7¾" 22.00
Chinex Classic, plate, dinner; w/decal, 9¾" 8.50
Chinex Classic, saucer, Brownstone 2.00
Circle, bowl, gr or pk, 4½" 8.00
Circle, pitcher, gr or pk, 60-oz 35.00
Circle, plate, luncheon; gr or pk, 8¼" 4.00
Circle, sherbet, gr or pk, 4¾" 6.00
Cloverleaf, ashtray, blk, match holder in center, 5¾" 85.00
Cloverleaf, bowl, cereal; yel, 5" 35.00

Cloverleaf, candy dish, green, $55.00.

Photo courtesy Gene Florence

Cloverleaf, sugar bowl, gr, ftd, 3⅝" 10.00

Cloverleaf, tumbler, gr, ftd, 10-oz, 5¾" 25.00
Colonial, bowl, berry; gr, 4½" 18.00
Colonial, bowl, soup; pk, low, 7" 65.00
Colonial, cheese dish, gr 225.00
Colonial, pitcher, crystal, 54-oz, 7" 30.00
Colonial, platter, gr, oval, 12" 22.00
Colonial, sugar bowl, crystal, 4½" 10.00
Colonial, tumbler, lemonade; pk, 15-oz 65.00
Colonial Block, butter tub, gr or pk 45.00
Colonial Block, creamer, gr or pk 12.00
Colonial Block, sherbet, gr or pk 10.00
Colonial Fluted, creamer, gr 6.50
Colonial Fluted, cup, gr 5.00
Columbia, cup, crystal 8.50
Columbia, cup, pk 25.00
Columbia, plate, luncheon; pk, 9½" 35.00
Columbia, tumbler, water; crystal, 9-oz 30.00
Coronation, bowl, nappy; Royal Ruby, hdld, 6½" ...12.00
Coronation, bowl, pk, no hdls, 4¼" 75.00
Coronation, plate, luncheon; pk, 8½" 4.50
Coronation, sherbet, gr 75.00
Cremax, bowl, cereal, 5¾" 3.50
Cremax, sugar bowl, decal decor, open 8.00
Cube, bowl, dessert; pk, 4½" 6.50
Cube, coaster, pk, 3¼" 7.00
Cube, plate, luncheon; gr, 8" 7.00
Cube, saucer, pk 2.50
Cube, tumbler, gr, 9-oz, 4" 72.50
Diamond Quilted, bowl, cream soup; blk, 4¾" 20.00
Diamond Quilted, cake salver, gr or pk, 10" dia 60.00
Diamond Quilted, compote, gr or pk, 6x7¼" 45.00
Diamond Quilted, cup, bl or blk 17.50
Diamond Quilted, ice bucket, bl or blk 85.00
Diamond Quilted, plate, luncheon; bl or blk, 8" 12.00
Diamond Quilted, plate, sherbet; gr or pk, 6" 4.00
Diamond Quilted, tumbler, gr or pk, ftd, 9-oz 12.50
Diana, ashtray, pk, 3½" 3.50
Diana, bowl, amber, scalloped edge, 12" 20.00
Diana, bowl, cream soup; crystal, 5½" 8.00
Diana, cup, crystal 3.00
Diana, plate, pk, 9½" 16.00
Diana, saucer, amber 100.00
Dogwood, bowl, cereal; Cremax, 5½" 5.00
Dogwood, plate, bread & butter; Monax, 6" 21.00
Dogwood, plate, cake; gr, heavy solid ft, 13" 115.00
Dogwood, plate, dinner; pk, 9¼" 37.50
Dogwood, saucer, gr 6.50
Doric, bowl, vegetable; pk, oval, 9" 35.00
Doric, candy dish, gr, w/lid, 8" 40.00
Doric, candy dish, 3-part, Delphite 12.00
Doric, cup, pk 9.00
Doric, sherbet, Delphite, ftd 7.00
Doric, tray, gr, hdls, 10" 18.00
Doric, tumbler, pk, 9-oz, 4½" 65.00
Doric & Pansy, creamer, pk or crystal 75.00
Doric & Pansy, cup, gr or teal 16.00
Doric & Pansy, plate, dinner; pk or crystal, 9" 12.00
Doric & Pansy, sugar bowl, gr or teal, open 110.00
English Hobnail, candlestick, gr or pk, rnd base, 9" ..40.00
English Hobnail, cigarette jar, gr or pk, w/lid 22.50
English Hobnail, cup, turq or ice bl 25.00
English Hobnail, marmalade, gr or pk, w/lid 20.00
English Hobnail, mayonnaise, gr or pk, 6" 20.00
English Hobnail, plate, gr or pk, rnd, 8" 12.50

English Hobnail, shakers, gr or pk, rnd, ftd, pr 77.50
English Hobnail, tidbit, turq or ice bl, 2-tier 75.00
Fire-King Philbe, bowl, vegetable; crystal, oval, 10" ..50.00
Fire-King Philbe, creamer, bl, ftd, 3¼" 130.00
Fire-King Philbe, plate, sandwich; gr or pk, 10" 65.00
Fire-King Philbe, sherbet, bl, 4¾" 75.00
Fire-King Philbe, sugar bowl, gr or pk, ftd, 3¼" 110.00
Fire-King Philbe, tumbler, crystal, ftd, 10-oz, 5¼" ...30.00
Floral, bowl, vegetable; pk, oval, 9" 20.00
Floral, candlesticks, pk, 4", pr 75.00
Floral, comport, pk, 9" 800.00
Floral, relish, gr, 2-part, oval 20.00
Floral, tray, pk, closed hdls, sq, 6" 17.50
Floral & Diamond Band, bowl, berry; gr, 4½" 9.00
Floral & Diamond Band, creamer, pk, sm 10.00
Floral & Diamond Band, plate, luncheon; gr or pk, 8" ..42.50
Floral & Diamond Band, sherbet, pk 7.00
Floral & Diamond Band, tumbler, water; pk, 4" 20.00
Florentine No 1, bowl, cereal; crystal or gr, 6" 22.00
Florentine No 1, bowl, crystal or gr, flat, 9" 27.50
Florentine No 1, butter dish, yel or pk, w/lid 160.00
Florentine No 1, coaster/ashtray, yel, 3¾" 20.00
Florentine No 1, cup, pk 9.00
Florentine No 1, plate, dinner; crystal or gr, 10" 16.00
Florentine No 1, plate, salad; crystal or gr, 8½" 7.50
Florentine No 1, sugar bowl, crystal or gr, ruffled ...18.00
Florentine No 2, bowl, cereal; crystal or gr, 6" 30.00
Florentine No 2, bowl, cream soup; yel, 4¾" 22.00
Florentine No 2, coaster, pk, 3¼" 16.00
Florentine No 2, creamer, crystal or gr 8.00
Florentine No 2, custard cup, crystal or gr 60.00
Florentine No 2, plate, dinner; crystal, gr or yel, 10" ..15.00
Florentine No 2, plate, salad; crystal, gr or pk, 8½" ...8.50
Florentine No 2, shakers, yel, pr 50.00
Flower Garden w/Butterflies, ashtray, amber or crystal ..165.00
Flower Garden w/Butterflies, candlesticks, blk, 8", pr ..300.00
Flower Garden w/Butterflies, candlesticks, pk, gr or bl-gr, 8", pr ..135.00
Flower Garden w/Butterflies, cup, pk, gr or bl-gr 65.00
Flower Garden w/Butterflies, plate, amber or crystal, 8" ..15.00
Flower Garden w/Butterflies, plate, pk, gr or bl-gr, 10" ..42.50
Fortune, bowl, dessert; pk or crystal, 4½" 9.00
Fortune, candy dish, pk or crystal, flat, w/lid 25.00
Fortune, plate, luncheon; pk or crystal, 8" 22.00
Fruits, saucer, gr 5.50
Fruits, sherbet, pk 7.00
Fruits, tumbler, gr, 12-oz, 5" 135.00
Georgian, butter dish, gr, w/lid 72.50
Georgian, creamer, gr, ftd, 4" 15.00
Georgian, sherbet, gr 12.00
Hex Optic, bucket reamer, gr or pk 55.00
Hex Optic, cup, gr or pk, 2 style hdls, ea 4.50
Hex Optic, pitcher, gr or pk, ftd, 48-oz, 9" 45.00
Hex Optic, shakers, gr or pk, pr 27.50
Hex Optic, sugar shaker, gr or pk 195.00
Hex Optic, tumbler, gr or pk, ftd, 7" 12.00
Hobnail, pitcher, crystal, 67-oz 25.00
Hobnail, plate, luncheon; pk, 8½" 3.50
Hobnail, sugar bowl, crystal, ftd 4.00
Homespun, coaster/ashtray, pk or crystal 6.50
Homespun, cup, pk or crystal 10.00
Homespun, saucer, pk or crystal 4.00
Homespun, tumbler, pk or crystal, ftd, 15-oz, 6¼" ...27.50
Indiana Custard, bowl, cereal; French Ivory, 6½" 24.00
Indiana Custard, butter dish, French Ivory, w/lid 60.00

Indiana Custard, plate, bread & butter; French Ivory, 5¾" 6.50
Indiana Custard, plate, dinner; French Ivory, 9¾" 27.50
Indiana Custard, sugar bowl, French Ivory 12.00
Iris, bowl, fruit; crystal, str edge, 11" 60.00
Iris, bowl, soup; crystal, 7½" 160.00
Iris, bowl, soup; irid, 7½" 60.00
Iris, candlesticks, crystal, pr 42.50
Iris, creamer, gr or pk, ftd 110.00
Iris, goblet, wine; crystal, 3-oz, 4½" 17.00
Iris, plate, dinner; crystal, 9" 55.00
Iris, tumbler, crystal, flat, 4" 135.00
Jubilee, bowl, fruit; pk, flat, 11½" 195.00
Jubilee, candy jar, pk or yel, 3-ftd, w/lid 325.00
Jubilee, cup, yel 12.00
Jubilee, plate, luncheon; pk, 8¾" 27.50
Jubilee, tray, cake; yel, hdls, 11" 45.00
Lace Edge, bowl, cereal; pk, 6½" 24.00
Lace Edge, bowl, pk, plain, 9½" 26.00
Lace Edge, candy jar, pk, ribbed, w/lid 50.00
Lace Edge, plate, dinner; pk, 10½" 33.00
Lace Edge, platter, pk, 12¾" 37.50
Lace Edge, sugar bowl, pk 22.50
Laced Edge, bowl, basket; bl or gr opal 225.00
Laced Edge, bowl, soup; bl or gr opal, 7" 80.00
Laced Edge, bowl, vegetable; bl or gr opal, 9" 95.00
Laced Edge, candlesticks, bl or gr opal, dbl, pr 165.00
Laced Edge, creamer, bl or gr opal 40.00
Laced Edge, mayonnaise, bl or gr opal, 3-pc 135.00
Laced Edge, plate, dinner; bl or gr opal, 10" 85.00
Laced Edge, saucer, bl or gr opal 15.00
Laced Edge, tumbler, bl or gr opal, 9-oz 55.00
Lake Como, bowl, cereal; wht, 6" 25.00
Lake Como, platter, wht, 11" 70.00
Lake Como, saucer, regular; wht 12.00
Lake Como, sugar bowl, wht, ftd 32.50
Laurel, bowl, lg berry; French Ivory, 9" 22.00
Laurel, candlesticks, wht opal or Jade Green, 4", pr 40.00
Laurel, cup, French Ivory 7.00
Laurel, saucer, French Ivory 3.00
Laurel, tumbler, French Ivory, flat, 12-oz, 5" 50.00
Lincoln Inn, ashtray, colors other than cobalt or red 12.00
Lincoln Inn, bowl, cereal; cobalt or red, 6" 13.00
Lincoln Inn, comport, cobalt or red 30.00
Lincoln Inn, plate, colors other than cobalt or red, 12" 15.50
Lincoln Inn, tumbler, colors other than cobalt or red, flat, 9-oz ...19.50
Lorain, bowl, cereal; crystal or gr, 6" 45.00
Lorain, cup, yel 15.00
Lorain, plate, dinner; crystal or gr, 10¼" 45.00
Lorain, saucer, yel 6.00
Lorain, sugar bowl, crystal or gr, ftd 16.00
Madrid, ashtray, amber, sq, 6" 225.00
Madrid, bowl, salad; gr, 8" 17.50
Madrid, bowl, sauce; pk, 5" 6.50
Madrid, butter dish, gr, w/lid 90.00
Madrid, candlesticks, amber, 2¼", pr 22.00
Madrid, jam dish, bl, 7" 40.00
Madrid, plate, dinner; gr, 10½" 40.00
Madrid, plate, relish; amber, 10½" 15.00
Madrid, saucer, gr 5.00
Madrid, tumbler, amber, 9-oz, 4¼" 15.00
Manhattan, bowl, pk, closed hdls, 8" 25.00
Manhattan, candy dish, pk, 3-leg 12.00
Manhattan, creamer, crystal, oval 10.00
Manhattan, plate, dinner; crystal, 10¼" 20.00

Manhattan, plate, salad; crystal, 8½" 15.00
Manhattan, relish, crystal, 4-part, 14" 18.00
Manhattan, sugar bowl, crystal, oval 10.00
Mayfair Federal, bowl, sauce; gr, 5" 12.00
Mayfair Federal, creamer, crystal, ftd 10.50
Mayfair Federal, cup, crystal 5.00
Mayfair Federal, saucer, crystal 2.50
Mayfair/Open Rose, bowl, cream soup; pk, 5" 52.50
Mayfair/Open Rose, bowl, vegetable; bl, 10" 70.00
Mayfair/Open Rose, cookie jar, pk 52.50
Mayfair/Open Rose, cookie jar, yel 895.00
Mayfair/Open Rose, cup, pk 18.00
Mayfair/Open Rose, pitcher, pk, 60-oz, 8" 55.00
Mayfair/Open Rose, plate, cake; gr, ftd, 10" 150.00
Mayfair/Open Rose, plate, cake; gr, hdld, 12" 40.00
Mayfair/Open Rose, relish, bl, 4-part, 8⅜" 65.00
Mayfair/Open Rose, saucer, pk, w/cup ring 32.50
Mayfair/Open Rose, sugar bowl, gr or yel, ftd 210.00
Miss America, bowl, cereal; pk, 6¼" 25.00
Miss America, bowl, vegetable; crystal, oval, 10" 15.00
Miss America, butter dish, pk, w/lid 595.00
Miss America, cup, gr 12.00
Miss America, goblet, water; crystal, 10-oz, 5½" 21.00
Miss America, pitcher, pk, w/ice lip, 65-oz, 8½" 185.00
Miss America, plate, salad; Royal Ruby, 8½" 150.00
Miss America, saucer, Royal Ruby 65.00
Miss America, tumbler, iced tea; pk, 14-oz, 5¾" 85.00
Moderntone, bowl, cream soup; amethyst, 4¾" 20.00
Moderntone, cup, cobalt or amethyst 11.00
Moderntone, platter, cobalt, oval, 11" 47.50
Moderntone, saucer, cobalt 5.00
Moderntone, tumbler, cobalt, 9-oz 37.50
Mt Pleasant, bonbon, pk or gr, rolled-up, hdld, 7" 16.00
Mt Pleasant, cup, pk or gr 9.50
Mt Pleasant, mayonnaise, amethyst, blk or cobalt, 3-ftd, 5½" 30.00
Mt Pleasant, plate, cake; pk or gr, 2-hdl, 10½" 16.00
New Century, bowl, cream soup; gr or crystal, 4¾" 20.00

Photo courtesy
Gene Florence

New Century, butter dish, green, $55.00.

New Century, creamer, gr or crystal 8.50
New Century, cup, pk, cobalt or amethyst 20.00
New Century, plate, grill; gr or crystal, 10" 12.00
New Century, saucer, pk, cobalt or amethyst 7.50
New Century, sugar bowl, gr or crystal 8.00
Newport, bowl, cream soup; amethyst, 4¾" 18.00
Newport, creamer, cobalt 16.00
Newport, plate, dinner; cobalt, 8¾" 30.00
Newport, shakers, amethyst, pr 40.00
Newport, sugar bowl, cobalt 16.00
No 610 Pyramid, bowl, pickle; crystal, 9½x5¾" 20.00
No 610 Pyramid, relish, gr, 4-part, hdld 50.00
No 610 Pyramid, sugar bowl, yel 40.00

Photo courtesy
Gene Florence

No. 610 Pyramid, bowl, pink, oval, handles, 9½", $35.00.

No 612 Horseshoe, bowl, berry; yel, 4½" 23.00
No 612 Horseshoe, butter dish, gr, w/lid 775.00
No 612 Horseshoe, creamer, yel, ftd 18.00
No 612 Horseshoe, plate, grill; gr, 10½" 100.00
No 612 Horseshoe, tumbler, gr, ftd, 12-oz 150.00
No 616 Vernon, cup, gr 17.50
No 616 Vernon, plate, luncheon; crystal, 8" 6.00
No 616 Vernon, tumbler, gr or yel, ftd, 5" 37.50
No 618 Pineapple & Floral, ashtray, crystal, 4½" 17.50
No 618 Pineapple & Floral, bowl, salad; amber or red, 7" 10.00
No 618 Pineapple & Floral, plate, dinner; gr, 9½" 35.00
No 618 Pineapple & Floral, sherbet, crystal, ftd 22.00
No 618 Pineapple & Floral, tumbler, amber or red, 8-oz, 4¼" 25.00
Normandie, creamer, irid, ftd 8.00
Normandie, cup, pk 8.50
Normandie, plate, dinner; amber, 11" 33.00
Old Cafe, bowl, berry; crystal or pk, 3¾" 5.00
Old Cafe, bowl, cereal; Royal Ruby, 5½" 13.00
Old Cafe, saucer, crystal or pk 3.00
Old Cafe, tumbler, juice; Royal Ruby, 3" 14.00
Old Cafe, tumbler, water; Royal Ruby, 4" 20.00
Old English, compote, pk, gr or amber, 3½x7" 22.00
Old English, egg cup, crystal only 8.00
Old English, sandwich server, pk, gr or amber, center hdl 55.00
Old English, vase, pk, gr or amber, ftd, 12" 60.00
Ovide, creamer, gr 4.50
Ovide, cup, blk 6.50
Ovide, tumbler, Art Deco 85.00
Oyster & Pearl, bowl, Royal Ruby, heart-shaped, 1 hdl, 5¼" 17.00
Oyster & Pearl, plate, sandwich; pk or crystal, 13½" 12.00
Parrot, bowl, berry; gr, 5" 25.00
Parrot, creamer, amber, ftd 65.00
Parrot, cup, gr or amber 40.00
Parrot, plate, salad; gr, 7½" 35.00
Parrot, platter, amber, oblong, 11¼" 75.00
Parrot, saucer, gr or amber 15.00
Parrot, shakers, gr, pr 250.00
Parrot, tumbler, gr, 12-oz, 5½" 160.00
Patrician, bowl, cereal; pk, 6" 24.00
Patrician, butter dish, amber or crystal, w/lid 90.00
Patrician, jam dish, gr 40.00
Patrician, plate, salad; pk, 7½" 15.00
Patrician, shakers, gr, pr 60.00
Patrician, sugar bowl, amber, crystal, pk or gr 9.00
Patrician, tumbler, gr, ftd, 8-oz, 5¼" 60.00
Patrick, bowl, console; yel, 11" 125.00
Patrick, cheese & cracker set, pk 150.00
Patrick, goblet, water; yel, 10-oz, 6" 70.00
Patrick, mayonnaise, pk, 3-pc 195.00
Patrick, saucer, yel 12.00
Patrick, tray, pk, 2-hdl, 11" 75.00
Petalware, pitcher, crystal w/pastel bands, 80-oz 25.00
Petalware, plate, dinner; Monax, 9" 9.00

Petalware, plate, salad; pk, 8" 5.00
Petalware, saucer, Cremax 3.50
Primo, bowl, yel or gr, 4½" 18.00
Primo, creamer, yel or gr 12.00
Primo, cup, yel or gr 12.00
Primo, plate, cake; yel or gr, 3-ftd, 10" 30.00
Primo, plate, dinner; yel or gr, 10" 22.00
Primo, sugar bowl, yel or gr 12.00
Princess, ashtray, gr, 4½" 70.00
Princess, bowl, salad; pk, octagonal, 9" 35.00
Princess, cake stand, gr, 10" 30.00
Princess, coaster, pk 70.00
Princess, creamer, pk, oval 15.00
Princess, plate, dinner; pk, 9½" 25.00
Princess, relish dish, topaz or apricot, divided, 7½" 100.00
Princess, saucer (same as sherbet), topaz or apricot 3.00
Princess, tumbler, water; gr, 9-oz, 4" 26.00
Queen Mary, ashtray, crystal, rnd, 3½" 3.00
Queen Mary, bowl, cereal; pk, 6" 25.00
Queen Mary, candy dish, crystal, w/lid 22.00
Queen Mary, cigarette jar, pk, oval, 2x3" 7.50
Queen Mary, comport, crystal, 5¾" 8.00
Queen Mary, creamer, pk, oval 7.50
Queen Mary, shakers, crystal, pr 19.00
Queen Mary, sugar bowl, pk, oval 7.50
Queen Mary, tumbler, water; pk, 9-oz, 4" 15.00
Raindrops, plate, luncheon; gr, 8" 5.50
Raindrops, tumbler, gr, 10-oz, 5" 9.00
Ribbon, bowl, berry; blk, 8" 35.00
Ribbon, candy dish, gr, w/lid 38.00
Ribbon, plate, luncheon; blk, 8" 14.00
Ribbon, plate, sherbet; gr, 6¼" 2.50
Ring, bowl, soup; crystal, 7" 10.00
Ring, creamer, crystal, ftd 4.50
Ring, ice bucket, w/decor or gr 35.00
Ring, plate, sherbet; crystal, 6¼" 2.00
Ring, sandwich server, w/decor or gr, center hdl 27.50
Ring, sugar bowl, crystal, ftd 4.50
Ring, tumbler, water; w/decor or gr, ftd, 5½" 10.00
Ring, vase, crystal, 8" 17.50
Rock Crystal, candelabra, crystal, 3-light, pr 52.50
Rock Crystal, candy dish, other than crystal, w/lid 75.00
Rock Crystal, comport, red, 7" 95.00
Rock Crystal, cup, crystal, 7-oz 17.50
Rock Crystal, jelly dish, other than crystal, scalloped/ftd, 5" 27.50
Rock Crystal, pitcher, red, w/lid, 9" 675.00
Rock Crystal, relish dish, red, 2-part, 11½" 75.00
Rock Crystal, saucer, crystal 7.50
Rock Crystal, shakers, other than crystal, 2 styles, pr 125.00
Rock Crystal, stem, cordial; other than crystal, ftd, 1-oz 45.00
Rock Crystal, stem, red, 7-oz 52.50
Rock Crystal, sugar bowl, crystal, open, 10-oz 15.00
Rose Cameo, bowl, gr, str sides, 6" 22.00
Rose Cameo, sherbet, gr 12.00
Rosemary, creamer, gr, ftd 12.50
Rosemary, plate, dinner; pk 20.00
Rosemary, sugar bowl, gr, ftd 12.50
Roulette, bowl, fruit; pk or gr, 9" 15.00
Roulette, pitcher, crystal, 65-oz, 8" 30.00
Roulette, plate, luncheon; pk or gr, 8½" 6.00
Roulette, sherbet, crystal 3.50
Roulette, tumbler, pk or gr, ftd, 10-oz, 5½" 30.00
Round Robin, bowl, berry; gr or irid, 4" 5.00
Round Robin, cup, irid, ftd 5.50

Round Robin, sherbet, gr 5.00
Roxana, bowl, berry; yel, 5" 11.00
Roxana, plate, sherbet; yel, 6" 7.50
Royal Lace, bowl, nut; pk or gr 400.00
Royal Lace, bowl, vegetable; crystal, oval, 11" 25.00
Royal Lace, butter dish, pk, w/lid 160.00
Royal Lace, creamer, bl, ftd 55.00
Royal Lace, cup, bl 35.00
Royal Lace, pitcher, crystal, str sides, 48-oz 40.00
Royal Lace, saucer, bl 12.50
Royal Lace, shakers, pk, pr 65.00
Royal Lace, sugar bowl, bl 25.00
Royal Ruby, cigarette box/card holder, crystal w/Ruby lid, 6x4" ...65.00
Royal Ruby, creamer, ftd 9.00
Royal Ruby, goblet, ball stem 10.00
Royal Ruby, sugar bowl, ftd 7.50
S Pattern, bowl, cereal; crystal, 5½" 5.00
S Pattern, plate, dinner; yel, amber or crystal w/trim, 9¼" 9.00
S Pattern, tumbler, yel, amber or crystal w/trim, 10-oz, 4¾" 8.00
Sandwich, bowl, berry; amber or crystal, 4¼" 3.50
Sandwich, bowl, teal bl, hexagonal, 6" 14.00
Sandwich, cup, teal bl 8.50
Sandwich, decanter, pk or gr, w/stopper 110.00
Sandwich, plate, dinner; pk or gr, 10½" 20.00
Sandwich, saucer, teal bl 4.50
Sandwich, shakers, amber or crystal, pr 17.50
Sandwich, sugar bowl, red, lg 45.00
Sandwich, wine, red, 4-oz, 3" 12.50
Sharon, bowl, cereal; amber, 6" 22.00
Sharon, bowl, vegetable; pk, oval, 9½" 32.00
Sharon, candy jar, gr, w/lid 160.00
Sharon, jam dish, amber, 7½" 40.00
Sharon, plate, bread & butter; pk, 6" 7.50
Sharon, plate, dinner; gr, 9½" 22.50
Sharon, sherbet, amber, ftd 13.00
Sharon, tumbler, pk, thin, 9-oz, 4⅛" 45.00
Ships, cup, bl & wht, Moderntone (plain) 11.00
Ships, dinner; bl & wht, 9" 32.00
Ships, pitcher, bl & wht, w/lip, 86-oz 70.00
Ships, saucer, bl & wht 17.00
Ships, tumbler, juice; bl & wht, 5-oz, 3¾" 12.00
Sierra, bowl, cereal; pk, 5½" 15.00
Sierra, butter dish, gr, w/lid 67.50
Sierra, creamer, pk 20.00
Sierra, sugar bowl, pk 20.00
Spiral, bowl, berry; gr, 4¾" 5.00
Spiral, creamer, gr, flat or ftd 7.50
Spiral, platter, gr, 12" 30.00
Spiral, sugar bowl, gr, flat or ftd 7.50
Spiral, tumbler, gr, ftd, 6" 15.00
Starlight, bowl, pk, closed hdls, 8½" 20.00
Starlight, bowl, salad; crystal or wht, 11½" 25.00
Starlight, plate, luncheon, crystal or wht, 8½" 5.00
Starlight, shakers, crystal or wht, pr 22.50
Strawberry, bowl, berry; pk or gr, 4" 9.00
Strawberry, bowl, salad; crystal or irid, deep, 6½" 15.00
Strawberry, olive dish, crystal or irid, 1 hdl, 5" 9.00
Strawberry, sherbet, crystal or irid 6.50
Sunburst, bowl, berry; crystal, 8½" 18.00
Sunburst, cup, crystal 6.00
Sunburst, saucer, crystal 2.00
Sunburst, tray, crystal, sm oval 12.00
Sunflower, plate, dinner; gr, 9" 20.00
Sunflower, tumbler, pk, ftd, 8-oz, 4¾" 28.00

Swirl, bowl, console; pk, ftd, 10½" 20.00
Swirl, creamer, Delphite, ftd 12.00
Swirl, cup, pk 10.00
Swirl, plate, dinner; pk, 9¼" 15.00
Swirl, saucer, pk 3.50
Swirl, sugar bowl, Delphite, ftd 12.00
Tea Room, bowl, finger; gr 55.00
Tea Room, ice bucket, pk 52.50
Tea Room, mustard, pk, w/lid 125.00
Tea Room, relish, gr, divided 25.00
Tea Room, tray, gr, center hdl 195.00
Tea Room, vase, crystal, ruffled rim, 9½" 16.00
Tea Room, vase, pk, ruffled rim, 11" 275.00
Thistle, cup, gr, thin 25.00
Thistle, plate, luncheon; pk, 8" 15.00
Thistle, saucer, pk or gr 9.50
Tulip, creamer, amber, crystal or gr 18.00
Tulip, cup, amber, crystal or gr 12.00
Tulip, plate, amethyst, bl, 9" 37.50
Tulip, sugar bowl, amber, crystal or gr 18.00
Twisted Optic, bowl, colors other than bl or canary yel, 9" 15.00
Twisted Optic, bowl, console; bl or canary yel, 19½" 35.00
Twisted Optic, candlesticks, colors other than bl or canary yel, 8" pr 27.50
Twisted Optic, creamer, bl or canary yel 12.50
Twisted Optic, mayonnaise, bl or canary yel 35.00
Twisted Optic, powder jar, bl or canary yel, w/lid 65.00
Twisted Optic, sugar bowl, colors other than bl or canary yel 6.50
US Swirl, bowl, berry; gr, 4½" 5.50
US Swirl, comport, gr 20.00
US Swirl, pitcher, pk, 48-oz, 8" 55.00
US Swirl, plate, salad; gr, 8" 5.50
Victory, bonbon, amber, pk or gr, 7" 11.00
Victory, bowl, vegetable; blk or bl, oval, 9" 95.00
Victory, candlesticks, amber, pk or gr, 3", pr 30.00
Victory, plate, dinner; amber, pk or gr 20.00
Victory, saucer, blk or bl 12.00
Vitrock, bowl, fruit; wht, 6" 5.50
Vitrock, plate, luncheon; wht, 8¾" 4.50
Vitrock, sugar bowl, wht 5.00
Waterford, bowl, cereal; crystal, 5½" 17.00
Waterford, coaster, crystal, 4" 3.50
Waterford, plate, salad; crystal, 7" 6.00
Waterford, plate, sherbet; pk, 6" 7.00
Waterford, shakers, crystal, 2 styles, ea pr 8.50
Waterford, sugar bowl, pk 12.50

Windsor Diamond, tumblers, pink, 3", $25.00; 5", $32.00.

Windsor, bowl, salad; crystal, 10½" 15.00
Windsor, coaster, gr, 3¼" 20.00
Windsor, comport, crystal 10.00
Windsor, plate, cake; pk, ftd, 10¾" 20.00
Windsor, plate, dinner; gr, 9" 25.00

Windsor, shakers, pk, pr **36.00**
Windsor, tumbler, crystal, 12-oz, 5" **9.00**

Desert Sands

As early as the 1850s, the Evans family living in the Ozark Mountains of Missouri produced domestic clay products. Their small pot shop was passed on from one generation to the next. In the 1920s it was moved to North Las Vegas, Nevada, where the name Desert Sands was adopted. Succeeding generations of the family continued to relocate, taking the business with them. From 1937 to 1962 it operated in Boulder City, Nevada; then it was moved to Barstow, California, where it remained until it closed in the late 1970s.

Desert Sands pottery is similar to Mission Ware by Niloak. Various mineral oxides were blended to mimic the naturally occurring sand formations of the American West. A high-gloss glaze was applied to add intensity to the colorful striations that characterize the ware. Not all examples are marked, making it sometimes difficult to attribute. Marked items carry an ink stamp with the Desert Sands designation. Paper labels were also used.

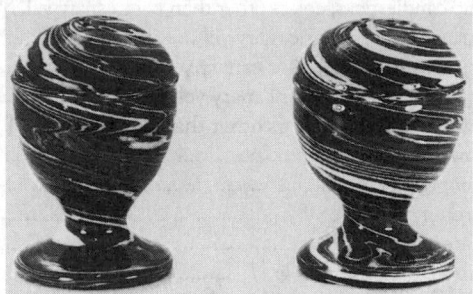

Shakers, three-color swirl, footed, $30.00 for the pair.

Ashtray, 6½" **25.00**
Bowl, console; hand thrown, 9½" **65.00**
Bowl, incurvate rim, 3" **18.00**
Butter dish **60.00**
Candle holder, 3" **18.00**
Mug **32.00**
Tumbler **22.00**
Vase, bulbous, flared rim, 3½" **35.00**
Vase, inverted cylinder, slim, 5" **25.00**
Vase, waisted form, flared rim, 2½" **25.00**
Vase, 3-color swirl, T Evans, 4¼" **30.00**

Dickota

The Dickota Pottery, a name coined from Dickinson, North Dakota, where it was founded as a brickyard, began operations in the early 1930s. In 1934 potters formerly associated with the North Dakota School of Mines and Charles Hyten from Nyloak began their own operation there. Hyten developed a line of swirled ware which was marked 'Dickota Badlands.' Vases, bowls, and ashtrays in a mottled glaze were also made. A variety of marks were used, all of which contain the Dickota name. The company closed in the late 1930s. For further information we recommend *Collector's Encyclopedia of the Dakota Potteries, Identification & Values,* by Darlene Hurst Dommel (Collector Books).

Ashtray, sundogs relief border, orange gloss, 4" **45.00**

Bookends, mountain goats, 4½x4½", pr **450.00**
Creamer & sugar bowl, soft olive gr **75.00**
Figurine, hippo, incised mk, 1½" **100.00**
Paperweight, shield shape, 2¾" **45.00**
Pitcher, water; Peacock Pink, pk & wht mottled glaze, 5" **65.00**
Teapot, Cableware, blk gloss glaze, 3¾" **200.00**

Photo courtesy Darlene Hurst Dommel

Vase, pine green high-fire glaze, 3x6", from $35.00 to $50.00; Vase, airbrush blended yellow to blue, 7", from $50.00 to $60.00.

Vase, Badlands, sgn HL, 3" **125.00**
Vase, Badlands, 6" **175.00**
Vase, bud; Peacock Blue, bl & wht mottled glaze, 6½" **35.00**
Vase, bud; rusty orange gloss, 6½" **25.00**
Vase, matt yel w/bl spray on top, 7" **85.00**

Documents

Although the word 'document' is defined in the general sense as 'anything printed or written, etc., relied upon to record or prove something. . .,' in the collectibles market, the term is more diversified with broadsides, billheads, checks, invoices, letters and letterheads, land grants, receipts, and waybills some of the most sought after. Some documents in demand are those related to a specific subject such as advertising, mining, railroads, military, politics, banking, slavery, nautical, or legal (deeds, mortgages, etc.). Other collectors look for examples representing a specific period of time such as colonial documents, Revolutionary or Civil War documents, early western documents, or those from a specific region, state, or city.

Aside from supply and demand, there are five major factors which determine the collector value of a document. These are:

1) Age — Documents from the eastern half of the country can be found that date back to the 1700s or earlier. Most documents sought by collectors usually date from 1700 to 1900. Those with 20th-century dates are still abundant and not in demand unless of special significance or beauty.

2) Region of origin — Depending on age, documents from rural and less-populated areas are harder to find than those from major cities and heavily populated states. The colonization of the West and Mid-West did not begin until after 1850, so while an 1870s billhead from New York or Chicago is common, one from Albuquerque or Phoenix is not, since most of the Southwest was still unsettled.

3) Attractiveness — Some documents are plain and unadorned, but collectors prefer colorful, profusely illustrated pieces. Additional artwork and engravings add to the value.

4) Historical content — Unusual or interesting content, such as a letter written by a Civil War soldier giving an eyewitness account of the Battle of Gettysburg or a western territorial billhead listing numerous animal hides purchased from a trapper, will sell for more than one with mundane information.

5) Condition — Through neglect or environmental conditions, over many decades paper articles can become stained, torn, or deteriorated. Heavily damaged or stained documents are generally avoided altogether. Those with minor problems are more acceptable, although their value will decrease anywhere from 20% to 50%, depending upon the extent of damage. Avoid attempting to repair tears with scotch tape — sell 'as is' so that the collector can take proper steps toward restoration.

Foreign documents are plentiful; and though some are very attractive, resale may be difficult. The listings that follow are generalized; prices are variable depending entirely upon the five points noted above. Values here are based upon examples with no major damage. Common grade documents without significant content are found in abundance and generally have little collector value. These usually date from the late 1800s and early 1900s. It should be noted that the items listed below are examples of those that meet the criteria for having collector value. There is little demand for documents worth less than $5.00. For more information we recommend *Owning Western History* by our advisor Warren Anderson. His address and ordering information may be found in the Directory under Utah.

Key:
illus — illustrated   vgn — vignette

Account book, general store, completely filled, 1852-1905, EX **75.00**
Appointment, NJ justice of peace, sgn Gov GC Ludlow, 1882 .....**27.50**
Bank note, Bank of Selma AL, $1000, goddess vgn, 1863 ....**95.00**
Bank note, Commercial Bank of Columbia SC, $10, 1850 ....**20.00**
Bank note, GA, Civil War era, $5, dtd 1858, EX **20.00**
Bill of lading, CA Fast Freight Line, NY to CA, 1880, 9x14" **18.00**
Bill of sale, 3 Negro slaves, New Orleans, 1840 ....**400.00**
Billhead, BF Tuttle & Co, Petaluma, purchase of lumber, 1862, 7x9" .**18.00**
Book, dr's visiting; names/descriptions of cases, IN, 1875 ....**55.00**
Certificate, for foreigners to join militia, 1864 ....**75.00**
Certificate, man born free, MD, 1838, 7x4½" **75.00**
Certificate, pharmacist renewal, SD state seal, 1920s, 4x8" **9.00**
Certificate of discharge, WWII, Army Infantry, w/service record .**28.00**
Certificate of service, Continental Army, partly printed **25.00**
Check, Cashier of City Bank, NY, unused, 1840, M **5.00**
Check, IN-MD Development Co, blk on wht w/orange vgn, 1905 .**8.00**
Check, 10th Ward Savings Assoc, St Louis, MO, 1872, 3x8" **9.00**
Confederate money, $20 bill, worn **15.00**
Contract, US Treasury Dept Certificate, medical services, 1862 .**100.00**
Court martial, orders for Union soldier to be shot, 1863, 2-pg **50.00**
Debt repayment, free man of color, handwritten in Spanish, 1801 ..**300.00**
Discharge, Civil War Union soldier, eagle vgn, 8x10" **35.00**
Envelope, 5¢ air rate, w/stamp showing beacon on mtn top, 1928 ..**12.00**
Expense account, disbursement for voyage, Cuba to Europe, 1841-42 .....**60.00**
General orders, Corps of Sharpshooters, 1862, VG **20.00**
Invoice, US Arsenal at Schuykill NY, preprinted, 1837, 8x12" **18.00**
Land contract, PA, dtd 1862, 18x13", EX **25.00**
Land office patent, for 160 acres, dtd 1878, EX **20.00**
Ledger, pharmacy; details of prescriptions/supplies/etc, 1884-85 ...**80.00**
Letter, details of San Francisco earthquake, 1907, 12-pg **385.00**
Letter, mining engineer requests payment, CO, 1897, 8x11" **17.00**
Letter, Union soldier's, war news, describes killing, 1862, 3-pg ..**175.00**
List, 12th MO Cavalry survivors, Civil War era, 12x6" **20.00**
Muster pay roll, St Joseph Vols, MI, B Company, 1861, 30x22", EX ..**150.00**
Muster roll, Civil War OH Volunteer Infantry, dtd 1865, VG **38.00**
Notice, MA society of meeting at tavern, 1803, 4½x5" **25.00**
Notice, marriage of MA residents, 1798, 2¼x6¼" **15.00**
Order form, Treasury Department, for morphine sulphate, 1946 ..**50.00**
Order of reconciliation in New Orleans district, sgn de Casa, 1800 .**135.00**
Orders, discharge; 20th KY Vols, sgn Brig Gen Wm Sidell, 1862 .**75.00**
Pamphlet, Mormon doctrine, Kingdom of God, IA, 1900, EX **10.00**

Pay order, CT citizen for support of state pauper, 1794, EX **12.50**
Pay order, payment of expenses for prisoners, CT, 1777, 9x6" **100.00**
Pay order, Revolutionary War, partly printed, 3 signatures **20.00**
Pay roll, railroad employes occupations/wages, 1880s, EX **12.00**
Pay voucher, 33rd IN Vols, Coburn's Infantry, 1862, VG+ **50.00**
Promissory note, Revolutionary War, partly printed, 7x4", EX **40.00**
Receipt, cattle sale, Kansas City Stock Yards, 1905, 8x11" **12.00**
Receipt, Navy Dept, purchase of corn, 1863, 5½x8" **40.00**
Report, annual; home for disabled soldiers, 1879, 120-pg **45.00**
Report, debts owed, New Orleans, sgn Governor de Lemos, 1797 .**135.00**
Report, Steward's Weekly Return of Provisions, 1862, EX **50.00**
Requisition, for stationery, 6th ME Volunteers, 1863, EX **40.00**
Summons, CT man to appear in court, 1790s, 8x6" **25.00**
Tax stamp, Internal Revenue, Mfg Tobacco, 1880s, 7x14½", EX .**30.00**
Telegram, Spanish-Am war, re: fish order for soldiers, 1899 ....**12.50**
Volunteer enlistment papers, 9 month soldiers, unissued **5.00**

Dollhouses and Furnishings

Dollhouses were introduced commercially in this country late in the 1700s by Dutch craftsmen who settled in the East. By the mid-1800s, they had become meticulously detailed, divided into separate rooms, and lavishly furnished to reflect the opulence of the day. Originally intended for the amusement of adults of the household, by the latter 1800s their status had changed to that of a child's toy. Though many early dollhouses were lovingly hand fashioned for a special little girl, those made commercially by such companies as Bliss and Schoenhut are highly valued.

Furniture and furnishings in the Biedermeier style featuring stenciled Victorian decorations often sell for several hundred dollars each. Other early pieces made of pewter, porcelain, or papier-mache are also quite valuable. Certainly less expensive but very collectible, nonetheless, is the quality, hallmarked plastic furniture produced during the '40s by Renwal and Acme, and the 1960s Petite Princess line produced by Ideal. In the listings that follow, dollhouses are litho paper on wood, unless otherwise noted. For more information, see *Schroeder's Collectible Toys, Antique to Modern*. Our advisor for this category is Barbara Rosen; she is listed in the Directory under New Jersey. See also Miniatures.

Furniture

Armoire, Mattel Littles **8.00**
Armoire, Tomy Sellers Homes **10.00**

Bathroom set, green and white stenciled paperboard, Tootsietoy, VG in EX box, $100.00.

Bathroom set, dk ivory, hard plastic, 4-pc, Marx, ¾" scale **20.00**
Bathroom tub, pk, turq or rose, Plasco, ea **4.00**
Bed, w/cover & pillow, Mattel Littles, MIB **15.00**
Bedroom set, dk ivory, hard plastic, Marx, ¾" scale **40.00**
Buffet, reddish brn, Jaydon **4.00**
Carpet Sweeper, Renwal **85.00**

Chair, club; bl w/brn base, Renwal, #76 ....8.00
Chair, dining room; brn, Plasco 3.00
Chair, dining room; yel, Superior, ¾" scale 3.00
Chair, living room; Mattel Littles 4.00
Chest of drawers, pk, hard plastic, Marx, ¾" scale 5.00
Clock, kitchen; ivory or red, Renwal, ea 20.00
Cradle, bl, Ideal 40.00
Cradle, pk, w/spread insert, Renwal, #119 ....30.00
Desk, teacher's; bl, Renwal, #34 ....25.00
Highboy, yel, hard plastic, Marx, ½" scale 3.00
Hutch, red, Allied 4.00
Lamp, floor; red w/ivory shade, Renwal, #70 ....15.00
Lowboy, red, Marx Little Hostess 10.00
Nightstand, Ideal, brn 6.00
Piano, marbleized brn, Renwal, #74 ....30.00
Playpen, pk, soft plastic, Marx, ¾" scale 3.00
Playpen, Wolverine 8.00
Scale, red, Renwal, #10 ....10.00
Sink, pk w/lt bl, Renwal, #T96 ....5.00
Sofa, brocade, Ideal Petite Princess, #4407-3 ....25.00
Sofa, ivory w/brn base, Renwal #78 ....18.00
Sofa, Mattel Littles 8.00
Sofa, red, Strombecker, ¾" scale 10.00
Sofa, yel or red, hard plastic, ¾" scale, ea 5.00
Stove, pk, no-base style, Plasco 3.00
Stove, wht, Donna Lee 6.00
Table, coffee; Ideal 10.00
Table, coffee; Tomy Smaller Homes 10.00
Table, kitchen; ivory, Renwal, #67 ....5.00
Table, living room; gold, Tootsietoy 20.00
Table, picnic; wht, Ideal 20.00
Toilet, ivory, hard plastic, Marx, ½" scale 3.00
Vanity, pk, Allied 3.00
Washing machine, bl or pk w/bear decal, Renwal, #31, ea 30.00

Houses

Schoenhut, Dutch Colonial style, yellow with red roof and green shutters, VG base, 22x25x24", $750.00.

Bliss, 2-story, Colonial mansion, hinged dbl doors, 18x16", G ...300.00
Bliss, 2-story, 4 bow windows, sm porch w/2 columns, 13x9", EX ...650.00
Christian Hacker, 2-story, balcony/porch, 1910s, 23x23", EX .3,520.00
Mansford, 2-story Victorian w/belvedere, 49" sq base, EX 2,800.00
Marx, split-level w/pool, 60-pc furniture set, EX 125.00
Marx, 2-story, tin, wht clapboard/stone, red roof, 14x38", VG ...100.00
McLoughlin, Dolly's Play House, 2-room fold-up, EX (worn box) .375.00
Meritoy, Cape Cod, tin, clapboard/stone/red roof, 1949, 21", M ...150.00
Rich, Arts & Crafts-style bungalow, cb, 1930s, 31x21", VG 200.00

Schoenhut, 2-story, brick/stone/red roof, 23x23", G 1,045.00
T Cohn, tin, bl shutters/red roof, furnished, 1951, 16x24", VG ..200.00
Wolverine, Colonial mansion, no garage, ½" scale, EX 50.00

Dolls

To learn to invest your money wisely as you enjoy the hobby of doll collecting, you must become aware of defects which may devaluate a doll. In bisque, watch for eye chips, hairline cracks and chips, or breaks on any part of the head. Composition should be clean, not crazed or cracked. Vinyl and plastic should be clean with no pen or crayon marks. Though a quality replacement wig is acceptable for bisque dolls, composition and hard plastics should have their originals in uncut condition. Original clothing is a must except in bisque dolls, since it is unusual to find one in its original costume.

It is important to remember that prices are based on condition and rarity. When no condition is noted, dolls are assumed to be in excellent condition with the exceptions of American Character, Cameo, Celebrity Dolls, Kestner, Madame Alexander, and Shirley Temple, which are generally priced in mint condition. Cabbage Patch values are for dolls mint in the box. In relation to bisque dolls, excellent means having no cracks, chips, or hairlines, being nicely dressed, shoed, wigged, and ready to to be placed into a collection. For a more thorough study of the subject, refer to *Talking Toys of the 20th Century* by Kathy and Don Lewis; *Collector's Encyclopedia of American Composition Dolls, 1900 – 1950*, by Ursula R. Mertz; and *Modern Collectible Dolls*, Vols. I, II, and III and *Doll Values, Antique to Modern, Third Edition*, by Patsy Moyer, our advisor for this category. Mrs. Moyer is listed in the Directory under Arizona. Several other book are referenced throughout this category. All are published by Collector Books.

Key:
bjtd — ball-jointed
blb — bent limb body
bsk — bisque
c/m — closed mouth
hh — human hair
hp — hard plastic
jtd — jointed
MIG — Made In Germany
NC — no clothes
NRFB — never removed from box
o/c/e — open closed eyes
o/c/m — open closed mouth

OC — original clothes
o/m — open mouth
p/e — pierced ears
pnt — painted
pwt — paperweight eyes
RpC — replaced clothes
ShHd — shoulder head
ShPl — shoulder plate
SkHd — socket head
str — straight
trn — turned

American Character

AC or Petite, mama, compo/cloth, mohair or hh wig, crier, OC, 16" ..275.00
Annie Oakley, hp walker, embr on skirt, OC, 14" 400.00
Bottletot, compo/cloth, o/c/e, pnt hair, bent limbs, OC, 18" 325.00
Carol Ann Beery, compo Patsy type, cm/, o/c/e, OC, 13" 415.00
Freckles, face changes, 1966, OC, 13" 40.00
Pre-teen Tressy, grow hair, Am Char 63, 1963, OC, 14" 55.00
Puggy, jtd compo, scowling, pnt hair, cowboy OC, 12" 485.00
Ricky Jr, vinyl baby boy, 1954-56, OC, 13" 50.00
Sally, compo/cloth, crier, o/c/e, OC, 16" 350.00
Sally Joy, compo ShHd, cloth body, o/c/e, curly wig, OC, 24" 400.00
Talking Marie, record player in body, battery-op, 1963, OC, 18" .90.00
Tiny Tears, hp/vinyl, 1950-62, OC, 8" 50.00
Toodle-Loo, plastic, rooted hair, pnt eyes, c/m, OC, 1961, 18" ..190.00
Vinyl head, mk Am Character, OC, 20" 80.00

Annalee

Barbara Annalee Davis has been making her dolls since 1950.

What began as a hobby, very soon turned into a commercial venture. Her whimsical creations range from tiny angels atop powder puff clouds to funky giant frogs, some 42" in height. In between there are dolls for every occasion (with Christmas being her specialty), all characterized by their unique construction methods (felt over flexible wire framework) and wonderful facial expressions. Naturally, some of the older dolls are the most valuable (though more recent examples are desirable as well, depending on scarcity and demand), and condition, as usual, is very important. To date your doll, look at the tag. If made before 1986, that date is only the copyright date. (Dolls made after 1986 do carry the manufacturing date.) Dolls from the '50s have a long white red-embroidered tag with no date. From 1959 to '64, that same tag had a date in the upper right-hand corner. From 1965 until '70, it was folded in half and sewn into the seam. In 1970, a satiny white tag with a date preceded by a copyright symbol in the upper right-hand corner was used. In '75, the tag was a long white cotton strip with a copyright date. This tag was folded over in 1982, making it shorter. Our advisor for Annalee dolls is Jane Holt; she is listed in the Directory under New Hampshire.

Angel, 1987, 10" 45.00
Ballerina bunny, pk tutu, 1980, 18" 125.00
Bowler, 1984, 7" 65.00
Bunny girl, pick, 1982 ....45.00
Bunny girl, wht, 1977, 18" 80.00
Bunny girl w/flowerpot, 1985, 7" 35.00
Bunny w/butterfly, 1977, 7" 50.00
Caroller boy, 1982, 10" 60.00
Caroller girl, 1984, 8" 50.00
Cat w/mouse & mistletoe, 1982, 18" 120.00
Colonial girl, head pick, 1976 ....100.00
Cross Country Santa skier, 1979, 7" 75.00
Dentist mouse, 1984, 7" 50.00
Devil mouse, 1983, 7" 50.00
Drummer boy, 1986, 12" 60.00
Elf, red, 1987, 10" 35.00
Frog boy, 1979, 18" 150.00
Gnome, 18" 150.00
Gnome, 1979, 10" 60.00
Graduation girl, 1985, 7" 40.00
Hiker mouse, 1981, 7" 60.00
Indian boy & girl, 1987, 7", pr 60.00
Jack Frost elf w/5" snowflake, 1981, 10" 90.00
Jogger boy, 1983, 7" 35.00

Monkey (comes in chartreuse, blue, and hot pink), 1970, 10", $325.00 each.

Monkey boy or girl, 1983, 12", ea 180.00
Mr & Mrs Bob Cratchet, 1984, 18", pr 200.00
Mr & Mrs Santa Claus w/basket, 1974, 30", pr 250.00
Mrs Santa, wired card holder, pk & wht stripe, 1966, 18" .100.00
Nurse w/needle, 1979, 7" 60.00

PJ baby, 1983, 3" 75.00
Scarecrow, 1977, 10" 100.00
Sweetheart mouse, 1982, 7" 35.00
Swimmer w/inner tube, 1979, 7" 80.00
Toy soldier, 1988, 18" 85.00
Tree top, gold, w/star, 1989, 12" 50.00
Woodchopper mouse, 1981, 7" 60.00

Armand Marseille

Alma, ShHd, 15" 250.00
AM, Floradora, ShHd, 20" 350.00
AM, Floradora, SkHd, 27" 500.00
AM, My Dearie, SkHd, 1908, 14" 300.00
AM, ShHd, boy, 14" 250.00
AM, SkHd, 16" 275.00
AM, Sunshine, ShHd, 1910, 24" 525.00
AM 248, mk GB (Geo Borgfeldt), o/m, 1912, 10" 325.00
AM 253, SkHd, googly eyes, 1915, 16" 2,100.00
AM 255, SkHd, intaglio eyes, 7½" 900.00
AM 310/7/0 Just Me, SkHd, bl o/c/e to side, c/m, 9" 1,050.00
AM 320, SkHd, c/m, googly eyes, 6½" 650.00
AM 324, googly eyes, 7" 465.00
AM 328, baby, SkHd, closed dome, 1922, 14" 275.00
AM 341, My Dream Baby, flange, c/m, 18" 550.00
AM 347, SkHd, 1909, 16" 365.00
AM 351, My Dream Baby, flange, o/m, 6" 150.00
AM 362, Teenie Weenie, baby, closed dome, wht, 15" 550.00
AM 370, 16½" 275.00
AM 370n, Kiddiejoy, girl, SkHd, c/m, molded hair, 20" ...2,600.00
AM 390, My Dearie, 23" 465.00
AM 390, SkHd, o/m w/4 teeth, jtd compo, orig Scottish outfit, 9" .130.00
AM 390, SkHd, 16" 300.00
AM 390n, nun, SkHd, brn o/c/e, o/m w/teeth, OC, 20" 300.00
AM 390n, SkHd, 1915, 27" 550.00
AM 402, SkHd, pnt bsk, 14" 300.00
AM 500, Infant Berry, molded hair, 1908, 8" 765.00
AM 600, SkHd, flange, c/m, 1910, 10" 1,200.00

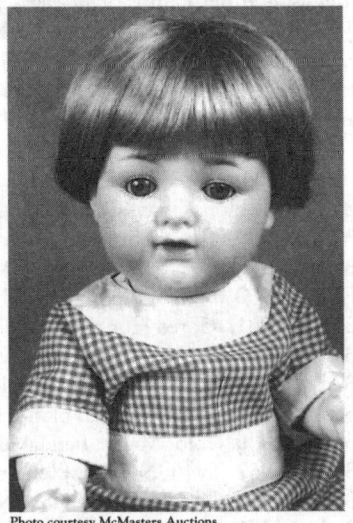

AM 990, Happy Tot, baby, socket head, blue sleep eyes, open mouth with two upper teeth, replaced wig, re-dressed, 16", $400.00.

Photo courtesy McMasters Auctions

AM 966, baby SkHd, flirty eyes, 14" 350.00
AM 975, Sadie, baby, SkHd, 1914, 9" 250.00
AM 990, Happy Tot, baby, SkHd, 1910, 16" 450.00
AM 992, baby, SkHd, 1914, 22" 700.00
AM 1894, boy, SkHd, brn o/c/e, o/m w/teeth, rprs, RpC, 23" .400.00

AM 3200, ShHd, some trn, 22" 450.00

Arranbee

Baby, cloth body, OC or appropriate RpC, 1930s-40s, 16" 125.00
Cinderella, hp & vinyl, silver/pk dress, 14", M, scarce 825.00
Debu' Teen, compo ShHd, cloth body, hh wig, OC, 14" 225.00
Dream Baby, compo/cloth, 1972+, OC, 14" 250.00
Little Bo Peep, w/papier-mache lamb, ca 1935, OC, 8½" 225.00
Littlest Angel, hp walker, R&B mk head, 7-pc body, nude, 10" ...50.00
Nancy, vinyl & hp, wig, 1951-52, OC, 14" 150.00
Nancy Lee, compo, o/c/e, wig, OC, 1939+, 17" 300.00
Nancy Lee, o/c/e, mohair or hh wig, OC, 12" 195.00
Nancy Lee Baby, plastic, p/e, crying look, 1952, OC, 15" 145.00
Nanette, plastic, synthetic wig, o/c/e, c/m, OC, 14" 350.00
Sonja Skater, compo, 1945, OC, 14" 275.00

Barbie Dolls and Related Dolls

Though the face has changed three times since 1959, Barbie is still as popular today as she was when she was first introduced. Named after the young daughter of the first owner of the Mattel Company, the original Barbie had a white iris but no eye color. These dolls are nearly impossible to find, but there is a myriad of her successors and related collectibles just waiting to be found.

For further information we recommend *The Barbie Doll Years, Third Edition*, by Patrick C. Olds; *The Story of Barbie, Second Edition*, by Kittarah B. Westenhouser; *The World of Barbie Dolls* and *The Wonder of Barbie, 1976 – 1986*, by Paris, Susan, and Carol Manos; *The Collector's Encyclopedia of Barbie Dolls and Collectibles* by Sibyl DeWein and Joan Ashabraner; *Barbie Exclusives, Books 1 and 2*, by Margo Rana; *A Decade of Barbie Dolls and Collectibles, 1981 – 1991*, by Beth Summers; *Barbie, The First Thirty Years*, by Stefanie Deutsch; *Thirty Years of Mattel Fashion Dolls, The Barbie Doll Boom, 1986 – 1995, Collector's Encyclopedia of Barbie Doll Exclusives and More*, all by J. Michael Augustyniak; *Collector's Guide to 1990s Barbie Dolls, Identification & Values*, by Maria Martinez-Esguerra; and *Skipper — Barbie Doll's Little Sister*, by Scott Arend, Karla Holzerland, and Trina Kent. *Barbie Fashion, Vol I and II*, by Sarah Sink Eames, gives a complete history of the wardrobes of Barbie, her friends, and her family. *Schroeder's Toys, Antique to Modern*, is another good source for current market values. You may also be interested in *Collector's Guide to Barbie Paper Dolls* by Lorraine Meiszala; and *Collector's Guide to Barbie Doll Vinyl Cases* by Connie Craig Kaplan. All these are published by Collector Books.

Allan, 1964-67, bendable legs, M 165.00
Barbie, #1, blond ponytail, MIB 9,950.00
Barbie, 1959-60, #2, brunette ponytail, MIB 8,500.00
Barbie, 1960, #3, blond ponytail, NM 950.00
Barbie, 1960, #4, blond ponytail, MIB 1,100.00
Barbie, 1961, #5, red hair, ponytail, MIB 1,300.00
Barbie, 1961, Bubble Cut, brunette hair, EX+ 190.00
Barbie, 1963, Fashion Queen, complete w/8 wigs & stand, NM .275.00
Barbie, 1964, Swirl Ponytail, blond, NM 450.00
Barbie, 1966, Color Magic, bendable legs, NM 650.00
Barbie, 1967, Twist 'N Turn, blond w/orig pk swimsuit, NM 265.00
Barbie, 1971, Growin' Pretty Hair, NM 250.00
Barbie, 1971, Hair Happenin's, red hair, MIB 1,200.00
Barbie, 1972, Ward's issue, MIB 525.00
Barbie, 1973, Newport, NRFB 175.00
Barbie, 1974, Sun Valley, EX 50.00
Barbie, 1977, Fashion Photo, MIB 85.00
Barbie, 1979, Kissing, EX 16.00
Barbie, 1980, Hispanic, MIB 70.00

Barbie, 1986, Celebration, Sears, MIB 90.00
Barbie, 1988, Holiday, MIB 1,000.00
Barbie, 1989, Gift Giving, MIB 30.00
Barbie, 1989, Golden Greetings, FAO Schwarz, MIB 250.00
Barbie, 1989, Peach Pretty, K-Mart, MIB 35.00
Casey, 1967, Twist 'N Turn, MIB 150.00
Chris, 1967-70, blond, NM 125.00
Francie, 1966, bendable legs, blond, orig swimsuit, NM 200.00
Francie, 1972, Malibu, MIB 35.00
Julia, 1969, Talking, MIB 150.00
Ken, #1, 1961, str legs, flocked hair, NM 165.00
Ken, 1962, pnt hair, MIB 225.00

Ken, 1965, bendable legs, MIB, $350.00.

Ken, 1965, bendable legs, NM 225.00
Midge, 1963, str legs, MIB 150.00
Midge, 1965, bendable legs, MIB 400.00
PJ, 1970, Talking, NM 165.00
Ricky, 1965, MIB 175.00
Skipper, 1965, bendable legs, red hair, NM 100.00
Todd, 1966, NM 125.00
Tutti, 1967, NM 85.00

Barbie Gifts Sets and Related Accessories

When no condition is indicated, the items listed below are assumed to be mint and in the original box or package (if one was issued). Items in only excellent condition may be worth 40% to 60% less.

Gift Set, Skipper on Wheels Set, #1032, Sears, 1965, MIB, $600.00.

Clothes, Arabian Nights, Barbie, #864, NRFB 500.00
Clothes, Barbie Q, #962-0, complete, NM 60.00

Clothes, Career Girl, #954-1, complete, NM 130.00
Clothes, Country Music, #1055, NRFB 195.00
Clothes, Hearts 'N Flowers, Skipper, #1945, complete, NM 165.00
Clothes, Knitting Pretty, #957-5, complete, EX 195.00
Gift set, Birthday Fun at McDonald's, 1993, NRFB 50.00
Gift set, Francie Rise & Shine, 1971, NRFB 1,000.00
Gift set, Skipper on Wheels, 1965, MIB 600.00
House, Deluxe Family House, 1966, complete, VG 135.00
House, Magical Mansion, 1990, NRFB 1,000.00
Vehicle, Dream Vette, 1982, pk, NRFB 50.00
Vehicle, Dune Buggy, 1970, pk, Irwin, NRFB 300.00
Vehicle, Ferrari, 1988, wht, MIB 50.00

Belton

Concave head, 2 or 3 hole, EX bsk, o/c/m or c/m w/wig, 8" 800.00
Concave head, 2 or 3 hole, EX bsk, o/c/m or c/m w/wig, 10" ...1,200.00
Concave head, 2 or 3 hole, EX bsk, o/c/m or c/m w/wig, 13" ...1,600.00
Concave head, 2 or 3 hole, EX bsk, o/c/m or c/m w/wig, 15" ...1,900.00
Concave head, 2 or 3 hole, EX bsk, o/c/m or c/m w/wig, 16" ...2,000.00
Concave head, 2 or 3 hole, EX bsk, o/c/m or c/m w/wig, 17" ...2,000.00
Concave head, 2 or 3 hole, EX bsk, o/c/m or c/m w/wig, 20" ...2,800.00
Concave head, 2 or 3 hole, EX bsk, o/c/m or c/m w/wig, 22" ...3,000.00
Concave head, 2 or 3 hole, EX bsk, o/c/m or c/m w/wig, 23" ...3,200.00
Concave head, 2 or 3 hole, EX bsk, o/c/m or c/m w/wig, 26" ...3,800.00

Betsy McCall

Doll, Am Character, in Playtime outfit, 14", EX 250.00
Doll, Am Character, orig outfit, multi-jtd, 22", MIB 250.00
Doll, orig outfit w/pk tissue & booklet, 8", MIB 225.00
Doll, wearing pk Prom Time formal, 8", EX 135.00
Outfit, April Showers, complete, EX 35.00
Outfit, fur stole & mink, MIB 150.00
Outfit, Sunday Best, 1957, complete, EX 85.00
Pattern, McCall's #2247, uncut 25.00

Boudoir Dolls

Boudoir dolls, often called flapper dolls, were popular during the 1920s and 1930s, but they continued to be made up into the '40s as well. These dolls are rarely marked, but most were made in the United States, France, Italy, and Germany. Dolls of this type have silk or felt painted face masks, elaborate costumes, and are of excellent quality. The less expensive ones have composition heads and clothes that are stapled or nailed onto the body. Our advisor for this category is Bonnie Groves; she is listed in the Directory under Texas.

Anita, compo head & hands, cloth body, nude, '20s, EX, $50 to ..85.00
Anita, compo head & hands, silk floss wig, OC/shoes, VG, $150 to ..200.00
Black, from $150 to 300.00
Cloth, music box inside, all orig, Fr, 30", EX, minimum value ...500.00
Cloth, silk face, mohair wig, nude, shoes & stockings, 30", VG ...85.00
Common, std doll mk WKS Inc, crazed, EX clothes, 28" 45.00
Compo, common carnival type, all orig, 1940s, 28", VG, $50 to ..125.00
Compo, jtd arms, mk Sterling, all orig, 30", VG 150.00
Compo, sleep eyes, bald, nude, 30", G 50.00
Compo ShPl, compo arms/high-heeled ft, WKS Inc, EX clothes, 30" .200.00
Doll head on hat stand, VG, from $65 to 135.00
Etta, all cloth, all orig, 30", VG, from $95 to 250.00
Finely pnt features, average clothes & quality, 28", from $85 to .125.00
Finely pnt features, average clothes & quality, 32", from $100 to .150.00
Finely pnt features, EX clothes/quality, glass eyes, 28", $145 to ..200.00
Finely pnt features, EX clothes/quality, glass eyes, 32", $150 to ..250.00
Finely pnt features, standard quality, dressed, 16" 125.00
French, silk face, bks limbs, OC, 30", VG 200.00
French, silk face/costume, bsk arms & legs, 21", VG, from $150 to ..200.00
Glass eyed, 27", EX, from $145 to 200.00
Lenci, 18-26", from $800 to 1,500.00
Shoes for doll, EX, from $25 to 45.00
Smoker, Anita, head only, VG 50.00
Smoker, Blossom, Argentine costume, all orig, 30", EX 350.00
Smoker, cloth, 16" 285.00
Smoker, cloth, 25" 475.00
Smoker, compo, 28" 375.00
Smoker, jtd compo, all orig, 25", G 300.00
Smoker, jtd compo, nude bald, 15", G-, from $50 to 100.00
Smoker, Lenci, all orig, moth damage 500.00
Unmk, silk face, wht mohair, RpC (old pattern), orig shoes, 30", EX ..200.00

Cameo Dolls

Annie Rooney, compo, yarn wig, legs pnt blk, OC, 12", minimum ...475.00
Baby Bo Kaye, bsk/cloth, molded hair, o/m, OC, 17" 2,500.00
Baby Bo Kaye, celluloid/cloth, molded hair, o/m, glass eyes, OC, 12" ..400.00
Baby Mine, vinyl/cloth, o/c/e, 1962-64, OC, 16" 100.00
Betty Boop, compo/wood, 1932, OC, 11" 650.00
Bsk, molded hair, glass o/c/e, 2 teeth, jtd limbs, OC, 5" 1,500.00
Joy, compo/wood, molded hair, pnt features, OC, 10" 300.00
Miss Peep, vinyl, pin-jtd shoulders/hips, 1947-70s+, OC, 15" 45.00
Newborn, vinyl & hp, 1962 ....40.00
Pinkie, compo/wood, molded hair, pnt features, OC, 10" 375.00
Scootles, compo, o/c/e, OC, 15" 700.00

Celebrity

Silk face, hand-painted features, mohair wig, original silk and taffeta dress and jewelry, French, VG, $450.00.

Brooke Shields, Prom Party, LJN, 1983, 3rd issue, rare, 11½", NRFB, $200.00.

Al Lewis (Grandpa Munster), Remco, 1964, 6", MIB 200.00
Andy Gibb, Ideal, 1979, 7½", NRFB 50.00
Barbara Eden (I Dream of Jeannie), Remco, 1972, 6½", NRFB ..100.00
Bobby Orr, Regal, 1975, 12", rare, MOC 800.00
Debbie Boone, Mattel, 1978, 11", MIB 50.00
Desi Arnez (Ricky Ricardo), Applause, 1988, 17", MIB 50.00
Diana Ross, Mego, 1977, wht & silver dress, 12", NRFB 125.00
Elvis Presley (Burning Love), World Doll, 1984, 21", MIB 110.00
Groucho Marx, Effanbee, 1983, 17", MIB 90.00
Jaleel White (Urkel), Hasbro, 1991, cloth & vinyl, 17", MIB 50.00
Jimmy Osmond, Mattel, 1978, 9", MIB 65.00
Joe Namath, Mego, 1970, 11½", rare, MIB 400.00
Mae West, Effanbee, 1982, Great Legends, 18", MIB 120.00
Marie Osmond, Mattel, 1976, 30", MIB 115.00
Michael Jackson, LJN, 1984, 11½", NRFB 70.00
Mr T, Galoob, 1983, 1st edition, bib overalls, 12", MIB 60.00
Pam Dawber (Mork & Mindy), Mattel, 1979, 8½", MIB 50.00
Princess Diana, Danbury Mint, 1985, pk dress, 15", MIB 110.00
Redd Foxx, Shindana, 1977, cloth, talker, MIB 45.00
Sally Fields (Flying Nun), Hasbro, 1967, 12", MIB 200.00
Selena, Arm Enterprises, 1996, 11½", MIB 45.00
Soupy Sales, Sunshine Dolls, 1965, 6", NRFB 235.00
Three Stooges, Collins, set of 3, 13", MOC 140.00
Twiggy, Mattel, 1967, 11½", rare, MIB 350.00
WC Fields, 1980, 16", M 85.00

China, Unmarked

Boy, marked 784 #9 on shoulder plate, painted blue eyes, closed mouth, molded blond hair, bisque lower arms, 23", EX, $800.00; Covered Wagon style, sausage curls, leather arms, original dress, 21", minor damage/flakes, 700.00.

Photo courtesy McMasters Auctions

Adelina Patti, center part, curls at temples, 1860s, 18" 450.00
Biedermeier or Bald Head, takes wig, RpC, 20" 700.00
Common Hairdo, blond or blk hair, RpC, after 1905, 12" 145.00
Common Hairdo, blond or blk hair, RpC, after 1905, 8" 80.00
Curly Top, loose ringlet curls, RpC, 1845-60s, 16" 500.00
Dolly Madison, modeled ribbon & bow, RpC, 1870-80s, 14" 275.00
Dolly Madison, modeled ribbon & bowl, RpC, 1870-80s, 21" 600.00
Glass Eyes, various hairstyles, RpC, 1840s-70s, 14" 1,600.00
Man or Boy, glass eyes, side part, RpC, 14" 2,200.00
Man or Boy, pnt eyes, side part, RpC, 16" 1,400.00
Pet Name, molded shirtwaist w/name on front, RpC, 1905, 19" .265.00
Pierced Ears, various hairstyles, RpC, 18" 675.00
Spill Curls, w/or w/out headband, RpC, 14" 400.00
Wood Body, articulated/slim hips, RpC, 1840s-50s, 12" 1,600.00
Wood Body, jtd hips, covered-wagon hairdo, 1840s-50s, 15" ..1,900.00

Cloth

A cloth doll in very good condition will display light wear and soiling, while one assessed as excellent will be clean and bright.

Alabama Indestructible Doll, baby, 1900-25, 19", VG 2,000.00
Alabama Indestructible Doll, Black child, 1900-25, 23", VG ..6,800.00
Averill Mfg Corp, Dolly Dimple, 1923, 11", EX 385.00
Babyland Rag by Horsman, litho face, 24", VG 550.00
Beecher, Julia Jones, Missionary Ragbabies, 1893-1910, 16", G .1,725.00
Bing Art, compo head, 1921-32, 12", VG 175.00
Bing Art, pnt hair on cloth or felt, 13", VG 275.00
Bruckner for Horsman, blk, printed/molded mask, 1901-30+, 14", VG ..425.00
Chad Valley, cat, 1917-30+, 12", G 75.00
Chad Valley, child w/glass eyes, 1917-30+, 14", VG 625.00
Colonial Toy Mfg Co, Kitty Puss, poseable limbs & tail, 1916, VG .400.00
Kamkins by LR Kampes Studio, 1919-28, 19", VG 600.00
Krueger, Richard; child, 1917+, 20", VG 240.00
Martha Chase, baby, 1889-1930+, 19", EX 700.00
Martha Chase, Mad Hatter, 1889-1930+, 15", EX 2,000.00

Orphan Annie, embroidered features, yarn hair, orange flannel body, unmarked, 20", EX; Along with Sandy (her dog), 11", VG, $700.00 for the pair.

Photo courtesy McMasters Auctions

Petzold, Dora; Germany, 26", VG 850.00
Russian, pnt stockinette head, Made in Soviet Union, '20s, 7", EX ..70.00
Topsy-Turvy, oil-pnt head, VG 650.00

Eegee

Annette, vinyl, teen type, rooted hair, pnt eyes, 1963, OC, 11½" ..55.00
Babette, vinyl/cloth, o/c/e, rooted hair, 1970, OC, 15" 40.00
Baby Tandy Talks, vinyl/cloth, pull-string talker, 1963, OC, 14" .35.00
Flowerkin, mk F-2 on head, 1962, 15", MIB, 7 made, ea 60.00
MaMa, compo/cloth, crier, swing legs, pnt eyes, 1920s, OC, 16" 250.00
Miss Charming, compo, Shirley Temple look-alike, 1936, OC, 19" .450.00
Posi Playmate, vinyl, bendable limbs, rooted hair, o/c/e, 12", MIB ..20.00

Effanbee

Bernard Fleischaker and Hugo Baum became business partners in 1910, and after two difficult years of finding toys to buy, they decided to manufacture dolls and toys of their own. The Effanbee trademark is a blending of their names, Eff for Fleischaker and bee for Baum. The company still exists today. For more information we recommend *Effanbee Dolls* by Pat Smith, and *Collector's Encyclopedia of American Composition Dolls, 1900 – 1950*, by Ursula R. Mertz.

Anne Shirley, compo, 1936-40, OC, 14", EX 300.00
Baby Effanbee, compo/cloth, OC, 12-13", EX 165.00
Barbara Joan, compo, separated fingers, OC, 1936-39, 15", EX ..675.00
Charlie McCarthy, compo ShHd, pnt eyes, string-op, OC, 17" ..500.00
Coquette, Naughty Marietta, compo/cloth, OC, 1915+, 12" 400.00
Happy Birthday Doll, music box in body, w/bracelet, 17", MIB ..700.00
Honey Walker, hp, jtd knees/ankles, OC, 14" 400.00

Ice Queen, compo, o/m, skater outfit, 17" **850.00**
Lamkins, compo/cloth, crier, o/c/e, o/m, OC, 16" **475.00**
Marilee, compo, ShHd, bl tin sleep eyes, o/m/teeth, wig, RpC, 29" .**650.00**
Mary Ann, compo, o/c/e, wig, o/m, 1932+, OC, 19" **350.00**
Mary Jane, bsk, o/c/e, wooden limbs, OC, 20" **700.00**
Mary Lee, compo, o/c/e, o/m/teeth/felt tongue, RpC, 16" **265.00**
Mary Lee, compo, o/m, on Patsy Joan body, 16" **250.00**
Patsy Ann, jtd vinyl, rooted hair, o/c/e, freckles, OC, 15" **250.00**
Patsy Baby, compo, o/c/e, OC, 9" **325.00**
Patsy Lou, compo, o/c/e, c/m, pnt hair, 5-pc body, 22" **525.00**
Suzanne, jtd compo, o/c/e, wig, c/m, magnets in hands, OC, 14" ..**300.00**

Half Dolls

Half dolls were never meant to be objects of play. Most were modeled after the likenesses of lovely ladies, though children and animals were represented as well. Most of the ladies were firmly sewn on to pincushion bases that were beautifully decorated and served as the skirts of their gowns. Other skirts were actually covers for items on milady's dressing table. Some were used for parasol or brush handles or for tops to candy containers or perfume bottles. Most popular from 1900 to about 1930, they will most often be found marked with the country of their origin, especially Bavaria, Germany, France, and Japan. You may also find some fine quality pieces marked Goebel, Dressel and Kester, KPM, and Heubach.

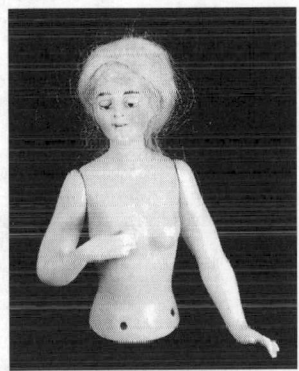

Germany, bisque with jointed shoulders, adult face, original mohair wig, jointed arms, marked KPM, 4½", $350.00.

Germany, arms & hands attached, common type, 3" **25.00**
Germany, arms & hands attached, common type, 5" **35.00**
Germany, arms & hands attached, common type, 8" **55.00**
Germany, arms & hands completely away, 3", from $85 to **145.00**
Germany, arms & hands completely away, 5", from $100 to **285.00**
Germany, arms & hands completely away, 8", from $165 to **650.00**
Germany, arms & hands completely away, 12", from $200 to **950.00**
Germany, arms extended, hands attached, 3" **50.00**
Germany, arms extended, hands attached, 5" **85.00**
Germany, arms extended, hands attached, 8" **125.00**
Japan mk, 3" **20.00**
Japan mk, 5" **30.00**
Japan mk, 8" **50.00**

Handwerck

Child, #69, #79, #89, or #99, o/m, RpC, 18" **725.00**
Child, #69, #79, or #89, o/m, RpC, 13" **475.00**
Child, #79 or #89, c/m, RpC, 15" **1,700.00**
Child, #109, #119, #139, or #199, o/m, RpC, 22" **750.00**

Child, #109, #199, #139, or #199, o/m, RpC, 15" **500.00**
Child, #189, o/m, RpC, 15", NM **800.00**
Child, no mold #, bsk Skhd, o/m, o/c/e, p/e, wig, RpC, 25" **700.00**

Hertel, Schwab and Company

#127, character child, dome w/molded hair, o/c/e, o/m, RpC, 15" ..**1,350.00**
#131, character, solid dome, pnt c/m, RpC, 18" **1,300.00**
#136, character face, o/m, Made in Germany, RpC, 24" **1,200.00**
#140, character, glass eyes, o/m laughing, RpC, 12" **3,400.00**
#141, character, pnt/e, o/c/m, RpC, 24" **7,500.00**
#142, bsk head, compo bent-leg baby, o/c/e, RpC, 9" **300.00**
#150, bsk head, toddler body, RpC, 14" **500.00**
#154, bsk head, c/m, RpC, 21" **2,700.00**
#154, character, solid dome, molded hair, glass eyes, o/m, RpC, 20" ..**1,900.00**
#167, K&H character, o/c or o/m, RpC, ca 1912, 15" **2,000.00**

Heubach

#6688, ShHd, character child, solid dome, intaglio eyes, RpC, 10" .**625.00**
#6969, SkHd, glass eyes, c/m, sq mk, RpC, 12" **1,850.00**
#7325, ShHd, character child, sunburst, c/m, nude, 17", VG ..**1,150.00**
#7602, long face pouty, pnt eyes & hair, c/m, RpC, 16" **2,200.00**
#7616, SkHd or ShHd, molded tongue, glass eyes, RpC, 13" ...**1,600.00**
#7644, pnt eyes, o/c laughing/m, sunburst or sq mk, RpC, 14" **865.00**
#7711, flapper, glass eyes, o/m, RpC, 13" **900.00**
#7850, Coquette, o/c/m, RpC, 11" **750.00**
#8316, boy, grinning, o/c/m w/8 teeth, o/c/e, RpC, 19" **4,800.00**
#8774, Whistling Jim, smoker/whistler, molded hair, RpC, 13" .**1,200.00**
#9355, glass eyes, o/m, sq mk, RpC, 13" **850.00**
#11010, Revalo, o/c/e, o/m, for Gebr Ohlaver, RpC, 19" **700.00**
Adult, o/m, glass eyes, RpC, 14" **4,500.00**
Adult, smile pnt eyes, RpC, 15" **3,500.00**
Heubach mk, no mold #, o/c/m, dimples, RpC, 18" **4,450.00**

Horsman

Angelove, plastic/vinyl, made for Hallmark, 1974, OC, MIB **25.00**
Baby Butterfly (Oriental), compo head & hands, pnt features, 12" ..**225.00**
Betty, vinyl 1-pc body & limbs, 1951, 14", MIB **60.00**
Betty Jo, compo, OC, 16" **225.00**
Cindy Kay, vinyl child w/long legs, 1950s+, 15", MIB **80.00**
Dolly Rosebud, compo head/limbs, dimples, o/c/e, 1926-30, OC, 18" ..**175.00**
Gold Metal, compo/cloth, upper & lower teeth, 1930s, OC, 21" ..**200.00**
Jeanie Horsman, compo/cloth, pnt hair, o/c/e, OC, 1937, 14" **225.00**
Peterkin, compo/cloth, pnt or o/c/e, c/m smiling, OC, 11" **300.00**

Ideal

Two of Ideal's most collectible lines of dolls are Chatty Cathy and Tammy. For more information, refer to *Chatty Cathy Dolls* by Kathy and Don Lewis, *Collector's Guide to Tammy, The Ideal Teen,* by Cindy Sabulis and Susan Weglewski, and *Collector's Guide to Ideal Dolls, Second Edition,* by Judith Izen.

April Showers, vinyl, battery-op, 1968, 14", M **28.00**
Baby Tenderlove, 1971, OC, 16", VG **25.00**
Belly Button Baby, vinyl, rooted hair, wht, 9½", M **18.00**
Black Flexy, pnt eyes, c/m, OC, 13½", NM **325.00**
Bud (Tammy), MIB, minimum value **300.00**
Captain Lazer, vinyl, light-up eyes, laser gun, 1967, 12", M **265.00**
Cinderella, compo, flirty eyes, o/m w/teeth, hh, 13", M, minimum ...**300.00**
Deanna Durbin, compo, felt tongue, o/c/e, OC, 15", NM, minimum .**500.00**
Kissy, vinyl toddler, o/c/e, wht, OC, 1961-64, 22½", M **75.00**

Mary Hartline, hard plastic, fully jointed, blond nylon wig, all original, 16", MIB, $700.00.

Photo courtesy McMasters Auctions

Misty (Tammy), MIB 100.00
Peter Playpal, vinyl, gold o/c/e, freckles, OC, 1960-64, 38", M ..850.00
Pinocchio, compo/wood, OC, 1939, 8", NM 300.00
Pos'n Misty & Her Telephone Booth, MIB 125.00
Pos'n Pete, MIB 125.00
Strawman, cloth, yarn hair, all orig, 1939, 17", NM 800.00
Tammy's Mom, MIB 65.00
Tickletoes, compo/cloth/rubber, squeaker, OC, 14", NM 150.00
Tiffany Taylor, vinyl, pnt eyes, teenager, 1974-75, 19", M 45.00
Tiffany Taylor, vinyl, rooted hair, high-heeled, 1974-76, 14", M .30.00

Jumeau

The Jumeau factory became the best known name for dolls during the 1880s and 1890s. Early dolls were works of art with closed mouths and paperweight eyes. When son Emile Jumeau took over, he patented sleep eyes with eyelids that drooped down over the eyes. This model also had flirty (eyes that move from side to side) eyes and is extremely rare. Over 98% of Jumeau dolls have paperweight eyes. The less-expensive German dolls were the downfall of the French doll manufacturers, and in 1899 the Jumeau company had to combine with several others in an effort to save the French doll industry from German competition.

Open mouth, jointed French body, clothes possibly original, marked 1907 Jumeau, 29", $2,300.00.

Photo courtesy McMasters Auctions

#200 character child, RpC, 15", minimum value 36,000.00
#230 character child, o/m, RpC, 16" 1,450.00
#1907, mk Jumeau, o/c or set/e, o/m, jtd Fr body, RpC, 14" 1,850.00
Adult, c/m, RpC, 20" 6,000.00
Adult, o/m, RpC, 14" 2,200.00
Depose Jumeau, poured bsk head w/compo & wood body, RpC, 14" .5,000.00
Depose/E 8 J, bsk SkHd, o/c/e, c/m, p/e, RpC, 19" 5,750.00
EJ Bebe, bsk SkHd, o/c/e, c/m, p/e, str wrists, RpC, 17" 9,000.00
Fashion type, # on swivel head, stamped kid body, RpC, 14" ..2,800.00
Fashion type, #d swivel head, wood body, bsk arms, RpC, 16" ...5,100.00
Long Face Triste Bebe, #d head, o/c/e, c/m, p/e (appl), RpC, 19" ...18,500.00
Phonograph type, bsk head, o/m, phonograph in torso, RpC, 20" ..7,800.00
Portrait, RpC, 15" 3,450.00
Portrait, RpC, 18" 5,650.00
Princess Elizabeth, bsk SkHd w/EX color, flirty eyes, RpC, 18" ..2,100.00
R Bebe, o/c/e, c/m, jtd compo, str wrists, wig, p/e, RpC, 22" 5,100.00
Tete Jumeau, c/m, RpC, 19" 4,600.00
Tete Jumeau, o/m, RpC, 21" 2,725.00

Kammer and Reinhardt

#100, character baby, dome head, jtd body, o/c/m, RpC, 11" 650.00
#101, Peter or Marie, pnt eyes, c/m, RpC, 7-8", ea 1,600.00
#112, pnt o/c/m, RpC, 14" 9,700.00
#114, Hans or Gretchen, pnt/e, c/m, RpC, 10", ea 2,900.00
#115, solid dome, pnt hair, o/c/e, c/m, RpC, 15" 5,000.00
#117A, glass eyes, c/m, RpC, 16" 4,100.00
#121, toddler, SkHd, o/c/e, o/m w/teeth, jtd compo, 16" 525.00
#122, o/c/e, bent-leg baby, RpC, 11" 700.00
#126, Mein Liebling baby, flirty eyes, bent-leg baby, RpC, 14" ..750.00
#135, baby body, o/c/e, o/m, RpC, 13" 850.00
#191, Dolly face, o/c/e, o/m, jtd child, RpC, 17" 865.00
#192, o/c/e, o/m, jtd child, RpC, 9" 1,000.00
K*R (no mold #), SkHd, glass eyes, o/m, RpC, 12" 550.00

Kestner

Johannes D. Kestner made buttons at a lathe in a Waltershausen factory in the early 1800s. When this line of work failed, he used the same lathe to turn doll bodies. Thus the Kestner company began. It was one of the few German manufacturers to make the complete doll. By 1860, with the purchase of a porcelain factory, Kestner made doll heads of china and bisque as well as wax, worked-in-leather, celluloid, and cardboard. In 1895 the Kestner trademark of a crown with streamers was registered in the U.S. and a year later in Germany. Kestner felt the mark was appropriate since he referred to himself as the 'king of German dollmakers.'

C, ShHd, brn o/c/e, o/m w/teeth, OC, 12" 400.00
K, ShHd, o/c/e, o/m w/teeth, wig, kid body, 24" 325.00
Unmk, solid dome SkHd, 5-pc compo baby body, 11" 300.00
6, ShHd w/trn head, o/c/e, c/m, bsk ½-arms, RpC, 16" 500.00
7, solid dome SkHd, pnt eyes, o/c/m, bent limbs, 10½" 250.00
154, ShHd, brn o/c/e, o/m w/teeth, mohair wig, DEP, 24½" 450.00
154, ShHd, o/c/e, o/m, bsk ½-arms, hh wig, OC, 10½" 175.00
154, SkHd/ShHd, kid w/bsk ½-arms, o/m w/teeth, DEP, 17" 725.00
167, SkHd, jtd compo, o/c/e, o/m w/teeth, H1/4 MIG/12 1/4, 24" .800.00
168, SkHd, o/m, MID/G7, 26" 1,000.00
208, Shhd, o/c/e, c/m, jtd bsk, 4½", MIB mk Dolly Dimples 160.00

Lenci

Characteristics of Lenci dolls include seamless, steam-molded felt heads, quality clothing, childishly plump bodies, and painted eyes that glance to the side. Fine mohair wigs were used, and the middle and fourth fingers were sewn together. Look for the factory stamp on the foot, though paper labels were also used. The Lenci factory continues today, producing dolls of the same high quality. Values are for dolls in near mint condition — no moth holes, very little fading.

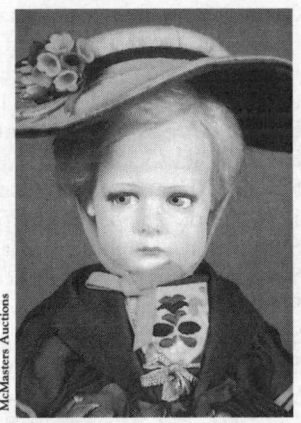

Girl, swivel head, closed mouth, original felt clothes with shawl, apron, hat, leather shoes, original tag, 17", EX, $1,200.00.

Photo courtesy McMasters Auctions

Aviator girl, w/felt helmet, 18"	3,200.00
Child, mini, 9"	400.00
Child, Oriental, 17"	3,600.00
Child, 1920s-30s, softer face, elaborate costume, 13"	1,750.00
Child, 1940s-50s, hard face, less intricate costume, 13"	400.00
Child, 1940s-50s, hard vace, less intricate costume, 17"	600.00
Flower girl, ca 1930, 20"	1,000.00
Glass eyes variation, 16"	1,600.00
Glass eyes variation (flirty), 20"	2,800.00
Lady, flapper or boudoir body, long slim limbs, 17"	1,050.00
Madame Butterfly, ca 1926, 17"	3,200.00
Mascotte, swing legs, may have loop on neck, 8½"	325.00
Pan, hooved ft, 10"	2,000.00
Smoker, pnt eyes, 28"	2,400.00

Liddle Kiddles

From 1966 to 1971, Mattel produced Liddle Kiddle dolls ranging in size from ¾" to 4". They were all poseable and had rooted hair that could be restyled. There were various series of the dolls, among them Animiddles, Zoolery Jewelry Kiddles, extraterrestrials, and Sweet Treats, as well as many accessories. To learn more about these dolls, we recommend *Liddle Kiddles, Identification and Value Guide*, by our advisor for this category, Paris Langford, who is listed in the Directory under Louisianna. Please send an SASE for information or contact Paris by e-mail: bbean415@aol.com.

Alice in Wonderliddle Playset, #5077, 1968, NRFB, with booklet and hang tag, $225.00.

Photo courtesy Paris Langford

Aqua Funny Bunny, #3532, loose, EX	20.00
Aqua Funny Bunny, #3532, MIP	100.00
Bunson Burnie, #3501, NRFB	275.00
Flower or Heart pin, M	45.00
Gardenia Kologne, #3710, complete, loose, EX	100.00
Gardenia Kologne, #3710, MIP	75.00
Hot Dog Stand, EX	55.00
Howard Biff Boodle, #3502, complete, loose, EX	100.00
Howard Biff Boodle, #3502, NRFB	300.00
Jewelry Treasure Box, M	60.00
Kiddles 'N Kars, MOC	150.00
Lady Lace, #A3840, NRFB	75.00
Liddle Kiddles' Klub House, EX	50.00
Liddle Kiddles Doll Box, complete, M	75.00
Liddle Lion Zoolery, #3661, complete, M	200.00
Lilac Locket, #3540, complete, loose, EX	35.00
Lilac Locket, #3540, MIP	75.00
Lucky Lion, #3635, complete, M	45.00
Luvvy Duvvy Kiddle, #3596, MIP	75.00
Olivia Orange Cola, M	60.00
Peter Paniddle, #3547, NRFB	350.00
Romeo & Juliet, #3782, complete, loose, EX	65.00
Romeo & Juliet, #3782, MIP	175.00
Santa Kiddle, #3595, MIP	65.00
Sheila Skediddle, w/pusher, M	35.00
Sheila Skediddle, w/pusher, MIB	100.00
Snap Happy Living Room, MIB	45.00
Suki'n Outfit, MIP	25.00
Sweet Treat Frosty Mint Kone, MOC	100.00
Teeter Time Baby, complete, M	65.00
Vanilly Lilly, #2819, MIP	25.00

Madame Alexander

Beatrice Alexander founded the Alexander Doll Company in 1923 by making an all-cloth, oil-painted face, Alice in Wonderland doll. With the help of her three sisters, the company prospered; and by the late 1950s there were over six hundred employees making Madame Alexander dolls. The company still produces these lovely dolls today. For more information, refer to *Collector's Encyclopedia of Madame Alexander Dolls* by Pat Smith and *Madame Alexander Collector's Doll Price Guide* by Linda Crosey.

Alice in Wonderland, hard plastic, synthetic wig, sleep eyes, closed mouth, 1949 – 52, 17", $425.00.

Photo courtesy McMasters Auctions

Alice in Wonderland, swivel waist, Wendy Ann, compo, '30s, 13"	425.00
Anatolia, str leg, #524, 1987 only, 8"	65.00

Aunt Agatha, hp, Wendy Ann, #434, 1957, 8", minimum value .1,100.00
Baby Lynn, cloth/vinyl, 1973-76, 20" 135.00
Ballerina, compo, Little Betty, 1935-41, 9" 400.00
Babbie, cloth, 1934-36, 16", minimum value 775.00
Baseball Girl, #16300, baseball outfit w/ball glove, 8" 58.00
Bessy Bell, plastic/vinyl, Classic Series, Wendy Ann, 1988, 14" ...75.00
Bobby, hp, Wendy Ann, #347, 1957 only, 8" 600.00
Bride, compo, Tiny Betty, 1935-39, 7" 275.00
Bride, hp, Dreams Come True, Cissy, 1955 only, 20", minimum 1,000.00
Bridesmaid, hp, Lissy, 1956-59, 12", minimum value 600.00
Carnival in Venice, porc, 1990-91, 21" 500.00
Cinderella, hp, Margaret, poor outfit, 1950-51, 14" 600.00
Clarabell Clown, 1951-53, 19" 350.00
Cookie, compo/cloth, 1938-40, 19", EX 650.00
Crete, str leg, wht face, #529, 1987 only, 8" 70.00
Danish, compo, Tiny Betty, 1937-41, 7" 325.00
Dilly Dally Sally, compo, Tiny Betty, 1937-42, 7" 300.00
Dolly Dryper, vinyl, 1952 only, 11", w/7-pc layette 325.00
Easter Doll, hp, Wendy Ann, for West Coast, 1968, 8", minimum .1,100.00
Elixe, hp/vinyl, jtd ankles & knees, 1963-64, 18" 300.00
Fairy Princess, compo, Little Betty, 1939-41, 9" 325.00
Flora McFlimsey, vinyl head, Cissy, 1953 only, 15" 600.00
Gainsboro, hp/vinyl, Jacqueline, bl & wht gown, #2184, 1968, 21" ..650.00
Ginger Rogers, compo, Wendy Ann, 1940-45, 14-21", minimum value .2,500.00
Goldilocks, compo, Tiny Betty, 1938-42, 7-8" 300.00
Graduation, hp, Lissy, 1957, 12" 800.00
Hansel, hp, str-leg walker, Wendy Ann, #470, 1955 only, 8" 550.00
Honeybea, vinyl, 1963 only, 12" 175.00
India, hp, bend-knee walker, Wendy Ann, #775, 1965, 8" 175.00
Jack & Jill, compo, Tiny Betty, 1938-43, 7", ea 275.00
Jane Withers, compo, closed mouth, 1937, 12-13½", minimum ...1,000.00
Juliet, compo, Portrait, Wendy Ann, 1945-46, 21", minimum value .2,500.00
Karen Ballerina, compo, Margaret, 1946-49, 15", minimum value ..850.00
Klondike Kate, hp, Portrette Cissette, 1963 only, 10", minimum .1,400.00
Little Bitsey, vinyl nurser, Sweet Tears, 1967-68, 9" 150.00
Little Shaver, cloth, 1940-44, 10", minimum value 450.00
Littlest Kitten, vinyl, lacy outfit w/bonnet, 1963, 8", minimum .300.00
Madeline, hp, jtd elbows & knees, 1950-53, 17-18", minimum value ..700.00
Maid of Honor, compo, Wendy Ann, 1940-44, 18", minimum value ..700.00
Margo, hp, Cissette, in formal, 1961 only, 10-11", minimum .450.00
Mary Ann, plastic/vinyl, red/wht dress, w/tag, 1965, 14" 275.00
Mary Mine, cloth/vinyl, 1977-89, 21" 125.00
Melanie, compo, Wendy Ann, 1945-47, 21", minimum value .2,300.00
Michael, plastic/vinyl, Janie, of Peter Pan set, 1969 only, 11" 375.00
Miss Victory, compo, magnets in hands, Princess Elizabeth, 20" ..750.00
Mrs Buck Rabbit, cloth/felt, mid-1930s 625.00
Netherlands Boy, hp, str leg, mk Alex, #577, 1974-75, 8" 75.00
Nurse, compo, Tiny Betty, 1937, 1941-43, 7" 275.00
Old Fashioned Girl, compo, Betty, 1945-47, 13", minimum value .550.00

Pamela, hp, 1962-63, 12", in case, minimum value 1,000.00
Persia, compo, Tiny Betty, 1936-38, 7" 300.00
Pitty Pat, cloth, 1950s, 16" 475.00
Princess Alexandria, cloth/compo, 1937 only, 24", minimum value .275.00
Princess Elizabeth, compo, o/m, 1937-41, 18-19" 700.00
Queen, hp, Margaret, wht gown, short cape, 1954 only, 18" 975.00
Queen Isabella, hp, Americana Series, #329, 1992 only, 8" 125.00
Red Riding Hood, compo, Tiny Betty, 1936-42, 7" 275.00
Renoir, hp, Margaret, 1950 only, 14", minimum value 875.00
Royal Evening, hp, Margaret, 1953 only, 18", minimum value ...125.00
Rusty, cloth/vinyl, 1967-68 only, 20" 300.00
Samson, Bible Series, #14582, 1995 only, 8" 100.00
Scarlett O'Hara, compo, Wendy Ann, 1945, 1947, 21" 1,600.00
School Girl, compo, Tiny Betty, 1936-43, 7" 275.00
Sir Winston Churchill, hp, Margaret, w/hat, 1953 only, 18" ...1,200.00
Sleeping Beauty, compo, Princess Elizabeth, 1938-40, 15-16" 475.00
Snow White, compo, pnt eyes, Princess Elizabeth, 1937-39, 13" .475.00
Soldier, compo, Wendy Ann, 1943-44, 14" 775.00
Sound of Music, Maria, Nancy Drew, sm set, 1971-73, 12" 300.00
Spanish Girl, hp, bend-knee walker, Wendy Ann, 1962-65, 8" ..150.00
Special Girl, cloth/compo, 1942-46, 23-24", minimum value 500.00
Sugar Darlin', cloth/vinyl, 1964 only, 14-18", from $75 to 125.00
Sulky Sue, Wendy Ann, mk Alexander, #445, 1988-90, 8" 75.00
Sweet Tears, vinyl, 1965-74, 9" 95.00
Timmy Toddler, plastic/vinyl, 1960-61, 23" 150.00
Tippy Toe, cloth, 1940s, 16" 600.00
Victoria, hp, Cissy, 1954 only, 20", minimum value 1,900.00
WAAC (Army), compo, Wendy Ann, 1943-44, 14", minimum value ..750.00
Wendy Bride, compo, Wendy Ann, 1944-46, 14-22", from $325 to .500.00
Yolanda, Brenda Starr, 1965 only, 12" 395.00

Mattel

Baby First Step, 1967, MIB, L6 ....150.00
Baby Secret, vinyl, red hair, pull-string talker, 1965, 18" 45.00
Baby Small Talk, MIB 75.00
Casper the Talking Ghost, 1961, MIB 100.00
Linus the Lionhearted, nonworking talker, 1965, 21", VG 90.00
Mork, w/talking space pack, 1979, 8", NRFB 35.00
Sister Belle, plastic/cloth, yarn hair, talker, OC, 17" 25.00
Sister Small Talk, 1968, plastic & vinyl, blond hair, EX 55.00
Talking Baby Tenderlove, working, OC 20.00
Timey Tell, MIB, L6 ....110.00

Papier-Mache

Cloth body, bright coloring, wig, 1920s & later, RpC, 8" 80.00
Cloth body, ShHd, blond wig, OC, 14" 250.00
Cloth body, wooden limbs, glass eyes, RpC, 1840s-60s, 24" 2,200.00
Cloth body, wooden limbs, long curls, RpC, 1840s-60s, 12" 650.00
Cloth body, wooden limbs, pnt eyes, RpC, 1840s-60s, 21" 1,150.00
Cloth body, wooden limbs, pnt eyes, RpC, 1840s-60s, 9" 450.00
Cloth body & limbs, bright color, Fr costume, 1920s, 9" 125.00
Clown, cloth body w/compo pnt features/molded hair, RpC, 8" .235.00
Coiled braids over ears, RpC, 20", minimum 2,200.00
German, pnt eyes, c/m, 1870s-90s, EX clothes, 18" 375.00
Kid body, pnt hair, glass eyes, bamboo teeth, Fr-type, RpC, 16" ..1,750.00
Kid body, wooden limbs, center part, sausage curls, RpC, 14" 575.00
Kid body, wooden limbs, molded bonnet, RpC, 15", minimum ...2,000.00
Kid body, wooden limbs, molded comb, braided coronet, RpC, 16" .3,300.00
Kid body, wooden limbs, top knot hair w/side curls, 10" 800.00
M&S Superior, kid or leather arms/boots, ShHd, RpC, 17" 425.00
M&S Superior, ShHd, glass eyes, kid arms/boots, RpC, 12" 600.00
M&S Superior, ShHd, molded hair, cloth body w/kid arms, RpC, 17" ..425.00

Princess Elizabeth, McGuffey Ana, composition head, sleep eyes, open mouth with teeth, human hair wig, 1930, outstanding condition, MIB, $2,100.00 at auction.

Photo courtesy McMasters Auctions

Parian

Alice in Wonderland (head band) style, RpC, 12"	400.00
Countess Dagmar, head band, cluster curls on forehead, RpC, 25"	800.00
Empress Eugenie, molded bodice, pnt eyes, unmk, RpC, 25"	750.00
Fancy hairdo w/ribbons/flowers/etc, glass eyes, p/e, RpC, 16"	1,700.00
Fancy hairstyle, swivel neck, glass eyes, RpC, 15"	2,625.00
Man w/parted pnt hair, glass eyes, cloth body, RpC, 16"	2,825.00
Man w/parted pnt hair, pnt eyes, RpC, 16"	950.00
Molded hat, pnt hair, glass eyes, RpC, 16"	2,825.00
Undecorated, plain style, RpC, 13"	175.00
Wigged, solid-dome head, molded ears, ca 1850s, RpC, 16"	850.00

Schoenhut

Albert Schoenhut left Germany in 1866 to go to Pennsylvania to work as a repairman for toy pianos. He eventually applied his skills to wooden toys and later designed an all-wood doll which he patented on January 17, 1911. These uniquely jointed dolls were painted with enamels and came with a metal stand. Some of the later dolls had stuffed bodies, voice boxes, and hollow heads. Due to the changing economy and fierce competition, the company closed in the mid-1930s.

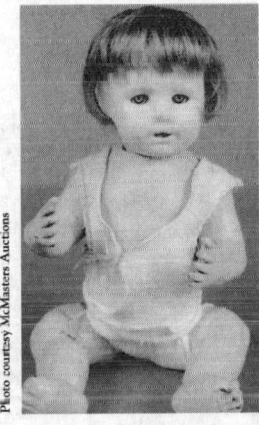

Photo courtesy McMasters Auctions

Wooden socket head with brown decaled sleep eyes, open mouth with two teeth, mohair wig, rare five-piece bent-limb wooden baby body, dressed in knit undies, Patent Jan. 17th 1911, general wear with some color fading, 13", $900.00.

Bent-leg body, wig or pnt hair, RpC, 14"	550.00
Character face, intaglio eyes, o/c/m, cvd hair, RpC, 19"	3,000.00
Character face, intaglio eyes, wig, 1911-23, RpC, 14"	1,700.00
Dolly face, o/c/m, mohair wig, spring-jtd, decal eyes, RpC	600.00
O/c/e, o/m, wig, RpC, 13"	600.00
Toddler, baby head, jtd body, pnt eyes, hair or wig, RpC, 14"	750.00
Tootsie Wootsie, o/c/m/tongue/2 teeth, pnt eyes, RpC, 15"	3,400.00
Walkable 1-pc legs, mechanism in body, RpC, 14"	700.00

SFBJ

By 1895 Germany was producing dolls at much lower prices than the French dollmakers could, so to save the doll industry, several leading French manufacturers united to form one large company. Bru, Raberry and Delphieu, Pintel and Godshaux, Fleischman and Bodel, Jumeau, and many others united to form the company Society Francaise de Fabrication de Bebes et Jouets (SFBJ).

20, molded pnt shoes & eyes, 5-pc body, Paris/12, 10"	365.00
60, French WWI nurse, 5-pc body, SFBJ/13/0, 8½"	475.00

60, o/m w/teeth, o/c/e, hh wig, RpC, 12"	450.00
60, SkHd, compo w/str legs, o/m, curved arms, 15"	650.00
227, closed dome, o/m, inset eyes, pnt hair, 15"	2,100.00
229, compo w/swivel head, o/c/m, inset eyes, 18"	5,000.00
230, compo walker, p/e, o/m, inset eyes, 16"	1,600.00
235, closed dome, molded hair, o/c/m & eyes, 16"	1,700.00
236, laughing Jumeau, o/m, o/c/e, dbl chin, 20"	2,200.00
238, compo w/swivel head, o/m, inset eyes, Paris/6, 15"	3,800.00
245, boy, o/c/m, lg glass googly eyes, pnt shoes, 8"	1,400.00
247, Twirp, SkHd, o/c/m & eyes, 2 teeth, 21"	3,000.00
252, pouty, c/m, inset eyes, papier-mache body, 11"	2,800.00
266, character, bsk head, closed dome, o/c/m, 20"	4,200.00
301, bsk SkHd on compo, o/m, inset eyes, 22"	1,200.00
301, bsk SkHd on compo, o/m, inset eyes, 28"	1,700.00

Shirley Temple

Prices are suggested for dolls complete and in mint condition. Add up to 25% (depending on her outfit) if mint with box. A played-with doll in only very good condition would be worth only about half of listed values.

Bsk, 6", pnt, molded hair, Japan	250.00
Celluloid, 5", Japan	185.00
Celluloid, 8", Japan	245.00
Compo, 11", cowgirl, G	950.00
Compo, 11", jtd body, gr o/c/e, o/m w/teeth, mohair wig, 1934-40	950.00
Compo, 13"	700.00
Compo, 17", Ideal, OC tagged dress, VG	550.00
Compo, 17-18", Ideal, from $875 to	950.00
Compo, 25", cowgirl	1,500.00
Plastic/vinyl, 12", 1982-83	40.00

Vinyl, 12", Ideal, hazel sleep eyes, open/closed mouth with six upper teeth, five-piece body, original clothes, 1950s, M, $225.00.

Photo courtesy McMasters Auctions

Vinyl, 16", 1973	125.00
Vinyl, 17", Montgomery Ward, 1972	165.00
Vinyl, 19", 1950s	400.00
Vinyl, 36", 1950s	1,600.00

Simon and Halbig

Simon and Halbig was one of the finest German makers to operate during the 1870s into the 1930s. Due to the high quality of the makers, their dolls still command large prices today. During the 1890s a few Simon & Halbig heads were used by a French maker, but these are extremely rare and well marked S&H.

CM Bergmann, SkHd, o/m w/teeth, Simon & Halbig, RpC, 32"	1,500.00
Handwerck, SkHd, o/m, 1895, G/S&H/1, 16"	450.00

409, SkHd, o/m, S&H, 24"	**685.00**
719, SkHd, bjtd, o/m, S12H/DEP, rpl wig, RpC, 20"	**3,300.00**
769, SkHd, c/m, S&H DEP, 17"	**2,600.00**
940, SkHd, swivel on ShPl, o/c/m, S 2 H, 14"	**1,500.00**
1039, SkHd, flirty bl eyes, jtd walker, p/e, wig, 22"	**1,100.00**
1498, SkHd, c/m, 5-pc baby body, period RpC, 13", EX	**1,100.00**

Steiner

Jules Nicholas Steiner established one of the earliest French manufacturing companies (making dishes and clocks) in 1855. He began with mechanical dolls with bisque heads and open mouths with two rows of bamboo teeth; his patents grew to include walking and talking dolls. In 1880 he registered a patent for a doll with sleep eyes. This doll could be put to sleep by turning a rod that operated a wire attached to its eyes.

Photo courtesy McMasters Auctions

Le Parisien, bisque socket head, cardboard pate, wig, paperweight eyes, closed mouth, jointed compo body, nicely dressed, 18½", $3,600.00.

#128, child, compo body, o/c/e, o/m, 9", M	**175.00**
#240, newborn, solid dome, c/m, o/c/e, RpC, 16"	**600.00**
#246, character, dome, glass eyes, o/c laughing/m, teeth, OC, 9"	**.700.00**
#401, ShHd, dome, pnt eyes, o/c laughing/m/teeth/tongue, RpC, 15"	**.475.00**
A or C Series, bsk SkHd w/cb pate, wig, pwt eyes, c/m, RpC, 14"	**.8,500.00**
A Series, child, cb pate, c/m, pwt eyes, jtd, RpC, 9"	**3,100.00**
A Series, Le Parisien, o/m, RpC, 23"	**2,500.00**
Bebe, unmk, bulgy pwt eyes, o/m/teeth, p/e, RpC, 1870s, 18"	**.5,500.00**
Bourgoin, c/m, 1870s, RpC, 17"	**5,200.00**
C Series, o/m w/teeth, pwt eyes, RpC, 23"	**6,200.00**
Le Parisien, bsk SkHd w/cb pate, jtd compo, o/m, p/e, RpC, 10"	**3,600.00**
Le Petit Parisien, bsk SkHd, glass eyes, c/m, p/e, RpC, 13"	**3,500.00**
Motschmann type, bsk head, twill body, glass eyes, c/m, RpC, 14"	**4,800.00**

Terri Lee

Jerri Lee, hp, caracul wig, 16"	**125.00**
Jerri Lee, in Spring Coat outfit	**300.00**
Jerri Lee, w/chaps & gun belt, all orig	**375.00**
Mary Jane, Terri Lee look-alike, hp walker, 16", MIB	**265.00**
Terri Lee, Brownie uniform, incomplete accessories	**385.00**
Terri Lee, compo, 1946-47, 16"	**80.00**
Terri Lee, early pk coat w/lt bl piping	**325.00**
Terri Lee, lt rose formal w/pk net skirt	**450.00**
Terri Lee, pedal-pusher outfit	**250.00**
Terri Lee, pk terry cloth bathrobe	**250.00**

Terri Lee, pnt hp, 1947-50, 16", MIB	**500.00**
Terri Lee, red school dress w/wht collar	**300.00**
Terri Lee, wht lace blouse & navy pleated skirt	**300.00**
Tiny Terri Lee, OC, 10", M in red/wht cb case	**185.00**

Vogue

This is the company that made the Ginny doll. Composition was used during the '40s, but vinyl was the preferred material throughout the decade of the '50s. An original mint-condition composition Ginny would be worth a minimum of $450.00 on the market today (played-with about $90.00). The last Ginny came out in 1969. Another Vogue doll that is becoming very collectible is Jill, whose values are steadily climbing. For more information, we recommend *Collector's Guide to Vogue Dolls* by Judith Izen and Carol Stover. Our advisor for Jill dolls is Bonnie Groves; she is listed in the Directory under Texas.

Binny Baby, 20", MIB	**55.00**
Ginny International, vinyl, 1977, OC, minimum value	**45.00**
Jan, vinyl, basic bra & girdle, VG	**54.00**
Jan/Jill desk & chair, gr, VG, from $50 to	**135.00**
Jan/Jill wardrobe, gr, VG, from $50 to	**135.00**
Jeff, nude, VG, from $25 to	**45.00**
Jeff, vinyl, bl suit 10", VG	**125.00**
Jeff, vinyl, in shorts outfit, 10", VG, from $65 to	**85.00**

Photo courtesy Bonnie Groves

Jill, blond ponytail, pink tulle formal, original accessories, replaced hair wreath, 1959, 10½", EX, $200.00.

Jill, hp, cotton street dress, all orig, 10½", EX, $85 to	**135.00**
Jill, hp, leotard, 1957, 10½", MIB	**250.00**
Jill, hp, nude, haircut, 10½", G-	**20.00**
Jill, hp, 1957-62, 10½", MIB	**190.00**
Jill, in peach flowered formal, all orig, EX, from $135 to	**200.00**
Jill, in ribbon hat outfit, complete, 1958, EX	**175.00**
Jill, in 1960 street dress, scarce, incomplete, EX, from $65 to	**80.00**
Jill, vinyl, History Land, all orig, EX, from $85 to	**200.00**
Jill bed, VG, from $50 to	**85.00**
Jill chromium head pendant, MIP, from $50 to	**150.00**
Jill coke bottle, accessory to jeans outfits, scarce, from $12 to	**20.00**
Jill cotton dress, EX, from $35 to	**50.00**
Jill Dream Cozy Bed Set (bedding), MIP, from $35 to	**50.00**
Jill dress, semiformal, MIP, from $50 to	**75.00**
Jill felt coat, EX, from $45 to	**65.00**

Jill jewelry, MIP, from $35 to 50.00
Jill shoes, MIP 25.00

Wax, Poured Wax

Bartenstein, 2-faced, laughing/crying, 1880s-90s, RpC, 15" 900.00
Man, trn ShHd, molded top hat, set eyes, wood arms, RpC, 17" 1,000.00
ShHD, inserted hair, glass eyes, wax limbs, cloth body, RpC, 13" ..1,100.00
Wax over compo or papier-mache, inserted hair, RpC, 14" 1,000.00
Wax over ShHd, o/m, glass eyes, RpC, 11", EX 200.00

Door Knockers

Door knockers, those charming precursors of the doorbell, come in an intriguing array of shapes and styles. The very rare ones come from England. Cast-iron examples made in this country were often produced in forms similar to the more familiar doorstop figures.

Our listings are prices realized at auction. Most were in exceptional condition. See Doorstops for suggestions on pricing examples in lesser conditions.

Butterfly, mc, EX details, Judd, 4½x4¼", EX 440.00
Butterfly w/floral bkplate, mc, Waverly Pat Appl For, 3½", NM .715.00
Butterfly w/floral bkplate, mc, Waverly...#70139, 1926, 3½", NM .415.00
Cardinal on twigs, mc, EX details, 5x3", M 315.00
Cat & fiddle, brass, M 195.00
Christmas wreath, gr w/red trim, 3½" dia, NMIB 250.00
Clipper ship on waves, mc, Judd, 7⅜x2⅞", NM 245.00
Drake's flagship, CI, EX....95.00
Flower basket, country style, mc w/pk trim, #15, 4x3", M 90.00
Flower basket, mc, cast in 2 pcs, NMIB 220.00
Flower basket, orange & bl w/gold, Made in France, 4" dia, M ...825.00
Flower basket, w/vine & flower as knocker, mc, 4x3", MIB 135.00
Flower basket w/bow, mc, EX details, Judd #616, 4x3", M 90.00
Flower basket w/bow, pastels, unmk, 4¾x3", EX 110.00
Flower basket w/rope of flowers as knocker, mc, 7x4½", EX 660.00
Flowers in vase, mc, cast-on bkplate, Hubley, 3¾x2¼", EX 300.00
Ivy basket, mc, w/ivy bkplate, Hubley #123 Made in USA 300.00
Lady's hand, NP 60.00

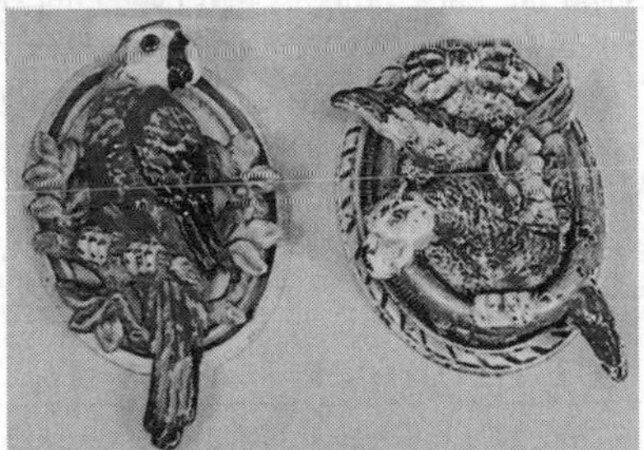

Parrot on branch, multicolor paint on cast iron, Hubley, 4¾x2¼", M, $110.00; Parrot with wings spread (rarely found) perched on ring, multicolor paint on cast iron, unmarked, 4x3", EX, $185.00.

Parrot bkplate w/separate flowered knocker, 3¾x2½", MIB 100.00
Parrot on twigs, mc, EX details, 4½x3", M 125.00
Sir Frances Drake, NM 140.00
Urn of flowers w/bow on rectangular base, mc, Hubley, 4x2", M .200.00
Woman w/bonnet profile, Judd #613, over-pnt bkplate, 4x3", EX .330.00
Woodpecker & tree, brass, M 185.00

Doorstops

Although introduced in England in the mid-1800s, cast-iron doorstops were not made to any great extent in this country until after the Civil War. Once called 'door porters,' their function was to keep doors open to provide better ventilation. They have been produced in many shapes and sizes, both dimensional and flat-backed, and in the past few years have become a popular, yet affordable collectible. While cast-iron examples are the most common, brass, wood, and chalk were also used. An average price is in the $100.00 to $200.00 range, though some are valued at more than $400.00. Doorstops retained their usefulness and appeal well into the '30s.

The prices below reflect market values in the East where doorstops are at a premium. For other areas of the country, it may be necessary to adjust prices down about 25%. When no condition code is present, items are assumed to be in exceptional original condition, flat-backed unless noted full-figured, and cast iron unless another material is mentioned. To evaluate a doorstop in only very good to excellent paint, deduct at least 35%. Values for examples in poor to good paint drop dramatically. For further information we recommend *Doorstops, Identification and Values*, by Jeanne Bertoia.

Key:
ff — full figured

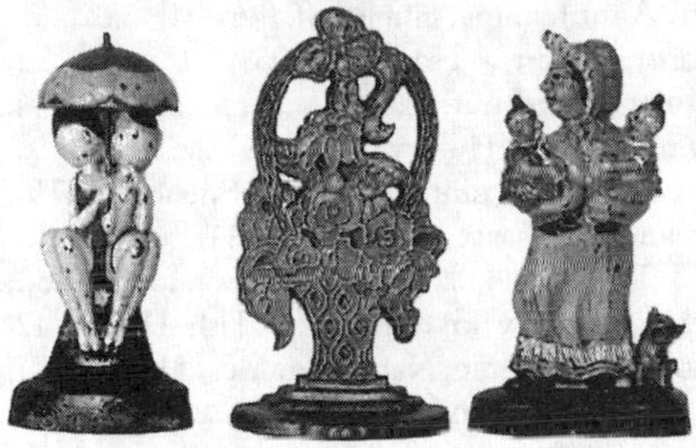

Bathing beauties, multicolor paint, c Fish 250, EX, $880.00; Flower Basket, multicolor paint, marked Lacs 745 W, EX+, $575.00; Mrs. Sloper, multicolor paint, EX, $770.00.

Basket of Kittens (3), M Rosenstein, 1932, 10x7" 425.00
Bellhop, bl uniform, #1244, 8⅞x4⅝" 300.00
Bellhop, carries bag, 7½x5⅛" 425.00
Bobby Blake, holds teddy bear, Hubley #46, 9½x5¼" 475.00
Boston Terrier, blk & wht, sitting, ff, 9½x7" 350.00
Cape Cod Cottage, Hubley #444, 5½x7¾" 175.00
Cat, grooming itself, Sculptured Metal Studios, 10¼x7½" 475.00
Cat by Flower, bl cat, yel flower, 5x6¼" 150.00
Chameleon, Sherwin Williams Paint Co, 1¼x8" 150.00
Cherubs, fighting for grapes, 10x6⅜" 450.00
Colonial Dame, pk & bl dress, bl shawl, Hubley #37, 8x4½" 250.00
Colonial Woman, pk dress, blk purse, Littco, 10¼x5¾" 175.00
Cottage w/Fence, Nat'l Foundry #32, 5¾x8" 150.00
Covered Wagon, 2 horses, Hubley #375, 9½x5⅛" 200.00
Cricket, narrower antennas than bootjack, 2x9" 85.00
Doberman Pinscher, ff, Hubley, 8x8½" 400.00
Donald Duck, holds stop sign, Disney, 1971, 8⅜x5¼" 250.00
Duck, wedge, yel on bl base, Hubley, 5x3¾" 275.00
Dutch Girl, w/shoulder yoke, Littco, #33, label, 13x10" 450.00
English Bulldog, ff, head turned to right, Hubley, 5⅞x8½" 175.00
Fawn, gr on dk gr base, Taylor Cook #6, 1930, 10x6" 300.00
Frog on Mushroom, ff, solid, gr on yel mushroom, 4½x3⅝" 200.00
George Washington, bl jacket, ff, 15x6½" 525.00
Giraffe, wedge, mk S-110, 13½x5¼" 275.00
Gnome, gr pants, red shirt & hat, ff, 14½x6¼" 500.00
Halloween Girl, wht costume w/orange pumkin, 13¾x9¾" 750.00

Horse, blk w/brn saddle, Nat'l Foundry #12, 8x10" 175.00
Little Dutch Woman, bl & wht dress, ff, solid, 4x2⅜" 125.00
Maiden, bl dress, carries flower basket, 8⅞x3¾" 400.00
Modernistic Cat, ff, blk, Hubley, 9¾x5" 425.00
Monkey on Barrel, Taylor Cook #3, 1930, 8⅜x4⅞" 425.00
Owl, on stump, Hubley #254, 10x4½" 250.00
Pansy Bowl, Hubley #256, 7x6½" 150.00
Parrot, big bl head, Taylor Cook #4, 1930, 10½x4⅞" 435.00
Peacock, male w/tail spread, 6¼x6¼" 200.00
Peasant Girl, fruit basket on head, Hubley #5, 8¾x5" 225.00
Pekingese, ff, gold-tone, faces left, Hubley, 14½x9" 650.00
Peter Rabbit, stands eating carrot, Hubley #96, 9½x4¾" 425.00
Police Boy, in diaper, w/dog, whistling, 10⅝x7¼" 450.00
Poppy Basket, CH Co #E110, 10½x9½" 325.00
Rooster, wht w/red crown, Spencer, 13¼x11" 575.00
Rose Basket, Hubley #121, 11x8" 200.00
Sailor, hands on hips w/rope, keg between legs, 11⅜x5" 475.00
Scottish Highlander, stands w/spear, 15½x13" 300.00
Setter, ff, pointing, Hubley, 8¾x15⅞" 250.00
Skier, bl & wht outfit holding 2 skis, ff, 12½x5" 475.00
Sleeping Cat, ff, blk, Nat'l Foundry, 3⅜x9⅝" 300.00
Small Mammy, Aunt Jemima, Hubley, ff, 8½x4½" 250.00
Spanish Guitarist, gr shirt, yel sash, ff, 11x3⅜" 800.00
Squirrel, on stump, eating nut, 9x6⅜" 200.00
St Bernard, lying down, ff, Hubley, 3½x10½" 375.00
Terrier, wedge, blk & wht, running on base, Spencer, 4x7" 225.00
Tropical Woman, fruit basket on head, 12x6¼" 275.00
Turkey, mc, 13x11" 700.00
Twin Doormen in Livery, worn orig pnt, mk Fish, Hubley, 12" .1,760.00
White Cockatoo, on bl stump, Nat'l Foundries, 11¾x5¼" 175.00
Windmill, AA Richardson, 8x5⅝" 175.00
Witch, on broom w/bat overhead, 7x7" 325.00
Yawning Child, nude on knees, ff, 9x5" 300.00

Dorchester Pottery

Taking its name from the town in Massachusetts where it was organized in 1895, the Dorchester Pottery Company made primarily utilitarian wares, though other types of items were made as well. By 1940 a line of decorative pottery was introduced, some of which was painted by hand with scrollwork or themes from nature. The buildings were destroyed by fire in the late 1970s, and the pottery was never rebuilt. In the listings that follow, the decorations described are all in cobalt unless otherwise noted. Our advisor for this category is Dale MacLean; he is listed in the Directory under Massachusetts.

Key: CAH — Charles A. Hill (noted artist)

Bowl, Clematis flower, N Ricci, stamped mark, 3⅛x8½", $400.00.

Bottle, scent; Full Scroll, spherical mk, 5½x4½" 250.00
Bottle, scent; Whale, deep bl, scroll stopper, CAH, 5", VG 250.00
Bowl, cereal; Apple, CAH, 5¾" 100.00
Bowl, cereal; Pine Cone, CAH, 5¾" 75.00
Bowl, cereal; Whale, CAH, w/bl swirl underplate, EX 125.00
Bowl, Colonial Lace, sgn CAH, stamped, 2x5¾" 100.00
Bowl & underplate, Whale, sgn CAH, 2¼x5½", 7½" 150.00
Candlestick, Half Scroll, deep bl, CAH, 5½" dia 175.00
Candy dish, Clown, striped perimeter, CAH, 4" dia 100.00
Casserole, Whale, sgn CAH/N Ricci, stamped, 4¾x8" 300.00
Chamberstick, Pine Cone, sgn CAH, stamped, 1¼x5¾" 150.00
Coffee set, Blueberry, sgn CAH, pot+mug+sugar bowl 250.00
Cookie jar, Poppy, layered bl, CAH, 7½x7¼" 400.00
Creamer & sugar bowl, Blueberry, CAH, 3", 3¼" 150.00
Creamer & sugar bowl, Whale, late CAH, 3", 3½" 200.00
Cup, coffee; Pine Cone 50.00
Cup & saucer, demitasse; Blueberry, CAH, EX 50.00
Cup & saucer, Whale, deep bl, swirl saucer, CAH, 2¾", 6¼" 60.00
Cup & saucer, Yel-Ware Scroll, CAH, 2¾", 6⅛" 200.00
Decanter, Pine Cone, sperical cap w/bl florals, mk, 9x7" 250.00
Dish, Eagle & Star, med to lt bl, Nixon Inauguration mk, hdls ..300.00
Jar, Darts & Loops, deep bl, Joseph McCune, 3¾x4" 250.00
Jar, Pine Cone, realistic, RT, 4½x4" 225.00
Mug, Captain, blended bl, Knesseth Denisons, 4¾", EX 125.00
Mug, Clown, Happy Day, sgn CAH, 2¾" 125.00
Mug, Clown & Stripe, sgn CAH, stamped, 4½" 175.00
Mug, Colonial Lace, Blended Blue, Joseph McCune, 4¾" 100.00
Mug, Eight Bells, Knesseth Denisons, deep bl, 4¾", EX 125.00
Mug, Full Scroll, deep bl, CAH, 4½" 100.00
Mug, Sacred Cod, deep bl, CAH, 4½" 75.00
Nut dish, Striped & Scroll, CAH, 3¾", EX 100.00
Pitcher Pussy Willow, sgn CAH/N Ricci, stamped, 5½x4¼" 300.00
Plate, Daffodil, speckled bl petals, CAH, 7¼" 225.00
Plate, Whale, blended bl waves, CAH, 10¼" 275.00
Shot pourer, Rooster, blended bl, Knesseth Denisons, 2½" 125.00
Soap holder, Colonial Lace, Joseph McCune, 5½" dia 200.00
Star dish, Pine Cone, bsk glaze, CAH, 8", EX 125.00
Star dish, Star, deep bl, 5-pointed, unmk, 7¾" dia 150.00
Sugar bowl, Lighthouse, blended bl, Knesseth Denisons, 3½" 150.00
Sugar bowl, Pomegranate, blended bl, Knesseth Denisons, 3⅛" .150.00
Sugar bowl, Sacred Cod, med & deep bl, med lustre, CAH, 3x4" .100.00
Sugar jar, Lace, bulbous, sgn JM, stamped, 3¼x3" 150.00
Syrup, Grape, sgn CAH, stamped, 5½x5" 140.00
Toby jug, Quaker Oats replica, early orig label, 8x7½" 250.00
Vase, Blended Blue, speckled, high lustre, label, 4¼", EX 100.00
Vase, Pine Cone, trumpet shape, CAH, 3½x3" 100.00
Vase, 2-tone bl, 4-sided, crimped mouth, bulbous, mk, 4½x5" ...100.00

Dorflinger

Christian Dorflinger was born in Alsace, France, and came to this country when he was ten years old. When still very young, he obtained a job in a glass factory in New Jersey. As a young man, he started his own glassworks in Brooklyn, New York, opening new factories as profits permitted. During that time he made cut glass articles for many famous people including President and Mrs. Lincoln, for whom he produced a complete service of tableware with the United States Coat of Arms. In 1863 he sold the New York factories because of ill health and moved to his farm near White Mills, Pennsylvania. His health returned, and he started a plant near his home. It was there that he did much of his best work, making use of only the very finest materials. Christian died in 1915, and the plant was closed in 1921 by consent of the family.

Dorflinger glass is rare and often hard to identify. Very few pieces were marked. Many only carried a small paper label which was quickly discarded; these are seldom found today. Identification is more accurately made through a study of the patterns, as colors may vary. Our advisor for this category is Ruth Jordan; she is listed in the Directory under New York.

Champagne, Kalani Lily, 5½" **98.00**
Cocktail set, 6" beaker w/pnt rooster, +6 martinis w/hens **290.00**
Creamer & sugar bowl, cut daisy pattern, 4¼", 3" **112.50**
Grapefruit bowl, Kalana Lily **100.00**
Grapefruit compote, Kalana Poppy, 4¾" **75.00**
Parfait, Renaissance, faceted teardrop stem, 6 for **195.00**
Pitcher, Kalana Lily, 7", from $300 to **400.00**
Sherbet, Kalana Lily, 4" **80.00**
Vase, cut hobstars/fans, trumpet form, mini, 6" **195.00**
Vase, gold etch decor, cylindrical, sgn Honesdale, 10¾" **400.00**
Vase, sweet pea; Kalana Pansy, 3¼x6" **110.00**

Dragon Ware

Dragon ware is fairly accessible and is still being made today. The new Dragon ware is distinguishable by the lack of detail in the dragon. In the older pieces, much care is given to the slipwork dragon's eyes, scales, and wings. In the new ware, the dragon is flat and lacks detail.

Colors are primary, referring to background color, not the color of the dragon. The primary color of a new piece has more shine than that of the older ware. Old colors are vibrant but for the most part not shiny (except for the lustre colors). New colors include green, lavender, yellow, pink, blue, pearlized, and orange as well as the classic blue/black. Old colors include orange, green, yellow, blue, pearlized, and blue/black. In addition to lustre finishes, you will find some background colors that are applied unevenly (and without shine), producing a cloud effect behind the dragon.

Many Dragon ware cups have lithophanes in the bottoms, often the face of a geisha girl. Nude lithophanes are scarcer but can sometimes be found in cups and saki cups. New pieces may also have lithophanes, but they are lacking in detail and tend to be flat.

Items listed below are unmarked unless noted otherwise. Ranges are given for pieces that are currently being produced. (Be sure to examine unmarked items well; in particular, look for good detailing in the dragon. New pieces should not command the prices of the older ware, so use the low end of the range to evaluate any pieces you feel may be new.) Our advisor for this category is Suzi Hibbard; she is listed in the Directory under California.

Key:
MIJ — Made in Japan   MIOJ — Made in Occupied Japan

Cup and saucer, $20.00.

Aladdin lamp, orange, 3-leg, 6" **35.00**
Aladdin lamp, violet lustre, 6¾" **20.00**
Ashtray, gr, 3⅜" x 2⅛" **10.00**
Bowl, nappy; brn, beaded edge, 12-sided, MIJ **30.00**

Candy dish, gray, on ped, no mk, 5" **45.00**
Child's cup & saucer, orange, no mk **20.00**
Child's tea set, Little Hostess, lustre, MIJ, 21-pc, +case **175.00**
Chocolate pot, gray, MIJ, 7" **30.00**
Cigarette box, gray, MIJ, 5x3½" **20.00**
Compote w/candlesticks, MIJ **150.00**
Condiment set, gray, no mk, tray w/8pcs including lids **150.00**
Creamer & sugar bowl, orange, MIJ **15.00**
Cup, saucer & pie plate, gray, lithophane, no mk **15.00**
Cup & saucer, demitasse; gray, no mk **12.50**
Cup & saucer, nude lithophane, no mk **75.00**
Dish, gray, 4-compartment, wicker hdl, Nippon **75.00**
Dresser box, ftd, MIJ, 4½ x 5¼" **50.00**
Ewer, gray, MIJ, 4" **30.00**
Ice bucket, earthenware w/wicker hdl, MIJ, 8" **250.00**
Ice bucket, gray earthenware, dog head on lid, hdls, MIJ, 8" **200.00**
Juice set, elephant decanter & 4 cups, bl & wht **250.00**
Lamp, Aladdin; gr lustre, souvenir of Washington, DC, 6¾" **12.50**
Lamp, Aladdin; peach lustre, souvenir of Rock City, 6¾" **12.50**
Lamp gray, 13¾", w/cloth cord **60.00**
Lamp hurricane; cobalt, 3½" **25.00**
Lamp oil; orange; 3-leg, Chinatown, San Francisco, 7½" **12.50**
Lighter, gray, 7¼" **25.00**
Plate, brn, Nippon like (no mks), 7½" **15.00**
Sake cups, bl, lithophanes, set of 6 ....**75.00**
Sake set, dispenser w/kitten in center, bl cloud, w/6 cups **100.00**
Sake set, gray, no mk, dispenser w/6 cups w/lithophanes **60.00**
Sake set, gray, whistling, w/6 whistling cups **60.00**
Shakers, coffee/tea style, blk, pr **15.00**
Shakers, gray, M in wreath mk, on tray **30.00**
Shakers, gray, souvenir w/Niagara Falls, 3", pr **12.50**
Sherbet set, cloverleaf plate w/sherbet cup, brn/yel, MIJ **60.00**
Shoe, gray, no mk, 3¾" L **30.00**
Tea set, bl cloud, dragon spouts, lithophanes, Kutani, 24-pc **375.00**
Tea set, blk & orange lustre, no mk, 24-pc **275.00**
Tea set, gr, dragon spouts, MIJ, 24-pc **250.00**
Tea set, gr, no mk, 17-pc **125.00**
Tea set, gray, dragon spouts, MIJ, 24-pc **225.00**
Tea set, gray, MIJ, 15-pc **175.00**
Vase, additional slip in yel, MIJ, 4¾" **17.50**
Vase, amethyst glass, 6" **25.00**
Vase, brn, MIJ, 4" **10.00**
Vase, bud; bl lustre, MIOJ, 7" **10.00**
Vase, bud; pk, souvenir, Florida, MIJ, 5" **7.50**
Vase, gray, hdls, Nippon, 6" **260.00**
Vase, orange, floating dragon head, no mk, 5" **20.00**
Vase, red, hdls, GNCO, 6¼" **15.00**
Vinegar & oil bottles, brn, mk O&V, on tray (missing mustard) ...**45.00**
Vinegar bottle, gray, no mk **22.50**
Wall pocket, bl & yel lustre, MIJ, 8½" **30.00**

Dresden

The term Dresden is used today to indicate the porcelains that were produced in Meissen and Dresden, Germany, from the very early 18th century well into the next. John Bottger, a young alchemist, discovered the formula for the first true porcelain in 1708 while being held a virtual prisoner at the palace in Dresden because of the King's determination to produce a superior ware. Two years later a factory was erected in nearby Meissen with Bottger as director. There fine tableware, elaborate centerpieces, and exquisite figurines with applied details were produced. In 1731, to distinguish their product from the wares of such potters as Sevres, Worcester, Chelsea, and Derby, the Meissen company adopted their famous crossed swords trademark. During the next century, several potteries were producing porcelain in the 'Meissen style' in Dresden itself. Their wares were often marked with imitations of Meissen's crossed swords.

The Carl Theime factory produced dinnerware as well as decorative pieces in the Meissen style from 1872 until 1972. Openwork pieces were their specialty. Their mark was an intertwined 'SP' with the word Dresden below. Other companies followed suit, and in 1883 began using the crown mark along with the Dresden indication. There were several variations of this mark employed over the years. Many of these companies produced Meissen-type wares well into the 20th century. See also Meissen.

Photo courtesy William Brinkley

The Presentation, four finely dressed figures in colorful costumes with much lace trim, $1,100.00.

Bowl, floral encrusted, held up by 4 cherubs, 7½x10½" L 250.00
Card holders, flower shape, set of 4 ....155.00
Compote, floral relief, mc on wht, rtcl rim, 9x6½", NM 265.00
Compote, 18th C couple in garden, flowers & gold, rtcl rim, 4x7⅜" 130.00
Compote, 18th C couple on base support rtcl bowl, 3-pc, 23x15x12" ..750.00
Figurine, ballerina, in pk/wht dress w/appl flowers, 7" 225.00
Figurine, lady w/flower basket, 1890s, 9" 175.00
Figurine, peasant & sleeping lover, lamb/kid/children/bee, 10" ..700.00
Plate, courting scene, 3 more w/gold scrolls in border, 9½" 200.00

Dresser Accessories

Dresser sets, ring trees, figural or satin pincushions, manicure sets — all those lovely items that graced milady's dressing table — were at the same time decorative as well as functional. Today they appeal to collectors for many reasons. The Victorian era is well represented by repousse silver-backed mirrors and brushes and pincushions that were used to display ornamental pins for the hair, hats, and scarves. The hair receiver — similar to a powder jar but with an opening in the lid — was used to hold long strands of hair retrieved from the comb or brush. These were wound around the finger and tucked in the opening to be used later for hair jewelry and pictures, many of which survive to the present day. (See Hair Weaving.)

Celluloid dresser sets were popular during the late 1800s and early 1900s. Some included manicure tools, pill boxes, and buttonhooks, as well as the basic items. Because celluloid tends to break rather easily, a whole set may be hard to find today. (See also Plastics.) With the current interest in anything Art Deco, sets from the '30s and '40s are especially collectible. These may be made of crystal, Bakelite, or silver, and the original boxes just as lavishly appointed as their contents.

Curling iron heater, traveling, lid w/holder, La Favorite, 3" 65.00
Nail file, Nouveau style, sterling, Holmes & Edwards 50.00
Set, German crystal & silver, 6-pc 300.00

Set, Nouveau silver (Alvin), 8-pc 550.00
Set, Queen Anne, jade blk, New Martinsville, complete 275.00
Set, silver w/gr enamel vignettes, Austria, 1920s, 7-pc 1,875.00
Tray, perfume; gold w/mirrored top, 4 dolphin ft, 14½x12½" 90.00

Dryden

Dryden Pottery was founded fifty years ago in Ellsworth, Kansas, by Jim Dryden, a WWII veteran with financing from a G.I. loan. A mention on the front page of the *Wall Street Journal* resulted in substantial orders from Macy's of New York and Fred Harvey Restaurants and gift shops in all the stations of the Santa Fe Railroad.

In the late 1940s and early 1950s, some six hundred stores stocked Dryden pottery. Stiff competition from occupied Japan and Europe forced wholesale prices so low that the only profit from the pottery was from direct sales to the traveling public. Tourists watched potters at work. These sales were profitable, but in 1955 the new transcontinental highway 70 through Kansas missed Ellsworth. The pottery had to move. Hot Springs, Arkansas, with its hundreds of thousands of tourists was chosen as the new location.

Since 1970 more and more of the production is wheel thrown and hand sculpted in an all-out attempt to follow the example of the world-famous Rookwood Pottery (1880 – 1967). Beautiful matt and gloss glazes plus one-of-a-kind originals make Dryden Pottery highly collectible.

Kansas pieces have a golden tan clay base. Most are signed and numbered like those made in Arkansas. Rare and specialty pieces have sold for over $200.00. Arkansas pieces have a white clay base. Expect to find molded pieces dating from the 1940s through the 1970s. Pieces from the '70s to the present are primarily wheel thrown, hand-sculpted originals with beautiful matt and gloss glazes. These pieces are often dated. Our advisor for this category is Ralph Winslow; he is listed in the Directory under Missouri.

Kansas Dryden (1946 – 1956)

Ashtray, #17A, Boot Hill, brn 38.00
Berry set, #C2, yel, 7-pc 125.00
Bookends, Scotty dog, 2-color, 4", pr 60.00
Coffee cup, #899B, brn, squat 10.00
Creamer & sugar bowl, #900, gr 35.00
Figurine, buffalo, gray, rare 200.00
Figurine, elephant, #10, brn, 11" 85.00
Figurine, elephant, #313, Salina KS, 3" 50.00
Figurine, lion, yel, rare 75.00
Figurine, panther, brn, 18" 100.00
Flower frog, pelican, #720, gr 45.00
Lamp, Genie; bl, 2¾" 35.00
Pitcher, #180, Camdenton MO, maroon 25.00
Pitcher, #950, Valley Forge, gr 35.00
Pitcher, #99, Fargo ND, 4½" 30.00
Pitcher, blk w/drip glaze, KFMC 1946 ....38.00
Planter, #X, 10" 35.00
Planter, cow, blk, 5¾" 50.00
Planter, elephant, #313, Salina KS, 3" 50.00
Planter, pony, #5, blk 75.00
Shakers, #70, Rio Grand Valley, brn, pr 35.00
Spoon holder, Salina KS, yel 35.00
Spoon holder, 3-leg, maroon 25.00
Syrup, #94, Claremore OK, yel 30.00
Tankard, #49, w/#4 tumblers, yel 120.00
Vase, #Y, rooster, pk 45.00
Vase, #104, Ellsworth KS, blk, 3" 45.00
Vase, #190, aqua, 6½" 35.00

Vase, #7R, pk 30.00
Vase, #7X, deer, 8½" 50.00
Vase, #800, yel, 10" 75.00
Vase, #955, leaf, aqua, 5" 40.00
Vase, Bull Shoals, sq, maroon, 6" 80.00
Wall pocket, #956, gr 25.00

Arkansas Dryden (1956 to Present)

Bowl, muted gr, 9" 20.00
Candle holder, #L01-74, brn, 4½" 15.00
Jardiniere, wheel thrown, aqua, 10" 50.00
Mug, wheel thrown, L01-77, face, 3¾" 25.00
Mug, wheel thrown, snake hdl, 3¾" 35.00
Nude, lady, brn 45.00
Pitcher, open hdl, gr, 9" 45.00
Tankard, aqua, 11" 32.00
Teapot, muted colors, 5½" 35.00
Tumbler, aqua, 6" 12.00

Vase, white with brown decor,
turquoise interior, 7", $35.00.

Vase, aqua, 9" 35.00
Vase, wheel thrown, brn, 7" 35.00
Vase, wheel thrown, bulbous, sculpted, 6" 50.00
Vase, wheel thrown, gr, 3" 15.00
Vase, wheel thrown, pinched top, brn, 15" 90.00
Vase, wheel thrown, sculpted, pk, 6" 45.00

Duncan and Miller

The firm that became known as the Duncan and Miller Glass Company in 1900 was organized in 1874 in Pittsburgh, Pennsylvania, a partnership between George Duncan, his sons Harry and James, and his son-in-law Augustus Heisey. John Ernest Miller was hired as their designer. He is credited with creating the most famous of all Duncan's glassware lines, Three Face. (See Pattern Glass.) The George Duncan and Sons Glass Company, as it was titled, was only one of eighteen companies that merged in 1891 with U.S. Glass. Soon after the Pittsburgh factory burned in 1892, the association was dissolved, and Heisey left the firm to set up his own factory in Newark, Ohio. Duncan built his new plant in Washington, Pennsylvania, where he continued to make pressed glassware in such notable patterns as Bagware, Amberette, Duncan Flute, Button Arches, and Zippered Slash. The firm was eventually sold to U.S. Glass in Tiffin, Ohio, and unofficially closed in August 1955.

In addition to the early pressed dinnerware patterns, today's Duncan and Miller collectors enjoy searching for opalescent vases in many patterns and colors, frosted 'Satin Tone' glassware, acid-etched designs, and lovely stemware such as the Rock Crystal cuttings. Milk glass was made in limited quantity and is considered a good investment. Ruby glass, Ebony (a lovely opaque black glass popular during the '20s and '30s), and, of course, the glass animal and bird figurines are all highly valued examples of the art of Duncan and Miller.

Expect to pay at least 25% more than values listed for other colors, for ruby and cobalt, as much as 50% more in the Georgian, Pall Mall, and Sandwich lines. Pink, green, and amber Sandwich is worth approximately 30% more than the same items in crystal. Milk glass examples of American Way are valued up to 30% higher than color, 50% higher in Pall Mall. Chartreuse Canterbury is worth 10% to 20% more than crystal. Add approximately 40% to 50% to listed prices for opalescent items. Etchings, cuttings, and other decorations will increase values by about 50%. For further study we recommend *The Encyclopedia of Duncan Glass*, by Gail Krause; she is listed in the Directory under Pennsylvania. Several Duncan and Miller lines are shown in *Elegant Glassware of the Depression Era* by Gene Florence. Also refer to *Glass Animals and Figural Flower Frogs of the Depression Era* by Lee Garmon and Dick Spencer; they are both listed under Illinois. See also Glass Animals. Our advisor is Roselle Schleifman; she is listed in the Directory under New York.

Byzantine, crystal, cocktail 12.00
Byzantine, crystal, plate, 8½" 5.00
Byzantine, crystal, tumbler, juice 16.00
Byzantine, crystal, wine 22.50
Cadena, topaz, cordial 80.00
Cadena, topaz, sherbet, low 15.00
Canterbury, amber, bowl, berry; 5" 7.00
Canterbury, amber, goblet, water 10.00
Canterbury, amber, plate, 7½" 7.00
Canterbury, chartreuse, goblet, water 12.00
Canterbury, crystal, bowl, fruit 8.00
Canterbury, crystal, goblet, 9-oz 8.00
Canterbury, crystal, plate, w/lily-of-the-valley cutting, 8¼" 15.00
Canterbury, crystal, plate, 7¾" 6.00
Canterbury, crystal, relish, 3-part 18.00
Canterbury, crystal, sherbet, low 6.00

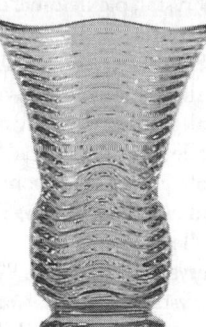

Caribbean, blue vase,
footed, 10", $135.00.
Photo courtesy Gene Florence

Caribbean, bl, bowl, salad; 9" 75.00
Caribbean, bl, creamer 25.00
Caribbean, bl, pitcher, milk; 16-oz 250.00
Caribbean, bl, relish, 6" dia 25.00
Caribbean, bl, shakers, metal lids, 5", pr 110.00
Caribbean, bl, tumbler, ftd, 5½" 50.00
Caribbean, crystal, bowl, grapefruit; ftd, hdls, 7¼" 20.00
Caribbean, crystal, bowl, tab hdls, 9½" 35.00
Caribbean, crystal, candlestick, bl prisms, 7¼" 65.00
Caribbean, crystal, cruet 70.00
Caribbean, crystal, goblet, 3-oz, 4¼" 25.00
Caribbean, crystal, plate, rolled edge, 7¼" 5.00
Caribbean, crystal, relish, 5-part 40.00
Caribbean, crystal, tumbler, iced tea; ftd, 11-oz ..27.50
Cerice, crystal, comport, #5831, 6" 27.50

Cerice, crystal, cordial, #15071 ....40.00
First Love, crystal, ashtray, #30, 5x3¼" 24.00
First Love, crystal, bowl, #117, 7x13" 62.50
First Love, crystal, bowl, flared rim, #111, 3¾x10" 55.00
First Love, crystal, candle holder 28.00
First Love, crystal, candy dish, #115, 6½", w/5" lid 65.00
First Love, crystal, champagne/sherbet 16.00
First Love, crystal, comport, #115, 5x5½", from $35 to 45.00

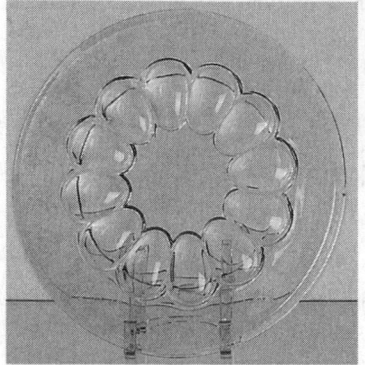

First Love, crystal egg plate, #30, 12", $125.00.

Photo courtesy Gene Florence

First Love, crystal, goblet, water 24.00
First Love, crystal, goblet, wine 28.00
First Love, crystal, mayonnaise, #111, ftd, 5½" 35.00
First Love, crystal, nappy, w/hdl, 6" 22.00
First Love, crystal, plate, torte; #111, 13" 57.50
First Love, crystal, plate, 7½" 18.00
First Love, crystal, relish, 3-part, w/hdls, 8" 38.00
First Love, crystal, sugar bowl, 2½" 14.00
First Love, crystal, tray, celery/relish; oblong, #30, 12" 70.00
First Love, crystal, vase, ftd, 12" 145.00
Hobnail, bl opal, goblet, 9-oz 40.00
Hobnail, bl opal, hat, 6" 195.00
Indian Tree, crystal, pickle/olive dish, 8½" 40.00
King Arthur, crystal, pitcher, water; w/6 tumblers 125.00
Language of Flowers, crystal, relish, 3-part, rnd 25.00
Lily of the Valley, crystal, ashtray, 3" 18.00
Lily of the Valley, crystal, candy dish, w/lid 75.00
Lily of the Valley, crystal, cordial 75.00
Lily of the Valley, crystal, mayonnaise 30.00
Lily of the Valley, crystal, plate, 8" 20.00
Lily of the Valley, crystal, wine 40.00
Mardi Gras, crystal, cake stand, 9" 140.00
Mardi Gras, crystal, claret jug 80.00
Mardi Gras, crystal, vase, slim, 10" 45.00
Mardi Gras, crystal, water bottle 50.00
Nautical, bl, ashtray, 6" 25.00
Nautical, bl, creamer 30.00
Nautical, bl, high ball 27.50
Nautical, bl, plate, 8" 20.00
Nautical, crystal, cigarette holder 15.00
Nautical, crystal, ice bucket 55.00
Nautical, crystal, relish, 2-part, hdls 22.50
Nautical, crystal, tumbler, whiskey & soda; 8" 12.00
Puritan, crystal, cup, ftd 7.00
Puritan, crystal, plate, dinner; 10" 25.00
Puritan, gr, compote, 5½x7" 40.00
Puritan, pk, compote, 5½x7" 50.00
Puritan, pk, cup 10.00
Puritan, pk, cup & saucer, demitasse 25.00
Sailfish (novelty cutting), crystal, tumbler, sea horse 28.00

Sandwich, crystal, bowl, fruit; flared rim, 12" 70.00
Sandwich, crystal, bowl, fruit; 5" 10.00
Sandwich, crystal, cake plate, ped ft 85.00
Sandwich, crystal, candelabra, 1-light, prisms, 10", pr 160.00
Sandwich, crystal, candy dish, ftd, w/lid, 8½" 55.00
Sandwich, crystal, coaster 10.00
Sandwich, crystal, cocktail, 3-oz, 4¼" 15.00
Sandwich, crystal, creamer 9.00
Sandwich, crystal, cup & saucer 16.00
Sandwich, crystal, deviled egg plate 85.00
Sandwich, crystal, fan vase, ftd 40.00
Sandwich, crystal, goblet, 9-oz, 6" 18.00
Sandwich, crystal, pitcher, water; ice lip 135.00
Sandwich, crystal, plate, cracker; w/ring, 13" 30.00
Sandwich, crystal, plate, torte; 12" 50.00
Sandwich, crystal, plate, 13" 55.00
Sandwich, crystal, plate, 8" 10.00
Sandwich, crystal, relish, 2-part, oval, 7" 20.00
Sandwich, crystal, relish, 3-part, 6x10" 27.50
Sandwich, crystal, relish, 5-part 30.00
Sandwich, crystal, shakers, metal lids, pr 18.00
Sandwich, crystal, sherbet/ice cream 10.00
Sandwich, crystal, sugar bowl 8.00
Sandwich, crystal, syrup jar 65.00
Sandwich, crystal, tumbler, iced tea; ftd 18.00
Sandwich, crystal, tumbler, juice; ftd 13.00
Sandwich, crystal, tumbler, water; ftd, 9-oz 14.00
Sandwich, crystal, vase, ftd, #41, 10" 90.00
Sandwich, crystal, vase, ruffled, 4¼x6" 35.00
Sanibel, bl opal, mint dish, 7" 40.00
Sanibel, pk opal, leaf swan, 6½" 95.00
Sanibel, yel opal, muffin tray, 13" 80.00
Sanibel, yel opal, plate, salad 40.00
Spiral Flutes, amber, gr or pk, almond, ftd, 2" 12.00
Spiral Flutes, amber, gr or pk, bowl, almond; 2" 13.00
Spiral Flutes, amber, gr or pk, bowl, cereal; 6½" 32.50
Spiral Flutes, amber, gr or pk, bowl, 9" 27.50
Spiral Flutes, amber, gr or pk, candlestick, 7½" 55.00
Spiral Flutes, amber, gr or pk, cigarette holder, w/cutting 70.00
Spiral Flutes, amber, gr or pk, creamer, oval 8.00
Spiral Flutes, amber, gr or pk, cup, bouillon; 2-hdl 15.00
Spiral Flutes, amber, gr or pk, ice tub, w/hdls 52.00
Spiral Flutes, amber, gr or pk, mug, 9-oz 27.50
Spiral Flutes, amber, gr or pk, plate, luncheon; 8⅜" 4.00
Spiral Flutes, amber, gr or pk, plate, 7½" 4.00
Spiral Flutes, amber, gr or pk, tumbler, flat, 8-oz 30.00
Spiral Flutes, amber, gr or pk, vase, 10½" 30.00
Tear Drop, crystal, bonbon, 4-hdl, 6" 12.00
Tear Drop, crystal, bowl, crimped, low ft, 12" 40.00
Tear Drop, crystal, bowl, dessert; 6" 6.00
Tear Drop, crystal, bowl, salad; 9" 27.50
Tear Drop, crystal, butter dish, ¼-lb 27.00
Tear Drop, crystal, candy basket, hdls, oval, 7½x5½" 75.00
Tear Drop, crystal, champagne, 5-oz 10.00
Tear Drop, crystal, cheese compote 18.00
Tear Drop, crystal, coaster/ashtray, rolled rim, 3" 7.00
Tear Drop, crystal, cordial 18.00
Tear Drop, crystal, cup, demitasse; 2½-oz 10.00
Tear Drop, crystal, goblet; wine; 3-oz 18.00
Tear Drop, crystal, mustard jar, w/lid, 4¼" 35.00
Tear Drop, crystal, olive dish, 2-part, 6" 15.00
Tear Drop, crystal, plate, bread & butter; 6" 4.00
Tear Drop, crystal, plate, dinner; 10½" 35.00
Tear Drop, crystal, sherbet, low 6.00

Tear Drop, crystal, sweetmeat, center hdl, 6½" 35.00
Tear Drop, crystal, tray, hdls, 10" 8.00
Tear Drop, crystal, tumbler, flat, 14-oz 17.50
Tear Drop, crystal, tumbler, juice; ftd 8.00
Terrace, cobalt or red, bowl, ftd, 4¾x10¼" 125.00
Terrace, cobalt or red, cup & saucer 47.50
Terrace, cobalt or red, pitcher 825.00
Terrace, cobalt or red, plate, 8½" 25.00
Terrace, cobalt or red, relish, 2-part, w/hdls, 6" 45.00
Terrace, cobalt or red, tumbler 45.00
Terrace, crystal or amber, bowl, 3½" sq 17.50
Terrace, crystal or amber, cheese stand, 3x5¼" 25.00
Terrace, crystal or amber, claret, #5111½ 45.00
Terrace, crystal or amber, cordial, #5111½, 1-oz 42.50
Terrace, crystal or amber, mayonnaise, crimped, 3½x5½" 32.00
Terrace, crystal or amber, plate, w/hdls, 11" 40.00
Terrace, crystal or amber, plate, 6" sq 14.00
Terrace, crystal or amber, vase, ftd, 10" 115.00

Durand

Durand art glass was made by the Vineland Flint Glass Works of Vineland, New Jersey. Victor Durand Jr. was the sole proprietor. The division called the 'fancy shop' was geared to the production of fine hand-blown art glass in the style of Tiffany and Steuben. Lustered glass and opal glass were used as a base to create such patterns as King Tut, Heart and Vine, Peacock, Feather, and Egyptian Crackle. Cased glass was used to produce cut designs. Production of art glass began in 1924 and continued until 1931. Although most of this art glass was unsigned, when it was, it was generally signed within the pontil 'Durand' or 'Durand' written across the top of a large letter V, all in silver script. The numbers that sometimes appear along with the signature indicate the shape and height of the object. Owner Victor Durand employed the owner and several workers from the failed Quezal Art Glass and Decorating Co. This is why early Durand may sometimes look similar to Quezal art glass. In 1926 Durand art glass was awarded a medal of honor at the Sesquicentennial International Exposition in Philadelphia, Pennsylvania. Our advisor for this category is Edward J. Meschi, author of *Durand — The Man and His Glass* (Antique Publications); he is listed in the Directory under New Jersey.

Console bowl, yellow amber-gris with blue-outlined white feathers on applied pedestal foot, 9x11", $1,250.00.

Bowl, feathers, red/opal on red over clear, 3x12½" 825.00
Bowl, heart & vines, bl on dk bl, acorn form w/amber ft, 7" 1,700.00
Bowl, hearts & vines, wht on bl irid, 2x4¼" 575.00
Candlesticks, leaf & flower cutting, yel lustre, 3½x3½", pr 525.00
Champagne, Optic Ribbed, amethyst, 4" 175.00
Champagne, ruby red w/Spanish Yellow stem, red ft, 5½" 325.00
Champagne, Spanish Yellow w/gr trim, 7" 125.00
Cocktail, feathers, bl/opal on bl over crystal, crystal stem/ft, 5" ..300.00
Compote, feathers, red/opal on red over crystal, ftd, 6½x8" 675.00

Compote, feathers, wht/opal on gr over crystal, ftd, 6½x8" 525.00
Finger bowl, amethyst, 2½x4½", +6" plate 225.00
Finger bowl, red w/wht trim, 2½x4½" 100.00
Finger bowl, Spanish Yellow w/gr trim, 2½x5", +6" plate 225.00
Flower spill, feathers, red/opal on crystal, 8" 900.00
Goblet, feathers, opal on gr over crystal, crystal stem/ft, 6½" 325.00
Goblet, feathers, opal on red over crystal, crystal stem/ft, 6" 325.00
Goblet, feathers, opal on royal bl, amber stem/base, 7" 375.00
Goblet, feathers, yel lustre, bl & wht band at rim, 7" 325.00
Goblet, geometric zipper, bl over crystal, crystal stem, 7" 425.00
Goblet, geometric zipper, bl over crystal, crystal stem/ft, 7" 425.00
Goblet, geometrics, gr over crystal, crystal stem/ft, 7" 350.00
Goblet, Optic Ribbed, bl w/Spanish Yellow stem, bl ft, 8½" 325.00
Iced tea, feathers, gr/opal on gr over yel lustre, appl ft, 6" 375.00
Iced tea, Optic Ribbed, red, 6" 75.00
Iced tea, Spanish Yellow w/gr trim, 6" 75.00
Jar, bl irid w/bl threading, yel florette on lid, 9x10" 1,900.00
Jar, feathers, opal/bl on gold, thread-wrapped, glass lid, 7" 1,600.00
Jar, gold, classic form, rosette on lid, #1964-6, 7" 1,050.00
Lamp, torchere; leaves/threads; brass ft w/acanthus leaves, 16" ..1,000.00
Parfait, feathers, red/opal on red over crystal, crystal ft, 5½" 400.00
Pitcher, red crystal crackle, appl hdl, 8½" 1,575.00
Plate, King Tut, swirl center & rim, opal & bl uptrn rim, 8" ...1,200.00
Sherbet, emerald gr w/wht scalloped edge, 2½", +plate 175.00
Sherbet, feathers, wht on Spanish Yellow w/bl & wht trim, 4" ...325.00
Sherbet, gold w/wrapped-in fused gold threads, 3x4¼" 350.00
Sherbet, yel lustre w/gr trim, 5" 125.00
Vase, amber w/bl irid surface, down-trn rim, 8x8" 1,265.00
Vase, amber w/gold irid, bulbous base w/indent, 15" 1,150.00
Vase, amber w/gold irid, shouldered w/flared rim, 6x6" 375.00
Vase, bl crystal crackle, hard ribbed, w/lustre, 10" 1,250.00
Vase, bl irid, cylinder w/flared rim, widened base, #1714, 7½" ...675.00
Vase, bl irid, waisted rim, 9¼" 800.00
Vase, bl irid w/bl threading, #1812-8, 7½", NM 825.00
Vase, dk bl irid w/gold & bl threading allover, att, ftd, 9" 625.00
Vase, Egyptian Crackle, gr/wht on lustre-amber, 10x12" 1,800.00
Vase, feathers, bl & opal on bl to clear, appl ft, 8" 925.00
Vase, feathers, bl/opal on bl over clear, 8" 1,050.00
Vase, feathers, opal & red on red to clear, appl ft, 12" 1,150.00
Vase, geometric cuttings, red to crystal, 10" 1,375.00
Vase, gold, classic form, #1710-10, 10" 875.00
Vase, gold, ribbed w/flared rim, #1818-7, 7½" 700.00
Vase, gold, shouldered w/waisted rim, unmk, 8½" 500.00
Vase, gr crystal crackle w/lustre, 10½" 1,150.00
Vase, grapes & vines cut band, opal on yel lustre, 6½" 625.00
Vase, hearts, opal/bl on gold, thread-wrapped, ftd, 10" 900.00
Vase, hearts, opal/gr on gold, gold threading, 6½" 800.00
Vase, hearts & vines, bl w/gold ped ft, #20120-12, 12" 1,725.00
Vase, hearts & vines, opal on bl irid, can neck w/2 rings, 10" .1,750.00
Vase, hearts & vines, opal on bl irid, gold disk ft, 8x3" 1,200.00
Vase, hearts & vines, opal on bl irid, ovoid, #1968-6, 6" 900.00
Vase, hearts & vines allover, opal on bl irid, #1812-7, 7½" 1,000.00
Vase, King Tut, bl irid w/bl-opal swirled veins, ruffled, 7" 900.00
Vase, King Tut, gr on gold, amber-bl base, trumpet form, 14" .2,250.00
Vase, King Tut, gr w/bl waves, #1722-6, 5½" 900.00
Vase, King Tut, opal on gold irid, corseted form, 10" 600.00
Vase, King Tut, silver/gold on emerald, bulb w/trumpet top, 17" ..3,450.00
Vase, Lady Gay Rose w/gold King Tut decor, 9" 1,750.00
Vase, Optic Ribbed, amethyst w/appl ft, 8" 575.00
Vase, Optic Ribbed, deep amethyst, appl ft, 16" 1,525.00
Vase, Optic Ribbed, lt amethyst, 6" 425.00
Vase, red hard-ribbed Moorish crackle w/lustre, 7½" 1,875.00
Vase, red ribbed crackle over crystal w/lustre, 6" 1,750.00
Vase, royal bl irid w/lav, intense color, 9½" 900.00

Durant Kilns

The Durant Pottery Company operated in Bedford Village, New York, in the early 1900s. Its founder was Mrs. Clarence Rice; she was aided by L. Volkmar to whom she assigned the task of technical direction. (See also Volkmar.) The art and table wares they produced were simple in form and decoration. The creative aspects of the ware were carried on almost entirely by Volkmar himself, with only a minimal crew to help with production. After Mrs. Rice's death in 1919, the property was purchased by Volkmar, who chose to drop the Durant name by 1930. Prior to 1919 the ware was marked simply Durant and dated. After that time a stylized 'V' was added.

Vase, gr mottled, bulbous w/flared rim, dtd 1922, 5¼x5¾" 200.00
Vase, gr/yel mottled matt, rnd/ftd, Volkmar/1913, 6½" 500.00
Vase, thick Persian Blue, ribbed cylinder w/waisted neck, 12", EX .550.00

Easter

Eggs, bunnies, chicks, and baskets have all become basic elements of Easter celebrations; and the older, more interesting examples are being collected (often for nostalgic reasons) and displayed during the holidays to make the festivities brighter.

Ducks and chicks do not command prices as high as rabbits, and German rabbits with clothes are much more valuable than the plain brown ones. Papier-mache rabbits made in the 1940s – 50s and marked USA are less pricey than composition bunnies made in Germany. In the listings that follow, unless noted otherwise, values are given for candy containers in very good to excellent condition. Our advisor for this category is Jenny Tarrant; she is listed in the Directory under Missouri.

Candy Containers

Mr. and Mrs. Bunny candy containers, papier-mache, Germany, 1920s, 10", $750.00 for the pair.

Photo courtesy Dunbar Gallery

Boy w/chick, papier-mache, Germany, 6½" 155.00
Chick, coated cb, Germany 95.00
Chick, egg-shape body, papier-mache, 6½" 45.00
Chick w/cloth clothing, papier-mache & cb, 6½" 105.00
Duck, papier-mache, egg shape, W Germany, 6½" 65.00
Hen on nest, papier-mache, Germany, 6" 50.00
Rabbit, appl eyes, papier-mache, Germany, 7¾" 360.00
Rabbit, cb, spring neck, W Germany 85.00
Rabbit, compo, dressed, Germamy, 5-7", ea 225.00
Rabbit, compo, dressed, Germany, 3-4", ea 155.00
Rabbit, compo, Germany, 5-7", ea 125.00
Rabbit, papier-mache, plain, USA, 7-11", ea 85.00

Rabbit clown, papier-mache, on mica egg, 4" 1,265.00
Rabbit clown, papier-mache, 6" 990.00
Rabbit lady, pressed cb, glass eyes, 8" 330.00
Rabbit pulling twig cart, papier-mache, 6x8" 100.00

Miscellaneous

Figurine, Ballooning Bunnies, Fitz & Floyd 85.00
Figurine, Mother Rabbit, Fitz & Floyd 65.00
Figurine, rabbit, compo, Germany, 1½" 48.00
Roly-poly, goose, dresssed, celluloid, Germany 150.00
Transfer-o-s, Mickey Mouse, PAAS, 1930s, unused 75.00
Wind-up toy, bunny pulling cart, tin litho, Ohio Art 75.00

Egg Cups

Egg cups, one of the fastest growing collectibles of the '90s, have been traced back to the ruins of Pompeii. Since then, they have been made in almost every country and in almost every conceivable material (ceramics, glass, metal, papier-mache, plastic, wood, ivory, even rubber and straw). Popular categories include Art Deco, Black Memorabilia, Chintz, Characters/Personalities, Golliwoggs, Railroadiana, Steamship, Souvenir Ware, etc.

Still being produced today in most countries, egg cups appeal to collectors on many levels. Prices can range from quite inexpensive to many thousands of dollars. Those made prior to 1840 are scarce and sought after, as are the character/personality egg cups of the 1930s.

For a more thorough study of egg cups we recommend that you refer to *Egg Cups: An Illustrated History and Price Guide* (Antique Publications) by Brenda Blake, our advisor for this category. You will find her address listed in the Directory under Maine.

Key:
bkt — bucket, a single cup without a foot
dbl — two-sided with small end for eating egg in shell, large end for mixing egg with toast and butter
fig — figural, an egg cup actually molded into the shape of an animal, bird, car, person, etc.
hoop — hoop, a single open cup with waistline
set — tray or cruet (stand, frame or basket) with two to eight cups
sgl — single, with a foot; goblet shaped

Photo courtesy Carole Bess White

Bucket, hand-painted mountain scenic in multicolor with tan lustre, Noritake mark, 3", $35.00; Figural, chicken, tan and yellow lustre, red mark, 2½", $25.00.

Advertising/Souvenir

Bkt, British Airways, bl & wht, Royal Doulton 14.00

Bkt, Raffles Hotel, maroon bands, Churchill, 1990s 12.00
Dbl, Centenary, B&O Railroad, Lamberton 400.00
Dbl, Mountains & Flowers, Great Northern Railroad 100.00
Dbl, Texaco **285.00**
Dbl, USN (Navy), bl anchor & band, Tepco 20.00
Dbl, Wyoming Seminary, bl seal & trim 15.00
Fig, Harrods' Doorman, Wade, 1990s 38.00
Sgl, Aristocrat, Chicago/Burlington/Quincy Railroad 150.00
Sgl, Bless This House, Lancaster PA, red heart 9.00
Sgl, CAAC (China National Airlines) 12.00
Sgl, Cadbury's Creme Egg, lg, brn rim, 1989 ....12.00
Sgl, Lazarus Stores 89th Anniversary on Fiesta turq egg cup, 1940 .100.00
Sgl, Moxie Girl 150.00
Sgl, Plymouth Rock, Plymouth MA, Germany, ca 1900 ....40.00
Sgl, Souvenir of Indianapolis IN, HP, Made in Japan 10.00
Sgl, St Paul's Cathedral, pk lustre, ca 1900 ....25.00

American China/Pottery

Dbl, Arizona, Eva Zeisel design, Hall China, 1950s 25.00
Dbl, Autumn, mc fruit basket, Lenox 45.00
Dbl, Autumn Leaf, Hall's Autumn Leaf Collector's Club gift, 1997 ....60.00
Dbl, Breakfast Nook, windows w/flower trellis, WS George 20.00
Dbl, Chick, Juvenile, Roseville, ca 1917 ....300.00
Dbl, Colonial, bl, Stangl, 1926 ....12.00
Dbl, Desert Rose, Franciscan, 1942 on 22.00
Dbl, fruit in basket design, MA Hadley 22.00
Dbl, Hankscraft, or horizontal ring design 15.00
Dbl, Ivy Vine, Harker 12.00
Dbl, Rustic, plaid, Blue Ridge, 1950s 25.00
Dbl, Starburst, Franciscan, 1954 ....38.00
Dbls, Bride & Groom, Cleminson, pr 50.00
Sgl, Florida, Lenox, 1922 ....45.00
Sgl, Lei Lani, maroon lotus flower, Vernon Kilns, ca 1940, lg 65.00
Sgl, Redware, Stahl, lg 150.00
Sgl, Shearwater, gr glaze, ca 1950 ....38.00

Art Deco

Bkt, Crocus, Clarice Cliff 95.00
Dbl, Wash Band, bl, Susie Cooper, 1930s 45.00
Set, chrome stand w/6 tulip cups 80.00
Sgl, Cottage design over wide gr band, Clarice Cliff, 1930s 240.00
Sgl, geometric design, pewter insert, Shelley, 1930s 95.00
Sgl, Orange Tree, Crown Ducal 60.00
Sgl, Tango, geometric motif, Royal Doulton, 1930s 60.00

Characters/Personalities

Bkt, Little Bo Peep, yel, Keele St Pottery 25.00
Fig, Margaret Thatcher, Spitting Image, Carlton, 1980s 65.00
Fig, Mickey Mouse on scooter, lustre, Walt Disney Prod, Japan .110.00
Fig, Minnie Mouse, orange ears, Foreign, 1930s 125.00
Fig, Popeye squatting, smoking pipe, Japan, 1930s 125.00
Fig, Princess Diana, Spitting Image, Carlton, 1980s 135.00
Fig, Ronald Reagan, Spitting Image, Carlton, 1980s 90.00
Fig, Snoopy, chef's hat 50.00
Fig, Swee' Pea, King Features Syndicate, 1980 ....70.00
Fig set, Muppets: Statler/Waldorf/Zoot/Sam, Sigma Tastesetter, '81 .240.00
Fig set, Snow White & 7 Dwarfs, stand by their cups, Japan, '37 ..1,400.00
Sgl, Paddington Bear, taking a walk, Coalport, late 1970s 25.00
Sgl, Prince Ranier/Princess Grace of Monaco, wedding, Limoges, 1950s 100.00
Sgl, Queen Elizabeth, 60th birthday, Coronet, 1986 ....25.00
Sgl, Snoopy Good Morning series 16.00

Sgl, Teletubbies, w/box & chocolate egg, 1998 ....8.00

Figurals

Airplane, yel, Honiton, 1960s 22.00
Black man's face, Germany, ca 1900 ....100.00
Chef, pk face, 1950s 12.00
Duck, yel, Royal Art Pottery 20.00
Golly, Robert's Golden Shred, plastic, ca 1959 ....55.00
Legs running, Carlton Ware, 1978 ....70.00
Legs walking, gr shoes, Carlton Ware 38.00
Miss Cutie Pie, Lefton 30.00
Model of antique car, yel, 1940s 28.00
Pirate, blk eye patch, 1980s 15.00
Santa Claus, appl nose & mustache 20.00
Set, Cottage Ware, 4 cottage-shape bkt cups on sq tray, Price Bros ..55.00
Shoe Shoe, plastic w/2 ft, Lego, 1985 ....10.00
Toilet, wht w/blk lid, 2 legs 15.00
Wellies, gr boots, Carlton Ware 150.00
Whistler, bl bird, gr beak, 1920s 85.00
Whistler, train, orange luster, 1920s 110.00

Foreign

Bkt, quails, brn, Tirschenreuth, ca 1880 ....18.00
Dbl, HP, sgn, Hutchenreuther 75.00
Dbl, peasant lady, yel & gr, floral panels, HB Quimper 55.00
Fig, Cardinal Tuck, red robe, Goebel 175.00
Set, majolica basket w/6 egg cups, leaf pattern, 1880s 475.00
Sgl, basketweave w/pk lustre, Belleek, 1st blk mk 250.00
Sgl, Canton, rain cloud border, 1st period, ca 1840 ....150.00
Sgl, celadon, Japan, ca 1910 ....28.00
Sgl, floral on hard paste w/gold, Sevres, LL in interlaced Ls, 1789 ....425.00
Sgl, romantic scene, part of mini dish set, Limoges, 1⅜" 22.00

Glass

Dbl, Cape Cod, crystal, Imperial, ca 1932 ....38.00
Dbl, Chalaine Blue, McKee 18.00
Dbl, Jade-ite, gr, from $35 to 40.00
Fig, Chicken, wht, str rim, Vallerysthal 28.00
Fig, Rooster, milk glass w/red trim, Westmoreland, 1930s 17.00
Sgl, amethyst, flared gallery rim, pressed, ca 1880 ....120.00
Sgl, Bohemian, o/l, wht to orange, ca 1890-1920 ....110.00
Sgl, cranberry w/gold edging, fluting 100.00
Sgl, Greek Key, Heisey 75.00
Sgl, Invt T'print, amberina 350.00
Sgl, ruby stained, eng Dolly 1926 ....60.00

Staffordshire

Bkt, Mabel Lucie Attwell, Shelley 100.00
Dbl, Castles, red transfer, Enoch Woods 30.00
Dbl, Cornish Kitchen Ware, bl bands, TC Green & Co, 1930s 30.00
Dbl, English Chippendale, Johnson Bros 25.00
Dbl, Friendly Village, Johnson Bros 22.00
Dbl, Manchu, bl & wht, Mason 25.00
Dbl, Mr Snowman w/dish hat, Royal Doulton, ca 1985 ....85.00
Dbl, Nantwich, chintz, blk, Royal Winton 220.00
Dbl, Tea Leaf, repro, Adams, 1970 ....95.00
Dbl, Vista, red transfer, Mason 32.00
Dbl, Watteau, brn transfer, Mason 25.00
Sgl, Black Cockerel, Good Morning, Devon 60.00
Sgl, blk basalt, English, 18th C 550.00

Sgl, Drabware, impressed, Minton, ca 1850 ....**135.00**
Sgl, Flow Blue, oriental scene, ca 1850 ....**250.00**
Sgl, Jasperware, Dance of the Hours, Wedgwood, 1995 ....**32.00**
Sgl, Mulberry, paneled, ca 1850 ....**275.00**
Sgl, Sarah's Garden, Wedgwood, 1990s **16.00**
Sgl, spatterware, bl & wht, early 19th C **200.00**
Sgl, The Kirkwood, goose-egg sz, Royal Doulton **22.00**
Sgl, Tower, bl, Copeland/Spode, ca 1930 ....**40.00**

Miscellaneous

Bkt, Bakelite, mottled, British NB Ware **6.00**
Hoop, Coats' & Clark's, coat of arms, gr, Dunn Bennett & Co, Ltd .**70.00**
Hoop, Cunard, Queen Mary, blk decor border **48.00**
Hoop, Straw, navy bl **20.00**
Set, Mauchline stand w/6 cups, ca 1860 ....**450.00**
Set, Sheffield SP, Georgian design w/urn finial, 6 cups, 1790s ...**1,000.00**
Sgl, ivory, trn & polished, late 19th C **65.00**
Sgl, rubber, smiley face **8.00**
Sgl, silver cup attached to model of Thonet chair, Fr, 1880s **100.00**
Sgl, Tartan Ware, plaid, 19th C **150.00**

Elfinware

Made in Germany from about 1920 until the 1940s, these minia-ture vases, boxes, salt cellars, and miscellaneous novelty items are char-acterized by the tiny applied flowers that often cover their entire surface. Pieces with animals and birds are the most valuable, followed by the more interesting examples such as diminutive grand pianos, candle holders, etc. Items covered in 'spinach' (applied green moss) can be valued at 75% to 100% higher than pieces that are not decorated in this manner. See also Salts, Open.

Vase, green 'spinach' and applied rose, 2¾", $50.00; Swan, green 'spinach' and applied rose, 2¼", $65.00.

Baby shoe, overall gr spinach & flowers, 4½" L **110.00**
Baby shoe, rose appl on lt bl, 4" **50.00**
Basket, loop hdl, sm **38.50**
Basket, overall gr spinach w/appl red rose, 3½x5" **120.00**
Box, oval, 3x4" **75.00**
Box, piano form, appl violets & roses, crown mk, 3x5" **195.00**
Box, piano form, 3" **55.00**
Candlestick, sm ring hdl, 2½" **55.00**
Card holder **27.50**
Cradle, much spinach, 3½" **82.50**
Furniture set, settee/table/2 chairs, w/moss & flowers, 1" H **95.00**
Salt cellar, bl floral on basketweave, 2-hdl **35.00**
Slipper, appl rose, 3½" L **40.00**
Slippers, dbl, lg **110.00**
Swan, 2½" **45.00**
Teapot, spinach & rose on front, Germany, 2" **40.00**
Vase, 3" **50.00**

Watering can, 6" **60.00**

Epergnes

Popular during the Victorian era, epergnes were fancy centerpieces often consisting of several tiers of vases (called lilies), candle holders, dishes, or a combination of components. They were made in all types of art glass, and some were set in ornate plated frames.

Lime opalescent lily and two baskets with rigaree, in Meriden frame with cherubs, 26", $625.00.

Amber w/appl sapphire bl trim, HP florals, 1-pc, 14⅜x7½" **400.00**
Bl o/l w/florals, lg lily in ftd bowl, 16x10¾" dia **395.00**
Bl o/l w/HP flowers & leaves, lift-out lily, 15¾x9½" **375.00**
Clear w/wht loops, 1-lily, hollow knop, 18x11¼" **110.00**
Cranberry, central lily, 2 baskets hang from clear arms, 24" **1,650.00**
Cranberry, lg jack-in-pulpit vase+3 sm in ruffled 11" bowl, 19" ..**1,150.00**
Crystal/etch/frosted lily w/emb cherubs; SP Meriden Cupid base ..**175.00**
Gr opal, 4 lilies stem from flower bowl, 23" **600.00**
Peachblow o/l, 2 5" vases+1 clear 12" on mirror, yel rigaree **650.00**
Pk o/l, 3-lily, heavy wire fr w/berries & leaves, 19x11" **350.00**
Pk shaded o/l lily in 12" bowl on SP ftd base, 18½" **495.00**
Red ruffled-edge satin glass bowl w/HP floral; SP fr, 16" **150.00**

Erickson

Carl Erickson of Bremen, Ohio, produced hand-formed glassware from 1943 until 1960 in artistic shapes, no two of which were identical. One of the characteristics of his work was the air bubbles that were cap-tured within the glass. Though most examples are clear, colored items were also made. Rather than to risk compromising his high standards by selling the factory, when Erickson retired, the plant was dismantled and sold.

Decanter, gr w/2 clear rings at neck, pinched, 1940s, 15½" **168.50**
Pitcher, smoke, 14" **100.00**
Vase, emerald gr, bulbous base, 18½x6¼" **150.00**
Vase, smoky clear w/controlled bubbles, 10½x5" **100.00**

Erphila

Ebeling and Ruess, an importing company in Philadelphia, began operations in 1886. The acronym 'Erphila' was frequently substituted for the manufacturer's mark on the imported items. It appears that the Erphila mark was used through the late 1930s and then again after WW II on products from U.S. Zone Germany as well as from other areas. The company imported from factories such as Fustenberg, W. Goebel, Villeroy and Boch, Heinrich, Keramos, and Schumann, to name a few.

Figurines, art pottery, and some utilitarian items can be found bearing the Erphila mark. Examples are hard to find. Early German marks (those prior to 1900) often contain the word 'Fayence.' After the turn of the century, a rectangular mark in green ink was used. Following WW I, porcelain items were imported from Czechoslovakia. These sometimes carried gold and silver labels. A small variety of marks were used in the 1920s and '30s, but they all contained the name Erphila. Sticker labels were also used. 'Bavaria,' 'Black Forest,' 'Italy,' and 'France' are found in combination with 'Erphila.'

Eheling and Ruess continue the importing business, but it appears that since the 1940s they are also using an 'E' and 'R' on a bell-shaped mark. Because this mark does not contain the name 'Erphila,' we do not consider it to be such. We assume that they stopped using this name sometime in the 1950s.

Basket, rust, sm, MIG, 4½" 32.00
Bookends, man & woman, mc, MIG, pr 75.00
Box, basket form w/fruit lid, 2 ring hdls, 6¼" 200.00
Bust, Shakespeare, natural colors, Germany, 2" 35.00
Candlestick, wht w/orange flowers, Czech, 5", pr 75.00
Charger, majolica, gr grapes in center, bl forest mk 120.00
Creamer, lady, wht & orange, Czech 125.00
Dish, hen on nest, mc, Czech, 4x7" 85.00
Dish, wheelbarrow shape w/child pushing, mc, MIG, 3x4" 50.00
Dresser doll, Madame Pompadour, yel dress, MIG, 5" 115.00
Figurine, beagle dog, mk Germany, 9" 52.50
Figurine, bear, gray, MIG, 1x3" 20.00
Figurine, bird on stump, yel & gray, MIG, 4¾" 35.00
Figurine, bulldog, blk & wht, 3¼x6½" 115.00
Figurine, cat, sleeping, blk & wht w/mc collar, Germany, 3½" L ..38.00
Figurine, Dalmatian dog, paws crossed, 5¼x10" 30.00
Figurine, dog, Chow, 4" 35.00

Figurine, elk, brown, MIG, 15x15", $450.00.

Figurine, elephant, gray, 5" L 45.00
Figurine, elephant, red, MIG, 4¼" 23.00
Figurine, horse rearing, bl, Czech, 7" 30.00
Figurine, lion on stool, MIG, 2½x3" 29.00
Figurine, Mrs Gump, wht & orange, MIG, 3" 35.00
Figurine, rabbits, sitting, natural colors, Germany, 2½" ...20.00
Figurine, tiger, natural colors, MIG, 1x3" 20.00
Mug, Toby, bl coat, rust hat, Sam Weller, MIG 110.00
Planter, lady in pleated dress, Czech, 8" 45.00
Plate, cake; carnations, MIG, 11" 30.00
Plate, cake; cherry chintz, MIG, 12" 52.00
Plate, grapes, majolica, MIG, 7¾" 72.50
Reamer, yel flower, 1-pc, mk, 8½" 95.00
Teapot, cat figural, gray & blk, MIG, 8" 120.00
Teapot, pig figural, pk & blk, MIG, 8" 150.00
Urn, cherub transfer scene, gold floral stencil, w/lid, 11" 60.00
Vase, bl iris, narrow neck, Czech, 8½" 68.00

Vase, floral w/raised enameling, 11½" 95.00

Eskimo Artifacts

While ivory carvings made from walrus tusks or whale teeth have been the most emphasized articles of Eskimo art, basketry and woodworking are other areas in which these Alaskan Indians excel. Their designs are effected through the application of simple yet dramatic lines and almost stark decorative devices. Though not pursued to the extent of American Indian art, the unique work of these northern tribes is beginning to attract the serious attention of today's collectors.

Basket, circular lidded box with whalebone polar bear and cub finial, inscribed 398, Omnik, Pt. Hope, Alaska, 4x4¼", $650.00.

Basket, animal hide crosses, 1940s, 6x6" 50.00
Basket, mc butterfly & bird, w/lid, 1970s, 6x5" 325.00
Basket, mc butterfly & dmn, w/lid, 1960s, 5x7" 325.00
Basket, yarn flower & crosses design, w/lid, 1900s, 10x11" 200.00
Basket, 2-color connecting dmns, w/lid, 1930s, 9x8" 300.00
Carving, ivory billikin, prehistoric, 2x½" 50.00
Carving, ivory rookery w/baleen birds & base, 1972, 4x2" 25.00
Carving, ivory tapalik (shaman) w/baby on bk, 1900s, 4½x1" 195.00
Carving, soapstone lady kneeling w/child, ca 1920, 6½" 300.00
Carving, soapstone mother & child, ca 1920, 5" 300.00
Carving, 5-pc ivory dance scene, 1975, 4x4" 500.00
Cribbage board, walrusk tusk w/scrimshaw scenes, ca 1900, 21x3" .275.00
Goggles, snow; cvd wood, ca 1870, 5x1" 550.00
Gun case, sealskin, 1880s, 52x8" 75.00
Harpoon points, cvd bone, prehistoric, 1-6", 6 for 100.00
Knife, old native coopper w/cvd bone hdl, 1880s, 14x2" 320.00
Ladle, cvd horn w/notched decor, 1-pc, 1920s, 9x10" 50.00
Mask, cvd ivory miniature on ivory stand, ca 1985, 6x5" 125.00
Mask, wood, thin/cvd contorted face w/teeth, 1870, 8½x5" 250.00
Mask, wooden Musk Ox ceremonial w/fish protrusions, 1920s, 21" .700.00
Moccasins, sealskin w/beads, trade-cloth toes, 1890s 80.00
Muklucks, fur & hide w/floral beadwork, 1940s, 12x10" 160.00
Pants, sealskin w/fur, 1880s, 42x15" 75.00
Pouch, sealskin w/decor, flap closure, 1880s, 7x8" 300.00
Spindle whorl, whalebone, excavated, 1880s, 7" 300.00
Ulu (lady's knife), scrimshawed ivory hdl, 1850s, 5x7" 150.00

Face Jugs, Contemporary

The most recognizable form of Southern folk pottery is the face jug. Rich alkaline glazes (lustrous greens and browns) are typical, and occasionally shards of glass are applied to the surface of the ware which during firing melts to produce opalescent 'glass runs' over the alkaline. In some locations clay deposits contain elements that result in areas of fluorescent blue or rutile; another variation is swirled or striped ware, reminiscent of 18th-century agateware from Staffordshire. Collector demand for these unique one-of-a-kind jugs is at an all-time high and is still escalating. Choice examples made by Burlon B. Craig and Lanier Meaders often bring over $1,000.00 on the secondary market. If you're interested in learning more about this type of folk pottery, contact the Southern Folk Pottery Collectors Society; their address is in the Directory under Clubs, Newsletters, and Catalogs. Our advisor for this category is Billy Ray Hussey; he is listed in the Directory under North Carolina.

Photo courtesy Southern
Folk Pottery Collectors Society

China teeth, inserted clay eyes, two-piece lips, applied lashes and lids, multicolor mottled high lustre glaze, signed M Rogers in script, ca 1982 – 84, 9", $325.00.

China plate teeth, 'pearl' eyes, blk slip, M Rogers, 3⅞" **90.00**
China pupils/teeth, orange-brn Albany slip, EJ Brown, 1960s, 7" .**450.00**
China teeth, appl face w/lg nose, J Brown, 1950s, flaw, 8" **110.00**
China teeth, Oriental-style, BR Hussey/RE Albright, 1976, 7⅞" ..**275.00**
China teeth, pierced pupils, brn-gr, JO Brown, 1920s, 8" **1,900.00**
Devil, china teeth, incised brow/mouth, horns, C Lisk, 7¾" **250.00**
Devil, rock teeth, blk/brn/gr, Lanier Meaders, 1973-74, 9" **2,800.00**
Medusa, 15 snake heads w/fangs, incising, M Rogers, 1986-88, 11" ..**425.00**
Wht clay eyes, rolled teeth, alkaline glaze, L Meaders, 10¼" ..**1,050.00**
1 china tooth, incised brows/lashes, dbl-dip line, L Brown, 7¼" .**250.00**

Fairings

Fairings are small, brightly colored 19th-century hard-paste porcelain objects, largely figural groups and boxes. Most figural fairings portray amusing (if not risque) scenes of courting couples, marital woes, and political satire complete with appropriate base captions.

Fairing boxes, also referred to as trinket boxes, sometimes had captions similar to figural fairings, and often there were similar figures on top. It was originally assumed that fairings were made in the Staffordshire area, and for many years they were referred to as Staffordshire fairings. But soon there were many European makers producing them as well, especially the boxes, since the Europeans could make them more cheaply. England encouraged these makers by not charging import duties. Both the figural fairings and the box fairings (trinket boxes) were made with the same consumers in mind.

Many early fairings were not marked; those that were had only a small incised or painted mark. Before 1850 the makers, especially Conte and Boehme of Possneck, Germany (who became the major maker of the boxes, indicated by 'C&B' in listings), used hand-incised numbers (for one article) and Roman numerals (for the size number). The painter often added his painted-on mark or number. After the 1850s both the article number and the maker's mark were impressed. The Conte and Boehme mark is the most familiar — a bent elbow (arm) holding a sword, laying on a shield.

After 1891 all wares shipped to the U.S. had to be clearly marked by the name of the country. For more information, we recommend *Victorian Trinket Boxes* by Janice and Richard Vogel, published by the authors (see Directory, Florida). Other good references are *Victorian Fairings* by W.S. Bristoe and *Victorian Fairings and Their Value* by Margaret Anderson.

Bank, pk cottage w/Present From Scarborough in gold, 4" W **150.00**
Box, A Child's Prayer, girl in bed, C&B mk **200.00**
Box, baby asleep on pillow, ruffled edge, 2½" **150.00**
Box, Be Good If You Can't Be Careful **135.00**
Box, boy seated, crying feeding cat, C&B mk, 4¾x3x2⅜" **240.00**
Box, carpenters working, 4x4x2½" **175.00**
Box, cat w/frog, English, 3" **90.00**
Box, child on bed pulls on pajamas, C&B mk, 4" **120.00**
Box, child w/dog, shoe in hand, C&B mk, 4⅝x3⅛x2⅛" **110.00**
Box, dove w/envelope, unmk, 4x3⅛x2½" **70.00**
Box, girl peeking through bushes at rabbit **125.00**
Box, Grandmama in chair w/ball, C&B mk **225.00**
Box, Greenaway-type girl w/muffs, C&B mk, 4⅝x3x2" **150.00**
Box, Happy Father, What 2?..., couple & twins, 1880s, 3½" **110.00**
Box, Looking Down Upon His Luck, couple w/twins, Germany, 3½" ...**100.00**
Box, monkey playing instrument **200.00**
Box, O Do Leave Me a Drop, 2 cats at box **175.00**
Box, Tug of War, girl & dog by fence tugging doll, 2¾x5¼" **185.00**
Box, Who Said Rats?, cat in draped bed, mice on table **165.00**
Box, 2 cats w/overturned bucket, chair shape, C&B mk, 4½" H ..**190.00**

Fans

The Japanese are said to have invented the fan. From there it went to China, and Portuguese traders took the idea to Europe. Though usually considered milady's accessory, even the gentlemen in 17th-century England carried fans! More fashionable than practical, some were of feathers and lovely hand-painted silks with carved ivory or tortoise sticks. Some French fans had peepholes. There are mourning fans, calendar fans, and those with advertising.

Fine antique fans (pre-1900) of ivory or mother-of-pearl have recently escalated in value. Those from before 1800 often sell for upwards of $1,000.00. Examples with mother-of-pearl sticks are most desirable; least desirable are those with sticks of celluloid. Our advisor for this category is Vicki Flanigan; she is listed in the Directory under Virginia.

Pierced ivory brise fan with carved and scrolling flowers, monogram, ca 1790, 10½", $1,200.00.

Blk Chantilly lace, ornate cvd/gilt MOP sticks, 1870s, 10½" **620.00**
Bone w/printed paper & hand-colored details, 1890s, 19½", EX ..**195.00**
Brise, ivory, cvd/pierced buildings & figures, Canton, 1840s, 9" .**450.00**

Brise, pierced horn, sticks: gilt/jewels/enamel, 1800s, 7" 660.00
Brussels lace over ivory satin, MOP sticks, ca 1870, 10" 350.00
Cabriolet, HP lovers, embr sequins, pnt ivory sticks, 1890s, 12" .475.00
Cabriolet, HP scene w/putti & gilt, ivory sticks, 1750s, 10" 1,540.00
Chromolitho w/mc vignettes, MOP sticks, silk tassle, 1860s, 11" .350.00
Gauze w/embr sequins, cvd/pierced ivory sticks, 1790s, 10" 1,540.00
HP litho bullfighting scenes, wooden sticks, 1840s, 10" 150.00
HP scene on silk, cvd/pnt wood ribs, late 1800s, 17½", EX 175.00
HP woodcut w/snow scene, ivory sticks, Japan, 19th C, 10½" 400.00
Ivory w/HP fabric covering ribs, in fr, 11½x19½" 275.00
Lace sprays on net, pierced/cvd MOP sticks, 1870s, 11" 620.00
MOP panels, HP lovers scene, ivory sticks, 1760, +provenance ..1,375.00
Pheasant feathers, tortoise shell sticks, 1910, 9" 127.00
Rosepoint lace, cvd/gilt MOP sticks, Continental, 1900, 12" 800.00
Silk w/HP scene, Brussels lace inserts, MOP sticks, 1890s, 13" ...300.00
18th-C courting scene (HP), cvd ivory sticks, late 1880s, 18½" .220.00

Farm Collectibles

Country living in the 19th century entailed plowing, planting, and harvesting; gathering eggs and milking; making soap from lard rendered on butchering day; and numerous other tasks performed with primitive tools of which we in the 20th century have had little first-hand knowledge. Our advisor for this category is Lar Hothem; his address is listed in the Directory under Ohio. See also Cast Iron; Woodenware; Wrought Iron.

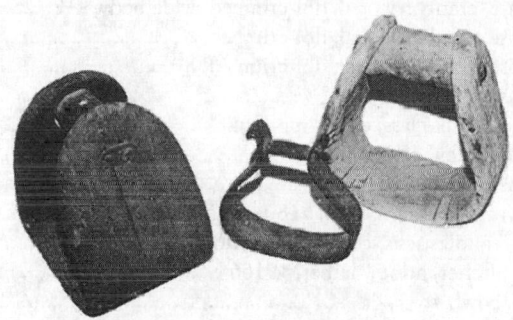

Stirrups, wood and iron, from $25.00 to $45.00.

Bench, harness maker's; plank seat/stake legs/treadle tensions, 43" ..120.00
Booklet, Wm Deering Farm Equipment, 1888 ....37.00
Corn sheller, Ott Bros, Wheeling WV, EX 275.00
Cream separator, Arcade, McCormick Deering, CI, 5¼", EX 900.00
Dryer, seed corn; CI, 10 prong, 20th C, 19" L 14.00
Egg carrier, wooden, Farmer's Friend...Pat 1898, 11x14x13" 240.00
Egg crate, old mustard pnt, 33x15x16½" 120.00
Hay hook, wrought iron w/wood hdl 5.00
Implement seat, Buckeye, CI, EX 125.00
Implement seat, Deering, CI, EX 125.00
Implement seat, Hoosier, CI, EX 125.00
Implement seat, Rock Island Plow Co, 2 stars, EX 140.00
Scoop, cranberry; steel tines, root hdl, old varnish, 16" 275.00
Stool, milking; red pnt, 1 leg under center of seat, 12x11x10" ...110.00
Wagon seat, 2-slat bk, trn finials, rush seat, 29x35x13" 415.00
Well dipper, CI, 6-segment, folding, 20th C, opens to 58" 65.00

Fenton

Frank and John Fenton were brothers who founded the Fenton Art Glass Company in 1906 in Martin's Ferry, Ohio. The venture, at first only a decorating shop, began operations in July of 1905 using blanks purchased from other companies. This operation soon proved unsatisfactory, and by 1907 they had constructed their own glass factory in Williamstown, West Virginia. John left the company in 1909 and organized his own firm in Millersburg, Ohio.

The Fenton Company produced over 130 patterns of carnival glass. They also made custard, chocolate, opalescent, and stretch glass. This company has always been noted for its various colors of glass and has continually changed its production to stay attune with current tastes in decorating. In 1925 they produced a line of 'handmade' items that incorporated the techniques of threading and mosaic work. Because the process proved to be unprofitable, the line was discontinued by 1927. Even their glassware made in the past twenty-five years is already regarded as collectible. Various paper labels have been used since the 1920s; only since 1970 has the logo been stamped into the glass. For further information we recommend *Fenton Art Glass Patterns, 1939 – 1980*, and *Fenton Art Glass, 1907 – 1939*, by Margaret and Kenn Whitmyer; *Fenton Glass, The Third Twenty-Five Years*, by William Heacock (with 1998 value guide); and *Fenton Glass: The 1980s Decade* by Robert E. Eaton, Jr. (1997 values). For information concerning Fenton Art Glass Collectors of America, Inc., see the Clubs, Newsletters, and Catalogs section of the Directory. See also Carnival Glass; Custard Glass; Stretch Glass.

Apple Blossom, compote, dbl-crimped 45.00
Apple Tree, vase, blk, crimped or flared, #1561, 10" 175.00
Apple Tree, vase, Moonstone, crimped, #1561, 1933, 10" 150.00
Aqua Crest, vase, dbl-crimped, 4½" 40.00
Aqua Crest, vase, ftd, #7554, 4" 30.00
Aqua Crest, vase, triple; short 20.00
Aqua Crest/Dmn Lace, cake stand, Fr opal, low 75.00
Basketweave, basket, blk, open edge, #1092, 1935-36, 5½" 35.00
Basketweave, bonbon, milk glass, open edge, #1093, 1934, 7" 30.00
Basketweave, plate, gr opal, 7½" 35.00
Beatty Waffle, rose bowl, gr opal, 4½" 50.00
Big Cookies, basket, Chinese Yellow, #1681, 10½" 175.00
Big Cookies, basket, gr transparent, #1681, 1933 ....125.00
Big Cookies, basket, lilac, #1681, 1933, 10½" 350.00
Big Cookies, basket, Moonstone, #1681, 1933, 10½" 325.00
Big Cookies, macaroon jar, Flame, #1681, 7" 300.00
Blueberry, vase, gr transparent, rare, #1562, 1933, 10" 85.00
Cactus, shakers, vaseline, pr 75.00
Cameo Opalescent, candy dish, w/lid, #10 ....125.00
Cannonball, pitcher, cobalt w/decor, #821 ....150.00
Coin Dot, basket, cranberry opal, #1435, 4½" 110.00
Coin Dot, basket, cranberry opal, #1437, 7" 115.00
Coin Dot, bowl, cranberry opal, #1427, 7" 85.00
Coin Dot, bowl, Fr opal, #1522, 10" 55.00
Coin Dot, candlesticks, cranberry opal, #1524, 5¾", pr 195.00
Coin Dot, creamer, cranberry opal, #1461, 4" 65.00
Coin Dot, hat, cranberry opal, #1492, 3¼" 80.00
Coin Dot, hat vase, Fr opal, #1455, 5" 45.00
Coin Dot, pitcher, cranberry opal, ice lip, #1467, 9½" 375.00
Coin Dot, tumbler, cranberry opal, #1449, 9-oz 55.00
Coin Dot, vase, cranberry opal, #1450, 5" 85.00
Coin Dot, vase, cranberry opal, #189, 10" 145.00
Coin Dot, vase, cranberry opal, 6½" 75.00
Coin Dot, vase, yel opal, dbl-crimped, 7½" 95.00
Coin Spot, boudoir lamp, Fr opal 225.00
Daisy & Button, cologne, Royal Blue 125.00
Daisy & Button, powder box, vaseline 95.00
Daisy & Button, top hat, yel 24.00
Daisy & Button, vase, gr pastel, fan form, #1959, 8" 45.00
Daisy & Fern, hurricane lamp, topaz 265.00

Daisy & Fern, pitcher, yel opal, water sz 275.00
Dancing Ladies, bowl, Chinese Yellow, oval, #900, 1932, 11" 250.00
Dancing Ladies, bowl, milk glass, oval, #900, 1933, 11" 100.00
Dancing Ladies, vase, Jade Green, crimped, #901, 1933-35, 9" ..250.00
Dancing Ladies, vase, Periwinkle Blue, sq, #901, 1934, 9" 300.00

Diamond Lace, epergne, French opal with aqua crest, #4801, $315.00.

Diamond Optic, basket, Jade Green, #1502, 1933 ....30.00
Diamond Optic, bonbon, Jade Green, flared, #1502, 1927, 6" 45.00
Diamond Optic, bonbon, Orchid, #1502, 1927, 6" 45.00
Diamond Optic, bonbon, rose, cupped, #1235, 1936-37 ....22.00
Diamond Optic, cologne, gr transparent, #1502, 1927 ....60.00
Diamond Optic, cup, Celeste Blue, #1502 ....28.00
Diamond Optic, finger bowl, Orchid, #1502, 1928 ....20.00
Diamond Optic, goblet, Jade Green, #1502, 1928, 11-oz 25.00
Diamond Optic, goblet, Orchid, #1502, 1928, 11-oz 28.00
Diamond Optic, ice pail, blk, #1616, 1928, 6½" 57.00
Diamond Optic, jug, ruby o/l, w/hdl, 6" 78.00
Diamond Optic, pitcher, ruby o/l 150.00
Diamond Optic, vase, Mandarin Red, #1502, 1933, 10" 110.00
Diamond Optic/Melon, mini lamp, mulberry, w/chimney 250.00
Dolphin, bonbon, ruby, flared, ftd, #1502, 6" 28.00
Dolphin, bowl, blk, oval, w/hdl, ftd, #1601 ....145.00
Dolphin, bowl, blk, rolled rim, #1504-A, 1928, 10" 65.00
Dolphin, bowl, Lilac, #1504-A, 1933, 9" 150.00
Dolphin, bowl, Lilac, deep, oval, #1608, 10½" 225.00
Dolphin, bowl, rose, rolled rim, #1600, 10" 190.00
Dolphin, comport, Tangerine, ftd, #1533, 6" 135.00
Dot Optic, creamer, cranberry opal, 4" 65.00
Dot Optic, pitcher, cranberry opal, water sz 275.00
Dot Optic, sugar shaker, bl opal 100.00
Dot Optic, sugar shaker, cranberry opal, #2293 ....80.00
Emerald Crest, bottle, oil; w/gr stopper #7269 (#860) 90.00
Emerald Crest, compote, dbl-crimped 35.00
Emerald Crest, flowerpot, #7299, w/attached saucer 67.50
Emerald Crest, plate, torte; #7216, 16" 65.00
Emerald Crest, vase, dbl-crimped, 4¼" 30.00
Fenton's 'Fishing Boat,' crystal 35.00
Flame, bowl, shallow, cupped, #601, 1924, 10" 120.00
Gold Crest, vase, #7350, 5½" 50.00
Goldenrod, vase, melon ribs, dbl-crimped, 4½" 110.00
Grape & Cable, bowl, rose, rolled rim, #920, 11" 225.00
Grape & Cable, bowl, Venetian Red, crimped, #920, 11" 300.00
Grecian Gold, iced-tea tumbler, cut w/grapes, #1352 ....45.00
Green Pastel, fairy lamp, 2-pc, #7390 ....100.00
Hobnail, ashtray, milk glass, #3810, 2-pc 18.00
Hobnail, basket, topaz opal, 7" 135.00
Hobnail, bonbon, gr opal, dbl-crimped, 5" 22.00
Hobnail, boudoir lamp, milk glass, pr 100.00
Hobnail, bowl, bl opal, dbl-crimped, 10" 65.00
Hobnail, bowl, cranberry opal, 10½" 65.00
Hobnail, butter dish, milk glass, ¼-lb 35.00
Hobnail, cake plate, milk glass, ftd, 12½" 34.00

Hobnail, candle holder, wht, ring hdl, ea 25.00
Hobnail, candlesticks, ruby, #3974, pr 28.00
Hobnail, candlesticks, yel opal, #3974, pr 75.00
Hobnail, cologne, bl opal, #3865 ....85.00
Hobnail, covered slipper, bl marble, #3700 ....45.00
Hobnail, creamer & sugar bowl, Fr opal, mini 20.00
Hobnail, creamer & sugar bowl, Fr opal, star shape 35.00
Hobnail, cruet, bl opal, #869 ....38.00
Hobnail, epergne, Fr opal, 4-pc 85.00
Hobnail, fan vase, bl opal, 6¼" 42.00
Hobnail, lamp, courting; amber, #3792, electric 85.00
Hobnail, lavabo, milk glass, #3867 ....130.00
Hobnail, mustard, bl opal, w/spoon, #3889 ....32.00
Hobnail, mustard, topaz opal 75.00
Hobnail, oil cruet, bl opal, w/stopper 38.00
Hobnail, pitcher, milk glass, juice sz 40.00
Hobnail, pitcher, yel opal, 5" 75.00
Hobnail, powder jar, bl opal, 1950s 55.00
Hobnail, punch set, milk glass, octagonal, #3820 ....500.00
Hobnail, shakers, bl opal, flat, pr 40.00
Hobnail, shakers, bl opal, ftd, pr 75.00
Hobnail, shakers, milk glass, ftd, pr 45.00
Hobnail, sherbet, dk amber, #3825, early 12.00
Hobnail, spoon holder, milk glass, #3612 ....70.00
Hobnail, tidbit, wht, 2-tier 55.00
Hobnail, vase, bl opal, dbl-crimped, #389, 3½" 24.00
Hobnail, vase, Colonial Green, #3653, 5" 15.00
Hobnail, vase, cranberry opal, dbl-crimped, wide body, 4½" 50.00
Hobnail, vase, cranberry opal, dbl-crimped, 6" 90.00
Hobnail, vase, cranberry opal, dbl-crimped, 8" 125.00
Hobnail, vase, Fr opal, mini, 4" 30.00
Hobnail, vase, milk glass, dbl-crimped, 11" 40.00
Hobnail, vase, ruby, 4½" 25.00
Hobnail, vase, topaz opal, ftd, 6" 55.00
Hyacinth, vase, Mandarin Red, #180, 1935 ....250.00
Ivory Crest, candlesticks, cornucopia form, 6", pr 70.00
Jacqueline, pitcher, honey amber, #9166 ....75.00
Jade Green, bowl, #847, 7" 30.00
Jade Green, bowl, cupped, #847, 1932, 6" 28.00
Jade Green, bowl, oval, #1563, 17" 95.00
Jade Green, cigarette holder, #556, 1934 ....95.00
Jade Green, pancake lamp, no decor, #G 70 ....150.00
Jade Green, puff box, #57 ....55.00
Jade Green, vase, flared, #184, 10" 90.00
Leaf Tiers, bowl, Jade Green, cupped, #1790, 1935, 8" 125.00
Lilac, comport, #1536 ....100.00
Lilac cased, shell bowl, #9020, 10" 100.00
Lily of the Valley, candlesticks, bl opal, #3974, pr 40.00
Mandarin Red, basket, wicker hdl, #1684, 1933-35 ....175.00
Mandarin Red, bowl, console; oval, #950 ....175.00
Mandarin Red, macaroon jar, #1684, 1933-35, 6½" 165.00
Mikado, cake plate, Mandarin Red, high ft, #919, 1934 ....350.00
Ming Green, bowl, crimped, 3-toed, #249, 9" 40.00
Ming Green, bowl, 8-sided, 9", w/liner 350.00
Ming Green, pitcher, rare blk hdl, #1653 ....165.00
Ming Pink, basket, wicker handle, #1684, 9" 125.00
Ming Pink, bowl, oval, #950, 11" 75.00
Ming Pink, console, oval 85.00
Ming Pink, macaroon jar, wicker hdl, 1684, 6½" 135.00
Mongolian Green, bowl, flared, #846, 1934, 8½" 47.00
Mongolian Green, vase, flared, #1093, 5½" 95.00
Peach Crest, jack-in-the-pulpit vase, 8½" 75.00
Peach Crest, shell bowl, #9020 ....95.00
Peach Crest, top hat 42.50

Peach Crest, vase, dbl-crimped, tall	50.00
Peacock, vase, Mandarin Red, 8"	150.00
Peacock, vase, milk glass, flared, #791, 1933, 8"	75.00
Pekin Blue, candlestick, #549, 1924, 8½", ea	85.00
Pekin Blue, cologne, #53, 1932, 5"	125.00
Periwinkle Blue, vase, sq top, #621, 1934, 8"	95.00
Poppy, student lamp, Colonial Green, #9107, 20"	170.00
Rose Crest, fan vase, ftd, 4½"	35.00
Rose Crest, vase, melon ribs, dbl-crimped, 8"	50.00
Rose Overlay, basket, 6½"	65.00
Royal Blue, cornucopia candlestick, #950, 1934, ea	50.00
Ruby, plate, leaf pattern etching, #1639, 6"	45.00
Sheffield, bowl, Halo etching, rolled rim, #1800, 12"	95.00
Sheffield, rose bowl, aquamarine, flat, 1936-38	20.00
Sheffield, tulip vase, ruby, 1936-38, 6½"	27.00
Sheffield, vase, bl, ftd	30.00
Silver Crest, basket, 7" dia	35.00
Silver Crest, bowl, dbl-crimped, 12"	37.00
Silver Crest, bowl, tricorn, 7½"	35.00
Silver Crest, bowl, 6-sided, #7338	38.00
Silver Crest, bowl, 68-oz, 9½"	46.00
Silver Crest, cake salver, ped ft, #7213, 13"	50.00
Silver Crest, candlesticks, 3¼", pr	37.00
Silver Crest, compote, 7" dia	30.00
Silver Crest, epergne, 4-part, #7308	125.00
Silver Crest, heart bowl, 1-hdl	27.00
Silver Crest, nut dish, 3-ftd	17.00
Silver Crest, plate, 8½"	20.00
Silver Crest, rose bowl, ftd, 6"	55.00
Silver Crest, tidbit, 2-tier, #7294	48.00
Silver Crest, top hat basket, hdld, 5"	45.00
Silver Crest, vase, fan form, #573, 8½"	35.00

Snow Crest, hat vase, amber, #1921, 7", $45.00.

Special Rose, bowl, Fr opal, #201	65.00
Spiral Optic, vase, gr opal	50.00
Stag & Holly, bowl, blk, rolled rim, #1608, 1916, 10"	150.00
Stag & Holly, bowl, rose, shallow or crimped, #1608, 1932, 10"	45.00
Stretch, fan vase, gr, ftd, 5¼"	35.00
Stretch, puff box, gr, #743	55.00
Tangerine, vase, #1530, 1928, 12"	150.00
Thumbprint, plate, ruby, 8"	20.00
Thumbprint, sherbet, ruby	14.00
Thumbprint, wine, ruby	20.00
Vasa Murrhina, basket, Blue Mist, #6458, 11"	95.00
Venetian Red, ashtray, 1927, #1566	85.00
Wisteria, bowl, oval, #6, 11"	95.00
Wisteria, candlestick, #749, 12", ea	160.00
Wisteria, pitcher, iced tea; #222	250.00

Fiesta

Fiesta is a line of dinnerware produced by the Homer Laughlin China Company of Newell, West Virginia, from 1936 until 1973. It was made in eleven different solid colors with over fifty pieces in the assortment. The pattern was developed by Frederick Rhead, an English Stoke-on-Trent potter who was an important contributor to the art-pottery movement in this country during the early part of the century. The design was carried out through the use of a simple band-of-rings device near the rim. Fiesta Red, a strong red-orange glaze color, was made with depleted uranium oxide. It was more expensive to produce than the other colors and sold at higher prices. Today's collectors still pay premium prices for Fiesta Red pieces. During the '50s the color assortment was gray, rose, chartreuse, and dark green. These colors are relatively harder to find and along with Fiesta Red and medium green (new in 1959) command the highest prices.

Fiesta Kitchen Kraft was introduced in 1939; it consisted of seventeen pieces of kitchenware such as pie plates, refrigerator sets, mixing bowls, and covered jars in four popular Fiesta colors.

As a final attempt to adapt production to modern-day techniques and methods, Fiesta was restyled in 1969. Of the original colors, only Fiesta Red remained. This line, called Fiesta Ironstone, was discontinued in 1973.

Two types of marks were used: an ink stamp on machine-jiggered pieces and an indented mark molded into the hollow ware pieces.

In 1986 HLC reintroduced a line of Fiesta dinnerware in five colors: black, white, pink, apricot, and cobalt (darker and denser than the original shade). Since then yellow, turquoise, seafoam green, 'country' blue, lilac, persimmon, sapphire blue, and chartreuse have been added. Collectors have found that the new line poses no threat to their investments.

In the listings below, 'original colors' indicates only three of the original six — light green, turquoise, and yellow (or those remaining after specific original colors have been priced). Red, ivory, and cobalt values are listed separately. Turquoise was the last original color to be introduced, so the items that were discontinued in 1946 are harder to find in that color (since it had a shorter production run), and values fall into the upper price range along with red, cobalt, and ivory. These are designated with an asterisk.

For more information we recommend *The Collector's Encyclopedia of Fiesta, Harlequin, and Riviera* (values updated in 1998) by Sharon and Bob Huxford (Collector Books).

Dinnerware

Ashtray, '50s colors	88.00
Ashtray, orig colors	47.00
Ashtray, red, cobalt or ivory	60.00
Bowl, covered onion soup; cobalt or ivory	750.00
Bowl, covered onion soup; red	750.00
Bowl, covered onion soup; turq, minimum value	8,000.00
Bowl, covered onion soup; yel or lt gr	600.00
Bowl, cream soup; '50s colors	72.00
Bowl, cream soup; med gr, minimum value	4,000.00
Bowl, cream soup; orig colors	42.00
Bowl, cream soup; red, cobalt or ivory	60.00
Bowl, dessert; '50s colors, 6"	52.00
Bowl, dessert; med gr, 6"	475.00
Bowl, dessert; orig colors, 6"	38.00
Bowl, dessert; red, cobalt or ivory, 6"	52.00
Bowl, fruit; '50s colors, 4¾"	40.00
Bowl, fruit; '50s colors, 5½"	40.00
Bowl, fruit; med gr, 4¾"	485.00
Bowl, fruit; med gr, 5½"	75.00
Bowl, fruit; orig colors, 4¾"	28.00
Bowl, fruit; orig colors, 5½"	28.00
Bowl, fruit; orig colors, 11¾"	300.00
Bowl, fruit; red, cobalt or ivory, 4¾"	35.00
Bowl, fruit; red, cobalt or ivory, 5½"	35.00

Bowl, fruit; red, cobalt or ivory, 11¾" * 300.00
Bowl, ftd salad; orig colors 300.00
Bowl, ftd salad; red, cobalt or ivory * 350.00
Bowl, ind salad; med gr, 7½" 105.00
Bowl, ind salad; red, turq or yel, 7½" 85.00
Bowl, nappy; '50s colors, 8½" 65.00
Bowl, nappy; med gr, 8½" 140.00
Bowl, nappy; orig colors, 8½" 40.00
Bowl, nappy; orig colors, 9½" 52.00
Bowl, nappy; red, cobalt or ivory, 8½" * 60.00
Bowl, nappy; red, cobalt or ivory, 9½" * 65.00
Bowl, Tom & Jerry; ivory w/gold letters 260.00
Bowl, unlisted salad; red, cobalt, or ivory, minimum value 500.00
Bowl, unlisted salad; yel 105.00
Candle holders, bulb; orig colors, pr 95.00
Candle holders, bulb; red, cobalt or ivory, pr * 130.00
Candle holders, tripod; orig colors, pr 465.00
Candle holders, tripod; red, cobalt or ivory, pr * 600.00
Carafe, orig colors 250.00
Carafe, red, cobalt or ivory * 300.00
Casserole, '50s colors 300.00
Casserole, French; standard colors other than yel 650.00
Casserole, French; yel 300.00
Casserole, med gr 725.00
Casserole, orig colors 150.00
Casserole, red, cobalt or ivory 200.00
Coffeepot, '50s colors 350.00
Coffeepot, demi; orig colors 340.00
Coffeepot, demi; red, cobalt or ivory * 435.00
Coffeepot, orig colors 195.00
Coffeepot, red, cobalt or ivory 245.00
Compote, orig colors, 12" 148.00
Compote, red, cobalt or ivory, 12" * 185.00
Compote, sweets; orig colors 75.00
Compote, sweets; red, cobalt or ivory * 90.00
Creamer, '50s colors 40.00
Creamer, ind; red 250.00
Creamer, ind; turq or cobalt 345.00
Creamer, ind; yel 70.00
Creamer, med gr 80.00
Creamer, orig colors 22.00
Creamer, red, cobalt or ivory 35.00
Creamer, stick hdld, orig colors 45.00
Creamer, stick hdld, red, cobalt or ivory * 70.00
Cup, demi; '50s colors 350.00
Cup, demi; orig colors 65.00
Cup, demi; red, cobalt or ivory 75.00

Egg cup: Red, cobalt, or ivory, $70.00; Original colors, $58.00; '50s colors, $160.00.

Lid, for mixing bowl #1-#3, any color, minimum value 785.00
Lid, for mixing bowl #4, any color, minimum value 1,000.00
Marmalade, orig colors 230.00
Marmalade, red, cobalt or ivory * 285.00

Mixing bowl, #1, orig colors 170.00
Mixing bowl, #1, red, cobalt or ivory * 225.00
Mixing bowl, #2, orig colors 110.00
Mixing bowl, #2, red, cobalt or ivory * 125.00
Mixing bowl, #3, orig colors 120.00
Mixing bowl, #3, red, cobalt or ivory * 130.00
Mixing bowl, #4, orig colors 130.00
Mixing bowl, #4, red, cobalt or ivory * 155.00
Mixing bowl, #5, orig colors 155.00
Mixing bowl, #5, red, cobalt or ivory * 185.00
Mixing bowl, #6, orig colors 200.00
Mixing bowl, #6, red, cobalt or ivory * 265.00
Mixing bowl, #7, orig colors 280.00
Mixing bowl, #7, red, cobalt or ivory * 350.00
Mug, Tom & Jerry; '50s colors 100.00
Mug, Tom & Jerry; ivory w/gold letters 65.00
Mug, Tom & Jerry; orig colors 60.00
Mug, Tom & Jerry; red, cobalt or ivory 85.00
Mustard, orig colors 200.00
Mustard, red, cobalt or ivory * 250.00
Pitcher, disk juice; gray, minimum value 2,500.00
Pitcher, disk juice; Harlequin yel 62.00
Pitcher, disk juice; red 450.00
Pitcher, disk juice; yel 45.00
Pitcher, disk water; '50s colors 275.00
Pitcher, disk water; med gr, minimum value 1,150.00
Pitcher, disk water; orig colors 125.00
Pitcher, disk water; red, cobalt or ivory 165.00
Pitcher, ice; orig colors 140.00
Pitcher, ice; red, cobalt or ivory * 160.00
Pitcher, jug, 2-pt; '50s colors 150.00
Pitcher, jug, 2-pt; orig colors 90.00
Pitcher, jug, 2-pt; red, cobalt or ivory 120.00
Plate, '50s colors, 6" 9.00
Plate, '50s colors, 7" 13.00
Plate, '50s colors, 9" 22.00
Plate, '50s colors, 10" 52.00
Plate, cake; orig colors 755.00
Plate, cake; red, cobalt or ivory * 885.00
Plate, calendar; 1954 or 1955, 10" 45.00
Plate, calendar; 1955, 9" 50.00
Plate, chop; '50s colors, 13" 100.00
Plate, chop; '50s colors, 15" 115.00
Plate, chop; med gr, 13" 275.00
Plate, chop; orig colors, 13" 35.00
Plate, chop; orig colors, 15" 48.00
Plate, chop; red, cobalt or ivory, 13" 55.00
Plate, chop; red, cobalt or ivory, 15" 75.00
Plate, compartment; '50s colors, 10½" 75.00
Plate, compartment; orig colors, 10½" 40.00
Plate, compartment; orig colors, 12" 50.00
Plate, compartment; red, cobalt or ivory, 10½" 40.00
Plate, compartment; red, cobalt or ivory, 12" 60.00
Plate, deep; '50s colors 55.00
Plate, deep; med gr 120.00
Plate, deep; orig colors 40.00
Plate, deep; red, cobalt or ivory 60.00
Plate, med gr, 6" 20.00
Plate, med gr, 7" 32.00
Plate, med gr, 9" 45.00
Plate, med gr, 10" 110.00
Plate, orig colors, 6" 5.00
Plate, orig colors, 7" 9.00
Plate, orig colors, 9" 12.00

Plate, orig colors, 10" 32.00
Plate, red, cobalt or ivory, 6" 7.00
Plate, red, cobalt or ivory, 7" 10.00
Plate, red, cobalt or ivory, 9" 18.00
Plate, red, cobalt or ivory, 10" 40.00
Platter, '50s colors 58.00
Platter, med gr 140.00
Platter, orig colors 35.00
Platter, red, cobalt or ivory 45.00
Relish tray, gold decor, complete 250.00
Relish tray base, orig colors 65.00
Relish tray base, red, cobalt or ivory * 85.00
Relish tray center insert, orig colors 42.00
Relish tray center insert, red, cobalt or ivory * 55.00
Relish tray side insert, orig colors 40.00
Relish tray side insert, red, cobalt or ivory * 48.00
Sauce boat, '50s colors 78.00
Sauce boat, med gr 155.00
Sauce boat, orig colors 45.00
Sauce boat, red, cobalt or ivory 75.00
Saucer, '50s colors 6.00
Saucer, demi; '50s colors 95.00
Saucer, demi; orig colors 18.00
Saucer, demi; red, cobalt or ivory 22.00
Saucer, med gr 12.00
Saucer, orig colors 4.00
Saucer, red, cobalt or ivory 5.00
Shakers, '50s colors, pr 45.00
Shakers, med gr, pr 140.00
Shakers, orig colors, pr 22.00
Shakers, red, cobalt or ivory, pr 30.00
Sugar bowl, ind; turq 350.00
Sugar bowl, ind; yel 120.00
Sugar bowl, w/lid, '50s colors, 3¼x3½" 72.00
Sugar bowl, w/lid, med gr, 3¼x3½" 160.00
Sugar bowl, w/lid, orig colors, 3¼x3½" 45.00
Sugar bowl, w/lid, red, cobalt or ivory, 3¼x3½" 55.00
Syrup, orig colors 325.00
Syrup, red, cobalt or ivory * 400.00
Teacup, '50s colors 38.00
Teacup, med gr 58.00
Teacup, orig colors 25.00
Teacup, red, cobalt or ivory 35.00

Teapot, medium: Original colors, $165.00; Red, cobalt, or ivory, $200.00.

Teapot, lg; orig colors 185.00
Teapot, lg; red, cobalt or ivory * 220.00
Teapot, med; '50s colors 325.00
Teapot, med; med gr, minimum value 1,000.00
Tray, figure-8; cobalt 90.00
Tray, figure-8; turq or yel 350.00
Tray, utility; orig colors 38.00

Tray, utility; red, cobalt or ivory * 42.00
Tumbler, juice; chartreuse, Harlequin yel or dk gr 460.00
Tumbler, juice; orig colors 40.00
Tumbler, juice; red, cobalt or ivory 45.00
Tumbler, juice; rose 65.00
Tumbler, water; orig colors 60.00
Tumbler, water; red, cobalt or ivory * 85.00
Vase, bud; orig colors 80.00
Vase, bud; red, cobalt or ivory * 110.00
Vase, orig colors, 10" 750.00
Vase, orig colors, 12", minimum value 1,000.00
Vase, orig colors, 8" 600.00
Vase, red, cobalt or ivory, 10" * 850.00
Vase, red, cobalt or ivory, 12", minimum value * 1,200.00
Vase, red, cobalt or ivory, 8" * 700.00

Kitchen Kraft

Covered jug, red or cobalt, $275.00.

Bowl, mixing; lt gr or yel, 6" 65.00
Bowl, mixing; lt gr or yel, 8" 82.00
Bowl, mixing; lt gr or yel, 10" 100.00
Bowl, mixing; red or cobalt, 6" 75.00
Bowl, mixing; red or cobalt, 8" 92.00
Bowl, mixing; red or cobalt, 10" 120.00
Cake plate, lt gr or yel 55.00
Cake plate, red or cobalt 65.00
Cake server, lt gr or yel 130.00
Cake server, red or cobalt 140.00
Casserole, ind; lt gr or yel 140.00
Casserole, ind; red or cobalt 155.00
Casserole, lt gr or yel, 7½" 85.00
Casserole, lt gr or yel, 8½" 100.00
Casserole, red or cobalt, 7½" 90.00
Casserole, red or cobalt, 8½" 110.00
Covered jar, lg; lt gr or yel 300.00
Covered jar, lg; red or cobalt 320.00
Covered jar, med; lt gr or yel 260.00
Covered jar, med; red or cobalt 280.00
Covered jar, sm; lt gr or yel 270.00
Covered jar, sm; red or cobalt 290.00
Covered jug, lt gr or yel 250.00
Fork, lt gr or yel 100.00
Fork, red or cobalt 125.00
Metal frame for platter 26.00
Pie plate, lt gr or yel, 9" 40.00
Pie plate, lt gr or yel, 10" 40.00
Pie plate, red or cobalt, 9" 45.00
Pie plate, red or cobalt, 10" 45.00
Pie plate, spruce gr 290.00
Platter, lt gr or yel 68.00
Platter, red or cobalt 78.00
Platter, spruce gr 350.00
Shakers, lt gr or yel, pr 95.00

Shakers, red or cobalt, pr **105.00**
Spoon, ivory, 12", minimum value **500.00**
Spoon, lt gr or yel **100.00**
Spoon, red or cobalt **125.00**
Stacking refrigerator lid, ivory **205.00**
Stacking refrigerator lid, lt gr or yel **70.00**
Stacking refrigerator lid, red or cobalt **80.00**
Stacking refrigerator unit, ivory **195.00**
Stacking refrigerator unit, lt gr or yel **45.00**
Stacking refrigerator unit, red or cobalt **55.00**

Fifties Modern

Postwar furniture design is marked by organic shapes and lighter woods and forms. New materials from war research such as molded plywood and fiberglass were used extensively. For the first time, design was extended to the masses and the baby-boomer generation grew up surrounded by modern shape and color, the perfect expression of postwar optimism. The top designers in America worked for Herman Miller and Knoll Furniture Company. These include Charles Eames, George Nelson, and Eero Saarinen.

Unless noted otherwise values are given for furnishings in excellent condition; glassware and ceramic items are assumed to be in mint condition. This information was provided to us by Richard Wright. See also Italian Glass.

Key:
fbrg — fiberglass	uphl — upholstered
lcq — lacquered	vnr — veneer

Armchair, aluminum fr w/'omega' sides, uphl bk/seat, no mk ..**1,300.00**
Armchair, Eames/Miller, orange fbrg shell on cat's-cradle base ..**400.00**
Armchair, Nelson/Miller, fbrg, 2-part shock-mt, 4-leg base **850.00**
Armchair, Rasmusen, Safari, bk tilts, ash-fr leather sling **350.00**
Armchair, Wormley/Dunbar, ash laminate, caned bk/leather seat ...**225.00**
Armchair, Wormley/Dunbar, walnut/Naugahyde, spindle sides, pr .**200.00**
Armchair rocker, Eames/Miller, fbrg on Eiffel Tower wire base ..**750.00**
Armchairs, Eames/Miller, Aluminum Group, swivel, vinyl, set of 4 .....**750.00**
Armchairs, Eames/Miller, Aluminum Group, swivel, wood, set of 4 .**1,100.00**
Bed fr, mahog vnr, panel headboard/sides, single, VG **200.00**
Bedroom suite, Heywood-Wakefield, Riviera, Champagne finish, 6-pc .**850.00**
Bench, Nelson/Miller, Primavera w/slatted platform top, 68" **800.00**
Bottle, Beatrice Wood, volcanic bl/yel, 4¾x2½" **1,300.00**
Bottle, Fantoni/Raymor, gr/orange-red flambe, flattened, 10x9" .**300.00**
Bowl, Lukens, bubbled/wavy pk glass, 2½x14" **200.00**
Buffet, Nelson/Miller, walnut vnr, 2 doors/4 drw, worn, 56" **700.00**
Buffet, Powell, walnut, 3 sliding linen-panel doors, 114" **2,900.00**
Cabinet, china; McCobb/Calvin, mahog vnr, sliding glass, 60x48" .**250.00**
Cabinet, Nelson/Miller, combed oak vnr, 2-door, 30x34" **1,300.00**
Chair, Aalto/Artek, molded C-shaped sides, reuphl, VG **2,300.00**
Chair, angular bronzed steel fr, wood armrests, uphl slat bk **500.00**
Chair, Bertoia/Knoll, Diamond, blk wire grid construction **300.00**
Chair, Eames/Miller, fbrg shell, birch rockers, wire base, VG ..**1,300.00**
Chair, Eames/Miller, fbrg shell on aluminum ped, 32", EX **90.00**
Chair, Eames/Miller LCM, red dyed & molded plywood seat/bk .**800.00**
Chair, Eames/Miller LCW, molded blond wood: seat/bk/legs, 27" ..**750.00**
Chair, Erwin & Estelle Laverne, Tulip style, wht fbrg **1,400.00**
Chair, Gould (Wegner style), wrought fr, string web seat/bk **500.00**
Chair, Hansen/Jacobsen, wool-uphl swan style, X base, EX **425.00**
Chair, Kopod-Larsen, wrap-around wood bk, leather seat, pr **325.00**
Chair, lounge; Gray, Trans-At, leather sling seat, wood fr, 40" ..**2,000.00**
Chair, lounge; Matheson, bentwood fr, webbed J-shape bk/seat .**500.00**
Chair, lounge; Risom/Knoll, bentwood birch fr, cotton webbing ..**1,600.00**

Chair, lounge; Wegner/Getama, cord on steel fr w/headrest, 44" ...**3,500.00**
Chair, Nelson/Miller, shaped fbrg w/arms, swag 4-leg base **700.00**
Chair & ottoman, Nelson/Miller, Coconut, naugahyde/chrome ..**7,000.00**
Chair & ottoman, Saarinen/Knoll, Grasshopper, reuphl, VG .**1,800.00**
Chairs, dining; Cherner, formed plywood, 2 w/arms+4 sides ...**1,600.00**
Chairs, dining; Italian, 6-slat ladder-bk, blk lacquer, 6 for **850.00**
Chairs, dining; Wear-Ever, vinyl seats/bks, aluminum fr, set of 4 ..**100.00**
Chairs, Eames/Miller DCM, 2-part molded wood, tube chrome, 4 for **950.00**
Chairs, McCobb/Winchedon, Planner Group, maple, 4 for **150.00**
Chairs, Panton, S style, blk uphl, rnd base, no mk, 4 for **2,200.00**
Chairs, Panton/Miller, molded plastic, stacking, mc, 6 for **850.00**
Chaise lounge, Mathsson/Mathsson, bentwood w/web uphl, 66" **1,600.00**

Chest, Charles Eames for Herman Miller, First Series ESU #200 Series, three-drawer, angle-iron corners, birch fronts, ca 1950, 33x24x16", $2,400.00.

Chest, Mont, 3-drw, sandblasted/pickled oak front, 34x46" **2,900.00**
Chest, Rhode, exotic vnr, 3 curve-front drws, inlaid base, 46" ...**750.00**
Clock, Miller, Built-in Wall, hour markers, hands, MIB **150.00**
Clock, Miller, Chronopak, walnut hemisphere on wire base, 7x6" **225.00**
Clock, Nelson/Miller, brass w/blk face, Lucite front, 6x5" dia **550.00**
Clock, Nelson/Miller, Zoo, neon orange bird-shape case, 11½" .**230.00**
Clock, wall; Nelson/Miller, Asterisk, brass/enamel, 10" dia **500.00**
Credenza, Risom, walnut vnr, door+4 drws, recessed legs, 54" **450.00**
Desk, child's, Russel Wright/Conant Ball, 3-drw bank, rfn **200.00**
Desk, Heywood-Wakefield, keyhole style, birch, 6 drw, +chair ..**750.00**
Desk, Nelson/Miller, oak vnr drop-front, aluminum legs, 41", VG ..**1,300.00**
Desk, Ponti/Singer, walnut, open shelf under top, rfn, 51" **3,750.00**
Desk, Risom, walnut vnr, side drw, dowel legs, 51" **450.00**
Desk, walnut vnr, 4 sm drw in right bank, wood pulls, 56", EX ..**600.00**
Dining suite, Wormley/Dunbar, walnut, caned seat/bks, 7-pc .**1,500.00**
Fabric, Dan Cooper, loose-weave cotton w/fish, 8 yds, EX **175.00**
Globe stand, Wormley/Dunbar, maple, for Rand McNally globe, 35" **450.00**
Lamp, Aulenti, Pipistrello, molded plastic shade/base, 24", VG .**475.00**
Lamp, desk; chrome w/semi-spherical shade, L-shape base, 13x10" **150.00**
Lamp, floor; Arco, chrome shade & arched armature, marble base .**1,800.00**
Lamp, floor; Light-o-lier, 3 blk shades/tripod base, 45" **950.00**
Lamp, floor; ½-bowl wht Murano shade, chrome shaft, marble base .**700.00**
Lamp, Nelson/Miller, Bubble, sprayed plastic over wire ball, VG ...**425.00**
Lamp, table; Evans, wide twisted brass ribbon base, 54" **150.00**
Lamp, table; Laurel, Portable, frosted wht glass mushroom, 14" .**325.00**
Lamp, table; O-on-trapezoid alabaster base, linen shade, 27", pr ...**550.00**
Light fixture, Henningsen PH, stacked wht-pnt metal circles **550.00**
Light fixture, Henningsen PH5, 3-tier, pnt metal, 9x24" dia **750.00**
Light fixture, Lightolier, cubic plexiglass/chrome, 17-light **150.00**
Light fixture, Nelson/Miller, parchment bubble over wire, 11x24" **550.00**
Light fixture, Venini, amethyst/wht stripes, onion shape, 14" **275.00**
Light fixture, Venini/att Vignelli, cased/brn & wht canes, 14" ...**275.00**
Light fixture, wht plastic cylinder in 14" slatted teak ball **150.00**
Light fixture, 8 sm balls on spokes, wht enamel center, 24" dia **80.00**

Loveseat, Heywood-Wakefield, naugahyde, open arms, 45", pr ..450.00
Ottman, Wormley/Dunbar, rnd w/orange-section seaming, 16x24" ..290.00
Ottoman, gray/wht chevron damask uphl, mahog base, 6-sided .300.00
Ottoman, Heywood-Wakefield, orange-section uphl, wood legs ..200.00
Plate, HV Poor, ceramic, mtn landscape, firing flaws, 9" 600.00
Plate rack, Nakashima, blk walnut, linen lined, 33x45x5" 850.00
Rug, Matisse/Smith & Sons, Mimosa, abstract, 57x36", VG ..2,900.00
Rug, shag pile rya, brn/rust geometrics on yel/orange, 6x4', EX ..150.00
Rug, Tapetes Banderantes, geometrics on red, 56x77" 500.00
Rug, Tapetes Banderantes, wool, mc lines/sqs on gr, 77x68" 650.00
Sconce, Evans, Brutal Look, soldered corseted iron pcs, pr 425.00
Screen, Shoji, 5-panel, fir/rice paper, 130x35", VG 1,000.00
Sculpture, Cubist-style head, marble, gray stone base, 11" 450.00
Sculpture, Gambone, clay elephant, frothy pastel glazes, 5x6x5", EX ..150.00
Seating unit, Nelson/Miller, 1-arm sofa+table w/2 cushions, 124" 1,100.00
Serving cart, McCobb/Calvin, walnut top, chrome legs, 2-drw ..350.00
Settee, Plattner/Knoll, curved uphl bk/seat, wire base 650.00
Shelf unit, McCobb/Calvin, mahog vnr w/brass fr, 4-drw, 49x38" ...400.00
Shelving unit, Eames/Miller, ESU 400, 6-color panels, 58x47" ..12,000.00
Sideboard, Wormley/Dunbar, #4579B, walnut/mahog, Chinese hdw, 69" ..1,400.00
Sofa, att Knoll, walnut fr, webbed foundation, blk fabric, 81" .4,000.01
Sofa, Eames/Miller, Compact, slab seat/blk, naugahyde, 72", VG .1,000.00
Sofa, Wormley/Dunbar, tufted reuphl, Xd mahog base, 89", VG ..1,100.00
Stool, Eames/Miller, Time Life, trn walnut w/concave seat, 15" ..1,300.00
Storage unit, Nakashima, spindles-over-linen front, 30x90x17" ..4,000.00
Table, coffee; Danish walnut, hanging corner shelf, 50" 175.00
Table, coffee; Dunbar, walnut slat fr, blk top, 2-shelf, 53", EX ...425.00
Table, coffee; Eames/Miller, Surfboard, wire base, 89", VG 1,500.00
Table, coffee; Plattner/Knoll, 36" dia glass top, wire base 275.00
Table, coffee; Plattner/Knoll, 43" dia glass top, wire base 500.00
Table, coffee; Ponti/Singer, terrazzo on walnut fr, 60", VG 1,400.00
Table, coffee; 42" dia glass top, aluminum propeller base 575.00
Table, dining; Belman/Knoll, Popsicle Stick, birch, 48" dia, VG ..2,000.00
Table, dining; Juhl/Bovirke, rosewood, 59", 14 chairs, VG 1,700.00
Table, dining; Nelson/Miller, laminate top, chrome legs, 54" 475.00
Table, dining; Noguchi, Rudder, free-form, 3rd leg is fin-shape ..3,250.00
Table, dining; Saarineen/Knoll, Tulip, wht laminate 78" oval ...2,300.00
Table, dining; Saarineen/Knoll, Tulip, 42" dia wht marble top ..650.00
Table, dining; Wormley/Dunbar, maple vnr/bleached mahog, 66", G 260.00
Table, Eames/Miller, Surfboard, plywood/wire, rstr, 89", G 1,300.00
Table, Eames/Miller CTM, 34" dia plywood top, chrome legs, 16", EX ..450.00
Table, Eames/Miller CTW, blk lacquered top, bentwood legs, 35" ..800.00
Table, end; Heywood-Wakefield, Champagne, w/shelf, 28x21x15", pr ..225.00
Table, end; Keal/Brown-Saltman, blond maple, recessed top, pr .175.00
Table, Evans/Powell, 41" dia walnut top, flared wire base, 27" .1,000.00
Table, extension; Risom/Drexel, walnut, overhang top, 40x58x29" ..400.00
Table, Frankl/Johnson, 2 tiers w/cork top on mahog, 24x36x33", G ..325.00
Table, lamp; mahog vnr, 6-sided, 3-panel base, 22x28", pr 2,400.00
Table, make-up; Rhode, wood vnr, 3 sm drw+4 cubby holes, 57" ..400.00
Table, McCobb/Calvin, faux wht marble 20" sq top, 15" 300.00
Table, Noguchi/Knoll, 30" dia laminate top on Xd wire base, 47" ...1,200.00
Table, Rhode/Miller, 27" free-form glass top, 3 leather legs 2,000.00
Table, side; Schultz/Knoll, 16" dia petal top, ped base, rpt 150.00
Table, trestle; Nakashima, cherry w/blk walnut trim, 72x42" ..5,000.00
Table, Wormley/Dunbar, 21x25" tile top, brass legs, 17" 800.00
Table, 33" sq blk lacquer top, 2 Xd tube chrome legs, 30" 100.00
Tables, stack; France/Daverkosen, teak, lg: 16x18x18", 3 for 200.00
Vanity, Nelson/Miller, walnut, 3-part, pop-up mirror, 88", EX .1,300.00

Finch, Kay

Kay Finch and her husband, Braden, operated a small pottery in Corona Del Mar, California, from 1939 to 1963. The company

remained small, employing from twenty to sixty local residents who Kay trained in all but the most requiring tasks, which she herself performed. The company produced animal and bird figurines, most notably dogs, Kay's favorites. Figures of 'Godey' type couples were also made, as were tableware (consisting of breakfast sets) and other artware. Most pieces were marked.

After Kay's husband, Braden, died in 1962, she closed the business. Some of her molds were sold to Freeman-McFarlin of El Monte, California, who soon contracted with Kay for new designs. Though the realism that is so evident in her original works is still strikingly apparent in these later pieces, none of the vibrant pastels or signature curliques are there.

Kay Finch died on June 21, 1993. Prices for her work have been climbing.

The New Kay Finch Ceramics Identification Guide (published in 1996), containing many reprints of original catalog pages, is available from Frances Finch Webb; she is listed in the Directory under California. For further information we recommend *The Collector's Encyclopedia of California Pottery, Second Edition,* by Jack Chipman and *Collectible Kay Finch* by Richard Martinez and Jean Frick (Collector Books). Another fine reference is *Kay Finch Ceramics, Her Enchanted World* (Schiffer), written by our advisors for this category, Mike Nickel and Cynthia Horvath; they are listed in the Directory under Michigan. See also Clubs and Newsletters.

Note: Original model numbers are included in the following descriptions — three-digit numbers indicate pre-1946 models. After 1946 they were assigned four-digit numbers, the first two digits representing the year of initial production. Prices below are for figurines decorated in multiple colors, not solid glazes.

Ashtray, pk, #4730, 4¼" 50.00
Bank, Winkie the pig, #185, 3¾x4" 150.00
Cookie jar, Cookie Puss, #4614, 11¾", minimum value 2,500.00
Cup & saucer, Briar Rose 35.00
Figurine, angel, #114a, #114b, or #114c, ea 50.00
Figurine, angel, wide-wing, #140A, 4" 200.00
Figurine, bear, Sleepy, #5004, 4½" 275.00
Figurine, birds, Mr & Mrs Bird, #434 & #453, 4½", 3", pr 225.00
Figurine, burro (prospector's), #475, lg, minimum value 850.00

Figurine, camel, #464,
4½x5½", $450.00.

Figurine, camel, Ship of the Desert, #464, 5½" 450.00
Figurine, cat, Ambrosia, #155, 10½", minimum value 700.00
Figurine, cat, Hannibal, #180, 10¼" 900.00
Figurine, cat, Jezebel, #179, 6" 225.00
Figurine, cats, Muff & Puff, #182 & #183, pr 195.00
Figurine, choir boy, #210, 7½" 125.00
Figurine, choir boy, kneeling, #211, 5½" 75.00
Figurine, dog, Afghan, sitting, #5553, 5¼" 550.00
Figurine, dog, Airedale, standing, #4832, 5x5" 550.00
Figurine, dog, cocker spaniel, blk, #5201, 8" 500.00
Figurine, dog, cocker spaniel, Vickie, #455, 11" 1,000.00
Figurine, dog, Pekingese, #154, 14" L 550.00

Figurine, dog, Pomeranian, Mitzi, #465, 10" 1,500.00
Figurine, dog, poodle begging, #5262, 8" 650.00
Figurine, dog, pups, Yorky; #170 & #171, pr 650.00
Figurine, ducks, Mama & Papa, #471 & #472, pr 650.00
Figurine, ducks, Peep & Jeep, #178a & #178b, 3", pr 100.00
Figurine, elephant, Peanuts, #191, 8½" 350.00
Figurine, elephant, Popcorn, #192, 6¾" 300.00
Figurine, elephant, Violet, Queen of Circus, #190, 17", minimum ...3,500.00
Figurine, Godey Couple, #122, 9½", pr 200.00
Figurine, Godey Couple, #160, 7½", pr 125.00
Figurine, hippo, #5109, 5" 600.00
Figurine, lamb, prancing, #168, 10½", minimum value 900.00
Figurine, lamb, standing, #109, 5½" 125.00

Happy monkey, minimum value $1,000.00.

Figurine, monkey, Jocko, #4842, 4" 250.00
Figurine, monkey, Monkeyshines, #4962, 9½" 950.00
Figurine, owl, Hoot, #187, 8½" 195.00
Figurine, owl, Toot, #188, 5¾" 100.00
Figurine, owl, Tootsie, #189, 3¾" 50.00
Figurine, penguin, Pete, #466, 7½" 450.00
Figurine, pig, Grampa, #163, 10x16" 1,500.00
Figurine, pig, Porky, #5055, 2¾x3" 275.00
Figurine, pig, Sassy, #166, 3¾" 95.00
Figurine, pig, Smiley, 6¾x8" 375.00
Figurine, rabbit, Cuddles, #4623, 11" 900.00
Figurine, rooster, Chanticleer, #129, 10¾" 500.00
Figurine, rooster & hen, Butch, #177, & Biddy, #178, he: 8½", pr 200.00
Figurine, squirrel family, Mama, Papa & Baby, #108a, b & c, 3-pc ...200.00
Figurine, stallion, no base, #213, 21" 3,500.00
Flower bowl, swan, #4956, 6½" 100.00
Heart box, #5051 ....75.00
Planter, Baby Block w/bear, 6½" 100.00
Platter, canape; hibiscus design, #5414, 16" 100.00
Soup tureen, turkey figural, #5361 ....495.00
Stein, w/afghan hdl 650.00
Wall pocket, girl, #5502, 11" 450.00
Wall pocket, Santa face, #5373, 9½" 450.00

Findlay Onyx and Floradine

Findlay, Ohio, was the location of the Dalzell, Gilmore, and Leighton Glass Company, one of at least sixteen companies that flourished there between 1886 and 1901. Their most famous ware, Onyx, is very rare. It was produced for only a short time beginning in 1889 due to the heavy losses incurred in the manufacturing process.

Onyx is layered glass, usually found in creamy white with a dainty floral pattern accented with metallic lustre that has been trapped

between the two layers. Other colors found on rare occasions include a light amber (with either no lustre or with gilt flowers), light amethyst (or lavender), and rose. Although old tradepaper articles indicate the company originally intended to produce the line in three distinct colors, long-time Onyx collectors report that aside from the white, production was very limited. Other colors of Onyx are very rare, and the few examples that are found tend to support the theory that production of colored Onyx ware remained for the most part in the experimental stage. Even three-layered items have been found (they are extremely rare) decorated with three-color flowers. As a rule of thumb, using white Onyx prices as a basis for evaluation, expect to pay two to five times more for colored examples.

Floradine is a separate line that was made with the Onyx molds. A single-layer rose satin glassware with white opal flowers, it is usually priced in the general range of colored Onyx.

Chipping around the rims is very common, and price is determined to a great extent by condition. Our advisors for this category are Betty and Clarence Maier; they are listed in the Directory under Pennsylvania.

Floradine

Bowl, fluted, squat bulbous base, 4" 950.00
Celery vase, fluted cylinder neck, bulbous body, 6½", EX 1,000.00
Celery vase, NM 1,800.00
Creamer, bulbous, 4⅝" 950.00
Mustard pot, NM 1,550.00
Mustard pot, 3¾", EX 1,000.00
Spooner, 4¾" 1,285.00
Sugar bowl, bulbous, w/lid, 5½" 1,200.00
Sugar shaker 1,500.00
Syrup pitcher 2,500.00
Toothpick holder, 2½" 1,500.00
Tumbler, slightly bulbous, 3⅝" 1,000.00

Onyx

Bowl, wht w/raspberry decor, fluted top, 2½x4½" 2,000.00
Bowl, wht w/silver decor, 2¾x8" 350.00
Butter dish, wht w/silver decor, 3x6" 1,250.00
Covered dish, wht w/silver decor, 5½" 1,000.00
Creamer, wht w/silver decor..485.00
Mustard, wht w/raspberry decor, hinged metal lid, 3¼" 2,900.00
Pitcher, water; wht w/silver decor, 8" 1,200.00
Shaker, wht w/silver decor, minor wear, 2¾" 650.00
Shaker, wht w/silver decor, Pat 2/23/1889, 2⅝" 800.00
Spooner, wht w/orange decor, 3¾" 950.00
Spooner, wht w/silver decor, 4½x4" 525.00
Sugar bowl, wht w/silver decor, 5½", EX 475.00
Sugar shaker, wht w/silver decor, 5½", from $450 to 545.00
Syrup, wht w/silver decor, 7¾", from $850 to 1,150.00
Toothpick holder, wht w/silver decor, 2½" 500.00
Tumbler, wht w/apricot decor, 3½" 2,000.00
Tumbler, wht w/silver decor, bbl shape, 3½" 450.00

Fire Marks

The earliest American fire marks date back to 1752 when 'The Philadelphia Contributionship for the Insurance of Houses From Loss By Fire' (the official name of this company, still in business!) used a plaque to identify property they insured. The first fire marks were made of cast iron; later, sheet brass, lead, copper, tin, and zinc were also used. The insignia of the insurance company appeared on each mark, and they would normally reward the volunteer fire department who managed to be the first on the scene to battle the fire. (Altercations occasionally broke out between firefighting companies vying for the chance to earn the reward!)

Fire marks were first used in Great Britain about 1780 and were more elaborate than U.S. marks. The first English examples were made of lead and carried a policy number. They were used to identify insured property to the fire brigades maintained by the insurance companies.

During the latter half of the 19th century, municipalities replaced the volunteer fire companies and fire brigades with paid fire departments. No longer was there a need for fire marks, so the companies discontinued their use. Some companies still use fire marks for advertising purposes. Reproductions may be purchased for decorative purposes. See *The Fire Mark Circle of America,* listed under Clubs, Newsletters, and Catalogs in the Directory.

Prices listed are for legitimate fire marks for the most part. Fantasy items and reproductions are identified when possible. Many fire marks have been and continue to be widely reproduced in cast iron and aluminum. They are sold legitimately as decorator items and collectible reproductions. Fantasy items, on the other hand, are not reproductions, as they depict items that never existed in the first place. They are of modern fabrication and never existed in their present form prior to their recent production. They appear in cast iron, aluminum, and other mediums.

Baltimore Equitable Society...MD, CI, old pnt, 1794, 9⅜x10" ...750.00
Eagle Hose #2, CI, lt rust, 11" H (fantasy item, ca 1960) 18.00

Eagle Ins. Co., Cincinnati, Ohio, eagle above banner, cast iron with gold on black, 8x12", $850.00 (not known to have been reproduced).

FA (Fire Assoc), CI, EX (up to 15 legitimate variations), $100 to .1,000.00
Invicta & famous wht horse of Kent, lead, 8¾x6½" 385.00
Liverpool & London & Globe, tin, common, modern, M 50.00
Mutual Assurance of Phila, gr tree type on wooden shield 100.00
Mutual Assurance of Phila, gr tree type on wooden shield, repro .15.00
Mutual Insurance, angel flying over Charleston, repro, 9½x7½" ..15.00
Mutual Insurance, angel flying over Charleston, 9½x7½" 750.00
Philadelphia Contributorship, metal hands on wooden shield, EX 75.00
Phoenix Hartford, tin, lt pnt loss/rust, 8¾x4¼" 275.00
Protector Fire Ins Co London, copper, 1835, VG 85.00
United Fireman's Ins Co Phila PA, CI, 11⅜x8¾", VG 100.00
Valiant Hose #2, pnt CI, 10½", repro 18.00
Valiant Hose #2, pnt CI (fantasy item, ca 1960s) 18.00

Firefighting Collectibles

Firefighting collectibles have always been a good investment in terms of value appreciation. Many times the market will be temporarily affected by wild price swings caused by the 'supply and demand principle' as related to a small group of aggressive collectors. These collectors will occasionally pay well over market value for a particular item they need or want. Once their desires are satisfied, prices seem to return to their normal range. It has been noticed that during these periods of high prices, many items enter the marketplace that otherwise would remain in collections. This may (it has in the past) cause a

price depression (due again to the 'supply and demand principle' of market behavior).

The recent phenomena of Internet buying and selling has caused wild swings in prices for some fire collectibles. The cause of this is the ability to reach into vast national and international markets. It appears that this has resulted in a significant escalation in prices paid for select items. The every-day, average items have shown an increase in selling price as well. The bottom-line items languish price wise, but at least seem to change hands. This marketplace is growing by leaps and bounds, and many outstanding items have appeared recently in the fire antiques and collectibles field. But when all is said and done, the careful purchase of quality, well-documented firefighting items will continue to be an enjoyable hobby and an excellent investment opportunity.

Today there is a large, active group of collectors for fire department antiques (items over 100 years old) and an even larger group seeking related collectibles (those less than 100 years old). Our advisors for this category (except grenades) are H. Thomas and Patricia Laun; they are listed in the Directory under New York. (SASE required.)

Fire grenades preceded the pressurized metal fire extinguishers used today. They were filled with a mixture of chemicals and water and made of glass thin enough to shatter easily when thrown into the flames. Many varieties of colors and shapes were used. Not all the grenades listed contain salt-brine solution, some, such as the Red Comet, contain carbon tetrachloride, a powerful solvent that is also a health hazard and an environmental threat. (It attacks the ozone layer.) It is best to leave any contents inside the glass balls. The source of grenade prices are mainly auction results; current retail values will fluctuate. Our fire grenades advisor is Larry Meyer; he is listed in the Directory under Illinois.

Key:
ALF — American LaFrance   s&a — soda & acid
CCL4 — carbon tetrachloride

Alarm, Gamewell Fire Alarm Station, oval, red, Pat...1924, 9" ..110.00
Alarm box, CI, Gamewell Fire Alarm-Telegraph Station, rpt, VG .200.00
Alarm box, Gamewell...Alarm Station, Hercolite, 1924, complete .135.00
Axe, presentation; German, silver-tone, blk hdl, 13" 175.00
Axe, Viking style, pnt hdl, EX 325.00
Badge, Allentown FD #379, copper shield shape 95.00
Badge, C of H FD & Philadelphia-style hand tub on shield shape ..120.00
Badge, Humane #1, Norristown PA 35.00
Badge, KI City-7-FD, hydrant/hose carriage/etc 60.00
Badge, presentation, 14k gold, eagle atop banner/etc, 1913 ....700.00
Badge, President...Fireman's League, gold-tone w/eagle, 1958, 2" .65.00
Badge, VFA-Philad'a 1875 & hydrant on shield, silver 100.00
Badge, 75 Assoc-Veteran Firemen-NY, steel shield shape, 2¼" 75.00
Bed key, CI, 19th C, VG 140.00
Bell, apparatus; brass, acorn finial, 10" dia, VG 350.00
Bell, brass muffin type w/trn wood hdl, 5" dia, VG 250.00
Bell, engine; chrome-plated, w/clapper, 10" dia 400.00
Bell, muffin; trn wooden hdl, Pat dates/carrying ring, 4", G 350.00
Belt, parade; leather, Liberty, red & wht, VG 65.00
Box, ballot; walnut w/sliding door, blk & wht marbles, EX 100.00
Bucket, leather, blk & gold letters: Old North, 14", VG 140.00
Bucket, leather, maroon & gold letters, dtd 1839, 13"+hdl 275.00
Buckle, brass, appl hose wagon, Ridabock & Co, ca 1890, 2¼x3" ...80.00
Card case, Gamewell, plastic fire-box shape, 1929, 4¾", EX 200.00
Catalog, Gamewell, Municipal Fire Alarm Systems, rare, 1913, EX .300.00
Certificate, Firemen's Pension Fund of Philadelphia, 1916, 8x12" ..40.00
Clamp, hose; red-pnt metal, mk La France, 1¾x3½" dia 65.00
Cup, presentation; coin silver, florals & scrolls 475.00
Emblem, shirt; metal, Goodwill #7, Phila 25.00
Emergency light, apparatus; Sireno Signal, 3 red lights, 10" 50.00
Extinguisher, apparatus; ALF & Foamite Corp, nickel, complete, G ..150.00

Extinguisher, apparatus; Mack Childs 220.00
Extinguisher, Atlas, cone shaped, EX 195.00
Extinguisher, Captain Fyr-Fyter, copper, pony-sz 130.00
Extinguisher, DB Dmith...Indian Pat-Utica NY, copper, 18" 60.00
Extinguisher, First Aid Chicago, copper, s&a 45.00
Extinguisher, Miller-Peerless Pump Type..., nickel, 27", EX 55.00
Extinguisher, Mini-Max, conical, EX 120.00
Extinguisher, Rameses, tin tube, dry powder, 22", G 45.00
Extinguisher, Red Comet, CCL4, wall mt plastic holder, EX 25.00
Extinguisher, Simplex, conical, EX 130.00
Extinguisher, Standard Fire Trumpet, tin tube, powder, 22", EX ..70.00
Extinguisher, Sur Stop, CCL4, wall-mt metal holder, M 80.00
Extinguisher holder, apparatus; Ahrens Fox, brass, 12" 85.00
Finial for helmet, brass, lion figural, 5", EX 170.00
Flag, Boston Fire Dept, 22x26", EX 50.00
Frontispc, leather, Cosgould SFE SFD, shield w/hose & star, 8", EX .225.00
Frontispc, leather, Fire Ward CS, 8", EX 275.00
Frontispc, leather, high-front shield, Niagara-2-WFD, MA, 8" ..110.00
Frontispc, leather, wht high-front shield, 1st Asst..., MA, 8" 100.00
Gas mask kit, M-S-A all service Model S w/canister, EX 30.00
Gauge, Amoskeag Mfg, NP brass, Pat 1859, 6½" dia 600.00
Gauge, Stutz Fire Engine, Dbl Springs, US Gauge Co, NP, 9x12" ..150.00

Gong, Gamewell, 15" brass bell in 36" oak ball-top case, EX, $3,850.00.

Gong, Gamewell, chrome, center wind, 6" 95.00
Gong, Gamewell, Moses Crane oak case, 8" bell, ca 1880, 22" ..1,800.00
Gong, Gamewell, Moses Crane oak case, 8½" brass bell 1,800.00
Gong, Gamewell, oak case, flat top, 15" brass bell, 1880, 38", EX+ .2,800.00
Gong, Gamewell, wooden case, ball top, 15" brass bell, 26", VG 3,800.00
Gong, Gamewell Fire Station, oak flat top, 18" bell, EX 3,800.00
Grenade, Auto-Fyr-Stop, clear, wall mt, from $35 to 45.00
Grenade, Babcock, Manf'd by Fire...M'fg Co, cobalt, 7½" 1,300.00
Grenade, Dri-Gas Grenade, Diamond pattern, Chattanooga, w/bracket ...130.00
Grenade, Eddison's Electric Fire Exterminator, aqua 3,000.00
Grenade, Grenades Du Progres..., yel orange-amber, 5⅝" 275.00
Grenade, Hayward's...Pat Aug 8 1871, smoky ice bl, 6⅛" 550.00
Grenade, Hayward's...Pat Aug 8 1972, dk yel-olive, 6⅛" 375.00
Grenade, Hayward's...Pat August 8 1861, turq bl, 6⅜" 300.00
Grenade, Hayward...No 407 Broadway NY, yel-olive, 6" 750.00
Grenade, HSN, yel topaz, globular w/lg dmns, sb, 7" 100.00
Grenade, Magic Fire Extinguisher Co, yel-amber, 6¼" 425.00
Grenade, Red Comet Fire Grenade, red, hangs from ceiling, $15 to ..25.00
Grenade, Rockford Kalamazoo Automatic..., med cobalt, 11" 425.00
Grenade, Shur-Stop, magenta liquid, wall mt, from $25 to 35.00
Hat, parade; HP portrait of Marquis de Lafayette, rstr 1,300.00
Hat, parade; red pressed felt w/gold letters, 1819, VG 1,400.00
Helmet, aluminum, Fireman's Fund, Cairns & Bros, VG 200.00

Helmet, leather, high eagle, Anderson & Jones, 84-comb, EX ...450.00
Helmet, leather, high eagle, Asst Engineer SFD, Cairns, VG 460.00
Helmet, leather, high eagle, Asst Foreman-1-1769, 64-comb, G .360.00
Helmet, leather, high eagle, Gouverneur-FD, Cairns, G 375.00
Helmet, leather, high eagle, Hose-1-LFD, torch mt, EX 450.00
Helmet, leather, high eagle, Oak Hill Boston, lacking front, VG .300.00
Helmet, leather, high eagle, Treasurer-4-SCO, Cairns, EX 425.00
Helmet, leather, high eagle, Van Nest-Hose-2-De, Cairns, EX ..450.00
Helmet, leather, high eagle, WA-1-FFD, Smith Mfg, G 200.00
Helmet, leather, high eagle, Windsor Hose 3, Cairns, G 200.00
Helmet, leather, high fox, Hampden Fire Co, 1867, EX 800.00
Helmet, leather, high lion, metal frontpc: Fairmount FD 2 ....625.00
Helmet, leather, high sea horse, Cataract Steamer 1836, EX ..1,000.00
Helmet, leather, low front, Aide-Fire Comm'r 8829, VG 250.00
Helmet, leather, low front, Dunbarton FD, Cairns, EX+ 200.00
Helmet, leather, Olsen, 1 lg comb, 7" front w/lg red B 325.00
Helmet, leather, war-baby style, 2-MFD, VG 175.00
Helmet, presentation; leather, high eagle, Engineer NFD, Smith, M .2,900.00
Holder, key; brass, steam engine & horses eng, 9x4½" 150.00
Indicator, Gamewell, oak case, 38", EX 1,800.00
Keg, Hazelton's High Pressure Chemical..., amber, 11½x4½" ...275.00
Kerchief slide, metal shield form, EX 200.00
Key, alarm box; Gamewell...USA, flat Christmas tree cut 7.50
Ladder, wooden, folding type, 144", VG 100.00
Ladder holders, apparatus; red pnt, 19", pr 30.00
Lamp, apparatus; candle-lit, solid brass, Putnam 31, 21" 3,100.00
Lamp, apparatus; 6 eng panels, Jersey City, Devoursney, 1870, 20" .2,000.00
Lamp, apparatus; 6-sided, bl/clear/red panels, 15½", EX 1,200.00
Lamp, engine; Excelsior 2, SP w/red & clear glass, 1850s, 22" .2,000.00
Lamp, engine; HPM 1, sea-horse finial, ca 1873, 20½" 2,000.00
Lantern, Dietz Fire King, red pnt, copper bottom, 14", G 140.00
Lantern, Dietz King, brass, clear globe 200.00
Lantern, Dietz King, NP brass w/red globe, VG 225.00
Lantern, Dietz Underwriters Mill, red globe, ca 1914, G 45.00
Lantern, Eclipse, brass, clear globe, ca 1870, 14"+hdl, G 700.00
Lantern, hand; Vulture No 4/Quincy, 1851, brass, EX+ 850.00
Lantern, wrist; brass, Chief Engineer WHFD, 14"+hdl, EX 1,100.00
Lantern, wrist; Joseph S Abbott eng globe, ca 1884 ....1,500.00
Letter opener, Gamewell Fire Alarm Tel Co, brass, 9" 300.00
Lithograph, Grand Canal Celebration, Hook & Ladder Co, 12x18" 20.00
Match safe, Gutta Percha & Rubber Mfg NY, w/3 orig matches, 2¾" ..150.00
Match safe, sterling, ...Home Insurance...NY, horses/steamer, 2½" 500.00
Nozzle, Akro-Ball, Akron, chrome, rubber hdls, w/tip, 20" 160.00
Nozzle, Boston Woven Hose & Rubber Co, brass w/red cord, 30" .70.00
Nozzle, brass, riveted leather body, 2-man type, 35", G 375.00
Nozzle, distributor; Elkhart, brass, 7" 180.00
Nozzle, Wooster, brass w/rubber hdls, lacks 2½" tip, 20" 70.00
Pipe, NP w/leather straps, from steamer, 39" 395.00
Pipes, Amoskeag Mfg...1880 No 9, brass, 17", pr 480.00
Play pipe, brass, polished/lacquered, 2½" tip, 30" 80.00
Play pipe, Underwriter, brass & copper, 1½" tip, 39½" 75.00
Play pipe, Underwriter, Wooster, brass w/red twine, tip mk: 1⅛, 30" 75.00
Rattle, alarm; dbl-reed, wooden w/weighted end, VG 160.00
Register, alarm; Foote Pierson & Co...NJ, brass, EX 50.00
Register, Gamewell, 1902, w/orig key & punch cup, VG 300.00
Repeater, Gamewell, cased 5-station, complete, mtd on slate, VG .1,650.00
Siren, Sirenlite #50, Sterling Siren Model 30, w/bracket 230.00
Siren, Sterling Siren Fire Horn, hand-crank, working, EX 500.00
Staff, warden's, wood w/cvd flame top, red/gold pnt, 66" 2,500.00
Strainer, suction; NP, 5" (inside) dia 50.00
Switchboard, Gamewell, on walnut stand, 17x15½" 550.00
Telephone, Gamewell Police Patrol, aluminum 250.00
Torch, apparatus; brass, for whale oil, bases removed, pr 200.00
Torch, apparatus; brass, w/wicks, 12", pr 425.00

Torch, apparatus; NP brass, orig screw-on top, acorn finial, pr ...400.00
Transmitter, Gamewell, complete w/code wheels, 38", EX 2,300.00
Trumpet, presentation; SP, emb steamer/etc, 1900, 20" 2,750.00
Trumpet, presentation; SP, eng Reading Telegram..., 22" 1,100.00
Trumpet, speaking; solid brass, 18", VG 300.00
Trumpet, working; NP, Chief on inside plaque, 18" 450.00
Trumpet, working; NP, Foreman Eng Co, 18" w/tassel 425.00
Watch fob, brass, red Gamewell alarm box/etc, 1½", VG 375.00
Whistle, City Police & Fire..., nickel & brass, VG 80.00

Fireplace Implements

In the colonial days of our country, fireplaces provided heat in the winter and were used year round to cook food in the kitchen. The implements that were a necessary part of these functions were varied and have become treasured collectibles, many put to new use in modern homes as decorative accessories. Gypsy pots may hold magazines; copper and brass kettles, newly polished and gleaming, contain dried flowers or green plants. Firebacks, highly ornamental iron panels that once reflected heat and protected masonry walls, are now sometimes used as wall decorations. By Victorian times the cook stove had replaced the kitchen fireplace, and many of these early utensils were already obsolete; but as a source of heat and comfort, the fireplace continued to be used for several more decades. See also Wrought Iron.

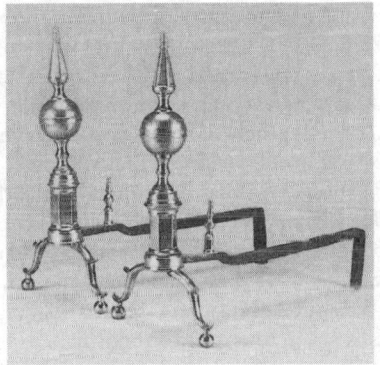

Andirons, brass, Federal, with faceted steeple finial above sphere on columnar supports, cabriole legs with ball feet, ca 1800, $1,100.00.

Andirons, brass, belted, ball top, Hunneman, 1800s, 17" 1,380.00
Andirons, brass, fire dog, penny ft, urn finials, 13" 385.00
Andirons, brass, ribbed/faceted finials, ball ft, 18", G 200.00
Andirons, brass, trn top/columns, ball ft, 14¼" 100.00
Andirons, brass, trn/faceted tops, scroll legs, ball ft, 22" 550.00
Andirons, CI, Hessian soldier figural, 20½" 300.00
Andirons, CI, open scrollwork, 14" 125.00
Andirons, gilt bronze, Louis XVI style, pomegranate finials, 9x12" 1,200.00
Broiler, wrought iron, drip pan, heart hdl, 10½x16" 525.00
Broiler, wrought iron, rotary style, old rpr, 12½" dia 135.00
Crane, wrought iron, hook on end w/diagonal arm brace, 60" 75.00
Ember tongs, brass hdl, 19" L 125.00
Fender, brass, 3-bar design above pierced skirt, 42" L 200.00
Fender, brass w/cast leafy detail & ball finials, 48" L 160.00
Fork, wrought steel, eng geometrics, ca 1800, 15¼" 175.00
Griddle, rotating type, wrought iron, 4-legged, 22" 100.00
Screen, brass & wire, D-shape, scroll-decor middle, 24x36x15" .500.00
Screen, Victorian trn walnut, cvd/pierced crest, 19th C, 53x27" ..800.00
Surround, Regency gilt bronze, lion chenets & scrolling, 41" ..2,300.00
Trammel, wrought iron, 3-prong hook, 24" 195.00
Trammel, wrought-iron chain type, 18th C, worn 145.00
Trammel, wrought-iron ratchet type, 19th C, extends to 56" 375.00
Waffle iron, CI heart shape, long hdl, hinged, 29⅜" 400.00

Fishing Collectibles

Collecting old fishing tackle is becoming more popular every year. Though at first most interest was geared toward old lures and some reels, rods, advertising, and miscellaneous items are quickly gaining ground. Values are given for examples in excellent or better condition and should be used only as a guide. For more information we recommend *The Fishing Lure Collector's Bible* by R.L. Streater with Rick Edmisten and Dudley Murphy, *Fishing Lure Collectibles* by Dudley Murphy and Rick Edmisten, and *Collector's Guide to Creek Chub Lures & Collectibles* by Harold E. Smith, M.D. (Collector Books). Our advisor for this category is Randy Hilst, an appraiser and collector whose address and phone number are listed in the Directory under Illinois. (SASE required.)

Key:
GE — glass eyes   PE — painted eyes

Bobber, Ideal, ball end, mc, 10", EX 115.00
Bobber, Kingfish, mc, w/instructions, EX+ on card 15.00
Catalog, South Bend, mc charts, 1939, EX+ 75.00
Decoy, Blue Catfish, Carl Christenson, GE, 10¼", EX+ 75.00
Decoy, Golden Sucker, Dennis Wolf, cvd tail, GE, 10", EX+ 195.00
Decoy, Northern Pike, Carl Christenson, GE, 9¾", EX+ 75.00
Fly holder, leather, Sport King, 6x4½", EX 35.00
Fly rod line dressing, Weber Floatline, metal container, EX+ 35.00
Hooks, Reds' Automatic, 12 on counter display card, MOC 120.00
Lure, Baby Chub Wiggler #200, Creek Chub Bait, ca 1917, EX ...30.00
Lure, Bass Nabber, metal diving tail, 1 treble, 1940, 2¾" 55.00
Lure, Black Sucker #1300, ca 1925, 5¾", EX 700.00

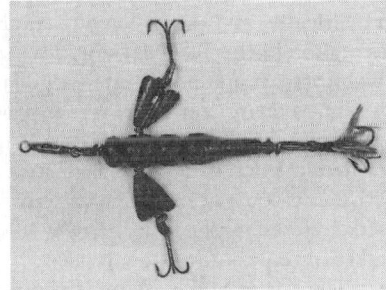

Lure, Comstock 1883 Patent Type 1 flying helgramite, 2⅞", old paint, sparse feathers, rare, $2,500.00.

Lure, Crystal Minnow, luminous, ca 1883, 1¼", EX 800.00
Lure, Fin Tail Shiner #2100, Creek Chub, 2 trebles, 1930, 4" 50.00
Lure, Flat Plug, 1 treble/1 single, 1930, 2⅜" 75.00
Lure, fly; Oreno Frog, frog spot, sm, EX+ 75.00
Lure, fly; Oreno Mouse, tan body, front whiskers, blk PE, EX 75.00
Lure, fly; Trout-Oreno 971, Rainbow, PE, EX 20.00
Lure, Kazoo Wobbler #6637, Shakespeare, ca 1935, 3¾", EX 60.00
Lure, Kent Floater, Pflueger, stamped logo, ca 1910, 2¼", EX 350.00
Lure, Moonlight Pollywog, Keeling, 2 trebles, 1926, 4" 50.00
Lure, Musky Gee-Wiz Frog, Al Star Bait, 1930, 5½" 225.00
Lure, Musky Trolling Minnow, South Bend, ca 1925, 5", EX 350.00
Lure, Pikie Minnow #700, Creek Chub, 3 trebles, 1920, 4¼" 25.00
Lure, Surface #200, Heddon, ca 1915, 4¾", EX 250.00
Lure, Surface Tom, Keeling, 2 trebles, 1920, 3¼" 40.00
Lure, Surface Wonder #42, Shakespeare, ca 1910, 4", EX 75.00
Outboard propeller, Paul Bunyan, Vari-Pitch, papers, EX+IB 45.00
Reel, Ambassadeur 1750A, papers, NMIB (box mk) 95.00
Reel, Atlas, portage, sliding click, raised pillar, EX 10.00
Reel, B Ocean, J Vom Hofe, ca 1918, EX 60.00
Reel, Bass Carter, mk, holds 80 yards, EX 10.00
Reel, Bronson, Fleetwing #2475, jeweled, level-wind, EX 9.00

Reel, Brookline #16, EX 8.00
Reel, Coronet #25, JA Coxe, aluminum, ca 1940, EX 40.00
Reel, Criterion #1961, Mod HO eng, EX 22.00
Reel, Empire City, sliding click & drag, mk, holds 80 yards, EX ...20.00
Reel, fly; Hendryx, brass, ca 1890, EX 20.00
Reel, fly; Rainbow, Meisselbach, aluminum, EX 25.00
Reel, fly; William Billinghurst, early 19th C, EX 225.00
Reel, Free Cast, South Bend, #666, mk, EX 14.00
Reel, Go-Ite Mfg, mk Go-Ite Real Reel Pat Pend, aluminum, EX ...20.00
Reel, Heddon #3-15, silver, EX 75.00
Reel, Heddon Pal #P-41, EXIB 10.00
Reel, Indian, raised pillar, mk, holds 60 yards, EX 16.00
Reel, Meek, BF & Son #3, EX 100.00
Reel, Meek & Milam, brass, handmade, ca 1850, EX 300.00
Reel, Milam, mk, Frankfort KY #1, EX 200.00
Reel, Oceanic #2859, Pflueger, Pat 1907 & 1923, EX 35.00
Reel, Orvis, silver, 1874 Pat in script, EX 200.00
Reel, Precision, Shakespeare, jeweled, 1914, EX 15.00
Reel, Samson, Union Hardware, holds 60-80 yards, EX 15.00
Reel, spinning; Dam Quick 550, rare right-handed model, EX 55.00
Reel, spinning; Malloch, brass, early, EX 130.00
Reel, Superex Automatic #775, Pflueger, Pat 1907, EX 30.00
Reel, Talbot, mk 'Kansas City MO,' silver, early 1900s, EX 90.00
Reel, Wards Sportking #60-6310, model 5-C (eng), EX 10.00
Reel, Whitecap #410, Langley, star drag, free spool, EX 20.00
Rod & reel combo, Stubby, hand brake, 23" L, 1921, EX 45.00
Texas Angler, trick hooking device, M in tube 30.00

Flags of the United States

Over the past few years the popularity of vintage flags has grown dramatically, and prices have risen greatly as a result. The pending restoration of the Fort McHenry Flag (The Star Spangled Banner) has also created greater public interest in flag collecting.

The brevity and imprecise language of the first Flag Act of 1777 allowed great artistic license for America's early flag makers. This resulted in a rich variety of imaginative star formations which coexisted with more conventional row patterns. In 1912 inviolate design standards were established for the new 48-star flag, but the banners of our earlier history continue to survive:

The 'Great Star' pattern — configured from the combined stars of the union, appeared in various star denominations for about 50 years, then gradually disappeared in the post-Civil War years.

The utilitarian 'scatter' pattern — created through the random placement of stars, is traceable to the formative years of our nation and remained a design influence through most of the 19th century.

The 'wreath' pattern — first appearing in the form of simple single-wreath formations, eventually evolved into the elegant double- and triple-wreath medallion patterns of the Centennial period.

Acquisition of specific star denominations is also a primary consideration in the collecting process. Pre-Civil War flags of 33 stars or less are very scarce and are typically treated as 'blue chip' items. Civil War-era flags of 34 and 35 stars also stand among the most sought-after denominations. Market demand for 36-, 37-, and 38-star flags is strong but less broad-based, while interest in the unofficial 39-, 40-, 41, and 42-star examples is largely confined to flag aficionados. The very rare 43 remains in a class by itself and is guaranteed to attract the attention of the serious collector.

Row-patterned flags of 44, 45, and 46 stars still turn up with some frequency and serve as a source of more modestly priced vintage flags. Ordinary 48-star flags flood the flea markets and are priced accordingly, while the short-lived 49 is regarded as a legitimate collectible. 13-star flags, produced over a period of more than 200 years, surface in many forms and must be assessed on a case-by-case basis.

Many flag buffs favor sizes that are manageable for wall display, while others are attracted to the more monumental proportions. Allowances are typically made for the normal wear and tear — it goes with the territory. But severe fabric deterioration and other forms of excessive physical damage are legitimate points of negotiation.

The dollar value of a flag is by no means based upon age alone. The wide price swings in the listing below have been influenced by a variety of determining factors related to age, scarcity, and aesthetic merit. In fact, almost any special feature that stands out as unusual or distinctive is a potential asset. Imprinted flags and inscribed flags; 8-point stars, gold stars, and added stars; extra stripes, missing stripes, tricolor stripes, and war stripes are all part of the pricing equation. And while political and military flags may rank above all others in terms of prestige and price, any flag with a significant and well-documented historical connection has 'star' potential (pardon the pun). Our advisor for this category is Ryan Cooper; he is listed in the Directory under Massachusetts.

13 stars, (4-5-4), sea captain's, ca 1860s, 74x140" 700.00
13 stars, circular pattern, hand sewn, 1860s, 29x40" 1,300.00
13 stars, hand/machine sewn, Centennial, 60x86" 450.00
13 stars, printed glazed muslin, 1880s, 7x11" 100.00
13 stars, 9 stripes, hand sewn, 1860s, 27x50" 1,300.00
15 stars, union jack from War of 1812, rare, 35x62" 23,000.00
15 stars, 15 stripes, all machine sewn, ca 1912, 48x72" 375.00
16 stars, Great Star, hand sewn, 1850s, 54x78" 6,800.00
19 stars, 16 orig+3, sewn scrap fabric, 39x66" 6,500.00
20 stars, oval pattern, ship's, 1818, worn, 64x128" 6,500.00
21 stars, Commissioning pennant, ship 'Herald,' 1819, 50-ft ...8,500.00
25 stars, oval pattern w/central star, ship's flag, 96x200" 6,700.00
25 stars, row pattern, Civil War, 90x175" 2,200.00
26 stars, Great Star, embr on sewn silk, 30x43" 7,500.00
29 stars, entirely hand sewn, poor condition, 43x68" 2,500.00
30 stars, gold stars/fringe, silk, delicate, 52x68" 2,500.00
31 stars, Great Star, Lincoln related, printed, 11x14" 285.00
31 stars, row pattern, hand-stitched bunting, 104x247" 2,500.00
32 stars, dbl wreath of inset stars, hand sewn, 36x48" 5,200.00
33 stars, Great Star, hand-sewn muslin, 60x96" 4,200.00
33 stars, hand-/machine-sewn wool bunting, 66x92" 2,250.00
33 stars, in rows, printed bunting, 28x44", G- 700.00

34 stars in pentagonal clusters, all hand-sewn (exclusively a war flag, succeeded in 1863 by the 35 star flag as the Civil War raged on) $620.00.

34 stars, dbl-wreath pattern, printed silk, 18x28" 700.00
34 stars, Great Star, from Albany RR Depot, 116x175" 4,500.00
34 stars, printed linen, 3 sewn sections, 22x48" 500.00
34 stars, random pattern, hand sewn, 66x140" 1,200.00
35 stars, dbl-wreath pattern, printed, sized muslin, 19x28" 650.00

35 stars, recruiting, sewn bunting, 50x116" 1,300.00
35 stars, row pattern, hand/machine sewn, 96x180" 950.00
36 stars, cut-in, in rows, machined stripes, 25x50" 700.00
36 stars, parade, muslin print, 6x9" 190.00
36 stars, sailing ship's, inscribed & dtd, 75x142" 550.00
37 stars, medallion pattern, printed/sewn muslin, 48x87" 450.00
37 stars, printed silk, 32x40" 225.00
37 stars, row pattern, hand-sewn silk, poor, 60x80" 230.00
37 stars, row pattern, stitched bunting, 30x48" 450.00
38 stars, medallion-wreath pattern, printed cotton, 12x17" 225.00
38 stars, printed silk w/ribbon ties, 30x47" 150.00
38 stars, row pattern, clamp dyed in 3 sections, 60x120" 220.00
38 stars, row pattern, hand/machine-stitched bunting, 71x116" .250.00
38 stars, unique wreath pattern, sewn, 89x134" 500.00
38 stars, 1776-1876 pattern, printed linen, 27½x46" 1,800.00
39 stars, Centennial 'International Flag,' 16x24" 140.00
39 stars, row pattern, all machine-stitched bunting, 40x84" 350.00
39 stars, row pattern variation, printed silk, 12x24" 125.00
39 stars (6-5 pattern), printed gauze bunting, 19x34" 125.00
40 stars, row pattern, hand-sewn bunting, lg, 98x204" 270.00
40 stars, row pattern, printed/sewn British import, 55x106" 185.00
41 stars (rare), printed cotton sheeting, 15x24" 225.00
42 stars, row pattern, printed silk/fringe, poor, 24x36" 70.00
42 stars, sewn cotton, from Ft Hamilton NY, 120x177" 275.00
42 stars, 7-row pattern, printed cotton, 27x47" 125.00
43 stars, machine-sewn bunting, extremely rare, 29x70" 1,200.00
44 stars, machine-sewn cotton bunting, 53x82" 150.00
44 stars, triple-wreath pattern, printed cotton, 23x26" 175.00
45 stars, HP w/sewn stripes, 38x70" 120.00
45 stars, machine-sewn cotton bunting, 80x108" 55.00
45 stars, printed silk w/red ribbon ties, 32x46" 45.00
45 stars, row pattern variant, printed muslin, 9x13" 25.00
46 stars, machine-sewn wool bunting, 72x138" 60.00
46 stars, printed silk, GAR Post in gold, 32x45" 350.00
47 stars, unofficial, sewn bunting, 108x137" 350.00
48 stars, all crocheted, dtd 1941, 20x38" 85.00
48 stars, machine-sewn cotton bunting, 60x96" 30.00
48 stars, printed cotton w/GAR surprint, 11x16" 25.00
48 stars, sewn to form 'USA,' unauthorized WWI, 45x69" 300.00
48 stars, USN Union Jack, machine-sewn wool, 23x33" 35.00
48 stars in gold, sewn WWII casket flag, 58x118" 95.00
49 stars, embr, sewn stripes, 36x60" 45.00
49 stars, 3 uncut flags, printed cotton sheet, 37x36" 25.00
50 stars, early prototype 'June 1959,' 52x66" 220.00
50 stars, hand-knitted coverlet w/fringe, 30x51" 30.00
51 stars, printed flaglette for DC statehood, 4x6" 15.00

Florence Ceramics

Figurines marked 'Florence Ceramics' were produced in the '40s and '50s in Pasadena, California. The quality of the ware and the attention given to detail are prompting a growing interest among today's collectors. The names of these lovely ladies, gents, and figural groups are nearly always incised into their bases. The company name is ink stamped. Examples are evaluated by size, rarity, and intricacy of design. For more information we recommend *The Florence Collectibles* by Doug Foland, a coadvisor for this category. You will find him listed in the Directory under Oregon. Another source is *The Collector's Encyclopedia of California Pottery, Second Edition*, by Jack Chipman; he is listed in the Directory under California. Advise also came from Jerry Kline; he is listed in the Directory under Tennessee.

Abigail, 8" 185.00

Amber, 9¼" 700.00
Amelia, 8¼" 275.00
Angel, 7¾" 140.00
Annabel, 8" 675.00
Barbara, child, 8½", from $200 to 250.00
Bea, flower holder, 6¼" 85.00
Birthday Girl, 9" 750.00
Blue Boy & Pinkie, 12", 12", pr 800.00
Camille, hands, 8½" 325.00
Camille, plain, 8½" 185.00
Carol 700.00
Catherine, 7¾" 700.00
Charles, 8¾" 325.00
Charmaine, hands away, 8½" 300.00
Choir Boy, 6" 115.00
Cinderella & Prince Charming, from $2,500 to 3,000.00
Clarissa, hand in, 7¾" 175.00
Clarissa, hand w/articulated fingers, 7¾" 275.00
Colleen, 8" 285.00
Cynthia 750.00
David, 7½", from $100 to 175.00
Dear Ruth, lamp 1,250.00
Deborah 750.00
Delia, 7¼", from $150 to 175.00
Diana, powder box, 6¼" 450.00
Douglas, 8¼" 175.00
Edward, 7" 450.00
Elaine, matt finish, 6" 80.00
Elizabeth, 8½x7", from $350 to 450.00
Emily, flower holder, 8" 60.00
Gary, 8½" 200.00
Georgette, 10" 750.00
Gesille 750.00
Grandmother & I, from $2,000 to 2,200.00
Her Majesty, 7" 200.00
Irene, 6" 70.00
Jeanette, fancy, 7¾" 225.00
Jenevieve (Genevieve), plain, 8" 185.00
Jim, 6¼" 80.00
Joy, child, 6" 165.00
Karla (or Lisa) Ballerina, 7¼" 450.00
Kay, flower holder, 7" 60.00
Laura, 7½", from $150 to 190.00
Leading Man, 10½" 475.00
Leading Man & Prima Donna, 10½", 10", pr 1,450.00
Lillian, 7¼" 130.00
Linda Lou, red or teal, 7¾" 375.00
Louise, 7¼", from $80 to 145.00
Love Letter 1,500.00
Madam Pompadour, 12½" 450.00
Madam Pompadour/Louis XV, 12½", 12½", pr 900.00

Marie Antoinette and Louis XVI, $750.00 for the pair.

Photo courtesy Doug Foland

Mark Anthony & Cleopatra	3,000.00
Mary, seated, 7½"	600.00
Masquerade, 8¼"	900.00
Matilda, 8½"	175.00
Melanie, 7½"	150.00
Musette, 8¾"	495.00
Our Lady of Grace, 9¾"	190.00
Pamela, 7¼"	325.00
Portrait	1,500.00
Priscilla, & John Alden, pr	650.00
Rebecca, aqua dress w/violet trim, 7"	325.00
Rebecca, other colors, 7"	250.00
Roberta, 8½"	375.00
Sarah, 7½"	130.00
Scarlett, hands away, 8¾"	450.00
Scarlett, no hand away, 8¾"	200.00
Scarlett & Rhett, no hand away, 8¾", 9", pr	550.00
Shirley, hands away, 8"	375.00
Shirley, no hand away, 8"	225.00
Story Hour w/Boy & Girl, 8"	1,250.00
Story Hour w/Girl, 8"	1,050.00
Sue, 6"	75.00
Sue Ellen, 8¼"	200.00
Victor, 9¼"	325.00
Victoria, 8¼x7"	550.00
Vivian, 10"	395.00
Wendy, flower holder, 6¼"	70.00
Wynkin & Blynkin, 5½", 5½", pr	500.00

Florentine Cameo

Although the appearance may look much like English cameo, the decoration on this type of glass is not wheel cut or acid etched. Instead a type of heavy paste — usually a frosty white — is applied to the face to create a look very similar to true cameo. It was produced in France as well as England; it is sometimes marked 'Florentine.'

Pitcher, orange w/wht bird & grass, 8", +4 4¾" tumblers	300.00
Tumbler, bl w/wht flowers, 3¾"	35.00
Vase, allover flowers in dotted bands w/fringe below, 12"	250.00
Vase, bl w/wht butterfly & berries, 8"	110.00
Vase, cobalt wht wht daisies & pheasant, 3¾"	50.00

Flow Blue

Flow Blue ware was produced by many Staffordshire potters; among the most familiar were Meigh, Podmore and Walker, Samuel Alcock, Ridgway, John Wedge Wood (who often signed his work Wedgewood), and Davenport. It was popular from about 1825 through 1860 and again from 1880 until the turn of the century. The name describes the blurred or flowing affect of the cobalt decoration, achieved through the introduction of a chemical vapor into the kiln. The body of the ware is ironstone, and Oriental motifs were favored. Later issues were on a lighter body and often decorated with gilt. For further information we recommend *The Collector's Encyclopedia of Flow Blue China* by Mary Frank Gaston (Collector Books).

Albany, bowl, vegetable; w/lid	275.00
Albany, gravy boat, w/tray	295.00
Albany, plate, Johnson Bros, 7½"	32.00
Aldine, bone dish, Grindley	38.00
Aldine, sugar bowl, w/lid, Grindley	145.00

Amoy, bowl, vegetable; Davenport, w/lid	450.00
Amoy, cup plate, Davenport	130.00
Amoy, plate, Davenport, 10½"	175.00
Amoy, platter, Davenport, 16"	650.00
Amoy, teapot, full panel Gothic, Davenport, 10"	1,200.00
Argyle, bowl, vegetable; w/lid; Ford	175.00
Argyle, cup & saucer, coffee; Grindley	95.00
Argyle, plate, Grindley, 10"	100.00
Argyle, platter, Grindley, 17"	375.00
Argyle, platter, Grindley, 19⅝"	500.00
Argyle, relish, Ford	140.00
Ashburton, bowl, dessert; Grindley, 5¾"	38.00
Ashburton, creamer, Grindley	75.00
Ashburton, platter, Grindley, 16"	285.00
Astral, gravy boat, Grindley, w/undertray	240.00
Astral, platter, Grindley, 11"	160.00
Baltic, bowl, fruit; Grindley	45.00
Baltic, bowl, soup; Grindley	75.00
Baltic, bowl, vegetable; oval, Grindley	135.00
Baltic, bowl, vegetable; w/lid, Grindley	235.00
Baltic, butter pat, Grindley	35.00
Baltic, creamer & sugar bowl, Grindley	195.00
Baltic, cup & saucer, Grindley	75.00
Baltic, gravy boat, Grindley	195.00
Baltic, plate, Grindley, 10"	95.00
Baltic, plate, Grindley, 8"	75.00
Baltic, platter, Grindley, 14"	195.00
Baltic, platter, Grindley, 18"	295.00
Baltic, sugar & creamer, Grindley	195.00
Bamboo, sauce plate, Dimmock	135.00
Bamboo, soup tureen, Alcock	1,700.00
Brooklyn, bowl, vegetable; w/lid	350.00
Brooklyn, platter, 13x9"	300.00
Burleigh, bowl, vegetable; w/lid, Burgess & Leigh	85.00
Burleigh, sauce tureen, w/ladle, Burgess & Leigh	595.00
Candia, cup & saucer, Cauldon	110.00
Candia, plate, Cauldon, 10"	95.00
Candia, soup tureen, w/lid, unmk, lg	950.00
Cashmere, cup, Ridgway & Morley	135.00
Cashmere, plate, dinner; Ridgway & Morley, 10½"	250.00
Cashmere, waste bowl, Ridgway & Morley, 3x5¼"	400.00
Cattle Scenery, bowl, Adams, ca 1850, 4x7½"	150.00
Chapoo, bowl, soup; Wedge Wood, 8⅜"	165.00
Chapoo, plate, Wedge Wood, 8⅜"	165.00
Chapoo, plate, Wedge Wood, 9"	180.00
Chapoo, platter, Wedge Wood, 18", NM	800.00
Chapoo, teapot, Wedge Wood	865.00
Chatsworth, platter, 13½", EX	250.00
Chinese, plate, Dimmock, 6¾"	88.00
Chinese, sugar bowl, Dimmock	400.00
Chinese, teapot, Dimmock	785.00
Chusan, pitcher, milk; Holdcroft, 8"	625.00
Chusan, teacup, hdld, Holdcroft, ca 1830	195.00
Clarence, cup & saucer, Johnson Bros	70.00
Clarence, sugar bowl, w/lid, Johnson Bros	100.00
Clover, platter, 16½"	175.00
Conway, bowl, vegetable; New Wharf Pottery, 8⅞"	70.00
Conway, creamer, New Wharf Pottery	165.00
Conway, plate, New Wharf Pottery, 10"	90.00
Conway, platter, New Wharf Pottery, 10½"	140.00
Coronet, plate, Samson Hancock, 10⅜"	95.00
Coronet, plate, Samson Hancock, 8½"	65.00
Coronet, plate, Samson Hancock, 9½"	75.00
Dainty, plate, Maastrich, 9½"	100.00

Dainty, plate, Maddock, 8" 65.00
Del Monte, butter dish 295.00
Delft, plate, Petrus Regout, 7¼" 35.00
Delft, soup plate, Minton, 10½" 90.00
Delft, waste bowl, Minton 70.00
Duchess, bowl, Grindley, w/lid, 5½x11" 180.00
Duchess, plate, Grindley, 9½" 70.00
Elipse, creamer & sugar bowl 495.00
Fairy Villas, sugar bowl 295.00
Florida, bowl, vegetable; w/lid, Johnson Bros 450.00
Florida, creamer, Johnson Bros 150.00
Florida, cup & saucer, Johnson Bros 90.00
Florida, plate, Johnson Bros, 9" 80.00
Florida, relish, Grindley 110.00
Formosa, plate, Mayer, 8½" 80.00
Formosa, teapot, Mayer, 8⅝", NM 500.00
Gainsborough, pitcher, 7¾" 395.00
Georgia, bowl, berry; Johnson Bros, ind 35.00
Georgia, platter, Meakin, 12¼x9¼" 175.00
Gothic, bowl, vegetable; w/lid 680.00
Grace, bowl, rimmed soup; 9" 85.00
Grace, platter, 15½" 275.00
Granada, butter dish, Alcock, 3-pc 250.00
Haddon, butter pat, Grindley 30.00
Haddon, charger, Grindley, 12½" 395.00
Haddon, pitcher, Grindley, 8" 300.00
Haddon, plate, Grindley, 10" 110.00
Haddon, platter, Grindley, 14" 325.00
Hindustan, creamer, Maddock 350.00
Hindustan, relish, Maddock 300.00

Hong Kong, wash bowl and pitcher, Meigh, 1845, $1,550.00.

Hong Kong, chamber pot, w/lid, Meigh, EX 700.00
Hong Kong, plate, Meigh, 8¼" 95.00
Hong Kong, plate, Meigh, 9¼" 135.00
Hong Kong, waste bowl, Meigh 450.00
Ideal, chamber pot, Grindley 250.00
Indian, plate, Meigh, 7¼" 80.00
Indian, teapot, Meigh, lg 1,150.00
Indian, waste bowl, Meigh 350.00
Indian Jar, cup & saucer 130.00
Iris, bowl, vegetable; w/lid, Royal Staffordshire 250.00
Kaolin, creamer, Podmore Walker 335.00
Kaolin, waste bowl, Podmore Walker 335.00
Kyber, plate, Adams, 10" 125.00
Kyber, platter, Adams, 18x14" 455.00
La Belle, charger, 12½" 275.00
La Belle, chop plate, Wheeling, 11" 200.00
La Belle, custard ramekin 295.00
La Belle, gravy boat 375.00
La Belle, ice cream tray, 13" 350.00
La Belle, ice pitcher, w/silver lid 2,495.00
La Belle, syrup, w/metal lid & underplate 495.00

La Francaise, bowl, soup; French China, 9" 50.00
La Francaise, creamer & sugar bowl, French China 38.00
La Francaise, cup & saucer, French China 40.00
La Francaise, gravy boat, w/underplate, French China 95.00
Lahore, plate, Phillips, 8½" 100.00
Lahore, platter, Phillips, 18" 585.00
Leighton, bowl, vegetable; w/lid, hexagonal, Burgess & Leigh ...185.00
Lonsdale, bowl, cereal; Ford, 6⅛" 48.00
Lonsdale, platter, EX gold, Ridgway, 16" 265.00
Lorne, bowl, vegetable; w/lid, oval, Grindley 295.00
Lorne, gravy boat, Grindley 130.00
Lorne, plate, Grindley, 8" 60.00
Lorne, platter, Grindley, 12" 135.00
Lorraine, creamer, Ridgway 150.00
Madras, cup & saucer, hdld, Alcock, oversz 175.00
Madras, plate, Doulton, 9½" 110.00
Madras, sauce ladle, Doulton 250.00
Mandarin, plate, Pountney, 9¼" 75.00
Mandarin, sauce bowl, w/lid, Pountney, 2-cup 295.00
Manilla, creamer, Podmore Walker 495.00
Manilla, gravy boat, Podmore Walker 320.00
Manilla, platter, Podmore Walker, 20" 976.00
Manilla, teapot, Podmore Walker 1,100.00
Marechal Neil, bone dish 60.00
Marechal Neil, platter, 12" 150.00
Marguerite, bone dish, Grindley 50.00
Marguerite, cup & saucer, Grindley 75.00
Marguerite, platter, Grindley, 18" 365.00
Marie, butter pat, Grindley 32.00
Marie, gravy boat & undertray, Grindley 250.00
Meissen, bowl, soup; Libertas, 7¼" 50.00
Melbourne, gravy boat, Grindley, w/underplate 210.00
Melbourne, plate, Grindley, 9" 70.00
Melbourne, platter, Grindley, 16" 350.00
Melbourne, sauce tureen, Grindley 325.00
Mongolia, bowl, berry; Johnson Bros 375.00
Mongolia, bowl, Johnson Bros, 7⅛" 60.00
Mongolia, cup & saucer, Johnson Bros 105.00
Mongolia, plate, Johnson Bros, 8" 80.00
Morning Glory, plate, 8½" 90.00
Morning Glory, platter, Ashworth, 11x8½" 95.00
Morning Glory, waste bowl, gold lustre decor, 3⅜x5⅝" 100.00
Nankin, bowl, vegetable; Davenport, w/lid 895.00
Neptune, pitcher, sea dragon hdl, bearded man under spout, 7¾" ..250.00
Non-Pareil, bone dish, Burgess & Leigh 75.00
Non-Pareil, bowl, berry; Burgess & Leigh, 5" 35.00
Non-Pareil, bowl, vegetable; rectangular, Burgess & Leigh, 9½" ...350.00
Non-Pareil, bowl, vegetable; w/lid, Burgess & Leigh, 5x12x7½" ...600.00
Non-Pareil, butter dish, Burgess & Leigh, 3½x8" 350.00
Non-Pareil, chop plate, Burgess & Leigh, 11½" 275.00
Non-Pareil, cup & saucer, Burgess & Leigh, 4 for 700.00
Non-Pareil, cup & saucer, demitasse; Burgess & Leigh, 2", 4¾" .175.00
Non-Pareil, gravy boat, Burgess & Leigh, 4x7½" 250.00
Non-Pareil, plate, Burgess & Leigh, 5¾" 35.00
Non-Pareil, plate, Burgess & Leigh, 7¾" 60.00
Non-Pareil, plate, Burgess & Leigh, 8¾" 75.00
Non-Pareil, plate, Burgess & Leigh, 9¾" 110.00
Non-Pareil, platter, Burgess & Leigh, 12¼" 475.00
Non-Pareil, platter, Burgess & Leigh, 15½x13" 600.00
Non-Pareil, soup plate, flanged, Burgess & Leigh 120.00
Non-Pareil, sugar bowl, w/lid, Burgess & Leigh, 6¼x8x5" 375.00
Non-Pareil, tureen, w/lid, Burgess & Leigh, 7x12" 325.00
Normandy, bowl, potato; Johnson Bros 225.00
Normandy, bowl, serving; oval, Johnson Bros 175.00

Normandy, bowl, vegetable; w/lid, Johnson Bros 325.00
Normandy, charger, Johnson Bros 100.00
Normandy, cup & saucer, Johnson Bros 95.00
Normandy, fish sauce, Johnson Bros 260.00
Normandy, gravy boat w/undertray, Johnson Bros 195.00
Normandy, ladle, Johnson Bros, sm 285.00
Normandy, plate, Johnson Bros, 10½" 75.00
Normandy, plate, Johnson Bros, 8" 65.00
Normandy, platter, bacon; Johnson Bros, ind 145.00
Normandy, platter, Johnson Bros, 14" 250.00
Normandy, platter, Johnson Bros, 9¾" 160.00
Normandy, tureen, w/lid, Johnson Bros 400.00
Normandy, waste bowl, Johnson Bros, 5⅞x3¼" 160.00
Orchid, bowl, soup; flanged, Maddock, 10⅜" 72.50
Orchid, plate, Maddock, 9" 55.00
Oregon, bowl, berry; Mayer 100.00
Oregon, cup & saucer, Mayer 175.00
Oregon, platter, Mayer, 10¾x8⅛" 300.00
Oregon, relish, Mayer, 9" 285.00
Oriental, bowl, soup; Ridgway, 9" 125.00
Oriental, plate, L&Co, 9½" 70.00
Oriental, shaving mug, unmk 140.00
Osborne, bowl, berry; Ridgway, ind 35.00
Osborne, creamer, Ridgway 150.00
Osborne, cup & saucer, Grindley 70.00
Osborne, pitcher, water; Ridgway 150.00
Ovando, drainer, Meakin, 13½x9¼" 500.00
Ovando, platter, Meakin, 12½" 250.00
Paisley, bowl, soup; Mercer, 8⅞" 80.00
Paisley, bowl, vegetable, w/lid, Mercer 200.00
Paris, bowl, New Wharf Pottery, 8" 55.00
Paris, plate, New Wharf Pottery, 8" 55.00
Pelew, cup & saucer, Challinor 180.00
Queen, plate, Rathbone, 9" 95.00
Regent, bowl, vegetable; w/lid, Meakin, 11" 375.00
Regent, platter, Meakin, 14" 350.00
Regent, sauce tureen, w/lid, underplate & ladle, Meakin, 8" 900.00
Rhone, teapot, Furnival 800.00
Roma, soup, Wedgwood, 9½" 70.00
Royal, butter dish, Furnival, w/insert 750.00
Sabraon, creamer, 5¼" 375.00
Sabraon, sauce tureen 625.00
Savoy, sugar bowl, Stoke, w/lid 120.00
Scinde, bowl, dessert; Alcock, 5" 50.00
Scinde, bowl, rectangular, Alcock, 1½x7½x5½" 300.00
Scinde, bowl, vegetable; Alcock, 8" 450.00
Scinde, creamer, Alcock, 6¼" 450.00
Scinde, cup & saucer, handleless; Alcock 200.00
Scinde, cup plate, Alcock, 4¼" 200.00
Scinde, gravy boat, Alcock, 5½" 425.00
Scinde, plate, Alcock, 10½" 175.00
Scinde, plate, Alcock, 8" 110.00
Scinde, plate, Alcock, 9½" 135.00
Scinde, plate, dessert; Alcock, 7½" 85.00
Scinde, platter, Alcock, 16" 800.00
Scinde, platter, Walker, 11" 450.00
Scinde, sugar bowl, w/lid, Alcock, rpr, 7½" 550.00
Scinde, teapot, Alcock, 9" 900.00
Scinde, waste bowl, Alcock, 3¼x5¼" 500.00
Sevres, butter pat, Wood & Son 25.00
Shapoo, plate, 7⅜" 65.00
Shell, cup & saucer, handleless; Challinor 175.00
Shell, plate, Challinor, 10¼" 135.00
Shell, teapot, Alcock 750.00

Temple, bowl, rectangular, unmk, 2¾x8x6¼" 325.00
Temple, bowl, vegetable; unmk, 2⅛x9¾x7¾" 240.00
Temple, bowl, vegetable; w/lid, 9" 650.00
Temple, creamer & sugar bowl, unmk, prof rpr 500.00
Temple, cup & saucer, hdl, Podmore Walker 225.00
Temple, plate, Podmore Walker, 10" 150.00
Temple, plate, Podmore Walker, 8¾" 125.00
Temple, platter, Podmore Walker, 13¾x10½" 300.00
Temple, platter, Podmore Walker, 15¾x12¼" 425.00
Temple, soup plate, Podmore Walker, 9¾" 175.00
Tonquin, cup, ped ft, hdl, 12-panel, Adams, rare 185.00
Tonquin, plate, Adams, 9" 160.00
Tonquin, plate, Heath, 7⅞" 125.00
Tonquin, sugar bowl, Heath 275.00
Touraine, bone dish, Stanley 70.00
Touraine, bowl, vegetable; 8" 110.00
Touraine, butter pat 45.00
Touraine, creamer 225.00
Touraine, cup & saucer, Stanley 100.00
Touraine, gravy boat, Alcock 200.00
Touraine, plate, Alcock, 6½" 45.00
Touraine, platter, 12" 185.00
Touraine, sauce dish 48.00
Touraine, soup, 8½" 125.00
Trent, cup & saucer, New Wharf Pottery 65.00
Vermont, cup & saucer, demitasse 110.00
Virginia, butter pat, Maddock 45.00
Virginia, cup & saucer, Maddock 60.00
Virginia, plate, Maddock, 9¾" 85.00
Virginia, platter, Maddock, 20" 750.00
Virginia, sauce bowl, Maddock 35.00
Waldorf, bowl, vegetable; New Wharf Pottery, 9" 115.00
Waldorf, cup & saucer, New Wharf Pottery 125.00
Waldorf, waste bowl, New Wharf Pottery 200.00
Watteau, pitcher, Doulton, 10½" 450.00
Watteau, plate, Doulton, 10½" 120.00
Watteau, plate, Doulton, 6½" 75.00
Watteau, soup, Doulton, 7½" 80.00
Waverly, bowl, vegetable; w/lid, oval, Maddock 275.00
Waverly, butter pat, Maddock 50.00
Waverly, platter, Maddock, 17" 350.00
Yeddo, plate, Ashworth, 10⅜ 120.00
Yeddo, soup plate, Ashworth, 10" 110.00

Flue Covers

When spring housecleaning started and the heating stove was taken down for the warm weather season, the unsightly hole where the stovepipe joined the chimney was hidden with an attractive flue cover. They were made with a colorful litho print behind glass with a chain for hanging. In a 1929 catalog, they were advertised at 16¢ each or six for 80¢. Although scarce today, some scenes were actually reverse painted on the glass itself. The most popular motifs were florals, children, animals, and lovely ladies. Occasionally flue covers were made in sets of three — one served a functional purpose, while the others were added to provide a more attractive wall arrangement. They range in size from 7" to 14", but 9" is the average.

For further information we recommend *Flue Covers, Collector's Value Guide*, by Jim Meckley II, available from Collector Books or your local bookstore.

Asian Beauty, brunette w/flowers/long pins in hair, 7", from $70 to .80.00
Autumn, scenic countryside landscape, 6½x8¼", from $50 to 60.00

Basket of Strawberries, 7x8¼", from $75 to 85.00
Bouquet's End, roses in vase w/falling petals, 7x8¼", from $85 to ..95.00
Branch of Cherries, Victorian girl holds branch, 7x8½", from $75 to .85.00
Buddies, 3 Black boys sitting on cotton bales, 9½", from $250 to ...300.00
Cherub & Stars, cherub portrait w/in starry border, 8", from $55 to .60.00
Elizabeth, blond Victorian girl in pk, 9½", from $85 to 95.00
Feline Love, lady w/rose in hair holds kitten, 7¾", from $90 to ..100.00
Fetching Water, 3 children at well, 9¼", from $55 to 65.00
Fisherman, sailboat scene, 9¼", from $60 to 70.00
Flapper, lady in cloche hat w/flower, 7¾", from $75 to 85.00
Fur Muff, Victorian lady w/hat & muff, 7¾", from $75 to 85.00

Girl in pink beside table with
vase of flowers, 9½", $65.00.

Grandpa's Story, wht-bearded man reads to girl, 11¾", from $90 to .100.00
Laddie, collie portrait, 9½", from $75 to 85.00
Lady in Red, lady in red-hooded cloak, 14", from $150 to 175.00
Lovely Display, pk roses & buds, 9½", from $70 to 80.00
My Friend Barney, girl in red holds pup w/bl bow, 8", from $85 to ..95.00
Pink Chapeau, girl w/long hair wearing pk hat, 7¾", from $65 to 75.00
Pink Wisteria, dainty pk flowers in vase, 8¼x7", from $50 to 60.00
Playmates, girl in pk, boy in bl in reserve, 9x9", from $75 to 85.00
Serenade, man plays guitar to lady, 10¼", from $50 to 60.00
Sir Winston, racehorse portrait, 9½", from $70 to 80.00
Summer Leisure, lady & child w/book & parasol, 9½", from $85 to ..95.00
Tattling to Mother, Victorian child whispering, 9½", from $85 to ..95.00
Teeter-Totter, 3 children & pup at play, 9½", from $70 to 80.00
Tresses, lady w/abundant long hair, yel border, 7¾", from $55 to .65.00
Under the Oak Tree, courting couple by tree, 9¼", from $55 to ...65.00
Waltz, Victorian boy & girl dancing, 9x6½", from $75 to 85.00
Wig, Colonial lady in long wht wig, 6", from $50 to 60.00

Folk Art

That the creative energies of the mind ever spark innovations in functional utilitarian channels as well as toward playful frivolity is well documented in the study of American folk art. While the average early settler rarely had free time to pursue art for its own sake, his creative energy exemplified itself in fashioning useful objects carved or otherwise ornamented beyond the scope of pure practicality. After the advent of the Industrial Revolution, the pace of everyday living became more leisurely, and country folk found they had extra time. Not accustomed to sitting idle, many turned to carving, painting, or weaving. Whirligigs, imaginative toys for the children, and whimsies of all types resulted. Though often rather crude, this type of early art represents a segment of our heritage and as such has become valued by collectors.

Values given for drawings, paintings, and theorems are 'in frame' unless noted otherwise. See also Baskets; Decoys; Frakturs; Samplers; Trade Signs; Weather Vanes; Wood Carvings.

Airplane, made from scraps of iron, open wings, 1910, 21" W 150.00

Birdhouse, seacoast style w/mansard roof & cupola, ME, 24" ..1,800.00
Calligraphy, lion attacks deer, Prof JM Witlach...1911, 30x40" .2,500.00
Cutout, wht paper on blk, animals/landscape, ca 1900, 12x13" .1,100.00
Cvg, limestone, lion's head, ca 1870, 13x13x12" block 1,850.00
Cvg, sandstone, monkey seated w/folded arms, E (Popeye) Reed, 5" ..195.00
Diorama, ship scene, wood/pnt/paper/cellophane/string, 6⅝" 100.00
Drawing, ink/graphite, 19th-C gentleman, eglomise fr, 7x6" 385.00
Featherwork floral pc, 19th C, eglomise fr, 20x14" 450.00
Marching stick, patriotic, red/wht/bl bands, 1800s, 36" 350.00
Painting on masonite, Woman in Pk Dress, Mose Tolliver, 20x17" ..330.00
Snake, coiled, wrought iron, imp decor, 19th C, 3½x7x4" 3,335.00
Spencerian calligraphy, eagle & banner, red/bl, 5x7¾"+fr 385.00
Spencerian drawing, 2 sailing ships & lighthouse, 15x22"+fr 75.00
Spencerian penmanship certificate, birds/flowers/etc, 1866, 23x18" 465.00
Theorem on velvet, flowers in bowl, mc, fr, 21x34" 165.00
Totem, highly figured/cvd/grained, Bobby Quinlin, 1991, 81" ...165.00
Towel holder, cvd lady w/arms out holds bar, mc pnt, 1900s, 9x14" .9,775.00
Valance, pnt/stencil wood, farmhouse/boats/foliage, 1870s, 42" .3,740.00
Watercolor & pencil drawing, girl on decor floor, 1867, 7x5"+fr ..880.00
Watercolor on paper, bowl of strawberries, Am school, 1854, 6x7" .2,990.00
Watercolor on paper, fruit basket, 7x9", EX 400.00
Watercolor on paper, lady w/fancy bonnet, old fr, 8x7½" 440.00
Watercolor/ink on paper w/pinpricks, stylish couple, 8x6½" 220.00

Whirligig, folk-painted,
full-bodied faceless family of four, $2,900.00.

Whirligig, Indian woman, pnt wood/horsehair/copper, 19th C, 24" 27,600.00
Whirligig, policeman, pnt aluminum, late 1920s, 9" 575.00
Whirligig, soldier swings swords, worn mc pnt, ca 1900, 14½" .1,500.00

Fostoria

The Fostoria Glass Company was built in 1887 at Fostoria, Ohio, but by 1891 it had moved to Moundsville, West Virginia. During the next two decades, they produced many lines of pressed patterned tableware and lamps. Their most famous pattern, American, was introduced in 1915 and was produced continuously until 1986 in well over two hundred different pieces. From 1920 to 1925, top artists designed tablewares in colored glass — canary (vaseline), amber, blue, orchid, green, and ebony — in pressed patterns as well as etched designs. By the late '30s, Fostoria was recognized as the largest producer of handmade glassware in the world. The company ceased operations in Moundsville in 1986.

Many items from both the American and Coin Glass lines are currently being reproduced by Lancaster Colony. In some cases the new glass is superior in quality to the old. Since the 1950s, Indiana Glass has produced a pattern called 'Whitehall' that looks very much like Fostoria's American, though with slight variations. Because Indiana's is not handmade glass, the lines of the 'cube' pattern and the edges of the items are sharp and untapered in comparison to the fire-polished originals. Three-footed pieces lack the 'toe' and instead have a peg-like foot, and the rays on the bottoms of the American examples are narrower than on the Whitehall counterparts. The Home Interiors Company offers several pieces of American look-alikes which were not even produced in the United States. Be sure of your dealer and study the books suggested below to become more familiar with the original line.

Coin Glass reproductions are flooding the market. Among items you may encounter are an 8" round bowl, 9" oval bowl, 8¼" wedding bowl, 4½" candlesticks, urn with lid, 6¼" candy jar with lid, footed comport, sugar and creamer; there could possibly be others. Colors in production are crystal, green, blue, and red. The red color is very good, but the blue is not the original color, nor is the emerald green. Buyer beware!

For further information see *Elegant Glassware of the Depression Era* by Gene Florence; *Fostoria Glassware, 1887 – 1982*, by Frances Bones; *Fostoria Stemware, The Crystal for America* and *Fostoria Tableware, 1924 – 1943*, both by Milbra Long and Emily Seate; and *Fostoria, Books I and II*, by Ann Kerr, *Glass Animals and Figural Flower Frogs of the Depression Era* by Lee Garmon and Dick Spencer offers an in-depth look at that particular aspect of Fostoria's production. (See also Glass Animals.) Their addresses are listed in the Directory under Illinois. Our advisor is Deborah Maggard; she is listed in the Directory under Ohio.

American, ashtray, sq, 5" 40.00
American, bell 365.00
American, bonbon, 3-ftd, 8" 17.50
American, bowl, boat shape, 8½" 15.00
American, bowl, cream soup; 2-hdl, 5" 45.00
American, bowl, deep, 10" 35.00
American, bowl, float; oval, 11½" 45.00
American, bowl, lily pond; 12" 65.00
American, bowl, nappy; 6" 15.00
American, bowl, rose; 3½" 20.00
American, butter dish, w/lid, ¼-lb 35.00
American, cigarette box, w/lid, 4¾" 37.50
American, compote, w/lid, 5" 25.00

American, creamer, rare, $400.00.

Photo courtesy Gene Florence

American, goblet, fruit; #2056, hex ft, 4½-oz, 4¾" 90.00
American, hotel washbowl & pitcher (extremely rare) 3,500.00
American, jam pot, w/lid 60.00
American, pitcher, w/o ice lip, ½-gal 260.00
American, plate, salad; 7" 10.00
American, ring holder 200.00
American, shakers, 3", pr 20.00
American, tray, ice cream; oval, 13½" 160.00
American, tray, sq, 10" 110.00
American, tumbler, iced tea; hdld 225.00
American, vase, flared, 8" 80.00
Baroque, bl, bowl, jelly; w/lid, 7½" 90.00
Baroque, bl, ice bucket 125.00
Baroque, bl, sherbet, 5-oz, 3¾" 27.50
Baroque, crystal, bowl, celery; 11" 45.00
Baroque, crystal, bowl, punch; ftd 350.00
Baroque, crystal, candlesticks, 4", pr 25.00
Baroque, crystal, compote, 6½" 17.50
Baroque, crystal, plate, torte; 14" 13.00
Baroque, yel, bowl, cereal; 6" 32.00

Baroque, yel, bowl, hdld, 10" 40.00
Baroque, yel, pitcher, w/ice lip, 7" 400.00
Baroque, yel, tumbler, water; 9-oz, 4¼" 25.00
Buttercup, bottle, syrup; #2586, sani-cut 250.00
Buttercup, bowl, #2364, flared, 12" 60.00
Buttercup, bowl, salad; #2364, 9" 50.00
Buttercup, candlestick, #2324, 4" 17.50
Buttercup, candlestick, duo; #6023, 5½" 35.00
Buttercup, cheese stand, #2364, 5¾x2⅞" 20.00
Buttercup, compote, #6030, 5" 30.00
Buttercup, pitcher, #6011, 53-oz, 8⅞" 265.00
Buttercup, plate, #2337, 8½" 17.50
Buttercup, plate, crescent salad; #2364, 7¼x4½" 45.00
Buttercup, plate, torte; #2364, 14" 45.00
Buttercup, saucer, #2350 ....5.00
Buttercup, stem, claret/wine; #6030, 3½-oz, 6" 32.50
Buttercup, stem, cordial; #6030, 1-oz, 3⅞" 40.00
Buttercup, vase, #6021, ftd, 6" 75.00
Camelia, bonbon, 3-ftd, 7¼" 25.00
Camelia, bowl, hdld, oval, 10" 45.00
Camelia, bowl, hdld, 4½" 15.00
Camelia, bowl, lily pond; 11¼" 45.00
Camelia, bowl, salad; 8½" 32.00
Camelia, candlestick, triple; 7¾" 50.00
Camelia, compote, 4⅜" 25.00
Camelia, plate, cracker; 10¾" 30.00
Camelia, plate, dinner; sm, 9½" 35.00
Camelia, plate, torte; 14" 45.00
Camelia, salver, ftd, 12¼" 75.00
Camelia, stem, sherbet; #6063, low, 6-oz, 4⅛" 12.00
Camelia, stem, water; #6063, 9½-oz, 6⅞" 25.00
Camelia, tray, for ind shakers, 4¼" 17.50
Camelia, tray, relish; 2-part, 7⅜" 18.00
Century, ashtray, 2¾" 10.00
Century, bowl, cereal; 6" 22.50
Century, bowl, flared, 8" 25.00
Century, bowl, rolled edge, ftd, 11" 40.00
Century, bowl, serving; oval, 9½" 32.50
Century, candy jar, w/lid, 7" 37.50
Century, mayonnaise, divided, w/2 ladles, 4-pc 35.00
Century, plate, cake; hdld, 10" 22.00
Century, plate, cracker; 10¾" 20.00
Century, plate, crescent salad; 7½" 35.00
Century, preserve, w/lid, 6" 35.00
Century, salver, ftd, 12¼" 50.00
Century, stem, sherbet; 5½-oz, 4½" 12.00
Century, tray, for ind shakers, 4¼" 14.00
Century, vase, bud; 6" 18.00
Chintz, bell, dinner 85.00
Chintz, bottle, salad dressing; #2083, 6½" 350.00
Chintz, bottle, syrup; #2586, sani-cut 395.00
Chintz, bowl, #2496, 8½" 65.00
Chintz, bowl, #6023, ftd 50.00
Chintz, bowl, vegetable; #2496, 9½" 75.00
Chintz, candlestick, dbl; #6023, ...45.00
Chintz, compote, #2496, 5½" 37.50
Chintz, cruet, oil; #2496, w/stopper, 3½-oz 110.00
Chintz, plate, cake; #2496, hdld, 10½" 45.00
Chintz, plate, upturned edge, 17½" 175.00
Chintz, sauce boat liner, #2496, oblong, 8" 30.00
Chintz, stem, claret/wine; #6026, 4½-oz, 5⅜" 55.00
Chintz, tumbler, tea; #6026, ftd, 13-oz 35.00
Coin, amber, ashtray, #1372/114, rnd, 7½" 25.00
Coin, amber, lamp, patio; #1372/459, oil, 16⅝" 160.00

Coin, amber, lamp chimney, courting; #1372/292, hdld 45.00
Coin, amber, vase, bud; #1372/799, 8" 22.00
Coin, bl, ashtray, #1372/110, w/lid, 3" 25.00
Coin, bl, candy jar, #1372/347, w/lid, 6¼" 50.00
Coin, bl, jelly dish, #1372/448 ....25.00
Coin, bl, lamp, coach; #1372/321, electric, 13½" 195.00
Coin, bl, salver, #1372/630, ftd, 6½" 150.00
Coin, bl, sugar bowl, #1372/673, w/lid 45.00
Coin, crystal, bowl, #1372/199, ftd, 8½" 50.00
Coin, crystal, cigarette box, #1372/374, w/lid, 5¾x4½" 40.00
Coin, crystal, cruet, #1372/531, w/stopper, 7-oz 55.00
Coin, crystal, tumbler, dbl old fashioned; #1372/23, 10-oz, 5⅜" ...30.00
Coin, gr, bowl, wedding; #1372/162, w/lid 135.00
Coin, gr, nappy, #1372/499, hdld, 5⅜" 40.00
Coin, gr, urn, #1372/829, w/lid, ftd, 12¾" 200.00
Coin, olive, candy box, #1372/354, w/lid, 4⅛" 30.00
Coin, olive, tray, condiment; #1372/738, 9⅝" 75.00
Coin, ruby, cigarette urn, #1372/381, ftd, 3⅜" 40.00
Coin, ruby, stem, sherbet; #1372/7, 9-oz, 5¼" 70.00
Corsage, bowl, #2537, ftd, 9½" 145.00
Corsage, bowl, finger; #869 ....30.00
Corsage, bowl, sauce; #2440, oval, 6½" 65.00
Corsage, candlesticks, #2496, 5½", pr 60.00
Corsage, candy dish, #2496, w/lid, 3-part 100.00
Corsage, cup, #2440 ....18.00
Corsage, pitcher 250.00
Corsage, plate, cake; #2440, hdld, 10½" 32.50
Corsage, plate, cracker; #2496, 11" 35.00
Corsage, stem, cocktail; #6014, 3½-oz, 5" 22.00
Corsage, stem, oyster cocktail; #6014, 4-oz, 3¾" 17.50
Corsage, tidbit, #2496, 3-ftd 15.00
Corsage, tray, relish; #2496, 2-part 22.50
Corsage, tumbler, water; #6014, 9-oz, 5½" 22.00
Corsage, vase, #2470, ftd, 10" 135.00
Fairfax #2375, amber, bowl, cereal; 6" 12.00
Fairfax #2375, amber, cigarette box 18.00
Fairfax #2375, amber, plate, dinner; 10¼" 6.00
Fairfax #2375, amber, sugar bowl, tea 8.00
Fairfax #2375, gr or topaz, cup, AD 17.50
Fairfax #2375, gr or topaz, platter, oval, 10½" 25.00
Fairfax #2375, rose, bl or orchid, baker, oval, 10½" 38.00
Fairfax #2375, rose, bl or orchid, plate, canape 18.00
Fairfax #2375, rose, bl or orchid, sauce boat 45.00
Heather, bowl, cereal; 6" 25.00
Heather, bowl, lily pond; 11¼" 45.00
Heather, bowl, serving; oval, 9½" 45.00
Heather, candlestick, triple, 7¾" 50.00
Heather, creamer, 4¼" 15.00
Heather, ice bucket 75.00
Heather, plate, bread & butter; 6" 7.00
Heather, plate, cake; hdld, 10" 30.00
Heather, plate, salad; 7½" 10.00
Heather, preserve, w/lid, 6" 65.00
Heather, stem, parfait; #6037, 6-oz, 6⅛" 25.00
Heather, sugar bowl, ind 15.00
Heather, tray, utility; hdld, 9⅛" 33.00
Heather, vase, #4121, 5" 50.00
Heather, vase, flip; #2660, 8" 95.00
Hermitage, amber, gr or topaz, bowl, fruit; #2449½, 5" 8.00
Hermitage, amber, gr or topaz, decanter, #2449, w/stopper, 28-oz ..50.00
Hermitage, amber, gr or topaz, plate, #2449½, 8" 10.00
Hermitage, bl or wisteria, bowl salad; #2449½, 7½" 20.00
Hermitage, bl or wisteria, icer, #2449 ....30.00
Hermitage, bl or wisteria, tray, relish/celery; #2449, 11" 25.00

Hermitage, crystal, ashtray, #2449 ....3.00
Hermitage, crystal, compote, #2449, 6" 12.00
Hermitage, crystal, pitcher, #2449, 3-pt 30.00
Hermitage, crystal, tumbler, #2449½, 2-oz, 2½" 4.00
Jamestown, amber or brn, pickle dish, #2719/540, 8⅜" 21.00
Jamestown, amber or brn, salver, #2719/630, 7x10" 60.00
Jamestown, amber or brn, stem, goblet; #2719/2, 9½-oz, 5¾" 10.00
Jamestown, amber or brn, tray, muffin; #2719/726, hdld, 9⅜" 26.00
Jamestown, amber or brn, tumbler, tea; ftd, 12-oz, 6" 10.00
Jamestown, amethyst, crystal or gr, butter dish, #2719/300, ¼-lb .24.00
Jamestown, amethyst, crystal or gr, tumbler, tea; ftd, 11-oz, 6" 21.00
Jamestown, bl, pk or ruby, bowl, dessert; #2719/421, 4½" 16.00
Jamestown, bl, pk or ruby, bowl, salad; #2719/211, 10" 45.00
Jamestown, bl, pk or ruby, creamer, #2719/681, ftd, 3½" 25.00
Jamestown, bl, pk or ruby, plate, torte; #2719/567, 14" 60.00
Jamestown, bl, pk or ruby, sauce dish, #2719/635, w/lid, 4½" 35.00
Jamestown, bl, pk or ruby, stem, sherbet; #2719/7, 6½-oz, 4¼" ...16.00
Jamestown, bl, pk or ruby, tumbler, juice; #2719/88, 5-oz, 4¾" ...25.00
June, crystal, baker, oval, 10" 50.00
June, crystal, creamer, tea 25.00
June, crystal, parfait, 5¼" 45.00
June, rose or bl, bowl, mint; 3-ftd, 4½" 42.00
June, rose or bl, compote, #2400, 5" 60.00
June, rose or bl, plate, luncheon; 8¾" 18.00
June, rose or bl, shakers, ftd, pr 175.00
June, rose or bl, vase, fan; ftd, 8½" 210.00
June, topaz, bowl, dessert; hdld, lg 65.00
June, topaz, plate, torte; 14" 65.00
Kashmir, bl, baker, 9" 45.00
Kashmir, bl, ice bucket 90.00
Kashmir, bl, plate, luncheon; 9" 12.00
Kashmir, bl, stem, water; ftd, 10-oz 30.00
Kashmir, bl, stem, wine; 2½-oz 40.00
Kashmir, yel or gr, bowl, cream soup 22.00
Kashmir, yel or gr, candlesticks, 9½", pr 85.00
Kashmir, yel or gr, pitcher, ftd 275.00
Kashmir, yel or gr, sauce boat, w/liner 75.00
Kashmir, yel or gr, stem, juice; ftd, 5-oz 15.00
Lido, bonbon, 3-ftd, 7⅜" 17.00
Lido, bottle, oil; w/stopper, 3½-oz 85.00
Lido, bowl, #2545 Flame, oval, 12½" 45.00
Lido, bowl, 1-hdl, 4⅜" 14.00
Lido, candlesticks, 5½", pr 44.00
Lido, compote, 4¾" 17.50
Lido, creamer, ind 11.00
Lido, plate, cake; hdld, 10" 30.00
Lido, plate, torte; 14" 40.00
Lido, shaker, 2¾", ea 25.00
Lido, stem, cocktail; #6017, 3½-oz, 4⅞" 18.00
Lido, sugar bowl, ind 10.00
Lido, tumbler, iced tea; #6017, ftd, 12-oz, 6" 22.00
Lido, tumbler, sham; #4132, 4-oz, 3½" 10.00
Lido, tumbler, sham; #4132, 9-oz, 3¾" 13.00
Mayflower, bowl, #2560, crimped, 11½" 60.00
Mayflower, bowl, finger; #869 ....25.00
Mayflower, bowl, fruit; #2560, 13" 55.00
Mayflower, bowl, salad; #2560, 10" 45.00
Mayflower, candlestick, duo; #2560, 5⅛" 40.00
Mayflower, pitcher, #4140, flat, 60-oz, 7½" 265.00
Mayflower, plate, #2560, 7½" 10.00
Mayflower, plate, torte; #2560, 14" 40.00
Mayflower, stem, claret; #6020, 5½-oz, 6⅛" 35.00
Mayflower, stem, cocktail; #6020, 3½-oz, 4⅞" 18.00
Mayflower, stem, cordial; #6020, 1-oz, 3¾" 40.00

Mayflower, tray, #2560, for ind sugar & creamer, 7½" 15.00
Mayflower, tumbler, iced tea; #6020, ftd, 12-oz, 6⅜" 25.00
Mayflower, vase, #5100, ftd, 10" 110.00
Meadow Rose, bowl, flared, 12" 62.50
Meadow Rose, bowl, hdld, 8½" 65.00
Meadow Rose, candlesticks, 4", pr 50.00
Meadow Rose, candy dish, w/lid, 3-part 110.00
Meadow Rose, creamer, ftd, 4¾" 25.00
Meadow Rose, jelly dish, w/lid, 7½" 65.00
Meadow Rose, pitcher, #5000, ftd, 48-oz 350.00
Meadow Rose, plate, cracker; 11" 30.00
Meadow Rose, sauce dish liner, oval, 8" 30.00
Meadow Rose, stem, water; #6016, 10-oz, 7⅝" 30.00
Meadow Rose, stem, wine; #6016, 3¼-oz, 5½" 40.00
Meadow Rose, tray, #2375, center hdl, 11" 35.00
Meadow Rose, tray, relish; 3-part, 10x7½" 45.00
Meadow Rose, vase, #4108, 5" 75.00
Navarre, bowl, #2496, hdld, 4⅜" 14.00
Navarre, bowl, flared, #2496, 12" 65.00
Navarre, bowl, nut; #2496, 3-ftd, 6¼" 20.00
Navarre, candy box, #2496, w/lid, 3-part 125.00
Navarre, ice bucket, #2375, 4⅜" 125.00
Navarre, plate, cake; #2496, hdld, 10" 50.00
Navarre, sauce dish, #2496, 6½x5¼" 125.00
Navarre, stem, claret; #6106, 4½-oz, 6½" 47.50
Navarre, syrup, #2586, metal cut-off top, 5½" 395.00
Navarre, tray, relish; #2496, 4-part, 10" 52.50

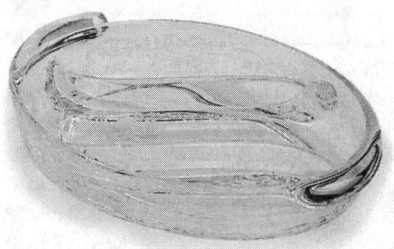

Romance, three-part relish, #2364, 10", $59.00.

Romance, bowl, #2594, hdld, oval, 13½" 55.00
Romance, bowl, rimmed soup; #2364, 8" 90.00
Romance, bowl, salad; #2364, 10½" 45.00
Romance, candlestick, #6023, 2-light, 5½" 35.00
Romance, compote, #2364, 8" 40.00
Romance, ice tub, #4132, 4¾" 70.00
Romance, plate, #2337, 8" 15.00
Romance, plate, cracker; #2364, 11¼" 25.00
Romance, saucer, #2350 ....5.00
Romance, stem, goblet; #6017, 9-oz, 7⅜" 25.00
Romance, stem, wine; #6017, 3-oz, 5½" 35.00
Romance, tumbler, #6017, ftd, 9-oz, 5½" 21.00
Romance, vase, #2614, 10" 85.00
Romance, vase, #4143, ftd, 6" 55.00
Royal, amber or gr, bowl, console; #2329, 11" 25.00
Royal, amber or gr, bowl, cream soup; #2350½, ftd 18.00
Royal, amber or gr, candy box, w/lid, ftd, ½-lb 165.00
Royal, amber or gr, ice bucket, #2315 ....25.00
Royal, amber or gr, nappy, #2350, 9" 32.00
Royal, amber or gr, plate, Mah Jongg (canape); #2321, 8¾" 35.00
Royal, amber or gr, platter, #2350, 15½" 85.00
Royal, amber or gr, stem, wine; #869, 2¾-oz 30.00
Seville, amber, bowl, #2297, flared, deep, 12" 30.00
Seville, amber, bowl, soup; #2350, 7¾" 20.00
Seville, amber, candy jar, #2250, w/lid, ftd, ½-lb 95.00

Seville, amber, cup, AD; #2350 ....25.00
Seville, amber, plate, #2350, rnd, 15" 35.00
Seville, amber, tumbler, #5084, ftd, 2-oz 35.00
Seville, gr, bowl, #2315, flared, ftd, 10½" 30.00
Seville, gr, bowl, cream soup; #2350, flat 16.00
Seville, gr, ice bucket; #2378 ....55.00
Seville, gr, saucer, AD; #2350 ....5.00
Sun Ray, bowl, almond; ftd, ind 12.00
Sun Ray, bowl, rolled edge, 13" 40.00
Sun Ray, candy jar, w/lid 45.00
Sun Ray, creamer, ftd 12.00
Sun Ray, jelly jar, w/lid 28.00
Sun Ray, plate, torte; 15" 65.00
Sun Ray, plate, 6" 5.00
Sun Ray, shakers, 4", pr 45.00
Sun Ray, sweetmeat, hdld, divided 30.00
Sun Ray, tumbler, juice; ftd, 5-oz, 4⅝" 15.00
Trojan, rose, bottle, salad dressing; #2983 ....500.00
Trojan, rose, candlesticks, 2394, 2", pr 44.00
Trojan, rose, goblet, cordial; #5099, ¾-oz, 4" 95.00
Trojan, rose, mayonnaise, #2375, w/liner 60.00
Trojan, rose, plate, chop; #2375, 13" 50.00
Trojan, rose, sugar pail, #2378 ....175.00
Trojan, topaz, bowl, fruit; #2375, 5" 18.00
Trojan, topaz, cheese & cracker set, #2375, #2368 ....65.00
Trojan, topaz, plate, cream soup/mayonnaise liner; #2375, 7½" 8.00
Trojan, topaz, sauce plate, #2375 ....40.00
Trojan, topaz, vase, #2417, 8" 120.00
Versailles, bl, bowl, mint; 3-ftd, 4½" 40.00
Versailles, bl, goblet, claret; #5099 or #5098, 4-oz, 6" 150.00
Versailles, pk or gr, baker, #2375, 9" 55.00
Versailles, pk or gr, compote, #2400, 8" 65.00
Versailles, pk or gr, ice bucket, #2375 ....65.00
Versailles, pk or gr, vase, #4100, 8" 135.00
Versailles, yel, candlesticks, #2395, 3", pr 44.00
Versailles, yel, plate, canape; #2375, 6" 32.00
Versailles, yel, sugar bowl lid only, #2375½ 125.00
Vesper, amber, baker, #2350, oval, 9" 70.00
Vesper, amber, candy jar, #2331, w/lid, 3-part 110.00
Vesper, amber, ice bucket, #2378 ....70.00
Vesper, amber, platter, #2350, 12" 60.00
Vesper, amber, vase, #2292, 8" 95.00
Vesper, bl, candlesticks, #2394, 3", pr 85.00
Vesper, bl, plate, #2287, center hdld, 11" 55.00
Vesper, bl, tumbler, #5100, ftd, 2-oz 60.00
Vesper, gr, bowl, cream soup; #2350, flat 25.00
Vesper, gr, compote, 8" 40.00
Vesper, gr, cup, AD; #2350 ....40.00
Vesper, gr, stem, cordial; #5093, ¾-oz 75.00

Fostoria Glass Specialty Company

The Fostoria Glass Specialty Company was founded in Fostoria, Ohio, in 1899. In 1910 they were purchased by General Electric. The new owners had an interest in developing a high-quality lustre-type art glass able to complete with the very successful glassware produced by Tiffany. They hired Walter Hicks, who had previously worked for Tiffany, to help develop the line they called Iris. Their efforts were extremely successful. The art glass they developed was cased and iridescent, very similar to Steuben's Aurene. Colors included green, tan, white, blue, yellow, and rose. It was made in several patterns, including Heart and Leaf, Leaf and Tendrils, Heart and Spider Webbing, and Lustred Dot. Although the main thrust of their production was lamp shades, vases and bowls were made as well. Iris was made for only four years, since gold was required in its production and manufacturing costs were very high. It was marked with only a paper label, without which identification is sometimes difficult. Look for a pronounced, well-finished pontil that shows the glass layers represented. Most items show a layer of white, which Fostoria called Calcite, as did Steuben. Very little has been written on the history of this company, but for more information refer to *The Collector's Encyclopedia of Art Glass* by John Shuman (Collector Books), and *Fostoria Ohio Glass, Vol II*, by Melvin L. Murray (self published).

Our advisor for this category is Frank W. Ford; he is listed in the Directory under Massachusetts.

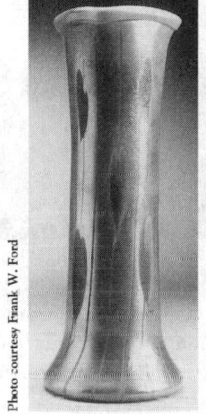

Photo courtesy Frank W. Ford

Vase, Iris, gold lustre with emerald green leaf and vine decor, square folded top (distinguishes it from Durand and other makers), 12", $2,000.00.

Rose bowl, Iris, gold lustre leaves on opal, ovoid **500.00**
Shade, festoons, gr on opal, 7" **250.00**
Shade, leaves & vines, gr & gold on opal, 4-sided **250.00**
Shade, stylized leaves & vines on pearly wht, gold int, bell form .**270.00**
Vase, Iris, gold lustre, pinched-in sides, narrow neck, ftd, 4½" ...**600.00**

Frakturs

Fraktur is a German style of black letter text type. To collectors the fraktur is a type of hand-lettered document used by the people of German descent who settled in the areas of Pennsylvania, New Jersey, Maryland, Virginia, North and South Carolina, Ohio, Kentucky, and Ontario. These documents recorded births and baptisms and were used as bookplates and as certificates of honor. They were elaborately decorated with colorful folk-art borders of hearts, birds, angels, and flowers. Examples by recognized artists and those with an unusual decorative motif bring prices well into the thousands of dollars; in fact, some have sold at major auction houses well in excess of $5,000.00. Frakturs made in the late 1700s after the invention of the printing press provided the writer with a prepared text that he needed only to fill in at his own discretion. The next step in the evolution of machine-printed frakturs combined woodblock-printed decorations along with the text which the 'artist' sometimes enhanced with color. By the mid-1800s, even the coloring was done by machine. The vorschrift was a handwritten example prepared by a fraktur teacher to demonstrate his skill in lettering and decorating. These are often considered to be the finest of frakturs. Those dated before 1820 are most valuable.

The practice of fraktur art began to diminish after 1830 but hung on even to the early years of this century among the Pennsylvania Germans ingrained with such customs. Our advisor for this category is Frederick S. Weiser; he is listed in the Directory under Pennsylvania. (Mr. Weiser has provided our text, but being unable to physically examine the frakturs listed below cannot vouch for their authenticity, age, or

condition. When requesting information, please include a self-addressed stamped evelope.) These prices were realized at various reputable auction galleries in the East and Midwest. Unless otherwise noted, values are for examples in excellent condition. Note: Be careful not to confuse frakturs with prints, calligraphy, English-language marriage certificates, Lord's Prayers, etc.

Key:
lp — laid paper   wc — watercolored
pr — printed   wp — wove paper
p/i — pen and ink

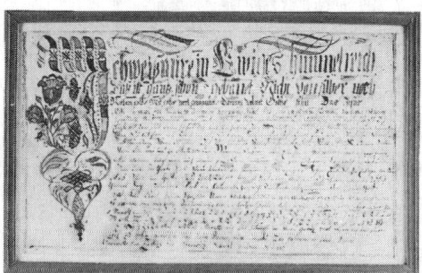

Watercolor and ink on paper, dated 1818, 7¾x13¼", in frame, $800.00.

P/i/wc, birds/flowers/vines, style of Mayer, PA, 1813, 16x18" ..**2,500.00**
P/i/wc, family register/flowers, Sullivan, 1880s, 19x16" **300.00**
P/i/wc, flowers/urns, Schuller, PA, 17x14" **650.00**
P/i/wc, heart/mermaids/birds/vines, PA, 1766, 16⅝x19¾" **1,050.00**
P/i/wc, heart/tulip/suns/wreaths/fans/text, PA, 1787, 18x21" ..**13,000.00**
P/i/wc/lp, flowers/foliage, OH, 1847, stains/fold, 5⅜x7¾" **1,485.00**
P/i/wc/lp, flowers/leaves/hearts, early 19th C, 6x4⅞" **365.00**
P/i/wc/lp, tulip/compass stars, mc, stain, 6⅝x3"+modern fr **330.00**
P/i/wc/wp, lady's profile/flowers/birds/star, PA, 1831, 11x8" ..**21,000.00**
P/i/wc/wp, primitive tulips/birds/etc, 1847, 8½x7"+fr **880.00**
P/i/wp, 3-color, OH, 1833, 5x8¼"+fr, EX **825.00**
Pr/wc, heart/vines/flowers/etc, PA, 1829, 11x14"+old fr **425.00**
Pr/i/wc, 4-color, OH, 1809, 14x15" **660.00**
Pr/p/i/wc, parrots/heart/suns/etc, Krebs, PA, 1786, 12½x16" ...**1,450.00**
Pr/p/i/wc/lp, J Bauman, Ephrata, 1816, 13x16"+ fr **600.00**
Pr/p/i/wc/lp, vining floral, dtd 1794, 12x15½"+fr **715.00**
Pr/wc, angels/birds/blessing, Ritter, PA, rstr, 16x12"+fr **500.00**
Pr/wc, facing angels/eagles/birds, PA, 1830, 16x12⅝" **175.00**
Pr/wc, Gerburts und Tasfuschein, Ebner, PA, 1822, 16x13½" **175.00**
Pr/wc, heart/bird/flowers/cherub/verse, Mayer, PA, 1808, 13x16" ..**2,000.00**
Pr/wc, heart/eagle/cherubs/etc, PA, 1841, 12½x14⅝"+fr **300.00**
Pr/wc, heart/flowers/deer, PA, 1902, prof rstr, 13x16½" **425.00**
Pr/wc/lp, angels/cherub/birds, Ritter, PA, 1839, 15x12½" **100.00**
Wc/lined paper, tulips, B Witmer, 1855, 5¼x7⅞"+fr **1,800.00**

Miscellaneous

Art work, silhouettes of couple, p/i/wc, early 1800s, 6x7", pr **400.00**
Bookplate, p/i/wc/wp, tulips, 4-color, PA, 1827, 10x12" **330.00**
Bookplate, pr/wc, Bixler portrait/Adam/Eve/angels, PA, 5¾x3¼" .**1,000.00**
Bookplate, w/i/wc/lp, 1792, 2½x2⅜"+modern fr **440.00**
Family register, p/i/wc/lp, PA, 1850s, 6x9", 2-pg **50.00**
House blessing, p/i/wc, text/flowers/birds, PA, 1859, 16x20" **500.00**
Valentine, pencil/crayon/p/i/ledger paper, verses, 12x12" **1,750.00**
Vorschrift, p/i/wc, scrolls/tulips, red/blk, 1826, 8x12⅝"+fr **425.00**

Frames

Styles in picture frames have changed with the fashion of the day, but those that especially interest today's collectors are the deep shadow boxes made of fine woods such as walnut or cherry, those with Art Nouveau influence, and the oak frames decorated with molded gesso and gilt from the Victorian era. Our advisor for this category is Michael Hinton; he is listed in the Directory under Pennsylvania.

Note: Unless another date is given, mirrors described in the following listings are from the 19th century.

Cast iron, polychromed military theme with crossed sabers, cannon, and eagle crest, original paint, $200.00.

Blk walnut & gold leaf, 1871 Pat date, 24x20" oval image, 35x31" .**1,150.00**
CI, cherubs & flowers castings, ornate oval, 10x11" **220.00**
CI, cherubs & scrolls, oval opening, 9½x11", EX **220.00**
CI, eagle & shield, old blk rpt w/mc details, Pat 1862, 20x12" ...**550.00**
CI, lily castings, 10x7½", M **275.00**
CI, 2 Nouveau ladies & scrolls, ornate casting, 14x14½" **350.00**
Cvd & pnt split baluster, brn w/blk pnt details, 19th C, 20x16" .**460.00**
Ebonized stripes w/gilt liner, shadowbox, 1950s, 33x28" **150.00**
Gold-wash metal, Art Nouveau, 1897 Pat, 8x5" **65.00**
Gutta percha, oval, dtd 1855, 5¼x4¾" **60.00**
Mosiac floral w/half-circle top, easel bk, 3x2⅛" **35.00**
Polychrome w/artificial graining, 1930s, 19x13" **90.00**
Walnut, gilt fillet, ebonized bands, 13¾x16", pr **90.00**
Wood w/appl crosses at corners & oak leaves, gilt trim, 13x15" **35.00**

Frances Ware

Frances Ware, produced in the 1880s by Hobbs, Brockunier and Company of Wheeling, West Virginia, is either clear or frosted with amber-stained rim bands. The most often found pattern is Hobnail, but Swirl was also made. For more information, refer to *Hobbs, Brockunier & Co. Glass*, by Neila and Tom Bredehoft. Our advisors for this category are Betty and Clarence Maier; they are listed in the Directory under Pennsylvania.

Hobnail, clear; bowl, 7½", from $65 to **75.00**
Hobnail, clear; butter dish, from $80 to **95.00**
Hobnail, clear; creamer, from $40 to **60.00**
Hobnail, clear; finger bowl, 4", from $25 to **35.00**
Hobnail, clear; pitcher, water; from $125 to **175.00**
Hobnail, clear; spooner **45.00**
Hobnail, frosted; bowl, ftd, berry pontil, 6x10" **150.00**
Hobnail, frosted; bowl, oblong, 8" **75.00**
Hobnail, frosted; bowl, sq, 7½" **70.00**
Hobnail, frosted; bowl, 2½x5½" **40.00**
Hobnail, frosted; bowl, 4½" **30.00**
Hobnail, frosted; bowl, 8" dia **75.00**

Hobnail, frosted; bowl, 9" **85.00**
Hobnail, frosted; butter dish, from $80 to **120.00**
Hobnail, frosted; chandelier, amber font, brass fr, 14" dia **950.00**
Hobnail, frosted; cruet, from $425 to **500.00**
Hobnail, frosted; pitcher, milk **150.00**
Hobnail, frosted; pitcher, water; sq top, 8½" **175.00**
Hobnail, frosted; plate, sq, 5¾" **25.00**
Hobnail, frosted; sauce dish, sq, 4" **28.00**
Hobnail, frosted; shakers, very rare, pr **300.00**

Hobnail, frosted; sugar bowl, from $65.00 to $85.00.

Hobnail, frosted; syrup, pewter lid **375.00**
Hobnail, frosted; toothpick holder **60.00**
Hobnail, frosted; tray, cloverleaf, 12", from $90 to **125.00**
Hobnail, frosted; tumbler, water **45.00**
Swirl, clear; syrup **90.00**
Swirl, frosted; bowl, 3¾" H **40.00**
Swirl, frosted; cruet **295.00**
Swirl, frosted; mustard jar, from $90 to **125.00**
Swirl, frosted; pitcher, water **250.00**
Swirl, frosted; shakers, pr **165.00**
Swirl, frosted; sugar bowl, w/lid **80.00**
Swirl, frosted; sugar shaker, orig lid **195.00**
Swirl, frosted; syrup, Pat dtd **295.00**
Swirl, frosted; tumbler **45.00**

Franciscan

Franciscan is a trade name used by Gladding McBean and Co., founded in northern California in 1875. In 1923 they purchased the Tropico plant in Glendale where they produced sewer pipe, gardenware, and tile. By 1934 the first of their dinnerware lines, El Patio, was produced. It was a plain design made in bright, attractive colors. El Patio Nouveau followed in 1935, glazed in two colors — one tone on the inside, a contrasting hue on the outside. Coronado, a favorite of today's collectors, was introduced in 1936. It was styled with a wide, swirled border and was made in pastels, both satin and glossy. Before 1940 fifteen patterns had been produced. The first hand-decorated lines were introduced in 1937, the ever-popular Apple pattern in 1940, Desert Rose in 1941, and Ivy in 1948. Many other hand-decorated and decaled patterns were produced there from 1934 to 1984.

Dinnerware marks before 1940 include 'GMcB' in an oval, 'F' within a square, or 'Franciscan' with 'Pottery' underneath (which was later changed to 'Ware.') A circular arrangement of 'Franciscan' with 'Made in California USA' in the center was used from 1940 until 1949. At least forty marks were used before 1975; several more were introduced after that. At one time, paper labels were used.

The company merged with Lock Joint Pipe Company in 1963, becoming part of the Interpace Corporation. In July of 1979 Franciscan was purchased by Wedgwood Limited of England, and the Glendale plant closed in October 1984.

Note: due to limited space, we have used a pricing formula, meant to be only a general guide, not a mechanical ratio on each piece. Rarity varies with pattern, and not all pieces occur in all patterns. Our advisors for this category are Mick and Lorna Chase (Fiesta Plus); they are listed in the Directory under Tennessee. See also Gladding McBean.

Coronado

Both satin (matt) and glossy colors were made including turquoise, coral, celadon, light yellow, ivory, and gray (in satin); and turquoise, coral, apple green, light yellow, white, maroon, and redwood in glossy glazes. High-end values are for maroon, yellow, redwood, and gray. Add 10 – 15% for gloss.

Bowl, casserole; w/lid, from $85 to	125.00
Bowl, cereal; from $15 to	20.00
Bowl, cream soup; w/underplate, from $40 to	50.00
Bowl, fruit; from $12 to	18.00
Bowl, nut cup; from $16 to	18.00
Bowl, onion soup; w/lid, from $45 to	60.00
Bowl, rim soup; from $28 to	32.00
Bowl, salad; lg, from $35 to	50.00
Bowl, serving; oval, 10½", from $30 to	45.00
Bowl, serving; 7½" dia, from $20 to	25.00
Bowl, serving; 8½" dia, from $18 to	20.00
Bowl, sherbet/egg cup; from $15 to	18.00
Butter dish, from $35 to	45.00
Cigarette box, w/lid, from $75 to	90.00
Creamer, from $12 to	15.00
Cup & saucer, demitasse; from $28 to	45.00
Cup & saucer, jumbo	35.00
Demitasse pot, from $125 to	195.00
Fast-stand gravy, from $28 to	40.00
Jam jar, w/lid, from $65 to	80.00
Pitcher, 1½-qt, from $35 to	60.00
Plate, chop; 12½" dia, from $25 to	35.00
Plate, chop; 14" dia, from $35 to	45.00
Plate, crescent hostess; w/cup well, no established value	
Plate, crescent salad; lg, no established value	
Plate, ind crescent salad; from $25 to	35.00
Plate, 10½", from $20 to	25.00
Plate, 6½", from $6 to	10.00
Plate, 7½", from $9 to	12.00
Plate, 8½", from $12 to	15.00
Plate, 9½", from $15 to	18.00
Platter, oval, 10", from $20 to	25.00
Platter, oval, 13", from $30 to	45.00
Platter, oval, 15½", from $45 to	60.00
Relish dish, oval, from $20 to	35.00
Shakers, pr, from $20 to	35.00
Sugar bowl, w/lid, from $15 to	25.00
Teacup & saucer, from $12 to	15.00
Teapot, from $65 to	95.00
Tumbler, water; no established value	
Vase, 8", no established value	

Desert Rose

Ashtray, ind	20.00
Ashtray, oval	125.00
Ashtray, sq	295.00
Bell, Danbury Mint	125.00
Bell, dinner	125.00
Bowl, bouillon; w/lid	325.00

Bowl, cereal; 6"	15.00
Bowl, divided vegetable	45.00
Bowl, fruit	12.00
Bowl, mixing; lg	195.00
Bowl, mixing; med	185.00
Bowl, mixing; sm	175.00
Bowl, porringer	295.00
Bowl, rimmed soup	28.00
Bowl, salad; 10"	115.00
Bowl, soup; ftd	32.00
Bowl, vegetable; 8"	32.00
Bowl, vegetable; 9"	40.00
Box, cigarette	125.00
Box, egg	195.00
Box, heart shape	165.00
Box, rnd	165.00
Butter dish	45.00
Candle holders, pr	145.00
Candy dish, oval	295.00
Casserole, 1½-qt	85.00
Casserole, 2½-qt, minimum value	600.00
Coffeepot	125.00
Coffeepot, ind	395.00
Compote, lg	75.00
Compote, low, no established value	
Cookie jar	295.00
Creamer, ind	40.00
Creamer, regular	22.00
Cup & saucer, coffee; no established value	
Cup & saucer, demitasse	55.00
Cup & saucer, jumbo	65.00
Cup & saucer, tall	45.00
Cup & saucer, tea	18.00
Egg cup	35.00
Ginger jar	225.00
Goblet, ftd	195.00
Gravy boat	32.00
Heart	145.00
Hurricane lamp, no established value	
Jam jar	125.00
Long 'n narrow, 15½x7¾"	495.00
Microwave dish, oblong, 1½-qt	285.00
Microwave dish, sq, 1-qt	215.00
Microwave dish, sq, 8"	245.00
Mug, bbl, 12-oz	50.00
Mug, cocoa; 10-oz	135.00
Mug, 7-oz	32.00
Napkin ring	65.00
Piggy bank	295.00
Pitcher, jug; no established value	
Pitcher, milk	95.00
Pitcher, syrup	75.00
Pitcher, water; 2½-qt	125.00
Plate, chop; 12"	75.00
Plate, chop; 14"	175.00
Plate, coupe dessert	95.00
Plate, coupe party	295.00
Plate, coupe steak	195.00
Plate, divided; child's	195.00
Plate, grill	125.00
Plate, side salad	40.00
Plate, TV	175.00
Plate, 10½"	18.00
Plate, 6½"	6.00

Plate, 8½"	18.00
Plate, 9½"	20.00
Platter, turkey; 19"	295.00
Platter, 12¾"	45.00
Platter, 14"	65.00
Porringer	295.00
Relish, oval, 10"	35.00
Relish, 3-section	75.00
Shaker & pepper mill, pr	295.00
Shakers, rose bud, pr	24.00
Shakers, tall, pr	75.00
Sherbet	25.00
Soup ladle, no established value	
Sugar bowl, open, ind	125.00
Sugar bowl, regular	32.00
Tea canister	225.00
Teapot	125.00
Thimble	75.00
Tidbit tray, 2-tier	195.00
Tile, in fr	75.00
Tile, sq	65.00
Toast cover	195.00
Trivet, fluted, rnd	325.00
Tumbler, juice; 6-oz	55.00
Tumbler, 10-oz	32.00
Tureen, soup; flat bottom	495.00
Tureen, soup; ftd, either style	695.00
Vase, bud	75.00

For other hand-painted patterns, we recommend the following general guide for comparable pieces (based on current values):

Cafe Royal	-20%
Daisy	-20%
October	-20%
Forget-Me-Not	Same as Desert Rose
Meadow Rose	Same as Desert Rose
Desert Rose	Base Line Values
Apple	+10%
Ivy	+40%
Strawberry Fair	+20%
Strawberry Time	+20%
Fresh Fruit	+20%
Bountiful	+20%
Poppy	+50%
Original (small) Fruit	+50%
Wild Flower	200% or more!

There are several Apple items that are so scarce they command higher prices than fit the above formula. The Apple ginger jar is valued at $600.00+, the 4" jug at $195.00+, and any covered box in Apple is at least 50% more than Desert Rose.

There is not an active market in Bouquet, Rosette, or Twilight Rose, as these are scarce, having been produced only a short time. Our estimate would place Bouquet and Rosette in the October range (-20%) and Twilight Rose in the Ivy range (+40%).

Apple Pieces Not Available in Desert Rose

Bowl, batter; minimum value	450.00
Bowl, str sides, lg	55.00
Bowl, str sides, med	45.00
Casserole, stick hdl & lid, ind	65.00
Coaster	65.00

Jam jar, redesigned	425.00
Shaker & pepper mill, wooden top, pr	395.00
½-apple baker, from $195 to	225.00

El Patio, 1934 – 1954

This line includes a few pieces not offered in Coronado and the colors differ, but per piece these two patterns are valued about the same.

Franciscan Fine China

The main line of fine china was called Masterpiece. There were at least four marks used during its production from 1941 to 1977. Almost every piece is clearly marked. This china is true porcelain, the body having been fired at a very high temperature. Many years of research and experimentation went into this china before it was marketed. Production was temporarily suspended during the war years. More than 170 patterns and many varying shapes were produced. All are valued about the same with the exception of the Renaissance group, which is 25% higher.

Bowl, vegetable; serving, oval	50.00
Cup	20.00
Plate, bread & butter	18.00
Plate, dinner	30.00
Plate, salad	25.00
Saucer	12.00

Starburst

Ashtray, ind	20.00
Ashtray, oval, lg	50.00
Bonbon/jelly dish	35.00
Bowl, crescent salad	40.00
Bowl, divided, 8"	25.00
Bowl, fruit; ind	13.00
Bowl, salad; ind	25.00
Bowl, soup/cereal	13.00
Bowl, vegetable; 8½"	45.00
Butter dish	45.00
Candlesticks, pr, from $175 to	200.00
Casserole, lg	100.00
Chop plate, from $55 to	65.00
Coffeepot	150.00
Creamer	15.00
Cup & saucer	25.00
Gravy boat, from $20 to	30.00
Gravy boat, w/attached undertray	40.00
Gravy ladle	30.00
Jug, water; 10"	90.00
Mug	60.00
Oil cruet	75.00
Pepper mill	150.00
Pitcher, water; 10"	85.00
Pitcher, 7½", from $50 to	75.00
Plate, dinner	12.00
Plate, 11"	45.00
Plate, 6"	6.00
Plate, 8"	8.00
Platter, 15"	80.00
Shakers, bullet shape, lg, pr	50.00
Shakers, sm, pr	20.00
Snack/TV tray w/cup rest, 12½", from $75 to	100.00
Sugar bowl	25.00
Tumbler, 6-oz, from $40 to	50.00

Vinegar cruet 75.00

Frankart

During the 1920s Frankart, Inc., of New York City, produced a line of accessories that included figural nude lamps, bookends, ashtrays, etc. These white metal composition items were offered in several finishes including verde green, jap black, and gunmetal gray. The company also produced a line of caricatured animals, but the stylized nude figurals have proven to be the most collectible today. With few exceptions, all pieces were marked 'Frankart, Inc.' with a patent number or 'pat. appl. for.' All pieces listed are in very good original condition unless otherwise indicated. Our advisor for this category is Walter Glenn; he is listed in the Directory under Georgia.

Floor ashtray, three nudes hold
6" ash ball, 25", $1,600.00.

Aquarium, nude sits atop wrought-iron stand, aqua, sq, 14" 850.00
Ashtray, ballet girl in center of 8" rnd onyx tray, 10" 525.00
Ashtray, dancing nude holds tray on side, box on base, 10" 550.00
Ashtray, nude on pointe, 3 trays form ballerina's tutu, 10" 525.00
Ashtray, nude on tiptoe arches bk, holds 4" tray 475.00
Ashtray, seated nude w/matchbox holder, 5½" 450.00
Ashtray, stylized duck holds tray in outstretched wings, 5" 275.00
Bookends, caricatured cowboys in chaps, 8", pr 250.00
Bookends, nude sits atop human skull, 8", pr 450.00
Bookends, standing nude, arms bk to support, 7½", pr 285.00
Bookends, standing nude peeks around books, 8", pr 425.00
Bookends, stylized parrot on arched perch, 7", pr 275.00
Bowl, fruit; 2 bk-to-bk kneeling nudes hold 8" dish, 6" 875.00
Clock, 2 nudes kneel & hold 10" rnd glass clock, 12½" 2,200.00
Incense burner, standing nude holds tray in front, 10" 475.00
Lamp, kneeling nude gazes into 5" rnd globe, 7" 875.00
Lamp, seated nude, leg extended, 2" cylinders on sides, 8" 1,275.00
Lamp, standing nude silhouettes against glass fan, 10" 1,450.00
Lamp, 2 bk-to-bk dancing nudes hold sq glass cylinder, 13" 1,525.00
Lamp, 2 bk-to-bk nudes hold 8" ball globe, 21" 1,250.00
Lamp, 2 kneeling nudes embrace 8" crackle glass globe, 9" 975.00
Lamp, 2 nudes flank rectangular glass panel, 10½" 1,550.00
Mirror, kneeling nude holds 6" gold-bk mirror, 11" 650.00
Smoke set, seated nude, cigarette box on base, tray in ea arm, 9" ...650.00
Smoke stand, nude sits atop wrought-iron stand, 36" 650.00
Vase, dancing nude holds 10" flower vase on hip, 12½" 1,150.00
Vase, 2 bk-to-bk standing nudes hold 7" glass vase, 13" 850.00

Frankoma

The Frank Pottery, founded in Oklahoma in 1933 by John Frank, became known as Frankoma in 1934. The company produced decorative figurals, vases, and such, marking their ware from 1936 to 1938 with a pacing leopard 'Frankoma' mark. These pieces are highly sought. The entire operation was destroyed by fire in 1938, and new molds were cast — some from surviving pieces — and a similar line of production was pursued. The body of the ware was changed in 1955 from a honey tan (called 'Ada clay,' referring to the name of the town near the area where it was dug) to a red brick clay (known as Sapulpa), and this, along with the color of the glazes (over fifty have been used), helps determine the period of production. A Southwestern theme has always been favored in design as well as in color selection.

In 1965 they began to produce a limited-edition series of Christmas plates, followed by a bottle vase series in 1969. Considered very collectible are their political mugs, bicentennial plates, Teenagers of the Bible plates, and the Wildlife series. Their ceramic Christmas cards are also very popular items with today's collectors.

Frankoma celebrated their 50th anniversary in 1983. On September 26 of that same year, Frankoma was again destroyed by fire. Because of a fire-proof wall, master molds of all 1983 production items were saved, allowing plans for rebuilding to begin immediately.

Frankoma filed for Chapter 11 in April 1990, and eventually sold to a Maryland investor in February of 1991, thereby ending the family-ownership era. For a more thorough study of the subject, we recommend that you refer to *Frankoma Treasures* and *Frankoma and Other Oklahoma Potteries* by Phyllis and Tom Bess, our advisors; you will find their address in the Directory under Oklahoma.

Ashtray, arrowhead shape, turq, red clay, #453, 1953, 7" 15.00
Ashtray, Tulsarama, Desert Gold, red clay, 1957, 7¾" 35.00
Ashtrays, Dutch shoe shape, Clay Blue, 1958-60, #466, 6", pr 75.00
Baker, Mayan Aztec, Prairie Green, Ada clay, #7U, 1949-72, ind .45.00
Bank, collie head, med bl, 1971, 7¾" 125.00
Bank, mallard shape, Autumn Yellow, #382, 1980-83, 4¾" 45.00
Bell, 50th Anniversary, Owen & Opel, Desert Gold, red clay, 1¾" ..35.00
Bookend, bucking bronco, Prairie Green, #423, 1942-49, 5½", ea .175.00
Bowl, Cork Bark, Desert Gold, red clay, #B4, 1960-61, 9" 25.00
Bowl, cresent; Desert Gold, red clay, #211, 1950-69, 12½" 40.00
Bowl, Desert Gold, red clay, #214, 1950-69, 12" 30.00
Bowl, mint; Desert Gold, #34, 1936-38, sm, 3" 60.00
Bowl, Prairie Green, red clay, #45, 1955-78, 12" 40.00
Bowl, shell shape, Peacock Blue, #213, 1942-49, 14" 35.00
Candle holder, Aladdin lamp shape, wht, #309, 1968-70, 8½" 50.00
Candle holder, Lamp of Knowledge, White Sand, red clay, 5½" ..45.00
Candle holder, monk w/basket on bk, #308, 1934-35, 4½" 350.00
Canteen, Prairie Green, #59, incised mk 60.00
Canteen, thunderbird design, Prairie Green, Ada clay, #59K, 5" ..95.00
Cookie jar, swan lid, Prairie Green, #99, 1942, 10" 1,000.00
Figurine, fan dancer, Woodland Moss 500.00
Figurine, puma seated, White Sand 75.00
Flower frog, mermaid, Desert Gold, 1933-34, 7" 5,000.00
Flower frog, swan, ivory, 1936-38, 4" 350.00
Flower holder, hobby horse, Peacock Blue, #182, 1942, 3½" 200.00
Flowerabrum, Prairie Green, #58, ca 1942, 11½" 150.00
Humidor, ivory, w/lid, 1934-35, 6½" 300.00
Jar, Indian; Prairie Green, 27" circumference 300.00
Jug, Iowa Sunshine, Prairie Green, Ada clay, 1950s, 6½" 50.00
Jug, juice; Royal Blue, w/stopper, #90, 1936-42, 1-qt 85.00
Medallion, Texas cowboy, Osage Brown, prancing leopard logo, 2" .300.00
Medallion, woman, ivory, prancing leopard logo, 1936-37, 1¾" .250.00
Mug, Political; Nixon-Ford, Coffee Brown, 1974 ....500.00
Mug, War God; Desert Gold, red clay 50.00
Pitcher, Aztec decor, Old Gold, mini 30.00
Pitcher, snail shape, Old Gold, #558, 1942-51, mini, 2" 30.00
Planter, basket shape, Mountain Haze, #188, 1989-91, 4½" 25.00

Planter, turtle shape, Robin Egg Blue, #396, 1983-92, 7" **50.00**
Plate, Braille System, rubbed bsk, limited edition, 1977, 9" **125.00**
Plate, Cherokee Alphabet **47.50**
Plate, Conestoga wagon, pale bl, limited edition, 8½" **125.00**
Plate, dinner; Aztec, Desert Gold **15.00**
Plate, Oklahoma Eastern Star, Desert Gold, Ada clay, 7" **30.00**
Sculpture, Camel, irid blk, 1934-35, 6" **1,500.00**
Sculpture, Coati-Mundi, early Desert Gold, 1933-38, 4⅜" **3,000.00**
Sculpture, Cowboy, Osage Brown, 1934-35, 7½" **1,200.00**
Sculpture, Coyote Pup, Prairie Green, #105, 1934-38, 7¾" **2,000.00**
Sculpture, Harlem Hoofer, Pompeian Bronze, #127, 1934-35, 13" ..**4,000.00**
Sculpture, Indian Bowl Maker, Osage Brown, mk Taylor, 1934, 6¾" ..**2,500.00**
Sculpture, Ponytail Girl, red clay **95.00**
Sculpture, Prancing Colt, Prairie Green, #117, 1935-52, 8" **900.00**
Sculpture, Sitting Puma, red clay **55.00**
Sculpture, Squirrel, Willard Stone, #104, 1986-present, 6" **10.00**
Shakers, bbl shape, Prairie Green, Ada clay, #97H, 1950-61 ....**25.00**
Shakers, bull shape, Silver Sage, #166H, 1942, 2", pr **95.00**
Shakers, horseshoe shape, White Sand, red clay, 3" **30.00**
Shakers, oil derrick shape, Desert Gold, red clay, 1957, 3", pr **35.00**
Sign, #2, tepee, Prairie Green, Ada clay, 6½" **1,500.00**
Sugar bowl, Silver Sage, 2-hdl, w/lid, #92A, 1942 ....**75.00**
Table bell, brn satin, #817, 1982-69, 6" **30.00**
Teapot, Wagon Wheel, Prairie Green, #94T, 1942-76, 6-cup **75.00**
Teapot, Westwind, Desert Gold, #6J, 1966-69, 2-cup **25.00**
Toothbrush holder, Flame, #401, 1980-91 ....**20.00**
Tray, cracker; Royal Blue, grooved bottom, ca 1942, 6x6¾" **500.00**
Trivet, Lazybones, Desert Gold, red clay, #4TR, 1957 ....**65.00**
Vase, cornucopia; Peach Glow **30.00**
Vase, fan; shell shape, Desert Gold, Ada clay, 1942-65, #54, 6" ...**50.00**
Vase, Grecian, Prairie Green w/floral silver o/l **500.00**
Vase, Prairie Green, Ada clay, #28 ....**60.00**
Vase, Ram, Prairie Green, Ada clay, #38, sm **75.00**
Vase, ram's head, jade, #74, 1934-38, 9¼" **175.00**
Vase, redbud glaze, #502, 1950-51, 2¾" **65.00**
Vase/honey jar, Desert Gold, Ada clay, #832, 1950s, 6½" **55.00**
Wall pocket, Dutch shoe, Desert Gold, red clay, 1955, 8½" **50.00**
Wall pocket, Indian head, early bl, 1936-38, 3" **300.00**
Wall pocket, wagon wheel, Desert Gold, Ada clay, 1949-53, 7" ...**50.00**

Fraternal Organizations

Fraternal memorabilia is a vast and varied field. Emblems representing the various organizations have been used to decorate cups, shaving mugs, plates, and glassware. Medals, swords, documents, and other ceremonial paraphernalia from the 1800s and early 1900s are especially prized. Our advisor for Odd Fellows is Greg Spiess; he is listed in the Directory under Illinois. Information on Masonic and Shrine memorabilia has been provided by David Smies, who is listed under Kansas. Assistance concerning Elks collectibles was provided by David Wendel; he is listed in the Directory under Missouri.

Elks

Cuff links, enameled, pr **6.00**
Flask, ceramic, emb symbols, wht w/brn, dtd 1912, 4½x2½" **140.00**
Inkwell, elk's-head base, rack is pen holder, O of E, 1800s **165.00**
Medal, 1901 convention, 2x4" **18.00**
Note pad & pencil, Ladies' Night, 1916, EX **40.00**
Ribbon, Syracuse Lodge...1885, w/2½" bronze pin **10.00**
Watch button, celluloid, w/2 1933 ribbons **25.00**
Watch fob **20.00**
Watch fob/cigarette case, sterling w/gold symbols **95.00**

Masons

Apron, metallic embr on wht satin & bl velvet, 12x14" +fringe ...**22.00**
Ashtray, brass, sq & compass, 1934 ....**22.00**
Book, Richardson's Monitor, 1950 ....**25.00**
Chairs, red/blk grpt w/yel stripes/gold emblems, 1 arm+5 sides ..**1,150.00**
Decoration, CI, compass, T-sq & C emblems, 1800s, 7x6x1¼" **65.00**
Game, Build, Whitehall Games Inc, 1980 ....**15.00**
Ring, 14k gold, 32nd Degree **150.00**
Rug, emblem & Lodge name & #, Oriental type, 49x36" **290.00**
Settle, old gray over wht w/pnt symbols, plank seat, 99" L **500.00**

Odd Fellows

Badge, memorial; Rebeka Lodge, ornate, 1894 ....**27.50**
Banner, symbols on bl, gold braid, 30x18", EX **100.00**
Collar, cream w/red trim, 4 rosettes, VG **4.00**
Cookie mold, symbols, CI, 1820s, 5x6½" **275.00**
Mask, Goliath, horsehair beard/mustache, ca 1900 ....**195.00**
Mask, pnt wire mesh w/cloth cap, ca 1900, EX **50.00**
Match safe, brass, symbols & emb ribbon, late 1800s, 2¼" **95.00**
Medal, Grand Lodge...San Francisco, 1904, w/purple ribbon **22.00**
Sash, red & wht stripes, stars on bl at top, 1890s, 39x5" **53.00**
Symbol, 3 cvd/pnt rings linked together, 19th C, 20" L **175.00**
Tankard, Justice/allegorical gray transfer w/mc, 4" **50.00**

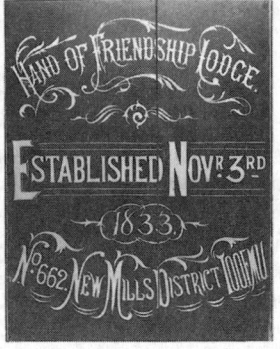

Triptych, Past Grands from 1833 to 1946, gilt and black paint, 32" H, $990.00.

Turban, EX **7.50**
Wristwatch, symbols on dial, silver case, Waltham, NM **250.00**

Shrine

Badge, enameled, 2-pc, MN, 1908 ....**13.50**
Cane, wood, Nile Temple, Seattle, 1936 ....**40.00**
Chalice, cranberry glass w/silver sword hdls, 1908 ....**92.50**
Cigar cutter, Crowe Chicago, pocket sz **28.00**
Cup, Indian head in relief, mc pnt on glass, 1903 ....**45.00**
Earrings, Bakelite ivory cabochon w/orange ball drop, pr **35.00**
Goblet, ruby stained, St Paul MN, 1908 ....**36.00**
Measure, dbl liquor; cranberry & clear glass, St Louis, 1909 ....**72.00**
Paperweight, spelter figure, 5" **45.00**
Pin, sword w/set-in rhinestones, sterling **4.00**
Tile, desert scene w/camel/pyramids/etc, 6x6" **50.00**
Tumbler, officers & donkey on milk glass, sq, 1917 ....**120.00**
Tumbler, Pittsburgh, 1900 ....**63.00**
Wine, all symbols, dtd 1899 ....**75.00**

Miscellaneous

Eastern Star, spoon, sterling, ca 1950s **38.50**
Eastern Star, wreath pin, enamel star/seed pearls on 10k gold **35.00**

Knights of Columbus, sword, w/canvas case 95.00
Moose, fob, 14k w/tooth 45.00

Fraunfelter

Charles Fraunfelter organized his company in Zanesville, Ohio, in 1915. It was known as the Ohio Pottery Company until 1923. During this period their main product was a line of utilitarian articles for chemical laboratories made of hard-paste porcelain. In 1918 they used the same body to produce a brown and white line called 'Petruscan.' By 1920 a line of hotel ware was added. The company organized in 1923 and became known and Fraunfelter China Company; but after the death of Fraunfelter in 1925, the business fell into hard times and eventually closed altogether in 1939.

Casserole, fruit & floral band, 3x8x6", w/lid & chrome holder 40.00
Casserole, Royalite decal, in chrome holder 25.00
Coffee set, flower panels/gold lustre, percolator+cr/sug+6 cups 85.00
Coffee urn, Poppy, chrome trim, Royal Rochester, 14½" 65.00
Cup, demitasse; gold band at rim, in silver chrome holder 25.00
Custard cup, brn lustre, #11, mk 10.00
Teapot, brn ribs, 5½" 15.00
Teapot, cobalt w/gold trim, ind 95.00
Teapot, floral silver o/l on ivory, repousse lid, 6", +trivet 75.00
Teapot, Manhattan style, dk gr w/gold, ind 35.00
Teapot, New York style, dk turq w/gold, 5-cup 75.00
Vase, gold stylized trees on wht, sgn Lessell, #98, 9½" 375.00
Vase, gr luster w/gold & blk Oriental decor, #80, 4½" 45.00

Fruit Jars

As early as 1829, canning jars were being manufactured for use in the home preservation of foodstuffs. For the past twenty-five years, they have been sought as popular collectibles. At the last estimate, over four thousand fruit jars and variations were known to exist. Some are very rare, perhaps one-of-a-kind examples known to have survived to the present day. Among the most valuable are the black glass jars, the amber Van Vliet, and the cobalt Millville. These often bring prices in excess of $5,000.00 when they can be found. Aside from condition, values are based on age, rarity, color, and special features. Our advisor for this category is John Hathaway; he is listed in the Directory under Maine.

Ball Perfect Mason, olive-amber, smooth base, ca 1910 – 20, one-quart, M, $160.00.

A&DH Chambers Union...PA (base), aqua, wax sealer, tin lid, qt ..30.00
Acme Seal (script), clear, regular mouth, qt 50.00
Allen's Patent June 1871, aqua w/clear lid, orig clamp, qt 185.00
Anchor Mason's Patent, sun-colored amethyst, qt 45.00
Atlas (Strong Shoulder), cornflower bl, qt 40.00
Atlas (Strong Shoulder), yel-gr, pt 65.00
Atlas E-Z Seal, amber w/amber lid, qt 60.00
Atlas E-Z Seal, amber w/milk glass lid, qt 55.00

Atlas E-Z Seal, bl, qt 18.00
Atlas E-Z Seal, bl or gr, pt 18.00
Atlas EZ Seal (no hyphens), aqua, ½-pt 25.00
Atlas Good Luck, clear, full wire bail, ½-pt 25.00
Atlas Jr Mason, clear, ½-pt 18.00
Atlas Mason Improved, sky bl, qt 25.00
Atlas Mason Improved Patent CN 520, apple gr, qt 30.00
Atlas Special Mason, aqua, qt 10.00
AW Pitts, PA (base), aqua, wax sealer, tin lid, ½-gal 28.00
Ball (in tail of M) Mason, lt bl, pt 20.00
Ball (script) Mason's Patent 1858, aqua, qt 15.00
Ball (slanted L's) Perfect Mason, aqua, qt 12.00
Ball Ideal, Ball bl, full wire bail, ½-pt 75.00
Ball Ideal Rev Patd July 14 1908, lt gr, dimple neck, pt 12.00
Ball Improved Ghost Mason, aqua, pt 20.00
Ball Mason, lt olive gr, pt 30.00
Ball Mason (3 loop), aqua w/sm amber swirl, qt 25.00
Ball Mason (3-tapered), clear, pt 53.00
Ball Mason's Patent 1858, aqua, pt 12.00
Ball Perfect Mason, Ball bl, ½-pt 125.00
Ball Perfect Mason, emerald gr, qt 100.00
Baltimore Glass Works, aqua, w/repro stopper, qt 390.00
Banner (circled by patent dates), aqua, qt 148.00
Banner (circled by patent dates), aqua, ½-gal 175.00
Bosco Double Seal, clear, qt 43.00
Bostwick Perfect Sealer (script), clear, orig closure, pt 90.00
Brackett's Perfection, aqua, qt 425.00
Brighton, clear, pt 25.00
Burlington BG Co R'D 1876, clear, ½-gal 48.00
Canton Domestic, clear, ½-gal 125.00
Carrols True Seal (w/star in stippled fr), clear, pt 35.00
Clarke...Cleveland O, aqua, orig closure, ½-gal 125.00
Clyde (script), clear, qt 12.00
Cohansey Glass Mfg Co, aqua, bbl-shaped base, wax sealer, ½-gal .98.00
Cohansey Mfg Co Pat Mch 20 77 (base), aqua, bbl shape, qt 128.00
Commonwealth, clear, qt 88.00
Crown Cordial & Extract & Co New York, aqua, ½-gal 25.00
Crown Cordial & Extract & Co New York, clear, ½-gal 12.00
Daisy (in circle), clear, pt 12.00
Double Safety, sun-colored amethyst, qt 9.00
Double Seal, clear, qt 20.00
Gem Wallagerburg, clear, ½-gal 20.00
Geo D Brown, lt aqua, repro clamp 48.00
Green Mountain (in fr), clear, qt 12.00
Green Mountain CA Co (in circle), aqua, pt 12.00
Hero Improved, aqua, qt 28.00
Ideal, aqua, qt 18.00
Jewel (block letters in fr), clear, qt 15.00
Jewel Jar (block letters in fr), clear, qt 15.00
Kerr Self Sealing Mason, amber, qt 30.00
Keystone Mason Fruit Jar Patent Nov 30th 1858, aqua, ½-gal 25.00
King (on banner below crown), clear, twin side clamps, qt 10.00
Lafayette (script), aqua, ½-gal 175.00
Lafayette (script), clear, rare, ½-gal 190.00
Leotric, clear, sm mouth, qt 20.00
Lipton Fruit Growers & Preserver, lt gr, pt 220.00
Mason (in str line), amber, pt 100.00
Mason Jar of 1872, aqua, ½-gal 45.00
Mason Patent Sept 24th 1872, aqua, qt 83.00
Mason's (Cross) Improved, aqua, qt 5.00
Mason's (Cross) Patent Nov 30th 1858, amber, ½-gal 225.00
Mason's (Cross) Patent Nov 30th 1858, lt apple gr, qt 70.00
Mason's CFJ Improved, aqua, midget 25.00
Mason's CFJ Patent Nov 30th 1858, lt gr, pt 35.00

Mason's CFJ Patent Nov 30th 1858, sky bl, qt 295.00
Mason's II Patent Nov 30th 1858, aqua, qt 35.00
Mason's III Patent Nov 30th 1858, aqua, qt 125.00
Mason's Patent, teal, ½-gal 25.00
Mason's Patent Nov 30th 1858, sun-colored amethyst, qt 35.00
Mason's Patent Nov 30th 58, aqua, midget 60.00
Millville Atmospheric, aqua, repro clamp, 68-oz 55.00
New Gem, sun-colored amethyst, qt 35.00
Peerless, aqua, ½-gal 135.00
Penn (The), aqua, wax sealer, tin lid, ftd base, qt 68.00
Penn (The), aqua, wax sealer, tin lid, ftd base, ½-gal 125.00
Potter & Bodine Philadelphia (script), aqua, orig lid, ½-gal 195.00
Potter & Bodine Philadelphia (script), aqua, w/lid, qt 123.00
Queen (circle by patent dates), aqua, qt 33.00
Rau's Improved Pat Applied For, clear, groove ring, qt 45.00
Schaffer Jar Rochester NY, aqua, dome lid, orig closure, qt 350.00
St Louis Syrup & Preserving Co St Louis MO, aqua, qt 35.00
Standard (arched), aqua, wax sealer, tin lid, qt 25.00
Standard (slanted), gr, wax sealer, tin lid, qt 20.00
Superior AG Co (in circle), aqua, qt 12.00
TM Lighting, amber w/touch of gr, ½-gal 135.00
TM Lighting Registered US Patent Office, cornflower bl, pt 100.00

Fry

Henry Fry established his glassworks in 1901 in Rochester, Pennsylvania. There, until 1933 when it was sold to the Libbey Company, he produced glassware of the finest quality. In the early years they produced beautiful cut glass; and when it began to wane in popularity, Fry turned to the manufacture of occasional pieces and oven glassware. He is perhaps most famous for the opalescent pearl glass called 'Foval.' It was sometimes made with blue or jade green trim in combination. Because it was in production for only a short time in 1926 and 1927, it is hard to find. Our advisor for this category is Ron Damaska; he is listed in the Directory under Pennsylvania. See also Kitchen Collectibles, Glassware.

Baker, Pearl Ovenware, oval, w/lid, 1932, 12" 75.00
Basket, cut, hobstars & notching, t'print hdl, 5¼x4¼" 300.00
Basket, cut, pinwheel & notching, rnd, sm 350.00
Bean pot, Pearl Ovenware, 1924, 2-pt 60.00
Bowl, berry; Foval, Delft bl ft, Rockwell silver o/l 300.00
Bowl, cut, hobstars, strawberry fields, rim w/lg fans, 9" 185.00
Candlesticks, bl appl spiral looping, collar & ring, 10¾", pr 275.00
Candlesticks, Foval, spiral stems & Delft bl wafers, 11", pr 300.00
Coffeepot, Foval, Delft bl knob & hdl, 11" 200.00
Comport, Foval w/Delft bl trim & festooning, 5½" 350.00
Compote, cut, X-hatching & stars, 3" 180.00
Compote, Foval w/Delft bl appl to lip & stem, 4¼x9½" 220.00
Compote, royal bl, baluster stem, 5x8½" 200.00
Creamer & sugar bowl, Foval, Delft bl hdls, #2000 ....200.00
Creamer & sugar bowl, Reliance, cut 215.00
Cup & saucer, Foval, Delft bl trim 40.00
Cup & saucer, tea; Foval, tall, #9003 ....80.00
Custard cup, Pearl Ovenware, cut leaf band, 1927 ....20.00
Egg cup, Foval, jade ft, #2300 ....115.00
Ferner, Albert, ftd 250.00
Meatloaf, Pearl Ovenware, emb grapes, w/lid, 1928, 9" 40.00
Muffin pan, Pearl Ovenware, 6-compartment, 1956, 9" 60.00
Nappy, cut, flashed hobstars, snowflake-like center, hdl, 6" 125.00
Pitcher, cut, lg pinwheels over notched prisms, 8" 240.00
Relish dish, Trojan, cut, oval, 10" 150.00
Roaster, Pearl Ovenware, w/lid, 1946, 14" dia 140.00
Teapot, Foval, English, 6-cup 300.00

Tray, cut, flashed hobstars, 3-ftd, 10½" dia 150.00
Vase, cut, hobstars & sm panels of cane, trumpet form, 18" 375.00
Vase, jack-in-pulpit; Foval w/Delft bl trim, #821, 10" 250.00

Fulper

Throughout the 19th century (for perhaps as long as one hundred years) the Fulper pottery in Flemington, New Jersey, produced utitarian and commercial wares. But it was during the span from 1909 to 1935 (the Arts & Crafts period in particular) that they became prominent producers of beautifully glazed art pottery. Although most pieces were cast and not hand decorated, their graceful, classical shapes combined with wonderful experimental glaze combinations made each piece a true work of art.

The company also made dolls' heads, Kewpies, figural perfume lamps, and powder boxes. Examples prized most highly by collectors today are those that were produced before the devastating fire of 1929 and the subsequent takeover by Martin Stangl. (See Stangl Pottery.)

Several marks were used: a vertical in-line 'Fulper' being the most common, a horizontal mark, Flemington, Rafco, Prang, and paper labels (on earlier pieces). Most Fulper is marked although unmarked pots that surface can be identified by shape and glaze characteristics. Values are determined by size, desirability of glaze, and rarity of form. Lamps with colored glass inserts are rare and avidly sought by collectors. Our advisor for this category is Douglass White; he is listed in the Directory under Florida.

Bowl, bl crystalline, scalloped, ribbed, ftd, 6½x11" 350.00
Bowl, bl/cream/gr flambe over bl matt, flat rim flange, 10" 180.00
Bowl, Effigy, cat's eye flambe, mustard matt/brn ext, 8x11" 750.00
Bowl, leopard skin crystalline, 2x5", set of 6 ....425.00
Candlesticks, ivory/Fr gloss, 4-sided w/rnd base, 10½", pr 700.00
Lamp base, Chinese Bl crystalline, classic shape, 17x8½" 1,000.00
Lamp base, frothy bl crystalline, faceted sides, ftd, 12" 325.00
Pilgrim flask, Flemington Gr flambe, disc w/ornate hdls, 10" 750.00
Temple jar, mirror blk crystalline, 13½", NM 2,100.00
Vase, bl/gr/yel flambe over Famille Rose, rim hdls, 9x7½" 550.00
Vase, bl/ivory sheer flambe drip on mustard matt, 3¾x3¾" 175.00
Vase, brn/cream/tan crystalline drip, sqd shoulder hdls, 12½" .1,400.00
Vase, caramel/gr under gr/gray crystalline, spherical, 5½" 550.00
Vase, cat's eye flambe, classic shape, stilt pull, 13x6" 600.00
Vase, cat's eye flambe, cylindrical w/sm bulb neck, 5½" 400.00
Vase, cat's eye/Chinese Bl flambe, squat gourd shape, 4x6" 175.00
Vase, Chinese Bl dripping flambe, incurvate cylinder, 7x4¾" 325.00
Vase, Chinese Bl matt crystalline drip, cylindrical, 13x4" 1,600.00
Vase, Chinese Bl/ivory flambe, incurvate cylinder, 14x11" 2,900.00

Vase, copperdust crystalline with embossed decor, corseted with closed-in top, #592, 11½x9", $6,500.00; Vase, Elephant's Breath flambe over mustard matt, ovoid, #425, 12¼x9", $3,250.00.

Vase, copperdust crystalline, rnded-off panels, #592, 12x9" **6,500.00**
Vase, copperdust crystalline froth, angle hdls, 5x6" **425.00**
Vase, copperdust crystalline to gr, rim-to-low-width hdls, 10 .....**550.00**
Vase, cream/purple/taupe crystalline drip over mocha, 12" **650.00**
Vase, cream/tan/brn flambe over bl & gunmetal, 7x5" **325.00**
Vase, cucumber crystalline, spherical, 6x7" **1,300.00**
Vase, cucumber crystalline/matt, ovoid w/appl ring hdls, 13x8" ..**1,000.00**
Vase, cucumber gr to Flemington Gr flambe, #600l, 15x7" **3,250.00**
Vase, dk brn/gray matt crystalline, Vasekraft, 4x3" **375.00**
Vase, elephant's breath flambe over mustard, #425, 12x9" **3,250.00**
Vase, Flemington Gr flambe, rim-to-low-width buttresses, 14" .**2,400.00**
Vase, gr frothy matt, 5½x8" **500.00**
Vase, gr to cobalt crystalline flambe, rim-to-shoulder hdls, 8" **300.00**
Vase, gr/turq crystalline, ovoid, 9x6" **350.00**
Vase, gunmetal flambe, 3x2½" **150.00**
Vase, gunmetal froth/hare's-fur drip on bl crystalline, 13x11" .**3,750.00**
Vase, hammered leopard skin crystalline, horizontal hdls 12x11" .**1,200.00**
Vase, ivory/elephant's breath flambe, base: emb mushrooms, 10" .**1,425.00**
Vase, ivory/gunmetal/mahog flambe, ribbed, hdls, 12½x8" **650.00**
Vase, ivory/mahog/mirror blk flambe, ribbed w/hdls, 12x7½" .**1,000.00**
Vase, lav/tan/leopard skin crystalline flambe, dbl-gourd, 11" ..**2,700.00**
Vase, leopard skin crystalline, baluster, 10¾x4½" **450.00**
Vase, leopard skin crystalline, lg rim-to-width hdls, 8x1½" **550.00**
Vase, leopard skin crystalline, rim-to-width angle hdls, 6½x8" ..**550.00**
Vase, leopard skin crystalline, sphere w/3 rim hdls, 6½x7½" **650.00**
Vase, lt gr crystalline, squat body, long trumpet neck, 11" **425.00**
Vase, mahog/gr lustre flambe, short-neck bottle form, 9" **1,100.00**
Vase, mirror blk crystalline, 5x3" **200.00**
Vase, mirror blk over rose famille, short neck, bulbous body, 8" .**450.00**
Vase, mirror blk to copperdust crystalline, scroll hdls, 15x7" ...**1,300.00**
Vase, mirror blk to Flemington Gr flambe, ovoid, 5½x3" **400.00**
Vase, mirror blk/copperdust crystalline, emb dots at neck, 7x5" .**600.00**
Vase, mirror gr over mahog flambe, shoulder hdls, 8x6¾" **300.00**
Vase, rose matt w/gr/bl drip, spherical w/3 sm rim hdls, 6½" **400.00**
Vase, turq crystalline/moss flambe, 6-sided classic shape, 11" **300.00**
Vase, yel over brn/bl/gr flambe, bulbous w/waisted neck, 8" **550.00**

Furniture

American 17th- and 18th-century furniture played an important role in our country's environment. Aside from its utility, furniture was a symbol indicating wealth, taste, and station in life of the owner. Each period brought about distinct design changes that created a recognizable form for that particular time frame. Our earliest furniture was handmade by the cabinetmaker with apprentices and journeymen who learned every phase of the craft from the master cabinetmaker. The end of the Civil War brought the Industrial Revolution and mechanization of furniture manufacturing. With it came the ornate Victorian period and the many revival styles. These were followed in the 20th century by Art Deco and Art Nouveau and more revival of our earliest periods.

It is important for the buyer of antique and collectible furniture to approach each piece from the point of view of the prevailing taste of that particular time frame. Pieces from lesser cabinetmakers should be recognized simply as old furniture, as age alone does not equal value.

The marketplace has completely recovered from the recession; however, the fashion in the marketplace has changed...Victorian and turn-of-the-century and Jacobean oak may never hit the highs of years past. Still rising are the well made and collectible mahogany pieces from the first half of the 20th century. Making new inroads in collectibility are the designs of the '50s and '60s, which are still quite affordable. Traditional mahogany furniture from the 20th century and machine made in the style of Hepplewhite, Sheraton, and Duncan Phyfe

is still enjoying great popularity as is its English counterparts. Turn-of-the-century European inlaid and carved furniture is also rising in value. Commonplace oak furniture is still selling well below its highs of a few years ago. Items that have sold at auction for at least 25% lower than their normal market values will be designated with (*). Items listed in the lines that are designated with (**) are pieces in the best of form and of museum quality.

Please note: If a piece actually dates to the period of time during which it originated, we will use the name of the style only. For example: 'Hepplewhite' will indicate an American piece from roughly the late 1700s to 1815. The term 'style' will describe a piece that is far removed from the original time frame. 'Hepplewhite style' refers to examples from the turn of the century. When the term 'repro' is used it will mean that the item in question is less than thirty years old and is being sold on a secondary market. When only one dimension is given for blanket chests, dry sinks, tables, settees, sideboards, and sofas, it is length.

Condition is the most important factor to consider in determining value. It is also important to remember that *where* a piece sells has a definite bearing on the price it will realize, due simply to regional preference. Our advisor for this category is Suzy McLennan Anderson, ISA, of Heritage Antiques, whose address is listed in the Directory under New Jersey. (Photo and SASE required; no phone appraisals.) To learn more about furniture, we recommend *The Collector's Encyclopedia of American Furniture* (there are three in the series), and *Furniture of the Depression Era* by Robert and Harriet Swedberg; *Heywood-Wakefield Modern Furniture* by Steve and Roger Rouland; *Antique Oak Furniture* by Conover Hill; *American Oak Furniture, Books I and II* and *Victorian Furniture, Our American Heritage, Books I and II* by Kathryn McNerney; and *Collector's Guide to Oak Furniture* by Jennifer George. See also Art Deco; Art Nouveau; Arts and Crafts; Fifties Modern; Nutting, Wallace; Shaker; Stickley.

Key:

Am — American	Geo — Georgian
bj — bootjack	grpt — grainpainted
brd — board	hdbd — headboard
Chpndl — Chippendale	hdw — hardware
Co — Country	Hplwht — Hepplewhite
cvd — carved	mar — marriage
cvg — carving	NE — New England
c&b — claw and ball	QA — Queen Anne
do — door	rswd — rosewood
drw — drawer	trn — turning
Emp — Empire	uphl — upholstered/upholstery
Fed — Federal	vnr — veneer
Fr — French	Vict — Victorian
ftbd — footboard	W/M — William and Mary
G — good	: — over (example: 1 do: 2 drw)
Geo — Georgian	

Armoires, See Also Wardrobes

Chestnut Fr Provincial 'Bretagne' w/cvg, 19th C, 89x51x20" .**1,980.00**
Chestnut Fr Provincial, canted/molded cornice, much cvg, 88x52" **2,500.00**
Chestnut Provincial Louis XV, dbl do, 92x60x26" **6,000.00**
Fruitwood Louis XVI, cartouch panel do, scrolls, 87x42x26" ..**2,200.00**
Mahog Am Classic w/figure, cornice:2 do:3 drw, 87x66x28" ...**5,775.00**
Mahog Am Late Classical, 2 figured do, drws in base, 1830s, 92" .**3,400.00**
Mahog Am Late Classical w/fine figure, 2-do, 1840s, 90x79" ..**3,500.00**
Rswd Am Rococo, 1-do, arched cornice w/crest, drw **6,000.00**
Walnut Am, dbl-do, cvd crest/frieze, 2-drw, 1850s, 106x61x20" **3,575.00**
Walnut Am w/foliate/shell-cvd crest atop bonnet, 1-do/1-drw ..**3,400.00**

Beds

American carved mahogany four-poster bed, foliate carved headboard, acanthus carved finials, 106x72", ca 1840 – 50, $4,000.00.

Brass, plain, early 20th C, 69x42" **350.00**
Brass, Vict, fancy, 69x58" **1,400.00**
Canopy, mahog Fed, tall cvd posts, 77x52" **2,500.00**
Cherry Sheraton-style, cvd swags/tassels, 59" posts, full sz **550.00**
Convent, trn walnut, ca 1900, 79" posts, 42" W **770.00**
Field, birch Sheraton NE, orig canopy fr, 66x70x57" **4,950.00**
Half-tester, walnut & burl Am, serpentine beads, arched hdbd .**6,875.00**
Half-tester, walnut Am Renaissance, arched hdbd, Sampson, 102" ..**2,000.00**
Hired man's, poplar, old pnt, 29x74" **200.00**
Low post, mahog vnr Classical cvd, ca 1835-45, 56x78x59" **1,100.00**
Low post/folding, old Spanish brn pnt, trn posts, 1800s, 34x78x53" **700.00**
Mahog Am Late Classical w/Gothic arched panels, 59x61" **1,300.00**
Maple Sheraton w/pine hdbd, extended rails, 59" H, full sz **1,650.00**
Rope, curly maple, cut-out eagle hdbd, OH, 1840s, 53x70x53" .**3,000.00**
Rope, maple, sq posts, trn finials, molded hdbd, rfn, 49" W **110.00**
Rope, 4-post cannon-ball style, shaped pine hdbd, 46x71x50" ...**200.00**
Sleigh, figured mahog, 59x69x45" **2,000.00**
Tall post, cherry/hardwoods, trn/cvd posts, rpl fr, single **550.00**
Tall post, mahog Classical vnr, trn ft, ca 1825-35, 98x81x59" ...**7,000.00**
Tall post, mahog Fed w/leaf cvgs, 2-brd hdbd, 90x72x52" **3,850.00**
Tall post, maple Co Hplwht w/old rfn, rpl fr, 76x71x50" **1,265.00**
Tall post, poplar Co Sheraton, rpr, 79x72x52" **600.00**
Tall post, W&M, barley-twist posts, ball ft, uphl hdbd, 94x69" **3,575.00**
Tester, mahog Am Late Classical, acanthus posts, stepped, 107" ..**6,600.00**
Tester, pine Sheraton, bold trns, 49x76" **600.00**
Tester, tiger maple Sheraton, red stain, 79x70x50" **1,000.00**
Trundle, pine hdbd w/sq posts, wooden wheels, 18x53x42" **100.00**
Walnut Am laminated/cvd, arched hdbd w/crest, 1850s **3,000.00**
Walnut figured vnr Vict, trn/molded details, single sz **220.00**
Walnut Vict Baroque Revival w/figured vnr panels, 88x71x61" ...**1,300.00**
Walnut w/burl vnr Vict, appl moldings, cvd details, 80x72x58" .**440.00**
4-poster, cherry Co, trn posts, scroll-eared hdbd, 1830s, 97" ...**4,400.00**
4-poster, shaped hdbd w/trn blanket roll attached, 46x72x51" ...**250.00**
4-poster, walnut, spool trns, 67x56" w/76" rails **385.00**

Benches

Co Sheraton Windsor, trn spindles/posts/rungs, rush seat, 73" ...**770.00**
Cobbler's, leather seat, iron tacks, compartments, 19th C, 50" ...**325.00**
Louis XIV w/old caned bk & seat, EX cvg, velvet cushion, 78" ...**3,200.00**
Pine, 2-tier, str legs, orig gr pnt, New England, 27x48x21" **1,265.00**
Rswd Am Rococo w/cvd medallion, cabriole legs, 1850s, 16x43x20" .**770.00**
Settle, bamboo Windsor, 1-brd plank seat w/old rpr, crest, 77" ..**1,045.00**

Settle, PA decor, stencil/freehand flowers/etc, trn legs, 79" **4,950.00**
Water, birch/pine w/old red, trn ft, 5-shelf, 52x64x12½" **1,400.00**
Water, pine Co, 3-shelf, plank ends w/cutouts, 19th C, 42x52" .**525.00**
Water, primitive pine, gray pnt, str apron, low shelf, 23x56" **650.00**
Window, mahog vnr Classical cvd, uphl seat, 1835-45, 18x48x16" ..**2,185.00**

Blanket Chests, Coffers, Trunks, and Mule Chests

Euro mc pnt w/crest/vintage/etc, worn/damage, 56" L **990.00**
Hardwood/pine Chpndl w/rpt brn grpt, 6-brd type, 2-drw, 38" ..**2,300.00**
Immigrant's, dome top, rose decor, rpl trn ft, 1805, 30" **990.00**
Mahog vnr w/cedar-lined compartments, Lane, 47⅜" **150.00**
Oak English, paneled front/ends, 2-drw, 18th C, 30x52x22" **550.00**
Pine w/old dk pnt & mc florals, 6-brd, 2 dvtl drw, 42" **880.00**
Pine w/old red, 6-brd type, 2 dvtl drw, rpl brasses, 36" **2,500.00**
Pnt splotches & swirls, red on putty, bj ends, till, 20x44x16" **700.00**
Poplar w/mc floral on dk gr rpt, dvtl bracket ft, apron, 32" **635.00**
Poplar/chestnut, old rpt w/HP flowers, trn legs, till, 37" **550.00**
Poplar/chestnut Co Hplwht w/worn red, 2 dvtl drw, 38x41x20" **1,375.00**
Walnut Co, dvtl case, bracket ft, scroll detail, w/till, 50" **635.00**
Walnut/poplar, stylized floral/compass star/etc, att Yoder, 44" .**4,400.00**

Bookcases

Lawyer's, walnut step-bk, dbl 4-pane do:4 panel do, rfn, 97x59" .**2,400.00**
Mahog Am, highly cvd, cabriole legs, ca 1890, 72x60", pr **12,000.00**
Mahog vnr, 3 stacked sections, Wernicke, OH, 36x34" **330.00**
Mahog vnr, 3 stacked sections, Wernicke, OH, 50x35" **380.00**
Mahog vnr, 4 stacked sections w/base & top, Wernicke, OH, 61x34" ..**440.00**
Quarter-sawn figure, paw ft, apron, glass do, Golden Oak era, 58" .**400.00**
Quarter-sawn oak, 3 stacked sections w/base & top, Camden, 45x34" ..**300.00**
Rswd vnr Gothic Revival, dbl do:2 dvtl drw, rfn, 85x49" **935.00**
Walnut Fr Gothic cvd, 19th C, 69x38x18" **2,100.00**
Walnut Vict, appl moldings/cvd details, 2-drw, 2 glass do, 68x55" **2,000.00**

Cabinets

Breakfront, mahog Chpndl style, 82" **1,500.00**
China, quarter-sawn oak, compo details, curved glass, 64x40" ...**525.00**
China, quarter-sawn oak, curved glass sides, center do, 60x38" ..**330.00**
Curio, Edwardian w/inlay, 2 glass do w/cathedral moldings, 70x45" ..**1,000.00**
Curio, Fr, Marjorelle, ormolu, 19th C **2,500.00**
Curio, mahog Fr-style w/scenic panels, curved glass, 58x28x17" .**1,850.00**
Curio, mahog Late Emp, bow-front **600.00**
Curio, vnr Fr-style w/inlay, rstr pntings, glass shelves, 59" **550.00**
Mahog Edwardian-style, open shelves/drw/pullouts, 20th C, 33x55" .**1,100.00**
Music, rswd Am Renaissance w/inlay, panel do, 46x25x20" **1,550.00**
Music, rswd Edwardian w/inlay, broken arch pediment, 59x22" ..**1,100.00**
Music, rswd Rococo cvd, lift top, fitted int, 19th C, 30x22x16" .**660.00**
Music, walnut, bow-front, brass trim **450.00**
Oak Flemish, cvd facade, figural pilasters, rstr, 39x31x23" **3,575.00**
Oak Vict, ornate cvgs, crown crest, 2 glass do/panels, 82x52x20" .**1,750.00**
Parlor, rswd Am Renaissance w/marquetry inlay, 1865, 57x77x19" **11,000.00**
Press, cherry Late Fed w/inlay, drws in base, Fr ft, 75x41" **2,200.00**
Vernis Martin, HP figures w/instruments, ormolu mts, 55x27" ..**1,500.00**
Vernis Martin, 2 HP nude youths w/flute & book, ormolu, 59" .**1,900.00**
Vitrine, satinwood Biedermeier w/inlay, glass shelves, 52x32" **1,600.00**

Candlestands

Birch Co Chpndl w/red traces, 1-brd top, tripod base, 27x19" dia ..**275.00**
Cherry Chpndl cleaned down, tripod base, snake ft, 1-brd, 26" ..**440.00**
Cherry Hplwht, sq top w/notched corners, 3 spider legs, 38" **450.00**
Cherry Hplwht, tripod base, snake ft, 2-brd, rfn, 28x17x16" **990.00**

Co, X-shaped base, mortised fr, pegs & early nails, 34x13x12" ..1,200.00
Curly maple Hplwht, tripod w/spider legs, att NY, 28x17x17" ..6,300.00
Tilt-top, birch Hplwht, tripod base, rpr/rfn, 28x21" dia 300.00
Tilt-top, mahog Am Hplwht, tripod base w/spider legs, 38x17x17" ..385.00
Tilt-top, mahog Fed, 8-sided, vase/ring-trn post, spider legs 1,500.00
Tilt-top, mahog Hplwht, tripod base, snake ft, rprs, 26x21x16" .330.00
Tilt-top, walnut Chpndl, tripod base w/snake ft, old rpr, 28x22" ...1,100.00
Tilt-top, walnut PA Chpndl, tripod w/snake ft, birdcage, 30" dia ..2,400.00
Windsor, dished style w/3 splayed legs, old rfn, 1780s, 36x13" .1,850.00

Chairs

Queen Anne side chair, block
and ring turnings, Spanish feet,
early red paint, New England,
1700s, ** (museum quality),
39½", $1,100.00.

Arm, bamboo Windsor w/old blk pnt & yel striping, 35" 1,375.00
Arm, Chpndl-style wing-bk, brn leather uphl, modern repro, 44" ..550.00
Arm, Co QA, old red rpt, rpl rush seat, 44" 880.00
Arm, Co Windsor bow-bk, trn legs, rfn/rpl, 39x18" 415.00
Arm, English Regency pnt-decor Sheraton, cane seat, 19th C ..1,200.00
Arm, Fr-style wing-bk w/cvd walnut fr, reuphl brocade, 43" 440.00
Arm, fruitwood Biedermeier, laminated bk, reuphl, worn, 32" ...195.00
Arm, Louis XVI w/cvd fr, cane bk & seat (G), 20th C, 31" 220.00
Arm, mahog English Gainsborough-style, serpentine crest, 19th C ..470.00
Arm, mahog Geo III-style, shaped bk/seat, cotton reuphl 600.00
Arm, oak Charles II-style, uphl bk/seat, 19th C 2,200.00
Arm, rswd Am Rococo, foliate crest, uphl bk/seat, worn 935.00
Arm, Sheraton, wing-bk, trn front legs, worn uphl, rprs, 45" 990.00
Arm, walnut Venetian cvd, old uphl, ca 1700, minor rstr 2,750.00
Arm, walnut Vict w/rswd grpt, fruit & foliage crest, reuphl, 43" .250.00
Arm, Windsor, fan-bk, knuckle arms, mk PS Byrn 1708, 44" ..3,960.00
Arm, 4-slat bk, sausage trns, old rpt, rpl rush seat, 44" 220.00
Arm & rocker, Old Hickory, bentwood, caned seat/bk, pr 500.00
Bergere, giltwood Bell Epoque cvd in Louis XVI style, old uphl 2,500.00
Campeachy, mahog Am Classical, reeded/paneled crest, uphl, 40" ..5,720.00
Chaise, walnut English-style, paw ft, wool uphl, repro, 77" 360.00
Corner, mahog Chpndl-style, c&b ft, reuphl velvet seat, 30" 635.00
Corner, maple QA, 4 cabriole legs, trn arm posts, slip seat, 29" ..3,300.00
Corner, shaped arms, trn legs, rush seat, early, rprs, 27x15" 350.00
Corner, walnut Chpndl, cabriole legs, slipper ft, rstr, 32" 3,600.00
Corner, walnut QA, crest:shaped slats:compass seat, rfn, 30x17" .3,000.00
Corner, yew/walnut English Chpndl, scroll arms/crest, uphl seat .1,100.00
Invalid's, mahog Geo, Pat mechanical action, 1830s 2,100.00
Lolling, mahog, H stretcher, reuphl in wool, old finish, 45" 2,750.00
Lolling, mahog Hplwht Martha Washington, rprs/rfn, 43½" ...1,100.00
Mahog Chpndl wing bbl-bk, reuphl, 44" 1,595.00
Mahog Fed in Sheraton taste, wing-bk, leather uphl, 1800s 3,000.00
Mahog QA, wing-bk, cabriole legs, reuphl/rpl leg, 43" 1,650.00
Rocker, nursing; trn/tapered bk posts, plank bottom, trn legs, rfn .75.00

Rocker, sewing; olive gray w/PA decor, wear, 27½" 275.00
Rocker/arm, arrow comb-bk, bamboo Windsor base, old rpt, 41" ..200.00
Rocker/arm, bamboo Windsor, comb-bk, step-down crests 350.00
Rocker/arm, bamboo Windsor, comb-bk w/old brn rpt, rprs, 44" ..495.00
Rocker/arm, Co 4-slat ladder-bk, EX cvg, splint seat, 38" 275.00
Rocker/arm, half-spindle ladder-bk, scroll arms, brn rpt, 43" 250.00
Rocker/arm, Windsor, high-bk, old mustard grpt over red, 44" ...660.00
Side, bamboo Co Windsor, spindle-bk, yoke crest, rfn, 37" 440.00
Side, Indian, teak w/old worn patina, elephant/birds cvgs, 48" ...220.00
Side, laminated rswd Am Rococo, Belter, Fountain Elms, uphl, 38" * ..6,000.00
Side, mahog Am Classical, crest rail, eagle splat, 1810s 1,100.00
Side, mahog Vict w/floral needlepoint seat, rprs, 34" 235.00
Side, maple Co, banister-bk, trn details, splint seat, rfn, 46" 275.00
Side, maple/ash Windsor, 7-spindle sack-bk, PA, 1780s, 38" ..2,300.00
Side, Neoclassical cvd/gilded, anthemion bk, caned seat 1,240.00
Side, oak Baroque Revival, much cvg, leather seat/bk, 1890s, 47" ..600.00
Side, walnut Fr-style Euro, cvd details, reuphl/rfn, 19th C 150.00
Side, Windsor, fan-bk, H stretcher, saddle seat, rfn, 36" 275.00
Side, Windsor, fan-bk w/old blk rpt, trn legs, saddle seat, 37" 300.00
Side, Windsor, pnt/cvd fan-bk, bamboo trn legs, ca 1800, 36" ..4,600.00
Side, Windsor, sack-bk, trn/knuckle arms, blk rpt, repro, 38" .2,200.00
Side, Windsor, 7-spindle bow-bk, saddle seat, rpt, 36" 330.00
Walnut Am Neo-Greco, mc Egyptian/Classical elements, 1875, 32" ...1,980.00
Walnut Vict Sleepy Hollow, finger cvg & flowers, reuphl, 41" ...100.00

Chair Sets

Dining, cherry/burl vnr Gothic Revival, reuphl/rfn, 2 arm+2 side ..660.00
Dining, mahog Chpndl-style, needlepoint seats, 2 arm+6 side ..1,275.00
Dining, mahog Regency-style, uphl seats, 2 arm+6 side 3,300.00
Dining, mahog/parcel gilt Fr Neoclassical, 2 arm+10 side 11,000.00
Dining, oak English ladder-bk w/cvgs, 1 arm+7 side 1,200.00
Dining, oak Renaissance-style, acanthus-cvd legs, 2 arm+6 side ...770.00
Dining, oak Vict, cornucopia crests, uphl bks/seats, 2 arm+10 ..2,500.00
Dining, rswd Regency, curved crest/trn legs/uphl seat, 8 for 4,000.00
Dining, walnut Baroque Revival, brocade uphl, 2 arm+4 side 825.00
Dining, walnut QA, vasiform splat, cvd knees, 8 for 8,000.00
Kitchen, Windsor style, plank seat, rfn, 35", 4 for 300.00
Side, Baroque Revival, cvd/trn details, old finish, 44", 4 for 200.00
Side, blk lcq English w/MOP & chinoiserie pnt motifs, 4 for 660.00
Side, cherry Chpndl, sq legs, slip seats, shaped crest, 4 for 2,475.00
Side, cherry ladder-bk, rush seats, 20th C, 45", 5 for 385.00
Side, curly maple Sheraton, trn legs, rpl seats, 4 for 1,300.00
Side, fruitwood Euro, curved bks w/openwork slats, reupl, 4 for ..550.00
Side, hardwood press-bk w/trn spindles, 6 for 600.00
Side, mahog English Chpndl, sq legs, slip seats, 37", pr 990.00
Side, mahog English Regency, shell cvgs, reuphl seats, 6 for ...1,400.00
Side, mahog Hplwht-style, shield-shape spindle-bks, reuphl, 8 for ..2,650.00
Side, mahog QA-style, slip seats, cabriole legs, repro, 8 for 1,650.00
Side, PA decor on orig red grpt, 33", 6 for 1,485.00
Side, rswd Am Rococo, petit-point seat/bk, 1850s 500.00
Side, walnut Vict w/burl vnr crests, rpl cane seats, 34", 6 for 500.00
Side, walnut W&M Revival, orig leather uphl, 19th C, 34", 4 for ...220.00
Side, walnut w/figured vnr apron, balloon bk, sabre legs, 6 for ...450.00
Side, Windsor, balloon bks/saddle seats/H stretchers, 1860, 4 for ...500.00
Side, Windsor, fan-bks, bulbous trns, saddle seats, rfn, 4 for 2,650.00
Side, Windsor, 9-spindle bks, saddle seats, old pnt, 1810, 4 for ..5,175.00

Chests (Antique), See Also Dressers

Birch Chpndl, 4 grad dvtl drw, sanded top/rfn, 37x38" 1,700.00
Birch Hplwht bow-front w/flame vnr drw fronts, 4 grad drw, 34x38" .2,200.00
Butler's, mahog vnr Chpndl-style, 4-drw, pull-out shelf, 30x30" ...300.00
Case of 14 drws, oak w/some quarter-sawn figure, 1900s, 79x31" .1,125.00

Cherry Chpndl, 20 grad drw, high ogee ft, rstr ft, 66x38" ...**3,960.00**
Cherry Chpndl-style, 3 grad drw, handmade repro, 49x38" **770.00**
Cherry CT River Valley Chpndl, 4 dvtl grad drw, rfn, 39" **2,200.00**
Cherry Hplwht w/figured vnr & inlay, Fr ft, 5-drw, 39x38" **1,800.00**
Cherry QA, 2 short:5 grad dvtl drw, minor rprs, 51x36" **4,125.00**
Cherry Sheraton, 4 dvtl drw w/beading, trn legs, rfn, 41x40" ...**1,550.00**
Cherry/curly maple Co Sheraton, 4 drw w/beading, rfn/rpl, 37x40" ..**825.00**
Cherry/curly maple/mahog Hplwht, 6-drw, Fr ft, rprs, 47x46" **825.00**
Cherry/curly maple/walnut Fed, 4 dvtl drw, rprs, 53x46" **770.00**
Cherry/mahog vnr Hplwht bow-front, 4 dvtl drw w/inlay, 36x42" .**3,575.00**
China, mahog, c&b ft, curved glass in do & 2 sides, 20th C, 55" ..**660.00**
Floral marquetry Fr Louis XV-style bombe, 4-drw, 1900s, 43" ..**2,200.00**
Louis XV-style parquetry/marquetry, marble top, bombe form, 36x58" ..**8,500.00**
Mahog Am Rococo, mirror w/swan supports, marble top:5-drw .**1,200.00**
Mahog English Chpndl, 5-dvtl drw, orig brasses, 35x37x20" ...**1,875.00**
Mahog English Regency w/figure & oak inlay, 5-drw, 48x46" **715.00**
Mahog Fed bow-front w/figured vnr facade, 4-drw w/beading, 35" **990.00**
Mahog Geo III of Chpndl design, 3 short:3:3-drw base, 66x43" **2,200.00**
Mahog Hplwht bow-front w/bird's-eye vnr facade, 4-drw, 39x42" .**3,300.00**
Mahog Hplwht-style w/inlay, 4 dvtl drw, 20th C, 33x31" **715.00**
Maple Chpndl, 2 short:4 grad drw, bracket ft, rfn, 44x36" **3,400.00**
Maple Chpndl, 4 grad dvtl drw, ogee ft, rprs/rfn, 36x35" **3,200.00**
Maple W&M, 5 dvtl grad drw, rpl/old rfn, trn ft, MA, 43x35" ..**5,225.00**
Oak Euro, mortised & pinned, rail & post, 3-drw, 41x60x27" .**4,800.00**
Olive wood vnr English QA w/oyster burl inlay, 4-drw, rfn, 41" .**2,750.00**
On chest, cherry Chpndl, 9 grad drw, bracket ft, CT, 74x39" .**7,700.00**
On chest, mahog English Hplwht w/inlay, 8-drw, rfn, 79x41" .**1,870.00**
Pine Chpndl, 5 grad drw, high bracket base, old red pnt, 50" ..**7,000.00**
Pine Co, 2 short:6 drw, paneled sides, apron, 35x41x16" **200.00**
Pine Co, 4 grad dvtl drw, ball trn ft, red stain, 38x32" **275.00**
Sugar, cherry Am, divided int, KY or TN, 1815-25, 34x26x17" ...**5,280.00**
Tall, birch, cornice:6 thumb-molded drw:bracket base, rfn, 55x36" .**4,255.00**
Walnut Am Renaissance, arched mirror, marble top, 99x48" .**1,750.00**
Walnut Chpndl, chamfered corners w/lamb's tongue, 9-drw, 69x48" .**4,000.00**
Walnut Chpndl, 6 dvtl grad drw, rpl ogee ft, rfn, 47x39" **1,100.00**

Cupboards, See Also Pie Safes

Architectural, pine Co English (or Irish) w/pnt traces, 72x34" ..**990.00**
Architectural corner, pine English, 2-pc, 20th C, 87x60" **1,300.00**
Cherry Co, 8-pane dbl do:3 drw:2 panel do, rpl hinges, 87x46" .**3,400.00**
Cherry Co Emp, panel dos, 3 dvtl drw, 2-pc, rprs, 85x47" **1,400.00**
Corner, brn grpt w/faux-flame mahog do panels, 2-pc, 81x45" .**6,250.00**
Corner, cherry Co, panel dos, cornice, 1-pc, rprs, 91x48" **900.00**
Corner, cherry Co, 1-pane dos:2 dvtl drw:2 panel do, 95x59" .**2,300.00**
Corner, cherry Co, 2 6-pane do:drw/2 panel do, 1-pc, 78x46x49" .**4,675.00**
Corner, cherry Southern Hplwht, 12-pane do:dbl do, rpl ft, 90x44" .**5,225.00**
Corner, cherry/poplar Co, 1-pc, rstr/rfn, 79x42" **1,500.00**
Corner, cherry/poplar Co, 2 8-pane do:2 drw:2 do, 2-pc, 91x54" ..**3,000.00**
Corner, pine w/old red pnt, 2 3-pane do:dbl do, 2-pc, 78x38" .**3,575.00**
Corner, pine/poplar, cornice:2 8-pane do:2 panel do, 1-pc, 49" **2,200.00**
Corner, walnut Co, 2 5-pane do:2 drw:2 panel do, 1-pc, 82x48" **3,000.00**
Euro Baroque Revival, cvd ft/post/molding, drw:dbl do, worn, 38" ..**1,700.00**
Indian, teak serpentine front, animal cvgs, worn patina, 37x35" ...**600.00**
Jelly, pine/poplar w/grpt, 2 do:panel dos, gallery, 59x45" **500.00**
Jelly, pine/poplar w/red-grn grpt, panel do, 2 dvtl drw, 50x41" ...**770.00**
Jelly, walnut Co, cut-out ft, 1 brd-&-batten do, 76x35" **1,150.00**
Kitchen, golden oak, 2 do:3 drw:shelf:2 do:drw, 2-pc, 83x38" .**1,320.00**
Mahog traditional-style w/inlay, 2-pc, 20th C, 79x34" **990.00**
Pewter, cornice:2 9-pane do:shelf:3 drw:2 panel do, 1780s, 86x56" .**5,500.00**
Pewter, pine Co w/red pnt, 3-shelf top:1-brd do, rpr, 72x36" .**2,100.00**
Pewter, pine/poplar W&M, panel dos, rstr, ca 1700, 81x56" ...**6,050.00**
Pewter, primitive NE softwood, 1-do, 1-pc, rfn, 75x48" **650.00**
Pine w/orig flame grpt, paneled stiles & do, 63x44" **4,600.00**

Pine/poplar Co, old gr/olive-tan pnt, 1-brd dos, 1-pc, 75x37" .**1,125.00**
Pine/poplar Co, yel-brn grpt, dbl 8-pane do:2 drw:2 do, 91x51" .**2,750.00**
Step-bk, cherry, 2 6-pane do:shelf:2 drw:2 panel do, 2-pc, 89" .**4,070.00**
Step-bk, pine w/brn/yel grpt, panel dos, minor rprs, 79x41" ...**1,200.00**
Step-bk, poplar/curly maple Co, 2 do:shelf:2 drw:2 do, 2-pc, 81" ...**1,600.00**
Step-bk, walnut, 2 do:6 drw:shelf:2 do, rprs, 2-pc, 81x48" **1,200.00**
Step-bk, walnut, 2 6-pane do:2 drw:2 panel do, 1-pc, 81x46" .**2,000.00**
Walnut Baroque Revival w/appl ornaments, 20th C, 51x50x25" ...**250.00**
Walnut Co, cut-out ft, panel dos, CI thumb latch w/knob, 84x46" ..**1,800.00**
Walnut Euro, 2 dvtl drw, galleried cornice, 3-pc, 1890s, 90x45" ...**770.00**
Walnut Euro Renaissance Revival court, 3-section, rfn, 90x45" .**600.00**

Desks

Bow-front, burl walnut English, 4-drw ends, central drw, 54" .**1,550.00**
Butler's, mahog Chpndl, dbl do:desk drw:3 drw, 81x44" **3,500.00**
Butler's, rswd vnr, scrolled base, Gothic arch cutouts, 38x40" **990.00**
Davenport, mahog Emp, rstr/rpr **450.00**
Davenport, mahog Geo III, 4-drw **1,250.00**

English carved and burl walnut Davenport desk, original leather surface, lower section in four-drawer compartment with false drawers, carved legs, scroll feet, ca 1850, 33x22x22", $1,980.00.

Fall-front, mahog Chpndl, 4-grad drw:bracket ft, 1770, 43x39" * ..**16,000.00**
Lady's, mahog Hplwht w/vnr X-banding, Fr ft, 2-pc, 53x40x20" .**3,650.00**
Lap, rswd, brass bound, slant-lid, 1850s **450.00**
Mahog Chpndl-style, c&b ft, 4 serpentine drw, worn, 42x36x19" ..**330.00**
Partner's, mahog Chpndl style, 31x62x30" **975.00**
Partner's, oak Am, leather top, 4 long+2 pencil drw ea side, 84" **1,100.00**
Plantation, cherry Co, table base w/trn legs, bookcase top, 86" ...**1,400.00**
Postmaster's, walnut, paneled, fitted int, Moore's Pat, 62x42" ...**5,060.00**
QA style, 5-drw, old red pnt w/gold, cabriole legs, 20th C, 48" **770.00**
Roll-top, mahog Am, fitted int, ped ends w/3 drw ea, 45x60" .**2,200.00**
Roll-top, oak, 9-drw, fitted int, Derby Desk, 43x48x30" **715.00**
Roll-top, walnut Vict w/burl vnr, 3-drw base, 2-pc, 92x40" **1,875.00**
Slant front, cherry Chpndl, fitted int, 42x35" **4,500.00**
Slant front, cherry Co Hplwht, 2 dvtl drw, 32x24x18" **495.00**
Slant front, cherry Hplwht, 4 dvtl drw w/beading, 42x38" **2,751.00**
Slant front, maple Chpndl w/some curl, 4 dvtl drw, 1779, 40x35" ..**4,400.00**
Slant front, oak Geo III, fitted int, 4 long drw, 43x36x18½" **300.00**
Walnut Fr-style, 3-drw, brass pulls, Baker, 29x60x24" **250.00**
Walnut Renaissance Revival, shoe ft, cut-out ends, 3-drw, 36" L **250.00**
Walnut Renaissance Revival, 3-drw, 2-do, worn finish, 1900s, 57" .**360.00**
Walnut VA Chpndl, 8-drw, ogee ft, orig finish/rstr, 55x43x43" ...**7,150.00**

Dressers (Machine Age), See Also Chests

Golden Oak era w/serpentine facade, 5-drw, rfn, 75x37" **425.00**
Oak Welsh, 3 shelf:3 drw:3 openings & shelf:sq ft, 74x56" **3,200.00**

Walnut Vict, appl cvgs, 2 handkerchief:3 long drw, mirror, 75" .**450.00**
Walnut Vict w/figured vnr, cvd details, 3-drw, marble top, 85" ..**825.00**
Walnut Vict w/figured vnr, fruit pulls, marble top, 40"+mirror ..**600.00**

Dry Sinks

Co w/dbl-lift breadbrd top, old yel pnt, 34x35x18" **700.00**
Grpt softwood w/cupboard base, 1-drw:dbl do, 1870s, 35x43x20" ..**850.00**
High-top, softwood, dbl do top:sink & drw:dbl do, 1850s, 79x55" ..**475.00**
Pine/poplar Co, old pnt, panel dos, dvtl drw, 36x49x21", EX **800.00**
Poplar, hutch-type shelf, drw, old rfn/rstr, 44x42x18" **500.00**
Poplar Co, 1-brd ends, panel dos, 2-drw, brn grpt, 34"+crest ...**1,045.00**

Hall Pieces

Chair, oak Elizabethan Revival, cvd foliate bks, 1890s, pr **525.00**
Chair, oak English 'Modern Gothic,' cvd splat, 1880s **350.00**
Hall tree, Golden Oak era, quarter-sawn figure, lift lid, 78" **580.00**
Table, mahog Early Renaissance Revival, frieze drw, trestle base .**500.00**
Table, continental rswd, apron, ped base, scroll ft, 51" **1,200.00**

Highboys

Maple American Chippendale carved highboy chest in two parts, bonnet top, urn finials, three top drawers, the center shell-carved over graduated drawers, cabriole legs, paw feet, ca 1750 – 80, 81x39x19", $6,600.00.

Cherry QA, 3 short:5 grad:4 drw, bonnet top, cvd fan, rstr, 81" ..**8,250.00**
Curly maple QA, 3 short:6 long:3 short drw, cvd fans, 79" ...**23,000.00**
Curly maple QA, 4 grad drw/scroll apron/cabriole legs, rprs, 70" ..**4,125.00**
Curly maple QA, 5 grad drw:long drw:3 drw, cvd fans, 2-pc, 73" .**7,000.00**
Mahog QA style, 3 short:5:3 short drw, Drexel label, 82" **1,300.00**
Walnut/pine/burl vnr W&M w/herringbone X-banding, 62x35" .**9,350.00**

Lowboys

Oak English in Geo-style, 3 banded drw, 19th C, 29x30x20" **700.00**
Oak W&M, trn legs, ball ft, scrolled apron, drw, rfn, 30x31x18" ..**440.00**
Walnut QA-style, quartered top w/herringbone inlay, 18th C, 30" ..**3,100.00**
Walnut vnr English W&M w/inlay, 3 dvtl drw, rstr/rpl, 39x34x22" .**2,000.00**
Walnut/burl vnr W&M w/herringbone cross banding, Am, 29x31" ..**11,550.00**
Walnut/maple QA, cabriole legs, apron, 4-drw, rstr, 31" **2,650.00**

Pie Safes

Pine Co, old bl-gr pnt, pinwheel-punched tin, 46x40x19" **2,400.00**
Pine Co, old natural, punched panels, cornice, 45x39" **1,265.00**
Poplar w/old bl, 12 punched panels, nailed drw, mortised fr, 59x40" ..**1,550.00**
Softwood & pierced tin, hangs, 4 iron brackets, 29x55x20" **180.00**

Softwood & pierced tin, molded gallery, 1850-70s, 25x24x12" ..**300.00**
Walnut Co, dvtl drw:2 3-panel punched tin do, 58x39x15" **990.00**

Secretaries

Cherry Chpndl, 4 dvtl drw, fitted int, ogee ft, 2-pc, 83" **8,800.00**
Chinoiserie w/gold on blk, w/bookcase, 20th C, 96x42x19" **880.00**
Mahog Emp w/flame-grain vnr, 2-pc, NH label, 76x39x19" **1,200.00**
Mahog English Gothic Revival, panel dos, 2-pc, 88x40x21" ...**2,850.00**
Mahog Geo II w/bookcase:hinged lid:4 grad drw, 1780s, 86x42x25" .**6,600.00**
Mahog Governor Winthrop w/bookcase, Monitor...NY, 80x31" ...**715.00**
Mahog Hplwht-style w/inlay, bookcase:slant lid:3 drw, repro, 82" .**1,300.00**
Mahog Hplwht-style w/inlay, pull-out desk, leather top, 82x37" ...**1,760.00**
Pine/poplar Co Hplwht, old brn grpt on yel, dvtl drw, 2-pc, 74" ..**1,800.00**
Walnut Co, dbl do:2 do:hinged lid:3 drw, 2-pc, 80x37" **1,300.00**
Walnut Co Vict, trn legs, dvtl drw, slant lid, 82x43x19" **1,000.00**
Walnut Vict, cylinder top, olive-wood vnr/cvgs, 93x35" **1,300.00**
Walnut Vict, 2 1-pane do:fall front:3-drw base, 89x40" **1,500.00**

Settees

Beech Fr Provincial cvd in Louis XV style, old uphl, 67" **2,400.00**
Fr Louis XV, rfn blond wood fr w/cvd details, muslin uphl, 51" .**1,450.00**
Fruitwood Charles X cvg in Egyptian style, 1830s, 78" **3,850.00**
Mahog Chpndl-style, detailed cvg, old uphl, rpr, ca 1900, 42" ...**770.00**
Mahog Vict w/cvg, brocade reuphl, 47" **525.00**
Mahog w/inlay, brocade reuphl, 20th C, rprs/rfn, 48" **115.00**
PA softwood, half-spindle bk, plank seat, 8-leg, 34x70" **400.00**
Walnut Vict, cvd rose crest, velvet reuphl w/tufted bk, 54" **465.00**
Walnut Vict w/cvd crest, open arms, oval bk, reuphl, 56" **715.00**

Settles, See Benches

Shelves

Bakery, pine w/old pnt traces, Bamby Bread..., 50x37x11" **880.00**
Clock, poplar w/worn red & blk grpt, 24½", VG **250.00**
Corner, walnut, truncated sides, glass shelves, hangs, 50x24" ..**3,200.00**
Etagere, rswd Am Rococo, laminated/cvd, center mirror, 96" ..**10,000.00**
Standing, pine, old brn pnt cut-out ends, rprs, 30x25x9½" **465.00**
Standing, primitive, dvtl, 3-shelf, bj ends, 42x32x8½" **475.00**
Wall, dvtl pine w/old bl, 25x32x7" **2,000.00**
Wall, poplar w/cherry stain, cutouts, crest, 4-shelf, 42x24x13" ...**660.00**
Wall, walnut, chip-cvd details, appl ornaments, 18x14" **190.00**
Wall bracket, giltwood Wm IV, cvd floral support, 1835, 20x18x14" ..**660.00**

Sideboards

English Regency mahogany and ebony inlaid sideboard, arched backsplash, pedestal ends, ca 1820, 54x90x25", $2,100.00.

Buffet, oak Jacobean-style, much cvg, mirror, 60x82x26" **3,300.00**
Cherry Am (Southern), 3-do/2-drw, splashbrd, 1850s, 54x66x22" ..**500.00**
Corner, mahog Geo III w/inlay, 1 drw:2+4 false drw, 39x59x41" .**2,750.00**
Mahog Am Classical, 3 frieze drw, 4 columns, paw ft, 72" **1,300.00**
Mahog Am Late Classical, drw:2 panel do, 1850s, 38x36x18" **825.00**
Mahog Emp w/figure, trn ft/pilasters, 2 panel do/2 drw, 42x55" ..**550.00**
Mahog Euro, marble inserts & top, 3-drw, high bk, 20th C, 62x73" ...**1,000.00**
Mahog Fed w/inlay, 4-drw, 4 cupboards, 6 tapered legs, 40x66x27" .**39,000.00**
Mahog Hplwht w/inlay, 4-do, 5 dvtl drw, att Baltimore, 40x79" .**16,500.00**
Mahog Sheraton w/flame-grained mahog vnr, rpl brasses, 49x45" .**1,300.00**
Mahog vnr Emp, dbl-ped base, 2-do, 3-drw, EX cvg, 68x75" **850.00**
Mahog vnr English Hplwht-style w/X-banding/ebony inlay, 55" .**1,100.00**

Sofas

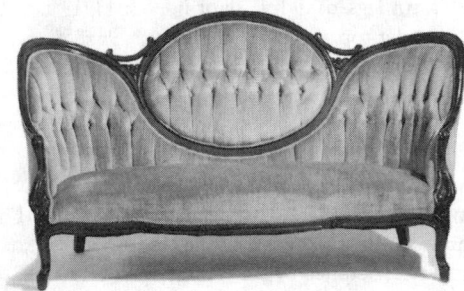

Early Empire carved mahogany sofa, turned back rail with ornate carving, paw feet with casters, ca 1830 – 40, 91", $1,750.00.

Birch Co w/rolled arms & curved bk, trn legs, reuphl, 84" **825.00**
Chpndl-style camel-bk w/c&b ft, reuphl (worn), 77" **300.00**
Mahog Am Vict, serpentine crest, acanthus ft, 1850s, 82" **600.00**
Mahog Chpndl camel-bk, scroll arms, over-uphl seat rail, 1770s, 79" ..**17,250.00**
Mahog Chpndl camel-bk w/inlay, old rfn, ca 1800, 37x76x27" ..**42,550.00**
Mahog Chpndl-style, camel-bk, fine uphl, 83" **880.00**
Mahog Duncan Phyfe style, red & gold silk uphl, 20th C, 81" ...**660.00**
Mahog Emp, paw ft w/acanthus/fruit detail, reuphl/rfn, 67" **550.00**
Mahog Emp, rfn serpentine fr, reuphl striped velvet, 95" **360.00**
Mahog English Chpndl, velvet reuphl, rprs, 66" **330.00**
Mahog Fed att to Duncan Phyfe, partial rstr, 60" **12,650.00**
Mahog Philadelphia Hplwht camel-bk, serpentine fr, reuphl, 67" ...**5,000.00**
Mahog Vict w/appl cvgs, fruit crest, reuphl/rprs, 75" **500.00**
Mahog vnr Classical cvd crest ends, paw ft, uphl, 92x35x17" .**1,600.00**
Mahog vnr Emp, cvd foliage crest, velvet reuphl, 76" **220.00**
Olive wood & mahog English Vict, folds into bed, reuphl, 84" ..**350.00**
Rswd Am Late Classical, curving bk, scroll arms, 1835, 35x76" ..**2,700.00**
Rswd Am Rococo cvd/laminated, att JH Belter, 1850-60 ....**3,000.00**
Satinwood, uphl, geometric brass nailheads, att Tiffany, 78" ..**21,000.00**
Walnut Vict, finger-cvd, vintage crest, reuphl brocade, 67" **525.00**
Walnut Vict w/cvd detail, velvet reuphl, minor rprs, 59" **450.00**

Stands

Canterbury, rswd George III w/cvg & inlay, 1800s, 20x17x15" ..**2,100.00**
Canterbury, rswd Regency cvd lyre form, drw in base, 17x19x13" .**1,600.00**
Cherry Hplwht, 1-drw w/trn wood knob, rfn, 39x19½x17" **200.00**
Cherry/birch Co Hplwht, tilt-top, tripod base, rfn, 27x18x15" ...**450.00**
Cherry/curly maple Sheraton, rope-cvd legs, 2-drw, 39x20x17" .**2,200.00**
Curly maple Hplwht, dvtl drw, 2-brd top, old brass, 26x18x18" ..**1,200.00**
Curly/bird's-eye maple Sheraton, 2-drw, 1-brd top, 28x19x16" .**1,650.00**
Hardwood Co Hplwht, tripod base, trn column, oval top, 39x20x15" ..**2,035.00**

Sewing, cherry, ogee drw, pincushion top, rpr, 7½" **110.00**
Sewing, walnut Am Renaissance, cvd moldings, 1890s, 30x17" .**935.00**
Sewing, walnut Vict Eastlake, trn/cvd details, 2-drw, 30x16x24" .**360.00**
Sewing, walnut vnr w/inlay, lyre base, 8-sided top, 39x18" **110.00**
Walnut Co, dvtl drw, 2-brd top, worn finish, 29x24x18" **200.00**
Windsor, old bright gr pnt, New England, 1800s, 29x15x15", EX .**1,265.00**

Stools

Footstool, beech Louis XVI-style, reeded legs, uphl **135.00**
Footstool, pine w/old blk pnt & mc striping, bj ft, 8x15" **250.00**
Footstool, primitive w/bj ends, legs tenoned through top, 16" **110.00**
Footstool, stag horn base, needlepoint top, 11x12x11" **110.00**
Footstool, Vict cowhide uphl w/burl walnut fr **240.00**
Footstool, walnut Am Classical cvd, uphl seat, 1830s **550.00**
Footstools, mahog Am Rococo, reuphl, on casters, 1850s, pr ..**1,155.00**

Tables

Banquet, mahog 3-part Duncan Phyfe-style, scimitar legs, 80" ..**1,500.00**
Center, mahog cvd Classical, beaded skirt, rfn, 1825, 28x36" dia ..**8,000.00**
Center, mahog English Regency-style w/leather top, 29x45" dia ..**360.00**
Center, walnut Vict, ornately cvd base, marble top, 30x41x32" ..**2,475.00**
Center hall, mahog, marble top, 19th C, 20x34" dia **525.00**
Coffee, mahog w/inlay & glass tray top, 20th C, 25x26x16" **415.00**
Conference, mahog English Late Vict, leather top, 3-drw, 106" ..**6,150.00**
Console, mahog Am, serpentine top, appl shell cvgs, paw ft **825.00**
Dining, golden oak quarter-sawn, ped w/4 paw ft, 48"+leaves **800.00**
Dining, mahog Geo III, 2-part, tilt-top, ped ft, 38x72x36"+leaf ..**5,750.00**
Dining, oak Am in Renaissance style, center ped, 5 leaves **2,200.00**
Dining/drop-leaf, birch QA, cabriole legs, rfn, 1760s, 47" **4,000.00**
Dining/drop-leaf, mahog Wm IV, removable D-ends, 1835, 100" .**2,860.00**
Dressing, cherry/maple Co, curly crest, 2 dvtl drw, rfn, 36x39" ..**1,800.00**
Dressing, curly birch Co, 2 dvtl drw, simple crest, rfn, 36" **495.00**
Dressing, curly maple/hardwood, 2-drw, gallery, rfn, 33x30" **385.00**
Dressing, mahog English Hplwht w/inlay, drw:dbl do, 34x16x16" .**1,600.00**
Drop leaf, butterfly; maple/pine, trn legs, 1-brd top, 48x48" **2,860.00**
Drop-leaf, cherry, rpl top, swing-leg, rfn, 20th C, 44"+leaves **250.00**
Drop-leaf, cherry Sheraton-style Pembroke, 2-drw, 20th C, 36"+leaves .**450.00**
Drop-leaf, cherry/mahog Fed Pembroke, cvd legs/drw, 40"+leaves ...**450.00**
Drop-leaf, curly maple/birch Co Hplwht, pine apron, 42"+leaves **825.00**
Drop-leaf, mahog English Chpndl Pembroke, dvtl drw, 28"+leaves .**580.00**
Drop-leaf, mahog Sheraton, att Duncan Phyfe NY, 36"+12" leaves * .**15,400.00**
Drop-leaf, maple/cherry Chpndl, swing-leg, rfn/rpl, 48"+leaves .**400.00**
Drop-leaf, QA w/old red, dvtl apron, swing-leg, 42"+leaves* ..**28,600.00**
Drop-leaf, walnut PA QA, swing-leg, rprs, 48"+leaves **4,400.00**
Drop-leaf, walnut Southern Sheraton, swing-leg, drw, 47"+leaves ...**800.00**
Game, English Chpndl, acanthus cvgs, c&b ft, false drw, 38x35" .**2,000.00**
Game, mahog Chinese Chpndl, 39x35x18" **3,000.00**
Game, mahog Hplwht, cvd inlay, swing-leg **1,250.00**
Game, mahog Hplwht, swing-leg, D-shaped apron, 38x34x17" .**1,750.00**
Game, mahog Hplwht demilune w/inlay, rprs, 29x36x18" **2,100.00**
Game, mahog vnr Sheraton style **800.00**
Harvest, walnut, trn legs, 1-brd top, 30x96x28" **2,000.00**
Hutch, pine Co, old dk gr pnt, 3-brd top, 30x70x35", EX **1,375.00**
Hutch, pine Co, rpt w/stencil over red, lift lid, 3-brd top, 52" .**1,100.00**
Library, mahog Geo III-style Chpndl taste, leather top, 1840s, 58" .**6,050.00**
Library, mahog w/shelf, cvd cabriole legs, 2-drw, 20th C, 45" **880.00**
Library, rswd Vict, shaped/molded top/apron, foliate legs, 60" ...**3,850.00**
Marble top, polished steel w/cast foliage apron, 34x79x22" **3,100.00**
Marble top, walnut Am Renaissance, trn ped in cage, 4-leg, 35" .**935.00**
Marble top, walnut Eastlake Vict w/walnut burl, 39x31x21" **660.00**
Oak Jacobean-style, 4 pullouts, 17x11x11" **120.00**
Parlor, rswd vnr Vict Renaissance Revival, rpr, 30x46x27" **1,870.00**

Parlor, Vict, oval marble top w/cvg, 30x42" **950.00**
Parlor, walnut Eastlake Vict, 29x32x22" **325.00**
Pier, mahog Am Late Classical, marble top, scrolls, 37x41x20" ..**1,980.00**
Refectory, oak/pine Vict, reeded apron, trn legs, 32x95x41" **600.00**
Sawbuck, pine, 2-brd top, old dk finish, 26x19x32" **660.00**
Stand, rswd Vict, cvd Rococo ornaments, marble top, 33x17x15" ..**2,900.00**
Tavern, cherry QA, porringer top, handmade repro, 26x33x23" ...**880.00**
Tavern, maple Co QA, dvtl drw, 2-brd breadbrd top, worn ft, 38" ..**2,750.00**
Tavern, maple/pine QA, dvtl drw, 2-brd breadbrd top, apron, 42" ..**1,375.00**
Tavern, pine/birch Co QA, rfn 2-brd top, rpt red base, 30½" **990.00**
Tea, birch/maple Co QA, 2-brd porringer top, 27x30x22" **1,650.00**
Tea, cherry Chpndl, tilt top, c&b ft, birdcage, rfn, 28x33" dia ..**1,870.00**
Tea, cherry QA, overhanging top, cabriole legs, ped ft, 39x37x22" .**23,000.00**
Tea, mahog English Chpndl, tripod base, c&b ft, tilt-top, 33" dia ...**850.00**
Tea, mahog QA, dvtl drw, quatrefoil top, rfn/sm rprs, 30x22" .**3,025.00**
Tea, maple Co Chpndl, 1-brd tilt-top, tripod base, rprs, 27" dia ...**2,090.00**
Tilt-top, mahog English Regency, 4-part base, 38x39x46" **770.00**
Tray, mahog, 2 trn removable legs, closed: 30x31x21" **660.00**
Trestle, oak Jacobean style, rfn/rstr, 62" **550.00**
Wine tasting, pine Co fr tilt-top, shoe ft, 47x43" dia **745.00**
Work, cherry Co Sheraton, rope-cvd/trn legs, 2-brd, 36" **300.00**
Work, ebonized Fr-style w/ped base, inlay top, 20th C, 23" dia ..**220.00**
Work, maple Co QA, rnd legs, shaped apron, 2-brd top, 26x32x26" .**4,125.00**
Work, rswd Am Rococo, much cvg, hinged lid/mirror/drw, 32x22x17" ..**880.00**
Work/drop-leaf, pine/maple Co Chpndl, dvtl drw/breadbrd top, 48" ..**880.00**
Writing, Louis XV, marble: red w/wht base, rpr, 35x82x37" .**23,000.00**
Writing, mahog Geo III-style, demilune top, drw, 37x39" **990.00**
Writing, pine/cherry Fr Provincial, leather top, drw, 36x28" **715.00**

Wardrobes, See Also Armoires

Golden Oak era, panel dos:2 dvtl drws, cvd cornice, 94x44" **440.00**
Kas, butternut/poplar/cherry, dvtl/raised panels, PA, rstr, 83x70" ..**2,000.00**
Kas, Dutch cvd rswd/ebonized Baroque form, cvd busts, 74x68" * .**13,000.00**
Linen press, cherry Chpndl, 2 do:3 grad drw:bracket ft, 2-pc, 80" ..**6,325.00**
Linen press, poplar w/brn combed grpt, 3 dvtl drw, 2-pc, 85x57" **2,000.00**
Mahog English w/inlay, bow-front, late 1800s, 94x80x30" **990.00**
Mahog vnr, cabriole legs, 2-do (1 w/int drws), Marvels, 52x40" .**220.00**
Poplar Co w/mustard grpt, 2-drw, 2 panel do, OH, 82x48" **990.00**
Poplar w/red pnt, 2 panel do, pegs inside, KY, ca 1850, 79x48" ...**2,645.00**
Walnut Eastlake Vict, panel drw:do, 82x34" **600.00**
Walnut Eastlake Vict w/figured vnr, dbl do:2 drw, 88x60" **880.00**
Walnut PA, 3-pc, panel dos:3 dvtl drw, rattail hinges, 89x73" ...**4,400.00**
Walnut Vict Rococo Revival, appl cvgs, 3-do/3-drw, 111x92" ..**1,550.00**

Washstands

Bird's-eye maple Am Late Classical, marble top, 1830s, 36x27x19" .**4,000.00**
Cherry, shelf w/dvtl drw, rpl top, 29"+gallery **200.00**
Cherry Biedermeier demilune corner, marble top, 35x26x21" .**1,500.00**
Cherry Sheraton-style, base shelf, dvtl drw, 20th C, 39x21x18" .**250.00**
Corner, mahog Hplwht bow-front w/ebony inlay, shelf, 42" **990.00**
Corner, mahog Hplwht bow-front w/inlay, shelf, 44x26" **965.00**
Corner, mahog Hplwht w/figure/curly maple vnr, dvtl drw, 41x34" **995.00**
Corner, pine Co, bow-front, conforming do & dvtl drw, rprs, 35" ..**165.00**
Fruitwood Biedermeier w/ebony, marble top:dwr:2 do, 19th C ..**2,970.00**
Italian Neoclassical parquetry inlay, marble top, 1790, 29x16" ..**1,980.00**
Mahog English Chpndl, 4-drw facade, dvtl gallery, 31x21" **800.00**
Mahog Hplwht w/inlay, fitted top for accessories, 1785, 40x22x15" .**800.00**
Mahog stain, trn legs, base shelf, dvtl drw, rpl top, 28"+crest **100.00**
Pine/poplar Sheraton, old yel rpt w/gold floral, dvtl drw, 39" **200.00**
Poplar Co Sheraton, dvtl drw, bow-front apron, rfn, 37x18x12" ...**250.00**
Walnut Vict, scalloped apron, 3 dvtl drw, 36½x39x16" **385.00**
Walnut Vict, 3-drw, fruit pulls, Masonite bk, 34x29x15" **275.00**

Walnut/poplar Co Vict, 3 dvtl drw, brass pulls, rprs, 27"+crest ..**275.00**
Walnut/poplar Co Vict, 3 dvtl drw, shaped gallery top, 38x29" .**220.00**

Miscellaneous

Bookmill, oak, Danners Revolving....Dec 11 1877, 59x23" **880.00**
Bookmill, oak, revolving, panel dos, 1910x, 27x46" dia **415.00**
Parlour suite, burl walnut Am Renaissance, settee+6 chairs ...**6,600.00**
Parlour suite, rswd Am Neo-Greco, griffin arms, settee+2 chairs ...**3,750.00**
Parlour suite, walnut Vict, reuphl, 70" settee+corner+2 sides **935.00**
Pedestal, mahog Fr Emp-style Neoclassical, gilt cvg, 44" **495.00**
Pedestal, rswd inlay Neoclassical w/gilt capitals, 45x12x12" **990.00**
Pedestal, walnut Am Renaissance Revival w/gilt, 19th C, 23" ..**5,725.00**
Pedestal, walnut Vict, foliate relief cvgs, 1890s, 41x12" **500.00**
Planter, rswd Regency-style, urn finials, 19th C, 14x42x17" ...**1,100.00**
Sink, walnut Am Renaissance, marble top w/splash-bk, 48x36x20" ...**770.00**
Trolley, walnut English Late Vict, 3-tier, 1890s, 45x48x22" ...**2,200.00**

Galena

Potteries located in Galena, Illinois, area were generally plain utility wares with lead glaze and often found in a pumpkin color with some slip decoration or splashes of other colors. These potteries thrived from the early 1830s until sometime around 1860. In the listings that follow, all items are made of red clay unless noted otherwise.

Bowl, mixing; dk gr w/orange spots, stacking rim, 6x9½" **175.00**
Figure, dog, open front legs, brn mottle, 9", VG **675.00**
Jar, preserving; gr w/orange spots, 10", VG **120.00**
Jug, gr gloss w/orange spots, ovoid, chips/hairlines, 11" **215.00**
Jug, gr w/orange spots, ovoid, ribbed strap hdl, 10", EX **330.00**

Galle

Emile Galle was one of the most important producers of cameo glass in France. His firm, founded in Nancy in 1874, produced beautiful cameo in the Art Nouveau style during the 1890s, using a variety of techniques. He also produced glassware with enameled decoration, as well as some fine pottery — animal figurines, table services, vases, and other objets d'art. In the mid-1880s he became interested in the various colors and textures of natural woods and as a result began to create furniture which he used as yet another medium for expression of his artistic talent. Marquetry was the primary method Galle used in decorating his furniture, preferring landscapes, Nouveau floral and fruit arrangements, butterflies, squirrels, and other forms from nature. It is for his furniture and his cameo glass that he is best known today. All Galle is signed.

In the listings below, 'fp' indicates items that have been fire polished. Our advisor for this category is Don Williams; he is listed in the Directory under Missouri.

Cameo

Atomizer, floral, brn on caramel, gilt mts, 8¾" **900.00**
Bottle, scent; floral, red/frost, oblong, flat-top stopper, 4" **1,200.00**
Bottle, scent; poppies, amber on almond frost, fp, 5½" **1,400.00**
Bowl, floral, bl on yel, 2½x6" **1,200.00**
Bowl, grasshopper/leaves, purple/yel/wht, 4-lobe rim, 3½x6" ..**2,000.00**
Box, apple blossoms, wine on amber, fp, 2¼x4" dia **1,750.00**
Decanter, clematis, purple on frost, purple stopper, 6½" **1,700.00**
Lamp, desk; 7" shade: mums on citron; gilt scroll base, 9" **1,500.00**

Lamp, floral, dk bl on lt amber 8" cone shade/base, 16" 6,500.00
Lamp base, maple leaves, amber/brn on citron, fp, 11" 825.00

Vase, wild flowers, red to cranberry on frosted yellow, signed, 16", $9,500.00.

Vase, apple blossoms, red/amber/wine on yel, spherical, 5½" ..2,875.00
Vase, berry branches, purple on gr-gray, ovoid, 6" 750.00
Vase, bleeding hearts, pk on frost/bl, message at neck, 5" 2,350.00
Vase, blown-out clematis, 4-layer, 7x5" 7,750.00
Vase, branches, tan on frost, 2 red/ruby cabochon berries, 4" ..1,300.00
Vase, clematis, amethyst on gray/yel frost, 25½" 5,700.00
Vase, clematis, on frost/purple, emb silver mts, hdls, 8½" 1,650.00
Vase, clematis, purple on purple frost, neck hdls, 10½x8" 4,000.00
Vase, dragonfly/aquatic plants, amber on aqua/frost, 7" 2,200.00
Vase, ferns, wine/lime on lt apricot/lime, banjo shape, 7" 650.00
Vase, floral, brn/orange on bright bl, 8x4" 2,500.00
Vase, floral, gr/lav on pk/wht/lav, bun base, stick neck, 24" 3,220.00
Vase, floral, orange on frost, stick neck, 12½" 1,200.00
Vase, floral, tan on citron/orange mottle, stick neck, 5¾" 575.00
Vase, floral (leafy), red on turq-bl frost, 2¼x4½" 750.00
Vase, floral (spiky), purple/gr on gr/yel, stick neck, 24" 1,850.00
Vase, grapes, amber/brn on pk/brn/clear/yel, 7½x4" 1,100.00
Vase, grapes, gold-brn on burgundy/frost, stick neck, 18" 2,000.00
Vase, hydrangea, lilac/gr on pk/lilac, 3" 500.00
Vase, iris, lav-bl/purple on citron, slender, 10½" 1,600.00
Vase, iris, yel/purple on lt opal (EX detail), 14x3" 2,800.00
Vase, irises (lg), purple on clear frost, slim ovoid, 12½" 2,300.00
Vase, lake fr w/trees, bl/gr/lav/purple on bl-gray, 12" 2,650.00
Vase, lake scene, brn on peach/gr, elongated bottle form, 11" .1,400.00
Vase, lake/mtns, amethyst on gray/amber frost, shouldered, 7½" ..2,100.00
Vase, mums/dk foliage, lav-bl on citron, disc shape, 5½" 4,300.00
Vase, nasturtiums, amber/tan on pk/amber, fp, ftd/hdls, 11" 4,100.00
Vase, nasturtiums/pods, amber on pk/amber frost, 2½" 375.00
Vase, poppies, orange on clear, slim cylinder w/disc ft, 12" 1,150.00
Vase, Queen Anne's lace, cut/pnt on clear/gr, bottle shape, 8" 1,100.00
Vase, rhododendrons, red/amber/maroon on yel, spherical, 4¼" ...2,300.00
Vase, seed pods, gr/lime on apricot/frost, hexagonal, 12" 1,200.00
Vase, seed pods drip from rim, lime on pk/opal, banjo form, 7" ..650.00
Vase, trees/boats, gr/brn on peach/pk, paper label, 14x7" 3,100.00
Vase, trees/castle beyond, blk/brn-red on amber-gray, 13½" ...2,750.00
Vase, trees/lake, brn on gray/amber frost, shouldered, 18" 5,400.00
Vase, trees/river, brn/gr on gray, tapered cylinder, 17½" 3,700.00
Vase, vines/foliage, gr on pk/frost, cylinder w/bun base, 13" 1,000.00
Vase, wisteria, purple on lime/purple, bottle shape, 15" 1,600.00

Enameled Glass

Bowl, mums/gilt on smoky amber, gold on ruffled rim, 6x10" 900.00

Cordial, wild flowers, wine/brn/pk on smoke, 2" 175.00
Vase, fuchsias, mc/gold on gr, rain texture, str sides, 11" 2,000.00
Vase, Japonesque floral on topaz, ribbed, 3 ftd, 6" 300.00
Vase, thistle pods on amber, swirl ribs, 17¾" 2,415.00

Marquetry, Wood

Cabinet, mahog, cvd & inlaid florals & scenic, mk, 36x25" 4,675.00
Music stand, gladiolas, scalloped top+2 tiers, rtcl notes, 34" ...2,200.00
Table, 2-tier, foliate inlay top/shelf, 29x23" L, EX 2,500.00
Table, 2-tier, jonquils, curved y-legs, 30x30x20" 2,530.00
Vitrine, flowers: top/sides/front panel, glass door, 53x24" 6,500.00

Pottery

Boats (2/connected), mc/blk/silver on gilt-sponged wht, sm 350.00
Bowl, rooster form on shield tray, flowers/gilt on wht, 11" L ...1,100.00
Pitcher, man at table on brn w/gold, flat-sided, 8¾" 825.00
Pitcher, swirled w/HP pansy & gilt, duck spout, 9", NM 1,265.00
Plaque, HP peacock, shield shape w/seashell border, 12x14" 575.00
Plaque, Limoges-style cattle scene, 12½" 750.00

Miscellaneous

Atomizer, bl o/l cut w/florals & birds, label, 4½", NM 400.00
Bottle, scent, rabbits etched on pk o/l, rnd lay-down, 5½" 450.00
Decanter, intaglio fir tree w/gold needles on amber, sqd, 7" 400.00

Gambling Memorabilia

Gambling memorabilia from the infamous casinos of the West and items that were once used on the 'floating palace' riverboats are especially sought after by today's collectors.

Roulette wheel, G. Caro, Paris, ca 1890, 32" diameter, EX, $1,800.00.

Ashtray, sterling silver, suits in corners, Armstrong, 3x3", EX 40.00
Book, A World of Luck, Time-Life, M 32.00
Book, Gambling & Gambling Devices, JP Quinn, 1912, 308-pg, EX ...120.00
Book, Gambling Secrets, Joseph E Mayer, 1911, EX 90.00
Box, blk laquer w/4 etched silver cards, 5x6½x1½", EX 100.00
Card press, maple w/turq buttons & beaded rose, VG 275.00
Card shuffler/dealer, automatic, common, 1940s, 5x5x5" 20.00
Card trimmer, shears style, unmk, ca 1910, 12¾x6½" 1,200.00

Chip, Bakelite, US Anchor, 1½" dia, 100 in orig box 65.00
Chip, bone, w/design or color border, 1mm thick, set of 100 ....75.00
Chip, clay compo w/litho inlay of crest & seal 8.50
Chip, clay or metal, w/casino name, minimum value 3.00
Chip, dealer; clay w/goat head in relief 50.00
Chip, ivory w/fancy numeral cvgs, set of 5 ....210.00
Chip, MOP, cvd decor, rectangular, English, ca 1800, 2¼" L 32.00
Chip, MOP, cvd designs, ca 1900, 5 for 60.00
Chip, MOP, cvd figures/openwork, European, 1700s, 1" sq 12.50
Chip, plastic, wood or rubber, no design, set of 100 ....5.00
Chip rack, lazy susan (carousel) type, w/lid, no chips 10.00
Cover, card table; hand-woven wool, India, 1880, 36x36", EX 90.00
Dice, red Lucite, 2", pr, EXIB 125.00
Dice cage, Chuck-A-Luck, w/dice, ca 1930 ....75.00
Dice cage, hide drums, heavy chrome, 9x14" 300.00
Dice cup, leather 40.00
Dice cup, leather, w/5 celluloid die 55.00
Dice cup, resembles cigar lighter, w/5 dice, Japan, 4½" 22.00
Game, Put & Take, tin, w/roulette wheel, 1920s, 5" dia, VG 50.00
Keno goose, polished walnut bowl between posts, 13x24" 750.00
Match book, Golden Nugget Gambling Hall, Lion, unused, EX 4.00
Money clip, sterling silver, enameled King of Hearts, ca 1930, EX ..65.00
Photo postcard, Bank Club, Reno Nevada, 1920s-30s, G 10.00
Punch board, Best Hand, 240 punches, 7½x10½", M 35.00
Put-n-Take top, brass, eng Take 1, Put 2..., 1950s, ½x1⅛" 17.50
Roulette wheel, walnut & base metal, 18" dia, VG 92.00
Spinner, sterling w/red & blk letters, .12 troy oz, EX 35.00
Spoon, silver w/Monte Carlo crest HP finial, table in bowl, 5½" ..50.00
Table, crap; casino style, felt layout, ca 1930, VG rstr 2,200.00
Table, gaming; inlaid top & sides, 8-drw, 36" dia, EX 2,000.00
Tally card, Casino De Monte-Carlo cover, Fr, ca 1907, M 22.00
Tip board, Spark Plug (horse) reserves, 10x11", EX 22.50
Watch, roulette; Roulette Ideal, beveled crystal, 1890s, EX 325.00
Wheel, HC Evans Big 6, horse race, mirrored glass/wood/metal, 60" .3,000.00
Wheel, roulette; wood, table-top type, 21" dia, EX 900.00
Wheel, wood, #1-30, w/clicker, wall mt, 25" dia 90.00
Wheel, wood, old varnish, yel lines, wooden arrow, 20th C, 24" dia .245.00
Whist scorer, MOP w/silver & enamel, 1880s, 2" dia, EX 90.00

Gameboards

Gameboards, the handmade ones from the 18th and 19th century, are collected more for their folk art quality than their relation to games. Excellent examples of these handcrafted 'playthings' sell well into the thousands of dollars; even the simple designs are often expensive. If you are interested in this field, you must study it carefully. The market is always full of 'new' examples. Well-established dealers are often your best sources; they are essential if you do not have the expertise to judge the age of the boards yourself. Our advisor for this category is Louis Picek; he is listed in the Directory under Iowa.

Checkers, painted pine, black, brown, and yellow, America, late 1800s, 20x20", EX, $1,100.00.

Carom, 2-sided, mc pnt w/gold, early 1900s, 28½" sq 90.00
Checkers, cvd/pnt pine, ca 1900, 12½x18¾" 315.00
Checkers, HP oilcloth on wooden fr, PA, 21x23" 550.00
Checkers, pine w/bl sqs & border on pk, 20x20" 330.00
Checkers, pine w/old maroon & olive pnt, gold & blk trim 415.00
Checkers, playing sq center of lg grpt brd, 19th C, 18x37" 4,025.00
Checkers ea side, red & yel sqs, 2 trays on 1 side, 21x30", G 450.00
Checkers/geometric maze, pnt wood, appl gallery, 13x13" 195.00
Checkers/parcheesi, pnt landscape border, oversz, 37x37" 1,100.00
Cribbage, brass peg holes, anchor & 1907 dk wood inlay, 17x4" .250.00
Unknown game, poplar w/orig blk & mc pnt, OH, 19th C, 25x25", NM 1,265.00

Games

Collectors of antique games are finding it more difficult to find their treasures at shows and flea markets. Most of the action these days seems to be through specialty dealers and auctions. The appreciation of the art on the boards and boxes continues to grow. You see many of the early games proudly displayed as art, and they should be. The period from the 1850s to 1910 continues to draw the most interest. Many of the games of that period were executed by well-known artists and illustrators. The quality of their lithography cannot be matched today. The historical value of games made before 1850 has caused interest in this period to increase. While they may not have the graphic quality of the later period, their insights into the social and moral character of the early 19th century are interesting.

Twentieth-century games invoke a nostalgic feeling among collectors who recall looking forward to a game under the Christmas tree each year. They search for examples that bring back those Christmas-morning memories. While the quality of their lithography is certainly less than the early games, the introduction of personalities from the comic strips, radio, and later TV created new interest. Every child wanted a game that featured their favorite character. Monopoly, probably the most famous game ever produced, was introduced during the Great Depression.

For further information, we recommend *Schroeder's Collectible Toys, Antique to Modern*, available from Collector Books. Our advisor for personality-related games is Norm Vigue; he is listed in the Directory under Massachusetts. Miscellaneous games are under the advice of Paul Fink, listed under Connecticut.

$64,000 Question, Lowell, 1955, EX (EX box) 50.00
All Star Baseball, Cadaco, 1969, VG (VG box) 40.00
Apple's Way, Milton Bradley, 1974, VG (VG box) 20.00
Arrest & Trial, Transogram, 1963, NMIB 75.00
Ask Me Another, Marx, 1928, EX (EX box) 350.00
Axis & Allies, Milton Bradley, 1948, VG (VG box) 20.00
Battle Line, Ideal, 1964, NM (NM box) 75.00
Battle-Cry, Milton Bradley, 1961, VG (VG box) 30.00
Beyond the Stars, House of Ideas, 1964, NMIB 35.00
Bicycle Race, McLoughlin Bros, 1890, EXIB 925.00
Billionaire, Parker Bros, 1973, VG (VG box) 35.00
Blockade, Corey Games, 1941, VG (VG box) 85.00
Booby-Trap, Parker Bros, 1965, VG (VG box) 20.00
Break the Bank, Betty-B, 1955, few coins missing, EX (EX box) ..50.00
Bust-Em Target Game, Marx, 1930, NM (EX box) 125.00
Careers, Parker Bros, 1955, EX (VG+ box) 25.00
Children's Hour, Parker Bros, 1961, EX (EX box) 20.00
Circus Boy Adventure, 1956, VG (VG box) 85.00
Clean Sweep, Schaper, 1967, EX (EX box) 50.00
Clue, Parker Bros, 1963, EX (EX box) 25.00
Comic Card Game, Milton Bradley, 1972, NM (EX box) 30.00
Conflict, Parker Bros, 1940, EX (EX box) 150.00
Crazy Eights, card game, Whitman, 1951, NM (NM box) 10.00

Crow Hunt, Parker Bros, 1930, VG (VG box) 65.00
Deputy, Milton Bradley, 1960, NM (NM box) 90.00
Dice Ball, Milton Bradley, 1934, VG (VG box) 65.00
Dogfight, Milton Bradley, 1963, VG (VG box) 40.00
Down You Go, Selchow & Righter, 1954, VG (VG box) 20.00
Dunce, Schaper, 1955, EX (EX box) 30.00
Finance & Fortune, Parker Bros, 1936, NM (EX box) 45.00
Fish Pond, Milton Bradley, 1920, EX (EX box) 75.00
Flag, card game, McLoughlin Bros, 1887, VG (VG box) 60.00
Flip a Basket, Hasbro, 1969, EX (EX box) 35.00
Flying the Bean, Parker Bros, 1941, NM (NM box) 100.00
Forest Friends, Milton Bradley, 1956, VG (VG box) 20.00
Game of Diamonds & Hearts, McLoughlin Bros, 1886, EX (EX box) .175.00
Game of Hide & Seek, McLoughlin Bros, 1895, EX (EX box) ..2,200.00
Game of Merry Christmas, JH Singer, EX (G box) 925.00
Game of Politics, Parker Bros, 1952, VG (VG box) 40.00
Game of States & Cities, card game, Parker Bros, 1947, VG (VG box) .10.00
Game of the Authors, card game, Parker Bros, 1897, VG (VG box) .40.00
Game of Zulu, McLoughlin Bros, EXIB 900.00
Going to the Fire, Milton Bradley, 1920s, VG (VG box) 125.00
Gold Fever, Idea Makers Inc, 1975, VG (VG box) 50.00
Hearts, card game, Whitman, 1951, NM (EX box) 10.00
Hippety-Hop, Corey Games, 1940, VG (VG box) 65.00
Hokum, card game, Parker Bros, 1927, VG (VG box) 15.00
Horse Racing, Milton Bradley, 1953, VG (VG box) 45.00
Hurdle Races, Milton Bradley, 1920s, VG (VG box) 175.00
Jackpot, Milton Bradley, 1974, VG (G box) 10.00
Last Straw, Schaper, 1966, NMIB 25.00
Lolli Plop Skill Game, Milton Bradley, 1962, NM (EX box) 20.00
Long Bomb Football, Mattel, 1982, MIB 50.00
Long Shot Horse Race, Parker Bros, 1962, NM (EX box) 40.00
Lost Gold, Parker Bros, 1975, NM (EX box) 20.00
Lucky Stars, Ideal, 1960s, EX (EX box) 25.00
Mad Magazine, Parker Bros, 1979, VG (G box) 20.00
Magnetic Fish Pond, Parker Bros, 1930, EXIB 75.00
Make-A-Million, card game, Parker Bros, 1945, VG (VG box) ...30.00
Mansion of Happiness, Henry P Ives, 1864, EXIB 250.00
Midget Auto Race, Lowe, 1941, NM (EX box) 35.00
Mixies, card game, Ed-U, 1956, NM (NM box) 10.00
Monopoly Deluxe, Parker Bros, 1964, EX (EX box) 65.00
Mosquito, Milton Bradley, 1966, NMIB 40.00
Mostly Ghostly, Cadaco, 1975, EX (EX box) 20.00
Moving Pictures, Milton Bradley, 1930s, EX (EX box) 145.00
Mystic Skill Game of Voodoo, Ideal, 1954, EX (EX box) 65.00
Night Before Christmas, Parker Bros, 1896, EXIB 850.00
Old Maid, Milton Bradley, 1900s, EX (EX box) 45.00
Parcheesi, Selchow & Righter, 1938, VG (VG box) 10.00

Pathfinder, Milton Bradley, 1977, EX (EX box) 50.00
Peg Baseball, Parker Bros, 1930s, EX (EX box) 85.00
Pirate Plunder, All-Fair, 1950s, VG (VG box) 50.00
Pirates & Travelers, trifold w/boxed pcs, 1911, EX 120.00
Pit, card game, Parker Bros, 1919, VG (VG box) 20.00
Pro-Football, Milton Bradley, 1964, VG (VG box) 45.00
Puff Balls, Spears, 1960s, NMIB 25.00
Pursuit, Game Maker Inc, 1940s, EX 75.00
Ropes & Ladders, Parker Bros, 1954, few pcs missing, VG (VG box) ..20.00
Sandlot Slugger, Milton Bradley, 1968, VG (VG box) 40.00
Shariland, Transogram, 1959, VG (VG box) 45.00
Sharpshooter, Cadaco, 1965, EX (EX box) 35.00
Smack-A-Roo, Mattel, 1964, EX (EX box) 40.00
Snoopy, card game, Ideal, 1965, NM (EX box) 25.00
Solarquest, Western Publishing, 1986, EX (EX box) 30.00
Soldiers, target game, J Pressman, EX (EX box) 100.00
Space Race, Beswick/England, EX (EX box) 100.00
Spin the Spin-nik, Fun Craft, 1960s, NM (EX box) 75.00
Square Mile, Milton Bradley, 1962, VG (VG box) 35.00
Stump the Stars, Ideal, 1962, VG (VG box) 20.00
Swoop, Whitman, 1969, NM (NM box) 30.00
Tantalizer, Northern Signal, 1965, VG (VG box) 40.00
Targets in Space, Spear/England, EX (EX box) 400.00
Ten-To-Tal, Selchow & Righter, EX (EX box) 45.00
Tiddle Tennis, Schonlat, 1930s, EX (EX box) 45.00
Tiddly Winks, Whitman, 1958, NM (EX box) 20.00
Toppling Tower, Ideal, 1967, EX (EX box) 35.00
Touring, Parker Bros, 1926, EX (VG box) 30.00
Tradewinds, Parker Bros, 1960, VG (VG box) 60.00
Tug of War, Chafee/Selchow, 1898, VG+ (VG+ box) 425.00
Twin Target, Milton Bradley, 1920s, VG (VG box) 225.00
Two for the Money, Hasbro, 1955, VG (worn box) 25.00
Universe Game, Parker Bros, 1967, NM (EX box) 60.00
Video Village, Milton Bradley, 1960, VG (VG box) 20.00
Which Witch?, Milton Bradley, 1970, EX (EX box) 75.00
Wildlife, ES Lowe, 1971, VG (VG box) 40.00
Wings Air Mail, Parker Bros, 1920s, EXIB 35.00
You Don't Say, Milton Bradley, 1963, EXIB 20.00
Zoo Game, Milton Bradley, 1920s, EX (worn box) 55.00

Personalities, Movies, and TV Shows

Addams Family, card game, Milton Bradley, 1965, NM (EX box) .30.00
Adventures of Sir Lancelot, Lisbeth Whiting, 1957, VG (VG box) .140.00
Alvin & the Chipmunks Acorn Hunt, Hasbro, 1960, EX (EX box) ...55.00
Amos & Andy Card Party, A Davis, 1930, unused, MIB 200.00
Art Linkletter's House Party, Whitman, 1968, NM (NM box) 50.00
Ben Casey MD, transogram, 1961, NM (EX box) 30.00
Bewitched, Gem Games, 1965, EX (EX box) 125.00
Bionic Woman, Parker Bros, 1976, VG (VG box) 30.00
Bonanza, Parker Bros, 1964, EX (EX box) 40.00
Candid Camera, Lowell, 1963, EX (EX box) 65.00
Carol Burnett, card game, Milton Bradley, NM (NM box) 25.00
Charlie's Angels, Milton Bradley, 1977, NM (EX box) 25.00
CHiPs, Milton Bradley, 1977, VG (VG box) 30.00
Daniel Boone, card game, Ed-U, 1965, NM (NM box) 15.00
Dick Tracy Master Detective, 1961, EX (EX box) 50.00
Dragnet, Transogram, 1955, NM (EX box) 50.00
Emmett Kelly's Circus, All-Fair, 1950s, NM (VG box) 75.00
Fall Guy, Milton Bradley, 1982, EX (EX box) 20.00
Flintstones, Milton Bradley, 1971, NM (EX box) 30.00
Frosty the Snowman, Parker Bros, 1979, VG (VG box) 25.00
Game of Captain Kangaroo, Milton Bradley, 1956, EX (EX box) .50.00
Game of General Hospital, Cardinal Industries, 1982, VG (VG box) 50.00

Rival Policemen, McLoughlin Bros, MIB, sold in 1995 for $4,500.00.

Game of Jack & the Beanstalk, McLoughlin Bros, 1898, VG (G box) .865.00
GI Joe Navy Frogman, Hasbro, 1965, NMIB 75.00
Great Grape Ape, Milton Bradley, 1975, EX (VG box) 15.00
Hardy Boys Treasure Game, Parker Bros, 1957, NMIB 95.00
Howdy Doody, card game, Russell, 1950s, EX (EX box) 45.00
Hunt for Red October, TSR, 1988, VG (VG box) 20.00
Knight Rider, Parker Bros, 1983, NM (EX box) 20.00
Kojak, Milton Bradley, 1975, VG (VG box) 25.00
Lone Ranger, Parker Bros, 1938, VG (VG box) 95.00

Lost in Space, Milton Bradley, 1965, EX+ in box, $135.00.

Magilla Gorilla, Ideal, 1964, NMIB 150.00
McHale's Navy, Transogram, 1962, few pcs missing, EX (EX box) .30.00
Mickey Mouse Target, Marks Bros, 1930s, EX 125.00
Mork & Mindy, card game, 1979, VG (VG box) 35.00
Murder She Wrote, Warren, 1985, EX (EX box) 35.00
Newlywed Game, Hasbro, 1969, NMIB 20.00
Patty Duke, Milton Bradley, 1964, EX (EX box) 45.00
Petticoat Junction, Standard Toycraft, 1965, NMIB 165.00
Popeye the Sailor Shipwreck, Funland, EX (EX box) 200.00
Road Runner, Milton Bradley, 1968, EX (EX box) 35.00
Robin Hood, Parker Bros, 1973, VG (VG box) 30.00
Sherlock Holmes, Cadaco, 1974, NMIB 30.00
Skipper, Mattel, 1964, NMIB 70.00
Snoopy, card game, Milton Bradley, 1974, MIB 15.00
Star Trek, Milton Bradley, 1979, VG (VG box) 75.00
Superman, Merry Mfg, 1964, rare, EX (EX box) 250.00
Tammy, Ideal, 1965, 2nd issue, NM (NM box) 50.00
Terminator 2 — Judgement Day, Milton Bradley, 1991, VG (VG box) ..25.00
Three Musketeers, Milton Bradley, 1950, NMID 60.00
Tom & Jerry, Transogram, 1965, NMIB 100.00
Twiggy, Milton Bradley, 1960s, NM (NM box) 85.00
Wagon Train, Milton Bradley, 1960, EX (EX box) 50.00
Wally Gator Game, Transogram, EX (EX box) 65.00
Waltons, Milton Bradley, 1974, VG (VG box) 20.00
Wizard of Oz, Cadaco, 1974, VG (VG box) 40.00
Yoda the Jedi Master, Kenner, 1981, EX (EX box) 50.00
Yogi Bear Score-O-Matic, 1960, EX (EX box) 75.00

Garden City Pottery

Founded in 1902 in San Jose, California, by the end of the 1920s this pottery had grown to become the largest in Northern California. During that period production focused on stoneware, sewer pipe, and red clay flowerpots. In the late '30s and '40s, the company produced dinnerware in bright solid colors of yellow, green, blue, orange, cobalt, turquoise, white, and black. Royal Arden Hickman, who would later gain fame for the innovative artware he modeled for the Haeger company, designed not only dinnerware but a line of Art Deco vases and bowls as well. The company endured hard times by adapting to the changing needs of the market and during the '50s concentrated on production of

garden products. Foreign imports, however, proved to be too competitive, and the company's pottery production ceased in 1979.

Because none of the colored glazed products were ever marked, to learn to identify the products of this company, you'll need to refer to *Sanford's Guide to Garden City Pottery*, by Jim Pasquali, who is listed in the Directory under California.

Baker, Wide-Ring, solid color, w/lid, 4" 30.00
Bean pot, plain, solid color, angle handles, recessed lid, 1-qt 25.00
Bowl, mixing; Conical, solid color, #36 ....15.00
Bowl, mixing; Swirl, solid color, #18 ....40.00
Bowl, mixing; Wide-Ring, solid color, #5 ....50.00
Bowl, Swirl, solid color, low, 14" 45.00
Canister, Wide-Ring, solid color, 7½" 50.00
Casserole, Narrow-Ring, solid color, w/lid, 9" 50.00
Cookie jar, shouldered Deco shape, solid color, 7½" 75.00
Pitcher, plain, solid color, 1-qt 35.00
Shakers, rocket shape, pr 45.00
Teapot, Deco style, spherical w/'pelican-bill' spout, 4-cup 60.00
Vase, Deco styling, solid colors, assorted, ea 65.00
Vase, Florist, solid color, str ribbed sides, 11" 75.00
Vase, U-shape flattened pillow form, solid color, 4½x10" 65.00

Gas Globes and Panels

Gas globes and panels, once a common sight, have vanished from the countryside but are being sought by collectors as a unique form of advertising memorabilia. Early globes from the 1920s (some date back to as early as 1912), now referred to as 'one-piece globes,' were made of molded milk glass and were globular in shape. The gas company name was etched or painted on the glass. Few of these were ever produced, and this type is valued very highly by collectors today.

A new type of pump was introduced in the early 1930s; the old 'visible' pumps were replaced by 'electric' models. Globes were changing at the same time. By the mid-teens a three-piece globe consisting of a pair of inserts and a metal body was being produced in both 15" and 16½" sizes. Collectors prefer to call globes that are not one-piece or plastic 'three-piece glass' (Type 2) or 'metal body, glass inserts' (Type 3). Though metal-body globes (Type 3) were popular in the 1930s, they were common in the 1920s, and some were actually made as early as 1915. Though rare in numbers, their use spans many years. In the 1930s Type 2 and Type 3 globes became the replacements of the one-piece globe. The most recently manufactured gas globes are made with a plastic body that contains two 13½" glass lenses. These were common in the '50s but were actually used as early as 1932.

Note: Standard Crowns with raised letters are one-piece globes that were made in the 1920s; those made in the 1950s (no raised letters), though one-piece, are not regarded as such by today's collectors. Our advisor for this category is Scott Benjamin; he is listed in the Directory under Ohio.

Type 1, Plastic Body, Glass Inserts (Inserts 13½") — 1931 – 1950s

Ashland Diesel 300.00
DX Ethyl 350.00
Falcon 1,200.00
Frontier Gas, Rarin' To Go, w/horse 900.00
Hornet, Capcolite body, 13½", NM 350.00
Kendal Deluxe, Capcolite body w/red pnt, 13½" 275.00
Marathon, no runner 200.00
Marine, sea horse, EX color 850.00
Never Nox Ethyl 450.00
Shamrock, oval body 350.00

Spur, Oval body 350.00
Texaco Diesel Chief, Capcolite body, 13½", NM 800.00
Texaco Sky Chief 325.00
Viking, pictures Viking ship 750.00
66 Flite Fuel, Phillips, shield shape, all plastic 500.00

Type 2, Glass Frame, Glass Inserts (Inserts 13½") — 1926 – 1940s

Amaco, glass body, 12½", NM 375.00
Champlin Preston, 3-pc glass 450.00
Golden 97 Ethyl, hull glass body, 12½", NM 450.00
Gulf, hull body, 13½", NM 450.00
Indian Gas, Red Dot 750.00
Kanotex, w/sunflower, gill body 650.00
Koolmotor, clover shape, gr bkground 1,500.00
Mobil Gas 450.00
Red Crown, milk glass 400.00
Skelly Anomarx w/Ethyl 500.00
Sky Chief, gill body, 13½", NM 450.00
Standard Crown, bl 650.00
Texaco Diesel Chief 900.00
Texaco Star, blk outline on 'T' 450.00
White Flash, gill body 450.00
White Rose, boy, glass body 1,500.00

Type 3, Metal Frame, Glass Inserts (Inserts 15" or 16½") — 1915 – 1930s

Blue Sunoco, 15" 550.00
Cities Services Oils, 1929, 15" fr 750.00
Crown, crown pictured, 16½", EX 1,500.00
Esso Extra, 15" 500.00

Mobilgas, red metal body, winged horse, 15", NM, $750.00.

Mobilfuel Diesel, lg horse, high profile 850.00
Pure, porc body, 15" 750.00
Purol Pep, porc body 750.00
Richfield, w/eagle 700.00
Rocor, w/eagle 800.00
Socony, milk glass inserts on metal 1,400.00
Sunland Ethyl, 15" 750.00
Tidex, 16½" 550.00
Tydol, 16½" 600.00

Type 4, One-Piece Glass Globes, No Inserts, Co. Name Etched, Raised, or Enameled — 1912 – 1931

Diamond 1,200.00
Iowa Gas 2,000.00
Musgo 5,000.00
Pierce Pennant, etched 3,200.00
Red Crown, rnd, etched 3,600.00

Sinclair, etched, milk glass 1,200.00
Sinclair Aircraft, etched 4,500.00
Skelly 1,000.00
Texaco, milk glass, emb letters, brass collar 1,400.00

Gaudy Dutch

Inspired by Oriental Imari wares, Gaudy Dutch was made in England from 1800 to 1820. It was hand decorated on a soft-paste body with rich underglaze blues accented in orange, red, pink, green, and yellow. It differs from Gaudy Welsh in that there is no lustre (except on Water Lily). There are seventeen patterns, some of which are War Bonnet, Grape, Dahlia, Oyster, Urn, Butterfly, Carnation, Single Rose, Double Rose, and Water Lily. For further information we recommend *The Collector's Encyclopedia of Gaudy Dutch & Welsh* by John Shuman, available from Collector Books. Unless otherwise noted, values are given for items with minimal wear and no obvious damage.

Butterfly, coffeepot, 11" 4,400.00
Butterfly, cup & saucer, butterfly on side 825.00
Butterfly, cup & saucer, handleless, EX 660.00
Butterfly, plate, butterfly on side, 8¼" 990.00
Butterfly, plate, wide spread decor in center, 9⅞", M 1,870.00
Butterfly, plate, 8⅜", EX 385.00
Butterfly, sugar bowl 1,870.00

Butterfly, teapot, $2,500.00.

Butterfly, waste bowl 1,485.00
Butterfly Variant, deep dish, 10" 1,000.00
Carnation, coffeepot 1,430.00
Carnation, cup plate 715.00
Carnation, plate, deep, sm feather border, 10" 855.00
Carnation, plate, 8⅜", M 850.00
Carnation, soup plate, 8½" 770.00
Carnation, sugar bowl 800.00
Dahlia, cup & saucer, handleless 825.00
Dahlia, plate, 8" 880.00
Dahlia, plate, 8⅜" 990.00
Dahlia, sugar bowl 900.00
Double Rose, creamer 660.00
Double Rose, cup & saucer 600.00
Double Rose, plate, 10", M 1,100.00
Double Rose, plate, 9¾" 855.00
Double Rose, platter, 11½" 3,400.00
Dove, plate, plain border, 6¼", M 550.00
Dove, plate, 9¾" 880.00
Dove, teapot 1,100.00
Dove, toddy plate 700.00
Dove, waste bowl, 6⅜" 770.00
Grape, cream pitcher 765.00

Grape, cup & saucer, 4-color 525.00
Grape, cup plate 650.00
Grape, plate, 8", M 550.00
Grape, plate, 9¾" 660.00
Grape, soup plate, 8¾" 500.00
Grape, teapot 700.00
Grape, waste bowl 400.00
Leaf, bowl, unusual shape, 8¾" 1,100.00
Leaf, sugar bowl, w/lid 1,100.00
Oyster, plate, orange pattern, 9¾", M 1,430.00
Oyster, plate, 5⅝" 400.00
Oyster, plate, 8½" 515.00
Primrose, sugar bowl, w/lid 990.00
Primrose, teacup & saucer, handleless 770.00
Primrose, waste bowl 825.00
Single Rose, cup & saucer 515.00
Single Rose, plate, 7¼", M 550.00
Single Rose, plate, 9½" 600.00
Single Rose, sugar bowl, w/lid 715.00
Single Rose, teapot, M 1,650.00
Strawflower, plate, mk Riley, 8¼" 880.00
Strawflower, plate, 8½" 900.00
Strawflower, plate, 9" 915.00
Sunflower, creamer 500.00
Sunflower, cup & saucer, handleless 880.00
Sunflower, plate, 7½", M 675.00
Sunflower, plate, 8¼", M 660.00
Urn, creamer 385.00
Urn, cup & saucer, M 490.00
Urn, cup plate 465.00
Urn, plate, 7½" 550.00
Urn, plate, 8¼", M 685.00
War Bonnet, cup & saucer, NM 755.00
War Bonnet, cup plate 715.00
War Bonnet, plate, shallow, 8⅛", M 1,000.00
War Bonnet, plate, 6⅜" 635.00
War Bonnet, teapot, M 2,310.00
War Bonnet, waste bowl, 5, M 1,100.00
Zinnia, plate, 6⅜" 660.00

Gaudy Ironstone

Gaudy Ironstone was produced in the mid-1800s in Staffordshire, England. Some of the ware was decorated in much the same colors and designs as Gaudy Welsh, while other pieces were painted in pink, orange, and red with black and light blue accents. Lustre was used on some designs, omitted on others. The heavy ironstone body is its most distinguishing feature.

Bowl, vegetable; Floral, 1¾x8⅝x6⅞" 300.00
Bowl, vegetable; Floral, 8-sided, w/lid, 7¼x9" 1,450.00
Coffeepot, Floral, 8-sided, sq hdl, rosette finial, unmk, 10" 525.00
Coffeepot, Pinwheel, triangular finial, scroll hdl, 9⅛" 575.00
Coffeepot, Seeing Eye, scroll hdl, 9⅞", EX 340.00
Creamer, Seeing Eye, scrolled arched hdl, 5¾" 975.00
Cup & saucer, Floral, 3½", 5¾", NM 90.00
Cup & saucer, handleless; Floral, 3¾", 5⅞", NM 200.00
Cup & saucer, handleless; Floral Variant, ftd, 4", 5¾" 80.00
Cup & saucer, handleless; Seeing Eye, 3⅝", 5⅞", from $275 to ..300.00
Plate, Floral, #5, 8¾", NM 115.00
Plate, Floral, 10-sided, #5, 8⅛", pr 525.00
Plate, Floral, 8¼", NM 115.00
Plate, Seeing Eye, Niagara shape, mk, 1856, 6¾", pr 550.00
Plate, Seeing Eye, Niagara shape, registry mk, dtd 1856, 5", pr ...575.00
Plate, Seeing Eye, Niagara shape, Walley, mk, 1856, 8½" 250.00
Plate, Seeing Eye, Niagara shape, Walley, mk, 1856, 9½", NM ..200.00
Plate, Seeing Eye, 10-sided, #5, 8½", pr 575.00
Plate, Seeing Eye, 10-sided, mk Pearl White, 5⅜" 160.00
Plate, Seeing Eye, 10-sided, mk Pearl White, 6⅜" 210.00
Plate, Seeing Eye, 12-sided, unmk, 9¾" 250.00
Platter, Floral, unmk, 15½x12⅛", NM 1,025.00
Platter, flowers & butterfly w/bl scrolls & orange rim, 21" 350.00
Platter, Pinwheel, 11⅞x9⅛", NM 175.00
Soup plate, Pinwheel, 14-sided, mk Ironstone, 10¾", pr 375.00
Sugar bowl, Seeing Eye, scroll hdls, w/lid, unmk, 7", EX+ 875.00
Sugar bowl, Strawberry, 8-sided, married teapot lid, 8¼" 625.00
Waste bowl, Seeing Eye, Niagara shape, 3¼x4⅝", EX 225.00
Waste bowl, Seeing Gye, unmk, 3¼x5½", EX 175.00

Gaudy Welsh

Gaudy Welsh was an inexpensive hand-decorated ware made in both England and Wales from 1820 until 1860. It is characterized by its colors — principally blue, orange-rust, and copper lustre — and by its uninhibited patterns. Accent colors may be yellow and green. (Pink lustre may be present, since lustre applied to the white areas appears pink. A copper tone develops from painting lustre onto the dark colors.) The body of the ware may be heavy ironstone, creamware, earthenware, or porcelain; even style and shapes vary considerably. Patterns, while usually floral, are also sometimes geometric and may have trees and birds. Beware! The Wagon Wheel pattern has been reproduced.

Our advisor for this category is Cheryl Nelson; she is listed in the Directory under Minnesota. For further information we recommend *The Collector's Encyclopedia of Gaudy Dutch & Welsh* by John Shuman, available from Collector Books.

Note: The Bethedsa pattern is very similar to a Davenport jug pattern. No porcelain Gaudy Welsh was made in Wales.

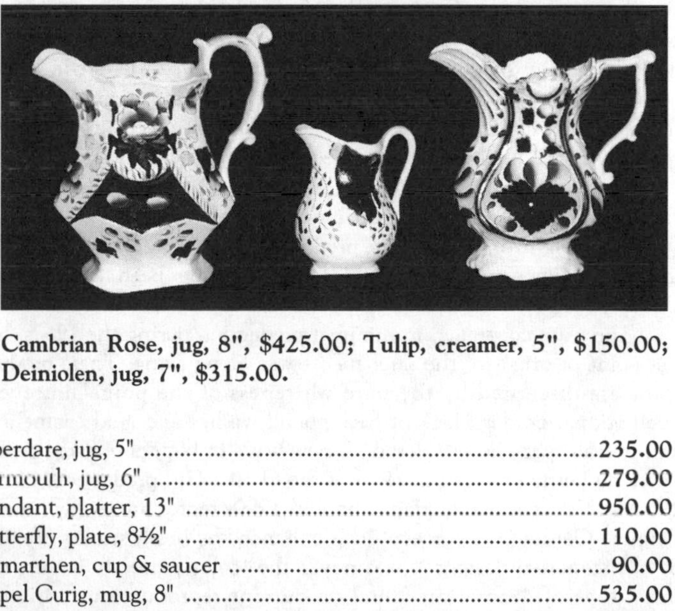
Photo courtesy Cheryl Nelson

Cambrian Rose, jug, 8", $425.00; Tulip, creamer, 5", $150.00; Deiniolen, jug, 7", $315.00.

Aberdare, jug, 5" 235.00
Barmouth, jug, 6" 279.00
Bondant, platter, 13" 950.00
Butterfly, plate, 8½" 110.00
Camarthen, cup & saucer 90.00
Capel Curig, mug, 8" 535.00
Cardiff, jug, 7" 400.00
Castle, cup & saucer 80.00
Castle, waste bowl 90.00
Cheyenne, bowl, gr, rare 775.00
Chinoiserie, cup & saucer 75.00

Columbine, plate, 8" 65.00
Conwy, mug, 2½" 195.00
Cynon, mug, 2½" 185.00
Drape, cup & saucer 80.00
Feather, plate, 10" 170.00
Honeysuckle, cup & saucer 90.00
Jewel, plate, 8" 180.00
Leek, plate, 8" 160.00
Morning Glory, cup & saucer 90.00
Nightingale, creamer 240.00
Penilyn, plate, flo, 6" 210.00
Pennant, plate, 8" 175.00
Ragland, jug, 6" 450.00
Rainbow, creamer 190.00
Rainbow, mug, 2" 175.00
Scallop, jug, 3", minimum value 200.00
Tassel, jug, 10" 470.00
Trumpet, plate, 10" 150.00
Tulip, tea set, 24-pc 1,000.00
Urn, jug, 7¼" 395.00
Wheatstock, plate, 8" 215.00

Geisha Girl

Geisha Girl Porcelain was one of several key Japanese china production efforts aimed at the booming export markets of the U.S., Canada, England, and other parts of Europe. The wares feature colorful, kimono-clad Japanese ladies in scenes of everyday Japanese life, surrounded by exquisite flora, fauna, and mountain ranges. Nonetheless, the forms in which the wares were produced reflected the late 19th- and early 20th-century Western dining and decorating preferences: tea and coffee services, vases, dresser sets, children's items, planters, etc.

Over one hundred manufacturers were involved in Geisha Girl production. This accounts for the several hundred different patterns, well over a dozen border colors and styles, and several methods of design execution. Geisha Girl Porcelain was produced in wholly hand-painted versions, but most were hand painted over stenciled outlines. Be wary of Geisha ware executed with decals. Very few decaled examples came out of Japan. Rather, most were Czechoslovakian attempts to hone in on the market. Czech pieces have stamped marks in broad, pseudo-Oriental characters. Items with portraits of Oriental ladies in the bottom of tea or sake cups are *not* Geisha Girl Porcelain, unless the outside surface of the wares are decorated as described above. These lovely faces, formed by varying the thickness of the porcelain body, are called lithophanes and are collectible in their own right.

The height of Geisha Girl production was between 1910 and the mid-1930s. Some post-World War II production has been found marked Occupied Japan.

The ware continued in minimal production during the 1960s, but the point of origin of the later pieces was Hong Kong. These productions are discerned by the pure whiteness of the porcelain; even, unemotional borders; lack of background washes and gold enameling; and overall sparseness of detail. A new wave of Nippon-marked reproduction Geisha emerged in 1996. If the Geisha Girl productions of the 1960s – 80s were overly plain, the mid-1990s repros are overly ornate. Original Geisha Girl porcelain was enhanced by brush strokes of color over a stenciled design; it was never the 'color perfectly within the lines' type of decoration found on current reproductions. Original Geisha Girl porcelain was decorated with color washes; the reproductions are in heavy enamels. The backdrop decoration of the current reproductions feature solid, thick colors, and the patterns feature too much color; period Geisha ware had a high ratio of white space to color. The new pieces also have bright shiny gold in proportions greater than

most period Geisha ware. The Nippon marks on the reproductions are wrong. Some of the Geisha ware created during the Nippon era bore the small precise decaled green M-in-Wreath mark, a Noritake registered trademark. The reproduction items feature an irregular facsimile of this mark. Stamped onto the reproductions is an unrealistically large M-in-Wreath mark in shades of green ranging from an almost neon to pine green with a wreath that looks like it has seen better days, as it does not have the perfect roundness of the original mark. Reproductions of mid-sized trays, chunky hatpin holders, an ornate vase, a covered bottle, and a powder jar are among the current reproductions popping up at flea and antique markets.

Many of our descriptions contain references to border colors and treatments. This information is given immediately preceding the mark and/or size. Our advisor for this category is Elyce Litts; she is listed in the Directory under New Jersey.

Key:

#2 — Torii Nippon	#42 — Vantine
#4 — T in Cherry Blossom	#68 — SGK China, Occupied
#11 — diaper mk	Japan
#12 — Royal Kaga, Nippon	J #1 — Yachi
#15 — Green, M-in-Wreath,	J #2 — Yachi tsukuru
Nippon	J #6 — Tashiro
#16 — SNB, Nippon	J #16 — Kutani
#19 — Japan	J #19 — Ozan
#20 — Made in Japan	J #36 — Made by Kato
#35 — Plum Blossom	J #46 — Yasutera

Platter, Parasol B, red border with green circles and gold lacing, 9½x6¼", $65.00.

Photo courtesy
Elyce Litts

Basket vase, Bamboo Trellis, gr hdl & brn ft w/gold, 8½" 150.00
Berry set, Dragon Boat, cobalt w/gold, master+5 ind 85.00
Biscuit jar, Court Lady, cobalt w/blk-outlined reserves, J#1 ....75.00
Biscuit jar, Oni Dance B, red-orange w/gold mums, ftd 85.00
Bowl, berry; River's Edge, gr/orange/gold, 5" 20.00
Bowl, Footbridge B, red w/yel, 8" 35.00
Box, Garden Bench B, red sides, 6-sided, #20, 6" 35.00
Butter pat, Flower Gathering B, red-orange, 3¼" 12.00
Cocoa pot, Garden Bench C, cobalt w/gold, cylindrical, 6½" 55.00
Cocoa pot, Parasol B: Torii & Parasol, cobalt w/gold, fluted, #16 .65.00
Compote, Boat Festival, river scene, ftd, #4, 6" H 55.00
Creamer, Boy w/Scythe, cobalt w/gold, #20 ....15.00
Creamer, Paper Carp, red-orange w/gold, J#16 ....20.00
Creamer & sugar bowl, Ribbon Parasol, red-orange w/gold 35.00
Cup & saucer, demi; Basket A, apple gr, allover patterns 20.00
Cup & saucer, tea; Peacock on Flowered Stone Roof, cobalt/gold .25.00
Dresser tray, Blind Man's Bluff on cobalt, scalloped, 11½x8½" ...85.00
Egg cup, Duck Watching, gold border, mk 22.00
Egg cup, Parasol Modern: Processional Parasol, pale cobalt 7.00
Hair receiver, Footbridge A 35.00
Hatpin holder, Rendezvous, vine & leaves, J#16 ....100.00
Humidor, Battledore, scalloped, bl w/gold line 125.00
Jug, Battledore, apple gr, fluted edge & base, ribbed, 5" 40.00

Luncheon set, Garden Bench D, mc border, pot+6 c/s+6 plates .225.00
Manicure jar, Parasol C: Parasol, red #19, 2¼" 20.00
Marmalade, Cloud A, red-orange w/yel, ribs, w/tray, J#6, 5" 45.00
Match holder, Garden Bench A, bl-gr, hanging 35.00
Mint dish, Bamboo Trellis, red-orange w/gold buds 12.00
Mug, Gardening, red w/gold line, 3x3" 45.00
Napkin ring, Templea, oval, #15A 30.00
Nappy, Mother & Daughter, dk turq, lobed 35.00
Pin tray, Duck Watching B, pine gr w/wht, uneven edge, #34 ......15.00
Plate, Bamboo Tree, pine gr, chrysanthemum shape, 7" 15.00
Plate, Fan A, red-orange w/gold, 7" 20.00
Plate, Inside the Treehouse, apple gr, fluted swirl, 8½" 35.00
Plate, Kite B, red w/gold lacing, scalloped sdge, J#16, 7" 28.00
Powder jar, Pug, brick red, 4¼" 35.00
Sauce dish, Mother & Son, red w/gold, emb leaves, #19, 6" 16.00
Shakers, Bouncing Ball, bl-gr, pr 22.00
Sugar bowl, Garden Bench G, cobalt w/gold, J#16 ....32.00
Sugar bowl, Mother & Daughter, 2 reserves, red w/gold 20.00
Tea set, Visitor to the Court, cobalt w/gold trim, #19, 3-pc 65.00
Teacup & saucer, Bicycle Race, red-orange w/gold 30.00
Teacup & saucer, Cloud B, red-orange w/yel 15.00
Toothpick holder, Circle Dance, red, cylindrical 15.00
Vase, Bamboo Trellis, red-orange, #14, 4½", pr 30.00

Georgia Art Pottery

In Cartersville, Georgia, in August 1935, W.J. Gordy first fired pottery turned from regional clays. By 1936 he was marking his wares 'Georgia Art Pottery' (GP) or 'Georgia Art Pottery' (GAP) and continued to do so until 1950 when he used a 'Hand Made by WJ Gordy' stamp (HM). Since 1970 he has signed his pottery. Known throughout the world for his fine glazes, he won the Georgia Governor's Award in 1983. Examples of his wares are on display in the Smithsonian. His father W.T.B. and brother D.X. are also well-known potters.

Ashtray, pk, bl & wht irid, 1½x4½" 34.00
Cruet, flared rim, bulbous, WJ Gordy, 4¾x3" 85.00
Flower vase, pk, 19 holes, Gordy, 5x5" 102.50
Jug, Rebecca, cobalt mottle, sgn WJG, 7" 140.00
Mug, aqua bl-gr, 4⅛" 50.00
Pitcher, gr, sgn WJ Gordy, 3¼" 66.00
Pitcher, Rebecca, yel-gr, sgn WJG, 7¼" 140.00
Stein, mirror blk, cylindrical, DX Gordy, ca 1937-39, 5" 100.00
Vase, brn to tan striated semigloss, rim-to-hip hdls, 8" 227.50
Vase, cobalt, ruffled rim, 2¼x3¼" 65.00
Vase, frothy wht over pk, scalloped rim, sgn WJG, 3" 70.00

German Porcelain

Unless otherwise noted, the porcelain listed in this section is marked simply 'Germany.' Products of other German manufactures are listed in specific categories. See also Bisque; Pink Paw Bears; Pink Pigs; Elfinware.

Platter, 18th century courting couple, brass-mounted, Heinrich & Co, Selb, early 20th century, 21½x12⅜", $400.00.

Bowl, roses & gold wreaths, sq paneled mold, mk, 10½" 50.00
Bowl, vegetable; emb shells, HP house/moon in center 30.00
Charger, lady's portrait on turq w/gold scrolls, 12" 110.00
Charger, roses/gold scrolls on cobalt, IPF, 13" 125.00
Figurine, dancer holds skirt high, Herwig & Co, 1930s 350.00
Figurine, fan dancer, Herwig & Co, 1930s, 12" 325.00
Plate, Grecian lady, wine rim w/gold flowers, 9", in gilt fr 175.00
Vase, dk brn w/rust stripes & mc dots on matt, MIG, 3½" 22.50

Gladding McBean and Company

This company was established in 1875 in Lincoln, California. They first produced only clay drainage pipes, but in 1883 architectural terra cotta was introduced, which has been used extensively in the United States as well as abroad. Sometime later a line of garden pottery was added. They soon became the leading producers of tile in the country. In 1923 they purchased the Tropico Pottery in Glendale, California, where in addition to tile they also produced huge garden vases. Their line was expanded in 1934 to included artware and dinnerware.

At least fifteen lines of art pottery were developed between 1934 and 1942. For a short time they stamped their wares with the Tropico Pottery mark; but the majority was signed 'GMcB' in an oval. Later the mark was changed to 'Franciscan' with several variations. After 1937 'Catalina Pottery' was used on some lines. (All items marked 'Catalina Pottery' were made in Glendale.) For further information we recommend *The Collector's Encyclopedia of California Pottery, Second Edition*, by our advisor for this category, Jack Chipman. He is listed in the Directory under California.

Pitcher, orange, marked GMcB, 9x9", NM, $100.00.

Photo courtesy Michael John Verlangieri

Candle holder, Tropico Art Ware, wht 30.00
Carafe, orange/gr, in metal holder 40.00
Compote, Avalon Art Ware, turq & ivory, #C724, 8" 32.50
Cornucopia, Coronado Art Ware 35.00
Cup & saucer, Ruby Art Ware 45.00
Figurine, Samoan woman w/child, satin wht, 13" 250.00
Teapot, El Patio, wht 150.00
Tile, angelfish, 6x6" 75.00
Tumbler, orange/gr, in metal holder 18.00
Vase, bud; turq/wht, 6" 45.00
Vase, Coronado Art Ware, ivory satin, ftd, 10½" 135.00
Vase, Ox Blood Art Ware, #C290, 11" 750.00
Vase, Ox Blood Art Ware, turq to maroon, 9½" 350.00
Vase, Ruby Art Ware, bulbous w/flared rim, blk mk, 6" 165.00
Vase, turq/wht, 4" 40.00

Glass Animals and Figurines

These beautiful glass sculptures have been produced by many

major companies in America, in fact, some are still being made today. Heisey, Fostoria, Duncan and Miller, Imperial, Paden City, Tiffin, and Cambridge made the vast majority, but there were many others involved on a lesser scale. Some, but not all, marked their animals.

As many of the glass companies went out of business, molds were often sold to others still active who used them to reproduce their own line of animals. While some are easy to recognize, others can be very confusing. For example, Summit Art Glass now owns Cambridge's 6½", 8½", and 10" swan molds. We recommend *Glass Animals of the Depression Era* by Lee Garmon and Dick Spencer, if you're thinking of starting a collection or wanting to identify and evaluate the glass animals you already have. Both are our advisors for this category and are listed in the Directory under Illinois.

Note: Heisey Collectors of America stopped using the plug horse and have adopted the rabbit paperweight as the new yearly mascot.

Cambridge

Bashful Charlotte, flower frog, crystal, 11½"	175.00
Bashful Charlotte, flower frog, gr, 11½"	375.00
Bashful Charlotte, flower frog, Moonlight Blue, 11½"	525.00
Bashful Charlotte, flower frog, Peachblo, 6½"	150.00
Bird, crystal satin, 2¾" L	35.00
Blue jay, flower holder, crystal	135.00
Bridge hound, ebony, 1¼"	50.00
Buddha, amber, 5½"	225.00
Draped Lady, flower frog, amber, 8½"	195.00
Draped Lady, flower frog, Dianthus, 8½"	175.00
Draped Lady, flower frog, Gold Krystol, 8½"	250.00
Draped Lady, flower frog, ivory, oval base, 8½"	800.00
Draped Lady, flower frog, lt pk, 8½"	125.00
Draped Lady, flower frog, Moonlight Blue, 13"	860.00
Draped Lady, flower frog, pk, 13½"	190.00
Eagle, bookend, crystal, 5½x4x4", ea	95.00
Heron, crystal, lg, 12"	135.00
Lion, bookend, crystal, ea	185.00
Mandolin Lady, flower frog, dk amber	450.00
Mandolin Lady, flower frog, lt emerald	400.00

Melon Boy flower holder, emerald green, $425.00.

Photo courtesy National
Cambridge Collectors, Inc.

Owl, lamp, ivory w/brn enamel, ebony base, 13½"	1,100.00
Rose Lady, flower frog, amber, 8½"	200.00
Rose Lady, flower frog, Dianthus, 8½"	275.00
Rose Lady, flower frog, gr, 8½"	200.00
Scottie, bookends, crystal, hollow, pr	175.00
Sea gull, flower block, crystal	60.00
Swan, amber, #1 style, 10½"	875.00
Swan, Carmen, #3 style, 8½"	350.00
Swan, Carmen, 6½"	225.00
Swan, Crown Tuscan, 3"	50.00
Swan, crystal, #1 style, 10½"	180.00

Swan, ebony, 3"	65.00
Swan, ebony, 8½"	165.00
Swan, ebony, 10½"	250.00
Swan, emerald, 8½"	125.00
Swan, milk glass, #3 style, 8½"	350.00
Swan, milk glass, 8½"	275.00
Swan, yel, 8½"	175.00
Turkey, bl, w/lid	550.00
Turkey, gr, w/lid	475.00
Turtle, flower holder, ebony	225.00
Two Kids, flower frog, amber satin, 9¼"	400.00

Duncan and Miller

Donkey, cart & peon, crystal, 3-pc set	475.00
Duck, ashtray, crystal, 4"	25.00
Duck, ashtray, red, 7"	125.00
Goose, crystal, fat, 6x6"	375.00
Heron, crystal	150.00
Mallard duck, cigarette box, crystal, #30, w/lid, 3½x4½"	50.00
Swan, ashtray, crystal w/bl neck, 4"	35.00
Swan, candle holder, red, 7", ea	80.00
Swan, wheat cutting, 11"	200.00
Swordfish, bl opal, rare	500.00
Sylvan swan, bl or pk, 5½"	125.00
Sylvan swan, yel opal, 5½"	120.00
Tropical fish, ashtray, pk opal, 3½"	50.00

Fenton

Airedale, Rosalene	75.00
Alley cat, pk carnival, mk, 11"	100.00
Alley cat, Teal Marigold, 11"	85.00
Bunny, lt bl	16.00
Butterfly, candle holder, ruby carnival, 1989 souvenir, 7½", ea	85.00
Donkey, custard, HP daisies, 4½"	45.00
Filly, Rosalene, head front	115.00
Fish, bookend, Rosalene, ea	95.00
Fish, paperweight, red carnival, ltd ed, 4½"	65.00
Gazelle, Rosalene	115.00
Giraffe, Rosalene	110.00
Happiness Bird, Rosalene	40.00
Peacock, bookends, crystal satin, 5¾", pr	175.00
Plug Horse, HCA, Rosalene	50.00
Turtle, flower block, amethyst, 4" L	85.00

Fostoria

Buddha, bookends, blk, pr	525.00
Cardinal head, Silver Mist, 6½"	175.00
Chanticleer, blk, 10¾"	600.00
Chinese Lute, ebony w/gold, 12½"	300.00
Colts, Silver Mist, standing	45.00
Deer, milk glass, sitting or standing, ea	55.00
Dolphin, bl, 4¾"	35.00
Duck, mama, crystal	30.00
Duckling, amber frost, head bk, #2632/405, 2½"	35.00
Duckling, crystal, head down (+)	20.00
Eagle, bookend, crystal, 7½", ea	150.00
Elephant, bookend, ebony, 6½", ea	150.00
Elephant, crystal	65.00
Goldfish, crystal, horizontal, rare	145.00
Goldfish, crystal, vertical	110.00
Lady bug, bl, lemon or olive gr, 1¼", ea	50.00

Owl, bl, lemon or olive gr, 2¾", ea 50.00
Pelican, amber, 1991 commemorative 55.00
Penguin, crystal, sq base, 4⅝" 75.00
Polar bear, crystal, 4⅝" 65.00
Rebecca at Well, candle holder, crystal frost, ea 125.00
Seal, topaz, 3⅞" 125.00
Squirrel, amber, sitting 45.00
Stork, bl, lemon or olive gr, 2", ea 50.00

Heisey

Asiatic pheasant, crystal, 7½" L 325.00
Bull, crystal, sgn, 4x7½" 1,800.00
Bunny, crystal, head down, 2½" 225.00
Clydesdale, crystal, 7½x7" 400.00
Colt, amber, rearing 650.00
Colt, cobalt, kicking 1,500.00
Colt, crystal, kicking 200.00
Cygnet, baby swan, crystal, 2½" 225.00

Dolphin candlestick, cobalt, #110, $1,250.00 each.

Photo courtesy Neila Bredehoft

Dolphin, candlesticks, crystal, #110, pr 350.00
Dolphin, candlesticks, Moongleam, #110, pr 800.00
Duck, ashtray, crystal 90.00
Duck, ashtray, Marigold 400.00
Duck, flower block, Flamingo 200.00
Duck, flower block, Hawthorne 295.00
Elephant, amber, lg or med, ea 1,850.00
Elephant, crystal, lg or med, ea 450.00
Filly, crystal, head bkwards 1,800.00
Fish, bookend, crystal, ea 145.00
Fish, candlestick, crystal, 5", ea 225.00
Fish, match holder, crystal, 3x2¾" 180.00
Flying Mare, crystal 3,000.00
Frog, cheese plate, Marigold 285.00
Giraffe, crystal, head bk 275.00
Giraffe, crystal, head forward 240.00
Giraffe, crystal, head to side 275.00
Goose, crystal, wings half 100.00
Hen, crystal, 4½" 350.00
Horse head, bookend, crystal, ea 175.00
Horse head, cigarette box, crystal, #1489, 4½x4" 55.00
Irish setter, ashtray, crystal 30.00
Irish setter, ashtray, Flamingo 45.00
Kingfisher, flower block, Flamingo 225.00
Mallard, crystal, wings down 350.00
Mallard, crystal, wings up 200.00
Piglet, crystal, standing 100.00
Plug horse, amber 600.00
Pouter pigeon, crystal, 7½" L 800.00
Rabbit, paperweight, crystal, 2¾x3¾" 225.00

Ram head, stopper, crystal, 3½" 160.00
Ringneck pheasant, crystal, 11¾" 175.00
Rooster, crystal, 5½x5" 350.00
Rooster, vase, crystal, 6½" 110.00
Rooster head, cocktail shaker, crystal, 1-qt 75.00
Scottie, crystal 135.00
Sow, crystal, 3x4½" 800.00
Swan, crystal 1,450.00
Swan, ind nut, crystal, #1503 ....25.00
Swan, pitcher, crystal 800.00
Tiger, paperweight, crystal, 2¾x8" 900.00
Tropical fish, crystal, 12" 2,000.00
Wood duck, crystal 800.00

Imperial

Angelfish, bookend, amber (crystal or frosted), ea 100.00
Asiatic pheasant, amber 425.00
Bull, amber, very rare 725.00
Bulldog-type pup, milk glass, 3½" 65.00
Champ terrier, caramel slag, 5¾" 95.00
Chick, milk glass, head down 10.00
Chick, milk glass, head up 10.00
Clydesdale, amber 400.00
Clydesdale, Salmon 275.00
Clydesdale, Verde Green 150.00
Colt, amber, balking 140.00
Colt, amber, standing 125.00
Colt, caramel slag, balking 140.00
Colt, Horizon Blue, kicking 35.00
Colt, Sunshine Yellow, standing 75.00
Cygnet, blk, 2½" 55.00
Cygnet, caramel slag 55.00
Cygnet, Horizon Blue 25.00
Dog, Airedale, caramel slag 115.00
Dog, Airedale, Ultra Blue 65.00
Donkey, caramel slag 55.00
Donkey, Meadow Green carnival 45.00
Donkey, Ultra Blue 65.00
Duck, Ultra Blue, standing, 2⅝" 45.00

Eagle bookend, crystal, #777/3, rare, $200.00.

Photo courtesy Gene Florence

Elephant, caramel slag, med 65.00
Elephant, caramel slag, sm 85.00
Elephant, Meadow Green carnival, #674, med 75.00
Elephant, Nut Brown, sm 120.00
Filly, satin, head forward 85.00
Filly, Verde Green, head bkward 155.00
Fish, bookend, ruby, ea 340.00
Fish, candlestick, Sunshine Yellow, 5", ea 50.00
Fish, match holder, Sunshine Yellow satin, 3" 20.00

Flying mare, amber, NI mk, extremely rare 1,500.00
Gazelle, blk, 11" 350.00
Giraffe, amber, ALIG mk, extremely rare 350.00
Horse head, bookend, pk, rare, ea 300.00
Mallard, caramel slag, wings down 200.00
Mallard, caramel slag, wings half 35.00
Mallard, caramel slag, wings up 40.00
Mallard, Horizon Blue, wings down, HCA, 4½" 35.00
Mallard, lt bl satin, wings down 35.00
Marmote Sentinel (woodchuck), caramel slag, 4½" 60.00
Owl, Hootless; caramel slag 50.00
Owl, Jade Green slag, shiny 85.00
Owl, jar, caramel slag, 16½" 65.00
Owl, milk glass 48.00
Owl, purple slag, shiny 85.00
Piglet, amber, sitting 40.00
Piglet, amber, standing 40.00
Piglet, ruby, standing 35.00
Plug horse, pk, HCA, 1978 ....40.00
Rabbit, paperweight, Horizon Blue, 2¾" 110.00
Ring-neck pheasant, amber, extremely rare 300.00
Rooster, amber 475.00
Rooster, pk, fighting 175.00
Scolding bird, Cathay Crystal 175.00
Scottie, milk glass, 3½" 55.00
Swan, purple slag, shiny 95.00
Terrier, Parlour Pup, amethyst carnival, 3½" 45.00
Terrier, Parlour Pup, Sunshine Yellow carnival 45.00
Tiger, paperweight, caramel slag 150.00
Tiger, paperweight, Jade Green slag, 8" L 95.00
Wood duck, caramel slag 65.00
Wood duck, Ultra Blue satin 45.00
Wood duckling, caramel slag, sitting, 4½" 75.00
Wood duckling, floating, Sunshine Yellow satin 20.00
Wood duckling, standing, Sunshine Yellow satin 15.00
Wood duckling, standing, Ultra Blue 45.00

L.E. Smith

Camel, cobalt 95.00
Camel, crystal 50.00
Elephant, condiment set, amber, set of 3 ....85.00
Goose, crystal, 2½" 25.00
Goose Girl, gr or flame, 6", ea 50.00
Horse, bookend, amber, rearing, ea 38.00
Horse, bookend, blk, rearing, ea 65.00
Horse, bookend, ruby, rearing, ea 55.00
Queen fish, aquarium, gr, 7x15" 225.00
Scottie, pipe rest, fired-on blk, 5½" L 10.00
Sparrow, crystal, head up, 3½" 15.00
Swan, soap dish, crystal 25.00

New Martinsville

Bear, mama, crystal, 4x6" 225.00
Bear, papa, crystal frost 225.00
Bunny, crystal, head up, scarce, 1" H 60.00
Chick, orange-red 65.00
Duck, crystal, standing, Viking's Epic Line, 9" 35.00
Elephant, bookend, crystal, 5½", ea 90.00
Gazelle, leaping, crystal w/frosted base, 8¼" 65.00
German shepherd, lamp base, pk 125.00
Hen, crystal, 5" 75.00
Nautilus shell, bookend, crystal frost, 6", ea 35.00

Pelican, crystal 95.00
Pig, mama, crystal 325.00
Rooster w/crooked tail, crystal, 7½" 85.00
Seal, candle holders, crystal, pr 125.00
Seal w/ball, bookends, crystal, 7", pr 140.00
Starfish, bookends, crystal, pr 170.00
Swan, sweetheart candy dish, red, 5" 35.00
Tiger, crystal frost, head down, 7¼" 200.00
Wolfhound, crystal, 7" 95.00

Paden City

Bunny, cotton-ball dispenser, bl frost, ears bk 125.00
Bunny, cotton-ball dispenser, milk glass, ears bk 95.00
Chinese pheasant, bl 150.00
Dragon swan, crystal, 9¾" L 225.00
Eagle, bookends, crystal, pr 300.00
Horse, crystal (sun trn), rearing 150.00
Pheasant, Chinese; crystal, 13¾" 100.00
Pheasant, head bk, crystal, 12" 110.00
Pheasant, head bk, lt bl, 12" 175.00
Pony, blk, 12" 350.00
Pony, crystal, 12" 100.00
Rooster, Barnyard; bl, 8¾" 200.00
Rooster, Barnyard; crystal, 8¾" 85.00
Rooster, Chanticleer; bl, 9½" 200.00
Rooster, Chanticleer; crystal, 9½" 95.00
Squirrel on curved log, crystal, 5½" 65.00

Tiffin

Pheasant paperweights, female with head down, upright male, crystal, $400.00 for the pair ($650.00 for a pair in Copen Blue).

Cat, Sassy Suzie, blk satin w/pnt decor, #9448, 11" 175.00
Cat, Sassy Suzie, milk glass 300.00
Fawn, flower floater, Citron Green 325.00
Fawn, flower floater, Copen Blue 500.00
Fish, crystal, solid, 8¾x9" 350.00
Frog, candle holders, blk satin, pr 225.00
Owl, lamp, cobalt, 1934-29 ....1,250.00
Pheasants, Copen Blue, paperweight bases, male & female pr 650.00

Viking

Angelfish, blk, 6½" 150.00
Bird, candy dish, med gr, w/lid, 12" 95.00
Bird, moss gr, tail up, 12" 40.00
Bird, orange, #1311, 10" 55.00
Bird, ruby, #1310, 12" 85.00
Cat, gr, sitting, 8" 55.00
Dog, orange 45.00
Dolphin, candle holders, pk, hexagonal ft, 9½", pr 150.00
Duck, crystal, fighting, head up or down, Viking's Epic Line, ea ..45.00
Duck, orange, rnd, ftd, 5" 35.00

Duck, vaseline, 5"	35.00
Egret, amber, #1315, 12"	45.00
Egret, orange, 12"	45.00
Hound dog, crystal, 8"	50.00
House, Crystal Mist, 4"	35.00
Owl, amber, Viking's Epic Line	45.00
Owl, paperweight, amber	50.00
Rabbit (Thumper), crystal, 6½"	35.00
Rooster, avocado, Viking's Epic Line	55.00
Seal, Persimmon, 9¾" L	25.00
Swan, orange, fluted, 6½x4"	45.00
Swan, Yellow Mist, paper label, 6"	50.00

Westmoreland

Bird in flight, Amber Marigold, wings out, 5" W	35.00
Butterfly, Blue Mist, 2½"	25.00
Butterfly, crystal, 4½" W	45.00
Butterfly, pk, 2½"	20.00
Butterfly, Smoke, 2½"	20.00
Owl, dk bl, shiny eyes, 5½"	45.00
Pig, amberina	85.00
Porky Pig, milk glass, hollow, 3" L	20.00
Robin, crystal, 5⅛"	20.00
Robin, pk, 5⅛"	25.00
Robin, red, 5⅛"	27.50
Starfish, candle holders, milk glass, 5", pr	45.00
Turtle, ashtray, crystal	15.00
Turtle, cigarette box, crystal	45.00
Turtle, flower block, gr, 7 holes, 4" L	55.00
Wren, Crystal Mist, 2½"	17.50
Wren, lt bl, 2½"	22.50
Wren, Pink Mist, 2½"	22.50
Wren, red, 2½"	22.50
Wren on perch, lt bl on wht, 2-pc	40.00

Miscellaneous

American Glass Co, horse, crystal, jumping	55.00
Co-Operative Flint, elephant, crystal, 13"	375.00
Co-Operative Flint, elephant, pk, tusks rpr, 13"	400.00
Co-Operative Flint, elephant, pk, 4½x7"	85.00
Federal, Mopey dog, crystal, 3½"	10.00
Haley, horse, milk glass, jumping	50.00
Haley, pheasant, crystal, 1940s, 12"	30.00
Haley, thrush, crystal	30.00
Haley, thrush, Robin's Egg Blue	85.00
Indiana, panther, amber, walking	300.00
Indiana, panther, bl, walking	400.00
Indiana, powter pigeon, bookend, crystal frost, ea	40.00
LG Wright, trout, crystal	150.00
LG Wright, turtle, amber	125.00
New Martinsville by Mirror Images, baby bear, ruby	95.00
New Martinsville by Mirror Images, mama bear, ruby	150.00
New Martinsville by Mirror Images, wolfhound, ruby carnival	150.00
Pilgrim, whale, crystal, #924, w/labels, in '64 World's Fair box	45.00
Unknown, flamenco dancers, crystal frost, mk copyright, 10½"	225.00

Glass Knives

Glass knives were manufactured from about 1920 to 1950, with distribution at its greatest in the late '30s and early '40s. Colors generally followed Depression glass dinnerware: crystal, light blue, light green, pink (originally called rose), and more rarely amber, forest green, and white (opal). Many glass knives were hand painted in fruit or flower designs. Knife blades were ground to a sharp edge. Today knives are usually found with blades nicked through years of use or reground, which is acceptable to collectors as long as the original knife shape is maintained.

Many glass knives were engraved for gift-giving, personalized with the recipient's name, and on occasion, with a greeting. Originally presented in boxes, most glass knives were accompanied by a paper insert extolling the virtues of the knife and describing its care.

Boxes printed with World's Fair logos are fun to find, though not rare. Butter knives, which are smaller than other glass knives, typically were made in Czechoslovakia and sometimes match the handle patterns of glass salad sets. Knife lengths often vary slightly because the knives were snapped off the molded glass and the end ground during manufacture.

Several styles of knives (i.e. Vitex, Dur-X, Cryst-O-Lite) were manufactured by the thousands and therefore are found more often. Prices have become volatile due to the popularity of on-line, Internet auctions, and the competition that results.

Our advisor for this category is Michele Rosewitz; she is listed in the Directory under California.

Values reflect knives with minor blade roughness or resharpening.

Aer-Flo, crystal, 7½"	50.00
Aer-Flo, pk, 7½"	85.00
BK Co, crystal, HP, 9¼"	35.00
BK Co, gr, HP, 9¼"	50.00
Block, crystal, 8¼", MIB	30.00

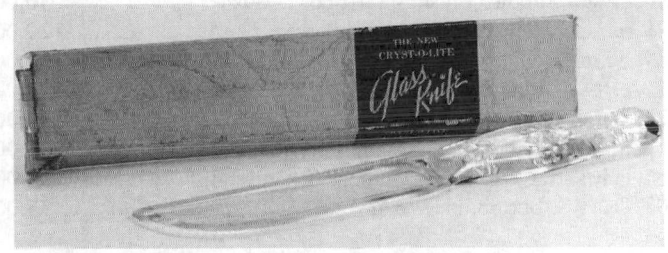

Cryst-O-Lite, crystal, MIB, $16.00.

Block, pk, 8¼"	35.00
Dur-X, 3-Leaf, bl, 8½ or 9", ea	40.00
Dur-X, 5-Leaf, bl, 9"	45.00
Dur-X, 5-Leaf, pk, 9"	40.00
Dur-X 3-Leaf, gr, 8½" or 9", ea	35.00
Imperial Candlewick, crystal, 8½"	400.00
Rosespray style, crystal, 8¼", MIB	40.00
Rosespray style, gr, 8¼", MIB	125.00
Steel-ite, gr, 8½"	75.00
Stonex, crystal, 8½"	35.00
Stonex, gr, 8½", MIB	85.00
Stonex, opal, 8½"	275.00
Thumbguard, crystal, HP, 9"	35.00
Vitex (Star & Dmn), bl, 8½" or 9", ea	30.00
Vitex (Star & Dmn), crystal, 8½" or 9", ea	20.00
Vitex (Star & Dmn), pk, 8½" or 9", ea	30.00

Glass Shoes

Little shoes made of glass can be found in hundreds of styles, shapes, and colors. They've been made since the early 1800s by nearly every glasshouse, large and small, in America. To learn more about them, we recommend *Shoes of Glass* (newly updated) by our advisor Libby Yalom, who is listed in the Directory under Maryland. Numbers in the listings refer to her book. Another reference is *Collectible Shoes of Glass* by Earlene Wheatley, published by Collector Books.

#12, Daisy & Button, amber, Patd Oct 19/86, med 50.00
#13, Fine Cut, crystal, front opening, 3 lace holes ea side 55.00
#17, Daisy & Button, bl, no lace holes, mesh sole, 3x5⅞" 60.00
#50, Fine Cut, crystal, dmn mesh sole mk HT, 2¾x5⅛" 52.00
#53, Fine Cut, amber, no laces, unmk, 2⅝x4⅜" 50.00
#101, Cane, crystal, high front, mesh sole, 1880s, 2¼x4⅝" 48.00
#116, milk glass, bow on front, slightly concave sole, 2⅜x4¾" 49.00
#128, crystal w/scalloped edge, tassel, 4⅜x4¼" 85.00

#161, Finecut roller skate, aqua, 3x4", $75.00.

#136, cuffed boot w/spur, blk, att Challinor-Taylor, 3¼x4" 60.00
#203, baby's, crystal w/gold-pnt laces, bow & flowers, 3⅞" 30.00
#262, scalloped near top, bl, mesh sole, 6 lace holes, 6" L 105.00
#276, crystal, stippled finish, sm flat bowl, 2½x4⅜" 30.00
#322, mc spangle w/wht int, crystal rigaree, 3¾x5" 120.00
#359, burmese coloring (frosted/shaded), ruffled, 2½x6⅜" 100.00
#371, pk & wht latticinio, crystal ruffle/heel, wht sole, 6⅝" 100.00
#427, Dutch shoe, crystal, 1⅞x4" 40.00
#489, boot w/strap & spur, crystal, R on side, 2½x2¼" 20.00
#581, lady's shoe-&-leg bottle on hassock, crystal, 12¾" 225.00
#602, Daisy & Button, bl, 2¼x4⅜" 35.00

Glidden

Genius designer Glidden Parker established Glidden Pottery in 1940 in Alfred, New York, having been schooled at the unrivaled New York State College of Ceramics at Alfred University. Glidden pottery is characterized by a fine stoneware body, innovative forms, outstanding hand-milled glazes, and hand decoration which make the pieces individual works of art. Production consisted of casual dinnerware, artware, and accessories that were distributed internationally.

In 1949 Glidden Pottery became the second ceramic plant in the country to utilize the revolutionary Ram pressing machine. This allowed for increased production and for the most part eliminated the previously used slip-casting method. However, Glidden stoneware continued to reflect the same superb quality of craftsmanship until the factory closed in 1957. Although the majority of form and decorative patterns were Mr. Parker's personal designs, Fong Chow and Sergio Dello Strologo also designed award-winning lines.

Glidden will be found marked on the unglazed underside with a signature that is hand incised, mold impressed, or ink stamped. Interest in this unique stoneware is growing as collectors discover that it embodies the very finest of mid-century high style. Our advisor is David Pierce; he is listed in the Directory under Ohio.

Ashtray, Garden, teardrop form, #184 ....35.00
Ashtray, Green Mesa, #274-U 35.00
Ashtray, Safex, dbl sq 30.00
Boat, Sandstone, #4034 ....125.00
Bowl, Charcoal & Rice, free-form 100.00
Bowl, Plaid, #27 ....35.00

Photo courtesy David Pierce

Bowl, Sandstone, pedestal foot, $200.00.

Bowl, Sage & Sand, #17 ....20.00
Bowl, Turquoise Matrix, #38 ....30.00
Bowl, Viridian, lug soup, #467 ....25.00
Candlebench, Afrikans 50.00
Candlebench, Chi Chi Poodle 35.00
Candlebench, Mexican Cock 40.00
Casserole, Feather, engobe, #167 ....20.00
Casserole, Menagerie, Hippo, #163 ....55.00
Casserole, Mexican Cock, #163 ....50.00
Casserole, Pear, #165 ....45.00
Casserole, Ric Rac, bl-gray, #167 ....25.00
Casserole, Viridian, #165 ....40.00
Casserole, Will o' the Wisp, #163 ....50.00
Coaster, Flourish, #19 ....15.00
Coaster, Mexican Cock, #19 ....10.00
Creamer & sugar bowl, Alfred Stoneware, #802 & #803 ....100.00
Creamer & sugar bowl, Boston Spice, #1430 & #1440 ....70.00
Creamer & sugar bowl, Feather, engobe, #144 & #133 ....50.00
Creamer & sugar bowl, Flourish, #144 & #133 ....80.00
Creamer & sugar bowl, Yellowstone, #1430 & #1440 ....50.00
Cup & saucer, Boston Spice, #1441A & #442 ....25.00
Cup & saucer, Feather, engobe, #441A & #442 ....20.00
Cup & saucer, Pear, #141 & #142 ....25.00
Cup & saucer, Yellowstone, #141 & #142 ....15.00
Pitcher, Boston Spice, #617 ....75.00
Pitcher, Glidden Blue, #615 ....100.00
Pitcher, Turquoise Matrix, #617 ....60.00
Planter, Charcoal & Rice, bird form 100.00
Planter, Yellowstone, #122 ....20.00
Plate, Handsome Fish, #410 ....40.00
Plate, Marine Fantasia, #431 ....60.00
Plate, Plaid, #65 ....25.00
Plate, Sage & Sand, #433 ....15.00
Plate, Snowdrop, #33 ....75.00
Teapot, Yellowstone, #240 ....65.00
Tumbler, Turquoise Matrix, #127 ....20.00
Vase, Cobalt, #87 ....35.00
Vase, Early Pink, #128 ....45.00
Vase, Flourish, #5 ....50.00
Vase, Gulfstream Blue, #4020 ....300.00

Goebel

F.W. Goebel founded the F&W Goebel Company in 1871, located in Rodental, Germany. They produced thousands of different decorative and useful items over the years, the most famous of which are the Hummel figurines first produced in 1935 based on the artwork of a Franciscan nun, Sister Maria Innocentia Hummel.

The Goebel trademarks have long been a source of confusion because **all** Goebel products, including Hummels, of any particular time period bear the same trademark, thus leading many to believe all Goebels are Hummels. Always look for the Hummel signature on actual Hummel figurines (these are listed in a separate section).

There are many, many other series — some of which are based on artwork of particular artists such as Disney, Charlot Byj, Janet Robson, Harry Holt, Norman Rockwell, M. Spotl, Lore, Huldah, and Schaubach. Miscellaneous useful items include ashtrays, bookends, salt and pepper shakers, banks, pitchers, inkwells, and perfume bottles. Figurines include birds, animals, Art Deco pieces, etc. The Friar Tuck monks and the Co-Boy elves are especially popular.

The date of manufacture of a particular piece is determined by the trademark. The incised date found underneath the base on many items is the **mold copyright** date. Actual date of manufacture may vary as much as twenty years or more from the copyright date.

Most Common Goebel Trademarks and Approximate Date Used:
Crown mark (may be incised or stamped, or both): 1923 – 1950
Full bee (complete bumble bee inside the letter 'V'): 1950 – 1957
Stylized bee (dot with wings inside the letter 'V'): 1957 – 1964
3-Line (stylized bee with three lines of copyright info to the right of the trademark): 1964 – 1972
Goebel bee (word Goebel with stylized bee mark over the last letter 'e'): 1972 – 1979
Goebel (word Goebel only): 1979 – present

Our advisors for this category are Gale and Wayne Bailey; they are listed in the Directory under Georgia.

Perfume bottle, Spanish dancer figural, yellow dress, red shawl, glass dauber, full bee mark, #XF156/30, $210.00.

Photo courtesy Monsen and Baer

Cardinal Tuck (Red Monk)

Ashtray, ZF43/0 ....225.00
Bank 500.00
Calendar holder 325.00
Egg timer, single 250.00
Match holder 275.00
Pipe stubber 295.00
Pitcher, S141/0, stylized bee, 4" 135.00
Pourer 230.00
Shakers, pr, w/Bibles & tray 250.00

Charlot BYJ Redheads and Blonds

Atta Boy, Charlot BYJ 7 ....85.00
Bongo Beat, 3-Line mk, 5" 127.50
Camera Shy, BYJ 79, Goebel 100.00
Daisies Won't Tell, 3-Line mk, BYJ 24 ....65.00
Just in Time, 4¾" 55.00
Kibitzer, BYJ 23, 3-Line mk, 4¼" 125.00
Kneeling in Prayer, BYJ 59 ....60.00

Let It Rain, BYJ 51 ....125.00
Off Key, BYJ 22, stylized bee 66.00
Purr-fect Friend 57.50
Say A-h-h-h, 4x5" 125.00
Sleepy Head, BYJ 11 ....80.00
Swinger, BYJ 62 ....85.00
Way To Pray, BYJ 46 ....75.00
Wishing You Sunny Days 60.00
You're a Perfect Pair 77.50

Co-Boy Figurines

Al, playing trumpet, 6" 60.00
Bert, Jim, Tommy, Bob, ea 75.00
Brad Clock, Goebel 225.00
Carol, Jack, Connie, ea 85.00
Herbie 85.00
Niels, 7½" 70.00

Cookie Jars

Cardinal, stylized bee, K 29, from $1,750 to 2,000.00
Cat, Goebel W Germany, from $100 to 125.00
Dog, Goebel W Germany, from $100 to 125.00
Friar Tuck, K 29 Made in W Germany 1957, from $375 to 475.00
Lion, Goebel W Germany, from $70 to 80.00
Owl, Goebel W Germany, from $70 to 80.00
Panda Bear, Goebel W Germany, from $70 to 80.00
Parrot, Goebel W Germany, from $70 to 80.00
Pig, Goebel W Germany, from $100 to 125.00

Friar Tuck (Brown Monk)

Ashtray, RF142, pierced for hanging 150.00
Bank, SD29, full bee 100.00
Calendar & pen holder 120.00
Candle holders, stylized B, 3", pr 75.00
Cigarette box, RX110, TM-3 ....150.00
Cookie jar, full bee 450.00
Egg cup, E95/A, stylized bee 48.00
Goblet, figural stem 50.00
Honey pot 295.00
Liquor tot, KL94, stylized bee, 1⅞" 32.00
Matchbox holder, stylized bee 100.00
Mug, T74/0, full bee 35.00
Mug, T74/0, stylized bee, 4" 25.00
Mustard, S183, full bee, 3¾" 35.00
Oil & vinegar cruets, 3-Line mk, pr 250.00
Pipe stubber, RX107 ....65.00
Pitcher, M43A 60.00
Pitcher, S141-3/0 ....135.00
Pitcher, S141/11, rare 400.00
Shakers, full bee, pr 35.00
Shakers, w/Bible, stylized bee, pr 110.00
Stein, T74/111 ....450.00
Stopper, NM 50.00
Sugar bowl, M43B 60.00
Sugar bowl, Z37 ....47.00
Tray, M42D 20.00

Shakers

Bride & groom, Goebel, 3½", pr 48.00
Cat & dog, crown mk, 2⅝", pr 65.00

Chef w/spon & 2 pots (shakers), M-31, from $120 to 160.00
Ducks, pr 16.50
Flower (skunk), Disney, 2½", pr 125.00
Man w/4-leaf clover-type badge on chest, red scarf, 3", pr 40.00
Poodles, blk & wht, ca 1960, 3½", pr 18.00
Quail chicks, Goebel, tallest: 2½", pr 15.00
Rabbit sits in (separate) basket, #71003, 4x4" 60.00
Swiss boy & girl, Goebel, 2¾", pr 20.00
Thumper, Disney, pr 125.00
Turkeys, P98, pr 42.50

Miscellaneous

Beehive Honey Pot, H125/0, stylized bee 35.00
Bell, Angel, 1976, 3x2½" 55.00
Bust, Elvis Presley, Goebel, 1977, 8½" 45.00
Card/bud holder, musician, crown mk, ca 1935, 3" 120.00
Cocker spaniel, playing, Goebel 35.00
Decanter, comical huntsman w/snooty dog, Crown mk, 10" 175.00
Figurine, ballerina, sgn Huldah, 9¼" 260.00
Figurine, blk panther, 20" L 120.00
Figurine, blue jay, CV80, Goebel bee, 7" 100.00
Figurine, Center Court 1903, lady tennis player, 8½" 225.00
Figurine, fish, orange & blk on gr ped, stylized bee, 5¾x6" 60.00
Figurine, lady w/book, sgn Hahn, #503, bee in V, 7" 200.00
Figurine, Mickey Mouse as sorcerer, 5¼" 137.50
Figurine, St Bernard puppy, 6½x11" 140.00
Figurine, Thumper, Goebel bee, Disney #131, sm 35.00
Figurine, Tinkerbell, full bee, 5½" 350.00
Figurine, wedding couple dancing, 3-Line mk, 7" 270.00
Figurine, wht stallion, Goebel, 18x14" 400.00
Figurine/bookend, Benjamin Franklin, 8x4x3¼" 75.00
Flower frog, antelope, Deco style, VT756, 8x6x3" 85.00
Inkwell, clown, XS458 ....150.00
Kitten w/ball, gray w/red, Goebel bee, CK364 ....25.00
Perfume lamp, terrier dog, #58022-18, 7x3½x4" 125.00
Planter, stork, KZ944, dbl crown, 4x7" 80.00
Reamer, jester (clown?), crown mk, 4½" 200.00
Sugar bowl, cat figural, 5x3" 65.00
Thumper, figural ashtray, Dis 8, full bee, 4" 200.00
Vase, Bambi, Disney, full bee, 5½" 285.00

Goldscheider

The Goldscheider family operated a pottery in Vienna for many generations before seeking refuge in the United States following Hitler's invasion of their country. They settled in Trenton, New Jersey, in the early 1940s where they established a new corporation and began producing objects of art and tableware items. (No mention was made of the company in the Trenton City Directory after 1950, and it is assumed that by this time the influx of foreign imports had taken its toll.) In 1946 Marcel Goldscheider established a pottery in Staffordshire where he manufactured bone china figures, earthenware, etc., marked with a stamp of his signature. Larger artist-signed examples are the most valuable with the Austrian pieces bringing the higher prices.

A wide variety of marks has been found: 1.) Goldscheider USA Fine China; 2.) Original Goldscheider Fine China; 3.) Goldscheider USA; 4.) Goldscheider-Everlast Corp.; 5.) Goldscheider Everlast Corp. in circle; 6.) Goldscheider Inc. in circle; 7.) Goldcrest Ceramics Corp. in circle; 8.) Goldcrest Fine China; 9.) Goldcrest Fine China USA; 10.) A Goldcrest Creation; and 11.) Created by Goldscheider USA.

Our advisors are Randy and Debbie Coe; they are listed in the Directory under Oregon.

Tray, two birds at side, 8½", $125.00.

Bookends, girl standing on books, England, 1940s, 7x3½", pr 145.00
Bust, Black maid, scarf about hair, 2nd as drape, 1888, 19" 1,500.00
Bust, Mother Sorrow, sgn Jacob, 10x5x4" 175.00
Figurine, Balinese dancing girl, B Baldwin, 1940s, 17" 275.00
Figurine, bird on pine cone, Deco air-brushed style, 8", pr 195.00
Figurine, Borzoi dog, recumbent, Austria, 17" 450.00
Figurine, Chinese actor & actress, Everlast mk, 12½", pr 350.00
Figurine, girl playing violin, book at ft, #861, 9" 145.00
Figurine, girl w/fan, gr M (Myott) mk, 1940s, 7½x5½" 85.00
Figurine, Grecian dancer, 1940s, 13" 250.00
Figurine, Lady Caller, sgn P Procher, 6½", NM 85.00
Figurine, lady w/gray hair, bl coat/hat/etc, sgn YW, 1925, 15½" ...3,500.00
Figurine, lady w/muff, #802, USA mk, 8½" 125.00
Figurine, Marie Antoinette, Peggy Porscher, 6½" 95.00
Figurine, New Bonnet, lady in bl-gr w/new hat, 5¾" 65.00
Figurine, Oriental musicians, Everlast, 1930s, 10½", 10¼", pr 145.00
Figurine, Royal Blackamoor, couple, 15" 650.00
Figurine, temple dancer, 8" 85.00
Figurine, White Christmas, lady w/muff, P Porcher, 6¼" 85.00
Figurine, 2 dogs pulling at joined leash, orange/wht, 4½x5½" 75.00
Lamp, lady seated beside stick column, Vienna, 16" 750.00
Plaques, boy & girl, #8814-2/#88152, Austria, 1937-41 mk, 4", pr .125.00
Wall mask, beige face w/bl ringlets, 5" 350.00

Gonder

Lawton Gonder grew up with clay in his hands and fire in his eyes. Gonder's interest in ceramics was greatly influenced by his parents who worked for Weller and a close family friend and noted ceramic authority, John Herold. In his early teens Gonder launched his ceramic career at the Ohio Pottery Company while working for Herold. He later gained valuable experience at American Encaustic Tile Company, Cherry Art Tile, and the Florence Pottery. Gonder was plant manager at the Florence Pottery until fire destroyed the facility in late 1941.

After years of solid production and management experience, Lawton Gonder established the Gonder Ceramic Art Company, formerly the Peters and Reed plant, in South Zanesville, Ohio. Gonder Ceramic Arts produced quality art pottery with beautiful contemporary designs which included human and animal figures and a complete line of Oriental pottery. Accentuating the beautiful shapes were unique and innovative glazes developed by Gonder such as flambe (flame red with streaks of yellow), 24k gold crackle, antique gold, and Chinese crackle. (These glazes bring premium prices.)

All Gonder is marked with the company name and mold number. They include 'Gonder U.S.A' in block letters, 'Gonder' in script, 'Gonder Original' in script, and 'Gonder Ceramic Art' in block letters. Paper labels were also used. Some of the early Gonder molds closely resemble RumRill designs that had been manufactured at the Florence Pottery; and because some RumRill pieces are found with similar (if not identical) shapes, matching mold numbers, and Gonder glazes, it is speculated that some RumRill was produced at the Gonder plant. In 1946 Gonder started another company which he named Elgee (chosen for his initials LG) where he manufactured lamp bases until a fire in 1954 resulted in his shifting lamp production to the main plant. Operations ceased in 1957.

Our values are for items in mint condition, unless noted otherwise. Our advisor for this category is Ron Hoopes; he is listed in the Directory under Ohio.

Ashtray, copper color, #219, 9¾x7½" 56.00
Basket, #L-19 ....95.00
Basket, shell form, lt yel, #674, 8" 25.00
Bowl, Argenta, #1510, 8½" 167.50
Bowl, dolphin, #556 ....75.00
Butter warmer, gr-yel, w/orig candle, #996, 4½", 3-pc 26.00
Candle holders, floral form, #E-14, pr 25.00
Cookie jar, Ye Olde Oaken Bucket, #974, 8" 65.00
Cookie jar, yel, #P-24 ....125.00

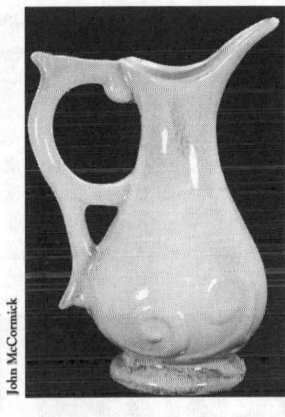

Ewer, pale aqua to tan, J-25, 11", $75.00.

Photo courtesy John McCormick

Creamer, beige, #P-33 ....30.00
Ewer, gr shell, #508 ....175.00
Ewer, shell & starfish form, dk gr w/brn drip, #508, 13½" 175.00
Figurine, Chinese coolies, turq, 1 w/head up/1 down, 8", pr 62.00
Figurine, elephant, stylized, lt gray, #108, 7½x10" 250.00
Figurine, Oriental man & lady w/yoke & planters, 13", pr 45.00
Figurine, panther, gr, recumbent, #210, 19" L 175.00
Figurine, swan, gr, #511, lg 85.00
Pitcher, #917 ....60.00
Pitcher, wht, #E-60 ....45.00
Planter, gazelle figural 60.00
Planter, gondola, yel & pk, #550 ....25.00
Planter, Madonna, gr & pk, #E303 ....23.00
Planter, red flambe, #E-5 ....75.00
Shakers, La Gonda, aqua, pr 22.00
Teapot, purple, #P-31 ....85.00
Teapot, yel, #P-31 ....85.00
Tile, hunting dog decal, sq 20.00
Tray, Argenta, 4½" 30.00
Vase, bl, dbl swirl, #510, 11x8", NM 110.00
Vase, bl w/pk overspray, #H-62, 10" 23.00
Vase, blk & wht, #410, 8" 36.00
Vase, cornucopia; wine, #521, 7x11" 20.00
Vase, deer head, lt bl, #518, 10" 68.00
Vase, deer head, wht crackle, 10" 198.00
Vase, egret stands on 1 leg, bird flies beyond, 8½" 62.00
Vase, fish figural, brn shaded to aqua gr, #422, 9" 60.00
Vase, gold crackle, #E-4 ....95.00
Vase, gold crackle, hdls, #H-56, 8½" 28.00
Vase, gold crackle, trumpet neck, up-trn hdls, #604, 10" 40.00

Vase, gold crackle over turq, pk int, 7¼x4¼" 60.00
Vase, gray, hdls, #H-5, 9" 48.00
Vase, gray-bl w/wht accents, hdls, #H-77, 8½" 33.00
Vase, leaf, #E-67 ....60.00
Vase, leaf, pk, #584, 11x9" 36.00
Vase, lt bl w/purple, #H-56, 8¼", NM 30.00
Vase, lt gray w/pk int, #H-73, 8" 25.00
Vase, pk w/gray, H-165, 7", pr 46.00
Vase, ribbon candy design, yel w/brn streaking, #517, 10½" 18.00
Vase, swan, blended gray/mauve/pk, #J-31, 9x9" 48.00
Vase, swan form, #511 ....75.00
Vase, yel, #H-84 ....45.00
Vase, yel, #J-35, 11" 60.00
Vase, yel & mauve, tulip shape, H-68, 9x6" 14.00

Goofus Glass

Goofus glass is American-made pressed glass with designs that are either embossed (blown out) or intaglio (cut in). The decorated colors were aerographed or hand applied and not fired on the pieces. The various patterns exemplify the artistry of the turn-of-the-century glass crafters. The primary production dates were ca 1908 to 1918. Goofus was produced by many well-known manufacturers such as Northwood, Indiana, and Dugan. Our advisor for this category is Steve Gillespie of the *Goofus Glass Gazette*; he is listed in the Directory under Missouri. See also Clubs and Newsletters.

Bowl, Butterfly, pattern decor, Dugan, 9" 65.00
Bowl, Carnations, 9" 25.00
Bowl, Daisy & Web, opal 65.00
Bowl, Deer & Carnation, Northwood, 9" 65.00
Bowl, Greek Key & Sunflower, gr glass, Northwood, 9" 65.00
Bowl, Jeweled Heart, Dugan, 9" 55.00
Bowl, Monk Drinking From Tankard, 7" 65.00
Bowl, Moth, pattern decor, rare 65.00
Bowl, nappy; Poppy, pattern decor, Northwood 35.00
Bowl, Nasturtium, Indiana, 9" 30.00
Bowl, Pears, brn on gold, allover decor 75.00
Bowl, Rose on crackle pnt 45.00
Bowl, Two Fruits & Olympic Torch, pattern decor, 9", rare 95.00
Bowl, Wheel & Block, opal 45.00
Dish, Sunflower, gr glass, Northwood, 7" 65.00
Dresser item, Cabbage Rose decanter 65.00
Dresser item, Cabbage Rose powder jar 30.00
Dresser item, Gibson Girl powder jar 50.00
Dresser item, Rose on Basketweave hair receiver, rare 125.00
Dresser item, Rose on Basketweave hatpin holder, rare 65.00
Lamp, Cabbage Rose, matching chimney, 12" 150.00
Lamp, Cabbage Rose, umbrella shade, 18" 400.00
Lamp, Daisy, w/matching chimney, 18" 300.00

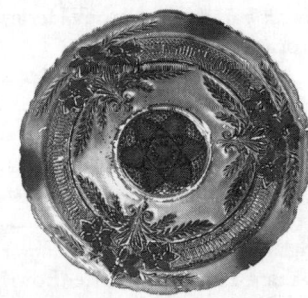

Plate, gold with red flowers, 10½", EX, $30.00.

Lamp, Poppy, ball shade, 18"	275.00
Plate, Butterfly, Dugan, rare, 11"	125.00
Plate, Carnation, 11"	25.00
Plate, chop; Bird & Strawberry, 12"	125.00
Plate, Chrysanthemum, 3-color combination, 11"	65.00
Plate, Monk Drinking From Tankard, 7"	125.00
Plate, Roses-in-Snow (Goofus version), 11"	35.00
Plate, Thistle, rare, 5"	65.00
Shakers, Cabbage Rose, orig lids, pr	75.00
Syrup, Cabbage Rose	150.00
Vase, Asters in Basket, 12½"	95.00
Vase, Bird in Berry Patch, 12", M	95.00
Vase, Cabbage Rose, milk glass, 7"	25.00
Vase, Cabbage Rose, 15"	95.00
Vase, Lady w/Veil, 12"	125.00
Vase, Lovebirds in Hollyhock, 12"	85.00
Vase, Peacock in Tree, 15"	150.00
Vase, Poppy, 5"	15.00
Vase, Statue of Liberty, rare, 12"	150.00

Goss and Crested China

William Henry Goss received his early education at the Government School of Design at Somerset House, London, and as a result of his merit was introduced to Alderman William Copeland, who owned the Copeland Spode Pottery. Under the influence of Copeland from 1852 to 1858, Goss quickly learned the trade and soon became their chief designer. Little is known about this brief association, and in 1858 Goss left to begin his own business. After a short-lived partnership with a Mr. Peake, Goss opened a pottery on John Street, Stoke-on-Trent, but by 1870 he had moved to his business to a location near London Road. This pottery became the famous Falcon Works. Their mark was a spread-wing falcon (goss-hawk) centering a narrow, horizontal bar with 'W.H. Goss' printed below.

Many of the early pieces made by Goss were left unmarked and are difficult to discern from products made by the Copeland factory, but after he had been in business for about fifteen years, all of his wares were marked. Today unmarked items do not command the prices of the later marked wares.

Adolphus William Henry Goss (Goss's eldest son) joined his father's firm in the 1880s. He introduced cheaper lines, though the more expensive lines continued in production. Shortly after his father's death in 1906, Adolphus retired and left the business to his two younger brothers. The business suffered from problems created by a war economy, and in 1936 Goss assets were held by Cauldon Potteries Ltd. These were eventually taken over by the Coalport Group, who retained the right to use the Goss trademark. Messrs. Ridgeway Potteries bought all the assets in 1954 as well as the right to use the Goss trademark and name. In 1964 the group was known as Allied English Potteries Ltd. (A.E.P.), and in 1971 A.E.P. merged with the Doulton Group. Now it remains to be seen if Goss ware will ever be produced again. Our advisor for this category is Patrick Herley; he is listed in the Directory under New York.

Abergavenny Ancient Jar, Fowey	8.00
Ann Hathaway's Cottage, sm	55.00
Blackpool Tower, Blackpool	55.00
Burns Cottage, sm	115.00
Flask, conical, Conway	4.75
Hastings Kettle, Cerne Abbey	7.50
Horse-shaped Norwegian Beer Bowl, Norway	31.00
Jug, Dorchester, Wymondham	9.50
Jug, Gloucester, Norwich	9.00

Lloyd George's Early Home (no annex)	135.00
Maltese fire gate, Valleta	21.50
Milk bucket, Swiss, Lucerne crest	18.00
Mortar, Hythe Gromwellian	15.00
Munich Beer Seidel, Munich	50.00
Portland Lighthouse, Wargham	37.50
Queen Elizabeth's Riding Shoe, South Sea	34.50
Ramsgate Romano, British ewer	21.50
Reculver's Towers, Kent/Herne Bay	120.00
Shakespeare bust, sm	51.00
Shakespeare's House, separate base	95.00
St Nicholas Chapel	170.00
Teapot stand, circular, Eastbourne	11.50
Urn, Ramsgate, Chichester	9.50
Vase, amphora, 1911 Coronation, 4"	47.50
Vase, Southwold, 6"	42.50

Crested China

Arcadian, Alexander, Tower Bridge, City of London	25.00
Arcadian, Black boy in bed	120.00
Arcadian, ewer, Wembly	18.00
Arcadian, Old Curiosity Shop	25.00
Arcadian, teddy bear, Cinque Port of Rye	17.50
Arcadian, The Globe, Swanage	25.00
Carlton, bust, Edward VII	75.00
Carlton, ewer, Wembley, 2"	7.50
Carlton, vase, 2-hdl, Cornwall	6.00

Figures, all rare: Boxer, Shelley, $155.00; Fisher Girl, Carlton, $65.00; Irish Colleen, Carlton, $115.00; Comical horse and jockey, Carlton, $120.00; Footballer, Grafton, $185.00.

Grafton, figurine, baby sitting	10.00
Grafton, Fireman's Helmet, Basingstoke Crest	17.50
Grafton, vase, Banbury, 2"	5.50
Shelley, rose bowl, Stafford, silver, #147	32.50
Waterfall, de la Pole Statue, Hull	14.95
Willow Art, Chesterfield, Parrish Church, Chesterfield	27.50
Willow Art, Hay Castle, 3½"	47.50
Willow Art, match striker, Great Yarmouth	9.50
Wyknot, A Prehistoric Skull, Cheddar	10.50

Gouda

Gouda is an old Dutch market town in the province of South Holland. Famous for its cheese, Gouda's ceramics industry had its beginnings in the early 16th century and was fueled by the growth in the popularity of smoking tobacco. Initially learning their craft from immigrant potters from England who had settled in the area, the clay pipe makers of Gouda were soon regarded as the best. While some authorities give 1898 (the date the Zuid-Holland factory began operations) as

Gouda

the initial date for the manufacturing of decorative pottery in Gouda, C.W. Moody, author of *Gouda Ceramics*, indicates the date was ca 1885. Gouda was not the only town in the Netherlands making pottery; Arnhem, Schoonhoven, and Amsterdam also had earthenware factories, but technically the term 'Gouda pottery' refers only to pieces made within the town of Gouda. Today, no Gouda-style factories are active within the city's limits, but in the first quarter of the 20th century there were several firms producing decorative pottery in Gouda — the best known being Zuid, Regina, Zenith, Ivora, and Goedewaagen.

This information was provided to us by Adela Meadows; she is listed in the Directory under California.

For further information we recommend *The World of Gouda Pottery* by Phyllis T. Rituo (Front & Center Press, Weston, Massachussets).

Ashtray, glossy, w/matchbook holder, Ponseau, date tree, 6" dia .330.00
Bowl vase, floral, mc on blk, mc int, Regina, 6¾x4" 250.00
Bowl vase, floral on rust w/gold, wht int, Regina, 6¾x4" 240.00
Candlestick, rust/brn/gr on blk, attached bobeche, lg hdl, 11½" 225.00
Candlesticks, scrolls/floral, Blanca, house mk, 15", pr 635.00
Dutch shoe, mc, glossy, Maas, 5½" 120.00
Ginger jar, vivid floral, high dome lid, mk Gouda, 16½" 990.00
Jug, Ivora, floral, #120, 5¼" 330.00
Pitcher, Arce Royale, glossy, high hdl, 9½" 180.00
Pitcher, floral on oyster, Areo Royale, 6½x5½" 290.00

Vases, mirror image birds on stylized leaves, W.P. Hartgring, marked, ca 1908, 16¾", $4,250.00 for the pair.

Vase, blk w/wide mc floral band, ftd gourd shape, mk, 6" 110.00
Vase, floral in reserve, geometric bands, Oud, 14x5" 440.00
Vase, Nouveau flowers, 3 bulbous sections, Royal Goedewaagen, 6¾" .55.00
Wall pocket, shoe, floral on wht, 10x4" 350.00

Graniteware

Graniteware, made of a variety of metals with enamel coatings, derives its name from its appearance. The speckled, swirled, or mottled effect of the vari-colored enamels may look like granite — but there the resemblance stops. It wasn't especially durable! Expect at least minor chipping if you plan to collect.

Graniteware was featured in 1876 at Phily's Expo. It was mass produced in quantity, and enough of it has survived to make at least the common items easily affordable. Condition, color, shape, and size are important considerations in evaluating an item; cobalt blue and white, green and white, brown and white, and old red and white swirled items are unusual, thus more expensive. Pieces of heavier weight, seam constructed, riveted, and those with wooden handles and tin or matching graniteware lids are usually older.

For further study we recommend *The Collector's Encyclopedia of Graniteware, Colors, Shapes, and Values*, Books I and II, by our advisor, Helen Greguire. Both are available from the author and from Collector Books. For information on how to order, see her listing in the Directory under South Carolina. For the address of the National Graniteware Society, see the section on Clubs, Newsletters, and Catalogs.

Basin, bl & wht med mottle, 4⅜x12¾", G+ 70.00
Biscuit sheet, brn & wht med mottle, Onyx Ware, 12-cup, 11" L, NM ...1,100.00
Bowl, Snow on the Mountain, Elite-Austria, 3⅝x2¾", NM 265.00
Bread pan, cobalt & wht lg mottle, seamed ends, 3x9¾x4¾", NM .345.00
Bucket, bl & wht lg swirl w/blk, w/lid, bail hdl, 5¼x4¾", G+ 195.00
Bucket, slop; bl & wht med mottle w/blk, wht int, 10", G+ 125.00
Candle holder, red solid w/blk, shell form w/ring, 1½x5¾", NM ..195.00
Casserole, gr to lt gr, cream int, w/lid, 3x5", NM 85.00
Clock, Delft-style windmill scene, 8-day, Germany, 7x7", M 450.00
Coffee biggin, gray lg mottle, seamed, 9¾x5⅜", NM 495.00
Coffee biggin, red solid w/blk, squatty, 5-pc, 10½", NM 110.00
Coffee boiler, bl-gray & wht lg swirl, Lava Ware, 10¼", G+ 395.00
Coffee carrier, bl checks on wht w/cobalt, mk BB 3 18195 Depose, NM .395.00
Coffeepot, aqua solid w/blk, wht int, Pyrex insert, 1930s, 9", NM 65.00
Coffeepot, gr & wht med relish w/blk, gray basket, mk, 7¾", NM ...235.00
Coffeepot, red & wht lg swirl w/blk, seamed, old, 9½x5½", G+ 2,750.00
Colander, bl & wht lg swirl w/cobalt, Bl Dmn Ware, 5x9¾", NM ..350.00
Creamer, bl & wht lg mottle int/ext w/blk, 1989, 3¼", M 395.00
Crumb tray, violets & leaves on lt bl w/brn trim, 9x10", G+ 395.00
Cuspidor, bl & wht med mottle, seamless, 5x9", G+ 225.00
Cuspidor, wht w/cobalt trim, 2-pc, mk Sweden, 2½x8", NM 95.00
Dipper, Windsor; bl & wht lg mottle w/blk hdl, 6½" dia, G+ 120.00
Double boiler, bl & wht lg swirl w/blk, w/insert, 7¼", NM 395.00
Dust pan, red solid, 13⅜x10½", NM 245.00
Egg pan, red solid, for 7, hdls, 1⅛x9⅞", M 110.00
Fry pan, blk w/wht speckles, cold hdl, 1920s, 8½" dia, G+ 40.00
Fry pan, lt bl & wht lg swirl, CI base, 2⅛x10½", G+ 245.00
Fry pan, yel & wht lg mottle w/blk, 1950s, 8⅛" dia, M 145.00
Funnel, bl & wht lg swirl w/blk, 4½x3¼", NM 200.00
Grater, cream w/gr hdl, flat, 1x6½x4½", NM 175.00
Kettle, cream w/gr, 16 ribs, w/lid, 6x7⅜", NM 40.00
Measure, lav-bl & wht lg swirl w/blk, seamed, 9⅞x6½", G+ 625.00
Measuring cup, lav-cobalt med swirl, strap hdl, 1-cup, 2⅛", G+ .800.00
Milk can, cobalt & wht lg swirl, matching lid, 9x4⅞", NM 895.00
Milk can, gr & wht lg swirl w/cobalt, matching lid, 9x4¾", G+ ...1,250.00
Muffin pan, dk brn & wht fine mottle, 8-cup, 14¼" L, NM 145.00
Muffin pan, gray lg mottle, 12-cup, Agate Seconds, 12½", G+ ...250.00
Muffin pan, lt bl & wht fine mottle w/cobalt, 8-cup, 13⅜", NM .595.00
Mug, farmer's; bl & wht lg swirl w/blk, seamless, 4½", G+ 265.00
Mug, mush; dk gr & wht lg mottle w/cobalt, Chrysolite, 5", G ...125.00
Mug, red & wht lg swirl w/red, wht int, 1970s, 3⅛", M 30.00
Oyster measure, gray lg mottle, emb 1 qt liq'd, 4¼" dia, NM 325.00
Pie plate, brn & wht med mottle w/blk, 9⅝", G+ 15.00
Pie plate, shaded violet, wht int, Thistle Ware, 9", NM 65.00
Pitcher, milk; brn w/wht sm mottle, wht int, DRGM, 8½x5⅜", NM .225.00
Pitcher, water; bl & wht lg swirl w/blk, seamless, 9x4", G+ 525.00
Plate, yel & red lg mottle w/blk, 3-compartment, 1970, 11¾", M ...25.00
Platter, brn & wht lg swirl over cobalt & wht lg swirl, 11" L, NM .295.00
Pudding pan, bl & wht med mottle w/blk, oblong, 2x10½x7½", G+ .115.00
Rice boiler, bl & wht lg swirl w/blk, w/lid & insert, NM 485.00
Roaster, cream w/gr, oval, w/lid, 8¾"+hdls, NM 145.00
Sauce pan, creamy yel w/brn flecks & brn trim, 1980s, 7½" dia, M ..25.00
Scoop, American Gray lg mottle, riveted hdl, 8½" L, G+ 265.00

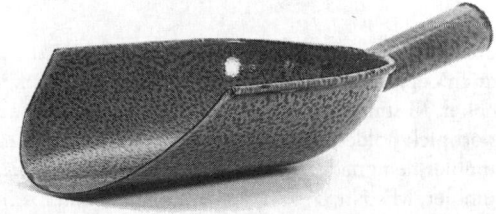

Scoop, American Gray medium mottle, 13" L, NM, $245.00.

Soup plate, fruit & flowers on wht w/cobalt, 1980s, 9", M 30.00
Spoon, brn w/wht flecks, 1990, 12⅛" L, M 5.00
Sugar bowl, bl solid w/blk, wht int, w/lid, 5¼", NM 295.00
Tea steeper, lt bl solid, seamless, Elite Austria..., 4½", G+ 65.00
Teakettle, bl & wht lg swirl w/blk, bail hdl, 7x8", NM 395.00
Teakettle, gr & wht lg mottle w/blk, wht int, 1960s, 6½", G+ ...125.00
Teakettle, gr & wht relish w/NP, Manning Bowman, 10x6½", M ..695.00
Teakettle, pk & wht lg marbleized w/blk, Bakelite knob, 9" dia, NM ..525.00
Teapot, bl-gr shading to off-wht w/blk, seamed, 8x4⅝", NM 225.00
Teapot, burgundy w/mc chicken wire pattern, wht int, Austria, 6", NM ...750.00
Teapot, dk aqua-gr & wht lg swirl w/blk, ca 1970, 8x5", G+ 45.00
Teapot, floral on wht, metal trim & mts, 9¾", M 295.00
Teapot, gray & lt gray relish int/ext, Romania, ca 1990, 5", M 25.00
Teapot, gray lg mottle w/metal trim, squatty, 7¼x6⅛", M 425.00
Teapot, red & wht lg swirl w/bl trim, seamed, 1960s, 8x5", M 115.00
Teapot, wht w/blk, glass insert in lid, metal ft, 1920s, 10", M 185.00
Tray, mc flowers w/red rim, Tiger Special...Japan, 1980s, 14", M .45.00
Trivet, bl & wht scallop design, unmk, ⅜x6¾" dia, G 140.00
Tube mold, cobalt solid w/wht int, ribbed style, 8¼" dia, G+ 95.00
Wash basin, gr & wht lg mottle w/blk, wht int, 11¾", G+ 155.00
Wash pitcher & bowl, gr & wht lg swirl w/cobalt, Emerald Ware, G+ .695.00
Water carrier, gray lg mottle, pouring lip, bail hdl, 8x8½", NM .425.00

Green Opaque

Introduced in 1887 by the New England Glass Company, this ware is very scarce due to the fact that it was produced for less than one year. It is characterized by its soft green color and a wavy band of gold reserving a mottled blue metallic stain. It is usually found in satin; examples with a shiny finish are extremely rare. Values depend to a large extent on the amount of the gold and stain remaining.

Bowl, EX stain, 4x8", NM 650.00
Bowl, M stain & gold, 4x8" 1,150.00
Box, powder; stain & gold on bowl & lid, 4x6¼" 1,150.00
Celery vase, worn stain & gold, 6½" 450.00
Cruet, orig stopper, M stain & gold 1,950.00
Mug, EX stain & gold, 2¼" 500.00
Mug, M stain & gold, 2½" 700.00

Punch cup, 2½", M mottling,
$750.00.

Punch cup, M stain & gold 750.00
Punch cup, worn stain & gold, 2½" 225.00
Shaker, M stain & gold, 2½" 400.00
Toothpick holder, M gold trim 1,150.00
Tumbler, lemonade; w/hdl, M stain & gold, 5" 950.00
Tumbler, M stain, 3½" 800.00
Vase, flared, M stain & gold, 6" 900.00
Vase, 14-rib ovoid w/flaring rim, VG stain & gold, 6" 500.00

Greenaway, Kate

Kate Greenaway was an English artist who lived from 1846 to 1901. She gained worldwide fame as an illustrator of children's books, drawing children clothed in the styles worn by proper English and American boys and girls of the very early 1800s. Her book, *Under the Willow Tree*, published in 1878, was the first of many. Her sketches appeared in leading magazines, and her greeting cards were in great demand. Manufacturers of china, pottery, and metal products copied her characters to decorate children's dishes, tiles, and salt and pepper shakers as well as many other items. Our advisor is James Lewis Lowe, Director of the Kate Greenaway Society; he is listed in the Directory under Pennsylvania. See also Napkin Rings.

Vase, barrel form with three applied figures, $4¼", $225.00.

Almanac, 1886, wht leather, Sangorski/Sutcliffe 475.00
Almanac, 1890, London, Routledge, NM 200.00
Biscuit jar, ceramic, boy w/tinted features, w/lid 165.00
Book, A Apple Pie, Warne, 1940, w/dust jacket, VG 28.00
Book, Birthday Book for Children, Greenaway illus, 1880, VG .160.00
Book, Day in a Child's Life, Routledge, 1st ed, VG 150.00
Book, Greenaway's Babies, Saafield Muslin Book, 1907, G+ 40.00
Book, Kate Greenaway Pictures, London, Warne, 1st ed, 1921, VG ..300.00
Book, Kate Greenaway's Alphabet, London, 1880, EX 190.00
Book, Language of Flowers, Routledge, 1st ed, picture board, VG ..100.00
Book, Marigold Garden, Greenaway illus, London, 1888, VG 60.00
Book, Mother Goose, London, later print of 1st ed, VG 150.00
Book, Pied Piper of Hamlin, Greenaway illus, NM 85.00
Book, pnt; Little Folks, hardcover, early, EX 70.00
Book, Under the Willow, Routledge, 1st ed, orig cloth 165.00
Butter pat, children playing transfer, pre-1910 ....40.00
Engraving, Harper's Bazaar, Jan 1879, full-pg 25.00
Figurine, seated girl tugs on lg hat, bsk, pre-1910, sm 75.00
Inkwell, boy & girl, bronze 215.00
Match holder, ornate SP, girl in fancy clothes, Tufts 195.00
Pencil holder, pnt porc, pre-1910 ....100.00
Pickle castor, bl; SP fr w/2 girls, blown-out florals 455.00
Plate, ABC, girl in lg hat, Staffordshire, 7" 105.00
Plate, children at play, fruits, birds & flowers, 9" 100.00
Scarf, Greenaway illus on silk, early, EX 65.00
Stickpin holder, SP, girl figural, Meriden, 4" 125.00
Tea set, semiporc, floral motif, pre-1910, 3-pc, child sz 95.00
Toothpick holder, bsk, girl sits on stump, basket on bk 40.00
Toothpick holder, clear glass, 2 girls by basket 100.00
Wall pocket, ceramic, 6 girls on open book form, 6x9x3" 137.00

Greentown Glass

Greentown glass is a term referring to the product of the Indiana

Tumbler and Goblet Company of Greentown, Indiana, ca 1894 to 1903. Their earlier pressed glass patterns were #75 (originally known as #11), a pseudo-cut glass design; #137, Pleat Band; and #200, Austrian. Another line, Dewey, was designed in 1898. Many lovely colors were produced in addition to crystal. Jacob Rosenthal, who was later affiliated with Fenton, developed his famous chocolate glass in 1900. The rich, shaded opaque brown glass was an overnight success. Two new patterns, Leaf Bracket and Cactus, were designed to display the glass to its best advantage, but previously existing molds were also used. In only three years Rosenthal developed yet another important color formula, Golden Agate. The Holly pattern was designed especially for its production. The dolphin covered dish with a fish finial is perhaps the most common and easily recognized piece ever produced. Other animal dishes were also made; all are highly collectible. There have been many repros — not all are marked! The symbol (+) at the end of some of the following lines was used to indicate items that have been reproduced.

Our advisors for this category are Jerry and Sandi Garrett; they are listed in the Directory under Indiana. See the Pattern Glass section for clear pressed glass; only colored items are listed here.

Animal dish, bird w/berry, amber (+) 325.00
Animal dish, bird w/berry, cobalt 650.00
Animal dish, bird w/berry, emerald gr (+) 325.00
Animal dish, bird w/berry, Nile Green 2,000.00
Animal dish, cat on hamper, canary, tall (+) 650.00
Animal dish, cat on hamper, chocolate, low 700.00
Animal dish, cat on hamper, Nile Green, tall (+) 1,500.00
Animal dish, cat on hamper, wht opaque, tall 500.00
Animal dish, dolphin, amber, beaded edge 800.00
Animal dish, dolphin, chocolate, smooth edge 450.00
Animal dish, dolphin, clear, beaded edge 350.00
Animal dish, dolphin, emerald gr, sawtooth edge (+) 725.00
Animal dish, dolphin, Golden Agate, beaded edge 1,000.00
Animal dish, dolphin, wht opaque, sawtooth edge (+) 750.00
Animal dish, fighting cocks, chocolate 2,500.00
Animal dish, fighting cocks, cobalt 2,200.00
Animal dish, hen on nest, canary 450.00
Animal dish, hen on nest, cobalt 600.00
Animal dish, hen on nest, Golden Agate 1,500.00
Animal dish, rabbit, amber (+) 200.00
Animal dish, rabbit, clear 200.00
Animal dish, rabbit, wht opaque (+) 225.00
Austrian, bowl, canary, rectangular, 8¼x5¼" 225.00
Austrian, butter dish, chocolate, child sz 750.00
Austrian, compote, canary, 4½" dia 225.00
Austrian, cordial, emerald gr 260.00
Austrian, creamer, canary, no rim, lg 225.00
Austrian, creamer, cobalt, child sz 300.00
Austrian, nappy, canary, w/lid 265.00
Austrian, sugar bowl, chocolate, w/lid, 2½" 195.00
Austrian, tumbler, amber 300.00
Austrian, wine, amber 300.00
Brazen Shield, butter dish, bl 275.00
Brazen Shield, cake stand, bl, 9⅜" or 10⅜", ea 250.00
Brazen Shield, sugar bowl, bl w/lid 200.00
Brazen Shield, tumbler, bl 90.00
Cactus, butter/cheese dish, chocolate, ped ft 850.00
Cactus, celery vase, chocolate, 7½", NM 500.00
Cactus, compote, chocolate, 5¼" dia 165.00
Cactus, compote, chocolate, 9¼" 285.00
Cactus, mug, chocolate, hdld 75.00
Cactus, nappy, chocolate 180.00
Cactus, syrup, chocolate, metal thumb-lift lid, 6" 225.00
Cactus, tumbler, bl-wht opal rim 350.00

Cactus, tumbler, chocolate, 5" 70.00
Cord Drapery, bowl, cobalt, ftd, 6¼" 175.00
Cord Drapery, cake plate, amber, ftd 180.00
Cord Drapery, mug, amber, ftd 175.00
Cord Drapery, spooner, amber 150.00
Cord Drapery, syrup jug, chocolate 225.00
Cord Drapery, water tray, emerald gr 275.00
Cupid, creamer, chocolate 375.00
Cupid, spooner, chocolate 350.00
Cupid, spooner, Nile Green 400.00
Cupid, sugar bowl, wht opaque, w/lid 150.00
Dewey, bowl, berry; chocolate, 8" 285.00
Dewey, bowl, emerald gr, 8" 90.00
Dewey, butter dish, cobalt, 4" 375.00
Dewey, butter dish, Nile Green, 4" dia 250.00
Dewey, creamer, wht opaque, 4" 100.00
Dewey, mug, teal bl 200.00
Dewey, pitcher, amber 165.00
Dewey, sauce, amber 40.00
Dewey, serpentine tray, Golden Agate, sm 1,650.00
Dewey, sugar bowl, canary, w/lid, 2¼" dia 85.00
Diamond & Bow, plate, cut, chocolate, 6" sq 750.00
Early Diamond, dish, cobalt, rectangular, 8x5" 200.00
Early Diamond, tumbler, cobalt 200.00
Greentown Daisy, butter dish, frosted clear 65.00
Greentown Daisy, mustard pot, chocolate, w/lid 225.00
Greentown Daisy, sugar bowl, chocolate, w/lid 240.00
Herringbone Buttress, bowl, clear w/bl opal edge, 5¼" 775.00
Herringbone Buttress, bowl, emerald gr, 9¼" 300.00
Herringbone Buttress, butter dish, emerald gr, ped ft 600.00
Herringbone Buttress, cordial, emerald gr, 3" 275.00
Herringbone Buttress, mug, chocolate 85.00
Herringbone Buttress, shaker, emerald gr 325.00
Herringbone Buttress, vase, emerald gr, 8" 250.00
Herringbone Buttress, wine, olive gr 210.00

**Holly Amber, Water pitcher, 9",
$3,000.00; Compote, 8¼", $2,750.00.**

Holly Amber, bowl, rectangular, 10x4" 1,500.00
Holly Amber, bowl, 7½" 2,600.00
Holly Amber, cake stand 2,600.00
Holly Amber, cruet 2,250.00
Holly Amber, mug, 4" (+) 425.00
Holly Amber, plate, sq, 7½" 950.00
Holly Amber, spooner 800.00
Holly Amber, toothpick holder (+) 450.00
Holly Amber, vase, ped ft, 8" 2,200.00
Leaf Bracket, butter dish, cobalt 1,300.00
Leaf Bracket, celery tray, chocolate, 11" 135.00
Leaf Bracket, shaker, chocolate 165.00

Mug, Deer & Oak Tree, chocolate 750.00
Mug, Dog & Child, chocolate 750.00
Mug, Outdoor Drinking, chocolate, 4½" 175.00
Mug, Pepper Box, chocolate 350.00
Mug, Serenade, emerald gr 125.00
Novelty, Connecticut skillet, Nile Green 650.00
Novelty, corn vase, amber, 4⅝" 250.00
Novelty, Dewey bust, wht opaque, w/base 250.00
Novelty, ribbed covered dish (Dewey base w/lid), teal bl 250.00
Novelty, Scotch thistle, chocolate 1,175.00
Pattern #75 (formerly #11), bowl, emerald gr, rectangular, 8x6½" ..90.00
Pattern #75 (formerly #11), toothpick holder, emerald gr 95.00
Pitcher, Ruffled Eye, emerald gr 200.00
Pitcher, water; Paneled, chocolate 600.00
Pleat Band, compote, chocolate, plain stem, smooth rim, 4¼" ...175.00
Pleat Band, wine, canary 200.00
Scalloped Flange, vase, chocolate 95.00
Shuttle, butter dish, chocolate 1,250.00
Shuttle, creamer, chocolate 650.00
Shuttle, mug, gr 450.00
Shuttle, spooner, chocolate 500.00
Shuttle, tumbler, canary 400.00
Teardrop & Tassel, butter dish, cobalt 265.00
Teardrop & Tassel, compote, Nile Green, w/lid, 4⅝" 450.00
Teardrop & Tassel, compote, Nile Green, w/lid, 6½" 500.00
Teardrop & Tassel, spooner, cobalt 165.00
Teardrop & Tassel, sugar bowl, wht opaque, w/lid 150.00
Toothpick holder, picture fr, amber 250.00
Toothpick holder, picture fr, Nile Green 425.00
Toothpick holder, witch head, Nile Green (+) 200.00
Tumbler, Paneled, chocolate 500.00
Tumbler, Sawtooth, chocolate 125.00
Tumbler, Uneeda Biscuit, chocolate, tall 150.00

Grueby

William Henry Grueby joined the firm of the Low Art Tile Works at the age of fifteen and in 1894, after several years of experience in the production of architectural tiles, founded his own plant, the Grueby Faience Company, in Boston, Massachusetts. Grueby began experimenting with the idea of producing art pottery and had soon perfected a fine glaze (soft and without gloss) in shades of blue, gray, yellow, brown, and his most successful, cucumber green. In 1900 his exhibit at the Paris Exposition Universelle won three gold medals.

Grueby pottery was hand thrown and hand decorated in the Arts and Crafts style. Vertically thrust stylized leaves and flowers in relief were the most common decorative devices. Tiles continued to be an important product, unique (due to the matt glaze decoration) as well as durable. Grueby tiles were often a full inch thick. Obviously incompatible with the Art Nouveau style, the artware was discontinued soon after 1907. The ware is marked in one of several ways: 'Grueby Pottery, Boston, USA'; 'Grueby, Boston, Mass.'; or 'Grueby Faience.' The artware is often artist signed. Our advisor for this category is David Rago; he is listed in the Directory under New Jersey.

Bowl, lt gr (heavy/curdled), appl vertical leaves, DEW, 7x9½" ...1,500.00
Candle holder, dk bl, appl vertical leaves, 8¾x3¾" 1,400.00
Paperweight, scarab, EX curdled matt gr, 4x1½", NM 700.00
Paperweight, scarab, gr matt, 3x2" 700.00
Paperweight, scarab, mustard, 3x2" 700.00
Paperweight, scarab, teal matt (leathery), 3½x2½" 475.00
Tile, candlestick, gray/cream on rust, sgn LC, 6", NM 1,800.00
Tile, knight on horsebk, 4-color (leathery), 8", in wide fr 4,000.00

Tile, landscape w/trees & stream, mc, 4", NM 850.00
Tile, mermaid, red clay on mustard ground, 6", EX 175.00
Tile, sailing ship, 4-color, 4", in wide oak fr 425.00
Tile, sailing ship, 6-color, 7½", in wide oak fr 1,500.00
Tile, swan/mtns, 5-color, 4" 650.00
Tile, tulip/leaves, gr tones w/yel flower, no mk, 6" 1,035.00
Tile, tulip/leaves, 3-color, 6" 1,700.00
Tile, water lilies, ivory/orange/lt gr on dk gr, 6", EX 1,300.00
Vase, bl mottle, upright lily-of-valley sprigs, RE, 10x4" 38,000.00
Vase, brn curdled matt, cvd upright ribs, 6¾x4" 2,800.00
Vase, dk bl, stylized leaves, bulb w/waisted neck, 3¾" 1,800.00
Vase, dk cucumber gr, horizontal ridges, 9x4" 1,400.00
Vase, dk gr, appl leaves, cup top, gourd body, #101, 9" 3,500.00
Vase, dk gr, incised verticals, 5½x4" 1,400.00
Vase, gr, appl leaves at bulb bottom, cvd stems/buds, RE, 7½" ..2,200.00
Vase, gr, appl/emb leaves & buds, lobed rim, 8x4", NM 3,500.00
Vase, gr, cut-bk arched panels, WP/#113, 7x5" 2,000.00
Vase, gr, leaves at base, low angle, long flared neck, 8x4½" 2,600.00
Vase, gr, sculpted leaves w/cvd buds between, 4½x5", NM 1,300.00
Vase, gr, squat w/cylindrical neck, 6x3¾" 950.00
Vase, gr, squat w/rolled rim, 3½x5½" 950.00
Vase, gr, tooled leaves, Erikson, ovoid, 5¼x3" 1,200.00
Vase, gr, tooled/appl leaves, gourd shape, Seaman, 8x4½" 7,000.00

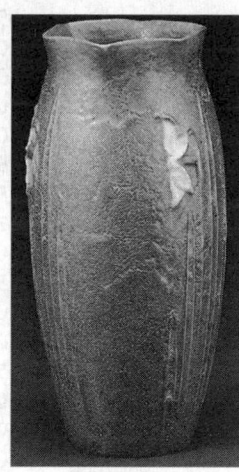

Vase, tooled and applied yellow daffodils on green, six-sided rim, circular stamp, 11¼x5¼", $7,750.00.

Vase, gr, 6 hdls curl at rim between upright leaves, 9½" 9,000.00
Vase, gr (frothy), 3 appl leaves, tips shape rim, 7¾x4¾" 1,900.00
Vase, gr (leathery), 7 broad recessed leaves, sgn EP, 11x11" .25,000.00
Vase, gr (thick), flaring sides, 4" 850.00
Vase, gr w/bl-gr 5-petal flowers, broad leaves, sm rstr, 6x9" 4,100.00
Vase, gr w/yel buds between lg leaves, lobed rim, 9", NM 1,900.00
Vase, gr w/yel daffodils, hex rim, EX mold/glaze, 11x5½", NM ..7,750.00
Vase, gr w/yel daffodils & slender leaves, lobed rim, 12" 8,500.00
Vase, honey (thick/textured), cylindrical, 7x3" 1,700.00
Vase, lt bl, leaves/wht crocus buds, 6¼x3½" 18,000.00
Vase, lt gr w/mottling at rim, 5 cvd vertical lines, 7½" 975.00
Vase, oatmeal, cylindrical, paper label, drilled, 8x11¼" 920.00
Vase, pumpkin matt, molded leaves, ovoid, 3½x3¾" 2,000.00
Vase, wht, leaves around base, squat w/can neck, 4¾x5" 1,500.00

Gustavsberg

Gustavsberg Pottery, founded near Stockholm, Sweden, in the late 1700s, manufactured faience, creamware, and porcelain in the English taste until the end of the 19th century. During the 20th century, the factory has produced some inventive modernistic designs, often signed by their artists. Wilhelm Kage (1889 – 1960) is best remembered for

Argenta, a stoneware body decorated in silver overlay, introduced in the 1930s. Usually a mottled green, Argenta can also be found in cobalt blue and white. Other lines included Cintra (an exceptionally translucent porcelain), Farsta (copper-glazed ware), and Farstarust (iron oxide geometric overlay). Designer Stig Lindberg's work, which dates from the 1940s through the early 1970s, includes slab-built figures and a full range of tableware. Some pieces of Gustavsberg are dated.

Ashtray, Argenta, silver o/l, 1x4¼" sq 50.00
Bowl, Agenta, gr w/silver fish & trailing bubbles, #59, 1⅛x6" 150.00
Figurine, cat, Lisa Larson, 4½" 75.00
Jar, sqd floral bands, bl/gr on hammered ivory, w/lid, 6x7" 450.00
Plate, Argenta, floral, 5½" 75.00
Toothpick holder, Argenta, silver o/l at top, 2½x2¾" 50.00
Tray, Art Nouveau Cintra sea nymphs, 1911 mk, 11½x6¾" 250.00
Tray, Swedish Am Line, cobalt w/silver o/l oceanliner, 3x6" 75.00
Vase, Argenta, floral silver o/l, #1029, 4x1¾" 120.00
Vase, Argenta, gr w/silver inlay stylized feathers, 7⅛x5¾" 355.00
Vase, bl heart shape w/tiny pipestem neck, Friberg, 5" 765.00
Vase, bl-gr mottling, silver o/l fish w/bubbles, 4⅝x3½" 250.00
Vase, bud; Argenta, turq w/silver floral o/l, 6" 95.00
Vase, pks & bls w/gold Deco decor, sgn JE, dtd 1929, 4x6½" 165.00
Vase, stylized floral relief, bl on gr, no mk, 1921, 10x7" 575.00
Vase, taupe matt w/gr, dbl gourd, tiny opening, 6x3", NM 210.00
Vase, Thalia, Lisa Larson, 1961, 10x3½" 200.00

Gutta Percha

Gutta percha is the plastic substance from the latex of several types of Malaysian trees. It resembles rubber but contains more resin. A patent for the use of this material in manufacturing an early type of plastic was issued in the 1850s.

Dresser set, dtd 1879, EX in orig case 150.00
Frame, Pat 1863, opening sz: 6½x4½" 165.00
Plaque, James Garfield, attached to hinged lidded box, 5x5" 275.00

Hagen-Renaker

Best known for their line of miniature animal figures, Hagen-Renaker was founded in Monrovia, California, in 1946. It is estimated that perhaps as many as eighty different dogs were produced. In addition to the animals, they made replicas of characters from several popular Disney films under license from the Disney Studio. The firm relocated in San Dimas in 1962, where they remain active to the present time. Their wares are sometimes marked with an incised 'HR,' a stamped 'Hagen-Renaker' or part of the name, or paper labels. For more information, we recommend *The Collector's Encyclopedia of California Pottery, Second Edition,* by Jack Chipman, *Charlton Standard Catalog of Hagen-Renaker, Second Edition,* and *Disneyana Collector's Guide to Californian Pottery, 1938 – 1960,* by Devin Frick and Tamara Hodge. Another source of information is Hagen-Renaker Collectors Club (HRCC), listed in the Directory under Clubs, Newsletters, and Catalogs.

Figurine, Bennie, Basset hound, gloss, 1954, 6¼" 50.00
Figurine, Bennie, Basset hound, matt, 1954, 6¼" 65.00
Figurine, buckskin mare & colt, MOC, pr 20.00
Figurine, Butch, Cocker Spaniel, 1¾" or 5¼", ea from $50 to 60.00
Figurine, Cornball, Dachshund pup, 2" L, NM 40.00
Figurine, crow, #889, 1¼x2" 15.00
Figurine, Cutting Steer, 3½" 75.00
Figurine, Daschie (dog), Disney, w/sticker, 1⅟₁₆" 175.00
Figurine, Drafter, horse, #459, 2¾" 80.00
Figurine, Dumbo, elephant, 3¾x3½" 300.00
Figurine, fawn waking, brn, #32, 1½" 12.00
Figurine, German Shepherd pup, discontinued, 1" 10.00
Figurine, Harry, burro 45.00
Figurine, Hereford bull, mini 40.00
Figurine, Khitti Kat, playing kitten w/right paw up, 2½" 45.00
Figurine, Lady (dog), mini, Disney, 1¼" 50.00

Figurine, Mischief, yearling with head down, B-680, 4", $300.00.

Photo courtesy Gayle Roller

Figurine, Monrovia, skunk, #A-095 ....11.00
Figurine, Nobby, English Bulldog pup, crouched, 1¾x3" 40.00
Figurine, owl, Designer's Workshop, adult, 5½" 60.00
Figurine, Puss 'n Boots, Designer's Workshop, San Marcos, 6½" ...100.00
Figurine, raccoon on fence, #3094 ....10.00
Figurine, saddle horse, palomino w/4 wht socks, #A-146 ....36.00
Figurine, Si & Am (cats), Disney, 1955-59, pr 180.00
Figurine, Siamese cat, creeping, #A-175, 1¼" 20.00
Figurine, Sparkle, Persian kitten on side, 2 paws up, 2¼" 30.00
Figurine, Specialties Girl w/pony, blond, mk/sticker, 2¾x4" 25.00
Figurine, Spooky, Dalmatian, San Marcos, 5½" 75.00
Figurine, Starlite, wht cat, ca 1958-75, 6½", NM 40.00
Figurine, Trusty (dog) from Lady & Tramp, Disney 80.00
Plaque, fish on irregular shape, bright enameling, 8x19" 200.00
Shadow boxes, Victorian man & lady in oval, 5x4½", pr 50.00

Hagenauer

Carl Hagenauer founded his metal workshops in Vienna in 1898. He was joined by his son Karl in 1919. They produced a wide range of stylized sculptural designs in both metal and wood.

Bust of Chinese man, bronze/walnut, 5" 900.00
Figure, woman w/arms raised, orig blk surface, mk, 10x5½" 750.00
Figure, wooden lady reclining on silver base, mk, 7x24x4" 1,500.00
Horse head, streamline style, ebony/steel, mk, 9x6x3" 650.00
Paperweight, Deco fish, heavy yel brass 125.00

Hair Weaving

A rather unusual craft became popular during the mid-1800s. Human hair was used to make jewelry (rings, bracelets, lockets, etc.) by braiding and interlacing fine strands into hollow forms with pearls and beads added for effect. Wreaths were also made, often using hair from deceased family members as well as the living. They were displayed in deep satin-lined frames along with mementoes of the weaver or her departed kin. The fad was abandoned before the turn of the century. The values suggested below are for mint condition examples. Any fraying of the hair greatly lowers value. For further information, we recommend *Collector's Encyclopedia of Hairwork Jewelry* by C. Jeanenne Bell (Collector Books). See also Mourning Collectibles.

Bracelet, simple plaited braid w/palette-worked hair, 1830s **445.00**
Bracelet, woven over flexible core, cross-over style, 1870s **550.00**
Bracelet, 3 braided tubes, gold glass w/hair compartment, 1860s ...**525.00**
Bracelet, 3 rows in 2 weaves, gold clasp w/citrine, 1850-80 ....**300.00**
Brooch, gold oval mt w/curl & woven flowers under glass, 1⅛" ..**350.00**
Brooch, jet fr mt w/hair swirl under glass, 1860-80, 1" sq **150.00**
Earrings, acorn shape w/gold mts, 1850-70, 1¼", pr **375.00**
Earrings, elongated table-worked hair w/gold mts, 1840-70, 2⅝", pr ..**425.00**
Floral arrangement, on wood base, glass dome, 19th C, 10x10" ..**110.00**
Necklace, crossover-style flat-weave choker, gold mts, 1850s, 15" **500.00**
Necklace, 3 flat rows in 2 weaves, gold-filled mts, 1860s, 14" **450.00**
Pendant, carnelian w/crystal hair compartment in center, 1830s ..**500.00**
Pendant, cross of table-worked hair balls w/gold mts, 1850s, 2¼" .**400.00**
Ring, gold buckle motif, opens for hair compartment, 1850-80 ..**895.00**
Ring, palette-worked flowers in oval, gold mts, 1790-1830 ....**500.00**
Watch chain, G fittings **80.00**
Watch chain, spiraling tube weave, gold-filled mts, 1830s, 13" ..**150.00**
Watch chain, 4 rows sewn together form flat chain, 1880s, 17" **90.00**
Watch fob, 14k & enamel mts, Victorian, 12½" **125.00**
Wreath, flowers & curls, mc hair, thick, in gilt 27" sq fr **1,300.00**
Wreath, 3-color, ca 1840, EX, in shadow-box fr, 12x16" **375.00**

Hall

The Hall China Company of East Liverpool, Ohio, was established in 1903. Their earliest product was whiteware — toilet seats, mugs, jugs, etc. By 1920 their restaurant-type dinnerware and cookingware had become so successful that Hall was assured of a solid future. They continue today to be one of the country's largest manufacturers of this type of product.

Hall introduced the first of their famous teapots in 1920; new shapes and colors were added each year until about 1948, making them the largest teapot manufacturer in the world. These and the dinnerware lines of the '30s through the '50s have become popular collectibles. For more thorough study of the subject, we recommend *The Collector's Encyclopedia of Hall China* by Margaret and Kenn Whitmyer; their address may be found in the Directory under Ohio.

Acacia, custard, Radiance **15.00**
Acacia, marmite, w/lid **40.00**
Beauty, bowl, salad; 9½" **35.00**
Beauty, drip jar, Thick Rim, w/lid **30.00**
Blue Blossom, butter dish, Zephyr style, 1-lb **750.00**
Blue Blossom, jug, Donut **250.00**
Blue Bouquet, bowl, fruit; 5½" **7.50**
Blue Bouquet, bowl, salad; 7¾" **20.00**
Blue Bouquet, cake plate **35.00**
Blue Bouquet, creamer, Modern **20.00**
Blue Bouquet, French baker, fluted **22.00**
Blue Bouquet, leftover, sq **125.00**
Blue Bouquet, soup tureen **310.00**
Blue Bouquet, teapot, Boston, 6-cup **175.00**
Blue Crocus, bowl, str-sided, 6" **18.00**
Blue Crocus, shakers, hdld, pr **60.00**
Blue Floral, bowl, 6¼" **12.00**
Blue Floral, casserole **30.00**
Blue Garden, ball jug, #2 ....**125.00**
Blue Garden, syrup, Sundial **175.00**
Blue Willow, bowl, finger; 4" **27.00**
Blue Willow, teacup, Chinese; 2 styles, ea **22.00**
Cactus, bowl, Radiance, 10" **40.00**
Cactus, creamer, New York **22.00**
Cactus, shakers, Five Band, pr **44.00**

Cactus, syrup, Five Band **95.00**
Cameo Rose, butter dish, ¼-lb **300.00**
Cameo Rose, cup **9.00**
Cameo Rose, gravy boat, w/underplate **32.00**
Cameo Rose, plate, 8" **8.50**
Cameo Rose, sugar bowl, w/lid **22.00**
Cameo Rose, tidbit tray, 3-tier **55.00**
Christmas Tree & Holly, coffeepot **225.00**
Christmas Tree & Holly, cup **18.00**
Christmas Tree & Holly, mug, Irish coffee; 3-oz **35.00**
Christmas Tree & Holly, saucer **4.00**

Crocus, creamer and sugar bowl, $50.00.

Crocus, bottle, water; Zephyr style **1,200.00**
Crocus, bread box, metal **55.00**
Crocus, custard **22.00**
Crocus, gravy boat, D style **35.00**
Crocus, mug, tankard style **75.00**
Crocus, pretzel jar **225.00**
Eggshell, bean pot, New England, #3, dot pattern **95.00**
Eggshell, bowl, Ribbed, plaid or swag pattern, 8½" **25.00**
Eggshell, mustard, dot pattern **35.00**
Eggshell, pretzel jar, dot w/ivory body **110.00**
Game Bird, casserole **30.00**
Game Bird, creamer **15.00**
Game Bird, teapot, Grape, Thorley **225.00**
Heather Rose, bowl, vegetable; w/lid **30.00**
Heather Rose, cookie jar, Flare **45.00**
Heather Rose, jug, Rayed **14.00**
Heather Rose, pickle dish, 9" **18.00**
Heather Rose, platter, oval, 13¼" **25.00**
Heather Rose, teapot, London **35.00**
Homewood, bowl, soup; flat, 8½" **10.00**
Homewood, saucer **1.50**
Mums, bowl, fruit; D style, 5½" **5.50**
Mums, bowl, salad; 9" **22.00**
Mums, creamer, Art Deco **20.00**
Mums, custard, Radiance **22.00**
Mums, gravy boat, D style **32.00**
Mums, pretzel jar **190.00**
Mums, teapot, Rutherford **225.00**
No 488, ball jug, #3 ....**125.00**
No 488, bowl, rnd, 9¼" **37.50**
No 488, canister, Radiance **350.00**
No 488, cookie jar, Radiance **375.00**
No 488, jug, Medallion **70.00**
No 488, mug, Tom & Jerry **18.00**
No 488, platter, oval, 11¼" **25.00**
No 488, soup tureen **325.00**
Orange Poppy, baker, French, fluted **22.00**
Orange Poppy, bowl, cereal; C style, 6" **16.00**

Orange Poppy, cake plate 35.00
Orange Poppy, custard 7.00
Orange Poppy, leftover, loop hdl 100.00
Orange Poppy, match safe, metal 85.00
Orange Poppy, plate, C style, 9" 22.00
Orange Poppy, shaker, Teardrop, ea 25.00
Orange Poppy, teapot, Boston 220.00
Pastel Morning Glory, coffeepot, Terrace 70.00
Pastel Morning Glory, cup, St Denis 35.00
Pastel Morning Glory, gravy boat, D style 35.00
Pastel Morning Glory, jug, Donut 150.00
Pastel Morning Glory, pie baker 40.00
Pastel Morning Glory, sugar bowl, New York or Modern, w/lid, ea .25.00
Primrose, ashtray 10.00
Primrose, pie baker 22.00
Primrose, saucer 1.50
Red Poppy, bowl, fruit; D style, 5½" 5.50
Red Poppy, bowl, salad; 9" 14.00
Red Poppy, clock, metal, teapot shape 150.00
Red Poppy, drip jar, #1188, open 37.00
Red Poppy, jug, milk or syrup; Daniel, 4" 47.00
Red Poppy, plate, D style, 10" 60.00
Red Poppy, recipe box, metal 50.00
Red Poppy, soap dispenser, metal 80.00
Red Poppy, tablecloth, plastic, 54x100" 110.00
Red Poppy, teapot, Aladdin 175.00
Sears' Arlington, bowl, fruit; 5¼" 4.00
Sears' Arlington, creamer 9.00
Sears' Arlington, plate, 10" 6.00
Sears' Fairfax, bowl, flat soup; 8" 9.00
Sears' Fairfax, cup 5.00
Sears' Fairfax, plate, 10" 7.00
Sears' Monticello, bowl, cereal; 6¼" 12.00
Sears' Monticello, cup 6.00
Sears' Monticello, plate, 8" 4.50
Sears' Monticello, platter, oval, 11¼" 13.00
Sears' Monticello, sugar bowl, w/lid 15.00
Sears' Mount Vernon, bowl, fruit; 5¼" 6.00
Sears' Mount Vernon, bowl, oval, 9¼" 20.00
Sears' Mount Vernon, coffeepot, all china 200.00
Sears' Mount Vernon, plate, 8" 4.00
Sears' Richmond/Brown-Eyed Susan, bowl, fruit; 5¼" 4.50
Sears' Richmond/Brown-Eyed Susan, pickle dish, 9" 5.00
Sears' Richmond/Brown-Eyed Susan, plate, 7¼" 5.00
Sears' Richmond/Brown-Eyed Susan, platter, oval, 15½" ..22.00
Serenade, bean pot, #4, New England 100.00
Serenade, bowl, rnd, D style, 9¼" 22.00
Serenade, creamer, Art Deco 18.00
Serenade, platter, D style, 13¼" 22.00
Serenade, pretzel jar 125.00
Serenade, sugar bowl, New York, w/lid 25.00
Silhouette, ball jug, #3 ....125.00
Silhouette, casserole, Medallion 40.00
Silhouette, coaster 9.00
Silhouette, creamer, Modern 15.00
Silhouette, gravy boat, D style 35.00
Silhouette, jug, Simplicity 175.00
Silhouette, match safe 80.00
Silhouette, mug, beverage 45.00
Silhouette, pitcher, Federal, crystal 120.00
Silhouette, plate, D style, 6" 6.50
Silhouette, sifter 75.00
Silhouette, tea tile, 6" 110.00
Springtime, ball jug, #3 ....110.00

Springtime, casserole, Thick Rim 27.00
Springtime, platter, oval, D style, 15" 25.00
Springtime, teapot, French 115.00
Teapot, Albany, Mahogany w/gold, 6-cup 95.00
Teapot, Basket, Lemon w/platinum, 6-cup 140.00
Teapot, Biggin, Stock Brown, 2-cup 110.00
Teapot, Birdcage, maroon w/gold, 6-cup 400.00
Teapot, Boston, red, 6-cup 175.00
Teapot, Boston, wht w/gold lettering, 2-cup 45.00
Teapot, Car, turq w/platinum, 6-cup 650.00
Teapot, Dripless, Marine Blue w/gold, 6-cup 125.00
Teapot, French, Seaspray w/gold, 2-cup 40.00
Teapot, Globe, emerald gr w/gold, 6-cup 125.00

Teapot, Kansas, green with gold, six-cup, $225.00.

Photo courtesy Margaret and Kenn Whitmyer

Teapot, Manhattan, red, 8-cup 500.00
Teapot, Moderne, Marine blue w/gold, 6-cup 45.00
Teapot, Parade, yel w/gold, 6-cup 45.00
Teapot, Star, cobalt w/gold, 6-cup 125.00
Teapot, Star, Delphinium w/gold, 6-cup 75.00
Teapot, Streamline, red, 6-cup 140.00
Teapot, Surfside, Cadet Blue, 6-cup 275.00
Teapot, Teamaster, Canary w/gold, 6-cup 145.00
Teapot, Washington, Marine Blue w/gold, 12-cup 65.00
Teapot, Windshield, maroon w/Gold Dot, 6-cup 95.00
Teapot, Windshield, turq w/gold, 6-cup 65.00
Tulip, bowl, oval, D style 27.00
Tulip, bowl, Radiance, 7½" 18.00
Tulip, coffeepot, Perk 60.00
Tulip, drip jar, Thick Rim, w/lid 27.00
Tulip, waffle iron, metal 85.00
Wildfire, bowl, cereal; D style, 6" 16.00
Wildfire, cake plate 60.00
Wildfire, coffeepot, w/lid 55.00
Wildfire, egg cup 125.00
Wildfire, pie baker 50.00
Wildfire, teapot, Boston 225.00
Wildfire, tidbit, 3-tier 75.00
Yellow Rose, bowl, vegetable; rnd, D style, 9¼" 30.00
Yellow Rose, casserole, Radiance 27.00
Yellow Rose, creamer, Norse 15.00
Yellow Rose, onion soup 40.00
Yellow Rose, saucer, D style 2.00

Zeisel Designs, Hallcraft

Arizona, bottle, vinegar 40.00
Arizona, bowl, coupe soup; 9" 18.00
Arizona, butter dish 150.00
Arizona, platter, 15" 30.00
Bouquet, candlestick, 8" 50.00
Bouquet, percolator, electric, MJ shape 160.00
Bouquet, saucer, AD 3.00
Bouquet, vase 45.00

Buckingham, candlestick, 4½"	27.00
Buckingham, casserole, 2-qt	37.00
Buckingham, egg cup	40.00
Buckingham, onion soup, w/lid	45.00
Caprice, ashtray	6.00
Caprice, bottle, vinegar	35.00
Caprice, creamer	9.00
Caprice, marmite, w/lid	30.00
Fantasy, bowl, cereal; 6"	7.00
Fantasy, jug, 3-qt	30.00
Fantasy, platter, 17"	40.00
Fantasy, sugar bowl, w/lid	20.00
Fern, ashtray	6.00
Fern, cup	5.00
Fern, ladle	10.00
Fern, relish, 4-part	27.00
Frost Flowers, bowl, celery; oval	22.00
Frost Flowers, egg cup	35.00
Frost Flowers, gravy boat	27.00
Frost Flowers, marmite, w/lid	35.00
Harlequin, bowl, salad; lg, 14½"	40.00
Harlequin, cookie jar	150.00
Holiday, bowl, coupe soup; 9"	18.00
Holiday, sugar bowl, AD; open	12.00
Lyric, bowl, cereal; 6"	10.00
Lyric, butter dish	150.00
Mulberry, cup	6.00
Mulberry, platter, 17"	40.00
Peach Blossom, ashtray	8.00
Peach Blossom, platter, 12¼"	22.00
Peach Blossom, vase	32.00
Pinecone, ashtray	6.00
Pinecone, plate, 8"	6.50
Pinecone, tidbit, 3-tier, E style	65.00
Spring, jug, 3-qt	30.00
Sunglow, bowl, fruit; 5¾"	6.00
Sunglow, bowl, vegetable; divided	27.00
Sunglow, plate, 8"	6.00
Sunglow, teapot, 6-cup	95.00

Hallmark

Hallmark introduced a line of artplas (molded plastic) ornaments in 1973 which quickly became popular with collectors. The Hallmark Keepsake Ornament Collectors Club was organized in 1987 and offered exclusive limited edition ornaments to club members. Hallmark has produced miniature ornaments since 1988 and added a line of Easter (now known as Spring) ornaments beginning in 1991. All these ornaments are very collectible.

The magazine, *The Ornament Collector*, edited by Rosie Wells, our advisor for this category, is available if you want more information on ornament collecting. Rosie also publishes a yearly official *Secondary Market Price Guide on Hallmark Ornaments*. Her address is listed in the Directory under Clubs, Newsletters, and Catalogs and again under Illinois. Values are for ornaments in mint condition and with their original boxes.

1979, QX 155-9, Here Comes Santa, Motorcar, 1st in series, MIB .650.00
1980, QX 137-4, Frosty Friends, A Cool Yule, 1st in series, MIB ..675.00
1981, QX 422-2, Rocking Horse, 1st in series, MIB 495.00
1982, QXC 460-3, Tin Locomotive, 1st in series, MIB 750.00
1984, QX 448-1, Nostalgic Houses & Shops, Victorian Dollhouse, MIB ..215.00
1984, QX 459-1, Classical Angel, dtd, ltd ed, MIB 50.00

1986, QX 403-3, Nostalgic Houses & Shops, Xmas Candy Shoppe, MIB ..300.00
1987, QX 481-7, Light Shines at Xmas Collector's Plate, MIB 75.00
1988, QXC 570-4, Hold On Tight, Keepsake Club Miniature, MIB .75.00
1988, QXM 563-4, Old English Village Family Home, mini, MIB ..45.00
1989, QX 449-2, Baby's 1st Christmas, Teddy Bear Years, MIB 80.00
1991, QLX 719-9, Star Trek Starship Enterprise, MIB 400.00
1991, QX 556-9, Winnie-the-Pooh, MIB 55.00
1991, QXM 582-7, Tiny Tea Party Set, porc, dtd, mini set, MIB ..175.00
1993, QK 107-2, Santa Claus Folk Art Americana, Showcase, MIB ...225.00
1995, QEO 806-9, Springtime Barbie, Easter, 1st in series, MIB ...35.00

1996, QCX 416-1, Wizard of Oz, Keepsake Club Members only, MIB, $45.00.

1996, QX 631-1, Madame Alexander Cinderella, 1st in Series, MIB ..35.00
1996, QXM 402-4, Vehicles of Star Wars, set of 3, MIB 35.00
1997, QX 626-5, The Lone Ranger, tin lunch box, MIB 35.00

Halloween

The origin of Halloween can be traced back to the ancient practices of the Druids of Great Britain who began their New Year on the 1st of November. The Druids were pagans, and their New Year's celebrations involved pagan rites and superstitions. They believed that as the old year came to an end the devil would gather up all the demons and evil in the world and take them back to Hell with him. Witches were women who had sold their souls to the devil and, with their black cat in attendance, flew up through their chimneys on brooms. When the Roman Catholic Church came into power in 700 A.D., they changed the holiday into a religious event called 'All Saints Day,' or 'Allhallows.' The evening before, October 31, became 'Allhallows Eve' or 'Halloween.' Today Halloween is strictly a fun time, and Halloween items are fun to collect. Pumpkin-head candy containers of papier-mache or pressed cardboard, noisemakers, postcards with black cats and witches, costumes, and decorations are only a sampling of the variety available.

For further information we recommend *More Halloween Collectibles, Anthropomorphic Vegetables and Fruits of Halloween*, by Pamela E. Apkarian-Russell (Schiffer).

Our advisor for this category is Jenny Tarrant; she is listed in the Directory under Missouri. See Clubs and Newsletters for information concerning *Trick or Treat Trader*, a quarterly newsletter. Unless noted otherwise, values are for items in excellent condition.

Key: JOL — Jack-o'-lantern

American

Most American items were made during the 1940s and '50s, though a few date from the 1930s as well. Lanterns are constructed either of flat cardboard or pressed cardboard pulp similar to the material used to make egg cartons. Values of American-made Halloween items have risen dramatically over the past several years.

Decoration, pumpkin w/horn nose, metal, USA, 1950s, 6" 35.00
Diecut, cat 30.00
Diecut, witch 45.00
Jack-o'-lantern, pressed cb pulp w/orig face, 4" 95.00
Jack-o'-lantern, pressed cb pulp w/orig face, 4½" 125.00
Jack-o'-lantern, pressed cb pulp w/orig face, 5" 145.00
Jack-o'-lantern, pressed cb pulp w/orig face, 5½" 165.00
Jack-o'-lantern, pressed cb pulp w/orig face, 6" 185.00
Jack-o'-lantern, pressed cb pulp w/orig face, 6½" 195.00
Jack-o'-lantern, pressed cb pulp w/orig face, 7" 225.00
Jack-o'-lantern, pressed cb pulp w/orig face, 7½" 245.00
Jack-o'-lantern, pressed cb pulp w/orig face, 8", minimum value ...275.00
Lantern, cat, pressed cb pulp w/orig face 245.00
Lantern, cat (full body), pressed cb pulp, 7x6½" 350.00
Lantern, cb w/tab sides, any 95.00

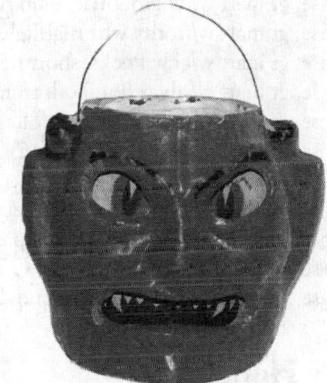

Lantern, devil's face, papier-mache pulp, USA, rare, $485.00.

Photo courtesy Jenny Tarrant

Lantern, devil, pressed cb pulp w/orig face, 5x6" 350.00
Lantern, pumpkin man (full body), pressed cb pulp 350.00
Plastic cat pushing JOL, 1950s, 5" 150.00
Plastic cat w/JOL, 1950s, 3½" 30.00
Plastic clown, 1950s 95.00
Plastic donkey on wheels w/JOL, 1950s, 5" 75.00
Plastic girl cat on wheels w/spring head, 1950s, 9", NM 335.00
Plastic pumpkin, witch on 1 side, cat on other, 1950s, sm 38.00
Plastic pumpkin candy holders, 1950s, 5" + ...45.00
Plastic scarecrow w/stem, 1950s 75.00
Plastic shovel (witch or cat), 1950s 90.00
Plastic snowman w/pipe, orange, 1950s 95.00
Plastic witch holding pumpkin, 1950s, 3½" 30.00
Plastic witch on bike, 1950s, 6" 450.00
Plastic witch on lg rocker, 1950s, 6" 450.00
Plastic witch on rocker, 1950s, 4" 125.00

German

As a general rule, German Halloween collectibles date from 1900 through the early '30s. They were made either of composition or molded cardboard, and their values are higher than American-made items.

Diecut, cat, emb cb, from $55 to 95.00
Diecut, cat w/saxaphone, emb cb, 12", NM 100.00
Diecut, Devil, emb cb, from $95 to 150.00
Diecut, JOL playing drums, emb cb, 1920s, 7½", EX 150.00
Diecut, pumpkin, emb cb, from $95 to 125.00

Diecut, pumpkin lady, emb cb, 7½" 125.00
Diecut, witch, emb cb, from $95 to 125.00
Figurine, veggie man w/hands on tummy, compo, 1910, 2", EX .105.00
Jack-o'-lantern, compo w/orig insert, 3" 225.00
Jack-o'-lantern, compo w/orig insert, 3½" 250.00
Jack-o'-lantern, compo w/orig insert, 4" 275.00
Jack-o'-lantern, compo w/orig insert, 4½" 325.00
Jack-o'-lantern, compo w/orig insert, 5" 350.00
Jack-o'-lantern, molded cb w/orig insert, 3" 110.00
Jack-o'-lantern, molded cb w/orig insert, 3½" 120.00
Jack-o'-lantern, molded cb w/orig insert, 4" 155.00
Jack-o'-lantern, molded cb w/orig insert, 4½" 165.00
Jack-o'-lantern, molded cb w/orig insert, 5" 200.00
Jack-o'-lantern, molded cb w/orig insert, 5½" 225.00
Jack-o'-lantern, molded cb w/orig insert, 6" 275.00
Jack-o'-lantern, molded cb w/orig insert, 6½" +, minimum value ...300.00
Jack-o'-lantern, on ped, molded cb w/orig insert, 7½", VG 525.00
Lantern, cat, cb, molded nose w/bow under chin, 3" 275.00
Lantern, cat, cb, molded nose w/bow under chin, 4" 325.00
Lantern, cat, cb, molded nose w/bow under chin, 5" 375.00
Lantern, cat, cb, simple rnd style 225.00
Lantern (ghost, skull, Devil, witch, etc), molded cb, 3-4", minimum ...375.00
Lantern (ghost, skull, Devil, witch, etc), molded cb, 5" +, minimum ..425.00
Lantern (skull, Devil, witch, etc), compo, 3", minimum value ...375.00
Lantern (skull, Devil, witch, etc), compo, 4", minimum value ..425.00
Lantern (skull, Devil, witch, etc), compo, 5", minimum value ...550.00
Ornament, witch's head, pnt blown glass, ca 1910, 4" 275.00
Pipe, JOL, wooden mouthpc, 1920s, 5", EX 125.00

Candy Containers

Cat, compo, Gemany, 3" 175.00
Cat, compo, Germany, 4" 240.00
Cat, compo, Germany, 5" 285.00
Cat, compo, glass eyes, Germany, 4" 250.00
Cat, compo, glass eyes, Germany, 5" 275.00
Cat, compo, glass eyes, Germany, 6" 325.00
Cat, compo w/mohair, Germany, 5" 350.00
Cat, compo w/mohair, Germany, 6" 400.00
Cat, papier-mache, tin plug, USA, 5" 150.00
Clown w/up, cb JOL head, tin legs/ft, felt suit, 1920, 10", NM ..2,100.00
Devil rabbit, papier-mache, EX 150.00
Devil's head, compo, red, slide pull, Germany, 1920s, 3½", EX ..350.00
Figure, compo, on top of candy box, Germany, 3½" 225.00
Figure, compo, on top of candy box, Germany, 4" 285.00
Figure, compo, on top of candy box, Germany, 5" 315.00
Ghoul, man/woman 2-faced, compo, Germany, ca 1910, 3¾", EX ..330.00
Goblin on pumpkin w/cat, papier-mache, Germany, 6", EX 300.00
Pumkin-head baby, pressed cb & papier-mache, 3", VG 190.00
Pumkin-head lady, papier-mache, base mk Germany, 5½", EX ..385.00
Pumkin-head witch, papier-mache, head removes, 7½", EX 715.00
Witch, orange & blk, crepe paper & compo, 6", VG+ 190.00
Witch, pumpkin people, Devil, ghost, etc, compo, Germany, 3" ..225.00
Witch, pumpkin people, Devil, ghost, etc, compo, Germany, 4" ..300.00
Witch, pumpkin people, Devil, ghost, etc, compo, Germany, 5" ..375.00
Witch, pumpkin people, Devil, ghost, etc, compo, Germany, 6" ..425.00
Witch or pumpkin person, compo, head removes, Germany, 4" ...275.00
Witch or pumpkin person, compo, head removes, Germany, 5" ...325.00
Witch or pumpkin person, compo, head removes, Germany, 6" ...365.00
Witch or pumpkin person, compo, head removes, Germany, 7" ...425.00

Noisemakers

Pan knocker, paper/tin, orange, Chein, 1910, 10", EX 410.00

Pumpkin face w/rachet, pnt cb, wood hdl, 6½", EX 250.00
Pumpkin head man w/rachet, papier-mache & wood, 8" 250.00
Ratchet, cb ball-shaped blk cat head, 1920s, 3x6" L, EX 245.00
Ratchet, cb JOL in top hat, wood, 8" L, EX 350.00

Hampshire

The Hampshire Pottery Company was established in 1871 in Keene, New Hampshire, by James Scollay Taft. Their earliest products were redware and stoneware utility items such as jugs, churns, crocks, and flowerpots. In 1878 they produced majolica ware which met with such success that they began to experiment with the idea of manufacturing art pottery. By 1883 they had developed a Royal Worcester type of finish which they applied to vases, tea sets, powder boxes, and cookie jars. It was also utilized for souvenir items that were decorated with transfer designs prepared from photographic plates.

Cadmon Robertson, brother-in-law of Taft, joined the company in 1904 and was responsible for developing their famous matt glazes. Colors included shades of green, brown, red, and blue. Early examples were of earthenware, but eventually the body was changed to semiporcelain. Some of his designs were marked with an M in a circle as a tribute to his wife, Emoretta. Robertson died in 1914, leaving a void impossible to fill. Taft sold the business in 1916 to George Morton, who continued to use the matt glazes that Robertson had developed. After a temporary halt in production during WWI, Morton returned to Keene and re-equipped the factory with the machinery needed to manufacture hotel china and floor tile. Because of the expense involved in transporting coal to fire the kilns, Morton found he could not compete with potteries of Ohio and New Jersey who were able to utilize locally available natural gas. He was forced to close the plant in 1923.

Interest is highest in examples with monochrome glazes, and it is the glaze, not the size or form, that dictates value. The souvenir pieces are not particularly of high quality and tend to be passed over by today's collectors.

Bowl, cobalt matt, emb cabbage leaves w/wht edges, 3x4¼" 225.00
Bowl, gr matt, cvd geometrics/arched panels, 2½x5½" 375.00
Bowl, gr matt, low, incurvate, 6" 460.00
Bowl, gr matt, 6 water lilies w/vertical stems, #57, 3x9¾" 750.00
Candle holder, gr matt, baluster, 3¼x7" 200.00
Creamer, experimental volcanic glaze 110.00
Ewer, flowing gr matt, leaf-shape rim, squat body, 10" 400.00
Inkwell, gr matt, cylindrical, stepped shoulder, 3½x4" 350.00
Lamp, fairy; cobalt matt, orig frosted shade, 5x4½" 325.00
Lamp, gr matt, emb water lily buds, 5 slim hdls, electrified, 19" ..1,600.00
Lamp, gr matt, shaped ribbon hdls, B&H oil font, 8x10" 650.00
Lamp, gr matt, tapering form, hdls, 8½x12" 1,035.00
Lamp, taupe matt, emb panels w/stylized trees, 13x7" 1,100.00
Pitcher, gr matt w/gray flecks, 5½x5" 100.00
Stein, gr matt, sgn LE, 5¾" 225.00

Vase, embossed flowers under dripping pink and blue matt, 8x6", $800.00.

Vase, aqua matt w/cobalt mottle, tulip buds, closed mouth, 7" ...500.00
Vase, aqua to deep cerulean bl matt, #108, 12x4½" 750.00
Vase, bl/wht feathered matt w/emb upright leaves, 7x4" 600.00
Vase, blk, emb Greek-Key design, soft shoulders, rstr, 4⅛x6" 100.00
Vase, bronze-like brn w/emb leaves & buds, 6½x3¾" 425.00
Vase, cerulean bl, emb water lilies on short stems, #42, 7x5" 900.00
Vase, cobalt/navy/bl mottle w/mauve, trumpet neck, #111, 9" ...750.00
Vase, cocoa-brn matt, trumpet neck, 9¾x6¼" 400.00
Vase, cucumber & olive mottle, cylindrical, 8⅛x3¾" 425.00
Vase, forest gr/tan/brn/ivory mottle, emb leaves, #86, 7x4½" 450.00
Vase, gr matt, emb blade-like leaves, #98, 7⅛x4¼" 475.00
Vase, gr matt, emb corn & husk, short baluster, 5¾x5½" 850.00
Vase, gr matt, emb dandelions, flat rim, 5¾x5" 700.00
Vase, gr matt, emb foliage, 2 buttress hdls, #39, 5¾x7¾" 425.00
Vase, gr matt, emb leaves & stems w/buds, M in circle, 7" 550.00
Vase, gr matt, geometrics & ovals, 2½x5½" 375.00
Vase, gr matt, incised decor, C Robertson's mk, 2½x5½" 345.00
Vase, gr matt, 3-hdld trumpet form, 5x5¼" 225.00
Vase, gr matt w/crackle, closed-flat mouth, #38, 7¼x3¾" 275.00
Vase, gr matt w/dk gr mottle, emb ribbon at neck, 10¾x5" 650.00
Vase, gr matt w/frothy wht highlights, cvd foliage, 6¼x3½" 635.00
Vase, gr matt w/gray flecks, short neck, unmk, 6x3¾" 250.00
Vase, gr matt w/silver floral o/l, trumpet neck, 5x4" 750.00
Vase, gr matt w/wht froth, cvd foliage, 6¼x3½" 635.00
Vase, gr/brn matt, shouldered, 6½" 500.00
Vase, ivory/brn matt, possibly experimental, 3½x3½" 400.00
Vase, ochre-brn matt, long trumpet neck, squat body, 9½" 450.00
Vase, taupe matt, emb broad leaf panels, mfg flaw, 6x7" 300.00
Vase, tobacco brn, raised leaves, C Robertson, #132, 3x6" 460.00
Vase, wht w/mocha flecks over 2nd drip flowing to base, #542, 5" .350.00

Handel

Philip Handel was best known for the art glass lamps he produced at the turn of the century. His work is similar to the Tiffany lamps of the same era. Handel made gas and electric lamps with both leaded glass and reverse-painted shades. Chipped ice shades with a texture similar to overshot glass were also produced. Shades signed by artists such as Bailey, Palme, and Parlow are highly valued.

Teroma lamp shades were created from clear blown glass blanks that were painted on the interior (reverse painted), while Teroma art glass (the decorative vases, humidors, etc. in the Handel Ware line) is painted on the exterior. This type of glassware has a 'chipped ice' effect achieved by sand blasting and coating the surface with fish glue. The piece is kiln fired at 800 degrees F. The contraction of the glue during the cooling process gives the glass a frosted, textured effect. Some shades are sand-finished, adding texture and depth.

Both the glassware and chinaware decorated by Handel are rare and command high prices on today's market. Many of Handel's chinaware blanks were supplied by Limoges.

Key:
chp — chipped/lightly sanded

Handel Ware

Humidor, boy in nightshirt writing in snow: Good Luck, 8x8" ...275.00
Humidor, bull moose, pipe on lid, #4129T, 7½x6" 900.00
Humidor, fisherman's portrait, emb curlicues, #4060, 7½x6" 275.00
Humidor, flowers & Tobacco, HP/emb, opal w/gr ground, att, 5" .400.00
Humidor, horse/hound sgn Godwin, pewter lid w/pipe 900.00
Humidor, hunting dog, sgn Kelsey, copper-look lid w/pipe 1,100.00
Humidor, moose head, metal lid w/match bbl, 5½x5" 850.00

Tazza, mums, rose on pk to yel, stem: yel to bl w/purple, 8x6" 800.00
Vase, cameo floral, gold-amber on clear, Palme/#4258, 11", EX ..1,150.00
Vase, Teroma, wooded scene, no mk, 8", NM 690.00

Lamps

Table lamp, reverse-painted 18" domed #6868 shade with landscape, bronzed-metal base with tree trunk design, signed, 22", $6,500.00.

Base only, bronze 3-light shouldered baluster shape, 22½" 275.00
Boudoir, rvpt 7" bell-shape meadow shade; ribbed std, 14" 2,645.00
Boudoir, rvpt 7" dome pond lilies shade (EX); VG baluster std .1,800.00
Boudoir, rvpt 7" evening scene shade; tree trunk std, 14" 3,300.00
Boudoir, rvpt 7" Mt Fuji scene shade; reed std w/filigree ft 3,000.00
Boudoir, rvpt 7" ships/windmills #6356 shade; ribbed std, 15" 2,400.00
Chandelier, 6-sided glass w/geometric bronzed metal o/l, 23" .2,500.00
Desk, ldgl lily shade; lily pad base w/bud on curving stem, 14" ...920.00
Desk, ldgl 7½" bell shade w/dmn band; harp std adjusts, 19" ...1,495.00
Desk, pnt/chp 8" foliage/urn cylinder shade; bronzed std 1,700.00
Desk, rvpt 7" scenic shade; bronze bell-form harp std, 19" 3,250.00
Evening, trees/4 dancers, blk on orange, upright cylinder, 11" ...475.00
Globe, Teroma, birds in flight, spherical, 10½x10" 2,100.00
Hall, HP macaws, bl on amber opal sphere, metal tassel, 10" 650.00
Hanging, HP 10" parrots globe shade; orig hdw, overall: 15" 225.00
Piano, HP shade w/2 zigzag lines on rust; C-std, 13x10" 1,000.00
Shade, birds, irid orange int, ball shape, #7004, 3", EX 1,495.00
Shade, ldgl 28" ladderwork hex shade; metal tree o/l apron 1,800.00
Table, etch/HP 18" jungle parrot #7686 shade; emb std, 28" ...4,000.00
Table, HP 12" tam-o'-shanter leaves/scrolls shade; hex base 800.00
Table, ldgl 16" dogwood-band shade (EX); bronze-patina std .2,700.00
Table, ldgl 16" flower-band shade; bronze std, no mk, 22½" ...1,800.00
Table, ldgl 18" floral shade; bronze vasiform std w/4 hdls 800.00
Table, ldgl 25" 8-panel rvpt-band shade, no mk; metal std, G .2,700.00
Table, Mission style, 2-arm metal base w/hanging slag shades, 18" ...1,650.00
Table, molded 14" #7617 shade w/dmn ext; bronzed metal std ..1,500.00
Table, rvpt 15" basketweave wild rose shade; sq-base std 2,200.00
Table, rvpt 15" roses-on-basketweave shade (EX); sqd std 2,185.00
Table, rvpt 16" roses shade; bronze reeded floral base, 22" 3,400.00
Table, rvpt 16" scene/bridge shade; lobed bronze std, 23" 4,890.00
Table, rvpt 16" water/trees shade; brn std w/wide ribbing 3,450.00
Table, rvpt 18" daffodil sgn #7122 shade; bronzed metal std ...7,000.00
Table, rvpt 18" Egyptian ruins/ships shade (NM); rpl std 5,000.00
Table, rvpt 18" exotic birds on blk #7026 shade; 3-part std ...11,500.00
Table, rvpt 18" moon/trees shade sgn FU; forest-emb std, 23" .9,400.00
Table, rvpt 18" nightscape shade; textured vasiform std 4,000.00
Table, rvpt 18" trees hex ribbed shade sgn HR; unmk std 4,200.00
Table, rvpt/chp purple leaves shade #6730; textured std 2,400.00
Table, rvpt/chp 15" scenic shade; bronze-patina sgn std 2,700.00
Table, rvpt/chp 18" exotic birds sgn Palme shade; 3-shaft std ..11,500.00
Table, rvpt/chp 18" floral-band shade; coppered std, 22" 3,900.00
Table, rvpt/chp 18" trees shade; bronze metal baluster std 2,800.00
Table, slag 18" paneled shade w/metal tree o/l; tree std 8,500.00
Torchere, etched/pnt heraldic shade (VG); orig base, 67" 400.00

Harker

The Harker Pottery was established in East Liverpool, Ohio, in 1840. Their earliest products were yellow ware and Rockingham produced from local clay. After 1900 whiteware was made from imported materials. The plant eventually grew to be a large manufacturer of dinnerware and kitchenware, employing as many as three hundred people. It closed in 1972 after it was purchased by the Jeannette Glass Company. Perhaps their best-known lines were their Cameo wares, decorated with white silhouettes in a cameo effect on contrasting solid colors. Floral silhouettes are standard, but other designs were also used. Blue and pink are the most often found background hues; a few pieces are found in yellow. For further information we recommend *The Collector's Guide to Harker Pottery* by Neva Colbert. Our advisor for this category is Ted Haun; he is listed in the Directory under Indiana.

Photo courtesy Neva Colbert

Modern Tulip: Pie baker, $15.00; Creamer, $8.00; Water jug, $25.00.

Amy, hi-rise jug 22.00
Amy, plate, emb edge, 6" 5.00
Antique Auto, cup & saucer, jumbo 22.00
Bamboo, plate, luncheon 8.00
Bermuda, plate, luncheon 8.00
Birds & Flowers, cup & saucer 7.00
Black-Eyed Susan, cake/pie lifter 20.00
Black-Eyed Susan, tidbit tray, 1-tier 6.00
Black-Eyed Susan, tidbit tray, 3-tier 20.00
Blue Grapes, pie baker 15.00
Blue Rhythm, plate, dinner 10.00
Bridal Rose, bowl, vegetable; swirl 11.00
Brim, bowl, mixing 36.00
Cabbage Rose, dresser tray, turq 100.00
Cabbage Rose, plate, dinner 10.00
Calender plate, Christmas, 1907 ....80.00
Calender plate, Washington's Headquarters, 1913 ....25.00
Calico Tulip, condiment jar set, w/lids & rack, set of 4 ....39.00
Carnivale, custard 10.00
Carnivale, salad fork server 20.00
Cherry Trim, sugar bowl, Embassy 10.00
Chesterton (Bermuda Blue), gravy boat 14.00
Chesterton (Celadon), creamer & sugar bowl 12.00
Chesterton (Charcoal), platter, 13" 8.00
Chesterton (Silver-Gray), cup & saucer 10.00
Chesterton (Silver-Gray), gravy jug 14.00
Chesterton (Teal), plate, luncheon 8.00
Frogs & Scarecrow, plate 30.00
Green Blush, tray, on Dixie shape 20.00
Green Blush, tumbler 10.00
Ivy, platter, Olympic 14.00
Jessica, bowl, mixing 40.00
Lisa, Regal jug 30.00

Lotus, plate, dinner 10.00
Lovelace, cake lifter 13.00
Mallow, bowl, mixing 40.00
Mallow, refrigerator jar, sq, w/lid 33.00
Manila, brush vase 10.00
Modern Tulip, hi-rise jug 30.00
Modern Tulip, teapot, Modern Age 30.00
Monterey, casserole, w/lid 36.00
Pansy, casserole w/lid 36.00
Pastel Roses, shaving mug 30.00
Peacock Alley, jug 25.00
Petit Point, bowl, mixing 40.00
Petit Point, jug, rnd, w/lid 45.00
Playmates, dish, cylindrical, stamped w/Embellished Bow & Arrow ..40.00
Quaker Maid, creamer & sugar bowl 10.00
Queen Elizabeth II, commemorative plate, 1957 ....25.00
Red Apple, waffle set, platter & 2 jugs, complete 75.00
Rose, platter, Olympic 14.00
Rosebud, shakers, skyscraper shape, pr 22.00
Spanish Gold, plate, luncheon 25.00
Strawberries & Gold, demitasse set 200.00
Tahiti, jug, w/lid 50.00
Tulip, pie baker 25.00
White Rose, bowl, utility 12.00
Wild Rose, cake/pie lifter 20.00

Harlequin

Harlequin dinnerware, produced by the Homer Laughlin China Company of Newell, West Virginia, was introduced in 1938. It was a lightweight ware made in maroon, mauve blue, and spruce green, as well as all the Fiesta colors except ivory (see Fiesta). It was marketed exclusively by the Woolworth stores, who considered it to be their all-time best seller. For this reason they contracted with Homer Laughlin to reissue Harlequin to commemorate their 100th anniversary in 1979. Although three of the original glazes were used in the reissue, the few serving pieces that were made were restyled, and collectors found the new line to be no threat to their investments.

The Harlequin animals, including a fish, lamb, cat, penguin, duck, and donkey, were made during the early 1940s, also for the dime-store trade. Today these are very desirable to collectors of Homer Laughlin china.

In the listings that follow, use the values designated 'high' for all colors other than turquoise and yellow. Unless priced, for medium green, double the 'high' values on all items other than flat items and small bowls. *The Collector's Encyclopedia of Fiesta* (Collector Books), by Sharon and Bob Huxford contains a more thorough study of this subject and includes specific pricing for many medium green examples.

Animals, maverick, gold trim 55.00
Animals, non-standard color 275.00
Animals, standard color 175.00
Ashtray, basketweave, high 58.00
Ashtray, basketweave, low 35.00
Ashtray, regular, high 53.00
Ashtray, regular, low 38.00
Bowl, '36s oatmeal; high 26.00
Bowl, '36s oatmeal; low 16.00
Bowl, '36s; high 40.00
Bowl, '36s; low 26.00
Bowl, cream soup; high 30.00
Bowl, cream soup; low 22.00
Bowl, cream soup; med gr, minimum value 600.00

Bowl, fruit; high, 5½" 11.00
Bowl, fruit; low, 5½" 8.00
Bowl, ind salad; high 42.00
Bowl, ind salad; low 28.00
Bowl, mixing; Kitchen Kraft, mauve bl, 8" 125.00
Bowl, mixing; Kitchen Kraft, red or lt gr, 6", ea 90.00
Bowl, mixing; Kitchen Kraft, yel, 10" 125.00
Bowl, nappy; high, 9" 40.00
Bowl, nappy; low, 9" 26.00
Bowl, oval baker, high 40.00
Bowl, oval baker, low 27.00

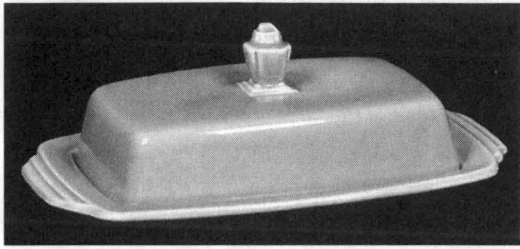

Butter dish, ½-lb, Cobalt, $300.00; High, $135.00; Low, $115.00.

Candle holders, high, pr 285.00
Candle holders, low, pr 240.00
Casserole, w/lid, high 160.00
Casserole, w/lid, low 95.00
Creamer, high lip, any color, ea 130.00
Creamer, ind; high 35.00
Creamer, ind; low 20.00
Creamer, novelty, high 40.00
Creamer, novelty, low 28.00
Creamer, regular, high 20.00
Creamer, regular, low 14.00
Cup, demitasse; high 110.00
Cup, demitasse; low 42.00
Cup, lg, any color, ea 180.00
Cup, tea; high 11.00
Cup, tea; low 9.00
Egg cup, dbl, high 28.00
Egg cup, dbl, low 20.00
Egg cup, single, high 35.00
Egg cup, single, low 25.00
Marmalade, high 240.00
Marmalade, low 200.00
Nut dish, basketweave, high 18.00
Nut dish, basketweave, low 13.00
Perfume bottle, any color, ea 120.00
Pitcher, service water; high 105.00
Pitcher, service water; low 70.00
Pitcher, 22-oz jug, high 68.00
Pitcher, 22-oz jug, low 40.00
Pitcher, 22-oz jug, med gr, minimum value 250.00
Plate, deep; high 30.00
Plate, deep; low 20.00
Plate, deep; med gr 75.00
Plate, high, 6" 5.50
Plate, high, 7" 8.00
Plate, high, 9" 14.00
Plate, high, 10" 36.00
Plate, low, 6" 4.00
Plate, low, 7" 6.00

Plate, low, 9" 10.00
Plate, low, 10" 24.00
Platter, high, 11" 25.00
Platter, high, 13" 32.00
Platter, low, 11" 18.00
Platter, low, 13" 22.00
Platter, med gr, 11" 200.00
Platter, med gr, 13" 250.00
Sauce boat, high 35.00
Sauce boat, low 22.00
Saucer, demitasse; high 28.00
Saucer, demitasse; low 15.00
Saucer, demitasse; med gr, minimum value 125.00
Saucer, high 4.00
Saucer, low 2.00
Saucer/ashtray, high 63.00
Saucer/ashtray, low 50.00
Shakers, high, pr 26.00
Shakers, low, pr 18.00
Sugar bowl, w/lid, high 32.00
Sugar bowl, w/lid, low 20.00
Sugar bowl, w/lid, med gr, minimum value 100.00
Syrup, red or yel 175.00
Syrup, Spruce gr or mauve 300.00
Teapot, high 145.00
Teapot, low 85.00
Tray, relish; mixed colors 300.00
Tumbler, car decal 65.00
Tumbler, high 58.00
Tumbler, low 45.00

Hatpin Holders

Most hatpin holders were made from 1860 to 1920 to coincide with the period during which hatpins were in vogue. The taller types were required to house the long hatpins necessary to secure the large hats that were in style from 1890 to 1914. They were usually porcelain, either decorated by hand or by transfer with florals or scenics, although some were clever figurals. Glass examples are rare, and those of slag or carnival glass are especially valuable.

If you are interested in collecting or dealing in hatpins or hatpin holders, you will enjoy *Hatpins and Hatpin Holders* by Lillian Baker, with beautiful color illustrations and current market values. For information concerning the International Club for Collectors of Hatpins and Hatpin Holders, see the Clubs, Newsletters, and Catalogs section of the Directory. Our advisor for this category is Robert Larsen; he is listed in the Directory under Nebraska. (SASE required.)

Adams, jasperware, wht on bl, ca 1891-1914, 4", NM 250.00
Bavaria, china, silver floral on wht, 4¾" 235.00
Bsk, cameo on bell form, 12-hole, 2¼" 245.00
Bsk, pk & wht w/gr cameo ea side, 7-hole, unmk, 4½" 225.00
Carnival glass, Grape & Cable, purple, 7x2½" 375.00
China, slipper form, wall mt 250.00
Chocolate glass, emb florals, ftd, ca 1905, 7⅞x2⅝" 600.00
Custard glass w/bl wash, ftd, ca 1905, 7½" 1,200.00
Custard glass w/pk wash, ftd, ca 1905, 7½" 1,400.00
Flow blue, Victorian scenes, Watteau 175.00
Limoges, lav floral on wht w/much gold, 16-hole, unmk, 5" 125.00
Limoges, roses on wht w/gold, sq top, 5¼" 125.00
Porc, classical figure & peacock on wht, cylindrical, 3⅝" 375.00
Pressed glass, Daisy & Button, clear, silver top, rare, 8" 600.00
Royal Bayreuth, Corinthian, bl mk, 4¾", +4" saucer 375.00

Photo courtesy Robert Larsen

Royal Bayreuth, rooster figural, red and gray, $1,200.00.

Royal Bayreuth, poppy figural, pk, ca 1908, 4½" 1,200.00
RS Germany, orange poppies, gr mk 135.00
RS Prussia, calla lilies, gr to dk gr 235.00
RS Prussia, 3-hdl, floral decor, ca 1910, 4½" 600.00
Ruby glass, HP daisies & gold sprays 165.00
Satin glass, HP, 6 pin holes, ca 1910, 4½" 550.00
Sterling golf bag form, 2 putters form legs, mk, 1895, 3" 200.00
Vienna Austria, Nouveau floral, HP w/much gold, 4¾" 110.00

Hatpins

A hatpin was used to securely fasten a hat to the hair and head of the wearer. Hatpins, measuring from 4" to 12" in length, were worn from approximately 1850 to 1920. During the Art Deco period, hatpins became ornaments rather than the decorative functional jewels that they had been. The hatpin period reached its zenith in 1913 just prior to World War I, which brought about a radical change in women's headdress and fashion. About that time, women began to scorn the bonnet and adopt 'the hat' as a symbol of their equality. The hatpin was made of every natural and manufactured element in a myriad of designs that challenge the imagination. They were contrived to serve every fashion need and complement the milliner's art. Collectors often concentrate on a specific type: hand-painted porcelains, sterling silver, commemoratives, sporting activities, Carnival glass, Art Nouveau and/or Art Deco designs, Victorian Gothics with mounted stones, exquisite rhinestones, engraved and brass-mounted escutcheon heads, gold and gems, or simply primitive types made in the Victorian parlor. Some collectors prefer the long pin-shanks while others select only those on tremblants or nodder-type pin-shanks.

If you are interested in collecting or dealing in hatpins, see the information in the Hatpin Holders introduction concerning a reference book and a national collectors' club. Our advisor for this category is Robert Larsen; he is listed in the Directory under Nebraska. (SASE required.)

Key: cab — cabochon

Amethyst stone set in gilt-over-brass mt, ¾", 8" pin 110.00
Basse-taille enameled head over-pnt w/roses, gold trim, 1½" 175.00
Brass, Nouveau style w/4 topaz-colored stones, 2¾", 12" pin 100.00
Brass heart-shape fr w/many brilliants, 1905, 1¾" top 110.00
Eagle head figural w/31 pave-set rhinestones, ca 1876, 1¾x1¼" .175.00
Garnet, cab, 1" on 5½" gilt pin 150.00
Jet glass, faceted, soldered into wire fr, Czech, 1870s, $155 to 275.00
Mosaic, in brass button-sleeve mt w/gold trim, 1", 8" pin 95.00
Plique-a-jour, mc Nouveau enamel w/opal center, 1¼x1½" 675.00

Porc, transfer & gold o/l on ball form, 1895, 1¼", 8½" pin 160.00
Rhinestones, prong-set, on domed 1¼" brass filigree top 125.00
Satsuma, HP birds & leaves, 1½", on 10½" steel pin 375.00
Silver, lady's emb portrait, mk front, ⅞", on 7½" pin 175.00
Silver, scarab figural w/mc enamel, Germany, 1½x1¼" 110.00
Silver alloy (oxidized) w/faceted amethyst glass, 1900s, 7½" 125.00
Sterling, dbl mold, Nouveau lady's head, hollow, 1x11¼" 145.00
Sterling, Gibson girl w/repousse, ca 1900, 1½", on pin 125.00
Sterling w/pearl & tortoise-shell inlay 160.00
Vanity, brass w/red stone, ornate filigree, w/puff & mirror **1,400.00**
Vanity, gilt over brass w/simulated stone, ca 1913, 1¾" 900.00
Vanity, Nouveau moth w/red faceted stone & rhinestones, 1½" .**1,500.00**
1908 Liberty nickel, Pat Nov 22 1904 on bk, on 9" nickel shank ...125.00

Haviland

The Haviland China Company was organized in 1840 by David Haviland, a New York china importer. His search for a pure white, nonporous porcelain led him to Limoges, France, where natural deposits of suitable clay had already attracted numerous china manufacturers. The fine china he produced there was translucent and meticulously decorated, with each piece fired in an individual sagger.

It has been estimated that as many as 60,000 chinaware patterns were designed, each piece marked with one of several company backstamps. 'H. & Co.' was used until 1890 when a law was enacted making it necessary to include the country of origin. Various marks have been used since that time including 'Haviland, France'; 'Haviland & Co. Limoges'; and 'Decorated by Haviland & Co.' Various associations with family members over the years have resulted in changes in management as well as company name. In 1892 Theodore Haviland left the firm to start his own business. Some of his ware was marked 'Mont Mery.' Later logos included a horseshoe, a shield, and various uses of his initials and name. In 1941 this branch moved to the United States. Wares produced here are marked 'Theodore Haviland, N.Y.' or 'Made In America.'

Though it is their dinnerware lines for which they are most famous, during the 1880s and 1890s they also made exquisite art pottery using a technique of underglaze slip decoration called Barbotine, which had been invented by Ernest Chaplet. In 1885 Haviland bought the formula and hired Chaplet to oversee its production. The technique involved mixing heavy white clay slip with pigments to produce a compound of the same consistency as oil paints. The finished product actually resembled oil paintings of the period, the texture achieved through the application of the heavy medium to the clay body in much the same manner as an artist would apply paint to his canvas. Primarily the body used with this method was a low-fired faience, though they also produced stoneware. For further information we recommend Mary Frank Gaston's *Encyclopedia of Limoges Porcelain*, which offers examples and marks of the Haviland Company.

Bonbon basket, pk floral w/gold, Fantaisie Romeo form, 1904-20s 175.00
Bowl, covered vegetable; Ranson, rnd 85.00
Bowl, Drop Rose, pk w/gold, hdls, low, 9¼" 145.00
Chocolate pot, floral/gilt, emb mold, Theodore, 10" 110.00
Chocolate pot, gold band & hdl, 1893-1930, 5" 100.00
Chocolate pot, pk & gr roses w/gold, L France, 1888-1896, 10" .175.00
Creamer & sugar bowl, gold bands on wht, 1850-65 mk, 7", 8", pr ..185.00
Hair receiver, floral w/gold, 1893-1930 mk, 5" L 175.00
Jardiniere, terra cotta, sculpted flowers, 1873-82 ....**2,200.00**
Pitcher, Deco 'Farewell' cat figural, yel/wht, Limoges, 8⅝" 700.00
Pitcher, duck figural, Sandoz, 1904-1920s 750.00

Pitcher, water, emb & HP floral w/gold, 1850-65 mk, 10" 140.00
Vase, appl roses & leaves on pillow form, Limoges, 16x10x5½" ..**1,200.00**
Vase, Barbotine, bird on blooming cherry branch, 16x9½" 600.00
Wash bowl & pitcher, red band on wht w/gold, 1865-75, 12", 15½" .**1,100.00**

Hawkes

Thomas Hawkes established his factory in Corning, New York, in 1880. He developed many beautiful patterns of cut glass, two of which were awarded the Grand Prize at the Paris Exposition in 1889. By the end of the century, his company was renowned for the finest in cut glass production. The company logo was a trefoil form enclosing a hawk in each of the two bottom lobes with a fleur-de-lis in the center. With the exception of some of the very early designs, all Hawkes was signed. (Our values are for signed pieces.)

Bowl, allover eng, bulbus, ped ft, 5x7½" 120.00
Bowl, buttons lattice, 4 vesica hobstars/rayed bull's eye, 2x9" .**1,275.00**
Bowl, Greek Key rim, 9⅜" 140.00
Bowl, Venetian, 9" 215.00
Carafe, ship's; Grecian pattern of Russian & tusks, 7½" 400.00
Chalice, blazing stars w/dmn-faceted amber centers, 7¾" 160.00
Cheese & cracker, florals w/hobstar eclipses, heavy, 10" 140.00
Creamer & sugar bowl, hobstars, 2½" 125.00
Decanter, 8-panel, hollow pointed stopper, sgn 2X, 14" 200.00
Pitcher, cider; Brunswick, 6½" 475.00
Pitcher, flattened dmns on ball shape, 5" dia 125.00
Tray, Pueblo, hobstars, beveled rnds w/interlocking devices, 11" ..**13,800.00**
Tumbler, Brunswick, 4", set of 6 ....370.00

Vase, engraved school of fish and a crab, hammered metal top, two scrolled arms, signed, 15½", $700.00.

Vase, amethyst, eng floral, deep ribbing, sterling ft, 12x4" 350.00
Vase, pnt gr w/eng 3-toed dragon, 8x3" 200.00

Head Vases

Vases modeled as heads of lovely ladies, delightful children, clowns, Madonnas — even some animals — were once popular as flower containers. Today they represent a growing area of collector interest. Most of them were imported from Japan, although some American potteries produced a few as well.

For more information, we recommend *Head Vases, Identification and Values,* by Kathleen Cole and *The World of Head Vase Planters* by Mike Posgay and Ian Warner.

Child, #609, girl graduate, 5¼" 40.00
Child, Inarco, boy as fireman, #5 red hat, 5" 75.00
Child, Inarco #E1579, girl praying, blond hair, 6" 45.00
Child, Inarco #E2965, girl in yel scarf w/pigtails, 7" 58.00

Child, Inarco #E3155, Indian boy, blond, 5½" 40.00
Child, Inarco #E3155, Swiss boy, brn hat, blond hair, 5½" 40.00
Child, Inarco #E4392, baby boy w/phone, Hello Gran'pa! on bib, 6" ..45.00
Child, Japan, girl in pk hat, gift in hand, gold trim, 5½" 50.00
Child, Napco #CX2348B, Christmas girl w/gift, blond, 5½" 75.00
Child, unmk, baby in pk bonnet w/bl roses, blond hair, 6" 45.00
Child, Velco, girl in hat w/parasol, blond curls, 5½" 75.00
Clown, Inarco #E6730, red hair, yel/bl hat & collar, 5½" 50.00
Clown, unmk, orange/wht/bl/blk face, bl/wht ruffled collar, 4" 45.00
Lady, Brinn #T1821, allover curls, bl/wht floral bust, 7" 50.00
Lady, Enesco, fur collar, short blond hair, 6" 65.00
Lady, Inarco #E1062, gold crown, frosted updo, pearls, 6" 75.00
Lady, Inarco #E1611, Dutch hat, hand under chin, gold trim, 5½" ...300.00
Lady, Inarco #E190/M, blk hat, blond, hand to chin, pearls, 5" 50.00
Lady, Inarco #E191/m/c, peach hat w/plume, blond updo, 5½" 45.00
Lady, Inarco #E191/m/c, plumed hat, blond, pearls, 5½" 45.00
Lady, Inarco #E2104, bow in blond hair, hand to face, 7" 125.00
Lady, Inarco #E2104, frosted hair over eye, hand to face, 7" 250.00
Lady, Inarco #E2966, frosted updo, blk bodice, pearls, 11" 450.00
Lady, Inarco #E3523, blond, wht ruffled collar, gold trim, 7" 250.00
Lady, Japan, blk hat, long blond hair, pk hand to face, 5" 45.00
Lady, Japan, gr perforated hat, brn updo, hand to face, 7" 75.00
Lady, Japan, yel hat/wht bow, redhead, gr/wht bodice, 5½" 35.00
Lady, Lefton's #1843, hat/bow, short blond hair, 5½" 50.00
Lady, Mary Lou, Betty Lou Nichols, 5½" 450.00
Lady, Nancy, Betty Lou Nichols, 6" 295.00
Lady, Napco #C 7498, frosted hair, bl hat w/bow, pearls, 11" 450.00
Lady, Napco #CX5409, poinsettia at neck, blk/wht hat, 4½" 65.00
Lady, Napco #C3282A, wht hat, blond updo, hand, blk/gold trim, 6" .50.00
Lady, Napco #C5708, colonial-style banana curls, 6" 175.00
Lady, Napco #C7474, frosted, pearls/brooch on blk bodice, 9" ...150.00
Lady, Parma #A219, lt frosted sidesweep, gr bodice, pearls, 8½" ...300.00

Lady in long white curls, ruffled bodice with bow and gold trim, Relpo #K1335, 8", $160.00.

Photo courtesy Kathleen Cole

Lady, Relpo #K1175L, gr hat/plaid bow, hands under chin, 5" 50.00
Lady, Relpo #K1817, short frosted hair, wht frilly collar, 5½" 65.00
Lady, Relpo #K1931, blk band in long hair, bodice, 8½" 300.00
Lady, Relpo #1783, gr hat tied at neck, gr sundress, 7½" 250.00
Lady, Replo #A1197, bl floral pillbox, gloved hands to face, 5" 55.00
Lady, Rubens #4121, pk bows in braided hair, cold-pnt, 6" 45.00
Lady, Rubens #4135, pk cape hood over blond hair, 5½" 65.00
Lady, Rubens #483, blond upsweep, pk ruffled collar, hand, 6½" .55.00
Lady, Rubens #495, wht picture hat, blond updo, hands clasped, 6" .65.00
Lady, Rubens #500, wht hat, yel curls, gold/pearl trim, 5½" 45.00
Lady, Shawnee #896, islander w/bowl on head, draped shoulder, 6" .45.00
Lady, unmk, blk exotic hair/eyes, gr bodice w/sequin trim, 7¼" 65.00
Lady, unmk, blk/wht '40s hat, yel hair, high collar, 6" 45.00
Lady, unmk, cartoon features, pk/gr floral hat, pearls, 5½" 45.00
Lady, unmk, head/neck, looking up, airbrushed pageboy, 6" 32.50
Lady, unmk, hugging hat, blond, wht collar up, gold trim, 6½" 65.00
Lady, unmk, pk & gr turban/bodice, sideways glance, open smile, 8" .225.00
Lady, unmk, pk bow atop flip hairdo, pk bodice, pearls, 7½" 300.00

Lady, unmk, pk fan collar, blond updo, sq base, 6½" 75.00
Lady, unmk, pk/wht hat w/V cutout, blond updo, looking up, 7" ..125.00
Lady, unmk, yel poofed hat/bodice, blk hair, gold trim, 7½" 55.00
Lady, Vcagco, blond in wht/peach head scarf, thick lashes, 6" 55.00
Oriental, Lee Wards, geisha in blk & wht w/gold trim, 5" 50.00
Religious, Napco #R7076, Virgin Mary w/baby Jesus, 6½" 42.50
Religious, Relpo #C1811, nun, pale bl, 5" 27.50
Religious, unmk, monk boy praying, 6" 45.00
Teen girl, Enesco, gr turtleneck, bows in side ponytails, 4½" 40.00
Teen girl, Napco #C8493, yel bow/long hair, pearl earring, 5½" ..65.00
Teen girl, Relpo #2031, 2 gr bows, gr/wht/yel bodice, pearls, 6" ...55.00
Teen girl, unmk, sunglasses atop blond head w/ponytails, 7½" ...350.00
Teen girl, Velco, head cocked on shoulder, pk leaf hat, blond, 5" ...50.00

Heisey

A.H. Heisey began his long career at the King Glass Company of Pittsburgh. He later joined the Ripley Glass Company which soon became Geo. Duncan and Sons. After Duncan's death Heisey became half-owner in partnership with his brother-in-law, James Duncan. In 1895 he built his own factory in Newark, Ohio, initiating production in 1896 and continuing until Christmas of 1957. At that time Imperial Glass Corporation bought some of the molds. After 1968 they removed the old 'Diamond H' from any they put into use. In 1985 HCA purchased all of Imperial's Heisey molds with the exception of the Old Williamsburg line.

During their highly successful period of production, Heisey made fine handcrafted tableware with simple, yet graceful designs. Early pieces were not marked. After November 1901 the glassware was marked either with the 'Diamond H' or a paper label. Blown ware is often marked on the stem, never on the bowl or foot.

For information concerning Heisey Collectors of America, see the Clubs, Newsletters, and Catalogs section of the Directory. See also Glass Animals.

Cabochon, crystal, bowl, dessert; #1951, 4½" 4.00
Cabochon, crystal, butter dish, #1951, ¼-lb 25.00
Cabochon, crystal, creamer, #1951 ....9.00
Cabochon, crystal, mint dish, #1951, slanted sides, ftd, 5¾" 22.50
Cabochon, crystal, plate, sandwich; #1951, 14" 18.00
Cabochon, crystal, stem, cordial; #6091, 1-oz 22.50
Cabochon, crystal, stem, sherbet; #6091, 5½-oz 4.00
Cabochon, crystal, tray, #1951, for creamer & sugar bowl, 9" 45.00
Cabochon, crystal, tumbler, beverage; #6092, blown, 10-oz 8.00
Cabochon, crystal, tumbler, iced tea; #6091, ftd, 12-oz 8.00
Cabochon, crystal, vase, #1951, flared, 3½" 22.00
Charter Oak, crystal, candle holder, #130 Acorn, 1-light, ea 100.00
Charter Oak, crystal, plate, salad; #1246 Acorn & Leaves, 7" 8.00
Charter Oak, crystal, tumbler, #3362, flat, 12-oz 12.50
Charter Oak, gr, pitcher, #3362, flat 100.00
Charter Oak, gr, stem, oyster cocktail; #3362, low ft, 3½-oz 17.00
Charter Oak, marigold, stem, parfait; #3362, 4½-oz 50.00
Charter Oak, orchid, stem, cocktail; #3362, 3-oz 45.00
Charter Oak, orchid, stem, saucer champagne; #3362, 6-oz 40.00
Charter Oak, pk, candlestick, #129 Tricorn, 3-light, 5", ea 65.00
Charter Oak, pk, plate, dinner; #1246 Acorn & Leaves, 10½" 37.50
Charter Oak, pk, stem, goblet; #3362, high ft, 8-oz 30.00
Chintz, crystal, bowl, mint; ftd, 6" 20.00
Chintz, crystal, creamer, 3 dolphin ft 20.00
Chintz, crystal, plate, dinner; sq, 10½" 45.00
Chintz, crystal, stem, saucer champagne; #3389, 5-oz 14.00
Chintz, crystal, stem, wine; #3389, 2½-oz 17.50
Chintz, crystal, tray, celery; 13" 18.00

Chintz, yel, bowl, flower; hdls, ftd, 8½" 65.00
Chintz, yel, cruet, oil; 4-oz 125.00
Chintz, yel, platter, oval, 14" 65.00
Chintz, yel, stem, oyster cocktail; #3389, 4-oz 20.00
Chintz, yel, sugar bowl, ind 28.00
Chintz, yel, tumbler, iced tea; #3389, 12-oz 30.00

Photo courtesy Gene Florence

Crystolite, crystal, ashtray, rare, $150.00.

Crystolite, crystal, ashtray, w/match book holder, 5" 45.00
Crystolite, crystal, bottle, cologne; w/#108 stopper, 4-oz 65.00
Crystolite, crystal, bowl, dessert/sauce; 8" 30.00
Crystolite, crystal, bowl, preserve; 5" 20.00
Crystolite, crystal, candle block, swirl, 1-light 20.00
Crystolite, crystal, candy dish, swan shape, 6½" 45.00
Crystolite, crystal, creamer, ind 17.00
Crystolite, crystal, mustard jar, w/lid 40.00
Crystolite, crystal, pitcher, syrup; Drip Cut 135.00
Crystolite, crystal, plate, shell shape, 7" 24.00
Crystolite, crystal, plate, torte; 11" 40.00
Empress, Alexandrite, bowl, mint; dolphin ft, 6" 325.00
Empress, Alexandrite, bowl, nasturtium; dolphin ft, 7½" 425.00
Empress, cobalt, bowl, flower; dolphin ft, 11" 395.00
Empress, cobalt, candy dish, dolphin ft, w/lid, 6" 425.00
Empress, gr, bowl, preserve; hdls, 5" 27.50
Empress, gr, bowl, relish; Triplex, 10" 65.00
Empress, gr, plate, 12" 65.00
Empress, pk, bonbon, 6" 20.00
Empress, pk, bowl, relish; center hdl, 3-part, 7" 45.00
Empress, pk, grapefruit dish, w/sq liner 30.00
Empress, pk, mustard jar, w/lid 75.00
Empress, pk, tray, celery; 10" 16.00
Empress, yel, bowl, floral, hdls, ftd, 8½" 50.00
Empress, yel, cup, AD 50.00
Empress, yel, plate, 8" 20.00
Empress, yel, saucer, AD 10.00
Greek Key, crystal, bottle, oil; w/#6 stopper, 2-oz 110.00
Greek Key, crystal, bottle, water 185.00
Greek Key, crystal, bowl, almond; ftd, 5" 35.00
Greek Key, crystal, bowl, banana split; ftd, 9" 40.00
Greek Key, crystal, candy dish, w/lid, 1-lb 140.00
Greek Key, crystal, hair receiver 125.00
Greek Key, crystal, horseradish jar, w/lid, sm 110.00
Greek Key, crystal, nappy, 4" 20.00
Greek Key, crystal, plate, 5½" 25.00
Greek Key, crystal, puff box, #1, w/lid 85.00
Greek Key, crystal, spooner, lg 75.00
Greek Key, crystal, stem, claret; 4½-oz 170.00
Ipswich, cobalt, bowl, flower; ftd, 11" 365.00
Ipswich, crystal, candy jar, w/lid, ¼-lb 150.00
Ipswich, crystal, stem, goblet; knob stem, 10-oz 30.00
Ipswich, crystal, tumbler, soda; ftd, 12-oz 35.00
Ipswich, gr, stem, saucer champagne; knob stem, 5-oz 40.00

Ipswich, gr, tumbler, soda; ftd, 5-oz 70.00
Ipswich, pk, finger bowl, w/underplate 59.00
Ipswich, pk, tumbler, str rim, flat, 10-oz 60.00
Ipswich, yel, creamer 50.00
Ipswich, yel, sherbet, knob in stem, ftd, 4-oz 25.00
Ipswich, yel, tumbler, cupped rim, flat, 10-oz 50.00
Lariat, crystal, basket, ftd, 8½" 165.00
Lariat, crystal, bowl, celery; 13" 40.00
Lariat, crystal, bowl, salad; hdls, 10½" 38.00
Lariat, crystal, cheese dish, w/lid, 8" 60.00
Lariat, crystal, cup 15.00
Lariat, crystal, plate, salad; 7" 12.00
Lariat, crystal, platter, oval, 15" 60.00
Lariat, crystal, stem, claret; blown, 4-oz 28.00
Lariat, crystal, stem, cocktail; pressed, 3½-oz 20.00
Lariat, crystal, stem, sherbet; low, 6-oz 10.00
Lariat, crystal, sugar bowl 20.00
Lariat, crystal, tumbler, iced tea; ftd, 12-oz 24.00
Lodestar, Dawn, bowl, crimped, 11" 95.00
Lodestar, Dawn, bowl, sauce; #1626, 4½" 40.00
Lodestar, Dawn, candlesticks, 2-light, 5¾", pr 600.00
Lodestar, Dawn, creamer, w/hdl 90.00
Lodestar, Dawn, plate, 14" 90.00
Lodestar, Dawn, tumbler, juice; 6-oz 45.00
Lodestar, Dawn, vase, #1626, 8" 140.00
Minuet, crystal, bell, dinner; #3408 ....85.00
Minuet, crystal, bowl, floral; ftd, 11" 95.00
Minuet, crystal, bowl, relish; triple, 7" 35.00
Minuet, crystal, bowl, salad; 13½" 75.00
Minuet, crystal, compote, #5010, 5½" 35.00
Minuet, crystal, ice bucket, dolphin ft 150.00
Minuet, crystal, plate, luncheon; 8" 20.00
Minuet, crystal, stem, sherbet; #5010, 6-oz 15.00
Minuet, crystal, stem, wine; #5010, 2½-oz 50.00
Minuet, crystal, tray, social hour; 15" 75.00
Minuet, crystal, tumbler, iced tea; #5010, 12-oz 60.00
Minuet, crystal, vase, #4196, 8" 85.00
New Era, crystal, bowl, flower; 11" 60.00
New Era, crystal, cup, AD 60.00
New Era, crystal, plate, 9x7" 25.00
New Era, crystal, stem, claret; 4-oz 18.00
New Era, crystal, stem, cordial; 1-oz 45.00
New Era, crystal, tray, celery; 13" 35.00
New Era, crystal, tumbler, soda; 14-oz 15.00
Octagon, crystal, bowl, cream soup; hdls 10.00
Octagon, crystal, plate, 6" 4.00
Octagon, gr, candlestick, 1-light, 3", ea 35.00
Octagon, gr, plate, 14" 35.00
Octagon, marigold, bowl, nut; hdls, ind 65.00
Octagon, marigold, frozen dessert dish, #500 ....50.00
Octagon, orchid, creamer, hotel sz 35.00
Octagon, orchid, sugar bowl, #500 ....45.00
Octagon, pk, bowl, mint; #1229, 6" 15.00
Octagon, pk, plate, salad; #1229, 10" 20.00
Octagon, yel, bowl, compote, #1229, ftd, 8" 35.00
Octagon, yel, plate, sandwich; center hdl, 10½" 40.00
Old Colony, crystal, nappy, 4½" 7.00
Old Colony, crystal, plate, rnd, 10½" 28.50
Old Colony, gr, cup, AD 50.00
Old Colony, gr, sugar bowl, dolphin ft 50.00
Old Colony, gr, tumbler, soda; #3380, ftd, 10-oz 25.00
Old Colony, marigold, compote, #3368, ftd, 7" 95.00
Old Colony, marigold, tumbler, bar; #3380, ftd, 2-oz 35.00
Old Colony, pk, bowl, floral; ftd, hdls, 8½" 47.00

Old Colony, pk, stem, sherbet; #3380, 6-oz 11.00
Old Colony, pk, vase, ftd, 9" 130.00
Old Colony, yel, bowl, flared, ftd, 13" 40.00
Old Colony, yel, stem, claret; #3390, 4-oz 27.50
Old Sandwich, cobalt, beer mug, 12-oz 250.00
Old Sandwich, cobalt, tumbler, bar; ground bottom, 1½-oz 100.00
Old Sandwich, crystal, bottle (cruet), catsup; w/#3 stopper 12.00
Old Sandwich, crystal, pilsner, 8-oz 14.00
Old Sandwich, gr, cup 125.00
Old Sandwich, gr, stem, claret; 4-oz 55.00
Old Sandwich, pk, candlestick, 6", ea 100.00
Old Sandwich, pk, plate, sq, 7" 27.00
Old Sandwich, pk, tumbler, 10-oz 40.00
Old Sandwich, yel, creamer, 12-oz 170.00
Old Sandwich, yel, saucer 15.00
Old Sandwich, yel, sundae, 6-oz 30.00
Orchid, crystal, bell, dinner; #5022 or #5025 ....135.00
Orchid, crystal, bowl, jelly; Waverly shape, ftd, 6½" 60.00
Orchid, crystal, bowl, salad; Waverly shape, 9" 160.00
Orchid, crystal, candlestick, Mercury shape, 1-light 40.00
Orchid, crystal, cigarette holder, w/lid 160.00
Orchid, crystal, decanter, sherry; oval, 1-pt 225.00
Orchid, crystal, mayonnaise, hdl, 6½" 65.00
Orchid, crystal, plate, Queen Ann shape, 15½" 100.00
Orchid, crystal, plate, salad; 7" 22.00
Orchid, crystal, stem, wine; #5022 or #5025, 3-oz 75.00
Orchid, crystal, tray, celery; 12" 50.00
Orchid, crystal, vase, bud; ftd, 8" 200.00
Plantation, crystal, bowl, celery; 13" 50.00
Plantation, crystal, bowl, salad; 9" 135.00
Plantation, crystal, candle block, 1-light 90.00
Plantation, crystal, cigarette box, w/lid 180.00
Plantation, crystal, creamer, ftd 35.00
Plantation, crystal, marmalade, w/lid 140.00
Plantation, crystal, nappy, 5" 20.00
Plantation, crystal, plate, salad; 8" 32.00
Plantation, crystal, shakers, pr 70.00
Plantation, crystal, stem, claret; blown, 4½-oz 65.00
Plantation, crystal, tumbler, juice; blown, ftd, 5-oz 40.00
Plantation, crystal, vase, flared, ftd, 5" 90.00
Pleat & Panel, crystal, compote, w/lid, high ftd, 5" 35.00
Pleat & Panel, crystal, nappy, 4" 5.00
Pleat & Panel, crystal, plate, 6" 4.00
Pleat & Panel, crystal, platter, oval, 12" 15.00
Pleat & Panel, gr, bowl, vegetable; oval, 9" 35.00
Pleat & Panel, gr, pitcher, ice lip, 3-pt 145.00
Pleat & Panel, gr, plate, dinner; 10¾" 47.50
Pleat & Panel, gr, tray, spice; compartments, 10" 30.00
Pleat & Panel, pk, bowl, lemon; w/lid, 5" 40.00
Pleat & Panel, pk, marmalade, 4¾" 25.00
Pleat & Panel, pk, plate, bread; 7" 8.00
Pleat & Panel, pk, stem, saucer champagne; 5-oz 14.00
Provincial, crystal, bonbon, upturned sides, hdls, 7" 12.00
Provincial, crystal, bowl, floral; 12" 35.00
Provincial, crystal, creamer, ftd 20.00
Provincial, crystal, nappy, hdld, rnd, 5½" 15.00
Provincial, crystal, plate, snack; hdls, 7" 12.00
Provincial, crystal, stem, oyster cocktail; 3½-oz 15.00
Provincial, crystal, sugar bowl, ftd 20.00
Provincial, crystal, vase, candle; #4233, 3-light, 5" 95.00
Provincial, Limelight Green, candy box, w/lid, ftd, 5½" 550.00
Provincial, Limelight Green, mayonnaise set, plate, ladle & bowl, 7" ...150.00
Provincial, Limelight Green, nappy, 4½" 70.00
Provincial, Limelight Green, plate, luncheon; 8" 50.00

Provincial, Limelight Green, vase, violet; 3½" 95.00
Queen Ann, crystal, bowl, cream soup 15.00
Queen Ann, crystal, bowl, floral; hdls, ftd, 8½" 35.00
Queen Ann, crystal, bowl, lemon; w/lid, oval, 6½" 40.00
Queen Ann, crystal, bowl, preserve; hdls, 5" 12.00
Queen Ann, crystal, bowl, relish; triple, 10" 20.00
Queen Ann, crystal, candlestick, dolphin ft, 6", ea 50.00
Queen Ann, crystal, creamer, ind 15.00
Queen Ann, crystal, plate, cream soup liner 6.00
Queen Ann, crystal, plate, muffin; upturned sides, 12" 30.00
Queen Ann, crystal, plate, 7" 8.00
Queen Ann, crystal, saucer 3.00
Queen Ann, crystal, tray, celery; 10" 12.00
Ridgeleigh, crystal, ashtray, rnd, 4" 22.00
Ridgeleigh, crystal, bottle, rock & rye; w/#104 stopper 100.00
Ridgeleigh, crystal, bowl, floral; 11½" 50.00
Ridgeleigh, crystal, bowl, jelly; divided, hdls, 6" 14.00
Ridgeleigh, crystal, mustard jar, w/lid 50.00
Ridgeleigh, crystal, nappy, scalloped 12.00
Ridgeleigh, crystal, nappy, sq, 9" 65.00
Ridgeleigh, crystal, plate, sandwich; 13½" 50.00
Ridgeleigh, crystal, plate, scalloped, 6" 10.00
Ridgeleigh, crystal, stem, cordial; blown, 1-oz 160.00
Ridgeleigh, crystal, stem, saucer champagne; blown, 5-oz 25.00
Ridgeleigh, crystal, stem, soda; no knob in stem, ftd, 12-oz 50.00

Rose, crystal, water pitcher, Waverly blank, 73-ounces, $575.00.

Photo courtesy Gene Florence

Rose, crystal, bowl, jelly; Waverly shape, ftd, 6½" 45.00
Rose, crystal, bowl, relish; Waverly shape, 3-part, 11" 77.50
Rose, crystal, bowl, salad dressing; Queen Ann shape, 7" 50.00
Rose, crystal, butter dish, Cabochon shape, w/lid, ¼-lb 295.00
Rose, crystal, creamer, Waverly shape, ftd 35.00
Rose, crystal, finger bowl, #3309 ....95.00
Rose, crystal, ice bucket, Queen Ann shape, dolphin ft 295.00
Rose, crystal, plate, salver; Waverly shape, ftd, 12" 225.00
Rose, crystal, stem, wine; #5072, 3-oz 115.00
Rose, crystal, tray, celery; Waverly shape, 12" 60.00
Rose, crystal, vase, violet; Waverly shape, ftd, 4" 120.00
Saturn, crystal, bottle, bitters; w/short tube, blown 35.00
Saturn, crystal, bowl, pickle; 7" 15.00
Saturn, crystal, candle block, 2-light 95.00
Saturn, crystal, mustard, w/lid & paddle 60.00
Saturn, crystal, shakers, pr 45.00
Saturn, Limelight Green, bowl, baked apple 75.00
Saturn, Limelight Green, bowl, salad; 11" 140.00
Saturn, Limelight Green, creamer 180.00
Saturn, Limelight Green, plate, 6" 35.00
Saturn, Limelight Green, stem, parfait; 5-oz 110.00
Saturn, Limelight Green, tumbler, soda; 12-oz 150.00
Stanhope, crystal, bottle, oil; w/ or w/o rnd knob, 3-oz 275.00
Stanhope, crystal, bowl, salad; 11" 65.00

Stanhope, crystal, candy box, w/lid, w/ or w/o rnd knob **180.00**
Stanhope, crystal, celery tray, hdls, w/ or w/o T knobs, 12" **25.00**
Stanhope, crystal, jelly dish, hdl, w/or w/o rnd knobs, 6" **25.00**
Stanhope, crystal, plate, 7" **10.00**
Stanhope, crystal, stem, goblet; pressed, 9-oz **35.00**
Stanhope, crystal, stem, oyster cocktail; #4083, 4-oz **25.00**
Stanhope, crystal, stem, wine; pressed, 2½-oz **20.00**
Stanhope, crystal, tray, relish; hdls, 5-part, 12" **45.00**
Stanhope, crystal, tumbler, soda; #4083, 12-oz **25.00**
Stanhope, crystal, vase, hdls, w/or w/o T knobs, 9" **65.00**
Twist, crystal, bottle, French dressing **55.00**
Twist, crystal, claret, 4-oz **15.00**
Twist, crystal, saucer **3.00**
Twist, gr, bowl, nasturtium; rnd, 8" **75.00**
Twist, gr, mayonnaise **45.00**
Twist, gr, sugar bowl, zigzag hdls, w/lid **60.00**
Twist, pk, cup, zigzag hdls **25.00**
Twist, pk, nappy, 4" **22.00**
Twist, pk, stem, sherbet; 2-block stem, 5-oz **18.00**
Twist, yel, bowl, floral; 4-ftd, oval, 12" **65.00**
Twist, yel, plate, cream soup liner **15.00**
Victorian, crystal, bottle, rye; 27-oz **160.00**
Victorian, crystal, bowl, punch **265.00**
Victorian, crystal, celery tray, 12" **30.00**
Victorian, crystal, cigarette box, 4" **50.00**
Victorian, crystal, compote, cheese; for center sandwich **40.00**
Victorian, crystal, plate, buffet/punch bowl liner, 21", from $100 to .**110.00**
Victorian, crystal, plate, liner for finger bowl, 6" **10.00**
Victorian, crystal, plate, sandwich; 13" **80.00**
Victorian, crystal, stem, saucer champagne; 5-oz **17.50**
Victorian, crystal, stem, wine; 2½-oz **22.00**
Victorian, crystal, tumbler, old fashioned; 8-oz **30.00**
Victorian, crystal, vase, ftd, 6" **55.00**
Waverly, crystal, bowl, chocolate; w/lid, 5" **70.00**
Waverly, crystal, bowl, fruit; 9" **22.00**
Waverly, crystal, bowl, ice; hdls, 6½" **50.00**
Waverly, crystal, candle block, 1-light, rare **100.00**
Waverly, crystal, candle epergnette, deep, 6" **22.00**
Waverly, crystal, celery tray, 12" **18.00**
Waverly, crystal, compote, low ftd, 6" **20.00**
Waverly, crystal, cruet, w/#122 stopper, 3-oz **60.00**
Waverly, crystal, plate, luncheon; 8" **8.00**
Waverly, crystal, plate, sandwich; 14" **35.00**
Waverly, crystal, stem, cocktail; #5019, 3½-oz **10.00**
Waverly, crystal, vase, fan shape, ftd, 7" **40.00**
Yeoman, crystal, bowl, cream soup; hdls **12.00**
Yeoman, crystal, plate, grapefruit; 6½" **5.00**
Yeoman, gr, bowl, pickle/olive; rectangular, 8" **25.00**
Yeoman, gr, parfait, 5-oz **25.00**
Yeoman, gr, stem, fruit cocktail; 4-oz **9.00**
Yeoman, marigold, bowl, fruit; low, 12" **55.00**
Yeoman, marigold, plate, bouillon underliner; 6" **15.00**
Yeoman, orchid, bowl, fruit; oval, 9" **55.00**
Yeoman, orchid, sugar bowl, w/lid **60.00**
Yeoman, pk, cup **20.00**
Yeoman, pk, nappy, 4½" **7.50**
Yeoman, yel, bowl, preserve; oval, 6" **17.00**
Yeoman, yel, saucer **7.00**
Yeoman, yel, tumbler, whiskey; 2½-oz **10.00**

Heubach

Gebruder Heubach is a German porcelain company that has been in

operation since the 1800s, producing quality figurines and novelty items. They are perhaps most famous for their doll heads and piano babies, most of which are marked with the circular rising sun device containing an 'H' superimposed over a 'C.' Items with arms and hands positioned away from the body are more valuable and color of hair and intaglio eyes affect price as well. Our advisor for this category is Grace Ochsner; she is listed in the Directory under Illinois. See also Dolls, Heubach.

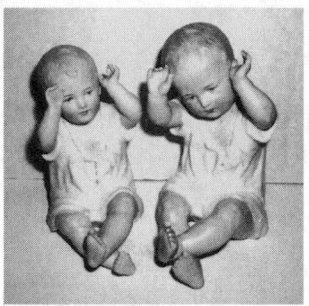

Babies, 4", $325.00; 5", $375.00.

Photo courtesy Grace Ochsner

Angry baby w/clenched hands sits before open eggshell, 5" **450.00**
Baby crawling on tummy, wht gown, bsk, 8" **550.00**
Baby in wht gown sitting & reaching for toes, 8", from $550 to .**650.00**
Baby seated in pk dress, 5", from $250 to **350.00**
Bicyclist, 11½" **450.00**
Blond boy straddling bench blowing bubbles, 9" **500.00**
Blond girl in pk pleated dress w/gr sash, 5¾" **425.00**
Blond girl stands before wicker chair, intaglio eyes, 12" **1,250.00**
Blond girl w/kitten in muff, intaglio eyes, 16" **1,100.00**
Boy in dk bl sweater, tan pants, on tummy, holds ball, 5" L **425.00**
Boy in pk swimsuit seated on stump at edge of water, 12" **550.00**
Boy in tattered suit, broom resting between ft, 8" **450.00**
Boy w/parasol, 5" **235.00**
Boy w/red hat & eyeglasses sits w/arms Xd on chair bk, 7" **675.00**
Bust of Victorian girl leaning on log, mk, 6" **625.00**
Dog, wht shaggy fur, begging pose, intaglio eyes, 9" **950.00**
Dog on haunches, wht w/tan collar, mk, 9x3⅝" **325.00**
Dutch boy, seated, yoke on shoulders, basket ea side, 5" **325.00**
Dutch boy & girl stand bk to bk, unmk, 5¼x3" **275.00**
Dutch children sitting, mk, 7¼", pr **425.00**
Dutch girl w/attached basket, flirty pose, mk, 7½" **325.00**
Dutch girl w/bucket in apron, bl & wht, 6" **275.00**
Farmer boy (& girl), 12½", pr **750.00**
Girl in bunny costume before lg pk egg, eyes to side, 7½" **525.00**
Girl stands beside vase, mk, 6½" **325.00**
Girl w/fruit baskets, unmk, 12½" **265.00**
Humidor, Jasper, gr, Indian chief on lid, 5" **275.00**
Man w/ax & lady w/baby, bsk, 12½", pr **895.00**
Nude baby running & looking bk w/fear, intaglio eyes, 7" **500.00**
Nude boy w/clenched fist, pouty face, vase at bk, 6" **400.00**
Pup w/muzzle, impressed mk, 5" **225.00**
Shepherdess w/flock, figural planter, mk, 4x10¾x2¾" **275.00**
Snow baby dressed as bear, seated, 3" **225.00**
Vase, anemones, pk on gray, gr mk, 8⅝x3" **275.00**
Vase, lady's profile w/in Nouveau floral reserve on bl, 4½" **350.00**

Hickman, Royal Arden

Born in Willamette, Oregon, Royal A. Hickman was a genius in all aspects of design interpretation. Mr. Hickman's expertise can be seen in the designs of the lovely Heisey figurines, Kosta crystal, Bruce Fox aluminum, Three Crowns aluminum, Vernon Kilns, and Royal Haeger Pottery, as well as handcrafted silver, furniture, and paintings.

Because Mr. Hickman moved around during much of his lifetime, his influence has been felt in all forms of the media. Designs from his independent companies include 'Royal Hickman Pottery and Lamps' (sold through Ceramic Arts Inc., of Chattanooga, Tennessee), 'Royal Hickman's Paris Ware,' 'Royal Hickman — Florida,' and 'California Designed by Royal Hickman.' The following listings will give examples of pieces bearing the various trademarks. Our advisor for this category is Doris Frizzell; she is listed in the Directory under Illinois. (SASE required.) See also Garden City Pottery; Royal Haeger.

Bruce Fox Aluminum

Banana leaf, sgn Royal Hickman-RH 6, 22½" L	35.00
Dish, lobster, sgn Bruce For-RH #37, lg	85.00
Dish, 3-point leaf, sgn Royal Hickman, 15½" L	30.00
Ivy tray, #362, 13"	25.00
Platter, fish, EX detail, sgn Royal Hickman-RH 3, 13x9"	85.00
Silent butler, dog's head, sgn, 8x5½"	65.00
2-acorn oak tray, 14½"	30.00
5-point leaf tray, 14"	30.00
7-point leaf tray, sgn Royal Hickman, 14"	35.00

California, Designed by Royal Hickman

Bowl, red & blk highlights, #607, 9½"	50.00
Figurine, deer, apple gr w/wht spots, appl eyes, 15"	45.00
Figurine, giraffe w/young, pk w/blk spots	75.00
Gravy boat & leaf tray	75.00
Lamp base, flying geese, 17"	250.00
Punch bowl, Tom & Jerry, w/8 mugs	350.00
Swan, red & blk highlights, #643, 17"	125.00
Vase, fluted, purple, #602, 9¼"	50.00

Miscellaneous Signatures

Vase, fish figural, Petty Crystal Glaze, #467	45.00
Vase, lg heart, sgn Royal Hickman, Italy, #3775	95.00
Vase, rooster figural, Petty Crystal Glaze, #565	125.00
Vase, sea horse shape, sgn Royal Hickman USA, #468, 8"	35.00

Royal Hickman — Florida

Vase, free-form, #578, 14"	50.00
Vase, horse's head, gray w/wht mane, 13¾"	150.00
Vase, leaf, gray, #547, 8½"	45.00
Vase, pouter pigeon, blk cascade, #599, 8½"	60.00
Vase, swan, head down, blk cascade, #3624-R, 14"	75.00

Royal Hickman — Guadalajara, Mexico

Vase, 3 dolphin figures, 14k gold decor, gold crown label, 13"	200.00

Higgins

Contemporary glass artists Frances and Michael Higgins have been designing high-quality glassware since the late 1940s. Their designs are often created by fusing layers of glass together, though sometimes colored ground glass is used to 'paint' the decoration onto the surface. Molds are used, and through a process called 'slumping,' the glass is fired to a very high temperature, causing it to soften and take on the predetermined shape. Their work is ultramodern and is more readily found in metropolitan areas.

The earliest mark was an engraved signature on the bottom of the glass — either 'Frances Stewart Higgins' or 'Michael Higgins' or both, which was dropped in favor of just 'Higgins' with a raised 'Higgins Man.' From approximately 1957 to 1964, the Higgins signature was embossed in gold on top. After 1964 up to the present the signature again appears on the bottom and is engraved in the glass. Our advisor is Dennis Hopp; he is listed in the Directory under Illinois.

Ashtray, orange & gr psychedelic florals, 11½x7"	40.00
Bowl, bl daisy, 4½"	40.00
Bowl, bl pulled feathers, 7" sq	45.00
Bowl, gr, orange & bl check w/bubbles, free-form, 9"	110.00
Bowl, gr sun ray w/bubbles, 5½"	40.00
Bowl, radiating wedges of lustred wht/ochre on gray, 12"	125.00
Bowl, wht & chartreuse stripes w/gold seaweed, 13" dia	90.00
Charger, bl & gr spikes on purple, 12½"	100.00
Charger, gr w/chartreuse spikes, 17½"	175.00
Charger, purple w/bl & gr triangles, 12"	100.00
Pendant, trees & setting sun, 2x3"	50.00
Plate, gr, orange & red fire flower, 6½" dia	40.00
Plate, pk & lav pulled leaf, 6½"	50.00
Plate, purple w/bl & gr spikes, paper label, 12½"	100.00

Tray, purple and green geometric triangles on lavender, 14x9½", $125.00.

Tray, red, orange & avocado stick man, 7x14"	125.00
Tray, turq dot rays on clear, 10" sq	85.00
Vase, radiating red lines on mottled clear/orange, 4x6"	250.00
Wall pocket, cobalt, leaf-shaped dangles, brass hanger, 38x7½"	325.00
Wall pocket, orange & red rays on clear, 10"	165.00

Historical Glass

Glassware commemorating particularly significant historical events became popular in the late 1800s. Bread trays were the most common form, but plates, mugs, pitchers, and other items were also pressed in clear as well as colored glass. It was sold in vast amounts at the 1876 Philadelphia Centennial Exposition by various manufacturers who exhibited their wares on the grounds. It remained popular well into the 20th century.

In the listings that follow, L numbers refer to a book by Lindsey, a standard guide used by many collectors. Our advisor for this category is Darlene Yohe; she is listed in the Directory under Arkansas. See also Bread Plates; Pattern Glass.

Bank, Liberty Bell	38.00
Bottle, Columbus, lay-down, metal screw lid	350.00
Bottle, Granger, L-266	110.00
Bottle, Grover Cleveland bust, clear & frosted, L-318, lg	225.00
Bust, Dewey, Manila 1898, 5"	145.00
Butter dish, Garfield Drape	85.00
Celery, Independence Hall	65.00
Compote, George Peabody	75.00

Creamer, Peace & Plenty, milk glass, pontil scar, 4⅝", NM 475.00
Cup, Harrison & Morton, bl 235.00
Cup plate, Bunker Hill 30.00
Flask, John Paul Jones 20.00
Glass, ale; Centennial 55.00
Goblet, Emblem Centennnial, L-61 ....45.00
Goblet, Pittsburgh Centennial 95.00
Hat, Uncle Sam, no pnt, L-110 ....35.00
Jar, Statue of Liberty, L-530 ....70.00
Lamp, Emblem, L-62 ....195.00
Match holder, T Roosevelt, etched, top hat form 90.00
Mug, Assassination 60.00
Mug, beer; Philadelphia Centennial 65.00
Mug, Bumper to the Flag, honeycombed, Murdock & Adams #273 ...250.00
Mug, Christopher Columbus, L-1 ....45.00
Mug, Martyrs, Lincoln & Garfield portraits 65.00
Mug, McKinley 30.00
Mug, Tennessee, L-102 ....55.00
Mustard dish, Dewey bust, w/Xd flags on lid, milk glass, 4¼" 55.00
Paperweight, Columbian Expo, lady w/upswept hair, US Glass, frosted ..145.00
Paperweight, George Washington, frosted center, rnd, Gillinder ..295.00
Paperweight, Memorial Hall, frosted, L-495 ....150.00
Paperweight, Plymouth Rock, L-18 ....90.00
Pickle dish, E Pluribus Unum 45.00
Pin tray, McKinley bust, frosted base, L-297 ....110.00
Pitcher, Garfield Drape, scarce 145.00
Plate, Atlantic City Lighthouse, Egg & Dart border, 5¼" 22.00
Plate, CA Gold Rush, Eureka 50.00
Plate, Columbus, milk glass, 9½" 65.00
Plate, Dewey, clear/frosted, sm 15.00
Plate, Frieda Hepel, Egg & Dart border, 5¼" 40.00
Plate, Grant, Patriot & Soldier, amber, sq, 9½" 50.00
Plate, Mary Had a Little Lamb, Egg & Dart border, 5¼" 25.00
Plate, McKinley 35.00
Plate, Old Glory, Egg & Dart border, 5¼" 32.00
Plate, Old State House, L-32 ....50.00
Plate, Texas Campaign, lt bl, 9½" 195.00
Plate, Yankee Doodle, Egg & Dart border, 5¼" 35.00
Platter, Carpenter's Hall 65.00
Shaker, Centennial, boot 27.00
Shot glass, Bryan & McKinley, 1896, NM 130.00
Spooner, Log Cabin, L-184 ....115.00
Statuette, Lincoln, frosted, Gillinder 385.00
Statuette, Ruth the Gleaner, frosted, 1876 Phila Expo, Gillinder .175.00
Sugar shaker, Proclaim Liberty Throughout the Land 195.00
Tumbler, Admiral Dewey, L-398 ....55.00
Tumbler, America, L-48 ....25.00
Tumbler, Lincoln Tribute, L-282 ....25.00
Tumbler, Louisiana Purchase, L-107 ....35.00
Tumbler, McKinley, L-337 ....50.00
Tumbler, Pan American Buffalo Exposition 22.00
Tumbler, Rock of Ages, L-227 ....25.00
Tumbler, whiskey; Bumper to Flag, Union Forever, flint 225.00
Tumbler, 5 stars & Flag w/13 stars & rifle 175.00
Wine, Washington Centennial 65.00

Hobbs, Brockunier & Co.

Hobbs and Brockunier's South Wheeling Glass Works was in operation during the last quarter of the 19th century. They are most famous for their peachblow, amberina, Daisy and Button, and Hobnail pattern glass. The mainstay of the operation, however, was druggist items and plain glassware — bowls, mugs, and simple footed pitchers with shell handles.

For further information we recommend *Hobbs, Brockunier & Co. Glass, Identification and Value Guide*, by Neila and Tom Bredehoft (Collector Books). See also Frances Ware.

Bitters bottle, Dew Drop, ruby 220.00
Bottle, water; Opal Swirl #325, ruby 385.00
Bowl, berry; Leaf & Flower #339, amber stain on satin, 8" 60.00
Butter dish, Oglebay #332, crystal, w/lid 85.00
Can, molasses; Polka Dot, sapphire, #98, 16-oz 185.00
Comport, Blackberry, opal, high ft, w/lid 200.00
Comport, Tree of Life w/Hand, crystal, ftd, 10" 95.00
Creamer, Mario #341, crystal w/ruby or amber stain 60.00

Cruet, Hobnail, cranberry opal with original crystal stopper, 7¼x4½", $485.00.

Ice bowl, Daisy & Button #101, canary, w/drainer 120.00
Pickle jar, Viking, satin highlights 165.00
Pitcher, Hobnail, pk satin, att, 7x6", EX 150.00
Pitcher, Maltese & Ribbon, amber ribbon on crystal, 1-qt 100.00
Sugar bowl, Dolphin, crystal w/sand-blast decor, w/lid 375.00
Sugar sifter, Peach Blow, shaded amberina plated w/opal 1,200.00
Syrup pitcher, Hobnail, amber, pewter top mk Pat Jan 29 84 .....285.00
Tumbler, Venetian, wht loopings w/red or bl threading, minimum value 850.00

Holt Howard

Novelty ceramics marked Holt Howard represent one of the newest areas of collectibles on today's market, and dealers report a good amount of market activity. Made from the '50s into the '70s, they're not only marked, but most are dated as well. There are several lines to reassemble — the rooster, the white cat, figural banks, Christmas angels and Santas, to name only a few — but the one that most Holt Howard collectors seem to gravitate toward is the pixie line. For more information see *Garage Sale and Flea Market Annual* (Collector Books). Our advisors for this category are Pat and Ann Duncan; they are listed in the Directory under Missouri.

Angel, cb cone body w/pk feathers, ceramic head, from $20 to 30.00
Ashtray, Kozy Kitten one on sq plaid base, 4 corner rests, from $60 to .75.00
Ashtray, lady w/bottle 110.00
Bank, Dandy-Lion, bobbing head, from $140 to 160.00
Bowl, cereal; Rooster, 6" 25.00
Candle holder, boy on shoe 22.00
Candle holder, Ponytail Girl on figure-8 base w/flower candle cup .60.00
Candle holders, kneeling camels, jeweled blankets, gilt bridles, pr ..35.00
Candlestick, winking Santa-head candle cup on red saucer base ..20.00
Cigarette holder, Rooster pnt on wood, wall mt, holds several packs 150.00
Cocktail olives, Pixieware, winking gr head finial 150.00
Cocktail shaker, bartender theme, +4 tumblers 75.00
Coffeepot, Rooster emb 100.00
Cookie jar, Kozy Kitten head form, from $40 to 50.00

Decanter, Pixieware, flat-head stopper w/red nose, minimum value 200.00
Demitasse pot, flared cylinder, holly & berries on wht, from $50 to .65.00
Desk accessory, eagle w/wings wide on marble base, holds 1 pen ..100.00
Dish, Christmas tree form, divided, 13⅞" 25.00
Dish, Rooster figural, open body receptacle 30.00
Egg cup, dbl; Rooster figural 40.00
Hors d'oeuvre, Pixieware, pierced body, tall hairdo, minimum value ...200.00
Hurricane lamp, Santa figural w/candle holder in hat, from $25 to ...35.00
Italian dressing bottle, Pixieware minimum value 300.00
Jam & jelly jar, Rooster emb 75.00
Letter holder, Kozy Kitten w/coiled wire bk 75.00
Match holder, pk mouse w/cane, unmk, 6" 48.00
Mug, Christmas tree w/Santa hdl 10.00
Mustard jar, Pixieware, yel head finial on lid, from $45 to 75.00
Onions jar, Onions If You Please on sign held by butler, minimum ..200.00
Pitcher, juice; winking Santa, fan-like beard, +6 mugs 95.00
Planter, camel 20.00
Planter, stylized deer head w/antlers, red nose 25.00
Russian dressing bottle, Pixieware, minimum value 300.00
Shakers, bunnies in wicker baskets, pr 45.00
Shakers, holly girl w/poinsettia w/P or S at center, pr, from $15 to ...20.00
Shakers, Kozy Kitten head form, in wireware napkin holder fr, $50 to ...75.00
Shakers, Pixieware, Salty & Peppy, flat head, pnt wood hdl, pr 65.00
Shakers, pk mouse w/red bow, 1958, 4¼", pr 40.00
Shakers, Ponytail Girl, from $60 to 75.00
Shakers, Rooster emb, pr 10.00
Shakers, Rooster figural, tall, pr, from $25 to 30.00
Shakers, Salty & Peppy raccoons, pr 30.00
Soup tureen, tomato form, lg, from $85 to 100.00
Spice set, Kozy Kitten, stacking 175.00
Syrup, Rooster emb on front, tail hdl 40.00
Tape measure, Kozy Kitten on cushion 85.00
Tray, dbl; Ponytail Girl between 2 flower cups 65.00
Votive candle holder, pig, pastel, dtd 1958, 5½" 45.00
Votive candle holder, Santa, dtd 1968, 3" 20.00

Homer Laughlin

The Homer Laughlin China Company of Newell, West Virginia, was founded in 1871. The superior dinnerware they displayed at the Centennial Exposition in Philadelphia in 1876 won the highest award of excellence. From that time to the present, they have continued to produce quality dinnerware and kitchenware, many lines of which are becoming very popular collectibles. Most of the dinnerware is marked with the name of the pattern and occasionally with the shape name as well. The 'HLC' trademark is usually followed by a number series, the first two digits of which indicate the year of its manufacture. For further information we recommend *The Collector's Encyclopedia of Fiesta, Eighth Edition*, by Sharon and Bob Huxford; *The Collector's Encyclopedia of Homer Laughlin China* by Joanne Jasper; and *Collector's Guide to Homer Laughlin's Virginia Rose* by Richard G. Racheter (all available from Collector Books). Another fine source of information is *Homer Laughlin, A Giant Among Dishes,* by Jo Cunningham (Schiffer). Our advisors for Virginia Rose are Jack and Treva Hamlin; they are listed in the Directory under Ohio.

Our values are base prices. Very desirable patterns on the shapes named in our listings may increase values by as much as 70%. See also Blue Willow; Fiesta; Harlequin; Riviera.

Dinnerware

Amberstone, ashtray, rare 30.00
Amberstone, tea server 52.00

Americana, bowl, cream soup 75.00
Americana, platter, rnd, 13" 40.00
Carnival, plate, 6½" 3.00
Carnival, teacup 6.00
Casualstone, bowl, salad; jumbo, 10" 38.00
Casualstone, pitcher, disk type 45.00
Conchita, sugar bowl, w/lid 32.00
Conchita, tumbler, fired-on design, 10-oz 20.00
Dogwood, bowl, fruit; gold trim, 5¾" 8.00
Dogwood, sauce boat, gold trim 28.00

Eggshell Georgian, teapot, $65.00.

Epicure, coffeepot, 10" 150.00
Epicure, nut dish, 4" 35.00
Hacienda, bell 95.00
Hacienda, butter dish, ½-lb 140.00
Hacienda, platter, 10" 34.00
Hacienda, teapot, rare 160.00
Jubilee, bowl, fruit 5.00
Jubilee, casserole 40.00
Max-i-cana, bowl, lug soup; 4½" 40.00
Max-i-cana, casserole 135.00
Max-i-cana, creamer, lg 26.00
Mexicana, bowl, deep, 2½x5" 44.00
Mexicana, egg cup, torpedo shape 38.00
Mexicana, sauce boat liner 32.00
Mexicana, syrup jug, Century, w/lid 425.00
Newell (various decals), bowl, fruit; 5" 4.00
Newell (various decals), plate, 10" 10.00
Newell (various decals), sugar bowl, w/lid 15.00
Pastel Nautilus, bowl, vegetable; oval 12.00
Pastel Nautilus, platter, 13" 15.00
Priscilla, bowl, vegetable; gold trim, rnd, 8" 25.00
Priscilla, plate, gold trim, 10" 15.00
Priscilla, sugar bowl, gold trim, w/lid 25.00
Rhythm, plate, rare, 8" 18.00
Rhythm, tidbit, 3-tier 40.00
Rhythm Rose, creamer 9.00
Rhythm Rose, cup & saucer, AD 18.00
Serenade, creamer 18.00
Serenade, pickle dish 20.00
Skytone, egg cup 11.00
Suntone, bowl, nappy; 8½" 9.00
Tango, bowl, baker; oval, 9" 12.00
Tango, shakers, pr 12.00
Virginia Rose, bowl, fruit; 5½" 8.00
Virginia Rose, bowl, oatmeal; 6" 15.00
Virginia Rose, bowl, vegetable; gold or silver trim, w/lid, 9" 125.00
Virginia Rose, bowl, vegetable; scarce, 7½" 32.00
Virginia Rose, creamer 20.00
Virginia Rose, egg cup, dbl 75.00
Virginia Rose, mug, coffee; gold or silver trim 65.00

Virginia Rose, pitcher, milk; 5" 80.00
Virginia Rose, plate, 9" 10.00
Virginia Rose, platter, 13" 35.00
Virginia Rose, platter/gravy liner, 9" 32.00
Virginia Rose, sauce boat 30.00
Virginia Rose, shakers, scarce, pr 150.00
Virginia Rose, tray, hdls, 8" 35.00
Wells (various decals), bowl, vegetable; oval, 9" 18.00
Wells (various decals), creamer 12.00
Wells (various decals), platter, 11" 18.00
Yellowstone (various decals), butter dish 32.00
Yellowstone (various decals), sauce boat 10.00

Art China

American Beauty, charger, 10" 150.00
American Beauty, mug 125.00
American Beauty, tankard 360.00
American Floral, tankard 360.00
Currant, bowl, ruffled, 2x10" 165.00
Currant, chocolate pot 295.00
Currant, humidor, wooden lid, 5x6" 225.00
Currant, mug 85.00
Currant, pitcher, Dutch jug, 10" 165.00
Currant, pitcher, str sides, 6½" 140.00
Currant, plate, scalloped, 10" 90.00
Currant, vase, hdls, 8" 125.00
Currant, vase, 7" 110.00
Dreamland, plaque, 10" 190.00
Dreamland, plate, open hdls, 10" 210.00
Dreamland, vase, 3½" 150.00
Flow Blue, bonbon, gold trim 180.00
Flow Blue, bowl, 17th-C child, w/gold trim, ruffled 180.00
Flow Blue, chocolate cup & saucer 180.00
Flow Blue, cuspidor, lady's, gold trim, 5½x8" 360.00
White Pets, bread tray 175.00
White Pets, pitcher, milk 215.00
White Pets, stein 180.00
White Pets, vase, hdls, 8" 275.00

Hull

The A.E. Hull Pottery was formed in 1905 in Zanesville, Ohio, and in the early years produced stoneware specialities. They expanded in 1907, adding a second plant and employing over two hundred workers. By 1920 they were manufacturing a full line of stoneware, art pottery with both airbrushed and blended glazes, florist pots, and gardenware. They also produced toilet ware and kitchen items with a white semiporcelain body. Although these continued to be staple products, after the stock market crash of 1929, emphasis was shifted to tile production. By the mid-'30 interest in art pottery production was growing, and over the next fifteen years, several lines of matt pastel floral-decorated patterns were designed, consisting of vases, planters, baskets, ewers, and bowls in various sizes.

The Red Riding Hood cookie jar, patented in 1943, proved so successful that a whole line of figural kitchenware and novelty items was added. They continued to be produced well into the '50s. (See also Little Red Riding Hood.) Through the '40s their floral artware lines flooded the market, due to the restriction of foreign imports. Although best known for their pastel matt-glazed ware, some of the lines were high gloss. Rosella, glossy coral on a pink clay body, was produced for a short time only; and Magnolia, although offered in a matt glaze, was produced in gloss as well.

The plant was destroyed in 1950 by a flood which resulted in a devastating fire when the floodwater caused the kilns to explode. The company rebuilt and equipped their new factory with the most modern machinery. It was soon apparent that the matt glaze could not be duplicated through the more modern processes, however, and soon attention was concentrated on high-gloss artware lines such as Parchment and Pine and Ebb Tide. Figural planters and novelties, piggy banks, and dinnerware were produced in abundance in the late '50s and '60s. By the mid-'70s dinnerware and florist ware were the mainstay of their business. The firm discontinued operations in 1985.

Our advisor, Brenda Roberts, has compiled a lovely book, *The Collector's Encyclopedia of Hull Pottery*, with full-color photos and current values, available from Collector Books. You will find her address in the Directory under Missouri. Another informative book is *Collector's Guide to Hull Pottery, The Dinnerware Lines*, by Barbara Loveless Gick-Burke, also available from Collector Books.

Special note to Hull collectors: reproductions are on the market in all categories of Hull pottery — matt florals, Red Riding Hood, and later lines including House 'n Garden dinnerware.

Bank, Corky Pig, pastels, 5" 105.00
Blossom Flite, basket, #T-2, 6" 80.00
Blossom Flite, cornucopia, #T-6, 10½" 105.00
Blossom Flite, ewer, #T-13, 13½" 180.00
Blossom Flite, teapot, #T-14 ....145.00
Blossom Flite, vase, #T-7, 10½" 135.00

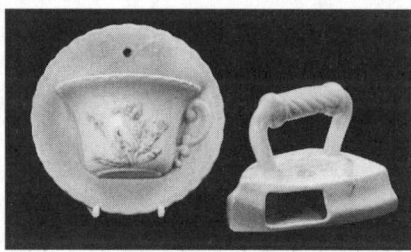

Bow-Knot wall pockets: Cup and saucer, B-24, 6", $260.00; Flatiron, unmarked, 6¼", $280.00.

Bow-Knot, candle holder, #B-17, 4" 120.00
Bow-Knot, cornucopia, #B-5, 7½" 180.00
Bow-Knot, jardiniere, #B-19, 9⅜" 1,075.00
Bow-Knot, vase, #B-11, 10½" 500.00
Bow-Knot, wall pocket, pitcher form, #B-26, 6" 260.00
Butterfly, basket, matt, #B-17, 10½" 335.00
Butterfly, ewer, matt, #B-11, 8¾" 175.00
Butterfly, serving tray, wht matt & turq w/gold, #B-23, 11½" 115.00
Butterfly, vase, #B-14, 10½" 95.00
Butterfly, vase, bud; #B-1, 6¼" 65.00
Butterfly, window box, #B-7, 12¾" 70.00
Calla Lily, bowl, #500/32, 10" 200.00
Calla Lily, vase, gr & creme, angle hdls, #560/33, 13" 450.00
Calla Lily, vase, gr to pk, angle hdls, #500/33, 8" 180.00
Camellia, basket, hanging, pk, #132, 7" 315.00
Camellia, candle holder, #117, 6½" 150.00
Camellia, cornucopia, pk, #101, 8½" 175.00
Camellia, vase, bud; pk, low hdls, #129, 7" 135.00
Camellia, vase, pk, low hdls, scalloped rim, #143, 8½" 180.00
Cinderella Kitchenware (Blossom), creamer, #28, 4½" 45.00
Cinderella Kitchenware (Blossom), pitcher, #29, 16-oz 50.00
Cinderella Kitchenware (Bouquet), bowl, mixing; #20, 7½" 50.00
Cinderella Kitchenware (Bouquet), pitcher, #22, 64-oz 175.00
Classic, vase, #5, 6" 35.00
Classic, vase, hdls, #4, 6" 35.00
Crescent Kitchenware, casserole, divided, w/lid, #35, 11½" 65.00

Crescent Kitchenware, creamer, #B-15, 4¼" 22.00
Crescent Kitchenware, shakers, #B-4/#B-5, 3½", pr 40.00
Debonair, cookie jar, pk w/blk stripe, #O-8, 8¾" 155.00
Dogwood, bowl, low, pk to turq, sm hdls, #521, 7" 180.00
Dogwood, vase, pk to turq, ornate hdls, #510, 10½" 360.00
Early Art, vase, mc w/emb ribs, stoneware, #26, 8" 85.00
Early Utility, bowl, gr w/emb ribs, rolled rim, #30, 7" 30.00
Early Utility, bowl, yel w/brn band, #106, 6" 25.00
Early Utility, flowerpot w/saucer, gr, #538, 4" 36.00
Early Utility, tankard, emb scene, yel w/brn wash, #492, 9½" 275.00
Ebb Tide, basket, shell form w/fish hdl, unmk, 6¼" 140.00
Ebb Tide, candle holder, #E-13, 2¾" 32.00
Ebb Tide, ewer, shell form w/fish hdl, #E-10, 14" 260.00
Fiesta, basket, pk & wht, #44, 6½" 65.00
Fiesta, flowerpot, blk, #40, 4¼" 30.00
Fiesta, jardiniere, floral on wht, ftd, #43, 6" 40.00
Floral, bowl, salad; #49, 10" 75.00
Floral, pitcher, #46, 6" 55.00
Floral, shakers, #44, 3½", pr 40.00
Gingerbread Man, cookie jar, gray 450.00
Gingerbread Man, cup, brn, child's 80.00
Gingerbread Man, server, Sand, 10x10" 165.00
Imperial, urn vase, blk, #454, 5" 22.00
Iris, jardiniere, pk to bl, #413, 5½" 185.00
Iris, vase, bud; pk to bl, hdls, #410, 7½" 195.00
Iris, vase, cream to pk, hdls, #402, 8½" 235.00
Magnolia, glossy; ewer, #H-11, 8½" 150.00
Magnolia, glossy; teapot, #H-20, 6½" 175.00
Magnolia, glossy; vase, low hdls, #H-13, 10½" 170.00
Magnolia, glossy; vase, ring hdls, #H-7, 6½" 60.00
Magnolia, glossy; vase, swan hdls, #H-16, 12½" 250.00
Magnolia, matt; candle holder, low hdls, #27, 4" 50.00
Magnolia, matt; dbl cornucopia, #6, 12" 195.00
Magnolia, matt; ewer, #18, 13½" 380.00
Magnolia, matt; vase, low hdls, #16, 15" 500.00
Magnolia, matt; vase, low hdls, #9, 10½" 195.00
Magnolia, matt; vase, open hdls, #21, 12½" 450.00
Mardi Gras, bowl, mixing; pk, emb ribs, flared rim, unmk, 10¼" ..45.00
Mardi Gras/Granada, ewer, emb floral on yel to pk, #31, 10" 160.00
Mardi Gras/Granada, vase, pk to bl, hdls, #49, 9" 60.00
Mardi Gras/Granada, vase, yel, low hdls, #49, 9" 55.00
Mirror Almond, bowl, soup/salad; 6½" 7.00
Mirror Almond, jug, 2-qt 30.00
Mirror Almond, plate, luncheon; 9⅜" 7.00
Mirror Almond, stein 7.00
Mirror Brown, bake 'n serve dish, #573 ....10.00
Mirror Brown, baker, rectangular, #567 ....35.00
Mirror Brown, bean pot, w/lid, 2-qt 40.00
Mirror Brown, bowl, divided vegetable; #542, 7x10⅞" 14.00
Mirror Brown, bowl, salad; w/rooster imprint, oval, #508 ....75.00
Mirror Brown, casserole, oval, w/chicken lid, 2-qt 60.00
Mirror Brown, casserole, w/duck lid, #5770, 2-qt 75.00
Mirror Brown, coffee cup, #597, 7-oz 4.00
Mirror Brown, Dutch oven, #565, 2-pc 35.00
Mirror Brown, gravy boat & underplate, #540 ....42.00
Mirror Brown, jug, water; #509, 80-oz 30.00
Mirror Brown, pie plate, #566, 9½" 20.00
Mirror Brown, plate, steak; oval, #541, 9x11⅞" 16.00
Mirror Brown, server, w/hdl, #873H 85.00
Mirror Brown, spoon rest, w/Spoon Rest imprint, #594 ....35.00
Novelty, baby shoes, brn, unmk, 3½" 65.00
Novelty, candle holder, Bandana Duck, #77, 3½x3½" 40.00
Novelty, colt figurine, blk & wht, unmk, 5½" 65.00
Novelty, dog w/yarn planter, #88, 5½x8" 32.00

Novelty, flower wall pocket, #71 ....60.00
Novelty, goose planter, #411, 12¼" 40.00
Novelty, kitten doorstop, yel w/pk bow, #61, 7½" 320.00
Novelty, parrot planter, #60, 9½" 45.00
Novelty, shrimp planter, yel, 1940, #201, 5" 40.00
Nuline Bak-Serve, pitcher, bl, B-29, 8½" 120.00
Orchid, bookends, bl, #316, 7", pr 1,350.00
Orchid, ewer, pk to bl, #311, 13" 725.00
Orchid, vase, bl, hdls, #302, 6" 165.00
Orchid, vase, pk to bl, hdls, #304, 10¼" 410.00
Parchment & Pine, basket, #S-3 ....120.00
Parchment & Pine, bowl, console; #S-9 ....135.00
Parchment & Pine, creamer, #S-2 ....45.00
Parchment & Pine, ewer, #S-7, 14¼" 240.00
Poppy, basket, yel to pk, #601, 12" 900.00
Poppy, lamp base, unnamed design, yel, unmk, 9" 510.00
Poppy, vase, turq to pk, hdls, #606, 10½" 425.00
Rosella, lamp base, unmk, 6¾" 260.00
Rosella, vase, #R-2, 5" 95.00
Rosella, vase, heart shape, #R-8, 6½" 140.00
Royal Imperial, jardiniere, #75, 7" 55.00
Royal Woodland, bowl, console; turq w/gray, #W-29, 14½" 95.00
Serenade, bonbon basket, #S-5, 6¾" 145.00
Serenade, pitcher, #S-21, 10½" 220.00
Serenade, teapot, #S-17, 5" 195.00
Serenade, vase, #S-12, 14" 140.00
Sueno Tulip, ewer, pk to bl, #101-33, 9" 500.00
Sueno Tulip, vase, bud; pk to bl, #106-33, 6" 130.00
Sueno Tulip, vase, cream to bl, hdls, #106-33, 6" 125.00
Sunglow, ewer, #90, 5½" 45.00
Sunglow, pitcher, #55, 7½" 145.00
Sunglow, salt shaker, #54, 2¾", ea 15.00
Sunglow, vase, hdls, #95, 8½" 75.00
Thistle & Pinecone, vase, pk, hdls, #52, 6½" 125.00
Tokay, cornucopia, #10, 11" 75.00
Tokay, ewer, #13, 12" 290.00
Tokay, vase, #6, 10" 100.00
Tuscany, basket, #6, 8" 85.00
Tuscany, bowl, fruit; #7, 9½" 165.00
Tuscany, consolette, #16, 15¾" 185.00
Tuscany, cornucopia, #1, 6½" 48.00
Utility, flowerpot, emb basketweave on gr, 4" 40.00
Water Lily, bowl, console; #L-21, 13½" 220.00
Water Lily, cornucopia, dbl; #L-27, 12" 215.00
Water Lily, creamer, #L-19, 5" 80.00
Water Lily, jardiniere, #L-24, 8½" 340.00
Water Lily, vase, hdls, #L-8, 8½" 160.00
Wildflower, basket, #W-16, 10½" 360.00

Wildflower, cornucopia vase, W-10, 8½", $78.00.

Wildflower, ewer, #W-19, 13½" 450.00
Wildflower, ewer, #W-2, 5½" 75.00

Wildflower, vase, angle hdls, #W-1, 5½" 50.00
Wildflower (# series), bowl, console; #70, 12" 425.00
Wildflower (# series), candle holder, dbl; #69, 4" 150.00
Wildflower (# series), sugar bowl, high hdls, open, #74, 4¾" 275.00
Woodland, glossy; cornucopia, #W-2, 5½" 45.00
Woodland, glossy; ewer, #W-6, 6½" 80.00
Woodland, glossy; flowerpot/saucer, #W-11, 5¾" 125.00
Woodland, glossy; jardiniere, #W-7, 5½" 85.00
Woodland, glossy; vase, dbl bud; #W-13, 8½" 120.00
Woodland, matt; basket, #W-22, 10½" 975.00
Woodland, matt; cornucopia, #W-5, 6½" 75.00
Woodland, matt; ewer, #W-24, 13½" 950.00
Woodland, matt; flowerpot/saucer, #W-11, 5¾" 185.00
Woodland, matt; vase, dbl bud; #W-15, 8½" 215.00
Woodland, matt; vase, low hdls, petal ft, #W-16, 8½" 225.00
Woodland, matt; vase, yel to gr, hdls, post-1950, #W-16, 8½" ...195.00

Hummel

Hummel figurines were created through the artistry of Berta Hummel, a Franciscan nun called Sister M. Innocentia. The first figures were made about 1935 by Franz Goebel of Goebel Art Inc., Rodental, Germany. Plates, plaques, and candy dishes are also produced, and the older, discontinued editions are highly sought collectibles. Generally speaking, an issue can be dated by the trademark. The first Hummels, from 1935 to 1949, were either incised or stamped with the 'Crown WG' mark. The 'full bee in V' mark was employed with minor variations until 1959. At that time the bee was stylized and represented by a solid disk with angled symetrical wings completely contained within the confines of the 'V.' The three-line mark, 1964 – 1972, utilized the stylized bee and included a three-line arrangement, 'c by W. Goebel, W. Germany.' Another change in 1972 saw the 'stylized bee in V' suspended between the vertical bars of the 'b' and 'l' of a printed 'Goebel, West Germany.' Collectors refer to this mark as the 'last bee' or 'Goebel bee.' The mark in use from 1979 to 1990 omits the 'bee in V.' The current mark, New Crown, in use since 1991 is a small crown with 'WG' initials, a large 'Goebel,' and a small 'Germany' signifying a united Germany. For further study we recommend Hummel, An Illustrated Handbook and Price Guide, by Ken Armke; Hummel Figurines and Plates, A Collector's Identification and Value Guide, by Carl Luckey; The No. 1 Price Guide to M.I. Hummel by Robert L. Miller; and The Fascinating World of M.I. Hummel by Goebel. These books are available through your local book dealer. See also Limited Edition Plates.

Key:
ce — closed edition   LB — last bee
CM — crown mark   MB — missing bee
cn — closed number   oe — open edition
FB — full bee   tw — temporarily withdrawn
NC — new crown mark   3L — three-line mark
SB — stylized bee

#III, 110, Let's Sing, box, CM, ce, 6¼" 540.00
#III/53, Joyful, box, 3L, ce, 5¾" 180.00
#III/58, Playmates, box, CM, ce, 6¾" 540.00
#III/63, Singing Lesson, box, CM, ce, 6¾" 540.00
#10/III, Flower Madonna, color, FB, ce, 12½" 575.00
#100, Shrine, table lamp, CM, ce, 7½" 5,760.00
#103, Farewell, table lamp, CM, ce, 7½" 5,760.00
#105, Adoration w/Bird, CM, ce, 4¾" 5,040.00
#107, Little Fiddler, plaque w/wood fr, CM, ce, 6x6" 3,600.00
#109/0, Happy Traveler, SB, ce, 5" 160.00
#11 2/0, Merry Wanderer, CM, ce, 4¼" 325.00

#111/I, Wayside Harmony, SB, ce, 5¼" 290.00
#112, Just Resting, CM, ce, 5½" 505.00
#114, Let's Sing, ashtray, 3L, ce, 3½x6¼" 120.00
#118, Little Thrifty, bank, CM, ce, 5¼" 360.00
#12/I, Hear Ye, Hear Ye, FB, ce, 6" 320.00
#121A, Wayside Harmony, bookend on wooden base, CM, ce .3,600.00
#123, Max & Moritz, LB, ce, 5¼" 190.00
#125, Vacation Time, plaque, MB, tw, 4x4¾" 135.00
#127, Doctor, CM, ce, 5" 325.00
#128, Baker, FB, ce, 5" 250.00
#13/0, Meditation, CM, ce, 5½" 505.00
#130, Duet, 3L, ce, 5¼" 240.00
#132, Star Gazer, NC, oe, 5" 165.00
#134, Quartet, plaque, SB, ce, 5½x6¼" 270.00
#135, Soloist, 3L, ce, 4¾" 130.00
#137A, Child in Bed (looking left), plaque, CM, ce, 3x3" 3,600.00
#140, The Mail Is Here, plaque, CM, ce, 4¼x6¾" 470.00

#141/III/0, Goebel bee in V mark, ca 1972, style B (no bird in tree), $160.00.

#141, Apple Tree Girl, FB, ce, 6½" 430.00
#142, Apple Tree Boy, CM, ce, 6½" 575.00
#143/0, Boots, SB, ce, 5¼" 215.00
#145, Little Guardian, LB, ce, 4" 130.00
#147, Angel Shrine, font, NC, oe, 3x5" 40.00
#150/0, Happy Days, FB, ce, 5" 380.00
#152A, Umbrella Boy, CM, ce, 8" 2,880.00
#153, Auf Wiedersehen, CM, ce, 7" 650.00
#154, Waiter, CM, ce, 6½" 610.00
#16/2/0, Little Hiker, MB, ce, 4" 100.00
#163, Whitsuntide, MB, ce, 6¾" 245.00
#166, Boy w/Bird, ashtray, FB, ce, 3¼x6" 200.00
#169, Bird Duet, SB, ce, 4" 150.00
#17/0, Congratulations, CM, ce, 5¾" 430.00
#170/I, School Boys, NC, oe, 7½" 950.00
#171, Little Sweeper, 3L, ce, 4¼" 135.00
#173/0, Festival Harmony (flute), 3L, ce, 8" 290.00
#174, She Loves Me, She Loves Me Not, FB, ce, 4¼" 250.00
#176/I, Happy Birthday, CM, ce, 5½" 575.00
#179, Coquettes, SB, ce, 5" 325.00
#180, Tuneful Good Night, plaque, SB, ce, 5x4¾" 250.00
#181, Old Man Reading Newspaper, cn, 6¾" 10,800.00
#183, Forest Shrine, SB, ce, 9" 505.00
#185, Accordion Boy, MB, ce, 5" 160.00
#19, Prayer Before Battle, ashtray, CM, cn, 5½" 3,600.00
#190, Old Woman Walking to Market, cn, 6¾" 10,800.00
#192, Candlelight, candle holder, long candle, SB, ce, 7" 430.00
#196/0, Telling Her Secret, NC, oe, 5¼" 240.00
#198/I, Home From Market, FB, ce, 5½" 290.00
#2/I, Little Fiddler, FB, ce, 7¾" 470.00
#200, Little Goat Herder, CM, ce, 5½" 470.00

#201 2/0, Retreat to Safety, SB, ce, 4"	200.00
#205, MI Hummel Dealer's Plaque (German), FB, ce, 5½x4¼"	720.00
#207, Heavenly Angel, font, CM, ce, 3x5"	250.00
#209, MI Hummel Dealer's Plaque (Swedish), FB, ce, 5½x4"	2,880.00
#21/II, Heavenly Angel, SB, ce, 8½"	430.00
#211, MI Hummel Dealer's Plaque (English), FB, ce, 5½x4"	14,400.00
#218/0, Birthday Serenade, FB, ce, 5¼"	630.00
#22/I, Angel w/Bird, font, FB, ce, 3½"	290.00
#223, To Market, table lamp, SB, ce, 9½"	470.00
#226, The Mail Is Here, 3L, ce, 4¼x6"	505.00
#227, She Loves Me, She...Not, table lamp, LB, ce, 7½"	290.00
#23/I, Adoration, 3L, ce, 6½"	325.00
#230, Apple Tree Boy, table lamp, FB, ce, 7½"	650.00
#231, Birthday Serenade, table lamp, FB, ce, 9¾"	1,440.00
#237, Star Gazer, plaque, FB, cn, 4¾x5"	7,200.00
#238C, Angel w/Trumpet, SB, ce, 2"	70.00
#239A, Girl w/Nosegay, SB, ce, 3½"	70.00
#24/III, Lullaby, candle holder, FB, ce, 6¼"	685.00
#242, Joyous Angel News w/Trumpet, font, cn	1,080.00
#256, Knitting Lesson, 3L, ce, 7½"	450.00
#257, For Mother, SB, ce, 5"	450.00
#26, Child Jesus, font, CM, ce, 3x5¾"	250.00
#260, Lg Nativity Set (wooden stable), 3L, ce, 16-pc	3,930.00
#260K, Little Tooter (lg nativity set), 3L, ce, 5⅛"	150.00
#264, Heavenly Angel (annual plate, 1971), 3L, ce, 7½"	540.00
#266, Globe Trotter (annual plate, 1973), LB, ce, 7½"	145.00
#27/I, Joyous News, FB, ce, 2¾"	180.00
#28/III, Wayside Devotion, FB, ce, 8¾"	720.00
#284, Feeding Time (annual plate, 1984), MB, ce, 7½"	125.00
#300, Bird Watcher, LB, ce, 5"	190.00
#305, The Builder, SB, ce, 5½"	720.00
#308, Little Tailor, 3L, ce, 5½"	720.00
#311, Kiss Me, LB, ce, 6"	250.00
#315, Mountaineer, 3L, ce, 5"	200.00
#322, Little Pharmacist, SB, ce, 6"	540.00
#332, Soldier Boy, SB, ce, 6"	720.00
#336, Close Harmony, SB, ce, 5½"	720.00
#34, Singing Lesson, ashtray, CM, ce, 3½"-6¼"	325.00
#342, Mischief Maker, 3l, ce, 5"	540.00
#344, Feathered Friends, 3L, ce, 4¾"	540.00
#348, Ring Around the Rosie, 3L, ce, 6¾"	2,520.00
#355, Autumn Harvest, MB, ce, 5"	170.00
#358, Shining Light, 3L, ce, 2¾"	125.00
#36/I, Child w/Flowers, font, FB, ce, 3½x4½"	200.00
#360A, Boy & Girl, wall vase, SB, ce, 4½x6"	380.00
#362, I Forgot, FB, ce, 5½"	2,880.00
#372, Blessed Mother, 3L, ce, 10¼"	2,160.00
#377, Bashful, LB, ce, 4¾"	175.00
#380, Daisies Don't Tell, LB, ce, 5"	720.00
#383, Going Home, LB, ce, 5"	1,440.00
#384, Easter Time, 3L, ce, 4"	720.00
#386, On Secret Path, 3L, ce, 5¼"	720.00
#389, Girl w/Sheet of Music, 3L, ce, 2½"	125.00
#391, Girl w/Trumpet, 3L, ce, 2½"	125.00
#393, Dove, font, 3L, ce, 2¾x4¼"	1,440.00
#395, Shepherd Boy, LB, ce, 6¾"	2,160.00
#397, The Poet, NC, oe, 6¼"	180.00
#399, Valentine Joy, MB, ce, 5¾"	215.00
#4, Little Fiddler, MB, ce, 5¼"	180.00
#403, An Apple a Day, MB, ce, 6½"	240.00
#406, Pleasant Journey, MB, ce, 7⅛x6½"	1,980.00
#411, Do I Dare, LB, ce, 6"	2,160.00
#413, Whistler's Duet, MB, ce, 4¼"	360.00
#415, Thoughtful, MB, ce, 4½"	190.00

#422, What Now?, MB, ce, 5¼"	250.00
#44B, Out of Danger, table lamp, FB, ce, 9"	305.00
#45/I, Madonna w/Halo, color, CM, ce, 10½"	215.00
#47/II, Goose Girl, FB, ce, 7"	505.00
#48/V, Madonna, plaque, SB, ce, 8¾x10¾"	720.00
#50/0, Volunteers, CM, ce, 5½"	610.00
#52/I, Going to Grandma's, CM, ce, 6"	900.00
#54, Silent Night, candle holder, SB, ce, 3½x4¾"	340.00
#59, Skier, FB, ce, 6"	290.00
#6/II, Sensitive Hunter, CM, ce, 7¼"	1,080.00
#65/I, Farewell, FB, ce, 4¾"	325.00
#67, Doll Mother, LB, ce, 4½"	175.00
#69, Happy Pastime, FB, ce, 3½"	215.00
#7/0, Merry Wanderer, 3L, ce, 6"	270.00
#70, Holy Child, 3L, ce, 7"	235.00
#71/I, Stormy Weather, MB, ce, 6"	365.00
#73, Little Helper, FB, ce, 4¼"	180.00
#75, White Angel, font, 3L, ce, 4"	45.00
#79, Globetrotter, MB, ce, 5"	160.00
#8, Book Worm, SB, ce, 4¼"	250.00
#81/0, School Girl, SB, ce, 5"	215.00
#83, Angel Serenade (w/lamb), FB, ce, 5½"	360.00
#85/0, Serenade, CM, ce, 5"	290.00
#88/I, Heavenly Protection, MB, ce, 6½"	365.00
#91A&B, Angels at Prayer, fonts, CM, ce, 3⅜x5"	290.00
#92, Merry Wanderer, plaque, SB, ce, 4½x5"	160.00
#94 3/0, Surprise, CM, ce, 4"	325.00
#95, Brother, 3L, ce, 5½"	200.00
#97, Trumpet Boy, 3L, ce, 4½"	130.00
#98, Sister, FB, ce, 5¾"	250.00
III/38/I, Angel, Joyous News w/Lute, FB, ce, 2½"	180.00

Hutschenreuther

The Porcelain Factory C.M. Hutschenreuther operated in Bavaria from 1814 to 1969. After the death of the elder Hutschenreuther in 1845, his son Lorenz took over operations, continuing there until 1857 when he left to establish his own company in the nearby city of Selb. The original manufactory became a joint stock company in 1904, absorbing several other potteries. In 1969 both Hutschenreuther firms merged, and that company still operates in Selb. They have distributing centers in both France and the United States.

Candle holder, lg angel, color, 12"	275.00
Cup & saucer, demi; gray & blk random dmns on wht, angle hdl	40.00
Figurine, cardinal, red	85.00
Figurine, cockatoo, 11"	100.00
Figurine, Deco dancer w/flowing hair, arms out, Tutter, 11½"	750.00
Figurine, Deco girl running w/Borzoi, wht w/gold trim	225.00
Figurine, lady playing flute, US Zone	195.00
Figurine, leopard crouched/looking bk, K Tutter, 11¼" L	345.00
Figurine, Madonna & Child	135.00
Figurine, skater in bl doing sit spin	195.00
Figurine, 2 tigers on base, pnt porc, 1920s, 9½" L	800.00
Plate, Catalina Orchid, 11" sq	65.00
Plate, yel chrysanthemums, gold rim, 7¾"	16.00

Imari

Imari is a generic term which covers a broad family of wares. It was made in more than a dozen Japanese villages, but the name is that of the port from whence it was shipped to Europe. There are several types of Imari. The most common features a design with panels of birds, florals, or people surrounding a central basket of flowers. The colors used in this type are underglaze blue with overglaze red, gold, and green enamels. The Chinese also made Imari wares which differ from the Japanese type in several ways — the absence of spur marks, a thinner-type body, and a more consistent control of the blue. Imari-type wares were copied on the Continent by Meissen and by English potters, among them Worcester, Derby, and Bow. Unless noted otherwise, our values are for Japanese ware.

Biscuit jar, ca 1900-20, 7½" 200.00
Bowl, apple blossoms/foliage, mc, scalloped, 19th C, 11" L 195.00
Bowl, birds & foliage, flower petal border, 19th C, 9¼" 385.00
Bowl, floral central reserve/garden reserves, 18th C, 11½" 625.00
Bowl, shishi among peonies, deep, 19th C, 16¼" 2,000.00
Bowl, 4 cloud reserves w/lion & people, 19th C, 4¼x9", EX 260.00
Charger, bamboo/peonies/chrysanthemums, 18th C, 18½" 1,500.00
Charger, central floral reserve/6 border reserves, 12" 190.00
Charger, floral reserves, shallow, mid 19th C, 24" dia, VG 1,750.00
Charger, floral/bird/butterfly, gold trim, late, 12" 110.00
Charger, pine & floral reserve, sm rim reserves, ca 1900, 16" ..1,150.00
Charger, scenic, bl & rust w/mc, bl & wht reserve, 1830-50, 18" ..495.00
Charger, 3 lady-in-garden reserves, late, 12½" 120.00
Jar, cranes/pines/peonies, 3-lobe collar, late 17th C, 16" 1,000.00
Plate, Chrysanthemum, bl/red/gr w/gold mk, 9½", 6 for 400.00
Plate, floral vase & sprigs, 2 borders, gold trim, 18th C, 9" 140.00
Umbrella stand, birds & florals, cylindrical, 24" 1,100.00

Imperial Glass Company

The Imperial Glass Company was organized in 1901 in Bellaire, Ohio, and started manufacturing glassware in 1904. Their early products were jelly glasses, hotel tumblers, etc., but by 1910 they were making a name for themselves by pressing quantities of carnival glass, the iridescent glassware that was popular during that time. In 1914 NuCut was introduced to imitate cut glass. The line was so popular that it was made in crystal and colors and was reintroduced as Collector's Crystal in the 1950s. From 1916 to 1920 they used the lustre process to make a line called Imperial Jewels. Free-Hand ware, art glass made entirely by hand using no molds, was made from 1922 to 1928.

The company entered bankruptcy in 1931 but was able to continue operations and reorganize as the Imperial Glass Corporation. In 1936 Imperial introduced the Candlewick line, for which it is best known. In the late thirties the Vintage Grape Milk Glass line was added, and in 1951 a major ad campaign was launched, making Imperial one of the leading milk glass manufacturers.

In 1940 Imperial bought the molds and assets of the Central Glass Works of Wheeling, West Virginia; in 1958 they acquired the molds of the Heisey Company and in 1960 the molds of the Cambridge Glass Company of Cambridge, Ohio. Imperial used these molds, and after 1951 they marked their glassware with an 'I' superimposed over the 'G' trademark. The company became a subsidiary of Lenox in 1973; subsequently an 'L' was added to the 'IG' mark. In 1981 Lenox sold Imperial to Arthur Lorch, a private investor (who modified the L by adding a line at the top angled to the left, giving rise to the 'ALIG' mark). He in turn sold the company to Robert F. Stahl, Jr., in 1982. Mr. Stahl filed for Chapter 11 to reorganize, but in mid-1984 liquidation was ordered, and all assets were sold. A few items that had been made in '84 were marked with an 'N' superimposed over the 'I' for 'New Imperial.'

For more information, we recommend *Imperial Glass Encyclopedia, Vols I and II*, edited by James Measell. Our advisor is Joan Cimini; she is listed in the Directory under Ohio. See also Candlewick; Carnival Glass; Glass Animals and Figurines; Stretch Glass.

Basket, Crocheted Crystal, 12" 60.00
Basket, ruby slag, #475, mini 55.00
Basket bowl, Katy, bl opal 225.00
Bottle, cordial; Cape Cod, Ritz Blue, #160/256, 18-oz 250.00
Bowl, berry; Katy, bl opal, flat rim 30.00
Bowl, Cape Cod, crystal, hdls, #160/51F, 6" 33.00
Bowl, cereal; Katy, bl opal, deep 65.00
Bowl, dessert; Cape Cod, crystal, lug hdl, #160/197, 4½" 40.00
Bowl, Dmn Quilt, blk, crimped, 7" 20.00
Bowl, Grape, caramel slag, #47c, 10" 90.00
Bowl, jelly; Beaded Block, bl opal, hdld 45.00
Bowl, Katy, bl opal, 5⅞" 37.50
Bowl, mayonnaise; Crocheted Crystal, 5¼" 12.50
Bowl, Pillar Flutes, lt bl, 10" 35.00
Bowl, Pipe, ruby slag, #1605, 7½" 40.00
Bowl, Rose, jade slag, #52c, 8" 58.00
Bowl, Rose, jade slag, #62c, 9" 75.00
Bowl, salad; Cape Cod, crystal, #7608A, 11" 90.00
Bowl, salad; Crocheted Crystal, 10½" 27.50
Bowl, soup; Katy, gr opal, 7" 80.00
Bowl, vegetable; Katy, bl opal, 9" 95.00
Cake stand, Crocheted Crystal, ftd, 12" 40.00
Candle holder, Cape Cod, crystal, #160/170, 3" 26.50
Candle holder, Crocheted Crystal, dbl, 4½" 17.50
Candlesticks, Dolphin, caramel slag, 3779, 5", pr 70.00
Candlesticks, Free-Hand, clear w/red knops & threads, 11", pr ...1,400.00
Champagne, Cape Cod, amber, #1602 ....25.00
Claret, Cape Cod, Azalea, #1602 ....20.00
Cocktail, Cape Cod, crystal, #160b 12.00
Cocktail, Cape Cod, ruby, #160 ....27.00
Comport, Cape Cod, crystal, #160F, 5¼" 27.50
Comport, Katy, milk glass, 4¾" 45.00
Cordial, Collector's Crystal, crystal, #612 ....14.00
Cordial, Fancy Colonial, pk, #582, 1-oz 50.00
Creamer, Cape Cod, crystal, #160/30 ....12.00
Creamer, Crocheted Crystal 35.00
Cruet, Collector's Crystal, caramel slag, #505 ....50.00
Cruet, Octagon, jade, w/stopper, #505 ....80.00
Cup, Katy, bl opal 35.00
Cup & saucer, Pillar Flutes, lt bl 25.00
Decanter, bourbon; Cape Cod, crystal, #160/260 ....80.00
Decanter, Cask #1, Antique Blue 55.00
Decanter, Grape, Heather, #8 ....55.00
Goblet, Cape Cod, Evergreen, #160, 14-oz 55.00
Goblet, Chroma, ruby, #123 ....30.00
Gravy bowl, Cape Cod, crystal, #160/202, 18-oz 70.00
Hors d'oeuvre dish, Crocheted Crystal, rnd, 4-part, 10½" 30.00
Ivy ball, Reeded (Spun), red, crystal ft, 4" 65.00
Jar, vanity; Reeded (Spun), pk, #701, 7⅝" 45.00
Ladle, punch; Cape Cod, crystal 25.00
Lamp, hurricane; Crocheted Crystal, 11" 37.50
Mayonnaise, Katy, bl opal, w/underplate 120.00
Mayonnaise, Katy, gr opal, 3-pc 135.00
Mint dish, Cape Cod, crystal, heart shape, #160/49, 5" 25.00
Nappy, Pansy, caramel slag, hdl, 5" 40.00
Pitcher, Cape Cod, crystal, #160/24, 2-qt 125.00
Pitcher, Dew Drop, opal, #624, 56-oz 65.00
Pitcher, Windmill, red slag, satin 55.00
Plate, cheese & cracker; crystal, ftd, 12" 35.00
Plate, Crocheted Crystal, 14" 22.50
Plate, dinner; Cape Cod, crystal, #160/10D, 10" 37.50
Plate, Katy, bl opal, 6" 20.00
Plate, salad; Katy, bl opal, 8" 32.00
Platter, Katy, gr opal, 13" 175.00

Punch bowl, Crocheted Crystal, 14" 65.00
Punch cup, Crocheted Crystal, closed hdl 5.00
Relish, Cape Cod, crystal, 5-part, #160/102, 11" 75.00
Relish, Crocheted Crystal, 3-part, 11½" 25.00
Shakers, Cape Cod, crystal, #160/109, pr 20.00
Shakers, Cape Cod, Fern Green, #160/117, pr 75.00
Shakers, Cape Cod, Sunshine Yellow, #160/117, pr 75.00
Sherbet, Cane #666½ (Huckabee), pk, ftd 25.00

Stem, Fancy Colonial, green,
#582, one-ounce, $45.00.

Stem, cocktail; Crocheted Crystal, 4½" 12.50
Stem, cordial; Cape Cod, crystal, #1502, 1½-oz 10.00
Sugar bowl, Crocheted Crystal 15.00
Sugar bowl, Crocheted Crystal 12.50
Sugar bowl, Katy, bl opal 42.50
Toothpick holder, Octagon, caramel slag, #505 ....18.00
Tumbler, Katy, gr opal, 9-oz 55.00
Tumbler, whiskey; Cape Cod, crystal, #160, 2½-oz 12.50
Vase, bud; Free-Hand, hearts/vines, lt gr on opal, 8½" 350.00
Vase, bud; peach & butterscotch w/mirror finish, 10" 225.00
Vase, Cape Cod, crystal, urn form w/hdls, #160/186, 10½" 165.00
Vase, Free Hand, marigold irid, shouldered w/flared rim, 7" 175.00
Vase, Free-Hand, Drag Loops, bl on wht, 11½x5" 875.00
Vase, Free-Hand, gold w/pk & orange irid, ovoid, 10" 350.00
Vase, Free-Hand, hearts/vines, bl on orange irid, 9" 350.00
Vase, Free-Hand, hearts/vines, gr on wht opaque, 8¾" 650.00
Vase, Free-Hand, hearts/vines, opal on cobalt, gold int, 10½" 700.00
Vase, Free-Hand, hearts/vines, orange on cobalt, bulbus, 6" 600.00
Vase, Free-Hand, hearts/vines, wht on cobalt, label, 4⅝x6" 650.00
Vase, Free-Hand, hearts/vines, wht on jade gr, orange int, 10" ...850.00
Vase, Free-Hand, swags, bl opal on olive irid, 11½" 800.00
Vase, Katy, bl opal, #743n, 5½" 60.00
Vase, Katy, bl opal, #743x, 4½" 45.00
Vase, Katy, red, #743b, 5¼" 65.00
Vase, Mosaic, cobalt shaded & swirled w/opal, orange int, 6½" .490.00
Vase, Reeded, cobalt, squat, 5¾" 65.00
Vase, Reeded (Spun), red, 9" 75.00

Imperial Porcelain

The Blue Ridge Mountain Boys were created by cartoonist Paul Webb and translated into three-dimension by the Imperial Porcelain Corporation of Zanesville, Ohio, in 1947. These figurines decorated ashtrays, vases, mugs, bowls, pitchers, planters, and other items. The Mountain Boys series were numbered 92 through 108, each with a different and amusing portrayal of mountain life. Imperial also produced American Folklore miniatures, twenty-three tiny animals one inch or less in size, and the Al Capp Dogpatch series. Because of financial difficulties, the company closed in 1960.

American Folklore Miniatures

Cat, 1½" 50.00
Cow, 1¾" 45.00
Hound dogs 60.00
Plaque, store ad, Am Folklore Porcelain Miniatures, 4½" 450.00
Sow 45.00

Blue Ridge Mountain Boys by Paul Webb

Ashtray, #101, man w/jug & snake 120.00
Ashtray, #103, hillbilly & skunk 120.00
Ashtray, #105, baby, hound dog, & frog 125.00
Ashtray, #106, Barrel of Wishes, w/hound 115.00
Ashtray, #92, 2 men by tree stump, for pipes 125.00
Box, cigarette; #98, dog atop, baby at door, sq 150.00
Dealer's sign, Handcrafted Paul Webb Mtn Boys, rare, 9" 700.00
Decanter, #100, outhouse, man, & bird 125.00
Decanter, #104, Ma leaning over stump, w/baby & skunk 125.00
Decanter, man, jug, snake, & tree stump, Hispch Inc, 1946 ......125.00
Figurine, #101, man leans against tree trunk, 5" 125.00
Figurine, man on hands & knees, 3" 125.00
Figurine, man sitting, 3½" 110.00
Figurine, man sitting w/chicken on knee, 3" 125.00
Jug, #101, Willie & snake 95.00
Mug, #94, Bearing Down, 6" 95.00
Mug, #94, dbl baby hdl, 4¼" 95.00
Mug, #94, ma hdl, 4¼" 95.00
Mug, #94, man w/bl pants hdl, 4¼" 95.00
Mug, #94, man w/yel beard & red pants hdl, 4¼" 95.00
Mug, #99, Target Practice, boy on goat, farmer, 5¾" ...95.00
Pitcher, lemonade 200.00
Planter, #100, outhouse, man, & bird 125.00
Planter, #105, man w/chicken on knee, washtub 125.00
Planter, #110, man, w/jug & snake, 4½" 95.00
Planter, #81, man drinking from jug, sitting by washtub 95.00
Shakers, Ma & Old Doc, pr 110.00

Miscellaneous

Items in this section that are designated 'IP' are miscellaneous novelties made by Imperial Porcelain; the remainder are of interest to Paul Webb collectors, though made by an unknown manufacturer. Prints on calendars and playing cards are signed 'Paul Webb.'

Artist board, babies or mtn women, sgn Paul Webb, 30x30" 275.00
Artist board, mtn boys only, sgn Paul Webb, 30x30" 275.00
Calendar, 1954, 12 sgn scenes, Brown & Bigelow, complete 65.00
Figurine, cat in high-heeled shoe, 5½" L 65.00
Hot pad, Dutch boy w/tulips, rnd, IP 30.00
Ink blotters, sgn scenes, ea 15.00
Mug, #29, man hdl, sgn Paul Webb, 4¾" 50.00
Planter, #106, dog sitting by tub, IP 95.00
Playing cards, ad: Rafe Oiling Gun, Brown & Bigelow, MIB 75.00
Shakers, pigs, 5", pr 95.00
Shakers, standing pigs, IP, 8", pr 110.00

Indian Tree

Indian Tree is a popular dinnerware pattern produced by various potteries since the early 1800s to recent times. Although backgrounds and borders vary, the Oriental theme is carried out with the gnarled, brown branch of a pink-blossomed tree. Among the manufacturers' marks, you may find represented such notable firms as Coalport, S. Hancock and Sons, Soho Pottery, and John Maddock and Sons. See also Johnson Brothers.

Bowl, fruit; Morley, sm **8.00**
Bowl, Myott, 8" **20.00**
Bowl, soup; rimmed, Maddock, 9" **22.00**
Cup & saucer, AD; Minton **25.00**
Cup & saucer, Spode **35.00**
Gravy boat, w/attached underplate, Spode **88.00**
Jar, Sadler, fancy shape, w/lid, 4½" **55.00**

Maddock pieces: Plates, 8", $8.00; 10", $12.50; 6", $5.00; Cup and saucer, $22.50.

Pitcher, milk; Coalport **75.00**
Plate, Copeland Spode, 9", 12 for **425.00**
Platter, John Maddock & Son, 14" **35.00**
Platter, well & tree, 21" **305.00**
Teapot, Burgess & Lee **60.00**

Inkwells and Inkstands

Receptacles for various writing fluids have been used since ancient times. Through the years they have been made from countless materials — glass, metal, porcelain, pottery, wood, and even papier-mache. During the 18th century, gold or silver inkstands were presented to royalty; the well-known silver inkstand by Philip Syng, Jr., was used for the signing of the Declaration of Independence, and impressive brass inkstands with wells and pounce pots (sanders) were proud possessions of men of letters. When literacy vastly increased in the 19th century, the dip pen replaced the quill pen, and inkwells and inkstands were widely used and produced in a broad range of sizes in functional and decorative forms from ornate Victorian to flowing Art Nouveau and stylized Art Deco designs. However, the acceptance of the ballpoint pen literally put inkstands and inkwells 'out of business.' But their historical significance and intriguing diversity of form and styling fascinate today's collectors.

For further information we recommend *Collector's Encyclopedia to Inkwells, Books I and II,* by Veldon Badders (Collector Books). See also Bottles, Ink.

Brass, column shape on low ftd base, early 1900s, 3½" W **70.00**
Brass, rnd contour type, swivel lid, distressed look, 1890s **60.00**
Bronze, modeled w/ducks, sgn A Tithe, Austria, 1920, 4x13x6" ...**500.00**
Bronzed CI, lady's head in clover shape, glass insert, 6" dia **225.00**
Copper, hammered dome w/flat lid, 1910-15, 3½" dia **45.00**
Glass, amber w/deep dimple ea side, polished, 4x2½" sq **325.00**
Glass, blown amethyst funnel type w/cleaning hole, Am, 1850s, 3" ...**175.00**
Glass, blown aqua jar w/ball-shaped stopper, Am, late 1800s, 5" ..**375.00**
Glass, gr irid w/irid threads, bronze floral base, DRGM, 3½" **350.00**
Glass, ladybugs/grass, mc/brn on opal, flared w/mushroom cap ...**325.00**
Glass, pillow-shape cut crystal w/SP collar & lid, 1900-15, 4" **195.00**
Glass, pressed swirl design w/matching lid, late 1800s, 1½" sq **60.00**

Glass, 3-step shape w/hinged brass collar, cut knob, Am, 1900 ..**140.00**
Porc, couple atop scroll-ft box w/gold, Fr, 1840-50, 5½" L **650.00**
Porc, eagle figural, worn mc pnt w/gold, mk DB, 5⅛" **140.00**
Porc, HP seated clown w/pen holder at ft, Fr, 1900s, 4¼" L **150.00**
Porc, yel w/floral panels, Aladdin, Fr, 4¾" W **225.00**
Redware, gr glaze, Am, early 1900s, 2¾" dia **30.00**
Seashells mtd in plaster w/pressed-glass bottle & 1931 calendar ...**80.00**
Soapstone, hand-cvd incised decor, Am, early 1900s, 2½" sq **25.00**
Stoneware, tiered bulbous body, Am, 1950-60, 3" **50.00**
Wht metal, cast tree-trunk w/porc inset, late 1800s, 1½" dia **55.00**
Wood, cvd dog's head w/log-shaped pen rest, German (?), 1890, 5" L .**300.00**
Wood, cvd nut on lg leaf, German, 1890-1900, 5" L **140.00**

Insulators

The telegraph was invented in 1844. The devices developed to hold the electrical transmission wires to the poles were called insulators. The telephone, invented in 1876, intensified their usefulness; and by the turn of the century, thousands of varieties were being produced in pottery, wood, and glass of various colors. Even though it has been rumored that red glass insulators exist, none have ever been authenticated. Many insulators are embossed with patent dates.

Of the more than 3,000 types known to exist, today's collectors evaluate their worth by age and rarity of color. Aqua and green are the most common colors in glass, dark brown the most common in porcelain. Threadless insulators (for example, CD #701.1) made between 1850 and 1865, bring prices well into the thousands, if in mint condition.

In the listings that follow, the CD numbers are from an identification system developed in the late 1960s by N.R. Woodward.

Those seeking additional information about insulators are encouraged to contact Line Jewels NIA #1380 (whose address may be found in the Directory under Clubs, Newsletters, and Catalogs) or attend a club-endorsed show. (For information see Directory under Florida for Jacqueline Linscott.) In the listings that follow those stating 'no name' have no company identification but do have embossed numbers, dots, etc. Those stating 'no embossing' are without raised letters, dots, or any other markings.

Key:
* (asterisk) — Canadian
BE — base embossed
CB — corrugated base
CD — Consolidated Design
FDP — flat drip points

RB — rough base
RDP — round drip points
SB — smooth base
SDP — sharp drip points

CD 267, Cable #4, SB, emerald green, $500.00.

Photo courtesy Jacqueline Linscott

Threaded Pin-type and Threadless Glass Insulators

CD 104, National Insulator Co, BE, aqua **250.00**
CD 106, Ericsson, RDP, clear **10.00**
CD 113, Armstrong's No 13, SB, straw **10.00**

CD 115*, Dominion-10, RDP, dk straw 15.00
CD 118, no emb, SB, carnival 250.00
CD 120, Patent/Dec 19, 1871, SB, ice bl 10.00
CD 121, C&P Tel Co, SB, gr 20.00
CD 121, OVG Co, SB, aqua 5.00
CD 122, Kerr No 2, SB, clear 2.00
CD 122, McLaughlin, RDP, apple gr 6.00
CD 123.2, Chester/NY, SB, aqua 3,500.00
CD 125, WU/5, SB, bl 25.00
CD 128, Hemingray, E-14-B, SB, opal 50.00
CD 128, Hemingray, SB, off-clear 2.00
CD 128, Kerr CSC, SB, clear 3.00
CD 130, Cal Elec Works/Parent, SB, ice aqua 350.00
CD 133, City Fire Alarm, SB, lt aqua 75.00
CD 133.2, Homer Brooke's Pat, SB, lt bl 25.00
CD 134, Good, SB, bl aqua 15.00
CD 135, WGM Co, SB, lt purple 30.00
CD 136, B&O, Pat Jan 25th 1870, SB, aqua 10.00
CD 139, Brookfield Postal Tel Co, SB, lt aqua 12.00
CD 139, Combination/Safety, SB, aqua 7,500.00
CD 143, CNR, SB, aqua 5.00
CD 143, Hemingray, RDP, carnival 15.00
CD 143.5, THE Co, SB, lt gr 60.00
CD 144*, no name, horizontal ridges, SB, gr 75.00
CD 147, Hemingray, Pat Oct 8, 1907, SB, aqua 1.00
CD 154, AA, RDP, aqua 40.00
CD 154, Gayner No 44, SB, bl-aqua 2.00
CD 155, Kerr DP.1, SB, off-clear 3.00
CD 158.1, Chester, inner skirt emb, SB, aqua 1,250.00
CD 160, Maydwell-14, FDP, Gingerale 5.00
CD 162, Hamilton Glass Co, RDP, lt gr 40.00
CD 163, Armstrong, SB, clear 1.00
CD 164, Maydwell-20, SDP, clear 2.00
CD 166, California, SB, sage gr 5.00
CD 168, Hemingray No 510, CB, carnival 30.00
CD 170, no name, SB, gr-aqua 10.00
CD 175, Hemingray-25, SB, clear 10.00
CD 183, Hemingray-71, CB, clear 5.00
CD 188, B, SB, dk aqua 10.00
CD 188, Brookfield, SB, emerald gr 30.00
CD 196, HB Co, Pat May 2, 1893, SDP, ice aqua 75.00
CD 197, Whitall Tatum No 15, SB, clear 3.00
CD 203, Kerr TW, SB, clear 1.00
CD 206, no name, SDP, straw 250.00
CD 210, Postal, SB, emerald gr 10.00
CD 213, Hemingray-43, RDP, bl 15.00
CD 220, Hemingray-67, SB, lt lemon 40.00
CD 230, Hemingray-512, SB, lt citrine 25.00
CD 235, Pyrex-662, SB, carnival 30.00
CD 240, Pyrex-131, SB, clear 15.00
CD 251, NEGM Co, SB, ice bl 20.00
CD 252, Knowles Cable/Insulator, SB, aqua 10.00
CD 252, M&E, SB, aqua 40.00
CD 252, No 2 Cable, SB, aqua 5.00
CD 253, Knowles Cable/Insulator, SB, milky aqua 150.00
CD 254, No 3 Cable, SB, lt bl 50.00
CD 256, Manhattan, SB, aqua 35.00
CD 257, Hemingray No 60, RDP, clear 15.00
CD 258, Cable, SDP, dk aqua 175.00
CD 263, Columbia, SB, squa 60.00
CD 263, Pat'd May 12 1891/Columbia, SB, dk aqua 75.00
CD 267, NeGM, SB, yel-gr 220.00
CD 267, No 4 Cable, SB, emerald gr 500.00
CD 269, Jumbo, SB, dk aqua 300.00

CD 282, Knowles Boston, SB, aqua 200.00
CD 286, Locke, SB, lt bl 50.00
CD 292.5, Boston, SB, bl 300.00
CD 294, NEGMCo, SB, aqua 40.00
CD 299.1, prism, SB, lt aqua 250.00
CD 306, Lynchburg, SDP, aqua 200.00
CD 317, Chambers, SB, gr 300.00
CD 325, Pyrex-401, SB, clear 15.00
CD 326, Pyrex TM Reg US Pat Off Made in USA, SB, clear 25.00
CD 724, Chester NY, BE, dk cobalt 5,000.00
CD 728, no emb, SB, lt bl 125.00
CD 734, McMicking, SB, lt aqua 60.00
CD 742, no emb, SB, lt gr 100.00
CD 743, no name, SB, deep amber 400.00
CD 782, TMCo, SB, aqua 3,000.00

Irons

History, geography, art, and cultural diversity are all represented in the collecting of antique pressing irons. The progress of fashion and invention can be traced through the evolution of the pressing iron.

Over seven hundred years ago, implements constructed of stone, bone, wood, glass, and wrought iron were used for pressing fabrics. Early ironing devices were quite primitive in form, and heating techniques included inserting a hot metal slug into a cavity of the iron, adding hot burning coals into a chamber or pan, and placing the iron directly on hot coals or a hot surface.

To the pleasure of today's collectors, some of these early irons, mainly from the period of 1700 to 1850, were decorated by artisans who carved and painted them with regional motifs typical of their natural surroundings and spiritual cultures.

Beginning in the mid-1800s, new cultural demands for fancy wearing apparel initiated a revolution in technology for types of irons and methods to heat them. Typical of this period is the fluter which was essential for producing the ruffles demanded by the 19th-century ladies. Hat irons, polishers, and numerous unusual iron forms were also used during this time, and provided a means to produce crimps, curves, curls, and special fabric textures. Irons from this era are characterized by their unique shapes, odd handles, latches, decorations, and even revolving mechanisms.

Also during this time, irons began to be heated by burning liquid and gaseous fuels. Gradually the new technology of the electrically heated iron replaced all other heating methods, except in the more rural areas and undeveloped countries. Even today the Amish communities utilize gasoline fueled irons.

In the listings that follow, prices are given for examples in best possible as-found condition. Damage, repairs, plating, excessive wear, rust, and missing parts can dramatically reduce value. For further information we recommend *Irons by Irons* and *More Irons by Irons* by our advisor Dave Irons; his address and information for ordering these books are given in the Directory under Pennsylvania.

Alcohol, Manning-Bowman...USA, tank missing, 1900s, 7¼" ...150.00
Box, Bless-Drake Salamander, top lifts, 1890s, 6", from $200 to .300.00
Box, charcoal, Junior Carbon...1911..., top lifts, 6", from $150 to ..200.00
Box, English, #10, brass, lift-up gate, 1890s, 7¾", from $100 to ..150.00
Box, English, brass, lift-out gate, 1850s, 5⅝", from $200 to 300.00
Charcoal, tall chimney, vents adjust, damper, 1900, 11½" 125.00
Electric, General Electric, travel, ca 1950, 6¼", MIB, from $30 to ...40.00
Electric, KM Knapp Monarch, travel, ca 1940, 6⅜", from $30 to .50.00
Electric, Prilect Traveling, orig tin box, 1925, 4⅞", from $70 to ..100.00
Electric, Universal Stroke Sav-R, ca 1950, 9", from $10 to 20.00
Flat, blk/wht agate, Codin (European), ca 1900, 7⅛", from $120 to ...150.00

Flat, cast, BG (Fr), belled-out hdl, late 1800s, 6", from $30 to **50.00**
Flat, cast, Wapak #4, ca 1900, 5⅛", from $10 to **20.00**
Flower, J Alente NY, brass/iron, late 1800s, 9½", from $100 to ..**125.00**
Fluter, combination, Pat'd Aug 2, 70, Knapp, 6⅝", from $100 to ...**150.00**
Fluter, combination/revolving, Pat 1876, 5½", from $300 to **500.00**
Fluter, Dudley Fluter Patd...1876, red pinstripes/decals, 6¾" **500.00**
Fluter, Geneva Hand...1866, rocker, brass base, 5¾", from $150 to ...**200.00**
Fluter, machine, Pat May_ 187_, pnt pinstripes/flowers, 6" **175.00**
Fluter, The Erie, Griswold, rocker, clip-on hdl, 5½", from $100 to ..**150.00**
Gasoline, Dmn...Akron Lamp Co..., ca 1900, 7½", from $50 to ...**75.00**
Gasoline, Rex-Patent, like charcoal iron, 1900, 10", from $300 to ...**500.00**
Goffering, dbl, European, iron bbls & std, CI base, 1850s, 11½" ...**400.00**
Goffering, English, brass, tripod base, 1850s, 10⅜" **250.00**
Goffering, European, wrought iron, monkey tail, tripod, 1800s, 11" .**500.00**
Goffering, single; English, brass, flared ft, 1850s, 11", minimum ...**250.00**
Hat, tolliker, solid cast, wood hdl, late 1800s, 4", from $80 to **100.00**
Iron heater, laundry stove, Union, holds 6 irons **300.00**
Iron heater, pyramid type, holds 3 irons **125.00**
Iron heater, stove top, Centennial, mechanical **300.00**
Little, French, PG, 4" **60.00**
Little, Ober, dbl point, 4" **150.00**
Little, swan (cast), no pnt, 1⅞" **90.00**
Little, tri-bump hdl, 2⅛" **45.00**
Little, wire hdl, Mexican, 2¾" **40.00**
Little, wood grip, #25, 4½" **110.00**
Little, wood grip, The Pearl, 3⅞" **90.00**
Mangle board, horse hdl, cvd geometric designs **500.00**
Natural gas, Wright Pat Aug 22 1911, 7", from $70 to **100.00**
Ox Tongue, European, #2, brass, lift-up gate, 1850s, 5½" **250.00**
Pan, Greek, rnd pan w/high ridges in bottom, 1900s, 18", from $150 to **200.00**
Pleating board, wire cups, New Victorian Pleater **50.00**
Poking stick, European, decor shaft, early 1800s, 9½", from $150 to .**175.00**
Polisher, AJ Bellamy..., steep sides, late 1800s, 6⅛", from $70 to .**100.00**
Polisher, Sweeney...Nov 17 96 #4..., 7", from $150 to **200.00**
Seam, Pat Apd For, hdl opens, late 1800s, 6¾", from $200 to **300.00**
Sleeve, Pat'd June 15 1897, flat toe, 9⅞", from $150 to **200.00**
Sleeve, Sensible..Sept 6 1887 on hdl, 6⅞", from $60 to **80.00**
Slug, Danish, brass w/Rococo & designs, 1750, minimum **500.00**
Slug, European, brass cutwork/eng o/l plate, 1850s, 7", minimum ..**750.00**
Slug, Pat Apd For, swan figural w/swan latch, 1877, 7", minimum .**750.00**
Steam, N Rubenstein's..., thumb valve, ca 1900, 10¼", from $70 to ..**100.00**
Trade card, Enterprise **45.00**

Ironstone

During the last quarter of the 18th century, English potters began experimenting with a new type of body that contained calcinated flint and a higher china clay content, intent on producing a fine durable whiteware — heavy, yet with a texture that would resemble porcelain. To remove the last trace of yellow, a minute amount of cobalt was added, often resulting in a bluish-white tone. Wm. and John Turner of Caughley and Josiah Spode II were the first to manufacture the ware successfully. Others, such as Davenport, Hicks and Meigh, and Ralph and Josiah Wedgwood, followed with their own versions. The latter coined the name 'Pearl' to refer to his product and incorporated the term into his trademark. In 1813 a 14-year patent was issued to Charles James Mason, who called his ware Patented Ironstone. Francis Morley, G.L. Asworth, T.J. Mayer, and other Staffordshire potters continued to produce ironstone until the end of the century. While some of these patterns are simple to the extreme, many are decorated with in-mold designs of fruit, grain, and foliage on ribbed or scalloped shapes. In the 1830s transfer-printed designs in blue, mulberry, pink, green, and black became popular; and polychrome versions of Oriental wares were manu-

factured to compete with the Chinese trade. See also Mason's Ironstone. Our advise for this category comes from Home Place Antiques, whose address is listed in the Directory under Illinois.

Bowl, berry/sauce; Rolling Star, Edwards **30.00**
Bowl, soup; Ceres, Elsmore & Forster, 9¾" **55.00**
Bowl, soup; Fig, Wedgwood, 9½" **55.00**
Bowl, soup; Full Ribbed, Panhurst, 8¾" **32.00**
Bowl, Square Ridged, octagonal, Wedgwood & Co **120.00**
Bowl, Tracery, oval, Johnson Bros, 6¼" **20.00**
Bowl, vegetable; Bow & Tassel, oval, Burgess & Merideth, w/lid, lg ...**110.00**

Bowl, vegetable; Ceres, with lid, Elsmore & Forster, 11", $195.00.

Bowl, vegetable; Tulip Sydenham, T&R Boote, w/lid, 8" **225.00**
Bowl, vegetable; Wheat & Hops, W Taylor, w/lid, 10¼" L **145.00**
Chamber pot, Corn & Oats, w/lid **175.00**
Chamber pot, Portland, Elsmore & Forster, w/lid **75.00**
Chamber pot, President, J Edwards, w/lid **125.00**
Coffeepot, Ceres, w/lid, Elsmore & Forster, 10¾" **265.00**
Coffeepot, Grape Octagon, pk lustre accents, Walley, 10" **65.00**
Coffeepot, Laurel Wreath, Elsmore & Forster, 11¼" **325.00**
Coffeepot, Lily, H Burgess **295.00**
Coffeepot, Wheat & Clover, Tompkinson Bros, 10⅝" **245.00**
Compote, New York, 9½" dia **225.00**
Creamer, octagonal w/paneled sides, Meigh & Son, 5⅛" **85.00**
Creamer, Wheat & Clover, Turner & Tompkinson, 7⅜" **125.00**
Cup plate, Fig, Davenport, 4¼" **55.00**
Cup plate, Gothic, 12-sided, Alcock, 4¼" **25.00**
Cup plate, Niagara Falls, Shaw, 3⅞", EX **70.00**
Jug, hot beverage; Octagon, w/lid, Boote, 10" **950.00**
Ladle, sauce; Boote's 1851, unmk, 7¼" **60.00**
Ladle, sauce; flower on hdl, paneled bowl, no mk **65.00**
Mold, jelly; scalloped, 5x7¾" dia **75.00**
Mug, Chinese, Anthony Shaw, 3½" **95.00**
Pitcher, milk; Olympic, Elsmore & Forster, 9⅜" **145.00**
Pitcher, President, J Edwards, 8⅝" **155.00**
Pitcher, Sydenham, 9" **195.00**
Plate, Lily of the Valley, James Edwards & Son, 10½" **28.00**
Plate, Sharon Arch, Davenport, 10½" **32.00**
Plate, Sydenham, T&R Boote, 10½" **40.00**
Plate, Wheat & Clover, Turner & Tomkinson, 8⅜" **35.00**
Platter, Ceres, Elsmore & Forster, oval, 16" **85.00**
Platter, Cupid/nymph by fire pot emb in center, Sebring, 18" **175.00**
Platter, De Soto, Thos Hughes, 11⅝x9" **65.00**
Platter, Nosegay, Baker & Co, 13½" **50.00**
Platter, Tracery, oval, Johnson Bros, 11" **50.00**
Relish, Ceres, w/rope, Elsmore & Forster **78.00**
Relish, Wheat, Meakin **30.00**
Sugar bowl, Wheat on Ceres shape, w/lid, Elsmore & Forster, 7¾" ...**150.00**
Tea/coffeepot, Bow & Tassel Variant, Bridgwood & Sons, 8½" .**150.00**
Teacup & saucer, Baltic, Thulme **65.00**
Teacup & saucer, Leaf & Crossed Ribbon, Livesley Powell **55.00**
Teapot, Corn & Oats **275.00**
Teapot, Wheat & Hops, sm **245.00**

Toddy bowl, Ceres, open, Elsmore & Forster 350.00
Tureen, giblet; Grape Octagon, +lid/ladle/underplate 280.00
Tureen, sauce; Scalloped Decagon, Wedgwood, +base, EX 100.00
Tureen, sauce; St Louis, Edwards, +ladle/base/undertray 225.00
Tureen, soup; Dominion, water lily bud finial, Baker & Co, +base ...295.00
Tureen, soup; Octagon, T&R Boot, 1850, EX 550.00
Underplate, Columbia, Clementson, 14¼x10½" 85.00
Wash bowl, New York, Clementson, 13½" 85.00
Wash bowl, Victory, John Edwards 115.00
Wash bowl & pitcher, Divided Gothic, John Alcock, 11¼" 200.00
Wash bowl & pitcher, mini, 3¼x3¾", 1⅜" 85.00
Wash bowl & pitcher, Sydenham, T&R Boote, 13" dia, 11¼" ...400.00
Wash pitcher, Corn & Oats 175.00
Wash pitcher, Hebe, John Alcock, 11⅞" 145.00
Waste bowl, Sydenham, flared rim, unmk, 4x6½" 120.00
Waste bowl, Tuscan, unmk, 3⅛x5¼" 80.00

Patterned Ironstone

Bowl, vegetable; No 21, purple transfer, 2x9⅜x6⅝" 45.00
Coffeepot, Canella, brn transfer, Challinor, 14", EX 95.00
Coffeepot, Paradise, purple transfer, Livesley Powell, 9", NM 230.00
Coffeepot, Tyrol, purple transfer, Wedgwood, rpr, 10" 75.00
Cup & saucer, Cleopatra, bl transfer 60.00
Cup plate, Gipsy, bl transfer, 4" 35.00
Pitcher, Laurel Wreath, Washington transfer, 9¼" 1,250.00
Pitcher, milk; floral pattern (unidentified), unmk, 6" 300.00
Plate, Andalusia, pk transfer, Wm Adams, 6" 50.00
Plate, Bologna, pk transfer, Adams, 11¾" 90.00
Plate, Corinthia, pk transfer, E Challinor, 10" 30.00
Plate, Corinthia, pk transfer, E Challinor, 8¾" 50.00
Plate, Farm, dk bl transfer, England, 10½" 50.00
Plate, Feather, gr transfer w/red & yel polychrome, #2, 8¼" 45.00
Plate, Lozere, dk bl transfer, E Challinor, 10⅝" 50.00
Plate, Palestine, purple transfer, Adams, 10¾" 50.00
Plate, Parisian Chateau, blk transfer, Ralph Hall, 10⅜" 80.00
Plate, Spanish Festivities 1798, dk bl transfer, G Jones, 9¼" 65.00
Plate, Wild Rose 1784, dk bl transfer, G Jones England, 9¼" 75.00
Plate, Wiseton Hall Nottinghamshire, med bl transfer, 8½" 100.00
Plate, Zamara, gr transfer w/mc details, F Morley, 8¼" 45.00
Platter, Aurora, red transfer, F Morley, 15x11½" 180.00
Platter, Gipsy, bl transfer, 15x11¾" 80.00
Platter, Lady of the Lake, dk bl transfer, rectangular, 15x11⅜" ..325.00
Soup plate, Corsica, purple transfer, mk EC, 9¾" 50.00
Sugar bowl, Cleopatra, bl transfer, w/lid, 7¼" 75.00
Sugar bowl, Laurel Wreath, Washington transfer, w/lid 600.00
Teapot, Laurel Wreath, Washington blk transfer, Elsmore & Forster 1,200.00
Teapot, Wilton, pk transfer w/mc, Albion Pottery, +underplate ...225.00
Waste bowl, Cleopatra, bl transfer, paneled sides, 4x5⅞" 65.00

Italian Glass

Throughout the 20th century, one of the major glassmaking centers of the world was the island of Murano. From the Stile Liberte work of Artisi Barovier (1890 – 1920s) to the early work of Ettore Sottsass in the 1970s, they excelled in creativity and craftsmanship. The 1920s to '40s featured the work of glass designers like Ercole Barovier for Barovier and Toso, and Vittorio Zecchin, Napoleone Martinuzzi, and Carlo Scarpa for Venini. Many of these pieces are highly prized by collectors.

The 1950s saw a revival of Italy as a world-reknown design center for all of the arts. Glass led the charge with the brightly colored work of Fulvio Bianconi for Venini, Dino Martens for Aureliano Toso and Ercole Barovier for Barovier and Toso. The best of these pieces are

extremely desirable. The '60s and '70s have also seen many innovative designs with work by the Finnish Tapio Wirkkala, the American Thomas Stearns, and many other designers.

Unfortunately, amongst the great glass, there was a plethora of commercial ashtrays, vases, and figurines produced that, though having some value, do not compare in quality and design to the great glass of Murano.

Venini: The Venini company was founded in 1921 by Paolo Venini, and he led the company until his death in 1959. Major Italian designers worked for the firm, including Vittorio Zecchin, Napoleone Martinuzzi, Carlo Scarpa, and Fulvio Bianconi. After his death, his son-in-law, Ludovico de Santillana, ran the factory and employed designers like Toni Zucchieri, Tapio Wirkkala, and Thomas Stearns. The company is known for creative designs and techniques including Inciso (finely etched lines), Battuto (carved facets), Sommerso (controlled bubbles), Pezzato (patches of fused glass), and Fascie (horizontal colored lines in clear glass). Until the mid-'60s, most pieces were signed with acid-etched 'Venini Murano ITALIA.' In the '60s they started engraving the signatures. The factory still exists.

Barovier: In the late 1920s, Ercole Barovier took over the Artisti Barovier and started designing many different vases. In the 1930s he merged with Ferro Toso and became Barovier and Toso. He designed many different series of glass including the Barbarico (rough, acid-treated brown or deep blue glass), Eugenio (free-blown vases), Efeso, Rotallato, Dorico, Egeo (vases incorporating murrine designs), and Primavera (white etched glass with black bands). He designed until 1974. The company is still in existence. Most pieces were unsigned.

Aureliano Toso: The great glass designer Dino Martens was involved with the company from about 1938 to 1965. It was his work that produced the very desirable Oriente vases. This technique consisted of free-formed patches of green, yellow, blue, purple, black, and white stars and pieces of zanfirico canes fused into brilliantly colored vases and bowls. His El Dorado series was based on the same technique but was not opaque. He also designed pieces with alternating groups of black and white filigrana lines. Pieces are unsigned.

Seguso: Flavio Poli became the artistic director of Seguso in the late 1930s and remained until 1963. He is known for his Corroso (acid-etched glass) and his Valve series (elegant forms of two to three layers of colored glass with a clear glass casing).

Archimede Seguso: In 1946 Archimede Seguso left the Seguso Vetri D'Arte to open a new company and designed many innovative pieces. His Merlatto (thin white filigrana suspended three dimensionally) series is his most famous. The epitome of his work is where a colored glass (yellow or purple) is windowed in the merlotti. His Macchia Ambra Verde is yellow and spots on a gold base encased in clear glass. The A Piume series contained feathers and leaves suspended in glass. Pieces are unsigned.

Alfredo Barbini: Barbini was a designer known for his sculptures of sea subjects and his amorphic-shaped vases with an inner core of red or blue glass with a heavy layer of finely incised outer glass. He worked in the 1950s to 1960s, and some pieces are signed.

Vistosi: Although this glassworks was started in the 1940s, fame came in the 1960s and '70s with the birds designed by Allesandro Pianon and the early work of the Memphis school designer, Ettore Sottsass. Pieces may be signed.

AVEM: This company is known for its work in the 1950s and '60s. The designer, Ansolo Fuga, did work using a solid white glass with inclusions of multicolored murrines.

Cenedese: This is a postwar company led by Gino Cenedese with Alfredo Barbini as designer. When Barbini left, Cenedese took over the design work and also used the free-lanced designs of Fulvio Bianconi. They are known for their figurines and vases with suspended murrines.

Cappellin: Venini's original partner (1921 – 25), Giacomo Cappellin, opened a short-lived company (1925 – 32) that was to become extremely important. His chief designer was the young Carlo Scarpa who was to create many masterpieces in glass both for Cappellin and then Venini.

Ettore Sottsass: Sottass founded the Memphis School of Design in the 1970s. He is an extremely famous modern designer who designed several series of glass for the Vistosi Glass Company. The pieces were created in limited editions, signed and numbered, and each piece was given a name.

Our advisor for this category is Howard Lockwood, publisher of *Vetri: Italian Glass News*. For further information concerning Mr. Lockwood or this publication, see the Directory under New Jersey.

Venini Glass

A Bugne: gr cylindrical vase 6,310.00
Battuto: pale gr vase 13,126.00
Battuto: tall bl vase by T Scarpa 6,199.00
Bird: J shape, bl-gr, copper legs 1,823.00
Bottle, red & gr narrow vertical canes, stopper 1,094.00
Bottle, yel & aubergine vertical canes 948.00
Bottle, yel & bl vertical stripes, stopper 948.00
Cornucopia: pk laguna vase w/gold inclusions 1,536.00
Corroso: red bowl w/appl decor 2,300.00
Fasce, bl bottle w/2 wide yel stripes 802.00
Fasce Murrine: wht cylinder, murrine bands 9,480.00
Fasce Ritorta: bowl, amethyst, bl & gray 576.00
Fasce Ritorte: cylinder vase, red, bl & turq bands 6,769.00
Fazzoletto: lg, pk & wht zanfirico 3,450.00
Fazzoletto: med sz, yel & wht zanfirico 355.00
Fenecio: clear & gr perfume bottle 1,064.00
Figurine, female, wht filigrana 2,875.00
Fish, lav w/yel & mustard decor 1,840.00
Forato: bl & violet single-holed vase 1,750.00
Forato: bl cased w/pk single-holed vase 640.00
Hourglass: gr & red 241.00
Inciso: cylindrical, steel bl w/amber layer 1,056.00
Inciso: flaring vase, clear over gr 690.00
Inciso: triangular bottle, bl, w/stopper 575.00
Latticino: cylinder, pk & wht canes 615.00
Latticino: gray vase w/wht canes 576.00

Murrine: red and black checkered vase, $54,693.00.

Photo courtesy Howard Lockwood

Murrine: 3-sided vase, gr & blk 8,751.00
Obelisk: 8-sided, smoke-gray 176.00
Occhi: blk & wht, sq 3,646.00
Occhi: red cigar-shaped vase, designed by T Scarpa 8,022.00
Pennalatte: yel & tan stripes, designed by C Scarpa 21,877.00
Pezzato: cigar shaped, red, bl, clear & gr patches 6,199.00
Pezzato: cylinder vase w/aubergine, turq, gray & clear ...7,475.00

Pezzato: vase, red, bl, beige & gr patches 13,856.00
Pitcher & tumbler, red & bl canes 875.00
Scozzese: cylinder vase, turq vertical stripes 10,560.00
Soffiati: bl compote, ftd 577.00
Soffiati: red Veronese vase 690.00
Tessuto: 2 halfs - red/clear & blk/red 2,552.00
Torso: female torso w/raised arms, amber 6,325.00
Wirkkala Correnno: plate, bl & deep bl 620.00
Wirkkala: bowl, wht mezza filigrana 219.00

Non-Venini Glass

Archimede Seguso, A Piume: teardrop vase, peach w/4 feathers .4,025.00
Archimede Seguso, Alarante: pierced hdld pitcher, yel w/gr int .676.00
Archimede Seguso, Losanghe: cylindrical, wht & caramel sqs ..2,875.00
Archimede Seguso, Merletto: bl w/wht merletto panels 15,314.00
Archimede Seguso, Merletto: purple w/botom half wht, purple dots ..12,762.00
Archimede Seguso, Sommerso: ribbed vase, amber over deep yel 747.00
Archimede Seguso, Sommerso: ribbed vase, clear, cranberry & purple .1,265.00
Artisti Barovier, Mosaic: goblet-shaped ped vase, bl murrines 28,750.00
Aureliano Toso, A Trina: pigeon, wht, blk & copper aventurine 747.00
Aureliano Toso, Bianca/Nera: vase, blk & wht spiralling canes .440.00
Aureliano Toso, Eldorado: vase w/appl collar 14,585.00
Aureliano Toso, Mezza Filigrana: lamp base 230.00
Aureliano Toso, Mezza Filigrana: leaf-formed dish 172.00
Aureliano Toso, Oriente: flared vase 9,775.00
AVEM, Anse Volante: irid gr pitcher, flaring hdl 4,084.00
Barbini, Inciso; thick-walled clear bowl w/red int 1,940.00
Barbini, Sasso: ftd w/inciso cut & int red decor 8,022.00
Barbini, Sasso: vase w/inciso cut & int red decor 5,834.00
Barbini, Scavo: gray polar bear 952.00
Barovier, Efeso: amber cylindrical vase 193.00
Barovier, figurine: drum major iridized clear w/bl trim ...517.00
Barovier, Intarsio: amber & yel patches 5,377.00
Barovier, Intarsio: red, bl, amber, clear triangular patches 7,187.00
Barovier, iridized flared vase w/ribs 2,688.00
Barovier, Rugiadoso: leaf-shaped bowl, clear/wht 230.00
Barovier, Spidereo: wasited vase, windows lined in aubergine .2,880.00
Barovier, Spina: bowl, mauve & opaline herringboned pattern .1,840.00
Cenedese, aquarium block w/3 fish 2,415.00
Cenedese, owl, clear & blk sommerso glass 275.00
Cenedese, Scavo: La Fornace: mc, glass workers 5,175.00
Cenedese, Scavo: vase, lt bl 880.00
Cenedese, Scavo: vase w/appl woman carrying fruit 3,450.00
Fratelli Toso, Murrine: bottle vase w/single target murrine 4,609.00
Fratelli Toso, Murrine: mc Kiku vase 13,856.00
Fratelli Toso, Murrine: mc vase of murrines 9,845.00
Fratelli Toso, Nerox: metallic black w/blk/red & yel/gr 20,149.00
Fratelli Toso, Nerox: metallic blk vase w/clear glass blots 9,480.00
Salviati, Gasparil Birds, stylized, clear, pr 275.00
Seguso Vetri D'Arte, fish, gray glass on appl ft 676.00
Seguso Vetri D'Arte, Pulegoso, gr leaf bowl 292.00
Seguso Vetri D'Arte, Shell, lt bl amorphic shape 1,458.00
Seguso Vetri D'Arte, Siderale: vase, gr & yel concentric circles ...17,502.00
Seguso Vetri D'Arte, Sommerso: flared vase, crimson w/violet int .1,380.00
Seguso Vetri D'Arte, Sommerso: tall, purple int cased in red ..6,760.00
Seguso Vetri D'Arte, Valva: bl int, red & clear layers 8,751.00
Seguso Vetri D'Arte, Valva: gray cased in pale amber 2,300.00
Sottsass, Alcor: vase, clear, wht & bl 3,090.00
Sottsass, Alioth: vase, bl, yel & gr 3,200.00
Sottsass, Altair: vase, bl w/wht appl hdl 2,530.00
Tagliapietra, Incalmo: bl top, wht base 862.00
Tagliapietra, Incalmo: turq bl w/folded blk rim 1,725.00
Vistosi, bird, J shape, bl, copper legs 1,035.00

Vistosi, bird, J shape, gr, copper legs 1,350.00
Vistosi, bird, ovoid, bl, copper legs 1,610.00
Vistosi, bird, spherical, red, no protrusions 2,185.00

Ivory

Ivory is the dentine portion of any mammalian tooth, although only the larger teeth and tusks are of commercial value. The material used for carving and utilitarian objects comes primarily from elephants but also from the mammoth, walrus, hippopotamus, sperm whale, boar, and warthog.

There are a number of laws domestically and internationally to protect endangered animals including the elephant, walrus, and whale. However, ivory taken and used before the various enactment dates is legal within the country in which it is located and can be shipped internationally with a permit. Ivory from the mammoth, hippopotamus, wart hog, and boar is exempted from all bans.

Ivory has been used and valued since Neolithic times. It is a product of every culture and every continent. In the current market, European and Japanese carvings command the highest prices. Indian and African carvings are less in demand. Our advisor for this category is Robert Weisblut; he is listed in the Directory under Maryland.

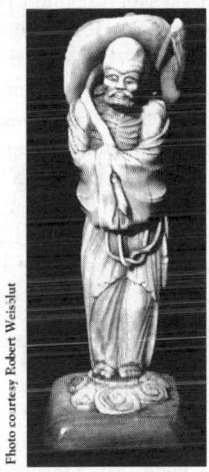

Carving of Chinese Lohan, 18th century, 7", $800.00.

Photo courtesy Robert Weisblut

Bijin w/flower basket, Tokyo School, Meiju period, 12½" 2,070.00
Box, quail covey amidst millet, in manner of Okatomo, Meiji, 8¾" 6,900.00
Chess set, king & queen on thrones: 8", 32 pcs in fitted case ..5,000.00
Frame, cvd dragon, scroll & heart, oval, easel bk, 6" 70.00
Man w/2 boys, monkey on hurdy-gurdy, Japan, 1900, 5½" 425.00
Parasol hdl, rats & monkey on branch, 6¾" 165.00
Pie crimper, gazelle form, openwork cutting wheel, 20th C, 7½" ..225.00
Plaque, 3 ladies, putti & herm, Germany, 1800s, 5½x7", +fr 600.00
Quan Yin w/peach & longevity symbols by sm deer, 12", $1,000 to ...1,200.00
Table screen, mtn scene, openwork borders, China, 19th C, 11", pr ..1,380.00
Tusk, gods climbing among foliage, India, 1800s, 9" 175.00
Tusk, scrolling vines w/bird surmount, 18" L, pr 935.00
Vase, children beneath wisteria view pond, Yusai, Meiji, 9⅜" ...1,265.00
Vase, cvd as stalk of bok-choy w/grapes & bugs, mc stain, 9" ..1,250.00

Jack-in-the-Pulpit Vases

Popular novelties at the turn of the century, jack-in-the-pulpit vases were made in every type of art glass produced. Some were simple, others elaborately appliqued and enameled. They were shaped to resemble the lily for which they were named.

Amberina, Invt T'print, fold-down rim w/amber ruffle 13½" 275.00
Bl Hobnail, ribbed, aqua to gr, ruffled rim w/gr trim, 11" 150.00
Chartreuse Dmn Quilt w/rainbow hobnail, ruffled, 7½" 150.00
Cranberry to pk w/clear edging, 7¾x4½" 165.00
Cranberry w/wht opal edge, clear wafer ft, Hobbs, 9x5" 325.00
Lt gr w/wht opaque trumpet cased w/yel, appl gr bands, 9⅝" 75.00
Pk w/wht int & HP bellflowers, 7" 75.00
Purple stretch w/butterscotch pulled feathers on base, 14" 270.00
Spangle, bl/yel/brn on wht w/silver flecks, swirled, Mt WA, 6" ..250.00
Spatter, mc w/allover silver mica flecks, crystal rim, 5½" 250.00
Tomato top w/yel melon-rib body, crimped rim, Sandwich, 4" ...125.00
Yel w/butterscotch int, 7½" 90.00

Jackfield

Jackfield has come to be a generic term used to refer to wares with a red clay body and a high-gloss black glaze. It originated at Jackfield in Stropshire, England; however, it was produced in the Staffordshire district as well. While some pieces are decorated with relief motifs or painted-on florals and gilding, many are unadorned. Teapots produced in the eighteenth century were known locally as 'black decanters.' These pots and figural dogs and roosters are the items most often found.

Coffeepot, blk w/metal mts, bird finial, camel spout, 12½" 350.00
Creamer, cow figural, gold trim, w/lid, 5½x6" 165.00
Pitcher, blk w/HP bird/initials/1763, appl hdl, 6½", EX 110.00
Teapot, fruit & vines, globular, crabstock hdl & spout, 1765, 8" .230.00

Jewelry

Jewelry as objects of adornment has always been regarded with special affection. Today prices for gems and gemstones crafted into antique and collectible jewelry are based on artistic merit, personal appeal, pure sentimentality, and intrinsic value. Note: In general, diamond prices have gone up more than 20% in the past year, and platinum is becoming popular again, so retail prices are rising. Diamond prices vary greatly depending on cut, color, clarity, etc., and to assess the value of any diamond of more than a carat in weight, you will need to have information about all of these factors. Values given here are for diamond jewelry with a standard commercial grade of diamonds that are most likely to be encountered.

Our advisor for fine jewelry is Rebecca Dodds; her address may be found in the Directory under Florida. If you are interested in collecting or dealing in jewelry, you will find that authority Lillian Baker has several fine books available on the subject — *100 Years of Collectible Jewelry: 1850 – 1950; Art Nouveau and Art Deco Jewelry;* and *Fifty Years of Collectible Fashion Jewelry: 1925 – 1975.* These books are complete with beautiful full-color illustrations and current market values. Other fine sources of information are *Collectible Costume Jewelry* by Cherri Simonds, *Costume Jewelry, A Practical Handbook & Value Guide,* by Fred Rezazadeh, *Collector's Encyclopedia of Hairwork Jewelry, Identification & Values,* by C. Jeanenne Bell, and *Collector's Guide to Hair Combs, Identification and Values,* by Mary Bachman (all available from Collector Books). See also Plastics.

Key:

cab — cabochon	g-t — gold-tone
ct — carat	k — karat
dmn — diamond	plat — platinum
dwt — penny weight	r/stn — rhinestone
Euro — European cut	stn — stone
fl — filigree	tw — total weight
gf — gold filled	wg — white gold

gp — gold plated   yg — yellow gold
grad — graduated   ygf — yellow gold filled
gw — gold washed

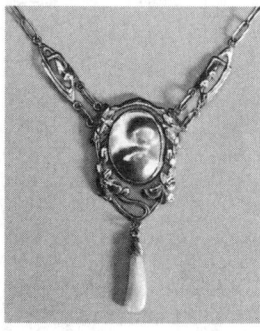

Necklace, Kalo, 14k foliate design around suggestive abalone and freshwater pearl pendant, 9¼", $3,165.00.

Bar pin, 10k yg w/fancy scroll eng, 2.3 grams 35.00
Bar pin, 14k yg w/1 rnd sapphire & 2 sm dmns, Deco fl 195.00
Bar pin, 14k 3-color gold, crescent & star center w/sm dmns 300.00
Bracelet, Art Silver Shop, gp, hammered, w/lg citrine 125.00
Bracelet, bangle; ivory w/dragon cvg 285.00
Bracelet, bangle; sterling fl w/3 lg mc stones, 1930s 75.00
Bracelet, bangle; 14k yg w/21 sm opals 590.00
Bracelet, charm; 14k yg woven wire, ¼" W, w/8 charms 195.00
Bracelet, cuff; Wm Spratling, sterling, rtcl edge, X-bands 235.00
Bracelet, cultured pearls, 3-row 5.5mm w/gold spacers 385.00
Bracelet, Geo Jensen, sterling, floral links w/lapis cabs 700.00
Bracelet, gf w/locket-like medallion w/Nouveau lady's profile 75.00
Bracelet, Jondell, sterling, thick C-form, Mexican #925 ....65.00
Bracelet, Kalo, sterling, floral links, moonstone cabs, EX 600.00
Bracelet, Sheena Thomas, sterling, thick/lg, architectural 225.00
Bracelet, ygf, open links w/emb decor, 8 charms/locket 220.00
Bracelet, 14k wg fl w/sm dmn & peridots, 1920s 400.00
Bracelet, 14k yg, flat-sided rnd link, box clasp, 50.8 grams 715.00
Bracelet, 14k yg, open florentine links, 84.5 grams 550.00
Bracelet, 14k yg stiff band w/fct topaz & half pearls 330.00
Bracelet, 14k yg open links w/gold & jeweled charms 525.00
Bracelet, 18k yg, Lover's Knot w/3 .5 dmns 385.00
Bracelet, 18k yg, snake w/sapphire/ruby cab eyes, 15.2 dwt 1,400.00
Brooch, cameo, tower & bridge landscape, 10k rose-gold fr, 2" ..110.00
Brooch, Danecraft, sterling flower wreath, 1¼" dia 45.00
Brooch, Geo Jensen, sterling, bird in foliage wreath, 1¾" 175.00
Brooch, Geo Jensen, sterling, rtcl oval w/leaves & berries, 2" 395.00
Brooch, gf peacock w/fl & enamel, Victorian 25.00
Brooch, plat, Euro .40ct dmn in bar+40 sm dmns/8 sapphires .1,450.00
Brooch, silver basket w/mc paste stns, early 125.00
Brooch, sterling spray of ivy leaves 25.00
Brooch, 14k yg floral branch w/mc enamel & 3 sm dmns 300.00
Brooch, 14k yg flower & lily pad w/1 pearl & 1 half-pearl 335.00
Brooch, 14k yg w/blk & wht tracery on shield shape 225.00
Brooch, 14k yg w/1.20ct Euro dmn w/6 sm dmns, circular 4,200.00
Brooch, 18 yg abstract w/.35ct dmn, plat/dmn spray accent 695.00
Brooch, 18k yg Georgian design w/5 fct aquamarines, 1930s ...1,000.00
Brooch, 9k yg sword w/ruby/rose dmn & sapphire 150.00
Brooch/lavalier, lg garnet amid sm, heart-shape memorial type, 3" ...575.00
Cuff links, Hans Hanson, 14k yg, pillow shape, pr 275.00
Cuff links, sterling horseman on 1" polished wood circle 30.00
Cuff links, 14k yg w/rectangular flat onyx stones, pr 150.00
Earrings, yg, dmn studs, .77ct tw, prong-set w/gold heads 635.00
Lavalier, plat, 3 rose-cut/8 mine-cut dmns (1ct tw) 580.00
Lavalier, 14k yg w/chain, dmn w/fl, Art Nouveau 175.00
Lavalier, 14k yg w/chain, ruby w/fl, Art Nouveau 150.00
Locket, baby's, eng 14k yg on 14k yg chain 150.00

Necklace, cherry-amber faceted grad beads w/14k spacers, 17" ...125.00
Necklace, coral & fluted onyx beads/gold spacers, 14k clasp 245.00
Necklace, cultured pearls, 1-strand, 3.5-7mm, wg clasp, 19" 300.00
Necklace, garnet grad beads, 1-strand, 16" 125.00
Necklace, Kalo, sterling, link-joined cherries/leaves, 15" 365.00
Necklace, lapis lazuli, 64 grad beads, 18" 110.00
Necklace, lapis lazuli, 76 matched beads, vermeil clasp, 28" 165.00
Necklace, Persian turq nuggets, strand of 41 grad 125.00
Necklace, 8mm gold beads (14 dwt), EX 175.00
Pendant, Art Metal Shop, sterling, hammered leaf form, 1¾" 75.00
Pendant, Kalo, sterling, lg lapis cab, 1¼x¾" 600.00
Pendant, lg Bohemian garnet in low-k yg on 14k chain 150.00
Pendant, 14k yg multistrand fine chain w/lg smoky topaz 355.00
Pin, see brooch
Ring, Cartier, plat, 5x25ct tourmaline fr w/dmn melees 1,750.00
Ring, champagne dmn, 1.38ct solitaire, Tiffany mt 3,500.00
Ring, Cire Perdu, 14k yg w/lg pearl 85.00
Ring, Jabeli, 18k yg & wg w/20 dmns (1.75 ct tw) 2,000.00
Ring, Kalo, 14k yg, lg oval jade cab 475.00
Ring, plat, 1.6ct sapphire amid 2 dmn melees 700.00
Ring, plat w/.65ct old Euro-cut dmn+6 single dmns, Art Deco ..800.00
Ring, plat w/14k yg mts, .10ct Euro dmn+10 sm dmns 250.00
Ring, plat w/3.75ct mine-cut dmn/2 .30ct bag dmns/18 sm dmns 14,000.00
Ring, yg, .5ct brilliant-cut dmn w/.08ct dmns & 14 sm melee dmns ...1,100.00
Ring, yg, 1ct oval sapphire amid 18 rnd/marquise dmns, '60s ..2,200.00
Ring, 10k, emerald-cut 10mmx8mm synthetic alexandrite 75.00
Ring, 10k wg, engr crystal w/sm dmn 150.00
Ring, 10k yg, ¾x1" hardstone cameo, Victorian 225.00
Ring, 14k wg, attached 10mm solid gold nugget atop 85.00
Ring, 14k wg, 12.8x8.4mm blk opal & 6 sm dmns 1,100.00
Ring, 14k yg, 18mm fct citrine in free-form setting 150.00
Ring, 14k yg, 18x13mm onyx stone in bezel setting 65.00
Ring, 14k yg, 2ct mine-cut dmn in 6-prong setting 3,600.00
Ring, 14k yg, 3 bl 4x6mm topaz+4 .04ct tw rnd dmns 195.00
Ring, 14k yg, 4 8mm cultured pearls/6 half pearls 165.00
Ring, 14k yg, 5 5mm cab gr jade stns 60.00
Ring, 14k yg, 7 dmns (tw .56) in snowflake pattern 465.00
Ring, 14k yg designed as wizard, .50 ct dmn 585.00
Ring, 14k yg figural butterfly, 4 opals/20 dmns in wings 350.00
Ring, 14kt yg w/polished free-form lapis lazuli stone 500.00
Ring, 15k rose gold/silver, 5 Euro dmns (3 brn)+8 sm, 1.36 ct tw ...650.00
Ring, 18k wg, .40ct sapphire+30 dmns tw .50ct 700.00
Ring, 18k wg, sq w/sm dmns surrounding center .33ct dmn 550.00
Ring, 18k yg, 12ct amethyst in wg basket mt w/yg flowers 500.00
Ring, 18k yg, 2 dmns & ½ct paste gemstone 125.00
Stickpin, amethyst 8x6mm in yg, .03ct dmn 95.00
Stickpin, Kalo, sterling, cvd malachite scarab 225.00
Stickpin, yg horseshoe, 3 heart-shaped opals & 1 ruby 135.00
Stickpin, 14k yg w/.4ct dmn 100.00

Costume Jewelry

Rhinestone jewelry has become a very popular field of collecting. Rhinestones are foil-backed leaded crystal stones with a sparkle out-shining diamonds. Copyrighting jewelry came into effect in 1955. Pieces bearing a copyright mark (post-1955) are considered 'collectibles,' while pieces (with no copyright) made before then are regarded as 'antiques.' Fur clips are two-pronged, used to anchor fur stoles. Dress clips have a spring clasp and are used at the dress neckline. Look for signed and well-made, unmarked pieces for your collections and preserve this American art form. Our advisor for costume jewelry is Marcia Brown, who is the host of the video *Hidden Treasures, A Collector's Guide to Antique and Vintage Jewelry of the 19th and 20th Centuries*. She is listed in the Directory under Oregon.

Bracelet, bangle, brass w/eng dragon, India 20.00
Bracelet, bangle; ygf, ⅜" W 15.00
Bracelet, Boucher, Blkamoor bust, enamel on g-t w/faux gems 90.00
Bracelet, Coro, g-t feathers form links 45.00
Bracelet, Florenza, pastel pk plastic beads/r/stns, +earrings 90.00
Bracelet, Jomaz, Buddha, gr/bl enamel, gr/wht stns, 1¾" 85.00
Bracelet, Lisner, faux coral 30.00
Bracelet, silver-tone w/bl glass cab stns 25.00
Bracelet, Sorrento, 5 tiger-eye sections w/guard chain, 7" 45.00
Bracelet, sterling clamp type w/Calla Lily design 40.00
Bracelet, sterling crossover w/amethyst ends, dtd 1953 ....35.00
Bracelet, Trifari, sterling w/r/stns & bl stns, 1930s 75.00
Brooch, Ciner, faux turq on g-t loose knot 125.00
Brooch, Coro, enameled flowers, 4" L 20.00
Brooch, Coro, g-t bird w/bl stn, lg 55.00
Brooch, Coro, sterling, 5 twisted flowers, 3½" 45.00
Brooch, Coro, 3-color stns, 5 levels, 2" dia 40.00
Brooch, Corocraft, sterling vermeil birds & flowers 235.00
Brooch, Florenza, g-t fl w/faux jade stn 75.00
Brooch, Jeanne, rooster figural, g-t w/red & wht r/stns, lg 70.00
Brooch, Judy-Lee, gr & citrine r/stns, circular, lg 65.00
Brooch, KJ Lane, grasshopper 70.00
Brooch, Kramer, crescent w/amethyst r/stns, lg, +earrings 150.00
Brooch, Miriam Haskell, gp shield w/lions 55.00
Brooch, Napier, sterling, geometric design, clip type, 1¼" 45.00
Brooch, Ora, g-t flower form w/center pearl, +earrings 45.00
Brooch, Robert, g-t leaves & faux pearls, lg 250.00
Brooch, Rubenstein, wht stns, pearl center on g-t, 1⅜" 75.00
Brooch, Sarah Coventry, Santa figural 50.00
Brooch, Schreiner, wht opaque/cloudy bl stns, clear r/stns 90.00
Brooch, Trifari, butterfly, wht plastic 35.00
Brooch, Trifari, elephant figural, sm 20.00
Brooch, Trifari, gold fl circle w/gr r/stns 45.00
Brooch, Trifari, sterling, bird of paradise, enameling, 3½" 375.00

Brooch, Weiss, open gold-tone metal with ruby red rhinestones, matching earrings (not shown), $65.00.

Photo courtesy Marcia Brown

Brooch, Weiss, trembling butterfly, blk stns, 2" 135.00
Dress clip, Trifari, sterling w/r/stns, 1930s, 4" 95.00
Dress clip, Vendome, lg ruby-red center stn, pr 75.00
Earrings, Coro, lg aquamarine drops 30.00
Earrings, Eisenberg, typical lacy pattern 85.00
Earrings, Eisenberg Ice, rnd, marquise & pave stns 45.00
Earrings, Laguna, red glass beads form cluster 30.00
Earrings, Miriam Haskell, prong-set clear/red stns, w/red drops ..110.00
Earrings, Pennino, lg faux pearl & sm r/stns on g-t 50.00
Earrings, shell cameo, ygf, sm, pr 12.00
Earrings, Trifari, sm g-t mts w/gr cabs & pave-set r/stns 90.00
Fur clip, Trifari, chess set (King, Queen, Rook), +earrings 600.00
Fur clip, Vendome duette, aurora borealis stns 125.00
Necklace, Amco, ygf w/3 shell cameos, 1940s 60.00
Necklace, Emmons, chain w/plastic bead drops 20.00
Necklace, Hobe, 4-strand plastic beads, +earrings 65.00

Necklace, Indian-head penny in r/stn & gp fr, w/chain 350.00
Necklace, KJ Lane, 8-strand choker of 2-tone & gold beads 395.00
Necklace, Lisner, mc r/stns, chain extension, hook latch 65.00
Necklace, Miriam Haskell, baroque pearls, 17", +earrings 150.00
Necklace, Miriam Haskell, glass bead strand w/pk flowers, +earrings ...55.00
Necklace, Monet, gp chain 25.00
Necklace, Napier, pave-set stns/silver-metal pendant, +earrings ..65.00
Necklace, Trifari, plastic flower inserts & r/stns, +bracelet 70.00
Necklace, Trifari, 1-strand faux turq beads 65.00
Pin, see brooch
Ring, Eisenberg, chevron design, fl faux sapphire & clear r/stn ..175.00
Ring, Judy-Lee, gr marquise stn w/sm gr r/stns 35.00

Johnson Brothers

A Staffordshire-based company operating since well before the turn of the century, Johnson Brothers has produced many familiar lines of dinnerware, several of which are becoming very collectible. Some of their patterns were made in both blue and pink transfer as well as in polychrome. One of the more familiar lines is Friendly Village, which is still being produced, though the line is much more limited than it once was.

Values below range from a low base price for lines that are still in production (i.e., Friendly Village) or less collectible to a high that would apply to very desirable patterns such as Old Britain Castles, Wild Turkeys, Strawberry Fair, Historic America, Rose Chintz, Chintz — Victorian, etc. Mid-range lines include Coaching Scenes, Millstream, Old English Countryside, Rose Bouquet (and there are others).

For more information on marks, patterns, and pricing, we recommend *Johnson Brothers Dinnerware Pattern Directory and Price Guide* by our advisor, Mary J. Finegan, who is listed in the Directory under North Carolina.

Bowl, cereal/soup; sq, rnd or lug, from $10 to 12.00
Bowl, soup; sq or rnd, 7", from $12 to 14.00
Bowl, vegetable; oval, from $30 to 40.00
Butter dish, from $50 to 60.00
Cake plate, minimum value 60.00
Coffee mug, from $15 to 20.00
Demitasse set, from $20 to 24.00
Gravy boat, from $40 to 48.00
Pitcher/jug, from $45 to 55.00
Plate, buffet; 10½-11", minimum value 30.00
Plate, dinner; from $14 to 18.00
Plate, salad; sq or rnd, from $10 to 14.00
Platter, med, 12-14", from $45 to 55.00
Sugar bowl, open, from $30 to 35.00
Teacup & saucer, from $15 to 19.00
Teapot or coffeepot, minimum value 90.00
Turkey platter, 20½", minimum value 200.00

Josef Originals

Figurines of lovely ladies, charming girls, and whimsical animals marked Josef Originals were designed by Muriel Joseph George of Arcadia, California, from 1945 to 1985. Until 1960 they were produced in California, but costs were high and copies of her work were being made in Japan. To remain competitive, she and her partner, George Good, contracted with the Katayama Company in Japan to build a factory to produce her designs to her approval. Muriel retired in 1982; however, George Good continued production of her work as well as new ones of his staff's creation. The company was sold in late 1985; the name is currently owned by Applause, and a limited amount of figurines bear the name. Those made during the ownership of Muriel George are the most collectible. They can be recognized by these characteristics: The girls have a high-gloss finish, black eyes, and most are signed. Brown eyes date from 1982 to 85. Applause uses a red-brown eye. The animals were mainly done in a matt finish and have labels. Later animals have a flocked coat. Prices are given for figurines (with black eyes unless specified otherwise) in perfect condition. Our advisors, Jim and Kaye Whitaker, are the authors of two books: *Josef Originals, Charming Figurines*, and *Josef Originals, A Second Look*. They are listed in the Directory under Washington.

Aquarius, Zodiac Girls series, Japan, 4¾", from $40 to 50.00
Birthstone dolls, March Aquamarine & April Diamond, Japan, 3½", ea 25.00
Boxer Dog, Champions series, Japan, 5" 22.00
Buggy Bugs series, various poses, wire antenna, Japan, 3¼", ea 9.00
Bunny, jumping rope, Bunny Hutch series, Japan, 4" 10.00
Cat wall plaque, California, 4", from $45 to 50.00
Christmas angel praying by decorated tree night light, 7" 50.00

Couple music box, mauve gown, blue cape Japan, 5¼", from $80.00 to $90.00.

Photo courtesy Jim and Kaye Whitaker

Dalmatian, Kennel Club series, Japan, 3½" 10.00
Elephant, sitting, Japan, 3¾" 20.00
England, Small World series, brn eyes, holding umbrella, Japan, 4½" 35.00
Farmer's Daughter, girl w/hen & basket of eggs, Japan, 5" 40.00
First Date, young lady in gr gown holding fan, Japan, 9" 106.00
Girl cutting cake, Japan, 6", from $45 to 50.00
Happiness Is — Mud Pies, girl making mud pies, Japan, 5¼" 35.00
Hunter, standing horse, Japan, 6" 35.00
It's a Wonderful World series figurines, Japan, 3½", ea 45.00
Jeanne, Colonial Days series, Japan, 9" 125.00
Lara's Theme music box, Japan, 6" 55.00
Lipstick, First Time series, Japan, 4½", from $35 to 40.00
Love Letter from Love Story, Romance series, Japan, 8" 125.00
Mary Ann & Mama, California, 4", 7", pr 125.00
Melody, Sweet Memories series, lady by Victrola, Japan, 6½" 75.00
Mice, Christmas, Japan, 2¾", ea 9.00
Missy, girl in bonnet, several colors, California, 4" 40.00
Monkey dressed as doctor, Japan, 3" 10.00
Nanette, half-doll w/jewels, several colors, California, 5½" 55.00
New Home, special Occasions series, girl w/key, Japan, 4½" 35.00
Nurse, Career Girls series, nurse in yel holding baby, Japan, 5¾" .60.00
Pixie, Christmas Helper, painting toy, Japan, 4¾" 25.00
Pixies, various poses, gr trimmed in red & gold, Japan, 2"-3¼", ea .20.00
Poodle family, Japan, set of 3, mini, 1¼-2½" 12.00
Puerto Rico, Little International, Japan, 4" 35.00
Rose, Flower Girl series, girl w/flower hat, Japan, 4¼" 30.00
Rose Garden series, brn eyes, Japan, 6 different, 5¼", ea 60.00
Ruby, Little Jewels series, girl w/ruby in crown, Japan, 3½" 25.00
Santa, kiss on forehead, Japan, 4¾" 45.00
Secret Pal, girl w/fan, various colors, California, 3½" 30.00
Skunk w/perfume atomizer, Japan, 2½" 12.00

Sports Angels series, playing various sports, Japan, 2¾", ea 25.00
Tawny, Character Cat, Siamese, Japan, 4" 17.00
Three Coins in Fountain music box, girl by fountain, Japan, 6¼" ..75.00
Tony, First Love series, Japan, 5", from $40 to 45.00
Warm Hello, Thinking of You series, girl on phone, Japan, 5" 45.00
Wee Ching/Wee Ling, Chinese Children, w/dog & cat (widely copied) 60.00
Wee Folk, various poses, Japan, 4½", ea 12.00
Wee Three, cats in basket, California, 3" 40.00
Yorkshire, Kennel Klub series, Japan, 3", from $15 to 20.00

Judaica

The items listed below are representative of objects used in both the secular and religious life of the Jewish people. They are evident of a culture where silversmiths, painters, engravers, writers, and metal workers were highly gifted and skilled in their art. Most of the treasures shown in recently displayed exhibits of Judaica were confiscated by the Germans during the late 1930s up to 1945; by then eight Jewish synagogues and fifty warehouses had been filled with Hitler's plunder. Judaica is currently available through dealers, from private collections, and the annual auction held in Israel.

Atarah, Continental, embr flowing pattern, late 1800s, 31½" 220.00
Atarah, Continental silver, repetitive floral, 1890s, 31" 440.00
Broadside, Mizrahi party entering government, Palestine, 1930s 195.00
Charity box, Israel, pictorial tin of Bikur Holim Hospital, 1940s 120.00
Game, Tashbizon Ivri Mekori (scrabble-like), Israel, 1950s, EXIB .220.00
Hallah cover, Continental, embr cloth, ca 1900, 14x15¼", VG ...100.00
Hannukah/sabbath lamp, Palestinian silver, filigree, 1930s, 7" ...660.00
Kiddush/Havdalah goblet, Am silver, 5 panels, 1950s, 6⅛" 9,350.00
Mezuah, Am silver, openwork musicians/flowers/etc, 1950s, 7½" 13,200.00
Mezuah, Catriel ebony & silver, house form, 1993, 6¼x2¾" 770.00
Passover plate, Continental faience, Pessah/flowers, 18th C, 9¼" .900.00
Passover Seder plate, Tepper ceramic, blk/wht, 20th C, 9¾" 145.00
Platter, Continental silver, biblical scenes, ca 1900, 19¾x15½" 550.00
Sabbath candelabra, Polish brass, 5-light, 1850s, 18" 385.00
Skull cap, Polish silver threaded, symmetrical pattern, 1900s, 6" .165.00
Spice container, Am pewter & glass, triangular, 20th C, 3¾" 220.00
Spice container, Continental silver, bird form, 1890s, 6¼" 715.00
Spice container, Mid Eastern SP, pomegranate form, 20th C, 3¾" ...220.00
Spice container, Near East gilt/silvered metal, fruit form, 5" 600.00
Spice tower, Am brass/copper/silver, 2 stars, 1980s, 8¾" 300.00
Spice tower, Am silver, angels/animals, gilt studs, 1950s, 5⅝" ...17,600.00
Spice tower, Am sterling, 6-sided, wire stem, 1900s, 7¼" 300.00
Spice tower, German silver, fruit motifs, 1890s, 7½" 300.00
Symbolic tool set, Jerusalem stone & olivewood, ca 1900, 4-pc+box ...220.00
Torah binder, German, mc tones, undyed linen band, ca 1862, 136" ..330.00
Wall carpet, Palestinian, Vision of Herzl, ca 1900, 44x24", EX ..300.00

Jugtown

The Jugtown Pottery was started about 1920 by Juliana and Jacques Busbee, in Moore County, North Carolina. Ben Owen, a young descendant of a Staffordshire potter, was hired in 1923. He was the master potter, while the Busbees experimented with perfecting glazes and supervising design and modeling. Preferred shapes were those reminiscent of traditional country wares and classic Oriental forms. Glazes were various: natural-clay oranges, buffs, 'tobacco-spit' brown, mirror black, white, 'frog-skin' green, a lovely turquoise called Chinese blue, and the traditional cobalt-decorated salt glaze. The pottery gained national recognition, and as a result of their success, several other local potteries were established. Jugtown is still in operation; however, they no longer use their original glaze colors which are now so collectible.

Bowl, Chinese Blue, Korean shape, 1940s, 3¼x9½" 500.00
Bowl, Chinese Blue, 2x4¼", pr 425.00
Candle holder, Tobacco Spit, lotus-leaf form, 1940s-50s, 2x4" 80.00
Candlestick, gr-bl, V Owens, 1953-64, 17½", NM 375.00
Chip 'n dip, orange & gr spotted, 1940s-50s, 2x10¾" 150.00
Creamer & sugar bowl, Frog-Skin Green......................................90.00
Punch set, turq pastel, V Owens, 1962-64, 10½" bowl+6 3" cups 300.00
Ring jug, cobalt on salt glaze, flower top, 1950s-60s, 10¾x12" ...175.00
Tea bowl, Chinese Blue, 1940s, 1½x4½" 100.00
Teapot, turq pastel, V Owens, 1962-64, 7½x9½", NM 325.00
Vase, brn speckle over red clay, 4 sm shoulder hdls, 9x6" 650.00
Vase, Chinese Blue, mk, 9¼x8", NM 750.00
Vase, Chinese Blue, ovoid, 5x4½" 450.00
Vase, Chinese Blue, ovoid w/closed-in rim, 7½", NM 850.00
Vase, Chinese Blue & gunmetal, ovoid, 6x5" 400.00
Vase, Chinese Blue flambe, 3¾x2½" 325.00
Vase, Chinese Blue mottle, horizontal hdls, 11x9" 3,200.00
Vase, Chinese Blue w/red veins, ovoid, 6x3½" 550.00
Vase, Frog-Skin Green, Ben Brown clay, 4-hdl, late 1920s, 8¼" 750.00
Vase, frothy wht semimatt, ovoid, 4¼x3" 150.00
Vase, thick wht drip, brn clay exposed at bottom, 7x5" 450.00
Vase, top: mustard matt, bottom: clear, hdls, 9x7" 850.00
Vase, turq mottle, shouldered, 1940s, 5¾" 200.00
Vase, wht frothy semimatt, ovoid, 4¼x3" 150.00
Vase, wht semimatt, ovoid, rim hairline, 7x5" 300.00
Vase, wht semimatt, wide angled shoulder, 3½x5" 225.00
Vase, wht semimottled slip, incurvate rim, 1930s-40s, 3¾" 100.00

K. P. M. Porcelain

The original KPM wares were produced from 1823 until 1847 by the Konigliche Porzellan Manfaktur, located in Berlin, Germany. Meissen used the same letters on some of their porcelains, as did several others in the area. In addition to the initials, the mark sometimes contains a crowned eagle with a scepter. Watch for items currently being imported from China; they are marked KPM with the eagle, but the scepter is not present. Our advisor for this category is Don Williams; he is listed in the Directory under Missouri.

Plaque, lady rests against tree, ornately carved frame with integral tree and branches, plaque: 9x6", frame: 16x13¼" (both marked), $8,500.00.

Bowl, serving; spring flowers, gold rim/strap hdl, 11" dia 225.00
Cup & saucer, swan, gilt on bsk, anthemion border on saucer 400.00
Figurines, she in Empire dress, he in long coat, gilt, 8½", pr 600.00
Plaque, artist painting pot, lady looking on, Knoillez, 8x6" 2,600.00
Plaque, bust portrait of lady, 4½x7", matted/fr to 14x18" 1,750.00
Plaque, Heaven's Angel, sgn, scepter mk, 6¼x9¼" 3,750.00
Plaque, lady's portrait, Wagner, cvd/gilt fr, scepter mk, 15x8" ..6,500.00

Plaque, lady w/sword, 12½x7½", +new fr 4,000.00
Plaque, maiden seated on stone wall, sceptre mk, 9¾x7⅜"+fr ..3,500.00
Plaque, outdoor scene w/Vikings & lady, Raup, 10x12", +fr 4,500.00
Plaque, peasant girl w/harp before stone wall, 14x19", +fr 7,500.00
Plaque, Rapunzel, seated by window, 9x7", orig ornate fr 3,250.00
Plaque, recumbent lady reading book, 15x10", +new fr 4,500.00
Plaque, seminude attended by seamstress & maid, 9x6", +fr 3,250.00
Plaque, ¾-view: Ruth w/sheaf of wheat, sgn Koch, 10x6", +fr .2,750.00
Plate, mythological scene, gr border w/gold flowers, 9½" 85.00
Stein, leaf design, inlaid, hunter thumb lift, 1860s, 1-litre 350.00

Kayserzinn Pewter

J.P. Kayser Sohn produced pewter decorated with relief-molded Art Nouveau motifs in Germany during the late 1800s and into the 20th century. Examples are marked with 'Kayserzinn' and the mold number within an elongated oval reserve. Items with three-dimensional animals, insects, birds, etc., are valued much higher than bowls, plates, and trays with simple embossed florals, which are usually priced at $100.00 to about $200.00, depending on size.

Basket, emb floral, Xd hdls w/flower bud finial, 9x11½" 325.00
Bowl, butterflies & squash, lobed, 4x10" 250.00
Bowl, emb Nouveau decor, ftd, w/lid, #4037, 6½" dia 300.00
Bowl, serving; emb foliage, mk, 2½x13½" 100.00
Crumber, emb thistles, #4508, no brush 75.00
Inkwell, leaf shape w/emb bees, no insert 295.00
Pitcher, emb/appl satyr's mask, iris on side, branch hdl, 12" 450.00
Platter, emb pheasants, 16" 160.00

Keeler, Brad

Keeler studied art for a time in the 1930s; later he became a modeler for a Los Angeles firm. By 1939 he was working in his own studio where he created naturalistic studies of birds and animals which were marketed through giftware stores. They were decorated by means of an airbrush and enhanced with hand-painted details. His flamingo figures were particularly popular. In the mid-'40s, he developed a successful line of Chinese Modern housewares glazed in Ming Dragon Blood, a red color he personally developed. Keeler died of a heart attack in 1952, and the pottery closed soon thereafter. For more information, we recommend *The Collector's Encyclopedia of California Pottery, Second Edition*, by Jack Chipman.

Bowl, lettuce leaves w/vegetables in center, 5-compartment, 18" ...100.00
Dish, divided, lobster form, 14" 85.00
Dish, duck figural, w/lid, #324, 6x7x5½" 150.00
Dish, lobster claw form, 9" 45.00
Figurine, bird, #17, 6" 45.00
Figurine, bird, Exotic Series, #707, 15" 275.00
Figurine, bluejay, #19 ....85.00
Figurine, bunny, #787, 5½x2¼x4" 65.00
Figurine, cockatoo, #26, 10" 125.00
Figurine, cockatoo, 6" 75.00
Figurine, duck, gr head, #50 ....45.00
Figurine, fawn, #880 ....50.00
Figurine, flamingo, #2, 9¾" 175.00
Figurine, flamingo, #3, 7¼" 125.00
Figurine, heron, wht w/pk, #714, paper label 100.00
Figurine, pheasants, #38A&B, pr 125.00
Figurine, rooster, crowing, #746, 18x12" 350.00
Figurine, Siamese cat, #798 ....100.00

Figurine, Siamese cat on red pillow, 3x3x3"	40.00
Planter, Pride & Joy, pk kitten, 3¾x6"	110.00
Platter, fish shape, 12½x7⅞"	50.00
Tray, red pepper in lettuce, 14"	60.00

Keen Kutter

Keen Kutter was the brand name chosen in 1870 by the Simmons Firm for a line of high-grade tools and cutlery. The trademark was first applied to high-grade axes. A corporation was formed in 1874 called Simmons Hardware Company. In 1922 Winchester merged with Simmons and continued to carry a full line of hardware plus the Winchester brand. The merger terminated in March of 1929 and converted back to the original status of Simmons Hardware Co. It wasn't until July 1, 1950, that Simmons Hardware Co. was purchased by Shapleigh Hardware Company. All Simmons Hardware Co. trademark lines were continued, and the business operated successfully until its closing in 1962. Today the Keen Kutter logo is owned by the Val-Test Company of Chicago, Illinois. For further study we recommend *Keen Kutter Collectibles*, an illustrated price guide by our advisors for this category, Jerry and Elaine Heuring, available at your favorite bookstore or public library. The Heurings are listed in the Directory under Missouri. See also Knives.

Auger bit set, in logo-shaped canvas roll up	275.00
Auger bits, KS9, w/wooden box & paper label	120.00
Axe, #5, plain pattern	55.00
Axe, hunter's	30.00
Bit, screwdriver bit set of 3, for a brace	40.00
Bottle, oil; clear or bl, 5½x2"	80.00
Brace, KA6, 5" sweep	55.00
Butt gauge, K85, w/marking both sides	90.00

Calendars, tin pad type, contains hardware store name and address, 16x6", $125.00 each.

Photo courtesy Jerry and Elaine Heuring

Calipers, 9" inside	50.00
Can opener, w/bottle opener attachment, rare	150.00
Catalog, 1942 Keen Kutter/Diamond Edge w/29 sections	275.00
Chisel, narrow blade, mortising, ⅛"	25.00
Clock, electric, red w/15" wht dial, 18¾" dia	1,000.00
Concrete edger, brass w/wood hdl	125.00
Corkscrew	30.00
Dividers, various szs, 6", 7", 8", & 10", ea	45.00
Draw knife, K10 blade, w/logo, 10"	45.00
Fence, attachment for plane w/logos	100.00
File, flat, single cut	10.00
Flashlight	75.00
Food chopper, K23	15.00
Fork, spading; long bent hdl, 4-tine	35.00
Garden tool rack, octagon shape, 37¼"	200.00

Gas can, mk w/logo, 2½-gal	25.00
Glass cutter	50.00
Gouge, 1½"	35.00
Grinder, hand; logo on stone, CI holder, 7" wheel	200.00
Hammer, ball pein, 16-oz	45.00
Hammer, blacksmith's	55.00
Hammer, claw; 16-oz	40.00
Hatchet, broad or bench; 5" to 6", ea	75.00
Hatchet, sportsman w/flying duck	325.00
Ice pick	80.00
Invoice, w/logo & hardware store name/address, used	10.00
Knife, butcher	15.00
Knife, pocket; Office Knife, K02220, M	200.00
Knife purse, for pocketknife, logo on brass button	50.00
Knife steel, emblem-shaped guard	40.00
Kraut cutter, CI, logo on side, logo on wood at top	90.00
Lapel pin, pin-bk style, w/logo, ⅞" dia	65.00
Level, CI, 24"	200.00
Magazine ad, 1907 Saturday Evening Post, shows tools	30.00
Minnow bucket	160.00
Nail puller	55.00
Padlock, trunk lock, logo lift, w/key	175.00
Plane, iron block, K220	40.00
Plane, iron K3, corrugated bottom	150.00
Plane, rabbett; KK78, iron	200.00
Plane, smooth; wooden bottom, K23, adjustable 9"	60.00
Pliers, needle nose	35.00
Price tag, rnd, tie-on	5.00
Puzzle, w/orig box	1,250.00
Radio, Keen Tone, electric	400.00
Razor, straight; K15, logo in hdl & on blade	40.00
Razor hone, K20, w/metal box	70.00
Reel, Keen Kaster	45.00
Rule, boxwood, 4-fold, K680, 24"	45.00
Safety razor, colored plastic hdl, in orig box	30.00
Saw, back; K44	50.00
Saw, mitre; w/CI mitre box	300.00
Saw, hand; K816, 28" blade w/logo	50.00
Scissors, Stork, bird form	150.00
Scissors, 7½"	8.00
Screwdriver, hardwood hdl	25.00
Screwdriver, offset, K7	70.00
Screwdriver rack, 5½x24x10½"	150.00
Shotgun, 16-gauge, mk Keen Kutter	350.00
Showcase, for scissors or shears, on ped, slant top	800.00
Sign, tin, w/hardware store name, 9¾x27¾"	150.00
Spade, ditch	25.00
Square, combination, mk on blade, maroon hdl	100.00
Square, framing	30.00
Square, 4-square, 10"	75.00
Tape measure, metallic, 50-ft	75.00
Tool box, oak, dbl-door, 31"	750.00
Vise, hand-held type, K49, 7"	200.00
Wagon, Jet, red, boy's	250.00
Wrench, adjustable crescent; K10	40.00
Wrench, alligator; K20	40.00
Wrench, bicycle; K94	75.00
Wrench, pipe; 18"	30.00
Yardstick, sliding; w/hardware store advertisement	35.00

Kellogg Studio

Stanley Kellogg (1908 – 1972) opened the Kellogg Studio in

Petoskey, Michigan, in 1948. It remained in operation until 1976, producing a wide range of both decorative and functional ceramics including dinnerware, vases, and figurines. Most pieces are glazed in rich, solid colors and are marked 'Petoskey' as well as 'S. Kellogg Studio' or 'Kellogg's.' Stanley Kellogg began as a sculptor, and it was while working on an outdoor monument with the great Swedish-American sculptor, Carl Milles, that Stanley suffered the back injury which forced him to turn to studio work. In addition to naturalistic treatments of Michigan wildlife, Kellogg developed some angular, architectural forms in his molded art pottery. Our co-advisors for this category are Walter P. Hogan and Wendy L. Woodworth; they are listed in the Directory under Michigan.

Bowl, bl w/flower-frog lid, 3¼" dia 30.00
Bowl, chartreuse, 8-sided asymmetrical, 2½x4" 35.00
Dish, bl teardrop form w/tiny flower-frog insert, 3½" 10.00
Figurine, Great Horned Owl on branch, brn & ivory, 7¼" 65.00
Figurines, mama duck, 7", w/2 different 3½" ducklings 50.00
Flower-frog vase, yel matt, spherical w/pentagonal rim, 3¼" 30.00
Jar, rust/brn streaked, flowers etched on lid, rnd, 4" 35.00
Plate, maple leaf theme, 10" 10.00
Table set, sky bl, rnd cr/sug+sq shakers+8x4" rectangular tray 75.00
Vase, burgundy, bulbous w/cylindrical top, slanted rim, 5" 25.00
Vase, gunmetal blk, narrow hourglass shape, 13" 80.00

Kelva

Kelva was a trademark of the C.F. Monroe Company of Meriden, Connecticut; it was produced for only a few years after the turn of the century. It is distinguished from the Wave Crest and Nakara lines by its unique Batik-like background, probably achieved through the use of a cloth or sponge to apply the color. Large florals are hand painted on the opaque milk glass; and ormolu and brass mounts were used for the boxes, vases, and trays. Most pieces are signed. Our advisors for this category are Dolli and Wilfred Cohen; they are listed in the Directory under California.

Whisk broom holder, blue, $1,950.00.

Photo courtesy Wilfred Cohen

Biscuit jar, floral, wht on peach, SP lid & hdl, rare 900.00
Box, floral bouquets, pk on gray, 3x6" 700.00
Box, lilies on pk, 8-sided, 4x6" 550.00
Box, lilies on red, sq, 3x4x4" 500.00
Box, parrot tulips, pk/wht on gr, 8-sided, 4x6" 600.00
Box, poppies, pk on bright bl, oval, 5½x4" 495.00
Box, starflower w/pk stems on med gr, 6-sided, 3½x4" 500.00
Ferner, wild roses on gr, 8" dia 595.00
Humidor, Cigars & flowers on gr, 5x3½" 995.00
Pin tray, wild roses on gr, hexagonal, ormolu rim/hdls 200.00
Vase, daisies on gr, ormolu hdls, 9" 1,000.00
Vase, floral on pk, gold scrolls, SP ormolu ft, 8½x3½" 650.00

Vase, wild roses/gold scrolls/drapes on bl, SP base, 8½" 650.00

Kenton Hills

Kenton Hills Porcelain was established in 1940 in Erlanger, Kentucky, by Harold Bopp, former Rookwood superintendent, and David Seyler, noted artist and sculptor. Native clay was used; glazes were very similar to Rookwood's of the same period. The work was of high quality, but because of the restrictions imposed on needed material due to the onset of the war, the operation failed in 1942. Much of the ware is artist signed and marked with the Kenton Hills name or cipher and shape number.

Ashtray, horse head form, brn/bl glossy, Seyler, #182, 6" 110.00
Vase, bl-gr aventurine, U-shape, 5¾x5" 325.00
Vase, brn stripes & dots on gr, WE Hentschel, #105, 4" 375.00
Vase, gazelles/geometrics on gr, Hentschel, #134, 6½", NM 550.00
Vase, squeeze-bag brn dots/lines on pk matt, 4x4½" 300.00

Kentucky Derby Glasses

Kentucky Derby glasses are the official souvenir glasses sold at Churchill Downs filled with mint juleps on Derby Day. Many folks from all over the country who attend the Derby take home the souvenir glass, and thus the collecting begins. The first glass (1938) is said to have either been given away as a souvenir or used for drinks among the elite at the Downs. This one, the 1939 glass, two glasses from 1940, the 1940 – 41 aluminum tumbler, the 'Beetleware' tumblers from 1941 – 44, and the 1945 short, tall, and jigger glasses are the rarest, most sought-after glasses, and they command the highest prices. Some 1974 glasses incorrectly listed the 1971 winner Canonero II as just Canonero; as a result, it became the 'mistake' glass for that year. Also, glasses made by the Federal Glass Company (whose logo is a tiny shield with an F inside) were used for extra glasses for the 100th running in 1974. There is also a 'mistake' and a correct Federal glass, making four to collect for that year.

In order to identify the year of a pre-1969 glass, since it did not appear on the front of the glass prior to then, simply add one year to the last date listed on the back of the glass. This may seem to be a confusing practice, but the current year's glass is produced long before the Derby winner is determined. Our advisor for this category is Betty Hornback; she is listed in the Directory under Kentucky.

1940, aluminum 800.00
1940, French Lick, aluminum 800.00
1941-44, Beetleware, from $2,500 to 4,000.00
1945, jigger 1,000.00
1945, regular 1,400.00
1945, tall 425.00
1946-47, ea 100.00
1948, clear bottom 190.00
1948, frosted bottom 200.00
1949 ....190.00
1950 ....425.00
1951 ....550.00
1952, Gold Cup 190.00
1953 ....150.00
1954 ....185.00
1955 ....135.00
1956, 4 variations, ea from $150 to 250.00
1957, gold & blk on frosted 110.00
1958, Gold Bar 175.00
1958, Iron Leige 200.00

1959-60, ea	80.00
1961	100.00

1962, Churchill Downs, red, gold, and black on clear glass, $70.00.

1963-64, ea	50.00
1965	70.00
1966	55.00
1967-69, ea	50.00
1970	55.00
1971	45.00
1972	40.00
1973	45.00
1974, Federal (ea), from $125 to	150.00
1974, mistake	18.00
1974, regular	16.00
1975	12.00
1976	14.00
1976, plastic	12.00
1977	10.00
1978-79, ea	12.00
1980	18.00
1981-82, ea	12.00
1983	9.00
1984-85, ea	10.00
1986	12.00
1986 (1985 copy)	18.00
1987-89, ea	9.00
1990-92, ea	8.00
1993-96, ea	6.00
1997-98, ea	4.00
1999	3.00

Kew Blas

Kew Blas was a trade name used by the Union Glass Company of Summerville, Massachusetts, for their iridescent, lustered art glass produced from 1893 until about 1920. The glass was made in imitation of Tiffany and achieved notable success. Some items were decorated with pulled leaf and feather designs, while others had a monochrome lustre surface. The mark was an engraved 'Kew Blas' in an arching arrangement.

Cordial, red-gold, distended stem, 5"	325.00
Decanter, gold w/EX irid, ribbed/pnt stopper, 15"	1,450.00
Tumbler, gold, pinched sides, 3"	275.00
Vase, amber w/pulled gr int decor, wide trumpet form, 4x5"	800.00
Vase, feathers, gold on opal-cased amber, 7"	980.00
Vase, feathers, gr on amber irid, tooled/spiked rim, 10"	520.00
Vase, feathers, gr/gold on wht, gold rim int, 6½x7"	1,450.00
Vase, gold irid lustre w/splotches & spots, goblet form, 8¼"	750.00
Vase, gold w/lav irid, ribbed ovoid w/flared rim, att, 3¼"	200.00

King's Rose

King's Rose was made in Staffordshire, England, from about 1820 to 1830. It is closely related to Gaudy Dutch in body type as well as the colors used in its decoration. The pattern consists of a full-blown, orange-red rose with green, pink, and yellow leaves and accents. When the rose is in pink, the ware is often referred to as Queen's Rose.

Coffeepot, dome lid, pearlware, 11¼"	650.00
Creamer, pk band w/emb dmns, 4½"	200.00
Creamer, Queen's Rose, pearlware, 4½"	230.00
Cup & saucer, pk/red/gr/yel, NM	180.00
Cup & saucer, Queen's Rose, pearlware, 2⅛x3⅜", 5½", EX	130.00
Cup & saucer, vine border w/sm roses, 2¼x3⅝", 5½", NM	150.00
Pitcher, milk; pearlware, 5⅜"	300.00
Plate, orange stripes on rim, 6¾"	110.00
Plate, orange stripes on rim, 8¼"	250.00
Plate, pk border, 7½", EX	130.00
Plate, pk border w/emb dmns, 8⅛"	185.00
Plate, Queen's Rose, pearlware, scalloped rim, unmk, 7⅜"	95.00
Plate, Queen's Rose, 5¼"	75.00
Plate, Queen's Rose, 6⅝"	85.00
Plate, toddy; 4¾"	275.00
Sugar bowl, Queen's Rose, pearlware, dmn shape, w/lid, 5⅝"	250.00
Teapot, pk border, emb shell-design body, C hdl, 6⅛", EX	85.00
Teapot, Queen's Rose, pearlware, 5⅝"	350.00

Kitchen Collectibles

During the last half of the 1850s, mass-produced kitchen gadgets were patented at an astonishing rate. Most were ingeniously efficient. Apple peelers, egg beaters, cherry pitters, food choppers, and such were only the most common of hundreds of kitchen tools well designed to perform only specific tasks. Today all are very collectible.

For further information we recommend *Kitchen Glassware of the Depression Years* and *Anchor Hocking's Fire-King & More,* both by Gene Florence; and *Kitchen Antiques, 1790 – 1940,* by Kathryn McNerney. See also Appliances; Butter Molds and Stamps; Cast Iron; Cookbooks; Copper; Glass Knives; Molds; Pie Birds; Primitives; Reamers; String Holders; Tinware; Trivets; Wooden Ware; Wrought Iron.

Cast-Iron Kitchen Ware

Be aware that cast-iron counterfeit production is on the increase. Items with phony production numbers, finishes, etc., are being made at this time. Many of these new pieces are the popular cornstick pans. To command the values given below, examples must be free from damage of any kind or excessive wear. Waffle irons must be complete with all three pieces and the handle. The term 'EPU' in the description lines refers to the Erie PA, USA mark. The term 'block mark' refers to the lettering in the large logo that was used ca 1920 until 1940; 'slant logo' refers to the lettering in the large logo ca 1900 to 1920. Victor was Griswold's first low-budget line (ca 1875). Skillets #5 and #6 are uncommon, while #7, #8, and #9 are easy to find. For further information contact our advisor, Grant S. Windsor (SASE required); he is listed in the Directory under Virginia. See also Keen Kutter; Clubs and Newsletters.

Aebleskiver pan, Griswold #32, Diamond Erie trademk	200.00
Baster, Wagner #9, drip-drop, lg	75.00
Bunt cake pan, Griswold	1,000.00
Cake mold, lamb, Griswold #866	100.00
Cake pan, Danish; Griswold #31, full writing	150.00

Cornbread pan, Wagner, tea sz 60.00
Cornstick pan, Griswold, Erie #273 ....25.00
Cornstick pan, Griswold #262 ....65.00
Cornstick pan, Puritan 100.00
Deep fat fryer, Griswold, w/basket 45.00
Dutch oven, Griswold #12, w/trivet 650.00
Gem pan, Griswold #8, EPU, slant trademk 250.00
Golf ball pan, Griswold #9, full writing 150.00
Griddle, Griswold #9, block mk, hdl type 35.00
Griddle, Griswold #9, Erie/slant logo, oval type 175.00
Heat Regulator, Griswold #300, dbl-sided 325.00
Kettle, Griswold #6, flat bottom, w/lid, scarce 650.00
Kettle, Griswold #8, Maslin shape, 6-qt 75.00
Lemon squeezer, Griswold #2, CI 125.00

Photo courtesy Grant S. Windsor

**Muffin pan, Griswold #13 Turk Head,
Pattern #60, $1,600.00.**

Muffin pan, Griswold #240 ....475.00
Patty mold, Griswold #3, combination set, MIB 150.00
Popover pan, Griswold #10, #949, no cutouts 30.00
Popover pan, Griswold #18, wide hdl 65.00
Popover pan, Wagner 'R' 45.00
Roaster, Oval; Griswold #5, full writing top, w/trivet ...475.00
Roaster, Wagner #5, w/trivet 275.00
Scotch bowl, Griswold #5, block mk 60.00
Skillet, dbl; Wagner 125.00
Skillet, egg; Griswold #129, sq w/hdl on corner 40.00
Skillet, Griswold, 5-in-1 Breakfast 150.00
Skillet, Griswold #2, block mk, no heat ring 425.00
Skillet, Griswold #4, wood hdl, block mk, no ring, pattern #758 ....600.00
Skillet, Griswold #5, block mk, w/heat ring 500.00
Skillet, Griswold #6, Victor (full writing) 325.00
Skillet, Griswold #7, block mk, w/smoke ring 35.00
Skillet, Griswold #9, block mk, no heat ring 30.00
Skillet, Griswold #10, block mk, no smoke ring 50.00
Skillet, Griswold #12, sm trademk 65.00
Skillet, Griswold #14, bailed hdl 1,200.00
Skillet, Griswold #775 Sq Toy 175.00
Skillet, Victor #8, full markings 45.00
Skillet, Wagner #4, #1054, w/smoke ring 50.00
Skillet, Wagner #5, wood hdl 125.00
Skillet, Wagner #9, smooth bottom 55.00
Skillet, Wagner #10, heat ring 55.00
Skillet, Wagner #11, pie logo 475.00
Skillet, Wapak Indian #9 ....125.00
Skillet grill, Griswold #299 ....100.00
Skillet lid, Griswold #12, low dome, full writing top ...250.00
Skillet lid, Griswold #3, raised letters, low dome 550.00
Skillet lid, Griswold #5, low dome, full writing top ...500.00
Skillet lid, Griswold #8, high dome, full writing top 50.00
Teakettle, Wagner, child sz 200.00
Trivet, Griswold #8 Dutch oven 25.00

Waffle iron, French; Griswold #8, 3-section 1,200.00
Waffle iron, Griswold #11, sq, high base 100.00
Waffle iron, Wagner #9 ....50.00
Whole wheat stick pan, Griswold #27 ....275.00

Egg Beaters

Egg beaters are unbeatable. Ranging from hand-helds, rotary crank, and squeeze power to Archimedes up-and-down models, egg beaters are America's favorite kitchen gadget. A mainstay of any kitchenware collection, in recent years egg beaters have come into their own — nutmeg graters, spatulas, and can openers will have to scramble to catch up! At the turn of the century, everyone in America owned an egg beater. Every household did its own mixing and baking — there were no pre-processed foods. And every inventor thought he/she could make a better beater. Thus American ingenuity produced more than one thousand egg beater patents, dating back to 1856, with several hundred different models being manufactured over the years. As true examples of Americana, egg beaters have risen in value over the past couple of years, with a half dozen mixers valued at $2,000.00 and more, including the cast-iron, rotary-crank 'Dodge Race Course egg beater.' But the vast majority stay under $50.00, while the values of the super rare beaters continue upward. And just when you think you've seen them all, new ones always turn up, usually at flea markets or garage sales. For further information, we recommend our advisor (author of the definitive book on egg beaters) Don Thornton, who is listed in the Directory under California. (SASE required.)

A&J, all metal, sm, 9¾" 10.00
A&J, center drive, pk & gray wooden hdls, 12" 12.00
Aluminum Beauty Pat'd April 20, 1920, rotary crank, 10½" ...15.00
Beats Eggs, Cream...No 825 Androck, hand-held fan type, 11" ...5.00
Dover...Patd May 6th 1873...1891..., CI rotary crank, 11¼" ...55.00
Express or 'Fly Swatter,' Pat Oct 25, 1887, 11½" ...1,800.00
Holt's Egg Beater & Cream Whip, CI, Pat August 22 '99-Apr 6 '00, 9" ...240.00
Jaquette Phila PA, CI & wire, dbl hdls, Pat No 3, 10½" ...1,000.00
Jiffy Whip...Krasbert & Sons Mfg, rotary crank turbine, 11¾" ...25.00
K-C (soap bubble), 1930s, 10" 75.00
Keystone Mfg, Pat Dec 15 '85, Philadelphia PA, wall mt, EX ...425.00
Quik Whip Reg US Pat Off..Pending, metal, squeeze power, 11¾" ...295.00
Star Egg Beater April 19, 59 Oct 16, 60, CI rotary crank, 10½" ...900.00
Turbine Beater Androck Made in USA, rotary crank, 11½" ...18.00
Vandeusen Egg Whip, CA Chapman...1894, all metal, hand held, 11" ...15.00
Whipwell...USA Pat Mch 23 1920..., rotary crank, wood hdl, 11" ...25.00

Glass

Batter jug, amber, Paden City, w/lid 250.00
Batter jug, blk, Fenton 175.00
Batter jug, cobalt, McKee 125.00
Bottle, water; Forest Green, w/lid 30.00
Bowl, cobalt, 8½" 40.00
Bowl, custard, flared sides, 8" 18.00
Bowl, Delphite, horizontal ribs, Jeannette, 5½" 65.00
Bowl, Jade-ite, vertical ribs, Jeannette, 9¾" 25.00
Bowl, Jade-ite, w/decor, Hocking, 6½" 15.00
Bowl, mixing; blk, 7⅜" 55.00
Bowl, mixing; Delphite, vertical ribs, Jeannette, set of 4 ...260.00
Bowl, mixing; gr, paneled, 11½" 35.00
Bowl, mixing; pk, Hex Optic, flat rim, 9" 30.00
Bowl, pk, no spout, 2-hdl, 9" 25.00
Bowl, Skokie Green, McKee, 9" 20.00
Bowl, wht w/red fired-on Dutch figures, 7" 10.00
Butter box, gr, rectanglar, 2-lb 200.00

Butter box, pk, emb B, Jeannette, 2-lb 180.00
Butter dish, amber, Federal, 1-lb 35.00
Butter dish, Delphite, rectangular, McKee 285.00
Butter dish, gr, Block Optic, Hocking 55.00
Butter dish, pk, bow-hdld lid 60.00
Canister, blk letters on milk glass, McKee, 48-oz 55.00
Canister, caramel, matching lid, 40-oz 75.00
Canister, clear w/gr 'Taverne' scene decal 35.00
Canister, custard, Coffee in blk enamel, sq sides, metal lid 40.00
Canister, Delphite, Coffee, Jeannette, 40-oz 375.00
Canister, dk amber, emb Tea, tin lid 75.00
Canister, Dutch boy decal on clear, sq sides, lg 20.00
Canister, frosted, Owens-Illinois, tin lid, 40-oz 20.00
Canister, Jade-ite (lt or dk), screw-on kid, rnd, Jeannette, 40-oz ..95.00
Canister (sugar), dk amber, ribbed sphere, tin lid 125.00
Casserole, dk amber, oval, Cambridge, w/lid 55.00
Casserole, gr, Pyrex 25.00
Casserole, wht clambroth, oval, Pyrex 125.00
Cookie jar, gr, LE Smith 125.00
Cookie jar, Peacock Blue, LE Smith 100.00
Cruet, frosted w/rooster decal, clear stopper 15.00
Cup, soup; fired-on color 4.00
Curtain tie bks, Feathered, dk amber, pr 25.00
Decanter, gr, pinched teardrop shape, Hocking 45.00
Decanter, yel opaque, pinched sides, Mckee 110.00
Egg cup, amber, Paden City 10.00
Fork & spoon set, cobalt 55.00
Gravy boat, gr, Cambridge, w/tray 85.00
Gravy boat, pk, 2-spout, Cambridge 45.00
Gravy boat, red, Imperial, w/tray 175.00
Grease jar, Red Tulips on milk glass, Vitrock 25.00
Ladle, Chalaine Blue, screw-on hdl 200.00
Marmalade, Emerald-Glo, w/lid & spoon 25.00
Measuring cup, caramel, 2-spout, McKee, 1-cup 600.00
Measuring cup, Chalaine Blue, no hdl, 4-cup 1,500.00
Measuring cup, Chalaine Blue, 2-spout, 1-cup 800.00
Measuring cup, clambroth, Hocking, 2-cup 150.00
Measuring cup, clear, McKee Glasbake Scientific, 2-cup 25.00
Measuring cup, cobalt, 3-spout, Hazel Atlas, 1-cup 400.00
Measuring cup, gr, dry measure (no spout), Cambridge, 1-cup ...275.00
Measuring cup, gr, 20-oz 150.00
Measuring cup, gr, 3-spout, Federal 45.00
Measuring cup, gr, 3-spout, no hdl, Federal 35.00
Measuring cup, milk glass, Glasbake, McKee 75.00
Measuring cup, pk, ¼-cup 45.00
Measuring cup, Ultramarine, 1-cup 55.00
Measuring cup, Vitrock (milk glass), Hocking, 2-cup 40.00
Measuring pitcher, Chalaine Blue, ftd, 4-cup 450.00
Measuring pitcher, Delphite, McKee, 4-cup 550.00
Measuring pitcher, Delphite, sunflower in base, Jeannette, 2-cup ...80.00
Measuring pitcher, gr, 36-oz 160.00
Measuring pitcher, Jade-ite, 2-cup 22.00
Measuring pitcher, pk, slick hdl 45.00
Mug, Chalaine Blue 30.00
Mug, clambroth 35.00
Mug, yel, Hazel Atlas 35.00
Napkin holder, blk, Paden City, Party Line 150.00
Napkin holder, milk glass, Slen-dr-fold 55.00
Parfait, gr, Paden City 18.00
Pitcher, amber, w/lid, Chesterfield 95.00
Pitcher, batter; pk, Jenkins 175.00
Pitcher, Skokie Green, McKee, 2-cup 20.00
Pretzel jar, pk, Hocking 95.00
Refrigerator dish, Chalaine Blue, 7¼" sq 125.00

Refrigerator dish, clambroth, oval, Hocking, 8" 35.00
Refrigerator dish, fired-on yel w/clear glass lid, Pyrex, 7x9" 10.00
Refrigerator dish, gr, Tufglas, 5⅞" sq 25.00
Refrigerator dish, milk glass (Vitrock), Hocking, 8x8" 35.00
Refrigerator dish, pk, indented hdls, 4x4" 25.00
Refrigerator dish, yel opaque, Hocking, 6x6" 22.50
Rolling pin, Chalaine Blue, shaker top 1,750.00
Rolling pin, clambroth, wooden hdls 150.00
Rolling pin, Peacock Blue 275.00
Scoop, gr, sm 40.00
Shaker, fired-on color, colored metal lid, ea 6.00
Shakers, Forest Green, pr 20.00
Spoon & fork, salad; gr frost, Heisey 100.00
Sugar cube tray, yel, Cambridge 75.00
Sugar shaker, amber, Paden City, metal lid 225.00
Sugar shaker, Jade-ite (dk), metal lid, Jeannette 75.00
Sundae, gr, fluted 25.00
Teakettle, clear, Glasbake 35.00
Tumbler, pk, Mission Juice 30.00
Tumbler, Rena line, gr, Paden City 12.00
Tumbler/egg cup, Skokie Green, McKee 15.00
Water bottle, red, plain or ribbed, Hocking 200.00
Water dispenser, cobalt, LE Smith 450.00

Miscellaneous

Cream whip/mayonnaise mixer, Holt-Lion Co, Tarrytown NY, aqua pint jar, smooth base, hand-beater closure, all original, M, $375.00.

Apple corer, Ateco Std, dk gray tin tube type 8.00
Apple corer, silver T-shape 35.00
Apple peeler, CI, 5-geared, mk Pat Pending 95.00
Apple peeler, Goodell Turntable 98, CI, EX 65.00
Apple peeler, Hudson Pat 1882, CI 85.00
Apple peeler, Reading #78, CI, 12" 145.00
Apple peeler, wooden table-top style, branded JS on clamp, 14" ..250.00
Apple segmenter, JCB, tin, tall strap hdl 95.00
Biscuit cutter, Egg Baking Powder 225.00
Biscuit cutter, Kreamer, strap hdl 10.00
Cake decorator, tin tubular shape, 18 different points, 1900s, 7" ..45.00
Cake spatula, porc w/floral decals & gold trim, mk MIG 10.00
Can opener, CI bull's head figural, pnt traces, 5¾" 55.00
Can opener, CI bull's head figural, tail forms hdl, 1800, 6⅜" 65.00
Can opener, CI fish figural, ca 1900, 5⅛" 70.00
Can opener, Pet Milk, tin, rnd 20.00
Cheese drainer, tin, rnd, ftd, hdl 125.00
Cherry seeder, Family Cherrystoner (dbl), CI, EX 40.00
Cherry seeder, New Standard, CI 110.00
Chopper, flat steel blade, maple hdl, 8¾", G 45.00
Churn, Dazey #10, beveled edge, 1-qt 1,350.00
Churn, Dazey #10, bull's-eye, 1-qt 1,300.00

Churn, Dazey #20 ....**200.00**
Churn, Dazey #30, Pat 1922 ....**225.00**
Churn, Dazey #40 ....**140.00**
Churn, Dazey #400, heavy tin, 4-gal **200.00**
Churn, Dazey #60 ....**165.00**
Churn, Dazey #80 ....**250.00**
Churn, Elgin, 2-qt **125.00**
Churn, syllabub; Wonder Merger, tin **110.00**
Churn, unmk, glass, 1-gal **75.00**
Cottage cheese mill, dvtl wood **250.00**
Doughnut cutter, Dover, dk tin **12.00**
Egg poacher, copper, tin-lined, 3-compartment **185.00**
Egg separator, Town Talk Flour Has No Equal, dk tin **20.00**
Egg timer, bellhop, ceramic, gr, Japan, 4½" **60.00**
Egg timer, cat w/ribbon at neck, ceramic, mk Germany **85.00**
Egg timer, Colonial lady w/bonnet, ceramic, mc, Germany, 3¾" ..**65.00**
Flour scoop, Pillsbury, tin, sifting type **95.00**
Flour sieve, Kno-Bugs, tin, can shape, bottom sifter, w/lid **25.00**
Flour sifter, Bromwell, pnt tin, ca 1940s-50s, EX **15.00**
Flour sifter, Duplex, gray tin, center wood hdl, 1922, 6¾" **30.00**
Flour sifter, Ernshaw, tin scoop shape **150.00**
Flour sifter, Rumford Baking Powder, 1950s, scarce, EX **75.00**
Fly trap, glass, hanging type **35.00**
Funnel, Dover, tin **12.00**
Grater, All in One Pat Pending, tin, ca 1940, 10½x4¼" **25.00**
Grater, cheese; iron & tin w/wood top, 3-ftd, mk MIG **15.00**
Grater, chocolate; Edgar, Nov 10, 1896 ....**275.00**
Grater, nutmeg; Gem, rotary **135.00**
Grater, nutmeg; tin & wood half cylinder, 5¼x3", VG **85.00**
Grater, tin, hand punched, w/hdl, on brd **125.00**
Grater, vegetable; Schroeter, iron, tin bk, wood hdl, old bl pnt **40.00**
Grinder, herb; CI, rnd blade w/sq hole center, boat-like base, 17" ..**750.00**
Grinder, meat; Favorite #27, Pat Feb 18, 1896, complete **12.00**
Grinder, meat; Universal #323, cast metal, from $12 to **15.00**
Ice cream maker, White Mountain Junior, EX **395.00**
Juicer, Handy Andy, heavy aluminum, 3-leg, rnd base, crank hdl ...**28.00**
Lemon squeezer, wooden, hinged **55.00**
Measure cup, Rumford, tin **85.00**
Milk can, tin w/lid & bail hdl, sm, 1-pt **50.00**
Noodle cutter, Titantonios, CI, clamps to table **55.00**
Pie crimper, brass, dbl wheels, rare **135.00**
Pie crimper, iron shank hdl w/brass 2½" wheel, 7" **150.00**
Pie crimper, lg iron wheel w/wood hdl, handmade **110.00**
Pie crimper, wood hdl, brass collar & 1½" wheel, 8", EX **120.00**
Pie crimper, wood w/2" wheel, 7¼", EX **75.00**
Pie crimper, wrought iron, star & rosettes on wheel, 1790s, 6⅜" ..**300.00**
Pot scrubber, chain, iron hdl, 1893 ....**70.00**
Potato baker, Rumford, tin **75.00**
Potato masher, CI, lacy rnd mashing end **20.00**
Potato masher, old grid wire style w/wood hdl **7.50**
Potato peeler, Hamlinite, Pat July 20-20 ....**85.00**

Knives

Knife collecting as a hobby began in earnest during the 1960s when government regulations required for the first time that knife companies mark their product with the country of origin. The few collectors and dealers cognizant of this change at once began stockpiling the older knives made before this law was enacted. Another impetus to the growing interest in this area came with the Gun Control Act of 1968, which severely restricted gun trading. Frustrated gun dealers transferred their attention to knives. Today there are collectors' clubs in many of the states.

The most sought-after pocketknives are those made before WWII.

However, Case, Schrade, and Primble knives of a more recent manufacture are also collected. Most collectors prefer knives 'as found.' Do not attempt to clean, sharpen, or in any way 'improve' on an old knife.

The prices quoted here are for knives in mint condition. If a knife has been used, sharpened, or blemished in any way, its value decreases. Knives in excellent condition generally are valued at half the prices listed below. The newer the knife, the greater the reduction in value. For further information refer to *The Standard Knife Collector's Guide, 2nd Edition*, by Ron Stewart and Roy Ritchie; and *Sargent's American Premium Guide to Knives and Razors, Identification and Values, 3rd Edition*, by Jim Sargent. Our advisor for this category is Bill Wright; he is listed in the Directory under Indiana.

Key:
bd — blade
imi — imitation
jack — jackknife
s/b — slant button
wb — winterbottom

Case, B1098, waterfall hdl, 1-bd, Tested XX, 5½" **500.00**
Case, C91050SAB, onyx hdl, 1-bd, Tested XX, 5⅛" **650.00**
Case, GS233, gold-stone hdl, 2-bd, Tested XX, 1920-40, 2⅝" ...**300.00**
Case, R1093, candy-stripe hdl, 1-bd, Tested XX, 5" **400.00**
Case, 1202, grafting/budding, wood hdl, 2-bd, Tested XX, 3⅜" ..**400.00**
Case, 2136, blk compo hdl, 1-bd, Tested XX, 4⅛" **140.00**
Case, 22087, slick blk hdl, 2-bd, 10 Dot, 1970, 3¼" **30.00**
Case, 2383, slick blk hdl, 3-bd, Tested XX, 3½" **325.00**
Case, 31093, toothpick, yel compo, hi-pull, 1-bd, Tested XX, 5" ..**250.00**
Case, 5207, stag hdl, 2-bd, Tested XX, 3½" **450.00**
Case, 52086, stag hdl, 2-bd, Tested XX, 1920-40, 3¼" **450.00**
Case, 5375, stag hdl, 3-bd, 10 Dot, 4¼" **85.00**
Case, 5488, stag hdl, 4-bd, Tested XX, 4⅛" **1,200.00**

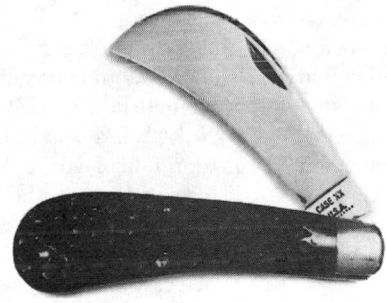

Case, #61011, jigged wood scales, one blade, 10 Dot, 4", $30.00.

Case, 61011, Rogers bone hdl, 1-bd, Tested XX, 4" **210.00**
Case, 6185, red bone hdl, 1-bd, XX, 1940-64, 3⅝" **110.00**
Case, 62027, gr bone hdl, 2-bd, Tested XX, 1920-40, 2¾" **135.00**
Case, 62063½, gr bone hdl, 2-bd, Tested XX, 1920-40, 3⅛" **120.00**
Case, 62096, toothpick, gr bone hdl, 2-bd, Tested XX, 3⅛" **400.00**
Case, 6214, gr bone hdl, 2-bd, XX, 1940-55, 3⅜" **125.00**
Case, 6250, red bone hdl, 2-bd, 1940-64, 4⅜" **350.00**
Case, 6269LP, gr bone hdl, 2-bd, XX, 3" **150.00**
Case, 6345, gr bone hdl, 3-bd, Tested XX, 3⅝" **250.00**
Case, 6347SHPU, bone hdl, 3-bd, XX, 3⅞" **75.00**
Case, 6380, whittler, gr bone hdl, 3-bd, XX, 3⅞" **600.00**
Case, 6392, gr bone hdl, 3-bd, XX, 4" **210.00**
Case, 64052, bone hdl, 4-bd, XX, 3½" **90.00**
Case, 6445R, utility, gr bone hdl, 4-bd, Tested XX, 3¾" **225.00**
Case, 6488, 2nd-cut stag hdl, 4-bd, USA, 4⅛" **500.00**
Case, 8201, pearl hdl, 2-bd, XX, 1940-64, 2⅝" **110.00**
Case, 8201, pearl hdl, 2-bd, XX, 2⅝" **110.00**
Case, 8264TF, pearl hdl, 2-bd, Tested XX, 1920-40, 3⅛" **185.00**
Case, 8364SC, pearl hdl, 3-bd, Tested XX, 3⅛" **250.00**

Case, 9201, pearl hdl, 2-bd, 10 Dot, 2⅝" 30.00
Case, 92058, faux pearl hdl, 2-bd, Tested XX, 1920-40, 3¼" 125.00
Case, 92210, cracked ice hdl, 2-bd, Tested XX, 1920-40, 3⅜" 500.00
Keen Kutter, Coke bottle, ebony hdl, 1-bd, 5¼" 200.00
Keen Kutter, Congress, pearl hdl, 2-bd, file, 2½" 75.00
Keen Kutter, dog-leg jack, walnut hdl, 1-bd, 3⅜" 60.00
Keen Kutter, equal-end jack, cocobolo hdl, 1-bd, 3¼" 25.00
Keen Kutter, K16, Congress, brn bone hdl, 4-bd, 3½" 90.00
Keen Kutter, peanut, cracked ice hdl, 2-bd, 2⅞" 35.00
Keen Kutter, sleeveboard pen, pearl hdl, 2-bd, EC Simmons, 2⅞" ..45.00
Keen Kutter, stockman pen, cracked ice hdl, 3-bd, 4" 85.00
Keen Kutter, Texas toothpick, brn bone hdl, 1-bd, EC Simmons, 5" ...175.00
Keen Kutter, whittler, stag hdl, 3-bd, swell center, 3¾" 300.00
Pal, Barlow, bone hdl, 2-bd, tang stamp, 3½" 100.00
Pal, bone hdl, 2-bd, swell center/shield, tang stamp, 3" 35.00
Pal, faux onyx hdl, 1-bd, tang stamp, bail, 3" 20.00
Pal, jack, faux onyx hdl, 2-bd, swell end, tang stamp, 3⅜" 50.00
Pal, serpentine jack, lt bone hdl, 2-bd, tang stamp, 3⅝" 60.00
Queen, Rogers stag hdl, 2-bd, Queen City, 4½" 90.00
Queen, 13, Rogers bone hdl, 1-bd, Queen Big Q, 4⅛" 55.00
Queen, 18, jack, wb bone hdl, 2-bd, Big Q, 3⅝" 50.00
Queen, 24, trapper, wb bone hdl, 2-bd, Queen Steel, 4" 35.00
Queen, 33, Congress, Rogers bone hdl, 4-bd, Big Q, 3½" 120.00
Queen, 38, pen, wb bone hdl, 2-bd, Queen Steel, 3" 70.00
Queen, 46, fisherman's, wb bone hdl, 2-bd, Queen Steel, 5" 35.00
Queen, 57, pearl hdl, 3-bd, 3⅜" 30.00
Queen, 6105, stag hdl, 2-bd, swell center, Queen, 3½" 35.00
Remington, bow tie, R653, bone hdl, 1-bd, 3⅞" 400.00
Remington, RB47, Barlow, brn bone hdl, 2-bd, 3⅜" 200.00
Remington, RG44, brn bone hdl, 2-bd, 3⅜" 150.00
Remington, RH73, jack, brn bone hdl, 2-bd, 3⅛" 130.00
Remington, R1045, jack, pyremite hdl, 2-bd, 3⅜" 175.00
Remington, R105A, onyx hdl, 2-bd, 3⅜" 150.00
Remington, R1061, jack, redwood hdl, 2-bd, 3⅜" 90.00
Remington, R1073, bone hdl, 2-bd, 3⅜" 150.00
Remington, R1240, Barlow, brn bone hdl, 1-bd, 5" 300.00
Remington, R135, pyremite hdl, 3-bd, 3½" 150.00
Remington, R1383, lock-bk, brn bone hdl, 1-bd, fishscaler, 4¼" ..450.00
Remington, R1535, florist, faux ivory hdl, 1-bd, 3¾" 100.00
Remington, R1653, peanut, brn bone hdl, 2-bd, 2⅞" 125.00
Remington, R181, jack, redwood hdl, 2-bd, 3¾" 150.00
Remington, R1915LP, candy-stripe hdl, 2-bd, 3⅜" 150.00
Remington, R213, jack/easy opener, bone hdl, 2-bd, 3⅝" 180.00
Remington, R258, cocobolo hdl, 2-bd, 3⅝" 150.00
Remington, R3054, stockman, pearl hdl, 3-bd, 4" 400.00
Remington, R3059, stockman, all metal, 3-bd, 4" 250.00
Remington, R31, redwood hdl, 2-bd, 3⅛" 90.00
Remington, R3273, cattle, equal-end, brn bone hdl, 3-bd, 3¾" .250.00
Remington, R333, equal-end, brn bone hdl, 2-bd, 3¾" 175.00
Remington, R503, bone hdl, 2-bd, 3½" 180.00
Remington, R563, brn bone hdl, acorn shield, 2-bd, 3¼" 150.00
Remington, R7284, lobster, pearl hdl, 2-bd, bail, 3" 100.00
Remington, R732, blk compo hdl, 1-bd, 4½" 120.00
Remington, R803, hawkbill, bone hdl, 1-bd, 3" 100.00
Remington, R8034, bartender's, pearl hdl, 2-bd, 2⅞" 250.00
Remington, R953, toothpick, brn bone hdl, 1-bd, 5" 225.00
Remington, R973, jack, faux bone hdl, 2-bd, 4¼" 275.00
Western States, A127, amber cream compo hdl, 1-bd, 5¼" 65.00
Western States, C208, jack, candy stripe pyralin hdl, 2-bd, 3⅝" ..75.00
Western States, lobster, pearl hdl, 2-bd, 2½" 45.00
Western States, S203B, gr sparkle hdl, 2-bd, bail, 2½" 25.00
Western States, 12229½, peanut, pearl hdl, 2⅞" 20.00
Western States, 2230, pearl o/l compo hdl, 2-bd, 4½" 125.00
Western States, 422, bone hdl, 2-bd, shield, 3⅝" 50.00

Western States, 6100, bone hdl, 1-bd, buffalo skull etch, 5⅜" 300.00
Western States, 6211½, Barlow, bone hdl, 2-bd, 3⅜" 100.00
Western States, 6242, serpentine jack, bone hdl, 2-bd, 3⅜" 30.00
Western States, 8344, pearl hdl, 3-bd, 2⅞" 40.00
Winchester, 1608, cocobolo hdl, 1-bd, 3⅜" 70.00
Winchester, 1922, stag hdl, 1-bd, 3⅛" 120.00
Winchester, 1936, toothpick, brn bone hdl, 1-bd, 5" 350.00
Winchester, 2059, Senator, celluloid hdl, 1-bd, 3¼" 100.00
Winchester, 2204, NP silver hdl, 2-bd, 3⅛" 75.00
Winchester, 2330, pen, pearl hdl, 2-bd, 3¼" 125.00
Winchester, 2380, dr's, pearl hdl, 2-bd, 3¼" 400.00
Winchester, 2691, trapper, cocobolo hdl, 2-bd, 3⅞" 300.00
Winchester, 2847, pen, brn bone hdl, 2-bd, 3¼" 125.00
Winchester, 2991, peanut, brn bone hdl, 2-bd, 2⅞" 140.00
Winchester, 3345, whittler, pearl hdl, 3-bd, 3¼" 225.00
Winchester, 3382, lobster, pearl hdl, 3-bd, 3" 150.00

Kosta

Kosta glassware has been made in Sweden since 1742. Today they are one of that country's leading producers of quality art glass. Two of their most important designers were Elis Bergh (1929 – 1950) and Vicke Lindstrand, artistic director from 1950 to 1973. Lindstrand brought to the company knowledge of important techniques such as Graal, fine figural engraving, Ariel, etc. He influenced new artists to experiment with these techniques and inspired them to create new and innovative designs. Today's collectors are most interested in pieces made during the 1950s and '60s. Our advisor for this category is Abby Malowanczyk; she is listed in the Directory under Texas.

Bowl, bl-cut-to-clear ovals/disks, Lindstrand/56693, 5x6½" 575.00
Bowl, wht opaque threads on clear, LH 1004, Lind/Strand, 5⅜" ...230.00
Decanter, pheasant form, eng feathers, Lindstrand/8218, 8" 465.00
Obelisk, 2 sides w/petroglyphs eng on bl, 3rd clear, Warff, 5" 700.00
Paperweight, mushroom; clear/bubbles, amber ft, Warff/97323, 4" ...200.00
Rose bowl, emb floral panels on clear satin, 1936, 7x7" 485.00
Sculpture, etched running horses, V Lindstrand, 4x20x1¾" 750.00
Sculpture, iceberg, aqua w/etched elk, V Lindstrand WL 90002, 6" 200.00

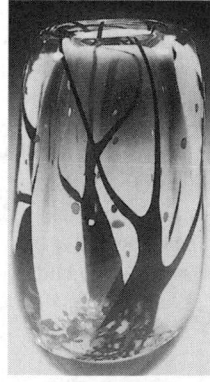

Vase, Autumn, stylized black-brown trees with multicolored falling leaves, designed by Vicke Lindstrand, Kosta LU 2011 on base, 7", $3,100.00.

Vase, clear w/emerald int cut to clear w/circles, B-2779, 6" 285.00
Vase, clear w/3 gr patches cut w/circles, Lindstrand/46190, 8½" ...660.00
Vase, flattened teardrop on base, bl int, Lindstrand 1962/63, 6" ...250.00
Vase, maypole dancers, ftd bottle form, Lindstrand/LG-2309, 12" 225.00
Vase, sq w/stylized cut base, V Lindstrand/46116, 11x4" 625.00

Vase, vertical brn/bl stripes cased in clear, LCI, 12" **425.00**

Kutani

Kutani, named for the Japanese village where it originated, was first produced in the seventeenth century. The early ware, Ko Kutani, was made for only about thirty years. Several types were produced before 1800, but these are rarely encountered. In the nineteenth century, kilns located in several different villages began to copy the old Kutani wares. This later, more familiar type has large areas of red with gold designs on a white ground decorated with warriors, birds, and flowers in controlled colors of red, gold, and black.

Box, mc floral w/gold, 3 gold ft, 20th C, 2x4¾" **65.00**
Cup, pomegranates & archaic signs **300.00**
Cup & saucer, gold dragon decor, geisha lithophane **25.00**
Inkwell, cherry blossoms w/gold, 7x4" **200.00**
Jardiniere, pheasants, 19th C, rpr, 11⅛x11½" **160.00**
Plate, floral diapering w/gold, 19th C, 8¼" **250.00**
Tea set, Oriental ladies, lakeside pagoda, 1900-20s, 3-pc **85.00**
Vase, orange floral w/gold, bulbous base, 6x5" **120.00**

Labels

Before the advent of the cardboard box, wooden crates were used for transporting products. Paper labels were attached to the crates to identify the contents and the packer. These labels often had colorful lithographed illustrations covering a broad range of subjects. Eventually the cardboard box replaced the crate, and the artwork was imprinted directly onto the carton. Today these paper labels are becoming collectible — primarily for the art, but also for their advertising appeal. Our advisor for this category is Cerebro; their address is listed in the Directory under Pennsylvania.

Can, Big Chief Malt Syrup, uniformed man smoking cigar, 1929, EX **30.00**
Can, Campus Peaches, college buildings/pennant, 1936, EX **15.00**
Can, Cobcut, hand cutting corn off cob, 1930, M **10.00**
Can, Delight Malt Syrup, man smiling at can, 1929, EX **18.00**
Can, Duff's Molasses, gingerbread man, 1929, EX **5.00**
Can, Easter Peaches, Easter lilies/peaches, 1936, VG **20.00**
Can, Fairview, old car on country road, 1911, M **12.00**
Can, Fountain Oysters, fountain/basket of oysters, 1933, M **20.00**
Can, Gold Camel, camel on desert/pyramid, 1922, EX **40.00**
Can, La Choy Chow Mein Noodles, 1924, EX **7.00**
Can, Light House Peas, clipper ship, 1923, EX **18.00**
Can, Masperos Coffee, woman drinking coffee, 1914, EX **30.00**
Can, South Shore Peaches, golfers/country cub/golf bag, 1934, EX ..**30.00**
Can, Vadco Talcum Powder, skyscraper, 1923, EX **30.00**
Cigar box, inner lid; Bleriot, man/airplane, 1909, EX **60.00**
Cigar box, inner lid; Commodore Watson, battle ships, 1898, EX **150.00**
Cigar box, inner lid; Cyro, Roman wearing toga, 1915, M **12.00**
Cigar box, inner lid; El Stymo, Indian sharing w/ladies, 1910, M .**25.00**
Cigar box, inner lid; Elk, nature scene, 1911, EX **150.00**
Cigar box, inner lid; Junio, 1903, M **15.00**
Cigar box, inner lid; Lime Kiln Club, Black men at meeting, 1883, EX ...**500.00**
Cigar box, outer; Adolphus Busch, 1913, M **200.00**
Cigar box, outer; Grand Knight, knight in gold armor, 1896, M ..**35.00**
Cigar box, outer; Motorist, Mercury driving through flames, 1922, M ..**35.00**
Cigar box, outer; Shetland Ponies, 1931, M **50.00**
Cigar box, outer; Volumo, field/port/town, 1907, M **12.00**
Cigar box, outer; Washington, portrait, silver, 1895, EX **100.00**
Cigar box, outer; woman/plantation, 1895, M **12.00**

Crate, apple; Airship, 1920, M **250.00**
Crate, apple; Dainty Maid, girl w/apple, 1930, M **12.00**
Crate, apple; Sebastopol Queen, apple queen w/wand, 1950, M **2.00**
Crate, California Orange, Boulevard, estate/valley/hills, 1947, M ...**25.00**
Crate, California Orange, Memory, hacienda, 1920, M **9.00**
Crate, California Orange, Reindeer, buck/mountains/lake, 1920, M .**15.00**
Crate, California Orange, Vital, woman playing tennis, 1930, EX ...**175.00**

**Crate, Champ Louisiana Sweet
Potatoes, 1930s, 9x9", $4.00.**

Crate, Florida Citrus, Blue & Gray, generals clasp hands, 1930, M **15.00**
Crate, Florida Citrus, Chest of Gold, chest of oranges, 1940, M **4.00**
Crate, Florida Citrus, Merry Christmas, 1920, M **35.00**
Crate, lemon; First American, Indian brave/teepee, 1916, M **150.00**
Crate, lemon; Paula, senorita w/fan, 1930, EX **18.00**
Crate, lemon; Southern Cross, mission/stars, 1930, M **80.00**
Crate, pear; B-Wise, owl on bl background, 1930, M **16.00**
Crate, pear; Grand Prize, California mission, 1915, M **15.00**
Crate, pear; Tie-It-On, dog w/pear tied to tail, 1930, M **6.00**

Labino

Dominick Labino was a glass blower who until mid-1985 worked in his studio in Ohio, blowing and sculpting various items which he signed and dated. A ceramic engineer by trade, he was instrumental in developing the heat-resistant tiles used in space flights. His glassmaking shows his versatility in the art. While some of his designs are free-form and futuristic, others are reminiscent of the products of older glasshouses. Because of problems with his health, Mr. Labino became unable to blow glass himself; he died January, 10, 1987. Work coming from his studio since mid-1985 has been signed 'Labino Studios, Baker,' indicating ware made by his protegee, E. Baker O'Brien. In addition to her own compositions, she continues to use many of the colors developed by Labino.

Bowl, gold-red, tooled base, 1976, 3¼x7¾" **400.00**
Bowl, opaque pulls in amber, 1977, 7" **800.00**
Cordial, red to amber, twisted air-bubble stem, 1969, 6½" **1,000.00**
Emergence, dbl veil & encased air, 1976, 6" **6,100.00**
Panel, gr w/brn, 18x18" **800.00**
Paperweight, bl w/purple clouds, opal/brn swirls, conical, 4" **325.00**
Paperweight, coiled snake in amethyst & gr, 1969, 2¾" **225.00**
Paperweight, peach w/air bubbles & veil, 1971, lg **400.00**
Sculpture, abstract form w/long amber bubble, 1971, 7" **750.00**
Sculpture, angular anvil form, bubbles/veils of color, '72, 10" **750.00**
Sea Kingdom, clear w/bl fish, 1979, 4" **4,800.00**
Vase, bl w/brn design & bubbles, 1968, 5½" **750.00**
Vase, clear w/silver loopings, 1968, 10" **1,700.00**
Vase, emerald w/bubble inclusions, 1970, 5½" **450.00**
Vase, gr/opal w/bl eruptions & bubbles, spherical, 1970, 4½" **600.00**

Vase, iron red opaque, hdls, ovoid, 1967, 6½" **825.00**
Vase, marbled gr, bottle form, 1968, 6½" **400.00**
Vase, mc design w/veil, sq, 1984, 4½" **650.00**
Vase, purple w/everted rim, 1966, 7½" **400.00**
Vase, red irid w/appl ribbed leaves & prunts, 1970, 6¼" **900.00**
Vase, red-amber opal, melon ribbed, 1970, 4½" **270.00**
Vase, silver schmelz, wide rim, 1968, 6" **1,300.00**
Vase, silver schmelz w/lav & gr swirls, wide mouth, 1968, 7½" ..**1,500.00**
Vase, striated red, pierced-through hole hdl, 1980, 4" **260.00**
Vase, thick/clear w/bl stripes, yel-pk core, #7-1392, 7½" **800.00**

Lace, Linens, and Needlework

Two distinct audiences vie for old lace and linens. Collectors seek out exceptional stitchery like philatelists and numismatists seek stamps or coins — simply to marvel at its beauty, rarity, and ties to history. Collectors judge lace and linens like figure skaters and gymnasts are judged: artist impression is half the score, technical merit the other. How complex and difficult are the stitches and how well are they done? The 'users' see lace and linens as recyclables. They seek pretty wearables or decorative materials. They want fashionable things in mint condition, and have little or no interest in technique. Both groups influence price.

Undiscovered and underpriced are the eighteenth-century masterpieces of lace and needle art in techniques which will never be duplicated. Their beauty is subtle. Amazing stitches often are invisible without magnification. To get the best value in any lace, linen, or textile item, learn to look closely at individual stitches, and study the design and technique. The finest pieces are wonderfully constructed. The stitches are beautiful to look at, and they do a good job of holding the item together. Our advisor for this category is Elizabeth M. Kurella; she is listed in the Directory under Michigan.

Key: embr — embroidered

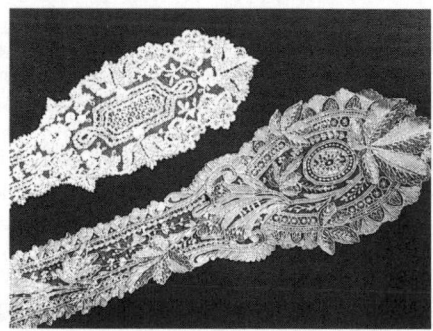

Photo courtesy Lace Merchant

19th-century lappets, both about 30" long and about 3" – 4" wide at the bottom, Left: Pointe de Gaze needle lace, Right: Belgin bobbin lace, each about $125.00 to $150.00.

Bedspread, crewel, wool on cotton homespun, cutwork hem, 102x72" ..**350.00**
Bedspread, crochet, Popcorn stitches (sqs/triangles), 102x124" ..**325.00**
Bedspread, crochet, stars form 4½" circles, 90x92" **135.00**
Bedspread, crochet, 8" pinwheels, 82x66"+fringe **80.00**
Blanket, twill-woven wool plaid, rust/gr/sage/yel, 1840, 82x70" .**800.00**
Bridal veil, 8" L teardrop, 14" needle-lace border, rprs **1,100.00**
Doiley, Battenberg, grapes & leaves, 10" dia **75.00**
Dresser scarf, embr mc floral on wht w/crochet edge, 17x45" **25.00**
Hand towel, embr mc flowers on wht, 8x14", from $10 to **15.00**
Handkerchief, hairpin lace **45.00**
Lappet, Argentan needle lace, joined, ca 1740, G **475.00**

Mat, embr flowers & leaves on wht w/crochet edge, oval, 19x11" ...**36.00**
Napkin, simple embr flowers & border, 10½" sq **5.00**
Needlework panel, landscape/flowers, wool/silk on silk, 19x16" ..**1,200.00**
Needlework panel, wool on felt, bird in tree w/berries, 18x20" ...**300.00**
Needlework pc, petit point, Asian couple, 1920s, 3x4", pr **65.00**
Pillowcase, crochet edge, pr **35.00**
Runner, Battenberg flowers, scalloped, 14x38" **175.00**
Runner, crochet, butterflies down center, tassels, 11x25" **70.00**
Runner, filet lace, Grecian women w/instruments, 10x23" **95.00**
Runner, filet lace, ladies w/flower baskets, 16x50" **135.00**
Runner, lace & needlework, wht & mc floss scene, 13x52" **215.00**
Sham, red embr, child in bed w/angel holding cover, 27" sq **70.00**
Shams, 16" Battenberg center, buttoned bk, 30x30"+ruffle, pr ...**155.00**
Sheet, natural linen, embr MS 1862 in red, rolled hem, 86x88" ...**50.00**
Show towel, homespun w/cutwork stars/ladies & embr, 60x18" .**360.00**
Show towel, X-stitch flowers/animals/birds/name/1847, 8x18" ...**165.00**
Table pc, Battenberg lace, 14" dia **70.00**
Table pc, tatted lace, 11" dia **60.00**
Tablecloth, Battenberg inserts, 110", +12 napkins **350.00**
Tablecloth, homespun, gold & wht check, hand hemmed, 40x68" ...**220.00**
Tablecloth, ivory w/ecru lace in center, 4 lace inserts, 90" dia ...**125.00**
Tablecloth, linen, ecru, Cluny lace medallions, 136" L **225.00**
Tablecloth, machine lace, floral pattern, 72x100" **245.00**
Tablecloth, turkey-red fringed linen, 1890s, 87x60" **110.00**
Tablecloth, wht lawn, 82x65", +6 napkins w/cutwork & embr ..**115.00**
Tablecloth, wht w/floral needle lace openwork, banquet sz **450.00**
Tablecloth, 4" Cluny lace insert center, 10" lace border, 48" dia ..**265.00**

Lacy Glassware

Lacy glass became popular in the late 1820s after the development of the pressing machine. It was decorated with allover patterns — hearts, lyres, sheaves of wheat, etc. — and backgrounds were completely stippled. The designs were intricate and delicate, hence the term 'lacy.' Although Sandwich produced this type of glassware in abundance, it was also made by other eastern glassworks as well as in the Midwest. By 1840, its popularity on the wane and a depressed economy forcing manufacturers to seek less expensive modes of production, lacy glass began to be phased out in favor of pressed pattern glass.

For more information read *Sandwich Glass* by Ruth Webb Lee. When no condition is indicated, the items listed below are assumed to be without obvious damage; minor roughness is normal. See also Salts, Open.

Bowl, Hairpin, shallow, 8⅛" **385.00**
Bowl, Heart & Lyre rim, Plaid center, shallow, 8⅜" **635.00**
Bowl, Industry, 6¼", EX **150.00**
Bowl, Princess Feather, shallow, 10" **465.00**
Bowl, Quatrefoil, 9⅝" **165.00**
Bowl, Rayed Peacock Eye, 1¾x7½" **110.00**
Bowl, Tulip & Acanthus, 7½" **140.00**
Compote, Heart, appl knop stem, 3½x4¾" **400.00**
Compote, Heart, bladed stem, rnd base w/pontil, 4x6" **425.00**
Compote, leaves/shields, dbl-knop stem, 4x6" **375.00**
Compote, Roman Rosette bowl, Hairpin base, 3x6", EX **475.00**
Compote, Roman Rosette bowl, on stem w/cup plate base, 4x6" ..**2,250.00**
Dish, bull's-eye rim, Midwestern, rectangular, 9" **100.00**
Dish, bull's-eye rim, C scrolls/zigzags, star center, 8" **600.00**
Dish, Gothic Arch, rectangular, 6¼x8¼" **275.00**
Plate, Midwestern rope border, 6" **70.00**
Plate, Roman Rosette, 9⅜" **165.00**
Plate, toddy; Grape Vine & Harp (Satyr), 4¼", pr, EX **250.00**
Sugar bowl, flower basket/2-headed eagle/shield, lid, 6", VG ..**3,300.00**

Sugar bowl, Gothic Arch, bright bl, 5¼" 1,200.00
Taster, Sunflower, ftd, 2¼" 150.00
Tureen, cobalt, Sandwich, mini, 2x3" 1,200.00
Whiskey taster, bl opaque, flaking on base, 1¾" 325.00
Whiskey taster, emerald gr, petal ft, 1¾" 425.00

Lalique

Beginning his lengthy career as a designer and maker of fine jewelry, Rene Lalique at first only dabbled in glass, making small panels of cire perdue (wax casting) to use in his jewelry. He also made small flacons of gold and silver with his glass inlays, which attracted the attention of M.F. Coty, who commissioned Lalique to design bottles for his perfume company. The success of this venture resulted in the opening of his own glassworks at Combs-la-Ville in 1909. In 1921 a larger factory was established at Wingen-sur-Moder in Alsace-Lorraine. By the '30s Lalique was world renown as the most important designer of his time.

Lalique glass is lead based, either mold blown or pressed. Favored motifs during the Art Nouveau period were dancing nymphs, fish, dragonflies, and foliage. Characteristically the glass is crystal in combination with acid-etched relief. Later some items were made in as many as ten colors (red, amber, and green among them) and were occasionally accented with enameling. These colored pieces, especially those in black, are highly prized by advanced collectors.

During the '20s and '30s, Lalique designed several vases and bowls reminiscent of American Indian art. He also developed a line in the Art Deco style decorated with stylized birds, florals, and geometrics. In addition to vases, clocks, automobile mascots, stemware, and bottles, many other useful objects were produced. Most items made before his death in 1945 were marked 'R. Lalique'; later the 'R' was deleted even though some of the original molds were still used. Numbers found on the bases of some pieces are catalog numbers. Beware of fraudulent pieces that have began to surface in increasing numbers. Our advisor for this category is John Danis; he is listed in the Directory under Illinois.

Key:

cl/fr — clear and frosted	RL — signed R. Lalique
L — signed Lalique	RLF — signed R. Lalique, France
LF — signed Lalique France	

Ashtray, Soudan, zigzag design, cl/fr, LF, 4½x4½" 195.00
Ashtray, 8 beaded indents, opal, LF, 7½" dia 175.00
Beaker, oak leaves, cl/fr, LF, 4¼x3½" 75.00
Bottle, scent; Baptiste, waves/spirals, cl/fr, L in script, 2½" 155.00
Bottle, scent; Calendale, fr w/gr wash, Molinard Lalique, 4½" ...1,000.00
Bottle, scent; Cassis, red, currant berry stopper, RL, 4¾" 7,185.00
Bottle, scent; Cigales, cl/fr w/amber wash, RL, 5½" 3,300.00
Bottle, scent; Dahlia, fr w/blk enamel, button stopper, LF, 3⅜" .145.00
Bottle, scent; Flausa, cl/fr w/pk wash, after 1914, 4¾" 4,000.00
Bottle, scent; Jaytho, tulips, cl/fr w/amber wash, RL, 4" 1,100.00
Bottle, scent; Je Revins, dk bl w/turq cap, for Worth, 12" 900.00
Bottle, scent; Le Jade, jungle birds, bright gr, RL, 3¼" 2,185.00
Bottle, scent; Palerme, cl teardrop w/pearls, RL/Maison, 4⅝" 440.00
Bottle, scent; Poesie d'Orsay, maidens, cl w/amber wash, 6" 3,850.00
Bottle, scent; Quatre Cigales, cicadas ea corner, RLF, 5¾" 1,150.00
Bottle, scent; Salamandres, cl/fr, L in block, 3¾" 1,320.00
Bottle, scent; Sans Adieu, gr w/pine cone stopper, RLF, 5¾" ..1,350.00
Bottle, scent; Tzigane, cl/fr, RL, 3¾", MIB 880.00
Bowl, Dahlia #1, blossom ft, opal, RLF, 3½x9" 1,100.00
Bowl, Marguerites, flower heads, gr wash, RLF, 2¼x13" 935.00
Bowl, Perruches, 20 lovebirds, bl patina, RL/F, 9¾" 1,500.00
Bowl, Pinsons, bird, cl/fr, Cristal LF, 9¼" 250.00
Bowl, resting on fr base w/4 birds, LF, 3x5" 165.00
Bowl, 5 lg flowers in relief, cl, LF, 14" 220.00
Bowl, 6 opal sunflowers on ext, RLF, 2¼x8½" 175.00
Box, Emiliane, floral, cl w/sepia wash, 4" dia 230.00
Box, Pappillons, 3 butterflies on lid, mk L Depose, 2x3" 920.00
Bracelet, Rondelles, gr glass discs on extensible cord 1,840.00
Ceiling light bowl, birds/berries/foliage, sepia, LF, 13½" 485.00
Cigarette lighter, lion's head, LF, 4½x4" 155.00
Coupe-Vasque, Coquilles, shells, bl opal, RLF, 3½x9½" 500.00
Display decoration, free-standing cl wedge w/fr trademk, LF, 5" L 145.00
Figurine, Danseus, cl/fr, LF, 9½x4½" 400.00
Figurine, elephant, on plinth, fr, LF, 6x6" 415.00
Figurine, Leda & Faune, maidens w/animals, fr, LF, 4½", pr 200.00
Figurine, Madonna & Child, cl/fr on blk sq plinth, LF, 14" 700.00
Figurine, Naiade, mermaid w/coiled tail, RLF, 5¼" 3,100.00
Figurine, Perdrix Inquiete, cl/fr, LF, 5¼x5½" 385.00
Figurine, turtle, Caroline, amber opaline, LF, 2x6" 200.00
Inkstand, Biches, deer, red-amber, RL, #427, 3¾", w/6" tray ...2,500.00
Jar, Epines, thorns, sepia patina, RL, F on base, 3½" 460.00
Necklace, Feuilles de Lievre, 20 gr leaf forms, restrung 2,000.00
Necklace, Fleurettes, 11 1¼" floral-banded bbl beads 1,300.00
Necklace, Fleurs et Rinceaux, 12 1¼" bl beads on bl cord 2,300.00
Ornament, table; Luxembourg, 3 cherubs, cl/fr, LF, 8" 800.00
Pendant, Trefles, clovers, opal w/bl wash, L, #1656, 2¼" 900.00
Stopper, L'Air du Temps for Ricci, lovebirds, 6x12" 100.00
Tester, Les Fleurs d'Orsay, 5 receptacles, fr, 8¾" L, EX 1,200.00

Vase, Bacchantes, opalescent, France, 9¾", $5,500.00 (signed Lalique, France, $1,500.00).

Vase, Bacchantes, cl/fr, LF, 5", NM 400.00
Vase, Biches, wildflowers, cl/fr, L Crystal F, 6½x4½" 600.00
Vase, burnt amber w/lg wing-shaped hdls, RLF, 12½" 800.00
Vase, Claude, tall slim neck, cl/fr, LF, 13¾" 385.00
Vase, Courlis, sea terns, red-amber, shouldered, RLF, 6½" 3,600.00
Vase, Danaides, nudes w/urns, opal, cylindrical, RLF, 7" 1,400.00
Vase, Esterel, leaves, fr w/bl wash, RLF, 6" 1,600.00
Vase, fern fronds on teal frost, ovoid, RL, 8" 600.00
Vase, lappet panels, cl fan form, LF, 6¼" 300.00
Vase, Laurier, spiked leaves/berries, cl cylinder, RL, #947, 7" 315.00
Vase, Lierre, ivy leaves, bl-gray wash on cl, RLF, 7x6" 600.00
Vase, Oleron, fish, gray fr oval, RLF, #1008, 3½" 460.00
Vase, Palme, ferns, bl-gray wash, spherical, RL, 4½" 400.00
Vase, Perruches, lovebirds, electric bl, fr/polished, RLF, 10" .10,000.00
Vase, Ronces, branches, fr, RL, #946, 9¼" 575.00
Vase, 6 Figurines at Masques, nudes/grotesques, fr, LF, 9½" 2,400.00

Lamps

The earliest lamps were simple dish containers with a wick that hung over the edge or was supported by a channel or tube. Grease and oil from animal or vegetable sources were the first fuels used. Ancient pottery lamps, crusie, and Betty lamps are examples of these early types.

In 1784 Swiss inventor Ami Argand introduced the first major improvement in lamps. His lamp featured a tubular wick and a glass chimney. During the first half of the 19th century, whale oil, burning fluid (a highly explosive mixture of turpentine and alcohol), and lard were the most common fuels used in North America. Many lamps were patented for specific use with these fuels.

Kerosene was the first major breakthrough in lighting fuels. It was demonstrated by Canadian geologist Dr. Abraham Gesner in 1846. The discovery and drilling of petroleum in the late 1850s provided an abundant and inexpensive supply of kerosene. It became the main source of light for homes during the balance of the 19th century and for remote locations until the 1950s.

Although Thomas A. Edison invented the electric lamp in 1879, it was not until two or three decades later that electric lamps replaced kerosene household lamps. Millions of kerosene lamps were made for every purpose and pocketbook. They ranged in size from tiny night or miniature lamps to tall stand or piano lamps. Hanging varieties for homes commonly had one or two fonts (oil containers), but chandeliers for churches and public buildings often had six or more. Wall or bracket lamps usually had silvered reflectors. Student lamps, parlor lamps (now called Gone-with-the-Wind lamps), and patterned glass lamps were designed to complement the popular furnishing trends of the day. Gaslight, introduced in the early 19th century, was used mainly in homes of the wealthy and public places until the early 20th century. Most fixtures were wall or ceiling mounted, although some table models were also used.

Few of the ordinary early electric lamps have survived. Many lamp manufacturers made the same or similar styles for either kerosene or electricity, sometimes for gas. Top-of-the-line lamps were made by Pairpoint, Phoenix, Tiffany, Bradley and Hubbard, and Handel. See also these specific sections.

When buying lamps that have been converted to electricity, inspect them very carefully for any damage that may have resulted from the alterations; such damage is very common, and when it does occur, the lamp's value may be lessened by as much as 50%. Lamps seem to bring much higher prices in some areas than others, especially the larger cities. Conversely, in rural areas they may bring only half as much as our listed values. One of our advisors for lamps is Carl Heck; he is listed in the Directory under Colorado. Advice for miniature lamps comes from Bob Culver (who is listed in the Directory under Michigan), and Jeff Bradfield (in Virginia) is our advisor for pattern glass lamps. See also Stained Glass.

Key: col — cut overlay

Aladdin Lamps, Electric

From 1908 Aladdin lamps with a mantle became the mainstay of rural America, providing light that compared favorably with the electric light bulb. They were produced by the Mantle Lamp Company of America in over eighteen models and more than one hundred styles. During the 1930s to the 1950s, this company was the leading manufacturer of electric lamps as well. Still in operation today, the company is now known as Aladdin Industries LLC., located in Nashville, Tennessee. For those seeking additional information on Aladdin Lamps, we recommend *Aladdin — The Magic Name in Lamps*, *Aladdin Electric Lamps Collector's Manual & Price Guide #3*, and *Aladdin Collector's Manual and Price Guide #18*, all written by our advisor for Aladdins, J. W. Courter; he is listed in the Directory under Kentucky. Mr. Courter has also published a book called *Angle Lamps, Collector's Manual and Price Guide*.

Bed, #832 SS, Whip-o-lite pleated shade **275.00**
Bedroom, M-59, Colonial Modern candlestick **50.00**

Bedroom, P-51, ceramic 25.00
Boudoir, E-410, glass, early 60.00
Boudoir, G-40, Alacite, 1952 ....40.00
Boudoir, M-148, metal, 1937 ....40.00
Bridge, #2051 ....225.00
Bridge, #2073, walnut 300.00
Bridge, #7092, swing arm, reflector 175.00
Bridge/table combination, #7091 ....225.00
Figurine, G-16, lady, crystal, etched 750.00
Figurine, G-234, pheasant 275.00
Floor, #3281, Alacite ring, no candle arms, w/night light 250.00
Floor, #3334, reflector 175.00
Floor, #3358, IES reflector 225.00
Floor, #3690, reflector, candle arms 200.00
Floor, #3761, torchere 275.00
Floor, #4886C, Certified, Circline flourescent tube 200.00
Floor, C-130, Colonial, amber or gr bowl, sm 250.00
Glass Urn, G-213A, Alacite, closed 225.00
Pin-up, G-352, Panel & Scroll, Alacite 85.00
Ranch House, G-378C, Alacite Bullet, illuminated urn 325.00
Table, E-200, Vogue Ped, gr 375.00
Table, G-140, Moonstone 80.00
Table, G-179, Opalique 150.00
Table, G-2, marble-like glass 325.00
Table, G-20 ....200.00
Table, G-223, Alacite 50.00
Table, G-25, glass 150.00
Table, G-265, Alacite 50.00
Table, G-84, Velvex, minimum value 450.00
Table, M-367, iron base, spun glass shade 15.00
Table, M-495, brass metal 20.00
Table, MT-509, Magic Touch, ceramic base 300.00
Table, P-401, ceramic 50.00
Table, P-417, ceramic 40.00
TV, TV-425, metal w/foil shade 25.00

Aladdin Lamps, Kerosene

Caboose Model B, B-400, brass font, w/shade 250.00
Crystal Vase Model #12, red Venetian Art-Craft, 10¼" 400.00
Crystal Vase Model #12, variegated tan, 12" 175.00
Floor Model #12, bl & gold, w/burner, no shade 200.00
Floor Model B, #1254, bronze & gold, 1933-35 ....175.00
Floor Model B, B-267, oxidized bronze, 1935 ....175.00
Floor Model B, B-284, silver & gold, 1937-38 ....200.00
Florentine Vase Model #12, Rose Moonstone, 8½" 2,600.00
Foreign Table Model #8, London 275.00
Foreign Table Model C, B-139, aluminum font 50.00
Hanging Model #2, w/#203 shade 450.00
Hanging Model #23, aluminum hanger & font, wht paper shade ..75.00
Hanging Model #7, w/#416 shade 600.00
Hanging Model B, inside chain, parchment shade 375.00
Practicus, parlour, polished brass or Old English 600.00
Shelf Model #23 Lincoln Drape, clear, 1975-82 ....100.00
Tabel Model #5, satin brass or nickel 225.00
Table Model #11, nickel 120.00
Table Model #23, A-4181, Designer Marble, porc base, brn 90.00
Table Model #23 Short Lincoln Drape, cobalt, 1987 ....125.00
Table Model A, Venetian, #99, clear 300.00
Table Model B, Beehive, B-81, gr crystal 125.00
Table Model B, Cathedral, #108, gr crystal 125.00
Table Model B, Colonial, #105, gr 175.00
Table Model B, Corinthian, B-106, clear font, amber ft 125.00
Table Model B, Majestic, B-120, wht moonstone 375.00

Table Model B, Orientale, B-130, ivory 175.00
Table Model B, Queen, B-95, wht moonstone, oxidized bronze base ...375.00
Table Model B, Quilt, B-92, wht moonstone & rose moonstone ..325.00
Table Model B, Short Lincoln Drape, B-61, amber crystal 2,500.00
Table Model B, Simplicity, B-76A, Alacite, plain 150.00
Table Model B, Solitaire, B-70, wht moonstone 2,200.00
Table Model B, Tall Lincoln Drape, B-76, cobalt, scalloped ...1,800.00
Table Model B, Treasure, B-137, bronze 125.00
Table Model B, Vertique, B-88, yel moonstone 600.00
Table Model B, Washington Drape, B-40, gr crystal, rnd base 125.00
Table Model B, Washington Drape, B-43, clear, plain stem 80.00
Table Model B, Washington Drape, B-48, gr crystal, bell stem ..350.00
Table Model B, Washington Drape, B-50, clear, filigree stem ...100.00
Wall Bracket Model #1, no shade 600.00
Wall Bracket Model #23, B-180, aluminum font 70.00
Wall Bracket Model #6, no shade 200.00

Angle Lamps

The Angle Lamp Company of New York City developed a unique type of kerosene lamp that was a vast improvement over those already on the market; they were sold from about 1896 until 1929 and were expensive for their time. Our Angle lamp advisor is J.W. Courter; he is listed in the Directory under Kentucky. See the narrative for Aladdin Lamps for information concerning popular books Mr. Courter has authored.

Gas adaptor, polished brass, no glass, EX 850.00
Hanging, #224, nickel, rose floral, no glass, EX 750.00
Hanging, #263, polished brass, old glass, EX 475.00
Hanging, #284, antique brass, no glass, EX 500.00
Hanging, #352, polished brass, 3-burner, no glass, EX 600.00
Hanging, dbl, leaf & vine, nickel, EX 375.00
Wall, #103, nickel, old glass, NM 265.00
Wall, #104, grape pattern, nickel, no glass, EX 275.00
Wall, #125, Pinwheel, nickel, no glass, EX 350.00
Wall, #285, antique brass, old glass, EX 1,000.00
Wall, Classic #3, antique gold, no glass, EX 1,000.00
Wall, dbl, grape pattern, brass, old glass, EX 950.00
Wall, Leaf & Vine, nickel, old glass, EX 400.00
Wall cone, tin, blk pnt, no glass 200.00

Chandeliers

Queen Anne, brass with six removable S-scroll candle arms, 21x27½" diameter, $3,100.00.

Argand, bronze, 2-arm, floral band, patterned chain, 33x26" ..1,500.00
Bronze & crystal w/Rococo inspiration, 8-light, 40x20" 1,600.00
Bronze Neoclassical style, 6-light, orig patina, ca 1900 ....3,850.00
Deco brass w/gilt, 6-arm, glass shades, 39" drop, 26" dia 1,350.00
Fr Provincial tole-piente florals, 12-light, 36x36" dia 1,500.00
Gilt bronze, 12-light, cut cranberry center bowl, 27x34" 3,000.00

Gilt bronze, 5 scroll arms, hexagonal cups, 17x9½", pr 600.00
Regency-style, patinated bronze, 3-light, late 1800s, 27" 1,875.00
SP bronze Regency w/crystals/prisms, 5-light, 1800s, 38x17" ..6,500.00

Decorated Kerosene Lamps

When only one color is given in a two-layer cut overlay lamp description, the second layer is clear; in three-layer examples, the second will be white, the third clear.

Col (2-layer) amethyst, stepped marble base, brass stem, 12" 415.00
Col (2-layer) bl, bl opaque stem insert, marble base, 14" 1,760.00
Col (2-layer) bl w/gilt traces, marble base, 8" 330.00
Col (2-layer) clambroth/bl, wht base, 8¾" 300.00
Col (2-layer) cranberry, cut ruby stem, grape-etch shade, 23" .1,250.00
Col (2-layer) cranberry, gr stem insert, marble/brass base, 14" 500.00
Col (2-layer) cranberry, rpl gilt metal base, brass collar, 13" 275.00
Col (2-layer) cranberry, wht base, Sandwich, 13" 800.00
Col (2-layer) cranberry, wht stem, cranberry cut-floral shade, 19" .1,700.00
Col (2-layer) emerald gr, gr opaque w/gold stem, 13", NM 7,000.00
Col (2-layer) gr w/worn gilt, marble base, 8½" 330.00
Col (2-layer) lime gr font w/worn gilt, dk lime gr base, 11" 385.00
Col (2-layer) red, Star & Quatrefoil, Sandwich, 17", pr 550.00
Col (2-layer) ruby, wht opaque base, brass mts, 14" 770.00
Col (2-layer) violet-bl, marble base, att Sandwich, 14" 1,000.00
Col (3-layer) bl, brass connector/collar, 10" 300.00
Col (3-layer) bl font w/gilt, wht opaque base, 13⅜" 770.00
Col (3-layer) bl font w/worn gilt, marble base, brass stem, 10" ...600.00
Col (3-layer) cobalt, w/blk opaque base, 21¼" 1,650.00
Col (3-layer) pk, brass stem, 3-layer floral shade, 20" 1,450.00
Col (3-layer) pk font, fiery opal base, 13½" 880.00
Col (3-layer) pk font w/gilt, gr opaque stem, marble base, 14" ...1,045.00
Col (3-layer) pk w/gilt, stepped marble/brass base, 12" 550.00
Col (3-layer) red, gr opaque base w/gold, Sandwich, 13" 1,900.00
Col (3-layer) red, wht base, Sandwich, 22", NM 1,200.00
Col (3-layer) red w/gilt, cut/etch shade, prisms, Sandwich, 33" .3,500.00
Col (3-layer) tomato checkerbrd font, wht base, chimney, 14" ..1,050.00
End-of-day clambroth base, clear font w/wht loopings, 10" 1,400.00
Jade gr waisted font w/gold on brass stem, marble base, 9" 650.00
Lt gr craquelle font w/gilt, wht base, brass collar, 10" 330.00
Reed Oval threaded font, cranberry/wht, wht base, 8", EX 550.00
Victorian ladies etched/HP herons on opal, Sandwich, 25½" .1,100.00
Wht font w/gold & gr foliage, marble base, 11½" 400.00
Yel satin w/floral, umbrella shade/rnd font, metal ft, 21" 3,000.00

Fairy Lamps

Baby's head, emerald gr frost, pyramid sz, 4½x2⅝" 175.00
Burmese, cherry branch, on burmese cup, Webb, Cricklite, lg ..1,000.00
Burmese, fall flowers, 2 domes+2 sm lily vases+5" vase, 10½" ..3,800.00
Burmese, ivy, clear Clarke's cup, 4" 750.00
Burmese, 2 3½" domes w/Clarke's cups on silver 2-arm std 425.00
Burmese, 3½" dome, Clarke's cup, on cut glass stick base 550.00
Burmese, 3½" dome in 2¼x5" crimped bowl base, Clarke's cup .700.00
Burmese, 3¾" dome w/berries/leaves, Clarke's porc cup 900.00
Burmese, 7½" petticoat base w/crimped edge, Webb Queen's, 5½" ...775.00
Dmn Quilt, turq, clear Clarke's base, 4¾" 195.00
Dmn Quilt pk MOP, on clear Clarke's base, 5" 275.00
Eyewinker, gr, LG Wright 35.00
Nailsea, bl, bowl-form base w/crimped edge, Clarke's cup, 5" 550.00
Nailsea, chartreuse, clear Clarke's base, 3" 200.00
Nailsea, med bl, dome shade, ruffled 4-lobe bowl, 3-part, 7x7" ..900.00
Peachblow, crimped, Clarke's cup w/pressed cande holder, 5" 600.00
Pk Drapery, ball shade, cylinder base, 8½" 250.00

Stippled Star, gr, 3-pc, ca 1960s **65.00**
Sweetheart, 3-pc, ca 1960s **65.00**

Gone-With-the-Wind and Banquet Lamps

Bl w/mc HP florals, Best Duplex burner, brass mts, 21⅜" **200.00**
Col (2-layer) bl w/leafy vines, brass acorn base, Sandwich, 20" ..**900.00**
Onyx/brass/iron std w/allegoricals & 4 claw ft, rpl shade, 35" **385.00**
Orchids on 10" ball shade & teardrop bottom, 27" **500.00**

Photo courtesy John A. Shuman III

Poppies embossed on red satin, brass fittings, cast-iron base with claw feet, 1890s, 25½", $1,200.00.

Rose w/emb cherub faces, std w/3-D putti, alabaster stem, 28" ...**300.00**
Roses emb, ruby/gr on wht swirl globe shade & body, 10" **175.00**
Roses on pk & wht 11" ball shade & squat vase-shaped base **400.00**
Shade w/putti decal, cast font above Cupid on fancy base, 30" ...**385.00**
Wht opaque w/HP, brass-plated base, Consolidated burner, 30" ..**180.00**

Hanging Lamps

Brass w/clear glass panels w/mc jewels, 1890s, 26x10x13" **325.00**
Burmese, shiny, swirled cylinder, 9x7", EX, fancy metal hdw **650.00**
Citron Swirl MOP melon-rib ball shade in brass fr, complete **450.00**
Cranberry w/wht enameling, brass fr w/shell & drop-in front ..**2,250.00**
Milk glass w/transfer, brass fr, prisms, B&H burner, 36"+chain ..**450.00**
Wht opaque w/HP dome shade, ornate brass fr, prisms, 48" **575.00**

Lanterns

Hall, gilt brass, 5 curved glass panes, 35x15" dia, EX **770.00**
Onion, tin w/red glass globe, brass burner, 10x5⅜", EX **395.00**
Royal Dietz, clear Popcorn globe, tin w/brass cap, 14¾x7" **120.00**
Skater's, brass w/clear cylinder globe, Pat Dec 24 '85, 9x4" **200.00**
Skater's, Perko Wonder Junior, brass, polished, 6¾" **160.00**
Skater's, tin, amethyst globe, 7" **525.00**
Skater's, tin, cornflower bl globe, 7⅛" **300.00**
Skater's, tin, emerald gr globe, 6½" **440.00**
Wood, tin candle socket, hinged door, bail hdl, 12" **450.00**

Lard Oil/Grease Lamps

Betty, copper, 4¼", w/hanger **140.00**
Betty, tin, crimped edge shelf, rnd, pan, 7" **360.00**
Betty, wrought iron, w/hanger & pick, 4¼" **275.00**
Crusie, wrought iron w/jam spike of twisted design, 7½x4½" **75.00**
Kettle, brass, heavy iron gimbal hanger, 6½" **220.00**
Kettle, iron/brass, pencil std, 3-ftd saucer base, 9" **300.00**

Rush, wrought iron, w/candle socket counterweight, 9½" **385.00**

Miniature Lamps, Kerosene

Miniature oil lamps were originally called 'night lamps' by their manufacturers. Early examples were very utilitarian in design — some holding only enough oil to burn through the night. When kerosene replaced whale oil in the second half of the nineteenth century, 'mini' lamps became more decorative and started serving other purposes. While mini lamps continue to be produced today, collectors place special value on the lamps of the kerosene era, roughly 1855 to 1910. Four reference books are especially valuable to collectors as they try to identify and value their collections: *Miniature Lamps* by Frank and Ruth Smith, Schiffer Publishing, 1968 (referred to as SI); *Miniature Lamps II* by Ruth Smith Schiffer Publishing 1982 (SII); *Miniature Victorian Lamps* by Margorie Hulsebus, Schiffer Publishing, 1996; and *Price Guide for Miniature Lamps* by Marjorie Hulsebus, Shiffer Publishing, 1998 (contains 1998 values for all the above books). References in the following listings correlate with each lamp's plate number in the Smith books. Our advisor is Bob Culver; he is listed in the Directory under Michigan.

Acanthus, clear, SI-230 ....**200.00**
Artichoke, gr & yel **395.00**
Basketweave, flared top, SI-277 ....**200.00**
Bull's Eye, clear w/cranberry eyes **80.00**
Daisy Cub, SI-482, orig, no shade, NM **50.00**
Florette, bl opaque, SI-388 ....**545.00**
Gothic Arch, clear, SI-164 ....**225.00**
Grecian Key, clear, SI-169 ....**90.00**
Hobnail, cranberry, swirl font, orig brass burner/ring, 11¼" **495.00**
Leon, milk glass, SI-177 ....**200.00**
Little Jewel, gr, SI-44 ....**1,050.00**
Maltese Cross, SI-214 ....**150.00**
Manila, cobalt, SI-30 ....**110.00**
Milk glass w/angel decor, SI-325 ....**345.00**
Owl, gr pnt, SI-497, rare **1,250.00**
Pk Dmn Quilt ruffled 4-lobe U-shape shade & bowl base, 8" **595.00**
Pk emb satin, ruffled melon-rib shade/hdld cup font, ormolu ft .**1,300.00**
Reclining Elephant, S-488, rpl ball shade **350.00**
Snail, milk glass w/HP decor, SI-242 ....**325.00**
Sunflower, #206 ....**300.00**
Vapo-Cresolene, SI-630 ....**70.00**
Wht satin w/lime & pk pull-ups, 6", w/chimney, Northwood **225.00**

Motion Lamps

Animated motion lamps were made as early as 1920 and as late as 1980s. They reached their peak during the 1950s when plastic became widely used. They are characterized by action created by the heat of a light bulb which causes the cylinder to revolve and create the illusion of an animated scene. Some of the better-known manufacturers were Econolite Corp., Scene in Action Corp., and LA Goodman Mfg. Co. As with many collectible items, prices are guided by condition, availability, and collector demand. Collectors should be aware that reproductions of cars, trains, sailing ships, fish, and mill scenes are being made. Values are given for original lamps in mint condition. Any damage or flaws seriously reduce the price. Our advisors for motion lamps are Kaye and Jim Whitaker; they are listed in the Directory under Washington.

Antique Autos, Econolite, 1957, 11" **150.00**
Aquarium, glass bowl for fish-motion below in stand, 1931 ....**300.00**
Davy Crockett **200.00**
Disneyland Express, Econolite, 1955, 11" **195.00**
Elvgrin Pin-Up Girls **400.00**

Firefighters, LA Goodman, 1957, 11" 195.00
Fireplace, Econolite, 1958, 11" 150.00
Forest Fire, Econolite, 1955, 11" 100.00
Forest Fire, Rotovue Jr, 1949, 10" 100.00
Forest Fire, Scene in Action, 1931, 10" 130.00
Fountain of Youth, Rotovue Jr, 1950s, 10" 100.00
Fresh Water Fish, Econolite, 1950s, 11" 95.00
Indian Chief, Gritt Inc, 1920s, 11" 115.00
Indian Maiden, Gritt Inc, 1920s, 11" 120.00
Japanese Twilight, Scene in Action, 1931, 13" 185.00
Jet Planes, Econolite 175.00
Merry Go Round, Rotovue Jr, 1949, 10" 100.00
Michelob Advertising Lamp, Christmas design, 13" 95.00
Miss Liberty, Econolite, 1957, 11" 250.00
Niagara Falls, Econolite, 1955, 11" 95.00
Niagara Falls, Rotovue Jr, 1949, 10" 75.00
Niagara Falls, Scene in Action, 1931, 10" 100.00
Op Art Lamp, Visual Effects, 1970s, 13" 45.00
Oriental Fantasy, LA Goodman, 1957, 11" 95.00
Oriental scene, Econolite, 1959, 11" 105.00
Sailboats, LA Goodman, 1954, 14" 110.00
Sailing Ships, Econolite 150.00
Seattle World's Fair, Econolite 175.00
Seven Up 75.00
Snow scene, LA Goodman 95.00
Steamboats, Econolite, 1957, 11" 110.00
The Bar Is Open, Visual Effects, OP Art, 1970s, 13" 35.00
Totville Train, Econolite, 1948, 11" 150.00
Tropical Fish, Econolite, 1954, 11" 95.00
White Christmas, flat front, Econolite, 11" 160.00

Pattern Glass Lamps

The letter/number codes in the following descriptions refer to *Oil Lamps*, Books I and II by Katherine Thuro (book, page, item number of letter). Our advisor for this section is Jeff Bradfield who is listed in the Directory under Virginia.

Buckle, brass/iron base, T-1-113E 185.00
Bull's Eye, flat finger lamp, T1-270A 85.00
Chapman, T1-141J 85.00
Coin Dot, bl opal, on bl leaf & jewel base, 8¾" 750.00
Cross Diamond Band, stem lamp, T1-315H 110.00
Depressed Oval Band, stem lamp, amber, T2-109Q 160.00

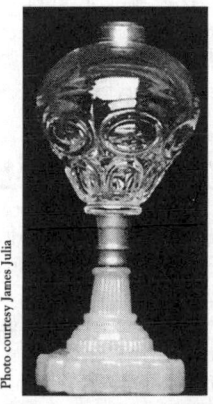

Double Bull's Eye, blue opaque base, 1865 – 70, 10", EX, $300.00.

Photo courtesy James Julia

Eason, clear opal w/blk stem & ft, stand lamp, 8¾", T1-236L 450.00
Erin Fan, ped base, orig burner, T1-274C 90.00
Feather Duster, stand lamp, 8", T1-224F 90.00
Heart, gr custard, finger lamp, 5½", T1-260A 325.00

Heart, yel opaque, finger lamp, 3¼" 225.00
Hobbs Coin Dot, bl opal, clear stem/ft, 9⅛", T2-102M 700.00
Hobbs Coin Dot, cranberry opal, clear stem/ft, 8½", T2-102M ..700.00
Hobbs Coin Dot, wht opal, clear stem/ft, 9", T2-102M 400.00
Invt T'print, cranberry/wht spatter, mc Detroit base, 9", T1-310A ..425.00
King's Crown, stand lamp, 8½", T1-320-3 ....120.00
Loop, hex base, ped ft, orig burner, 9¾", T1-333-8 .....130.00
Markham Swirl Band, cranberry opal, T1-280H 450.00
Markham Swirl Band, opal cobwebs, bl finger hold, T2-101L 550.00
Olympic, sq bl glass Gem base, 8½", T1-143B 350.00
One-O-One, finger lamp, T1-280B 120.00
Peacock Feather, amber, stem lamp, T1-282B 200.00
Peacock Feather, bl, ftd, hand lamp 400.00
Peanut, ped base, T1-304A 110.00
Ribbed, flattened acorn shape, mk P&A Mfg Co, T1-88A 85.00
Ring Punty, Sawtooth & Eye, milk glass ped base, T2-24F 110.00
Seaweed, cranberry opal, clear stem/ft, stand lamp, 8" 1,100.00
Sharon Panel base, w/Rib font, T1-265L 110.00
Sheldon Swirl, clear opal, #1 burner, stand lamp, 7½", T2-120C .250.00
Sheldon Swirl, cranberry opal, #0 burner/chimney, 7½", T2-120C .750.00
Snowflake, cranberry opal, ftd finger lamp, 5", T2-104C 1,150.00
Snowflake, wht opal, finger lamp, 3" 400.00
Teardrop w/Eyewinker, Plume font, T1-250D 130.00
Tulip (bl) font, sq milk glass base, T2-41I 240.00
Tulip font, bl base, 12" to top of brass collar, T2-41I ...195.00
Windows, bl opal, clear base, stand lamp, Eason, 10" ...800.00
Windows, cranberry opal, clear base, Eason, hand lamp, 5" 1,250.00

Peg Lamps

Blown, spherical, tin drop burner, 4¼", pr 500.00
Free-blown, orig collar, appl peg, 5" 100.00
Pk Dmn Quilt MOP ruffled shade/rnd font; brass stick, 14" 650.00
Pk ribbed Bristol o/l ruffled 6" shade; brass std, 17" 600.00
Pk Swirl MOP 5" ruffled shade & ball font, 11" 695.00
Stippled cranberry w/gold cherries on shade/font, 112" 565.00

Reverse-Painted Lamps

Classique, 14" cottages textured shade; Arts & Crafts std, 21" .1,100.00
Jefferson, 16" scenic dome shade (EX colors); gr-patina std 1,950.00
Jefferson, 18" costal storm shade; emb vase std w/lg hdls 2,200.00
Jefferson, 18" landscape cone sgn shade (VG); glass base 1,800.00
Moe Bridges, 14" scenic shade; unmk tooled std, 20½" 1,300.00
Moe Bridges, 15" scenic, blk on red shade; petal-etch std 1,200.00
Moe Bridges, 7" scenic shade; copper-plated base, 13" 375.00
Moe Bridges, 8" scenic shade; mkd brn baluster base 1,000.00
Pittsburgh, 14" trees/meadow shade; thistle-emb hammered std ...1,100.00
Pittsburgh, 16" Lakes of Killarney shade; leaf-emb std, 23" 2,050.00
Pittsburgh, 17" 2 ships/high seas shade; hdld vase-like std 2,000.00

Whale Oil/Burning Fluid Lamps

Amethyst, 3-printie block, pressed base, orig burner, 8", pr 5,000.00
Amethyst sq base, 8-sided baluster stem w/knop, 10¼" 2,860.00
Bl & clambroth tulip form, orig burner, 13¼", pr 2,800.00
Canary, hexagonal w/3-printie font, w/burner, 8½" 550.00
Clambroth acanthus font, bl opaque sq base, 11¾" 935.00
Clear blown cone font w/beehive wafer, pressed base, 9" 160.00
Clear blown font, candlestick-shaped base w/rnd ft, 9" 220.00
Clear blown font, 4-sided lacy base, Sandwich, 4½", EX 120.00
Clear blown font w/cut panels, pressed sq ft w/8-sided stem, 11" .250.00
Clear blown font w/wafer, pressed hex base, 7½" 60.00
Clear blown font w/wafers, lacy base, open burner, 8¼" 195.00

Clear blown font w/2 wafers, pressed step base, 8¼" **150.00**
Clear blown/pressed cone font, paw ft, scroll base, 11" **500.00**
Clear blown/pressed cone font w/9 cut panels, step base, 12", pr ...**600.00**
Clear blown/pressed font w/fan cuttings, att Pittsburgh, 11¼", EX ..**275.00**
Clear blown/pressed font w/swag & tassel drapery, 11½", EX, pr .**300.00**
Clear eng glass bowl on stepped ped, 1800s, 10" **60.00**
Clear frosted blown font w/cut floral, pressed sq base, 9", EX **170.00**
Clear Loop hexagonal font w/flat bottom, arched hdl, 4⅝" **190.00**
Clear pressed base, hollow blown stem, deep socket w/3 wafers, 10½" .**235.00**
Clear pressed waterfall base, blown stem, pewter collar, 9⅜" **250.00**
Clear/frosted figural stem, blown font, drip pan, 12", pr **220.00**
Cobalt hex base & loop font w/wafer, 9¾", NM **1,265.00**
Cobalt hex waterfall base, arch/panel fans w/wafer, 10", pr **3,300.00**
Emerald gr, pressed paneled font, 8-sided extension, 10¾" **2,500.00**
Gr, blown, teardrop stem, saucer base, rpl collar, 7⅛" **200.00**
Jade gr, Star & Punty, brass collar, 10¾", NM **4,750.00**
Lt jade, blown/pressed, brass collar/connector, 13⅜" **7,000.00**
Sapphire bl, Loop, 8-sided std, sq base, 10", pr **1,200.00**
Tin, conical font w/tin burner, single wick, weighted base, 11" ..**300.00**
Wht, blown/pressed, Lion & Basket of Flowers, 8" **175.00**
Wht & deep clambroth, Star & Punty, rpl collar, 11" **1,000.00**

Miscellaneous

Argand, LB Wilbor NY, patinated bronze, 2-arm, 20x16x7" **800.00**
Astral, col (bl/red/wht) stem, marble base, prisms, 28" **2,850.00**
Astral, Cornelius & Co...1854, brass Rococo, etch shade, 25" ...**1,000.00**
Bronzed maid w/vines sprouting 3 petal fixtures, Moreau, 30" **660.00**
Marriage, DC Ripley Pat Pending, wht & bl opaque, 11½" **880.00**
Marriage, wht w/bl fonts & match holder lid, frosted shades, 21" ..**3,600.00**
Metal lady on lily pad lifts metal shade w/clear panels, 23" **220.00**
Pittsburgh, molded 12" textured gold irid shade; bronzed std **300.00**
Sconces, SP Georgian style, acanthus chased, 3-arm, 18x15", pr ...**1,100.00**
Slag, gilt o/l Oriental scene, CI std w/ram heads, Mosaic, 23" **770.00**
Solar, Archer & Warner, columnar brass w/etch shade, prisms, 24" ...**900.00**

Lang, Anton

Anton Lang (1875 – 1938) was a German studio potter and an actor in the Oberammergau Passion Plays early in the 20th century. Because he played the role of Christ three times, tourists brought his pottery back to the U.S. in suitcases, which accounts for the prevalence of smaller examples today. During 1923 – 1924 Anton Lang and the other 'Passion Players' toured the U.S. selling their crafts. Lang would occasionally throw pottery when the cast passed through a pottery center such as Cincinnati, where Rookwood was located. The pots thrown at Rookwood are easy to identify as Lang hand signed the side of each piece and they have a 1924 Rookwood mark on the bottom. Lang visited the U.S. only once, and contrary to popular belief, he was never employed by Rookwood. His pottery, marked with his name in script, is fairly scarce and highly valued for its artistic quality. His son Karl (1903 – 1990) also a gifted potter, designed most of the Art Deco shapes and conducted glaze experiments. Only pieces bearing a hand-written signature (not a facsimile) are certain to be Anton Lang originals instead of the work of Karl or the Langs' assistants. Anton and Karl also made pieces together; Karl might design a piece and Anton decorate it. Postcards, programs, print, and photographs depicting Lang are also collectible. Karl was managing the day-to-day operations of the pottery by 1934, and he continued to operate it as Anton Lang Pottery after his father's death in 1938. The pottery is now owned and operated by Karl's daughter, Barbara Lampe, who took over for her father in 1975. The facsimile 'Anton Lang' signature was used until 1995 when the name was changed to Barbara Lampe Pottery. Her mark is an interlocked 'BL'

in a circle. Pieces with a facsimile signature and an interlocked 'UL' in a circle were made by Lampe's former husband, Uli Lampe, and date from 1975 to 1982. Our advisor for this category is Clark Miller; he is listed in the Directory under Minnesota.

Wall plaque, white squeeze bag on brown, facsimile signature, 11½", $125.00.

Photo courtesy Clark Miller

Book, Reminiscences, autographed & hand dtd, 1930 ....**65.00**
Bowl, bl Vienna Secession-style decor on gr, hand sgn, 4x4" **225.00**
Bowl, brn geometric design on buff, 2x5¾" **65.00**
Bowl, forest gr w/blk, twig hdls & appl leaves, hand sgn, 3½x5" ...**175.00**
Bowl, turq, 1¾x2½" **32.50**
Chamberstick, windmill, HP blk/gr on tan, hand sgn, 6x4½" **150.00**
Cup & saucer, flowers on bl, hand sgn **50.00**
Figurine, Joseph, Mary & Child, Deco style, mc, 12x8x5" **500.00**
Figurine candle holders, gargoyles, orange, 7½x7½", pr **500.00**
Holy water font, doves in relief, bl matt, hand sgn, 5½x3½" **125.00**
Lamp, Deco style, orange, 9x5½" **225.00**
Photo, Am tour, autographed & hand dtd 1924, 3½x5¼" **35.00**
Photo, Lang as Christ, autographed & hand dtd 1900, 6x4" **25.00**
Photo, Lang as Christ, autographed & hand dtd 1922, 9½x7½" ...**50.00**
Pitcher, floral, mc/HP on tan, hand sgn, 6¾x6" **150.00**
Pitcher, flower emb on gunmetal, 4¾x4¾" **75.00**
Pitcher, fuzzy bl bands on tan, 4x4" **35.00**
Postcard, Lang Passion Play scene **5.00**
Postcard, Lang throwing pot **7.50**
Postcard, Lang throwing pot, autographed **15.00**
Print, Passion Play scene, autographed & hand dtd 1922, 9½x7" .**50.00**
Program, Oberammergau in Am Home Art Exhibition, 1923-24 .**50.00**
Stereoview card, Anton Lang as Christ **7.50**
Tile, Anton Lang as Christ, bsk, dtd, hand sgn, 4¼" dia **225.00**
Vase, Deco style, blk w/bl int, 7¾x7¼" **275.00**
Vase, maroon w/turq int, flared top, 5" **50.00**
Vase, mauve w/gr int, 3¾x3" **35.00**
Vase, red/orange w/turq int, ribbed, 3¼x3¼" **35.00**
Vase, sgrafitto decor, wht on brn w/yel int, hand sgn, 4x4" **175.00**
Vase, turq over maroon w/yel int, hand sgn, 11¼x5¼" **325.00**
Wall plaque, frog skin, 6⅝x1⅜" **30.00**
Wall pocket, Deco style, brn, 7½x3½" **175.00**

Le Verre Francais

Le Verre Francais was produced during the 1920s by Schneider at Epinay-sur-Seine in France. It was a commercial art glass in the cameo style composed of layered glass with the designs engraved by acid. Favored motifs were stylized leaves and flowers or geometric patterns. It was marked with the name in script or with an inlaid filigrane. Our advisor for this category is Don Williams; he is listed in the Directory under Missouri.

Cameo

Bowl, centerpc; beetles & geometrics, orange/brn, 4½x10" **700.00**

Bowl vase, Deco flowers/tassels, brn on orange frost, 7x9" 900.00
Night-light base, poppies/pods, brn on red to yel, w/cap, 3" 375.00
Vase, bleeding hearts, brn/red on yel, ftd classic form, 18" 1,725.00
Vase, blossoms, swag panels, orange/brn-gr, 15½" 1,035.00
Vase, Deco fans/spires, red/orange/gr on wht mottle, 7x4" 650.00
Vase, ducks in flight, bl/brn on yel/wht, ovoid, 13" 1,300.00
Vase, floral 'trees,' red on yel/orange, ovoid on amber ft, 12" ..1,375.00
Vase, foliage, red to gr on yel-amber, bulb w/flared neck, 3" 550.00
Vase, foxglove stalks, orange/wine on pk, Charder, 19" 1,725.00
Vase, horseshoe crabs, orange mottle on yel, 11½" 975.00
Vase, iris, red on yel mottle, bun ft, 17½" 1,450.00
Vase, leaves/vines, wht-spotted amber on orange, bun ft, 22" .1,350.00
Vase, pendant poppies & seed pods, brn on orange/yel, 22" 1,495.00
Vase, seed clusters/leaves, orange/aubergine-brn, 19½" 865.00
Vase, trailing florals, lav/amber on pastels, Charder, 16" 1,100.00
Vase, trailing florals, lav/purple on pk, rim hdls, 15x4" 1,495.00
Vase, upright pussy willow stems, orange/brn on amber, 12x9" ..1,265.00
Vase, 3 lg beetles, brn on orange mottle, bun ft, 16" 2,000.00
Vase, 3 lg beetles/Deco borders, brn on orange, bun ft, 17" 2,000.00

Leeds, Leeds Type

The Leeds Pottery was established in 1758 in Yorkshire and under varied management produced fine creamware, often highly reticulated and transfer printed, shiny black-glazed Jackfield wares, polychromed pearlware, and figurines similar to those made in the Staffordshire area. Little of the early ware was marked; after 1775 the impressed 'Leeds Pottery' mark was used. From 1781 to 1820, the name 'Hartley Greens & Co.' was added. The pottery closed in 1898.

Today the term 'Leeds' has become generic and is used to encompass all polychromed pearlware and creamware, wherever its origin. Thus similar wares of other potters (Wood for instance) is often incorrectly called 'Leeds.' Unless a piece is marked or can be definitely attributed to Leeds by confirming the pattern to be authentic, 'Leeds-Type' would be a more accurate nomenclature.

Key:
cw — creamware   pw — pearlware

Coffeepot, Batavian Ware, bl transfer on pw, 1800s, 11" 750.00
Coffeepot, mc floral, pear shape, floral finial, 1795, rstr, 10½" ...700.00
Coffeepot, mc floral, reeded spout, leaf hdl, ca 1775, rstr, 8¾" ...925.00
Coffeepot, Tea Party/Shepherd blk transfers, ca 1790, 10¼", EX ..865.00
Mug, lady & family crest transfer, pk lustre bands, 3½x4" 110.00
Pitcher, Enterprise & Boxer, blk transfer w/pk lustre band, 4½" 2,000.00
Pitcher, pw, mc floral, mini, 3½", NM 50.00
Pitcher, pw, mc floral, stains, 8⅝" 275.00
Plate, Am sailing ship, blk transfer w/mc, 9¾", NM 300.00
Plate, Am ship, blk transfer w/mc, emb floral, 10", EX 100.00
Plate, castle scene, blk transfer w/mc, 10", EX 110.00
Plate, cw, emb gr grapes center, feather border, 4⅜" 430.00
Plate, 3-masted ship, blk transfer, blk floral border, 9¾" 200.00
Platter, pw, bl/wht Oriental decor, bl feather edge, rpr, 21" 500.00
Strainer/dish, cw, twist hdl, scrolled rim, 7¾", NM 225.00
Teapot, cw, Prince of Orange portraits, ribbed hdl, rstr lid, 5" 450.00
Teapot, mc rose, emb floral hdl terminals, 4¾" 3,000.00

Lefton China

The Lefton China Company was the creation of Mr. George Zoltan Lefton who migrated to the United States from Hungary in 1939. In 1941 he embarked on a new career and began shaping a business that sprang from his passion for collecting fine china and porcelains. Though his funds were very limited, his vision was to develop a source from which to obtain fine porcelains by reviving the postwar Japanese ceramic industry, which dated back to antiquity. As a trailblazer, George Zoltan Lefton soon earned the reputation as 'The China King.'

Counted among the most desirable and sought-after collectibles of today, Lefton items such as Bluebirds, Miss Priss, Angels, all types of dinnerware and tea-related items are eagerly acquired by collectors. As is true with any antique or collectible, prices may vary, dependent on location, condition, and availability. For additional information on the history of Lefton China, its factories, marks, products, and values, readers should consult the *Collector's Encyclopedia of Lefton China, Books I and II*, and the *1999 Lefton Price Guide* by our advisor, Loretta DeLozier, who is listed in the Directory under Iowa.

Figurine, eagle, #802, 11", $100.00.

Photo courtesy Loretta DeLozier

Angel, February, #130 ....40.00
Animal, Bambi, pearl lustre w/stones, #473, 8¼", pr 45.00
Animal, beaver, bsk, #4747, 5" 38.00
Animal, cat, pearl lustre w/stones, #316, 6¼" 18.00
Animal, Christmas dog, #2036, 3" 8.00
Animal, Christmas mice, #02477, 2½" 12.00
Animal, deer, #521, 5⅝", pr 40.00
Animal, dog, Love Eyes, #6862, 3¼" 12.00
Animal, elephant family, #594, 3-pc set 45.00
Animal, poodle w/2 babies, pk w/stones, #80063, 6" 45.00
Animal, rabbit, bsk, #5057, 5" 36.00
Animal, raccoon, #4752, 5" 42.00
Animal, sheep family, #117, 3-pc set 45.00
Ashtray, Gold Wheat, #20124, nested set of 4 ....15.00
Baby set (bowl & mug), Bluebirds, #435 ....95.00
Bank, Hubert the Lion, #13384 ....25.00
Bank, owl w/rhinestone eyes, #90195, 6½" 50.00
Bell, angels spelling Noel, #90283, 3½", 4-pc set 50.00
Bell, Christmas, #80109, 4½" 20.00
Bird, angel on leaves w/cardinal, #852, 6" 55.00
Bird, bobwhite, #300, 5¼" 36.00
Bird, long-tail rooster, #1057, 10", pr 125.00
Bird, owl, #7556, 12" 75.00
Bookends, parakeets, #90581, 5", pr 50.00
Bowl, gr bsk w/cherub, #837 ....150.00
Box, Flower Garden, #2152, 5" dia 80.00
Box, pin; pk w/rhinestones, #90254, 2¼" 35.00
Bust, Jefferson, #1136, 5½" 35.00
Butter dish, Mr Toodles, #3294 ....165.00
Cake plate, Green Heritage, #719 ....42.00
Canister set, Rustic Daisy, #4115, 4-pc set 90.00
Cheese dish, Honey Bee, #1285 ....55.00
Coffeepot, Blue Paisley, #1972 ....135.00
Coffeepot, Brown Heritage Fruit, #20591 ....165.00
Coffeepot, Green Heritage, #3065 ....165.00

Coffeepot, Magnolia, #2518 ....165.00
Coffeepot, Violet Chintz, #660 ....185.00
Cookie jar, Apple, #20487, 6" 65.00
Cookie jar, Dainty Miss, #040 ....200.00
Cookie jar, Honey Bee, #1279 ....110.00
Cookie jar, Miss Priss, #1502 ....150.00
Cookie jar, Winking Santa, #90148 ....180.00
Creamer & sugar bowl, Elegant Rose, stacking, #2564 ....70.00
Creamer & sugar bowl, Miss Priss, #1508 ....65.00
Cup & saucer, Grapes, #911 ....45.00
Cup & saucer, Green Heritage, #3067 ....35.00
Cup & saucer, Green Holly, #2047 ....22.00
Cup & saucer, Red Cardinal, #01248 ....25.00
Cup & saucer, Rose Chintz, #662 ....35.00
Cup & saucer, tea; Blue Paisley, #2339 ....22.00
Cup & saucer, tea; Rose Chintz, #656 ....32.00
Cup & saucer, tea; To a Wild Rose, #2566 ....28.00
Decanters, dk gr glassware w/gold, #4107, 5-pc set 120.00
Dish, latticed, w/lilacs & stones, #232, 6" 32.00
Egg cup, Bluebirds, #286 ....60.00
Figurine, bloomer girl w/umbrella, wht, #10531, 4" 65.00
Figurine, Chinese figure sitting, #1008, 4½", pr 45.00
Figurine, Colonial man & woman, #2256, 10½", pr 350.00
Figurine, Don Quixote & Sancho Panza, #4721, 8" 110.00
Figurine, modern dancers, #80103, 5½", pr 65.00
Figurine, Napoleon on horse, #4908, 11" 285.00
Figurine, old man w/dog & gun holding rabbit, #237, 6½" 60.00
Figurine, Pussy Cat Pussy Cat, #1474, 5" 55.00
Figurine, Rock a Bye Baby in Treetop, #1104, 8" 180.00
Figurine, Siamese dancers, #493, 6½", pr 95.00
Figurine, veterinarian w/dog, #1858, 8" 65.00
Jam jar, Dutch girl, #2697 ....95.00
Jam jar, Grapes, #4852, 5" 25.00
Jam jar, Mr Santa, #1651, 6½" 30.00
Mug, Teddy Roosevelt, #2191, 4½" 45.00
Music box, girl w/instrument & dog, Jingle Bells, #7066, 6½" 40.00
Pitcher & bowl, Pink Dogwood, #04311, 4¾" 15.00
Planter, bulldog w/puppy, #046, 5" 40.00
Planter, Forget Me Not, #5356 ....15.00
Planter, Gingham Elephant, #50090 ....32.00
Planter, girl w/cart, #50048, 5" 30.00
Planter, Ice Pink, bsk, #1030, 4" 15.00
Planter, milk china, #827 ....25.00
Planter, wht, violets & stones, sponge gold, #153, 5" 22.00
Planter, wht w/golden rose, #2707, 4½" 16.00
Plaque, My Guests Like My Kitchen Best, #60329, 8" 28.00
Plate, Americana, #963, 10½" 35.00
Plate, Dogwood Design, #2818, 7¼" 18.00
Plate, Magnolia, #2522, 7½" 22.00
Plate, salad; Berry Harvest, #305, 8" 28.00
Shakers, Bluebirds, #282, pr 40.00
Shakers, comical animal, #30404, pr 18.00
Shakers, Dainty Miss, #439, pr 45.00
Shakers, dogs, dressed, stone eyes, #30404, pr 20.00
Shakers, Green Holly, egg shape, pr 15.00
Shakers, turkeys, #1991, pr 28.00
Sleigh, Green Holly, #1346, 8" 55.00
Sleigh, wht china w/pk roses, #321, 7" 105.00
Snack set, rose, #100, 8" 30.00
Snack set, 4 colors, #2579, 8" 22.00
Spoon rest, Black chef, nodder, #90413, 5" 135.00
Teapot, Bluebirds, musical, #734 ....250.00
Teapot, Cabbage Cutie, #2123 ....85.00
Teapot, Fleur De Lis, #1799 ....65.00

Teapot, Golden Lily Design, #20027 ....65.00
Teapot, Honey Bee, #1278 ....125.00
Teapot, Poinsettia, #4388 ....175.00
Teapot, Spring Violets, #2439 ....125.00
Tidbit tray, Green Heritage, #1153, 2-tier 75.00
Tidbit tray, Green Holly, #1364, 2-tier 45.00
Tidbit tray, Rose Chintz, #649, 2-tier 75.00
Tray, Rose Chintz, #651 ....30.00
Vase, bag, Forget-Me-Not, #7290 ....32.00
Vase, Cameo, ewer shape, #1875, 8" 22.00
Vase, dbl hands, pk w/roses, #903, 7" 45.00
Vase, head form, #1226, 6" 55.00
Vase, head form, blk, wht & gold, #50507, 6½" 65.00
Vase, Pineapple, #7283, 5½" 60.00
Vase, rabbit's head, pk w/stones, #70244, 7½" 30.00
Vase, wht w/bl grapes, #2186, 7½" 18.00
Wall pocket, Dainty Miss, #6767 ....95.00
Wall pocket, Pepper, #50574, 4½" 30.00

Legras

Legras and Cie was founded in St. Denis, France, in 1864. Production continued until the 1930s. In addition to their enameled wares, they made cameo art glass decorated with outdoor scenes and florals executed by acid cuttings through two to six layers of glass. Their work is signed 'Legras' in relief and in enamel. Our advisor for this category is Don Williams; he is listed in the Directory under Missouri.

Cameo

Vase, etched and carved woodland and lake scene on gray shaded with violet, coral, brown, and green, signed, 22", $2,000.00.

Bowl, autumn leaves at rim, brn on wht, 3x9¾"+7" SP stand 425.00
Box, floral, cut/pnt on textured frost, 3x5" dia 450.00
Lamp, base/shade w/snowy woodland & birds on topaz, 12" 4,000.00
Vase, aquatic plants, wine/gr on tan/orange, 13" 325.00
Vase, berries/leaves, pk & clear, quatra form, 5¼", NM 300.00
Vase, berries/vines, wine on apricot/frost, cylndrical, 8" 550.00
Vase, floral, lt/dk gr/amethyst on yel opal, 19½" 2,000.00
Vase, floral, pk/maroon on clear, bulbous, 8½" 575.00
Vase, floral branches, maroon/pk on clear, flared, 12" 650.00
Vase, geraniums, pk/gr on opal amber, triangle rim, 12" 425.00
Vase, holly/berries, gr/red on peach & citron, dimpled, 4¾" ...1,200.00
Vase, honeysuckle, wine/amber on amber opal, 5¾" 750.00
Vase, leafy branches, pk/maroon on clear, ovoid, 10¾" 635.00
Vase, magnolia leaves, gr/brn on pastels, pillow form, 9x8" 800.00
Vase, maple leaves, cranberry to pk frost, stick neck, 15" 750.00
Vase, pine trees/lake, dk gr on pk/frost, cylindrical, 12" 1,200.00
Vase, shepherd/flock silhouette on bl/peachblow, slim, 14" 1,500.00

Vase, shepherd/flock/trees/mtns on peachblow, flat-sided, 6" 600.00
Vase, trees, cut/pnt on gr/bl mottle, rectangular, 4¼x5¼" 1,265.00

Enameled Glass

Rose bowl, grapes & vines HP on frost, 9" 165.00
Tray, winter scene, quatreform, in fitted wood fr, 5x9" 345.00
Vase, floral central motif on clear frost w/cobalt at rim, 14" 460.00
Vase, flower reserve, frost to yel/orange mottle, bulbous, 6" 100.00
Vase, leaf band at rim, maroon on frost, 9¾x3" 200.00
Vase, poppies w/gold on gr satin, trumpet form, 12¼" 635.00
Vase, river scenic on rose, pillow form, 4½" 350.00
Vase, trees/boats on yel/gr, 15¾x4" 900.00
Vase, wisteria, yel/pk w/gr butterflies on frost/bl, 12" 100.00

Lenox

Walter Scott Lenox, former art director at Ott and Brewer, and Jonathan Coxon founded The Ceramic Art Company of Trenton, New Jersey, in 1889. By 1906 Cox had left the company, and to reflect the change in ownership, the name was changed to Lenox Inc. Until 1930 when the production of American-made Belleek came to an end, they continued to produce the same type of high-quality ornamental wares that Lenox and Coxon had learned to master while in the employ of Ott and Brewer. Their superior dinnerware made the company famous, and since 1917 Lenox has been chosen the official White House china. Our advisor for this category is Mary Frank Gaston. See also Ceramic Art Company.

Ashtray, flying pheasant, 8" dia 22.00
Ashtray, gold ship, Am Export, 1960, 5½" 40.00
Bonbon, pk shell, gr mk, 4½" 25.00
Bowl, Cattail, w/gold, 7¼" 25.00
Bowl, fruit; Oakleaf 20.00
Bowl, rimmed soup; Kingsley 50.00
Bowl, salad/cereal; Springdale 35.00
Bowl, vegetable; Hancock, w/lid 195.00
Bowl, vegetable; Wyndcrest, oval 75.00
Box, cherry blossoms on gr, w/lid & pr of ashtrays, #3018 ....95.00
Candlesticks, Westfield, pr 75.00
Candy dish, Holiday, 9¾" 35.00
Chocolate pot, Belleek, mc daisies, 11", +6 c/s 425.00
Cigarette lighter, pk w/gold, Ronson wick type, gold wreath mk ..75.00
Coffee set, roses w/gold, ped ft, 3-pc 550.00
Creamer, Kelly 60.00
Cup, Westfield 45.00
Cup & saucer, Amethyst 30.00
Cup & saucer, Black Royale 42.50
Cup & saucer, Cattail, w/gold 30.00
Cup & saucer, Charleston 42.50
Cup & saucer, Classic Edition 50.00
Cup & saucer, demitasse; sterling rim 115.00
Cup & saucer, demitasse; Trent 45.00
Cup & saucer, Hannah 30.00
Cup & saucer, Holiday 40.00
Cup & saucer, Lace Point 42.50
Cup & saucer, Maywood 30.00
Cup & saucer, Mystic 35.00
Cup & saucer, Orleans 30.00
Cup & saucer, Poppies on bl 30.00
Cup & saucer, Weatherly 35.00
Cup & saucer, Wyndcrest 36.00
Figurine, horse head, Deco style, dtd 1929 ....275.00

Flower holder, Celadon, #1781, 12" 95.00
Lamp, boudoir; Deco lady w/hoop skirt & fan forms shade, 9" ...410.00
Lamp, nude sits atop column, wht porc on chrome base, 1930s, 14" ..400.00
Leaf dish, heavy gold, #3005, 2x10½" 75.00
Pitcher, Belleek, cherries on gr/bl, 6½x7" 175.00
Plate, bread & butter; Citation Gold 9.00
Plate, bread & butter; Flirtation 20.00
Plate, bread & butter; Hannah 10.00
Plate, bread & butter; Kelly 12.00
Plate, bread & butter; Oakleaf 17.00
Plate, bread & butter; Orleans 10.00
Plate, dinner; Brandywine 40.00
Plate, dinner; Carlbee, pk, 10½" 55.00
Plate, dinner; Cattail, w/gold trim, 10" 25.00
Plate, dinner; Citation Lace 33.00
Plate, dinner; Country Garden 35.00
Plate, dinner; Fairfield 30.00
Plate, dinner; Forever 20.00
Plate, dinner; Hannah 25.00
Plate, dinner; Harrison 25.00
Plate, dinner; Kelly 24.00
Plate, dinner; Moonlight Mood 35.00
Plate, dinner; Olympia, 10" 26.00
Plate, dinner; Orleans 25.00
Plate, dinner; Rosemont 42.50
Plate, dinner; Weatherly 30.00
Plate, mallard duck among rushes, gold trim, sgn Nosek, 10" 225.00
Plate, salad; Cattail, w/gold, 8" 14.00
Plate, salad; Citation Gold 12.00
Plate, salad; Fruits of Life 16.00
Plate, salad; Goldenrod 15.00
Plate, salad; Holiday 19.00
Plate, salad; Maywood, 8¼" 10.00
Plate, salad; Orleans 15.00
Platter, Belvidere, 13⅞" 80.00
Platter, Cattail, w/gold, 13" 50.00
Platter, Kelly, lg 140.00
Platter, Oak Leaf, platinum trim, 13½" 75.00
Platter, Westfield, oval, lg 135.00
Relish plate, dbl, leaf-emb rim & int, center hdl, 15½" 125.00
Sugar bowl, Eternal 58.00
Swan, blk mk, 8½" 95.00
Swan, wht, open bk, gr mk, lg 55.00
Teapot, Virginia, gold hdls, 11" +cr/sug 450.00

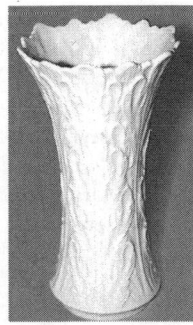

Vase, embossed foliage on white, 8½", $50.00.

Vase, band of lg birds/mtns, porc, gr ink mk, 10½" 260.00
Vase, Belleek, lady in long wht gown by pk tree, 12" 500.00
Vase, Belleek, lilacs, lav/wht/yel, sgn LWD, 7" 200.00
Vase, Belleek, peacocks on bl, sgn Hipple on base, 12" 700.00
Vase, Belleek, springer spaniel, sgn Baker, wreath mk, 8¼" 800.00
Vase, flowering branch w/birds in relief on sage gr, 9¼" 95.00
Vase, Lenox Rose, 13" 275.00

Vase, Romeo & Juliet, from Ispanky sculpture, ltd ed, 9½" 195.00

Letter Openers

Made in a wide variety of materials and designs, letter openers make an interesting collection, easy to display and easy on the budget as well. For further information we recommend *Collector's Guide to Letter Openers, Identification & Values*, by Everett Grist (Collector Books); Mr. Grist is listed in the Directory under Tennessee.

Alpaca w/abalone bottle-opener hdl, fish w/open mouth 30.00
Bakelite hdl, butterscotch w/HP flowers, Ocean City MD 25.00
Bakelite hdl w/nickel blade, Chicago World's Fair, 1934 ....75.00
Brass, armadillo 12.00
Brass, Falstaff, mk Peerage England 15.00
Brass, grasshopper, paperweight hdl 20.00
Bronze, pheasant 8.00

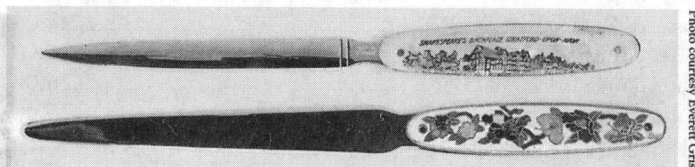

Photo courtesy Everett Grist

Celluloid and steel, Shakespeare's Birthplace, Stratford-Upon-Avon, Made in Germany, $25.00; Cloisonne enamel, brass, and steel, $20.00.

CI, Amish man or woman, w/label, ea 20.00
Gold-plated w/jeweled hdl 8.00
Horn, cvd whale w/ivory eye, mk Hawaii 25.00
Ivory, cvd camel motif 60.00
Ivory, cvd crocodile 85.00
Ivory w/silver hdl, Art Nouveau, swallow motif, Victorian 125.00
Jade-ite, smooth w/curved ends, no decor 85.00
Lucite hdl w/metal blade, dolphin shape w/encapsulated seashells ..35.00
Mother-of-Pearl, cvd pineapple-style hdl, Victorian 65.00
Pewter, dancing frog, Metzke 1979 ....12.00
Plastic, clear bathing beauty w/flocked suit 20.00
Plastic/steel, cigarette lighter atop ruler blade, Mardi Gras '67 ...40.00
Porc, HP rose motif on short key shape, sgn R Riddle 45.00
Pot metal, gold-colored lobster w/red-pnt detail 8.00
Resin, Egyptian head, made in USA 5.00
Silver, open floral hdl, eng VS Bergen, mk 830 Silver, Victorian .65.00
Silver, Smokey the Bear, mk Silver Holland 45.00
Steel, Siam enameled cross & shield 20.00
Sterling w/cvd gr onyx hdl, Mexico 45.00
Tortoise shell, bird's claw holding movable marble, Victorian ...125.00
Wood, cvd duck, African 20.00
Wood, cvd Indian chief 22.00

Libbey

The New England Glass Company was established in 1818 in Boston, Massachusetts. In 1892 it became known as the Libbey Glass Company. At Chicago's Columbian Expo in 1893, Libbey set up a ten-pot furnace and made glass souvenirs. The display brought them worldwide fame. Between 1878 and 1918, Libbey made exquisite cut and faceted glass, considered today to be the best from the brilliant period. The company is credited for several innovations — the Owens bottle machine that made mass production possible and the Westlake machine which turned out both electric light bulbs and tumblers automatically. They developed a machine to polish the rims of their tumblers in such a way that chipping was unlikely to occur. Their glassware carried the patented Safedge guarantee. Libbey also made glassware in numerous colors, among them cobalt, ruby, pink, green, and amber. Our advisor for this category is Mike Roscoe; he is listed in the Directory under Ohio.

Bonbon, cut, feathered leaf & cane, oval, 5" 75.00
Bowl, Comet, cut, 9" 925.00
Bowl, cranberry cut to clear w/daisies & lattice, 14" 200.00
Bowl, cut, hobstars & crosshatching, 8" 135.00
Bowl, cut, Lovebird, 4½x9" 300.00
Candlesticks, cut, teardrop stem, faceted knob/ray base, 10", pr .500.00
Candy barrel, cut, strawberry dmn fan/X-hatching, w/lid, 7" 550.00
Champagne, Empire, eng, jade gr knob on stem, ca 1933, 5½" ..150.00
Cups, punch; cut hobstars/notched ladders/fans/etc, 8 for 245.00
Flower center, cut, hobstar & X-hatching, faceted collar, 6x10" ...425.00
Maize, butter dish, bl husks on irid 650.00
Maize, butter dish lid, gr husks on custard 165.00
Maize, celery vase, clear w/amber staining & bl leaves, 6" 235.00
Maize, celery vase, gr husks on custard 200.00
Maize, condiment set, custard, 3 pcs on tray w/metal lid 600.00
Maize, pickle castor, amber stain 595.00
Maize, pickle castor, gr husks on custard, SP fr 550.00
Maize, pitcher, bl husks on clear w/amber irid, clear hdl, 9" 600.00
Maize, pitcher, clear irid w/amber stain, 8½" 550.00
Maize, shakers, gold-edged bl husks on custard, pr 250.00
Maize, sugar shaker, yel/gold leaves on custard, 5¾" 345.00
Maize, toothpick holder, gold-edged gr husks on custard 400.00
Maize, tumbler, bl husks on irid 235.00
Maize, vase, yel/gold leaves on custard, 6½" 250.00
Pitcher, cut, allover notching w/hobstars at top, 9" 325.00
Pitcher, cut, hobstars, strawberry, dmn & fan, bulbous, 7" 300.00
Punch cup, appl amethyst pods & stems, 3" 125.00
Salt cellar, geometric cuttings on boat form 65.00
Shakers, Columbia Exhibition 1893, lay-down egg shape, 2¾", pr ...350.00
Stem, champagne, squirrel, wht opal, 6" 200.00
Stem, claret, bear, blk, 5½" 155.00
Stem, claret, bear, wht opal 165.00
Stem, cordial, kangaroo, blk 110.00
Stem, cordial, monkey, blk 150.00
Stem, cordial, monkey, wht opal, 5" 130.00
Stem, cordial, whippet/greyhound, wht opal 175.00
Stem, goblet, cat, wht opal 200.00
Stem, sherbet, rabbit, wht opal, 2½" 160.00
Stem, sherbet, squirrel, wht opal, 4" 150.00
Tray, cut, Sonora, oval, 12" L 275.00
Tray, ice cream; cut, pinwheel center, hobstars/X-hatching, 12" ..575.00
Tumbler, amberina, ribbed, att, 3¾" 95.00
Tumbler, cut, hobstars, notched prism, 3¾", set of 6 ....210.00
Vase, amberina, #3013, EX color, 4⅝x6" 1,250.00
Vase, amberina, EX color, lt ribbing, flared, 11½x2" 950.00
Vase, amberina, slim/ribbed w/flared rim, ftd, att, 7½" 750.00
Vase, clear w/gr 'zipper' design, ribbed trumpet form, 10" 150.00
Vase, cut, hobstar panels, notched prisms, 12" 125.00
Vase, cut, hobstars, fans, notching, scalloped ped ft, 14" 600.00
Vase, cut, hobstars/decor dmns, prisms/bull's-eye rows, 10" 175.00
Vase, jack-in-pulpit; amberina, down-trn rim, long neck, 16" .1,250.00
Vase, lily; amberina, #3006, 11" 700.00
Vase, lily; amberina, 15" 825.00
Vase, Zipper, amber w/int gr dotted lines, ribbed, Nash, 6" 260.00

Little Pals, #7600, MIB 1,800.00
Little Riders 170.00
Little Traveler, #7602, MIB 900.00
Lovers in the Park, couple on bench, 11" 950.00
Martin Luther King, #7528, MIB 250.00
Matrimony 585.00
Missy, #4951 ....650.00
My Baby, #1331 ....995.00
My New Pet, #5549, MIB 125.00
Perfect Performance 300.00
Picture Perfect, #7612 ....270.00
Pisces, #06223 ....145.00
Pocket Full of Wishes 330.00
Princess & Unicorn 1,950.00
Pulling Doll Carriage, #5044 ....175.00
Sitting Pretty, #5699 ....225.00
Sorrowful Mother, #5849 ....895.00
Spanish Policeman, #4889 ....175.00
Summer Stroll, #7611, MIB 450.00
Tailor Made, #6489, MIB 140.00
Virgo, #06215 ....145.00
Voyage of Columbus 880.00
Young Bach, #1801 ....750.00
Young Mozart, #5915, MIB 1,400.00

Lobmeyer

J. and L. Lobmeyer, contemporaries of Moser, worked in Vienna, Austria, during the last quadrant of the 1800s. Most of the work attributed to them is decorated with distinctive enameling; favored motifs are people in 18th-century garb.

Basket, 2 18th-C couples/florals, eng/gilt, 13x8" 1,500.00
Bowl, cameo tulips, wine on clear w/etched florals, 6½" 375.00
Creamer & sugar, peasants/castles/etc, 3-ftd, sgn, 3¼"; 2¼" 1,500.00
Cup, demi; flowers/scrolls, wht/yel on chartreuse w/gold, ftd 300.00
Vase, crystal w/cvd feathers, free-form, 3½" 700.00
Wine glass, colonial man w/sword, mc on clear panels, sgn, 5⅜" .675.00

Locke Art

By the time he came to America, Joseph Locke had already proven himself many times over as a master glass maker, having worked in leading English glasshouses for more than seventeen years. Here he joined the New England Glass Company where he invented processes for the manufacture of several types of art glass — amberina, peachblow, pomona, and agata among them. In 1898 he established the Locke Art Glassware Co. in Mt. Oliver, Pittsburgh, Pennsylvania. Locke Art Glass was produced using an acid-etching process by which the most delicate designs were executed on crystal blanks. Most examples are signed simply 'Locke Art,' often placed unobtrusively near a leaf or a stem. Other items are signed 'Jo Locke,' some are dated, and some are unsigned. Most of the work was done by hand. The business continued into the 1920s. For further study we recommend *Locke Art Glass, Guide for Collectors*, by Joseph and Janet Locke, available at your local bookstore.

Our advisor for this category is Richard Haigh; he is listed in the Directory under Virginia.

Bonbon dish, almond, 5" 295.00
Champagne, Poppy, sgn 135.00
Comport, Pineapple Grape, sgn 495.00
Cordial, Shamrock, sgn 135.00

Decanter, Shamrock, sgn 495.00
Goblet, Violets, sgn 150.00
Pitcher, Grape & Linis, sgn, +6 tumblers 1,400.00
Pitcher, Ivy, sgn 600.00
Sherbet, Fern, ftd, w/underplate 395.00
Tumbler, Crescent, sgn 135.00
Vase, Poppy, sgn, 5" 550.00

Locks

The earliest type of lock in recorded history was the wooden cross bar used by ancient Egyptians and their contemporaries. The early Romans are credited with making the first key-operated mechanical lock. The ward lock was invented during the Middle Ages by the Etruscans of Northern Italy; the lever tumbler and combination locks followed at various stages of history with varying degrees of effectiveness. In the 18th century the first precision lock was constructed. It was a device that utilized a lever-tumbler mechanism. Two of the best known of the early 19th-century American lock manufacturers are Yale and Sargent, and today's collectors value Winchester and Keen Kutter locks very highly. Factors to consider are rarity, condition, and construction. Brass and bronze locks are generally priced higher than those of steel or iron. Our advisor for this section is Joe Tanner; he is listed in the Directory under Washington.

Key:
bbl — barrel   st — stamped

Brass Lever Tumbler

Ames Sword Co, Perfection st on shackle, 2¾" 65.00
Automatic, emb, flat key, 2⅛" 15.00
Belknap, emb, 3⅛" 25.00
Blue Grass, emb, 3" 85.00
Chubbs Patent London, st, 6⅛" 350.00
Cleveland 4 Way, Cleveland 4 Way emb on front, 3⅝" 90.00
Cotterill, st High Security key, 5⅛x3⅛" 290.00
Crusader, shield, swords emb on body, 2¾" 45.00
Duplex Yale & Towne Mfg Co, st, 2⅞" 125.00
Geo B Bahr & Co Lou KY, st, 3⅛" 45.00
Good Luck, emb, 2¾" 45.00
GW Co, 1929, emb, 3" 60.00
Jackson's, st Jackson's on front, 2½" 20.00
JWM, emb, bbl key, 2⅝" 25.00
Keen Kutter, shape of KK emblem, KK emb on front, 4¾" 125.00
Mercury, Mercury emb on body, 2¾" 75.00
Our Very Best, OVB emb on body, 2⅞" 150.00
P Fister Cin O, st, 2½" 60.00
Romer & Co, Romer & Co st on dust cover, 3" 55.00
Ruby, Ruby emb in scroll on front, 2¾" 20.00
Safe, Safe emb in scroll on front, 2⅜" 20.00
Simmons, emb, 2¼" 18.00
Sphinx, sphinx & pharaoh head emb on front, 2¾" 35.00
Tooker & Reeves (seal lock), st, 5¼" 400.00
W Bohannan & Co, SW emb in scroll on front, 2⅜" 30.00
Watch, emb, flat key, 3" 30.00
Winchester, Winchester emb on front, 3" 160.00

Combinations

Canton Lock Co, emb, iron, 3⅜" 425.00
Clark, st, brass, 2¼" 300.00
Edwards Mfg Co No-Key, st on lock, brass, 2¾" 60.00

Junkunc Bros Mfrs, all st on bk, brass, 1⅞" 30.00
Karco st on body, 2½" 50.00
No Kee, st, brass, 2" 45.00
Number or letter disc, st, 4-disk, brass, 4½" 250.00
Number or letter disk, st, 3-disk, iron, 2" 20.00
Number or letter disk, st, 4-disk, brass, 3½" 170.00
Number or letter disk type (4 disks), brass, 2¾" 130.00
Permutation Lock Den Co, emb, brass, 3⅝" 400.00
Quaint Mfg Co, st on lock case, 4¼" 200.00
Sq lock case of steel, st Pat Germany, 4-wheel, 3¼" 110.00
Sutton Lock Co st on body, 3" 200.00
Turman's Keyless, st, brass, 2¼" 160.00
WA Harrison, Inc, st, brass, 2½" 60.00
Your Own st on body, 3⅞" 325.00

Eight-Lever Type

Armory, brass, Armory 8-Lever st on front 30.00
Blue Chief, st, steel, 4½" 25.00
Electric, steel, Electric st on front 30.00
Goliath, steel, Goliath 8-Lever st on front 25.00
Mastodon, st, brass, 4½" 30.00
Mastodon, st, steel, 4½" 15.00
Miller, steel, Miller 8-Lever st on front 18.00
Samson, brass, 8-Lever st on front 18.00

Iron Lever Tumbler

Airplane, st, 2¾" 40.00
Bear, emb, 2⅝" 25.00
Bronco, emb, 3¼" 45.00
Bulldog, word Bulldog & face of dog emb on front, 2¾" 30.00
Caesar, emb, 2¾" 15.00
Dragon, word Dragon & dragon emb on front, 2⅞" 25.00
Eagle, word Eagle emb on body, 4⅜" 40.00
Eagle, 4 dice emb on front, 2¾" 40.00
HC Jones (trick lock), st, 4¼" 470.00
Indian Head, Indian head emb on front, 3" 90.00
Jupiter, word Jupiter/star & moon emb on front, 3¼" 18.00
King Korn, words King Korn emb on body, 2⅞" 40.00
Lever Buckle Co, emb, 4½" 45.00
Mars, emb, 2¼" 20.00
Nineteen O Three, 1903 emb on front, iron, 3⅞" 90.00
Owl, emb, 2¼" 30.00
Red Chief, words Red Chief emb on body, 3¾" 90.00
Rugby, football emb on body, 3" 20.00
S Andrews, st, 2⅝" 200.00
Star Lock Works, st, 3⅛" 50.00
Unique, word Unique emb on front, 3¼" 120.00
Victory, emb, 3⅛" 45.00
W Bohannon, Brook NY WB, st, 3¼" 35.00
Woodland, emb, 2⅜" 30.00
Yale & Towne, lion face emb on front, shackle mk Y&T, 3" 110.00

Lever Push Key

Achilles, emb, iron, 3⅝" 50.00
Belknaps 6-Lever, emb, iron, 2¼" 40.00
California, emb, brass, 2½" 20.00
Champion, emb Champion 6-Lever, brass push-key type, 2¼" 25.00
Cherokee, emb, 6-lever, iron, 2½" 170.00
Columbia, emb Columbia 6-Lever, brass push-key type, 2¼" ...35.00
Crank, emb, iron, 2⅞" 25.00
Crescent, 4-lever, emb, iron, 2" 40.00

Duke, emb 6-Lever, 2⅛" 45.00
Eagle 3-Lever, emb, brass, 2" 50.00
Eclipse, 4-lever, emb, brass, 2½" 20.00
Empire, emb, 6-lever, brass, 2½" 20.00
Fordloc, emb, iron, 3¼" 40.00
Harvard, emb Harvard 4-Lever, brass push-key type, 2" 50.00
IXL, emb IXL on body, 2¼" 75.00
Jewett Buffalo, emb, brass, 2¼" 150.00
McIntosh, emb, 6-lever, iron, 2½" 90.00
McIntosh, emb McIntosh on body, 2¼" 90.00
Morley, emb, iron, 2½" 30.00
Nugget 4-Lever, emb, brass, 2" 50.00
SB Co, emb SB Co on body, 3¼" 60.00
Smith & Egge Mfg Co, Smith & Egge stamped on front, 3" 75.00
Ten Star, emb Ten Star 6-Lever, 2¼" 45.00
Vulcan, emb, iron, 2¾" 20.00

Logo — Special Made

Brass pancake push key emb US Internal Revenue, 2¼" 185.00
Canada Custom, emb, iron, 2¾" 130.00
Coca-Cola, st, brass, 2⅝" 40.00
Conoco, st, brass, 2⅝" 25.00
Delco Products, st, brass 20.00
Georgia Power Co, st, brass, 3" 15.00
Hawaiian Elec, st, brass, 3" 30.00
Heart-shape brass lever type st Board Education, bbl key, 3½" 65.00
International Harvester Co, emb, brass, 2½" 100.00
John Deere, st, brass 50.00
Okla State Pen, st, brass, 2⅝" 50.00
Oliver, emb, iron, 2½" 80.00
Ordinance Dept, st, brass, 2⅞" 20.00
Public Service Co, st, brass, 2⅞" 20.00
Sq brass pin-tumbler case st Regd US Mail, int counter, 2¾" 140.00
Sq Yale-type brass pin tumbler, st Shell Oil Co on body, 3⅛" 25.00
Swift & Co, st, iron, 2¼" 20.00
Texaco, emb, brass, 2¾" 60.00
University of Okla, st, brass, 2⅞" 40.00
USBIA, st, brass, 3¾" 80.00
USGS, emb, iron, 2½" 40.00
USMC, st, brass, 2½" 20.00
Winchester, emb, iron, 2⅞" 140.00
Zoo, st, iron, 2½" 25.00

Pin-Tumbler Type

Carbin, brass, Corbin in oval st on body, 3⅝" 25.00
Corbin, emb, iron, 2¾" 20.00
Eagle, emb, iron, 2¾" 20.00
Fulton, emb Fulton on body, 2⅝" 30.00
Hope, brass, emb Hope on body, 2½" 20.00
Il-A-Noy, emb, iron, 2¾" 35.00
Il-A-Noy, emb Il-A-Noy on body, 2½" 40.00
Rich-Con, emb, iron, 2⅞" 50.00
Sargent, brass, emb Sargent on body, 3" 15.00
Sargent, emb, iron, 2¾" 15.00
Shapleigh, emb Shapleigh on body, 2⅝" 30.00
Simmons, emb, iron, 2⅝" 30.00
Yale, brass, emb Yale on body, Made in England on shackle, 3" ...30.00
Yale, brass, emb Yale on body, Yale & Towne on shackle, 2⅝" 25.00

Scandinavian (Jail House) Type

Bull Dog, emb, brass, 2½" 80.00

Locks (continued)

JHW Climax Co, iron, 2⅞"	50.00
Nrarvck (Russian), st, iron, 4"	160.00
R&E Co, emb, iron, 3¼"	40.00
Romer, st, iron, 4"	70.00
Star, emb line on bottom, iron, 3¾"	100.00
99 Miller, emb 99, brass, 1¾"	80.00
999 Miller, emb 999, brass, 2½"	70.00

Six-Lever Type

Eagle, brass, Eagle Six-Lever st on body	18.00
Edwards, iron, Edwards st on body	18.00
Miller Six-Lever, st, brass, 3⅞"	20.00
Oak Leaf Six-Lever, st, iron, 3¼"	15.00
Olympiad Six-Lever, st, iron, 3¾"	25.00
SHCo Simmon Six-Lever, emb, iron, 3⅞"	70.00
Yale, brass, Yale emb on front	12.00

Story and Commemorative

Canteen, US emb on lock, lock: canteen shape, 2"	500.00
CI, emb ornate scroll motif throughout body of lock, 3½"	170.00
CI, emb skull/X-bones w/florals, NH Co on bk, 3¼"	200.00
CQD/sinking ship Titanic & SOS waves emb on brass, 2¾"	120.00
Eagle & stars/shield & stars, emb CI, Eagle Liberty, 2½"	300.00
Mail Pouch emb on lock, lock in shape of mail pouch, 3⅛"	225.00
Missouri Seal, brass, 2¼"	150.00
National Hardware Co (NHCo), emb Mercury figure, iron, 2"	170.00
National Hardware Co (NHCo), emb SK, iron, 3½"	425.00
New York to Paris, brass, 2⅝"	200.00
Russell & Erwin (R&E), emb Aztec figure, iron, 2¼"	200.00
Russell & Erwin (R&E), emb bird, iron, 2⅞"	400.00
Russell & Erwin (R&E), emb Ganesha form, iron, 3"	325.00
Russell & Erwin (R&E), emb vase, iron, 3¼"	600.00
1901 Pan Am Expo, brass, emb w/buffalo, 2⅝"	175.00
1904 World's Fair, iron & brass, 3⅝"	300.00

Warded Type

Aetna, emb, brass, 2¼"	35.00
Cruso Chicken, emb, brass, 2¾"	35.00
Enders, st, brass, 1½"	25.00
G&B, st, brass, 3"	15.00
Hex, iron, sq lock case, emb US on bk, 2⅛"	95.00
Jewel, emb, iron, 2½"	18.00
Lucky, emb, brass, 2½"	45.00
Navy, iron pancake ward key, bk: scrolled emb letters, 2½"	40.00
Red Cross, brass sq case, emb letters, 2"	10.00
Rex, steel case, emb letters, 2⅝"	18.00
Ruby, emb, brass, 2⅛"	20.00
Safe, brass sq case, emb letters, 1⅞"	8.00
Sampson, emb, iron, 2½"	20.00
Secure, iron pancake type, emb letters, 2⅝"	20.00
Shapleigh, st, brass, 2"	18.00
Texas, emb, brass, 2½"	50.00
Try Me, iron pancake type, emb letters, 2½"	25.00
Twister, st, brass, 2⅞"	12.00
Van Guard, emb, iron, 2⅞"	18.00

Wrought Iron Lever Type (Smokehouse Type)

Bramah's Patent VR, 5"	60.00
DM&Co, bbl key, 4¼"	20.00
MW&Co, bbl key, 2⅝"	10.00
MW&Co, flat key, 3½"	20.00
R&E, 4½"	40.00
S&Co, bbl key, 3"	8.00
Waines, 4⅜"	40.00
WT Patent, 3¼"	20.00

Loetz

The Loetz Glassworks was established in Klostermule, Austria, in 1840. After Loetz's death the firm was purchased by his grandson, Johann Loetz Witwe. Until WWII the operation continued to produce fine artware, some of which made in the early 1900s bears a striking resemblance to Tiffany's, with whom Loetz was associated at one time. In addition to the iridescent Tiffany-style glass, he also produced threaded glass and some cameo. The majority of Loetz pieces will have a polished pontil. Our advisor for this category is Don Williams; he is listed in the Directory under Missouri.

Vases: Globular, yellow-amber with violet iridescence and oil spots, paper label, 8½", $575.00; Globular with dimpled sides and three-crimp rim, cobalt with silvery turquoise iridescent oil spots, 4¼", $750.00.

Bowl, amberina, Invt T'print, folded-in rim, 3¾x9"	210.00
Bowl, cameo, 8 Deco tulip panels, amethyst on wht, 4x8"	1,700.00
Bowl, emerald w/threading, 3 branch ft, ruffled, 4x8"	175.00
Bowl, gr irid w/emb web motif, squatty w/free-form rim, 4x6"	145.00
Bowl, irid ripples, hexagonal; bronze std w/floral drops, 8½"	1,000.00
Bowl, purple irid w/swirls, incurvate/pleated rim, 4½x10"	150.00
Cracker jar, gr w/threading, metal mts, swirl lid, 7½"	85.00
Creamer, opal irid w/amethyst trailings, silver spout/hdl, 4"	250.00
Flask, gold w/oil spots, jack-in-pulpit rim, 10"	635.00
Ink well, chartreuse w/amethyst threading, brass cap, 2½" sq	160.00
Rose bowl, wine w/blk flowers, 8 yel ovals, 3 ball ft, 7	1,000.00
Vase, amber irid w/gold spots/red ribbons, ovoid, 10½"	5,175.00
Vase, amber w/irid bl-gold waves, U form w/pinched sides, 4"	1,200.00
Vase, amber/clear mottle w/silver irid, triangular body, 13"	750.00
Vase, amberina to gold irid, ribbed, squat twisted base, 12"	225.00
Vase, apricot w/wine & opal pulled leaves on stems, 14"	750.00
Vase, bl irid w/twig pattern, cylindrical, 5"	250.00
Vase, clear w/bl/gr/gold, combed waves, ribbed cylinder, 12"	975.00
Vase, cobalt irid w/swirls, 4½"	330.00
Vase, cobalt w/oil spots, 4 dimples, 4-lobe rim, 7"	690.00
Vase, cranberry w/irid spots & random threading, free-form, 4"	250.00
Vase, cranberry w/yel swirls, low width, tri-lobe rim, 13"	500.00
Vase, emerald gr cased, partial silver o/l, ogee sides, 5"	150.00
Vase, flamingo figural, irid gold/purple/gr, 16½"	750.00
Vase, gold, dimpled shoulder, folded tricorn rim, 3¼"	3,000.00
Vase, gold w/bl-gold pulled motif, pinched sides, hdls, 5"	1,800.00

Vase, gold w/rows of chains, 3 silver o/l prunts w/trails, 7" **2,000.00**
Vase, gold w/3 appl flowers, angle shoulder, 5¾" **500.00**
Vase, gr irid, tricon rim, 3⅛" **500.00**
Vase, gr irid w/etched florals, cylinder, att, 8¾" **175.00**
Vase, gr opal w/oil spots, tapered, 4" **100.00**
Vase, gr w/orange pnt outline flowers & oil spots, ribbed, 4" **225.00**
Vase, jack-in-pulpit; bl-gold irid/gr w/bark texture, 14" **400.00**
Vase, lt gr w/6 gold trailing prunts, 3-lobe rim, 10x4½" **250.00**
Vase, ochre w/irid, twisted/ruffled cylinder, wide base, 13" **350.00**
Vase, oil spots/gilt trailings on red, dimpled, 4-lobe rim, 8" **550.00**
Vase, paperweight; pk w/pulled gr mica design, stick neck, 6" **225.00**
Vase, Papillon, clear w/gold spots & lustre irid, 9¾" **400.00**
Vase, peacock feathers on gr w/bl irid texture, 13" **850.00**
Vase, purple irid w/random spots in strapwork bronze holder, 5" ..**125.00**
Vase, purple/brn irid w/oil drops, 7½x4½" **1,150.00**
Vase, rainbow, wht int, bottle form w/clear shells at neck, 11" ...**325.00**
Vase, rainbow irid w/oil spots, ovoid, 6¾" **900.00**
Vase, red-gold w/swirled veins, dimpled/ruffled, 7x14" **1,450.00**
Vase, royal bl w/oil spots, ormolu hdls w/leafy swags, 9" **900.00**
Vase, silver o/l floral on bl w/oil spots, #1268, 5" **1,200.00**
Vase, silver o/l scrolls on bl irid, long conical neck, 12" **1,000.00**
Vase, silver o/l w/borders & swirls, bl-gr irid, 3¼" **1,095.00**
Vase, striated agate w/wht 'lace,' pk int, 4-lobe rim, 7½" **285.00**
Vase, textured irid w/3-pinch bottom, no mk, 7" **275.00**
Vase, yel above bright bl irid on ftd U form, 7x6" **1,200.00**

Lomonosov Porcelain

Founded in Leningrad in 1744, the Lomonosov porcelain factory produced exquisite porcelain miniatures for the Czar and other Russian nobility. One of the first factories of its kind, Lomonosov produced mainly vases and delicate sculptures. In the 1800s Lomonosov became closely involved with the Russian Academy of Fine Arts, a connection which has continued to this day as the company continues to supply the world with these fine artistic treasures. In 1992 the backstamp was changed to read 'Made in Russia,' instead of 'Made in USSR.' Some dealers may be pricing items marked 'Made in USSR' at 75% to 100% above prices listed below.

Baikal duck, #6438 ....**12.50**
Bear, standing, #6448 ....**12.50**
Buck, #6547 ....**122.00**
Chipmunk, running, #8521, mini **6.50**
Ermine w/egg, #6562 ....**28.00**
Foal, brn, #6497 ....**24.50**

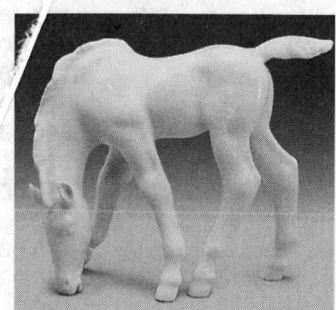

Foal, #6512, lg, $53.00.

Fox, #6541 ....**14.00**
Gazelle, #6530 ....**10.00**
Leopard cub, #6576 ....**14.50**
Lynx, #6550 ....**33.00**

Magpie, #6963 ....**36.50**
Magpie, wht, #2644 ....**38.00**
Moose, #6438 ....**123.00**
Otter, #6538 ....**26.50**
Pig, #9241, mini **9.50**
Seagull, #6579 ....**27.50**
Snow Bunting, #6557 ....**8.50**
Spitz, #9528, mini **15.50**
Squirrel, #7404, mini **4.50**
Tiger, #6479, lg **105.00**
Yakut w/dog, #6244 ....**75.50**

Longwy

The Longwy workshops were founded in 1798 and continue today to produce pottery in the north of France near the Luxembourg-Belgian border under the name 'Societe des Faienceries de Lonswy et Senelle.' The ware for which they are best known was produced during the Art Deco period, decorated in bold colors and designs. Earlier wares made during the first quarter of the 19th century reflected the popularity of Oriental art, cloisonne enamels in particular. The designs were executed by impressing the pattern into the moist clay and filling in the depressions with enamels. Examples are marked 'Longwy,' either impressed or painted under glaze.

Bowl, divided, 4 oval reserves w/clouds & rays, 12" L **150.00**
Charger, deer, blk on dk bl, incised mk/label, 15" dia **575.00**
Plaque, heron in swamp on cobalt, oval, 8x7" **135.00**
Tile, Deco lady in garden, 4-color, Primavera, 8x8" **395.00**
Vase, foliage, mc on crackled ivory, mk, 8¾x6½" **345.00**
Vase, leaves & swirls, yel/brn on blk/wht, Catteau, 10" **550.00**

Lonhuda

William Long was a druggist by trade who combined his knowledge of chemistry with his artistic ability in an attempt to produce a type of brown-glazed slip-decorated artware similar to that made by the Rookwood Pottery. He achieved his goal in 1889 after years of long and dedicated study. Three years later he founded his firm, the Lonhuda Pottery Company. The name was coined from the first few letters of the last name of each of his partners, W.H. Hunter and Alfred Day. Laura Fry, formerly of the Rookwood company, joined the firm in 1892, bringing with her a license for Long to use her patented airbrush-blending process. Other artists of note, Sarah McLaughlin, Helen Harper, and Jessie Spaulding, joined the firm and decorated the ware with nature studies, animals, and portraits, often signing their work with their initials. Three types of marks were used on the Steubenville Lonhuda ware. The first was a linear composite of the letters 'LPCO' with the name 'Lonhuda' impressed above it. The second, adopted in 1893, was a die-stamp representing the solid profile of an Indian, used on ware patterned after pottery made by the American Indians. This mark was later replaced with an impressed outline of the Indian head with 'Lonhuda' arching above it. Although the ware was successful, the business floundered due to poor management. In 1895 Long became a partner of Sam Weller and moved to Zanesville where the manufacture of the Lonhuda line continued. Less than a year later, Long left the Weller company. He was associated with J.B. Owens until 1899, at which time he moved to Denver, Colorado, where he established the Denver China and Pottery Company in 1901. His efforts to produce Lonhuda utilizing local clay were highly successful. Examples of Denver Lonhuda are sometimes marked with the LF (Lonhuda Faience) cipher contained within a canted diamond form. For further information we recommend *Collector's*

Encyclopedia of Colorado Pottery by Carol and Jim Carlton; they are listed in the Directory under Colorado.

Bowl, banana boat; tiny blossoms, 4-ftd, hdls, 5½x9½" 185.00
Bowl, roses on brn, S McLaughlin, 4x4" 160.00
Mug, blkberries & blossoms on gray matt, att Leffler, 4" 150.00
Napkin ring, floral on brn, 2x2" 100.00

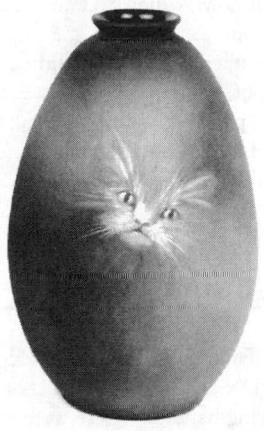

Vase, kitten's face on gray matt, signed C. Leffler, marked, 9½", $3,250.00.

Vase, roses on brn, EX art, sgn M Taylor, 5x4" 160.00
Vase, standard, apple blossoms, #350LF, 7x8" 240.00
Vase, thistles/leaves, bk: flower, mk, 7½" 275.00
Vase, tulips on brn, integral hdls, 6x9" 650.00

Lotton

Charles Lotton is a contemporary glass artist. He began blowing glass and developing original designs thirty years ago and now has work on display in many major glass museums and collections, among them the Smithsonian, the Art Institute of Chicago, the Museum of Glass, and the Chrysler Museum. He has become famous for his unique lamps. Every piece is signed and dated. His three sons, David, Daniel, and John, each work in their own studios. All four artists produce distinctive work. They sell their glass at antique shows and in their showroom in Lansing, Illinois. For further information read *Lotton Art Glass* by Charles Lotton and Tom O'Conner; see the Directory under Illinois. The values that follow are actual prices realized from a recent auction.

Bottle, scent; pk/wht floral w/gr leaves, John 1998, 4x2½" 65.00
Bottle, scent; pulled/feathered bls, Daniel 1997, 8x5½" 300.00
Bowl, Multi Flora, Charles 1990, 7⅝x8¾" 850.00
Bowl, Multi Flora on pk, invt rim, John 1998, 5x6" 390.00
Ornament, brn/gr/gold stripes on beige, Daniel, 3¼" dia 50.00
Paperweight, King Tut, Charles 730.00
Paperweight, pk/wht floral on blk, John 1988, 10¼x6¼" 690.00
Paperweight, wht-bl flowers w/wht vines, Mark 1998, 2¼x2¾" 80.00
Paperweight, 5 pk impatiens on aventurine ground, 1984, 4¾" ..250.00
Vase, dk bl hearts/gr vines on yel, Lotton 1977, 5¼" 227.50
Vase, jack-in-pulpit; blk w/mc irid crackle int, David 1992, 7" ..220.00
Vase, midnight bl pulls on red, Lotton 1975, 3¾" 315.00
Vase, Zipper, irid lt & dk bls, Charles 1997, 10¾x7" 1,100.00
Vase, 5 pk flowers w/gr leaves on dk to lt orange, 1984, 9" 500.00
Vase, 6 pk impatiens w/gr leaves, 1984, 6¾" 300.00

Lotus Ware

Isaac Knowles and Issac Harvey operated a pottery in East Liver-

pool, Ohio, in 1853 where they produced both yellow ware and Rockingham. In 1870 Knowles brought Harvey's interests and took as partners John Taylor and Homer Knowles. Their principal product was ironstone china, but Knowles was confident that American potters could produce as fine a ware as the Europeans. To prove his point, he hired Joshua Poole, an artist from the Belleek Works in Ireland. Poole quickly perfected a Belleek-type china, but fire destroyed this portion of the company. Before it could function again, their hotel china business had grown to the point that it required their full attention in order to meet market demands. By 1891 they were able to try again. They developed a bone china, as fine and thin as before, which they called Lotus. Henry Schmidt from the Meissen factory in Germany decorated the ware, often with lacy filigree applications or hand-formed leaves and flowers to which he added further decoration with liquid slip applied by means of a squeeze bag. Due to high production costs resulting from so much of the fragile ware being damaged in firing and because of changes in tastes and styles of decoration, the Lotus Ware line was dropped in 1896. Some of the early ware was marked 'KT&K China'; later marks have a star and a crescent with 'Lotus Ware' added. For further information we recommend *Collector's Encyclopedia of Knowles, Taylor & Knowles China* by Mary Frank Gaston, our advisor for this category.

Bonbon/nappy, sm floral on wht w/gold, ftd, 8" L 325.00
Bottle, scent; pierced/scrolled, twig hdl, folded rim, 3½" 650.00
Bowl, appl floral branches, netting, 3¾x4¾" 175.00
Bowl, Columbia, appl lacy openwork w/gold, 4¾" H 900.00
Bowl, floral branches w/gold, fishscale shoulder, mk, 4¾" H 400.00
Bowl, gold emb floral branches, beaded ruffled rim, 4x4¾" 175.00
Bowl, gold floral & rtcl ornaments on yel, gr mk, 4" H 500.00
Bowl, gold rtcl medallions, HP florals, gold netting, 6½" L 600.00
Bowl, pastel cornflowers, sgn, gold ruffled rim, 4½" H 450.00
Chocolate jug, emb florals, no enameling or gold, 9" 550.00
Chocolate jug, gold-paste floral, 9" 750.00
Creamer & sugar bowl, chestnut design, gold-paste floral 500.00
Cup & saucer, tea; Sonoma, sculpted leaf design, ftd cup 135.00
Ewer, pk floral, gold-specked twig hdl, 6½" 375.00
Flower bowl, gold leaves w/red & bl highlights, 4½" 650.00
Jug, Globe, roses w/much gold, 5x7" 750.00
Pin tray, draped nude, fan behind her, HP, rare, 6" L 1,300.00
Pitcher, netting, 2¾" 100.00
Pitcher, netting on wht, tied bamboo hdl, squat, 3½" 150.00
Pitcher, pk floral branches w/gold, bamboo hdl w/gold, 4½" 275.00
Rose bowl, flowers/leaves, lav on wht, beaded lav rim, 4x4" 350.00
Rose jar, lt gr w/rtcl wht trim, rtcl dome lid, 4" 650.00
Rose jar, wht w/allover bead swags & medallions, petal ft, 8" ..1,700.00
Rose jar, wht w/rtcl lid, ornamental side mts, ftd, 7x6" 1,350.00
Salt cellar, gold lustre int..80.00
Shell tray, roses & gold transfer, 5x5½" 350.00
Syrup, acanthus leaf shoulder, scroll hdl, floral rim, 4½" 225.00
Syrup, morning glories, pk/wht on pk, serpentine hdl, 3" 225.00
Teapot, emb floral, gilt cut-out rim, 3¾", +cr/sug 525.00
Vase, Etruscan, appl flowers, filigree hdls, whtware, 10" 1,350.00
Vase, lily form, bl/pk/ivory shaded w/gold trim, 8" 1,100.00
Vase, roses in yel & pk, blk hdls w/emb masks below, 8" 425.00
Whiskey jug, Meredith's Diamond Club, Pure Rye Whiskey, 7½" .150.00

Lu Ray Pastels

Lu Ray Pastels dinnerware was introduced in the early 1940s by Taylor, Smith, and Taylor of East Liverpool, Ohio. It was offered in assorted colors of Persian Cream, Sharon Pink, Surf Green, Windsor Blue, and Chatham Gray in complete place settings as well as many service pieces. It was a successful line in its day and is once again finding favor with collectors of American dinnerware. For further information we recommend *Collector's Guide to Lu Ray Pastels* by Bill and Kathy Meehan. Our advisor for this category is Shirley Moore; she is listed in the Directory under Oklahoma.

Bowl, '36s oatmeal 50.00
Bowl, coupe soup; flat 15.00
Bowl, cream soup 55.00
Bowl, fruit; Chatham Gray, 5" 16.00
Bowl, fruit; 5" 5.00
Bowl, lug soup; tab hdld 19.00
Bowl, mixing; 10¼" 85.00
Bowl, mixing; 5½" 85.00
Bowl, mixing; 7" 85.00
Bowl, mixing; 8¾" 85.00
Bowl, salad; any color other than yel 65.00
Bowl, salad; yel 55.00
Bowl, vegetable; oval, 9½" 20.00
Butter dish, any color other than Chatham Gray, w/lid 50.00
Butter dish, Chatham Gray, rare color, w/lid 90.00
Calendar plates, 8", 9" & 10", ea 40.00
Casserole 95.00
Chocolate cup, AD; str sides 80.00
Chocolate pot, AD; str sides 360.00
Coaster/nut dish 65.00
Coffee cup, AD 20.00
Coffeepot, AD 200.00
Creamer 8.00
Creamer, AD, ind 40.00
Creamer, AD, ind, from chocolate set 92.00
Egg cup, dbl 24.00
Epergne 110.00
Gravy boat 28.00
Jug, water; ftd 110.00
Muffin cover 90.00
Muffin cover, w/8" underplate 105.00
Nappy, vegetable; rnd, 8½" 20.00
Pitcher, any color other than yel, bulbous w/flat bottom 95.00
Pitcher, juice 150.00
Pitcher, yel, bulbous w/flat bottom 75.00
Plate, cake 70.00
Plate, Chatham Gray, rare color, 7" 16.00
Plate, chop; 15" 38.00
Plate, grill; compartment 28.00
Plate, 10" 20.00
Plate, 6" 3.00
Plate, 7" 12.00
Plate, 8" 15.00
Plate, 9" 10.00
Platter, oval, 11½" 16.00

Platter, 13", $19.00.

Relish dish, 4-part 95.00
Sauce boat, any other color than yel, fixed stand 35.00

Sauce boat, yel, fixed stand 22.50
Saucer, coffee; AD 8.50
Saucer, coffee/chocolate 30.00
Saucer, cream soup 22.50
Saucer, tea 3.00
Shakers, pr 16.00
Sugar bowl, AD; w/lid, from chocolate set 92.00
Sugar bowl, AD; w/lid, ind 40.00
Sugar bowl, w/lid 15.00
Teacup 8.00
Teapot, curved spout, w/lid 95.00
Teapot, flat spout, w/lid 160.00
Tray, pickle 28.00
Tumbler, juice 45.00
Tumbler, water 65.00
Vase, bud 325.00

Lunch Boxes

    Early 20th-century tobacco companies such as Union Leader, Tiger, and Dixie sold their products in square, steel containers with flat, metal carrying handles. These were specifically engineered to be used as lunch boxes when they became empty. (See Advertising, specific companies.) By 1930 oval lunch pails with colorful lithographed decorations on tin were being manufactured to appeal directly to children. These were made by Ohio Art, Decoware, and a few other companies. In 1950 Aladdin Industries produced the first 'real' character lunch box — a Hopalong Cassidy decal-decorated steel container now considered the beginning of the kids' lunch box industry. The other big lunch box manufacturer, American Thermos (later King Seely Thermos Company) brought out its 'blockbuster' Roy Rogers box in 1953, the first fully lithographed steel lunch box and matching bottle. Other companies (ADCO Liberty; Landers, Frary & Clark; Ardee Industries; Okay Industries; Universal; Tindco; Cheinco) also produced character pails. Today's collectors often tend to specialize in those boxes dealing with a particular subject. Western, space, TV series, Disney movies, and cartoon characters are the most popular. There are well over five hundred different lunch boxes available to the astute collector. For further information we recommend *The Illustrated Encyclopedia of Metal Lunch Boxes* by Allen Woodall and Sean Brickell. Our advisor for this category is Allan Smith; he is listed in the Directory under Texas. In the following listings, lunch boxes are metal unless noted vinyl or plastic, and values include thermoses only when they are mentioned within the descriptions.

Action Jackson, 1973, w/thermos, NM 200.00
Alf, 1987, plastic, red, w/thermos, NM 18.00
America on Parade, 1976, w/thermos, EX 60.00
Animaniacs, vinyl, hot pk, EX 20.00
Apple's Way, 1975, w/thermos, M 180.00
Atom Ant, 1966, w/thermos, EX 275.00
Batman & Robin, 1966, G 95.00
Battle of the Planets, 1979, w/thermos, M 200.00
Beauty & the Beast, vinyl, pk & purple softee, w/thermos, VG 20.00
Bedknobs & Broomsticks, 1972, VG 30.00
Bionic Woman, running, 1978, EX 85.00
Bonanza, 1963, gr rim, EX 185.00
Brady Bunch, 1970, VG 110.00
Bugaloos, Aladdin, 1971, EX 125.00
Cabbage Patch Kids, plastic, 1983, yel, w/thermos, EX 10.00
Captain Astro, 1966, EX 300.00
Cartoon Zoo, 1962, G 80.00
Chan Clan, 1973, w/thermos, EX 115.00
Color Me Happy, 1984, EX 150.00

Daniel Boone, 1955, w/thermos, M 550.00
Daniel Boone, 1965, w/thermos, M 450.00
Disney Express, 1979, w/thermos, M 100.00
Doctor Dolittle, 1967, w/thermos, EX 150.00
Dudley Do-Right, 1962, w/thermos, EX 650.00
Emergency, 1977, dome top, w/thermos, EX+ 175.00
Fall Guy, 1981, w/thermos, EX 35.00
Flag-O-Rama, 1954, EX 600.00
Flintstones & Dino, 1962, orange, VG 95.00
Flintstones Movie, plastic, 1994, rock shape, w/thermos, NM 15.00
Fraggle Rock, 1984, EX 25.00
Gene Autry, 1954, w/thermos, EX 500.00
Globetrotters, 1959, dome top, w/thermos, M 600.00
Gremlins, 1984, VG+ 16.00
Gunsmoke, 1962, w/thermos, EX 335.00
Happy Days, 1976, VG 30.00
Hong Kong Phooey, 1975, w/thermos, EX 90.00
Howdy Doody, 1954, EX 400.00
Indiana Jones & the Temple of Doom, 1984, w/thermos, VG 30.00
Jungle Book, 1966, w/thermos, M 250.00
King Kong, 1977, w/thermos, EX 60.00
Land of the Giants, 1968, w/thermos, M 350.00
Lawman, 1961, w/thermos, M 350.00
Lone Ranger, 1954, EX 400.00
Luggage Tweed, 1957, bl, EX 75.00
Man From Uncle, 1966, w/thermos, EX 200.00
Masters of the Universe, plastic, 1983, bl, VG 10.00
Mickey Mouse Club, 1977, red trim, w/thermos, M 120.00
Mork & Mindy, 1979, VG 35.00
Munsters, 1965, w/thermos, NM 475.00
NFL, 1977, w/thermos, EX 25.00
Peanuts, vinyl, 1969, red, w/thermos, M 130.00
Pebbles & Bamm-Bamm, 1971, w/thermos, EX 100.00
Pete's Dragon, 1978, w/thermos, EX 60.00
Pinocchio, 1971, VG 60.00
Popeye, 1980, w/thermos, VG 40.00
Popeye & Son, plastic, 1987, yel, 3-D, M 55.00
Porky's Lunch Wagon, 1959, dome top, EX 400.00
Scooby Doo, plastic, w/thermos, EX 50.00
Secret Wars, 1984, VG 40.00
Snow White & the Seven Dwarfs, Disney, 1975, w/thermos, EX .75.00
Sport Goofy, 1983, VG 20.00
Strawberry Shortcake, vinyl, 1980, checked design, VG 35.00
Superman, 1967, VG 130.00
Talespin, plastic, 1986, bl, w/thermos, EX 25.00
Teenage Mutant Ninja Turtles, vinyl, 1988, bl softee, EX 8.00
Track King, 1975, w/thermos, EX 350.00
Transformers, plastic, red, w/thermos, EX 10.00
Universal Movie Monsters, Aladdin, 1979, w/thermos, EX 100.00
Wild Frontier, 1977, EX 60.00
World of Teddy Ruxpin, plastic, 1990, w/thermos, EX 10.00

Lutz

From 1869 to 1888, Nicholas Lutz worked for the Boston and Sandwich Company where he produced the threaded and striped art glass that was so popular during that era. His works were not marked; and since many other glassmakers of the day made similar wares, the term Lutz has come to refer not only to his original works but to any of this type.

Cup & saucer, yel/wht/gold latticinio 100.00
Finger bowl, cranberry, amber reeded crimped rim, 5½", +tray ..160.00

Tumbler, 3-color latticinio, 3¾" 120.00

Maddux of California

One of the California-made ceramics now so popular with collectors, Maddux was founded in the late 1930s and during the years that followed produced novelty items, TV lamps, figurines, planters, and tableware accessories. Our advisor for this category is Doris Frizzell; she is listed in the Directory under Illinois. (SASE required.)

#206A, planter, Chinese Bell Tower, 8" 20.00
#221, vase, swan, wht, 12" 20.00
#225, vase, horse's head top, str-sided body, aqua, 12" 18.00
#300, figurine, puppy, 6x5½" 15.00
#400/401, flamingo, pr 50.00
#515, planter, flamingo, pk, 10½" 45.00
#519, TV lamp, rooster, orange, 13" 75.00
#527, Chinese pheasant, 11½" 20.00
#528, planter, 2 birds in flight, pk & blk, 10" 20.00
#529, vase, 2 flamingos, 5" 40.00
#536, planter, bird in flight, 11½" H 20.00
#627, TV lamp, stallion, 13" 35.00
#628, planter, swallow, pk & gray 35.00
#808, TV lamp, pearl-tone shell, 13" 40.00
#810, TV lamp, stallion, prancing, on base, 12" 65.00
#825, TV lamp, swans, 10x11½x5¾" 55.00
#826, TV lamp, cockatoos 65.00
#828, TV lamp, swan planter, wht porc, 12½" 40.00
#829, TV lamp, deer (2), running, natural, 10½" 45.00
#839, TV lamp, mallard, flying, natural colors, 11½" 45.00
#841, TV lamp, head of Christ, 3-D planter 45.00

#510, black swan planter, 11", $18.00.

#844, TV lamp, prairie schooner (covered wagon), 11" 45.00
#846, TV lamp, nativity scene, 3-D planter 45.00
#859, TV lamp, Toro (bull), ft on mound, 11½" 50.00
#887, TV lamp, Persian Glory (horse head), 11½" 50.00
#889, TV lamp, Malibu shell, pearl-tone, 10¼" 20.00
#892, TV lamp, Colonial ship, 10½" 40.00
#894, TV lamp, Toro (bull), charging, walnut, 11½" 50.00
#895, TV lamp, dbl swan, 11½" 50.00
#896, TV lamp, bassett hound, 12" 155.00
#897, TV lamp, mare & foal, wht porc 60.00
#907, doe, walnut, wht porc, tangerine, 12½" 15.00
#912/913, Chinese pheasants, airbrushed colors, 11", pr 30.00
#914, stag, standing, natural colors, 12½" 20.00
#923, swans (2), blk matt, 10½" 25.00
#924, stag, standing, natural colors, 12½" 15.00
#925/926, horses, rearing/charging, pr 20.00
#928/929, mallards, male/female, natural colors, 9½", pr 40.00
#932, rooster, 10½" 30.00

#969, Early Birds, blk matt, tangerine, 14½", pr **25.00**
#970, flamingo, flying, natural colors, 11" **45.00**
#971, flamingo, winging, natural colors, 12" **45.00**
#972/973, bull, red, head up/head down, 11" L, pr **75.00**
#982, horse, prancing **20.00**
#984, elephant, sitting, 18" **25.00**
#1019, swan console bowl (set), porc wht, 11½" **20.00**
#1047, Contempo bowl (set), wht satin, 16½" **15.00**
#1051, candlestick, dbl, 12" **25.00**
#1067, shell console bowl (set), pk, 16" **15.00**
#2015, Antique Gold, hdls, 12" **15.00**
#2102, bowl, ftd **10.00**
#2217, cream can, Paul Revere Milc Co, Maddux **75.00**
#3006, TV lamp/planter, half-circle **25.00**
#3009, serving tray/lazy susan, pearlized, 2-tiered, 6-pc **25.00**
#3017, seashell bowl, wht **15.00**
#3051, bowl, red tomato w/gr dbl leaves, w/lid, 16" L **48.00**
#3095A, bowl, ped w/6 ind servers **25.00**
#3251-L, tray, serving; 2-tier **20.00**
#3275, gr pepper relish, w/lid & side bowls **12.00**
#3302, bank, cat, yel **35.00**
#3304, planter, bird **20.00**
#7001, ashtray, 12" dia **10.00**
#7134, ashtray, fish, 6" L **20.00**
#7204, ashtray, pig form, natural colors, 7" L **12.00**
Ashtray set, yel & red, metal caddy w/6 ind ashtrays **20.00**
Bank, smiling pig, red or gr, 12" L **25.00**
Bowl, cabbage leaf design, 4x13" L **30.00**
Cats, Deco style, blk matt, 12½" facing pr **50.00**
Cockatoos, on branch w/appl flowers, 11" **40.00**
Cookie jar, Bear, #2101 ....**75.00**
Cookie jar, Beatrix Potter Rabbit **100.00**
Cookie jar, Cat **65.00**
Cookie jar, Clary Hippy **300.00**
Cookie jar, Clown, very lg, from $325 to **395.00**
Cookie jar, Grape Cylinder **45.00**
Cookie jar, Humpty Dumpty, #2113 ....**300.00**
Cookie jar, Koala **75.00**
Cookie jar, Queen, #2104, from $125 to **140.00**
Cookie jar, Raggedy Ann, #2108, from $250 to **300.00**
Cookie jar, Scottie **75.00**
Cookie jar, Snowman **75.00**
Cookie jar, Squirrel, #2110, C Romanelli **100.00**
Cookie jar, Strawberry **35.00**
Cookie jar, Walrus **65.00**
Cookie jar, 3 baby birds on lid, #3233 ....**65.00**
Ducklings, 3 on grassy base **20.00**
Flamingo Line, single flamingo planter, 6" **20.00**
Planter, horse, rearing, 10 7½" **22.00**
Wall pocket, bird in metal holder (resembles cage), 7x7"+cage **35.00**

Magazines

Magazines are collected for their cover prints and for the information pertaining to defunct companies and their products that can be gleaned from the old advertisements. In the listings that follow, items are assumed to be in very good condition unless noted otherwise. Our advisor for this category is Charles Zayic; he is listed in the Directory under Maine. See also Movie Memorabilia; Parrish, Maxfield.

Key:
M — mint condition, in original wrapper
EX — excellent condition, spine intact, edges of pages clean and straight
VG — very good condition, the average as-found condition

American Boy, 1909, July, Wright Brothers article, EX **25.00**
American Magazine, 1909, August, Jack London story, VG+ **40.00**
Atlantic Monthly, 1862, July, Nathaniel Hawthorne story, VG+ ..**50.00**
Collier's, 1914, September 12, Leyendecker cover, G **10.00**
Esquire, 1936, June, Ernest Hemingway story, VG **40.00**
Esquire, 1943, January, Alberto Varga calender for 1943, EX **80.00**
Family Circle, 1939, December 15, Scarlett & Rhett cover, NM .**50.00**
Family Circle, 1939, June 30, Scarlett O'Hara cover, NM **75.00**
Harper's Weekly, 1905, February 18, Thomas Hardy poem, EX **20.00**
Inside Sports, 1979, October 1, 1st issue, Yankees cover, EX **50.00**
Liberty, 1938, February 18, Battle of the Fairs article, EX **10.00**
Liberty, 1938, February 5, Lombard article, EX **9.00**
Liberty, 1938, July 30, more Lindbergh case info, EX **10.00**
Liberty, 1938, September 17, EX **9.00**
Liberty, 1941, August 9, Bob Feller cover portrait, EX **20.00**
Liberty, 1942, March 14, Walt Disney cover, EX **20.00**
Life, 1936, December 28, Margaret Mitchell article, NM **40.00**
Life, 1940, March 11, Vivien Leigh article, NM **40.00**
Life, 1942, December 21, lonely war wife cover, EX **8.00**
Life, 1944, June 26, Statue of Liberty cover, G **8.00**
Life, 1947, September 29, Johnny Lujack cover, EX....................**20.00**
Life, 1953, June 8, Roy Campanella cover, EX **25.00**

Life, 1964, March 6, Cassius Clay cover, NM, $35.00.

Life, 1971, November 12, Bobby Fischer cover, EX+ **6.00**
Life, 1972, June 16, '50s revival news, EX **10.00**
Life, 1979, December, Special Issue, decade in pictures, NM **10.00**
Life, 1984, August, The Fifties, EX **10.00**
Life, 1988, Fall, 150 Yrs of Photography, NM **6.50**
Life, 1988, May, Rhett & Scarlett Return, EX **10.00**
Life, 1989, Fall, Special Issue, The '80s, EX **8.00**
Life, 1991, Fall, Pearl Harbor December 7 1941-1991, NM **6.00**
Lippincott's Monthly, 1887, August, athlete's union article, VG .**100.00**
Literary Digest, 1933, November, G **3.00**
Look, 1939, December 19, 2-pg article & illus of Gone w/Wind, M .**40.00**
Look, 1939, October 10, Joe DiMaggio cover portrait, VG+ **30.00**
Newsweek, 1969, September 15, Joe Namath/Jets cover, EX **55.00**
Newsweek, 1970, December 28, Rockwell Santa cover, VG **6.00**
Newsweek, 1970, November 9, Muhammad Ali cover, EX **65.00**
Pacific Monthly, 1907, November, Sinclair Lewis poem, EX **30.00**
Pic, 1946, November, JF Kennedy cover portrait, EX **30.00**
Reader, The; 1907, January, Harrison Fisher cover art, VG **25.00**
Redbook, 1935, February, William Saroyan story, EX **25.00**
Saturday Evening Post, 1910, October 1, Robinson cover art, VG+ ..**20.00**
Saturday Evening Post, 1930, May 31, F Scott Fitzgerald story, EX **25.00**
Saturday Evening Post, 1942, March 14, How To Blockade Japan, EX ..**4.00**
Saturday Evening Post, 1948, July 10, Post-War USA cover, EX **3.00**
Saturday Evening Post, 1955, March 26, Life in Middle '50s, VG ..**3.00**
Saturday Evening Post, 1969, January 25, A Miller article, EX **6.00**

Seaside Library, Vol 3, No 64, ca 1880, Jules Verne story, EX 50.00
Sport Magazine, 1948, April 4, Ted Williams cover, EX 75.00
Sport Magazine, 1949, August, Jackie Robinson cover, EX 50.00
Sport Magazine, 1951, August, Yogi Berra cover, EX 30.00
Sport Magazine, 1952, February, Sugar Ray Robinson cover, EX ..25.00
Sport Magazine, 1954, July, Stan Musial cover, EX 45.00
Sport Magazine, 1955, September, Duke Snider cover, EX 35.00
Sport Magazine, 1956, October, Mickey Mantle cover, EX 65.00
Sporting News, 1967, May 6, Whitney Ford/Yankees cover, EX ...25.00
Sporting News, 1970, March 28, Kareem Jabhar/Bucks cover, EX ..35.00
Sports Illustrated, 1956, June 11, Sam Snead cover, EX 40.00
Sports Illustrated, 1960, October 2, Roger Maris/Yankees cover, EX ..60.00
Sports Illustrated, 1962, June 4, Willlie Mays/Giants cover, EX ...60.00
Sports Illustrated, 1966, December 4, Lew Alcinder/UCLA cover, EX ..30.00
Sports Illustrated, 1977, November 28, Larry Bird/Indiana cover, EX ..50.00
Sports Illustrated, 1990, 35 Years of Covers, EX 25.00
Sports Illustrated for Kids, 1989, January 1, Jordan cover, EX 30.00
Time, 1978, March 6, Cheryl Tiegs cover, EX 7.50
Time, 1988, March 14, Clark Kent & Superman article, EX 7.00
Time, 1989, Fall, 150 Yrs of Photo Journalism, NM 7.50
Town & Country, 1948, July, Salvadore Dali cover art, VG 30.00
True Romance, 1955, October, Marilyn Monroe cover, EX 75.00
True Story, 1939, December, Bund Love Camp, EX 7.50
Who's Who in Baseball, 1926, Max Carey cover, EX 120.00
Wide World, 1934, December, KKK cover art, EX 25.00
Woman's Home Companion, 1933, September, Charlie Chaplin cover, EX .30.00
Youth's Companion, 1895, October 3, Mark Twain article, EX ...40.00
Youth's Companion, 1906, March 15, Robert Frost sgn poem, EX ..25.00

Majolica

Majolica is a type of heavy earthenware, design-molded and deco-rated in vivid colors with either a lead or tin type of glaze. It reached its height of popularity in the Victorian era; examples from this period are found in only the lead glazes. Nearly every potter of note, both here and abroad, produced large majolica jardinieres, umbrella stands, pitchers with animal themes, leaf shapes, vegetable forms, and nearly any other design from nature that came to mind. Few, however, marked their ware. Among those who did were Minton, Wedgwood, Holdcroft, and George Jones in England; Griffin, Smith and Hill (Etruscan) in Phoenixville, Pennsylvania; and Chesapeake Pottery (Avalon and Clifton) in Baltimore.

Color and condition are both very important worth-assessing fac-tors. Pieces with cobalt, lavender, and turquoise glazes command the highest prices. For further information we recommend *The Collector's Encyclopedia of Majolica* by Mariann Katz-Marks (see Directory, Penn-sylvania). Unless another condition is given, the values that follow are for pieces in mint condition. Our advisor for this category is Hardy Hudson; he is listed in the Directory under Florida.

Basket, Blackberry, sm 225.00
Basket, Pond Lilly, att Holdcroft 385.00
Basket, Sunflower & Begonia Leaf 600.00
Bowl, Pond Lily, ftd, Holdcroft 350.00
Bowl, sauce; Daisy, Etruscan 350.00
Bread platter, Begonia, Etruscan 300.00
Bread tray, Pond Lily & Fern, Holdcroft 400.00
Butter pat, Floral & Berry on cobalt 165.00
Butter pat, Morning Glory on Napkin 125.00
Butter pat, Prunus, Wedgwood 140.00
Butter pat, Shell & Seaweed (w/seaweed), Etruscan 275.00
Cake stand, Pond Lily, 3 storks on ft, 6x9¼" 500.00
Cake stand, Shell & Fishnet, Fielding 500.00

Candle holder, girl w/doll, Continental 125.00
Card holder, Picket Fence, EX color, Minton 500.00
Compote, Begonia, 6x10" 275.00

Compote, water lily support-ed by sea nymph on dolphin, shell-form base, Holdcroft, 12¼", NM, $1,495.00.

Creamer, floral on cobalt, Geo Jones 375.00
Ewer, wing; Pompeiian, mermaid hdl & putto, Minton 1,800.00
Fork & spoon, salad; Argenta Prunus, Wedgwood 250.00
Game dish, bird on lid, EX color, rpr lid, Geo Jones 2,500.00
Game dish, fox on lid, goose on yel basket base 2,800.00
Humidor, alligator w/red cape, 5" 600.00
Humidor, bear w/bl smoking jacket 550.00
Humidor, bison w/gray smoking jacket & pipe, rare, 8" 630.00
Humidor, Black face w/straw hat, bl collar, BB #338 ....450.00
Humidor, Black jockey 450.00
Humidor, coiled snake 135.00
Humidor, dog w/padlock on collar 200.00
Humidor, dog w/red smoking jacket 375.00
Humidor, Indian w/red hat & bl tassel, 11½" 350.00
Humidor, monkey seated on drum 200.00
Knife rest, ear of corn, Continental 75.00
Knife rest, pickle, Continental, NM 75.00
Match striker, monkey, lg 385.00
Mug, Sunflower, cobalt 200.00
Mug, Water Lily, Etruscan 275.00
Nut dish, squirrel, Geo Jones 1,800.00
Pitcher, Bird & Fan, Wardles, 8½" 375.00
Pitcher, cat w/fiddle figual, 9" 700.00
Pitcher, Corn, pewter top, EX color, English registry mk, 9" 400.00
Pitcher, Dogwood, w/ice lip, Holdcroft, 10" 375.00
Pitcher, Floral, dragon hdl, 10" 300.00
Pitcher, honey bear figural, att Holdcroft, 10½" 1,100.00
Pitcher, Lily of the Valley w/Butterfly, 8½" 300.00
Pitcher, monkey figural w/duck hdl, 13" 745.00
Pitcher, owl figural, EX color, 9½" 400.00
Pitcher, owl figural, 6½" 250.00
Pitcher, parrot figural, EX color, 10" 350.00
Pitcher, pelican figural, rare sz, 11" 1,300.00
Pitcher, Pineapple, 8½", NM 275.00
Pitcher, pug dog figural, 9" 400.00
Pitcher, rooster figural, St Clements, 11" 165.00
Pitcher, Wild Rose, butterfly spout, Etruscan, 9½" 450.00
Plate, Bird & Branch, cobalt, Eureka, 9½" 330.00
Plate, Bird & Fruit, 9" 150.00
Plate, crescent shape, Geo Jones, 9½" 400.00
Plate, oyster; raised center shell, EX color, Geo Jones 2,000.00
Plate, Picket Fence & Basket, Geo Jones, 7" 400.00
Plate, Pond Lily, EX color, Geo Jones, 9" 745.00
Plate, Water Lily, unmk Holdcroft, 9" 250.00
Platter, Bird & Fan on wht w/brn rim, Wardles, 13" 350.00
Platter, Cattail & Fish, Holdcroft, 26" 2,600.00
Platter, Sunflower & Floral, Wardles, 12½" 300.00

Sardine box, Fish, cobalt 800.00
Sardine box, Fish & Shell on turq 750.00
Sardine box, Oak Leaf & Acorn 465.00
Spittoon, Pineapple 750.00
Strawberry server, figural flower cups for cr/sug 1,300.00
Sweetmeat dish, monkey w/fish & basket, 5½" 600.00
Syrup, Pineapple, pewter lid, 6" 450.00
Syrup, Sunflower on cobalt, Etruscan 650.00
Tea set, Fish & Seaweed on cobalt, 3-pc 900.00
Teapot, Blackberry, Holdcroft 385.00
Teapot, Chinaman, cobalt, rpr 750.00
Teapot, Floral & Basket on turq 350.00
Teapot, Fruit, brn, 6" 300.00
Teapot, Isle of Man, rope hdl & base, 10" 880.00
Teapot, monkey, yel, rprs 700.00
Teapot, monkey figural hdl, cobalt, Geo Jones 4,500.00
Teapot, Pineapple, unusual bail hdl, 8" 550.00
Teapot, Shell & Seaweed, Etruscan 800.00
Toothpick holder, deer & fox scenic 85.00
Tray, Fan & Wheat, cobalt, 10½x9½" 355.00
Tray, Wild Rose & Rope, brn, 12" 200.00
Umbrella stand, Crane, Bamboo, Ribbon & Bow, att Fielding, 24" ..2,300.00
Umbrella stand, Stork in Cattails, gr & pk, 21" 750.00
Vase, Art Nouveau lady, Continental, 8½" 175.00
Vase, Shell on Coral, 4½" 140.00
Vase, soldier figural, cobalt, 6½" 110.00
Vase, spill; Winged Sea Horse Shell, 4½" 195.00
Waste bowl, Pineapple 415.00

Malachite Glass

Malachite is a type of art glass that exhibits strata-like layerings in shades of green, similar to the mineral in its natural form. Some examples have an acid-etched mark of Moser/Carlsbad, usually on the base. However, it should be noted that in the past fifteen years there have been reproductions from Czechoslovakia with a paper label.

Photo courtesy Monsen and Baer

Bottle, molded winged cherubs with flower garlands, floral stopper, unsigned, 6⅜", $325.00.

Ashtray, tigers in relief, Bohemian, 2½x6½", pr 150.00
Bottle, bluebells cvg, dauber lacking, Czech, 6¾" 522.50
Bottle, cherries cluster, bird on cherry branch top, 4½" 660.00
Bottle, stylized flowers, flower-basket stopper, Czech, 9" 1,650.00
Vase, 4 ribbed panels alternate w/seminudes, Schvelot, 9½" 485.00

Mantel Lustres

Mantel lustres are decorative vases or candle holders made from all types of glass, often highly decorated, and usually hung with one or more rows of prisms. In the listings that follow, values are given for a pair.

Amber cut to clear w/t'prints & fans, w/prisms, Bohemian, 11" .275.00
Bl w/gold bands & blk Deco designs, prisms, 13½" 400.00
Ruby, florals/gilt, 2 rows of prisms, 14" 650.00
Ruby bristol w/HP gold rosettes & wht beads, prisms, 14" 650.00

Mantua

A glasshouse was established in Mantua Township, Ohio, in 1821 for the purpose of manufacturing bottle-glass. Two years later the proprietor, David Ladd, left Mantua, re-establishing and enlarging his glasshouse in Kent, Ohio. Besides bottle-glass, flint glass items such as bowls, pitchers, decanters, etc., were also blown in green, aquamarine, amber, and amethyst shades — some with decorative devices that were seldom attempted outside the area. Though plain ware was common, several patterns were used as well — 16-rib, 32-rib, broken rib, swirled, corrugated, 15-diamond.

Bottle, globular, honey-amber, 16 vertical ribs, sm stain, 5¼" 770.00
Chestnut flask, amber, 16 swirled ribs, 6⅛", NM 330.00
Chestnut flask, amber, 16 vertical ribs, sheared lip, 5⅛", NM 220.00
Chestnut flask, gr, 15 vertical ribs, 4¾", NM 275.00
Nurser, aqua, 15-Dmn, minor damage/stain, 5⅞" 50.00
Pitcher, yel-topaz, 32 vertical ribs, classic form, 5¾" 3,250.00
Pitkin flask, gr, 16 broken-swirl ribs, half-post neck, 6" 550.00
Pitkin flask, peacock gr, 32 broken-swirl ribs, half-post neck, 7" ..500.00

Maps and Atlases

Maps are highly collectible, not only for historical value but also for their sometimes elaborate artwork, legendary information, or data that since they were printed has been proven erroneous. There are many types of maps including geographical, military, celestial, road, and railroad. Nineteenth-century maps, particularly of U.S. areas, are increasing in popularity and price. Rarity, area depicted (i.e. Texas is more sought after than North Dakota), and condition are major price factors. Our advisor for this category is Murray Hudson; he is listed in the Directory under Tennessee.

Key: hc — hand colored

Atlases

CS Hammond's Illus...for Young Am, mc, 1956, 96-pg, EX 20.00
Darke County, Griffing, Gordon & Co, 31 maps/no eng, 1888 ..175.00
Funk & Wagnalls...World & Gazetteer, 1923, 175-pg, VG 25.00
GF Cram's Universal..., mc, Gray/NY, 1894, 560-pg, EX 365.00
GF Cram's Unrivaled Family...World, 1883, 1st ed, 124-pg, EX .375.00
GF Cram...Illustrating Spanish Am War, mc, 1899, 52-pg, EX ..150.00
Hammond Space Age World, for BF Goodrich, 1967, 32-pg 25.00
HC Tunison's Peerless Universal...World, NY, 1896, 232-pg, EX ..425.00
JB Lippincott Popular Family...World, 1886, dbl-pg maps, 26-pg, EX ..150.00
JM Miller 20th C...Commercial...Historical World, 1902, 341-pg, VG .150.00
Madison County, JA Caldwell, 11 G maps/25 eng, 1875, EX 110.00
People's Illust...Family...World, Chicago, 1884, 366-pg, EX 350.00
Rand McNally Old Lady's Pocket...World, mc, 1886, 128-pg, VG .100.00
Rand McNally Standard...World, Chicago, mc, 1887, 192-pg, EX .350.00
Union County, Harrison/Sutton/Hare, 22 G maps/24 eng, 1877 .175.00

Maps

Ancient Greece, hc, published 1894, 14x11" 25.00
City of Sandusky, Doolittle, NY, 1918, hc, 17x18"+fr 300.00

City of WA, Cowperthwait, 1850, 12½x15½"	75.00
CO/WY/DK/MT, Mitchell, c 1874, dbl-pg, EX	80.00
DE & MD, Johnson, 3 vignettes, 12x15"	65.00
GA & AL, Wm Bradley, Atlanta/Savannah insert, 13x21"	60.00
Honduras, Thomas Jefferys, London, 1775, 23x30½", EX	400.00
Louisiana, hc, F Lucas Jr, Baltimore, 19th C, 11⅛x17⅜"	550.00
MS, Frank Gray, c 1878, 26x16", EX	85.00
NB, Frank Gray, c 1874, 12x15", EX	75.00
NC&SC, Asher & Adams, 1872, 16x22"	80.00
NM, sketch of Public Surveys, blk/wht, 1855, 7½x10½"	85.00
NY City, SA Mitchell, 1877, 14x21", EX	55.00
OH, Frank Gray, dbl, w/inserts, c 1877, EX	65.00
OH, Johnson, NY, view of capital building in corner, 1866, 22x19"	75.00
OH & IN, SA Mitchell, c 1877, 14x21", EX	55.00
PA, Mitchell, EX color, 1840s, EX	75.00
PA, SA Mitchell, w/lg insert, c 1871, 14x21", EX	50.00
Pacific Ocean, Bradford, 1835, 8x10" +info sheet	75.00
Philadelphia streets, ca 1900, 26x18"	45.00
Philadelphia/Camden, Wm Bradley, 1886, dbl, 13x21"	50.00
Plan of Havana, hc, dtd 1739 in cartouche, German, 9¼x11¼"	500.00
Polar Regions, hc, list N Pole as unknown region, 1893, 11x14"	40.00
TX, Johnson, c 1863, 17x23"	225.00
US, Bradford, outline color, 1835, EX+	125.00
US, Johnson, bright colors, c 1864, 17x23"	150.00
US Geologic Survey Indian Territory, Tishomingo Quadrangle, 1903	75.00
WI, Asher & Adams, 1872, EX	85.00
World, Rand NcNally's, 1883, 22x15", VG	50.00
World in Hemispheres, Mitchell, 1867, 11x13"	90.00

Marblehead

What began as therapy for patients in a sanitarium in Marblehead, Massachusetts, has become recognized as an important part of the Arts and Crafts Movement in America. Results of the early experiments under the guidance of Arthur E. Baggs in 1904 met with such success that by 1908 the pottery had been converted to a solely commercial venture. Simple vase shapes were sometimes incised with stylized animal and floral motifs or sailing ships. Some were decorated in low relief; many were plain. Simple matt glazes in soft yellow, gray, wisteria, rose, tobacco brown, and their most popular, Marblehead blue, were used alone or in combination. The Marblehead logo is distinctive — a ship with full sail and the letters 'M' and 'P.' The pottery closed in 1936.

Bowl, bl shaded, flaring, 4x7", +frog	275.00
Bowl, brn speckled, 2¾x5¼"	325.00
Bowl, mauve w/lav int, flaring, 3¾x7½"	350.00
Bowl, pk, 7"	220.00
Bowl, yel w/gr to bl int, flaring, 4½x7¾"	275.00
Chamberstick, bright yel, ring hdl, saucer base, 4x4½"	275.00

Cider set, dark green with gray-brown at rims and handles, signed AB (Arthur Baggs), Pitcher, 8", from $600.00 to $800.00; six 3½" mugs, $200.00 each.

Hanging basket, bl-lav, bowl form w/3 hdls, 3½x5½"	175.00
Humidor, stylized floral, dk bl on speckled sand, 5x4"	4,100.00
Match safe, gr, hexagonal, w/lid & striker, 3x2", NM	350.00
Plate, camels/nomads band, bl/yel on wht, 7½"	950.00
Tile, Egyptian figure in profile, cvd/emb, bl-gr, 7½x4½"	460.00
Tile, flower basket, Arts & Crafts style, mc on blk, 6"	600.00
Tile, sailing ship, mc, 6", in wide oak fr	435.00
Vase, band of flowers on long stems, brn on gr, Tutt, 7x4"	4,000.00
Vase, berries/leaves (cvd), dk gr/red on speckled gr, 3½x3"	1,500.00
Vase, bl, ovoid, 6¾"	375.00
Vase, bl, tapered ovoid, 9"	700.00
Vase, bl-gray microcrystalline, 8x4½"	450.00
Vase, bl-gray speckle, closed-in rim, 9x7"	900.00
Vase, columns w/geometric capitals (cvd), lt brn/sand, 6x4"	4,750.00
Vase, dk bl, ovoid, 7x4¼"	600.00
Vase, dk bl, shouldered, incurvate, 8x6½"	700.00
Vase, dk bl, swollen cylinder, 7"	600.00
Vase, dk bl, tapered w/flared rim, no mk, 6x4½"	150.00
Vase, dk gr, waisted cylinder, 7"	500.00
Vase, foliage (cvd), mc on bl speckled, minute rpr, 7x4"	2,300.00
Vase, geometric device (full-length), dk brn on gr, sgn, 4½"	3,000.00
Vase, gr/brn speckled, ovoid, 7x4"	400.00
Vase, gray, bulbous w/flaring rim, flat lid, 4¼x4¾"	600.00
Vase, gray, paper label, 3¾x4½"	400.00
Vase, leaves (cvd), gr/yel/bl speckled, Baggs, 5x3"	6,500.00
Vase, moths at top (cvd/pnt), gray on gr, 7x5"	4,000.00
Vase, peacock feathers, brn on gr mottle, 8½x4"	400.00
Vase, pk, 3¾x4½"	300.00
Vase, purple, swollen form, 9"	1,200.00
Vase, tobacco brn, waisted cylinder, 4½"	475.00
Vase, trees, bl on gray-gr, cylinder w/flared rim, 14"	12,500.00
Vase, trees (full-length), gr on brn, early, 6¼x3¾", EX	1,600.00
Vase, trees/flowers, yel on bl speckled, 5¼x3¼"	1,500.00
Vase, trees/slim trunks, 2-tone bl-gray on gray, Tutt, 3½"	1,600.00
Vase, trefoils at shoulder (cvd), long stems, 2-color, 5½x3½"	2,500.00
Vase, yel, tube shape widens at base, 6"	210.00
Vase, yel, waisted cylinder, 9"	750.00
Wall pocket, 3-panel (1 w/emb flower), dk bl, 5½x7"	500.00

Marbles

Marbles have been popular with children since the mid-1800s. They've been made in many types from a variety of materials. Among some of the first glass items to be produced, the earliest marbles were made from a solid glass rod broken into sections of the proper length which were placed in a tray of sand and charcoal and returned to the fire. As they were reheated, the trays were constantly agitated until the marbles were completely round. Other marbles were made of china, pottery, steel, and natural stones. Below is a listing of the various types, along with a brief description of each.

Agates: stone marbles of many different colors — bands of color alternating with white usually encircle the marble; most are translucent.

Ballot Box: handmade (with pontils), opaque white or black, used in lodge elections.

Bloodstone: green chalcedony with red spots, a type of quartz.

China: with or without glaze, in a variety of hand-painted designs — parallel bands or bull's-eye designs most common.

Clambroth: opaque glass with outer evenly spaced swirls of one or alternating colors.

Clay: one of the most common older types; some are painted while others are not.

Comic Strip: a series of twelve machine-made marbles with faces of comic strip characters, Peltier Glass Factory, Illinois.

Crockery: sometimes referred to as Benningtons; most are either blue or brown, although some are speckled. The clay is shaped into a sphere, then coated with glaze and fired.

End of the Day: single-pontil glass marbles — the colored part often appears as a multicolored blob or mushroom cloud.

Goldstone: clear glass completely filled with copper flakes that have turned gold colored from the heat of the manufacturing process.

Indian Swirls: usually black glass with a colored swirl appearing on the outside next to the surface, often irregular.

Latticinio Core Swirls: double-pontil marble with an inner area with net-like effects of swirls coming up around the center.

Lutz Type: glass with colored or clear bands alternating with bands which contain copper flecks.

Micas: clear or colored glass with mica flecks which reflect as silver dots when marble is turned. Red is rare.

Onionskin: spiral type which are solidly colored instead of having individual ribbons or threads, multicolored.

Peppermint Swirls: made of white opaque glass with alternating blue and red outer swirls.

Ribbon Core Swirls: double-pontil marble — center shaped like a ribbon with swirls that come up around the middle.

Rose Quartz: stone marble, usually pink in color, often with fractures inside and on outer surface.

Solid Core Swirls: double-pontil marble — middle is solid with swirls coming up around the core.

Steelies: hollow steel spheres marked with a cross where the steel was bent together to form the ball.

Sulfides: generally made of clear glass with figures inside. Rarer types have colored figures or colored glass.

Tiger Eye: stone marble of golden quartz with inclusions of asbestos, dark brown with gold highlights.

Vaseline: machine-made of yellowish-green glass with small bubbles.

Prices listed below are for marbles in near-mint condition unless noted otherwise. When size is not indicated, assume them to be of average size, ½" to 1". Polished marbles have greatly reduced values. (We do not list tinted marbles because there is no way of knowing how much color the tinting has, and intensity of color is an important worth-assessing factor.)

For a more thorough study of the subject, we recommend *Antique and Collectible Marbles, 3rd Edition; Machine-Made and Contemporary Marbles, 2nd Edition;* and *Big Book of Marbles,* all by our advisor, Everett Grist; you will find his address in the Directory under Tennessee.

Agate, contemporary, carnelian, 1¾"	160.00
Banded Opaque, gr & wht, 2"	1,200.00
Banded Opaque, red & wht, 1¾"	1,200.00
Banded Opaque, red & wht, ¾"	95.00
Banded Transparent Swirl, bl, ¾"	75.00
Banded Transparent Swirl, lt gr, 1¾"	750.00
Bennington, bl, 1¾"	40.00
Bennington, bl, ¾"	5.00
Bennington, brn, 1¾"	30.00
Bennington, fancy, 1¾"	80.00
Bennington, fancy, ¾"	10.00
China, decorated, glazed, apple, 1¾"	1,200.00
China, decorated, glazed, rose, 1¾"	2,000.00
China, decorated, glazed, wht w/geometrics, 1¾"	125.00
China, decorated, unglazed, geometrics & flowers, ¾"	300.00
Clambroth, opaque, bl & wht, 1¾"	2,600.00
Clambroth, opaque, bl & wht, ¾"	300.00
Clambroth Swirl, red/wht, Germany, 1900, ⅞"	475.00
Comic, Andy Gump	100.00
Comic, Betty Boop	200.00
Comic, Cotes Bakery, advertising	900.00

Comic, Kayo, rare	300.00
Comic, Little Orphan Annie	150.00
Comic, Moon Mullins	300.00
Comic, set of 12	1,500.00
Comic, Skeezix	150.00
Comic, Tom Mix	2,000.00
Cork Screw, machine-made, common, ⅝"	5.00
End of Day, bl & wht, 1¾"	400.00
Goldstone, ¾"	35.00
Indian Swirl, 1¾"	2,500.00
Indian Swirl Lutz-type, gold flakes, ¾"	600.00
Line Crockery, clay, 1¾"	75.00
Mica, bl, ¾"	35.00
Mica, gr, 1¾"	800.00
Onionskin, w/mica, 1¾"	1,500.00
Onionskin, w/mica, ¾"	110.00
Onionskin, 16-lobe, unusual, 1¾"	1,800.00
Onionskin, ¾"	90.00
Onionskin, 4-lobe, 1¼"	450.00
Opaque Swirl, gr, ¾"	75.00
Opaque Swirl Lutz-type, bl, yel, gr, ¾"	325.00
Peppermint Swirl, opaque, red, wht, & bl, 1¾"	2,000.00
Peppermint Swirl, opaque, red, wht, & bl, ¾"	125.00
Pottery, 1¾"	75.00
Ribbon Core Lutz-type, red, 1¾"	1,800.00
Slag, bl, machine-made, sm	3.00
Slag, bl, machine-made, 1½"	150.00
Solid Opaque, gr, 1¾"	800.00
Solid Opaque, ¾"	75.00
Sulfide, angel face w/wings, 1¾", M	1,000.00
Sulfide, baboon playing bass fiddle, 2⅛"	1,200.00
Sulfide, bear cub on all 4s, detailed, 1¼", NM+	400.00
Sulfide, billy goat, 1½"	100.00
Sulfide, bird, 2", EX	150.00
Sulfide, boar, 1⅞"	165.00
Sulfide, camel, 1-hump, on grassy mound, 1½"	200.00
Sulfide, child sitting, 1¾"	600.00
Sulfide, child w/sailboat, 1¾"	800.00
Sulfide, circus bear, 2"	140.00
Sulfide, crane w/fish, 1¾"	600.00
Sulfide, crucifix, 1¾"	600.00
Sulfide, deer, 1¼"	175.00
Sulfide, dog howling, 1⅜", M	140.00
Sulfide, dog on grass mound, HP/3-color, pontil, 1¼"	3,500.00
Sulfide, dog w/bird in mouth, 1¾", M	900.00
Sulfide, dove, 1⅝", M	165.00
Sulfide, eagle w/closed wings, 1⅞"	200.00
Sulfide, elephant, standing, sea gr glass, 1¾"	400.00
Sulfide, elephant w/long trunk, 1¼"	140.00
Sulfide, figure-8, 1¾"	400.00
Sulfide, fish, 1¾"	175.00
Sulfide, fox, 1½", EX	130.00
Sulfide, George Washington, bust, 2⅜"	650.00
Sulfide, hen, 1⅛", M	150.00
Sulfide, horse rearing, 1⅞"	175.00
Sulfide, horse standing, 2", EX	130.00
Sulfide, Jenny Lind bust, 1¾"	900.00
Sulfide, lamb, 1¾"	125.00
Sulfide, lion, standing male, 1½"	125.00
Sulfide, Little Boy Blue, 1¾", M	700.00
Sulfide, monkey, seated on drum, 1⅜", M	200.00
Sulfide, Nipper dog, 1¾", EX	350.00
Sulfide, owl, w/closed wings, 1¾"	150.00
Sulfide, papoose, 1¾", M	700.00

Sulfide, parrot, 1½", EX 100.00
Sulfide, peasant boy, on stump w/legs crossed, 1½" 600.00
Sulfide, poodle on hind legs, 1⅛" 100.00
Sulfide, rabbit running, lg/offset/sm bubble, 1½", M- 110.00
Sulfide, razor-bk hog, 1½" 150.00
Sulfide, rooster, 1¾" 150.00
Sulfide, Santa Claus, 1¾" 700.00
Sulfide, sheep grazing, 1¼" 135.00
Sulfide, squirrel, standing, 1¾", EX 170.00
Sulfide, woman (Kate Greenaway), 1½" 450.00

Marine Collectibles

Vintage tools used on sea-going vessels, lanterns, clocks, and memorabilia of all types are sought out by those who are interested in preserving the romantic genre that revolves around the life of the sea captains, their boats and their crews; ports of call; and the lure of far away islands. See also Steamship Collectibles; Telescopes; Scrimshaw; Tools.

Bell, yacht; bronze, bronze dolphin base, wood stand, 8½" dia ...1,500.00
Binnacle, sky light; brass, Negus NY, Ritchie Pembross 3,250.00
Binnacle, wood w/brass hood, floor standing, Kelvite, 58" 1,100.00
Cannon, line throwing; brass, CC Galbraith & Son NY, 42", EX ...1,300.00
Cannon, solid brass, Lantanka, 48", on customized stand 1,400.00
Cask, rum; brass-bound oak, EX, 20½"+spigot, w/stand 325.00
Chair, yacht, teak, w/CI tripod base, leather seat, 32" 300.00
Chest, seaman's; gray pnt, nailed, iron bands, w/till, 14x19x13" ...150.00
Chronometer, US Navy, Hamilton, dtd 1941, complete, EX ..1,300.00
Desk, captain's traveling; rosewood, brass bound, 19x12x7½" 500.00
Dial, Butterfield type, brass w/eng bird, 2⅝", +box 3,000.00
Dial, equinoctial; Universal, Dollond, London, ca 1780, EX 350.00
Dial, sun; Augsburg Universal equatorial, L Grassi, 1750s, 2⅝" .850.00
Fid, rope working; cvd whale bone, trn ball end, 10" 150.00
Lamp, lighthouse buoy; copper/brass, AGG New Jersey, 36" ...1,200.00
Mallet, cvd whalebone, 9¾", VG 475.00
Octant, ebony/brass/ivory, lacking minor pcs, ca 1820, 16" 700.00
Octant, G Heath-Erith-Kent, ebony/brass/ivory, 1850s, 12" 625.00
Octant, Moon From Dollonds...London, ebony/brass/ivory, 12" .600.00
Octant, Seth Winslow-1811, ebony/brass/ivory, rpl eyepc, 17" ..550.00
Pantograph, Cary London, brass & ivory, EX in mahog case 755.00
Sculpture, figurehead of cherub, gilt on metal, 16x8½" 400.00
Sextant, Cardiff & Dock, brass w/silver scales, EX in case 600.00
Sextant, Cary London, brass w/gold scale/platinum vernier scale ..2,000.00
Sextant, Made by Cornelius Knudsen Denmark, brass/silver, VG .460.00
Sextant, WF Cannon...High St, London, brass, EX in case 550.00
Telegraph, pilot house engine order; brass, US Coast Guard, EX ..800.00
Telegraph, solid brass, Chadburn & Son, 45"+hdl, VG 1,100.00
Trumpet, captain's hailing; solid brass, eng name, 18", VG 450.00
Wheel, ship's; walnut/maple, Am, 66" dia 1,500.00

Martin Bros.

The Martin Bros. were studio potters who worked from 1873 until 1914, first at Fulham and later at London and Southall. There were four brothers, each of whom excelled in their particular area. Robert, known as Wallace, was an experienced stonecarver. He modeled a series of grotesque bird and animal figural caricatures. Walter was the potter, responsible for throwing the larger vases on the wheel, firing the kiln, and mixing the clay. Edwin, an artist of stature, preferred more naturalistic forms of decoration. His work was often incised or had relief designs of seaweed, florals, fish, and birds. The fourth brother, Charles, was their business manager. Their work was incised with

their names, place of production, and letters and numbers indicating month and year.

Though figural jars continue to command the higher prices, decorated vases and bowls have increased in value. Our advisor for this category is David Rago; he is listed in the directory under New Jersey.

Bird jar, head cocked, mustard/bl/gr/brn matt, 1898, 10½" ...16,250.00
Bird jar, minor rstr, 5x3" 4,400.00
Bird jar, open mouth, Xd-eyes, 1911, rstr, 11x6½" 16,250.00
Bird vessel, grotesque, brn/bl/gr/gray, wood base, 8x3½" 7,475.00

Double-faced jug, two smiling faces, teeth exposed, off-center spout, tan, brown, and white, marked, $75.00.

Humidor, 2-faced, orange-brn tones, rstr lid, 1903, 7x6¼" 6,800.00
Jug, sea creatures/plants, grays/brns/bl, 4-sided, 1896, 9½" 3,250.00
Paperweight, dragon w/curled tail, brn/gr, 1882, 2½x4½" 2,600.00
Pitcher, iguanas & lizards, 4-sided, 1875, rstr, 7½x6½" 2,300.00
Salt cellar, toothy fish & flowers, bl/brn/gr, sq, 3¼x5" 3,000.00
Toby jug, seated man, brn & caramel, RW Martin, 1903, 10x5½" ..4,900.00
Vase, dragons, blk & gray on copperdust, slim, 1901, 11½" 2,900.00
Vase, flying dragons, gray on brn, classic form, 1896, 8¾" 2,300.00
Vase, plumes/florals, bl/brn on gray-gr, RW/#680, 4¼x3½" 200.00

Mary Gregory

Mary Gregory glass, for reasons that remain obscure, is the namesake of a Boston and Sandwich Glass Company employee who worked for the company for only two years in the mid-1800s. Although no evidence actually exists to indicate that glass of this type was even produced there, the fine colored or crystal ware decorated with figures of children in white enamel is commonly referred to as Mary Gregory. The glass, in fact, originated in Europe and was imported to this country where it was copied by several eastern glasshouses. It was popular from the mid-1800s until the turn of the century. It is generally accepted that examples with all-white figures were made in the U.S.A., while gold-trimmed items and those with children having tinted faces or a small amount of color on their clothing are European. Though amethyst is rare, examples in cranberry command the higher prices. Blue ranks next; and green, amber, and clear items are worth the least. Watch for new glass decorated with screen-printed children and a minimum of hand painting. The screen effect is easily detected with a magnifying glass.

Box, amber, boy, hinged lid, 3¼x3⅜" 245.00
Box, blk, boy w/bouquet by tree/butterfly, oval, 4" L 375.00
Box, sapphire bl, lady in fancy dress & hat, 4" dia 375.00
Cruet, cranberry, girl feeding rooster, flat-sided, 7" 425.00
Decanter, golden amber, girl, amber bubble stopper, 9½x3⅝" 185.00
Dresser set, vaseline, girl in foliage, 2 9" bottles+powder box 395.00
Flask, lady's; gr, girl, 3½" 295.00
Goblet, sapphire bl, boy (girl), 5⅞x2⅝", pr 245.00
Paperweight, blk, boy & girl, rectangular, 4" L 295.00

Perfume, cobalt, children/angels/flowers, crown top, 10", pr **600.00**
Pitcher, sapphire bl, girl w/watering can, tankard, 10¾x4⅛" **495.00**
Pitcher, water; clear, girl, tinted hands/hair **225.00**
Vase, amber, girl, heart shape, ftd, 7x5" **295.00**
Vase, amber, girl, ruffled trumpet neck, 8x3½" **175.00**
Vase, blk, boy w/ball on string, blown-out neck ring, ftd, 8" **245.00**
Vase, blk, girl & boy pick apples, ped ft, gold trim, 9¾" **350.00**
Vase, blk, girl in wreath of bl forget-me-nots, 10" **195.00**
Vase, clear, boy (girl), gold trim, ca 1900, 8⅝", pr **90.00**
Vase, cobalt, boy & lilies of valley, clear trim ea side, 7" **145.00**
Vase, cobalt, boy standing in foliage, gold trim, 2½" **325.00**
Vase, cranberry, girl holding flower, 10x5" **295.00**
Vase, emerald, boy picking flowers, 12" **135.00**
Vase, gr bristol, boy carrying tray of flowers, ftd, 11" **210.00**
Vase, lime, girl w/butterfly net, cylndrical, 10½" **175.00**

Mason's Ironstone

In 1813 Charles J. Mason was granted a patent for a process said to 'improve the quality of English porcelain.' The new type of ware was in fact ironstone which Mason decorated with colorful florals and scenics, some of which reflected the Oriental taste. Although his business failed for a short time in the late 1840s, Mason re-established himself and continued to produce dinnerware, tea services, and ornamental pieces until about 1852, at which time the pottery was sold to Francis Morley. Ten years later, Geo. L. and Taylor Ashworth became owners. Both Morley and the Ashworths not only used Mason's molds and patterns but often his mark as well. Because the quality and the workmanship of the later wares do not compare with Mason's earlier product, collectors should take care to distinguish one from the other. Consult a good book on marks to be sure. The Wedgwood Company now owns the rights to the Mason patterns and is reproducing Vista. Note: Blue Vista is generally valued at 15% to 20% above prices for pink/red.

Bowl, Blossom, mc on bl, 8-sided, 1890 mk, 10¼", +12" plate ...**275.00**
Bowl, Floral & Urn, bl, scallop w/gold, 1813-25 mk, 7" **175.00**
Bowl, Red Scale, blk w/mc on wht, 1890-1900 mk, 3¼x8¼" **200.00**
Bowl, serving; American Marine, bl, scalloped, 1890-1900 mk, 9" .**150.00**
Bowl, serving; Vista, red, triangular, 1925-30 red mk, 10½" **350.00**
Bowl, soup; Old Japan Vase, mc on wht, 1875 mk, 10¼", 6 for ..**225.00**
Bowl, vegetable; Strathmore, ca 1920, 11x7" **225.00**
Bowl, Vista, red, scalloped, 1890-1900 red mk, 6", 4 for **50.00**
Butter dish, Vista, brn, 1925-30 brn mk, 2½x6½" **100.00**
Casserole, Real Old Canton, bl, w/lid, 1890 bl mk, 7x11x10", NM .**300.00**
Chamberpot, Red Scale, blk w/mc on wht, 1840 mk, 5¼x4" **400.00**
Coffeepot, Vista, bl, 1890-1900 mk, 8½x8" **375.00**
Coffeepot, Vista, brn, 1890-1900 brn mk, 9½", w/6" trivet **275.00**
Compote, fruit; Floral, mc on blk, 1890-1900 blk mk, 5½x12" ...**300.00**
Compote, Strathmore, red w/mc, 1890-1900 red mk, 2½x8¾" ...**150.00**
Coupe soup, Vista, red, 1890-1900 mk, 6", w/6½" undertray **100.00**
Cup & saucer, American Marine, bl, 8-sided, 1890-1900 mk **60.00**
Cup & saucer, chowder; Vista, red, 1925-30 red mk, 3", 7¼" **80.00**
Cup & saucer, demi; Bandana, blk w/mc, 1862 mk, 2", 4¾" **225.00**
Cup & saucer, demi; Vista, red, 1890-1900 red mk **40.00**
Egg cup, Vista, brn, ftd, 1925-30 brn mk, 4" **60.00**
Gravy boat, American Marine, brn, scalloped ft, #16, 4½x7¼" **80.00**
Jug, Blue Willow, 1890 bl mk, 7x6" **350.00**
Jug, Pheasants, bl w/mc, cobalt serpent hdl, 1815-20 mk, 6" **37.50**
Jug, Red Scale, blk w/mc on wht, 8-sided, 1840 mk, 4¼x3½" **350.00**
Jug, Red Scale, blk w/mc on wht, 8-sided, 1840 mk, 6x4½" **375.00**
Jug, Vista, brn, 8-sided, 1890-1900 mk, 6½x5" **125.00**
Jug, Vista, red, 8-sided, 1925-30 red mk, 4½x4" **150.00**
Jug, Vista, red, 8-sided, 1925-30 red mk, 7x6", NM **175.00**

Plate, American Marine, bl, 1890-1900 bl mk, 10" **125.00**
Plate, American Marine, bl, 1890-1900 bl mk, 8" **70.00**
Plate, American Marine, blk w/gr & yel, 1890-1900 mk, 9¼", NM **50.00**
Plate, Colored Pheasant, mc on cream, 1890 mk, 10½" **80.00**
Plate, Dbl Landscape, mauve w/mc on cobalt w/gold, 1862-75 mk, 8" **125.00**
Plate, salad; Vista, brn, 1890-1900 brn mk, 7¾", 4 for **100.00**
Plate, salad; Vista, red, 1925-30 red mk, 7¾", 4 for **100.00**
Plate, Singing Birds, bl, scalloped/crimped, 1890-1900 mk, 10½" ...**90.00**
Plate, The Capitol, red, H Fennell, 1890-1900 mk, 10½" **100.00**
Plate, Turkey Vista, red, 1925-30 red mk, 10¾", 3 for **375.00**
Plate, Vista, red, scalloped, 1890-1900 red mk, 9¾", 4 for **150.00**
Platter, American Marine, dk bl, 1890-1900 mk, 15" **225.00**
Platter, American Marine, red, scalloped, 1890-1900 red mk, 15" ...**225.00**
Platter, Old Japan Vase, mc on wht w/gold, 1862 mk, 9¾" **125.00**
Platter, Vista, red, Oak-pattern rim, 1890-1900 mk, 17" **350.00**
Platter, Vista, red, scalloped rim, 1890-1900 red mk, 11¼", NM ..**90.00**
Platter, Vista, red, 1890-1900 red mk, 14¼" **125.00**
Shakers, Vista, red, 8-sided, 1890-1900 red mk, 4" **100.00**
Teapot, Landscape Portraits, mauve w/mc on wht, 1835-40 mk, 3" .**300.00**
Teapot, Vista, red, 1925-30 red mk, 6¾x9½" **250.00**
Tray, Flying Birds, blk w/mc on wht, 1890 mk, 10¼" **125.00**
Trivet, Vista, brn, 1925-30 brn mk, 5¾" dia **80.00**
Tureen, Vista, red, 8-sided, scalloped, 10x14", +15" undertray ...**425.00**
Tureen, Vista, red, 8-sided, scalloped, 1925-30 mk, 6x8"+tray ...**300.00**
Washbowl & jug, Blue Willow, 1890 bl mk, 3½x11", 7½" **600.00**

Massier

Clement Massier was a French artist-potter who in 1881 established a workshop at Golfe Juan, France, where he experimented with metallic lustre glazes. (One of his pupils was Jacques Sicardo, who brought the knowledge he had gained through his association with Massier to the Weller Pottery Company in Zanesville, Ohio.) The lustre lines developed by Massier incorporated nature themes with allover decorations of foliage or flowers on shapes modeled in the Art Nouveau style. The ware was usually incised with the Massier name, his initials, or the location of the pottery. Massier died in 1917.

Vase, sunflowers in iridescent tones and flat yellow ochre on violet and green iridescent, long neck, ear handles, ca 1900, 14¼", $1,250.00.

Charger, pine trees w/lake in distance, gold/wine lustre, 13" ...**1,300.00**
Ewer, floral, wht irid & gold w/pk & yel, CM, 12" **475.00**
Vase, gr/brn flambe, lg cut-out 'wing' hdls, imp mk, 11x7" **70.00**
Vase, grapes/leaves, purple/yel on gr to bl, 7½x4½" **600.00**

Match Holders

John Walker, an English chemist, invented the match more than one hundred years ago, quite by accident. Walker was working with a mixture of potash and antimony, hoping to make a combustible that could be used to fire guns. The mixture adhered to the end of the wooden stick he had used for stirring. As he tried to remove it by scraping the stick on the stone floor, it burst into flames. The invention of the match was only a step away! From that time to the present, match holders have been made in amusing figural forms as well as simple utilitarian styles and in a wide range of materials. Both table-top and wall-hanging models were made — all designed to keep matches conveniently at hand. The prices in this category are very volatile due to increased interest in this field and the fact that so many can be classified as a cross or dual collectible.

Caution: as prices for originals continue to climb, so do the number of reproductions. Know your dealer. Our advisor for this category is Ron Damaska; he is listed in the Directory under Pennsylvania. See also Advertising.

Brass, pig figural, short legs, open top, 1800s, 2x4½" 150.00
Brass, pressed, fishing pole & creel, wall hanging, 5x3¼" 150.00
Brass, Punch figural, Go to Bed, 6½" 375.00
Bronze, lion figural, front striker/cigar holder, sgn, 4" 895.00
Bsk, boy w/butterfly net 75.00
China, bulldog's head, brn w/blk details, Carlsbad Austria, 2⅛" ...100.00
China, shoe form, striker on sole 35.00
CI, Bacchus face, grotesque, wall hanging, EX orig 165.00
CI, lacy urns (pr), dtd 1867, 7½" 95.00
CI, scroll design, arched top, 2 compartments/1 lid, 7x4" 95.00
CI, shoe, Regent MFG Co, Chicago adv, wall hanging, EX orig pnt ..250.00
CI, shoe form, EX orig pnt, 5" 50.00
CI, soldier figural, EG Zimmerman, 4¾" 175.00
Compo, Pillsbury Mills advertising, loaf shape, souvenir, 2¾" 125.00
Conta & Boehme, porc, baby in basinet box, striker under lid, 5" ..250.00
Conta & Boehme, porc, boots w/bootjack striker, 4½" 125.00
Conta & Boehme, porc, girl w/boat, HP 245.00

German porcelain, hunter figural, table top with side striker, $195.00.

Photo courtesy Ron Damaska

Glass, amber, hand holding container 85.00
Glass, Lady Liberty, dtd 1876, 4½" 125.00
Lacquerware, boots form, striker base, England 150.00
Majolica, Black man figural, side striker, cigar holder, table top, 7" 350.00
Majolica, stork figural, side striker, cigar holder, table top, 11" ..495.00
Schafer & Vater, bsk, Don't Scratch Me Scratch..., cats 245.00
Schafer & Vater, bsk, Scratch My Bald Head, man standing 245.00
Schafer & Vater, bsk, Scratch My Patch, hobo 225.00
Stoneware, advertising, cone shape on tray 125.00
White metal, bank building form, box holder w/ashtray, 4" 95.00
White metal, box w/Cupid decor, striker under lid 145.00

Match Safes

Before the invention of the safety match in 1855, matches were carried in small pocket-sized containers because they ignited so easily.

Aptly called match safes, these containers were used extensively until about 1920, when cigarette lighters became widely availabe. Some incorporated added features (hidden compartments, cigar cutters, etc.), some were figural, and others were used by retail companies as advertising giveaways. They were made from every type of material, but silverplated styles abound. Both the advertising and common silverplated cases generally fall in the $50.00 to $100.00 price range.

Beware of reproductions and fakes; there are many currently on the market. Know your dealer. Our advisor for this category is Ron Damaska; he is listed in the Directory under Pennsylvania. See also Advertising.

Brass, emb sailing ship scene in rope-like fr, rectangular 60.00
Celluloid, Buckwalter Stoves, w/orig matches 125.00
NP, emb fleur-de-lis in repeating pattern, oval 40.00
Silveroid, emb Nouveau florals, eng initials 85.00
SP, eng leaf & berry branch, Pairpoint 75.00
Sterling, elk in relief, Battin & Co 150.00
Sterling, emb cherubs w/instruments, mk Kerr 175.00
Sterling, emb game birds in grassy-fr oval, rectangular 150.00
Sterling, emb Indian portrait in reserve, rope-like trim 175.00
Sterling, emb leaves & vines, eng initial in oval reserve, Gorham .125.00
Sterling, emb linear decor, Battin & Co 95.00
Sterling, emb scrolls, eng floral center, rectangular 100.00
Sterling, eng swirling floral, Birmingham 1902 ....100.00
Sterling, nude in surf, crane above, 2½" 275.00

McCoy

The third generation McCoy potter in the Roseville, Ohio, area was Nelson, who with the aid of his father, J.W., established the Nelson McCoy Sanitary Stoneware Company in 1910. They manufactured churns, jars, jugs, poultry fountains, and foot warmers. By 1925 they had expanded their wares to include majolica jardinieres and pedestals, umbrella stands and cuspidors, and an embossed line of vases and small jardinieres in a blended brown and green matt glaze. From the late '20s through the mid-'40s, a utilitarian stoneware was produced, some of which was glazed in the soft blue and white so popular with collectors today. They also used a dark brown mahogany color and a medium to dark green, both in a high gloss. In 1933 the firm became known as the Nelson McCoy Pottery Company. They expanded their facilities in 1940 and began to make the novelty artware, cookie jars, and dinnerware that today are synonomous with 'McCoy.' More than two hundred cookie jars of every theme and description were produced.

More than a dozen different marks have been used by the company; nearly all incorporate the name 'McCoy,' although some of the older items were marked 'NM USA.' For further information consult *The Collector's Encyclopedia of McCoy Pottery* (with recently updated values) by Sharon and Bob Huxford or *McCoy Pottery Collector's Reference & Value Guide, Vol. I and II*, by Margaret Hanson, Craig Nissen, and Bob Hanson (all published by Collector Books). Also available is *Sanfords Guide to McCoy Pottery* by Martha and Steve Sanford. (Mr. Sanford is listed in the Directory under California.)

Alert! Stimulated by the high prices commanded by desirable cookie jars, a broad spectrum of 'new' cookie jars are flooding the marketplace in three categories: 1) Manufacturers have expanded their lines with exciting new designs to attract the collector market. 2) Limited editions and artist-designed jars have proliferated. 3) Reproductions, signed and unsigned, have pervaded the market, creating uncertainty among new collectors and inexperienced dealers. After McCoy closed its doors in the late 1980s, an entrepreneur in Tennessee tried (and succeeded for nearly a decade) to adopt the McCoy Pottery name and mark. This company reproduced old McCoy designs as well as some classic designs of other defunct American potteries, signing their wares 'McCoy' with a mark which very closely approximated the old McCoy mark. Legal action finally put a stop to this practice, though since then this company has used other fradulent marks as well: Brush-McCoy (the compound name was never used on Brush cookie jars) and B.J. Hull.

Cookie Jars

Animal Crackers	100.00
Apollo Age, minimum value	1,000.00
Apple, 1950-64	50.00
Apple, 1970	60.00
Apple, 1972	50.00
Apple on Basketweave	70.00
Asparagus	50.00
Astronauts	850.00
Bananas	140.00

Barnum's Animals, $350.00.

Barrel, Cookies sign on lid	125.00
Baseball Boy	300.00
Basket of Eggs	50.00
Basket of Potatoes	40.00
Bear, cookie in vest, no 'Cookies'	75.00
Betsy Baker (+)	275.00
Black Kettle, w/immovable bail, HP flowers	40.00
Blue Willow Pitcher	50.00
Bobby Baker	60.00
Bugs Bunny, cylinder	200.00
Burlap Bag, red bird on lid	70.00
Caboose	200.00
Cat on Coal Scuttle	250.00
Chairman of the Board (+)	550.00
Chef (+)	110.00
Chilly Willy	50.00
Chipmunk	125.00
Christmas Tree, minimum value	800.00
Churn, 2 bands	35.00
Circus Horse	250.00
Clown Bust (+)	75.00
Clown in Barrel, yel, bl or gr	85.00
Clyde Dog	250.00
Coalby Cat	375.00
Coca-Cola Can	100.00
Coca-Cola Jug	85.00
Coffee Grinder	45.00
Coffee Mug	45.00
Colonial Fireplace	85.00
Cookie Bank, 1961	165.00
Cookie Boy	225.00
Cookie Cabin	80.00

Cookie Jug, dbl loop	35.00
Cookie Jug, single loop, 2-tone gr rope	25.00
Cookie Jug, w/cork stopper, brn & wht	40.00
Cookie Log, squirrel finial	45.00
Cookie Mug	45.00
Cookie Pot, 1964	40.00
Cookie Safe	65.00
Cookstove, blk or wht	35.00
Corn	175.00
Corn, yel or wht, 1977	85.00
Covered Wagon	95.00
Cylinder, w/red flowers	45.00
Dalmatians in Rocking Chair (+)	375.00
Davy Crockett (+)	600.00
Dog on Basketweave	90.00
Drum, red	90.00
Duck, stylized, yel	150.00
Duck on Basketweave	90.00
Dutch Boy	45.00
Dutch Girl, boy on reverse, rare	250.00
Dutch Treat Barn	50.00
Eagle on Basket	50.00
Early American Chest (Chifferobe)	85.00
Elephant	200.00
Elephant w/Split Trunk, rare, minimum value	300.00
Engine, blk	175.00
Flowerpot, plastic flower on top	500.00
Football Boy (+)	250.00
Forbidden Fruit	75.00
Freddy Gleep (+)	500.00
Friendship 7	200.00
Frog on Stump	75.00
Frontier Family	60.00
Fruit in Bushel Basket	80.00
Gingerbread Boy	75.00
Globe	325.00
Grandfather Clock	90.00
Granny	110.00
Hamm's Bear (+)	225.00
Happy Face	80.00
Hen on Nest	95.00
Hillbilly Bear, rare, minimum value (+)	900.00
Hobby Horse (+)	150.00
Hocus Rabbit	45.00
Honey Bear, rustic glaze	80.00
Hot Air Balloon	40.00
Ice Cream Cone	45.00
Indian, brn (+)	350.00
Indian, majolica	400.00
Jack-O'-Lantern	600.00
Kangaroo, bl	300.00
Keebler Tree House	70.00
Kettle, bronze, 1961	40.00
Kissing Penguins	80.00
Kitten on Basketweave	90.00
Kittens (2) on Low Basket, minimum value	600.00
Kittens on Ball of Yarn	100.00
Koala Bear	85.00
Kookie Kettle, blk	35.00
Lamb on Basketweave	90.00
Leprechaun, minimum value (+)	1,800.00
Liberty Bell	75.00
Little Clown	75.00
Lollipops	80.00

Mac Dog 95.00
Mammy, Cookies on base, wht (+) 150.00
Mammy w/Cauliflower, G pnt, minimum value (+) 1,100.00
Milk Can, Spirit of '76 ....75.00
Modern 65.00
Monk 50.00
Mother Goose 175.00
Mouse on Clock 40.00
Mr & Mrs Owl 95.00
Mushroom on Stump 55.00
Nursery, decal of Humpty Dumpty 85.00
Oaken Bucket 25.00
Orange 55.00
Owl 50.00
Pear, 1952 ....85.00
Pears on Basketweave 70.00
Penguin, yel or aqua 250.00
Pepper, yel 40.00
Picnic Basket 75.00
Pig, winking 300.00
Pineapple 80.00
Pineapple, Modern 90.00
Pirate's Chest 125.00
Popeye Cylinder 200.00
Potbelly Stove, blk 30.00
Puppy, w/sign 60.00
Quaker Oats, rare, minimum value 500.00
Raggedy Ann 110.00
Red Barn, cow in door, rare, minimum value 350.00
Rooster, wht, 1970-1974 ....60.00
Rooster, 1955-1957 ....95.00
Round w/HP Leaves 45.00
Sad Clown 85.00
Snoopy on Doghouse (+) 200.00
Snow Bear 65.00
Spaniel in Doghouse, bird finial 250.00
Stagecoach, minimum value 800.00
Strawberry, 1955-57 ....65.00
Strawberry, 1971-75 ....40.00
Teapot, 1972 ....65.00
Tepee, slat top 350.00
Tepee, str top (+) 300.00
Tilt Pitcher, blk w/roses 50.00
Timmy Tortoise 45.00
Tomato 60.00
Touring Car 100.00
Traffic Light 50.00
Tudor Cookie House 125.00
Tulip on Flowerpot 225.00
Turkey, gr, rare color 300.00
Turkey, natural colors 250.00
Upside Down Bear, panda 50.00
WC Fields 200.00
Wedding Jar 90.00
Windmill 100.00
Wishing Well 40.00
Woodsy Owl 275.00
Wren House, side lid 175.00
Yosemite Sam, cylinder 200.00

Miscellaneous

Bank, Liberty Bell, bronze in color 50.00
Basket, hanging; pipe form, 1970s 50.00

Caddy, buffalo figural, Swank 50.00
Caddy, dresser; Am Eagle, Swank 55.00
Cat dish, emb letters on yel, late 1930s 50.00
Creamer, dog, tail forms hdl, mk, 1950s 150.00
Dog dish, emb bird dog on brn, 1940s, lg 95.00
Jar, strawberry; quail on top, mk, 1950 ....40.00
Novelty, birdbath, w/pk bird, mk, 1950 ....40.00
Pencil holder, cowboy boot form, 1973 ....50.00
Planter, Basketweave, dbl, 1953 ....25.00
Planter, bunny w/carrot, mk, rare 100.00
Planter, carriage, blk w/wht & orange wheels & umbrella, mk, 1955 .200.00
Planter, cradle, unmk 30.00
Planter, fish, pk w/gr fins, mk, 1955 ....500.00
Planter, goose w/cart, mk, 1943 ....30.00
Planter, lamb, wht w/big bl bow, mk, 1953 ....50.00
Planter, lamb w/lg bl bow, mk, 1953 ....50.00
Planter, pear form on leaf base, mk, 1957 ....65.00
Planter, quail family among leaves, mk, 1955 ....55.00
Planter, rooster, mk, 1951 ....30.00
Planter, stork beside basket, 1956 ....50.00
Planter, triple-lily, 1950 ....60.00
Planter/bookends, hunting dog w/bird in mouth, mk, 1955, pr ...130.00
Spoon rest, penguin, gr, mk, 1953 ....100.00
Tankard, wht w/hunting scene, mk #7 & #14, 1970 ....50.00
Teapot, Sunburst Gold, mk, w/lid, 1957 ....85.00

Vase, fan form with leafy base, medium and dark green, 1954, $125.00.

Violet pot & saucer, dk gr, 1961 ....16.00
Violet pot & saucer, emb decor, 1950 ....30.00
Wall pocket, bellows, 1956 ....90.00
Wall pocket, bird on birdbath, 1949, 8" 100.00
Wall pocket, iron on trivet 75.00
Wall pocket, leaf, ivory to red, 1950 ....50.00
Wall pocket, lily, mk, 7½" 65.00
Wall pocket, Mexican emb on gr conical form, 1941 ..60.00
Wall pocket, owls on trivet, 1953 ....75.00
Wall pocket, pear on leaves, 1953 ....60.00
Wall pocket, red or bl grape cluster among leaves, 7x6" ...85.00
Wall pocket, umbrella form, yel, mk, 1955 ....75.00
Window box, gr stones, rectangular, 1954, lg 20.00

McCoy, J. W.

The J.W. McCoy Pottery Company was incorporated in 1899. It operated under that name in Roseville, Ohio, until 1911 when McCoy entered into a partnership with George Brush, forming the Brush-McCoy Company. During the early years, McCoy produced kitchenware, majolica jardinieres and pedestals, umbrella stands, and cuspidors. By 1903 they had begun to experiment in the field of art pottery and, though never involved to the extent of some of their contemporaries, nevertheless produced several art lines of merit. Their first line was Mt. Pelee, examples of which are very rare today. Two types of glazes were used, matt green and an iridescent charcoal gray. Though the line was primarily mold formed, some pieces evidence the fact that while the clay remained wet and pliable it was pulled and pinched with the fingers to form crests and peaks in a style not unlike George Ohr.

The company rebuilt in 1904 after being destroyed by fire, and other artware was designed. Loy-Nel Art and Renaissance were standard brown lines, hand decorated under the glaze with colored slip. Shapes and artwork were usually simple but effective. Olympia and Rosewood were relief-molded brown-glaze lines decorated in natural colors with wreaths of leaves and berries or simple floral sprays. Although much of this ware was not marked, you will find examples with the die-stamped 'Loy-Nel Art, McCoy,' or an incised line identification.

Corn Line, mug, unmk	**70.00**
Loy-Nel Art, jardiniere, Nouveau mold, cherries, 9x10"	**300.00**
Loy-Nel Art, jardiniere, tulips, 8"	**250.00**
Loy-Nel Art, spittoon, brn w/yel floral, 1905	**300.00**
Loy-Nel Art, vase, leaves/cherries, 13½x5"	**210.00**
Loy-Nel Art, vase, poppies/buds, 12½"	**270.00**
Matt Green, umbrella stand, unmk, 1910, 21"	**550.00**
Olympia, bowl, pretzel; unmk, 1905	**500.00**
Olympia, mug, mk, 1905	**200.00**
Olympia, punch bowl, mk, 1905	**600.00**
Rosewood, jardiniere, unmk, pre-1903, 9"	**450.00**

McKee

McKee Glass was founded in 1853 in Pittsburgh, Pennsylvania. Among their early products were tableware of both the flint and nonflint varieties. In 1888 the company relocated to avail themselves of a source of natural gas, thereby founding the town of Jeannette, Pennsylvania. One of their most famous colored dinnerware lines, Rock Crystal, was manufactured in the 1920s. Production during the '30s and '40s included colored opaque dinnerware, Sunkist reamers, and 'bottoms up' cocktail tumblers as well as a line of black glass vases, bowls, and novelty items. All are popular items with today's collectors, but watch for reproductions. The mark of an authentic 'bottoms up' tumbler is the patent number 77725 embossed near the rim. The company was purchased in 1916 by Jeannette Glass, under which name it continues to operate. See also Animal Dishes with Covers; Depression Glass; Kitchen Collectibles; Reamers.

Bottoms Up, coaster, crystal	**50.00**
Bottoms Up, tumbler, butterscotch opal	**125.00**
Bottoms Up, tumbler, custard	**90.00**
Bottoms Up, tumbler, Jade-ite	**125.00**
Bottoms Up, tumbler, Jade-ite, w/coaster	**305.00**
Bottoms Up, tumbler, legs apart, att	**175.00**
Bottoms Up, tumbler, milk glass	**100.00**
Candelabra, Rock Crystal, 3-light, pr	**55.00**
Candy dish, Rock Crystal, rnd, w/lid	**60.00**
Decanter, Pillared, clear flint, 13¼", pr	**350.00**
Pitcher, Prescut, Sunburst, crystal	**95.00**
Pitcher, Rock Crystal, 7½"	**125.00**
Plate, cake; Rock Crystal, scalloped edge, 11½"	**20.00**
Tankard jug (pitcher), Toltec, 8½"	**130.00**
Vase, Rock Crystal, red, ftd, 11"	**195.00**
Vase, Sarah, jade gr, 8"	**150.00**
Whiskey, Rock Crystal, 2½-oz	**18.00**
Wine, Rock Crystal, red, 2-oz	**55.00**

Medical Collectibles

The field of medical-related items encompasses a wide area from the primitive bleeding bowl to the X-ray machines of the early 1900s. Other closely related collectibles include apothecary and dental items. Many tools that were originally intended for the pharmacist found their way to the doctor's office, and dentists often used surgical tools when no suitable dental instrument was available. A trend in the late 1700s toward self-medication brought a whole new wave of home-care manuals and 'patent' medical machines for home use. Commonly referred to as 'quack' medical gimmicks, these machines were usually ineffective and occasionally dangerous. Our advisor for this category is Jim Calison; he is listed in the Directory under New York.

Bullet extractor, scissors-like, Civil War era, 4½"	**60.00**
Cup, dosage; etched glass, WC Freund..., gilt rim, 2⅝"	**25.00**
Cupboard, oak, 24 dvtl drws in base, ca 1880, 95x73x14"	**1,600.00**
Dr's bag, alligator leather, ca 1900, EX	**85.00**
Dr's bag, blk leather, 2 compartments, brass locks, EX	**95.00**
Ear trumpet, japanned tin, jointed shaft, curved ear-pc, 1860s, 10"	**265.00**
Ear trumpet, jointed tin, ring-shaped ear-pc, curved shaft, 9½"	**335.00**
Ear trumpet, leather over brass, curved ear-pc, 1800s, 8½"	**1,250.00**
Enema set, brass syringe, tubing, ivory rectal pc, EXIB	**165.00**
Fleam, brass casing, 3-blade, mk Jessup Cast Steel, 1860s	**66.00**
Fleam, horn casing w/brass insert, Wm Jackson... mk on 2 blades	**78.00**
Fleam, wrought-iron curved shaft, single blade, 1850s, 6"	**135.00**
Forceps, lithotomy; steel scissors-like paddle, Mathieu a Paris, 9"	**50.00**
Forceps, unplated steel, locking device on side, 1860s, 5½"	**58.00**
Knife, amputation; ebony hdl, Mathieu, Paris, 1860s, 11⅝"	**136.00**
Lancet, ivory hdl, gooved shaft, Clark, 1860s, 6⅜"	**50.00**
Lancet, spring; brass, 1-blade, M in leather-covered case	**150.00**
Leech carrier, blown glass w/pontil, 2¼"	**60.00**
Machine, electromagnetic; mahog/brass box, Davis & Kidder, 1850s	**215.00**
Mirror, dental; removable ebonite hdl, 7½"	**18.00**
Mold, suppository; oval shape, makes 12 rectal/2 vaginal, 7" L	**265.00**
Mouth gag, scissors-like hdls, rubber mouthpc, Allen & Hanbury	**15.00**
Packet, first aid: US Army, brass, Bauer & Blk, 1918, unopened	**20.00**
Perforator, obstetric; scissors-like spade shape, Reynders & Co, 13"	**45.00**
Pneumometer (spirometer), tube w/spout, Oliver-Pell London, NMIB	**145.00**
Retractor, S-shaped blades, Mathiew Paris, 4⅝"	**25.00**
Saw, amputation; pistol-grip ebony hdl, Heuberger in Wein, 1850s	**400.00**
Saw, amputation; 8-sided ebony hdl, Gangeret, 1800s, 20"	**715.00**
Scaler, dental; ebony hdl, steel shaft, dmn-shaped tip, 1860s	**55.00**
Stethoscope, monaural; ebonized wood, Collin, 6⅜"	**210.00**
Syringe, irrigation; pewter, wooden-hdld plunger, 1860s, 9"	**45.00**
Table, examination; quarter-sawn oak w/appl cvgs, 39x40x22"	**550.00**
Tenaculum, folding, w/tortoise-shell cover, 1860s, 4¾"	**40.00**
Tenaculum, smooth ebony hdl, Sharp & Smith, 1860s, 6½"	**35.00**
Thermometer, doctor's pocket; in Catlin case, 1930s	**48.00**
Tongue depressor, bone, thumb-shaped hdl, 7"	**42.00**
Tooth elevator, Pied-de-Biche type, Charrier, 1840s, 6"	**195.00**
Tooth elevator, steel shaft, ebony hdls, 1850s, 5⅛", pr	**220.00**
Tooth extractor, unplated steel, check hdls, Brinkerhoff, 1850s	**35.00**
Tooth extractor, wrought-iron flared hdls, early 1800s, 6¼"	**50.00**
Tooth key, hardwood hdl w/decor, steel shaft, 1850s, 4½"	**215.00**
Tooth key, horn hdl, steel shaft, single claw, LAFAV, 1850s, 5"	**235.00**
Tourniquet, field; leather-covered pad, brass body, 1860s	**195.00**
Tracheostomy tube, silver & bone, mk Mathieu	**30.00**
Trocar, bulbous hardwood hdl, Mega Vicor on canule, 6¾"	**32.00**

Trocar, 8-sided ebony hdl, silver canule, 1860s, 4½" 36.00
Vaccinator, tortoise-shell cover, folds, mk Dalleas, 3⅝" 60.00

Meissen

The Royal Saxon Porcelain Works was established in 1710 in Meissen, Saxony. Under the direction of Johann Frederick Bottger, who in 1708 had developed the formula for the first true porcelain body, fine ceramic figurines with exquisite detail and tableware of the highest quality were produced. Although every effort was made to insure the secrecy of Bottger's discovery, others soon began to copy his ware; and in 1731 Meissen adopted the famous crossed swords trademark to identify their own work. The term 'Dresden ware' is often used to refer to Meissen porcelain, since Bottger's discovery and first potting efforts were in nearby Dresden. See also Onion Pattern.

Box, bl & wht scenic, dtd 1926 ....185.00
Box, red dragon, sm 125.00
Bust, lady in lilac cap w/appl flowers, yel ribbon, 5" 150.00
Centerpiece, cat & kittens by vase w/flowers/etc, rstr, 9x11x8" ..600.00
Compote, appl/HP flowers, 2 nude youths by stump stem, 12" .1,000.00
Compote, coat-of-arms reserves w/gold, rtcl rim, 9x11" 275.00
Figurine, boy & girl in Napoleonic dress, Xd swords, 6" 700.00
Figurine, cherub in purple robe on ice skates, Xd swords, 5½" 600.00
Figurine, cherub preparing tea, Xd sword, 4", NM 900.00
Figurine, cherub w/crutches, Xd swords mk, rstr, 8½" 400.00
Figurine, cherubs toss flowers, Xd swords mk, ca 1900, 5½" 500.00
Figurine, Chinese lady dancer, Xd swords mk, late 19th C, 6½" .650.00
Figurine, dancing couple in period dress, Xd swords, 8", 9", pr ..1,430.00
Figurine, Dutch lady w/apples, Xd swords, 7" 600.00
Figurine, lady w/lamb, beside tree trunk, ca 1775-79, 7½" 600.00
Figurine, maiden w/mirror & spy glass (allegorical), 1900s, 11" ..1,300.00
Figurine, man (& lady) on stump w/grapes, #16 & 127-1, 5", pr ...650.00
Figurine, woman selling vegetables, 5½" 600.00
Figurine, 18th-C guitar player, Xd swords, 6" 700.00
Figurine, 3 figures, dog in parlor, blanc de chein, 8½x11" 1,000.00
Jar, putti reserves on dk bl, ormolu mts, w/lids, mk, 15", pr 1,600.00

Mercury Glass

Mercury glass was made popular during the 1850s when the New England Glass Company displayed an assortment of items at the New York Crystal Palace Exhibition. It enjoyed a short revival at the turn of the century. Mercury glass was made with two thin layers, either blown with a double wall or joined in sections, with the space between the walls of the vessel filled with a mixture of tin, lead, bismuth, and perhaps some mercury, though some authorities say that because mercury was so costly, it was soon replaced with silver nitrate. The opening was sealed to prevent air from dulling the bright color. Though most examples are silver, red, blue, green, and gold can be found on occasion.

Remember that the value of this type of glass hinges greatly on the condition of the 'mercury' lining. In the listings that follow, all examples are silver unless noted another color.

Note: Be aware that during the 1998 holiday season many department stores offered mercury glass items (mostly in silver, but some in gold) — vases, candlesticks, place card holders, and huge Christmas balls.

Bowl, 3 clear appl ft, 4¾x9½" 120.00
Candlestick, grape leaves w/wreath & Gothic etchings, 7¾" 240.00
Candy container, gun form, 7½" L 28.50
Chalice, 5¾x4" 120.00
Compote, 7½x7" 255.00

Curtain pins, eng vintage, pewter collars, NE Glass, 3½", pr 300.00
Mug, clear hdl, 3" 30.00
Ornament, organ grinder monkey 30.00
Rose bowl, Czechoslovakia, 10" 200.00
Salt cellar, ped ft, 2¾" 46.00
Shade, dmn pattern, bl, 5" dia 300.00
Tie backs, 2½x4", pr 85.00
Vase, eng vintage, 5½x4¾" 105.00
Vase, HP floral w/berries & gold, 6½" 175.00
Vase, HP rose, 10½x4" 255.00
Vase, tapered beaker form, 8¼x6¼" 60.00

Merrimac

Founded in 1897 in Newburyport, Massachusetts, the Merrimac Pottery Company primarily produced gardenware. In 1901, however, they introduced a line of artware that is now attracting the interest of collectors. Marked examples carry an impressed die-stamp or a paper label, each with the firm name and the outline of a sturgeon, the translation of the Indian word Merrimac.

Vase, green matt with hand-applied leaf decoration, ca 1907, 4½x4½", $800.00.

Bowl, gr matt w/gray, lily pads/water lilies, cvd/appl, 5x9" 1,600.00
Stein, textured gr & blk w/flowing gr 1 side, 4⅛x5⅛" 325.00
Vase, dk bl-gr crystalline, modeled/appl feathers, rpr, 8" 3,000.00
Vase, dk gr matt, 3 raised floral forms, sm rprs, 11½x6" 1,725.00
Vase, gr, bulbous, 2½", NM 250.00
Vase, gr matt, aquatic plants, tooled/appl, 8x5", EX 3,250.00
Vase, gr/gunmetal w/EX feathering, squat w/flared neck, 4x3½" ...450.00
Vase, mustard crystalline drip over speckled matt, 7x6", NM 450.00
Vase, orange/gr semigloss, stilt chips, 4" 300.00

Metlox

Metlox Potteries was founded in 1927 in Manhattan Beach, California. Before 1934 when they began producing the ceramic housewares for which they have become famous, they made ceramic and neon outdoor advertising signs. The company went out of business in 1989.

Well-known sculptor Carl Romanelli designed artware in the late 1930s and early 1940s (and again briefly in the 1950s). His work is especially sought after today.

Some Provincial dinnerware lines can be confusing. There are three 'rooster' lines, Red Rooster (red, orange, and brown) and California Provincial (dark green and burgundy), and there are three 'homestead' lines, Colonial Heritage (red, orange, and brown like the Red Rooster pieces), Homestead Provincial (dark green and burgundy like California Provincial), and Provincial Blue (blue and white). For further information we recommend *Collector's Encyclopedia of Metlox Potteries* by our advisor Carl Gibbs, Jr.; he is listed in the Directory under Texas.

Cookie Jars

Photo courtesy Ermagene Westfall

Topsy, red polka dots, minimum value, $800.00; Mammy, Cook, red trim, from $750.00 to $850.00.

Apple, Golden Delicious, 9½"	150.00
Barrel, w/Cookie lid (Cookie Barrel), 11"	125.00
Barrel, w/Red Apple lid (Apple Barrel), 3¾-qt, 11"	50.00
Basket, natural, w/fruit lid (Fruit Basket), 4-qt	50.00
Basket, natural, w/gr apple lid	50.00
Basket, wht, w/basket lid	45.00
Basket, wht, w/red apple lid	50.00
Bear, Circus, minimum value	350.00
Bear, Panda, w/lollipop, minimum value	350.00
Bear, Teddy, bsk, 3-qt	45.00
Beaver, Bucky	175.00
Calf, Ferdinand, minimum value	750.00
Cat, Ali	225.00
Cat, Katy	95.00
Children of the World, Cookie Creations Series, 2-qt	125.00
Clown, wht w/blk accents	200.00
Cookie Boy, 9"	350.00
Cookie Girl, bsk, 2½-qt	65.00
Cow, purple w/pk flowers & butterfly, yel bell, 2½-qt	450.00
Cow, yel, no flowers, orange-wht butterfly, orange bell, minimum	550.00
Dina-Stegosaurus, French Blue	175.00
Dog, Fido, cream	125.00
Dog, Scottie, blk	125.00
Duck, Sir Francis Drake	50.00
Duck Blues	125.00
Egg Basket	175.00
Flamingo, minimum value	475.00
Goose, Lucy	150.00
Grapefruit, 3-qt	175.00
Hen, bl	300.00
Hippo, Bubbles, lt gray & gr, minimum value	450.00
Intaglio	200.00
Kitten (Tattle-Tale), says Meow	125.00
Lighthouse, minimum value	375.00
Mammy, Cook, bl	575.00
Mediereè, beige, 2½-qt	45.00
Merry Go Round, orange, yel & wht	375.00
Mona-Monoclonius, rose	175.00
Mouse Mobile, bsk	125.00
Noah's Ark, color glaze	175.00
Owl, wht, 2½-qt	50.00
Pear, gr	200.00
Pig, little	325.00
Pinocchio, 3-qt, 11"	400.00
Pretty Anne, 2½-qt	175.00
Rabbit, clover bloom finial	225.00

Rabbit, Mrs Bunny holding carrot	150.00
Raccoon, Cookie Bandit, bsk, 2¾-qt	90.00
Rag Doll, girl, 2½-qt	175.00
Rex-Tyrannosaurus Rex, lavender (experimental)	200.00
Rose, 2¾-qt	425.00
Santa, standing, solid chocolate, minimum value	900.00
Scout, Brownie, minimum value	750.00
Space Rocket, 12⅞", minimum value	1,000.00
Squirrel, on stump, glaze decor	100.00
Squirrel, w/acorn, stain finish	325.00
Topsy, solid bl apron	550.00
Tulip Time, Cookie Creations Series, 2-qt	85.00
Turtle, Flash	650.00
Watermelon	375.00
Woodpecker, on acorn, 3-qt	375.00

Dinnerware

#200 series/Poppy Trail, butter dish, w/lid	55.00
#200 series/Poppy Trail, cup, jumbo	25.00
#200 series/Poppy Trail, gravy/sauce boat	28.00
#200 series/Poppy Trail, grease jar, w/lid	50.00
#200 series/Poppy Trail, pitcher, ice lip, lg	60.00
#200 series/Poppy Trail, plate, chop; 12"	35.00
#200 series/Poppy Trail, shakers, ftd, pr	24.00
#400 series/Pintoria, bowl, serving	100.00
#400 series/Pintoria, saucer	30.00
#500 series/Yorkshire, candle holder	25.00
#500 series/Yorkshire, cream soup	45.00
#500 series/Yorkshire, cup, demitasse	25.00
#500 series/Yorkshire, egg cup, dbl	30.00
#500 series/Yorkshire, relish, hdld, 5-part	55.00
Antique Grape, butter dish, w/lid	60.00
Antique Grape, mug, 8-oz	24.00
Antique Grape, shakers, pr	26.00
Blueberry Provincial, bowl, salad; 11⅛"	70.00
Blueberry Provincial, bread server, 9½"	60.00
Blueberry Provincial, pitcher, 2¼-qt	70.00
Blueberry Provincial, plate, bread & butter; 6½"	8.00
California Aztec, coffeepot, w/lid	275.00
California Aztec, jam & jelly	65.00
California Aztec, platter, 13"	70.00
California Golden Blossom, bowl, vegetable; w/lid	95.00
California Golden Blossom, butter dish, w/lid	70.00
California Golden Blossom, pitcher, water	90.00
California Ivy, creamer, 6-oz	25.00
California Ivy, egg cup	35.00
California Ivy, mug, 7-oz	24.00
California Ivy, pepper mill	55.00
California Ivy, plate, dinner; 10¼"	15.00
California Ivy, tumbler, 13-oz	30.00
California Peach Blossom, plate, dinner	17.00
California Peach Blossom, sugar bowl, w/lid	35.00
California Provincial, bowl, salad; 11⅛"	100.00
California Provincial, cookie jar, w/lid	110.00
California Provincial, egg cup	45.00
California Provincial, lazy susan, 7-pc, complete	275.00
California Provincial, oil cruet, w/lid, 7-oz	42.00
California Provincial, pitcher, water; 2¼-qt	95.00
California Provincial, salad fork & spoon set	85.00
Chantilly Blue, cup	10.00
Chantilly Blue, platter, oval, lg	45.00
Colonial Heritage, ashtray, 10"	35.00
Colonial Heritage, bowl, salad	80.00

Colonial Heritage, bowl, vegetable; w/lid, rnd, med 95.00
Colonial Heritage, buffet server, rnd 70.00
Colonial Heritage, butter dish, w/lid 65.00
Colonial Heritage, coffee carafe, w/lid 130.00
Colonial Heritage, platter, oval, lg 50.00
Homestead Provincial, bread server, 9½" 85.00
Homestead Provincial, pitcher, milk; 1-qt 75.00
Homestead Provincial, plate, dinner; 10" 20.00
Homestead Provincial, soup tureen, w/lid 500.00
Homestead Provincial, sugar bowl, w/lid, 8-oz 40.00
Jamestown, buffet server, rnd 60.00
Jamestown, cookie jar, w/lid 75.00
Jamestown, plate, dinner 12.00
La Mancha, gravy boat, 12-oz 30.00
La Mancha, plate, bread & butter; 6½" 8.00
La Mancha, sugar bowl, w/lid, 12-oz 28.00
Lavender Blue, butter dish, w/lid 55.00
Lavender Blue, creamer, 10-oz 22.00
Lavender Blue, shakers, pr 24.00
Lotus, cup, 7-oz 12.00
Lotus, plate, chop; 17" 75.00
Navajo, bowl, salad; 12" 90.00
Navajo, coaster 22.00
Navajo, sauce boat 35.00
Navajo, shakers, pr 36.00
Navajo, tumbler, 10-oz 32.00
Provincial Blue, canister, coffee; w/lid 80.00
Provincial Blue, casserole, kettle; w/lid, 2-qt, 12-oz 135.00
Provincial Blue, cup, 6-oz 13.00
Provincial Blue, match box 95.00
Provincial Blue, mustard cruet, w/lid, 4-oz 35.00
Provincial Blue, pepper mill 65.00
Provincial Blue, plate, chop; 12¼" 85.00
Provincial Blue, tumbler, 11-oz 40.00
Provincial Rose, canister, flour; w/lid 75.00
Provincial Rose, platter, rectangular, 13" 45.00
Red Rooster Provincial, ashtray, 10" 35.00
Red Rooster Provincial, bowl, salad; 11⅛" 90.00
Red Rooster Provincial, canister, sugar; w/lid 80.00
Red Rooster Provincial, creamer, 6-oz 28.00
Red Rooster Provincial, gravy, 1-pt 45.00
Red Rooster Provincial, pepper mill 55.00
Sculptured Daisy, butter dish, w/lid 55.00
Sculptured Daisy, creamer, 6-oz 25.00
Sculptured Daisy, platter, oval, 9½" 35.00
Sculptured Daisy, teapot, w/lid, 7-cup 100.00
Sculptured Grape, bowl, vegetable; w/lid, med, 1-qt 95.00
Sculptured Grape, saucer, 6⅛" 5.00
Sculptured Grape, sugar bowl, w/lid, 10-oz 38.00
Sculptured Zinnia, coffeepot, w/lid, 8-cup 95.00
Sculptured Zinnia, creamer, 10-oz 25.00
Sculptured Zinnia, plate, salad; 7½" 10.00
Woodland Gold, bowl, salad; 11" 65.00
Woodland Gold, canister, flour; w/lid 80.00
Woodland Gold, cup, 7-oz 10.00
Woodland Gold, teapot, w/lid, 6-cup 100.00
Woodland Gold, tumbler, 12-oz 28.00

Disney Figurines

Bambi, jumbo 1,500.00
Bambi, w/butterfly 250.00
Bird, Boy or Girl (Cinderella), ea 250.00
Brer Rabbit, planter 4,250.00

Bruno (Cinderella), sitting 200.00
Cinderella, in formal 450.00
Doc (Snow White), miniature, 2" 250.00
Donald Duck, wall planter 400.00
Dopey (Snow White) 250.00
Dormouse (Alice in Wonderland) 500.00
Dumbo, standing 225.00
Figaro (Pinocchio), standing 225.00
Flower (Bambi), med 100.00
Huey, Dewey or Louie, playing baseball, ea 275.00
Jiminy Cricket 600.00
Limey (Lady & the Tramp), 1½" 250.00
Mad Hatter (Alice in Wonderland) 275.00
Mamma Mouse (Cinderella) 200.00
Mermaid (Peter Pan) 475.00
Michael (Peter Pan) 180.00
Mickey Mouse 400.00
Nana (Peter Pan) 250.00
Panchito (Three Caballeros) 350.00
Peter Pan 450.00
Pinocchio 450.00
Pluto, sniffing 250.00
Prince Charming (Cinderella) 400.00
Sleepy (Snow White) 250.00
Snow White 500.00
Three Little Pigs, toothbrush holder 400.00
Thumper (Bambi), lg 95.00
Thumper (Bambi), planter, lg 275.00
Timothy Mouse (Dumbo), aka Dumbo Mouse, miniature, 1¼" ..250.00
Tinker Bell (Peter Pan) 500.00
Tweedle Dee or Tweedle Dum (Alice in Wonderland), ea 250.00
Wendy (Peter Pan) 400.00
White Rabbit (Alice in Wonderland) 275.00

Miniatures

Baby the Indian Elephant, balancing on a ball, 6½", $145.00 minimum value.

Photo courtesy
Jack Chipman

Caterpillar 30.00
Chimpanzee, ashtray 85.00
Crocodile, 9" 110.00
Giant Anteater 125.00
Giraffe, 5¾" 125.00
Indian Rhinoceros 125.00
Nine-banded Armadillo, 1¾" 125.00
Shark, 6" 90.00

Nostalgia Line

Reminiscent of the late 19th and early 20th centuries, the Nostalgia line contained models of locomotives, gramaphones, early autos, stage coaches, and baby carriages. There were also wagons and carts pulled by horses or donkeys, sometimes with separate drivers and passengers. The line was produced from the late 1940s through the 1960s.

American Royal Horse, Circus/Draft Horse, lg, 11x8" **150.00**
American Royal Horse, Clydesdale, 9x9" **200.00**
American Royal Horse, Currier & Ives, 11x7¾" **125.00**
American Royal Horse, Mustang, lg, 10x8" **125.00**
Barrel wagon, 11x8" **100.00**
Budweiser beer wagon, 12½" **500.00**
Cutter sleigh, 8½" **85.00**
Hansom cab, 13x7x5¼" **80.00**
Ivy harp **100.00**
Locomotive **65.00**
Merrie Oldsmobile **85.00**
Roman fountain bowl & centerpc **315.00**
Victoria carriage, 10½" **100.00**

Poppets

From the mid-'60s through the mid-'70s, Metlox produced a line of
'Poppets,' eighty-eight in all, representing characters ranging from royalty and professionals to a Salvation Army group. They came with a
name tag; some had paper labels, others backstamps.

Babe, baseball player, 7¾" **55.00**
Chimney sweep, 7¾" **55.00**
Cigar Store Indian, 8¾" **55.00**
Doc, w/4" bowl **45.00**
Florence, nurse w/4" bowl **55.00**
Grace, princess **45.00**
Grover, bass drum man, 6¾" **55.00**
Hawaiian girl, 4¾" **35.00**
Huck, fishing boy, 6½" **45.00**
Leroy, king **45.00**
Nellie, girl w/bird, 8⅝" **55.00**
Ronnie, choir boy #2 ....**45.00**
Sam, little boy, 5¾" **35.00**

Mettlach

In 1836 Nicholas Villeroy and Eugene Francis Boch, both of whom
were already involved in the potting industry, formed a partnership and
established a stoneware factory in an old restored abbey in Mettlach,
Germany. Decorative stoneware with in-mold relief was their specialty,
steins in particular. Through constant experimentation, they developed
innovative methods of decoration. One process, called chromolith,
involved inlaying colorful mosaic designs into the body of the ware.
Later underglaze printing from copper plates was used. Their stoneware
was of high quality, and their steins won many medals at the St. Louis
Expo and early world's fairs. Most examples are marked with an incised
castle and the name 'Mettlach.' The numbering system indicates size,
date, stock number, and decorator. Production was halted by a fire in
1921; the factory was not rebuilt.

Key:
L — liter   PUG — print under glaze
POG — print over glaze   tl — thumb lift

#1032, coasters, dwarfs scenes (6), PUG, 5", NM, 6 for **700.00**
#1044, plaque, etch/glaze: bird & floral, 13" **360.00**
#1044/1066 & 1067, plaques, water pump/water wheel, Reiss, 17", pr ..**1,400.00**
#1044/5164, plaque, PUG: Cochem Castle, 17½" **465.00**
#1044/5165, plaque, Delft: Stolzenfels Castle, 17½" **300.00**
#1091, plaque, 3 lions, bl border, 20½" **1,400.00**
#1146, stein, etch: students, inlaid lid, .5L **660.00**
#1154, stein, etch: 3 hunt scenes, bock tl, inlaid lid, 1L **950.00**

#1163, stein, etch: musicians, Warth, inlaid lid, flaw, .5L **440.00**
#1289, vase, etch/glaze: repeating design, 3-ftd, 10¾" **465.00**
#1405, plaque, etch: woman, 10½" **400.00**
#1475, stein, etch: dwarfs digging, inlaid lid, .5L **695.00**
#1490, plaque, etch/glaze/relief: lady w/lg hat, 35" **8,800.00**
#1525, stein, relief: fox in jacket w/grapes, inlaid lid, .25L **290.00**
#1526, stein, HP: hunter w/rabbit behind, pewter lid, 1L **400.00**
#1526, stein, transfer/HP: Nurnberger Tucher Bier, 1L **350.00**
#1526/1108, stein, PUG: boch & people, barmaid lid, .5L **275.00**
#1526/1502, stein, PUG: military scene, inlaid lid, .5L **475.00**
#1643, stein, etch: tapestry/university student, pewter lid, 1L **450.00**
#1655, stein, etch: dancing scene, inlaid lid, .5L **400.00**
#1675, stein, etch: Heidelberg castle, inlaid lid, .5L **500.00**
#1687, stein, character: Heidelberg bbl, inlaid lid, .5L, NM **400.00**
#1700, vase, etch: floral, 3½" **250.00**
#1728, vase, etch/glaze: repeating design, 7½" **250.00**
#1804, vase, etch/glaze: repeating design, 9½" **300.00**
#1808, vase, etch/glaze: repeating design, 6" **230.00**
#1817, stein, etch: bicycle scenes, Schultz, lion/crown lid, 3.1L ..**3,400.00**
#1855, stein, etch/glaze: Post eagle, SP lid, .5L, NM **660.00**
#1909/1236, stein, PUG: Dutch children, pewter lid, .5L **465.00**
#1914, stein, etch: 4F Turner design, inlaid lid, .5L **750.00**
#1932, stein, etch: cavaliers toasting, Warth, inlaid lid, .5L **635.00**
#1934, stein, etch: military uniforms, Wilhelm I tl, .5L **1,200.00**
#1986, stein, etch: 2 ladies, crown inlaid lid, .5L **600.00**
#1997, stein, etch/PUG: Geo Ehret, inlaid lid, .5L **275.00**
#2001F, etch/relief: architecture, inlaid, lid, .5L, NM **600.00**
#2012, stein, Art Nouveau, ship inlaid lid, .25L, NM **260.00**
#2036, stein, character: owl, inlaid lid, .5L **1,150.00**
#2050, stein, etch: wedding, slipper/hearts lid, .5L, NM **1,500.00**
#2112/#2113, plaques, etch: dwarfs on branches, 16½", pr **2,300.00**
#2134, stein, etch: dwarf sitting in nest, pewter lid, .3L **825.00**
#2140753, stein, PUG: military scene, star lid, .5L **800.00**
#2142, plaque, etch: Bismark on horsebk, 15", NM **800.00**
#2148, plaque, etch/relief: Snow Wht & 7 Dwarfs, Schlitt, 16" .**1,100.00**
#2180/955, stein, PUG: cavaliers drinking, Schlitt, 3.3L **800.00**
#2184/966, stein, PUG: dwarfs, inlaid lid, .5L **300.00**
#2184/967, stein, PUG: dwarfs, inlaid lid, .3L **475.00**
#2184/967, stein, PUG: dwarfs, inlaid lid, .5L **600.00**
#2205, stein, etch: Diana/hunters, squirrel lid, boar tl, 5.2L, NM .**1,300.00**
#2206, stein, etch: Gasthaus scene, inlaid lid, 3L **1,500.00**
#2217, stein, transfer/HP: Muessel Brewing..., .4L, NM **260.00**
#2223, stein, etch: man on horsebk, pewter lid, 5.5L **3,465.00**
#2277, stein, etch: Wartburg Castle, inlaid lid, .3L **465.00**
#2286, stein, etch: drinking scene, inlaid lid, 2.6L **1,850.00**
#2301, vase, etch/relief: children, 15½" **1,375.00**
#2303, stein, PUG: Bartholomay's Rochester Beer, pewter lid, 3" ..**255.00**
#2303, stein, PUG: plain, new pewter lid, 3" **100.00**
#2324, stein, etch: rugby game, football finial, .5L **2,200.00**
#2327/1172, beaker, PUG: dwarf, Schlitt, .25L **200.00**
#2327/1200, beaker, PUG: Vancouver, rare, .25L **260.00**
#2362, plaque, etch: Heidelberg castle, lt gold wear, 17½" **1,200.00**
#2382, stein, etch: Thirsty Rider, Schlitt, tower form, .5L, NM .**600.00**
#2388, stein, character: stacked pretzels, pretzel hdl/lid, .5L **425.00**
#2391, stein, etch/relief: Lohengrin wedding, gargoyle hdl, 1L .**1,100.00**
#2430, stein, etch: cavalier drinking, inlaid lid, 3L **1,775.00**
#2500, stein, etch: drunken cavaliers, inlaid lid, 1L **850.00**
#2541, vase, PUG: hops & leaves, Nouveau style, 9¼" **250.00**
#2547, stein, relief: 3 drinking scenes, inlaid lid, .3L **160.00**
#2588, vase, etch: Art Nouveau, 10¾" **1,000.00**
#2686, stein, cameo: bicyclists, inlaid lid, 2.5L, NM **1,500.00**
#2768, stein, etch: couples walking, inlaid lid, .5L **695.00**
#2797, stein, etch: Richard Wagner, inlaid lid, 4.1L **3,800.00**
#2800, stein, etch: Art Nouveau, inlaid lid, .5L **450.00**

#2817, coaster, etch: cavalier serving, 4½" 230.00
#2828 stein, etch/glaze: Wartburg, castle lid, .5L, NM 1,275.00
#2829, stein, etch/glazed relief: Rodenstein, inlaid lid, .5L 1,100.00
#2870, mustard pot, w/lid, 3½" 125.00
#2898, plaque, etch: Spring, girl w/flowers, 17½", NM 2,400.00
#2917, stein, etch/glaze: Munich child, lion/shield lid, .5L, NM .1,585.00
#2935, stein, etch: Art Nouveau, inlaid lid, .25L 635.00
#2960/I, plate, etch: Art Nouveau, 15", NM 475.00
#2999, vase, etch: Art Nouveau, 9¼" 645.00
#3135, stein, etch: eagle/Am flags, inlaid lid, rpr, .5L 600.00
#3170, stein, etch: people walking, Hohlwein, .5", EX 350.00
#3170, stein, etch: winter scene, Hohlwein, inlaid lid, .5L 1,150.00
#3225/1290, plaque, PUG/HP: eagle/crests, 13x11" 695.00
#3272, plate, cameo: 4 girls, sgn Stahl, 6½" 315.00
#328, stein, relief: drunken man/chair, Foltz, early, .5L, NM 350.00
#3321/II, teapot, Art Deco clovers, sm rpr, 7" 485.00
#3330, trivet, etch: Art Nouveau, 8" 465.00
#3347, vase, relief: repeating floral, 3¼x3¼" 250.00
#3452, bowl, etch/glaze: repeating design, w/lid, 3" 200.00
#3480, stein, relief: cavaliers & Gambrinus, inlaid lid, .5L 465.00
#4515, biscuit jar, etch: Art Deco, w/lid, 6½" 350.00
#7002, vase, Phanolith, ladies/man, Stahl, 2-hdl, rpr, 9½" 350.00
#7018, vase, Phanolith, ladies/birds/flowers, Stahl, 13½" 825.00

Microscopes

The microscope has taken on many forms during its 250-year evolutionary period. The current collectors' market primarily includes examples from England, those surplused from institutions, and continental beginner and intermediate forms which sold through Sears Roebuck & Company and other retailers of technical instruments. Earlier examples have brass maintubes which are unpainted. Later, more common examples are all black with brass or silver knobs and horseshoe-shaped bases. Early and more complex forms are the most valuable; these always had hardwood cases to house the delicate instruments and their accessories. Instruments were never polished during use, and those that have been polished to use as decorator pieces are of little interest to most avid collectors. Our advisor for this category is Dale Beeks; he is listed in the Directory under Iowa.

Baker, 224 High Holborn London, brass, 1840s, 17" 1,200.00

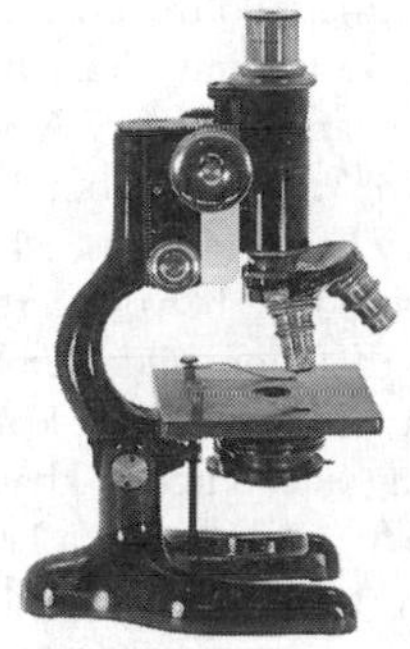

Bausch & Lomb, all black with stage clips and substage condenser lens, 1930s, complete with two lenses, $175.00.

Bausch & Lomb, blk, horseshoe base, 1915, EX 225.00
Bausch & Lomb, brass, Pat Aug 24 '97, 12x4⅛x6", NM in crate ..235.00
Bausch & Lomb, brass, tripod base, 1876, 16", EX, +case 600.00
Bausch & Lomb, rack & pinion focus, triple nosepc, EX, +case .350.00
Bulloch, Chicago, brass, complex, Y base, 1880, 15", +case 1,100.00
E Leitz Wetzlar, brass, revolving 3-power turret, EX in case 195.00
English, student, brass, ca 1870, 12", +case/accessories 595.00
German, student, rnd base, ca 1860, G, +case 125.00
Grunow, New Haven, iron & brass, 15", EX, +case 1,100.00
Gundlach, brass, Y base, 1879, 14", EX 325.00
Gundlach Manhattan, student, all brass, 11", EX 165.00
McAllister, chain-drive focus, 14", G, +case 325.00
Smith & Black, brass, binocular, London #3243, EX, +mahog box 1,350.00
Spencer Lens Co, brass, horseshoe base, 13", EX 195.00
Stamp, magnifier, brass, 3-leg, 1½", G 40.00
Watson, English binoculars form, 1880, 18", EX, +case 1,250.00

Midwestern Glass

As early as 1814, blown glass was made in Ohio. By 1835 glasshouses in Michigan were producing similar pattern-molded types that have long been highly regarded by collectors. During the latter part of the 19th century, all six of the states of the Northwest Territory were mass producing the pressed-glass tableware patterns that were then in vogue. Various types of art glass were produced in the area until after the turn of the century. Items listed here are attributed to the Midwest by certain physical characteristics known to be indigenous to that part of the country. See also Findlay Onyx; Greentown Glass; Libbey; Mantua; Zanesville Glass. Our advisor for this category is Mark Vuono; he is listed in the Directory under Connecticut.

Bottle, clear, globular, 12 ribs, folded rim, pontil, 8⅜" 300.00
Bottle, club; bl-aqua, 24 vertical ribs, rolled mouth, 7⅞" 220.00
Bottle, club; dk gr-aqua, 24 left-swirl ribs, red pontil, 7⅝" 450.00
Bottle, club; yel w/amber tone, 16 left-swirl ribs, pontil, 9" 3,600.00
Bottle, dk bl-aqua, 24 right-swirl ribs, pontil, 7⅝" 375.00
Bottle, dk root beer-amber, 24 vertical ribs, pontil, 7⅜" 5,750.00
Bottle, golden yel w/amber tone, globular, pontil, 7⅜" 450.00
Bottle, honey-olive, globular, 25 melon ribs, 8" 250.00
Bottle, lt bottle-glass gr, globular, pontil, 7" 150.00
Bottle, med amber, globular, 24 left-swirl ribs, 8¼" 550.00
Chestnut flask, aqua, 21 broken swirl ribs, flared lip, 5" 220.00
Chestnut flask, dk amber, flared lip, pontil, flake, 5¼" 160.00
Chestnut flask, dk aqua, 16 vertical ribs, pontil, 4¼" 200.00
Chestnut flask, dk aqua, 24 broken right swirl ribs, 6¾" 575.00
Chestnut flask, golden yel-amber, 24 right-swirl ribs, 6¼" 550.00
Chestnut flask, Grandfather, med amber, 24 vertical ribs, 8", NM ..1,300.00
Chestnut flask, med golden amber, 24 vertical ribs, pontil, 5" 230.00
Chestnut flask, yel-olive, 24 vertical ribs, pontil, 6¼" 350.00
Grandmother's flask, dk red-amber, 24 vertical ribs, 6⅞" 1,500.00
Jug, deep amber, flared lip, pontil, 5⅝" 425.00
Pan, clear, 16 vertical ribs, folded rim, pontil, 1⅜x3" 130.00
Pitkin flask, dk emerald gr, 15 broken right-swirl ribs, 6¼" 1,150.00
Pitkin flask, lt apple gr, 20 broken right-swirl ribs, 4¾" 450.00
Pitkin popcorn flask, yel-amber, 30 broken right-swirl ribs, 6¾" ..1,450.00
Salt cellar, clear, 24 vertical ribs, pontil, 1½x3⅛" 550.00
Tumbler, olive gr, broken blister, 4" 715.00

Militaria

Because of the wide and varied scope of items available to collectors of militaria, most tend to concentrate mainly on the area or areas that interest them most or that they can afford to buy. Some items represent a major investment and because of their value have been reproduced. Extreme caution should be used when purchasing Nazi items. Every badge, medal, cap, uniform, dagger, and sword that Nazi Germany issued is being reproduced today. Some repros are crude and easily identified as fakes, while others are very well done and difficult to recognize as reproductions. Purchases from WWII veterans are usually your safest buys. Reputable dealers or collectors will normally offer a money-back guarantee on Nazi items purchased from them. There are a number of excellent Third Reich reference books available in bookstores at very reasonable prices. Study them to avoid losing a much larger sum spent on a reproduction. Our advisor for this category is Ron Willis; he is listed in the Directory under Oklahoma.

Key: insg — insignia

Imperial German

Backpack, Army, gray canvas w/brn trim, mk, dtd 1915, EX **15.00**
Badge, Bavarian pilot, silver w/Imperial Crown & wreath, EX ..**415.00**
Badge, wound; gilt metal, stamped construction, EX **110.00**
Belt buckle, enlisted, NP inset on brass field, In Treue Fest **20.00**
Belt buckle, enlisted, NP on brass field, Gott Mit..., EX **15.00**
Boots, Cavalry, blk leather high tops, pull-on straps, pr, EX **100.00**
Coat, dress frock; Navy, dk bl wool w/silver bullion, 1890s, EX ..**165.00**
Gas mask, w/filter & gray canister, strap & loop, EX **50.00**
Helmet, officer's dress; winged eagle on leather, EX **800.00**
Helmet, spike; Artillery NC, brass mts, eagle frontplate, EX **795.00**
Helmet, spike; enlisted, gray metal mts, no cockades, G **125.00**
Helmet, trench; Model 1916, dk field gray, G **70.00**
Holster, Lugar; dk brn leather, w/belt loops/buckle/etc, EX **150.00**
Medal, Iron Cross, 1st class, 1813, w/sew-on loops **330.00**
Medal, 1914 Iron Cross, 2nd Class, w/ribbon, EX **25.00**
Postcard, propaganda; British 'Dum-Dum' bullets, EX **15.00**
Sleeve insg, Medical Service, yel embr on bl wool oval, M **20.00**
Statue, Baron Carl von Weber portrait, wht bsk, ca 1860, 12" **95.00**

Third Reich

Arm band, Deutscher Volkssturm Wehrmacht, printed, EX **20.00**
Badge, combat; Luftwaffe Flak Artillery, silver w/eagle, NM **175.00**
Badge, combat; Luftwaffe Paratrooper, diving eagle/wreath, M ..**300.00**
Badge, combat; Navy Submarine, gray metal w/gold traces, G **90.00**
Badge, combat; Navy Submarine, NM gilt finish, hall mk **135.00**
Badge, Luftwaffe Flak Personnel specialist, bl-gray field, NM **15.00**
Badge, Luftwaffe radio operater/air gunner's, 2-rivet, mk B&N ..**150.00**
Badge, Luftwaffe 4-Yr...Service, silver w/mini eagle device, EX **30.00**
Badge, Naval minesweeper's, EX **165.00**
Badge, proficiency; Army handworker, rose embr on gray wool **20.00**
Badge, proficiency; Hitler Youth leader, EX gilt finish, RZM **40.00**
Badge, 75 General Assault, 4-rivet, JFS in emb letters **85.00**
Banner, Army vehicle identification, printed cross on wht w/red, M **85.00**
Booklet, RAD Membership, early pattern, stylized Weimar eagle, EX ..**15.00**
Breeches, tropical; Army, khaki cotton, zinc buttons, NM **145.00**
Cap, DAF overseas; Bevo insg, bl piping, cotton lining, EX **85.00**
Cap, overseas; SS Panzer officer's, Bevo insg, aluminum tress **385.00**
Cap, side; Army Eastern Volunteer, gray cotton w/bl piping, EX ..**400.00**
Cap, SS Panzer M-43, single button, lined blk wool, EX` **110.00**
Cap, visor; Forestry officer's, bullion eagle cockade, EX **185.00**
Collar tabs, Army Artillery, silver bullion on red wool, pr **35.00**
Collar tabs, SS, heavy silver bullion, pr **120.00**
Collar tabs, Waffen SS Unterscharfuhrer, embr gray runics, pr **45.00**
Flight suit, Nazi Luftwaffe, sheepskin-lined, 2-pc, VG **450.00**
Frontplate, Police Shako eagle, gray metal w/screw posts, EX **24.00**
Gas mask, Army Luftschutz, rubberized canvas, rpt canister, G **30.00**
Hat, summer visor; Luftwaffe Flak Artillery enlisted, EX **200.00**
Helmet, desert camo, M35 style w/liner, scarce, EX **295.00**
Helmet, Luftwaffe chicken wire, M34/40 style, EX **550.00**
Helmet, M-35 Luftschutz beaded combat, NM pnt **195.00**
Helmet, M42 w/1st pattern SS runes, w/liner, EX **1,400.00**
Insignia, cap; Waffen SS Mtn Troup, edelweiss on blk wool, M **25.00**
Jacket & trousers, Waffen SS, reverses from autumn to wht, EX ...**300.00**

Kit, rifle cleaning; Army, tobacco-tin style, dtd 1937, G **25.00**
Knife, Hitler Youth, eng blade, blk checkered grips, NP hilt, EX ..**200.00**
Medal, Iron Cross, 1st Cross, 1939, in case **140.00**
Pin, RAD troop membership, shovel & wht insg w/enamel, EX ...**35.00**
Postcard, Luftwaffe aircraft image of Ju-87 on airfield, EX **15.00**
Raincoat, Navy U-Boat, rubberized fabric, blk buttons, 1943, EX ..**235.00**
Shako, Police, blk compo, leather liner, NM **45.00**
Stickpin, Wound Badge, NM blk finish, 1936 ....**22.00**
Tunic, Africa Korps, olive/brn cotton twill, Bevo eagle, EX **300.00**
Tunic, Army NC field, gray wool, M-36 style, EX **110.00**
Tunic, Army Panzer enlisted, M1944, gray wool w/collar tabs, NM ...**850.00**
Tunic, Hitler Youth, brn cotton twill, gold-washed buttons, EX ...**255.00**

Japanese

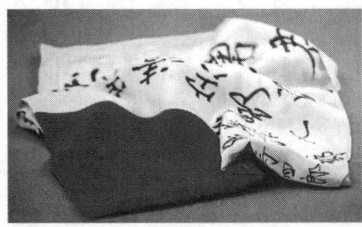

Flag, red ball on white silk, original Japanese characters, WWII era, EX, **$50.00.**

Badge, visor hat; WWII, Navy cadet, gilt brass w/anchor & rope, VG **85.00**
Badge, WWII Military veteran, silver w/gilt star insg **65.00**
Bayonet, WWII, Arisaka, stamped to Jinsen Arsenal, EX **38.00**
Bayonet, WWII, Type 30, 1st pattern, wood grips, G **30.00**
Helmet, flight; WWII, brn leather w/hard shell earphone flaps, G ..**110.00**
Helmet, WWI, Army, pnt steel w/star insg, VG+ **140.00**
Helmet, WWII, Home Guard, late war, EX **25.00**
Medal, Order of Rising Sun, 7th class, silver w/mc enamel, M ...**150.00**
Medal, Order of Rising Sun breast star, silver & gold, M **2,600.00**
Medal, Order of Sacred Treasure, 3rd class, neck badge, EX **300.00**
Medal, WWII era Red Cross, silver w/ribbon, EX **30.00**
Postcard, WWII, artillery crew in jungle, EX **15.00**
Sake cup, China incident, wht porc w/brn helmet/cherry blossoms ..**15.00**
Sword, practice; WWII, wood, Samauri type w/tsuba, 35" **45.00**
Sword, WWII, police, short pattern, brass hilt, EX polish, G **65.00**
Sword, WWII officer's parade dress, EX gilt, eng cherry blossoms .**125.00**

Russia/Soviet

Badge, Auxiliary Police, enamel on gilt, pin-bk, 1990, EX **15.00**
Badge, KGB Academy Graduation, gilt & enamel, 1990, M **15.00**
Badge, Submarine Military Academy Graduation, ca 1980, M **20.00**
Badge, 30th Anniversary of Liberation of Mongolia, mc enamel ..**45.00**
Beret, Navy Landing Force, blk wool, w/insg, ca 1980, NM **20.00**
Beret, Paratrooper, bl wool w/red side flash, insg, 1980s **46.00**
Book, identification; gilded emb red cover, 1980s, unissued **15.00**
Cap, flight; WWI pilot, blk leather w/ear protectors, EX **50.00**
Cap, folding side; officer's, khaki wool w/red piping, 1990 ....**20.00**
Cap, sable fur w/ear flaps, ca 1975, M **40.00**
Cap, visor; Army enlisted, khaki wool, 1983, M **30.00**
Cap, visor; Red Army, winter type, gray wool w/ear flaps, 1930, M ...**300.00**
Cap, visor; Red-Wht Civil War era, Shlem-pattern wool, EX **125.00**
Cap, WWII sailor, blk wool w/wht piping, blk silk ribbon **98.00**
Card, KGB identification, gilt on red-grained cover, unissued **15.00**
Dagger, dress; Air Force officer, dbl-edged, gilt guard, 1986, M ..**120.00**
Dagger, Navy officer, dbl-edged blade, gilt guard, 1954, EX **155.00**
Helmet, Army, gr pnt w/brn leather strap, ca 1960, EX **50.00**
Helmet, tank crew, padded, blk cotton w/fleece, G **50.00**
Knife, survival; cosmonaut, 2-blade, compo grips, 1980s, M **50.00**
Medal, Capture of Berlin, bronze, w/ribbon, EX **25.00**

Medal, Civil War Awaloff, bronze, St George & dragon, 1910 .....50.00
Medal, Defense of Caucasus, bronze, w/ribbon, NM 30.00
Medal, Defense of Kiev, gilded, w/ribbon, ca 1965, M 40.00
Medal, Victory Over Germany, brass, w/ribbon, EX 20.00
Medal, 10 Yr Distinguished Service, gilded, w/ribbon, M 20.00
Medal, 30th Anniversary of Space Exploration, bronze, w/ribbon ..45.00
Medal, 40th Anniversary of WWII, w/ribbon, M 30.00
Saber, WWII Cavalry, brass mts, CCCP/hammer/sickle, EX 265.00

United States

Arm band, WWI stretcher bearer, red cross on wht twill 20.00
Badge, WWII AAF flying instructor's wings, yel embr on khaki, M 15.00
Blanket, Spanish-Am War, Army, bl-gray wool, VG 65.00
Breeches, WWI, Army, khaki twill, metal buttons, faded, G 15.00
Bullet mold, iron, 36 caliber conical cavity, ca 1860, scarce 100.00
Button, Civil War, Union Dragon, Model 1851 officer's, coat sz ..35.00
Canteen, aluminum w/khaki collar, screw cap, dtd 1918 ....15.00
Cap, overseas; WWII Army officer's, khaki wool & leather, EX ...15.00
Chevron, WWII, petty officer 1st Class, silver/gold on bl wool 15.00
Coat, WWII Army officer, ¾-length, khaki wool, G 45.00
Collar disks, WWI, office of Indian Affairs, bronze, pr 385.00
Drum, snare; Pre-Civil War, Porter Blanchard...NH, 16x17", VG 600.00
Flight jacket, WWII, AAF heated coverall style, complete 165.00
Hat, campaign; WWI Army, khaki wool w/gold bullion cord, VG ...45.00
Haversack sling, Spanish-Am War, blk letter w/brass fittings, EX ...30.00
Helmet, WWI Infantry, khaki sand finish, pine-tree insg, EX 65.00
Helmet Liner, Vietnam War era, khaki finish, w/decal, EX+ 15.00
Insignia, shoulder; Vietnam War era 117 Gun Ship, coiled snake ..40.00
Jacket, pilot's, Flying Tigers, type A2, leather, w/silk printed map .1,600.00
Kepi, Civil War style w/brass infantry horn mtd on top, ca 1900 ..85.00
Leggings, WWI, leather, khaki canvas, bronzed metal fittings, EX 20.00
Medal, WWI, Dunkirk, NY Service, bronze, EX 25.00
Medal, WWI, State of OR Service, bronze cross, w/ribbon, NM ..25.00
Money belt, WWI, Army, 3-pocket, khaki twill, NP buckle, EX ..15.00
Overshoes, WWII, Army, early-style winter, rubberized twill, EX ..25.00
Pea coat, WWI, Navy enlisted, dk bl wool, compo buttons, VG ..35.00
Saddle bags, US Cavalry, McClellan, blk, ca 1885, EX 1,500.00
Signal light, WWII Army, hand-held lamp, Bakelite grips, EX 22.00
Uniform, WWII Navy, wool tunic w/havelock & trousers 24.00

Milk Glass

Milk glass is the current collector's name for milk-white opaque
glass. The early glassmaker's term was Opal Ware. Originally attempted
in England in the 18th century with the intention of imitating china,
milk glass was not commercially successful until the mid – 1800s. Pieces
produced in the U.S.A., England, and France during the 1870-1900 period are highly prized for their intricate detail and fiery, opalescent edges.

For further information we recommend *Collector's Encyclopedia of
Milk Glass, An Identification & Value Guide,* by Betty and Bill New-
bound. Another highly recommended book is *The Milk Glass Book* by
Frank Chiarenza and James Slater. Our advisor for this category is Rod
Dockery; he is listed in the Directory under Texas. Several standard col-
lectors' books have been referenced in our listings: Belknap (B), Collec-
tor's Encyclopedia by Newbound (CE), Ferson (F), Millard (M), and
Milk Glass Book (MGB). See also Animal Dishes with Covers; Bread
Plates; Historical Glass; Westmoreland.

Bookends, horse head, Indiana Glass, 6", M, pr 50.00
Bottle, dresser; Pansy, w/stopper, CE-1b, 10" 35.00
Bottle, dresser; wreath decor, satin finish w/gold, CE-17b, 10½" ..35.00
Bottle, Lady Bust, MGB-13, 5" 150.00

Bowl, Daisy Ray design, hdld, CE-26, 8x4¾" 20.00
Bowl, fruit; openwork edge w/basketweave, ped, CE-88 ....75.00
Bowl, Scroll & Eye, shallow, Challinor Taylor, CE-32a, 6¾" 30.00
Butter dish, Lace & Dewdrop, deep, CE-317, 6½x6" 40.00
Butter dish, Versailles, CE-315, 6¾x4" 80.00
Butter dish, Wild Rose, invt rose on bottom, w/lid, CE-82 ....75.00
Cake stand, HP mc rings on ped, HP floral trim on top, CE-107 ..50.00
Candlesticks, Jewel & Dewdrop, Kemple, CE-66b, pr 30.00
Candlesticks, rope hdld, emb tassels on sides, CE-64, pr 50.00
Candy dish, HP floral lid, divided 3-section base, CE-45, 6½" 40.00
Compote, basketweave design, CE-100b, 10¼x8" dia 135.00
Compote, bird ped, CE-87, 4⅛x7" dia 50.00
Compote, grape design, Anchor Hocking, CE-29 ....10.00
Compote, Lace & Dew Drop, Kemple, w/lid, CE-98b, 8½" 40.00
Creamer, Cow & Wheat, 3-ftd, CE-295, 4⅝" 125.00
Creamer, owl, glass eyes, bl, Challinor Taylor, F-6, 3⅝", M 45.00
Creamer, Sunflower, CE-299c/F-313, 4½" 45.00

Covered dish, Stagecoach, Fostoria, F-222, $250.00.

Goblet, Dewberry, Kemple, CE-218a, 6" 15.00
Goblet, Jewel & Dewdrop, Kemple, CE-218b, 6" 20.00
Jar, Old Abe Eagle, F-568, 6½", M 135.00
Ladle, curved hdl, ice lip, CE-223, 13¾" 55.00
Pitcher, Birds on Branch, CE-320/F-519, 7" 110.00
Pitcher, Owl, glass eyes, Challinor Taylor, CE-313, 7½" 185.00
Plaque, coupe; Eagle & Shield, mk MarCor, CE-251, 15" 50.00
Plaque, coupe; HP roses/leaves/couple w/gold, CE-249, 16" 60.00
Plate, Club & Shell border, Columbus bust, CE-270, 9¾" 45.00
Plate, Club & Shell border, Kemple, HP cherries, CE-260d, 9½" .18.00
Plate, Contrary Mule, B-12b 35.00
Plate, Diamond & Shell border, HP winter scene, CE-269d, 7" ...25.00
Plate, Easter Chicks, F-492 ....50.00
Plate, Easter Opening, B-7d, 7½" 75.00
Plate, Easter Rabbits, Dithridge, late 1800s, B-3f, 6¾" 55.00
Plate, Flower & Scroll, 8⅜" 15.00
Plate, Gothic, B-9b 25.00
Plate, Gray Ghost Streamer (lure), Lacy Heart border, Kemple, 6½" 12.00
Plate, H-Circle (Wicket) border, plain, Atterbury, 1890, 7½" 25.00
Plate, H-Circle border, Kemple, Colonial Folks decal, CE-263b, 8¼" .22.00
Plate, Lotus Flower edge, 7⅝" 15.00
Plate, No Easter W/out Us, Dithridge, F-30, 6¼" 55.00
Plate, Owl Lovers, M-31a, 7½" 65.00
Plate, Pennsylvania Turnpike, MGB-203, 8¼" dia 95.00
Plate, Rabbit & Horseshoe, Pat 1902, B-7a, 7½" 50.00
Plate, Serenade, M-1a, 6½" 45.00
Plate, Yacht & Anchor, M-28b, 7½" 35.00
Plate, 3 Bears, M-16a, 7½" 40.00
Plate, 3 Kittens, M-16b, 9" 35.00
Plates, Petalware, ribbon edge, fruit decor, CE-254, 8" dia 15.00
Rolling pin, blown glass, w/cork, CE-224b, 15" 120.00
Salt cellar, Cradle, MGB-315, 1⅞x2⅞" 75.00
Spooner, Lily (Sunflower), Atterbury, CE-299d, 4½" 45.00
Spooner, Strawberry, Bryce, flint glass, CE-304c/F-323 ....70.00

Stein, Monk design, CE-79, 4" **80.00**
Sugar bowl, Viking, 5 heads (4 ft/1 finial), CE-307, 8", minimum ...**750.00**
Toothpick holder, Bearded Old Man Grape Carrier, MGB-367, rare .**300.00**
Tray, Easter, w/verse, F-199, 10" L **40.00**

Miniatures

There is some confusion as to what should be included in a listing of miniature collectibles. Some feel the only true miniature is the salesman's sample; other collectors consider certain small-scale children's toys to be appropriately referred to as miniatures, while yet others believe a miniature to be any small-scale item that gives evidence to the craftsmanship of its creator. For salesman's samples, see specific category; other types are listed below. See also Dollhouses and Furnishings; Children's Things.

Armchair, mahog QA w/red velvet slip seat, 20th C, 24½" **140.00**
Blanket chest, bracket ft, scalloped apron, grpt, 8x9x12" **425.00**
Blanket chest, cherry & walnut, worn rfn, bracket ft, 20" L **880.00**
Blanket chest, poplar, dvtl case, molded-edge top, rfn, 19" **330.00**
Blanket chest, poplar, old rfn, bracket ft, minor damage, 15" **195.00**
Blanket chest, red stain, cut-out apron, butt hinges, 22" L **275.00**
Bureau, pine w/red stain, glove drw+3 drws, trn pulls, 1875, 17" ..**520.00**
Bureau, walnut w/mirrored top, 2-drw w/porc knobs, 14x6x4" ...**298.00**
Candelabra, unmk pewter, Nouveau-style shaft, 4-arm, 1890s, 3" ...**10.00**
Candlestick, brass w/CI weighted base, flared drip pan, 4", pr **35.00**
Chest, cherry Hplwht-style w/inlay, 4-drw, 29½x27¼x16" **550.00**
Chest, mahog English Hplwht w/flame vnr facade, 30x24x19" ..**990.00**
Chest, mahog/cherry, 5-drw, bracket ft, rfn, 17x12" **500.00**
Chest, walnut, 2 dvtl cockbeaded drws, crest, trn legs, rfn, 17" ..**660.00**
Cookware, blk iron kettle, frying pan, pot & coal scuttle, MIB **75.00**
Dry sink, walnut w/old red, paneled do, CI latch, 26x15x24" ..**3,850.00**
Dry sink, 2-tier, old red pnt, cutouts on sides, 23x25x15" **450.00**
Mirror, Hitchcock-style, 2-part w/rvpt scene in top, 7¾x5" **575.00**
Powder keg, wooden bbl form w/old red pnt, wooden stopper, 4½" .**100.00**
Sea chest, lt brn pnt w/dk brn squiggles, canted front, 8¼" **500.00**
Settee, Am Classical, highly cvd mahog, 1850s, 25x38x24" **1,500.00**
Strainer, bentwood & fine fabric, iron tacks, 2x3⅞" **250.00**
Table, rswd & maple Regency, rayed multiwood top, 5¾x6¾" ...**725.00**
Table, tea; mahog, old rpr to base of column, 19th C, 11x9" **660.00**
Taper sticks, unmk pewter, baluster shafts, lt wear, 3½", pr **290.00**

Minton

Thomas Minton established his firm in 1793 at Stoke on Trent and within a few years began producing earthenware with blue-printed patterns similar to the ware he had learned to decorate while employed by the Caughley Porcelain Factory. The Willow pattern was one of his most popular. Neither this nor the porcelain made from 1798 to 1805 was marked (except for an occasional number series), making identification often impossible.

After 1805 until about 1816, fine tea services, beehive-shaped honey pots, trays, etc., were hand decorated with florals, landscapes, Imari-type designs, and neoclassic devices. These were often marked with crossed 'L's. It was Minton that invented the acid gold process of decorating (1863), which is now used by a number of different companies. From 1816 until 1823, no porcelain was made. Through the '20s and '30s, the ornamental wares with colorful decoration of applied fruits and florals and figurines in both bisque and enamel were usually left unmarked. As a result, they have been erroneously attributed to other potters. Some of the ware that was marked bears a deliberate imitation of Meissen's crossed swords. From the late '20s through the '40s, Minton made a molded stoneware line (mugs, jugs, teapots, etc.) with florals or figures in high relief. These were marked with an embossed scroll with an 'M' in the bottom curve. Fine parian ware was made in the late 1840s, and in the '50s Minton experimented with and perfected a line of quality majolica which they produced from 1860 until it was discontinued in 1908. Their slogan was 'Majolica for the Millions,' and for it they gained widespread recognition. Leadership of the firm was assumed by Minton's son Herbert sometime around the middle of the 19th century. Working hand in hand with Leon Arnoux, who was both a chemist and an artist, he managed to secure the company's financial future through constant, successful experimentation with both materials and decorating methods. During the Victorian era, M.L. Solon decorated pieces in the pate-sur-pate style, often signing his work; these examples are considered to be the finest of their type. After 1862 all wares were marked 'Minton' or 'Mintons,' with an impressed year cipher.

Many collectors today reassemble the lovely dinnerware patterns that have been made by Minton. Perhaps one of their most popular lines was Minton Rose, introduced in 1854. The company itself once counted forty-seven versions of this pattern being made by other potteries around the world. In addition to less expensive copies, elaborate hand-enameled pieces were also made by Aynsley, Crown Staffordshire, and Paragon China. Solando Ware (1937) and Byzantine Range (1938) were designed by John Wadsworth. Minton ceased all earthenware production in 1939.

Dinnerware values given in the following listings are for items that were produced from 1870 to 1950. Current production pieces bring lower prices on the resale market. See also Majolica; Pate-Sur-Pate.

Plaque, five armed female figures stand below reclining Cupid, Louis Solon, 1880, 8½x15½", in ebony frame, $9,200.00.

Bowl, soup; Spot & Wreath, 1840 mk **35.00**
Coffeepot, Dainty Sprays **85.00**
Cup, Haddon Hall, bone china, mk **10.00**
Hot plate, Rose, ftd, 6¼" sq **80.00**
Pitcher, flowers & birds int/ext, #9666, 4x6" **95.00**
Plate, dinner; Ancestral, 10¾" **35.00**
Sugar bowl, Rose **48.00**
Thimble, Spring Bouquet **12.50**
Tile, bulldog, bl on wht, mk, 6x6" **40.00**
Vase, foliate/geometric bl transfer band on yel, hdls, 24" **460.00**

Mirrors

The first mirrors were made in England in the 13th century of very thin glass backed with lead. Reverse-painted glass mirrors were made in this country as early as the late 1700s and remained popular throughout the next century. The simple hand-painted panel was separated from the mirrored section by a narrow slat, and the frame was either the dark-finished Federal style or the more elegant, often-gilded Sheraton.

Mirrors changed with the style of other furnishings; but whatever type you purchase, as long as the glass sections remain solid, even broken or flaking mirrors are more valued than replaced glass. Careful resilvering is acceptable if excessive deterioration has taken place. In the listings that follow, items are from the 19th century unless noted otherwise. The term 'style' (example: Federal style) is used to indicate a mirror reminiscent of but made well after the period indicated. Obviously these retro styles will be valued much lower than their original counterparts. Our advisor for this category is Michael Hinton; he is listed in the Directory under Pennsylvania.

Key:
Chpndl — Chippendale	QA — Queen Anne
Emp — Empire	Vict — Victorian
Fed — Federal	vnr — veneer
Hplwht — Hepplewhite	

Brass Fr Rococo, beveled glass, easel bk, 19th C, 12" **200.00**
Cheval, Arts & Crafts oak, added varnish, 58x26" **500.00**
Convex, rnd molded fr w/eagle bracket, twin candle arms, 28" ..**1,760.00**
Gilt Am Classical, trn foliate cvd fr, 1840s, 39x25¼" **500.00**
Gilt Classical, free-standing pilasters, 2-part, 44x27" **1,650.00**
Gilt Fed, eagle finial, cornucopias & flowers, rpt, 40½" **2,500.00**
Gilt Fed, molded cornice, rvpt floral tablet, rstr, 38x23" **1,000.00**
Gilt gesso Classical, split baluster, spiral moldings, 1830s, 48x23" ..**455.00**
Gilt gesso Fed, molded cornice, appl rosets/spirals, 1820s, 37x22" ..**925.00**
Gilt gesso Fed, rvpt landscape scene, ca 1820, 26x13" **650.00**
Giltwood Fed, Parker & Clover...NY label, rvpt scene, 29x14" ..**2,000.00**
Girondole, gilded, figural masks, 3-light candle arms, 43", pr ..**2,500.00**
Mahog & gilt gesso Chpndl w/phoenix & cresting, 1790s, 40x22" ..**800.00**
Mahog Chpndl scroll w/gilt liner, old rpr, 40x21" **2,100.00**
Mahog Chpndl scroll w/gilt phoenix, rfn, 31x17" **1,400.00**
Mahog Classical cvd, overhanging cornice w/gilt, 1830s, 38x20" **600.00**
Mahog Fed, trn columns/2-part glass, rprs, 46x24" **300.00**
Mahog Fed vnr/stencil/split baluster, rpl glass, 1830s, 37x17" .**1,150.00**
Mahog Fed w/figure, brass rosettes, 2-part, 50" **350.00**
Mahog Hplwht scroll, X-banded vnr fr w/inlay, 26x15" **400.00**
Mahog vnr Chpndl scroll, gilt phoenix, 28x18" **1,000.00**
Mahog w/robust shell & foliate pierced cvg, 50x58" **1,500.00**
Mahog/maple Classical, cornice, veneer frieze, 2-part, 1825, 49x26" .**450.00**
Over-mantel, Biedermeier inlaid curly maple, 1850s, 59x31" ..**2,500.00**
Over-mantel, Biedermeier maple/bird's-eye maple w/gilt, 29x46" **500.00**
Over-mantel, gilded Am Renaissance, arched fr, 1850s, 64x48" ...**500.00**
Over-mantel, gilded Napoleon III, cartouch crest, 1850, 84x39" ..**2,500.00**
Over-mantel, gilded/gesso Vict w/foliate crest, 19th C, 55x55" ..**750.00**
Over-mantel, pine Geo III, Greek Key design, 3-part, 42x61" ...**1,300.00**
Over-mantel, rswd & gilt w/bronze mts, Paris, 19th C, 72x48" ..**2,000.00**
Pier, gilded/cvd, marble top console table in Rococo style, 103" ..**2,000.00**
Rswd Vict Baroque Revival w/inlay, cvd details, 106x73" **1,750.00**
Walnut Chpndl gilt gesso, ca 1750s, rstr, 46x24" **1,250.00**
Walnut Chpndl scroll, gilt gesso, rstr, 1770s, 46x24" **1,500.00**
Walnut Chpndl scroll, orig finish, worn silvering, 23x13" **700.00**
Walnut Geo I w/gilt, pierced fr, early 18th C, 48x28" **1,900.00**
Walnut QA scroll, gilt Prince of Wales feather, rprs, 37x14" **700.00**
Walnut vnr Chpndl w/parcel gilt, Am, 18th C, rstr, 37x15" **575.00**
Walnut vnr QA scroll, appl gilded ornaments, 47x19" **2,500.00**
Walnut vnr QA scroll, appl ornaments, old gold rpt, 31x13" ..**1,100.00**

Mocha

Mochaware is utilitarian pottery made principally in England (and to a lesser extent in France) between 1780 and 1840 on the then prevalent creamware and pearlware bodies. Initially, only those pieces decorated in the seaweed pattern were called 'Mocha,' while geometrically decorated pieces were referred to as 'Banded Creamware.' Other types of decorations were called 'Dipped Ware.' During the last thirty to forty years the term 'Mocha' has been applied to the entire realm of 'Industrialized Slipware' — pottery decorated by the turner on his lathe using coggle wheels and slip cups.

Mocha was made in numerous patterns — Tree, Seaweed or Dandelion, Rope (also called Worm or Loop), Cat's-eye, Tobacco Leaf, Lollypop or Balloon, Marbled, Marbled and Combed, Twig, Geometric or Checkered, Banded, and slip decorations of rings, dots, flags, tulips, wavy lines, etc. It came into its own as a collectible in the latter half of the 1940s and has become increasingly popular as more and more people are exposed to the rich colorings and artistic appeal of its varied forms of abstract decoration.

The collector should take care not to confuse the early pearlware and creamware Mocha with the later kitchen yellow ware, graniteware, and ironstone sporting mocha-type decoration that was produced in America by such potters as J. Vodrey, George S. Harker, Edwin Bennett, and John Bell. This type was also produced in Scotland and Wales and was marketed well into the 20th century.

Mugs: Wavy lines on brown, 5¾", NM, $650.00; Black seaweed on greenish-tan with broad blue band at top, 6", NM, $650.00; Repeated twig pattern in black and blue on light green with blue and brown banding, tiny nick on inner rim, 6", $1,000.00.

Bowl, bl band, 3 blk stripes on wht, rnd ft, 2⅞x5¾" **325.00**
Bowl, earthworm in bl/brn, 3x6¼" **450.00**
Bowl, scroddled mc band, rnd gallery-type ft, rpr, 2¼x4⅞" **175.00**
Chamber pot, bl sponging on wht band, brn stripes, child's, 7" ..**250.00**
Chamber pot, earthworm, blk & wht on bl bands, leaf hdl, 8¾" ...**300.00**
Jar, earthworm & cat's eyes, 3-color on bl band, rprs, 5" **595.00**
Mug, bl bands & blk lines, strap hdl, 4¾" **450.00**
Mug, cream band & 2 blk stripes, flared rim, 4x3¼" **260.00**
Pepper pot, bl & wht stripes w/brn band, wht leaves/dots, 4¾" ..**715.00**
Pepper pot, seaweed, blk on orange band, 2 yel bands, w/lid, 4" .**900.00**
Pitcher, earthworm, 3-color on bl, blk & bl stripes, 5", VG **250.00**
Pitcher, milk; earthworm, bl/blk/tan stripes, bl band, 6¾" **1,150.00**
Pitcher, milk; seaweed, blk on brn band, blk & gr stripes, 6" ..**1,100.00**
Pitcher, water; blk sponging on cream band, bl/blk stripes, 9⅝" ..**2,500.00**
Salt cellar, cream band & 2 blk stripes, ftd, master, 2¼x3" **275.00**
Salt cellar, seaweed, blk on brn band, blk stripe, 3" dia **550.00**
Salt cellar, wavy lines, wht on gray band w/blk stripes, 2½x3" ...**335.00**
Shaker, seaweed, blk w/tan bands, blk stripes, 4⅛", EX **220.00**
Tankard measure, seaweed, blk on gray band, blk/bl stripes, pt ..**140.00**
Waste bowl, seaweed, blk on amber band, gr lip band, 4¾", G ...**275.00**

Molds

Food molds have become popular as collectibles — not only for their value as antiques, but because they also revive childhood memories of elaborate ice cream Santas with candy trim or barley sugar figurals adorning a Christmas tree. Ice cream molds were made of pewter and came in a wide variety of shapes and styles. Chocolate molds were made in fewer shapes but were more detailed. They were usually made of tin, copper, and occasionally of pewter. Hard candy molds were usually metal, although primitive maple sugar molds (usually simple hearts, rabbits, and other animals) were carved from wood. (Unless otherwise indicated, those in our listings are cast aluminum or stainless steel.) Cake molds were made of cast iron or cast aluminum and were most common in the shape of a lamb, a rabbit, or Santa Claus. Our advisors for this category are Dale and Jean Van Kuren; they are listed in the Directory under New York.

Chocolate Molds

Astronaut	75.00
Basketball w/ridge lines & laced end, 20th C, 2-part, 6" dia	125.00
Bear, standing, 5"	175.00
Boy on bicycle, 9"	250.00
Bulldog	35.00
Cartoon cat w/long neck	250.00
Champagne bottle, Germany, 4¾"	30.00
Charlie Chaplin	255.00
Chick w/hat, 5½"	45.00
Chicken, S&Co, #173	55.00
Circus elephant, 2-part, 4¼"	125.00
Egg w/emb stork & baby medallion, 3x2x2"	55.00
Girls (3), folding, US Pat Pending, 9½"	125.00
Heart w/Cupid, S&Co #1102	40.00
Hen on Basket, lg	60.00
Indian, 5¼"	85.00
Jack-o-lantern, 2-pc, folding	95.00
Lion, 2-pc, 6½"	65.00
Lions, standing, 4 sections	135.00
Mickey Mouse	125.00
Model T, Germany, 7½"	125.00

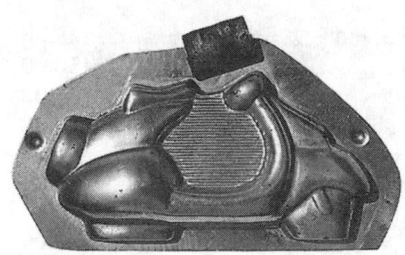

Moped, #16057, two-piece with clamp, 3¼x6", $60.00.

Owl	55.00
Rabbit, Eppelsheimer & Co, lt rust, 11¼"	150.00
Rabbit, late 1800s, 12"	250.00
Rabbit, running, 10½"	75.00
Rabbit, 2-pc, Anton Reiche, Dresden Germany, 18½"	300.00
Rabbit, 3-part, tin mold in steel fr, 13½"	220.00
Rabbit in convertible	145.00
Rabbit in suit, 6"	40.00
Rabbit on lg egg, 8½"	75.00
Rabbit w/basket, 2-pc, MIG, 7½"	105.00
Rabbits (3), German, 5x8"	95.00
Ram	85.00
Santa, side hinge, 4½"	95.00
Santa in sleigh w/reindeer, wht metal, makes 15, Elsreimer, 14x18"	115.00
Scottie	65.00
Scottish girl in kilt, 10"	140.00
Smokey the Bear, metal, 8½"	58.00
Squirrel, tin, 9½"	100.00
Teddy bear, 11½"	395.00
Train, lg	95.00

Hard Candy Molds

Battleships in waves, TM-256, groove for stick, 2½x1¼"	55.00
Castle w/flag, groove for stick, 1¾x1½"	80.00
Hand, TM-31, groove for stick, 1¾x1¼"	60.00
Lion, 3-part, TM-40, groove for stick, 4x5"	115.00
Locomotive, 3-part, TM-14, groove for stick, 3½x6"	125.00
Mouse, TM-37, groove for stick, 2¼x1¼"	90.00
Rabbits, baby in cart, TM-41, groove for stick, 4½x3½"	130.00
Rat, TM-238, groove for stick, 2½x1"	80.00
Teddy bear, walnut, rtcl, 2-part, makes 6, 1½x12"	130.00

Ice Cream Molds

Airplane, E&Co, 5"	95.00
American flag, E&Co #1160	60.00
Blimp, E&Co	85.00
Cabin cruiser	85.00
Chick & egg, #599	85.00
Child w/nosegay, E&Co, 4¾"	80.00
Christmas tree, E&Co #1154	125.00
Draped nude, 5¼"	200.00
Duck, #167	55.00
Elephant, E&Co	45.00
Eskimo in parka, E&Co, 5"	60.00
Father Christmas, E&Co #991	125.00
Football player, S&Co	60.00
Horse, E&Co #639	55.00
Knights of Columbus seal, #1138	50.00
Lemon, #357	25.00
Peach, #164	90.00
Rooster, 4¼"	50.00
Rose, 2-part, 3½"	85.00
Sailboat, S&Co	85.00
Steamer, #513	110.00
Stork w/baby, #1151	125.00
Stork w/baby, Edd Hoffman, Chicago	80.00
Turkey, 4¼"	40.00
Vegetable, #209	55.00
Wedding ring, 3¾" dia	65.00

Maple Sugar Molds

Beaver, hand cvd, EX detail, 5x9"	125.00
Fruit & foliage, hardwood, 2-part, 5½x8"	50.00
Heart w/face, hand cvd, in orig tin case, 1800, 5½"	425.00
Hearts (2), varnished, 3x18"	140.00
House w/cvd windows & doors, separate sides & roof, 5½"	110.00
Indian on horse, well cvd, 2-part	95.00
Openwork on rnd fluted cups, CI, 12 in 11x16" fr	115.00
Porcupine figure (2) on cvd paddle form, 1800s, 8¾" w/hdl	175.00
Rnd w/hdl on side, open spout opposite, crudely cvd, 11¾" dia	130.00
Strawberry, deeply cvd pine, dvtl, 1830s, 1¾x5½x9"	165.00
6 cutouts, birds/fish/etc, 1-pc, 16x3"	170.00

Miscellaneous

Aluminum, lady finger, England, 4", set of 6, MIB	15.00
Aluminum, lamb, 12"	65.00
Bronze, for cast pewter spoons, 8"	250.00
CI, bird on branch on oval, scalloped border, 5" L	95.00
CI, cloverleaf, for doughnuts, Pat The Ace Co	115.00
CI, fish shape, 1¾x9x8¾"	120.00
Copper, eagle w/arrows & laurel, 7¾" dia	385.00
Copper/tin, ear of corn, worn, 6x4"	125.00
Pewter, 4-parts: grapes/eagles & swags/rabbit/basket, 5x6"	250.00
Tin, apples/plums/grapes, scalloped sides, 4½x8½"	85.00
Tin, fish shape, 2½x10½x7½"	135.00

Tin, melon, 2-part, mk Kreamer, 4x5¼x2½" 40.00
Tin, overlapping circles, fluted sides, 3¾x7x5" 45.00
Wood, cvd floral, high tin sides, curved heart form, 7" 275.00

Monart

Scottish glassmaker, John Moncrief was fascinated by the technique of suspending colored enamels within the molten glass during the glassmaking process. Recognizing the potential of the process (which he had observed while in France), he began his own business in Perth, Scotland, in 1924. The glassware he created was called Monart. Several commercial lines were along the fine artware pieces designed with scrolls or feathers suspended within the glass. Nearly all examples are unmarked, most having originally carried a paper label.

Vase, cluthra type, dk bl/med bl w/goldstone, 6x5" 150.00
Vase, earth tone mottle, opal spatter base, mk Scotland, 12" ..1,250.00
Vase, red mottle w/maroon stripes & opal mottling, 4½" 130.00

Monmouth

The Monmouth Pottery Company was established in 1892 in Monmouth, Illinois. Their primary products were salt-glazed stoneware crocks, churns, jugs, bristol, spongeware, and brown glaze. In 1906 they were absorbed by a conglomerate called the Western Stoneware Company. Monmouth became their #1 plant and until 1930 continued to produce stoneware marked with their maple leaf logo. Items marked 'Monmouth Pottery Co.' were made before 1906. Western Stoneware Co. introduced a line of artware in 1926. The name chosen for the artware was Monmouth Pottery. Some stamps and paper labels add ILL to the name.

Churn, bristol, 2-gal 250.00
Churn, salt glazed, 3-gal 350.00
Cookie jar 50.00
Cooler, ice water; bl & wht sponge, w/lid & spigot, 8-gal 2,000.00
Cooler, ice water; bl & wht sponge, 5-gal 2,000.00
Cow & calf, brn, mk Monmouth Pottery Co 2,000.00

**Crock, bristol glaze,
ten-gallon, $100.00.**

Crock, bristol, 20-gal 100.00
Crock, bristol, 60-gal 700.00
Crock, bristol & Albany glaze, 1-qt 100.00
Crock, early dull bristol w/cobalt stencil 300.00
Crock, salt glazed, hand decor, base mk, 2-gal 125.00
Jug, bristol, rectangle mk, 5-gal 250.00
Pig, brn, mk Monmouth Pottery Co 1,000.00
Snuff or preserve jar, wax seal 350.00
Vase, bl matt, incised shoulder band, 16x10" 495.00

Monot and Stumpf

The firm of Monot and Stumpf was organized in 1868, the merger of the E.S. Monot and F. Stumpf glassworks. It was located in Pantin, France. They produced fine art glass of various types until ca 1892, when the company reorganized and became known as the Cristallerie de Pantin.

Banquet lamp, pk opal swirl shade/font; brass swirl std, 27" 775.00
Bowl, pk opal, ribbed, 3¾x7¾" 175.00
Salt cellar, lav-pk opal, gold lustre int, fluted, 1⅝" 78.00
Salt cellar, wht opal w/gold lustre int, Pantin, 1½x1¾x2⅛" 65.00
Vase, pk opal to clear w/gold irid, HP florals, hdls, 10¾" 175.00

Mont Joye

Mont Joye was a type of acid-cut French cameo glass produced by Cristallerie de Pantin in Paris around the turn of the century. It is accented by enamels. Our advisor for this category is Don Williams; he is listed in the Directory under Missouri.

Cracker jar, violets/gold leaves on textured frost, att 450.00
Vase, floral, plum to gr w/gold, mk, 11½" 660.00
Vase, grapes & leaves, pk to clear w/mc & gold, 13x3¾" 600.00
Vase, lg poppies, lav/yel/gilt on gray-gr, bun base, 16", pr 1,650.00
Vase, mums, yel/lav/wht on ruby to clear, 15", pr 1,300.00
Vase, Nouveau floral in gold on irid textured cylinder, 11½" 850.00
Vase, sweet peas, gold on lt gr, ornate rim, 12" 300.00
Vase, swirls/sm flowers, lime on leaf-texture frost, sq, 12x5" 650.00
Vase, violets/gilt stem on textured frost, pinched/ruffled, 5" 225.00

Moon and Star

Moon and Star was originally produced in the 1880s by John Adams & Company of Pittsburgh. In the 1960s, Joseph Weishar of Wheeling, West Virginia, owner of the Island Mould & Machine Company, reproduced some of the original molds and incorporated the pattern into approximately forty new and different items. Two of the largest distributors of this line were L.E. Smith of Mt. Pleasant, Pennsylvania, who pressed their own glass, and L.G. Wright of New Martinsville, West Virginia, who had theirs pressed by Fostoria, Fenton, and Westmoreland. Both companies carried a large and varied assortment of shapes and colors. Several other companies were involved in its manufacture as well, especially of the smaller items.

Over the years the glassware has been pressed in amberina (yellow shading to orange- or ruby-red), green, amber, crystal, light blue, and ruby. Pieces in ruby and light blue are most collectible and harder to find than the other colors, which seem to be abundant. Purple, pink, cobalt, amethyst, tan slag, and light green and blue opalescent were made, too, but on a lesser scale.

Current L.E. Smith catalogs contain a small assortment of pieces that are still available in crystal, pink, cobalt (lighter than the old shade), and these colors with an iridized finish. A new color, teal green, was introduced in 1992, a water set in sapphire blue opalescent was pressed in 1993, and the new color in 1994 was cranberry ice. Items are currently being pressed in various colors by the Weishar Company, who add their mark to the new glassware which is made primarily for collectors. Our values are given for ruby and light blue unless noted otherwise. For amberina, green, and amber, deduct 20%.

Ashtray, moons at rim, star in base, 6-sided, 5½" 18.00

Basket, allover pattern, scalloped rim, 9" **75.00**

Butter dish, allover pattern, scalloped ft, 6x5½" **45.00**

Candle holders, allover pattern, flared & scalloped ft, 6", pr **50.00**

Cheese dish, patterned base, plain clear lid, 9½" **70.00**

Compote, allover pattern, w/lid, 8x10" **65.00**

Decanter, bulbous w/allover pattern, plain neck, 32-oz, 12" **130.00**

Goblet, water; plain rim & ft, 5¾" **20.00**

Jelly dish, plain flat rim, disk ft, patterned lid, 6¾x3½" **35.00**

Nappy, allover pattern, crimped rim, 2¾"x6" **18.00**

Relish tray, moons form scalloped rim, star base, rectangular, 8" ..**35.00**

Salt cellar, allover pattern, scalloped, sm flat ft **8.00**

Shade, ruffled dome shape w/allover pattern, amber, 10" **100.00**

Shakers, allover pattern, metal lids, 4x2", pr **25.00**

Sherbet, plain rim & stem, 4¼x3¾" **25.00**

Soap dish, allover pattern, oval, 2x6" **12.00**

Sugar bowl, allover pattern, sm flat ft, w/lid, 5¼x4" **40.00**

Sugar/cheese shaker, allover pattern, metal lid, 4½x3½" **45.00**

Syrup, allover pattern, metal lid, 4½x3½" **65.00**

Toothpick holder, allover pattern, scalloped rim, ftd **10.00**

Tumbler, iced tea; no pattern at rim or ft, 11-oz, 5½" **22.00**

Tumbler, no pattern at rim or disk ft, 5-oz, 3½" **20.00**

Tumbler, no pattern at rim or disk ft, 7-oz, 4½" **22.00**

Moorcroft

William Moorcroft began to work for MacIntyre Potteries in 1897. At first he was the chief designer but very soon took over their newly created Art Pottery department. His first important design was the Aurelian Ware, part transfer and part hand painted. Very shortly thereafter, around the turn of the century, he developed his famous Florian Ware, with heavy slip, done in mostly blue and white. Since the early 1900s there has been a succession of designs, most of them very characteristic of the company. Moorcroft left MacIntyre in 1913 and went out on his own. He had already established his name, having won prizes and gold medals at the St. Louis World's Fair as well as in Paris. In 1929 Queen Mary, who had been collecting his pottery, made him 'Potter to the Queen,' and the pottery was so stamped up until 1949. William Moorcroft died in 1945, and his son Walter ran the company until recent years. The factory is still in existence. They now produce different designs but continue to use the characteristic slipwork. Moorcroft pottery was sold abroad in Canada, the United States, Australia, and Europe as well as in specialty areas such as the island of Bermuda.

Moorcroft went through a 'Japanese' stage in the early teens with his lovely lustre glazes and Oriental shapes and decorations. During the mid-teens he began to produce his most popular Pomegranate Ware, and Wisteria (often called 'Fruit'). Around that time he also designed the popular Pansy line as well as Leaves and Grapes. Soon he introduced a beautiful landscape series called variously Hazeldine, Moonlit Blue, Eventide, and Dawn. These wonderful designs along with Claremont (Mushrooms) seem to be the most sought after by collectors today. It would be possible to add many other designs to this list.

During the 1920s and '30s, Moorcroft became very interested in highly fired Flambe (red) glazes. These could only be achieved through a very difficult procedure which he himself perfected in secret. He later passed the knowledge on to his son.

Dating of this pottery is done by knowledge of the designs, shapes, signatures, and marks on the bottom of each piece; an experienced person can usually narrow it down to a short time frame. Prices escalated for this 'rediscovered' pottery in the late 1980s but has now leveled off. This is true mainly of the pre-1935 designs of William Moorcroft, as it is items from that era that attract the most collector interest. Prices in the listings below are for pieces in mint condition unless noted otherwise; no reproductions are listed here. Advisors for this category are Wilfred and Dolli Cohen; they are listed in the Directory under California.

Bowl, anemones on cobalt, 4½" **165.00**

Bowl, Eventide, sunset scene, WM, MIE, 3x8" **1,400.00**

Bowl, hibiscus, bright yel w/red & gr on gr, mks, 1½x5" **30.00**

Bowl, hibiscus (3) on gr, WM, MIE, 3x6" **160.00**

Bowl, Moonlit Blue, trees on bl, mk, MIE, #195Y, 5½x7" ...**1,200.00**

Bowl, pansies on gr to wht, mk, WM, #56, 3x4½" **395.00**

Bowl, pomegranates on cobalt, WM, 1928-49, 3x7" **450.00**

Bowl, spring flowers, mc on gr, bl ext, rstr, 3½x12" **275.00**

Box, anemones, lt to bl, cylindrical, mk, 1945, 3½" H **260.00**

Candlesticks, anemones, dk bl, mk, 4¼", pr **450.00**

Charger, heron & reeds, dk bl against sunset, WM, 14" dia **220.00**

Creamer, orchids, mc on lt gr to dk bl, 3" **260.00**

Humidor, Spanish design, screw-on lid, WM, early mk, 4½x5" ..**1,800.00**

Jar, grapes & leaves, mc on gr to bl, w/lid, WM, MIE, 5½x5" **375.00**

Jar, temple; Eventide, w/lid, 11x8½" **6,000.00**

Jar, wisteria on cobalt, w/lid, MIE, #769Y, 8½", NM **450.00**

Jardiniere, pomegranates on cobalt, WM, 6x8" **650.00**

Lamp base, grape & leaf flambe, unmk, 12" **850.00**

Lamp base, grapes & leaves on gr to bl-gr, 1928-49, 10" **650.00**

Pitcher, irises, yel/pk on bl to gr, bulbous, 5x6" **350.00**

Pitcher, orchids on gr, mk, 4½" **250.00**

Plate, mushrooms on gr, WM, MIE, 10" **150.00**

Plate, penguin, WM 106/150, 10¼" **125.00**

Sugar bowl, orchids, mc on gr to dk bl, 2½x3" **200.00**

Vase, anemones, mauve/wine on cobalt, classic shape, 12x5½" ..**800.00**

Vase, anemones on cobalt, shouldered, 6" **300.00**

Vase, anemones on cobalt & gr, bulbous w/flared rim, 10" **600.00**

Vase, anemones on gr to cobalt, 5" **300.00**

Vase, clematis on gr to bl, MIE, 1949-86, 6" **250.00**

Vase, clematis on tan to bl, WM, 6" **200.00**

Vase, cornflowers, powder bl, hdls, 1917, 12¾" **4,850.00**

Vase, Florian, white stylized floral on cobalt, 8x7½", **$925.00.**

Vase, freesia, mc on lt gr to bl, WM, 6x7½" **550.00**

Vase, grape & leaf flambe, script sgn/imp mk, 9½" **950.00**

Vase, grapes, swollen top, rnd ped base, 6" **325.00**

Vase, Hazeldine, trees, gr/gray on gr, mk, 1913, 4½x7" **1,600.00**

Vase, hibiscus, red/yel on bl, MIE, 4" **100.00**

Vase, hibiscus on cobalt & gr, bulbous, 7½" **450.00**

Vase, Moonlit Blue, landscape on cobalt, WM, MIE, #M94, 8½" ...**2,395.00**

Vase, orchid band on cobalt, shouldered, 5¼" **325.00**

Vase, orchids, mc on bl to red flambe, mk, 3½" **220.00**

Vase, orchids on bl-gr to cobalt, paper label, 5" **250.00**

Vase, orchids on gr to bl, 3" **210.00**

Vase, pansies on cobalt, England, 4" **250.00**

Vase, pomegranates, WM, ca 1928-49, 4½" **325.00**

Vase, pomegranates on bl to brn, MIE/paper label, #d, 9" **650.00**

Vase, pomegranates on cobalt, fluted cylinder, 1913-16, 13" ..**1,500.00**

Vase, pomegranates on cobalt, shouldered, MIE, #101, 12", NM ...**475.00**

Vase, pomegranates on cobalt, silver #10015 neck/rim, #101, 12" ...**1,300.00**

Vase, spring flowers on gr to bl, WM, 1928-49, 9" **750.00**

Vase, swans, blk & wht on gr pond, WM, MIE, 7" **220.00**

Vase, tulips on purple to bl, MH/WM, MIE, 7½" **125.00**

Vase, wisteria band on bl, WM, MIE, 8" **450.00**
Vase, wisteria on cobalt, MIE, #74, 12" **850.00**

Moravian Pottery and Tile Works

The Moravian Pottery and Tile Works, Doylestown, Pennsylvania, was founded by Dr. Henry Chapman Mercer in 1898. He discovered the art and science of tile making on his own, without training from the existing American or European tile industry. This, along with his diverse talents as an author, anthropologist, historian, and artist, led Dr. Mercer to create something very unique. He approached tile design with an historic point of view, and he created totally new production methods that ultimately became widely accepted by manufacturers of handcrafted tile. The subject matter for the designs he preferred included nature and the arts, colonial tools and artifacts, storytelling, and medieval themes. Both of these 'new' approaches (to design and production) allowed Dr. Mercer to become extremely influential in the development of pottery and tile in the Arts & Crafts Movement in America.

After Mercer's death in 1930, the Tile Works was managed by Frank Swain until 1954. In 1967 it was purchased by the Bucks County Dept. of Parks & Recreation. Tiles are being produced there today in the handmade tradition of Mercer; they are marked with a conjoined MOR and dated. Collectors look for the early tiles (mostly pre-1940), the preponderance of which bear no backstamps. These tiles were made using both red and white clays and are also referred to as 'Mercer' tiles. Our advisor for this category is Karen Guido; she is listed in the Directory under Connecticut.

Aquarius, zodiac, gr w/red flush high glaze, V border, 4" **60.00**
Cancer, pierced & notched, gr high glaze, red clay, 4¼" **75.00**
Column Base stove tile, yel/gr w/red high glaze, 5½x7", NM **225.00**
Cutting Tree, bl/cream w/red flush high glaze, 4" **70.00**
Dipping Candles, bl/wht unglazed, filigree border, 4" **65.00**
Doylestown Rotary 1924-49, bl/cream w/red flush high glaze, 4" ..**45.00**
Dragon lg brocade, red clay w/bl high glaze, 5x4" **78.00**
Lattice Border Margam Abbey, cream/bl, red clay, 5½x2½" **52.00**
Mayflower ship, bl/wht unglazed, circle & flower border, 4" **65.00**
Plus Ultra, cream/bl high glaze, red clay, 5" **100.00**
Prioress, gr/yel high glaze, red clay, 4", NM **80.00**
Priscilla, red clay w/gr high glaze, 4" **70.00**
Reaper, gr/cream w/red flush high glaze, 4" **85.00**
Sagittarius sm brocade, olive gr high glaze **50.00**
Taurus, gr matt & red clay, 3x4" **40.00**
Wheel of Castle Acre, bl w/red flush, 2¾" **30.00**

Morgantown Glass

Incorporated in 1899, the Morgantown Glass Works experienced many name changes over the years. Today 'Morgantown Glass' is a generic term used to identify all glass produced there. Purchased by Fostoria in 1965, the factory was permanently closed in 1971.

Adam etch, crystal/gr; stem, goblet; #7606½ Athena, 9-oz **120.00**
Adonis etch, topaz; stem, goblet; #7604½ Heirloom, 9-oz **70.00**
Am Beauty etch, crystal; tumbler, iced tea; #8701 Garret, 14-oz ..**45.00**
Am Beauty etch, rose; stem, goblet; #7565 Astrid, 10-oz **125.00**
Art Moderne, cobalt/crystal; stem, cordial; #7640, 1½-oz **155.00**
Baden etch, crystal/blk; jug, ftd, #49 Jubilee, 54-oz **500.00**
Barley #7637, gr/cased Alabaster/gr; tumbler, ftd, 13-oz **95.00**
Candlespheres, Old Amethyst; #8 Mars, pr **300.00**
Carlton frostie etch, crystal; punch bowl, #21, 12" **650.00**
Cherry Blossom etch, topaz; stem, goblet; #7577 Venus, 9-oz **75.00**

Crinkle, crystal; Tiajuana, juice/martini, #1962, 34-oz **70.00**
Crinkle, peacock bl; tumbler, juice; flat, #1962, 6-oz **26.00**
Eileen etch, crystal/gold #32 band; goblet; #7673 Lexington, 9-oz .**125.00**
Faun etch, crystal/blk; champagne, #7640 Art Moderne, 5½-oz .**160.00**

Floret etch icer/insert (the only icer to ever surface), crystal, $110.00.

Photo courtesy Jerry Gallagher

Golf Ball, cobalt/crystal; stem, goblet; #7643, 9-oz **58.00**
Golf Ball, rose/gr finial; candy dish, flat, #2938 Helga, 5" **745.00**
Golf Ball, ruby/crystal; stem, goblet; #7643, 9-oz **58.00**
Guest set, Golden Iris; hdls, pulled spout, #23 Margaret **450.00**
Kyoto etch, crystal/gr; stem, goblet; #7634 Tiburon, 9-oz **150.00**
LeMons, cobalt/platinum; stem, goblet; #7640 Art Moderne, 9-oz ..**250.00**
LMX (El Mexicano), Rose Quartz; Ockner jug, #1933, 54-oz **340.00**
LMX (El Mexicano), Seawood; decanter, liquor; w/stopper, #1933 ..**275.00**
Marilyn etch, crystal/rose; stem, champagne; #7636 Square, 5½-oz ..**135.00**
Melon, frosted/blk hdl, Aurora etch; jug, #20069 ....**725.00**
Monroe #7690, Old Amethyst/crystal; stem, cordial, 1½-oz **145.00**
Nasreen etch, topaz/crystal; stem, claret; #7665 Laura, 5-oz **95.00**
Old English #7678, Stiegel Green/crystal; stem, iced tea; 12-oz **58.00**
Palm Optic, Anna Rose/gr; stem, wine; #7614 Hampton, 3-oz **95.00**
Palm Optic, Venetian Green; stem, goblet; #7577 Venus, 9-oz **50.00**
Peacock Optic, gr or rose; stem, goblet; #7638 Avalon, 9-oz **48.00**
Pickardy etch, crystal; stem, goblet; #7646 Sophisticate, 9-oz **60.00**
Pygon #7623, crystal/blk; sherbet, 5-oz **110.00**
Reyer Thistle, crystal; stem, wine; #7668 Galaxy, 2½-oz **45.00**
Rosamonde etch, pnt crystal/Golden Iris; tumbler, #9074, 10-oz ..**165.00**
Sharon etch, crystal/platinum; candlespheres, #8 Mars, pr **325.00**
Square #7636, claret, DC Thorpe decor, 4½-oz **265.00**
Tinker Bell, crystal; guest set, #24 Maria, 4-pc, very rare **785.00**
Versailles, crystal; stem, goblet; #7711 Callahan, 10-oz **50.00**
Yale, #7684, cobalt or ruby; stem, goblet; 9-oz **165.00**

Continental Line

Ashley #4354, Golden Iris/crystal rim; basket, ftd, 10" dia **375.00**
Jennie #20, Aquamarine/crystal hdl; basket, bonbon; 4½" dia **500.00**
Patrick #4358, all crystal; basket, flower; 8-crimp, 6" dia **325.00**
Vienna #71, Stiegel Green; bowl, console; Italian base, 12" **1,000.00**

Sunrise Medallion Etch

#37 Barry, crystal; jug, ftd, 80-oz **635.00**
#53 Serenade, Azure; vase, bud; bulbous, ftd, 10" **480.00**
#7630 Ballerina, rose; stem, goblet; 9-oz **85.00**
#7654½ Legacy, crystal/Moonstone; stem, cocktail; 3-oz **195.00**
#7664 Queen Anne, crystal; stem, goblet; 10-oz **125.00**

Mortars and Pestles

Mortars are bowl-shaped vessels used for centuries for the purpose of grinding drugs to a powder or grain into meal. The masher or grinding device is called a pestle.

Ash burl, ca 1800, 7x6¼", w/trn pestle 275.00
Bronze, circular base w/flared rim, 1800s, 3½x4", w/7" pestle 190.00
Bronze, incised lines, 1800s, 3x4", w/pestle 115.00
Ironstone, wht, mini 45.00
Walnut w/19 incised lines, trn, 19th C, 6½x4½", w/10" pestle ..115.00
Wood, ovoid w/rnd base, 7x5¾", +pestle w/'button' finial 100.00
Wood, trn ovoid w/old red pnt, 12½", w/pestle 160.00

Mortens Studio

Oscar Mortens was already established as a fine sculptural artist when he left his native Sweden to take up residency in Arizona. During the 1940s he developed a line of detailed animal figures which were distributed through the Mortens Studios, a firm he co-founded with Gunnar Thelin. Thelin hired and trained artists to produce Mortens' line, which he called Royal Designs. More than two hundred dogs were modeled and over one hundred horses. Cats and wild animals such as elephants, panthers, deer, and elk were made, but on a much smaller scale. Bookends with sculptured dog heads were shown in their catalogs, and collectors report finding wall plaques on rare occasions. The material they used was a plaster-type composition with wires embedded to support the weight. Examples were marked 'Copyright by the Mortens Studio' either in ink or decal. Watch for flaking, cracks, and separations. Crazing seems to be present in some degree in many examples. When no condition is indicated, the items listed below are assumed to be in near-mint condition, allowing for minor crazing.

Airedale, standing, blk & tan, #741, 5¾x4¾" 95.00
Bassett Hound, standing, blk & wht w/tan, #878, 3¼x5¼" 95.00
Bookends, lions, recumbent, pr 150.00
Boston Bull Terrier pup, blk & wht, rnd stamp, #838, 3½" 75.00
Boxer, male, fawn, rnd & oval stickers, #780, 6½" 100.00
Boxer dog, sitting, 4½" 70.00
Boxer pup, sitting, rnd stamp, #823, 3" 65.00
Chihuahua, rnd sticker, #777A, 5½", EX+ 85.00
Chihuahua pup, sitting, blk & tan, #865, 3½" 65.00
Chinchilla Persian cat, cream, rnd & oval stickers, #912, 6" L ...100.00
Cocker Spaniel, begging, red, #764, 5" 75.00
Cocker Spaniel pup, sitting, blk, #820, 3¼" 65.00
Collie, sitting, tan & cream, #791, 5¾" 95.00
Collie, standing, tan & cream, #759A, 6" 100.00
Collie, wall plaque 195.00
Dachshund, red, #886B, 3½x6" L 85.00
Dalmatian pup, sitting, #812, 3¼" 65.00
English Bulldog pup, cream & blk, #832 ....75.00
English Setter, wall plaque, #9507 ....160.00
Fox Terrier, tan & cream, smooth coat, #772B, 5¼" 75.00
French Poodle, cream, French cut, #788, 3½x4" 95.00
German Shepherd, sitting, gray & blk, #756, 6½" 100.00
German Shepherd, standing, tan & blk, #755, 6½" 100.00
German Shepherd pup, cream & blk, #844, 3½" 65.00
Horse, blk, running, #112E 100.00
Horse, chestnut, running, #550, 3¾x5½" 85.00
Horse, filly, chestnut brn, #716, 8½" 95.00
Horse, golden-brn, running, #724, 7" L 100.00
Horse, gray, #652, 4½x5" 85.00
Horse, palomino, rearing, 9" 110.00
Horse, stallion, rearing, blk, #662, 4¾" 95.00
Irish Setter pup, 3" 35.00
Lion, recumbent, 4x6" 135.00
Lynx 175.00
Pekingese, standing, red & tan, #740, 4½x3½" 100.00
Persian cat, standing, gray & cream, #908 ....95.00

Wire Hair Terrier, begging, #557, rare, 3" 165.00

Morton Pottery

Six potteries operated in Morton, Illinois, at various times from 1877 to 1976. Each traced its origin to six brothers who immigrated to America to avoid military service in Germany. The Rapp brothers established their first pottery near clay deposits on the south side of town where they made field tile and bricks. Within a few years, they branched out to include utility wares such as jugs, bowls, jars, pitchers, etc. During the ninety-nine years of pottery operations in Morton, the original factory was expanded by some of the sons and nephews of the Rapps. Other family members started their own potteries where artware, gift-store items, and special-order goods were produced. The Cliftwood Art Pottery and the Morton Pottery Company had showrooms in Chicago and New York City during the 1930s. All of Morton's potteries were relatively short-lived operations with the Morton Pottery Company being the last to shut down on September 8, 1976. For a more thorough study of the subject, we recommend *Morton's Potteries: 99 Years, Vols. I and II*, by Doris and Burdell Hall; their address can be found in the Directory under Illinois.

Morton Pottery Works — Morton Earthenware Co. (1877 – 1917)

Bean pot, yel ware, ind, ½-pt 30.00
Bean pot, yel ware, ind, ¼-pt 20.00
Coffeepot, brn Rockingham, ind, ¾-pt 40.00
Coffeepot, brn Rockingham, 5-pt 130.00
Pie baker, yel ware, 10" 125.00
Teapot, pear shape, yel ware, 1-cup 50.00
Teapot, Rebecca at the Well, brn Rockingham, 8½-pt 150.00
Teapot, restaurant, brn, nesting, w/lid, 3-pc 60.00

Cliftwood Art Potteries, Inc. (1920 – 1940)

Figurine, Billiken doll, brn, 11" 100.00
Figurine, bulldog, Nero, gray drip, 11" 95.00
Figurine, German Shepherd reclining, brn drip, 11" 150.00
Lamp, ball-shape jug w/single hdl, pk/orchid drip, 7" ...70.00
Lamp, dougnut shape w/clock insert, brn drip, 11" 150.00
Lamp, Egyptian design, snake/fish hdls, cobalt, 30" ...125.00
Lamp, Egyptian design, 2-hdl, bl/gray drip, 8¼" 60.00
Pretzel jar, bbl shape, brn drip, 7½" 75.00
Vase, bud; brn drip, 6" 25.00
Vase, fan shape w/brass-knuckle hdls, cobalt, 9" 40.00
Vase, heron figural, turq matt, 6" 20.00
Vase, tree trunk form, Herbage Green, 8¼" 60.00

Midwest Potteries, Inc. (1940 – 1944)

Figurine, baseball player, batter, gray uniform, 7¼" ..300.00
Figurine, baseball player, catcher, wht uniform, 6¾" ..275.00
Figurine, baseball player, umpire, blk suit & cap, 6¼" ..250.00

Figurine, canary pair on stump, yellow with gold decor, 4½", $30.00.

Photo courtesy Doris and Burdell Hall

Figurine, cockatoo, gr/yel/brn spray, 8½" 25.00
Figurine, crane, gr/yel spray, 11" 35.00
Figurine, flying fish, bl/yel spray, 9" 35.00
Figurine, flying sea gull, wht/gold decor, 12" 40.00
TV lamp, owl w/spread wings, Kron mk, 12" 75.00
TV lamp, Pug & Poodle, Kron mk, 14" 90.00
TV lamp, Siamese cats (pr), Kron mk, 13" 65.00
TV lamp, Teddy bear, Kron mk, 10" 80.00

Morton Pottery Company (1922 – 1976)

Bookends, books (2 open), pr 14.00
Bookends, 4 closed books w/Atlas attached, pr 20.00
Bookends, 4 closed books w/baby shoes attached, pr 18.00
Christmas item, Santa cigarette box, hat is ashtray 25.00
Christmas item, Santa w/gold bell stands by blk cauldron 22.00
Christmas item, Santa-face plate, 12" 50.00
Head vase, '20s hairstyle, wide floppy-brim hat 60.00
Head vase, '40s hairstyle, pillbox hat 50.00
Head vase, Betty Grable type 35.00
Planter, dog figure on pr rockers 18.00
Planter, hen figure on pr rockers 16.00
Planter, horse figure on pr rockers 16.00
Planter, pig figure on pr rockers 18.00
Planter, rooster figure on pr rockers 16.00

American Art Potteries (1947 – 1963)

TV lamp, rearing horse, green and black, #327, 9x8x6", $40.00.

Photo courtesy Doris and Burdell Hall

Figurine, deer w/antlers, leaping, wht w/gold, #502 ....40.00
Figurine, fawn, leaping, gr/brn spray, #503 ....30.00
Figurine, horse, leaping, brn/tan spray, #504 ....35.00
Figurine, squirrel sitting erect, brn/gr spray, #311 ....20.00
Figurine, tiger roaring, natural spray colors, #456 ....40.00
Planter, elephant w/curved trunk, #94E 18.00
Planter, lamb w/pk bow, #456D 25.00
Planter, swan, pk/mauve w/gold, #391G 27.00
TV lamp, doe w/fawn, gr/yel spray, #322J 40.00
TV lamp, fish w/extended dorsal fin, bl/wht spray, #328U 30.00

Mosaic Tile Co.

The Mosaic Tile Company was organized in 1894 in Zanesville, Ohio, by Herman Mueller and Karl Langenbeck, both of whom had years of previous experience in the industry. They developed a faster, less-costly method of potting decorative tile, utilizing paper patterns rather than copper molds. By 1901 the company had grown and expanded with offices in many major cities. Faience tile was introduced in 1918, greatly increasing their volume of sales. They also made novelty ashtrays, figural boxes, bookends, etc., though not to any large extent. Until they closed during the 1960s, Mosaic used various marks that included the company name or their initials — 'MT' superimposed over 'Co.' in a circle. See also Tiles.

Bowl, console; bl-gr, hand thrown, low, 1½x11x7" 16.00
Box, dog figure reclines on lid, gr gloss/rust matt, 3½x8" 265.00
Box, turtle form, brn-gr w/bl inside, 4¼x3" 48.00
Brush holder, lav, fireplace form, mk 70.00
Figurine, bear, blk on dk gr matt, 5½x9½" 155.00
Tile, African boy profile w/yel halo on cobalt, 5¾"+fr 295.00
Tile, Lincoln in low relief, bl & wht, 6-sided, 3½" 50.00
Tile, sailboat in low relief, bl & wht, 6" 20.00
Tile, Teddy Roosevelt, mc transfer, 4¼" 140.00
Tile, Vice President Marshall, wht on bl, 6-sided, 1916 ....50.00

Moser

Ludwig Moser began his career as a struggling glass artist, catering to the rich who visited the famous Austrian health spas. His talent and popularity grew and in 1857 the first of his three studios opened in Karlsbad, Czechoslovakia. The styles developed there were entirely his own; no copies of other artists have ever been found. Some of his original designs include grapes with trailing vines, acorns and oak leaves, and richly enameled, deeply cut or carved floral pieces. Sometimes jewels were applied to the glass as well. Moser's animal scenes reflect his careful attention to detail. Famed for his birds in flight, he also designed stalking tigers and large, detailed elephants, all created in fine enameling.

Moser died in 1916, but the business was continued by his two sons who had been personally and carefully trained by their father. The Moser company bought the Meyr's Neffe Glassworks in 1922 and continued to produce quality glassware.

When identifying Moser, look for great clarity in the glass; deeply carved, continuous engravings; perfect coloration; finely applied enameling (often covered with thin gold leaf); and well-polished pontils. Our advisor for this category is Don Williams; he is listed in the Directory under Missouri. Items described below are enameled unless noted otherwise.

Bottle, scent; cobalt w/floral, matching stopper, 9½" 220.00
Bowl, amber w/gold warrior band, faceted, 4½x9" 460.00
Bowl, lav to clear, intaglio floral, oval, 7½" 480.00
Bowl, sapphire bl w/clear appl ft, HP/gilt floral, 8" 200.00
Box, amber, gilt warrior band, floral on lid, 1¾x3½" dia 250.00
Cordial, frosted w/gilt etched cherubs & animals, dk bl rim 80.00
Cracker jar, amethyst to pk, poppies/gold bees, silver mts 625.00
Cruet, wine; amethyst to clear, gold band w/flowers, 7¾" 195.00
Decanter, gr to clear, gold scrolls/swags, acorn stopper, 9" 400.00
Decanter, pk to wht to clear w/t'prints & leaves, 10" 250.00
Ewer, clear w/yel netted scrolls & ruby panels, gilt trim, 12" 275.00
Fernery, dk amethyst w/Invt T'print & florals, 7" dia 400.00
Finger bowl, amber w/gold ovals & flowers, jewels, +plate 200.00
Finger bowl, pk rims, scrolls/flowers, 4-fold rim, +plate 475.00
Pitcher, topaz w/floral, teal-bl angle hdl/3 prunts, 7½" 375.00
Pokal, amethyst, cut/faceted, floral w/gold, 8", pr 1,200.00
Sherbet, lt gr w/raised gold florals, 4¼", +underplate 225.00
Tumbler, amethyst to clear, intaglio floral, 8 panels, 4¾" 175.00
Tumbler, juice; cranberry w/butterflies/flowers 75.00
Vase, amber w/2 bl salamanders, bl drips at rim, metal ft, 12" 325.00
Vase, amethyst to clear, gilt/cut lotus/fish at arched rim, 16" 1,300.00
Vase, amethyst to clear, intaglio poppy, metal rim, sqd, 4" 225.00
Vase, amethyst to clear, pansies/gilt ferns, cylinder, 12" 400.00
Vase, bands of bl/yel/ivory w/florals alternate, 11½" 385.00
Vase, clear to apricot w/gold trim, sq, 12" 250.00
Vase, clear w/opal panel w/lady's portrait, allover gilt, 9" 150.00

Vase, cobalt, florals/gold, 12½" **220.00**
Vase, cranberry, stylized gilt florals, 12½" **275.00**
Vase, cranberry w/gold florals & scrolls, stick neck, 11" **165.00**
Vase, dk gr to clear, vaseline ft, much gold, 14" **300.00**
Vase, electric bl w/appl fish, pnt plants, ribbed/ftd, 9½" **450.00**
Vase, gr w/daisies, gold rim band, 12" **300.00**
Vase, heavy crystal w/allover mc butterflies & flowers, 4" **125.00**
Vase, jewels/seed pearls in gold cartouche w/gold filigree, 12½" .**300.00**
Vase, opal w/appl salamander & icicles, 3 ball ft, 11" **500.00**
Vase, red Venetian, goddess Diana w/much gold, trumpet form, 10" ..**450.00**
Vase, rubena swirl w/florals, 14½" **165.00**
Vase, ruby to clear, facet cuttings, ped ft, sgn, 4" **125.00**
Vase, teal w/gold leaves+2 acorns, flared stick neck, 13½" **475.00**
Vase, vaseline w/gold Amazon women band, goblet form, 6" **400.00**
Vase, wht frost to cranberry, florals, 10" **300.00**

Moss Rose

Moss Rose was a favorite dinnerware pattern of many Staffordshire and American potters from the mid-1800s. In America the Wheeling Pottery of West Virginia produced the ware in large quantities, and it became one of their bestsellers, remaining popular well into the '90s.

Bone dish, unmk, gold edge **32.00**
Butter pat, Meakin **16.00**
Cake plate, open hdls, unmk **60.00**
Coffeepot, dolphin hdl, 7" **70.00**
Creamer, child sz **25.00**
Cup & saucer, child sz **20.00**
Cup & saucer, demitasse; ornate hdl & ft **20.00**
Gravy tureen, w/lid & undertray, Haviland **125.00**
Plate, Powell Bishop, 9" **25.00**
Plate, unmk, 7½" **10.00**
Platter, rectangular, Meakin, 14x10" **42.00**
Shaving mug, unmk **35.00**

Sugar bowl with lid, Alfred Meakin, 5", $50.00.

Tea set, child sz, 15-pc **275.00**
Tea set, Japan, 16-pc+lids **75.00**
Tray, tiered, unmk **32.00**
Wash pitcher & bowl, Meakin, 12½" **400.00**
Wash pitcher & bowl, unmk, 11" pitcher+13½" bowl **300.00**

Mother-of-Pearl Glass

Mother-of-Pearl glass was a type of mold-blown satin art glass popular during the last half of the 19th century. A patent for its manufacture was issued in 1886 to Frederick S. Shirley, and one of the companies who produced it was the Mt. Washington Glass Company of New Bedford, Massachusetts. Another was the English firm of Stevens and Williams. Its delicate patterns were developed by blowing the gather into a mold with inside projections that left an intaglio design on the surface of the glass, then sealing the first layer with a second, trapping air in the recesses. Most common are the Diamond Quilted, Raindrop, and Herringbone patterns. It was made in several soft colors, the most rare and valuable is rainbow — a blend of rose, light blue, yellow, and white. Occasionally it may be decorated with coralene, enameling, or gilt. Watch for 20th-century reproductions, especially in the Diamond Quilted pattern. Our advisors for this category are Betty and Clarence Maier; they are listed in the Directory under Pennsylvania. See also Coralene.

Basket, Herringbone, pk, crimped/ruffled, pinched hdl, 5¾" **290.00**
Bonbon, Dmn Quilt, wht/clear alternate, wide ruffle, Pat, 9" **450.00**
Bowl, Dmn Quilt, bl, 3 frosted thorny ft, ruffled, 4½x5⅞" **395.00**
Bowl, Dmn Quilt, lt bl w/mica, vaseline appl ft, 4x5½" **175.00**
Bowl, Dmn Quilt, wht, appl stems/flowers, att Webb, 5x6" **550.00**
Bowl, Herringbone, bl w/pk int, melon ribs, ruffled, 2¼x4½" **300.00**
Bowl, salad; Ribbon, shaded gold, 8¾", +spoon & fork **695.00**
Celery vase, Dmn Quilt, bl, tightly crimped rim, 4¾" **235.00**
Creamer, Dmn Quilt, rainbow, sq top, frosted hdl, 2¾" **950.00**
Creamer & sugar bowl, Ribbon, sky bl, 2½"; 2⅛" **375.00**
Cruet, Dmn Quilt, bl, floral, camphor thorn hdl/stopper, 7½" **725.00**
Cruet, Herringbone, rainbow, dbl-knob neck, cut stopper, 8" .**1,500.00**
Cruet, Herringbone, rainbow (EX color), 3-lobe rim, 8" **1,350.00**
Cup & saucer, Invt T'print, pk, camphor hdl, cup: 3" **175.00**
Ewer, Dmn Quilt, pk, melon ribs, crimped/ruffled, 11" **175.00**
Ewer, Herringbone, pk, tricon rim, pear form, camphor hdl, 9" ..**225.00**
Ewer, Herringbone, rainbow, bulb w/knob neck, 3-lobe rim, 10" ..**750.00**
Finger bowl, Dmn Quilt, yel, crimped, 2¼" H, +6½" tray **225.00**
Jam dish, Dmn Quilt, bl, tightly ruffled, +SP holder, Webb **295.00**
Lamp, Dmn Quilt, rainbow ruffled 10" shade/font; brass base .**2,800.00**
Lamp, Swirl, yel 6" ruffled shade; 3-ftd brass base w/prisms **195.00**
Pitcher, Dmn Quilt, bl, bulbous w/heart-shape lip, 8½" **250.00**
Pitcher, Dmn Quilt, yel, squat w/sqd rim, camphor reed hdl, 5" .**300.00**
Plate, Drape, rose to wht, mk Pat, 7" **145.00**
Rose bowl, Dmn Quilt, rainbow, crystal vertical stripes, 3" **400.00**
Rose bowl, Dmn Quilt, rainbow, mk Pat, 3" **600.00**
Rose bowl, Dmn Quilt, rose, mk Pat, 3½" **200.00**
Rose bowl, Dmn Quilt, rose, mk Pat, 4" **450.00**
Rose bowl, Dmn Quilt, shaded brn, 8-crimp, Webb, 3x3" **375.00**
Rose bowl, Herringbone, bl, 6-crimp, 4x3⅜" **185.00**
Rose bowl, Ribbon, bl, irregular ruffled rim, 3" **100.00**
Rose bowl, Ribbon, bl, 9-crimp rim, 2½x3¾" **235.00**
Rose bowl, Ribbon, wht on clear frosted wafer ft, 3x2½" **110.00**
Rose bowl, Swirl, red to almond, pleated rim, Stevens & Wms, 5" ..**400.00**
Sweetmeat, Flower & Acorn, med bl, squatty, silver mts **275.00**
Toothpick holder, Dmn Quilt, bl, ruffled rim, camphor trim, 3" ...**250.00**
Toothpick holder, Dmn Quilt, rainbow, 2¼" **675.00**
Tumbler, Coin Spot, pk/bl rainbow, 3¾" **200.00**
Tumbler, Dmn Quilt, bright yel, Mt WA, 4" **165.00**
Tumbler, Dmn Quilt, pk, bird on branch/berries, 4" **150.00**
Tumbler, Dmn Quilt, rainbow w/floral branch, 3½" **885.00**
Tumbler, Herringbone, dk to lt pk, 3¾x2⅝" **175.00**
Vase, Coin Spot, bl, ruffled, 8x4½" **375.00**
Vase, Coin Spot, pk/wht, gold floral/butterfly, stick neck, 12" ...**450.00**
Vase, Coin Spot, rainbow, ribbed/squatty, 3-fold rim, 14" **1,250.00**
Vase, Dmn Quilt, bl, 3-lobe rim w/amber trim, 7" **160.00**
Vase, Dmn Quilt, pk, camphor leaf hdls, cup rim, 10½" **150.00**
Vase, Dmn Quilt, pk, ftd ovoid w/knob neck, crimped flange, 7½" .**225.00**
Vase, Dmn Quilt, rainbow, bulbous w/knob neck, 3-lobe rim, 6" ..**650.00**
Vase, Dmn Quilt, rose, pear-form body, stick neck, 7¾" **300.00**
Vase, Dmn Quilt, rose to pk, ruffled, M hdls, Mt WA, 6½x6" **750.00**
Vase, Dmn Quilt, shaded rose, ruffled trumpet neck, Mt WA, 9" ..**400.00**
Vase, Herringbone, apricot w/floral & gilt, bottle form, 6" **200.00**

Vase, Herringbone, lt bl w/threading, Northwood/England, 8" ..450.00
Vase, Herringbone, wht w/clear threading o/l, pk int, 7" 275.00
Vase, jack-in-pulpit; Dmn Quilt, rainbow, clear base, Pat, 10" ..450.00
Vase, jack-in-pulpit; Raindrop, butterscotch, frosted ruffle, 7⅜" ..200.00
Vase, Moire, pk, 4" 175.00
Vase, Muslin, wht, melon rib, frosted edge, Mt WA, 6x5½" 425.00
Vase, peachblow o/l w/3 appl wht flowers, gr/amber branch, 8" ..300.00
Vase, Raindrop, amber, bulbous w/ruffled tricon rim, 8" 125.00
Vase, Raindrop, apricot, melon ribs, camphor tricon rim, 5½" ...250.00
Vase, Raindrop, bl, frosted at top, 7½x4¼" 165.00
Vase, Raindrop, butterscotch, flared petal rim, brass ft, 7½" 210.00
Vase, Raindrop, dk gold, crimped camphor edge, Mt WA, 9x3½" .285.00
Vase, Raindrop, med bl, melon ribs, Mt WA, 5x4" 275.00
Vase, Ribbon, chartreuse, frosted wafer ft, 2½x2¾" 185.00
Vase, Ribbon, chartreuse, rectangular rim over emb ring, 2½" ...185.00
Vase, Ribbon, chartreuse w/gold prunus, bulbous base, Webb, 4" ..375.00
Vase, Snowflake, pk w/yel flowers, camphor hdls, 5½" 350.00
Vase, Swag, pk, lg/ornate camphor twig hdls, bulbous, 5" 375.00
Vase, Swirl, bl, melon ribs, ruffled rim, ormolu ft, 7x3" 195.00
Vase, Swirl, lav bl w/rose o/l, stick neck, Stevens & Wms, 9" 600.00
Vase, Swirl, pk, folded ruffled rim, 8½" 400.00
Vase, Swirl, rubena verde, stick neck, Stevens & Wms, 7½" 425.00
Vase, Verre Moire, pk, shouldered, 8x5" 450.00

Movie Memorabilia

Movie memorabilia covers a broad range of collectibles, from books and magazines dealing with the industry in general to the various promotional materials which were distributed to arouse interest in a particular film. Many collectors specialize in a specific area — posters, pressbooks, stills, lobby cards, or souvenir programs (also referred to as premiere booklets). In the listings below, a one-sheet poster measures approximately 27" x 41", three-sheet: 41" x 81", and six-sheet: 81" x 81". Window cards measure 14" x 22". Values are for examples in NM condition unless noted otherwise. See also Autographs; Cartoon Art; Paper Dolls; Personalities; Sheet Music.

Lobby card, *Forbidden Planet*, MGM, 1936, 11x14", complete set of eight, $1,300.00.

Insert card, Bad Boy, Audie Murphey, 1949 ....70.00
Insert card, Beach Ball, Edd Byrnes/Supremes/etc, 1965 ....60.00
Insert card, Big Combo, Cornel Wilde, 1955 ....70.00
Insert card, Bonnie Parker Story, Dorothy Provine, 1958 ....55.00
Insert card, Dr at Sea, Bardot pinup, 1956 ....50.00
Insert card, Dr Strangelove, Sellers/Scott, Kubrick, 1963 ....80.00
Insert card, Entertainer, L Olivier/J Plowright, 1960 ....45.00
Insert card, Fuller Brush Girl, Lucille Ball/Eddie Albert, 1950 ......55.00
Insert card, Hills of Home, E Gwenn/D Crisp/J Leigh, 1948 ....50.00
Insert card, Home of the Brave, James Edwards, 1949 ....55.00
Insert card, I Shot Jesse James, Don Barry, 1950 ....55.00
Insert card, Machine Gun Kelly, Charles Bronson, 1958 ....55.00
Insert card, Mrs Pollyfax Spy, Frazetta art, 1971 ....27.50
Insert card, Nob Hill, G Raft/J Bennett, 1945 ....70.00
Lobby card, Auntie Mame, Rosalind Russell, 1958 ....10.00

Lobby card, Bad Sister, Humphrey Bogart, 1931, rare 1,200.00
Lobby card, College Holiday, Martha Raye, 1936, jumbo sz 80.00
Lobby card, Damn Yankees, 1958 ....20.00
Lobby card, Duck Hunter, Billy Bevan, 1922 ....75.00
Lobby card, God's Little Acre, Aldo Ray/Robert Ryan, 1958 ....55.00
Lobby card, Howards of VA, Cary Grant, 1940 ....60.00
Lobby card, Left Hand of God, H Bogart/G Tierney, 1955 ....15.00
Lobby card, More Than a Secretary, Jean Arthur, 1936 ....35.00
Lobby card, Naked City, Barry Fitzgerald, 1947 ....32.00
Lobby card, Silver Lining, Maureen O'Sullivan, 1931 ....37.50
Lobby card, Smile Please, Harry Langdon, 1924 ....165.00
Lobby card, Soldier Arms, Charlie Chaplin, 1918, EX 150.00
Lobby card, Stagefright, R Todd/J Wyman/A Sim, 1950 ....35.00
Lobby card, There Goes My Girl, Ann Southern, RKO, 1937 ......17.50
Lobby card, Viva Marie, Bridgette Bardot, 1965 ....8.00
Lobby card set, Buster Keaton Story, D O'Connor, 1957, ½-sheet ..42.50
Lobby card set, Colossus of NY, 1958 ....175.00
Lobby card set, Devil's Harvest, marijuana film, 1948 ....185.00
Lobby card set, Human Desire, Glenn Ford/Gloria Graham, 1954 ..60.00
Lobby card set, Kill the Umpire, Wm Bendix, 1950 ....115.00
Lobby card set, Li'l Abner, color reissue, 1948 ....45.00
Lobby card set, Macabre, printed insurance policy, 1958 ....65.00
Lobby card set, White Savage, Maria Montez, 1949 reissue 45.00
Movie book, Gone w/the Wind, soft cover, 1st edition 40.00
Poster, All These Women, Bibi Andersson, 1964, 1-sheet 55.00
Poster, Apartment, J Lemmon/S MacLaine, 1960, 1-sheet 55.00
Poster, Bambi, Cartoon artwork, 1966 re-release, 6-sheet 65.00
Poster, Blondie Goes Latin, A Lake/P Singleton, 1940, 1-sheet, EX ..70.00
Poster, Brannigan, John Wayne, 1971, 1-sheet 32.50
Poster, Calaboose, Hal Roach comedy, Jimmy Rogers, 1943, 27x41" ...40.00
Poster, Call of South Seas, Allan Lane/Janet Martin, 1-sheet 50.00
Poster, Captain Lightfoot, Rock Hudson, 1955, 1-sheet 48.00
Poster, Cardinal, Bass design, Preminger, 1964, 1-sheet 60.00
Poster, Dixie, Bing Crosby, litho art, 1943, 3-sheet, EX 80.00
Poster, Fabulous Suzanne, Rudy Vallee, 1946, 27x41" 35.00
Poster, Father's Little Dividend, S Tracy/E Taylor, 1951, 3-sheet ..125.00
Poster, Gambling Daughters, dice scene, 1943, 1-sheet 55.00
Poster, Girl in Every Port, Groucho Marx, Wm Bendix, 1952, 14x36" ..40.00
Poster, Grand Prix, James Garner/Eve Marie Saint, ½-sheet 55.00
Poster, Great American Pastime, Tom Ewell, 1956, 14x36" 35.00
Poster, I Was a Teenage Werewolf, M Landon, 1957, 1-sheet, EX 275.00
Poster, It Comes Up Love, Gloria Jean, D O'Connor, 1942, 27x41" ...45.00
Poster, It's In the Bag, Fred Allen, Jack Benny, 1952, 14x36" 40.00
Poster, Lady Sings the Blues, Diana Ross, 1972, 1-sheet 50.00
Poster, Movie Man, Jimmy Dorsey, 1948, 27x41" 45.00
Poster, Movie Struck, Laurel & Hardy, 1952, 27x41" 45.00
Poster, Mr Magoo's Holiday Festival, 1970, 1-sheet 35.00
Poster, My Son John, H Hayes/R Walker, 1952, 1-sheet 70.00
Poster, Night Wind, dog in field, stone litho, 1948, 1-sheet 65.00
Poster, Pickup Alley, Anita Ekberg, 1957, 1-sheet 30.00
Poster, Searchers, John Wayne, 1956, ½-sheet 350.00
Poster, Sergeant York, Gary Cooper, 1941, 1-sheet 475.00
Poster, Sound of Laughter, Crosby, Hope & Kaye, 1963, 27x41" ..35.00
Poster, Speedway, Elvis Presley/Nancy Sinatra, 1968, 40x60" 90.00
Poster, Stallion Road, R Reagan/A Smith, 1947, 1-sheet 95.00
Poster, Suddenly Last Summer, E Taylor in swimsuit, 1960, 3-sheet 275.00
Poster, Swingin' on a Rainbow, Harry Langdon images, 1943, 14x36" ..40.00
Poster, Undead, Roger Corman horror design, 1957, 1-sheet 135.00
Poster, Washington Melodrama, F Morgan, D Dailey, 27x41" 30.00
Poster, Wind & Lion, S Connery/C Bergen, 1975, 1-sheet 65.00
Poster, Woman's Prison, Cleo Moore & Ida Lupino, 1955, ½-sheet .50.00
Poster, Young Ideas, Mary Astor/Herbert Marshall, 1943, 1-sheet ..38.00
Pressbook, Further Perils of Laurel & Hardy, 1967, EX 25.00
Pressbook, Hey There It's Yogi Bear, 1964 ....22.50

Program, Fantasia **65.00**
Program, Gone w/the Wind premiere, December 15, 1939, M ...**100.00**
Souvenir book, Big Fisherman, hardcover, 1959 ....**25.00**
Souvenir book, On a Clear Day, Barbra Streisand, EX **15.00**
Souvenir book, Ten Commandments, color plates **20.00**
Title card, South Pacific, Mitzi Gaynor, 1959 ....**25.00**
Window card, Big Country, Gregory Peck/Charlton Heston, 1958 ..**48.00**
Window card, China, A Ladd/L Young, 1943 ....**80.00**
Window card, Daddy Long Legs, F Astaire/L Caron, 1955 ....**40.00**
Window card, Desiree, M Brando/J Simmons/M Oberon, 1954 ....**55.00**
Window card, Hustler, P Newman/J Gleason, 1961 ....**70.00**
Window card, It Happened to Jane, D Day/J Lemmon, 1958 ....**30.00**
Window card, King Creole, Elvis Presley, 1958, rare **150.00**
Window card, Lady Refuses, Betty Compson, 1921 ....**85.00**
Window card, Lost World, Claude Rains, 1960 ....**70.00**
Window card, Patton, George C Scott, 1970 ....**40.00**
Window card, Rosemary's Baby, M Farrow, 1968 ....**48.00**
Window card, Sweepstakes, Eddie Quillan comedy, 1930 ....**55.00**
Window card, War & Peace, Audrey Hepburn/Henry Fonda, 1956 ....**60.00**
Window card, White Christmas, Crosby/Kaye/Clooney/Ellen, 1954 ...**80.00**

Mt. Washington

The Mt. Washington Glass Works was founded in 1837 in South Boston, Massachusetts, but moved to New Bedford in 1869 after purchasing the facilities of the New Bedford Glass Company. Frederick S. Shirley became associated with the firm in 1874. Two years later the company reorganized and became known as the Mt. Washington Glass Company. In 1894 it merged with the Pairpoint Manufacturing Company, a small Brittania works nearby, but continued to conduct business under its own title until after the turn of the century. The combined plants were equipped with the most modern and varied machinery available and boasted a working force with experience and expertise rival to none in the art of blowing and cutting glass. In addition to their fine cut glass, they are recognized as the first American company to make cameo glass, an effect they achieved through acid-cutting methods. In 1885 Shirley was issued a patent to make Burmese, pale yellow glassware tinged with a delicate pink blush. Another patent issued in 1886 allowed them the rights to produce Rose Amber, or amberina, a transparent ware shading from ruby to amber. Pearl Satin Ware and Peachblow, so named for its resemblance to a rosy peach skin, were patented the same year. One of their most famous lines, Crown Milano, was introduced in 1893. It was an opal glass either free-blown or pattern-molded, tinted a delicate color and decorated with enameling and gilt. Royal Flemish was patented in 1894 and is considered the rarest of the Mt. Washington art glass lines. It was decorated with raised, gold-enameled lines dividing the surface of the ware in much the same way as lead lines divide a stained glass window. The sections were filled in with one or several transparent colors and further decorated in gold enamel with florals, foliage, beading, and medallions.

Our advisors for this category are Betty and Clarence Maier; they are listed in the Directory under Pennsylvania. See also Amberina; Cranberry; Salt Shakers; Burmese; Crown Milano; Mother of Pearl; Royal Flemish; etc.

Biscuit jar, florals on almond, egg form, floral-emb mts, 7½" **500.00**
Biscuit jar, gold acorns & leaves on pnt burmese, SP mts **900.00**
Biscuit jar, gold spider mums on peach & ivory, sqd, 6" **600.00**
Biscuit jar, gold wild roses, pk/yel shadow leaves, bowl form **950.00**
Biscuit jar, lace/tassels at shoulder, wht on pk/almond, 5" **375.00**
Biscuit jar, roses on opal, scalloped gr bands, SP mts, 7x7½" **725.00**
Bowl, cameo, griffins/scrolls/etc, bl on wht, 4x8" dia **1,475.00**
Bowl, columbines, wht/pk/gilt on frost, hdld oval, 12" L **225.00**

Bowl, snowball blossoms, wht on pnt burmese, scalloped, 6x7" ..**600.00**
Box, monk w/wine, mc on gr on opal w/gold, SP trim, 5¼" **550.00**
Box, rose on gr on opal w/gold, emb floral/ribbon, 4½x7" ...**1,750.00**
Candlesticks, portrait on maroon, SP mts, #6139, 8x4", pr ...**1,750.00**
Hatpin holder, forget-me-nots, mushroom form, 3x5½" **450.00**
Lamp, cameo, woman/baskets of flowers, 10" floral shade, 21" ..**8,500.00**
Lamp, 12" melon-rib floral shade/font; lg figural base, 24" **2,600.00**
Letter holder, wild roses on opal, emb floral, gilt mt w/cherub ...**875.00**
Mustard, oak leaves on pk on opal, metal lid/hdl, 3" **85.00**
Pitcher, wht w/bl wash ext, HP floral/gold, sq mouth, 9" **550.00**
Rose bowl, ivy/floral/gilt on clear, ribbed, folded rim, 4" **485.00**
Rose bowl, pansies, bl/lav on beige satin w/gold, 3½x4" **400.00**
Shaker, cockleshell, forget-me-nots on wht w/pk edge, 2¾" **600.00**
Shakers, Chick in Egg, floral on coral or lt pk, 2¼", pr **700.00**
Shakers, ferns/flowers on almond, fig shape, 2½", pr **325.00**
Shakers, floral on pk or gr, egg shape, 2¼", pr **150.00**
Shakers, leaves/berries on pk or bl, tomato shape, pr **175.00**
Sugar shaker, bouquets on tan-shaded frost, fig shape, 4" **1,450.00**
Sugar shaker, daisies, pastel on crystal frost, fig shape, 4" **1,700.00**
Sugar shaker, floral on pk on opal, sgn Canty, egg shape, 4¾" ...**425.00**
Sugar shaker, floral on pnt burmese, SP lid, tomato shape, 3x3½" ...**600.00**
Sugar shaker, leaves on lt bl, ostrich egg shape, 4¼" **475.00**
Syrup, violets on wht, 7½" **1,250.00**
Vase, Colonial, gold vines/bow on wht gloss, slim form, 12" **550.00**
Vase, floral, lt tones/gold on clear w/ribs, rim pulled 2X, 11" **635.00**
Vase, floral on apricot to almond satin, floriform neck, 9" **475.00**
Vase, jack-in-pulpit; lustreless wht, scattered flowers, 9½" **300.00**
Vase, Napoli, frog among bulrushes, 4-color w/gold, 8½x5" **1,000.00**
Vase, Napoli, mums/gold, ext: gold web, ribbed, #880, 10" **1,450.00**
Vase, Napoli, 2 chickens/gilt raindrops, scroll rim hdls, 8" **1,400.00**
Vase, windmill scene on pk opal w/gold, 9x5½" **375.00**

Mulberry China

Mulberry china was made by many of the Staffordshire area potters from about 1830 until the 1850s. It is a transfer-printed earthenware or ironstone named for the color of its decorations, a purplish-brown resembling the juice of the mulberry. Some pieces may have faded out over the years and today look almost gray with only a hint of purple. (Transfer printing was done in many colors; technically only those in the mauve tones are 'mulberry'; color variations have little effect on value.) Some of the patterns (Corean, Jeddo, Pelew, and Formosa, for instance) were also produced in Flow Blue ware. Others seem to have been used exclusively with the mulberry color. Our advisor for this category is Mary Frank Gaston.

Abbey, creamer **195.00**
Abbey, cup & saucer, handleless **70.00**
Abbey, pitcher, 8-sided, 7¼" **75.00**
Athens, gravy boat, Meigh **85.00**
Athens, pitcher, 6½" **85.00**
Athens, platter, Meigh, 15½" **225.00**
Bochara, bowl, vegetable; w/lid **375.00**
Bochara, plate, Edwards, 10" **80.00**
Bochara, platter, Edwards, 14" **200.00**
Bochara, platter, Edwards, 15¼" **250.00**
Bochara, sauce tureen, w/lid & ladle, John Edwards **650.00**
Calcutta, plate, 8½" **60.00**
Calcutta, teapot **275.00**
Castle Scenery, pitcher, 8" **425.00**
Corean, bowl & pitcher, NM **1,100.00**
Corean, cup & saucer, lg **100.00**
Corean, pitcher, 1½-qt, 8¾" **475.00**

Corean, plate, 8"	55.00
Corean, platter, Podmore Walker, 13½"	250.00
Corean, sauce boat	115.00
Corean, sugar bowl, Clementson	375.00
Cyprus, creamer, Davenport	250.00
Cyprus, platter, Davenport, 16"	300.00
Flora, platter, Walker, 15⅜"	250.00
Game, pitcher, 9", VG	185.00
Heath's Flower, platter, 14"	335.00
Hong, pitcher, 2-qt	500.00
Jeddo, bowl, covered vegetable; Gothic shape, Adams	550.00
Jeddo, cup & saucer, Adams	95.00
Jeddo, pitcher, Adams, 2-qt	435.00
Longport, plate, T&J Mayer, 9½"	25.00
Marble, creamer, 5½"	75.00
Medina, cup & saucer	65.00
Medina, sugar bowl, Furnival	195.00
Nankin, bowl, covered vegetable; 8-sided, Davenport, lg	395.00
Ning-Po, creamer, Hall	375.00
Ning-Po, platter, Hall, 15½"	275.00
Panama, creamer, Challinor	245.00
Pelew, bowl, vegetable; w/lid, Challinor	525.00
Pelew, cup & saucer, handleless; Challinor	75.00
Pelew, plate, Challinor, 7½"	45.00
Pelew, waste bowl, Challinor, 5½"	225.00
Peruvian, cup & saucer, handleless	70.00
Peruvian, honey dish, Wedge Wood	90.00
Rhone Scenery, coffeepot, Podmore Walker	400.00
Rhone Scenery, cup & saucer, Podmore Walker	70.00
Rhone Scenery, sauce tureen, w/underplate	250.00
Rose, fish sauce boat, hdls, Walker, rare	375.00
Rose, platter, Challinor, 14x11"	185.00
Seaweed, potty	270.00
Shapoo, cup plate	65.00
Susa, plate, Meigh, 10½"	55.00
Sydenham, creamer	130.00
Temple, bowl, vegetable; Podmore Walker, 7"	200.00
Temple, plate, Podmore Walker, 9¾"	90.00
Temple, tea tile, Podmore Walker	95.00
Tivoli, teapot	325.00
Vincennes, bowl, vegetable; w/lid	375.00
Vincennes, cup & saucer, handleless, Alcock, ca 1860	75.00
Vincennes, plate, 9½"	75.00
Vincennes, relish	180.00
Washington Vase, bowl & pitcher	750.00
Washington Vase, creamer, Podmore Walker	250.00
Washington Vase, plate, Podmore Walker, 10"	80.00
Washington Vase, plate, Podmore Walker, 9"	75.00
Washington Vase, sugar pot, lion's head hdls	240.00
Washington Vase, waste bowl, Podmore Walker	215.00
Wreath, bowl, covered vegetable; 11"	425.00

Muller Freres

Henri Muller established a factory in 1900 at Croismare, France. He produced fine cameo art glass decorated with florals, birds, and insects in the Art Nouveau style. The work was accomplished by acid engraving and hand finishing. Usual marks were 'Muller,' 'Muller Croismare,' or 'Croismare, Nancy.' In 1910 Henri and his brother Deseri formed a glassworks at Luneville. The cameo art glass made there was nearly all produced by acid cuttings of up to four layers with motifs similar to those favored at Croismare. A good range of colors was used, and some later pieces were gold flecked. Handles and decorative devices were sometimes applied by hand. In addition to the cameo glass, they also produced an acid-finished glass of bold mottled colors in the Deco style. Examples were signed 'Muller Freres' or 'Luneville.' Our advisor for this category is Don Williams; he is listed in the Directory under Missouri.

Cameo

Vase, aquatic plants/seashells, red on frost, 6"	1,650.00
Vase, crane/exotic trees/mtns, dk gr on yel/gr, dbl-gourd, 5"	1,800.00
Vase, cranes/water plants, red on frost, ftd egg shape, 5½"	1,200.00
Vase, Deco curvilinear design, champagne aventurine/amethyst, 8"	1,380.00
Vase, ferns/scrolls at rim, bl/amber-gr on pk spatter, 16"	2,600.00
Vase, forest w/deer at lake's edge, blk on red, 13½"	3,000.00
Vase, lakeside scene, blk/gr/orange/wht, flared rim, 9"	1,500.00
Vase, marsh/dragonflies, turq on yel/wht/bl mottle, 7½"	1,450.00
Vase, narcissus, gr on pk/almond mottle w/bl, 10½"	3,000.00
Vase, orchids, cut/HP on orange/wine, ovoid w/bun ft, 14"	1,840.00
Vase, trees, lake beyond, purple-blk on mauve/lav, hdls, 11x8"	6,000.00
Vase, trees/water, gr/blk-gr on lav mottle, pillow form, 5"	3,000.00
Vase, windmill on yel/brn, EX detail, 8¾x4"	1,450.00
Vase, wisteria, bl-blk on citron, elongated neck, 11½"	975.00

Miscellaneous

Bowl, yel-orange mottle w/red & royal bl rim, ftd, 2½x9"	500.00
Lamp, ceiling; Deco foliage in relief, clear/frosted, 14½" dia	1,600.00
Vase, dk gr, emb Deco African/elephant, pillow form, 5¾"	700.00
Vase, mottled orange/red/aubergine swirls, flared rim, 6½"	230.00
Vase, orange/rust/cobalt mottle, squatty, 3½"	135.00
Vase, red-orange to royal bl, clear cased, ftd, 13"	750.00

Muncie

The Muncie Pottery was established in Muncie, Indiana, by Charles O. Grafton; it operated there from 1922 until about 1935. The pottery they produced is made of a heavier clay than most of its contemporaries; the styles are sturdy and simple. Early glazes were bright and colorful. In fact, Muncie was advertised as the 'rainbow pottery.' Later most of the ware was finished in a matt glaze. The more collectible examples are those modeled after Consolidated Glass vases — sculptured with lovebirds, grasshoppers, and goldfish. Their line of Art Deco-style vases bear a remarkable resemblance to the Consolidated Glass Company's Ruba Rombic line. Vases, candlesticks, bookends, ashtrays, bowls, lamp bases, and luncheon sets were made. A line of garden pottery was manufactured for a short time. Items were frequently impressed with MUNCIE in block letters. Letters such as A, K, E, or D and the numbers 1, 2, 3, 4, or 5 often found scratched into the base are finishers' marks.

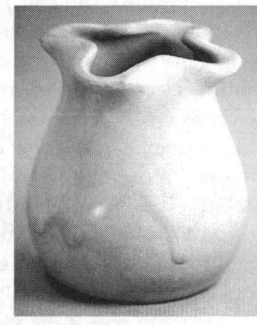

Vase, green/lavender drips with ruffled top, #413, 4", $65.00.

Basket, bl/rose, rnd w/hdl, #175, 6½x7½"	825.00

Basket, gr/rose, oval w/hdl, #174, 7½x12" 550.00
Bookends, owls, matt gr/rose, #257, 5x6½", pr 325.00
Canoe, matt bl/rose, w/insert, #255, 11½" 275.00
Pitcher, blk matt, #428, 6" 75.00
Vase, bittersweet, pillow form, hdls, #192-9, 8½x9" 300.00
Vase, bl gloss, pillow form, hdls, #192-6, 5½x6" 110.00
Vase, goldfish, gr/lav, pillow form, #189, 7x8" 450.00
Vase, gr/lav, ruffled top, #404, 6" 75.00
Vase, katydids, matt gr, pillow form, #194, 4½x6" 325.00
Vase, lovebirds, lt gr, pillow form, #193, 8½x9" 400.00
Vase, matt bl/rose, pillow form, #191-6, 4½x6" 110.00
Vase, matt gr, hdls, #143, 5½x7" 175.00
Vase, matt gr/rust, pillow form, #191-9, 7½x9" 235.00
Vase, Ruba Rombic, fan shape, gr/lav, #300, 7x8" 775.00
Vase, Ruba Rombic, matt bl/rose, #301, 6" 650.00

Musical Instruments

The field of automatic musical instruments covers many different categories ranging from watches and tiny seals concealing fine early musical movements to huge organs and orchestrions which weigh many hundreds of pounds and are equivalent to small orchestras. Music boxes, first made in the early 19th century by Swiss watchmakers, were produced in both disk and cylinder models. The latter type employs a cylinder with tiny pins that lift the teeth in the comb of the music box (producing a sound much like many individual tuning forks), and music results. The value of a cylinder music box depends on the length and diameter of the cylinder, the date of its manufacture, the number of tunes it plays (four or six is usually better than ten or twelve), and its manufacturer. Nicole Freres, Henri Capt, LeCoultre, and Bremond are among the most highly regarded, and the larger boxes made by Mermod Freres are also popular. Examples with multiple cylinders, extra instruments (such as bells or an organ section), and those in particularly ornate cabinets or with matching tables bring significantly higher prices. While smaller cylinder boxes are still being made, the larger ones (over 10" cylinders) typically date from before 1900. Disk music boxes were introduced about 1890 but were replaced by the phonograph only twenty-five years later. However, during that time hundreds of thousands were made. Their great advantage was in playing inexpensive interchangeable disks, a factor that remains an attraction for today's collector as well. Among the most popular disk boxes are those made by Regina (USA), Polyphon, Mira, Stella, and Symphonion. Relative values are determined by the size of the disks they play, whether they have single or double combs, if they are upright or table models, and how ornate their cases are. Especially valuable are those that play multiple disks at the same time or are incorporated into tall case clocks.

Player pianos were made in a wide variety of styles. Early varieties consisted of a mechanism which pushed up to a piano and played on the keyboard by means of felt-tipped fingers. These use sixty-five note rolls. Later models have the playing mechanism built in, and most use eighty-eight note rolls. Upright pump player pianos have little value in unrestored condition because the cost of restoration is so high. 'Reproducing' pianos, especially the 'grand' format, can be quite valuable, depending on the make, the size, the condition, and the ornateness of the case. 'Reproducing' pianos have very sophisticated mechanisms and are much more realistic in the reproduction of piano music. They were made in relatively limited quantities. Better manufacturers include Steinway and Mason & Hamlin. Popular roll mechanism makers include Ampico, Duo-Art, and Welte. The market for all types of player pianos has been weak for several years.

Coin-operated pianos (Orchestrions) were used commercially and typically incorporate extra instruments in addition to the piano action. These can be very large and complex, incorporating drums, cymbals, xylophones, bells, and hundreds of pipes. Both American and European coin pianos are very popular, especially the larger and more complex models made by Wurlitzer, Seeburg, Cremona, Weber, Welte, Hupfeld, and many others. These companies also made automatically playing violins (Mills Violin Virtuoso, Hupfeld), banjos (Encore), and harps (Whitlock); these are quite valuable.

Collecting player organettes is a fun endeavor. Roller ograns, organettes, player organs, grind organs, hand organs — whatever the name — are a fascinating group of music makers. Some used wooden barrels or cobs to operate the valves, or metal and cardboard discs or paper strips, paper rolls, metal donuts, or metal strips. They usually played from 14 to 20 keys or notes. Some were presser operated or vacuum type. Their heyday lasted from the 1870s to the turn of the century. Most were reed organs, but a few had pipes. Many were made in either America or Germany. They lost favor with the advent of the phonograph, as did the music box. Some music boxes wre built with little player organs in them. Any player organette in good working condition with some music and in their original finish should be worth from $300.00 to $1,200.00, depending on the model. Generally the more keying it has and the larger and fancier the case, the more desirable it is. Rarity plays a part too. There are a handfull of individuals who make new music rolls for these player organs. Some machines are very rare, and music for them is nearly impossible to find. For further information on player organs we recommend *Encyclopedia of Musical Instruments* by Bowers. Our advisor for player organs is James R. Wilkins; he is listed in the Directory under Texas.

Unless noted, prices given are for instruments in fine condition, playing properly, with cabinets or cases in well-preserved or refinished condition. In all instances, unrestored instruments sell for much less, as do those with broken or missing parts, damaged cases, and the like. On the other hand, particularly superb examples in especially ornate case designs and those that have been particularly well kept will often command more. Our advisor for mechanical instruments other than player organs is Martin Roenigk; he is listed in the Directory under Arkansas.

Key:
c — cylinder   d — disk

Mechanical

Regina music box, oak case, double comb, ca 1890, 10x22x20", EX, with 30 discs, $3,700.00.

Bird, automated, in cage, 22", unrstr 850.00
Bird, automated, sterling silver case, bird-shaped key, ca 1925 ..1,100.00
Bird, automated, tortoise shell case, fusee, Bruguier, ca 1865 ..3,500.00
Birds (2), automated, in cage, 21", unrstr 1,650.00
Box, Cuff; Capital Style B, w/8 cuffs, lt rstr 6,800.00
Box, Etouffoirs en Acier, 10¾" c, 6-tune 800.00
Box, German Symphonion, 13¾" d, walnut veneer 22" case ...2,700.00
Box, interchangable 11" c, w/writing table, EX 6,500.00
Box, Langdorf Longue Marche, 7 12½" c, EX 9,500.00
Box, Mermod Freres, interchangeable, oak case, 4 18" c 13,500.00
Box, Mermod Freres, 11¼" c, 2½" d, 10-tune 1,500.00

Box, Mermod Freres Ideal Soprano, 14¾" c, 6-tune 3,400.00
Box, Mira, 18½" d, console w/decal, EX 11,500.00
Box, Nichole Freres, 13¼" c, 8-tune, ebony wood case 2,100.00
Box, Nicole Freres (art), 10¾" c, 6-tune, VG 1,500.00
Box, Regina, phone-style 240 console, 15½" d/records, mahog ..11,000.00
Box, Regina, 12" d, mahog cabinet 1,600.00
Box, Regina, 15½" d, curved front, changer, oak case, rstr 19,500.00
Box, Regina, 15½" d, heavily cvd case 6,800.00
Box, Regina, 15½" d, single comb, pinstriped case, EX 2,600.00
Box, Regina, 20¾" d, dbl comb, oak desk style, ca 1910 ....12,000.00
Box, Regina, 27" d, single auto changer, walnut case, EX rstr ..20,000.00
Box, Regina, 27" d, 2 c, eng walnut case, single play 13,000.00
Box, Regina Style 50, 15½" d, cvd mahog case, 10½x21x19", +60d 5,700.00
Box, Stella, 17¼" d, dbl comb, mahog case, table model, EX ..4,500.00
Box, Swiss, 6½" c, 4-tune, veneer 21" case 450.00
Box, Swiss Sublime Harmony, 8⅛" c, dbl comb, 17" case 1,100.00
Calliope, National, 53-note, w/ext blower, EX orig 7,900.00
Calliope, Tangley, roll operated, EX 7,500.00
Nickelodeon, Coinola Cupid, rstr 6,500.00
Nickelodeon, Coinola CX, walnut case, w/xylophone, EX orig .7,000.00
Nickelodeon, Seeburg E, w/xylophone, rstr 9,000.00
Nickelodeon, Seeburg K, w/xylophone, eagle front 11,000.00
Nickelodeon, Seeburg L, rstr 7,500.00
Nickelodeon, Seeburg Late G, 1926, rstr 55,000.00
Orchestrelle, Aeolian W, EX, +200 rolls 4,900.00
Orchestrion, Coinola CX, w/11 instruments 18,000.00
Orchestrion, Coinola Style #0 Midget, oak case, art glass, rstr ...8,000.00
Orchestrion, Coinola X, oak case, full rstr 14,000.00
Orchestrion, Cremona J, rstr 45,000.00
Orchestrion, Link R, rstr 12,900.00
Orchestrion, Link RX, art glass, EX orig 17,500.00
Orchestrion, Pierre Eich Solophone, 104 pipes, EX, +36 rolls ..38,000.00
Orchestrion, Seeburg G, NM 45,000.00
Orchestrion, Seeburg KT Special Replica, 1970s, M 15,000.00
Orchestrion, Wurlitzer CX, Grecian style, rstr 23,500.00
Organ, band; Artisan, 46-key, +15 rolls 16,000.00
Organ, band; Wurlitzer #105, new case 10,500.00
Organ, band; Wurlitzer #153, on trailer, EX 42,000.00
Organ, band; Wurlitzer #153, rstr 42,000.00
Organ, band; Wurlitzer Caliola, rstr 12,900.00
Organ, Bijou Orchestrone, 20-note paper roll, Am 1,000.00
Organ, Concert Rollar, 6" wooden roller cobs, NY 950.00
Organ, dance; Bursen, rstr 17,500.00
Organ, fairground; Gavioli, 65-key, 240 pipes, EX 42,000.00
Organ, Gem Rollar, 6" wooden roller cob, built in NY, 6" 600.00
Organ, Grand Rollar, 15" roller cob, 32-note 4,000.00
Organ, Mandolina or Celestina, 20-note paper roll, Am 1,000.00
Organ, military band; Wurlitzer #148, w/brass trumpets, EX orig ..28,000.00
Organ, monkey; Molinari, 26-key, EX 4,500.00
Organ, monkey; Molinari, 47-key, w/orig cart, EX 11,500.00
Organ, Ruth Model 35-B, 67 keyless, Germany, ca 1900, rstr ..95,000.00
Organette, Amorette, zinc d, 16-note, Germany, 22.5 cm 600.00
Organette, Amorette, zinc d, 18-note, 26.5 cm 750.00
Organette, Amorette, zinc d, 24-note, 30.5 cm 1,000.00
Organette, Ariosa, zinc donut d, 18-note, Germany 750.00
Organette, Ariston, 13" cb d, 24-key 1,200.00
Organette, Grand Roller, G, +8 13" wooden cobs 2,500.00
Organette, Musical Casket, 14-note paper roll, AM 500.00
Organette, Organina, walnut case, paper rolls 375.00
Organette, Phonix, zinc donut d (several szs), 24-key, Germany ..1,500.00
Organette, 14-note, G orig, +5 paper rolls 375.00
Organette, 22-note, Celestina, G orig, +10 paper rolls 700.00
Organette, 22-note, Concert Roller, G, +5 6¾" wooden cobs 750.00
Organette, 22-note, floor model, paper roll 1,800.00

Organette, 22-note, Gem Roller Organ, G, +6 6¾" wooden cobs 550.00
Piano, baby grand; Baldwin Welte, mahog case, 38x61x56", EX ..2,800.00
Piano, baby grand; Hardman Welte reproducing, G orig 1,700.00
Piano, barrel; Victor Chlappa, 34-key c (2), EX orig 1,400.00
Piano, grand; Knabe Ampico, 62", EX orig 1,200.00
Piano, grand; Marshall & Wendall Ampico, 60", EX orig 1,800.00
Piano, grand; Wurlitzer Recordo, retubed, rfn, 56" 1,500.00
Piano, grand; Wurlitzer/Apollo Ampico, art case, 73", rstr ...11,000.00
Piano, upright; Ampico B, Marshall & Wendall, EX 2,200.00
Piano, upright; Chickering Ampico, EX orig 1,500.00
Piano, upright; Steinway Duo-Art, brn mahog, M rstr 6,500.00
Piano/pipe organ, Reproduco, EX orig 6,500.00
Pianocorder, Marantz, +50 cassettes, EX 3,000.00
Toy, QRS Play-A-Sax, w/3 rolls 125.00
Toy, Rolmonica, Bakelite case, w/5 rolls 100.00
Toy, Zilotone, Chein, clown, w/6 discs 350.00

Non-Mechanical

Grand piano, panel inscribed C. Bechstein, Hof-liefenant, sr. maj. Des Kaiser V. Konigs, Berlin, ca 1880, closed: 38x79x57", EX, $3,500.00.

Accordion, Hohner, 3-row buttons, red, Corona #HA3522, MIB ..375.00
Banjo, Bacon Peerless Plectrum, 1920, rstr, M 1,500.00
Banjo, Gibson RB-175, long neck, 5-string, 1954, NM, +case ...550.00
Banjo-mandolin, Weymann #40, maple shell, dk-stained neck ..125.00
Drum, bass; 1930s-40s, 14x24" dia, NM 165.00
Drum, Carl Fischer NY, orig varnish & transfers, rprs, 17" 330.00
Fiddle, cherry wood, handmade, ca 1860, 22x6", EX 250.00
Fife, Am, B-flat, German silver, ebonite band/inlays, 14" 45.00
Flugelhorn, CW Moritze, brass w/German-silver trim, 1880s 850.00
Flute, Graves, fruitwood, ivory mts, 1 brass key, 1850s, 21" 1,200.00
Flute, maple wood w/incised cvg, 7-hole, 16", EX 150.00
Guitar, classical; Solar-Gonzalez, rosewood, 1965, +case 1,350.00
Guitar, Gibson L-12, sunburst, 1939, EX, w/hard case 1,650.00
Guitar, Guild F-47, 1972, VG, orig hard case 1,200.00
Guitar, Martin 00-18G, classic w/X-brace, 1938, EX 950.00
Guitar, steel; Megna #M-199-3-J LA, CA amplifier, 1950s, complete 750.00
Guitar, steel; National, 1940s, EX in case 195.00
Harmonica, Hohner Chromonica, MIB 125.00
Harpsicord, Am, rosewood, scroll & lyre rest, 1860s, 38x81" ..2,500.00
Mandolin, Gibson Style A-Jr, snakehead, brn face, NM 675.00
Piano, J Osborn, Boston, classical mahog/mahog vnr, 1820, 67" .1,850.00
Piccolo, unstamped German Grenadilla, ivory band, NP mts 50.00
Ukelele, Wayman Soprano, mahog, EX 150.00
Viola, Mathias Thomas model, 2nd half 20th C 2,450.00
Violin, Amati Model by Jerome Thibouville Lami, early 1900s ..2,250.00
Violin, Andreas Morelli by K Hermann, early 1900s 2,650.00

Mustache Cups

Mustache cups were popular items during the late Victorian period, designed specifically for the man with the mustache! They were made in silverplate as well as china and ironstone. Decorations ranged from simple transfers to elaborately applied and gilded florals. To properly position the 'mustache bar,' special cups were designed for the 'lefties.' These are the rare ones!

Clydesdale mare & name w/gold, left handed **90.00**
Floral spray w/pk ribbon, decaled, scrolled blank & hdl **40.00**
Knights & angels w/gold, Royal Bavaria, +saucer **67.50**
Lady w/flowers transfer, lg **45.00**
Pk lustre w/gold leaves **60.00**
Roses, red on gr, Germany **60.00**
SP, cut/beaded decor, Eureka Silver, 1901, +saucer **70.00**
SP, floral eng, Barbour, EX **85.00**
SP, floral eng, very little wear, oversz **85.00**

Nailsea

Nailsea is a term referring to clear or colored glass decorated in contrasting spatters, swirls, or loops. These are usually white but may also be pink, red, or blue. It was first produced in Nailsea, England, during the late 1700s but was made in other parts of Britain and Scotland as well. During the mid-1800s a similar type of glass was produced in this country. Originally used for decorative novelties only, by that time tumblers and other practical items were being made from Nailsea-type glass. See also Lamps; Witch Balls.

Bell, marriage; wht satin w/pk loopings, 11½x6½" **125.00**
Bottle, gemel; aqua w/wht loopings, sheared lip, 7" **85.00**
Bottle, wine; cranberry w/wht loopings, stopper, 12½" **245.00**
Flask, amber w/wht loopings, flared mouth, 4½" **230.00**
Flask, amber w/wht loopings, 13 right-swirl ribs, 5" **275.00**
Flask, clear to cranberry w/wht loopings, teardrop, 8" **165.00**

Flask, white with red and blue loopings, sheared mouth, pontilled base, mid to late 1800s, one-pint, $290.00.

Flask, wht w/red & bl loopings, rolled lip, 9x5½" **300.00**
Flask, wht w/red-pk loopings, sheared/tooled lip, 8" **125.00**
Pipe, wht w/red-pk loopings, appl red bowl rim, 28", M **400.00**
Pitcher, tankard; clear w/wht & lt bl loopings, clear hdl, 8x4" ...**150.00**
Powder horn, milk glass w/yel-gr loopings, clear rigaree, 13" **150.00**
Rolling pin, aquamarine w/bl to sapphire bl loopings, 13" **275.00**

Nakara

Nakara was a line of decorated opaque milk glass produced by the C.F. Monroe Company of Meriden, Connecticut, for a few years after the turn of the century. It differs from their Wave Crest line in several ways. The shapes were simpler; pastel colors were deeper and covered more of the surface; more beading was present; flowers were larger; and large transfer prints of figures, Victorian ladies, cherubs, etc., were used

as well. Ormolu and brass collars and mounts complemented these opulent pieces. Most items were signed; however, this is not important since the ware was never reproduced. Our advisors for this category are Dolli and Wilfred R. Cohen; their address is listed in the Directory under California.

Ashtray, flowers on gr hexagonal bowl, ormolu mts, sm **200.00**
Bonbon, daisies/beaded scrolls on pk to yel, wire hdl, 6" dia **595.00**
Box, Bishop's Hat, floral, wht/pk on yel, ormolu ft, 5x5½" **550.00**
Box, Collars & Cuffs/pk azaleas on bright bl, 8½x8½" **2,600.00**
Box, glass lid w/floral, rtcl all-brass base, ftd, 3½x7" **1,750.00**
Box, iris, purple on biscuit, octagonal, 3¼x6" **750.00**
Box, lady's portrait on gr, 2¾x4½" **650.00**
Box, Princess Louise on pk/yel, ftd, sqd, 4x4½" **750.00**
Box, Queen Louise in garden on gr, wild rose fr, 3x8" **975.00**
Box, ring; man & lady on yel & pk, 2½x2¾" **975.00**
Box, roses, pk on purple, 4x8" dia **895.00**
Box, 3 Greenaway girls at tea, lace decor, 3x6" **1,050.00**
Hair receiver, children have tea, wht beadwork, dmn shape **585.00**
Humidor, frog reading newspaper on bl, metal lid, 6¾" **1,050.00**
Match holder, tiny beaded flowers on gr, ormolu rim, 2" dia **495.00**
Photo receiver, Indian Chief on yel/olive, 2½x4" L **750.00**
Plaque, Queen Louise in wht reserve on bl, ormolu mt **3,500.00**
Toothpick holder, beaded ovals/pk flowers on gr, ormolu mts **650.00**
Tray, dresser; daisies, pk/wht on gr, ormolu hdls, 6" dia **225.00**
Vase, wild roses/scrolls on beige, 4-ftd ormolu base, 9" **795.00**

Napkin Rings

Napkin rings became popular during the late 1800s. They were made from various materials. Among the most popular and collectible today are the large group of varied silverplated figurals made by American manufacturers. Recently the larger figurals in excellent condition have appreciated considerably. Only those with a blackened finish, corrosion, or broken and/or missing parts have maintained their earlier price levels. When no condition is indicated, the items listed below are assumed to be all original and in very good to excellent condition. Check very carefully for missing parts, solder repairs, or marriages.

A timely warning: inexperienced buyers should be aware of excellent reproductions on the market, especially the wheeled pieces and cherubs. However, these do not have the fine detail and patina of the originals and tend to have a more consistent, soft pewter-like finish. These are appearing at the large, quality shows at top prices, being shown along with authentic antique merchandise. Beware! For further information we recommend *Figural Napkin Rings* (Collector Books) by Lillian Gottschalk and Sandra Whitson. Our advisor for this category is Deborah Maggard; she is listed in the Directory under Ohio.

Key:
gw — gold washed   SH&M — Simpson, Hall &
R&B — Reed & Barton   Miller

Barrel ring held by Xd branches & leaf **65.00**
Beaver sits on leaves & branches, Toronto #110 ....**155.00**
Boy in harness pulls ring on wheels, Wilcox #01577 ....**625.00**
Boy rolls ring, lady watches, oblong base, Tufts #1597 ....**500.00**
Boy w/bat & ball by ring, rectagular base, Babcock #202 ....**295.00**
Bulldog sits chained to doghouse, sq base, SH&M #207 ....**350.00**
Bulldog stands beside ring **225.00**
Cat atop ring arches bk at dog, rnd base, Rogers #296 ....**295.00**
Cherub holds spear while riding on bk of fish, Meriden #157 .....**395.00**
Cherub w/feather in hat sits atop ring **225.00**
Chick by ornate ring on wishbone **85.00**

Chick pulls cart holding ring 245.00
Dog chases bird up ring, oval base, R&B #1110 ....150.00
Dog on ea side of sachel-shaped ring, Van Bergh #97 ....295.00
Dog on hind legs plays horn, ball-ftd sq base, Hartford #017 ......275.00
Dog on hind legs watches bird on ring, Aurora #27 ....225.00
Dog stands w/emb ring on bk, unmk 275.00
Eagle on ea side of ring, Meriden 70.00
Fairy w/butterfly, Wilcox #2206 ....250.00
Fan forms base for 2 butterflies holding ring 125.00
Flower at side of ring on leafy base 65.00
Frog rests on rock, rocky base 135.00
Frog w/glass eyes on sm leaf, fly on hammered ring 350.00
Giraffe nibbles vine tied to ring, Manhattan #239 ....395.00
Girl w/pigtails holds ring, no base, Meriden Britania #280 ....325.00
Girl w/rifle on shoulders, sq-ft base, SH&M #205 ....450.00
Goat by 6-sided ring 150.00
Greenaway boy by fence, raised base, Tufts #1593 ....350.00
Greenaway boy w/cookie, dog begs, rectagular base, Rogers 350.00
Greenaway boy w/drumstick on hands & knees, ring on bk, #243 ..350.00
Horse rearing/pulling wheeled ring, Meriden #219 ....550.00
Horseshoe on ring, w/emb horse's head & Good Luck, SH&M ..100.00
Lion reclines w/ring on bk 200.00
Man in top hat w/cane, 8-sided base, Wilcox #4300 ....165.00
Monkey playing sax attached to ring 205.00
Owl on sq base w/leaves, sm owls on ring, SH&M #204 ....395.00
Peacock sits atop decor ring, Meriden #151 ....295.00
Poodle (lg) on hind legs by ring on rectangular base, Tuffs #1616 ..295.00
Rabbit sitting under log tree, ring above, R&B #1520 ....210.00
Rooster beside ring, Rogers #11 ....165.00
Sailor w/anchor beside ring, R&B #1346 ....395.00
Sled w/ring atop, old-fashioned type, Wilcox #01532 ....95.00
Squirrel climbs tree, ring atop, rnd base, R&B #1150 ....195.00
Standing cat reaches for fly on top of ring, unknown maker 275.00
Stork harnessed to fancy cart w/ring, SH&M, 6" L 600.00
Tennis raquet & ball support ring, EX 185.00

Nash

A. Douglas Nash founded the Corona Art Glass Company in Long Island, New York. He produced tableware, vases, flasks, etc. using delicate artistic shapes and forms. After 1933 he worked for the Libbey Glass Company.

Bowl, Chintz, orange & yel, raised & scalloped rim, 7" 165.00
Compote, gold irid, scalloped, low ft, sgn, 3½x6¼ 500.00
Goblet, Chintz, bl/gr stripes, 6½" 125.00
Goblet, gold irid, knop stem, 6¾" 250.00
Parfait, Chintz, bl lines alternate w/gr-threaded clear, 7" 200.00
Vase, Chintz, bl/gr stripes & swags on clear, 9½x4½" 425.00
Vase, Chintz, orange stripes & yel-amber pulled threads, 5¼" 175.00

Vase, Chintz, deep red oval with alternating wide and narrow silver lustre stripes, signed Nash RD 66, 5½", $980.00.

Vase, Chintz, silver-bl veins on dk red, gourd form, 8½" 850.00
Vase, Chintz, silver-bl veins on dk red, shouldered, 7" 600.00
Vase, floriform; irid w/textured/molded leaves, #548, 5x7" 925.00

Natzler, Gertrude and Otto

The Natzlers came to the United States from Vienna in the late 1930s. They settled in Los Angeles where they continued their work in ceramics, for which they were already internationally recognized. Gertrude created the forms; Otto formulated a variety of interesting glazes, among them volcanic, crystalline, and lustre. Our advisor for this category is Abby Malowanczyk; she is listed in the Directory under Texas.

Bottle, burnt-orange/amber mottle, 16½" 5,250.00
Bottle, sang/gr hare's fur reduction w/melt fissures, 10" 4,500.00
Bottle, yel semi-matt over brn clay, 11x5¼" 2,600.00
Bowl, apple gr/mahog brn flambe, sm rnd ft, 6½x2¼" 2,000.00
Bowl, copper crystalline pooled at bottom int, 1½x10½" 6,000.00
Bowl, dripping turq crystalline, sm ft, 2¾" 2,700.00
Bowl, EX golden flambe, sm ft, 3x4¼" 1,700.00
Bowl, EX turq crystalline, sm ft, 3¼x8¼" 5,500.00
Bowl, fine volcanic turq, sm rnd ft, 2¼x4¾" 2,100.00
Bowl, lt bl gloss, ftd/flaring, 2½x6¼" 1,400.00
Bowl, mahog/umber Mariposa matt, sm ft, 3½x6½" 1,800.00
Bowl, mottled Persian bl semi-matt, sides pressed in, 5x12x9" ...1,900.00
Bowl, sang-de-boeuf lustre, 2x5" 1,700.00
Bowl, speckled gray semimatt, sm ft, 2½x4¾" 1,000.00
Bowl, thick dripping orange matt, semispherical, sm ft, 5½" ...3,000.00
Bowl, turq over red clay, 3x4" 950.00
Bowl, verte de wine on red clay, flattened sides, 2x5½" 475.00
Bowl, yel/brn hare's fur semi-matt, 2 sides uptrn, 2½x7" 2,000.00
Dish, pk lustre/gunmetal crystalline, flaring, ¾x4¾" 1,000.00
Vase, chartreuse gloss over red clay, ftd, deep/flaring, 3½" 1,200.00
Vase, copper crater reduction gray-blk matt, ftd cylinder, 9" ...1,600.00
Vase, dawn celadon reduction w/melt fissures, cylinder, 5½" ..1,900.00
Vase, flowing burnt apple gr, 3-part/4-sided form, 19" 2,100.00
Vase, Ikebana, gr lustre, slab built, sgn Otto, 2¼x4x3" 650.00
Vase, ivory celadon reduction w/melt fissures, finger mks, ftd, 4" .3,500.00
Vase, turq/rose/moss gr speckled matt, 4½x4½" 1,700.00

New England Glass Works

Founded in 1818 by Deming Jarves in Boston, Massachusetts, the New England Glass Company produced cut, blown three-mold, freeform, and pressed glass of the highest quality. They were recognized for their fine decorative accomplishments, using etching, gilding, and engraving to emphasize their wares. For more than fifty years, they produced prize-winning pressed glass dinnerware sets. Because they refused to compromise the quality of their product by using the cheaper lime-based glass that flooded the market in the 1860s, the company fell into financial trouble and by 1877 was forced to close. However, William Libbey, who had been the sales manager there since 1870, leased the premises and resumed operations with his father, Edward Drummond Libbey, as full partner. In 1892 the firm became known as The Libbey Glass Company. See also Amberina; Libbey.

Candlesticks, caryatid form, deep opal, att, 1875, 9", pr, EX ...2,500.00
Candlesticks, lt bl opaque, baluster stem, 1850s, 7", pr, EX 750.00
Pitkin flask, dk amber, 36 broken-swirl ribs, half-post neck, 6" ..440.00
Pitkin flask, olive, 36 broken-swirl ribs, half-post neck, 5" 360.00
Pitkin flask, olive, 36 broken-swirl ribs, half-post neck, 6" 495.00

Pitkin flask, olive, 36 swirled ribs, half-post neck, 7¼" **385.00**
Vase, blown, teal gr & clear, flared rim, appl ring, 6½" **2,500.00**

New Geneva

In the early years of the 19th century, several potteries flourished in the Greensboro, Pennsylvania, area. They produced utilitarian stoneware items as well as tile and novelties for many decades. All failed well before the turn of the century.

Pitchers: Free-hand floral, brown on reddish clay, 4¾", $650.00; Free-hand floral, brown on buff clay, 7¾", $800.00.

Flowerpot, buff clay w/Albany slip, attached saucer, 4½" **75.00**
Flowerpot, buff w/Albany slip stripes, attached base, 8½" **495.00**
Pitcher, redware, brn Albany slip, 8⅞" **55.00**

New Martinsville

The New Martinsville Glass Company took its name from the town in West Virginia where it began operations in 1901. In the beginning years, pressed tablewares were made in crystal as well as colored and opalescent glass. Considered an innovator, the company was known for their imaginative applications of the medium in creating lamps made entirely of glass, vanity sets, figural decanters, and models of animals and birds. In 1944 the company was purchased by Viking Glass, who continued to use many of the old molds, the animals molds included. They marked their wares 'Viking' or 'Rainbow Art.' Viking recently ceased operations and has been purchased by Kenneth Dalzell, president of the Fostoria Company. They, too, are making the bird and animal models. Although at first they were not marked, future productions are to be marked with an acid stamp. Dalzell/Viking animals are in the $50.00 to $60.00 range. Values for cobalt and red items are two to three times higher than for the same item in clear. See also Depression Glass; Glass Animals and Figurines.

Ashtray, Moondrops, colors other than cobalt or red **17.00**
Basket, Janice, cobalt or red, 9x6½" **145.00**
Bonbon, Janice, crystal, hdls, 4¾x7" **25.00**
Bonbon, Janice, crystal, hdls, 4x6" **12.00**
Bonbon, Radiance, cobalt or red, 6" **30.00**
Bowl, Janice, cobalt or red, flared rim, 12" **70.00**
Bowl, Janice, crystal, flared, 9½" **35.00**
Bowl, Muranese, peachblow, 8-lobed ruffled rim, 3¼x5¼" **165.00**
Bowl, Prelude, crystal, 3-ftd, 11" **50.00**
Bowl, Radiance, amber or crystal, crimped rim, 12" **30.00**
Bowl, Radiance, amber or crystal, 2-part, 7" **18.00**
Bowl, Radiance, cobalt or red, crimped rim, 10" **45.00**
Bowl, soup; Moondrops, cobalt or red, 6¾" **90.00**
Cake salver, Prelude, crystal, 5½x11" **55.00**
Candlesticks, dbl; Prelude, crystal, 6", pr **70.00**
Candlesticks, Moondrops, cobalt or red, ruffled, 5", pr **35.00**
Candlesticks, Radiance, cobalt or red, 8", pr **100.00**
Comport, Moondrops, colors other than cobalt or red, 4" **18.00**
Comport, Radiance, amber or crystal, 6" **22.00**

Creamer, Janice, crystal, 6-oz **20.00**
Cruet, Radiance, cobalt or red, ind **75.00**
Cup, Janice, cobalt or red **30.00**
Cup, Radiance, amber or crystal **12.00**
Cup & saucer, Janice, red **20.00**
Ice tub, Janice, crystal, ftd, 6" **85.00**
Ladle, punch; Radiance, amber or crystal **95.00**
Mayonnaise, Moondrops, colors other than cobalt or red, 5¼" **32.00**
Pitcher, berry cream; Janice, crystal, 15-oz **37.50**
Pitcher, Oscar, red **95.00**
Pitcher, Radiance, cobalt, 64-oz **225.00**
Plate, bread & butter; Moondrops, red, 6¼" **10.00**
Plate, Janice, crystal, 13" **30.00**
Plate, luncheon; Radiance, cobalt or red **18.00**
Plate, salad; Janice, red, 8" **12.00**
Plate, salad; Moondrops, cobalt or red, 7⅛" **14.00**
Plate, torte; Prelude, crystal, 15" **60.00**
Platter, Janice, cobalt or red, oval, 13" **70.00**
Relish, Prelude, crystal, 3-part, hdls, 10" **45.00**
Server, Prelude, crystal, center hdl **55.00**
Sherbet, Janice, crystal **12.00**
Sugar bowl, Janice, crystal, tall **15.00**
Tray, Prelude, crystal, center hdl, 11" **35.00**
Tumbler, Amy, ftd, #34 ....**22.50**
Tumbler, Janice, cobalt or red **27.50**
Tumbler, Moondrops, cobalt or red, 7-oz, 4⅜" **16.00**
Vase, bud; Prelude, crystal, pewter base, 10" **30.00**
Vase, Janice, crystal, cupped, 3-toed, 8" **50.00**
Vase, Prelude, crystal, crimped rim, 11" **60.00**
Vase, Radiance, cobalt or red, flared, 10" **65.00**
Whiskey, Moondrops, cobalt, 2-oz **20.00**

Newcomb

The Newcomb College of New Orleans, Louisiana, established a pottery in 1895 to provide the students with first-hand experience in the fields of art and ceramics. Using locally dug clays — red and buff in the early years, white-burning by the turn of the century — potters were employed to throw the ware which the ladies of the college decorated. Until about 1910 a glossy glaze was used on ware decorated by slip painting or incising. After that a matt glaze was favored. Soft blues and greens were used almost exclusively, and decorative themes were chosen to reflect the beauty of the South. The year 1930 marked the end of the matt-glaze period and the art-pottery era.

Various marks used by the pottery include an 'N' within a 'C,' sometimes with 'HB' added to indicate a 'hand-built' piece. The potter often incised his initials into the ware, and the artists were encouraged to sign their work. Among the most well-known artists were Sadie Irvine, Henrietta Bailey, and Fannie Simpson.

Newcomb pottery is evaluated to a large extent by two factors: design and condition. In the following listings, items are assumed matt unless noted otherwise. Our advisor for this category is David Rago; he is listed in the Directory under New Jersey.

Bowl, floral (stylized), 4-color gloss, Butler, WW20, 3x6" **4,000.00**
Bowl, gr matt, incurvate, 4¼x5½" **500.00**
Bowl, jonquil band under rim on bl, sgn, 1926, 3½x6" **1,000.00**
Bowl, morning-glory vine at rim on bl, Simpson, 4½x6¾" **1,500.00**
Bowl vase, oaks/moss/sky, Simpson, 1918, 3¼x4" **1,700.00**
Brush pot, blk irid w/ochre int, sgn Graner, 3" **300.00**
Mug, 5 rabbits among trees, glossy, AR/JM/Q, sm firing line, 4" .**4,300.00**
Plate, band w/3 flowers on bl-gr gloss, Irvine, 7" **2,400.00**
Vase, berries, pk on purple, Irvine, 1929, 2¼x2¾" **900.00**

Vase, berries/leaves, pk/gr on bl, Irvine, 11x4"	2,500.00
Vase, bl-gray matt, dbl-gourd, 7x4¼"	600.00
Vase, bl/rose matt under bl/red/gr drip, Meyer, NC, 8½"	800.00
Vase, cotton plants (EX work), wht cvd on bl, Ryan, 1904, 6x4"	5,750.00
Vase, daffodil shoulder band, Irvine, 4¼x7"	1,800.00
Vase, daffodils under gr/bl w/irid highlights, JM/Mason/#89, 6"	1,500.00
Vase, Deco pleated draping cvd on bl-gr, bulbous, 1930s, 7x7"	1,400.00
Vase, distinct finger ridges, rose drip on dk bl, Meyer, 6½"	425.00
Vase, Espanol design cvd top/bottom, 3-color, Irvine, 4x4½"	1,400.00
Vase, floral shoulder band (abstract) on lt purple, 5x5½"	1,600.00
Vase, floral sprays w/vertical stems, gr/bl, CN/HQ8, 8x5"	2,300.00
Vase, florals at flaring rim on bl, Bailey, 4½x2½"	900.00
Vase, florals/column band, 4-color gloss, LeBlanc, rstr, 4¼x5"	3,000.00
Vase, florals/leaves below neck band on bl, Irvine, 5x5"	1,500.00
Vase, horizontal ridges, turq semimatt, Kenneth Smith, 7½x6"	550.00
Vase, incised lines on gold semimatt, Gonzales, 7½x4"	1,100.00
Vase, irises at shoulder, Charlaron, 5½x6"	2,200.00
Vase, jonquils on bl semimatt, AF Simpson, 1907, 10½"	5,775.00
Vase, jonquils/long stems on dk bl, Benson, 9½x3¼"	4,000.00
Vase, lily of valley, glossy bls/gr/wht, ML Dunn, #CT85, 2½"	1,500.00
Vase, lily pads/upright leaves, gr matt, AVL/JM, 6x3¼"	1,600.00
Vase, magnolia band on lt & med bl/bl-gr, Bailey, 5"	6,500.00
Vase, moon/moss/oak trees, Arco, 1903, 5x4½"	3,500.00
Vase, moon/moss/oak trees, Irvine, spherical, 3¾x5½"	1,900.00
Vase, moon/moss/oak trees, Irvine, 1925, 12x5"	7,000.00
Vase, moon/moss/oak trees, Irvine, 8x3½"	2,900.00
Vase, moon/moss/oak trees, Simpson, 1920, 6½x6½"	4,500.00
Vase, moon/moss/trees/cabin/river, S Irvine, #148, 1928, 8½"	7,750.00
Vase, moss/oak trees, Irvine, 3¾x3¾"	1,500.00
Vase, moss/oak trees (5), detailed, exposed clay, Simpson, 5x6"	4,600.00
Vase, moss/trees (EX color), Irvine, #RX13, 2½x3" (rare sz)	2,100.00
Vase, pine cones/needles, rose/gr on dk bl, Bailey, 10½"	4,500.00
Vase, pine trees/needles/long trunks (EX art), LeBlanc, 12"	6,000.00
Vase, squash blossom band, 3-color gloss, Wells, 5½x3"	3,250.00
Vase, Transitional, daisy chain on rare mauve, Mason, 5x4", NM	1,700.00
Vase, Transitional, floral, wht/gr on bl, Irvine, 7x3¾"	2,100.00
Vase, tulips (stylized), bl & gr, #BC86, 7⅞"	3,500.00
Vase, wheat sheaves (full-length) cvd on dk bl, Bailey, 9½x3"	3,750.00
Vase, wine berries, Joseph Meyers, cylindrical, 6¼"	2,200.00

Newspapers

People do not collect newspapers simply because they are old. Age has absolutely nothing to do with value — it does not hold true that the older the newspaper, the higher the value. Instead, most of the value is determined by the historic event content. In most cases, the more important to American history the event is, the higher the value. In over two hundred years of American history, perhaps as many as 98% of all newspapers ever published **do not** contain news of a significant historic event. Newspapers not having news of major events in history are called 'atmosphere.' Atmosphere papers have little collector value. (See price guide below.)

To learn more about the hobby of collecting old and historic newspapers, be sure to visit our web sight on the Internet at: http://www.historybuff.com/. The e-mail address for the NCSA: info@historybuff.com. See Newspaper Collector's Society of America in Clubs and Newsletters for more information.

1800-1820, Atmosphere editions	7.00
1821-1859, Atmosphere editions	5.00
1836, Texas declares independence	60.00
1845, Annexation of Texas	35.00

1846, Start of Mexican War	30.00
1846-1847, Major battles of Mexican War	20.00
1847, End of Mexican War	30.00
1848, Gold discovered in California	60.00
1859, John Brown's raid on Harper's Ferry	45.00
1860, Lincoln elected 1st term	150.00
1861, Lincoln's inaugural address	175.00
1861-1865, Atmosphere editions: Confederate titles	50.00
1861-1865, Atmosphere editions: Union titles	7.00
1861-1865, Major battles of Civil War	75.00
1862, Emancipation Proclamation	135.00
1863, Gettysburg Address	250.00
1865, April 29 edition of Frank Leslie's	350.00
1865, April 29 edition of Harper's Weekly	300.00
1865, Capture & death of J Wilkes Booth	100.00
1865, Fall of Richmond	100.00
1865, NY Herald, Apr 15 (Beware: reprints abound)	900.00
1865, Titles other than NY Herald, Apr 15	400.00
1866-1900, Atmosphere editions	4.00
1876, Custer's Last Stand	150.00
1881, Billy the Kid killed	200.00
1881, Garfield assassinated	50.00
1881, Gunfight at OK Corral	225.00
1882, Jesse James killed	200.00
1898, Sinking of Maine	40.00
1901, McKinley assassinated	60.00
1903, Wright Brother's flight	300.00
1906, San Francisco earthquake, other titles	30.00
1906, San Francisco earthquake, San Francisco title	500.00
1912, Sinking of Titanic	250.00
1915, Sinking of Lusitania	125.00

1927, June 13, Lindbergh arrives in Paris, New York Journal, $75.00.

Photo courtesy Rick Brown Archives

1927, Babe Ruth hits 60th home run	70.00
1929, St Valentine's Day Massacre	150.00
1929, Stock market crash	90.00
1931, Al Capone found guilty	35.00
1931, Jack 'Legs' Diamond killed	35.00
1933, Machine Gun Kelley captured	35.00
1934, Baby Face Nelson killed	40.00
1934, Bonnie & Clyde killed	125.00
1934, Dillinger killed	150.00
1934, Pretty Boy Floyd killed	35.00
1937, Hindenberg explodes	65.00
1941, Honolulu Star-Bulletin, Dec 7, 1st extra (+)	600.00
1941, Other titles, Dec 7, w/Pearl Harbor news	35.00
1948, Chicago Daily Tribune, Nov 3, Dewey Defeats Truman	900.00
1961, Alan Shephard 1st astronaut in space	20.00
1961, Roger Maris hits 61st home run	25.00
1962, Death of Marilyn Monroe	30.00

Nicodemus

Chester Nicodemus moved from Dayton, Ohio, to Columbus in 1930 and started teaching at the Columbus Art School. During this time he made vases and commissioned sculptures, water fountains, and limestone and wood carvings. In 1941 Chester left the field of teaching to pursue pottery making full time, using local red clay containing a large amount of iron. Known for its durability, he called the ware Ferro-stone. He made teapots and other utility wares, but these goods lost favor, so he started producing animal and bird sculptures, nativity sets, and Christmas ornaments, some bearing Chester's and Florine's names as personalized cards for his customers and friends. Chester died in 1990.

His glaze colors were turquoise or aqua, ivory, green mottle, pussy willow (pink), and golden yellow. The glaze was applied so that the color of the warm red clay would show through, adding an extra dimension to each piece. Examples are usually marked with his name incised in the clay, but paper labels were also used. For more information we recommend *Sanford Guide to Nicodemus, His Pottery and His Art*, by our advisor for this category, James Riebel; he is listed in the Directory under Ohio.

Ashtray, Bryn Mawr name & logo, 4" **58.00**
Bank, rabbit figural, gr mottle, 4" **350.00**

Figurine, duck, turquoise, #114, from $75.00 to $100.00; Penguin, Optimist, #91, from $75.00 to $100.00.

Figurine, bull, Indiana University **695.00**
Figurine, collie **195.00**
Figurine, girl kneeling **195.00**
Figurine, robin, 5" **195.00**
Pitcher, honey; 4" **55.00**

Niloak

During the latter part of the 1800s, there were many small utilitarian potteries in Benton, Arkansas. By 1900 only the Hyten Brothers Pottery remained. Charles Hyten, a second generation potter, took control of the family business around 1902. Shortly thereafter he renamed it the Eagle Pottery Company. In 1909 Hyten and former Rookwood potter Arthur Dovey began experimentation on a new swirl pottery. Dovey previously worked for the Ouachita Pottery Company of Hot Springs and produced a swirl pottery there as early as 1906. In March 1910 the Eagle Pottery Company introduced Niloak,

kaolin spelled backwards. During 1911 Benton businessmen formed the Niloak Pottery corporation. Niloak, connected to the Arts and Crafts Movement and known as 'Mission' Ware, had a national representative in New York by 1913. Niloak's production centered on art pottery characterized by accidental, swirling patterns of natural and artificially colored clays. Many companies through the years have produced swirl pottery, yet none achieved the technical and aesthetic qualities of Niloak. Hyten received a patent in 1928 for the swirl technique. Although most examples have an interior glaze, some early Mission Ware pieces have an exterior glaze as well; these are extremely rare. Swirl/Mission Ware production continued steadily until the Depression when hard times and sagging sales caused Hyten to produce more traditional wares. In 1931 Niloak introduced Hywood Art Pottery, a glazed ware (sometimes similar in shape to Weller's Nile) of mostly hand-thrown vases. Soon thereafter, Niloak introduced castware as its primary production and renamed the line Hywood by Niloak. Throughout its existence, the company produced utilitarian items as well as artware.

In 1934 Hyten's company found itself facing bankruptcy. Hardy L. Winburn, Jr., along with other Little Rock businessmen, raised the necessary capital and were able to provide the kind of leadership needed to make the business profitable once again. Both lines (Eagle and Hywood) were renamed 'Niloak' in 1937 to capitalize on this well-known name. The pottery continued in production until 1947 when it was converted to the Winburn Tile Company, which exists to this day in Little Rock.

Be careful not to confuse the swirl production of the Evans Pottery of Missouri with Niloak. The significant difference is the dark brown matt interior glaze of Evans pottery. For further information we recommend *Collector's Encyclopedia of Niloak Pottery* by David Edwin Gifford (Collector Books). Our advisors for this category are Lila and Fred Shrader; they are listed in the Directory under California.

Mission Ware

Ashtray, str sides, 1½x5½" **135.00**
Bookends, wedge shape, weighted, 4x4", pr **425.00**
Bowl, flared rim, early mk, 3¼" **125.00**
Bowl, flat float shape, 3¼x11¼" **235.00**
Bowl, powder; ball-shaped finial on lid, 2nd art mk, 3x4¾" **295.00**
Bud vase, stick neck w/flared base, 8½" **165.00**
Chamberstick, w/finger ring, 5½" **240.00**
Cracker jar, ink stamp, 7x6½" **800.00**
Figurine, elephant, molded, unmk, 2" **570.00**
Gear shift knob, unmk, 2" **275.00**
Inkwell, bottle neck, squat, 2½" dia **165.00**
Jar, rose; w/lid & pierced insert, bulbous w/high shoulders, 8½" .**625.00**
Lamp base, bulbous w/flared base, 8½"+old metal fittings **415.00**
Mug, finger rest hdl, bbl shape, 4½" **175.00**
Mug, hdl, str sides, 4½" **160.00**
Pin dish, 1½x3½" **89.00**
Pitcher, cyindrical ewer form w/elongated graceful hdl, 9½" **300.00**
Punch bowl, on ped base, 10x14" **1,200.00**
Tankard, cylindrical w/hdl & slightly flared base, 13" **555.00**
Tumbler, bbl shape, shot sz, 2¼" **110.00**
Vase, baluster shape w/flared mouth, tan, brn & cream, 9¼" **325.00**
Vase, bbl shape, mini, 1½" **105.00**
Vase, bean pot shape w/2 sm hdls, 3½" **135.00**
Vase, bulbous w/high shoulders, 8" **200.00**
Vase, bulbous w/long neck, flared rim, mk Patent Pend'g, 6½" ..**200.00**
Vase, conical, flared ft, mini, 2" **110.00**
Vase, cylindrical, bottle neck, flared rim, 1st art mk, 10" **276.00**
Vase, shouldered cylinder, bright colors, 2nd art mk, 14¼" **550.00**
Vase, teardrop shape w/2" neck opening, 10½" **325.00**

Miscellaneous

Key:
HN — Hywood by Niloak   NB — Niloak (block letters) mark
N — N Mark   NI — Niloak (impressed) mark

Ashtray, bath tub shape, 2 rests, matt, N, 3¾" 29.00
Ashtray, wood tub shape w/detailed staves, 2 rests, glossy, NB, 4" 23.00
Ashtray, wooden shoe shape, 1 rest, NB, 2½x5" 28.00
Basket w/3" simulated rope hdl, matt, N, 7½" 42.00
Bowl, overlapping petals, matt, NB, 12" dia, +bird flower frog ...135.00
Bowl, rnd bottom, 3¾" holes on collar, 4x8¼" 65.00
Box, woven design, matt, NB, 3½x5" 58.00
Candlestick, hand-thrown, matt, 6" 85.00
Cornucopia, graceful lines, matt, NB, 8" L 56.00
Creamer, right-angle hdl, glossy, NI, 4½" 15.00
Ewer, lg graceful hdl & extended spout, glossy, 16" 150.00
Figurine, deer leaping over foliage, matt, 5" 25.00
Figurine, elephant, stylized, very rnd, matt, 2½x2¾" 55.00
Figurine, frog w/open mouth on lily pad, glossy, NI, 3¾" 33.00
Figurine, razorbk hog, w/or w/o U of A, matt, 4½" 110.00
Figurine, Scottie dog w/bow at neck, matt, N, 3½" 42.00
Flower frog, bird in flight, matt, 6" 49.00
Jug, label remnant: Slim's XX Honey, glossy, N, mini, 3½" 32.00
Pitcher, utilitarian shape w/recessed lid, 6½" 65.00
Planter, camel w/saddle baskets resting, gr matt, NB, 4" 38.00
Planter, duck, nesting, glossy, NI, 3¾" 31.00
Planter, elephant w/elongated trunk, well detailed, matt, N, 6½" L ...80.00
Planter, rooster, strutting & crowing, NB, 9" 48.00
Relish, triangular w/3 compartments, glossy, 9x9x9" 55.00
Tumbler, imp daisies, matt, N, 3½" 16.00
Vase, fan shape w/calla lily decor, glossy, NB, 7½" 26.00
Vase, ribbed w/elongated well-detailed hdls, glossy, HN, 7½" 21.00

Nippon

Nippon generally refers to Japanese wares made during the period from 1891 to 1921, although the Nippon mark was also used to a limited extent on later wares (accompanied by 'Japan'). Nippon, meaning Japan, identified the country of origin to comply with American importation restrictions. After 1921 'Japan' was the acceptable alternative. The term does not imply a specific type of product and may be found on items other than porcelains. For further information we recommend *The Collector's Encyclopedias of Nippon Porcelain* (there are five in the series) by our advisor, Joan Van Patten; you will find her address in the Directory under New York. In the following listings, items are assumed hand painted unless noted otherwise. Numbers included in the descriptions refer to these specific marks:

Key:
#1 — China E-OH   #5 — Rising Sun
#2 — M in Wreath   #6 — Royal Kinran
#3 — Cherry Blossom   #7 — Maple Leaf
#4 — Double T Diamond in   #8 — Royal Nippon, Nishiki
      Circle   #9 — Royal Moriye Nippon

Ashtray, pipe & matches on brn, bl #2, 5" sq 200.00
Ashtray, sampan scenic, 4-rest, gr #2, 4½" sq 160.00
Basket vase, mc roses w/much gold, unmk, 7" 475.00
Bottle, cologne; river scenic, earth tones & cobalt, #2, 5¼" 275.00
Bowl, berries & leaves, gold on wht, scalloped rim, #7, 9¾" 225.00
Bowl, floral, wht on cream to tan, 6-sided gold rim, #2, 7¼" 150.00
Bowl, landscape scenic, sgn Kimu, #2, 12½" L 425.00

Bowl, peanuts in relief, hdls, gr #2, 7" 175.00
Bowl, punch; mc grapes, ftd, scroll hdls, gr #2, 12¾x13" 1,000.00
Bowl, river scenic, oval, hdls, #2, 9½" 160.00
Bowl, roses (lg yel) on wht, tub hdls, #2, 7½" 275.00
Bowl, roses, pk & yel w/gold, scalloped rim, #7, 9¾" 325.00
Bowl, Wedgwood, cream on bl, hdls, gr #2, 7¼" 400.00
Box, cigarette; Am Indian portrait on brn, #2, 4¼" L 300.00
Box, cigarette; sampan scenic, gr #2, 4¾" L 250.00
Box, jewelry; irises on wht, gr #2, 4¾" sq 150.00
Box, powder; floral band on wht, gr #2, 5½" dia 80.00
Box, powder; lady's portrait reserve on lid, bl #7, 5¼"dia 400.00
Box, trinket; scenic reserve, heart shape, #7 ....100.00
Cake plate, mc floral w/cobalt & gold rim, 10½", +4 6½" 450.00
Cake plate, mc roses w/gold, sm hdls, #7, 11¼" 350.00
Cake plate, rose band on wht w/gold, pierced hdls, red mk, 10½" ...95.00
Candlesticks, Deco floral on blk, 6-sided, #2, 8", pr 425.00
Cheese dish, Deco floral on wht, slant lid, #2, 7¾" L 200.00
Chocolate pot, moriage dragon, HP mk, 10¼", +4 c/s 450.00
Chocolate pot, river scenic w/gold, #7, 10" 350.00
Cookie jar, gold on wht, 6-sided, RC mk, w/underplate, 8" 400.00
Cookie jar, roses, mc on wht w/much gold, ftd, #7, 7½" 525.00
Cracker jar, Deco florals on wht w/gold, #2, 9½" 250.00
Creamer & sugar bowl, gold o/l on wht, rnd ft, HP mk, w/lid 75.00
Creamer & sugar bowl, river scenic, ftd, w/lid, gr #2 ....200.00
Creamer & sugar bowl, roses, pk & red on wht w/gold, #3, w/lid ..140.00
Creamer & sugar bowl, roses, pk on gold w/turq enamel dots, #7 ..375.00
Cup & saucer, bouillon; bird & flowers on wht, 2-hdl, #7 ....50.00
Demitasse set, pk & gold band on wht, #5, tray+pot+cr/sug+4 c/s ..375.00
Dresser set, geometric decor, bl #7, 11¼" tray+4 pcs 800.00
Ewer, Deco flowers on cobalt, invt funnel shape, #6, 10" 350.00
Ewer, floral reserve on gold w/much o/l, slim, #7, 9¾" 500.00
Ewer, roses w/gold on wht lobed shape, ornate hdl, #6, 9¼" 375.00
Ferner, man on camel in desert scene, hdls, ftd, #2, 5¾x10½" ...500.00
Ferner, moriage dragon on brn, ftd, #7, 7½" 400.00
Ferner, river scenic, triangular, 3-ftd, #2, 8" 325.00
Hair receiver, roses, mc on gr, #7, 5" dia 80.00
Humidor, Am Indian on running horse relief, brn tones, #2, 6" ..1,300.00
Humidor, Deco-style geometric decor, 6-sided, #2, 5½" 425.00
Humidor, figures in early auto on wht, gr #2, 6½" 1,300.00
Humidor, flowers on gold w/enamel dots, #7, 5½" 900.00
Humidor, fox hunt scenic band on gr, sq, #7, 6½" 675.00
Humidor, Grecian ladies (14) relief, vintage relief lid, #2, 7½" ..1,800.00
Humidor, man on camel relief on brn tones, rnd, #2, 7½" 1,100.00
Humidor, moriage pipes on blended tones, #7, 7" 800.00
Humidor, sampan in sunset, earth tones, #2, 5" 450.00
Lamp base, sampan scenic reserve on cobalt, unknown mk, 17" .375.00
Lemon dish, bluebirds on wht, gold trim, #5, 5½" 30.00
Luncheon set, pk flowers among brn band on wht, bl #2, 72-pc ..1,300.00
Match holder, gold o/l on wht, hanging, #2, 4½" L 160.00
Nut set, violets on wht w/gold, #7, 7½" bowl +4 3½", ind 250.00
Pitcher, lemonade; roses, mc on cream w/gold, #7, 6" 235.00
Pitcher, roses on wht w/gold, 6-sided, RC mk, 7" 250.00

Plaque, hand-painted portrait of monk, 9½", $660.00.

Plaque, Am Indian portrait, geometric rim, #2, 8"	325.00
Plaque, buffalo (2) in relief, gr #2, 10½"	700.00
Plaque, bulldog portrait, gr #2, 10"	600.00
Plaque, gull & lg wave, fancy gold border, #7, 11½"	400.00
Plaque, lion's portrait in relief, brn tones, #2, 10½"	1,400.00
Plaque, sampan scenic, narrow gold border, #7, 10"	325.00
Plaque/charger, palm scenic, gr #2, 14"	400.00
Plate, poppies & flowers, gold rim, #7, 7½"	150.00
Plate, river scenic, cobalt & gold rim, gr #2, 8½"	275.00
Smoke set, playing cards on brn to gr, #2, 6" humidor+5 pcs	1,350.00
Snack set, flowers & birds in band on wht, #7, cup & tray	85.00
Stein, dogs in relief, twisted leash forms hdl, #2, 7"	950.00
Stein, figures in sunset scene, gold hdl, cylindrical, #2, 7"	650.00
Stein, monk drinking, vintage border, cylindrical, #2, 7"	750.00
Stein, spring-like landscape w/cottage, #2, 7"	650.00
Sugar shaker, roses on wht w/gold, #7, 4"	150.00
Syrup, floral (dainty) w/gold on wht, gr #2, 5¾"	95.00
Tankard, elk in relief, horn hdl, #2, 11½", +4 5" mugs	4,300.00
Tea set, butterflies, bl on wht, #5, child sz, 15-pc	300.00
Tea set, floral band on wht, HP mk, child sz, 21-pc	250.00
Tea set, palm scenic w/gold, bl #7, 5" pot+cr/sug	250.00
Tea set, river scenic w/gold, #2, 6½" pot+cr/sug+4 c/s	475.00
Tea strainer, flowers & gold, unmk, 6"	200.00
Tray, Capitol Building (WA DC) in center, floral band, #7, 8¾"	200.00
Urn, cattle drinking in landscape, gold hdls, #2, 16½"	2,500.00
Urn, swan scenic w/much gold, artist sgn, w/lid, #2, 19"	8,000.00
Vase, Anna Potocka reserve on gold & wht, hdls, #7, 7½"	900.00
Vase, cloisonne, red leaves on blk, bulbous, gold Nippon mk, 4"	350.00
Vase, Egyptian figure on brn cylinder, geometric bands, #2, 8½"	325.00
Vase, fisherman w/baskets at shore, hdls, gr #2, 8¼"	6,000.00
Vase, floral, mc on wht, cylinder w/bottle neck, #7, 9"	235.00
Vase, floral in relief, high hdls, #7, 8½"	650.00
Vase, floral on sq shouldered form w/sm gold hdls, #2, 9¾"	375.00
Vase, floral reserve & band on cobalt w/gold o/l, #2, 7½"	700.00
Vase, floral w/cobalt & gold, low hdls, #7, 9½"	325.00
Vase, floral w/coralene beading, RS Nippon mk, 7"	425.00
Vase, gold o/l scenic band & reserve on cobalt, hdls, #7, 7½"	600.00
Vase, grapes, mc on bl w/gold angle hdls, #2, 8½"	400.00
Vase, irises on slim ewer form w/gold, bl #3, 11"	400.00
Vase, moriage trees in landscape, hdls, #7, 9"	500.00
Vase, rose tapestry, sm gold hdls, gr #7, 6"	750.00
Vase, roses, pk on gold w/turq enamel dots, hdls, #7, 7"	500.00
Vase, roses (lg pk), bottle neck, #2, 6½"	200.00
Vase, roses (lg/mc) on tan, gold hdls, bottle neck, #7, 12"	500.00
Vase, roses (3 lg pk) in landscape, cylindrical, sm neck, #7, 12"	500.00
Vase, roses w/much gold, gourd shape w/hdls, #6, 8¾"	400.00
Vase, scenic tapestry, cylindrical, bl #7, 6¼"	650.00
Vase, silver o/l flowers on cobalt, shouldered, gr RC mk, 6½"	500.00
Vase, swan scenic w/moriage cattails, bulbous, hdls, #7, 9"	450.00
Vase, Wedgwood, cream on bl, hdls, gr #2, 8"	625.00
Vase, windmill scenic, earth tones, loving cup form, #2, 5½"	150.00
Whiskey jug, river reserve on keg form, gr #2, 5½"	750.00
Wine jug, Deco-style night scene, bl #7, 11"	950.00
Wine jug, English coaching scene reserve on gr, bl #7, 9½"	950.00

Nodders

So called because of the nodding action of their heads and hands, nodders originated in China where they were used in temple rituals to represent deity. At first they were made of brass and were actually a type of bell; when these bells were rung, the heads of the figures would nod. In the 18th century, the idea was adopted by Meissen and by French manufacturers who produced not only china nodders but bisque as well.

Most nodders are individual; couples are unusual. The idea remained popular until the end of the 19th century and was used during the Victorian era by toy manufacturers. For further information we recommend *Figural Nodders, Identification & Value Guide*, by Hilma R. Irtz, available from Collector Books or your local bookstore. Our advisor for non-German nodders is Barry Larkins; he is listed in the Directory under Florida.

Photo courtesy Hilma R. Irtz

Chinese man and lady, painted bisque, Germany, early 1900s, 4½" each, from $200.00 to $250.00 for the pair.

Bag sorter, wood, blk stenciled detail, red trim, 16", VG	550.00
Black boy on turtle's bk, pnt & fired bsk, 2¾x3½"	85.00
Black man sits on watermelon eating a slice, porc, Germany, 4½"	375.00
Bluebird, baby; pnt zinc, early 1900s, emb Germany, 2½"	95.00
Camel, fabric covered papier-mache & wood, glass eyes, 8x6½"	175.00
Cat, flocked papier-mache, orange, w/necklace, Japan, 7¾"	50.00
Doe, pewter, EX detail, 3½x3½"	150.00
Donkey, strutting, celluloid, made in Occupied Japan, lg	85.00
Donkey, 2 milk can shakers on bk, Vcagco Ceramics, 4¼x6¼"	75.00
Dutch child, holding skirt w/both hands, glazed porc, Germany	225.00
Jewish man w/holding red cloth, Portugal, 1900s	150.00
Pig, plastic, emb Germany, 2x4"	75.00
Santa Snoopy, pnt papier-mache, United Feature Syndicate, 3"	125.00
Skeleton, wax-dipped wood-pulp compo, pnt, Germany, 1900s, 5¼"	150.00
Turk w/sword, bsk, Germany	95.00
Turtles (2) sitting on log, cvd wood, unknown origin, 2½", L	15.00
Weight lifter, pnt & fired bsk, Germany, 1900s, 5½"	225.00

German Comic Characters

During the early 1930s, Germany produced a collection of small figure dolls, approximately 2" to 4" high, representing the most popular comic strip and cartoon characters of that time. They were made of bisque with brightly painted details and clearly stamped with their appropriate names and 'Germany' on their backs. Generally, their movable heads were attached with an elastic string going through their bodies, hence the name 'nodders,' but there were some characters produced earlier that were frozen with no movable parts. The most popular ones came in boxed sets, but the lesser-known characters were sold separately, making them rarer and harder to find today. We have listed the most valuable characters from the series here; those not mentioned below are valued at $125.00 and under. Our advisor for German character nodders is Doug Dezso; he is listed in the Directory under New Jersey. He will answer questions (as long as an SASE is included) on German character nodders only.

Ambrose Potts	350.00
Auntie Blossom	150.00
Auntie Mamie & Uncle Willie, ea	250.00
Bill, Dock, Avery, Max or Pop Jenks, ea	200.00
Buttercup	250.00
Chubby Chaney	250.00
Corky	475.00
Fanny or Rudy Nebbs, ea	250.00
Ferina	350.00

Grandpa Teen	350.00
Happy Hooligan	625.00
Harold Teen	150.00
Jeff Regus, med or lg, ea	250.00
Jeff Regus, sm	175.00
Josie	425.00
Junior Nebbs	625.00
Lilacs	425.00
Lillums	150.00
Little Annie Rooney, movable arms, complete	300.00
Little Egypt	350.00
Lord Plushbottom	150.00
Ma and Pa Winkle, ea	350.00
Marjorie	425.00
Mary Ann Jackson	250.00
Min Gump	150.00
Mr Bailey	150.00
Mr Bibb	400.00
Mushmouth	175.00
Mutt, med or lg, NM, ea	250.00
Mutt, sm, ea	175.00
Nicodemus	350.00
Old Timer	350.00
Our Gang, 6-pc set, MIB	1,200.00
Pat Finnegan	400.00
Patsy	425.00
Pete the Dog	250.00
Scraps	250.00
Widow Zander	400.00
Winnie Winkle	150.00

Noritake

The Noritake Company was first registered in 1904 as Nippon Gomei Kaisha. In 1917 the name became Nippon Toki Kabushiki Toki. The 'M in wreath' mark is that of the Morimura Brothers, distributors with offices in New York. It was used until 1941. The 'tree crest' mark is the crest of the Morimura family.

The Noritake Company has produced fine porcelain dinnerware sets and occasional pieces decorated in the delicate manner for which the Japanese are noted. (Two dinnerware patterns are featured below, and a general range is suggested for others.)

Authority Joan Van Patten has compiled two lovely books, *The Collector's Encyclopedia of Noritake, Vols. I and II,* with many full-color photos and current prices; you will find her address in the Directory under New York. In the following listings, examples are hand painted unless noted otherwise. Numbers refer to these specific marks:

Key:
#1 — Komaru   #3 — N in Wreath
#2 — M in Wreath

Azalea

The Azalea pattern was produced exclusively for the Larkin Company, who gave the lovely ware away as premiums to club members and their home agents. From 1916 through the '30s, Larkin distributed fine china which was decorated in pink azaleas on white with gold tracing along edges and handles. Early in the '30s, six pieces of crystal hand painted with the same design were offered: candle holders, a compote, a tray with handles, a scalloped fruit bowl, a cheese and cracker set, and a cake plate. All in all, seventy different pieces of Azalea were produced. Some, such as the fifteen-piece child's set, bulbous vase, china ashtray,

and the pancake jug, are quite rare. One of the earliest marks was the Noritake 'M in wreath' with variations. Later the ware was marked 'Noritake, Azalea, Hand Painted, Japan.' Our advisor is Peggy Roush; she is listed in the Directory under Florida.

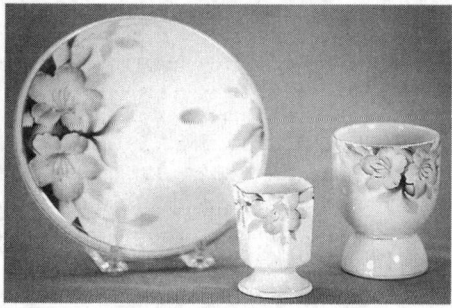

Tea tile, #169, $40.00; Toothpick holder, #192, $135.00; Egg cup, #120, $30.00.

Basket, mint; Dolly Varden, #193	195.00
Bonbon, #184, 6¼"	50.00
Bowl, #12, 10"	42.50
Bowl, candy/grapefruit; #185	195.00
Bowl, deep, #310	68.00
Bowl, fruit; shell form, #188, 7¾"	385.00
Bowl, oatmeal; #55, 5½"	28.00
Bowl, vegetable; divided, #439, 9½"	295.00
Bowl, vegetable; oval, #101, 10½"	60.00
Bowl, vegetable; oval, #172, 9¼"	58.00
Butter chip, #312, 3¼"	145.00
Butter tub, w/insert, #54	48.00
Cake plate, #10, 9¾"	40.00
Candy jar, w/lid, #313	695.00
Casserole, gold finial, w/lid, #372	540.00
Casserole, w/lid, #16	115.00
Celery/roll tray, #99, 12"	55.00
Cheese/butter dish, #314	135.00
Child's set, #253, 15-pc	2,500.00
Coffeepot, AD; #182	595.00
Compote, #170	98.00
Condiment set, #14, 5-pc	65.00
Creamer & sugar bowl, #7	45.00
Creamer & sugar bowl, AD; open, #123	140.00
Creamer & sugar bowl, gold finial, #401	155.00
Creamer & sugar bowl, ind, #449	395.00
Creamer & sugar shaker, #122	158.00
Cruet, #190	195.00
Cup & saucer, #2	20.00
Cup & saucer, AD; #183	150.00
Cup & saucer, bouillon; #124, 3½"	24.50
Egg cup, #120	30.00
Gravy boat, #40	48.00
Jam jar set, #125, 4-pc	155.00
Mayonnaise set, scalloped, #453, 3-pc	495.00
Mustard jar, #191, 3-pc	60.00
Pickle/lemon set, #121	24.50
Pitcher, milk jug; #100, 1-qt	195.00
Plate, #4, 7½"	10.00
Plate, bread & butter; #8, 6½"	10.00
Plate, breakfast; #98	28.00
Plate, cream soup; #363	175.00
Plate, dinner; #13, 9¾"	28.00
Plate, grill; 3-compartment, #38, 10¼"	165.00

Plate, scalloped sq, salesman's sample 950.00
Plate, soup; #19, 7⅛" 25.00
Platter, #17, 14" 60.00
Platter, #186, 16" 475.00
Platter, #56, 12" 58.00
Platter, cold meat/bacon; #311, 10¼" 215.00
Refreshment set, #39, 2-pc 48.00
Relish, #194, 7⅛" 85.00
Relish, oval, #18, 8½" 20.00
Relish, 2-part, #171 ....58.00
Relish, 2-part, loop hdl #450 ....425.00
Relish, 4-section, #119, rare, 10" 150.00
Saucer, fruit; #9, 5¼" 10.00
Shakers, bell form, #11, pr 30.00
Shakers, bulbous, #189, 8" 115.00
Shakers, ind, #126, pr 27.50
Spoon holder, #189, 8" 115.00
Syrup, #97, w/underplate & ladle 135.00
Tea tile 40.00
Teapot, #15 ....110.00
Teapot, gold finial, #400 ....495.00
Toothpick holder, #192 ....135.00
Vase, bulbous, #452 ....1,150.00
Vase, fan form, ftd, #187 ....185.00
Whipped cream/mayonnaise set, #3, 3-pc 38.50

Tree in the Meadow

Another of their dinnerware lines has become a favorite of many collectors. Tree in the Meadow features a hand-painted scene with a large dark tree in the foreground, growing near a lake. There is usually a cottage in the distance. Sometimes referred to as Tree by the Lake, this line was made during the 1920s and '30s and seems today to be in good supply. Various interesting forms are seen, and reassembling a complete set should be an enjoyable undertaking. Our advisor is Peggy Roush; she is listed in the Directory under Florida.

Basket, Dolly Varden 125.00
Bowl, cream soup; 2-hdl 35.00
Bowl, fruit; shell form, #210 ....300.00
Bowl, oatmeal 15.00
Bowl, soup 20.00
Bowl, vegetable; 9" 35.00
Butter pat 15.00
Butter tub, open, w/drainer 35.00
Cake plate 35.00
Candy dish, 5½" 400.00
Celery dish 35.00
Cheese dish 45.00
Coffeepot 200.00
Compote 50.00
Condiment set, 5-pc 45.00
Creamer & sugar bowl, demitasse 40.00
Cruets, vinegar & oil; cojoined, #319 ....360.00
Cup & saucer, breakfast 25.00
Cup & saucer, demitasse 35.00
Egg cup 30.00
Gravy boat 50.00
Jam jar/dish, 4-pc 70.00
Lemon dish 15.00
Mayonnaise set, 3-pc 50.00
Relish, divided 35.00
Sugar bowl, #204 ....25.00
Tea set, 3-pc 100.00

Miscellaneous

Ashtray, flowers on shaded cream, 4 rests, #2, 5¾" 50.00
Ashtray, Indian chief portrait, geometric rim, 6-sided, #2, 6½" ..160.00
Bowl, exotic birds on wht, Deco-style band, #2, 7¼" 90.00
Bowl, floral reserve w/orange lustre, bl rim, hdls, #2, 9¼" 65.00
Bowl, irises on wht, bl rim w/gold hdls, #2, 10½" 85.00
Bowl, river scenic, 8-sided, red #2, 6½" 35.00
Bowl, roses, pk on wht w/gold border & hdls, gr #2, 11" W 150.00
Bowl, 3 floral reserves w/gold on wht, 3 pierced hdls, #2, 6¼" ...30.00
Candlesticks, exotic bird on branch, bl rims & ft, #2, 8¼", pr 240.00
Candy jar, river reserve & band on gold lustre, #2, 6½" 225.00
Celery tray, celery stalks on cream, #2, 12", +6 3¾" salts 140.00
Cheese dish, yel band w/Deco flowers on wht, slant lid, #2, 8" L ..100.00
Chocolate pot, gold o/l on wht, #2, 9" 140.00
Chocolate set, exotic birds on wht w/gold, #2, 9½" pot+5 c/s 300.00
Cigarette holder, flowers on bell shape, bird finial, #2, 5" 200.00
Compote, floral on cream w/gold hdls, ftd, #2, 9¾" 80.00
Compote, swans in river scenic, hdls, #2, 9" W 85.00
Condensed milk container, Deco floral on wht w/gold, #2, 5¼" .160.00
Condiment set, exotic birds on red, #2, 3 pcs on 6¾" tray 150.00
Egg cup, windmill & river scenic, earth tones, #2, 3½" 40.00
Humidor, camel scene at sunset, gr #2, 5¾" 375.00
Humidor, owl on branch in relief, #2, 7" 525.00
Jam jar, bl & gold lustre, rose finial, #2, w/spoon & tray, 5¼" 80.00
Lemon dish, flowering branch on yel, red #2, 6½" L 40.00
Lemon dish, lemons & leaves, tan lustre rim, #2, 5¾" 40.00
Mantel set, Deco floral on cream w/gold, #2, 9" bowl+pr sticks ..425.00
Mustard set, roses, pk & yel on wht, #2, 3", 4-pc 35.00
Napkin ring, mc roses, #2, 2¼" W 45.00
Nappy, roses, pastels on cream, 1-hdl, #2, 5" 40.00
Night light, lady praying figural, lustre dress, #2, 9¾" 1,800.00
Plaque, river scenic w/swans, earth tones, #2, 6½" 115.00
Plate, windmill & river landscape, bright colors, #2, 7½" 65.00
Playing card holder, horse on tan lustre, ftd, #2, 3¾" 150.00
Sauce dish, flowers & bird on wht w/tan lustre, #2, 4½", +spoon .50.00
Sauce dish, roses on tan w/orange lustre, #2, 5", +ladle & tray 80.00
Shakers, river scenic, earth tones, #2, 2½", pr 16.00
Shaving mug, river scenic, earth tones w/gold, #2, 3¾" 120.00
Spooner, river scenic w/red-roofed cottage, #2, 8" L 70.00
Sugar shaker, floral band on wht, gold top, #2, 6½" 30.00
Syrup, trees, river & red-roofed cottage scene, #2, 4¼"+tray 85.00
Tea set, river scenic, #2, child sz, 3½" pot+8 pcs 225.00
Tile, river scenic, canted corners, #2, 5" 55.00
Toast rack, bl lustre w/bird finial, #2, 5½" L 125.00
Tray, river scenic w/swans, bl #1, 12" 80.00
Vase, lg open roses, pastel tones w/gold, hdls, #2, 11¼" 250.00
Vase, peacock feathers on tan, ruffled rim, slim, #1, 8", pr 180.00
Vase, river scenic, jack-in-pulpit shape, #2, 7¾" 180.00
Vase, roses on long stems on wht, hdls, #2, 8½" 165.00
Vase, tulip figural, purple & gr, #2, 5¼" 250.00
Vase, Wedgwood type, wht flowers on bl, hdls, #1, 9½" 475.00
Wall pocket, butterflies on tan lustre, red #2, 9" 125.00

Various Dinnerware Patterns, ca. 1933 to Present

So many lines of dinnerware have been produced by the Noritake company that to list them all would require a volume in itself. In fact, just such a book is available — *The Collector's Encyclopedia of Early Noritake* by Aimee Neff Alden (Collector Books). And while many patterns had specific names, others did not, so you'll probably need the photographs the book contains to help you identify your pattern. Outlined below is a general guide for the more common pieces and patterns. The high side of the range will represent lines from about 1933 until the mid-'60s (including those marked 'Occupied Japan'), while the lower side should be used to evaluate lines made after that period.

Bowl, berry; ind, from $8 to	10.00
Bowl, soup; 7½", from $10 to	15.00
Bowl, vegetable; rnd or oval, ca 1945 to present, from $25 to	35.00
Butter dish, 3-pc, ca 1933-64, from $35 to	50.00
Creamer, from $15 to	25.00
Cup & saucer, demi; from $10 to	17.50
Gravy boat, from $35 to	45.00
Pickle or relish dish, from $15 to	25.00
Plate, bread & butter; from $8 to	12.00
Plate, dinner; from $15 to	30.00
Plate, luncheon; from $10 to	18.00
Plate, salad; from $10 to	15.00
Platter, 12", from $25 to	40.00
Platter, 16" (or larger), from $40 to	60.00
Shakers, pr, from $15 to	25.00
Sugar bowl, w/lid, from $15 to	30.00
Tea & toast set (sm cup & tray), from $15 to	25.00
Teapot, demi pot, chocolate pot, or coffeepot, ea, from $45 to	60.00

Norse

The Norse Pottery was established in 1903 in Edgerton, Wisconsin, by Thorwald Sampson and Louis Ipson. A year later it was purchased by A.W. Wheelock and moved to Rockford, Illinois. The ware they produced was inspired by ancient bronze vessels of the Norsemen. Designs were often incised into the red clay body. Dragon handles and feet were favored decorative devices, and they achieved a semblance of patina through the application of metallic glazes. The ware was marked with model numbers and a stylized 'N' containing a vertical arrangement of the remaining letters of the name. Production ceased after 1913. Our advisor for this category is John Danis; he is listed in the Directory under Illinois.

Bowl, incised waves, 3-ftd, #55, 2½x4½"	200.00
Chamberstick, linear decor, blk w/gr & gold, #69, 6x5"	475.00
Jardiniere, incised snake, 3 Viking head ft, verdigris, #62, 7x9"	500.00
Jug, emb serpents on blk w/gold & gr, mk, #47, 8", w/stopper	550.00
Vase, lg lizard on side, gold wash, #25, 12"	1,000.00
Wall pocket, salamanders, 8¾", NM	400.00

North Dakota School of Mines

The School of Mines of the University of North Dakota was established in 1890, but due to a lack of funding it was not until 1898 that Earle J. Babcock was appointed as director, and efforts were made to produce ware from the native clay he had discovered several years earlier. The first pieces were made by firms in the East from the clay Babcock sent them. Some of the ware was decorated by the manufacturer; some was shipped back to North Dakota to be decorated by native artists. By 1909 students at the University of North Dakota were producing utilitarian items such as tile, brick, shingles, etc., in conjunction with a ceramic course offered through the chemistry department. By 1910 a ceramic department had been established, supervised by Margaret Kelly Cable. Under her leadership, fine artware was produced. Native flowers, grains, buffalo, cowboys, and other subjects indigenous to the state were incorporated into the decorations. Some pieces have an Art Nouveau – Art Deco style easily attributed to her association with Frederick H. Rhead, with whom she studied in 1911. During the '20s the pottery was marketed on a limited scale through gift and jewel-

ry stores in the state. From 1927 until 1949 when Miss Cable announced her retirement, a more widespread distribution was maintained with sales branching out into other states. The ware was marked in cobalt with the official seal — 'Made at School of Mines, N.D. Clay, University of North Dakota, Grand Forks, N.D.' in a circle. Very early ware was sometimes marked 'U.N.D.' in cobalt by hand. For more information refer to *Collector's Encyclopedia of Dakota Potteries* by Darlene Hurst Dommel (Collector Books). Our advisor for this category is William M. Bilsland III; he is listed in the Directory under Iowa.

Bowl, floral, mc on brn clay, Tollefson, 9½"	210.00
Bowl, oxen/covered wagons pnt/tooled around ext, JM/Huck, 6½"	950.00
Jar, oak leaves/acorns cvd on shaded gr matt, MLM/1931, 6x6"	365.00
Lamp base, gr to brn, sgn Taft 1930, ink mk, 10"	165.00
Planter bookends, ivy, dk gr over moss matt, Whitman, 3¾", pr	750.00
Plate, Deco flower/bull's eye, brn tones on beige, 1933, 9½"	375.00
Vase, band of leaves cvd on bl gloss, squat, 4x4½"	150.00
Vase, daffodils, lt brn cvd on dk brn, Cunningham, 1950, 9x5"	1,700.00
Vase, daffodils cvd on rust w/brn bkground, Skyberg, 7¾x5½"	1,900.00
Vase, geometric bands, yel/dk brn on brick red, Mattson, 4½x3"	600.00
Vase, geometrics/narrow band, gr/brn on yel, VB Arnold, '15, 7"	750.00

Vase, gourd form with incised brown oak leaves on light yellow-green matt, signed R. Sheppard, ink mark, 7½", $850.00.

Vase, horizontal stripes, gr on mustard, Mattson, 3¼x3¼"	325.00
Vase, lg oak trees cvd allover, Huckfield, 11x5½"	4,000.00
Vase, lines cvd on shoulder, yel/brn matt, Mattson/Slater, 4½"	150.00
Vase, Nouveau floral on long sems, 4-color, Mattson, 7x7½"	650.00
Vase, shoulder cvg on rose matt, sgn MP, 6"	300.00
Vase, triangles/birds/rainbow, yel/blk on brick, Aescadius, 4"	475.00

North State

In 1924 the North State Pottery of Sanford, North Carolina, began small-scale production, the result of the extreme fondness Mrs. Rebecca Copper had for potting. With the help of her husband and the abundance of suitable local clay, the pottery flourished and became well known for lovely shapes and beautiful glazes. The pottery was in business for thirty-five years; most of its ware was sold in gift and craft shops throughout North Carolina.

Jug, Chrome Red, thumb-grooved hdl, WN Owens, 1930s, att, 5⅝"	150.00
Jug, salt glaze (uncommon), thumb-grooved hdl, 1926-27, 5⅛"	175.00
Pansy pot, red-brn dbl-dip, earthenware, 1950s, 4", pr	50.00
Pitcher, Rebekkah, gr over yel-orange, ca 1960, 9⅝"	130.00
Vase, Chrome Red, folded top, WN Owens, 1930s, att, 4⅛"	75.00
Vase, dk red matt, corseted w/wrap-around hdls, sm rstr, 10x7"	550.00
Vase, salt glaze, tin-oxide int, ca 1926, 5"	200.00
Vase, 2-tone aqua, horizontal ribs, lg hdls, bulbous, att, 8"	160.00

Northwood

The Northwood Company was founded in 1896 in Indiana, Pennsylvania, by Harry Northwood, whose father, John, was the art director for Stevens and Williams, an English glassworks. Northwood joined the National Glass Company in 1899 but in 1901 again became an independent contractor and formed the Harry Northwood Glass Company of Wheeling, West Virginia. He marketed his first carnival glass in 1908, and it became his most popular product. His company was also famous for its custard, goofus, and pressed glass. Northwood died in 1923, and the company closed. See also Carnival; Custard; Goofus; Opalescent; Pattern Glass.

Bowl, Intaglio, red strawberries with much gold, scalloped edge, 10¼", $48.00.

Berry set, Leaf Umbrella, cranberry, 7-pc 600.00
Bowl, fruit; Royal Ivy, cranberry & canary craquelle, 9" 240.00
Bowl, sauce; Regal, bl, 4½" 20.00
Bowl, sauce; Regent, amethyst w/gold 40.00
Bowl, sauce; Royal Oak, rubena 55.00
Bowl, stretch, jade bl, rolled rim, 8" 75.00
Butter dish, Regal, gr 110.00
Butter dish, Royal Oak, frosted crystal 55.00
Cookie jar, Cherry Thumbprint, clear w/ruby & gold 150.00
Creamer, Regal, bl 60.00
Creamer, Royal Ivy, clear & frosted 80.00
Creamer, Royal Oak, frosted crystal 75.00
Cruet, Leaf Mold, cranberry spatter 595.00
Cruet, Leaf Umbrella, mauve 325.00
Cruet, Netted Oak, gr w/gold 295.00
Cruet, Royal Ivy, rainbow spatter 795.00
Epergne, bl opal, 4-trumpet (fluted/stippled), 17x11" 1,200.00
Pickle castor, Royal Ivy, clear spatter craquelle 695.00
Pitcher, Leaf Umbrella, bl opaque, 72-oz 650.00
Pitcher, Leaf Umbrella, cranberry, water sz 425.00
Pitcher, Maple Leaf, vaseline, water sz 300.00
Pitcher, Peach, gr w/gold, water sz, +6 tumblers 400.00
Pitcher, Regent, amethyst, water sz, +6 tumblers 800.00
Pitcher, Royal Ivy, cased spatter, water sz 350.00
Pitcher, Royal Ivy, rubena, water sz 300.00
Pitcher, Royal Oak, rubena, water sz 295.00
Shakers, Nestor, bl, pr 100.00
Shakers, Royal Ivy, cased spatter, orig tops, pr 250.00
Shakers, Royal Oak, rubena frost, MOP lids, pr 250.00
Spooner, Wreath & Shell, vaseline opal 110.00
Sugar bowl, Cherry Thumbprint, clear w/ruby & gold, w/lid 100.00
Sugar bowl, Memphis, gr 85.00
Sugar shaker, Daisy & Fern, cranberry, 9-panel 190.00
Sugar shaker, Leaf Mold, cranberry spatter w/gold flakes 360.00
Sugar shaker, Leaf Umbrella, cranberry, orig lid 495.00
Sugar shaker, Leaf Umbrella, cranberry spatter 395.00
Sugar shaker, Royal Ivy, rubena frost 225.00
Sugar shaker, Royal Oak, rubena 315.00
Sugar shaker, Royal Oak, rubena frost 295.00
Syrup, Leaf Mold, cranberry spatter, satin 495.00
Table set (creamer/spooner/butter/open sugar), Peach, gr w/gold ..350.00
Toothpick holder, Royal Ivy, rubena 95.00

Toothpick holder, Royal Oak, rubena frost 135.00
Tumbler, Royal Ivy, rubena 100.00
Tumbler, Royal Oak, rubena frost 100.00
Vase, Pull Up, gr/chartreuse/aqua swirls on wht, 4¼x3⅝" 175.00

Norweta

Norweta pottery was produced by the Northwestern Terra Cotta Company of Chicago, Illinois. Both matt and crystalline glazes were employed, and terra cotta vases were also produced. It was made for approximately ten years, beginning sometime before 1907. Not all was marked.

Plaque, advertising, children at play, mustard gloss, 15" L, EX ...**350.00**
Tile, stylized cherub w/plaque, terra cotta, 4x5", NM 60.00
Trivet, floral & stylized ovals in ivory matt, 6½" dia, EX 70.00
Vase, cream matt w/orange highlights, 20x16" 1,200.00
Vase, lav over cream matt, bottle neck, flared rim, 5½" 140.00
Vase, vertical leaves, gr & brn matt, mk, 4x6½" 500.00
Vase, wht/bl crystalline, bulbous base, 10x6" 1,600.00

Nutcrackers

The nutcracker, though a strictly functional tool, is a good example of one to which man has applied ingenuity, imagination, and engineering skills. Though all were designed to accomplish the same end, hundreds of types exist in almost every material sturdy enough to withstand sufficient pressure to crack the nut. Figurals are popular collectibles, as are those with unusual design and construction. Patented examples are also desirable. Our advisor for this category is Earl MacSorley; he is listed in the Directory under Connecticut. For more information we recommend *Ornamental and Figural Nutcrackers* by Judith A. Rittenhouse.

Bloodhound face, brass, pliers style, 6½" 125.00
Cat, full figure, brass, signed Cheshire, 5¼" 75.00
Cat face, cvd wood, glass eyes, 7¼" 250.00
Elephant, brass, pliers style, 5¼" 75.00
Frisbie, CI lever on brd, Patd May 17, 1859 ....75.00
Grandfather's clock, brass, pliers style, 5¼" 80.00
Lady's legs, brass, 4¾" 40.00
Man's face w/glasses, cvd wood, 8" 140.00
Monkey face, cvd wood, glass eyes, 8" 175.00
Prize Cutter, S Lee, 3-function, CI, Patd 1863, 14", mtd on brd .150.00
Rabbit head, cvd wood, long ears, glass eyes, 8¼" 140.00
Rooster head, cvd wood, glass eyes, 9¼" 125.00
Sargent #10 or #12, CI, on brd 12.00

Nutting, Wallace

Wallace Nutting (1861 – 1941) was America's most famous photographer of the early 20th century. A retired minister, Nutting took more than 50,000 pictures, keeping 10,000 of his best and destroying the rest. His popular and bestselling scenes included Exterior Scenes (apple blossoms, country lanes, orchards, calm streams, and rural American countrysides), Interior Scenes (usually featuring a colonial woman working near a hearth), and Foreign Scenes (typically thatch-roofed cottages). His poorest selling pictures, which have become today's rarest and most highly collectible, are classified as Miscellaneous Unusual Scenes and include categories not mentioned above: animals, architecturals, children, florals, men, seascapes and snow scenes. Process Prints are 1930s machine-produced reprints of twelve of Nutting's most popular pictures. These have minimal value and can be detected by using a magnifying glass.

Nutting sold literally millions of his hand-colored platinotype pictures between 1900 and his death in 1941. He started in Southbury, Connecticut, and later moved his business to Framingham, Massachusetts. The peak of Wallace Nutting picture production was 1915 – 25. During this period Nutting employed nearly two hundred people, including colorists, darkroom staff, salesmen, and assorted office personnel. Wallace Nutting pictures proved to be a huge commercial success and scarcely an American household was without one by 1925.

While attempting to seek out the finest and best early American furniture as props for his colonial interior scenes, Nutting became an expert in early American antiques. He published nearly twenty books in his lifetime, including his 10-volume State Beautiful series and various other books on furniture, photography, clocks, stools, chairs, settles, settees, tables, stands, desks, mirrors, beds, chests of drawers, cabinet pieces, and treenware. He made furniture as well, which he clearly marked with a distinctive paper label that was glued directly onto the piece, or a block or script signature brand which was literally branded into the furniture.

The overall synergy of the Wallace Nutting name — on pictures, books, and furniture — has made anything 'Wallace Nutting' quite collectible.

Our advisor for this category is Michael Ivankovich, author of many books concerning Nutting. Those currently available are *The Collector's Guide to Wallace Nutting Pictures; The Wallace Nutting Expansible Catalog; The Alphabetical and Numerical Index to Wallace Nutting Pictures; The Guide to Wallace Nutting Furniture, Wallace Nutting General Catalog, Supreme Edition; Wallace Nutting: A Great American Idea; Wallace Nutting's Windsors: Correct Windsor Furniture;* and *The Guide to Wallace Nutting-Like Photographers of the Early 20th Century.* Also available through Mr. Ivankovich is *The History of The Sawyer Pictures* by Carol Begley Gray. Mr Ivankovich's address and ordering information are listed in the Directory under Pennsylvania.

Prices below are for pictures in good to excellent condition. Mat stains or blemishes, poor picture color or frame damage can decrease value significantly.

Wallace Nutting Pictures

Although Wallace Nutting was widely recognized as the country's leading producer of hand-colored photographs during the early 20th century, he was by no means the only photographer selling this style of picture. Throughout the country literally hundreds of regional photographers were selling hand-colored photographs from their home regions or travels. The subject matters of these photographers was very comparable to Nutting's, including interior, exterior, foreign, and miscellaneous unusual scenes. The key determinants of value include the collectibility of the particular photographer, subject matter, condition, and size. Keep in mind that only the rarest pictures in the best condition will bring top prices. Discoloration and/or damage to the picture or matting can reduce value significantly.

Several photographers operated large businesses, and although not as large or well known as Wallace Nutting, they sold a substantial volume of pictures which can still be readily found today. The vast majority of their work was photographed in their home regions and sold primarily to local residents or visiting tourists. It should come as little surprise that three of the major Wallace Nutting-like photographers — David Davidson, Fred Thompson, and the Sawyer Art Co. — each had ties to Wallace Nutting.

Among the Ferns, 14x17"	165.00
Barre Brook, 13x16"	125.00
Billows of Blossoms, 14x17"	120.00
Bonnie May, 16x20"	40.00
Chair for John, 12x16"	130.00
Comfort & a Cat, 14x17"	325.00

Dog-On-It, 7x11"	1,265.00
Eventful Journey	650.00
Flowery Path, 13x16"	395.00
Garden of Larkspur, 13x16"	85.00
Hint of September, 15x22"	75.00
Hollyhocks (floral scene), 8x10"	525.00
Larkspur, 13x16"	175.00
Litchfield Minster, 11x14"	165.00
Meandering Battenkill, 10x16"	155.00
Mission Corner, 10x12"	275.00
Old Cabinet Maker, 12x14"	4,500.00
Pennsylvania Arches, 14x17"	300.00
Plymouth Curves, 11x17"	145.00
Pride of the Lane, 13x17"	165.00
Roses & Larkspur, 13x16"	1,200.00
Sheffield Basket, 13x16"	580.00
Street Border, 12x16"	240.00
Sunshine & Music, 13x16"	225.00
Untitled blossomes (blossoms & stone wall), 7x9"	75.00
Untitled interior (girls by fire), 8x12"	125.00
Venice's Chief Glory, 14x17"	575.00
Way It Begins, 14x17"	625.00
Wealth of October, 15x22"	90.00
Zinnias, 13x16"	500.00

Wallace Nutting Books

England Beautiful, gr cover, 1st edition	55.00
Furniture of the Pilgrim Century, 1st ed	140.00
Ireland Beautiful, gr cover, 1st edition	50.00
New York Beautiful, tan cover, 2nd edition	45.00
Photographic Art Secrets	28.00
Virginia Beautiful, tan cover, 2nd edition	40.00
Wallace Nutting Biography, w/dust jacket	140.00

Wallace Nutting Furniture

Armchair, sack bk	825.00
Armchair, Windsor, low-bk, #414, block brand, paper label	525.00
Candlestand, Windsor, tripod, #17, block brand	525.00
Chair, side; Windsor, bent-rung bow-bk, bamboo trns, #305, block brand	800.00
Chair, side; 4-rung ladder-bk, #392, block brand	475.00
Hutch table, pine	825.00
Mirror, gold, 3-feather, #761, impressed brand	575.00
Stool, Windsor, rnd, 3104, block brand	300.00
Table, oak refractory, #601, block brand	935.00
Table, trestle	500.00

David Davidson

Second to Nutting in overall production, Davidson worked primarily in the Rhode Island and Southern Massachusetts area. While a student at Brown University around 1900, Davidson learned the art of hand-colored photography from Wallace Nutting, who happened to be the minister at Davidson's church. After Nutting moved to Southbury in 1905, Davidson graduated from Brown and started a successful photography business in Providence, Rhode Island, which he operated until his death in 1967.

Blossom Lane	35.00
Daughter of Sheffield, 13x16"	275.00
Lamb's May Feast	130.00
Porch Beautiful	60.00
Puritan Lady, 12x16"	75.00

Snowbound Brook	55.00
Village Maiden, 14x17"	180.00
Ye Olden Tyme, 13x16"	300.00

Sawyer

A father and son team, Charles H. Sawyer and Harold B. Sawyer, operated the very successful Sawyer Art Company from 1903 into the 1970s. Beginning in Maine, the Sawyer Art Company moved to Concord, New Hampshire, in 1920 to be nearer their primary market of New Hampshire's White Mountains. Charles H. Sawyer briefly worked for Nutting in 1902 – 03 while living in southern Maine. Sawyer's production volume ranks #3 behind Wallace Nutting and David Davidson.

Autumn Glory, 9x12"	50.00
Echo Lake, Franconia Notch, 13x16"	55.00
Gosport Church	90.00
Lafayette Slides, 13x15"	90.00
Majestic Nature	55.00
Rock Garden, Cape Cod, 16x20"	165.00
Winchester Bridge	210.00

Fred Thompson

Frederick H. Thompson and Frederick M. Thompson were another father and son team that operated the Thompson Art Company (TACO) from 1908 to 1923, working primarily in the Portland, Maine, area. We know that Thompson and Nutting had collaborated because Thompson widely marketed an interior scene he had taken in Nutting's Southbury home. The production volume of the Thompson Art Company ranks #4 behind Nutting, Davidson, and Sawyer.

Apple Tree Road	45.00
Covered Bridge, 9x12"	75.00
Fireside Fancy Work	140.00
Nature's Carpet	50.00
Neath the Blossoms, 7x9"	65.00
Portland Head	240.00
Roasting Apples, 10x12"	55.00
Spinning Days, 14x17"	95.00

Charles Higgins

Working out of Bath, Maine, some of Higgins's finest pictures rivaled Nutting's best. No firm connection has been found between Higgins and Wallace Nutting.

Charles R. Higgins, Colonial Stairway	65.00
Florian A Baker, Rushing Waters	50.00
Haynes, Untitled Waterfalls	20.00
Lane, 9x12"	95.00
Rocky Shore, 8x14"	55.00
Untitled seascape, 7x11"	65.00

Minor Wallace-Like Photographers

Hundreds of other smaller local and regional photographers attempted to market hand-colored pictures comparable to Nutting's during the 1900 – 30s time period. Although quite attractive, most were not as appealing to the general public as Wallace Nutting pictures. However, as the price of Wallace Nutting pictures has escalated, the work of these lesser-known Wallace Nutting-like photographers have become increasingly collectible.

A partial listing of some of these minor Wallace Nutting-like photographers include Babcock; J.C. Bicknell; Blair; Ralph Blood (Portland, Maine); Bragg; Brehmer; Brooks; Burrowes; Busch; Carlock; Pedro Cacciola; Croft; Currier; Depue Bros; Derek; Dowly; Eddy; May Farini (hand-colored colonial lithographs); Geo. Forest; Gandara; Gardner (Nantucket, Bermuda, Florida); Gibson; Gideon; Gunn; Bessie Pease Gutmann (hand-colored colonial lithographs); Edward Guy; Harris; C Hazen; Knoffe; Haynes (Yellowstone Park); Margaret Hennesey; Hodges; Homer; Krabel; Kattleman; La Bushe; Lake; Lamson (Portland, Maine); M. Lightstrum; Machering; Rossiler Mackinae; Merrill; Meyers; William Moehring; Moran; Murrey; Lyman Nelson; J. Robinson Neville (New England); Patterson; Owen Perry; Phelps; Phinney; Reynolds; F. Robbins; Royce; Fred'k Scheetz (Phila...Pennsylvania); Shelton; Standley (Colorado); Stott; Summers; Esther Svenson; Florence Thompson; Thomas Thompson; M.A. Trott; Sanford Tull; Underhill; Villar; Ward; Wilmot; Edith Wilson; and Wright.

A very general breakdown of prices for works by these minor Wallace Nutting-like photographers would be as follows:

The same pricing guidelines that apply to Wallace Nutting pictures typically apply to Wallace Nutting-like pictures
    1.) Exterior scenes are the most common.
    2.) Some photographers sold colonial interior scenes as well.
    3.) Subject, matter, condition, and size are all important determinants of value.

Larger pictures, greater than 14x17", from $75 to over	200.00
Medium pictures, from 11x14" to 14x17", from $50 to over	200.00
Smaller pictures, 5x7" to 10x12", from $10 to	75.00

Miscellaneous Nutting Memorabilia

Advertising sign, paper, 11x16"	125.00
Catalog, furniture, 1927-28	65.00
Christmas card, 4x5"	150.00
Miniature exterior scene, 4x5"	65.00
Pirate print, Swimming Pool, unsgn	10.00
Silhouette, Girl Sits at Vanity, 4x4"	45.00
Silhouette, Girl w/Powder Puff, 4x4"	70.00

Occupied Japan

Items marked 'Occupied Japan' have become popular collectibles in the last few years. They were produced during the period from the end of World War II until April 18, 1952, when the occupation ended. By no means was all of the ware exported during that time marked 'Occupied Japan'; some was marked 'Japan' or 'Made In Japan.' It is thought that because of the natural resentment felt by the Japanese toward the occupation, only a fraction of these wares carried the 'Occupied' mark. Even though you may find identical 'Japan'-marked items, because of its limited use, only those with the 'Occupied Japan' mark are being collected to any great extent. Values vary considerably, based on the quality of workmanship. Generally, bisque figures command much higher prices than porcelain, since on the whole they are of a finer quality.

For those wanting more information, we recommend *The Collector's Encyclopedia of Occupied Japan Collectibles* (there are six in the series) by Gene Florence; he is listed in the Directory under Kentucky. Our advisor for this category is Florence Archambault; she is listed in the Directory under Rhode Island. She represents the Occupied Japan Club, whose mailing address may be found in the Directory under Clubs, Newsletters, and Catalogs. All items described in the following listings are assumed ceramic unless noted otherwise.

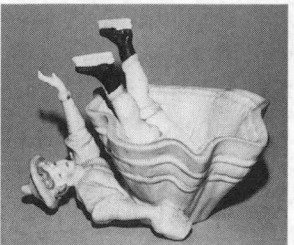

Figurine, tumbled ice skater, marked Ardalt, 4x5½", $75.00.

Photo courtesy Florence Archambault

Ashtray, baseball glove, metal, emb mk 15.00
Ashtray, Indian head shape, metal, souvenir White Pine Lodge ...15.00
Ashtray, peacock decor in center, metal 6.00
Bank, elephant, floral decor on bk, 2¼x3¾" 30.00
Bell, chef w/rolling pin, 3" 25.00
Bowl, fruit decor, lattice edge, 5½" 17.50
Bowl, soup; Livonia (Dogwood), 8⅞" 9.00
Box, dragon (ornate) decor, w/lid, metal, crown mk, 4x7" 27.50
Box, peacock on red bkground, emb w/flag, CKS in emblem, metal ..17.50
Butter pat, cottage decor, T in circle mk 12.50
Candy dish, 3-part, metal, w/hdl, emb T in chicken-shaped emblem ..20.00
Cigarette box, bobbing bird picks up cigarette, wooden 50.00
Cigarette box, pagoda scene, T over M mk 30.00
Cigarette lighter, camel, sitting, metal, emb mk on base 20.00
Cigarette lighter, horse head, metal, emb mk 20.00
Clock, birdcage design, impressed mk 250.00
Cookie jar, cottage shape, T in circle mk 75.00
Creamer, iris decor, sm 12.50
Crum butler, Washington DC souvenir, metal 7.50
Cup & saucer, house scene, luster 15.00
Cup & saucer, Phoenix Bird, bl & wht 25.00
Cup & saucer, thatch house river scene, mk MIOJ 17.50
Dinnerware set, Sango China, floral pattern & rim, serves 4 ......200.00
Figurine, angel w/mandolin, 6⅜" 35.00
Figurine, bird on branch, 7⅞" 40.00
Figurine, boy & girl tending sunflower, bsk, 5⅜" 60.00
Figurine, boy sitting on fence w/cat below, 4" 15.00
Figurine, bride & groom, 6⅛" 50.00
Figurine, Colonial man playing violin, bsk, 9" 60.00
Figurine, courting couple w/lambs, 8¼x9¼" 350.00
Figurine, cuckoo clock w/bird on top, pendulums on strings, 5" ...15.00
Figurine, Dutch lady at well, 4½" 12.50
Figurine, elephant, gray, impressed mk on ft, 4" 30.00
Figurine, elk, celluloid-sprayed silver, 7x7½" 15.00
Figurine, girl w/teddy bear in basket, 5⅜" 25.00
Figurine, horse & sulky, metal, emb camel mk 30.00
Figurine, lady w/dog & gun, bsk, 6" 35.00
Figurine, Little White Riding Hood, 4⅛" 15.00
Figurine, man w/lady in rickshaw, celluloid, wood base, 2" 20.00
Figurine, mermaid w/orange tail on rocks 30.00
Figurine, monkey in brn suit, red circle w/cross mk, 3½" 35.00
Figurine, puppies (3) in basket, 3" 15.00
Figurine, yel coach led by 2 wht horses, 3" 10.00
Flower frog, wht w/7 mc dots, rnd, 4½" dia 20.00
Gravy boat, Livonia (Dogwood) 17.50
Ice bucket, Lacquerware, Maruni, gold & pearl stork decor, 7⅝" ..60.00
Incense burner, elephant, wht w/gold decor, 2½" 20.00
Incense burner, Mexican man, seated, 4" 30.00
Lamp base, lady's head, purple flower in hair, 10" 55.00
Match safe, brn w/yel & wht flowers w/bl leaves, 2-tiered, 6¼" 40.00
Mug, elephant, trunk forms hdl, brn, 4¾" 20.00
Mug, Santa form, hat forms hdl, 3" 35.00
Music box, Geisha dancer, 4-drw, 12x5" 175.00

Pin, Scottie dog in bl jacket, celluloid, incised mk 15.00
Planter, buggy, bl, arch symbol, 5¼" 10.00
Planter, cupid on sled, bsk, paper label, 5" 45.00
Planter, elephant, raised trunk 15.00
Planter, heart w/angel playing accordion, 3⅝" 12.00
Planter, shell form, lady holding basket, bsk, 5½x6½" 55.00
Planter, woodpecker eyeing frog 5.00
Plaque, Dutch boy w/2 baskets, chalkware, 7½" 22.50
Plate, Hibiscus, open lace edge, 8¼" 22.50
Plate, Lacquerware, pagoda scene, sq w/cut corners, 6" 40.00
Platter, Livonia (Dogwood), 13½" 30.00
Shakers, clowns on drums, pr 40.00
Shakers, cowboy boots, metal, emb mk inside heel 20.00
Shakers, penguin shape, metal, pr 22.50
Shakers, strawberry shape, on leaf tray, set 20.00
Shelf sitter, boy holding hat, 5¼" 20.00
Shelf sitter, boy w/horn, 3¾" 15.00
Shelf sitter/planter, Oriental lady 20.00
Sugar bowl, Lily of the Valley, pk 12.50
Sugar bowl, windmill shape, w/lid, 3⅞" 20.00
Tape measure, pig form, celluloid 50.00
Teapot, floral w/draping ivy, gold trim 40.00
Teapot, gray w/yel blooming water lillies 30.00
Teapot, windmill shape 50.00
Tray, lobster in center, 3-part 40.00
Tray, sailfish decor, shell shaped, sgn, 3" dia 10.00
Vase, bud; Indian chief stands beside tree, 3⅝" 10.00
Vase, Lacquerware, gold fern decor, 13" 150.00
Vase, urn; emb grapes, emb mk 15.00
Wall pocket, peacock on branch decor 30.00

Ohr, George

George Ohr established his pottery in the 1880s in Biloxi, Mississippi. The first pottery burned down and was subsequently rebuilt. Ohr, among other things, was a master of the wheel. This mastery enabled him to create unique forms of unbelievable thinness, verging at times on Abstraction and looking far ahead toward many art movements of the 20th century. In addition to Abstraction, by studying Ohr, one can discover elements of Expressionism and Fauvism (the wild use of color often seemingly at odds with the piece being glazed) and Dada (meaning shock the bourgeosie). An Ohr piece may be rooted in the functional form of a teapot, but following his manipulation it becomes a sculpture for which the functional form serves only as a take-off point for the finished piece. Ohr was also a master of glazes. Highly esteemed are his volcanic and gunmetal glazes. He was not well received in his day and sold few pieces of his art pottery — a van Gogh-like tale. Ohr decorated his pieces with snakes and lizards and sometimes with asymmetrical handles. He believed that like all things on earth, no two things should be alike. This dictum was applied to his pottery making. He signed his pieces either in impressed letters or florid script. In the early 1900s Ohr ceased making pottery and became a motorcycle dealer and ultimately sold automobiles. His pottery was stored away to be rediscovered many years later. Ohr died in 1918. Our advisor for this category is Fer-Duc, Inc.; whose address is listed in the Directory under New York.

Bowl, amber/brn/gr speckle, folded/dimpled free-form, 2½x5" ...2,400.00
Bowl, amber/gunmetal speckle, pinched/folded free-form, 6½" ...2,600.00
Bowl, blk drips on gr, ca 1890, 2⅜x2⅝" 425.00
Bowl, blk w/skin-like texture, 3x5½" 650.00
Bowl, bsk, dimpled sides, line in mfg, 4" H 750.00
Bowl, incurvate w/even pleats, bsk, 5" dia 1,600.00
Candlestick, gunmetal, shaped std, thick rnd base, 4½x3¾" 375.00

Chamberstick, bsk, deep in-body twist, folded hdl, 5½x4¾" 375.00
Chamberstick, gunmetal/gr, deep in-body twist, 3¾x4½" 900.00
Cup, gr/cobalt/raspberry marble, int: cobalt/raspberry, 2½" 1,500.00
Jar, gunmetal/brn mottle, incised shoulder/base design, 4", NM .700.00
Jardiniere, gunmetal matt, lg shoulder bulge, 3½" 450.00
Jug, bsk-fired wht clay, from St Louis Expo, 4x3" 450.00
Match holder, amber gloss, relief lion's head, 4¼" dia 800.00
Pitcher, gr speckled, scalloped rim, ear hdl, 3x5½" 1,600.00
Pitcher, gr/raspberry/gunmetal speckles, squat, 2¾x5" 1,100.00
Pitcher, gr/red speckled, lg dimples, pinched spout, 4x5" 4,500.00
Pitcher, gunmetal, pinch spout/pinch over cut-out hdl, 3¾" ..1,700.00
Pitcher, gunmetal/gr mottle, dimpled, ftd, 3x5¼" 1,000.00
Pitcher, half currant/half mauve speckled, organic shape, sm ..3,750.00
Puzzle mug, brn/gunmetal mottle, dimpled, 3½x4¾" 850.00
Teapot, brn spots on ochre, flared body, 4x6" 300.00
Teapot, teal gr speckle, snake spout, sm flaw, 3¼x6½" 2,000.00
Vase, bl-gr/red-cobalt mottle on pk, ornate hdls, rstr, 9" ..12,000.00
Vase, brn gloss, in-body twist, folded rim/hdls, rstr, 3x4" 1,100.00
Vase, brn w/rough texture, int: gr/brn, bulbous, 3½" 320.00
Vase, bsk, hourglass shape w/folded ribbon hdls, 6x4½" 1,400.00
Vase, bsk scroddled clay, folded/crinolated rim, 4x4¾" 1,100.00
Vase, bud; matt blk crystalline, in-body twist, 5¼x2½" 1,400.00
Vase, dk aventurine/gunmetal, folded top, 5¼x4½", NM 800.00
Vase, dk bl/lt gr/mahog flambe, ftd baluster, 6x3¼" 850.00
Vase, gr/blk gloss w/red clay exposed, collar neck, 3½" 500.00
Vase, gr/blk/gunmetal, shouldered w/cylinder neck, 3½" 550.00
Vase, gunmetal, can neck/wide body, 4 lg horizontal ribs, 3½" ...700.00
Vase, gunmetal, crimped, row of dents, beaded band, 3", NM 850.00
Vase, gunmetal, extreme shoulder angle, crimped rim, flaw, 4½" ...2,000.00
Vase, gunmetal/blk/gr, flaring shoulder, 3" 500.00
Vase, gunmetal/gr mottle, classic shape, 8½x3¼" 2,200.00
Vase, gunmetal/khaki speckle, under-rim pinched twist, 6x5½" ...1,800.00
Vase, mahog/aventurine/gunmetal, folded rim, str sides, 5x4½" .850.00
Vase, mustard gunmetal drip on olive & brn, incurvate rim, 4" ..475.00
Vase, pk/bl/gr mottled gloss, gourd shape, 4¾x3¾" 1,300.00
Vase, pk/wht/bl mottled gloss, tapered/shouldered, 3¼x3¼" ...1,100.00
Vase, pnt swirls, brn on cream, bulbous w/can neck, 3" 550.00
Vase, raspberry, gunmetal int, shaped rim, dimpled, 2½x3½" .1,600.00
Vase, raspberry/wht/amber mottle, pinched rim, ribbon hdls, 6" 13,000.00
Vessel, dk bl-gr/gunmetal, lobed/pinched rim, 3½x4½" 1,100.00

Old Ivory

Old Ivory dinnerware was produced during the late 1800s by Herman Ohme, of Lower Salzbrunn in Silesia. The patterns are referred to by the numbers stamped on the bottom of many items. (Though not every piece is numbered, the vast majority bears the tiny blue fleur-de-lis/crown mark with Silesia or Germany beneath. Handwritten numbers signify something other than pattern.) Patterns #16 and #84 are the easiest to find and come in a wide variety of table items. Values are about the same for both patterns. Other floral designs include pink, yellow, and orange roses; holly; and lavender flowers — all on the same soft ivory background. The ware was not widely distributed; its two main distribution points were in Maine and, to a lesser extent, Chicago. Our prices are intended to represent a nationwide average, though you may have to pay a little more in some areas. Novice collectors should be aware of copy-cat versions from the turn of the century that are much heavier and of a coarser material. They are marked 'Old Ivory' without the blue trademark. They are not included in this listing.

For further information we recommend *Collector's Encyclopedia of Old Ivory China, The Mystery Explored,* by Alma Hillman (our advisor), David Goldschmitt, and Adam Szynkiewicz (Collector Books). Ms. Hillman is listed in the Directory under Maine.

Basket, #145, hdld 250.00
Bone dish, #11 ....400.00
Bouillon cup saucer, #11, 3½" 200.00
Bowl, berry; #16 or #84, 5" 35.00
Bowl, berry; #27 (rare pattern), 9½" master +10 sm 350.00
Bowl, cereal; #16 or #84, 6½" 65.00
Bowl, ice cream; #16 or #84, 4½x5" 35.00
Bowl, nappy; #15, 6½" 135.00
Bowl, soup; #16 or #84, 7½" 165.00
Bowl, vegetable; #16 or #84, w/lid 1,095.00
Butter dish, #84, w/lid & insert, 7½" 700.00
Butter pat, #16 or #84 ....125.00
Cake plate, #15, open hdls, 10¾" 125.00
Cake plate, #16 or #84, open hdls, 10" ...130.00
Cake plate, #62 (Holly) 300.00
Celery tray, #16 or #84, 11x5½" 125.00
Charger, #82, 13" 425.00
Chocolate set, #15, pot +4 c/s 850.00
Cracker jar, #16 or #84 ....450.00
Creamer & sugar bowl, #16 or #84, w/lid ...175.00
Cup & saucer, #75 ....75.00
Cup & saucer, #76 ....85.00
Cup & saucer, demi; #15 ....95.00
Demitasse pot, #15, 7½" 500.00
Gravy boat, #16 or #84, attached base, 8½" L 800.00
Hair receiver, 2½x4" dia 300.00
Mayonnaise & underplate, #73, 6½" 200.00
Mustard pot, #57, 3¾" 325.00
Pickle dish, #4, 8½" 95.00
Pitcher, water; #28, 8" 1,200.00
Plate, #11, dinner; 9¾" 250.00
Plate, #16 or #84, 6⅛" 35.00
Plate, #16 or #84, 8¼" 60.00
Plate, #17, dinner; 9¾" 400.00
Plate, #40, peach roses on Empire blank, mk, 6¼" 45.00
Plate, #62 (Holly), 6¼" 75.00
Plate, #75, scalloped edge, 8" 85.00
Plate, #76, luncheon 95.00

Plate, #82, Alice mold, 9¾", $250.00.

Plate, #84, 8" 60.00
Platter, #75, open hdls, 11½" 175.00
Porringer, #33 ....110.00
Teapot, #15 ....500.00
Tile, #16 or #84, 6¼" dia 225.00
Toothpick holder, #16 or #84 ....250.00
Toothpick holder, #73 ....265.00
Tray, bun; #204, 10" 265.00
Waste bowl, #7, mk, 2½x9x7" 225.00

Old Paris

Old Paris porcelains were made from the mid-18th century until about 1900. Seldom marked, the term refers to the area of manufacture rather than a specific company. In general, the ware was of high quality, characterized by classic shapes, colorful decoration, and gold application.

Bottle, scent; cavalier figural, ca 1840, 10½" 385.00
Bowl, centerpc; ornate hdls, pendant fruit, reserves, 21" L 650.00
Bowl, floral w/gold, 1850s, 4x12" 275.00
Bowl, vegetable; cutout ends, 1850s, 12½x9½", pr 500.00

Centerpiece bowl, young rustics in landscape reserves on turquoise with gilt and applied flowers, 9x18", $1,500.00.

Coffeepot, putti w/flower baskets, gold borders, 1815, 10x5" ...1,045.00
Compote, floral cartouches on wht w/gold, 1850s, 8x9¾" 550.00
Compote, gold & wht, rtcl base/bowl, ca 1840, 7½x10", pr 950.00
Compote, rtcl bowl w/foliage, magenta & wht w/gold, 1850s, lg ...750.00
Corbeilles, bl, gilt & floral decor, 7x9" dia, pr 400.00
Sauce tureen, salmon & gilt, acorn finial, attached stand, 7x10x6" .400.00
Shell dish, fluted, peach & bl rim w/gold foliage, 1840s, 9½" 450.00
Urn, cobalt & gilt, caryatid hdls, ca 1815, 9¼", pr 1,000.00
Vase, floral on cobalt, 19th C, 10½" 250.00
Vase, meadow flowers/morning glories allover, 13" 425.00
Vase, Turkish prince portrait/Eiffel Tower, bl decor, 10½" 250.00
Veilleuse, European village reserve on gr w/gold, 19th C, 9" 275.00

Old Sleepy Eye

Old Sleepy Eye was a Sioux Indian chief who was born in Minnesota in 1780. His name was used for the name of a town as well as a flour mill. In 1903 the Sleepy Eye Milling Company of Sleepy Eye, Minnesota, contracted the Weir Pottery Company of Monmouth, Illinois, to make steins, vases, salt crocks, and butter tubs which the company gave away to their customers. A bust profile of the old Indian and his name decorated each piece of the blue and gray stoneware. In addition to these four items, the Minnesota Stoneware Company of Red Wing made a mug with a verse which is very scarce today.

In 1906 Weir Pottery merged with six others to form the Western Stoneware Company in Monmouth. They produced a line of blue and white ware using a lighter body, but these pieces were never given as flour premiums. This line consisted of pitchers (five sizes), steins, mugs, sugar bowls, vases, trivets, and mustache cups. These pieces turn up only rarely in other colors and are highly prized by advanced collectors. Advertising items such as trade cards, pillow tops, thermometers, paperweights, letter openers, postcards, cookbooks, and thimbles are considered very valuable. The original ware was made sporadically until 1937. Brown steins and mugs were produced in 1952. Our advisor for this category is Jim Martin; he is listed in the Directory under Illinois.

Banner, center portrait & western scenes, 22" sq, EX 1,450.00
Barrel, flour; orig paper label, 1920s 1,800.00
Barrel, grapevine-effect banding 3,500.00

Barrel, oak w/brass bands 4,500.00
Blanket, horse; w/logo, EX 2,500.00
Butter crock, Flemish bl & gray 750.00
Cabinet, bread display; Old Sleepy Eye etched in glass 950.00
Calendar, 1904, NM 375.00
Cookbook, Indian on cover, Sleepy Eye Milling Co, 4¾x4", NM ...300.00
Cookbook, loaf of bread shape, NM 210.00
Coupon, for ordering cookbook 250.00
Coupon, for ordering pillow top 200.00
Dough scraper, tin/wood, To Be Sure, EX 435.00
Fan, chief cb diecut, minor rub on tassle, EX 210.00
Flour sack, cloth, mc Indian, red letters 345.00
Flour sack, paper, Indian in blk, blk lettering, NM 125.00
Ink blotter 125.00
Label, bbl end; mc Indian portrait, 16", NM 160.00
Letter opener, bronze 900.00
Match holder, pnt 1,000.00
Match holder, wht 1,050.00
Mug, bl & gray, 4¼" 360.00
Mug, bl & wht, 4¼" 220.00
Mug, verse, Red Wing, EX 1,625.00
Paperweight, bronzed company trademk 560.00
Pillow cover, Sleepy Eye & tribe meet President Monroe 750.00
Pillow cover, trademk center w/various scenes, 22", NM 1,800.00
Pin-bk button, Indian, rnd face 350.00
Pitcher, #1, 4" 300.00
Pitcher, #2 ....350.00
Pitcher, #3 ....315.00
Pitcher, #3, w/bl rim 1,375.00
Pitcher, #4 ....400.00
Pitcher, #5 ....435.00
Pitcher, bl & gray, 5" 325.00
Pitcher, bl on cream, 8", M 345.00
Pitcher, standing Indian, good color, #5 size 1,560.00
Postcard, colorful trademk, 1904 Expo Winner 185.00
Ruler, wooden, 15" 700.00
Salt crock, Flemish bl & gray, 4x6½" 700.00
Sheet music, in fr 300.00
Sign, self-fr tin, Old Sleepy Eye Flour, 20x24" 2,500.00
Sign, tin litho die-cut Indian, ...Flour & Cereals, 13½" 1,650.00
Spoon, demitasse; emb roses in bowl, Unity SP 105.00
Spoon, Indian-head hdl 125.00
Stein, bl & wht, 7¾" 800.00
Stein, brn, 1952, 22-oz 300.00
Stein, brn & wht 1,500.00
Stein, brn & yel, Western Stoneware 1,500.00
Stein, cobalt 1,250.00
Stein, Flemish bl & gray 700.00
Stein, ltd edition, 1979-84, ea 125.00
Sugar bowl, bl & wht, 3" 750.00
Thermometer, front rpl 800.00
Vase, cattails, all cobalt 1,450.00
Vase, cattails, bl & wht, good color, 9" 800.00
Vase, cattails, brn on yel, rare color 1,500.00
Vase, cattails, gr & wht 5,000.00
Vase, Indian & cattails, Flemish, 8½" 470.00

O'Neill, Rose

Rose O'Neill's Kewpies were introduced in 1909 when they were used to conclude a story in the December issue of *Ladies' Home Journal*. They were an immediate success, and soon Kewpie dolls were being produced worldwide. German manufacturers were among the earliest and also used the Kewpie motif to decorate chinaware as well as other items. The Kewpie is still popular today and can be found on products ranging from Christmas cards and cake ornaments to fabrics, wallpaper, and metal items.

For further information we recommend *Doll Values, Antique to Modern*, by Patsy Moyer (Collector Books). Our advisor for this category is Kitty Watson; she is listed in the Directory under Oklahoma. In the following listings, 'sgn' indicates that the item is signed Rose O'Neill. Doll values are for examples in mint condition. © in circle is also a good mark on items. Unsigned items can be of interest to collectors; many are authentic and collectible, some are too small to sign.

Ad, Jell-O, blk & wht, ca 1915 ....**6.00**
Ad, Kewpies & ice cream, sgn Rose O'Neill, color, full pg **45.00**
Ashtray, brass Kewpie figure at side of slag tray **225.00**
Bell, brass, Kewpie figural hdl, 3" **95.00**
Bell, sterling, figural, sgn, 4" **198.00**
Book, Kewpies in Action, M Leuzzi, 1971 ....**150.00**
Booklet, Jell-O Girl & Kewpie-like fairies, 1910s, NM **60.00**
Bowl, cereal; 5 action Kewpies, Royal Rudolstadt, sgn, 6¼" **115.00**
Candle holder, dbl; metal, seated Kewpie between, wht pnt, mk ..**1,700.00**
Color book, Adventures & Kewpies, 1962, M, from $65 to **70.00**

Clock, Kewpies, jasperware, white on blue, signed, Germany, 5½x5½", $625.00.

Cup, 5 action Kewpies, Royal Rudolstadt, sgn O'Neill Wilson, lg ...**100.00**
Display case, tin, Kewpie-Garter advertising, 12½x13¾", $550 to ...**700.00**
Doll bed, poster style w/Kewpie decals on gr, orig **450.00**
Dress, pk, Kewpies, child's sz 6, from $75 to **100.00**
Figurine, bsk, Doodle Dog, sgn, 3", minimum value **1,850.00**
Flannel, Kewpies (2), sgn Rose O'Neill, ca 1914, 5x5¾" **135.00**
Game, Kewpie Doll, Parker Bros, 1963, MIB, from $95 to **120.00**
Hatpin, sterling silver Kewpie, on orig cb holder **125.00**
Hatpin holder, bl/wht jasper, Kewpies, mk, 4½", NM, minimum ..**425.00**
Hood ornament, Kewpie, metal, mk, rare, 6½" **2,500.00**
Inkwell, dbl; metal, Kewpie in middle, mk **2,300.00**
Kewpie, brass door knocker, mk Elpec England, 5" **150.00**
Kewpie, bsk, American Doughboy, WWI, sticker, sgn ft, 5½" **900.00**
Kewpie, bsk, Blunderboo, falling, sgn, 1¾", from $395 to **525.00**
Kewpie, bsk, Confederate Soldier, 4" **400.00**
Kewpie, bsk, Doodle Dog, blk/brn spots, sgn, 5" (rare sz) **4,200.00**
Kewpie, bsk, Doodle Dog, molded onto bathtub, sgn, 1¾x3¼" ..**2,700.00**
Kewpie, bsk, Drummer, sgn, 3½" **2,750.00**
Kewpie, bsk, Farmer w/flowers, sgn, 4½" **500.00**
Kewpie, bsk, Hottentot, jtd arms, 7¾", from $875 to **925.00**
Kewpie, bsk, Huggers, 2½" **125.00**
Kewpie, bsk, Jester, wht hat on head, sgn, 4½", minimum value ..**850.00**
Kewpie, bsk, jtd hips & shoulders, 5" **525.00**
Kewpie, bsk, jtd shoulders, molded clothing, sgn, 8", minimum ..**950.00**
Kewpie, bsk, jtd shoulders, molded clothing, 10" **625.00**
Kewpie, bsk, jtd shoulders, 10" **625.00**
Kewpie, bsk, kneeling, sgn, 4" **900.00**
Kewpie, bsk, lady bug on toe, sgn, w/orig bug, 3½" **750.00**

Kewpie, bsk, Mayor, arms folded, sgn, 6" **600.00**
Kewpie, bsk, non-jtd, bl wings, pnt hair, 5" **175.00**
Kewpie, bsk, on bk, kicking 1 ft, 4" **400.00**
Kewpie, bsk, on tummy, arms & legs out, sgn, 4" **450.00**
Kewpie, bsk, on tummy, heart sticker, sgn, 4" **550.00**
Kewpie, bsk, reading book on lap, sgn, 3½" **825.00**
Kewpie, bsk, seated in lg fancy gr chair, sgn, 4" **850.00**
Kewpie, bsk, seated w/gray cat, 2¼" **850.00**
Kewpie, bsk, sitting, 'O' mouth, hands on ears, sgn, 3½" **2,000.00**
Kewpie, bsk, sitting, bug on extended right arm, sgn, 4", $875 to .**950.00**
Kewpie, bsk, sitting, heart label, sgn, 3½" **525.00**
Kewpie, bsk, Soldier vase, sgn, 6½", minimum value **950.00**
Kewpie, bsk, stradling goose, sgn/#d, rare, 3½", from $5,500 to ...**6,200.00**
Kewpie, bsk, Thinker, sgn, 6" **500.00**
Kewpie, bsk, w/baby bottle & baby Kewpie, sgn, 3½" **2,900.00**
Kewpie, bsk, w/blk cat, Japan, 1920s, lg **375.00**
Kewpie, bsk, w/rabbit, sgn, 2½" **400.00**
Kewpie, bsk head/glass eyes, cloth body, sgn, 12", minimum ...**3,000.00**
Kewpie, bsk shoulder head, cloth body, sgn, 6-7", from $600 to ..**850.00**
Kewpie, carnival chalk, jtd shoulders, sgn, 13" **165.00**
Kewpie, celluloid, Black, Germany, 2", from $95 to **115.00**
Kewpie, celluloid, Bride & Groom, Japan, sgn, 4" **75.00**
Kewpie, celluloid, Bride & Groom, Germany, sgn, 3" **150.00**
Kewpie, celluloid, Japan, 5" **90.00**
Kewpie, celluloid, jtd arms, heart label, Germany, sgn, 12", minimum ...**325.00**
Kewpie, compo, flexo jtd, segmented arms/legs, sticker, 27", $6,000 to ...**7,000.00**
Kewpie, compo, Hottentot, jtd arms, red wings, decal, 1946, 11" ...**575.00**
Kewpie, compo head, cloth body, 14" **325.00**
Kewpie, hard plastic, jtd neck/shoulders/hips, sleep eyes, sgn, 12" ..**435.00**
Kewpie, hard plastic, 1-pc, 1950s, 8" **120.00**
Kewpie, papier-mache (compo type), Twin Children's Shoes, 32" ..**1,000.00**
Kewpie, plush, vinyl mask, Knickerbocker, 1960s, 6" **40.00**
Kewpie, vinyl, Black, striped pajamas, 11", MIB **100.00**
Kewpie, vinyl, jtd shoulders only, 9" **40.00**
Kewpie, vinyl, Ragsy, 1-pc w/molded clothes, sgn, 8", minimum ..**85.00**
Kewpie, vinyl, Thinker sitting down, 1-pc, 1971, 4" **25.00**
Kewpie, vinyl head & limbs, cloth body, 16" **185.00**
Knife rest, Sheffield SP Kewpie, w/trademk **275.00**
Lamp base, Kewpies, metal, cast steel on sq base, 5½" **1,200.00**
Napkin ring, SP Kewpie, mk, from $250 to **275.00**
Paper dolls, 1963, M in folder, from $65 to **70.00**
Perfume holder, china, Kewpie figural, 1-pc, opening at bk of head ..**1,100.00**
Place card holder, bsk, Kewpie playing mandolin, 3" **350.00**
Plate, 6 Kewpies, Royal Rudolstadt, 7" **115.00**
Scootles, Cameo for Maxine Ltd Editions, 1973, 16" **150.00**
Shakers, ceramic, Japan, pr, from $50 to **60.00**
Sheet, magazine; Kewpies in airplane, sgn Rose O'Neill **35.00**
Soap figure, Kewpie, w/colored label w/rhyme, 1917, 4", M **110.00**
Stickpin, sterling, Kewpie Thinker, mk, from $85 to **100.00**
Sunday Magazine cover, man & woman, 1908, matted/fr, 12x16" ..**110.00**
Talcum container, compo, 1-pc, 7", M **95.00**
Tea set, Action Kewpies, c O'Neill Wilson, Germany, 22-pc ..**1,300.00**
Tea set, Kewpies w/gold, O'Neill/Bavaria, child's, 15-pc **900.00**
Thermometer, metal, Kewpie on knees, mk, 7½" **2,100.00**
Toy, celluloid, Kewpie crawling, w/up, mk Occupied Japan, $185 to ...**250.00**
Tray, Kewpies make lemonade, tin litho, 13x10½", VG, $500 to ...**575.00**

Onion Pattern

The familiar pattern known to collectors as Onion acquired its name through a case of mistaken identity. Designed in the early 1700s by Johann Haroldt of the Meissen factory in Germany, the pattern was a mixture of earlier Oriental designs. One of its components was a stylized peach, which was mistaken for an onion; as a result, the pattern became known by that name. Usually found in blue, an occasional piece may also be found in pink and red. The pattern is commonly associated with Meissen, but it has been reproduced by many others including Villeroy and Boch and Royal Copenhagen.

Blue Danube is a modern line of Onion-patterned dinnerware produced in Japan and distributed by Lipper International of Wallingford, Connecticut. At least 100 items are available in porcelain; it is sold in most large stores with china departments.

Bowl, rim soup; England, late	25.00
Bowl, soup/cereal; Lipper, from $12 to	15.00
Butter dish	120.00
Cache pot, gold borders, Meissen, 1890s, 5½"	245.00
Canister, German type	100.00
Canister set, vertical ribs, w/oil & vinegar	1,200.00
Chamberstick, flower hdl, Meissen X swords	165.00
Coffeepot, from $50 to	65.00
Coffeepot, graniteware	65.00
Coffeepot, 1800s, 9½"	400.00
Cup & saucer, bouillon; Meissen	65.00
Egg cup, dbl; Lipper, from $12 to	15.00
Funnel, loop hdl, lg	125.00
Funnel, sm	38.00
Humidor, pearlware, bulbous, hdls on shoulders, 8x6"	400.00
Knife, dessert; patterned hdl, brass blade, 6 for	145.00
Knife rest	18.00
Meat cleaver, Germany	125.00
Mug, Lipper, from $12 to	15.00
Mug, shaving; w/matching brush	85.00
Pestle	150.00
Plate, dinner; Lipper, from $15 to	18.00
Plate, Meissen, 6¼"	35.00
Plate, Meissen, 9½"	60.00
Plate, Meissen, 10½"	75.00
Platter, Meissen, 11"	175.00
Platter, Meissen, 17½"	400.00
Platter, Meissen, 21½"	475.00
Platter, scalloped oval, Xd swords, 1880s, 23x18"	550.00
Reamer, red, old, unmk Germany	110.00
Rolling pin, heavy, old, EX quality, 18"	325.00
Shell dish, Meissen, 1900, 7¾"	125.00
Skimmer, wooden hdl, unmk	200.00
Soup tureen, w/tray, Lipper, from $225 to	250.00
Spoon, serving; Meissen, 10"	135.00
Spoon rest, Meissen	175.00
Sugar bowl, Xd swords, lg	195.00
Tenderizer	175.00
Tureen, shell hdls, dome lid, 1900, 10½" H	665.00
Whisk	115.00

Opalescent Glass

First made in England in 1870, opalescent glass became popular in America around the turn of the century. Its name comes from the milky-white opalescent trim that defines the lines of the pattern. It was produced in table sets, novelties, toothpick holders, vases, and lamps. Note that American-made sugar bowls have lids; sugar bowls of British origin are considered to be complete without lids. For further information we recommend *The Standard Encyclopedia of Opalescent Glass, Third Edition*, by Bill Edwards and Mike Carwile (Collector Books).

Alaska, bowl, master; canary	110.00
Alaska, sugar bowl, wht, w/lid	90.00
Alaska, tray, emerald	110.00
Alhambra, tumbler, vaseline	65.00
Argus (Thumbprint), compote, bl	85.00
Ascot, sugar bowl, canary, open	85.00
Aurora Borealis, vase, novelty; gr	45.00
Barbells, bowl, bl	40.00
Basketweave (Open Edge), nappy, gr	25.00
Beaded Cable, rose bowl, gr, ftd	45.00
Beaded Drapes, bowl, vaseline, ftd	55.00
Beaded Fleur De Lis, bowl whimsey, wht	70.00
Beaded Ovals in Sand, butter dish, gr	265.00
Beaded Stars & Swag, plate, advertising; bl	250.00
Beads & Curlycues, bowl, novelty; gr, ftd	46.00
Beatty Honeycomb, butter dish, bl	200.00
Beatty Rib, match holder, bl	50.00
Beatty Rib, mustard jar, wht	110.00
Beatty Swirl, pitcher, bl	155.00
Beatty Swirl, spooner, wht	45.00
Blackberry, nappy, bl	40.00
Blocked Thumbprint & Beads (Fishscale & Beads), nappy, gr	40.00
Blown Drape, pitcher, wht	200.00
Blown Twist, tumbler, bl	65.00
Boggy Bayou, vase, wht	30.00
Brideshead, tray, canary, oval	115.00
Bubble Lattice, sugar bowl, cranberry	275.00
Bull's Eye, bowl, bl	50.00
Button & Braids, pitcher, wht	125.00
Button Panels, bowl, bl	45.00
Calyx, vase, vaseline	60.00
Cashews, rose bowl, wht	35.00
Chippendale, basket, canary	60.00
Chrysanthemum Base Swirl, bowl, master; wht	45.00
Chrysanthemum Base Swirl, toothpick holder, cranberry	300.00
Circled Scroll, shakers, bl, pr	250.00
Coinspot, sugar shaker, cranberry, 9-panel, 5"	350.00
Coinspot (variants, average pricing), pitcher, gr	245.00
Colonial Stairsteps, creamer, bl	75.00
Compass, bowl, bl, scarce	80.00
Consolidated Criss-Cross, bowl, master; cranberry	250.00
Consolidated Criss-Cross, celery vase, wht	135.00
Consolidated Criss-Cross, pitcher, wht	400.00
Contessa, pitcher, amber	250.00
Coral Reef, bottle, bitters; wht	95.00
Corinth, vase, bl, 8-13", ea	35.00
Coronation, pitcher, bl	195.00
Curtain Optic, guest set, wht, 2-pc	80.00
Daffodils, oil lamp, gr	295.00
Daisy & Fern, bowl, finger; wht	55.00
Daisy & Fern, pickle castor, bl	315.00
Daisy & Fern, pitcher, bl, 3 shapes, ea	290.00
Daisy & Fern, rose bowl, gr, ftd	55.00
Daisy & Fern, sugar shaker, wht	165.00
Daisy May (Leaf Rays), bonbon, wht	28.00
Diamond & Daisy, bowl, novelty; gr	40.00
Diamond Maple Leaf, bowl, gr, hdld	70.00
Diamond Optic, compote, wht	40.00
Diamond Point, vase, gr	45.00
Diamond Point Columns, vase, wht, rare	150.00
Diamond Spearhead, compote, gr, tall	350.00
Diamond Wave, vase, cranberry, 5"	75.00
Diamonds, vase, wht, decor, 6"	75.00
Dolly Madison, plate, bl, scarce, 6"	110.00
Dolly Madison, tumbler, gr	75.00

Dolphins & Herons, tray, novelty; wht, ftd 95.00
Double Greek Key, spooner, bl 100.00
Dragon Lady (Diamond Compass), vase, bl 95.00
Duchess, butter, canary 165.00
Dugan's #1013 (Wide Rib), vase, gr 75.00
Ellen, vase, bl 50.00
English Drape, vase, wht 40.00
Everglades, shakers, bl, pr 275.00
Everglades, tumbler, canary 90.00
Feathers, vase, bl 35.00
Fenton #100, bowl, vaseline 50.00
Fenton #370, nappy, amber 55.00
Fern, creamer, bl 125.00
Fern, pitcher, wht, various styles, ea 150.00
Fishnet, epergne, wht, 1-lily, 2-pc 125.00
Flora, spooner, bl 95.00
Fluted Bars & Beads, vase, novelty; wht 50.00
Fluted Scrolls (Klondyke), creamer, bl 75.00
Fluted Scrolls w/Vines, vase, wht, ftd 45.00
Four Pillars, vase, gr 70.00
Frosted Leaf & Basketweave, butter dish, vaseline 275.00
Gonterman (Adonis) Swirl, sugar bowl, amber 210.00
Grape & Cable, bowl, centerpc; bl 275.00
Greek Key & Ribs, bowl, bl 60.00
Greek Key & Scales, bowl, novelty; gr 75.00
Hearts & Clubs, bowl, wht, ftd 40.00
Herringbone, tumbler, bl 100.00
Hilltop Vines, chalice, novelty; wht 40.00
Hobnail, Hobbs; tray, water; wht 95.00
Hobnail (Northwood), butter dish, wht 130.00

Hobnail in Square, water pitcher, white opalescent, $220.00.

Hobnail in Square, bowl, master; wht 70.00
Hobnail 4-Footed, spooner, cobalt 90.00
Honeycomb (Blown), cracker jar, wht 225.00
Honeycomb & Clover, creamer, bl 85.00
Honeycomb & Clover, pitcher, bl 275.00
Idyll, butter dish, wht 195.00
Inside Rubbing, compote, jelly; bl 65.00
Inside Rubbing, spooner, bl 75.00
Interior Panel, vase, fan; bl 55.00
Iris w/Meander, pitcher, bl 390.00
Iris w/Meander, sugar bowl, gr 145.00
Jack-in-the-Pulpit (Dugan), vase, bl, 4½" 50.00
Jackson, butter dish, wht 130.00
Jefferson Spool, vase, bl 50.00
Jefferson Wheel, bowl, gr 50.00
Jewel & Flower, creamer, bl 75.00
Jewelled Heart, compote, gr 150.00
Jewelled Heart, tumbler, gr 65.00
Jolly Bear, bowl, gr 250.00

Keyhole, bowl, gr, scarce 90.00
Lattice Medallion, bowl, bl 45.00
Laura (Single Flower Framed), nappy, gr, scarce 35.00
Leaf & Beads, bowl whimsey, bl 45.00
Leaf & Leaflets (Long Leaf), bowl, wht 45.00
Leaf Rosette & Beads, bowl, gr, scarce 260.00
Little Nell, vase, bl 40.00
Lords & Ladies, creamer, canary 70.00
Many Loops, bowl, wht 25.00
Mary Ann, vase, bl, rare 295.00
National Swirl, pitcher, gr 260.00
Netted Roses, plate, wht 100.00
Northwood Block, celery vase, canary 55.00
Old Man Winter, basket, gr, sm 100.00
Opal Open (Beaded Panels), rose bowl, novelty; bl 50.00
Over-All Hob, pitcher, vaseline 195.00
Palisades, bowl, novelty; bl 45.00
Palm & Scroll, rose bowl, gr, ftd 40.00
Palm Beach, compote, jelly; bl 175.00
Panelled Flowers, rose bowl, wht, ftd 45.00
Peacock Tail, tumbler, gr, rare 90.00
Pearl & Scales, compote, bl 65.00
Pinecones & Leaves, bowl, wht 70.00
Plain Panels, vase, gr 40.00
Polka Dot, pitcher, bl, rare 250.00
Popsicle Sticks, bowl, wht, ftd 30.00
Pressed Coinspot (#617 or Concave Columns), card tray, gr 95.00
Prince Williams, sugar bowl, bl, open 65.00
Princess Diana, butter dish, bl 100.00
Pump & Trough, pump, wht 100.00
Quilted Pillow Sham, butter dish, bl, oval 100.00
Ray, vase, wht 35.00
Reflecting Diamonds, bowl, gr 40.00
Regal (Northwood), bowl, sauce; gr 40.00
Regal (Northwood), pitcher, bl 300.00
Reverse Drapery, vase, wht 35.00
Reverse Swirl, custard cup, cranberry 150.00
Rib & Big Thumbprint, vase, bl 45.00
Ribbed Optic, tumble-up, gr 80.00
Richelieu, sugar bowl, canary, open 60.00
Richelieu, triple sweet dish, bl 70.00
Ring Handle, ring tray, bl 100.00
Rose (Rose & Ruffles), bowl, vaseline, w/lid, lg 150.00
Ruffles & Rings, bowl, novelty; gr 45.00
S-Repeat, tumbler, bl 65.00
Scottish Moor, cracker jar, bl 350.00
Scroll w/Acanthus, butter dish, wht 175.00
Seaweed, pitcher, cranberry 600.00
Seaweed, syrup, wht 135.00
Shell, Beaded; bowl, master; gr 100.00
Shell & Dots, bowl, novelty; bl 52.00
Single Lily Spool, epergne, vaseline 250.00
Somerset, pitcher, juice; wht, 5½" 50.00
Spanish Lace, celery vase, bl 120.00
Spanish Lace, creamer, bl 95.00
Spanish Lace, liqueur jug, wht 195.00
Spatter, tumbler, cranberry 75.00
Spool, compote, wht 35.00
Star Base, bowl, bl, sq 40.00
Stork & Rushes, mug, bl 95.00
Stripe, pitcher, cranberry 450.00
Stripe, vase, wht 60.00
Sunburst on Shield (Diadem), bowl, novelty; wht, 7½" 70.00
Sunburst on Shield (Diadem), nappy, bl, rare 150.00

Swag w/Brackets, pitcher, bl 250.00
Swag w/Brackets, spooner, gr 75.00
Swirl, shot glass, bl 80.00
Swirl, spooner, wht 40.00
Target, vase, gr 110.00
Thousand Eye, spooner, wht 75.00
Thread & Rib, epergne whimsey, vaseline 850.00
Three Fingers & Panel, bowl, sauce; wht, rare 25.00
Tokyo, creamer, bl 65.00
Tree of Love, compote, wht 50.00
Tree Trunk, vase, gr 45.00
Triangle, match holder, bl 75.00
Twig, vase whimsey, gr 100.00
Twister, bowl, bl 50.00
Victoria & Albert, butter dish, wht, w/lid 110.00
Victorian Hamper, basket, canary, hdl 70.00
Waterlily & Cattails (Fenton), bowl, sauce; wht 25.00
Waterlily & Cattails (Fenton), butter dish, gr 350.00
Waterlily & Cattails (Northwood), tumbler, bl, rare 100.00
Wheel & Block, plate, novelty; gr 65.00
Wide Rib, vase, wht 50.00
Wild Bouquet, bowl, sauce; gr 35.00
William & Mary, compote, bl 65.00
Wilted Flowers, basket, bl, hdld 75.00
Windows (Plain), tumbler, wht 35.00
Windows (Swirled), mustard jar, cranberry 150.00
Windows (Swirled), plate, cranberry, 2 szs 250.00
Windows (Swirled), sugar bowl, bl 195.00
Woven Wonder, rose bowl, wht 40.00
Wreath & Shell, ivy ball, wht, rare 85.00
Wreath & Shell, lady's spittoon, canary 95.00
Wreath & Shell, spooner, bl 110.00
Zipper & Loops, vase, wht, ftd 35.00

Orientalia

The art of the Orient is an area of collecting currently enjoying strong collector interest, not only in those examples that are truly 'antique' but in the 20th-century items as well. Because of the many aspects involved in a study of Orientalia, we can only try through brief comments to acquaint the reader with some of the more readily available examples. We suggest you refer to specialized reference sources for more detailed information. See also specific categories.

Key:
Ch — Chinese   hdwd — hardwood
cvg — carving   Jp — Japan
drw — drawer   Ko — Korean
Dy — Dynasty   lcq — lacquer
E — export   mdl — medallion
FR — Famille Rose   rswd — rosewood
FV — Famille Verte   tkwd — teakwood

Blanc de Chine

Figure, Quanyin on cushion, hollow molded, 19th C, 8¼" 1,850.00
Vase, 7 boys at play, trumpet neck, 18th C, 16½" 2,300.00

Blue and White Porcelain

Bottle, dragon amid clouds, Yuan Dy, 9⅝" 7,000.00
Bottle, flowers & sprays on flat shoulder, late Ming Dy, 10" 800.00
Bottle, phoenix/peonies/lappets/foliage, hdls, Yuan Dy, 7½" ...3,000.00

Charger, Arita, seaside landscape, Jp, 1870s, 25" 935.00
Stem cup, floral sprays, Yuan Dy, 3⅝" 2,000.00
Stem cup, peony scrolls/foliage, floral int, Yuan Dy, 4⅜" 4,000.00
Teapot, E, melon form w/appl leaf & squirrel, Ch, 6" 525.00
Vase, E, landscape w/hills & river, Ch, 1870s, 24" 200.00
Vase, flowering prunus, bottle form, 15th C, 9¾" 2,500.00

Bronze

Bowl, lotus; winding stem w/2 crabs on lily pad, Meiji, 6½" 550.00
Censer, mask ring hdls, gold splashes, wooden lid, 18th C, 6" .5,750.00
Mirror, feline reliefs among grapes, Tang Dy, 5⅞" 750.00
Model, dragon descending, gilt, Tang Dy, 4⅜" 1,500.00
Stand, dragon relief, 3 scroll ft, open bottom & top, 6x9½" 150.00
Vase, cast blossoms, drilled for lamp, Meiji, 14" 100.00

Celadon

Bowl, hot water, eng peonies & central flower, Ming Dy, 8⅝" ...800.00
Bowl, sea gr w/6 notches along rim, early Ming Dy, 7¼" 600.00
Guan (jar), eng cellwork & band, incised swords, w/lid, 11½" .1,400.00

Furniture

Bookcase, Jumu, 2 doors, 2 drws, 2 shelves, Shuge, 70x31x17", pr .1,725.00
Cabinet, cvd tkwd, 2-door base, glass door in top, 20th C, 72" 360.00
Desk, lcq hdwd w/cvd dragons, soapstone mts, 3-drw, 57x42x28" ..2,500.00

Etagere, hand-carved teakwood, three drawers and seven shelves, 1800s, 62x49x14", $5,000.00.

Hat stand, HP persimmons on gray, Ch, 19th C, 11½x4½" dia ..150.00
Screen, cvd dragon fr w/stone inlay, Ch, 2 74x36" panels 1,200.00
Screen, cvd lcq, mc scenes on brn, wear, 4-part, ea: 71x16" 360.00
Stools, Jumu, simple form, hoof ft, Fangdeng, 19th C, 17x17", pr ..800.00
Table, sewing, Ch E lcqwork w/gilt, trestle base, 1840s 1,500.00
Table, tea/traveling; Huanghuali, reeded top, 19th C, 36" dia ..1,750.00
Tabouret, cvd wood w/marble top/MOP floral inlay, 19th C, 19x24" ...275.00
Trunk, pigskin, brass front latch, bail hdls, Ch, 29¾" 250.00

Hardstones

Jade, bird finial, lt gr, Shang Dy, 1⅜" 2,300.00
Jade, brush washer, lt brn mottle, Guangxu Period, 6" 1,265.00
Jade, cvd hand, moss-embedded-in-melting-snow color, 8" 150.00
Jade, photo fr, dk gr, 13x10½" 230.00
Jade, sleeve weight, gr mottle, lion form, Ming Dy, 2½" 2,300.00
Jade, vase, mottled gr, cvd phoenix/etc, baluster, w/lid, 14" 8,050.00
Nephrite jade, pendant, gray-gr mottle, Chimera, Song Dy, 2" ..745.00

Rock crystal, vase, fine cvd Buddhist symbols, w/lid & stand, 12" .**10,925.00**

Lacquer

Lacquerware is found in several colors, but the one most likely to be encountered is cinnabar. It is often intricately carved, sometimes involving hundreds of layers built one at a time on a metal or wooden base. Later pieces remain red, while older examples tend to darken.

Box, flowering gilt branches, shell inlay, Meiji, 2⅝x5x4" **2,300.00**
Box, picnic; floral, blk/gold, slide top, 3-compartment, 12x12x7" .**230.00**
Figure, dignitary w/long mustache & beard, cvd wood/gilt, 15" ..**160.00**
Kobako, cranes/pines/Juji in gilt, 19th C, 3¾", NM **2,600.00**
Kobako, gold & silver valley scene, Meiji, 2x4½x3¼" **1,600.00**
Shrine, int w/seated Bodhisattva on lotus, gilt, Jp, 14" **325.00**
Tea safe, E, w/pewter canisters, Ch, 1800s, 11x8" **300.00**

Netsukes

A netsuke is a miniature Japanese carving made with two holes called the Himitoshi, either channeled or within the carved design. As kimonos (the outer garment of the time) had no pockets, the Japanese man hung his pipe, tobacco pouch, or other daily necessities from his waist sash. The most highly valued accessory was a nest of little drawers called an Inro, in which they carried snuff or sometimes opium. The netsuke was the toggle that secured them. Although most are of ivory, others were made of bone, wood, metal, porcelain, or semiprecious stones. Some were inlaid or lacquered. They are found in many forms — figurals the most common, mythological beasts the most desirable. They range in size from 1" up to 3", which was the maximum size allowed by law. Many netsukes represented the owner's profession, religion, or hobbies. Scenes from the daily life of Japan at that time were often depicted in the tiny carvings. The more detailed the carving, the greater the value.

Careful study is required to recognize the quality of the netsuke. Many have been made in Hong Kong in recent years; and even though some are very well carved, these are considered copies and avoided by the serious collector. There are many books that will help you learn to recognize quality netsukes, and most reputable dealers are glad to assist you. Use your magnifying glass to check for repairs. In the listings that follow, netsukes are ivory unless noted otherwise; 'stain' indicates a color wash.

Badger with inlaid eyes, sepia wash and black pigment, 19th century, 1½", $1,265.00.

Baby boy on hands & knees, mc stains, Masakatsu, 19th C, 1¾".**575.00**
Blind men mt elephant, sepia stain, Masayuki, Meiji, 1¾" **1,265.00**
Courtier crouching/smiling/playing drum, late 19th C, 1¼" **315.00**
Dog & pups, movable collar, inlaid eyes, Mitsuharu, 1890s, 2" .**1,095.00**
Frog, boxwood w/stain, sgn Sigemasa, 19th C, 1¾" **1,495.00**
Groom washing horse, wood w/inlay/stain, Taiso period, 1¾" **925.00**
Karako (2), children w/instruments, sgn Kagetoshi, 19th C, 1½" ...**920.00**
Man w/grain basket, mc stains, age crack, 19th C, 1½" **345.00**
Mandarin duck, folded wings, sepia wash/inlaid eyes, 19th C, 1½" ...**700.00**
Matsuri revelers & musicians, wash/stain, sgn, Meiji, 2" **575.00**

Monkey mother & baby on peach branch, horn inlay, 1890s, 2" ...**1,035.00**
Monkey w/fruit, inlaid teeth, Masanao, 1" **1,265.00**
Nio mending Waraji of Asakusa temple, sepia wash, Meiji, 1¾" ...**925.00**
Okame (goddess of mirth) w/fan, sepia wash, Meiji, 1¼" **490.00**

Porcelain

Chinese export ware was designed to appeal to Western tastes and was often made to order. During the 18th century, vast amounts were shipped to Europe and on westward. Much of this fine porcelain consisted of dinnerware lines that were given specific pattern names. Rose Mandarin, Fitzhugh, Armorial, Rose Medallion, and Canton are but a few of the more familiar.

Bowl, E, FR, peony scrolls on lemon yel, 5½", pr **2,645.00**
Bowl, FV, alternating reserves, Ch, 19th C, 4¼x10¼" **635.00**
Bowl, FR, lt wear, 19th C, 13¼" **975.00**
Bowl, punch; Rose Canton, Ch, 19th C, 21", NM **3,450.00**
Charger, E, armorial, floral spray border, Ch, 18th C, 14" **750.00**
Cup & saucer, E, FR, 20th C, 9 for **135.00**
Plate, E, Judgement of Paris reserve/scenes, Ch, 18th C, 9" **5,000.00**
Plate, E, Rebecca at wht Well, Ch, 18th C, 9" **5,000.00**
Plate, soup; E, FR, early 20th C, 10 for **200.00**
Salt cellar, E, mc court reserves w/gold, 18th C, 3⅛" **460.00**
Teapot, lobed form/reeded strap hdls w/gold, Ch, 1800s, 5½" **515.00**
Vase, E, FR, floral sprays on powder bl, Kangxi, 17¾" **1,495.00**
Vase, E, FV, mtd as lamp, 13¼x4½" **220.00**
Vase, E, FV, mtns/butterflies/flowers in panels, Kangxi, 10¼" .**2,070.00**
Vase, Tobacco Leaf, mdt as lamp on wood base, 15½x6", pr **400.00**
Warming dish, Hundred Butterfly, sepia w/gold, Ch, 19th C, 9¾" .**350.00**

Pottery

Jar, gr glaze, std form w/molded lions/tigers, Han Dy, 12" **1,500.00**
Jar, granary; gr glazed, bear ft, integral lid, Han Dy, 12" **575.00**
Jar, hill; gr glaze, bear ft, cvd figures/etc, Han Dy, 9" **1,500.00**
Model, entertainer dancing/holding tambourine, Sichuan, 17¼" **2,500.00**
Model, equestrienne astride standing horse, Tang Dy, 12" **750.00**
Model, guard dog, red, Han Dy, 23¼x21½" **3,000.00**
Model, horse, std legless 2-part form, Han Dy, 17¾" **700.00**
Model, recumbent hound, gray, Han Dy, on wood stand, 7¼" L .**2,000.00**
Model, sleeping boar, gray, Han Dy, 6½" L, on wood stand **1,500.00**

Rugs

The 'Oriental' or Eastern rug market has enjoyed a renewal of interest in recent years as collectors have become aware of the fact that some of the semiantique rugs (those sixty to one hundred years old) may be had at a price within the range of the average buyer.

Afshar, red border, salmon spandrels on dk bl, lt wear, 59x74" ...**990.00**
Bakhtiari, brn border & gold ground, airbrush effect, 55x84" **330.00**
Bergama, hooked lattice w/geometrics, mc on olive, 1890s, 50x54" .**350.00**
Bijar, bl border & pk spandrels on burgundy, 52x82" **3,000.00**
Fetti Chinese, beige border & dk bl bround, lt wear, 75x103" **330.00**
Heriz, med bl border, dk salmon grd, damage, 34x116" **1,400.00**
Heriz, midnight bl borders/wht spandrels on wine, 125x216" ..**5,500.00**
Indo-Persian, red border & spandrels on ivory, 37x65" **165.00**
Isphahan Tree of Life, pictorial, bl border on ivory, 52x81" **2,300.00**
Karabagh, dk bl w/dk red border, 56x99" **1,425.00**
Kashan, dk bl border/ground w/dk salmon spandrels, 106x144" ..**5,775.00**
Kerman, dk bl border on burgundy, lt wear, 53x96" **450.00**
Kerman, red w/midnight bl border, lt wear, 114x168" **935.00**
Kuba-Shirvan prayer, ivory border on blk, 40x84" **2,300.00**

Laver Kerman, mc tree w/pk border, red spandrels on ivory, 104x142" .3,000.00
Mahajarin Sarouk, dk bl border on rust, 34x58" 770.00
Persian Turkoman, ivory/dk bl/brn on burgundy, 50x79" 400.00
Sarouk, burgundy w/midnight bl border, 50x81" 1,595.00
Sarouk, camel border on plum, 21x38" 165.00
Serebend, ivory border & spandrels on red, stain, 52x78" 715.00
Shervan prayer, serrated boteh, mc on midnight bl, 1880s, 63x40" .1,265.00
Tabriz, camel border, dk bl spandrels on rust, 57x74" 3,000.00
Tabriz, dk bl border, lt bl spandrels on red, 48x72" 825.00
Tabriz, lt gold overall w/lt bl secondary borders, 115x156" 5,775.00
Tekke prayer, ivory/dk bl/rust on maroon, 45x56", EX 500.00
Turkish Kazak, brn & tans w/ivory border & bl, 30x56", EX 425.00
Zeigler Mahal, rust red/dk bl w/ivory border, 50x79", VG 500.00

Snuff Bottles

The Chinese were introduced to snuff in the 17th century, and their carved and painted snuff bottles typify their exquisite taste and workmanship. These small bottles, seldom measuring over 2½", were made of amber, jade, ivory, and cinnabar; tiny spoons were often attached to their stoppers. By the 18th century, some were being made of porcelain, others were of glass with delicate interior designs tediously reverse painted with minuscule brushes sometimes containing a single hair. Copper and brass were used but to no great extent.

Amethyst teardrop, ca 1900, 3¼" 350.00
Bl glass w/blk o/l, 19th C, 2⅞" 125.00
Bubbled suffused ground w/ruby o/l, 1800-60, 2⅛" 325.00
Fossiliferous limestone, 19th C, 2⅛" 525.00
Gr jade w/brn inclusions, 19th C, 2⅞" 350.00
Lapis lazuli w/cvg, ca 1900, 2⅛" 275.00
Malachite fish form, ca 1900, 2⅞" 200.00
Molded porc w/HP lion & ball, ca 1900, 3" 80.00
Moss agate, w/malachite top, 2½" 60.00
Quartz, chalcedony w/relief-cvd horse, 19th C, 2⅛" 500.00
Quartz-agate w/brn inclusions, 19th C, 3" 225.00

Rock crystal, reverse-painted landscape scene, signed, 19th century, 2¼", $1,100.00; Chinese Hornbill, carved figural scenes, with chain and hardwood stand, 8", $900.00.

Rvpt glass, warriors on horsebk, 19th C, 4" 225.00
Rvpt glass, 11 children playing, 19th C, 3" 150.00
Wood, well-cvd horse ea side, 19th C, 3" 400.00
Yi-Hsing pottery, script on front, 19th C, 2⅛" 1,000.00

Textiles

Panel, phoenix/etc, silk/velvet/metallic threads, 1800s, 22x23" .600.00
Panel, rampant dragon & pearl, silk, ca 1700, 13x17" 700.00
Robe, priest's; woven silk, beige/bl/etc, Late Edo period, 76" ..1,500.00

Woodblock Prints, Japanese

Framed prints are of less value than those not framed, since it is impossible to inspect their condition or determine whether or not they have borders or have been trimmed.

Beautiful Woman, Utagawa Kunisada, ca 1900, 9½x14" 450.00
Bifan & Attendant, Kikumaro, oban, 1820-30, 15x9½" 330.00
Biographies of Loyal & Faithful Samurai, Yoshitora, 1866, 14x10" ..400.00
Calling the Waitress, Kunisada, 19th C, 10x14½" 400.00
Courtesan/servant/musician, Okumura Masanobu, dai oban yoko-e ..2,300.00
Courtesans & boy beside standards, Utamaro, oban tate-e 1,380.00
Evening on Veranda, Toyahara Chikanobu, triptych, 19th C, 29x14" 950.00
Executioner, Tiro Kiyonaga, 18th C, 9¾x14¾" 400.00
General Surveying Battlefield, Kobayashi Kiyochika, 19th C, 10x14" .500.00
Ladies in Waiting of Chyoda Palace, Toyochara Chikanobu, triptych ..950.00
Man in lg room w/wall of fusuma, Kuniyoshi, triptych 575.00
Porter & Daughter, Toyahara Kunichika, 19th C, 9¼x14" 300.00
Scene from Kabuki, Kuniyoshi, ca 1850, diptych, 14x19½" 1,000.00
Tiger & bamboo, Kikugawa Eizan, kakemono-e 630.00
View of path leading to village, Hiroshige ga, oban tate-e 315.00
Woman Admiring Sword, Toyokuni, 18th C, 10x14½" 400.00
Woman w/Dog, Tori Kiynaga, 18th C, 9¼x14½" 400.00
Workers among buildings & trees, Hiroshige, 19th C, 8x13" 150.00

Miscellaneous

Altar coffer, wood, cvd panels/apron, Ch, 19th C, 15½x37x7" ..300.00
Box, brass & porc w/pnt reserve, Ch, 4x7" dia 55.00
Figure, temple; gilt/pnt decor cvd wood, Ch, 19th C, 45" 3,000.00
Painting, wedding procession on rice paper, 19th C, 48x19" 200.00
Rvpt glass, mother & child landscape, Ch, 19th C, 16x12", pr .1,200.00
Scroll painting, Old Fisherman, 19th C, unfr, 70x18" 225.00
Scroll painting, Pine Tree w/Red Blossoms, 51x13" 125.00
Scroll painting, 3 Figures Seated in Snow, unknown age, 46x16" 125.00
Tsuba, copper Mokume, sgn Sakashu, rnded hexagon, no decor, 8" 430.00
Tsuba, Hizen School, gold Nunome iron, gibbon/branch, 18th C, 8" ..1,000.00
Tsuba, pierced/cvd silver, 2 water dragons, Omori Teruhide, 7" 1,500.00
Tsuba, Tembo style, iron w/gold highlights, heavy punchwork, 8" 115.00
Watercolor on silk, old man w/children, Jp, 14x10" 85.00

Orrefors

Orrefors Glassworks was founded in 1898 in the Swedish province of Smaaland. Utilizing the expertise of designers such as Simon Gate, Edward Hald, Vicke Lindstrand, and Edwin Ohrstrom, it produced art glass of the highest quality. Various techniques were used in achieving the decoration. Some were wheel engraved; others were blown through a unique process that formed controlled bubbles or air pockets resulting in unusual patterns and shapes. Our advisor for this category is Abby Malowanczyk; she is listed in the Directory under Texas.

Bottle vase, Ariel, bubbles, aubergine/clear, 1815E Ohrstrom, 7⅜" ..500.00
Bowl, Ariel, air stripes, amber/bl in clear, Ohrstrom, 4½" 400.00
Bowl, Ariel, bl stripes, #191A?/E Ohrstrom, 2⅜x7¼" 600.00
Bowl, Ariel, rows of bubbles, dk bl/clear, Ohrstrom/#452, 4x8" ..800.00
Bowl, Graal, cvg, gray/wht in clear, Hald/#2092L, 3½x8" 680.00
Bowl, leopard among cut bars, #4688-13 Gunnar Cyren, 6x8" ..1,380.00
Compote, on solid ped w/trapped teardrop, 6¾x12" 350.00
Decanter, Romeo serenading/Juliet on balcony, sq, #880, 12½" .345.00
Vase, angelfish (2), bubbles overall, LA 1916, 10" 345.00
Vase, Ariel, air panels/gray feathers in clear, Ohrstrom, 7½" ..2,500.00
Vase, Ariel, bubbles, clear/aubergine/amber, #431L/Lunding, 5½" .750.00
Vase, draped nude, sq sides, Palmquist 5078 6B, 1949, 9½" 490.00
Vase, etched nude, Lindstrand/1418.92.138, 13½x6", pr 850.00
Vase, Graal, aquatic scene, global, #2265D II Hd, 4½" 600.00

Vase, Graal, bl verticals/peach bands in clear, Hald, #194, 8" .2,000.00
Vase, Graal, fish, clear/brn/gr, #2770D/E Hald, 1953, 5¾" 800.00
Vase, pheasants etched in Modernistic taste, ca 1950, 9½" 250.00
Vase, seminude Japanese dancer eng, Gate/#1387, 10x11" 1,800.00
Vase, teal bl, cylinder, heavy-walled, Palmquist, 7x7" 175.00
Vase, Veiled, clear to pk, bl rim, Expo 2641 Landberg, 11½" 288.00

Ott and Brewer

The partnership of Ott and Brewer began in 1865 in Trenton, New Jersey. By 1876 they were making decorated graniteware, parian, and 'ivory porcelain' — similar to Irish belleek though not as fine and of different composition. In 1883, however, experiments toward that end had reached a successful conclusion, and a true belleek body was introduced. It came to be regarded as the finest china ever produced by an American firm. The ware was decorated by various means such as hand painting, transfer printing, gilding, and lustre glazing. The company closed in 1893, one of many that failed during that depression. In the listings below, the ware is belleek unless noted otherwise. Our advisor for this category is Mary Frank Gaston.

Basket, crisscross indents, gold leaves, twig hdl, mk, 4" 550.00
Bowl, berry; yel lustre w/gilt scalloped rim, +5½" saucer 200.00
Bowl, Cactus, gold thistles inside & out, mk, 3¼x10½" 1,100.00
Bowl, chrysanthemum sprays, gold on cream, ca 1886, 3x7½" ...400.00
Bowl, wht lustre w/gold scalloped rim, 2½x5½" 250.00
Cup & saucer, pk lustre w/gold rim, mk, 2½", 5½" 200.00
Ewer, gold stylized leaves, cactus hdl, 8½" 1,225.00
Humidor, wht w/brn staves, gold hdl, Tiffany & Co/mk 425.00
Teapot, Tridacna, yel w/gold, wht loop hdl, mk, 4" 400.00
Tete-a-tete set, wht to pk w/gold, 4x4½" pot+cr/sug 500.00
Tray, gold-paste floral, sq, ruffled rim, 8¼" 465.00

Overbeck

The Overbeck Studio was established in 1911 in Cambridge City, Indiana, by four Overbeck sisters. It survived until the last sister died in 1955. Early wares were often decorated with carved designs of stylized animals, birds, or florals with the designs colored to contrast with the background. Others had tooled designs filled in with various colors for a mosaic effect. After 1937, Mary Frances, the last remaining sister, favored handmade figurines with somewhat bizarre features in fanciful combinations of color. Overbeck ware is signed 'OBK,' frequently with the designer's and potter's initials under the stylized 'OBK.'

Vase, white stylized crows on blue-gray matt, signed, 6x6", $5,500.00.

Bowl, 3 panels w/cvd geometrics, pk on gr, EF, 2x3", EX 750.00
Box, geometric-cvd top, olive/bl matt, EF, 3½" dia 1,300.00
Figural group, farm scene, calf & 2 children, 5x4½" 1,300.00

Figurine, Black lady w/skillet, old man w/(rstr) cane, 4½" & 5", pr ...700.00
Figurine, lady (& man) in fancy attire, 5" & 4½", pr 275.00
Figurine, photographer w/camera, 2¾" 800.00
Figurine, singing farmer, 5½" 175.00
Vase, 3 cut-bk panels w/flowers, 3-color, EF, sm rpr, 6" 1,400.00
Vase, 3 cut-bk panels w/stylized trees, gray/wine/brn, EF, 7½" ...2,600.00
Vase, 3 panels w/Japanese-style lady, 3-color, 3x2¾", NM 1,100.00
Vase, 3 panels w/stylized birds, dusty pk on mauve, 5½x5" 2,800.00

Overlay Glass

Art glass having layers of more than one type or color of glass is sometimes called overlay or cased glass. Very often glassware of this type has applied decorations such as fruit, flowers, leaves, or ruffles (rigaree), such as is commonly identified with Stevens and Williams. See also Stevens and Williams.

Bowl, bl w/pk int, ruffled 4-lobe rim, clear ft, 5x5x8¾" 210.00
Candlestick, rose w/wht int, clear rigaree/branch stem, 8½" 225.00
Flower bowl, pk w/wht int, thorns, clear wishbone ft, 3½" 75.00
Pitcher, Drape, shaded raspberry w/wht int, clear hdl, 6" 200.00
Pitcher, shaded orange, cream int, clear hdl, ruffled, 7" 165.00
Pitcher, shaded rose, clear reeded hdl, 7½" 165.00
Rose bowl, threaded wht w/bl int, appl vaseline decor/ft, 4½" 165.00
Vase, bl w/wht int, flowers, ribs, clear rim/hdl/leaves, 5x4½" 95.00
Vase, pk w/wht int, clear rigaree up sides of stick neck, 6½" 65.00
Vase, pk w/wht int, clear thorns/edge/ft, 5x3" 110.00
Vase, pk w/wht int, flowers, amber ft, trn-down 4-lobe rim, 7" 125.00
Vase, shaded pk w/wht int, sm flowers & bee, 7x3⅝" 120.00
Vase, wht w/bl int, HP floral, ormolu ft, wide ruffle, 7" 100.00
Wine cruet, orange w/wht int, Gin on metal stopper, sqd, 9" 185.00

Overshot

Overshot glass is characterized by the beaded or craggy appearance of its surface. Earlier ware was irregularly textured, while 20th-century examples tend to be more uniform.

Bowl, lt bl w/appl rigaree & flower, 4x6" 225.00
Ice bucket, cranberry, emb ice pattern, w/int wafer drain, 6½" ...150.00
Pitcher, bl w/opal spots, bl reeded hdl, att Hobbs, 8" 200.00
Pitcher, clear, rope twist hdl, ice bladder, 10½" 80.00
Pitcher, cranberry, bulbous, water sz 350.00
Pitcher, red/gold snake spirals body & forms hdl, ftd, 13" 275.00
Pitcher, tankard; cranberry, clear reeded hdl, pewter lid, 9" 175.00
Tumbler, cranberry, gold rim, 3½" 45.00
Vase, rubena w/appl flowers & leaves, ruffled, hdls, 10x7" 200.00

Owen, Ben

Ben Owen worked at the Jugtown Pottery of North Carolina from 1923 until it closed in 1959. He continued in the business in his own Plank Road Pottery, stamping his ware 'Ben Owen, Master Potter,' with many forms made by Lester Fanell Craven in the late 1960s. His pottery closed in 1972. He died in 1983 at the age of 81.

Bean pot, Tobacco Spit Brown, rnded hdls, w/lid, 1960s, 7½" ...175.00
Birdhouse, warm to bright orange, mk, 1960s, 9½" 300.00
Bowl, salt glaze, Dogwood Blossom, Korean style, 1960s, 2⅞x8⅝" ...750.00
Candle saucers, wht slip, stoneware, sgn, 1960s, 1¾x7½", pr 150.00
Candlesticks, orange gloss, mk, 9", pr 275.00

Candlesticks, warm to bright orange, sgn, 1960s, 12", pr **250.00**
Casserole, orange, w/lid, mk, early 1960s, 4⅝x9" **130.00**
Chamberstick, gr spots on orange gloss, sgn, 1960s, 2⅛x8" **325.00**
Cracker/coffee bean jar, brn-orange, earthenware, early 1960s, 10" ..**400.00**
Creamer & sugar bowl, yel w/ash specks, w/lid, 1960s, 3¾" **80.00**
Cup, Tobacco Spit Brown gloss, earthenware, 1960s, 3⅛" **20.00**
Egg cup, Tobacco Spit Brown, sgn, 1960s, 2⅞" **70.00**
Jar, apothecary; Frogskin Green, sgn, 1960s, 4½" **90.00**
Lamp, Asion oil-bottle; Pumpkin Brown, sgn, 1960s, 12⅝" **800.00**
Lamp, oil bottle; Tobacco Spit Brown, drilled, 10" **500.00**
Mug, Tobacco Spit Brown, curved bbl form, 1960s, 4" **30.00**
Pie plate, warm orange, earthenware, 1960-61, 2¼x10½" **150.00**
Pitcher, Frogskin Green, pulled hdl, sgn, 1960s, 9" **275.00**
Pitcher, salt glaze w/fly ash patina, sgn, 1960s, 3½" **130.00**
Platter, bent-ring; orange, hdls, sgn, 1960s, 3¼x14¾x12" **175.00**
Pot, cobalt on salt glaze, knob lid, circle mk, 1960s, 3¾" **120.00**
Tea bowl, wht slip, earthenware, att, 1960s, 1½x4¾" **70.00**
Vase-lamp, Pumpkin Brown, shouldered, bottle neck, sgn, 1960s, 14" .**200.00**

Owens Pottery

J.B. Owens founded his company in Zanesville, Ohio, in 1891, and until 1907, when the company decided to exert most of its energies in the area of tile production, made several quality lines of art pottery. His first line, Utopian, was a standard brown ware with underglaze slip decoration of nature studies, animals, and portraits. A similar line, Lotus, utilized lighter background colors. Henri Deux, introduced in 1900, featured incised Art Nouveau forms inlaid with color. (Be aware that the Brush McCoy Pottery acquired many of Owens' molds and reproduced a line similar to Henri Deux, which they called Navarre.) Other important lines were Opalesce, Rustic, Feroza, Cyrano, and Mission, examples of which are rare today. The factory burned in 1928, and the company closed shortly thereafter. Values vary according to the quality of the artwork and subject matter. Examples signed by the artist bring higher prices than those that are not signed. For further information we recommend *Owens Pottery Unearthed* by Kristy and Rick McKibben and Jeanette and Marvin Stofft. Mrs. Stofft is listed in the Directory under Indiana.

Utopian, vase, kitten portrait, multicolor on shaded brown to gray background, marked, 8", $2,800.00.

Aborigine, vase, geometrics on gr matt, squat bottle form, 5" **375.00**
Aqua Verdi, vase, textured, 4 neck hdls, 8" **550.00**
Feroza, vase, brn to gunmetal, 6" **200.00**
Lightweight, stein, grapes on brn, sgn Herold, #795, 8" **475.00**
Lightweight, vase, chick in grass, 4 ft, sgn, 5x4" **400.00**
Lotus, jardiniere, mushrooms, #230, 3" **275.00**
Lotus, vase, bee over grass blades, sgn, 4" **400.00**
Lotus, vase, irises (EX art), sgn, 16½" **1,400.00**
Lotus, vase, toadstools, 2-hdl mug form, #235, 5" **450.00**
Matt Green, vase, cvd Greek Key at rim, #10, 11½x9" **650.00**
Matt Utopian, vase, floral, elongated bottle form, 7½" **450.00**

Matt Utopian, vase, poppy, 12½" **600.00**
Matt Utopian, vase, 2 lg pansies, artist sgn, 14½" **650.00**
Opalesce, ewer, floral, 5½" **350.00**
Tile, mtn landscape, 5-color, 11¾", in new fr **2,700.00**
Utopian, candlestick, floral, #948, 7" **175.00**
Utopian, jug, ear of corn, sgn Steele, 8x4½" **250.00**
Utopian, vase, floral, 3-sided petticoat shape, 3" **125.00**
Utopian, vase, floral, 7x4½" **190.00**
Utopian, vase, pansies, #010, 10x5" **275.00**
Utopian, vase, rose petals, sgn HS, #887, 9x4" **225.00**
Utopian, vase, roses, H Robinson, #804, 6½x2¼" **150.00**
Utopian, vase, roses, S Timberlake, #1031, 11½x5" **375.00**
Utopian, vase, roses, sgn, 11" **300.00**
Utopian, vase, sweet peas, 8" **225.00**
Venetian, bowl, gold irid, undulating surface, 3¾x7" **350.00**

Pacific Clay Products

The Pacific Clay Products Company got its start in the 1920s as a consolidation of several smaller southern California potteries. The main Los Angeles plant had been founded in 1890 to make kitchen stoneware, ollas, and similar items. Terra cotta and brick were later produced.

In 1932 Hostess Ware, a vividly colored line of dinnerware, was introduced to compete with Bauer's Ring Ware. Coralitos, a lighter-weight, pastel-hued dinnerware line was first marketed in 1937, and a similar but less expensive line called Arcadia soon followed. Art ware including vases, figurines, candlesticks, etc., was produced from 1932 to 1942, at which time the company went into war-related work and pottery manufacture ceased. A limited amount of hand-decorated dinnerware was also made. For further information we recommend *The Collector's Encyclopedia of California Pottery, 2nd Edition*, by our advisor, Jack Chipman; he is listed in the Directory under California.

Bowl, salad; Apricot, ftd, low, 8" **125.00**
Bust, Madonna, pastel gr matt, B Lundy, #902, 8" **90.00**
Cake plate, Apache Red w/geometric decor, Hostessware, 14" ...**275.00**
Candelabrum, 3-branch, brn, unmk, 10" L **75.00**
Candle holder, turq, stepped sq base, 3" **45.00**
Carafe, Apache Red, w/hdl **75.00**
Cup & saucer, demitasse; Coralitos **25.00**
Figurine, fan dancer, ivory, 15½", minimum value **500.00**
Flower holder, cockatoo figural, yel, #3802 ....**200.00**
Leaf dish, aqua/wht, 12½x10" **35.00**
Planter, Jack, ivory matt, #907, 5" **50.00**
Plate, dinner; Coralitos, 10" **15.00**
Platter, emb fish, Hostessware line, 15" **165.00**
Sand jar, Apache Red, circular 1100 mk, 20½" **500.00**
Teacup & saucer, royal bl, w/decor, minimum value **100.00**
Vase, bird figural, hand-decor, stamped mk, ca 1939, 8¼" **100.00**
Vase, Deco style, yel, #3107, 7" **75.00**
Vase, fluted shell form, deep purple w/turq int, #3349, 8" **85.00**
Vase, prow of sailing ship, pk, #4000, 13½", minimum value **300.00**
Vase, turq, hdls, #3807 ....**75.00**
Vase, wht w/bl leaf decor at corners, #3603, 12" **150.00**

Paden City

The Paden City Glass Company began operations in 1916 in Paden City, West Virginia. The company's early lines consisted largely of the usual pressed tablewares, but by the 1920s production had expanded to include colored wares in translucent as well as opaque glass in a variety of patterns and styles. The company maintained its high standards of handmade perfection until 1949, when under new management much of the work formerly done by hand was replaced by automation. The Paden City Glass Company closed in 1951; its earlier wares, the colored patterns in particular, are becoming very collectible.

Paden City Glass is not always easily recognized by collectors or dealers, as it was almost never marked. It is believed this was so the glass could be sold to decorating companies. The company assigned both line numbers and names to many of its blanks or sets of glassware. Colors were sometimes given more than one name, and etchings were named as well. All this makes identification of items offered for sale through mail order difficult, and labels prepared by dealers are often confusing.

A review of literature available on Paden City reveals the following names for the company's plate etchings: Ardith; California Poppy; Cupid; Delilah Bird (Peacock Reverse); Eden Rose; Frost; Gazebo; Gothic Garden; Lela Bird; Nora Bird; Orchid (three variations); Peacock and Rose (Peacock and Wild Rose); Samarkand; Trumpet Flower; Utopia. Names given to cuttings made on Paden City blanks are Yorktown and Lazy Daisy. It is not clear whether the names originated with Paden City or with secondary decorating companies.

Our advisors for this category are George and Mary Hurney; they are listed in the Directory under Illinois. (Note: their interest is only in Paden City glassware, not the pottery.) See also Glass Animals and Figurines; Kitchen Collectibles, Glass.

This list gives company line numbers with corresponding line names. This information was obtained from Hazel Marie Weatherman's *Price Trends 2* and Jerry Barnett's *Paden City: The Color Company*.

#69, #69½ — Georgian, Aristocrat
#90 — Breton, Chevalier
#154 — Rena
#191 — Party Line
#198 — Ross
#199 — Inna
#202 — Virginia
#203 — Webb
#204 — Etta
#205 — Estelle
#206 — Pineapple
#209 — Edna
#210 — Skidoo, Spire
#215 — Hotcha
#220 — Cantina, Largo
#221 — S.S. Dreamship, Maya
#300 — Archaic
#330 — Luli
#400 — City Lights
#411 — Vaara, Mrs B
#412 — Crow's Foot (Square)
#444 — Vale
#555 — Vermillion
#700 — Simplicity
#701 — Lazy Daisy
#777 — Secrets
#836 — Future
#881 — Wotta Line, Gadroon
#890 — Crow's Foot (Round)
#895 — Lucy
#900 — Nadja
#991 — Penny Line
#994 — Popeye and Olive
#1503 — Trance
#1504 — Chaucer
#2000 — Mystic

And, finally, a listing of colors with alternate names or descriptive phrases:

Amber — (dull)
Cheriglo — (delicate) pink
Cobalt Blue — Royal Blue
Crystal — (clear, no tint)
Dark Green — forest green
Dark Amber — (honey color)
Light Blue — Copen, Neptune

Mulberry — amethyst
Opal — opaque white
Primrose — (amber with reddish tint)
Red — ruby
Rose — (dark pink)
Yellow — (pale, soft)

Orchid, mayonnaise set, yellow, three-piece, $75.00.

Photo courtesy Gene Florence

Black Forest, bowl, berry; blk 125.00
Black Forest, vase, blk, squat, 6½" 175.00
Black Forest, vase, blk, 10" 295.00
Crow's Foot, bowl, amber, sq, 11" 30.00
Crow's Foot, bowl, red, sq hdls, 8½" 50.00
Crow's Foot, bowl, whipped cream; blk, 3-ftd 27.50
Crow's Foot, cake plate, red, low ped, sq 85.00
Crow's Foot, cheese stand, red, 5" 25.00
Crow's Foot, creamer, yel, flat 6.50
Crow's Foot, gravy boat, red, ped ft 125.00
Crow's Foot, plate, dinner; pk, 10½" 40.00
Crow's Foot, plate, dinner; red, 9¼" 30.00
Crow's Foot, tumbler, red, 4¼" 75.00
Crow's Foot, vase, amber, flared, 11¾" 65.00
Cupid, bowl, fruit; gr or pk, ftd, 9¼" 250.00
Cupid, cake plate, gr or pk, 11¾" 165.00
Cupid, comport, gr or pk, 6¼" 185.00
Cupid, creamer, gr or pk, ftd, 4½" 125.00
Cupid, plate, gr or pk, 10½" 110.00
Cupid, sugar bowl, gr or pk, ftd, 5" 125.00
Gazebo, bowl, bl, bead hdls, 9" 65.00
Gazebo, bowl, crystal, #555, 9" 45.00
Gazebo, bowl, crystal, fan hdls, 9" 45.00
Gazebo, cake stand, crystal, #555, 3¾x10½" 125.00
Gazebo, candlestick, crystal, 5¼" 45.00
Gazebo, cheese dish, bl, w/lid 175.00
Gazebo, crystal, vase, 10¼" 75.00
Gazebo, mayonnaise, crystal bead hdls 25.00
Gazebo, plate, crystal, #555, 11" 50.00
Gazebo, punch cup, crystal, #555, 4-oz 12.00
Gazebo, server, bl, center hdl, 11" 65.00
Gothic Garden, candy tray, lt gr, hdld, #300, 11" 145.00
Largo, server, ruby, center hdl, #220 ....95.00
Lela Bird, cake plate, 10" 125.00
Nora Bird, candlesticks, pk or gr, pr 80.00
Nora Bird, candy dish, pk, w/lid, #300 ....300.00
Nora Bird, creamer, pk or gr, rnd hdl, 4½" 45.00
Nora Bird, cup, pk or gr 55.00
Nora Bird, ice tub, pk or gr, 6" 135.00
Nora Bird, sugar bowl, pk or gr, pointed hdls, 5" 42.50
Nora Bird, tumbler, pk or gr, ftd, 4¾" 65.00

Nora Bird, tumbler, pk or gr, 3" 40.00
Orchid, bowl, red or bl, hdls, 8½" 110.00
Orchid, bowl, yel, gr or amber, 4⅞" sq 22.00
Orchid, cake stand, yel, gr or pk, sq, 2" H 75.00
Orchid, creamer, red or bl 55.00
Orchid, creamer, yel, gr or pk 40.00
Orchid, mayonnaise set, red or bl, 3-pc 130.00
Orchid, sandwich server, crystal or gr, center hdl 65.00
Orchid, sugar bowl, red or bl 55.00
Orchid, vase, red or bl, 8" 160.00
Orchid, vase, yel or crystal, 10" 125.00
Peacock & Wild Rose, bowl, any color, flat, 8½" 125.00
Peacock & Wild Rose, bowl, console; any color, 14" 195.00
Peacock & Wild Rose, candlesticks, any color, 5", pr 165.00
Peacock & Wild Rose, ice bucket, any color, 6" 175.00
Peacock & Wild Rose, pitcher, any color, 5" 250.00
Peacock & Wild Rose, vase, any color, 2 styles, 10", ea 250.00
Peacock Reverse, bowl, any color, 4⅞" sq 40.00
Peacock Reverse, bowl, console; any color, 11¾" 125.00
Peacock Reverse, candy dish, any color, 6½" sq 175.00
Peacock Reverse, plate, sherbet; any color, 5¾" 22.50
Peacock Reverse, server, center hdl, any color 75.00
Peacock Reverse, tumbler, any color, flat, 4" 75.00
Penny Line, goblet, amethyst, low ft 18.50
Penny Line, sherbet, amethyst, low ft 12.50
Penny Line, tumbler, iced tea; amethyst, 12-oz 22.50
Penny Line, tumbler, iced tea; red, 12-oz 22.50

Paintings on Ivory

Miniature works of art executed on ivory from the 1800s are assessed by the finesse of the artist, as is any fine painting. Signed examples and portraits with identifiable subjects are usually preferred.

Portraits of Swedish lady and man, in plain gold frames, marked CGH, Stockholm 180⅞, 2¾", $825.00 for the pair.

Battle scene, EX detail, 4¾x6"+brass fr 525.00
Benjamin Franklin, in oval brass fr, 2¾x2½" 500.00
Caroline Bonaparte w/crown & jewels, sgn, easel-bk fr, 2⅞" 220.00
Child w/dog, red dress, pk roses, 5¼x4"+fr 660.00
Child w/lt brn hair, identified, 1841-44, 2¼x1¾" 1,155.00
Dutch village scene, sgn Wauwermann, in inlaid ivory fr, 5x6" ..330.00
Girl in wht dress, braided hair border, pendant fr, 1¾" 7,475.00
Lady, medallion sz, 1⅝" 165.00
Lady, wht polka-dot dress w/lace trim, gold case w/hair, 2⅝" 900.00
Lady (identified), sgn, dtd 1822, in gilt case, 3x2½" 140.00
Lady (identified), 4¾x3¾"+ornate gilt gesso fr 485.00
Lady holding spaniel, 1½x2", in etched ivory fr, 3x3½" 275.00
Lady in blk dress w/lace collar, jet jewelry, 3x2½" 990.00

Lady in blk dress w/wht lace/pk ribbon, gold case, sm rpr, 2½" ...825.00
Lady in high blk collar, identified/dtd 1825, 4⅞"+brass fr 355.00
Lady w/cloth hat, sgn RH, gilt fr w/crest, 2⅝x2⅛" 195.00
Lady w/wht lacy bonnet & shawl, gold case, 2x1½" 465.00
Man, blk frock coat/waistcoat, gold spectacles, gold case, 2⅜" .1,200.00
Man in blk frock, waistcoat & tie, gold cane, 2⅜x2" 440.00
Man in formal coat & tie, att I Sheffield, 1800s, 2½" 1,100.00
Man w/beard in blk jacket, vest & bow tie, in brass fr, 3x2" 170.00
Man w/bl frock coat, frilly wht neckpc, gold case, 2½" 500.00
Man w/blk frock coat & wht neck wear, 2⅝x2⅛" 330.00
Man w/ship & lighthouse in bkground, faded colors, 3⅝x3⅛" ...990.00
Officer w/decorations, sgn Caban, ebonized fr, 6¼x4¾" 220.00
Washington Memorial w/lady at tomb, eglomise fr, 4¾" 770.00

Pairpoint

The Pairpoint Manufacturing Company was built in 1880 in New Bedford, Massachusetts. It was primarily a metalworks whose chief product was coffin fittings. Next door, the Mt. Washington Glassworks made quality glasswares of many varieties. (See Mt. Washington for more information concerning their artware lines.) By 1894 it became apparent to both companies that a merger would be to their best interest.

From the late 1890s until the 1930s, lamps and lamp accessories were an important part of Pairpoint's production. There were three main types of shades, all of which were blown: puffy — blown-out reverse-painted shades (usually floral designs); ribbed — also reverse painted; and scenic — reverse painted with scenes of land or seascapes (usually executed on smooth surfaces, although ribbed scenics may be found occasionally). Cut glass lamps and those with metal overlay panels were also made. Scenic shades were sometimes artist signed. Every shade was stamped on the lower inside or outside edge with 1) The Pairpoint Corp., 2) Patent Pending, 3) Patented July 9, 1907, or 4) Patent Applied For. Bases were made of bronze, copper, brass, silver, or wood and are always signed.

Because they produced only fancy, handmade artware, the company's sales lagged seriously during the Depression, and as time and tastes changed, their style of product was less in demand. As a result, they never fully recovered; consequently part of the buildings and equipment was sold in 1938. The company reorganized in 1939 under the direction of Robert Gundersen and again specialized in quality hand-blown glassware. Isaac Babbit regained possession of the silver departments, and together they established Gundersen Glassworks, Inc. After WWII, because of a sharp decline in sales, it again became necessary to reorganize. The Gundersen-Pairpoint Glassworks was formed, and the old line of cut, engraved artware was reintroduced. The company moved to East Wareham, Massachusetts, in 1957. But business continued to suffer, and the firm closed only one year later. In 1970, however, new facilities were constructed in Sagamore under the direction of Robert Bryden, sales manager for the company since the 1950s.

In 1974 the company began to produce lead glass cup plates which were made on commission as fund-raisers for various churches and organizations. These are signed with a 'P' in diamond and are becoming quite collectible. See also Napkin Rings.

Glass

Bell, pk-cased wht w/daisies, clear hdl w/wht swirls, 12" 275.00
Box, gold lily on opal, emb scrolls etc at edges, 7½" L 175.00
Box, pansies w/emb scroll center, ribbed, hinged lid, 6" dia 325.00
Candlestick, gr w/cut floral, 11" 120.00
Candlestick, grapevines, etch/cvd on amethyst, 16" 325.00
Candlesticks, crystal, hollow blown stem, 16", pr 250.00
Compote, SP, on cobalt & clear ped w/bubble ball, 6½x12" 200.00

Console set, Tavern, floral, 3-color on clear, bowl+3" sticks **575.00**
Cracker jar, floral sprays/gold scrolls, melon ribs, emb lid **550.00**
Decanter, cut, dmn point/wheat, notched hdl, stopper, 10" **525.00**
Lamp, cut, Viscaria, SP mts & prisms, 20x10" **1,250.00**
Vase, clear w/cut floral, netting, brass/onyx mt w/paw ft, 14" **175.00**
Vase, Tavern, sailing ship on clear w/tiny bubbles, 6" **300.00**
Vase, Tavern, vase of flowers, clear w/tiny bubbles, 5½x4½" **225.00**

Lamps

GWTW, lilies on ribbed ball shade & squat body, 10½" **475.00**
Puffy 4" lilac shade; sgn Pairpoint metal base w/hdl, 7¾" **1,700.00**
Puffy 6" rose tree shade w/butterfly; tree trunk base, 11" **8,000.00**
Puffy 9" floral shade w/wht scrolls, ribbed; slim std, 16" **3,800.00**
Puffy 9" roses/lattice Stratford shade; sgn/#C3057 std, 15" **2,780.00**
Puffy 14" hummingbird/roses shade; brass std #E3032, 20" **6,900.00**
Puffy 14" rose bouquet shade (EX color); SP Nouveau 3-leg std .**10,000.00**
Puffy 16" hummingbird & rose shade; SP torch-shape std, 25" ..**10,450.00**
Puffy 16" pansies/bk: roses San Reno shade; std #B3000, 23" ..**9,000.00**
Rvpt 6½" goldenrod on sponged yel shade; matching base, 11" .**1,150.00**
Rvpt 7" sqd floral shade; cherub base w/onyx ft, 14½" **1,300.00**
Rvpt 8" floral-band shade; metal baluster std, 14½" **700.00**
Rvpt 9" Deco floral flared-cone Danvers shade; VG sgn/# std **750.00**
Rvpt 9¾" scenic-band Berkely shade sgn Ambero; #D3024 std ..**1,650.00**
Rvpt 10" urn-w/flowers Copley shade; wood std w/brass o/l, 13" .**1,500.00**
Rvpt 16" camels/Arabs Chesterfield shade; Gothic motif std ..**9,500.00**
Rvpt 16" ducks/sunrise Guba shade; 3-dolphin copper std, 21" .**4,450.00**
Rvpt 16" forest/bridge Copley shade; mahog/metal std, 20" **1,440.00**
Rvpt 16" Garden of Allah Pisa-style shade; sgn/#B3037 std **8,000.00**
Rvpt 16" Springfield shade w/Deco lilies & flowers; emb std ...**4,650.00**
Rvpt 17" farm scene Exeter shade; ftd trumpet form std, 23" ...**2,300.00**
Rvpt 18" Treasure Island sgn Duran shade; urn-on-disk std **6,750.00**
Rvpt 20" sea gull Copley shade & base sgn Rae, 24" **9,500.00**

Pairpoint Limoges

Limoges china blanks were imported from France in strict accordance with Pairpoint specifications. They were decorated by Pairpoint in designs that ranged from simple to elaborate florals and scenics. Called Crown Point French China in old Pairpoint and Mt. Washington catalogs, these are easily identified. Look for the Pairpoint name over a crown with the Limoges name below. You may also find similar ware marked 'Pairpoint Minton.'

Gravy boat & underplate, Dresden, mc flowers on wht **175.00**
Plate, harbor scene w/ship, sgn Tripp, fuchsia rim, 7½" **550.00**
Vase, ducks/rayed sun/bk: duck, cylinder w/scroll hdls, 15" **750.00**
Vase, water lilies on beige, dk gr trim on hdls/ruffle rim, 7x7" **425.00**

Paper Dolls

No one knows quite how or when paper dolls originated. One belief is that they began in Europe as 'pantins' (jumping jacks) and were frequently worn as part of the costume. By the late 1790s, they were being mass produced. During the 19th century, most paper dolls portrayed famous dancers and opera stars such as Fanny Elssler and Jenny Lind. In the late 1800s, the Raphael Tuck Publishers of England produced many series of beautiful paper dolls; retail companies used them as advertisements to further the sale of their products. Around the turn of the century, many popular women's magazines began featuring a page of paper dolls.

Most familiar to today's collectors are the books with dolls on cardboard covers and clothes on the inside pages. These made their appear-

ance in the late 1920s and early '30s. The most collectible (and the most valuable) are those representing celebrities, movie stars, and comic-strip characters of the '30s and '40s.

When no condition is indicated, the dolls listed below are assumed to be in mint, uncut, original condition. Cut sets will be worth about half price if all dolls and outfits are included and pieces are in very good condition. If dolls were produced in die-cut form, these prices reflect such a set in mint condition with all costumes and accessories.

For further information we recommend *A Collector's Guide to Magazine Paper Dolls* (Collector Books) and *Tomart's Price Guide to Lowe and Whitman Paper Dolls,* both by Mary Young, our advisor for this category; she is listed in the Directory under Ohio. We also recommend *Schroeder's Collectible Toys, Antique to Modern* (Collector Books).

Airline Stewardess, Lowe #4913, 1957, uncut, M **35.00**
Ann Sheridan, Whitman #986, 1944, uncut, M **200.00**
Ava Gardner, Whitman #965, 1949, uncut, M **125.00**
Baby Show, Lowe #1021, 25 dolls, 1940, uncut, M **100.00**
Beauty Contest, Lowe #1026, 1941, uncut, M **100.00**
Betty Grable, Whitman #962, 1946, M **175.00**
Blondie, Whitman #982, 1940, uncut, M **150.00**
Bobbsey Twins, Lowe #1254, 1952, uncut, M **75.00**
Carmen Miranda, Whitman #995, 1942, uncut, M **175.00**
Cinderella, Saalfield #2590, 1950, uncut, M **75.00**
Claudette Colbert, Saalfield #2451, 1943, uncut, M **200.00**
Cradle Crowd, Whitman #1173, 1948, uncut, M **50.00**
Debbie Reynolds, Whitman #1948, 1962, uncut, M **80.00**
Dolls of Many Lands, Whitman #3046, 1931, MIB **85.00**
Dream Girl, Merrill #3448, 1947, uncut, M **75.00**
Elizabeth Taylor, Whitman #968, 1949, uncut, M **135.00**
Faye Emerson, Saalfield #2722, 1952, uncut, NM **85.00**
Flintstones, A Great Big Punch Out, Whitman #1982, 1961, uncut, M **95.00**
Glenn Miller-Marion Hutton, Lowe #1041, 1942, uncut, M **400.00**
Green Acres, Whitman #4773, 1968, uncut, NMIB **60.00**
Haley Mills, That Darn Cat, Whitman #1955, 1965, uncut, M **50.00**
Here Comes the Bride, Lowe #2562, 1955, uncut, M **30.00**
Hollywood Personalities, Lowe #1049, 1941, uncut, M **300.00**
Honeymooners, Lowe #2560, 1956, uncut, M **300.00**
Jeanette MacDonald, Merrill #3460, 1941, uncut, M **250.00**
Judy Garland, Whitman #996, 1945, uncut, M **225.00**

Julia, Saalfield #6055, 1970, uncut, $55.00.

Lana Turner, Whitman #988, 1942, uncut, M **200.00**
Little Lulu, Whitmann #1970, 1971, uncut NM **30.00**
Lola Talley, Whitman #971, 1942, uncut, M **125.00**
Margaret O'Brien, Whitman #963, 1946, uncut, M, from $75 to .**125.00**
Mary Martin, Saalfield #2492, 1944, uncut, NM **150.00**
Mother Goose, Whitman #987, 1937, uncut, M **25.00**
Munsters, Whitman #1959, 1966, uncut, EX **100.00**
Natalie Wood, Whitman #2086, 1958, uncut, M **125.00**
Our Gang, Whitman #900, 1931, uncut, M **200.00**

Patti Page, Lowe #2406, 19057, uncut, M **75.00**
Petunia & Patches, Saafield #2160, 1937, uncut, M **175.00**
Popeye, Whitman #980, 1937, uncut, M **350.00**
Rainbow Dolls, Whitman #990, 1934, uncut, M **95.00**
Rosemary Clooney, Lowe #2569, 1956, uncut, M **85.00**
Sheree North, Saafield #4420, 1957, uncut, NM **90.00**
Shirley Temple, Saafield #2112, 1934, uncut, M **200.00**
Sonja Henie, Merrill #3475, 1939, uncut, M **275.00**
Turnabout Dolls, Lowe #1025, 1943, uncut, M **50.00**
Twinkle Twins, Lowe #521, 1944, uncut, M **25.00**
Walt Disney Silly Symphony Cut-out, Whitman #989, 1933, uncut, M .**400.00**
Wedding Party, Saafield #2721, 1951, uncut, NM **50.00**
Winnie the Pooh, Whitman #947, 1935, uncut, M **100.00**

Paperweights

Glass paperweight collecting has become a feverish passion, growing in intensity in the past few years. Perhaps it is because there many glass artists in the marketplace today who are creating beautiful examples, and a beginning collector can pick up these lovely objets d'art for under $100.00. Hundreds of glass artisans in the U.S. and factories in China, Italy, and Scotland produce 'gift range' paperweights. Collectors have the choice of forming their collections strictly from that price range, or they can choose to select pieces that can run into the thousands of dollars — or anywhere in between. Additionally, astute collectors are beginning to piece together collections of the old Chinese paperweights that were imported into this country during the 1930s. These were basically unrefined imitations of the lovely and unique French weights of the mid 1800s. When viewed some seventy years later, however, one can appreciate the beauty and craftsmanship these weights exhibit. Murano weights, especially those from the 1960s and '70s, represent another area of concentrated interest. Prices are beginning to escalate in both categories. Collectors who have a larger budget for these exquisite 'glass balls' may form their collection with only antique French paperweights from the classic period (1845 – 1860), the wonderful English or American weights from the 1850s, or choose to collect the high quality contemporary artistry of master glass artists such as Ayotte, the Banfords, Buzzini, Ebelhare, Grubb, Kontes, S. Lundberg, Rosenfeld, G. Smith, Tarsitano, the Trabuccos, or Stankard. The door is wide open for everyone to begin collecting in whatever price range they can afford, and the Paperweight Collector's Association, Inc. with chapters in many states can be of great assistance to collectors at all levels.

Baccarat, St. Louis, and Clichy (names synonymous with classic French paperweights) as well as some American factories stopped making paperweights between the 1880s and 1910 due to a decline in their popularity. In the 1950s Baccarat and St. Louis resumed their production. Other factories producing high quality millefiori and lampworked weights today include Perthshire and Caithness/Whitefriars (Scotland). In the 1960s smaller furnaces were developed that allowed more freedom for the individual glassmaker to design and fabricate a piece from the fire to the annealing kiln. As a result, many new studios began to spring up. The success of these ventures is evident in the creative glass produced by Lundberg Studios, Orient & Flume, and Correia Studios, to name only a few.

Books on paperweights abound, but *The Encyclopedia of Glass Paperweights* (Hollister), *Paperweights of the World, 2nd Edition, With Updated Value Guide* (Flemming & Pommerencke), and *All About Paperweights* (Selman) are three excellent selections for the beginning collector.

Many factors determine value, particularly of antique weights, and auction-realized prices of contemporary weights usually differ from issue price. Competition among new collectors entering the field has greatly influenced prices. As the number of collectors increases, available antique weights decrease per capita, forcing prices upwards. Antique paperweights have steadily increased in value as has the work of many now-deceased glass artists (i.e., Paul Ysart, Joe St. Clair, Charles Kazian, Del Tarsitano).

In the listings that follow, the dimension given at the end of the line is diameter. Prices are for weights in perfect or near-perfect conditon. Our advisors for this category are Betty and Larry Schwab, The Paperweight Shoppe; they are listed in the Directory under Illinois.

Key:
con — concentric	jsp — jasper
(d) — deceased	latt — latticinio
fct — faceted	mill — millefiori
gar — garland	o/l — overlay
grd — ground	sil — silhouette

Ayotte, Rick

Photo courtesy Betty and Larry Schwab

Bird and flowers, blues and yellow on clear, 3½", from $900.00 to $1,100.00.

Frog on lily pad w/wht lily/4 tadpoles, sgn, 1987, 3⅞", $900 to ..**1,200.00**
Monarch butterfly on flowering branch, 1984, 3⅜" **1,000.00**
Ruby-throated hummingbird w/flowers/leaves, 1984, 3¼" **1,000.00**
Vermillion flycatcher on flowered branch, 1984, 3⅜", $1,000 to ..**1,200.00**
3 yel jackets/hive/3 blossoms/etc on bl grd, 1985, 3½", $1,000 to .**1,200.00**

Baccarat, Antique

Close pack mill mushroom, bl/wht torsade, 3", from $1,500 to ..**1,800.00**
Dbl clematis, red/gr w/stems & buds, star-cut base, 2½", $1,500 to ..**1,800.00**
Dbl clematis w/star-dust cane/gr leaves, star-cut base, 3", $1,800 to .**2,000.00**
Pansy, purple & yel w/gr leaves, yel bud, star-cut base, 2½" **550.00**
Stag & trees etching on amber flashed grd, 5/1 fcts, 3", $1,200 to ...**1,500.00**

Baccarat, Modern

Gridel goat on butterscotch, 1978, 3", from $500 to **700.00**
Herbert Hoover sulfide, bl fct o/l, 3¼", MIB, from $80 to **120.00**
Patrick Henry sulfide, bl fct o/l, 3⅛", MIB, from $80 to **120.00**
Sea horse in underwater scene on bl-gr grd, sgn, 1975, 3¼", $600 to **800.00**
Thomas Paine sulfide on gr/wht fct o/l, 1975, 3¼", from $80 to .**100.00**
Zodiac bull sulfide, fct, dk bl grd, 2⅞", from $80 to **100.00**

Banford, Bob

Asters, yel to wht to clear fct o/l w/purple asters, 3", $800 to ..**1,000.00**
Magnum bouquet of 5 flowers surrounding pansy, waffle base .**2,000.00**
2 Clichy-style pansies, star centers, buds, leaves, 3½" **750.00**

Banford, Ray

Basket irises, purple in yel/clear to wht flowers, 3¼", $1,200 to ...**1,500.00**
Cabbage roses, red/wht/to clear, grid base, 3¼", up to **2,200.00**

Buzzini, Chris

Asters/mullein/morning glories w/leaves, sgn, 3⅛", $850 to **1,000.00**
Morning glories (2) w/(3) buds & leaves, 1988, 3⅛", $800 to .**1,000.00**
Orchid w/root system, 1988, 3", from $700 to **900.00**

Clichy, Antique

Looped mill w/central cane, indented top fct, 3" **250.00**
Looped mill w/pastry/complex canes, lg central cane, 2¾" **650.00**
Nosegay, 5 gr leaves w/3 mill canes, mini, 2⅛" **450.00**
Scramble type w/gr/wht/red Clichy rose canes included, 2⅝" **900.00**
Washington sulfide on red grd, 3¼", nick **800.00**

Deacons, John

Bl translucent o/l w/3 wht flowers/gr stems, sgn, 2¾", $250 to **300.00**
Poinsettia on wht latt basket, multi-fcts, star-cut, 3", $275 to **300.00**
Rose & wht dbl o/l w/pk/mauve/bl flowers, sgn, 3¼", $275 to **300.00**
10-petal pk flower on wht basket w/cane ring, 2¾", $250 to **350.00**
10-petal pk/wht flower w/leaves on wht latt basket, '96, 3", $275 to ...**325.00**

Kaziun, Charles

Gold bee on rose, 3 leaves, mill/latt on cobalt, ftd, 2", $600 to ..**800.00**
Gr snake w/yel/wine stripes by red rose, 3 leaves, 2", $900 to ..**1,200.00**
Lime/pk/wht mill w/hearts & shamrocks, ftd, 1½", $800 to **1,000.00**
Perfume, fct body/stopper, turq aventurine w/yel flower, 3", up to ..**1,500.00**
Pk/wht flower & wreath, 3 leaves, aventurine grd, 1¾", $900 to **1,200.00**
Rabbit/flowers in wreath, border: 8 chartreuse mill, 1¾", up to ...**1,200.00**
Spider lily on gold-dusted cobalt grd, ped, 1⅜x2", from $500 to ..**600.00**

New England Glass, Antique

Mc crown, center cane, 2½", from $1,800 to **2,000.00**
Nosegay, 4 gr leaves w/3 mill canes, 2", from $275 to **375.00**
Plymouth Rock molded, clear, made for 1876 Centennial, $75 to ...**100.00**

Perthshire

Flower on gr/wht/bl latt, single fct, sgn, 1981, 3¼", from $475 to ..**500.00**
Heather sprig w/gar on dk bl grd, 1978 label, 2⅝", from $200 to .**250.00**
Lampwork flower in cane ring overlaid w/basket canes, top fct, 2" ..**400.00**
Tudor Rose, 1975, ltd 400, 3¼", from $550 to **650.00**
3-D bouquet, 12/1 facets, fancy cut base, 1999, ltd 150, 3" **675.00**

Rosenfeld, Ken

Bouquet, 4 pk/yel flowers, 2 buds, 1992, 2¾" **350.00**
Pk rose & bud w/stems/leaves, 1998, mini, 2½" **250.00**
Snake, desert grd, rocks, flowers, 1993, 3½", from $800 to **1,000.00**
Upright bouquet, buds, berries, sculptural cube, 3¼x2½" **700.00**

Sandwich Glass

Clematis w/bud & gar, swirling wht latt grd, 5/1 fcts, 2⅞" **600.00**
Cross flower w/star cane, gr tips/leaves on clear grd, 2¾" **550.00**
Dbl clematis on swirling latt grd, 3¼", from $1,200 to **1,500.00**
Poinsettia, red w/gr leaves & stem, 2⅞", from $750 to **850.00**

Weedflower, mc petals, gold-stone center cane, 2¾", $1,000 to ..**1,200.00**

Smith, Gordon

Frog on desert grd w/plants & rocks, 1995, 3⅜", from $600 to ...**700.00**
Lady slippers, 2 w/gr leaves on dk gr flashed grd, '84, 3", $400 to ..**500.00**
Strawberries (2) w/flower/bud on dk bl grd, 1983, 2¾", $400 to .**500.00**

South Jersey

Millville umbrella, ftd, 3½" H, from $500 to **600.00**
Rose, orange, crimped, ftd, 3x2⅞", from $150 to **250.00**
Rose, wht & shaded bl, att W Valla, ftd, 3¼x2¾", from $150 to ..**250.00**
Rose, yel, ftd, att W Valla, 3¼x3½", from $150 to **250.00**

St. Louis, Modern

Bl & wht swirl, 1971, 3⅛", from $450 to **500.00**
Bl/wht/red canes form carpet grd, 1982, 3⅛" **475.00**
Doily pattern w/6 pk clusters of canes on bl grd, 1972, 3⅛" **325.00**
Eagle sulfide, red to wht 5/1 fct o/l on dk bl, 3¼", from $350 to .**450.00**
Piedouche, wht carpet grd, 1992, ltd 150, from $1,600 to **1,800.00**
Pistachio/wht dbl o/l, mushroom w/con mill canes, '70, $550 to ..**700.00**
Snake coiled on bed of upset muslin, 5/1 fct, 1969, 3¼", $500 to ...**550.00**

Stankard, Paul

Arethusa orchid, pk/orange w/roots on bl, sgn/'82, 3⅛", $1,100 to .**1,400.00**
Blood root, flower & bud w/leaves/roots, sgn/'82, 3¼", $1,200 to ...**1,400.00**
Blueberry & Spirit, pk blossoms/roots/nude male, 3¼", $2,400 to ..**2,600.00**
Cymbidium epiphytic orchid, wht grd, sgn/'85, 3¼", $1,200 to **1,400.00**
Desert flowers & bud on cobalt, sgn/'83, 3¼", from $900 to **1,100.00**
Flowering arbutus branch w/gr leaves, 1985, 3⅛", $900 to **1,100.00**
Indian Pipes/Spirit, 3 wht flowers/nude, S1594, 3", $23,000 to ..**24,000.00**
Mixed bouquet w/trailing branches on clear grd, sgn, 1986, 3¼" .**2,000.00**
Morning glories (2), bl & wht, lt gr grd, sgn, 1984, 3¼" **1,400.00**
Mtn hawthorn blossoms, pk w/roots on clear, '83, 3⅛", $1,100 to .**1,500.00**

Tarsitano, Debbie

Bouquet w/4 ribbons, honeycomb fcts, star-cut, 2¾", $550 to **750.00**
Lg pk rose, star-cut base, sgn, 3", from $500 to **600.00**
Pansy, mc w/center mill cane/bl bud, star-cut, 2¾", from $600 to .**800.00**
Tulip bouquet in hand, clear grd, sgn, 3¼" **450.00**
3 pk flowers/2 buds/3 lily-of-valley sprays, '83, 3¼", from $600 to ..**800.00**
5-layer purple dahlia, star-cut base, sgn, 3⅛", from $1,500 to ..**2,000.00**

Tarsitano, Delmo

Peaches on branch w/leaves, 6/1 fct, sgn, 2¾", from $900 to ...**1,200.00**
Peaches on brn branch w/gr leaves on cobalt grd, 3", $800 to .**1,100.00**
Strawberries w/flowers & leaves, 3⅛", from $700 to **1,000.00**

Trabucco, Victor

Lav roses, 3 on gr/brn leafy stem, VT cane, '94, 3¾", $1,000 to .**1,100.00**
Lg mixed bouquet, seamless, sgn, 1985, 3¾", from $1,000 to ..**1,400.00**
Lg mixed bouquet, seamless, sgn, 1985, 4¾", from $1,400 to ..**1,800.00**
Lg purple flower/2 lily-of-valley sprays, sgn, '86, 3¼", $600 to **700.00**
Magnum camelia bouquet, 1996, 3⅞", from $1,200 to **1,600.00**
Mc mixed flowers & leaves on cobalt, 1985, 3⅞", $900 to **1,200.00**
Mixed bouquet, multi-fct to sit upright, sgn, '88, 4½", $1,000 to ...**1,200.00**
Morning glories w/buds & leaves, sgn, 1983, 3¾", from $600 to .**800.00**
Purple flower w/2 pk/7 wht flowers, 1986, 3¼", from $600 to **800.00**

Raspberries & roses, red/wht in clear, VT leaf cane, 3¾", $800 to ...900.00
Strawberries/flowers/bud, irregularly sculpted, fct, 1983, 3⅝" 800.00
Whiptail lizard on pebble grd, sgn, 1983, 3", from $900 to 1,100.00

Whitefriars

Coronation Jubilee, 6/1 fcts, 1977, 3¼", from $350 to 450.00
Red/wht/bl mill, magnum, 4⅛", from $350 to 400.00

Miscellaneous

Bohemian, mc mill canes on swirling yel latt grd, 2⅜", $100 to .200.00
Bohemian, sulfide roses bouquet in mc gar on bl, 3¾", $500 to ..600.00
Degenhart, John; window weight, from $500 to 800.00
Donofrio, Jim; tree frog among bamboo shoots & flower, 1994, 3½" ..475.00
Ebelhare, Drew; concentric Piedouche, 1993, 2⅛", from $400 to ...600.00
Gillinder & Sons, hand w/turtle, 4¼", from $400 to 700.00
Grubb, R; bl o/l swirl to wht to clear w/rose/2 buds, 3⅛", $400 to ..500.00
Karg, Rolano; tall sculpture, confusion twist 250.00
Kontes, J; pears/flower on wht muslin on cobalt grd, 3", $2,200 to 2,600.00
Pairpoint type, red roses w/in dbl o/l, 6/1 fct, 2¾", from $300 to ...400.00
Parabelle, trefoil gar on muslin, 1990, ltd 75, 2⅞", from $250 to ...350.00
Parsley, J; pk/flowers/buds on cobalt, 1989, 2¾", from $500 to ...600.00
Parsley, J; wildflowers/pods/leaves on gr flash grd, 2⅝", $500 to .600.00
Somerville, Am flag & USA w/in mc flower gar, 4", $300 to 400.00
Somerville, Fr flag w/RF & sm flower gar, 3¾", NM, $250 to 400.00

Parian Ware

Parian is hard-paste unglazed porcelain made to resemble marble. First made in the mid-1800s by Staffordshire potters, it was soon after produced in the United States by the U.S. Pottery at Bennington, Vermont. Busts and statuary were favored, but plaques, vases, mugs, and pitchers were also made.

Box, winged griffins in corners, bronze mts, 9½" 700.00
Bust, Captain Matthew Webb, JS Crapper of Hanley, 1875, 25" .750.00
Bust, Goddess of Sunflower, minor stain, 8⅜" 100.00
Bust, Lafayette, 8" 300.00
Bust, Washington, 11½" 350.00
Figurine, Diana in wrist shackles, on plinth, 13½" 295.00
Figurine, girl w/flower basket, pastels w/gold, 16" 225.00
Figurine, Matchmaking, owls on tree branch, English, ca 1871, 7¾" 195.00
Figurine, seated nude, 13" 200.00
Figurine, 2 children w/wreath & flowers, J&TB, 10¾" 250.00
Syrup, Good Samaritan, scroll hdl, Jones & Walley, 1841, 6¼", EX ...65.00

Parrish, Maxfield

Maxfield Parrish (1870 – 1966), with his unique abilities in architecture, illustrations, and landscapes, was the most prolific artist during 'The Golden Years of Illustrators.' He produced art for more than one hundred magazines, painted girls on rocks for the Edison-Mazda division of General Electric, and landscapes for Brown & Bigelow. His most recognized work was 'Daybreak' that was published in 1923 by House of Art and sold nearly two million prints. Parrish began early training with his father who was a recognized artist, studied architecture at Dartmouth, and became an active participant in the Cornish artist colony in New Hampshire where he resided. Due to his increasing popularity, reproductions are now being marketed. For further information we recommend *Collector's Value Guide to Early 20th Century American Prints* by Michael Ivankovich. Bobby Babcock, our advisor for this category, is listed in the Directory under Texas.

Blotter, Lamp Seller of Bagdad, Edison-Mazda, 1922, 5¾x3¼" ..150.00
Book, Arabian Nights, 1st edition, 1909 ....200.00
Book, Dream Days, 1902 ....200.00
Book, Early Years, Skeeter's, all editions, ea 300.00
Book, Knave of Hearts, spiral bound, 1925 ....1,000.00
Book, Knickerbocker's History of New York, 1900 ....400.00
Book, Mother Goose in Prose by L Frank Baum, 1897, EX 2,000.00
Book plate, Lantern Bearers 35.00
Calendar, Business Man's, Dodge Publishing, 6x8" 150.00
Calendar, Egypt, Edison-Mazda, 1922, complete, 37½x18" 4,500.00
Calendar, Enchantment, Edison-Mazda, 1926, complete, 37½x18" .4,000.00
Calendar, Friendship, Dodge Publishing, 6x8" 150.00
Calendar, Golden Hours, Edison-Mazda, 1929, complete, 19x8½" 950.00
Calendar, Golden Hours, Edison-Mazda, 1929, complete, 37½x18" .1,500.00
Calendar, Moonlight, Edison-Mazda, 1934, complete, 19x8½" 1,200.00
Calendar, Solitude, Edison-Mazda, 1932, complete, 19x8½" ..1,500.00
Calendar, Spirit of Night, Edison-Mazda, 1919, complete, 19x8½" .4,500.00
Calendar, summer landscape, B&B, complete, 22x14" 295.00
Calendar, summer landscape, B&B, complete, 23x28" 375.00
Calendar, summer landscape, B&B, complete, 30x24" 400.00
Calendar, summer landscape, B&B, 10x12" 200.00
Calendar, Sunrise, Edison-Mazda, 1933, complete, 19x8½" 1,100.00
Calendar, Waterfall, Edison-Mazda, 1931, complete, 37½x18" .2,900.00

Calendar top, Edison-Mazda, Venetian Lamplighter, cropped, 6¼x10½", $450.00; 14⅛x23⅝", $1,700.00.

Photo courtesy Michael Ivankovich

Calendar top, Enchantment, 1926, 10½x6¼" 750.00
Calendar top, Reveries, Edison-Mazda, 1927, 22½x14½" 950.00
Calendar top, Spirit of the Night, 1919, 10½x6¼" 1,200.00
Calendar top, Venetian Lamplighter, 1924, 22½x14½" 1,000.00
Calendar top, winter landscape, B&B, 10x12" 300.00
Calendar top, winter landscape, B&B, 22x14" 325.00
Calendar top, winter landscape, B&B, 23x28" 425.00
Calendar top, winter landscape, B&B, 24x30" 500.00
Calendar top, winter landscape, B&B, 9x10" 200.00
Greeting card, summer landscape, B&B 60.00
Greeting card, winter landscape, B&B 150.00
Magazine cover, Century, from $150 to 500.00
Magazine cover, Life, from $100 to 800.00
Magazine insert, Djer Kiss Elves, 1918, 9x14" 125.00
Magazine insert, Pandora's Box, 1908, 9x11" 85.00
Magazine insert, Swift's Premium Ham, 1921, 9x12" 125.00
Menu, Broadmoor, 1920s, 11x15" 250.00
Playing cards, Contentment, 1928, full deck, w/box 300.00
Playing cards, In the Mountains, 1971, full deck, w/box 140.00
Playing cards, Waterfall, 1931, full deck, w/box 300.00
Poster, Century Magazine, 1902, 14x20" 1,500.00
Poster, Jack & Beanstalk, Ferry Seed, 1923, 21x28" 3,500.00
Poster, New Hampshire Winter Paradise, 1939, 24x29" 1,200.00
Print, Autumn, 1905, 10x12" 250.00
Print, Canyon, 1924, 6x10" 225.00
Print, Cleopatra, 1917, 28x24½" 2,500.00

Print, Daybreak, 1922, 18x30"	500.00
Print, Dreaming, 1928, 18x30"	1,350.00
Print, Gardener, 1907, 12x19"	450.00
Print, Knave of Hearts, Fool in Green, bookplate	150.00
Print, Knave of Hearts, Frog & Prince, bookplate	150.00
Print, Knave of Hearts, Prince, bookplate	150.00
Print, Knave of Hearts, 2 Chefs at the Table, bookplate	150.00
Print, Morning, 1926, 12x15"	350.00
Print, Royal Gorge, 1925, 16½x20"	900.00
Print, Rubaiyat, 1917, 8x30"	1,000.00
Print, Stars, 1927, 12x20"	1,250.00
Print, Sugar Plum Tree, Scribner's & Sons, 1905, 11x16"	800.00
Print, White Birch, 1930, 9x11"	150.00
Puzzle, Lady Violetta & the Knave, 1926	295.00
Tape measure, 2 knaves, Edison-Mazda advertisement	250.00
Tie rack, Old King Cole, Pyraglass, 1909	950.00

Pate-Sur-Pate

Pate-sur-pate, literally paste-on paste, is a technique whereby relief decorations are built up on a ceramic body by layering several applications of slip, one on the other, until the desired result is achieved. Usually only two colors are used, and the value of a piece is greatly enhanced as more color is added.

Box, nude sits by water, wht on bl w/gold, Limoges, 5½" dia	200.00
Plaque, angelic artist draws angel, Barriere/Limoges, 4" dia	425.00
Plaque, classical figure relief, gray/wht, Albione Birks, 5½"	100.00
Plaque, lady w/lg dog, wht on deep bl, Barriere/Limoges, 6x8"	425.00
Vase, ribboned portrait medallions, wht/rose on teal, hdls, 7"	325.00

Pattern Glass

Pattern glass was the first mass-produced fancy tableware in America and was much prized by our ancestors. From the 1840s to the Civil War, it contained a high lead content and is known as 'flint glass.' It is exceptionally clear and resonant. Later glass was made with soda lime and is known as nonflint. By the 1890s pattern glass was produced in great volume in thousands of patterns, and colored glass came into vogue. Today the highest prices are often paid for these later patterns flashed with rose, amber, canary, and vaseline; stained ruby; or made in colors of cobalt, green, yellow, amethyst, etc. Demand for pattern glass declined by 1915, and glass fanciers were collecting it by 1930. No other field of antiques offers more diversity in patterns, prices, or pieces than this unique and historical glass that represents the Victorian era in America.

Our advisor for this category is Darlene Yohe; she is listed in the Directory under Arkansas. For a more thorough study on the subject, we recommend *The Collector's Encyclopedia of Pattern Glass* by Mollie Helen McCain and *Standard Encyclopedia of Pressed Glass, 1860 – 1930, Identification & Values* by Bill Edwards and Mike Carwile, both available from Collector Books. See also Bread Plates; Cruets; Historical Glass; Salt and Pepper Shakers; Salts, Open; Sugar Shakers; Syrups; specific manufacturers such as Northwood.

Note: Values are given for open sugar bowls and compotes unless noted 'w/lid.'

Actress, butter dish	100.00
Actress, cheese dish	240.00
Actress, goblet, frosted bowl	98.00
Admiral Dewey, See Dewey; See Also Greentown Dewey	
Adonis, compote, w/lid, 8"	100.00

Adonis, creamer	27.50
Adonis, relish	10.00
Alabama, butter dish, ruby stain	145.00
Alabama, relish, 5x8"	22.00
Alaska, celery tray	70.00
Alaska, spooner	45.00
Almond Thumbprint, cordial, flint	42.50
Almond Thumbprint, egg cup, flint	48.00
Almond Thumbprint, spooner, nonflint	16.00
Almond Thumbprint, tumbler, flint	62.50
Amazon, butter dish, etched decor	75.00
Amazon, champagne	32.50
Amberette, See Klondike	
Apollo, pitcher, water	80.00
Apollo, salt cellar	20.00
Arched Grape, butter dish, nonflint	48.00
Arched Grape, wine, nonflint	26.00
Argus, ale glass, flint	80.00
Argus, egg cup, nonflint	25.00
Argus, mug, appl hdl, flint	75.00
Argus, pitcher, water; flint	375.00
Art, banana stand	98.00
Art, bowl, 9¾"	40.00
Art, compote, 7" dia	55.00
Art, creamer, ruby stain	95.00

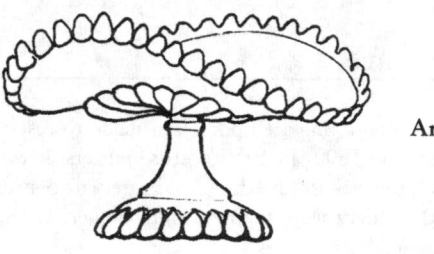

Art

Art, goblet	65.00
Ashburton, carafe	178.00
Ashburton, celery vase, scalloped	138.00
Ashburton, champagne	60.00
Ashburton, honey dish	18.00
Ashburton, sauce dish	7.50
Ashburton, tumbler, water; ftd	95.00
Atlas, champagne, 5½"	35.00
Atlas, marmalade	50.00
Atlas, wine	32.00
Austrian, bowl, 8"	48.00
Austrian, plate, 10"	42.00
Austrian, sugar bowl, w/lid	42.50
Austrian, tumbler	22.50
Austrian, wine	32.00
Balder, See Pennsylvania	
Baltimore Pear, bowl, 8"	22.00
Baltimore Pear, compote, high std, 7"	85.00
Baltimore Pear, pickle dish	22.50
Baltimore Pear, sugar bowl, w/lid	55.00
Barberry, celery vase	38.00
Barberry, egg cup	24.00
Barberry, plate, bl, 6"	48.00
Barley, bowl, scalloped oval, 8½"	17.50
Barley, compote, 8x8½"	32.50
Barley, creamer	25.00
Barley, goblet	35.00
Barrel Huber, See Huber	

Basket Weave, cup & saucer, amber 30.00
Basket Weave, egg cup 16.00
Basket Weave, goblet 24.00
Basket Weave, wine 22.50
Beaded Band, creamer 32.00
Beaded Band, pitcher, water 78.00
Beaded Grape, bowl, 5½" sq 17.50
Beaded Grape, cake stand, 6x9" sq 55.00
Beaded Grape, relish, 4x7" 22.50
Beaded Grape, wine 32.00
Beaded Grape Medallion, egg cup 35.00
Beaded Grape Medallion, goblet 32.00
Beaded Grape Medallion, relish, w/lid 150.00
Beaded Medallion, butter dish 45.00
Beaded Medallion, goblet 25.00
Beaded Medallion, tumbler 48.00
Beaded Mirror, See Beaded Medallion
Beaded Swirl, creamer, flat 27.00
Beaded Swirl, punch cup, gr 14.00
Beaded Tulip, goblet 38.00
Beaded Tulip, tray, 9" dia 27.50
Bearded Head, See Viking
Bellflower, bowl, scalloped, 4½x8" 78.00
Bellflower, celery vase 115.00
Bellflower, cordial, knob stem 120.00
Bellflower, wine, plain stem, str sides 95.00
Bigler, celery vase 90.00
Bigler, champagne 90.00
Bigler, wine 60.00
Bird & Strawberry, bowl, flat, 9" 50.00
Bird & Strawberry, butter dish 85.00
Bird & Strawberry, punch cup 24.00
Bleeding Heart, bowl, 8" 36.00
Bleeding Heart, creamer, appl hdl 60.00
Bleeding Heart, creamer, molded hdl 32.00
Bleeding Heart, tumbler, ftd 78.00
Block & Fan, butter dish, ruby stain 90.00
Block & Fan, goblet, ruby stain 125.00
Block & Fan, ice tub, ruby stain 50.00
Block & Fan, orange bowl 48.00
Blue Jay, See Cardinal Bird
Bow Tie, butter pat 27.50
Bow Tie, goblet 65.00
Bow Tie, punch bowl 110.00
Bow Tie, spooner 32.00
Bridal Rosette, cup 7.50
Bridal Rosette, plate, 10" 22.00
Broken Column, biscuit jar 80.00
Broken Column, carafe 80.00
Broken Column, plate, 8" 42.50
Broken Column, relish 25.00
Buckle, bowl, flint, 8" 58.00
Buckle, egg cup, nonflint 27.50
Buckle, wine, flint 78.00
Buckle w/Star, goblet 30.00
Buckle w/Star, mustard jar 80.00
Buckle w/Star, tumbler 55.00
Buckle w/Star, wine 22.50
Bull's Eye, bottle, bitters 82.50
Bull's Eye, carafe 50.00
Bull's Eye, creamer 120.00
Bull's Eye, goblet 67.50
Bull's Eye, mug, appl hdl, 3½" 110.00
Bull's Eye & Fan, creamer 25.00

Bull's Eye & Fan, goblet 32.00
Bull's Eye & Fan, relish 24.00
Bull's Eye Band, See Reverse Torpedo
Bull's Eye in Heart, See Heart w/Thumbprint
Bull's Eye w/Diamond Point, celery vase 175.00
Bull's Eye w/Diamond Point, creamer, appl hdl 180.00
Bull's Eye w/Diamond Point, honey dish 35.00
Bull's Eye w/Diamond Point, wine 125.00
Button Arches, cake stand, ruby stain 175.00
Button Arches, creamer 20.00
Button Arches, punch cup 10.00
Button Band, bowl, 10" 32.00
Button Band, goblet 42.50
Cabbage Rose, cake stand, 12½" 55.00
Cabbage Rose, mug 62.50
Cabbage Rose, wine 40.00
Cable, bowl, ftd, 8" 48.00
Cable, egg cup 65.00
Cable, honey dish 17.50
Cable, plate, 6" 80.00
California, See Beaded Grape

Cane

Cane, celery vase 34.00
Cane, relish, 8" 22.00
Cane, spooner, apple gr 38.00
Cape Cod, compote, w/lid, 12x8" 140.00
Cape Cod, decanter 175.00
Cape Cod, plate, open hdls, 10" 50.00
Cape Cod, plate, 10" 45.00
Cardinal Bird, butter dish, 3 birds in base 125.00
Cardinal Bird, creamer 35.00
Cardinal Bird, spooner 40.00
Cathedral, bowl, berry; 8" 42.50
Cathedral, creamer, vaseline, tall 45.00
Cathedral, tumbler 25.00
Centennial, See Liberty Bell
Chain w/Star, creamer 27.50
Chain w/Star, spooner 27.50
Chandelier, creamer 35.00
Chandelier, violet bowl 42.50
Classic, pitcher, water; collared base 265.00
Classic, plate, Warrior, 10" 155.00
Coin, See US Coin
Colorado, banana stand 36.00
Colorado, mug 25.00
Colorado, punch cup 20.00
Columbian Coin, mug, frosted coins 125.00
Columbian Coin, syrup, frosted coin 325.00
Columbian Coin, tumbler, maiden's blush 12.00
Comet, creamer 165.00
Comet, goblet 88.00
Comet, mug 125.00
Compact, See Snail

Connecticut, celery vase 28.00
Connecticut, tumbler, lemonade; hdl 22.50
Connecticut, wine 37.50
Cord & Tassel, creamer 22.00
Cord & Tassel, wine 45.00
Cord Drapery, creamer, bl 130.00
Cord Drapery, mug 40.00
Cord Drapery, tray 175.00
Cord Drapery, tumbler, bl 70.00
Cordova, creamer 35.00
Cordova, finger bowl 20.00
Cottage, creamer 30.00
Cottage, creamer, amber 65.00
Cottage, plate, 7" 22.50
Croesus, bowl, purple, 8" 155.00
Croesus, butter dish 90.00
Croesus, pitcher, water; gr 275.00
Crow's Foot, See Yale
Crown Jewels, See Chandelier
Crystal Wedding, creamer 35.00
Crystal Wedding, nappy 27.50
Crystal Wedding, wine 98.00
Cube w/Fan, See Pineapple & Fan
Cupid & Venus, cordial 90.00
Cupid & Venus, goblet 78.00
Cupid & Venus, jelly jar 78.00
Currant, butter dish 70.00
Currant, spooner 22.00
Currier & Ives, creamer 35.00
Currier & Ives, pitcher, milk 55.00
Currier & Ives, sauce dish, flat or ftd 12.50
Currier & Ives, tumbler, ftd 42.00
Cut Log, champagne 12.00
Cut Log, mug 22.50
Cut Log, pitcher, water; ruby stain 250.00
Dahlia, bowl, bl 30.00
Dahlia, pitcher, bl 125.00
Daisy & Button, banana boat, gr 32.00
Daisy & Button, bread tray 22.00
Daisy & Button, creamer 17.50
Daisy & Button, plate, leaf shape, 5" 12.50
Daisy & Button w/Crossbars, creamer, ind 22.00
Daisy & Button w/Crossbars, punch cup 15.00
Daisy & Button w/Crossbars, tumbler, amber 27.00
Daisy & Button w/Thumbprint Panels, goblet, amber stain 50.00
Daisy & Button w/Thumbprint Panels, goblet, bl stain 45.00
Daisy & Button w/V Ornament, celery vase 32.00
Daisy & Button w/V Ornament, compote, amber, 8" 55.00
Dakota, celery tray 48.00
Dakota, compote, eng, high std, w/lid, 8" dia 200.00
Dakota, wine, ruby stain 58.00
Deer & Pine Tree, goblet 60.00
Deer & Pine Tree, mug, lg 48.00
Deer & Pine Tree, spooner 80.00
Deer & Pine Tree, waste bowl 85.00
Delaware, creamer 50.00
Delaware, pitcher, water; rose w/gold 110.00
Delaware, tumbler, gr w/gold 42.00
Dewey, parfait 48.00
Dewey, pitcher, water 70.00
Dewey, See Also Greentown Dewey
Diagonal Band, creamer 32.00
Diagonal Band, pitcher, water 45.00
Diamond Medallion, See Grand

Diamond Point, bowl, w/lid, nonflint, 7" 22.00
Diamond Point, champagne, flint 130.00
Diamond Point, claret, flint 95.00
Diamond Point, plate, flint, 6" 32.00
Diamond Quilted, celery tray, amethyst 65.00
Diamond Quilted, champagne, turq 40.00
Diamond Thumbprint, bowl, 8" 88.00
Diamond Thumbprint, tumbler 88.00
Diamond Thumbprint, tumbler, bar; 3¾" 145.00
Dinner Bell, See Cottage
Doric, See Feather
Double Leaf & Dart, See Leaf & Dart
Drapery, butter dish 42.50
Drapery, sugar bowl, w/lid 40.00
Egg in Sand, goblet 28.00
Egg in Sand, pitcher, water 36.00
Egg in Sand, relish 15.00
Egyptian, compote, high std, sphinx base, w/lid, 8" dia 265.00
Egyptian, creamer 50.00
Egyptian, plate, 12" 88.00
Egyptian, sugar bowl 32.50
Elephant, See Jumbo
Emerald Green Herringbone, See Florida
Empress, butter dish 65.00
Empress, creamer, gr w/gold 48.00
Esther, creamer, ind 165.00
Esther, goblet 55.00
Etched Dakota, See Dakota
Excelsior, cordial, flint 45.00
Excelsior, spooner, flint 75.00
Excelsior, tumbler, ftd, flint 42.50

Eyewinker

Eyewinker, bowl, 6½" 28.00
Eyewinker, celery vase 42.50
Eyewinker, plate, 7" sq 25.00
Fairfax Strawberry, See Strawberry
Feather, cake stand, 8½" dia 42.50
Feather, cordial 120.00
Feather, pickle dish 18.00
Festoon, marmalade 35.00
Festoon, tumbler 22.00
Fine Cut, cake stand 40.00
Fine Cut, goblet, vaseline 45.00
Fine Cut, wine, pk stain 65.00
Fine Cut & Block, champagne, amber 68.00
Fine Cut & Block, pitcher, amber 88.00
Fine Cut & Diamond, See Grand
Fine Cut & Feather, See Feather
Fine Rib, spoon holder 55.00
Fine Rib, wine 45.00
Fingerprint, See Almond Thumbprint
Fishscale, bowl, 6" 38.00

Fishscale, cake stand 38.00
Fishscale, pitcher 60.00
Flamingo Habitat, cheese dish, blown 115.00
Flamingo Habitat, creamer 45.00
Flamingo Habitat, wine 48.00
Florida, celery vase 32.00
Florida, nappy, gr 27.50
Florida, tumbler, gr 42.00
Flower Pot, butter dish 55.00
Flower Pot, goblet 45.00
Frosted Circle, cake stand, 9½" 50.00
Frosted Circle, sugar bowl, w/lid 65.00
Frosted Circle, wine 42.50
Frosted Leaf, sugar bowl, w/lid 180.00
Frosted Leaf, tumbler 45.00
Frosted Lion, See Lion
Frosted Ribbon, See Ribbon
Frosted Roman Key, butter dish, flint 55.00
Frosted Roman Key, goblet, flint 55.00
Frosted Stork, sauce bowl 30.00
Frosted Stork, spooner 60.00
Galloway, butter dish 65.00
Galloway, finger bowl 25.00
Galloway, vase, 11" 32.00
Garfield Drape, cake stand 80.00
Garfield Drape, goblet 40.00
Garfield Drape, honey dish 18.00
Gem, See Nailhead
Georgia, bonbon, ftd 28.00
Georgia, creamer 35.00
Georgia, mug 30.00
Good Luck, See Horseshoe
Grand, spooner 20.00
Grand, sugar bowl 18.00
Grape & Festoon w/Shield, mug, 1⅞" 20.00
Grape & Festoon w/Shield, pitcher, water 78.00
Grape & Festoon w/Stippled Leaf, relish 20.00
Grape & Festoon w/Stippled Leaf, sugar bowl, w/lid 50.00
Grasshopper, celery vase 65.00
Grasshopper, compote, w/lid, 8¼" 75.00
Grasshopper, tumbler, amber, ftd 72.50
Greek Key, goblet 90.00
Greek Key, punch cup 20.00
Guardian Angel, See Cupid & Venus
Hairpin, champagne, flint 78.00
Hairpin, tumbler, flint 65.00
Halley's Comet, creamer 42.00
Halley's Comet, tumbler 28.00
Hamilton, butter dish 72.50
Hamilton, egg cup 45.00
Hand, honey dish 16.00
Hand, mug 42.00
Hawaiian Lei, cake stand 40.00
Hawaiian Lei, cup & saucer 42.50
Heart w/Thumbprint, finger bowl 42.50
Heart w/Thumbprint, mustard jar, SP lid ...100.00
Heart w/Thumbprint, sugar bowl, pewter rim, ind 30.00
Herringbone Band, See Ripple
Herringbone Buttress, See Greentown, Herringbone Buttress
Hickman, butter dish 38.00
Hickman, pitcher, water 60.00
Hidalgo, rose bowl 30.00
Hidalgo, tumbler 30.00
Hinoto, egg cup 40.00

Hinoto, wine 68.00
Holly, goblet 125.00
Holly, pickle dish, oval 32.00
Holly, sugar bowl, w/lid 130.00
Holly, wine 150.00
Holly Amber, See Greentown, Holly Amber
Honeycomb, celery vase, flint 65.00
Honeycomb, champagne, flint 45.00
Honeycomb, pitcher, milk; flint 85.00
Hops & Barley, See Wheat & Barley
Horn of Plenty, butter pat, flint 24.00
Horn of Plenty, relish, oval, flint, 7x5" 90.00
Horn of Plenty, tumbler, water; flint 65.00
Horseshoe, creamer 45.00
Horseshoe, doughnut stand 100.00
Horseshoe, sugar bowl, w/lid 95.00
Huber, celery vase 40.00
Huber, egg cup 30.00
Hummingbird, tray, water 55.00
Hummingbird, wine 95.00
Idaho, See Snail
Illinois, olive dish 20.00
Illinois, pitcher, milk; sq 65.00
Iowa, goblet 27.50
Iowa, olive dish 18.00
Iowa, spooner 7.50
Iris w/Meander, See Opalescent Glass
Ivy in Snow, mug, ruby stain 50.00
Ivy in Snow, plate, 10" 32.00
Jacob's Ladder, creamer 38.00
Jacob's Ladder, goblet 70.00
Jacob's Ladder, pitcher, water; appl hdl 145.00
Jersey Swirl, butter dish, bl 70.00
Jersey Swirl, marmalade jar 50.00
Jersey Swirl, wine, bl 48.00
Jewel w/Dewdrop, compote, high std, 8" dia 80.00
Jewel w/Dewdrop, mug, 3½" 35.00
Jewel w/Dewdrop, sugar bowl, w/lid 68.00

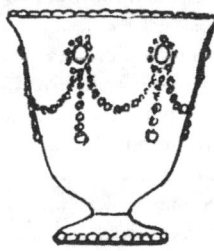

Jewel with Festoon

Jewel w/Festoon, punch cup 24.00
Jewel w/Festoon, sauce bowl 14.00
Jewel w/Moondrop, cake plate 58.00
Jewel w/Moondrop, mug 50.00
Jeweled Moon & Star, celery vase 25.00
Jeweled Moon & Star, platter 50.00
Job's Tear, See Art
Jumbo, butter dish, elephant finial 725.00
Jumbo, creamer, Barnum head hdl 300.00
Jumbo, sugar bowl, Barnum head hdls, elephant finial 475.00
Kentucky, cake stand, 9½" 42.50
Kentucky, punch cup, gr 16.00
Kentucky, spooner 35.00
King's Crown, cake stand, 10" 80.00

King's Crown, goblet	32.50
King's Crown, tumbler, ruby stain, 3¾"	37.50
Klondike, bowl, frosted w/amber stain, 7" sq	185.00
Klondike, bowl, spearhead rim, 8"	78.00
Klondike, goblet	100.00
Klondike, vase, frosted w/amber stain, trumpet form, 10"	300.00
La Clede, See Hickman	
Lace, See Drapery	
Lawrence, See Bull's Eye	
Leaf, See Maple Leaf	
Leaf & Dart, pitcher, water	80.00
Leaf & Dart, tumbler, ftd	27.50
Leaf Bracket, See Greentown, Leaf Bracket	
Leaf Medallion, See Northwood, Leaf Medallion	
Liberty Bell, butter dish	98.00
Liberty Bell, creamer, appl hdl	100.00
Liberty Bell, plate, closed hdls, 10"	85.00
Lily of the Valley, honey dish	15.00
Lily of the Valley, relish, sm	25.00
Lincoln Drape, egg cup	70.00
Lincoln Drape, goblet	150.00
Lincoln Drape, spooner	70.00
Lion, compote, low std, 5" dia	60.00
Lion, cordial	195.00
Lion, creamer	70.00
Lion, marmalade jar, lion finial	145.00
Lion, wine	195.00
Log Cabin, bowl, w/lid, 3⅝x9x5¼"	120.00
Log Cabin, creamer, 4¼"	140.00
Loop, creamer, flint	38.00
Loop, goblet, flint	25.00
Loop & Dart, bowl, oval, 9"	32.50
Loop & Dart, relish	22.50
Loop & Dart, wine	38.00
Louisiana, goblet	32.00
Louisiana, wine	37.50
Maine, creamer	32.00
Maine, mug	37.50
Maine, wine, gr	75.00
Manhattan, creamer, ind	25.00
Manhattan, plate, 10¾"	22.50
Manhattan, tumbler, iced tea	30.00
Maple Leaf, goblet, vaseline	160.00
Maple Leaf, pitcher	48.00
Maryland, cake stand, 8"	45.00
Maryland, platter	32.50
Maryland, spooner	30.00
Mascotte, cheese dish	67.50
Mascotte, tumbler	30.00
Massachusetts, banana boat, 6½"	58.00
Massachusetts, creamer	32.00
Massachusetts, punch cup	17.50
Medallion, relish, amber, 7x5"	24.00
Medallion, sugar bowl, amber, w/lid	45.00
Melrose, compote, 5¾x7½"	27.50
Melrose, wine	22.00
Michigan, goblet, bl stain	42.00
Michigan, sauce bowl	12.50
Minerva, compote, low std, 8"	130.00
Minerva, relish, oblong, 6x9"	60.00
Minerva, waste bowl	55.00
Minnesota, cup	17.50
Minnesota, pitcher, tankard, ruby stain	215.00
Minor Block, See Mascotte	

Missouri, pitcher, water tankard; gr	75.00
Missouri, sauce bowl, gr	12.50
Moon & Star, tumbler, flat	88.00
Morning Glory, champagne, flint	385.00
Morning Glory, wine, flint	95.00
Nail, pitcher, etched	115.00
Nail, tumbler	18.00
Nailhead, plate, 9" sq	25.00
Nailhead, wine	38.00

Nailhead

New England Pineapple, creamer, flint	275.00
New England Pineapple, decanter, 1-pt	150.00
New Hampshire, mug, rose stain, lg	48.00
New Hampshire, sugar bowl, rose stain, w/lid, breakfast sz	20.00
New Hampshire, wine, flared	20.00
New Jersey, celery tray	25.00
New Jersey, goblet	42.50
New Jersey, tumbler	27.50
O'Hara Diamond, cup & saucer, ruby stain	65.00
O'Hara Diamond, plate, 7"	24.00
O'Hara Diamond, tumbler	28.00
Oaken Bucket, See Wooden Pail	
One Hundred & One, creamer	55.00
One Hundred & One, pitcher, water; appl hdl	150.00
One Hundred & One, spooner	40.00
One-O-One, See One Hundred & One	
Oregon #1, butter dish, flat	42.50
Oregon #1, cake stand, 10"	58.00
Oregon #1, compote, high std, 6"	32.00
Oregon #1, goblet	35.00
Palmette, cup plate	57.50
Palmette, egg cup	42.00
Palmette, wine	115.00
Panelled Daisy, celery vase	38.00
Panelled Daisy, goblet	28.00
Panelled Forget-Me-Not, mustard jar	42.50
Panelled Forget-Me-Not, pitcher, water; amethyst	175.00
Panelled Forget-Me-Not, spooner	38.00
Panelled Star & Button, mug, mini	18.00
Panelled Star & Button, salt cellar, master	17.50
Panelled Thistle, basket	75.00
Panelled Thistle, bowl, 7"	48.00
Pavonia, cake stand, etched, 10"	78.00
Pavonia, creamer, eng	40.00
Pennsylvania, goblet	22.50
Pennsylvania, punch cup	12.00
Pennsylvania, tumbler, clear w/gold	27.50
Pigmy, See Torpedo	
Pillow Encircled, creamer	26.00
Pillow Encircled, sauce dish	12.50
Pineapple & Fan, pitcher, water	80.00

Pineapple & Fan, vase, trumpet form, 10" 35.00
Pioneer, See Westward Ho
Pleat & Panel, goblet 35.00
Pleat & Panel, plate, 7" sq 20.00
Plume, bowl, w/lid, 8" 45.00
Plume, goblet 35.00
Polar Bear, goblet 100.00
Polar Bear, waste bowl 95.00
Popcorn, celery vase 22.00
Popcorn, wine 32.50
Portland, creamer 45.00
Portland, jam jar, clear w/gold, SP lid 42.00
Portland, sugar bowl, w/lid 55.00
Powder & Shot, creamer, bulbous, flint 110.00
Powder & Shot, goblet 50.00
Prayer Rug, See Horseshoe
Pressed Leaf, spooner 25.00
Pressed Leaf, wine 42.00
Primrose, tray, water; 11" dia 35.00
Primrose, wine 32.00
Princess Feather, cake plate, closed hdls, 9" 58.00
Princess Feather, creamer 40.00
Princess Feather, pitcher, water 130.00
Priscilla, bowl, str sides, flat, 3½x8" 40.00
Priscilla, pitcher, water 135.00
Question Mark, bowl, oblong, 7" 22.00
Question Mark, bread tray 32.00
Recessed Pillared Red Top, See Nail
Red Block, mug 48.00
Red Block, pitcher, water; 8" 235.00
Red Block, rose bowl 75.00
Red Top, See Button Arches
Reverse Torpedo, cake stand, high std 80.00
Reverse Torpedo, goblet 90.00
Reverse Torpedo, tumbler 35.00
Ribbed Ivy, egg cup 40.00
Ribbed Palm, bowl, 7" 335.00
Ribbed Palm, egg cup 40.00
Ribbon, goblet 32.50
Ribbon, platter, 13" 60.00
Ribbon Candy, cake stand 50.00
Ribbon Candy, cordial 58.00
Ripple, ice tub 60.00
Ripple, wine 37.50
Ripple Band, See Ripple
Rochelle, See Princess Feather
Roman Rosette, creamer 32.00
Roman Rosette, pitcher, milk; ruby stain 145.00
Roman Rosette, shakers, pr 35.00
Rose in Snow, pitcher 130.00
Rose in Snow, platter, bl 90.00
Rose in Snow, tumbler 48.00
Rosette, champagne 42.50
Rosette, plate, 7" 17.50
Royal Ivy, See Northwood
Royal Oak, See Northwood
Ruby Thumbprint, See King's Crown
S-Repeat, condiment tray, amethyst 40.00
S-Repeat, toothpick holder, amber 6.00
S-Repeat, wine, apple gr 47.50
Sawtooth, compote, flint, 7½x7½" 55.00
Sawtooth, goblet, flint 60.00
Sawtooth, spooner, nonflint 60.00
Sawtooth Band, See Amazon

Scalloped Daisy Red Top, See Button Arches
Scroll w/Flowers, cake plate 32.00
Scroll w/Flowers, compote, w/lid 75.00
Sedan, See Panelled Star & Button
Seneca Loop, See Loop
Shell & Jewel, pitcher 78.00
Shell & Jewel, sugar bowl, w/lid 48.00
Shell & Jewel, tumbler, bl 42.00
Shell & Tassel, oyster dish 235.00
Shell & Tassel, relish, canary, 5x8" 130.00
Sheraton, goblet, bl 48.00
Sheraton, wine 22.00
Shoshone, banana boat 50.00
Shoshone, mug 25.00
Shoshone, plate, gr 34.00
Shuttle, goblet 65.00
Shuttle, pitcher, amber 138.00
Shuttle, spooner, scalloped 48.00
Shuttle, tumbler 48.00
Skilton, celery vase 38.00
Skilton, goblet 35.00
Skilton, pickle dish 17.50
Snail, banana stand 160.00
Snail, cake stand 180.00
Spades, See Medallion
Spirea Band, relish 20.00
Spirea Band, spooner, vaseline 32.50
Spirea Band, wine, bl 36.00
Sprig, compote, low std, w/lid, 5" 50.00
Sprig, sugar bowl, w/lid 150.00
Star & Feather, creamer 35.00
Star & Feather, plate, amber, 7" 20.00
Stars & Stripes, creamer 22.50
Stars & Stripes, wine 18.00
States, cocktail 27.50
States, nappy, hdls, clear w/gold 25.00
States, pickle tray 17.50
Stippled Chain, egg cup 32.00
Stippled Chain, goblet 24.00
Stippled Forget-Me-Not, cake stand 42.50
Stippled Forget-Me-Not, cup & saucer 40.00
Stippled Grape & Festoon, compote, low std, 8" 45.00
Stippled Grape & Festoon, goblet 35.00
Strawberry, salt cellar, gr 185.00
Strawberry, spooner 35.00
Sunk Honeycomb, cup & saucer, ruby stain 40.00
Sunk Honeycomb, mug, souvenir 27.50
Sunk Honeycomb, tumbler, eng 25.00
Sunk Honeycomb, wine, eng 20.00
Swan, cake stand 110.00
Swan, compote, 8" 160.00
Teardrop & Tassel, pitcher, bl 190.00
Teardrop & Tassel, relish 36.00

Tennessee

Tennessee, celery vase 35.00
Tennessee, creamer 32.00
Tennessee, mug 42.50
Texas, creamer 50.00
Texas, goblet 95.00
Texas, vase, 9" 37.50
Theatrical, See Actress
Thousand Eye, nappy, bl, 5" 45.00
Thousand Eye, pitcher, water; 1-gal 98.00
Thousand Eye, plate, folded corners, 6" sq ...32.00
Three Face, butter dish, plain 195.00
Three Face, compote, high std, w/lid, 8" dia ...300.00
Three Face, cracker jar 1,350.00
Three Face, pitcher, water; etched 550.00
Three Panel, butter dish, vaseline 60.00
Three Panel, goblet, bl 45.00
Three Panel, spooner 16.00
Thumbprint, See Argus
Thumbprint Band, See Dakota
Thunderbird, See Hummingbird
Torpedo, banana stand 60.00
Torpedo, jelly compote, w/lid 45.00
Torpedo, sugar bowl, w/lid 98.00
Tree of Life, See Portland
Tree of Life w/Hand, cake stand, frosted base, 11½" ...130.00
Tree of Life w/Hand, mug, 3" 120.00
Tree of Life w/Hand, spooner 40.00
Triangular Prism, goblet 22.00
Tulip w/Sawtooth, creamer, flint 88.00
Tulip w/Sawtooth, wine, flint 30.00
Two Panel, bowl, gr, oval, 9" 47.50
Two Panel, wine 30.00
US Coin, bowl, berry; frosted, 7" 325.00
US Coin, bread tray, frosted, 8x10" 250.00
US Coin, butter dish, clear 500.00
US Coin, celery tray, frosted 350.00
US Coin, compote, frosted, 7x7" 195.00
US Coin, compote, w/lid, frosted, 6x9" 350.00
US Coin, pickle dish, frosted, 7½x3¾" 220.00
US Coin, sugar bowl, frosted, w/lid 400.00
US Coin, tumbler, frosted 200.00
Utah, creamer 32.00
Utah, tumbler 18.00
Valencia Waffle, bread plate 35.00
Valencia Waffle, butter dish, gr 58.00
Valencia Waffle, goblet, amber 37.50
Vermont, goblet, gr w/gold 52.50
Vermont, vase, gr w/gold 48.00
Viking, butter dish 110.00
Viking, creamer 60.00
Viking, pitcher, water; 8¾" 110.00
Waffle, bar tumbler 100.00
Waffle, champagne 135.00
Waffle & Thumbprint, cordial, flint 95.00
Waffle & Thumbprint, goblet, knop stem, flint ...67.50
Waffle & Thumbprint, tumbler, whiskey; flint ...95.00
Washington, creamer 195.00
Washington, egg cup 42.50
Washington, wine 125.00
Wedding Ring, goblet, flint 115.00
Wedding Ring, tumbler 82.50
Westward Ho, marmalade jar, w/lid 195.00
Westward Ho, platter, 13" 165.00
Wheat & Barley, jelly dish, amber, 4½" 32.00

Wheat & Barley, plate, amber, hdls, 9" 45.00
Wheat & Barley, shakers, pr 40.00
Wildflower, butter dish 47.50
Wildflower, creamer, bl 37.50
Wildflower, sugar bowl, w/lid 40.00
Willow Oak, goblet 32.00
Willow Oak, plate, hdls, 9" 37.50
Wisconsin, bonbon, hdls, 4" 25.00
Wisconsin, creamer 55.00
Wisconsin, cup & saucer 55.00
Wooden Pail, pitcher 110.00
Wooden Pail, spooner 32.50
Wyoming, bowl, ftd, 7" 45.00
Wyoming, mug 65.00
Wyoming, tumbler, flat 26.00
X-Ray, carafe, gr w/gold 145.00
X-Ray, goblet, gr 37.50
X-Ray, tumbler 16.50
Yale, cake stand 55.00
Yale, goblet 47.50
Yale, relish, oval 12.00
Zipper, creamer 50.00
Zipper, pitcher, water, ½-gal 42.50
Zipper, tumbler 22.50

Paul Revere Pottery

The Saturday Evening Girls were a social group of young Boston ladies who met to pursue various activities, among them pottery making. Their first kiln was bought in 1906, and within a few years it became necessary to move to a larger location. Because their new quarters were near the historical Old North Church, they chose the name Paul Revere Pottery. With very little training, the girls produced only simple ware. Until 1915 the pottery operated at a deficit, then a new building with four kilns was constructed on Nottingham Road. Vases, miniature jugs, children's tea sets, tiles, dinnerware, and lamps were produced, usually in soft matt glazes often decorated with incised, hand-painted designs from nature. Examples in a dark high gloss may also be found on occasion.

Several marks were used: 'P.R.P.'; 'S.E.G.'; or the circular device, 'Boston, Paul Revere Pottery' with the horse and rider.

The pottery continued to operate; and even though their product sold well, the high production costs of the handmade ware caused the pottery to fail in 1946. Our advisor for this category is Hardy Hudson; he is listed in the Directory under Florida.

Creamer, wild rose border, white on blue with gray background and black outlines, FR/255-6-09, SEG, 2⅞", $550.00.

Bowl, bl-gray satin drip, experimental, PRP, 2¾x8¼" 275.00
Bowl, daffodil band int, 2-tone yel, SEG/1916, 10" 800.00
Bowl, ducks band, wht on bl-gray, SEG/1910, 2¼x4¼" 550.00

Bowl, floral, yel w/blk outlines, SEG/DH, 2¼x6¾" 500.00
Bowl, floral band, w/lg hdl, SEG/DH/1912, 2¼x6¾" 550.00
Bowl, gr matt, sgn EM, #016, 2¼x8¼" 150.00
Bowl, landscape, mc on gr, sgn FL, SEG/10-19, 2½x8¾" 1,495.00
Bowl, rose semi-gloss, SEG/1122 EG, 2½x5" 100.00
Bowl, stylized floral, gr/bl/wht on brn, PRP/1924, 2½x6" 550.00
Bowl, tree clusters/landscape band on bl, SEG/1914, 6" 550.00
Bowl, trees, lt gr on lt bl, PRP, 3x6¾" 500.00
Bowl set, 1 ea: brn, gr, ochre, PRP, largest: 3x7½", 3 for 300.00
Cup & saucer, stylized flowers, bl/gr on tan, SEG/AM/18-8-12 ..750.00
Egg cup, chicks on Scarab Blue, SEG, 1½" 425.00
Honey pot, bees in bands on lid & base, SEG/RM, 5½x5½" ...2,000.00
Humidor, bl matt w/pk int, spherical, PRP, 6" 400.00
Inkwell, brn, ET, SEG/11/19, 2½x4x2¾" 375.00
Lamp base, yel & bl, A3-28, paper label, 10x4" 300.00
Pitcher, squirrel band on cream, SEG/SG/1911, 4½", EX 865.00
Plate, mice/inscription, wht/celadon/brn, SEG/1911, 6½" 1,300.00
Plate, pine cone band, brn/gr on wht, SEG/1917, 6½" 250.00
Plate, tortoise walking to water, SEG/12-19/DH, 6¼" 1,000.00
Plate, trees on gr, SEG/1912, 7½" 650.00
Plate, windmill band, bl/gr, wht center, SEG/1911, 7½" 950.00
Ring tray, tree band, bl-gray/gr on bl-gray, SEG, 4" 275.00
Teapot, sailboats on waves, brn/wht/yel, SEG/1918 ....1,200.00
Tile, Badger House, Corner, mc on terra cotta, ink mk, 3¾" 750.00
Trivet, goose standing on hill on dk bl, PRP/1924, 5½" dia 550.00
Trivet, house/setting sun on bl-gray, PRP/1924, 4¼" dia 425.00
Trivet, house/trees (EX design), SEG/1920, 6½" dia 1,300.00
Triver, ship, 3-color w/blk outline, imp mk, 9/26, 5¾" dia 300.00
Vase, floral band, mc on bl, SEG/obscured date, 5¾x3¼" 1,850.00
Vase, flowing med gr microcrystalline, closed rim, PRP, 7x7" 350.00
Vase, gr satin, SEG, 1920, 10½x5¾" 250.00
Vase, med bl semimatt, shouldered cylinder, 1925, 10x5" 400.00
Vase, orange/brn gloss & matt, bottle shape, PRP, 4x3" 225.00
Vase, squirrels/bl stripe on wht crackle, SEG/1912, 3¾" 550.00

Pauline Pottery

Pauline Pottery was made form 1883 to 1888 in Chicago, Illinois, from clay imported from the Ohio area. The company's founder was Mrs. Pauline Jacobus, who had learned the trade at the Rookwood Pottery. Mrs. Jacobus moved to Edgerton, Wisconsin, to be near a source of suitable clay, thus eliminating shipping expenses. Until 1905 she produced high-quality wares, able to imitate with ease designs and styles of such masters as Wedgwood and Meissen. Her products were sold through leading department stores, and the names of some of these firms may appear on the ware. Not all are marked; unless signed by a noted local artist, positive identification is often impossible. Marked examples carry a variety of stamps and signatures: 'Trade Mark' with a crown, 'Pauline Pottery,' and 'Edgerton Art Pottery' are but a few.

Bowl, 3-lobe, 3-hdl, 10" 850.00
Ginger jar, stylized leaves, gold-lined on caramel & gr, 9", EX ...800.00
Tea caddy, spiderweb in flow bl on wht, paneled, 5x3½" 350.00
Teapot, leaves & branches, mc w/gold, 5x6" dia, EX 350.00
Vase, trees, brn/gr/bl gloss, 10½" 1,200.00

Peachblow

Peachblow, made to imitate the colors of the Chinese Peachbloom porcelain, was made by several glasshouses in the late 1800s. Among them were New England Glass, Mt. Washington, Webb, and Hobbs, Brockunier and Company (Wheeling). Its pink shading was achieved through action of the heat on the gold content of the glass. While New England's peachblow shades from deep crimson to white, Mt. Washington's tends to shade from pink to blue-gray. Many pieces were enameled and gilded. While by far the majority of the pieces made by New England had a satin (acid) finish, they made shiny peachblow as well. Wheeling glass, on the other hand, is rarely found in satin. In the 1950s Gundersen-Pairpoint Glassworks initiated the reproduction of Mt. Washington peachblow, using an exact duplication of the original formula. Though of recent manufacture, this glass is very collectible. Our advisors for this category are Betty and Clarence Maier; they are listed in the Directory under Pennsylvania.

Bottle, scent; Webb, gold prunus/butterfly, opal cased, 5" 750.00
Bowl, Webb, gold prunus/trim, 2½x4" 325.00
Carafe, Wheeling, conical w/molded collar ring, 8" 850.00
Celery vase, NE Glass, scalloped sq top, thin walls, 7" 785.00
Celery vase, Webb, floral, gold scalloped rim, waisted, 5¼" 300.00
Creamer, NE Glass, asters, ribbed, 2½" 450.00
Creamer, NE Glass, ribbed, wht hdl, 2¾" 350.00
Cruet, Gundersen, bulbous, 7" 300.00
Cruet, Gundersen, bulbous w/long neck, 8x3½" 875.00
Cruet, NE Glass, bulbous, tricon spout, almond hdl/stopper, 5½" .800.00
Cruet, Sandwich, scissor-cut rim, amber hdl & stopper, 6" 700.00

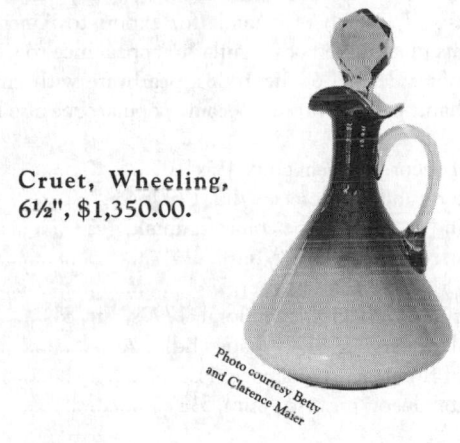

Cruet, Wheeling, 6½", $1,350.00.

Photo courtesy Betty and Clarence Maier

Cruet, Wheeling, amber reed hdl/faceted stopper, bulbous, 6¾" .1,200.00
Lamp, hall; pansies, ovoid, 5¾"; brass fixtures, 14" to mt 325.00
Peach, Webb, amber stem, 3" 500.00
Pear, NE Glass, long stem, 5½" 125.00
Pear, Wheeling, stem shortened, 5½x3" 800.00
Pitcher, flared rim, clear hdl, 7½" 135.00
Pitcher, Gundersen, Hobnail, 5½" 500.00
Pitcher, tankard; Gundersen, almond reeded hdl, 6½" 225.00
Spittoon, lady's; NE Glass, waisted neck w/wavy rim, 2¾x5¼" ..750.00
Sugar bowl, NE Glass, fluted top, sm low hdls, 3" 750.00
Syrup, Wheeling, amber hdl, thumb-lift hinged cap, EX color .3,200.00
Toothpick holder, NE Glass, 3-lobe top, 2¼" 485.00
Tumbler, Gundersen, 4" 150.00
Tumbler, Mt WA, 3¾" 1,500.00
Tumbler, NE Glass, 3¾" 175.00
Tumbler, Wheeling, 3⅞" 450.00
Tumbler, whiskey; NE Glass, 3½" 300.00
Vase, bird/floral branch, blk/rust/gold, crimped amber rim, 12" ..275.00
Vase, bl to wht o/l, HP/gold floral, clear rim, flattened, 7" 325.00
Vase, gold lines/rings w/bird head & flowers, stick neck, 12" ..3,250.00
Vase, lily; NE Glass, 15" 1,100.00
Vase, Morgan; Wheeling, in plastic griffin holder, 9¾" 1,450.00
Vase, Morgan; Wheeling, no stand, 7¾" 1,300.00

Vase, Mt WA, floral/bl shadow foliage, dbl-gourd stick neck, 8" .3,700.00
Vase, Mt WA, gourd shape, 8x4" **2,775.00**
Vase, NE Glass, flared neck w/ring, bulbous body, 3¼" **550.00**
Vase, NE Glass, gourd shape w/cup rim, 10½x5" **1,250.00**
Vase, Webb, bulbous w/stick neck, 12½" **450.00**
Vase, Webb, gold bird/floral, gold hdls, bottle form, 12½" **450.00**
Vase, Webb, gold ferns/vines cascade from rim, 4½" **175.00**
Vase, Webb, gold floral/insects, bulb w/can neck, ruffled, 5" **300.00**
Vase, Webb, gold leaves/floral at neck, stick neck, 9½", pr **525.00**
Vase, Webb, gold prunus/berries, wide invt cone form, 6½" **600.00**
Vase, Webb, gold vines/wht flowers, stick neck, 7", pr **550.00**
Vase, Webb, gold vintage 1 side, 7", pr **350.00**
Vase, Webb, pinched sides, stick neck, 8" **300.00**
Vase, Wheeling, bulbous w/elongated neck, 10½" **1,275.00**
Vase, Wheeling, crimped/ruffled rim, 18½" **3,000.00**
Vase, Wheeling, dbl gourd, 7" **1,800.00**
Vase, Wheeling, stick neck, 8¼" **1,000.00**
Vase, Wheeling, tapered w/sqd rim, 3½" **325.00**
Vase, Wheeling, teardrop shape w/stick neck, 9" **1,100.00**

Pearlware

Developed by Wedgwood in the late 1770s primarily for their din-nerware lines, pearlware was soon being made by many other Staffordshire potteries as well. Much of it made for export to America. It is characterized by its blue-white body, similar in appearance to true porcelain. During the first decade of the 1800s, pearlware with chinoiserie decorations and hand-painted flowers became popular. See also Leeds.

Bowl, bl Oriental decor, wear/sm chip, 4½x10" **195.00**
Fruit basket, rope rim/hdls w/florets, w/lid, 1790s, 9⅝" **925.00**
Pepper pot, gr band at waist, stripe collar/ft, unmk, 4½" **150.00**
Pitcher, bl sunburst-style decor, rstr, mini, 3⅛" **100.00**
Plate, bl & wht Oriental decor, Turner, 7¾" **165.00**
Sauceboat, boar's head, underglaze bl floral, 1790s, rstr, 8⅜" **750.00**
Sugar bowl, floral, underglaze bl, C-shaped hdl, 3¾" **100.00**
Tall pot, bl & wht floral, sm rpr/damage, 11" **360.00**
Teapot, bl Oriental decor, prof rstr, mini, 3½" **100.00**

Peking Cameo Glass

The first glasshouse was established in Peking in 1680. It produced glassware made in imitation of porcelain, a more desirable medium to the Chinese. By 1725 multilayered carving that resulted in a cameo effect lead to the manufacture of a wider range of shapes and colors. The factory was closed from 1736 to 1795, but glass made in Po-shan and shipped to Peking for finishing continued to be called Peking glass. Similar glassware was made through the first half of the 20th century. See also Orientalia.

Vases, peony flowers, red on white, gourd shapes, 1800s, 10", $1,200.00 for the pair.

Belt buckle, Daoist scene, red on wht, rectangle, 1800s, 2¾" **875.00**
Bowl, floral, bl on wht, 1940s, 3x6¼" **75.00**
Bowl, lotus form w/peony branch panels, yel on wht, 1800s, 6" ..**800.00**
Cup, dragon panels in high relief, yel on wht, 1800s, 4½" **800.00**
Cup & saucer, clouds/dragons, bl on wht, 1800s **200.00**
Inkwell, scroll/sword/flower/basket/fan, gr on blk, '40s, 2x3" **70.00**
Snuff bottle, bats & coins, red on wht, 1940s, 2⅜" **95.00**
Snuff bottle, cabbage form, gr to wht, 1950s, 2" **85.00**
Snuff bottle, dragons, blk on wht, 1940s, 2⅜" **105.00**
Urn, 3 wht panels w/blk floral or fruit motif, w/lid, 1800s, 9" **400.00**
Vase, birds & flowers, orange on wht, ca 1940, 9½" **145.00**
Vase, dragon panels, bl on wht, stick neck, 1800s, 9⅛" **1,400.00**
Vase, floral/butterflies, cobalt on wht, 1800s, 11½" **1,100.00**
Vase, rams in landscape, lappet bands, cobalt on wht, 1800s, 9" .**1,750.00**
Vase, rooster/plants/flowers, cobalt on wht, dbl gourd, late, 9¾" .**200.00**

Peloton

Peloton glass was first made by Wilhelm Kralik in Bohemia in 1880. This unusual art glass was produced by rolling colored threads onto the transparent or opaque glass gather as it was removed from the furnace. Usually more than one color of threading was used, and some items were further decorated with enameling. It was made with both shiny and acid finishes.

Bowl, wht w/brn & yel strings, ribbed, 3 clear thorn ft, 6x6½" ...**325.00**
Bowl, 3-point rim w/rigaree, ribbed w/3 clear shell ft, 4¾x6" **400.00**
Cracker jar, lt bl w/pastel strings, ribbed, spherical, SP mts **785.00**
Cruet, bl w/mc strings, swirl mold, faceted ball stopper, 7" **500.00**
Rose bowl, shaded bl w/mc strings, 4-point rim, 4x4" **395.00**
Rose bowl, wht w/strings in brn tones, 8-point rim, ftd, 6x5" **325.00**
Vase, clear w/bl threading, HP foliage/florals, 4¼x2½" **175.00**
Vase, clear-cased lav-pk w/mc strings, ruffled gourd form, 6½" ...**250.00**
Vase, pk w/mc strings, pinched middle, 3½x3x3⅞" **225.00**
Vase, pk w/wht int, mc strings, bulb w/can neck, hdls, 6x5" **450.00**
Vase, wht o/l w/pastel strings, ribbed cylinder, ruffled, 4½" **225.00**
Vase, wht w/mc strings, ribbed, sqd ruffled rim, clear ft, 4" **200.00**
Vase, wht w/mc strings, tricorner, 4x4¾" **295.00**

Pennsbury

Established in the 1950s in Morrisville, Pennsylvania, by Henry Below, the Pennsbury Pottery produced dinnerware and novelty items, much of which was sold in gift shops along the Pennsylvania Turnpike. Henry and his wife, Lee, worked for years at the Stangl Pottery before striking out on their own. Lee and her daughter were the artists responsible for many of the early pieces, the bird figures among them. Pennsbury pottery was hand painted, some in blue on white, some in multicolor on caramel. Pennsylvania Dutch motifs, Amish couples, and barbershop singers were among their most popular decorative themes. Sgraffito (hand incising) was used extensively. The company marked their wares 'Pennsbury Pottery' or 'Pennsbury Pottery, Morrisville, PA.'

In October of 1969 the company closed. Contents of the pottery were sold in December of the following year, and in April of 1971, the buildings burned to the ground. Items marked Pennsbury Glenview or Stumar Pottery (or these marks in combination) were made by Glenview after 1969. Pieces manufactured after 1976 were made by the Pennington Pottery. Several of the old molds still exist, and the original Pennsbury Caramel process is still being used on novelty items, some of which are produced by Lewis Brothers, New Jersey. Production of Pennsbury dinnerware was not resumed after the closing. Our advisor for this category is Shirley Graff; she is listed in the Directory under

Ohio. Note: prices may be higher in some areas of the country — particularly on the East Coast, the southern states, and Texas. Values for examples in the Rooster pattern apply to both black and red variations.

Ashtray, Don's Be So Doppich, 5"	20.00
Ashtray, Rooster, 4"	20.00
Bookends, eagles, 8¼", pr	90.00
Bowl, divided vegetable; Rooster, 9½x6¼"	50.00
Bowl, Dutch Talk, 9"	85.00
Bowl, pretzel; Amish Couple	85.00
Bowl, pretzel; Gay Ninety	85.00
Bowl, Rooster, pie edge, 6½"	50.00
Bowl, Rooster, 9"	45.00
Bowl, vegetable; Rooster, 2-part	40.00
Bread plate, Sheafs of Wheat, oval or rnd	40.00
Butter dish, Rooster, ¼-lb	50.00
Cake stand, Amish, 4½x11½"	85.00
Cake stand, Harvest or Hex, 4½x11½"	80.00
Candlesticks, hummingbird on flower, 3-D, 5", pr	150.00
Candy dish, Folkart, heart shape	25.00
Canister, Hex, Flour, 7½"	110.00
Canister, Rooster, Sugar, 7½"	110.00
Casserole, Hex, w/lid, 9" dia	50.00
Chip 'n dip, Folkart	80.00
Coaster, Fisherman, 4½", set of 4	80.00
Coffeepot, Folkart, 2-cup, 6½"	25.00

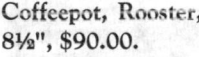
Coffeepot, Rooster,
8½", $90.00.

Cookie jar, Folkart	100.00
Creamer & sugar bowl, Amish	30.00
Cup & saucer, Folkart	12.00
Egg cup, Folkart	16.00
Figurine, Magnolia Warbler	250.00
Mug, beer; Fisherman	45.00
Mug, beverage; Rooster, 4½"	35.00
Mug, coffee; Rooster	35.00
Pie pan, Rooster, 9"	65.00
Pitcher, Delft Toleware, bl, 5"	55.00
Pitcher, Tulip, 3-qt, 9¾"	45.00
Plaque, Amish Sayings, 7x5"	25.00
Plaque, Eagle, 22"	175.00
Plaque, It Is Whole Empty, 4" dia	35.00
Plaque, Pea Hen, 6" dia	40.00
Plaque, Pennsylvania Railroad 1856, Tiger Locomotive, 8x5⅝"	48.00
Plaque, Rooster, 4" dia	25.00
Plate, Family Wagon, 8"	30.00
Plate, Rooster, 10"	35.00
Plate, Rooster, 8"	18.00
Platter, Rooster, 11"	48.00
Relish tray, Rooster, 14½x11½"	85.00
Snack tray & cup, Folkart or Hex	20.00
Sugar bowl, Amish man & lady, 4½"	20.00
Tea tile, skunk, Why Be Disagreeable, 6"	40.00

Teapot, Rooster, 6-cup	95.00
Tureen, Rooster, w/ladle nook	120.00
Wall pocket, Bellows, eagle, 10"	65.00

Pens and Pencils

The first metallic writing pen was patented in 1809, and soon machine-produced pens with steel nibs gradually began replacing the quill. The first fountain pen was invented in 1830, but due to the fact that a suitable metal for the tips had not yet been developed, they were not manufactured commercially until the 1880s. The first successful commercial producers were Waterman in 1884 and Parker with the Lucky Curve in 1888.

The self-filling pen of 1890 featured the soft, interior sack which filled with ink as the metal bar on the outside of the pen was raised and lowered. Variations of the pumping mechanism were tried until 1932 when Parker introduced the Vacumatic, a sackless pen with an internal pump. Our advisors for this category are Judy and Cliff Lawrence; they are listed in the Directory under Florida. For those seeking additional information, a catalog is published monthly by the Pen Fancier's, whose address can be found in the Directory under Clubs, Newsletters, and Catalogs.

Key:
AF — aeromatic filler	GPT — gold-plated trim
BF — button filler	HR — hard rubber
CF — capillary filler	LF — lever filler
CPT — chrome-plated trim	NPT — nickel-plated trim
ED — eyedropper filler	PF — plunger filler
GFM — gold-filled metal	TD — touchdown filler
GFT — gold-filled trim	VF — vacumatic filler

Fountain Pens

Blackbird Self-Filling, 1917, blk HR, NPT, LF, EX	45.00
Carter INX, 1929, coral marbleized, GFT, LF, EX	300.00
Conklin Crescent Filler, 1901, GFM, GFT, EX	450.00
Conklin Endura, 1926, lady's, red woodgrain HR, GFT, LF, EX	100.00
Conway Stewart #475, 1939, bl marbleized, GFT, LF, EX	105.00
Mont Blanc #149 Diplomat, 1978, blk, GFT, suction filler, NMIB	275.00
Moore, 1941, blk, GFT, LF, EX	75.00
Parker Bl Dmn Vacumatic, 1941, gold pearl stripes, GFT, VF, EX	90.00
Parker Bl Dmn Vacumatic, 1945, silver pearl stripes, wht GFT, VF, EX	80.00
Parker Bl Dmn 51, 1946, bl, Lustraloy cap, GFT, VF, EX	80.00
Parker Duofold, 1934, blk, GFT, BF, EX	100.00
Parker Duofold Jr, 1925, red, GFT, BF, EX	125.00
Parker Duofold Jr, 1928, red, GFT, BF, EX	125.00
Parker Duofold Jr, 1930, burgundy-red & blk, GFT, BF, EX	150.00
Parker Duofold Special, 1924, red, GFT, BF, rare, EX	250.00
Parker Duofold Sr, 1927, Mandarin Yel, GFT, BF, EX	1,500.00
Parker Duofold Sr, 1930, Mandarin Yel, GFT, BF, EX	1,300.00
Parker Duofold Sr, 1930, red, GFT, BF, EX	400.00
Parker Lady Duofold, 1923, blk HR, GFT, lg imprint, BF, EX	99.00
Parker Lady Duofold, 1930, Gr Jade marbleized, GFT, BF, G	70.00
Parker Lucky Curve, 1918, sterling, BF, NM	500.00
Parker Lucky Curve, 1921, lady's, blk chased HR, NPT, BF, EX	135.00
Parker Pastel, 1927, Naples Bl, GFT, BF, NM	175.00
Parker Pastel, 1931, Bl Moire, GFT, BF, EX	175.00
Parker Vacumatic, 1938, red pearl stripes, GFT, VF, NM	250.00
Parker Vacuum Filler, 1933, blk, GFT, VF, rare, EX	400.00
Parker VS, 1947, bl w/Lustraloy cap, wht GFT, BF, EX	90.00
Parker 17 (English), 1952, bl, GFT, AF, EX	100.00
Parker 51, 1948, blk w/GFM cap, GFT, VF, NM	190.00
Parker 51, 1952, bl, GFM cap, GFT, AF, EX	190.00

Parker 51 Special, 1956, maroon, chrome cap, CPT, AF, NM **65.00**
Parker 61, 1957, blk, 2-tone GFM cap, GFT, capillary filler, EX .**350.00**
Parker 61 Demonstrator, transparent, Lustraloy cap, wht GFT, M ..**450.00**
Parker 61 Prototype, 1954, blk, Lustraloy cap, 1st ed badge, GFT, EX .**1,100.00**
Parker 61 Signet, 1965, GFM, GFT, CF, EX **400.00**
Parker 75, 1965, sterling, GFT, AF, M **200.00**
Parkette, 1934, blk, GFT, LF, EX **35.00**
Pelikan #400, 1969, blk w/gr-blk stripe, GFT, suction filler, NM ..**195.00**
Sheaffer #2, 1921, blk chased HR, GFT, LF, EX **80.00**
Sheaffer #46 Special, 1918, blk chased HR, GFT, LF, EX **129.00**
Sheaffer #46 Special Desk, 1931, Gr Jade marbleized, GFT, LF, EX ..**90.00**
Sheaffer #8 Self-Filling, 1920, blk HR, 14k gold trim, LF, EX **495.00**
Sheaffer Lifetime, 1924, Gr Jade marbleized, GFT, LF, NM **495.00**
Sheaffer Lifetime, 1934, emerald pearl marbleized, GFT, LF, EX ..**450.00**
Sheaffer Lifetime, 1934, pearl & blk marbleized, GFT, LF, EX ...**255.00**
Sheaffer Lifetime #1500 Sentinel, 1946, blk, banded cap, GFT, LF, NM **149.00**
Sheaffer Lifetime Triumph, 1945, blk, GFT, LF, NM **125.00**
Sheaffer Lifetime Triumph, 1946, emerald stripes, GFT, PF, EX ...**125.00**
Sheaffer PFM I, 1959, maroon/chrome, Palladium alloy nib, TD, NM ...**105.00**
Sheaffer PFM III, 1959, blk, GFT, TD, EX **250.00**
Sheaffer Statesman Tuckaway, 1949, maroon, GFT, TD, M **69.00**
Sheaffer Triumph TM, 1952, maroon, GFT, TD, EX **62.50**
Sheaffer Triumph TM Crest, 1951, maroon, GFM cap, GFT, TD, EX .**95.00**
Sheaffer Vacuum, 1936, silver pearl marbleized, CPT, LF, EX **80.00**
Wahl #5, 1925, GFM, GFT, LF, EX **595.00**
Wahl-Eversharp Executive Skyline, 1945, maroon, GFT, LF, EX ..**295.00**
Wahl-Eversharp Gold Seal, 1931, blk, GFT, LF, EX **595.00**
Wahl-Eversharp Gold Seal Doric, 1940, red marbleized, GFT, LF, EX ...**450.00**
Wahl-Eversharp Skyline, 1945, brn, GFT, LF, EX **62.50**
Waterman, 1949, bl, chrome cap, CPT, LF, M **49.00**
Waterman Ideal #412, 1906, sterling filigree, ED, EX **400.00**
Waterman Ideal #5, 1934, red circle & point, blk, GFT, LF, G ..**225.00**
Waterman Ideal #52, 1925, blk chased HR, gold bands, LF, EX .**135.00**
Waterman Ideal #52, 1930, blk chased HR, NPT, LF, NM **110.00**
Waterman Ideal #52½V, blk chased HR, GFT, LF, EX **49.00**
Waterman Ideal #7, 1932, blk, GFT, LF, EX **298.00**
Waterman Ideal #92, 1936, gr-gold specked marbleized, GFT, LF, NM .**119.00**
Waterman Ideal Ink-View, 1937, blk, wht GFT, EX **200.00**
Waterman Ideal Silver Ray Ink-View, 1937, blk striped pearl, GFT, EX .**295.00**
Waterman Stateleigh Taperite, 1945, gray, GFM cap, GFT, LF, M .**150.00**
Williamson, 1910, pearl & gold filigree, ED, EX **595.00**

Mechanical Pencils

Eversharp, 1928, red woodgrain HR, NPT, EX **90.00**
Eversharp, 1941, bl & blk marbleized, NPT, EX **25.00**
Eversharp Gold Seal Doric, 1933, blk, GFT, EX **115.00**
Eversharp Gold Seal Doric, 1935, lav marbleized, GFT, EX **72.50**
Norma, 1947, 4-color, chrome, CPT, G **35.00**
Parker Duofold, 1931, Modern Blk & pearl marbleized, GFT, EX ..**135.00**
Parker Duofold, 1941, bl pearl & blk stripes, GFT, EX **52.00**
Parker Duofold Sr, 1928, Gr Jade marbleized, GFT, EX **198.00**
Parker Golf, 1931, Modern Blk & pearl marbleized, GFT, EX **135.00**
Parker Lady Duofold, 1930, Gr Jade marbleized, GFT, BF, G **70.00**
Parker Pastel, 1927, magenta, GFT, NM **90.00**
Parker 45 Signet, 1960, GFM, GFT, NM **65.00**
Parker 51, 1944, blk w/sterling cap, GFT, EX **129.00**
Parker 51, 1944, mustard w/GFM cap, GFT, NM **250.00**
Parker 51, 1946, blk, Lustraloy cap, GFT, M **79.00**
Parker 51, 1957, bl, Lustraloy cap, wht GFT, EX **49.00**
Parker 51 Repeater, 1956, beige, Lustraloy cap, wht GFT, EX **49.00**
Parker 61 Liquid Lead, 1960, red, Lustraloy top, GFT, M **49.00**
Parker 61 Liquid Lead, 1965, turq, Lustraloy top, GFT, M **49.00**
Sheaffer, 1920, GFM, GFT, G **79.00**

Sheaffer, 1934, emerald marbleized, GFT, EX **90.00**
Sheaffer #400, 1946, emerald stripes, GFT, EX **45.00**
Sheaffer Crest, 1946, emerald stripes, GFM top, GFT, G **62.50**
Sheaffer Lifetime, 1925, blk, GFT, EX **50.00**
Sheaffer Lifetime, 1925, Gr Jade marbleized, GFT, EX **79.00**
Sheaffer PFM IV, blk w/chrome-gold band, GFT, TD, NM **325.00**
Sheaffer PFM IV, 1959, blk, chrome-gold banded top, GFT, M ...**90.00**
Superite, 1925, GFM, GFT, EX **45.00**
Swan Fyne Point, 1925 GFM, GFT, G **72.50**
Wahl Skyline Repeater, 1945, blk, blk-silver striped top, EX **55.00**
Wahl-Eversharp, 1925, GFM, EX **16.00**
Wahl-Eversharp, 1925, GFM, GFT, EX **16.00**
Wahl-Eversharp, 1925, red HR, NPT, EX **135.00**
Wahl-Eversharp, 1925, 18k GFM, GFT, EX **40.00**
Wahl-Eversharp Doric, 1933, Cathay marbleized, wht GFT, M ...**62.50**
Wahl-Eversharp Skyline Repeater, 1945, blk, GFT, EX **35.00**
Wahl-Eversharp Skyline Repeater, 1945, maroon, GFT, M **45.00**
Wahl-Eversharp Skyline Repeater, 1946, brn w/GFM derby, M ...**72.50**
Wahl-Eversharp Symphony Deluxe, 1950, blk, banded cap, GFT, EX ..**45.00**
Wahl-Eversharp Symphony Repeater, 1950, blk, banded cap, GFT, EX **45.00**
Waterman Ideal, 1928, bl-gr ripple HR, GFT, M **90.00**
Waterman Ideal, 1928, sterling filigree, EX **360.00**
Waterman Ideal, 1930, red-gold marbleized, GFT, EX **62.50**
Waterman Ideal, 1936, red-specked silver marbleized, wht GFT, EX ..**80.00**
Waterman Ideal Lady Patricia, 1934, onyx, GFT, EX **55.00**

Sets

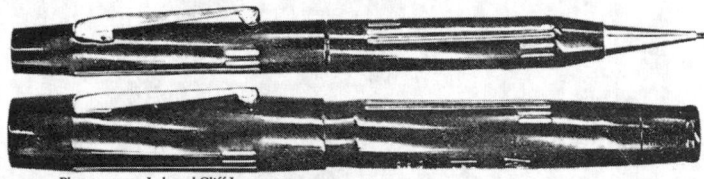

Photo courtesy Judy and Cliff Lawrence

Chilton Wingflow pen and pencil set, 1935, black with inlaid gold, gold-filled trim, touchdown filler, EX, $500.00.

Parker Bl Dmn 51, 1946, blk w/GFM caps, GFT, VF, EX **179.00**
Parker Vacumatic Jr, 1937, blk, GFT, VF, EX **180.00**
Parker 51, 1957, beige, Lustraloy caps, wht GFT, AF, EX **90.00**
Parker 51 Demi-sz, 1947, blk w/GFM caps, GFT, VF, M **240.00**
Parker 51 Signet, GFM, GFT, AF, EX **269.00**
Sheaffer Lifetime Pen/Pencil Combo, 1932, pearl/blk, GFT, LF, EX ..**295.00**
Sheaffer Snorkel Admiral, 1953, red, GFT, TD, M **80.00**
Sheaffer Triumph Snorkel Sentinel, 1953, powder bl, GFT, TD, M ..**149.00**
Sheaffer Triumph Tuckaway, 1948, blk, GFT, PF, M **125.00**
Waterman Ideal, 1938, gold filigree, GFT, LF, EX **695.00**
Waterman Ideal #52, 1924, red HR, GFT, LF, EX **375.00**

Personalities, Fact and Fiction

One of the largest and most popular areas of collecting today is character-related memorabilia. Everyone has favorites, whether they be comic-strip personalities or true-life heroes. The earliest comic strip dealt with the adventures of the Yellow Kid, the smiling, bald-headed Oriental boy always in a nightshirt. He was introduced in 1895, a product of the imagination of Richard Fenton Outcault. Today, though very hard to come by, items relating to the Yellow Kid bring premium prices.

Though her 1923 introduction was unobtrusively made through only one newspaper, New York's *Daily News*, Little Orphan Annie, the vacant-eyed redhead in the inevitable red dress, was quickly adopted by hordes of readers nationwide, and before the demise of her creator, Harold Gray, in 1968, she had starred in her own radio show. She made two feature films, and in 1977 'Annie' was launched on Broadway.

Other early comic figures were Moon Mullins, created in 1923 by Frank Willard; Buck Rogers by Philip Nowlan in 1928; and Betty Boop, the round-faced, innocent-eyed, chubby-cheeked Boop-Boop-a-Doop girl of the early 1930s. Bimbo was her dog and KoKo her clown friend.

Popeye made his debut in 1929 as the spinach-eating sailor with the spindly-limbed girlfriend, Olive Oyl, in the comic strip *Thimble Theatre*, created by Elzie Segar. He became a film star in 1933 and had his own radio show that during 1936 played three times a week on CBS. He obligingly modeled for scores of toys, dolls, and figurines, and especially those from the '30s are very collectible.

Tarzan, created around 1930 by Edgar Rice Burroughs, and Captain Midnight, by Robert Burtt and Willfred G. Moore, are popular heroes with today's collectors. During the days of radio, Sky King of the Flying Crown Ranch (also created by Burtt and Moore) thrilled boys and girls of the mid-1940s. Hopalong Cassidy, Red Rider, Tom Mix, and the Lone Ranger were only a few of the other 'good guys' always on the side of law and order.

But of all the fictional heroes and comic characters collected today, probably the best loved and most well known is Mickey Mouse. Created in the late 1920s by Walt Disney, Micky (as his name was first spelled) became an instant success with his film debut, Steamboat Willie. His popularity was parlayed through wind-up toys, watches, figurines, cookie jars, puppets, clothing, and numerous other products. Items from the 1930s are usually copyrighted 'Walt Disney Enterprises'; thereafter, 'Walt Disney Productions' was used.

For more information we recommend *Schroeder's Collectible Toys, Antique to Modern*, by Sharon and Bob Huxford. For those interested in Disneyana, we recommend *Stern's Guide to Disney Collectibles* (there are three in the series), and *The Collector's Encyclopedia of Disneyana* by David Longest and Michael Stern. *Cartoon Toys & Collectibles* by David Longest; *Collector's Guide to TV Toys and Memorabilia*, Second Edition, by Greg Davis and Bill Morgan; *Collector's Reference & Value Guide to the Lone Ranger* by Lee Felbinger; and *G-men and FBI Toys and Collectibles* by Harry and Jody Whitworth are other great publications. All are available from Collector Books. Our advisor for this category is Norm Vigue; he are listed in the Directory under Massachusetts. See also Autographs; Banks; Big Little Books; Children's Books; Comic Books; Cookie Jars; Dolls; Games; Lunch Boxes; Movie Memorabilia; Paper Dolls; Pin-Back Buttons; Posters; Puzzles; Rock 'N Roll Memorabilia; Toys.

Addams Family, key chain, Thing, EX 5.00
Agent Zero, camera/pistol, Mattel, 1964, plastic, EX+ 45.00
Alf, lap tray, Let's Do Lunch, 1987, metal, EX 15.00
Alice in Wonderland, note paper, Whitman, 1951, 9½x8", EX ...95.00
Andy Brown, sparkler, Germany, eyes spark, tin, 1930s, 7", NM ..725.00
Andy Gump, record & mask, Listerine premium, EX (EX card) .100.00
Archies, stencil set, 1983, MOC 15.00
Astro Boy, music box, Japan, ceramic, gold trim, 1980s, NM 175.00
Bambi, bicycle ornament, Bambi, celluloid, 1940s, M 125.00
Bambi, mirror, molded plastic fr, 1960s, 20x24", EX 175.00
Banana Splits, pajama bag, Animal Creations Ltd, 1970, 18", NM ..600.00
Banana Splits, pillow, Fleegle, 1960s, 10", minor fading o/w EX ...50.00
Batman, bicycle license plate, emb metal, 1966, 4x7", NM 50.00
Batman, clip-on tie, Omega, red w/yel letters, 11", NMIB 100.00
Batman, gloves, Wells Lamont Corp, faux leather, 1966, MIP ...100.00
Batman, night light, Snap-It, hard plastic, 1966, 2x3", NM 35.00
Batman, poncho & mask, 1976, MIP 35.00
Batman, sleeping bag, various scenes, 1975, sm tears o/w EX 30.00
Batman, slippers, 1966, faux bl leather, boot-type, M 125.00

Batman, String Art Kit, Smith, 1976, MIB (sealed) 45.00
Batman, wastebasket, litho tin w/'Duo' image, 1966, 10", VG 65.00
Ben Casey, nurse kit, Transogram, 1962, complete, NM (EX box) ..30.00
Betty Boop, display, cb stand-up, life-sz, EX 30.00
Betty Boop, fan, image of Betty w/moving eyes, prewar, 12", NM ..400.00
Betty Boop, mask, Bimbo, celluloid, 6x6", NM 175.00
Bonanza, cup, litho tin, Adam, 1960s, 3½" dia, EX 30.00
Bonanza, sweatshirt, Norwich, portraits/logo/map, 1960-63, VG+ ..150.00
Bugs Bunny, purse, Mighty Star, cloth w/felt, 1971, 17", NM 20.00
Bugs Bunny, sleeping bag, w/Bugs & friends, 1977, VG 15.00

Bugs Bunny, ceramic planter, copyright Leon Schlesinger, Shaw, 5", $85.00.

Captain America, pendant, Dell Plastics, yel vinyl, 7", EX (EX pkg) 65.00
Casey Jr, pencil sharpener, WDP, Bakelite, 1940, 1¾", NM 90.00
Casper the Ghost, chalkboard, 12x18", MIP (sealed) 40.00
Charlie McCarthy, pencil sharpener, Bakelite, rnd, EX 50.00
Curious George, magic slate, Fairchild, 1969, 12x9", M 10.00
Dale Evans, skirt, vinyl fringe & trim, 1950s, child sz, VG 65.00
Davy Crockett, bank, plaster figure, VG 125.00
Davy Crockett, coonskin hat, image of Davy, 1950s, EX 25.00
Davy Crockett, flashlight, tin w/plastic top, 1950s, 3", EX 25.00
Davy Crockett, Thunderbird Moccasin Kit, Blaine, 1950s, NMIB ..175.00
Dennis the Menace, mug, red-pnt plastic, 1962, EX 12.00
Dick Tracy, belt buckle, gold or silver, 1960s, EX 20.00
Dick Tracy, film, Trick or Treat, 8mm, 1960s, EX (EX box) 50.00
Dick Tracy, flashlight, bl & red w/etched image, pocket sz, NMIB ...75.00
Dick Tracy, magnifying glass, Larami, 1979, MOC 20.00
Dick Tracy, note pad, Tracy & Rick Fletcher signature, 7x3½", M ..15.00
Dick Tracy, wallet, blk vinyl, w/6 Crimestopper cards, 1973, NM ..20.00
Ding Dong School, record player, Miss Frances on front, EX 130.00
Disney, binoculars, WDP, Disney on Ice, 1970s, 6", M 10.00
Disney, Cockamamies Skin Transfers, 1961, MIB 20.00
Disney, globe, Rand McNally, characters on globe, 1950s, EX ...150.00
Disney, mold set, Model Craft, 1950s, EXIB 125.00
Disney, piano, Jaymar, wooden, decal images, 1960s, 9x16", EX ..85.00
Disney, record player, Bakelite, decaled characters, 1950s, VG ..110.00
Disney, shovel, Ohio Art, scene w/characters, 1930s, 26", VG ...175.00
Disney, suitcase, vinyl w/allover character design, EX 15.00
Disney, tray, England, various characters, 1950s, 12½x16", VG ...45.00
Disneyland, charm bracelet, Little Miss Disneyland, 1950s, MIB .35.00
Disneyland, coin purse, WDP, Tinkerbell, vinyl, mk, 1960s, M ...30.00
Disneyland, metal tooling kit, NM 35.00
Disneyland, pencil case, cb, Mickey as engineer, 1950s, VG+ 20.00
Disneyland, pennant, wht on red w/bl trim, 1950s, EX 40.00
Disneyland, tray, litho tin, aerial view of Disneyland, EX 150.00
Disneyland, xylophone, Original Concert Grand, w/stand, NMIB ..135.00
Donald Duck, bank, Leeds, sitting, ceramic, 1940s, 7½", EX 110.00
Donald Duck, bicycle ornament, jtd celluliod, 1940s, M 125.00
Donald Duck, blotter, Nu-Blue Sunoco, as Ben Franklin, 1939, NM ...25.00
Donald Duck, camera, WDP/Herbert George, 3x5", M (VG box) ..75.00
Donald Duck, charm, enamel, long-billed figure, 1930s, EX 65.00
Donald Duck, lamp, Glowies, Universal Lamp, 1969-71, 9½", MIB .75.00

Donald Duck, pencil sharpener, celluloid, 1930s, 2¾", EX **400.00**
Donald Duck, photo album, playing guitar, leather, 8x14", NM ...**75.00**
Donald Duck, pnt box, Page of London/WDP, 1970s, 5x9", EX ...**25.00**
Donald Duck, roly poly, celluloid, jtd, 4¼", EX+ **325.00**
Donald Duck, rug, Donald & nephews in a band, 1950s, 43x60", EX ...**150.00**
Donald Duck, soap, Cussons/England, molded figure, scarce, MIB ...**150.00**
Dr Dolittle, periscope, Bar-Zim, NMIP **30.00**
Dr Dolittle, projector, Ugly Mugly, Remco, w/movie slides, NMIB ..**50.00**
Dumbo, pencil sharpener, Bakelite, WDP, 1930s, 1¾", NM **125.00**
Elvira, make-up kit, MOC **20.00**
ET, night light, chest glows, MIB **35.00**
ET, pillow, bl or purple, EX **20.00**
ET, sponge ball, 1982, M **6.00**
Felix the Cat, drum, litho tin, scarce, 1930s, EX **185.00**
Felix the Cat, sparkler, Nifty, litho tin, 5", NM (worn box) **3,200.00**
Flash Gordon, compass, silver plastic w/yel wristband, 1950s, MOC ...**65.00**
Flintstones, coin purse, Barney, 1975, NM **25.00**
Flintstones, gumball machine, Hasbro, plastic Fred head, 8", EX .**50.00**
Gabby Hayes, hat, wool, EX+ **135.00**
Garfield, gumball machine, Superior, 1988, EX **20.00**
Garfield, mug, figural hdl: Garfield clutching side, 4¾" **14.00**
Garfield, necklace, Avon, MIB **10.00**
Garfield, night light, 2 variations, MOC, ea **15.00**
Goofy, bank, Playpals, vinyl head form, 1971, 12", NM **25.00**
Green Hornet, charm bracelet, w/5 charms, NMOC **100.00**
Green Hornet, wallet, Mattel, vinyl, M **100.00**
Happy Days, guitar, Fonzie, 1976, MIB (sealed) **75.00**
Herman & Katnip, kite, Saalfield, cb, 1960s, MIP **25.00**
Hopalong Cassidy, bedspread, chenille, 1950, NM **300.00**
Hopalong Cassidy, bicycle horn, w/hdlbar clamp, EX **200.00**
Hopalong Cassidy, ear muffs, red **175.00**
Hopalong Cassidy, laundry bag, plastic, orig container & card ...**850.00**
Hopalong Cassidy, money clip, Bar 20 w/dial, EX **75.00**
Hopalong Cassidy, neckerchief slide, steer head, lg, EX **60.00**
Hopalong Cassidy, party plate, EX **15.00**
Hopalong Cassidy, pennant, EX **25.00**
Hopalong Cassidy, pocketknife, blk & wht, 1950s, 3½", VG **45.00**
Hopalong Cassidy, spurs, metal w/name screened on leather, EX+ ..**225.00**
Hopalong Cassidy, tablet, EX **35.00**
Hopalong Cassidy, tie rack, EX **225.00**
Hopalong Cassidy, wallpaper section, 40x18" **175.00**
Hopalong Cassidy, wrist cuffs, blk, sm **220.00**

Howdy Doody, Uke, plastic, Emenee, ca 1950, copyright Kagran, 17", MIB, $130.00.

Howdy Doody, boxing gloves, Parvey, 1950s, 6", NMIB **325.00**
Howdy Doody, catcher's mitt, brn vinyl w/silver image, 1950s, VG ..**100.00**
Howdy Doody, handkerchief, mc, Howdy w/lasso, 1950s, 8x8", EX **25.00**
Howdy Doody, sparkler, Ja-Ru, 1987, MOC **10.00**
Howdy Doody, stationary, Graphic Products, w/envelopes, 1971, MIB .**25.00**
Howdy Doody, suitcase, cb, 1955 World's Fair, 10x14", VG **300.00**
Hugga Bunch, tray, litho metal, 1984, VG **10.00**

Incredible Hulk, switchplate, glow-in-the-dark, 1976, MIP **25.00**
Incredible Hulk, wallet, vinyl, 1976, unused, NM **20.00**
James Bond, wallet, mk Glidrose Productions, vinyl, 1966, NM ...**80.00**
Jetsons, film, 8mm, 1960s, NMIB **15.00**
Joe Carioke, pencil sharpener, Bakelite, 1940s **50.00**
King Kong, jewelry box, M **30.00**
Lassie, Trick Trainer, Mousely Inc, 1956, scarce, NM (EX box) ...**275.00**
Li'l Abner, tattoos, Orange Crush premium, set of 8, 1950, MOC ..**20.00**
Little Orphan Annie, coin purse, vinyl, 1930s, 3x2", EX **25.00**
Little Orphan Annie, mug, Ovaltine, stoneware **50.00**
Little Orphan Annie, teapot, porcelain, mk, 1930s, 3", M **70.00**
Lone Ranger, mask & neckerchief, VG+ **115.00**
Lone Ranger, party horn, tin, 5", NM **30.00**
Lone Ranger, pnt box, Milton Bradley, 1938, M **80.00**
Ludwig Von Drake, gumball machine, WDC, plastic, NM **25.00**
Marvel Super Heroes, bumper sticker, 1978, 4x14", M **15.00**
Marvel Super Heroes, notebook, Mead, 1970s, unused, M **25.00**
Mary Poppins, purse, vinyl, NM **80.00**
Maverick, wallet & key case, Warner Bros, plastic, 1958, NM+ .**100.00**
Mickey Mouse, banjo, wood & litho tin, 1932, 22", EX **435.00**
Mickey Mouse, bank, Animals Plus, vinyl, 12", NM **25.00**
Mickey Mouse, bank, Crown, compo, 6", VG+ **75.00**
Mickey Mouse, belt, Pyramid Belt, 50th Birthday, 1978, MIB **30.00**
Mickey Mouse, bicycle bell, WDP, chrome w/decal, 1960s, NM ..**40.00**
Mickey Mouse, birthday candle holders, Cypress/WDE, 1930s, NMIB .**250.00**
Mickey Mouse, blackboard easel, Pressman, 1950s, unused, MIB ..**100.00**
Mickey Mouse, camera, Mick-A-Matic, plastic head figure, MIB .**50.00**
Mickey Mouse, cane, wood w/compo head, 1930s, 32", EX **225.00**
Mickey Mouse, drum, Ohio Art/WDE, litho tin, 6" dia, NM **195.00**
Mickey Mouse, globe, tin, EX+ **225.00**
Mickey Mouse, guitar, Carnival, Mousegetar, 1960s, 30", EX **25.00**
Mickey Mouse, gumball machine, Hasbro, head on base, 1968, NM .**50.00**
Mickey Mouse, kaleidoscope, VG **50.00**
Mickey Mouse, lantern, WDP, figural, battery-op, 1977, MIB **100.00**
Mickey Mouse, magnifier, Monogram, 1980s, MOC **5.00**
Mickey Mouse, milk pitcher, figural, pottery, 1930s, 7", EX **175.00**
Mickey Mouse, mirror, plastic, drum shape, 24", NM **150.00**
Mickey Mouse, music box, western style, Schmidt, M **75.00**
Mickey Mouse, night light, plastic, TV shape, 1950s, 6", EX **90.00**
Mickey Mouse, Nintendo video game, hand-held, 1980s, MIB **25.00**
Mickey Mouse, ornament, bsk, pie-eyes, early, 5½", EX+ **275.00**
Mickey Mouse, pencil box, plastic rocket shape, 1970s, EX **10.00**
Mickey Mouse, pin, mc celluloid figure, EX **75.00**
Mickey Mouse, playing cards, no mk, bl box, 1930s, VG (VG box) ..**30.00**
Mickey Mouse, pnt box, Page of London/WDP, 1970s, M **50.00**
Mickey Mouse, recipe card, Bell Bread premium, 1934, 3½x5", M ...**38.00**
Mickey Mouse, sled, pressed steel & wood, 30½", G **115.00**
Mickey Mouse, spoon, Wm Rogers/Post Toasties premium, 1930s, EX ...**25.00**
Mickey Mouse, swim mask, Ideal, yel w/blk ears, 1970s, M **40.00**
Mickey Mouse, wall plaque, ceramic, as band leader, 1970s, M ..**100.00**
Mickey Mouse & Minnie, bookends, Determined, 1970, 6½", EX .**95.00**
Mickey Mouse & Minnie, hairbrush, Hughes/WD, wooden, 1930s, EX **50.00**
Mickey Mouse & Minnie, party horn, Marks Bros/WDE, 7", NM ..**150.00**
Mickey Mouse Club, blanket, emb, 1950s, 106x84", EX **175.00**
Mickey Mouse Club, kaleidoscope, wht w/gr trim, 1970s, 8", M ...**25.00**
Mickey Mouse Club, Newsreel, Mattel, 1950s, complete, EXIB .**150.00**
Mickey Mouse Club, telescope, WDP, 1970s, 9", MIP **25.00**
Mickey Mouse Club, umbrella, clear plastic, ft as hdl, M **75.00**
Mickey Mouse Club, wallet, w/Donald Duck, NMIB **75.00**
Mickey Mouse Club, Western Wagon, 1950s, EX, minimum value .**250.00**
Minnie Mouse, brush & comb set, Reed & Barton, SP, 1980s, MIB ..**40.00**
Minnie Mouse, gumball machine, WDP, NM **25.00**
Minnie Mouse, soap dish, ceramic, EX **20.00**
Minnie Mouse, wall plaque, Disneyland, ceramic head, 1970s, M ..**100.00**

Mother Goose, dish set, Ideal, plastic, 1940s, 26-pc, MIB **150.00**
Mother Goose, jack-in-the-box, plays theme song, NM **25.00**
Mutt & Jeff, drum, Converse, litho tin, faux signature, 12", VG ...**250.00**
Our Gang, note pad, 1930s-40s, 5x9", EX **40.00**
Peanuts, beach bag, Beagle Beach, Colgate premium, 9x8", M **20.00**
Peanuts, bookmark, Snoopy on doghouse, plastic, 4", M **8.00**
Peanuts, fishing rod & reel, Snoopy, Zebco, plastic, VG **10.00**
Peanuts, jump rope, Snoopy, wht plastic, M **15.00**
Peanuts, megaphone, Charlie Brown, Chein, 1970, rare, EX **25.00**
Peanuts, pajama bag, Snoopy, plush, Commonwealth, 18", M **15.00**
Peanuts, wallet, Snoopy & Woodstock, wht vinyl, NM **25.00**
Peter Pan, bell, Tinkerbell, souvenir, 1950s, 3", EX **60.00**
Peter Pan, outfit, Cadillac Toys, belt, hat & sheath, 1950s, EX **25.00**
Peter Pan, pin, Captain Hook, 1950s, EX **35.00**
Peter Pan, towel set, Gildex, 1950s, M (worn pkg) **65.00**

Pinocchio Ride-On Rocker, American, 1940s, M, $165.00.

Photo courtesy Dunbar Gallery

Pinocchio, charm, silver-tone metal head shape, 1940s, M **10.00**
Pinocchio, fork & spoon set, SP, 1940s, EX **85.00**
Pinocchio, mask, Figaro, Gillette Blue Blade, 1939, VG **8.00**
Pinocchio, stationery, Whitman, cb folder, 1939, EX **85.00**
Pinocchio, tablet, Jiminy Cricket, Westab, 1961, 5x3", NM **10.00**
Pinocchio & Jiminy Cricket, shovel, litho tin, 1940s, 16", EX **85.00**
Planet of the Apes, squirt gun, Cornelius, AHI, plastic, 1970s, M ...**145.00**
Popeye, boxing gloves, Everlast, red, 1950s, MIP **55.00**
Popeye, harmonica, metal w/mc detail, 4", EX (EX box) **165.00**
Popeye, lantern, pnt tin & glass figure, 11", EX **125.00**
Popeye, mug, Espirit/Sales Aweigh! King Features, 1980s, M **28.00**
Popeye, pencil sharpener, litho tin, 3", EX **325.00**
Popeye, watering can, T Cohn, litho tin, 7", EX **350.00**
Porky Pig, gum machine, Banko Matic, plastic, 1970s, 9½", EXIB ..**25.00**
Raggedy Ann, jewelry box, 1972, 9", VG **15.00**
Rambo, walkie-talkies, LarGo, 1985, complete w/headband, MOC .**30.00**
Rat Fink, key chain, figural, yel, EX **25.00**
Reg'lar Fellers, microscope set, complete, NMIB **275.00**
Ripley's Believe It or Not, kaleidoscope, cb, 1950s, EX (EX box) .**60.00**
Rocketeer, backpack, leather-like, AMC Theatres promo, NM .**125.00**
Rocketeer, belt, turq or bl, EX, ea **30.00**
Rocketeer, sleeping bag, EX **45.00**
Rocketeer, tape & book set, MIP (sealed) **10.00**
Rocketeer, umbrella, Pyramid Handbag Co, NM **100.00**
Rocketeer, wallet, Pyramid Handbag Co, EX **40.00**
Rocky & Bullwinkle, telescope, Larami, 1970s, MOC **25.00**
Rookies, helmet, plastic w/sticker on top, 1970s, VG **15.00**
Rootie Kazootie, drum, litho tin, 1950s, 8" dia, EX **125.00**
Roy Rogers, bank, ceramic, Roy on Trigger, 8", NM **275.00**
Roy Rogers, binoculars, decaled, 5", NM **100.00**
Roy Rogers, fountain pen, name in script on side, EX **150.00**
Roy Rogers, hunting knife w/sheath w/compass, EX **450.00**
Roy Rogers, neckerchief slide, hat shaped, yel plastic, EX **75.00**
Roy Rogers, pants & chaps, brn & orange, 1950s, EX **65.00**
Roy Rogers, Quick Shooter hat, Ideal, MIB **385.00**

Shirley Temple, scrapbook, spiral-bound, Saafield, 1936, EX **50.00**
Simpsons, bulletin board, Roseart, cork, mc image, 16x20", EX ...**15.00**
Simpsons, Fun Dough Model Maker, MIB **20.00**
Sleeping Beauty, bubble wand, 1950s, unused, MIP **40.00**
Sleeping Beauty, sewing set, Transogram, 1959, unused, EX+ **65.00**
Smurfs, banner, Happy Smurfday, MIP **20.00**
Smurfs, chalkboard, Smurfette, EX **25.00**
Smurfs, coin purse, To Paint a Rainbow Life, cloth, EX **10.00**
Smurfs, sand bucket & shovel, plastic, EX **10.00**
Smurfs, sewing cards, MIB (sealed) **25.00**
Snow White & the Seven Dwarfs, birthday card w/LP record, M **40.00**
Snow White & the Seven Dwarfs, handkerchief, 1930s, 9x9", NM .**23.00**
Spider-Man, bicycle, Am Flyer Jr Roadmaster, 1978, 42", VG ...**165.00**
Spider-Man, sunglasses, Nasta, 1986, MOC **10.00**
Superman, belt buckle, Pioneer, bronze w/emb image, 1940s, EX ..**450.00**
Superman, kite, Hi-Flyer, 1984, MIP **30.00**
Superman, smock, Miss Boutique, red vinyl w/mc image, 1976, M ...**45.00**
Sylvester the Cat, roly poly, EX **25.00**
Texas Ranger, outfit, Leslie Henry, box only, VG **35.00**
Thor, sew-on patch, blk cloth w/yel border, 1970s, 3", NM **6.00**
Three Little Pigs, switchplate, plastic, 1950s, MIP **35.00**
Three Stooges, flasher rings, Curly, Larry or Moe, NM, ea **20.00**
Tom & Jerry, guitar, Mattel, musical w/up, 1965, EX **40.00**
Tom & Jerry, jack-in-the-box, Mattel, M **100.00**
Universal Monsters, iron-on transfers, set of 6, 1964, MOC **200.00**
Weird-Ohs, magic slate, 1963, 11x8", M (sealed) **35.00**
Welcome Back Kotter, record player, 1976, EX **100.00**
Welcome Back Kotter, wastebasket, metal, oval, VG+ **40.00**
Who Framed Roger Rabbit, party favor bags, plastic, MIP **20.00**
Who Framed Roger Rabbit, tray, Jessica figure, M **70.00**
Winky Dink, outfit, yel, red & wht felt, scarce, EX **85.00**
Winnie the Pooh, lamp, plastic, Eeyore pulls Pooh in wagon, EX ...**55.00**
Winnie the Pooh, night light, ceramic, EX **40.00**
Wizard of Oz, bath beads, Ansehi, set of 12 w/tray, 1976, EXIB ...**75.00**
Wizard of Oz, jack-in-the-box, Scarecrow, 1967, NM **50.00**
Wizard of Oz, Magic Kit, Fun Inc, complete, 1960s, NMIB **50.00**
Wizard of Oz, sunglasses, Scarecrow, Multi-Kids/Lowe, 1989, MOC **20.00**
Wizard of Oz, trinket box, ruby slippers, Presents, 1989, MIB **15.00**
Wonder Woman, mirror, Avon, plastic figural hdl, 1978, NM (EX box) .**20.00**
Wonder Woman, sunglasses, Nasta, 1988, MOC **20.00**
Woody Woodpecker, film, 8mm, 1960s, NMIB **15.00**
Woody Woodpecker, harmonica, plastic figure, early, 6", EX **30.00**
Woody Woodpecker, jack-in-the-box, Mattel, M, from $100 to ...**150.00**
Woody Woodpecker, kazoo, Linden, red plastic figure, 1960s, 7", EX .**25.00**
Woody Woodpecker, mug, brn plastic w/pnt face, 1965-73, NM .**15.00**
Wyatt Earp, guitar, 24", EX **125.00**
Wyatt Earp, spur set, plastic, Selco, NMOC **50.00**
Wyatt Earp, tablet, Hugh O'Brien on cover, M **25.00**
Yogi Bear, mug, pnt plastic, NM **20.00**
Yogi Bear, night light cover, 1960s, 7", EX **20.00**
Yogi Bear, riding stick, AJ Renzi, wood w/plastic head, 34", EX ...**55.00**
Zorro, cape, Carnival Creations, w/card, EX **65.00**
Zorro, cup, Melmac, wht w/image, EX **25.00**
Zorro, gloves, w/ring, M **60.00**
Zorro, key chain/flashlight, plastic, 1950s, EX **60.00**
Zorro, ring, silver & blk, EX **15.00**
Zorro, rug, mc cotton pile, 1950s, EX **185.00**
Zorro, sword, WDP, EX **20.00**
Zorro, wallet, brn or wht vinyl w/Zorro & horse, EX **70.00**

Peters and Reed

John Peters and Adam Reed founded their pottery in Zanesville,

Ohio, just before the turn of the century, using the local red clay to produce a variety of wares. Moss Aztec, introduced about 1912, has an unglazed exterior with designs molded in high relief and the recesses highlighted with a green wash. Only the interior is glazed to hold water. Pereco (named for Peters, Reed and Company) is glazed in semi-matt blue, maroon, cream, and other colors. Orange was also used very early, but such examples are rare. Shapes are simple with in-mold decoration sometimes borrowed from the Moss Aztec line. Wilse Blue is a line of high-gloss medium blue with dark specks on simple shapes. Landsun, characterized by its soft matt multicolor or blue and gray combinations, is decorated either by dripping or by hand brushing in an effect sometimes called Flame or Herringbone. Chromal, in much the same colors as Landsun, may be decorated with a realistic scenic, or the swirling application of colors may merely suggest one. Vivid, realistic Chromal scenics command much higher prices than weak, poorly drawn examples. (Brush-McCoy made a very similar line called Chromart. Neither will be marked; and due to the lack of documented background material available, it may be impossible make a positive identification. Collectors nearly always attribute this type of decoration to Peters and Reed.) Shadow Ware is usually a glossy, multicolor drip over a harmonious base color but occasionally seen in overall matt glaze. When the base is black, the effect is often iridescent.

Perhaps the most familiar line is the brown high-glaze artware with the 'sprigged'-type designs. Although research has uncovered no positive proof, it is generally accepted as having been made by Peters and Reed. It is interesting to note that many of the artistic shapes in this line are recognizable as those made by Weller, Roseville, and other Zanesville area companies. Several other lines were produced including Mirror Black, Persian, Egyptian, Florentine, Marbleized, etc., and an unidentified line which collectors call Mottled-Marbleized Colors. In this high-gloss line, the red clay body often shows through the splashed-on multicolors.

In 1922 the company became known as the Zane Pottery. Peters and Reed retired, and Harry McClelland became president. Charles Chilcote designed new lines, and production of many of the old lines continued. The body of the ware after 1922 was light in color. Marks include the impressed logo or ink stamp 'Zaneware' in a rectangle.

Bowl, centerpc; Wilse Blue, w/candlesticks	125.00
Bowl, emb branch, deep gr matt, unmk, 3x8"	150.00
Candlestick, Brown Ware, bell shape w/appl wreath	60.00
Candlestick, Moss Aztec, slim, #64, 8½"	85.00
Jar, Landsun, variegated gr, #1, w/lid, 3"	80.00
Jardiniere, Chromal scenic, 8"	600.00
Lamp, wht w/long gr & rust runs, Zaneware, 11½"	400.00
Lamp base, Shadow Ware, 7"	225.00
Pitcher, Brown Ware, floral, sq rim, slim, 9"	125.00
Planter, Marbleized, 10½"	300.00

Vase, Chromal, log cabin scenic, 13½", $1,500.00.

Vase, bl gloss w/blk/turq/yel abstracts, 12x7"	150.00
Vase, Brown Ware w/appl flowers, hdls, 4"	50.00
Vase, Brown Ware w/appl wreath, 10"	175.00
Vase, Chromal (realistic), 13x7"	1,500.00
Vase, gr matt, 8"	150.00
Vase, Landsun, gr, bl & brn geometric design, #45, 5"	75.00
Vase, Moss Aztec, leaves w/trailing stems, #172, 8"	125.00
Vase, Moss Aztec, lg flowers, brn w/gr wash, Ferrell, 8"	180.00
Vase, Pereco, emb Nouveau floral, gr matt, 18x8", NM	350.00
Vase, rust gloss w/blk/yel/gr/brn dripping abstracts, Zane, 12"	210.00
Vase, Wilse Blue, #612, 8½"	80.00
Wall pocket, Egyptian figural, gr matt	250.00

Pewabic

The Pewabic Pottery was formally established in Detroit, Michigan, in 1907 by Mary Chase Perry Stratton and Horace James Caulkins. The two had worked together since 1903, firing their ware in a small kiln Caulkins had designed especially for use by the dental trade. Always a small operation which relied upon basic equipment and the skill of the workers, they took pride in being commissioned for several important architectural tile installations.

Some of the early artware was glazed a simple matt green; occasionally other colors were added, sometimes in combination, one over the other in a drip effect. Later Stratton developed a lustrous crystalline glaze. (Today's values are determined to a great extent by the artistic merit of the glaze.) The body of the ware was highly fired and extremely hard. Shapes were basic, and decorative modeling, if used at all, was in low relief. Mary Stratton kept the pottery open until her death in 1961. In 1968 it was purchased and reopened by Michigan State University. Several marks were used over the years: a triangle with 'Revelation Pottery' (for a short time only); 'Pewabic' with five maple leaves; and the impressed circle mark.

Ashtray, gr/rose/platinum metallic, 4½"	110.00
Bowl, burgundy gloss, int: gold lustre, 2x5"	450.00
Tile, Arts & Crafts flower, bl on gray, 3", +orig fr	210.00
Tile, geometric cvg, bl/gr, canted corners, label, 5½" sq	325.00
Vase, bl matt w/slight lustre, early mk, shouldered, 3½"	300.00
Vase, bl metallic, bulbous w/long neck, paper label, 7½"	550.00
Vase, bl-gr crystalline, classic shape, 9¾x5¾"	2,000.00
Vase, bl-gr irid drip over gold/purple mottle, rstr rim, 6x4½"	400.00
Vase, blk, gr & lav lustre, squat, circular mk, 3½x5¼"	450.00
Vase, bright metallic bl/gr/purple, shouldered, 11½"	2,100.00
Vase, brn/bl/tan matt dripping over gr/brn, maple leaf mk, 7"	550.00
Vase, celadon irid drips on bl lustre, sm flaw, 5½x4"	750.00
Vase, cobalt lustre, bulbous w/can neck, sm flaw, 9x7"	1,000.00
Vase, dk bl lustre, classic shape, mk, 8x6"	750.00
Vase, flowing fire-orange/gr, sm rim, 8½x4"	1,800.00
Vase, gold/gr/burgundy lustre, tapered shoulder, 8x5"	1,300.00
Vase, gr/purple/red lustre, stovepipe neck, 4x3"	300.00
Vase, leathery fire-orange/gr, can neck, shouldered, 9¾"	1,900.00
Vase, leaves cvd in relief on gr matt, 8x6"	5,750.00
Vase, metallic bl/gunmetal/purple, imp mk, 5½x5"	750.00
Vase, metallic gold/bl/gray, lip rpr, 5½x5"	200.00
Vase, mirror purple, corseted shoulder, circular mk, 5x5"	700.00
Vase, oatmeal matt, flaring bowl form, sgn WB, 7½"	260.00
Vase, red/gold irid drip over Chinese Blue & red, 7½x5"	1,600.00
Vase, turq & taupe lustre, bulbous, circular mk, 5½x5½"	650.00

Pewter

Pewter is a metal alloy of tin, copper, very small parts of bismuth and/or antimony, and sometimes lead. Very little American pewter contained lead, however, because much of the ware was designed to be used as tableware, and makers were aware that the use of lead could result in poisoning. (Pieces that do contain lead are usually darker in color and heavier than those that have no lead.) Most of the fine examples of American pewter date from 1700 to the 1840s. Many pieces were melted down and recast into bullets during the American Revolution in 1775; this accounts to some extent why examples from this period are quite difficult to find. The pieces that did survive may include buttons, buckles, and writing equipment as well as the tableware we generally think of.

After the Revolution makers began using antimony as the major alloy with the tin in an effort to regain the popularity of pewter, which glassware and china was beginning to replace in the home. The resulting product, known as britannia, had a lustrous silver-like appearance and was far more durable. While closely related, britannia is a collectible in its own right and should not be confused with pewter.

Key: tm — touch mark

Coffeepots: Roswell Gleason touchmark, Dorchester, Massachusetts, pear shape, ca 1840, 12", EX+, $450.00; Rufus Dunham touchmark, Westbrook, Maine, ca 1840, minor pitting, 12", $400.00.

Bowl, SE (Samuel Ellis) tm, pit/scratch/rpr, 13¼" 165.00
Bucket, unmk, arched swing hdl, ftd, early 1800s, 5½x7⅞" 120.00
Candlesticks, Sellew & Co Cincinnati tm, 8", pr 550.00
Candlesticks, unmk, domed bases, baluster shafts, 9x3¾", pr 100.00
Coffeepot, Boardman tm, triple-belly, ca 1830, 11½" 550.00
Coffeepot, Dunham partial tm, flower finial, rpr, 8¼" 165.00
Coffeepot, Homan & Co tm, cast flower finial, sm dents, 8¾" ...125.00
Coffeepot, Sellew & Co, Cincinnati tm, sm hole, 10¾" 250.00
Commode, unmk Am, cylindrical w/flared sides, flattened rim, 11¾" ..80.00
Flagon, communion; Smith & Feltman Albany tm, sm dents, 12" .200.00
Flagon, communion; unmk Am, ear hdl, bent lip, 10½" 140.00
Funnel, unmk Am, rnd w/long spout, wire loop, late 1800s, 9x6" .150.00
Ladle, cream; Yates tm, curved hdl, 6¾" 50.00
Ladle, J Weeks tm, some wear, 13¼" 165.00
Lamp, oil; dbl bull's eye, unmk, 19th C, 8¼" 750.00
Lamp, unmk, wide flat lard oil burner, dents, 6⅜", EX 150.00
Lamp, unmk Am, fluid burner (needs rpr), 5¾" 125.00
Pitcher, att Boardman & Hart, globular, domed lid, 1850s, 10" .350.00
Pitcher, R Dunham tm, 6¾" 360.00
Pitcher, Sellew & Co Cincinnati, hinged lid, rpr, 8¾" 220.00
Plate, Boardman & Co NY eagle tm, wear, 10¾" 275.00
Plate, Harbeson Phila tm, wear/scratches, 7⅞" 275.00
Plate, London tm w/Neptune-like figure, ca 1800, 7¾" 65.00
Plate, TD Boardman, eagle tm, worn/battered, 7⅝" 195.00
Plate, unmk, minor wear/dents, 7½", 4 for 220.00
Plate, unmk Am, ca 1800, 5" (rare sz) 130.00
Plates, unmk, normal wear/scratches, 8", 4 for 200.00

Platter, fish; Engel Block 1735, angel tm, repro, 24x10" 125.00
Porringer, att Samuel Hamlin, flowered hdl, 2x5⅜" 660.00
Porringer, RG tm (att Roswell Gleason), crown hdl, 4⅜" 200.00
Porringer, TD & SB tm, cast crown hdl, 5" 525.00
Porringer, unmk, cast flower hdl, sm crack, 5½" 275.00
Porringer, unmk Am, crown-shaped pierced hdl, 1800s, 4¼" 340.00
Spoons, unmk, rnd bowl w/rectangular hdls, 6¾", pr 80.00
Tall pot, Boardman & Co tm, sq hdl, curved spout, dome lid, 12" .600.00
Tall pot, Dixon & Son tm, wooden finial wafer, 12½", EX 220.00
Tall pot, Whitlock Troy NY tm, lt wear/pitting, 10¾" 250.00
Tankard, English tm, eng RM on underside, ca 1810, 1-pt 150.00
Teapot, A Grisowld eagle tm, some battering/rprs, 6¾" 195.00
Teapot, B&P tm, rprs, rare, 6½" 415.00
Teapot, G Richardson Warranted tm, rpr hdl, 7¼" 200.00
Teapot, L Boardman Warranted tm, rprs, 7½" 140.00
Teapot, McQuilkin tm, dents, 8⅞" 220.00
Teapot, Putnam tm, sm holes in hdl, 8¾" 250.00
Teapot, R Gleason tm, battered, 9" 110.00
Teapot, Sellew & Co Cincinnati tm, wear/split, 8" 165.00
Teapot, Smith & Co tm, rprs, 8½" 165.00
Teapot, Trask (partial) tm, 9¼" 200.00
Teapot, unmk Am, resoldered finial, 8½" 85.00
Teapot, unmk Continental, C-shaped hdl, removable lid, 4½" ..340.00

Pfaltzgraff

Pfaltzgraff has operated in Pennsylvania since the early 1800s making redware at first, then stoneware crocks and jugs, yellow ware, and spongeware in the '20s, artware and kitchenware in the '30s, and stoneware kitchen items through the '40s. To collectors, they're best known for their Gourmet Royal (circa 1950s), a high-gloss dinnerware line of solid brown with frothy white drip glaze around the rims, and their giftware line called Muggsy, comic-character mugs, ashtrays, bottle stoppers, children's dishes, pretzel jars, cookie jars, etc. It was designed in the late 1940s and continued in production until 1960. The older versions have protruding features, while the features of later examples were simply painted on.

Their popular Village line, an almond-glazed pattern with a brown-stenciled folk-art tulip design, was discontinued a few years ago, and is today becomming very collectible. Yorktowne and Folk Art, though still in production, are being issued in a more limited assortment than in past years, so discontinued items in those lines are attracting much interest as well. For more information on their dinnerware, we recommend *The Flea Market Trader* and *The Garage Sale and Flea Market Annual*, both by Collector Books.

Christmas Heritage, bowl, soup/cereal; #009, 5½", from $2 to 3.50
Christmas Heritage, cheese tray, #533, 10½x7½", from $5 to 7.00
Christmas Heritage, mug, ped ft, #290, 10-oz 4.50
Christmas Heritage, plate, dinner; #004, 10", from $4 to 5.50
Gourmet Royale, ashtray, #321, 7¾", from $12 to 15.00
Gourmet Royale, bean pot, #11-3, 3-qt 35.00
Gourmet Royale, bowl, mixing; 6", from $8 to 10.00
Gourmet Royale, bowl, soup; 2¼x7¼", from $6 to 8.00
Gourmet Royale, casserole, stick hdl, 1-qt 18.00
Gourmet Royale, casserole, stick hdl, 3-qt 30.00
Gourmet Royale, casserole-warming stand 10.00
Gourmet Royale, creamer, #382, from $5 to 7.00
Gourmet Royale, flour scoop, sm, from $12 to 15.00
Gourmet Royale, jug, #384, 32-oz, from $32 to 36.00
Gourmet Royale, mug, #392, 16-oz, from $12 to 14.00
Gourmet Royale, platter, #320, 14", from $20 to 25.00
Gourmet Royale, roaster, #325, oval, 14", from $30 to 35.00

Gourmet Royale, shirred egg dish, #360, 6", from $10 to **12.00**
Gourmet Royale, tray, tidbit; 2-tier, from $15 to **18.00**
Heritage, butter dish, #002-028, from $6 to **8.00**
Heritage, cake/serving plate, #002-529, 11¼" dia, from $10 to **15.00**
Heritage, cup & saucer, #002-002, 9-oz **3.00**
Heritage, soup tureen, #002-160, 3½-qt, from $35 to **45.00**
Village, baker, #237, sq, tab hdls, 9", from $9 to **12.00**
Village, baker, #24, oval, 10¼", from $8 to **10.00**
Village, beverage server **28.00**
Village, bowl, fruit; #008, 5" **4.00**
Village, bowl, mixing; #453, ½ to 3-qt, 3-pc set, from $40 to **50.00**
Village, bowl, rim soup; #012, 8½" **6.00**
Village, bowl, serving; #010, 7" **10.00**
Village, bowl, soup/cereal; #009, 6" **4.50**
Village, bowl, vegetable; #011, 8¾" **15.00**
Village, butter dish **8.00**
Village, candlesticks, pr **14.00**
Village, canister set **60.00**
Village, casserole, #315, w/lid, 2-qt **30.00**
Village, coffee mug, #89F, 10-oz **5.50**
Village, cup & saucer **3.50**
Village, gravy boat, #443, w/saucer, 16-oz, from $10 to **15.00**
Village, ped mug, #90F, 10-oz **4.50**
Village, plate, dinner **4.50**
Village, spoon rest, #515, 9" L **7.50**
Yorktowne, baker, #247, oval, 14" **25.00**
Yorktowne, bowl, salad; #220 ....**28.00**
Yorktowne, candle holders, #574, 5¼", pr **14.00**
Yorktowne, canister, Flour, str sides, lug hdl, 8" **20.00**
Yorktowne, casserole, #325, 3½-qt **40.00**
Yorktowne, clock, #925 ....**45.00**
Yorktowne, crock, ice; #650 ....**28.00**
Yorktowne, gravy boat, #433, 23-oz **15.00**
Yorktowne, jug, Toby; #418, 18-oz **25.00**
Yorktowne, loaf pan, #235, lug hdl, 2-qt **15.00**
Yorktowne, mug, demi; #284 ....**12.00**
Yorktowne, napkin holder **12.00**
Yorktowne, plate, #003, 7" **2.50**
Yorktowne, platter, #017, 16" **25.00**
Yorktowne, souffle, #406, 1-qt **12.00**
Yorktowne, teapot, #550, 42-oz **30.00**
Yorktowne, trivet, #518, lug hdl, rnd **12.00**

Muggsy Line

Ashtray **125.00**
Bottle opener, head, ball shape **85.00**
Canape holder, Carrie, lift-off hat, from $125 to **150.00**
Cigarette server **125.00**
Clothes sprinkler bottle, Myrtle, Black, from $225 to **260.00**
Clothes sprinkler bottle, Myrtle, wht, from $195 to **225.00**
Cookie jar, character face, minimum value **250.00**
Jar, utility; Handy Harry, hat forms lid **200.00**
Mug, action figure, Black **125.00**
Mug, action figure (golfer, etc), ea from $65 to **85.00**
Mug, character face, ea **38.00**
Shot mug, character face **50.00**
Tumbler **60.00**

Phoenix Bird

Blue and white Phoenix Bird china has been produced by various Japanese potteries from the early 1900s. With slight variations the design features the Japanese bird of paradise and scroll-like vines of Kara-Kusa, or Chinese grass. Although some of their earlier ware is unmarked, the majority is marked in some fashion. More than one hundred different stamps have been reported, with 'Made in Japan' the one most often found. Coming in second is Morimura's wreath and/or crossed stems (both having the letter 'M' within). The cloverleaf with 'Japan' below very often indicates an item having a high-quality transfer-printed design. Among the many categories in the Phoenix Bird pattern are several shapes; therefore (for identification purposes), each has been given a number, i.e. #1, #2, etc. Newer items, if marked at all, carry a paper label. Compared to the older ware, the coloring of the new is whiter and the blue more harsh; the design is sparse with more ground area showing. Although collectors buy even 'new' pieces, the older is, of course, more highly prized and valued.

For further information we recommend *Phoenix Bird Chinaware, Books I – IV*, written and privately published by our advisor, Joan Oates; her address is in the Directory under Michigan. Join Phoenix Bird Collectors of America (PBCA) and receive the *Phoenix Bird Discoveries* newsletter, an informative publication that will further your appreciation of this chinaware. See Clubs, Newsletters, and Catalogs for ordering information.

Batter jug, teardrop lid, $75.00.

Photo courtesy Joan Oates

Bonbon dish, rattan hdl **65.00**
Bouillon, 2-hdl **15.00**
Bowl, berry; #3, 5-scallop **75.00**
Cake tray, #3, rnd w/hdls **68.00**
Celery tray, #1, 13½" L **125.00**
Child's tea set, #2, 3-pc **125.00**
Child's tureen cover, oval **25.00**
Coaster **25.00**
Coffeepot 'B,' post-1970 ....**55.00**
Condensed milk, #2, w/lid & underplate **130.00**
Dresser tray, 8¼x5¼" **45.00**
Gravy boat, #2, attached underplate, Nippon **85.00**
Ice cream dish, oval, invt scallops **35.00**
Jug, batter; w/teardrop lid **75.00**
Mustard pot, #2, w/lid **55.00**
Nut cup, 3-ftd, Seto **25.00**
Pitcher, lemonade; bulbous **165.00**
Plate, dessert; 7¼" **12.00**
Plate, dinner; 9¾" **45.00**
Plate, luncheon; fine quality, 8½" **25.00**
Shakers, 6-sided, Occupied Japan, pr **35.00**
Tankard, water; bell shape, 6½" **145.00**
Teapot, #11-B, Q-hdl, flat base **48.00**
Tureen, vegetable; rnd, w/lid **155.00**

Phoenix Glass

Founded in 1880 in Monaca, Pennsylvania, the Phoenix Glass

Company became one of the country's foremost manufacturers of lighting glass by the early 1900s. They also produced a wide variety of utilitarian and decorative glassware, including art glass by Joseph Webb, colored cut glass, Gone-with-the-Wind style oil lamps, hotel and barware, and pharmaceutical glassware. Today, however, collectors are primarily interested in the 'Sculptured Artware' produced in the 1930s and '40s. These beautiful pressed and mold-blown pieces are most often found in white milk glass or crystal with various color treatments or a satin finish.

Phoenix did not mark their 'Sculptured Artware' line on the glass; instead, a silver and black (earliest) or gold and black (later) foil label in the shape of the mythical phoenix bird was used.

Quite often glassware made by the Consolidated Lamp and Glass Company of nearby Coraopolis, Pennsylvania, is mistaken for Phoenix's 'Sculptured Artware.' Though the style of the glass is very similar, one distinguishing characteristic is that perhaps 80% of the time Phoenix applied color to the background leaving the raised design plain in contrast, while Consolidated generally applied color to the raised design and left the background plain. Also, for the most part, the patterns and colors used by Phoenix were distinctively different from those used by Consolidated.

In 1970 Phoenix Glass became a division of Anchor Hocking which in turn was acquired by the Newell Group in 1987. Phoenix has the distinction of being one of the oldest continuously operating glass factories in the United States. For more information refer to *Phoenix and Consolidated Art Glass, 1926 – 1980*, written by our advisor, Jack D. Wilson, who is listed in the Directory under Illinois. See also Consolidated Glass.

Key: mg — milk glass

Aster, vase, pearlized on lt tan, 7"	85.00
Bachelor Button, vase, mg design on pk bkground, rare, 7"	250.00
Bachelor Button, vase, wht pearlized, 7"	225.00
Bittersweet, vase, lt bl wash, orig Reuben Line label	175.00
Bluebell, vase, pearlized design on lt pk, 7"	125.00
Cosmos, vase, bl on mg, 7½"	150.00
Cosmos, vase, ivory pearlized, 7½"	125.00
Daisy, vase, bl over mg, 9x9"	425.00
Dancing Girl, vase, gr on mg, 12"	475.00
Diving Girl, vase, brn shadow, 14"	375.00
Fern, vase, bl & gr on wht-reverse decor, label, 7"	230.00
Fern, vase, bl on crystal, 7"	85.00
Fern, vase, bl stain on mg, 7"	100.00
Fern, vase, Reuben Blue on crystal frost, 7"	275.00
Flying Geese, vase, bl stain on mg	220.00
Flying Geese, vase, brn stain on mg	220.00
Freesia, fan vase, brn wash on mg	125.00
Freesia, vase, frosted design on pk ground, 8"	150.00
Jewel, vase, maroon pearlized, 4¾"	85.00
Jewel, vase, wht w/lt bl design, 4¾"	85.00
Jonquil, platter, lt bl frost, crystal, 14" dia	400.00
Lacy Dewdrop, candy dish, dk bl stain on mg, w/lid, 6"	100.00
Lacy Dewdrop, compote, pk decor on mg	145.00
Lily, bowl, console; slate bl on frost, design both sides, 14½"	395.00
Madonna, vase, brn shadow, 10½"	275.00
Madonna, vase, pearlized on tan, 10½"	200.00
Philodendron, vase, amber, 11½"	125.00
Philodendron, vase, brn shadow finish, 11½"	175.00
Philodendron, vase, tan shadow on mg, #246, 11½"	190.00
Philodendron, vase, wht w/frosted design, 11½"	125.00
Phlox, ashtray, slate bl pearlized	225.00
Phlox, candy dish, bl frosted	175.00
Phlox, cigarette box, brn stain on mg, 2x5x4"	140.00

Star Flower, vase, bl & mg, 7"	145.00
Strawberry, candle holders, bl on mg, 4¼", pr	275.00
Thistle, umbrella vase, lime gr pearlized, 18"	575.00

Thistle umbrella vase, burgundy pearlized, 18", $650.00.

Photo courtesy Jack D. Wilson

Thistle, vase, med gr pearlized	575.00
Thistle, vase, powder bl pearlized	600.00
Tiger Lily, bowl, amethyst frosted, 11½"	350.00
Tiger Lily, bowl, pk frosted, 11½"	300.00
Tiger Lily, bowl, wht frost, 11½"	155.00
Tropical Fish, vase, Reuben Blue, 9"	630.00
Wild Geese, vase, lime-gr pearlized, 9¼"	225.00
Wild Geese, vase, pk geese in wht-reverse decor, 9x12"	230.00
Wild Geese, vase, red pearlized, 9¼"	275.00
Wild Geese, vase, tan shadow on mg, oval, 9¼"	230.00
Wild Rose, lamp, brn shadow on mg, 10½"	150.00
Wild Rose, vase, amber, 10½"	175.00
Wild Rose, vase, frost on aqua wash, rare, 10½"	250.00
Wild Rose, vase, frost on rose wash, 10½"	175.00
Zodiac, vase, mg, no decor, 10½"	175.00
Zodiac, vase, pearlized on lt bl, 10½"	895.00

Phonographs

The phonograph, invented by Thomas Edison in 1877, was the first practical instrument for recording and reproducing sound. Sound wave vibrations were recorded on a tinfoil-covered cylinder and played back with a needle that ran along the grooves made from the recording, thus reproducing the sound. Very little changed about this art of record making until 1885, when the first replayable and removable wax cylinders were developed by the American Graphaphone Company. These records were made from 1885 until 1894 and are rare today. Edison began to offer musically recorded wax cylinders in 1889. They continued to be made until 1902. Today they are known as brown wax records. The first disc records and disc machines were offered by the inventor Berliner in 1894. They were sold in America until 1900, when the Victor company took over. In the 1890s, all machines played 7" diameter disc records; the 10" size was developed in 1901. By the early 1900s there existed many disc and cylinder phonograph companies, all offering their improvements. Among them were Berliner, Columbia, Zonophone, United States Phono, Wizard, Vitaphone, Amet, and others.

All Victor I's through VI's originally came with a choice of either brass bell, morning-glory, or wooden horns. Wood horns are the most valuable, adding $1,000.00 (or more) to the machine. Spring models were produced until 1929 (and even later). After 1929 most were electric (though some electric-motor models were produced as early as

1910.) Unless another condition is noted, prices are for complete, original phonographs in at least fine to excellent condition. Note: Edison coin-operated cylinder players start at $7,000.00 and may go up to $20,000.00 each. All outside-horn Victor phonographs are worth at **least** $1,000.00 or more, if in excellent original condition. Machines that are complete, still retaining all their original parts, and with the original finish still in good condition are the most sought after. Our advisor for this category is J.R. Wilkins; he is listed in the Directory under Texas. Unless noted, values are for examples in excellent condition, sold at popular, repeated buying prices.

Key:
cyl — cylinder   NP — nickel plated
mg — morning glory   rpd — reproducer

Aretino, disc, orig gr mg horn, 3" center spindle **750.00**
Berliner Trade Mark, disc, Clark-Johnson rpd, brass horn **5,000.00**
Bing Kiddyphone, disc, Bing rpd, cone horn, circular case **250.00**
Brunswick, cvd upright case w/moldings, lg **350.00**
Busy Bee Grand, disc, orig rpd, red mg horn, w/decal **700.00**
Cameraphone, disc, orig rpd, tortoise-shell resonator, oak **550.00**
Colibri, disc, box camera type, Colibri rpd, soundbox, w/case **350.00**
Columbia, BF Peerless, cyl, Lyric rpd, NP horn, M case **800.00**
Columbia AA, cyl, eagle rpd, blk horn, oak **1,000.00**
Columbia AB (McDonald), cyl, eagle rpd, brass horn, 2 mandrels ...**1,400.00**
Columbia AH, disc, Columbia rpd, brass bell horn, no decal ..**1,000.00**
Columbia AJ, disc, Columbia rpd, blk/brass bell horn, top crank ...**1,200.00**
Columbia AK, disc, orig rpd, brass bell horn, 7¼" turntable **800.00**
Columbia AO, cyl, D rpd, brass bell horn **500.00**
Columbia AZ, cyl, Lyric rpd, repro blk/brass horn **500.00**
Columbia BE Leader, cyl, Lyric rpd, mg, 6" mandrel, serpentine ...**650.00**
Columbia BI Sterling, disc, Columbia rpd, oak horn **2,250.00**
Columbia BK Jewel, cyl, Lyric rpd, orig horn, striping **450.00**
Columbia Grafonola, disc, orig rpd, inside horn, mahog, upright ..**200.00**
Columbia Grafonola Mignon, disc, inside horn, floor model **200.00**
Columbia K, disc, orig rpd, front mt **1,000.00**
Columbia P Premium, disc, orig rpd, red horn **625.00**
Columbia Q, cyl, Q rpd, repro cone horn, oak w/banner **350.00**
Columbia Q Busy Bee, cyl, D rpd, 14" blk cone horn, keywind ..**300.00**
Columbia Regent Desk, disc, Columbia rpd, inside horn, mahog ..**400.00**
Edison Amberola VI, cyl, Dmn B rpd/inside horn, oak table top ..**450.00**
Edison Amberola X, cyl, Dmn B rpd, inside horn, NM **400.00**
Edison Amberola 30, cyl, Dmn C rpd, inside horn, oak, NM **375.00**
Edison Concert, cyl, D rpd, brass horn/stand, 5" mandrel **2,500.00**
Edison Concert A, cyl, automatic, rpd, 36" brass horn, w/stand ..**3,000.00**
Edison Concert C, cyl, R rpd, 30" brass bell, floor stand, M **2,500.00**
Edison Dmn Disc A100, DD rpd, inside horn, Moderne golden oak ..**350.00**
Edison Dmn Disc B80, DD rpd, inside horn, table model **350.00**
Edison Dmn Disc S19, DD rpd, inside horn, oak, upright **250.00**
Edison Fireside A, cyl, Dmn B rpd, oak Music Master horn **2,250.00**
Edison Fireside A, cyl, K rpd, maroon horn/crane **1,000.00**
Edison Fireside B, cyl, Dmn B rpd, blk cygnet horn, 4-min **1,000.00**
Edison Gem D Maroon, cyl, K rpd, maroon Fireside horn, w/crane ..**1,800.00**
Edison Gem D Maroon, cyl, K rpd, 20" maroon horn **1,800.00**
Edison Gem E Maroon, cyl, all orig **2,000.00**
Edison Home, cyl, H rpd, metal cygnet horn, 2/4-min **675.00**
Edison Home A, cyl, C rpd, 14" blk/ brass horn, gr oak/banner ..**500.00**
Edison Home A Suitcase, cyl, C rpd, 14" repro horn, decal **550.00**
Edison Home E, cyl, O rpd, oak cygnet horn, oak case **1,800.00**
Edison Opera, cyl, Dmn A rpd, Music Master horn, mahog, rstr ..**5,000.00**
Edison Opera A, cyl, L rpd, mahog Music Master horn, mahog **5,000.00**
Edison Standard, cyl, C rpd, brass bell horn **475.00**
Edison Standard, cyl, Y rpd, brass bell horn, 2/4-min **400.00**
Edison Standard A Suitcase, cyl, old-style rpd, 14" brass bell **550.00**

Edison Standard C, cyl, C rpd, mg horn, repeating attachment ..**700.00**
Edison Standard D, cyl, K rpd, blk cygnet horn **1,000.00**
Edison Triumph, cyl, O rpd, oak cygnet horn, NM **2,500.00**
Edison Triumph, cyl, O rpd, wood cygnet, 2/4-min repeater ...**2,800.00**
Edison Triumph A, cyl, O rpd, Music Master cygnet, striping .**2,850.00**
Edison Triumph D, cyl, H rpd, 23" bell horn, 2/4-min **1,000.00**
Edison Triumph G, cyl, opera case **7,500.00**
Fern-O-Grand Baby Grand, disc, inside horn, piano shape **950.00**
Kalamazoo Duplex, disc, Kalamazoo rpd, 2 lg horns **3,300.00**
Klingsor, disc, Klingsor rpd, inside horn, stained glass doors ...**2,000.00**
Pathe Actuelle, disc, cone horn, mahog console **1,000.00**
Pathe Coq, cyl, ebonite rpd, aluminum horn, walnut cover **425.00**
Puck Lyre, cyl, floating rpd, sm Puck horn **450.00**
Regina Hexaphone #102, cyl, Hexaphone rpd, oak horn, rstr .**7,500.00**
Regina Hexaphone #103, cyl, Hexaphone rpd, oak horn, rstr .**7,500.00**
Regina Hexaphone #104, cyl, Hexaphone rpd, oak horn, rstr .**8,500.00**
Standard A, disc, Standard rpd, bl mg horn, decal **650.00**
Standard X, disc, Standard rpd, front mt brass bell w/support **600.00**
Thorens Excelda, disc, Excelda rpd, internal horn, camera type .**285.00**
United Symphony, disc, United rpd, inside horn, table model ...**250.00**
Victor I, disc, Exhibition rpd, repro brass bell, oak case **1,000.00**
Victor II, disc, Exhibition rpd, metal horn **1,200.00**
Victor II, disc, Exhibition rpd, oak horn & case **2,500.00**
Victor IV, disc, Exhibition rpd, mahog horn & case **2,200.00**
Victor M Monarch, disc, Exhibition rpd, 11" horn, oak/composite .**1,500.00**
Victor MS Monarch Specialty, disc, Exhibition rpd, oak horn .**2,500.00**
Victor R Royal, disc, Exhibition rpd, 9½" brass bell, oak **1,000.00**
Victor Schoolhouse XXV, disc, orig oak horn, oak, upright **3,000.00**
Victor Type Z, disc, Exhibition rpd, brass bell horn **1,400.00**
Victor VI, disc, Exhibition rpd, mahog horn & case **5,000.00**
Victor VV-VI, disc, Exhibition rpd, inside horn, oak, table top .**200.00**
Victor VV-X, disc, Exhibition rpd, inside horn, table top **500.00**
Victor VV-50, disc, #2 rpd, inside horn, oak, portable **150.00**
Victor VV-70, disc, #4 rpd, inside horn, table top **325.00**
Victor VV-8-30, disc, Orthophonic rpd, inside horn, credenza .**1,000.00**
Vitaphone, disc, w/horn, minimum value **1,000.00**
Zonophone, disc, front mt w/horn, from $1,000 to **3,000.00**
Zonophone A, disc, Concert rpd, brass horn, glass sides **2,500.00**
Zonophone Grand Opera, brass horn, rear mt **2,000.00**
Zonophone Parlor, disc, brass bell horn, rear crank **1,100.00**

Photographica

Photographic collectibles include not only the cameras and equipment used to 'freeze' special moments in time but also the photographic images produced by a great variety of processes that have evolved since the daguerrean era of the mid-1800s. For the most part, good quality images have either maintained or increased in value. Poor quality examples (regardless of rarity) are not selling well. Interest in cameras and stereo equipment is down, and dealers report that average-priced items that were moving well are often completely overlooked. Though rare items always have a market, collectors seem to be buying only if they are bargain priced.

Our advisor for this category is John Hess; he is listed in the Directory under Massachusetts.

Albumens

Manitou (town in CO Rockies), WH Jackson, 1880s, 4⅛x6⅝" **60.00**
Niguel Sheep Ranch Near San Luis Rey, titled, 1890, 5x8" **60.00**
Pebble Beach, Johnson, ca 1890, 5¼x8¼" **165.00**
Union soldier w/feather in cap, 8x10" **165.00**
Walnut Grove Dam view, Rothrock, ca 1889, 4½x7⅜" **250.00**

Ambrotypes

An ambrotype is a type of photograph produced by an early wet-plate process whereby a faint negative image on glass is seen as positive when held against a dark background.

Quarter plate, fireman, hand-colored, EX in case, $375.00.

4th plate, lady sits w/sm bouquet, sad appearance, +case 45.00
4th plate, man w/horse & carriage, tinted, 1850s, +leather case .350.00
6th plate, man seated bkwards in chair, ruby, +case 45.00
6th plate, 2 girls, identified 40.00
6th plate, 2 men seated in formal pose 50.00
9th plate, lady in blk cloak & gloves, +case 40.00
9th plate, man holding cased image 75.00
9th plate, military man, ruby ambro 35.00
9th plate, Union soldier seated, artillery insignia 125.00

Cabinet Photos

Artilleryman in 5-button sack coat, full view, 1880s 20.00
Barbershop scene w/3 Black barbers & 1 Black shoeshine boy 100.00
General store interior, well stocked shelves 25.00
Horse-drawn float, Stockton CA, 1905 ....45.00
Indian War soldier w/badge, mid-chest view, FL, VG 25.00
John G Owens, armless guitar player w/wife 125.00
Man on high-weel bicycle 20.00
Maude Granger, actress, hand-colored 35.00
Military camp scene, tinted, post-Civil War 75.00
Mining camp scene w/smelter 40.00
Nude woman bound w/rope to column, face hidden 200.00
Queen Victoria in later years, seated w/hands folded, VG 45.00
Sharpshooter w/medals, Western hat, long fur coat & cane 65.00
Sutherland sisters (7), ea w/extremely long hair, Pittsburgh 70.00
Threshing crew, Avery steam tractor 60.00
War Eagle (Indian) in full costume & blanket, 1898, 5x4" 50.00
West Point Cadet, chest view, Pach Bros NY, 1870s, VG 15.00

Cameras

Collecting antique cameras is very popular, and values have continued to move upward as the high-quality items have become harder to find. Most of the pre-1900 cameras will be found in the large format view cameras or studio camera types. There are quite a few of these that can be found in a well-worn condition, but there is a large difference in value between an average-wear item and an excellent or mint-condition camera. It is rare indeed to find one of these early cameras in mint condition.

The types of cameras are generally classified into large format, medium format, early folding and box types, 35 mm single-lens-reflex (SLR), 35mm rangefinders, twin-lens reflex (TLR), miniature or subminiature, novelty, and even a few others. Collectors may specialize in a type, a style, a time period, or even in high-quality examples of the same camera.

In the 1900 to 1940 period, large quantities of box cameras of various makes and folding bellows type cameras were produced by many manufacturers, and the popular 35mm camera was introduced in the 1930s. Most have low values because they were made in vast numbers, but mint-condition cameras are prized by collectors. In the 1930 to 1955 period, the 35mm rangefinders and the SLR's and TLR's became the cameras of choice. The most prized of these are the early German or Japanese rangefinders such as the Leica, Canon, or Nikon. Earlier, German optics were favored, but after WWII, Japanese cameras and optics rivaled and/or even exceeded the quality of many German optics.

Now there are thousands of different cameras to choose from, and collectors have many options when selecting categories. Quality is the major factor; values vary widely between an average-wear working camera and one in mint condition, or one still in the original box and unused. This brief list suggests average prices for good working cameras with average wear. The same camera in mint condition will be valued much higher, while one with excessive wear (scratches, dents, corrosion, poor optics, nonworking meters or rangefinders) may have little value.

Note: To date, no appreciable collector's market has developed for most old movie cameras or projectors. The Polaroid type of camera has little value, although a few models are gaining in popularity among collectors, and values are expected to increase. Note that there are many fakes and copies that have been made of several of the classic cameras such as the German Leica, and caution is advised in purchasing one of these cameras at a price too good to be true. Consult a specialist on high-priced classics if good reference material is not available. Our advisor for this category is Gene Cataldo; he is listed in the Directory under Alabama. (SASE required.)

Agfaflex, various models, from $50 to 100.00
Ansco Standard Speedex, f6.3 lens, 1950 ....15.00
Ansco Super Speedex, 75/3.5 lens, 1953-58 ....150.00
Anthony Climax Detective Camera, late 1880s 1,500.00
Asahi Pentax, orig 1957 ....275.00
Asahi Pentax Spotmatic, many models, from $50 to 150.00
Blair Baby Hawk-eye, 1897 box camera 300.00
Canon IIB, 1949-52 ....250.00
Canon III, 1952 ....275.00
Canon S, 1938-46 (usually Nikkor lenses), from $3,000 to 5,500.00
Conley, folding plate, many models, 1900-20, from $75 to 300.00
Eastman Baby Brownie, NY World's Fair, 1939 ....200.00
Eastman Baby Brownie Special, 1939-54 ....10.00
Eastman Beau Brownie, varied colors, 1930-33, from $50 to 150.00
Eastman Kodak Box, orig 1888-89 ....3,000.00
Eastman Kodak Jiffy models, from $10 to 20.00
Eastman Kodak No 2C Brownie Box, 1917-34 ....12.00
Eastman Kodak Premo, folding, many models, from $12 to 150.00
Eastman Kodak Retina, many models, Germany, from $35 to 550.00
Eastman No 1 Kodak, 1889-95 ....1,000.00
Exakta, German made, various models, 1933-78, from $50 to 800.00
FED, 35 mm, Russian made, various models, from $50 to 150.00
Graflex, many models, 1902-73, from $100 to 900.00
Konica Baby Pearl, folding cameras, 1934-46 ....125.00
Konica II, 35mm rangefinder, 1955 ....90.00
Leica II, 1932-48, from $250 to 350.00
Leica IIIa, 1935-50, from $200 to 275.00
Leica IIIf, 1950-56, from $250 to 500.00
Minolta, folding cameras, 1934, from $150 to 300.00
Minolta-35, rangefinder, several models, from $300 to 600.00
Minox, orig made in Riga, Latvia 800.00
Minox B, chrome, 1958-71 ....125.00
Minox II, made in Wetzlar, Germany 400.00
Nikon F, SLR, 1960s, from $150 to 250.00
Nikon I, 1948, from $5,000 to 10,000.00

Nikon S, 1951-54, from $300 to **600.00**
Olympus OM Series, many models, from $75 to **225.00**
Olympus Pen, half-fr, many models, from $50 to **125.00**
Olympus Six, prewar **175.00**
Olympus-35, many models, from $40 to **100.00**
Polaroid 195, w/Tominon f3.8 lens **200.00**
Polaroid 95, 1948-53, from $10 to **20.00**
Praktica FX, 1952 ....**45.00**
Praktica Nova, 1965 ....**50.00**
Rolleicord/Rolleiflex, many models, from $75 to **800.00**
Sears (Seroco, Marvel, Perfection, Towers & others), from $10 to ..**500.00**
Voigtlander Bessa, early folding cameras, 1931-50, from $30 to ...**50.00**
Voigtlander Bessamatic, 35mm, 1959 ....**135.00**
Voigtlander Vitessa L, 1954 ....**250.00**
Zeiss Contaflex Super, 1960 ....**120.00**
Zeiss Contax III, 1936-42 ....**250.00**
Zeiss Contessa-35, 1950 ....**175.00**
Zeiss Ikoflex 1a, TLR, 1953 ....**100.00**
Zeiss Ikonta A, folder, 1933-40 ....**80.00**

Carte De Visites

Among the many types of images collectible today are carte de visites, known as CDVs, which are 2¼" x 4" portraits printed on paper and produced in quantity. The CDV fad of the 1800s enticed the famous and the unknown alike to pose for these cards, which were circulated among the public to the extent that they became known as 'publics.' When the popularity of CDVs began to wane, a new fascination developed for the cabinet photo, a larger version measuring about 4½" x 6½". Note: A common portrait CDV is worth only about 50¢ unless it carries a revenue stamp on the back; those that do are valued at about $2.00 each.

Admiral Dot, 13 years old, 25" high, $20.00; Admiral Dot with Miss Minnie Warren and unknown gentleman, EX, $20.00.

Abraham Lincoln, 1860 beardless 'Cooper Union' pose, G, minimum **195.00**
Actress in Tyrolean dress & apron, long braids, Fredericks, NY ...**35.00**
Alice Nielson Scottish Soprano, Brady, 1870s **45.00**
Barnum midgets, beautifully dressed lady & w/2 men **50.00**
Benjamin Grotz Brown (Senator), Brady, EX **45.00**
Boxers (2) w/fists drawn, full view, 1870s, VG **35.00**
Boy w/dog, full view, MA **22.50**
Captain Gay, USA, bust view **65.00**
Cavalryman w/knee-high boots/gauntlets/forage cap **80.00**
Chinese lady w/long nails & bound ft, traditional dress ...**65.00**
Col SW Owens, asleep by tent, bottle nearby, Gardner, 1860s ..**300.00**
East Indian man in turban w/umbrella, London **22.00**
Empress Carlotta of Mexico, standing in beautiful gown ...**75.00**
Gentleman beside table w/books (unidentified), 1880s, 4¼x2½" .**15.00**
Herr Anton Rubenstein, ¾-profile, London **125.00**
Hunter w/slouch hat, dbl-bbl shotgun, Cooper, London ...**25.00**
Juan Roland & 2 daughters, Los Angeles, ca 1880, 3¾x2⅛" **60.00**
Lewis C Parmelee, Pvt Co H, 7th NY State Militia, standing **65.00**
Man w/pet goat, Civil War mt **55.00**
Mr Skinny Man & His Family, Eisenmann, NY, fading ...**22.00**

Murderer in chains (identified) **80.00**
President Andrew Johnson, photo of engraving **35.00**
President Lincoln w/wife & sons, photo of engraving **25.00**
Teenage girl w/kittens, dove on table, dog at ft, 1880s, VG **85.00**
Ulysses S Grant seated, Brady/Anthony, NM **125.00**
Union General George McClellan, full standing view **75.00**
Union General Robert Anderson, ¾-standing view **125.00**
Union General Winfield Scott, seated view, NY, G **55.00**
Union Major w/frock coat (unidentified), Bogardus, ¾-view **125.00**
Union Navy officer w/raincloth-covered hat, NY **50.00**

Daguerreotypes

Among the many processes used to produce photographic images are the daguerreotypes (made on a plate of chemically treated metal) — the most-valued examples being the 'whole' plate which measures 6½" x 8½". Other sizes include the 'half' plate, measuring 4½" x 5½", the 'quarter' plate at 3¼" x 4¼", the 'sixth' plate at 2¾" x 3¼", the 'ninth' at 2" x 2½", and the 'sixteenth' at 1⅜" x 1⅝". (Sizes may vary slightly, and some may have been altered by the photographer.)

4th plate, church & village green, 1850s, +patriotic case **1,200.00**
4th plate, family/horse/carriage/Greek Revival house, 1850s, +case ..**1,500.00**
6th plate, baby girl in chair, pleated dress, +case **40.00**
6th plate, boy seated w/book, tinted **85.00**
6th plate, lady in Gothic chair, pre-Civil war, +case **60.00**
9th plate, lady w/pearl necklace **30.00**

Photos

Photogravure, ES Curtis, Yokuts Basketry, 15½x11", +fr **550.00**
Sepia, dressing station of troops in Mesopotamia, ca 1915, 7x9" ..**20.00**
Sepia, Scots marching through town, Jordan, 1918, 7x9" **25.00**
Silver gelatin, CA farm w/olive grove, Waite, ca 1890, 5x8" **80.00**
Silver gelatin, family eating fruit, CA, ca 1910, 7½x9⅝" **75.00**
Silver gelatin, Ocean Park market int, ca 1910, 6x8⅜" **75.00**
Silver gelatin, President McKinley on 5th St, 1900, 7⅝x4½" **75.00**
Silver gelatin, storefront w/merchandise/13 figures, 1910, 6x8" ..**175.00**

Stereoscopic Views

Stereo cards are photos made to be viewed through a device called a stereoscope. The glass stereo plates of the mid-1800s and photo prints produced in the darkroom are among the most valuable. In evaluating stereo views, the subject, date, and condition are all-important. Some views were printed over a thirty- to forty-year period; 'first generation' prices are far higher than later copies, made on cheap card stock with reprints or lithographs, rather than actual original photographs.

It is relatively easy to date an American stereo view by the color of the mount that was used, the style of the corners, etc. From about 1854 until the early 1860s, cards were either white, cream-colored, or glossy gray; shades of yellow and a dull gray followed. While the dull gray was used for a very short time, the yellow tones continued in use until the late 1860s. Red, green, violet, or blue cards are from the period between 1865 until about 1870. Until the late '70s, corners were square; after that they were rounded off to prevent damage. Right now, quality stereo views are at a premium.

Atlantic City boardwalk & steel pier, Keystone, 1920s **10.00**
Black chiclren playing at station depot, 1896, Campbell **20.00**
Bret Harte w/book at table, flat mt **100.00**
Broadway on rainy day, flat mt **40.00**
Daybreak on Vimy Ridge, strewn bodies, April 9, 1917 ....**15.00**
Firing Line at Passchendale, British view, WWI era **10.00**

Japanese pontoon troops at Tokyo leaving for Manchuria, 1904 ..**10.00**
McKinley's Old Comrade Inauguration Parade, WA DC, w/100+ vets ...**15.00**
RR bridge destruction, red mt, Taylor & Huntington, post-Civil War ..**125.00**
Soldiers (5) & lady w/parasol by tents, ca 1870, flat mt, EX **20.00**
Soldiers Nat'l Cemetery VA, row after row of graves **10.00**
Theodore Roosevelt portrait in floral wreath, Keystone, VG **15.00**
Trossel's Barnyard Gettysburg, dead horses/etc, flat mt **175.00**
Troup D of Rough Riders on way to Cuba **22.00**
Union line before Petersburg, Taylor & Huntington, post-Civil War ..**120.00**

Tintypes

Tintypes, contemporaries of ambrotypes, were produced on japanned iron and were not as easily damaged.

Half plate, boy w/rock in hand, tinted **50.00**
4th plate, Corporal & Sergeant shaking hands, w/case **185.00**
4th plate, Union soldier w/musket, frock coat, EX in case **175.00**
6th plate, cadet w/forage cap w/A insignia, seated, w/case **120.00**
6th plate, Indian Wars musician w/kepi, lg horn, belt & bag **55.00**
6th plate, stagecoach w/driver & 16+ passengers **65.00**
6th plate, Union soldier in greatcoat, patriotic mat **85.00**
6th plate, Union soldier w/hands folded, gilt buttons/tinted **125.00**

Union Cases

From the mid-1850s until about 1880, cases designed to house these early images were produced from a material known as thermoplastic, a man-made material with an appearance much like gutta percha. Its innovator was Samuel Peck, who used shellac and wood fibers to create a composition he called Union. Peck was part owner of the Scoville Company, makers of both papier-mache and molded leather cases, and he used the company's existing dies to create his new line. Other companies (among them A.P. Critchlow & Company; Littlefield, Parsons & Company; and Holmes, Booth & Hayden) soon duplicated his material and produced their own designs. Today's collectors may refer to cases made of this material as 'thermoplastic,' 'composition,' or 'hard cases,' but the term most often used is 'Union.' It is incorrect to refer to them as gutta percha cases.

Sizes may vary somewhat, but generally a 'whole' plate case measures 7" x 9⅛" to the outside edges, a 'half' plate 4⅞" x 6", a 'quarter' plate 3¾" x 4¾", a 'sixth' 3⅛" x 3⅝", a 'ninth' 2⅜" x 2⅞", and a 'sixteenth' 1¾" x 2". Clifford and Michele Krainik and Carl Walvoord have written a book, *Union Cases*, which we recommend for further study. Another source of information is *Nineteenth Century Photographic Cases and Wall Frames* by Paul Berg. Values are for examples in excellent condition unless noted otherwise.

Half plate, The Wedding Procession, K-10, EX, $425.00.

Half plate, WA Monument, K-4, couple ambrotype **450.00**
16th plate, K-637, w/lady tintype **75.00**

16th plate, scroll, w/lady ambrotype, VG **45.00**
16th plate, spray of flowers, K-628, G **45.00**
4th plate, Parting of Hafed & Hinda, K-35, VG **200.00**
4th plate, Roger de Coverly & Gypsies, K-29, couple tintype, VG .**100.00**
4th plate, Union & Constitution, K-27, EX **150.00**
6th plate, Chess Players, man's portrait daguerreotype **175.00**
6th plate, Fireman Saving Child, K-118, EX **115.00**
6th plate, Geometric, K-224, w/2 tintypes **75.00**
6th plate, Geometric, K-226, w/lady daguerreotype, VG **125.00**
6th plate, roses, lilies & basket of flowers, K-203, VG **85.00**
6th plate, Shield, Crossed Cannon & Flags w/Liberty Cap, EX ..**175.00**
9th plate, American Gothic, K-374, EX **50.00**
9th plate, Chess Players, K-338, 2 children tintypes **75.00**
9th plate, Geometric, K-467, VG **55.00**
9th plate, patriotic theme, K-368, EX **85.00**
9th plate, Scroll, K-507, VG **60.00**
9th plate (dbl), Children w/Toys, R-29 ....**135.00**

Miscellaneous

Album, celluloid w/emb brass/celluloid, brass bound, 9x11" **50.00**
Album, Philippines WWII officer's, Army & local life, 178 photos ..**150.00**
Lantern slide, Indians w/masks, Riley & Riley, NY **10.00**
Magic lantern, pnt tin, kerosene lamp base, JS, EXIB **75.00**
Magic lantern, tin & CI, Ernst Plank, EX, +glass slides/wood box ..**100.00**
Magic lantern, tin & CI, kerosene lamp, glass slides, JS, 9", EXIB ..**100.00**
Stanhope, alabaster bbl, Niagara Falls scene **30.00**
Stanhope, binoculars, French Expo, EX **75.00**
Stanhope, cross, bone, WWI, troups in trenches, ca 1914, EX **50.00**
Stanhope, inkwell, ivory, chalet form, German views **50.00**
Stanhope, needle case, vegetal ivory, bathing scene **125.00**
Stanhope, pen, rhinestones, Lord's Prayer **45.00**
Stanhope, pipe, cvd wood, 4 Port Erin views, 1", EX **50.00**
Stanhope, pipe, rhinestones, Lord's Prayer **45.00**
Stanhope, ring, aluminum, nude **65.00**
Stanhope, ring, man's, 2 female nude views, EX **295.00**
Stanhope, tape measure, bbl form w/ivory finial, 1 view **65.00**
Stereopticon, aluminum/mahog, Monarch B Keystone 1904, from $35 to **45.00**
Stereopticon, aluminum/wood, Underwood/Underwood, 1901, from $35 to .**45.00**

Piano Babies

A familiar sight in Victorian parlors, piano babies languished atop shawl-covered pianos in a variety of poses: crawling, sitting, on their tummies, or on their backs playing with their toes. Some babies were nude and some wore gowns. Sizes ranged from about 3" up to 12". The most famous manufacturer of these bisque darlings was the Heubach Brothers of Germany, who nearly always marked their product; see Heubach for listings. Watch for reproductions. These guidelines are excerpted from one of a series of informative doll books by Pat Smith, published by Collector Books.

Blk, bsk, 4", EX quality **425.00**
Blk, bsk, 4", med quality **300.00**
Blk, bsk, 8", EX quality **525.00**
Blk, bsk, 8", med quality **375.00**
Blk, bsk, 12", EX quality **995.00**
Blk, bsk, 12", med quality **595.00**
Blk, bsk, 16", EX quality, minimum value **995.00**
Blk, bsk, 16", med quality **925.00**
Bsk, molded hair, unjtd, molded-on clothes, 4", EX quality **475.00**
Bsk, molded hair, unjtd, molded-on clothes, 4", med quality **225.00**
Bsk, molded hair, unjtd, molded-on clothes, 8", EX quality **895.00**

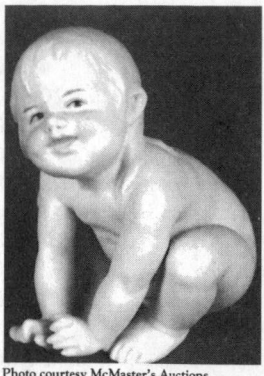

Bisque child with blue intaglio eyes, laughing open-closed mouth, molded and painted hair, crouched with hands in front of feet, nude, Gebruder Heubach, 6", $375.00.

Photo courtesy McMaster's Auctions

Bsk, molded hair, unjtd, molded-on clothes, 8", med quality **395.00**
Bsk, molded hair, unjtd, molded-on clothes, 12", EX quality **975.00**
Bsk, molded hair, unjtd, molded-on clothes, 15", med quality **525.00**
Bsk, w/animal/pot/flowers/etc, 4", EX quality **425.00**
Bsk, w/animal/pot/flowers/etc, 8", EX quality **550.00**
Bsk, w/animal/pot/flowers/etc, 12", EX quality **995.00**
Bsk, w/animal/pot/flowers/etc, 16", EX quality, minimum value **1,100.00**

Pickard

Founded in 1893 in Edgerton, Wisconsin, the Pickard China Company was originally a decorating studio, importing china blanks from European manufacturers. Some of these early pieces bear the name of those companies as well as Pickard's. Trained artists decorated the wares with hand-painted studies of fruit, florals, birds, and scenics and often signed their work. In 1915 Pickard introduced a line of 23k gold over a dainty floral-etched ground design. In the 1930s they began to experiment with the idea of making their own ware and by 1938 had succeeded in developing a formula for fine translucent china. Since 1976 they have issued an annual limited edition Christmas plate. They are now located in Antioch, Illinois.

The company has used various marks. The earliest (1893 – 1894) was a double-circle mark, 'Edgerton Hand Painted' with 'Pickard' in the center. Variations of the double-circle mark (with 'Hand Painted China' replacing the Edgerton designation) were employed until 1915, each differing enough that collectors can usually pinpoint the date of manufacture within five years. Later marks included the crown mark, 'Pickard' on a gold maple leaf, and the current mark, the lion and shield. Work signed by Challinor, Marker, and Yeschek is especially valued by today's collectors. For further information we recommend *Collector's Encyclopedia of Pickard China* by Alan B. Reed, available from Collector Books.

Charger, poppies on etched border, sgn F Walt, 1905-10 mk, 12¼" ..**275.00**
Chocolate pot, nasturtiums, E Challinor, 1903-05 mk, 6¼" **525.00**
Creamer & sugar bowl, apple blossoms on gr w/gold, w/lid, 1910 mk ...**225.00**
Cup & saucer, chocolate; Raised Gold Daisy, Haviland blank **60.00**
Cup & saucer, roses, yel & pk on yel w/gold, Blaha, 1898-1903 mk ..**135.00**
Mug, monk w/tankard & candle, Aldrich, 1898-1903 mk, 6" ...**300.00**
Pitcher, grapes on yel to maroon, Seidel, 1903-05 mk, 8" **400.00**
Pitcher, lemons, sgn Schoner, 1903-05 mk, 6¾" **450.00**
Pitcher, milk; irises, sgn Gibson, 1905-10, Limoges blank, 6½" ..**285.00**
Plate, chop; autumn foliage border, sgn EF, 1903-05, 12½" **275.00**
Plate, poppies, pk & wht, sgn Challinor, 8½" **145.00**
Plate, tulips, sgn Wight, 1905-10, Haviland blank, 8¾" **125.00**
Punch bowl, Strawberry Sprays, sgn LeRoy, 14" **2,200.00**
Shakers, Aura Linear Argenta, sgn H (Hiecke), pr **195.00**
Sugar shaker, turq & gold, 1910-12 mk, w/matching salt shakers ..**195.00**
Teapot, gold etch, +cr/sug **260.00**

Teapot, pk flower on wht w/gold, Wight, T&V blank, 1905-10, 7½" ..**100.00**
Vase, courting couple in garden w/gold, 7½" **195.00**
Vase, cow in pastoral scene, Aldrich, sm gold hdls, 1903-05 mk, 6" ..**750.00**
Vase, lilies on yel, sgn Schoner, waisted, 1905-10, 9" **215.00**

Pickle Castors

Pickle castors, which were both functional and decorative, became popular after the Civil War, reaching their peak about 1885. By 1900 they had virtually disappeared from factory catalogs. Numerous styles were available. They consisted of a decorated, silverplated frame that held either a fancy clear pressed-glass insert or one of decorated colored art glass — the latter being popular in the more affluent Victorian households and more desirable with collectors today.

In the listings below, the description prior to the semicolon refers to the jar (insert), and the remainder of the line describes the frame. Unless a color is mentioned, all glassware is clear. When no condition is indicated, the silverplate is assumed to be in very good to excellent condition; glass jars are assumed near-mint. Our advisor for this category is Deborah Maggard; she is listed in the Directory under Ohio.

Warning: Watch for reproduction frames from Taiwan!

Key: rsl — resilvered

Rubena crystal, ornate quadruple plated Derby frame, 11" to top of handle, $725.00.

Photo courtesy John A. Shuman III

Bead & Drape, red satin; ftd SP fr, +tongs **395.00**
Bl satin w/enameling, egg shape; Tufts rsl fr **550.00**
Bl satin w/floral; ornate Rogers stand on 4 legs, 11", +tongs **875.00**
Bull's Eye, icicle trim, Hobnail bands, 4"; fr, +tongs **275.00**
Cane & Rosette; rstr fr **175.00**
Cane; ornate ftd SP fr **350.00**
Cobalt w/florals & gold; rsl Benedict fr, 10½" **500.00**
Cone, pk satin cased, rstr Tufts SP fr **450.00**
Cranberry, Invt T'print, HP florals; orig SP fr, 9½" **295.00**
Cranberry w/HP florals, ribbed egg shape; ornate Meriden fr, 9" ...**450.00**
Cranberry w/HP windmill & foliage; Pairpoint SP fr **450.00**
Cranberry w/mc floral; ornate Tufts fr, +tongs **450.00**
Crown Milano, florals on Hobnail; Pairpoint fr, 9", +tongs **1,500.00**
Cupid & Venus; SP fr **295.00**
Daisy & Button, canary; bird finial, scroll-top fr, +tongs **350.00**
Dmn Point, honey amber; Forbes SP fr, +tongs **225.00**
Dmn Quilt, cranberry, emb ivy border; rstr Middletown fr, +fork ...**315.00**
Florette, pk; rstr Tufts fr **400.00**
Herringbone, frosted wht to pk; Rogers sq ruffled fr, +tongs **695.00**
Invt Baby T'print, cranberry w/floral; mk fr w/lg C-hdl to side ...**600.00**
Invt T'print, cranberry, gold butterfly, etc; Meriden fr **550.00**
Invt T'print, cranberry w/coralene beading; ornate fr **675.00**
Invt T'print, cranberry w/floral; ornate C-shape mt, +tongs **650.00**
Invt T'print, cranberry w/gold; Barbour SP fr, +tongs **495.00**

Invt T'print, cranberry; SP fr, +tongs 400.00
Invt T'print, red, 4"; emb florals on base/lid of fr, +tongs 600.00
Invt T'print, sapphire bl w/mc floral; orig SP fr, +tongs 600.00
MOP Dmn Quilt, pk, 4"; branch/ivy vine fr mk Hartford, 9¾" ..600.00
MOP Raindrop, wht to pk; Simpson Hall Miller fr, 12" 1,395.00
Optic Rib, cranberry w/daisies; SP fr 395.00
Peachblow, ovoid, 4¼"; rope/floral-hdl fr, 9¾", +tongs 875.00
Peachblow w/floral; birds on base of fr, ornate finial, 9" 600.00
Ribbed Pillar, frosted pk spatter, Northwood; orig SP fr 450.00
Shell & Seaweed, pk cased, HP floral; Aurora fr, 9½" 1,150.00
Swirled Windows, bl opal; orig rsl fr, +tongs 365.00
Torquay, pigeon blood; orig SP fr 350.00
Wht satin, HP rose apple blossoms; rstr fr 325.00

Pierce, Howard

Collectors of Howard Pierce's work have witnessed new trends and higher prices this year. Values are topping the scales on almost all his work, due in part, perhaps, because of his death on February 28, 1994. Pierce designed a line of pins which he first produced in 1941. The originals were in pewter, but a short time later, he made them in a copper finish. Some painted pins and figurines were created as well. These items bear the early 'Howard Pierce' mark. While most researchers believed just last year that examples of this jewelry would be in the $100.00 to $175.00 range, dealers and collectors thought differently; and it has not been uncommon to find the gavel dropping at about $200.00 for most examples. (If any pin is more plentiful than any other, it would be the lamb.) Almost all animals have seen a substantial rise in value. The vases with bisque inserts, even though they have increased about 10% over last year's values, have not seen the growth one would expect, given that few were produced.

Howard Pierce and his wife Ellen (Van Voorhis) opened his Claremont, California, studio in 1941, where they worked side by side. Howard was one of few artists who attempted to work with so many varied materials: Polyurethant, Wedgwood-type Jasperware, ash from Mt. St. Helens' eruption, gold leaf and a gold leaf-type (the latter being created for Sears, Roebuck & Company), rough-textured as well as high-gloss porcelain, cement, pewter, copper, aluminum, bronze, and hydrocal.

Pierce had ambivalent feelings about experimental glazes. He tested glazes on a large scale, especially during the later years of his career, but most of the time he did not like what he had created. Today's collectors actively seek them out. Some of these glazes are deep purple, pale blue, iridescent pink, green, and a very dark cobalt that sometimes appears ebony in recessed details. Scratched-in numbers sometimes found on these items correspond to Howard's formula book. Howard preferred gray, white, or brown glazes. Though he liked the leopards and tigers with hand-painted stripes and spots, because they were so time consuming, less than a dozen of each were ever produced. His porcelain angels, though popular sellers (especially those with Black faces), also had a short production run, due to the fact that their wings were often damaged in the kiln.

Because of his poor health, in 1992 Howard and Ellen destroyed all the molds they had ever created. Still the artist in Howard needed to create, so in 1993 (only a year before he died) they purchased a small kiln and began making miniature versions of their original products. These pieces are simply stamped 'Pierce.' Some collectors are speculating that in a short time, these miniature pieces will be more costly than their larger counterparts, since their production time was so limited.

For further information we recommend *Collector's Encyclopedia of Howard Pierce Porcelain* by Darlene Hurst Dommell (Collector Books). Our advisor for this category is Susan Cox; she is listed in the Directory under California.

Bank, turtle figural, blk gloss w/gr gloss shell, 3x8" 175.00
Bowl, bl w/teal, fluted, 4½x7" 145.00
Candle holders, comma shapes, gray speckled, 2¾", pr 115.00
Figurine, angels, wht w/Black faces, 3¾" to 5¾", 3-pc set 300.00
Figurine, angels, wht w/wht faces, 3¾" to 5¾", 3-pc set 200.00
Figurine, bear cub, head up, brn hi-gloss, 4¾x5¾" 65.00
Figurine, birds (3) on raised branch, bl, mk, 4x7" 120.00
Figurine, circus horse on base, bl, 6¼x7½" 215.00
Figurine, coyote, lava glaze, 5¾x2¾" 125.00
Figurine, dachshund, stylized, brn gloss, 3¼x10" 135.00
Figurine, frog, lt/dk gr, mk Howard Pierce Porcelains, 5" 145.00
Figurine, gazelle head, mk Howard Pierce, rare, 16½x5" 325.00
Figurine, giraffe, short legs, stylized, brn, 10x4" 95.00
Figurine, girl w/dog on base, mk, 4½x3¼" 135.00
Figurine, hippo, volcanic glaze, mk St Helens, 6½" 135.00
Figurine, owl in tree, gray gloss, sm Pierce mk, 1993-94 pc, 5¼" ..38.00
Figurine, pelican, bill away from body, brn-wht, 8½x6" 155.00
Figurine, porcupine, blk-wht, rare, 4½x6" 165.00
Figurine, raccoon, textured brn, 5x5¼" 175.00
Figurine, tiger w/HP stripes, rare, 12" 550.00
Magnet, turtle, bl, 2¼" 95.00
Pin, crane, pewter, mk, 4" 195.00
Sign, gold leaf, Howard at top, Pierce below, rare, 5½" 300.00
Sign, Howard Pierce in script on tree bark, Porcelain in block, 6" .225.00
Vase, deer & tree on blk base, 7½x5" 145.00

Pigeon Blood

Pigeon blood glass, produced in the late 1800s, may be distinguished from other dark red glass by its distinctive orange tint.

Biscuit jar, Florette, metal lid 325.00
Biscuit jar, melon ribbed, SP mts, 7" 400.00

Biscuit jar, Torquay, 11", $375.00.

Bowl, Venecia, w/floral decor, 8½" 125.00
Bride's basket, ruffled; SP fr 650.00
Butter dish, Torquay 225.00
Creamer, arched ribs, clear hdl, 4½" 260.00
Pitcher, water; Bulging Loops 425.00
Pitcher, water; Torquay, metal rim & hdl 425.00
Spooner 150.00
Syrup, Globule, glossy 1,150.00
Tumbler, Bulging Loops 95.00
Vase, gold vines/leaves, bulbous w/4-scallop top, 4¾x4½" 145.00

Pilkington

Founded in 1892 in Manchester, England, the Pilkington pottery experimented in wonderful lustre glazes that were so successful that when they were displayed at exhibition in 1904, they were met with critical acclaim. They soon attracted some of the best ceramic technicians and designers of the day who decorated the lustre ground with flowers, animals, and trees; some pieces were more elaborate with scenes of sailing ships and knights on horseback. Each artist signed his work with his personal monogram. Most pieces were dated and carried the company mark as well. After 1913 the company became known as Royal Lancastrian.

Their Lapis Ware line was introduced in the late 1920s, featuring intermingling tones of color under a matt glaze. Some pieces were very simply decorated while others were painted with designs of stylized leafage, scrolls, swirls, and stripes. The line continued into the '30s. Other pieces of this period were molded and carved with animals, leaves, etc., some of which were reminiscent of their earlier wares.

The company closed in 1938 but reopened in 1948. During this period their mark was a simple P within the outline of a petaled flower shape. Our advisor for this category is David Ehrhard; he is listed in the Directory under California.

Bookends, dolphins, 5½", pr 350.00
Bowl, Lapis, Wm S Mycock, geometric design 225.00
Bowl, stylized mc shamrocks, 3 closed hdls, 2x4½" 325.00
Tile, broad leaves, silver on red irid, 6x3" +oak fr 400.00
Vase, floral, yel on bl irid, wht leaf band, 1920, 4¾x5¼" 435.00
Vase, gold lustre w/mc highlights, long bottle neck, 7" 350.00
Vase, gr & bl mottled matt, mks, 5" 80.00
Vase, Lapis, GM Rogers, bulbous, bold design 195.00
Vase, lt gr/lt bl flambe froth, #2462, 8½x5½" 150.00
Vase, orange matt, 6" 160.00
Vase, stylized upright feathers, blk on orange/yel, 13x6½" 900.00

Pillin

Polia Pillin was born in Poland in 1909. She came to the U.S. as a teenager and showed an interest and talent for art which she studied in Chicago. She married William Pillin, who was a poet and potter. They ultimately combined their talents and produced her very distinctive pottery from the 1950s to the mid-1980s. She died in 1993.

Polia Pillin won many prizes for her work, which is always signed Pillin with the loop of the 'P' over the full name. Some undecorated pieces are signed W&P, due to her husband's collaboration.

Her work is prized for its art, not for the shape of her pots, which for the most part are simple vases, dishes, bowl, and boxes. Wall plaques are rare. She pictured women with hair reminiscent of halos, girls, an occasional boy, horses, birds, and fish. After viewing a few of her pieces, her style is unmistakable. Some of her early work is very much like that of Picasso.

Her pieces are somewhat difficult to find, as all the work was done without outside help, and therefore limited in quantity. In the last few years, more and more people have become interested in her work, resulting in escalating prices. Our advisors for this category are Dolli and Wilfred Cohen; they are listed in the Directory under California.

Bowl, lady w/2 cats on wht, irregular shape, 2¾x8" 550.00
Box, lady w/bird, mc on gr & brn, 2x4" dia 375.00
Bust, lady w/2 stylized birds, mc 425.00
Covered dish, lady w/mandolin, mc on shaded bl, 2x4" dia 375.00
Dish, 2 dancing harlequins on brn, 6" dia 350.00
Jug, blistered yel/brn gloss, sgn, 7¾x5" 350.00
Plate, lady & bird, 7¾" 850.00
Vase, abstract figure on all 4 sides, 11½x3¾" 975.00
Vase, birds, mc, 5" 595.00

Vase, dancing women, mc on mottled pk & yel, 7½" 750.00
Vase, dbl portraits of girls & rooster on dk yel, pinched, 5" 450.00
Vase, dk gr/bl crystalline, 1950s, 9¾" 250.00
Vase, gr/olive matt texture, wide gourd w/tiny neck, 13" 375.00
Vase, horse & 2 ladies, wht on peacock & rust, 9x7" 850.00
Vase, horses, lady w/balloons, mc on bl, can form, 4½" 495.00
Vase, horses, mc on wht to brn, pear form, 6" 550.00
Vase, horses, 2 frolicking, mk, 4¾" 450.00
Vase, ladies, mc on bl, rectangular, 9", NM 850.00
Vase, ladies (2 full length) mc on yel/brn, slim form, 15" 1,500.00
Vase, ladies (2) seining for fish, bulbous, 4¼" 475.00
Vase, lady & horse, 6" 625.00
Vase, lady w/bird, 2 ladies dance, mc on bl, 4½x5" 495.00
Vase, lady w/birds, ball form, 6" 550.00
Vase, lt to dk brn crystalline, bulbous w/can neck, 8½" 270.00
Vase, lt to dk gr gloss, bulbous w/sm opening, 6½" 200.00
Vase, nudes, 6" 750.00
Vase, Oriental-look bl & gr gloss w/red highlights, 11½x12" 1,000.00
Vase, rooster on bl, cylindrical, 7" 495.00
Vase, scarlet flambe gloss, spherical w/short neck, 9½x7" 425.00
Wine cup, rooster, gr w/mc, 2½" 325.00

Pin-Back Buttons

Buttons produced up to the early 1920s were made of a celluloid covering held in place by a ring (or collet) to the back of which a pin was secured. Manufacturers used these 'cellos' to advertise their products. Many were of exceptional quality in both color and design. Buttons were produced in sets featuring a variety of subjects. These were given away by tobacco, chewing gum, and candy manufacturers, who often packed them with their product as premiums. Usually the name of the button maker or the product manufacturer was printed on a paper placed in the back of the button. Often these 'back papers' are still in place today. Much of the time the button maker's name was printed on the button's perimeter, and sometimes the copyright was added. Beginning in the 1920s, a large number of buttons were lithographed on tin; these are referred to as tin 'lithos.' Nearly all pin-back buttons are collected today for their advertising appeal or graphic design. There are countless categories to base a collection on.

The following listing contains non-political buttons representative of the many varieties you may find. Our advisor for this category is Michael J. McQuillen; he is listed in the Directory under Indiana.

UMW of A – 8 Hours, red, white, and blue cello, early style, 1¾", VG-, $25.00.

Aunt Jemima Breakfast Club, Eat A Better Breakfast, 1950s, 4", M ..35.00
Barnet Lightning Rods, cello, 1¼", VG 80.00
Cadillac 30, 1911, $1700, blk/yel on wht, 1½", EX 690.00
Captain Marvel, litho, 1950s, ⅞", EX 50.00
Cycol, The Navy Uses., wht/red/gr, 2" dia, NM 185.00
Dennis the Menace, 1960s, ⅞", M 22.00
DuPont Smokeless Powder, cello, 1¼", VG 100.00
Elmore, 1907 auto, sepia, 1" dia, EX 635.00

Esso, Dr Seuss, 1950s, 1¼", EX	65.00
Esso, Santa, 1950s, 1¼", EX	35.00
Hupmobile, 1911 auto/Memphis dealer, oval, EX	750.00
Indian Motorcycle Agent, Indian profile, mc, 1¼", EX	880.00
Nat'l Matches Camp, Perry OH, cello, 1941, lg	29.00
New Haven RR Club, cello, oval, 1970s, 1¼"	4.00
Oliver Chilled Plows, cello, 1¼", EX	70.00
Peters Shells, cello, ⅞", EX	65.00
Quality Sausage, 3 Little Pigs, tin litho, 1¼", VG	65.00
Sampson Windmills, cello, 1¾", EX	65.00
Seven-Up, enameled, 1950s, EX	30.00
Shmoo, metal, hallmk, 1960s, 1", EX	27.00
Smokey Bear, Join Smokey's Campaign, Prevent., 1960s, 1", M	20.00
St Louis Browns, w/ball & glove, ⅞" litho, EX	35.00
The White, early buggy-type auto, sepia, 1¼", G	745.00
1910 Detroit Electric, image of auto, 1¼" dia, EX	690.00

Pink Lustre Ware

Pink lustre was produced by nearly every potter in the Staffordshire district in the late 18th and first half of the 19th centuries. The application of gold lustre on white or light-colored backgrounds produced pinks, while the same over dark colors developed copper. The wares ranged from hand-painted plaques to transfer-printed dinnerware. Design features in the phrase immediately following the item (i.e. cup, plate, etc.) are in pink lustre unless otherwise specifically described within the line.

Pitcher, classical figures, enamel and purple lustre, England, ca 1825, restored, 9¼", $250.00.

Compote, man gives children food/He That Refuseth, 4x5", EX	65.00
Creamer & sugar bowl, wide band w/floral, ribbed, 5", 5¾"	90.00
Cup & saucer, girl & cat, pk transfer w/mc, line	65.00
Cup & saucer, goat & cherub transfer, blk w/mc, NM	60.00
Cup & saucer, House pattern on wide band, lg	100.00
Cup & saucer, Picket Fence reserve	100.00
Cup plate, House pattern, 4" dia	50.00
Desk set, Greek Key borders, tray & 3 covered pots, 1810s	650.00
Jug, commemorative; Princess Charlott/Prince Leopold, 6"	375.00
Mug, House pattern, emb basketweave, fluted band, 3¾"	180.00
Pitcher, HP florals, 1820s, 8¼"	525.00
Pitcher, mc oval reserves/sailing ship, pearlware, 9½", NM	675.00
Plaque, Queen Caroline, rectangle, 1820s, 4½x5¼"	375.00
Sugar bowl, purple transfer genre scene, hdls, w/lid, 4½"	45.00

Pink Paw Bears

These charming figural pieces are very similar to the Pink Pigs described in the following category. They were made in Germany dur-ing the same time frame. The cabbage green is identical; the bears themselves are whitish-gray with pink foot pads. You'll find some that are unmarked while others are marked 'Germany' or 'Made in Germany.' In theory, the unmarked bears are the oldest, made prior to 1890 when the McKinley Tariff Act required imports to be marked with the country of origin. Those marked 'Made In' were probably produced after the revision of the Act in 1914.

1 by bean pot	135.00
1 by graphophone	150.00
1 by honey pot	145.00
1 by top hat	125.00
1 in front of basket	135.00
1 in roadster (car identical to pk pig car)	185.00
1 on binoculars	150.00
1 peaking out of basket	135.00
1 sitting in wicker chair	150.00
2 in hot air balloon	150.00
2 in purse	165.00
2 in roadster	165.00
2 on pin dish	120.00
2 on pin dish w/bag of coins	145.00
2 peering in floor mirror	150.00
2 sitting by mushroom	125.00
2 standing in wash tub	135.00
3 in roadster	190.00
3 on pin dish	145.00

Pink Pigs

Pink Pigs on cabbage green were made in Germany around the turn of the century. They were sold as souvenirs in train depots, amusement parks, and gift shops. 'Action pigs' (those involved in some amusing activity) are the most valuable, and prices increase with the number of pigs. Though a similar type of figurine was made in white bisque, most serious collectors prefer only the pink ones. They are marked in two ways: 'Germany' in incised letters, and a black ink stamp 'Made in Germany' in a circle. The unmarked pigs are the oldest, made prior to 1890 when the McKinley Tariff Act required imports to be marked with the country of origin. Those marked 'Made In' were probably produced after the revision of the Act in 1914.

One in green suitcase bank, gold trim, $110.00.

1 beside gr drum, wall-mt match holder	95.00
1 beside purse	75.00
1 beside shoe	75.00
1 beside stump, camera around neck, toothpick holder	145.00
1 beside wastebasket	75.00
1 coming out of cup	95.00
1 coming out of suitcase	95.00

1 coming through gr fence, post at sides, open for flowers **95.00**
1 driving touring car **165.00**
1 going through purse **90.00**
1 holding cup by fence **140.00**
1 in case looking through binoculars **145.00**
1 in gr Dutch shoe **75.00**
1 in Japanese submarine, Japan imp on both sides **125.00**
1 in money sack bank **85.00**
1 in roadster **145.00**
1 lg pig sitting behind 3" trough **95.00**
1 on binoculars **135.00**
1 on binoculars, gold trim **150.00**
1 on chair **110.00**
1 on gr trinket dish, leg caught in lobster claw **110.00**
1 on horseshoe-shaped dish w/raised 4-leaf clover **95.00**
1 on keg playing piano **150.00**
1 on shoulder of gr ink bottle **115.00**
1 playing accordion on side of tray, wht bear ea side **150.00**
1 pushing head through wooden gate **95.00**
1 putting letter in mailbox **110.00**
1 reclining on horseshoe ashtray **85.00**
1 riding train, 4½" **165.00**
1 sits, holds orange Boston Baked Beans pot match holder **125.00**
1 sits by high-top boot **110.00**
1 sitting in bathtub **135.00**
1 sitting on log, mk Germany **110.00**
1 standing in front of cracked open egg **95.00**
1 standing in gr tub **95.00**
1 w/attached toothpick holder **75.00**
1 w/front ft in 3-part dish containing 3 dice, 1 ft on dice **125.00**
1 w/tennis racket stands beside vase, Lawn Tennis, 3¾" **125.00**
1 wearing chef's costume, holds frypan, w/basket **125.00**
2, mother & baby in bl blanket in tub, rabbit on board atop **110.00**
2, mother in tub gives baby a bottle, lamb looks on, 4x3½" **125.00**
2, 1 at telephone booth, 1 inside, 4½" **125.00**
2 at confession, 4½" **110.00**
2 at wishing well **110.00**
2 behind trough, unmk **95.00**
2 by eggshell **95.00**
2 dancing, in top hat, tux & cane **135.00**
2 in basket, Merry Squeelers, 3½x3" **135.00**
2 in bed, Good Night on footboard, 4x3x2½" **145.00**
2 in carriage **125.00**
2 in open car **150.00**
2 in open trunk, 3¾" **125.00**
2 on basket, head raising lid, plaque on front **110.00**
2 on cotton bale, 1 peers from hole, 1 over top **135.00**
2 on seesaw on top of pouch bank **125.00**
2 on top hat **125.00**
2 on tray hugging, 3x4½" **125.00**
2 sitting at table playing card game 'Hearts' **170.00**
2 under toadstool **125.00**
3, 1 on lg slipper playing banjo, 2 dancing on side **165.00**
3, 2 sit in front of coal bucket, 3rd inside **125.00**
3 at trough, 4½" L **98.00**
3 dressed up on edge of dish **125.00**
3 sm pigs behind oval trough, mk, 2¾x2½x1¾" **95.00**
3 w/baby carriage, father & 2 babies, Wheeling His Own **125.00**
3 w/carriage, mother & 2 babies, Germany **125.00**

Pisgah Forest

The Pisgah Forest Pottery was established in 1920 near Mount Pis-

gah in Arden, North Carolina, by Walter B. Stephen, who had worked in previous years at other locations in the state — Nonconnah and Skyland (the latter from 1913 until 1916). Stephen, who was born in the mountain region near Asheville, was known for his work in the Southern tradition. He produced skillfully executed wares exhibiting an amazing variety of techniques. He operated his business with only two helpers. Recognized today as his most outstanding accomplishment, his Cameo line was decorated by hand in the pate-sur-pate style (similar to Wedgwood Jasper) in such designs as Fiddler and Dog, Spinning Wheel, Covered Wagon, Buffalo Hunt, Mountain Cabin, Square Dancers, Indian Campfire, and Plowman. Stephen is known for other types of wares as well. His crystalline glaze is highly regarded by today's collectors.

At least nine different stamps mark his wares, several of which contain the outline of the potter at the wheel and 'Pisgah Forest.' Cameo is sometimes marked with a circle containing the line name and 'Long Pine, Arden, NC.' Two other marks may be more difficult to recognize: 1) a circle containing the outline of a pine tree, 'N.C.' to the left of the trunk and 'Pine Tree' on the other side; and 2) the letter 'P' with short uprights in the middle of the top and lower curves. Stephen died in 1961, but the work was continued by his associates. Our advisor for this category is R.J. Sayers; he is listed in the Directory under North Carolina.

Ginger jar, Oxblood, stylized hdls, w/lid, mk, ca 1931, 6½" **300.00**
Mug, Cameo, fiddler & dog, wht on gr, 1949 Stephen, 3½" **200.00**

Mug, Cameo, clog dancers, ivory on blue, Walter Stephen, marked on base, 3⅜", $165.00.

Teapot, Cameo, wagon on prairie, wht on bl, porc, 1949 Stephen, 4⅜" ..**650.00**
Vase, Aubergine-wine, low & wide, Stephen, ca 194?, 3½" **60.00**
Vase, Augergine-wine, Ku shape, #47, Stephen, ca 1947, 5¾" ...**100.00**
Vase, bl shoulder transitioning to purple, 7x5½" **115.00**
Vase, bl to purple, ovoid, 5½x7" **110.00**
Vase, brn/purple flambe, bulbous, 1925, 6x6½" **475.00**
Vase, Cameo, masonic symbols/dedications, wht on med bl, 7x5½" ...**400.00**
Vase, Cameo, wagon scene, wht on pk can neck, gr below, 4½" ...**200.00**
Vase, Cameo, wagon train band on moss gr, 1963, 4x4" **300.00**
Vase, crystalline, bl & wht on celadon flambe, stilt pull, 5x7" ...**300.00**
Vase, crystalline, bl & wht on cream/moss flambe, mfg chip, 7½" ..**375.00**
Vase, crystalline, bl-gr, waisted neck, 1936, 6x4¼" **300.00**
Vase, crystalline, bl/gr/wht, classic shape, 1949, 8x5" **500.00**
Vase, crystalline, celadon, 1936, 8x6½", EX **600.00**
Vase, crystallinc, ccladon/caramel, 8x5¾" **300.00**
Vase, crystalline, celadon/mauve/ivory, classic shape, 10" **800.00**
Vase, crystalline, cream & camel, Oriental style, 1950s, 5⅝" **375.00**
Vase, crystalline, gr on speckled oatmeal, 1935, 9x5½" **690.00**
Vase, crystalline, gr/red lustre, bulbous, 1938, 6x4½" **500.00**
Vase, crystalline, wht w/silver & some bl, pk int, Stephen, 4x6" ..**375.00**
Vase, crystalline, wht w/some bl, pk int, Stephen, 1953, 4x6" **375.00**
Vase, crystalline, wht/sky bl/camel, Ku shape, #47, Stephen, 5¾" ..**375.00**
Vase, Dogwood Blossom, N Jones, triangle mk, ca 1939, 5" **300.00**
Vase, turq crackle w/pk int, 6½", pr **125.00**

Pittsburgh Glass

As early as 1797, utility window glass and hollow ware were being produced in the Pittsburgh area. Coal had been found in abundance, and it was there that it was first used instead of wood to fuel the glass furnaces. Because of this, as many as 150 glass companies operated there at one time. However, most failed due to the economically disastrous effects of the War of 1812. By the mid-1850s those that remained were producing a wide range of flint glass items including pattern-molded and free-blown glass, cut and engraved wares, and pressed tableware patterns. Our advisor for this category is Mark Vuono; he is listed in the Directory under Connecticut.

Bottle, bar; dk amethyst, 8-Rib Pillar mold, marble stopper 3,250.00
Candlestick, Pillar mold, bulbous hollow stem, 10⅛" 2,000.00
Candlesticks, cobalt, hexagonal, pewter inserts, chip, 9", pr ...1,870.00
Candlesticks, fiery opal/bl opaque, dolphin base, pontil, 6", pr ..7,800.00
Celery vase, cut strawberry/dmns fans, foliate rim, knop stem, 8" .140.00
Compote, cut floral, 8 panels, reverse baluster stem, 5x4¾" 330.00
Compote, cut Gothic arches/waffles/fans, stepped ft, 7x8" 330.00
Compote, cut strawberry dmns/sawtooth/rays/fans, ftd, 8x8¾" ...500.00
Compote, cut strawberry/dmns/fans, knop stem, appl ft, 6x8½" .195.00
Compote, fiery opal loop bowl, clear baluster stem/ft, 4⅜x6" ..1,870.00
Compote, hollow baluster stem, folded lip w/eng vintage, 6x6½" .85.00
Compote, Pillar mold, appl ft & bowl, rough finial, 12½" 1,265.00
Creamer & sugar bowl, Pillar mold, 4" & 4x4¾" 250.00
Cruet, Pillar mold, appl ft, hollow hdl, pewter hinged lid, 10½" ...525.00
Decanter, blown, wheel-eng eagle w/shield, appl rings, 8½" 1,430.00
Decanter, cut panels & fans, appl ft & rings, w/stopper, 8½" 125.00
Jar, Pillar mold, wide ft, baluster stem, 8-rib, w/lid, 17¾" 1,265.00
Pitcher, appl ft, hollow hdl, tooled lip, 7½" 250.00
Pitcher, appl ring, hollow hdl, 8⅜" 385.00
Pitcher, cobalt, hollow hdl, tooled lip, 7¾" 4,180.00
Pitcher, Pillar mold, appl hdl, sm open blister, 6½" 415.00

Sugar bowl, Pillar mold, dome lid, pontiled base, ca 1850, 10½", EX, $550.00.

Sugar bowl, cobalt, 12 vertical ribs, pontil, 7⅛" 5,750.00
Sugar bowl, strawberry dmns/roundels/rays, ftd, w/lid 2,500.00
Sugar bowl, wheel-eng flowers/floliage, ftd, eng lid, 8" 2,475.00
Sugar bowl, 12-rib, tam-type finial, solid base, 1825-40, 7⅜" 500.00
Tumbler, golden honey-amber, 6-sided, pontil, 3½" 450.00
Vase, appl ft w/cut star, knob stem, cut panels in bowl, 8" 250.00
Vase, Pillar mold & drapery swags, hourglass stem, 10¼" 360.00

Plastics

The term 'collectible plastics' is defined as those types produced between 1868 (when synthetic plastics were invented) and the period immediately following WWII. There are several, and we shall mention each one and attempt briefly to acquaint you with their characteristics:

1) Pyroxylin (Celluloid, Loalin, French Ivory, Pyralin). Chemical name: cellulose nitrate. Earliest form, invented in 1868 by John Wesley Hyatt; highly flammable; yellows with age; much used in toiletry articles. Fairly lightweight, many articles of pyroxylin were made by heating and molding thin sheets.

2) Cellulose Acetate (Tenite, Similoid). Made in attempt to produce a product similar to cellulose nitrate but without the flammability. Had limited use in the costume jewelry trade; most often encountered as car knobs and handles of the '30s and '40s. Surfaces tend to crack with age and exposure to light. Always molded, never cast. Colors varied; imitation horn and marble were most popular; imitation coral is seen in molded 'floral' jewelry.

3) Casein Plastics (Ameroid, Galalith, Dorcasine, Casolith). Invented in 1904 using milk proteins. Use limited to buttons and buckles due to warping and lengthy curing time. Made in a wide range of colors; very easy to laminate or to carve from stock rods or sheets, but never molded.

4) Phenol Formaldehyde (Bakelite, Catalin, Marblette, Agatine, Gemstone, Durite, Durez, Prystal). Invented by L.H. Baekland in 1908; used extensively in the '30s. There are two major types: cast and molded. Molded types include Durez and Bakelite, dark-toned, wood flour-filled plastics that were used extensively for early telephones (still used when non-conductivity of heat and electricity is vital). The most popular name in cast phenolics was Catalin, trade name of the American Catalin Corporation of New York. Made in a wide range of colors; widely used for costume jewelry, cutlery handles, decorative boxes, lamps, desk sets, etc. Heavyweight material with a slightly 'greasy' feel; very hard but can be carved with files, grinding tools, and abrasive cutters. Buffs to high, durable polish. Cast phenolics were used primarily from 1930 to around 1950 when they proved too labor-intensive to be economical.

5) Urea Formaldehyde (Beetleware, Plaskon, Duroware, Hemocoware, Uralite). Invented around 1929, this was lighter in color than phenol formaldehyde, thus used for injection-molded products in pastel colors. Lightweight, not strong; shiny rather than glossy. It cannot be carved and was used mainly for cheap radio and clock cases, never for jewelry.

The period between the two World Wars produced acrylic resins such as Lucite and vinyl. Polystryene made its appearance then, and furfural-phenols were in use in industrial applications. Though a great future was predicted for ethyl cellulose, by the late '30s it was still in the experimental phase. For most purposes the field of decorative plastics from the first half of the century can be narrowed down to the five major types listed above. Of these, cellulose acetate is rarely encountered. Casein is limited to button and belt buckle manufacture; urea is easily identifiable as a cheap, brittle material. Pyroxylin is the celluloid of which so many vanity sets were made. Molded phenolics such as Bakelite were dark in color and used for utilitarian objects; cast phenolics such as Catalin were used most notably for jewelry (please don't call it Bakelite), cutlery handles, desk sets, and novelties.

Dealers and collectors should be aware of '70s reproduction Marblette animal napkin rings (they have no eye rods and no age patina) and molded acrylic bracelets in imitation of carved Catalin ones (look for a seam line or lack of definition in carved areas). As prices rise, copies become more common. In 1986 the mass production of inlaid polka-dot bracelets using old-stock findings but without the precision fit (or patina) of the originals was seen.

In 1988 and continuing to the present, a large number of 'collage' pieces appeared in vintage clothing and antique stores on the West and East coasts. These are over-sized, glued-together assemblages of old Catalin stock parts including buttons with the shanks filed off, poker chips, etc., made into brooches or pendants, sometimes hung on necklaces of re-strung Catalin beads. They can be recognized by their aesthetically jumbled, 'put-together' look; and although some may claim they are old, they are not. For further information we recommend *Celluloid Treasures of the Victorian Era, Identification & Values*, by Joan Van Patten and Elmer and Peggy Williams; *Celluloid Collectibles* by Shirley Dunn; and *Celluloid Collector's Reference and Value Guide*, by Keith Lauer and Julie Robinson. All are published by Collector Books.

Bakelite

Cigarette box, half-cylinder, rotates open, dk brn	45.00
Clock, mantel; wind-up alarm, Deco design, dk brn	60.00
Penholder, streamlined, blk	22.50
Radio, Silvertone Compact, Sears, dk brn, 1936-37	250.00
Roulette wheel, dk brn, 1930s	80.00
Watch, lady's handbag; Westclox, blk, 2¾" dia	100.00

Catalin

Barometer, Taylor, amber & dk gr, rectangular, 4"	45.00
Bottle opener, chrome plate, red, gr or amber hdl	10.00
Bracelet, bangle; apple-juice clear, floral bk-cvg	150.00
Bracelet, bangle; deep cvg, w/rhinestones	90.00
Bracelet, bangle; elaborate floral cvg, wide	85.00
Bracelet, bangle; lt geometric cvg, wide	45.00
Bracelet, bangle; scratch cvd, narrow	22.00
Bracelet, bangle; scratch cvd, wide	27.00
Bracelet, bangle; stylized floral cvg, wide	45.00
Bracelet, bangle; uncvd, wide	11.00
Bracelet, bangle; 2-color stripes	80.00
Bracelet, bangle; 4-color (or more) stripes	150.00
Bracelet, cellulose acetate chain, 7 cvd figural charms	250.00
Bracelet, clamper; inlaid geometric designs	200.00
Bracelet, clamper; w/inlaid rhinestones	50.00
Bracelet, curved/flat links, uncvd	45.00
Bracelet, stretch; orig elastic, deeply cvd	65.00
Buckle, latch type, mc, novelty or figural applique	65.00
Buckle, latch type, mc, uncvd	25.00
Buckle, latch type, 1-color, stylized floral or geometric	30.00
Buckle, latch type, 1-color w/rhinestones, Deco	30.00
Buckle, slide type, mc, uncvd	20.00
Buckle, slide type, 1-color, uncvd	6.00
Buttons, card of 6, red or blk laminated, 1½" rod	18.00
Buttons, card of 6, uncvd octagonal, amber, 1" dia	10.00
Carving set, knife, fork, steel	30.00
Checkers, red & blk, full set, in box	35.00
Chess set, hand cvd, red & blk, leather box	300.00
Cigarette box, chrome inserts, cylindrical, 4½"	45.00
Cigarette lighter, imitation amber, sterling tip, orig case	25.00
Clock, New Haven, wind-up alarm, amber, Deco, 3⅝"	60.00
Clock, Seth Thomas, wind-up alarm, maroon case, 3½"	60.00
Clothesline, Jigger, red anchors, 10 pins, metal box	10.00
Cocktail recipes, Ben Hur, mtd on fighting roosters	45.00
Corkscrew, chrome, red, gr or amber hdl, ea	12.50

Crib toy, cat, $195.00.

Crib toy, Tykie Toy, boy, girl, clown, kitten, etc, ea	195.00
Crib toy, Tykie Toy, elephant, laolin head/Catalin body	195.00
Crib toy, Tykie Toy, 1½" rings (12) on 2⅞" ring, 1940s	100.00
Crib toy, Tykie Toy Tales (book about these toys), 1946	45.00
Dice, ivory or red, ¾", pr	2.00
Dice cup, leather or cork lined	40.00
Dominoes, red or gr, full set, w/wooden box	50.00
Drawer pull, 2-color, octagon, w/inlaid dot	3.00
Dress clip, novelty, figural, animal or vegetable	50.00
Dress clip, 1-color, w/rhinestones, Deco design	30.00
Earrings, novelty, figural animal or vegetable, pr	35.00
Earrings, uncvd discs, pr	8.00
Flatware, chrome plate, 1-color hdl	2.00
Flatware, stainless, 1-color hdl	3.00
Flatware, stainless, 1-color hdl, 3-pc matched place setting	10.00
Flatware, stainless, 2-color hdl, wood box, 36-pc set	250.00
Gavel, lathe trn, ivory	25.00
Gavel, lathe trn, red, w/presentation box, dtd 1946	40.00
Inkwell, Carvacraft Great Britain, amber, dbl well	115.00
Knife, cvd red, gr or amber hdl	6.00
Lamp base, red, amber & blk, Deco design, 8"	44.00
Letter opener, chrome/Catalin, Deco design	20.00
Mah-Jong set, tiles, rails, 6-color, complete, w/box	150.00
Nail brush, Ducky, duck shape, translucent eye rod	50.00
Napkin ring, amber, red or gr, 2" dia band	8.00
Napkin ring, chicken w/inlaid beak	35.00
Napkin ring, lathe trn, amber, red or gr, 1¾" dia	10.00
Napkin ring, rabbit w/inlaid eye rod	40.00
Napkin ring, Scottie w/inlaid eye rod	40.00
Necklace, cellulose acetate chain, animal figurals	300.00
Necklace, cvd red & amber beads, 18"	65.00
Ozone generator, Air-Clear, dk amber, streamlined case	75.00
Pencil sharpener, Bambi, Walt Disney Productions, 1" dia	55.00
Pencil sharpener, Goofy, rnd & fluted, 1½"	50.00
Pencil sharpener, gun, tank or plane w/decal, from $50 to	80.00
Pencil sharpener, mantel clock, Germany 2"	50.00
Pencil sharpener, Scottie, yel, silhouette shape	22.00
Pencil sharpener, Walt Disney's train, figural, 1¾"	85.00
Penholder, amber & blk striped, Deco design	35.00
Penholder, Scottie, red w/blk base	45.00
Picture frame, red, gr or amber, 6" sq	35.00
Pin, animal, resin wash w/glass eye, sm	90.00
Pin, animal or vegetable, inlaid or appl in several colors, sm	125.00
Pin, animal or vegetable, 1-color sm	80.00
Pin, mc Deco design, sm	60.00
Pin, novelty or patriotic figual, 1-color, sm	65.00
Pin, novelty or patriotic figural, resin wash/inlay/appl, lg	200.00
Pin, novelty or patriotic figural, resin wash/inlay/appl, sm	135.00
Pin, novelty or patriotic figural, 1-color, sm	65.00
Pin, stylized floral cvg, sm	40.00
Pin, w/danglers, animal or vegetable, 1-color	135.00
Pin, w/danglers, geometric form, 1-color	50.00
Pin, w/danglers, novelty or patriotic, 1-color	150.00
Pitcher, glass, red, gr or amber hdl, syrup sz	18.00
Poker chip rack, cylindrical, w/50 chips, 2½"	85.00
Powder box, amber & blk fluted cylinder, 2½"	50.00
Ring, inlaid Deco stripe design, 2-color	45.00
Ring, uncvd, 1-color	20.00
Ring case, hinged-lid style, amber or maroon	150.00
Safety razor, Schick Injector, amber hdl	18.00
Salad servers, Chase chrome, ivory, blk or brn, pr	45.00
Shakers, ball shape or half-cylinder shape, 1½", pr	30.00
Shakers, mushroom shape, amber & ivory, 1⅞", pr	35.00
Shakers, Washington Monument, 3¼", pr	35.00

Shaving brush, red, gr or amber, w/holder **40.00**
Spoon, iced tea; chrome, w/Catalin knob, 6-pc set **25.00**
Steering knob, chrome clamp **18.00**
Stirrer, iced tea; shovel blade, Catalin hdl, 6-pc set **45.00**
Strainer, red, gr or amber hdl, 5" dia **6.00**
Swizzle stick holder, amber or red, Rheingold Lager decal **95.00**
Thermometer, Taylor, amber & dk gr, rectangular, 4" **45.00**

Celluloid

Autograph album, Victorian lady, 4½x6", from $175 to **225.00**
Box, collar & cuff; lady's portrait, 6x6¼x6¼", from $300 to **350.00**
Box, handkerchief; Mucha print, 3x5½x5½", from $175 to **225.00**
Box, letter; Victorian girls, 2x5x7½", from $100 to **150.00**
Box, sewing; harvest scene, 4x9x7½", from $175 to **200.00**
Brush, Victorian lady bk, ornate hdl, 8½", from $90 to **125.00**
Glove case, Victorian scene, 3¼x11¼x3½", from $250 to **300.00**
Jewel case, mother/child reserve, gilt lock, 3x8x5", from $185 to ..**250.00**
Jewel case, Victorian children, velvet trim, musical, 4x10x6" **250.00**
Manicure set, Victorian scene, 9-pc in 4x13x11" case, from $325 to ...**400.00**
Mirror, hand; ornate bk, 9¾x4", from $100 to **150.00**
Mirror, shaving; emb classic figures, trifold, 12¼x20½" **500.00**
Photo album, Victorian child, musical, 12x9½", from $600 to ...**700.00**
Photo album, Victorian scene, upright, 8½x10½", from $450 to ..**525.00**
Shaving set, ivoroid, 5-pc in 3½x9x7" box, from $350 to **400.00**
Whisk broom holder, lady in plumed hat, from $125 to **175.00**

Playing Cards

Playing cards can be an enjoyable way to trace the course of history. Knowledge of the art, literature, and politics of an era can be gleaned from a study of its playing cards. When royalty lost favor with the people, Kings and Queens were replaced by common people. During the periods of war, generals, officers, and soldiers were favored. In the United States, early examples had portraits of Washington and Adams as opposed to Kings, Indian chiefs instead of Jacks, and goddesses for Queens.

Tarot cards were used in Europe during the 1300s as a game of chance, but in the 18th century they were used to predict the future and were regarded with great reverence.

The backs of cards were of no particular consequence until the 1890s. The marble design used by the French during the late 1800s and the colored wood-cut patterns of the Italians in the 19th century are among the first attempts at decoration. Later the English used cards printed with portraits of royalty. Eventually cards were decorated with a broad range of subjects from reproductions of fine art to advertising.

Although playing cards are becoming popular collectibles, prices are still relatively low. Complete decks of cards printed earlier than the first postage stamp can still be purchased for less than $100.00. In the listings, below decks are without boxes unless the box is specifically mentioned. Our advisor for this category is Ray Hartz; he is listed in the Directory under Pennsylvania. Another fine source of information is the American Antique Deck Collectors Club, 52 Plus Joker; see Directory under Clubs, Newsletters, and Catalogs.

Key:
AC — ad card   SC — score card
C — complete   std — standard
cts — courts   ws — wide scenic
J — joker   XC — extra card

Advertising

Alfa Romeo Motori, steering wheel aces, Modiano, 52+2J+XC, NMIB ...**45.00**

Am Hoist & Derrick, Brown & Bigelow, 1920s, 52+J+XC, NMIB ..**30.00**
Anheuser-Bush Spanish Am War II, 52+J, VG+, torn box **590.00**
Bailey Banks & Biddle, Russell, 1916, 52+special J, VGIB **67.50**
Bernhard Altmann Cashmere, Lang cts & pips, 52, EXIB **50.00**
Fifth Ave, United Drugs, special aces, wide, 52+J+XC, EXIB **25.00**
Florsheim Shoes, narrow, 1926, 52+special J+XC, VGIB **77.50**
GE Refrigerator, narrow, sphinx/refrigerator bks, 52+2XC, NMIB .**72.50**
Gold Seal Champagne, Urbana Wines, 1909, 52+J+XC, G+, broken box .**65.00**
Hard-A-Port, blk bks, costumed ladies, Wylie, 1886, 52+J, G **500.00**
Home Rubber, USPC, ca 1910, 52+J+2XC, EXIB **82.05**
Kinney Bros Transparent Tobacco Insert Cards, 1890, 52C, EX ..**1,550.00**
Luden's Cough Drops, cough drop box shapes, 52+2J, NMIB **27.50**
Mobil Oil Co, 2 decks, wooden case w/logo, complete, EX **90.00**
Monarch Bicycle, USPC, 1895, 52+special J+XC, EXIB **985.00**
Portina Cigars, Dougherty, pinochle, 1894 tax stamp, M, sealed ..**70.00**
RG Dun Cigars, Duragone, gr bks, MIB, sealed **16.50**
Robins Conveying Belts, red bks, 1920s, 52+special J, EXIB **95.00**
Royal Stag Canadian Whiskey, 1980, dbl deck, 104+4J, MIB **10.00**
Saks & Co, NY City, Dondorf, 1935, 52+cat J+XC, EXIB **250.00**
Schering Medical II, Coricidin, nonstd cts, 1966, 52+J+booklet, NM .**20.00**
Smoke Union-Made Cigars, Standard, 1913, 52 no J, VG+ **45.00**
Wills Tobacco Commemorative, royalty, 1986, 52+2J+XC, MIB ...**65.00**

Foreign Manufacturers

Belgium, Motorcycle Playing Cards, 1920s, unused, MIB, $100.00.

Photo courtesy Dunbar Gallery

Australia, Barribal, Owen King, ltd ed, 1980-90, 52+4J+2XC, NMIB ..**88.00**
Austria, Hausermann Natural Aluminum, 1925, 52 no J, NMIB ..**150.00**
Austria, Jugenstil Art Nouveau, Piatnik, 1980s, dbl deck, MIB **16.50**
Austria, Nonstd Piatnik cts, 1920s-30s, 52+Jolly J, VG, no box ...**80.00**
England, Cavalier, E&G Goldsmid, satire repro, 51/52, NMIB ..**137.50**
England, For Queen & Country, Kimberley, 1890s, 52+XC, no J, G- .**60.00**
England, Mayfair, Waddington, lady bks, 52+J, VG-, G box **228.00**
England, Pasha, Goodall, bl bks, 1885, 52+early J, EX-, no box .**132.00**
England, Queen Victoria Jubilee, Goodall, 1897, 52, EX, no box .**35.00**
England, Royal Marriage, Diana/Charles, dbl deck, 1981, MIB **22.00**
England, Veniant Omnes, Goodall, battleship bks, 52+J+XC, VGIB ..**32.50**
Finland, Lapland Drinking Team, cartoon J/bks/cts, MIP **22.00**
France, Ballet Petrouchka, Grimaud, ballet cts, 52+2J+XC, NMIB ...**20.00**
France, Grandprix, Grimaud, colorful pips/cts, 1973, 52+J, NMIB **20.00**
France, Grands Navigateurs, Grimaud, special cts, 1976, 52+J, MIB .**16.50**
Germany, My Fair Lady, Stadtische 1967, 32+18XC, EX in bag ..**55.00**
Germany, Operettenkarte, Becker, 1984, special cts, 52+2J+XC, NMIB .**15.00**
Germany, std pattern by CL Wust, 2-way cts, 1860s, 52, EX **110.00**
Germany, 18th-C reversible cts, Altenburger, dbl deck, NMIB **26.00**
India, Unique 555, Playwell, ruler cts, 52+2J+XC, NMIB **32.00**
Israel, Jacob's Bible Cards, Lion/Tel-Aviv, non-std cts, MIB **15.00**
Italy, Club, Modiano, stylish cts, 52+2J, NM, torn box **16.50**
Japan, Diana, Nintendo, all plastic, 58mmx101mm, 52+2J, NMIB .**15.00**
Mexico, Bullfighting, Guerrero, Llopis, 1940s, MIB, sealed **35.00**
Spain, Am Civil War, Fournier, Miciano, 1961, 52+2J+booklet, NMIB ..**38.50**
Spain, Am's Colonizers & Discoverers, Fournier, 1954, 52+XCs, MIB **27.50**
Spain, Nude in Art, Fournier, 52+2J, NMIB **22.00**

Spain, Political Twin Pack, Fournier, 104 caricatures, MIB **33.00**
Switzerland, Vues et Costumes Suisses, Muller, 1891, 52+SC, NMIB .**175.00**

Odd Sizes

Circular Coon Cards, Sutherland, 3-headed cts, 1925, 52+J, VGIB .**1,375.00**
Clark's Tiles, mini cards on plastic tiles, 1927, 51/52+XCs **45.00**
Elf #93, NYCC, red Cupid bks, 52 no J, EX, broken box **16.50**
Fauntleroy Mini, USPC, 1930, 52+Fauntleroy J, VG, leather case ...**10.00**
Round Rio Rita, Waddington, 1930, 52+J, EX, torn box **65.00**
Round Waterproof Playing Cards, Globe, 1890, 52+J, VG, torn box .**180.00**

Older Decks, Narrow, American

Bijou #1, USPC, bl bks, 1905, 50/52 no J, EXIB **22.00**
Celluloid, red bks, 1928, 52 no J, EX-, taped box **55.00**
Congress #606, Carnival Days, Deco bks, 52 no J, EX-, broken box .**12.00**
Forcolar, no-revoke deck, 1947, 52 no J, VGIB **28.00**
Kem Cards, statue bks, narrow, dbl deck, 1935, VGIB **12.00**
Trophy Whist #39, USPC, std cts, 1895-99, 52 no J, VGIB **30.00**

Older Wide Decks

Bicycle #808, autocycle red bk, 1916, 52 no J, EXIB **175.00**
Bicycle #808, chainless red bk, ca 1915, 52 no J, VG, OB **150.00**
Bicycle #808, Cupid gr bk, ca 1895, 52+J, VG-, no box **110.00**
Bicycle #808, league bl bk, 1894 stamp, 10-4-17, MIB, sealed **65.00**
Bicycle #808, racer bl bk, 1940s, tax stamp, MIB, sealed **45.00**
Bicycle #808, thistle bl bk, 1914, 52 no J, EX+IB **38.00**
Card Fabrique Co, ca 1883, 50/52, no J, stained, C, w/fabric wrap ..**45.00**
Congress, Minuet, dancing couple bks, 1901, 52+J, EX+, torn box .**70.00**
Congress #606, Berenice, ca 1914, 52+J+2XC, EX+, NM box **50.00**
Congress #606, Bridge, 1899, 52+Bridge J, VG+, EX box **55.00**
Congress #606, Gee, boy w/watermelon, 1910, 52+J+XC, NMIB .**118.00**
Congress #606, Julia Marlowe, 1907, 52+J+SC+XC, VG- w/holder ..**65.00**
Congress #606, Martha Washington, 1901, 52 no J, NMIB **55.00**
Congress #606, Rowdy, bulldog bks, 1913, 52+J, EX-, VG box **90.00**
Court of Music, special cts, ca 1910, 52 no J+XC, VG+, VG box ..**248.00**
Nat'l Club #75, red pattern bks, 1907, 52 no J, VG+, EX box **35.00**
Par Auction, Milton Bradley, ca 1920, 52+2XC, VG, torn box ...**22.00**
Steamboat #99, pattern bks, 1930s, 52+steamboat J, NMIB **55.00**
Waldorf #230X, Boating, Dougherty, 1915, 52+J, EXIB **85.00**

Souvenir

Am Indian, Lazarus, 1903, blanket bks, ws, 52+J+XC, G+, G box .**165.00**
Among Wht Mtns, Chisolm Bros, photos, ws, 1910, 52+J+SC, NMIB ..**33.00**
Brazil Centennial of Independence, ws, 1922, 52 no J, M, G box .**90.00**
Cinema by de la Rue, Paramounts star cts, narrow, 1935, 52, VGIB ..**95.00**
Florence Scenic, Fotometalgrafica, ws, 1975, 52+2J+SC, NMIB ..**22.50**
Forbidden City, Boxer Rebellion, ws, 1901, 52+J+XC, EX+ **275.00**
Jeffries Championship, fighters, 1909, 52+J+XC, EX+ **410.00**
Midwinter Internat'l Expo, Winters, pk bks, 1894, 52+bear J, VG+ .**250.00**
Nation's Capital, ws, 1909, 52 no J, VGIB **27.50**
Ocean to Ocean, Canada, Goodall, ws, 1905, 52+J+XC, EXIB **45.00**
Paris Expo, Tom Jones, statue bks, 1900, 52+statue J, EXIB **135.00**
Stage #65, picture aces & cts (current stars), 1896, EX+ **90.00**
Views of Pittsburg, May Drugs, photos, ws, 1905, 52 no J, VGIB ..**38.50**
Western Aces, western film stars, 1960, postcard sz, 52+12 aces, EX+ ..**50.00**

Political

The most valuable political items are those from any period which

relate to a political figure whose term was especially significant or marked by an important event or one whose personality was particularly colorful. Posters, ribbons, badges, photographs, and pin-back buttons are but a few examples of the items popular with collectors of political memorabilia.

Political campaign pin-back buttons were first mass produced and widely distributed in 1896 for the president-to-be William McKinley and for the first of three unsuccessful attempts by William Jennings Bryan. Pin-back buttons have been used during each presidential campaign ever since and are collected by many people. The scarcest are those used in the presidential campaigns of John W. Davis in 1924 and James Cox in 1920.

Contributions to this category were made by Michael J. McQuillen, monthly columnist of *Political Parade,* which appears in *AntiqueWeek* newspapers; he is listed in the Directory under Indiana. Our advisor for this category is Paul J. Longo; he is listed under Massachusetts. See also Autographs; Broadsides; Historical Glass; Watch Fobs.

Button, 1889 commemorative of 100th Anniversary of Washington's inauguration, bronze or copper, scarce, $125.00.

Ballot, Nat'l Republican ticket, Grant/Colfax, 1868, 4x12" **75.00**
Bottle opener, Carter, smiling face w/hdl **20.00**
Broadside, FD Roosevelt, 1932-45, woven silk, 12x15" **125.00**
Broadside, Fillmore/Donelson, Know Nothing Party, cloth, 1856 ..**300.00**
Cane, McKinley head cvd hdl, all wood, EX **95.00**
Engraving, Taft/Sherman & Cabinet, w/portraits, 1909 ....**95.00**
Envelope, I Like Ike, NM **15.00**
Handkerchief, Cleveland/Thurman in horseshoe wreath, 18½x19½" ...**150.00**
Handkerchief, Tippecanoe & His Grandson Too, red & bl on cotton ..**350.00**
Handkerchief, Tippecanoe & Morton Too, red & bl on wht cotton **275.00**
Handkerchief, Washington commemorative, red/wht/bl, 1876, 24x17" .**400.00**
Invitation packet, Reagan/Bush inaugural, 1981, 6-pc in envelope ..**15.00**
Jug, Taft/Sherman photo, mini, EX **100.00**
Key holder, Truman, leather **60.00**
License plate, Goldwater, Au H20 beneath name, 1964, M **25.00**
License plate, Rebel Power, humorous soldier in gray, M **6.00**
License plate attachment, Hoover for President **35.00**
Match holder, Teddy & bear, worn pnt **65.00**
Match safe, Grover Cleveland head figural, hinged lid **225.00**
Mug, Mamie Eisenhower's face form, ivory w/brn hdl **40.00**
Paperweight, McKinley, full-face, glass **50.00**
Pitcher, FD Roosevelt, Happy days, Stangl **250.00**
Plate, T Roosevelt, 1905 Lewis & Clark Expo, Rowland & Marsellus .**150.00**
Postcard, T Roosevelt Charges to White House, flasher **35.00**
Postcard, Taft/Sherman dbl jugate, 1908, VG **25.00**
Poster, FD Roosevelt portrait, 1932, 12x17", EX **65.00**
Poster, Richard Nixon presidential campaign, mc, 24x18", M **15.00**
Print, Garfield, Lincoln, McKinley, In Memorium, 1901 ....**85.00**
Ribbon, Blaine/Logan, 1884 ....**75.00**
Ribbon, Jackson, Benevolent Society, EX **500.00**
Ribbon badge, McKinley/Hobart jugate, cello, 1896, 9" overall .**250.00**
Sheet music, Harding's the Man for Me, custom fr **85.00**
Sheet music, President George Bush March, photo cover, 1988, M ..**10.00**
Soda can, Goldwater, full **20.00**
Spoon, T Roosevelt on horsebk as hdl, sterling **150.00**

Stud, McKinley sits on struggling WJ Bryan, brass, 1896 ....**350.00**
Textile, James G Blaine portrait, red/bl/brn on cotton, 25x18" ..**225.00**
Ticket stub, Republican Nat'l Convention, 1916 ....**25.00**
Token, Henry Clay, 1844, EX **35.00**
Torch, Harrison campaign, tin top-hat holders, 56", pr **500.00**
Tumbler, Roosevelt for/Fairbanks, etched portraits, 3¾" **100.00**
Tumbler, Willkie, 1940 ....**30.00**
Watch fob, Calvin Coolidge, foliate pot metal w/cello inset **125.00**

Pin-back Buttons

Dewey, elephant figure, celluloid, ¾" dia **18.00**
FDR, Gallant Leader, litho, ⅞", EX **10.00**
Gay, Lesbian & Bisexual Rights March, WA DC, 1993, 2¼", M **4.00**
Hughes w/flag & shield, ½", EX **10.00**
I'm On the Way, elephant walking to White House, cello, ⅞", EX ..**40.00**
Ike & Dick Junior Club, litho, 2¼", EX **40.00**
Kennedy, He Will Win, flasher, 2½" **25.00**
Robert Van Wyck, NY City Mayor, 1900s, ⅞" **15.00**
Roosevelt for Humanity, litho, ⅞", EX **10.00**
State Senator James A C Johnson of NJ **30.00**
Wilson, Peace, Prosperity, celluloid, 1912, ⅞" **12.00**
Wings for America, Willkie, plane, litho, 1", EX **12.00**

Pomona

Pomona glass was patented in 1885 by the New England Glass Works. Its characteristics are an etched background of crystal lead glass often decorated with simple designs painted with metallic stains of amber or blue. The etching was first achieved by hand cutting through an acid resist. This method, called first ground, resulted in an uneven feather-like frost effect. Later, to cut production costs, the hand-cut process was discontinued in favor of an acid bath which effected an even frosting. This method is called second ground. Our advisors for this category are Betty and Clarence Maier; they are listed in the Directory under Pennsylvania.

Bowl, Cornflowers, 1st ground, scalloped base, 3½x8½" **650.00**
Butter dish, Acanthus Leaf, 1st ground, gold stain, 4½x8" dia ...**1,265.00**
Carafe, Cornflowers, 2nd ground, ribbed neck, T'print body, 8" ...**385.00**
Celery, 1st ground, floral/gold band, appl ft, ruffled, 5" **625.00**
Champagne, 2nd ground, amber rim, 4¼" **325.00**
Cruet, Invt T'print, 2nd ground, gold neck/hdls/stopper, 7" **385.00**
Finger bowl, Cornflowers, 2nd ground, amber stain, 5½" **150.00**
Finger bowl, 1st ground, gold irid fluted top, 2½x5" **85.00**
Pitcher, Honeycomb, 1st ground, mc florals, rope hdl, 7½" **700.00**
Pitcher, tankard; 1st ground, leaves at rim, amber hdl, 9" **325.00**
Punch cup, Cornflowers, 1st ground, amber stain, 2¾" **150.00**
Punch cup, 1st ground, amber hdl/rim, 2½" **85.00**
Rose bowl, 2nd ground, bl flowers, 5x5¼" **450.00**
Sugar bowl, Cornflowers, 1st ground, ruffled amber rim, 2¾" **175.00**
Toothpick holder, 1st ground, amber stain, tricorn, 2" **350.00**
Toothpick holder, 1st ground, amber stan, fan form, 2¾" **475.00**
Tumbler, Cornflowers, 2nd ground, amber & bl stain, 3¾x2⅝" .**145.00**
Tumbler, Dmn Quilt/Cornflowers, 2nd ground, bl stain, 3¾" **200.00**
Tumbler, lemonade; Cornflowers, 1st ground, hdl **325.00**
Vase, Invt T'print, 1st ground, ruffled, rigaree collar, 4½" **70.00**

Porcelier

The Porcelier Company, originally from East Liverpool, Ohio, started business in the late 1920s and moved to Greensburg, Pennsylva-

nia, in the early 1930s. The company flourished until the late 1940s and finally closed its doors due to labor disputes in 1954.

They produced an endless line of vitrified porcelain products including furniture coasters, electric appliances, dripolators, and light fixtures. These products were sold in many stores under a variety of names and carried over ten different types of marks and labels.

The prices below are for items in excellent condition with no chips, cracks, or excessive wear. To learn more about this subject, we recommend *Collector's Guide to Porcelier China* by Susan F. Grindberg (Collector Books). If you have any questions or information regarding Porcelier, please contact our advisor, Jim Barker; he is listed in the Directory under Pennsylvania. (Queries require SASE.)

Beverage cooler, high or low bbl **100.00**
Beverage cooler, rectangular **85.00**
Bowl, spaghetti; Basketweave Wild Flowers **250.00**
Canisters, Barock-Colonial, #2014, gold, ea **50.00**
Casserole, lt yel, w/knobbed lid, 8½" dia **30.00**
Coffeepot, Colonial (Silhouette), 6-cup **75.00**
Coffeepot, Flight, 8-cup **50.00**
Coffeepot, Ribbed Betty, 6-cup **35.00**
Creamer & sugar bowl, Serv-All Line, #3007 or 3009, platinum ..**35.00**
Decanter, Quilted Floral Cameo **40.00**

Photo courtesy Susan E. Greenberg

Dripolator, Basketweave Wild Flowers six-cup pot with decorated dripper, $75.00.

Lamp, dresser; Dutch boy **55.00**
Lamp, table; Antique Rose, gold trim **70.00**
Light fixture, drop ceiling w/orig globe **78.00**
Light fixture, porch; blk w/gold trim, glass globe **80.00**
Liqueur set, Ringed, decanter w/6 lg shot glasses **75.00**
Mug, beer; Ringed, solid **20.00**
Mug, Wildlife, gold trim **35.00**
Percolator, Black-Eyed Susan, #710 ....**85.00**
Percolator, Golden Wheat, #120 ....**70.00**
Percolator, Scalloped Wild Flowers **125.00**
Pitcher, batter; Serv-All Line, #3014, gold, red, or blk **100.00**
Pitcher, Flight, disc form **85.00**
Powder jar, ivory w/gold trim, w/lid **85.00**
Pretzel jar, Barock-Colonial, ivory, red, or bl **105.00**
Sandwich grill, Scalloped Wild Flowers **300.00**
Shakers, HP floral, pr **25.00**
Tankard, Field Flowers, 6-cup **35.00**
Teapot, Barock-Colonial, #2011, gold **45.00**
Teapot, Latticework, 4-cup **30.00**
Teapot, Periwinkle, 4-cup **30.00**
Toaster, Basketweave Wild Flowers **900.00**
Urn, Silhouette, electric **125.00**
Waffle iron, Scalloped Wild Flowers **300.00**

Wall sconce, floral, w/shade 47.00

Postcards

Postcards are often very difficult to evaluate, since so many factors must be considered — for instance the subject matter or the field of interest they represent. For example: a 1905 postcard of the White House in Washington D.C. may seem like a desirable card, but thousands were produced and sold to tourists who visited there, thus the market is saturated with this card, and there are few collectors to buy it. Value: less than $1.00. However, a particular view of a small town of which only five hundred were printed could sell for far more, provided you find someone interested in the subject matter pictured on that card. Take as an example a view of the courthouse in Hillsville, Virginia. This card would appeal to those focusing on that locality or county as well as courthouse collectors. Value: $3.00.

The ability of the subject to withstand time is also a key factor when evaluating postcards. Again using the courthouse as an example, one built in 1900 and still standing in the 1950s has been photographed for fifty years, from possibly a hundred different angles. Compare that with one built in 1900 and replaced in 1908 due to a fire, and you can see how much more desirable a view of the latter would be. But only a specialist would be aware of the differences between these two examples.

Postcard dealers can very easily build up stocks numbering in the 100,000s. Greeting and holiday cards are common and represent another area of collecting that appeals to an entirely different following than the view card. These types of cards range from heavily embossed designs to floral greetings and, of course, include the ever popular Santa Claus card. These were very popular from about 1900 until the 1920s, when postcard communication was the equivalent of today's quick phone call or e-mail. Because of the vast number of them printed, many have little if any value to a collector. For instance, a 1909 Easter card with tiny images or a common floral card of the same vintage, though almost one hundred years old, are virtually worthless. It's the cards with appeal and zest that command the higher prices. One with a beautiful Victorian woman in period clothing, her image filling up the entire card, could easily be worth $3.00 and up. Holiday cards designed for Easter, Valentines Day, Thanksgiving, and Christmas are much more common than those for New Year's, St. Patrick's Day, the 4th of July, and Halloween. Generally, then, they're worth less, but depending on the artist, graphics, desirability, and eye appeal, this may not always be true. The signature of a famous artist will add significant value — conversely, an unknown artist's signature adds none.

In summary, the best way to evaluate your cards is to have a knowledgeable dealer look at them. For a list of dealers, send a SASE to the International Federation of Postcard Dealers, P.O. Box 1765, Manassas, VA 20108. **Do not** expect a dealer to price cards from a list or written description as this is not possible. For individual questions or evaluation by photocopy (front and back), you may contact our advisor, Jeff Bradfield, 90 Main St., Dayton, VA 22821. You **must** include a SASE for a reply.

Posters

Advertising posters by such French artists as Cheret and Toulouse-Lautrec were used as early as the mid-1800s. Color lithography spurred their popularity. Circus posters by the Strobridge Lithograph Co. are considered to be the finest in their field, though Gibson and Co. Litho, Erie Litho, and Enquirer Job Printing Co. printed fine examples as well. Posters by noted artists such as Mucha, Parrish, and Hohlwein bring high prices. Other considerations are good color, interesting subject matter and, of course, condition. The WWII posters listed below are

among the more expensive examples; 80% of those on the market bring less than $50.00. See also Movie Memorabilia; Rock 'N Roll.

Advertising

A La Place Clichy, cascading rugs, Paris, 1891, 46x30", NM ..**1,600.00**
Ah! Une Whitworth (bicycle), lady & policeman, 1897, 51x36", NM **1,600.00**
Bertozzi Parmigiano-Reggiano, 3 judges sniffing, 1930, 55x39", NM **4,350.00**
Cachou Lajounie, lady smoker w/breath sweetener, '20, 58x38", NM .**2,300.00**
Champagne Masse Pere & Fils, man in wine cellar, 47x32", M ..**700.00**
Columbia, lady w/bicycle, Barreau, Paris, 1897, 31x19", EX **800.00**
Edison Records, dancing couple, mc, 1920s, 26x30", NM **460.00**
Greyhound Lines, Cash Bonus for Everyone ..., 1936, 38x28", VG .**385.00**
Greyhound Lines, How To Stretch Xmas Dollar, 1932, 39x28", EX .**550.00**
Greyhound Lines, What a Glorious Vacation, 1940, 39x28", EX+ .**600.00**
If You See It in Sun..., lady in blk, inscr Rhead, 1895, 42x27" ..**1,265.00**
Impermeables Perfecta, man in warm coat, 47x31", EX **460.00**
Kymris...Bicyclette, brunette dreaming, 1900, 49x36", EX **515.00**
L'Astrolin, Pierrot pnts moon, Champenois, 59½x40", EX **3,000.00**
La Royale (car wax), Arc de Triomphe/cars, 46¾x31", M **430.00**
PKZ (clothing), beautiful man's overcoat, Zurich, 1923, 35x50", NM ..**4,600.00**
Remoncourt, lady reading mineral water ad, 1900, 48x36", NM .**1,850.00**
Source des Roches, girl examines water glass, 1899, 17x19", NM ...**700.00**
Strand-Hotel, lady by table, yel/purple, 1930, 47x33", NM **1,500.00**
Thermogene, gr man w/orange heating pad, Brussels, 38x29", NM ..**1,380.00**
Woodroffe's Engagement Rings, couple, Petty & Sons, 60x40", EX .**1,265.00**

Circus

Downie Bros. Circus, clown face surrounded by many circus characters, full-color litho, 41x28", EX, $400.00.

Barnum & Bailey, Berta Beeson, High Wire, Strobridge, 1920s .**920.00**
Barnum & Bailey, man/women highdivers, 1898 ....**8,625.00**
Barnum & Bailey, Versatile Performers, Equestrian Exploits ...**1,725.00**
Barnum & Bailey portraits, Greatest Show, Strobridge, 40x30" ...**1,400.00**
Carson & Barnes, clown/elephants/horses/etc, mc, paper, 34x42", VG **50.00**
Elephant w/outstretched trunk, Erie, 1930s, EX **920.00**
Ringling Bros, Barnum & Bailey, leopard snarling, mc, 43x28½" **200.00**
40 Horse Team/Ponderous Tableau Bandwagon, Strobridge, 1903 .**3,000.00**

Literary

Harper's April/Joan of Arc, 1895, 17½x12½", EX **460.00**
Harper's August, man in swimsuit/lady in gr, 1896, 19x14", M ..**920.00**
Harper's Christmas, Santa & lady in bl, 1895, 25½x20", EX+ **315.00**
Harper's February, man in orange/lady in brn, 1896, 20x11", NM **345.00**
Harper's July, lady in bl, 1896, 18¾x13¾", EX **575.00**
Harper's March, lady in blk gown, 1896, 18½x11", NM **575.00**
Harper's May, lady w/2 cats, 1896, 17¾x11¾", NM **1,150.00**
Harper's November, wealthy couple, 1895, 16⅝x11¾", EX+ **925.00**
June Century, Napoleon in Egypt, Grasset, 1895, 21x15", NM ..**430.00**

Lippincott's February, lady w/valentine on bed, 1896, 17x12", NM ..300.00
Lippincott's June, lady in red w/magazine, 1896, 16x11½", NM .345.00
Lippincott's May, man w/pipe & servant, 1896, 17x12", NM 315.00
Scribner's Fiction Number, man/porter, McManus, 1895, 23x15", NM ...460.00
Scribner's for Xmas, lady w/holly, 1895, 19¾x13⅝", NM 1,725.00

Magic

Carter The Great, The Modern Priestess of Delphi, three sections glued together, 78x42", $500.00.

Carter Beats the Devil, magician plays devil in poker, 22x14", NM- ...405.00
Chang & Fak-Hong's United.Buddha, man & snake, 25x17", EX 315.00
George/Supreme Master..., gr statue on ped, Otis, 1929, 27x20", EX ..285.00
Great Chang & Fak-Hong's United, Noe Ark, Valencia, 30x43", EX .375.00
Houdini, ca 1925, 72x96", M 8,500.00

Travel

A Chile!, lady in orange swimsuit w/parasol, 1930, 42x29", EX .975.00
Am Airlines, cowgirl in lg hat, Kauffer, 1948, 40x30", NM 575.00
Annecy La Plage, Fr mtn/lake scene, 1935, 39x25½", M 1,035.00
Arandora Star, launching scene, 39¾x24¾", EX 375.00
Budapest, speeding train, Semizky, Kloss & Son, 1930, 37x25", NM ...800.00
Connecticut, New Haven RR, countryside scene, 1935, 42x28", EX ..515.00
Cunard Holidays, departure scene, 1925, 39⅝x24½", NM 575.00
Czechoslovakia, mtn climbers, gr sky, Dolezal, 1930, 27x25", M ..500.00
Gulf Coast, IL Central, summer scene, ca 1930, 42x28", VG+ ...920.00
Imperial Airways/Reliability, lion in wind, 30x20", NM 515.00
Juni Festival Budapest, Danube scene, 37½x24¾", NM 635.00
Las Vegas, Night & Day photo montage, TWA, 1950s, 25x15", NM 460.00
Mission Ange, mtns/speeding train, Brown & Bigelow, 40x30" NM ..1,380.00
Ratische Bahn, Swiss mtn/lake, Wolfenberger, 1916, 51x36", NM 1,600.00
Rodeo Parade, N Pacific RR, Indian chief/parade, 40x30", NM 1,100.00
Ski in Sun in France, Fr Railway, blond skier, 1957, 39x24", M .545.00
Sun Valley ID, lady in red w/skis, ca 1940, 37¾x25¼", EX+ ..1,955.00
This Summer Sun Valley, lady skater, 38¾x25¾", M 2,185.00
Thoroughbreds, NY Central RR, 3 locomotives, 1927, 1924", EX+ .1,035.00
Visit India, Rajah on elephant, Purvis, 39½x50", NM 1,600.00

War

WWI, After Welcome Home — a Job, soldier, 1919, 41x28", EX 515.00
WWI, Boys Come Over Here..., D Allen & Sons, 1916, 40x50", EX 400.00
WWI, Brighten His Days, Jewish Welfare Board, mc, 1917, 38x21" 2,750.00
WWI, Buy Liberty Bonds, minuteman w/gun, Ickes, 1917, 41x27", NM .700.00
WWI, Come Lad Slip Across..., D Allen & Sons, 1916, 40x50", EX 700.00
WWI, Full Speed Ahead!, Uncle Sam & locomotive, 1920, 26x19" 925.00
WWI, Humanity Knows No Creed, mother/child, 1917, 28x21", NM ..2,185.00
WWI, Join US School Garden Army, girl w/plants, 1918, 30x20", M 2,070.00
WWI, Treat 'Em Rough...Tanks, Black Tom (cat), 1918, 19x14", EX 575.00
WWII, Am's Answer! Production, hand w/wrench, 1942, 30x41", EX ..1,850.00

WWII, Clear the Way, Christy, EX 250.00
WWII, Corn Food of Nation, lady & corn products, 30x21", NM 485.00
WWII, Let Him...Wake Unharmed!, boy & dog, 1942, 40x31", NM ..200.00
WWII, Let's Give Him Enough..., Rockwell, 1942, 28⅜x40⅜", NM .635.00
WWII, Medical Dept US Army, medic & soldier, 25x19", NM 1,265.00
WWII, US Army Build Men, orange soldier, Niagara, 1917, 30x20", EX .460.00
WWII, We French Workers Warn You, Shahn, 28½x40", NM .545.00
WWII, Well Boy...Your Bit, Australian bonds, 1919, 30x20", EX .975.00

Miscellaneous

Audio DNA, Peter Max, features many rock musicians, mtd, 24x36" ...450.00
Buffalo Bill on White Horse, mtd on linen, ca 1900, 48x32" ..3,750.00
Bull's-Eye, Robin Hood, work incentive, Mather, 1929, 44x36", EX+ 800.00
Chaise lounge, Schultz, Leisure Group, vinyl mesh on wht fr, 69" 650.00
Concerts Bridgeport Symphony..., conductor, Laing, 1930, 22x14", NM ..450.00
Dance party (Bill Graham's Fillmore), Wes Wilson, '66, 22x14" .100.00
Eastern Ski Championships, man jumping, 1935, 33¾x22", EX .975.00
Engage Yur Butler..., man w/tray, ca 1930, 22x14", EX 485.00
Indianapolis 500 Mile Race, Oilzum, top 4 winners, 1947, 25x17" ..200.00
Internat'l Overseas Exhibition, Lang, English, '31, 40x24", NM ..325.00
Making Sure...a Hit!, lady/horse, work incentive, '29, 44x36", EX .300.00
Man Must Moon, Peter Max, ode to Apollo II landing, '69, mtd .200.00
Watch Out for Old Man Accident, WPA, 1931, 22x14", NM ...545.00
Young Judea, children clasping hands, 22x17½", EX+ 635.00

Pot Lids

Pot lids were pottery covers for containers that were used for hair dressing, potted meats, etc. The most common were decorated with colorful transfer prints under the glaze in a variety of themes, animal and scenic. The first and probably the largest company to manufacture these lids was F. & R. Pratt of Fenton, Staffordshire, established in the early 1800s. The name or initials of Jesse Austin, their designer, may sometimes be found on exceptional designs. Although few pot lids were made after the 1880s, the firm continued into the 20th century.

American pot lids are very rare. Most have been dug up by collectors searching through sites of early gold rush mining towns in California. Minor rim chips are expected and normally do not detract from listed values. When no condition is given, assume that the value is based on an example in such condition.

American

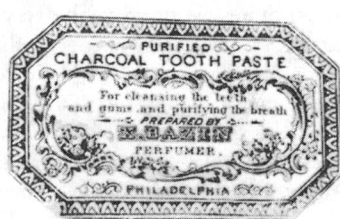

Purified Charcoal Tooth Paste Prepared by X Bazin Perfumer, black transfer, 3¾x2⅜", M, $110.00.

Capitol at Washington Worsley..., lav, 3½", EX, +base 850.00
Charcoal Tooth Paste...Jules Hauel..., blk, 2¾", EX 300.00
Chlorine Detergent...Royce & Esterly..., eagle, bl, 2¾" 600.00
Cold Cream of Roses...Caswell Massey..., red, flake, 2½" 170.00
Dr EJ Coxe's Copaina, Sarsaparilla..., blk, rprs, 3", +base 300.00
Dr EJ Coxe's Extract...Sarsaparilla..., blk, 3¼", EX, +base 450.00
Genuine Beef Marrow...X Baxin..., blk, 3", EX 300.00
Hazard, Hazard & Co Violet Cold Cream...NY, brn transfer, 2¾" 200.00
Hide & Seek, mc transfer, 4" 100.00
Highest Permium...Jules Hauel World's Fair..., blk, 3½" 575.00

Highest Premium...Jules Hauel World's Fair..., blk, 3½" 575.00
Improved Cold Cream of Roses...X Bazin..., blk, stain, 2⅜" 170.00
Jules Hauel Perfumer..., Franklin profile, purple, chip, 3½" 350.00
Jules Hauel Perfumer..., Franklin profile, red, chip, 3¾" 350.00
Jules Hauel Saponaceous Shaving Compound..., red transfer, 4" ...200.00
Odonto or Oak Bark...Tooth Paste..., red, 3¼", +base 475.00
Roussel's Premium Shaving Cream..., gray transfer, 3", EX 220.00
Roussel's Cold Cream of...X Bazin's..., bird/floral, blk, 2¾" 270.00
Superior Cold Cream...Melvin & Badger...Boston, bl, 2½" 375.00
Superior Purified Bear's Grease...TH Peters..., blk, 3", VG 500.00
Superior Rose Tooth Paste...X Bazin..., red, 2¼" 100.00
Taylor's Saponaceous Compound..., man shaving, bl, 3¼" 425.00
Taylor's Saponaceous Compound..., purple, 3½", EX, +base 575.00
Washington Crossing Delaware...Taylor..., blk, 3" 650.00
Whorsley Wholesale Perfumer..., Capital building, blk, 3⅝" 600.00
Wms Swiss Violet Shaving..., violet/brn/gr, lt stain, 3¾" 525.00
World's Fair...Charcoal Tooth Paste...Jules Hauel..., blk, 2½"..300.00
Wright's Gold Medal Ambrosial Shaving Cream, monks, blk, 3⅜" 1,000.00
X Bazin Saponaceous Shaving Compound..., blk, 3¾", EX 375.00

English

Cherry Toothpaste...F Newbury..., sailboat, blk/wht, 2¾", EX 75.00
Children sailing boat in tub, mc, minor rstr, 3", +fr 120.00
Contrast, bulldog & greyhound, mc, 4⅛", +fr 100.00
Dutch battle, windmill burning, Pratt, Wouvermann, 6" L 85.00
Harbour of Hong Kong, mc, 4", +fr 100.00
May Dancers at Swan Inn, mc, 4⅛", +base 110.00
Ning Po River, mc, minor scratches, 4⅛" 90.00
Nipirama Trinadado, ships scene, mc, 4⅜", EX 250.00
Peace, family w/sheep, mc, 4", EX 120.00
Pulling a Tooth, mc, w/matching base, rare, 4", EX 675.00
Residence of Hathaway...Avon, mc, 4⅛", EX 70.00
Shakespeare House Henley St...Avon, mc, 4⅛", +fr 70.00
Swinton's English Primrose, cobalt/wht, 2⅝", +base 185.00
Transplanting Rice, Oriental farm scene, mc, 4", +fr 80.00
Volunteers, old man & children, mc, 3", in wood fr 120.00
War, injured horse, mc, 4¼"+fr, EX 110.00
Wimbledon July 2nd 1860, mc, minor chips, 4¼", +fr 110.00

Powder Horns and Shot Flasks

Though powder horns had already been in use for hundreds of years, collectors usually focus on those made after the expansion of the United States westward in the very early 1800s. While some are basic and very simple, others were scrimshawed and highly polished. Especially nice carvings can quickly escalate the value of a horn that has survived intact to as high as $400.00. Those with detailed maps, historical scenes, etc., bring even higher prices.

Metal flasks were introduced in the 1830s; by the middle of the century they were produced in quantity and at prices low enough that they became a viable alternative to the powder horn. Today's collector regards the smaller flasks as the more desirable and valuable, and those made for specific companies bring premium prices.

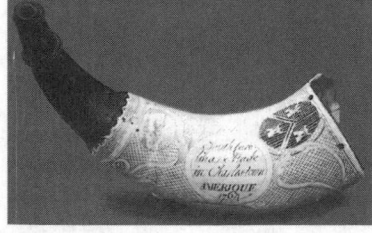

Horn, ships at sea, Charleston harbor, etc., engravings, dated 1764, 9½", EX, $6,300.00.

Flask, brass, Ames, fouled anchor/USN, 1843, EX 450.00
Flask, brass, stamped shells on pear shape, complete, 8" 55.00
Flask, brn boar hide body cover, nickel mts, Dixon, 1880s, EX 85.00
Flask, copper, straw & leaf design, Dixon & Sons, 9¼" 110.00
Flask, copper (plain), external spring, brass spout, 1870s, G 35.00
Flask, copper w/pistols/eagle/cannon/etc, dk patina, brass spout .195.00
Horn, brass, oak leaves/acorn/stag, WH Hawksley, 8" 125.00
Horn, brass, wild game relief, Dixon & Sons...Improved Pat, 8" .125.00
Horn, British Artillery priming, brass spout, 1812 period, 12", G ...125.00
Horn, convex wood base plug, hanging loop finial, 7½", G 20.00
Horn, cvd wood base w/iron staple finial, walnut plug, 15" 110.00
Horn, cvd wood spout, iron wire finial, mellow color, 16" 110.00
Horn, eng coat of arms/town map on cow horn, 1750s, 12½", VG ..2,400.00
Horn, eng eagle & pistol, brass end cap, 13", EX 200.00
Horn, eng face/ship/sea serpent, dtd 1820, w/plug, 5¾" 450.00
Horn, eng Indian-related decor, wood base, 8" 150.00
Horn, eng initials on mellow yel w/blk tip, pine plug, 16", EX ...500.00
Horn, eng map of fort/roads/stag hunt scene, 18th C, 10½" 2,750.00
Horn, eng Meeting House/Ship Rochester, trimmed/crack, 9¼" .825.00
Horn, eng name/sailing ships/Union Jack/Am flag, 1775, 13", VG ...2,000.00
Horn, eng stags/foliage/geometrics/name, ca 1800, 11¼" 650.00

Pratt

Prattware has become a generic reference for a type of relief-molded earthenware with polychrome decoration. Scenic motifs with figures were popular; sometimes captions were added. Jugs are most common, but teapots, tableware, even figurines were made. The term 'Pratt' refers to Wm. Pratt of Lane Delph, who is credited with making the first examples of this type, though similar wares were made later by other Staffordshire potters. Pot lids and other transfer wares marked Pratt were made in Fenton, Staffordshire, by F. & R. Pratt & Co. (See Pot Lids.)

Bottle, scent; figure reserve on orange peel, ca 1800, 3⅛" 260.00
Creamer, mc & pk lustre, emb floral decor, 4¾" 220.00
Figurine, cowherd w/cow & calf, mc, 1800-20, 5½x7½", EX 550.00
Figurine, cradle, pearlware, typical palette, 11¾", EX 2,415.00
Figurine, gentleman & cow, dog at ft, rstr, 1800s, 5¾x6" 1,265.00
Figurine, lady w/mandolin, rocky base, minor rstr, ca 1795, 9½" ...1,035.00
Figurine, maiden w/cow & calf, on oval base, 5¾x6" 2,500.00
Figurine, ram & lady gardener on oval base, rstr, 6x5½" 1,725.00
Figurine, stag, bocage on free-form oval base, 4½x5½" 750.00
Figurine, Winter allegory, cut-corner base, ca 1800, 9¼" 460.00
Mirror/window rest, bearded man in turban, rstr, 5¾" 600.00
Snuff box, dog on pillow figural, rstr, 1790s, 1⅞" 1,150.00
Toby jug, underglaze palette, minor hat rstr, 1790s, 8¼" 1,000.00

Precious Moments®

Known as 'America's Hummels,' Precious Moments® are a line of well-known collectibles created by Samuel J. Butcher and produced by Enesco, Inc. These pieces have endeared themselves to many because of the inspirational messages they portray. Over 300,000 club members have joined the national club since 1982.

The collection is twenty-one years old as of 1999. Each piece is produced with a different mark each year. This mark, not the date, is usually the link to the value of the piece. Most mold changes result in increased values, and when a piece is retired or suspended, its price increases as well. As an example, 'God Loveth a Cheerful Giver' retailed for $9.50 in 1980; it was retired in 1981 and has a secondary market price now of $850.00 to $950.00. The majority of the collection has increased in value from its original retail.

Rosie Wells Enterprises, Inc., our advisor for this category, is in her seventeeth year of publishing news on the Precious Moments® collection, as well as a secondary market price guide. She has hosted international conventions for Precious Moments® collectors since 1983. Her address is in the Directory under Clubs, Newsletters, and Catalogs. Items listed below are assumed to be in mint condition with the original box.

Bride and Groom, E-3114: No mark, $90.00; Triangle mark, $80.00; Hourglass mark, $70.00; All other marks from $50.00 to $55.00 each.

#102466, Reindeer, ornament, dtd 1986, missing mk 175.00
#102466, Reindeer, ornament, dtd 1986, Olive Branch mk 175.00
#12068, Voice of Spring, 1st issue/4 Seasons, 1985, Cross mk, $250 to . 295.00
#12068, Voice of Spring, 1st issue/4 Seasons, 1985, Dove mk 275.00
#12092, Winter's Song, 4th issue/4 Seasons, 1986, Dove mk 135.00
#12092, Winter's Song, 4th issue/4 Seasons, 1986, Flower mk ... 160.00
#139475, Love Makes World..., 1985 Century Circle, Ship mk .. 500.00
#16012, Baby's 1st Trip, 4th ed/Baby's 1st, suspended, Dove mk 300.00
#16012, Baby's 1st Trip, 4th ed/Baby's 1st, suspended, Flower mk . 265.00
#520322, Make a Joyful Noise, Easter Seals, 1989, Bow/Arrow mk, 9" ... 900.00
#529567, Sam Butcher, Population sign, 1992, G Clef mk 185.00
BC861, Fishing for Friends, 1986 Birthday Club, Dove mk 145.00
BC861, Fishing for Friends, 1986 Birthday Club, Olive Branch mk 125.00
E-0001, But Love Goes on Forever, 1991 Club Gift, no mk, $155 to 175.00
E-0001, But Love Goes on..., 1991 Club Gift, Triangle mk, $140 to . 150.00
E-1374G, Make a Joyful Noise, goose girl, Cedar Tree mk 35.00
E-1374G, Make a Joyful Noise, goose girl, no mk 110.00
E-2011, Come Let Us Adore Him, retired 1981, no mk, from $250 to . 300.00
E-2827, I Get a Kick Out of You, retired 1986, Fish mk 220.00
E-2827, I Get a Kick Out of You, retired 1986, Olive Branch mk 190.00
E-2841, Baby's 1st Picture, 2nd ed, Baby's 1st, Cross mk 185.00
E-2841, Baby's 1st Picture, 2nd ed, Baby's 1st, Flower mk 160.00
E-5202, Thank You for Coming to My Ade, suspended 1984, Cross mk . 110.00
E-5202, Thank You for Coming to My Ade, suspended 1984, no mk 155.00
E-9268, Nobody's Perfect, smiling 'error,' retired 1990, Hourglass mk 525.00

Pre-Columbian Artifacts

The term 'pre-Columbian' loosely refers to some time prior to 1492, when Columbus arrived in America. In particular, it indicates pre-1492 artifacts of Central and South America, some of which can be dated as early as 4000 B.C. Artifacts representing the cultures of the Inca, Mayan, and Aztec Indians are avidly sought by the collector. These may be made of precious metals, hardstones, or pottery. Some were used in rituals and religious rites; some such as bowls and other utensils, though strictly utilitarian, nevertheless convey through form and decoration the craftsmanship of these early tribes.

Bottle, water; blkware, dbl rattlesnakes, 9x7" 75.00
Bowl, blk & cream on red clay, 4½x8" 70.00
Bowl, blk & red on cream clay, 3-leg, 5x10" 150.00

Bowl, geometric, blk on red clay, Mimbres, 3x6¾" 1,000.00
Bowl, geometrics, blk on cream on red clay, 3-leg, 3½x6½" 75.00
Bowl, red-on-cream pottery, rpr, 3x10" 125.00
Bowl, tadpole, blk on wht clay, spirit release hole, Mimbres, 7" .. 1,300.00
Bowl, 5-point star design, blk & cream, 2x5" 55.00
Idol, seated female w/legs out, hands to chest, 12x9" 450.00
Idol, seated hunchbk w/headdress & ear spools, 8x5" 175.00
Jar, red-on-cream stairsteps, no rstr, 4x8" 80.00
Jar, water; plainware, rpr neck, 7x8" 100.00
Mortar, cvd stone w/radiating design, 6x6" 110.00
Sewing kit, basketry container w/spindles & cvd beads, 14" L 150.00
Stone cvg, human face, wide nose & mouth, 6x4" 80.00
Stone cvg, human head, stylized features, 9x5" 150.00

Primitives

Like the mouse that ate the grindstone, so has collectible interest in primitives increased, a little bit at a time, until demand is taking bites instead of nibbles into their availability. Although the term 'primitives' once referred to those survival essentials contrived by our American settlers, it has recently been expanded to include objects needed or desired by succeeding generations — items representing the cabin-'n-cornpatch existence as well as examples of life on larger farms and in towns. Through popular usage, it also respectfully covers what are actually 'country collectibles.'

From the 1600s into the latter 1800s, factories employed carvers, blacksmiths, and other artisans whose handwork contributed to turning out quality items. When buying, 'touchmarks,' a company's name and/or location and maker's or owner's initials, are exciting discoveries.

Primitives are uniquely individual. Following identical forms, results more often than not show typically personal ideas. Using this as a guide (combined with circumstances of age, condition, desire to own, etc.) should lead to a reasonably accurate evaluation. For items not listed, consult comparable examples. Authority Kathryn McNerney has compiled several lovely books on primitives and related topics: *Primitives, Our American Heritage; Collectible Blue and White Stoneware;* and *Antique Tools, Our American Heritage.* You will find her address in the Directory under Florida. See also Butter Molds and Stamps; Boxes; Copper; Farm Collectibles; Fireplace Implements; Kitchen Collectibles; Molds; Tinware; Weaving; Woodenware; and Wrought Iron.

Washing machine, Favorite, R. Ward Mfg Co. stamp on pine rocker-style machine, 41x32x21", EX, $260.00.

Bed warmer, brass, chased sunburst decor, wood hdl, 43" L 250.00
Bed warmer, brass & copper, long wooden hdl, 42", VG 125.00
Bed warmer, copper, eng lid, trn wooden hdl, 43" L 220.00
Bellows, old red pnt w/gold & blk vintage, old leather, 18" 220.00
Bellows, orig yel pnt w/mc fruit stencil, prof rstr leather, 18" 880.00
Bellows, turtle-bk, old red pnt w/mc decor, poor leathers, 17" 120.00
Bellows, turtle-bk, smoked wht pnt w/mc floral stencil, 18" 360.00
Bellows, turtle-bk w/HP fruit & foliage, rstr leather, 17" 450.00

Broom, splint w/wire binding, cvd wood hdl, 38" **130.00**
Candle box, 2-tier compartments, plank bk, rfn, 15¾x11x5" **225.00**
Candle mold, pewter & wood, 18-tube, 18x22x6½", EX **1,200.00**
Candle mold, tin, 2-tube, gallery rim, wire loop, 3x2x11" **110.00**
Candle mold, tin, 3-tube, gallery rim, ribbon hdl, 11x4x3" **100.00**
Candle mold, tin, 4-tube, flared gallery rim, ribbon hdl, 10x6x5" ...**140.00**
Candle mold, tin, 4-tube, strap hdl, 10½" **100.00**
Candle mold, tin, 6-tube, C-shaped hdl, 5¾x5x2½" **900.00**
Candle mold, tin, 8-tube, curved ft, ear hdl, 11¼" **300.00**
Candle mold, tin, 12-tube, dbl hanging rings, 6⅞x5⅝x4½" **475.00**
Candle mold, tin, 24-tube, dbl-ear hdls, 11¾" **300.00**
Candle mold, tin, 24-tube, pine base w/old red, NY stencil, 13" ..**1,760.00**
Cheese carrier, Windsor style, rnd hoop w/32 spindles on fr, 31" L ..**700.00**
Cheese sieve, tin heart shape, hanging ring, 6" **360.00**
Cheese sieve, woven splint, EX age & patina, 27" dia **465.00**
Cheese slicer, wrought iron, rpl wire blade, wood hdl, 18x23" **65.00**
Cheese strainer, pnt wood, canted sides, 19th C, 8x19x19" **800.00**
Churn, coopered wood, cylindrical w/iron bands, 19th C, 46" w/hdl ..**260.00**
Churn, pnt wood w/metal straps, dasher type, 18½", VG **155.00**
Churn, rocking bbl shape on sawbuck stand, 19th C, 33" **150.00**
Foot warmer, tin w/punched heart design, wooden fr, 9x8x6" **195.00**
Hair curler, scissors style, wrought iron, 19th C, 10¼" L **35.00**
Knife, chopping; wrought iron, appl iron shaft w/wood hdl **20.00**
Pastry board, tin on wood, wall mt, 22x22", +maple rolling pin .**200.00**
Peel, wrought iron w/ram's horn hdl, pitted, 46" **110.00**
Pelt stretcher, wooden, various szs, 6 for **60.00**
Pipe tongs, wrought steel, Ft Wm Henry Capt...1756, 17¼" ..**9,200.00**
Rack, candle drying; revolving, 8 chamfered arms, 40x44" **400.00**
Rack, drying; mortised/chamfered, shoe ft, bl rpt, 39x25" **220.00**
Rack, drying; pine, orig red-brn stain, mortised/chamfered, 30x30" ...**415.00**
Rack, drying; pine w/old dk patina, A fr w/7 rods, 42x48" **825.00**
Rack, drying; pine w/old red over gr, 3-drw, wire nails, 45x40" ..**495.00**
Rack, plate drying; hanging, softwood, cut-out hdl, dvtl, 8x27" ...**95.00**
Rake, wood, rnd wooden teeth, old red pnt, 72x26" **60.00**
Rolling pin, tin, wooden hdls, minor dents, 16½" **450.00**
Scouring board, arched top, dtd 1837, 29x4¾x3⅛" **150.00**
Sieve, bean; wood, slatted, movable sides, ca 1867 ....**195.00**
Slaw board, poplar w/heart cutout, old patina, 9x20" **250.00**
Slaw board, softwood, hanging hole, iron blade, 7x26" **70.00**
Sock stretchers, branded 10½ w/Co name, 40" L, pr, EX **45.00**
Spice cabinet, hanging, 7 drws w/3 compartments, 1890s, 3x12" .**190.00**
Sugar nippers, brass/wood/wrought iron, scissors type, 11¾" **325.00**
Sugar nippers, iron, on board, ca 1850 ....**400.00**
Sugar nippers, rod iron, J Nibb, 8½" **150.00**
Tongs, ember; iron, acorn finial, notched hdl, 15" **350.00**
Washboard, CI w/heart cutout at top, PA, 19th C, 23x13" **755.00**
Washboard, National, metal rubs **30.00**
Washboard, pine, 9-slat, recessed top panel, weathered, 1890s, 25" .**100.00**
Washboard, wooden, 16-dowel scrubbing surface, 22" L **95.00**

Prints

The term 'print' may be defined today as almost any image printed on paper by any available method. Examples of collectible old 'prints' are Norman Rockwell magazine covers and Maxfield Parrish posters and calendars. 'Original print' refers to one achieved through the efforts of the artist or under his direct supervision. A 'reproduction' is a print produced by an accomplished print maker who reproduces another artist's print or original work. Thorough study is required on the part of the collector to recognize and appreciate the many variable factors to be considered in evaluating a print. Prices vary from one area of the country to another and are dependent upon new findings regarding the scarcity or abundance of prints as such information may arise. Although

each collector of old prints may have their own varying criteria by which to judge condition, for those who deal only rarely in this area or newer collectors, a few guidelines may prove helpful. Staining, though unquestionably detrimental, is nearly always present in some degree and should be weighed against the rarity of the print. Professional cleaning should improve its appearance and at the same time help preserve it. Avoid tears that affect the image; minor margin tears are another matter, especially if the print is a rare one. Moderate 'foxing' (brown spots caused by mold or the fermentation of the rag content of old paper) and light stains from the old frames are not serious unless present in excess. Margin trimming was a common practice; but look for at least ½" to 1½" margins, depending on print size.

When no condition is indicated, the items listed below are assumed to be in very good to excellent condition. See also Nutting, Wallace; Parrish, Maxfield.

Audubon, John J.

Audubon is the best known of the American and European wildlife artists. His first series of prints, 'Birds of America,' was produced by Robert Havell of London. They were printed on Whitman water-marked paper bearing dates of 1826 to 1838. The Octavo Edition of the same series was printed in seven editions, the first by J.T. Bowen under Audubon's direction. There were seven volumes of text and prints, each 10" x 7", the first five bearing the J.J. Audubon and J.B. Chevalier mark, the last two, J.J. Audubon. They were produced from 1840 through 1844. The second and other editions were printed up to 1871. The Bien Edition prints were full size, made under the direction of Audubon's sons in the late 1850s. Due to the onset of the Civil War, only 105 plates were finished. These are considered to be the most valuable of the reprints of the 'Birds of America Series.'

In 1971 the complete set was reprinted by Johnson Reprint Corp. of New York and Theaturm Orbis Terrarum of Amsterdam. Examples of the latter bear the watermark G. Schut and Zonen. In 1985 a second reprint was done by Abbeville Press for the National Audubon Society.

Although Audubon is best known for his portrayal of birds, one of his less-familiar series, 'Vivaparous Quadrupeds of North America,' portrayed various species of animals. Assembled in corroboration with John Bachman from 1839 until 1851, these prints are 28" x 22" in size. Several octavo editions were published in the 1850s. In the following listing, all measurements are actual print size unless stated otherwise.

Moose Deer, hand colored, John T. Bowen, Double Elephant Folio Edition, plate LXXVI, 21¼x27", EX, $3,750.00.

American Oyster Catcher, Bowen, 6x9" **500.00**
Black Vulture, #108, Havell, 25½x37½" **5,500.00**
California Hare, Bowen, 21x27" **5,500.00**
Canvasback Duck w/View of Baltimore, Amsterdam edition, 25x37" ..**2,500.00**
Common Mouse, JT Bowen, plate XC, 19½x25¼" **6,000.00**
Crow, Bowen, 1st ed, 1840, 9x6" (sight) **300.00**
Curlew Sandpiper, Bien, 1860, 15x18¾" **400.00**
Florida Cormorant, Amsterdam edition, 26x39" **500.00**
Gannet, #326, Havell, 26x39" **16,000.00**
Mallard Duck, #385, Bien, 26¾x37½" **10,000.00**
Maryland Marmot, lg folio, 22x27" **1,500.00**

Meadowlark, Bowen, 6x9" **700.00**

Polar Bear, Hitchcock litho, Bowen, 6½x9" **400.00**

Purple Finch, #4, Havell, 25x37" **4,500.00**

Summer or Wood Duck, Amsterdam edition, 29½x19" **3,000.00**

Swamp Hare, #37, Bowen, 1850s, 7x10" **250.00**

Ursos-Ferox, Lewis & Clark Grizzly Bears Males, Bowen, 22x27" ...**4,500.00**

White Wolf, Bowen, 21x27" **3,500.00**

Whooping Crane, #227, Amsterdam, 37x25" **1,500.00**

Wild Turkey, Bowen, 6x9" **2,000.00**

Currier and Ives

Nathaniel Currier was in business by himself until the late 1850s when he formed a partnership with James Merrit Ives. Currier is given credit for being the first to use the medium to portray newsworthy subjects, and the Currier and Ives views of 19th-century American culture are familiar to us all. In the following listings, 'C' numbers correspond with a standard reference book by Conningham. Values are given for prints in very good condition; all are colored unless indicated black and white. Unless noted 'NC' (Nathaniel Currier), all prints are published by Currier and Ives. Our advisors for this category are John and Barbara Rudisill (Rudisill's Alt Print Haus); they are listed in the Directory under Maryland.

Morning in the Woods, NC, 1852, C-4196, large folio, $2,800.00.

Abigail, NC, 1846, C-9, sm folio **85.00**

Accommodation Train, 1876, C-32, sm folio **400.00**

Am Fireman, Always Ready; 1858, C-152, med folio **1,300.00**

Am Forest Game, 1866, C-156, lg folio **1,000.00**

Am Game, 1866, C-163, lg folio **750.00**

Am Prize Fruit, 1862, C-183, lg folio **1,800.00**

Arguing the Point, NC, 1855, C-265, lg folio **5,200.00**

Arkansas Traveler, 1870, C-270, sm folio **275.00**

Autumn in Adirondacks (Lake Harrison), undtd, C-323, sm folio .**350.00**

Autumn on Lake George, undtd, C-324, sm folio **250.00**

Beautiful Brunette, undtd, C-453, sm folio **75.00**

Beautiful Persian, undtd, C-457, sm folio **75.00**

Beauty of New England, undtd, C-462, sm folio **65.00**

Benjamin Franklin, Statesman..., NC, 1847, C-499, sm folio **500.00**

Between Two Fires, 1879, C-511, sm folio **300.00**

Black-Eyed Beauty, undtd, C-549, sm folio **65.00**

Bombardment of Fort Pulaski...April, 1862, C-595, sm folio **350.00**

Boss of the Track, 1881, C-619, sm folio **225.00**

Burning of Chicago, 1871, C-738, sm folio **600.00**

Burning of Clipper...Golden Light, NC, undtd, C-740, sm folio .**450.00**

Burning of the Steamship Austria, Sept 13, undtd, C-748, sm folio ..**275.00**

Cares of a Family, NC, 1856, C-814, lg folio **3,500.00**

Catherine, NC, 1845, C-849, sm folio **90.00**

Caught on a Fly, 1879, C-864, sm folio **300.00**

Champion Stallion Directum, 1893, C-975, sm folio **300.00**

Chicago in Flames, Scene at Randolph...; undtd, C-1027, sm folio .**600.00**

Chicky's Dinner, undtd, C-1029, sm folio **175.00**

Christ Walking on the Sea, undtd, C-1071, sm folio **30.00**

City of New York, NC, 1855, C-1102, lg folio **3,000.00**

Clara, undtd, C-1127, sm folio **75.00**

Clipper Ship in a Hurricane, undtd, C-1155, sm folio **650.00**

Coming in 'On His Ear,' 1875, C-1221, sm folio **250.00**

Cottage Dooryard, Evening; NC, 1855, C-1265, med folio **400.00**

Cross Matched Race, 1891, C-1306, med folio **550.00**

Custer's Last Charge, 1876, C-1333, sm folio **350.00**

Darktown Yacht Club, Hard...Breeze; 1885, C-1439, sm folio ...**275.00**

Day of Marriage, 1847, C-1459, NC, sm folio **100.00**

Declaration Committee, 1876, C-1530, sm folio **300.00**

Disputed Heat, Claiming Foul; 1878, C-1587, lg folio **1,800.00**

Distanced, 1878, C-1589, sm folio **225.00**

Drive Through the Highlands, undtd, C-1627, med folio **700.00**

Dude Swell, 1883, C-1635, sm folio **230.00**

Dutchman & Hiram Woodruff, 1871, C-1640, sm folio **700.00**

Easter Flowers, 1869, C-1655, sm folio **50.00**

Elizabeth, NC, 1846, C-1698, sm folio **95.00**

English Snipe, 1871, C-1744, sm folio **375.00**

English Winter Scene, undtd, C-1745, sm folio **525.00**

Express Train, 1870, C-1792, sm folio **2,000.00**

Fall of Richmond...April 2..., 1865, C-1822, sm folio **300.00**

First Trot of the Season, 1870, C-1998, lg folio **2,000.00**

Flowers, NC, undtd, C-2058, sm folio **125.00**

Fording the River, NC, undtd, C-2081, med folio **550.00**

Fr Revolution, Burning...Carriages...; NC, 1848, C-2139, sm folio .**125.00**

Fruit & Flowers Piece, 1863, C-2160, med folio **400.00**

Gap of Dunloe, undtd, C-2219, sm folio **100.00**

Gen Tom Thumb, Smallest Man Alive; NC, 1849, C-2305, sm folio ...**200.00**

General Lewis Cass, NC, 1846, C-2288, sm folio **95.00**

Girl I Love, 1870, C-2376, sm folio **75.00**

God Bless Our Home, undtd, C-2392, sm folio **250.00**

Good Times on the Old Plantation, undtd, C-2451, sm folio **900.00**

Grand Horse St Julien, 1881, C-2488, sm folio **325.00**

Grand National Whig Banner, NC, 1844, C-2511, sm folio **400.00**

Grand Pacer Richball, 1890, C-2519, sm folio **300.00**

Grand Racer Kingston, Toy Spendthrift...; C-2521, 1891, lg folio .**1,500.00**

Great Conflagration at Pittsburgh, NC, undtd, C-2581, sm folio .**650.00**

Great Salt Lake, Utah; undtd, C-2649, sm folio **400.00**

Group of Lilies, undtd, C-2670, sm folio **150.00**

Happy Home, NC, undtd, C-2713, sm folio **100.00**

Happy Little Pups, undtd, C-2717, sm folio **150.00**

Harvesting, The Last Load; undtd, C-2750, sm folio **325.00**

Haunted Castle, undtd, C-2756, sm folio **90.00**

Hero & Flora Temple, NC, 1856, C-2800, lg folio **1,800.00**

Home of the Deer, undtd, C-2867, med folio **500.00**

Hooked, 1874, C-2928, sm folio **500.00**

Horse Fair, undtd, C-2940, sm folio **300.00**

Hues of Autumn on Racquet River, undtd, C-2982, sm folio **300.00**

Husking, 1861, C-3008, lg folio **10,000.00**

Impending Crisis, Caught in the Act; 1860, C-3033, med folio .**250.00**

Imported Messenger, 1880, C-3042, sm folio **300.00**

Ingleside Winter, undtd, C-3112, sm folio **600.00**

Jane, undtd, C-3181, sm folio **80.00**

Jolly Dog, 1878, C-3287, sm folio **200.00**

Just Married, undtd, C-3321, sm folio **100.00**

King of the Forest, undtd, C-3333, sm folio **200.00**

Kitties Among the Roses, 1873, C-3352, sm folio **175.00**

Lakeside Home, 1869, C-3423, med folio **350.00**

Leaders, 1888, C-3471, lg folio **1,000.00**

Liberty, 1876, C-3486, sm folio **200.00**

Lieutenant Gen Winfield Scott..., undtd, C-3495, sm folio **125.00**

Life in the Country, Evening; 1862, C-3508, med folio **850.00**

Life of a Hunter, Catching a Tartar; 1861, C-3521, lg folio **5,000.00**

Lion Hunter, NC, undtd, C-3554, sm folio 165.00
Little Bo Peep, undtd, C-3577, sm folio 175.00
Little Ellen, undtd, C-3614, sm folio 95.00
Little Jamie, undtd, C-3642, sm folio 95.00
Little Students, undtd, C-3720, sm folio 150.00
Little Willie, undtd, C-3738, sm folio 90.00
Loss of Steamship Swallow, NC, 1845, C-3779, sm folio 425.00
Lottie, undtd, C-3785, sm folio 75.00
Maiden Rock, Mississippi River; undtd, C-3891, sm folio 500.00
Marriage Certificate, NC, 1848, C-4000, sm folio 100.00
Mill-Cove Lake, undtd, C-4123, sm folio 400.00
Mink Trapping, Prime; 1862, C-4139, lg folio 10,000.00
Moonlight, The Ruins; undtd, C-4184, sm folio 95.00
Moose & Wolves, A Narrow Escape; undtd, C-4185, sm folio ...300.00
Moosehead Lake, undtd, C-4186, sm folio 250.00
Mother's Wing, 1866, C-4239, med folio 250.00
Mountain Rumble, undtd, C-4244, sm folio 175.00
My Boyhood's Home, 1872, C-4276, sm folio 200.00
My Highland Boy, NC, undtd, C-4305, sm folio 95.00
My Little Favorite, undtd, C-4315, med folio 125.00
My Love & I, 1872, C-4343, sm folio 125.00
My Pet Bird, undtd, C-4348, med folio 175.00
My Pony & Dog, undtd, C-4350, sm folio 150.00
New Fashioned Girl, undtd, C-4422, sm folio 225.00
Niagara Falls, From Goat Island; undtd, C-4457, med folio 350.00
Noontide a Shady Spot, undtd, C-4501, sm folio 175.00
Old Farm Gate, 1864, C-4555, lg folio 1,400.00
Old Forge Bridge, undtd, C-4559, sm folio 225.00
Old Oaken Bucket, 1872, C-4577, sm folio 225.00
On a Point, NC, 1855, C-4592, med folio 600.00
Outward Bound, Going Out Under..., undtd, C-4666, sm folio .700.00
Pacing for a Grand Purse, 1890, C-4677, lg folio 1,500.00
Parson's Colt, 1879, C-4706, sm folio 250.00
Patriot of 1776, 1876, C-4725, sm folio 200.00
Pennsylvania Railroad Scenery, undtd, C-4745, sm folio 750.00
Played Out, 1871, C-4794, sm folio 325.00
Pride of the Garden, 1873, C-4914, sm folio 175.00
Pride of the West, 1870, C-4918, sm folio 75.00
Puzzled Fox, 1872, C-4984, sm folio 350.00
Quail Shooting, NC, 1852, C-4989, lg folio 3,000.00
Rabbits in Woods, undtd, C-5036, sm folio 250.00
Raspberries, 1870, C-5065, sm folio 175.00
Rattling Heat, 1891, C-5068, med folio 650.00
River Side, undtd, C-5163, sm folio 225.00
Robinson Crusoe..., 1874, C-5189, sm folio 200.00
Rocky Mountains, undtd, C-5195, sm folio 900.00
Scene on the Susquehanna, undtd, C-5415, sm folio 300.00
Scholar's Rewards, 1874, C-5425, sm folio 225.00
Shall I?, undtd, C-5477, very sm folio 1,000.00
Shooting on the Prairie, undtd, C-5498, sm folio 700.00
Single, NC, 1845, C-5527, sm folio 175.00
Snipe Shooting, NC, 1852, C-5577, lg folio 3,000.00
Source of the Hudson..., undtd, C-5627, sm folio 325.00
Split Rock, St John River; undtd, C-5663, sm folio 275.00
Stable Scene No 2, NC, undtd, C-5686, sm folio 500.00
Stella & Alice Grey,...Whalebone; NC, 1855, C-5811, lg folio .1,850.00
Straw-Yard Winter, undtd, C-5837, med folio 975.00
Striped Bass, 1872, C-5844, sm folio 350.00
Summer Morning, undtd, C-5869, sm folio 175.00
Sunday in the Olden Time, undtd, C-5883, sm folio 175.00
Sunrise on Lake Saranac, 1860, C-5895, lg folio 2,800.00
Surrender of General Lee., 1865, C-5909, sm folio 250.00
Sylvan Lake, undtd, C-5940, sm folio 200.00
Tomb of Washington, Mt Vernon VA; undtd, C-6112, sm folio .150.00

Trinket..., 1879, C-6152, sm folio 300.00
Trotting Cracks at the Forge, 1869, C-6169, lg folio 8,000.00
Vase of Flowers, undtd, C-6363, sm folio 175.00
Velocipede, 1869, C-6365, sm folio 1,400.00
View of the Houstanic, 1867, C-6443, lg folio 1,400.00
View of the Hudson..., 1846, C-6421, sm folio 300.00
Virginia Water Windsor Park, undtd, C-6475, sm folio 150.00
Washington at Prayer, NC, undtd, C-6517, sm folio 150.00
Washington at Princeton, NC, 1846, C-6518, sm folio 450.00
Washington Family, undtd, C-6531, sm folio 100.00
Watkin's Glen NY, undtd, C-6573, sm folio 350.00
Wedding Day, NC, undtd, C-6599, sm folio 125.00
West Point Foundry, Hudson River, NY; 1862, C-6617, med folio 1,500.00
White Squadron US Navy, 1893, C-6644, lg folio 1,200.00
William Tell, Son's Head; undtd, C-6712, sm folio 125.00
Winter Morning, 1861, C-6740, med folio 2,100.00
Woodcock Shooting, 1870, C-6775, sm folio 550.00
Yacht Vesta..., undtd, C-6817, sm folio 400.00
Young Brood, 1870, C-6840, sm folio 250.00
Young Mother, NC, undtd, C-6860, sm folio 100.00

Fox, R. Atkinson

A Canadian who worked as an artist in the 1880s, R. Atkinson Fox moved to New York about ten years later, where his original oils were widely sold at auction and through exhibitions. Today he is best known, however, for his prints, published by as many as twenty printmakers. More than thirty examples of his work appeared on Brown and Bigelow calendars, and it was used in many other forms of advertising as well. Though he was an accomplished artist able to interpret any subject well, he is today best known for his landscapes. Fox died in 1935. Our advisor for Fox prints is Pat Gibson whose address is listed in the Directory under California.

Venetian Garden, #7, 15½x19", $165.00.

Capital & Labor, #50, 10x6" 195.00
Day's Work Done, The; #626, 11x8" 225.00
Feeding Ground, #285, 15x5" 195.00
Garden of Nature, #189, 18x10" 145.00
Home of the West Wind, #423, 16x23" 200.00
Lake Louise, Alberta, #402, 11x14" 175.00
Magic Forest, #330, 16x12" 165.00
Morning Call, The; #481, 8x12" 190.00
Music of the Waters, #218, 20x16" 150.00
Nature's Treasures, #91, 14x22" 145.00
Old Ironsides, #195, 8x12" 135.00
Playmate Guardian, #24, 9x7" 100.00
Returning From Pasture, #502, 9x7" 120.00
Sunrise, Coast of Maine, #526, 7½x10½" 175.00
Surf Fishing, #799, 4x3" 250.00
Waiting for Their Master, #484, 8x6" 175.00

Gutmann, Bessie Pease

Delicately tinted prints of appealing children sometimes accompanied by their pets, sometimes asleep, often captured at some childhood activity are typical of the work of Gutmann; she painted lovely ladies as well and was a successful illustrator of children's books. Her career spanned the earlier decades of this century. Our advisor for this category is Earl MacSorley; he is listed in the Directory under Connecticut.

Betty, #787, 14x18"	275.00
Bobby, #789, 14x18"	250.00
Bride, #629	600.00
Butterfly, #632, 14x18"	175.00
Fairest of the Flowers, #659, 14x18"	350.00
Friendly Enemies, #215, 11x14"	75.00
Happy Dreams, #800, 14x20"	250.00
Hearing, #119, 9x12"	200.00
Little Bit of Heaven, #650, 14x18"	75.00
Little Bo Peep, #200, 11x14"	125.00
Little Miss Muffet, #204, 11x14"	200.00
Lorelei, #645, 14x18"	1,000.00
Mighty Like a Rose, #642, 14x18"	275.00
My Darling, #610, 14x18"	450.00
Nitey Nite, #826, 14x21"	95.00
On the Up & Up, #796, 14x18"	150.00
Seeing, #211, 11x14"	200.00
Sunbeam, #730	200.00
Television, #821, 14x21"	125.00
To Have & To Hold, #625, 14x18"	375.00
Wedding March, #653, 14x18"	500.00

Icart, Louis

Louis Icart (1888 – 1950) was a Parisian artist best known for his boudoir etchings in the '20s and '30s. In the '80s prices soared, primarily due to Japanese buying. The market began to readjust in 1990, and most etchings now sell at retail between $1,400.00 and $2,500.00. Value is determined by popularity and condition, more than by rarity. Original frames and matting are not important, as most collectors want the etchings restored to their original condition and protected with acid-free mats.

Beware of the following repro and knock-off items: 1. Pseudo engravings on white plastic with the Icart 'signature.' 2. Any bronzes with the Icart signature. 3. Most watercolors, especially if they look similar in subject matter to a popular etching. 4. Lithographs where the dot-matrix printing is visible under magnification. Some even have phony embossed seals or rubber stamp markings. Items listed below are in excellent condition unless noted otherwise. Our advisor is William Holland, author of *Louis Icart: The Complete Etchings*, and *The Collectible Maxfield Parrish*; he is listed in the Directory under Pennsylvania.

Pals, 1923, touches of hand coloring, laid down, 16¾x21¼", matted and framed, $3,200.00.

Autumn Swirls, 1924, 17x12"+fr	1,200.00
Belle Rose, 1933, 16x21", M	2,200.00
Chronicles of Women: Strategist, 1917, 10x6⅞"	700.00
Cinderella, 1927, 15½x19¼", VG	1,800.00
Coursing II, 1929, 15½x25"	3,200.00
Don Juan, 1928, 21¼x14⅛"	1,250.00
Eve, 13x19"	1,850.00
Fair Dancer, 1939, 20x23"	1,800.00
French Doll, lady smoking & admiring doll, 14x18"	1,150.00
Hiding Place, 1927, 19x15"+fr	1,850.00
Hydrangeas, 1929, 16⅞x21"	2,070.00
Joan of Arc, 1929, 21½x15⅛"	1,500.00
Lady of the Camelias, 1927, 17x20½"	1,450.00
Laughing, 1930, 12x17"	1,650.00
Laziness, 1925, 15½x19½"	1,850.00
Leda & the Swan, 1937, 20½x31"	6,500.00
Lilies, 1934, 28½x20"	3,600.00
Louise, 1927, 21x14"	1,800.00
Love Letters, 1926, 14½x19"	1,500.00
Manon, 1927, 20¾x13⅞"	1,400.00
Modern Eve, 1933, 21x16½", M	5,000.00
My Model, 1932, 22x17"	1,700.00
Old Yarn, 1924, 17x21"+fr	700.00
On the Champs Elyees, 1938, 16x22"	2,200.00
Orange Seller, 1929, 18¼x14"+fr	1,200.00
Orchids, 1937, 28⅜x19⅜"+fr	4,800.00
Pekinese Buddha, 1926, 14x19½"	1,000.00
Pink Lady, HP touches, 1933, 8⅝x11"+fr	800.00
Puppies, 1925, 17x22⅛"	1,950.00
Seville, HP touches, 1928, 20x13¼"	1,150.00
Silk Robe, 1926, 15½x19"	1,950.00
Sleeping Beauty, 1927, 15½x19¼", VG	1,800.00
Snow, 1922, 29½x14¼"+fr	1,150.00
Speed, 1927, 15¼x25½"	4,000.00
Spilled Oranges, 1921, 15¾x11¾", VG	1,250.00
Springtime, 1924, 18x14¼" +fr	1,265.00
Swallows, 1926, 19⅜x11¾", VG	1,150.00
Swimsuit, 14x10"+fr	1,350.00
Symphony in Blue, 1936, 23½x20"	1,950.00
Venus, 1928, 14x19½"	1,900.00
Waltz Echos, 1938, 19⅜x19½"+fr	4,025.00
Waterfall, 1936, 21x9"	2,900.00
White Underwear, 1925, 15½x19½"	1,900.00
Winter Bouquet, 1924, 16½x11¾"	1,900.00
Wistfulness, 17½x22½"	1,500.00
Zest, 1928, 20x15"	2,450.00

Kurz and Allison

Louis Kurz founded the Chicago Lithograph Company in 1833. Among his most notable works were a series of thirty-six Civil War scenes and one hundred illustrations of Chicago architecture. His company was destroyed in the Great Fire of 1871, and in 1880 Kurz formed a partnership with Alexander Allison, an engraver. Until both retired in 1903, they produced hundreds of lithographs in color as well as black and white. Our advisor for these prints is Robert Wieland; he is listed in the Directory under Florida.

Battle of Atlanta, lg folio, VG	395.00
Battle of Bull Run, lg folio, VG	425.00
Battle of Bunker Hill, ca 1900, 17½x25"	400.00
Battle of Cedar Creek, lg folio, VG	395.00
Battle of Champion Hills, 1997, 17⅝x25"+fr, EX	400.00
Battle of Chattanooga, lg folio, VG	395.00

Battle of Corinth, MS; lg folio, VG 395.00
Battle of Fort Donelson, 1887, 17½x25", EX 500.00
Battle of Franklin, Chicago; 1891, 19½x26½", VG 350.00
Battle of Franklin, TN; lg folio, VG 395.00
Battle of Gettysburg, 1884, 17¾x25"+fr, EX 400.00
Battle of Kenesaw Mountain, lg folio, VG 395.00
Battle of Lookout Mountain, lg folio, VG 395.00
Battle of Pea Ridge, lg folio, VG 495.00
Battle of Princeton, lg folio, VG 395.00
Battle of Williamsburg, VA; lg folio, VG 395.00
Battle of Wilson's Creek, MO; lg folio, VG 395.00
Declaration of Independence, ca 1900, 17½x25⅛", EX 450.00
Fort Pillow Massacre, lg folio, VG 495.00

McKenney and Hall

Our advisor for McKenney and Hall prints is Robert Wieland; he is listed in the Directory under Florida.

Chippewqa Mother & Child, 1843, sm folio 255.00
Chittee-Yoholo, Seminole Chief, 1845, octavo, 9¼x6" 200.00
Kish-Kal-Wa a Shawanoe Chief, EC Biddle, 17½x12½" 500.00
Little Crow, Sioux Chief, Greenough, 1838, lg folio 200.00
Oche-Finceco, Rice & Clark, Phila, 1845, 19½x13¾" 300.00
Ong-Pa-Ton-Ga/Big Elk, Omaha Chief, 1838, lg folio 230.00
Petalesharro, Pawnee Brave, 1845, octavo, 9x6" 330.00
Sha-Ha-Ka, Mandan Chief, 1838, lg folio 230.00
Sum-Ma-Nu, Flat Head Boy, Bowen, 1838, 19½x13¾" 250.00

Prang, Louis

Battle of Antietam, 1887, 15x21½" 300.00
Battle of Fredericksburg: Laying Pontoons., 1886, 7¾x12½" 350.00
Battle of Port Hudson, ca 1887, 15x21½" 300.00
Battle of Shiloh, after Thulstrup, ca 1886, 14⅞x21½" 300.00
Sheridan's Ride, after Thulstrup, ca 1888, 14⅞x21½" 300.00
Siege of Atlanta: Gen Sherman…Inspecting, 1888, 7¾x12½" ..350.00

Yard Longs

Values for yard-long prints are given for examples in **near mint** condition, full length, nicely framed, and with the original glass. To learn more about this popular area of collector interest, we recommend *Those Wonderful Yard-Long Prints and More*, *More Wonderful Yard-Long Prints*, Book 2, and *Yard-Long Prints*, Book 3, by our advisors Bill and June Keagy, and Charles and Joan Rhoden. They are listed in the Directory under Indiana and Illinois respectively. A word of caution: watch for reproductions; **know your dealer.**

1913 Pompeian Beauty art panel, advertising and calendar on back, $350.00.

Photo courtesy June and Bill Keagy

At the North Pole, Jos Hoover & Son, c 1904 ....400.00
Battle of the Chicks, Ben Austrian, c 1920 ....250.00
Dogwood & Violets, Paul DeLongpre 300.00
Home Sweet Home, Paul DeLongpre, c 1901 ....300.00
La France Roses, by Paul DeLongpre, Spiehler's Perfumes, c 1903 .350.00
Mother & Child, for Nat'l Stockman & Farmer, 1913 ....450.00
Nasturtiums, pnt for Mandervill & King, Seedsmen, Rochester NY ...250.00
Our White House Queen for 1911, ad for White House Shoes ..500.00
Pabst Malt Extract, Jewel calendar, 1908 ....550.00
Piggies in Clover, 10 pigs playing in clover, c 1904 ....750.00
Pompeian Art Panel, Irresistible, sgn Clement Donshea, 1930 ...450.00
Schlitz Malt Extract Indian Girl, 1909 ....550.00
Selz Good Shoes, sgn Christy, lady holding roses, 1928 ....550.00
Selz Good Shoes, sgn Christy, lady holding yel plume fan, 1926 .550.00
Selz Good Shoes, sgn Christy, lady w/fur-trimmed red cape, 1930 .550.00
Selz Good Shoes, sgn Gene Pressler, 1924 ....550.00
Shower of Pansies, Muller Luchsinge & Co, c 1895 ....200.00
Temptation Candy Girl, lady in lt gr dress holding candy box ...500.00
Untitled Fruit, by J Califano, c 1903 ....250.00
Yard of Cherries, Guy Bedford, c 1906 ....200.00
Yard of Cherries & Flowers, LeRoy 200.00
Yard of Dogs, c 1903 ....200.00
Yard of Kittens, sgn Guy Bedford 300.00
Yard of Mixed Flowers, by Guy Bedford 200.00
Yard of Roses, Newton A Wills, c 1898 ....200.00
Yard of Sweet Peas, Heinmuller, ca 1905 ....200.00

Purinton

Founded in 1936 in Wellsville, Ohio, Purinton Pottery relocated in 1941 in Shippenville, Pennsylvania, and began producing hand-painted wares that are today attracting the interest of collectors of 'country-type' dinnerware. Using bold brush strokes of vivid color, simple yet attractive patterns such as Apple, Fruit, Tea Rose, and Pennsylvania Dutch were manufactured in tableware sets and accessory pieces. For more information we recommend *Purinton Pottery* by our advisor, Susan Morris; she is listed in the Directory under Oregon.

Ashtray, Apple, center hdl, 5½" 40.00
Baker, Intaglio, 7" 30.00
Baker, Maywood, 7" 25.00
Baker, Pennsylvania Dutch, 7" 45.00
Baker, Petals, 7" 35.00
Bean pot, Intaglio, 3¾" 50.00
Bean pot, Provincial Fruit, w/warming stand, 5¾", 9" w/stand 65.00
Bottle, night; Fruit, 1-qt, 7½" 45.00
Bottle, vinegar; Fruit, cobalt trim, 1-pt, 9½" 35.00
Bottles, oil/vinegar; Apple, 1-pt, 9½", pr 95.00
Bowl, cereal; Provincial Fruit, 5¼" 10.00
Bowl, dessert; Intaglio, 4" 8.00
Bowl, fruit; Apple, plain border, 12" 35.00
Bowl, fruit; Petals, 12" 50.00
Bowl, fruit; Saraband, 12" 25.00
Bowl, range; Fruit, red trim, w/lid, 5½" 45.00
Bowl, range; Grapes, w/lid, 5½" 45.00
Bowl, range; Normandy Plaid, w/lid, 5½" 50.00
Bowl, salad; Maywood, 11" 25.00
Bowl, spaghetti; Normandy Plaid, 14½" 55.00
Bowl, vegetable; Intaglio, divided, 10½" 30.00
Bowl, vegetable; Peasant Garden, open, 8½" 80.00
Bowl, vegetable; Tea Rose, open, 8½" 40.00
Butter dish, Apple, 6½" 65.00

Candle holder, Intaglio style, star shaped, 6" 65.00
Candy dish, Apple, 5¾" 75.00

Canister, coffee; Heather
Plaid, 7½", $40.00.

Photo courtesy Susan Morris

Canister, Apple, rare cobalt trim, oval, 9" 75.00
Canister, Fruit, rnd, wooden lid, 7½" 65.00
Canister, tea; Pennsylvania Dutch, 5½" 100.00
Coffee server, Seaform, 9" 125.00
Coffeepot, Apple, w/drip-filter, 8-cup, 11" 110.00
Coffeepot, Apple, 8-cup, 8" 90.00
Coffeepot, Chartreuse, 8-cup, 8" 75.00
Coffeepot, Fruit, drip style, 8-cup, 11" 85.00
Coffeepot, Ivy-Red blossom, drip-filter, 8-cup, 11" 85.00
Coffeepot, Maywood, 8-cup, 8" 65.00
Coffeepot, Petals, 8-cup, 8" 75.00
Cookie jar, Fruit, red trim, oval, 9" 60.00
Cookie jar, Mountain Rose, wooden lid, sq, 9½" 100.00
Cookie jar, Pennsylvania Dutch, slant-top, wooden lid, 7x7" 125.00
Creamer, Fruit, 3" 15.00
Creamer, Intaglio, 3½" 20.00
Creamer, Ivy — Yellow Blossom, 3½" 15.00
Creamer & sugar bowl, Normandy Plaid, mini, 2", set 30.00
Cruet, oil/vinegar, Fruit, open apple/gr grapes, sq, 5" 55.00
Cup, Normandy Plaid, 2½" 10.00
Cup, Tea Rose, 2½" 20.00
Decanter, Intaglio, mini, 5" 35.00
Decanter, Ivy — Red Blossom, no holes in top, mini, 2½" 12.00
Decanter, Mountain Rose, 5" 45.00
Dish, jam & jelly; Apple, 5½" 45.00
Dish, jam & jelly; Intaglio, 5½" 40.00
Dish, jam & jelly; Pennsylvania Dutch, 5½" 65.00
Jar, grease; Heather Plaid, w/lid, 5½" 60.00
Jar, grease; Normandy Plaid, w/lid, 5½" 60.00
Jar, marmalade; Apple, 4½" 50.00
Jar, marmalade; Mountain Rose, 4½" 65.00
Jar, marmalade; Palm Tree, 4½" 125.00
Jardiniere, Ming Tree, 5" 40.00
Jug, Dutch; Chartreuse, 2-pt, 5¾" 55.00
Jug, Dutch; Heather Plaid, 2-pt, 5¾" 45.00
Jug, honey; Shooting Stars, 6¼" 35.00
Jug, honey; Ivy-Yellow Blossom, 6¼" 35.00
Jug, Intaglio, 5-pt, 8" 75.00
Jug, Kent; Fruit, 1-pt, 4½" 30.00
Jug, Kent; Mountain Rose, 1-pt, 4½" 45.00
Jug, Kent; Normandy Plaid, 1-pt, 4½" 30.00
Jug, Oasis; Ribbon Flower, 9½", minimum value 500.00
Jug, Rebecca; Daisy, 7½" 50.00
Jug, Rebecca; Pennsylvania Dutch, 7½" 75.00
Mug, beer; Normandy Plaid, 16-oz, 4¾" 40.00
Mug, beer; Palm Tree, 16-oz, 4¾" 85.00
Mug, juice; Apple, 6-oz, 2½" 20.00

Mug, juice; Fruit, 6-oz, 2½" 15.00
Mug, juice; Ivy — Red Blossom, 6-oz, 2½" 15.00
Mug, juice; Maywood, 6-oz, 2½" 15.00
Pitcher, Apple, Rubel mold, 5" 75.00
Pitcher, gravy; Intaglio, TS&T mold, 3¾" 65.00
Planter, basket; Palm Tree, 6¼" 100.00
Planter, basket; Pennsylvania Dutch, 6¼" 85.00
Planter, Ming Tree, 5" 35.00
Planter, Tea Rose, 5" 65.00
Plate, breakfast; Peasant Garden, 8½" 100.00
Plate, chop; Apple, scalloped border, 12" 40.00
Plate, chop; Fruit, 12" 35.00
Plate, chop; Heather Plaid, 12" 25.00
Plate, chop; Intaglio, 12" 25.00
Plate, chop; Mountain Rose, 9¾" 25.00
Plate, dinner; Ming Tree, 9¾" 20.00
Plate, dinner; Saraband, 9¾" 8.00
Plate, lap; Crescent FLower, 8½" 35.00
Plate, salad; Pennsylvania Dutch, 6¾" 25.00
Platter, grill; Apple, indentations, 12" 45.00
Platter, grill; Chartreuse, 12" 30.00
Platter, meat; Normandy Plaid, 12" 30.00
Platter, meat; Pennsylvania Dutch, 12" 65.00
Platter, meat; Provincial Fruit, 11" 40.00
Saucer, Apple, 5½" 3.00
Saucer, Heather Plaid, 2½" 3.00
Shakers, Fruit, range style, cobalt trim, 4", pr 40.00
Shakers, Peasant Garden, jug style, mini, 2½", pr 65.00
Shakers, pour & shake; Apple, 4¼", set 50.00
Shakers, pour & shake; Pennsylvania Dutch, 4¼", pr 100.00
Shakers, stacking; Apple, 2¼", pr 50.00
Shakers, stacking; Saraband, 2¼", pr 25.00
Sugar bowl, Fruit, w/lid, 4" 25.00
Sugar bowl, Heather Plaid, w/lid, 4" 30.00
Teapot, Fruit, 2-cup, ind, 4" 45.00
Teapot, Intaglio, 6-cup, 6½" 65.00
Tcapot, Maywood, 6-cup, 6½" 45.00
Teapot, Saraband, 6-cup, 6½" 40.00
Tray, relish; Fruit, pottery hdl, 3-part, 10" 55.00
Tray, relish; Normandy Plaid, 3-part, 12" 45.00
Tray, roll; Normandy Plaid, 11" 35.00
Tray, tidbit; Intaglio, 10" 45.00
Tray, tidbit; Seaform, 9x10" dia 75.00
Tumbler, Pennsylvania Dutch, 12-oz, 5" 35.00
Tumbler, Provincial Fruit, 12-oz, 5" 20.00
Vase, cornucopia; Ivy — Red Blossom, 6" 25.00
Vase, pillow; Maywood, NAPCO mold, 6¾" 25.00
Wall pocket, Apple, 3½" 50.00
Wall pocket, Chartreuse, 3½" 35.00

Purses

Purses from the early 1800s are often decorated with small, brightly colored glass beads. Cut steel beads were popular in the 1840s and remained stylish until about 1930. Purses made of woven mesh date back to the 1820s. Chain-link mesh came into usage in the 1890s, followed by the enamel mesh bags carried by the flappers in the 1920s. Purses are divided into several categories by (a) construction techniques — whether beaded, embroidered, or a type of needlework; (b) material — fabric or metal; and (c) design and style. Condition is very important. Watch for dry, brittle leather or fragile material. For those interested in learning more, we recommend *Antique Purses, A History, Identification, and Value Guide, Second Edition,* by Richard Holiner; *More Beautiful Purses,* and

Combs and Purses, both by Evelyn Haertigi of Carmel, California, and *Vintage Vanity Bags & Purses* by Roselyn Gerson. An interesting related book is *Vintage Contemporary Purse Accessories* also by Roselyn Gerson. Our advisor for this category is Veronica Trainer; she is listed in the Directory under Ohio.

Key: W&D — Whiting & Davis

Mesh, multicolor geometric floral design, green and black enamel Whiting & Davis frame, fringe, 6½", $155.00.

Beaded, blk & bl checkerboard design, metal fr, 8¾x6¾" 50.00
Beaded, blk & silver, allover loopy fringe, drawstring, 5x10" 85.00
Beaded, mc geometric, fringe, drawstring, 11½x6¾" 100.00
Beaded, mc geometric w/much blk fringe, drawstring, 12x8" 140.00
Beaded, mc river scene, ornate fr, fringe, Germany, 8x13" 375.00
Beaded, mc roses, fringe, emb metal fr, 14¼x8" 350.00
Beaded, rose/butterflies on blk, fringe, drawstring, 11x7" 150.00
Beaded, wht w/long fringe, drawstring, 8½x5¼" 50.00
Cloisonne vanity, wht & gold-tone, compartments, 5x2½x¾" ..450.00
Crocheted, red/wht/bl flag form, WWII era, 10x6" 45.00
Gold-tone vanity w/stones & pearls, tassel, 4x3¼x¾" 450.00
Leather, tooled, blk & brn, strap hdl, Jemco, 7x6" 90.00
Leather, tooled, clutch type, Meeker, 5x9" 85.00
Leather vanity, mirrored lid, Lili-Staly, 4x7x5" 325.00
Lucite vanity, clear w/gold & sparkles, carryall lid, Willardy, 7" .350.00
Lucite vanity, tortoise, compartments, Willardy Orig, 4x7x4" 250.00
Lucite vanity, wht marbleized/compartments, Elgin, 3¾x4½x4¼" .350.00
Mesh, Bead-Lite, floral, fringe, gilt W&D fr, 7x4" 85.00
Mesh, birds on branches, fringe, metal fr, Mandalian, 8x5" 125.00
Mesh, blk & silver diagonal stripes, W&D metal fr, 12x7" 250.00
Mesh, blk & wht spider web, W&D fr, 7x6" 95.00
Mesh, gold, fringe, W&D fr, 7x4" 85.00
Mesh, gold & wht geometric, fringe, W&D vanity fr, 4x7½" 55.00
Mesh, gold w/fringe, Napier fr w/attached compact, 8x4" 110.00
Mesh, gold-tone, w&D snake hdl, taffeta lined, 9x6" 75.00
Mesh, landscape scenic, fringe, metal fr, Germany, 10x7" 145.00
Mesh, peacock, fringe, gilt W&D fr, 7x6½" 95.00
Mesh, silver-tone rings, attached compact, 1900s, 5x8" 200.00
Mesh, silvertone, W&D metal fr, chain hdl, silk lined, 6x5" 65.00
Mesh vanity, filigree lid w/stones, silk lined, mirror, 3" dia 175.00
Mesh vanity, mc enamel, powder well/mirrored lid, 4½x2½" dia ..400.00
Mesh vanity, mc geometric w/floral W&D fr, 8¼x4" 125.00
Nylon, yel & brn drawstring bag, 1930s, 12x10", EX 15.00
Rhinestones, hand set, Czechoslovakia, sm 85.00

Puzzles

'Jigsaw' puzzles have been around almost as long as games. The first examples were handcrafted from wood, and they are extremely difficult to find. Most of the early examples featured moral subjects just as the board games did. By the 1890s jigsaw puzzles had become a major form of home entertainment. During the Depression years jigsaw puzzles were set up on card tables in almost every home. The early wood examples are the most valuable.

Cube puzzles, or blocks, were often made by the same companies as the board games. Again, early examples display the finest quality lithography. While all subjects are collectible, some (such as Santa blocks) often command prices higher than games from the same period. Our advisor for this category is Norm Vigue; he is listed in the Directory under Massachusetts. In the listings all items are jigsaw puzzles unless noted otherwise.

Personalities, Movies, and TV Shows

Adventures in Gulliver, fr-tray, Whitman, 1969, 14x11", NM 35.00
Alien-Nostromo Flight, HG Toys, 1979, EX (VG+ box) 15.00
Beatles in Pepperland, 100 pcs, MIB (sealed) 200.00
Broken Arrow, Built-rite, 1958, NM (EX box) 20.00
Bullwinkle, Whitman, 1960, EX (EX box) 25.00
Captain Marvel, Fawcett, 1941, EX (EX box) 75.00
Chipmunks, fr-tray, Whitman, 1964, EX 25.00
Cinderella, 1950s, EX (EX canister) 30.00
Circus Boy, fr-tray, 1958, VG 50.00
Defenders of Earth, 1986, EX (EX box) 10.00
Donald & Mickey on the Moon, fr-tray, Playskool, EX 10.00
Dr Dolittle, fr-tray, Whitman, 1967, 14x11", NM 16.00
Dr Seuss, Random House, 1979, 60 pcs, NMIB 15.00
Eddie Cantor, Einson, 1933, NMIB 30.00
Flipper, Whitman, 1965, NMIB 20.00
Frankenstein Jr, Whitman, 1968, 99 pcs, EX (EX box) 30.00
GI Joe, Milton Bradley, 1985, 221 pcs, MIB 15.00
Goofy, fr-tray, Whitman, 1963, 14x11", NM 20.00
Henry, Fairchild, 1973, 100 pcs, NMIB 25.00
Jetsons, fr-tray, Whitman, 1962, EX 35.00
Kaptain Kool & the Kongs, fr-tray, 1978, MIP (sealed) 15.00
Krazy Ikes, fr-tray, 1969, 14x11", EX 14.00
Little King, Jaymar, 1930s, EX (EX box) 50.00
Mighty Mouse, Whitman, 1972, 100 pcs, NMIB 20.00
Mr Magoo, fr-tray, Jaymar, 1967, 10x13", EX 15.00
Pebbles, fr-tray, Whitman, 1963, 14x11", EX 25.00
Princess of Power, fr-tray, 1985, 14x11", EX 10.00
Robin Hood, Jaymar, 1973, NMIB 15.00
Superman, fr-tray, Whitman, 1965, 14x11", EX 25.00
Superman, Whitman, 1966, 150 pcs, EX (EX box) 25.00
Tarzan, Whitman, 1968, EX (EX box) 20.00
Tom & Jerry, Whitman, 1969, NMIB 15.00
Wacky Races, fr-tray, Whitman, 1969, 14x11", EX 30.00
Welcome Kotter, fr-tray, 1977, MIP 20.00
Winnie the Pooh, fr-tray, Whitman, 1979, 14x11", EX 8.00
Yogi Bear, Whitman Jr, 1960s, 63 pcs, NMIB 25.00

Miscellaneous

Animal Picture Cubes, McLoughlin, 1897, set of 6, VG (VG box) .135.00
Autumn Scene, cb, 100 pcs, 1930s, EX (EX box) 10.00
City of Worchester Picture Puzzle, McLoughlin, 1889, EX (EX box) .1,000.00
Colorful Venice, cb, Tuco, 350 pcs, 1930s, EX (EX box) 10.00
Darkest Hour, plywood, 500 pcs, 1920s, EX (rpl box) 110.00
Day In the Fields, Madmar/Blue Ribbon, 500 pcs, 1930s, EX (EX box) ...100.00
Garden Glories, cb, Tuco, 200 pcs, 1940s, EX (EX box) 8.00
Holland Windmill, plywood, 94 pcs, 1930s, 2 rpl pcs, EX (EX box) ..15.00
May Day, wood, 564 pcs, early 1900s, 11x8", EX 85.00
Old Ironsides, plywood, Glengarry, 310 pcs, 1930s, EX (EX box) .50.00
PAR Picture Puzzle, 750 pcs, EXIB 375.00
Southern Home, plywood, 272 pcs, 1930-40, EX (rpl box) 40.00
Sunset Ridge, Milton Bradley/Piedmont, 200 pcs, 1930s, EXIB 30.00

Tranquility, plywood, Perx Puzzle, 142 pcs, 1930s, EX (EX box) ..**25.00**
Venice, plywood, R Purrington, 400 pcs, 1930s, EX (EX box) **80.00**

Quezal

The Quezal Art Glass and Decorating Company of Brooklyn, New York, was founded in 1901 by Martin Bach. A former Tiffany employee, Bach's glass closely resembled that of his former employer. Most pieces were signed 'Quezal,' a name taken from a Central American bird. After Bach's death in 1920, his son-in-law, Conrad Vohlsing, continued to produce a Quezal-type glass in Elmhurst, New York, which he marked 'Lustre Art Glass.' Examples listed here are signed unless noted otherwise.

Bottle, scent; gold w/purple & bl irid, mk Melba, 8x2" **400.00**
Bowl, gold w/purple irid, 16 int ribs, flared rim, 1½x2½" **400.00**
Compote, horizontal leaves/swirls, gr/gold on wht opal, 5½" ...**2,400.00**

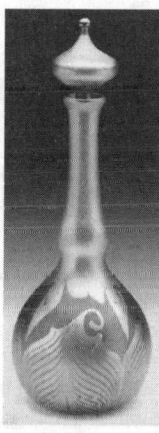

Decanter, green and gold double-hooked feathers on green, gold iridescent elongated neck, with stopper, Martin Bach design, 11½", $3,850.00.

Finger bowl, gold, scalloped, 4¼", on ribbed pod-form tray **425.00**
Finger bowl, gold w/red-bl irid, ribbed, scalloped, 5" **250.00**
Lamp, cast-metal lady figural base, gold irid mk shade, 18½" ..**1,250.00**
Lamp, desk; bronze lion base, curved arm, feather shade, 13x16" .**1,035.00**
Lamp, lily; 3 red-gold ribbed shades; lily pod base, 14" **2,500.00**
Shade, Calcite w/gold rickrack band, gold int, ribbed, 5" **225.00**
Shade, leaves, gr/gold on opal, gold threading, 5¼" **225.00**
Shade, wht w/allover gold wispy 'ferns,' irid int, 5x7" **525.00**
Vase, Agate, obsidian-type tan/yel/brn/gr striations, 5½" **1,380.00**
Vase, bl irid, shouldered, 4¼" **475.00**
Vase, feathers, gr/gold on translucent amber, 4½x4½" **900.00**
Vase, floriform; leaves, gold/gr on opal, petal cup, att, 15" **920.00**
Vase, gold, waisted flared rim, 8" **500.00**
Vase, leaves, gold/gr on cased oval, flared 3-fold rim, 6" **1,600.00**
Vase, leaves, gr w/gold on ivory, in 3-arm Gorham stand, 10" **800.00**
Vase, Nouveau floral silver o/l on rainbow irid, 6½" **950.00**
Vase, red-gold, ribbed cylinder, 9" **550.00**
Vase, swirls at shoulder, leaves below, opal/gr/gold, 9¾" **3,500.00**
Vase, wht spatter on clear w/blk base, #20120-12 K, 11½" **385.00**

Quilts

Quilts, while made of necessity, nevertheless represent an art form which expresses the character and the personality of the designer. During the 17th and 18th centuries, quilts were considered a necessary part of a bride's hope chest; the traditional number required to be properly endowed for marriage was a 'baker's dozen'! American colonial quilts reflect the English and French taste of our ancestors. They would include the classifications known as Lindsey-Woolsey and the central medallion appliqué quilts fashioned from imported copper-plate printed fabrics.

By 1829 spare time was slightly more available, so women gathered in quilting bees. This not only was a way of sharing the work but also gave them the opportunity to show off their best handiwork. The hand-dyed and pieced quilts emerged, and they are now known as sampler, album, and friendship quilts. By 1845 American printed fabric was available.

In 1793 Eli Whitney developed the cotton gin; as a result, textile production in America became industrialized. Soon inexpensive fabrics were readily available, and ladies were able to choose from colorful prints and solids to add contrast to their work. Both pieced and appliquéd work became popular.

Pieced quilts were considered utilitarian, while appliquéd quilts were shown with pride of accomplishment at the fair or used when itinerant preachers traveled through and stayed for a visit. Today many collectors prize pieced quilts and their intricate geometric patterns above all other types. Many of these designs were given names: Daisy and Oak Leaf, Grandmother's Flower Garden, Log Cabin, and Ocean Wave are only a few. Appliquéd quilts involved stitching one piece — carefully cut into a specific form such as a leaf, a flower, or a stylized device — onto either a large one-piece background fabric or an individual block. Often the background fabric was quilted in a decorative pattern such as a wreath or medallions.

Amish women scorned printed calicos as 'worldly' and instead used colorful blocks set with black fabrics to produce a stunning pieced effect. To show their reverence for God, the Amish would often include a 'superstition' block which represented the 'imperfection' of man!

One of the most valuable quilts in existence is the Baltimore Album quilt. Made between 1840 and 1860 only three hundred or so still exist today. They have been known to fetch over $100,000.00 at prominent auction houses in New York City. Usually each block features elaborate appliqué work such as a basket of flowers, patriotic flags and eagles, the Oddfellow's heart in hand, etc. The border can be sawtooth, meandering, or swags and tassels.

During the Victorian period the crazy quilt emerged. This style became the most popular quilt ever in terms of sheer numbers produced and popularity. The crazy quilt was formed by random pieces put together following no organized lines and was usually embellished by elaborate embroidery stitches. Fabrics of choice were brocades, silks, and velvets.

Another type of embellishment, highly prized and rare today, is trapunto. These quilts were made by first stitching the outline of the design onto a solid sheet of fabric which was backed with a second having a much looser weave. White was often favored, but color was sometimes used for accent. The design (grapes, flowers, leaves, etc.) was padded through openings made by separating the loose weave of the underneath fabric; a backing was added and the three layers quilted as one.

Besides condition, value is judged on intricacy of pattern, color effect, and craftsmanship. Examine the stitching. Quality quilts have from ten to twelve stitches to the inch. A stitch is defined as any time a needle pierces through the fabric. So you may see five threads but ten (stitches) have been used. In the listings that follow, examples rated excellent have minor defects, otherwise assume them to be free of any damage, soil, or wear. Values given here are auction results; retail may be somewhat higher. Our advisor is Craig Ambrose; he is listed in the Directory under Iowa.

Key:
dmn — diamond	hq — hand quilted, quilting
embr — embroidered	mp — machine pieced
hs — hand sewn, sewing	ms — machine sewn

Amish

Basket variant, 7-color w/wool indigo border, ca 1800, 92x71" ..**550.00**

Bricks, wine/blk/gr wool, quilted wine border, ca 1930, 37x33" .5,175.00
Flying Geese, dk solid colors, PA, 90x102", M 895.00
Grandmother's Flower Garden, solid dk colors, 101x103", M 895.00
Sq blk/royal bl/teal/gray patches, lav border, 1900s, 54x35" 2,400.00
Triple Irish Chain, solid dk colors, 93x105", M 895.00
4-color dmns alternate w/lt bl & khaki, IN, worn/fragile, 66x82" .400.00
9-Square, purple/blk/gr, fine hq, ca 1900, PA, 40x35", EX 200.00

Appliquéd

Appliqué album quilt, various motifs with names in each corner on white cotton background, ca 1867, 84x86", EX, $2,100.00.

Blossoms & leaves, pk & gr w/brn embr stems, scalloped, 88x27" .250.00
Floral medallions, mc on wht, swag border, EX quilting, 82x90" ...425.00
Floral medallions, red/gr/goldenrod, faded, 71x82" 200.00
Floral medallions (15) in grid, red/wht/gr, 79x84" 600.00
Floral medallions w/vines (stylized), gr/red/orange/wht, 78x81" .715.00
Floral/vintage w/pc-work, mc on wht, EX quilting, wear, 78x81" ..500.00
Hand variant, mc tulip-like design, ca 1900, 82" sq, VG 250.00
Nasturtiums, red & gr on wht, scalloped border, 1900s, 90x76" .300.00
Oak Leaf variant, mc calicos on wht, 19th C, 36x29" 575.00
Poinsettia-like flowers, mc on wht, ms binding, 88x90", EX 300.00
Star of Bethlehem, plain/printed cottons on wht, 19th C, 85x88" ...800.00
Sunbursts/medallions (reversible), mc on wht, lt wear, 78" sq 500.00
Tulip in Pot, lav/gr/wht, lav binding, scalloped, 1900s, 44x42" ..225.00
Tulips, birds & foliage, mc calicos on wht, 19th C, 93x95" 1,000.00

Pieced

Am flags, red/wht/bl, Remember the Main/etc applique, 1898, 70" sq .6,300.00
Barn Raising Log Cabin variant, mc calicos, ca 1890, 70x68", VG ..600.00
Bear Paw, pk & gr calico, EX color, 90x90" 440.00
Bowtie sqs in mc prints on wht, stain, 70x80" 250.00
Bowtie sqs in mc prints on wht w/dk bl calico ground, 66x85", EX .450.00
Centennial theme w/stars/stripes/etc, red/wht/bl, 1876, 83x75" .750.00
Double Irish Chain, bl/pk calicos, sawtooth border, 72x80", EX ..450.00
Double Wedding Ring, mc on cream, ca 1930, 80x72", EX 300.00
Flower Baskets, mc on red, feather quilting, 82x85", EX 450.00
Flying Geese, navy/wht/ecru, well quilted, unused, 1899, 71x79" .660.00
Geometrics (repeating), various calicos, late 1800s, 83x72", G .250.00
Grandmother's Flower Garden, mc on wht, ms binding, 70x83", EX 385.00
House, various bl prints, lt wear/stains, 66x88" 900.00
Irish Chain, red/gr calico, pk calico binding, 80x80", EX 500.00
Irish Chain, red/wht/bl calico, wear, rebound, 82x82" 225.00
Irish Chain w/Sawtooth border, bl/wht, rpr, 82" sq 250.00
LeMoyne Star, dk solids/prints, worn, PA, 74x90", G 250.00
LeMoyne Star, mc calicos on red & gr, ca 1890, 80x67", EX 500.00
Log Cabin, Sunshine & Shadow, red/bl-gray/pk/wht, 65x73" 300.00
Log Cabin, Sunshine & Shadow, worn, 64x82" 350.00
Log Cabin, 6 concentric designs w/red eye centers, 46" sq, VG ..300.00
Log Cabin in Concentric Dmns, mc prints/wht/red, ms/hq, 83x88" ..500.00
Lone Star, goldenrod/yel/wht sateen, 82x84", EX 350.00

Lone Star, red/bl/orange/yel/lav/lt bl/wht, 1900s, 86x86" 675.00
Lone Star, wht/bl cotton, fine hq, ca 1900, 30x27" 250.00
Mini 9-Patch, pk & gr calico w/mc prints on dk bl, 64" sq, EX ...365.00
Morning Star, purple/bl/gr print, ca 1900, 80x86", EX 225.00
Navajo rug design, mc on wht, ca 1900, 77x69", EX 500.00
Nine-Patch, bl & wht calico, lt wear/stains, 76x84" 250.00
Nine-Patch, gr/pk floral calico, feather hq, 78x88", EX 350.00
Nine-Patch w/crazy quilt border, calicos on gr, 19th C, 82x77" .500.00
Northumberland Star, red/purple/wht/blk, ca 1900, 76" sq 325.00
Pineapple, red & wht w/fine red hs, early 20th C, 96x82" 500.00
Pinwheel, bl & wht, PA, lt stain, ca 1920, 80x82" 250.00
Pinwheels & mini 9-Block, mc, sm holes/wear, 72x84" 165.00
Postage stamp sqs, mc bright prints/wht, red binding, 67x78" 450.00
Rolling Pinwheel, dk bl print/wht, ca 1900, fine hq, 80x80", EX ..325.00
Sawtooth, bl/wht/amethyst/khaki silks/cottons, sgn/1841, 96x100" ..700.00
Sawtooth medallion, yel/wht, feather quilting, 76x78" 375.00
Star, mc prints/pk calico, sm stain, 80x83", EX 440.00
Star medallions, mc calico on wht, EX hs, stain, 84x84" 1,200.00
Star medallions (9 bold), mc on wht, fading, 74x88" 275.00
Star of Bethleham variant, mc on wht cotton, 1890s, 76x80" 800.00
Starflowers w/star borders, red/gr/wht, fine hq, 74x92" 350.00
Sunflower, mc prints/pk/bl, EX color, 66x82", EX 350.00
Variegated Hexagons, mc solids/prints, ca 1900, 78x84", NM 450.00
Wedding Ring, mc on wht, scalloped border, 79" sq, EX 200.00
Wheel, red/bl/purple/blk/wht/yel, ca 1890, 74x82" 450.00

Quimper

Quimper pottery bears the name of the Breton town in northwestern France where it has been made for over three hundred years. Production began in 1690 when Jean-Baptiste Bousquet settled into a small workshop in the suburbs of Quimper, at Locmaria. There he began to make the hand-painted, tin enamel-glazed earthenware which we know today as faience. By the last quarter of the 19th century, there were three factories working concurrently: Porquier, de la Hubaudiere (the Grand Maison), and Henriot. All three houses produced similar wares which were decorated with scenes from the everyday life of the peasant folk of the region. Their respective marks are an AP or a P with an intersecting B (similar to a clover), an HB, and an HR (which became HenRiot after litigation in 1922).

The most desirable pieces were produced during the last quarter of the 19th century through the first quarter of the 20th century. These are considered to be artistically superior to the examples made after World War I and II with the exception of the Odetta line, which is now experiencing a renaissance among collectors here and abroad.

Most of what was made was faience, but there was also a history of utilitarian gres ware (stoneware) having been produced there. In 1922 the Grande Maison HB revitalized this ware and introduced the line called Odetta, examples of which seemed to embody the bold spirit of the Art Deco style. The companion faience pieces of this period and genre are classified as Modern Movement examples and frequently bear the name of the artist who designed the mold.

Currently there are two factories still producing Quimper pottery. La Societe Nouvelle des Faienceries de Quimper is owned by Sarah and Paul Jenessens along with a group of American investors. Their mark is a stamped HB-Henriot logo. The other, La Faiencerie d'art Breton, is operated by the direct descendents of the HB and Henriot families. Their pieces are marked with an interlocked F and A conjoined with an inverted B. Other marks include HQF which is the Henriot Quimper France mark and HBQ, the HB Quimper mark. If you care to learn more about Quimper, we recommend *Quimper Pottery: A French Folk Art Faience* by Sandra V. Bondhus, our advisor for this category, whose address can be found in the Directory under Connecticut.

Ashtray, Breton sailor w/accordion, HBQ, 5x5" 90.00
Ashtray, couple by dmn-shape tray, Sevellec, HQ, 4x5½x4" 160.00
Bell, peasant lady forms hdl, flower garland base, HQ, 5" 325.00
Bottle, liquor; Breton lady figure, hand on hip/hat spout, HQ, 11" ..240.00
Bottle, man figural, top of hat is stopper, HQ, 7¾" 200.00
Bowl, man w/walking stick/flowers, cut corners, HRQ, 6½" 60.00
Bowl, peasant lady & florals, oyster-shell shape, HQF, 4¾" 40.00
Bowl, peasant man w/pipe, scalloped, HRQ, 2x6" 85.00
Bowl, peasant man/floral sprigs, bl dots, HQF, 3x10" 170.00
Bowl, vegetable; peasant man/mc floral sprigs, HQF, 9½" 85.00
Box, man on top of bbl form, Galland, HQ, rstr, 7½" 160.00
Box, peasant couple, mc on creme, red plaid base, HQ, 3x5½" ..180.00
Bust, Bigouden lady, wht coif, ribbons, Le Bozec, HQ, 8x9" 350.00
Bust, Breton man, pk clay, Le Gall, HQ, 7½x8½" 185.00
Butter tub, peasant lady, floral band w/bluets, HRQ, 3½x3¼" ...180.00
Butter/jam dish, peasant, sponged hdls, HQF, 3x4½" 130.00
Cake plate, lady & fir tree, bl roses in garland, HBQF, 11" 95.00

Charger, Demi-fantasie lady with cane, blue
croisille panels with red dotwork alternating with
dogwood blossoms, HQ159, 12½", NM, $350.00.

Charger, Decor Riche, peasants at well, HQ, 23½" 4,550.00
Cigarette holder, brn camel, palm-tree corners, HQF, 3x3½" 245.00
Cigarette/match holder, peasant man, Ivoire Corbeille, HQF, 3x2" .190.00
Coffeepot, Pecheur, man w/sailboat at sunset, HBQ, rstr, 10" 380.00
Compote, fruit; lady w/in flower garland, rstr, HBQ, 13" L 110.00
Compote, peasant lady/fir tree/etc, ped ft, HBQF, 4x10" 150.00
Creamer, peasant lady's face, ribbons form hdl, Quimper, 3½" ...130.00
Creamer, peasant man/florals, sponged hdl, HQF, 4½" 100.00
Creamer, peasant man/florals/dots/sponged hdl, HQF, 3¼" 60.00
Cruets, man & lady/bl dots, sponged stopper, HQF, 7", pr 155.00
Cup, custard; peasant man/floral, HQF, 3x2½" 30.00
Cup & saucer, conch shell & sea flora on blk, HQ 50.00
Cup & saucer, floral w/bluets, hexagonal, HRQ, 3", 3 for 220.00
Dinnerware, flower vase, mc w/brn sponging, HBQF, 26-pc set .375.00
Dish, ermine-tail shape, peasant man, cobalt sponging, HQF, 4" .70.00
Egg cup, swan figural tray, 6 cygnet cups, HRQ, 8½x15" 2,100.00
Figurine, Bebe a la Pomme, girl w/apple, LV Blandin, HQ, 12" ..550.00
Figurine, best man & maid of honor, JES, HQ, 3¼" 200.00
Figurine, biniou & bombarde players, JES mk, prof rstr, 3¼" 250.00
Figurine, boy & 2 girls arm-in-arm, JES, HQ, 2½" 150.00
Figurine, boy seated, B Savigny, HBQ, old rpr, 6½x7½" 80.00
Figurine, boy w/hands folded, bright mc, Bachelet, HQ, 10½" ...450.00
Figurine, bride & groom, JES, HQ, 3¼" 180.00
Figurine, couple dancing gavotte, Micheau-Vernez, HQ, 14" 600.00
Figurine, Femme a la Quenouille, Nicot, HQ, 8½" 85.00
Figurine, lady w/hands in apron pockets, HQ, 6¾" 135.00
Figurine, lady w/jug, straw bonnet, Made in France, 3" 145.00

Figurine, lady w/umbrella & basket, Made in France (Henriot), 3" ...150.00
Figurine, Lannik, man w/walking stick, HQF, 4" 125.00
Figurine, Loik, man w/arms folded, bright colors, HQ, 12" 275.00
Figurine, Louisik, holding wht cloth w/rose border, HQ, 4½" 140.00
Figurine, mother & father of bride, JES, HQ, 3½" 220.00
Figurine, peasant lady, mc w/wht coif, Sevellec, HQF, 3½" 120.00
Figurine, peasant lady, radiant coif, Galland, HQ, 6" 350.00
Figurine, peasant lady w/attached basket at her ft, HQ, 7½" 250.00
Figurine, peasant lady w/basket, Galland, HQ, 6" 120.00
Figurine, peasant man w/walking stick, Galland, HQ, 6" 155.00
Figurine, Retour de Peche, sailor returning, HBQ, 4¾" 150.00
Figurine, Ste Anne des Bretons w/anchor & daughter, HBQ, 5" ..185.00
Figurine, Ste Vierge, Mary w/Jesus, HBQ, 6¾" 200.00
Figurine, Ste Yves, scroll in hand, mc, HR, 19th C, 6½" 825.00
Figurine, Yann (John), mc, Henriot, 4" 200.00
Figurine, Youenn, mc clothes, gr base, HQ, 4½" 140.00
Figurine, 2 girls & boy, Sevellec Village Breton series, HQ, 3" ...190.00
Figurine, 3 sailers arm-in-arm, Sevellec, HQ, 6x7¼" 625.00
Hors d'oeuvre, 3 compartments w/lady in ea, JE, HQ, 10½" W ..175.00
Inkwell, duck figural, natural mc, QF, lid missing, 3x5½" 275.00
Inkwell, man w/bl lattice corners, no insert, HBQ, 1¾x2¼" sq 65.00
Knife rest, lady reclining figural, Maillard, HQ, 4½" 180.00
Knife rest, peasant man/floral sprays/bluets/sponging, HQF, 3½" .30.00
Knife rest, shrimp figural, HQCM, 4½", pr 150.00
Mustard jar, plump lady figural, w/wooden spoon, HQ, 5½" 185.00
Mustard pot, lady holding lid of bbl, Galland, HQ, 5½" 160.00
Pitcher, lady w/garlands, pinched spout, bl hdl, HQF, 3½" 45.00
Pitcher, plump lady figural, hat ribbons form hdl, HQ, rstr, 3½" ..85.00
Pitcher, plump lady figural, ribbons form hdl, HQ, 8" 250.00
Pitcher, 1st Period Porquier Beau, flowers, PB, 10¾x8½", NM ..1,450.00
Plate, Celtic, Modern Movement palette, sgn PF, HBQ, 9" 120.00
Plate, Christmas; Mistral Bl, Noel 1980, cut corners, HBQF, 9" ...20.00
Plate, Eskimo, mc w/gr scalloped rim, HQF, 4½", pr 200.00
Plate, fish shape w/speckles, peasant man, HQF, 4¾" 60.00
Plate, fisherman w/net & basket, bl border, HQF, 4½" 45.00
Plate, Fleur-de-Lis, ruffled rim, HB Quimper, 8", NM 140.00
Plate, forget-me-nots/a-la-touche florals, scalloped, HQF, 5" 55.00
Plate, Malicorne, bird at fountain, PBX, 9¾" 195.00
Plate, man w/pipe, tree/garland border, scallop, HBQ, rstr, 7" 40.00
Plate, Normandy man w/pipe, bl banded rim, HQF, 4" 45.00
Plate, Normandy man (woman), bl scallop, HQF, hanging, 5", pr .100.00
Plate, oyster; bowl & 6 shells, man & lady/florals, HRQ, 10" 600.00
Plate, pears on branch, bl sponged border, HQF, 8", NM 65.00
Plate, red croisille geometrics, HQF, doll's sz, 2¼" 55.00
Platter, floral sprays, w/bl & red decor, hdls, HBQ, 19x12" 220.00
Platter, peasant couple/floral sprays/bluets/bud chain, HQ, 6¼" .130.00
Platter, peasant man/florals, garland rim, HQF, 11¼" 145.00
Porringer, a-la-touche floral, yel/bl bands, HRQ, 5¾" L 55.00
Porringer, bl strutting goose, sponged bl hdls, HRQ, 5¾" L 90.00
Porringer, Fleur-de-Lis, 2-tone bl, HBQ, pierced, 7¼" 75.00
Porringer, peasant man w/walking stick on yel, HBQF, 5¾" 35.00
Salt cellar, dbl swan figural, man/floral sprig, HQ, 2½x4" 140.00
Shaker, lady's head, wht coif, necklace, (Galland), HQF, 2¾" ...100.00
Smoke set, peasants at sunrise/sunset, HBQ, 8" tray+5 pcs 525.00
Tea & toast set, man & bluets, Marshall Field QF, teacup & tray .140.00
Teapot, man w/florals/bl dots, HBQF, 4½", NM 80.00
Trivet, lady w/lacy coif/collar, 8-sided, Modern Movement, HQ, 9½" ..125.00
Tureen, man w/flower garland lid, garland base, HQF, 5x7" 150.00
Tureen, peasant lady, a-la-touche florals, w/lid, HBQF, 6x5¾" 150.00
Tureen, Regency, apple & leaf finial, red glaze, HQF, 10½x13" .160.00
Vase, crescent form w/dolphin support, peasant man, HQF, 4½" ...250.00
Vase, man & a-la-touche petals, yel/brn banded rim, HBQ, 3½x2" ..40.00
Vase, peasant, Modern Movement, HBQ, 7¼" 95.00
Vase, peasant couple, fan shape, butterfly ft, HQF, 5x8" 130.00

Wall pocket, man w/pipe/bl roses/red dots, HBQF, 9¾x4¼" 220.00

Radford

Pottery associated with Albert Radford (1882 – 1904) can be categorized by three periods of production. Pottery produced in Tiffin, Ohio (1896 – 1899), consists of bone china (no marked examples known) and high-quality jasperware with applied Wedgwood-like cameos. Tiffin jasperware is often impressed 'Radford Jasper' in small block letters. At Zanesville, Ohio, Radford jasperware was marked only with an incised, two-digit shape number, and the cameos were not applied but rather formed within the mold and filled with a white slip. Zanesville Radford ware was produced for only a few months before the Radford pottery was acquired by the Arc-en-Ciel company in 1903. Production in Zanesville was handled by Radford's father, Edward (1840 – 1910), who remained in Zanesville after Albert moved to Clarksburg, West Virginia, where the Radford Pottery Co. was completed shortly before Albert's death in 1904. Jasperware was not produced in Clarksburg, and the molds appear to have been left in Zanesville, where some were subsequently used by the Arc-en-Ciel pottery. The Clarksburg, West Virginia, pottery produced a standard glaze, slip-decorated ware, Ruko; Thera and Velvety, matt glazed ware often signed by Albert Haubrich, Alice Bloomer, and other artists; and Radura, a semimatt green glaze developed by Albert Radford's son, Edward. The Clarksburg plant closed in 1912.

Pottery marked 'E. Radford, Burslem,' or 'E. Radford, England,' includes a variety of earthenware designed by Edward Radford (1883 – 1968), first for H.J. Wood and later for himself in Burslem (production ending in 1948). A variety of floral patterns, cottage or tavern scenes, and Art Deco motifs distinguish this ware. His father, Edward Thomas Radford, worked at the Pilkington Tile and Pottery Co. in Manchester, England, and appears to have been a brother of Albert Radford. Our advisor for this category is James L. Murphy; he is listed in the Directory under Ohio.

Jasper

Bowl, muses & vintage, fluted rim, imp mk 295.00
Ewer, appl grapes/raspberries, Old Man Winter hdl, #17, 9" 350.00
Letter holder, lady w/bow & target scene, bark trim, #61 ....500.00
Mug, floral, 4½" 165.00
Pitcher, tankard, vintage, lt bl, #26, 12" 200.00

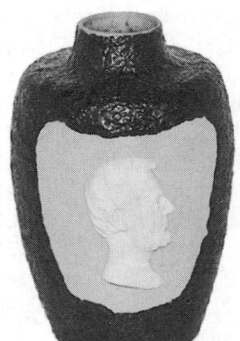

Vase, bust of Lincoln, reverse: eagle, bark trim, #12, 7", from $300.00 to $350.00.

Vase, #15, rare, 7" 295.00
Vase, bust of Washington; eagle reverse, bark trim, #12, 7" 265.00
Vase, cherubs & lion, #15, 6½" 325.00
Vase, cherubs on flying eagles, #23, 9½" 475.00
Vase, lady by fire, grapes reverse, #55, 3½" 100.00

Vase, lady kneeling w/bird, gray, #24, 10½x4½" 250.00
Vase, lady kneels w/arms up, bird in hand, bark trim, #24, 9" 600.00
Vase, lady sits, trees & dog, bark trim, #14, 7" 310.00
Vase, lady w/dog, #22, 10x6" 250.00
Vase, lady w/flowers, grapes reverse, #59, 4" 165.00

Miscellaneous

Jardiniere, Ruko, tulips, 8½x9" 250.00
Pitcher, dog & goose scenic panels, pine tree hdl, 10½" 160.00
Plate, E Radford, HP floral, gr matt, 5x9" 27.50
Teapot, E Radford, HP floral, gr matt, 4½" 75.00
Vase, Radura, 4-hdl, scalloped rim, 10" 400.00
Vase, Ruko, floral, standard glaze, 15" 325.00
Vase, Thera, floral, mc on gr, #1453, 12½" 700.00
Vase, Velvety, mums, mc on gr matt, sgn, bottle form, 10¼x3" .550.00

Radios

Vintage radios are very collectible. There were thousands of styles and types produced, the most popular of which today are the breadboard and the cathedral. Consoles are usually considered less marketable, since their size makes them hard to display and store. For those wishing to learn more about antique radios, we recommend *The Collector's Guide to Antique Radios, Volumes I* through *IV,* by Sue and Marty Bunis, available from your local bookstore or Collector Books. They are also the authors of *A Collector's Guide to Transistor Radios, Second Edition.* For information on novelty radios, refer to *Collector's Guide to Novelty Radios, Books I and II,* by Marty Bunis and Robert Breed. Values are given for radios in near mint to mint condition. Our advisor for this category is James Fred; he is listed in the Directory under Indiana.

Key:
BC — broadcast	s/r — slide rule
pb — push button	SW — short wave
phono — phonograph	tbl/m — table model
R/P — radio-phonograph	

A-C Dayton #R-12, tbl/m, mahog, battery, 1924 ....130.00
Admiral #Y3379 Fiesta, tbl/m, clock, plastic, AM, AC, 1963 ....15.00
Admiral #5F11, portable, plastic, BC, AC/DC/battery, 1949 ....35.00
Admiral #7T10, tbl/m, plastic, BC, AC/DC, 1947 ....40.00
Admiral #985-6Y, tbl/m, plastic, SW, BC, AC, 1937 ....70.00
Air Castle #629, tbl/m, wood, 6 pb, 4 knobs, 1937 ....90.00
Air-Way #G, tbl/m, wood, 3-dial front panel, battery, 1923 ....1,400.00
Airline #62-437, tbl/m, wood, movie dial, 4 knobs, 1936 ....80.00
Airline #84WG-2714F, console/phono, wood, BC/FM, AC, 1948 .80.00
American Bosch #18, console, wood, sliding doors, 1929 ....225.00
American Bosch #809, tbl/m, wood, cloth grill, AC/DC, 1937 ....45.00
Apex #106, console, wood, highboy, storage, 3 knobs, 1926 ....145.00
Arvin #442-A, tbl/m, plastic, midget, BC, AC/DC, 1941 ....75.00
Arvin #746P, portable, plastic, hdl, 1953 ....75.00
Atlantic #31AC, Colonial-style grandfather, wood, AC, 1931 ..400.00
Atwater Kent #601, tbl/m, plastic, s/r dial, BC, AC/DC, 1947 .....50.00
Atwater Kent #84D, cathedral, wood, cloth grill, DC, 1931 ....425.00
Aydar #976, console, wood, airplane dial, 4 knobs, AC, 1935 ....140.00
Bendix #69M9, console/phono, wood, s/r dial, BC/FM, AC, 1949 .60.00
Bremer-Tully #8-21, console, wood, cloth grill, AC, 1928 ....135.00
Bush & Lane #40, console, wood, dbl doors, 1929 ....175.00
Chelsea, Super Six tbl/m, wood, 3 window dials, battery, 1925 ..130.00
Cleveland #A-5, tbl/m, wood, 3-dial front, 5 tubes, 1925 ....125.00
Continental #C-45, tbl/m, alarm clock, plastic, BC, AC, 1957 ....30.00
Crosley, Travo Deluxe, tbl/m, Deco case, cloth grill, 1932 ....100.00

Crosley #6-60, tbl/m, wood, thumbwheel dial, battery, 1927 ....85.00
Crosley #656, tombstone style, wood, rnd dial, 4 knobs, AC 130.00
Crosley 22-AS, tbl/m, phono w/lift-top lid, wood, 3 knobs 25.00
Crosley 66-T, tbl/m, wood, 4 knobs, BC/SW, 1946 ....55.00
Delco #1107, tombstone, wood, airplane dial, BC/SW, AC, 1935 .125.00
Dewald #580, tbl/m, wood, 3 knobs, AC, 1933 ....85.00
Eagle #K-2, tbl/m, wood, fold-down front door, battery, 1926 ....145.00

Emerson AU-190, Catalin, scalloped gold dial, three vertical sections, cloth grill, three knobs, 1938, minimum value $1,000.00.

Photo courtesy Sue and Marty Bunis

Emerson #CG-294, console/phono, wood, lift top, BC/SW, AC, 1939 .70.00
Emerson #L-559, tbl/m, wood, chest-type, lift top, AC, 1932 .....225.00
Emerson #17, tbl/m, plastic, Deco, 2 knobs, AC/DC, 1935 ....135.00
Emerson #341, tbl/m, wood, s/r dial, tuning eye, BC, AC 50.00
Emerson #550, tbl/m, wood, s/r dial, BC, AC/DC, 1947 ....40.00
Emerson #642, tbl/m, plastic, hdl, 2 knobs, BC, AC/DC, 1950 ....45.00
Emerson #813, tbl/m, plastic, gold grill, logo, ftd, BC, 1955 ....25.00
Fada #260V, tbl/m, ivory plastic, Deco bars, BC, AC/DC, 1936 ..100.00
Fada #43, cathedral, wood, scalloped top, ornate front 300.00
Farnsworth #CC-70, console, wood, pb, 4 knobs, 7 tubes, 1941 .100.00
Ferguson #3, tbl/m, wood, 3 dial, 4 tubes, battery, 1925 ....125.00
Garod #5A2-Y, tbl/m, plastic, s/r dial, BC, AC/DC, 1946 ....55.00
GE #FB-52, cathedral, wood, cloth grill, battery 100.00
GE #J-614, tbl/m, plastic, s/r dial, 2 knobs, BC/SW, AC/DC 35.00
GE #LF-115, console, walnut, s/r dial, pb, BC/FM/SW, 1940 .....120.00
GE #221, tbl/m, wood, s/r dial, BC/SW, AC/DC, 1946 ....40.00
General Television #27C5, tbl/m, plastic, BC, AC/DC, 1948 ....45.00
Grantline #5610, end tbl/m, wood, s/r dial, BC, AC/DC, 1948 ....90.00
Grunow #1241, console, wood, rnd dial, BC/SW, AC, 1935 ....150.00
Hoffman #A-700, portable, s/r dial, BC, AC/DC/battery, 1947 ....35.00
Hyman #V-60 Bestone, tbl/m, wood, rectangular case, battery ...115.00
Jewel #5310, portable, plastic, hdl, BC, battery, 1953 ....25.00
King #FF, tbl/m, 2-tone metal, 3 knobs, AC, 1929 ....85.00
Lafayette #BB-27, tbl/m, wood, pb, tuning eye, AC/DC, 1939 .....65.00
Lafayette #FE-156, console, phono, wood, BC/SW, AC, 1940 .....125.00
Magic-Tone #504, tbl/m, bottle shape, BC, AC/DC, 1947 ....350.00
Majestic #31, cathedral, walnut, shouldered, 2 knobs, 1931 ....225.00
Mantola #24B6, tbl/m, wood, sq dial, hdl, BC, AC/DC, 1947 ......45.00
Meissner #9-1065, portable, phono, recorder, PA system, 1946 ....35.00
Mohawk #110, tbl/m, wood, high domed top, battery, 1925 ....185.00
Motorola #12-Y-1, console, walnut, tuning eye, BC/SW, AC, 1937 ...150.00
Motorola #51X17, tbl/m, Catalin, 2 knobs, hdl, BC, AC, 1941 ....40.00
Motorola #61E, tbl/m, plastic, 5 pb, 2 knobs, BC, AC/DC, 1939 .65.00
Motorola #81C, console, wood, s/r dial, 6 pb, BC/SW, AC, 1939 ..125.00
Olympic #7-421W, tbl/m, plastic, 2 knobs, BC, AC/DC, 1949 ....70.00
Paragon #DA-2, tbl/m, oak, detector/2-stage amplifier, 1921 ..1,100.00
Philco #17-D, console, wood, highboy, 6 legs, BC/SW, AC, 1933 ....145.00
Philco #38-10, console, wood, 4 knobs, BC/SW, AC, 1938 ....110.00
Philco #39-118, console, wood, s/r dial, 5 pb, BC, AC/DC, 1939 .110.00
Philco #41-315, console, walnut, s/r dial, 8 pb, BC/SW, 1941 ....150.00
Philco #50-921, tbl/m, ivory plastic, BC, AC/DC, 1950 ....50.00

Philco #53-1754, console, phono, wood, s/r dial, AC, 1953 ....50.00
Pilot #63, tombstone, wood, rnd dial, BC/SW, AC, 1934 ....140.00
Puritan #515, tbl/m, wood, s/r dial, 2 knobs, BC, AC/DC, 1947 ...35.00
RCA #R-22-W, tbl/m, wood, 5 tubes, AC/DC, 1933 ....100.00
RCA #16T4, tbl/m, wood, s/r dial, 5 pb, BC/SW, AC, 1940 ....75.00
RCA #2-X-61, tbl/m, plastic, dial on top, BC, AC/DC, 1953 ....40.00
RCA #5X3, tbl/m, wood, 3 knobs, BC/SW, AC, 1936 ....85.00
RCA #56X10, tbl/m, plastic, s/r dial, BC/SW, AC/DC, 1946 ....40.00
RCA #7K1, console, wood, tuning eye, 4 knobs, BC/SW, 1937 .125.00
RCA #812K, console, wood, s/r dial, tuning eye, BC/SW, AC, 1937 ..175.00
RCA #9C7FE, tbl/m, alarm clock, s/r dial, ftd, BC, AC 20.00
RCA #95X6, tbl/m, wood, 2 knobs, cloth grill, BC, AC/DC, 1938 ..60.00
Regal #205, tbl/m, plastic, s/r dial, BC, AC/DC, 1947 ....40.00
Sentinal #194UTI, tbl/m, ivory plastic, 2 knobs, AC/DC, 1940 ...50.00
Silvertone #6138, console, wood, s/r dial, 8 pb, tuning eye 125.00
Sonora #DD-14, tbl/m, wood, s/r dial, BC/SW, AC/DC, 1939 .....35.00
Sparton #27, console, wood, ½-rnd dial, dbl doors, 1932 ....130.00
Stewart-Warner #C51T1, tbl/m, plastic, BC, AC/DC, 1948 ....40.00
Sylvania #1202, tbl/m, plastic, aluminum panel, BC, AC/DC 20.00
Troy #C-170-PC, console, phono, wood, lift-top, AC, 1938 ......110.00
Ware #X, tbl/m, walnut, meter, 3-dial panel, battery, 1925 ....120.00
Westinghouse #WR-14, cathedral, 2-tone wood, 3 knobs, 1931 ...125.00
Zenith #L-515, tbl/m, alarm clock, plastic, ftd, 5 knobs, BC 35.00
Zenith #11, tbl/m, walnut, thumbwheel dial, battery, 1927 ....150.00
Zenith #4-G-903, portable, plastic, flip-over dial, BC, 1949 ....25.00
Zenith #6-S-511, tbl/m, plastic, pb, hdl, BC/SW, AC, 1941 ....55.00

Novelty Radios

Avon Skin-So-Soft, NMIB 35.00
Bozo the Clown, plastic, 6", EX 85.00
Bullwinkle, PAT World Prod, 3-D plastic, 6¼x11⅞" 250.00
Buster the Talking Monkey, Stellar #4221, w/clock, 8x12" 100.00
Cadillac Convertible, 1963 model, AM, MIB 45.00
Champion Spark Plug, MIB 100.00
Charlie McCarthy, Majestic, 1930s, Bakelite & metal, 7", EX ..2,000.00
Coca-Cola Vending Machine, China, 1989, MIB 65.00
Cracker Jack, 2-sided, scarce, NM 125.00
Elvis on Stage, M 75.00
Folger's Coffee Can, plastic, 4", NM 75.00
Gumby, Lewco, 1970s, NM 150.00
Hershey Syrup Bottle, MIB 75.00
Hopalong Cassidy, Arvin, 1950, blk version, 8", EX 500.00
Lone Ranger, Airline, 1950, wht w/mc image on Silver, NM ..1,100.00
Michelin Man, Italy, 1960s, rare, NM 400.00
Mickey Mouse, sitting in a chair, EX 45.00
Oscar the Grouch, MIB 45.00
Pepsi-Cola Fountain Despenser, 7", EX 225.00
Planters Cocktail Nuts Can, MIB 55.00
Raid Bug, clock radio, M 225.00
Red Goose Shoe, VG 50.00
Snoopy's Dog House, Determined, 1975, NM 65.00
V8 Can, NM 50.00
Welch's Grape Fruit Can, M 45.00

Transistor Radios

Post-World War II baby boomers, now approaching their fiftieth year, are rediscovering prized possessions of youth, their pocket radios. The transistor wonders, born with rock 'n roll, were at the vanguard of miniaturization and futuristic design in the decade which followed their introduction to Christmas shoppers in 1954. The tiny receiving sets launched the growth of Texas Instruments and shortly to follow abroad, Sony and other Japanese giants.

The most desirable sets include the 1954 four-transistor Regency TR-1 and colorful early Sony and Toshiba models. Certain pre-1960 models by Hoffman and Admiral represented the earliest practical use of solar technology and are also highly valued. To avoid high tariffs, scores of two-transistor sets, boys' radios, were imported from Japan with names like Pet and Charmy. Many early inexpensive transistor sets could be heard only with an earphone. The smallest sets are known as shirt-pocket models while those slightly larger are called coat-pockets. Early collectible transistor radios all have civil defense triangle markings at 640 and 1240 on the frequency dial and nine or fewer transistors. Very few desirable sets were made after 1963. Model numbers are most commonly found inside. Our advisor for this category is Mike Brooks; he is listed in the Directory under California and welcomes questions. (Please include a SASE.)

Admiral #Y2273, vertical, 6 transistors, AM, battery, 1963 ....20.00
Arvin #61R13, vertical, 6 transistors, AM, battery, 1961 ....30.00
Bulova 250, 4 transistors 300.00
Channel Master #6479, horizontal, 14 transistors, AM/FM, battery ..20.00
Crown TR-610, 6 transistors 55.00
Dewald Playmate, 6 transistors 180.00
Dumont #900, horizontal, 9 transistors, AM, battery 40.00
Firestone 4C29, transistors & tubes 200.00
GE #P830E, vertical, 6 transistors, stand, AM, battery 30.00
Global GR-711, 6 transistors 100.00
Global GR-900, 6 transistors 125.00
Hi-Lite #STW-6, horizontal, clock, 6 transistors, AM, battery 15.00
Hoffman Home & Travel Solaradio, any color 800.00
Kowa #KT-66, vertical, 6 transistors, Japan, AM, battery 45.00

Kowa KT-91, plastic, nine transistors, window dial with large sunburst panel, AM, battery, 1962, from $175.00 to $200.00.

Photo courtesy Sue and Marty Bunis

Minute Man GT-170, 6 transistors 90.00
Mitchell #1103, vertical, 4 transistors, AM, battery 450.00
National #T-21, vertical, 7 transistors, MW/SW, battery 30.00
Nec NT 6Z0, 6 transistors 60.00
Penny's #1132, horizontal, 6 transistors, logo, AM, battery 35.00
RCA #9-BT-9J, horizontal, 6 transistors, AM, battery 45.00
Regency TR-1, jade, 4 transistors 500.00
Seminole #806, horizontal, 8 transistors, AM, battery 25.00
Sony TR-55 (first Sony) 1,200.00
Sony TR-6, 6 transistors 450.00
Sony TR-8 Micro 300.00
Soundsign #SD-1670, vertical, 6 transistors, AM, battery 15.00
Toshiba #6TP-314A, vertical, 6 transistors, AM, battery 110.00
Toshiba 5TR-193 'Lace' 400.00
Toshiba 8TP-90, 8 transistors 400.00
Toshiba 9TM-40, 9 transistors 300.00
Webcor #310, horizontal, 10 transistors, AM/FM, battery 35.00

Railroadiana

Collecting railroad-related memorabilia has become one of America's most popular hobbies. The range of collectible items available is almost endless; not surprising, considering the fact that more than 175 different railroad lines are represented. Some collectors prefer to specialize in only one railroad, while others attempt to collect at least one item from every railway line known to have existed. For the advanced collector, there is the challenge of locating rarities from short-lived railroads; for the novice, there are abundant keys, buttons, and passes. Among the most popular specializations are dining-car collectibles — flatware, glassware, dinnerware, etc., in a wide variety of patterns and styles. Railroad blankets are also collectible. Most common are Pullman blankets. The early ones had a cross-stitch pattern; these were followed by one in a solid cinnamon color; both are marked clearly with the Pullman name. These are now valued at $125.00 up to $175.00 in good condition. Pullman, in the 1920s, put out a blue blanket, marked Pullman, specifically for ethnic use. There is one in the Sacramento railroad museum. Other railroads had their own 'marked' blankets that are even more desirable, such as the Soo line, the Chessie, and one marked 'Pheasant' (which was a private car on the Milwaukee Line that was reserved to carry special parties for hunting trips).

As is true in most collecting fields, scarcity and condition determine value. There is more interest in some railway lines than in others; generally speaking, it is greater in the region serviced by the particular railroad. Reproductions abound in railroadiana collectibles — from dinnerware and glassware to lanterns, keys, badges, belt buckles, timetables, and much more. Repro hand-executed, reverse-painted glass signs have been abundant throughout the country, most of them read 'Santa Fe,' but some say 'Whites Only.' Beware! Also railroad drumheads are coming out of collections. A drumhead is a large (approximately 24" diameter) glass sign in a metal case. They were used on the back end of all railroad observation cars to advertise a special train or a presidential foray, etc. They're now beginning to surface, and a good one like the Flying Crow from the Kansas City Southern Railroad will go for $2,500.00, as will many others. When items of this value come out, the counterfeiters are right there. It is important to 'Know Thy Dealer.' For a more thorough study, we recommend *Railroad Collectibles, Third Revised Edition*, by Stanley L. Baker. The values noted for most of our dinnerware, glassware, linen, silverplate, and timetables are actual selling prices. However, because prices are so volatile, the best pricing sources are often monthly or quarterly 'For Sale' lists. Two you may find helpful may be ordered from Golden Spike, P.O. Box 422, Williamsville, NY 14221, and Grandpa's Depot and Caboose, 1616 17 St., Suite 562, Denver, CO 80202. Our co-advisors for this category are Fred and Lila Shrader (See Directory, California), and John White (Grandpa's Depot, see Colorado).

Key:
BL — bottom logo   SL — side logo
BS — bottom stamped   SM — side mark
FBS — full back stamp   TL — top logo
NBS — no back stamp   TM — top mark
NTL — no top logo

Dinnerware

Many railroads designed their own china for use in their dining cars or company-owned hotels or stations. Some railroads chose to use stock patterns to which they added their name or logo; others used the same stock patterns without the added identification.

Ashtray, ATSF, California Poppy, 3 rests, NBS, 5" 110.00
Ashtray, C&O, Silhouette, SL, NBS, 7¼x3¼" 125.00
Ashtray, GN, Mtns & Flowers, BS, 4¼" sq 135.00
Bowl, berry; B&O, Centenary, BS, 4¼" 75.00
Bowl, berry; GN, Mtns & Flowers, BS, 5¼" 88.00
Bowl, berry; UP, Winged Streamliner, NBS, 5½" 45.00
Bowl, bouillon; SP, Prairie Mtn Wildflowers, w/o hdls, NBS 65.00
Bowl, cereal; B&O, Centenary, BS, 6½" 120.00
Bowl, cereal; N&W, Yellowbird, NBS, 6" 85.00
Bowl, cereal; PRR, Broadway, BS, 6½" 65.00
Bowl, rim soup; B&O, Centenary, BS, 9" 160.00
Bowl, rim soup; SP, Imperial, TL, 9" 195.00
Bowl, serving; WP, Feather River, NBS, 6¾" 350.00
Butter pat, ATSF, Mimbreno, BS, 3¼" 135.00
Butter pat, B&O, Centenary, BS, 3½" 125.00
Butter pat, CMStP&P, Peacock, NBS, 3" 135.00
Butter pat, CP, Halifax, BS, 4" 165.00
Butter pat, FEC, Mistic, NBS, 3" 25.00
Butter pat, NYNH&H, New England, TM, 3¼" 65.00
Butter pat, Pullman, Indian Tree, TM, 3½" 125.00
Butter pat, UNC, Oak Leaves, BS, 3" 115.00
Chocolate pot, ATSF, California Poppy, BS, w/lid 255.00
Coffeepot, UP, Historical, BS, w/lid 535.00
Creamer, C&NW, Flambeau, w/hdl, NBS, ind, 2¾" 165.00
Creamer, CP, Empress, BS, 4" 75.00
Creamer, CP, Empress, w/hdl, BS, ind, 2¼" 68.00
Creamer, KCS, Roxbury, w/o hdl, NBS, ind, 2½" 18.00
Creamer, PRR, Keystone, w/hdl, SL, NBS, ind, 2¼" 95.00
Creamer, PRR, Purple Laurel, NBS, 4" 85.00
Cup, bouillon; ATSF, Mimbreno, w/hdls, BS 245.00

Cup and saucer, The Philip E. Thomas 1838, 150 Year Commemorative, Baltimore & Ohio, $125.00.

Cup & saucer, ATSF, Adobe, cup SL, both NBS 110.00
Cup & saucer, ATSF, Mimbreno, BS 225.00
Cup & saucer, C&O, Chessie, SL 195.00
Cup & saucer, C&O, Train Ferry, cup SL, both NBS 125.00
Cup & saucer, CMStP&P, Peacock, NBS, demitasse 335.00
Cup & saucer, MP, Eagle, TL, saucer BS, demitasse 225.00
Cup & saucer, SP, Prairie Mtn Wildflower, NBS, demitasse 245.00
Cup & saucer, Wabash, Banner, TL, NBS 295.00
Egg cup, GN, Glory of the West, sm ped, NBS, 2½" 335.00
Egg cup, UP, Winged Streamliner, sm ped, NBS, 2½" 110.00
Gravy boat, ATSF, California Poppy, NBS 195.00
Gravy boat, D&RGW, Prospector, SL 235.00
Gravy boat, UP, Desert Flower, BS 175.00
Hot food cover, PRR, Keystone, SL, 6" 225.00
Ice cream dish w/tab hdl, ATSF, California Poppy, NBS 135.00
Ice cream dish w/tab hdl, MStP&SSM, Logan, BS, 5½" 135.00

Mustard pot, FEC, St Johns, BS, w/lid, 3" 435.00
Pitcher, FEC, Mistic, NBS, 6" 45.00
Plate, Alaska, McKinley, TL, 5½" 365.00
Plate, ATSF, Adobe, TM, 9½" 87.00
Plate, ATSF, Bleeding Blue, TM, 5½" 150.00
Plate, ATSF, Griffin, BS, 9¾" 375.00
Plate, B&O, Capitol, TL, 9" 125.00
Plate, C&O, Chessie, TL, 9¾" 285.00
Plate, CMStP&P, Traveler, NBS, 9½" 175.00
Plate, divided; B&O, Centenary, BS, 11" 265.00
Plate, grill; SRR, Piedmont, BS, 9¾" 105.00
Plate, IC, Coral, NBS, 5½" 35.00
Plate, NYNH&H, Indian Tree, BS, 8" 90.00
Plate, PRR, Broadway, BS, 9" 175.00
Plate, Pullman, Calumet, TM, 6½" 83.00
Plate, service; MP, State Flowers, TL, NBS, 10½" 250.00
Plate, service; N&W, Dogwood, TM, NBS, 10½" 135.00
Plate, UP, Zion, BS, 9½" 375.00
Plate, WP, Feather River, NBS, 9½" 245.00
Platter, ATSF, California Poppy, NBS, 7x5" 28.00
Platter, B&O, Capitol, TL, NBS, 15½x10½" 350.00
Platter, CMStP&P, Peacock, NBS, 8x6½" 55.00
Platter, CN, Truro, TM, NBS, 6½x4½" 26.00
Platter, D&RG, Curecanti, TL, w/scallop corners, 10½x8" 410.00
Platter, NYC, Mercury, BS, 8½x7½" 165.00
Platter, SP, Harriman Blue/Morgan, TL, 10x7" 175.00
Platter, SRR, Piedmont, BS, 9x7" 49.00
Platter, UP, Portland Rose, NBS, 10x7½" 350.00
Relish, ACL, Flora of the South, BS, 9½x4½" 265.00
Relish, CMStP&P, Galatea, NBS, 7½x3½" 115.00
Relish, NYC, Mercury, BS, 9½x5" 85.00
Sauce boat, KCS, Roxbury, NBS 35.00
Sherbet, ATSF, Mimbreno, ped ft, NBS 175.00
Sugar bowl, D&RGW, Blue Adam, w/lid, NBS 125.00
Sugar bowl, UP, Zion, BS, w/lid 295.00
Teapot, FEC, Mistic, NBS, w/lid, 36-oz 75.00
Teapot, UP, Portland Rose, FBS 755.00

Glassware

Ashtray, B&O, clear w/bl logo & Capitol dome, 4½" 25.00
Ashtray, Erie, winged logo/100th Anniversary, bl & gold, 3½" sq ..20.00
Ashtray, Erie logo in bl & wht, 3½" 24.00
Ashtray, Pullman, oval, fits onto passenger car wall, mk 40.00
Bottle, milk; Fred Harvey, Newton KS emb in clear, scarce, ½-pt ..45.00
Bottle, milk; MKT (MO/KS/TX), red pnt, scarce, ½-pt 40.00
Bottle, milk; NP, emb SM, ½-pt 110.00
Champagne, ATSF, cut banner w/Santa Fe, 3½" 150.00
Claret, NYC, frosted 20th Century Ltd SL, knob stem, 4" 39.00
Cordial, ATSF, etched Santa Fe in cursive, stem, 3¼" 45.00
Cordial, NYC blk logo, 4½" 85.00
Cruet, Santa Fe, Daylight w/ball & wing logo 200.00
Goblet, UP, frosted shield, pinstripe, ped ft, 5½" 20.00
Iced tea, ATSF, Santa Fe in wht enamel (cursive), 5½" 20.00
Mug, BN, gr name, blk slogan, 1972 ....12.00
Roly-poly, PRR, frosted train encircles glass, 3½" 15.00
Salt cellar, C&S, heavy glass, oval, 2¼x1½" 200.00
Shot glass, Pullman, etched SL, 2¼" 65.00
Stem, water; UP, wht shield, 6½" 18.00
Stem, wine; CMStP&P, etched box logo SM, hollow-cut stem, 5" .75.00
Tumbler, Burlington Rte, 4½" 15.00
Tumbler, juice; WP frosted logo, 3¾" 65.00
Tumbler, MP, eagle logo in wht enamel, 4½" 18.00
Tumbler, NYC, wht enamel, 5½" 15.00

Tumbler, old fashioned; IC, Main Line of America, 4½" **28.00**
Tumbler, SR, diesel engine & Southern Serves South, 3½" **15.00**
Wine, IC, etched dmn logo, stem, 3¾" **65.00**

Keys

Switch keys are brass with hollow barrels and round heads with holes for attaching to a key ring. They were used to unlock the padlocks on track-side switches when the course of the tracks had to be changed. (Switches were padlocked to prevent them from being thrown by accident or vandals, a situation that could result in a train wreck.) A car key used to open padlocks on freight cars and the like is very similar to the switch key, except the bit is straighter instead of being specifically curved for a particular railroad and its accompanying switch locks. A second type of 'car' key was used for door locks on passenger cars, Pullmans, etc.; this type was usually of brass, but instead of having a hollow barrel, they were shaped like an old-fashioned hotel door key. In order for a key to be collectible, the head must be marked with a name, initials, or a railroad identification, with 'switch' generally designated by 'S' and 'car' by 'C' markings. Railroad, patina 'not polished,' and the presence of a manufacturer's mark other than Adlake all have a positive effect on pricing and collectibility.

A new precedent was set in 1995 when a Denver and South Park 'car' key went at a Missouri auction for $2,500.00. The key was marked DSP&P (an early Colorado road that stopped running in 1898); it was brass and had a hollow barrel and straight bit. Switch keys that only recently brought $15.00 to $17.00 are now bringing $35.00.

Switch, Burlington Rte, brass **35.00**
Switch, C&O, brass **30.00**
Switch, D&TSL, brass **25.00**
Switch, DL&W, brass **40.00**
Switch, ELRR, brass **25.00**
Switch, GTW, brass **35.00**
Switch, KCS, brass **35.00**
Switch, M&StL, brass **38.00**
Switch, UP, brass **32.00**
Switch, W&LE, brass **35.00**

Lamps

Inspector's, CMStP&P, clear lens, EX **65.00**
Inspector's, NYCS on clear globe, unmk Dietz Acme, EX **65.00**
Marker, tail end; Omaha Ry, 4 lenses, wall mk **150.00**
Switch, Armspear Mfg, 4 lenses, EX **165.00**
Switch, unmk Adlake, 4-toed, 4 lenses, lt rust **150.00**
Track walker's, hand type, unmk, EX **75.00**
Vertical, Adlake, red & clear lenses, steel, worn pnt, sm **50.00**
Wall candle, unmk, brass, removable glass chimney, 1907 ....**65.00**

Lanterns

Before 1920 kerosene brakemen's lanterns were made with tall globes, usually 5⅜" high. These are most desirable to collectors and are usually found at the top of the price scale. Short globes from 1921 through 1940 normally measure 3½" in height, except for those manufactured by Dietz, which are 4" tall. (Soon thereafter, battery brakemen's lanterns came into widespread usage; these are not highly regarded by collectors and are generally not railroad marked.)

All lanterns should be marked with the name or initials of the railroad — look on the top, the top apron, or the bell base (if it has one). Globes may be found in these colors (listed in order of popularity): clear, red, amber, aqua, cobalt, and two-color.

ATSF, Dressel, etched red globe, short **75.00**

B&O, Adams & Westlake, twist-off pot, Pat 1895, VG **150.00**
BR, Handlan, clear unmk globe, short **85.00**
C&A, Adams & Westlake, mk 5⅜" globe, rprs, Pat 1909 ....**125.00**
C&EI, Adams & Westlake, amber mk globe, short **125.00**
C&EI, Handlan, emb clear globe, tall **150.00**
C&NW, Adlake, clear etched globe, short **95.00**
CCC&StL, Adams & Westlake, bell bottom, unmk globe, tall ..**150.00**
D&H on apron, Adlake Reliable, clear globe, tall, EX **175.00**
FP&E, Adlake, clear unmk globe, short, scarce, EX **125.00**
ICR, ET Wright, clear 5½" globe, Pat 1908, EX **125.00**
M&StL, Armspear, clear mk Safety Always globe, tall **300.00**
MOPAC, Handlan, clear unmk globe, short **75.00**
NKP, Adlake, etched amber globe, short **200.00**
NYC, Dietz Vesta, clear unmk globe, short **65.00**
OSL, Adlake, clear unmk globe, tall **225.00**
PC&StL, brass top w/twist-off bell, clear unmk globe, VG **150.00**
Penn Central, Adlake, red globe, short **70.00**
Pennsylvania System (in keystone), Handlan, clear mk globe, tall ...**200.00**
RI, Adams & Westlake Adams, mk red cast globe, Pat 1909, EX ...**185.00**
TX & Pacific, Adlake Kero, red mk globe, TM, short **100.00**
UP, Adams & Westlake, clear unmk globe, short **85.00**

Linens and Uniforms

Apron, CA Zephyr printed over Pullman logo **25.00**
Blanket, CMStP&P in rectangle, beige & brn, wool, 60x86" **165.00**
Blanket, Pullman, bl-gray wool, EX **175.00**
Coat, conductor's; CI&L, brass buttons, pre-1940 ....**85.00**
Hand towel, CI&L, The Hoosier woven in bl center stripe **8.50**
Hand towel, Pullman, bl stripe w/date, 24x16", from $12 to **24.00**
Headrest, ACL, Florida Vacationland, purple on gray **24.00**
Headrest cover, GN & goat, orange on tan, 14x18" **29.00**
Headrest cover, L&N, red logo on wht, 14x18" **26.00**
Headrest cover, PRR, train passing Capitol, brn on tan **18.00**
Jacket, C&NW cook's, logo on front, M **15.00**
Napkin, Burlington Rte in script, wht on wht, 23" sq **27.00**
Napkin, C&NW center logo, wht on wht, 23" sq **28.00**
Napkin, FW&DC, wht w/red sewn letters in corner **10.00**
Napkin, SL&SF, Frisco in script, wht on wht, 23" sq **30.00**
Napkin, UP, pk on pk w/UP & rose woven in ea corner **38.00**
Pants, CA Zephyr, wht w/purple stripe, button fly **2.50**
Pillowcase, UP, blk shield on wht, 32x22" **11.00**
Sheet, UP, stamped shield logo, 81x64" **16.00**
Tablecloth, Burlington Rte, wht-on-wht logo, 43x45" **35.00**
Tablecloth, CN, wht w/logo woven on bl stripe, 45x48" **28.00**
Tablecloth, NYC, 2-tone rust w/wht letters, 40x43" **30.00**
Tablecloth, SCL, wht-on-wht logo, VG **25.00**
Towel, dish drying; Burlington Rte, bl on wht, G **15.00**
Uniform, CNR conductor's, dk charcoal w/gold stripes, 1970s **95.00**
Vest, conductor's, Amtrak, bl & blk **15.00**

Locks

Brass switch locks (pre-1920) were made in two styles: heart-shaped and Keen Kutter style. Values for the heart-shaped locks are determined to a great extent by the railroad they represent and just how its name appears on the lock. Most in demand are locks with large embossed letters; if the letters are small and incised, demand for that lock is minimal. For instance, one from the Union Pacific line (even with heavily embossed letters) may go for only $45.00, while the same from the D&RG railroad could easily sell for $250.00. Old Keen Kutter styles (brass with a 'pointy' base) from Colorado & Southern and Denver & Rio Grande could range from $600.00 to $1,200.00.

Steel switch locks (circa 1920 on) with the initials of the railroad incised in small letters — for example BN, L&H, and PRR — are usually valued at $20.00 to $28.00.

Brass heart shape with cast and stamped letters StPM&M RR, Union Brass company, 1870s, rare, $300.00.

Master, SCL, brass, heavy duty, w/brass mk key & 8" chain 45.00
Shanty, CRR, steel, w/brass unmk key 55.00
Shanty, N&W, steel 40.00
Switch, Central of GA, steel, w/8" chain, M 25.00
Switch, CRR, brass 175.00
Switch, CRR, Keline steel, w/brass mk key 50.00
Switch, ETV&G, brass, w/mk key, rare 325.00
Switch, N&W, cast brass, w/mk key 115.00
Switch, P&R, brass, ornate 225.00
Switch, UP, cast brass 125.00
Switch, VSRR (on dust cover), brass, Yale 95.00

Silverplate

The value of silverplate, hollow ware or flatware, is influenced by the location of the logo or railroad name and, of course, by condition. A side- or top-marked piece is preferable to one with a bottom mark. Examine a prospective purchase carefully. Some unmarked flatware has been 'enhanced' with a rather crude stamping of the railroad's name. Authentic railway markings were done at the time of manufacture and were generally executed in a flawless manner.

Bread tray, D&H, TL, BS, Internat'l, 9½x5" 85.00
Butter pat, B&A, BS, Reed & Barton, 4" 110.00
Butter pat, GN, TM&BS, Internat'l, 3½" 55.00
Candle holder, PRR, raised Keystone TL, Internat'l, 1" 125.00
Coffeepot, CP, Elkington, flip lid, TM, 5½" 85.00
Coffeepot, NYC, flip lid, TM, flat NYC finial, 1948, 14-oz 75.00
Coffeepot, Pullman, BS, Internat'l, 12-oz 135.00
Coffeepot, Rio Grande (unmk), artichoke finial of 1941, 8-oz 50.00
Corn holder, CI&L, Monon TM 95.00
Corn holder, Pullman Co TM, Pfleghar 75.00
Creamer, CStPM&O, hinged lid, SL, Gorham, 8-oz 160.00
Creamer, MOPAC, flip lid, 1927 BS, 6-oz 75.00
Creamer, New Haven, BS, Reed & Barton, 1926, 2-oz 75.00
Finger bowl, Santa Fe, hand chased, emb floral, 1910s, 4½" 350.00
Fork, cocktail; ATSF, Cromwell, TM, Internat'l 22.00
Fork, cocktail; C&O, American, BM in cursive, Internat'l 26.00
Fork, dinner; B&A, TM w/arrow logo, Internat'l 55.00
Fork, place; Fred Harvey, Albany, International 18.00
Hot food cover, CRI&P, pierced w/knob, SM, 5½" dia 95.00
Ice bucket, FEC incised logo SM & BS, Internat'l, 4x7" dia 650.00
Knife, butter; B&O, Clovelly, TM, Reed & Barton 24.00
Knife, dinner; Fred Harvey, Cromwell, TM, Internat'l 25.00
Knife, place; CA Zephyr 18.00

Ladle, gravy; PRR, Kings, raised Keystone TL, Internat'l 135.00
Liquor jigger, Pullman Co SM, dbl jiggers, 4" 125.00
Mustard, Canadian Nat'l, flip lid, Elkington, SM 75.00
Pie server, D&H, Regent, incised TL, Gorham 210.00
Place set, Fred Harvey, Albany, knife/fork/spoon, BS 50.00
Spoon, bouillon; GM&O, Broadway, TM, Internat'l 25.00
Spoon, demitasse; B&O, Clovelly, TM, Reed & Barton 29.00
Spoon, grapefruit; ATSF, Cromwell, TM, Internat'l 35.00
Spoon, iced-tea; SL&SF, Sierra, BM in cursive, Reed & Barton ..19.00
Spoon, serving; D&H, Providence, TL, Gorham 155.00
Spoon, serving; UP, Westfield, Meriden, BS 40.00
Spoon, soup; WP, Hutton, BM w/feather, Internat'l 27.00
Stirrer, cocktail; SAL, Chester, TM in cursive, Gorham 78.00
Sugar bowl, CI&L, Monon SL, BS, w/lid & hdls, Internat'l, 8-oz ...245.00
Sugar bowl, Reading, SL, w/lid & hdls, Raleigh 295.00
Sugar tongs, L&N, Cromwell, SL, Internat'l 110.00
Sugar tongs, SL&SF, Dartmouth, SL, Wallace 145.00
Syrup, New Haven, w/diffuser, 1935, 2-oz, G 65.00
Tea strainer, B&O, TM, Reed & Barton, 5¾" L 137.00
Teaspoon, ACL, Zephyr, TM, Internat'l 18.00
Teaspoon, NYC, Century, BM, Internat'l 15.00
Thermos-type w/hdl, CB&Q, SL Burlington Rte, Stanley, 7" 210.00
Tray, MOPAC, buzz-saw logo, silver on copper, 1937 BS, 11" 75.00
Tray, tip; SP, Sunset logo TM, BS, Internat'l, 6" dia 145.00
Vase, bud; GN SM, BM, 7½" 148.00

Miscellaneous

Annual passes continue to be favored over trip and one-time passes. Their value is contingent upon the specific railroad, its length of run, and the appearance of the pass itself. Many were tiny works of art enhanced with fancy calligraphy and decorated with unique vignettes.

Timetables continue to gain in popularity and offer the collector vast information about the glory days of railroading. Pins and badges bearing the name or logo of a railroad are also popular collectibles. The novice needs to be cautious about signs (metal as well as cardboard) and belt buckles. Reproductions flourish in these areas.

Ashtray, CMStP&P, metal, Milwaukee Road around rim, 5" 72.00
Badge, breast; BART (CA), Police, gold-tone w/enamel 355.00
Badge, breast; IC/Gulf, Police, 5-point ball-tip star, 1980s 82.00
Badge, breast; PRR watchman, Clover 'German silver,' '40s 76.00
Badge, breast; W MD Ry Police, 'German silver' star, '40s 170.00
Badge, cap; B&M Conductor, gold w/blk, contoured 80.00
Badge, cap; CPR, old style beaver & shield, Scully, 1920s, NM .125.00
Badge, CN porter's, emb letters on silver, anodized ground 60.00
Badge, dining car; CNR, maple leaf, pin-bk, ca 1930, NM 45.00
Badge, hat; CPR steward's, 1" emb letters on brass, 4" 65.00
Badge, lapel; BR, red & blk logo 12.00
Badge, UP brakeman's, blk plastic w/lg silver letters 15.00
Badge, waiter's, CP Hotels, bl enamel letters, 1⅜" dia 30.00
Bell, locomotive; yoke & cradle, bell: 17" dia 985.00
Berth key, silver color, T shape, scarce 50.00
Blotter, City of Los Angeles, desk sz 45.00
Book, Mt Washington in Winter, 1871, 1st ed, 363-pg 140.00
Book, RR Transportation...Exposition...St Louis, 1904, 11x16" .195.00
Booklet, ATSF, Cool Summer Way to California, 1914 ....39.00
Booklet, D&RG, Camping in the Rockies, 1911 ....17.00
Booklet, D&SL, Moffat Road, text/pictures of tunnel, open: 16" .45.00
Booklet, GN, promoting Chicago RR Fair, 1948, 4x9" foldout 17.00
Booklet, L&N, New Orleans w/fold-out map, 1920s, 32-pg 34.00
Booklet, Penn Central, Maintenance of Ways, '50-70s, 8½x15" ..50.00
Bookmark, T&P, aluminum, emb heart shape, 2½" 38.00
Box, cigar; Fred Harvey, La Corona Belvedere, 1953 customs label ..50.00

Brochure, GN, illus, 1920s, EX **35.00**
Brochure, SP, Lake Tahoe, 1927, EX **35.00**
Bucket, MP, MP Lines, heavy metal, 1-gal **27.00**
Button, BR&P, brass, Waterbury, ⅞" **4.00**
Button, PRR, Waterbury, ⅝" **3.00**
Button, StLTermRR Co, brass, Waterbury, ⅞" **8.00**

Calendar prints, Great Northern Railway, Glacier National Park: Night Shoots, Blackfoot Brave, 1928; Little Plume Blackfoot Indian Chieftan, 1928; Many Mules, 1931; each 22x10", EX, $200.00 for the set.

Calendar, B&A, fish illus on heavy stock, 1903, 9x11" **37.00**
Calendar, D&RGW, 1948, complete pad, NM **110.00**
Calendar, KCS, brn metal, complete, 1953 ....**35.00**
Calendar, PA RR, 1936, frontal image of train, 29x29", EX+ **100.00**
Calendar, UP, celluloid, 1925-1939, pocket sz, ea **12.00**
Catalog, American Ry Supply Co, illus, 46-pg, 7½x9" **130.00**
Clipboard, CSS&SB, metal w/felt bk, 5½x8¼" **25.00**
Coaster, UP, paper w/Winged Streamliner imprint **3.00**
Coffee can, Fred Harvey, girl in red, key wind, 1940s, 1-lb **150.00**
Compact, Frisco Line, celluloid top, Cleopatra Vanity Box Co, EX ...**125.00**
Coupon, NP Railroad, breakfast, EX **35.00**
Fire extinguisher, Wabash, brass, w/holder **70.00**
First-aid kit, PRR, metal box/lid/bandages, 4¾x2x2¾" **33.00**
Fold-out, Pullman, compartments shown, mc, 1920s, long type ...**40.00**
Hat, CNR porter's, w/silver pebbled badge **70.00**
Jug, GN Ry, stoneware, 2-gal, EX **250.00**
Jug, Pullman, Deodorizer, stoneware, ½-gal **125.00**
Knife, MO-KS-TX Lines, Katy Serves the Southwest Well **35.00**
Knife, office; Hamilton (RR) Watch Co, advertising & logo **120.00**
Lapel pin, UP skeleton, gold or silver, ea **4.00**
Letterhead, ATSF, Chico logo, unused, 8½x11" **4.00**
Letterhead, Fred Harvey...CA Western...Office, 8x10" **5.00**
Lighter, cigarette; ATSF & Chico, Zippo, MIB **104.00**
Lighter, cigarette; NH logo & NH Pres McGinnis signature, Zippo ..**50.00**
Lighter, Hulcher RR Service, Emergency, Virden IL **10.00**
Magazine, Maine Line, Aug 1960 ....**5.00**
Map, Ry system of PA, stamp by Ry Supt IB Brown, 1897, 37x58" ..**65.00**
Match book, IC, commemorating 90 yrs, w/logo, 1941, unused **12.00**
Match holder, IA Central, wooden, hangs, Easter 1901 .....**100.00**
Menu, ATSF, Fred Harvey service, Grand Canyon scenes, 1940s ..**10.00**
Menu, Fred Harvey, La Fonda, dbl-fold, single card, 1937, 5½x8" ..**15.00**
Menu, GN, Banner Tours, single card, 1939, 9x5½" **11.00**
Menu, GN, breakfast w/OW Reis Indian cover, 1943 ......**37.00**
Menu, UP, City of Los Angeles, 1956 ....**12.00**
Mile post marker **4.00**
Note pad, BN, Burlington Northern & logo, unused, 5x7" **7.00**
Order pad, waiter's; SCL, unused **12.00**
Paper clip holder, Milwaukee Road **18.00**
Paperweight, C&O, Chessie playing card embedded in glass ...**12.00**
Paperweight, CMStP&P, bronze-like bear, 3½" **225.00**
Paperweight, railroad spike, US Steel **31.00**
Paperweight, SOO top logo under magnifying glass, 3½" **24.00**
Pass, M&StL, 1894 ....**20.00**
Pass, MStP&SSM, 1918 ....**17.00**
Pass, N&W, emb blk logo, 1917 ....**16.00**

Pass, UP&OSL, Pacific Hotel, rate card, scarce **50.00**
Pass, UPS, cream w/blk lettering, Overland logo, 1895 .....**65.00**
Pass, Yosemite Valley RR, annual, 1928 ....**33.00**
Patch, CNR, locomotive & cars, 5-color, 4x2½" **5.00**
Pen, ball point; ATSF, Santa Fe, 1970s, in orig box **25.00**
Pencil, mechanical; Burlington Rte **25.00**
Pencil, mechanical; Thank You for Routing C&NW **25.00**
Pencil, various RR, eraser type, unused, ea, up to **5.00**
Pencil, various RR, no eraser, unused, ea, up to **3.00**
Pencil clip, various, metal w/plastic RR logo, '50s, ea, up to ...**5.00**
Photo, Northern Pacific, Montana Roundup, hand-tinted, 27x40", VG+ ..**100.00**
Photo, RR car int, 1870s, lg **115.00**
Pin, PRR Veteran's Assoc, ½" dia **9.00**
Pin-bk, Am Federation of RR Workers, litho, 1/28, ⅞" dia **14.00**
Pin-bk, Great Northern Safety, celluloid, NM **15.00**
Pin-bk, Rock Island, 1959, celluloid **15.00**
Place mat, ATSF, brn on tan, route map **12.00**
Plate, builder's; Pullman **30.00**
Playing cards, Alaska RR, dbl deck, ca 1990, M in wrappers **22.00**
Playing cards, C&O, Chessie & Peake, dbl deck, unopen plastic case ..**65.00**
Playing cards, C&O, Chessie & Peake, dbl deck, unopened box ..**45.00**
Playing cards, D&RGW, scenics, slipcase, 2¼" **64.00**
Playing cards, D&RGW, souvenir, all-different views, 1925, EXIB ..**50.00**
Playing cards, IC, scenes, 2¼", w/box **42.00**
Playing cards, Intercolonial Ry, Goodall, 1915, EX in case **40.00**
Playing cards, Milwaukee Road, ca 1957, MIB, sealed **25.00**
Playing cards, NP Monad, dbl deck, unopened plastic case **65.00**
Playing cards, NYC, Pacemaker, 2½", w/slipcase **89.00**
Playing cards, Pullman, 1950s, 2¼", unopened box **23.00**
Playing cards, Quanah, Acme & Pacific, Chief bks, 1948, NM **60.00**
Playing cards, SOO, dbl deck, unopened plush box w/logo **42.00**
Playing cards, Western Carloading, dbl deck, 2¼", orig case **16.00**
Playing cards, Wht Pass & Yukon Rte, 1905, 52+4 cards, VGIB ..**70.00**
Pocket watch, Hamilton, 21 jewel, 18 sz, open face **179.00**
Pocket watch, Hamilton 992, 21 jewel, open face, 1907 ....**440.00**
Portfolio, C&O, Chessie, Peake, Chessie & kittens, orig envelope ..**45.00**
Postage stamps, 3¢ US, sheet of 50, 1952 B&O 125th Anniversary .**7.50**
Postcard, IC, steam engine illus, silver metallic **15.00**
Postcard, NP, buffet table & Black waiters illus, w/logo **18.00**
Postcard, SP, Streamliner on Coast Rte illus **3.00**
Receipt, CRI&P, freight of household goods, 1880, 8½x9" **5.00**
Receipt, MP, letterhead on yel, freight of goods, 1890, 7x9" ..**10.00**
Rule book, D&RGW, Rates, Rules & Regulations for Conductors, '50 .**15.00**
Ruler, D&RGW logo w/passenger train on plastic, 12" **22.00**
Ruler, KCS, Port Arthur Rte, wood, blk map, 15" **35.00**
Ruler, MP, wooden **12.50**
Ruler, Soo Line, Ship & Travel, metal **15.00**
Sack, Fred Harvey, wht cloth w/lg brn letters **3.00**
Sign, BN, stainless steel, 2-pc, 75x24", 69x24", EX **50.00**
Sign, IA RR Co, 38x26" **60.00**
Sign, Milwaukee Road, 22¾x16¾" **50.00**
Sign, Private Parking CRI&P, 24x18" **55.00**
Sign, Ry Express, 2-sided porc, 13x40", EX **250.00**
Sign, S Pacific Sunset Route, pressed paper, seminude, 17x10", VG ..**100.00**
Sign, Southern Railway, sf tin, High Bridge KY River, 26x38", EX ...**80.00**
Sign, Southern RR Tickets, reverse glass, gold on blk, 5x29", EX ..**75.00**
Spittoon, ATSF, brass **120.00**
Stamp, Brookville St RR System, CI/brass, gold/blk/red pnt, 11x7" ..**45.00**
Stationery & envelope, CRI&P, Rte of Rockies, Rock Island Lines ..**5.00**
Stationery & envelope, UP, Winged Streamliner, unused, 6x8" ..**4.00**
Stirrer, Commodore, gr glass, Right at Grand Central Terminal ..**25.00**
Stock certificate, B&O, vignette, issued/canceled, 1928 ....**9.00**
Stool, step; CN, metal w/raised logo, 14x14x12" **125.00**
Stool, step; GN, metal emb, Morton Mfg, 10x15x13½" **350.00**

Stool, step; Pullman, metal emb, Utica **165.00**
Swizzle stick, plastic, figural w/logo (no moving parts), up to **4.50**
Swizzle stick, Pullman, bl plastic w/Pullman Co in gold **5.00**
Swizzle sticks, plastic, plain w/RR name on shank, ea, up to **1.50**
Tag, baggage; SRR, brass, 1¾" sq **67.00**
Tag, collar; CNR, gold, Scully **20.00**
Tag, personnel; British Columbia Electric Ry, Bakelite/aluminum ...**27.50**
Thermometer, CNW, IA division **30.00**
Ticket punch, MKT, Poole Bros **132.00**
Timetable, Des Moines & Fort Dodge, 1886 ....**50.00**
Timetable, employee; Alaska RR, system, 1/92 ....**19.00**
Timetable, employee; C&NW, Wisconsin Division, 4/30/50 ....**9.00**
Timetable, employee; GN, Willmar Division, 10/11/08 ....**26.00**
Timetable, employee; GN, Willmar Division, 10/30/56 ....**10.00**
Timetable, employee; Sante Fe, 1975 ....**7.00**
Timetable, Grand Trunk Ry, local, blk/wht, 1947 ....**7.00**
Timetable, public; A&WP, 11/20/54 ....**12.00**
Timetable, public; B&O, 7/13/30, w/map & bus information **14.00**
Timetable, public; Central of GA, w/map, 1956, 18-pg **11.00**
Timetable, public; Chicago Great Western, 3/1/46 ....**12.00**
Timetable, public; L&N, 1956-57 ....**10.00**
Timetable, public; PRR, w/NY World's Fair info, 1939 ....**15.00**
Timetable, Sante Fe, Big System Map, 1888, EX **50.00**
Timetable/map, B&O, 1899, EX **40.00**
Token, IC, Diamond logo: For 100 Yrs..., 1951 issue **12.00**
Token, NH, Compliments of Dining Service, 1¹⁄₁₆" dia **12.00**
Water can, Burlington Rte **60.00**
Wax sealer, American Express Co, brass head, CI hdl **98.00**
Wax sealer, CRI&P, brass head, trn wood hdl **285.00**
Whistle, brass w/bell, 3 chambers/3 chimes, Powel, 19" **873.00**

Razors

As straight razors gain in popularity, prices of those razors also increase. This carries with it a lure of investment possibilities which can encourage the novice or speculator to make purchases that may later prove to be unwise. We recommend that before investing serious money in razors, you become familiar with the elements which make a razor valuable. As with other collectibles, there are specific traits which are desirable and which have a major impact on the price of a piece.

The following information is based on the second edition of *The Standard Guide to Razors* by Roy Ritchie and Ron Stewart (available from R&C Books, P.O. Box 151, Combs, KY 41729, $9.95 +$2.50 S&H, autographed). It describes the elements most likely to influence a razor's collector value and their system of calculating that value. (Their book is a valuable reference guide to both the casual and serious collector of razors.)

There are four major factors which determine a razor's collector value. These are the brand and country of origin, the handle material, the art work found on the handles or blades, and the condition of the razor. Ritchie and Stewart freely admit that there are other factors that may come into play with some collectors, but these are the major players in determining value. They have devised a system of evaluation which is based on these four factors.

The most important factor is the value placed on the brand and country of origin. This is the price of a common razor made by (or for) a particular company. It has plain handles, probably made of plastic, no art work, and is in collectible condition. It is the beginning value. Hundreds (thousands?) of these values are provided in the 'Listings of Companies and Base Values' chapter in the book.

The second category is that of handle material. This covers a wide range of materials, from fiber on the low end to ivory on the high end. The collector needs to be able to identify the different handle materials when he sees them. This often takes some practice, since there are some very good plastics that can mimic ivory quite successfully. Also, the difference between genuine celluloid and plastic can become significant when determining value. A detailed chart of these values is supplied in the book. The listing below can be used as a general guide.

The third category is the most subjective. Nevertheless, it is an extremely important factor in determining value. This category is artwork, which can include everything from logo art to carving and sculpture. It may range from highly ornate to tastefully correct. Blade etching as well as handle artistry are to be considered. Perhaps what some call the 'gotta have it' or the 'neatness' factors properly fall into this category. You must accurately determine the artistic merits of your razor when you evaluate it relative to this factor. Again, the book we referenced earlier provides a more complete listing of considerations than is used here.

Finally, the condition is factored in. The book's scales run from 'parts' (10% +/-) to 'Good' (150% +/-). Average (100% +/-) is classified as 'Collectible.'

Samplings from charts:

Chart A — Companies and Base Values:

Abercrombie & Finch, NY **12.00**
Aerial, USA **24.00**
Boker, Henri & Co, Germany **14.00**
Brick, F, England **9.00**
Case Mfg Co, Spring Valley, NY **40.00**
Chores, James **8.00**
Dahlgren, CW; Sweeden **14.00**
Diane, Japan **10.00**
Electric Co, NY **15.00**
ERN, Germany **12.00**
Faultless, Germany **11.00**
Fox Curlery, Germany **10.00**
Griffon XX, Germany **10.00**
Henckels, Germany **15.00**
Holley Mft Co CT **27.00**
International Cutlery Co NY/Germany **11.00**
IXL, England **14.00**
Jay, John; NY **10.00**
KaBar, Union Cut Co, USA **28.00**
Kanner, J; Germany **10.00**
Kern, R&W; Canada/England **10.00**
LeCocltre, Jacque; Switzerland **12.00**
Levering Razor Co, NY/Germany **18.00**
McIntosh & Heather, OH **12.00**
Merit Import Co, Germany **9.00**
National Cut Co, OH **11.00**
Oxford Razor Co, Germany **10.00**
Palmer Brothers, Savannah, GA **20.00**
Primble, John; Indian Steel Works, Louisville, KY **24.00**
Queen City, NY **30.00**
Quigley, Germany **12.00**
Rattler Razor Co **10.00**
Robeson Cut Co, USA **28.00**
Salamander Works, Germany **11.00**
Sodercin, Ekilstuna, Sweden **11.00**
Taylor, LM; Cincinnati, OH **14.00**
Tower Brand, Germany **16.00**
Ulmer, Germany **10.00**
US Barber Supply, TX **11.00**
Vinnegut Hdw Co, IN **11.00**
Vogel, ED; PA **8.00**
Wade & Butcher, England **24.00**
Weis, JH; Supply House, Louisville, KY **15.00**
Yankee Cutlery Co, Germany **11.00**

Yazbek, Lahod, OH 9.00
Zacour Bros, Germany 9.00
Zepp, Germany 9.00

Chart B, as described below, is an abbreviated version of the handle materials list in *The Standard Guide to Razors*. It is an essential category in the use of the appraisal system developed by the authors.

Ivory	550%
Tortoise Shell	500%
Pearl	400%
Stag	400%
Bone	300%
Celluloid	250%
Composition	150%
Plastic	100%

Chart C deals with the artistic value of the razor. As pointed out earlier, this is a very subjective area. It takes study to determine what is good and what is not. Taste can also play a significant role in determining the value placed on the artistic merit of a razor. The range is from superior to nonexistent. Categories generally are divided as follows:

Exceptional	650%
Superior	550%
Good	400%
Average	300%
Minimal	200%
Plain	100%
Nonexistant	0%

Chart D is also very subjective. It determines the condition of the razor. You must judge accurately if the appraisal system is to work for you.

Good   150%

Does not have to be factory mint to fall within this category. However, there can be no visible flaws if it is to be calculated at 150%.

Collectible   100%

May have some flaws that do not greatly detract from the artwork or finish.

Parts   10%

Unrepairable, valuable as salvageable parts.

Razors may fall within any of these categories, ie. collectible + 112%.

Now to determine the value of your razor, multiply A times B, then multiply A times C. Add your two answers and multiply this sum times D. The answer you get is your collector value. See the example below.

(a) Brand and Origin Base Value	(b) Handle Material % Value	(c) Artwork % Value	(d) Condition % Value	(e) Collector Value
Wade & Butcher England $24.00	Iridescent Pearl Handles 24 x400% $96.00	Carved handles 24 x 350% $84.00	Cracked handle at pin Collectible- 80%	$96+$84=$180 $180 x 80%= $144.00

Reamers

The reamer market is very active right now, and prices are escalating rapidly. They have been made in hundreds of styles and colors and by as many manufacturers. Their purpose is to extract the juices from lemons, oranges, and grapefruits. The largest producer of glass reamers was McKee, who pressed their products from many types of glass — custard; Delphite and Chalaine Blue; opaque white; Skokie Green; black; caramel and white opalescent; Seville Yellow; and transparent pink, green, and clear. Among these, the black and the caramel opalescents are the most valuable.

The Fry Glass Company also made reamers that are today very collectible. The Hazel Atlas Crisscross orange reamer in pink is valued at $275.00 to $300.00 or more — the same in blue, $375.00. Hocking produced a light blue orange reamer and, in the same soft hue, a two-piece reamer and measuring cup combination. Both are considered rare and very valuable with currently quoted estimates at $400.00 and up for the former and $800.00 and up for the latter. In addition to the colors mentioned, red glass examples — transparent or slag — are rare and costly. Prices vary greatly according to color and rarity. The same reamer in crystal may be worth three times as much in a more desirable color.

Among the most valuable ceramic reamers are those made by American potteries. The Spongeband reamer by Red Wing is valued in excess of $500.00; Coorsite reamers with gold or silver trim are worth $300.00 and up. Figurals are popular — Mickey Mouse and John Bull may bring $600.00 to $1,000.00. Others range from $55.00 to $350.00. Fine china one- and two-piece reamers are also very desirable and command very respectable prices.

A word about reproductions: A series of limited edition reamers is being made by Edna Barnes of Uniontown, Ohio. These are all marked with a 'B' in a circle. Other repoductions have been made from old molds. The most important of these are Anchor Hocking two-piece two-cup measure and top, Gillespie one-cup measure with reamer top, Westmoreland with flattened handle, Westmoreland four-cup measure embossed with orange and lemons, Duboe (hand-held darning egg), and Easley's Diamonds one-piece.

Our advisor for this category is Dee Long; she is listed in the Directory under Illinois. For more information concerning reamers and reproductions, contact our advisor or the National Reamer Collectors Association (see Clubs, Newsletters, and Catalogs). Be sure to include an SASE when requesting information.

Ceramic

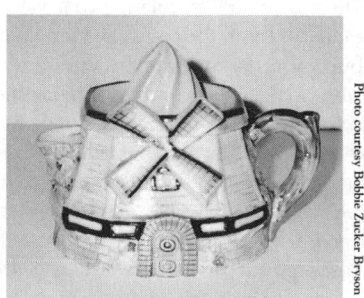

Photo courtesy Bobbie Zucker Bryson

Windmill, multicolor, Japan, two-piece, 4½", $150.00.

Baby's, 2-pc, pk w/wht kitten in bl pajamas, mc top, Japan, 4" **95.00**
Black man's head on saucer, Japan, 3½" **325.00**
Camel, kneeling, 2-pc, lustre w/lt gr top, 4¼" **225.00**

Child's, lustre w/red & yel flowers, octagonal, Japan, 3¼" 200.00
Child's, 2-pc, orange lustre w/red, bl & yel flowers, 2" 200.00
Clown, saucer, orange & wht, German/Goebel, 5" dia 250.00
Clown, seated, hat w/mc vertical stripes, Japan, 5½" 100.00
Clown (cross-eyed) w/maroon vest, 7½" 225.00
Clown figural, mc, Japan 100.00
Clown head in orange shell, 3-pc 125.00
Clown head pitcher, 'twisted' cone, 5½" 100.00
Dog, 2-pc, beige w/red & blk trim, 8" 225.00
Duck figural, orange & gr on wht pearlized body 110.00
Elephant, 2-pc, wht w/red & bl trim, 4¼", from $150 to 200.00
Floral, red & blk, Japan, 2-pc, 5½" 70.00
Floral (overall), German, 2-pc, 3½" 125.00
Floral (overall), str sided, Japan, 2-pc, 5" 75.00
Jiffy Juicer, maroon, Pat 2, 130, 775, 9-20-38, 5¼" 85.00
Lemon, 2-pc, yel w/gr leaves, wht top, Germany, 3¼" 70.00
Pitcher, 2-pc, cream w/lav lilies, Universal Cambridge, 9" 185.00
Plaid design, Japan, 2-pc, 2¼" 80.00
Puddinhead, 2-pc, 6¼" 175.00
Red Wing USA, yel, 6¾" 125.00
Saucer, cream, tan & maroon w/bl trim, England, 3¼" dia 90.00
Saucer, 2-pc, France, Ivoire Corbelle, Henriot Quimper #1166, 4¼" 350.00
Saucer type, lg hooded spout, Corns China Co, 6¼" 120.00
Saucer type, mc flowers, china, 4½" 200.00
Sourpuss, 4¾" 100.00
Swan, 2-pc, cream w/rose flowers & gr base, Japan, 4¼" 80.00
Teapot, 2-pc, wht w/yel & maroon flowers, Nippon, 3¼" 90.00
Teapot, 2-pc, yel, tan & wht, England/Shelley, 3½" 125.00
Toby-style man, gray hair, gr jacket, lavender hat, 4¾" 250.00
Toby-style man w/mustache, blk coat, mc tie, brn hat 395.00
Wht w/cobalt & gold, Germany, 2-pc, 3½" 200.00
Windmills, bl & wht, Germany, 2-pc, 3½" 140.00

Glass

Cambridge, lt pk 200.00
Federal, amber, tab hdl, lg 300.00
Federal, pk, ribbed, loop hdl 35.00
Fenton, blk, pitcher base, 2-pc 1,400.00
Fenton, elephant decor on clear base, 2-pc, baby sz 75.00
Fenton, gr, Ming pattern 600.00
Fleur-de-Lis, red/orange slag 425.00
Foreign (emb), gr or pk, 2-pc 50.00
Fry, dk amber 325.00
Hazel Atlas, cobalt w/tab hdl, orange reamer 295.00
Hazel Atlas, gr, Circle pitcher w/reamer top, 2-pc 70.00
Hazel Atlas, gr, tab hdl, sm 25.00
Hazel Atlas, yel, pitcher base, 2-pc 350.00
Hocking, Vitrock, tab hdl 75.00
Indiana, amber, hdls, spout opposite 300.00
Indiana, crystal, horizontal hdl 20.00
Indiana, dk amber 325.00

Jeannette, Delphite, lg 1,200.00
Jeannette, dk Jade-ite, lg 35.00
Jeannette, pk, Hex Optic bucket style 45.00
Lindsay, pk 425.00
McKee, blk, 2-spout 900.00
McKee, Skokie Green, lg or sm 35.00
Mckee, yel opaque, grapefruit 225.00
McKee (emb McK), custard, 6" 35.00
Orange Juice Extractor, blk 400.00
Sunkist, blk 750.00
Sunkist, Chalaine Blue 295.00
Sunkist, chocolate 750.00
Sunkist, custard 50.00
Sunkist, milk glass 20.00
Sunkist, yel opaque, McKee 55.00
US Glass, yel, pitcher form 750.00
Valencia, milk glass 100.00
Westmoreland, dk amber, 2-pc 200.00
Westmoreland, pk, 2-pc, baby sz 175.00

Records

Records of interest to collectors are often not the million-selling hits by 'superstars.' Very few records by Bing Crosby, for example, are of any more than nominal value, and those that are valuable usually don't even have his name on the label! Collectors today are most interested in records that were made in limited quantities, early works of a performer who later became famous, and those issued in special series or aimed at a limited market. Vintage records are judged desirable by their recorded content as well; those that lack the quality of music that makes a record collectible will always be 'junk' records in spite of their age, scarcity, or the obsolescence of their technology.

Records are usually graded visually rather than aurally, since it is seldom if ever possible to first play the records you buy at shows, by mail, at flea markets, etc. Condition is one of the most important determinants of value. For example, a nearly mint-condition Elvis Presley 45 of 'Milk Cow Blues' (Sun 215) has a potential value of over $1,500.00. A small sticker on the label could cut its value in half; noticeable wear could reduce its value by 80%. A mint record must show no evidence of use (record jackets, in the case of EPs and LPs, must be equally choice). Excellent condition denotes a record showing only slight signs of use with no audible defects. A very good record has noticeable wear but still plays well. Records of lesser grades may be unsaleable, unless very scarce and/or highly sought-after.

While the value of most 78s and 45s does not depend upon their being in appropriate sleeves (although a sleeveless existence certainly contributes to damage and deterioration!), this is not the case with most EPs (extended play 45s) and LPs (long-playing 33⅓ rpm albums), which **must** have their jackets (cardboard sleeves), in nice condition, free of disfiguring damage, such as writing, stickers, or tape. Often, common and minimally-valued 45s might be collectible if they are in appropriate 'picture sleeves' (special sleeves that depict the artist/group or other fanciful or symbolic graphic and identify the song titles, record label, and number), e.g. many common records by Elvis Presley, The Beatles, and The Beach Boys.

Promotional copies (DJ copies) supplied to radio stations often have labels different in designs and/or colors from their commercially-issued counterparts. Labels usually bear a designation 'Not for Sale,' 'Audition Copy,' 'Sample Copy,' or the like. Records may be pressed of translucent vinyl; while most promos are not particularly collectible, those by certain 'hot' artists, such as Elvis Presley, The Beach Boys, and The Beatles, are usually premium disks.

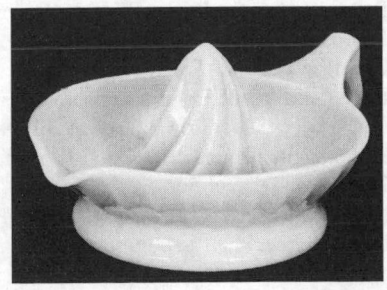

Jeannette, Delphite Blue, small, $95.00.

Many of the most desirable and valuable 45s have been 'bootlegged' (counterfeited). For example, there are probably more fake Elvis Presley *Sun* records in circulation than authentic copies — certainly in higher grades! Collectors should be alert for these often deceptive counterfeits.

Our advisor for this category is L.R. Docks, author of *American Premium Record Guide*, which lists 60,000 records by over 7,000 artists, now in its fifth edition. He is listed in the Directory under Texas. In the listings that follow, prices are suggested for records that are in excellent condition; worn or abused records may be worth only a small fraction of the values quoted, and may not be saleable at all.

Key:
Bru — Brunswick   Para — Paramount
Ch — Champion   Orch — Orchestra
Col — Columbia   Vi — Victor
Edi — Edison   Vo — Vocalion

Rare Buddy label, Vernon Dalhart, Wreck of the '1256,' Aluminum Specialty Co. (and five other companies), from $30.00 to $50.00.

Photo courtesy Les Docks

Blues, Rhythm and Blues, Rock 'N Roll, Rockabilly

Adams, Charlie; Black Land Blues, Col 21524, 45 rpm **10.00**
Allen, Ira; Nursery Rock, Mav-Rick 105, 45 rpm **75.00**
Amerson, Doug; Bop Man Bop, IntraState 25, 45 rpm **50.00**
Armstrong, May; Joe Boy Blues, Vo 1129, 78 rpm **100.00**
Banks, Mack; Be Boppin' Daddy, Fame 580, 45 rpm **40.00**
Barrix, Billy; Cool Off Baby, Chess 1662, 45 rpm **300.00**
Bees, Toy Bell, Imperial 5314, 45 rpm **60.00**
Belew, Carl; Cool Gator Shoes, Decca 30947, 45 rpm **12.00**
Bilbro, DH; Chester Blues, Vi 23831, 78 rpm **75.00**
Blakely, Wellington; Sailor Joe, Vee Jay 104, 45 rpm **25.00**
Bledsoe, Steve; Dumb Dumb Bunny, Witch 102, 45 rpm **30.00**
Boone, Alonzo; Kansas City Blues, Supertone 9428, 78 rpm **400.00**
Boyd, Robert; Boyd's Bounce, Wasco 201, 45 rpm **100.00**
Brown, Buster; Fannie Mae, Fire 1008, 78 rpm **100.00**
Burley, Dan; Shotgun House Rag, Circle 1022, 78 rpm **20.00**
Burns, Sonny; A Real Cool Cat, Starday 209, 45 rpm **40.00**
Byrd, Roy; Curly Haired Baby, Federal 12061, 45 rpm **50.00**
Carroll, Jimmy; Big Green Car, Fascination 2000, 45 rpm **30.00**
Carter, George; Hot Jelly Roll Blues, Para 12750, 78 rpm **200.00**
Carter, Wilf; Montana Slim, Camden 527, LP **20.00**
Checkers, Flame in My Heart, King 4558, 45 rpm **75.00**
Climbers, My Darlin' Dear, J&S 1652, 45 rpm **150.00**
Clouds, I Do, Cobra 1005, 45 rpm **200.00**
Cooley, Spade; Sagebrush Swing, Col 9007, 10" LP **30.00**
Covelle, Buddy; Lorraine, Coral 62181, 45 rpm **100.00**
Crawford, James; Flood & Thunder, Gennett 6536, 78 rpm **100.00**
Curry, Earl; Hobo, Post 2011, 45 rpm **30.00**
Cymbal, Johnny; Mr Bass Man, Kapp 3324, LP **30.00**
Dawson, Ronnie; Rockin' Bones, Rockin' Records 1, 45 rpm **60.00**
Deberry, Jimmy; Take a Little Chance, Sun 185, 45 rpm **150.00**
Dickson, Tom; Death Cell Blues, Okeh 8590, 78 rpm **150.00**

Dietzel, Elroy; Rock-N-Bones, Bo-Kay 101, 45 rpm **50.00**
Douglas, Mel; Cadillac Boogie, San 1506, 45 rpm **30.00**
Drifters, The World Is Changing, Crown 108, 45 rpm **80.00**
Eay, Eddie; Dancin' Girl, Echo 5911, 45 rpm **50.00**
Echo Valley Boys, Wash Machine Boogie, Island ½, 45 rpm **100.00**
Evans, Paul; Guaranteed 1000 Fabulous Teens, LP **50.00**
Falcons, I Miss You Darling, Cash 1002, 45 rpm **150.00**
Fisher, Sonny; Pink & Black, Starday 244, 45 rpm **40.00**
Five Chances, I May Be Small, Chance 1157, 45 rpm **300.00**
Five Wings, Johnny Has Gone, King 4778, 45 rpm **50.00**
Flamingos, Blues in a Letter, Chance 1133, 45 rpm **400.00**
Foster, Evelyn; Beating Blues, Ch 15590, 78 rpm **250.00**
Fox, Eugene; Sinner's Dream, Checker 792, 45 rpm **40.00**
Gales, My Eyes Keep Me in Trouble, JVB 34, 45 rpm **250.00**
Gazelles, Honest, Gotham 315, 45 rpm **40.00**
Gene & Eunice, Rock & Roll Sock Hop, Score 4018, LP **150.00**
Glen, Emery; Back Door Blues, Col 14472-D, 78 rpm **75.00**
Groves, Carl; Let's Rock Tonight, MAV 468, 45 rpm **50.00**
Handy Jackson, Got My Application Baby, Sun 177, 45 rpm **150.00**
Hardy, Bill; Rockin' at the Zoo, Rita 1001, 45 rpm **20.00**
Harmonica Frank, Rockin' Chair Daddy, Sun 205, 45 rpm **150.00**
Harris & Harris, Teasing Brown, Vi V38594, 78 rpm **250.00**
Henry, Robert; Old Battle Ax, King 4646, 45 rpm **150.00**
Hess, Bennie; Wild Hog Hop, Major 1001, 45 rpm **75.00**
Hite, Mattie; Texas Twist, Col 14503-D, 78 rpm **75.00**
Hooper, Jess; All Messed Up, Meteor 5025, 45 rpm **150.00**
Horton, Johnny; Honky Tonk Man, Col B-2130, EP **75.00**
Hot Shot Love, Wolf Call Boogie, Sun 196, 78 rpm **80.00**
JB & His Hawks, Pet Cream Man, Chance 1160, 45 rpm **200.00**
Jimmie & Walter, Before Long, Sun 180, 45 rpm **150.00**
Johnson, Buster; Undertaker Blues, Ch 16718, 78 rpm **300.00**
Johnson, Porkchop; Pork Chop Stomp, Ch 15796, 78 rpm **250.00**
Keghouse, Keghouse Blues, Okeh 8583, 78 rpm **75.00**
Kidds, Are You Forgetting Me, Imperial 5335, 45 rpm **175.00**
King, Albert; Bad Luck Blues, Parrot 798, 45 rpm **75.00**
Larks, My Reverie, orange vinyl, Apollo 1184, 45 rpm **500.00**
Limelighters, Cabin Hideaway, Joz 795, 45 rpm **25.00**
Louis, Joe Hill; Dorothy May, Checker 763, 45 rpm **150.00**
Lumkin, Bobby; One Way Ticket, Felco 102, 45 rpm **50.00**
Maltais, Gene; The Raging Sea, Lilac 3159, 45 rpm **60.00**
Marcels, Blue Moon, Colpix 416, LP **50.00**
McDonald, Tee; Beef Man Blues, Decca 7018, 78 rpm **75.00**
McGinnis, Wayne; Rock & Roll Rhythm, Meteor 5035, 45 rpm .**30.00**
McLarey Butch; Rockin' Hall, Kliff 103, 45 rpm **60.00**
Memphis Mose, Pig Meat Papa, Bru 7102, 78 rpm **150.00**
Mitchell, Lee; Rootie Tootie Baby, Sharp 0862, 45 rpm **60.00**
Mitchell, Walter; Pet Milk Blues, JVB 75827, 78 rpm **50.00**
Mixers, You Said You're Leaving Me, Bold 101, 45 rpm **100.00**
Moon Mulligan, Jenny Lee, Coral 61994, 45 rpm **50.00**
Murphy, Don; Mean Mama Blues, Cosmopolitan 2264, 45 rpm ...**40.00**
North, Hattie; Honey Dripper Blues, Vo 1433, 78 rpm **150.00**
Ontarios, Memories of You, Big Town 121, 45 rpm **80.00**
Orchids, Oh Why, King 4661, 45 rpm **100.00**
Pelicans, Chimes, Imperial 5307, 45 rpm **300.00**
Pharoahs, Walking Sad, Fascination 001, 45 rpm **75.00**
Play Boy Thomas, Too Much Pride, Swing Time 340, 45 rpm **75.00**
Pope, Jenny; Bull Frog Blues, Vo 1522, 78 rpm **150.00**
Powers, Jett; Go, Girl Go, Design 811, 45 rpm **50.00**
Prager, Billy; Do It Bop, Crystal 106, 45 rpm **20.00**
Primettes, Tears of Sorrow, LuPine 120, 45 rpm **50.00**
Prowlers, Rock Me Baby, Aragon 302, 45 rpm **40.00**
Reed, Jimmy; High & Lonesome, Chance 1142, 45 rpm **150.00**
Reed, Lulu; Moody & Blue, King 604, LP **120.00**
Rockin' Dukes, My Baby Left Me, OJ 1007, 45 rpm **100.00**

Romeos, I Beg You Please, Apollo 461, 45 rpm 125.00
Ross, Lucy; Cotton Belt Blues, Ch 15775, 78 rpm 130.00
Sabres, Always Forever, Cal-West 45947, 45 rpm 100.00
Schoolboy Cleve, Strange Letter Blues, Feature 3013, 45 rpm 50.00
Sha-Weez, No One To Love Me, Aladdin 3170, 45 rpm 250.00
Sheppards, Love, Theron 112, 78 rpm 75.00
Smith, Eithel; Jelly Roll Mill, Ch 16613, 78 rpm 250.00
Smith, Sammy; Alaska Rock, Wee Rebel 102, 45 rpm 40.00
Snow, Eddie; Ain't That Right, Sun 226, 45 rpm 80.00
Spaulding, Henry; Cairo Blues, Bru 7085, 78 rpm 125.00
Stayton, Jimmy; Hot Hot Mama, Blue Hen 220, 45 rpm 100.00
Stone, Jeff; Everybody Rock, Sarg 151, 45 rpm 40.00
Sweet Papa Stovepipe, Mama's Angel Child, Para 12404, 78 rpm ...125.00
Sysom, Bobby; Big Time Mama, Blue Moon 304, 45 rpm 50.00
Taro, Frankie; Susy Ann, G&G 111, 45 rpm 40.00
Topps, Tippin', Red Robin 126, 45 rpm 40.00
Turks, Emily, Money 211, 45 rpm 20.00
Utah Carl, Lovin' You, Starday 301, 45 rpm 15.00
Vibes, Stop Torturing Me, Chariot 105, 45 rpm 200.00
Vocaltones, My Girl, Apollo 488, 45 rpm 50.00
Wayne, Billy; I Love My Baby, Hill Crest 778, 45 rpm 40.00
Wayne, Roy; Honey Won't You Listen, Clif 101, 45 rpm 50.00
Williamson, James; The Woman I Love, Chance 1131, 45 rpm .200.00
Wilson, Jackie; Lonely Teardrops, Bru 55105, 78 rpm 75.00
Young, George; Can't Stop Me, Mercury 71259, 45 rpm 20.00

Country and Western

Allen, Lee & Austin; Chattanooga Blues, Col 14266-D, 78 rpm ..100.00
Ashley, Clarence; Little Sadie, Col 15522-D, 78 rpm 60.00
Baker, Buddy; Box Car Blues, Vi 21549, 78 rpm 15.00
Bentley Boys, Henhouse Blues, Col 15565-D, 78 rpm 50.00
Boggs, Dock; Country Blues, Bru 131, 78 rpm 50.00
Brooks, Billy; Freight Train Blues, Col 15614-D, 78 rpm 30.00
Cain, Albert; Runnin' Wild, Okeh 45557, 78 rpm 40.00
Carpenter, Boyden; Hobos Convention, Ch 16519, 78 rpm 25.00
Carson, Rosa Lee; Drinker's Child, Okeh 45005, 78 rpm 12.00
Carter, Floyd; Flemington Kidnap Trial, Oriole 8847, 78 rpm 10.00
Childre, Lew; Moonshine Blues, Ch 16011, 78 rpm 50.00
Crawford, Alvin; I Sit Broken Hearted, Superior 2528, 78 rpm 30.00
Dave & Howard, Bay Rum Blues, Vi 23566, 78 rpm 75.00
Davis Trio, Sleepy Hollow, Para 3238, 78 rpm 20.00
Denmon, Morgan; Drunkard's Dream, Okeh 45327, 78 rpm 12.00
Duncan Boys, Kentucky Stomp, Supertone 9676, 78 rpm 30.00
Fletcher & Foster, Travelin' North, Ch 16121, 78 rpm 50.00
Gaydon, Whit; Tennessee Coon Hunt, Vi V40315, 78 rpm 20.00
Georgia Wildcats, She's Waiting for Me, Vi 23640, 78 rpm 50.00
Halton Bros, Hook & Line, Ch 16628, 78 rpm 75.00
Harper, Oscar & Doc; Bitter Creek, Okeh 45385, 78 rpm 50.00
Holmes, George; A Mother's Plea, Superior 2525, 78 rpm 20.00
Home Town Boys, Home Town Rag, Col 15762-D, 78 rpm 40.00
Johnson, Gene; TB Blues, Timeley Tunes 1550, 78 rpm 75.00
Johnson & Harvey, Birdie, Ch 16449, 78 rpm 60.00
Kelly, Pat; Down by the Railroad Track, Para 3319, 78 rpm 40.00
Lancaster, GE; Tennessee Yodel, Superior 2538, 78 rpm 40.00
Lewis, Archie; Miss Handy Hanks, Ch 16677, 78 rpm 30.00
Lunsford, Frank; Hobo's Return, Ch 16287, 78 rpm 30.00
Major, Jack; Tennessee Mountain Girl, Bru 252, 78 rpm 20.00
Marlow, Andy; My Little Lady, Ch 15875, 78 rpm 20.00
Mattox, Jimmie; Good Bye Mama, Gennett 7227, 78 rpm 50.00
Maynard, Ken; Cowboy's Lament, Col 2310-D, 78 rpm 100.00
Moonshiners, Fulton County, Vi V40284, 78 rpm 25.00
Morgan, Everett; Texas Home, Ch 16616, 78 rpm 40.00
Nichols Bros, She's Killing Me, Vi 23582, 78 rpm 100.00

Owens, EB; Sweet Carlyle, Col 15414-D, 78 rpm 20.00
Patrick, Luther; Cornbread, Gennett 6448, 78 rpm 20.00
Pine Mountain Boys, Wild Woman Blues, Vi 23605, 78 rpm 100.00
Price, Ray; Jealous Lies, Bullet 701, 78 rpm 50.00
Red Mountain Trio, Dixie, Col 15369-D, 78 rpm 15.00
Renfro Valley Boys, Loreena, Para 3321, 78 rpm 40.00
Rice, Davis & Thomas; Circus Day Rag, QRS 9019, 78 rpm 50.00
Saxton Bros, Going-A-Courtin', Superior 2537, 78 rpm 35.00
Scotty the Drifter, Gooseberry Pie, Decca 5296, 78 rpm 10.00
Smallwood, Lester; Cotton Mill Girl, Vi V40181, 78 rpm 60.00
Spangle & Pearson, Patrick County Blues, Okeh 45287, 78 rpm ..60.00
Stratton, Harley; Red River Valley, Superior 2588, 78 rpm 20.00
Texas Night Hawks, Possum Rag, Okeh 45363, 78 rpm 30.00
Three Stripped Gears, Alabama Blues, Okeh 45571, 78 rpm 100.00
Walter Family, Shaker Ben, Ch 16653, 78 rpm 60.00
Weber, Sam; My Ozark Mountain Home, Superior 2822, 78 rpm ...50.00
White Mountain Orch, Leather Britches, Vi V40185, 78 rpm 30.00
Williams, Hank; Pan American, Sterling 210, 78 rpm 100.00
Wooten, Kyle; Lumber Camp Blues, Okeh 45511, 78 rpm 50.00

Jazz, Dance Bands, Personalities

Alabama Jazz Pirates, Canned Heat Blues, Bell 1182, 78 rpm 250.00
Arkansas Trio, Boll Weevil Blues, Edi 51373, 78 rpm 10.00
Astaire, Fred; Cheek to Cheek, Bru 7486, 78 rpm 10.00
Banta, Frank; My Sugar, Vi 19705, 78 rpm 8.00
Bell, Anna; Hopeless Blues, QRS 7007, 78 rpm 150.00
Bobby's Revelers, Mojo Blues, Silvertone 3552, 78 rpm 75.00
Brown, Henry; Blues Stomp, Para 12934, 78 rpm 200.00
Call, Bob; Thirty-one Blues, Bru 7137, 78 rpm 100.00
Campus Boys, Rainbow Man, Banner 6425, 78 rpm 10.00
Candy & Coco, Kingfish Blues, Vo 2833, 78 rpm 30.00
Checker Box Boys, Outside, Broadway 1262, 78 rpm 8.00
Club Wigwam Orch, Alabamy Bound, Domino 3458, 78 rpm 15.00
Cotton Pickers, After Awhile, Gennett 6380, 78 rpm 75.00
Cuban Dance Players, I'll Fly to Hawaii, Challenge 210, 78 rpm ..60.00
Davis, Wilmer; Gut Struggle, Vo 1034, 78 rpm 100.00
Deppe, Louis; Southland, Gennett 20021, 78 rpm 30.00
Dixie Stompers, Goose Pimples, Harmony 545-H, 78 rpm 15.00
Eaton, Charlie; Bucket of Blood, Herwin 93017, 78 rpm 150.00
Ellis, Gay; True Blue Lou, Harmony 981-H, 78 rpm 10.00
English, Sharlie; Transom Blues, Para 12610, 78 rpm 100.00
Finnie, Ethel; Hula Blues, Ajax 17027, 78 rpm 30.00
Frazier, Jake; Jake's Weary Blues, Ajax 17117, 78 rpm 40.00
Gibson, Cleo; Nothing But Blues, Okeh 8700, 78 rpm 50.00
Golden Gate Serenaders, On! Baby, Gennett 6487, 78 rpm 15.00
Green Parrot Inn Orch, At Sundown, Ch 15322, 78 rpm 50.00
Hall, Wendell; Headin' Home, Col 1028-D, 78 rpm 8.00
Harlem Trio, Fuzzy Wuzzy, Herwin 93012, 78 rpm 200.00
Henderson, Bertha; Six Thirty Blues, Para 12511, 78 rpm 150.00
High Steppers, Please, Crown 3394, 78 rpm 15.00
Hot Dogs, Steady Roll, Silvertone 3574, 78 rpm 150.00
Jamaica Jazzers, West Indies Blues, Okeh 40117, 78 rpm 75.00
Jelly Whippers, SOB Blues, Herwin 92018, 78 rpm 200.00
Jolly Three, Ain't Got a Dime, Vo 03955, 78 rpm 30.00
Kay, Dolly; A Good Man Is Hard To Find, Vo 15664, 78 rpm 40.00
King David's Jug Band, Sweet Potato Blues, Okeh 8901, 78 rpm ..150.00
Langford, Frances; Moon Song, Bluebird 5016, 78 rpm 12.00
Lee, Chauncey C; Banjo Rag, Okeh 40321, 78 rpm 100.00
Lill's Hot Shots, Drop That Sack, Vo 1037, 78 rpm 120.00
Lumpkin, Guy; Decatur Street Rag, QRS 7078, 78 rpm 200.00
Melody Four, I'm Crazy 'Bout My Baby, Vi 23289, 78 rpm 50.00
Midnight Rounders, Bull Fiddle Rag, Vo 1237, 78 rpm 150.00
Moonlight Revelers, Memphis Stomp, Grey Gull 1786, 78 rpm ...50.00

Moskowitz, Joseph; Operatic Rag, Vi 17978, 78 rpm **20.00**
New Orleans Feetwarmers, Maple Leaf Rag, Vi 24150, 78 rpm **75.00**
Night Owls, Pump Tille, Silvertone 3549, 78 rpm **125.00**
Old Southern Jug Band, Hatchet Head Blues, Vo 14958, 78 rpm ..**150.00**
Original Memphis Five, Pacific Coast Blues, Bell P-153, 78 rpm ..**30.00**
Owens, Red & His Gang; Hard Luck, Ch 16423, 78 rpm **125.00**
Preer, Evelyn; Muddy Water, Banner 1972, 78 rpm **8.00**
Randall, Duke & His Boys; Squeeze Me, Ch 15491, 78 rpm **300.00**
Rhythm Aces, Jazz Battle, Bru 4244, 78 rpm **100.00**
Riffers, Rhapsody in Love, Col 14677-D, 78 rpm **40.00**
Russell's Roving Revelers, Ch 15701, 78 rpm **35.00**
Sara Martin's Jug Band, Blue Devil Blues, Okeh 8188, 78 rpm ...**125.00**
Scare Crow, Traveling Blues, Gennett 7209, 78 rpm **200.00**
Searcy Trio, Kansas Avenue Blues, Okeh 8360, 78 rpm **75.00**
Sioux City Six, Flock O' Blues, Gennett 5569, 78 rpm **150.00**
Sizzlers, Diga Diga Doo, Edi 52463, 78 rpm **30.00**
South Street Ramblers, Endurance Stomp, QRS 7019, 78 rpm ..**150.00**
Sunset Dance Orch, High Society, Ch 15038, 78 rpm **60.00**
Thomas' Devils, Boot It, Boy, Bru 7064, 78 rpm **150.00**
Triangle Harmony Boys, Sweet Patootie, Gennett 6275, 78 rpm ..**300.00**
Underwood, Sugar; Dew Drop Alley Stomp, Vi 21538, 78 rpm ...**100.00**
Vicksburg Blowers, Monte Carlo Joys, Gennett 6089, 78 rpm **200.00**
Washboard Trio, Washboard Rag, Para 12682, 78 rpm **150.00**
West, Theadore; Hot Jelly Blues, Ajax 17118, 78 rpm **40.00**
Williams, Mary Lou; Night Life, Bru 7178, 78 rpm **150.00**
Williams & Moore, Block & Tackle Blues, QRS 7016, 78 rpm ..**200.00**
Yankee Six, Jimtown Blues, Okeh 40348, 78 rpm **50.00**

Red Wing

The Red Wing Stoneware Company, founded in 1878, took its name from its location in Red Wing, Minnesota. In 1906 the name was changed to the Red Wing Union Stoneware Company after a merger with several of the other local potteries. For the most part they produced utilitarian wares such as flowerpots, crocks, and jugs. Their early 1930s catalogs offered a line of art pottery vases in colored glazes, some of which featured handles modeled after swan's necks, snakes, or female nudes. Other examples were quite simple, often with classic styling. After the addition of their dinnerware lines in 1935, 'Stoneware' was dropped from the name, and the company became known as Red Wing Potteries, Inc. They closed in 1967.

The pottery was reopened several years ago, and handmade and decorated salt-glazed stoneware is again being produced. Each piece is stamped with the potters' initials and the year of production.

Our artware advisors are Wendy and Leo Frese (Three Rivers Collectibles); they are listed under Texas. For further study we recommend *Red Wing Stoneware, An Identification and Value Guide,* and *Red Wing Collectibles* by Dan and Gail DePasquale and Larry Peterson; and *Red Wing Art Pottery, Books I and II,* by B.L. Dollen. All are published by Collector Books. Another good reference is *Red Wing Art Pottery* by Ray Reiss (privately published).

Commercial Art Ware and Miscellaneous

Ash receiver, donkey, maroon, #876 ....**250.00**
Ash receiver, pelican, lt gr, #880, NM **150.00**
Ashtray, angelfish, dk gr, #933 ....**125.00**
Ashtray, duck, aqua, ind **75.00**
Ashtray, duck, bright yel, from 'Plain' dinnerware line **75.00**
Ashtray, wing, maroon, 75th Anniversary **50.00**
Basket, wht w/lt gr int, #348, 6½" **35.00**
Bowl, brn, 3-ftd, #M5014, 10½" **15.00**
Bowl, console; persimmon w/cream int, #B1406, 2¾" **30.00**

Bowl, Gondola, Bell Kogan, #B1420, w/pr candle holders **50.00**
Bowl, gr w/gray int, low, #1278, 1¾" H **25.00**
Bowl, lt gr & brn blend, scalloped, ped ft, #691, 7½" **30.00**
Bowl, Murphy, Orchid, #M1572, 10" **50.00**
Bowl, Murphy Free-Form, lt gr w/wht int, #M1463 ....**25.00**
Bowl, wht, ped ft, #M5006, 3¼" **30.00**
Bowl, yel w/brn int, #1348, 2" **35.00**
Candle holder, Ceramastone, burnt orange **35.00**
Candle holders, Fondoso, wht, pr **100.00**
Candle holders, gr w/yel int, #B1411, 2", pr **30.00**
Candle holders, pk w/gray int, 5" sq, pr **30.00**
Candle holders, Textura, pk w/gray int, Bell Kogan, #B2113A, pr ..**30.00**
Casserole, chicken figural, pk, #250, ind, 6x8" **75.00**
Casserole, fish figural, ivory, #248, NM **90.00**
Console set, Oxford (blk matt w/wht stippling), #2303, 3-pc **100.00**
Cornucopia, gray w/pk int, #1097, 5½", pr **40.00**
Ewer, cobalt, bl circle stamp, #52, NM **150.00**
Ewer, Continental, man's face & serpent details, #220, 10" **50.00**
Ewer, Magnolia, w/Pompeiian finish, #1020, 10½" **95.00**
Figurine, accordion man, HP, #B1417, 10" **150.00**

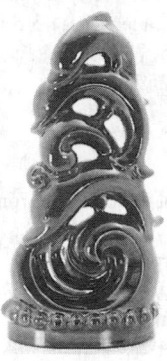

Figurine, four piggyback dolphins on wave, purple with pink, 9", $70.00.

Flowerpot, wht w/lt gr int, #677, 4" **20.00**
Jardiniere, Brushware, emb lilies & cattails, unmk, 15" **275.00**
Pitcher, Green Glazed Ware, bl circle stamp, 1931, #179, 10" ...**200.00**
Planter, Anniversary (maroon & gray), #2308 ....**60.00**
Planter, bl fleck, #642, 11" **25.00**
Planter, brn w/yel int, #B2017, 4¾" **25.00**
Planter, burgundy w/gray int, #1378, 5½" **28.00**
Planter, gr w/yel int, #B1402, 3¾" **20.00**
Planter, gr w/yel int, #1516 ....**20.00**
Planter, maroon w/gray int, #B2016, 4¼" **40.00**
Planter, pk flecks, #431 ....**25.00**
Planter, pk speckled, #1265 ....**30.00**
Planter, Polka Dot, Dutch Blue, #677, 1938, 5x6" **75.00**
Planter, potbelly stove, pk matt w/yel int, #765, 7" **75.00**
Planter, swan, rust w/yel int, #278, 3¼" **30.00**
Planter, swan, wht, #259, 5¼" **40.00**
Planter, swan, yel flecks, #444, 1956, 9", minimum value **200.00**
Planter, wht, #M1495, 3" **40.00**
Planter, wht w/gr int, #B1391, 3¼" **15.00**
Planter/jardiniere, brn fleck w/wht int, #445, 10" **55.00**
Shoe vase, blk, #638, lg **125.00**
Teapot, lady figural, cobalt, #260 ....**300.00**
Vase, beige, brass hdls, #M1599, 9¾" **40.00**
Vase, beige, brass hdls, #M1609, 10½" **40.00**
Vase, Belle, olive gr w/dk gr int, #874, 6½" **30.00**
Vase, Belle 100, pk gloss w/brn int, #765, 7" **40.00**
Vase, Belle 100, Red Wing (Rumrill glaze), flake/line, #785, 10" ..**100.00**
Vase, Birch Tree, dk gr w/golden yel panels, bl circle stamp, #163 ...**100.00**
Vase, Brushware, gr int, #133, 10½" **130.00**

Vase, bud; gr, bl circle ink stamp, #188, 9" 100.00
Vase, children dancing in high relief, #1159 ....75.00
Vase, Colonial Mug, blk, #5033, 6" 500.00
Vase, cornucopia; gray gloss w/brn int, tropical leaves, #1294, 10" ...50.00
Vase, cornucopia; Lustre Burgundy, #1284, 10½" 75.00
Vase, cornucopia; olive gr, #1152, 9" 40.00
Vase, crackled turq w/bronze int, #1290, 10" 50.00
Vase, Desert Flower, chartreuse, lt gray int, #B-2002, 8" 25.00
Vase, Egyptian, wht w/gr highlights, #159, 9" 90.00
Vase, face, pk w/wht int, #1151, 8" 90.00
Vase, Floral, wht w/lt gr int, #1294, 8" 40.00
Vase, gr w/wht int, 3-hdl, #1167 ....35.00
Vase, Leaf, Slate Blue, #1112 ....25.00
Vase, Lion, Blended glaze, Blue Circle Union mk, #164S, 7½" ..300.00
Vase, Lustre Burgundy, gray int, Belle Kogan, #B-1400, 1951, 5" 30.00
Vase, Lustre Burgundy w/gray int, #1114, 7" 60.00
Vase, Lustre Rachelle (pk gloss), hdls, #753, 6" 50.00
Vase, Lustre Tan w/gr int, #1103D, 8¼" 45.00
Vase, Manhattan, bl w/pk int, #537, 12" 40.00
Vase, maroon, #B2015, 4¾" 65.00
Vase, Nokomis, #196, 10½" 650.00
Vase, persimmon w/gr int, 75-yr label, #B1429, 8" 55.00
Vase, Pompeiian, wht w/brn highlights, #1096, 9" 40.00
Vase, sand w/gr int, 1-hdl, #1356, 7½" 30.00
Vase, Sgraffito, HP w/tan speckle overglaze, #M4008, 11½" 75.00
Vase, shell form, wht w/gr int, #1562, 6" 25.00
Vase, Spiral, lt brn w/lt gr int, #1632, 8" 40.00
Vase, Star, lt gr, #656, 9½" 40.00
Vase, Textura, forest gr w/yel int, hairline, #B2100, 8" 15.00
Vase, Textura, pk glossy w/gray int, #B-2113, 7" 30.00
Vase, Travertine, Citron Yellow, #1377, 11" 60.00
Vase, urn style, lt gray, #M5000, 8" 40.00
Vase, Wheat Stalk, gray-gr w/brn highlights, pk int, #1106 ....50.00
Vase, wht w/gr int, hdls, #1168, 7" 50.00
Vase, wht w/gr int, ped ft, #M5007, 4¾" 35.00
Vase, wht w/lt gr int, #B1934, 7½" 25.00
Vase, wht w/lt gr int, #730, 7½" 45.00
Vase, yel w/brn int, 1-hdl, #1346, 7½" 30.00
Vase, yel w/brn int, 4-hdl, #1355, 7½" 25.00
Vase, yel w/gr int, #B2001, 8¼" 48.00
Window box, Magnolia, #1234, 12", NM 40.00

Cookie Jars

Be aware that there is a very good reproduction of the King of Tarts. Except for the fact that the new jars are slightly smaller, they are sometime difficult to distinguish from the old. Our advisor for this section is Charlie Snyder; he is listed in the Directory under Kansas.

Bob White, unmk, from $100 to 135.00
Carousel, unmk, from $900 to 950.00
Crock, wht 80.00
Dutch Girl (Katrina), yel w/brn trim, from $175 to 200.00
Friar Tuck, cream w/brn, mk, from $200 to 225.00
Friar Tuck, gr, mk, from $250 to 300.00
Friar Tuck, yel, unmk 175.00
Grapes, cobalt or dk purple, ea, from $575 to 600.00
Grapes, gr, from $250 to 275.00
Jack Frost, unmk, short 750.00
Jack Frost, unmk, tall, from $850 to 900.00
King of Tarts, mc, mk (+) 975.00
King of Tarts, pk w/bl & blk trim, mk 1,000.00
King of Tarts, wht, unmk, from $450 to 500.00
Peasant design, emb/pnt figures on aqua, from $275 to 300.00

Peasant design, emb/pnt figures on brn 275.00
Pierre (chef), bl, unmk 195.00
Pierre (chef), brn, unmk, from $250 to 300.00
Pierre (chef), pk, mk 400.00
Pineapple, yel 200.00

Dinnerware

Dinnerware lines were added in 1935, and today collectors scramble to rebuild extensive table services. Although interest is obvious, right now the market is so volatile, it is often difficult to establish a price scale with any degree of accuracy. Asking prices may vary from $50.00 to $200.00 on some items, which indicates instability and a collector market trying to find its way. (One guide currently on the market, for instance, lists Midnight Rose dinner plates at $15.00 to $20.00, while another terms them 'rare,' and values them at $145.00 each.) Sellers seem to be unfamiliar with pattern names and proper identification of the various pieces that each line consists of. There were many hand-decorated lines; among the most popular are Bob White, Tropicana, and Round-up. But there are other patterns that are just as attractive and deserving of attention. The Dollen books referenced both have dinnerware sections, and Ray Reiss has published a book called *Red Wing Dinnerware, Price and Identification Guide*, which shows nearly one hundred patterns on its back cover alone.

Town and Country, designed by Eva Zeisel, was made for only one year in the late 1940s. Today many collectors regard Zeisel as one of the most gifted designers of that era and actively seek examples of her work. Town and Country was a versatile line, adaptable to both informal and semiformal use. It is characterized by irregular, often eccentric shapes, and handles of pitchers and serving pieces are usually extensions of the rim. Bowls and platters are free-form comma shapes or appear tilted, with one side slightly higher than the other. Although the ware is unmarked, it is recognizable by its distinctive shapes and glazes. White (often used to complement interiors of bowls and cups), though an original color, is actually more rare than Bronze (metallic brown, also called gunmetal), which enjoys favored status; Gray is unusual. Other colors include Rust, Dusk Blue, Sand, Chartreuse, Peach, and Forest Green. Pieces have also shown up in Mulberry and Ming Green and are considered quite rare. (These are Red Wing Quartelle colors!) Note: Eva Zeisel recently gave permission to reissue a few select pieces of Town and Country; these are being made by World of Ceramics. In 1996 salt and pepper shakers were reproduced in **new** colors not resembling Red Wing colors. In 1997 the mixing bowl and syrup were reissued. All new pieces are stamped EZ96 or EZ97 and are visibly different from the old, as far as glaze, pottery base, and weight.

Our advisor for the general dinnerware lines is Doug Podpeskar; he is listed in the Directory under Minnesota. Karen Silvermintz (see Texas) and Charles Alexander (see Indiana) advise on the Town and Country dinnerware.

Key:
c/s — cobalt on stoneware   RW — Red Wing
MN — Minnesota   RWUS — Red Wing Union
NS — North Star   Stoneware

Brittany, teapot, $125.00.

Blossom Time, bowl, Concord shape, 8½" 12.00
Blossom Time, butter dish, ¼-lb 30.00
Blossom Time, cup & saucer, Concord shape 12.00
Blossom Time, plate, bread & butter 8.00
Blossom Time, platter, Concord shape, 13¼" 20.00
Blossom Time, saucer 4.00
Bob White, bowl, divided vegetable 32.00
Bob White, bowl, nappy 30.00
Bob White, bowl, sauce 12.00
Bob White, casserole, lg, 4-qt 55.00
Bob White, casserole, w/lid & stand, sm, 2-qt 45.00
Bob White, creamer, 7" 30.00
Bob White, cup & saucer 20.00
Bob White, gravy, w/lid 40.00
Bob White, hors d'oeuvre bird 50.00
Bob White, pitcher, water; 60-oz 50.00
Bob White, plate, 10½" 12.50
Bob White, plate, 6½" 6.00
Bob White, platter, 13 ....45.00
Bob White, shakers, tall, pr 35.00
Bob White, sugar bowl, w/lid 20.00
Bob White, tumbler, water 125.00
Brittany, bowl, cereal 15.00
Brittany, casserole, w/lid, 8½" 80.00
Brittany, chop plate, 12" 30.00
Brittany, creamer, 4" 25.00
Brittany, cup & saucer 15.00
Brittany, saucer 8.00
Brittany, shakers, 2½", pr 30.00
Capistrano, bowl, divided vegetable 28.00
Capistrano, plate, dinner; 10" 15.00
Capistrano, plate, 6½" 8.00
Crazy Rhythm, creamer & sugar bowl 45.00
Crazy Rhythm, tidbit tray, 2-tier 22.00
Frontenac, bowl, cereal 10.00
Frontenac, butter dish 20.00
Frontenac, plate, dinner 10.00
Frontenac, plate, salad 6.00
Lexington Rose, bowl, nappy 15.00
Lexington Rose, bowl, sauce 8.00
Lexington Rose, bowl, 8" 15.00
Lexington Rose, casserole, w/lid 35.00
Lexington Rose, creamer 15.00
Lexington Rose, cup & saucer 12.00
Lexington Rose, gravy boat 30.00
Lexington Rose, plate, bread & butter 6.00
Lexington Rose, platter, 13" 35.00
Lexington Rose, sugar bowl, w/lid 20.00
Lotus, casserole, w/lid 30.00
Lotus, cup & saucer 12.00
Lotus, egg plate, w/lid 90.00
Lotus, platter, 13" 35.00
Magnolia, bowl, fruit; 5¼" 5.50
Magnolia, cup & saucer 12.00
Magnolia, plate, dinner; 10" 14.00
Magnolia, rim soup 16.50
Midnight Rose, teapot 125.00
Midnight Rose, tidbit tray, 3-tier 27.50
Orleans, bowl, buffet 50.00
Orleans, French casserole 48.00
Pepe, bowl, divided vegetable 28.00
Pepe, plate, dinner; 10" 15.00
Pepe, shakers, pr 25.00
Pepe, tray, serving; 1-tier 25.00

Provincial Oomphware, bowl, 11½" 40.00
Provincial Oomphware, pitcher, water; 2-pt 45.00
Random Harvest, bowl, salad; 12" 45.00
Random Harvest, cup & saucer 15.00
Random Harvest, gravy boat 35.00
Random Harvest, plate, dinner 18.00
Random Harvest, sugar bowl, w/lid 20.00
Round-Up, casserole, lg 200.00
Round-Up, cup & saucer 55.00
Round-Up, plate, dinner 50.00
Round-Up, shakers, pr 95.00
Round-Up, teapot 240.00
Tampico, gravy boat 35.00
Tampico, mug, coffee 40.00

Town and Country, casserole, Sand, stick handle, with lid, large, $125.00.

Town & Country, bean pot, Rust, w/lid, minimum value 400.00
Town & Country, bowl, mixing; Dusk Blue 125.00
Town & Country, bowl, vegetable; Sand, 8" 35.00
Town & Country, bowl, 5" 15.00
Town & Country, creamer & sugar bowl, w/lid, minimum value .60.00
Town & Country, cruets, mixed colors, orig stoppers, pr 160.00
Town & Country, mug, coffee 75.00
Town & Country, pitcher, Peach, 3-pt 150.00
Town & Country, plate, Bronze, 10½" 45.00
Town & Country, plate, 10½" 30.00
Town & Country, shakers, Shmoo shape, mixed colors, pr 75.00
Town & Country, teapot, Sand 275.00
Village Green, bowl, cereal 17.50
Village Green, casserole stand, 8" 25.00
Village Green, shakers, pr 22.50
Village Green, warmer 25.00

Stoneware

Bean pot, Albany slip, MN, ½-gal 150.00
Bean pot, Albany slip, MN, ½-gal 135.00
Bean pot, Albany slip, NS, 1-gal 135.00
Bean pot, brn & wht, bail hdl, RWUS, ½-gal 95.00
Bowl, Greek Key, bl & wht, from 6" to 10", ea, from $125 to 175.00
Butter jar, Albany slip, high, MN, 1-gal 100.00
Butter jar, Albany slip, high, NS, 1-pt 175.00
Butter jar, Albany slip, low, MN, 1-lb 85.00
Butter jar, Albany slip, low, MN, 2-lb 60.00
Butter jar, Albany slip, low, RW, 2-lb 60.00
Butter jar, salt glaze, low, RW, 10-lb 75.00
Butter jar, wht, high, MN, 1-gal 45.00
Butter jar, wht, low, MN, 10-lb 60.00
Butter jar, wht, low, RW, 1-lb 70.00
Chamber pot, Albany slip, MN 300.00
Chamber pot, wht, fancy hdl, RW, 9", w/lid 150.00

Churn, #10/birch leaves, c/s, Union oval, 10-gal	1,500.00
Churn, #2/red wing on wht, Union oval, 2-gal	300.00
Churn, #3/parrot, c/s, MN, 3-gal	4,500.00
Churn, #4/leaf, c/s, RW, 4-gal	1,500.00
Churn, #5/red wing on wht, Union oval, 5-gal	300.00
Churn, #6/bird, c/s, RW, 6-gal	1,900.00
Churn, #6/butterfly, c/s, RW, 6-gal	1,750.00
Cooler, #3/Ice Water/red wing on wht, new Union trademk, 3-gal	1,000.00
Cooler, #4/daisy, c/s, RW, 4-gal	3,200.00
Cooler, #4/dbl leaves, c/s, RW, 4-gal	3,250.00
Cooler, #5/flower/Ice Water, c/s, RW, 6-gal	9,000.00
Crock, #10/elephant ear leaves, c/s, MN, 10-gal	175.00
Crock, #10/leaf, c/s, MN, 10-gal	750.00
Crock, #12/red wing on wht, RWUS, 12-gal	125.00
Crock, #2/birch leaves, c/s, RWUS, 2-gal	65.00
Crock, #20/elephant ear leaves, c/s, MN, 20-gal	275.00
Crock, #25/leaves, c/s, MN, 25-gal	1,250.00
Crock, #25/leaves, c/s, Union oval, 25-gal	750.00
Crock, #3/dbl P, c/s, MN, 3-gal	700.00
Crock, #3/dbl P, c/s, unmk, 3-gal	250.00
Crock, #3/drop 8, c/s, RW, 3-gal	550.00
Crock, #30/butterfly, c/s, stenciling, RW, 30-gal	2,300.00
Crock, #30/lily, c/s, stenciling, RW, 30-gal	2,500.00
Crock, #30/red wing on wht, RWUS, 30-gal	375.00
Crock, #4/dbl P, c/s, MN, 4-gal	540.00
Crock, #40/leaves, c/s, unmk, 40-gal	1,200.00
Crock, #5/elephant ear leaves, c/s, MN, 5-gal	125.00
Crock, #5/leaf, c/s, RW, 5-gal	600.00
Crock, #6/butterfly, c/s, 5-gal	750.00
Crock, #6/P, c/s, RW, 6-gal	600.00
Cuspidor, bl & wht sponging, unsgn	650.00
Cuspidor, brn & wht, MN, lg	475.00
Cuspidor, molded seam, bl & wht sponging, RW, 10" dia	750.00
Cuspidor, molded seam, brn & wht, unsgn	225.00
Flowerpot, Albany slip, geometric decor, MN, 7"	350.00
Jar, packing; wht, bail hdl, MN, 3-lb	90.00
Jar, preserve; Albany slip, RW, 1-gal	550.00
Jar, preserve/snuff; Albany slip, MN, 1-gal	75.00
Jar, preserve/snuff; Albany slip, RW, 4-gal	275.00
Jar, safety valve; wht, RW, 1-qt	200.00
Jar, wax sealer, Albany slip, NS, 1-gal	325.00
Jar, wax sealer, Albany slip, RW, 1-qt	60.00
Jug, beehive; #3/red wing on wht, Union oval, 3-gal	375.00
Jug, beehive; #4/birch leaves, c/s, Union oval, 4-gal	650.00
Jug, beehive; #5, Albany slip, RW on hdl, 5-gal	950.00
Jug, beehive; #5/birch leaves, c/s, Union oval, 5-gal	1,750.00
Jug, bl bands on wht, cone top, MN, 1-gal	400.00
Jug, bl bands on wht, cone top, RW, 1-gal	450.00
Jug, common, Albany slip, molded in middle, NS, 1-gal	200.00
Jug, common, Albany slip, seamed at bottom, dome top, MN, 1-gal	100.00
Jug, common, wht, MN, 1-gal	80.00
Jug, common, wht, MN, ½-gal	75.00
Jug, fancy, wht w/brn ball top, RW, 1-gal	200.00
Jug, fancy, wht w/brn ball top, RW, ½-gal	225.00
Jug, fancy, wht w/brn ball top, RW, ½-pt	175.00
Jug, fancy, wht w/brn ball top, unmk, 1-pt	50.00
Jug, fruit; Albany slip, wide mouth, MN, ½-gal	100.00
Jug, molded seam, Albany slip, 'bird' in bottom mk, RW, 1-gal	125.00
Jug, molded seam, Albany slip, bail hdl, MN, ½-gal	250.00
Jug, molded seam, Albany slip, bail hdl, RW, 1-gal	400.00
Jug, molded seam, bl sponging on wht, bail hdl, MN, 1-gal	1,500.00
Jug, molded seam, wht, bail hdl, MN, 1-qt	175.00
Jug, molded seam, wht, bail hdl, MN, ½-gal	100.00
Jug, molded seam, wht, bail hdl, RW, 1-gal	150.00

Jug, molded seam, wht, bail hdl, RW, 1-qt	150.00
Jug, molded seam, wht, wide mouth, RW, 1-qt	100.00
Jug, shoulder; #3/birch leaves, c/s, MN, 3-gal	175.00
Jug, shoulder; #3/red wing on wht, Union oval, 3-gal	100.00
Jug, shoulder; Albany slip, cone top, RW, 2-gal	650.00
Jug, shoulder; brn & salt glaze, ball top, RW, 1-gal	225.00
Jug, shoulder; brn & salt glaze, cone top, NS, 2-gal	400.00
Jug, shoulder; brn & salt glaze, cone top, RW, 1-gal	175.00
Jug, shoulder; brn & salt glaze, cone top, RW, 2-gal	350.00
Jug, shoulder; brn & salt glaze, dome top, MN, 2-gal	175.00
Jug, shoulder; brn & salt glaze, dome top, RW, 1-gal	225.00
Jug, shoulder; brn & salt glaze, funnel top, MN, 1-gal	125.00
Jug, shoulder; brn & salt glaze, funnel top, MN, 2-gal	175.00
Jug, shoulder; brn & salt glaze, wide mouth, NS, 1-gal	450.00
Jug, shoulder; red wing on wht, Albany slip std top, 2-gal	500.00
Jug, shoulder; wht, cone top, RW, ½-gal	115.00
Jug, shoulder; wht, cone top, RW, 2-gal	70.00
Jug, shoulder; wht, dome top, MN, 1-gal	75.00
Jug, shoulder; wht, funnel top, MN, 2-gal	85.00
Jug, shoulder; wht, std top, MN, 1-qt	115.00
Jug, shoulder; wht, std top, MN, 2-gal	100.00
Jug, shoulder; wht, std top, RW, 1-qt	125.00
Jug, shoulder; wht, std top, RW, ½-gal	75.00
Jug, shoulder; wht, std top, short, MN, 1-qt	150.00
Jug, syrup; wht, cone top, pour spout, MN, 1-gal	100.00
Jug, syrup; wht, pour spout, MN, 1-gal	75.00
Jug, threshing; #5/red wing on wht, RWUSCo oval, 5-gal	1,100.00
Milk pan, Albany slip, MN, any sz, from $100 to	125.00
Milk pan, Albany slip, RW, 7"	55.00
Milk pan, bl, RW, 7"	150.00
Pipkin, Albany slip, unmk, 1-pt	90.00
Pipkin, brn & wht, MN, 2-pt	275.00
Pitcher, mustard; Albany slip, NS	325.00
Pitcher, Russian milk; Albany slip, MN, 1-gal	110.00
Spittoon, bl bands on salt glaze, German style, MN	825.00
Spittoon, bl bands on salt glaze, German style, unmk	650.00
Spittoon, salt glaze, unmk	325.00
Success filter, bands, c/s, incised decor, MN, 4-gal	1,000.00
Umbrella stand, bl & wht sponging, unmk	1,450.00
Wash bowl & pitcher, lt bl to wht, emb lily decor, RW	875.00

Redware

The term redware refers to a type of simple earthenware produced by the Colonists as early as the 1600s. The red clay used in its production was abundant throughout the country, and during the 18th and 19th centuries redware was made in great quantities. Intended for utilitarian purposes such as everyday tableware or use in the dairy, redware was simple in design and decoration. Glazes of various colors were used, and a liquid clay referred to as 'slip' was sometimes applied in patterns such as zigzag lines, daisies, or stars. Plates often have a 'coggled' edge, similar to the way a pie is crimped or jagged, which is done with a special tool. In the following listings, EX (excellent condition) indicates only minor damage. Our advisor for this category is Barbara Rosen; she is listed in the Directory under New Jersey.

Bank, jug shape, blk pnt w/gold stripe, PA, 19th C, 4¾x2¾"	325.00
Bank, onion shape, orange-brown w/splotches, 4⅝x3⅜"	550.00
Bank, onion shape, orange-red, diagonal slot, 2½x2¼"	400.00
Bowl, orange mottle, PA, 2x8½"	130.00
Bowl, red-orange w/gr & brn mottling, PA, 4½x9½"	450.00
Bowl, skimming; lt gr glazed int, 3¼x20", EX	400.00
Bowl, 3-line yel slip, coggled rim, old chips, 2¾x13"	770.00

Creamer, gray tint, galleried lip, wear, 4¼" 85.00
Crock, dk brn mottle, PA, 19th C, mini, 2¾x2¾" 90.00
Crock, orange-brn, flared rim, PA, 19th C, 4¼x5¼", EX 275.00
Cuspidor, dk brn, funnel top, PA, 1⅞x3¾" 700.00
Herb pot, brn-gr ovoid, appl hdl, w/lid, 3¼", EX 500.00
Jar, dk brn/blk, str sides, sgn B Dodge Portland, 5¾", NM 1,200.00
Jar, gr & brn speckles w/dk splotches, tooled squiggle, 6" 3,500.00
Jar, gr & brn spots w/dk speckles, 8", VG 2,600.00
Jar, gr-gray w/gr spots & brn mottle, ME, 9", EX 1,700.00
Jar, lt gr w/dk gr speckles, C-shaped hdls, ovoid, 10½x8" 4,500.00
Jar, orange-brn w/brn mottle, w/lid, 7¼", EX 500.00
Jar, orange-brn w/brn splotches, str sides, 8½", EX 200.00
Jar, orange-brn w/yel & gr slip dots, att Seymour, 8x7", NM ...3,600.00
Jar, red & gr, constricted neck, Day's Ferry label, 5¾" 950.00
Jug, dk brn, ovoid, loop hdl, 3½", EX 500.00
Jug, gr & orange mottle, incised shoulder bands, 8" 1,300.00
Jug, gr & orange spots, ovoid, hdl, att ME, 9", EX+ 1,400.00
Jug, gr w/red speckles, long appl hdl, 19th C, 9", EX 400.00
Jug, gr w/red-brn highlights, incised bands, hdl, 11", VG 350.00
Jug, gr-brn w/blk mottling, appl hdl w/t'print, 12¾", EX 700.00
Mold, Turk's head, brn w/mica flakes, 2⅝x6", NM 325.00
Mug, lt brn & gr, 2 incised bands, appl hdl, ca 1800, 4¾" 2,200.00
Pie plate, orange-brn w/yel & gr slip lines, PA, 7¼" 525.00
Pie plate, orange-brn w/6 yel slip lines, 19th C, PA, 7½" 225.00
Pitcher, gr speckles, appl hdl, ME, 5¾", EX 1,900.00
Pitcher, gr w/orange spots, appl hdl, 7½", EX 600.00
Pitcher, gr w/orange spots & ring of wht slip, 10¾", NM 1,000.00
Pitcher, yel w/gr splotching, ovoid, 19th C, 6¼x4⅛" 1,000.00
Plate, orange w/3 yel slip lines, PA, 8" 800.00
Plate, orange-brn, 2 yel slip lines & 5 manganese dots, PA, 5" ...700.00
Plate, orange-red w/2 yel slip lines, PA, 8½" 375.00
Plate, yel slip squiggles & dots, notched edge, 11½" 300.00
Shaving mug, dk streaky brn, 2nd int cup opposite hdl, 4¼", EX .350.00
Stew pot, red-orange w/gr, glossy, w/lid, 5½" 550.00
Stew pot, red-orange w/gr, John Safford...No 2, 1835-75, 5¾" .2,400.00

Regal China

Located in Antioch, Illinois, the Regal China Company opened for business in 1938. Products of interest to collectors are James Beam decanters, cookie jars, salt and pepper shakers, and similar novelty items. The company closed its doors sometime in 1993. The Old Mac-Donald Farm series listed below is especially collectible, so are the salt and pepper shakers.

Note: Where applicable, prices are based on excellent gold trim. (Gold trim must be 90% intact or deductions should be made for wear.) See also Decanters.

Alice in Wonderland

Cookie jar 3,200.00
Creamer, White Rabbit 600.00
Pitcher, King of Hearts, milk sz 650.00
Shakers, matching colors, rare, pr 675.00
Shakers, Tweedledee & Tweedledum, pr 850.00
Shakers, wht w/gold trim, pr 675.00
Sugar bowl, White Rabbit, w/lid 600.00
Teapot, Mad Hatter 2,500.00

Cookie Jars

Cat 425.00
Churn Boy 275.00

Clown, gr collar 675.00
Davy Crockett 550.00
Dutch Girl 675.00
Dutch Girl, peach trim 800.00
Fifi Poodle 650.00
Fisherman 650.00
French Chef 375.00
Goldilocks (+) 375.00
Harpo Marx 1,200.00
Hobby Horse 250.00
Hubert Lion 775.00
Humpty Dumpty, red 325.00
Little Miss Muffett 385.00
Majorette 675.00
Oriental Lady w/Baskets 600.00
Peek-a-Boo (+) 1,500.00
Quaker Oats 125.00
Three Bears 285.00

Toby Cookies, unmarked, $750.00.

Photo courtesy Ermagene Westfall

Tulip 300.00
Uncle Mistletoe 850.00

Old McDonald's Farm

Butter dish, cow's head 220.00
Canister, flour, cereal, coffee; med, ea 220.00
Canister, pretzels, peanuts, popcorn, chips, tidbits; lg, ea 300.00
Canister, salt, sugar, tea; med, ea 220.00
Canister, soap, cookies, lg, ea 300.00
Cookie jar, barn 275.00
Creamer, rooster 110.00
Grease jar, pig 175.00
Pitcher, milk 400.00
Shakers, boy & girl, pr 75.00
Shakers, churn, gold trim, pr 90.00
Shakers, feed sacks w/sheep, pr 195.00
Spice jar, assorted lids, sm, ea 100.00
Sugar bowl, hen 125.00
Teapot, duck's head 250.00

Shakers

A Nod to Abe, 3-pc nodder 300.00
Bendel, bears, wht w/pk & brn trim, pr 100.00
Bendel, bunnies, wht w/blk & pk trim, pr 135.00
Bendel, kissing pigs, gray w/pk trim, lg, pr 375.00
Bendel, love bugs, burgundy, lg, pr 165.00
Bendel, love bugs, gr, sm, pr 65.00
Cat, sitting, eyes closed, wearing hat, wht w/gold bow, pr 225.00

Clown, pr	450.00
Dutch Girl, pr	275.00
Fifi, pr	450.00
Fish, mk C Miller, 1-pc	55.00
French Chef, wht w/gold trim, pr	175.00
Humpty Dumpty, pr	140.00
Peek-a-Boo, peach trim, rare, lg, pr	575.00
Peek-a-Boo, red dots, lg, pr (+)	500.00
Peek-a-Boo, red dots, sm, pr	250.00
Peek-a-Boo, w/burgundy trim, rare, sm, pr	350.00
Peek-a-Boo, wht solid, lg, pr	400.00
Peek-a-Boo, wht solid, sm, pr	200.00
Peek-a-Boo, wht w/gold trim, lg, pr	450.00
Pig, pk, mk C Miller, 1-pc	95.00
Tulip, pr	50.00
Van Telligen, bears, brn, pr	28.00
Van Telligen, boy & dog, wht, pr	65.00
Van Telligen, boy & girl, boy (Black) & dog, pr	125.00
Van Telligen, bunnies, solid colors, pr	28.00
Van Telligen, ducks, pr	35.00
Van Telligen, Dutch boy & girl, pr	45.00
Van Telligen, Mary & lamb, pr	55.00
Van Telligen, sailor & mermaid, pr	195.00

Relief-Molded Jugs

Early relief-molded pitchers (ca 1830s – 40s) were made in two-piece molds into which sheets of clay were pressed. The relief decoration was deep and well defined, usually of animal or human subjects. Most of these pitchers were designed with a flaring lip and substantial footing. Gradually styles changed, and by the 1860s the rim had become flatter and the foot less pronounced. The relief decoration was not as deep, and foliage became a common design. By the turn of the century, many other types of pitchers had been introduced, and the market for these early styles began to wane.

Watch for recent reproductions; these have been made by the slip-casting method. Unlike relief-molded ware which is relatively smooth inside, slip-cast pitchers will have interior indentations that follow the irregularities of the relief decoration. Values below are for pieces in excellent condition. Our advisor for this category is Kathy Hughes; she is listed in the Directory under North Carolina.

Key: Reg — Registered

Argos, gr, Brownfield, Apr 29, 1864, 8"	175.00
Bird & Butterfly, tan & wht, Minton, ca 1830, 6"	375.00
Bundle of Faggots, drabware, metal lid, Ridgway, Reg Oct 1, 1835, 8"	250.00
Cain & Abel, tan stoneware, Edward Walley, ca 1850, 10"	325.00
Chelsea Pensioners, wht stoneware, unknown, ca 1845	350.00
Chrysanthemum, gr & wht, Ridgway, ca 1860, 9¼"	275.00
Cupids at Play, buff & brn, Turner, ca 1800, 9½"	475.00
Diana, gr stoneware, Edward Walley, Reg June 21, 1850, 10"	425.00
Garibaldi, unknown, ca 1870, 13"	250.00
Good Samaritan, buff & tan, Jones & Walley, 1841, 8"	375.00
Good Samaritan, wht stoneware, unknown, ca 1850, 9¾"	400.00
Idle Apprentices, wht & bl, unknown, 1840, 7"	250.00
Julius Caesar, gray, appl laurel wreath, Meigh, 1839, 8¼"	450.00
King Soloman, drabware, Wood & Brownfield, Reg Sept 30 1841, 7½"	300.00
Love & War, purple on wht parian, Samuel Alcock, ca 1845, 7¾"	425.00
Mermaid & Cupid, Minton, gr & wht parian, ca 1911, 6"	700.00
Now I'm Grandpapa, unknown, ca 1850, 8½"	400.00
Peel & Cobden, yel earthenware, unknown, ca 1846	250.00

Princess Charlotte/Prince Leopold, gold/bl salt glaze, 2¾"	300.00
Princess Charlotte/Prince Leopold, minor rstr, 6"	275.00
Punch, purple on wht parian, Samuel Alcock, ca 1845, 8¾"	475.00
Punch, Samuel Alcock & Co, ca 1845, 8¾"	450.00
Royal Children, bl earthenware, unknown, ca 1848	325.00
Shakespeare, wht on purple parian, Samuel Alcock, ca 1850, 6"	475.00
Sir Robert Peel, tan earthenware, ca 1846	175.00
Sir Walter Scott commemorative, gray-gr, Minton, 8"	350.00
Stag, gray-gr, Enoch & Edward Wood, ca 1840, 9¼"	350.00
Stag, purple on wht parian, Samuel Alcock, ca 1845, 8⅛"	425.00

Tulip, white stoneware, Dudson, ca 1860, 8", $250.00.

Photo courtesy Kathy Hughes

Tulip, bl & wht, Dudson, 1860, 7"	175.00
Youth & Old Age, ca 1845, Copeland-Garret, gray-gr, 8¾"	250.00

Restraints

Since the beginning of time, many things from animals to treasures have been held in bondage by hemp, bamboo, chests, chains, shackles, and other constructed devices. Many of these devices were used to hold captives who awaited further torture, as if the restraint wasn't torturous enough. The study and collecting of restraints enables one to learn much about the advancement of civilization in the country or region from which they originated. Such devices at various times in history were made of very heavy metals — so heavy that the wearer could scarcely move about. It has only been in the last sixty years that vast improvements have been made in design and construction that afford the captive some degree of comfort. Our advisor for this category is Joseph Tanner; he is listed in the Directory under Washington.

Key:
bbl — barrel	lc — lock case
d-lb — double lock button	NST — non-swing through
K — key	ST — swing through
Kd — keyed	stp — stamped

Foreign Handcuffs

Australian, Saf Lock, ST, takes pin-tumbler K in side, stp	160.00
Czechalaviak, ST, Ralken flat key, modern ST	100.00
Deutsche Polizei, ST, middle hinge, folds, takes bbl-bit K	80.00
East German, aluminum, single lg hinge, ST, bbl key	60.00
East German, heavy steel, NP single lg hinge, NST, bbl key	90.00
English, Chubb, NST, hi-security 10-slider lock mechanism	300.00
English, Chubb Arrest, steel, ST, multi-bit solid K	250.00
English, Latrobe, aluminum alloy, center chain, ST, dbl-bit K	160.00
French Lapegy, ST, aluminum alloys, takes flat bitted K	75.00
French Revolved, oval, ST, takes 2 Ks: bbl & pin tumbler	150.00
German, Swartiger, steel, NST, bbl K goes in at end of cuffs	400.00
German, 3-lb steel set, 2⅝" thick, center chain, bbl K	175.00

German Clejuso, oval design, ST, dbl-cuff weight, 22-oz 100.00
German Clejuso, sq lc, adjusts/NST, d-lb on side, bbl K 100.00
German Darby, adjusts, well finished, NST, sm 120.00
German Hamburg 8, non-adjust NST, center bar/post w/K-way ...250.00
Hiatt, English Darby, like US CW Darby, stp Hiatt & #d 75.00
Hiatt, solid state, 2 separate cuffs joined bk to bk, stp/#d 165.00
Hiatt English non-adjust screw K Darby style, uses screw K 100.00
Hiatt Figure 8, swings open to insert/withdraw wrists 125.00
Italian, stp New Police, modern Peerless type, ST, sm bbl K 35.00
Plug 8, remove plug before inserting external threaded K 200.00
Russian modern ST, blued bbl key, unmk, crude 80.00
Spanish, stp Alcyon/Star, modern Peerless type, flat K 65.00
Spanish, stp Alcyon/Star, modern Peerless type, ST, sm bbl K 45.00

Foreign Leg Shackles

East German, aluminum, lg hinge, cable amid 4 cuffs, bbl key 80.00
German Clejuso, sq lc, adjusts/NST, d-bl on side, bbl K 125.00
German Clejuso Darby type, adjusts/NST/plated, uses screw K ..160.00
Hiatt English combo manacles, handcuff/leg irons w/chain 275.00
Hiatt English non-adjust screw K Darby style, uses screw K 100.00
Hiatt Plug leg irons, same K-ing as Plug-8 cuffs, w/chain 225.00

U.S. Handcuffs

Adams, teardrop lc, bbl Kd, NST, usually not stp 170.00
American Munitions, modern/rnd, sm bbl Kd, ST bow, stp 45.00
Bean Giant, sideways figure-8, solid center lc, dbl-bit K 450.00
Bean Patrolman, kidney-bean form, d-lb on lc, NST, stp T 100.00
Bean-Cobb, sm rnd lc, removable cylinder, d-lb, NST, 1899 ....90.00
Cavenay, looks like Marlin Daley but w/screw K, NST 160.00
Civil War padlocking type, various designs w/loop for lock 200.00
Colt, modern ST bow, sm bbl Kd, stp w/Colt & Co name 160.00
Flash Action Manacle, like Bean Giant w/ST, K-way center 250.00
Flexibles, steel segmented bows, NST Darby type, screw K 150.00
Guardian, modern ST, NP steel, bbl K 60.00
H&R Super, ST, shaft-hinge connector takes hollow titted K ...100.00
Harvard, takes sm bbl K, ST, stp Harvard Lock Co 65.00
Judd, NST, used rnd/internally triangular K, stp Mattatuck 120.00
Lilly Hand Iron, 2" strap iron (8" L), oval bands, NST, sq K 500.00
Marlin Daley, NST, bottle-neck form, neck stp, dbl-titted K 200.00
Mattatuck, NST, propeller-like K-way, stp Mattatuck/etc 90.00
Palmer, 2" steel bands, 2 K-ways (top & center), NST stp 300.00
Peerless, ST, takes sm bbl K, stp Mfg'ered by Peerless Co 40.00
Peerless, ST, takes sm bbl K, stp Mfg'ered by S&W Co 75.00
Peerless Big Guy, modern ST, bbl key 50.00
Phelps, NST, twist chain between cuffs, Tower look-alike 250.00
Pratt combo, 1 cuff connnects w/nipper/claw, ST, mk Pratt 275.00
Providence Tool Co, stp, NST, Darty screw K style 120.00
Rankin, steel NST, mk screw K 225.00
Romer, NST, takes flat K, resembles padlock, stp Romer Co 250.00

Strauss, ST, takes lg solid bitted K, stp Strauss Eng Co 85.00
Tower, NST, bottom K, solid/flat-fitted K goes in cuff edge 100.00
Tower bar cuffs, cuffs separate by 10-12" steel bar 120.00
Tower Dbl Lock, NST, takes bbl-bitted K, usually stp Tower 60.00
Tower Detective Pinkerton, NST, sq lc, bbl-bitted K, no stp 120.00
Tower Single Lock, NST, bbl-bit K, K-way slanted on lc, sm 70.00
Tower-Bean, NST, sm rnd lc, takes tiny bbl-bitted K, stp 75.00
Tri-lock, heavy polymer & stainless steel, ST, triple lock 200.00
Walden 'Lady Cuff,' NST, takes sm bbl K, lightweight, stp 300.00

U.S. Leg Shackles

American Munitions, as handcuffs 55.00
Civil War or prison ball & chain, padlocking or rivet type 300.00
Cloc spike, 30" L opening for ankle w/padlock & 2 spikes 500.00
H&R Supers, as handcuffs 400.00
Harvard, as handcuffs 75.00
Judd, as handcuffs 135.00
Leg lock brace, metal brace, ankle to knee, lever locked 225.00
Oregon boot, break-apart shackle on above ankle support 700.00
Palmer, as handcuffs but w/detachable chain, NST 425.00
Peerless Big Guy, modern ST, bbl key 60.00
Providence Tool Co, stp, NST 150.00
Strauss, as handcuffs 125.00
Tower, bottom K, as handcuffs 100.00
Tower ball & chain, leg iron w/chain & 6-lb to 50-lb ball 250.00
Tower Detective, as handcuffs 150.00

Various Other Restraining Devices

African slave Darby-style cuffs, heavy iron/chain, handmade 130.00
African slave Darby-style leg shackles, heavy/hand forged 160.00
African slave padlocking or riveted forged iron shackles 135.00
Argus iron claw, twist T to open & close 40.00
Darby neck collar, rnd steel loop opens w/screw K 200.00
English figure-8 nipper, claws open by lifting top lock tab 80.00
Gale finger cuff, knuckle duster, non-K, mk GFC 125.00
German nipper, twist hdl opens/closes cuff, stp Germany/etc 75.00
Jay Pee, thumb cuffs, mk solid body, bbl K 15.00
Mighty-Mite, thumb cuffs, solid body, ST, mk, bbl K 75.00
Phillips nipper, claw, flip lever on top to open 80.00
Thomas Nipper, claw, push button top to open 80.00
Tower Lyon, thumb cuffs, solid body, NST, dbl-bit center K 170.00

Reverse Painting on Glass

Verre eglomise is the technique of painting on the underside of glass. Dating back to the early 1700s, this art became popular in the 19th century when German immigrants chose historical figures and beautiful women as subjects for their reverse glass paintings. Advertising mirrors of this type came into vogue at the turn of the century.

Country house in winter, gold pnt fr, 10½x12½" 75.00
Dutch landscape w/windmill, flakes, fr, 15x23" 110.00
Equestrian figure in colorful uniform in landscape, fr, 15x12" 600.00
Lady's portrait, colorful clothes, brn bkground, fr, 15x12" 500.00
Man's portrait, long overcoat, wht wig, old rpr, 18x14" 415.00
Vase of flowers, mc w/minor flaking, gilt fr, 10x8" 110.00

Rhead

Associated with many companies during his career — Weller,

**Smith & Wesson Model 90, nickel, silver and blue,
3½" diameter, NMIB with two keys, $75.00.**

Vance Avon, Arequipa, A.E. Tile, and finally Homer Laughlin China — Fredrick Herten Rhead organized his own pottery in Santa Barbara, California, ca 1913. Admittedly more of a designer than a potter, Rhead hired help to turn the pieces on the wheel but did most of the decorating himself. The process he favored most involved sgraffito designs inlaid with enameling. Egyptian and Art Nouveau influences were evidenced in much of his work. The ware he produced there was often marked with a logo incorporating the potter at the wheel and 'Santa Barbara.'

Vase, dk gr w/exposed brn clay, mk w/pottery at wheel, 7" **1,900.00**
Vase, med/lt gr matt w/brn exposed, Santa Barbara #28/#50, 4" ...**1,400.00**

Richard

Richard, who at one time worked for Galle, made cameo art glass in France during the 1920s. His work was often multilayered and acid cut with florals and scenics in lovely colors. The ware was marked with his name in relief. Our advisor for this category is Don Williams; he is listed in the Directory under Missouri.

Cameo

Lamp, 7½" dome shade w/mtns/castle; 3-D bird on metal base ..**2,500.00**
Toothpick holder, trumpet flowers, purple on frost **250.00**
Vase, church/mtns/river, pk/red/burgundy-blk, 8" **575.00**
Vase, floral, amethyst on lt gl, 4" **550.00**
Vase, floral, cobalt on orange, 4½" **275.00**
Vase, floral stalks, bl-blk on gold-yel, ftd, slim, 6½" **525.00**
Vase, floral stalks/2 insects, bl-blk on yel, 3½" **350.00**
Vase, holly/berries, bl-blk on red, ftd, squat base, 4¼" **575.00**
Vase, mtn lake/trees/castle, cobalt on orange, 13½" **2,300.00**
Vase, thistle blossoms, brn on lt gr, 6¼x2¼" **400.00**

Ridgway

As early as 1792, the Ridgway brothers, Job and George, produced fine quality earthenwares in Shelton, Staffordshire, marking their products Ridgway, Smith & Ridgway, and later Job & George Ridgway. Around 1800 the brothers split, and each had his own firm, both at Shelton. They were joined in the business by various members of the Ridgway family, and, in fact, their descendants still operate there today.

The two firms created by the split were the Bell Works and the Cauldon Pottery. Bell produced stone china and earthenware decorated with blue transfer printing. Their mark was 'J. & W. Ridgway' or 'J. & W. R.' (John and William) until 1848 when 'William Ridgway' was used. The Cauldon Pottery made earthenware, stone china, and high quality porcelains fine enough to win them the distinction of being appointed potters to the Queen. From 1830 their wares attest to this fact, bearing the Royal Arms mark with 'J.R.' within the crest. In 1960 '& Co.' was added. Most examples of Ridgway's wares found today are transfer-printed historical scenes. See also Staffordshire, Historical; and Flow Blue.

Biscuit jar, Coaching Days, brn rattan hdl, 6½" **245.00**
Coffeepot, Coaching Days, 8" **200.00**
Cup & saucer, Coaching Days **38.00**
Cup & saucer, Royal Vista **25.00**
Mug, Coaching Days, Broken Trade, 4" **35.00**
Mug, Polar Bear & Cat, silver lustre trim, 4½" **50.00**
Pitcher, Coaching Days, 5½" **70.00**
Pitcher, Coaching Days, 9½" **120.00**

Plaque, Taking Up the Mails, yel, 12" **135.00**
Plate, Coaching Days, 10" **45.00**
Plate, Coaching Days, 9" **35.00**
Platter, Liberty Cap & Flag, red transfer w/bl & gr, 12" **225.00**
Punch bowl, flowers & birds, blk transfer w/mc, 7x16" **145.00**
Teapot, Coaching Days, 5½" **175.00**
Tray, Coaching Days, 12" dia **65.00**

Rie, Lucie

Lucie Rie was born in 1902. She moved to London in 1938 and shared her studio with Hans Coper from 1946 to 1958. Her ceramics look modern; however they are based on shapes from many world cultures dating back to Roman times. Lucie Rie is best known for the use of metallic oxides in her clay and glazes. She specializes in the hand throwing of thin porcelain bowls, which is a very difficult process. Her works are in the world's best museums. All of her ceramics are impressed with a seal mark on the bottom, a cojoined 'R & L' within a rectangular reserve.

Bowl, wht matt w/bronze-colored rim, funnel shape, 3½x5¼" ...**1,800.00**
Bowl, yel crackle w/bronze band, sm ft, 3¾x7¾" **2,750.00**
Vase, lt gr/raspberry on brn, ftd cylinder, trumpet neck, 8" **4,500.00**
Vase, wht matt w/gr lines & runs, flared top/gourd body, 111", NM **6,500.00**

Riviera

Riviera was a line of dinnerware introduced by the Homer Laughlin China Company in 1938. It was sold exclusively by the Murphy Company through their nationwide chain of dime stores. Riviera was unmarked, lightweight, and inexpensive. It was discontinued sometime prior to 1950. Colors are mauve blue, red, yellow, light green, and ivory. On rare occasions, dark blue pieces are found, but this was not a standard color. For further information we recommend *The Collector's Encyclopedia of Fiesta* (1998 values) by Sharon and Bob Huxford, available from Collector Books.

Batter set, complete **285.00**
Batter set, ivory, w/decals, complete **170.00**
Bowl, baker; 9" **28.00**
Bowl, cream soup; w/liner, ivory **95.00**
Bowl, fruit; 5½" **12.00**
Bowl, nappy; 7¼" **28.00**
Bowl, oatmeal; 6" **40.00**
Bowl, utility; ivory **50.00**
Butter dish, cobalt, ¼-lb **250.00**
Butter dish, colors other than cobalt or turq, ¼-lb **135.00**
Butter dish, turq, ¼-lb **290.00**
Butter dish, ½-lb **140.00**

Casserole, with lid, $110.00.

Creamer 12.00
Cup & saucer, demitasse; ivory 80.00
Jug, open, ivory, 4½" 95.00
Jug, w/lid 130.00
Pitcher, juice; mauve bl 210.00
Pitcher, juice; yel 120.00
Plate, deep 24.00
Plate, 10" 55.00
Plate, 6" 8.00
Plate, 7" 12.00
Plate, 9" 18.00
Platter, closed hdls, 11¼" 28.00
Platter, cobalt, 12" 70.00
Platter, 11½" 25.00
Platter, 15" 60.00
Sauce boat 27.00
Saucer 4.00
Shakers, pr 20.00
Sugar bowl, w/lid 20.00
Teacup 11.00
Teapot 145.00
Tidbit, ivory, 2-tier 75.00
Tumbler, hdl 75.00
Tumbler, hdl, ivory 145.00
Tumbler, juice 52.00

Robj

Robj was the name of a retail store that operated in Paris for only a few years, from about 1925 to 1931. Robj solicited designs from the best French artisans of the period to produce decorative objects for the home. These were executed mostly in porcelain but there were glass and earthenware pieces as well. The most well known are the figural bottles which were particularly popular in the United States. However, Robj also promoted tea sets, perfume lamps, chess sets, ashtrays, bookends, humidors, powder jars, cigarette boxes, figurines, lamps, and milk pitchers. Robj objects tend to be whimsical, and all embody the Art Deco style. Items listed below are ceramic unless noted otherwise. Our advisors for this category are Randall Monsen and Rod Baer; their address is listed in the Directory under Virginia.

Bottle, Scotsman in uniform, mc, 10½", VG 250.00
Cocktail shaker, golfer figural, bl & wht 1,250.00
Decanter, lady in gr dress w/wht apron, 10¾" 260.00
Decanters, set of 5 figurals including Napoleon, ea 10" ...1,150.00
Inkwell, Blackamoor in gold/wht robe holds well, no lid, 6" ...275.00

Decanters, two figures, one in black cloak, second figure in white, marked, 10½", $345.00 each.

Rock 'N Roll Memorabilia

Memorabilia from the early days of rock 'n roll recalls an era that many of us experienced firsthand; these listings are offered to demonstrate the many and various aspects of this area of collecting. Beware of reproductions! Many are so well done even a knowledgeable collector will sometimes be fooled.

Our advisor for Elvis memorabilia is Rosalind Cranor, author of *Elvis Collectibles* and *Best of Elvis Collectibles* (Overmountain Press); she is listed in the Directory under Virginia. The remainder is under the advisement of Bob Gottuso, author of Beatles and Kiss sections in *Garage Sale Gold* by Tomart; see Pennsylvania. For more information we recommend *Rock-N-Roll Treasures* by Joe Hilton and Greg Moore (Collector Books).

AC DC, program, 1986, from $20 to 25.00
Aerosmith, concert ticket, Jackson MS, 1/7/78, unused 25.00
Allman Brothers, concert ticket, Forum, 5/15/79, unused 35.00
Allman Brothers, ticket, 1980, unused, M 18.00
Bath Festival, program, 1970, Bath UK, 6/27-28/70, VG+ 400.00
Beach Boys/Crickets, poster, Girls on Beach, 1965, 1-sheet 65.00

Beatles, brunch bag, vinyl, zipper opening, Aladdin/NEMS, 1965, 8x8", M, $450.00; Thermos, M, $180.00.

Beatles, airbed, yel w/bl vinyl backing, faces & autographs, EX ..900.00
Beatles, banks, Yel Submarine, complete set 3,000.00
Beatles, belt buckle, gold-tone metal, w/band photo, EX 50.00
Beatles, Big 6 guitar, mc plastic, complete, 32", EX 660.00
Beatles, book calendar, blk/wht photos ea month, spiral, '64, 9x11" .190.00
Beatles, bubble bath, red plastic, Paul figural, VG+ 115.00
Beatles, concert ticket, Candlestick Park, 8/29/66, unused 450.00
Beatles, diary, color cover, stories, blk & wht pictures, '60s, M 65.00
Beatles, Disk-Go-Case, lt bl w/wht hdl, rnd, plastic, sticker, EX ..180.00
Beatles, doll, inflatable, cartoon image, set of 4 w/mailer 135.00
Beatles, Flip Your Wig game, MIB 180.00
Beatles, glass tumbler, picture of John, 20% gold rim gone 160.00
Beatles, Halloween costume, Ringo, Ben Cooper, VG+ (VG+ box) 740.00
Beatles, headband, Better Ware USA, Love the Beatles, MIP 65.00
Beatles, jelly glass, George, clear w/orange decor, 5½", EX 160.00
Beatles, lunch box, bl, w/thermos, EX 750.00
Beatles, pillow, full-figure pose w/instruments, 12", EX+ 300.00
Beatles, poster, John, Avedon for Look, 1968, 31x22½" 150.00
Beatles, poster, Ringo, w/dove, Avedon for Look, 1968, mtd, 31x22" ..70.00
Beatles, program, 1964 US tour, 24 pgs, EX 45.00
Beatles, Sgt Pepper doll, George, Applause, EX orig, 22" 65.00
Beatles, talc powder, Margo of Mayfair, full, 1964, NM 600.00
Beatles, ticket, 8/12/64, New Royal Theatre, unused, NM 125.00
Beatles, toy, Yel Submarine, Corgi, NMIB 700.00
Beatles, wallet, beige vinyl, Standard Plastics, no comb 90.00

Beatles, 3-ring binder, Yel Submarine, hard cover, 1969, M 350.00
Black Sabbath, concert ticket, Forum, 4/4/78, unused 45.00
Bob Dylan, poster, House of Blues, Atlanta, 8/96, 11x17", NM 50.00
Bob Dylan, poster, Milton Glaser for Columbia Records, mtd, 33" ..150.00
Bob Dylan/Tom Petty, program, 1986 True Confessions tour, NM 35.00
Bob Dylan/Wallflowers, poster, San Jose Arena, 11/14/97, NM ...50.00
Cars, program, 1984, NM, from $12 to 18.00
Charlatans/Youngbloods, 7/13-16/67, Avalon Ballroom, NM 20.00
Cheap Trick, bow tie, wht print on blk, EX 28.00
Chicago, ticket, Chicago Stadium, 1974, unused, NM, from $25 to .30.00
Chubby Checker, insert card, Don't Knock the Twist, 1962 ....55.00
Country Joe & Fish, postcard, Avalon Ballroom, 2/3-4/67, NM ...20.00
Crosby, Stills, Nash & Young, postcard, Fillmore West, 11/69, NM ..35.00
Dave Clark 5, lobby card set, Having a Wild Weekend, 1965 ......80.00
Dave Clark 5, movie poster, Having a Wild Weekend 150.00
Doors, concert ticket, KRNT Theatre, 9/27/67, unused 295.00
Doors, promo button, 1960s, 1½" dia 45.00
Doors, stationery, 1960s, NM 95.00
Eagles, program, 1976, NM 20.00
Eagles/Jimmy Buffett, poster, Aloha Stadium, 9/30/79, NM 145.00
Elton John/Kinks/Ballin' Jack, poster, Fillmore West, 11/70, NM ...75.00
Elvis Presley, Army hat, paper, GI Blues promo, 1960 ....35.00
Elvis Presley, ashtray, facsimile sgn photo in glass, 1956, EPE 400.00
Elvis Presley, belt, leather, EPE, 1956 ....700.00
Elvis Presley, belt buckle, pewter, 1935-1977 ....20.00
Elvis Presley, binder, Love Me Tender zipper model, EPE, 1956 ...1,000.00
Elvis Presley, book, Elvis & Me, by Priscilla Presley, paperbk, M 4.00
Elvis Presley, calendar, 1980 Elvis Memorial, w/Aloha Hawaii photo .7.50
Elvis Presley, ceramic tile, 'Best Wishes, EP,' EPE, 1956, 6" sq ...850.00
Elvis Presley, coaster, facsimile sgn photo in glass, EPE, 1956 ....150.00
Elvis Presley, concert ticket stub, Cleveland, 7/10/75 ....95.00
Elvis Presley, EP Board Game, EPE, 1956, orig box 1,000.00
Elvis Presley, Fan Club Membership Package, complete, 1956 ...400.00
Elvis Presley, pen, From Elvis & the Colonel, Las Vegas promo ...25.00
Elvis Presley, pencil sharpener, EPE, 1956 ....210.00
Elvis Presley, pennant, 'I Love Elvis,' EX 75.00
Elvis Presley, photo, Elvis Special Concert edition, 14x7" 15.00
Elvis Presley, poster, Jailhouse Rock, half sheet 300.00
Elvis Presley, poster book, Vol 1, all color, 8x16" 15.00
Elvis Presley, scarf, Vegas...Hotel/RCA Summer Festival, 28" 350.00
Elvis Presley, souvenir menu, Hilton, Las Vegas, 1971, 4-pg, 9x12" .95.00
Elvis Presley, statuette, bronze figural, EPE, 1956, 8" 550.00
Elvis Presley, Teddy Bear Perfume, Teen-Age Inc, 1957, orig box .250.00
Fleetwood Mac, backstage pass, 1982, EX 5.00
Fleetwood Mac, concert ticket, Forum, 12/11/79, unused 35.00
Grateful Dead, key chain, metal, ticket shape, MOC 8.00
Grateful Dead, postcard, Fillmore West, 12/31/70, NM 30.00
Grateful Dead, ticket, 1977 ....10.00
Gregg Allman, slingshot, Epic promotion, I'm No Angel, EX 35.00
Ike & Tina Turner, postcard, Spirit concert, Winterland, 10/70, NM ..25.00
Ike & Tina Turner, postcard, Winterland, 1970, unused, NM, from $8 to .10.00
Janis Joplin/Big Brother, postcard, Avalon Ballroom, 5/5-7/67, NM ..35.00
Jimi Hendrix, concert flyer, 5/9/70, Ft Worth, 8½x11½", NM ...295.00
Jimi Hendrix, poster, CNE Coliseum Toronto, 2/28/68, NM ..1,250.00
Jimi Hendrix/Jefferson Airplane, postcard, Fillmore West, NM 45.00
Joe Cocker, concert contract, Marquee Club, London, sgn, 6/25/68 .195.00
KISS, Ace doll, Mega, 12", MIB 285.00
KISS, Gene doll, Mego, 12", MIB 260.00
KISS, Gene silver coin, 1997, M 25.00
KISS, jacket, blk polyskin, 1978, M (sealed) 50.00
KISS, jacket, Production Staff, fleece pullover, 1996 Reunion ...115.00
KISS, On Tour game, complete, EX 90.00
KISS, song book, Destroyer, VG 25.00
KISS, tour book, 1977-78 Love Gun tour 40.00
Led Zeppelin, concert ticket, Detroit, 10/30/80, unused 150.00
Led Zeppelin, poster, Song Remains the Same, 1976, 1-sheet 25.00
Led Zeppelin, program, 8/11/79, Knebworth Park, VG+ 195.00
Lenny Bruce/The Mothers, postcard, Fillmore West, 6/24-25/66, NM .25.00
Michael Jackson, puffy stickers, 1980s, MIP 3.00
Michael Jackson, scarf, MJ License, 1983, 21x22", EX 13.00
Miller Blues Band, 7/6-9/67, Avalon Ballroom, NM 50.00
Monkees, backstage pass, 20th Anniversary Tour, EX 8.00
Monkees, beach ball, Pool It!, 1980s, inflatable, EX 25.00
Monkees, bracelet, MOC 50.00
Monkees, 45 rpm record carrying case, EX 325.00
Neil Young w/Crazy Horse, program, 1987 North American tour, EX 35.00
New Kids on the Block, party banner, MIP 5.00
Quicksilver, postcard, Avalon Ballroom, 4/21-22/67, NM 20.00
Rolling Stones, concert pin-bk button 1.00
Rolling Stones, flyer, Tokyo Dome, 3/12-17/97, 7x10", NM 45.00
Rolling Stones, Halloween poster, 10/94, uncut printer's proof, NM .295.00
Rolling Stones, pennant, 1960s, EX 75.00
Rolling Stones, program, Exile on Main Street, 1972 US tour, EX ...75.00
Rolling Stones, program, 1966 US tour, EX 145.00
Shawn Cassidy, notebook, face on cover, M 5.00
Stevie Ray Vaughn, poster, PA Beach Club Gardner, 8/13/89, NM .195.00
Supremes, flyer, Lincoln Center, 10/15/65, 6x9", NM 95.00
Ten Years After, concert contract, Marquee Club, London, 2/6/68 .150.00
Van Halen, binoculars, VH logo, EX 15.00
Various artists, poster, Fillmore West, 8/13-25/68, 7x9", NM 50.00

Rockingham

In the early part of the 19th century, American potters began to prefer brown- and buff-burning clays over red because of their durability. The glaze favored by many was Rockingham, which varied from a dark brown mottle to a sponged effect sometimes called tortoise shell. It consisted in part of manganese and various metallic salts and was used by many potters until well into the 20th century. Over the past two years, demand and prices have risen sharply, especially in the East. For further information we recommend *Collector's Guide to Rockingham, The Enduring Ware,* by Mary Brewer. See also Bennington.

Teapot, Rebecca at the Well, American, late 19th century, 8", $300.00.

Baker, flat bottom, rnded rim, 3x13⅛x10⅞" 300.00
Book flask, Spiritual Manifestations By, 1850s, 7", EX 350.00
Bowl, emb panels, 4½x6" 75.00
Bowl, mush; flared sides, #169, 2¼x8" 60.00
Bowl, mush; flared sides, flat bottom, 2⅝x9⅜" 70.00
Bowl, str paneled sides, brn w/gr accents, 12-sided, 3x7⅛" 210.00
Boxl, mixing; mini, 1¾x4¼", EX 55.00
Creamer, cow figural, tail hdl, 5⅜x7x3", EX 350.00
Doorknob, 8-sided, w/brass fitting, 2" dia 50.00
Inkwell, recumbent dog figural, 4x6¼x2⅞", EX 350.00

Mold, Turk's head, minor wear, 3x8" 125.00
Mold, Turk's head, swirled int, scalloped rim, 9¼" 125.00
Mug, hdld cylinder, 3⅞x3¾" 65.00
Pie plate, 10" 135.00
Pitcher, emb lady in reserve, emb face on arched hdl, 7¼" 145.00
Pitcher, emb peacock & palm tree, C-shaped hdl, 8", EX 160.00
Pitcher, hexagonal, paneled sides, 10" 260.00
Pitcher, XXX Ale, hound hdl, drain-hole spout, w/lid, 10" 150.00
Plate, flared sides, illegible mk, 1⅛x8½" 85.00
Soap dish, scallops descend from rim on side, oval, 5" L 75.00
Soap dish, vertical ribs, pierced top, 2¼x4¾x3½" 90.00
Spittoon, funnel-shaped top, oval reserves, 4¼x7¼" 225.00

Rockwell, Norman

Norman Rockwell began his career in 1911 at the age of seventeen doing illustrations for a children's book entitled *Tell Me Why Stories*. Within a few years he had produced the *Saturday Evening Post* cover that made him one of America's most beloved artists. Though not well accepted by the professional critics of his day who did not consider his work to be art but 'merely' commercial illustration, Rockwell's popularity grew to the extent that today there is an overwhelming abundance of examples of his work or those related to the theme of one of his illustrations.

The figurines described below were issued by the Rockwell Museum and Museum Collections Inc. (formerly Rockwell Museum). Our advisors for this category are Barb Putratz, who is listed in the Directory under Minnesota, and Joe Genens, listed under Wisconsin.

A Walkin' & a Whistlin', Museum Collections Inc, 1986 ....70.00
Adventures Between Adventures, 1986 ....100.00
All Wrapped Up, 1984 ....100.00
Almost Grown Up, 1982 ....175.00
America's Artist, ltd ed 5,000, 1983 ....195.00
Another Masterpiece by Norman Rockwell, ltd ed 5,000, 1985 .210.00
Apple for the Teacher, Museum Collections Inc, 1986 ....70.00
Artist, Museum Collections Inc, ltd ed 2,500, 1986 ....195.00
At the Circus, 1982 ....190.00
Authorized Collectors Center (ad stand), ltd ed 5,000, 1981 ....150.00
Baby's First Step, 1979 ....175.00
Barefoot Boy, Museum Collections Inc, ltd ed 5,000, 1986 ....110.00
Bedtime, LCF seriess, ltd ed 1,000, 1982 ....225.00
Bedtime, 1979 ....80.00
Bicycle Boys, 1981 ....120.00
Big Race, 1984 ....100.00
Birthday Party, 1980 ....150.00
Bobbing for Apples, 1982 ....120.00
Bored of Education, 1984 ....95.00
Bottom of the Sixth, Museum Collections Inc, ltd ed 5,000, 1986 ..200.00
Boy Meets His Dog, 1986 ....100.00
Braving the Storm, 1982 ....115.00
Bride & Groom, 1981 ....140.00
Bringing Home the Christmas Tree, 1982 ....125.00
Celebration, 1982 ....190.00
Census Taker, Museum Collections Inc, ltd ed 2,500, 1986 ....200.00
Checking His List, 1980 ....90.00
Christmas Prayers, 1985 ....95.00
Circus Comes to Town, 1982 ....125.00
Circus Strongman, 1986 ....100.00
Cobbler, LCF Series, ltd ed 1,000, 1982 ....225.00
Cobbler, 1979 ....90.00
Collect Fine Porcelain Figurines (ad stand), 1984 ....140.00
Country Doctor, 1982 ....95.00
Courageous Hero, 1982 ....185.00
Dollhouse for Sis, 1979 ....80.00
Downhill Racer, 1981 ....120.00
Drawing a Blank, Museum Collections Inc, ltd ed 2,500, 1987 ..165.00
Dreams in the Antique Shop, Museum Collections Inc, 1986 ....80.00
Dreams in the Antique Shop, 1982 ....100.00
Drummer's Friend, 1982 ....125.00
Final Touch, 1983 ....95.00
First Car in Town, ltd ed 2,500, 1985 ....235.00
First Haircut, 1979 ....150.00
First Prom, 1979 ....125.00
For a Good Boy, LCF series, ltd ed 1,000, 1983 ....225.00
For a Good Boy, 1980 ....90.00
Freedom of Fear, ltd ed 5,000, 1982 ....350.00
Freedom of Speech, ltd ed 5,000, 1982 ....350.00
Freedom of Want, ltd ed 5,000, 1982 ....350.00
Freedom of Worship, ltd ed 5,000, 1982 ....350.00
Giving Thanks, 1982 ....200.00
Goin' Fishin', 1984 ....95.00
Going Out, Museum Collections Inc, ltd ed 2,500, 1986 ....210.00
Good Food, Good Friends, 1982 ....225.00
Happy Birthday, Dear Mother, 1979 ....140.00
Helping Mother, 1982 ....120.00
High Hopes, 1983 ....150.00
High Stepping, 1982 ....110.00
Home for Fido, Museum Collections Inc, 1986 ....75.00
Homerun Slugger, 1982 ....145.00
Kite Maker, 1982 ....135.00
Late Night Dining, Museum Collections Inc, 1986 ....80.00
Letterman, Museum Collections, ltd ed 2,500, 1986 ....165.00
Lighthouse Keeper's Daughter, LCF Series, ltd ed 1,000, 1982 ...225.00
Lighthouse Keeper's Daughter, 1979 ....85.00
Little Mother, 1980 ....175.00
Little Patient, 1981 ....120.00
Little Salesman, 1982 ....185.00
Little Shaver, 1982 ....185.00
Lovely in Lipstick, Museum Collections Inc, 1988 ....75.00
Memories, LCF series, ltd ed 1,000, 1983 ....225.00
Memories, 1980 ....90.00
Model, ltd ed 15,000, 1986 ....150.00
Mom's Helper, ltd ed 15,000, 1986 ....120.00
Mother's Little Helpers, 1981 ....140.00
Music Lesson, 1980 ....90.00
Music Master, 1980 ....90.00
Mysterious Malady, 1986 ....100.00
New Arrival, 1981 ....160.00
No Fishin', No Nothin', Museum Collections Inc, 1986 ....80.00
Off to School, 1981 ....115.00
Out Fishin', Museum Collections Inc, ltd ed 25,000, 1985 ....100.00
Outward Bound, ltd ed 5,000, 1984 ....200.00
Painter & the Pups, ltd ed 5,000, 1986 ....205.00
Partygoers, Museum Collections Inc, ltd ed 2,500, 1986 ....165.00
Pest, 1982 ....125.00
Playing Pirates, ltd ed 2,500, 1984 ....235.00
Practice Makes Perfect, Museum Collections Inc, ltd ed 2,500, 1987 ..170.00
Pride of Parenthood, 1986 ....100.00
Puppy Love, 1983 ....95.00
Report Card, Museum Collections Inc, 1986 ....80.00
Ringing in Good Cheer, 1981 ....125.00
Rosie the Riveter, Museum Collections Inc, ltd ed 2,500, 1987 .165.00
Santa Takes a Break, Museum Collections Inc, ltd ed 3,500, 1987 ..110.00
Saturday's Hero, 1984 ....105.00
Secrets, ltd ed 5,000, 1986 ....185.00
Sneezing Spy, Museum Collections Inc, ltd ed 2,500, 1986 ....160.00
Soda Jerk, ltd ed 5,000, 1986 ....205.00

Space Age Santa, 1984 ....115.00
Space Pioneers, 1982 ....185.00
Special Treat, 1982 ....100.00
Spirit of America, ltd ed 5,000, 1982 ....185.00
Spring Fever, 1981 ....100.00
Stereoscope, 1986 ....100.00
Student, 1980 ....165.00
Summer Fun, 1982 ....120.00
Sunday Morning, Museum Collections Inc, ltd ed 2,500, 1986 ..225.00
Surprise Treat, 1984 ....95.00
Sweet Dreams, 1981 ....190.00
Sweet Sixteen, 1979 ....125.00
Tattoo Artist, Museum Collections Inc, ltd ed 2,500, 1987 ....170.00
Tipping the Scale, Museum Collections Inc, 1986 ....75.00
Toymaker, LCF series, ltd ed 1,000, 1982 ....225.00
Toymaker, 1979 ....95.00
Trumpeter, Museum Collections Inc, ltd ed 2,500, 1986 ....200.00
Vacation, 1982 ....115.00
Vacation's Over, 1981 ....140.00
Visiting the Vet, Museum Collections Inc, 1988 ....85.00
Waiting for Santa, 1982 ....135.00
Washing Our Dog, 1981 ....140.00
We Missed You Daddy, 1981 ....190.00
Weighty Matters, ltd ed 5,000, 1986 ....180.00
Wet Behind the Ears, Museum Collections Inc, 1986 ....80.00
While the Audience Waits, 1981 ....100.00
Winter Fun, 1982 ....95.00
Words of Wisdom, 1982 ....130.00
Wrapping Christmas Presents, 1980 ....130.00

Rogers, John

John Rogers (1829 – 1904) was a machinist from Manchester, New Hampshire, who turned his hobby of sculpting into a financially successful venture. From the originals he meticulously fashioned of red clay, he had bronze master molds made from which plaster copies were cast. He specialized in five different categories: theatrical, Shakespeare, Civil War, everyday life, and horses. His large detailed groupings portrayed the life and times of the period between 1859 and 1892. In the following listings, examples are assumed to be in very good to excellent condition. Our advisor for this category is George Humphrey; he is listed in the Directory under Maryland.

Fetching the Doctor, signed John Rogers, $750.00.

Balcony 1,500.00
Bath 2,000.00
Bubbles 2,000.00
Charity Patient 650.00
Checker Players, sm 1,200.00
Chess 800.00

Country Post Office 750.00
Courtship in Sleepy Hollow, Pat date 550.00
Fighting Bob, ca 1889 ....1,100.00
First Ride 725.00
Frolic at the Old Homestead, 1887, 22½" 800.00
Home Guard 800.00
Mail Day 2,000.00
One More Shot 550.00
Peddler at the Fair 800.00
Picket Guard 750.00
Referee 600.00
Rip Van Winkle - At Home 325.00
Shaughraun & Tatters 700.00
Slave Auction 2,000.00
Speak for Yourself John 500.00
Taking the Oath & Drawing Rations, sgn, 23" 525.00
Washington 1,250.00
Watch on the Santa Maria 1,000.00
Weighing the Baby, 20½", EX 600.00
Wounded Scout, ca 1864 ....750.00

Rookwood

The Rookwood Pottery Company was established in 1879 in Cincinnati, Ohio. Its founder was Maria Longworth Nichols Storer, daughter of a wealthy family who provided the backing necessary to make such an enterprise possible. Mrs. Storer hired competent ceramic artisans and artists of note, who through constant experimentation developed many lines of superior art pottery. While in her employ, Laura Fry invented the airbrush-blending process for which she was issued a patent in 1884. From this, several lines were designed that utilized blended backgrounds. One of their earlier lines, Standard, was a brown ware decorated with underglaze slip-painted nature studies, animals, portraits, etc. Iris and Sea Green were introduced in 1894 and Vellum, a transparent mat-glaze line, in 1904. Other lines followed: Ombroso in 1910 and Soft Porcelain in 1915. Many of the early artware lines were signed by the artist. Soon after the turn of the 20th century, Rookwood manufactured 'production' pieces that relied mainly on molded designs and forms rather than freehand decoration for their esthetic appeal. The Depression brought on financial difficulties from which the pottery never recovered. Though it continued to operate, the quality of the ware deteriorated, and the pottery was forced to close in 1967.

Unmarked Rookwood is only rarely encountered. Many marks may be found, but the most familiar is the reverse 'RP' monogram. First used in 1886, a flame point was added above it for each succeeding year until 1900. After that a Roman numeral added below indicated the year of manufacture. Impressed letters that related to the type of clay utilized for the body were also used — G for ginger, O for olive, R for red, S for sage green, W for white, and Y for yellow. Artware must be judged on an individual basis. Quality of the artwork is a prime factor to consider. Portraits, animals, and birds are worth more than florals; and pieces signed by a particularly renowned artist are highly prized. Our advice for this category comes from Fer-Duc Inc., whose address is listed in the Directory under New York.

Aerial Blue

Vase, poppies, K Shirayamadani, #562, 1896, rstr, 9½" 1,000.00
Vase, sailboat, bottle shape, Strafer, 1895, 5¾x2½" 3,700.00

Aventurine

Vase, broad shouldered, gr/lime hi-glaze, #6310, 1932, 5" 475.00

Vase, cherry hi-glaze, #6311, 1939, drilled, 7½" **550.00**
Vase, cherry red hi-glaze, #5675, 1930, 4", pr **850.00**
Vase, ducks/reeds/water, mc, #6550, 1939, 6" **400.00**
Vase, gold/brn/gr, #1656D, 1920, 9½" **425.00**
Vase, gray/orange/mahog, 1932, mini, 4" **550.00**
Vase, orange & gr, #6823, 1943, X, 8" **250.00**
Vase, red hi-glaze, S, 1935, 5½" **600.00**
Vase, rooks emb at shoulder on gr, #2705, 1924, 7" **700.00**

Cameo

Ewer, flowers, wht/gold on gray, tooled gold neck, Wilcox, 10" .**700.00**
Pitcher, roses, AM Valentien, #13 W, 1889, 6" **450.00**
Vase, floral, brn & wht on pk, AB Sprague, #519, W, 1899, 5½" ...**400.00**
Vase, girls (3) hold hands, HE Wilcox, #484D W, 1891, 7x9" .**2,100.00**

Iris

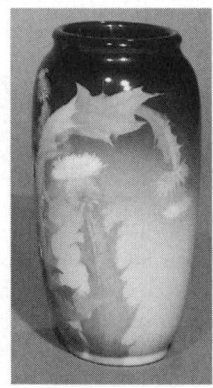

Vase, thistles on white, Fred Rothenbusch, #892C, 1904, 8⅝", $6,500.00.

Vase, bleeding hearts, L Linderman, #917D, 1906, 6½" **1,000.00**
Vase, calla lilies on bl to amber, Sax, 1903, 12¾x5¾" **3,750.00**
Vase, clover on stem, F Rothenbusch, #916E, 1904, 4½" **750.00**
Vase, floral, V Demarest, #604E, 1901, 6" **950.00**
Vase, floral on gr to lav, E Diers, #732B W, 1904, 10½" **1,600.00**
Vase, floral on ivory to lav, S Sax, #906E, 1900, X, 4" **650.00**
Vase, floral trefoils/long leaves, Reed, 1902, 9x5" **1,800.00**
Vase, floral w/lg leaves, L Asbury, #900C, 1907, 8", NM **750.00**
Vase, flowers/buds, I Bishop, #941E W, 1905, 6½" **1,100.00**
Vase, flowers/long stems, C Schmidt, #926D, 1901, 7" **1,200.00**
Vase, geese (3) in fading sky, L Asbury, #604D W, 1909, 7", NM ..**850.00**
Vase, geese in flight, AR Valentien, #S1410B, 1898, rpr, 12½" ..**7,000.00**
Vase, grapes & leaves, S Sax, #950D, 1906, 8½" **1,400.00**
Vase, irises, Diers, 1902, 8½x6" **1,500.00**
Vase, irises (EX art) on shaded mauve, Schmidt, 1901, 8½x4" .**4,000.00**
Vase, irises on gr (EX art), C Schmidt, #907C W, 1910, 14" ..**13,000.00**
Vase, irises on long stems, M Daly, #909C W, 1900, 9½" **1,900.00**
Vase, irises on purple to ivory, S Sax, #932D W, 1902, 9" **1,600.00**
Vase, irises/buds on gr to blk, C Baker, #907E, 1907, 9" **7,000.00**
Vase, landscape: trees, K Shirayamadani, #952 D, 1906, 8½" .**1,600.00**
Vase, landscape: trees/grass, Shirayamadani, 1906, 8x3¾" **3,250.00**
Vase, maple leaf branch on wht to gray, Zettel, 1902, 8¾" **1,500.00**
Vase, parrot tulips, Lawrence, 1902, X, 14½x9" **7,500.00**
Vase, pine cones, K Van Horne, #915E, 1907, 5½" **850.00**
Vase, pine cones/needles, L Asbury, #907E W, 1906, 8½" **2,400.00**
Vase, Queen Anne's lace, S Sax, #825C, 1906, flaw, 9½" **2,500.00**
Vase, rose on long stem, AR Valentien, #904B, 1902, 13½" ...**1,600.00**
Vase, swans on cobalt-to-blk lake, C Schmidt, #S1772, 1904, 10½" .**14,000.00**
Vase, thistles, Van Horne, 1908, 7x3¾" **850.00**
Vase, wild grapes on blk to bone, Van Horne, 1910, 6¾x3¾" .**1,800.00**
Vase, wild rose/buds, J Zettel, #937, 1902, 9" **900.00**

Limoges

Bowl, butterflies w/gold, NJ Hirschfield, #166 G, 1883, 7" **375.00**
Coffeepot, ducks/grasses, ML Nichols, Turkish shape, 1882, 11½" ..**2,000.00**
Flask, pilgrim; butterfly & flowers w/gold, Rookwood 1882, 6½" .**375.00**
Flask, pilgrim; geese/waterfowl/reeds, AR Valentien, #882, 7" ...**800.00**
Jug, birds in flight & egrets w/gold, unknown artist, 1882, 5" **270.00**
Jug, butterfly on smeared gr, AR Valentien, #52 G, 1884, 12" ...**700.00**
Pitcher, butterfly w/gold, spider & web, #65 R, 1882, 9½" **650.00**
Plate, bird/reeds w/gold, NJ Hirschfield, #87, 1882, 6½", NM **180.00**
Vase, bats on brn/tan w/gold, ML Nichols, #102 G, 1882, 9½" ..**3,750.00**
Vase, birds among reeds, M Rettig, #126B, 1883, 9", NM **750.00**
Vase, butterfly w/bamboo, leaves & gold, M Daly, att, 8" **650.00**

Mat

Note: Both incised mat and painted mat are listed here. Incised mat descriptions are indicated by the term 'cvd' within the line; the others are for the hand-painted mat ware.

Bowl, cvd floral, red/gr/bl on bl, Hentschel, 1915, 6½" **400.00**
Mug, cvd/modeled peacock feather, grs/bl, sgn, 1905, 4¾x5" **400.00**
Stein, emb poppies, gr/rose on rose, Pons, 1907, 6x5½" **500.00**
Tray, rose & leaves, K Shirayamadani, #1640, 1912, 6½" **350.00**
Vase, cvd abstract floral, brn w/butterfat drip, Todd, 3½" **500.00**
Vase, cvd chevrons at neck, caramel, AM, date obscured, 7x6" .**550.00**
Vase, cvd daffodils, frothy gr on brn, Lincoln, 1905, 6¾" **600.00**
Vase, cvd fir branches on bl-gray, Pons, 1908, 5x3¾" **375.00**
Vase, cvd floral, gr/rose mottle, Hentschel, #1133, 1910, 10" **865.00**
Vase, cvd floral at shoulder, 5-color, Todd, 1916, 9x5" **900.00**
Vase, cvd floral band, 5-color, Todd, 1914, 3¾x5" **650.00**
Vase, cvd floral/leaves, red/gr on rust, Todd, 1914, 11" **1,200.00**
Vase, cvd geometric neck band, yel, #2318, 1923, 9½" **260.00**
Vase, cvd grapes/leaves, purple/gr on mustard, Toohey, 5x4" **700.00**
Vase, cvd lotus, 3-color (EX glaze), Hentschel, 1915, 11x7" ...**1,100.00**
Vase, cvd stylized leaves, blk on olive/moss, Hentschel, 9" **1,400.00**
Vase, cvd/pnt Greek Key, 4-color, Wilcox, 1904, 10x5" **2,600.00**
Vase, cvd/pnt poppies & leaves, Fechheimer, 1905, 7½x2¾" ..**2,100.00**
Vase, daffodils, K Shirayamadani, S, 1942, 6½" **1,200.00**
Vase, floral, bl/orange on brn/bl, Hentschel, #1844, 1921, 5½" ..**700.00**
Vase, floral, mc on bl, L Abel, #1356D, 1922, 9" **1,100.00**
Vase, floral, mc on bl to rose, S Coyne, #1660F, 1927, 6" **600.00**
Vase, floral, mc on brn mottle, C Covalenco, #614D, 1925, 11" ..**1,500.00**
Vase, floral, mc on gr, S Coyne, #2070, 1925, 7½" **600.00**
Vase, floral, mc on lt bl, MH McDonald, S, 1938, 5½", NM **700.00**
Vase, floral, mc on mottled gr & bl, L Abel, #2720, 1925, 6½" ..**650.00**
Vase, floral, mc on purple to gr, J Jensen, #2720, 1920, 6" **750.00**
Vase, floral, mc on yel/orange, J Jensen, #2831, 1929, 5½" **750.00**
Vase, floral, purple/gr on lt brn, J Jensen, #2078, 1930, 5" **600.00**
Vase, floral branch, mc on gr, MH McDonald, #2723, 1924, 6" .**450.00**
Vase, geometrics, W Rehm, #6195E, 1930, X, 5½" **600.00**
Vase, papyrus (stylized), 5-color, Todd, 1926, 6x3½" **2,200.00**
Vase, seed pods on ribbing, squeezebag, Hentschel, 1927, 5x5" .**375.00**
Wall pocket, #1635, 1908, cicada form, gr, 9" **1,200.00**
Wall pocket, cvd floral, pk to gr, tapered, 1913, 12x4" **300.00**

Porcelain

Bowl, roses over 6-point star, WE Hentschel, #2239, 1920, 6½" ..**450.00**
Bowl w/kingfisher flower frog, mc flowers, L Eppley, 1927, 13" dia ..**900.00**
Tea set, floral, 8" rattan-hdl pot, S Sax, #S1844, 1910, 3-pc ...**1,000.00**
Vase, berries/leaves, K Shirayamadani, #654D, 1926, 4½" **1,400.00**
Vase, circles/geometrics/etc, mc, L Holkamp, #6660F, 1952, 5" dia ..**450.00**
Vase, floral, cvd/pnt, bl/lav, Wareham, bottle form, '52, 12" **750.00**

Vase, floral, mc on yel to gr, MH McDonald, S, 1942, 7½" 500.00
Vase, floral, modern style, W Hentschel, #2785, 1924, 13" 1,700.00
Vase, floral, sgraffito/pnt, unknown artist, #6133F, 1946, 4½" ...250.00
Vase, floral (swirling), A Conant, #2448, 1921, 14½", NM 6,000.00
Vase, floral branches, W Hentschel, #935C, 1922, 9½" 1,200.00
Vase, floral wreath under flame-pnt celadon, Epply, 6x5" 700.00
Vase, geometrics, gray/bl on wht, Menzel, 1952, 7¾x4" 450.00
Vase, geometrics, mc, L Epply, #2917E, 1930, X, 6" 600.00
Vase, gr/purple/rust drip, Toohey, #S2009, 1920, drilled, 16" ..3,750.00
Vase, grapes/leaves, bl/brn on wht, Jensen, 1943, 6½" 1,200.00
Vase, impressionistic design, ET Hurley, #2548, 1924, 8½" 800.00
Vase, Jewel, apple blossoms, wht froth overglaze, Hurley, 7" ...2,500.00
Vase, Jewel, apple blossoms on pumpkin, Sax, 1924, 5x3¼" ...1,400.00
Vase, Jewel, Art Deco horse heads on dk bl, Jensen, 1933, 6" .2,200.00
Vase, Jewel, birds & foliage, ET Hurley, #339B/#4761, 1925, 14" 4,500.00
Vase, Jewel, dogwood, Shirayamadani, 1929, 5x7" 2,600.00
Vase, Jewel, floral, brn/bl on bone, Jensen, 1944, 8x4" 800.00
Vase, Jewel, floral, S Sax, #1110, 1923, 5½" W 1,000.00
Vase, Jewel, floral band (low), purple/gr on blk, Sax, 8x4" 8,000.00
Vase, Jewel, floral/berries on bl to pk, Rothenbusch, 1924, 6x3" ...1,600.00
Vase, Jewel, floral/geometrics on apple gr, Sax, 1930, 7½" 3,750.00
Vase, Jewel, lg Deco floral, Sax, 930, 6x5½" 2,100.00
Vase, Jewel, pears/leaves, yel/brn on gray, Barrett, 6", pr 950.00
Vase, Jewel, rose/leaves on bone, Jensen, 1945, 6½x4" 550.00
Vase, Jewel, stylized bison, brn/blk/bone, Jensen, 1944, 10x6" ..2,600.00
Vase, Jewel, trees/water scene, MH McDonald, #892C, 1935, 9" ..950.00
Vase, Jewel, whiplashes, wht/brn on dk bl, Jensen, 1933, 6x5" ..1,400.00
Vase, Jewel, women, Jensen, 1932, 8x4" 2,600.00
Vase, leaves, wht w/brn on peach, WE Hentschel, #6206F, 1931, 5" ...950.00
Vase, leaves pnt/cvd, gr on pk, RE Menzel, #6737, 1942, 5" 550.00
Vase, mottled gr/navy/bl/wht w/drips, R Menzel, S, 1951, X, 7½" ...550.00
Vase, parrots on rose to bl, K Shirayamadani, #892C, 1930, 9" 3,000.00
Vase, roses, pk on pk/bl shaded mottle, Sax, 1932, 3¾x6" 1,000.00
Vase, wild roses, H Wilcox, #230S, 1921, 9½" 1,900.00

Sea Green

Vase, three ducks in flight, multicolor on green to gray, signed M.A. Daly, #S1603C, 1901, 10", $9,500.00.

Lamp, lotus blossoms w/appl copper leaves, Shirayamadani, 18" ...33,350.00
Vase, floral w/leaves & stems, M Mitchel, #921, 1901, 6" 850.00
Vase, frogs (8) hopping, AR Valentien, #786D, 1896, 8", NM 1,600.00
Vase, irises, SP bronze at top, M Daly, #S1574 G, 1900, 12½" ...12,000.00
Vase, sailing ships, S Laurence, #S1735, 1903, drilled, 14½" ..8,000.00
Vase, serpent w/lt sgraffito, M Daly, #184/#765, 1895, 5½" 3,250.00
Vase, thistles, R Fechheimer, #589F, 1901, 7½" 3,000.00

Standard

Basket, daisies, gondola-shape, Shirayamadani, 1888, 8x15½" ...600.00

Ewer, mums, yel/orange/gr, AB Sprague, #495, 1893, 8½" 650.00
Ewer, oak leaves, Toohey, #611, 1899, 11x8" 375.00
Ewer, roses, yel on brn to gr, C Schmidt, #639D, 1897, 6½" 550.00
Ewer, silver o/l, floral, HR Strafer, #R198, 1892, 7", NM 3,500.00
Humidor, pipes/matches/cigars, Baker, 1896, w/lid, 5½x6" 600.00
Inkwell, silver o/l, feather & clover, C Baker, #586C, 1899, 10" ..1,600.00
Jug, wheat stalks, Gorham silver stopper, Baker, 1895, 10x5" 275.00
Stein, man's portrait, M Daly, #775, 1896, rstr insert, 9½" 1,600.00
Vase, berries/leaves, Sprague, 1890, 7x3½" 300.00
Vase, clover buds on yel to brn, AM Valentien, 1894 10x7" 650.00
Vase, daffodils on blk to dk gr, Shirayamadani, #829, 1889, 9" ..2,000.00
Vase, dogwood blossoms in heavy relief, #163, 1887, 14x8" 800.00
Vase, floral, mc on brn to gr, AB Sprague, #537C, 1899, 16" .1,700.00
Vase, floral, mc on orange to brn, L Asbury, #753, 1899, 6½" 757.00
Vase, floral/gourds/leaves, K Shirayamadani, #2997, 1928, 14" ...1,700.00
Vase, gooseberries/leaves, Rothenbusch, ruffled, 1897, 4x3½" ...375.00
Vase, holly leaves/berries, J Zettel, #636W, 1892, 6" W, NM 400.00
Vase, hyacinths, SE Coyne, #901, 1903, drilled, 9½" 600.00
Vase, leaves, mc on brn, L Asbury, #504E, 1895, 7½" 600.00
Vase, maple leaves, Shirayamadani, #496, 1893, 13x5½" 1,900.00
Vase, mums, H Altman, #534C, 1903, X, 7½" 325.00
Vase, mums, ovoid, flaring rim, Shirayamadani, 1892, 13" ...1,000.00
Vase, nasturtiums, Hurley, #972, 1902, 11x4¾" 450.00
Vase, palm leaves, Matt Daly, #S1411C, 1898, X, 13½" 1,100.00
Vase, portrait, Rembrandt style, A Van Briggle, 1897, 6¾" 800.00
Vase, roses, Lincoln #932, 1903, 10x4" 850.00
Vase, roses, Toohey, bulbous w/hdls, 1889, 5¾x4¾" 550.00
Vase, silver o/l, clover & leaves, C Steinle, #R148, 1892, 4" ...4,500.00
Vase, silver o/l, daisies, Hurley, #785, 1901, 10½x5" 1,500.00
Vase, silver o/l, pansies, Baker, 1892, 8x4", NM 1,300.00
Vase, water lilies & poppies, K Shirayamadani, 1890, W, 17" .6,000.00
Vase, wild roses, Shirayamadani, #186, 1889, 11½x6" 2,200.00

Vellum

Plaque, birch trees, grays/ivory, Hurley, 1913, 11x9", +fr 3,600.00
Plaque, birch trees/lake at dusk, Diers, 1926, 6x8", gilt fr 2,200.00
Plaque, Frozen Stream, Coyne, 1926, 10x12", orig gilt fr 5,750.00
Plaque, landscape, artist sgn, 1913, firing line, 8x11" 2,600.00
Plaque, sailboats (lg), Diers, 1926, 9½x4½", orig gilt fr 5,500.00
Plaque, Snow Clad Hillside, Epply, 8x6", orig fr 1,250.00
Plaque, snow scene w/trees/sky, S Sax, 8x6" 1,500.00
Plaque, snowy landscape, L Epply, 1916, 9x11"+fr 3,500.00
Plaque, trees/riverbank scene, ET Hurley, 1915, 9½x5½" 2,600.00
Plaque, winter scene, Rothenbusch, 9x5", orig fr 1,900.00
Vase, birch trees/meadow, Diers, 1923, 7x4", NM 1,800.00
Vase, birch trees/misty meadow, Hurley, 1914, 10x5" 1,900.00
Vase, Canadian geese band on gr, Hurley, 1911, 9x 5½" 4,500.00
Vase, Canadian geese/trees, K Shirayamadani, #1667, 1910, 11" .4,000.00
Vase, cherry blossoms, Diers, 1926, 7x2" 200.00
Vase, cherry blossoms on orange to bl, Asbury, 1925, 6x6" 900.00
Vase, cvd geese, lt bls/yels, Noonan, 1907, 7" 1,400.00
Vase, dogwood on gr to pk, Noonan, 1908, 8x3½" 700.00
Vase, evergreens/moon/snow, L Asbury, #1652D, 1910, 9½" .3,000.00
Vase, fish, aquamarine on pk to gr, Noonan, 1908, 7½x3¾" ...1,200.00
Vase, fish (2 lg) on aqua & lt gr, ET Hurley, #942C, 1907, X, 7" ...900.00
Vase, fish (4 lg) among coral, E Noonan, #1358E, 1908, 7", NM ...700.00
Vase, fish among coral, E Noonan, #1120, 1909, 5" 1,500.00
Vase, floral, mc on bl, MH McDonald, #1660E, 1918, 7½", NM ...400.00
Vase, floral, mc on ivory w/pk & bl, C Steinle, #995#, 1916, 5½" .600.00
Vase, floral, wht/gr on bl, Hurley 1928, 8x4¾" 1,095.00
Vase, floral (indistinct), Shirayamadani, w/hdls, 1935, 8½", pr ...1,600.00
Vase, floral (trailing), L Asbury, #922D, 1924, 7½" 2,100.00
Vase, florals at shoulder on rose to yel-red, Lincoln, 9" 865.00

Vase, irises on gr to lav w/purple, S Coyne, #904CC, 1910, 10½" ..**3,250.00**
Vase, mallards over water, K Shirayamadani, #950C, 1907, 10½" .**4,000.00**
Vase, mistletoe, Asbury, St Louis Expo label, 5x4½" **700.00**
Vase, morning glories, Diers, 1925, 6x4½" **800.00**
Vase, mums, pk/purple/gr on dk bl to bone, Conant, 1916, 6" ...**950.00**
Vase, mushrooms on lav, unknown artist, #2066, 1916, 7½" ..**1,100.00**
Vase, palm trees/river, Denzler, 1915, 7¾x3½" **1,700.00**
Vase, palm trees/water, Hurley, #935, 1907, 9½x5" **5,700.00**
Vase, poppies, pk on gray, Lincoln, 1907, 8½x3" **475.00**
Vase, poppy on leafy stem, Sax, 1904, 6¼x3" **700.00**
Vase, prunus branches, Hurley, 1912, 9½" **1,200.00**
Vase, river scene (autumnal), Hurley, 1931, 7½x4½" **1,600.00**
Vase, rook/moon on bl to gr, SE Coyne, #951D, 1908, 9" **4,000.00**
Vase, roses, pk on gr, E Diers, #939C, 1907, 9" **1,300.00**
Vase, roses/flower garlands, F Rothenbusch, #1356E, 1924, 7½" ..**1,400.00**
Vase, sailboat scene, L Asbury, #1658F, 1912, 6½" **1,200.00**
Vase, sailboat scene on gr to rose, Schmidt, 1923, 8x3¾" **3,000.00**
Vase, snowy forest/lake, Coyne, 1921, 6x3" **1,100.00**
Vase, spruce trees/lake, Lincoln, 1912, 6x3" **1,400.00**
Vase, trees, dk silhouettes on shaded gr, Coyne, 1911, 9½x3¾" ...**2,300.00**
Vase, trees, F Rothenbusch, #925C, 1929, 11" **6,000.00**
Vase, trees in snow, L Asbury, #907D, 1916, 12" **6,000.00**
Vase, trees landscape, F Rothenbusch, #1358D, 1916, 9" **1,300.00**
Vase, trees/lake/meadow, Hurley, 1940, 5¾" **1,400.00**
Vase, trees/mtn, E Diers, #30E, 1918, 9" **2,100.00**
Vase, trees/mtns (EX colors), Rothenbusch, 1924, 9x5" **2,200.00**
Vase, tulips panels (3) at shoulder, S Sax, #932E, 1907, 8" **600.00**
Vase, Venetian sailboats scene, C Schmidt, #907C, 1920, 15" ..**10,000.00**
Vase, wisteria, bl on shaded bl, Hurley, 14x6" **5,000.00**
Vase, wisteria on branches, E Diers, #2720, 1925, 6½" **1,600.00**

Wax Mat

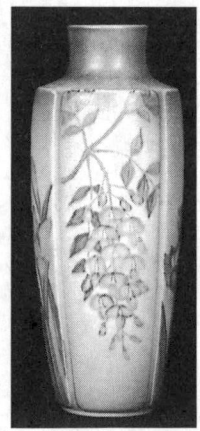

Vase, four floral panels (each different) on lavender to pale yellow, Kataro Shirayamadani, #2932, 1937, 14", $5,500.00.

Vase, bellflowers, purple on turq, McDonald, 1931, 9x5", pr ..**2,500.00**
Vase, dogwood branches on lt brn, Barrett, 1925, 8x4½" **450.00**
Vase, floral, dk pk on pk, Jones, stick neck, 1930, 7x3" **550.00**
Vase, floral, pk on shaded pk, McDonald, hdls, 1929, 7x3¾" **750.00**
Vase, floral, purple/brn on yel, Jensen, 1930, 12x5" **900.00**
Vase, floral, red/pk/gr on yel & gr, Jensen, 1926, 8x5" **550.00**
Vase, floral, yel/gr on lt yel, Hurley, 1934, 5¾x4" **800.00**
Vase, floral abstract on gray-gr mottle, Jensen, 1930, 9x4" **900.00**
Vase, floral at shoulder, bl/yel/gr on pk/bl, Jones, 1926, 5" **550.00**
Vase, floral/fruit, mc on pk, Asbury, 1931, 7¾x5" **1,200.00**
Vase, floral/leaves, red/gr on shaded brn, Lincoln, 1926, 8½" .**1,100.00**
Vase, hearts/leaves, red/gr on feathered bl, Lincoln, '20, 9" **650.00**
Vase, hibiscus, pk on turq, Shirayamadani, 1933, 8x8" **2,300.00**
Vase, hibiscus, pk/gr on yel, Jones, hdls, 1927, 6x4½" **700.00**

Vase, poppies, red on yel, Shirayamadani, hdls, 1940, 7x6" **1,100.00**
Vase, roses, red/gr on yel, Barrett, 1926, 9x4" **750.00**
Vase, tulips, red on yel, Jensen, lg hdls, 1928, 9x7" **1,500.00**

Miscellaneous

Basket, #2059, 1926, pk & gr mat, 6" dia **150.00**
Basket, hanging; #S1732, 1905, gr mat, 9x10" dia, NM **400.00**
Bookends, #2275, 1920, rook, brn mat, 5", pr **325.00**
Bookends, #2565, 1929, owl, brn mottle, McDonald, 7x5½", pr ...**425.00**
Bookends, #6023, 1929, roots/leaves relief, lt gr/rust, 6", pr **500.00**
Bookends, #6252, 1926, lady in long gown, 3-color mat, 7", NM, pr ..**400.00**
Bowl, #2145, 1919, leaves, brn mat, mfg flaw, 3½x8" **260.00**
Bowl, #2399, 1919, leaves, bl/gr mat, 3½x9" **260.00**
Bowl, #6313, 1936, bl hi-glaze, 3½x8" **200.00**
Bowl vase, #494B, 1913, Greek Key band, maroon/lt gr, 5x8" **550.00**
Box, #6568, 1944, lt bl hi-glaze, 5½" **210.00**
Candlesticks, #1248, 1921, flower form, pk mat, 7", pr **250.00**
Card holder, #2952, 1927, bl crystalline ped base, 3½x3" **200.00**
Clock, #7039, 1950, panther on base, gunmetal gray, 7½" **260.00**
Compote, #S2205, 1955, red hi-glaze, floral medallion, crimped top ..**200.00**
Cup & saucer, #2816, 1950, mottled gray & ivory hi-glaze, 5" **70.00**
Figurine, #2832, 1949, pheasant, mc, 9x14" **300.00**
Figurine, #6170, 1934, deer, wht mat, sgn Abel, 6" **200.00**
Flower frog, #2336, 1921, satyr w/turtle, brn mat, 7" **425.00**
Jardiniere, #117, 1905, garland wreath, gr mat, 11½x13" **900.00**
Jardiniere, #180, 1910, cvd upright leaves, brn/gr mat, 9x9" **500.00**
Paperweight, #6149, 1943, pelican, celadon hi-glaze, 6" **200.00**
Pitcher, #2494, 1921, gr & pk mat, 4½" **140.00**
Sconce, #1688, 1910, pr of owls emb, gr/brn mat, rpr, 11x6" **900.00**
Tile, #B950A, emb classical figures, wht on bl mat, 8x19", NM .**900.00**
Tile, #1378Y/84, Faience, recessed sailing ship, 8", +fr **865.00**
Tile, #417/#3246Y/#G414, satyrs w/grapes, mc faience, 27" W, NM .**1,500.00**
Tile, clover leaf, aqua/dk bl/cream, 4", in wide oak fr **150.00**
Tile, garden steps/pool/trees, mc, 12", in wide oak fr **2,300.00**
Tile, geometric emb, gray/brn on med bl, 4", in wide oak fr **130.00**
Tile, grapes/leaves, brn/gr mat, 6" **250.00**
Tile, owl w/coat-of-arms, 3-color, 7½x8½", EX **300.00**
Tile, semicircular w/emb floral sprays, 3-color, 4½x9", EX **200.00**
Tile, ship w/sails, cut-bk, 3-color, 6", orig oak fr **200.00**
Tile, trees/water/mtns, smooth/curdled glazes, 12", +fr **2,100.00**
Trivet, #3077, 1930, parrot among flower branch, 6" sq **300.00**
Urn, #2300, 1920, hand thrown, aqua hi-glaze, w/lid, 11½" **750.00**
Vase, #1710, 1924, poppies, yel mat, 11x6" **950.00**
Vase, #1795, 1927, rooks emb, bl mat, 5-sided, 4¾x3" **325.00**
Vase, #1889, 1922, pine cones, caramel mat, 6½" **375.00**
Vase, #1895, 1921, bamboo trees emb, yel mat, 6½" **350.00**
Vase, #1907, 1914, floral, gr to rose mat, cylindrical, 5" **170.00**
Vase, #1908, 1917, leaf panels & solid areas, bl/gr, 4¾" **250.00**
Vase, #2010, 1922, cat lilies emb, med/lt bl mat, 14" **350.00**
Vase, #2014, 1917, peacock feathers emb, gr & pk mat, 7x5" **375.00**
Vase, #2097, 1919, swans emb, gr mat, 3½" **250.00**
Vase, #2099, 1924, leaf & berry on gr crystalline mat, 4½" dia ..**150.00**
Vase, #2220, 1916, floral, gr & pk mat, 7" **250.00**
Vase, #2396, 1919, Grueby-like leaves cmb, lt brn mat, 11½" **750.00**
Vase, #2421, 1921, geometric incising, pk/gr mat, 10" **425.00**
Vase, #2433, 1920, geometric emb, gr mat, 9½" **550.00**
Vase, #2592, 1946, cream hi-glaze over banded cattails, 5" **150.00**
Vase, #2854, 1932, floral incising, purple mat, 4½" **275.00**
Vase, #6260, 1932, sunflowers, gr crystalline, 4½" **290.00**
Vase, #6316, 1932, purple/brn hare's fur, porc, 3¾x4" **275.00**
Vase, #6457, 1938, flowers & butterflies, wht mat, 5" **100.00**
Vase, #6493, 1938, emb shoulder decor, pk/gr mat, hdls, 8" **350.00**
Vase, #6509, 1935, butterflies on yel mat, 4½" **290.00**

Vase, #670, 1916, cvd band on trumpet neck, purple mat, 8½x7" ..**375.00**
Vase, #6831, 1945, geese against clouds, pk semigloss, 6" **200.00**
Vase, #77C, 1929, yel mat, hdls at neck, X, 5½" **270.00**
Vase, #935C, 1907, cvd trailings at shaped/swollen top, 8½" **550.00**

Rorstrand

The Rorstrand Pottery was established in Sweden in 1726 and is today Sweden's oldest existing pottery. The earliest ware, now mostly displayed in Swedish museums, was much like old Delft. Later types were hard-paste porcelains that were enameled and decorated in a peasant style. Contemporary pieces are often described as Swedish Modern. Rorstrand is also famous for their Christmas plates.

Urn, Royal Palace scene w/claret & gilt accents, 1902, 40" **7,150.00**
Vase, brn & gunmetal crystalline over brn gloss, 6x8" **450.00**
Vase, brn/gr matt, rim w/2 arched extensions, Nylund, 12" **425.00**
Vase, matt, bulbous, 6" **40.00**
Vase, poppies, pk & gr on blk, A Erikson, 1904, rpr, 16½" **750.00**

Rose Mandarin

Similar in design to Rose Medallion, this Chinese Export porcelain features the pattern of a robed mandarin, often separated by florals, ladies, genre scenes, or butterflies in polychrome enamels. It is sometimes trimmed in gold. Elaborate in decoration, this pattern was popular from the late 1700s until the early 1840s.

Bowl, scalloped rim, 9½" **385.00**
Cache pot, court figures reserves, squirrel/grape border, 8½" **700.00**
Coffeepot, 19th C, 10¼" **1,500.00**
Mug, 2 intertwined straps form hdl, 3¾" **160.00**
Platter, lt wear, 19th C, 15¾" **1,100.00**
Platter, well & tree; rstr, 19th C, 17½" **1,150.00**
Punch bowl, Butterflies, 6¾x16¼" **1,760.00**
Sauce boat, intertwined hdl, 19th C, 8¼" **300.00**
Shrimp dish, 19th C, lt wear, 10⅝" **430.00**
Umbrella stand, wrapped bamboo form, 19th C, 24" **1,495.00**

Rose Medallion

Rose Medallion is one of the patterns of Chinese export porcelain produced from before 1850 until the second decade of the 20th century. It is decorated in rose colors with panels of florals, birds, and butterflies that form reserves containing Chinese figures. Pre-1850 ware is unmarked and is characterized by quality workmanship and gold trim. From about 1850 until circa 1860, the kilns in Canton did not operate, and no Rose Medallion was made. Post-1860 examples (still unmarked) can often be recognized by the poor quality of the gold trim or its absence. In the 1890s the ware was often marked 'China'; 'Made in China' was used from 1910 through the 1930s.

Bowl, hot water; w/lid, 10" dia, EX **330.00**
Bowl, kidney shape, 11" **440.00**
Bowl, scalloped rim, 19th C, 9¾" **700.00**
Bowl, vegetable; fruit finial, almond shape, NM **300.00**
Bowl, w/lid, 19th C, 9¼", EX, pr **750.00**
Brush box, lady w/golden hair, w/lid, 7½x3½" **400.00**
Charger, 13⅝" **500.00**
Chop plate, mk China, ca 1895, 11" **225.00**
Chop plate, 16¼" **550.00**

Compote, 4x7½", EX **175.00**
Creamer, 3-ftd, 3⅝", EX **175.00**
Cup & saucer, birds & people, China **30.00**
Cup & saucer, bouillon **55.00**
Cup & saucer, set of 4 ....**200.00**
Garden seat, 19th C, lt wear, 18¾" **1,725.00**
Jar, temple; gilt foo dogs & lion mask hdls, domed lid, 16", pr ..**2,750.00**
Plate, fluted rim, scalloped edge, 8½", EX **175.00**
Plate, Made in China, 6" **17.00**
Plate, Made in China, 9½" **50.00**
Platter, lt wear, 19th C, 15" **350.00**
Platter, 19th C, 18⅜" **400.00**
Punch bowl, late 19th C, 16" **1,035.00**
Punch bowl, 19th C, 14½" **1,380.00**
Shakers, 3", pr **75.00**
Sugar bowl, intertwined hdls, fruit finial, 5" **300.00**
Teapot, domed lid, 8½" **660.00**
Tureen, soup; 19th C, 11x14" **2,185.00**

Vases: Trumpet neck, 11", $500.00; Bottle neck, 11", $800.00.

Vase, dbl gourd form, 19th C, 12¼" **800.00**
Vase, gilt-metal mts, converted to lamp, 17½", pr **1,500.00**
Vase, w/lid, lt wear, 19th C, 19", on hardwood stand, pr **2,750.00**
Wash basin, gold trim, 19th C, 16¼", EX **350.00**

Roselane

As collectors begin considering California pottery, many turn their attention toward the products created by William 'Dock' Fields and his wife, Georgia. In 1938 they started Roselane Pottery which they operated together from their home. Less than two years later they had moved the operation to Pasadena, California, and then, onto Baldwin Park, California, where it remained for six years. William died in 1973, Georgia sold the company to Prather Engineering Corporation, and they moved it to Long Beach, California. By 1977 Roselane no longer existed.

Various items were created over the years such as candlesticks, ashtrays, bowls, wall pockets, and sculptured high-gloss animals on wooden bases. Lines included the Sparkler series, Aqua Marine, and Chinese Modern. Collectors today are looking for the sculptured, high-glazed animals on walnut bases. Being stylistic in nature, this series was not well received by the public, and was soon discontinued. Roselane surpassed many companies with their deer groups. These lightweight deer, extremely fragile, have become regarded as masterpieces. Many have multiple figures on one base. The glazes are usually muted, and the deer can most often be found in pale blue, ivory, brown, or pale green. Paper labels as well as a variety of other marks were used. Even if the label is missing and there is no other mark, experience and a well-trained eye will make it easily possible to distinguish Roselane creations from those of other companies. Our advisor for this category is Susan Cox; she is listed in the Directory under California.

Bowl, Chinese Key, sq w/ped ft, late 1940s, 2½x6¼" **25.00**

Bowl, gray, pk int w/snowflakes, 9" dia 75.00
Candle holder, gray/wine, sq center base w/vertical ribs, #C1, 2½" .24.00
Dealer sign, Roselane in emb letters, dk aqua, 3x12½" 350.00
Figurine, angelfish, Sparkler, 4½" 25.00
Figurine, Basset hound, sitting, Sparkler, 4" 18.00
Figurine, boy w/dog, 5½" 25.00
Figurine, Bulldog, fierce look, Sparkler 25.00
Figurine, cat, sitting, head turned right, Sparkler 40.00
Figurine, Chihuahua, sitting, paw raised, Sparkler, 6½" 25.00
Figurine, cockatoo, gray, 8½" 28.00
Figurine, deer (2) on base, lt gr, 5¼" 50.00
Figurine, deer w/head down, yel, 6" 45.00
Figurine, elephant, jeweled headpc, Sparkler, 6" 25.00
Figurine, elephant, stylized, on wooden base 175.00
Figurine, fawn, recumbent, Sparkler, 4" L 25.00
Figurine, fish, pink, from Aqua Marine line, 7½" 85.00
Figurine, fox, on mk walnut base, 9" 180.00
Figurine, horse, wht, stylized, wood base, burned mk, 9", minimum ...175.00
Figurine, kangaroo mama w/babies, Sparkler 35.00
Figurine, nurse, holding baby, beige/brn satin matt, mk, 4½" 25.00
Figurine, owl, Sparkler, 7" 30.00
Figurine, pheasant, seed pearl eyes, stylized, tail up, 7¾" 35.00
Figurine, raccoon, plastic eyes, mk USA, sm 25.00
Figurine, roadrunner, Sparkler 50.00
Figurine, Siamese cat, sitting, Sparkler, 6½" 27.00
Figurine, Whippet, sitting, 7½" 28.00
Vase, Chinese style, emb Chinese Key design, 9¾" 45.00

Rosemeade

Rosemeade was the name chosen by Wahpeton Pottery Company of Wahpeton, North Dakota, to represent their product. The founders of the company were Laura A. Taylor and R.J. Hughes, who organized the firm in 1940. It is most noted for small bird and animal figurals, either in high gloss or a Van Briggle-like matt glaze. The ware was marked 'Rosemeade' with an ink stamp or carried a 'Prairie Rose' sticker. The pottery closed in 1961. Our advisor for this category is Bryce L. Farnsworth; he is listed in the Directory under North Dakota. For more information we recommend *Collector's Encyclopedia of the Dakota Potteries* by Darlene Hurst Dommel.

Ashtray, gopher figural, Gopher State, Minnesota 165.00
Ashtray, palomino pony, standing 400.00
Bank, bear, blk, 3" 500.00
Bank, log cabin, 2" 500.00
Bathtub, model from DeMores Chateau, Medora, ND 175.00
Bell, tea; Art Nouveau tulip form, 3¾" 150.00
Bell, tea; flamingo figural 275.00
Bookends, wolfhounds, pr 280.00
Candle holders, Prairie Rose, pr 200.00
Cotton dispenser, rabbit, wht, HP pk ears & eyes 150.00
Creamer & sugar bowl, corn design, 2½", pr 55.00
Dealer sign, 7¼" L 1,900.00
Figurine, deer, leeping, 3½", ea 150.00
Figurine, doe, bronze, 7¼" 75.00
Figurine, fighting cocks, mini, pr 400.00
Figurine, model, Mount Rushmore 600.00
Figurine, model, world's largest book 550.00
Figurine, palomino, cut-out foliage, 9½" 500.00
Figurine, panda bear 1,075.00
Figurine, pheasant rooster, 14" 525.00
Figurine, Sacred White Buffalo, solid, 2½x3¼" 150.00
Figurine, skunk, 2¾x4" 30.00

Rosenthal

Glaze tester, wht 275.00
Perching bird (for vase edge), bluebird 235.00
Perching bird (for vase edge), robin 175.00
Perching bird (for vase edge), yel finch 235.00
Pin, horse head 1,575.00
Pitcher, ball shape 45.00
Pitcher, braided hdl, 3¾" 60.00
Shakers, bear, lt brn, pr 75.00
Shakers, bobwhite, pr 50.00
Shakers, chickadees, pr 300.00
Shakers, cucumbers, pr 55.00
Shakers, deer, leaping, pr 90.00
Shakers, Devil's Finger cactus, pr 110.00
Shakers, dolphins, pr 65.00
Shakers, elephants, standing, pr 90.00
Shakers, mallards, pr 80.00
Shakers, mice, 1 sitting/1 lying down, pr 60.00
Shakers, Paul Bunyan & Babe the Blue Ox, pr 150.00
Shakers, pheasants, tails up, pr 50.00
Shakers, quail, w/feather topknot, pr 100.00
Shakers, spaniels, begging, pr 85.00
Shakers, tulips, 2¼", pr 60.00
Shakers, turkeys, 3", pr 75.00
Spoon rest, money bag 135.00
Spoon rest, pheasant, flying, 3¼x5½" 55.00
Spoon rest, Prairie Rose 65.00
TV lamp, palomino, 9½" 525.00
Vase, fan shape on ped base, pk/gray 50.00
Vase, peacock, 8" 200.00
Vase, wheat design, 5" 55.00
Wall pocket, deer 75.00
Watering can, rabbit design 50.00

Rosenthal

In 1879 Phillip Rosenthal established the Rosenthal Porcelain Factory in Selb, Bavaria. Its earliest products were figurines and fine tablewares. The company has continued to operate to the present decade, manufacturing limited edition plates. Our advisor for this category is Raphael Wise; he is listed in the Directory under Florida.

Cake plate, mc roses, hdls, 11" 60.00
Chocolate set, roses, artist sgn, pot+6 c/s 465.00

Compote, fruit and flowers with gold trim, 6½x14", $225.00.

Figurine, bird on limb, yel, 6" 135.00
Figurine, boxer dog, standing, 7" L 550.00
Figurine, Brittany spaniel, 9" 650.00
Figurine, foal, recumbent, 5½" 65.00
Figurine, German shepherd 250.00
Figurine, harem dancer, artist sgn, 10" 600.00
Figurine, Harlequin, Great Dane, 9½" L 750.00
Figurine, Pointer, dog, 10½" L 600.00

Figurine, poodle, 8" L 450.00
Hatpin holder, gr w/silver o/l 235.00
Lamp, owl figural, brn & gray w/yel glass eyes, 7" 250.00
Nappy, courting couple on lilac, scalloped, 1891-1907 mk, 9½" ...95.00
Plaque, Medieval woman holding falcon, 9½x8" 380.00
Plate, peacock, sgn Knapp, shallow, hdls, 1920s 300.00
Tray, dresser; floral, early Xd swords mk, 11½" 115.00
Vase, lady's portrait on wine w/gold, sgn R Viehl, 8" 550.00
Vase, roses, ruby/pk w/mc foliage, shouldered, 7" 110.00

Roseville

The Roseville Pottery Company was established in 1892 by George F. Young in Roseville, Ohio. Finding their facilities inadequate, the company moved to Zanesville in 1898, erected a new building, and installed the most modern equipment available. By 1900 Young felt ready to enter into the stiffly competitive art pottery market. Roseville's first art line was called Rozane. Similar to Rookwood's Standard, Rozane featured dark blended backgrounds with slip-painted underglaze artwork of nature studies, portraits, birds, and animals. Azurean, developed in 1902, was a blue and white underglaze art line on a blue blended background. Egypto (1904) featured a matt glaze in a soft shade of old green and was modeled in low relief after examples of ancient Egyptian pottery. Mongol (1904) was a high-gloss oxblood red line after the fashion of the Chinese Sang de Boeuf. Mara (1904), an iridescent lustre line of magenta and rose with intricate patterns developed on the surface or in low relief, successfully duplicated Sicardo's work. These early lines were followed by many others of highest quality: Fudjiyama and Woodland (1905 – 06) reflected an Oriental theme; Crystalis (1906) was covered with beautiful frost-like crystals. Della Robbia, their most famous line (introduced in 1906), was decorated with designs ranging from florals, animals, and birds to scenes of Viking warriors and Roman gladiators. These designs were worked in sgraffito with slip-painted details. Very limited but of great importance to collectors today, Rozane Olympic (1905) was decorated with scenes of Greek mythology on a red ground. Pauleo (1914) was the last of the artware lines. It was varied — over two hundred glazes were recorded — and some pieces were decorated by hand, usually with florals.

During the second decade of the century until the plant closed forty years later, new lines were continually added. Some of the more popular of the middle-period lines were Donatello, 1915; Futura, 1928; Pine Cone, 1931; and Blackberry, 1933. The floral lines of the later years have become highly collectible. Pottery from every era of Roseville production — even its utility ware — attests to an unwavering dedication to quality and artistic merit.

Examples of the fine art pottery lines present the greatest challenge to evaluate. Scarcity is a prime consideration. The quality of artwork varied from one artist to another. Some pieces show fine detail and good color, and naturally this influences their values. Studies of animals and portraits bring higher prices than the floral designs. An artist's signature often increases the value of any item, especially if the artist is one who is well recognized.

The market is literally flooded with imposter Roseville that is coming into the country from China. An experienced eye can easily detect these fakes, but to a novice collector, they may pass for old Roseville. Study the marks. If the 'USA' is missing or appears only faintly, the piece is most definitely a reproduction. Also watch for lines with a mark that is not correct for its time frame; for example, Luffa with the script mark, and Woodland with the round Rozane stamp from the 1917 line.

For further information consult *The Collector's Encyclopedia of Roseville Pottery, First and Second Series*, by Sharon and Bob Huxford (Collector Books); *Collector's Compendium of Roseville Pottery, Volumes I and II*, by R.B. Monsen (see Directory, Virginia); and *Roseville in All Its*

Splendor With Price Guide by Jack and Nancy Bomm (self-published). Note: Reference names in the Futura descriptions that follow have developed via communication among collectors (Monsen follows up on this in Volume I). The values we list for that line were prices realized at auction. Futura prices tend to be volatile, and only when there were multiple sales for a particular piece did we choose to include it here.

Apple Blossom, basket, #309, 8" 250.00
Apple Blossom, bud vase, #379, 7" 125.00
Apple Blossom, vase, #381, 6" 110.00
Artwood, vase, 8" 95.00
Aztec, pitcher, squatty, bl/wht, 5" 275.00
Azurean, mug, floral 475.00
Azurean, vase, grapes, W Myers, 14" 1,250.00
Baneda, bowl, gr, 3½x10" 400.00
Baneda, vase, gr, 6" 350.00
Baneda, vase, red, 5½" 250.00
Baneda, vase, red, 8" 500.00
Bittersweet, basket, #807-8, 8½" 150.00
Bittersweet, basket, #808, 6" 150.00
Bittersweet, basket, #810, 10" 225.00
Bittersweet, vase, #972, 5" 125.00
Blackberry, basket, angled w/curved hdl 800.00
Blackberry, bowl, hdld, 8" 325.00
Blackberry, hanging basket, 4½x6½" 850.00
Blackberry, vase, squatty w/angled hdls, 4" 300.00
Bleeding Heart, basket, #360, 10" 350.00
Bleeding Heart, ewer, #963, 6" 175.00
Bleeding Heart, plate, #381-10, 10½" 175.00
Bleeding Heart, vase, #138, 4" 120.00
Burmese, candlestick, blk, #75-B 60.00
Bushberry, bowl, #411, 4" 85.00
Bushberry, cornucopia vase, #154, 8" 150.00
Bushberry, ewer, #1, 6" 140.00
Bushberry, wall pocket, #1291, 8" 350.00
Capri, Late Line; ashtray, #599-3, 13" 50.00
Capri, Late Line; bowl, #529-9, 9" 25.00
Capri, Late Line; shell bowl, #C-1120, 13½" 60.00
Carnelian (dripware), fan vase, textured, 8" 125.00
Carnelian I, flower frog, 4½" 75.00
Carnelian I, pillow vase, 5" 90.00

Carnelian II vases: Small angle handles, 9x8", $550.00; Trumpet neck with ornate handles, 10", $350.00.

Carnelian II, basket, 4x10" 300.00
Carnelian II, bowl vase, hdld, 5" 300.00
Carnelian II, planter, 3x8" 120.00
Ceramic Design, jardiniere, mc geometrics on cream, ftd, 4" 95.00
Cherry Blossom, bowl vase, hdld, 6" 350.00
Cherry Blossom, candle holders, flared base, curved hdls, 4", pr .450.00
Cherry Blossom, lamp base, ball shape w/hdls 750.00
Chloron, vase, emb floral, bulbous w/2 sm hdls, 7" 600.00
Chloron, vase, ftd, 12" 450.00

Clemana, candle holders, 4½", pr	300.00
Clemana, vase, #112-7, 7½"	300.00
Clemana, vase, #759-14, 14"	700.00
Clematis, basket, #388, 8"	160.00
Clematis, bowl, #445, 4"	60.00
Clematis, console bowl, #458-10, 14"	125.00
Clematis, ewer, #18, 15"	350.00
Clematis, vase, #108, 8"	125.00
Colonial, pitcher, twig hdl, bl sponging, 11"	250.00
Colonial, toothbrush holder, bl sponging w/gold trim, 5"	95.00
Columbine, basket, #368, 12"	400.00
Columbine, bowl, #401, 6"	135.00
Columbine, ewer, #18, 7"	175.00
Corinthian, ashtray, 2"	100.00
Corinthian, bud vase, dbl; gate type, 7"	100.00
Corinthian, vase, 6"	95.00
Cornelian (spongeware), toothbrush holder, 5"	70.00
Cosmos, basket, 12"	500.00
Cosmos, bowl vase, #376, 6"	200.00
Cosmos, hanging basket, 7"	250.00
Creamware, mug, Biblical scene, 5"	175.00
Cremona, candle holder, 4"	85.00
Cremona, fan vase, 5"	125.00
Cremona, flower frog	75.00
Dahlrose, bowl, oval, angled hdls, 10" W	200.00
Dahlrose, bud vase, 8"	250.00
Dahlrose, candlesticks, 3½", pr	175.00
Dahlrose, hanging basket, 7½"	175.00
Dawn, vase, #828, 8"	200.00
Decorated Utility Ware, pitcher, floral design, 4"	50.00
Dogwood I, bowl, 2½"	75.00
Dogwood I, vase, 6"	125.00
Dogwood II, boat planter, 6"	175.00
Dogwood II, wall pocket, dbl	300.00
Dogwood II, window box w/liner, 5½x13½"	175.00
Donatello, basket, pointed hdl, 15"	400.00
Donatello, bud vase, dbl; 5"	75.00
Donatello, candlestick, 8"	175.00
Donatello, incense burner, cone top, 3½"	350.00
Donatello, powder jar, 2x5" dia	300.00
Dutch, pitcher & bowl set, 9", 12" dia	750.00
Earlam, candlestick, 4"	275.00
Earlam, planter, 5½x10½"	150.00
Earlam, vase, hdld, 6"	175.00
Egypto, pitcher, seal mk, 5"	400.00
Egypto, pitcher, 7"	300.00
Egypto, vase, seal mk, 11"	700.00
Falline, bowl, hdld, 11" W	250.00
Falline, vase, 6"	350.00
Falline, vase, 8"	450.00
Ferella, bowl w/frog, 5"	400.00
Ferella, vase, angled hdls, 4"	250.00
Ferella, vase, angled vessel w/curved hdls, 9"	450.00
Florane, basket, 8½"	150.00
Florane, bowl, 8" dia	85.00
Florane, bowl vase, 3½"	85.00
Florane, vase, #81, 7"	85.00
Florane, vase, #82, 9"	110.00
Florane, vase, 12½"	150.00
Florentine, basket, 8"	200.00
Florentine, bowl, 9" dia	75.00
Florentine, hanging basket, 9"	175.00
Florentine, lamp, w/dbl sockets	350.00
Florentine, window box, 11½"	200.00

Foxglove, candle holder, #1150, 4½"	110.00
Foxglove, conch shell, #426, 6"	150.00
Foxglove, hanging basket, 6½"	300.00
Foxglove, tray, 8½"	110.00
Foxglove, vase, #659, 3"	85.00
Freesia, basket, #390-7, 7"	150.00
Freesia, flowerpot, #670, 5"	150.00
Freesia, tea set (pot/creamer/sugar), #6	400.00
Freesia, vase, #122, 8"	150.00
Fuchsia, basket w/frog, #350, 8"	475.00
Fuchsia, bowl vase, #346, 4"	175.00
Fudji, vase, cone shape, 9"	1,200.00
Futura, jardinere, leaves, hdls, 9" dia	325.00
Futura, jardiniere, leaves, hdls, 14" dia	400.00
Futura, vase, Arches, #411-14, from $2,400 to	2,800.00
Futura, vase, Balloons Globe, #404-8, from $1,000 to	1,300.00
Futura, vase, Bamboo Leaf Ball, #387-7, from $600 to	800.00
Futura, vase, Beehive, #406-8, from $600 to	700.00
Futura, vase, Beer Mug, #381-6, from $250 to	325.00
Futura, vase, Big Blue Triangle, #388-9	450.00
Futura, vase, Black Flame, #391-10, from $650 to	850.00
Futura, vase, Bomb, #394-12, from $1,000 to	1,100.00
Futura, vase, Bottle, #384-8	435.00
Futura, vase, Chinese Pillow, #430-9, from $1,000 to	1,300.00
Futura, vase, Christmas Tree, #390-10, from $450 to	500.00
Futura, vase, Cone, #401-8	450.00
Futura, vase, Egg w/Leaves, #428-8, from $400 to	500.00
Futura, vase, Emerald Urn, #398-9	600.00
Futura, vase, Football Urn, $409-9, from $1,000 to	1,200.00
Futura, vase, Half-Egg or 3-Leg Bowl, #197-6	600.00
Futura, vase, Jukebox, #386-8	600.00
Futura, vase, Little Blue Triangle, #383-8, from $300 to	375.00
Futura, vase, Mauve Thistle, #427-8, from $850 to	1,000.00
Futura, vase, Pink Twist, #425-8, from $450 to	550.00
Futura, vase, Red V (Victory), #3999-7, from $350 to	450.00
Futura, vase, Sand Toy, #189-4-6, from $400 to	500.00
Futura, vase, Sea Gull, #408-10, from $1,000 to	1,200.00
Futura, vase, Shooting Star, #392-10, from $800 to	1,100.00
Futura, vase, Space Capsule, #432-10, from $600 to	650.00
Futura, vase, Spittoon, #403-7, from $700 to	900.00
Futura, vase, Square Cone, #397-6, from $325 to	365.00
Futura, vase, Stepped Egg, #424-7, from $600 to	750.00

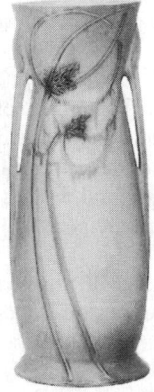

Futura vase, Tall Thistle, two long open buttresses, 15½", from $1,200.00 to $1,500.00.

Futura, vase, Telescope, #382-7, from $350 to	400.00
Futura, vase, Tombstone, #426-6, from $275 to	375.00
Futura, vase, Twist, #398-6½, from $300 to	350.00
Futura, vase, 2-Pole Pink Bud, #84-4, from $275 to	375.00
Futura, vase, 4-Ball, #393-12, from $650 to	850.00

Futura, wall pocket, 8", from $475 to	550.00
Gardenia, basket, #608, 8"	275.00
Gardenia, cornucopia vase, dbl; #622, 8"	160.00
Gardenia, ewer, #617, 10"	225.00
Gardenia, vase, #689-14, 14½"	300.00
Holland, powder jar, w/lid, 3"	125.00
Holland, tankard, #2, 9½"	175.00
Imperial I, basket, 11"	250.00
Imperial I, bud vase, 12"	200.00
Imperial I, comport, 6½"	135.00
Imperial I, planter, 14x16"	150.00
Imperial II, bowl, 4½"	250.00
Imperial II, vase, #475, 8"	400.00
Iris, case, #914, 4"	110.00
Iris, console bowl, #362-10, 3½x12½"	175.00
Iris, ewer, #926	300.00
Iris, pillow vase, #922-8, 8½"	200.00
Iris, wall shelf, 8"	375.00
Ivory II, bowl, #550, 6"	50.00
Ivory II, cornucopia, #2, 5½"	60.00
Ivory II, vase, Carnelian shape, 10"	135.00
Ixia, basket, #346, 10"	300.00
Ixia, console bowl, 3½x10½"	125.00
Ixia, vase, #853, 6"	115.00
Jonquil, basket, 10"	500.00
Jonquil, bowl, angled body w/curved hdls, 4"	150.00
Jonquil, candlestick, 4"	125.00
Jonquil, flowerpot w/frog, 1-pc, 5½"	300.00
Jonquil, vase, 8"	300.00
Juvenile, bowl, rabbit heads, 5½"	135.00
Juvenile, chamber pot, chicks, w/hdl & lid	750.00
Juvenile, milk pitcher, ind; standing rabbits	150.00
La Rose, bowl, 3"	110.00
La Rose, bud vase, dbl, gate type	125.00
La Rose, vase, 6"	100.00
Laurel, vase, 10"	400.00
Laurel, vase, 6½"	225.00
Laurel, vase, 8"	325.00
Lombardy, jardiniere, 3-ftd, 6½"	200.00
Lombardy, vase, 3-ftd, 6"	200.00
Lotus, candle holders, #L5, 2½", pr	125.00
Lotus, vase, #L3, 10"	250.00
Luffa, bowl, hdld, 4"	150.00
Luffa, jardiniere, angled hdls, 5¼" base dia	350.00
Luffa, vase, 7"	275.00
Lustre, basket, pointed hdl, 10"	150.00
Lustre, candle holder, 8"	60.00
Magnolia, bud vase, dbl, #186, 4½"	125.00
Magnolia, mug, #3, 3"	150.00
Magnolia, tea set (pot/creamer/sugar), #4	350.00
Magnolia, vase, #86, 4"	75.00
Mara, vase, filigree design, 13"	2,000.00
Mara, vase, 5½"	1,650.00
Matt Green, bud vase, dbl, gate type, 5x8"	50.00
Matt Green, planter/liner, sq, ftd, 4x8"	250.00
Mayfair, candlestick, #115-1, 4½"	20.00
Mayfair, jardiniere, #1109-4, 4"	40.00
Mayfair, pitcher, #1105, 8"	140.00
Mayfair, planter, #1113, 8"	60.00
Mayfair, vase, #1106-12, 12½"	75.00
Ming Tree, bowl, #526-9, 4x11½"	110.00
Ming Tree, candle holders, #551, pr	125.00
Ming Tree, vase, #582, 8"	140.00
Mock Orange, bowl, #900, 4"	85.00

Mock Orange, pillow vase, #930-8, 7"	115.00
Mock Orange, planter, tall ftd box shape	150.00
Moderne, comport, #297-6, 6"	175.00
Moderne, vase, #299, 6½"	200.00
Moderne, vase, #788, 6½"	25.00
Mongol, vase, #C-16, 10½"	1,250.00
Mongol, vase, long trumpet neck, 16"	1,150.00
Mongol, vase, str-sided, 15"	1,100.00
Monticello, basket, 6½", from $500 to	600.00
Monticello, vase, bl, 6"	350.00
Morning Glory, basket, wht, 10½"	500.00
Morning Glory, bowl vase, hdld, wht, 4"	350.00
Morning Glory, candlestick, gr, 5"	200.00
Moss, candle holders, #1107, 4½", pr	200.00
Moss, jardiniere, 6x6½"	300.00
Moss, vase, #774, 8"	225.00
Mostique, hanging basket, geometrics, 7"	225.00
Mostique, vase, flared, geometrics on cream, 6"	85.00
Mostique, vase, str-sided, geometrics, 6"	100.00
Normandy, jardiniere, 7"	250.00
Olympic, pitcher, Ulysses at the Table of Circle, 7"	2,250.00
Olympic, vase, ftd cone shape, 13"	3,000.00
Orian, comport, #272-10, 4½x10½"	125.00
Orian, vase, 7"	175.00
Panel, candlestick, 8"	275.00
Panel, fan vase, w/nude, 6"	600.00

Panel, vase, nude figures, white on green, 6", $600.00.

Pasadena, planter, #526, 7"	50.00
Pauleo, bowl, 3"	500.00
Pauleo, vase, flared squatty body w/tall trumpet neck, 19"	1,250.00
Pauleo, vase, ftd cylinder, 12"	650.00
Peony, basket, #376, 7"	150.00
Peony, bowl, #427, 4"	125.00
Peony, ewer, #8, 10"	200.00
Peony, mug, #2-3½, 3½"	125.00
Persian, bowl, 3 hdls, 3½"	150.00
Persian, sugar bowl & creamer, angled, ftd	175.00
Pine Cone, basket, #353-11, bl, 11"	425.00
Pine Cone, bowl, #632, brn	150.00
Pine Cone, cornucopia vase, #128, gr, 8"	200.00
Pine Cone, fan vase, #472, brn, 6"	250.00
Pine Cone, pitcher, #425, bl, 9"	650.00
Pine Cone, tray, dbl, no mk, gr, 13"	275.00
Poppy, basket, #347, 10"	275.00
Poppy, bowl, #642-3, 3½"	85.00
Poppy, vase, 6½"	110.00
Primrose, bowl, hdld, 4"	125.00
Raymor, bean pot, #194	70.00
Raymor, butter dish, #181, w/lid, 7½"	100.00
Raymor, casserole, #183, med, 11"	85.00
Raymor, corn server, ind; #162, 12½"	50.00

Raymor, plate, luncheon; #153 ....20.00
Raymor, swinging coffeepot, #176 ....350.00
Rosecraft, vase, bowl, 2½" 120.00
Rosecraft Black & Colors, bowl, hdld, bl, 5" 125.00
Rosecraft Black & Colors, comport, blk, 4x11" 125.00
Rosecraft Black & Colors, flowerpot, yel, 4½" 150.00
Rosecraft Hexagon, bowl vase, 4" 325.00
Rosecraft Hexagon, candlestick, 8" 250.00
Rosecraft Panel, covered jar, 10" 550.00
Rosecraft Panel, window box, 6x12" 300.00
Rosecraft Vintage, bowl, 6" dia 100.00
Rosecraft Vintage, vase, 5" 125.00
Rozane Light, card holder, playing cards, #7, 3½" 375.00
Rozane Light, jardiniere, ftd, 5" 200.00
Rozane Light, pillow vase, ftd, M Timberlake, 7" ...375.00
Rozane Royal, mug, ear of corn, artist sgn, Royal seal mk, 6" 300.00
Rozane Royal, pillow vase, cherries on gr/wht, W Myers, 10x10" .1,000.00
Rozane Royal, tankard, Royal seal mk, 15½" 500.00
Rozane Royal, vase, gourd shape, Rozane Ware seal, 8½" 250.00
Rozane Royal, vase, integral hdls, seal mk, 8" 250.00
Rozane Royal, vase, pillow form, unmk, 7" 350.00
Rozane Royal, vase, Rembrandt portrait, sgn Williams, 14½" .1,700.00
Rozane 1917, basket, pk, 6" 150.00
Rozane 1917, bowl, gr, 3" 75.00
Rozane 1917, vase, yel, 7" 135.00
Rozane 1940s, bud vase, #862, 4" 165.00
Rozane 1940s, jug, #888, 4½" 225.00
Rozane 1940s, vase, #398, 6" 95.00
Russco, bud vase, dbl; 8½" 125.00
Russco, vase, trumpet form, 7" 150.00
Silhouette, ashtray, #799 ....85.00
Silhouette, candle holders, #751, 3", pr 125.00
Silhouette, planter vase, #756, 5" 95.00
Silhouette, wall pocket, #766, 8" 175.00
Snowberry, basket, #1BK, 8" 200.00
Snowberry, basket, #1BK-12, 12½" 225.00
Snowberry, bud vase, #1BV, 7" 75.00
Snowberry, console bowl, #1BL1, 10" W 115.00
Snowberry, pillow vase, #IRB-6, 6" 125.00
Sunflower, bowl, hdls, 7½" dia 650.00
Sunflower, jardiniere, 9" 700.00
Sunflower, vase, 10" 800.00
Sunflower, window box, 3½x11" 450.00
Teasel, basket, #349, 10" 300.00
Teasel, vase, #882, 6" 165.00
Thorn Apple, candle holders, #1117, 2½", pr 150.00
Thorn Apple, cornucopia, 6" 100.00
Thorn Apple, hanging basket, 7" 400.00
Thorn Apple, vase, #308, 4" 125.00
Topeo, bowl, 2½" 150.00
Topeo, candlestick, dbl, 5" 125.00
Topeo, vase, 9" 300.00
Tourmaline, cornucopia vase, 7" 100.00
Tourmaline, flower frog 50.00
Tourmaline, pillow vase, 6" 125.00
Tourmaline, vase, 6" 150.00
Tuscany, candle holders, 4", pr 125.00
Tuscany, fan vase, hdld, ftd, 8" 150.00
Tuscany, vase, squatty trumpet shape w/hdls, 4" 95.00
Velmoss, vase, 12½" 400.00
Velmoss, vase, 9½" 300.00
Velmoss II, cornucopia vase, dbl, 8½" 225.00
Velmoss Scroll, candlestick, 9" 200.00
Velmoss Scroll, compote, 4x9" dia 175.00

Velmoss Scroll, jardiniere w/ped, 30" 1,250.00
Vista (Forest), bowl, str sides, 8½" 220.00
Vista (Forest), vase, rtcl buttress hdls, 10" 375.00
Vista (Forest), vase, 17½" 950.00
Vista (Forest), window box, orig liner, 11½" L, NM 1,200.00
Water Lily, basket, #382, 12" 400.00
Water Lily, cookie jar, #1, 10" 450.00
Water Lily, hanging basket, USA, 9" 225.00
Water Lily, vase, #73, 6" 115.00
White Rose, basket, #364, 12" 325.00
White Rose, bowl, #653, 3" 115.00
White Rose, ewer, #993, 15" 425.00
White Rose, vase, #987-9, 9" 200.00
Wincraft, basket, #209, 12" 175.00
Wincraft, ewer, #216, 8" 120.00
Wincraft, vase, #282, 8" 175.00
Windsor, candlesticks, 4½", pr 300.00
Windsor, console bowl/planter, w/frog, 16" W 300.00
Windsor, vase, 7" 500.00
Wisteria, bowl vase, hdld, 5" 350.00
Wisteria, console bowl, 12" 400.00
Wisteria, vase, 7½" 600.00
Woodland, vase, iris, 15" 1,300.00
Woodland, vase, iris, 8" 1,100.00
Zephyr Lily, bowl, #671, 4" 110.00
Zephyr Lily, cornucopia vase, #203, 6" 100.00
Zephyr Lily, ewer, #24, 15" 400.00
Zephyr Lily, fan vase, #205-6, 6½" 115.00

Rowland and Marsellus

Though the impressive back stamp seems to suggest otherwise, Rowland and Marsellus were not Staffordshire potters but American importers who commissioned various English companies to supply them with the transfer-printed historical ware that had been a popular import commodity since the early 1800s. Plates (both flat and with a rolled edge), cups and saucers, pitchers, and platters were sold as souvenirs from 1890 through the 1930s. Though other importers — Bawo & Dotter, and A. C. Bosselman & Co., both of New York City — commissioned the manufacture of similar souvenir items, by far the largest volume carries the R. & M. mark, and Rowland and Marcellus has become a generic term that covers all 20th-century souvenir china of this type. Their mark may be in full or 'R. & M.' in a diamond. Though primarily made with blue transfers on white, other colors may occasionally be found as well. Our advisor for this category is David Ringering. He is listed in the Directory under Oregon.

Key:
r/e — rolled edge   v/o — view of
s/o — souvenir of

Creamer, Plymouth, mk as Burbank 45.00
Cup & saucer, Brooklyn, s/o 95.00
Cup & saucer, Lenox MA, s/o 85.00
Cup & saucer, mush; Take ye a cup o' kindness..., gr 45.00
Cup & saucer, Yale, s/o 95.00
Plate, Asbury Park NJ, v/o, 9" 35.00
Plate, Battle of Lake Erie, fruit & flower border, 9¾" 60.00
Plate, Butte MT, s/o, r/e, 10" 80.00
Plate, Cape Cod, fisherman's portrait, 9" 40.00
Plate, Charles Dickens, r/e, 10" 75.00
Plate, coupe; Chicago, Marshall Field & Co, v/o, 6" 50.00
Plate, coupe; Cooperstown NY, s/o, 6" 60.00
Plate, coupe; Harrisburg, s/o, 10" 60.00

Plate, coupe; Tuscon AZ, 5 scenes, v/o, 6" 50.00
Plate, Decator IL, s/o, r/e, 10" 75.00
Plate, Henry Addressing VA Assembly, fruit/flower border, 9¾" .60.00
Plate, Hermitage, fruit & flower border, 9¾" 50.00
Plate, Lookout Mountain, TN, s/o, r/e, 10" 70.00
Plate, Lynn MA, 9" 35.00
Plate, Miami, s/o, Chief Osceola, 10" 70.00
Plate, Portland OR, Lost Lake center scene, s/o, r/e, 10" 80.00
Plate, Ride of Paul Revere, fruit & flower border, 9¾" 60.00
Plate, Valley Forge (PA), 1777-78, r/e, 10" 55.00
Sugar bowl, Plymouth, Am pilgrims 55.00
Tumbler, Ottawa Canada 85.00
Tumbler, Tacoma WA, s/o 85.00
Tumbler, Thousand Islands, v/o 85.00

Royal Bayreuth

Founded in 1794 in Tettau, Bavaria, the Royal Bayreuth firm originally manufactured fine dinnerware of superior quality. Their figural items, produced from before the turn of the century until the onset of WWI, are highly sought after by today's collectors. Perhaps the most abundantly produced and easily recognized of these are the tomato and lobster pieces. Fruit, flower, people, animal, bird, and vegetable shapes were also made. Aside from figural items, pitchers, toothpick holders, cups and saucers, humidors, and the like were decorated in florals and scenic motifs. Some, such as the very popular Rose Tapestry line, utilized a cloth-like tapestry background. Transfer prints were used as well. Two of the most popular are Sunbonnet Babies and Nursery Rhymes (in particular, those decorated with the complete verse).

Caution: Many pieces were not marked; some were marked 'Deponiert' or 'Registered' only. While marked pieces are the most valued, unmarked items are still very worthwhile. Our advisors for this category are Larry Brenner from New Hampshire and Dee Hooks from Illinois; they are listed in the Directory under their home states.

Figurals

Ashtray, elk, bl mk 350.00
Ashtray, mountain goat, bl mk 450.00
Bowl, grapes, wht satin, unmk, lg 275.00
Bowl, poppy, apricot, open hdls, bl mk, 9½" 675.00
Bowl, poppy, orchid, bl mk, w/lid, lg 250.00
Bowl, poppy, orchid, bl mk, w/lid, sm 185.00
Bowl, poppy, orchid, ftd, bl mk, 2¾x4½" 200.00
Bowl, poppy, wht MOP, rnd, ftd, bl mk, 8" 325.00
Bowl, tomato, bl mk, w/lid, lg 150.00
Box, card; Devil & Cards, bl mk 500.00
Candle holder, basset, bl mk 525.00
Candlestick, clown, yel, bl mk, tall, w/match holder 2,500.00
Candlestick, Devil & Cards, bl mk 350.00
Candy dish, grape, wht, bl mk 50.00
Candy dish, lobster, bl mk, 5½" 180.00
Card tray, Devil & Cards, bl mk 300.00
Compote, poppy, wht or orchid MOP, bl mk 595.00
Cup & saucer, demi; apple, bl mk 210.00
Cup & saucer, demi; Devil & Dice, bl mk 200.00
Cup & saucer, demi; rose, bl mk 495.00
Cup & saucer, demi; spiky shell, wht MOP, bl mk 150.00
Gravy boat, poppy, wht MOP, unmk 250.00
Match holder, Devil & Cards, bl mk, wall hanging 600.00
Match holder, poppy, red, wall hanging, unmk 395.00
Mustard, poppy, red, bl mk 225.00
Mustard, spiky shell, w/spoon, bl mk 200.00

Mustard, tomato, bl mk 175.00
Nappy, poppy, red, bl mk 150.00
Nappy, poppy, wht MOP, bl mk 175.00
Nappy, poppy, yel, bl mk 200.00
Nut set, pansy, pk lustre, bl mk, 5-pc 1,100.00
Pitcher, alligator, albino, unmk, cream sz 295.00
Pitcher, alligator, mc, bl mk, cream sz 425.00
Pitcher, apple, red, bl mk, water sz 925.00
Pitcher, apple, unmk, cream sz 175.00
Pitcher, bell ringer, bl mk, cream sz 325.00
Pitcher, bull, blk w/red horns, bl mk, cream sz 300.00
Pitcher, butterfly, open wings, bl mk, cream sz 425.00
Pitcher, cat, blk, bl mk, cream sz 250.00
Pitcher, cat hdl, blk or wht, bl mk, cream sz 350.00
Pitcher, clown, red, bl mk, cream sz 350.00
Pitcher, coachman, bl mk, cream sz 325.00
Pitcher, coachman, bl mk, milk sz 400.00
Pitcher, conch shell w/lobster hdl, unmk, cream sz 75.00
Pitcher, crow, albino, unmk, cream sz 175.00
Pitcher, dachshund, bl mk, cream sz 350.00
Pitcher, dachshund, bl mk, water sz 1,200.00
Pitcher, Devil & Cards, bl mk, souvenir of LA, cream sz 250.00
Pitcher, Devil & Cards, face cards, bl mk, cream sz 275.00
Pitcher, duck, bl mk, cream sz 300.00
Pitcher, eagle, bl mk, cream sz 350.00
Pitcher, elk, bl mk, cream sz 200.00
Pitcher, elk, bl mk, milk sz 350.00
Pitcher, elk, bl mk, water sz 700.00
Pitcher, fish head, unmk, milk sz 400.00
Pitcher, frog, unmk, cream sz 175.00
Pitcher, grapes, lav MOP, bl mk, cream sz 275.00
Pitcher, grapes, lav MOP, bl mk, milk sz 375.00
Pitcher, grapes, wht MOP, bl mk, water sz 800.00
Pitcher, hawk, unmk, cream sz 650.00
Pitcher, kangaroo, brn, bl mk, cream sz 6,000.00
Pitcher, lamplighter, bl mk, cream sz 375.00
Pitcher, lemon, bl mk, cream sz 250.00
Pitcher, melon, bl mk, cream sz 350.00
Pitcher, monkey, gr, bl mk, milk sz 600.00
Pitcher, mountain goat, bl mk, cream sz 335.00
Pitcher, mouse, gray, mk registered, cream sz 2,100.00
Pitcher, oak leaf, bl mk, cream sz 325.00
Pitcher, oak leaf, wht MOP, bl mk, cream sz 375.00
Pitcher, orange, bl mk, cream sz 295.00
Pitcher, owl, mc, unmk, cream sz 395.00
Pitcher, owl, unmk, cream sz 350.00
Pitcher, parakeet, red, unmk, cream sz 295.00
Pitcher, perch, bl mk, cream sz 425.00
Pitcher, poodle, gray, bl mk, cream sz 375.00
Pitcher, poppy, apricot MOP w/gr hdl, milk sz 410.00
Pitcher, poppy, orchid MOP, bl mk, milk sz 395.00
Pitcher, poppy, red, bl mk, cream sz 250.00
Pitcher, poppy, red, bl mk, milk sz 325.00
Pitcher, poppy, wht MOP, bl mk, cream sz 325.00
Pitcher, robin, unmk, cream sz 185.00
Pitcher, rose, pk, bl mk, cream sz 395.00
Pitcher, Santa Claus, red, bl mk, cream sz 4,000.00
Pitcher, shell w/coral hdl, unmk, cream sz 115.00
Pitcher, spiky shell, MOP, bl mk, cream sz 225.00
Pitcher, squirrel, bl mk, water sz (rare) 6,500.00
Pitcher, St Bernard, unmk, cream sz 220.00
Pitcher, water buffalo, blk, bl mk, cream sz 250.00
Pitcher, water buffalo, gray, cream sz 250.00
Plate, lettuce leaf, w/hdl, bl mk, 7½" dia 25.00

Plate, poppy, yel, bl mk, 6" 200.00
Plate, tomato, bl mk 100.00
Relish, spiky shell, MOP, bl mk, 8" 85.00
Shakers, chile pepper, long, unmk, pr 300.00
Shakers, chile pepper, short, unmk, pr 300.00
Shakers, grape, purple, bl mk, pr 200.00
Shakers, tomato, ftd, unmk, pr 275.00
Sugar bowl, grapes, purple, bl mk, w/lid 200.00
Sugar bowl, lobster, bl mk, w/lid, lg 175.00
Sugar bowl, poppy, orchid, bl mk, w/lid 275.00
Sugar bowl, poppy, red, bl mk, w/lid 250.00
Teapot, poppy, red, bl mk 350.00
Teapot, poppy, wht MOP, bl mk, rare 475.00
Teapot, tomato, bl mk, lg 275.00
Toothpick holder, elk, bl mk 165.00
Toothpick holder, spiky shell, MOP, bl mk 200.00
Tray, dresser; clown, yel, bl mk 1,850.00
Wall vase, grapes, wht, unmk 350.00

Nursery Rhymes

Bell, Jack & Beanstalk, w/rhyme & clapper, bl mk 350.00
Box, Jack & Jill, bl mk, w/lid 250.00
Coffeepot, Jack & Jill, bl mk 365.00

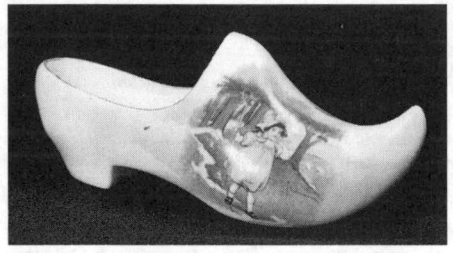

Dutch shoe, Little Bo Peep, blue mark, $375.00.

Leaf dish, Little Jack Horner, bl mk 150.00
Mug, Jack & Beanstalk, w/verse, bl mk, lg 175.00
Mug, Ring Around the Rosies, bl mk 135.00
Pitcher, Little Miss Muffett, bl mk, milk sz 215.00
Pitcher, Miss Muffet w/verse, dbl hdl, bl mk, cream sz 300.00
Plate, Jack & Beanstalk, bl mk, 6" 150.00
Plate, Jack & Jill, bl mk, 6" 150.00
Plate, Little Bo Peep, bl mk, 6¼" 175.00
Sugar bowl, Little Boy Blue, bl mk 215.00
Vase, Babes in Woods, bl mk, 4" 385.00

Scenics and Action Portraits

Ashtray, cockfight, w/stirrup, bl mk 250.00
Box, fox hunt on lid & base, bl mk 175.00
Box, peacock scene, bl mk 145.00
Box, trinket; musicians, bl mk 150.00
Cake plate, Arab scene, bl mk, 10½" 200.00
Candlestick, penguin & stork, yel, scabbard shape, bl mk, 7" 400.00
Charger, goose girl, bl mk, 13" 325.00
Chocolate pot, farm scene w/horses, bl mk 350.00
Cup & saucer, Brittany girl, bl mk 110.00
Cup & saucer, demi; boys & turkeys, unmk 95.00
Humidor, penguin on sides & lid, lime gr, bl mk, 7½" 475.00
Jar, powder; fox hunt, ftd, bl mk, rare 225.00
Jug, fox hunt, bl mk, mini 150.00
Mug, cavalier, 3-hdl, bl mk 75.00
Nappy, girl w/candle, bl mk 75.00

Pitcher, Brittany woman clam digger, bl mk, cream sz, 4½" 65.00
Pitcher, castle scene w/roses, bl mk, cream sz 125.00
Pitcher, cockfight, bl mk, 6" 135.00
Pitcher, farmer & turkeys, bl mk, cream sz 195.00
Pitcher, fisherman, bl mk, milk sz 175.00
Pitcher, goats, bl mk, cream sz 165.00
Pitcher, peasant musicians, bl mk, cider sz, 6½x7¼" 350.00
Pitcher, polar bear, bl mk, water sz, 6¼" 2,800.00
Pitcher, The Hunt, boat shape, bl mk, cream sz 75.00
Pitcher, toasting cavalier, bl mk, cream sz, 4½" 95.00
Pitcher, water at sunset, bl mk, 7" 125.00
Pitcher, woman & sheep, unmk, cream sz 75.00
Plate, hunter w/gun & dog, bl mk, 9" 200.00
Plate, musicians, bl mk, 7½" 65.00
Stein, candle girl, bl mk 165.00
Toothpick holder, colonial couple & dog, rnd, bl mk 150.00
Toothpick holder, Corinthian, blk & wht, bl mk 40.00
Toothpick holder, dogs on moose in water, bl mk 210.00
Toothpick holder, goose girl, 3-hdl, bl mk 200.00
Toothpick holder, penguin, bl mk 175.00
Vase, candle girl, bl mk, 4½" 80.00
Vase, Corinthian, bl mk, 4½" 35.00
Vase, cows & trees, bl mk, 6" 150.00
Vase, dbl bud; woman & sheep, bl mk 70.00
Vase, Dutch children, 4-hdl, unmk, mini 125.00
Vase, fox hunt, bl mk, 3" 175.00
Vase, highland sheep, hdls, bl mk, 4" 125.00
Vase, lady w/horse, cobalt, bl mk, 10" 800.00
Vase, musicians, 3-sided, bl mk, 5½" 135.00
Vase, polar bear, urn shape, bl mk, mini, 4" 3,200.00
Vase, swan, hdls, bl mk, 4½" 265.00
Vase, toasting cavalier, silver rim, bl mk, 3" 125.00

Sunbonnet Babies

Ashtray, laundry, rnd, bl mk 175.00
Bell, sewing, unmk 400.00
Candle holder, fishing, shield bk, bl mk 675.00
Creamer & sugar bowl, bl mk 600.00
Pie plate, bl mk, 6" 150.00
Pitcher, mending, bl mk, cream sz 275.00
Pitcher, sweeping, bl mk, cream sz 275.00
Plate, ironing, bl mk, 6" 175.00
Shoe, fishing, bl mk 700.00
Sugar bowl, fishing, w/lid, bl mk 300.00
Tea tile, bl mk 165.00
Vase, ironing, ruffled top, bl mk, 3⅝" 350.00

Tapestries

Basket, Rose Tapestry, 3-color, bl mk, 4¾x5¼" 395.00
Box, dresser; Rose Tapestry, 3-color, bl mk 350.00
Box, Rose Tapestry, wht, bl mk, 3" 295.00
Creamer, cow, pinched spout, bl mk 265.00
Creamer & sugar bowl, Prince & His Lady, bl mk 550.00
Hair receiver, Rose Tapestry, bl mk 325.00
Hatpin holder, lady w/lg hat, bl mk 750.00
Hatpin holder, violets, bl mk 500.00
Match holder, cavaliers, wall hanging, bl mk 425.00
Match holder, sheep, wall hanging, bl mk, #1059 ....485.00
Mug, Rose Tapestry, 3-color, gold hdl, bl mk, 3⅜" 325.00
Nappy, sheep scenic, cloverleaf, hdld, bl mk 225.00
Pitcher, Rose Tapestry, pk, pinched spout, bl mk, cream sz 350.00
Pitcher, Rose Tapestry, 3-color, corset shape, bl mk, cream sz 325.00

Pitcher, sheep scenic, bl mk, 4" 355.00
Shoe, violets, low style, orig lace, gr mk 650.00
Toothpick holder, castle scene, bl mk, rare 500.00
Tray, Colonial Curtsy, bl mk, 11¾x8¼" 450.00
Tumbler, lake scene w/deer, bl mk 350.00
Vase, The Bathers, bl mk, 8¼" 525.00
Vase, Victorian lady's portrait, bk: landscape, 7" 500.00

Royal Bonn

Royal Bonn is a fine-paste porcelain, ornately decorated with scenes, portraits, or florals. The factory was established in the mid-1800s in Bonn, Germany; however, most pieces found today are from the latter part of the century.

Charger, emb mold, mc irises, sgn, ca 1890 mk, 13" 190.00
Clock, floral w/gold, open escapement, pendulum, 12½x14½" ..1,480.00
Clock, La Cruz, pk & yel floral on porc, Ansonia, 12x9x5", NM ..430.00
Clock, La Normandie, Ansonia, 13½x13x6" 750.00
Clock, La Rambl, lg mc roses, Ansonia, 1885-1895, 12x10", NM ..650.00
Jardiniere, Nouveau florals, sm rpr, 12x20x14" 125.00
Tile, mixed floral on wht w/gold, 1920s, 7" dia 65.00
Umbrella stand, irises & much color, 18" 450.00
Vase, crocus on wht w/gold, hdls, bulbous, 12" 90.00
Vase, pastel floral w/gold, bottle form w/ornate hdls, 23½" 950.00
Vase, purple & yel iris, ornate rim-to-ft hdls, 12½" 140.00
Vase, rose/forget-me-not garlands, emb gold swags, 6½" 325.00
Vase, roses on lt to dk bl, ped ft, 10" 325.00
Vase, Warwick Castle, hdls, ca 1900, 10" 165.00

Royal Copenhagen

The Royal Copenhagen Manufactory was established in Denmark in about 1775 by Frantz Henrich Muller. When bankruptcy threatened in 1779, the Crown took charge. The fine dinnerware and objects of art produced after that time carry the familiar logo, the crown over three wavy lines. For further information we recommend *Royal Copenhagen Porcelain, Animals and Figurines*, by Robert J. Heritage (Schiffer). See also Limited Edition Plates.

Figurines, falcons: #1661, 16", $650.00; #263, 8½", $325.00.

Figurine, Agnate & the Mermaid, #4187, 22½x10" 1,050.00
Figurine, Airedale, #3139, 6x7" 165.00
Figurine, baboon, #2152, 7x5" 265.00
Figurine, barn owls (pr fused), #283, 13½x8" 665.00
Figurine, basset hound, wht w/brn, #4616, 4x6" 195.00
Figurine, blacksmith, #4502, 9x4" 275.00

Figurine, boy at lunch, #865, 4x7" 155.00
Figurine, boy w/teddy bear, #3468, 7x3½" 205.00
Figurine, bull, #1195, 8½x11" 665.00
Figurine, burro w/baskets, #607, 5x6½" 315.00
Figurine, fawn, asleep, #2649, 4½x5½" 195.00
Figurine, fox on hollow mound, #546, 6¼x5" 155.00
Figurine, Giant Panda, #5298, 4½x9" 275.00
Figurine, girl w/butterfly, #1495, 4x4½" 175.00
Figurine, Great Dane, #1679, 4½x9" 225.00
Figurine, hunter on rock, #1087, 8¼x6" 465.00
Figurine, jaguar cub, #4659, 3x8½" 175.00
Figurine, Jersey cow, sitting, #4683, 3½x9" 310.00
Figurine, lynx, #1329, 4½x6¼" 215.00
Figurine, Mandarin duck pr, male & female, #1863, 7½" 415.00
Figurine, Nathan the Wise, #1413, 13½x5¾" 665.00
Figurine, Neptune riding a fish, #2347, 5x5" 315.00
Figurine, Old English Sheepdog, #4952, 8x8" 365.00
Figurine, Pan on tortoise, #858, 4x3½" 76.00
Figurine, Pekingese, snarling, #2565, 7x9" 515.00
Figurine, penguin, #417, 9x5" 225.00
Figurine, perch, #1138, 2x6½" 145.00
Figurine, pheasant, #2394, 8x4" 275.00
Figurine, Pigmy Hippopotamus, #309, 7½x14" 745.00
Figurine, polar bear, #4753, 8x12" 315.00
Figurine, Princess & Hans Clodhopper, #1473, 9x9" 1,075.00
Figurine, Proposal, #1680, 10x5" 485.00
Figurine, schnauzer, #2871, 5¾x3½" 150.00
Figurine, sea lions, #2519, 4¼x4" 145.00
Figurine, Snowy Owl, #1829, 16" 825.00
Figurine, squirrel w/nut, #982, 2½" 65.00
Figurine, tiger, reclining, #714, 5½x12" 365.00
Figurine, vixen w/cubs, #1788, 4¾x5" 275.00
Platter, sm bl floral on wht, 14¼" 125.00
Sauce boat, Flora Danica, 9¼" L 1,225.00
Tureen, sm bl floral on wht, fluted, hdls, 3⅞x12x7¼" 175.00
Vase, snail eyeing clover, ca 1894-1900, 4" 255.00
Vase, 2 swans in flight, pre-1923, 4" 90.00

Royal Copley

Royal Copley is a decorative type of pottery made by the Spaulding China Company in Sebring, Ohio, from 1942 to 1957. They also produced two other major lines — Royal Windsor and Spaulding. Royal Copley was primarily marketed through five-and-ten cent stores; Royal Windsor and Spaulding were sold through department stores, gift shops, and jobbers. Items trimmed in gold are worth 25% to 50% more than the same item with no gold trim.

For more information we recommend *Collector's Guide to Royal Copley Plus Royal Windsor & Spaulding, Books I and II*, by our advisor for this category, Joe Devine; he is listed in the Directory under Iowa.

Ashtray, straw hat w/bow, 5" 25.00
Bank, pig, striped shirt, paper label, 7½", from $65 to 75.00
Bank, rooster, paper label, 7½", from $65 to 75.00
Bank, Teddy bear, paper label, 7½", from $90 to 100.00
Creamer & sugar bowl, leaf hdls, 3" 23.00
Figurine, Blackamoor, paper label, 8½", from $25 to 30.00
Figurine, cat, blk w/pk bow, paper label, 8", from $40 to 45.00
Figurine, cockatoo, 8¼", from $40 to 45.00
Figurine, dog, brn tones w/dk ears, paper label, 8", from $30 to 35.00
Figurine, hen, paper label, 7" 40.00
Figurine, kingfisher, paper label, 5" 45.00
Figurine, lark (skylark), paper label, 6½" 20.00

Figurine, mallard duck, head erect, paper label, 9¼" 45.00
Figurine, swallow w/extended wings, paper label, 7", from $70 to .80.00
Figurine, vireo, paper label, 4½" 15.00
Figurine, wren, paper label, 6¼" 20.00
Pitcher, decal on wht, 6" 16.00
Pitcher, Pome Fruit, cobalt, 8" 62.00
Planter, barefoot boy or girl, paper label, 7½", ea 30.00
Planter, cat & cello, paper label, 7½", from $85 to 95.00
Planter, coach, paper label, 3¼" 18.00
Planter, cockatiel, paper label, 8½", from $45 to 55.00
Planter, cocker spaniel head, 5", from $28 to 30.00
Planter, cocker spaniel w/basket, paper label, 5½", from $20 to 22.00
Planter, dog pulling wagon, paper label, 5¾", from $35 to 40.00
Planter, dogwood, oval, 3½" 15.00
Planter, duck & mailbox, paper label, 6¾", from $65 to 75.00
Planter, duck on stump, paper label, 8" 40.00
Planter, Dutch boy or girl w/bucket, paper label, 6", ea 25.00
Planter, floral arrangement, 3½x7", from $10 to 12.00
Planter, hat w/flowers along band, 7" 45.00
Planter, hummingbird on flower, paper label, 5¼", from $55 to ...65.00
Planter, Indian boy & drum, paper label, 6½", from $20 to 24.00
Planter, kitten & boot, paper label, 7½", from $50 to 55.00
Planter, Oriental boy or girl w/lg vase, paper label, 4¾", ea 15.00
Planter, philodendron, ftd, paper label, 4¼", from $10 to 12.00
Planter, poodle resting, paper label, 6½x8½", from $50 to 60.00
Planter, pouter pigeon, paper label, 5¾", from $20 to 24.00
Planter, tanager on stump, gr stamp, 6¼", from $20 to 25.00
Planter, Teddy bear, blk & wht, paper label, 8", from $90 to 95.00
Planter, Tony, wide-brim hat, mustache, label, 8¼", from $65 to .70.00
Planter, woodpecker beside stump, 6¼", from $21 to 23.00
Vase, Floral Elegance, 8" 26.00
Vase, ivy, ftd, paper label, 7" 12.00
Vase, Lord's Prayer decal, cylindrical, 8" 45.00
Vase, mare & foal, 8½", from $30 to 35.00
Vase, Oriental style, emb dragon, ftd, paper label, 5½" 15.00
Vase, stylized leaf, paper label, 8¼" 11.00
Vase/planter, gazelle, 9" 34.00
Wall pocket, Blackamoor prince, wht turban, 8" 45.00
Wall pocket, girl w/wide-brim hat, 7½" 37.00
Wall pocket, rooster, 6¾", from $40 to 45.00

Royal Crown Derby

The Royal Crown Derby company can trace its origin back to 1848. It first operated under the name of Locker & Co. but by 1859 had became Stevenson, Sharp & Co. Several changes in ownership occurred until 1866 when it became known as the Sampson Hancock Co. The Derby Crown Porcelain Co. Ltd. was formed in 1876, and these companies soon merged. In 1890 they were appointed as a manufacturer for the Queen and began using the name Royal Crown Derby.

In the early years, considerable 'Japan ware' decorated in Imari style, using red, blue, and gold in Oriental patterns was popular. The company excelled in their ability to use gold in the decoration, and some of the best flower painters of all time were employed. Nice vases or plaques signed by any of these artists will bring thousands of dollars: Gregory, Mosley, Rouse, Gresley, and D'esir'e Leroy. We have observed porcelain plaques decorated with flowers signed by Gregory selling at auction for as much as $12,000.00. If you find a signed piece and are not sure of its value, if at all possible, it would be best to have it appraised by someone very knowledgeable regarding current market values.

As is usual among most other English factories, nearly all of the vases produced by Royal Crown Derby came with covers. If they are

missing, deduct 40% to 45%. There are several well illustrated books available from antique booksellers to help you learn to identify this ware. The back stamps used after 1891 will date every piece except dinnerware. The company is still in business, producing outstanding dinnerware and Imari-decorated figures and serving pieces. They also produce custom (one only) sets of table service for the wealthy of the world.

Cup & saucer, Imari, 1932, 2½x3¼", 5½" 100.00
Cup & saucer, Mikado, garden scene 28.00
Figurine, frog, cobalt/gold/rust/wht, bone china, 3¼x4¼" 100.00

Jar, fruits and beading in relief on cream with enamel and gilt flowers, globular, marked, ca 1888, 9", $750.00.

Lighter, Old Imari, Ronson, #1128 ....65.00
Plate, flower bouquet, leaf & scroll border, 10½" 50.00
Plate, Imari, 9½" 82.50
Sugar bowl, Mikado, gold trim, 5¾x3" 28.00

Royal Doulton, Doulton

The range of wares produced by the Doulton Company since its inception in 1815 has been vast and varied. The earliest wares produced in the tiny pottery in Lambeth, England, were salt-glazed pitchers, plain and fancy figural bottles, etc. — all utility-type stoneware geared to the practical needs of everyday living. The original partners, John Doulton and John Watts, saw the potential for success in the manufacture of drain and sewage pipes and during the 1840s concentrated on these highly lucrative types of commercial wares. Watts retired from the company in 1854, and Doulton began experimenting with a more decorative product line. As time went by, many glazes and decorative effects were developed, among them Faience, Impasto, Silicon, Carrara, Marqueterie, Chine, and Rouge Flambe. Tiles and architectural terra cotta were an important part of their manufacture. Late in the 19th century at the original Lambeth location, fine artware was decorated by such notable artists as Hannah and Arthur Barlow, George Tinworth, and J.H. McLennan. Stoneware vases with incised animal drawings, gracefully shaped urns with painted scenes, and cleverly modeled figurines rivaled the best of any competitor.

In 1882 a second factory was built in Burslem which continues even yet to produce the famous figurines, character jugs, series ware, and table services so popular with collectors today. Their Kingsware line, made from 1899 to 1946, featured flasks and flagons with drinking scenes, usually on a brown-glazed ground. Some were limited editions, while others were commemorative and advertising items. The Gibson Girl series, twenty-four plates in all, was introduced in 1901. It was drawn by Charles Dana Gibson and is recognized by its blue and white borders and central illustrations, each scene depicting a humorous or poignant episode in the life of 'The Widow and Her Friends.' Dickensware, produced from 1911 through the early 1940s, featured illustrations by Charles Dickens, with many of his famous characters. The Robin Hood series was introduced in 1914; the Shakespeare series #1, portraying scenes from the Bard's plays, was made from 1914 until World War II. The Shakespeare series #2 ran from 1906 until 1974 and was decorated with featured characters. Nursery Rhymes was a series that was first produced in earthenware in 1930 and later in bone china. In 1933 a line of decorated children's ware, the Bunnykin series, was introduced; it continues to be made to the present day. About 150 'bunny' scenes have been devised, the earliest and most desirable being those signed by the artist Barbara Vernon. Most pieces range in value from $60.00 to $120.00.

Factors contributing to the value of a figurine are age, demand, color, and detail. Those with a limited production run and those signed by the artist or marked 'Potted' (indicating a pre-1939 origin) are also more valuable. After 1920 wares were marked with a lion — with or without a crown — over a circular 'Royal Doulton.' Our advisor for this category is Nicki Budin; she is listed in the Directory under Ohio.

Animals and Birds

Airedale, HN1024, sm 275.00
Boxer, CH Warlord of Mazelain, HN2643, from $145 to 195.00
Bulldog, HN1044 ....350.00
Cairn, begging, HN2589 ....80.00
Cat, HN999, blk & wht 225.00
Cavin Terrier, HN1035 ....125.00
Chow, K-15 ....130.00
Cocker Spaniel, K-9 ....100.00

Ashstead Applause, Collie, HN1058, medium size, 5x7", $175.00.

Dachshund, K-17 ....80.00
Doberman, HN2645, med 165.00
Elephant, HN2644, 5½" 155.00
English Cocker Spaniel, HN1137, med 135.00
English Setter, HN1050, med 165.00
Fox, recumbent, HN147 ....235.00
Hare, recumbent, K-37 ....130.00
Kitten, HN2582 ....90.00
Mallard on rock, HN853 ....285.00
Pekingese, HN1012 ....100.00
Penguin, K22 ....225.00
Penguin & chick, K-20 ....265.00
Persian Cat, HN2539 ....175.00
Piglet, HN2653 ....235.00
Scottish Terrier, K-18 ....125.00
Yellow Bird, HN145 ....265.00

Bunnykins

Beaker, Feeding the Baby/Leapfrog, 2-hdl, sgn Barbara Vernon ...95.00
Beaker, Pressing Trousers/Leapfrog, sgn Barbara Vernon 95.00
Beaker, Windy Day/Broken Umbrella, 1-hdl, special bkstamp 35.00
Beaker pad, Raising Hat 175.00
Bowl, baby's, Greetings, sgn Barbara Vernon, A mk, sm 135.00
Bowl, oatmeal/cereal; Apple Picking 20.00
Bowl, oatmeal/cereal; Bathtime 40.00
Bowl, oatmeal/cereal; Bedtime Story 20.00
Bowl, oatmeal/cereal; Letterbox, sgn Barbara Vernon 50.00

Bowl, oatmeal/cereal; Playing on the River 20.00
Bowl, oatmeal/cereal; Television Time 40.00
Egg cup, Sheltering Under an Umbrella, ca 1937 ....130.00
Figurine, Aerobic Bunnykins 225.00
Figurine, Brownie 65.00
Figurine, Cooling Off, DB3 ....155.00
Figurine, Father 50.00
Figurine, Jockey 250.00
Figurine, Mr Easter Parade 65.00
Figurine, Playtime 65.00
Figurine, Rock & Roll Bunnykins, 1991 ....180.00
Figurine, Santa Bunnykins, DB17 ....45.00
Figurine, Tally Ho!, DB78, 1988 only 175.00
Figurine, Uncle Sam, mc 125.00
Mug, Daisy Chains/Smelling Flowers 35.00
Mug, Disturbing Sleeping Father/Pea Shooter 35.00
Mug, Engine Pulling a Carriage/To the Station 35.00
Mug, Feeding the Baby/Cycling, sgn Barbara Vernon 85.00
Mug, Swinging/Skipping, sgn Barbara Vernon 85.00
Mug, Unravelling Knitting/Trying on Knitting, 2-hdl hug-a-mug 32.00
Mug, Windy Day/Broken Umbrella, 2-hdl hug-a-mug 30.00
Plate, baby's, Baking, Golden Jubilee, w/orig spoon, MIB 65.00
Plate, baby's, Christmas Menu 90.00
Plate, baby's, Game of Golf 100.00
Plate, baby's, Going Shopping, sgn Barbara Vernon, A mk 55.00
Plate, baby's, Orange Vendor, sgn Barbara Vernon 80.00
Plate, Bathtime, 7½" 30.00
Plate, Conducting the Orchestra, sgn Barbara Vernon, 8½" 165.00
Plate, Dressing Up, 7½" 55.00
Plate, Geography Lesson, sgn Barbara Vernon, 8¾" 175.00
Plate, Getting Dressed, sgn Barbara Vernon, 8½" 235.00
Plate, Mrs Moppet's Tea Room, sgn Barbara Vernon, 8½" 165.00
Plate, Orange Vendor, 7½" 55.00
Plate, porridge; Family Cycling 110.00
Plate, porridge; Spring Cleaning 110.00
Plate, Raft, 7½" 55.00
Plate, Ring-A-Ring o' Roses, 7½" 55.00
Plate, Santa Claus, sgn Barbara Vernon, A mk, 7½" 115.00
Plate, See-Saw, 7½" 55.00
Plate, Visiting the Cottage, sgn Barbara Vernon, 7½" 75.00
Plate, Watering the Flowers, 7½" 55.00
Saucer, Chicken Pulling a Cart, sgn Barbara Vernon 75.00
Saucer, Convalescing, sgn Barbara Vernon 45.00
Saucer, fruit; Apple Picking, special bkstamp 55.00
Saucer, fruit; Baking, sgn Barbara Vernon 80.00
Saucer, Going Shopping, sgn Barbara Vernon 60.00
Saucer, Greetings, sgn Barbara Vernon, A mk 170.00
Saucer, Orange Vendor, sgn Barbara Vernon 60.00
Teacup, Family w/Pram/Raising Hat, sgn Barbara Vernon, A mk .75.00
Teacup, Unravelling Knitting/Skipping Game 17.00

Character Jugs

'Ard of 'Earing, D6588 ....1,250.00
'Arrict, D6526, tiny 200.00
'Arry, D6249, mini 100.00
Apothecary, D6574 ....65.00
Auld Mac, D5823, lg 135.00
Beefeater, D6206, lg, gr hdl 140.00
Blacksmith, D6578, sm 65.00
Bootmaker, D6586, mini 65.00
Buz Fuz, D5838, sm 95.00
Cap'n Cuttle, D5842, sm 110.00
Captain Ahab, D6500, lg 120.00

Captain Henry Morgan, D6467, lg	125.00
Captain Hook, D6605, mini	375.00
Cardinal, D6258, tiny	250.00
Cavalier, D6114, lg	145.00
Charles I, lg	375.00
Chelsea Pensioner, lg	155.00
Davy Crockett & Santa Anna, D6729, lg	95.00
Dick Turpin, D5495, mask up, gun hdl, lg	150.00
Dick Whittington, D6375, lg	395.00
Drake, D6115, lg	145.00
Farmer John, D5788, lg	160.00
Farmer John, sm	80.00
Gaoler, D6570, lg	150.00
Gladiator, D6553, sm	350.00
Gondolier, D6592, sm	365.00
Gone Away, D6545, mini	60.00
Granny, D5521, lg, A	100.00
Grant & Lee, D6698	275.00
Guardsman, D6582, mini	65.00
Gulliver, D6563, sm	475.00
Gunsmith, D6573, lg	110.00
Guy Fawkes, Canada Ltd Ed, lg	195.00
Henry Doulton, sm	85.00
Jarge, D6288, lg	350.00
Jester, D4446, sm	125.00
Jimmy Durante, retired	150.00
Jockey, D6625, lg	350.00
Johnny Appleseed, D6372, lg	335.00
Lord Nelson, D6336, lg	375.00
Lumberjack, D6610, lg	115.00
Mad Hatter, D6598, lg	150.00
Mae West, lg	125.00
Mephistopheles (devil), D5757, lg	625.00
Michael Doulton, sm	60.00
Mikado, D6507, sm	325.00
Mine Host, D6513, mini	55.00
Mr Pickwick, D5839, sm	140.00
Night Watchman, D6569, lg	115.00
Old Charlie, D6144, tiny	95.00
Old King Cole, D6036, lg	265.00
Parson Brown, D5486, lg	140.00
Pied Piper, D6514, mini	60.00
Punch & Judy Man, D6593, sm	465.00
Queen Elizabeth/Philip of Spain, sm, pr	195.00
Regency Beau, D6565, mini	650.00
Robin Hood, D6205, plain hdl, lg	165.00
Robinson Crusoe, D6539, sm	65.00
Sairey Gamp, D6045, mini	55.00
Sam Johnson, D6289, lg	335.00

Sam Weller, D6064, lg	165.00
Sancho Panza, D6518, mini	65.00
Santa Claus, D6668, doll hdl, lg	175.00
Scaramouche, D6558, lg	775.00
Simon the Cellarer, D5504, lg	150.00
Simple Simon, D6374, lg	675.00
Smuggler, D6616, lg	120.00
Snaker Charmer, lg	175.00
St George, D6618, lg	295.00
Tam O'Shanter, D6640, mini	60.00
Toby Philpots, D5736, lg	155.00
Tony Weller, D6044, mini	70.00
Touchtone, D5613, lg	275.00
Town Crier, D6544, mini	135.00
Ugly Duchess, D6599, lg	625.00
Veteran Motorist, D6633, lg	135.00
Vicar of Bray, D5615, lg	225.00
Viking, D6526, mini	140.00
Walrus & Carpenter, D6502, sm	75.00
Washington, lg	75.00
WC Fields, D6674, lg	135.00
Yachtsman, D6602, lg	125.00

Figurines

Alice, HN2158	150.00
Alison, HN2326	140.00
Amy, HN3316	550.00
Angela, HN2389	140.00
Anne Boleyn, HN3232	525.00
Antoinette, HN1851, blk base	1,750.00
Bachelor, HN2319	275.00
Barbara, HN1421	1,600.00
Belle, HN2340	90.00
Bluebeard, HN2105, 2nd version	450.00
Boudoir, HN2542	450.00
Camilla, HN1711	1,400.00
Captain Cook, HN2889	345.00
Catherine of Aragon, HN3233	525.00
Centurion, HN2726	250.00
Charlie Chaplin, HN2771	395.00
Chief, HN2892	225.00
Christine, HN1840	1,050.00
Christine, HN2792	265.00
Cinderella, HN3677	350.00
Columbine, HN2738	810.00
Cookie, HN2218	175.00
Countess Spencer, HN3320	425.00
Cup of Tea, HN2322	220.00
Drummer Boy, HN2679	495.00
Fate, HN1782, wall mask, ltd edition, 1935, 10½"	1,850.00
First Waltz, HN2862	225.00
Flower Seller's Children, HN1406, yel	550.00
Geraldine, HN2348	145.00
Gollum, HN2913	160.00
Grand Manner, HN2723	225.00
Granny's Heritage, HN2031	675.00
Greta Garbo, HN1593, wall mask, ca 1935, 7⅝"	500.00
Gwynneth, HN1980	350.00
Harlequin, HN2737	810.00
Heart to Heart, HN2276	395.00
Helmsman, HN2499	225.00
His Royal Highness Prince Philip, HN2386	495.00
Home Again, HN2167	175.00

Sancho Panza, D6456, copyright 1945, large, $145.00.

Huckleberry Finn, HN2927 .... 130.00
Huntsman, HN2492 .... 245.00
Jane, HN2806 .... 195.00
Janet, HN1537 .... 225.00
June, HN1691 .... 900.00
Kate Hardcastle, HN1718 .... 1,175.00
Kate Hardcastle, HN1719 .... 650.00
Lady April, HN1965, gr 925.00
Leading Lady, HN2269 .... 225.00
Lilac Time, HN2137 .... 375.00
Linda, HN2106 .... 140.00
Little Boy Blue, HN2062 .... 150.00
Lynne, HN2329 .... 175.00
Madame Pompadour, HN1817, wall mask, ca 1938, 7¾" 1,100.00
Marlene Dietrich, HN1591, wall mask, 1930s, 8" 300.00
Mary Had a Little Lamb, HN2048 .... 125.00
Memories, HN1856 .... 850.00
Memories, HN2030 .... 425.00
Mendicant, HN1365 .... 225.00
Milkmaid, HN2057 .... 195.00
Minuet, HN2019 .... 265.00
Mirabel, HN1744 .... 1,650.00
Nina, HN2347 .... 185.00
Old King, HN2134 .... 450.00
Owd Willum, HN2042 .... 260.00
Paisley Shawl, HN1988 .... 225.00
Pecksniff, HN1891 .... 395.00
Pecksniff, HN2098 .... 275.00
Phillipine Dancer, HN2439 .... 750.00
Phyllis, HN1420 .... 895.00
Piper, HN2907 .... 250.00
Please Keep Still, HN2967 .... 130.00
Potter, HN1493 .... 495.00
Prince of Edinburgh, HN2386 .... 450.00
Prince of Wales, HN2883 .... 450.00
Priscilla, HN1340 .... 495.00
Priscilla, HN1495 .... 650.00
Professor, HN2281 .... 175.00
Promenade, HN3072 .... 245.00
Quality Street, HN1211 .... 1,750.00
Reverie, HN2306 .... 285.00
Roseanna, HN1926 .... 425.00
Rosebud, HN1983 .... 575.00
Ruth, HN2799 .... 195.00
Sandra, HN2275 .... 180.00
Sara, HN2265 .... 225.00
Soiree, HN2312 .... 175.00
Southern Belle, HN2229 .... 260.00
St Agnes, HN1786, wall mask, ca 1935, 11" 1,000.00
Stayed at Home, HN2207 .... 195.00
Suzette, HN1577 .... 850.00
Suzette, HN2026 .... 400.00
Sweet & 20, HN1610 .... 450.00
Sweet Anne, HN1590, wall mask, ca 1935, 8" 400.00
Sweet 17, HN2734 .... 225.00
Taking Things Easy, HN2680 .... 245.00
Tall Story, HN2248 .... 275.00
Tete A Tete, HN798 .... 2,450.00
Toymaker, HN2250 .... 375.00
Uncle Ned, HN2094 .... 450.00
Viking, HN2375 .... 295.00
Votes for Women, HN2816 .... 275.00
Windflower, HN1763 .... 595.00
Winston Churchill, HN3433, second version 360.00

Wistful, HN2396 .... 235.00

Flambe

Figurine, cat, seated, 11" 250.00
Figurine, Confucious, HN3314, 9" 95.00
Figurine, Dog of Fo, #48 .... 190.00
Figurine, drake, standing, #806, 6" 285.00
Figurine, duck, #112, 1½" 70.00
Figurine, fox, recumbent, #12, 5" 375.00
Figurine, goose, 6⅛" 125.00
Figurine, guinea, #69 .... 595.00
Figurine, guinea hen 595.00
Figurine, hippo, 3¼x6¾" 1,350.00
Figurine, monkeys, pr embracing, #486, 2¾" 365.00
Figurine, rabbit, ears tucked, #43 .... 475.00
Figurine, tiger, slinking, sgn Noke, 9½" 1,150.00
Figurine, tiger, stalking, 6x14" 750.00
Figurine, wizard, #3121, 10" 200.00
Pitcher, mottled red & bl, SP trim, ca 1900, 8¼" 550.00

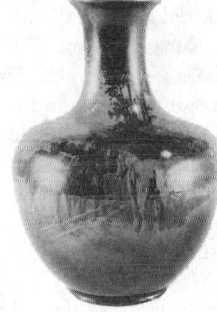

Vase, Sung, farmhouse in landscape, A. Eaton, signed Noke, 13¾", $1,725.00.

Vase, desert landscape silhouette, 7x4¼" 250.00
Vase, landscape, 14x7" 585.00
Vase, landscape scene in underglaze blk, mk, ca 1900, 4¼" 175.00
Vase, red & yel mottle, H Nixon, ca 1930, 6¾" 315.00
Vase, shepherd & sheep landscape, ca 1895, 5¾" 550.00
Vase, veined, bulbous, mid-1900s, 16¾" 775.00

Series Ware

Ashtray, Ships, Trading Ketch, mc, 5¼" sq 78.00
Bowl, Bobby Burns, 7½" 150.00
Bowl, Gypsies, 5" 160.00
Bowl, salad; Bayeux Tapestry, Battle of Hastings, 6" 98.00
Candlestick, King Arthur's Knights, mc, D2961, 1924, 6½" 98.00
Candlestick, Ships, Trading Ketch, mc, 1924, 6½" 110.00
Candlesticks, Woodlands, 7", pr 85.00
Chop plate, Under the Greenwood Tree, 13½" 270.00
Creamer, Nursery Rhymes, Little Man, 1905, 3¼" 98.00
Cup & saucer, Mad Hatter 125.00
Ewer, Babes in Woods, mk, 9" 1,250.00
Fern pot, Dutch People, 5" 110.00
Loving cup, King Arthur's Knights, mc, D2961, 6" 385.00
Mug, King Arthur's Knights, 2 knights, dtd 1921, 5½" 265.00
Nut dish, Dickensware, Sam Weller 50.00
Pitcher, Eglington Tournament, D2792, 13½" 525.00
Pitcher, Egyptian A, blk & wht figures on red, D3619, 7½" 335.00
Pitcher, Jackdaw of Rheims, sgn Noke, D2532, 4" 275.00
Pitcher, Shakespeare, Ophelia, milk sz, 7" 150.00
Pitcher, Shakespeare, Romeo, 4½" 90.00
Plaque, Babes in Woods, girl w/basket, P Jones, 9¾x7¾" 1,525.00

Plate, Australia Gum Trees, Gum Trees & Settlement, mc, 10½" ..75.00
Plate, Australian Views, Aborigines w/Weapons, 10½" 50.00
Plate, Babes in Woods, mk, 10" **450.00**
Plate, Canadian Maple Tree, Rose & Thistle, D4653, 10⅝" 135.00
Plate, Canadian Views, Niagara Falls, D6476, 10½" **75.00**
Plate, Canadian Views, Vermillion Lake & Mt Rundle, 10½" 60.00
Plate, Castles & Churches, Rochester Castle, mc, 10⅜" 85.00
Plate, Castles & Churches, Windsor Castle, litho, 10⅜" 95.00
Plate, Flowers, nasturtiums, D3786, dtd 1915, 8½" 135.00
Plate, Flowers, prunus, pk on dk gr, dtd 1917, 8½" 75.00
Plate, Gibson Girl, 1904, 10½" 130.00
Plate, Gibson Widow & Friends, She Finds Consolation, 10½" .130.00
Plate, Golf, Caddy Blowing Ball, 10" **400.00**
Plate, Gondoliers, lady w/fan & gentleman, D3039, 10½" 165.00
Plate, Home Waters, barges at pier, Grace, 1913, 8¼" 60.00
Plate, Home Waters, sailboats & townscape, Grace, 13" 150.00
Plate, Nautical History B, Sir Francis Drake, D2737, 1907, 8" 50.00
Plate, Old Rustic Inns, Cobham, 10" 60.00
Plate, Professionals, Parson, 1934, 10⅜" 75.00
Plate, Shakespeare, Portia, mc, 7⅜" 80.00
Stein, Night Watchman, front view, D4746, 5" 95.00
Tile, Canterbury Pilgrims 125.00
Toothpick holder, Woodland, mc transfer, D5815, 1938, 2½" ...110.00
Tumbler, Nursery Rhymes, Little Bo Peep 95.00
Vase, Babes in Woods, children in garden, 5½" 650.00
Vase, Babes in Woods, mother & child in snow, mk, 11½" 1,575.00
Vase, Babes in Woods, 2 children look in tree, 10" 750.00
Vase, Rembrandt Ware, oval portrait, A Eaton, ca 1900, 13½" ..1,250.00
Vase, Welsh Ladies, 2 ladies by fence, mk, 3⅜" 120.00

Stoneware

Biscuit jar, cows & sm girls, H Barlow, SP trim, 1878, 6½" 1,750.00
Biscuit jar, geese & grasses, F Barlow, SP trim, 1881, 7" 800.00
Biscuit jar, leaves, SP rim & lid, Lambeth, 1878, 8" 230.00
Candlesticks, foliage, E Simmance, early 1900s, 7⅜", pr 350.00
Crock, utility; mustard yel & beige panels, 1858-90, 6x5" 130.00
Figurine, man clutching robe, sgn Noke, rstr, 1895, 17½" 635.00
Inkwell, baby figural, Suffragette Movement, 1908, 3⅜" 450.00
Jug, Bellarmine-style, salt glaze, orange-peel texture, 10½" 200.00
Jug, monks scenes, Lambeth, 7¾" 115.00
Mug, hunters relief, wht/brn/tan, 3-hdl, dtd 1899, 1⅜" 425.00
Pepper shaker, advertising, brn & tan salt glaze, 4½" 90.00
Pitcher, hunters relief, wht/tan/brn, missing lid, ca 1900, 6" 325.00
Pitcher, lions frieze, Hannah Barlow, 1877, 8⅝" 1,000.00
Pitcher, Victoria, silver lip w/London hallmk, Lambeth, 5¼" 250.00
Vase, Carrara Ware, pk roses, pre-1891, 8⅞" 235.00
Vase, cats band, scroll & leaf border, H Barlow, 1885, 6⅝" 800.00
Vase, deer grazing, leaf & flower border, EE Stormer, 1891, 7" ...700.00
Vase, emb florets, incised foliage, F Butler, 1879, 11" 450.00
Vase, pigs on stippled ground, Hannah Barlow, 1895, 12" 850.00
Watch stand, dragon on fr on bk, sgn, unmk, 19th C, 5⅛" 300.00

Toby Jugs

Best Is None Too Good, D6107 ....445.00
Double XX (Man on Barrel), D6266 ....365.00
Falstaff, D6063 ....95.00
Fat Boy, D6264 ....275.00
Honest Measure, D5108, 4¼" 135.00
Jolly Toby, D6109 ....130.00
Mr Micawber, D6262 ....260.00
Sherlock Holmes, D6661 ....135.00
Winston Churchill, D6172, sm 115.00

Royal Dux

The Duxer Porzellan Manufactur was established by E. Eichler in 1860. Located in what is now Duchcov, Czechoslovakia, the area was known as Dux, Bohemia, until WWI. The war brought about changes in both the style of the ware as well as the mark. Prewar pieces were modeled in the Art Nouveau or Greek Classical manner and marked with 'Bohemia' and a pink triangle containing the letter 'E.' They were usually matt glazed in green, brown, and gold. Better pieces were made of porcelain, while the larger items were of pottery. After the war the ware was marked with the small pink triangle but without the Bohemia designation; 'Made in Czechoslovakia' was added. The style became Art Deco, with cobalt blue a dominant color.

Bust, young woman with flowing hair, hair and bodice strewn with flowers and foliage, ca 1900, marks, 20¾", NM, $3,000.00.

Figurine, bird dog w/pheasant, 20" L 695.00
Figurine, clown playing accordion, bls & grs, 12" 600.00
Figurine, English setter w/game bird in mouth, 6x13" 195.00
Figurine, hound on base, brn on wht oval, 11" L 225.00
Figurine, lady dancing, cobalt gown, gold shoes & trim, 10" 240.00
Figurine, nude sits bkwards on horse, stylized, wht porc, 13" 400.00
Figurine, nude sitting on 1 leg, 2nd up, holds bottle, wht, 8" 300.00
Figurine, Oriental man w/lantern, mc w/gold, mk, 20" 170.00
Flower frog, nude on lotus base, 13" 900.00
Vanity bust, lady w/lg hat looks over shoulder, E Strobach, 6" ...375.00
Vase, floral, pk triangle mk, 12" 285.00

Royal Flemish

Royal Flemish was introduced in the late 1880s and was patented in 1894 by the Mt. Washington Glass Company. Transparent glass was enameled with one or several colors and the surface divided by a network of raised lines suggesting leaded glasswork. Some pieces were further decorated with enameled florals, birds, or Roman coins. Our advisors for this category are Betty and Clarence Maier; they are listed in the Directory under Pennsylvania.

Cracker jar, gold griffin on window panels, SP mts 1,700.00
Cracker jar, Roman coins/tringular panels, metal mts, 8" 2,250.00
Cracker jar, thistles/gold lines on frost, emb mts, sq, 7" 1,750.00
Cracker jar, 4 Roman coins on maroon/rust, rpl lid 1,500.00
Ewer, heraldic band under neck, typical colors/gold flowers, 9½" ..1,200.00
Ewer, rnd-top panels w/gold mums on bl to/lav, 12x5½" 3,000.00
Ewer, St Geo & dragon, rope hdl about neck, flattened sides, 11" .5,500.00
Jar, 4 jeweled butterflies w/bl & purple mums, no lid, 6x6½" ..4,000.00
Tankard, band w/leaves & jewel berries, lines/circles below, 7" .3,050.00
Vase, coat of arms/gold lines, neck w/2 ornate bands, hdl, 12" ..2,000.00
Vase, gold mums/3 jeweled butterflies on frost, 4½x5" 1,300.00
Vase, gold/red raspberries on frost, elongated neck, 10x4" 1,850.00

Vase, jeweled berries, bl w/wine & gold, split-neck hdls, 9" 4,500.00
Vase, owl on branch, gold scrolls, scrolled reed hdls, 9x8" 15,000.00
Vase, pansies/gold sun rays & vines, gold leaf hdls, 5½" 2,000.00
Vase, plants/shellfish/6" fish on bl & gr sections, 14x4½" 13,000.00
Vase, St Geo & dragon, long neck w/hdls, dome lid, 16x8½" ..10,000.00
Vase, violets/scrolls on non-sectioned ground, hdls, 6½x6" 1,050.00
Vase, winged creature, much gold, wine/tan/brn/gr, 14x4½" ...5,000.00
Vase, winged serpent dragon, pinwheel stars, wine/gr, 11x8" ..3,500.00
Vase, 5 snow geese fly over sun on bl/gr/tan, gold stars, 14" 9,000.00

Royal Haeger, Haeger

In 1871 David Henry Haeger, a young son of German immigrants, purchased a brick factory at Dundee, Illinois, and began an association with the ceramic industry that his descendants have pursued to the present time. David's bricks rebuilt Chicago after their great fire in 1871. By 1914 the company had ventured into the field of commercial artware. Vases, figurines, lamp bases, and gift items in pastel matt glazes were marked with the logo of the company name written over the bar of an 'H.' From 1929 to 1933, they produced dinnerware which they marketed through Marshall Fields. Items produced before the mid-'30s are sometimes found with a paper label; such pieces are of special interest. 'Royal Haeger,' their premium line designed in 1938 by Royal Hickman, is highly regarded by collectors today. The mark 'Royal Haeger' (in raised lettering) was used during the '30s and '40s; later a paper label in the shape of a crown was used.

Fast becoming popular is the Earth Graphic Wraps line, first introduced in the mid-'70s. These one-of-a-kind pieces are decorated with raised free-forms on backgrounds of marigold, white, fern, and brown, in both matt and glossy finishes.

The Macomb plant, built in 1939, primarily made vases and planters for the florist trade. A second plant, built there in 1969, produces lamp bases. For more information we recommend *Haeger Potteries Through the Years* by our advisor for this category, David Dilley (L-W Books); he is listed in the Directory under Indiana.

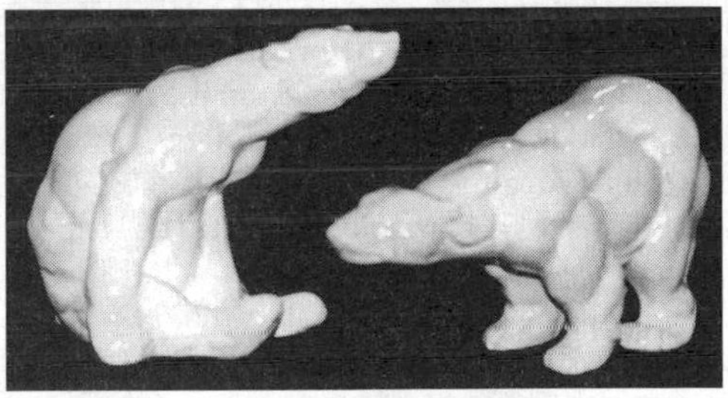

Photo courtesy Barbara and Norman Haas

R-375B (7¼x8½") and R-376B (5½x10"), polar bears, $250.00 minimum value for the pair.

#2058X, ashtray, Earth Graphic Wrap, brn, 6¾" 15.00
#3172X, planter, Earth Graphic Wrap, brn 40.00
#4187, vase, Earth Graphic Wrap, wht, 13" 100.00
#500H, planter, Earth Graphic Wrap, Marigold Agate, 8x12" ...125.00
#8188, pitcher/vase, Earth Graphic Wrap, brn, 9" 65.00
F-17, wild goose, wings up, 6½" 10.00
R-102, rooster, head up, 12" 75.00
R-106, tray, rnd, fluted, 16½" W 30.00
R-1096, Douglas ashtray, 7" 15.00
R-1119, horse planter, 7" 30.00
R-1131, leopard, head turned, tail up, sitting, 8" 75.00
R-1139, wraparound vase, 7" 24.00
R-114, open leaf vase, 9" 40.00
R-1152, golf club ashtray, 5" 15.00
R-1161, window box, 13½" 25.00
R-1170, mask planter, 11" 40.00
R-1181, candle holder, fluted, 3½", ea 15.00
R-1204, leaf bowl, single, 9" 18.00
R-1221, butterfly vase, 7½" 24.00
R-1239, bronco TV planter, 12" 125.00
R-1253, Little Sister, 11½" 25.00
R-1283, fawn ashtray, 8½" 18.00
R-129, bowl, ftd, 14" 24.00
R-1316, dbl-leaf wall pocket, 11½" 45.00
R-1331, greyhound planter, 12" 50.00
R-1337, dbl swirl bowl, 11" 20.00
R-1360, shell bowl, 15" 30.00
R-1375, wicker basket, 12½" 25.00
R-138, leaf vase, single, 12½" 45.00
R-1396, boxer (dog), 11" 75.00
R-141, maple leaf bowl, pointed edges, 14" 45.00
R-1416, planter, oblong, w/stand, 14" 40.00
R-1440, poodle, 8" 75.00
R-1451, rooster vase, 4" 25.00
R-1456, bow tie vase, 3" 25.00
R-1469, feeding bird, 3½" 15.00
R-1493, candle holder, 3-leg, 4", ea 20.00
R-1500, dbl loop vase, modern, 8" 40.00
R-156, angelfish, head up, med, 6½" 50.00
R-158, Inebriated Duck, fallen, 10" 50.00
R-164, pheasant hen, 6" 85.00
R-164-S, dbl wall pocket 65.00
R-171, stallion, head up, 8" 36.00
R-180, Macaw parrot, 14" 200.00
R-206, fish platter, lg, 7" 20.00
R-224, Daisy bowl, 12" 40.00
R-230, cog wheel ashtray, 7" 15.00
R-234, colt, long legs, 12" 150.00
R-271, sailfish vase, 9" 45.00
R-284, trout flower vase, 7" 75.00
R-299, snail shell vase, 11" L 35.00
R-310, swan bowl, lg, 13" L 45.00
R-313 & R-314, panther figures, pr 300.00
R-320, elm leaf vase, 12" 30.00
R-329, conch shell bowl, 7" 45.00
R-347, angelfish planter, w/mermaid on bk, 13", minimum value ...500.00
R-350, pheasants on ped, 14" 40.00
R-36, swan vase, neck down, bill on breast, solid base, 16" 75.00
R-364, flower block, nude w/seal, 13" 125.00
R-370, Dutch cup bowl, 19" 20.00
R-376D, polar bear, standing, 5½" 125.00
R-402, dappled horse, 6" 35.00
R-413, kneeling fawn, 7½" 35.00
R-438, rosebud candle holder, 3½", ea 15.00
R-447, shell ashtray, 4½" 15.00
R-457, 3-leaf dish, w/bird in center, 9"L 40.00
R-479, prospector w/burros, 11½" 150.00
R-488, pillow vase, 7⅛" 35.00
R-495, blk panther, tail curled, 24" 60.00
R-508, dolphin vase, 18" 90.00
R-513, dolphin ashtray, 6" 20.00
R-525, dbl tulip flowerpot, 10" 16.00
R-541, turtle ashtray, 7½" 25.00
R-575, Rose of Sharon basket, 7" 65.00
R-590, Hawaiian candy box, rnd, 2-pc, 8" 50.00
R-631, leopard cigar box, sm, 7" 75.00
R-638, leopard bookend planter, 15", ea 75.00

R-641, stallion bookend/planter, 8½" **40.00**
R-664, polar bear candy box, 7½" **85.00**
R-687, fish cigar box, 4" **40.00**
R-701, seashell vase, 11" **40.00**
R-713, swan vase, 8" **25.00**
R-718, ram head bookends, 5½", pr **75.00**
R-736, dachshund, 14½" **85.00**
R-752, fish planter, 8½" **24.00**
R-758, Egyptian cat **50.00**
R-767, Madonna, from $15 to **20.00**
R-776, sleeping cocker spaniel, 6" **45.00**
R-790, fighting cock, left, 11½" **75.00**
R-808, mountain lion **300.00**
R-831, resting stag planter, 15" **75.00**
R-852, triple ball planter, 11" **30.00**
R-858, snail bowl **16.00**
R-875, colt planter, 14" **150.00**
R-883, dbl racing horse planter, 18" **175.00**
R-901, swordfish vase, 6" **30.00**
R-917, Peter Pan vase, 10" **65.00**
R-947, duckling candle holder, 5" **20.00**
R-957, swan soap dish, 6" **20.00**
R-967, starfish bowl, 14" **75.00**
R-977, shell flower block, 7" **35.00**

Royal Rudolstadt

The hard-paste porcelain that has come to be known as Royal Rudolstadt was produced in Thuringia, Germany, in the early 18th century. Various names and marks have been associated with this pottery. One of the earliest was a hay-fork symbol associated with Johann Frederich von Schwarzburg-Rudolstadt, one of the first founders. Variations, some that included an 'R,' were also used. In 1854 Earnst Bohne produced wares that were marked with an anchor and the letters 'EB.' Examples commonly found today were made during the late 1800s and early 20th century. These are usually marked with an 'RW' within a shield under a crown and the words 'Crown Rudolstadt.' Items marked 'Germany' were made after 1890.

Bowl, mc floral w/gold rim, sgn Hut, 9½" **65.00**
Butter dish, mc floral on wht w/gold, dome lid, ca 1900 ....**85.00**
Celery dish, pk roses, pierced hdls, mk **45.00**
Dresser set, floral, box+hair receiver+hatpin holder+10" tray **200.00**

Ewer, duck in landscape on body, 11", $200.00.

Ewer, fall flowers w/gold on ivory, gr band w/lilac rings, 15" **185.00**
Ewer, floral on wht, ruffled rim, gold hdl, 13½" **175.00**
Ewer, floral w/gold on yel, gold hdl about neck, 10½" **140.00**
Figurine, poodle beside baby on pillow w/gold, 2½x4x4" **75.00**
Lamp, Delft, windmill pnt on globe, 23" **750.00**

Nappy, violets w/gold, gold hdl, 6" **38.00**
Plate, Happifats, 5" **45.00**
Plate, oyster; pastel floral on wht w/gold, ca 1900, 8½" **50.00**
Plate, pk roses on ivory to bl-gray w/gold, 8½" **35.00**
Plate, wht roses on pale lav w/gold, 8½" **35.00**
Plate, 3 roses, gold trim, 6¼" **25.00**
Tray, dresser; lilies on wht w/gold, 16x6¼" **70.00**
Tray, roses w/gold, shamrock shape, 8½" **60.00**
Vase, floral banquets on pk to cream, pierced hdls, 14¼" **395.00**
Vase, floral w/gold on wht, hdls, 8¼" **50.00**
Vase, poppies on brn to gr, yel at ft, rtcl rim, 7x2½" **85.00**

Royal Vienna

In 1719 Claude Innocentius de Paquier established a hard-paste porcelain factory in Vienna where he made highly ornamental wares similar to the type produced at Meissen. Early wares were usually unmarked; but after 1744, when the factory was purchased by the Empress, the Austrian shield (often called 'beehive') was stamped on under the glaze. In the following listings, values are for hand-painted items unless noted otherwise. Decal-decorated items would be considerably lower.

Note: An influx of Japanese reproductions on the market have influenced values to decline on genuine old Royal Vienna. Buyer beware! On new items the beehive mark is over the glaze, the weight of the porcelain is heavier, and the decoration is obviously decaled. Our advisor for this category is Madeleine France; she is listed in the Directory under Florida.

Bowl, wht snowflake carnations on bl-gr w/gold, 10" **150.00**
Box, portrait on cobalt w/much gold, bl mk, 2x4" dia **350.00**
Candlesticks, portraits on maroon w/gold, 5½", pr **700.00**
Charger, 3 maids & Cupid attend lady on dk gr w/gold & jewels, 16" .**2,500.00**
Cup & saucer, Hector, Paris & Flitera on red, sgn Hept **250.00**
Cup & saucer, scene on cobalt w/gold **165.00**
Demitasse pot, ladies in garden, +cr/sug, 4 c/s, 15" tray **995.00**
Mug, Rosina, lady's portrait, sgn Gorref, 2", +bowl saucer **195.00**
Plate, battle scene w/horses, blk-gr rim w/heavy gold, 10" **400.00**
Plate, lady w/rose in hair, gr border w/gold scrolls, 9½" **135.00**
Plate, monk/ldgl window, rim: gilt scenes/scrolls, 9", pr **200.00**
Tazza, monk w/Bible, cobalt/gold scroll rim w/cherubs, 9" **700.00**
Teapot, lovers in reserve on bl w/gold, hdls, late, 17" **525.00**
Urn, 3 ladies on gr w/gold, sgn Noseck, ornate hdls, 15½x6" ..**1,600.00**
Vase, allegorical scene on cobalt, sgn, hdls, w/lid, 14" **1,300.00**
Vase, lady's portrait & flowers on mc, hdls, 8" **200.00**

Roycroft

Near the turn of the century, Elbert Hubbard established the Roycroft Printing Shop in East Aurora, New York. Named in honor of two 17th-century printer-bookbinders, the print shop was just the beginning of a community called Roycroft, which came to be known worldwide. Hubbard became a popular personality of the early 1900s, known for his talents in a variety of areas from writing and lecturing to manufacturing. The Roycroft community became a meeting place for people of various capabilities and included shops for the production of furniture, copper, leather items, and a multitude of other wares which were marked with the Roycroft symbol, an 'R' within a circle below a stylized cross. Hubbard lost his life on the Lusitania in 1915; production in the community continued until the Depression.

Interest is strong in the field of arts and crafts in general and in Roycroft items in particular. Copper items are evaluated to a large extent by the condition and type of the original patina. The most desirable patina is either the dark or medium brown; brass-wash, gunmetal, and silver-wash patinas follow in desirability. The acid-etched patina and the smooth (unhammered) surfaced Roycroft pieces are later (after 1925) developments and tend not to be attractive to collectors. In the listings that follow, values reflect the worth of items in excellent original condition unless otherwise described and marked unless noted to the contrary. Our advisor for this category is Bruce Austin; he is listed in the Directory under New York.

Key: h/cp — hammered copper

Hammered copper vases: Tall shaft with riveted bottom, fine original patina, 11", $1,500.00; Incised florals with trailing stems, #212, fine original patina, 10½", $1,200.00.

Andirons, twists/curlicues, rnd link chain, #9, no mk, 27x13" ...2,400.00
Ashtray, h/cp, imp mk, 4½" dia 90.00
Book, Abe Lincoln & Nancy Hanks, Hubbard, string/rope bound 100.00
Book, Essay on Silence, Hubbard, tooled leather cover, EX 375.00
Bookend, wood w/burned mk, tombstone shape, stepped base, 7x8" ..350.00
Bookends, h/cp, emb peacock on verdigris panel, 4x6" 450.00
Bookends, h/cp, emb/etched sailing ship medallion, rare, 4¾" ...375.00
Bookends, h/cp, half-circle w/circle top, appl loop, 4½" 200.00
Bookends, h/cp, riveted strap w/lines & loose ring, 5x4½" 600.00
Bookends, h/cp, rnd w/tooled owl design, 5x5½" 450.00
Bookends, h/cp, sm tooled flowers in top corners, 4½x5" 450.00
Bookends, h/cp, sq, 1 w/emb floral, 1 open, 8½x6" 475.00
Bookends, h/cp, triangular w/tooled roses in pot, 3½x6½" 300.00
Bookends, h/cp, ½-circle w/repousse poppy etc, #305, 5½" 850.00
Bookmark, fabric w/Roycroft sewn in, bl & wht, 19" 40.00
Bookstand, Little Journeys, keyed-thru tenons, recoated 550.00
Bookstand, wood w/dvtl joints, cvd mk ea end, 4½x5½x18" 900.00
Bowl, fern; h/cp, 3 ball ft, rfn, 3¼x7" 450.00
Bowl, fruit; h/cp, incised trefoils, #810, 3¼x9" 1,000.00
Bowl, h/cp, incurvate, mk, 6" dia 375.00
Bowl, h/cp, Italian polychrome, inset panels w/gr enamel, 4½" ..290.00
Bowl, h/cp, 2½x4½" 250.00
Bowl, h/cp, 5-crimp petal top, 2½x5" 375.00
Box, Goodie, mahog w/copper hinges & hdls, 23" L 900.00
Calendar, 1908, in wood fr, Hunter design, 9x8", VG 1,100.00
Candle holders, h/cp, 3 cups on horizontal bar, 3x8", pr 300.00
Candle sconce, h/cp, flame-shape bk, 8¼x4¾", pr 475.00
Candlesticks, brass-washed h/cp, petal base, pencil std, 8", pr 425.00
Candlesticks, brass-washed h/cp, twisted stems, 13x5", pr 800.00
Candlesticks, h/cp, hollow cylinder shaft, #406, 7x3½", pr 475.00
Candlesticks, h/cp, Princess, 2-strap std, sq base, 7¾", pr 600.00
Candlesticks, h/cp, 2-strap std, sq base, Kipp #403, 8", pr 650.00
Candlesticks, h/cp, 2-strap std on raised sq base, Kipp, 8", pr 600.00
Candlesticks, h/cp, 4 upright riveted straps, curved ft, 12" 1,100.00
Chair, Morris; slide slats, rstr seat/bk, #045 ....7,500.00
Chairs, dining; 2 bk slats, new leather seats, #027, 5 for 7,000.00
Chamberstick, brass-washed h/cp, trumpet ft, hdl, 3½x4½" 175.00

Clown bean bag, in polka-dot outfit, paper tag, 8" 100.00
Crumber set (tray & knife), h/cp, 6x12" 175.00
Desk mat, tooled leather w/leaf border, #2021, 12x18" 1,100.00
Flower holder, h/cp strap holds glass tube insert, 8½" 175.00
Humidor, h/cp, emb trefoil, #626, minor wear, 9½x6¼" 600.00
Incense burner, h/cp, w/box of incense cones 650.00
Inkwell, h/cp, riveted base, glass insert, bell shape 325.00
Inkwell, h/cp, scalloped edge, radial border hammering, 4⅛" 325.00
Inkwell, h/cp, sq, widens at base, 2½x3" 300.00
Lamp, desk; h/cp, 6" helmet shade, flaring ft, rfn, 14" 1,000.00
Lamp, h/cp dome shade, sq std on sq base, 14" 2,500.00
Lamp, h/cp w/brass wash, sm sq red glass 'windows,' 14x9" 3,000.00
Lamp, h/cp 6" dome shade & simple std, 16", VG 600.00
Letter holder, h/cp, lg poppy emb on front, 6x7" 1,100.00
Letter opener, h/cp, bent-up/folded hdl, 8" 110.00
Letter opener, h/cp, curved blade, 9" 100.00
Mat, leather w/tooled design, no mk, 6" sq 250.00
Mat, leather w/tooled design at edge, imp mk, 6" dia 650.00
Mirror, narrow oak fr, no mk, 27½x23½" 300.00
Note pad, Cordova Shops, tooled leather w/'Shopping List' 600.00
Nut bowl set, h/cp, w/matching trays, service for 6 ....900.00
Pen tray, h/cp, hammered design at border, 9½" L 300.00
Pen tray, h/cp, 2 florals ea end, raised bar for pens, 8½" 110.00
Picture fr, oak, cvd orb mk on front, 20x24" 1,200.00
Plate, dinner; gr/brn geometrics & orb mk on wht, set of 6 .....1,600.00
Poker chip set, h/cp & wood, complete w/chips, #1109, 7x4½" ..750.00
Pouch, Spanish steerhide, tooled grapes/leaves, folds, no mk, 6" ...250.00
Scissors holder, leather w/tooled oak leaves/acorns, 4" 110.00
Sconce, h/cp, spade-shaped bks, 8½x3", pr 800.00
Shakers, red/gr geometrics on wht, Buffalo, 3", pr 450.00
Smoke set, h/cp, glass-lined bowl w/rivets, +matchbook, mk 900.00
Table, dining; buttressed split ped, #016, 48" dia, +3 leaves 4,000.00
Table, library; 2-drw, shelf, orig hdw, orb mk, 48" 2,000.00
Table, oak, sq 12" top, flaring legs, wide apron, rfn 850.00
Tray, h/cp, finely detailed border design, 10" dia 400.00
Tray, h/cp, incurvate, shallow, early mk, 5" dia 170.00
Tray, h/cp, recessed center, 6" dia, VG 100.00
Tray, h/cp, rectangular, 7½" 110.00
Vase, Am Beauty, h/cp, long trumpet neck, shouldered, 18" ...1,800.00
Vase, Am Beauty, h/cp, tall cylinder neck, new patina, 21x8" ...1,700.00
Vase, brass-washed h/cp, incurvate, some wear to wash, 4¾" 375.00
Vase, h/cp, appl nickel dbl-band decor, cylindrical, 6" 1,500.00
Vase, h/cp, ovoid, 5¾x2¼" 800.00
Vase, h/cp, rim w/4 leaf-like designs, 8½" 1,200.00
Vase, h/cp, tooled flowers w/gr enamel, cylindrical, 7" 2,100.00
Vase, h/cp, 4 tapered sides, ea w/8 sm cutouts at top, 7" 6,500.00
Vase, h/cp w/silver appl initials, 4½" 150.00
Vase holder, brass-washed h/cp, 4-leaf, #248, Steuben vase, 6" ..750.00
Vase holder, h/cp spiral, rpl insert, #103, 4x2¾" 400.00
Walking stick, wood w/leather strap, burned mk, dtd 1903, 35" .500.00

Rubena

Rubena glass was made by several firms in the late 1800s. It is a blown art glass that shades from clear to red. See also Art Glass Baskets; Cruets; Sugar Shakers; Salts; specific manufacturers.

Butter dish, Invt T'print crystal top/Daisy & Button base, 7" dia ..200.00
Cracker jar, cut fans & strawberries, silver lid, 7x6" 1,150.00
Cracker jar, cut panels, gold florals, silver lid, 6" 200.00
Decanter, Hobnail, tricon rim, clear Hobnail stopper, 12½" 200.00
Jam pot, Swirl, cylindrical w/plain SP lid & hdl, 5½" 165.00
Pickle caster, Invt Baby T'print w/mc florals, SP Derby fr, 11¾" ..400.00

Pitcher, florals, clear reeded hdl, Mt WA, 8x5" 325.00
Pitcher, Hobnail opal, sqd rim, gr hdl, 8" 400.00
Pitcher, Invt T'print, Hobbs Brockunier, 4" 150.00
Pitcher, wht spiral stripes, sq ruffled pleated rim, 8x6½" 275.00
Vase, HP pansies w/gold, ground pontil, 6½" 250.00

Rubena Verde

Rubena Verde glass was introduced in the late 1800s by Hobbs, Brockunier, and Company of Wheeling, West Virginia. Its transparent colors shade from red to green. Our advisor for this category is Mike Roscoe; he is listed in the Directory under Michigan. See also Art Glass Baskets; Cruets; Sugar Shakers; Salts.

Bowl, Hobnail, ruffled, 5" 150.00
Butter dish, vaseline knob & underplate, 7" dia 650.00
Celery vase, Invt T'print, 6" 235.00
Cracker jar, lg daisies, beaded bail, floral-emb lid, 8" 300.00
Cruet, Invt T'print, ball or tepee, ea 485.00
Vase, floral, sq fluted top, 6x3" 150.00
Vase, jack-in-the-pulpit 135.00

Ruby Glass

Produced for over one hundred years by every glasshouse of note in this country, ruby glass has been used to create decorative items such as one might find in gift shops, utilitarian bottles and kitchenware, figurines, and dinnerware lines such as were popular in the Depression era. For further information and study, we recommend *Ruby Glass of the 20th Century* by our advisor, Naomi Over; she is listed in the Directory under Colorado.

Bank, owl figural, Anchor Hocking, 1981, 7" 165.00
Basket, Daisy & Button, oval, Fenton 18.00
Bonbon, crimped, 7¼" 27.50
Bottle, beer; Royal Ruby, Anchor Hocking, 1950, 32-oz 32.00
Bowl, cereal; Old Cafe, Anchor Hocking, 1940s, 5½" 14.00
Bowl, scalloped, 4-toed, Cambridge, 6" 66.00
Cake plate, Sandwich, Indiana, 1960s-70s, 13" 95.00
Candlestick, swan neck, Viking, 6¼" 27.50
Candlesticks, metal stem, 8½", pr 110.00
Comport bonbon, Dmn Optic, #1502, 7½" 42.50
Console set, Tiara's Sunset Leaf, Indiana, bowl+pr 5" sticks 50.00
Cup, measuring; 16-oz 32.00
Cup & saucer, sq, Anchor Hocking, 1950s 10.00
Figurine, bird, Swedish Glass, 4" 17.50
Lamp, fairy; Sweetheart, LG Wright, 1974-81, 4½" 35.00
Marmalade, Eyewinker, LG Wright, 1974-81, 8¾" 35.00
Nappy, Royal Ruby, Anchor Hocking, 6½" 9.00
Paperweight, pear, Viking, 8½" 45.00
Pickle dish, Anchor Hocking, 1940s, 6" 17.50
Pickle dish, Royal Ruby, Anchor Hocking, 1940s, 7" 20.00
Pie shell, Pyrex, 9½" 55.00
Pitcher, High Point, Anchor Hocking, 1940s, 80-oz 50.00
Pitcher, reeded, Imperial, 80-oz 110.00
Plate, Oyster & Pearl, Anchor Hocking, 13½" 45.00
Plate, Royal Ruby, Anchor Hocking, 9" 9.00
Saucer, American, McBeth-Evans, 1930-36, scarce 28.00
Sherbet, plain stem, Anchor Hocking, ca 1942 ....7.50
Tumbler, Hobnail, Anchor Hocking, 1930s, 4½" 10.00
Vase, Hoover, Anchor Hocking, 9" 22.00
Vase, Rachel, Anchor Hocking, 1940s, 10" 45.00

Vase, Swirl cornucopia, Duncan & Miller, #121, 14" 150.00

Ruby-Stained Glass

Ruby-flashed or ruby-stained glass was made through the application of a thin layer of color over clear. It was used in the manufacture of some early pressed tableware and from the Victorian era well into the 20th century. These items were often engraved on the spot with the date, location, and buyer's name.

Souvenir toothpick holders: Button Arches, $26.00; Truncated Cube, dated 1896, $45.00.

Bowl, berry; Ruby T'print, boat shape, master+4 sm ind 160.00
Creamer, Buttons & Arches, 1907 souvenir, 2½" 22.50
Match holder, Button Arches 15.00
Mug, Bordered Elipse, 3⅛" 32.00
Mug, Button Arches, child sz 35.00
Mug, Lacy Medallion, 1900, 3¾" 30.00
Mug, Scalloped Daisy, 1918, 2½" 27.50
Pitcher, Button Arches, Pan Am Expo 155.00
Punch cup, Masonic Temple 1893, 2¾" 27.50
Spooner, Button Arches, Asbury Park 1900, 4" 32.50
Toothpick holder, Beaded Swag, inscr, dtd 1908, 2" 27.50
Tumbler, Button Arches, from $30 to 40.00
Wine, Button Arches 36.00

Rugs, Hooked

Hooked rugs are treasured today for their folk-art appeal. Rug making was a craft that was introduced to this country in about 1830 and flourished its best in the New England states. The prime consideration when evaluating one of these rugs is not age but artistic appeal. Scenes with animals, buildings, and people; patriotic designs; or whimsical themes are preferred. Those with finely conceived designs, great imagination, interesting color use, etc., demand higher prices. Condition is, of course, also a factor. Marked examples bearing the stamps of 'Frost and Co.,' 'Abenakee,' 'C.R.,' and 'Ouia' are highly prized. Note: the rugs listed here are made of rag unless noted otherwise. See also Orientalia, Rugs.

Cat sits on checked rug, mc w/blk border, braided edge, 35x23" ..1,450.00
Cottage scene, mc, ca 1936, 37x36", EX 300.00
Cow in landscape w/foliage, 6-color, lt damage, 25x38" 600.00
Fishscale design, red/gr/blk, lt wear, prof rpr, 31x63" 770.00
Floral, leaf & boteh, mc on ecru, New England, 1800s, 74x44" ...4,600.00
Floral w/geometric border, mc on ecru, Am, 19th C, 64x35" ..2,875.00
Flower, red w/gr leaves on tan w/brn mottled border, 66x33" ..1,000.00
Flower basket on tan, bl/gr/blk borders, Boston, 37x30" 350.00
Flowers & vines, mc on gr w/gold & ivory, 40x28", EX 350.00
Foliate medallions, mc on gray, early 1900s, 21½x80⅜" 485.00
Geometric sqs, gray/purple/charcoal/lt brn/blk, 1880s, 30x31" ..1,265.00

Grenfell, dog sled underway, label, 19x32", VG 925.00
Grenfell, 2 people w/dog sled, label, 27x39" 2,185.00
Hen & rooster w/7 eggs in nest, 19th C, 24x41" 9,200.00
Horse in landscape, mc borders, 29x50", EX 1,800.00
Pointer, blk/brn dog on mc geometric ground, dtd 1901, 30x35" 4,140.00
Roses & tulips, mc on tan, Waldaboro style, 54x28½", EX 800.00
Sailing scene on brn w/mc border, 39x53" 650.00
Stage cartouch, mc on raspberry red, early 1900s, 24x35" 490.00
Urn of flowers, mc on gray w/blk border, semicircular, 40x23" ...220.00

RumRill

George Rumrill designed and marketed his pottery designs from 1933 until his death in 1942. During this period of time, four different companies produced his works. Today the most popular designs are those made by the Red Wing Stoneware Company from 1933 until 1936 and Red Wing Potteries from 1936 until early 1938. Some of these lines include Trumpet Flower, Classic, Manhattan, and Athena, the Nudes.

For a period of months in 1938, Shawnee took over the production of RumRill pottery. This relationship ended abruptly, and the Florence Pottery took over and produced his wares until the plant burned down. The final producer was Gonder. Pieces from each individual pottery are easily recognized by their designs, glazes, and/or signatures. It is interesting to note that the same designs were produced by all three companies. They may be marked RumRill or with the name of the specific company that made them. You will find information on RumRill in these books: *Red Wing Art Pottery, Books I and II,* by B.L. and R.L. Dollen (Collector Books). Our advisors for this category are Wendy and Leo Frese; they are listed in the Directory under Texas.

Vase, #630, Dutch Blue, 7",
from $95.00 to $110.00.

Ball jug, #547, brn & orange, 7" 51.00
Ball jug, #547, orange 47.00
Bowl, #274, deep bl (rare color) 75.00
Bowl, #311-7, cream matt 65.00
Bowl, #445, bl-gr w/tan highlights, Sylvan design, 4x8½" 65.00
Bowl, #448, wht, scalloped rim 75.00
Bowl, console; #414 ....65.00
Bowl, console; #571, Athena, lt bl, nude hdls, 11", minimum 500.00
Candle holder, #597, wht 55.00
Ewer, #184, Indian, brn/orange mottle, 7" 50.00
Figurine, #B11, upright bird, semi-matt wht 40.00
Flower frog, #563, Athena, wht, NM 850.00
Pitcher, #547, gr mottle, ball shape 75.00
Pitcher, #565, orange w/wht int, wood hdl, NM 50.00
Planter, #277, lt bl 30.00
Planter, log form 55.00
Vase, #H-54, gr drip glaze 45.00
Vase, #H-67, Dutch Blue, 9" 22.50

Vase, #183, Grecian, Lilac (violet/gr blend), 8" 75.00
Vase, #215, elephant hdls, bl circle stamp, 6" 125.00
Vase, #291, 6" 55.00
Vase, #300, Fluted, Dutch Blue, 8½" 75.00
Vase, #320, Fluted, Goldenrod (gr over pumpkin), 5½" 50.00
Vase, #367, tan-gr 50.00
Vase, #507, speckled orange over ivory glaze, 7½" 90.00
Vase, #514, yel w/Seafoam White int 65.00
Vase, #558, bl, 3" 35.00
Vase, #587, gr 56.00
Vase, #637, Dutch Blue 67.00
Vase, #663, Neoclassic, Seafoam White w/lt gr int, 8" 250.00
Vase, #697, Neoclassic, slate bl, 7½" 150.00
Vase, #706, yel, 2-hdl 35.00

Ruskin

This English pottery operated near Birmingham from 1989 until 1935. Its founder was W. Howson Taylor, and it was named in honor of the renowned author and critic, John Ruskin. The earliest marks were 'Taylor' in block letters and the initials 'WHT,' the smaller W and H superimposed over the larger T. Later marks included the Ruskin name.

Bowl, red/purple/gray hi-glaze, mks, 1924, 1½x5" 100.00
Bowl vase, lt bl/purple/cream/gr mottle, mks, 1909, 3" 325.00
Pedestal, red/purple/gray hi-glaze, mks, 2½x4" 300.00
Vase, bl crystalline on tan/orange/mint gr, mks, 1932, 5½" 475.00
Vase, blk/gr/tan mottled hi-glaze, gourd shape, mks, 1906, 7" 650.00
Vase, cream & bl crystalline, gourd shape, mks, 1930, 5" 210.00
Vase, lt bl irid lustre w/mc highlights, shouldered, 1925, 8½" ...300.00
Vase, lt bl irid w/mc highlights, mks, 1914, 8½", EX 170.00
Vase, mc mottle hi-glaze (very fine), mks, 1910, 6¼" 850.00
Vase, pk & cream mottle, gourd shape, mk, no date, 7" 280.00
Vase, purple/wht/bl mottle, flared cylinder, mks, 1921, 8" 500.00
Vase, purple/wht/dk gr hi-glaze (fine), mks, ?? date, 7½" 750.00
Vase, red & wht hi-glaze, mks, 1922, 9½", EX 400.00
Vase, red/wht/gray hi-glaze, mks, 1932, 8", +3½x6" ped 900.00
Vase, red/wht/purple hi-glaze, 1 angle hdl, mks, 1933, 8½" 300.00
Vase, wht & purple hi-glaze, flared cylinder, mks, 1923, 7½" ...450.00
Vase, yel lustre, mks, 1916, 14", NM 325.00

Russel Wright Dinnerware

Russel Wright, one of America's foremost industrial designers, also designed several lines of ceramic dinnerware, glassware, and aluminum ware that are now highly sought-after collectibles. His most popular dinnerware then and with today's collectors, American Modern, was manufactured by the Steubenville Pottery Company from 1939 until 1959. It was produced in a variety of solid colors in assortments chosen to stay attune with the times. Casual (his first line sturdy enough to be guaranteed against breakage for ten years from date of purchase) is relatively easy to find today — simply because it has held up so well. During the years of its production, the Casual line was constantly being restyled, some items as many as five times. Early examples were heavily mottled, while later pieces were smoothly glazed and sometimes patterned. The ware was marked with Wright's signature and 'China by Iroquois.' It was marketed in fine department stores throughout the country. After 1950 the line was marked 'Iroquois China by Russel Wright.' For those wanting to learn more about the subject, we recommend *The Collector's Encyclopedia of Russel Wright, Second Edition,* by our advisor, Ann Kerr. She is listed in the Directory under Ohio.

American Modern

To calculate values for American Modern, double the values listed for these colors: Canteloupe, Glacier Blue, Bean Brown, and White. Chartreuse is represented by the low end of our range; Cedar, Black Chutney, and Seafoam by the high end; and Coral and Gray near the middle.

Bowl, lug soup; from $15 to **20.00**
Bowl, salad; from $100 to **165.00**
Bowl, vegetable; from $20 to **25.00**
Butter dish, w/lid, from $250 to **275.00**
Carafe (jug), from $250 to **300.00**
Coaster, from $20 to **30.00**
Coffee cup cover, from $175 to **200.00**
Coffeepot, 8½", from $200 to **300.00**
Hostess set w/cup, from $125 to **150.00**
Ice box jar, w/lid, from $200 to **250.00**
Plate, dinner; 10", from $10 to **12.00**
Plate, 8", from $12 to **15.00**
Relish, divided, from $200 to **225.00**
Salad fork & spoon set, from $150 to **175.00**
Sauce boat, from $35 to **50.00**
Saucer, from $3 to **4.00**
Stack server, from $250 to **300.00**
Sugar bowl, from $15 to **20.00**
Teapot, wht, 10", rare, from $200 to **215.00**
Tumbler, child's, from $95 to **135.00**

Casual

To price Brick Red, Aqua, and Canteloupe, double our values; for Avacado, use the low end of the range. Oyster and Charcoal are valued at 50% more than the prices listed.

Bowl, cereal; 5", from $12 to **15.00**
Bowl, gumbo soup; 11½-oz, from $35 to **50.00**
Bowl, vegetable; open, 36-oz, 8⅛", from $30 to **50.00**
Butter dish, ¼-lb, from $250 to **350.00**
Carafe, wine/coffee; from $225 to **300.00**
Casserole, 2-qt, 8", from $40 to **60.00**
Casserole, 3-qt, rare, from $175 to **185.00**
Coffeepot, AD; w/lid, from $100 to **200.00**
Coffeepot, w/lid, from $150 to **300.00**
Creamer, stacking; from $15 to **18.00**
Gravy boat w/attached tray, from $165 to **200.00**
Mug (orig), 13-oz, from $95 to **165.00**
Pepper mill, from $200 to **225.00**
Pitcher, redesigned, from $200 to **300.00**
Plate, bread & butter; 6½", from $5 to **8.00**
Plate, dinner; 10", from $10 to **12.00**
Platter, ind, 10¼", from $75 to **100.00**
Shakers, stacking; from $20 to **25.00**
Teapot, restyled, from $200 to **300.00**

Glass

Unless otherwise described, values are given for glassware in Coral and Seafoam; other colors are 10% to 15% less.

Bartlett Collins, cocktail, 3", from $12 to **15.00**
Bartlett Collins, shot glass, 2", from $20 to **25.00**
Bartlett Collins, Zombie, from $25 to **30.00**
Imperial Flair, tumbler, iced tea; 14-oz, from $65 to **70.00**
Imperial Flair, tumbler, juice; 6-oz, from $50 to **75.00**

Imperial Flair, tumbler, water; 11-oz, from $65 to **70.00**
Imperial Pinch, tumbler, iced tea; 14-oz, from $50 to **75.00**
Imperial Pinch, tumbler, juice; 6-oz, from $45 to **60.00**
Imperial Pinch, tumbler, water; 11-oz, from $50 to **65.00**
Imperial Twist, old fashioned, from $65 to **85.00**
Imperial Twist, tumbler, iced tea; from $60 to **75.00**
Imperial Twist, tumbler, juice; from $45 to **60.00**
Old Morgantown/Modern, cocktail, 3-oz, 2½", from $30 to **50.00**
Old Morgantown/Modern, cordial, 2-oz, 2", from $50 to **75.00**
Old Morgantown/Modern, dessert dish, 2x4", from $50 to **75.00**
Old Morgantown/Modern, tumbler, iced tea; 5¼", from $40 to **60.00**
Old Morgantown/Modern, tumbler, juice; 8-oz, 3¾", from $30 to **40.00**
Old Morgantown/Modern, tumbler, water; 12-oz, 4½", from $40 to .**50.00**
Snow Glass, saucer, from $100 to **150.00**
Snow Glass, tumbler, water; 10-oz, from $200 to **300.00**

Highlight

Bowl, cereal or soup; 2 sizes, ea, from $50 to **100.00**
Bowl, vegetable; rnd, from $100 to **150.00**
Creamer, from $50 to **100.00**
Cup, from $25 to **50.00**
Plate, bread & butter; from $10 to **15.00**
Plate, dinner; $25 to **30.00**
Platter, oval, lg, from $75 to **125.00**
Platter, oval, sm, from $50 to **75.00**
Platter, rnd, sm, from $60 to **70.00**
Shakers, 2 szs, pr, from $75 to **125.00**

Spun Aluminum

Russel Wright's aluminum ware may not have been especially well accepted in its day — it tended to damage easily and seems to have had only limited market appeal — but today's collectors feel quite differently about it, as is apparent in the suggested values noted in the following listings.

Bain Marie server, from $400 to **500.00**
Beverage set, from $400 to **500.00**
Bowl, fruit; rattan hdl, from $150 to **175.00**
Bun warmer, from $100 to **150.00**
Cheese knife, from $100 to **125.00**
Flower ring, from $150 to **175.00**
Ice fork, from $75 to **100.00**
Peanut scoop, from $100 to **115.00**
Pitcher, rnd hdl, from $175 to **200.00**
Relish, w/glass inserts & ice-pool bottom, from $200 to **225.00**
Relish rosette, lg, from $200 to **300.00**
Sandwich humidor, from $125 to **150.00**
Tea set, from $500 to **700.00**
Tidbit tray, 2-tier, from $150 to **200.00**
Vase, rnd ball, lg, from $200 to **225.00**

Sterling

Ashtray, from $100 to **125.00**
Bouillon, 7-oz, from $15 to **20.00**
Bowl, salad; 52-oz, 10", from $14 to **35.00**
Celery, 11¼", from $30 to **35.00**
Creamer, ind; 3-oz, from $15 to **18.00**
Fruit, 5", from $10 to **12.00**
Plate, luncheon; 9", from $10 to **12.00**
Plate, salad; 7½", from $10 to **12.00**
Platter, oval, 13⅝", from $30 to **35.00**
Relish, divided, 16½", from $75 to **100.00**

Sauce boat, 9-oz, from $30 to 50.00
Sugar bowl, w/lid, 10-oz, from $25 to 40.00
Teapot, 10-oz, rare, from $150 to 250.00

Miscellaneous

Bauer, ash bowl, 5½", from $500 to 1,000.00
Bauer, corsage vase, 5", from $500 to 1,000.00
Bauer, flowerpot, 4½", from $350 to 750.00
Bauer, pillow vase, from $750 to 1,000.00
Country Garden, bread tray, from $200 to 250.00
Country Garden, creamer, from $75 to 100.00
Country Garden, ladle, from $150 to 175.00
Country Garden, patterned items, no established value
Country Garden, pitcher, 5-cup, from $300 to 325.00
Country Garden, platter, from $150 to 175.00
Country Garden, skillet server, from $250 to 300.00
Country Garden, sugar bowl, from $250 to 300.00
Flair, bowl, vegetable; oval, shallow, from $15 to 20.00
Flair, platter, #710, from $20 to 25.00
Harker White Clover, ashtray, decorated, from $50 to 65.00
Harker White Clover, cup, from $12 to 15.00
Harker White Clover, gravy, from $40 to 50.00
Harker White Clover, plate, dinner; 9¼", from $14 to 16.00
Home Decorator, bowl, vegetable; from $18 to 20.00
Home Decorator, cup, from $8 to 10.00
Home Decorator, plate, dinner; from $10 to 12.00
Home Decorator, plate, salad; from $10 to 12.00
Ideal Adult Kitchen Ware, bowl, leftover; w/lid, from $25 to 30.00
Ideal Adult Kitchen Ware, dish, salad/dessert; from $10 to 15.00
Ideal Adult Kitchen Ware, tumbler, 2 szs, ea, from $20 to 25.00
Ideal Children's Toy Dishes, boxed set, from $150 to 250.00
Ideal Children's Toy Dishes, place setting items, ea, from $10 to .15.00
Knowles Esquire, bowl, divided; from $65 to 100.00
Knowles Esquire, bowl, fruit; 5½", from $10 to 12.00
Knowles Esquire, centerpiece server, from $150 to 175.00
Knowles Esquire, plate, dinner; from $15 to 20.00
Knowles Esquire, platter, oval, 13", from $25 to 45.00
Linens, matkin, w/label 25.00
Linens, napkin, w/label 15.00
Linens, tablecloth, w/label, 54x78", from $125 to 150.00
Meladur, bowl, cereal; from $10 to 12.00
Meladur, plate, dessert; 6¼", from $8 to 10.00
Oceana serving item, leaf relish tray, from $800 to 900.00
Oceana serving item, relish, 1-hdl, from $700 to 800.00
Oceana serving item, salad bowl, fluted, from $700 to 800.00
Oceana serving item, snail relish, lg, from $800 to 850.00
Oceana serving item, wave salad bowl, from $700 to 800.00
Pinch cutlery, fork, from $75 to 85.00
Pinch cutlery, knife, from $100 to 150.00
Pinch cutlery, knife (orig), from $100 to 125.00
Pinch cutlery, serving pcs, ea, from $125 to 150.00
Residential, bowl, divided vegetable; from $30 to 50.00
Residential, sugar bowl, w/lid, from $15 to 20.00
Theme Formal, bowl, from $150 to 165.00
Theme Formal, coffeepot, no established value
Theme Formal, cup & saucer, no established value
Theme Formal, plate, dinner; 10", no established value
Theme Formal glassware, cordial, 3-oz, from $175 to 260.00
Theme Formal glassware, goblet, 8-oz, 5", from $200 to 225.00
Theme Formal lacquerware, bowl, rice; from $300 to 325.00
Theme Formal lacquerware, plate, from $175 to 200.00
Theme Informal, mug, from $125 to 150.00
Theme Informal, rice bowl, from $250 to 275.00

Russian Art

Before the Revolution in 1917, many jewelers and craftsmen created exquisite marvels of their arts, distinctive in the extravagant detail of their enamel work, jeweled inlays, and use of precious metals. These treasures aptly symbolized the glitter and the romance of the glorious days under the reign of the Tsars of Imperial Russia. The most famous of these master jewelers was Carl Faberge (1852 – 1920), goldsmith to the Romanovs. Following the tradition of his father, he took over the Faberge workshop in 1870. Eventually Faberge employed more than five hundred assistants and set up workshops in Moscow, Kiev, and London as well as in St. Petersburg. His specialties were enamel work, clockwork automated figures, carved animal and human figures of precious or semiprecious stones, cigarette cases, small boxes, scent flasks, and his best-known creations, the Imperial Easter Eggs — each of an entirely different design. By the turn of the century, his influence had spread to other countries, and his work was revered by royalty and the very wealthy. The onset of the war marked the end of the era. Very little of his work remains on the market, and items that are available are very expensive. But several of his contemporaries were goldsmiths whose work can be equally enchanting. Among them are Klingert, Ovchinnikov, Smirnov, Ruckert, Loriye, Cheryatov, Kuzmichev, Nevalainen, Adler, Sbitnev, Third Artel, Wakewa, Holmstrom, Britzin, Wigstrom, Orlov, Nichols, and Plincke. Most of them produced excellent pieces similar to those made by Faberge between 1880 and 1910.

Perhaps the most important bronze Russian artist was Eugenie Alexandrovich Lanceray (1847 – 87). From 1875 until 1887, he modeled many equestrian groups of falconers and soldiers ranging in height from about 20" to 30". Some of them bear the Chopin foundry mark; they are presently worth from $4,000.00 up. Other excellent artists were Schmidt Felling (19th century), who specialized in mounted figures of cossacks wearing military uniforms, and Nicholas Leiberich (late 19th century), who also specialized in equestrian groups. Most of the pieces made by the above artists were signed and had the foundry mark (Chopin, Woerfell, etc.).

Russian porcelain is another field where Imperial connections have undoubtedly added to the interest of collectors and museums worldwide. The most important factories were Imperial Russian Porcelain, St. Petersburg (or Petrograd or Leningrad, 1744 – 1917); Gardner, Moscow (1765 – 1872); Kuznetsoff, St. Petersburg and Moscow (1800 – 1900); Korniloff, St. Petersburg (1800 – 1900); and Babunin, St. Petersburg (1800 – 1900).

Icon, Christ Enthroned, 17th century, 45x35", $14,950.00.

Photo courtesy Jackson's Auctioneers and Appraisers

Angel, cast bronze, 16th C, 3¼x1¾" 625.00
Badge, silvered bronze, Nicholas Military Imperial Academy 290.00
Box, florals/scrolls/dots, mc pnt on silver, mk 84/mask, 7" L 900.00

Box, silver & mc enamel, hinged lid, 1900s, 2" dia 450.00
Box, silver & mc enamel, St Petersburg, ca 1900, 2½" dia 625.00
Box, silver w/gold-wash int, dome top, dtd 1889, 4¾" L 250.00
Case, cigarette; silver, peasant scene, cabochon thumbpc, 1900s ..425.00
Case, cigarette; silver, 2 swans on lid, Moscow, ca 1908, 4¼" 550.00
Champagne, silver, chased cone on dome base, Moscow, 1900, 8" ..450.00
Cross, altar; mc cloisonne enamel, 2-pc, 19th C, 12x7" 650.00
Cross, baptismal; gold & enamel, Save & Protect, Imperial, 2¼" ...200.00
Cross, baptismal; silver-gilt, Let God..., 17th C, 2¼"+chain ...1,250.00
Cross, Encolpion; bronze, 16th C, 3¾x2¼" 1,250.00
Cross, pectoral; cast bronze w/enamel, 18th C, 6½x3¾" 225.00
Cup & saucer, floral w/gold on wht china, 19th C, mk 100.00
Cup & saucer, silver, eng cottage scene, Baskakov, ca 1890 ....550.00
Cup holder, enameled silver, mk 84 KC, 4¾" 775.00
Egg, cobalt glass w/silver o/l, St Petersburg, 2-part, 3¼" 185.00
Icon, Almighty, 1600s, school of Ushakov, 13x10" 4,700.00
Icon, Ascension of Lord, 1800s, 16th-C style, 21x17¾" 2,200.00
Icon, Blessed Silence, cast bronze w/mc enamel, 19th C, 5x6" ...400.00
Icon, Feodoruvskaya Mother of God, gilt bronze, 18th C, 4x3" ...300.00
Icon, Head of John the Baptist, fine/rare cvg, 18th C, 13½x8" ..1,000.00
Icon, John the Theologian, Palekh school, ca 1900, 12x14½" ...2,500.00
Icon, Joy to All Who Sorrow, cast bronze triptych, 18th C, 5x4" ...225.00
Icon, Kazan Mother of God, Holy Polyect borders, 19th C, 33x28" ..2,000.00
Icon, Lord Almighty, o/l w/SP metal riza, 1800s, 12x10½" 220.00
Icon, November, saints depicted, late 1800s, 19x15" 1,300.00
Icon, Passion, on rnd wood panel, 1800s, 14" dia 300.00
Icon, Pokrov, cast bronze, 17th C, rare, 5¼x3" 400.00
Icon, Sleeping Virgin, bl/gr/wht/yel enamels, ca 1800 ....3,000.00
Icon, St George, cast bronze, 18th C, 4x2¾" 400.00
Icon, St Helen, SP metal riza w/3 red stones, 1800s, 13x11" 880.00
Icon, St Sergius of Radonezh w/Saints, bronze, 19th C, 5½x4¾" ..425.00
Incensor, repousse/chased SP 2-pc orb on 3 ball ft, 18th C, 8" ...500.00
Jar, mushroom; majolica, yel basket, mushroom finial, 1889, lg ..250.00
Kovsh, enamel on silver, mk 84 MC, eng initials, 4½" 1,380.00
Medal, bronze, 300 Yrs Romanov Rule 100.00
Napkin rings, silver & enamel, hallmk 84, ca 1908, 12 for 2,000.00
Plate, dinner; dbl eagle on wht porc, 1918 era 115.00
Postcard, Tsar Nicolas photograph 100.00
Purse, silver, eng & appl gold monograms, Fontikov, 1808, 8½" ...850.00
Salt cellar, enamel on silver, mk 84 AA HC, ca 1889, w/spoon .150.00
Salt cellar, gilt metal w/mc enamel, hallmks, ca 1940, 1¼x1¾" .110.00
Salt cellar, silver, 3-ball ft, hallmk Moscow/1890, 2" 100.00
Salt cellar, silver w/mc enamel, SK (Kazakou), 3 ball ft, 1½" 200.00
Shot glass, silver, eng, ftd, hallmk Moscow, 1896, 4" 165.00
Spoon, enamel on silver, mk 88 AA, ca 1891, 5" 125.00
Spoon, Russian Othodox ceremonial; gold-plated, chased, 1794 ..275.00
Spoon, silver & neillo, SAS/Moscow, 1863, 6¾" 100.00
Spoon, silver w/bl & wht enamel, Miliukov, tea sz 135.00
Spoon, silver-gilt & neillo, M Ch, hallmk Moscow, 1847 ....450.00
Sugar scoop, silver-gilt & mc enamel, Klingert, ca 1900, 4¼" 325.00

Sabino

Sabino art glass was produced by Marius-Ernest Sabino in France during the 1920s and '30s. It was made in opalescent, frosted, and colored glass and was designed to reflect the Art Deco style of that era. In 1960, using molds he modeled by hand, Sabino once again began to produce art glass using a special formula he himself developed that was characterized by a golden opalescence. Although the family continued to produce glassware for export after his death in 1971, they were never able to duplicate Sabino's formula.

Blotter, 3 flags & shield, brass parts to hold paper, 3½" 250.00

Bottle, lappet leaves on wht opal sphere, w/stopper, mk, 5¼" 175.00
Bottle, perfume; draped nudes on sides, pineapple stopper, 4" ...140.00
Bottle, scent; Petalia, overlapping petals, bud stopper, 5½x3" 85.00
Bowl, Roman scenes in relief, blk-pnt ground, mk, 1930, 4½x9½" .4,000.00
Box, 3 mermaids/ocean waves on lid, silk-covered base, 9" 1,500.00
Dish, seaweed design, smoky gray, 3-ft, 4x1" 56.00
Figurine, butterfly, open wings, opal, 2⅝" H 56.00
Figurine, Capelan fish, opal, 1 of 6 in series, 2¾", MIB 40.00
Figurine, cat, opal, head turned to left, sm version, 1¾" 51.00
Figurine, cherub, 2" 40.00
Figurine, clustered snail shells, opal, 4x2" 110.00
Figurine, Egyptian Goddess, opal, 5" on ⅞" base 160.00
Figurine, elephant w/raised trunk, opal, 2¼" 57.00
Figurine, flying bird, opal, sgn base, 1¼x2¾" 60.00
Figurine, Madonna, Sabino Paris & paper label, 5" 125.00
Figurine, nude silhouette, 1 hand over head, opal, 7" 270.00
Figurine, rabbit, crouched, opal, 1⅞x1⅜" 48.00
Figurine, snail, opal, 3x1¾" 48.00
Figurine, squirrel, 3" 65.00
Figurine, stork/heron, opal, 8" 315.00
Figurine, tropical fish, 4¾" 110.00
Knife rest, frog & bull (from fable), 1½x4" dia 50.00
Lamp, mushroom; mc streaks in base, 11" dia shade, 21" 640.00
Lamp, opal globe, bronze base, frosted shade, 6½x5½" dia 495.00
Mask, Triton, 10½x15" 2,500.00
Paperweight, fisherman sits by tree, opal, sgn, 4½x1¾" 66.00
Paperweight, hunter, 2 sided w/rabbit & pheasant, 1¼x2" 54.00
Vase, bumblebees on honeycomb & floral lattice, 7x7" 460.00
Vase, gold-amber, flared trumpet form, mk, 6" 260.00
Vase, La Danse, 14x8⅝" 1,525.00
Vase, La Ronde, 10½x6½" 3,200.00
Vase, Ovale Deux Femmes, 7x9½" 3,050.00

Salesman's Samples and Patent Models

Salesman's samples and patent models are often mistaken for toys or homemade folk art pieces. They are instead actual working models made by very skilled craftsmen who worked as model-makers. Patent models were made until the early 1900s. After that, the patent office no longer required a model to grant a patent. The name of the inventor or the model-maker and the date it was built is sometimes noted on the patent model. Salesman's samples were occasionally made by model-makers, but often they were assembled by an employee of the company. These usually carried advertising messages to boost the sale of the product. Though they are still in use today, the most desirable examples date from the 1800s to about 1945.

Many small stoves are incorrectly termed a 'salesman's sample'; remember that no matter how detailed one may be, it must be considered a toy unless accompanied by a carrying case, the indisputable mark of a salesman's sample.

Tractor model, clockwork driven, aluminum, white metal and brass, Unique Time Saving Tractor Patent Pending, 27", with fitted wooden case, $2,700.00.

Alligator anchor, brass, wings fold out at top, Pat 91, 4¾" 150.00
Bed, 4-post w/inlaid curved headboard, 10x10½x6½" 95.00
Book, advertising blotters, 200 mc illus of 1926 blotters 125.00
Bottle, baby's, Evenflo, glass, 3½" 30.00
Box of artist's paints, fitted int, wood w/brass mts, 5x13" 200.00
Fire extinguishers, glass, in metal holder, wood case: 11" L 275.00
Golf bag, brn & wht simulated alligator skin, 1950s, 13", M ...285.00
Horse collar 125.00
Knife, hunting; Puma logo, clip-point blade, 20¾" L+holder ..1,950.00
Ladder, metal & wood, 46", extended: 72", VG 140.00
Oil salesman's sample case, 7 bottles w/cork tops, 13x9x2" 285.00
Sawmill, wooden w/early red, iron gears/etc, 19th C, 19" L 500.00
Shoe, Red Cross, boy's 35.00
Steam engine, 1 vertical piston w/beam, lg flywheel, 15x8½" 495.00
Tin container, Axtell Grease, Standard Oil 95.00

Salt Glaze

As early as the 1600s, potters used common salt to glaze their stoneware. This was accomplished by heating the salt and introducing it into the kiln at maximum temperature. The resulting gray-white glaze was a thin, pitted surface that resembles the peel of an orange.

Bottle, floral branches, garlic neck, ovoid, ca 1750, 8⅜" 1,035.00
Bowl, mc birds & vines, ca 1760, rpr, 8⅞" 1,150.00
Coffee cup, mythical beasts/etc in panels, ca 1750s, 2¾" 500.00
Coffeepot, mc floral on pear shape, 1750s, rstr, 3" 1,850.00
Jug, cream; mc floral landscape on pear shape, 2⅞" 920.00
Jug, cream; mythical beasts/etc, rstr, ca 1750s, 6" 1,035.00
Jug, peony/fence/willow on pear shape, ca 1760, rstr, 5¼" 2,400.00
Mug, mc floral on bbl form, 1750s, 2½", EX 500.00
Plate, King of Prussia, eagle & bust portrait, 1756, 9¼" 635.00
Plate, mc floral landscape, emb flower/vine border, 1860s, 9¼" .490.00
Plate, mc nymph scene, sgn P Visseur 1769, emb rim, 9⅝" 4,300.00
Platter, flared vignettes, cut corners, ca 1755, 9¾x9¾" 750.00
Sauce boat, mask & paw ft, shells/flowers/etc, bl wash, 1750, 6" ..545.00
Stand, pierced/tapering base, ca 1755, mini, 1⅛x2¼" dia 230.00
Teapot, appl flowers, bird finial, 3 mask & claw ft, 1740s, 3⅝" ..865.00
Teapot, engine-trn bands to collar & base, 1750s, mini, 2⅝" 460.00
Teapot, Frederick King of Prussia mc portrait, 1760, 3¼", NM .5,750.00
Teapot, mask head spout, lion finial, dragon hdl, ca 1740, 5½" .1,380.00
Teapot, mc floral, crab-stock hdl, globular, 1765, 3¾" 975.00
Teapot, mc floral & vines, globular, ca 1760, rstr, 3½" 515.00
Toddy dipper, punched spout, tapered stem, 1750s, 1⅝" 1,100.00
Tumbler, floral decor, scratch bl, 1750s, 3" 920.00
Vase, campana form, mask-head hdls, trn banding, ca 1750, 6¾" .1,350.00
Wall pocket, flowering tree in pot relief, ca 1760, rstr, 8¾" 1,100.00

Salt Shakers

The screw-top salt shaker was invented by John Mason in 1858. Around 1871 when salt became more refined, some ceramic shakers were molded with perforated tops.

Today's Victorian glass salt shaker collectors' interests primarily encompass art glass of all types and colored glass, with preference given to hand-painted cranberry and ruby glass forms. Also, examples in rubena, opalescent, and custard glass are very desirable in both decorated and undecorated styles.

If you would like to learn more about Victorian glass salt shakers, we recommend *The World of Salt Shakers, Second and Third Editions*, written by Mildred and Ralph Lechner; their address may be found in the Directory under Virginia. (Mildred and Ralph deal only in Victorian glass shakers. Please do not contact them with questions pertaining to novelty types; **written queries require a long self-addressed stamped envelope.**) Values listed are for old, original shakers in excellent condition unless otherwise noted in the description.

Ribbed Barrel Burmese, hand decorated, original two-piece metal lids, Mt. Washington/Pairpoint, ca 1886 – 90, $1,200.00 for the pair.

Photo courtesy Mildred and Ralph Lechner

Arched Plumes, wht opaque w/HP floral & gold, ca 1899-1905, 3¼" .20.00
Aster & Leaf, emerald gr, ca 1895, 3" 100.00
Baby Optic Rib, clear w/HP floral, ca 1893-97, 2x1¾" 90.00
Bead & Panel, gr opal, 6-sided, 1901-03, 3" 95.00
Beaded Belt, wht opalware, waisted form, ca 1899-1907, 2¼" 35.00
Box-in-Box, ruby stain, ca 1894, 2⅞" 65.00
Bulb, Stretched; bl w/HP rose-bud branches, 1887-94, 3¼" 180.00
Butterfly & Tassel, bl opaque, ca 1894-1900, 3" 40.00
Cactus (Fenton), vaseline, 1959-63, 2⅞" 30.00
Columbia, Tarentum's; clear, ca 1898-99, 2⅝" 16.00
Cord & Pleat, cobalt, ca 1896-99, 2½" 70.00
Corn, pk (triple cased), ca 1894-1901, 3⅛" 140.00
Cylinder, Optic Honeycomb; bl/ma, sq shoulders, 1886-95, 2¾" ..150.00
Dewdrop, vaseline opal, short/bulbous, 1965-69, 2¾" 25.00
Diamond, Pressed; vaseline, cylinder, Central Glass, 1885-91, 2¾" ...80.00
Diamond Cork, reverse amberina, 2-pc top, 1884-87, 2⅝" 240.00
Douglas, ruby stain w/etch fleur-de-lis & stars, ca 1903, 2⅞" 40.00
Fancy Heart, gr opaque, step ft, 1859-903, 2⅞" 110.00
Feather Band (Wreath), clear, ca 1910, 3½x2⅜" 20.00
Fleur-de-Lis, Petite; wht opal, ca 1898-1904, 2⅛" 16.00
Forget-Me-Not, butterscotch opaque, 1886-91, 2" 110.00
Franklin Panel, wht opal, 6 vertical ribs, ca 1900-10, 4" 15.00
Harbor Light, wht opal, rnd bulging base, ca 1930-40, 5½" 32.00
Honeycomb, Large; amethyst, ca 1889-96, 3⅛" 90.00
Ice Cube, wht opal w/HP floral, ca 1896-1904, 2⅛x1⅞" 40.00
Ivy Scroll (Jefferson), bl w/gold leaves, 1900-05, 2¾" 140.00
Jefferson Optic, clear electric bl w/HP floral, 1905-10, 2⅞" 110.00
Lorraine (Flat Diamond Box), ruby stain, ca 1893, 3⅛" 65.00
Louisiana, clear, ca 1898, 2⅝x1¾" 35.00
Mary Ann, clear w/HP Cupid & flowers, silver top, 1897-1905, 2½" ..85.00
Net & Scroll, gr opaque, ca 1894-1900, 2⅞x2⅛" 50.00
Optic Treasure, amber w/HP floral, ca 1887-91, 3⅞" 85.00
Paneled Prism, bl w/wht speckles, 1887-90, 2¾x1½" 165.00
Panelled Holly, wht opal, pr 170.00
Peg Leg, Round; bl opaque, bulbous, 1894-1901, 2¼" 55.00
Reverse Swirl, bl opaque & wht spatter, ca 1888-90, 2½" 85.00
Rib, Optic 8; olive-amber w/HP floral, 2-pc top, 1887-92, 3⅝" ..215.00
Ridge Swirl, cobalt, ca 1900, 3x1⅝" 40.00
Seaweed, vaseline opal, 1890s, 3" 85.00
Spirea Band, bl opaque opaline, ftd cylinder, ca 1891, 3⅞" 80.00
Staggered Beads, amber, pillar shape, ca 1903-14, 2⅝" 30.00
Swirl, blk opaque, ca 1954, silver-tone plastic top, 1954, 2⅛" 12.00
Synora Lace, opalware, ca 1901, 3¼x2¾" 20.00
Teardrop, clear, ca 1899, 3¼x1⅞" 27.50
Thousand Eye, Ringed Center; vaseline, ca 1878-88, 3⅛" 75.00

Tulip Spray, wht opaque, ca 1899-1910, 3⅛x2½" **20.00**
Wheat Sheaf, emb Near Cut on inside bottom, ca 1910-20, 2¾" .**20.00**
Zippered Block, ruby stain, ca 1887, 2⅞x1½" **65.00**

Novelty Salt Shakers

Those interested in novelty shakers will enjoy *Salt and Pepper Shakers, Volumes I, II, III,* and *IV,* by Helene Guarnaccia, and *The Collector's Encyclopedia of Salt and Pepper Shakers, Figural and Novelty, Volumes I* and *II,* by Melva Davern. Both are available at your local library or from Collector Books. Note: 'Mini' shakers are no taller than 2". Instead of having a cork, the user was directed to 'use tape to cover hole.' Our advisor for novelty salt shakers is Judy Posner; she is listed in the Directory under Pennsylvania. See also Regal; Rosemeade; Occupied Japan; Shawnee; other specific manufacturers.

Advertising, Bert & Harry, blk suits, Piels Beer, 1950s, 4", pr **195.00**
Advertising, Campbell Kids, plastic, F&F, 4½", pr **70.00**
Advertising, Chicken of Sea Tuna, Am pottery, pr **25.00**
Advertising, Esso/Esso Extra gas pumps, EX, pr **40.00**
Advertising, Firestone US Rubber, tire shape, EX, pr **65.00**
Advertising, Greyhound, metal bus shape, EX, pr **100.00**
Advertising, Ken L Ration cat & dog, plastic, F&F, 1950s, pr **28.00**
Advertising, Seagrams 7, plastic, 1950s, 3¾", pr **35.00**
Advertising, Smokey Bear (fat), H-475 mk, 3¾", pr **125.00**
Advertising, Sunshine Bakers, pnt porc, Japan, 2¾", pr **29.00**
Advertising, Tappan Chefs, Japan, 4¼", pr **25.00**
Animals, alligators, shiny, EX pnt details, 2½", pr **18.00**
Animals, cats on 8 balls, Japan (unmk), 4", pr **35.00**
Animals, dinosaurs, Japan, 1950s, 3½", pr **65.00**
Animals, lambs, shiny, Napco label, 3", pr **22.00**
Animals, monkey couple, fancy clothes, Japan, 2¾", pr **25.00**
Animals, pups (stacking), dressed up, vintage import, pr **50.00**
Animals, rabbit couple, he w/razor, she w/mirror, Japan, 5", pr **65.00**
Animals, rabbits, wht porc, EX details, Nanco label, 4", pr **28.00**
Animals, rainbow trout, shiny porc, realistic, 5¼", pr **24.00**
Animals, sea horses, Leyden Arts, California, 4¼", pr **28.00**
Animals, skunks, shiny, Japan, 2¾", pr **24.00**
Animals, skunks w/flowers, holes in eyes & nose, Japan, 2¾", pr ..**24.00**
Anthropomorphic, candy cane men, Japan label, 4¾", pr **50.00**
Anthropomorphic, spoon & fork people, Japan, 5", pr **35.00**
Character, Ben Franklin & scroll, Parkcraft series, pr **28.00**
Character, Donald & Daisy Duck, shaking hands, Japan, 4", pr **45.00**
Character, Donald Duck, Dan Brechner...WD-32 1961, pr **195.00**
Character, Dumbo in flight, late 1940s, 1¾", pr **85.00**
Character, Ferdinand, cold pnt, unmk, 3½", NM **85.00**
Character, Goofy in car, pnt bsk, Japan, 1930s, 4x4", pr **350.00**
Character, Grumpy & Sneezy, Tokyo Disneyland, 1980s, 3½", pr ...**125.00**
Character, Humpty Dumpty, unmk Am, 2½x2¾", pr **45.00**
Character, JFK in rocker, Japan, Arrow 1962 NYC, pr **65.00**
Character, Kayo & Moon Mullins, pnt chalkware, 3", NM **60.00**
Character, Mickey Mouse as chef, Japan, WDP, 2¾", pr **28.00**
Character, Old King Cole & fiddler, majolica type, Japan, pr **45.00**
Character, Pebbles & Bamm-Bamm, Harry James, 4", pr **65.00**
Character, Pinocchio, pnt porc w/gold, 1940s, 5", pr **165.00**
Character, pixies, Elbee Art, 3", pr **18.00**
Character, Pluto w/bone (w/cup & saucer), cold pnt, 3¼", pr **125.00**
Character, scarecrow couple, Am pottery, 3", pr **28.00**
Character, Snow White, Japan, 1930s, pr **150.00**
Character, Tinker Bell, porc bell shape, Disneyland, pr **50.00**
Character, White Rabbit w/heart pendant, Japan, 3½", pr **89.00**
Character, Woody Woodpecker & Winny, W Lantz 1990, pr **95.00**
Character, Yosemite Sam, Lego label, 1960s, pr **150.00**
Character, Zodiac Girl (single), red Japan stamp, 4½" **55.00**

Comic, gr smiley faces, Have a Happy Day, TreasureCraft, pr **30.00**
Comic, happy smiley ft, unmk, 1960s, 3½", pr **22.00**
Comic, monks, shiny porc, gr #s on bases, 3½", pr **22.00**
Comic, outhouse couple, Japan label, 1950s, 4½", pr **45.00**
Inanimate objects, barns, Twin Winton, 4¼", pr **39.00**
Inanimate objects, fireplace & logs, unglazed bottom, 2½", pr **18.00**
Inanimate objects, golf bag & ball, H-151, Japan label, pr **24.00**
Inanimate objects, golf bag & ball, unmk, bag: 3¼", pr **22.00**
Inanimate objects, gun & bullet, unmk, vintage, 4" L, pr **24.00**
Mini, paint can & brush, 1950s, can: 1½", pr **24.00**
Mini, pillow on bed, unglazed bottom, unmk, 2" W, pr **22.00**
Nodder, elephant w/clown & pup, Pat TT, 5", pr **395.00**
Nodder, Indian couple in emb drum base, Japan, 4½", pr **80.00**
Nodder, 4-eyed man & woman in bbl, Pat TT, 3¾", pr **95.00**
People, caveman & wife, mc ceramic, unmk, 4", pr **59.00**
People, child in top hat (stacks), red Japan mk, 5", pr **45.00**
People, children under mushroom, Japan label, 3½", pr **24.00**
People, Colonial couple, Japan, 3½", pr **17.00**
People, Eskimos, Napco International Kissers series, pr **24.00**
People, lady in swimsuit on alligator, Japan, 4¼x5" **65.00**
People, soldier & princess embrace, red Japan mk, 3¼", pr **32.00**
People, sq dance couple, interlocking, unmk, 4¼", pr **28.00**
People, Strasburg railroad engineer & conductor, Japan, 4¼", pr .**35.00**
Souvenir, Hawaii suitcases, unmk (att TreasureCraft), 2¼", pr **24.00**
Souvenir, PA Turnpike, 3-pc metal chromolitho set **35.00**

Salts, Open

Before salt became refined, processed, and free-flowing as we know it today, it was necessary to serve it in a salt cellar. An innovation of the early 1800s, the master salt was placed by the host and passed from person to person. Smaller individual salts were a part of each place setting. A small silver spoon was used to sprinkle it onto the food.

If you would like to learn more about the subject of salts, we recommend *5,000 Open Salts,* written by William Heacock and Patricia Johnson, with many full-color illustrations and current values. Our advisor for this category is Chris Christensen; he is listed in the Directory under California. In the listings below, the numbers refer to *Open Salts* by Johnson and Heacock and *Pressed Glass Salt Dishes* by L.W. and D.B. Neal. Lines with 'repro' within the description reflect values for reproduced salts.

Key:
EPNS — electroplated nickel silver   HM — hallmarked

Animals, Figurals, and Novelties

Bird & Berry, colors, mk Degenhart, HJ-932, minimum value **25.00**
Bird & Berry, colors, unmk Degenhart, HJ-933, minimum value .**15.00**
Chicken, covered, milk glass, Westmoreland, HJ-949, M **18.00**
Squirrel on stump, various colors, sgn Boyd, HJ-929, repro **10.00**

Squirrel on stump, amber glass, HJ-4671, $85.00.

Swan pulling cart, caramel, St Clair, HJ-941, repro 35.00
Wheelbarrow, bl, Greentown, HJ-4669, M 200.00
Wheelbarrow, sgn St Clair, repro, minimum value 20.00

Art Glass

Crown Milano, HJ-46, M 175.00
Daum Nancy, flowers, mk, HJ-11 ....1,200.00
Daum Nancy, winter scene, sgn 1,400.00
Le Gras, sterling base, sgn, HJ-12, M 1,100.00
Monot Stumpf, HJ-19 to HJ-22, M, ea 100.00
Quezal, sgn, HJ-18, 1" dia, M 275.00
Tiffany, ruffled, sgn LCT Favrile, HJ-32, M 200.00
Webb, cranberry, acorn design, HJ-84, M 1,200.00

China and Porcelain

KPM, dbl, boy between 2 bowls, HJ-1155 or HJ-1156, M, ea 300.00
KPM, dbl, w/cherub, mk, HJ-1107, M 300.00
Lenox, silver o/l, HJ-1815, M 60.00
Limoges, HP, mk, HJ-1275 ....15.00
Meissen, sq, HJ-1595, ind, M 60.00
Nippon, HP buckets, HJ-1446 to HJ-1457, ind, M, ea 15.00
Pickard, sq, HJ-1569, M 65.00
Royal Bayreuth, claw, HJ-1667, ind 95.00
Royal Bayreuth, sheep, ped ft, HJ-1666, M 125.00
Royal Bayreuth, Sunbonnet Babies, M 200.00
Royal Copenhagen, oval, HJ-1672, ca 1920, M 45.00

Cut Glass

Amethyst, etched, Hawkes, HJ-2038, M 75.00
Bl cut to clear, ped ft, HJ-67, M 150.00
Clear, etched, rnd, Hawkes, HJ-3268 to HJ-3269, M, ea 35.00
Clear, ped ft, mk Libbey, HJ-2995, M 35.00
Heart, club, spade, diamond, HJ-3033 to HJ-3035, M, 4 for 200.00
Waterford, sgn, HJ-3459, not old, ind, M 20.00
Zippered, HJ-3088-3089, M 15.00

Lacy Glass

Barlow/Kaiser #1450, clear, Lyre or Harp, prof rpr 35.00
Neal BF-1F, opal, sm edge chips, underfilled, rare, 3" 350.00
Neal BF-1F, violet-bl opaque, rpr 300.00
Neal BS-2, opal, Beaded Scroll, Sandwich, NM 350.00
Neal BS-3, med bl opaque w/lt mottling, lt roughness 1,000.00
Neal BT-3, Lafayette boat, purple-bl opal, NM 1,500.00
Neal CD-2, scrolled sides & legs, w/lid, EX 800.00
Neal CD-2A, lt roughness 1,900.00
Neal CN-1B, fiery opal, Crown, Sandwich, NM 400.00
Neal DD-1, sm chip/roughness, extremely rare 650.00
Neal EE-3B, Dbl Eagle, deep fiery opal, EX 950.00
Neal EE-3B, Dbl Eagle, wht (chalk) opaque, mold roughness .1,300.00
Neal EE-7, shallow spall 250.00
Neal EE-8A, 3 eagles around sides, 1 in base, VG 450.00
Neal GA-3, Gothic Arch, Pittsburgh area, EX 110.00
Neal HN-11, med amber, French, minor edge chips, rare, 3" 250.00
Neal JY-2, wear/minor flakes, rare, 3" 100.00
Neal LE-2, lyre, med bl, minor roughness 850.00
Neal LE-3, peacock bl, sm crack 425.00
Neal NE-1, fiery opal, New England, NM 350.00
Neal NE-1A, wht opaque, New England, NM 200.00
Neal OL-14, med amethyst, NM 450.00
Neal OL-32, chip 160.00

Neal OL-34, Philadelphia area, NM 110.00
Neal OO-5, lt roughness 375.00
Neal OP-17, lt bl mottling, sm spall 800.00
Neal PO-4, Peacock Eye, peacock bl, flake 1,100.00
Neal PP-3, Peacock Eye, opaque violet, ped ft, 2x3", NM 2,500.00
Neal RD-12A, nick 70.00
Neal RD-22, moderate roughness 225.00
Neal RP-3, silver opaque bl, lt mottling 350.00
Neal RP-9, lt amethyst, 2", NM 1,300.00
Neal SC-2, moderate roughness 200.00
Neal SL-1, dk gr, roughness 325.00
Neal SL-14, purple-bl, roughness 400.00
Neal WN-1A, extremely rare, roughness 350.00

Pottery and Faience

Niloak, rnd, mk, HJ-1735, 1½", M 75.00
Quimper, dbl, w/dog or pig, HJ-1134, M 100.00
Royal Doulton, HM, emb animals, HJ-1859, M 75.00
Staffordshire, bl on tan, ped ft, HJ-4577, ca 1850, M 125.00
Staffordshire, Toby, w/pepper, mc, old, (+), 5¼", M, set 350.00
Wedgwood, chariots, gr & wht, sgn HM, M 225.00

Pressed Pattern Glass, Clear

Apollo, HJ-3576, master, M 30.00
Atlas, HJ-2933, ind, M 15.00
Beaded Grape Medallion, HJ-2522, ind, M 25.00
Bryce Bros #900, HJ-2800, ind, M 10.00
Cobb, HJ-2803, ind, M 10.00
Cordova, HJ-3057, ind, M 15.00
Early American Sandwich, w/saucer, Duncan, HJ-2687, M 25.00
Empress, HJ-2938, ind, M 40.00
Eureka, HJ-3611, master, M 30.00
Fine Cut & Block, HJ-2100, M 30.00
Liberty Bell, HJ-2689, ind, M 65.00
Ovoid Panels, HJ-3531, master, M 30.00
Pillow, Heisey, HJ-2697, ind, M 45.00
Prismatic, HJ-2671, ind, M 10.00
Puritan, HJ-2804, ind, M 8.00
Spiral Flutes, HJ-3549, master, M 15.00
Tree of Life, 'Salt,' ped ft, HJ-3581, M 110.00
3 Face, HJ-4430 to HJ-4431, ind, repro, M, ea 15.00

Pressed Pattern Glass, Colored

Bagware, bl, amber, or vaseline, HJ-449, ind, M, ea 20.00
Big Pansy, gold trim, HJ-153, repro 30.00
Candlewick, cranberry flashed, HJ-285, ind, M 30.00
Dewdrop, amber, HJ-513, ind, M 35.00
Fostoria #95, gr, HJ-333, M 30.00
Grape Leaf, gr, Fostoria, HJ-415, ca 1940, M 30.00
Lords & Ladies, vaseline or opal, English, HJ-137, M, ea 75.00
Maple Leaf (Leaf & Rib), bl or amber, HJ-435, ind, M, ea 20.00
Moon & Star, red, gr or amber, HJ-870, repros, ca 8.00
Pattee Cross, gold trim, HJ-185, ind 25.00
Pressed Diamond, bl, amber, or vaseline, HJ-427, ind 15.00
Triangle, bl, amber, or vaseline, HJ-442, ind, ea 25.00
Triangle, larger sz, all colors are repros, ea 5.00
Wildflower, turtle base, all colors, HJ-506, M, ea 125.00

Silverplate

American, Derby, lattice holder, cranberry liner, HJ-319, M 75.00

American, lattice holder, clear liner, ind, M 15.00
American, Meriden, Victorian, overshot insert, HJ-4215, M 75.00
American, Tiffany, emb, cobalt liner, HJ-658, M 75.00
English, cabbage on leaf w/spoon, HJ-4276, ind, M 45.00
German, oval, cobalt liner, ftd, HJ-747, M 35.00

Sterling and Continental Silver

Gorham, circular with three cast griffin feet, gilt interior, marked, ca 1865, 1¾x2½", set of four for $1,320.00.

American, Kerr, Art Nouveau, ped ft, cobalt liner, HJ-702, M ..125.00
American, Udall & Ballow, oval, emb, ped ft, HJ-4078, M 125.00
American, Wm Kerr, rnd, ped ft, HJ-4090, ca 1900, M 75.00
Austria, dbl, cranberry, w/hdl, HJ-4751, M 300.00
Austria, oblong, ped ft, HJ-3956, ca 1970, ind, M 30.00
London, A&P Bateman, oval, ped ft, HJ-3857, pr 600.00
Russian, chair, HJ-4735, M 500.00
Tiffany, sq, HJ-3973, ca 1900, ind, ¾", M 50.00

Other Types

Abalone shell over copper, w/spoon, Mexico, HJ-2011, M 20.00
Celluloid, Viking salt & horn pepper, w/spoon, HJ-207, set 55.00
Cloisonne, w/pepper, HJ-1995, not old, M, set 30.00
Dbl, bl opaque, ped ft, French, HJ-144 ....95.00
Dbl, pressed, clear, hdl, HJ-3805 to HJ-3807, M, ea 20.00
Dbl, pressed, figural hdl, HJ-3777, M 55.00
Intaglio, bl, common variety, HJ-253, M 20.00
Intaglio, bl, kitten, HJ-223, M 45.00
Intaglio, clear, HJ-256, M 20.00
Stone, rose quartz, HJ-1955, M 60.00
Venetian glass, swans, cranberry w/gold flecks, M 35.00

Samplers

American samplers were made as early as the colonial days; even earlier examples from 17th-century England still exist today. Changes in style and design are evident down through the years. Verses were not added until the late 17th century. By the 18th century, samplers were used not only for sewing experience but also as an educational tool. Young ladies, who often signed and dated their work, embroidered numbers and letters of the alphabet and practiced fancy stitches as well. Fruits and flowers were added for borders; birds, animals, and Adam and Eve became popular subjects. Later houses and other buildings were included. By the 19th century, the American Eagle and the little red schoolhouse had made their appearances.

Many factors bear on value: design and workmanship, strength of color, the presence of a signature and/or a date (both being preferred over only one or the other, and earlier is better), and, of course, condition.

ABCs/deer/flowers, cotton mesh, sgn, 14½x13½" 220.00
ABCs/flower band/zigzag border, homespun, 1796, 14x14" 2,145.00
ABCs/flowers/berries/records, homespun, sgn, 1826, 18x21" ...4,400.00
ABCs/flowers/fruit/verse, homespun, sgn, OH, 1826, 19x20"+old fr ..4,400.00
ABCs/flowers/verse, homespun, 1794, 13x11"+fr 1,400.00
ABCs/flowers/verse, wool on coarse-weave foundation, 1840, 17x17" .300.00

ABCs/genealogical info/verse/flowers, homespun, 1828, 17x17", EX ...600.00
ABCs/house/flowers, homespun, sgn, wear/damage, 18x16" 685.00
ABCs/initials/foliage/animals, homespun, early 19th C, 16x12" .500.00
ABCs/man/lady/trees/birds, sgn, homespun, EX color, 15x15" ...1,100.00
ABCs/sailing ship/bird, homespun, sgn, 1837, 13x16"+rpl fr 600.00
ABCs/verse/animals/flowers, homespun, sgn, 1854, 20x15", VG ..460.00
ABCs/verse/animals/trees, homespun, 180_, 16x14", VG 575.00
ABCs/verse/birds/flowers/horses, homespun, stain, 1808, 20x12" ...935.00
ABCs/verse/flowers/animals, homespun, 182_, 18⅝x16¼" 800.00
ABCs/verse/flowers/family names, homespun, 1806, 12x10"+fr .525.00
ABCs/verse/foliage/birds/etc, sgn, ca 1850s, 12x10" 700.00
ABCs/verse/ribbons/flowers, homespun, 1820, 16⅝x17⅛" ...1,500.00
ABCs/verses/flowers, linsey woolsey, sgn, 1888, 12x15"+fr, EX ...2,185.00
ABCs/vines/flowers/birds/etc, homespun, 1833, 17x26"+new fr .475.00
Adam & Eve/house/trees/dogs/flowers, homespun, 1793, 15x15" .1,925.00
Flower basket/birds/foliage, homespun, 1833, 27x28" 1,850.00
Flower/ribbon-like bow/strawberries, linen, 1826, 8x10" 2,150.00
Landscape/verse/animals/vines, homespun, curly fr, 21x21" 715.00
Text, flowers on linen, 1794, 11x11" 675.00
Verse/Adam & Eve/house/fruit/animals, homespun, 1830s, 25x24" .2,650.00
Verse/fruit/animals/house/etc, sgn, 1839, 16x12" 1,500.00
Verses/fruit/foliage/hearts/etc, sgn, 1850s, PA, 20x25" 1,265.00

Sandwich Glass

The Boston and Sandwich Glass Company was founded in 1820 by Deming Jarves in Sandwich, Massachusetts. Their first products were simple cruets, salts, half-pint jugs, and lamps. They were attributed with being one of the first to perfect a method for pressing glass, a step toward the manufacture of the 'lacy' glass which they made until about 1840. Many other types of glass were made there — cut, colored, snakeskin, hobnail, and opalescent among them. After the Civil War, profits began to dwindle due to the keen competition of the Western factories which were situated in areas rich in natural gas and easily accessible sand and coal deposits. The end came with an unreconcilable wage dispute between the workers and the company, and the factory closed in 1888.

In 1907 the vacant glasshouse was purchased and refurbished by the Alton Manufacturing Company. They specialized in lighting fixtures, but under the direction of an ex-Tiffany glassblower and former Sandwich resident James H. Grady, they also produced a line of iridescent art glass called Trevaise, examples of which are very rare today. It was often decorated with pulled feathers, whorls, leaves, and vines similar to the glassware produced by Tiffany, Quezal, and Durand. Examples that surface on today's market range in price from $1,500.00 to $2,000.00. Trevaise was made for less than one year. Due to financial problems, the company closed in 1908. (This information was provided by the Sandwich Glass Museum.) See also Cup Plates; Lacy Glass; Salts, Open; other specific types of glass.

Bottle, scent; amber, pressed pattern, pointed stopper, 7½" 250.00
Bottle, scent; amethyst, paneled/corseted form, 6" 700.00
Bottle, scent; bl 3-layer o/l w/grape & leaf cuttings, 7" 1,500.00
Bottle, scent; blown molded oval panels, lily stopper, 7" 120.00
Bottle, scent; canary, Star & Punty, w/stopper, 7" 525.00
Bottle, scent; cobalt, monument form, smooth base, 6⅜", EX 120.00
Bottle, scent; dk sapphire bl, 2-pc mold, 12-panel, w/stopper, 7" ..250.00
Bottle, scent; Elongated Loop, petticoat shape, 7½" 250.00
Bottle, scent; fiery bl opal w/opaque bl neck/mouth, T'print, 5⅝" .300.00
Bottle, scent; GI-7, dk sapphire bl, tam-o'-shanter stopper, 6¾" ...180.00
Bottle, scent; GI-7 type 2, med amethyst, 5¾" 200.00
Bottle, scent; GI-7 type 4, sapphire bl, 5⅝", NM 90.00
Bottle, scent; GI-7 type 4, sapphire bl, 6⅞" 110.00
Bottle, scent; lt violet-bl, GI-3 type 1, 5½" 240.00

Bottle, scent; sapphire bl w/purple tone, 12-sided, 7¼" 250.00
Bottle, scent; teal bl w/fiery bl opal, 12-sided, 5½" 350.00
Bottle, scent; Tulip, G gold, orig stopper, 5¼" 175.00
Bottle, scent; 12-sided, smooth base, 7⅛" 160.00
Bowl, Chrysanthemum Leaf, nonflint, 4½" 30.00
Candlestick, canary, hex pressed socket & base, 7¾" 120.00
Candlesticks, B-4037, canary, loop base, 1850s, 7", pr 375.00
Candlesticks, clambroth, Dolphin, 2-step base, 9½", EX, pr 800.00
Celery vase, dk bl, Loop, 9", EX 400.00
Compote, Ribbed Ivy, ped ft, scalloped rim, flint, 7½x8½" 130.00
Cruet, amethyst, mold blown, single horizontal rib, 5¾" 350.00
Decanter, GI-29, dk sapphire bl, pontil, w/stopper, ½-pt 700.00
Decanter, Lee #51-1, Waffle & Sunburst, w/stopper 250.00
Hat whimsey, GIII-7, 24 vertical ribs, 2¼" 300.00
Inkwell, domed cylinder, clear w/pk & wht stripes, 2¾" 2,300.00
Jug, fuchsia on opal, att Chamberlain, slim, w/stopper, 6½" 285.00
Pomade, bear figural, blk amethyst, 4", EX 250.00
Smoke bell, cranberry, clear appl ring, ruffled rim, 7" 400.00
Smoke bell, eng floral & cobalt rim, 7" 300.00
Smoke bell, eng grapes & red rim, 7⅜" 120.00
Smoke bell, fiery opal w/robin's-egg bl rim, 5¾" 220.00
Smoke bell, Greek border, ruffled rim, 7½" 325.00
Smoke bell, milk glass w/appl bl ruffled rim, pontil, 7¼" 300.00
Smoke bell, milk glass w/mc HP raspberries/florals, 3¼" 275.00
Smoke bell, milk glass w/robin's-egg bl ruffled rim, pontil, 6" 350.00
Spill holder, electric bl, hex w/star design, 5⅛" 1,200.00
Spill holder, Loop, low stem, 4¾" 45.00
Spoon holder, Ribbed Ivy, ped ft, scalloped rim, flint 25.00
Spoon holder, wht fiery opal, Loop, 5½" 150.00
Sugar bowl, Cable & Ring, flint 45.00
Sugar bowl, Magnet & Grape, flint, 5⅛x4¼" 65.00
Tumbler, Morning Glory, emb pattern, ftd, ca 1850, 5" 200.00
Vase, amethyst, 12-Panel, rolled rim, 7½x5½" 1,300.00
Vase, sapphire bl, Arch bowl w/wafer on stepped hex ft, 11¼" ..2,000.00
Vase, sapphire bl, Arch pattern, gauffered rims, 11¼", pr 3,750.00
Vase, tulip; gray-bl, paneled fonts w/wafer on 8-sided base, 10" ..4,750.00

Sarreguemines

Sarreguemines, France, is the location of Utzschneider and Company, founded in 1770, producers of majolica, transfer-printed dinnerware, figurines, and novelties which are usually marked 'Sarreguemines.'

Butter dish, fruit decor, w/lid 385.00
Compote, ivy & flowers in relief on turq, sm rpr 400.00
Ewer, Etna, mauve w/brn/gold crystalline, emb decor, 5½x7½" ..350.00
Pitcher, brn & tan crystalline, imp mk, 7" 150.00
Pitcher, John Bull's face, #3257, 6½" 330.00
Pitcher, judge's face, #4502, 6½" 550.00
Pitcher, man's face, bulging eyes, red hat, #8715, 5½" 440.00
Pitcher, man's face, rosy cheeks & chin, #3818, 6" 195.00
Pitcher, man's face w/teeth, #3181, 8½" 275.00
Pitcher, man's smiling face, 8½" 300.00
Pitcher, man's winking face, 8½" 300.00
Pitcher, pig figural, 9½" 330.00
Radish plate, radishes & leaves on wht majolica, ca 1900, 13" L ..200.00
Tureen, corn, w/lid, rpr hdl, 13½" L 165.00
Vase, Secessionist, teal, rtcl, 6-sided, 6-ftd, att Dachsel, 6¾" 325.00

Satin Glass

Satin glass is simply glassware with a velvety matt finish achieved through the application of an acid bath. This procedure has been used by many companies since the 20th century, both here and abroad, on many types of colored and art glass. See also Mother-of-Pearl; Webb.

Bottle, lt bl o/l w/floral, shallow/sq body, 2½x2¼", pr 450.00
Bottle, rose-red to gr, opal int, Gorham cap, ball shape, 4" 350.00
Cracker jar, lav w/gold floral & sq garden reserve, 6½" 175.00

Ewer, pink with hand-painted decoration, 9¾", $130.00.

Ewer, apricot to opal w/lilacs & berries, bulbous, 7¾" 175.00
Ewer, pk, flowers/butterflies, ribbed acorn body, 11" 150.00
Ewer, shaded bl o/l w/gold floral, melon ribs, 13" 225.00
Match striker, rose to pk o/l, heavy, 3x3" dia 145.00
Pitcher, Cone, pk w/wht int, frosted hdl, 6½" 125.00
Rose bowl, bl w/bird & floral, camphor hdls, 4½" 100.00
Rose bowl, bl w/wht int, morning glories, petal ft, 5" 145.00
Rose bowl, bright gr w/florals, pinched rim, 5x5½" 295.00
Rose bowl, yel to wht, berries/leaves, pinched rim, 4½" W 145.00
Vase, amber, melon ribbed, 8½" 110.00
Vase, bl w/gold roses, cylindrical w/crimped rim, 8", pr 350.00
Vase, bl w/netted gold scrolls, dimpled sides w/florals, 7" 175.00
Vase, bl w/wht & gold floral, ftd U-form w/crimped rim, 8" 175.00
Vase, gold shaded w/gold leaves & butterfly, 5x2½" 225.00
Vase, pk, petit-point enamel flowers, 5x3¼" 135.00
Vase, rainbow, swirl, shouldered w/stick neck, 7¾" 150.00
Vase, yel w/wht int, bulbous w/stick neck, pontil, 7½" 145.00

Satsuma

Satsuma is a type of fine cream crackle-glaze pottery or earthenware made in Japan as early as the 17th century. The earliest wares, made at the original kiln in the Satsuma province, were enameled with only simple florals. By the late 18th century, a floral brocade (or nishikide design) was favored, and similar wares were being made at other kilns under the direction of the Lord of Satsuma. In the early part of the 19th century, a diaper pattern was added to the florals. Gold and silver enamels were used for accents by the latter years of the century. During the 1850s, as the quality of goods made for export to the Western world increased and the style of decoration began to evolve toward becoming more appealing to the Westerners, human forms such as Arhats, Kannon, geisha girls, and samurai warriors were added. Today the most valuable pieces are those marked 'Kinkozan,' 'Shuzan,' 'Ryuzan,' and 'Kozan.' The genuine Satsuma 'mon' or mark is a cross within a circle — usually in gold on the body or lid, or in red on the base of the ware. Character marks may be included.

Caution: Much of what is termed 'Satsuma' comes from the Showa Period (1926 to the present); it is not true Satsuma but a simulated type, a cheaper pottery with heavy enamel. Collectors need to be aware that much of the of the 'Satsuma' today is really Satsuma style and should not carry the values of true Satsuma.

Bottle, maple branches w/group of shrike, gold mk, 7¼" 375.00

Bowl, dessert; seasonal landscapes on sepia, Meiji, 4¾" **285.00**
Ewer, blk dragon w/red details on dk brn w/mc florals, 13x10½" ...**400.00**
Figurine, girl in gold brocade robe, w/dog, 7" **200.00**
Jar, chrysanthemums & temples, Taniguchi, Meiji period, 10" ...**375.00**
Teacup & saucer, seated bijin on gilt-pnt sepia, Meiji, 4 for **170.00**
Teapot, child entertains family, bk: parade, melon ribs, 2" **130.00**
Urn, figures, foo dog finial, scroll hdls/ft, w/gold, 12¾", NM **225.00**
Vase, feathers, HP w/gold on cobalt, 1915, 15" **125.00**
Vase, ladies w/parasols/fans, geometrics, pillow form, 16" **210.00**
Vase, mc & gilt decor on cream, baluster, Meiji period, 10" **375.00**

Scales

In today's world of pre-measured and pre-packaged goods, it is difficult to imagine the days when such products as sugar, flour, soap, and candy first had to be weighed by the grocer. The variety of scales used at the turn of the century was highly diverse; at the Philadelphia Exposition in 1876, one company alone displayed over three hundred different weighing devices. Among those found today, brass, cast-iron, and plastic models are the most common. Fancy postal scales in decorative wood, silver, marble, bronze, and mosaic are also to be found.

A word of caution on the values listed: these values range from a low for those items in fair to good condition to the upper values for items in excellent condition. Naturally, items in mint condition could command even higher prices, and they often do. Also, these are **retail** prices that suggest what a collector will pay for the object. When you sell to a dealer, expect to get much less. The values noted are averages taken from various auction and other catalogs in the possession of the Society members. Among these, but not limited to, are the following: Joel L. Malter & Co., Inc., Encino, CA; *Collector's Journal of Ancient Art*, Joel L. Malter & Co., Inc.; Nobody's Bizness But Our Own, Storrs, CT; Craig A. Whitford Numismatic Auctions; *Auktion Alt Technic*, Auction Team, Koln, Germany.

Those seeking additional information concerning antique scales are encouraged to contact the International Society of Antique Scale Collectors, whose address can be found in the Directory under Clubs, Newsletters, and Catalogs.

Key:
ap — arrow pointer	h — hanging
bal — balance	hcp — hanging counterpoise
bm — base metal	hh — hand held
br — brass	l+ — label with foreign coin values
Brit — British	lb w/i — labeled box with instruc-
Can — Canadian	tions
Col — Colonial	lph — letter plate or holder
CW — Civil War	pend — pendulum
cwt — counterweight	PP — Patent Pending
Engl — English	st — sterling
eq — equal arm	tt — torsion type
Euro — European	ua — unequal arm
FIS — Fairbanks Infallible Scale Co.	wt — weight

Analytical (Scientific)

Am, eq, mahog w/br & ivory, late 1800s, 14x16x8", $200 to **400.00**

Assay

Am, eq, mahog box w/br & ivory, plaque/drw, 1890s, $400 to .**1,000.00**

Coin: Equal Arm Balance, American

Blk japanned metal, eagle on lid, late 19th C, $125 to **225.00**
Col, oak 6-part box, Col moneys, Boston, 1720-75, $600 to ...**1,200.00**
Post Col to CW, oak 6-part box, l+, 1843, $400 to **1,000.00**

Coin: Equal Arm Balance, English

Charles I, wooden box w/11 Brit wts, 1640s, $900 to **1,500.00**
1-pc wood box, rnd wts, label, Freeman, 1760s, $250 to **450.00**
6-pc oak box, coin wts label, Thos Harrison, 1750s, $200 to **450.00**

Coin: Equal Arm Balance, French

Solid wood box, 12 sq wts, J Reyne, Bourdeau, 1694, $400 to .**1,000.00**
Solid wood box w/recesses, 5 sq wts, A Gardes, 1800s, $250 to ..**800.00**
1-pc oval box, nested/fractional wts, label, 18th C, $250 to **400.00**
1-pc oval box, no wts, label of Fr/Euro coins, 18th C, $150 to **250.00**
1-pc walnut box, nested wts, Charpentier label, 1810, $275 to ..**675.00**

Coin: Equal Arm Balance, Miscellaneous

Amsterdam, 1-pc box, 32 sq wts, label, late 1600s, $850 to **2,500.00**
Cologne, full set of wts & full label, late 1600s, $1,200 to **2,800.00**
German, wood box, 13+ wts beneath main wts, label, 1795, $650 to .**900.00**

Counterfeit Coin Detectors, American

Allender Pat, lb w/i, cwt, Nov 22, 1855, 8½", $350 to **650.00**
Allender PP, rocker, labeled box, cwt, 1850s, 8½", $450 to **750.00**
Allender PP, rocker, no box or cwt, 1850s, 8½", $250 to **375.00**
Allender PP, space for $3 gold pc, lb w/i, cwt, 1855, $350 to **750.00**
Allender PP, space for $3 gold pc, no box or cwt, 1855, $275 to ...**375.00**
Allender Warranted, rocker, no box or cwt, 1850s, 8½", $350 to .**475.00**
McNally-Harrison Pat 1882, rocker, cwt, JT McNally, $275 to ..**500.00**
McNally-Harrison Pat 1882, rocker, cwt & box, FIS, $400 to **750.00**
McNally-Harrison...1882, rocker, CI base, no cwt/box, $250 to .**400.00**
Thompson, Z-formed rocker, Berrian Mfg, 1877 Pat, $175 to **350.00**

Counterfeit Coin Detectors, Dutch

Rocker, Ellinckhuysen, brass, +copy of 1829 Patent, $150 to **165.00**

Counterfeit Coin Detectors, English

Folding, Guinea, self-rising, labeled box, 1850s, $175 to **225.00**
Folding, Guinea, self-rising, wood box/label, ca 1890s, $125 to ..**175.00**
Folding, Guinea, self-rising, wooden box, pre-1800, $175 to **275.00**
Rocker, simple, no maker's name or cb, end-cap box, $85 to **125.00**
Rocker, w/maker's name & cb, end-cap box, $120 to **150.00**

Postal

In the listings below an asterisk (*) was used to indicate that any one of several manufacturers' or brand names might be found on that particular set of scales. Some of the American-made pieces could be marked Pelouze, Lorraine, Hanson, Kingsbury, Fairbanks, Troemner, IDL, Newman, Accurate, Ideal, B-T, Marvel, Reliance, Howe, Landers-Frary-Clark, Chatillon, Triner, American Bank Service, or Weiss. European/U.S.-made scales marked with an asterisk (*) could be marked Salter, Peerless, Pelouze, Sturgis, L.F.&C., Alderman, G. Little, or S&D. English-made scales with the asterisk (*) could be marked Josh. & Edmd. Ratcliff, R.W. Winfield, S. Mordan, STS (Samuel Turner, Sr.), W.&T. Avery, Parnall & Sons, S&P, or H.B. Wright. There may be other manufacturers as well.

Brit/Can Bal, eq, br or CI on base, *, 4"-15", $100 to **750.00**

Engl Bal, eq/Roberval, gilt or st, on stand, *, 3"-8", $500 to	....2,500.00
Engl Bal, eq/Roberval, plain to ornate, *, 3"-8", $100 to	.........2,500.00
Engl Spring, candlestick, br or st, *, 3½"-15", $100 to	.............500.00
Engl Spring, CI, br or NP fr, Salter, ozs/lbs, 7"-10", $25 to	.........200.00
Engl Steelyard, ua, 1- or 2-beam, h lph, *, 4"-15", $100 to	......1,500.00
Euro pend, gravity, br, CI or NP fr on base, oz/grams, $75 to	......350.00
Euro pend, gravity, 2-arm, bm, br or NP, *, 6"-9", $50 to	.........300.00
Euro/US Spring, br or NP, pence/etc, h or hh, *, 4"-17", $10 to	...100.00
US Pend, gravity, metal, pnt face, ap, hcp, sm, $20 to	................100.00
US Spring, pnt base metal, *, 2½"-8", $10 to	..................................80.00
US Spring, pnt bm, *, mtd on inkstand, 2½"-8", $75 to	.............250.00
US Spring, pnt bm, rnd glass-covered face, *, 8"-10", $25 to	......100.00
US Spring, SP, oblong base, *, 2½"-8", $100 to	................................200.00
US Spring, st, oblong base, *, 2½"-8", $200 to	............................500.00
US Steelyard, ua, CI, *, 5"-13" beam, 4½"-12" base, $25 to	.......100.00

Schafer and Vater

Established in 1890 by Gustav Schafer and Gunther Vater in the Thuringia region of southwest Germany, by 1913 this firm employed over two hundred workers. The original factory burned in 1918 but was restarted and production continued until WWII. In 1972 the East German government took possession of the building and destroyed all of the molds and the records that were left.

You will find pieces with the impressed mark of a nine-point star with a script 'R' inside the star. On rare occasions you will find this mark in blue ink under glaze. The items are sometimes marked with a four-digit design number and a two-digit artist mark. In addition or instead, pieces may have 'Made in Germany' or in the case of the Kewpies, 'Rose O'Neil copyright.' The company also manufactured items for sale under store names, and those would not have the impressed mark.

Schafer and Vater used various types of clays. Items made of hard-paste porcelain, soft-paste porcelain, jasper, bisque, and majolica can be found. The glazed bisque pieces may be multicolored or have an applied colored slip wash that highlights the intricate details of the modeling. Gold accents were used as well as spots of high-gloss color called jewels. Metallic glazes are coveted. You can find the jasper in green, blue, pink, lavender, and white. New collectors gravitate toward the pink and lavender shades.

Since Schafer and Vater made such a multitude of items, collectors have to compete with many cross-over collections. These include shaving mugs, hatpin holders, match holders, figurines, figural pitchers, Kewpies, tea sets, bottles, naughties, etc.

Reproduction alert: In addition to the crudely made Japanese copies, some English firms are beginning to make figural reproductions. These seem to be well marked and easy to spot. Our advisor for this category is Joanne M. Koehn; she is listed in the Directory under Minnesota.

Animal dish, Pig 'N Whistle, #9239, 5¼"	....................150.00
Ashtray/nodder, Baby Napoleon, #8638, 4x11x8"	............375.00
Bell, Dutch cook figural, pk, 4¼"	....135.00
Bottle, liquor; I'm So Discouraged, boy crying by wall	..............100.00
Bottle, liquor; One of the Boys	....165.00
Bottle, Never Drink Water, Scotch boy, #3938	....................85.00
Decanter, Life Saver (Butcher's Boy), bl	..............................385.00
Decanter, Now You Pull One	....350.00
Figurine, A Present for You, lady held in lg hand, #9410, 6"	......300.00
Figurine, bathing beauty w/cat	....295.00
Figurine, Castle Walk, couple dancing, 5½"	.........................240.00
Figurine, Don't Tell Anyone, #8055, 4"	...............................175.00
Figurine, Everybody's Doing It, children hold hands, 4"	.............80.00
Figurine, Grizzly Bear, couple dancing, #9870, 6"	................220.00
Figurine, lady sits w/knees up, fancy hat, 4½"	.......................300.00

Figurine, Mr Adam, comic Blk man w/lg leaf, 7½"	....................325.00
Figurine, Oriental baby w/mouth open wide, unmk, 3"	..............230.00
Figurine, Plantadge & puppy, w/hat, unmk, 3"	.......................140.00
Figurine, Sailor Dreadnought, barefoot sailor, #7278, NM	.........255.00
Figurine, Tango, dancing couple, #9271, 6"	..........................195.00
Flask, Apache Dance, couple dancing, 6¼", M	........................195.00
Flask, Bowling Man, man emb on brn, 5¼"	............................150.00
Flask, Hausdok, man pointing, bl/wht, #6226, 11¼"	...............375.00
Flask, Just a Little Nip, dog biting lady, 4¾"	........................185.00
Flask, monk w/wine bottle, 6½", M	......................................320.00
Flask, Mr Cocktail, #2596, 8¼"	....265.00
Flask, One of the Boys, man in tux on high stool, 6¾"	...............175.00
Flask, Present From Isle of Man, 7⅜"	...................................255.00
Flask, What a Night, slumped man walking, 5¼"	....................160.00
Hatpin holder, bear & tower form, mk, 4¾x3½"	.....................250.00
Jam pot, Jasper, classical ladies, wht on bl, 5¼"	....................95.00
Match holder, Don't Pull Too Hard, w/striker, 3¾"	.................185.00
Match holder, goose (clothed) figural, #22, 6¼"	....................185.00
Match holder, Here's a Scrape, lady w/legs in air, 4¼", M	..........230.00
Match holder, If a Match You Want..., bulldog, w/striker, #8480	...545.00
Match holder, man w/bug on nose, unmk, 4½"	.......................230.00
Match holder, Weather Forecast..., baby crying, #9625, 4"	.........185.00
Match holder/nodder, Hookums, unmk, 4¼"	..........................335.00
Match holder/nodder, What a Night, stooped man, 5"	...............335.00

Match striker, Scratch Your Match on My Patch, $175.00.

Photo courtesy Joanne M. Koehn

Nipper, Camel	....150.00
Nipper, Girl in Hand	....150.00
Nipper, Good Sip	....175.00
Nipper, Night Cap	....150.00
Nipper, Sailor w/Life Preserver	.....................................265.00
Nipper, Squire	....135.00
Nipper, Turkey Trot	....275.00
Pincushion/nodder, Oriental lady, #1357, 3½"	.....................400.00
Pitcher, Black boy, 3½"	....220.00
Pitcher, Black man, bug-eyed, 5"	....................................195.00
Pitcher, elf on pig, 4½"	....325.00
Pitcher, jester w/cymbals, bl, 4¾"	...................................115.00
Pitcher, Little Red Riding Hood & Wolf, bl, 5"	.....................125.00
Pitcher, mandolin player, 3½"	....140.00
Pitcher, Oriental lady & baby, #6821, 5¼"	.........................185.00
Pitcher, pig figural, cream sz	....135.00
Swinger, googly child w/lg swinging ft	..............................175.00
Vase, jewels on pk Jasperware, allover Tiffany irid, 7¼"	.............95.00

Scheier

The Scheiers began their ceramics careers in the late 1930s and soon thereafter began to teach their craft at the University of New Hampshire. After WWII they cooperated with the Puerto Rican government in establishing a native ceramic industry, an involvement which would continue to influence their designs. In the '50s they retired and moved to Mexico; they currently reside in Arizona.

Bowl, brn-yel flambe satin matt, sm rnd ft, 3x6" 300.00
Bowl, mahog to umber flambe, sm rnd ft, 3½x6" 200.00
Charger, zebra/foliage in bl enamel on med bl, 12" 500.00
Vase, figures relief in fish-shape reserves, bl/blk, 14x11" 700.00
Vase, men/fish incising, mahog on gray/gr, ftd cylnder, 7" 450.00

Schlegelmilch Porcelain

Authority Mary Frank Gaston has completed four volumes of *The Collector's Encyclopedia of R.S. Prussia* with full-color illustrations and current values. Mold numbers appearing in some of the listings refer to these books.

Key: RM — red mark

E.S. Germany

Fine chinaware marked 'E.S. Germany' or 'E.S. Prov. Saxe' was produced by the E.S. Schlegelmilch factory in Suhl in the Thuringia region of Prussia from sometime after 1861 until about 1925.

Bowl, divided; Hortense & Josephine, hdl 150.00
Bowl, divided; lady w/dove & lady w/peacock, center hdl, 9" 300.00
Bowl, divided; 2 ladies w/roses w/turq & gold, center hdl, mk, 15" L ...500.00
Bowl, lady's portrait, wine & gr border w/gold, mk, 10" 225.00
Bowl, pansies, steeple mold, circle mk 100.00
Bowl, roses on apple gr, artist sgn, RM, 3x10" 160.00
Bowl, windmill/water/boat/etc, hdls, mk, 1¾x7¼" 125.00
Celery dish, Niagara Falls souvenir, mk, 12" L 175.00
Chocolate pot, Napoleon portrait, mk 375.00
Chocolate pot, roses reserve on gr w/gold, mk, 8¾" 350.00
Cracker jar, lady holding rose & flowers, mk, 4½x8½" 350.00
Cup & saucer, demi; lady & roses, MOP lustre, ornate 175.00
Cup & saucer, demi; Madame LeBrun & Napoleon 125.00
Cup & saucer, Napoleon, florals/gold eagle, ftd, 3½" 125.00
Cup & saucer, pk & wht wild roses on wht, mk 35.00
Ewer, Diana, Venus & 3 Graces, Tiffany irid, mk, 9½" 550.00
Ewer, mythological scenes on turq w/gold, gold hdl, mk, 17" ..1,200.00
Inkwell, mythological scenic reserve & roses, mk, 3⅞" 350.00
Jar, birds & flowers, mk 475.00
Plate, Gibson girl portrait, cobalt border w/gold, mk, 7¾" 300.00
Plate, Goddess of Fire portrait, pierced border w/gold, mk, 8½" .350.00
Plate, lady w/swallows, pk poppies, pierced rim w/gold, mk, 11¼" ..350.00
Plate, lake & tree scenic, earth tones, mk, 7½" 75.00
Plate, Marie portrait, w/cameo portraits in border, mk 300.00
Plate, mythological scene, wine finish w/gold, mk, 12" 325.00
Plate, pk roses w/gold, 8-sided, mk, 10" 135.00
Plate, Portia & Shylock, sgn W Paget, gold border, mk, 9½" 700.00
Toothpick holder, classical scene, RM 100.00
Vase, lady w/doves reserve w/gold, mk, 11" 550.00
Vase, lady w/rose portrait on pk to wine w/gold, mk, 9½" 375.00
Vase, pk & wht lg stylized roses, gold hdls, mk, 8" 150.00

R.S. Germany

In 1869 Reinhold Schlegelmilch began to manufacture porcelain in Suhl in the German province of Thuringia. In 1894 he established another factory in Tillowitz in upper Silesia. Both areas were rich in resources necessary for the production of hard-paste porcelain. Wares marked with the name 'Tillowitz' and the accompanying 'R.S. Ger-

many' phrase are attributed to Reinhold. The most common mark is a wreath and star in a solid color under the glaze. Items marked 'R.S. Germany' are usually more simply decorated than R.S. Prussia. Some reflect the Art Deco trend of the 1920s. Certain hand-painted floral decorations and themes such as 'Sheepherder,' 'Man With Horses,' and 'Cottage' are especially valued by collectors — those with a high-gloss finish or on Art Deco shapes in particular. Not all hand-painted items were painted at the factory. Those with an artist's signature but no 'Hand Painted' mark indicate that the blank was decorated outside the factory.

Berry set, acorns & oak leaves w/gold, 7-pc 200.00
Bowl, cottage scene on brn tones, mk, 10½" 275.00
Bowl, floral w/cobalt border & gold, mold #8, 7¾" 250.00
Bowl, marbled bl & orange pearl lustre, clover shape, mk, 7" 30.00
Bowl, mc mums on ivory, mold #2, mk, 10" 225.00
Bowl, orange tulips, pierced hdls, mk, 9" 75.00

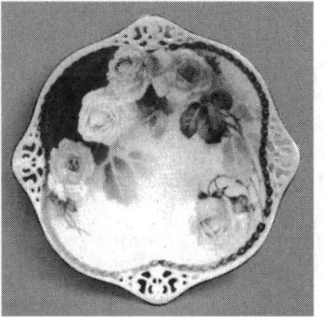

Bowl, roses, openwork on each side, 7", $70.00.

Photo courtesy Mary Frank Gaston

Bowl, roses, poppies, daisies & hydrangeas, scalloped, 9" 95.00
Bowl, snowballs on shaded gr, leaf form, mold #10, mk, 9x8" 200.00
Bowl, Summer portrait on wht satin, hdls, mold #25, mk, 13" L .1,700.00
Cake plate, floral w/pk & lustre border, leaf mold, unmk, 11" 75.00
Cake plate, mc floral on beige w/open hdls, RM, 10" 45.00
Cake plate, orchids on shaded brn, smooth rim, mk, 10" 60.00
Celery tray, red & wht tulips, gr at rim, mk, 12" L 150.00
Charger, yel-wht roses w/gold tapestry at top, mk, 12½" 75.00
Cheese & cracker set, poppies, mk 75.00
Cheese server, pk roses w/gr leaves, RM 125.00
Chocolate pot, iris on gr, Deco mold, 9½", +4 cups 365.00
Chocolate pot, man w/2 horses & house, 10", NM 185.00
Chocolate pot, roses w/gold stems, mold #8, mk 375.00
Chocolate pot, snowballs & shadow leaves w/gold, mk, 10" 250.00
Chocolate set, wht lilies, pot+5 c/s, EX 450.00
Console set, gold & purple irid lustre, 3-pc set 150.00
Creamer & sugar bowl, irises, mk, w/lid, 2⅜", 4" 90.00
Cup, demitasse; calla lily on wht, mk 32.50
Cup & saucer, pk floral on wht w/heavy gold at rim, mk 90.00
Ewer, white poppies, ornate rim & hdl, mold #640, mk, 5½" 115.00
Mustard pot, wht tulips w/gold, w/lid & ladle, mk, 3⅛" 115.00
Pin dish, lady w/fan, RM 150.00
Pitcher, lemonade; lg flowers, Deco mold, gr mk, 6½" 250.00
Plate, apple blossoms, sgn Lenbach, mk, 8" 45.00
Plate, dogwood w/gold, mold #256, mk, 8½" 55.00
Plate, lg wht daisies, smooth rim, mk, 9¾" 80.00
Plate, lily of the valley w/lg gold leaves, smooth rim, mk, 6⅜" 30.00
Relish, bird of paradise, mk 250.00
Relish, poppy & sm bl flowers, pierced hdls, mk, 8½" L 60.00
Shaving mug, floral, steeple mold, unmk 100.00
Shaving mug, poppies, scalloped base, w/soap holder 95.00
Tankard, cottage scenic, pk/gr/orange 'glow' ground, mk, 14" .1,300.00
Tankard, poppies on shaded gr w/gold, slim, gold hdl, mk, 14¾" ..650.00
Teapot, Godey lady in panel, irid, 10", +cr/sug 225.00

Toothpick holder, orange flowers, hdls, gr mk 75.00
Tray, bun; medieval castle scene on lake w/sailboat, 13" 500.00
Trivet, heart shape w/parrot hdls, mk 100.00
Vase, mc mums on shaded gr w/much gold, mold #13, mk, 8¾" .400.00
Vase, wht poppies on shaded ground w/red & gold trim, hdls, 8" ..120.00

R.S. Poland

'R.S. Poland' is a mark attributed to Reinhold Schlegelmilch's factory in Tillowitz, Silesia. It was in use for a few years after 1945.

Cup, chocolate, dogwood & pine on irid, mold #509a, mk, 3" 70.00
Cup & saucer, pk flowers on wht, swirled body, mk 55.00
Mug, shaving; daffodils, mk 65.00
Relish, mc roses w/gold, mk, 4½x9" 35.00
Vase, Chinese pheasants, mold #15, mk, 9" 900.00
Vase, lg peach roses on shaded brn, Nouveau hdls, mold #956, mk, 12" ..550.00
Vase, lilac clematis on shaded brn, mold #907, 5⅞" 160.00
Vase, pastoral scene w/cobalt & gold, mold #3, 8½" 1,400.00

R.S. Prussia

Art porcelain bearing the mark 'R.S. Prussia' was manufactured by Reinhold Schlegelmilch from the late 1870s to the early 1900s in a Germanic area known until the end of WWI as Prussia. The vast array of mold shapes in combination with a wide variety of decorations is the basis for R.S. Prussia's appeal. Themes can be categorized as figural (usually based on a famous artist's work), birds, florals, portraits, scenics, and animals.

Bowl, roses and floral garlands on satin with gold, Ribbon and Jewel mold, marked, 10½", $325.00.

Photo courtesy Mary Frank Gaston

Bowl, azaleas w/gold, mold #211A 225.00
Bowl, floral, bl & ivory, scalloped rim, RM, 10" 95.00
Bowl, floral, mc on bl lustre, mold #329, mk, 10½" 125.00
Bowl, Hidden Image, bl border, 3x10" 595.00
Bowl, mc flowers w/gr & gold, mold #1, unmk, 10½" 200.00
Bowl, mc roses on wht to pk at rim w/gold, mold #9, unmk, 10¾" ..250.00
Bowl, mc roses on wht w/gold, center hdl, mold #23, 14½" L 450.00
Bowl, parrot center, silver o/l, roses border, mk, 6" 675.00
Bowl, relish; floral w/4 portrait medallions, mk, 14" L 440.00
Bowl, yel roses w/gr border w/gold Greek key, mold #29, 10½" ..350.00
Bowl in bowl, nasturtiums w/much gold, mold #211A 200.00
Box, pin; mill scene, dmn shape, unmk 150.00
Cake plate, floral w/cobalt to lt bl w/gold, mold #4, 11½" 325.00
Cake plate, pk & gr floral on wht pearlized, scalloped, RM, 11" .245.00
Cake set, pk & wht roses w/lt gr & lav, 7-pc 1,295.00
Cake set, pk roses on satin, RM, 7-pc 1,250.00
Celery dish, lilies of the valley, emb ferns & gold, RM, 12½" L 225.00
Chocolate pot, floral on wht, mold #7, unmk, 12" 350.00
Chocolate pot, mc floral, lg molded base 295.00
Chocolate pot, mc poppies on shaded gr, mold #12, 10" 600.00
Chocolate set, dogwood blossoms on pearlized lustre, pot+6 c/s ..1,100.00
Coffeepot, floral, mold #631, unmk 150.00

Coffeepot, pastel flowers w/gold, stippled mold, RM 795.00
Cracker jar, dbl portraits, lily mold, unmk 950.00
Cracker jar, mc floral on wht w/gold, mold #16, unmk, 5½x9" ..200.00
Cracker jar, surreal dogwood, RM 185.00
Creamer & sugar bowl, mc floral, ped ft, mold #607, 3½" 265.00
Creamer & sugar bowl, roses on wht w/gold, mold #607, 3½" 265.00
Creamer & sugar bowl, roses w/gold, mold #607, 3½" 185.00
Ferner, floral w/gold, mold #8, 2¾x8½" 275.00
Hatpin holder, swan in evergreens, mold #728, unmk 225.00
Match box, bl floral w/gold on wht, mk, 3½x2½" 85.00
Match safe, yel & red roses, wall type, unmk, 4¼" L 75.00
Nut dish, Carnation mold, pearlized finish 200.00
Pitcher, lemonade; yel & wht roses, mk 700.00
Plaque, cottage scene, 'glow' bkground, unmk, 7½" 550.00
Plate, Autumn scene, RM, 9" 1,200.00
Plate, lilies, 7¼" 75.00
Plate, mc floral, pie-crust mold, mk, 11" 285.00
Plate, pheasant w/swan & 3 bluebirds in flight, mk 650.00
Plate, pk & gr floral on wht pearlized, hdls, RM, 11" 195.00
Relish, pk roses on wht w/gold, mold #98, unmk, 9½x4¼" 115.00
Relish, roses on satin, 9½" 135.00
Shaving mug, pk roses on gr/wht, w/mirror, 4x4" 200.00
Shaving mug, surreal dogwood, swirl mold 125.00
Shaving mug, swan scene 350.00
Shaving scuttle mug, floral w/pk & gold, mold #6, unmk, 4" 250.00
Sweetmeat, dbl; 2 shell-mold #20 bowls in SP fr, unmk, 12" L ..200.00
Teapot, mc roses on pk to wht w/gold, mold #12, unmk, 6" 300.00
Toothpick holder, floral & gold stencil, mold #664, unmk, 2¾" ...225.00
Toothpick holder, pk & wht roses, mold #540 ....225.00
Toothpick holder, snowball flowers, swirl mold, RM 125.00
Tray, bun; roses & snowballs, cobalt border, mold #56, RM 200.00
Tray, dresser; floral on wht to gr, much gold, mold #6, 11½x7½" ..275.00
Vase, bl floral on ivory w/cobalt & gold, mold #21, 7" 300.00
Vase, Diana the Huntress, unmk, salesman's sample 275.00
Vase, mill & cottage scenes w/cobalt, mold #907, RM 350.00
Vase, pheasant scene, mold #918, unmk, 4⅜x2⅝" 495.00
Vase, pk roses, Tiffany finish w/gold, mold #6, unmk, 9" 600.00
Vase, Queen Louise portrait w/cobalt & gold, mold #20, mk ..1,400.00
Vase, windmill, hdls, mk, 9" 900.00

R.S. Suhl, Suhl

Porcelains marked with this designation are attributed to Reinhold Schlegelmilch's Suhl factory.

Bowl, lav & wht flowers w/gold, hdls, mk, 8⅛" 150.00
Bowl, mixed floral on wht, 6-scallop, 1 hdl, mold #182, mk, 11" ..425.00
Box, pk roses w/gold, egg shape, mk, 3½x5⅞x4" 1,100.00
Ewer, Josephine portrait w/gold, mold #1, illegible mk, 9" 800.00
Vase, floral on dk gr, ornate gold hdls, mold #12, 13½" 650.00
Vase, hummingbirds on wht satin, hdls, mold #3, unmk, 9½" .3,750.00
Vase, lilac clematis, gold hdls, mold #9, 7⅜" 250.00
Vase, pk & wht roses on blk, gold hdls, mold #4, mk, 9¼" 425.00
Vase, pk flowers/wht snowballs on blk, RSP mold #907, mk, 5" .200.00
Vase, pk lilies w/lg leaves on blk w/gold, mold #2, mk, 7⅛" 400.00
Vase, seaside scenic w/bk views of figures, mold #7, 8⅝" 1,200.00

R.S. Tillowitz

R.S. Tillowitz-marked porcelains are attributed to Reinhold Schlegelmilch's factory in Tillowitz, Silesia.

Cake plate, pears & grapes, pierced hdls, mk, 10⅞" 90.00
Celery tray, sm pk roses, ribbed body, mk, 13½" L 45.00

Chop plate, yel roses on shaded brn, smooth rim, mk, 11" **60.00**
Coffeepot, China Blau (china bl), mk, 8¾" **250.00**
Cup & saucer, wht flowers w/lg yel centers, mk **55.00**
Dessert set, bird & floral on wht w/gold, mk, lg+6 sm bowls **165.00**
Ginger jar, cobalt & wht floral w/gold trim, mk, 9" **300.00**
Gravy boat, pk roses in int, wht ext, gold rim, mk, 6½" L **35.00**
Relish, bird of paradise, basket hdl, mk **350.00**
Toothpick holder, wht w/silver trim **55.00**
Vase, pk & yel roses, salesman's sample, mk, 4⅜" **250.00**

Schneider

The Schneider Glass Company was founded in 1914 at Epinay-sur-seine, France. They made many types of art glass, some of which sandwiched designs between layers. Other decorative devices were appliqué and carved work. These were marked 'Charder' or 'Schneider.' During the '20s commercial artware was produced with Deco motifs cut by acid through two or three layers and signed 'LeVerre Francais' in script or with a section of inlaid filigrane. Our advisor for this category is Don Williams; he is listed in the Directory under Missouri. See also Le Verre Francais.

Compote, pk opaque mottle, red rim, 5-sided pulled rim, 2x9" ...**320.00**
Compote, pk/wine mottle, 14"; metal 3-leg base w/glass beads ...**980.00**
Compote, red w/amber streaks, purple/blk stem/ft, 6x15" **500.00**
Compote, red-orange, striped purple knob & disk ft, 3½x15" **350.00**
Compote, wine w/6-point tooled rim, blk stem/disk ft, 7½" **975.00**
Pitcher, yel w/suspended bubbles, orange hdl, att, 6" **250.00**
Tazza, purple/wht/bl mottle; on ornate bronze base, 12x12" **700.00**
Vase, orange w/3 yel prunts on bulbous bottom, stick neck, 22" .**800.00**
Vase, orange w/3 yel/brn triangular encased elements, 15½" ...**1,380.00**
Vase, orange/amber ribs in clear, long-neck bottle form, 20" **230.00**
Vase, tango red to orange, bulbous w/long cone neck, 11x4" **750.00**
Vase, wht to purple & gr mottle, cone form, wafer ft, 20x5" **450.00**
Vase, yel/pk/gr/orange/purple mottle, bun ft, 14½x4" **350.00**

Schoolhouse Collectibles

Schoolhouse collectibles bring to mind memories of a bygone era when the teacher rang her bell to call the youngsters to class in a one-room schoolhouse where often both the 'hickory stick' and an apple occupied a prominent position on her desk. Our advisor for this category is Kenn Norris; he is listed in the Directory under Texas.

Banner, FFA (Future Farmer's of America), bl & gold **50.00**
Blocks, American Spelling Blocks, w/alphabet, 64 pcs+wood case ..**95.00**
Book, Alice & Jerry Ride & Slides, 1941, EX **20.00**
Book, autograph, 5th grader, 1956 ....**6.00**
Book, Dick & Jane, Happy Days w/Our Friends, Scott Foresman, 1954, VG ..**60.00**
Book, Dick & Jane, Our New Friends, Scott Foresman, 1946, VG+ ..**60.00**
Book, Dick & Jane, We Read Pictures, Scott Foresman, 1951, VG ...**50.00**
Book, Fun w/Dick & Jane, Scott Foresman, 1946-47, NM, from $325 to ...**350.00**
Book, McGuffey's Sixth Reader, 1880 edition, EX **30.00**
Book, Our New Friends, 1940s **35.00**
Desk, master's, birch/poplar, 2 dvtl drw, pigeonholes, rfn, 30" W .**220.00**
Desk, master's, cherry Country Sheraton, trn legs, dvtl drw **770.00**
Desk, master's, Sheraton slant lid, old red pnt, 41x27x22" **350.00**
Desk, master's, walnut, 2 dvtl drw, fall-front lid, att Zoar **550.00**
Dictionary, Latin-English, Vest Pocket Library **10.00**
Emblems, FFA (Future Farmers of America), complete set **275.00**
Globe, Cartocraft 12"...Denoyer Geppert Chicago, 12", w/stand ..**300.00**
Globe, Denmoyer Geppert Chicago, metal, 4", on metal stand **70.00**
Globe, H Schedler's...12"...NJ&NY, c 1889, VG **275.00**

Globe, J Schedler's...3" Prize Medal Paris Exp 1867, on base **800.00**
Globe, Lorings Terrestrial, 1841, 12", on CI stand, EX **2,000.00**
Globe, New Terrestrial...T Harris & Son London, 19th C, in case ...**2,750.00**
Globe, Replogle Globes Chicago, mk 12 Inch Library Globe, EX ..**750.00**
Globe, terrestrial, pocket sz, 3", in lignum vitae case **1,750.00**

Plaque, George Washington profile, copper on black wood, donated by 'Seniors of 1932,' $45.00.

Photo courtesy Kenn Norris

Poster, Schools at War **100.00**
Spelling board, Richmond School...Muncie IN, 1940, 9¼x13" **65.00**
Student handbook, Union High School, 1954-55 ....**5.00**
Tellurium, G Philip & Son...London, 3" globe, ca 1830s **2,500.00**
War bond card (25¢) **20.00**
Yearbook, Carbon High, photos taken & pasted in by students, 1936 ...**75.00**

Pencil Boxes

Among the most common of school-related collectibles are the many classes of pencil boxes. Generally from the period of the 1870s to the 1940s, these boxes were made in hundreds of different styles. Materials included tin, wood (thin frame and solid hardwood), and leather; fabric and plastics were later used. Most pencil boxes were in a basic, rectangular configuration, though rare examples were made to resemble other objects such as rolling pins, ball bats, nightsticks, etc. They may still be found at reasonable prices, even though collectors have recently taken a keen interest in them. All boxes listed below are in very-good to near-mint condition. Our advisors for pencil boxes are Sue and Lar Hothem, authors of *School Collectibles of the Past*; they are listed in the Directory under Ohio.

Advertising giveaway, Security Shoes, tin, sliding lid, 8" **38.00**
Hardwood, 2-level, roses lid decal, lock on lower compartment, 9½" ...**40.00**
Hardwood, 4-level, floral decal on sliding lid, 9" **70.00**
Plastic, Sterling No 562, rectangular, world capitals, 1960, 7¾" ...**25.00**
Store display, Ti-Con-Der-Oga, cb, Dixon, partial contents, 7¾" ..**20.00**
Wallace Invader, tin, cylindrical, orange figure on bl, 7¾" **60.00**
Wood fr, School Companion, Octagon Soap premium, 7⅞" **40.00**

Schoop, Hedi

Swiss-born Hedi Schoop started her ceramics business in North Hollywood in 1940. With a talented crew of about twenty decorators, she produced figurines, figure-vases, console sets, TV lamps, and other decorative housewares — much of which was accented with gold or platinum trim. Schoop's pottery closed after a fire destroyed the building in 1958. Marks are impressed or printed. For further information we recommend *The Collector's Encyclopedia of California Pottery, Second Edition*, by our advisor, Jack Chipman; he is listed in the Directory under California.

Ashtray, ballerina in triangular form, 10" W **175.00**

Basket, pk to gray to plum w/sponged gold, 9x4x7½"	55.00
Bowl, Oriental style w/dragons	65.00
Cookie jar, Darner Doll	375.00
Cookie jar, Queen, rare	600.00
Figurine, Asian musician (& dancer), pr	200.00
Figurine, clown, ft wide apart, holds barbell aloft, 13"	250.00
Figurine, Conchita, scarf over hat, basket on sides, 12½"	155.00
Figurine, Debutante, flower holder, 12½"	150.00
Figurine, French peasant boy & girl, 13", pr	300.00
Figurine, girl w/basket & poodle, bl & gray, mk, 10"	145.00
Figurine, girl w/ponytail in pk & wht, flower basket holder	100.00
Figurine, lady w/flowers, cream/brn/yel/peach, 13"	140.00
Figurine, Oriental girl w/basket on hip, 12½"	125.00
Figurine, Oriental girl w/umbrella, gr, #200, 12"	125.00
Figurine, peasant lady, red scarf, bl flowing skirt, 13"	165.00
Figurine, Repose, lady seated, holding bowl, tinted bsk, 12"	200.00
Figurine, rooster, 13"	165.00
Lamp, TV; Comedy & Tragedy, 11x13"	400.00
Planter, butterfly, gr w/gold, pr	150.00
Planter, pinched irregular rim, 12" L	75.00
Plate, French poodle, sq	50.00
Tray, lady figural, skirt forms tray	135.00
Vase, catcus shape, much color, 6x8"	120.00
Vase, duck form	75.00
Vase, rooster, gr w/gold, 14", pr	275.00
Vase, stylized chicken, 9", pr	155.00
Wall pocket, girl angel w/fingers to lips, gr bow in hair	100.00

Schramberg

The Schramberg factory was founded in the early 19th century in Schramberg Wuttemberg, Germany. The pieces most commonly seen are those made by Schramberger Majolika Fabrik (SMF) dating from 1912 until 1989.

Pieces are stamped with the pattern name (i.e. Gobelin) and the number of the painter who executed it. The imprinted number identifies the shape. Marks may also include these names: Wheelock, Black Forest, and Mepoco.

Perhaps the most popular examples with collectors are those from the Gobelin line. Such pieces have a gray background with as many as ten other colors used to create that design. For example, Gobelin 3 pieces will be painted with green and orange leaves and yellow eyes along with other colors specific to that design.

Little is known of the designers who worked for Schramberg; however, Eva Zeisel was employed at the factory for nearly two years starting in the fall of 1928. Her duties included design, production, and merchandising. Our advisor is Ralph Winslow; he is listed in the Directory under Missouri.

Vase, black and orange leaves on white, SMF, #2822, $72.00.

Ashtray, G5	45.00
Basket, G5, SMF, 4"	50.00
Bowl, orange/pk/gr	50.00
Candle holder, G3	55.00
Inkwell	45.00
Lamp	125.00
Plate, G6, 10"	45.00
Vase, brn drip, 6"	30.00
Vase, floral, 3½"	75.00
Vase, floral, 5"	25.00
Vase, floral, 7"	42.00
Vase, G1, 8-color, 7"	85.00
Vase, G4, 7-color, 4½"	50.00
Vase, G7, 8"	75.00
Vase, w/lid, G5, 5"	45.00

Scouting Collectibles

Boy Scouts

Scouting was founded in England in 1907 by a retired Major General Lord Robert Baden-Powell. Its purpose is the same today as it was then — to help develop physically strong, mentally alert boys and to teach them basic fundamentals of survival and leadership. The movement soon spread to the United States, and in 1910 a Chicago publisher, William Boyce, set out to establish Scouting in America. The first World Scout Jamboree was held in 1911 in England. Baden-Powell was honored as the Chief Scout of the World. In 1926 he was awarded the Silver Buffalo Award in the United States. He was knighted in 1929 for distinguished military service and for his Scouting efforts. Baden-Powell died in 1941. For more information you may contact our advisor, R.J. Sayers, author of *Guide to Scouting Collectibles*, whose address (and ordering information regarding his book) may be found in the Directory under North Carolina. (Correspondence other than book orders requires SASE please.)

Armband, 1977, Nat'l Jamboree, Committee Staff, tan	10.00
Ashtray, Boy Power/Man Power, given to leaders	3.00
Bank, Cub Scout, compo bust of Cub	30.00
Belt buckle, 1957 Nat'l Jamboree, Max Silber issue of 800	65.00
Belt buckle, 1960 Nat'l issue, full 1st class	3.00
Belt buckle, 1973 Nat'l Jamboree, Max Silber issue of 2,000	60.00
Belt buckle, 1985 World Jamboree, Max Silber issue of 125	50.00
Belt buckle, 1989, limited edition, #d for staff	45.00
Blotter, Onward for God & Country, BSA, 1950s, w/scouts	5.00
Book, Collecting Boy Scout Rank Badges, Myers, 1990	10.00
Book, Lost Patrol, 1913, EX	17.50
Book, Official Scout Bible, 1930, leather, name in gold	15.00
Bookends, Official BSA, Cub Scout issue, pressed wood, 1940s, pr	15.00
Camera, Official Cub Scout, plastic, w/flash attachment	10.00
Canteen, 1930s, rnd type, Wear/Ever, first screw-in top	17.00
Cap, gr baseball type w/Staff patch, 1960s	5.00
Card, membership; plastic, 1915, ring at top, 4-pg	12.00
Cards, Bridge, Official dbl deck, Rockwell	15.00
Cards, Thank You Cards, set of 10, w/sm scout, 1950s, color	10.00
Compass, Pathfinder, 1950s, MIB w/instruction booklet	20.00
Compass, red plastic, 1930, 8-point side	12.00
Cup, collapsible; w/Tenderfoot logo on top, 1930-50	7.00
Decal, Full 1st Class, silver, 1930s	3.00
Decal, Historic Trails Award, red border	2.00
Decal/stickers, Follow the Rugged Road, set of 16	5.00
Drum, BSA, tin, 1908, tin, scouts along border, sm	75.00
First-aid kit, Johnson & Johnson, tin, sq, flip-lid type	8.00
Flag, Regional; 1930-60, 36x60", 1 per region, rare	100.00

Flashlight, Eveready, red head, 3-battery type 3.00
Gadget box, pressed wood, Nat'l Supply, Cub Scout emblem on top ..5.00
Game, Target Ball, marble shooting game, 1920 ....125.00
Gameboard, Progress, 1926, EX 95.00
Handerchief, Cub Scout, bl w/Cub promise 4.00
Hatchet, Bridgeport, 1-pc steel, hickory hdl, 2 types 30.00
Hikemeter (pedometer), w/compass in bk, belt hanger, 1930s 22.50
Jacket, gr poplin type, scout or leader sz, ea 15.00
Money clip, 1969 Nat'l Jamboree, gold in color w/logo 3.00
Neckerchief, 1920, full-sq, Full 1st Class 5.00
Pamphlet, Aids for Tenderfoot, 2nd Class & 1st Class Scouts 3.00
Pamphlet, Camp Fires & Camp Cookers, Palmer, 1930, Boycraft Mfg ..5.00
Pamphlet, Guide to Good Camping, BSA, 1954 ....2.00
Paperweight, wht marble, w/Tenderfoot emblem in center 5.00
Pennant, Official, bl felt, 1937 Jamboree, w/lg logo 75.00
Pennant, set: 1957 Nat'l Jamboree, 3 szs, w/logo 35.00
Pin, Strengthen the Arm of Liberty, stick-bk 3.00
Pin, 1st Class, safety-clasp bk, 1½" 7.00
Pitcher, water; ceramic, scout & Baden-Powel, English, 1920s 75.00
Plaque, Boy Scout Creed, 1924, fr 15.00
Plate, ceramic, Rockwell-Gorham, Campfire Story 40.00
Plate, ceramic, Rockwell-Gorham, Our Heritage 50.00
Postcard, Blazing a Trail, 1914, color, #4 in series 10.00
Postcard, Fr, special World Jamboree, 1937, campfire scene 10.00
Postcard, Official 1959 World Jamboree, w/logo 5.00
Postcard, Uncle Dan Beard, blk & wht, simulated autograph 5.00
Postcard, World Jamboree, 1957, w/Official stamp 4.00
Poster, Henry Aldridge Boy Scout, promotional, 3 issued, ea 25.00
Poster, Mr Scoutmaster, lobby cards, 1950s, set of 6 ....40.00
Poster, recruiting, Schuyler, 1946, EX 85.00
Record, Boy Scouts in Switzerland, 1920, 78 rpm 15.00
Record, Official BSA Scout Marches, 1950, 45 rpm 8.00
Ring, Boy Scout, sterling, w/onyx Tenderfoot logo 8.00
Ring, sterling, Explorer logo in center 10.00
Ring, 1957 Nat'l Jamboree, sterling, w/logo 25.00
Sheet music, Follow Old Glory, Am Jr Boy Scouts, color, 1917 ...12.00
Signal set, Official Scout Signaler, #1095, Flagon, metal 15.00
Tie bar, Nat'l Staff, gold bar, w/logo, clip-on 6.00
Tie bar, Veteran; Leader, for 5-50 years, ea 7.00
Tray, silver, Rockwell picture under glass, 1940s 20.00
Watch, Official BSA, Midget Radiolite Army Strap, #1364, 1919 ..75.00
Watch, Official BSA, New Haven, #1255, 1934 ....30.00
Watch fob, Boy Scout w/crossed rifles, 1920 ....45.00
Watch fob, Boy Scout w/rifle, silver, 1912 ....60.00
Watch fob, Official BSA, Scoutmaster's, gr enamel center, #308 .200.00
Watch fob, Official BSA, Troop Committee, wht enamel, #312 ..200.00
Woodcarving kit, complete, #1241 ....25.00

Girl Scouts

Collecting Girl Scout memorabilia is a hobby that is growing nationwide. When Sir Baden-Powell founded the Boy Scout Movement in England, it proved to be too attractive and too well adapted to youth to limit its great opportunities to boys alone. The sister organization, known in England as the Girl Guides, quickly followed and was equally successful. Mrs. Juliette Low, an American visitor to England and a personal friend of the father of Scouting, realized the tremendous future of the movement for her own country, and with the active and friendly cooperation of the Baden-Powells, she founded the Girl Guides in America, enrolling the first patrols in Savannah, Georgia, in March 1912. In 1915 National Headquarters were established in Washington, D.C., and the name was changed to Girl Scouts. The first National Convention was held in 1914. Each succeeding year has shown growth and increased enthusiasm in this steadily growing army of girls and young women who are learning in the happiest ways to combine patriotism, outdoor activities of every kind, skill in every branch of domestic science and high standards of community service. Today there are over 400,000 Girl Scouts and more than 22,000 leaders. Mr. Sayers is also our Girl Scout advisor.

Armband, Senior Service Scout 20.00
Badge, 1st Class, cloth & khaki twill 7.00
Book, Brownies, by Mildred A Wirt, 1949-53 ....3.00
Book, GSA Nature; for leaders 5.00
Camera, box type, Official GSA, Falcon, 1940 ....30.00
Catalog, Official GSA Uniform; 1930s 15.00
Cup, collapsible, GSA, aluminum, 1950 ....5.00
Diary, GSA, 1929 ....15.00
Doll, Girl Scout, Effanbee, 1965, MIB 30.00
Doll, GSA Uniform; Georgene Novelties, cloth, 1954, 13¼" 30.00
Dress, Brownie, w/orange necktie, membership card, 1950s, M 20.00
Flag, Official Brownie; 1930s, sm 25.00
Flags, signal; Official GSA, wooden hdls, 1920 ....15.00
Game, Troup, complete, orig box 30.00
Handbook, Official GSA, 1913 ....150.00
Magazine, Am Girl, 1920-30s, ea 10.00
Medal, Life Saving, bronze, 1916, Maltese cross 200.00
Medal, 3rd Liberty Loan, GSA, only 416 awarded 200.00
Pin, Brownie, elf shape, plastic & metal, 1920 ....20.00
Pin, Mariners program, sm anchor guard 15.00
Pin, Wing Scouting, 1941 ....35.00
Poster, Scouting Trains in Democracy, 1918, 20x30" 100.00
Sewing kit, red plastic, opens like purse, 1950s, complete, M 58.00
Uniform, Official GSA, full dress, lt gr, 1930s 50.00
Uniform, Official GSA, top & skirt, khaki, 1917-23, no badges ...75.00
Wings, Brownie, 1931 ....10.00

Scrimshaw

The most desirable examples of the art of scrimshaw can be traced back to the first half of the 19th century to the heyday of the whaling industry. Some voyages lasted for several years, and conditions on board were often dismal. Sailors filled the long hours by using the tools of their trade to engrave whale teeth and make boxes, pie crimpers (jagging wheels), etc., from the bone and teeth of captured whales. Eskimos also made scrimshaw, sometimes borrowing designs from the sailors who traded with them.

Beware of fraudulent pieces; fakery is prevalent in this field. Many carved teeth are of recent synthetic manufacture (examples engraved with information such as ship's or captain's names, dates, places, etc., should be treated with extreme caution) and have no antique or collectible value. A listing of most of these plastic items has been published by the Kendall Whaling Museum in Sharon, Massachusetts. If you're in doubt or a novice collector, it's best to deal with reputable people who **guarantee** the items they sell. Our advisor for this category is John Rinaldi; he is listed in the Directory under Maine. See also Powder Horns.

Whalebone box, sliding cover with carving of Venus in conch shell drawn by sea horses, inset with five South American coins, sides decorated with British ships, cannons, etc., ca 1834, 2½x6x3⅝", $3,450.00.

Photo courtesy Butterfield & Butterfield

Box, ditty; open-cvd whalebone, skirted lid, 1840s, 4¾x10¼x7" ...5,750.00
Clock tower, whale ivory/bone/teakwood base, much cvg, 1850, 8" 8,950.00
Corset stay, buildings w/flags/whales/steamship/etc, 14¼x1½" ..1,400.00
Crimper, hand forms hdl, cuff detail, whale ivory, 1840s, 2" wheel .2,750.00
Crimper, lady's leg, whale ivory, baleen spacer, 1840s, 2" wheel ...3,275.00
Crimper, 3-tined fork end & crimping wheel, 7" 450.00
Fid, trn top, incised lines, mushroom-shaped end, 1860s, 1⅝" dia ..575.00
Rolling pin, 5-pc wooden cylinder w/whale ivory hdls, 1850s, 16" .695.00
Tooth, Am bark/sm sailing vessels, geometrics/whale scene, 1830s, 6" ..3,350.00
Tooth, Am Eagle w/arrows/etc & Mary Queen of Scots, 1830s, 6½" ..6,985.00
Tooth, Am ship/eagle & arrows, mc stain, 1840s, 4⅝x2½" 1,925.00
Tooth, church/3-masted ship under sail, 19th C, 5" 700.00
Tooth, girl in fancy clothes (full view), EX age/color, 5½" 850.00
Tooth, Lady Liberty/lg Am shield, old chip, 19th C, 4½" 695.00
Tooth, lady w/flowing hair & dagger, 5" 400.00
Tooth, Victorian lady & lady w/plumed hat, 4½" 600.00
Walking stick, narhwal shaft, ivory knob/hdl, spiral cvg, 1850s, 39" ..5,500.00

Sebastians

Sebastian miniatures were first produced in 1938 by Prescott W. Baston in Marblehead, Massachusetts. Since then more than six hundred have been modeled. These figurines have been sold through gift shops all over the country, primarily in the New England states. In 1976 Baston withdrew his Sebastians from production. Under an agreement with the Lance Corporation of Hudson, Massachusetts, one hundred designs were selected to be produced by that company under Baston's supervision. Those remaining were discontinued. In the time since then, the older figurines have become very collectible. Price is determined by three factors: 1) in production/out of production; 2) labels — color of oval label, i.e. red, blue, green, etc.; Marblehead label, a green and silver palette-shaped label used until 1977; or no label; 3) condition. If there is no label and the varnish coat is quite yellowed, then it is considered to be of the Marblehead era. Dates are merely copyright dates and have no particular significance in regard to value. (Signed) 'P.W. Baston' should only have impact on price when the signature is an actual autograph. Most pieces are manufactured with an imprinted 'P.W. Baston' on the base. Baston died in 1984; the miniatures are now being done by P.W. Baston, Jr.

Adams Academy, w/steeple 150.00
Aunt Polly 23.00
Becky Thatcher 23.00
Best in the Midwest, paperweight 85.00
Betsy Ross 23.00
Chiquita Banana 300.00
Christmas Morning 30.00
Doctor Berry (boys' camp fund) 60.00
Elizabeth Monroe 115.00
First Days of Fall 37.50
Gathering Tulips 100.00
Grocery Store, Marblehead label 65.00
Hanna Dustin, pen stand 300.00
In Candy Store 23.00
Jack & Jill, bl label 35.00
Katrina Vontassel 23.00
Mrs Obocell 400.00
Obesious Wiggam Esq, MIB 200.00
Prince Philip 200.00
Princess Elizabeth 200.00
Ronald Reagan, Young Republican 85.00
Sam Weller 60.00
Sampling the Stew, Marblehead era 55.00

Scrooge 25.00
Skipping Rope 35.00
Stagecoach 60.00
Swanboat, Masons 300.00
Tom Sawyer 23.00
Weaver & Loom, Marblehead label 60.00
White House, gold 100.00

Sevres

Fine-quality porcelains have been made in Sevres, France, since the early 1700s. Rich ground colors were often hand painted with portraits, scenics, and florals. Some pieces were decorated with transfer prints and decalcomania; many were embellished with heavy gold. These wares are the most respected of all French porcelains. Their style and designs have been widely copied, and some of the items listed below are Sevres-type wares.

Bleu Celeste porcelain urns, couple in landscape featuring ruins, gold ring handles, late 19th century, 14", $2,750.00 for the pair.

Centerpc, floral reserves on cobalt, Greek-key hdls, ped, 11x14" ...1,200.00
Charger, peasant lady/child, sgn Furloud, emb gold rim, 17" 850.00
Clock, mantel; bsk figures depicting the Arts, mc florals, 12" 990.00
Cup & saucer, cherubs & crowned Louis Philippe monogram, pr ...135.00
Figurine, cupid on throne, bl/wht hard-paste biscuit, 6½" 1,725.00
Foot basin, floral reserves on bl w/gold, 8½x22x14½" 385.00
Urn, cherubs picking fruit, gilt-bronze mts, 14x8", EX, pr 1,100.00
Urn, court scenes on gilt bronze w/cobalt, Abmlet, 24½", pr ..3,500.00
Urn, courting scene reserve on cobalt w/gold, bronze hdls, 40" ..4,000.00
Urn, Nouveau lady's portrait in floral fr, bronze mts, 25½" 8,000.00
Urn, 18th-C couple in landscape, Morin, bronze mts, 27x11" ..3,500.00

Sewer Tile

Whimsies, advertising novelties, and other ornamental items were sometimes made in potteries where the primary product was simply tile.

Ashtray, chimney & hearth form w/tooled 'stones,' 10" L 150.00
Bank, boy's head, 4⅜" 415.00
Birdhouse, rnd mushroom-like shape, sm chips, 8½" 165.00
Figure, dog seated, brn variegated finish, tooled details, 12½" .1,300.00
Figure, dog seated, EX detail, OH, 11" 550.00
Figure, dog seated, flat head, folky details, 9", EX 415.00
Figure, dog seated, flat-head type, extensive tooling, 11½" 2,300.00
Figure, dog seated, raised paw, OH, 9⅜" 500.00
Figure, duck, solid body, hand molded/tooled, rstr bill, 14½" L ..825.00
Figure, eagle, wings down, 6¾" 55.00
Figure, eagle, wings wide, FOE 1944, sm chips, 8" 55.00
Figure, fawn, late, 11" 250.00
Figure, frog, late, 6¾" 160.00
Figure, frog, 4¾" 50.00
Figure, frog on rectangular base, mk Bobby, dtd 1924, flakes, 4½" L .685.00
Figure, horse head, simple style, 5⅝" 55.00

Figure, keg on stand, Ice Cold 100% Cider 5, 3¾" L 550.00
Figure, lion, wear & old rpr, 4⅝" 100.00
Figure, lion on oval base, att Mogadore OH, rprs, 15", pr 880.00
Figure, lion on rectangular base, dk glaze, 9½" 330.00
Figure, lion on rectangular base, old brn rpt, 10" 220.00
Figure, owl, initialed EJE, OH, 14" 1,430.00
Figure, pig, head up, curly tail, mk JD, 6½" L 220.00
Figure, stump, 2½" 100.00
Lamp base, tree & 4 stumps, nude & lion, sgn, 1926, 13¾" 2,650.00
Lamp base, tree w/bird, sm chips, 8⅝" 100.00
Planter, stump, sm bird in crook, chips, 12¼" 165.00
Planter, stump w/vine, artist sgn, 12½x12½" 165.00
Shakers, tooled tree bark, 3", pr 275.00

Sewing Items

Sewing collectibles continue to intrigue collectors, and fine 19th-century and earlier pieces are commanding higher prices due to increased demand and scarcity. Complete needlework boxes and chatelaines in original condition are rare, but even incomplete examples can be considered prime additions to any collection, as long as they meet certain criteria: boxes should contain fittings of the period; the chains of the chatelaine should be intact and contemporary with the style; and the individual holders should be original and match the brooch. As 19th-century items become harder to find, new trends in collecting develop. Needle books, many of which were decorated with horses, children, beautiful ladies, etc., have become very popular. Some were giveaways printed with advertisements of products and businesses. Even early pins are collectible; the first ones were made in two parts with the round head attached separately. Pin disks, pin cubes, and other pin holders also make interesting additions to a sewing collection.

Tape measures are very popular — especially Victorian figurals. These command premium prices. Early wooden examples of transferware and Tunbridge ware have gained in popularity, as have figurals of vegetable ivory, celluloid, and other early plastics. From the 20th century, tatting shuttles made of plastics, bone, brass, sterling, and wood decorated with Art Nouveau, Art Deco, and more modern designs are in demand — so are darning eggs, stilettos, and thimbles. Because of the decline in the popularity of needlework after the 1920s (due to increased production of machine-made items), novelty items were made in an attempt to regain consumer interest, and many collectors today also find these appealing.

Watch for reproductions. Sterling thimbles are being made in Holland and the U.S. and are available in many Victorian-era designs. But the originals are usually plainly marked, either in the inside apex or outside on the band. Avoid testing gold and silver thimbles for content; this often destroys the inside marks. Instead, research the manufacturer's mark; this will often denote the material as well. Even though the reproductions are well finished, they do not have manufacturers' marks. Many thimbles are being made specifically for the collectible market; reproductions of porcelain thimbles are also found. Prices should reflect the age and availability of these thimbles. For more information see *Sewing Tools & Trinkets* by Helen Lester Thompson from Collector Books.

Box, bird's-eye maple w/walnut, tiered, 1-drw, 1850s, 8x10x7" ..375.00
Box, Lehnware, brn w/floral reserves, 5-compartment, 11" L ..1,125.00
Darner, aqua glass egg form w/amber stem, 6¾" L 80.00
Darner, ebony w/ornate sterling hdl 75.00
Embroidery hoop holder, Priscilla, 1902 ....80.00
Embroidery machine, Marvel, ca 1918 ....22.50
Embroidery punch, sterling w/emb florals 65.00
Hoop, embroidery; wood, w/clamp for table 75.00
Kit, Lydia Pinkham, metal 15.00
Knitting ruler, celluloid w/floral decor, folding type 20.00

Measure, advertising, Fab Detergent 25.00
Measure, advertising, Sweet Rose Flour 45.00
Measure, brass, turtle figural, w/motto, 2x1½", EX 65.00
Measure, celluloid, alarm clock form, Germany, 2" 135.00
Measure, celluloid, cactus form w/sm bloom, 2¼" 155.00
Measure, celluloid, fish figural 100.00
Measure, celluloid, Geo Washington, no tape 12.00
Measure, celluloid, movie star, rare 125.00
Measure, celluloid, pear form w/fly pull, Germany, 2½", EX 120.00
Measure, celluloid, penguin figural, bl 120.00
Measure, metal, rabbit figural, Germany 325.00
Measure, tin, egg form w/fly pull, orig pnt, VG 100.00
Measure/pincushion, plaster, Little Red Riding Hood, nodder 65.00
Measure/pincushion, potbelly stove, pottery, Japan, 5" 20.00
Nanny's pin, w/orig thread in holder, w/opal 225.00
Needle holder, chatelaine; mk sterling, eng initials, 2⅛" 45.00
Needle holder, cvd ivory, w/13 sm tools, 6" 135.00
Needle holder, sterling, eng decor, cylindrical, #925, 2½x½" 35.00
Needle holder, sterling, floral w/red stones, France, 1900s, 2⅞" .135.00

Pincushion, sterling high-heel shoe, cushion top, ca 1890, 2¾" long, $200.00.

Pincushion, bronze, monkey figural w/EX pnt, Vienna, ca 1800, 3" ..550.00
Pincushion, bsk, head w/cushion base, glass eyes, #1909, 7½x4½" .60.00
Pincushion, leather, slipper w/braid trim, Turkey, ca 1890 ....20.00
Pincushion, metal, pig, sitting, Germany 275.00
Pincushion, porc, boy in top hat, yel lustre, Japan, 2¾" 25.00
Pincushion, porc, dog, Made in Japan, 4½" 22.00
Pincushion, porc, doll head center of satin cushion, 6x6", EX 70.00
Pincushion, porc, elephant, calico, jtd, Made in Japan, 2x3¾" 25.00
Pincushion, porc, Hummel-like girl figural, Japan 12.50
Pincushion, porc, Mickey Mouse figural, Japan, 1930s, 4¼" 160.00
Pincushion, porc, shoe, wht w/red & bl flowers, Occupied Japan, 2x3" ...25.00
Pincushion, silk w/much beadwork, Victorian, 8x11" 55.00
Pincushion, velvet heart shape, beaded, late 19th C, 2½x5" 75.00
Pincushion, velveteen calico cat, steel eyes, 19th C, 3¾" 415.00
Pincushion, velveteen mouse on ball, blk bead eyes, 19th C, 3½" ..375.00
Pinking machine, Singer, NMIB 37.50
Scissors, chatelaine; folding, sterling hdl, mini 35.00
Shuttle, blk Bakelite, EX 16.00
Shuttle, sewing machine; Boye #22R, M in wooden tube 23.00
Shuttle, tatting; mk Boyle Improved 3.00
Stand, seamstress'; wicker, stand-up, opens like book, ca 1910 ...375.00
Thimble, Adams, china, England 15.00
Thimble, Greif, 925 silver, Germany 80.00
Thimble, Ketcham & McDougall, sterling & 14k gold, initial, 1900 .115.00
Thimble, Ketchum & McDougall, sterling w/gold-plate band 65.00
Thimble, Rockwell, china, Japan 10.00
Thimble, Simons, sterling, Greek Key 25.00
Thimble, Simons, sterling, ovals 30.00
Thimble, Simons, sterling 'target' band 67.50
Thimble, Simons, 14k gold, panel design, ca 1900 ....195.00
Thimble, Simons, 14k gr gold 160.00
Thimble, Stern Bros, sterling, feathers 25.00
Thimble, unmk, aluminum, Stern & Co advertising 12.50
Thimble, unmk, sterling w/gold band & 5 turq stones, gold wash int .125.00
Thimble, unmk, 14k, 2 floral ovals+1 w/monogram, ⅞" 85.00

Thimble holder, silver, rtcl, hinged lid, Webster Co, NM **195.00**
Thimble holder, sweet grass, w/NP thimble & holder for scissors .**95.00**
Thimble/jigger, SP, emb Mexican & cactus, New Mexico **65.00**
Thimble/jigger, sterling, Only a Thimble Full inscr at top **125.00**
Thread holder, sterling, plain **125.00**

Sewing Machines

The fact that Thomas Saint, an English cabinetmaker, invented the first sewing machine in 1790 was unknown until 1874 when Newton Wilson, an English sewing machine manufacturer and patentee, chanced upon the drawings included in a patent specification describing methods of making boots and shoes. By the middle of the 19th century, several patents were granted to American inventors, among them Isaac M. Singer, whose machine used a treadle. These machines were ruggedly built, usually of cast iron. By the 1860s and '70s, the sewing machine had become a popular commodity, and the ironwork became more detailed and ornate.

Though rare machines are costly, many of the old oak treadle machines (especially these brands: Davis, Home, Household, National, New Home, Singer, Weed, Wheeler & Wilson, and Willcox & Gibbs) have only nominal value. Machines manufactured after 1875 are generally very common as most were mass produced. Values for these later sewing machines range from $50.00 to $100.00. Refer to *Toy and Miniature Sewing Machines (Books I and II)* by Glenda Thomas for more information. Our advisor for this category is Peter Frei; he is listed in the Directory under Massachusetts. In the listings that follow, unless noted otherwise, values are suggested for machines in excellent working order.

Child's, Artcraft, Jr Miss, metal on wood base, 1940s-50s, from $50 to .**75.00**
Child's, Artcraft, Little Mother, dk bl, w/orig box, from $65 to **85.00**
Child's, Baby Brother, gray-gr metallic, Japan, 1960s, from $75 to .**100.00**
Child's, Betsy Ross, electric, w/base & case, from $75 to **95.00**
Child's, Casige, Deco decor, cam drive, MIG-British Zone, $75 to ..**100.00**
Child's, Casige, sheet metal, cam drive, MIG, pre WWII, from $75 to ..**90.00**
Child's, Diana, bl plastic, battery or hand operated, China, $15 to **30.00**
Child's, F&W Automatic, iron/steel, floral decor, 1907-08, $200 to ...**300.00**
Child's, KAYanEE Sew Master, hand operated, sheet metal, from $75 to ..**100.00**
Child's, Marx Sew Big, die-cast metal, w/plastic table, 1960s **75.00**
Child's, Miss Durham #5810, die-cast metal/plastic, Japan, 1970s-80s ..**35.00**
Child's, Muller #19 Little Beauty, MIG, pre-WWII, from $175 to .**225.00**
Child's, Olympia, manual or battery operated, Japan, from $20 to ..**30.00**
Child's, Singer Sewhandy Model 20, 1950s, from $100 to **125.00**
Eldredge Automatic, 1880s, complete, EX..**145.00**
Essex, highly chromed, wood base, 1940s-50s, 8" L......................**130.00**
Florence, CI, belt driven, Pat Nov 12, 1850, 16" L, EX **260.00**
Grover & Baker, last Pat May 27, 1856.....................................**1,200.00**
Singer, leather sewing, floor model, heavy, EX.............................**300.00**
Singer, Pat 1846, MOP inlay in head, walnut fold-out case.........**800.00**
Singer Featherweight #210, w/attachments, EX in case **465.00**
Singer Featherweight #221-1, blk/gold, w/case & attachments....**300.00**
Wheeler & Wilson, 625 Broadway, EX...**125.00**

Shaker Items

The Shaker community was founded in America in 1776 at Niskeyuna, New York, by a small group of English 'Shaking Quakers.' The name referred to a group dance which was part of their religious rites. Their leader was Mother Ann Lee. By 1815 their membership had grown to more than one thousand in eighteen communities as far west as Indiana and Kentucky. But in less than a decade, their numbers began to decline until today only a handful remain. Their furniture is prized for its originality, simplicity, workmanship, and practicality. Few

pieces were signed. Some were carefully finished to enhance the natural wood; a few were painted.

Although other methods were used earlier, most Shaker boxes were of oval construction with overlapping 'fingers' at the seams to prevent buckling as the wood aged. Boxes with original paint fetch triple the price of an unpainted box; number of fingers and overall size should also be considered.

Although the Shakers were responsible for weaving a great number of baskets, their methods are not easily distinguished from those of their outside neighbors, and it is nearly impossible without first-hand knowledge to positively attribute a specific example to their manufacture. They were involved in various commercial efforts other than woodworking — among them sheep and dairy farming, sawmilling, and pipe and brick making. They were the first to raise crops specifically for seed and to market their product commercially. They perfected a method to recycle paper and were able to produce wrinkle-free fabrics. Our advisor for this category is Nancy Winston; she is listed in the Directory under New Hampshire. Standard two-letter state abbreviations have been used throughout the following listings.

Key:
bj — bootjack
CB — Canterbury
EF — Enfield
NL — New Lebanon
PH — Pleasant Hill
ML — Mt. Lebanon
SDL — Sabbathday Lake
WV — Watervliet

Set of six graduated boxes, two or three fingers, natural finish, oval, with lids, ranging from 3½" to 15" long, $2,900.00 for the set.

Basket, feather; splint w/woven lid, bentwood hdl, 9⅜x11¾" **190.00**
Basket, field; splint, stationary bentwood hdl, 12x16" **300.00**
Basket, sewing; 4-finger, bentwood hdl, silk lined, 3x9x7" **230.00**
Bed, walnut, rfn, KY, ca 1850, 33x76x34" **875.00**
Bench, kneeling; poplar, old natural patina, att, 6¾x36" **350.00**
Bench, meeting house; maple/pine, 18-spindle, 5-leg, 19th C, 73" .**450.00**
Bench, wash; 2-tier pine w/red stain, 63x42x18", EX **500.00**
Blanket chest, butternut w/orig red, ML, 1840s, 44x43x18" **1,850.00**
Blanket rack, softwood, arched shoe ft, dk stain, att ML, 52x32" .**400.00**
Bonnet, doll; w/inner liner & lt bl fringe, SDL, 3½x4", VG **450.00**
Box, Harvard type w/iron tacks, old rfn w/gr traces, 6" **175.00**
Box, sewing; hexagonal, w/pincushion & needle holder, SDL, 4½" ..**350.00**
Box, sewing; mahog/flame mahog veneer w/inlay, 2-drw, 9x9x6" ..**1,100.00**
Box, sewing; pine/maple, copper tacks, swivel hdl, 8½" **550.00**
Box, sewing; 2-tier, w/drw, spool compartment & pincushion, 7" .**165.00**
Box, trinket; bentwood, pnt oval, finger-like joints, 2x3½x2¾" .**400.00**
Box, 2-finger, blk w/decoupage int, 19th C, 1¾x5" **300.00**
Box, 3-finger, copper tacks, old natural patina, 9" L **550.00**
Box, 3-finger, iron tacks, old bl-gr pnt, 6⅜" L **660.00**
Box, 3-finger, worn gray over bl, 6⅜" **200.00**
Box, 4-finger, bentwood, 2x6x4¾" **295.00**
Box, 4-finger, copper tacks, old red pnt, 11½" L **1,430.00**
Box, 4-finger, pine/maple, copper tacks, 7¼", VG **165.00**
Broadside, Rules for Doing Good..., 1850s, fr: 13¾x10⅝" **135.00**

Cabinet, panel door over 3 drws, orig red wash, hangs, 24x16x7" ..**3,225.00**
Cabinet, pine w/red, hinged door, drw, hangs, 1850s, 37x12x8" **1,100.00**
Candle holder, tin, w/ejector & conical snuffer, 4⅜x7¼" dia **200.00**
Carrier, 3-finger, natural, lg loop hdl, 10½x12½x8" **395.00**
Chair, side; maple, 3-slat bk, yel traces, rpl seat, 1850, 41" **750.00**
Cloak, beige Fr-wove broadcloth, no label, full-length **160.00**
Clothes brush, wood hdl, blk bristles, SDL, 9¼" **75.00**
Cradle, adult; pine w/red wash, dvtl/nailed, MA, 19th C, 79" **975.00**
Cupboard, orange on pine, panel do, 2-shelf, ML, 1830s, 42x25" **3,225.00**
Cupboard, poplar w/brn grpt, 1-brd ends, gallery, IN, 33x28" **715.00**
Cupboard, red wash, panel do, 4-shelf int, ML, 1850s, 74x30" ..**19,550.00**
Cupboard over drws, cherry, built-in, rfn, 1830s, 77x31x16" ...**7,000.00**
Cupboard over drws, pnt pine, built-in, ML, 1850s, 68x21x14" .**975.00**
Desk, deaconess'; butternut/tiger maple, EF, 1830, rfn, 29x21x17" ..**7,000.00**
Dust pan, trn maple hdl, 19th C, 16½" **460.00**
Glove form, maple, detachable thumbs, 12x3½", pr **175.00**
Herb dryer, folding, wood w/rope hinges, 41x24x1" **170.00**
Measure, SDL stencil in oval on natural, 4¼x7¾" **200.00**
Rack, 17 trn pegs, old powder bl over dk bl-gr pnt, 94" L **625.00**
Rack, 7 cvd pegs, brn-pnt pine, NY, 19th C, 3¼x84" **700.00**
Rack, 8 trn pegs, tan pnt, 3x58", EX **850.00**
Rocker, #3, dk orig finish, splint seat, 33", VG **300.00**
Rocker, #3, tape bk & seat, old dk brn varnish, ML, 34" **385.00**
Rocker, #7, 4-slat, shawl bar, wool seat, ML, 42" **1,100.00**
Rocker, armchair; blk rpt, rpl tape seat, ML type, 37¼" **450.00**
Rocker, armchair; cherry w/dk stain, splint seat, NY, 1900, 85" .**500.00**
Rocker, armchair; maple, 4-slat w/shawl bar, rpl seat, ML, 43" ...**800.00**
Rocker, maple, old rfn w/red traces, rpl seat, CB, 40" **700.00**
Rocker, old dk finish, rpl tape seat, ML, 35¾" **425.00**
Rocker, sewing; maple/oak, 3-slat, splint seat, rfn, 35" **350.00**
Scarf, gray silk w/bl stripe, KY, 1950s, 30x30", EX **1,100.00**
Sieve, horsehair, att DL, minor age cracks, 11" dia **150.00**
Sieve, horsehair in wooden fr, natural color, 3x1½", G **95.00**
Stand, seed sorting; lipped top, trn legs, OH, 1850s, 31x21x21" ..**1,100.00**
Stand, sewing; 4 brass rods/pincushion/emery, 5½x4¾" **275.00**
Steps, nailed, mortised bk, arched cutouts, 2-step, 9¼x11¾x8" ..**200.00**
Steps, sewing; pine/poplar, arched sides, NL, 1850-75, 15x16x13" ..**2,645.00**
Sugar chest, figured maple/chestnut/walnut/oak, 43x47x26" ...**1,875.00**
Swift, yel stain, table-top style, 22" closed, G **350.00**
Table, ministry; maple/pine, ped posts ea end, 19th C, 72" L **700.00**
Umbrella swift, wooden, clamp base, old yel traces, MA, 25" **400.00**
Wardrobe, red wash, shaped sides/panel door/shelves, 1870s, 84x48" ..**5,175.00**

Shaving Mugs

Between 1865 and 1920, owning a personalized shaving mug was the order of the day, and the 'occupationals' were the most prestigious. The majority of men having occupational mugs would often frequent the barber shop several times a week, where their mugs were clearly visible for all to see in the barber's rack. As a matter of fact, this display was in many ways the index of the individual town or neighborhood.

During the first twenty years, blank mugs were almost entirely imported from France, Germany, and Austria and were hand painted in this country. Later on, some china was produced by local companies. It is noteworthy that American vitreous china is inferior to the imported Limoges and is subject to extreme crazing.

Artists employed by the American barber supply companies were for the most part extremely talented and capable of executing any design the owner required, depicting his occupation, fraternal affiliation, or preferred sport. When the mug was completed, the name and the gold trim were always added in varying degrees, depending on the price paid by the customer. This price was determined by the barber who added his markup to that of the barber-supply company. As mentioned

above, the popularity of the occupational shaving mug diminished with the advent of World War I and the introduction by Gillette of the safety razor. Later followed the blue laws forcing barber shops to close on Sundays, thereby eliminating the political and social discussions for which they were so well noted.

Occupational shaving mugs are the most sought after of the group which would also include those with sport affiliations. Fraternal mugs, although desirable, do not command the same price as the occupationals. Occasionally, you will find the owner's occupation together with his fraternal affiliation. This combination could add anywhere between 25% to 50% to the price, which is dependent on the execution of the painting, rarity of the subject, and detail. Some subjects can be done very simply; others can be done in extreme detail, commanding substantially higher prices. It is fair to say, however, that the rarity of the occupation will dictate the price. Mugs with heavily worn gold loose between 20% and 30% of their value immediately. This would not apply to the gold trim around the rim, but to the loss of the name itself. Our advisor for this category is Burton Handelsman; he is listed in the Directory under New York.

Civil War era, dk gray tin, side brush holder, strap hdl **120.00**
Comic, drunk & dog at lamppost, Made in Germany, 3⅝" **575.00**
Decorative, mtn scene w/church & lake, 5-color, EX **100.00**
Decorative, sheafs of grain, cottage scene, 4" **250.00**
Fraternal, Civil War Sons Assoc, medals, gilt band, VG **125.00**
Fraternal, Crown of Life & cross, EX gold, rpr **200.00**
Fraternal, eagle w/shield, Freedom/Charity/Friendship, T&V **95.00**
Fraternal, Modern Woodmen of Am & name, gold trim, 3¾" **130.00**

Occupationals: H Hemberger, MM Chor and lyre, purple wrap, T&V Limoges, 3⅝", $400.00; Jas McAndrew and man in NYC & HR Railroad station ticket booth, 3⅞", extremely rare, $5,300.00. (The lettering on the ticket booth contributed to this auction-realized price; without this detail, the value would have been about half as much.)

Occupational, baseball player, bats & ball, Germany, 3¾" **2,300.00**
Occupational, blacksmith, man shoeing horse, Germany, EX **750.00**
Occupational, bricklayer, man at wall, 3⅝" **900.00**
Occupational, carpenter, man planing brd, Germany, 3¾" **250.00**
Occupational, carpenter, man w/tools, EX gold, Germany **450.00**
Occupational, deliveryman, man in horse-drawn stake wagon, 3⅝" .**575.00**
Occupational, druggist, man waiting on lady, Germany **650.00**
Occupational, drum major, man in uniform w/baton, 3¾" **2,500.00**
Occupational, fireman, 2-horse fire wagon & name in gold, KPM ...**1,100.00**
Occupational, furniture maker, man at work, EX gold, M **650.00**
Occupational, house painter, man working, rustic decor, 3⅝" **525.00**
Occupational, hunter w/dog & ducks, 3¾x4" dia, VG **350.00**
Occupational, milkman, horse-drawn Dairy wagon, 3½" **425.00**
Occupational, minister, open Bible, CA Smith Supplies, EX ..**1,600.00**
Occupational, salesman, w/customer & new boots, 3¾", EX **750.00**
Occupational, stationary machinist, detailed machine, T&V, 4" ..**425.00**
Occupational, storekeeper, clerk w/lady, 3⅝" **450.00**

Occupational, storekeeper, music store street scene, 3¾" 650.00
Occupational, trainman, locomotive & tender, 3⅞" 250.00
Occupational, trainman, passenger car & name, Germany, 3¾" ...375.00
Occupational, trolleyman, trolley/NYRR Co, 3¾" 2,200.00
Occupational/fraternal, baker's emblem/B&CWIU of A, Bavaria, 4" .1,050.00
Patriotic, eagle & flags, mc w/gold, mk Germany, NM 200.00

Shawnee

The Shawnee Pottery Company operated in Zanesville, Ohio, from 1937 to 1961. They produced inexpensive novelty ware (vases, flowerpots, and figurines) as well as a very successful line of figural cookie jars, creamers, and salt and pepper shakers.

They also produced three dinnerware lines, the first of which, Valencia, was designed by Louise Bauer in 1937 for Sears & Roebuck. A starter set was given away with the purchase of one of their refrigerators. Second and most popular was the Corn line. The original design was called White Corn. In 1946 the line was expanded and the color changed to a more natural yellow hue. It was marketed under the name Corn King, and it was produced from 1946 to 1954. Then the colors were changed again. Kernels became a lighter yellow and shucks a darker green. This variation was called Corn Queen. (Our values are for Corn King unless White Corn is noted in the description; Corn Queen is slightly less in value than Corn King.) Their third dinnerware line, produced after 1954, was called Lobsterware. It was made in either black, brown, or gray; lobsters were usually applied to serving pieces and accessory items.

For further study we recommend these books: *The Collector's Guide to Shawnee Pottery* by Janice and Duane Vanderbilt, who are listed in the Directory under Indiana; and *Shawnee Pottery, An Identification and Value Guide*, by Jim and Dev Mangus, who are listed in Ohio.

Cookie Jars

Basketweave, floral decal, mk USA, 7½" 125.00
Dutch Boy (Jack), dbl striped pants, mk USA 550.00
Dutch Boy (Jack), gold & decals, mk USA 450.00
Dutch Boy (Jack), yel pants/patches/gold, mk USA 525.00
Dutch Girl (Jill), tulip, gold & decals, mk USA 375.00
Dutch Girl (Jill), tulip, mk USA 250.00
Dutch Girl (Jill), yel skirt, gold & decals, mk USA 350.00
Great Northern Girl, dk gr, mk Great Northern USA 1026 ...475.00
Jo Jo the Clown, mk Shawnee 12, 9½" 475.00
Jug, Pennsylvania Dutch, mk USA, 8¼" 275.00
Jumbo, sitting elephant, gold & decals, mk USA, 12" 950.00
Little Chef, caramel, mk USA, 8½" 175.00
Little Chef, mc, mk USA, 8½" 150.00
Muggsy, decals & gold , mk Patented Muggsy USA, 11¾" (+) ...850.00
Owl, mk USA, 11½" 150.00
Puss 'n Boots, gold/decals, short tail, mk, 10¼", (+) $550 to 800.00
Sailor Boy (Jack Tar), blond hair/gold/decals, mk USA, 12" (+) .1,200.00
Smiley the Pig, bee above left eye, w/gold & decals, mk USA (+) ...750.00
Smiley the Pig, bl neckerchief, mk USA (+) 150.00
Smiley the Pig, chrysanthemum, mk USA (+) 400.00
Smiley the Pig, gr neckerchief, mk USA (+) 180.00
Smiley the Pig, shamrocks on chest, mk USA (+) 400.00
Winnie the Pig, apples, mk USA (+) 525.00
Winnie the Pig, clover bud, mk Pat Winnie USA (+) 700.00
Winnie the Pig, peach collar, mk USA (+) 375.00
Winnie the Pig, peach collar/gold, mk USA (+) 900.00
Winnie the Pig, shamrocks, mk USA (+) 375.00
Winnie the Pig, shamrocks/red collar/gold, mk USA (+) 1,100.00

Corn Line

Bowl, fruit; mk Shawnee 92, 6" 40.00
Bowl, mixing; mk Shawnee 5, 5" 22.00
Bowl, mixing; mk Shawnee 6, 6½" 30.00
Bowl, mixing; mk Shawnee 8, 8" 40.00
Bowl, soup/cereal; mk Shawnee 94 ....45.00
Bowl, vegetable; mk Shawnee 95, 9" 50.00
Butter dish, mk Shawnee 72, w/lid 50.00
Casserole, mk Shawnee 73, ind 125.00
Casserole, mk Shawnee 74, lg 45.00
Cookie jar, Corn King, mk Shawnee 66, 10½" 300.00
Cookie jar, Corn Queen, mk Shawnee 66, 10¼" 300.00

Creamer, 70, $28.00.

Creamer, White Corn, mk USA, 12-oz 25.00
Cup, mk 90 ....30.00
Jug, mk Shawnee 71, 40-oz 65.00
Mug, mk Shawnee 69, 8-oz 45.00
Plate, mk Shawnee 68, 10" 36.00
Plate, salad; mk Shawnee 93, 8" 30.00
Platter, mk Shawnee 96, 12" 52.00
Saucer, mk 91 ....15.00
Shakers, 3¼", pr 26.00
Shakers, 5¼", pr 35.00
Sugar bowl/utility jar, mk Shawnee 78 ....30.00
Sugar shaker, White Corn, mk USA 55.00
Teapot, mk Shawnee 65, 10-oz 165.00
Teapot, mk Shawnee 75, 30-oz 75.00
Teapot, White Corn, mk USA, 30-oz 75.00
Tray, relish; mk Shawnee 79 ....35.00

Kitchen Ware

Bowl, batter; Snowflake, mk USA 20.00
Canister, Fern, w/lid, mk USA, 2½-qt 65.00
Canister, fruit decal, mk USA, 2-qt 50.00
Canister, HP, gold trim, mk USA, 2-qt 75.00
Casserole, fruit; mk Shawnee USA 83 ....40.00
Coffee maker, Sunflower, mk USA 145.00
Coffeepot, AD; ribbed, mk USA 35.00
Creamer, Dutch style w/red feather decor, mk USA 12 ......35.00
Creamer, elephant, gold & decals, mk Pat USA 325.00
Creamer, Fern, mk USA, 9-oz 30.00
Creamer, Pennsylvania Dutch, heart & flower decor, mk USA 12 .55.00
Grease jar, cottage, mk USA 8 ....350.00
Grease jar, Sahara, mk Kenwood USA 977 ....50.00
Grease jar, Snowflake, mk USA, 3½" 40.00
Ice server, pk elephant w/wht or blk collar, mk Shawnee 60 ......200.00
Jug, ball; emb fruit, mk Shawnee 80, 48-oz 75.00
Jug, ball; Snowflake, mk USA, 2-qt 45.00
Jug, Boy Blue, gold trim, mk Shawnee 46, 20-oz 175.00
Jug, flower decor, space saver, mk USA 35, 20-oz 22.00
Matchbox holder, Fern, mk USA 110.00
Pitcher, Chanticleer, gold & decal, mk Pat Chanticleer USA ...350.00

Pitcher, Flower & Fern, mk USA, 4-cup 22.00
Salt box, Flower & Fern, mk USA 85.00
Shakers, cottage, sm, pr 350.00
Shakers, farmer pigs, sm, pr 75.00
Shakers, flowerpots, sm, pr 24.00
Shakers, Muggsy, gold & decals, lg, pr, minimum value 400.00
Shakers, owls, gold trim, sm, pr 70.00
Shakers, Saucy, sm, pr 20.00
Shakers, Smiley & Winnie, clover bud, lg, pr 200.00
Shakers, Swiss Kids, lg, pr 40.00
Sugar bowl, wave pattern, open, mk USA 22.00
Sugar bowl/utility jar, clover bud, w/lid, mk USA 50.00
Teapot, cottage, mk USA 7, 5-cup, minimum value 650.00
Teapot, Elite, gold & decals, mk USA, 4-cup 65.00
Teapot, Fern, mk USA, 8-cup 50.00
Teapot, Fr drip-type, mk USA, 7-cup 60.00
Teapot, Laurel Wreath, bl, yel or gr, mk USA, 5-cup 45.00
Teapot, Pennsylvania Dutch, mk USA, 30-oz 200.00
Teapot, Sunflower, w/gold, mk USA, 7-cup 75.00
Teapot, tulip & gold, ribbed collar, mk USA 60.00
Tumbler, Stars & Stripes, mk USA, 3" 8.00
Utility bucket, rnd, gold trim, w/lid, mk USA 80.00

Lobster Ware

Bowl, mixing; mk USA 917, 7" 35.00
Casserole, Fr; mk USA 900, 10-oz 18.00
Creamer, jug style, mk USA 921 ....45.00
Hors d'oeuvre holder, mk USA, 7¼" 250.00
Mug, mk Kenwood USA 911, 8-oz 75.00
Patio plate & mug set, mk USA 913, 8-pc 275.00
Salad set, mk USA 924, 9-pc 130.00
Shakers, full body, mk USA & paper label 200.00
Spoon holder, dbl, mk USA 935, 8½" 225.00

Valencia

Ashtray 17.00
Candle holders, tripod, pr 35.00
Carafe, w/lid 45.00
Coffeepot, AD 30.00
Comport, 12" 24.00
Cup, cream soup 12.00
Egg cup 14.00
Jug, 2-pt 25.00
Nappie, lg, 9½" 25.00
Pie server 50.00
Plate, chop; 15" 26.00
Plate, compartment 22.00
Punch bowl, 12" 28.00
Relish tray 130.00
Vase, bud 12.00
Vase, flower; 10" 14.00
Waffle set, 5-pc 95.00

Miscellaneous

Ashtray, Flight, Hostess line, mk Shawnee USA 208, 11" 14.00
Ashtray, leaf, mc, mk USA 350 ....6.00
Ashtray, panther paw, blk & wht, mk USA 25.00
Bookends, flying geese, gold trim, mk Shawnee 4000 ....50.00
Bowl, console; wheat, oval, mk USA, 9½x6" 22.00
Candle holder, Aladdin's-lamp style, mk USA, 2¼" 10.00
Candle holder, magnolia blossoms, gold trim, mk USA, 3", pr 30.00

Cigarette box, emb arrowhead, mk Shawnee 500.00
Clock, trellis, gr & wht or brn & wht, ea 90.00
Dish, bonbon; mc, mk USA 352, rectangular, 5" 8.00
Figurine, deer, mini, no mk 95.00
Figurine, gazelle, gold trim, mk USA 614, 5" 80.00
Figurine, puppy, mini, no mk 24.00
Figurine, Southern girl, mk USA, 4½" 20.00
Flower frog, swan, high base, no mk, 4¼" 35.00
Jardiniere, crisscross pattern, mk Shawnee USA 456, 5½" 10.00
Lamp, Harvest King, no mk 50.00
Lamp, puppy, no mk 75.00
Lamp, wall; fruit, glazed bk, no mk 55.00
Planter, baby skunk, mk Shawnee 512 ....25.00
Planter, cat & sax, mk USA 729 ....30.00
Planter, cub bear & wagon, gold trim, mk Shawnee USA 731 .....35.00
Planter, fox & bag, mk Shawnee USA 50.00
Planter, frog on lily pond, mk USA 30.00
Planter, Irish setter, mk USA 10.00
Planter, kitten, mk USA 723 ....30.00
Planter, mouse & cheese, gold trim, mk USA 705 ....32.00
Planter, panda & cradle, mk Shawnee USA 2031 ....30.00
Planter, pony, mk Kenwood 1509 ....65.00
Planter, pony, mk Shawnee 506 ....35.00
Planter, poodle on bicycle, mk USA 712 ....30.00
Planter, puppy w/fly, no mk 12.00
Planter, rabbit w/turnip, mk USA 703 ....28.00
Planter, squirrel & nut, mk USA 713 ....25.00
Planter, terrier & doghouse, mk Shawnee USA 20.00
Planter/vase, fish, gold trim, mk USA 717 ....45.00
Planting dish, emb flowers, mk USA, 6½" 8.00
Pot & saucer, African Violet; mk Shawnee 533, 3" 8.00
Vase, bud; gold trim, mk USA 1125 ....14.00
Vase, cornucopia; mk Shawnee USA 865, 5" 14.00
Vase, emb flower, gold trim, mk USA, 3½" 22.00
Vase, swan, mini, mk USA 18.00
Vase, swirl, mk USA, 5" 12.00
Vase, wheat, gold trim, mk USA, 5" 20.00
Vase/pitcher, dolphin hdl, gold trim, mk Shawnee 828, 6½" 35.00
Wall pocket, grandfather clock, gold trim, mk USA 1261 ....45.00
Wall pocket, Little Bo Peep, mk USA 586 ....30.00
Wall pocket, Scottie dog, no mk, 9x5" 65.00

Shearwater

Since 1928 generations of the Peter, Walter, and James McConnell Anderson families have been producing figurines and artwares in their studio at Ocean Springs, Mississippi. Their work is difficult to date. Figures from the '20s and '30s won critical acclaim and have continued to be made to the present time. Early marks include a die-stamped 'Shearwater' in a dime-sized circle, a similar ink stamp, and a half-circle mark. Any older item may still be ordered in the same glazes as it was originally produced, so many pieces on the market today may be relatively new. However, the older marks are not currently in use. Currently produced Black and pirate figurines are marked with a hand-incised 'Shearwater' and/or a cipher formed with an 'S' whose bottom curve doubles as the top loop of a 'P' formed by the addition of an upright placed below and to the left of the S. Many are dated, '93, for example. These figures are generally valued at $35.00 to $50.00 and are available at the pottery or by mail order. New decorated and carved pieces are very expensive, starting at $400.00 to $500.00 for a 6" pot.

Bowl, aqua, ca 1930, 2x6½" 75.00
Bowl, bl & gr flambe, mk, 9" sq 60.00

Figurine, Don Quixote **150.00**
Figurine, pelican, Blue Rain, 7¼", NM **80.00**
Luncheon set, bl, gr, or purple flambe, service for 6, 24-pc **400.00**
Pitcher, turq & copper lustre, semicircle mk, 1940s, 5" **80.00**
Vase, bls & grs, 6" **50.00**
Vase, Blue Rain, rolled rim, bulbous, 1950s-60s, 6" **30.00**

Sheet Music

Sheet music is often collected more for its colorful lithographed covers, rather than for the music itself. Transportation songs (which have pictures or illustrations of trains, ships, and planes), ragtime and blues, comic characters (especially Disney), sports, political, and expositions are eagerly sought after. Much of the sheet music on the market today is valued at under $5.00; some of the better examples are listed here. For more information refer to *Sheet Music Reference and Price Guide, Second Edition*, by Anna Marie Guiheen and Marie-Reine A. Pafik. Values are given for examples in excellent to near-mint condition unless otherwise noted.

Ain't She Sweet?, Sophie Tucker photo, 1927 ....**20.00**
America First, Howard Kocian, Patriotic & WWI, 1916 ....**15.00**
As I Was Saying to the Duchess, Movie: Pinocchio, Disney, 1940 .**15.00**
Atlantic City Pageant, John Phillip Sousa, 1927 ....**15.00**
Barney Google, Barney Google & Spark plug photo, 1923 ....**40.00**
Benzine Buggy Man, Alex Kramer, advertising, 1908 ....**35.00**
Brazil, Bob Russel, Movie: Saludos Amigos (Disney), 1939 ....**15.00**

Mutt and Jeff in the Wild and Wooley West, cartoon cover, $25.00.

Breeze From Alabama, Scott Joplin, 1902 ....**50.00**
Carlotta, Cole Porter, Movie: Can Can, 1943 ....**5.00**
Cold, Cold Heart, Hank Williams, Tony Bennett photo, 1951 ......**3.00**
Consider Yourself, Lionel Bart, Musical: Oliver, 1960 ....**5.00**
Cute Little Things You Do, Will Rogers photo, 1931 ....**10.00**
Dance of the Brownies, Palmer Cox cover artist, 1895 ....**35.00**
Dear Old Dixie, Taylor & Heagney, 1906 ....**15.00**
Diane, Rapee & Pollack, Movie: 7th Heaven, 1927 ....**15.00**
Down Among the Sheltering Palms, Al Jolson photo, 1915 ....**15.00**
Dusty Roads, Rene & Rene, Nelson Eddy photo, 1935 ....**5.00**
Elevator Man, Irving Berlin, no date **15.00**
Fine Romance, Astaire & Rogers photo, 1936 ....**10.00**
Fishing the Moon, Musical: Green Bird, Elsa Ryan photo, 1907 ..**20.00**
Garden of My Dreams, Musical: Ziegfeld Follies, 1918 ....**20.00**
Go Fly a Kite, Movie: Star Maker, Bing Crosby photo, 1939 ....**10.00**
Grizzly Bear, Irving Berlin, Maude Raymond photo, 1910 ....**15.00**
Heartbreak Hotel, Elvis Presley photo, 1956 ....**35.00**
Heigh-Ho, Movie: Snow White, 1938 ....**10.00**
Ho Ho Song, Red Buttons photo, 1953 ....**5.00**
I Beg of You, Elvis Presley, 1957 ....**20.00**
I Can't Remember, Irving Berlin, Movie: Easter Parade, 1933 ....**5.00**

I Love You Honolulu, Harry Lauder photo, 1915 ....**10.00**
I'm At the Mercy of Love, Musical: Cotton Club Parade, 1936 ......**8.00**
I'm Popeye the Sailor Man, Movie: Popeye the Sailor, 1934 ....**25.00**
I've Got the Army Blues, Gilbert & Morgan, WWI, 1916 ....**15.00**
I Watch the Love Parade, Musical: The Cat & the Fiddle, 1931 ..**10.00**
If I Should Lose You, Movie: Rose of the Rancho, 1935 ....**10.00**
In the Mood, Movie: Glenn Miller Story w/signed photo, 1954 .**100.00**
Isle D'Amour, Ziegfeld Follies, 1936 ....**10.00**
It Must Be Love, Meyer, Pfeiffer cover artist, 1912 ....**10.00**
Just a Little Closer, Movie: Remote Control, 1930 ....**8.00**
Laughing Water, Starmer cover artist, Indian, 1903 ....**20.00**
Lincoln Centinnial Grand March, President Lincoln photo **50.00**
Majestic Rag, Ben Rawls & Royal Neel, Rag, 1914 ....**10.00**
Mary, Louis & Hirsch, Musical: Mary, George M Cohan, 1920 ....**10.00**
Mona, Rici & Kelly, Bob Hope photo, 1938 ....**5.00**
Mr Whitney's Little Jitney Bus, Gaskill, 1915 ....**20.00**
My Buddy, Kahn & Donaldson, Al Jolson photo, 1922 ....**10.00**
My Ideal, Frank Sinatra signed photo, 1930 ....**5.00**
My Mother's Waltz, Bing Crosby photo, 1945 ....**5.00**
Nelly Was a Lady, Stephen C Foster, 1849 ....**50.00**
Nobody, Movie: The 7 Little Foys, Bob Hope photo, 1933 ....**5.00**
Oklahoma Hills, Jack & Woody Guthrie, Jack Guthrie photo **10.00**
Original Rags, Scott Joplin, 1899 ....**50.00**
Painting the Roses Red, Movie: Alice in Wonderland, 1951 ....**10.00**
Polar Bear Polka, Albert Berg, 1865 ....**50.00**
Put Me Off at Buffalo, Harry & John Dillon, 1895 ....**20.00**
Robin Hood March, Movie: Robin Hood, D Fairbanks photo, 1922 .**10.00**
Saratoga Glide, Harry L Newman, Roy Sebree photo, Rag, 1909 .**10.00**
Seattle, Walter Augustyne, Indian, 1909 ....**25.00**
Side By Side, Harry Woods, Kay Starr signed photo, 1927 ....**10.00**
So This Is Love, Movie: Cinderella, 1949 ....**10.00**
Sound of Music, Rodgers & Hammerstein II, Movie: same, 1959 ...**5.00**
Spirit of '76, Cox, WWI, 1917 ....**15.00**
Sweet Cookie Mine, Frost & Jones, Sophie Tucker photo, 1917 ..**20.00**
Then I'll Be Reminded of You, Movie: Vagabond Lover, 1939 .....**15.00**
They're All My Friends, George M Cohan **15.00**
Thirteen Collar, Musical: Very Good Eddie, 1915 ....**15.00**
Titanic, Boland, 1912 ....**50.00**
United Nations March, ET Paull (also cover artist) **35.00**
We'll Always Remember Pearl Harbor, Bryan/Raskin/Marks, 1941 ..**15.00**
When I Lost You, Irving Berlin, Babe Foy photo, 1912 ....**25.00**
When Mama Pickaninny's Fast Asleep, John Martin, Black Face ...**25.00**
When You Wish Upon a Star, Movie: Pinocchio, 1940 ....**10.00**
Wilhelmina, Movie: Wabash Avenue, Betty Grable photo, 1950 ..**5.00**
Worlds Are in My Heart, Movie: Gold Diggers of 1935, 1935 ......**10.00**
You'd Better Love Me, Martin & Gray, Musical: High Spirits **5.00**
You Know How Talk Gets Around, Eddy Arnold photo, 1949 ....**5.00**
You're a Natural, Loesser & Sherwin, Movie: College Swing, 1938 .**5.00**
You're the Top, Cole Porter, Movie: Anything Goes, 1934 ....**5.00**

Shell-Work Collectibles

Not long after the natural beauty of the shell was discovered, man began to use them for decorative purposes of many types. Shells were used to decorate clothing and household items as well as jewelry, personal gifts, and souvenirs. Remains of shell necklaces have been found that date to a time prior to the great flood!

During Victorian times shell work became a hobby for the middle class. Shell-work jewelry became popular at that time, but very little has survived due to its delicate nature. Examples of love tokens, souvenirs, and whimsies from that era are listed below. For further information we recommend *Neptune's Treasures, A Study and Value Guide*, by our advisors, Carole and Richard Smyth. The Smyths are listed in the Directory under New York.

Box, ornate top, simple shell-band base, ca 1900, from $25 to ...**180.00**
Box, w/ or w/o heart pincushion, various szs, from $175 to **380.00**
Chest/jewelry box, ornate decor, from $150 to **250.00**
Desk boxes & letter holders, ea, from $125 to **300.00**
Hand mirror, from $100 to **200.00**
Love token, anchor shape w/sm pincushion heart, from $250 to ...**450.00**
Lucky shoe, overall decor, from $150 to **300.00**
Miniature, dresser, from $175 to **400.00**
Miniature, home (often made as bank), from $200 to **450.00**
Miniature, step-bk cupboard, from $250 to **400.00**
Needle case, from $150 to **300.00**
Notebooks and cards, ea from $15 to **85.00**
Painting on shell, from $25 to over **200.00**
Paperweight, often souvenir, ea, from $50 to **180.00**
Photograph in decor fr, 1890s portrait, from $125 to **250.00**
Pin holder, message on bk, rnd, oval or heart shape, $50 to **150.00**
Pincushion, crown shape, from $125 to **200.00**
Pocketbooks & handbags, ea, from $150 to **400.00**
Print in decor fr, various types, flat glass, from $150 to **500.00**
Purse, mini souvenir, from $50 to **100.00**
Religious article (cvd prayer, mini shrine, etc), from $50 to **250.00**
Star, horseshoe or roundel, scenic center, ea, from $125 to **300.00**

Shelley

In 1872 Joseph Shelley became partners with James Wileman, owner of Foley China Works, thus creating Wileman & Co. in Stoke-on-Trent. Twelve years later James Wileman withdrew from the company, though the firm continued to use his name until 1925 when it became known as Shelley Potteries, Ltd. Like many successful 19th-century English potteries, this firm continued to produce useful household wares as well as dinnerware of considerable note. In 1896 the beautiful Dainty White shape was introduced, and it is regarded by many as synonymous with the name Shelley. In addition to the original Dainty (6-flute) design, other lovely shapes were produced: Ludlow (14-flute), Oleander (petal shape), Stratford (12-flute), Queen Anne (with 8 angular panels), Ripon (with its distinctive pedestal), and the 1930s shapes of Vogue, Eve, and Regent.

Though often overlooked, striking earthenware was produced under the direction of Frederick Rhead and later Walter Slater and his son Eric. Many notable artists contributed their talents in designing unusual, attractive wares: Rowland Morris, Mabel Lucie Attwell, and Hilda Cowham, to name but a few.

In 1966 Allied English Potteries acquired control of the Shelley Company, and by 1967 the last of the exquisite Shelley China had been produced to honor remaining overseas orders. In 1971 Allied English Potteries merged with the Doulton group. Reports of Shelley China currently being produced have not been verified. Some Shelley patterns (Dainty Blue, Bridal Rose, and Blue Rock) have been seen on Royal Albert and Queensware pieces. Both of these companies are part of the Doulton Group. Our advisors for this category are Lila and Fred Shrader; they are listed in the Directory under California.

Key:
MLA — Mabel Lucie Attwell   W — Wileman, pre-1910
QA — Queen Anne shape

Advertising ashtray, Pimms in red on cream, 5" dia **75.00**
Advertising tray, Simons in blk on yel, 3½x5" **98.00**
Ashtray, bridge set of 4: dmn/spade/heart/club, lustre **46.00**
Ashtray, Thistle, 3½" dia **45.00**
Bowl, cereal; DuBarry, Duchess or Georgian, 6½" **18.00**
Bowl, cream soup; Blue Rock or Rosebud, Dainty shape, hdls, w/tray ..**85.00**

Bowl, flat soup; Blenheim, 7½" **18.00**
Bowl, float; Melody border (int/ext), earthenware, 3x10½" **125.00**
Bowl, fruit; Bridal Rose, Harebell or Oleander shape, 5½" **38.00**
Bowl, fruit; Lily of the Valley, 5½" **49.00**
Bowl, rimmed soup; Blue Iris, QA, 8¾" **78.00**
Bowl, rimmed soup; Lily of the Valley, Dainty shape, 8½" **78.00**
Bowl, vegetable; Duchess, 9½x7" **75.00**
Bowl, vegetable; Heavenly Blue, Dainty shape, oval, 9x7" ...**198.00**
Bowl, vegetable; Wild Flowers, 8" **125.00**
Butter dish, Harmony Drip Ware, 4x6½" **150.00**
Butter pat, Blue Iris, Dainty shape, 3¾" **110.00**
Butter pat, Blue Rock, Dainty shape, 3¾" **82.00**
Butter pat, Regency, 3¾" **52.00**
Cake plate, Drifting Leaves, tab hdls, 8½" dia **50.00**
Cake plate, My Garden, tab hdls, QA, 8½" sq **50.00**

Cake stand, Dainty Blue, scalloped rim, pedestal foot, $225.00.

Candle holders, Indian Peony, 2½", pr **128.00**
Candy dish, Celandine, Violets or Ludlow shape, 4½" dia **50.00**
Candy dish, Rock Garden (chintz), tab hdls, 4½" sq **55.00**
Chamber set, utility ware w/roses, bowl+pitcher+3 pcs **225.00**
Children's ware, cake plate, airplane, MLA, tab hdls, 8" sq **195.00**
Children's ware, feeding dish, Cowham, Pussy cat, 7" **135.00**
Children's ware, plate, motoring, MLA, 7¼" **105.00**
Chop plate, Regency (Dainty White w/gold trim), 14" **210.00**
Cigarette holder, Stocks, Dainty shape, 2¼" **45.00**
Coffeepot, Georgian, Gainsborough shape, 8-cup **255.00**
Coffeepot, Regency, 8-cup, 8¼" **265.00**
Comport, Intarsio, center ped, 3 S-curve supports, 7" **385.00**
Condiment set, Forget-Me-Not, shakers+mustard w/lid on tray .**275.00**
Coronation ware, candy dish, QEII, tab hdls, 1953, 4½" sq **42.00**
Coronation ware, cup & saucer, Edward VIII, Regent shape, 1937 .....**59.00**
Creamer & sugar bowl, Campanula, Dainty, open, med, +oval tray ..**145.00**
Creamer & sugar bowl, Duchess or Sheraton, med **110.00**
Creamer & sugar bowl, Lily of Valley, Dainty, open, med, +oval tray .**195.00**
Creamer & sugar bowl, Peony, Vincent shape, open, med **65.00**
Creamer & sugar bowl, Shamrocks, Dainty shape, med **165.00**
Crested ware, pitcher, W, mini, 3½" **42.00**
Crested ware, Welsh hat, Hoc Age Snowden, 2½" **47.00**
Cup & saucer, Black Crackle, QA **78.00**
Cup & saucer, Blue Iris on wht w/bl trim, QA **85.00**
Cup & saucer, Charm, Canterbury shape, mini **145.00**
Cup & saucer, Dainty White, demi **35.00**
Cup & saucer, Fantasy w/lt pk int, Dainty shape **95.00**
Cup & saucer, Indian Peony or Lyric, Gainsborough shape, demi ...**54.00**
Cup & saucer, Oleander, Morning Glory, Ludlow shape **59.00**
Cup & saucer, Rose Pansy Forget-Me-Not, Dainty shape **69.00**
Cup & saucer, Shamrock, Dainty shape, demi **67.00**
Cup & saucer, Summer Glory (in cup), ftd Oleander shape **94.00**
Dinner service, Duchess, service of 8, 7-pc place set, 56 pcs **865.00**
Egg cup, Blue Rock, Bridal Rose or Rosebud, Dainty shape, 2½" .**67.00**
Egg cup set, Shamrocks, Dainty shape, 4 sm 1¾" egg cups+stand ...**225.00**
Gravy boat, Hedgeware, w/attached underplate **110.00**

Hatpin holder, Moonlight, W, 5" 89.00
Horn (tumbler), Charm, no hdl, 4½" 50.00
Horn (tumbler), Rambler Rose, Dainty shape, hdl, 4½" 145.00
Horn (tumbler), Rose, Pansy, Forget-Me-Not, Dainty shape, hdl .125.00
Jam/honey pot, Campanula, Dainty shape, w/slotted lid, 4" 135.00
Jam/honey pot, Maytime, w/lid & attached underplate, 4" 175.00
Jam/honey pot, Moonlight, slotted lid, 4" 65.00
Menu plaque, fruit/vegetable decor, 5x7" 118.00
Muffin, Lily of the Valley, Dainty shape, w/lid, 8" 185.00
Mustard pot, Charm, slotted lid, 2½" 65.00
Napkin ring, Rosebud, unmk (Royal Albert?) 45.00
Plate, Blue Iris on wht w/bl trim, QA, 7" 55.00
Plate, Deerstalking series, So Astonished..., earthenware, 10" 190.00
Plate, Heather, gold trim, 8" 28.00
Plate, Lilac Time or Lily of the Valley, Dainty shape, 10¾" 125.00
Plate, Old Sevres in ⅝" sterling silver fr, 11" 125.00
Plate, Strawberry or Thistle, 6" 40.00
Platter, Dainty Blue or Heavenly Blue, 15x12" 295.00
Platter, Melody (chintz), oval, 10x8" 185.00
Relish, Blue Rock or Rosebud, Dainty shape, 6½x3½" 95.00
Shakers, Rosebud, Dainty/pear shape, unmk, 3¾", pr 135.00
Tea & toast set, Blue Rock, Dainty shape, 8" dia 56.00
Tea & toast set, Rose, Pansy, Forget-Me-Not, Dainty shape, 5x8" plate .135.00
Teapot, Black Leafy Tree, QA, W, lg, 8-cup 395.00
Teapot, Phlox, Regent shape, 6" 195.00
Teapot, Rose, Pansy, Forget-Me-Not, Dainty shape, 2-cup 445.00
Toast rack, Regency, 3-bar, 3x4½" 100.00
Tray, pin; Cloisonne, 3x5½" 110.00
Tray, sandwich; Glorious Devon, Dainty shape, tab hdls, 12x4½" ...175.00
Tray, triple; Regency, graceful long gold leaf hdl, 12" 235.00
Trio, Chevrons, Perth shape, 7" plate 45.00
Trio, Eastern Star, New Cambridge shape, 8" plate 88.00
Trio, Japan, monochrome, W, Alex shape, 7" plate 175.00
Trio, Phlox, Regent shape, 7" plate 55.00
Vase, bud; Indian Peony, flared collar, 5½" 72.00
Vase, Urbato, W, Rhead, tube-lined, cylindrical, hdls, 14" 535.00

Shenandoah

The Shenandoah Valley, extending from Virginia to Pennsylvania is well known for the fine pottery made there from the early 1800s until the turn of the century. It is characterized by bright, clear glazes in a variety of colors or in combination. Many small potteries were involved. Items marked 'Bell' indicate one of the larger companies.

Bowl, redware, brn w/splotches, 3⅜x8" 200.00
Bowl, redware, orange brn w/splotches, 4x9" 800.00
Bowl, redware, orange-brn w/splotches, 3x6⅛" 425.00
Cuspidor, redware w/cream slip, brn & gr glaze, 6¼", EX+ 470.00
Humidor, redware, emb ribs, rope hdls, w/lid, 7x6", EX 950.00
Jar, storage; redware, orange-brn w/splotches, 4¼" 600.00
Mold, Turk's head, redware, orange w/mottling, John Bell, 5x8½" ..1,300.00
Mug, typical form, brn & cream, John Bell, 3½" 1,050.00
Pitcher, redware, orange & yel mottle, ovoid, 6" 650.00
Pitcher, redware, orange-brn w/splotches, 7x5⅝" 625.00
Plate, redware, brn, John Bell Waynesboro, 1⅜x10½", NM 725.00
Pudding mold, redware, orange-brn int glaze, Bell, 5¼", EX 624.00
Pudding mold, redware, orange-brown w/mottled band, 4" 275.00

Silhouettes

Silhouette portraits were made by positioning the subject between a bright light and a sheet of white drawing paper. The resulting shadow was then traced and cut out, the paper mounted over a contrasting color and framed. The hollow-cut process was simplified by an invention called the Physiognotrace, a device that allowed tracing and cutting to be done in one operation. Experienced silhouette artists could do full-length figures, scenics, ships, or trains freehand. Some of the most famous of these artists were Charles Peale Polk, Charles Wilson Peale, William Bache, Doyle, Edouart, Chamberlain, Brown, and William King. Though not often seen, some silhouettes were completely painted or executed in wax. Examples listed here are hollow-cut unless another type is described and assumed to be in excellent condition unless noted otherwise.

Key:
bk — backing   p — profile
c/p — cut and pasted   wc — watercolor
fl — full length

Child, fl, c/p, blk paper w/gilt detail, 4½x3½" 250.00
Dr Johnson (stocky man), fl p, c/p, ink details, 8x6¼"+fr 275.00
Girl w/bird in hand & sun hat, fl, c/p, Edouart, 1842, 14x12"+fr ..2,300.00
Girl w/book, fl, c/p, gilt detail, stain, old fr, 8½x6¼" 385.00
Lady, p, cut-out litho dress w/hand-coloring, gilt fr, 6x5" 600.00
Lady, p, detailed collar/neck ribbon, collar lace, fr, 5x4" 500.00
Lady, p, hair/collar/bodice w/ink details, brass fr, 5¼x4½" 575.00
Lady, p, ink details, brass fr, 5¼x4½" 550.00
Lady, p, pen/ink/watercolor details, cloth bk, 4½x3½" 275.00
Lady, p, wc/ink details, much embellishing, fr, 5x4" 2,300.00
Lady, ½-figure, brushed ink bodice, old fr w/gilt, 5x4" 330.00
Lady in bonnet, p, 4x3¼"+brass fr 220.00
Man, p, blk ink w/wht details, identified, 1780-1836, 4¼x2¾" ...275.00
Man, p, high collar, ruffled shirt, early 19th C, 6x4½" 110.00
Man, p, pencil details, curly maple fr, 4¼x3⅞" 385.00
Man & woman, p, blk cloth bk, 6⅜x5⅝"+fr, pr 220.00
Man in top hat w/dog, fl p, c/p, ink/gilt details, 12x9½"+fr 550.00
Man w/bowler hat, fl, c/p, dress coat & vest, HP details, 10x7" ..200.00
Men (facing pr) in top hats, p, sgn Mary D Smith, 7⅝x11"+fr ...340.00
Washington, p, cloth bk, stains, in 7⅝x6½" lacquer fr 220.00
Youth, p, blk cloth bk, stains, 5x4"+modern fr 140.00

Silver

Coin Silver

During colonial times in America, the average household could not afford items made of silver, but those fortunate enough to have accumulations of silver coins (900 parts silver/100 parts alloy) took them to the local silversmith who melted them down and made the desired household article as requested. These pieces bore the owner's monogram and often the maker's mark, but the words 'Coin Silver' did not come into use until 1830. By 1860 the standard was raised to 925 parts silver/75 parts alloy and the word 'Sterling' was added.

Key:
fh — flat handle   t-oz — troy ounce

A Henderson, crumber, bright-cut decor, ca 1840, 12½" 250.00
A Himmel for Hyde & Goodrich, hot-milk jug, repousse, 14-t-oz ..1,300.00
Albany NY (att), creamer & sugar bowl, repousse band, 30-t-oz ...440.00
Asa Blanchard, KY; beaker, bbl form w/reeded banding, 5-t-oz .5,450.00
Baldwin Gardiner, Phila & NY; teapot, flower basket finial, 43-t-oz .975.00
Ball, Black & Co, NY; milk jug, helmet shape, 1860 ....150.00
Bennett & Caldwell, Phila; teapot, floral eng, 5" 600.00

C Bard & Son, Phila; tea set, chased vintage, 207-t-oz 6,600.00
E&D Kinsey, Cincinnati OH; soup ladle, Fiddle, 12" 250.00
E&S, NYC; mustard pot, repousse lotus, ear hdl, urn finial, 4-t-oz .385.00
Francis Bassett, bowl, flared rim, ped ft, monogram, 5½x7" 400.00
HB Heyer, NY; creamer & sugar bowl, vintage, serpent hdls 400.00
Henry Ball, NY; teapot, fruit basket finial, domed lid, 32-t-oz 700.00
J Shoemaker, sugar bowl, urn shape, monogram, 10½" 1,650.00
JB Jones, Boston; pitcher, classical details, 10", 26-t-oz 1,045.00
JH Connor, NY City; creamer, shell/foliage band, 1830s, 7" 315.00
John I Monell/Chas M Wms NY, tea set, 3-pc, 10" pot+cr/sug ..2,185.00
Jones, Ball & Poor, Boston; tray, eng foliage, 1840s, 15¼" 975.00
Joseph Lownes, Phila; creamer, neoclassical form, 5-t-oz 460.00
Joseph Richardson Jr/Nathaniel Richardson, ladle, 7-t-oz 860.00
Joseph T Rice, Albany NY; tea set, 9⅝" pot+cr/sug 2,530.00
L Allen, teapot, bird finial on domed lid, ca 1840s, 10½" 975.00
Lincoln & Foss, Boston; butter dish, domed lid, 14-t-oz 350.00
Lincoln & Foss W&G Boston Pure Coin, sugar bowl, 11.6-t-oz .330.00
Lincoln & Reed, Boston; christening cup, scroll hdl, monogram ..180.00
MEL (w/horse head & shield), serving spoon, 1850s, set of 5 ....65.00
Mulford & Wendell, Albany; sauce boat, repousse floral, 13.2-t-oz .330.00
Pat 1855 (w/star), ladle, chased shell bowl, leaf on hdl, 7" 50.00
S Kirk & Son, julep cups, monogrammed, set of 6, 17.75-t-oz 330.00
Silas, Sawin, Boston; mint julep beaker, 1820, 4" 330.00
Thomas Fletcher, Phila; creamer, baluster form, 10-t-oz 350.00
W Moulton, porringer, cast hdl w/monogram, 6.6-t-oz 990.00
Wm Homes, Boston; serving spoon, mid-rib hdl, monogram, 8¼" .200.00
Wm Jones, NY City; porringer, cast hdl, 6.6-t-oz 1,045.00

Flatware

Silver flatware is being collected today either to replace missing pieces of heirloom sets or in lieu of buying new patterns, by those who admire and appreciate the style and quality of the older ware. Prices vary from dealer to dealer; some pieces are harder to find and are therefore more expensive. Items such as olive spoons, cream ladles, lemon forks, etc., once thought a necessary part of a silver service, may today be slow to sell; as a result, dealers may price them low and make up the difference on items that sell more readily. Many factors enter into evaluation. Popular patterns may be high due to demand though easily found, while scarce patterns may be passed over by collectors who find them difficult to reassemble. If pieces are monogrammed, deduct 25% (for rare, ornate patterns) to 30% (for common, plain pieces). Place settings generally come in three sizes: dinner, place, and luncheon, with the dinner size generally more expensive. In general, dinner knives are 9½" long; place knives, 9" to 9⅛"; and luncheon knives, 8¾" to 8⅞". Dinner forks measure 7⅜" to 7½"; place forks, 7¼" to 7⅜"; and luncheon forks, 7" to 7¼". Our advisors for this category are Jo Killmer and Rick Spencer; they are listed in the Directory under Utah. See also Tiffany, Silver.

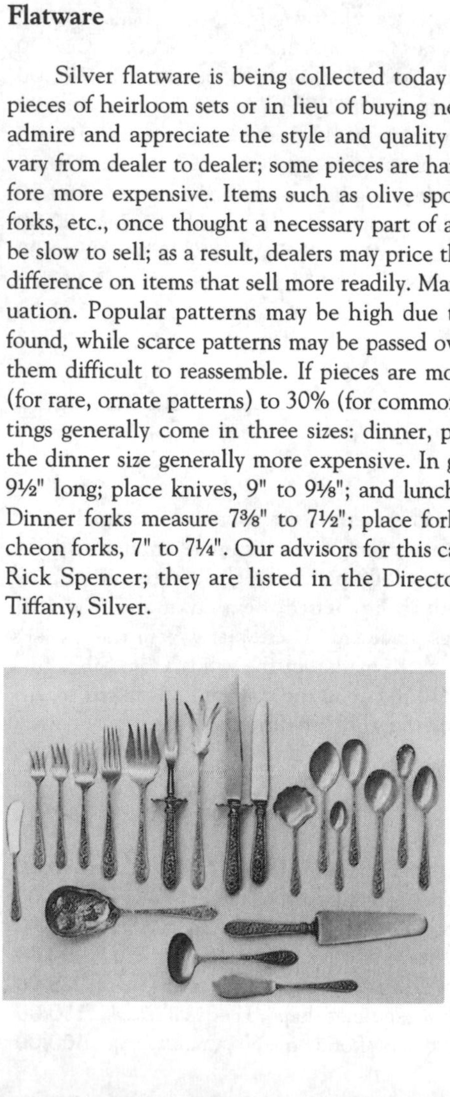

Corsage table service, Steiff, 87 pieces totalling 89 troy ounces weighable silver, $1,000.00 at auction.

Acanthus, G Jensen, caviar knife 85.00
Acanthus, G Jensen, oval soup 92.00
Acorn, G Jensen, cold-cut fork 75.00
Acorn, G Jensen, lemon fork 75.00
Acorn, G Jenson, demi spoon 45.00
Aegean Weave, G Jensen, bonbon sever 33.00
Afterglow, Oneida, master butter, fh 28.00
American Victorian, Lunt, gumbo soup 28.00
Autumn Leaves, Reed & Barton, iced tea spoon 38.00
Baltimore Rose, Schofield, teaspoon 22.00
Beaded, G Jensen, cream soup spoon 75.00
Belle Rose, Oneida, 4-pc set, place sz 75.00
Blossom Time, Internat'l, 4-pc set, dinner sz 110.00
Bridal Bouquet, Alvin, ind butter spreader, fh 20.00
Bridal Rose, Alvin, fish slice 495.00
Burgundy, Reed & Barton, 4-pc set, dinner sz 138.00
Buttercup, Gorham, cheese scoop 125.00
Buttercup, Gorham, cocktail fork 25.00
Buttercup, Gorham, rnd soup spoon 30.00
Cactus, G Jensen, dinner fork, 7⅝" 110.00
Cactus, G Jensen, teaspoon 84.00
Candlelight, Towle, bouillon spoon 30.00
Chantilly, Gorham, fruit spoon 24.00
Chantilly, Gorham, ice cream fork 35.00
Chantilly, Gorham, soup ladle 300.00
Chateau Rose, Alvin, place fork 26.00
Chippendale, Towle, cream soup 30.00
Chrysanthemum, Durgin, gravy ladle 225.00
Colfax, Durgin, dinner knife 39.00
Colonial Fiddle, Tuttle, oval soup 45.00
Copenhagen, Manchester, baby fork 22.00
Copenhagen, Manchester, 4-pc set, dinner sz 72.00
Corsage, Stieff, sugar spoon 25.00
Damask Rose, Oneida, teaspoon 20.00
Debussy, Towle, tablespoon, pierced 74.00
Dresden, Whiting, asparagus server 275.00
Dupleix, Christofle, dinner fork 58.00
El Grandee, Towle, 4-pc set, place set 120.00
Eloquence, Lunt, asparagus server 135.00
Eloquence, Lunt, place fork 44.00
English Shell, Lunt, iced tea spoon 25.00
Fairfax, Durgin, breakfast knife 38.00
Fairfax, Gorham, fork, 7¾" 25.00
Fanciful, Tiffany, fruit spoon 47.00
Federal Cotillion, F Smith, roast carving set, 3-pc 265.00
Fiddle Shell, Frank Smith, pie/cake server 48.00
Florentine Lace, Reed & Barton, place fork 39.00
Francis I, Reed & Barton, ice tongs 195.00
French Provincial, Towle, butter knife 25.00
French Provincial, Towle, lemon fork 13.00
French Regency, Wallace, steak knife 40.00
Frontenac, Internat'l, dessert fork, 3-tine 42.00
Frontenac, Internat'l, lettuce fork 150.00
Frontenac, Internat'l, tablespoon 52.00
George & Martha, Westmoreland, 4-pc set, luncheon sz 80.00
Georgian, Towle, luncheon knife 40.00
Grand Colonial, Wallace, luncheon fork 20.00
Grande Baroque, Wallace, master butter spreader 28.00
Grande Baroque, Wallace, tablespoon 65.00
Greenbriar, Gorham, cream soup 22.00
Hampton Court, Reed & Barton, 4-pc set, place sz 110.00
Horizon, Easterling, tomato server 60.00
Joan of Arc, Internat'l, baby spoon 22.00
Joan of Arc, Internat'l, bonbon 28.00

Joan of Arc, Internat'l, gravy ladle 65.00
John & Priscilla, Westmoreland, master butter, fh 26.00
Jonquil, Unger, olive spoon 95.00
King Albert, Whiting, ice cream fork 22.00
King Edward, Gorham, 4-pc set, dinner sz 120.00
King Richard, Towle, youth set 82.00
Lancaster, Gorham, lettuce fork 75.00
Laura, Bucellati, dinner fork 115.00
Les Six Fleurs, Reed & Barton, place spoon 45.00
Lily, Whiting, cream soup 34.00
Lily, Whiting, gravy ladle 225.00
Lily, Whiting, sardine fork 150.00
Lotus, Watson, berry server 70.00
Louis XV, Whiting, ice cream spoon 35.00
Louis XV, Whiting, stuffing spoon 275.00
Love Disarmed, Reed & Barton, salad serving spoon 225.00
Lucerne, Wallace, cream soup spoon 35.00
Lyric, Gorham, master butter spreader 19.00
Marie Antoinette, Gorham, tablespoon 60.00
Marlborough, Reed & Barton, bouillon spoon 34.00
Meadow Rose, Wallace, jelly server 28.00
Melrose, Gorham, olive fork 34.00
Milburn Rose, Westmoreland, 4-pc set, place sz 75.00
Minuet, Internat'l, tablespoon, pierced 58.00
Moonbeam, Rogers, 4-pc set, place sz 75.00
Mt Vernon, Lunt, fork, 7¼" 18.00
Norse, Internat'l, 4-pc set, dinner sz 75.00
Old Maryland, Kirk, candlesticks, pr 195.00
Old Master, Towle, cream soup spoon 34.00
Orange Blossom, Alvin, demi spoon 25.00
Parma, Bucellati, cracker scoop, pierced 250.00
Plymouth, Gorham, salad fork 32.00
Pointed Antique, Reed & Barton, bouillon spoon 30.00
Pointed Antique, Reed & Barton, 4-pc set, luncheon sz 110.00
Prelude, Internat'l, bonbon 30.00
Prelude, Internat'l, 4-pc set, luncheon sz 75.00
Pyramid, G Jensen, oval soup spoon 95.00
Queen Elizabeth, Towle, place spoon 36.00
Queen's Lace, Internat'l, 4-pc set, place set 79.00
Rambler Rose, Towle, cream soup spoon 26.00
Repousse, Kirk, berry spoon 135.00
Repousse, Kirk, pie server 250.00
Repousse, Kirk, 4-pc set, dinner sz 125.00
Romance of the Sea, Wallace, demi spoon 20.00
Rose, Stieff, berry spoon 150.00
Rose, Stieff, lemon fork 22.00
Rose, Stieff, pickle fork 20.00
Rose Point, Wallace, berry spoon 100.00
Rose Point, Wallace, master butter spreader 30.00
Rosepoint, Wallace, butter pick 26.00
Rosepoint, Wallace, 4-pc set, dinner sz 115.00
Royal Danish, Internat'l, baby-food pusher 35.00
Royal Danish, Internat'l, luncheon fork 20.00
Savannah, Reed & Barton, steak knife 40.00
Sea Rose, Gorham, fork, 7⅜" 21.00
Shell & Thread, Tiffany, demi spoon 44.00
Sir Christopher, Wallace, dinner knife 35.00
Sir Christopher, Wallace, teaspoon 13.00
Sir Christopher, Wallace, 4-pc set, place sz 105.00
Southern Charm, Alvin, 4-pc set, luncheon sz 75.00
Strasbourg, Gorham, meat fork 95.00
Tara, Reed & Barton, salad fork 32.00
Torchon, Bucellati, 4-pc set, dinner sz 369.00
Troubadour, Frank Whiting, 4-pc set, luncheon sz 95.00

Versailles, Gorham, gravy ladle 125.00
Versailles, Gorham, stuffing spoon 475.00
Violet, Wallace, chocolate spoon 35.00
Violet, Wallace, teaspoon 20.00
Wedgwood, Internat'l, cake server 35.00
Wild Rose, Internat'l, cold-meat fork 50.00
Wild Rose, Internat'l, cream soup 34.00
William & Mary, Lunt, cream ladle 22.00
William & Mary, Lunt, nut spoon 34.00
Young Love, Oneida, lemon fork 22.00
1810, Internat'l, 4-pc set, dinner sz 110.00

Hollow Ware

Until the middle of the 19th century, the silverware produced in America was custom made on order of the buyer directly from the silversmith. With the rise of industrialization, factories sprung up that manufactured silverware for retailers who often added their trademark to the ware. Silver ore was mined in abundance, and demand spurred production. Changes in style occurred at the whim of fashion. Repousse decoration (relief work) became popular about 1885, reflecting the ostentatious preference of the Victorian era. Later in the century, Greek, Etruscan, and several classic styles found favor. Today the Art Deco styles of this century are very popular with collectors.

In the listings that follow, manufacturer's name or trademark is noted first; in lieu of that information, listings are by country. Weight is given in troy ounces. See also Tiffany, Silver.

Key: t-oz — troy ounce

Ball Black & Co, bowl, chased vintage, CI detail, 15-t-oz 440.00
Bellis, plate, hand-hammered Arts & Crafts borders, 5½" 300.00
Black, Starr & Frost, NY; compotes, set of 4, 90-t-oz 3,400.00
Black, Starr & Frost, NY; tray, pierced/engr scrolls, 14", 24-t-oz ..770.00
Cartier, demitasse set, porc liners, pot+cr/sug+6 c/s, M in case ..300.00
Cartier, ice bucket, w/insulated liner, 10¼x9½" 1,500.00
Chicago Art Silver Shop, sauce boat, hammered, monogram 575.00
Chicago Art Silver Shop, sugar & creamer, hammered, #202 ....290.00
Chicago Art Silver Shop, tray, hammered, monogram, 13x7" 575.00
Elkington, teapot, melon ribs, emb floral/leaf spout, 1850s 175.00
F Whiting, nut dish, emb floral rim 80.00
Geo Jensen, bowl, flared, open-rib cup on dome ft, 4", +spoon ..750.00
Geo Jensen, dish, lt hammering, in rtcl cone base, 4", +spoon ...750.00
Gorham, bowl, vegetable; w/lid, 1909, 4½x11½x7½" 325.00
Gorham, pitcher, water; Renaissance Revival, 1887 mk, 36-t-oz ..1,870.00
Gorham, tea/coffee, hammered, 8-sided, ivory finials, 5-pc, EX .1,300.00
Gorham, tea/coffee set, eng florals, 2 pots+cr/2 sugars 2,400.00
Hardy & Hays, serving dish, strawberry clusters, 20th C, 12x14" .575.00
Internat'l, compote, chased/eng floral sprays, 1920s, 5x8" 150.00
Joseph Shoemaker, Philadelphia PA, cr/sug basin, 1798 ....2,500.00
Kalo, bowl, scalloped edge, #M138, 9¾x6" 425.00
Kirk & Son, child's bowl & plate, appl cherubs, monogram, 1911 .300.00
Kirk & Son, pitcher, water; floral repousse, 26-t-oz, 8⅛" 1,045.00
Kirk & Son, tea/coffee, ped ft, urn finials, 1925, 5-pc 925.00
Lebrucher & Co, Newark NJ; pitcher, chased floral/monogram, 38-t-oz 825.00
London, bacon warming tray, 5⅞x8⅜" w/5¼" hdl 300.00
London, creamer, Geo III, repousse flowers/parrot, 1784, 4¾" ...300.00
London, tankard, w/lid, eng monogram, rpr hinge, 8" 990.00
London 1899, muffineer, Georgian design w/crest 385.00
Pool, bowl, serving; Old English, 12" dia, 20-t-oz 240.00
Reed & Barton, bowl, poppies at pierced edge, 20th C, 1½x9¼" ..350.00
Reed & Barton, demitasse set, Heritage, 3-pc, 27-t-oz 575.00
Reed & Barton, lady's flask, Nouveau cherub/florals, 5½" 500.00
Reed & Barton, serving bowl, fluted/scalloped, paw ft, 4x13x9" .180.00

Shreve, tray, hammered, quarter-sawn oak base, 23x17" 700.00
T Edwards, Boston; sugar shaker, eng initials, 5" 1,200.00
Tane Silversmithy, tea/coffee service, melon forms, 4-pc, 120-t-oz ..650.00
TB, sauce boat, Geo III, 3 hoof ft, scroll hdl, 1770-75 ....770.00
Unmk, nut dishes, repousse lilies, 3½" dia, 6 for 140.00
Zimmerman, tea/coffee, spiral swirled, 2 pots+cr/sug, 54-t-oz 750.00

Silver Lustre and Silver Resist

Much of the ware known as silver lustre was produced in the 1800s in Staffordshire, England. This type of earthenware was entirely covered with the metallic silver glaze. It was most popular prior to 1840 when the technique of electroplating was developed and silverplated wares came into vogue. Later in the century, artisans used silver lustre to develop designs on vases and other decorative ware.

The process for decorating pottery with the silver-resist method involved first coating the design or that portion of the pattern that was to be left unsilvered with a water-soluble solution. The lustre was applied to the entire surface of the vessel and allowed to dry. Before the final firing, the surface was washed, removing only the silver from the coated areas. This type of ware was produced early in the 1800s by many English potteries, Wedgwood included.

Figurine, lion, detailed features, 9½x13¾", EX 700.00
Mug, English manner, magenta, 3⅛", EX 280.00
Pitcher, bird on branch, magenta transfer, 5¾" 550.00
Pitcher, floral, bl accents, rstr flake, 5" 275.00
Pitcher, floral, 3 purple transfers: Hope/Faith/Charity, 7" 100.00
Pitcher, floral on bl ground, 4½" 425.00
Pitcher, hunting scenes in bl, 4½" 450.00

Silver Overlay

The silver overlay glass made since the 1880s was decorated with a cut-out pattern of sterling silver applied to the surface of the ware.

Bottle, scent; clear, allover ornate o/l, bulbous, 7x3" 225.00
Bottle, scent; cranberry, allover o/l, onion form, 4½x5" 650.00
Bottle, scent; cranberry, allover o/l, stick neck, 6½" 600.00
Cocktail shaker, blk, triangular floral-panel o/l, Rockwell, 11" ..500.00
Vase, amber irid w/scroll & floral o/l, mk Sterling, 2½" 320.00
Vase, cobalt cased to wht opal, scroll & floral o/l, 6x3½" 460.00
Vase, dk gr, blown-out ribs amid lilies/strapwork o/l, 10" 750.00
Vase, dk gr floral o/l, att Alvin, ca 1910, 14¼" 1,320.00
Vase, rose-red, ornate floral/scroll o/l, 12x5" 1,300.00
Vase, rose-red w/opal int, floral/scrolls o/l w/crest, 12" 1,375.00

Silverplate

Silverplated flatware is fast becoming the focus of attention for many of today's collectors. Silver prices rose to over $7.00 an ounce in 1998, causing a slight increase in both sterling and silverplate prices on the secondary market. Demand is strong for early, ornate pieces, and prices have continued to rise steadily over the past five years. Our values are based on pieces in excellent or restored/resilvered condition. Serving pieces are priced to reflect the values of examples in complete original condition, with knives retaining their original blades. If pieces are monogrammed, deduct from 20% (for rare, ornate patterns) to 35% (for common, plain pieces). Our advisors for this category are Jo Killmer and Rick Spencer; they are listed in the Directory under Utah. See also Railroadiana, Silverplate.

Key:
CF — cocktail/seafood fork
DF — dinner/luncheon fork
DK — dinner/luncheon knife
FS — fruit/citrus spoon
IB — inverted butter spreader
ITS — iced tea spoon
OS — oval soup spoon
RS — round cream soup spoon
SF — salad/dessert fork
TS — teaspoon

Flatware

Alhambra, 1907, Rogers, berry spoon 30.00
Alhambra, 1907, Rogers, bouillon spoon 8.00
Alhambra, 1907, Rogers, cake server, hollow hdl 28.00
Alhambra, 1907, Rogers, demitasse spoon 8.00
Alhambra, 1907, Rogers, gravy ladle 19.00
Alhambra, 1907, Rogers, 8 ea: DF, DK, SF, CF, IB, 16 TS, set ...350.00
Beacon Hill, 1976, Internat'l Silver, cold meat fork 14.00
Beacon Hill, 1976, Internat'l Silver, sugar shell 4.00
Beacon Hill, 1976, Internat'l Silver, 8 ea: DF, DK, SF, TS, set ..120.00
Beethoven, 1971, Oneida, 12 ea: DF, DK, SF, TS, set 185.00
Bird of Paradise, 1923, Oneida, carving set, lg, 3-pc 45.00
Bird of Paradise, 1923, Oneida, jelly knife 8.00
Bird of Paradise, 1923, Oneida, lemon fork 20.00
Bird of Paradise, 1923, Oneida, sugar tongs 18.00
Bird of Paradise, 1923, Oneida, 12 ea: DF, DK, SF, TS, ITS, RS, IB, set ..325.00
Brittany Rose, 1948, Wm Rogers, master butter 4.00
Brittany Rose, 1948, Wm Rogers, sugar spoon 4.00
Brittany Rose, 1948, Wm Rogers, 8 ea: DF, DK, SF, TS, set 130.00
Centennial, 1972, Internat'l, 8 ea: DF, DK, SF, TS, IB, set 150.00
Charter Oak, 1906, 1847 Rogers, oyster ladle 140.00
Charter Oak, 1906, 1847 Rogers, sauce ladle 40.00
Charter Oak, 1906, 1847 Rogers, tablespoon 20.00
Charter Oak, 1906, 1847 Rogers, tomato server 195.00
Charter Oak, 1906, 1847 Rogers, 8 ea: DF, DK, SF, TS, OS, set ...850.00
Countess, 1969, Deep Silver, master butter knife 5.00
Countess, 1969, Deep Silver, pierced tablespoon 8.00
Countess, 1969, Deep Silver, sugar spoon 5.00
Countess, 1969, Deep Silver, 8 ea: DF, DK, SF, TS, CF, set 145.00
Exquisite, 1957, Rogers & Bro, pierced pie server 12.00
Exquisite, 1957, Rogers & Bro, sugar spoon 3.00
Exquisite, 1957, Rogers & Bro, tablespoon 8.00
Exquisite, 1957, Rogers & Bro, 12 ea: DF, DK, SF, OS, IB, CF, 24 TS, set....275.00
French Lace, 1983, Reed & Barton, 8 ea: DF, DK, SF, TS, OS, set .150.00
Garland, 1965, 1847 Rogers, bonbon server 10.00
Garland, 1965, 1847 Rogers, pierced tablespoon 10.00
Garland, 1965, 1847 Rogers, 8 ea: DF, DK, SF, TS, OS, set 175.00
Grenoble/Gloria, 1906, Wm A Rogers, demitasse spoon 8.00
Grenoble/Gloria, 1906, Wm A Rogers, olive spoon 35.00
Grenoble/Gloria, 1906, Wm A Rogers, pastry fork 28.00
Grenoble/Gloria, 1906, Wm A Rogers, preserve spoon 50.00
Grenoble/Gloria, 1906, Wm A Rogers, 12 ea: DF, DK, SF, TS, RS, set .725.00
Heraldic, 1916, 1847 Rogers, cold meat fork 12.00
Heraldic, 1916, 1847 Rogers, master butter 4.00
Heraldic, 1916, 1847 Rogers, sugar spoon 3.00
Heraldic, 1916, 1847 Rogers, tablespoon 6.00
Heraldic, 1916, 1847 Rogers, 8 ea: DF, DK, SF, TS, RS, set 180.00
Jubilee, 1953, Internat'l, cake server, hollow hdl 25.00
Jubilee, 1953, Internat'l, cold meat 14.00
Jubilee, 1953, Internat'l, steak knife 8.00
Jubilee, 1953, Internat'l, sugar shell 4.00
Jubilee, 1953, Internat'l, 8 ea: DF, DK, SF, ITS, IB, FS, CF, 16 TS, set ...300.00
Mayfair, 1923, Rogers & Bros, 8 ea: DF, DK, SF, TS, set 120.00
Milady, 1940, Oneida, 8 ea: DF, DK, SF, TS, RS, set 160.00
Moss Rose, 1949, National Silver, berry spoon 16.00
Moss Rose, 1949, National Silver, demitasse spoon 5.00

Moss Rose, 1949, National Silver, tablespoon 4.00
Moss Rose, 1949, National Silver, youth fork 5.00
Moss Rose, 1949, National Silver, youth knife 5.00
Moss Rose, 1949, National Silver, 12 ea: DF, DK, SF, TS, CF, set ..225.00
Narcissus, 1935, National Silver, 8 ea: DF, DK, SF, TS, set 115.00
Orleans, 1964, Deep Silver, cold meat fork 15.00
Orleans, 1964, Deep Silver, pierced tablespoon 9.00
Orleans, 1964, Deep Silver, 12 ea: DF, DK, SF, TS, OS, IB, CF, set .275.00
Pageant, 1927, Holmes & Edwards, 8 ea: DF, DK, SF, TS, set 125.00
Patrician, 1914, Oneida, bouillon spoon 6.00
Patrician, 1914, Oneida, ice cream fork 12.00
Patrician, 1914, Oneida, pickle fork 7.00
Patrician, 1914, Oneida, sugar tongs 20.00
Patrician, 1914, Oneida, 12 ea: DF, DK, SF, FS, RS, 16 TS, set .260.00
Queen Bess, 1946, Oneida, berry spoon 10.00
Queen Bess, 1946, Oneida, cold meat 10.00
Queen Bess, 1946, Oneida, cream ladle 8.00
Queen Bess, 1946, Oneida, sugar spoon 3.00
Queen Bess, 1946, Oneida, 16 ea: DF, DK, SF, RS, 32 TS, set ...250.00
Reflection, 1959, Internat'l, pierced olive spoon 8.00
Reflection, 1959, Internat'l, soup ladle 85.00
Reflection, 1959, Internat'l, 8 ea: DF, DK, TS, SF, FS, set 160.00
Royal Rose, 1939, Nobility, 8 ea: DF, DK, SF, TS, OS, set 130.00
Sharon, 1910, 1847 Rogers, egg spoon 10.00
Sharon, 1910, 1847 Rogers, master butter 14.00
Sharon, 1910, 1847 Rogers, pie server, hollow hdl 35.00
Sharon, 1910, 1847 Rogers, salad serving set (olive wood) 90.00
Sharon, 1910, 1847 Rogers, sardine fork 40.00
Sharon, 1910, 1847 Rogers, 12 ea: DF, DK, SF, TS, OS, IB, CF, set .520.00
Silver Tulip, 1956, Internat'l, pierced pie server 6.00
Silver Tulip, 1956, Internat'l, sugar spoon 3.00
Silver Tulip, 1956, Internat'l, 8 ea: DF, DK, SF, TS, set 75.00
Spring Garden, 1949, H&E, 12 ea: DF, DK, SF, TS, RS, CF, IB, set ..265.00
Spring Garden, 1949, Holmes & Edwards, baby fork 7.00
Spring Garden, 1949, Holmes & Edwards, baby spoon 7.00
Spring Garden, 1949, Holmes & Edwards, jelly server 7.00
Spring Garden, 1949, Holmes & Edwards, pickle fork 7.00
Spring Garden, 1949, Holmes & Edwards, roast-carving set, 2-pc ..45.00
Sylvia, 1934, 1847 Rogers, sugar spoon 4.00
Sylvia, 1934, 1847 Rogers, tablespoon 6.00
Sylvia, 1934, 1847 Rogers, tomato server 24.00
Sylvia, 1934, 1847 Rogers, 8 ea: DF, DK, SF, ITS, OS, set 190.00

Hollow Ware

Wine coolers, Rococo-style campana forms with elaborate shell, foliage, and scrollwork castings, 10½", $1,150.00 for the pair.

Basket, 4 cherubs as base, frosted glass bowl, Meriden, 8" 200.00
Bread basket, Reed & Barton, rtcl, eng Ritten House, 12" 65.00
Butter dish, oval lid pivots, ornate, scroll legs, 5x5x8" 65.00
Cafe-au-lait pot, att Casimir Rouyer, left-handed, wood hdl, 10" ...275.00
Cake basket, lappets/dmns/lunettes, bail hdl, Am, 1880s, 5x9½" ..195.00
Cake basket, ribbed, florals/vintage emb, 1870s, 9½x12x10" 85.00
Candelabra, Rococo style, 5-light, 22x20", pr 800.00
Candelabra, 2-arm, 1900s, English, mk SGEP, 16½", pr, EX 375.00

Candlesticks, wheel-cut glass hurricane shades, Fr, 19", pr 495.00
Centerpc, Neoclassical style w/gilt, 3 figures, 26x20" 3,850.00
Entree dish, telescoping, dome lid, English, 8½x13½" 450.00
Jardiniere, Continental, Neoclassical style, cobalt insert, 4x14x8" ..880.00
Pitcher, chased in Renaissance taste, Wilcox, 1878, 11½" 250.00
Punch set, chased floral/gadrooning, English, bowl/tray/18 cups ...750.00
Sugar bowl, w/spoon rack, 1890s, Toronto, w/lid, 9½" 65.00
Tea service, acanthus legs, etched flowers, Meriden, 5-pc 625.00
Toast rack, Xd golf clubs as rack, ball ea end, English, 5" 295.00
Tray, Georgian taste, pierced gallery, English, 22x15" 325.00
Tray, Reed & Barton, Georgian style, serpentine edge/hdls, 25" ...375.00
Tureen, Rogers & Bro Extra Plate, Waterbury CT, 15½" 415.00

Sheffield

Bowl, serving; w/reservoir, 10½" dia+hdls 110.00
Cake basket, shell-like rim decor, sq hinged hdl, 1890s, 10x12" .110.00
Cake basket, wirework body w/gadrooned edge, 1830s, 4½x11" .220.00
Candelabra, minor wear, sm rpr, 19", pr 400.00
Candelabra, 3-arm, flared base, 12½", pr 200.00
Candelabra, 3-light, egg & dart, 23", pr, +2 candlesticks 6,000.00
Candlesticks, telescoping stem, lt wear, 8⅛", pr 325.00
Cooler, wine; Georgian, scroll hdls, floral borders, 1830s, 11" 550.00
Covered vegetable, lid pivots, sm paw ft, w/drain, 15" 190.00
Epergne, Geo III, openwork basket, 4-arm, 17½" 1,100.00
Epergne, Waterford inserts, 1 lg & 4 sm bowls, rprs, 12¼" 1,875.00
Platter w/hot water reservoir, floral details, 25" L 600.00
Salt cellar, lion's head, cobalt insert, 3" 100.00
Serving dish, eng coat of arms, w/lid/liner/strainer, 14", pr 1,265.00
Serving dish, ornate cast hdl, paw ft, eng coat of arms, 10x15x9" ...425.00
Teapot, on stand, w/burner, 13½" overall 250.00
Tray, lt wear, 39" 385.00
Wine botle holder, dbl; w/wood bases, ivory castors, 16" L 276.00
Wine bottle coaster, wooden bottom, 7", pr 55.00

Cases

Plastic/Bakelite, fancy, minimum value 35.00
Pre-1920s, fancy wood, minimum value 50.00
Silvercloth pocket protector, from $2 to 6.00
1920s-50s, wooden, dbl drw, from $35 to 45.00
1920s-50s, wooden, single drw, from $25 to 35.00

Sinclaire

In 1904 H.P. Sinclaire and Company was founded in Corning, New York. For the first sixteen years of production, Sinclaire used blanks from other glassworks for his cut and engraved designs. In 1920 he established his own glass-blowing factory in Bath, New York. His most popular designs utilize fruits, flowers, and other forms from nature. Most of Sinclaire's glass is unmarked; items that are carry his logo: an 'S' within a wreath with two shields.

Basket, cut/eng flowers, Steuben blank, 17x12" 900.00
Bowl, amethyst, wheel-cvd floral vine, 4¾x7¾" 170.00
Bowl, canoe w/eng flowers, 11x7½" 185.00
Candlesticks, invt lip cut w/stars, low, 4" dia, pr 110.00
Compote, gr ribbed & opaque wht, 10" 200.00
Tray, eng leaves, 5-section, 10x14" 160.00
Tray, Snowflakes & Holly, rectangular, 8x10" 1,300.00
Vase, amber w/eng floral spray, fan form, 8" 150.00
Vase, eng bulbous bowl on pencil stem, 12" 465.00

Skookum Dolls

Representing real Indians of various tribes, stern-faced Skookum dolls were designed by Mary McAboy of Missoula, Montana, in the early 1900s. The earliest of McAboy's creations were made with air-dried apple faces that bore a resemblance to the neighboring Chinook Indian tribe. The name Skookum is derived from the Chinook/Siwash term for large or excellent (aka Bully Good) and appears as part of the oval paper labels often attached to the feet of the dolls.

In 1913 McAboy applied for a patent that described her dolls in three styles: a female doll, a female doll with a baby, and a male doll. In 1916 George Borgman and Co. partnered with McAboy, registered the Skookum trademark, and manufactured these dolls which were distributed by the Arrow Novelty Co. of New York and the HH Tammen Co. of Denver. The Skookum (Apple) Packers Association of Washington state produced similar 'friendly faced' dolls as did Louis Ambery for the National Fruit exchange.

The dried apple faces of the first dolls were replaced by those made of a composition material. Plastic faces were introduced in the 1940s, and these continued to be used until production ended in 1959. Skookum dolls were produced in a variety of styles, with the most collectible having stern, lined faces with small painted eyes glancing to the right, colorful Indian blankets pulled tightly across the straw- or paper-filled body to form hidden arms, felt pants or skirts over wooden legs, and wooden feet covered with decorated felt suede or masking tape.

Skookums were produced in sizes ranging from a 2" souvenir mailer with a cardboard address tag to 36" novelty and advertising dolls. Collectors highly prize 21" to 26" dolls as well as dolls that glance to their left. Felt or suede feet predate the less desirable brown plastic feet of the late 1940s and '50s. Our advisor is Glen Rairigh; he is listed in the Directory under Michigan.

Baby, looks left, cradle brd, beaded body/head covering, 10½" ..1,100.00
Baby, mc blanket, leather headband w/pnt decor, 4" 30.00
Baby, wrapped in mc blanket, feather in headband, 3½x3" 200.00
Baby mailer, 1½¢ postcard attached, feather/ribbon binding, 4" ...100.00
Baby mailer, 1½¢ postcard attached, rattan binding, 4" 105.00
Baby/child in loop basket, blanket wrap, necklace, 14" 200.00
Baby/child in loop basket, blanket wrap, unbraided hair, 12" 225.00
Boy, brn ft w/pnt decor, Bully Good label, 6½" 100.00
Boy, brn suede ft w/decor, headband, 10" 150.00
Boy, mc blanket, felt pants, leather shoes, 6½", VG 50.00
Boy, w/blanket/felt pants, brn plastic ft w/mk, wood beads, 9½" ...85.00

Chief with headdress, paper shoes with decoration, 12½", $250.00.

Photo courtesy Glen Rairigh

Family, chief w/mc feathers, 15", female w/baby, clothes match, 14" ..600.00
Family, man w/exposed right arm, 13½", female w/baby, 12½" ..900.00
Family, w/blankets/clothes/beads, 35", 33" w/10" baby in arms ..5,900.00
Female w/baby, floral skirt, glass bead necklace, 11½" 300.00
Female w/baby, w/blanket, purple felt ft/skirt, necklace, 11½" ...200.00
Female w/baby, w/blanket, worn paper ft, 12½", VG 150.00

Girl, cotton-wrapped legs, beaded ft decor, headband, 9½" 150.00
Girl, cotton-wrapped legs, pnt suede ft covers, Bully Good, 6½" ..100.00
Girl, w/blanket, felt skirt, decor felt ft, bandana, 10" 85.00
Girl, w/blanket/skirt, leather shoes, feather, label, 6½" 125.00
Mailer, baby in bl & yel cotton, Grand Canyon 10-1-52 ....25.00
Mailer, baby in patterned cotton on yel cb 25.00
Mailer, baby in red bandana on yel cb 55.00
Mailer, clay child in leather pouch, Yel Stone Park, 6-22-39 ....35.00

Slag Glass

Slag glass is a marbleized opaque glassware made by several companies from about 1870 until the turn of the century. It is usually found in purple or caramel (see Chocolate Glass), though other colors were also made. Pink is rare and very expensive. It was revived in recent years by several American glassmakers, L.E. Smith, Westmoreland, and Imperial among them. The listings below reflect values for items with excellent color. Our advisor for this category is Sharon Thoerner; she is listed in the Directory under California.

Almond, bear, LE Smith #6654A, 4½" 45.00
Almond, coal bucket, LE Smith #125A, 5" 25.00
Almond, slipper, LE Smith #80A, 6" 35.00
Almond, vase, bud; LE Smith #33A, 6½" 35.00
Caramel, Cherry, butter dish, w/lid, LG Wright Glass #7-2 ....110.00
Caramel, Cherry, tumbler, iced tea; LG Wright Glass, #7-15 ....25.00
Caramel, Hoot (Less) Owl, Imperial #18, 3½" 35.00
Caramel, pie wagon, Imperial #43890CS 300.00
Caramel, pony stallion, Imperial #12, 4x3½", minimum value 45.00
Caramel, Scotty bookend (single), Imperial 250.00
Pastel blue, Hobnail, shakers, Kanawha Glass #286ED, 5", pr ...35.00
Pastel blue, Thumbprint, pitcher, Kanawha Glass #204ED, 4½" ..35.00
Pastel green, Hobnail, basket, Kanawha Glass #296ED, 7" 45.00
Pastel green, pitcher, Kanawha Glass #264ED, 4¼" 25.00
Pink, Invt Fan & Feather, creamer 425.00
Pink, Invt Fan & Feather, pitcher, 7½" 1,200.00
Pink, Invt Fan & Feather, punch cup 315.00
Pink, Invt Fan & Feather, sauce dish, ball ft, 2½x4⅝" 165.00
Pink, Invt Fan & Feather, shakers, rare, pr 1,200.00
Pink, Invt Fan & Feather, spooner, 4¼" 425.00
Pink, Invt Fan & Feather, toothpick holder 500.00
Pink, Invt Fan & Feather, toothpick holder, ftd, 2⅜" 1,500.00
Pink, Invt Fan & Feather, tumbler, 4" 300.00
Purple, cake stand, baker's; Imperial #98, openwork at rim, 10" .150.00
Purple, Leaf & Orange Tree, rose bowl, Fenton #8223PS 80.00
Purple, rose bowl, Imperial #62C, crimped 50.00
Purple, syrup, Imperial #981 ....45.00
Purple, turkey, LG Wright Glass #70-17, lg, rare, minimum value ..700.00
Purple, vase, Imperial #194, ftd, 9½" 50.00
Red, Diamond Dot, basket, Kanawha Glass #324ED, 8¼" 65.00
Red, standing rooster, Kanawha Glass #869ED, 9½" 85.00
Ruby, butter dish, Fenton #868RX 85.00
Ruby, butter dish, Imperial #759 ....125.00
Ruby, epergne, Fenton #4401RX, sm 295.00
Ruby, Grape & Cable, tobacco jar, Fenton #9188RX 250.00
Ruby, grape bowl, Imperial #47C, crimped, 9" 75.00
Ruby, toothpick holder, Imperial #1 ....25.00
Ruby, vase, tricorn, Imperial, #192, 8½" 125.00

Smith Bros.

Alfred and Harry Smith founded their glassmaking firm in New

Bedford, Massachusetts. They had been formerly associated with the Mt. Washington Glass Works, working there from 1871 to 1875 to aid in establishing a decorating department. Smith glass is valued for its excellent enameled decoration on satin or opalescent glass. Pieces were often marked with a lion in a red shield. Our advisors for this category are Betty and Clarence Maier; they are listed in the Directory under Pennsylvania.

Bowl, gold prunus allover, beaded rim, melon ribs, 6" 375.00
Bowl, Moss Rose on beige, wht beaded rim, ribbed, 4x9" 675.00
Cracker jar, forget-me-nots at shoulder on wht, SP mts, 4½" 575.00
Cracker jar, gold ivy/floral, gr/pk leaves, melon ribs, 7½" 750.00
Cracker jar, long-stem rose on bl mottle, melon ribs, 6½" 650.00
Cracker jar, pansies on beige, bbl shaped, metal lid, 7x5" 750.00
Creamer & sugar, floral on bl to beige, SP mts, 4", 3¾" 750.00
Creamer & sugar, gold floral branches, metal mts, 3½", 2¾" 450.00
Creamer & sugar, violets on bl to beige, SP mts, 3¾", 3½" 750.00
Humidor, pansies on cream, melon-ribbed lid, 6¼x4" 850.00
Plate, Santa Maria, ship in tan & lt orange, 7¾" 550.00
Rose bowl, daisy sprays on beige, beaded rim, bulbous, 4½" 325.00
Rose bowl, gold prunus, jeweled, gold-beaded top, 2¼x3" 285.00
Rose bowl, pansies on beige, melon ribs, beaded top, 2½x3" 350.00
Sugar shaker, daisies on pnt burmese, 5½" 475.00
Sugar shaker, gold florals on ivory, melon ribs, gilt lid, 5" 425.00
Sugar shaker, Pillar Ribbed, wild roses, VG lid, 5¾" 495.00
Toothpick holder, Pillar Ribbed, wild roses, bead trim, 2¼" 250.00
Toothpick holder, violets, beaded top, ribbed, 2" 285.00
Vase, apple blossoms on glossy brn/rust, 10x9" 595.00
Vase, birds & florals, molded rings, 4¾" 125.00
Vase, daisies/World's Fair on ivory, 3 pinched sides, 4½" 400.00
Vase, fall/shadow gray leaves w/gold scrolls, melon ribs, 9" 550.00
Vase, florals w/buds, molded ring neck, 8" 125.00
Vase, lilacs/gold on ivory, tan neck/shoulder, beaded rim, 5" 645.00
Vase, storks on pk, waisted cylinder, mk New Bedford, MA, 5½" .425.00
Vase, Verona, irises w/gold on clear, int ribbing, 12½" 550.00
Vase, water lily on pk, 7" 195.00
Vase, wisteria on pnt apricot, w/gold, pinched sides, 5¼" 375.00
Vase, wisteria/gold outlines, melon ribs, bulb neck, 8½" 775.00
Vase, 2 circles behind birds on branches, cone shape, 6" 385.00

Snow Babies

During the last quarter of the 19th century, snow babies — little figurals in white snowsuits — originated in Germany. They were made of sugar candy and were often used as decorations for Christmas cakes. Later on they were made of marzipan, a confection of crushed almonds, sugar, and egg whites. Eventually porcelain manufacturers began making them in bisque. They were popular until WWII. These tiny bisque figures range in size from 1" up to 7" tall. Quality German pieces bring very respectable prices on the market today. Beware of reproductions. Our advisor for this category is Linda Vines; she is listed in the Directory under New Jersey.

2" babies: three on sled, one sits holding snowball, $60.00 each (Sled: $225.00).

Babies (2) sliding down brick wall, Germany, 2½" 130.00
Babies climbing on world, flat on top, open bk, Germany, 3" 200.00
Baby hiding under iceberg, Germany, 2" 140.00
Baby hugging brn bear, Germany, 2" 125.00
Baby inside glass snow dome, USA, 4" 75.00
Baby inside igloo, Santa on top, Germany, 2" 165.00
Baby inside igloo, Santa on top, Japan, 2" 65.00
Baby riding on snow bear, Germany, 2½" 135.00
Baby sitting, googly-eyed, oversz head, open bk, Germany, 2½" .185.00
Baby sitting or standing, Germany, 1", ea 45.00
Baby standing on lg snowball, Japan, 2½" 35.00
Baby w/seal & red ball, B Shackman, recent, 2" 25.00
Baby w/seal & red ball, Germany, 2" 135.00
Carollers (3) w/snow hats & sweaters, lantern, Germany, 2" 110.00
Child on skates, snow hat & sweater, pastel pants, Germany, 2" 90.00
Santa in boat by snow-topped lighthouse, Germany, 3" 125.00
Santa in silver car, toys in bk, Germany, 1½" 95.00
Santa standing w/angel, Germany, 2½" 100.00
Snow bear on hind legs, Germany, 2½" 80.00
Snow-topped house, Santa on top, Germany, 2½" 110.00

Snuff Boxes

As early as the 17th century, the Chinese began using snuff. By the early 19th century, the practice had spread to Europe and America. It was used by both the gentlemen and the ladies alike, and expensive snuff boxes and bottles were the earmark of the genteel. Some were of silver or gold set with precious stones or pearls, while others contained music boxes. In the following listings, the dimension noted is length. See also Orientalia, Snuff Bottles.

Brass w/stone inlay, oval, 2" 60.00
Enamel on copper, 2¼" dia 200.00
NP brass & wood w/MOP inlay, hinged lid, 1890s, ¾x3⅜x1¾" ...55.00
Oyster shell set in silver w/eng, 2½" 115.00
Silver, Rococo w/repousse, hinged lid, Danish, 18th C, 2¾" 250.00
Sterling, Wm IV, rectangular, Thos Shaw, 1835, 2¼x1¼" 220.00
Striped/polished oval stone set in silver, England, 2½" 265.00
Tortoise shell w/gold inlay, 3¾", VG 450.00

Soap Hollow Furniture

In the Mennonite community of Soap Hollow, Pennsylvania, the women made and sold soap; the men made handcrafted furniture. Rare today, this furniture was stenciled, grain painted, and beautifully decorated with inlaid escutcheons. These pieces are becoming very sought after. When well kept, they are very distinctive and beautiful. The items described in these listings were recently sold through Merle S. Mishlers Auctions, RD 2, Hollsopple, Pennsylvania. All are in excellent condition unless otherwise noted. Our advisor for this category is Anita Levi; she is listed in the Directory under Pennsylvania.

Chest, blanket; feathers on mustard & brn, MB/1897 ....1,400.00
Chest, blanket; grpt w/blk lid, fruit/florals w/gold, 1882 ....2,900.00
Chest, blanket; maroon w/gold stencil, rnd escutcheon, 1856 .2,000.00
Chest, blanket; poplar, orig red pnt w/blk/gold, att, 22x42" 3,850.00
Chest, blanket; red & blk, gold stencil MH 1871, 25x15x10", VG .6,200.00
Chest, blanket; red w/floral stencils, rpl hinges, FJ/1892, VG .3,800.00
Chest, blanket; rose decals, blk & brn graining, LK/1890 ....5,000.00
Chest, 4 lg/2 sm drws w/decor, enamel pulls, sgn, 1851, EX+ .4,600.00
Chest, 4lg/3 sm dwrs, stencil, enamel pulls, sgn, 1883, EX+ 5,400.00
Chest, 6-drw, brn w/mustard & decals, blk top & sides, Sala ...1,900.00

Chest, 6-drw, no pnt or decor, EX wood, G **475.00**
Chest, 7-drw, grpt w/blk, gold stencil, MH 1887, 47½x39½" **14,500.00**
Chest, 7-drw, maroon w/blk top/sides, rpt CKM/1879, G **550.00**
Chest of drws, bk brd, hidden lock, stencil, HS/1879 ....**5,500.00**
Chest of drws, brn grpt w/stencil, pnt pulls, 1883, EX+ **5,400.00**
Chest of drws, floral decals/fruit gilt stencil/grpt, MH/1879 ....**2,750.00**
Chest of drws, rosewood, 1841 ....**750.00**
Chest of drws, stenciling w/decals, dk brn, fancy bk brd **7,200.00**
Cradle, gilt stencils, mustard trim, maroon grpt **1,100.00**
Cupboard, corner; maroon w/blk, stencil, 1856 ....**11,500.00**
Cupboard, Dutch; 4 doors/2 drws, stencil/old rpt, 1875, 84x65" ..**8,000.00**
Dresser, Emp style, columns on 3 drws, HF/1874 ....**2,200.00**
Frame, gilt eagles, stenciled, blk **1,050.00**
Rope bed, cherry, red & brn finish, rare **2,300.00**
Stand, bedside; rpt mustard brn **400.00**

Soapstone

Soapstone is a soft talc in rock form with a smooth, greasy feel from whence comes its name. (It is also called Soo Chow Jade.) It is composed basically of talc, chlorite, and magnetite. In colonial times it was extracted from out-croppings in large sections with hand saws, carted by oxen to mills, and fashioned into useful domestic articles such as footwarmers, cooking utensils, inkwells, etc. During the early 1800s, it was used to make heating stoves and kitchen sinks. Most familiar today are the carved vases, bookends, and boxes made in China during the Victorian era. For further information we recommend *Collector's Digest Soapstone* by L-W Book Sales (1995 values).

Candle holder, gray, trapezoidal, 1½x2½x2½" **125.00**
Cigarette/match holder, phoenix birds/eng, red, 3½x4" **75.00**
Figure, Arhat seated, cat on side, 18th C, 5¼" **175.00**
Figure, bird in flowering tree, 7" **60.00**
Horse, rearing, flying mane, red-brn, 12x9" **170.00**
Vase, daisies/leaves, vintage rim, blk soapstone base, 11" **90.00**
Vase, rtcl flowers on ftd sq ped, 5", pr **85.00**

Soda Fountain Collectibles

The first soda water sales in the United States occurred in the very late 1790s in New York and New Haven, Connecticut. By the 1830s soda water was being sold in drug stores as a medicinal item, especially the effervescent mineral waters from various springs around the country. By this time the first flavored soda water appeared at an apothecary shop in Philadelphia.

The 1830s also saw the first manufacturer (John Matthews) of devices to make soda water. The first marble soda fountain made its appearance in 1857 as a combination ice shaver and flavor-dispensing apparatus. By the 1870s the soda fountain was an established feature of the neighborhood drug store.

The fountains of this period were large, elaborate marble devices with druggists competing with each other for business by having fountains decorated with choice marbles, statues, mirrors, water fountains, and gas lamps.

In 1903 the fountain completed its last major evolution with the introduction of the 'front' counter service we know today. (The soda clerk faced the customer when drawing soda.)

By this time ice cream was a standard feature, being served as sundaes, ice cream sodas, and milk shakes. Syrup dispensers were just being introduced as 'point-of-sale' devices to sell various flavorings from many different companies. Straws were commonplace, especially those made from paper. Fancy and unusual ice cream dippers were in daily use, and

they continued to evolve, reaching their pinnacle with the introduction of the heart-shaped dipper in 1927.

This American business has provided collectors today with an almost endless supply of interesting and different articles of commerce. One can collect dippers, syrup dispensers, glassware, straw dispensers, milk shakers, advertising, and trade catalogs. (Note: the presence of a 'correct' pump enhances the value of a syrup dispenser by 25%.)

Collectors need to be made aware of decorating pieces that are fantasy items: copper ice cream cones, a large copper ice cream dipper, and a copper ice cream soda glass. These items have no resale value. Our advisors for this category are Joyce and Harold Screen; they are listed in the Directory under Maryland. See also Advertising; Coca-Cola.

Straw jars, Clear, $200.00; Green with metal base (reproduced in clear, green, and blue glass but without the metal screw-on base), $425.00.

Bottle topper, Cherry Sparkle, cb **75.00**
Canister, malted milk; Borden's, aluminum, w/lid, ca 1940-50 ...**100.00**
Dipper, Benedict Indestructo #3, sz 24, MIB **250.00**
Dipper, Benedict Indestructo #4, sz 30 ....**125.00**
Dipper, Benedict Indestructo #16 ....**125.00**
Dipper, Canada Fisher Motor Co, Cold Dog, short bbl **1,500.00**
Dipper, Dover Mfg Co #16, dbl trigger **100.00**
Dipper, Ergo Ice Cream **160.00**
Dipper, Erie Specialty, Quick & Easy Model 8, rnd bowl **175.00**
Dipper, Gem Spoon Co, Trojan Model 20 ....**200.00**
Dipper, Gilchrist #31, banana split **700.00**
Dipper, Gilchrist #31, rnd bowl, szs 8 to 30 ....**35.00**
Dipper, Gilchrist #33, cone-shaped bowl, sz 10 ....**200.00**
Dipper, Hamilton Beach, sz 8 to 20 ....**20.00**
Dipper, Indestructo #13, rnd bowl, sz 12 ....**75.00**
Dipper, Jiffy Sandwich **525.00**
Dipper, United, banana split, sz 20 ....**800.00**
Dispenser, Birchola, ceramic ball shape, tall flared base, 14", G+ **1,550.00**
Dispenser, Cardinal Cherry, gr ball w/orig pump, 1920, 15", NM+ .**5,700.00**
Dispenser, Cherry Smash, red glass bowl, clamp base, 1930s, EX+ ...**475.00**
Dispenser, Fowler's Root Beer, ball shape w/top spigot, 14", EX ...**1,500.00**
Dispenser, Howel's Cherry-Julep, ball shape w/orig pump, 15", VG+ .**1,250.00**
Dispenser, Howel's Orange-Julep, ball shape w/orig pump, 15", EX .**1,250.00**
Dispenser, Johnson's Hot Fudge, w/lid & ladle **225.00**
Dispenser, Lash's Orangeade, metal canister w/fruit topper, 22", VG ..**500.00**
Dispenser, Lash's Orangeade, textured vaseline glass globe, VG .**200.00**
Dispenser, Mint Julep, stoneware base, bottle top, 18½x8½" dia ..**400.00**
Dispenser, Mission Beverages, cylinder w/porc base, orange/brn, VG+ .**190.00**
Dispenser, Mission Beverages, glass bottle on metal base, EX **200.00**
Dispenser, Mission Beverages, vaseline bbl, Bakelite base, NM ..**225.00**
Dispenser, Nesbitt, counter type w/jug & syrup-line glass **195.00**
Dispenser, Ward's Orange-Crush, beveled glass bowl, clamp base, NM ..**325.00**
Dispenser, Watts Ice Tea, w/base & lid, NM **135.00**
Festoon, Hendler's Chocolate Ice Cream, #128, 9-pc, NM+ **165.00**
Festoon, Hendler's Ice Cream, All Sodas 10¢, 5-pc pennant display, NM .**150.00**
Fountain glass, Bromo Seltzer, bl **30.00**
Fountain glass, Drink Moonshine, w/syrup line **125.00**

Fountain glass, Green River, yel w/syurp line 65.00
Fountain glass, Koedinger's Ginger Ale 100.00
Fountain glass, Nesbitt's 30.00
Fountain glass, Richardson's Real Orangeade, goblet 100.00
Fountain glass, Seven-Up, gr, sq logo 30.00
Fountain glass, Wahl's Bouillon, goblet style 100.00
Fountain glass, Zipp's Grape-O 125.00
Hot soda cup, Armour's Bouillon cubes 30.00
Hot soda cup, Bovox Makes Strength, monk image 30.00
Hot soda cup, Burnham's Clam Bouillon, monk image 30.00
Ice cream block press, NP brass, Sheffield Reg..., 5½x4x2" 50.00
Jar, Borden's Malted Milk, glass w/emb letters, 6½x4½" 125.00
Menu board, Hood's Ice Cream, metal 170.00
Mixer, Hamilton Beach, single head, 2-speed, gr porc, NM 165.00
Mixer, malt; Hamilton Beach, porc, 3-head, EX 250.00
Mug, Lash's Root Beer, ceramic, blk lettering/bl stripes on wht, NM+ .60.00
Straw holder, Illinois pattern, gr glass, sq, w/lid 400.00
Straw holder, Orange Julep, pressed-glass box, VG 425.00
Straw jar, paneled sides, NP brass lid & insert 95.00
Syrup bottle, Beef Tea, cranberry swirl glass, w/lid 300.00
Syrup bottle, Cherry Smash, w/cap, 1905-10, VG+ 350.00
Syrup bottle, Coffee, brn swirl glass, w/lid 300.00
Syrup bottle, Orange Julep, metal jigger cap, 13", VG 300.00
Syrup bottle, Wild Cherry, gold foil under glass, Pat Date/23/1862 ....600.00
Syrup jug, Cherry Smash, clear glass, emb, 1-gal, NM 100.00
Syrup jug, Cherry Smash, clear glass, paper label, 1-gal, EX 85.00
Syrup urn, Green River, ceramic, 1930s 500.00
Tumbler holder, Tuft's Artic soda, ornate metal 300.00

Spangle Glass

Spangle glass, also known as Vasa Murrhina, is cased art glass characterized by the metallic flakes embedded in its top layer. It was made both abroad and in the United States during the latter years of the 19th century, and it was reproduced in the 1960s by the Fenton Art Glass Company.

Vasa Murrhina was a New England distributor who sold glassware of this type manufactured by a Dr. Flower of Sandwich, Massachusetts. Flower had purchased the defunct Cape Cod Glassworks in 1885 and used the facilities to operate his own company. Since none of the ware was marked, it is very difficult to attribute specific examples to his manufacture. See also Art Glass Baskets; Fenton.

Creamer & sugar bowl, pk to wht o/l w/mica, wafer ft, 4", 3" 135.00
Ewer, pk mottle, ruffled rim, clear branch hdl, 9" 125.00
Ewer vase, bl w/mica, clear appl thorn hdl, 7⅜x3⅜" 115.00
Finger bowl, ribbed, irregular ruffled rim, 4¾", +tray 225.00
Pitcher, Drape, pk, 4-lobe rim, clear reed hdl, 8½" 300.00
Pitcher, rainbow on wht w/silver, swirled ribs, ruffled, Mt WA, 8" .575.00
Rose bowl, beige/pk/oxblood w/mica, 8-crimp, 3⅜x3¾" 100.00
Rose bowl, bl w/mica, 6-crimp, 3¾x3⅜" 100.00
Rose bowl, pk spatter, ribbed, wht spatter int, petal ft, 3¾" 110.00
Rose bowl, red o/l, mica coral-like motif, 3¾x3⅜" 100.00
Rose bowl, rose o/l w/heavy mica, 8-crimp, 3¾x3¼" 100.00
Tumbler, Dmn Quilt, orange/wht spatter w/mica, 3¾" 40.00
Vase, pk, melon ribbed, crimped/ruffled rim, 6" 90.00

Spatter Glass

Spatter glass, characterized by its multicolor 'spatters,' has been made from the late 19th century to the present by American glass houses as well as those abroad. Although it was once thought to have been made entirely by workers at the 'end of the day' from bits and pieces of leftover scrap, it is now known that it was a standard line of production. See also Art Glass Baskets.

Creamer, cranberry opal, clear hdl, melon ribs, 5" 175.00
Pitcher, cranberry w/wht, ribbed, sqd rim, 9" 200.00
Pitcher, rainbow cased, sqd rim, clear reed hdl, 8" 250.00
Pitcher, shaded cranberry w/wht, ribbed, pleated rim, 8" 150.00
Ring tree, orange & wht w/mc enameled dots & gold, 3½x3¼" ...65.00
Rose bowl, 3½" 75.00
Tumbler, Invt T'print, orange & wht spatter w/mica, 3¾" 40.00
Vase, mc on wht, wht int, 7½x3⅜" 110.00

Spatterware

Spatterware is a general term referring to a type of decoration used by English potters as early as the late 1700s. Using a brush or a stick, brightly colored paint was dabbed onto the soft-paste earthenware items, achieving a spattered effect which was often used as a border. Because much of this type of ware was made for export to the United States, some of the subjects in the central design — the schoolhouse and the eagle patterns, for instance — reflect American tastes. Yellow, green, and black spatterware is scarce and highly valued by collectors.

In the descriptions that follow, the color listed after the item indicates the color of the spatter. The central design is identified next, and the color description that follows that refers to the design. Our advisor is Diane Patalano; she is listed in the Directory under New Jersey.

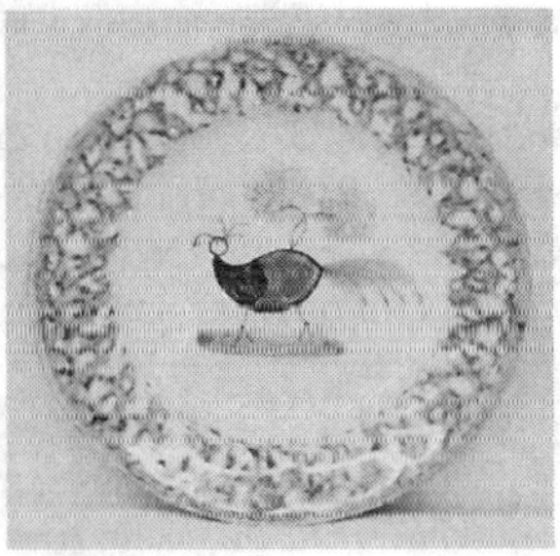

Plate, blue, Guinea Hen, red neck, yellow body, green tail, standing on green grass, black feet and comb, unmarked, 6½", $900.00.

Bowl, bl, Adam's Rose, red & gr, 5" dia, VG 235.00
Bowl, bl, Pineapple, 3-color, 3½x6½", EX 1,425.00
Bowl, sauce; bl, Peafowl, 3-color, 12-sided, 5⅝", NM 375.00
Creamer, bl, Fort, yel/red/brn/gr, minor wear, 5¾" 400.00
Creamer, bl, Thistle, red & gr, 4½" 330.00
Creamer, brn, Blue Flower, 3-color, C hdl, 4" 425.00
Creamer, red & bl Rainbow, 6¼", NM 210.00
Jar, brn/bl/wht/gr w/blk transfer label: Spaulding's..., 9¼" 350.00
Mug, bl, Peafowl, 4-color, stain, 3⅛" 715.00
Plate, bl, Fort, 4-color, 14-sided, 8½", NM 400.00
Plate, bl, Fort, 4-color, 9¾", NM 650.00
Plate, bl, Pansy, 4-color, 8⅝" 185.00
Plate, bl, Peafowl, 3-color, 8⅛" 300.00
Plate, bl, Profile Tulip, 3-color, 6½" 240.00
Plate, bl, Profile Tulip, 3-color, 8¾" 300.00
Plate, bl, Rose, 4-color, 8½" 275.00
Plate, bl, Star, 3-color, hairline, 8½" 275.00
Plate, bl, Star, 3-color, 12-sided, 8½", NM 320.00
Plate, bl, Wild Horses, blk transfer, 14-sided, 9" 175.00
Plate, gr, Columbine, gr no-center daisy border, red stripe, 5⅝" .110.00
Plate, gr & red, Columbine, 3-color, 8⅜" 125.00
Plate, gr w/red stripes, Rose, 4-color, 8½" 300.00
Plate, purple, Dogwood, 3-color, 8⅜" 110.00
Plate, red, Peafowl, 3-color, 9¼" 550.00

Plate, red, Peafowl, 4-color, 7⅜" 415.00
Plate, red, Peafowl, 4-color, 8⅜" 685.00
Plate, red, Tulip, 3-color, stain, 9" 250.00
Plate, red & yel Rainbow, flakes, 8¼" 1,375.00
Plate, red/bl, Bull's Eye & leaves, red & gr, 8¾", EX 150.00
Plate, red/bl/gr, Rainbow, 3-color bands, Adams, 8⅛" 475.00
Plate, toddy; bl & gr, Tulip, 3-color, 6½" 195.00
Plate, yel, Tulip, 3-color, rpr, 8½" 415.00
Plate, yel, Tulip, 3-color, wear/stain, 8" 1,980.00
Platter, red, Peafowl, 4-color, rpr, 15¾" 965.00
Soup plate, red, Star, red, 12-sided, 10¾" 435.00
Sugar bowl, bl, Fort, 3-color, crazing, chip, 4½" 385.00
Sugar bowl, bl, miniature, 4¼", NM 200.00
Sugar bowl, red & bl Rainbow, 8-sided, w/lid, prof rpr, 8¼" 250.00
Teabowl & saucer, bl, Fort, 3-color, stain, mini 300.00
Teabowl & saucer, bl, Holly Berry, 3-color, 3", 5⅞" 500.00
Teabowl & saucer, bl & gr variegated, Adams Rose, 3-color, 6" .195.00
Teabowl & saucer, gr, Columbine, 3-color, NM 165.00
Teabowl & saucer, gr, Peafowl, 3-color, 2¾", 4½" 300.00
Teabowl & saucer, red, Cluster of Buds, 3-color 250.00
Teabowl & saucer, red, Pansy, 3-color, NM 210.00
Teabowl & saucer, red, 4-Petal Open Tulip, 4-color, 2¾", 6" 500.00
Teabowl & saucer, red & bl Rainbow, Open Tulip, 3-color 975.00
Teapot, bl, Fort, 3-color, paneled, prof rpr, 8½" 1,100.00
Teapot, gr, Morning Glory, 3-color, 6¼", EX 525.00
Teapot, gr, Peafowl, 3-color, child sz, 4x6¼" 160.00
Toddy, red, Tulip, 4-color, lt wear, 6½" 770.00

Cut-Sponge

Bowl, bl, floral, 3-color, Baker & Co, 3⅛x6", NM 95.00
Bowl, red/bl, florets on blk vine, Staffordshire, 3⅝x7", EX 95.00
Bowl, vine w/gr leaves, red/bl florets, 6¾" 50.00
Creamer, bl dmns, vertical pleatings, scalloped 145.00
Cup & saucer, brn & gr, flowers, gr stripe rim, 5⅞", NM 30.00
Cup & saucer, red & gr designs & florets, dk bl band 100.00
Plate, bl dmn border w/yel rosettes & gr leaves, 8¾" 35.00
Plate, red & gr flowers w/bl stems, 3-color leaves, Adams, 9" 60.00
Plate, red dbl-sawtooth bands, yel & gr florets, 8½" 85.00
Plate, Virginia, purple/red/gr/bl florets, Adams, 1881, 6" 85.00
Soup plate, red & gr, leaves, bl flowers, lt wear, 10½" 110.00

Spelter

Spelter items are cast from commercial zinc and coated with a metallic patina. The result is a product very similar to bronze in appearance, yet much less expensive

Figure, dancing nude, silver enamel, 13" 125.00
Figure, Seated Shakespeare, bronze patina, 13½x8x5½" 300.00
Figure, warrior, bronze patina, blackened base, 16" 165.00
Lamp, pnt bronze nude reclines before amber slag-glass panel, 13" L ..150.00

Spode-Copeland

The Spode Works was established in 1770 in England by Josiah Spode I and continued to operate under that title until 1843. Their earliest products were typical underglaze blue-printed patterns. After 1790 a translucent porcelain body was the basis for a line of fine enamel-decorated dinnerware. Stone China was introduced in 1805, often in patterns reflecting an Oriental influence. In 1833 William Taylor Copeland purchased the company, having been Spode's business part-

ner. Copeland continued the business in much the same tradition as the Spode-Copeland partnership. Spode was the Royal Potter for years, providing many exquisite items for the Royal Families. They employed paintresses to decorate the merchandise by hand. Most of the Spode-Copeland wares were marked with one of several variations that incorporate the firm's name, making identification possible. The Spode Company merged with Worcester Royal Porcelain Company in 1976 and became Royal Worcester Spode Limited. This company was then purchased by Derby International in 1988. The two firms separated in 1989. The holding company is the Porcelain and Fine China Companies Limited, a division of Derby International. Spode china is still being manufactured today at exactly the same location where Josiah Spode I began in 1770. Robert Copeland, a descendent of William Taylor Copeland, resides in England. He writes books and gives lectures on Spode. Our advisor for this category is Don Haase; he is listed in the Directory under Washington.

Luncheon plate, Buchart, made especially for Madame Buchart of Buchart Gardens in 1930, $65.00.

Photo courtesy Don Haase

Bouillon cup & saucer, Blue Italian 45.00
Bread & butter, Billingsley Rose, 5½" 26.00
Butter dish, Mayflower, rectangular, w/lid 145.00
Butter pat, Blue Tower 32.00
Butter pat, Buttercup 25.00
Butter pat, Wicker Lane 25.00
Casserole, Fitzhugh, red, w/lid 125.00
Cereal, Blue Tower, 6¼" 28.00
Cereal, Christmas Tree, gr trim 28.00
Cereal, Wildflower 39.00
Chop plate, Florence, 13" dia 165.00
Coffeepot, Billingsley Rose, 6-cup 225.00
Coffeepot, Cowslip, 6-cup 175.00
Coffeepot, Fitzhugh, red 125.00
Coffeepot, Irene, bone, 8-cup 295.00
Comport, Cairo 345.00
Cream soup & saucer, Blue Tower 75.00
Cream soup & saucer, Dresden Rose Savoy, bone 135.00
Creamer, Buttercup, 4" 75.00
Creamer & covered sugar, Gainsborough, 3", 3½" 145.00
Creamer & covered sugar, Pink Tower, 4", 4½" 170.00
Cup & saucer, Tower, bl 45.00
Demitasse cup & saucer, Blue Tower 45.00
Demitasse cup & saucer, Pink Tower 45.00
Demitasse cup & saucer, Rosalie 39.00
Dessert plate, Buttercup, 8" 32.00
Dessert plate, Chelsea Garden, bone china 65.00
Dinner plate, Buttercup, 10½" 35.00
Dinner plate, Mayflower 65.00
Dinner plate, Wicker Lane 35.00
Dish warmer, Filigree (1810-33) 345.00
Footed salad, Mayflower 695.00

Footed salad, Ruins 495.00
Fruit, India Tree 25.00
Fruit, Pink Tower 28.00
Joke cup, Blue Fleur-de-Lis 145.00
Jubilee dish, India Tree 165.00
Jug, Blue Tower, bbl form, 5" 145.00
Jug, golfing subjects, wht on gr to sprigware, ca 1895, 4" 285.00
Luncheon plate, Fairy Dell, 8½" sq 42.00
Luncheon plate, Mayflower, 7½" sq 55.00
Luncheon plate, Pink Tower, 7½" sq 45.00
Luncheon plate, Wicker Rose, 8½" sq 42.00
Platter, Blue Tower, 11" 135.00
Platter, Florence, 13" 115.00
Platter, Gainsborough, 14½" 145.00
Platter, Mayflower, 24" 595.00
Punch bowl, Blue Tower, lg 695.00
Rim soup, Buttercup, 8½" 42.00
Rim soup, Castle (1815), 9" 195.00
Rim soup, Pink Camilia, 8½" 42.00
Rim soup, Ruins (1880), 9" 75.00
Salad plate, Blue Tower 35.00
Salad plate, Bridal Rose, bone 49.00
Salad plate, Primrose, bone 49.00
Sauce boat, Pink Tower, w/underplate 145.00
Shakers, Wickerdale, pr 110.00
Soup tureen, Blue Tower, w/ladle, lg 1,565.00
Sugar bowl, Buttercup 65.00
Sugar bowl, Fitzhugh, red, lg 65.00
Sugar bowl, Gainsborough, w/lid, lg 65.00
Syrup, Wicker Lane, 6" 75.00
Tea tile, Blue Tower 125.00
Teacup & saucer, Blue Ermine, tall 39.00
Teacup & saucer, Buttercup 39.00
Teacup & saucer, Chelsea Wicker, tall 35.00
Teacup & saucer, Mayflower, short 45.00
Teapot, Buttercup, 8-cup 225.00
Teapot, Fitzhugh, red, 8-cup 175.00
Teapot, Irene, 8-cup 395.00
Vegetable, Castle, rectangular 275.00
Vegetable, Hazel Dell, oval, 9½" 145.00
Vegetable, Seasons, ftd, w/lid, 11" 265.00
Vegetable, Wickerdale, 10" sq 155.00
Waste bowl, Old Salem, 5½" 45.00

Spongeware

Spongeware is a type of factory-made earthenware that was popular during the last quarter of the 19th century. It was decorated by dabbing color onto the drying ware with a sponge, leaving a splotched design at random or in simple patterns. Sometimes a solid band of color was added. The vessel was then covered with a clear glaze and fired at a high temperature. Blue on white is the most preferred combination, but green on ivory, orange on white, or those colors in combination may also occasionally be found. For further information we recommend *Collector's Encyclopedia of Salt Glaze Stoneware* by Terry Taylor, our advisor for this category, and Terry and Kay Lowrance, available from Collector Books.

Bowl, bl/wht, heart-shaped panels on sides, 5⅞x12⅛" EX 185.00
Bowl, bl/wht, molded fluting wear/flakes, 4x10½" 250.00
Bowl, bl/wht, oval, 13" 315.00
Bowl, mixing; bl/wht, lt wear/hairline, 5x10" 220.00
Bowl, mixing; bl/wht w/stripes, chip on ft, 5x11¼" 275.00
Creamer, bl/wht, 3", M 285.00

Creamer, flowing bl, bulbous, 4", EX 125.00
Crock, butter; bl/wht, wooden hdl, wire bail, no lid, 6¼x8¾" 275.00
Doorstop, dog figural, bl/wht, Whitehall, rare 875.00
Grandma's syrup jug, cobalt bl/wht, w/bail, smallest sz, M 1,200.00
Grandma's syrup jug, dk bl/wht, w/bail, sm to med 675.00
Jar, bl/wht, emb floral, scalloped rim, 5¾", NM 165.00
Jardiniere, bl/wht, emb foliage scrolls, worn gold, 9x10½" 200.00
Mug, bl/wht, molded hdl, 3⅝", NM 175.00
Mug, lt bl/wht, heavy stoneware, minor crazing, 5¼" 165.00
Mush cup & saucer, bl/wht, EX 300.00
Piggy bank, bl-gr/tan on cream, 3¾" 330.00
Pitcher, bl/wht, bl stripes, 6¾", NM 500.00
Pitcher, bl/wht, emb floral & panels, 8½", EX 200.00
Pitcher, bl/wht, paneled, 9" 375.00
Pitcher, brn/bl/cream, hairline, 10⅞" 185.00
Pitcher, cosmos; sponge top & bottom 380.00
Pitcher, dk bl/wht, slightly concave, 6¾" 325.00
Pitcher, lt bl/wht, Uhl, smallest sz 750.00
Pitcher, milk; bl/wht, 5⅛" 250.00
Pitcher, milk; flowing bl, emb scrolls, arched hdl, unmk, 7", EX ... 200.00
Pitcher, olive gr/wht w/bl edge band, 6½", EX 275.00
Plate, bl/wht, scalloped, lt stains, 9¼" 175.00
Plate, gr/red/wht, 8¼" 175.00
Platter, bl/wht, 13½" 350.00
Platter, flowing bl, oval, unmk, 12¼x8", EX 150.00
Soap dish, bl/wht w/bit of red, 4x6½", EX 175.00
Soap dish, red/bl on wht, 3½x4⅝" 175.00
Spittoon, bl/wht 135.00
Sugar bowl, gr/wht, minor wear/stains, 5¼" 100.00
Teapot, bl-gr/wht, sm chips, 6½" 330.00
Teapot, bl/wht, emb ribs, mismatched lid, 8½" 315.00
Teapot, bl/wht, w/lid 536.00
Umbrella stand, sponging w/bl bands at top & bottom, OH 1,200.00

Spoons

Souvenir spoons have been popular remembrances since the 1890s. The early hand-wrought examples of the silversmith's art are especially sought and appreciated for their fine craftsmanship. Commemorative, personality-related, advertising, and those with Indian busts or floral designs are only a few of the many types of collectible spoons. In the following listings, spoons are sorted by city, character, or occasion. Our advisor for this category is Margaret Alves; she is listed in the Directory under Connecticut.

Key:
B — bowl
emb — embossed
eng — engraved
ff — full figure

GW — gold wash
H — handle
HR — handle reverse

New Castle, PA, in bold script in bowl, fancy florals with knight's helmet finial, marked Sterling, 5⅞", $25.00.

Ann Arbor MI in B; wheat sheaves on H 35.00

Atlantic City NJ Convention Centre Building on H; plain B **30.00**
Battle Monument Baltimore in B; scroll H; sm **30.00**
Boston in B; coin w/head finial H; demi **20.00**
Boston Subway in B; buildings/etch on H; lg **40.00**
Buffalo etched in B; etched floral H **32.50**
Chicago in script H; Ft Dearborn etched in B **40.00**
Chicago in script in B; emb pansies on H & HR **35.00**
Chinatown SF cut-out H; plain B **25.00**
Columbus in pnt letters in B; emb floral H **25.00**
Columbus landing & 1492 in B; bird w/wreath H; lg **30.00**
Confederate Monument Lynchburg, VA in B; flower/peanut/etc H ..**40.00**
Deadwood SD in B; miner ff H **85.00**
Duluth MN, aerial bridge in B; grapes/leaves H **40.00**
Elysian MN etched in B; emb strawberries on H & HR **35.00**
Empire State Building cut-out H; plain B & HR **30.00**
Galesburg IL in B; scroll H; demi **20.00**
Gary SD in B; floral H & HR **25.00**
Grand Canyon view in B; swastika finial H **40.00**
Harrison ID in B; emb pine cones on H & HR **30.00**
Hawaiian dancers pnt in B; design on H **42.00**
Idaho state seal on H; plain B **25.00**
IL state seal on H; plain B; demi **8.00**
Jacob's Ladder Mt WA NH/train on bridge in B; pine cones H **40.00**
Joplin MO in B; emb floral H & HR **35.00**
Los Gatos, 2 cats etched in B; floral H **20.00**
Mining picks crossed on H; plain B **18.00**
MO state seal on H; simple HR; plain B **20.00**
Mormon Tabernacle in B; twisted/monogrammed H **30.00**
Mt Hood etched in B; emb floral H; simple HR **35.00**
Mt Hood relief in B; State Capitol/Rooster Rock H; Mt Hood HR ..**35.00**
Mt Ranier/mtns/trees in B; totem pole hdl **40.00**
Niagara Falls Canada in B, flower H; hearts on HR **35.00**
Niagara horseshoe & falls, scrolling w/Building 300-Ft High H, sm ..**35.00**
NY Grand Central Station/Statue of Liberty/etc in B; swirl H **40.00**
Old Stone Mill Newport RI in B; Indian bust H **40.00**
Pontiac MI in B; Indian head facing right H **35.00**
San Xavier Mission/Tucson AZ in B; Indian ff H; sm **35.00**
Santa Barbara, courthouse in B; scroll H **30.00**
Santa Claus in B; Christmas 1897/scrolls on H **40.00**
Sault St Marie MI, building in B; Indian head H **35.00**
Springfield IL state capitol eng in B; seal on H; scrolled HR **35.00**
St Louis Bridge in B; crown on H **32.50**
St Petersburg, FL in B; Black w/alligator ff H **165.00**
Steel Pier, Atlantic City NJ in B; Indian ff H **40.00**
Subway NY in B; NY City skyline/etc H, sites on HR; lg **60.00**
Trinidad CO on B; cut-out flowers on H **35.00**
Union Depot San Francisco in B; floral H; demi **24.00**
WA DC Capitol relief in B; Wht House/flag/etc on H & HR **32.00**
Walter Baker Ltd Dorchester MA in B; Baker Chocolate girl H; SP .**25.00**
Washoe Smelter, Anaconoa MT, Buffalo finial H; copper color, sm .**38.00**
Waterloo IA bridge in B; floral H **35.00**
Watertown SD in B; scroll H; plain HR **25.00**
Whist '05 in B; emb floral H & HR **35.00**
Yosemite/mtns H; plain B; demi **24.00**
1908 etched in B; graduate ff H; sm **35.00**

Sporting Goods

When sports cards became so widely collectible several years ago, other types of related memorabilia started to interest sports fans. Now they search for baseball uniforms, autographed baseballs, game-used bats and gloves, and all sorts of ephemera. Although baseball is America's all-time favorite, other sports have their own groups of interested col-

lectors. Our advice for this category comes from Paul Longo Americana. Mr. Longo is listed in the Directory under Massachusetts. See also Target Balls; Tennis Rackets.

Pin, N.Y. Yankees, pictures Mickey Mantle, Roger Maris, Yogi Berra, and Bill Skowron, 1960s, 3", rare, NM, $250.00.

Baseball, sgn Nolan Ryan, w/plaque **75.00**
Baseball glove, fielder's, full web, calf-skin leather, 1900s, EX **250.00**
Bat, Lou Gehrig store model, 1930s **500.00**
Book, Iowa Baseball Confederacy, Kinsella, 1st ed, w/dust jacket .**20.00**
Boxing card, John L Sullivan, Mecca Cigarettes, EX **85.00**
Letterhead, Cleveland Indians, +envelope w/logo **5.00**
License, hunting; CA, 1947 ....**40.00**
License, jockey's, City of NY, 1890s **40.00**
Money clip, PGA 1967 Championship **65.00**
Newspaper, National Auto Racing News, 1939 ....**10.00**
Pass, complimentary, White Sox game, 1934 ....**35.00**
Plate, Kentucky Derby, CBS TV Sterling Presentation, 1964 ....**250.00**
Postcard, Indianapolis 500, 1940s **10.00**
Postcard, Mickey Mantle, Holiday Inn, 1963, M **15.00**
Program, Brighton Beach Racing, July 4, 1892, in fr **125.00**
Program, Danbury Auto Races, 1931 ....**38.00**
Program, Indianapolis 500 race, 1924 ....**250.00**
Program, Milwaukee Braves, 1958 World Series **125.00**
Program, OH State Football, 1933, EX **45.00**
Program, Princeton-Brown, football, 1950 ....**20.00**
Program, Purdue vs Notre Dame, football, 1954 ....**30.00**
Program, Rangers Stanley Cup Playoff, 1982-83 ....**15.00**
Program, Sonja Henie, skating, 1938, EX **45.00**
Program/score card, Red Sox, 1955, VG **15.00**
Racing suit, worn by Bobby Allison, Goodyear, cloth, EX **300.00**
Racing suit, worn by Danny Sullivan, Miller Racing, cloth, EX .**500.00**
Score book, 1933 Washington vs White Sox, 1933, EX **50.00**
Score card, Cardinals, 1953 ....**20.00**
Score card, Detroit Senators, 1949 ....**20.00**
Score card, Philadelphia at Yankees, 1952 ....**20.00**
Score card, Yankees at White Sox, 1945 ....**25.00**
Ticket, Milwaukee Braves, 1954 ....**10.00**
Ticket, Rose Bowl, 1963 ....**20.00**
Yearbook, NY Mets, 1966 ....**60.00**
Yearbook, Rochester Red Wings, 1987 ....**5.00**

St. Clair

The St. Clair Glass Company began as a small family-oriented operation in Elwood, Indiana, in 1941. Most famous for their lamps, the family made numerous small items of carnival, pink and caramel slag, and custard glass as well. Later, paperweights became popular production pieces; many command relatively high prices on today's market. Weights are stamped and usually dated, while small production pieces are often unmarked. Lamps are in big demand (prices depend on size and whether or not they are signed) as are items signed by Paul or Ed St. Clair. For further information we recommend *St. Clair Glass Collector's Book* by Bonnie Pruitt, available from our advisor, Ted Pruitt, who is listed in the Directory under Indiana.

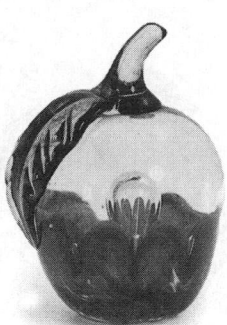

Apple, signed Maude & Bob, 1983, large, $100.00 (Small, $50.00).

Animal dish, dolphin, bl, Joe St Clair	175.00
Bell, ACGA 10th Annual Convention, bl carnival	75.00
Bell, carnival glass, from $90 to	100.00
Bell, Holly Carillon, cobalt carnival, sgn	35.00
Bird, bl & clear, lg, from $75 to	95.00
Candle holder, mc floral, sulfide, from $75 to	85.00
Candle holder/paperweight, pk floral, Joe St Clair	75.00
Covered dish, Reclining Colt, cobalt custard, from $135 to	160.00
Creamer, Holly Band, aqua opal	85.00
Doll, any color, from $30 to	40.00
Doorstop, mallard	375.00
Goblet, Hobstar, ice bl	25.00
Goblet, Roses in the Snow, cobalt	30.00
Goblet, Wildflower, amethyst carnival	45.00
Insulator, red, red carnival or marigold carnival, ea	110.00
Kewpie, chocolate carnival	110.00
Kewpie, flesh carnival	110.00
Lamp, 3-ball, sgn Joe & Bob St Clair	1,500.00
Paperweight, butterfly, controlled bubble, etched, from $250 to	350.00
Paperweight, flower in dome shape, Joe St Clair	60.00
Paperweight, Kewpie, windowed, from $175 to	200.00
Paperweight, rose, any color, Joe St Clair	1,000.00
Paperweight, sulfide, assassinated president, set of 4	525.00
Paperweight, sulfide, flower, windowed, Ed St Clair	300.00
Paperweight, sulfide, frog, from $140 to	165.00
Paperweight, sulfide, kitten, from $140 to	165.00
Paperweight, sulfide, Scottie	145.00
Paperweight, 5-lily, controlled bubbles	95.00
Plate, Kewpie, cobalt carnival	198.00
Plate, Lyndon B Johnson, from $20 to	25.00
Plate, Reagan/Bush, any color, from $30 to	35.00
Ring holder, clear w/yel flower	50.00
Statue, Scottie dog, custard or caramel, sgn Maude St Clair, ea	150.00
Statue, Scottie dog, dk amethyst (blk), Bob St Clair	300.00
Toothpick holder, Bicentennial sq, any color, from $27.50 to	30.00
Toothpick holder, cactus form, wht carnival	35.00
Toothpick holder, Holly Band, red carnival	20.00
Toothpick holder, Indian, bl & wht slag, sgn Joe St Clair	75.00
Toothpick holder, Indian, cobalt	25.00
Toothpick holder, Indian, yel carnival	25.00
Toothpick holder, kingfisher, cobalt carnival	18.00
Toothpick holder, paneled, red carnival	25.00
Toothpick holder, Santa Claus, Joe St Clair	150.00
Toothpick holder, sulfide, flower, from $65 to	75.00
Toothpick holder, wheelbarrow, caramel slag, Joe St Clair	40.00
Toothpick holder, witch, chocolate, from $50 to	75.00

Tumbler, Grape & Cable, red	30.00
Vase, paperweight base, clear trumpet neck, from $75 to	85.00

Staffordshire

Scores of potteries sprang up in England's Staffordshire district in the early 18th century; several remain to the present time. (See also specific companies.) Figurines and groups were made in great numbers; dogs were favorite subjects. Often they were made in pairs, each a mirror image of the other. They varied in heights from 3" or 4" to the largest, measuring 16" to 18". From 1840 until about 1900, portrait figures were produced to represent specific characters, both real and fictional. As a rule these were never marked.

The Historical Ware listed here was made throughout the district; some collectors refer to it as Staffordshire Blue Ware. It was produced as early as 1820, and because much was exported to America, it was very often decorated with transfers depicting scenic views of well-known American landmarks. Early examples were printed in a deep cobalt. By 1830 a softer blue was favored, and within the next decade black, pink, red, and green prints were used. Although sometimes careless about adding their trademark, many companies used their own border designs that were as individual as their names.

This ware should not be confused with the vast amounts of modern china (mostly plates) made from early in the century to the present. These souvenir or commemorative items are usually marketed through gift stores and the like. (See Rowland and Marcellus.) See also specific manufacturers. Our advisors for this category are Dave and Anne Middleton; they are listed in the Directory under New Jersey.

Key:
blk — black	l/b — light blue
gr — green	m/b — medium blue
d/b — dark blue	m-d/b — medium dark blue

Figures and Groups

A Lincoln, seated on horse, mc, old rstr, 15½"	1,100.00
Band of Hope, lady w/heart-shaped shield, child w/flag, 14"	350.00
Ben Franklin, mc w/fine details, rprs, 14½"	650.00
Ben Franklin (mistitled Geo Washington), red/blk/flesh, 15¾"	1,900.00
Bird, mc details, ca 1840, 4¼", EX	350.00
Bird nest w/2 eggs, bird atop, inkwell, mc, 3x3"	150.00
Blacksmith in striped shirt, 16½"	300.00
Boy w/dog (neck rpr), girl holds cat, gold trim, 8½", pr	150.00
Bust, lady w/draped shawl, earthenware, Enoch Wood, 15⅝"	850.00
Castle w/turrets & arched windows, mossy base, 4x4⅛x2½"	150.00
Castle w/2 turrets & lg clock, coleslaw grass, wear, 12"	100.00
Child on swimming swan, 8"	245.00
Cleopatra, asp to bosom, rocky base, 1800s, rstr, 12½"	200.00
Cobbler & wife, seated, she w/jug, att Ralph Hall, 12", pr	425.00
Cottage, money box/bank, 2-story, 2 chimneys, mc, 4", EX	225.00
Cottage, pastille burner, 2-story, mc w/mossy base, 6x4x3⅜"	225.00
Cottage, pastille burner, 2-story w/dbl gables, mc, 5¼"	225.00
Couple carrying flowers, 6"	100.00
Couple flank sq brick well, vase between, 7¾"	200.00
Couple in arbor bocage w/squirrel, ca 1820, 9⅛", EX	1,495.00
Couple seated under arbor w/appl flowers, 10½"	200.00
Couple seated under arched tree-shaped bk, mc w/gold, rpr, 6⅛"	200.00
Couple w/bird of paradise between them, 7½"	125.00
Couple w/clock below, 13"	175.00
Cow & calf, wht w/red-brn spots, oval base, 7x9x5"	500.00
Cow on rectangular base, creamer w/lid, ca 1800, 5⅛", NM	400.00
Death of Nelson, 3 male figures on base, mc, 8¾"	350.00

Dove keeper, man by birdhouse, spill vase behind, 9" 300.00
Eliza Cook, mc, flat bk, old rstr, 10" 450.00
Esmeralda & Gringoire w/violin, firing separation, 9¾" 200.00
Falconer, man w/lantern & bird, 8¼" 90.00
Flower sellers, lad in cocked hat/knee pants, & maid, 12", pr 495.00
Fruit seller, lady in laced bodice w/basket in ea hand, 14½" 275.00
Garibaldi, mc w/gold, 19⅜", EX 415.00
Garibaldi, plumed hat, orange coat, 11¼" 425.00
Girl dancing, 1 arm at waist/1 to forehead, 8½", EX 125.00
Girl w/vintage garland, mc w/worn gold, 13½", EX 300.00
Harvesters, dbl figure, 9½" 250.00
Hen on nest, covered dish, mc on basketweave, 6¼x7¼x5¾" 320.00
Hen on nest, covered dish, mc on orange base, 4¾x5¾x4¾" 350.00
Hen on nest w/egg cup insert, mc, rpr, 7½" 635.00
Highland hunter standing by fawn, 18" 275.00
Hunter on horseback, 15" 135.00
Hunter shields eyes, cobalt jacket, gilt trim, 16½" 400.00
IOGT Meeting (Independent Order of Good Templers), group, 11" ..110.00
Jester & dog, mc, flat bk, 11¼", EX 550.00
Lady w/book, bird on tree trunk at right, mc, 10" 150.00
Lady w/wheat, mc, rstr hat, flakes, 7¾" 150.00
Leopard, recumbent, on leafy oval base, 1850s, 7½" 315.00
Little Red Riding Hood, mc, flat bk, flake, 8½" 325.00
Man seated w/book & spectacles, mc w/some flaking, rprs, 8" 275.00
Mother carrying little girl, watering can in left hand, 10" 260.00
Old Maid & Old Batchelor, mc w/gold, 8x5⅝x2⅜", pr 525.00
Orlando, plumed hat, standing by vase, 18" 275.00
Prince & Princess Alexandra of Denmark's Engagement, titled, 15" ...365.00
Prince of Wales, hand on hip, dress uniform, 17¼" 260.00
Prince of Wales stands by setter dog, titled, 14½" 460.00
Queen Victoria & Prince Consort, mc, 10¼", pr 675.00
Queen Victoria & Prince of Wales, 16½", 17", pr, from $1,400 to ...1,600.00
Robert Burns, standing, title on base, 13" 200.00
Robert Burns & Highland Mary, couple seated under arch, 13" .200.00
Robert Burns & Highland Mary, mc, flat bk, 6¾" 250.00
Robin Hood, dbl figure w/spill vase, title on base, 14" 275.00
Shakespeare, mc w/gold, 9¼", NM 375.00
Shakespeare & 2 ladies, clock in base, mc, prof rstr, 10" 550.00
Sheep shearer w/sheep on lap, 8¾", VG 995.00
Simon, man w/arms crossed, on rocky base, 1790s, 9¾", EX 515.00
Soldier & wife, mc (bright), rstr, 7½", pr 700.00
Spring (allegorical lady), canary, 4½", NM 770.00
Spring (allegorical lady), pearlware w/brn & gr, 4¼", EX 220.00
Theatrical figures (2), minor rstr to mc pnt, rprs, 6½", pr 450.00
Tom King, man seated on wht horse, flaking/crazing, 9¼" 160.00
Uncle Tom w/Topsy seated on stump holding Little Eva, 9⅞" ...210.00
Washington bust, mc w/cobalt, blk base, Enoch Wood 1818, 8½" ...1,870.00

Dick Whittington, resting hand on marker stating IV Miles to London, flaw in making, 17", $250.00.

Winter (allegorical lady), canary, 4⅝", NM 660.00
Winter's Tale, couple beside tree trunk vase, mc, 12" 400.00

Woman w/rabbit in basket, cape about her shoulders, 13½" 165.00
Zebra, blk & gr, prof rstr, 6½" 225.00
Zebras w/Royal children, spill vases, 7", VG, pr 1,895.00

Historical

Coffeepot, Virginia Church, dark blue, minor restoration, replaced finial, 11", $600.00.

Basket, chestnut; Sarcophagi at Cacamo, m-d/b, Spode, 2¾x9" ...1,000.00
Basket, Sheltered Peasants, d/b, openwork, Hall, 3¾x11¾", NM 650.00
Bowl, Franklin's Tomb, d/b, Wood, w/hdl, 3½x5", NM 700.00
Bowl, Octagon Church Boston, d/b, Ridgway, rstr, 2x8¾" 400.00
Bowl, US Hotel Philadelphia, d/b, Tams/Anderson/Tams, 10⅝", EX ...4,000.00
Bowl, vegetable; fruit & birds still life, d/b, w/lid, 11", EX 440.00
Bowl, vegetable; Gentlemen's Cabin, l/b, Edwards, 10", EX 160.00
Bowl, vegetable; Moorish garden scene, d/b, w/lid, 12" 600.00
Bowl, vegetable; Quebec, d/b, shell border, 9½" sq 750.00
Bowl, vegetable; Tappan Zee From Greenburg, d/b, Wood, 9", NM .850.00
Bowl, vegetable; West Point...Academy, d/b, shell border, 10¾" L ...950.00
Bowl, vegetable; Woodlands Near Phila, d/b, w/lid, Stubbs, 6x12", EX 1,400.00
Bowl, vegetable; Yarmouth Isle of Wight, d/b, Wood, 10½", EX ..700.00
Cake stand, Boston State House, d/b, Rogers, 2x10⅝", NM 3,000.00
Coffeepot, Peekskill Landing, blk, Ridgway, 10¾", EX 225.00
Coffeepot, Wadsworth Tower, d/b, dome top, 11" 2,365.00
Creamer, Eagle on Urn, d/b, NM 800.00
Creamer, Garden Scenery, l/b, Mayer, 5¼" 110.00
Creamer, Oriental scene, d/b, 5⅛" 275.00
Cup, custard; Wadsworth Tower, d/b, shell border, Wood, 2⅜", NM ...200.00
Cup, invalid feeding; Basket of Flowers, d/b, old rstr, 2½x7¼" ...225.00
Cup, Utica NY, l/b, Meigh, 2¾" 80.00
Cup, 2 men in beached boat, m/b, unkown mfg, mfg flaw, 2¼" 75.00
Cup & saucer, Boston State House..., m-d/b w/copper lustre, Wood 1,000.00
Cup & saucer, Bride of Lannermoor, d/b, unknown mfg 135.00
Cup & saucer, Deer, m-d/b, unknown mfg, EX 115.00
Cup & saucer, Grecian, l/b 90.00
Cup & saucer, Seal of US, d/b, rare, NM 1,500.00
Cup plate, Anti-Slavery (Lovejoy/Tyrant's Foe), l/b, 4", NM 250.00
Cup plate, Castle Garden Battery NY, d/b, Wood, 3⅝", NM 200.00
Cup plate, Hyena, d/b, Hall Quadrupeds series, 4¼" 280.00
Cup plate, Swiss Lake & Village, l/b, Davenport, 4" 70.00
Dish, leaf; Fallow Deer, d/bl, Rogers & Son, 5¾" L, NM 250.00
Gravy boat, Catskill Mtns..., d/b, shell border, 4¾", EX 325.00
Invalid feeder, flower in vase, d/b, rprs, 3" 220.00
Pitcher, Erie Canal Aqueduct Bridge..., d/b, Wood, rpr, 7" 350.00
Pitcher, Falconry, brn, sm rstr, 8½" 140.00
Pitcher, hunting scene, d/b, old staple rstr, 6¼" 300.00
Pitcher, Lafayette at Franklin's Tomb, d/b, rstr, mini, 3¾" 500.00
Pitcher, Landing of Lafayette, d/b, Clews, prof rstr, 6¼" 550.00
Pitcher, Views of Erie Canal, d/b, Wood, flake, 6¾" 600.00
Pitcher, Virginia Church, d/b, minor rstr, mini, 3¾" 400.00
Pitcher, Washington, Independence, Truxton, d/b, prof rpr, 7⅝" ..600.00
Pitcher, Wells Cathedral Somersetshire, d/b, Hall, 10", EX 400.00

Plate, Am & Independence, d/b, Clews, 10½", EX 425.00
Plate, Am Villa, d/b, unknown mfg, 8½" 125.00
Plate, Arms of NY, d/b, Mayer, lt scratches, 10" 650.00
Plate, B&O RR (incline), d/b, shell border, Wood, 9⅛" 770.00
Plate, Baker's Falls, blk, 8¾" 125.00
Plate, Bank o/t US, Phila, d/b, eagle border, Stubbs, 10", NM 350.00
Plate, Battle of Chapultepeck, purple, Shaw, 9⅜" 425.00
Plate, Beaver, d/b, Hall's Quadrupeds series, 8¾" 300.00
Plate, Beehive, d/b, Stevenson & Wms, 6⅛" 160.00
Plate, Bishton Hall Staffordshire, med d/b, 10½", NM 250.00
Plate, Boston State House, m-d/b, Wood, 9¾", NM 175.00
Plate, British Views, d/b, fruit & flower border, Henshall, 8¼" ..170.00
Plate, British Views, d/b, fruit & flower border, Henshall, 9¾" ..225.00
Plate, Building, Sheep on Lawn, d/b, Clews States series, 8½" ...200.00
Plate, Bushey Park Middlesex d/b, Clews, 10" 350.00
Plate, Capitol at Washington, brn, Godwin, 10¾", pr 250.00
Plate, Capitol at Washington, d/b, shell border, rim flake, 6½" ..325.00
Plate, Castle & Cows, m-l/b, unknown mfg, 10½" 60.00
Plate, Castle Forbes, Aberdeenshire, d/b, grapevine border, 6⅝" ..100.00
Plate, City Hall, NY, d/b, Ridgeway Beauties of Am series, 9¾" ...280.00
Plate, City of Albany...NY, d/bl, shell border, 10⅛", NM 450.00
Plate, Dam & Waterworks Phila (side-wheeler), d/b, Henshall, 10" ...550.00
Plate, Dam & Waterworks Phila (stern-wheeler), d/b, Henshall, 10" .465.00
Plate, English landscape, d/b, Adams, 8⅞" 200.00
Plate, Entrance of Erie Canal...Albany, d/b, Wood, prof rstr, 10¼" .500.00
Plate, Erie Canal - De Witt Clinton Eulogy, d/b, 10" 475.00
Plate, Esholt House Yorkshire, d/b, grapevine border, 10" 225.00
Plate, Fairmount Near Phila, d/b, Stubbs eagle border, 10" 200.00
Plate, Fountain, m/b, Tay, flake, 10" 50.00
Plate, Franklin's Morals, d/b, att Davenport, 7⅝", NM 275.00
Plate, Gen Jackson Hero of New Orleans, carmine, 6¾" 1,900.00
Plate, Gilpins' Mills on Brandy, d/b, shell border, 9⅛" 1,200.00
Plate, Gracefield...Ireland, d/b, Adams, 10¼", NM 200.00
Plate, Guy's Cliff Warwickshire, d/b, grapevine border, 10⅛" 170.00
Plate, Harvard Collage, d/b, Acorn & Leaf border, rstr, 10" 150.00
Plate, Highlands at West Point..., d/b, Wood, 6½" 900.00
Plate, hot water; Death of Bear, m-d/h, Spode, 11½" 700.00
Plate, Hudson River View, d/b, shell border, Wood, 5¾", NM ...700.00
Plate, Hunting Series, d/b, Davenport, 9¾" 200.00
Plate, India Pattern, m-d/b, 8⅜" 65.00
Plate, Insane Hospital Boston, d/b, Beauties of Am, 7", NM 275.00
Plate, La Grange Residence of...Lafayette, d/b, Wood, 10", EX ..300.00
Plate, Landing of Fathers at Plymouth, m-d/b, Wood, 10" 200.00
Plate, Landing of Lafayette, d/b, Clews, 10⅛" 385.00
Plate, Landing of Lafayette, d/b, Clews, 5½", NM 200.00
Plate, Leopard & Antelope, d/b, unknown mfg, 7½" 190.00
Plate, Library, Phila, d/b, Ridgeway Beauties of Am, 8", NM 400.00
Plate, Ontario, l/b, Heath Lake Scenery series, 9¼" 60.00
Plate, Park Scenery, m-l/b, unknown mfg, 10", NM 50.00
Plate, Parke Theatre NY, d/b, acorn/oak leaf border, Stevenson, 10" .425.00
Plate, Pass in Catskill Mtns, d/b, shell border, 7½", NM 500.00
Plate, Picturesque Views...Sandy Hill, Hudson..., blk, Clews, 8" 95.00
Plate, Pine Orchard House..., d/b, shell border, 10¼" 600.00
Plate, Pittsfield Elm, d/b, Clews, 7⅞" 275.00
Plate, Rome (Tiber), m-d/b, Spode, 9¾" 110.00
Plate, Rural Homes, d/b, Woods, 7½", NM 85.00
Plate, Saltwood Castle, d/b, grapevine border, Wood, 6½" 375.00
Plate, Schuylkill Water Works, brn, Godwin, 9½", pr 135.00
Plate, Sheltered Peasants, d/b, Hall, 10⅛", pr 325.00
Plate, Shepherd Boy w/Flute, m/b, 7½" 65.00
Plate, Taymouth Castle..., d/b, grapevine border, 10¼", NM 150.00
Plate, Tiber, m/b, Spode, 8¼" 70.00
Plate, Transylvania University, d/b, shell border, rstr, 9⅛" 300.00
Plate, Trenton Falls, l/b, Enoch Wood, 7¾", NM 165.00

Plate, two stags, d/b, Wood Zoological series, 10¼" 275.00
Plate, unidentified Oriental view, d/b, 7½" 60.00
Plate, Union Line, d/b, Wood's shell border, 10", NM 500.00
Plate, Verona, m-l/b, Minton, 10½" 60.00
Plate, View Near Sandy Hill, blk, pk lustre border, 4¾", NM 200.00
Plate, View of Conway NH, red, Adams US Views, 9" 120.00
Plate, View of Trenton Falls, d/b, shell border, Wood, 6½" 200.00
Plate, View of Trenton Falls, d/b, shell border, Wood, 7½", NM ..275.00
Plate, Villa in Regent's Park London, d/b, Adams, 9" 165.00
Plate, Warleigh House Somersetshire, d/b, Hall, 8⅛" 190.00
Plate, Warwock Castle, d/b, grapevine border, 10" 150.00
Plate, Webster Vase, l/b, 10¼" 50.00
Plate, White House, Washington, d/b, shell border, rstr, 5⅝" 750.00
Platter, Ailanthus, brn w/mc, 15¼", NM 110.00
Platter, Albany, brn, Godwin, 10", EX 110.00
Platter, Alms House NY, d/b, Ridgway, 16¾", NM 550.00
Platter, Am Villa, d/b, BB&B, rstr, 16½" 260.00
Platter, Battle of Bunker Hill, d/b, vine border, 12¾" 3,500.00
Platter, Boston Mails...Saloon, blk, Edwards, 19⅞" 300.00
Platter, Camel, m-d/b, Rogers, 10½" 225.00
Platter, Castle Garden Battery NY, d/b, shell border, rstr, 18½" .600.00
Platter, Chinoiserie (no bridge), m-b, att Davenport, 12" 125.00
Platter, Chinoiserie (no bridge), m-b, att Davenport, 18½", NM ...180.00
Platter, Death of Stag, m-d/b, unknown mfg, 21", NM 475.00
Platter, Don Quixote, Shepherd Boy Rescued, d/b, 14", NM 700.00
Platter, Eton College, l/b, unknown mfg, 14⅝" 200.00
Platter, Fontill Abbey, d/b, bluebell border, Clews, 17", NM 900.00
Platter, Greek Statue, m-d/b, Rogers, 8" 180.00
Platter, Halifax, brn, Podmore Walker, 19¼" 600.00
Platter, Harper's Ferry, red, Adams US Views, 15½" 435.00
Platter, Hudson River, dk purple, Clews, 13⅜", NM 225.00
Platter, Huton on Canton River, m-d/b, Hamilton, 14½" 225.00
Platter, Italian, m/b, Spode, 14½" 200.00
Platter, Lake George, State of NY, d/b, shell border, 16½" 1,500.00
Platter, Landing of Lafayette, d/b, Clews, 12½", NM 800.00
Platter, Landing of Lafayette, d/b, Clews, 18⅞", NM 1,500.00
Platter, Mendenhall Ferry, d/b, Stubbs eagle border, 16½" 1,250.00
Platter, Monopteros, m-d/b, flake, mini, 5½" 50.00
Platter, Narrows From Fort Hamilton, l/b, Ridgway, rstr, 17½" ..200.00
Platter, Newburgh Hudson River, l/b, Clews, 18", NM 475.00
Platter, Octagonal Chinoiserie, m-d/b, unknown mfg, 12½", NM ..70.00
Platter, Philosopher, m/b, unknown mfg, 17" 425.00
Platter, Priory, l/b, E Challinor, 15½", NM 100.00
Platter, Rome (Tiber), m-d/b, Spode, 9⅜" 225.00
Platter, States...Dock w/Lg Bldg & Ships, d/b, Clews, 19", NM ..1,700.00
Platter, Tappan Bay From Greenburgh, d/b, shell border, rstr, 9¾" ..850.00
Platter, Tunbridge Castle, Surrey, d/b, Stevenson, 15", EX 700.00
Platter, View From Fort Putnam, blk, Am Scenery series, 15" 100.00
Platter, View of Greenwich, d/b, grapevine border, 14⅞" 750.00
Sauce tureen, Bank Savannah/Exchange Charleston..., s/b, 7x9", EX ...1,100.00
Sauce tureen, Battle of Buena Vista, l/b, Shaw, w/lid, 5⅜x7" ..1,000.00
Sauce tureen, Italian Scenery Terni, w/lid, 6¼", EX 450.00
Sauce tureen, Passaic Falls...NJ, d/b, 6½x7½"+tray 1,200.00
Sauce tureen, Persian, l/b, Ridgway, +8½" undertray 270.00
Sauce tureen, unidentified view, d/b, shell border, 6½x7¾" 500.00
Sauce tureen, unidentified view, d/b, 6½x7¼", +8" tray 800.00
Sauce tureen, Zebra, d/b, Rogers, old rstr, 7x8½" 225.00
Saucer, Washington, Scroll in Hand, d/b, Wood, 5¾", M 325.00
Soup, Arms of NY, d/b, Mayer, 2½x6½", NM 370.00
Soup, Beehive, d/b, 9⅞" 180.00
Soup, Bridge of Lucano, m-d/b, Wood Italian Scenery, 9¾" 140.00
Soup, Capitol Washington, brn, Godwin Am views, 10½", NM .120.00
Soup, City of Corinth, m/b, Spode Caramanian series, 10" 200.00
Soup, Dilston Tower..., d/b, bluebell border, Adams, 10", NM ...100.00

Soup, Octagon Church, Boston, d/b, Ridgeway Beauties of Am, 10" .425.00
Soup, Pine Orchard House..., d/b, shell border, Wood, 10⅛", NM 700.00
Soup, Springer Spaniel, m/b, floral border, 9¾" 300.00
Soup ladle, Sheltered Peasants, d/b, 11½" 650.00
Strainer, Quebec, brn, Podmore Walker, 12¾", EX 450.00
Sugar bowl, Landing of Lafayette, d/b, 6", EX 935.00
Sugar bowl, native riding zebra, d/b, w/lid, prof rpr, 7" 350.00
Tea set, bird & nest of eggs, d/b, teapot+cr/sug, 3-pc 1,650.00
Teapot, Eagle on Urn, d/b, Clews, 7", NM 1,700.00
Teapot, Gund Dogs, m-d/b, rstr flake, 5¼" 300.00
Teapot, Lafayette at Franklin's Tomb, d/b, Wood, EX 1,400.00
Tray, American Villa, d/b, prof rstr hdls, 9" 300.00
Tray, Castle Prison St Albans..., d/b, Hall, 10⅝", EX 175.00
Tray, Yale College, New Haven, l/b, Meigh, prof rstr, 9" 120.00
Undertray, Oxburgh Hall, d/b, acorn/oak leaf border, 10⅝" 650.00
Undertray, Upper Ferry Bridge Over...Schuylkill, d/b, Stubbs, 8", NM .225.00
Undertray, Woodlands Near Philadelphia, d/b, eagle border, 10¾" ..1,500.00
Wash bowl, Lafayette at Franklin's Tomb, d/b, Wood, 4¼x10¾" ...850.00
Waste bowl, Boston Harbor, d/b, Rogers, flake, 3¼x6¼" 400.00

Stained Glass

There are many factors to consider in evaluating a window or panel of stained glass art. Besides the obvious factor of condition, intricacy, jeweling, beveling, and the amount of selenium (red, orange, and yellow) present should all be taken into account. Remember, repair work is itself an art and can be very expensive. Our advisor for this category is Carl Heck; he is listed in the Directory under Colorado.

Lamps

American, 14x26", puffy fruit/grape clusters/birds, w/crown 800.00
Bigelow Kennard, 16" acorn-band shade, rstr 1,400.00
Bigelow Kennard, 9½x22" brickwork w/pine-cone band shade ..2,700.00
Ceiling, 20" shouldered brickwork shade w/'curtain-panel' apron ..750.00
Ceiling, 27" floral-on-gridwork umbrella-shaped dome shade .1,000.00
Duffner-Kimberly, 17" Colonial #501 shade: ribbed std 4,000.00
Duffner-Kimberly, 20" shade w/bows in apron; fluted std, EX .2,000.00
Duffner-Kimberly, 9x20" geometric shade w/ornate metal trim ...1,800.00
Unknown, 17x24" shade w/peonies on gridwork 1,400.00
Wilkinson, 23" water lily shade; tree trunk base w/lock, 30" ...7,500.00
Wilkinson, 26" brickwork/floral shade; ornate std w/leaves, 64" ...7,500.00

Windows

Center medallion w/beveled oval clear glass, 48x26", EX 400.00
Foliate design surrounds center anchor, jewels, 112x39" 3,000.00
Jesus & Samaritan woman at well central medallion, 1900s, 84x48" .1,045.00
Jesus & Ye That Labor & Are Heavy Laden..., ca 1900, 84x48" .990.00
Prairie School, stylized flowers, arched top, 45x13", VG 1,100.00
Tree of Life scene, ornate design, several layers, 56x37" 4,000.00

Stanford

The Stanford Pottery Co. was founded in 1945 in Sebring, Ohio. One of the founders was George Stanford, a former manager at Spaulding China (Royal Copley). They continued in operation until the factory was destroyed by a fire about 1961. They produced a Corn line, similar to that of the Shawnee Company, that is today very collectible. Most examples are marked (either Stanford Sebring Ohio or with a paper label), so there should be no difficulty in distinguishing one line from the other.

In addition to their Corn line, they produced planters and figurines, many of which were black trimmed with gold, made to be sold as pairs or sets. Wall pockets and vases were made as well. In 1949 they introduced a line called Tomato Ware, consisting of a cookie jar, grease jar, salt and pepper shakers, creamer and sugar bowl, mustard jar, marmalade jar, etc. These were shaped as bright red tomatoes with green leaves and stems (often used as lid finials), and were marketed under the name 'The Pantry Parade.' Our advisor for this category is Joe Devine; he is listed in the Directory under Iowa.

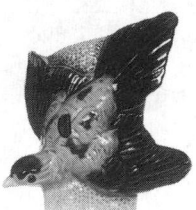

Wall pocket, bird, blue and cobalt with gold trim, 7", from $40.00 to $45.00.

Photo courtesy Glenn Hovinga

Ashtray, free-form, orange w/wht 'stucco,' #270-D, mk, 10x7" 12.00
Corn Line, butter dish 50.00
Corn Line, casserole 8" L 40.00
Corn Line, creamer & sugar bowl 50.00
Corn Line, pitcher, 7½" 60.00
Corn Line, plate, 9" L 32.00
Corn Line, relish tray 40.00
Corn Line, shakers, sm, pr 28.00
Corn Line, shakers, 4", pr 28.00
Corn Line, spoon rest 25.00
Corn Line, teapot 70.00
Planter, Dutch boy or girl by tulip, blk w/gold trim, ea 20.00
Planter, marching drummer, boy or girl, 7", ea 22.00
Planter, teddy bear, wht w/pk & bl trim, paper label, 7" 35.00
Tomato Ware, casserole, w/lid, 6x9" 55.00
Tomato Ware, cookie jar, 8" 70.00
Tomato Ware, creamer 28.00
Tomato Ware, grease jar, w/lid 34.00
Tomato Ware, marmalade jar 28.00
Tomato Ware, mustard jar 28.00
Tomato Ware, pitcher, 6½" 60.00
Tomato Ware, sugar bowl 28.00
Wall pocket, bird, bl & cobalt w/gold trim, 7", from $40 to 45.00
Wall pocket, cherry branch, red pie-crust edge, #299, mk, 6¼" 28.00

Stangl

Stangl Pottery was one of the longest-existing potteries in the United States, having as its beginning in 1814 the Sam Hill Pottery, becoming the Fulper Pottery which gained eminence in the field of art pottery (ca 1860), and then coming under the aegis of Johann Martin Stangl. The German-born Stangl joined Fulper in 1910 as chemical engineer, left for a brief stint at Haeger in Dundee, Illinois, and rejoined Fulper as general manager in 1920. He became president of the firm in 1928. Although Stangl's name was on much of the ware from the late '20s onward, the company's name was not changed officially until 1955. J.M. Stangl died in 1972; the pottery continued under the ownership of Wheaton Industries until 1978, then closed. Stangl is best known for its extensive Birds of America line, styled after Audubon; its brightly colored, hand-carved, hand-painted dinnerware; and its great variety of giftware, including its dry-brushed gold lines. For more information we recommend *Stangl Pottery* by Harvey Duke; for ordering information refer to the listing for Nancy and Robert Perzel, Popkorn Antiques (our advisors for this category), in our Directory under New Jersey.

Birds

#3250E, Drinking Duck	125.00
#3274, Penguin	500.00
#3275, Turkey	475.00
#3276, Bluebird, 5"	90.00
#3276D, Bluebirds, 8"	180.00
#3285, Rooster, wht & blk w/red & yel, early version, 4½"	100.00
#3286, Hen, late version	50.00
#3400, Lovebird, old version, 4½"	100.00
#3400, Lovebird, revised version	60.00
#3401, Wren, brn, revised version, 5"	60.00
#3401, Wren, tan, old version	250.00
#3401D, Wrens, brn, revised	135.00
#3401D, Wrens, early version, 6½"	350.00
#3402D, Orioles, old version, 6½"	300.00
#3402D, Orioles, revised version	125.00
#3404, Lovebirds Kissing	400.00
#3404D, Lovebirds, revised version, 6"	150.00
#3405, Cockatoo, sm, 6½"	60.00
#3405D, Cockatoos, old version, 10"	190.00
#3405D, Cockatoos, revised version, 9½"	150.00
#3406, Kingfisher, bl or teal	75.00
#3406D, Kingfishers, bl or teal, 5"	135.00
#3407, Owl	350.00
#3408, Bird of Paradise, 5"	125.00
#3443, Flying Duck, bl, 9"	275.00
#3443, Flying Duck, teal gr, 9"	300.00
#3444, Cardinal, dk red matt, 7"	135.00
#3444, Cardinal, pk, revised, 7"	100.00
#3444, Cardinal (female), pk, orig version, 6½"	165.00
#3445, Rooster, gray, 10"	250.00
#3445, Rooster, lt yel	200.00
#3446, Hen, gray	200.00
#3446, Hen, yel & brn, 7"	175.00
#3447, Prothonatary Warbler, yel & gr, 5"	80.00
#3448, Blue-headed Vireo, 4"	85.00
#3449, Paraquet, dk gr w/mc, 5½"	200.00
#3450, Passenger Pigeon	1,200.00
#3452, Painted Bunting, 5"	125.00
#3454, Key West Quail Dove, both wings up	750.00
#3454, Key West Quail Dove, single wing up, 10"	350.00
#3455, Shoveler Duck, rare, 12¼x14"	2,500.00
#3456, Cerulean Warbler, 4"	65.00
#3458, Quail, 7½"	1,300.00
#3490D, Redstarts, 9½"	225.00
#3491, Pheasant Hen	225.00
#3492, Cock Pheasant	225.00
#3518D, White-Crowned Pigeons, pr	750.00
#3580, Cockatoo, med, 9"	165.00
#3581, Chickadees, blk & wht	275.00
#3581, Chickadees, brn & wht	225.00
#3582D, Parakeets, bl	275.00
#3583, Parula Warbler, 4½"	60.00
#3584, Cockatoo, 11⅜"	300.00
#3585, Rufus Hummingbird, mc, 3½"	75.00
#3589, Indigo Bunting, 3½"	85.00
#3590, Carolina Wren	165.00
#3591, Brewer's Blackbird, 4"	150.00
#3592, Titmouse, 3"	65.00
#3593, Nuthatch, 3"	65.00
#3594, Red-Faced, Warbler, 3"	85.00
#3596, Gray Cardinal, 5"	90.00
#3597, Wilson Warbler, yel & blk, 3"	60.00
#3598, Kentucky Warbler, 3½"	60.00
#3599D, Hummingbirds	325.00
#3626, Broadtail Hummingbird, bl flowers, 6½"	150.00
#3627, Rivoli Hummingbird, w/pk flower	150.00
#3628, Reiffer's Hummingbird, 4½x6½"	125.00
#3629, Broadbill Hummingbird	125.00
#3634, Allen Hummingbird, 4"	85.00
#3635, Gold Finches, (group)	220.00
#3715, Blue Jay w/peanut, 10"	675.00
#3716, Blue Jay w/leaf	675.00
#3750, Western Tanager, 8½"	300.00
#3752D, Red-headed Woodpeckers, pk gloss, 8½"	325.00
#3752D, Red-Headed Woodpeckers, red matt, 8½"	350.00
#3754, White-Wing Crossbill, single	2,250.00
#3757, Scissor-Tailed Flycatcher, 11"	650.00
#3758, Magpie-Jay, 11x7"	1,200.00
#3810, Blackpoll Warbler	175.00
#3811, Chestnut-Backed Chickadee, 5"	165.00
#3812, Chestnut-Sided Warbler, 4½"	150.00
#3813, Evening Grosbeak, 5"	165.00
#3814, Black-Throated Green Warbler, 3"	165.00
#3815, Western Bluebird	400.00
#3848, Golden-Crowned Kinglet, 4½"	110.00
#3852, Cliff Swallow, 3½"	150.00
#3853, Golden-Crowned Kinglets, 5½x5"	600.00
#3922, European Finch	1,000.00
#3924, Yellow-Throated Warbler, 6"	425.00
#3925, Magnolia Warbler	2,000.00

Dinnerware

Orchard Song, pitcher, two-quart, 6½", $28.00.

Amber Glo, plate, 12½"	20.00
Amber Glo, shakers, pr	12.00
Antique Gold, pitcher, #4056, 8⅜"	25.00
Antique Gold, server, center hdl, 10"	13.00
Apple Delight, bowl, coupe soup; 7½"	20.00
Apple Delight, bowl, fruit; 5½"	12.00
Apple Delight, bowl, lug soup	12.00
Apple Delight, bowl, 9"	28.00
Apple Delight, creamer	10.00
Apple Delight, cup & saucer	12.00
Apple Delight, mug	24.00
Apple Delight, plate, bread & butter	5.00
Apple Delight, plate, 10"	20.00
Apple Delight, plate, 8"	10.00
Apple Delight, tea tile	15.00
Banquet, plate, 12"	150.00
Bittersweet, cup & saucer	11.00
Bittersweet, plate, 10"	13.00
Blueberry, bowl, lug soup	18.00
Blueberry, butter dish	45.00

Blueberry, clock, w/attached numerals 35.00
Blueberry, gravy liner 20.00
Blueberry, plate, 10" 22.00
Blueberry, platter, kidney shape 45.00
Blueberry, shakers, pr 24.00
Blueberry, teapot 125.00
Blueberry, tray, relish; long 35.00
Carnival, condiment tray, #415 ....20.00
Carnival, plate, 8" 10.00
Concord, cup 11.00
Concord, plate, 10" 18.00
Country Garden, bowl, cereal 20.00
Country Garden, bowl, salad; 10" 55.00
Country Garden, bowl, 8" 35.00
Country Garden, bread tray 50.00
Country Garden, chop plate, 12" 55.00
Country Garden, coaster 10.00
Country Garden, mug 45.00
Country Garden, pitcher, 1-qt 45.00
Country Garden, plate, 10" 22.00
Country Garden, teapot 85.00
Country Life, bowl, fruit; w/pony 75.00
Country Life, bowl, vegetable; mallard 130.00
Country Life, chop plate, farmhouse 250.00
Country Life, cup & saucer 65.00
Country Life, plate, farmer's wife, 10" 180.00
Country Life, shakers, pr 60.00
Cranberry, bowl, flat soup 22.00
Cranberry, plate, 10" 18.00
Festival, bowl, cereal 12.00
Festival, casserole, w/serving lid 60.00
Festival, plate, 6" 7.50
Flora, teapot, ind, 5¾" 75.10
Fruit, bowl, oval vegetable; 2-part 45.00
Fruit, chop plate, 12½" 50.00
Fruit, cruet, w/stopper 45.00
Fruit, egg cup 15.00
Fruit, pitcher, ½-pt 30.00
Fruit, server, center hdl 12.00
Fruit & Flowers, bowl, vegetable; 8" 40.00
Fruit & Flowers, cup & saucer 18.00
Fruit & Flowers, plate, 8" 18.00
Fruit & Flowers, shakers, pr 24.00
Garden Flower, coaster 16.00
Garden Flower, egg cup 15.00
Garden Flower, plate, 9½" 14.00
Golden Blossom, cup & saucer 10.00
Golden Blossom, pitcher, 2-qt 35.00
Golden Blossom, platter, 12" dia 20.00
Golden Harvest, bowl, divided vegetable 30.00
Golden Harvest, bowl, salad 30.00
Golden Harvest, cup & saucer 10.00
Golden Harvest, plate, 10" 13.00
Golden Harvest, plate, 6" 5.00
Golden Harvest, server, center hdl 8.00
Holly, bowl, salad; 10" 90.00
Jewelled Tree, cup & saucer, either style 40.00
Jewelled Tree, plate, dinner; 10" 50.00
Jewelled Tree, plate, 6" 22.00
Kiddieware, cup, Ginger Cat 180.00
Kiddieware, cup, Indian Campfire 100.00
Kiddieware, cup, Ranger 100.00
Kiddieware, dish, ABCs, divided, whiteware 80.00
Kiddieware, dish, Ducky Dinner, 3-part, w/cup 200.00

Kiddieware, dish, Kitten Kapers, 3-part 100.00
Kiddieware, dish, Our Barnyard Friends, 3-part 100.00
Kiddieware, plate, Peter Rabbit, Terra Rose 195.00
Magnolia, bowl, 8" 30.00
Magnolia, chop plate, 14¼" 40.00
Magnolia, creamer & sugar bowl, w/lid 22.00
Magnolia, plate, 10" 16.00
Magnolia, shakers, pr 20.00
Orchard Song, bowl, 12" 45.00
Orchard Song, bread tray 35.00
Orchard Song, plate, 12" 25.00
Orchard Song, plate, 6" 4.50
Orchard Song, server, center hdl 8.00
Provincial, bowl, lug soup; 5½" 12.00
Provincial, cup & saucer 12.50
Provincial, sugar bowl, w/lid 12.50
Rooster, creamer 15.00
Rooster, plate, 10" 30.00
Sculptured Fruit, cup & saucer 15.00
Sculptured Fruit, plate, 10" 14.00
Thistle, bowl, lug soup 15.00
Thistle, bowl, salad; 12" 90.00
Thistle, casserole, knob lid, ind 15.00
Thistle, coaster 20.00
Thistle, coffeepot, 8-cup 75.00
Thistle, plate, 10⅛" 18.00
Thistle, relish 25.00
Thistle, sugar bowl, w/lid 12.00
Town & Country, butter dish, bl, w/lid, ¼-lb 50.00
Town & Country, cheese & crackers, bl, dustpan shape 100.00
Town & Country, coffeepot, bl 100.00
Town & Country, pitcher, 2½-pt 65.00
Town & Country, plate, 10" 25.00
Town & Country, soap dish 45.00
Water Lily, coaster 25.00
Wild Rose, bowl, fruit; 5½" 15.00
Wild Rose, bread tray 45.00
Wild Rose, creamer 15.00
Wild Rose, cup & saucer 15.00
Wild Rose, plate, 10" 18.00
Wild Rose, plate, 8" 15.00
Yellow Tulip, bowl, divided, 10" 35.00
Yellow Tulip, bowl, 10" 45.00
Yellow Tulip, bowl, 11" 55.00
Yellow Tulip, bowl, 8" 35.00
Yellow Tulip, casserole, hdls, w/lid, 8" 65.00
Yellow Tulip, coaster 20.00
Yellow Tulip, cup & saucer 15.00
Yellow Tulip, platter, 14" 55.00

Miscellaneous

Ashtray, bird, Persian Yellow, hdld, #1323 ....150.00
Ashtray, deer, oval 65.00
Ashtray, duck, flying, oval, #3926b 25.00
Ashtray, mallard, sq, #3915 ....55.00
Ashtray, pheasant, oval, #3926 ....25.00
Ashtray, porpoise, sq 95.00
Ashtray, sailfish, boomerang 75.00
Ashtray, sailfish, rnd 75.00
Ashtray, Scottie, Antique Gold 65.00
Ashtray, woodcock, oval, #3926 ....75.00
Birdhouse, gray roof, terra cotta base 45.00
Plates, Sportsman series, inner raised rim, 10", set of 4 ....325.00

Vase, Sunflower, brn, Terra Rose, #3502, 11" 100.00
Wig stand, blond, w/ceramic base 250.00

Stanley Tools

The Stanley company was founded in Connecticut in 1854, and over the years has absorbed more than a score of tool companies already in existence. By the second decade of the 20th century, having long since solidified their position as *the* source for tools of the highest grade, the company enjoyed worldwide prestige. Through both World Wars, they were recognized as one of the nation's premier producers of wartime goods. Industrial arts classes introduced baby boomers to Stanley tools and provided yet another impetus to expansion and recognition. Overall, the company's growth and development has kept an easy pace along with the economy of the nation, and it continues today as a leader in the field of tool production.

Three factors to consider when evaluating a tool are these: age, completeness, and condition. One of their earliest trademarks (1854 – 1857) is 'A. Stanley,' found only on rulers. In the early '20s, their now-familiar 'sweetheart' trademark, the letters SW and a heart shape within the confines of a modified rectangle, was adopted. They continued to use this trademark until it was discontinued in 1933. Many other variations were used as well, some of which contain a patent date. A study of these marks will help you determine the vintage of your tools. Condition is extremely important, and though a light cleaning is acceptable, you should never attempt to 'restore' a tool by sanding, repainting, or replacing parts that may be damaged or missing. Tools listed below are for those in average 'as found' condition, ranging from very good to excellent. Note: Any common number $20.00 rule with the A. Stanley trademark is easily worth $500.00 plus!

For more information, we recommend *Antique and Collectible Stanley Tools*, written by our advisor, John Walter, who is listed in the Directory under Ohio.

Clapboard sliding marker, #88, mk on blade, ca 1909, EX 65.00
Gauge, butt; Type 1, ca 1897, 98% nickel finish, 1¾", EX 125.00
Gauge, jointer; #386, 99% nickel finish, 1920s, mk, EX+ 175.00
Gauge, mortise; #73, boxwood & brass, mk, 1920s, EX 150.00
Level, #37, 97% nickel finish, 1930s, 12", EX 75.00
Level, hexagon; #31, 1930s, 3" L, M 50.00
Level sights, #2, 1920s, M (G box) 100.00
Mitre box, #116, 1940s, EX (NM box) 75.00
Nosing tool, #5, S-casting w/cutter, 92% finish, 1895, VG+ 150.00
Plane, Bedrock smooth; #602, Type 7, 99% japanning, 1923, EX .750.00
Plane, beltmaker's; #11, B casting, 1892 cutter, ca 1900, VG 125.00
Plane, block; #60½, 99% japanning, 1940s, NM (EX box) 125.00
Plane, dado; #39¾, Pat cast in hdl, ca 1908, EX 225.00
Plane, jack; #26, Type 12, 98% japanning, ca 1912, EX+ 200.00
Plane, jack; Type 19, 99% japanning, NM (G box) 450.00
Plane, low angle block; #65, 1930s, M 100.00
Plane, plow; #46, Type 10, box of cutters, ca 1905, NM+ 450.00
Plane, rabbit; #92, 99% nickel finish, 1940s, NM (G box) 250.00
Plane, scrub; #40½, mk B casting, 97% japanning, 1900s, EX 150.00
Plane, smooth; #1, Type 6, 99% japanning, ca 1922, EX 1,200.00
Plane, smooth; #2, Type 15, ca 1931, 99% japanning, EX 350.00
Plane, smooth; #3C, Type 19, late 1940s, NM (EX+ box) 140.00
Plumb bob, #1, mk SR & L Co on spool, ca 1900, M 245.00
Ratcheting screwdriver, #215, 2" blade, mk on chuck, 1920s, VG ..90.00
Router, #271, w/instruction book, 1940s, M (EX box) 65.00
Router, #71, Type 3, 1 cutter, 98% finish, ca 1888, EX 85.00
Rule, caliper; #14, 2-fold, 6", fully bound, 1909, scarce, EX 700.00
Rule, carpenter's; #69, 4-fold, 12", 1910s, scarce Stanley mk, NM .175.00
Rule, combination; #036, 1-fold, 12", 1930s, EX 750.00

Scraper, #81, leftover SW blade, 99% japanning, ca WWII, NM .100.00
Spoke shave, rabbet; #68, 95% japanning, ca 1909, mk, EX 115.00
Spoke shave, reversible; #62, 97% japanning, ca 1909, EX 250.00
Square, try; #12, 2" blade, ca 1910, NM 250.00
Square, try; #12, 98% nickel finish, 12" blade, mk, 1920s, EX 125.00
Tool chest, #801, brass emblem on lid, 1920s, EX 275.00
Trammel points, #3, w/pencil-holder, ca 1930s, EX 175.00

Statue of Liberty

Long before she began greeting immigrants in 1886, the Statue of Liberty was being honored by craftsmen both here and abroad. Her likeness was etched on blades of the finest straight razors from England, captured in finely detailed busts sold as souvenirs to Paris fairgoers in 1878, and presented on colorfully lithographed trade cards, usually satirical, to American shoppers. Perhaps no other object has been represented in more forms or with such frequency as the universal symbol of America. Liberty's keepsakes are also universally accessible. Delightful souvenir models created in 1885 to raise funds for Liberty's pedestal are frequently found at flea markets, while earlier French bronze and terra cotta Liberties have been auctioned for over $100,000.00. Some collectors hunt for the countless forms of 19th-century Liberty memorabilia, while many collections were begun in anticipation of the 1986 Centennial with concentration on modern depictions. Our advisor for this category is Mike Brooks; he is listed in the Directory under California.

Smoking stand with electric lighter, ashtrays, and cigarette receptacle, light in torch, 1930s, 27x10½" diameter at base, $250.00.

Photo courtesy James Flanagan

Book, Inauguration of Statue of..., D Appleton & Co, NY, 1887 ..100.00
Booklet, Bartholdi Liberty, sm lithos/photos, accordian style 87.00
Booklet, Rays From Liberty's Torch, 1890 ....30.00
Bookmark, fabric, Bartholdi Souvenir, 1886 ....25.00
Bottle, milk glass, pewter lid, 10" 235.00
Bottle, seltzer; etched Liberty, A Doeink, Liberty, NY 35.00
Box, Liberty Hair Clipper, 1930s 25.00
Candy container, glass miniature w/metal statue top, 1920s 130.00
Card, admission to inauguration, 1886 ....70.00
Card, eng, Visit to Gauthier et Cie, Paris Foundry, 1883, VG 75.00
Charm bracelet, NY World's Fair 40.00
Cigar box label, Victory Day, WWI 6.00
Clock, figural, United, animated, very rare 350.00
Container, Yourex Silver Saver, rnd, cb, ca 1930 ....27.00
Cup, pewter, Germany, ca 1904 ....60.00
Cup, pewter, NY views, ca 19065, G- 15.00
Cup, sterling, Windsor Club, 1907, 2" 22.00
Doorknob, brass, Liberty in high relief, ca 1900 ....90.00
Envelope, NY World newspaper, postmk 1885, Liberty logo 55.00
Flyer, Statue of Liberty steamboat excursions, 1890s 25.00
Hanukkah menorah, Liberty-featured candle holders, M Anson ..1,800.00

Harper's Weekly, various litho prints, 1880s, ea, from $10 to **25.00**
Invitation to inauguration, by President Cleveland **150.00**
Letter, teen to military father re: parade on Broadway, 1886 ....**95.00**
Letter opener, Tat Hosiery Mills, 1930s **35.00**
Magic lantern side, harbor scene **30.00**
Medal, Central Valley Nat'l Bank **18.00**
Medal, Democratic National Convention, NY, 1924 ....**30.00**
Medal, Tasset, Paris, 1876 (earliest known) **100.00**
Napkin holder, sterling **15.00**
Paperweight, Port of NY, annual banquet, 1919 ....**45.00**
Paperweight, rnd, ca 1880s **100.00**
Photo, Liberty sketch, Centennial Photographic Co, 1876, VG ...**40.00**
Photo album, celluloid image on front, velvet bk, 10x8" **275.00**
Pin, enamel, 77th Div, WWI **12.00**
Pin-bk, No Beer, No Work, prohibition **15.00**
Pin-bk, 4th Liberty Loan Bond Salesman #d ID, oval, pot metal, 1917 ...**22.00**
Pipe, glazed clay, 1880s **90.00**
Plaque, bronze, Deco-style depiction, Yan Torno, 17" dia **125.00**
Plate, Austrian, various NY scenes, ca 1900 ....**45.00**
Plate, glass, eng statue, heart shape **22.00**
Plate, World Wide Art Studio, 1985, 8½" **10.00**
Plates, various makers, 1980s, ea, from $10 to **20.00**
Playing cards, Allied Nations, WWI, complete deck **20.00**
Pocket watch, Elgin, Liberty etched front/bk, gold, pre-1900s **180.00**
Postcards, hold-to-light, various, from $40 to **75.00**
Radio speaker stand, wht metal casting, Palcone, 17" **175.00**
Snow dome, glass w/wood base, fancy, contemporary **40.00**
Spoon, figural stem, sterling, Shiebler **75.00**
Statue, cast metal on marble base, June 13, 1885 ....**1,000.00**
Stereo card, head of Liberty, Paris, 1878 ....**80.00**
Straight razor, Liberty-etched blade, Sheffield, ca 1880 ....**75.00**
Tapestry, w/NY Harbor scene, 24x48" **85.00**
Ticket, lg souvenir of Gauthier et Cie (Liberty foundry), 1883 ..**105.00**
Tin, Liberty Brand Crystalized Ginger, 1920s, 3¾x2½" **33.00**
Tin, William's American Chewing Nuts, oval, British, 1930s, lg .**65.00**
Trade card, Columbia & Statue, July 4, 1885 ....**94.00**
Trade card, Frank Coe's Factory, 1887, G- **16.00**
Trade card, satirical, A&C Hams **70.00**
Trade card, satirical, Moline Plow **30.00**
Vase, frosted Liberty hand, Gillinder, 1876 Centennial **70.00**
Watercolor, View of Liberty, JW Goppard, 21x15" **220.00**

Steamship Collectibles

For centuries, ocean-going vessels with their venturesome officers and crews were the catalyst that changed the unknown aspects of our world to the known. Changing economic conditions, unfortunately, have now placed the North American shipping industry in the same jeopardy as the American passenger train. They are becoming a memory. The surge of interest in railroad collectibles and the railroad-related steamship lines has lead collectors to examine the whole spectrum of steamship collectibles. Our advisors for this category are Lila and Fred Shrader; they are listed in the Directory under California.

Key:
BM — back or bottom mark   SM — side mark
BS — back stamped   TL — top logo
NBS — no back stamp   TM — top mark
SL — side logo

Dinnerware

Ashtray, Cunard, yel, gray & blk stripe, BS, 5½" dia **49.00**

Ashtray, Pacific Far East, Philippine Bear TL, 5½" dia **68.00**
Bowl, berry; White Star, Brownfield-White Star, brn/turq, TM, 6" ..**555.00**
Bowl, cereal; Texaco, TL, 6" **110.00**
Bowl, flat soup; Pacific Far East Line, Philippine Bear, TL, 8½" ...**85.00**
Butter pat, United Fruit Line, Columbia, dk bl on wht, TM **85.00**
Butter pat, White Star Line (US), Port Huron, dk gr on wht, TL ..**75.00**
Creamer, D&C Nav Co, SL, dk bl on wht, w/hdl, ind, 2¾" **95.00**
Creamer, Luckenbach Line, house flag TL w/striping, 4½" **65.00**
Cup & saucer, Am President Lines, brn APL SL on cup, TL saucer ..**95.00**
Cup & saucer, Internat'l Mercantile..., cobalt & rust border, SL & TM .**135.00**
Cup & saucer, Prudential Lines, Santa Magdalena, turq border, TL ...**39.00**
Egg cup, Am President Lines, Eagle SL w/cobalt & red stripes, lg .**75.00**
Mug, coffee; Pickands-Mather, SL **95.00**
Plate, Algoma Central, Marine Division, house flag TL, 9½" **55.00**
Plate, Delta Queen Steamboat Co, ship's picture, brn border, 10" ..**22.00**
Plate, Dollar SS Line, house flag TL w/brn & blk stripes, 9½" ...**135.00**
Plate, Inland Steel Co, dmn-shape TL, 6½" **25.00**
Platter, Alaska SS, The Alaska Line, TL, 8x6" **78.00**
Platter, NYK Line, Mt Fuji scene, BM w/house flag, 7½x5" **45.00**
Shakers, QEII, wht w/gold band, BM, 4", pr **62.00**
Sugar bowl, Luchenbach Line, house flag TL w/striping, w/lid, 5" ..**168.00**
Teapot, North German Lloyd, anchor & key SL, ind **95.00**

Glassware

Ashtray, French Line, SS France, gold France on cobalt, 4" dia ...**22.00**
Ashtray, Matson, SS Lurline, silkscreen TL on dk glass **12.00**
Cocktail, stem; Matson, SL in wht silkscreen **18.00**
Cordial, United Fruit Lines, UFL cut SL **67.00**
Decanter, Norddeutscher Lloyd, cut anchor & key SL, w/stopper ..**335.00**
Goblet, stem; Mobil Oil Corp, red flying horse silkscreen SL **45.00**
Tumbler, Matson, SS Lurline, silkscreen SL, 5" **12.00**
Wine, stem; Savannah Line cut in script **85.00**

Linens

Bath towel, Dominion Line in wht script at ea end **72.00**
Blanket, CPSS, gray wool w/intertwined CPR over Steamshipm 48x80" ..**185.00**
Blanket, USLHS on gray & bl alternating stripes, wool, 54x80" ...**225.00**
Hand towel, Luckenbach Line woven in red on wht stripe, huck-type ..**20.00**
Hand towel, Maersk Line, red circle w/7-point star woven at ends ...**22.00**
Lap robe, Norddeutscher Lloyd, gr & bl wool w/logo, 48x36" **245.00**
Napkin, Norddeutscher Lloyd, wht on wht woven logo, 24" sq **35.00**
Pillow case, USCG bl stamp on border **7.00**
Tablecloth, Swedish-Am Line, 3-crown logo ea corner, 42x48" ...**32.00**

Silverplate

Creamer, Alaska SS SL & BM, Reed & Barton, 9-oz **125.00**
Creamer, US Lines, stars SL, BM, reeded hdl, 4-oz **67.00**
Cup holder, Am Export Line, BM, 3¼" **26.00**
Fork, salad; Texaco in boxed hexagon, BS **21.00**
Iced teaspoon, P&O SS Co, TM w/house flag encircled, Internat'l ..**22.00**
Knife, dinner; States Line, TL: S, Internat'l **12.00**
Sardine dish w/glass liner & lid, ball ft, QEII, SM/TM, 5½x4¼" ..**138.00**
Spoon, demitasse; Cunard, Romney, BM, Reed & Barton **29.00**
Spoon, serving; Cunard, BM, Meat written in English & Hebrew ..**29.00**
Sugar tongs, Red Star Line, King, Elkington, SM **72.00**
Wine bucket, NYK Line SL, BM: Nippon Yusen Kaisha, 8" **95.00**

Miscellaneous

Baggage tag, Rotterdam Lloyd, house flag logo, cb w/string **10.00**
Bell, SS Himalaya, Mediterranean Cruise, metal, 1952, 6" **120.00**

Brochure, Alaska SS, Steamers to All Alaska Points, 1908, 30-pg ..79.00
Brochure, Souvenir of Visit to White Star Liner, diecut, 1923 ...148.00
Button, uniform; White Star, brass rope design w/house flag, lg ...45.00
Calendar, Dollar SS Line, celluloid, wallet sz 38.00
Deck chair, wood w/footrest & cushion 765.00
Flare cylinder, watertight, w/hdld lid, 11" 89.00
Letter opener, Texaco, metal w/house flag emb on hdl 135.00
Map, Moore-McCormack Lines, voyage to S Am, fr souvenir, 25x18" ..45.00
Memorium card, Titanic, blk & silver borders, dedication, $195 to .485.00
Menu card, lunch; Calgaric, house flag on reverse, 8/27/33 ....27.00
Needle case, D&C Nav Co, Bakelite w/thimble cap & tassel, 2¼" ...85.00
Paperweight, Campania, glass souvenir, 1890s 65.00
Pen knife, Queen Mary, ship's portrait ea side, 3½" 48.00
Pennant, P&O Lines, SS Arcadia, lg 135.00
Playing cards, Eastern SS Lines, single deck in orig slip case 59.00
Puzzle, jigsaw; A Night To Remember, 1958, w/box 315.00
Ship's wheel, wood w/brass hub, 60" dia 650.00
Spittoon, Eastern SS Co, E House flag in ring, Buffalo Pottery, 5" .385.00
Swizzle stick, Cunard, Lucite, oar shape 4.00
Swizzle stick, figural (fish, lighthouse, ship, mermaid, etc), $1 to .15.00
Swizzle stick, nonfigural, contemporary cruise line 50
Telescope, US Navy Bu Ships, Mk-1, Bausch & Lomb, '41 ....112.00
Umbrella, P&O, wht w/rising sun logo, Canberra Final Season, 1997 .36.00
Whistle, ship's steam; M Edmund, brass, EX 1,500.00

Steins

Steins have been made from pottery, pewter, glass, stoneware, and porcelain, from very small up to the four-liter size. They may be decorated by etching, in-mold relief, decals, and occasionally they may be hand painted. Some porcelain steins have lithophane bases. Collectors often specialize in a particular type — faience, regimental, or figural, for example — while others limit themselves to the products of only one manufacturer. See also Mettlach.

Key:
L — liter   tl — thumb lift
lith — lithophane

Glass stein, red stain with engraved shepherd scene, matching glass inlaid lid, .75-L, $895.00.

Anheuser Busch by Ceramarte, Bald Eagle, lidded, .5L 400.00
Anheuser Busch by Ceramarte, Bavarian House, .5L 300.00
Anheuser Busch by Ceramarte, Bud Man, hollow head, .5L 470.00
Anheuser Busch by Ceramarte, Delft bl, .5L 350.00
Anheuser Busch by Ceramarte, Heidelberg, .5L 425.00
Burl, 3 cvd ft, lion tl, floral cvd lid, ca 1800, 8¼" 1,300.00
Character, alligator seated, porc, Schierholz, set-on lid, 1L 600.00
Character, alligator, porc, Bohne & Sohne, .5L 1,100.00
Character, apple w/snake, porc, Bohne & Son, rpl lid, .3L 400.00
Character, burger meister, porc, Schierholz, .5L, NM 750.00

Character, cat w/hangover, porc, Schierholz, .5L 600.00
Character, cavalier, pottery, #1439, old prof rpr, .5L 400.00
Character, devil, porc, Bohne & Sohne, inlaid lid, .5L 635.00
Character, dog coming from bbl, porc, lith, .5L, NM 450.00
Character, elephant, porc, Schierholz, sm rpr, .5L 825.00
Character, Indian, porc, Bohne & Sohne, .25L, EX 415.00
Character, lady w/clown hat, pottery, Diesinger #701, .5L, NM .415.00
Character, man, wealthy, stoneware, Merkelbach & Wick, .5L, NM ..265.00
Character, man on bbl, stoneware, Hauber & Reuther #63, .5L, NM ..525.00
Character, monkey, drunken, porc, Schierholz, chip, .5L 300.00
Character, monkey scratching (lid) on bbl, porc, lith, .5L, NM .575.00
Character, Munich child, porc, inlaid lid, 5½" 225.00
Character, Munich child, pottery, inlaid lid, .3L, NM 465.00
Character, Munich child, pottery, Reinemann, inlaid lid, 4¼" ..135.00
Character, Munich child on bbl, porc, Schierholz, .5L 1,000.00
Character, Munich child on bbl, porc, Schierholz, porc lid, .3L .250.00
Character, Nurnberg Tower, porc, Schierholz, .5L 575.00
Character, Nurnberg Tower, stoneware, mk TW, pewter lid, 2L ..1,200.00
Character, Perkeo on bbl, verse, porc, Schierholz, rpr, .5L 650.00
Character, pig singing, porc, Schierholz, inlaid lid, .5L 575.00
Character, pig smoking, porc, bl/wht, Schierholz, .5L, NM 1,325.00
Character, pig smoking, porc, tan, Schierholz, .5L 440.00
Character, pottery, Nurnberg Tower, pottery lid, ⅛L 250.00
Character, Sad Radish, porc, Schierholz, rpr, .5L 300.00
Character, skull, lg jaw, porc, Bohne & Sohne, inlaid lid, .5L 925.00
Character, skull on book, porc, Bohne & Sohne, inlaid lid, .5L .675.00
Character, Turkish man, porc, Schierholz, porc lid, rpr, .5L 550.00
Character, Wilhelm I, porc, Schierholz, .5L, NM 1,100.00
Character, woman, pottery, Merkelbach & Wick, inlaid lid, .5L .275.00
Glass, blown, amber, glass prunts, HP floral, pewter lid, .5L 220.00
Glass, blown, bl, Thumbprint, pewter base & lid, .5L 285.00
Glass, blown, clear, cut, porc inlay lid, copper tl, .5L 175.00
Glass, blown, clear, eng circles, glass/pewter inlay lid, .5L 350.00
Glass, blown, clear, eng circles, inlaid lid, .5L 275.00
Glass, blown, clear, eng floral, pewter lid, .75L 215.00
Glass, blown, clear, ornate cuttings, porc inlay lid, .5L, NM 160.00
Glass, blown, clear, wht enamel o/l, inlaid lid, 1850s, .25L 350.00
Glass, blown, gr, appl prunts, HP cavalier, dwarf finial/tl, 2L 360.00
Glass, blown, gr, HP crest, HP/inlaid gr lid, 1850s, 2L, NM 400.00
Military, brass, relief: Bismark portrait/leaves, lion lid, 1L 700.00
Military, pottery, transfer/HP: Unteroffizier..., pewter lid, .5L 270.00
Military, stoneware, transfer/HP: Iron Cross, Hindenburg lid, 1L .465.00
Military, stoneware, transfer/HP: soldiers, Iron Cross lid, .5L 285.00
Military, stoneware, transfer: Nurnberg, skyline relief lid, 1l 220.00
Occupational, porc, baker, lg scene, eagle finial, lith, .5L 400.00
Occupational, porc, gardener, lg scene, lith, .5L 500.00
Occupational, porc, sheepherder, lg scene, rpr, .5L 415.00
Occupational, porc, transfer/HP: diary, 10 scenes, 1932, .5L 885.00
Occupational, pottery, transfer/HP: sculptor, pewter lid, .5L 880.00
Pewter, appl cherub ft, eagle center, knight finial, 2L, 19" 250.00
Porc, HP: leaf & hops, Wagner, inlaid lid, 1899, .5L 635.00
Porc, transfer/HP: 4 men on highwheelers, crests, pewter lid, 1L ..1,250.00
Porc, transfer/HP: 4F Turner design, pewter lid, lith, .5L 230.00
Pottery, etch/relief: people/dog at table, JRW #1349, 1L 250.00
Pottery, etch: comic scene, Girmscheid #923, .3L 315.00
Pottery, etch: drinking scene, Hauber & Reuther #431, 1L 440.00
Pottery, etch: dwarfs, dwarf tl, Merkelbach & Wick #1175C, .5L ..255.00
Pottery, etch: festive scene, Hauber & Reuther #402, .5L 175.00
Pottery, etch: horsemen, Marzi & Remy #1621, inlaid lid, .5L ...300.00
Pottery, etch: men drinking, Girmscheid #1084A, .5L 355.00
Pottery, etch: people at table, JRW #1334, .5L, NM 165.00
Pottery, etch: people talking, JRW #1333, inlaid lid, rpr, 1L 165.00
Pottery, relief: drunken monks, Dumer & Breiden #547, 1L 485.00
Pottery, relief: Falstaff & animal heads, pewter lid, .5L 400.00

Pottery, relief: Heidelberg, glove/lion head hdl, music box, .5L ..**400.00**
Pottery, relief: monkeys w/books, skull lid, monkey hdl, .5L **450.00**
Pottery, relief: soccer scene, #2463, pewter lid, .5L **265.00**
Pottery, relief: target shooting, pewter jester/targets lid, .5L **165.00**
Pottery, transfer/HP: man on bicycle, pewter lid, .3L **375.00**
Regimental, porc, Barone Eugenio..., lion tl, glass lid, lith, .5L ..**700.00**
Regimental, porc, 116 Infantry...1907-09, roster, griffin tl, .5L ...**525.00**
Regimental, porc, 121 Infantry...1908-10, Wurtenburg tl, .5L **485.00**
Regimental, porc, 17 Infantry...1899-01, lion tl, prism lid, .5L ...**575.00**
Regimental, porc, 2 Ulan...1910-13, photo/4 scenes, lion tl, .5L .**1,200.00**
Regimental, porc, 21 Dragoon...1902-05, griffin tl, rpr, .5L **465.00**
Regimental, porc, 3 Comp...Victoria 1901-04, eagle tl, .5L **1,600.00**
Regimental, porc, 3 Comp...1903-06, floral tl, .5L, NM **1,600.00**
Stoneware, etch/glaze: orange ped w/balls, Capeller, 1904, .5L ..**1,200.00**
Stoneware, relief: bicycle scenes, relief lid, .5L **335.00**
Stoneware, relief: Konigsbacher...Bockfest 1905, hunt scenes, .4L **275.00**
Stoneware, relief: Lohengrin scene, vine hdl, pewter lid, 1L **485.00**
Stoneware, relief: Munich child/edelweiss, dtd 1894, pewter lid, .5L ...**275.00**
Stoneware, relief: people & vines, pewter lid, 1L **215.00**
Stoneware, transfer/HP: ...Turnfest 1908 Frankfurt, relief lid, .5L ..**375.00**
Stoneware, transfer/HP: bicyclist, 1904, pewter lid, .5L, NM **600.00**
Stoneware, transfer/HP: Brauerei Zum...Kindl, pewter lid, .5L ...**500.00**
Stoneware, transfer/HP: Munich child, Ringer, pewter lid, .5L ..**280.00**
Stoneware, transfer/HP: 125 Yrs Oktoberfest, pewter lid, 1L **800.00**
Third Reich, pottery, transfer/HP: Regt...1926, helmet lid, .5L ..**575.00**
Third Reich, pottery, transfer/HP: Unteroffizier..., helmet lid, 1L .**1,550.00**
Third Reich, stoneware, relief: swastica/monuments, .5L **600.00**
Third Reich, stoneware, transfer: ...Kriegsweihnachten 1941, .5L ..**575.00**

Steuben

Carder Steuben glass was made by the Steuben Glass Works in Corning, New York, while under the direction of Frederick Carder from 1903 to 1932. Perhaps the most popular types of Carder Steuben glass are Gold Aurene which was introduced in 1904 and Blue Aurene, introduced in 1905. Gold and Blue Aurene objects shimmer with the lustrous beauty of their metallic iridescence. Carder also produced other types of 'Aurenes' including Red, Green, Yellow, Brown, and Decorated, all of which are very rare. Aurene also was cased with Calcite glass. Some pieces had paper labels.

Other types of Carder Steuben include Cluthra, Cintra, Florentia, Rosaline, Ivory, Ivrene, Jades, Verre de Soie; there are many more.

Frederick Carder's leadership of Steuben ended in 1932, and the production of colored glassware soon ceased. Since 1932 the tradition of fine Steuben art glass has been continued in crystal.

Our advisor for this category is Thomas P. Dimitroff; he is in the Directory under New York. In the following listings, examples are signed unless noted otherwise.

Key: ACB — acid cut back

Basket, Blue Aurene, slim w/flared scalloped rim, 12x9" **3,000.00**
Basket, Gold Aurene w/purple/bl irid, #453, 6¾x6" **1,750.00**
Bottle, scent; Blue Aurene, #3425, blk stopper, petal finial, 7" ..**1,800.00**
Bottle, scent; Blue Aurene, dbl gourd, #6233, 4¼" **1,600.00**
Bottle, scent; Blue Aurene, deep melon ribs, 3 scroll ft, 5" **2,400.00**
Bottle, scent; Blue Aurene, peach/Alabaster flower stopper, 7" ...**1,800.00**
Bottle, scent; Gold Aurene, #1455, 8-lobe, 5" **800.00**
Bottle, scent; Gold Aurene, bell form, floral-emb stopper, 4" ..**1,100.00**
Bottle, scent; Gold Aurene, teardrop stopper, ftd, 7¾" **800.00**
Bottle, scent; Gold Aurene w/red irid, bell form, #1818, 5½" .**1,100.00**
Bottle, scent; opal w/Cintra accents & pk spirals, 12½" **2,650.00**
Bottle, scent; Verre-de-Soie w/gr threading, like #500A, 3½" **350.00**

Bowl, ACB Green Jade over Alabaster, Matsu-no-ke, global, 7" ..**1,050.00**
Bowl, ACB Plum Jade, Canton pattern, #2687, 4x8" **2,000.00**
Bowl, Blue Aurene, shouldered, 2½x5" **325.00**
Bowl, Calcite w/Blue Aurene int, stretched flange #3579, 15" ...**600.00**
Bowl, Calcite w/Gold Aurene int, eng vines on flange, 2x14" **800.00**
Bowl, Celeste Blue, fold-down rim, #3303, 6x14" **175.00**
Bowl, console; Cerise Ruby swirl, clear rib ft, 14", +sticks **800.00**
Bowl, Cyprian, 3-ftd, 2½x10½" **350.00**
Bowl, Flemish Blue, ribbed body & ft, 4x14" **175.00**
Bowl, Gold Aurene, mushroom form w/4-pillar base, #3080, 5x10" .**1,050.00**
Bowl, Gold Aurene, rolled-in rim, 3 pod ft, #2586, 2½x12" **450.00**
Bowl, Green Jade, int swirls, 6x7¾" **375.00**
Bowl, Grotesque, fan shape, 7x13" **175.00**
Bowl, Grotesque, Ivory, ftd, fan shape w/ruffled rim, 8½x11" **350.00**
Bowl, Grotesque, Ruby, #7277, 6½" **375.00**
Bowl, Plum Jade, rolled-in rim, 4x8" **450.00**
Bowl, Topaz, swirled, 3¾x8" **150.00**
Candlestick, clear w/4 gr prunts & rim, #3374, 10" **175.00**
Candlesticks, Gold Aurene/Calcite, wide bobeche, 6", pr **975.00**
Candlesticks, Pomona Green, knob stem w/raspberry prunts, 3¾", pr ..**350.00**
Compote, Gold Aurene, ruffled, ½-twist stem, #367 ....**1,000.00**
Compote, Gold Aurene w/red irid, #2839, 3¾x14½" **950.00**
Compote, Gold Aurene/Calcite, #5065, 3½x10" **250.00**
Compote, Gold Aurene/Calcite, ACB lilies on rolled rim, 7x12" ..**1,750.00**
Compote, Topaz, pear finial, like #3348, 9½" **525.00**
Cruet, Gold Aurene, appl neck ring, teapot spout, #2720, 5" ..**4,250.00**
Cup & saucer, Gold Aurene, #2780, cup: 2¼" **450.00**
Darner, Blue Aurene, 6½" **425.00**
Darner, Gold Aurene, 6½" **300.00**
Darner, vines, Blue Aurene, 5¾" **1,000.00**
Dish, Blue Aurene, gold ring hdl, #3997, ½x4" **750.00**
Figurine, angelfish, 10½x10" **750.00**
Figurine, dolphin leaping, pillar base, script mk, 9" **475.00**
Figurine, frog, appl eyes/ft, by Atkins, 4¾" L **400.00**
Figurine, owl, facing right, w/frosted eyes, by Pollard, 5½" **230.00**
Figurine, pelican, 6x7½" **625.00**
Figurine, porpoise, poised to dive, by Atkins, 12" L **865.00**
Finger bowl, Rosaline, #2883, 2¼" H, +6" underplate **175.00**

Goblet, black over crystal, engraved scrolling foliate pattern, #7181, 9", $550.00.

Goblet, Cluthra, bl to wht, hexagonal ft, 6½" **550.00**
Goblet, Gold Aurene, ½-twist stem, #705, mk Haviland, 6" **500.00**
Goblet, Gold Aurene w/red irid, ½-twist stem, 4½", +plate **750.00**
Goblet, Oriental Poppy, Pomona Green stem/base, #6615, 8" **750.00**
Lamp, ACB floral on Yellow Jade, rectangle 5¾" base, 20" **1,400.00**
Lamp base, Red Aurene w/gold-bl feathers at shoulder, 9" **2,500.00**
Mug, Matsu-no-ke, crystal w/Cintra rim, hdl w/tooled leaves, 6" ..**325.00**
Nut bowl, Calcite w/Gold Aurene ext, ruffled, 1¼x3½" **200.00**
Nut bowl, Gold Aurene, ruffled, #138, 1¼x3½" **175.00**

Nut bowl, Gold Aurene, 3 fleur-de-lys ft, #255 ....500.00
Nut bowl, Red-Gold Aurene, flanged/ruffled, 4-leg, Haviland, sm ..175.00
Plate, Cintra, duck/grasses center, textured/'hobnail' rim, 6" 300.00
Plate, Wisteria, 8½" 150.00
Plates, Audubon bird studies, 10", set of 6 ....3,000.00
Salt cellar, Blue Aurene, #3067, 1½x2½" 500.00
Salt cellar, Rosaline & Alabaster, ped ft 250.00
Sherbet, Marina Blue, etched birds at urn fountain, 2¼" 350.00
Tazza, Green Jade, swirl bowl/base, Alabaster disks on stem, 7" .325.00
Tumbler, Gold Aurene, mk Haviland, 3¾" 300.00
Tumbler, iced tea; Pomona Green, reeding, Topaz hdl/ft, 6" 100.00
Tumbler, iced tea; Rosaline, 4¾" 75.00

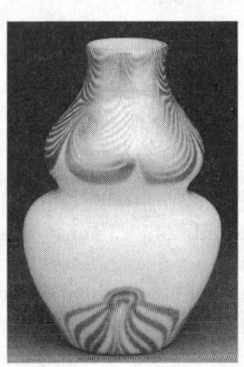

Vase, Alabaster double gourd with double-hooked Gold Aurene shoulder decoration, four green and gold pulled feathers below, #720, 5¾", $3,500.00.

Vase, ACB floral, Alabaster on Green Jade, #6078, 7" 1,450.00
Vase, ACB floral branches, Mayfair, Rosaline on Alabaster, 12" .1,900.00
Vase, ACB Green Jade on Alabaster texture, Alicia, ftd, 6" 500.00
Vase, ACB Rose Quartz w/flowers, #6078, spherical, 7" 2,650.00
Vase, amber transparent w/optic ribbing, #6287, 8" 310.00
Vase, Amberina, swirl, cylindrical, #6030, 6¾" 500.00
Vase, amethyst quartz, sculpted & acid etched, #6910, 7¼" 4,000.00
Vase, Aquamarine, ftd urn form, #938, 10½" 525.00
Vase, Blue Aurene, flared, ruffled, #723, 6" 475.00
Vase, Blue Aurene, ribbed, waisted body, flared rim, #7447, 6" .1,100.00
Vase, Blue Aurene, stick neck, #2556, 8" 325.00
Vase, Blue Aurene, thorny cylinder on disk base, #2741, 6" 575.00
Vase, Blue Aurene w/gold & opal vines, Carder, #2683, 8x8" .4,250.00
Vase, Blue Aurene w/mc irid, #2413, 6½x10" 1,500.00
Vase, Blue Aurene w/opal & caramel vine band, #6297 ....2,800.00
Vase, Bristol Yellow, ribbed fan form w/knob stem, 8½" 300.00
Vase, Bristol Yellow, swirled cylinder, #6030, 7" 250.00
Vase, Calcite w/Blue Aurene int, ruffled trumpet form, 10" 1,400.00
Vase, Celeste Blue, ftd trumpet form, 12" 225.00
Vase, Celeste Blue, swirled cylinder, #6030, 7" 225.00
Vase, Cluthra, amethyst, urn form w/M hdls, 10" 2,800.00
Vase, Cluthra, gr to wht, canteen form w/dbl hdl ea side, 10" .1,600.00
Vase, Cluthra, pink, classic form, #2683, 10" 1,850.00
Vase, Cluthra, pink, opal M hdls, 10" 1,550.00
Vase, Cluthra, wht w/Pomona Green, 2-prong shape, #6874, 10" .1,300.00
Vase, crystal, scroll hdls, 9½", +orig box & bag 575.00
Vase, Dmn Quilt, clear w/gr threading, 9¾" 250.00
Vase, floriform; Blue Aurene, #913, 5½" 650.00
Vase, Gold Aurene, classic form, #2683, 8" 900.00
Vase, Gold Aurene, distended ribbed neck, #245, 8" 900.00
Vase, Gold Aurene feathers on Alabaster above gr, #500, 8½" ..7,000.00
Vase, Gold Aurene w/bl irid, ftd U-form w/flared rim, #938, 11" ..750.00
Vase, Gold Aurene w/red irid, classic/ftd form, #3285, 12" 2,150.00
Vase, Gold Aurene w/red irid, flared rim, waisted body, 6" 575.00
Vase, Gold Aurene w/red irid, ribbed trumpet form, #913, 5¾" .525.00
Vase, Gold Aurene w/red irid, trumpet form, #2909, 12½" 950.00
Vase, Green Jade, 5 3-sided lilies on Alabaster base, #7063 ....900.00

Vase, Green Jade w/Alabaster 'M' hdls, #2939, 12" 1,250.00
Vase, Green Jade w/Alabaster 'M' shoulder hdls, #2939, 10" 950.00
Vase, Green Jade w/Alabaster ft, stick neck, #2556, 12½" 475.00
Vase, Green Jade w/Alabaster trim, tapered, 6" 200.00
Vase, Green Jade w/etched fir cones, spherical, #6078, 7" 1,000.00
Vase, Grotesque, ruby handkerchief-folded rim, #7090, 9" 400.00
Vase, Ivrene, classic form, #5133, 5" 500.00
Vase, Ivrene, classic form, #5133, 8" 650.00
Vase, Ivrene, ruffled, #7379, 7¾" 600.00
Vase, lily; Calcite w/Gold Aurene int, 8" 425.00
Vase, Moss Agate, allover bubbles, craquelle int, #6211, 6" 3,250.00
Vase, Pomona Green, ribbed fan form, 10½" 275.00
Vase, Pomona Green, Topaz knob stem/base, ribbed fan form, 8" ..325.00
Vase, Pomona Green, 3-prong stump, 5¾" 250.00
Vase, Red/Gold Aurene w/ivory & gr vines & leaves, #3426, 8" .3,450.00
Vase, Rosaline w/Alabaster dbl-knob stem, fan shape, 6" 500.00
Vase, Rosaline w/Alabaster stem & base, slim, 12" 600.00
Vase, Topaz, swirled, trumpet form, 6" 175.00
Vase, Topaz, swirled trumpet form w/3-lobe rim, #6441, 12" 250.00
Vase, Verre-de-Soie, #3045, 12" 375.00
Vase, Verre-de-Soie, wheel-cvd ferns/flowers, stick neck, 8" 200.00
Vase, Verre-de-Soie Dmn Quilt w/gr threaded rim, 4x8" 175.00

Stevengraphs

A Stevengraph is a small picture made of woven silk resembling an elaborate ribbon, created by Thomas Stevens in England in the latter half of the 1800s. They were matted and framed by Stevens, usually with his name appearing on the mat or often with the trade announcement on the back of the mat. He also produced silk postcards and bookmarks, all of which have 'Stevens' woven in silk on one of the mitered corners. Anyone wishing to learn more about Stevengraphs is encouraged to contact the Stevengraph Collectors' Association, whose address can be found in the Directory under Clubs, Newsletters, and Catalogs.

Are You Ready?, EX 300.00
Called to the Rescue, Heroism at Sea, EX 250.00
Coventry, 2 blk & wht scenes, fr, pr 110.00
Death of Nelson, G 195.00
Declaration of Independence, woven at Columbian Exhibition .225.00
First Innings, G 325.00
First Train Built by Geo Stephenson in 1825, 8⅞x11⅝" 150.00
God Speed the Plow, G 220.00
Good Old Days, coach & 4, matted & fr, 7½x10½", M 195.00
Good Old Days, orig mat, 6⅛x8¾" in fr, EX 220.00
Kenilworth Castle, orig matt & fr, 15½x22½" 175.00
Landing of Columbus, NM 250.00
Meet, orig mat, old fr, NM 250.00
Park in Coventry 75.00
Queen Victoria Jubilee, 1837-1887, unfr 55.00
Rescue at Sea, fr, VG 220.00
Victoria, Queen of Empire on Which the Sun Never Sets, unfr, EX ..195.00
Water Jump, fr, EX 225.00
Wellington & Blugher, EX 300.00

Miscellaneous

Bookmark, Behold the Man, blk fr, G 50.00
Bookmark, Dr Guthrie 50.00
Bookmark, Friend's Blessings 45.00
Bookmark, Garibaldi, United Italy 50.00
Bookmark, Home Sweet Home 75.00
Bookmark, Love's Remembrance, VG 75.00

Bookmark, Lt Gen US Grant, Richmond, 1865 ....75.00
Bookmark, To My Dear Sister 60.00
Postcard, Ann Hathaway's Cottage 40.00
Postcard, Shakespeare's Birthday 45.00

Stevens and Williams

Stevens and Williams glass was produced at the Brierly Hill Glassworks in Stourbridge, England, for nearly a century, beginning in the 1830s. They were credited with being among the first to develop a method of manufacturing a more affordable type of cameo glass. Other lines were also made — silver deposit, alexandrite, and engraved rock crystal, to name but a few. Our advisor for this category is Don Williams; he is listed in the Directory under Missouri.

Basket, rose o/l w/appl flowers, amber ft & hdl, 13½x7" 850.00
Bottle, scent; Pompeian Swirl, gold/rust w/turq int, 6½x4" 895.00
Bowl, wht w/pk int, 3-color leaves, 6 amber ft, 3x5" 135.00
Compote, shaded pk on alabaster stem/ft, plume mk, 4¾" 345.00
Finger bowl, gr-cut-to-clear grapes/vines, 5" dia 195.00
Pitcher, gr w/bl int, appl flowers, trn-down ruffle 7x4½" 385.00
Rose bowl, Arboresque, cranberry/wht, frosted ft, 4x3¾" 195.00
Rose bowl, cranberry w/appl vaseline base/ft/rigaree, 4¾x5½" ...350.00
Rose bowl, gold prunus on brn satin egg shape, pleated top, 5" ..375.00
Rose bowl, Pompeian Swirl, brn to gold, bl int, box pleated, 5" .850.00
Rose bowl, turq bl w/opal stripes, pleated/incurvate rim, 4½" 145.00
Vase, air trap swirls, amber to bl cased w/opal & yel, 7" 575.00
Vase, branching tree w/3 pk opal hobnail arms (vases), 11", pr ..425.00
Vase, florals, amethyst on amethyst frost, cylinder, att, 12" 500.00
Vase, gold prunus on shaded brn satin, pleated top, 5x3½" 395.00
Vase, pk o/l, intaglio daisy ea side & corner cuttings, 4" 225.00
Vase, pk o/l w/intricate intaglio shoulder band, wafer ft, 4" 195.00
Vase, pk/cream o/l, appl ruffled leaf, att, 3⅞x4⅛" 110.00
Vase, pk/wht cased w/appl amber leaves & petal ft, 10", pr 300.00
Vase, Pompeian Swirl, amberina, stick neck, 11x6½" 950.00
Vase, reverse peachblow w/crystal flowers, leafy ft, hdls, 9" 400.00
Vase, rubena verde Swirl MOP, bulbous w/cup neck, 9¾" 900.00
Vase, shaded bl o/l, appl plums/etc, amber ruffle, 9½" 550.00
Vase, Silveria, amethyst/gr w/gr veins, bulbous, 6½x5¼" 3,200.00
Vase, Silveria, amethyst/gr w/gr veins, hdld funnel shape, 7" ..3,200.00
Vase, wht w/pk int, 3-color appl leaves form ft, ruffled, 7" 265.00

Stickley

Among the leading proponents of the Arts and Crafts Movement, the Stickley brothers — Gustav, Leopold, Charles, Albert, and John George — were at various times and locations separately involved in designing and producing furniture as well as decorative items for the home. (See Arts and Crafts for further information.) The oldest of the five Stickley brothers was Gustav; his work is the most highly regarded of all. He developed the style of furniture referred to as Mission. It was strongly influenced by the type of furnishings found in the Spanish missions of California — utilitarian, squarely built, and simple. It was made most often of oak, and decoration was very limited or non-existent. The work of his brothers display adaptations of many of Gustav's ideas and designs. His factory, the Craftsman Workshop, operated in Eastwood, New York, from the late 1890s until 1915, when he was forced out of business by larger companies who copied his work and sold it at much lower prices. Among his shop marks are the early red decal containing a joiner's compass and the words 'Als Ik Kan,' the branded mark with very similar components, and paper labels.

The firm known as Stickley Brothers was located first in Bingham-

ton, New York, and then Grand Rapids, Michigan. Albert and John George made the move to Michigan, leaving Charles in Binghamton (where he and an uncle continued the operation under a different name). After several years John George left the company to rejoin Leopold in New York. (These two later formed their own firm called L. & J.G. Stickley.) The Stickley Brothers Company's early work produced furniture featuring fine inlay work, decorative cutouts, and leaned strongly toward a style of Arts and Crafts with an English influence. It was tagged with a paper label 'Made by Stickley Brothers, Grand Rapids,' or with a brass plate or decal with the words 'Quaint Furniture,' an English term chosen to refer to their product. In addition to furniture, they made metal accessories as well.

The workshops of the L. & J.G. Stickley Company first operated under the name 'Onondaga Shops.' Located in Fayetteville, New York, their designs were often all but copies of Gustav's work. Their products were well made and marketed, and their business was very successful. Their decal labels contained all or a combination of the words 'Handcraft' or 'Onondaga Shops,' along with the brothers' initials and last name. The firm continues in business today. Our advisor for this category is Bruce Austin; he is listed in the Directory under New York. Note: When only one dimension is given for tables, it is length. Cleaning diminishes values; ours are for furniture and metals with excellent original finishes unless noted otherwise.

Key:

b — brand	n — no mark
brd — board	p — paper label
d — red decal	t — Quaint metal tag
h/cp — hammered copper	vnr — veneer
hdw — hardware	w — work of...

Gustav Stickley

Coal bucket, #350, hammered copper with applied iron handle, raised oval design, 19x13", EX, $4,000.00.

Armchair, #310½, 3-slat bk, leatherette pad, d, 35x25", VG 450.00
Armchair, #314, H-bk, corbels, n, rfn/rstr, 40", VG 600.00
Armchair, #324, 3-slat bk, 5-slat sides, seat cushion, d, VG 1,600.00
Armchair, #376, high-bk w/11 spindles, n, rfn, 49", VG 4,500.00
Armchair, ladder-bk, d, rfn/new rush seats, 36" 650.00
Ashtray, h/cp, 4 recessed areas around bowl, cleaned, 7" dia, VG ..190.00
Bed, #912, peaked rail, full panel head/ft brd, d 8,000.00
Bed, #917, heavy w/3 wide slats to head/ft brd, d, '04 ....9,500.00
Bed, 12 spindles on head/ft brds, b, rfn, full sz 3,500.00
Book table, 2 shelves/6 spindles ea side, p, rfn, 29x23" 3,000.00
Bookcase, #718, 2 12-pane doors, keyed tenons, mk, 56x58" ..8,000.00
Bookcase, 2 12-pane doors, gallery top, d/p, 56x53" 8,000.00
Bowl, h/cp, 3 riveted ft, rolled rim, 3¾x6¾" 425.00
Box, shirtwaist; paneled top/sides, wrought hdw, p, 32" L 4,250.00
Chafing dish, #352, h/cp fr on 16" rnd oak base, n, EX 800.00
Chair, #308, H-bk, recovered seat, d, 41x17x16" 425.00

Chair, #353, by Ellis, 3 vertical bk slats, d, 40", VG 400.00
Chair, Morris; #2340, ash, bow arms, faceted pegs, n, rfn, VG ...5,000.00
Chair, Morris; #2341, 2-slat sides, sling seat, n, rfn, VG 3,000.00
Chair, Morris; #328, notched arms, corbels, d, 40x30x33" 1,700.00
Chair, sewing rocker; #2635, Thorndon, 2 bk slats, d, 31" 300.00
Chair, side; #1295, uphl bk/seat, orig leather/tacks, d/p 3,000.00
Chair, side; #1303, tacked leather bk/seat (some rpl), 37" 550.00
Chest, #621, 2 sm drw over 3, cast pulls, str apron, d, 42x36" .6,500.00
Chest, 2 drw over 2, swivel mirror, Ellis design, b, 33x48" 4,500.00
Chest, 5-drw: 2 over 3, V pulls, overhang top, d, 43x37", EX .3,000.00
China cabinet, #815, 2 doors ea w/8 panes, b/p, 64x42" 7,000.00
Costumer, #53, 2 tapered posts on shoe ft, 6 hooks, 71" 2,600.00
Cuspidor, h/cp, woodgrain pattern, 2½x9¼" 450.00
Desk, #729, fall-front, 2 drw over 3, retailer's p, 45x36", VG ..2,700.00
Desk, fall-front, drw, thru-tenons, n, rfn, 44x30" 425.00
Desk, fall-front; 2 drw over 1, full gallery int, d, 43x32" 2,000.00
Dresser, #911, 2 sm drw over 2, swivel mirror, d, 67x48" 11,000.00
Dresser, #913, 2 banks of 3 sm drw ea over 3, b, 51x36" 9,000.00
Footstool, #300, leather top, arched apron, n, 20" L, VG 1,000.00
Hall seat, #224, h-sides w/cutouts at top, panel bk, d, VG 4,000.00
Lamp, floor; 4-ftd oak w/triangle copper harp, mk, 58" 3,250.00
Lamp, piano; h/cp & iron, hanging yel glass sq shade, VG 6,000.00
Letter holder, revolving, cut-out hdl, dvtl, rfn, 9½x12" sq 700.00
Mirror, 4 triple hooks, 3-part glass, b, 28x42" 2,700.00
Rocker, #312½, 5-slat V-bk, thru-post built, d, rfn, G 1,100.00
Rocker, tall 3-slat bk, open arms, n, overcoat/reuphl, 43" 600.00
Rocker, 5-slat bk, open arms, drop-in spring seat, n, 37" 500.00
Rug, Drugget, Nile pattern, brn/gray on oatmeal, 51x82", VG ...750.00
Server, bksplash, overhang top, 2-drw, V-pulls, d, 42" 2,800.00
Settee, lower open arms, vertical bk slats, b, reuphl, 78" 3,250.00
Settle, #222, tall tapered posts, canted slats in side, d, 79" 15,000.00
Settle, #225, even arms, 1 bk slat, 5-slat sides, d, VG 4,750.00
Smoker's cabinet, h/cp pull on drw, door below, b, 29", VG ...2,200.00
Table, #466, 30" dia thru-tenon top, flush apron, p, overcoat .3,000.00
Table, #602, 17" dia top, notched X-stretchers, p, 18", VG 475.00
Table, #604, 20" dia top, notched X-stretchers, d, 26", VG 2,000.00
Table, #631, 3 pegs on ea splay leg, shoe-ft base, d, 86", VG ...1,400.00
Table, #654, 24" dia top, arched X-stretchers, n, rfn/rpl, 28" 700.00
Table, dining; #632, 48" dia, 5 tapered legs, 2 leaves, d/p, VG ...3,750.00
Table, dining; 5-leg extension, 48" dia top, p, rfn/re-vnr 2,100.00
Table, dining; 54" dia top, 5 post legs, n, rfn, +3 leaves 2,700.00
Table, dressing; #914, 2 sm drw, arched apron, mirror, d, 54x36" ..6,000.00
Table, library; #407, 40" dia top, keyed-thru tenons, d 7,500.00
Table, library; #616, 2-drw, corbels at legs, d, 54", VG 3,500.00
Table, library; #619, 3-drw, lower shelf, d, 66" 6,000.00
Table, library; #619, 3-drw/shelf, n, rfn/re-vnr, 6", G 3,000.00
Table, library; #652, drw/shelf, deep aprons, d, rpr, 30", G 900.00
Table, library; 48" hex top, X-stretchers w/finial, n, rfn 5,500.00
Table, 12-tile (Grueby) top, arched apron, n, rfn, 26x24" 9,500.00
Table, 30" dia top, rnd shelf, arched stretchers, rfn 800.00
Umbrella stand, #54, 4 tapering posts, p, liner gone/rfn 500.00

L. & J.G. Stickley

Armchair, #422, 6 vertical bk slats, d, 38" 650.00
Bookcase, 2 12-pane doors, keyed-thru tenons, gallery, 55x48" ...5,750.00
Chair, Morris; #798, 5-slat sides, thru-tenons, n, rfn, VG 4,000.00
Chair, side; 3-slat ladder-bk, rush seat, w, overcoat, 35" 200.00
Chairs, side; #800, 3-slat bk, drop-in seats, rfn, 4 for 1,600.00
Davenport/sleeping settle, broad slats, arched base rails, w, 79" ...5,750.00
Drink stand, 18" dia top, rnd shelf, X-stretchers, n, rfn, 29" 950.00
Frame, hanging, extended top, arched bottom, n, 30x33" 900.00
Magazine stand, #45, 4-shelf, slab sides taper, n, 42x19", VG .1,400.00
Magazine stand, pointed top rail, 4-shelf, n, 45x19" 1,100.00

Pedestal, 19" sq top w/long corbels, X-base, 36" 1,300.00
Rocker, open arms, chevron crest rail, 5 vertical slats, n, VG 600.00
Rocker, 6 bk slats, t, reuphl seat, 35x27x22" 650.00
Rocker, 6 slats in bk/6 under arms, w, overcoat, 37x29" 1,600.00
Settle, #14069-8, curved bk slats form 4 Vs, 2 in sides, d, 78" .5,250.00
Settle, #260, V-bk, flat open arms, 14 bk slats, d, 64", EX 1,900.00
Settle, #281, closely spaced bk/side slats, w, rpl seat, 76" 6,500.00
Settle, 5 broad bk splats, even arms, d, rfn, 72" 220.00
Sideboard, #735, plate rack, 2 doors, 2 drw over 2, n, 56" 5,000.00
Sideboard, #738, plate rail, 2-door/2-drw, copper hdw, b, 60", VG .3,000.00
Table, #538, 30" dia, apron/X-stretchers/thru-tenons, b, rfn, VG 1,100.00
Table, #559, 8-sided, arched X-stretchers, w, rfn, 20x18", VG .1,000.00
Table, #573, 24" dia top, sm rnd shelf, w, 29", VG 900.00
Table, #580, cut-corner 36" top, shelf, n, rfn, 30", VG 700.00
Table, dining; #717, 54" dia top, heavy sq ped w/4 ft, n, VG ..2,500.00
Table, game; #572, cut-corner 30" top, n, rfn, VG 600.00
Table, library; #521, drw w/copper hdw, shelf, d, 42" 1,500.00
Table, library; #522, 2-drw, corbel leg supports, n, 48", VG 1,400.00
Table, library; like #511, blind drw, arched apron, w, 48", VG ...850.00
Table, trestle; #594, lower shelf w/keyed-thru tenons, p, 72" .5,750.00
Table, trestle; leather top, keyed-thru tenons, w, rfn/rstr, 48" .2,500.00
Table, trestle; shaped plank cut-out sides, n, 48", VG 1,600.00
Table, 15" clip-corner octagon top, X-stretchers, d, rfn 700.00

Stickley Bros.

Magazine stand #4743, five shelves, one slat each side, original dark finish, stenciled number, 43x14x14", $650.00.

Armchair, English influence, cut-out bk slats (2)/apron, VG 500.00
Chair, Morris; #343, 3-slat sides, corbels, thru-tenons 3,000.00
Chairs, dining; #379 (4)/#380 (1), 3 vertical slats, t, VG 1,800.00
Ewer, #80, h/cp, long hammered iron hdl, p, 14½" 600.00
Hall chair, att, tall bk w/mirror & hooks, n, rfn, 74x17" 900.00
Magazine stand, #4602, 4-shelf, notched gallery, t, 47x16", VG .1,700.00
Magazine stand, 5-shelf, tall bk w/rnd cutouts, n, 49x12", VG ...950.00
Mirror, #7577, thru-tenons, iron hooks (1 rpl), n, 32x43", VG ..800.00
Mirror, space between side rails & fr, alligatored, 24x38" 650.00
Phone stand, #2886, open shelf, retailer's p, 30x20x18", VG 700.00
Settle, #3719, slatted bk/sides w/cut-out designs, t, 85" 2,900.00
Settle, att, even arms, 4 tapered posts, canted sides, 73", VG ..3,250.00
Sideboard, #8216, long drw over 3/2 cabinet doors, t, 55", VG ..2,000.00
Table, #2500, 24" dia top, thru-tenon X-stretcher base, t 900.00
Table, #2504, 26" dia top, sq apron/shelf, t, overcoat, 30" 750.00
Table, dining; #2424, 4 legs w/X-stretchers, 48" dia, G 1,000.00
Table, hall; arched apron, 2 slats ea side, n, rfn, 27x24x18" 750.00
Table, luncheon; #2674, angled apron, 36" sq top, n 500.00
Table, sq top, splay legs w/X-stretchers, n, rfn, 19x12" 350.00
Table, 12" sq top, b, 18", VG 260.00
Table, 24" dia top, shelf on X-stretchers, rfn, n, 30" 700.00
Vase, #246, h/cp, 3 shaped riveted hdls, loving-cup form, 10½" .600.00

Stiegel

Baron Henry Stiegel produced glassware in Pennsylvania as early as 1760, very similar to glass being made concurrently in Germany and England. Without substantiating evidence, it is impossible to positively attribute a specific article to his manufacture. Although he made other types of glass, today the term Stiegel generally refers to any very early ware made in shapes and colors similar to those he is known to have produced — especially that with etched or enameled decoration. It is generally conceded, however, that most glass of this type is of European origin. Our advisor for this category is Mark Vuono; he is listed in the Directory under Connecticut.

Bottle, bright amethyst, Dmn & Daisy over Flute, pontil, 5⅝" ..2,500.00
Bottle, med bright amethyst, 12-Dmn, pontil, 4⅞" 2,300.00
Creamer, emerald gr, 15-Dmn, crudely tooled rim, pontil, 3⅛" ..2,500.00
Creamer, emerald gr, 15-Dmn, ovoid w/appl hdl, pontil, 3⅛" .2,000.00
Creamer, sapphire bl, 20-ogival, solid hdl, pontil, 3⅞" 150.00
Flask, Dmn & Daisy, amethyst, 4¾" 500.00
Flask, pocket; med amethyst, 20-Dmn over flutes, pontil, 5¾" .2,100.00
Flip, emb basket & flowers, sheared rim, pontil, 7" 350.00
Flip, eng bird in heart w/in sunburst, pontil, 7" 400.00
Flip, eng bird w/sunburst, sheared mouth, pontil, mini, 3" 325.00
Flip, eng birds on heart w/in sunburst, pontil, 7⅞" 475.00
Flip, eng floral, sheared rim, pontil, 6¼" 300.00
Flip, eng floral (lg & sm), pontil, 8" 325.00
Flip, eng swags, graduated panels, pontil, hdl, 3½" 210.00
Pocket flask, emerald gr w/eng basket & floral, teardrop, 6⅜" 300.00
Sugar bowl, cobalt, Expanded Dmn, ftd, pontil, w/lid, 6" 1,100.00
Tankard, eng bird & sunburst, solid reeded hdl, ftd, 5¾" 500.00
Tankard, eng bird & tulip decor, cylindrical, pontil, 6¼" 475.00
Tankard, mc house/mtn scene on milk glass, cylindrical, 5½" 150.00
Tumbler, eng sunflower/floral/vines, lid w/appl finial, 10½" 750.00

Stocks and Bonds

Scripophily (scrip-awfully), the collecting of 'worthless' old stocks and bonds, gained recognition as an area of serious interest around the mid-1970s. Today there are an estimated 5,000 collectors in the United States and 15,000 worldwide. Collectors who come from numerous business fields mainly enjoy its hobby aspect, though there are those who consider scripophily an investment. Some collectors like the historical significance that certain certificates have. Others prefer the beauty of older stocks and bonds that were printed in various colors with fancy artwork and ornate engravings. Even autograph collectors are found in this field, on the lookout for signed certificates.

Many factors help determine the collector value: autograph value, age of the certificate, the industry represented, whether it is issued or not, its attractiveness, condition, and collector demand. Certificates from the mining, energy, and railroad industries are the most popular with collectors. Other industries or special collecting fields include banking, automobiles, aircraft, and territorials. Serious collectors usually prefer only issued certificates that date from before 1910. Unissued certificates are usually worth one-fourth to one-tenth the value of one that has been issued. Inexpensive issued common stocks and bonds dated between the 1930s and 1980s usually retail between $1.00 to $10.00. Those dating between 1890 and 1930 usually sell for $10.00 to $50.00. Those over one hundred years old retail between $25.00 and $100.00 or more, depending on the quantity found and the industry represented. Some stocks are one of a kind while others are found by the hundreds or even thousands, especially railroad certificates. Autographed stocks normally sell anywhere from $50.00 to $1,000.00 or more. A formal collecting organization for scripophilists is known as The Bond and Share Society with an American chapter located in New York City.

Our advisor for this category is Warren Anderson; he is listed in the Directory under Utah. In many of the following listings, two-letter state abbreviations immediately follow company name. All are in fine condition unless noted otherwise.

Key:
cp — coupon
I/C — issued/cancelled
I/U — issued/uncancelled
U — unissued
vgn — vignette

AK Exploration & Mining, AK Territory/1935, I/C 25.00
American Settlement, KS Territory/1856, eagle on bl, I/C 120.00
American Submarine Co, 1870, 3 vgns, I/C 145.00
American Voting Machine Co, ME/1917, torch vgn, I/U 20.00
Angelus Mill & Mining, AZ Territory/1903, 3 vgns, I/U 25.00
Annie C Gold Mining Co, NB/1896, 3 miners working vgn, 1896, I/U ..60.00
AZ Belmont Mining Co, AZ/1914, 3 vgns, I/U 25.00
Baltimore & Ohio RR, 1899, topless lady w/flag, I/C 12.00
Bell Mining, ID/1908, goddess vgn, bold title, I/U 25.00
Blk Hills Copper Co Ltd, AZ Territory/1905, 4 miners in shaft, I/U .35.00
Carmer Mining Co, CO/1890s, 3 miners vgn, sm banner title, U .10.00
Cashier Mining & Milling, WA/1903, 3 vgns, I/U 25.00
Champlain Construction, 1899, 3 RR vgns, U 15.00
Chicago & Alton RR, 1899, $1,000, eng train vgn, I/C 45.00
Chicago Goldfields Mining Co, AZ Territory/1907, miner vgn, I/U .30.00
City of Providence, RI/1892, $1,000, 3 eng vgn, U 38.00
Commercial Motor Body Corp, DE/1917, banner title, I/U 25.00
Conway's Theatre Ticket Offices Inc, DE/1919, angel vgn, I/U ...25.00
Dearborn Truck, DE/1920, eagle vgn on bl, I/C 50.00
Early Silver Mining, CO/1880s, miners vgn, U 20.00
Harvard Gold Mining Co, CO/1896, eagle vgn, I/U 45.00
Home Insurance, NY/1930, 3 vgns, ABNCo, I/C 15.00
Housatonic RR Co, CT/1880, 3 vgns, 1 State seal, 2 trains, U 20.00
IN Advertising Auto Speedway, IN/1921, Mercury vgn on gr, I/C .35.00
Ingersoll Warner Mercantile, KS/1906, Indians/train vgn, I/U 30.00
Jupitor Oil Co, WY/1918, 5 oil field scenes, I/U 15.00

Photo courtesy Warren Anderson

Las Vegas & Hot Springs Electric Railway Light & Power Company, 500 shares, $175.00 at auction.

Leon Gold Mining Co, CO/1895, 2 winged serpents/floral vase, I/U .45.00
Marmon Motor Car, IN/1930, allegorical figures vgn, ABNCo ..150.00
Mergenthaler Linotype Co, 1898, gr, 1 vgn, I/C 150.00
Mohawk & Malone RW, NY/1902, 2 vgns, cps, I/U 35.00
Montana Phonograph Co, 1889, vgn of early phonograph, U 35.00
Mutual Benefit Life Insurance Co, 1865, pelican vgn, U 80.00
Nat'l Gold & Silver Mining, SD/1919, 3 vgns, I/U 25.00
New Viola Co Ltd, England/ID/1890, ornate print, I/U 32.50
Oil Fields Corp, AR/1925, gusher vgn, brn seal, I/U 15.00
Oil Lease Development Co, DE/1923, eagle vgn, banner title, I/U .10.00
Parrot Silver & Copper, MT/1901, parrot/silver bar vgn, I/C 15.00
Pierce-Arrow Car, NY/1935, man & emblem vgns, ABNCo, I/C .135.00

Progressive Placer Co, AZ/1913, Miss Liberty vgn, I/U 20.00
Provo Mining Co, UT/1909, miners in tunnel vgn, I/U 25.00
Rosco Stock, UT Territory/1890, bull vgn, U 18.00
Sante Fe Dredging Co, NM/1914, elk vgn, I/U 20.00
Sea Island Co, GA/1866, 1 eagle vgn, 2 Blacks picking cotton, I/U .195.00
Sunset-Eclipse Gold Mining, WY/1902, blk on wht, I/U 35.00
Thompson & Tucker Lumber Co, TX/1904, construction site vgn, I/C ..85.00
Treasure Gold Mining, AZ Territory/1910, 3 vgns, I/U 25.00
TX Crude Oil, TX/191, gusher vgn, 6", I/U 25.00
Union Mutual Insurance Co, 1873, 3 vgns, I/C 65.00
US Car Co, 1894, train vgn, I/U 75.00
US Worsted, MA/1923, sheep herds vgn, ABNCo, I/C 40.00
Utah Bingham Mining Co, ME/1906, 3 miners in tunnel, I/U 25.00
Wells Fargo, 1863, sgn by founders, sm folio, I/C 1,300.00
1st Nat'l Bank of Ouray, CO/1889, miners vgn, blk/wht, I/C 35.00

Stoneware

There are three broad periods of time that collectors of American pottery can look to in evaluating and dating the stoneware and earthenware in their collections. Among the first permanent settlers in America were English and German potters who found a great demand for their individually turned wares. The early pottery was produced from red and yellow clays scraped from the ground at surface levels. The earthenware made in these potteries was fragile and coated with lead glazes that periodically created health problems for the people who ate or drank from it. There was little stoneware available for sale until the early 1800s, because the clays used in its production were not readily available in many areas and transportation was prohibitively expensive. The opening of the Erie Canal and improved roads brought about a dramatic increase in the accessibility of stoneware clay, and many new potteries began to open in New York and New England.

Collectors have difficulty today locating earthenware and stoneware jugs produced prior to 1840, because few have survived intact. These ovoid or pear-shaped jugs were designed to be used on a daily basis. When cracked or severely chipped, they were quickly discarded. The value of handcrafted pottery is often determined by the cobalt decoration it carries. Pieces with elaborate scenes (a chicken pecking corn, a bluebird on a branch, a stag standing near a pine tree, a sailing ship, or people) may easily bring $1,000.00 to $12,000.00 at auction.

After the Civil War there was a need and a national demand for stoneware jugs, crocks, canning jars, churns, spittoons, and a wide variety of other pottery items. The competition among the many potteries reached the point where only the largest could survive. To cut costs, most potteries did away with all but the simplest kinds of decoration on their wares. Time-consuming brush-painted birds or flowers quickly gave way to more quickly executed swirls or numbers and stenciled designs. The coming of home refrigeration and Prohibition in 1919 effectively destroyed the American stoneware industry.

Investment possibilities: 1) Early 19th-century stoneware with elaborate decorations and a potter's mark is expensive and will continue to rise in price. 2) Late 19th-century hand-thrown stoneware with simple cobalt swirls or numbers is still reasonably priced and a good investment. 3) Mass-produced stoneware (ca. 1890 – 1920) is available in large quantities, inexpensive, and has been slowly increasing in price over the last ten years.

Skillfully repaired pieces often surface; their prices should reflect their condition. Look for a slight change in color and texture. The use of a black light is also useful in exposing some repairs. Buyer beware! Hint: Buy only from reputable dealers who will guarantee their merchandise.

In the following listings, 'c/s' means 'cobalt on salt glaze'; all decoration described before this abbreviation is in cobalt. See also Bennington, Stoneware.

Batter pail, #4/tornado, c/s, att Whites Utica, 9½", NM 330.00
Batter pail, bird (long tail), c/s, att Whites Utica, rstr, 10½" 855.00
Churn, #4/triple flower, c/s, Ithaca NY, w/dasher, 16" 375.00
Churn, #4/1863 in heart wreath, c/s, Whites Utica, 16", NM .4,500.00
Churn, #5/flower w/dotted theme, c/s, N Clark Jr..., 5-gal, 17" ..685.00
Churn, #5/long-tail bird, c/s, T Harrington Lyons, chip, 19" ..9,350.00
Cooler, #3/bird & accents, c/s, S Hart Fulton, chip, rare, 13" 600.00
Cooler, #3/triple hops, c/s, Burger & Lang...NY, 13½", EX 500.00
Cooler, #5/flower & vine, c/s, Bennett & Chollar Homer, 16½" .750.00
Cream pot, #2/triple flower/bird, c/s, N Clark Rochester, 11", NM .5,400.00

Crock, tulips, cobalt on salt glaze, American, 15¼x10½", EX, $1,495.00; Churn, cow, cobalt on salt glaze, handles, 19th century, 22¾x10¼", EX, $3,100.00.

Crock, #1/bird (running), c/s, Whites Utica, line, 7" 600.00
Crock, #1/tornado, c/s, West Troy, 1870s, 7½", NM 145.00
Crock, #1/wreath/accents, c/s, Lyons, line, 7½" 300.00
Crock, #2/bird on plume, c/s, Flak & Van Arsdale...Ont, 10" 770.00
Crock, #2/flower/accents, c/s, Burger & Lang...NY, pail shape, 10" ...415.00
Crock, #2/horse at hitching post, c/s, JC Waelde North Bay, 9½" .7,150.00
Crock, #3/bird (dotted wings), c/s, N Clark NJ...NY, 10½", NM .525.00
Crock, #3/bird on flower branch, c/s, Whites Utica, 10½" 380.00
Crock, #3/bird on plume, c/s, Haxstun Ottman & Co...NY, 10¼", EX .715.00
Crock, #3/bird on plume, c/s, West Troy Pottery, chip, 10½" 300.00
Crock, #3/bird on stump, c/s, Brady & Ryan, rstr, 10½" 415.00
Crock, #3/bird on stump, Riedinger & Caire...NY, c/s, rstr, 10½" ..575.00
Crock, #3/fish (folky), c/s, W Hart Ogdensburgh, prof rstr, 11" ...1,495.00
Crock, #3/orchid (drooping), c/s, Whites Utica NY, sm chips, 10½" .375.00
Crock, #3/orchid (ornate), c/s, Whites Utica NY, 10¼", EX 495.00
Crock, #3/stag in landscape, c/s, Whites Utica, rstr, 11½" 2,100.00
Crock, #3/tornado, c/s, J Burger Jr...NY, 10", NM 300.00
Crock, #3/tulip (ribbed), c/s, Burger & Lang...NY, chip, 10" 220.00
Crock, #4 (script)/bird/dots, c/s, S Hart & Son..., 11" 520.00
Crock, #4/bird, c/s, Haxstun Ottman & Co...NY, 11½" 1,400.00
Crock, #4/bird, c/s, S Hart Fulton, tight line, 1870, 11½" 360.00
Crock, #4/bird (running), c/s, Whites Utica, line, 11½" 687.00
Crock, #4/flower/accents, c/s, N Clark Lyons, minor chips, 13" .770.00
Crock, #4/trumpet flower/sunflower, c/s, Harrington & Burger, 11" .1,650.00
Crock, #5/bird on lg plume, c/s, Hart Bros...NY, stain, 12" 415.00
Crock, #5/flower (triple), c/s, J Burger Jr...NY, line, 13" 880.00
Crock, #5/tulips (top to bottom), c/s, M Woodruff Cortland, 11½" ..365.00
Crock, cake; #4/bird, c/s, AO Whittemore...NY, 8", NM 990.00
Jar, #1/sunflower, c/s, F Stetzenmeyer & Co, chips, 10" 695.00
Jar, #2 (dbl)/flower (dbl)/accents, c/s, Lyons, flakes, 11½" 300.00
Jar, #2/deer & grasses, c/s, T Harrington Lyons, chips, 11½" ...2,650.00
Jar, #2/drooping iris, c/s, C Hart & Co Ogdensburgh, 11¼" 250.00
Jar, #2/floral vine, slip & c/s, Porter & Fraser...NY, 12", EX 135.00
Jar, #2/flower (dbl)/accents, c/s, Lyons, 10" 550.00
Jar, #2/tulip in fr, c/s, N&A Seymour Rome, 1830s, 11½" 200.00
Jar, #2/vine, slip decor, c/s, Edmands & Co, ca 1870, 11½" 220.00
Jar, #3/lovebirds/dots, c/s, S Hart Fulton, prof rstr, 12" 1,760.00
Jar, #3/man's profile in star, c/s, T Harrington Lyons, rpr, 13½" .3,500.00
Jar, #4/dots & dbl 4s, c/s, Hubbel & Chesebro Geddes NY, 13½", EX ..90.00

Jar, #4/flower (triple), c/s, Pottery Works...NY, 1870s, 15", EX ..415.00
Jar, #4/flower (triple), c/s, Whites Utica, wear/line, 13½" 250.00
Jar, preserve; #1/flower, c/s, Lyons, rpl wooden lid, 9", EX 275.00
Jar, preserve; #2/sunflower, c/s, John Burger, rpr, 10½" 825.00
Jar, preserve; #2/triple flower, c/s, S Hart Fulton, rstr, 10½" 210.00
Jar, preserve; #3/plume, c/s, N White, Utica, 13" 120.00
Jug, #1 1/2/flower basket, c/s, Fort Edward Pottery Co, 13" 1,550.00
Jug, #1/bird, c/s, Fort Edward Pottery, spider, 11½" 745.00
Jug, #1/pine tree, c/s, Whites Utica, 11" 165.00
Jug, #2/Bantam rooster in fr, c/s, JC Waelde North Bay, 14" ...5,280.00
Jug, #2/bird (paddle tail), c/s, NA White & Son...NY, 14" 2,400.00
Jug, #2/flower, c/s, Harrington & Burger Rochester, 14", NM 440.00
Jug, #2/flower (dbl), c/s, N Clark Jr...NY, 13½" 355.00
Jug, #2/flower & plume, c/s, Porter & Fraser...NY, 14" 220.00
Jug, #2/plume, c/s, Satterlee & Morey...NY, 11¼" 250.00
Jug, #2/robin on branch, c/s, Haxstun & Co...NY, line, 15" 580.00
Jug, #2/sunflower, c/s, John Burger Rochester, 14" 1,255.00
Jug, #3, accents at hdls, c/s, N Clark & Co Lyons, 11½" 155.00
Jug, #3/bird on twig, c/s, Haxstun Ottman & Co...NY, 16", NM .500.00
Jug, beehive; #5/dog, c/s, unsgn, rare, 1880s, 18" 1,375.00
Jug, molasses; #2/bird on floral plume, c/s, NY..., crack, 14" 580.00
Pitcher, #1/flower, c/s, Lyons, 11", NM 1,325.00
Pitcher, leaf decor, c/s, Whites Binghamton, prof rstr, 10½" 275.00

Store Memorabilia

Perhaps more so than any other yesteryear establishment, the country store evokes feelings of nostalgia for folks old enough to remember its charms — barrels for coffee, crackers, and big green pickles; candy in a jar for the grocer to weigh on shiny brass scales; beheaded chickens in the meat case outwardly devoid of nothing but feathers. Today mementos from this segment of Americana are being collected by those who 'lived it' as well as those less fortunate! Our advisor for this category is Charles Reynolds; he is listed in the Directory under Virginia. See also Advertising; Scales.

Display jar, clear glass with smooth base, original glass stopper, ca 1895 – 1910, 15", NM, $210.00.

Box, cracker; glass cover, old bl pnt, 8½" H 50.00
Broom holder, heavy wire, 23 loops, hanging, 19th C, 19x16" dia .180.00
Cabinet, bolt; oak, hex top w/6 banks of drw, 1880s, 65" 2,000.00
Cabinet, oak, 8-sided, metal base, ball/claw ft, revolves, 66" 500.00
Case, account ledger; McCaskey, swinging metal partitions 425.00
Case, scissors; 3-tiered revolving center, wood, Champlin 825.00
Case, shot; self-weighing, 10 compartments, Pat 5-10-1881 ....875.00
Counter jar, Colg'n's Taffy Tolu gum, clear, head finial, 11" 260.00
Desk, clerk's; walnut, slant front, 4-drw, attached top, 85" 1,430.00
Desk, storekeeper's; roll-top, oak 2,900.00
Dispenser, coffee bean; Red Pot Coffee, lg coffeepot shape 675.00
Dispenser, paper bag; pnt metal, chips, 30x9½" 325.00
Dispenser, shoe heel; Cat's Paw, tin 80.00
Display box, Adams Tutti Frutti Chewing Gum 100.00
Hat stand, maple, trn 38.00

Jar, licorice lozenges, mk Y&S, clear, Am, 1880-1900, 9¼" 50.00
Lamp, kerosene; emb SP, hanging, tin shade 475.00
Mannequin, papier-mache & wood w/CI boots, 1890s, 44x12x19" .700.00
Popcorn popper/peanut roaster, Holkum & Hoko, dk oak case ..2,400.00

Stoves

Antique stoves' desirability is based on two criteria: their utility and their decorative merit. It's the latter that adds an 'antique' premium to the basic functional value that could be served just as well by a modern stove. Sheer age is usually irrelevant. Decorative features that enhance desirability include fancy, embossed ornamentation, nickel-plated trim, mica windows, ceramic tiles, and (in cooking stoves) water reservoirs and high warming closets rather than mere high shelves. The less sheet metal and the more cast iron, the better. Look for crisp, sharp designs in preference to those made from worn or damaged and repaired foundry patterns. Stoves with a pastel porcelain finish can be very attractive; blue is a favorite, white is least desirable. Chrome trim, rather than nickel, dates a stove to circa 1933 or later and is a good indicator of a post-antique stove. Though purists prefer the earlier models trimmed in nickel rather than chrome, there is now considerable public interest in these post-antique stoves as well, and some people are willing to pay a good price for these appliance-era 'classics.' (Note: remember, not all bright metal trim is chrome; it is important to learn to distinguish chrome from the earlier, more desirable nickel plate.)

Among stove types, base burners (with self-feeding coal magazines) are the most desirable. Then come the upright, cylindrical 'oak' stoves, kitchen ranges, and wood parlors. Cannon stoves approach the margin of undesirability; laundries and gasoline stoves plunge through it.

There's a thin but continuing stream of desirable antique stoves going to the high-priced Pacific Coast market. Interest in antique stoves is least in the Deep South. Demand for wood/coal stoves is strongest in areas where firewood is affordable and storage of it is practical. Demand for antique gas ranges has become strong, especially in metropolitan markets, and interest in antique electric ranges is starting to surface. The market for antique stoves is so limited and the variety so bewildering that a consensus on a going price can hardly emerge. They are only worth something to the right individual, and prices realized depend very greatly on who happens to be in the auction crowd. Even an expert's appraisal will usually miss the realized price by a substantial percent.

In judging condition look out for deep rust pits, warped or burnt-out parts, unsound fire bricks, poorly fitting parts, poor repairs, and empty mounting holes indicating missing trim. Search meticulously for cracks in the cast iron. Our listings reflect auction prices of completely restored, safe, and functional stoves, unless indicated otherwise.

Base Burners

Art Garland 250, ca 1920, rstr 1,250.00
Imperial Universal 50, Cribben & Sexton, Chicago, 1913, rstr .4,000.00
Noble Crown, ca 1920, dismounted from base, rstr 1,300.00
Radiant Stewart 34, Fuller & Warren, Milwaukee, ca 1900, rstr .5,000.00
Retort 218, Marion IN, soft coal, 3 mica doors, 1914, rstr 2,400.00
Wehrle 100, Wehrle Co Newark OH, 1911, 14", rpl parts/rstr .4,000.00
Wehrle 100, 1911, rstr 9,000.00

Parlor

The term 'parlor stove' as we use it here is very general and encompasses at least eight distinct types recognized by the stove industry: cottage parlor, double-cased airtight, circulator, cylinder, oak, base burner, Franklin, and the fireplace heater.

Estate Oak F-316, no urn, ca 1915, G **425.00**
Fr enamel, Neoclassical ormolu mts, ca 1880s, 30½x22½" **500.00**
German Heater 119, oak stove, w/base/ft rails/urn, 1900, unrstr ...**25.00**
Ideal Garland 220, wood/coal, no urn, ca 1898, rstr **1,300.00**
Ideal Heater 417, Gem City Stove Mfg...IL, oak stove, 1925, G ..**175.00**
Peoria Oak, Culter & Proctor, oak stove, 1920, unrstr **25.00**
Round Oak D-18, complete, 1901, unrstr **300.00**
Round Oak D-18, w/extra half-section, figure missing, 1904, rstr ...**325.00**
Round Oak 18-T-31, 1940, G **225.00**
Round Oak 18-0-2, 1916, unrstr **100.00**

Ranges (Gas)

Alcazar, Milwaukee, 4-burner/1-oven, 1928, G **50.00**
Alcazar, pk & wht w/wood side, ca 1927, unrstr **40.00**
Detroit Jewel, 4-burner/1-oven, 1928, unrstr **15.00**
Magic Chef, wht, 6-burner/2-oven, high closet, 1933, G **800.00**
Magic Chef, wht, 6-burner/2-oven, high closet, 1938, rstr, up to .**12,000.00**
Magic Chef, wht, 6-burner/2-oven, high closet, 1938, unrstr ..**1,000.00**
O'Keefe & Merrit, 4-burner, cabinet base, ca 1929, G **110.00**
Prosperity, Wehrle/Sears, 4-burner/1-oven, 1929, G **35.00**
Quick Meal, bl, 4-burner, cabinet style, 1919, G **925.00**
Quick Meal, gray, 4-burner, canopy/high closet, 1924, unrstr **375.00**
Quick Meal, 4-burner/1-oven, 1928, unrstr **10.00**
Roper, 4-burner/1-oven, 1929, unrstr **20.00**
White Star, Detroit Vapor Stove Co, 4-burner/1-oven, 1929, unrstr ..**10.00**

Ranges (Wood and Coal)

Alpine Bride, CI, blk, ca 1920, rstr **300.00**
Brilliant Universal, bl, high closet, no reservoir, 1917, G **200.00**
Chambers, wht, 4-burner, ca 1949, G **250.00**
Glenwood F 107, CI, high shelf, 1910, rstr **1,100.00**
Globe, Kokomo IN, gray, ca 1925, G **150.00**
Kalamazoo Peerless, gray & wht, wood/coal/gas, G **875.00**
Magee 88, 2-oven/8-hole, CI, high closet/no reservoir, 1880, rstr .**5,500.00**

Stove Manufacturers' Toy Stoves

Buck's Jr Range, St Louis MO, new body/pnt/recast parts, 26" ...**850.00**
Charter Oak #503, GF Filley, St Louis MO, 14x12x25", EX ...**2,050.00**
Dainty, Reading Stove Works, PA, 7x13x8", VG **150.00**
Estate Fresh Air Oven, blk/wht enamel, NP, working gas range, 15" .**2,400.00**
Karr, Qualified, bl porc w/NP, Belleville IL, 1925, EX **2,500.00**
Karr Range, Belleville IL, bl porc, old model, 21½x13x9" **3,100.00**
Little Eva T Southard, NYC, 8½x14x11", G **350.00**
Little Fanny, CI, minor rust, EX **300.00**
Little Willie, EX **85.00**
Qualified Range, aluminum/tin, dial on door, 21½x13", EX **775.00**
Royal American, Bridgeford, Louisville KY, 14x12x10", G **950.00**

Toy Manufacturers' Toy Stoves

Arcade Hotpoint Range, pnt CI, tan & gr, VG **150.00**
Arcade Roper Range, pnt CI, gas type, door opens, 4½", EX **70.00**
Bing, cookstove, bl steel, brass trim, 16½", VG **600.00**
Crescent, cookstove, plated CI & steel, 4-burner, 11½", EX **230.00**
Eagle, Hubley, Lancaster PA, NP, recast parts **450.00**
Eagle, Kenton, CI, heavily scrolled, 4-ft, 11½x10", G **125.00**
Eclipse, CI, EX **175.00**
Kenton Royal, CI & steel, 4-burner, ornate, 10", VG **100.00**
Lionel, porc & CI, cream & gr, 4-leg, 32x26", EX **550.00**
Little Giant, unmk/unidentified, 7½x8½x11", EX orig **675.00**
Novelty, Kenton Hdwe, bl pnt/NP trim, rfn, 13x6½x8½" **600.00**

Pet, The Young Bros, Albany NY, 10½x6x8½" **165.00**
Rival, J&E Stevens, Cromwell CT, 14x9x16", M, +2 kettles ..**1,350.00**
Rival, no shelves, 12" L, EX **900.00**
Royal, Kenton, CI & steel, 4-burner/working grates, rpt, 10", G ..**50.00**
Royal, plated CI, stovepipe, shield shape, 16", G **85.00**
Susie Homemaker, VG+ **65.00**
Triumph, Kenton Hdwe, OH, 14x8½x19", G **195.00**

Stretch Glass

Stretch glass, produced from about 1916 through 1935, was made in an effort to emulate the fine art glass of Tiffany and Carder. The pressed or blown glassware was sprayed with a metallic salts mix while hot, then reshaped, causing a stretch effect in the iridescent finish. Pieces which were not reshaped had the iridized finish without the stretch, as seen on Fenton's #222 lemonade set and #401 guest set. Northwood, Imperial, Fenton, Diamond, Lancaster, Central, Vineland Flint, and the United States Glass Company were the manufacturers of this type of glass. See also specific companies.

Basket, Rose Ice, Imperial #300, 9¾" **65.00**
Bowl, aquamarine, oval, Fenton #1608, 10½" **225.00**
Bowl, bl, 3-ftd, Diamond, 8" **80.00**
Bowl, gr, Central, 9¼" **45.00**
Bowl, gr, flared rim, Diamond, 10" **40.00**
Bowl, Jade Blue, Northwood #620, 8½" **70.00**
Bowl, olive gr, flared, collar bottom, 3½x9½" **50.00**
Bowl, topaz, Northwood #648, 2⅜x13½" **75.00**
Bowl, wht, Imperial #719, 2x9⅜" **50.00**
Candlesticks, bl, Fenton #449, 8⅝", pr **85.00**
Candlesticks, gr, Central, 9¼", pr **95.00**
Candlesticks, gr, Diamond, wht enameling, 9", pr **80.00**
Candlesticks, Wisteria, Vineland Flint, 6¾", pr **95.00**
Candy dish, bl, Diamond #1, 8¾" **55.00**
Candy dish, Velva Rose, Diamond Optic, Fenton #568, ½-lb **60.00**
Cheese/cracker, smoke w/cut decor, Imperial #641 ....**75.00**
Compote, amberina, Imperial, 4½x6" **150.00**
Compote, bl, Adam's Rib, Diamond, 11¾" L **85.00**
Compote, topaz w/enameling, US Glass #314, 7" **50.00**
Compote, violet, sq base, Northwood #605 ....**80.00**
Console set, bl, Optic Swirl, Northwood **250.00**
Creamer & sugar bowl, vaseline, Fenton #3 ....**80.00**
Cup & saucer, gr, Florentine, Fenton **90.00**
Guest set, bl, Fenton #401, 2-pc **80.00**
Plate, bl, Diamond, pressed star base, 7⅝" **30.00**
Plate, bl, 8¾" **20.00**
Plate, gr, US Glass #310, 8½" **35.00**
Plate, salad; vaseline, Fenton, 8" **20.00**
Plate, topaz, Northwood #630, 6¾" **30.00**
Plate, topaz, openwork, US Glass #8076 ....**80.00**
Plate, wht, Colonial Panel, Imperial, 7" **12.00**
Vase, Jade Green, US Glass, 8½" **70.00**
Vase, tangerine, Fenton #1531, 14" **225.00**
Vase, topaz, Diamond Optic, Northwood #613 ....**85.00**

String Holders

Today, if you want to wrap and secure a package, you have a variety of products to choose from: cellophane tape, staples, etc. But in the 1800s, string was about the only available binder; thus the string holder, either the hanging or counter type, was a common and practical item found in most homes and businesses. Chalkware and ceramic figurals from the 1930s and '40s contrast with the cast and wrought-iron examples from the 1800s to make for an interesting collection. Our advisor for this category is Charles Reynolds; he is listed in the Directory under Virginia. See also Advertising.

Apple & blueberries, chalkware	50.00
Apple w/red berries, chalkware	50.00
Apple w/worm, chalkware, EX	100.00
Baby face, chalkware, lt wear	240.00
Beehive, CI, Pat 8/21/1856, 5x6½" dia	160.00
Chef, pnt CI, EX	50.00
Chef w/striped pants, chalkware	275.00
Cherries, chalkware, from $100 to	150.00
Clown w/string around tooth, chalkware, from $100 to	150.00
Dutch girl's head, bl dots, chalkware	75.00
Girl, sleeping, ceramic	100.00
I Hate Housework, ceramic	160.00
Jester, chalkware, from $100 to	150.00
Mammy, plaid apron, polka-dot shirt, ceramic, Japan	185.00
Mammy, Ty Me, chalkware	395.00
Man in top hat, head w/airbrushed accents, chalkware, 9"	45.00
Mouse, Josef Originals, ceramic, from $80 to	90.00
Owl, pottery	175.00
Pig w/flowers, ceramic, from $100 to	125.00
Strawberry face, chalkware	75.00

Sugar Shakers

Sugar shakers (or muffineers, as they were also called) were used during the Victorian era to sprinkle sugar and spice onto breakfast muffins, toast, etc. They were made of art glass, in pressed patterns, and in china. See also specific types and manufacturers (such as Northwood). Our coadvisors for this category are Jeff Bradfield and Dale MacAllister; they are listed in the Directory under Virginia.

Acorn, gr w/decor	275.00
Acorn, pk opaque w/mc floral	240.00
Argus Swirl, pk (Peach Bloom), scarce	260.00
Beatty Honeycomb, bl opal	250.00
Beatty Honeycomb, wht opal	200.00
Blown Twist, gr opal, wide waist	350.00
Bubble Lattice, wht opal	225.00
Challinor's Forget-Me-Not, gr opaque	225.00
Chrysanthemum Swirl, bl opal	325.00

Chrysanthemum Swirl, cranberry satin opalescent, 4½", $495.00.

Coinspot, cranberry opal, wide waist	250.00
Cone, bl	150.00
Cone, gr opaque	150.00
Cranberry, 12-panel cylinder, sterling top, 6¼"	275.00
Daisy & Fern, bl opal, Apple Mold	285.00
Daisy & Fern, bl opal, wide waist	295.00
Daisy & Fern, cranberry opal, bulbous	375.00
Fern, bl opal	350.00

Flower Mold, bl	395.00
Hobbs Swirl, cranberry opal	400.00
Invt T'print, bl, tapered	140.00
Late Block, Duncan	50.00
Little Shrimp, satin w/decor	350.00
Medallion Sprig, bl to clear	500.00
Northwood Venetian, cranberry	225.00
Parian Mold, cranberry	295.00
Parian Swirl, cranberry	295.00
Parian Swirl, gr w/decor	185.00
Parian Swirl, satin w/decor	150.00
Parian Swirl/Daisy & Fern, cranberry opal	300.00
Reverse Swirl, cranberry opal	485.00
Ribbed Lattice, bl opal	265.00
Ribbed Lattice, cranberry opal	350.00
Ribbed Lattice, wht opal	135.00
Ring Neck Coin Spot, bl opal	150.00
Ring Neck Optic, cranberry	195.00
Ring Neck Optic, gr	225.00
Satin, w/yel floral, melon ribs, Smith Bros	375.00
Seaweed, cranberry opal	500.00
Spanish Lace, bl opal, bulbous	250.00
Spanish Lace, vaseline opal	285.00
Swirl, cranberry opal	395.00
Tomato, wht satin w/decor, Mt WA	495.00

Sunderland Lustre

Sunderland lustre was made by various potters in the Sunderland district of England during the 18th and 19th centuries. It is often characterized by a splashed-on application of the pink lustre, which results in an effect sometimes referred to as the 'cloud' pattern. Some pieces are transfer printed with scenes, ships, florals, or portraits.

Bowl, West View of CI Bridge over River Wear/verse, 4x10½"	800.00
Creamer, cow figural, cloud pattern, 6½" L	250.00
Cup & saucer, cloud pattern	45.00
Egg stand, oval form w/6 egg cups, 1850s, 6½", EX	200.00
Jug, ship Northumberland/verse, brn transfer, rstr, 1850s, 7⅛"	550.00
Mustard jar, 4"	150.00
Plaque, Behold God Will Not Cast Away...Job 8:20, 8½"	285.00
Salt cellar, lt wear, 2"	50.00

Surveying Instruments

The practice of surveying offers a wide variety of precision instruments primarily for field use, most of which are associated with the recording of distance and angular measurements. These instruments were primarily made from brass; the larger examples were fitted with tripods and protective cases. These cases also held accessories for the instruments, and these can sometimes play a key part in their evaluation. Instruments in complete condition and showing little use will have much greater values than those that appear to have had moderate or heavy use. Instruments were never polished during use, and those that have been polished as decorator pieces are of little interest to most avid collectors. Our advisor for this category is Dale Beeks; he is listed in the Directory under Iowa.

Abney level, K&E, ca 1910, w/case	65.00
Alidade, coast-survey style high-post, CL Berger & Sons, '32	650.00
Alidade, telescopic, exploration type, 10"	425.00
Chain, 4-pole, Gurley NY, dirty, rust	120.00

Compass, FW & R King Balto, 1860s, 5" needle, 6" L	900.00
Compass, HM Poole, ca 1850	1,450.00
Compass, John Dupee, Boston, walnut case, ca 1760, 14"	1,955.00
Compass, pocket type, wooden housing, 3"	110.00
Compass, S Thaster & Son Boston, brass, 1850s, 3" dia, VG	175.00
Compass, telescopic vernier, Randolf	1,400.00
Compass, wooden, Am, unsgn, ca 1810, 12"	750.00
Jacob's staff, oak w/steel tip, octagonal	120.00
Level, combination, AS Aloe MO, 1930, 11¼" scope, 5" vial	350.00
Level, dumpy, Brunson, blk pnt	200.00
Level, engineer's, J Roach, ca 1875, 16½" scope	550.00
Level, wye, architect's, ca 1915, 11½" scope, 5" vial	300.00
Level, wye, builder's, 12" telescope	300.00
Level, wye, engineer's, Fennel Kassel, ca 1940, 18" scope	125.00
Level, wye, Gurley, ca 1880, 18"	550.00
Level, wye, Stackpole & Brother NY, 1875, 17½"	650.00
Level/transit, builder's, CL Berger & Sons, '40, 10½"	125.00
Level/transit, Henry Ware, Cincinnati OH, brass, 16" +stand	900.00
Plumb-bob, w/internal reel	200.00
Rod, #d stick, brass plate w/blk #s & letters, 0 in red, 81x2"	50.00
Solar attachment, Saegmuller; Bubb & Buff, 1940s, 6" scope	600.00
Staff, instrument; trn oak rod, brass end, iron drive point, 57"	100.00
Transit, blk pnt, ca 1930	225.00
Transit, CL Berger & Sons, 1945, 11" scope, 6¼"	450.00
Transit, FE Brandis NY, 1895, 10" scope, rfn, 6"	500.00
Transit, Keuffel & Esser NY, ca 1908, 11" scope, 5" vial	700.00
Transit, Mahn & Co MO, 1900, 11" scope, 4¼" compass, 6¼"	450.00
Transit, R Seelig Chicago, 1900s, 11¼" scope, 6¼" vial	500.00
Transit, Stackpole & Brother NY, ca 1855, 10½" scope, 6"	950.00
Transit, W&LE Gurley Troy NY, #1235	650.00
Tripod, transit type, telescopic legs	45.00

7506NR60EG, picture fr, European gold, sq, from $265 to	490.00
7550NR20029G, grapes, gold, med, from $500 to	555.00
7551NR100, butterfly, gold, from $1,500 to	1,530.00
7600NR109P, candle holder pin, from $200 to	450.00
7600NR121C, candle holder cup, from $490 to	500.00
7616NR000001, beaver mother, from $150 to	160.00
7619NR000002, Scotch terrier, from $100 to	115.00
7619NR000003, poodle, from $200 to	225.00
7620NR100000, walrus, from $175 to	195.00
7625NR50, partridge, from $140 to	155.00
7630NR40, hedgehog, med, from $175 to	215.00
7631NR30V2, mouse, sm, from $100 to	120.00
7631NR50, mouse, lg, from $750 to	1,065.00
7632NR30, turtle, sm, from $75 to	85.00
7633NR100000, Centenary swan, from $140 to	180.00
7637NR54, bear, sm, from $95 to	105.00
7637NR92, bear, king sz, from $2,250 to	2,750.00
7639NR55CG, butterfly, crystal & gold, from $250 to	320.00
7640NR100, Dumbo, 1990, from $1,140 to	1,250.00
7640NR60, elephant, lg, from $125 to	150.00
7641NR75V1, dachshund, from $130 to	155.00
7644NR41, blowfish, lg, from $160 to	175.00
7645NR100V2, falcon head, 2nd variation, lg, from $2,065 to	3,125.00
7647NR80, mallard, from $165 to	180.00
7658NR27, swan, mini, from $170 to	180.00
7659NR31, cat, mini, from $70 to	80.00
7678NR030, rabbit, recumbent, mini, from $70 to	80.00
92088, Christmas ornament, 1988, from $95 to	105.00
9406NR050001, Disneyworld 25th Anniversary paperweight, $180 to	215.00
9450005Z, toucan, on ped, sm, from $100 to	130.00
9540NR000031, Julia w/mandolin, from $70 to	80.00

Swarovski Crystal

The Swarovski family has been perfecting the glassmaker's art in Wattens, Austria, since 1895. Collectible figurines and desk items were introduced in 1977, and the Swarovski Collectors Society (SCS) was created in 1987. Featuring lead content of 30%+, these 'Silver Crystal' limited edition decorative accessories have attracted a following of over 200,000 dedicated collectors worldwide. Some designs were distributed regionally, making pursuit of retired items an interesting challenge that spans the globe. Most items have an etched mark on the underside. The first mark was a block-style SC. In 1989 the mark was changed to a Swan. Marks on larger items also include the name Swarovski. SCS figurines are further identified with the year and designer's initials. As the vigilance of Swarovski collectors has grown, their interest in all items of Swarovski manufacture has increased. In addition to Swarovski Silver Crystal, collectors also seek Trimlite, Giftware Suite, Swarovski Selections, Ebeling & Reuss, and private label productions by the Swarovski company. Prices listed below reflect the presence of complete original packing and enclosures, without which prices are compromised 10% to 35%.

CBNR2, elephant brooch, from $110 to	130.00
DO1X881CB, woodpeckers, #2, clear base, from $2,065 to	3,375.00
DO1X971, dragon, #11, from $440 to	490.00
D01X881M, woodpecker's mirror, from $80 to	185.00
SCMR88, cactus, from $115 to	140.00
69206, clown in cannon, from $100 to	115.00
7404NR30087, paperweight, Vitrail, rnd, med, from $80 to	90.00
7451NR60088, paperweight, carousel, Bermuda Blue, from $1,940 to	2,815.00
7467NR071000, dinner bell, lg, from $150 to	205.00
7474NR000027, town hall, from $220 to	240.00
7504NR030G, apple photo stand, gold, sm, from $150 to	175.00

Swastika Keramos

Swastika Keramos was a line of artware made by the Owens China Company of Minerva, Ohio, around 1902 – 04. It is characterized either by a coralene type of decoration (similar to the Opalesce line made by the J. B. Owens Pottery Company of Zanesville) or by the application of metallic lustres, usually in simple designs. Shapes are often plain and handles squarish and rather thick, suggestive of the Arts and Crafts style.

Ewer, comet & tree landscape, mc sky bkground, 10½"	850.00
Pitcher, broad leaves, gr on gold gloss, #704-L, 10", NM	180.00
Vase, scenic trees, metallic matt lustre, 11"	375.00
Vase, textured gr decor on wht over gold gloss, #7066, 7½"	160.00

Syracuse

Syracuse was a line of fine dinnerware and casual ware which was made for nearly a century by the Onondaga Pottery Company of Syracuse, New York. Early patterns were marked O.P. Company. Collectors of American dinnerware are focusing their attention on reassembling some of their many lovely patterns. In 1966 the firm became officially known as the Syracuse China Company in order to better identify with the name of their popular chinaware. Many of the patterns were marked with the shape and color names (Old Ivory, Federal, etc.), not the pattern names. By 1971 dinnerware geared for use in the home was discontinued, and the company turned to the manufacture of hotel, restaurant, and other types of commercial tableware.

Arcadia, cup & saucer, demitasse	30.00
Arcadia, plate, dessert; 7⅛"	18.00

Bombay, bowl, vegetable; gold trim, w/lid 98.00
Bombay, cup & saucer, gold trim 30.00
Bombay, platter, gold trim, 16" 65.00
Briarcliff, bowl, vegetable; w/lid 130.00
Briarcliff, cream soup 25.00
Briarcliff, platter, 12" 57.50
Circus, bowl, cereal; dog & ball, Union Pacific RR, 6" 70.00
Circus, plate, clown face, Union Pacific RR, 1951, 8½" 70.00

Cup and saucer, demitasse; blue with white leaves, $10.00.

Jefferson, bowl, vegetable; w/lid 98.00
Jefferson, cup & saucer 32.00
Jefferson, plate, dinner; 10¼" 30.00
Jefferson, rim soup 26.00
Lady Mary, plate, dinner; 9¾" 22.00
Lady Mary, sugar bowl 36.00
Madame Butterfly, bowl, dessert 8.00
Madame Butterfly, bowl, oval, 10¼" 30.00
Madame Butterfly, creamer & sugar bowl w/lid 45.00
Madame Butterfly, cup & saucer, demitasse 30.00
Madame Butterfly, deep plate, 9" 12.00
Madame Butterfly, gravy boat, attached underplate 40.00
Madame Butterfly, plate, dessert; 6¼" 10.00
Madame Butterfly, plate, 10" 15.00
Madame Butterfly, platter, 16" 50.00
Minuet, bowl, vegetable; oval 50.00
Minuet, cup & saucer 32.00
Minuet, plate, salad 17.50
Minuet, platter, med 82.50
Sharon, bowl, vegetable; oval, 10" 47.50
Sharon, plate, dinner 27.50
Sherwood, cup & saucer 18.00
Sherwood, gravy boat 68.00
Sherwood, plate, bread & butter 6.00
Sherwood, platter, 14" 65.00
Sherwood, platter, 16" rim, brass mts 35.00
Singing Cowboys, chop plate 60.00
Singing Cowboys, mug 25.00
Singing Cowboys, plate, 7½" 18.00
Stansbury, bowl, vegetable; w/lid 125.00
Stansbury, cream soup, w/underplate 30.00
Stansbury, plate, salad; 8" 16.00
Suzanne, bowl, Federal shape, oval, 10½" 50.00
Suzanne, cup & saucer, Federal shape 25.00
Suzanne, gravy boat 75.00
Suzanne, plate, Federal shape, 6½" 12.00
Suzanne, platter, Federal shape, 14" 50.00
Sweetheart, creamer 37.50
Sweetheart, cup & saucer 26.00
Sweetheart, plate, dinner; 10¼" 24.00
Sweetheart, plate, salad; 8" 14.00
Sweetheart, sugar bowl, w/lid 45.00

Syrups

Values are for old, original syrups. Beware of reproductions and watch handle area for cracks! See also various manufacturers (such as Northwood) and specific types of glass. Our coadvisors are Jeff Bradfield and Dale MacAllister; they are listed in the Directory under Virginia.

Alba, milk glass, w/decor 95.00
Baby Coinspot, wht opal 150.00
Baby Inverted Thumbrint, bl, Hobbs 175.00
Bubble Lattice, bl opal 450.00
Challinor's Forget-Me-Not, gr opaque 300.00
Chrysanthemum Base Swirl, wht opal 275.00
Coin Spot, bl opal 245.00
Coin Spot & Swirl, bl opal 175.00
Cone, pk cased 375.00
Daisy & Fern, bl opal, bulbous 285.00
Daisy & Fern, cranberry opal, LG Wright, 1960s 125.00
Daisy & Fern, cranberry opal, 1890s 350.00
Diamond Spearhead, vaseline opal 575.00
Empress, clear w/gold 225.00
Florette, pk satin 350.00
Flower & Pleat 195.00
Heisey Fancy Loop 150.00
Hobbs Hexagon Block, ruby stain 250.00
Hobnail, bl opal, Hobbs 325.00
Invt T'print, bl opal, tapered 225.00
Jeweled Moon & Star, w/decor 295.00
Klondike, amber stain 550.00
Lincoln Drape, appl hdl 345.00
Polka Dot, bl opal, bulbous 450.00
Reverse Swirl, bl opal 350.00
Reverse Swirl, canary yel 450.00
Reverse Swirl, cranberry opal 600.00
Ribbed Lattice, bl opal 395.00
Snail 165.00
Stars & Stripes, milk glass, orig pewter lid 150.00
Sunk Honeycomb, ruby stain, orig pewter lid 200.00
Sunset, bl opaque 250.00
Thousand Eye, bl 200.00
Windows Swirl, cranberry opal 800.00
Winged Scroll, gr 550.00

Target Balls

Prior to 1880 when the clay pigeon was invented, blown glass target balls were used extensively for shotgun competitions. Approximately 2¾" in diameter, these balls were hand blown into a three-piece mold. All have a ragged hole where the blowpipe was twisted free. Target balls date from approximately 1840 (English) to World War I, although they were most widely used in the 1870 – 1880 period. Common examples are unmarked except for the blower's code — dots, crude numerals, etc. Some balls were embossed in a dot or diamond pattern so they were more likely to shatter when struck by shot, and some have names and/or patent dates. When evaluating condition, bubbles and other minor manufacturing imperfections are acceptable; cracks are not. The prices below are for mint condition examples.

Amber w/emb ribs, horizontal or vertical 150.00
Bogardus' Glass Ball Pat'd April 10 1877, amber, Am 350.00
Bogardus' Glass Ball Pat'd April 10 1877, cobalt, 2¾" 800.00
Bogardus' Glass Ball Pat'd April 10 1877, other than amber, Am ..800.00

CTB Co, blk pitch, Pat dates on bottom, Am 250.00
Dmn Quilt w/o center band, yel-amber, 2¾" 250.00
Dmn Quilt w/plain center band, clear ground top, Am 150.00
Dmn Quilt w/plain center band, cobalt, 2⅝" 250.00
Dmn Quilt w/shooter emb in 2 panels, clear, English 300.00
Dmn Quilt w/shooter emb in 2 panels, gr or purple, English 500.00
EE Eaton Guns & C 53 State St Chicago, golden yel-amber, 2⅝" .1,000.00
Flesschenfabriek Boers & CP Delft, emb dmns, lt olive, 2⅝" 300.00
For Hockey's Pat Trap, gr, English 850.00
Glashuttenewotte Un Charlottenburg, clear, emb dmns, 2⅝" 700.00
Glashuttenewotte Un Charlottenburg, med yel-olive, 2⅝" 1,000.00
Great Western Gun Works, Pittsburgh, amber, Am 900.00
Gurd & Son, London, Ontario, amber, Canadian 500.00
Hobnail w/horizontal ribs along seams, yel-amber, 2¾" 800.00
Ilmenau (Thur) Sophiehutte, amber, Dmn Quilt, Germany 425.00
Ira Paine's Filled Ball Pat Oct 23 1877, amber, Am 250.00
Ira Paine's Filled Ball Pat Oct 23 1877, other than amber, Am ..800.00
Liddle & Keading Agents, dk bl-aqua, 2¾" 5,000.00
NB Glass Works Perth, other than pale gr, English 200.00
NB Glass Works Perth, pale gr, English 100.00
Plain, amber w/mold mks 65.00
Plain, clear w/mold mks 1,000.00
Plain, cobalt w/mold mks 150.00
Plain, dk grape amethyst w/mold mks, 2¾" dia 250.00
Plain, dk teal gr w/mold mks, 2¾" 300.00
T Jones, Gunmaker, Blackburn, pale bl, English 150.00
Van Cutsem A St Quentin, cobalt, 2¾" dia 100.00
WW Greener, St Mary's Works, various colors, English, ea 350.00

Related Memorabilia

Ball thrower, dbl; old red pnt, ME Card, Pat...78, 79, VG 900.00
Clay birds, Winchester, Pat May 29 1917, 1 flight in box 100.00
Pitch bird, blk DUVROCK 1.00
Shell, dummy, w/single window, any brand 35.00
Shell, dummy shotgun, Winchester, window w/powder, 6" 125.00
Shell set, dummy, Gamble Stores, 2 window shells, 3 cut out 125.00
Shell set, dummy, Winchester, 5 window shells 175.00
Shell set, dummy shotgun, Peters, 6 window shells+full box 175.00
Shotshell loader, rosewood/brass, Parker Bros, Pat 1884 ....50.00
Target, Am, sheet metal, rod ends mk Pat Feb 8 '21, set 25.00
Target, blk japanned sheet metal, Bussey Patentee, London 50.00
Target, BUST-O, blk or wht breakable wafer 20.00
Trap, DUVROCK, w/blk pitch birds 250.00
Trap, MO-SKEET-O, w/birds 150.00

Tea Caddies

Because tea was once regarded as a precious commodity, special boxes called caddies were used to store the tea leaves. They were made from various materials: porcelain, carved and inlaid woods, and metals ranging from painted tin or tole to engraved silver. Our advisor for this category is Tina Carter; she is listed in the Directory under California.

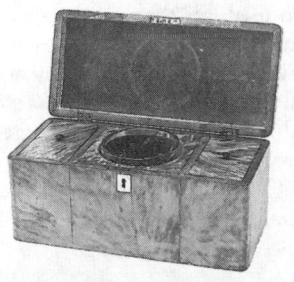

English tortoise-shell tea caddy, fitted compartments with lids, crystal mixing bowl, ivory-inlaid panel on lid, 1850s, 5x12x5¾", $1,000.00.

Ceramic, floral, bl & wht, German mk, rpr, 5½" 100.00
Cherry w/scrolled compass star cartouch & inlay, 12½" 2,300.00
Creamware w/floral decor, wear, 5¼" 700.00
Mahog w/brass bail & escutcheon, old finish, 9" 500.00
Papier-mache, lacquered w/inlaid MOP flowers & gilt, 6x11x8" ...700.00
SP, classic shape w/monogram, Wilcox, 4" 50.00
SP, hexagonal w/decor sides, 7" 50.00

Tea Leaf Ironstone

Tea Leaf Ironstone became popular in the 1880s when middle-class American housewives became bored with the plain white stone china that English potters had been exporting to this country for nearly a century. The original design has been credited to Anthony Shaw of Longport, who decorated the plain ironstone with a hand-painted copper lustre design of bands and leaves. Originally known as Lustre Band and Sprig, the pattern has since come to be known as Tea Leaf Lustre. It was produced with minor variations by many different firms both in England and the United States. By the early 1900s, it had become so commonplace that it had lost much of its appeal.

Items marked Red Cliff are reproductions made from 1950 until 1980 for this distributing and decorating company of Chicago, Illinois. Hall China provided many of the blanks.

Our advice for this category comes from Home Place Antiques, whose address is listed in the Directory under Illinois.

Baker, Wilkinson, 9½x6¾" 30.00
Bone dish, scalloped, Meakin 75.00
Bowl, vegetable; Cable, w/lid, Burgess 235.00
Bowl, vegetable; Empress, Adams, w/lid 125.00
Bowl, vegetable; Fish Hook, w/lid, Meakin, 10½x6½" 195.00
Bowl, vegetable; medallion finial & hdl, Mellor-Taylor 185.00
Bowl, vegetable; Pagoda, ribbed, hdls, w/lid, Wedgwood, 11x7" .225.00
Bowl, vegetable; Sunburst, ftd, w/lid, Shaw, 11½x5½", EX 225.00
Brush box, Cable, Burgess 325.00
Butter dish, Fish Hook, Meakin, w/drain 175.00
Butter dish, Little Cable, Furnival 200.00
Butter pat, Anthony Shaw & Sons, VG 16.00
Butter pat, Meakin, 2¾" sq 14.00
Cake plate, 8-sided, Adams Microtex, 11⅛x8¾" 45.00
Chamber pot, Bamboo, Alfred Meakin, w/lid 285.00
Chamber pot, Square Ridged, Mellor-Taylor, EX 325.00
Coffeepot, Bamboo, Meakin, 9" 225.00
Coffeepot, Chinese shape, Shaw, 10" 275.00
Compote, fruit; ped ft, Royal Ironstone, Meakin, 5½x8½", NM ..375.00
Creamer, Adams Microtex 60.00
Creamer, Morning Glory, Elsmore & Forster 285.00
Cup & saucer, Adams Microtex 35.00
Cup & saucer, handleless; Paneled, Shaw 95.00
Cup & saucer, Lily of the Valley, Shaw 125.00
Cup & saucer, ribbed below waist & around saucer, Wedgwood ..75.00
Cup & saucer, str sided, Meakin, 2¾", EX 85.00
Cup plate, Wilkinson, 3¼" 60.00
Egg cup, Boston, Meakin 350.00
Gravy boat, Bamboo, Alfred Meakin 75.00
Gravy boat, Laurel Wreath, Elsmore & Forster 95.00
Gravy boat, simple sq, unmk 65.00
Pitcher, hot water; Charles II-type, Mayer 250.00
Pitcher, Teaberry, NY shape, Clementson Bros, 8½" 395.00
Plate, Chinese shape, Shaw, 7⅞" 17.50
Plate, Chinese shape, Shaw, 9½" 45.00
Plate, gold lustre, Bridgewood, 7" 12.00
Plate, Meakin, 7⅞" 14.00

Plate, Meakin, 9¾"	35.00
Plate, Morning Glory, 9¾"	45.00
Plate, Red Cliff, 8¼"	18.00
Plate, Teaberry, 8"	35.00
Plate, Wedgwood, 8¼"	18.00
Platter, Brocade, Meakin, 12¾x9⅛"	45.00
Platter, rectangular, ribbed, Wedgwood, 12"	75.00
Platter, Square Ridged, Mellor-Taylor, 12x9½"	65.00
Platter, Wedgwood, 14x10¼"	65.00
Relish, Lily of the Valley, Shaw	175.00
Relish, oval, Shaw	75.00
Sauce tureen, Bamboo, Meakin, w/lid & ladle	365.00
Saucer, Lily of the Valley, mini, 4¼"	50.00
Shaving mug, leaf at hdl, Shaw	200.00
Shaving mug, wheel at top, sq ft, sq hdl	225.00
Soap dish, Cable, Anthony Shaw	275.00
Soap dish, gold lustre, Powell & Bishop	110.00
Soap dish, Lily of the Valley, Shaw, w/liner	425.00
Soup, flanged, Meakin, 8¾"	30.00
Sugar bowl, gold lustre, w/lid, unmk, EX	48.00
Sugar bowl, Lily of the Valley, Shaw, 5½x6½"	145.00
Sugar bowl, Morning Glory, Portland shape, Elsmore & Forster	225.00
Toothpick holder, Mellor-Taylor	145.00
Wash bowl, Meakin, 14¾"	235.00
Wash bowl & pitcher, Cable, Shaw	525.00
Wash bowl & pitcher, Lily of the Valley, Shaw, +2 pcs	675.00

Teapots

Teapots have become popular collectibles in recent years with a surge in tea shops featuring tea, teapots, and serving afternoon tea. Collectors should be aware of modern teapots which imitate older, similar versions. Study the types of pottery, porcelain, and china, as well as the marks. Multicolored, detailed marks over the glaze represent modern pieces. Teapots made in the last thirty years are quite collectible but generally don't demand the same prices as their antique counterparts.

A wide range of teapots can be found by the avid collector. Those from before 1880 are more apt to be found in museums or sold at quality auction houses. Almost every pottery and porcelain manufacturer in Asia, Europe, and America have produced teapots. Some are purely decorative and whimsical, while others are perfect for brewing a pot of tea. Tea drinkers should beware of odd-shaped spouts which sputter and drip. Reproductions to be aware of: majolica styles with modern marks, Blue Willow which has been made continuously for almost two centuries, and those marked Made in China (older teapots have 'chop marks' in Chinese).

Refer to various manufacturers' names for further listings. Our advisor for this category is Tina M. Carter, listed in the Directory under California. Her book, *Teapots*, is available at bookstores or direct from the author.

ALB, dripless, mottled, England, ca 1920	52.00
Anniversary, 50th; floral, Price Kensington	48.00
Automobile, silver lustre, Carlton Ware, England	495.00
Ballerina, music box & movement, Japan, ca 1960	30.00
Barge, brn, emb mk, Derbyshire, England, lg	75.00
Barge, emb floral decor, A Present..., ca 1800s	1,000.00
Basket, picnic teapot & 2 cups, hinged lid, padded, China	100.00
Belleek, Am, ornate detail, palette mk, ca 1900	850.00
Ben Franklin figural, ceramic w/metal hdl	65.00
Beswick Ware, Dicken's characters, England, ca 1930	75.00
Boston Tea Party, commemorative, Davison Newman, +cr/sug	45.00
Cast metal, scenes, octagonal, China, ca 1920	65.00
Charles & Diana, brn pottery, Wales CM, 2½"	78.00
Cloisonne, animal or designs, China, mini	35.00

Copper, Art Deco style, enamel decor, ball ft, China	38.00
Crinoline Lady, Made in Czechoslovakia	75.00
Crinoline Lady (Cinderella), Sadler, England, ca 1930	65.00
Cube, fleur-de-lis, Royal Crownford, England	25.00
Cube, HP, Made in Japan, ca 1940	20.00
Cube, Los Angeles Steamship Co, Clews, England	38.00
Duck, Peking; HP, wicker hdl, no mk, China, ca 1920	75.00
Edward VII commemorative, pk lustre, England, 2-cup	250.00
Granny, mc, Lingard or HJ Wood, England, 1930	55.00
Granny, Queensware, modern	35.00
Granny Ann, mk USA, Shawnee	80.00
Iced tea dispenser, USA, 2-pc, lg	175.00
Jim Beam, characters, ltd ed, Wade	48.00
Lefton, cozy set, violets, ca 1950	32.00
Lipton's, oval, ribbed, Fraunfelter, ca 1930	35.00
Lipton's, rnd, various colors, Hall China Co	30.00
Man in tux forms hdl, lady forms pot, ceramic, unmk, modern	35.00
Meakin, Alfred; blk trim, china relief, England	38.00
Pewter, New Amsterdam Silver Co, USA	35.00
Pottery, pk, mk Ford, USA, 1-cup	25.00
Rough glaze, buff sharkskin, tan, slip decor, Japan, 1920s	28.00
RS Prussia, scalloped hdl/edge, HP decor, unmk	75.00
Sadler, folklore, Robin Hood/King Arthur/etc, ca 1990	35.00
Salada Tea, promotional item, USA, 1-cup	25.00

Satsuma-style, shiny green with gold lustre blown-out elephants, dragon spout, elephant finial, Japan mark, 5½", $60.00.

Photo courtesy Carole Bess White

Silverplate, Rococo style, Community	70.00
Snow White w/Dwarfs, musical, Walt Disney Prod	75.00
Spode's Tower, bl/wht transfer, London shape, England, VG	58.00
Tiffin, tea liqueur, depot decanter, Germany, 1960	95.00
WWII, Esc to US by Royal Navy or Allied Fleets, brn, England	45.00
Yxing, padded box, chop mk, China repro	45.00

Teco

Teco artware was made by the American Terra Cotta and Ceramic Company, located near Chicago, Illinois. The firm was established in 1886 and until 1901 produced only brick, sewer tile, and other redware. Their early glaze was inspired by the matt green made popular by Grueby. 'Teco Green' was made for nearly ten years. It was similar to Grueby's, yet with a subtle silver-gray cast. The company was one of the first in the United States to perfect a true crystalline glaze. The only decoration used was through the modeling and glazing techniques; no hand painting was attempted. Favored motifs were naturalistic leaves and flowers. The company broadened their lines to include garden pottery and faience tiles and panels. New matt glazes (browns, yellows, blue, and rose) were added to the green in 1910. By 1922 the artware lines were discontinued; the company was sold in 1930.

Values are dictated by size and shape, with architectural and organic forms being more desirable. Teco is usually marked with a vertical impressed device comprised of a large 'T' to the left of the remaining three letters.

Bowl, gr, scalloped shoulder, 2¼x8" 275.00
Mug, gr, mk, 3¾" 125.00
Vase, aventurine, teardrop form, 4" 325.00
Vase, dk gr, gourd w/lobed rim & emb organic decor, 10x7" ...3,000.00
Vase, gr, bulbous w/ring neck, 4" 400.00
Vase, gr, bulbous w/sm neck, 5" 400.00
Vase, gr, dbl gourd w/in 4 curving buttresses, 6½x5½" 3,500.00
Vase, gr, rtcl interwoven blade leaves/tulips, 11x6" 5,500.00
Vase, gr, shouldered w/trumpet neck, 11½" 700.00
Vase, gr, str w/lobed rim, organic buttresses, Moreau, 13" 2,400.00
Vase, gr, 3-sided, paper label, 8x4" 950.00
Vase, gr, 4 finger-like lobes on invt cone, 9x4" 1,300.00
Vase, gr w/charcoal, tulip caged by 4 buttresses, 12", EX 2,400.00
Vase, gr/gunmetal w/emb calla lilies, cylindrical, 13x5" 850.00
Vase, lt gr, ovoid w/2 full-length buttress hdls, 5½x2¾" 700.00
Vase, mustard, cylinder w/full-length buttress hdls, 5½" 650.00
Vase, pea gr, daffodils on long stems, #60, 8½" 1,100.00
Wall pocket, gr, invt teardrop w/leaves, hdls, 15" 2,000.00
Wall pocket, gr, vertical leaves, 3 are hdls, 15x9" 2,000.00

Teddy Bear Collectibles

The story of Teddy Roosevelt's encounter with the bear cub has been oft recounted with varying degrees of accuracy, so it will suffice to say that it was as a result of this incident in 1902 that the teddy bear got his name. These appealing little creatures are enjoying renewed popularity with collectors today. To one who has not yet succumbed to their obvious charms, one bear seems to look very much like another. How to tell the older ones? Look for long snouts, jointed limbs, large feet and felt paws, long curving arms, and glass or shoe-button eyes. Most old bears have a humped back and are made of mohair stuffed with straw or excelsior. Cute expressions, original clothes, a nice personality, and, of course, good condition add to their value. Early Steiff bears in mint condition may go for a minimum of $100.00 per inch (for a small bear) up to $200.00 per inch (for one 20" high or larger). These are easily recognized by the trademark button within the ear. Our advisor for this category is Candace Gunther; she is listed in the Directory under California. For further information we recommend *Teddy Bears, Annalee's & Steiff Animals*, by Margaret Fox Mandel, available from Collector Books. See also Toys, Steiff.

Key: jtd — jointed

Unknown maker, teddy on trike, key wind, metal eyes, embroidered mouth and nose, worn, 7", $695.00.

Bears

Am, blond mohair, jtd, shoe button eyes, ca 1906, 16", M 2,800.00
Am, brn mohair, glass eyes, 1920s, 18", EX 300.00
Am, gold mohair, button eyes, jtd, straw stuffed, hump, 22" 415.00
Am, gold mohair, glass eyes, jtd, leather pads, 31", VG 275.00
Am, gold mohair w/integral polka dot dress, glass eyes, jtd, 28" ..100.00

Chad Valley, gold mohair, rexine pads, 14", M 375.00
East Germany, brn mohair, glass eyes, gold ribbon, 1950s, 10", NM .100.00
Germany, plush, glass eyes, straw stuffed, 1945-52, 11", EX 250.00
Germany, tan mohair, amber glass eyes, 1940-50, 6¾", VG 150.00
Ideal (?), blond mohair, jtd, button eyes, excelsior, 1910, 18", VG ..1,000.00
Knickerbocker, jtd, gold-yel, rnd ears, rpl eyes, 34", VG 400.00
Schuco, musical, yes/no, gold mohair, 16", M 2,000.00
Schuco, tipped, 1930s, 20", M 750.00
Steiff, beige mohair, brn floss nose/mouth, 1960s, 6", M 200.00
Steiff, Brennessal fabric, on wheels, button, 1904, 7", EX 750.00
Steiff, gold prickly mohair, w/button, 1907, 4", NM 975.00
Steiff, Jackie Jubilee Bear, button/tag, 1953, 13¾", M 2,600.00
Steiff, Orig Teddy, caramel mohair, button/tag, 14", EX 365.00
Steiff, Orig Teddy, complete ID, 16½", M 1,650.00
Steiff, Orig Teddy, dk brn mohair, chest tag, 1950, 6", NM 600.00
Steiff, Orig Teddy, gold mohair, 1950s, 3½", NM 250.00
Steiff, Orig Teddy, wht, no ID, 1950s, 3½", EX 285.00
Steiff, Record Teddy, wooden wheels, w/button, 1920s, 12", EX ...5,000.00
Steiff, rod type, mohair w/wax nose, rpl pads, ca 1903, 20", EX 3,500.00
Steiff, Zotty, complete ID, 14", M 1,600.00
Steiff, Zotty, complete ID, 8", M 425.00
Steiff, Zotty, frosted mohair, glass eyes, button, 1950s, 17", NM ...600.00
Steiff, Zotty, redwood mohair (unusual), button, 11", NM 325.00
Swiss, mohair, jtd, button eyes, Felpa..., 1950-60, 6½", M 125.00
Unmk, brn mohair, jtd, button eyes, embr nose/mouth, 11", G ..125.00
Unmk, frosted mohair, open mouth, 1940s, 21", NM 275.00
Unmk, gold mohair, jtd, brn glass eyes, rexine paws, 29", EX 150.00
Unmk, gold mohair, jtd, straw stuffed, hump, 22", G 100.00
Unmk, gold mohair, lg glass eyes, 1940s, 4½", EX 75.00
Unmk, wht mohair, plastic brads on outside, 5", EX 75.00
Unmk, yel mohair, glass eyes, embr nose, excelsior, 1920s, 27", G .300.00

Telephones

Since Alexander Graham Bell's first successful telephone communication, the phone itself has undergone a complete evolution in style as well as efficiency. Early models, especially those wall types with ornately carved oak boxes, are of special interest to collectors. Also of value are the candlestick phones from the early part of the century and any related memorabilia.

Am Electric, str shaft desk stand, 1903, 11", VG 135.00
Am Telecom, 1972, EX 40.00
Automatic Electric, dial, 1950s 15.00
Automatic Electric monophone, Bakelite, cradle type, 1920s, EX ..85.00
Danish Fr, Bakelite, 1913, EX 75.00
Fr, Bakelite, NP brass w/mc transfer, orig wiring, 13½" 110.00
Fr, w/eavesdropper 60.00
Kellogg, candlestick, Bakelite & metal, blk finish, 12" 110.00
Kellogg, wood, oak mt, Pat'd Nov 26, 1901 on speaker, 23", EX ...290.00
Leich, hand crank, wall type, EX orig 275.00
Leich Magneto 30.00
National Cash Register, EX 145.00
North Electric H-6, blk, 'Bogart' phone, EX 85.00
Stromberg, tapered desk stand, ca 1900, EX 650.00
Stromberg-Carlson, candlestick type 110.00
Stromberg-Carlson intercom, blk Bakelite, EX 50.00
Table model, golden oak, metal plate: Long Distance, 40", EX ..2,650.00
Western Electric, dial, desk stand, 1920s, 12", EX 250.00
Western Electric, oak, wall type, complete, EX 300.00
Western Electric, school wall intercom, brass/Bakelite, pr 100.00
Western Electric #202, blk metal cradle type, 1931, EX 120.00
Western Electric #500, blk cradle type, 1950s, EX 15.00

Blue Bell Paperweights

First issued in the early 1900s, bell-shaped glass paperweights were used as 'give-aways' and/or presented to telephone company executives as tokens of appreciation. The paperweights were used to prevent stacks of papers from blowing off the desks in the days of overhead fans. Over the years they have all but vanished — some taken by retiring employees, others accidentally broken. The weights came to be widely used for advertising by individual telephone companies; and as the smaller companies merged to form larger companies, more and more new paperweights were created. They were widely distributed with the opening of the first transcontinental telephone line in 1915. The bell-shaped paperweight embossed 'Opening of Trans-Pacific Service, Dec. 23, 1931,' in peacock blue glass is very rare, and the price is negotiable. In 1972 the first Pioneer bell paperweights were made to sell to raise funds for the charities the Pioneers support. This has continued to the present day. These bell paperweights have also become 'collectibles.' For further study we recommend *Blue Bell Paperweights, 1992 Revised Edition*, and its accompanying *1995 Addendum* by Jacqueline C. Linscott; she is listed in the Directory under Florida.

Bell of Pennsylvania 1879-1979, dk Peacock **40.00**
Bell System (front/bk), Region 12 (base emb), ruby red **40.00**
Bell System (front/bk), TPA Region 12 (base emb), ruby red carnival ..**50.00**
Bell System Chesapeake-Potomic Telephone...& Associated..., Ice Blue ..**150.00**
Bell Telephone Company, cobalt **175.00**
Break-Up of The Bell System, emerald gr **50.00**
Commemorating Florida's 1,000,000 Telephone, cobalt **200.00**
Compliments of Millville Kiwanis Club, Ice Blue **900.00**
Diamond Jubilee 1911-1986 - 75 Years of Community Service, lt bl ..**25.00**
Northern Louisiana Telephone Company, Peacock ....**open**
Opening of Trans-Pacific Service Dec 23, 1931, Peacock ....**open**
Pacific Bell/Nevada Bell, blk glass etched in gold & silver **75.00**
Pays 7% Mountain States Telephone, Peacock **225.00**
Save Time-Telephone/Save Steps—Telephone, Ice Blue **75.00**
Telephone Pioneers of America, Tea Rose **25.00**
The Central District & Printing Telegraph Company, Peacock .**500.00**
The Southwestern Bell Telephone Company, Peacock **175.00**
The Southwestern Telegraph & Telephone Company, cobalt ...**375.00**
Western Electric Company, (inkwell), cobalt **600.00**

Novelty Telephones

Bart Simpson, Columbia Tel-Com, 1990, MIB, $35.00.

AC Spark Plug, figural **35.00**
Alvin (of the Chipmunks) **60.00**
Beetle Bailey, 1983, MIB **95.00**
Bozo the Clown, 1980s, MIB **75.00**
Crest Sparkle, MIB **55.00**
Harley-Davidson motorcycle, lg **60.00**
Joe Cook, Seika, 1992 ....**60.00**

Keebler Elf, NM **100.00**
Kermit the Frog, touchtone, 1970s, EX **160.00**
Kermit the Frog, 1970s, MIB **225.00**
Little Green, Sprout **75.00**
Mickey Mouse, pnt plastic, Am Telecomm Corp, 1975, 10", EX+ ..**100.00**
Mickey Mouse, Western Electric, 1976, EX **135.00**
Oscar Mayer Weiner, EX **65.00**
Snoopy, Western Electric, 1976 ....**175.00**
Snoopy & Woodstock, pnt plastic, Am Telecomm Corp, 1976, NM **95.00**
Super Bowl XIX, full-sz football w/hand set, NM **70.00**
Superman, dial, early version **500.00**
Winnie the Pooh, sq base, from $225 to **250.00**

Related Memorabilia

Almanac, Bell Telephone, 1950 ....**10.00**
Booklet, How To Build Rural Telephone Lines, ca 1900 ....**15.00**
Coin saver, Bell Telephone, early attachment **75.00**
Shade, pnt glass bell shape, Telephone, wht w/bl, 14", EX **300.00**
Sign, Bell System, porc, flanged, roped bell, 16" sq, VG **200.00**
Sign, Bell System Public Telephone, convex porc, 7" dia **65.00**
Sign, Bell Telephone, 2-sided porc, 5½x12", EX **145.00**
Sign, Public Telephone, early Bell, rnd, EX **190.00**
Test box, portable, oak, w/carrying strap, all orig, EX **45.00**

Telescopes

Antique telescopes were sold in large quantities to sailors, astronomers, voyeurs, and the military but survive in relatively few numbers because their glass lenses and brass tubes were easily damaged. Even scarcer are antique reflecting telescopes, which use a polished metal mirror to magnify the world. Telescopes used for astronomy give an inverted image, but most old telescopes were used for marine purposes and have more complicated optics that show the world right-side up. Spyglasses are smaller, hand-held telescopes that collapse into their tube and focus by drawing out the tube to the correct length. A more compact instrument, with three or four sections, is also more delicate, and sailors usually preferred a single-draw spyglass. They are almost always of brass, occasionally of nickel silver or silver plate, and usually covered with leather, or sometimes a beautiful rosewood veneer. Solid wood barrel spyglasses (with a brass draw tube) tend to be early and rare. Before the middle of the 1800s, makers put their names in elaborate script on the smallest draw tube, but as 1900 approached, most switched to plain block printing. From the WWII era, British instruments by a variety of makers are commonly found, sharing a format of a 2" objective, 30" long with three draws extended, a tapered main tube, and sometimes having low- and high-power oculars and beautiful leather cases. U.S. Navy WWII spyglasses are quite common but have outstanding optics and focus by twisting the eyepiece, which makes them weather-proof. The Quartermaster (Q.M.) 16x spyglass is 31" long, with a tapered barrel and a 2½" objective. The Officer of the Deck (O.D.D.) is a 23" cylinder with a 1½" objective. Very massive, short, brass telescopes are usually gun sights or ship equipment and have little interest to most collectors. World War II marked the first widespread use of coated optics, which can be recognized by a colored film on the objective lens. Collectible post-WWII telescopes include early refractors by Unitron or Fecker and reflectors by Cave or Questar. Modern spotting scopes often use a prism to erect the image and are of great interest if made by the best makers, including Nikon and Zeiss. Several modern makers still use lacquered brass, and many replica instruments have been produced.

A telescope with no maker's name is much less interesting than a signed instrument, and 'Made in France' is the most common mark on old spyglasses. Dollond of London made instruments for two hundred years, and this is probably the most common name on antiques; but because of their important technical innovations and very high quality, Dollond telescopes are always valuable. Bardou, Paris, telescopes are also of very high quality. Bardou is another relatively common name, since they were a prolific maker for many years, and their spyglasses were sold by Sears. Alvin Clark and Sons were the most prolific early American makers, in operation from the 1850s to the 1920s, and their astronomical telescopes are of great historical import.

Spyglasses are delicate instruments that were subject to severe use under all weather conditions. Cracked or deeply scratched optics are impossible to repair and lower the value considerably. Most lenses are doublets, two lenses glued together, and deteriorated cement is common. This looks like crazed glaze and is fairly difficult to repair. Dents in the tube and damaged or missing leather covering can usually be fixed. The best test of a telescope is to use it, and the image should be sharp and clear. Any accessories, eyepieces, erecting prisms, or quality cases can add significantly to value. The following prices assume that the telescope is in very good to fine condition and give the objective lens (obj.) diameter, which is the most important measurement of a telescope.

Our advisor for this category is Peter Abrahams, who studies and collects telescopes and other optics. Please contact him, especially to exchange reference material. (See his comments concerning on-line auctions under Binoculars; they are applicable to telescopes as well.) Mr. Abrahams is listed in the Directory under Oregon. (Please include SASE with questions.)

Key: obj — objective lens

Adams, London, wooden bbl, rack & pinion fine focus, cased .1,300.00
Bardou & Son Paris, brass bbl, floor standing, on tripod, VG ..1,500.00
Bardou & Son Paris, 4-drw, 33X power, 36", VG 200.00
Chapman-London, 1-draw, 10-sided, 18th C, extends to 31", EX ...950.00
Dollond, London, captain's spy glass, 1-draw, SP, early, 29" 600.00
Dollond, London, 10-sided reverse-tapered wooden bbl, 18th C, 33" .1,100.00
Dollond, london, 2-draw, mahog/brass, 31", EX 1,100.00
Dollond, London, 2-draw, triple table mt, w/case/3 eyepcs 2,750.00
Gilbert & Wright, London, 3-draw, wooden, brass tripod, EX 1,050.00
Heath & Co...London for J Motion..., 1-draw, NP brass, 35", EX ...350.00
J Harris London Night or Day, 1-draw, wood bbl, 36", EX 350.00
T Cook & Sons, York & London, 5" main obj, lens, 80", EX 3,250.00
Unmk, 1-draw, wooden bbl, ca 1800, 48", EX 800.00
Unmk, 1-draw, wooden bbl, 11½x⅝" dia, EX 250.00
Unmk, 3-draw, brass bbl, good optics, polished, 29" 250.00
Unmk (finely made), 1-draw, brass, sliding lens covers, 37", EX ...400.00
Unmk night & day, 2-draw, brass & leather, fine optics, 19" 110.00
US Navy mks, 4-draw, wooden bbl, good optics, 36", VG 375.00
US Navy quartermaster's, polished brass, sharp optics, 1942, NM ...375.00
Wood-Abraham...Liverpool, rack & pinion focus adjust, tripod .700.00

Televisions

Many early TVs have escalated in value over the last few years. Pre-1943 sets (usually with only one to five channels) are often worth $500.00 to $5,000.00. Unusually styled small-screen wooden 1940s TVs are 'hot'; but most metal, Bakelite, and large-screen sets are still shunned by collectors. Color TVs from the 1950s with 16" or smaller tubes are valuable; larger color sets are not. One of our advisors for this category is Harry Poster, author of *Poster's Radio & Television Price Guide 1920 – 1990, 2nd Edition*; he is listed in the Directory under New Jersey. Another source of information is *Collector's Guide to Vintage Televisions* by Bryan Durbal and Glenn Bubenheimer (Collector Books).

Key: t/t — table-top

Admiral #17T12, mohog Bakelite, 1948, 7" screen 150.00
Admiral #19A11, Bakelite, t/t, dk brn, 1948, 7" screen 125.00
Airline, radio/phono/television combination, 1948, 7" screen ...100.00
Arvin #4080T, metal w/mahog front, 1950, 8" screen 150.00
Coronado #FA 43-8965, t/t, 1949, 7" screen 200.00
Crosley #9-419, DuMont chassis, 1949, 12" screen 100.00
Delco #TV 71A, wood, 1948, 7" screen 125.00
DuMont #183X, 1941, console, 14" screen, minimum value ...3,500.00
Espray, kit, 1947, 3" screen 400.00
Fada #799, t/t, 1948, 10" screen 125.00
Firestone #13-G-3, 1949, 7" screen 100.00
Garod #930TV, w/AM/FM, 1948, 10" screen 175.00
GE #10T1, Bakelite, 1948, 10" screen 100.00
GE #806, 1949, 10" screen 100.00
GE #811, console, 1949, 10" screen 125.00
GE #901, projection TV, radio, phono, 1946, 18x24" screen 300.00
Hallicrafters #T-54, metal cabinet, 1948, 7" screen 200.00
Hallicrafters #509, portable, 1948, 10" screen 150.00
HMV #907, w/radio, English, 9" screen, minimum value 4,000.00
Hospix, t/t, 1950, 8" screen 225.00
ITI Guest TV, metal cabinet, plexiglass front, 7" screen 250.00
Meck #XB-702, mahog, 1949, 7" screen 200.00
Motorola #TS 902, color, 1954, 15" screen, minimum value ...1,000.00
Motorola #19P1 Astronaut, all transistor, 1961, 19" screen 150.00
Motorola #7VT2, Bakelite, 1950, 7" screen 125.00
Motorola #773, portable, leatherette, 1949, 7" screen 150.00
Motorola VT #71, t/t, 1947, 7" screen 175.00
National #TV7M, metal, 1949, 7" screen 200.00
Olympic, t/t, Bakelite, 1949, 10" screen 100.00
Philco #48-1000, t/t, 1948, 10" screen 225.00
Philco #48-700, t/t, 1948, 7" screen 225.00
Philco #49-702, mahog, 1949, 7" screen 225.00
Philco #50-701, blk Bakelite, 1950, 7" screen 250.00
Pilot #TV-37, 1949, 3" screen 225.00
Raytheon/Belmont #22A21, 1947, 7" screen 400.00
RCA #TRK-120, w/radio, 1940, 12" screen, minimum value ..2,500.00
RCA #621 TS, walnut, 1946, 7" screen 400.00
RCA #630 TS, 1946, 10" screen 225.00
RCA #721, 1 channel, 1947, 10" screen 150.00
RCA #741 PCS, projection, 1947 ....425.00
Scott #6T11, projection, 1949 ....300.00
Sentinel #405TV, 1949, 7" screen 150.00
Silvertone #9116, upright portable, leatherette case, 7" screen ..150.00
Sony #8-301W, 1st Japanese transistor TV, 1961, 8" screen 300.00
Sparton #4900, mirror in lid, 1949 ....225.00
Stewart Warner #AVC-1, mirror in lid, 1949 ....250.00
Stromberg Carlson #TC 10H, Manhattan portable, 1958, 10" screen .125.00
Teletone #149, 1949, 7" screen 175.00
Temple #TV-1776, mahog, built-in magnifier, 7" screen 300.00
Viewtone #VP-100, 1947, 7" screen, minimum value 600.00
Western TV #V-00151, scanning disc, 1928, minimum value ...2,500.00
Zenith #24H21, 1950, 19" screen 175.00
Zenith #27F20, Broadmoor, 1948, 12" screen 200.00

Philco Predictas and Related Items

Made in the years between 1958 and 1960, Philco Predictas have become the icon for television of the modern age. Predictas are now 40 years old, yet their atomic-age styling is just as futuristic today as they were in 1958. The television has been called one of man's greatest inventions. As we move into the year 2000, the television will continue to evolve away from the bulky cathode-ray tube of today, and become more like the flat screen 'hang-on-the-wall' TV previously seen only on the 'Jetsons.' This evolution can be traced back to the Philco Predicta line of sets, which for the first time gave consumers a view of 'television from the world of tomorrow.' The Predicta line will continue to be highly collectible as we move into the new millenium.

The values given here are for as-found, average, clean, complete, unrestored sets, running or not, that have good picture tubes. Picture tubes that cannot be proven good or are known to be bad can cost up to $375.00 to replace. Predictas that have damaged viewing screens or missing parts will have a lower value. Our advisor for Predicta televisions is David Weddington; he is listed in the Directory under Tennessee.

G4242 'Holiday' 21" table top, wood cabinet, blond finish **425.00**
G4242 'Holiday' 21" table top, wood cabinet, mahog finish **375.00**
G4654 'Barber-Pole,' 21" console, boomerang front leg, mahog .**600.00**
G4654 'Barber-Pole' 21" console, boomerang front leg, blond **700.00**
G4710 'Tandem' 21" separate screen w/25-ft cable, blond finish **600.00**
G4710 'Tandem' 21" separate screen w/25-ft cable, mahog finish ..**525.00**
G4720 'Stereo Tandem' 21" separate screen, 4 brass legs, mahog ..**700.00**
G4720 'Stereo Tandem' 21" w/matching 1606S phono/amp, mahog ...**1,000.00**
H3406 'Motel' 17" t/t, metal cabinet, cloth grill, no antenna **275.00**
H3408 'Debutante' 17" t/t, cloth grill, antenna, UHF, charcoal .**350.00**
H3410 'Princess' 17" t/t, metal grill, plastic tuner window **375.00**
H3410 'Princess' 17" t/t, orig metal stand, brn finish **450.00**
H3412 'Siesta' 17" t/t, w/clock-timer above tuner, gold finish **500.00**
H4370 'Danish Modern' 21" console, 4 fin-shaped legs, mahog finish .**775.00**
H4370 'Danish Modern' 21" console, 4 fin-shaped legs, walnut finish .**800.00**
H4744 'Townhouse' 21" room-divider, walnut shelves, brass finish ..**1,000.00**
Stand, brass finish w/blk wood shelf, orig, for 17" t/t **125.00**
Stand, tubular steel, for 21" t/t, brass finish **125.00**
Stand, wood, for 21" t/t, mahog finish **150.00**
17 DRP4 picture tube, MIB, replacement for 17" t/t Predictas ...**160.00**
21EAP4 or 21FDP4 picture tube, MIB, replacement for 21" Predictas ..**200.00**

Tennis Rackets

Early tennis rackets (pre-1940) generally exhibit these characteristics: head shape — may be oval, flat-top, transitional flat-top, triangular (or other); throat wedge — the triangular section of wood at the junction of the head and the handle may be concave, convex, solid or laminated; handle — most from this era are not covered by leather and are either combed (grooved) or checkered wood, and some may have cork handles or enlargements at the butt end. Values vary, dependent on age, rarity, style, and condition. Brand and model are important, and all identifying decals should be legible and in good condition. Rackets from 1880 to 1940 range in price from $300.00 to $600.00 for rare models like the Hazel's Streamline down to $10.00 to $20.00 for more common models.

Our advisor for this category is Donald Jones; he is listed in the Directory under Georgia. In the listings that follow, values apply to examples in excellent condition.

Key:
cx-lam — convex laminated   tran — transitional
cx-s — convex solid

AJ Reach, Driver, concave wedge, combed hdl, oval head, 1920 .**75.00**
E Kent, Duchess, concave wedge, bulbous hdl, oval head, 1930 .**120.00**
Hazel's, Streamline, branched wedge, leather hdl, oval head, 1935 ...**500.00**
Horsman, Elberton, concave wedge, smooth hdl, flat-top head, 1885 ...**350.00**
Iver Johnson, Special, cx-s wedge, bulbous hdl, tran head, 1900 ...**175.00**
Magnon, Superior, concave wedge, combed hdl, oval head, 1928 ...**75.00**
Slazenger, Demon, cx-lam wedge, fishtail hdl, oval head, 1910 ..**250.00**
Spaulding, Park, cx-s wedge, combed hdl, flat-top head, 1895 ....**450.00**

Wright-Diston, Octagon, concave head, combed hdl, oval head, 1895 ...**120.00**
Wright-Ditson, Hub, cx-s wedge, checkered hdl, oval head, 1890 .**175.00**
Wright-Ditson, Star, cx-s wedge, combed hdl, oval head, 1904 ..**135.00**

Teplitz

Teplitz, in Bohemia, was an active art pottery center at the turn of the century. The Amphora Pottery Works was only one of the firms that operated there. (See Amphora.) Art Nouveau and Art Deco styles were favored, and much of the ware was hand decorated with the primary emphasis on vases and figurines. Items listed here are marked 'Teplitz' or 'Turn,' a nearby city. Our advisor for this category is Jack Gunsaulus; he is listed in the Directory under Michigan.

Basket, floral on gr w/gold, dbl hdls, ornate, 6x8" **295.00**
Bust, lady w/hair up, lacy gown, sgn/mk, 14" **1,800.00**
Chocolate pot, emb tomatoes, Ernst Wahliss **295.00**
Ewer, mums w/gold, dragon hdl, pear shape, 16x8" **630.00**
Jug, Gibson girl portrait, emb floral, Stellmacher, lg **375.00**
Plate, owls in flight, much gold, 7½" **125.00**
Vase, caped gentleman, Stellmacher, 7" **95.00**
Vase, cavalier w/gun & sword on gray, hdls, Stellmacher, 15" **450.00**
Vase, children's scene, mc on brn mottle, Stellmacher, 7½x6½" ..**200.00**
Vase, transfer portrait in wht reserve on irid bl/gr, 4½" **80.00**

Terra Cotta

Terra cotta is a type of earthenware or clay used for statuary, architectural facings, or domestic articles. It is unglazed, baked to durable hardness, and characterized by the color of the body which may range from brick red to buff.

Sculpture, two putti raising a conch shell, one on back of dolphin, one on crest of wave, signed F Durand, 19th century, 21", $700.00.

Bust, classical maiden, WW lines, London/1826, 27" **2,000.00**
Jar, storage; w/lid, 39" **990.00**
Jardiniere, majolica-style storks in relief, w/ped, 42x18" **770.00**
Sculpture, man struggling w/boulder, H Bargas, 12x20" **1,600.00**
Shelves, gr glaze, Baroque taste, mermaid supports, 20", pr **745.00**
Tile, classical urn w/eagle hdls, late 19th C, 20x14x4" **525.00**
Umbrella stand, mc appl grapes & leaves, 23x11½" **195.00**
Urn, capana form, Bacchic masks, made in 6 parts, 90", pr **3,300.00**

Thermometers

Few objects man has invented have been so eloquently expressed both functionally and artistically as the ubiquitous thermometer. Developed initially by Galileo as a scientific device, thermometers slowly evolved into decorative objet d'art, functional household utensils, and eye-catching advertising specialties. Most American thermometers manufactured early in the 20th century were produced by Taylor (Tycos), and today their thermometers remain the most plentiful on the market. Decorative thermometers manufactured before 1800 are now ensconced in the permanent collections of approximately a dozen European museums. Because of their fragility, few devices of this era have survived in private collections. Nowadays most antique thermometers find their way to market through estate sales.

Insofar as sheer beauty, uniqueness, and scientific accuracy, decorative thermometers are far superior to the ordinary and inexpensive versions which carry advertising. Decorative thermometers run the gamut from plain tin household varieties to the highly ornate creations of Tiffany and Bradley and Hubbard. They have been manufactured from nearly every conceivable material — oak, sterling, brass, and glass being the favorites — and have tested the artistry and technical skills of some of America's finest craftsmen. Ornamental models can be found in free-hanging, wall-mounted, or desk/mantel versions.

Since 1994 instrument prices have been escalating at a rate of 35% annually. This is due to their relative scarcity, infrequent trading, and absence of a 'knock-off' (retro) market. Look for this trend to continue indefinitely.

Thermometer prices are based on age, ornateness, and whether mercury or alcohol is used as the filler in the tube. A broken or missing tube will cut at least 40% off the value. Virtually all American-made thermometers available today as collectors' items were made between 1875 and 1940. The golden age of decoratives ended in the early 1940s as modern manufacturing processes and materials robbed them of their natural distinctiveness.

Key:
br — brass
Cen — Centigrade
Fah — Fahrenheit
mrc — mercury in tube
pmc — permacolor
R — rare

Rea — Reaumer
sc — scale
stl — stainless
strl — sterling
VR — very rare

Amadio, Fah, Corn Hill, desk, ivory pillar/compass, mrc, 1890, 10" ..850.00
Anonymous, cvd wood squirrel, glass Rea sc, mrc, 1905, 10" 800.00
Anonymous, desk, br conquistador figural, br sc, mrc 650.00
Anonymous, desk, love scene, silver metal, br Rea/Cen sc, mrc, 8" ..830.00
Anonymous, wall, giltwood fr, ivory, Fah sc, mrc, 1790, 10x3½" 3,100.00
Blk/Starr/Frost, desk, barometer, stl, Fah/Cen, mrc, '10, 11" ...2,200.00
Bradley & Hubbard, desk, br fr & Fah sc, mrc, 1895, 13x6" 2,800.00
Calley, desk, strl inkwell fr, porc Rea sc, mrc, 1899, 5x6" 3,200.00
Capendium, desk, handmade br/porc fr, Fah/Cen sc, rnd mrc, 4" ..850.00
Carpenter & Westley, desk, ivory w/glass dome mrc, 1880, 6" ...950.00
Casella London, wall, maxi/minimum, 2 units, wood, plastic sc .430.00
Cheshire Silversmiths, desk, br candelabra, mrc, 1875, 10" 4,500.00
Chevallier, L'ingre, wall, ivory/mahog, Rea/Cen sc, 1880, 11x3" 2,350.00
Clark, desk, ivory ped, crown, mrc, 1904, 7" 400.00
Cloister, inkwell, stl bk & base w/angels at side, 1901 ....1,050.00
Creswel, travel, ivory case/mirror, removable sc, mrc, 2½" 2,800.00
CW Wilder...NH, desk, Deco women, br Fah sc, mrc, R, 8" ...1,300.00
Desk, cvd walrus tusk, 2-tier disk base, inlay sc, 1860, 9" 430.00
Diamond, wall, br Fah sc on wood, R, 7½x1½" 525.00
Dixie, W (London); desk, gilt/br, Gothic, SP sc, mrc, 8" 790.00
Dollard London, desk, strl, br sc, mrc, 1908, R, 6" 750.00
Dollard London, hanging, mahog fr, strl sc, mrc, 1810, 18" 4,600.00
Dring & Fage, desk, marble, ivory sc, mrc, 1880, 6" 1,500.00
Farley, travel, walnut base mt, ivory Fah/Cen sc, mrc, 5" 900.00
Freeborn, desk, bronze w/3 lead decor, br sc, mrc, 8" 180.00
G Cooper, desk, bell shape w/cupola, strl, dial, 2x3" 400.00
Gilbert & Co, travel, silver eng sc, mrc, 1850, 8" 630.00

Gloucenter Scientific, stl case, glass front, pmc, 42" 1,500.00
Heath & Wing, figural calendar, br w/porc sc, mrc, 1870 ....930.00
J Waldstein, wall, br Rea sc on wood, mrc, 1900s, VR, 10½" 920.00
Kendal, desk, strl obelisk, br Fah sc, mrc, 1890, 8", $1,350 to .1,850.00
Moreau, desk, mahog, Rea/Cen, spiral tube, mrc, 1860, 6½x5½" ..1,725.00
Pairpoint, desk, strl picture fr, mrc, 1907, 5" 650.00
Reau, desk, sq incline base, floral top, mrc, 1895 ....180.00
Rowley & Sons, travel, ivory sc, mrc, 1894, 4", +case 350.00
Standard, wall, ivory Fah sc on ebony, mrc, 9" 750.00
Standard..., wall, br fr, enamel dial Fah sc, 1885, 9" dia 950.00
Taylor, ped, 3-sided, Fah sc, alcohol, 1900, R, 6" 3,200.00
Thermindex Switzerland, desk, Bakelite stand, Fah sc, 5" 725.00
Tiffany, desk, strl tetrahedron fr & Fah sc, mrc, 1910, 2x4" 4,000.00
Tiffany, gr glass w/pine needles, br sc/mrc, 1902, 8x12" 2,800.00
Tycos, maxi/minimum, japanned tin/br, mrc, T-5452, 8" 125.00
Unknown, cvd wood squirrel, glass Rea sc, mrc, 1905, 10", VR .800.00
Unknown, desk, alabaster w/eagle, Rea/Cen sc, mrc, 1895 ....875.00
Unknown, desk, br conquistador figural, br sc, mrc 650.00
Unknown, desk, love scene, silver metal, br Rea/Cen sc, mrc, 8" ...830.00
Unknown, England, desk, glass obelisk/8-sided, br Fah sc, mrc, 1880 ..1,259.99
Unknown, England, desk, marble ped fr, Cen, mrc, 1885, 6½" .930.00
Unknown, England, wall, br game bag fr, Fah sc, mrc, 1890, 9x5" ..1,650.00
Unknown, England, wall, rect wood fr, porc Cen sc, mrc, 1905, 5" .1,350.00
Unknown, pendant, strl case, ivory Fah sc, mrc, 1880, 5" 1,250.00
Unknown, wall, giltwood fr, ivory Fah sc, 1790, 10x3½" 3,100.00
VJD Inc, wall, clip Fah br sc, mrc, VR, 4" 1,650.00
W Pratt, desk, wood inlays, ivory sc, mrc, 1900, 6" 350.00
Warren Foundries, wall, umbrella w/dragon hdl, br sc, mrc, 12" .220.00
West, desk, Gothic design, br, 1900, 12" 1,360.00
WG Loveday, wall, Clearside, Fah sc, 5" dia 725.00
Whitehead & Hoag, Lambrecht's Polymeter, mrc, 9" 1,200.00
Zeradatha, desk, cast metal w/rotate sc, 1926, 7" 140.00

1000 Faces China

So named because of its many hand-painted faces, much of this chinaware was made during the '30s through the '50s (some even earlier). Though many pieces are unmarked, others are marked 'Made in Japan.' There are two primary patterns, 'Black Face' and the 'Gold' pattern, and variations exist. Both designs employ many colors. Dinner plates usually are decorated with an outer-most 'ring of color' (two or three hues) containing a simple design which is often flowers. The inner ring is usually comprised of many colors radiating from the center circle which may be done in a primary color (red, for instance) with a design such as a dragon or clouds painted in gold. 'Black Face' is distinguishable by its range of colors — primarily red, white, and yellow with some green and blue — and the black hand-painted faces. The 'Gold' pattern is also multicolored but is dominated by the gold throughout the design, and the faces themselves are gold as well. Other variations include '1000 Men in Robes' and '1000 Faces' with black or blue rims on the saucers and cups. These pieces seem to be very scarce. In the listings that follow, all items are marked 'Made in Japan' (MIJ) unless noted otherwise. Our advisor for this category is Suzi Hibbard; she is listed in the Directory under California.

Bowl, gold faces, petal shape, 6" 20.00
Cup & saucer, blk faces 40.00
Cup & saucer, demitasse; gold faces 25.00
Cup & saucer, gold faces, from $30 to 50.00
Cup & saucer, 1000 Geishas 40.00
Egg cup, bl faces 20.00
Ginger jar, gold faces, from $75 to 100.00
Lamp, gold faces, 8" vase base 125.00

Plate, blk, 10"	45.00
Plate, blk/gold, 6"	10.00
Salt cellar, bl faces, from $5 to	10.00
Shakers, bl faces, pr	20.00
Snack set, blk faces, kidney shape	45.00
Soup set, blk faces, 3-pc	75.00
Sweetmeat, blk faces, 9-pc set in lacquer box	175.00
Sweetmeat set, gold faces, 15-pc, serves 6	175.00
Tea set, blk faces, dragon spout, 7"	50.00
Tea set, demitasse; bl faces, 15-pc	125.00
Tea set, gold faces, 21-pc	225.00
Teapot, gold faces, dragon spout, 7"	50.00
Teapot, Men in Robes, 6-sided, Japanese mk	45.00
Teapot, 1000 Geishas, dragon spout	55.00
Vase, blk faces, 8"	60.00
Vase, gold, 8", from $75 to	100.00

Tiffany

Louis Comfort Tiffany was born in 1848 to Charles Lewis and Harriet Young Tiffany of New York. By the time he was eighteen, his father's small dry goods and stationery store had grown and developed into the world-renowned Tiffany and Company. Preferring the study of art to joining his father in the family business, Louis spent the next six years under the tutelage of noted artists. He returned to America in 1870 and until 1875 painted canvases that focused on European and North African scenes. Deciding the more lucrative approach was in the application of industrial arts and crafts, he opened a decorating studio called Louis C. Tiffany and Co., Associated Artists. He began seriously experimenting with glass, and eschewing traditionally painted-on details, he instead learned to produce glass with qualities that could suggest natural textures and effects. His experiments broadened, and he soon concentrated his efforts on vases, bowls, etc., that came to be considered the highest achievements of the art. Peacock feathers, leaves and vines, flowers, and abstracts were developed within the plane of the glass as it was blown. Opalescent and metallic lustres were combined with transparent color to produce stunning effects. Tiffany called his glass Favrile, meaning handmade.

In 1900 he established Tiffany Studios and turned his attention full time to producing art glass, leaded-glass lamp shades and windows, and household wares with metal components. He also designed a complete line of jewelry which was sold through his father's store. He became proficiently accomplished in silverwork and produced such articles as hand mirrors embellished with peacock feather designs set with gems and candlesticks with Favrile glass inserts.

Tiffany's work exemplified the Art Nouveau style of design and decoration, and through his own flamboyant personality and business acumen he perpetrated his tastes onto the American market to the extent that his name became a household word. Tiffany Studios continued to prosper until the second decade of this century when due to changing tastes his influence began to diminish. By the early 1930s the company had closed.

Serial numbers were assigned to much of Tiffany's work, and letter prefixes indicated the year of manufacture: A – N for 1896 – 1900, P – Z for 1901 – 1905. After that, the letter followed the numbers with A – N in use from 1906 – 1912; P – Z from 1913 – 1920. O-marked pieces were made especially for friends and relatives; X indicated pieces not made for sale.

Our listings are primarily from the auction houses in the East where Tiffany sells at a premium. All pieces are signed unless noted otherwise.

Glass

Bonbon, marigold cased, ext: opal rays, scalloped, 6"	650.00

Bottle, scent; gold, dbl gourd w/appl trailing prunts, 7"	2,400.00
Bowl, bl pastel w/opal ribs, stretch border, 2x6"	400.00
Bowl, bl-gold, open basketweave flaring rim, 3½x10½"	4,100.00
Bowl, floriform; leaves, gr on opal texture, ribbed, 6"	400.00
Bowl, flower; lily pads, gr on gold, 2-tier arranger insert, 11"	1,800.00
Bowl, gold, ribbed/scalloped flange, bulbous, 4 peg ft, 6"	1,000.00
Bowl, gold-spotted opal w/gr rim & 3 reeded rolled ft, 8"	1,600.00
Bowl, gr pastel, ribbed w/rice pattern, 2x7"	450.00
Bowl, lily pads, gr in clear, 2x6½"	575.00
Bowl, pk pastel, stretch border, 3x6¾"	700.00
Bowl, sapphire bl pastel, gold disk ft, 6"	995.00
Butter pat, bl-gold w/opal underside, scalloped	170.00
Candlestick, gold, swirl base, wide bobeche, 5x3½"	450.00
Compote, bl irid w/leaf & vine engr, scalloped, 4½x10"	2,750.00
Compote, bl stretched irid, morning-glory shape, 6x10"	2,500.00
Compote, floriform; leaves, gr on opal, gold int, 5x6¾"	1,265.00
Compote, floriform; opal w/amethyst rim, wht rays, 6", pr	2,000.00
Compote, pk & yel irid, LCT-Favrile, #H8908	935.00
Cordial, gold w/amethyst irid, pinched sides, 2", set of 4	600.00
Cordial, gold-bronze, pinched sides, 1¾"	150.00
Decanter, grapes eng on gold, stick neck, 11", +4 liqueurs	2,300.00
Finger bowl, aqua pastel, 5", +7" underplate	350.00
Goblet, aqua pastel, floriform, ribbed opal accents, 8"	335.00
Goblet, aqua pastel, 8½"	325.00
Goblet, gold cup w/4 leaf tips at base, pencil stem, 8"	750.00
Inkwell, eng Am eagle & shield, mk silver neck/lid, Dept of State	1,500.00
Jardiniere, lily pads on honey amber irid, #1521-9735M, 5x9"	1,600.00
Light shade, yel irid, #A1025, ca 1894	100.00

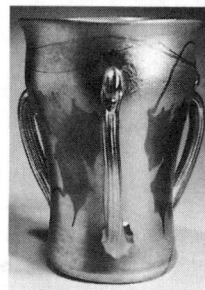

Loving cup, ambergris vasiform with three applied handles spacing green leaves amid vines, gold iridescence overall, #2024D, 8", $2,550.00.

Parfait, aqua pastel w/clear base, morning-glory form	225.00
Place setting, aqua pastel, scalloped 9" plate/sherbet/2 stems	1,100.00
Plate, pk pastel, 10 wedge-shape sections, 8¾"	545.00
Punch bowl, feathers, gr on gold, 12-rib, 2-part, 10½x14"	4,000.00
Salt cellar, bl-gold, ribbed/scalloped, waisted rim, 4 peg ft	350.00
Salt cellar, bl-gold, ribbed/tapered, waisted rim, 1¼"	300.00
Salt cellar, gold, ribbed w/waisted rim, 4-ftd, 1¾"	175.00
Salt cellar, red-gold irid, ruffled/ribbed, 1x2½", pr	330.00
Tile, cloverleaf, mustard yel/brn mottle, 3" sq	90.00
Tile, golden red, 4x4", mtd in 9½" sq gold metal fr	185.00
Tumbler, gold, 8 swirled/pulled prunts, ovoid w/flared rim, 3"	400.00
Vase, bl irid w/purple & gold, 2¾x2½"	800.00
Vase, bl-gold irid, trumpet shape, in gold enamel #152 base	425.00
Vase, bud; gold insert, bronze holder #1043, 15x5"	1,100.00
Vase, bud; gold irid, pinched ovoid, LCT, paper label, 3¾"	440.00
Vase, dk bl w/dk irid, gr/gold swirls at shoulder, 4x6"	2,900.00
Vase, feathered neck band on celadon opaque, gold int, 4"	1,495.00
Vase, floriform; bl-gold, ribbed, raised ribbed base, 7½"	1,100.00
Vase, floriform; feathers on gold, flared/crimped rim, 16"	5,400.00
Vase, floriform; gold, bulbous body w/4 pulled ft, 2½x3"	575.00
Vase, floriform; gold, ribbed shouldered cone, dome ft, 14"	1,300.00
Vase, floriform; leaves, lime/opal/gilt, ruffled, raised ft, 5"	1,500.00
Vase, floriform; leaves/threaded vines, gr on red-gold, 12"	2,500.00

Vase, floriform; red-gold irid, ribbed, scalloped rim, 8½" 1,350.00
Vase, gold, squatty, 4" 575.00
Vase, gold w/amethyst tint, ribs w/pinches at shoulder, 5" 600.00
Vase, gold w/EX irid, flared, shouldered, 11x10" 3,000.00
Vase, gold w/red irid, dimpled sides, 2¾" 300.00
Vase, leaves, gr/gold on wht irid lily, bronze ft #1048, 14" 2,300.00
Vase, oyster wht w/EX irid, sm hdls at mid point, 3½x2" 800.00
Vase, paperweight, narcissus, wht/gr on opal, 7¾" 675.00
Vase, paperweight, 10 narcissus in clear to brn/gr, 16" 17,250.00
Vase, pk pastel, clear ft w/etched floral, trumpet form, 9" 850.00
Vase, pulled/appl chevrons at shoulder on gold w/lav irid, 8" ..1,350.00
Vase, rose-cased wht w/mc vines & spots, dimpled, hdls, 8" 425.00
Vase, sea green w/bubbles, ribs & opal, #930V, 7x6" 700.00
Vase, wht top/bl irid body w/gold pulled border between, 6" ...3,000.00
Vase, yel & pk irid, gourd shape, LCT, #N7439 ....600.00
Wines, bl w/lav irid, tooled bodies & bases, 3½", 4 for 4,800.00

Lamps

Lamp prices seem to be getting stronger, especially for leaded lamps with brighter colors (red, blue, purples). Bases that are unusual or rare have brought good prices and added to the value of the more common shades that sold on them. Bases with enamel or glass inserts are very much in demand. Our advisor for Tiffany lamps is Carl Heck; he is listed in the Directory under Colorado.

Base, bronze & turtlebk tile, oil font, #6816, 17", $10,000 to ..12,000.00
Base, Cypriote, bl irid on gilt bronze ped, 18", from $700 to ...1,000.00
Base, Cypriote heart form on doré base w/ivory ball stem 1,500.00
Base, 3 scale-molded legs w/mammal ft, #S1630323, 11" 800.00
Bridge, ldgl 12" acorn-band shade, #429II 5-leg std, 57" 8,000.00
Candle, gold shade w/gr swirls; swirled rib std, 17", EX 1,600.00
Candle, leafy gr/wht/gold shade; bronze leaf/vine #4260 base ..3,400.00
Candle, 7" gold ruffled shade & swirled rib base, 14" 1,150.00
Candle, 7" gold ruffled shade; opal stem w/leaves; twist base ...1,300.00
Ceiling, ldgl 16" curved panel shade w/'wave' segments 2,185.00
Chandelier, 6-lily, gold shades (rpl), no mk, 13x20", $2,600 to ..3,000.00
Desk, bronze dome shade w/silver int; 2-socket #617 std, 18" .2,200.00
Desk, Gold Aurene ribbed Steuben shade; bronze harp std 1,700.00
Desk, gold bell-form shade w/feathers; pivoting harp std #418 ....2,000.00
Desk, linenfold 8" shade; harp std #613, 19½" 3,500.00
Floor, ldgl 25" curtain-border shade; std #376, 77" 44,850.00
Floor, pulled-feather 12" shade; 5-ftd std #423, 58" 6,500.00
Hanging, irid shade blown into bronze frwork, central tile 2,600.00
Lily, 10-light, wht opal shades; etched silver on bronze std, 22" ..6,600.00
Lily, 12-light, gold w/red & bl irid, ea sgn; #382 std, 21" 20,000.00
Lily, 12-light, ribbed/ruffled gold shades, 21½" 22,000.00
Lily, 3-stem, gold irid, in gold vase-like base #320, 7½" 4,200.00
Shade, ldgl, acorn band & gridwork, 14" 4,000.00
Student, cased gr irid 10" shade; single-post Manhattan std 4,800.00
Student, gold/opal pinch-side tulip shade; swing-arm std #25868 ...3,500.00
Student, 2 bell-form Loetz shades; #304 2-arm pencil std 2,300.00
Student, 2 ldgl 10" gridwork shades; dbl-post std w/font, 29" ...10,925.00
Table, ldgl 14" arrowroot shade; lg 3-arm paw-ft #289 std 18,400.00
Table, ldgl 16" acorn shade; bronze 4-leg urn base & font 5,500.00
Table, ldgl 16" acorn-band shade, EX; Grueby 4-hdl vase std .9,200.00
Table, ldgl 16" daffodil shade; 3-leg urn std #26870 (EX) 21,850.00
Table, ldgl 16" pansy shade (EX); ribbed/ftd #3602 std, 22" ..24,000.00
Table, ldgl 16" pomegranate-band shade; 4-ftd #9924 std 8,600.00
Table, ldgl 16" shade w/gr slag ovals; wishbone #444 std 8,700.00
Table, ldgl 16" triangles-band gridwork shade, EX; #534 std ...4,800.00
Table, ldgl 16" tulip shade; #9535 std w/turtle-bk tiles, 23" ..36,500.00
Table, ldgl 18" whirling leaf shade; dbl wishbone #440 std 8,350.00

Table, linenfold 20" 16-panel gold shade; slim gold doré std ...9,775.00

Metal Work

Items are bronze unless noted otherwise.

Tray, swirling Art Nouveau motif, with blue iridescent glass inserts, 7¾x3", $2,750.00.

Box, Vintage, caramel slag lined, #809, 2x4x6½" 300.00
Candlesticks, urn-form cups on tripod holders, #1213, 19", pr ...2,500.00
Clock, desk; Swiss mvt in gilt-metal/glass/bronze case, 6" 300.00
Clock, desk; Zodiac, keywind, gold dial, #1076, 4⅛x4¼" 1,380.00
Compote, gold irid on rtcl platform base w/4 dolphin ft, 4x5¾" .285.00
Compote, red enamel embellishments, gilded, #505, 8" dia 350.00
Desk set, American Indian, inkstand/stamp box/tray,+3 pcs ...1,380.00
Desk set, Byzantine, jewel inserts/beads/medallions, 3-pc 2,750.00
Desk set, Chinese, paper rack/stamp box/inkstand+4 pcs 2,800.00
Desk set, Grapevine, box #800/inkstand/scale #872+7 pcs 2,185.00
Desk set, Grapevine, gr slag inserts, 7-pc 1,955.00
Desk set, Grapevine, paper rack/bill file/2 boxes+8 pcs 2,750.00
Desk set, Pine Needle, etched decor, amber slag inserts, 6-pc .1,380.00
Desk set, Pine Needle, gold doré/slag inserts, 12-pc 2,550.00
Desk set, Russian, dk w/bl patina, 7-pc 4,025.00
Desk set, turq bl enamel inlay, inkstand/letter holder/knife 1,100.00
Desk set, Zodiac, paper rack/box/inkstand+5 pcs 1,300.00
Ferner, Marsh Marigold in relief, red/gr patina, 3½x11" 400.00
Figurine, pug dog, dk patina, no mk, 2" L 115.00
Frame, Abalone, some gr patina & shell inserts, 9x7" 1,495.00
Frame, etch blossoms w/gr slag inserts, easel bk, 7½x6¼" 925.00
Frame, Grapevine, amber slag lined, easel bk, #916, 14x12" ...1,380.00
Frame, Pine Needle, amber slag lined, oval int, #948, 9½x7½" ...1,300.00
Frame, Pine Needle, gr slag lined, easel bk, #947, 9x7½" 1,380.00
Inkstand, shell cover w/dolphin corners, #1842, 3x5¼x4¼" ...1,380.00
Inkstand, Zodiac, hinged lid, gold etched, #1072 ....600.00
Letter holder, American Indian, frog/serpent/geometrics, 6" 425.00
Letter holder, Venetian, 2-tier, #1643, 4½" 575.00
Note pad, Modeled Design, dk patina w/gr, mk 750.00
Plate/tray, etched decor, mk, #1746, 12" 315.00
Vase, bl/gr enameling, trumpet form, #165, 13x5¾" 900.00

Pottery

Bowl, amber/cream flambe, allover relief mushrooms, 5x7", NM ...2,700.00
Bowl, floral, dk gold on bark-like bronze finish, 5½" 1,600.00
Bowl, gr w/gunmetal, lily pad form, 3 frogs at base, 7x8" 18,000.00
Plate, dinner; exotic bird, marbleized border, mk, 12 for 1,100.00
Vase, brn/blk/gr mottled gloss, shouldered, 5½" 475.00
Vase, bronze-clad, leaves in relief, 5½x3¼" 2,000.00
Vase, bronze-clad w/emb floral, 2" 900.00
Vase, celadon/beige microcrystalline glaze, 3x3¼" 200.00
Vase, copper-clad, emb columbine, 8½x2¾" 2,000.00
Vase, fall leaves on gold w/red irid, shouldered, 4¾" 450.00
Vase, jonquil/leaves emb on shellac/moss satin matt, 12x4½" .5,000.00

Vase, maple leaves relief, unglazed, 20x11" **3,750.00**
Vase, silver-plated copper clad, emb poinsettias, 13x4" **1,800.00**
Vase, yel/amber/brn/cream crystalline mottle, 8x11½", EX **2,000.00**
Vase, 4 upright long-stem bulbs, blk/gr metallic gloss, 9½" **7,000.00**

Silver

Bowl, Art Modern, 2⅜x10⅜", 22-troy-oz **800.00**
Bowl, fluted border, w/lid, 3½x11½", 44-troy-oz **770.00**
Candelabrum, appl leaves, 2 shades, #16846, 14x14" **920.00**
Cigar box, bl enamel, hinged lid, #350, monogram, 6¼x3¾x2⅝" ..**865.00**
Demitasse set, Art Moderne taste, 9½" pot+cr/sug **1,760.00**
Hairbrush, floral & fern repousse, ca 1891-1902, 5½" **275.00**
Jug, water; monogram inscription, 1850s, 5½", 18½-troy-oz **1,200.00**
Pen tray, shell shape, 3" dia, +pen **175.00**
Salad server, gold wash, 9¾", 8 troy-oz **515.00**
Tazza, Japonesque Taste, 1870-75, 4½x13½" **2,000.00**

Tiffin Glass

The Tiffin Glass Company was founded in 1887 in Tiffin, Ohio, one of the many factories composing the U.S. Glass Company. Its early wares consisted of tablewares and decorative items such as lamps and globes. Among the most popular of all Tiffin products was the black satin glass produced there during the 1920s. In 1959 U.S. Glass was sold, and in 1962 the factories closed. The plant was reopened in 1963 as the Tiffin Art Glass Company. Products from this period were tableware, hand-blown stemware, and other decorative items.

Those interested in learning more about Tiffin glass are encouraged to contact the Tiffin Glass Collectors' Club, whose address can be found in the Directory under Clubs, Newsletters, and Catalogs. See also Black Glass; Glass Animals.

Ashtray, Twilight, cloverleaf, #9123/97, 5" 55.00
Banana flower arranger, #6814 ....130.00
Banana vase, #6101, 11" 125.00
Basket, Empress, Killarney gr, 13" **400.00**
Basket, Twilight, 9x5½" 295.00
Bell, Fuchsia, 5" 45.00
Bowl, Classic, hdls, 8x9¼" 110.00
Bowl, cream soup; Cadena, pk or yel 30.00
Bowl, finger; Flanders, pk, w/liner 75.00
Bowl, fruit/nut; June Night, 6" 35.00
Bowl, Fuchsia, crimped rim, 13" 75.00
Bowl, June Night, crimped rim, 12" 75.00
Bowl, salad; Cherokee Rose, 7" 37.50
Bowl, salad; Fuchsia, 9¾" 75.00
Bowl, wishbone; Twilight, ftd, 6½" 135.00
Cake plate, Cherokee Rose, center hdl, 12½" 125.00
Candlesticks, Cadena, pr 50.00
Candlesticks, Cherokee Rose, 2-light, #5902, pr 160.00
Candlesticks, Flanders, yel, either style, pr 80.00
Candlesticks, Killarney Green, 1-light, #6364, pr 100.00
Celery/relish, Flanders, 3-part 70.00
Champagne, Athens Diana 25.00
Champagne, Cadena, 6½" 17.00
Champagne, Chalet 40.00
Champagne, Fontaine, Twilight, lav bowl w/clear stem 45.00
Champagne, Majesty, Twilight 32.50
Champagne, Persian Pheasant, 5½-oz 30.00
Champagne, Twilight, cut, #17524 ....45.00
Claret, Fuchsia, 5¼" 37.50

Claret, La Fleur, yel, #15024 ....65.00
Claret, Persian Pheasant, 4½-oz 55.00
Cocktail, Athens Diana 30.00
Cocktail, Classic, 4-oz 27.50
Cocktail, Fuchsia 22.00
Cocktail, June Night, 3½-oz 27.00
Cocktail, Liege 12.00
Cocktail, Majesty, Twilight 37.50
Cocktail shaker, Fuchsia, metal top, 8" 235.00
Compote, Flanders, 3½" 65.00
Cordial, Cherokee Rose, 1-oz 50.00
Cordial, Classic, #185 ....70.00
Cordial, Coventry, #17623 ....29.00
Cordial, Flanders, 5" 55.00
Cordial, Persian Pheasant 65.00
Creamer, Cherokee Rose 30.00
Creamer, Classic, pk, flat 60.00
Creamer, June Night 17.50
Cup, Cadena, pk or yel 75.00
Cup & saucer, Athens Diana 24.00
Cup & saucer, Rosalind, yel, blown 45.00
Decanter, cvd roses, globe stopper, #3700 ....260.00
Goblet, Chalet 50.00
Goblet, Classic, #185 ....35.00
Goblet, Rosalind, yel 30.00
Goblet, Twilight 45.00
Jug, Athens Diana, #128 ....260.00
Jug, Rosalind, yel, #128 ....360.00
Martini jug, Twilight, 11½" 460.00
Oyster cocktail, Athens Diana 18.00
Parfait, cake; Classic, #185 ....70.00
Parfait, Flanders, pk, hdld, 5⅝" 165.00
Pickle dish, Fuchsia, 7⅜" 40.00
Pitcher, Cadena, ftd 250.00
Pitcher, Cherokee Rose 335.00
Pitcher, Classic, 61-oz 250.00
Plate, cracker; Deerwood, blk, gold edge 225.00
Plate, dinner; Cadena, pk or yel, 9¼" 35.00
Plate, dinner; Classic, 10" 85.00
Plate, dinner; Rosalind, yel, lg 50.00
Plate, lily; Cerise, 13" 65.00
Plate, luncheon; Cherokee Rose, 8" 18.50
Plate, luncheon; Fuchsia, 8⅛" 22.50
Plate, luncheon; June Night, 8" 20.00
Plate, luncheon; Rosalind, yel, 8" 20.00
Plate, salad; La Fleure, yel, 7¼" 15.00
Plate, sandwich; Fuchsia, 14¼" 50.00
Relish, Flanders, yel, 3-part 50.00
Relish, June Night, 3-part, 12½" 65.00
Saucer, champagne; Fuchsia, #17453, 7-oz 30.00
Shakers, Cherokee Rose, pr 100.00
Shakers, June Night, pr 175.00
Sherbet, Cadena, 4¾" 15.00
Sherbet, Cherokee Rose, #17399, 5½-oz 18.00
Sherbet, Fontaine, pk 32.50
Sugar bowl, Fuchsia, 2⅞" 40.00
Sugar bowl, June Night 25.00
Tumbler, iced tea; Cherokee Rose, #17403 ....35.00
Tumbler, iced tea; Empire, pk, ftd, 13-oz 65.00
Tumbler, iced tea; Flying Nun, crystal w/gr base, #185 ....60.00
Tumbler, juice; Classic, ftd, 5-oz, 3½" 22.00
Tumbler, juice; Fuchsia, flat, 4⅞" 27.50
Tumbler, juice; June Night, ftd, 5-oz 22.00
Tumbler, pilsner; Classic, ftd, 6½-oz 32.50

Tumbler, water; Flanders, yel, ftd 50.00
Tumbler, water; Fuchsia, ftd, 9-oz 20.00
Tumbler, water; Rosalind, yel, ftd, 9-oz 26.00
Tumbler, whiskey; Classic, ftd, #185, 2-oz 75.00
Vase, bud; etched roses, flat top, #19, 10" 40.00
Vase, bud; Fuchsia, 8¼" 35.00
Vase, Cadena, pk or yel, 9" 90.00
Vase, Flanders, fan form 85.00

Wall pocket, amethyst satin, 10x10¼", from $275.00 to $300.00.

Photo courtesy
Betty Newbound

Wine, Chalet 55.00
Wine, Classic, 3-oz 32.50
Wine, Flanders 45.00
Wine, Liege 18.00

Tiles

The history of tile making dates back to ancient Egypt and Assyria. For centuries tiles have played an important role as a decorative art form, as well as having a utilitarian function. Places such as palace walls, Islamic mosques, Roman floors, and medieval English churches were all adorned with tiles or glazed ceramic surfaces. Remnants of these tile installations can still be seen throughout the world.

The heyday of tile making in England and the United States dates back to circa 1860 through 1930 and envelops the Victorian, Art Nouveau, and Arts & Crafts Movements in both countries. These tiles comprise most of those seen on today's market.

Tiles are being collected today as individual art objects and are increasingly used as decorative accessories. They are also sought in order to restore homes, buildings, and furniture to original period condition. Many people are now incorporating antique and collectible tiles into their home-rebuilding projects for gardens, kitchens, bathrooms, fireplaces, stair risers, and floors.

Tiles must be judged on an individual basis. The condition of the tile face; the quality of the design; the rarity of the artist, company, or series; and the size of the tile or tile panel are just some of the factors to consider when assessing value. People, animals, and scenes are generally more desirable than florals and geometrics. Some glaze colors, such as true pale pink or bright red majolica, add value to Victorian tiles. Tiles may be more difficult to find than many other antiques or collectibles, partly because many were permanently installed. Unfortunately, many installations have been destroyed. These factors all have influence on the tile market, and it is not unusual for prices to vary greatly. See also Moravian; Grueby; Rookwood; other specific manufacturers. Our advisor for this category is Karen Guido; she is listed in the Directory under Connecticut.

Key:
bkg — background	pr mld — press molded
geo — geometric	srs — series
maj — majolica glaze	tbld — tube lined
plych — polychrome	tp — transfer printed

American

AETCO, encircled dog face, dk brn/wht tp, 6" 135.00
AETCO, fish on wave, cut-out border, mc maj, 6x5½" 155.00
AETCO, huntress on animal skin, gr maj, pr mld, 6" 245.00
AETCO, LA 24-tile panel (ea 4"), water lilies & pond, mc 1,640.00
AETCO, Republican State Convention, bl maj, 3½x1½", VG 87.00
Architectural Tiling Co, Black child playing, mc HP, 6" 35.00
Batchelder, parrot & pomegranate, bl patina glaze, 4" 150.00
Batchelder, thistle, bl patina glaze, pr mld, 3" 60.00
Beaver Falls, floral swirls, yel/gr maj, 6" 65.00
Burroughs Mountford, forest w/birds, HP, 6", VG 48.00
CALCO, mission scene, mc matt glaze, 11½x3½", VG 260.00
Decorative Art Tile Co, Arabian knight, mc, decal, 8" 100.00
Empire, tulip, high relief, gr/red matt glaze, 6" 200.00
Enfield, hunter w/rabbit & rifle, dk brn unglazed, 4½" 60.00
Flint Faience, witch on broomstick, unglazed, pr mld, 4½" 80.00
Franklin, Dutch girl & windmill, gray/red/blk, pr mld, 4" 45.00
Franklin, faience, 3 butterflies, mc, pr mld, 2x6" 25.00
Harris Strong, pr cut-out figures mtd on wood, mc, 41x9½" 660.00
Harris Strong, stylized forest scene, mc, tbld, orig fr, 6" 185.00
Harris Strong, 3-tile panel, houses/boats/animals, mc tbld, 18x6" 180.00
ITT, animals in roundels, brn/beige tp, 6" 160.00
Kensington, flowers, mottled mc maj, 6" 30.00
Low, female profile w/laurel leaves, lt olive-gr maj, 6" dia 155.00
Malibu, pillowed tile, brns, maj, 4½" 57.00
Matawan, octagonal geometric, cuenca mc, 6" 50.00
Mosaic, woodpecker Audubon srs, mc decal, 6" 25.00
Mueller, moth, cvd/pnt on lg dmn, triangles in corners, fr 220.00
Old Bridge, fleur-de-lys, mauve maj, pr mld, 3" 20.00
Providential, facing portraits, brn maj, ea 6", pr 475.00
Providential, female profile, gr maj, stove tile, 4" 165.00
Providential, female reclining, mottled mc maj, 6x12" 405.00
San Jose Potteries, calla lily, mc, 5¾" 170.00
San Jose Potteries, fish, mc, cuerda seca, ea 6", pr 300.00
Trent, chariot rider & horses, 2-tile, olive gold maj, 6x12", VG ...400.00
Trent, girl w/kerchief, olive gold maj, stove tile, 2¼" 95.00
US Encaustic, Hamlet & Ophelia, yel/cream maj, ea 6", pr 465.00
Wheatley, satyr, mc, pr mld, 6" 500.00
Wheeling, people stomping grapes, cream/blk tp, 4" 22.00

English

Wedgwood, Month series, June, boy and girl in field, brown and white transfer print, 6", $165.00.

Brown, Westhead & Moore, mule & dog, brn/wht tp, 6" 130.00
Campbell Brick & Tile, 4-pointed star, encaustic, mc tp, 6" 40.00
Copeland, month srs, February, mc HP, 6", VG 145.00
E Smith, floral & geo, brn/gr maj, pr mld, 6" 63.00
England, Art Nouveau lilies, mc maj, pr mld, 1902, 6" 153.00
Malkin Edge, Art Nouveau sqs, mc maj, 6" 85.00
Maw, 4 red flowers w/mc vines, tp, 6" 195.00
Minton & Co, AWN Pugin design, encaustic geo, mc, 6" 225.00
Minton Hollins, English History srs, Henry V, brn/beige tp, 6" 95.00
Mintons Ch Wrks, Shakespeare srs, Tempest plych tp, 6" 130.00

Sherwin & Cotton, Pope Pius X, photographic, sepia, 9x6" **410.00**
Sherwin & Cotton, roses, gold, 6" **65.00**
Steele & Wood, Blue Willow scene w/border, bl/wht, tp, 8", VG ..**150.00**
T&R Boote, canal scene, HP, 6" **60.00**
Webbs Tileries, putti, bl/wht tp, 6" **85.00**
Wedgwood, boy fishing scene, brn tp, 6" **120.00**
Wedgwood, calendar tile, 1913, brn tp, 5x3" **100.00**
Wedgwood, calendar tile, 1920, brn tp, 5x3" **143.00**

Other Countries

Delft, porc bottle mk, ship at sea, mc, pr mld, 4½" **90.00**
Longwy, women gathering flowers, mc, 8" **325.00**
Mexican, sgn Ruggerio, man w/sombrero, HP, 5¾" **65.00**
Villeroy & Boch, winter village scene, bl/wht tp, 6" **48.00**

Tinware

In the American household of the 17th and 18th centuries, tinware items could be found in abundance, from food containers to foot warmers and mirror frames. Although the first settlers brought much of their tinware with them from Europe, by 1798 sheets of tin plate were being imported from England for use by the growing number of American tinsmiths. Tinwares were often decorated either by piercing or painted designs which were both freehand and stenciled. (See Toleware.) By the early 1900s, many homes had replaced their old tinware with the more attractive aluminum and graniteware.

In the 19th century, tenth wedding anniversaries were traditionally celebrated by gifts of tin. Couples gave big parties, dressed in their wedding clothes, and reaffirmed their vows before their friends and families who arrived bearing (and often wearing) tin gifts, most of which were quite humorous. Anniversary tin items may include hats, cradles, slippers and shoes, rolling pins, etc. See also Primitives and Kitchen Collectibles.

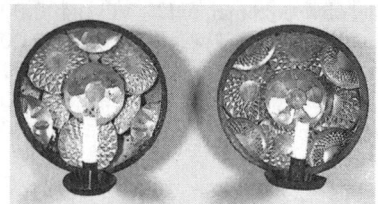

Mirror sconces, faceted reflection disks behind glass pane, crimped circular drip pan with candle holder, American, 19th century, 9¾" diameter, $6,600.00 for the pair.

Anniversary, loving cup, 2 funnels soldered, ca 1900, 7⅜" **45.00**
Anniversary, shoes, orig ribbons, dtd 1863, 9", pr **635.00**
Anniversary, top hat, 6¼" **300.00**
Baby feeder, short spout, bulb shape, rare, 4½" **350.00**
Can, pouring spigot on top, strap hdl, 4¾" **200.00**
Candle box, 2 tab hangers, 14x4½", EX **325.00**
Cheese drainer, dmn shape, punched designs, ftd **375.00**
Cheese mold, heart shape, handmade, early, 5½" **295.00**
Cheese strainer, heart form, ring ft & hdls, 4½" **250.00**
Cheese strainer, heart shape, 3-ftd, ribbon hdl, 19th C, 6⅜" ...**550.00**
Chocolate muddler, w/wooden stirrer **195.00**
Churn, wood dasher, side hdls, 13½" **325.00**
Coffeepot, gooseneck, punched band on hinged lid, 11" **190.00**
Coffeepot, tin w/copper bottom, lg **70.00**
Cookie press, tube shape, wooden pusher w/heart design **125.00**
Cup, emb decor, child sz **45.00**
Downspout ornament, circle w/emb pineapple & cutouts, 27" **250.00**
Egg poacher, oval shape on 4 ft, wire stem w/loop hdl, 7" **22.00**
Ladle, cup shape w/pour spout, long hook hdl, early **30.00**
Lunch basket, woven, hinged lid, top hdl **150.00**

Lunch bucket, oval, strap hdl, w/lid, sm **95.00**
Measure, raised rings, 1-pt **30.00**
Milk pan, Shaker style, minor rpr to lip, 6x16" **25.00**
Pastry sheet, w/shelf, w/dk tin rolling pin **650.00**
Pie crimper, wooden hdl, 6¾" **35.00**
Sconce, blk pnt, raised vine & scalloped crest, 14" **495.00**
Sconce, rnd reflecter w/sunburst decor, ca 1800, 13x9x5" **750.00**
Scones, 13 tube receivers for flags, ca 1876, 16½", pr, G **750.00**
Skimmer, molasses; wood & tin, 10x5¾"+4" hdl **50.00**
Sugar shaker, flared ft, rnd pierced lid, C hdl, ca 1890, 4" ...**50.00**
Teapot, pewter finial, 8" **105.00**
Toddy warmer, funnel shape, pouring lip, side hdl **100.00**
Wash bowl & pitcher **195.00**

Tobacciana

Tobacciana is the generally accepted term used to cover a field of collecting that includes smoking pipes, cigar molds, cigarette lighters, humidors — in short, any article having to do with the practice of using tobacco in any form. Perhaps the most valuable variety of pipes is the meerschaum, hand carved from hydrous magnesium, an opaque white-gray or cream-colored mineral of the soapstone family. (Much of this is today mined in Turkey which has the largest meerschaum deposit in the world, though there are other deposits of lesser significance around the globe.) These figural bowls often portray an elaborately carved mythological character, an animal, or a historical scene. Amber is sometimes used for the stem. Other collectible pipes are corn cob (Missouri Meerschaum) and Indian peace pipes of clay or catlinite. (See American Indian Art.)

Chosen because it was the Indians who first introduced the white man to smoking, the cigar store Indian was a symbol used to identify tobacco stores in the 19th century. The majority of them were hand carved between 1830 and 1900 and are today recognized as some of the finest examples of early wood sculptures. When found they command very high prices.

For further information on lighters, refer to *Collector's Guide to Cigarette Lighters* by James Flanagan. Ashtray collectors will enjoy *Collector's Guide to Ashtrays* by Nancy Wanvig. Our advisor for this category is Chuck Thompson; he is listed in the Directory under Texas. See also Advertising; Snuff Boxes.

Ashtray, Art Glass, intaglio cupids, 8-sided, 1920s, 3" **25.00**
Ashtray, Art Glass, sailfish in bowl, 6¾" **40.00**
Ashtray, brass, frog, top lifts, 2 rests, 5½" **14.00**
Ashtray, brass, ship's compass & wheel figural, 1930s, 6" **60.00**
Ashtray, brass, steer head, 3-ftd, 5" **25.00**
Ashtray, brass, winged dog holds tray in mouth, China, 3½" **32.00**
Ashtray, bronze, elephant head, sand casting, 6¼" **58.00**
Ashtray, ceramic, Black boy pushing ash bbl, 4" **42.00**
Ashtray, ceramic, Indian boy at teepee, smoker, 4¼" **25.00**
Ashtray, chalkware, Chattanooga Shoe Shine Boy, 5¼" **78.00**
Ashtray, chalkware, man w/gun on bull, 1950s, 5⅛" **25.00**
Ashtray, compo, seated Indian figural, glass ashtray insert, 5" **20.00**
Ashtray, copper, man lifting lady's skirt on bk, 3½x5½" **90.00**
Ashtray, copper-plated Indian arrowhead, Indian in center, 5⅝" **15.00**
Ashtray, marble, green, elephant on bk rim, 6" dia **50.00**
Ashtray, metal, nodder, Black boy w/cigar in mouth, Austria, 4⅞" **160.00**
Ashtray, pipe; glass, amethyst, Pat June 1923, 6⅝" **15.00**
Ashtray, pottery, Indian face in center, McMaster, 7⅜" dia **30.00**
Ashtray, soapstone, elephant figure on bk rim, gray, 4¼" **35.00**
Cheroot holder, meerschaum, cvd nude woman, 1880s, M **575.00**
Cheroot holder, meerschaum, 2 pool players, amber stem, 5" **140.00**
Cigar box opener, Faust **35.00**

Cigar box opener, John Ruskin 20.00
Cigar box opener, Sullivan 40.00
Cigar cutter, brass-plated w/emb floral & deer, table-top 135.00
Cigar cutter, gold-filled, w/bl sapphire 165.00
Cigar cutter, gold-plate w/snake emb, Art Nouveau 75.00
Cigar cutter, horn, bottle shape, sm 110.00
Cigar cutter, horn, curved, lg 165.00
Cigar cutter, metal, man w/top hat figural, 8¼" 400.00
Cigar cutter, New Currency 5 Cents 450.00
Cigar cutter, pearl hdl 95.00
Cigar cutter, Perforator 65.00
Cigar cutter, souvenir of Pan Am Expo, 1901, pocket sz 70.00
Cigar cutter, sterling w/eng florals 195.00
Cigar cutter, whale's tooth w/scrimshawed eagle's head 275.00
Cigar cutter, wood & metal, bull dog figural, 7¾" 400.00
Cigar cutter/watch fob, gold-filled blimp shape 110.00
Cigar cutter/watch fob, MOP 135.00
Cigar mold, wooden, EX 55.00
Cigar tray, These Are My Last, HP cigars/matches on porc 65.00
Cigarette box, leather book form, Philip Morris 16.00
Cigarette card, Duke's, NY From Brooklyn Bridge, 1885, EX 12.00
Cigarette cards, Allen & Ginter, bell-cut w/bird, album w/50, VG 245.00
Cigarette case, gold-tone cougar on lid, chrome base, 4¼" 50.00
Cigarette holder, Bakelite, gr or red 30.00
Cigarette holder, ivory, 3½" 40.00
Cigarette jar, cased glass, much gold, metal ormolu base 75.00
Cigarette pack, Camel Menthol Slide-o-matic 5.00
Cigarette pack, Camel 75th Birthday 12.00
Cigarette papers, Duke's Mixture, #8, wht, NM 20.00
Cigarette papers, Half & Half/A Cargo, NM 4.00
Cigarette papers, Half & Half/Lucky Strike, NM 10.00
Cigarette papers, Honest Long Cut, NM 30.00
Cigarette papers, Pride of Reidsville, gr, NM 60.00
Clock, Joe Camel pool player 50.00
Figure, Indian brave, wood & plaster, 72", EX 350.00
Figure, Indian chief, cvd wood, EX details & pnt, 1920s, 84" 3,850.00
Figure, Indian chief, cvd wood, headdress/feathered skirt, 28" ...2,850.00
Figure, Indian princess w/headdress, EX mc pnt, 1880s, 80" 17,250.00
Figure, Indian scout, cvd wood, old rpt, 1880s, 74" 19,550.00
Humidor, brass, La Palina Senators 48.00
Humidor, mahog, brass bound, dtd 1919 ....750.00
Humidor, majolica, Arab, Austria, 7½" 350.00
Humidor, majolica, Arab, mc, 6½" 300.00
Humidor, majolica, Blackamoor, mc, #d, 7½" 325.00
Humidor, majolica, boxer dog's head, #6933 over #43, 5" 350.00
Humidor, majolica, boy w/ear-flap hat, realistic colors, 5" 125.00
Humidor, majolica, Irish jockey figural, mc, 5" 195.00
Humidor, majolica, man's head, glossy, Japan, 6¾" 125.00
Humidor, pewter, claw & ball ft, EX detail, 7½" 75.00
Humidor, porc, devil, Victoria Carlsbad Austria, 4½", NM 285.00
Humidor, porc, drunken monkey, Shierholz, 7" 285.00
Humidor, porc, gentleman rabbit, Schierholz, rpr, 9¼" 265.00
Humidor, porc, monk's head form, brn & flesh tones, 6" 65.00
Humidor, pottery, dog face, emb, Staffordshire, pre-WWII, 5½" 425.00
Humidor, pottery, horses, lustre, Gray's Pottery Dunhill 65.00
Humidor, pottery, owl figural, yel/brn/cobalt gloss, 7" 350.00
Humidor, terra cotta, bowler, pnt, lt wear, 9¼" 850.00
Humidor, terra cotta, soldier & lady, pnt, JM (J Maresch), 11½" ...1,700.00
Humidor, wood, skull w/ivory snake, frog sits atop, 6" 595.00
Lighter, ATC cigarette case & lighter combo 20.00
Lighter, Calibri, polished chrome/gold, table sz 65.00
Lighter, Camel, brass-plated 12.50
Lighter, Camel advertising, chrome & brass 12.50
Lighter, cigar; Egyptian dog figural, brass, table sz 295.00

Lighter, cigar; hammered SP globe w/dragon hdl 175.00
Lighter, Dunhill, brass dueling pistol, 1930s, 4x6¼" 225.00
Lighter, Elgin, Am Lite-O-Matic, M 20.00
Lighter, Executive, Bakelite, Ellis, table sz, MIB w/booklet 350.00
Lighter, figural, Book of Smoking, Corona 20.00
Lighter, figural, cowboy boot w/spur, Evans 15.00
Lighter, figural, gun, Henry 42 caliber derringer, Swank 30.00
Lighter, fire pumper, cast metal, wheels trn, 4x4½" 125.00
Lighter, horse-head striker, USA 65.00
Lighter, Marvel Pocket Lighter, metal, w/Ray-O-Lite Fluid, MIB 35.00
Lighter, Mastercase by Ronson, chromium/blk enamel, 1933, 4¾" 40.00
Lighter, Partlow Kase Liter, polished chrome, MIB 20.00
Lighter, Ronson, Banker, 14k gold, engine-trn, 1950s 150.00
Lighter, Ronson, Princess, enameled florals on blk, 1950s 45.00
Lighter, USS Independence 100.00
Lighter, Zippo, chrome w/eng Joe Camel, M 50.00
Lighter, Zippo, Civil War, Cherokee rifleman, 1991 ....25.00
Lighter, Zippo, Landing on the Moon, 1969, from $25 to 30.00
Lighter, Zippo, whaling scene w/masted ship, 1980s 30.00
Photo, cigar store int, 1895, EX 12.50
Pipe box, wood w/old blk pnt, 1-drw, New England, 18th C, 22x9x5" .3,450.00
Pipe holder, compo Indian moccasin, 5½", EX 75.00
Plug cutter, Arrow 125.00
Plug cutter, Brighton #3, elf figural, 13" L, VG 275.00
Plug cutter, Cremo, CI V shape, 5¾x5½" 55.00
Plug cutter, Empire, Quebec 150.00
Plug cutter, Star, Pat 1885 ....75.00
Tobacco pouch, George Washington Cut Plug, cloth, NM 28.00
Tobacco pouch, Horse Shoe Plug, leather, EX 15.00
Tobacco pouch, Old North State Tobacco, cloth, 1½-oz, NM 25.00
Tobacco pouch, Thumper Sun Cured Tobacco, cloth, NM 5.00
Tobacco tag, Lucky Strike, rnd, EX 8.00
Tobacco tag, Peerless, diecut P, EX 6.00
Tobacco tag, Sailor's Hope, EX 6.00
Tobacco tag, Sentinel, octagonal, EX 5.00
Tobacco tag, Upper Ten, EX 3.00
Token, Ace Cigar Store, brass 3.00

Pipes

Bone/wood, hag in bonnet cvg 150.00
Clay, nude figural stem, 1880s, 4" 75.00
Meerschaum, curved stem w/silver mts, deep-cvd bowl, 12" 165.00
Meerschaum, hunter & dog, amber stem, 3½x8½", +case 250.00
Meerschaum, lion, 4¾", NM, +case 175.00
Meerschaum, turk's head, long stem, 16" 150.00
Meerschaum, Victorian lady's head w/fancy hat, 3x5" 125.00
Porc, owl figural bowl, E Bohne Sohne, 2¾" 575.00
Porc, sea captain figural, E Bohne Sohne, 2½" 325.00
Wood, Indian maiden bowl, 19th C, 11½" 1,100.00
Wood, man-in-top-hat bowl, inlaid eyes, 19th C, 2½x6¼" 1,380.00

Toby Jugs

The delightful jug known as the Toby dates back to the 18th century, when factories in England produced them for export to the American colonies. Named for the character Toby Philpots in the song *The Little Brown Jug*, the Toby was fashioned in the form of a jolly fellow, usually holding a jug of beer and a glass. The earlier examples were made with strict attention to details such as fingernails and teeth. Originally representing only a non-entity, a trend developed to portray well-known individuals such as George II, Napoleon, and Ben Franklin. Among the most-valued Tobies are those produced by Ralph Wood I in the late 1700s. By the mid-1830s Tobies were being made in America. See also Doulton; Lenox; Occupied Japan.

Quaker man and woman, painted majolica, Minton, ca 1868, 11¼", $4,600.00 for the pair.

Admiral Beatty, Dread Nought, Wilkinson, 1917, rstr, 10½" **500.00**
Admiral Jelhoe, Hell Five Jack, Wilkinson, 1918, 10" **500.00**
Captain Hook, full figure, England, 7" **75.00**
Field Marshall Haig, Push & Go, Wilkinson, 1917, 11" **400.00**
King Cole, Shorter mk, 1930s, 5" **55.00**
Man sits w/jug, mc pearlware, ca 1780-1800, minor rstr, 8¾" **250.00**
Parliament member, face w/wig, 5" **75.00**
President Wilson, Welcome! Uncle Sam, Wilkinson, 1918, 10¼" ...**1,150.00**

Toleware

The term 'toleware' originally came from a French term meaning 'sheet iron.' Today it is used to refer to paint-decorated tin items, most popular from 1800 to 1850s. The craft flourished in Pennsylvania, Connecticut, Maine, and New York state. Early toleware has a very distinctive look. The surface is dull and unvarnished; background colors range from black to cream. Geometrics are quite common, but florals and fruits were also favored. Items made after 1850 were often stenciled, and gold trim was sometimes added.

American toleware is usually found in practical, everyday forms — trays, boxes, and coffeepots are most common — while French examples might include candlesticks, wine coolers, jardinieres, etc. Be sure to note color and design when determining date and value, but condition of the paint is the most important worth-assessing factor. In the listings that follow, the dimension given for boxes and trays indicates length. Unless noted otherwise, values are for very good examples with average wear.

Box, floral, gold stencil on red, 1850s, 2⅝x4x2½" **110.00**
Box, floral, mc on blk, dome top, 10" **600.00**
Box, floral, mc on blk, oval, hinged lid, 5x7x5¼" **1,100.00**
Box, floral, mc on blk, ring-pull top, 5½x8¾x4½" **1,000.00**
Box, fruit, mc on blk, dome lid, ring-pull, 6x9½x5", G **300.00**
Box, match; floral, mc on blk, trefoil crest, hangs, 6" **300.00**
Box, Seed Box in gold w/mc bands & florals, 10x10x6½" **380.00**
Canister, floral, mc on blk w/red daubs, hinged lid, late, 6½" **100.00**
Chamberstick, floral, mc on dk brn japanning, 6½", EX **1,700.00**
Coffeepot, floral, mc on blk, old rprs/rpt, 10½" **220.00**
Coffeepot, floral, mc on blk, stick spout, hinged lid, 9" **1,600.00**
Coffeepot, floral, mc on blk, stick spout, hinged lid, 10" **2,900.00**
Coffeepot, floral, mc on blk japanning, wear, 1850s, 8½" **225.00**
Coffeepot, floral, mc on dk brn japanning, touch up, 10½" **600.00**
Mug, floral, mc on blk, 5¾" **965.00**
Tray, bread; floral, mc on blk, lt wear, 14x7" **770.00**
Tray, floral, mc on blk w/yel border, canted corners, 13x9" **1,100.00**
Tray, floral bouquet w/gold on blk, oval, late, 23½x18" **175.00**
Tray, fruit, mc (dk w/age) on blk, canted corners, 13x9", G **100.00**
Tray, Marco Polo (schooner) on blk w/gilt, 24½" **225.00**

Tray, ship in ice scene w/Am flag, dtd 1854, red & gr, 17" **330.00**

Tools

Before the Civil War, tools for the most part were handmade. Some were primitive to the point of crudeness, while others reflected the skill of those who took pride in their trade. Increasing demand for quality tools and the dawning of the age of industrialization resulted in tools that were mass produced. Factors important in evaluating antique tools are scarcity, usefulness, and portability. Those with a manufacturer's mark are worth more than unmarked items. When no condition is indicated, the items listed here are assumed to be in excellent condition. Our advisor for this category is Jim Calison; he is listed in the Directory under New York. See also Keen Kutter; Stanley; Winchester.

Auger, hollow, all brass except cutters (2) **145.00**
Auger, hollow, CI w/blk japanning, 1 cutter **55.00**
Ax, broad; W Hunt, 6", w/orig hdl **50.00**
Axe, Kent type, Fawnfoot hdl, minimum value **95.00**
Barking spud, spoon type, original hdl, 1800 ....**125.00**
Bowl maker's closed shaver, rnd, 3" dia **85.00**
Coach jack, hickory, iron joiners, minimum value **110.00**
Cobbler's soles cutter, iron, base-edge **30.00**
Colter plow, to cut turf **48.00**
Cooper's pull scraper, maple hdl, brass ferrule **45.00**
Cooper's stencil wheel, to mk bbl heads, minimum value **165.00**
Cutter, brass tubing **35.00**
Draw knife, DR Barton 1882, 22" overall, EX+ **85.00**
Draw knife, swan folding hdl **35.00**
Draw knife mast, 1830s **48.00**
Farrier's nail box, wood, metal base & hdl **45.00**
Fodder stripper, wood, 1-pc **23.00**
Gauge, carpenter's dbl marking; rosewood & brass, screw adjusting ...**75.00**
Gauge, marking; wood & brass, sgn Robt Maples...Sheffield, 7½" ...**65.00**
Gauge, mortising; cherry w/brass **65.00**
Hand-reaping hook, blacksmith signed, 1870 ....**120.00**
Hoopsetter, wood, concave base **52.00**
Jigsaw, treadle type w/ornate CI base, 41" **500.00**
Knife, leather cutting **12.00**
Level, Stratton Bros #1 grade, rosewood & brass, 30" **200.00**
Log measure, brass & wood, determines board ft **115.00**
Plane, compass; copy of Stanley 113, MIG, 1960, M **95.00**
Plane, H Chapin #204½ & A Rhode, wood/brass/iron, 10½" L **75.00**
Plane, jointer; wood bottom, adjustable fence guide, EX **185.00**
Rule, wood w/branch hinges, English **35.00**
Saw, trenching; maple, 1840s **85.00**
Spoke shave, Cincinnati Tool Co Hargrove on blade, 10½" **45.00**
Steamboat Engineer's wrench **55.00**
Stonemason's trimming axe, for sandstone, minimum value **70.00**
Tanner's stretching board, for sm game hides **20.00**
Tap & die auger, 1850s **145.00**
Tobacco spike, brass **45.00**
Violin maker's clamp, oak **75.00**

Toothbrush Holders

Most of the collectible toothbrush holders were made in prewar Japan and were modeled after popular comic strip, Disney, and nursery rhyme characters. Since many were made of bisque and decorated with unfired paint, it's not uncommon to find them in less-than-perfect paint, a factor you must consider when attempting to assess their values.

Our advisor for this category is Marilyn Cooper, author of *Pictorial Guide to Toothbrush Holders*; she is listed in the Directory under Texas.

Andy Gump & Min, bsk, Japan, 4" 85.00
Bear, chalkware, 6⅛" 55.00
Bell Hop w/Flowers, Japan, 5¼" 85.00
Big Bird, sitting, Taiwan, 4½" 80.00
Boy on Elephant, Japan, 6¼" 100.00
Cat w/Bass Fiddle, Japan, 6" 130.00
Clown, Juggling; Japan, 5" 85.00
Dog, Begging; Germany (5442), 3" 135.00
Dog w/Sad Face, Germany, 3¾" 100.00
Donkey, Japan (Goldcastle), 5¾" 100.00
Duck, Japan, 5½" 90.00
Dumbo, WDP, 3" 375.00
Elephant w/Tusk, Japan, 5½" 80.00
Frog w/Mandolin, Japan (Goldcastle), 6" 95.00
Halloween Policeman, Japan, 5" 110.00
Happy, Snow White & the Seven Dwarfs, WD, Japan, 3½" 625.00
Indian Chief, Japan, 4½" 325.00
Lone Ranger, chalkware, 4" 80.00
Mickey & Minnie, hands on hips, bsk, Japan, WED, 4¼" 350.00
Old King Cole, Japan, 5¼" 100.00
Orphan Annie & Sandy on Couch, bsk, Japan, 3¾" 135.00
Peter Rabbit, Germany, 6¼" 375.00
Pinocchio & Figaro, Shafford, 5¼" 550.00
Pluto, Japan, 4⅝" 200.00
Popeye, bsk, Japan, 5" 500.00
Schnauzer, Germany, 3⅛" 100.00
Skeezix, metal, USA, 6" 175.00
Soldier, Japan, 6¾" 95.00
Toonerville Trolley, bsk, Japan, 5½" 550.00

Toothpick Holders

Once common on every table, the toothpick holder was relegated to the china cabinet near the turn of the century. Fortunately, this contributed to their survival. As a result, many are available to collectors today. Because they are small and easily displayed, they are very popular collectibles. They come in a wide range of prices to fit every budget. Many have been reproduced and, unfortunately, are being offered for sale right along with the originals. These 'repros' should be priced in the $10.00 to $30.00 range. Unless you're sure of what you're buying, choose a reputable dealer. In addition to pattern glass, you'll find examples in china, bisque, art glass, and various metals. Toothpick holders in the listings that follow are glass unless noted otherwise. Values here are for originals. Our advisor for this category is Judy A. Knauer; she is listed in the Directory under Pennsylvania.

See also specific companies (such as Northwood) and types of glassware (such as Burmese, cranberry, etc.).

Arched Ovals 20.00
Baby Invt T'Print, amberina, 3-corner 275.00
Baby's Bootee, amber 50.00
Banded Portland, Maiden's Blush 55.00
Block, vaseline, hat form 55.00
Blocked Thumbprint Band 30.00
Box in Box 30.00
Box in Box, gr w/gold 42.00
Cat on Pillow, amber 60.00
Chrysanthemum Base Swirl, pk satin speckle 250.00
Colonial Stairsteps, bl opal, scarce 45.00

Daisy and Button, amber with metal bands, 2½", $20.00.

Daisy & Button, amber bbl w/brass bands 15.00
Daisy & Button, ruby stain buttons & rim 65.00
Daisy & Button w/V Ornament, bl 45.00
Delaware 100.00
Diamond Spearhead, gr opal 75.00
Diamond Spearhead, vaseline opal 80.00
Dmn Quilt, bl MOP, ruffled rim, camphor trim, 3" (+) 250.00
Dmn Quilt, fuchsia amberina, tricon rim, 2¼" (+) 275.00
Dog & Stump, bl (tail unbroken) 60.00
Double Ring Panel 30.00
Esther 35.00
Flora, gr 125.00
Florette, bl opaque 110.00
Florette, bl satin 55.00
Florette, pk, 2" 75.00
Frazier, cranberry w/gold & enamel 75.00
Holly, old 65.00
Idyll, gr opal 210.00
Intaglio Sunflower 35.00
Invt Baby T'print, amberina, crimped rim, 2¼" 200.00
Iris w/Meander, gr opal 80.00
King's Crown, ruby stained 30.00
Majestic, ruby stain 135.00
Michigan, floral decor & yel stain 85.00
Minnesota, clear w/gold 30.00
National's Eureka, ruby stain 80.00
Nevada 55.00
New Hampshire, clear w/etched advertising 45.00
New Jersey, clear w/EX gold 55.00
Oregon 85.00
Over-All Hob, wht opal 45.00
Paneled Grape, gr 75.00
Peerless, Heisey 40.00
Pineapple & Fan, gr w/gold, Heisey 150.00
Plain, scalloped panels, gr w/gold 20.00
Porcupine figural, rstr Meriden silver, 2⅛x3" L 100.00
Preparedness, glass figural 225.00
Pretty Maid (beware of repro) 65.00
Prize 40.00
Reverse Swirl, cranberry 110.00
Reverse Swirl, vaseline 135.00
Rib & Bead, ruby stain 55.00
Ribbed Drape, custard 350.00
Ribbed Spiral, bl opal 125.00
Ring-Neck Stripe, wht opal 125.00
Rising Sun 40.00
Saddle, bl 45.00
Scroll w/Acanthus, purple slag 310.00
Scroll w/Cane Band, ruby stain 110.00
Silver, eng florals, ped ft, 1890s, no mk, 3¼x1¾" 50.00
Sunbeam, gr w/gold 80.00
Sunk Daisy, clear w/gold 20.00
Sunk Honeycomb, ruby stain 45.00

Texas 35.00
Tokyo, wht opal 125.00
USA, clear w/gold 30.00
Vigilant, Fostoria 25.00
Zipper Slash, ruby stain 30.00

Torquay Pottery

Torquay is a unique type of pottery made in the South Devon area of England as early as 1867. At the height of productivity, at least a dozen companies flourished there, producing simple folk pottery from the area's natural red clay. The ware was both wheel-turned and molded and decorated under the glaze with heavy slip resulting in low-relief nature subjects or simple scrollwork. Three of the best-known of these potteries were Watcombe (1867 – 1962); Aller Vale (in operation from the mid-1800s, producing domestic ware and architectural products); and Longpark (1890 until 1957). Watcombe and Aller Vale merged in 1901 and operated until 1962 under the name of Royal Aller Vale and Watcombe Art Pottery.

A decline in the popularity of the early classical terra-cotta styles (urns, busts, figures, etc.) lead to the introduction of painted and glazed terra-cotta wares. During the late 1880s, white clay wares, both turned and molded, were decorated with colored glazes (Stapleton ware, grotesque molded figures, ornamental vases, large jardiniers, etc.). By the turn of the century, the market for art pottery was diminishing, so the potteries turned to wares decorated in colored slips (Barbotine, Persian, Scrolls, etc.).

Motto wares were introduced in the late 19th century by Aller Vale and taken up in the present century by the other Torquay potteries. This eventually became the 'bread and butter' product of the local industry. This was perhaps the most famous type of ware potted in this area because of the verses, proverbs, and quotations that decorated it. This was achieved by the sgraffito technique — scratching the letters through the slip to expose the red clay underneath. The most popular patterns were Cottage, Black Cockerel, Multi-Cockerel, and a scrollwork design called Scandy. Other popular decorations were Kerswell Daisy, ships, kingfishers, applied bird decorations, Art Deco styles, Egyptian ware, and many others. Aller Vale ware may sometimes be found marked 'H.H. and Company,' a firm who assumed ownership from 1897 to 1901. 'Watcombe Torquay' was an impressed mark used from 1884 to 1927.

Our advisors for this category are Jerry and Gerry Kline; they are listed in the Directory under Ohio. If you're interested in joining a Torquay club, you'll find the address of The North American Torquay Society under Clubs, Newsletters, and Catalogs.

Art Pottery

Bottle, scent; Cornish Violets, unmk, 2" 30.00
Bottle, scent; Devon Lavender, unmk, 3" 45.00
Bottle, scent; Devon Violets, Fornely Wallis, 2¾" 45.00
Bottle, scent; Devon Violets, Made in Great Britain, 2¼" 25.00
Bottle, scent; Devon Violets, unmk, w/crown stopper, 4½" 60.00
Bottle, scent; English Roses, unmk, 2½" 55.00
Bottle, scent; Sailboats, Paignton Breezes, unmk, 3" 75.00
Bowl, Cherries on bl w/cream int, attached underplate, 5" L 80.00
Bowl, Pheasant, faience, Torquay England, 2½x8" 225.00
Bowl, Sandringham, unmk Aller Vale, 4½" dia 75.00
Chamberstick, bl faience, 2 dimpled edges, illegible mk, 2½" 70.00
Chamberstick, Fruit, unmk, 4½" 80.00
Chamberstick, Moonlight, Watcombe, Isle of Wight, 4½" 135.00
Chamberstick, Thistle, Longpark, 1903-09, 4½" 125.00
Coffeepot, Crocus, Longpark, ca 1930-40, 7½" 195.00

Coffeepot, Sailboats in Rosy Sunset, 'Take Another Cup...,' 5" ...90.00
Creamer, Sea Gull, Royal Watcombe, 1935-62, mini, 2" 50.00
Cup & saucer, Crocus, Longpark, ca 1930-40, 3" 65.00
Egg cup plate, Polka Dot, Babbacombe, 6¼" 25.00
Hair receiver, Rosy Sunset, Watcombe, 1915-26, 3" 75.00
Jam dish, Sea Gull, Dartmouth, 5" W 45.00
Jam jar, Crocus, Longpark, 1930-40, 4¾" 55.00
Jam jar, Flamingo, Daison, 4½" 175.00
Jardiniere, Lemon & Cruet, heather decor, ruffled, 8x10" 375.00
Jardiniere, Parrots on branch, att Hele Cross, 4¾x6" 185.00
Jug, puzzle; Rosy Sunset, unmk, 'Come Try Your Skill,' 4¼" 150.00
Mug, Rosy Sunset, 'Sunshine Makes Shadows...,' unmk, 3" 75.00
Mustard jar, Sea Gull, Covelly, Babbacombe 40.00
Pin tray, Shamrock, Royal Devon, 3¼" 50.00
Pitcher, Cottage, Watcombe, faience, amber w/brn hdl, no motto, 3" 40.00
Pitcher, Forget-Me-Not, unmk, From Preston, 3" 45.00
Pitcher, Kingfisher, Royal Torquay, 1924-40, 4" 50.00
Pitcher, Kingfisher, Watcombe, 3½" 50.00
Pitcher, Rose on Trellis, Watcombe, 5¾" 170.00
Pitcher, Rosy Sunset, unmk, 4½" 68.00
Plate, bird in relief, unmk, 5½" 50.00
Plate, Sea Gull, St Ives, Babbacombe, 6½" 38.00
Shakers, Flamingo, att Daison, 2¾", pr 85.00
Sugar bowl, Cockington Forge, Watcombe, 2¾" dia 42.50
Sugar bowl, Sea Gull on rock, Land's End, ruffled top, 3½" 50.00
Teacup & saucer, Sea Gull, St Ives, Babbacombe 30.00
Teapot, Butterfly, water lily & reeds, Royal Torquay, '20s, 6½" .125.00
Vase, Barbotine, palm frond on bk, unmk Exeter, 4¼" 60.00
Vase, Butterfly, unmk, 2¼" 65.00
Vase, Dragon, unmk Longpark, ca 1920, 6¼" 525.00
Vase, finger; Scroll, unmk Aller Vale, 5¾" 150.00
Vase, Fruits, Watcombe, 1901-20, 4¼" 65.00
Vase, Iris, unmk, 3-hdl, 5" 75.00
Vase, Kingfisher on lt bl, Royal Watcombe, 7½" 165.00
Vase, Kingfisher on rich bl, unmk, pinched top, 4½" 65.00
Vase, Kingfishers, 1 in air/1 in nest, hdls, Watcombe, 14x4¼" ...375.00
Vase, Lemon & Cruet, lav & wht heather, twist hdls, 8¼" 180.00
Vase, Parrot on branch, Longpark, twist hdls, 12x4", pr 425.00
Vase, Pheasant against Rosy Sky, faience, Hele Cross, 11½" 225.00
Vase, Sailboats in Rosy Sunset, pinched top, unmk, 4" 75.00
Vase, Scroll on bl, Aller Vale, 7¾" 165.00
Vase, Scroll on lt bl, Aller Vale, 6" 150.00
Watering can, Sandringham, Aller Vale, 4¾" 250.00

Devon Motto Ware

Dresser tray, attributed to Longpark, 'A place for everything...,' 7¼x10¼", $200.00.

Ashtray, Cottage, Dartmouth, 'Du-ee Elp Yersel,' 3½x5" 40.00
Ashtray, Ship, Longpark, 'I'll Take the Ashes,' 4¾x3¼" 40.00
Basket, Cockerel, Royal Torquay, 'He Who Hesitates...,' 3½" 95.00
Beaker, Black Cockerel, Longpark, 'Suilence Is the Wise...,' 4½" .85.00
Beaker, Cottage, Dartmouth, 'Daun'ce Be 'fraid...,' 3" 50.00
Bowl, Cottage, Made in England, 'A Little Help's...,' 5½" 50.00
Bowl, porridge; Kingfisher, 'Help Yourself to Porrage' 40.00
Bowl, Ships, Longpark, 'Help Yersel an Dinna...,' 4½" 45.00

Butter dish, Thistle, Longpark, 'Frae Land o Burns...,' 3½x5" **98.00**
Candlestick, Scandy, unmk, ruffled, 'Last to Bed...,' 7½" **85.00**
Candlestick, Scandy, unmk Longpark, 'Hear All...,' 3½" **65.00**
Candlesticks, Cottage, Watcombe, faience, amber, 5¾", pr **135.00**
Chamberstick, Cottage, Longpark, 'Last in....' 1930-40, 2x4½" ..**125.00**
Chamberstick, Scandy, unmk, 'Blessed Are the Drowsy...,' 7½" .**225.00**
Chamberstick, Scandy, Watcombe, 'Goodnight & Joy Be...,' 6" **185.00**
Coffeepot, Sailboat, Longpark, 'Bornmouth Grawn Poeth,' 7" ...**175.00**
Cup & saucer, Cottage, 'Be Like a Sundial...,' 4x5½", 8¾" **150.00**
Cup & saucer, Kerswell Daisy, Aller Vale, 'It's Unca...,' 2½" **125.00**
Dust pan, Scandy, unmk, mini, 4½" **90.00**
Egg cup, Cottage, Dartmouth, 'New Laid,' 2¾" **30.00**
Egg cup, Cottage, unmk Watcombe, 'There's No Fun Like Work,' 3" ..**45.00**
Ewer, Ships, 'Time & Tide Wait...,' 6" **145.00**
Hatpin holder, Scandy, Longpark, 'Keep Me on the...,' 4½" **145.00**
Humdor, Shamrock, Longpark, 'Chosen Leaf of Bard...,' 5½" **95.00**
Inkwell, Scandy, Aller Vale, w/lid, 'Blot Out My Past...,' 2½" **98.00**
Jug, puzzle; Cottage, Dartmouth, 'Within This Jug...,' 4½" **95.00**
Loving cup, Scandy, Aller Vale, 'Little Duties...,' 4½" **85.00**
Match holder/striker, Cottage, Watcombe, 'Match for Any...,' 2" ..**110.00**
Mug, Cockerel, Longpark, 'Jack & Jill...,' 3" **75.00**
Pitcher, Babbacombe, 'Daun'ce Be 'Fraid...,' 4¼" **55.00**
Pitcher, Babbacombe, 'Elp Yersel' tu More...,' 3⅞" **50.00**
Pitcher, Cottage, unmk, 'Take a Wee Drop...,' mini, 1¾" **75.00**
Pitcher, Cottage, Watcombe, 'Waste Note Want...,' 3¾" **45.00**
Pitcher, flower design, faience, 'Brevity Is the Soul...,' 4¾" **65.00**
Pitcher, hot water; Primrose, unmk, 'May the Hinges...,' 8½" **175.00**
Pitcher, Kerswell Daisy, Aller Vale, 'For Every Evil...,' 6¾" **195.00**
Pitcher, Kingfisher, 'Fresh From the Cow,' 2¼" **50.00**
Pitcher, Kingfisher, Torquay, 'Time & Tide...,' 1925-30, 5½" **75.00**
Pitcher, Multi-Cockerel, Aller Vale, 'Guid Morn'...,' 4" **75.00**
Pitcher, Primrose, unmk, 'Shut Mouth Never...,' 3¼" **45.00**
Pitcher, Primrose, unmk, 'Straught Frae the Coo,' 3" **45.00**
Pitcher, Sailboat, 'There's No Wealth But Life,' 4¾" **65.00**
Pitcher, Scandy, unmk Aller Vale, 'Do What You Can...,' 7" **175.00**
Pitcher, Scandy on cobalt, Aller Vale, 'Be Canny...Cream,' 2½" ...**85.00**
Plate, Cottage, 'Be Like a Sundial...,' 9¾" **115.00**
Plate, Cottage, Dartmouth, 'E Can't Make a Silk...,' 6½" **50.00**
Plate, Cottage, Royal Watcombe, 'To Win a Smile...,' 6½" **55.00**
Plate, Dartmouth Cottage, 'To Thine Own Self...,' 6½" **50.00**
Powder jar, Scandy, illegible mk, 'Powder' on lid, 3⅝" **120.00**
Salt cellar, Cockerel, unmk Longpark, 'Be Canny...,' ped ft, 1¾" .**75.00**
Salt cellar, Scandy, unmk, open ft, 'Take Sum Saul' **45.00**
Sugar bowl, Cockerel, Longpark, Niver Say Die...,' 3¾" dia **45.00**
Teapot, Cottage, unmk Crown Devon, 'It's Unco Refreshing,' 3½" ..**135.00**
Toast rack, Crocus, Longpark, 'Giant's Causeway,' 3½x5¾" **90.00**
Vase, Cottage, Longpark, 'If You Can't Be Ainsy...,' 6⅛" **95.00**
Vase, Multi-Cockerel, 3 twist hdls, 'Do Noble Things...,' 3⅞" **75.00**
Vase, Passion Flower, unmk, 'He That Always Does...,' 10" **250.00**
Vase, Sailboat, Longpark, 'Welcome Is the Best Cheer,' 4" **45.00**

Toys

Toys can be classified into at least two categories: early collectible toys with an established history, and the newer toys. The antique toys are easier to evaluate. A great deal of research has been done on them, and much data is available. The newer toys are just beginning to be studied; relative information is only now being published, and the lack of production records makes it difficult to know how many may be available. Often warehouse finds of these newer toys can change the market. This has happened with battery-operated toys and to some extent with robots. Review past issues of this guide. You will see the changing trends for the newer toys. All toys become more important as collectibles when a fixed period of manufacture is known. When we know the numbers produced and documentation of the makers is established, the prices become more predictable.

The best way to learn about toys is to attend toy shows and auctions. This will give you the opportunity to compare prices and condition. The more collectors and dealers you meet, the more you will learn. There is no substitute for holding a toy in your hand and seeing for yourself what they are. If you are going to be a serious collector, buy all the books you can find. Read every article you see. Knowledge is vital to building a good collection. Study all books that are available. These are some of the most helpful: *Collecting Toys*, *Collecting Toy Soldiers*, and *Collecting Toy Trains, An Identification & Value Guide #3*, by Richard O'Brien; and *Toys of the Sixties, A Pictorial Guide*, by Bill Bruegman. Other informative books (published by Collector Books) are *Schroeder's Collectible Toys, Antique to Modern*, by Sharon and Bob Huxford; *Collector's Guide to Tinker Toys* by Craig Strange; *Classic Plastic Model Kits* by Rick Polizzi; *The Golden Age of Automotive Toys, 1925 – 1941*, by Ken Hutchison and Greg Johnson; *Motorcycle Toys, Antique & Contemporary*, by Sally Gibson-Downs and Christine Gentry; *Collector's Encyclopedia of Disneyana* by David Longest and Michael Stern; *Stern's Guide to Disney Collectibles, Vol I – 3*, by Michael Stern; *Modern Toys, American Toys, 1830 – 1980*, by Linda Baker; *Antique and Collectible Toys, 1970 – 1950*, *Toys, Antique & Collectible*, and *Cartoon Toys & Collectibles* all by David Longest; *Collectible Male Action Figures* by Paris and Susan Manos; *Collector's Guide to Bubble Bath Containers* by Greg Moore and Joe Pizzo; *G-Men and FBI Toys and Collectibles* by Harry and Jody Whitworth; *Breyer Animal Collector's Guide* by Felicia Browell; *Collector's Guide to Battery Toys, Identification & Values* by Don Hultzman; *Collector's Guide to TV Memorabilia, 1960s & 1970s, Second Edition*, by Greg Davis and Bill Morgan; *Matchbox Toys, 1948 – 1993*, *Matchbox Toys, 1974 – 1996, Second Edition*, and *Diecast Toys and Scale Models*, all by Dana Johnson.

Our advisor for all toys except Farm Toys, Guns, Schoenhut, Steiff, Toy Soldiers, and Trains is Jon Thurmond; he is listed in the Directory under Missouri. In the listings that follow, toys are listed by manufacturer's name if possible, otherwise by type. Measurements are given when appropriate and available; if only one dimension is noted, it is the greater one — height if the toy is vertical, length if it is horizontal. See also Children's Things; Personalities. For toy stoves, see Stoves.

Key:
b/o — battery operated
cl — celluloid
jtd — jointed

NP — nickel plated
w/up — wind-up

Company or Country of Manufacturer

Adams, Mr Magic Magic Set, 1960, NMIB **55.00**
Alps, Bongo the Drumming Monkey, b/o, 3 actions, 1960s, MIB **250.00**
Alps, Clown on Donkey, w/up, cl clown/litho tin donkey, 8", VG+ .**200.00**
AMT, 1960 Ford Starliner, 2-tone gr, M **125.00**
AMT, 1964 Pontiac Grand Prix, friction, 8¾", EX **60.00**
Arcade, Caterpillar Ten Tractor, pnt CI w/NP driver, 7½", EX .**700.00**
Arcade, Lawn Mower, push-type w/wooden hdl, CI cutter, 22", VG **55.00**
Arcade, Monocoupe, pnt CI w/NP prop, 8½", EX **500.00**
Arnold, Ocean Liner, pnt tin, 2-masted/2 stacks, w/up, 13½", EX ...**1,000.00**
Auburn Rubber, Building Bricks, 1950s, complete, EX (EX canister) ...**35.00**
Aurora AFX, Dodge Charger, bl, NM **20.00**
Aurora AFX, Dodge Fever Dragster, wht & yel, NM **20.00**
Aurora Cigarbox, Mako Shark, diecast w/plastic tires, M **45.00**
Aurora Cigarbox, Stingray, diecast w/rubber tires, NM **40.00**
Aurora Thunderjet, Cheetah #1403, gr, EX **35.00**
Aurora Thunderjet, Jaguar, red, VG **30.00**

Bandai, Chrysler Imperial Sedan, friction, 1961, 8", NMIB 275.00
Bandai, Cycling Daddy, b/o, 1960s, 10", NM 150.00
Bandai, Lincoln Mark III w/Shasta Trailer, friction, 1958, 22", M ...650.00
Bandai, Space Bus, b/o, NMIB 850.00
Billiken, Batman, litho tin w/vinyl cape, w/up, 8", MIB 100.00
Bing, Limousine Convertible, w/up, tin, glass windshield, 12", EX ..3,000.00
Bing, Speedboat, pnt tin w/compo figure, w/up, 1910, 11", VG+ ..550.00
Breyer, Foal, #909, woodgrain 75.00
Breyer, Indian Pony, matt alabaster, 1970-71 ....225.00
Breyer, Justin Morgan, matt red bay, 1977-89 ....40.00
Buddy L, Baggage Line Truck, blk/yel, 7", VG 2,300.00
Buddy L, Cement Mixer, gr, 9", VG 135.00
Buddy L, Mono Coupe, 10", NM 800.00
Buddy L, Sand Loader, yel w/blk buckets, 15", G 275.00
Buddy L, Town & Country Convertible, 19", EX 150.00
Budgie, Packard Convertible, diecast w/plastic wheels, 1950s, NM+ ..40.00
Budgie, VW Micro Bus, diecast w/metal wheels, 1950s, NM 30.00
Carette, Steam Launch, pnt tin, 16", VG (orig worn box) 900.00
Champion, Stake Truck, pnt CI, C-cab w/spoke wheels, 7½", VG ..275.00
Chein, Alligator w/Native Rider, 15", VG 200.00
Chein, Barnacle Bill Floor Puncher, 7", EX 700.00
Chein, Checkered Cab, 1924, 6", scarce, EX 400.00
Chein, Disneyland Melody Player, 7", NMIB 150.00
Cor-Cor, Airflow Sedan, pressed steel, 1930s, 16", EX 1,100.00
Cor-Cor, Graham Auto, pressed steel, aqua w/blk roof, rstr, 20" ..1,375.00

Corgi, Saint's Volvo, P-1800, 1965, MIB, $140.00.

Photo courtesy June Moon

Corgi, Disneyland Bus, #470, MIB 40.00
Corgi, Livestock Transporter, #484, MIB 60.00
Corgi, Range Rover Ambulance, #482, MIB 45.00
Corgi, Space Shuttle, #648, MIB 50.00
Corgi, Stunt Bike, #681, MIB 250.00
Corgi, US Army Rover, #500, MIB 400.00
Cragston, Air Control Tower #783, remote control, NMIB 200.00
Cragston, Dilly Dalmatian, b/o, MIB 250.00
Cragston, Melody Band Clown, b/o, tin, EX 115.00
Cragston, Patrol/Police Plane, remote control, 15½", NMIB 175.00
Daiya, Astro Captain, w/up, litho tin w/plastic arms, 6½", MIB .325.00
Dakin, Benji, 1978, cloth, VG 30.00
Dakin, Bull Dog, Dream Pets, EX 15.00
Dakin, Cool Cat, Warner Bros, w/beret, 1970, EX+ 40.00
Dakin, Dumbo, Disney, cloth collar, 1960s, MIB 25.00
Dakin, Porky Pig, Warner Bros, 1968, EX+ 30.00
Dent, Patrol Wagon, pnt CI, 2 horses/4 riders/driver, 21", VG ...953.00
Dinky, Citroen Dyane, #149, MIB 50.00
Dinky, Ford Capri, #165, MIB 100.00
Dinky, MG Midget, #108, diecast, MIB 200.00
Dinky, Plymouth Fury, #115, diecast, MIB 125.00
Dinky, Rolls Royce Phantom V, #124, diecast, MIB 90.00
Dinky, Sunbeam Alpine, #101, diecast, MIB 200.00
Distler, Monkey Driving Car, w/up, litho tin, 6", EX 600.00
Distler, Monkey Drummer, w/up, litho tin, 7½", EX 400.00
Duncan, Be a Sport Series Yo-Yo, 1970s, MIP 20.00
Duncan, Cattle Brand Yo-Yo, late 1970s, MOC, from $8 to 12.00
Elgo, Am Skyline, 1950s, complete, NM (VG box) 35.00
Ertl, Camaro GT #2653, diecast, bl, MIB 15.00
Ertl, 1980 Chevy Mountain Dew NASCAR Stocker, diecast, MOC 65.00

Falk, Ocean Liner, pnt tin, 3 stacks, w/up, 12", G+ 500.00
Fisher-Price, Bouncy Racer, #8, 1960, EX 40.00
Fisher-Price, Bunny Cart, #5, 1948, EX 75.00
Fisher-Price, Crackling Hen, #120, wht, 1958, EX 40.00
Fisher-Price, Looky Monk, #109, 1932, EX 700.00
Fisher-Price, Musical Sweeper, #100, 1950, EX 250.00
Fleischmann, Ocean Liner, pnt tin, 2 stacks, w/up, 10½", NM ..525.00
Gilbert, Mysto Magic Exhibition Set, 1920s, NM (EX box) 450.00
Girard, Deluxe Coupe, steel, w/up, b/o lights, 1934, 14", G 125.00
Haji, Automatic Racing Game, lever action, litho tin, NM (EX box) 200.00
Hartland Plastics, Annie Oakley, NM 275.00
Hartland Plastics, Brave Eagle, NM 200.00
Hartland Plastics, Bret Maverick, w/coffee dunn horse, NM 650.00
Hartland Plastics, Jockey, N, ...150.00
Hartland Plastics, Lone Ranger, NM 150.00
Hasbro, Mr Potato Head Funny-Face Kit, 1950s, NM (VG+ box) ..65.00
Hubley, Fire Pumper Truck, pnt CI w/NP driver, 11", VG 385.00
Hubley, Lindy NX 211 Ryan NYP, unpnt CI, 11", EX 875.00
Hubley, Maytag Washing Machine, late 1920s, red or bl, 7½", VG ...750.00
Hubley, Royal Circus Cage Wagon, 9½", VG 325.00
Ideal, Baby Stove, CI flat top w/stovepipe/burners, 8x16", EX ...525.00
Ideal, Fort Laramie Playset #4876, 1957, complete, VG (VG box) ...500.00
Ideal, Robert the Robot, remote control, plastic, 14", NMIB 500.00
Kelly Bros, Doll Carriage, wicker w/cloth parasol, VG 700.00
Kenner, Give-A-Show Projector Slides, 1963, complete, NMIB ..30.00
Kenner, See-A Show Viewer, 1966, Superman, complete, MIB (sealed) .85.00
Kenner, Spirograph, 1968, 1st issue, complete, EX (EX box) 25.00
Kenton, Dray Wagon, pnt CI, 2 horses, no driver, 11", M 550.00
Keystone, Aerial Ladder Truck, pressed steel, 12", G 550.00
Keystone, Coast-to-Coast Bus, pressed steel, rstr, 32" 1,400.00
Keystone, Locomotive, pressed steel, b/o lights, 1930s, 28", VG ..225.00
Keystone, Police Patrol Truck, pressed steel, caged bed, 27", G ..700.00
Keystone, Top-Wing, 25", VG 600.00
Keystone, US Army Truck, pressed steel w/canvas cover, rstr, 26" 450.00
Kilgore, Sea Gull, pnt CI w/NP wing prop & wheels, 7¾", VG 1,050.00
Kingsbury, Aerial Ladder Truck, pressed steel, clockwork, 13", G 325.00
Kingsbury, Aerial Ladder Truck, pressed steel, 35", VG 750.00
Kingsbury, Passenger Bus, pressed steel, clockwork, 16", NM ..3,600.00
Kingsbury, Roadster, pressed steel, 1930s, 12", EX 1,200.00
Kingsbury, Streetcar #781, pressed steel, 9", EX 200.00
Kingsbury, Tow Truck, pressed steel, w/up, b/o lights, 9", EX 400.00
KO, Buick, friction, bl w/chrome trim, 10½", EXIB 250.00
KO, Chief Robot Man, b/o bump-&-go, lights/sound, tin, 12", EX ..850.00
Lehmann, Autin Delivery Cart, litho tin, 1914-35, 4", VG 425.00
Lehmann, Balky Mule/Clown, litho tin, 1910, 8", EX 500.00
Lehmann, Cat & Mouse, litho tin, NM 1,400.00
Lehmann, Crocodile, litho tin, 9½", NM 400.00
Lehmann, EPL-1 Dirigible, litho tin w/cl props, 7½", EX 400.00
Lindstrom, Dodgem Car, w/up, litho tin, 1930s, 9½", EX 150.00
Lindstrom, Mammy, w/up, litho tin, 8", EX 275.00
Lindstrom, Skeeter-Bug, w/up, litho tin, NMIB 300.00
Linemar, Atomic Generator, b/o, NMIB 575.00
Linemar, Ball Playing Dog, b/o, 1950s, 9", M 175.00
Linemar, Donald Duck Dipsy Car, w/up, litho tin, 5", MIB 1,000.00
Linemar, Flower (Bambi), friction, litho tin, 1940s, 3", M 100.00
Linemar, Honeymoon Express, unused, MIB 250.00
Linemar, USAF Boeing YB-52 Strato Fortress, friction, 13", NMIB .350.00
Lionel, Donald Duck Hand Car #1107, w/up, 1930s, EX 1,000.00
Marklin, Cook Stove, tin & brass, claw ft, 11½x9½", EX 800.00
Marklin, Mercedes Benz 300SL, #5524/18, diecast, 1953, EX 90.00
Marusan, Cadillac Sedan, b/o, 1950, 11", NMIB 2,500.00
Marusan, Mercedes Benz Racer #8, friction, driver, 10", EX 225.00
Marx, Aero Oil Co Truck, friction, litho tin, 5½", NM 600.00
Marx, Aircraft Carrier, b/o, 20", EX 375.00

Marx, Alamo #3546 Playset, 1960, NMIB **900.00**
Marx, Alaska Playset #3708, 1959, complete, MIB **950.00**
Marx, Alley the Roaring Stalking Alligator, b/o, MIB **475.00**
Marx, Amos 'N Andy Fresh Air Taxi, w/up, litho tin, 8", G **525.00**
Marx, Archie Jalopy, w/up, plastic, 1975, MIB **125.00**
Marx, Armored Attack Playset, MIB **225.00**
Marx, Army Combat Playset #6017, complete, EXIB **200.00**
Marx, Boy's Camp #4103 Playset, 1956, EX (G box) **700.00**
Marx, Disneykins, Jungle Book, 2nd series, plastic 1960s, NM, ea ..**45.00**
Marx, Disneykins, plastic figures, 1960s, MIB, ea **22.00**
Marx, Fred Flintstone on Dino, b/o, 1961, 12", VG **350.00**
Marx, Magnetic Crane Truck, pressed steel, 1950, 18", EXIB **350.00**

Marx, Nutty Mad Tricycle, tin windup, celluloid witch on metal trike, ca 1960, MIB, $495.00.

Photo courtesy
Dunbar Gallery

Marx, Rollover Pluto, w/up, 1939, 9", EX **300.00**
Marx, US Army Flying Fortress, w/up, tin w/cl props, 19", NM **450.00**
Marx, Willys Jeep & Trailer, pressed steel, 22", EX (EX box) **250.00**
Matchbox, Diesel Road Roller #01-A, reg wheels, 1953, NM **43.00**
Matchbox, Revin' Rebel Dodge Challenger #01-1, 1-75 Series, 1982, M ..**6.00**
Matchbox, US Air Force Learjet #SB-01, Skybusters, MIB **4.00**
Matchbox, 1913 Cadillac #Y-06C, Models of Yesteryear, 1967, NM+ .**80.00**
Mattel, Dancing Dude, hand-crank, 8", NMIB **150.00**
Mattel, Hot Wheels Classic Cord, magenta, red line tires, '71, NM .**200.00**
Mattel, Hot Wheels Rumblers Choppin' Chariot, driver, 1971, NM ..**32.00**
Mattel, Hot Wheels Rumblers Road Hog, orange, driver, 1971, NM ..**15.00**
Mattel, Hot Wheels Sizzlers Anteater, metallic bl, EX+ **22.00**
Mattel, Hot Wheels Sizzlers Revin' Heaven, metallic orange, NMIB **40.00**
Mattel, Triple Thingmaker, EX (EX box) **145.00**
MB Daniel, Bowling Bank, b/o, 3 actions, 1960s, 10", M **125.00**
Meccano, Aeroplane Constructor, G (orig box) **300.00**
Mego, Baby Bertha, b/o, rare, MIB **1,250.00**
Metalcraft, Heinz Truck, steel, b/o lights, wht, 12", G **150.00**
Metalcraft, Shell Motor Oil Stake Truck, 12", VG **650.00**
Metalcraft, Sunshine Biscuit Truck, pressed steel, 1933, 11½", G ..**250.00**
Mettoy, G-A MTY Plane, tin, top wing single-prop, w/up, 16½", EX ..**300.00**
Mikuni, Dog Chasing Puppy, w/up, litho tin, 8", EX (EX box) ...**175.00**
MPC Fort Boone Playset, complete, unused, MIB **225.00**
MT, Animal Train, b/o, MIB **575.00**
MT, NASA Space Patrol, friction, litho tin, 6", EX **125.00**
MY, Circus Fire Engine, b/o, 1960s, 10", EX **225.00**
Nifty, Toonerville Trolley, w/up, litho tin, 1922, 7", EX **950.00**
Nylint, Pump-Mobile, w/up, litho tin, 9", EX (VG box) **350.00**
Remco, Casey's Car Wash Playset, complete, NMIB **125.00**
Remco, Movieland Drive-In Theater, 1959, complete, EX **150.00**
Rosko, Bartender, b/o, several actions, 11½", MIB **85.00**
Schuco, Donald Duck, w/up, tin w/plastic limbs, 1930s, 6", MIB .**875.00**
Schuco, Drinking Mouse, w/up, cloth w/tin ft, 5", EX **200.00**
Schuco, Ford Sedan #1945, w/up, red/cream, 4½", EX+ **135.00**
Schuco, Old Timer Renault, w/up, 7", EX (EX box) **100.00**
Schuco, Owl, Noah's Ark, 1950, 3", M **100.00**
Schuco, Tippy Dog, w/up, 5", NM (NM box) **275.00**
Schuco, Traffic Cop #4520, w/up, pnt tin, 5", NM (EX box) **375.00**
Schuco, Yes/No Bear, blk mohair, 1950, 5", NM **900.00**
Showa, USAF Sky Guard Jet, b/o, litho tin, 12", NM **500.00**
Smith-Miller, Auto Loader, NMIB **400.00**
Smith-Miller, GMC Bekins Truck, VG **400.00**

Smith-Miller, Mack PIE Truck, EX **750.00**
Spectra Star, Ghostbusters Yo-Yo, 1980s, MOC **7.00**
Steelcraft, Bulldog Mack Dump Truck, red/blk, 27", G **900.00**
Steelcraft, City Fire Dept Ladder Truck, 26", EX **1,500.00**
Steelcraft, City Fire Dept Mack Ladder Truck, 25", EX **1,100.00**
Steelcraft, GRAF Zepplin, 1930, 25½", G **225.00**
Strombecker, Picnic Set, early, ¾" scale, complete, MIB **125.00**
Sturditoy, Dump Truck #6, pressed steel, 1927, 25", G **650.00**
Sturditoy, Steam Shovel, pressed steel, 22", G **200.00**
Sturditoy, US Mail Truck, pressed steel, rstr, 26" **700.00**
Taiyo, Big Machine Race Car, b/o, NMIB **175.00**
TN, Aerial Ropeway, b/o, EXIB **165.00**
TN, Jet w/Ejecting Pilot, friction, 11", MIB **250.00**
TN, Trumpet Player, w/up, tin w/cloth clothes, 10", G **150.00**
Tonka, Jeep Surrey #350, 1963, M **100.00**
Tonka, Livestock Truck, 1952, NM **250.00**
Tonka, Power Boom Loader #115, 1960, EX **365.00**
Tonka, Sand Loader, 1961, EX **50.00**
Tonka, Thunderbird Express #37, 1960, EX **350.00**
Tonka, Trencher #534, 1963, EX **85.00**
Tonka, Winnebego Camper, 1968, VG **100.00**
Tootsietoy, Bleriot Plane #4482, 1910, NM **120.00**
Tootsietoy, Carrier #1036, NM **35.00**
Tootsietoy, Caterpillar Tractor #4646, 1931-39, NM **55.00**
Tootsietoy, DeSoto Airflow #0118, 1935-39, lt bl, NM **60.00**
Tootsietoy, Hudson Pickup Truck, 1947-49, rare, 4", NM **60.00**
Tootsietoy, Percolator Set, 3-pc on tray, 1920s, MIB **185.00**
Tootsietoy, Seaplane #4660, purple, NM **95.00**
Tootsietoy, US Army CJ3 Jeep, 1947, 4", NM **35.00**
Tootsietoy, 1935 Ford Roadmaster #9116, bl, M **70.00**
Topper, Motorized Monster Maker, 1960s, complete, M (EX box) .**185.00**
TPS, Acrobat Police Car, b/o, blk/wht, flashing light, 10", EX **55.00**
TPS, Circus Bugler, w/up, tin w/cloth costume, 10", NM (EX box) .**525.00**
TPS, Climbing Linesman, b/o, litho tin, 24", EXIB **300.00**
TPS, Wagon Fantasyland, w/up, litho tin, 12", MIB **350.00**
Transogram, Contruct-All #100, plastic, complete, NMIB **45.00**
Triang, Dump Truck, pressed steel, 12", EXIB **250.00**
Tyco, Blazer slot car, red/blk, VG **10.00**
Tyco, Javelin, red/wht/bl, EX+ **15.00**
Tyco, Jeep CJ7, red/bl, VG **12.00**
Tyco, Thunderbird #15, red/yel, VG **10.00**
Unique Art, Bambo the Monk, w/up, EXIB **275.00**
Unique Art, GI Joe & His Jouncing Jeep, w/up, litho tin, 7", G+ .**150.00**
Unique Art, Lincoln Tunnel, w/up, litho tin, 24", EX **300.00**
Wham-O, Shrink Machine, rare, MIB **85.00**
Wilkins, Back-to-Back Trap, pnt CI, w/horse & driver, 9", VG .**190.00**
Wilkins, Express Wagon, pnt CI, w/driver, 12½", VG **550.00**
Wilkins, Steamboat, pnt CI, 3 spoked wheels, 7½", G **135.00**
Wolverine, Ironing Set, 1940s, complete, MIB **35.00**
Wolverine, Zilotone, w/clown & 6 disks, EXIB **800.00**
Wyandotte, Construction Co Dump Truck, pressed steel, 2-tone, VG .**225.00**
Wyandotte, Greatest Show on Earth Truck & Trailer, 1930s, 11", EX .**500.00**
Wyandotte, Humphrey Mobile, w/up, litho tin, 1950, 9", EX **400.00**
Wyandotte, Monoplane, pressed steel w/wooden wheels, 10", EX **225.00**
Wyandotte, Woodie Station Wagon, maroon, 24", EX+ **525.00**
Y, Balloon Bunny, remote control, rare, MIB **375.00**
Y, Piggy Cook, w/up, litho tin, 5½", MIB **275.00**

Farm Toys

Anhydrous ammonia tank, IH, Ertl, #1550, 1/64th scale, MIB **2.50**
Bale throw wagon, John Deere, Ertl, #5755, 1/64th scale, MIB **3.50**
Baler, Hesston, Ertl, #2263, 1/64th scale, MIB **3.00**
Combine, John Deere, Ertl, #5604, 1/64th scale, MIB **10.00**

Cotton picker, John Deere, Ertl, #1000, 1/80th scale, MIB 6.50
Forage harvester, Hesston, Ertl, #2262, 1/64th scale, MIB 2.50
Forage wagon, New Holland, Ertl, #373, 1/64th scale, MIB 2.50
Grain cart, John Deere, Ertl, #5565, 1/64th scale, MIB 3.50
Mower conditioner, New Holland, Ertl, #322, 1/64th scale, MIB ...3.50
Rotary cutter, John Deere, Ertl, #200098, 1/16th scale, MIB 3.50
Rotary mower, John Deere, Ertl, #5600, 1/64th scale, MIB 3.50
Skid steer loader, John Deere, Ertl, #5622, 1/64th scale, MIB 4.50
Sprayer, John Deere, Ertl, #5553, 1/64th scale, MIB 3.00
Tractor, Fordson, Ertl, #2526, 1/43rd scale, MIB 5.50
Tractor, John Deere Model A, Arcade, pnt CI w/NP driver, 7", NM .875.00
Tractor, Massey-Ferguson 699, Ertl, #1120, 1/64th scale, MIB 3.00
Tractor, McCormick-Deering WD-40, Wheat Belt Works, 1/16, 9", MIB .265.00
Tractor, Oliver, Hubley, pnt CI, w/integral driver, 5½", EX 400.00
Tractor, Oliver Row Crop, Arcade, CI, rubber tires, 1939, 5½", EX 150.00
Wagon, John Deere, Vindex, pnt CI, 2 horses, no driver, 12½", VG .1,250.00
Wing disk, IH, Ertl, #1862, 1/64th scale, MIB 2.50
3-bottom plow, Case, Vindex, pnt CI, 10¼" 1,750.00

Guns: Cast-Iron Cap Guns (Caution: Some reproductions exist)

In years past, virtually every child played with toy guns, and the survival rate of these toys is minimal, at best. The interest in these charming toy guns has recently increased considerably, especially those in the western style, as collectors discover their scarcity, quality, and value. Toy gun collectibles encompass the early and the very ornate figural toy guns and bombs through the more realistic ones with recognizable character names, gleaming finishes, faux jewels, dummy bullets, engraving, and colorful grips. This section will cover some of the most popular cast-iron and diecast toy guns from the past one hundred years.

Our advisor is James Schleyer, internationally recognized collector and appraiser of toy guns. He has authored numerous books, articles, and newsletters on antique toy guns and holsters. He is the former editor for *Toy Gun Purveyors*, an international newsletter that fostered the collecting of these valuable and rare toys. His current book, *Backyard Buckaroos — Collecting Western Toy Guns*, contains nearly 2,500 photographs. Toy gun inquiries that include a SASE will be graciously answered. Send to: Toy Guns, Box 243-E, Burke, VA 22015.

In the listings below (*) was used to designate a classic example.

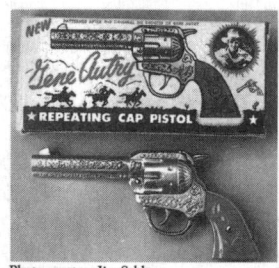

Gene Autry, engraved cast iron, with box, rare, $700.00.

American, cylinder revolves, Kilgore, 1940, 9⅜", EX (*) 500.00
Army 45 Auto, Hubley, 1945, 6½", M (*) 160.00
Atta Boy, single shot, 1935, 4", G- 40.00
Bango, eng, jewels, Stevens, 1940, 7½", VG 90.00
Big Bill, single shot, Kilgore, 1935, 4⅞", M 45.00
Big Horn, cylinder revolves, Kilgore, 1940, 8⅝", M (*) 550.00
Big Scout, single shot, Stevens, 1930, 9⅜", G- 135.00
Billy the Kid, single shot, Stevens, 1940s, 6¾", G- 115.00
Border Patrol, automatic, Kilgore, 1935, 4½", VG 65.00
Buc-A-Roo, single shot, Kilgore, 1940, 7¾", M 120.00
Buffalo Bill, single shot, Kenton, 1930, 13½", rare, VG 550.00
Buffalo Bill, single shot, Stevens, 1890, 11¾", rare, G- 250.00
Bull's Eye, eng, Kenton, 1940, 6½", M 350.00

Bulldog, single shot, Hubley, 1935, 6", G 35.00
Bunker Hill, single shot, National, 1925, 5¼", M 100.00
Captain, automatic, Kilgore, 1940, 4¼", VG 85.00
Champ, automatic, Star Medallion, Hubley, 1940, 5", EX 100.00
Chief, single shot, Dent, 1935, 7½", VG 85.00
Colt, single shot, Stevens, 1900, 5½", EX 65.00
Cowboy, Hubley, 1940, 8", VG 100.00
Cowboy King, Stevens, 1940, 9", M (*) 350.00
Dick, automatic, Hubley, 1930, 4⅛", VG 45.00
Doughboy, automatic, Kilgore, 1920, 4⅞", VG 125.00
Eagle, single shot, Hubley, 1935, 8½", VG 150.00
G-Man, automatic, Kilgore, 1935, 6", rare, M (*) 185.00
Gene Autry, dummy, Kenton, 1940, 8⅜", rare, M 350.00
Gene Autry, eng, Kenton, 1952, 6½", rare, VG 450.00
Gene Autry, eng, Kenton, 1952, 8⅜", rare, M 550.00
Gene Autry, repeater, nickel, Kenton, 1940, 8⅜", EX 275.00
Guard, bl finish, Kilgore, 1935, EX 100.00
Invincible, Kilgore, 1935, 5¼", G- 45.00
Lasso Em Bill, cylinder revolves, Kilgore, 1930s, 9", EX 250.00
Lawmaker, nickel, Kenton, 1940, 8⅜", rare, M (*) 350.00
Lone Eagle, cylinder revolves, Kilgore, 1930, 5¼", EX 130.00
Lone Ranger, nickel, Kilgore, 1940, 8¼", rare, M (*) 345.00
Long Boy, single shot, Kilgore, 1920, 11⅛", VG 135.00
Long Tom, cylinder revolves, 1940, 10⅜", M (*) 650.00
Mohican, single shot, Dent, 1930, 6¼", EX 60.00
National Auto, National, 1915, 3¾", G- 25.00
Officer's Pistol, automatic, Kilgore, 1940, 6", rare, M (*) 400.00
Patrol, Hubley, 1935-40, 6", M 75.00
Pawnee Bill, Stevens, 1940, 7⅝", VG (*) 235.00
Peacemaker, gold, Stevens, 1940, 8½", M 175.00
Pirate, dbl bbl, Hubley, 1940, 9⅜", M (*) 125.00
Police Chief, plastic grip, Kenton, 1940, 4⅝", EX 135.00
Presto, automatic, Kilgore, 1940, 5⅛", VG 65.00
Rodeo, single shot, Hubley, 1940, 7", EX 45.00
Scout, single shot, Stevens, 1890, 7", VG 75.00
Six Shooter, cylinder revolves, Kilgore, 1940, 6½", VG 100.00
Spitfire, automatic, Kilgore, 1940, 4⅝", EX 90.00
Texan, CI/nickel, cylinder revolves, Hubley, 1940, 9¼", M (*) .175.00
Texan Jr, CI, Hubley, 1940, 8⅛", VG (*) 100.00
Trooper Safety, repeater, Kilgore, 1925, 10¼", M 145.00
Two Time, rubber band, Kenton, 1929, 9¼", VG 155.00
Warrior, nickel, repeater, Kilgore, 1920s, 9", EX 175.00
Wild West, single shot, Kenton, 1920s, 11½", rare, M 275.00
101 Ranch, single shot, Hubley, 1930, 11½", VG 245.00
2 in 1, rubber band, Stevens, 1930, 9¼", VG 150.00
49-er, Stevens, 1940, 9", M (*) 325.00

Guns: Diecast and Miscellaneous Toy Guns

Alan Ladd, Geo Schmidt, 10¼", rare, EX 325.00
Annie Oakley, gold, Leslie-Henry, 9", very rare 850.00
Army 45 Auto, compo, non-working, Hubley, 1940 ....75.00
Army 45 Auto, dull gray finish, Hubley, 6½", M 95.00
Atomic Disintegrator, space gun, Hubley, 8", VG 445.00
Bonanza, cylinder revolves, Leslie-Henry 44, 10¼", M 185.00
Bronco, cylinder revolves, Kilgore, 9¼", VG 75.00
Buck'n Bronc, Geo Schmidt, 10½", EX 115.00
Buckle Gun, derringer, Mattel, 3", VG 95.00
Burke's Law Snub Nose, blk, Lone Star, 5", M 85.00
Champion, Leslie-Henry, 9", VG 125.00
Colt, Snub Nose Detective, Hubley, mini, M 30.00
Colt 45, cylinder revolves, bullets, Hubley, 14", VG 135.00
Colt 45, nickel w/ivory grips, cylinder revolves, 14", VG 135.00
Colt 45 1860, cylinder revolves, ivory grips, 14", M 245.00

Cowboy, cylinder revolves, gold, Hubley, 12", rare, EX 250.00
Cowboy, cylinder revolves, Hubley, 12", M 165.00
Cowhand 250, Nichols, 8½", VG 70.00
Coyote, Hubley, 8¼", M 65.00
Dale Evans, jewels, Geo Schmidt, 10½", rare, VG 400.00
Davy Crockett, Flintlock Buffalo Rifle, Hubley, 25", EX 175.00
Deputy, BB, copper grips, Schmidt, sm, 8½", EX 75.00
Dick Tracy, blk w/decal, steel clicker, Marx, EX 100.00
Dick Tracy Siren Pistol, red finish, Marx, VG 75.00
Dick Tracy Squad shotgun, cap & water, pump, Mattel 125.00
Eagle, nickel, cylinder revolves, Kilgore, 8", M 100.00
Fanner 'shootin' shell,' bullets, Mattel, 9", M 150.00
Fanner 45 'shootin shell,' Mattel, 11¼", rare, EX 325.00
Fanner 50, nickel, cylinder revolves, Mattel, 10⅝", EX 150.00
Flip Rifleman Ring Rifle, Hubley, 32", VG 285.00
G-Man, clicker pistol, tin w/jewel, Marx, 1935, M 75.00
G-Man, Sparking Wind-Up, steel, Marx, 5", VG 75.00
G-Man, Sparkling Machine Gun, tin, Marx, 26", VG 225.00
Gene Autry, nickel, Leslie-Henry, 9", M 175.00
Gene Autry 44, cylinder revolves, bullets, Leslie-Henry, 11", EX ...185.00
Grizzly, cylinder revolves, gold, Kilgore, 10¼", M 355.00
Hawk, automatic, amber grips, Hubley, 5", VG 35.00
Hawkeye, automatic, Kilgore, 4¼", M 45.00
Hopalong Cassidy, cameo grips, Geo Schmidt, 9", EX 325.00
Hopalong Cassidy, gold, Wyandotte, 9", M 650.00
Hopalong Cassidy, nickel, Wyandotte, 9", VG 350.00
Indian Scout Rifle, bullets, Mattel, 30", M 200.00
Lone Ranger, antique bronze, Actoy, 10", VG 175.00
Lone Ranger, tin clicker w/jewel, Marx, 8", M 95.00
Mare's Leg, Winchester lever-pistol, Marx, 14", EX 135.00
Mattel Snub-Nosed Detective, chrome, shootin' shell, EX 90.00
Maverick, Leslie-Henry, 10¼", VG 130.00
Maverick 45, cylinder revolves, Halco, 11", M 325.00
Me & My Buddy, tin clicker, Wyandotte, 1935-40, VG 100.00
Model 61, cylinder revolves, chrome finish, Nichols, rare, M 450.00
Model 61, cylinder revolves, steel-bl, Nichols, rare, M 365.00
Mountie, automatic, blk finish, Kilgore, 6", M 45.00
Mustang 500, nickel, Nichols, 12¼", EX 185.00
Paladin, nickel, repeater, Leslie-Henry, 9", rare, EX 285.00
Pet, nickel, Hubley, 1945-60, M 5.00
Pioneer, blk grips w/compass, Hubley, 10¼", EX 130.00
Pioneer, nickel, amber grips, Hubley, 10¼", M 100.00
Pirate, over-under bbls, Hubley, 1960, VG 45.00
Pony Boy, nickel, Esquire-Actoy, 10", EX 85.00
Rebel Scattergun, dbl bbl, Marx, 21", rare, M 800.00
Red Ranger, Wyandotte, 7¾", VG 45.00
Remington 36, cylinder revolves, bullets, Hubley, 8¼", EX 85.00
Ric-O-Shay, cylinder revolves, bullets, 12¼", M 125.00
Roy Rogers, copper grips, G Schmidt, 10¼", EX 225.00
Roy Rogers, cylinder revolves, diecast, eng, Kilgore, 10", M 385.00
Roy Rogers, gold, Leslie-Henry, 9", EX 375.00
Roy Rogers, nickel, diecast, Kilgore, 8", M 185.00
Scout Rifle, nickel, lever action , Hubley, 1960, EX 125.00
Sharps Carbine, Civil War Model, Marx, 1960, rare, EX 200.00
Stallion 32, Nichols, 8", VG 35.00
Stallion 38, cylinder revolves, bullets, Nichols, 9½", EX 115.00
Stallion 45 Mk II, cylinder revolves, bullets, Nichols, 12", M 300.00
Star, nickel, single shot, Hubley, 7", MIB 25.00
Sure Shot, nickel, Hubley, 8", EX 30.00
Texan, gold finish, cylinder revolves, diecast, Hubley, 9½", M ...175.00
Texan Jr, break action, diecast, Hubley, 9", VG 65.00
Texan Jr, side opener, diecast, Hubley, 9½", M 65.00
Thundergun, nickel, eng, Marx, 12½", M 225.00
Tightrope Snub Nose, nickel, Lone Star, EX 85.00

Trooper, snub nose, nickel, Hubley, 1950-60, EX 25.00
US Marshal, cylinder turns, antique bronze, Leslie-Henry, 11¼", VG .130.00
Wagon Train, antique bronze, Leslie Henry 44, 11¼", VG 135.00
Wells Fargo, nickel, Actoy, 11", M 155.00
Western, nickel, Hubley, 9", M 55.00
Wild Bill Hickok, Leslie-Henry, 9", VG 150.00
Wild Bill Hickok, Leslie-Henry 44, 11¼", EX 165.00
Winchester Carbine, shootin' shell, Mattel, 26", M 165.00
Winchester Saddle Gun, Mattel, 33", M 185.00
Wyatt Earp, Buntline Special, Actoy, 11", M 155.00
Wyatt Earp, nickel, long bbl, Hubley, 11", M 175.00
2 in 1, 2 interchanging bbls, Hubley, 6", EX 50.00

Guns: Early-Style Figural Guns and Bombs (Caution: reproductions exist)

Admiral Dewey Bomb, CI, Grey Iron, 1900, 1¾", VG 300.00
Butting Match, CI, Ives, 1885, 5", EX 450.00
Cannon, CI, Kenton, 1900, 4⅞", VG 500.00
Chinese Must Go, CI, Ives, 1880, 4¾", EX 550.00
Clown on Powder Keg, CI, Ives, 1890s, 3¾", VG 425.00
Devil's Head Bomb, CI, .22 blank, Ives, 1880, 2¼", VG 300.00
Dog's Head Bomb, CI, Ives, 1880, 2⅛", EX 265.00
Double Face Man, CI, Ives, 1890, 1⅝", VG 145.00
George Washington Bomb, CI, 1900, 1¼", EX 325.00
Hobo Bomb, CI, Ideal, 1890s, 2", G- 125.00
Liberty Bell Bomb, CI, 1876, 2⅜", EX 225.00
Lightening Express, CI, Kenton, 1900, 5", EX 650.00
Punch & Judy, CI, Ives, 1880s, 5¼", EX 850.00
Sea Serpent, CI, Stevens, 1890, 3½", G- 775.00
Yellow Kid Bomb, CI, Grey Iron, 1900, 1½", VG 180.00

Models

Adams, Vanguard #161, 1958, MIB 170.00
Addar, Evel Knievel #152, 1974, MIB (sealed) 120.00
Addar, Planet of Apes, Tree House Diorama #215, 1975, MIB (sealed) .50.00
Airfix, Henry VIII #2501, 1979, MIB 20.00
Airfix, Russian Vostok #5172, 1991, MIB (sealed) 20.00
Airfix, Space Warriors #5177, 1982, MIB 15.00
AMT, Munster Koach #901, 1964, orig issue, MIB 190.00
AMT, Star Trek, USS Enterprise #970, 1979, MIB 60.00
Arii, Barugon #26011, MIB 10.00
Arii, Gyoas #26010, MIB 10.00
Aurora, Alfred E Neuman #802, 1965, M (NM box) 360.00
Aurora, Dick Tracy #818, 1968, MIB 290.00
Aurora, Gladiator #406, 1964, MIB, from $165 to 200.00
Aurora, Indian Chief #417, Guys & Gals of All Nations, 1957, MIB .150.00
Aurora, James Bond #414, 1966, MIB 470.00
Aurora, Steve Canyon #H404, Famous Fighters series, 1958, MIB ..300.00
Aurora, Superboy #186, Comic series, 1974, MIB (sealed) 150.00
Bandai, Cosmo Zero (Super Star) #36132, 1980, MIB 12.00
Bandai, Thunderbird 2 #38602, 1971, MIB 40.00
Billiken, Frankenstein, 1988, MIB 240.00
Billiken, Predator, vinyl, 1991, MIB 90.00
Billiken, Thing, vinyl, 1984, MIB, from $175 to 200.00
Horizon, Dracula #4, 1988, MIB 25.00
Horizon, Joker #56, DC Comics, 1993, MIB 50.00
ITC Neanderthal Man #3808, 1959, MIB, from $60 to 80.00
Lunar Models, Batmobile #SF039, MIB 90.00
Lunar Models, Crawling Eye #FG44, 13", MIB 110.00
Monogram, Beer Wagon, 1995, M (NM sealed box) 25.00
Monogram, Hawker Harrier Jet, MIB 15.00
Monogram, Lion Diorama #102, 1961, MIB 40.00

Monogram, Space Buggy #194, 1969, MIB **110.00**
MPC, Street Hawk, Jesse Hawk's Mustang Coupe #687, 1984, MIB .**25.00**
Renwal, Family Coat-of-Arms #950, 1960s, MIB **50.00**
Renwal, Reptile Science, NM (VG+ box) **38.00**
Revell, Charlie's Angels Van #1130, 1977, MIB (sealed) **35.00**
Revell, CHiPs Helicopter #6102, 1980, MIB **20.00**
Revell, Moon Ship #1825, 1957, MIB, from $175 to **200.00**
Revell, Quarter Horse #1922, 1963, MIB **40.00**
Screamin', Ash #1100, Army of Darkness, 1993, MIB **60.00**
Screamin', Mary Shelly's Frankenstein #1400, 1994, MIB **35.00**
Tsukuda, King Kong #49, 1986, 16", MIB **70.00**

Pedal Cars and Ride-On Toys

Airplane, metal w/rubber tires, 26x53", EX orig **2,500.00**
Bearcat, Bartholomew, wood, high-gloss maroon, 1984, 31", NM ..**500.00**
BMC Special race car #8, rubber tires, 41", G **1,250.00**
Casey Jones locomotive, Garland, 40", G **580.00**
Diamond T dump truck, Am Nat'l, 1930, 58", G **2,550.00**
Dodge, Am Nat'l, 1920, 37", VG **2,500.00**
Fire chief car, Grendon, w/bell, 35", EX **2,500.00**
Ford convertible, Garton, 1937, rstr, from $1,000 to **1,800.00**
Garford dump truck, Am Nat'l, 49", VG+ **7,900.00**
Jeep Town & Country, Steger, wood/pressed steel, 43", EX **440.00**
Limousine convertible, Steelcraft, uphl 2-seater, rstr **2,550.00**
Murray Champion, str sides, pnt metal, rubber wheels, rstr **1,200.00**
Mustang, w/rear luggage rack, 40", EX **1,750.00**
Nellybelle, Roy Rogers'; semi-pro rstr, 1950s, EX **1,000.00**
Packard coupe, Am Nat'l, enclosed w/opening doors, 60", rstr ..**5,500.00**
Playload dump truck, Murray, 1961, Earth Mover logos, rstr ...**1,500.00**
Racer #7, Am Nat'l, 1910, 42", EX **2,500.00**
Special race car #8, BMC, 41", G **695.00**
Touring car, Mors, 1907, 45", EX **1,600.00**
1929 Lincoln, Am Nat'l Pedal Car Co, prof rstr **6,500.00**

Penny Toys

Touring car with chauffeur, bright paint, marked Germany, 4¾", NM, $450.00.

Airmail biplane, Germany/Levy, single prop, 3½", EX **525.00**
Auto garage w/sedan & racer, Germany/Kellerman, 3½", EX **330.00**
Bird in cage, Germany/Meier, 3½", EX **225.00**
Boat w/sailor at helm, 4⅝", EX+ **600.00**
Boy on sled, Germany, boy's pants read Chicago Ill, 2⅜", EX ...**230.00**
CAMPSA oil truck, Spain/RSA, 4¼", VG **275.00**
Cow on platform, German/Meier, neck bell/horns, disk wheels, 3", EX ...**225.00**
Dbl-decker bus, Germany/Distler, long-nose cab, 4¼", EX **275.00**
Dog on platform, Germany/Meier, w/collar, disk wheels, 2½", VG ...**275.00**
Elephant on platform, Germany/Distler, spoked wheels, 4", EX+ .**260.00**
Ferris wheel whistle, Germany, revolves, 4", VG **175.00**
Gas station & car, JDN, mk Gas & Oil, 3" car, EX **165.00**
Globe, Germany, revolves on tin base, 3½", VG **150.00**
Highchair w/child, Germany/Meier, 3¾", EX **250.00**
Jigger on base, Germany/Distler, crank-op, 3½", EX **400.00**
Lion on platform, Germany/Meier, spoked wheels, 3½", EX+ **600.00**
Man smoking pipe & pushing wheelbarrow, Germany, 2¾", EX ...**165.00**
Mantel clock, w/pendulum, moving hands, 2¼", EX **200.00**
Mobil gas station, Japan, w/race car, 2½x2" base, NM (EX box) ...**135.00**
Mouse in trap, Germany/Meier, lever action, 4¾", EX **200.00**

Steam engine, Germany/Distler, operating piston & wheel, 4", EX ..**385.00**
Tractor w/driver, Germany/Distler, 4¼", EX **300.00**
Train, Germany/Hess, locomotive/tender/3 passenger cars, 9¼", EX ..**275.00**
Watering can, Germany/Meier, spring-loaded lid, 3", VG **225.00**
Wheelbarrow, gr w/animal decor & gold trim, 4", VG **250.00**
Zeppelin string toy, Germany/Distler, 6", EX **950.00**

Pipsqueaks

Pipsqueak toys were popular among the Pennsylvania Germans. The earliest had bellows made from sheepskin. Later cloth replaced the sheepskin, and finally paper bellows were used.

Bird w/flapping wings, pnt compo/wood, 4", EX **120.00**
Chicken in cage, wood/paper/felt/feathers, 7", EX **140.00**
Girl holding lamb, pnt papier-mache, non-working, 4½", EX **745.00**
Horse in cage, dapple-gray flannel coat, glass eyes, 9", EX **475.00**
Peacock, pnt papier-mache, nonworking, 5¾" **265.00**

Pull Toys

Cow on platform, German, hide-covered w/glass eyes, 14", VG .**225.00**
Felix the Cat, Nifty/c Pat Sullivan, litho tin, w/2 red mice, EX ..**700.00**
General Lee Invasion Barge, Cass Toys, litho wood, 12", EXIB ..**100.00**
Goat bell toy, Gong Bell, 1890s, EX **550.00**
Goat on platform, 1880s, 5", EX **450.00**
Grasshopper, Hubley, pnt CI w/articulated legs, 9", VG **775.00**
Horse-drawn City Dairy milk wagon, litho tin/wood, 20", EX **385.00**
Horse-drawn coal dump cart, wood, blk mohair horse, EX **275.00**
Horse-drawn conestoga, Overland Trail 1849 on muslin top, 31", EX .**600.00**
Horse-drawn express wagon, Geo Brown, pnt tin, 1870s, 11", EX **1,500.00**
Horse-drawn Jackson Park Trolley, Bliss, paper on wood, 31", G ..**400.00**
Polar bear on platform, mohair w/glass eyes, mica platform, 11", EX ..**825.00**
Pony Circus, Gibbs, litho tin/wood, 13", G **300.00**
See-Saw, Gong Bell, CI, 6¼", EX **650.00**
Sunny Andy Street Railway, tin litho, 14", VG **220.00**
Teddy bear bell toy, Watrous, CI, 6", EX **400.00**

Robots

Acrobat Robot, SH, 1970s, 3 actions, plastic, b/o, 4½", EX **100.00**
Acrobot, Y, robot does acrobatics, plastic, b/o, EX **225.00**
Atom Robot, KO, 1960s, bump-&-go action, litho tin, b/o, 7", VG ...**300.00**
Atomic Fighter Robot, SH, 1950s, several actions, b/o, 11", EX ...**200.00**
Chief Robot Man, KO, 1950s, several actions, b/o, 12", NM **900.00**
Golden Gear Robot, SH, 1960s, several actions, b/o, 9", rare, NM ..**600.00**
Hi-Bouncer Moon Scout, Marx, 1968, b/o, 11", rare, NMIB ...**2,200.00**
Jupitor Robot, Yonezawa, 1950s, b/o, 13", rare, NMIB **2,000.00**
King Ding Robot, b/o, EX **325.00**
Laughing Clown Robot, b/o, NM **325.00**
Lunar Spaceman, Mego, 1960s, b/o, 12", EX **200.00**
Mando Robot, Japan, w/up, EX (EX box) **575.00**
Monster Robot, SH, 1970s, b/o, 10", EX **125.00**
Musical Drummer Robot, TN, 1950s, litho tin, b/o, 8", NM ...**8,000.00**
Pete the Spaceman, Bandai, 1960s, b/o, 5", MIB **200.00**
Pioneer PX-3 Robot Dog, litho tin, friction, 9", EX **475.00**
Planet Robot, KO, tin, bl w/red hands & feet, b/o, 9", MIB **2,700.00**
R-35 Robot, MT, 1950s, litho tin, b/o, 7½", NM **600.00**
Robert the Robot, Ideal, 1940s-50s, red & gray, b/o, 14", NMIB ..**400.00**
Robot Commander, b/o, EX (EX box) **500.00**
Rotator Robot, SH, 1960s, litho tin, b/o, 12", EX **250.00**
Rudy the Robot, Remco, 1968, b/o, 16", EX **225.00**
Sky Robot, SH, 1960s, plastic, b/o, 9", EX **125.00**
Star Strider Robot, SH, b/o, MIB **225.00**

Vision Robot, SH, 1960s, b/o, 12", EX 300.00

Schoenhut

Our advisor for Schoenhut Toys is Keith Kaonis, who has collected these toys for over twenty years. Because of his involvement with the publishing industry (currently *Collectors' Eye*, *Antique DOLL Collector*, and during the '80s, *Collectors' SHOWCASE*), he has visited collections across the United States, produced several articles on Schoenhut toys, and served a term as president of the Schoenhut Collectors' Club. Keith is listed in the Directory under New York.

The listings below are for Humpty Dumpty Circus pieces. All values are based on rating conditions of good to very good condition, i.e., very minor scratches and wear, good original finish, no splits, chips, no excessive paint wear or cracked eyes, and, of course, completeness and condition of clothes (if dressed figures).

Clowns with two-part heads (a cast face applied to a wooden head) were made from 1903 to 1915 and are most desirable — condition always is important. There have been nine distinct styles in fourteen different costumes recorded. Only eight costume styles apply to the two-part headed clowns. The later clowns had one-part heads whose features were pressed or wooden, and the costumes on the later ones, circa 1920, were no longer tied at the wrists and ankles.

Humpty Dumpty Circus Clowns and Other Personnel

Black Dude, reduced sz, from $300 to 600.00
Black Dude, 1-part head, purple coat, from $250 to 800.00
Black Dude, 2-part head, blk coat, from $500 to 700.00
Chinese Acrobat, 1-part head, from $200 to 500.00
Chinese Acrobat, 2-part head, rare, from $400 to 1,000.00
Clown, early, G, from $150 to 500.00
Clown, reduced sz, 1925-53, from $75 to 150.00
Gent Acrobat, bsk head, rare, from $300 to 600.00
Gent Acrobat, 2-part head, very rare, from $600 to 1,500.00
Hobo, reduced sz, from $300 to 600.00
Hobo, 1-part head, from $200 to 500.00
Hobo, 2-part head, curved-up toes, blk coat, from $500 to 1,000.00
Hobo, 2-part head, facet toe ft, from $400 to 800.00
Lady Acrobat, bsk head, from $300 to 600.00
Lady Acrobat, 1-part head, from $200 to 400.00
Lady Rider, bsk head, from $250 to 500.00
Lady Rider, 1-part head, from $200 to 400.00
Lady Rider, 2-part head, very rare, from $600 to 1,200.00
Lion Tamer, bsk head, rare, from $350 to 750.00
Lion Tamer, 1-part head, from $250 to 600.00
Lion Tamer, 2-part head, early, very rare, from $600 to 1,200.00
Ring Master, bsk, ca 1912-14, from $400 to 650.00
Ring Master, 1-part head, from $200 to 450.00
Ring Master, 2-part head, early, very rare, from $500 to 1,200.00

Humpty Dumpty Circus Animals

Humpty Dumpty Circus animals with glass eyes, ca. 1903 – 1914, are more desirable and can demand much higher prices than the later painted-eye versions. As a general rule, a glass-eye version is 30% to 40% more than a painted-eye version. (There are exceptions.) The following list suggests values for both GE (glass-eye) and PE (painted-eye) versions and reflects a low PE price to a high GE price.

There are other variations and nuances of certain figures: Bulldog — white with black spots or brindle (brown); open- and closed-mouth zebras and giraffes; ball necks and hemispherical necks on some animals such as the pig, leopard, and tiger, to name a few. These points can

affect the price and should be judged individually. Condition and rarity affect the price most significantly.

Alligator, GE/PE, from $200 to 500.00
Arabian Camel, 1 hump, GE/PE, from $250 to 750.00
Bactrian Camel, 2 humps, GE/PE, from $200 to 1,500.00
Brown Bear, GE/PE, from $200 to 900.00
Buffalo, cloth mane, GE/PE, from $300 to 1,000.00
Buffalo, cvd mane, GE/PE, from $200 to 900.00
Bulldog, GE/PE, from $400 to 1,600.00
Burro (made to go w/chariot & clown), GE/PE, from $200 to 700.00
Cat, GE/PE, rare, from $600 to 2,500.00
Cow, GE/PE, from $250 to 900.00
Deer, GE/PE, from $300 to 1,000.00
Donkey, GE/PE, from $75 to 200.00
Donkey w/blanket, GE/PE, from $90 to 400.00
Elephant, GE/PE, from $90 to 300.00
Elephant w/blanket, GE/PE, from $200 to 600.00
Gazelle, GE/PE, rare, from $700 to 3,000.00
Giraffe, GE/PE, from $200 to 800.00
Goat, GE/PE, from $150 to 400.00
Goose, PE only, from $200 to 600.00
Gorilla, PE only, from $1,200 to 3,000.00
Hippo, GE/PE, from $300 to 900.00
Horse, brn, saddle & stirrups, GE/PE, from $150 to 400.00
Horse, wht, platform, GE/PE, from $125 to 400.00
Hyena, GE/PE, very rare, from $1,000 to 4,000.00
Kangaroo, GE/PE, from $400 to 1,200.00
Lion, cloth mane, GE, from $500 to 1,200.00
Lion, cvd mane, GE/PE, from $250 to 900.00
Monkey, 1-part head, PE only, from $250 to 450.00
Monkey, 2-part head, wht face, from $300 to 900.00
Ostrich, GE/PE, from $200 to 750.00
Pig, 5 versions, GE/PE, from $200 to 700.00
Polar Bear, GE/PE, from $500 to 1,200.00
Poodle, cloth mane, GE only, from $300 to 500.00
Poodle, GE/PE, from $125 to 300.00
Rabbit, GE/PE, very rare, from $1,000 to 3,000.00
Rhino, GE/PE, from $250 to 1,000.00
Sea lion, GE/PE, from $400 to 1,200.00
Sheep (lamb) w/bell, GE/PE, from $200 to 700.00
Tiger, GE/PE, from $250 to 800.00
Wolf, GE/PE, very rare, from $600 to 5,000.00
Zebra, GE/PE, from $250 to 800.00
Zebu, GE/PE, rare, from $1,000 to 2,500.00

Humpty Dumpty Circus Accessories

There are many accessories: wagons, tents, ladders, chairs, pedestals, tight rope, weights, and more.

Menagerie, later, ca 1914-20, from $1,200 to 2,000.00
Menagerie tent, early, ca 1904, from $1,500 to 2,500.00
Oval litho tent, 1926, from $2,000 to 5,000.00
Sideshow panels, 1926, pr, from $2,000 to 5,000.00

Steiff

Margaret Steiff began making her stuffed felt toys in Germany in the late 1800s. The animals she made were tagged with an elephant in a circle. Her first teddy bear, made in 1903, became such a popular seller that she changed her tag to a bear. Felt stuffing was replaced with excelsior and wool; when it became available, foam was used. In addition to the tag, look for the 'Steiff' ribbon and the button inside the ear. For further information we recommend *Teddy Bears and Steiff Animals*, a full-color identification and value guide by Margaret Fox Mandel, available from Collector Books or your public library. See also Teddy Bears.

Adebar Stork, felt, chest tag, 1950, 24", rare, NM **1,275.00**
Basset Hound, red-brn & tan mohair, all ID, 1961, 5½", EX **125.00**
Bazi Dachshund, orig collar, chest tag, 1940, 5½", NM **110.00**
Bear, caramel mohair, raised script button, 1950, 3½", EX **265.00**
Bendy Bear, tan, all ID, 1970, 3½", M **55.00**
Bison, mohair w/felt horns, chest tag, 1950, 8", M **225.00**
Boar, blk w/brn face, all ID, 1950s, 11", M **175.00**
Cosy Fuzzy Fox, Dralon, all ID, 1968, 8½", NM **45.00**
Crabby Lobster, mohair & felt, all ID, 1963, 7", M **365.00**
Duck, chest tag, 1950, 4", NM **75.00**
Easter Bunny w/Basket, all ID, 1967, 9", rare, NM **465.00**
Fawn, velvet, all ID, 1950, 5", M **100.00**
Flossy Fish, all ID, 1968, 4", EX **65.00**
Froggy Frog, seated, velvet, all ID, 1968, 4½", M **135.00**
Grizzly Donkey, Dralon, all ID, 1968, 9½", M, from $75 to **100.00**
Hexie Dachshund, all ID, 1950, 5½", M **85.00**
Jocko Monkey, brn all ID, 1948, 5¾", NM **195.00**
Koala, tan, chest tag, 1950, 5", NM **300.00**
Lamby Lamb, orig ribbon, bell & chest tag, 4", EX **85.00**
Lora Parrot, mohair & felt, chest tag, 1968, 5", EX **110.00**
Molly Dog, brn/wht, orig ribbon/bell, all ID, 1949, 4", EX **200.00**
Murmy, all ID, 1950, 5", M **100.00**
Navy Goat, no ID, 1950s, 5", M **225.00**
Original Teddy, gold mohair, no ID, 1950s, 3½", NM **225.00**
Paddy Walrus, mohair, chest tag, 1950s, 4½", NM **100.00**
Peggy Penguin, all ID, 1959, 5", M **125.00**
Possy Squirrel, all ID, 1950s, 5", EX **95.00**
Robby Seal, chest tag, 1950, 5", M **85.00**
Slo Turtle, chest tag, 1950, 5", M **65.00**
Stork, felt, no ID, 1950, 6½", NM **110.00**
Tiger Cub, chest tag, 1950, 4", NM **125.00**
Turkey, raised script button, 1950s, 4¼", M **285.00**
Unicorn, split chest tag, brass button & stock tag, 1983, 7", M .. **125.00**
Walrus, raised script button & stock tag, 1950, 5", M **75.00**
Woolie Penguin, no ID, 1950, 2", M **65.00**
Zicky Goat, caramel, all ID, US Zone, 1948, 7½", M **285.00**
Zotty Bear, tan mohair, 1950, 8", NM, from $350 to **400.00**

Toy Soldiers and Accessories

Among the better-known manufacturers of 'dimestore' soldiers are Barclay, Manoil, and Jones, all of whom made hollow cast-lead figures; Grey Iron, who used cast iron; and Auburn, who made figures of rubber. They all measured about 3" to 3½" tall, and often accessories such as trucks, tanks, and airplanes were designed to add to the enjoyment of staging mock battles, parades, encampments, etc.

Britains is a very popular line, smaller and usually more detailed than the 'dimestores.' They've been made in England since 1893, and most of their boxed sets sell for a minimum of $100.00.

Some examples are very rare and therefore expensive, but condition is the driving force in making a value assessment. Percentages in the description lines refer to the amount of original paint remaining. Our advisors for this category are Stan and Sally Alekna; they are listed in the Directory under Pennsylvania. To learn more about this subject, we recommend *Toy Soldiers* by Richard O'Brien (Krause).

American Metal Toys, cow, standing, brn, NM **13.00**
American Metal Toys, doctor in wht, 98%, scarce **175.00**
American Metal Toys, mule, 99% **12.00**
Auburn Rubber, Marmon-Harrington tank, 3¼", NM **38.00**

Auburn Rubber, officer on horse, 99%, scarce **51.00**
Auburn Rubber, stretcher bearer, scarce, 95% **37.00**
Auburn Rubber, US Infantry officer, khaki, 94% **14.00**
Auburn Rubber, US Infantry private, 97% **13.00**
Barclay, AA gun truck, 4", 97% **53.00**
Barclay, aviator, khaki, 98% **22.00**
Barclay, boy, gray, 99% **15.00**
Barclay, cadet, 95% **16.00**
Barclay, cook w/roast, 96% **34.00**
Barclay, engineer, 97% **16.00**
Barclay, field cannon, closed hitch, 97% **18.00**
Barclay, fireman w/axe, 97% **28.00**
Barclay, Indian w/hatchet & shield, 99% **16.00**
Barclay, knight w/shield, 99% **23.00**
Barclay, knight w/sword across chest, 98% **34.00**
Barclay, machine gunner kneeling, short stride, tin helmet, 90% . **15.00**
Barclay, man skier, 99% **26.00**
Barclay, policeman, 99% **22.00**
Barclay, side dump truck, 1960s, 97% **14.00**
Barclay, soldier at port of arms, tin helmet, 99% **26.00**
Barclay, soldier running, tin helmet, 97% **32.00**
Barclay, soldier sitting w/rifle, tin helmet, 94%, scarce **35.00**
Barclay, tommygunner, tin helmet, 93% **17.00**
Britains, #1, Life Guards, 13-pc, EX+ **175.00**
Britains, #117, Egyptian Infantry, 1957-59, 8-pc, EXIB **250.00**
Britains, #227, US Infantry, 8-pc, G **130.00**
Britains, #312, Grenadier Guards, 8-pc, M (EX Soldiers box) **200.00**
Britains, #35, Royal Marine Artillery, 1925, 8-pc, G **350.00**
Britains, #75, Scots Guards, 7-pc, EX-M (EX box) **170.00**
Britains, #90, Coldstream Guards, 30-pc, EX (Whisstock box) .. **450.00**
Courtenay, Erle of Nassau, position Z-1, lying wounded, EX **500.00**
Courtenay, King of Castile, position 6, sword in hand, VG **550.00**
Grey Iron, Black man digging, scarce, 95% **29.00**
Grey Iron, cadet officer, 99% **36.00**
Grey Iron, Colonial mtd officer, 96% **47.00**
Grey Iron, conductor, 99% **16.00**
Grey Iron, cowboy w/lasso (lasso missing), 92%, scarce **49.00**
Grey Iron, Ethopian officer, very scarce, 90% **65.00**
Grey Iron, Indian chief w/knife, 98% **32.00**
Grey Iron, milkman, scarce, 98% **24.00**
Grey Iron, old man sitting, M **12.00**
Grey Iron, pirate w/sword & hook, 96% **34.00**
Grey Iron, ski trooper, no skis, 93%, scarce **41.00**
Grey Iron, trooper on horse, EX **9.00**
Grey Iron, US Cavalry officer, 98% **47.00**
Grey Iron, US Doughboy signaling, postwar, 98% **41.00**
Jones, British Marine firing musket at angle, 98% **28.00**
Jones, cow standing, 99% **10.00**
Jones, farmer, 99% **19.00**
Jones, Hession soldier on guard, 54mm, scarce, 98% **28.00**
Jones, 1775 officer w/sword at side, scarce, 95% **28.00**
Manoil, anti-aircraft gunner, 98% **32.00**
Manoil, Brahma bull, 99%, scarce **28.00**
Manoil, carpenter sawing lumber, 98% **28.00**
Manoil, combat soldier, scarce, 98% **40.00**
Manoil, cook's helper w/ladle, 95%, scarce **60.00**
Manoil, cowboy on blk horse, 97% **55.00**
Manoil, drummer, stocky version, 97%, scarce **39.00**
Manoil, farmer sewing grain, 97% **27.00**
Manoil, gas truck, 99% **32.00**
Manoil, hound, wht w/brn spots, 97% **27.00**
Manoil, machine gunner, seated, 95% **24.00**
Manoil, man chopping wood, 97% **22.00**
Manoil, marching soldier, thin, 98% **41.00**

Manoil, oil tanker, red & silver, 98% 43.00
Manoil, school teacher, 99%, scarce 54.00
Manoil, sedan, red plastic, scarce, M 25.00
Manoil, woman w/pie, 97% 30.00
Mignot, Ancient Frank Cavalry, 6-pc, M (EX box) 200.00
Mignot, Chasse, #0031, 31-pc, EX (EX box) 350.00
Mignot, French Army Machine Gun Unit (1914), 14-pc, EX 200.00
Mignot, Horse Guards Cavalry, #0247, 5-pc, M (M box) 260.00
Mignot, Polish Lancers, #0229, 6-pc, M (M box) 115.00
Mignot, Standard Bearers of Various Regiments, 6-pc, EX-M 300.00
Miller Plaster, stretcher bearer, few tiny scrapes, 97% 28.00

Trains

Electric trains were produced as early as the late 19th century. Names to look for are Lionel, Ives, and American Flyer. Identification numbers given in the listings below actually appear on the item.

Am Flyer, #K771 Operating Stockyard & Car, NMIB 150.00
Am Flyer, #23830 Piggyback Unloader & Car, NMIB 150.00
Am Flyer, #342 DC Switcher Locomotive, MIB 575.00
Am Flyer, #481 Silver Flash Diesel Locomotive, MIB 750.00
Am Flyer, #779 Oil Drum Loader, 1955-56, NM 150.00
Am Flyer, #874 Operating Boxcar, red, EX+ 150.00
Ives, #64 Canadian Pacific Boxcar, EX 250.00
Ives, #67 Ives Railway Line Caboose, EX 150.00
Lionel, #18303 Amtrak GGI Diesel Locomotive, LTI 1987-96, NMIB ...400.00
Lionel, #217 Caboose, peacock & red, prewar, EXIB 300.00
Lionel, #3360 Burro Crane, postwar, NMIB 600.00
Lionel, #6917 Jersey Central Caboose, NMIB 65.00
Lionel, #700 Pennsylvania Caboose, LTI 1987-96, NMIB 35.00
Lionel, #812 Suburban Landscape Villa, prewar, EX 510.00
Lionel, #8307 Southern Pacific Daylight, MPC 1970-86, MIB ...920.00
Lionel, #8413 Naperville Boxcar, LTI 1987-96, NMIB 15.00
Lionel, #9305 Santa Fe Operating Cowboy Car, 1970-96, EX 25.00
Marklin, #G800 Locomotive, blk/red, VG+ 160.00
Marklin, #3356 Crocodile Locomotive, NMIB 170.00
Marx, #M10000 Set, 5-pc, red/silver, EX 225.00
Marx, #4923 Set, 6-pc set, NM (in separate boxes) 150.00
MTH, #263 Steam Locomotive, blk w/nickel trim, MIB 320.00
MTH, #385 Locomotive & Tender, MIB 490.00
MTH, #840 Powerhouse, NMIB 410.00
Williams, Camelback 4-6-0 Locomotive, 3-rail, MIB 550.00
Williams, Union Pacific SD-45 Locomotive, MIB 195.00
Williams, USRS 4-6-2 Locomotive & Tender, MIB 375.00

Trade Signs

Trade signs were popular during the 1800s. They were usually made in an easily recognizable shape that one could mentally associate with the particular type of business it was to represent, especially appropriate in the days when many customers could not read!

Jeweler's, wooden pocketwatch form, gold paint with white faces, 19½" diameter, some repaint, $550.00.

Alcock's Tackle, emb tin fish w/red lettering, 26" L, EX 350.00
Boot, cvd wood, old gold rpt w/red & bl, OH, 1857, weathered, 28" .2,200.00
Clipper ship, bronze, throughly cvd, 26x21" 300.00
Dressmaking, pnt letters on brd, alligatored surface, 6x35" 215.00
Gunsmith, wooden dbl-bbl shotgun w/ramrod, 1800s, 100" 1,100.00
Pocket watch, wood w/gold/wht/blk pnt, J Fiske Boston, 24" 440.00
Pub, The Rifleman, 19th Century infantryman, tole pnt, 40x33" ..1,000.00
Shoe, cvd wood w/old gilt, ca 1800, on contemporary stand, 6x6" 515.00
Watch, cvd giltwood & metal, ca 1900, rstr, 22⅝" 1,250.00
Watches & Jewelry Rpr, pnt slate, Pat 1868, 6½x8½" 375.00

Tramp Art

'Tramp' is considered a type of folk art. In America it was primarily made from the end of the Civil War through the 1930s, though it employs carving and decorating methods which are much older, originating mostly in Germany and Scandinavia. 'Trampen' probably refers to the itinerant stages of Middle Ages craft apprenticeship. The carving techniques were also used for practice. Tramp art was spread by soldiers in the Civil War and primarily practiced where there was a plentiful and free supply of materials such as cigar boxes and fruit crates. The belief that this work was done by tramps and hobos as payment for room or meals is generally incorrect. The larger pieces especially would have required a lengthy stay in one place.

There is a great variety of tramp art, from boxes and frames which are most common to large pieces of furniture and intricate objects. The most common method of decoration is chip carving with several layers built one on top of another. There are several variations of that form as well as others such as 'Crown of Thorns,' an interlocking method, which are completely different. The most common finishes were lacquer or stain, although paints were also used. The value of tramp art varies according to size, detail, surface, and complexity. The new collector should be aware that tramp art is being made today. While some sell it as new, others are offering it as old. In addition, many people mistakenly use the term as a catchall phrase to refer to other forms of construction — especially things they are uncertain about. Our advisor is Matt Lippa; he is listed in the Directory under Alabama.

Box, chip-cvd, 3 built-up pyramids, hinged lid w/mirror, 9x9x16" ...330.00
Box, chip-cvd hearts & inlay, fabric panels, 1900s, 4x8x6", VG ..275.00
Box, 1-drw, crazed pnt, wht knob, pincushion top, 1920s, 4x10x7", EX .325.00
Box, 10 layers on top, 2 on front & sides, unfinished, 1900s, 5x10x6" ...150.00
Box, 3 to 4 layers, glass panel over wood lid, '20s, 4¾x13x8", G ..250.00
Box, 4-compartment, hearts/arrows/dmns/etc, ca 1900, 8x15x7", EX 425.00
Cradle, heart-shaped end, simply cvd, lacquered, ca 1900, doll sz .175.00
Cross, chip-cvd, mirrored medallions, gold pnt, '20s, 21x12x3½", VG 475.00
Cross, chip-cvd layers, tacks/velvet trim, 1890s, 23x14" on base ...350.00
Frame, chip-cvd (4 layers), brass tacks, 1900s, 11x7", VG 295.00
Frame, chip-cvd (4 layers), hearts/pyramids, 22x26½" 1,250.00
Frame, chip-cvd (6 layers), arrowheads/pyramids, 1900s, 13x16¼", VG 275.00
Frame, crested w/extended corners, 3-layer, 1910-20s, 14½x9¾" ..275.00
Frame, 4 layers/9 openings, dbl-X corners, old pnt, 1910s, 10x14", EX ..850.00
Shaving stand, 2 & 3 layers, swivel mirror, drw, ca 1911, 14x10x10" 595.00
Shelf, chip-cvd, made from crates, rstr crest, 1900s, 20x15x4½", EX 475.00
Shelf, chip-cvd scraps w/vine motif center, 1900s, 8x39x6½" 750.00
Shelf, fluted cvgs, 3-tier, wht pnt, ca 1910-20, 28x27x5", EX 195.00
Table, dbl ped, 4-layer base/8-layer top, 1930s, 27x28x13", EX ..875.00

Traps

Though of interest to collectors for many years, trap collecting has gained in popularity over the past ten years in particular, causing prices to appreciate rapidly. Traps are usually marked on the pan as to manufacturer, and the condition of these trademarks are important when determining their value. Grading is as follows:

Good: one-half of pan legible.
Very Good: legible in entirety, but light.
Fine: legible in entirety, with strong lettering.
Mint: in like-new, shiny condition.

Our advisor for this category is Boyd Nedry; he is listed in the Directory under Michigan. Prices listed here are for traps in fine condition.

Alaskan 'the wolf trap,' #9, dbl coil spring	95.00
All-Steel, #1, single long spring	85.00
Ampco self-setting gopher trap	18.00
Anti-cat Automatic, mousetrap	60.00
Arrow, #2, single under spring	30.00
Bell Trap, Canada #0, single long spring	30.00
Blake-Lamb, #40, dbl under spring	30.00
Briddell cush-in-grip, #1, long spring	40.00
Briddell cush-in-grip, single under spring	40.00
Bridger, #1, dbl coil spring	4.50
Bullock automatic self setter, #1	255.00
Butera Mfg, #1.500, coil spring	6.00
Champion, #2, dbl long spring	40.00
Cinch mole trap	18.00
Cooper Clutch, #2	75.00
Cosey Killer, pan type	40.00
Crago Clutch, #7	650.00
Critter Gitter, plastic mousetrap, live catch	20.00
CW Choghhill mousetrap, fits on fruit jar	40.00
Death Grip, mole trap, Brooklin Michigan, CI	65.00
Delusion, tin & wood mousetrap	60.00
Diamond #33, offset jaws, coil springs	40.00
Dwight #1, dogless, single long spring	365.00
Easy Setting, wood 4-hole choker mousetrap	22.00
Economy, #1, single long spring	25.00
Eleanchik, Frank J; #1½, dbl long spring	30.00
EZ Mole, Toledo Ohio	35.00
Fairy, revolving mousetrap	75.00
Family mousetrap, self-setting, wood & tin	60.00
Frost, JE; killer	30.00
Fut Set, rat trap, metal	20.00
Gabriel, fish & game trap	400.00
Gibbs, Harmon Live Bait, w/cage	275.00
Gibbs, King Bee, #0, single under spring	35.00
Gomber, L-shaped metal snap, rat trap	35.00
Goshen Killer	300.00
Half Moon, tin mousetrap	75.00
Handforged, blacksmith made, bear trap, 32" L	400.00
Hector, #0, single long spring, Pat 1904	70.00
Hercules, #1, single long spring	65.00
Herters, #41AX, bear trap	475.00
Hickory, wood snap rat trap	22.00
JVJ, gopher trap	45.00
KNAP, #1½, coil spring	10.00
Lamb Lamb Saver, ft gripper	10.00
Lomar, #4, dbl long spring	30.00
Mackenzie Dist Fur Co, #15, bear trap (new)	200.00
Mascotte, tin & wood mousetrap	60.00
Master Grip, by WW Stout, killer trap	210.00
McGill, 'all steel' mousetrap	10.00
Michigan Wire Goods, spear type, mole trap	20.00
Minting Tunnel Trap, metal	15.00
Nash Mole trap, CI choker, old	40.00
Nesbit, #1, emb date on pan, teeth, single long spring	600.00

Newhouse, #5, bear trap	550.00
Newhouse Bear trap, #15	575.00
Newhouse Bear trap, #6	765.00
Northwoods, #11, dbl long spring	6.00
Old Tom, mousetrap, fits on fruit jar	40.00
Orberto, #300, Iron Belt Minn	40.00
Peacock, killer, unmk	70.00
Pines Roach Trap, Chicago, glass	75.00
Pioneer, #1½, single long spring	8.00
PS&W, #1½, single long spring	15.00
PS&W 'Victoria,' #0, single long spring	95.00
Quigley, Van Kamp, wood snap mousetrap	15.00
Rev-o-Noc, stamped over Triumph, #1½, single long spring	40.00
Rival, WE Pratt Co, wood snap mousetrap	15.00
Runway, metal killer mousetrap	35.00
Save-a-Leg, Modern Animal Traps Inc, #210	60.00
Schroder's, CI spear-type mole trap	65.00
Sta-Kawt, #1, single long spring	16.00
Sure Hold, wood cone w/spikes, live trap	70.00
Taylor, TH Ketchem Mfg Co, killer	45.00
Taylor FC Special #1, single long spring	20.00
The Yankee, Plymouth Michigan, CI, mole trap	90.00
Trap Ease, wht plastic, mousetrap	15.00
Triumph, #4xt, triple clutch, dbl long spring	40.00
Triumph, #42x Ranger, w/teeth, dbl long spring	60.00
Unique, emb glass fly trap w/3 legs	95.00
Unique, plastic coon trap, w/setter	35.00
Verbail, chain trap, ft snare	125.00
Victor, #1½, stoploss, Niagara Falls Canada	22.00
Victor, #11, butterfly pan, single long spring	20.00
Victor, #3, dbl long spring	22.00
Victor Gladiator, metal snap rat trap	35.00

Trivets

Although strictly a decorative item today, the original purpose of the trivet was much more practical. They were used to protect table tops from hot serving dishes, and irons heated on the kitchen range were placed on trivets during use to protect work surfaces. The first patent date was 1869; many of the earliest trivets bore portraits of famous people or patriotic designs. Florals, birds, animals, and fruit were other favored motifs. Watch for remakes of early original designs. Some of these are marked Wilton, Emig, Wright, Iron Art, and V.M. for Virginia Metalcrafters. However, many of these reproductions are becoming collectible in the '90s. Expect to pay considerably less for these than for the originals, since they are abundant.

Brass

Heart supported by ovoid iron ft, 4¼x6"	225.00
Hearts & dmns cutouts, 9"	85.00
Lyre-shaped top, wrought-iron mts, 5x12x5"	115.00
Man O' War, racehorse	70.00
Musical note	75.00
Openwork star/dmn-shape center, scalloped, ball ft, 7" dia	40.00
Thistle design, 4-ftd, 7½x5½"	85.00
6-pointed star in hexagon, 3-ftd, 8½"	85.00

Cast Iron

Butterfly, 9½"	80.00
Christmas tree, Sanitary Co Am, Homefield PA..., 8½"	75.00
Dog among foliage, heart-shaped hdl, old break, 9"	130.00

Flatiron shape w/intersecting circles, 10¾" **50.00**

Geometric design with star-like center, four paw feet, 5½", $32.00.

George Washington's portrait, 9½" L **75.00**
Hearts form circle w/hdl, 8½" dia **50.00**
Hearts form oval, 5" **45.00**
Lyre, 7¼" **45.00**
Odd Fellows w/heart in hand, 8½" **65.00**
Uneedit, ornate, 7" **48.00**
Williams on face **28.00**

Wrought Iron

Dbl heart, shoe ft, blk pnt, 4½" **175.00**
Flatiron shape w/hdl, 13" **35.00**
Rectangular w/arched footed sides, 2½x6x6½" **35.00**
Round, 3 penny ft, 2¼x4½" dia **65.00**
Scrolled detail & tooling, spade ft, 9¾" L **250.00**
Shield shape, ftd, wooden hdl, 4⅜x10⅝" **65.00**
Tooled leaf detail, turned-up ft, 10½" L **330.00**
Triangular, w/wooden hdl, 9¼" **55.00**
10 bent iron rods, top rotates, 12" dia, 22" L **360.00**
3 splayed legs, hdl, 10x8" dia+hdl **150.00**
5-bar rectangle, 16x13x15" **120.00**

Trolls

The first trolls to come to the United States were molded after a 1952 design by Marti and Helena Kuuskoski of Tampere, Finland. The first trolls to be mass produced in America were molded from wood carvings made by Thomas Dam of Denmark. As the demand for these trolls increased, several U.S. manufacturers were licensed to produce them. The most noteworthy of these were Uneeda Doll Company's Wishnik line and Inga Dykin's Scandia House True Trolls. Thomas Dam continued to import his Dam Things line. Today trolls are enjoying a renaissance as baby boomers try to recapture their childhood. As a result, values are rising.

The troll craze from the '60s spawned many items other than troll dolls such as wall plaques, salt and pepper shakers, pins, squirt guns, rings, clay trolls, lamps, Halloween costumes, animals, lawn ornaments, coat racks, notebooks, folders, and even a car.

In the '70s, '80s, and '90s new trolls were produced. While these trolls are collectible to some, the avid troll collector still prefers those produced in the '60s. Remember, trolls must be in mint condition to receive top dollar. For more information we recommend *Collector's Guide to Trolls, Identification and Values*, by Pat Peterson. Our advisor for this category is Roger Inouye; he is listed in the Directory under California.

Ballerina, Dam, bright red hair, gr eyes, orig outfit, MIP **55.00**
Boy & Girl, Sun Rubber, 1964, pnt-on clothes, orange hair, EX, pr ...**150.00**
Bride-Nik, Uneeda Wishnik, MOC **20.00**
Christmas Stocking, Norfin, lg vinyl head, M, pr **6.00**
Doll face, Wishnik, petal-shaped red & wht costume, 7" **20.00**
Donkey, Dam, wht mane & tail, lg amber eyes, 9", G **50.00**
Elephant, bl hollow plastic, fuzzy hair, Japan, 1960s, 3", EX **25.00**
Eskimo, Dam, 1965, pnt-on clothes, brn hair & eyes, 5½", EX **75.00**

Giraffe, Dam, amber eyes, gray hair, 12", G **125.00**
Horse, Dam, 1964, long mane & tail, felt saddle, NM **45.00**
Judge, Uneeda Wishnik, gray hair, orange eyes, 5½", EX **30.00**
Kool-Aid Troll, pk hair, 5" **15.00**
Leprechaun, 1969, w/jacket, EX **25.00**
Lion, Dam, lg, M **125.00**
Moonitik, mohair body w/rubber ft & shake eyes, rare, 18" **100.00**
Nursenik, Uneeda Wishnik, 1970s, NM **25.00**
Santa, bank, 7" **68.00**
Sappy Claws, Dam, 7" **28.00**
Tarzan, Dam, long blk hair, dk amber eyes, leopard-skin costume, 3" ...**20.00**
Two-Headed Troll, pk & gr hair, VG+ **35.00**
Vampire, jointed, Hong Kong, 1966, 3", M **20.00**
Voodoo Doll, 1960s, cloth outfit, wht hair, red ruby eyes, M **15.00**
Weird Creature, real animal hair, 1960s, 3", MIB **30.00**
Werewolf Monster, 1960s, 3" **40.00**

Trunks

The first use of the term 'trunk' can be traced back to Egyptian times, when hollowed-out tree sections were used to transport goods of commerce. In the the days of steamboat voyages, stagecoach journeys, and railroad travel, trunks were used to transport clothing and personal belongings.

The most desirable trunks are flat-tops, 24" to 38" long, from the late 1800s, preferably in restored condition. Embossed dome-tops (rounded on top to better accommodate milady's finery) from the 1880s, 24" to 38" long, in complete original condition are very desirable as well. On the other hand, ca 1870s flush tin trunks, even in mint condition, inspire very little collector interest.

Unless the trunk is complete (retaining all original trays and compartments), its value is considerably lessened. If parts are absent or broken, the trunk is judged incomplete. All interiors differ; some had upper-lid compartments, others did not. Our advisor is Doris Harroff; she is listed in the Directory under Indiana.

Dome-top, emb decor, 1880s, 24" to 38", complete, from $75 to ..**175.00**
Dome-top, top & front pnt w/mc flowers on blk, mid-1800s, complete **2,000.00**
Flat-top, orig, 1880-1900, complete, rstr, from $300 to **425.00**
Flat-top, orig, 1880-1900, 24" to 38", complete, from $75 to **125.00**
Leather trim w/brass tacks on pine, 19x10x9" **110.00**
Stagecoach, flat or dome, pre-1860s, 24" to 38", rstr, up to **475.00**

Tuthill

The Tuthill Glass Company operated in Middletown, New York, from 1902 to 1923. Collectors look for signed pieces and those in an identifiable pattern. Condition is of utmost importance, and examples with brilliant cutting and intaglio (natural flowers and fruits) combined fetch the highest prices.

Bowl, cosmos & hobstars, 3¼x8" **160.00**
Bowl, vintage intaglio w/in hobnail gallery, oval, 9¾" **600.00**
Bowl, 5 flower sprays, 2½x9¼" **200.00**
Cake plate, hobstars, X-hatching, X-cut fans, low std, 10" **425.00**
Compote, candy; cherries cut allover bowl & base, 3¾x5" **155.00**
Plate, wild rose intaglio, 8¼" **295.00**
Vase, Primrose, stick form, 6¼" **135.00**

Twin Winton

Twin brothers Don and Ross Winton started this California-based company during the mid-1930s in Pasadena, California. In 1950 older brother Bruce Winton joined them. The company became a major producer of cookie jars, kitchenware, and household items until it closed in 1977. Besides their extensive line of very collectible cookie jars, they're also well known for their Hillbilly line — mugs, pitchers, bowls, lamps, ashtrays, decanters, and other novelty items, which evolved from the late 1940s through the early 1970s with a variety of decorating methods. The early designs had less details with a plain mug, and the later Japanese version was airbrushed with hand detailing on the face. Twin Winton continued to evolve and change with the market.

Don Winton was the only designer for Twin Winton and created literally thousands of designs for them. He is still sculpting in Corona del Mar, California, and collectors and dealers are continuing to find and document new pieces daily. To learn more about this subject, we recommend *Collector's Guide to Don Winton Designs* (Collector Books) by our advisor, Mike Ellis; he is listed in the Directory under California or visit the collector club web site at www.twinwinton.com.

Hillbilly Line, Men of the Mountain: mug, 5", $30.00; stein, 8", $40.00. Peanut Man cookie jar (rare), $1,800.00.

Photo courtesy Mike Ellis

Artist Palette Line, bowl, salad; 13" dia, rare, minimum value ...250.00
Artist Palette Line, cup & saucer, 3" dia, 6" dia 40.00
Bamboo Line, mug 30.00
Bamboo Line, stein, 8" 60.00
Bank, Dobbin, wood stain w/HP details, 8" 70.00
Bank, elf, wood stain w/HP details, 8" 70.00
Bank, kitten, wood stain w/HP details, 8" 70.00
Candle holder, Aladdin, lamp form, full pnt, 6½x9½" 65.00
Candle holders, Strauss, wood stain w/HP details, 10x5", pr 45.00
Candy jar, elephant, wood stain w/HP details, 6x9" 65.00
Candy jar, nut, squirrel finial, wood stain w/HP details, 8x9" 75.00
Canister set, bucket forms, 4-pc set 250.00
Canister set, Canisterville (house forms), 5-pc 525.00
Cookie jar, Apple, red & gr, 1971-72, 8x11" 180.00
Cookie jar, Baker, wood finish w/pnt details, 1966, 7x11" 400.00
Cookie jar, Bambi, full pnt, 8x10" 175.00
Cookie jar, Chipmunk, wood stain 75.00
Cookie jar, Church, rare 1,000.00
Cookie jar, Cookie Barn, Collector Series, fully pnt 175.00
Cookie jar, Cookie Catcher, wood stain w/pnt details, 8x13" 100.00
Cookie jar, Cookie Elf, gr, 8½x12" 65.00
Cookie jar, Cookie Time, wood stain w/pnt details, 7½x14" 45.00
Cookie jar, Dinosaur 400.00
Cookie jar, Duckling, wood stain w/pnt details, 8x11" 250.00
Cookie jar, Elf Bakery, wood stain w/pnt details, 8¾x12" 90.00
Cookie jar, Hen on Basket, wood stain w/pnt details, 8½" 125.00
Cookie jar, Howard Johnson, rare 3,500.00
Cookie jar, Lamb, Collector Series, fully pnt 175.00
Cookie jar, Lion & Lamb 400.00
Cookie jar, Ole King Cole 400.00
Cookie jar, Oriental Man, rare 800.00
Cookie jar, Owl, Collector Series, fully pnt 125.00
Cookie jar, Pirate Fox, Collector Series, fully pnt, 8½x11" 225.00

Creamer & sugar bowl, bull & cow 250.00
Creamer & sugar bowl, rooster & hen 250.00
Drawing (orig, pencil), Don Winton characters, from $100 to ..1,000.00
Espanimal (bookends/servers/planters), 4-pc animal, set 250.00
Figurine, angel blowing golden trumpet, early 1990s, 5" 40.00
Figurine, blond boy w/teddy bear, T-11, 3½" 125.00
Figurine, BooBoo Bear, made for Idea Inc, 4" 75.00
Figurine, boy skier, 7" 225.00
Figurine, cat, paw up in air, 3" 30.00
Figurine, Cocker Spaniel, wood stain w/HP details, 7" 50.00
Figurine, Godey lady, 6 orig designs made, 2½", ea, from $80 to ...100.00
Figurine, Mouseketeer girl w/sucker, T-2, 5½" 150.00
Figurine, Pan sitting on stump, 6½" 100.00
Figurine, Persian cat, 1940s, 10" 150.00
Figurine, Persian cat, 1940s, 5" 75.00
Figurine, rabbit, dtd 1940-43, 6" 45.00
Figurine, raccoon, 9" 100.00
Figurine, Snagglepuss, made for Idea Inc, 6" 60.00
Figurine, squirrel w/folded hands, 2¼x4" 30.00
Gnomes & Elves, elf in shoe, 7" 100.00
Gnomes & Elves, elf on snail pulling cart, 5" 100.00
Gnomes & Elves, garden gnomes, set of 7 ....200.00
Lamp, monkey figural, wood stain w/HP details 225.00
Lamp, seal figural, wood stain w/HP details, 12" 225.00
Men of the Mountains, bowl, hillbilly bather at side, 6x6" 80.00
Men of the Mountains, candy dish, w/lid 100.00
Men of the Mountains, hillbilly stein lamp, 15" 1,500.00
Men of the Mountains, napkin holder, hillbilly, 1969 ....150.00
Men of the Mountains, pitcher, hillbilly hdl, 1969, 7½" 70.00
Men of the Mountains, shakers, man & woman's heads on bbls, 4", pr ...40.00
Men of the Mountains, wall pocket 250.00
Miniature, cow, brn, #450, 2" 11.00
Miniature, mare, brn w/blk mane & tail, recumbent, #317, 1" 7.00
Miniature, skunk, sitting, #203, ¾" 5.00
Napkin holder, Bambi, wood grain w/HP details, 6x7" 85.00
Napkin holder, butler, wood grain w/HP details, 7x5" 100.00
Napkin holder, dog, wood stain w/HP details, 6x4" 150.00
Napkin holder, elephant, wood stain w/HP details, 6x4" 150.00
Napkin holder, horse, wood stain w/HP details, 6x4" 150.00
Napkin holder, poodle, wood grain w/HP details, 7x7" 75.00
Planter, rabbit crouching beside basket, 5x8" 85.00
Planter, rabbit w/cart, 7x10" 85.00
Shakers, bear (Ranger Bear), wood stain w/HP details, pr 40.00
Shakers, bucket, wood stain w/HP details, pr 30.00
Shakers, donkey, wood stain w/HP details, pr 40.00
Shakers, elephant (Sailor Elephant), wood stain w/HP details, pr ...35.00
Shakers, Kitten (Persian), wood stain w/HP details, pr 40.00
Shakers, Sheriff, wood stain w/HP details, pr 50.00
Shakers, snail, wood stain w/HP details, pr 125.00
Spoon rest, cow, wood grain w/HP details, 5x10" 80.00
Spoon rest, Dutch girl, wood grain w/HP details, 5x10" 80.00
Wall planter, lamb (head), wood grain w/HP details 100.00
Wall planter, puppy (head), wood grain w/HP details, 5½" 100.00

Typewriters

The first commercially successful typewriter was the Sholes and Glidden, introduced in 1874. By 1882 other models appeared, and by the 1890s dozens were on the market. At the time of the First World War, the ranks of typewriter-makers thinned, and by the 1920s only a few survived.

Collectors informally divide typewriter history into the pioneering period, up to about 1890; the classic period, from 1890 to 1920; and the modern period, since 1920. There are two broad classifications of early typewriters: (1) Keyboard machines, in which depression of a key prints a character and via a shift key prints up to three different characters per key; (2) Index machines, in which a chart of all the characters appears on the typewriter; the character is selected by a pointer or dial and is printed by operation of a lever or other device. Even though index typewriters were simpler and more primitive than keyboard machines, they were none-the-less a later development, designed to provide a cheaper alternative to the standard keyboard models that were selling for upwards of $100.00. Eventually second-hand keyboard typewriters supplied the low-price customer, and index typewriters vanished except as toys. Both classes of typewriters appeared in a great many designs.

It is difficult, if not impossible, to assign standard market prices to early typewriters. During the past decade, competition from a handful of wealthy overseas collectors has drastically affected the American market, and prices have become inflated on the rarer models. Some auction-realized prices have been astronomical. It is predicted that the market will drop again when this small group of collectors are satisfied and this atypical activity subsides. For now, we have updated values to reflect current market activity. Also, condition is a very important factor, and typewriters can vary infinitely in condition. A third factor to consider is that an early typewriter achieves its value mainly through the skill, effort, and patience of the collector who restores it to its original condition, in which case its purchase price is insignificant. Some unusual-looking early typewriters are not at all rare or valuable, while some very ordinary-looking ones are scarce and could be quite valuable. No general rules apply.

For further information we recommend *Antique Typewriters & Office Collectibles* by Darryl Rehr (Collector Books). When no condition is indicated, the items listed below are assumed to be in excellent, unrestored condition. Our advisor for this category is Mike Brooks; he is listed in the Directory under California.

American, CI pointer	175.00
American, indicator type, M	85.00
Automatic	1,000.00
Bennett, w/case	95.00
Bing #2, 1926	135.00
Blinkensderfer #6, oak case	200.00
Blinkensderfer Electric, 1903, extremely rare	7,000.00
Boston, index	13,000.00
Brooks	1,000.00
Caligraph #I, extremely early, poor cosmetic conditon, parts missing	2,000.00
Coffman, index	175.00
Crandall	1,000.00
Crown, index	1,000.00
Edison, index	1,000.00
Fitch	1,000.00
Geniatus Indicator	250.00
Hall, index	250.00
Hammond #12	75.00
Hammond Multiplex, for all languages, w/accessories, M	265.00
Jackson	2,500.00
Keystone	1,000.00
Lambert, decal name plate	550.00
Manhattan	250.00
Mignon #4	75.00
Molle	75.00
National	1,200.00
Niagara, index	3,500.00
Noiseless Portable	30.00
O'Dell #4, orig box	275.00
Oliver #5	110.00
Oliver Standard Visible #9, VG	60.00
Peoples, index	250.00
Pittsburg Visible #10	220.00

Postal #5	190.00
Rapid, minimum value	5,000.00
Rem-Blick	110.00
Royal #10, 1922, EX	50.00
Salter #6	350.00
Sholes & Glidden, w/decor	2,500.00
Simplex, various tin & wood index toys, ea, from $20 to	50.00
Smith #1 Premier, EX	115.00
Smith-Corona Cornet	35.00
Smith-Corona #4, portable, 1920s, in case	50.00
Sun, index	600.00
Travis	1,200.00
Underwood Standard, dtd 1912	28.00
World, index	250.00

Uhl Pottery

Founded in Evansville, Indiana, in 1849 by German immigrants, the Uhl Pottery was moved to Huntingburg, Indiana, in 1908 because of the more suitable clay available there. They produced stoneware — Acorn Ware jugs, crocks, and bowls — which were marked with the acorn logo and 'Uhl Pottery.' They also made mugs, pitchers, and vases in simple shapes and solid glazes marked with a circular ink stamp containing the name of the pottery and 'Huntingburg, Indiana.' The pottery closed in the mid-1940s. Those seeking additional information about Uhl pottery are encouraged to contact the Uhl Collectors' Society, whose address is listed in the Directory under Clubs, Newsletters, and Catalogs.

Jug, polar bear, brn	179.00
Pitcher, bl & wht spongeware, mk, 7½"	275.00
Pitcher, Grape, brn, bulbous, mk, #182	70.00
Pitcher, Lincoln, bl, 3½"	100.00
Vase, ycl, #6, 5"	50.00

Unger Brothers

Art Nouveau silver items of the highest quality were produced by Unger Brothers, who operated in Newark, New Jersey, from the early 1880s until 1909. In addition to tableware, they also made brushes, mirrors, powder boxes, and the like for milady's dressing table as well as jewelry and small personal accessories such as match safes and flasks. They often marked their products with a circle seal containing an intertwined 'UB' and '925 fine sterling.' In addition to sterling, a very limited amount of gold was also used. Note: This company made no pewter items; Unger designs may occasionally be found in pewter, but these are copies. Items dated in the mark or signed 'Birmingham' are English (not Unger).

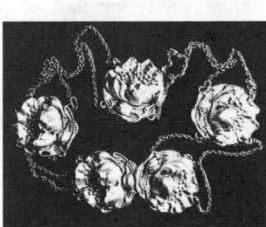

Belt, fits up to a 26" waist, $350.00.

Ashtray, smoking lady	375.00
Box, powder; cut w/hobstars, dmn & fan, angels/dolphins on lid	245.00
Coffee set, demitasse; Floral, 3-pc	1,000.00
Cuff links, lady figural, pr	195.00
Flask, knight's head	795.00
Hatpin, sterling, Art Nouveau, 8¾"	225.00

Thread case, ornate, mk 225.00
Vanity set, He Loves Me, mirror+2 brushes+jar w/cut lid, 1904 ...1,300.00

Universal

Universal Potteries Incorporated operated in Cambridge, Ohio, from 1934 to 1956. Many lines of dinnerware and kitchen items were produced in both earthenware and semiporcelain. In 1956 the emphasis was shifted to the manufacture of floor and wall tiles, and the name was changed to the Oxford Tile Company, Division of Universal Potteries. The plant closed in 1976. Our advisor for this category is Ted Haun; he is listed in the Directory under Indiana.

Ballerina, bowl, soup 6.00
Ballerina, egg cup 12.00
Bittersweet, cup & saucer 14.00
Bittersweet, plate, salad; 7" 12.00
Buttercup, coffeepot, modern shape 35.00
Calico Fruit, bowl, mixing; w/lid, 8¾" 47.00
Calico Fruit, bowl, mixing; 9⅛" 17.00
Calico Fruit, bowl, utility; w/lid, 5" 35.00
Calico Fruit, creamer 11.00
Calico Fruit, cup 8.50
Calico Fruit, plate, utility; 13" 30.00
Calico Fruit, shakers, pr 20.00
Calico Fruit, sugar bowl, w/lid 15.00
Calico Fruit, utility shaker 12.00
Cattail, bowl, 6¼" 7.00
Cattail, cake plate, Mt Vernon 25.00
Cattail, cake server 35.00
Cattail, cup & saucer 10.00
Cattail, scales, metal 37.00
Circus, bowl, soup; 7¾" 11.00
Circus, bowl, 5¼" 6.00
Circus, cup 9.00
Circus, plate, 9⅛" 9.00
Circus, platter, 13½" 25.00
Circus, saucer 3.00
Circus, shaker, bl bottom, 4¼" 8.00
Circus, spooner, 8¼" 23.00
Iris, bowl, fruit 8.00
Iris, bowl, lug soup 12.00
Iris, bowl, rnd vegetable; lg 18.00
Iris, creamer & sugar bowl, w/lid 25.00
Iris, cup & saucer 12.00
Iris, plate, bread & butter 4.00
Iris, plate, dinner 12.00
Rose Bouquet, pie server 20.00
Rose Bouquet, teapot, Mt Vernon 35.00
Woodvine, bowl, mixing; 4" 19.00
Woodvine, cup & saucer 8.00
Woodvine, gravy boat 12.00
Woodvine, pitcher, milk; 6½" 35.00
Woodvine, shakers, pr 12.00
Zinnias, casserole 13.00

Val St. Lambert

Since its inception in Belgium at the turn of the 19th century, the Val St. Lambert Cristalleries has been involved in the production of high-quality glass, producing some cameo. The factory is still in production. Our advisor for this category is Don Williams; he is listed in the Directory under Missouri.

Cameo

Bottle, scent; blossoms/swags, gr/red w/gold, screw top, 5¼" 375.00
Vase, bows/swags, dk gr on clear patterned frost, 13½" 385.00
Vase, cameo floral, dk gr on clear frost, 7¾" 1,200.00
Vase, mums on textured frost/amethyst w/gilt, 7½" 1,450.00
Vase, pansies, clear/chartreuse, bun base, 7½x2½" 1,200.00

Miscellaneous

Bottle, scent; cut floral on fern-texture clear, rpl stopper, 6½" ...220.00
Vase, cranberry w/amber casing, wht swirls w/gold mica, 11x5½" .125.00
Vase, cranberry w/amber casing & goldstone, emb swirls, 9x6" ..125.00
Vase, lime gr, elliptical, heavy walls, 5x6¾" 345.00

Valentines

These valentine listings have been separated into the following styles of cards: booklet, dimensional, flat, greeting, honeycomb paper puff, mechanical, and mechanical flat. All categories come in these styles.

The number preceding the dimensional cards is very important when determining the value of this type of card, along with the height, width, and depth.

As always, please remember the seven specifications when evaluating your card: condition, category, manufacturer, artist signature, age, and geographical location. Our advisor for this category is Katherine Kreider; she is listed in the Directory under Pennsylvania.

Key:
AS — artist signed   h — hanging
cl — celluloid   HCPP — honeycomb paper puff
dim — dimension/dimensional   htl — hold-to-light
e — early   mech — mechanical

Dimensional harp accented with Victorian children, dove, and violets, Made in Germany, early 1900s, 5x3x2½", EX, $35.00.

Photo courtesy
Katherine Kreider

Choked to death, cl, HP, h, late 1800s, 7½x9¼", EXIB 100.00
Dim, carriage pulled by horse, Tuck, e 1900s, 7x10½x5", EX 125.00
Dim, convertible, spoked wheels, 1920s, PIG, 10x10½x2", EX ..125.00
Dim, locomotive, Ambassador cards, 1960s, 7½x9½x5", EX 20.00
Dim, Pink locomotive, 1930s, 7x8x5", EX 150.00
Dim, 1D, Blk children in class, unsgn Brundage, PIG, 5¼x6x5", EX .50.00
Dim, 2D, holding hands motif, htl, PIG, e 1900s, 5x3x2¾", EX ...25.00
Dim, 3D, ship/sailboat combo, PIG, 1930s, 9½x5½x2¾", EX 95.00
Dim, 3D, swans pull shell carriage, PIG, e 1900s, 6¾x7¾", EX 75.00
Dim, 4D, cannon filled w/scraps, PIG, e 1900s, 8x4½x3¼", EX ...95.00
Dim, 4D, Greek lyre, PIG, e 1900s, 9x5½x3", EX 75.00
Dim, 5D, angels in flight, htl, PIG, 1900s, 8x4½x3¼", EX 75.00
Flat, arrow through heart, orig ribbon, h, e 1900s, 2x7¾", EX 45.00
Flat, box of kittens, unsgn JG Scott, 1920s, 4x3½", EX 10.00
Flat, Bull Terrier, easel bk, USA, 1940s, 9¾x4¼", EX 35.00
Flat, Charlie Chaplin, 1920s, 6x4½", EX 40.00
Flat, cowboy stick person, USA, 1940s, 5½x4¾", EX 10.00

Flat, golliwog w/queen of hearts, PIG, e 1900s, 4¾x5½", EX 30.00
Flat, Kewpie hanging heart, AS Rose O'Neill, e 1900s, 6x5½", EX ...75.00
Flat, Love-Line bus, unsgn C Twelvetrees, USA, 1920s, 1¾x8", EX ..15.00
Flat, Pore Lil'l Mose, Tuck, AS, e 1900s, 8x8", EX 150.00
Flat, Victorian lady w/muff, EP Dutton, h, PIB, e 1900s, 12½", EX 125.00
Flat w/dim, Collie & doghouse w/orig chain, MIG, 6¾x6x1½", EX 40.00
Flat w/dim, Dutch boy & girl w/pot of tulips, Tuck, 1910, 8x6x1", EX .50.00
Flat w/dim, lighthouse w/HCCP accent, 1920s, 10¾x6x2", EX 50.00
Flat w/dim, wooden boat, usgn CT, USA, 1940s, 10½x10x2", EX ..25.00
Flat/folded, African Am girl in bbl, 1940s, 3¼x2¾", EX 15.00
Gift-giving, candy container, heart shape, 1925, 5x2", EX 25.00
Greeting card, Gibson, 1912, NM in orig envelope 30.00
Greeting card, Kewpie, AS Rose O'Neill, Gibson mfg, 1910s, NM ..50.00
Greeting card, Little Bathing Beauty, 1940s, 3x3½", EX 5.00
Greeting card, over-sz Whitney, e 1900s, 10x8", EX 25.00
HCPP heart, Beistle, 1920s, USA, 12x12x6", EX 50.00
HCPP lamp, PIG, 1920s, 8x5x2¾", EX 50.00
HCPP w/dim, pedestal w/scrap, USA, 1920s, 4x3x2", EX 5.00
HCPP w/dim, phonograph, chromolitho, PIG, e 1900s, 10½x8x4", EX ...125.00
Mech, seesaw w/easel bk, PIG, 1920s, 5¼x7¼", EX 15.00
Mech-flat, dog, dressed animals, 1940s, 4x2¼", EX 8.00
Mech-flat, Goofy Gumpus, USA, 1940s, 4¾x4¾", EX 15.00
Mech-flat, kaleidoscope card w/HCPP hearts, PIG, 1920s, 6½x8", NM 20.00
Mech-flat, poodle in circus, casel bk, PIG, e 1900s, 7½x5¾", EX .40.00
Mech-flat, roadster convertible, unsgn CT, USA, 1920s, 3½x4", EX ..15.00
Mech-flat, Skippy, USA, 1930s, 7x6½", EX 25.00
Mech-flat w/dim, Bull mastif & cat, PIG, 1920s, 8½x8x2", EX 40.00
Novelty, Blk cherub fan, Tuck, e 1900s, 10¾x8¾", NM 95.00
Novelty, clockwork musical greeting card, ca 1959, 9½x7½x1", EX ..20.00
Novelty, pocketknife, Beistle, USA, 1920s, 7¼x1", EX 25.00
Novelty, puzzle purse valentine, handmade, e 1800s, 12" dia, VG ..400.00
Novelty, valentine sachet, English, late 1800s, 4x3", EX 25.00
Sailor's, handmade w/shells, e 1800s, 6½x4¾", EX 125.00

Van Briggle

The Van Briggle Pottery of Colorado Springs, Colorado, was established in 1901 by Artus Van Briggle, whose early career had been shaped by such notables as Karl Langenbeck and Maria Nichols Storer. His quest for several years had been to perfect a completely flat matt glaze, and upon accomplishing his goal, he opened his pottery. His wife, Anne, worked with him, and they, along with George Young, were responsible for the modeling of the wares. Their work typified the flow and form of the Art Nouveau movement, and the shapes they designed played as important a part in their success as their glazes. Some of their most famous pieces were Despondency, Lorelei, and Toast Cup. Increasing demand for their work soon made it necessary to add to their quarters as well as their staff. Although much of the ware was eventually made from molds, each piece was carefully trimmed and refined before the glaze was sprayed on. Their most popular colors were Persian Rose, Ming Blue, and Mustard Yellow.

Van Briggle died in 1904, but the work was continued by his wife. New facilities were built; and by 1908, in addition to their artware, tiles, gardenware, and commercial lines were added. By the '20s the emphasis had shifted from art pottery to novelties and commercial wares. Reproductions of some of the early designs continue to be made. The double AA mark has always been in use, but after 1920 the dates and/or shape numbers were dropped. Mention should be made here as well that the Anna Van Briggle glaze is a later line which was made between 1956 through 1968. Our advisor for this category is Michelle Ross; she is listed in the Directory under Michigan.

Bookends, squirrels, turq, 1950s, 7", pr 220.00
Bowl, console; Lady of Lake, turq/bl, 1940s, 10x15x11", $275 to 350.00

Bowl, floral, gr, #450, 1907, 3x6" 850.00
Bowl, holly, gr speckled matt w/exposed clay, 1906, 2x5½" 800.00
Bowl, leaves (spade), mulberry w/bl overspray, 1920s, 10½" dia .330.00
Candlestick, bl w/turq, 1930s, 4" 100.00
Figurine, elephant, brn w/gr & purple overspray, 1940s, 8" 110.00
Figurine, Indian maiden grinding corn, turq, 1940s, 5½" 135.00
Flower frog, turtle figural, turq/bl, 1930s, 6" dia 75.00
Mug, gr speckled matt, 1907, 4½" 325.00
Paperweight, elephant, turq, 1930s, 3½" 85.00
Plate, central leaf, turq/bl, 1907-12, 6¼" dia 195.00
Plate, grapes/leaves, rose w/slight overspray, 1910s, 8½" 300.00
Plate, lg poppy, red on bl-gr, 1907-11, 8½" 900.00
Tile, trees/mtns, 5-color, 6", in Arts & Crafts fr 2,300.00
Tile frieze, trees/hills, 4-color, 6 in oak fr, 18x12" 8,000.00
Vase, bears (2) hug rim, dk mahog, 1922-26, rstr base, 15" 2,100.00
Vase, butterfly, turq/bl, 1940s, 3" 40.00
Vase, daffodils (full-length), periwinkle froth, 1903, 14x6" 4,750.00
Vase, daffodils/long stems, turq/bl, 1920s, 13x5" 700.00
Vase, daffodils/swirled leaves, curdled brn, hdls, '06, 9½" 2,700.00
Vase, daisies/lg whiplash leaves, purple/red, 1918, 11x12" 1,500.00
Vase, Dos Cabezas, 2 women, mulberry/bl, 1919, 7¾" 2,970.00
Vase, Dos Cabezas, 2 women, 1902, mfg flaw, 8" 19,000.00
Vase, dragonflies at shoulder, maroon/bl matt, ca 1920-30s, 9½" ..300.00
Vase, dragonflies by incurvate rim, mauve/gr/turq, 1907-11, 7" ..900.00
Vase, floral, lt bl/gr, #503, 1923-26, 10" 275.00
Vase, floral, maroon/bl, shouldered w/tapered sides, 1920, 3½" ..250.00
Vase, floral, Persian Rose, 1950s, 5" 60.00
Vase, floral (stylized), dk bl-gr, 1916, 7½x4¼" 500.00
Vase, floral (stylized), turq, 1930s, 9½", from $110 to 125.00
Vase, floral/leaves, rose/gr on cream, gourd form, 1903, 5½" 900.00
Vase, floral/upright stems, burgundy, 1903, 10x4" 2,500.00
Vase, gr mottle, shouldered, 1905, 9x4½" 800.00
Vase, gr textured matt, 1910, 4x5½" 400.00
Vase, iris (long-stem), Fr Bl w/exposed clay, #671, 1908-11, 10" ..850.00
Vase, jonquils/leaves at shoulder, dk gr, 1902, 7x3½" 2,000.00
Vase, leaves, bl/lt gr, 1917, 4½" 330.00
Vase, leaves, mauve w/exposed clay, bulbous, 1908-11, 8x5½" ..1,200.00
Vase, leaves (curving), gr/brn matt, bottle form, 1920s, 11½" 250.00
Vase, leaves (EX mold), raspberry, gourd shape, #742, 8x5" 700.00
Vase, leaves (EX mold), teal bl, exposed clay, 1908-11, 7" 1,300.00
Vase, leaves (wide/triangular) in band, bl/turq, 1930s, 9x9" 475.00
Vase, leaves at shoulder, mulberry/bl-gr, hdls, #780, 1920s, 7½" ...330.00
Vase, leaves/berries at neck, rose/lt gr, bulb bottom, '04, 8" 1,750.00
Vase, leaves/sm flowers, brn/gr, hdls, #10, 1903, 8x7" 1,800.00
Vase, lilies/long stems, dk purple, 1903, 14x5¾" 4,750.00
Vase, Lorelei, bl/turq, 1920-25, 9½x4" 1,300.00
Vase, Lorelei, cadmium yel, 1907-11, sm rstr base chip, 9" 3,000.00
Vase, morning glories, yel matt, #228, 1903, 11x5", NM 4,000.00
Vase, mulberry, #838, 1920, 6", from $250 to 295.00
Vase, mulberry/bl matt, 1930s, 8" 195.00
Vase, peacock feathers, brn, spherical, 1905, 5½x6" 1,400.00
Vase, poppies, gr speckled matt w/exposed clay, 1903, 4x4" 2,000.00
Vase, poppies neck band w/long stems, purple/gr, 1908-11, 7x3½" .1,600.00
Vase, poppy (lg/long-stem), red/bl, ca 1920s, 8" 600.00
Vase, poppy pods/whiplash stems, gr/bl matt, #694, 1916, 7" 550.00
Vase, tulip (curved stem), lg leaf, gr w/purple, #175, 1903, 6" .2,000.00
Vase, turq, pinched rim w/twisted panels, 1940s 5" 60.00
Vase, turq/gr/purple mottle, baluster, #430, 1903, 6½x3½" 695.00

Vaseline

Vaseline, a greenish-yellow colored glass produced by adding uranium oxide to the batch, was produced during the Victorian era. It was made in smaller quantities than other colors and lost much of its popularity with the advent of the electric light. It was used for pressed tablewares, vases, whimseys, souvenir items, oil lamps, perfume bottles, drawer pulls, and doorknobs. Pieces have been reproduced, and some factories still make it today in small batches. Vaseline glass will fluoresce under an ultraviolet light.

Bottle, scent; pressed, w/pointed stopper, 6¾" 200.00
Bowl, dmn pattern w/cut fans at rim, 3½x8" 865.00
Candlestick, hexagonal, petal socket, 8½" 250.00
Card holder, hands 40.00
Celery boat, Daisy & Button, Hobbs Brockunier, 14" L 125.00
Coaster, starfish form 30.00
Compote, T-print w/Lattice 95.00
Sweetmeat, appl ruby loop edge, metal fr, 8x10" 125.00
Vase, swirl w/opal rice-like pattern, dimpled, ruffled, 4¾" 95.00

Verlys

Verlys art glass, produced in France after 1931 by the Holophane Company of Verlys, was made in crystal with acid-finished relief work in the Art Deco style. Colored and opalescent glass was also used. In 1935 an American branch was opened in Newark, Ohio, where very similar wares were produced until the factory ceased production in 1951. French Verlys was signed with one of three mold-impressed script signatures, all containing the company name and country of origin. The American-made glassware was signed 'Verlys' only, either scratched with a diamond-tipped pen or impressed in the mold. There is very little if any difference in value between items produced in France and America. Though some seem to feel that the French should be higher priced (assuming it to be scarce), many prefer the American-made product.

In June of 1955, about sixteen Verlys molds were leased to the A.H. Heisey Company. Heisey's versions were not signed with the Verlys name, so if an item is unsigned it is almost certainly a Heisey piece. The molds were returned to Verlys of America in July 1957. Fenton now owns all Verlys molds, but all issues are marked Fenton. Our advisor for this category is Don Frost; he is listed in the Directory under Washington.

Bowl, Leaves, clear etch, oval, 14½x11¾" 375.00
Bowl, Mary & Her Lamb, clear etch, oval, sgn C Schmitz, 1940, 13½" ..650.00
Bowl, Moderne, clear etch, 13½x9" 400.00
Bowl, Orchid, clear frosted, 14" 265.00
Bowl, Orchid, Dusty Rose, 14" 365.00
Bowl, Poppies, shallow, ftd, 13½" 300.00
Bowl, Round Fish, clear etch, rare, 8¼" 500.00
Bowl, Tassel, Directoire Blue, 11½" 300.00
Bowl, Thistle, topaz, 9" 250.00
Bowl, Water Lily, clear frosted, 14" 325.00
Bowl, Wild Duck, bl, 13½" 385.00
Candle holders, Eagles, 3½", pr 500.00
Charger, Birds & Bees, clear frosted, shallow bowl form, 11½" ..250.00
Plate & bowl, Sacre Mountain, clear etch, 11¾", 4x8¼" 475.00
Plate rest (trivet for Poissons fishbowl), clear etch, 11¾x7¾" 350.00
Vase, Alpine Thistle, clear frosted, 8¾x9" 230.00
Vase, Alpine Thistle, fiery opal, script mk, 9" 765.00
Vase, Eglantine, clear etch, 7½x6½" 450.00
Vase, Gems, 6½" 200.00
Vase, Lance (icicle), clear frosted 250.00
Vase, Laurel, opal, clear etch, 10½" 650.00
Vase, Lovebirds, clear frosted, 4½x6½" 175.00
Vase, Seasons, 8x5½" 800.00

Vernon Kilns

Vernon Potteries Ltd. was established by Faye G. Bennison in Vernon, California, in 1931. The name was later changed to Vernon Kilns; until it closed in 1958, dinnerware, specialty plates and figurines were their primary products. Among its wares most sought after by collectors today are items designed by such famous artists as Rockwell Kent, Walt Disney, Don Blanding, Jane Bennison, and May and Vieve Hamilton. Our advisor is Maxine Nelson, author of *Collectible Vernon Kilns* (now out of print); you will find her listed in the Directory under Arizona.

Ashtray, Mesa Verde Nat'l Park, CO, Jackson Hdwe 25.00
Ashtray, picture map of South Carolina 35.00
Ashtray, San Juan, Narrow Gauge Capitol of World, train scene .35.00
Ashtray, state Capital of CA, mc 35.00
Brown-Eyed Susan, picher, 1-pt, streamline, 6" 30.00
Brown-Eyed Susan, sauce boat 25.00
California Heritage, creamer, Raisin Purple 20.00
California Heritage, sugar bowl, Vineyard Green, w/lid 35.00
Casual California, carafe, pk, w/stopper 45.00
Casual California, coaster, lime gr 15.00
Casual California, egg cup, gray 25.00
Chatelaine, shakers, platinum, pr 90.00
Easter Fires, cup & saucer, demitasse; souvenir 65.00
Fantasia, bowl, mushroom, HP decor, rectangular, #120 ....375.00
Fantasia, bowl, mushroom, pk, #120 ....225.00
Fantasia, figurine, dancing hippo, arms out, #32 ....450.00
Fantasia, figurine, elephant w/trunk up, #27 ....250.00

Fantasia, figurine, hippo in tutu, #34, $450.00.

Fantasia, figurine, ostrich ballerina, #29 ....2,000.00
Fantasia, figurine, Pegasus, #21 ....450.00
Fantasia, satyr bowl, #124, gr 325.00
Frontier Days, tumbler, str sides, #5 ....90.00
Homespun, bowl, fruit 6.00
Homespun, bowl, oval vegetable; 2-pt 30.00
Homespun, bowl, tab-hdld, 6" 12.00
Homespun, butter dish 30.00
Homespun, carafe, w/stopper 50.00
Homespun, cup & saucer 12.00
Homespun, pitcher, 2-qt 47.50
Homespun, plate, 8" 8.00
Homespun, plate, 9¾" 10.00
Homespun, sugar bowl, yel, w/lid 12.00
Lei Lani, chop plate, 12" 55.00
Lei Lani, chop plate, 14" 125.00
Lei Lani, chop plate, 17" 195.00
Lei Lani, plate, 7" 27.00
Lei Lani, plate, 9" 35.00
Lei Lani, plate, 10¼" 45.00
Lei Lani, shakers, ultra shape, pr 45.00

Lei Lani, sugar bowl, w/lid 40.00
Lei Lani, tumbler 65.00
Mayflower, bowl, chowder 15.00
Mayflower, bowl, fruit; 5½" 8.00
Mayflower, bowl, serving; rnd, 9" 38.00
Mayflower, casserole, w/lid, 9¼" 65.00
Mayflower, creamer 15.00
Mayflower, cup & saucer 12.00
Mayflower, gravy boat 35.00
Mayflower, plate, bread & butter 8.00
Mayflower, plate, dinner; 10¼" 15.00
Mayflower, plate, salad; 7½" 12.00
Mayflower, platter, 14" 40.00
Mayflower, shakers, pr 24.00
Mayflower, sugar bowl, w/lid 25.00
Moby Dick, chop plate, bl, Rockwell Kent, 12" 145.00
Monterey, coffeepot 75.00
Organdie, bowl, salad; 10½" 75.00
Organdie, carafe, w/stopper 40.00
Organdie, syrup pitcher, Drip-Cut 60.00
Organdie, tumbler, water 25.00
Plate, Al Malaikah, Los Angeles, Shrine, 1950 ....30.00
Plate, Dwight D Eisenhower & Richard M Nixon 45.00
Plate, El Camino Real, CA missions, 14" 65.00
Plate, Ft Benning GA, various scenes, Belinda shape, 10½" 45.00
Plate, Galloping Goose, train scene, mc, 1940s, 10½" 65.00
Plate, General Douglas MacArthur 20.00
Plate, Lockheed Aircraft, air view of factory, 10½" 65.00
Plate, Martin Aircraft, China Clipper & other planes, 10½" 65.00
Plate, MI State Collage, scenes & seal, 1941 ....30.00
Plate, Southside Highschool...Anniversary, 1922-47, Monticeto shape 25.00
Plate, State Headquarters, NC Federation of Women's Club 25.00
Plate, University of Notre Dame, hand-tinted print 30.00
Plate, Will Rogers, portrait & scenes 20.00
Salamina, bowl, fruit; 5½" 55.00
Salamina, bowl, serving; 9" 150.00
Salamina, chop plate, 12" 285.00
Salamina, chop plate, 14" 325.00
Salamina, chop plate, 17" 500.00
Salamina, cup & saucer 100.00
Salamina, pitcher, 2-qt 775.00
Salamina, plate, bread & butter; 6½" 55.00
Salamina, plate, dinner; 10½" 135.00
Salamina, plate, luncheon; 9½" 95.00
Salamina, plate, salad; 7½" 75.00
Scenic America, cup & saucer, demitasse; Apache Trail, AZ 30.00
Shadow Leaf, creamer & sugar bowl 25.00
Shadow Leaf, cup & saucer 10.00
Shadow Leaf, plate, 7½" 6.00
Shadow Leaf, plate, 10" 10.00
Tweed, bowl, 9" 25.00

Winchester 73, pitcher
11½", $350.00.

Winchester 73, mug 45.00
Winchester 73, plate, dinner; 10" 75.00
Winchester 73, platter, 12½" 130.00
Winchester 73, salt cellar & pepper mill, pr 125.00
Winchester 73, tumbler 45.00

Villeroy and Boch

The firm of Villeroy and Boch, located in Mettlach, Germany, was brought into being by the 1841 merger of three German factories — the Wallerfangen factory, founded by Nicholas Villeroy in 1787; and Boch's father's factory in Septfontaines, established in 1767. Villeroy and Boch produced many varieties of wares, including earthenware with printed under-glaze designs which carried the well-known castle mark with the name 'Mettlach.' See also Mettlach.

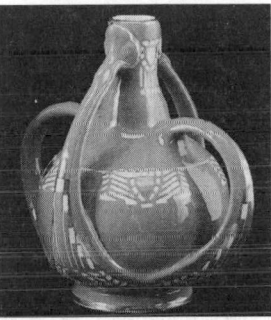

Vase, organic, geometric pattern in gold and bone on celadon, four-handled, faint mark, 9¼x7", $325.00.

Bottle, geometrics, 3-color, 2 rim-to-base-to-shoulder hdls, 9" ...325.00
Candlesticks, fruit & flowers, 4½", pr 50.00
Cup & saucer, Geranium, old style 30.00
Plaque, wealthy woman relief, much gold, 20½" 2,400.00
Plate, dinner; Geranium, old style 40.00
Plate, salad; Geranium, old style 20.00
Vase, florals, cherubs on neck, rtcl platinum trim, 1860s, 11", pr ..600.00

Vistosa

Vistosa was produced from about 1938 through the early '40s. It was Taylor, Smith, and Taylor's answer to the very successful Fiesta line of their nearby competitor, Homer Laughlin. Vistosa was made in four solid colors: mango red, cobalt blue, light green, and deep yellow. 'Pie crust' edges and a dainty five-petal flower molded into handles and lid finials made for a very attractive yet nevertheless commercially unsuccessful product. For further information, we recommend Collector's Guide to Lu-Ray Pastels by Kathy and Bill Meehan (Collector Books). Our advisor for this category is Ted Haun; he is listed in the Directory under Indiana.

Bowl, cream soup; from $20 to 25.00
Bowl, fruit; from $10 to 15.00
Bowl, nappy; from $40 to 50.00
Bowl, salad; ftd, 12", from $175 to 200.00
Bowl, soup; lug hdld, from $25 to 30.00
Chop plate, 12" 40.00
Chop plate, 15", from $40 to 50.00
Coffee cup, AD; from $30 to 35.00
Coffee saucer, AD; from $15 to 20.00
Creamer 20.00
Egg cup, ftd, from $25 to 35.00

Jug, water; 2-qt **85.00**
Plate, 6", from $10 to **15.00**
Plate, 7", from $12 to **18.00**
Plate, 9", from $15 to **20.00**
Plate, 10", from $50 to **60.00**
Sauce boat, from $150 to **175.00**
Shakers, pr **32.00**
Sugar bowl, w/lid **25.00**
Tea saucer, from $5 to **7.00**
Teacup, from $10 to **15.00**

Volkmar

Charles Volkmar established a workshop in Tremont, New York, in 1882. He produced artware decorated under the glaze in the manner of the early barbotine work done at the Haviland factory in Limoges, France. He relocated in 1888 in Menlo Park, New Jersey, and together with J.T. Smith established the Menlo Park Ceramic Company for the production of art tile. The partnership was dissolved in 1893. From 1895 until 1902, Volkmar located in Corona, New York, first under the name Volkmar Ceramic Company, later as Volkmar and Cory, and for the final six years as Crown Point. During the latter period he made art tile, blue under-glaze Delft-type wares, colorful polychrome vases, etc. The Volkmar Kilns were established in 1903 in Metuchen, New Jersey, by Volkmar and his son. Wares were marked with various devices consisting of the Volkmar name, initials, or 'Crown Point Ware.'

Bowl, modeled w/wide upright leaves, gr matt, 3x9" **450.00**
Bowl vase, brn/gr matt, 1910, 4¼x6½" **200.00**
Mug, gr matt, swollen form, ink mk, 4" **265.00**
Vase, gr/brn mottled matt, 4 slightly flattened sides, 3x4" **200.00**
Vase, thick gr matt, flared trumpet neck, 8x4" **400.00**

Vontury

Located in New Jersey, F.J. Von Tury is primarily a designer of architectural artware, tile and murals in particular, but he also produces a line of vases, bowls, and other decorative items. These are signed 'Vontury' in script. Impressionistic florals are favored.

Bowl, floral, hdls, 9½" **60.00**
Vase, floral, brn/bl/yel on gr, 8", pr **150.00**

Wade

The Wade Group of Potteries originated in 1810 with a small, single-oven pottery near Chesterton, just west of Burslem, England. This pottery, first owned by a Henry Hallen, was eventually taken over by George Wade who had opened his own pottery in the latter part of the 19th century on Hall Street, Burslem. In the early 19th century, George Wade combined the two businesses into one pottery — the George Wade Pottery, located on High Street, Burslem. This pottery was named the Manchester Pottery; it still stands and is in business today.

Both the original Hallen Pottery and the newer George Wade Pottery specialized in pottery items for the textile industry, then booming in northern England. In 1906 Wade's son, George Albert Wade, joined the company, and in 1919 the pottery name was changed to George Wade and Son Ltd.

George Wade's brothers, Albert and William, had interests in two other potteries, Wade Heath & Co. Ltd., founded in 1867 as Wade,

Colclough and Lingard (changed to Wade & Co. in 1887 and to Wade Heath & Co. Ltd. in 1927) and J. & W. Wade & Co., founded in the late 19th century with a name change also in 1927, to A.J. Wade & Co. Together the potteries manufactured decorative tiles, teapots, and other related dinnerware. In 1938 Wade Heath took over the Royal Victoria Pottery, also in Burslem, and began producing a wide range of figurines and other decorative items. The A.J. Wade & Co. pottery ceased production in 1970, but the main building was not sold and has reopened recently as The Pottery Store. The Royal Victoria Pottery is still in production but is now referred to as Hill Top.

In 1947 a new pottery was opened in Portadown, Northern Ireland, to produce both industrial ceramics and Irish porcelain giftware. In 1958 all the Wade potteries were amalgamated, becoming the Wade Group of Potteries. The most recent addition to the group is Wade (PDM) Limited, a marketing arm for the advertising ware made by Wade Heath at the Royal Victoria Pottery. Wade (PDM) Limited was incorporated in 1969. In 1989 the Wade Group of Potteries was bought out by Beauford Engineering. With this takeover, Wade Heath and George Wade & Son Ltd. were combined to form Wade Ceramics. Wade (Ireland) Ltd. and Wade (PDM) Ltd. became subsidiaries of Wade Ceramics. In 1990 Wade (Ireland) Ltd. changed its name to Seagoe Ceramics Limited. In April 1993, Seagoe Ceramics Limited ceased the production of table and giftware to concentrate on industrial ceramics. The pottery, although still owned by Beauford, is no longer part of the Wade Group.

For those interested in learning more about Wade pottery, we recommend *The World of Wade* and *The World of Wade Book 2* by Ian Warner and Mike Posgay; Mr. Warner is listed in the Directory under Canada.

Nursery Favourite, Old King Cole, $50.00.

Aquarian Set, Diver, 2¾" **28.00**
Bell's Whiskey Decanter, Charles & Diana Wedding, 75cl, empty ..**200.00**
Birdbath Pitcher, 10¼" **80.00**
British Character, Fish Porter **220.00**
British Character, Pearly King **175.00**
Burslem the Factory Cat **75.00**
Cellulose Figurine, Carnival, 7" **275.00**
Character Jug, Highwayman **200.00**
Character Jug, Toby Jim Jug **140.00**
Disney Blow-up, Scamp, 4⅛x5" **235.00**
Disney Series, Big Mama, 1¾" **37.00**
Disney Series, Thumper, 1⅞" **35.00**
Drum Box, Jem **95.00**
Grey Haired Rabbit, Wade Limited Edition **95.00**
Happy Family, Rabbit Baby, 1⅛" **12.00**
Irish Characters, Molly Malone **40.00**
Irish Porcelain, child's tankard **20.00**
Money Bank, Percy **145.00**
NatWest Piggy Bank, Annabel **34.00**
NatWest Piggy Bank, Baby Woody **27.00**
NatWest Piggy Bank, Maxwell **68.00**
NatWest Piggy Bank, Lady Hillary..**42.00**
Novelty Animal Figure, Baby Panda **170.00**

Novelty Animal Figure, Bernie & Poo 220.00
Novelty Animal Figure, Kitten on the Keys 250.00
Nursery Favourite, Bo-Peep, 2⅞" 65.00
Nursery Favourite, Queen of Hearts, 2⅞" 55.00
Nursery Rhyme Figure, Goldilocks, 4" 240.00
Posy Bowl, Barge, 1970s 30.00
Red Rose Tea (USA), Clown w/Pie 3.00
Red Rose Tea (USA), Gorilla, 1½" 5.50
Red Rose Tea (USA), Ringmaster 3.00
Ringstons Ltd Mini Maling Jug w/lid 55.00
Ringstons Ltd Tea Caddy, 1991 ....60.00
Romance Wall Plaque, 10½" 75.00
Tea Tidy, Jim Beam/Wade 20.00
Teapot, Bramble Ware 90.00
Tortoise Ashbowl, lg, 2x7¼" 50.00
Wade (PDM) Water Jug, VJ Dry Gin 25.00
Wade (PDM) Water Pitcher, Dewars Whiskey 40.00
Whim Tray, duck, bl 25.00
Whimsie on Why, Merryweather Farm 40.00
Whimsie on Why Village, Briar Row 35.00
Whimsie-Land Panda 25.00
Whimsie-Land Partridge 30.00
Whimsie-Land Retriever, 1¼x1⅝" 12.00
Zoolights, llama, yel 40.00

Wallace China

Dinnerware with a Western theme was produced by the Wallace China Company, who operated in California from 1931 until 1964. Artist Till Goodan designed three lines, Rodeo, Pioneer Trails, and Boots and Saddle, which they marketed under the package name Westward Ho. When dinnerware with a western theme became so popular just a few years ago, Rodeo was reproduced, but the new trademark includes neither 'California' or 'Wallace China.'

Our advisor for this category is Marv Fogleman; he is listed in the Directory under California. If you'd like to learn more about this company, we recommend *The Collector's Encyclopedia of California Pottery, Second Edition,* by Jack Chipman.

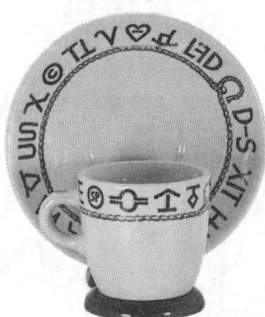

Rodeo, cup and saucer, $75.00.

Boots & Saddle, ashtray 60.00
Boots & Saddle, bowl, serving; oval 250.00
Boots & Saddle, plate, bread & butter 45.00
Boots & Saddle, plate, dinner 125.00
Boots & Saddle, shakers, pr 90.00
Boots & Saddle, sugar bowl, w/lid 125.00
Chuck Wagon, creamer, 3" 45.00
Chuck Wagon, platter, 12" 75.00
El Rancho, coffee mug 20.00
El Rancho, cup & saucer 40.00
El Rancho, platter, oval, 11½" 65.00

Rodeo, bowl, chili 65.00
Rodeo, bowl, serving; 9" 160.00
Rodeo, chop plate, 13" 295.00
Rodeo, plate, dinner 85.00
Rodeo, plate, 10½" 90.00
Rodeo, platter, 15" 300.00
Rodeo, saucer 20.00
Rodeo, shakers, pr 125.00
Westward Ho, ashtray, Pioneer Trail 50.00
Westward Ho, plate, Little Buckaroo, boy on horse, 9" 180.00
Westward Ho, shakers, 4", pr 125.00

Walley

The Walley Pottery operated in West Sterling, Massachusetts, from 1898 to 1919. Never more than a one-man operation, Walley himself handcrafted all his wares from local clay. The majority of his pottery was simple and unadorned and usually glazed in matt green. On occasion, however, you may find high- and semi-gloss green, as well as matt glazes in blue, cream, brown, and red. The rarest and most desirable examples of his work are those with applied or relief-carved decorations. Some pieces are marked 'WJW.'

Bowl, gr matt, closed-in rim, 3x5½" 475.00
Creamer, brn/gunmetal, grotesque hdl w/bl cabochon, 4x4½" 500.00
Vase, apple gr semimatt, ovoid imp w/broad leaves, 5x4" 375.00
Vase, brn to gr semigloss at base, WSH (Worcester Hospital), 8" .700.00
Vase, brn/gr mottle, 7x3½" 850.00
Vase, gr w/dripping gunmetal, shouldered, 10x7½" 850.00
Vase, gr/brn leathery gloss, spherical, small neck, 7x5" 2,200.00
Vase, gr/brn thick/dripping mottle, appl leaves, 7¾x4" 950.00
Vase, leaves on gr w/brn speckles, 6x4½" 345.00
Vase, mahog gloss, rnd w/collar rim, 7x7" 1,100.00
Vase, multi-gr frothy gloss, urn shape w/wing hdls, 9½x6¾" ...1,100.00
Vase, teal/bl glossy flambe, squat/shouldered, 3¼x4¼" 475.00
Vase, yel/gr mottled matt, doughnut rim, slight waist, 8x4½" .2,900.00

Walrath

Frederick Walrath was a studio potter who worked from around the turn of the century until his death in 1920. He was located in Rochester, New York, until 1918 when he became associated with the Newcomb Pottery in New Orleans, Louisiana.

Bowl, 3 sm frogs atop cvd/rtcl leaves, gr/yel matt, 3½x9" 2,500.00
Flower frog, seated nude w/urn on shoulder, gr matt, 8½x6" ...1,300.00
Jar, floral lid, dk mauve on mauve, 3x5" dia 1,100.00
Vase, water lilies, brn/gr on lt matt gr, shouldered, 7½x4½" ...2,000.00

Walter, A.

Almaric Walter was employed from 1904 through 1914 at Verreries Artistiques des Freres Daum in Nancy, France. After 1919 he opened his own business where he continued to make the same type of quality objets d'art in pate-de-verre glass as he had earlier. His pieces are signed A. Walter, Nancy H. Berge Sc.

Bowl, 3 snails evenly spaced around base, 3¾" 3,000.00
Covered dish, yel w/amber mouse on lid, 6¼" 2,875.00
Figure, Pan w/flute sits on stump, gr/frost, Mercier, 3½" 775.00
Paperweight, moth on flower cluster, 1¼x4" 1,750.00

Paperweight, salamander & offspring climb leafy mound, 3¾" ..2,750.00
Tray, fish, emerald gr on sea gr oval, 7⅜" 4,050.00
Vase, berry branches, gr/brn on cream, opaque, hdls, 4½" 4,350.00
Vase, lizard wrapped around stem of goblet form, 9" 6,300.00

Walters, Carl

Trained as a painter, Walters began designing ceramics about 1921. He is best known for his sculpted and painted animal forms.

Bowl, centerpc; appl grapes, dk gr, mk, chip, 14" 400.00
Pitcher, jeweled design on gold irid, mk, 7¾x6½" 400.00
Vase, lobster w/appl silver, 14½x6" 3,000.00
Vase, rooster form, red/bl/blk on wht, mks, 10¾x7¾" 230.00

Warwick

The Warwick China Company operated in Wheeling, West Virginia, from 1887 until 1951. They produced both hand-painted and decaled plates, vases, teapots, coffeepots, pitchers, bowls, and jardinieres featuring lovely florals or portraits of beautiful ladies done in luscious colors. Backgrounds were usually blendings of brown and beige, but ivory was also used as well as greens and pinks. Various marks were employed, all of which incorporate the Warwick name. For a more thorough study of the subject, we recommend *Warwick, A to W*, a supplement to *Why Not Warwick* by our advisor, Donald C. Hoffmann, Sr.; his address can be found in the Directory under Illinois. In an effort to inform the collector/dealer, Mr. Hoffmann now has a video available that identifies the company's decals and their variations by number.

Creamer & sugar bowl, brn to tan, floral, A-22, 4" 85.00
Dinnerware set, AB514, 8-place w/pattern # on cr/sug 350.00
Dinnerware set, A2003, 8-place w/pattern # on cr/sug 280.00
Dinnerware set, A2062, 8-place w/pattern # on cr/sug 300.00
Dinnerware set, B2001, Avon Rose, after 1945, 8-place w/#d cr/sug ..320.00
Dinnerware set, B2090, Bouquet Dresden, after 1945, 8-place, #d cr/sug ...325.00
Dinnerware set, B9294, 8-place w/pattern # on cr/sug 310.00
Dinnerware set, B9451, 8-place w/pattern # on cr/sug 300.00
Dinnerware set, D2100, 8-place w/pattern # on cr/sug 290.00
Dinnerware set, D573, Silver Moon, after 1945, 8-place w/#d cr/sug ..400.00
Marmalade jar, cream to brn, floral, A-6, 5" 90.00
Nut dish, gr to pk, roses, 3-ftd, B-30 ....90.00
Plate, brn to tan, lg decal, centered, fisherman, 10" 120.00
Plate, brn to tan, sm decal, friar w/hooded robe, 10" 115.00
Plate, brn to tan, sm decal, friar w/violin portrait, 10" 115.00
Plate, brn to tan, sm decal, Indian portrait, Chief White Horse, 10" ...130.00
Plate, brn to tan, sm decal, Indian portrait, Hattie Tom, 10" 150.00
Plate, brn to tan, sm decal, lady's portrait w/poppy in hair, 10" ..135.00
Plate, brn to tan, sm decal, monk holding wine cordial, 10" 115.00
Plate, brn to tan, sm decal, monk reading paper, 10" 95.00
Plate, russet to cream, sm decal, monk holding wine cordial, 10" ...130.00
Plate, russet to cream, sm decal, monk reading paper, 10" 125.00
Plate, russet to cream, sm decal, monk w/violin, 10" 125.00
Shaving mug, brn to tan, floral, A-6, 3½" 60.00
Vase, Bouquet #1, brn, floral, A-27, 11½" 235.00
Vase, Bouquet #1, brn, lady's portrait, A-17, 11½" 285.00
Vase, Bouquet #1, red, E-2, 11½" 265.00
Vase, Bouquet #2, brn, blond lady's (older) portrait, A-17, 10½" 290.00
Vase, Bouquet #2, brn, blond lady's (younger) portrait, A-17, 10½" .295.00
Vase, Bouquet #2, brn, lady w/sunflower, A-17, 10½" 350.00
Vase, Bouquet #2, brn, Madame Recamier portrait, A-17, 10½" ..295.00

Vase, Carol, brn, floral, A-27, 8" 250.00
Vase, Carol, brn, floral, A-40, 8" 275.00
Vase, Carol, brn, portrait, A-17, 8" 270.00
Vase, Carol, pk, portrait, H-1, 8" 315.00
Vase, Chrys #1, brn, floral, A-27, 15½" 180.00
Vase, Chrys #1, brn, floral, A-40, 15½" 190.00
Vase, Chrys #2, brn, floral, A-27, 13½" 175.00
Vase, Chrys #2, brn, Madame LeBrun portrait, A-17, 13½" 200.00
Vase, Chrys #3, brn, floral, A-17, 11½" 190.00
Vase, Chrys #3, brn, floral, A-6, 11½" 160.00
Vase, Narcis #1, brn, floral, A-6, 8¼" 200.00
Vase, Narcis #2, brn, portrait, A-17, 6¾" 265.00
Vase, Narcis #2, red, floral, E-2, 6¾" 240.00
Vase, Orchid, brn, Anna Potaka portrait, A-17, 10½" 325.00
Vase, Orchid, brn, floral, A-16, 10½" 300.00
Vase, Orchid, brn, floral, A-40, 10½" 275.00
Vase, Orchid, red, floral, A-2, 10½" 280.00
Vase, Pansy, brn, floral, A-4, 4" 110.00
Vase, Pansy, brn, floral, A-6, 4" 95.00
Vase, Pansy, red, floral, E-2, 4" 100.00
Vase, Peerless, brn, floral, A-6, 9½" 235.00
Vase, Peerless, floral, matt, M-6, 9½" 250.00
Vase, Queen, charcoal, floral, C-2, 12" 315.00
Vase, Queen, charcoal, floral, C-6, 12" 325.00
Vase, Rose, brn, floral, A-40, 8" 175.00
Vase, Rose, brn, floral, A-6, 8" 165.00
Vase, Rose, brn, portrait, A-17, 8" 225.00

Wash Sets

Before the days of running water, bedrooms were standardly equipped with a wash bowl and pitcher as a matter of necessity. A 'toilet set' was comprised of the pitcher and bowl, toothbrush holder, covered commode, soap dish, shaving dish, and mug. Some sets were even more elaborate. Through everyday usage, the smaller items were often broken, and today it is unusual to find a complete set.

Porcelain sets decorated with florals, fruits, or scenics were produced abroad by Limoges in France; some were imported from Germany and England. During the last quarter of the 1800s and until after the turn of the century, American-made toilet sets were manufactured in abundance. Tin and graniteware sets were also made.

Ironstone set by F Winkle & Co, England, Avon pattern, brown floral transfer, set includes: wash bowl, small and large pitchers, toothbrush holder, shaving mug, three-piece soap dish, covered chamber pot, $350.00.

English, bl-gr florals, pitcher/bowl/pot/toothbrush holder 395.00
Gertrude, semivitreous, Arts & Crafts floral, pitcher/bowl 625.00
Ironstone, wht w/gold trim, pitcher/bowl 225.00
Ironstone w/cobalt & gold, mk Warwick, 6-pc set 300.00

Old Paris, floral & scrollwork panels on wht, pitcher/bowl 595.00
W Hall & Co, Oriental Gardens, brn transfer, pitcher/bowl 215.00
Yellow ware, wht band w/blk stripes, pitcher/bowl/tumbler 130.00

Watch Fobs

Watch fobs have been popular since the last quarter of the 19th century. They were often made by retail companies to feature their products. Souvenir, commemorative, and political fobs were also produced. Of special interest today are those with advertising, heavy equipment in particular. Some of the more pricey fobs are listed here, but most of those currently available were produced in such quantities that they are relatively common and should fall within a price range of $3.00 to $10.00. Our advisor for this category is Tony George; he is listed in the Directory under California.

Am Legion, Akron OH, Indian w/canoe in tire, 1939 ....15.00
Armour Co, cow's head, silver-tone metal 35.00
Assoc Equipment Distributors, bl & gold on thin metal 5.00
Buffalo Spring, road machine shape, red & yel on silver 22.50
Cadillac, blk ducks, fabric strap, NM 200.00
Cadillac, wht swans, blk fabric strap, VG 100.00

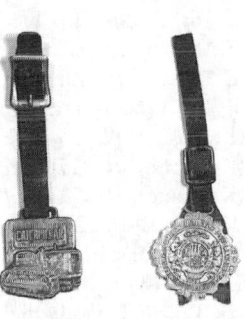

Caterpillar, J.P. Foster Co., $15.00; Compliments of Sov. Grand Lodge, St. Louis, $25.00.

Cherry Smash, cloisonne center w/cherries, EX 800.00
Columbia Tool Steel Co, Chicago IL, patriotic enameled shield ..18.00
Diamond Oilwell Jubilee, 75 Yrs of Progress, brass 10.00
Dry Farming Soil Expo, Tulsa OK, 1913 ....12.00
Ford emblem w/bl cloisonne, silver-tone trim, EX+ 50.00
Furniture Workers of Am Convention, Chicago IL, brass 25.00
Hamlight Lantern, lantern shape, NM 95.00
Harvard College 89, mc enamel, 1914, M 32.00
Homestake Mining Co Safety Award, sterling 12.00
IH (International Harvester), Oakland CA, red & blk enamel 15.00
J Menery Transfer Line 61 Baggage Rte, brass 17.50
Kellogg's Toasted Corn Flakes, stamped brass, rare, VG 135.00
Koch's Style Store for Men, OH, 1907 ....18.00
La Salle Extension University, Chicago, portrait 17.50
Mack, bulldog, circular, gold-tone metal 10.00
Manitowoc Shovels, Cranes & Draglines, hexagonal 17.50
Masters Photo Finishers of Am, film roll on arrow point 35.00
Maxwell House Coffee, brass w/red enamel 125.00
McCulloch Chain Saw, flying goose on waffled ground 8.00
Moose, silver 20.00
New Jersey Zinc Co, Gilman CO, zinc 22.50
NY-NJ Bridge Dedication, brass, 1931 ....25.00
Old Dutch Cleanser, Dutch Girl on yel center, EX 130.00
Pacific Livestock Expo, Portland OR, capital building 7.00
Salt Lake City, gold-tone metal, 1912 ....10.00
Santa Monica, beach scene on gold-tone metal, 1906 ....10.00
Scoopmobile Model LD-10, Portland OR 25.00
Scott-Madden Iron Works, St Louis MO, silver 30.00

Sun Ins Office of London, Western Dept, Chicago IL, 1907 ....22.50
Swift & Co, S-&-arrow symbol, red/wht/blk cloisonne, EX+ 120.00
Texas Cotton Assoc, FT Worth TX, bear & bull, bronze 17.50
Velvet Tobacco, pocket-tin shape, mc cloisonne, NM 140.00
Vickers Tractors, Jack Olding & Co Ltd, bl & wht enamel 42.50
Western Ranchman Outfitters, Cheyenne WY, bronc rider 30.00
WI state seal, SP brass 35.00

Watches

First made in the 1500s in Germany, early watches were actually small clocks, suspended from the neck or belt. By 1700 they had become the approximate shape and size we know today. The first watches produced in America were made in 1810. The well-known Waltham Watch Company was established in 1850. Later, Waterbury produced inexpensive watches which they sold by the thousands.

Open-face and hunting-case watches of the 1890s were often solid gold or gold-filled and were often elaborately decorated in several colors of gold. Gold watches became a status symbol in this decade and were worn by both men and women on chains with fobs or jeweled slides. Ladies sometimes fastened them to their clothing with pins often set with jewels. The chatelaine watch was worn at the waist, only one of several items such as scissors, coin purses, or needle cases, each attached by small chains.

Most turn-of-the-century watch cases were gold-filled; these are plentiful today. Sterling cases, though interest in them is on the increase, are not in great demand. Our advise for this category comes from Maundy International Watches, Antiquarian Horologists, price consultants, and researchers for many watch reference guides and books on horology. Their firm is a leading purveyor of antique watches of all kinds. They are listed in the Directory under Kansas. For character-related watches, see Personalities.

Key:

adj — adjusted	k/s — key set
brg — bridge plate design	k/w — key wind
d/s — double sunk dial	l/s — lever set
fbd — finger bridge design	mvt — movement
g/f — gold-filled	o/f — open face
g/j/s — gold jewel setting	p/s — pendant set
h/c — hunter case	r/g/p — rolled gold plate
HCI#P — heat, cold,	s — size
isochronism & position	s/s — single sunk dial
adjusted	s/w — stem wind
j — jewel	w/g/f — white gold-filled
k — karat	y/g/f — yellow gold-filled

Am Watch Co, 0s, 7j, #1891, 14k, h/c, Am Watch Co, M 350.00
Am Watch Co, 6s, 7j, #1873, y/g/f, h/c, Am Watch Co, M 95.00
Am Watch Co, 12s, 17j, #1894, 14k, o/f, Royal, M 225.00
Am Watch Co, 12s, 21j, #1894, 14k, h/c, M 575.00
Am Watch Co, 16s, 11j, #1872, p/s, silver h/c, Park Road, M 200.00
Am Watch Co, 16s, 15j, #1899, y/g/f, h/c, M 175.00
Am Watch Co, 16s, 16j, #1884, 5-min, 14k, Repeater, M 5,000.00
Am Watch Co, 16s, 17j, #1888, Railroader, M 975.00
Am Watch Co, 16s, 19j, #1872, 14k, h/c, Am Watch Woerd's Pat, M ...4,500.00
Am Watch Co, 16s, 21j, #1888, h/c, 14k, Riverside Maximus, M 1,500.00
Am Watch Co, 16s, 21j, #1899, y/g/f, l/s, o/f, Crescent St 325.00
Am Watch Co, 16s, 21j, #1908, y/g/f, o/f, Grade #645, M 325.00
Am Watch Co, 16s, 23j, #1908, o/f, 18k, Premier Maximus, MIB 12,000.00
Am Watch Co, 16s, 23j, #1908, y/g/f, o/f, adj, RR, Vanguard, M ...375.00
Am Watch Co, 16s, 23j, #1908, y/g/f, o/f, Vanguard Up/Down, EX ...650.00
Am Watch Co, 18s, #1857, silver h/c, Samuel Curtiss k/w, M .4,000.00

Am Watch Co, 18s, 11j, #1857, k/w, 1st run, PS Bartlett, M ..4,500.00

Am Watch Co, 18s, 11j, #1857, silver h/c, k/w, DH&D, EX ...1,100.00

Am Watch Co, 18s, 11j, #1857, silver h/c, k/w, s/s, Wm Ellery, EX ..250.00

Am Watch Co, 18s, 15j, #1877, k/w, RE Robbins, M 550.00

Am Watch Co, 18s, 15j, #1883, y/g/f, 2-tone, Railroad King, EX ...500.00

Am Watch Co, 18s, 17j, #1883, y/g/f, o/f, Crescent Street, M 175.00

Am Watch Co, 18s, 17j, #1892, HC, Canadian Pacific Railway, M ..950.00

Am Watch Co, 18s, 17j, #1892, y/g/f, o/f, Sidereal, rare 2,400.00

Am Watch Co, 18s, 17j, 25-yr, y/g/f, o/f, s/s, PS Bartlett, M 150.00

Am Watch Co, 18s, 21j, #1892, y/g/f, o/f, d/s, Crescent St, M 400.00

Am Watch Co, 18s, 21j, #1892, y/g/f, o/f, Grade #845, EX 200.00

Am Watch Co, 18s, 21j, #1892, y/g/f, o/f, Pennsylvania Special, M 3,000.00

Am Watch Co, 18s, 7j, #1857, silver case, k/w, CT Parker, M ..2,800.00

Auburndale Watch Co, 18s, 7j, k/w, l/s, Lincoln, M 1,500.00

Aurora Watch Co, 18s, 11j, k/w, silver h/c, M 300.00

Aurora Watch Co, 18s, 15 ruby j, y/g/f, s/w, 5th pinion, M 1,500.00

Ball (Elgin), 18s, 17j, o/f, silver, Official RR Standard, M 450.00

Ball (Hamilton), 16s, 21j, #999, g/f, o/f, l/s, M 500.00

Ball (Hamilton), 16s, 23j, #998, y/g/f, o/f, Elinvar, M 1,400.00

Ball (Hamilton), 18s, 19j, #999, g/f, o/f, l/s, EX 450.00

Ball (Hampden), 18s, 17j, o/f, adj, RR, Superior Grade, M 1,800.00

Ball (Illinois), 12s, 19j, w/g/f, o/f, M 300.00

Ball (Waltham), 16s, 17j, y/g/f, o/f, RR, Commercial Std, M 300.00

Ball (Waltham), 16s, 21j, o/f, Official RR Standard, M 550.00

Columbus, 6s, 11j, y/g/f hc, M 185.00

Columbus, 18s, 11-15j, k/w, k/s, M 500.00

Columbus, 18s, 15j, o/f, l/s, M 175.00

Columbus, 18s, 15j, y/g/f, o/f, Jay Gould on dial, G 700.00

Columbus, 18s, 21j, y/g/f, h/c, train on dial, Railway King, M 700.00

Columbus, 18s, 23j, 14k h/c, Columbus King, M 1,800.00

Cornell, 18s, 15j, s/w, JC Adams, EX 350.00

Cornell, 18s, 15j, silver h/c, k/w, John Evans, EX 350.00

Dudley, 12s, #1, 14k, o/f, flip-bk case, Masonic, G 2,600.00

Elgin, 6s, 11j, 14k, h/c, M 350.00

Elgin, 6s, 15j, 20-yr, y/g/f, h/c, s/s, EX 80.00

Elgin, 10s, 18k, h/c, k/w, k/s, s/s, Gail Borden, M 500.00

Elgin, 12s, 15j, 14k, h/c, EX 275.00

Elgin, 12s, 17j, 14k, h/c, GM Wheeler, M 250.00

Elgin, 16s, 15j, doctor's, 4th model, 18k, 2nd sweep hand, h/c, M ..1,400.00

Elgin, 16s, 15j, 14k, h/c, EX 500.00

Elgin, 16s, 21j, y/g/f, g/j/s, o/f, BW Raymond, EX 250.00

Elgin, 16s, 21j, y/g/f, g/j/s, 3 fbd, M 450.00

Elgin, 16s, 21j, y/g/f, o/f, l/s, RR, Father Time, M 400.00

Elgin, 16s, 21j, 14k, 3 fbd, grade #91, scarce, M 3,000.00

Elgin, 16s, 23j, up/down indicator, BW Raymond, EX 1,100.00

Elgin, 17s, 7j, k/w, orig silver case, Leader, M 150.00

Elgin, 18s, 11j, silver, h/c, k/w, gilded, MG Odgen, M 225.00

Elgin, 18s, 15j, o/f, d/s, k/w, silveroid, RR, BW Raymond 1st run, M ...1,500.00

Elgin, 18s, 15j, silver, k/w, k/s, h/c, HL Culver, M 300.00

Elgin, 18s, 15j, silver h/c, Penn RR dial, BW Raymond k/w mvt, M ..5,000.00

Elgin, 18s, 17j, silveroid h/c, BW Raymond, M 300.00

Elgin, 18s, 21j, y/g/f, o/f, Father Time, G 200.00

Elgin, 18s, 23j, y/g/f, o/f, 5-position, RR, Veritas, M 500.00

Fredonia, 18s, 11j, y/g/f, h/c, k/w, M 450.00

Hamilton, #4992B, 16s, 22j, o/f, steel case, G 200.00

Hamilton, #910, 12s, 17j, 20-yr, y/g/f, o/f, s/s, EX 70.00

Hamilton, #912, 12s, 17j, y/g/f, o/f, adj, EX 60.00

Hamilton, #920, 12s, 23j, 14k, o/f, M 600.00

Hamilton, #922MP, 12s, 18k case, Masterpiece (sgn), M 1,000.00

Hamilton, #925, 18s, 17j, y/g/f, h/c, s/s, l/s, M 200.00

Hamilton, #928, 18s, 15j, y/g/f, o/f, s/s, EX 175.00

Hamilton, #933, 18s, 16j, h/c, nickel plate, low serial #, M 700.00

Hamilton, #938, 18s, 17j, y/g/f, adj, M 650.00

Hamilton, #940, 18s, 21j, nickel plate, coin silver, o/f, M 350.00

Hamilton, #946, 18s, 23j, y/g/f, o/f, g/j/s, M 950.00

Hamilton, #947 (mk), 18s, 23j, 14k, h/c, orig/sgn, EX 4,500.00

Hamilton, #950, 16s, 23j, y/g/f, o/f, l/s, sgn d/s, M 1,200.00

Hamilton, #965, 16s, 17j, 14k, p/s, h/c, brg, scarce 1,000.00

Hamilton, #972, 16s, 17j, y/g/f, g/j/s, o/f, d/s, l/s, adj, EX 150.00

Hamilton, #974, 16s, 17j, 20-yr, y/g/f, o/f, s/s, EX 80.00

Hamilton, #992, 16s, 21j, y/g/f, o/f, adj, d/s, dbl roller, M 350.00

Hamilton, #992B, 16s, 21j, y/g/f, o/f, l/s, Bar/Crown, M 475.00

Hampden, 12s, 17j, w/g/f, o/f, thin model, Aviator, M 150.00

Hampden, 16s, 17j, o/f, adj, EX 60.00

Hampden, 16s, 17j, y/g/f, h/c, s/w, M 150.00

Hampden, 16s, 21j, g/j/s, y/g/f, NP, h/c, Dueber, ¾-mvt, M 280.00

Hampden, 16s, 23j, o/f, adj, dbl roller, Special Railway 500.00

Hampden, 16s, 7j, gilded, nickel plate, o/f, ¾-mvt, EX 60.00

Hampden, 18s, 15j, k/w, mk on mvt, Railway, M 1,000.00

Hampden, 18s, 15j, s/w, gilded, JC Perry, M 175.00

Hampden, 18s, 15j, silver, k/w, h/c, Hayward, M 225.00

Hampden, 18s, 15j, y/g/f, damascened, h/c, Dueber, M 200.00

Hampden, 18s, 21j, y/g/f, g/j/s, h/c, New Railway, M 325.00

Hampden, 18s, 21j, y/g/f, o/f, d/s, l/s, N Am Railway, M 400.00

Hampden, 18s, 23j, y/g/f, o/f, d/s, adj, New Railway, M 425.00

Hampden, 18s, 23j, 14k, h/c, Special Railway, M 950.00

Hampden, 18s, 7-11j, k/w, gilded, Springfield Mass 200.00

Howard, E; 6s, 15j, s/w, 18k h/c, Series VIII, G sz, M 1,475.00

Howard, E; 16s, 15j, s/w, 14k h/c, L sz, M 1,400.00

Howard, E; 18s, 15j, h/c, silver case, k/w, Series I, N sz, M 4,000.00

Howard, E; 18s, 15j, 18k h/c, k/w, Series II, N sz, M 4,500.00

Howard, E; 18s, 17j, 25-yr, y/g/f, o/f, orig case, split plate 800.00

Howard (Keystone), 12s, 23j, 14k, h/c, brg, Series 8, M 700.00

Howard (Keystone), 16s, 17j, y/g/f, o/f, Series 9, M 200.00

Howard (Keystone), 16s, 21j, y/g/f, o/f, RR Chronometer II, M .600.00

Howard (Keystone), 16s, 23j, y/g/f, o/f, Series 0, jeweled bbl, M ...725.00

Illinois, 0s, 7j, 14k, l/s, h/c, EX 250.00

Illinois, 8s, 13j, ¾-mvt, Rose LeLand, scarce, EX 275.00

Illinois, 12s, 17j, y/g/f, o/f, d/s dial, EX 50.00

Illinois, 16s, 17j, y/g/f, o/f, d/s, Bunn, EX 200.00

Illinois, 16s, 21j, g/j/s, h/c, Burlington, M 295.00

Illinois, 16s, 21j, o/f, d/s, Santa Fe Special, M 550.00

Illinois, 16s, 21j, y/g/f, o/f, d/s, Bunn Special, M 425.00

Illinois, 16s, 23j, y/g/f, o/f, d/s, 60-hr, Sangamo Special, M 2,400.00

Illinois, 16s, 23j, y/g/f, stiff bow, o/f, Sangamo Special, EX 900.00

Illinois, 18s, 11j, #1, silver, k/w, Alleghany, EX 100.00

Illinois, 18s, 11j, #3, o/f, s/w, l/s, Comet, G 100.00

Illinois, 18s, 11j, Forest City, G 100.00

Illinois, 18s, 15j, #1, adj, y/g/f, k/w, h/c, gilt, Bunn, M 775.00

Illinois, 18s, 15j, #1, k/w, k/s, silver hunter, Stuart, G 500.00

Illinois, 18s, 15j, k/w, k/s, gilt, Railway Regulator, M 900.00

Illinois, 18s, 15j, s/w, silveroid, G 50.00

Illinois, 18s, 17j, g/j/s, adj, B&O RR Special (Hunter), h/c, M ..1,650.00

Illinois, 18s, 17j, h/c, s/w, nickel plate, coin silver, Bunn, M 350.00

Illinois, 18s, 17j, o/f, d/s, adj, silveroid case, Lakeshore, G 100.00

Illinois, 18s, 17j, o/f, s/w, 5th pinion, Miller, EX 175.00

Illinois, 18s, 21j, g/j/s, g/f, o/f, A Lincoln, M 425.00

Illinois, 18s, 21j, g/j/s, o/f, adj, B&O RR Special, EX 1,350.00

Illinois, 18s, 21j, 14k, g/j/s, h/c, Bunn Special, M 1,100.00

Illinois, 18s, 23j, g/j/s, Bunn Special, EX 625.00

Illinois, 18s, 24j, g/j/s, adj, o/f, Chesapeake & Ohio, M 2,400.00

Illinois, 18s, 24j, g/j/s, Bunn Special, EX 625.00

Illinois, 18s, 26j, g/j/s, o/f, Ben Franklin USA, G 5,000.00

Illinois, 18s, 26j, 14k, Penn Special, M 7,000.00

Illinois, 18s, 7j, #3, Interior, G 50.00

Illinois, 18s, 7j, #3, silveroid, America, G 50.00

Illinois, 18s, 9-11j, o/f, k/w, s/s, silveroid case, Hoyt, M 150.00

Ingersoll, 16s, 7j, wht base metal, Reliance, G 40.00

Lancaster, 18s, 7j, o/f, k/w, k/s, eng silver case, EX	150.00
Marion US, 18s, h/c, k/w, k/s, ¾-plate, Asa Fuller, M	325.00
Marion US, 18s, 15j, nickel plate, h/c, s/w, Henry Randel, M	400.00
Melrose Watch Co, 18s, 7j, k/w, k/s, G	250.00
New York Watch Co, 18s, 7j, silver, h/c, k/w, Geo Sam Rice, EX	200.00
New York Watch Co, 19j, low sz #, wolf's teeth wind, M	1,850.00
Patek Philippe, 12s, 18j, 18k, o/f, M	2,000.00
Patek Philippe, 16s, 20j, 18k, h/c, M	3,300.00
Rockford, 16s, 17j, y/g/f, h/c, brg, dbl roller, EX	100.00
Rockford, 16s, 21j, #515, y/g/f, M	550.00
Rockford, 16s, 21j, g/j/s, o/f, grade #537, rare, M	1,500.00
Rockford, 16s, 23j, 14k, o/f, mk Doll on dial/mvt, M	2,400.00
Rockford, 18s, 15j, o/f, k/w, silver case, EX	450.00
Rockford, 18s, 17j, silveroid w/M mc dial, fancy mvt/hands, M	700.00
Rockford, 18s, 17j, y/g/f, o/f, Winnebago, M	375.00
Rockford, 18s, 21j, o/f, King Edward, M	600.00
Seth Thomas, 18s, 17j, #2, g/j/s, adj, Henry Molineux, EX	625.00
Seth Thomas, 18s, 17j, Edgemere, G	50.00
Seth Thomas, 18s, 25j, g/j/s, g/f, Maiden Lane, EX	2,450.00
Seth Thomas, 18s, 7j, ¾-mvt, bk: eagle/Liberty model, M	200.00
South Bend, 12s, 21j, dbl roller, Grade #431, M	225.00
South Bend, 12s, 21j, orig o/f, d/s, Studebaker, M	300.00
South Bend, 18s, 21j, g/j/s, h/c, Studebaker, M	1,200.00
South Bend, 18s, 21j, 14k, h/c, M	1,000.00
Swiss, 18s, 18k, h/c, 1-min, Repeater, High Grade, M	3,600.00

Waterford

The Waterford Glass Company operated in Ireland from the late 1700s until 1851 when the factory closed. One hundred years later (in 1951) another Waterford glassworks was instituted that produced glass similar to the 18th-century wares — crystal, usually with cut decoration. Today Waterford is a generic term referring to the type of glass first produced there.

Claret, Ashling	79.00
Claret, Colleen, tall	85.00
Cocktail, Colleen, 3½"	85.00
Cocktail, Colleen, 4⅞"	85.00
Cordial, Sheila	60.00
Flute, Ashling	79.00
Goblet, water; Sheila	85.00
Hock, Ashling	95.00
Old fashioned, Ashling	65.00
Sherbet, Ashling	79.00
Sherbet, Colleen, stemmed	85.00
Sherbet, Sheila	85.00
Sherry, Colleen	70.00
Tumbler, Ashling	79.00
Tumbler, Colleen, 9-oz	65.00
Tumbler, Donegal, 5¼"	60.00
Wine, Tyrone	85.00

Watt Pottery

The Watt Pottery Company was established in Crooksville, Ohio, on July 5, 1922. From approximately 1922 until 1935, they manufactured hand-turned stone containers — jars, jugs, milk pans, preserve jars, and various sizes of mixing bowls, usually marked with a cobalt blue acorn stamp. In 1936 production of these items was discontinued, and the company began to produce kitchen utility ware and ovenware such as mixing bowls, spaghetti bowls and plates, canister sets, covered

casseroles, salt and pepper shakers, cookie jars, ice buckets, pitchers, bean pots, and salad and dinnerware sets. Most Watt ware is individually hand painted with bold brush strokes of red, green, or blue contrasting with the natural buff color of the glazed body. Several patterns were produced: Apple, Autumn Foliage, Cherry, Dutch Tulip, Morning Glory, Rio Rose, Rooster, Tear Drop, Starflower, and Tulip, to name a few. Much of the ware was made for advertising premiums and is often found stamped with the name of the retail company.

Tragedy struck the Watt Pottery Company on October 4, 1965, when fire completely destroyed the factory and warehouse. Production never resumed, but the ware they made has withstood many years of service in American kitchens and is today highly regarded and prized by collectors. The vivid colors and folk art-like execution of each cheerful pattern create a homespun ambiance that will make Watt pottery a treasure for years to come.

For further study we recommend *Watt Pottery, An Identification and Price Guide*, by our advisors for this category, Sue and Dave Morris; they are listed in the Directory under Oregon. For the address of the *Watt's News* newsletter, see the section on Clubs, Newsletters, and Catalogs.

Apple, bean pot, hdld, #76, w/lid	175.00
Apple, bowl, cereal; #74	45.00
Apple, bowl, deep mixing; #63	50.00
Apple, bowl, ribbed, #05	60.00
Apple, bowl, salad; #73	85.00

Apple spaghetti bowl, #39, $175.00.

Apple, bowl, w/advertising, #8	55.00
Apple, casserole, Fr hdl, #18, ind, w/lid	225.00
Apple, casserole, ribbed, #601, w/lid	125.00
Apple, cookie jar, hdls, #503	450.00
Apple, creamer, #62	100.00
Apple, ice bucket, w/lid, no bottom mk	275.00
Apple, mug, #121	185.00
Apple, pie plate, w/advertising, #33	150.00
Apple, pitcher, w/ice lip, #17	275.00
Apple, shakers, hourglass form, w/advertising, pr	275.00
Autumn Foliage, bowl, mixing; #8	40.00
Autumn Foliage, mug, #121	200.00
Autumn Foliage, pie plate, #33	125.00
Autumn Foliage, platter, #31	110.00
Autumn Foliage, sugar bowl, #98, no lid	150.00
Banded, casserole, bl/wht bands, w/lid, 8" dia	50.00
Basketweave, casserole, brn, w/lid	30.00
Brown glaze, dog dish, #7	145.00
Butterfly, bowl, #8	275.00
Cherry, bowl, cereal; #52	55.00
Cherry, casserole, #3/19, w/lid	175.00
Cherry, cookie jar, #21	275.00
Cherry, pitcher, w/advertising, #15	175.00
Cherry, salt shaker, bbl shape	90.00
Dogwood, bowl, serving; 15" dia	110.00
Double Apple, baker, #96, w/lid, on wire stand	250.00

Double Apple, bowl, salad; #73	125.00
Dutch Tulip, bowl, mixing; #6	100.00
Dutch Tulip, casserole, #66, w/lid	250.00
Dutch Tulip, cheese crock, #80, w/lid	475.00
Dutch Tulip, pitcher, #15	250.00
Eagle, bowl, mixing; ribbed, #7	150.00
Goodies jar, #72, w/lid	350.00
Kitch-N-Queen, bowl, mixing; #7	40.00
Kitch-N-Queen, casserole, ribbed, #601, w/lid	125.00
Morning Glory, bowl, mixing; #7	125.00
Morning Glory, creamer, #97	500.00
Raised Pansy, pitcher, old style	225.00
Rio Rose, bowl, berry; 4" dia	30.00
Rio Rose, casserole, #3/19, w/lid	85.00
Rio Rose, Cut-Leaf; bowl, spaghetti; 15" dia	100.00
Rio Rose, Cut-Leaf; cup & saucer	150.00
Rooster, bowl, mixing; #8	85.00
Rooster, casserole, #67, w/lid	200.00
Rooster, creamer, #62	250.00
Rooster, pitcher, #16	165.00
Starflower, bowl, cereal; #74	30.00
Starflower, pie plate, w/advertising, #33	200.00
Tear Drop, bean server, #75, ind	30.00
Tear Drop, cheese crock, #80, w/lid	375.00
Tear Drop, pitcher, #15	60.00
Tulip, bowl, deep mixing; #63	75.00
Tulip, cookie jar, #503	400.00
Tulip, pitcher, #16	175.00
Woodgrain, pitcher, #613W	75.00

Wave Crest

Wave Crest is a line of decorated opal ware (milk glass) patented in 1892 by the C.F. Monroe Co. of Meriden, Connecticut. They made a full line of items for every room of the house, but they are probably best known for their boxes and vases. Most items were hand painted in various levels of decoration, but more transfers were used in the later years prior to the company's demise in 1916. Floral themes are common; items with the scenics and portraits are rarer and more highly prized. Many pieces have ornately scrolled ormolu and brass handles, feet and rims attached. Early pieces were often signed with a black mark; later a red banner mark was used, and occasionally a paper label may be found. However, the glass is quite distinctive and has not been reproduced, so even unmarked items are easy to recognize. Our advisors for this category are Dolli and Wilfred Cohen; they are listed in the Directory under California. Note: There is no premium for signatures on Wave Crest. Values are given for hand-decorated pieces (unless noted 'transfer') that are *not* worn.

Box, green floral top on white with lavender trim, oval, footed, 4½x8", $1,495.00.

Bonbon, Venetian scene, cracker jar shape (no lid), 7x6"	1,200.00
Box, asters on lt yel, emb lid edge & shoulder, oval, 5" L	300.00
Box, Baroque, Damask-like scrolls, 4 repeats around daisy, 7"	950.00

Box, Baroque Shell, 'drawing' of lady reserve on blk w/gold, 3x6"	500.00
Box, Baroque Shell, daisy bouquet, 4x7"	700.00
Box, blown-out shell lid, floral on bright bl, 4¼"	425.00
Box, blown-out zinnia lid, dk gr base w/emb flowers, 2½x4½"	850.00
Box, Cigarettes/flowers on yel, 4¼x3"	650.00
Box, Collars & Cuffs, Rococo w/florals, sq, 7x6½"	1,700.00
Box, daisies, emb floral/scrolls on yel, hinged, 3¼x5"	350.00
Box, Egg Crate, daisies, lav/pk on lt bl, ormolu ft, 5x7" L	600.00
Box, pansies/emb scrolls on lid, ivory, oval, 3" H	375.00
Box, Swirl, floral, lav/wht on almond, ormolu base/ft, 6" H	1,000.00
Box, Swirl, thistle/florals in brn/amethyst, 4x7"	400.00
Box, 2 cherubs in landscape/daisies on lt bl, 4x7½"	850.00
Box, 8-petal top w/pk floral bouquets, 3½x7¾"	600.00
Carafe, bridge/bk: lighthouse, sepia brn, reverse swirl neck	975.00
Cigarette holder, lt gr w/yel flowers w/in pnt star, 2¾"	450.00
Cracker jar, emb crests w/lg floral, ornate silver mts, 11x6"	675.00
Cracker jar, emb irregular panels w/pansies, ovoid, 9x6"	395.00
Cracker jar, Rococo, roses on bl, sq, metal mts, 6x5"	675.00
Cracker jar, Swirl, floral, pk on lt bl, 6½"	575.00
Cracker jar, Swirl, forget-me-nots, bowl form w/metal mts	650.00
Creamer, bird on fence/floral vine, squatty, metal mts/hdl	115.00
Creamer & sugar, Swirl, wild roses/beads on ivory, 4½"; 3½"	395.00
Fernery, Egg Crate, floral branches on almond, 6½" sq	200.00
Fernery, wild roses/netted scrolls on pk & yel, 7½" dia	200.00
Humidor, Puffy, Cigars/daisies, ormolu rims, sqd, 5x6"	1,000.00
Letter holder, clover, pk/gr on lt gr, 5½x6½"	495.00
Match holder, daisy spray, bl on pk/bl, ormolu ftd base, 2¾"	395.00
Plate, pond lily on shaded bl, openwork rim, 7"	750.00
Shaker, Erie Twist, mc floral, 2½"	150.00
Shakers, floral, tulip mold, 2½", pr	295.00
Spooner, Swirl, pansies on opal/pk, lg ornate SP hdls, 4"	625.00
Tray, daisies on pk, emb rosebuds/scrolls, 4½" dia	100.00
Tray, florals, urn form, hdld ormolu rim & ftd base, 3¼"	195.00
Tray, pin; daisies, blown-out shells, ormolu hdls/rim, 1½" H	100.00
Vase, daisies/foliage, emb acanthus bases, ormolu ft, 6", pr	300.00
Vase, floral, egg form w/long neck, ormolu hdls/trim/ft, 7"	275.00
Vase, rose buds/emb scrolls on bl, ormolu ftd base/rim, 7½"	250.00

Weapons

Among the varied areas of specialization within the broad category of weapons, guns are by far the most popular. Muskets are among the earliest firearms; they were large-bore shoulder arms, usually firing black powder with separate loading of powder and shot. Some ignited the charge by flintlock or caplock, while later types used a firing pin with a metallic cartridge. Side arms, referred to as such because they were worn at the side, include pistols and revolvers. Pistols range from early single-shot and multiple barrels to modern types with cartridges held in the handle. Revolvers were supplied with a cylinder that turned to feed a fresh round in front of the barrel breech. Other firearms include shotguns, which fired round or conical bullets and had a smooth inner barrel surface, and rifles, so named because the interior of the barrel contained spiral grooves (rifling) which increased accuracy. For further study we recommend *Modern Guns, Twelfth Edition*, by Russell Quertermous and Steve Quertermous, available at your local bookstore. All weapons but swords are under the advisement of Steve Howard, see the Directory under California. See also Militaria.

Key:
bbl — barrel	mag — magazine
cal — caliber	mgn — magnum
conv — conversion	mod — modified

cyl — cylinder	oct — octagon
f/l — flintlock	o/u — over/under
f/s — full stock	p/b — patch box
ga — gauge	perc — percussion
hdw — hardware	/s — stock
h/s — half stock	

Carbines

Winchester Model 1886, 45/90 caliber, 22" carbine barrel, full magazine, complete with saddle ring, EX, $5,500.00.

Ballard, 44 cal rimfire, 22" oct-to-rnd bbl, iron fr, G **400.00**
Burnside Civil War 5th Model, 54 cal, walnut/s, 21" rnd bbl, G ...**600.00**
Burnside, perc Civil War, 54 cal, walnut/s, 21" rnd bbl, VG ...**2,200.00**
Burnside 5th Model, 54 cal perc breechloader, G- **600.00**
Greene British, 54 cal, perc single shot, walnut/s, p/b, G **125.00**
Hall-North US 1833, breech loading perc, 52 cal, single shot, G ...**800.00**
Hall-North 1843, perc breech loader, 52 cal, 21" rnd bbl, VG ...**1,500.00**
IBM M-1, 30 cal, 20 rnd mag, repro bottom-folding/s, EX **275.00**
Inland M-1, 30 cal, cannons on stock, bbl dtd, 12-44, EX orig **500.00**
Japanese Type 38, 6.5mm cal, full length/s, 19" bbl, EX **250.00**
Joslyn Model 1864, 52 cal, breech loader, walnut/s, 22" bbl, G ..**550.00**
Lugar 1902, 30 cal, silver escutcheons, 11¾" bbl, VG+ **6,300.00**
Lugar 1902, 30 cal, walnut grips, wood base mag, 11¾" bbl, EX ..**10,000.00**
Nat'l Postal Meter M-1, 30 cal, dtd 43 bbl, flat bolt, EX **550.00**
Remington M 14R, 35 cal, str/s, 18½" bbl w/open sights, VG **650.00**
Savage 99 lever action, 303SAV cal, 20" rnd bbl, EX **500.00**
Sharps Metallic Cartridge Conv, 50-70 cal, 3-groove bbl, G **900.00**
Sharps New Model 1863, perc, 52 cal, 22" rnd bbl, EX **4,750.00**
Sharps New Model 1863 Conv, 50-70 cal, str/s, 22" bbl, VG ..**1,450.00**
Smith, 50 cal, perc breech loader, 21⅝" rnd bbl, EX **1,800.00**
Smith Civil War perc, 50 cal, walnut/s, VG **600.00**
Smith perc, 50 cal, walnut/s, 21⅝" rnd bbl, G **650.00**
Spencer Civil War, 52 cal rimfire, 22" rnd bbl, EX **1,000.00**
Spencer Repeating, 52 cal rimfire, 22" rnd bbl, G **900.00**
Springfield 1899 Krag, 30-40 cal, 22" bbl, VG+ **800.00**
Underwood M-1, 30 cal, flat bolt, flip safety, dtd 43 bbl, VG **600.00**
Winchester M3, 30 cal, sniper scope, NM **850.00**
Winchester M94 Eastern, 30 WCF cal, full mag, VG **300.00**
Winchester M94 Eastern, 32 WS cal, full mag, str/s, EX **200.00**
Winchester M94 SRC, 30 WCF cal, full mag, 20" bbl, EX **950.00**
Winchester M94 SRC, 30 WCF cal, full mag, 20" bbl, VG **550.00**
Winchester M 1866, 44RF cal, full mag tube, full NP w/20" bbl, EX .**4,000.00**
Winchester M 1894 Lever Action SRC, 30WCF cal, 20" bbl, VG ..**1,400.00**

Muskets

Am Revolutionary War Period f/l, cherry/s, 42" rnd bbl, VG ..**1,750.00**
British Long Land pattern Brn Bess, 71 cal, 46" rnd bbl, G **3,250.00**
Brown Bess, sea service, f/l, 75 cal, brass plates, 36" bbl, EX **4,250.00**
Colt M 1855 Revolving, 44 cal, rifled 31⅜" bbl, EX **6,300.00**
CS/Richmond VA Armory, 58 cal, walnut/s, 40" rnd bbl, G ..**5,000.00**
Model 1842 Palmetto Armory, 69 cal, walnut/s, 42" rnd bbl, VG .**4,000.00**
Remington 1863 Zouave Rifle, 58 cal perc, std configuration, EX .**2,250.00**
Savage Rifle, 58 cal perc, artillery type, 32" bbl, EX **500.00**
Springfield 1861, 58 cal perc, std issue rifle, VG **2,750.00**

US Special 1861, Lamson-Goodnow-Yale, 58 cal, rifled, G **800.00**
US 1795 Harper's Ferry f/l type 2, walnut/s, 45" rnd bbl, VG ..**2,100.00**
US 1816 Harper's Ferry f/l, transitional model, 69 cal, 42" bbl, G ...**700.00**
US 1816 Springfield Type II, altered to perc, 69 cal, 42" bbl, G .**325.00**
US 1816 Wickham Contract f/l, 69 cal, 42" rnd bbl, w/bayonet, VG **1,100.00**
US 1840 f/l, 69 cal, walnut/s, 42" rnd bbl, VG **500.00**
US 1861 Springfield, 58 cal, 3-band, rifled, walnut/s, G **550.00**
US 1863 Springfield, 58 cal single shot perc rifle, G- **500.00**
Wm Muir & Co 1861 Contract Rifle, 58 cal perc, mk lock, EX ..**1,700.00**

Pistols

Baby Browning Ltweight, 25 cal, NP slide w/anodized Dural fr, EX ...**200.00**
Beretta M70S Semi-Auto, 380 cal, blued, 3½" bbl, EX **225.00**
Beretta M71 Jaguar Semi-Auto, 22LR cal, blued, 3½" bbl, VG ..**120.00**
Colt Pre-Series 70 Semi-Auto, 38 super cal, compo grips, NM ...**600.00**
Colt Series 70 Gov't Model, 45 ACP cal, silver/walnut grips, EX **400.00**
Colt 1903 Pocket, 32 ACP cal, blued, walnut grips, 3¾" bbl, EX+ ..**325.00**
Colt 1903 Semi-Auto, 32 ACP cal, blued, checkered wood grips, EX+ ..**300.00**
Colt 1908 Pocket, 25 ACP cal, std configuration, VG **125.00**
Colt 1911 Commercial Semi-Auto, 45 ACP cal, wood grips, VG ..**250.00**
Colt 1911 Military, 45 ACP cal, custom NP w/ivory grips, VG ..**275.00**
CYQ P38 Semi-Auto, 9mm cal, rfn slide & grips, EX **275.00**
Desert Eagle Mark XIX Semi-Auto, 50 cal, 6¾" bbl, MIB **600.00**
FN Pocket, 25 ACP cal, Brownings Pat (like Colt 1908), EX **200.00**
H&R Self Loading, 32 ACP cal, blued, compo grips, 3½" bbl, VG ...**200.00**
Heckler & Koch P9S Semi-Auto, 45 ACP cal, 4" rifled bbl, EX ...**425.00**
Ithaca 1911A1 Semi-Auto, 45 ACP cal, NP, cvd pearl grips, EX .**300.00**
Lugar 1908 Semi-Auto, 42 code on link, chamber dtd 1940, EX ...**1,750.00**
Mauser HSC Pocket, 32 cal, Nazi mks, 2-pc wood grips, EX **325.00**
Mauser HSC Semi-Auto, 380 cal, blued, walnut grips, M **250.00**
Mauser M 1910 Pocket, 32 ACP cal, smooth wood grips, VG **125.00**
Remington M51 Pocket, 380 ACP cal, compo grips, 3½" bbl, VG ..**375.00**
Remington Rand Target, 45 ACP cal, 1911 fr, walnut grips, M ..**1,250.00**
Ruger Hawkeye Single Shot, 256 mag cal, 8½" bbl, VG+ **750.00**
S&H Stafford Warranted f/l, 58 smooth bore 9" rnd bbl, EX ..**5,000.00**
Savage 1910 Pocket, 32 cal, rubber grips, 3½" bbl, VG **110.00**
Seecamp Restricted Edition Stainless Steel Pocket, 32 cal, M **900.00**
Smith & Wesson M39-2 Semi-Auto, 9mm cal, NP, walnut grips, M ..**250.00**
Springfield Armory Nat'l Match Type, 45 cal, Remington Rand fr, EX ..**450.00**
Walther PPK/S Semi-Auto, 380 cal, 2 stainless mags, 3" bbl, EX ...**260.00**

Revolvers

Bacon Mfg Co pocket perc, 31 cal, 5-shot, walnut grips, G **225.00**
Colt Custom Single Action, 45 cal, bbl cut to 5¾", EX **1,500.00**
Colt Frontier 6-Shooter, 44-40 cal, NP, compo grips, 7½" bbl, EX .**4,000.00**
Colt SAA, 32 WCF cal, deluxe walnut grips, 5½" bbl, EX **2,500.00**
Colt SAA, 45 cal, blk compo grips, 4¾" bbl, EX **1,950.00**
Colt SAA, 45 cal, hard rubber grips, 5" bbl, EX **1,325.00**
Colt Sheriff's Model Lightning, 38 cal, 4½" etch bbl, NP, EX ..**1,200.00**
Colt 1st Generation SAA, 38 WCF cal, 5½" bbl, EX **1,900.00**
Colt 1855 Root Perc, 28 cal, 1-pc walnut grips, 3½" bbl, G **550.00**
Colt 1861 Navy, 36 cal, 6-shot, walnut grips, 7½" rnd bbl, EX ..**8,500.00**
Colt 1917 Military, 45 ACP cal, walnut grips, 5½" bbl, EX **400.00**
Eli Whitney Navy, 36 cal, 6-shot, 7½" oct bbl, EX **900.00**
Hopkins & Allen Dictator Spur Trigger, 32RF cal, NP, 2¾" bbl, VG ..**125.00**
R Jones Civil War Era Pinfire, 12mm cal, 6¼" rnd bbl, EX **550.00**
Remington Dbl Derringer, 41 cal rimfire w/3" bbls, MOP grips, VG ..**450.00**
Remington Smoot New Model #1, 30 cal rimfire short, 5-shot, EX ...**650.00**
Savage/North Navy, 36 cal, 7⅛" oct bbl w/flat-sided fr, VG **750.00**
Smith & Wesson 3rd Model DA, 44 WCF cal, lg fr, 6" keyhole bbl, G .**900.00**
Smith & Wesson Model 10, 38 special cal, 4-screw, EX **250.00**
Smith & Wesson Outdoorsman Target, 22 cal, blued fr, 6" bbl, EX+ .**425.00**

Smith & Wesson 1917 Commercial, 45 ACP cal, 5½" bbl, EX+ ..450.00
Smith & Wesson 1950 Target, 45 ACP cal, blued, 6½" bbl, M ..425.00
Smith & Wesson 38-44 Target, 38 Special cal, lg fr, 6½" bbl, M ..450.00
Smith & Wesson 5-screw Pre-29, 44 mag cal, 6½" ribbed bbl, EX+ 450.00
Starr Arms Co SA 1863 Army, 44 cal, 6-shot, 8" rnd bbl, VG ...600.00
Webley Mark VI Conv, 22LR cal, std fr, 7½" bbl, VG 450.00

Rifles

Browning Repro 1886, 45-70 cal, std grade, 26" oct bbl, EX 650.00
Browning Safari Grade Bolt Action, 7mm mag cal, 24" rnd bbl, EX 400.00
Christian Hawken KY, 50 cal, 45½" oct bbl, full/s, p/b, EX 1,500.00
Frank Wesson 2-trigger Single Shot, 22RF cal, 24" bbl, EX 850.00
Hamerli M300 Olympic Match, 7.5 Swiss cal, str pull, 29½" bbl, EX ..500.00
Henry Mauger KY, f/l, 55 cal smooth bore 44½" bbl, G 3,750.00
JP Beck KY, f/l, 66 cal smooth bore 43" oct bbl, VG 6,000.00
Remington M700BDL Deluxe Bolt Action, 200 Win mag cal, 24" bbl, EX ..400.00
Ruger Mini-14 Stainless Ranch, 223 cal, wood/s, MIB 325.00
Springfield 1898 Krag, 30-4 cal, 30" rnd bbl, EX 325.00
Stevens Crack Shot Boy's, 22 cal, 20" stepped rnd bbl, EX 165.00
Winchester M63 Semi-Auto, 22LR cal, 23" rnd bbl, pistol grips, VG ...375.00
Winchester 1890 Pump, 22LR cal, 24" oct bbl, ¾ mag, EX 350.00
Winchester 1892 Takedown Lever Action, 44 cal, 24" oct bbl, NM .4,500.00
Winchester 1894 Lever Action, 30 WCF cal, 26" oct bbl, EX 525.00
Winchester 1894 Lever Action, 32-40 cal, 26" bbl, G 300.00
Winchester 52A Target, 22LR cal, pistol grip, 28" rnd bbl, EX ..200.00

Shotguns

Browning A5 Semi-Auto, 12 ga, 30" solid rib bbl, EX 250.00
Browning Cigori Grade I o/u, 12 ga, 26" bbls, target forearm, VG ...300.00
Browning Sweet 16 A5 Semi-Auto, 16 ga, 26" mod bbl, VG 400.00
Ithaca Grade 2 Dbl Bbl, 12 ga, 20" bbls, pistol grip/s, EX 700.00
LC Smith Ideal Grade Featherweight Dbl Bbl, 20 ga, 26" bbls, VG .1,300.00
Lefever F Grade Damascus Dbl Bbl, 12 ga, 30" bbls, G 200.00
Parker CE Single Bbl Trap, 12 ga, 30" bbl, EX 1,300.00
Parker DHE Dbl Bbl, 16 ga, 30" bbls, eng receiver, EX 2,000.00
Parker GHE Dbl Bbl, 28 ga, 26" bbls on dbl O fr, EX 6,250.00
Parker VH Dbl Bbl, 12 ga, 30" bbls, pistol grip/s, EX 550.00
Winchester M12 Blk Dmn Pump, 16 ga, 26" full-choke bbl, VG ..1,600.00
Winchester M12 Deluxe Mag, 12 ga, 32" plain bbl, full choke, NM .700.00
Winchester M12 Pump, 20 ga, 28" full choke plain bbl, NM 700.00
Winchester M1894 Deluxe Lever Action, 30 WCF cal, 26" oct bbl, VG .2,200.00
Winchester M42 Custom Pump, 410 ga, 28" bbl, EX 2,000.00
Winchester M42 Pump, 410 ga, 26" plain bbl, mod choke, VG .600.00
Winchester M97 Pump, 12 ga, std grade, 30" full choke bbl, VG+ ..500.00
WW Greener Crown Grade Damascus Dbl Bbl, 12 ga, 30" bbls, VG .1,450.00

Swords

All swords listed below are priced 'with scabbard,' unless otherwise noted.

Ames 1840 Model, Civil War, musician's, EX 200.00

James Conning (Mobile) Confederate Cavalry saber, once owned by Leroy Tidwell of 39th Georgia Regiment, $13,750.00.

Ames 1850 Model, Civil War foot officer's, EX 935.00
German SS WWII presentation, Army NC type, SS runes/etc, EX ..330.00
German WWII Luftwaffe officer's, silver fittings, M 770.00
Lansfield & Lamb Lt Cavalry Saber, 35" blade, brass guard, G ...375.00
Model 1850 Presentation Grade Field Officer's, Fitch, NY, EX ..3,750.00
Polish Officer's, WII era, brass hilt w/crest, Solingen blade 150.00
S&K Heavy Cavalry Saber, 3-branch guard, 37" blade, VG+ 350.00
Scottish or English, full basket hilt, 34" dbl-edge blade, 1750s, VG ..850.00
1841 Pattern Light Artillery Saber, 33" curved blade, G 450.00

Weather Vanes

The earliest weather vanes were of handmade wrought iron and were generally simple angular silhouettes with a small hole suggesting an eye. Later copper, zinc, and polychromed wood with features in relief were fashioned into more realistic forms. Ships, horses, fish, Indians, roosters, and angels were popular motifs. In the 19th century, silhouettes were often made from sheet metal. Wooden figures became highly carved and were painted in vivid colors. E.G. Washburne and Company in New York was one of the most prominent manufacturers of weather vanes during the last half of the century. Two-dimensional sheet metal weather vanes are increasing in value due to the already heady prices of the full-bodied variety. Originality, strength of line, and patination help to determine value. When no condition is indicated, the items listed below are assumed to be in excellent condition.

Arrow, molded copper w/gilt traces, fine verdigris, 1800, 38x30" ..575.00
Banner & sun, sheet copper, att Howard, ca 1890s, 23x21" 2,300.00
Eagle, gilt copper, AL Jewell & Co, 1855-67, 21x25½", EX 3,750.00
Eagle, molded copper, gilt traces, Am, ca 1900, 19x33" 2,645.00
Eagle, molded copper, rstr gilt, ca 1900, dents, 21x25" 920.00
Eagle, molded copper, rstr gilt, ca 1900, dents, 27x31" 1,850.00
Eagle, molded copper w/verdigris, splits, 1900s, 18" H 925.00
Eagle & quill, molded copper, old pnt traces, 37x45" 2,675.00
God Is Love banner arrow, sheet metal, Am, 1890s, 38x56" ...1,850.00
Horse, copper & zinc, hollow, cut-out copper mane & tail, 13x12" ..1,500.00
Horse, sheet iron w/pnt details, old weathered surface, 14x20" ..2,500.00
Horse & sulky w/driver, gilt copper, Fiske, 25x46", EX 28,750.00
Horse jumping gate, copper w/verdigris, ca 1885, 26x34" 86,000.00
Horse running, copper, fine verdigris & bole, Blackhawk, 27" ..2,500.00
Horse running, copper, hollow body, rpr, 33", on CI arrow 440.00
Horse running, copper w/cast zinc ears, gilt traces, 27" 3,300.00
Horse running, molded copper, verdigris/gilt traces, 1880s, 30" L 2,500.00
Horse trotting, CI, rust bleeding through mustard, 1890s, 19x15" .31,050.00
Horse trotting, CI, rust/pnt traces, 1890, 26x34", VG 48,300.00
Horse trotting, copper w/CI head, fine verdigris, 1890s, 22x49" ..3,000.00
Horse trotting, copper w/gilt, ca 1900, 12x15½" 500.00
Rooster, cast zinc/sheet copper, gilt traces, Howard, 1890s, 27x25" ..3,100.00
Rooster, copper, hollow body, flat tail, gilt/pnt traces, 13" 500.00
Rooster, copper, pnt, dents/splits, ca 1900, 13x20" 260.00
Rooster, copper w/worn gilt, sm rpr, 23" 2,400.00
Rooster, copper w/yel sizing, verdigris/gold traces, 1890, 12x10" ...6,325.00
Rooster, sheet steel, old rpt, rpl rod, 33" 330.00
Sailing ship, cvd wood/zinc, att Frank Adams, ca 1930, 21x38" ..1,850.00
Sailing ship, 4-masted, metal & pnt (partial rpt) wood, 22x34" ..2,500.00
Swordfish, sheet steel silhouette, 15" 440.00

Weaving

Early Americans used a variety of tools and a great amount of time to produce the material from which their clothing was made. Soaked and dried flax was broken on a flax brake to remove waste material. It was then tapped and stroked with a scutching knife. Hackles further removed waste and separated the short fibers from the longer ones. Unspun fibers were placed on the distaff on the spinning wheel for processing into yarn. The yarn was then wound around a reel for measuring. Three tools used for this purpose were the niddy-noddy, the reel yarn winder, and the click reel. After it was washed and dyed, the yarn was transferred to a barrel-cage or squirrel-cage swift and fed onto a bobbin winder.

Today flax wheels are more plentiful than the large wool wheels since they were small and could be more easily stored and preserved. The distaff, an often-discarded or misplaced part of the wheel, is very scarce. French spinners from the Quebec area painted their wheels. Many have been stripped and refinished by those unaware of this fact. Wheels may be very simple or have a great amount of detail, depending upon the owner's ethnic background and the maker's skill.

Flax wheel, high-wheel type (wheel atop fr), complete, 51" 250.00
Flax wheel, oak, typical form, 33x21", VG 90.00
Hackle, shaped wooden base w/holes, tin sheathes, 4x15x4¼" ...100.00
Hackle, wood w/stepped top w/iron sheath & spikes, 14" 25.00
Loom, walnut fr, dbl harness, Gallinger, 51x44x49" 210.00
Niddy noddy, hardwood w/old yel pnt, age crack, 18¼" 110.00
Niddy noddy, pegged, tapered ends, early 1800s, 18⅝" 110.00
Spinning wheel, natural w/incised decor at base, 44", w/winder .200.00
Spinning wheel, old mustard pnt, copper tacks, 62", VG 150.00
Spinning wheel, wool; trn maple w/porc studs, 19" wheel, 35" ...165.00
Swift, cvd whalebone/whale ivory, 20" 500.00
Swift, wooden w/X base, old patina, 27½" 130.00
Yarn winder, bench base, 3 vertical posts, 19th C, 43" H 180.00
Yarn winder, gear-type measure, natural, 37½" H 100.00

Webb

Thomas Webb and Sons have been glassmakers in Stourbridge, England, since 1837. Besides their fine cameo glass, they have also made enameled ware and pieces heavily decorated with applied glass ornaments. The butterfly is a motif that has been so often featured that it tends to suggest Webb as the manufacturer. Our advisor for this category is Don Williams; he is listed in the Directory under Missouri. See also specific types of glass such as Alexandrite, Burmese, Mother of Pearl, and Peachblow.

Cameo

Bottle, floral vines/border, wht on red, silver mts, 5½" 1,600.00
Bottle, fuchsia/butterfly, wht on yel, ball form, 5", NM 1,200.00
Bottle, honeysuckle vine, red on wht, bulbous, 5½" 1,600.00
Bottle, lay-down; palm leaves/butterfly, wht on bl, 8" L 2,500.00
Bride's bowl, morning glories, red/wht; silver figural std, 13" ...1,950.00
Finger bowl+plate, floral/butterfly, red on textured frost 1,600.00
Lamp, floral/butterflies/bird, bl/wht shade/base, att, 18" 15,000.00
Vase, bud; bellflower/bk: butterfly, red/wht on citron, 4" 2,650.00
Vase, butterfly/cyclamen, wht on cinnamon, 5" 1,200.00
Vase, butterfly/passion flower, wht on peachblow, 9" 3,000.00
Vase, floral, bk: butterfly, wht on red, stick neck, 6" 1,250.00
Vase, Grape Picker (lady), wht on brn, sgn Woodall, 8½" 32,500.00
Vase, insect/apple blossoms, bk: fern, wht on red, 8x6" 6,000.00
Vase, Ivory, floral, bk: butterfly, stick neck, 8" 1,400.00
Vase, rose branches/line borders, wht on red, bulbous, 7" 2,500.00
Vase, roses, bk: branch, wht on red, bulbous, 7" 2,500.00
Vase, seashells, wht on red, bulbous w/flared rim, 5½" 2,645.00
Vase, seashells/seaweed, wht on red, bulb w/waisted neck, 5½" ..2,600.00
Vase, tulips, citron on clear texture, flared rim, 8¾" 500.00

Vase, vines, wht on textured confetti citron, 3¼" 450.00

Miscellaneous

Bottle, prunus/butterfly, gold on rose to amber, 5" 750.00
Finger bowl, pk-cased lime, deeply crimped rim, 5", +6" plate 150.00
Rose bowl, vines, MOP on rainbow, 3 camphor branch ft, 6x7" .1,450.00
Tray, butterfly/floral on bl to wht, clamshell form, 12" 245.00
Vase, bird, gold on bl opaque, wht int, 11" 200.00
Vase, bird/foliage on amber satin to wht cased, 10" 220.00
Vase, branches/butterfly, gold on shaded orange, hdls, 7x6" 195.00
Vase, branches/nests, gold/wht on apricot satin, hdls, 6" 125.00
Vase, deep purple w/bl & gold irid (Bronze), 8x4½" 175.00
Vase, floral, gold on pk-cased mauve w/shaded amethyst rim, 5" ..475.00
Vase, floral, gold on teal bl, shouldered, 5½" 275.00
Vase, floral on pk satin w/opal stripes, 5-lobe rim, att, 4x3" 195.00
Vase, floral swags/scrolls, gold on pk, wht int, 3 ball ft, 9" 165.00
Vase, floral/butterfly, gold on ivory opaque, 4x2½" 175.00
Vase, intaglio bug, Duberry Pink/cased, ftd disk w/hdls, 5" 675.00
Vase, leaves/berries/scrolls, gold on bl satin, ruffled, 7x4" 450.00
Vase, prunus/butterfly, gold on shaded brn satin, 9x4½" 495.00
Vase, prunus/butterfly, gold on yel, 3⅜x4" 275.00
Vase, thistles, gold on ruby w/wht int, 7" 385.00

Wedgwood

Josiah Wedgwood established his pottery in Burslem, England, in 1759. He produced only molded utilitarian earthenwares until 1770 when new facilities were opened at Etruria for the production of ornamental wares. It was there he introduced his famous Basalt and Jasperware. Jasperware, an unglazed fine stoneware decorated with classic figures in white relief, was usually produced in blues, but it was also made in ground colors of green, lilac, yellow, black, or white. Occasionally three or more colors were used in combination. It has been in continuous production to the present day and is the most easily recognized of all the Wedgwood lines. Jasper-dip is a ware with a solid-color body or a white body that has been dipped in an overlay color. It was introduced in the late 1700s and is the type most often encountered on today's market.

Though Wedgwood's Jasperware was highly acclaimed, on a more practical basis his improved creamware was his greatest success. Due to the ease with which it could be potted and because its lighter weight significantly reduced transportation expenses, Wedgwood was able to offer 'chinaware' at affordable prices. Queen Charlotte was so pleased with the ware that she allowed it to be called 'Queen's Ware.' Most creamware was marked simply 'Wedgwood.' ('Wedgwood & Co.' and 'Wedgewood' are marks of other potters.) From 1769 to 1780, Wedgwood was in partnership with Thomas Bentley; artwares of the highest quality may bear the 'Wedgwood & Bentley' mark indicating this partnership. Moonlight Lustre, an allover splashed-on effect of pink intermingling with gray, brown, or yellow, was made from 1805 to 1815. Porcelain was made, though not to any great extent, from 1812 to 1822. Bone china was produced before 1822 and after 1872. These types of wares were marked 'WEDGWOOD' (with a printed 'Portland Vase' mark after 1872). Stone china and Pearlware were made from about 1820 to 1875. Examples of either may be found with a printed or impressed mark to indicate their body type. During the late 1800s, Wedgwood produced some fine parian and majolica. Creamware, hand painted by Emile Lessore, was sold from about 1860 to 1875. From the 20th century, several lines of lustre wares — Butterfly, Dragon, and Fairyland (designed by Daisy Makeig-Jones) — have attracted the collector and, as their prices suggest, are highly sought after and admired.

Nearly all of Wedgwood's wares are clearly marked. 'WEDG-

WOOD' was used before 1891, after which time 'ENGLAND' was added. Most examples marked 'MADE IN ENGLAND' were made after 1905. A detailed study of all marks is recommended for accurate dating. See also Majolica.

Key:
WW — Wedgwood   WWMIE — Wedgwood Made in
WWE — Wedgwood England   England

Bidet, Queen's Ware, WW, early 1800s, 20¾" 350.00
Bough pot, Basalt, blk, rtcl body & lid, WW, 1790s, 5½" 750.00
Bowl, chalice; Fairyland Lustre, flame, Z5360, WWE, 10½" .13,800.00
Bowl, Fairyland Lustre, Daventry, #3427, WWE, 6½" 4,750.00
Bowl, Fairyland Lustre, Firbolgs, Z5200, WWE, 4¾" 1,500.00
Bowl, Fairyland Lustre, Poplar Trees, WWE, 9" 3,500.00
Bowl, Hummingbird Lustre, 8-sided, WWE, 8" 750.00
Bowl, Hummingbird Lustre, 8-sided, Z5294, WWE, 4¾" 400.00
Bowl, Hummingbird Lustre, 8-sided, Z5294, WWE, 9½" 700.00
Bowl, Jasper, blk, classical dancing hours, WWE, 1959, 10¼" ...1,000.00
Bowl, punch; Fairyland Lustre, Z4968, WWE, 9½" 4,000.00
Bust, Basalt, Locke, blk, integral plinth, WW, 1800s, 8¾" 600.00
Bust, Basalt, Mercury, blk, WW, 19th C, 8¾" 800.00
Bust, Basalt, Nelson, blk, circular socle, WW, 1798, 10½" 2,300.00
Bust, Basalt, Robert Burns, WW, mid 19th C, 8" 250.00
Bust, Basalt, Rousseau, blk, WW, 1850s, 6" 525.00
Candlesticks, Basalt, blk, floral sprays, WW, 1850s, 8", pr 925.00
Candlesticks, Basalt, blk sphinx form, WW, 19th C, 5", pr 2,400.00
Candlesticks, Stoneware, bl on wht, wreathed columns, WW, 4¾", pr 750.00

Chalice bowl, Flame Fairyland Lustre, Twyford Garlands with Fairy Gondola interior, WWE, ca 1920, 10½", $13,800.00.

Charger, Earthenware, 3-masted ship, A Powell, WWE, 1923, 18⅜" 1,035.00
Compote, Queen's Ware, banded border w/brn laurel, WW, 1790s, 12" ...350.00
Cup & saucer, Jasper, cobalt, Templetown children, WWE, 5⅛" ...700.00
Ewer, Basalt, blk, classical figures, WW, 1790, 10¼" 5,450.00
Figurine, Basalt, bear, blk, WWE, 1913, 4¾" 545.00
Figurine, Basalt, bulldog, blk, glass eyes, metal collar, WW, 5" ..375.00
Figurine, Basalt, cat, blk, glass eyes, WWE, 1913, 4¾" 575.00
Figurine, Basalt, cockatoo, blk, glass eyes, WWE, 1913, 4⅛" 635.00
Figurine, Basalt, rabbit, blk, glass eyes, WWE, 1913, 2½" 865.00
Figurine, Basalt, squirrel, blk, glass eyes, WWE, 1913, 5¼" 750.00
Figurine, Basalt, Venus Victrix, blk, RG Rendel, WWE, 20½" ...1,495.00
Figurine, Queen's Ware, Psyche, rocky base, WWE, 8½" 350.00
Game pie dish, Caneware, emb vintage, cabbage/carrot finial, WW, 8" .925.00
Group, Basalt, Cupid & Psyche, blk, free-form rocky base, WW, 8" ...1,725.00
Inkwell, Basalt, sphinx w/ink pot/liner/lid, WW, 19th C, 5¾ 1,265.00
Jug, Jasper, cobalt, Doric, pewter lid, WW, ca 1871, 8¾" 485.00
Jug, Queen's Ware, Garfield portrait/emblems, WW, 1881, 7¼" 750.00
Jug, Queen's Ware, thistle spray & border, WW, 20th C, 11½" .115.00
Jug, Stoneware, wht smear-glazed Gothic figures, WW, 1825, 8" ..515.00
Mug, Jasper, lt bl, Harry Barnard, WW, late 1800s, 5½" 925.00
Mug, Jasper, olive gr, Harry Barnard, WW, late 1800s, 5¼", NM 545.00
Necklace, Jasper, 17 lt bl beads w/wht leaves, 14k mts, WWE, 31" .700.00
Pitcher, Basalt, blk, pnt floral, bulbous, WW, 1850s, 6¾" 350.00
Plaque, Basalt, Hercules & Erymanthean Boar, blk, WW, 19th C, 5x7" .750.00
Plaque, Jasper, Adam Smith, lt bl, WW, 1787, 3x4" 230.00

Plaque, Jasper, Dancing Hours, cobalt, WW, late 1800s, 6x18" ..2,650.00
Plaque, Jasper, Dancing Hours, lt bl, WW, early 1800s, 6x18" .1,950.00
Plaque, Jasper, Minerva, gr, WW, early 1800s, 5x7½"+fr 430.00
Plate, Rosso Antico & Basalt, Egyptian symbols, WW, 1810, 7⅞" ..800.00
Platter, Queen's Ware, gr strawberry leaf & drop, WW, 19" 375.00
Sink, Earthenware, bl transfer Chinese Temple, WW, 1830, 14", NM .375.00
Slop pail, Queen's Ware, botanical flowers transfer, WW, 1885, 10" 750.00
Slop pail, Willow Ware, rattan hdl, w/lid, WWE, 1913, 9¼" 460.00
Sugar bowl, Jasper, bl, classical ladies, WWE, 4x5" 80.00
Sugar bowl, Rosso Antico & Basalt, hieroglyphics, w/lid, WW, 5" ...1,265.00
Teakettle, Basalt, blk, bamboo molded, WW, ca 1875, 6" 800.00
Teapot, Basalt, blk, beehive form, WW, ca 1810, 5½" 1,150.00
Teapot, Caneware, bamboo form, WW & Bentley, ca 1780, 4½" .3,000.00
Teapot, Jasper, Crimson, classical relief, WWE, ca 1920, 3½" ...1,725.00
Teapot, Queen's Ware, blk transfers, WW, 1780, 4½", NM ...1,265.00
Teapot, Queen's Ware, Chinese courtyard scene, WW, 1775, 5¾" ..1,725.00
Teapot, Rosso Antico, molded cabbage leaf, WW, early 19th C, 5" .1,500.00
Teapot, Rosso Antico & Basalt, hieroglyphics/etc, WW, 1810, 9" ...1,840.00
Vase, Basalt, blk, classical figure, WW, #943, 7¾" 3,220.00
Vase, Golconda Ware, floral/foliage w/gold, WW, ca 1885, 10¼" ..635.00
Vase, Hummingbird Lustre, Z5294, #2351, WWE, ca 1920, 8⅞" ..700.00
Vase, Jasper, bl, Portland, WW, 1840, 10⅛" 2,400.00
Vase, Jasper, blk, classical vignettes, WW, 1850s, 7¼" 975.00
Vase, Jasper, blk, pierced lid, WW, 1850s, 6½" 865.00
Vase, Jasper, blk, Portland, WW, ca 1900, 7¾" 700.00
Vase, Jasper, cobalt, hdls, WW, ca 1850s, 10½" 1,150.00
Vase, Jasper, dk bl, lion masks ea side, 7x3½" 225.00
Vase, Jasper, lt bl, ram's head/festoons, hdls, WW, 19th C, 12" .1,600.00
Vase, Lindsay Ware, Nouveau decor, hdls, WWE, 1902, 9" 575.00
Vase, potpourri; Pearlware, appl drapery swags, WW, 1790s, 7¾" 450.00
Vase, potpourri; Pearlware, floral transfers on gr, WW, w/lid, 16" ..1,725.00
Vase, Rhodian Ware, silver lustre/pnt floral, WWE, 1930s, 10¼" 260.00
Wine cooler, Terra Cotta, Triumph of Bacchus, WW, late 1700s, 10" .230.00

Weil Ware

Max Weil came to the United States in the 1940s, settling in California. There he began manufacturing dinnerware, figurines, cookie jars, and wall pockets. American clays were used, and the dinnerware was all hand decorated. Weil died in 1954; the company closed two years later. The last backstamp to be used was the outline of a burro with the words 'Weil Ware — Made in California.' Many unmarked pieces found today originally carried a silver foil label; but you'll often find a four-digit handwritten number series, especially on figurines. For further study we recommend *The Collector's Encyclopedia of California Pottery, Second Edition*, by our advisor, Jack Chipman. He is listed in the Directory under California.

Bowl, vegetable; Brentwood, w/lid, 10x11" 25.00
Butter dish, Bamboo, donkey mk 28.00
Creamer & sugar bowl, Bamboo, no lid 26.00
Cup & saucer, Blossom 18.00
Dish, relish; Brentwood, divided, 10½x6¼" 20.00
Figurine, lady in bl dress, parasol, paper bkstamp, 10½" 50.00
Figurine, lady in gr dress w/shawl, orig paper label, #1725, 11" 52.50
Figurine, lady in pk & bl dress w/pansies, #4035, M 46.00
Flower holder, lady pushing buggy 36.00
Flower holder, lady w/head scarf, unsgn, 10" 45.00
Gravy boat, Brentwood, w/underplate, 9x4", 10x6" 30.00
Planter, donkey cart 12.00
Plate, chop; Brentwood, 13" dia 30.00
Plate, Malay Blossom, gr, burro mk, 9¾" sq 15.00
Platter, serving; Rose, 13¼x9¼", M 25.00

Teapot, Bamboo 50.00
Vase, bud; Ming Tree, w/coralene, 6" 30.00
Vase, lady sitting against tree, roses in crossed arms, 8½" 50.00
Wall pocket, Asian lady, #4048, orig paper label, 10½x6½" 50.00
Wall pocket, Bamboo, vase form, mk, 5¾x4" 26.00
Wall pocket, Oriental lady on bench w/bowl ea side, 10½x7" 45.00

Weller

The Weller Pottery Company was established in Zanesville, Ohio, in 1882, the outgrowth of a small one-kiln log cabin works Sam Weller had operated in Fultonham. Through an association with Wm. Long, he entered the art pottery field in 1895, producing the Lonhuda Ware Long had perfected in Steubenville six years earlier. His famous Louwelsa line was merely a continuation of Lonhuda and was made in at least five hundred different shapes until 1924. Many fine lines of artware followed under the direction of Charles Babcock Upjohn, art director from 1895 to 1904: Dickens Ware (1st Line), under-glaze slip decorations on dark backgrounds; Turada, featuring applied ivory bands of delicate openwork on solid dark brown backgrounds; and Aurelian, similar to Louwelsa, but with a brushed-on rather than blended ground. One of their most famous lines was 2nd Line Dickens, introduced in 1900. Backgrounds, characteristically caramel shading to turquoise matt, were decorated by sgraffito with animals, golfers, monks, Indians, and scenes from Dickens novels. The work is often artist signed. Sicardo, 1903, was a metallic lustre line in tones of rose, blue, green, or purple with flowing Art Nouveau patterns developed within the glaze.

Frederick Hurten Rhead, who worked for Weller from 1903 to 1904, created the prestigious Jap Birdimal line decorated with geisha girls, landscapes, storks, etc., accomplished through application of heavy slip forced through the tiny nozzle of a squeeze bag. Other lines to his credit are L'Art Nouveau, produced in both high-gloss brown and matt pastels, and 3rd Line Dickens, often decorated with Cruikshank's illustrations in relief. Other early artware lines were Eoccan, Floretta, Hunter, Perfecto, Dresden, Etched Matt, and Etna.

In 1920 John Lessel was hired as art director, and under his supervision several new lines were created. LaSa, LaMar, Marengo, and Besline attest to his expertise with metallic lustres. The last of the artware lines and one of the most sought after by collectors today is Hudson, first made during the early 1920s. Hudson, a semimatt glazed ware, was beautifully artist decorated on shaded backgrounds with florals, animals, birds, and scenics. Notable artists often signed their work, among them Hester Pillsbury, Dorothy England Laughead, Ruth Axline, Claude Leffler, Sarah Reid McLaughlin, E.L. Pickens, and Mae Timberlake.

During the '30s Weller produced a line of gardenware and naturalistic life-sized figures of dogs, cats, swans, geese, and playful gnomes. The Depression brought a slow, steady decline in sales, and by 1948 the pottery was closed. For a more thorough study we recommend *The Collector's Encyclopedia of Weller Pottery* by Sharon and Bob Huxford, available at your local library or from Collector Books.

Eocean vase, multicolor storks on light gray to lavender, Chilcote, four-sided diamond shape, 10½", $3,000.00.

Alvin, vase, tree-trunk form, unmk, 8½" 75.00
Arcadia, emb overlapping leaves, #A-11, mk, 8½" 50.00
Arcadia, vase, leaves form body, #A-4, mk, 5½" 35.00
Ardsley, candle holders, lotus flower form, ink stamp, 3", pr 85.00
Ardsley, vase, cattails w/flowers at base, 2 mks, 11½" 275.00
Athens, vase, witch reserve & cat's heads, unmk, 10" 650.00
Atlas, bowl, star-shaped rim, mk, #C-3, 4" 60.00
Atlas, star dish, mk, #C-2, 2" 45.00
Aurelian, vase, floral, bottle neck, unmk, 9" 350.00
Aurelian, vase, floral, sgn EA, bulbous, hand mk, 7" 275.00
Aurelian, vase, floral, sgn TJW, cylindrical, mk, 16" 1,750.00
Auroro, vase, goldfish, sgn Hattie Mitchell, mk, 9" 1,750.00
Baldin, vase, apples form shoulder, mk, 7" 200.00
Baldin, vase, apples on branch along base on bl, unmk, 11" 500.00
Barcelona, ewer, stylized floral, ink mk, 9½" 275.00
Barcelona, vase, stylized floral, cylindrical, mk, 7" 175.00
Bedford, umbrella stand, long-stemmed flowers, matt, 20" 650.00
Besline, vase, floral, paper label, 11" 550.00
Besline, vase, floral, 7¾" 200.00
Blo' Red, vase, mk, 3½" 50.00
Blo' Red, vase, mk, 9" 130.00
Blossom, cornucopia, floral on gr, mk, 6" 45.00
Blue Drapery, jardiniere & ped, roses on bl, unmk, 33½" 1,000.00
Blue Drapery, vase, roses on bl, slim, unmk, 8" 85.00
Blue Ware, jardiniere, classical figures, unmk, 8½" 300.00
Blue Ware, vase, classical figures, flared cylinder, mk, 8½" 250.00
Bonito, vase, stylized floral, hdls, mk, 5" 145.00
Bonito, vase, stylized floral, sgn HP, hdls, mk, 11" 400.00
Bouquet, bowl, console; floral, #B-12, mk, 5x12½" 50.00
Breton, vase, emb floral band on brn, unmk, 7" 95.00
Brighton, bluebird on stump, mk, 7½" 700.00
Brighton, crow on base, unmk, 6½" 900.00
Brighton, parrot on perch, mk, 13½" 2,000.00
Brighton, swan flower frog, unmk, 4½" 400.00
Brighton, wall vase (dbl bud), bird amid 2 branches, unmk, 12" ...1,250.00
Brighton, woodpecker, unmk, 5" 250.00
Cactus, camel, mk, 4" 100.00
Cactus, duck, mk, 4½" 110.00
Camelot, vase, geometric decor, gourd shape, mk, 6" 200.00
Cameo, basket, floral, wht on gr, script mk, 7½" 60.00
Cameo, vase, wht on bl, hdls, unmk, 5" 35.00
Cameo Jewel, jardiniere, portrait cameos & jewels, mk, 8" 375.00
Cameo Jewel, umbrella stand, portrait cameos & jewels, mk, 22" ...900.00
Candis, bowl, console; ivory w/scroll & flower panel, mk, 11" 70.00
Candis, vase, gr w/ivory floral panel, mk, 9" 85.00
Chase, vase, hunt scene, silver on turq, mk, 12" 650.00
Chase, vase, hunt scene, wht on bl, bulbous, hand mk, 6½" 350.00
Chengtu, ginger jar, mk, 12" 225.00
Chengtu, vase, cylindrical, mk, 6" 60.00
Classic, fan vase, openwork at rim, 5" 55.00
Claywood, mug, floral, unmk, 4½" 100.00
Claywood, spittoon, floral, unmk, 4½" 150.00
Claywood, vase, spider web panels, cylindrical, unmk, 5½" 85.00
Colored Glaze, jardiniere, squirrels in relief, unmk, 8" 275.00
Coppertone, basket, emb floral, twig hdl, unmk, 8½" 225.00
Coppertone, bowl, fish in mold, frog on rib, 10" L 950.00
Coppertone, bowl, lobed, frog/lily & pads on side, 11" L 700.00
Coppertone, pitcher, fish hdl, ink mk, 7½" 950.00
Coppertone, vase, frogs & lily pads ea side of flared top, 8½" 950.00
Copra, vase, floral, ring hdls, mk, 10" 275.00
Cornish, bowl, leaves & sm berries, 4" 60.00
Creamware, Decorated; mug, decalcomania, 5" 75.00
Creamware, Decorated; pitcher, decalcomania, unmk, 5" 150.00
Creamware, hanging basket, rtcl pattern, unmk, 11½" 200.00

Creamware, planter, rtcl pattern, 4 integral ft, mk, 4" 85.00
Cretone, vase, stylized animal & flowers, mk, 8" 400.00
Darsie, flowerpot, emb tassels, mk, 3" 40.00
Darsie, vase, emb tassels, scalloped rim, mk, 5½" 50.00
Delsa, vase, floral, hdls, tall ft, mk, 6" 45.00
Dickens I, jardiniere, floral on brn, mk, 9" 325.00
Dickens I, jardiniere, trumpet flowers, mk, 8½" 325.00
Dickens I, mug, Admiral's portrait, mk, 5" 1,000.00
Dickens I, pillow vase, lady's portrait, mk, 7" 2,250.00
Dickens II, humidor, Captain, hand mk (inside), 7" 1,700.00
Dickens II, jug, Mt Vernon Bridge..., sgn UJ, mk, 5½" 700.00
Dickens II, mug, Black Bird (Indian) portrait, sgn UJ, 6" 750.00
Dickens II, mug, David Copperfield/several others, Upjohn, 5½" ..400.00
Dickens II, pitcher, men at table, sgn CW, mk, 4" 500.00
Dickens II, tankard, Dombey & Sons on dk brn gloss, 12½" 650.00
Dickens II, vase, deer head, #346M, 6½" 350.00
Dickens II, vase, female golfer, 8" 1,300.00
Dickens II, vase, figure in landscape, slim, glossy, 12½" 2,500.00
Dickens II, vase, hunter/haystack/fence w/decoys, 11" 700.00
Dickens II, vase, hunting dog, sgn EL Pickens, mk, 9" 1,750.00
Dickens II, vase, kitten, bottle neck, mk, 9" 1,500.00
Dickens II, vase, man's portrait on bl, JH, glossy, slim, 13½" ..1,250.00
Dickens II, vase, shepherd w/flock, mk, 15" 2,000.00
Dickens III, creamer, Charles Dickens on disk, #0034, mk, 4" ...225.00
Dickens III, mug, man w/pipe, unmk, 4" 300.00
Dickens III, mug, Master Belling, mk, 5" 600.00
Dickens III, teapot, Captain Cuttle/Florence Dombey, #5055, 7" 750.00
Dickens III, vase, Mr Weller Sr, Pickwick Papers, #15, unmk, 8" ..1,100.00
Dresden, vase, Dutch windmill/sailboats, 11" 700.00
Dunton, umbrella stand, birds among flowering branches, unmk, 23" .1,750.00
Dupont, bowl, flower baskets, Roma glaze, unmk, 3" H 50.00
Dupont, vase, flower baskets, cylindrical, mk, 10" 125.00
Dynasty, vase, gr drips over bl, ring hdls, unmk, 6" 50.00
Elberta, cornucopia vase, mk, 8" 85.00
Elberta, vase, mk, 6" 40.00
Eocean, basket, cherries on brn to wht, unmk, 6½" 450.00
Eocean, Late; vase, floral, sgn MT, 10½" 450.00
Eocean, mug, cherries, 6x5½" 140.00
Eocean, vase, cherries/leaves, 5½x4½" 170.00
Eocean, vase, egret pr, sgn, 11" 2,500.00
Eocean, vase, floral branches, sgn LJB, shouldered, mk, 13" 1,100.00
Eocean, vase, flowers, #S806, 4½x4¾" 220.00
Eocean, vase, flowers (EX art), Leffler, 16" 1,700.00
Eocean, vase, mushrooms (unusual subject), 4" 1,100.00
Etna, pitcher, floral, simple shape, mk, 6" 175.00
Etna, vase, carnations, 8x6¾" 290.00
Etna, vase, grapes on branch, shouldered, mk, 15" 650.00
Etna, vase, lizard along side, mk, 4½" 675.00
Evergreen, candlestick, script mk, 1½" 35.00
Evergreen, vase, uptrn hdls, flared rim, script mk, 10" 100.00
Fairfield, vase, cherubs band, unmk, 9½" 125.00
Flask, Old Kentuc, no mk, 5" 200.00
Flask, PAP Loyal Order of Moose, unmk, 4½" 185.00
Flask, Take a Plunge, unmk, 6" 135.00
Flemish, inkwell, floral, unmk, 4½x7" 500.00
Flemish, jardiniere, geometric decor, unmk, 8" 125.00
Flemish, umbrella stand, lg vining flowers, ink stamp, 22" 900.00
Fleron, bowl, ruffled rim, #J-6, 3" 85.00
Fleron, vase, ruffled rim, mk, 14½" 375.00
Florala, vase, dbl bud; floral, paper label, 5" 85.00
Florenzo, vase, stylized floral, emb ribs, ftd, mk, 7" 95.00
Floretta, tankard, fruit on branch, sgn CD, matt, unmk, 13½" ...550.00
Floretta, vase, cherries in reserve on gr, flared rim, unmk, 12" ..350.00
Floretta, vase, floral, pk on shaded brn, mk, 5½" 300.00

Floretta, vase, grapes emb on brn, bottle neck, mk, 7½" 150.00
Forest, jardiniere & ped, 28x11" 1,400.00
Forest, pitcher, glossy, mk, 5" 225.00
Forest, vase, cylindrical, unmk, 8" 175.00
Forest, window box, mk, 5½x14½" 450.00
Fruitone, vase, sq w/rnd rim, mk, 8½" 175.00
Fruitone, vase, 6-sided, mk, 8" 150.00
Garden ornament, gnome, mk, 14" 2,500.00
Garden ornament, gnomes on toadstool, mk, 17" 4,250.00
Geode, vase, stars & comets on wht, bulbous, mk, 5½" 500.00
Glendale, bowl, sea gulls, 15" dia 375.00
Glendale, vase, bird scene, classic shape, ink stamp/label, 12" 700.00
Glendale, vase, bird scenic, unmk, 6½" 450.00
Glendale, vase, pr birds, nest w/eggs, 9x8" 1,000.00
Gloria, vase, irises on gr, mk, 12½" 125.00
Golbrogreen, candle holder, ring hdl, unmk, 4½" 60.00
Goldenglow, candle holder, triple; script mk, 3½" 85.00
Graystone Garden Ware, jardiniere & ped, unmk, 18" 400.00
Greenbriar, pitcher, marbleized, unmk, 10" 225.00
Greenbriar, vase, marbleized, unmk, 6½" 135.00
Greora, vase, marbleized, angle hdls, mk, 9" 150.00
Greora, vase, marbleized, cylindrical, mk, 11½" 225.00
Hobart, candle holder, draped nude kneels beside, unmk, 6" 300.00
Hobart, girl w/flowers, bl, unmk, 8½" 350.00
Hobart, nude stands between 2-trunk dbl bud vase, pk, mk, 10" ..450.00

Hudson vase, pastoral landscape with houses, picket fence, and trees, signed McLaughlin, 9½", $2,700.00.

Hudson, Blue & Decorated; vase, floral, 6-sided, mk, 9½" 250.00
Hudson, Light; floral, sgn HP, shouldered, mk, 9" 450.00
Hudson, vase, butterflies/flowers, M Timberlake, 7", NM 1,300.00
Hudson, vase, dogwood at shoulder, sgn, 9" 450.00
Hudson, vase, floral, hdls, mk, 13½" 1,750.00
Hudson, vase, floral, Pillsbury, classic shape, unmk, 15" 1,600.00
Hudson, vase, floral, Timberlake, mk, 7" 350.00
Hudson, vase, irises, Axline, cylindrical, mk, 8½" 550.00
Hudson, vase, irises (EX art), Timberlake, 15" 3,500.00
Hudson, vase, landscape w/snow & fence, McLaughlin, 11½" ...4,250.00
Hudson, vase, lily of valley on bl to gr, sgn Hood, 9" 950.00
Hudson, vase, Rose of Sharon, sgn Pillsbury, 11½" 1,600.00
Hudson, vase, scenic, McLaughlin, hand mk, 12" 2,100.00
Hudson, vase, scenic, Pillsbury, ink mk, 8" 1,600.00
Hudson, vase, swan scenic, Pillsbury, cylindrical, 14½" 3,000.00
Hudson, vase, tiger stalking, mk, 8" 2,250.00
Hudson, White & Decorated; vase, fruit on branch, unmk, 7" ...200.00
Hudson-Perfecto, vase, Arab on horse, mk, 13" 3,750.00
Hudson-Perfecto, vase, floral, bulbous, mk, 5½" 400.00
Hudson-Perfecto, vase, floral, C Leffler, mk, 13½" 1,400.00
Hudson-Perfecto, vase, leaves & berries, HP, unmk, 4½" 175.00
Hunter, vase, birds in flight, sgn UJ, shouldered, #413, 7½" 950.00
Hunter, vase, duck swimming, ewer form, hand mk, 7" 575.00
Ivoris, bowl, console; flower along rim, w/frog, 3½x10" 95.00
Ivoris, powder box, w/lid, hand mk, 4" 50.00

Ivory (Clinton Ivory), jardiniere, floral panels, unmk, 5" 75.00
Ivory (Clinton Ivory), jardiniere, geometric decor, mk, 7½" 150.00
Ivory (Clinton Ivory), vase, leafy panels, cylindrical, 10" 85.00
Jap Birdimal, hair receiver, 4 Norse ships on dk bl, sgn VH, 2x4" ..190.00
Jap Birdimal, jardiniere, trees/moon on gray, 6½x7" 250.00
Jap Birdimal, mug, Oriental figure on brn, mk, 5" 1,000.00
Jap Birdimal, vase, birds on brn twisted form, unmk, 11" 800.00
Jap Birdimal, vase, geisha on teal (unusual color), LS, 10½" ...1,800.00
Jap Birdimal, vase, Oriental lady, unmk, 4" 400.00
Jap Birdimal, vase, scenic, bl on pk, mk, 14" 1,200.00
Jewell, mug, lady's portrait, jewels along base, mk, 6½" 475.00
Jewell, vase, geometric decor w/jewel centers, mk, 9" 500.00
Jewell, vase, Nouveau floral, 11" 800.00
Juneau, vase, mottled drip on pk, mk, 6½" 115.00
Kenova, vase, appl lizard, emb florals, 6" 850.00
Kenova, vase, emb trumpet flower vines, mk, 6½" 400.00
Klyro, bud vase, floral on brn, 6-sided, mk, 8½" 95.00
Klyro, planter, flowers on brn, openwork at top, sq, mk, 4" 60.00
Knifewood, humidor, hunting dog in landscape, unmk, 7" 550.00
Knifewood, jar, bird among foliage, w/lid, mk, 8" 700.00
Knifewood, vase, floral on brn, mk, 7" 250.00
L'Art Nouveau, bank, ear of corn shape, unmk, 8" 550.00
L'Art Nouveau, vase, floral, sq sides, mk, 12" 300.00
L'Art Nouveau, vase, lady in relief on brn, glossy, unmk, 12½" ..450.00
Lamar, vase, scenic, classic shape, unmk, 11½" 375.00
LaSa, vase, biplane, cylindrical, 9" 1,800.00
LaSa, vase, floral, bulbous, mk, 3½" 150.00
LaSa, vase/lamp base, palm trees, mk, 13½" 700.00
Lavonia, vase, slim w/3 low hdls, unmk, 9" 150.00
Lebanon, vase, Egyptian creatures, shouldered, unmk, 6" 600.00
Lido, vase, swirled shape, hdls, ruffled rim, mk, 6" 35.00
Lonhuda, pillow vase, cattle scene, #275, 11½" 4,400.00
Lorbeek, bowl vase, pleated shape, mk, 5" 100.00
Lorbeek, vase, pleated shape, mk, 8" 125.00
Lorber, vase, satyr in vineyard, mk, 13" 1,200.00
Louella, vase, floral on drapery, mk, 9½" 90.00

Louwelsa vase, detailed mums on brown to orange to green, signed A. Haubrich, #463X, 16", $1,500.00.

Louwelsa, Blue; floral, sgn LM, slim, bottle neck, mk, 10" 1,000.00
Louwelsa, Blue; vase, floral, cylindrical, mk, 10½" 1,100.00
Louwelsa, candle holder, floral, sgn MH, 4½" 150.00
Louwelsa, clock, half-circle seal, 10½x12½" 1,000.00
Louwelsa, ewer, floral, sgn, slim w/ornate hdl, 22½" 3,000.00
Louwelsa, ewer, floral, sgn JB, stick neck, half-circle mk, 6½" 225.00
Louwelsa, ewer, man's portrait, LJ Burgess, circle seal, 12½" ...1,500.00
Louwelsa, jardiniere, floral, ruffled rim, mk, 9½" 325.00
Louwelsa, mug, floral, sgn HM, slim, 8½" 325.00
Louwelsa, star dish, floral, w/lid, mk, 2½" 350.00
Louwelsa, vase, floral, sgn A Haubrich, hdls, 23½" 1,500.00
Louwelsa, vase, floral, sgn MM, rim-to-shoulder hdls, mk, 11" ...325.00
Louwelsa, vase, floral, squat, angle hdls, mk, 2" 100.00

Louwelsa, vase, grapes & leaves, sgn Lybarger, 17" 1,750.00
Louwelsa, vase, holly berries/leaves on bl, 7½" 900.00
Louwelsa, vase, pansies w/silver o/l, half-circle seal, 6½" 3,000.00
Lustre, candle holder, unmk, 4½" 45.00
Lustre, Cloudburst vase, unmk, 4½" 95.00
Malverne, pillow vase, emb leaves & buds, unmk, 8½" 125.00
Mammy Line, cookie jar, Mammy holding watermelon, mk, 11" .2,000.00
Mammy Line, syrup, mammy figural, mk, 6" 700.00
Manhattan, pitcher, floral, dk gr on gr, cylindrical, mk, 10" 100.00
Manhattan, vase, floral on gr, mk, 5½" 35.00
Marbleized, vase, cylindrical, mk, 10" 175.00
Marbleized, vase, flared rim, mk, 7½" 110.00
Marengo, vase, trees & mtns, 6-sided, unmk, 8" 300.00
Marvo, bud vase, emb foliage, ink stamp, 9" 70.00
Marvo, vase, emb floral w/much foliage, ink mk, 8½" 95.00
Matt, vase, leaves/berries on peach, LJ Burgess, 14" 1,000.00
Matt Louwelsa, vase, acorns/leaves, rust on tan, Pillsbury, 12" ...1,100.00
Melrose, basket, fruit branch, branch hdl, mk, 10" 225.00
Melrose, vase, flower branch, hdls, ruffled rim, unmk, 5" 85.00
Mi-Flo, vase, floral, angle hdls, #M-12, mk, 9½" 150.00
Minerva, vase, storks, cylindrical, mk, 8½" 600.00
Mirror Black, bud vase, unmk, 5½" 40.00
Mirror Black, wall vase, unmk, 6" 125.00
Modeled Etched Matt, vase, floral, sq sides, 10" 450.00
Monochrome, bowl, bl, incurvate rim, unmk, 3½x10" 45.00
Monochrome, comport, gr, mk, 10" 95.00
Montego, vase, gr runs over brn, angle hdls, mk, 8" 300.00
Muskota, elephant, mk, 7½x12½" 1,500.00
Muskota, foxy grandpa incense burner, mk, 4" 575.00
Muskota, geese flower frog, unmk, 6" 400.00
Muskota, girl w/flowers & hat, mk, 8" 425.00
Noval, bowl, apple hdls, unmk, 3½x9½" 80.00
Noval, candle holder, apples at base, mk, 9½" 150.00
Novelty, bumblebee, unmk, 2½" wingspan 175.00
Novelty, butterfly, bl or yel, unmk, 2", ea 175.00
Novelty, dragonfly, unmk, 3½" 175.00
Novelty, sitting dog ashtray, mk, 5" 110.00
Novelty, teapot wall vase, mk, 9" 150.00
Novelty, 3 pigs ashtray, unmk, 4" 150.00
Oak Leaf, basket, leaves on brn, twig hdl, #G-1, mk, 7½" 100.00
Oak Leaf, ewer, leaves on gr, angle hdl, mk, 8½" 75.00
Paragon, bowl vase, emb flowers & leaves, 4½" 125.00
Paragon, vase, emb flowers & leaves, script mk, 7½" 200.00
Parian, vase, floral tile-like design, unmk, 13" 150.00
Parian, wall pocket, floral tile-like design, unmk, 10" 250.00
Patra, basket, stylized floral hdl, mk, 5½" 175.00
Patra, vase, stylized floral panel, ftd, mk, 7" 125.00
Patricia, bowl, 8 duck heads along rim, mk, 13" 135.00
Patricia, vase, duck-head hdls, streaky brn, unmk, 5" 95.00
Pearl, bowl, roses & pearls on cream, mk, 3" H 125.00
Pearl, wall vase, roses & pearls on cream, mk, 8" 225.00
Perfecto (Matt Louwelsa), ewer, corn, A Haubrich, #580/4, 12" ...850.00
Perfecto (Matt Louwelsa), pillow vase, horse, Pillsbury, 10½" ...3,750.00
Perfecto (Matt Louwelsa), vase, lg peonies, England, 9x9" 650.00
Pumila, bowl, flower from, ink stamp, 3½" 35.00
Pumila, leaves form ruffled rim, ink stamp, 12" 125.00
Ragenda, vase, emb drape decor on bl, bulbous, mk, 9" 95.00
Ragenda, vase, emb drape decor on pk, shouldered, mk, 6½" 75.00
Roba, cornucopia, floral on brn, mk, 5½" 45.00
Roba, ewer, floral on swirled shape, twig hdl, mk, 6" 75.00
Roma, bowl, console; grapes, w/liner, unmk, 6½x18" 250.00
Roma, candlestick, floral, 3-light, 11½" 130.00
Roma, letter pocket, floral, unmk, 4½x7½" 300.00
Roma, vase, bud; grapevine, sq sides, unmk, 6½" 75.00

Roma, vase, floral, mk, 8½" **125.00**
Roma, vase, triple bud; floral, mk, 8" **130.00**
Rosemont, jardiniere, bird on branch, mk, 7" **350.00**
Rosemont, jardiniere, fruit basket reserves, unmk, 8" **200.00**
Rosemont, jardiniere & ped, floral on brn, mk, 25½" **550.00**
Rudlor, vase, floral, bead-like hdls (1 high/1 low), mk, 6" **50.00**
Sabrinian, basket, shells form base, mk, 7" **300.00**
Sabrinian, candle holder, dolphin stem, mk, 6½" **175.00**
Scandia, vase, 9¼" **280.00**
Senic, vase, river scene, sm hdls, #S-4, mk, 5½" **75.00**
Senic, vase, river scene on gr, #S-9, mk, 8" **100.00**
Sicardo, mug, floral, unmk, 3½" **500.00**
Sicardo, vase, floral, cylindrical, mk, 9" **1,000.00**
Sicardo, vase, floral, horn-like hdls, bulbous, mk, 6" **850.00**
Sicardo, vase, floral, long trumpet neck, mk, 15½" **1,700.00**
Sicardo, vase, floral, mk, 10½" **1,500.00**
Sicardo, vase, locust on side, sgn, mk, 3" **150.00**
Sicardo, vase, mums, sgn, 10½" **1,700.00**
Sicardo, vase, wheat, gold/mc irid, sgn, 9" **2,000.00**
Silvertone, basket, fruit, twig hdl, mk, 13" **450.00**
Silvertone, vase, floral, hdls, 8" **650.00**
Silvertone, vase, floral, ruffled rim, hdls, mk, 8½" **350.00**
Softone, vase, dbl bud; pk; script mk, 9" **28.00**
Souvenir, pin tray, rose along side of ruffled dish, mk, 2½" **150.00**
Souvenir, vase, Indian portrait, St Louis...Fair, 1904, 6½" **600.00**
Souvenir, vase, St Louis 1904, unmk, 3" **250.00**
Stellar, vase, stars on blk, bulbous, mk, 5" **500.00**
Suevo, vase, geometric bands on brn, unmk, 8" **150.00**
Sydonia, planter, mottled bl, mk, 5" **50.00**
Sydonia, vase, dbl, mottled bl, mk, 9½" **110.00**
Tivoli, vase, ivory w/blk rim, floral-banded ft, unmk, 9½" **125.00**
Trellis, wall shelf, turq, unmk, 10½" **200.00**
Turada, humidor, appl filigree on brn, mk, 5½" **350.00**
Turada, mug, appl filigree on brn, mk, #562/7 on base, 6" **325.00**
Turkis, vase, angle hdls, mk, 5½" **125.00**
Turkis, vase, ruffled rim, mk, 8" **150.00**
Tutone, basket, floral, mk, 7½" **120.00**
Tutone, vase, floral, 4-ftd, mk, 4" **70.00**
Underglaze Blue Ware, bowl, incurvate rim, w/frog, mk, 1½x6" ...**25.00**
Velva, bowl, floral panel, sm uptrn hdls, ftd, mk, 3½x12½" **75.00**
Velva, vase, floral panel, sm uptrn hdls, mk, 7½" **75.00**
Velvetone, batter jug, tricolor w/emb rings, mk, 10" **200.00**
Velvetone, pitcher, tricolor w/emb rings, mk, 10" **175.00**
Voile, fan vase, fruit tree, unmk, 5½" **100.00**
Voile, jardiniere, fruit trees, unmk, 6" **150.00**
Warwick, jardiniere, floral branch on woodgrain, mk, 7" **150.00**
Warwick, vase, floral branch on trunk form, branch hdls, mk, 4½" ..**85.00**
Wild Rose, candle holder, triple; floral, script mk, 6" **100.00**
Wild Rose, vase, floral, hdls, mk, 9½" **60.00**
Woodcraft, bowl, entwined branches, mk, 3½" **95.00**
Woodcraft, candle holder, tree form, mk, 8½" **125.00**
Woodcraft, owl lamp, 2-light, mk, 13½" **500.00**
Woodcraft, wall vase, bird among flowering branch, mk, 14½" ...**1,750.00**
Woodrose, vase, roses on tub form, mk, 4" **50.00**
Xenia, vase, floral, cylindrical, mk, 10½" **650.00**
Zona, baby plate, squirrels, rolled ABC rim, unmk, 7½" **135.00**
Zona, jardiniere, floral reserves among geometrics, unmk, 8½" ...**200.00**
Zona, pitcher, emb fruit branch, twig hdl, mk, 6" **85.00**
Zona, plate, dinner; fruited branch along rim, unmk, 10" **30.00**

Western Americana

The collecting of Western Americana encompasses a broad spectrum of memorabilia. Examples of various areas within the main stream would include the following fields: weapons, bottles, photographs, mining/railroad artifacts, cowboy paraphernalia, farm and ranch implements, maps, barbed wire, tokens, Indian relics, saloon/gambling items, and branding irons. Some of these areas have their own separate listings in this book. Western Americana is not only a collecting field but is also a collecting *era* with specific boundries. Depending upon which field the collector decides to specialize in, prices can start at a few dollars and run into the thousands.

Our advisor for this category is Bill Mackin, author of *Cowboy and Gunfighter Collectibles* (order from the author); he is listed in the Directory under Colorado.

Bit, Anchor brand, horsehead design, 1912, EX **220.00**
Bit, spade; spoonless, prison made, Walla Walla WA, 1930s, EX ...**400.00**
Branding iron, wrought iron w/dmn brand, 1900s, 33x20" **50.00**
Bridle & quirt, horsehair, prison made, EX **4,000.00**
Chaps, angora shotgun style w/tooled leather belt, 1910, 38" ..**1,100.00**
Chaps, shotgun; buck stitched & fringed, 18 conchos, 1900s, EX ...**850.00**
Coat, buffalo w/big horn sheep collar & cuffs, lg, EX **825.00**
Collar tips, eng sterling, mk EH Bohlin, 1940s **385.00**
Gauntlets, beaded & fringed floral pattern, 1920s, EX **880.00**
Gauntlets, horsehair, pr **85.00**
Key, jail; iron, 19th C **50.00**
Lap robe, horsehair w/wool backing **200.00**
Paperweight, Buffalo Bill w/rifle in fancy scout outfit, 1882 ....**325.00**
Reins, braided leather, ornate silver ferrules, fancy, 1930s **495.00**
Saddle, tooled/decor in German silver, boy sz, EX orig **225.00**
Saddle, US Military, w/saddlebags, all orig **880.00**
Saddlebags, perimeter stamping & EX patina, 1890s, pr **450.00**
Sombrero, Mexican; 9" crown w/gold brocade, 5" brim, 1870s ...**770.00**
Spurs, floral pattern, NP, Crockett, 1950s, pr **275.00**
Spurs, floral silver inlay, lg rowels, Mexican, 1900s, pr, EX **200.00**
Spurs, overlaid flying goose w/gooseneck shanks, Ray Anderson, pr ...**400.00**
Spurs, steerhead pattern w/arrow shank, Kelly Bros, 1930s, pr, G ...**900.00**

Western Pottery Manufacturing Company

This pottery was originally founded as the Denver China and Pottery Company; William Long was the owner. The company's assets were sold to a group who in 1905 formed the Western Pottery Manufacturing Company, located at 16th Street and Alcott in Denver, Colorado. By 1926, 186 different items were being produced, including crocks, flowerpots, kitchen items, and other stoneware. The company dissolved in 1936.

Seven various marks were used during the years, and values may be higher for items that carry a rare mark. Numbers within the descriptions refer to specific marks, see the line drawings. Prices may vary depending on demand and locale. Our advisors for this category are Cathy Segelke and Pat James; they are listed in the Directory under Colorado.

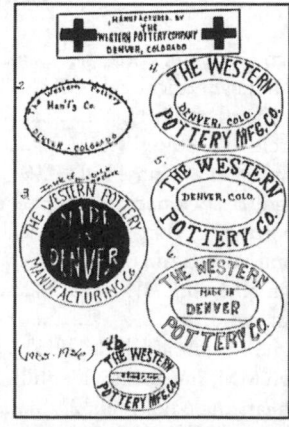

Churn, #2, hdl, 4-gal, M 75.00
Churn, #2, hdl, 5-gal, M 65.00
Churn, #2, no lid, 5-gal, G 80.00
Crock, #4, bail lip, 4-gal, G 55.00
Crock, #4, hdl, no lid, 8-gal, M 90.00
Crock, #4, ice water; bl/wht sponge pnt, 3-gal, NM 30.00
Crock, #4, 6-gal, EX 72.00
Crock, #4b, 20-gal, M 200.00
Crock, #4b, 22x17½", 15-gal, NM 150.00
Crock, #5, bail lip, 1½-gal, M 45.00
Crock, #5, no lid, 6-gal, M 70.00
Crock, #6, wire hdl, 10-gal, NM 100.00
Crock, #6, 3-gal, M 40.00
Crock, #6, 4-gal, M 50.00
Crock, #6, 5-gal, NM 60.00
Foot warmer, #6, M 60.00
Jug, #6, brn/wht, 1-gal, EX 25.00
Jug, #6, brn/wht, 5-gal, M 75.00
Rabbit feeder, #1, EX 25.00
Rabbit waterer, #1, M 25.00

Western Stoneware Co.

The Western Stoneware Co., Monmouth, Illinois, was formed in 1906 as a merger of seven potteries: Monmouth Pottery Co., Monmouth, IL; Weir Pottery Co., Monmouth, IL; Macomb Pottery Co. and Macomb Stoneware Co., Macomb, IL; D. Culbertson Stoneware Co., Whitehall, IL; Clinton Stoneware Co., Clinton, MO; and Fort Dodge Stoneware Co., Fort Dodge, IA.

Western Stoneware Co. manufactured stoneware, gardenware, flowerpots, artware, and dinnerware. Some early crocks, jugs, and churns are found with a plant number in the Maple Leaf logo. Plants 1 through 7 turn up. In 1926 an artware line was introduced as the Monmouth Pottery Artware. One by one each branch of the operation closed and today one branch remains. Western Stoneware Co. is still in operation in Monmouth on the site of the Weir Pottery Co. Our advisor for this category is Jim Martin; he is listed in the Directory under Illinois.

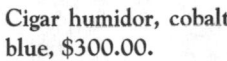
Cigar humidor, cobalt blue, $300.00.

Photo courtesy Jim Martin

Ashtray, Cardinal Brand Flower Pots 150.00
Birdbath, brn glaze 250.00
Churn, flowers on side, 3-gal 200.00
Churn, Maple Leaf mk, mini 600.00
Churn, Maple Leaf mk, 2-gal 175.00
Crock, Maple Leaf mk, 60-gal 600.00
Crock, Plant 1 mk, 5-gal 75.00
Jardiniere, Egret pattern, brushed gr 75.00
Jardiniere, Egyptian motif, brn-glazed int, 7" 75.00
Jug, Plant 3, 5-gal 200.00
Pitcher, bl & wht, sq, 1-qt 100.00

Pitcher, Cattail, bl & wht, 1-qt 150.00
Pitcher & bowl, Memphis pattern, bl & wht 350.00
Vase, Etruscan pattern, gr & wht 45.00
Water cooler, Cupid, bl & wht 650.00
Water cooler, Egyptian motif, 9¼x11", M 450.00

Westmoreland

Originally titled the Specialty Glass Company, Westmoreland began operations in East Liverpool, Ohio, producing utility items as well as tableware in milk glass and crystal. When the company moved to Grapeville, Pennsylvania, in 1890, lamps, vases, covered animal dishes, and decorative plates were introduced. Prior to 1920 Westmoreland was a major manufacturer of carnival glass and soon thereafter added a line of lovely reproduction art glass items. High-quality milk glass became their speciality, accounting for about 90% of their production. Black glass was introduced in the 1940s, and later in the decade ruby-stained pieces and items decorated in the Mary Gregory style became fashionable. By the 1960s colored glassware was being produced, examples of which are very popular with collectors today. Early pieces were marked with a paper label; by the 1960s the ware was embossed with a superimposed 'WG.' The last mark was a circle containing 'Westmoreland' around the perimeter and a large 'W' in the center. The company closed in 1985, and on February 28, 1996, the factory burned to the ground. See also Animal Dishes with Covers; Carnival Glass. Note: Though you may find pieces very similar to Westmoreland's, their Della Robbia has no bananas among the fruits relief.

Ashtray, Paneled Grape, milk glass, sq, lg 18.50
Basket, Della Robbia, crystal w/trim, 9" 175.00
Basket, English Hobnail, milk glass, 9" 32.00
Basket, Paneled Grape, milk glass, oval, hdld, 6½" 27.00
Basket, Pansy, milk glass, yellow 25.00
Bell, Beaded Bouquet, Yellow Mist 35.00
Bowl, Beaded Grape, milk glass, ftd, 9" 45.00
Bowl, Beaded Grape, milk glass, sq ft, w/lid, 5" 25.00
Bowl, centerpc; Thousand Eye, clear 40.00
Bowl, Della Robbia, crystal w/decor, rolled rim, 13" 125.00
Bowl, English Hobnail, milk glass, 6-pt, 8" 25.00
Bowl, Old Quilt, milk glass, flat, 4" 22.00
Bowl, Paneled Grape, milk glass, 9½" 45.00
Bowl, Paneled Grape, milk glass, oval, ftd, 12" 65.00
Bowl, Princess Feather, milk glass, 4½", w/underplate 16.00
Bowl, wedding; Roses & Bows, w/lid, 8" 100.00
Box, chocolate; Paneled Grape, milk glass, 6½" 50.00
Butter dish, Paneled Grape, milk glass, ¼-lb 30.00
Cake salver, Waterford, ruby stain 85.00
Cake stand, Paneled Grape, milk glass, ped ft 85.00
Cake stand, Paneled Grape, milk glass, skirted, 11" 85.00
Candle holders, Della Robia, lt lustre, single, pr 32.00
Candlesticks, Beaded Grape, milk glass, 4", pr 25.00
Candlesticks, Dolphin, milk glass, 4", pr 35.00
Candlesticks, Dolphin, milk glass, 9", pr 45.00
Candlesticks, English Hobnail, milk glass, 1-light, 3½", pr ..20.00
Candlesticks, Paneled Grape, milk glass, 4", pr 22.00
Candlesticks, Thousand Eye, clear, 3-ball, pr 35.00
Candy dish, Old Quilt, milk glass, sq, ftd, w/lid 22.00
Celery/spooner, Old Quilt, milk glass, ftd 25.00
Cheese dish, Old Quilt, milk glass 55.00
Chip & dip set, Paneled Grape, milk glass 25.00
Compote, Paneled Grape, Golden Sunset, 7" 30.00
Compote, Paneled Grape, milk glass, 4½" 15.00

Compote, shell; Dolphin, milk glass, 8" **35.00**
Creamer, Beaded Edge, milk glass, pnt decor, ftd **17.50**
Creamer & sugar bowl, Fruits, milk glass **15.00**
Creamer & sugar bowl, Paneled Grape, ice bl **65.00**
Creamer & sugar bowl, Paneled Grape, milk glass, ind **25.00**
Cruet, Paneled Grape, milk glass, w/stopper **25.00**
Cup, punch; Della Robbia, crystal w/decor **15.00**
Cup, punch; Fan & File, crystal, child sz **2.50**
Goblet, Ashburton, gr **6.00**
Goblet, Della Robbia, crystal w/trim, 8-oz, 6" **30.00**
Goblet, Old Quilt, milk glass, water sz **18.00**
Goblet, Paneled Grape, bl opal, water sz...............................**10.00**
Goblet, Paneled Grape, milk glass, wine sz **15.00**
Goblet, Princess Feather, crystal, 5¾" **13.00**
Gravy boat, Paneled Grape, milk glass, w/liner **60.00**
Honey dish, Beaded Grape, milk glass w/HP roses **65.00**
Ivy ball, English Hobnail, milk glass, crimped, 6½" **16.00**
Pitcher, Old Quilt, milk glass, water sz **40.00**
Pitcher, Paneled Grape, milk glass, juice sz **28.00**
Pitcher, Paneled Grape, milk glass, milk sz **45.00**
Planter, Paneled Grape, milk glass, 6x9" **35.00**
Plate, Beaded Edge, milk glass, peach, 7" **12.00**
Plate, Beaded Edge, milk glass, plain, 10½" **12.00**
Plate, Della Robbia, crystal w/decor, 7¼" **28.00**
Plate, Princess Feather, milk glass, 8" **8.00**
Relish, Paneled Grape, milk glass, 3-part **25.00**
Salt cellar, English Hobnail, milk glass, ftd **7.00**
Saucer, Beaded Edge, milk glass, plain **5.00**
Shakers, Della Robbia, crystal w/decor, pr **50.00**
Shakers, Paneled Grape, milk glass, ftd, pr **18.00**
Spooner, Old Quilt, milk glass, 4" **14.00**
Sugar bowl, Old Quilt, milk glass, lg **20.00**
Sugar bowl, Old Quilt, milk glass, sm **10.00**
Tumbler, Beaded Edge, milk glass, apple or blueberries, ftd, 5" **15.00**
Tumbler, Beaded Edge, milk glass, ftd, plain, 8-oz **8.00**
Tumbler, iced tea; Paneled Grape, milk glass, flat **15.00**
Urn, Waterford, ruby stain, w/lid, 12½" **95.00**
Vase, English Hobnail, milk glass, fan form, 5" **10.00**
Vase, rose bud; Paneled Grape, milk glass, 18" **22.00**

Wheatley, T. J.

In 1880 after a brief association with the Coultry Works, Thomas J. Wheatley opened his own studio in Cincinnati, Ohio, claiming to have been the first to discover the secret of under-glaze slip decoration on an unbaked clay vessel. He applied for and was granted a patent for his process. Demand for his ware increased to the point that several artists were hired to decorate the ware. The company incorporated in 1880 as the Cincinnati Art Pottery, but until 1882 it continued to operate under Wheatley's name. Ware from this period is marked 'T.J. Wheatley' or 'T.J.W. and Co.,' and it may be dated.

Matt green pieces dominate today's marketplace and will bring much more than the decorated pieces. The matt green pieces are seldom, if ever, marked or dated.

Lamp base, gr curdled matt, 4 buttresses under rim, 12x10½" .**2,600.00**
Mug, gr matt, in-mold shield, pretzel hdl, 7" **120.00**
Stein, coat of arms emb/Can't Loose, Fleischmann premium, 7½" .**100.00**
Vase, appl morning-glory spray on mottled ground, 20", VG **800.00**
Vase, gr curdled matt, bowl w/tall collar, 4 buttresses, 7x8" **2,800.00**
Vase, gr curdled matt, can w/4 angled buttresses, 11x7" **2,200.00**
Vase, silver o/l leaves, gr matt, wide base, 11x10" **2,500.00**
Vase, waves, striated gr matt, obscured mk, w/insert, 8½x9" ...**1,850.00**

Whieldon

Thomas Whieldon was regarded as the finest of the Staffordshire potters of the mid-1700s. He produced marbled and black Egyptian wares as well as tortoise shell, a mottled brown-glazed earthenware accented with touches of blue and yellow. In 1754 he became a partner of Josiah Wedgwood. Other potters produced similar wares, and today the term Whieldon is used generically.

Canister, tea; C scroll reserves/foliage on creamware, ca 1800, 4" ..**300.00**
Coffeepot, brn tortoise shell w/bl & gr, mismatched lid, 7½" **475.00**
Creamer, cauliflower mold, gr & clear, old rpr, 4¼" **365.00**
Mug, satyr's face, brn & gr, old rstr, 4½" **250.00**
Sugar bowl, cauliflower mold, gr & clear, w/lid, 3⅝x4⅜", EX .**3,245.00**
Tea caddy, cauliflower mold, gr & clear, no lid, 4¼" **550.00**
Teapot, landscape panels on creamware, lamb finial, 1760s, rpr, 5" .**8,000.00**

Wicker

Wicker is the basket-like material used in many types of furniture and accessories. It may be made from bamboo cane, rattan, reed, or artificial fibers. It is airy, lightweight, and very popular in hot regions. Imported from the Orient in the 18th century, it was first manufactured in the United States in about 1850. The elaborate, closely woven Victorian designs belong to the mid- to late 1800s, and the simple styles with coarse reedings usually indicate a post-1900 production. Art Deco styles followed in the '20s and '30s. The most important consideration in buying wicker is condition — it can be restored, but only by a professional. Age is an important factor, but be aware that 'Victorian-style' furniture is being manufactured today.

Key:
HB — Heywood Bros.   H/W — Heywood Wakefield

Child's chair, brown, minor imperfections, ca 1900, 37", $180.00.

Armchair, continuous arm, uphl seat, loose-weave apron, 32" ...**145.00**
Armchair, continuous arms, str apron, tight weave, 1910s **385.00**
Armchair, culiques/beadwork, rolled serpentine arms, 1880s **850.00**
Armchair, curliques/rolled arms, uphl bk/seat, HB, 1890s **1,150.00**
Armchair, loose weave, w/magazine holder/drink tray at arms **300.00**
Armchair, tight weave, mushroom seat, curliques, H/W, 1880s .**675.00**
Baby carriage, steel fr, old wht rpt w/gold, parasol cover, 36" **200.00**
Basket, arched hdl, early 1900s, 7½x9x5¾" **55.00**
Bench, photographer's; curliques, spindles, HB, 1890s **725.00**
Chair, side; ornate fan bk, pressed seat, fancy apron **220.00**
Chair, side; tight machine weave, uphl seat, 32x20" **210.00**
Desk, gallery top, wrapped legs, ball ft, drw **525.00**
Fern stand, bulbous top, flaring ped w/open sqs, 42", VG **325.00**

Footstool, tight-weave top & arpon, 4-leg, 23x17" dia 225.00
Lamp, table; tight-weave base, ornate-weave dome shade, 1890s, 16" .335.00
Loveseat, Am Victorian, rolled crest, scrolls, wht pnt, 44" 935.00
Recamier, low scrolling form, Am, late 19th C, 23x75x25" 715.00
Rocker, curlicue crest, cvd spindles at bk & arms, 39" 525.00
Rocker, platform, ornate-patterned bk, H/W, 48" 1,000.00
Rocker, shell-like patterned bk, wood seat, sm arms, 35" 245.00
Settee, curlique crest & apron, loose bk, cane seat, 32x36" 425.00
Settee, loose weave, half-cushioned bk & cushioned seat 325.00
Settee, tight weave, sturdy, for 2 children, 22½x31" 850.00
Sofa, tight weave w/dmn patterns, 3-cushion, flat arms, 1910s ..1,850.00
Table, rnd oak top, shelf, 30" dia 175.00
Table, tight-weave top, loose-weave apron, 3-leg, 30x31x21" 200.00
Table, tight-weave top, V-shaped woven magazine shelf, 24x22x16" ..295.00
Tea cart, tight weave, bottom shelf, front wheels, top tray 295.00
Tete-a-tete, fan bk, loose-weave apron, HB, 37x48x22" 3,200.00
Tray, breakfast; w/cup holder, paper rack on side, 1930s 130.00

Will-George

In 1934, after years of working in the family garage (in Los Angeles, California), William and George Climes founded the Will-George Company. They manufactured high-quality artware of porcelain and earthenware. Both brothers, motivated by their love of art pottery, had completed extensive education and training in manufacturing and decoration. In 1940 actor Edgar Bergen, a collector of pottery, developed a relationship with the brothers and invested in their business. With this new influx of funds, the company relocated to Pasadena. There they produced an extensive line of art pottery, but it was the bird and animal figurines they created that made them so well known. In addition they molded a large line of human figurines similar to Royal Doulton. The brothers, now with a staff of decorators, precisely molded their pieces with great care. They placed added emphasis on originality and detail, and as a result the products they created were high quality works of art that were only carried by exclusive gift stores.

In the late 1940s, after a split with Bergen, the company moved to San Gabriel to a larger, more modern location and renamed themselves The Claysmiths. There they mass produced many items, but due to the cheap, postwar imports from Italy and Japan that were then flooding the market, they liquidated the business in 1956. Our advisor for this category is Marty Webster. He is listed in the Directory under Michigan.

Bird figurine, Baltimore Oriole 155.00
Bird figurine, cardinal on branch, 10" 75.00
Bird figurine, cardinal on branch, 12½" 150.00
Bird figurine, eagle on rock, wht/brn, 10" 150.00
Bird figurine, flamingo, head to rear, 10" 75.00
Bird figurine, mallard duck w/spread wings, 7x11" 95.00
Bird figurine, parrot on branch, mc, 15" 200.00
Bird figurine, pheasant, female 110.00
Figurine, artist holding a palette, mc, 8" 95.00
Figurine, boy holding frog, on base, mc, 9" 95.00
Figurine, girl holding doll, on base, mc, 9" 125.00
Figurine, hula dancer, wht skirt, 12" 155.00
Figurine, monk, brn bsk, 4½" 50.00
Figurine, monk, brn bsk, 5½" 75.00
Pitcher, chicken figural, mc, 7" 125.00
Tumbler, chicken figural, mc, 4½" 50.00
Wine, chicken figural, mc, 5" 55.00

Willets

The Willets Manufacturing Company of Trenton, New Jersey, pro-

duced a type of belleek porcelain during the late 1880s and 1890s. Examples were often marked with a coiled snake that formed a 'W' with 'Willets' below and 'Belleek' above. Not all Willet's is factory decorated. Items painted by amateurs outside the factory are worth considerably less. High prices usually equate with fine artwork. In the listings below, all items are belleek unless noted otherwise. Our advisor for this category is Mary Frank Gaston; she is listed in the Directory under Texas.

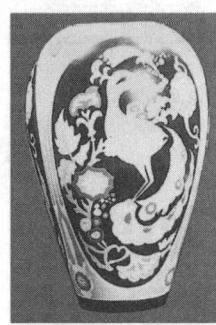

Vase, peacock reserve in pastels on black, signed, dated 1920, 13½", $550.00.

Bowl, gooseberries, hdls, sgn Moore, 7", pr; +6 5½" dia 700.00
Chalice, berries & leaves w/gold, prof decor, mk, 11½" 650.00
Chalice, monk w/cigar, gold trim, mk, 11½" 177.50
Chocolate pot, wht, no decor, brn mk, 9" 75.00
Clock, pk & gold floral & scroll designs, brn mk, 13½" 900.00
Loving cup, angels, gold hdls & decor, prof decor, mk, 8" 550.00
Muffineer, wht w/no decor, mk, 4½" 100.00
Mug, branch of apples & leaves, sgn, mk, 5½" 75.00
Mug, lady's portrait in reserve, bk: cherub, sgn Nosek, mk, 5¾" ..1,200.00
Mug, Princeton University Tiger, 5½" 56.00
Pitcher, cane design, lav tint w/gold sponging, red mk, 7" 350.00
Pitcher, devil-face spout, dragon hdl, no decor, 8½" 92.50
Pitcher, lady's head, hat brim forms spout, gold trim, 4½x5½" ...375.00
Pitcher, pk & gold floral, indented body, branch hdl, mk, 5¼" ..175.00
Pitcher, tankard; cavalier on bench, sgn Doering, 14" 1,100.00
Pitcher, tankard; floral on brn, dragon hdl, prof decor, mk, 13" .550.00
Pitcher, tankard; roses, ruby/pk/yel on mc, 11½" 150.00
Pitcher, violets w/gold, orange hdl, crimped rim, mk, 5" 75.00
Ring tree, floral w/brushed gold, mk, rare, 4½" 325.00
Salt cellar, floral w/gold, crimped rim, brn mk, 1½" 50.00
Vase, child's portrait in reserve w/gold, sgn Nosek, mk, 18½" .1,750.00
Vase, draped nude blowing bubbles, slim, prof decor, mk, 15½" .450.00
Vase, floral silver o/l, rim-to-hip hdls, gr mk, 12¾" 425.00
Vase, floral w/gilt, openwork design, scalloped ft, 12" 1,200.00
Vase, mc roses, gold uptrn hdls, prof decor, mk, 14" 850.00
Vase, wht tree-trunk form, unmk, 5" 250.00

Winchester

The Winchester Repeating Arms Company lost their important government contract after WWI and of necessity turned to the manufacture of sporting goods, hardware items, tools, etc., to augment their gun production. Between 1920 and 1931, over 7,500 different items, each marked 'Winchester Trademark U.S.A.,' were offered for sale by thousands of Winchester Hardware stores throughout the country. After 1931 the firm became Winchester-Western. Collectors prefer the prewar items such as we have listed below. Unless noted otherwise, values are for examples in excellent condition. Our advisor for this category is James Anderson; he is listed in the Directory under Minnesota. See also Knives.

Air rifle shot, lead, full tube, EX 20.00

Alarm clock, VG	175.00
Badge, worker's; #238, WWI era, EX+	90.00
Banner, oilcloth, w/target, horse & rider, 32x48", G+	235.00
Baseball bat, #2407, prof oil finish, EX	395.00
Baseball glove, fielder, 5-finger, mk The Winchester Store, EX	475.00
Baseball glove, mk Mark Sportsmen's Headquarters, G+	305.00
Bit brace, 10", G	125.00
Bread knife, stainless steel, blade #7337, G	40.00
Calendar, store; salesman's, 1926, VG+	425.00
Catalog, #18, 1918, Guns, Ammos & Sights, 213-pg, VG	65.00
Catalog, October 1898, rare, VG+	285.00
Clay bird thrower, standard sz, folds bk & locks, early, VG+	75.00
Counter mat, red rubber w/wht lettering, M	125.00
Diploma, Jr Rifle Corp, 1924, EX	47.00
Display, 5-panel, VG	850.00
Fan, hand; advertising for Schenck Hardware, 1920s, 7x9", G	75.00
Fishing plug, 3-hook, EX	350.00
Flashlight, shape of 20 gauge shell, VG+	45.00
Fly rod, bamboo, 108", NM	295.00
Golf club, Niblick #6640, wooden shaft, EX	165.00
Gun rack, 2-gun, branded banner, promotional, EX	45.00
Headlight, 5-cell, for hunting, no head band, 1930s, VG	25.00
Hoe, G	110.00
Ice pick, #9520	85.00
Jackknife, 2-blade, cocobolo hdl, nickel silver crest, 1920s	225.00
Knife, butcher; 6"	65.00
Lawn mower, VG	350.00
Level, wood, #9808, 18", EX	125.00
Lock, 6-lever, w/key, VG+	95.00
Pencil, bullet shape, pull-out, M	45.00
Pin, lapel; Winchester Jr Rifle Corp, bronze, M	45.00
Pocketknife, printer's block	65.00
Poster, Rabbit Hunting, paper, 1955, 26x40", folded o/w VG	50.00
Pressing iron, electric, w/cord	150.00
Printing block, catcher's mitt, EX	40.00
Putter, wedge type, EX	175.00
Rake, garden; EX	110.00
Reel, fishing; #2242, EX	125.00
Ruler, boxwood, 4-fold, W68, 24"	145.00
Scissors, #9012, 7", G+	42.00
Sign, pnt metal, horse & rider, 38" dia +hanging bracket, M	600.00
Spatula, kitchen; #7636, 15", EX	75.00
Stick pin, New Rival-Hunter's Choice, shotgun shape, brass, G	75.00
Tennis racquet, Ranger, Good as the Gun imprint, EX	375.00
Tube, rust remover; gray & red box, EX	40.00
Washboard, G	175.00
Wrench, telephone lineman's, Bell System, 13"	165.00

Windmill Weights

Windmill weights made of cast iron were used to protect the windmill's plunger rod from damage during high winds by adding weight that slowed down the speed of the blades.

Bull, Boss Bull, old worn pnt, 32-lb	1,800.00
Bull, Fairbury, no remaining pnt, 22½"	700.00
Crescent, Eclipse A13, Fairbanks Morse & Co, no pnt, 10½"	165.00
Crescent, Eclipse A13, Fairbanks Morse & Co, w/pnt, 10½"	415.00
Horse, Dempster, old blk pnt, 16½x17"	385.00
Horse, Demster, CI, pnt traces, 18⅜"	495.00
Rooster, Elgin A20, pnt traces, 20", on wooden base	1,265.00
Squirrel, Elgin Co, old worn pnt, 60-lb	2,500.00
W shape, Althouse Wheeler Co, stripped of pnt, 16" L	360.00

Wire Ware

Very primitive wire was first made by cutting sheet metal into strips which were shaped with mallet and file. By the late 13th century, craftsmen in Europe had developed a method of pulling these strips through progressively smaller holes until the desired gauge was obtained. During the Industrial Revolution of the late 1800s, machinery was developed that could produce wire cheaply and easily; and it became a popular commercial commodity. It was used to produce large items such as garden benches and fencing as well as innumerable small pieces for use in the kitchen or on the farm. Beware of reproductions. Our advisor for this category is Rosella Tinsley; she is listed in the Directory under Kansas.

Bacon rack, 6-prong, heavy wire, hook at top	18.00
Basket, calling card; heart-shaped hdls, glass plate, 7¼"	110.00
Basket, heavy wire in designs, ftd, hdld, 10" dia	95.00
Basket, ornate twisted wire, ftd, 1850s, 5"	110.00
Basket, petal-shaped sides, scalloped bottom, folding, 4½x7"	55.00
Biscuit pricker, heavy wire spikes, loop hdl, 2¼" dia	70.00
Bottle carrier, circular, top hdl, ftd	37.50
Broom holder (store), rnd, holds 24 brooms, hangs	175.00
Comb holder, twisted, fancy top, wall mt	125.00
Dish rack, ca 1890-1920, 16" dia	75.00
Egg tongs, heavy oval circular wire, squeeze hdl, 11" L	45.00
Fly cover, screen wire, wooden knob, 6½"	55.00
Glove, butcher's; woven wire mesh	24.00
Napkin ring, twisted wire, fancy design, pr	115.00
Pie rack, heavy wire, holds 6 pies	125.00
Plant stand, 2 lattice shelves w/scroll braces, wht pnt, 44x37"	325.00
Planter, corner; 3-tiered, wht pnt, 19th C, 49x28x20"	495.00
Rolling pin holder, heavy wire, hangs vertically, rare	65.00
Scrubber, wire ringlets, twisted wire hdl	45.00
Soap dish, twisted wire, fancy wire bk w/hanging loop	75.00
Soap saver, oblong screen-wire shape, wire & wood hdl	18.00
Tea ball, egg shape, ½" tin band ea side, 2¾"	28.00
Trivet, fine wire in circles, ftd, 14" dia	85.00
Trivet, tea; twisted wire, 6½" dia	45.00
Trivet, woven dmn center, 8" dia	20.00
Whisk, fancy twisted stem, target-shaped base, 1870s, 11½"	70.00
Whisk, twisted hdl, 8"	25.00

Witch Balls

Witch balls were a Victorian fad touted to be meritorious toward ridding the house of evil spirits, thus warding off sickness and bad luck. Folklore would have it that by wiping the dust and soot from the ball, the spirits were exorcised. It is much more probable, however, considering the fact that such beautiful art glass was used in their making, that the ostensive Victorians perpetrated the myth rather tongue-in-cheek while enjoying them as lovely decorations for their homes.

Purple amethyst ball resting on matching urn-form vase, South Jersey, 15" overall, $2,200.00.

Amber, sheared end, 5¾", on 1¼" stand 145.00
Amethyst, 6½", w/matching 7½" trumpet vase holder 1,600.00
Clear w/bl & wht loopings, sheared mouth, smooth base, 3½" ...325.00
Clear w/pk opaque loopings, 3" 170.00
Clear w/red, wht & bl loopings, open pontil, sm chips, 5½" 900.00
Clear w/red & wht loopings, vase holder, 11½" H 400.00
Clear w/wht loopings, open pontil, 5" 275.00
Clear w/wht loopings, Pittsburgh, 5", w/matching 14" vase/base ..2,650.00
Clear w/wht loopings, pontiled, 14", w/matching stand 750.00
Cobalt, sheared end, Am, 1860-85, 5½" 90.00
Cobalt, 5¼" dia, on clear blown 6¼" stand 300.00
Cranberry opal w/wht herringbone throughout, 3¾" 400.00
Deep grape amethyst, sheared end, Am, 1865-85, 3¾" 150.00
Golden amber, rolled rim, pontil, att South Jersey, 9¼" 225.00
Golden amber, sm pot stone, 5¼" 150.00
Gr-aqua w/wht loopings, 5" 250.00
Lt aquamarine w/wht loopings, 7", on matching trumpet base ...2,000.00
Lt vaseline w/wht loopings, open pontil, 4½" 100.00
Mercury glass, flared rim vase holder, NE Glass, 13", NM 150.00
Ruby cased, open pontil, 5" 200.00
Sapphire bl, sheared end, Am, 1865-85, 5¼" 160.00
Smoky clear w/mc splotches, 5½" 375.00
White opaque w/red/bl/yel glass fragments, 4½" 450.00
Wht opaque w/pk & lav loopings, 5¼" 800.00
Wht opaque w/red & bl glass fragments, 4" 200.00

Wood Carvings

Wood sculptures represent an important section of American folk art. Wood carvings were made not only by skilled woodworkers such as cabinetmakers, carpenters, etc., but by amateur 'whittlers' as well. They take the form of circus-wagon figures, carousel animals, decoys, busts, figurines, and cigar store Indians. Oriental artists show themselves to have been as proficient with the medium of wood as they were with ivory or hardstone. See also Carousel Animals; Decoys; Tobacciana.

Bears (2) hold center shelf, glass eyes, ca 1900, 7½x14½" 2,000.00
Bird mother & baby, orig mc pnt, metal ft, wooden base, 11" .1,100.00
Black man, pnt overalls/shirt, holding end of hoe, 19th C, 31" ...2,990.00
Candlestick, Candlestick Man, sgn Rev HL Hayes 1971, W VA, 10" 110.00
Cow, orig old blk & wht pnt, ca 1950s, unsgn, 5x7¼" 100.00
Draped maiden, mc pnt, minor losses, 21" 715.00
Dwarf w/ax & baskets, rstr, ca 1900, 9" 635.00
Eagle, bold relief cvg, old blk/wht rpt, 27½" L 1,300.00
Eagle, mahog, EX detail, open talons/beak, rpr, 27" 3,400.00
Eagle, realistic, glass eyes, 49½" 1,375.00
Eagle & flag, old mc rpt, sgn/dtd 1819, 22x29" 5,950.00
Eagle bracket, detailed cvg, old blk pnt, w/sm shelf, 14x9x8" ..3,685.00
Eagle head, old yel pnt, mtd on walnut brd, extends 10½" 1,400.00
Eagle w/Am flag, mc rpt, att John Bellamy, 10x27" 575.00
Elephant, orig gray pnt w/mc details, 3" 28.00
Fish, olive gr w/orange/yel/blk, wall mt, Jimmy Lewis, 1991, 35" ..70.00
Fish & frog in relief, mc, LA Plummer 1904, 25x40¼", VG .17,250.00
Indian dancing figure, articulated limbs, embr dress, 1850s, 14" ..9,200.00
Indian maiden, mc pnt, sgn Leroy Lewis, 1989, 28½" 195.00
Kangaroo w/joey, tropical wood w/old gray pnt, 1900s, 19" 50.00
Lawn ornament, policeman in uniform, Keep Off on hands, 1940s, 16" 65.00
Madonna & Child, poplar w/mc pnt, Lavell Nickoll (unsgn), 9¾" ..55.00
Man cvd from forked branch, mc pnt, 1930s, 18x10x3½" 155.00
Mask, carnival; Black man w/hair wig, Am, 19th C, 14" 75.00
Rooster, folky style, worn mc pnt, 6" 700.00
Uncle Sam, mc pnt, sgn Earnest Patton 1989 in pencil, 19½" 715.00
Watch case, cvd dbl rose & leaves, velvet lined, ca 1850, 3⅝" 50.00

Woodenware

Woodenware (or treenware, as it is sometimes called) generally refers to those wooden items such as spoons, bowls, food molds, etc., that were used in the preparation of food. Common during the 18th and 19th centuries, these wares were designed from a strictly functional viewpoint and were used on a day-to-day basis. With the advent of the Industrial Revolution which brought with it new materials and products, much of the old woodenware was simply discarded. Today original handcrafted American woodenwares are extremely difficult to find. See also Primitives.

Sugar bowl, turned maple, ca 1850s, fine original finish, 5½x5⅝", $650.00.

Bowl, ash burl, crudely cvd, ca 1800, 2⅛x4⅝" 125.00
Bowl, ash burl, dk finish w/stains, sm notch in rim, 6¼" dia 195.00
Bowl, ash burl, EX figure, scrubbed, trn detail, worn, 2x7" 385.00
Bowl, ash burl, EX figure, trn details, 10" 770.00
Bowl, ash burl, EX old patina, 1¾x4½x4¾" 300.00
Bowl, ash burl, flattened bottom, crude rim, 1800s, 5¾x14x12½" ...250.00
Bowl, ash burl, old brn patina, honest wear, 4¾x17x12" 1,100.00
Bowl, ash burl, old red & wht w/inside patina, worn, 7x21" 330.00
Bowl, ash burl, oval, cut-out rim hdls, dk stain, 3x9x8" 2,600.00
Bowl, ash burl, rfn, 1¾x4¼" 195.00
Bowl, ash burl, soft brn finish, lt wear, 4¾x12¾" 1,045.00
Bowl, ash burl, softly scrubbed, 5½x17¼" 1,400.00
Bowl, ash burl, trn rings, old rfn, worn int, 4¾x15" 495.00
Bowl, ash burl, uneven rim, ca 1800, 5⅛x12" 650.00
Bowl, ash burl, 8-sided base, worn old finish, 2x4¼" 250.00
Bowl, ash burl w/intense figure, putty-filled hole, 4⅜x14" 1,100.00
Bowl, bird's-eye maple w/old mustard, age crack, 17½" 150.00
Bowl, burl, trn scribe-line decor, rpr, 19th C, 4¼x12" 3,000.00
Bowl, burl, 19th C, age crack, 7¾x17¼" 1,600.00
Bowl, burl, 19th C, cracks, 6x11" 1,380.00
Bowl, cvd ft, cvd ribbed band, ca 1900, 5x12½" 1,150.00
Bowl, elongated w/rounded ends, wear/stains, 4½x24x9½" 140.00
Bowl, fitted lid w/trn finial, rpr crack, 6x6" 280.00
Bowl, poplar, trn, wht traces, CT, 6½x17¼" 330.00
Bowl, poplar, worn gr pnt over bl, 6¾x17x18" 400.00
Bowl, poplar, worn gray patina, 4½x14½x5¼" 140.00
Bowl, walnut, rnd w/flat bottom, cvd ribbed band, 3x5⅞" 350.00
Box, apple shape w/cvd stem hdl, gr pnt, 2½x2¾" 280.00
Box, trn pear shape, 3⅜x1⅞" 180.00
Butter paddle, burl bowl, brn pnt traces, 8½", EX 150.00
Butter paddle, curly chestnut, ring hdl, 12⅛" 220.00
Butter paddle, curly maple, heart hdl, 8" 500.00
Butter paddle, curly maple, horse-head hdl, age cracks, 10½" 415.00
Butter paddle, curly maple, stylized horse-head hdl, 10" 660.00
Butter paddle, curly maple, 2-tone, relief-cvd figure on hdl, 10" .770.00
Butter paddle, curly maple bowl, bird-head hdl, 14½" 580.00
Butter paddle, maple w/some curl, sleeping bird hdl, 6⅝" 1,155.00
Cookie board, arms of NY State, Excelsior, att J Conger, 11x11¼" 3,200.00
Cookie board, dancing couple, att Conger, mahog, 10¾" sq ...1,700.00
Cookie board, lion & stag, primitive cvgs, old patina, 4¼x6¼" ..440.00

Cookie board, man on horse, sgn Conger, mahog, 10½" sq 2,300.00
Cup, saffron; acorn shape, ivory finial, 2⅛x2¼" 85.00
Cup, saffron; Lehnware, floral on salmon, 5x2½" 600.00
Cup, saffron; Lehnware, strawberries/stripes on salmon, w/lid, 5" .1,050.00
Cup & saucer, Lehnware, strawberries on salmon, EX art, 1¼" 1,600.00
Cup & saucer, Lehnware, strawberries on salmon, ped ft, 3x2½" ..750.00
Cup & saucer, Lehnware, strawberries on salmon, 1891, 1⅛" 625.00
Dipper, curly maple, natural-shape bowl, rfn, 12" 110.00
Dough tray, pnt dvtl softwood, early 1800s, 31x39x22½" 2,500.00
Egg cup, Lehnware, floral on salmon, minor flakes, 2¾x1⅞" 375.00
Egg cup, sponged decor, rnd ft, 3⅛x1¾" 120.00
Firkin, gr pnt, staves/tacks, bentwood rim, w/lid, NE, 12" 290.00
Firkin, staved wooden bands, copper tacks, gray pnt, 6½" 300.00
Firkin, staved wooden bands, copper tacks, orig red, 6½" 360.00
Firkin, wooden bands, lt & dk gr pnt, bail hdl, 12x11½" 350.00
Jar, poplar, worn old sponge graining, 8" 360.00
Keg, staved, laced wooden bands, old bl rpt, wear, 15" 75.00
Measure, 2 lap joints on base, finger-jtd lid, old pnt, 7x14" 200.00
Pastry board, complete alphabet, brass ring hanger, 6x20⅛" 750.00
Pastry board, crudely cvd chicken in center, 7¼" sq 160.00
Pastry board, dbl-sided, hunter w/rifle/lady w/mandolin, 9x24", VG 180.00
Pastry board, man on stool milking cow, 9¾x6⅛" 325.00
Pie board, pine, 15" dia+5" hdl 185.00
Plate, curly poplar, old natural patina, Wm Ashton, 1880, 8⅜" .110.00
Rolling pin, curly maple, 18" 155.00
Salt cellar, Lehnware, bleeding hearts on salmon, 3x2⅜" 600.00
Salt cellar, Lehnware, strawberries on salmon, ped ft, 3x2⅜" 575.00
Salt cellar, ped ft, brn sponging, ca 1870s, 2½x2¾" 100.00
Scoop, cranberry; early mustard pnt, handmade 300.00
Scoop, hdl cvd from 1 pc, shovel-shape bowl, 17x7" 50.00
Spatula, curly maple, rfn, 13½" 100.00
Thread holder, bbl shape, trn int spools w/ivory inlay, 4¼x1½" .175.00
Trencher, cvd maple, rectangular hdls, flat bottom, 25" L 500.00
Trencher, old red & gr pnt, 10x11½" 150.00
Washing stick, cvd wood w/forked end, ca 1900, 30x3½" 70.00

Woodworking Machinery

Vintage cast-iron woodworking machines are monuments to the highly skilled engineers, foundrymen, and machinists who devised them, thus making possible the mass production of items ranging from clothespins, boxes, and barrels to decorative moldings and furniture. Though attractive from a nostalgic viewpoint, many of these machines are bought by the hobbyist and professional alike, to be put into actual use — at far less cost than new equipment. Many worth-assessing factors must be considered; but as a general rule, a machine in good condition is worth about 65¢ a pound (excluding motors). A machine needing a lot of restoration is not worth more than 35¢ a pound, while one professionally rebuilt and with a warranty can be calculated at $1.10 a pound. Modern, new machinery averages over $3.00 a pound. Two of the best sources of information on purchasing or selling such machines are *Vintage Machines — Searching for the Cast Iron Classics*, by Tom Howell, and *Used Machines and Abused Buyers* by Chuck Seidel from *Fine Woodworking*, November/December 1984. Prices quoted are for machines in good condition, less motors and accessories. Our advisor for this category is Mr. Dana Martin Batory, author of *Vintage Woodworking Machinery, An Illustrated Guide to Four Manufacturers*. See his listing in the Directory under Ohio for further information. No phone calls, please.

American Saw Mill Machinery Company, 1931

Band saw, Monarch Line, #X25, 30" built-in ball-bearing motor ..770.00
Mortiser, Monarch Line, #XI, hollow chisel, motorized 345.00
Sander, Monarch Line, #X8, ball-bearing drum & disk 560.00

Blue Star Products, 1939

Band saw, #1200, 12" floor model 85.00
Lathe, #1001, 72" bed, 12" swing 60.00
Table saw, #800, 8" 95.00

Boice-Crane Power Tools, 1937

Band saw, #800, 14" 100.00
Drill press, #1600, 15" 75.00
Lathe, #1100, gap bed 50.00
Scroll saw, #900, 24" 75.00

Crescent Machine Company, 1921

Band saw, 36" 975.00
Mortiser, hollow chisel 525.00
Universal Wood-Worker, #59, 5 machines in 1 .....2,050.00

Defiance Machine Works, 1910

Band saw, 28" 520.00
Table saw, #2, hand feed, 20" 650.00
Table saw, #2, power feed, 20" 1,100.00

Delta Manufacturing Company, 1939

Band saw, #768, 10" 50.00
Band saw, #890, 14" 70.00
Belt sander, #1400, 6" 35.00
Disk sander, belt drive, #1425, 12" 35.00
Drill press, bench, #645, 11" 30.00
Drill press, bench, #999, 14" 50.00
Drill press, floor, #1370, 17" 200.00
Drill press, floor, #989, 14" 70.00
Drill press, floor, high speed, #1370-H, 17" 200.00
Jointer, ball bearing, #290, 4" 35.00
Jointer, ball bearing, #654, 6" 50.00
Lathe, ball bearing, #1460, 12" 60.00
Lathe, timken bearing, #930, 11" 45.00
Lathe, timken bearing, #955, 9" 35.00
Scroll saw, multi-speed, #1440, 24" 50.00
Scroll saw, 4-speed, #1200, 24" 40.00
Shaper, ball bearing, reversible, #1180 .....30.00
Table saw, tilt top, #1160, 10" 95.00
Table saw, tilt top, #860, 8" 35.00
Unisaw, tilting-arbor, #1450, 10" 175.00

F.H. Clement Company, 1896

Band saw, 28", Improved 1,040.00
Band saw, 34", Patent Improved 635.00
Band saw, 42" 1,430.00
Jointer, Perfection, 8" 620.00
Lathe, pattern maker's; iron bed, Improved, 20" 815.00
Planer, #2½, dbl belted, Improved, 24" 1,465.00
Planer, #3, dbl surface, 26" 3,000.00
Sand belt machine, Improved 425.00
Sander, #1, spindle & drum 520.00
Sanding machine, surface; Improved 650.00
Shaper, #1, reversible, Improved 650.00

Table saw, dbl arbor, Improved, 16" 815.00

Gallmeyer & Livingston Company, 1927

Band saw, Union, 20" 390.00
Jointer, Union, motor on arbor, 8" 370.00
Table saw, Union #7, 7" 210.00

G.N. Goodspeed Company, 1876

Boring machine, upright 225.00
Planer, New & Improved, Pony, 24" 900.00
Table saw, 12" 200.00

Greenlee Bros. & Company, 1925

Tenoner, #530, sash, door & cabinet, ball-bearing 1,530.00

Hoyt & Brother Company, 1888

Band saw & resawing machine, #1194, 20" 1,700.00
Jointer, Perfection, 8" 450.00
Planer, matcher & surfacer, New Combined, #2, 24" 5,200.00
Sandpapering machine, The Boss, #5, 24" 1,600.00
Shingle machine, Grand Mogul, 2-block, automatic feed 2,210.00
Tenoning machine, #2 ....650.00

J.A. Fay & Egan Company, 1900

Jointer, New #2, 16" 1,550.00
Jointer, New #2, 24" 1,700.00
Jointer, New #4, extra heavy, 16" 1,625.00
Jointer, New #4, extra heavy, 24" 1,885.00
Molder, #1½, 4-sided, 4" 1,050.00
Molder, #2½, 4-sided, 7" 2,100.00
Mortiser, #5, dbl hollow chisel, horizontal 1,100.00
Saw, rip; #2, Improved Standard 1,175.00
Saw, rip; #3, self-feeding, X-lg 2,400.00

J.D. Wallace Company, 1940s

Band saw, 16" 210.00
Grinder & sander, disk; Wonder, 16" 165.00
Jointer, 4" 15.00
Lathe, 6x24" 115.00
Saw, circular (table saw); Universal, 7" 75.00
Saw, circular; plain, 7" 65.00

L. Power & Company, 1888

Mortiser & borer, #2 ....780.00
Shaper, single spindle, reversible 585.00
Table saw, self feed, 14" 715.00

Ober Manufacturing Company, 1889

Rip saw, self feed, 14" 725.00
Saw, swing cut-off, 18" 275.00
Shaper, saw & jointer combination 400.00

Oliver Machinery Company, 1922

Band saw, #17, 30" 925.00
Shaper, #483, high speed, dbl spindle 1,300.00

Table saw, #32, Variety, 12" 500.00

Parks Ball Bearing Machine Company, 1925

Jointer, H-133, Ideal, 12" 400.00
Sanding machine, H-165, Economy, 24" 230.00
Saw, H-97, swing cut-off, Alert, 12" 225.00

P.B. Yates Machine Company, 1917

Planer, #160, dbl surface, 20" 1,235.00
Saw, #232, swing cut-off, 16" 260.00

Powermatic, Inc., 1965

Band saw, #141, 14" 145.00
Jointer, #50, 6" 110.00
Lathe, #45, 12" 230.00
Mortiser, #10, hollow chisel 375.00
Planer, #100, 12" 200.00
Planer, #180, 18" 685.00
Planer, #225, 24" 1,600.00
Sander, #33, 6" belt 90.00
Scroll saw, #95, 24" 100.00
Table saw, #62, 10" 135.00
Table saw, #72, 12" 515.00

S.A. Woods Machine Company, 1876

Circular resawing machine, Joslin's Improved, 50" 2,275.00
Planer, panel; Improved, 20" 520.00
Planer, surface; Pat Improved, 30" 1,430.00

Sprunger Power Tools, 1950s

Band saw, 14" 60.00
Jigsaw, 20" 40.00
Lathe, gap bed, 10" 50.00
Table saw, tilt arbor, 10¼" 75.00

Worcester Porcelain Company

The Worcester Porcelain Company was deeded in 1751. During the first or Dr. Wall period (so called for one of its proprietors), porcelain with an Oriental influence was decorated in underglaze blue. Useful tablewares represented the largest portion of production, but figurines and decorative items were also made. Very little of the earliest wares were marked and can only be identified by a study of forms, glazes, and the porcelain body, which tends to transmit a greenish cast when held to light. Late in the '50s, a crescent mark was in general use, and rare examples bear a facsimile of the Meissen crossed swords. The first period ended in 1783, and the company went through several changes in ownership during the next eighty years. The years from 1783 to 1792 are referred to as the Flight period. Marks were a small crescent, a crown with 'Royal,' or an impressed 'Flight.' From 1792 to 1807 the company was known as Flight and Barr and used the trademark 'F&B' or 'B,' with or without a small cross. From 1807 to 1813 the company was under the Barr, Flight, and Barr management; this era is recognized as having produced porcelain with the highest quality of artistic decoration. Their mark was 'B.F.B.' From 1813 to 1840 many marks were used, but the most usual was 'F.B.B.' under a crown to indicate Flight, Barr, and Barr. In 1840 the firm merged with Chamberlain, and in 1852 they were succeeded by Kerr and Binns. The firm became known as Royal Worcester in 1862.

The production was then marked with a circle with '51' within and a crown on top. The date of manufacture was incised into the bottom or stamped with a letter of the alphabet, just under the circle. In 1891 Royal Worcester England was added to the circle and crown. From that point on, each piece is dated with a code of dots or other symbols. After 1891 most wares had a blush-color ground. Prior to that date it was ivory. Most shapes were marked with a unique number.

During the early years they produced considerable ornamental wares with a Persian influence. This gave way to a Japanesque influence. James Hadley is most responsible for the Victorian look. He is considered the 'best ever' designer and modeller. He was joined by the finest porcelain painters. Together they produced pieces with very fine detail and exquisite painting and decoration. Figures, vases, and tableware were produced in great volume and are highly collectible. During the 1890s they allowed the artists to sign some of their work. Pieces signed on the face by the Stintons, Baldwyn, Davis, Raby, Austin, Powell, Sedgley, and Rushton (not a complete list) are in great demand. The company is still in production. There is an outstanding museum on the company grounds in Worcester, England.

Note: Most pieces had lids or tops (if there is a flat area on the top lip, chances are it had one), if missing deduct 30% to 40%.

Bottle, scent; pear w/HP decor, ca 1907, 4¼" 630.00
Bowl, lg emb fall leaves/gold, openwork top edge, 1896, 9" 295.00

Centerpiece bowl, central tree trunk supports pierced basketweave dish, three figures between shell dishes, much gold, ca 1882, 14x11", NM, $1,725.00.

Coffee set, pine tree brn transfer, ca 1883, 11-pc on 20" tray ..2,875.00
Cracker jar, bamboo w/leaves & flowers, gold trim, 1887, 6¼" ...460.00
Cracker jar, floral sprays on ivory w/gilt, ribbed, 7½" 250.00
Cup & saucer, demitasse; rtcl, 1885 ....395.00
Cup & saucer, Japan pattern, Imari palette, ca 1770, 4¾" dia 500.00
Dinner set, Mansfield, serves 12, 98-pc 600.00
Ewer, floral in iron red w/gold, dragon hdl, #1048, 1887, 7¼" 300.00
Ewer, trophies of Arts & Hunt, salamander hdl, 1889 mk, 11½" ..700.00
Figurine, Capt Raimondo (horse) 995.00
Figurine, Grandmother's Dress, FG Doughty, #3081 ....200.00
Figurine, horse, Percheron 1,095.00
Figurine, Marian Coates w/Stroller 995.00
Figurine, Peter Pan, modeled by F Gertner, #3011, 7¾" 310.00
Figurine, Yankee, naturalistic colors, #836, 1902, 6¾" 345.00
Figurines, Joy & Sorrow, mc enameling, ca 1895, 9⅞", pr 1,725.00
Jardiniere, emb leaves on basketweave w/gold, #1947, 1899, 6½" ..200.00
Jug, mc floral & berries w/gold, #1229, ca 1889, 9⅜" 265.00
Jug, mc floral on bottle form w/gold dragon hdl, #260, 1889, 11½" ...400.00
Plate, roses on pk, 3-lobe rim, 1908, 9" 135.00
Plate, Tewkesbury scene, sgn Nicholls, 1953, 10¾" 225.00
Shell dish, tan to cream, gold at toothed edge, curled hdl 50.00

Sugar bowl, floral, appl flower finial, Dr Wall Period, 4½" 200.00
Teapot, floral vines/flower baskets, globular, 18th C, 5½", EX ...550.00
Teapot, melon form w/appl gold lotus leaves, 1888, 6" 450.00
Vase, floral sprigs, mc on ivory, rtcl hdls, stick neck, 12" 225.00
Vase, floral w/gilt, emb foliage, hdls, #1089, ca 1887, 10¼" 850.00
Vase, gilt birds amidst clouds, HS, 1890 mk, 11" 450.00
Vase, Patent Metallic, emb foliage, #850, ca 1881, 12½" 350.00

World's Fairs and Expos

Since 1851 and the Crystal Palace Exhibition in London, World's Fairs and Expositions have taken place at a steady pace. Many of them commemorate historical events. The 1904 Louisiana Purchase Exposition, commonly known as the St. Louis World's Fair, celebrated the 100th anniversary of the Louisiana Purchase agreement between Thomas Jefferson and Napoleon in 1803. The 1893 Columbian Exposition, known as The Chicago World's Fair, commemorated the 400th anniversary of the discovery of America by Columbus in 1492. (Both of these fairs were held one year later than originally scheduled.) The multitude of souvenirs from these and similar events have become a growing area of interest to collectors in recent years. Many items have a 'crossover' interest into other fields: i.e., collectors of postcards and souvenir spoons eagerly search for those from various fairs and expositions. For additional information collectors may contact World's Fairs Collectors Society (WFCS), whose address is in the Directory under Clubs, Newsletters, and Catalogs, or our advisor, Herbert Rolfes. His address is listed in the Directory under Florida.

Key:
T&P — Trylon & Perisphere   WF — World's Fair

1851 Crystal Palace, London (First World's Fair)

Cup, coffee; Crystal Palace picture, soft-paste porc 100.00
Pot lid, Crystal Palace pictured, 4" dia 300.00

1853 Crystal Palace, New York (First World's Fair in U.S.)

Medal, Crystal Palace on wht metal, 2" dia 75.00
Print, Crystal Palace, Moore & Crosby, 4⅜x7", matt: 8x11" 125.00

1876 Centennial, Philadelphia

Guide book (official catalog) 75.00
Kerchief, Memorial Hall, cotton, no stains or tears, 18½x24½" ...75.00
Package ticket (admission) 15.00
Stevengraph, Lincoln, 9½x1½", M 150.00

1893 Columbian, Chicago

Bell, acid-etched logo/florals/banners, spiral-emb hdl, 5¾" 185.00
Book, World's Columbian...Illus, Campbell, Jan 1892, 32-pg, NM ..17.50
Booklet, World Is Mine, Simmons Saw & Mfg Co, 5x3¼", NM ..12.50
Paperweight, sepia Ferris wheel view in glass, 3" dia 75.00
Playing cards, Columbian Souvenir, Clark, 54 in worn box 100.00
Punch cup, pressed glass, w/blk inscription, Libbey 85.00
Ticket, Chicago Day, w/stub 17.50

1894 California Mid-Winter, San Francisco

Coupon (ticket), San Francisco Day 35.00
Guide book 75.00

1898 Trans-Mississippi

Book, Snap Shots of Expo, 40-pg, 7x9" 20.00
Match safe, NP, female figure, expo bldgs 48.00
Pin-bk, Iowa Day Sept 21, 1898, celluloid, 1¼" 30.00
Pin-bk, PA Day, celluloid, 1¾" 40.00
Poster, panoramic view of expo, emb Nebraska Bldg, EX+ 22.50
Spoon, SP, Govt Bldg in bowl 24.00
Tray, bldg emb on pot metal, slight wear, 3½" 20.00

1901 Pan American

Bell, brass from wreck of the Battleship Maine, 3¾" 125.00
Elongated cent, 'Mfg & Liberal Arts/Pan-Am/1901,' 1894 cent 8.00
Encased cent, Good Luck/Lucky Penny, 1½" dia 12.50
Frying pan, image of buffalo w/Am flag behind, mini, 2¾" L 30.00
Medal, brass, US Govt Bldg, 1⅛" dia 10.00
Medal, Electric Tower/Niagara Falls, SP bronze, 1¼" dia 16.00
Pin tray, high-relief image of buffalo, 5" dia 32.00
Pin-bk button, robed female, Official, paper insert, 1¼" dia 17.00
Spoon, Indian/Niagara Falls on hdl, pan-shaped bowl, 1¼" 20.00

1904 St. Louis

Desk plaque, reverse-painted
view of Cascade Gardens,
mother-of-pearl and gilt frame,
5x6¾", EX, $180.00.

Flue cover, 1st Family of Land, sepia under glass, tin fr, 6¼" 450.00
Medal, bronze, 1904 St L Welcomes the Worlds, 2" dia 15.00
Mirror, Festival Hall, mc cello, rnd, 2¼" 235.00
Napkin ring, emb of Cascade Gardens, wht metal, 1¾" dia 15.00
Pin tray, pewter, image of Louis IX, 5½" dia 55.00
Pocketknife, designs in relief, aluminum case, 3½" L 45.00
Prosperity purse, W Millard Palmer Co, 2½x3¾" 15.00
Ribbon, RR & Transportation Day, bl on wht silk, 6" L 40.00
Token, commemorative; Roosevelt/Jefferson & others, 1¼" 18.00
Tray, advertising; India Tea, litho tin, hinged lid, 2½x4⅛" 120.00

1905 Lewis and Clark

Handkerchief, wht w/mc Foreign Exhibits Bldg, EX 15.00
Medal, brass, L&C Centennial...in wreath, EX 75.00
Pin-bk, 2 frogs under umbrella, mc on celluloid, mk, 1¾" 40.00
Postcard folder, mc views, Wolff & O'Brien, set of 24 ....20.00
Poster stamps, sheet of 12 ....20.00
Token, L&C, map of Louisiana, EX 24.00

1909 Alaska Yukon Pacific

Fob, watch; totem pole design, silver, 1¼x1½" 35.00
Folder, Invitation From Fraternal Brotherhood, mc, 5x6¾" 25.00
Handkerchief, silk, bird's-eye view of fair, mc, 15" sq, EX 40.00
Plate, china, Oregon State Bldg, mc transfer, 8" 90.00

Ribbon, wht silk w/red & bl letters, Japan Day, 2½x7½" 30.00
Tumbler, copper gilt on metal, 3 expo scenes & logo, 3½" 25.00

1915 Panama Pacific

Award ribbon, emb lettering & seal in gold & purple, 3½x7" 50.00
Bell, brass, wood hdl, Liberty Bell w/expo mks, 2½" 35.00
Cup, china, wht, scene of Govt Bldg, gold trim, mk England, 2½" ...60.00
Cup, collapsible; aluminum, emb North & South Am on lid, 2½" dia .32.50
Goblet, stemmed, gr glass, etched Louella & WF 1893, 3" 60.00
Napkin ring, celluloid, Tower of Jewels, cut-out design, 2x2" 20.00
Pen, quill; aluminum, mk Souvenir WCE 1893, rpr, 8½" L 20.00
Postcard, Festival Hall, Pacific Novelty Co, mc, unused 3.00
Postcard, Montana State Bldg, Pacific Novelty Co, mc, unused 3.00
Postcard, Official, mc views, Goldsmith, mk Series #1, ea 15.00
Postcard album, Official, Cardinell-Vincent Co, set of 19, M 35.00
Trade card, Horticultural Bldg, mc, Merrick's Spool Cotton 5.00
Tumbler, clear glass, Machinery Hall, frosted design, 3½" 40.00

1926 Sesquicentennial

Ashtray, metal, Liberty Bell emb, mk, 5½x3¼", EX 15.00
Book, Flags of Am, expo edition, 32-pg, 8x5½", EX 12.50
Brooch, Liberty Bell medallion, copper metal in gr fr, 1x1¼" 20.00
Compact, brass w/red & gr glass stones, fair mks, oval, EX 88.00
Mailing folder, Official Souvenir, 18 mc views in strip, 6" L 12.50
Pencil case, Liberty Bell on leather, 3x8", NM 25.00
Ribbon, silk, 150 Yrs of Am Independence, 6x4", EX 88.00
Tapestry, mc woven cloth, patriotic images, 1926, 24x48", EX 80.00
Train schedule, NYC Day, list of events, EX 10.00

1933 Chicago

Ashtray, emb Chrysler Bldg, copper, dtd 1933, 3x3" 7.50
Ashtray, tire; rubber, Firestone, amber glass, mk 50.00
Bank, Am Can Co, litho tin, bldgs in mc, dtd 1934, 3½x2" dia ...20.00
Booklet, Chinese Lama Temple, illus, 64-pg, 6x9¼" 20.00
Brochure, GM Bldg, mc, 1933 ....3.50
Fan, folding; wood & paper, fair/Oriental scenes, 10x15" open 45.00
Folder, The Doctor, painting from Petrolagar Exhibit 2.50
Guide, Official, illus information, w/map, 194-pg, 5½x9¼" 17.50
Map of MO, illus, commemorative of fair 7.50
Plate, china, Carillon Tower, blk on wht, dtd 1934, 8¼" 40.00
Plate, china, Federal Bldg/Court of States, 1833-1933, 9½" 75.00
Playing cards, Official, mc fair scenes on bks, complete+joker 37.50
Program, Wings of a Century, 12-pg+cover, 8½x11½" 15.00
Tray, Towers of Federal Bldg, litho tin, dtd 1933, mc, 4" dia 22.50

1935 California Pacific

Folder, Come to San Diego 1935, information & illus 7.50
Folder, Painted Desert Exhibit, illus, 3½x6" 5.00
Guide, Official Souvenir Program, illus, 1936, 56-pg, 6x9" 20.00
Guide, Official; daily events for 7/13/35, 5½x8½" 5.00
Match box holder, bl enameled brass, scenes of expo, 1x1½x½" 20.00
Tile, ceramic, expo scenes, emb letters at edge, mk, NM 60.00

1939 New York

Ashtray, clear glass in Syroco wood base, emb T&P design, 3" sq ..25.00
Book, NY WF Views, Quality Art Novelty Co, 48-pg, 9½x12" 30.00
Book, Official Guide; 1st edition, 256-pg, 5x8" 22.50
Elongated cent, 'World of Tomorrow,' & T&P design 10.00
Folder, Routes to WF, map of NY tunnel & fair schedule, T&P 7.50

Comb, amber plastic, in embossed gold-tone metal case with brass medallion in center, EX, $30.00.

Handkerchief, silk or rayon, dk bl w/mc WF scenes, 18" sq 35.00
Letter opener, bronzed metal, emb Christian Science Bldg, 8½" ..20.00
Medal, brass, T&P, Rockefeller Center on reverse, 1¼" dia 7.50
Pin, metal, robot shaped, mk Westinghouse, 1x⅞" 30.00
Pin, pickle shaped, gr, emb 'Heinz,' 1¼" dia 5.00
Pin-bk button, litho tin, mk Little Miss Junket, 1" dia 20.00
Polaroid viewer, front of Chrysler automobile shape 35.00
Sheet music, Yours for a Song, Official theme song, T&P cover ..30.00
Statue of Liberty, bronzed, T&P, 5½x2" sq 50.00

1939 San Francisco

Booklet, Famous Guide to SF & WF, indexed, illus, 144-pg, 5x7" .17.50
Comb case, red enamel, gold-toned emb WF designs, w/comb, 4½" ..22.50
Folder, general expo information, dtd 1939, illus, 3½x6" 5.00
Folder, Kirkland Travel Service, tours, illus, 4x9" 7.50
Folder, Treasure Island Night & Day, 16 mc lithos, 6x4" 10.00
Pillow sham, mc fair views, 17" sq, EX 18.00
Postcard, mc scenes of Court of the Moon 2.50
Wallet, leather w/WF mk & sailing ship, VG 20.00

1962 Seattle

Cup & saucer, wht ceramic w/pearlescent glaze & gold trim 22.00
Guide, Official 18.00
Plate, mc aerial view, cut-out border w/spikes at edge, 5" dia 8.00
Postcard, Eye of the Needle 3.00
Shakers, Space Needle form, ceramic, pr 30.00

1964 New York

Game, Official, 20x24" game sheet, M Bradley, 10x14½" box 35.00
Postcards, mc views of fair, unused, ea 2.50
Puzzle, fr tray; mc overview of fair, M Bradley, 10x14", NM 20.00
Shakers, Unisphere shape, silvered metal, 2", pr 17.50
Tray, metal, mc scene of Unisphere, rnd, 12" dia 12.50

Wright, Frank Lloyd

Born in Richland Center, Wisconsin, in 1869, Wright became a pioneer in architectural expression, developing a style referred to as 'prairie.' From early in the century until he died in 1959, he designed houses with rooms that were open, rather than divided by walls in the traditional manner. They exhibited low, horizontal lines and strongly projecting eaves, and he filled them with furnishings whose radical aesthetics complemented the structures to perfection. Several of his homes have been preserved to the present day, and collectors who admire his ideas and the unique, striking look he achieved treasure the stained glass windows, furniture, chinaware, lamps, and other decorative accessories made by Wright.

Key:
do — door   H — Heritage Henredon
drw — drawer   T — Taliesin design trim

Breakfront, H, mahog, 4 shelves ea side cabinet do, 10 drws, VG ..2,500.00
Cabinet, H, mahog, open top w/division, T, 26x20", VG 750.00
Cabinet, H, 2-do w/recessed hdls, T, 28x20x21", VG 1,100.00
Chair, angular bronzed steel fr, wood armrests, uphl slat bk 500.00
Chair, H, high uphl bk/U-shape seat, rfn, 40", VG, set of 6 ....2,800.00
Chair, H, uphl rectangle bk, U-shape seat/arms, 41", VG 1,000.00
Chair, side; 11-spindle bk, drop-in seat, att, 42", VG 1,300.00
Chair, uphl rectangle bk, U-shape seat/open arms, 41", VG, pr ..2,000.00

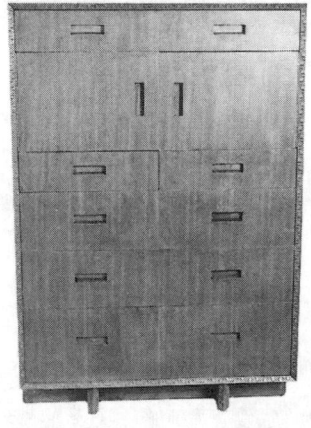

Chest of drawers, Henredon, mahogany, incised geometric decor, 52½x36½x20", EX original, $1,600.00.

Dresser, H, mahog, 10-drw, T, 33X65", VG 800.00
Figures, Indian couple, geometric style, dk red matt, 17" & 12" ..3,250.00
Light fixture, 19" ldgl shade w/raised geometric panels, VG ...22,000.00
Mirror, H, mahog, T, 48x35", EX 300.00
Print, Wasmuth, KC Rhodes, int/ext design, 22x14" 300.00
Table, dining; H, dbl V-slab base, T, 2 leaves, 76x65" 850.00
Theatre seat, angular metal fr w/uphl seat/bk, 34", VG 550.00
Wastepaper basket, att, 4 brass-fr sides w/wire grids 3,000.00

Wrought Iron

Until the middle of the 19th century, almost all the metal hand forged in America was made from a material called wrought iron. When wrought iron rusts it appears grainy, while the mild steel that was used later shows no grain but pits to an orange-peel surface. This is an important aid in determining the age of an ironwork piece.

Bird spit, wrought iron with brass inlay, tripod base signed and dated 1847, 18x17½", $850.00.

Bench, spiral crest, scrolled bk & decor, 19th C, 38x54x24" 300.00
Candlestand, 2-arm, 3 legs w/pad ft, brass mt at base, 59x18" 350.00
Coffin stand, Am, 19th C, 24¼x49¾x13" 145.00
Curling iron, box joint, curved hdls, ca 1800, 7½" 35.00
Fish spear, wraparound collar, incised lines, 11" 55.00
Fork, 2-tine, hdl pierced for hanging, dtd 1774, 7" 650.00
Gridiron, 10-bar, 4 sq legs w/pad-like ft, 19th C, 24x12" 275.00
Hinges, ram's horn strap type, beveled edges, old pnt, 28", pr 220.00
Hitching post, 4-sided w/trn finial, scalloped std, 18th C, 39" ...2,875.00
Kettle stand, gallery-like rim, 3 arched legs, 27" 110.00
Loom light, spring trammel w/splint holder & socket, 24" 770.00
Pan, long appl hdl mk W Foster, 2x10¾"+22¾" hdl 110.00
Pipe tongs, scissors type, loop hdls, ca 1900, 10¾" 75.00
Pot lid, appl snake-shaped curved hdl, 6-lobed radial design 130.00
Sconce, cut-out pinwheel design, ca 1800, 19½" 400.00
Silk shears, spring hdl, ca 1800, 5" 65.00
Spider pan, 3 appl legs, curved hdl, 7¼x11⅝"+26" hdl 230.00
Sugar break/cutter, scissors type, 10⅜" 230.00
Tray, circular, 2 sq hdls, Am, 19th C, 17" dia 150.00

Yellow Ware

Ranging in color from buff to deep mustard, yellow ware which almost always has a clear glaze can be slip banded, plain, Rockingham decorated, flint enamel glazed, or mocha glazed. Mocha-decorated pieces, especially those which are red or black decorated, are usually the most expensive and desirable pieces to own. The majority of pieces are plain and do not bear a manufacturer's mark. Yellow ware which was primarily produced in the United States, England, and Canada was popular from the mid-19th century to the early 20th century. A utilitarian ware, it was first domestically produced in New York, Pennsylvania, and Vermont. With more than thirty active potteries, East Liverpool, Ohio, became the center for yellow ware production. Although other wares have become more popular, yellow ware is still being produced today in both England and the United States. Because of advanced collectors attempting to complete their collections, prices continue to rise. Note: Because this is a utilitarian ware, it is often found with damage and heavy wear; this would of course decrease its value. For further information we recommend *Collector's Guide to Yellow Ware* by Lisa S. McAlister and *Collecting Yellow Ware, An Identification and Value Guide*, written by our advisor, John Michel and Lisa S. McAlister. Mr. Michel's address is in the Directory under New York.

Bank, dog seated on base, gr/brn runs, sm chip, 7½" 1,045.00

Pitcher, Seaweed on cream with brown rings, 5", $565.00.

Bedpan, plain, from $25 to 65.00
Bowl, Seaweed, blk on ivory band w/2 bl stripes, 7½x3½" 350.00
Creamer, cow shaped, plain, minimum value 2,000.00
Creamer, Seaweed, bl on wht band w/brn stripes, 4¾", NM 440.00

Creamer, Seaweed, gr on wht band w/blk stripes, 3⅞", EX 165.00
Cruet, Rockingham glaze, orig pottery stopper, 1900-30, 10" 450.00
Dish, pudding; bl & wht banded, 4" dia 85.00
Flask, fish form, tiny imperfections, 11x5½" 1,300.00
Humidor, dk gr Seaweed, brn bands, soft clay, 1840-60, 5" 550.00
Mold, turtle shape, 1800s, 6x8" 600.00
Nappy, flower or heart-shaped ft, American, 1800s 250.00
Pepper pot, Seaweed, gr & bl slip bands, 1800s 595.00
Pie plate, Rockingham glaze, heart-shaped ft 175.00
Pie plate colander, plain yel, dtd October 8, 1861 ....495.00
Pitcher, mocha-decor band, formed wide spout, 8", minimum value ..1,000.00
Platter, plain, rctl, Am, 1850-90 ....525.00
Spice jar, wht bands w/names of spices, w/lid, sm 275.00
Tea bowl, 2 wide wht bands, ftd, 6", from $95 to 150.00
Teapot, basketweave design, Jeffords, dtd November 13, 1879 ...500.00
Teapot, emb leaves & stars, English, ca 1840, 1-cup 550.00

Zanesville Glass

Glassware was produced in Zanesville, Ohio, from as early as 1815 until 1851. Two companies produced clear and colored hollow ware pieces in five characteristic patterns: 1) diamond faceted, 2) broken swirls, 3) vertical swirls, 4) perpendicular fluting, 5) plain, with scalloped or fluted rims and strap handles. The most readily identified product is perhaps the whiskey bottles made in the vertical swirl pattern, often called globular swirls because of their full, round bodies. Their necks vary in width; some have a ringed rim and some are collared. They were made in several colors; amber, light green, and light aquamarine are the most common. Our advisor for this category is Mark Vuono; he is listed in the Directory under Connecticut.

Bottle, golden amber, globular, 24 right-swirled ribs, rolled rim, 9½" (rare size), $1,400.00.

Bottle, club, amber, 24 broken swirl ribs, appl lip, 8½" 360.00
Bottle, club, aqua, 24 broken swirl ribs, appl threading, 8½" 330.00
Bottle, globular, amber, 24 swirled ribs, stain, 7" 500.00
Bottle, globular, amber, 24 swirled ribs, stain, 8" 880.00
Bottle, globular, amber, 24 swirled ribs, stain, 9¼" 1,045.00
Bottle, globular, amber, 24 swirled ribs, terminal ring, 7¼" 1,200.00
Bottle, globular, citron, 24 swirled ribs, stain, 7" 990.00
Bottle, globular, dk amber, 24 melon ribs, 7⅝" 1,800.00
Bottle, globular, honey-olive, 24 melon ribs, appl lip, 8⅜" 550.00
Bottle, globular, honey-olive, 24 swirled ribs, 7¾" 1,300.00
Bottle, globular, lt olive, 24 swirled ribs, 8" 2,200.00
Bowl, lt gr, appl ft & folded rim, lt wear, 4⅞x7¼" 1,650.00
Bowl, milk; lt yel, folded rim, 3x9½" 2,100.00
Chestnut flask, amber, 10-Dmn, EX impression, 4½" 1,875.00
Chestnut flask, amber, 10-Dmn, 5⅛" 1,155.00
Chestnut flask, amber, 24 broken swirl ribs, high neck, 5½" ...1,155.00

Chestnut flask, amber, 24 swirled ribs, sheared lip, 4½" 330.00
Chestnut flask, aqua, 10-Dmn, EX impression, 5", NM 1,100.00
Chestnut flask, aqua, 24 ribs, sheared lip, 4⅞" 250.00
Chestnut flask, citron, 24 broken swirl ribs, lt wear, 5¼" 500.00
Creamer, aqua, hollow hdl, tooled lip, 4¾" 2,475.00
Grandfather's flask, amber, 24 broken swirl ribs w/popcorn effect, 8" ..4,600.00
Grandfather's flask, amber, 24 vertical ribs, flake, 8⅛" 660.00
Grandmother's flask, amber, 24 vertical ribs, flake, 7" 575.00
Grandmother's flask, amber, 24 vertical ribs, lt stain, 6¾" 715.00
Mug, aqua, appl hdl, 5½" 1,155.00
Sugar bowl, aqua, w/gallery & lid w/folded lip, 5¾" 5,500.00
Tumbler, aqua, 24 tightly swirled ribs, 5⅝" 745.00

Zell

The Georg Schmider United Zell Ceramic Factories has a long and colorful history. Affectionately called 'Zell' by those who are attracted to this charming German-Dutch type tin-glazed earthenware, this type of ware came into production in the latter part of the last century.

While Zell has created some lovely majolica-like examples (which are beginning to attract their own following), it is the German-Dutch scenes that are collected with such enthusiasm. Typical scenes are set against a lush green background with windmills on the distant horizon. Into the scenes appear typically garbed girls (long dresses with long white aprons and lowland bonnet head-gear) being teased or admired by little boys attired in pantaloon-type trousers and short rust-colored jackets, all wearing wooden shoes. There are variations on this theme, and occasionally a collector may find an animal theme or even a Kate Greenaway-like scene.

A similar ware in both theme, technique, and quality but bearing the mark Haag or Made in Austria is included in this listing.

While Zell produced a wide range of wares and even quite recently (1970s) introduced an entirely hand-painted hen/rooster line, it is this early charming German-Dutch theme pottery that is coveted by increasing numbers of devoted collectors. Our advisors for this category are Fred and Lila Shrader; they are listed in the Directory under California.

Key:
KG — Kate Greenaway style   MIA — Made in Austria

Bowl, boy/girl scenes, Zell, Germany, set of 3, 7", 9½", 12" 295.00
Bowl, chickens, flat, Haag, 5½" 35.00
Bowl, rim soup; children & storyteller, KG, Zell, Baden, 8½" 78.00
Bowl, rim soup; rooster decor, W Germany, 1970s, 9" dia 28.00
Box, rooster decor on heart shape, W Germany, 1970s, 4" W 22.00
Canister, children/windmills, Cinnamon, w/lid, sq, Zell, Germany, 3" ..68.00
Clock case, cathedral w/3" clock, children/windmills, Baden, 10" 325.00
Coffeepot, mother & child walk to harbor, w/lid, Zell, Germany, 8" .145.00
Creamer, boy walking on path, hdl, Zell, Germany, 4" 23.00
Creamer, pear shape, hdl at right angle to spout, Zell, Baden, 4" ..55.00
Cup & saucer, boys strolling, harbor beyond, Zell, Baden, farmer sz ..78.00
Cup & saucer, girl offers fish to cat, Zell, Baden, child sz 58.00
Mug, costumed animals partying, hdl, Haag, 4½" 38.00
Pitcher, sm boy listening/watching older boy, Zell, Germany, 6" ..78.00
Plate, boy & girl in Alps setting, Zell, Baden, 7" 55.00
Plate, girls w/cart being teased by boys, Zell, Baden, 6" 62.00
Plate, majolica-like w/flowers on basketweave, open hdls, Zell, 10" ...58.00
Plate, majolica-like w/richly colored fruit on basketweave, Zell, 8" 52.00
Proverb plate, Not All Good Deeds Go Unpunished, dogs, MIA, 8½" ..55.00

Sugar bowl, costumed cats, w/hdls & lid, Haag, 3¾" 45.00
Tumbler, children on path w/rabbits, Zell, Baden, 6-oz, 4" 56.00
Vase, humorous donkey cart scene, bulbous, MIA, 4¾" 135.00
Wall plaque, boy & girl kissing, brass rtcl fr, 12" dia 275.00

Zsolnay

Only until the past decade has the production of the Zsolnay factory become more correctly understood. In the beginning they produced only cement; industrial and kitchen ware manufacture began in the 1850s, and in the early 1870s a line of decorative architectural and art pottery was initiated which has continued to the present time.

The city of Pecs (pronounced Paach) is the major provincial city of southwest Hungary close to the Yugoslav border. The old German name for the city was Funfkirchen, meaning 'Five Churches.' (The 'five-steeple' mark became the factory's logo in 1878.)

Although most Americans only think of Zsolnay in terms of the bizarre, reticulated examples of the 1880s and '90s and the small 'Eosine' green figures of animals and children that have been produced since the 1920s, the factory went through all the art trends of major international art potteries and produced various types of forms and decorations. The 'golden period,' circa 1895 – 1920, is when its Art Nouveau (Sezession in Austro-Hungarian terms) examples were unequaled. Vilmos Zsolnay was a Renaissance man devoted to innovation, and his children carried on the tradition after his death in 1900. Important sculptors and artists of the day were employed (usually anonymously) and married into the family, creating a dynasty.

Nearly all Zsolnay is marked, either impressed 'Zsolnay Pecs' or with the 'five steeple' stamp. Variations and form numbers can date a piece fairly accurately. For the most part, the earlier ethnic historical-revival pieces do not bring the prices that the later Sezession and second Sezession (Deco) examples do. Our advisor for this category is John Gacher; he is listed in the Directory under Rhode Island.

Flask, Old Ivory Ware, fully marked, #2902, 14" with stopper, EX, $750.00.

Photo courtesy John Gacher

Dish, dove w/snail figural, gold irid, red mk, 5x11" 625.00
Ewer, diagonal emb bands of train & smoke, irid, 17", NM 2,000.00
Ewer, orchids, yel/gr on gr/brn, vine/berry hdl, #5743, 29" 650.00
Figural group, chickens on base, sgn Sinko, 7½" 160.00
Inkwell, dk gr irid w/orange eyes, #21032 H, 7¼x9", NM 400.00
Pitcher, pine cones/branches, gold irid on bl/cream mottle, mk, 7" .350.00

Advisory Board

The editors and staff take this opportunity to express our sincere gratitude and appreciation to each person who has in any way contributed to the preparation of this guide. We believe the credibility of our book is greatly enhanced through their efforts. See each advisor's Directory listing for information concerning their specific areas of expertise.

You will notice that at the conclusion of some of the narratives the advisor's name is given. This is optional and up to the discretion of each individual. Simply because no name is mentioned does not indicate that we have no advisor for that subject. Our board grows with each issue and now numbers nearly 450; if you care to correspond with any of them or anyone listed in our Directory, you must send a SASE with your letter. If you are seeking an appraisal, first ask about their fee, since many of these people are professionals who must naturally charge for their services. Because of our huge circulation, every person who allows us to publish their name runs the risk of their privacy being invaded by too many phone calls and letters. We are indebted to every advisor and very much regret losing any one of them. By far, the majority of those we lose give that reason. Please help us retain them on our board by observing the simple rules of common courtesy. Take the differences in time zones into consideration; some of our advisors tell us they often get phone calls in the middle of the night. For suggestions that may help you evaluate your holdings, see the Introduction.

AAA Antique Shop
Nappanee, Indiana

Peter Abrahams
Lake Oswego, Oregon

Charles and Barbara Adams
Middleboro, Massachusetts

Geneva D. Addy
Winterset, Iowa

Stan and Sally Alekna
Lebanon, Pennsylvania

Charles Alexander
Indianapolis, Indiana

Margaret Alves
Shelton, Connecticut

Craig Ambrose
Des Moines, Iowa

James Anderson
New Brighton, Minnesota

Suzy McLennan Anderson
Holmdel, New Jersey

Tim Anderson
Provo, Utah

Warren R. Anderson
Cedar City, Utah

Dan Andrews
Rancho Palos Verdes, California

Dorothy Malone Anthony
Fort Scott, Kansas

Una Arnbal
Ames, Iowa

Bruce A. Austin
Pittsford, New York

Bobby Babcock
Austin, Texas

Veldon Badders
Hamlin, New York

Rod Baer
Vienna, Virginia

Wayne and Gale Bailey
Dacula, Georgia

Jim Barker
Allentown, Pennsylvania

Kit Barry
Brattleboro, Vermont

Henry Bartsch
Rockaway, Oregon

Mark Bassett
Lakewood, Ohio

Dana Martin Batory
Crestline, Ohio

D.R. Beeks
Mt. Vernon, Iowa

Scott Benjamin
LaGrange, Ohio

Phyllis and Tom Bess
Tulsa, Oklahoma

Robert Bettinger
Mt. Dora, Florida

John E. Bilane
Union, New Jersey

William M. Bilsland III
Cedar Rapids, Iowa

Brenda Blake
York Harbor, Maine

Clarence H. Bodine, Jr.
New Hope, Pennsylvania

Sandra V. Bondhus
Unionville, Connecticut

Clifford Boram
Monticello, Indiana

Jeff Bradfield
Dayton, Virginia

Larry Brenner
Manchester, New Hampshire

William J. Brinkley
McLeansboro, Illinois

Mike Brooks
Oakland, California

Jim Broom
Effingham, Illinois

David L. Brown
Victoria, British Columbia, Canada

Marcia Brown
White City, Oregon

Rick Brown
Newspaper Collector's Society of America
Lansing, Michigan

Nicki Budin
Worthington, Ohio

Robert C. Butz
Newbury Park, California

Jim Calison
Wallkill, New York

Carol and Jim Carlton
Englewood, Colorado

Tina M. Carter
El Cajon, California

Gene Cataldo
Huntsville, Alabama

Cerebro
East Prospect, Pennsylvania

Mick and Lorna Chase
Cookeville, Tennessee

Jack Chipman
Venice, California

Pat and Chris Christensen
Costa Mesa, California

Joan Cimini
Belmont, Ohio

Debbie and Randy Coe
Lafayette, Oregon

Wilfred and Dolli Cohen
Santa Ana, California

Marilyn Cooper
Houston, Texas

Ryan Cooper
Yarmouthport, Massachusetts

J.W. Courter
Kevil, Kentucky

Susan N. Cox
El Cajon, California

Rosalind Cranor
Blacksburg, Virginia

Bob Culver
Northville, Michigan

Ron Damaska
New Brighton, Pennsylvania

John Danis
Rockford, Illinois

Patricia M. Davis
Portland, Oregon

Loretta DeLozier
Bedford, Iowa

Joe Devine
Council Bluffs, Iowa

Doug Dezso
Maywood, New Jersey

David Dilley
Indianapolis, Indiana

Thomas P. Dimitroff
Corning, New York

Ginny Distel
Tiffin, Ohio

Rod Dockery
Ft. Worth, Texas

L.R. 'Les' Docks
San Antonio, Texas

Rebecca Dodds
Ft. Lauderdale, Florida

Maryanne Dolan
Pleasant Hill, California

Ron Donnelly
Tuscaloosa, Alabama

Robert A. Doyle, C.A.I., I.S.A.
Pleasant Valley, New York

James Dryden
Hot Springs National Park, Arkansas

Louise Dumont
Leesburg, Florida

Pat and Ann Duncan
Cape Fair, Missouri

Ken and Jackie Durham
Washington, DC

William Durham
Belvidere, Illinois

Rita and John Ebner
Columbus, Ohio

Bill Edwards
Madison, Indiana

Larry Egelhoff
Indianapolis, Indiana

J. David Ehrhard
Tujunga, California

Michael L. Ellis
Costa Mesa, California

Dr. Robert Elsner
Boynton Beach, Florida

Barbara Endter
Rochester, New York

Charlotte Safir
New York, New York

Martha and Steve Sanford
Campbell, California

R.J. Sayers
Brevard, North Carolina

Elizabeth Schaaf
Mentone, Alabama

Roselle Schleifman
Spring Valley, New York

Jim Schleyer
Burke, Virginia

Betty and Larry Schwab
Bloomington, Illinois

Roger R. Scott
Tulsa, Oklahoma

Virgil Scowden
Williamsport, Indiana

Joyce and Harold Screen
Baltimore, Maryland

Cathy Segelke
Merino, Colorado

Lila and Fred Shrader
Crescent City, California

Brenda and Jerry Siegel
St. Louis, Missouri

Karen Silvermintz
Dallas, Texas

David Smies
Manhattan, Kansas

Allan Smith
Sherman, Texas

Carole and Richard Smyth
Huntington, New York

Charlie and Rose Snyder
Independence, Kansas

Diane Snyder-Haug
St. Petersburg, Florida

Dick Spencer
O'Fallon, Illinois

Rick Spencer
Salt Lake City, Utah

Greg Spiess
Joliet, Illinois

Nancy Steinbock
Albany, New York

Stella's Collectibles
Torrance, California

Ron Stewart
Combs, Kentucky

Donna and Craig Stifter
Naperville, Illinois

Liz Stillwell
Pico Rivera, California

Dick Strickfaden
Pekin, Illinois

Pamela and Joseph Tanner
Spokane, Washington

Jenny Tarrant
St. Peters, Missouri

Terry Taylor
East Bend, North Carolina

Bruce Thalberg
Weston, Connecticut

Sharon Thoerner
Bellflower, California

Chuck Thompson
Houston, Texas

Don Thornton
Sunnyvale, California

Rosella Tinsley
Osawatomie, Kansas

Marlena Toohey
Longmont, Colorado

Veronica Trainer
Cleveland, Ohio

Dan Tucker
Toledo, Ohio

Valerie and Richard Tucker
Argyle, Texas

Robert Tuggle
New York, New York

John Tutton
Front Royal, Virginia

Hobart D. Van Deusen
Watertown, Connecticut

Jean and Dale Van Kuren
Clarence Center, New York

Joan F. Van Patten
Rexford, New York

Janice and Duane Vanderbilt
Indianapolis, Indiana

Norm Vigue
Goffstown, Massachusetts

Linda L. Vines
Upper Montclair, New Jersey

Stephen Visakay
West Caldwell, New Jersey

Mark Vuono
Stamford, Connecticut

John W. Waddell
Mineral Wells, Texas

Jim Waite
Farmer City, Illinois

John Walter
Marietta, Ohio

Judith and Robert Walthall
Huntsville, Alabama

Ian Warner
Brampton, Ontario, Canada

Kitty Watson
Guthrie, Oklahoma

Maret Webb
Phoenix, Arizona

Marty Webster
Saline, Michigan

David Weddington
Murfreesboro, Tennessee

Robert Weisblut
Wheaton, Maryland

Pastor Frederick S. Weiser
New Oxford, Pennsylvania

BA Wellman
Westminster, Massachusetts

Rosalie J. 'Rosie' Wells
Canton, Illinois

David Wendel
Poplar Bluff, Missouri

Kaye and Jim Whitaker
Lynnwood, Washington

John 'Grandpa' White
Denver, Colorado

Douglass White
Orlando, Florida

Margaret and Kenn Whitmyer
Gahanna, Ohio

Steven Whysel
Plantation, Florida

Robert Wieland
Ormond Beach, Florida

Doug Wiesehan
St. Charles, Missouri

James R. Wilkins
Duncanville, Texas

Don Williams
Kirksville, Missouri

Ron L. Willis
Moore, Oklahoma

Roy M. Willis
Lebanon Junction, Kentucky

Jack D. Wilson
Chicago, Illinois

Grant S. Windsor
Richmond, Virginia

Ralph Winslow
Laurie, Missouri

Nancy Winston
Northwood, New Hampshire

Jo Ellen Winther
Arvada, Colorado

Raphael C. Wise
West Palm Beach, Florida

Bill Wright
New Albany, Indiana

Libby Yalom
Adelphi, Maryland

Darlene Yohe
Stuttgart, Arkansas

Mary Young
Kettering, Ohio

Charles S. Zayic
Ellsworth, Maine

Chjarles Zayick
Ellsworth, Maine

Audrey Zeder
North Bend, Washington

Auction Houses

We wish to thank the following auction houses whose catalogs have been used as sources for pricing information. Many have granted us permission to reproduce their photographs as well.

A-1 Auction Service
2042 N. Rio Grande Ave., Suite 'E,' Orlando, FL 32804; 407-839-0004. Specializing in American antique sales

A&B Auctions, Inc.
Marlboro, MA; 508-480-0006 or fax 508-460-6101. Specializing in English ceramics, flow blue, pottery, and Mason's Ironstone

Absolute Auction & Realty, Inc./Pleasant Valley Auction Hall
Robert Doyle
PO Box 1739, Pleasant Valley, NY 12569. Antique and estate auctions twice a month at Pleasant Valley Auction Hall; Free calendar of auctions; Web site: www.auctionweb.com/aarny and absoluteauctionrealty.com

Alex G. Malloy, Inc.
PO Box 38, South Salem, NY 10590; 203-438-0396. Specializing in ancient and medieval coins, antiquities, numismatic literature; 4 mail bid auctions per year

Allard Auctions Inc.
Col. Doug Allard
PO Box 460, St. Ignatius, MT 59865-0460; 406-745-2951 or fax 406-745-2961

America West Archives
Anderson, Warren
PO Box 100, Cedar City, UT 84721; 435-586-9497; e-mail: awa@netutah.com. Publishes 26-page illustrated catalog 6 times a year that includes auction section of scarce and historical early western documents, letters, autographs, stock certificates, and other important ephemera, Subscription: $15 per year

Americana Auctions
c/o Glen Rairigh
12633 Sandborn, Sunfield, MI 48890. Specializing in Skookum dolls and antique auctions

Anderson Auctions/Heritage Antiques & Appraisal Services
Suzy McLennan Anderson
65 E. Main St., Holmdel, NJ 07733; 908-946-8801 or fax 908-946-1036. Specializing in American furniture and decorative accessories

Andre Ammelounx
The Stein Company
PO Box 136, Palatine, IL 60078; 847-991-5927 or fax 847-991-5947. Specializing in steins, catalogs available

Anthony J. Nard & Co.
U.S. Rt. 220, Milan, PA 18831; 717-888-9404 or fax 717-888-7723

Aston Macek Auctioneers and Appraisers
2825 Country Club Rd., Endwell, NY 13760-3349; Phone/fax: 607-785-6598. Specializing in and appraisers of Americana, folk art, other primitives, furniture, Shaker, fine art, porcelain, and china; Also have auctions on the Internet: ebay (folkman 2) and ehammer (folkman@stnylrun.com)

Bill Bertoia Auctions
2413 Madison Ave., Vineland, NJ 08360; 609-692-4092 or fax 609-692-8697. Specializing in toys, dolls, advertising, and related items

Bider's
241 S. Union St., Lawrence, MA 01843; 508-688-4347 or 508-683-3944. Antiques appraised, purchased, and sold on consignment

Brian Riba Auctions Inc.
PO Box 53, Main St., S. Glastonbury, CT 06073; 203-633-3076

Buffalo Bay Auction Co.
5244 Quam Circle, Rogers, MN 55374; 612-428-8480; or fax 612-428-8879; e-mail: buffalobay@aol.com. Specializing in advertising, tins and country store items.

Butterfield & Butterfield
220 San Bruno Ave., San Francisco, CA 94103; 415-861-7500 or fax 415-861-8951. Also located at: 7601 Sunset Blvd., Los Angeles, CA 90046; 213-850-7500 or fax 213-850-5843 and 441 West Huron St., Chicago, IL 60610; 312-377-7500 or fax 312-377-7501. Fine Art Auctioneers and Appraisers since 1865; Web site: www.butterfields.com

Butterfield & Dunning
441 W. Huron St., Chicago, IL 60610; 312-664-8400; www.butterfields.com

Cerebro
PO Box 327, E. Prospect, PA 17317-0327; 717-252-2400 or 800-69-LABEL; fax: 717-252-3685; e-mail: Cerebro@Cerebro.com. Specializing in antique advertising labels, especially cigar box labels, cigar bands, food labels, firecracker labels; holds semiannual auction on tobacco ephemera; consignments accepted

Charles E. Kirtley
PO Box 2273, Elizabeth City, NC 27096; 919-335-1262. Specializing in World's Fair, Civil War, political, advertising and other American collectibles

Cincinnati Art Gallery
225 E. Sixth St, Cincinnati, OH 45202; 513-381-2128. Specializing in American art pottery, American and European fine paintings, watercolors

Collector's Auction Services
R.D. 2, Box 431, Oil City, PA 16301; 814-677-6070. Specializing in advertising, oil and gas, toys, rare museum and investment-quality antiques

Collector's Sales & Service
PO Box 4037, Middletown, RI 02842; 401-849-5012 or fax 401-846-6156

Country Girls Estate & Appraisal Service
Diane Patalano
PO Box 144, Saddle River, NJ 07458

Dargate Auction Galleries
5607 Baum Boulevard, Pittsburgh, PA 15206; 412-362-3558
Specializing in estate auctions featuring fine art, antiques, and collectibles

David Rago
20th Century Design
Auction hall: 333 N. Main, Lambertville, NJ 08530; 609-397-9330; Gallery: 17 S. Main St., Lambertville, NJ 08530. Specializing in American art pottery and Arts & Crafts

Dunbar's Gallery
Leila and Howard Dunbar
76 Haven St., Milford, MA 01757; 508-634-8697 or fax 508-634-8698

Du Mouchelles
409 Jefferson Ave., Detroit, MI 48226

Early American Numismatics
Dana Linett, President
PO Box 2442, La Jolla, CA 92038

Early Auction Co.
123 Main St., Milford, OH 45150

Flying Deuce Auctions & Antiques
1224 Yellowstone Ave., Pocatello, ID 83201; 208-237-2002 or fax: 208-237-4544; e-mail: flying2@nicoh.com or Web site: www.flying2.com

Frank's Antiques & Auctions
2405 N. Kings Rd., Hilliard, FL 32046; 904-845-2870 or fax 904-845-4000. Specializing in antique advertising, country store items, rec room and restaurant decor as well as sporting collectibles, pottery and stoneware; catalogs issued

Freeman Fine Arts
1808 Chestnut St., Philadelphia, PA 19103; 215-563-9275 or fax 215-563-8236

Full House
Gene Willett
9090 Cherokee, Clarkston, MI 48348; 248-394-0313. Specializing in mail-bid playing card auctions

Garth's Auctions Inc.
2690 Stratford Rd., Box 369, Delaware, OH 43015; 740-362-4771

Glass-Works Auctions
James Hagenbuch
102 Jefferson, East Greenville, PA 18041; 215-679-5849. America's leading auction company in early American bottles and glass and barber shop memorabilia

Hake's Americana & Collectibles
Specializing in character and personality collectibles along with all artifacts of popular culture for over 32 years. To receive a catalog for their next 3,000-item mail/phone bid auction, send $5 to Hake's Americana, PO Box 1444M, York, PA 17405

Hanna-Whysel Auctioneers & Appraisers
Steven Whysel
3403 Bella Vista Way, Bella Vista, AR, 72714; 501-855-9600. Antiques and art auctions

Harmer Rooke Galleries
32 E. 57th St, 11th Floor, New York, NY 10022; 212-751-1900 or fax 212-758-1713

Henry/Pierce Auctioneers
1456 Carson Court, Homewood, IL 60430; 708-798-7508. Specializing in bank auctions

High Noon
9929 Venice Blvd., Los Angeles, CA 90034; 310-202-9010 or fax: 310-202-9011. Specialing in cowboy and western collectibles

History Buff's Auctions
Specializing in paper collectibles spanning 5 centuries; Contact at 517-887-1225; www./historybuff.com/auction or auction@historybuff.com

Horst Auctioneers
Horst Auction Center
50 Durlach Rd. (corner of Rt. 322 & Durlach Rd., West of Ephrata), Ephrata, Lancaster County, PA 17522; 717-859-1331 or 717-738-3080. Voices of Experience

Jack Sellner
Sellner Marketing of California
PO Box 308, Fremont, CA 94537; 510-792-9463

Jackson's, Auctioneers & Appraisers of Fine Art
2229 Lincoln St., Cedar Falls, IA 50613; 319-277-2256 or fax 319-277-1252. Specializing also in art pottery, jewelry, and decorative arts

James D. Julia
PO Box 830, Rt. 201, Skowhegan Rd., Fairfield, ME 04937; 207-453-7125 or fax 207-453-2502; e-mail: jjulia@juliaauctions.com; web site: www.juliaauctions.com

James R. Bakker Antiques, Inc.
James R. Bakker
370 Broadway, Cambridge, MA 02139; 617-864-7067. Specializing in American paintings, prints, and decorative arts

James J. Reeves
PO Box 219, 328 Allegheny St., Huntingdon, PA 16652; 814-643-5497 or fax 814-641-2600; Reeves5@vicon.net; www.JamesJReeves.com. Monthly mail-bid catalog dealing with stamps, coins, railroadiana, sports cards, comics, and all shippable antiques/collectibles

John Toomey Gallery
818 North Blvd., Oak Park, IL 60301; 708-383-5234 or fax 708-383-4828. Specializing in furniture and decorative arts of the Arts & Crafts, Art Deco, and Modern Design movements; Modern Design Expert: Richard Wright

Joy Luke Auctioneers & Appraisers
The Gallery
300 East Grove St., Bloomington, IL 61701; 309-828-5533 or fax 309-829-2266; web site: www.joyluke.com; e-mail: joyluke@aol.com

Kerry & Judy's Toys
7370 Eggleston Rd., Memphis, TN 31825-2112; 901-757-1722. Specializing in toys, 1920s – 1960s; consignments always welcome

Kit Barry Ephemera Auctions
88 High St., Brattleboro, VT 05301; 802-254-3634. Tradecard and ephemera auctions, fully illustrated catalogs with prices realized; consignment inquiries welcome

Kurt R. Krueger
160 N. Washington St., PO Box 275, Iola, WI 54945-0275

L.R. 'Les' Docks
Box 691035, San Antonio, TX 78269-1035. Providing occasional mail-order record auctions, rarely consigned; The only consignments considered are exceptionally scarce and unusual records.

Lloyd Ralston Toys
447 Stratford Rd., Fairfield, CT 06432

Majolica Auctions
Michael G. Strawser
200 North Main, PO Box 332, Wolcottville, IN 46795; 219-854-2859 or fax 219-854-3979. Issues color catalogs

Manion's International Auction House, Inc.
PO Box 12214, Kansas City, KS 66112; 913-299-6692 or fax 913-299-6792; e-mail: manions@qni.com URL: www.manions.com. Specializing in international militaria, particularly the US, Germany, and Japan. Extensive catalogs in antiques and collectibles, sports, transportation, political, and advertising memorabilia and vintage clothing and denim. Publishes 9 catalogs for each of the 5 categories per year. Request a free sample of past auctions, 1 issue of current auction for $7 or a 6-catalog subscription for $35.

Maritime Auctions
935 US Rt. 1, PO Box 322, York, ME 03909-0322; 207-363-4247 or fax 353-1415; Web site: www.maritiques.com; Auction: www.eswap.com

McMasters Doll Auctions
PO Box 1755, 5855 Glenn Highway, Cambridge, OH 43725; 740-432-4419 or fax 740-432-3191; or 800-842-3526

Michael Ivankovich Auctions, Inc.
PO Box 2458, Doylestown, PA, 18901; 215-345-6094. Specializing in early hand-colored photography and prints. Auction held 4 times each year, providing opportunity for collectors and dealers to compete for the largest variety of Wallace Nutting and Wallace Nutting-Like pictures available anywhere.

Michael John Verlangieri
Calpots.com
PO Box 844, Cambria, CA 93428; 805-927-4428. Specializing in fine California pottery; cataloged auctions (video tapes available); www.calpots.com

Monsen & Baer, Annual Perfume Bottle Auction
Monsen, Randall; and Baer, Rod
Box 529, Vienna, VA 22183; 703-938-2129 or fax 703-242-1357. Cataloged auctions of perfume bottles; will purchase, sell, and accept consignments; specializing in commercial, Czechoslovakian, Lalique, Baccarat, Victorian, crown top, factices, miniatures

Neal Auction Company
4038 Magazine St., New Orleans, LA 70115; 504-899-5329 or 1-800-467-5329; fax 504-897-3803

Noel Barrett Antiques & Auctions
PO Box 1001, Carversville, PA 18913; 215-297-5109 or fax 215-297-0457

New England Absentee Auctions
16 6th St., Stamford, CT 06905; 203-975-9055. Specializing in Quimper pottery

Norman C. Heckler & Company
79 Bradford Corner Rd., Woodstock Valley, CT 06282; 860-974-1634 or fax 860-974-2003. Auctioneers and appraisers specializing in early glass and bottles

Nostalgia Co.
21 S. Lake Dr., Hackensack, NJ 07601; 201-488-4536

Past Tyme Pleasures
Steve Howard
2491 San Ramon Blvd., San Ramon, CA 94583; 925-484-4488 or fax 925-484-2551. Offers 2 absentee auction catalogs per year pertaining to old advertising items

Phillips
406 E. 79th St., New York, NY 10021

Postcards International
Martin J. Shapiro
2321 Whitney Ave., Suite 102, PO Box 185398; Hamden, CT 06518; 203-248-6621 or fax 203-248-6628; www.vintagepostcards.com

Rafael Osona, Auctioneer & Appraiser
PO Box 2607, Nantucket, MA 02584; 508-228-3942. Specializing in Americana, fine arts, continental & marine antiques, Nantucket baskets, art, and memorabilia

Refinders
737 Barberry Rd., Highland Park, IL 60035; 708-831-1102 or 708-831-1160. Refinders will find your wants from 1860 to 1960

Richard Opfer Auctioneering, Inc.
1919 Greenspring Dr., Timonium, MD 21093; 410-252-5035; fax: 410-252-5863; web site: www.opferauction.com; e-mail: info@opferauction.com

Roan, Inc.
R.R. 4, Box 118, Cogan Station, PA 17728-9334

Rosen Estate Sales & Appraisals, Inc.
Kenna Rosen
9138 Loma Vista, Dallas, TX 75243; 972-503-1436; e-mail: kerosen@swbell.net. Specializing in quality estate sales

Schoolmaster Auctions and Collectibles
Kenn Norris
PO Box 4830; 513 N. 2nd St., Sanderson, TX 79848; 915-345-2640. Specializing in school-related items, barbed wire and related literature, and L'il Abner

Shot Glass Exchange
PO Box 219, Western Springs, IL, 60558; 706-246-1559. Publishes mail-auction catalog twice yearly

Skinner, Inc.
Auctioneers & Appraisers of Antiques and Fine Arts
The Heritage on the Garden, 63 Park Plaza, Boston, MA 02116; 617-350-5400 or fax 617-350-5429. Second address: 357 Main Street, Bolton, MA 01740; 978-779-6241 or fax 978-779-5144

Smith & Jones, Inc.
12 Clark Lane, Sudbury, MA 01776; 508-443-5517 or fax 508-443-8045. Specializing in Dedham dinnerware, Buffalo china and important American art pottery; Full-color catalogs available

Soldiers Trunk
60 Craigs Rd., Windsor, CT 06095; 203-688-0580. Specializing in American and foreign military items; 4 catalog issues for $20

SOLDUSA.COM, formerly Dixie Sporting Collectibles
1206 Rama Rd., Charlotte, NC 28211; 704-364-2900 or 877-SoldUSA; fax 704-364-2322; e-mail: gun1898@aol.com; Internet: www.sportauction.com. Specializing in fine sporting collectibles

Sotheby's
1334 York Ave., New York, NY 10021

Stanton's Auctioneers & Realtors
144 S. Main St., PO Box 146, Vermontville, MI 49096; 517-726-0181 or fax 517-726-0060. Specializing in all types of property, at auction, anywhere.

Steffen Historical Militaria
Roger S. Steffen
14 Murnan Rd., Cold Springs, KY 41076; 606-431-4499. Specializing in quality militaria, military art, rare books, antique firearms

Three Rivers Collectibles
Wendy and Leo Frese
PO Box 551542, Dallas, TX 75355; 214-341-5165. Annual Red Wing and Rum-Rill pottery and stoneware auctions

Toy Scouts, Inc.
137 Casterton Ave., Akron, OH 44303; 330-836-0668 or fax: 330-869-8668; e-mail: toyscouts@toyscouts.com or web site: www.toyscouts.com. Specializing in baby-boom era collectibles.

Tradewinds Auctions
Henry Taron
PO Box 249, Manchester-By-The-Sea, MA 01944-0249; 508-768-3327

Treadway Gallery, Inc.
2029 Madison Rd., Cincinnati, OH 45208; 513-321-6742 or fax 513-871-7722; web site: www.treadwaygallery.com. Specializing in American Art Pottery; American and European art glass; European ceramics; Italian glass; fine American and European paintings and graphics; and furniture and decorative arts of the Arts & Crafts, Art Nouveau, Art Deco, and Modern Design Movements. Modern Design expert: Thierry Lorthioir. Members: National Antique Dealers Association, American Art Pottery Association, International Society of Appraisers, American Ceramic Arts Society, Ohio Decorative Arts Society, Art Gallery Association of Cincinnati

Vogel Auction
4720 S.E. Fort King St., Ocala, FL 34470-1501; 352-694-5776; e-mail: Vogels@atlantic.net. Specializing in souvenir china

Vicki and Bruce Waasdorp
PO Box 434; 10931 Main St.; Clarence, NY 14031; 716-759-2361 or www.antiques-stoneware.com. Specializing in decorated stoneware

Weschler's
Adam A. Weschler & Son
905 E. St. N.W., Washington, DC 20004

Willis Henry Auctions
22 Main St., Marshfield, MA 02050

Directory of Contributors

When contacting any of the buyers/sellers listed in this part of the Directory by mail, you must include an SASE (stamped, self-addressed envelope) if you expect a reply. As hectic as our lifestyles are, the time it saves them is probably worth more to them than the price of a stamp. Not only that, but trying to decipher someone's handwritten name and address can be very frustrating. Sometimes even zip codes are unreadable, and even more time is required to double check zip code numbers. And in the end, if 'Rosen' becomes 'Rirer' and 'Ave. 5' becomes 'Ave. S,' even if the person you contacted was gracious enough to answer you, you probably won't ever know he did. Many of these people are professional appraisers and there will be a fee for their time and service. Find out up front. Include a clear photo if you want an item identified. Most items cannot be described clearly enough to make an identification without a photo.

If you call and get their answering machine, when you leave your number so that they can return your call, tell them to call back collect. And please take the differences in time zones into consideration. 7:00 AM in the Midwest is only 4:00 AM in California! And if you're in California, remember that even 7:00 PM is too late to call the East Coast. Most people work and are gone during the daytime. Even some of our antique dealers say they prefer after-work phone calls. Don't assume that a person who deals in a particular field will be able to help you with related items. They may seem related to you when they are not.

Please, we need your help. This book sells in such great numbers that allowing their names to be published can create a potential nightmare for each advisor and contributor. Please do your part to help us minimize this, so that we can retain them on our board and in turn pass their experience and knowledge on to you through our book. Their only obligation is to advise us, not to evaluate your holdings. Many of our people tell us that even with the occasional problem, they feel that the good outweighs the bad and makes all their hard work worthwhile.

Alabama

Cataldo, Gene
Gene's Cameras
2614 Artie St., S.W., Suite 37, Huntsville, 35805; 256-536-6893. Specializing in classic and used cameras

Donnelly, Ron
Saturday Heroes
6302 Championship Dr., Tuscaloosa, 35405. Specializing in Big Little Books, movie posters, premiums, western heroes, Gone With the Wind, character collectibles, early Disney; inquiries require SASE; no free appraisals

Lippa, Matt; and Schaaf, Elizabeth
Artisans
PO Box 256, Mentone, 35984; 256-634-4037. Specializing in folk art, quilts, painted and folky furniture, tramp art, whirligigs, windmill weights; further contacts: www.folkartisans.com or artisans@folkartisans.com

Walthall, Judith and Robert
PO Box 4465, Huntsville, 35815; 256-881-9198. Judith founded Peanut Pals in 1978. Robert is serving second term as president of Peanut Pals. Specializing in Planters Peanuts memorabilia; also Old Crow collectibles.

Arizona

Moyer, Patsy
1385 Iron Springs Rd., Suite #108, Prescot, 86301. Author (Collector Books) specializing in dolls

Nelson, Maxine
7657 E. Hazelwood St., Scottsdale, 85251. Specializing in Vernon Kilns; Author of *Collectible Vernon Kilns* (out of print). SASE appreciated for inquiries.

Webb, Maret
Vehr/Webb Studio Architects
4118 E. Vernon Ave., Phoenix, 85008-2333; 602-957-0653 or fax 602-957-1631. Specializing in Swarovski crystal; founder of Swan Seekers Network

Arkansas

Dryden, James
Dryden Pottery
PO Box 603, Hot Springs National Park, 71902; 501-627-4201. Specializing in hand-thrown artware vases, mugs, ovenware, etc.

Freyaldenhoven, Tony
PO Box 1295, Conway, 72033; 501-329-0628 or e-mail: camarket@cyberback.com. Specializing in Camark pottery

Musgrave, Marge
Look Nook Antiques
10757 Hwy. 5-S, Salesville, 72653-9698; 870-499-5283. Specializing in colored Victorian and art glass

Roneigk, Martin
Crescent Hotel & Spa
75 Prospect St., Eureka Springs, 72632; 800-671-6333 or mroenigk@aol.com. Specializing in mechanical musical instruments, music boxes, band organs, musical clocks and watches, coin pianos, orchestrions, monkey organs, automata, mechanical birds, and dolls, etc.

Yohe, Darlene
Timberview Antiques
PO Box 343, Stuttgart, 72160; 870-673-3437. Specializing in American pattern glass, historical glass, Victorian pattern glass, carnival glass, and custard glass

California

Aldrich, Jon Wm.
Jon Aldrich Antique Aero
PO Box 706, Groveland, 95321; 209-962-6121. Specializing in vintage aviation

Andrews, Dan
27105 Shorewood Rd., Rancho Palos Verdes, 90275; 310-541-5149 or e-mail: brewpub@earthlink.net. Specializing in beer cans, breweriana

Berg, Paul
PO Box 8895, Newport Beach, 92620. Author of *Nineteenth Century Photographica Cases and Wall Frames*

Brooks, Mike
7335 Skyline, Oakland, 94611; 510-339-1751 (evenings). Specializing in typewriters, transistor radios, early televisions, Statue of Liberty

Butz, Robert C.
Collector's Wedgwood
PO Box 462, Newbury Park, 91319. Specializing in Wedgwood; SASE required for reply

Carter, Tina M.
882 S. Mollison, El Cajon, 92020; 619-440-5043. Specializing in teapots, tea-related items, tea tins, children's and toy tea sets, plastic cookie cutters, etc.; Book on teapots available. Send $16 (includes postage) or $17 for CA residents, Canada: add $5, to above address

Chipman, Jack
California Spectrum
PO Box 1079, Venice, 90294-1079. Specializing in California ceramics; author of *Collector's Encyclopedia of California Pottery*, and *Collector's Encyclopedia of Bauer Pottery*, autographed copies available from author; either book: $28.45 ppd., +(CA) tax of $2.35

Christensen, Pat and Chris
1067 Salvador St., Costa Mesa, 92626. Specializing in open salts

Cohen, Wilfred and Dolli
Antiques & Art Glass
PO Box 27151, Santa Ana, 92799; 714-545-5673. Specializing in Wave Crest (C.F. Monroe); Victorian-era art and pattern glass (salt shakers, toothpick holders, syrups, cruets, sugar shakers, tumblers, biscuit jars, table and pitcher sets); art glass and cameo glass open salts; custard and ruby-stained glass; burmese, peachblow, and amberina glass; pottery by Moorcroft (pre-1935 only); Buffalo (Deldare and Emerald ware); Polia Pillin; Shelley China; Chintz China; and Clarice Cliff. Please include SASE for reply.

Conroy, Barbara J.
PO Box 2369, Santa Clara, 95055-2369; e-mail: restaurantchina@earthlink.net. Specializing in Commercial China; author and historian

Cox, Susan N.
800 Murray Drive, El Cajon, 92020; 619-697-5922; e-mail: Antiquefever@aol.com. Specializing in California pottery and Frankoma

Ehrhard, J. David
Psycho-Ceramic Restorations
7212 Valmont St., Tujunga, 91042. Specializing in restoration of ceramics, collects Susie Cooper and other British pottery, Mabel Lucie Attwell, 'Old Bill' china by Grimades, etc., Artist: Bruce Bairnsfather

Ellis, Michael L.
266 Rose Ln., Costa Mesa, 92627; 949-646-7112; fax 949-645-4919; toll free (book orders): 877-646-7119. Author (Collector Books) of *Collector's Guide to Don Winton Designs, Identification & Values*; specializing in Twin Winton

Enge, Delleen
Franciscan Dinnerware Matching Service
323 E. Matilija, Ste. 112, Ojai, 93023.

Fogleman, Marv
Marv's Memories
1814 W. Carriage Dr., Santa Ana, 92704. Specializing in Western Dinnerware, Metlox, Mikasa, and Franciscan

George, Tony
22431-B160 Antonio Pkwy., #252, Rancho Santa Margarita, 92688; 714-589-6075. Specializing in watch fobs

Giacomini, Mary Jane
PO Box 404, Ferndale, 95536-0404; e-mail: Giaco@humboldt1.com. Author of *American Bisque, A Collector's Guide With Prices*; specializing in American Bisque Pottery, cookie jars

Gibson, Pat
38280 Guava Dr., Newark, 94560; 510-792-0586. Specializing in R.A. Fox

Gunther, Candace (Candelaine)
Specializing in Steiff and Schuco bears and animals; send SASE for list; Phone: 616-796-4568; fax: 626-796-7172; e-mail: candelaine@aol.com

Harrison, Gwynne
PO Box 1, Mira Loma, 91752-0001; 909-685-5434. Specializing in Autumn Leaf (Jewel Tea)

Hibbard, Suzi
WanderWares
849 Vintage Ave., Fairfield, 94585. Specializing in Dragonware, 1000 Faces china, other Orientalia; inquiries should be accompanied by LSASE; also available at: SRHACS@Pacbell.net

Howard, Steve
Past Tyme Pleasures
2491 San Ramon Valley Blvd., Suite #1-204, San Ramon, 94583; 925-484-4488 or fax 925-494-2552. Specializing in antique American firearms, bowie knives, Western Americana, old advertising, and vintage gambling items

Inouye, Roger
1401 E. Santo Antonio Dr., Apt. 306, Colton, CA 92324. Specializing in Trolls

Main Street Antique Mall
237 E Main St., El Cajon, 92020; 619-447-0800

Maurer, Oveda L.
Oveda Maurer Antiques
34 Greenfield Ave., San Anselmo, 94960; 415-454-6439. Specializing in 18th-century and early 19th-century American furniture, lighting, pewter, hearthware, glass, folk art, and paintings

The Meadows Collection
Mark and Adela Meadows
PO Box 819, Carnelian Bay, 96104; 530-546-5516 or e-mail: meadows@cwo.com. Specializing in Gouda and Quimper; lecturers, authors of *Quimper Pottery, A Guide to Origins, Styles, and Values*, serving on the board of directors of the Associated Antiques Dealers of America; please include SASE for inquiries

Pardini, Dick
3107 N. El Dorado St., Dept. SAPG, Stockton, 95204-3412; 209-466-5550 (recorder may answer). Specializing in California Perfume Company items dating from 1886 to 1928 and 'go-with' related companies: buyer and information center. Not interested in items that have Avon, Perfection, or Anniversary Keepsake markings. California Perfume Company offerings must be accompanied by a photo, photocopy, or sketching along with a condition report and, most importantly, price wanted. Inquiries require large SASE and must state what information you are seeking; not necessary if offering items for sale.

Pasquali, Jim
479 Church #4, San Francisco, 94114; 415-861-4184. Author of book on Garden City Pottery

Roller, Gayle
PO Box 222, San Marcos, 92079-0222. Specializing in Hagen-Renaker

Rosewitz, Michele
3165 McKinley, San Bernardino, 92404; 909-862-8534; e-mail: rosetree@sprint-mail.com. Specializing in glass knives manufactured in the USA during the 1920s through the 1950s; all requests for information should include a SASE

Sanford, Steve and Martha
230 Harrison Ave., Campbell, 95008; 408-978-8408. Authors of 2 books on Brush-McCoy and *Sanfords Guide to McCoy Pottery* (available from the authors)

Shrader, Fred and Lila
Shrader Antiques
2025 Hwy. 199, Crescent City, 95531; 707-458-3525. Specializing in railroad, steamship, and other transportation memorabilia; Shelley china (and its predecessor, Foley China); Buffalo china and Buffalo Pottery including Deldare; Niloak, and Zell (and Haag)

Stella's Collectibles
Pieces of the Past
19032 S. Vermont Ave., Gardena, (Space 11), 90248; 310-316-7198; Julie's Antiques, Long Beach (Space 24); Westchester Faire Mall (Space 320); Enchanted Treasures, Lake Elsinore (Space 25); Collector's Corral, Lake Elsinore. Specializing in quality glass and china

Stillwell, Liz
Our Attic Antiques & Belleek
PO Box 1074, Pico Rivera, 90660; 323-257-3879 or 562-949-0592. Specializing in Irish and American Belleek

Thoerner, Sharon
15549 Ryon Ave., Bellflower, 90706; 562-866-1555. Specializing in covered animal dishes, powder jars with animal and human figures, slag glass

Thornton, Don
1345 Poplar Ave., Sunnyvale, 94087. Specializing in egg beaters; author of *Beat This: The Eggbeater Chronicles* (out of print, new edition coming in 1999); and *Apple Parers* ($59 ppd.)

Webb, Frances Finch
1589 Gretel Lane, Mountain View, 94040. Specializing in Kay Finch ceramics

Canada

Brown, David L.
Stevengraph Collectors Assn.
2103-2829 Arbutus Rd., Victoria, British Columbia, V8N 5X5; 250-477-9896. Specializing in Stevengraphs

Melis, Mirko
Marcelle Antiques
PO Box 53039, 5100 Erin Mills Pkwy., Mississauga, Ontario, L5M 4Z5; 905-689-1648. Specializing in American and European art glass, Russian works of art (enamels, porcelains, silver, etc.), English and Continental glass and china; member of Antique Appraisal Association of America, Inc., and AADA (Associated Antique Dealers of America, Inc.)

Mike's General Store
St. Anne's Rd., Winnepeg, Manitoba, R2M 273; 304-255-3464; e-mail: mikesgenellus.net

Warner, Ian
PO Box 93022, 499 Main St. S., Brampton, Ontario, L6Y 4V8; 905-453-9074 or fax 905-453-2931. Specializing in Wade porcelain and Swankyswigs, author of *The World of Wade, The World of Wade Book 2, Wade Price Trends*, and *The World of Head Vase Planters*, Co-author: Mike Posgay

Colorado

Carlton, Carol and Jim
8115 S. Syracuse St., Englewood, 80112; 303-773-8616. Specializing in Broadmoor, Coors, and other Colorado pottery

Heck, Carl
Carl Heck Decorative Arts
Box 8416, Aspen, 81612; phone/fax: 970-925-8011; www.carlheck.com. Specializing in original Tiffany lamps, art glass, windows, and chandeliers; also reverse-painted and leaded-glass table lamps, stained and beveled glass windows, bronzes, paintings, etc.; buy and sell; fee for written appraisals; please include SASE for reply

Mackin, Bill
Author of *Cowboy and Gunfighter Collectibles*; available from author: 1137 Washington St., Craig, 81625; 970-824-6717. Paperback: $25; other titles available; specializing in old and fine spurs, guns, gun leather, cowboy gear, Western Americana (collection in the Museum of Northwest Colorado, Craig)

Over, Naomi L.
8909 Sharon Lane, Arvada, 80002; 303-424-5922. Specializing in ruby glassware, author of *Ruby Glass of the 20th Century, Book II* (1999 values) available from author for $32.45 softbound or $42.45 hardbound, ppd. Naomi will attempt to make photo identifications for all who include a SASE with correspondence.

Segelke, Cathy; and James, Pat
970-847-3759 (Pat). Specializing in crocks, Western Pottery Mfg. Co. (Denver, CO)

Toohey, Marlena
703 S. Pratt Pky., Longmont, 80501; 303-678-9726. Specializing in black glass (buy, sell, or trade); book available from author for $20 ppd. (second book now available from author as well)

White, John 'Grandpa'
Grandpa's Depot
1616 17th St., Suite 267, Denver, 80202; 303-628-5590 or fax 303-628-5547. Specializing in railroad-related items; Catalogs available

Winther, Jo Ellen
8449 W. 75th Way, Arvada, 80005; 800-872-2345 or 303-421-2371. Specializing in Coors

Connecticut

Alves, Margaret
84 Oak Ave., Shelton, 06484; 203-924-4768. Specializing in souvenir spoons: plated, sterling, pre-1920s

Bondhus, Sandra V.
Box 100, Unionville, 06085; 860-678-1808. Author of *Quimper Pottery: A French Folk Art Faience*; specializing in Quimper pottery

FDS Antiques, Inc.
62 Blue Ridge Dr., Stamford, 06903-4923. Publishes *The 'No Nonsense' Antique Mall Directory*, a directory of antique malls, centers, and multi-dealer co-ops; over 4,700 listings listed according to state

Fink, Paul
Fun & Games
PO Box 488, Kent, 06757; 860-927-4001. Specializing in board games

Guido, Karen M.
Karen Michelle
PO Box 489, Bridgewater, 06752. Specializing in tiles; buy & sell; books on tiles available, many out of print; fee for written appraisal; please include SASE for inquiries

Kilbride, Mrs. Richard J.
81 Willard Terrace, Stamford, 06903; 203-322-0568. Has available for sale: *Art Deco Chrome, The Chase Era*, and *Art Deco Chrome, Book 2, A Collector's Guide, Industrial Design in the Chase Era*

MacSorley, Earl
823 Indian Hill Rd., Orange, 06477; 203-387-1793 (after 7:00 p.m.). Specializing in nutcrackers, Bessie Pease Gutmann prints, figural lift-top spittoons

Postcards International
Martin J. Shapiro
2321 Whitney Ave., Suite 102, PO Box 185398, Hamden, 06518; 203-248-6621 or fax 203-248-6628; www.vintagepostcards.com. Specializing in vintage picture postcards

Thalberg, Bruce
Mountain View Dr., Weston, 06883; 203-227-8175. Specializing in canes and walking sticks: novelty, carved, and Black

Van Deusen, Hobart D.
28 The Green, Watertown, 06795; 860-945-3456. Specializing in Canton, SASE required when requesting information

Vuono, Mark
16 6th St., Stamford, 06905; 203-357-0892 (10 a.m. to 5:30 p.m. E.S.T.). Specializing in historical flasks, blown 3-mold glass, blown American glass

District of Columbia

Durham, Ken and Jackie (by appointment)
909 26 St. N.W., Suite 502, Washington, D.C. 20037; web: www.GameRoomAntiques.com. Specializing in counter-top arcade machines, trade stimulators, and vending machines; 16-page illustrated list: $2; send SASE for free list of books on coin-operated machines

Griffith, Woody
1409 21st St., NW, #2D, Washington, D.C. 20036; 202-861-0937. Specializing in DeVilbiss perfumes and perfume lamps of all types

Nelson, Scott
1636 Nicholson St. N.W., Washington, D.C. 20011. Specializing in African Art

Florida

Bettinger, Robert
PO Box 333, Mt. Dora, 32756; 352-735-3575. Specializing in American art pottery

Cohen, Joel
Cohen Books & Collectibles
PO Box 810310, Boca Raton, 33481; 407-487-7888. Specializing in Disneyana

Dumont, Louise
318 Palo Verde Dr., Leesburg 34748. Specializing in cookie jars, Abingdon

Dodds, Rebecca
Silver Flute
Box 480644, Ft. Lauderdale, 33348. Specializing in jewelry

Elsner, Dr. Robert
29 Clubhouse Lane, Boynton Beach, 33436; 561-736-1362. Specializing in antique barometers and nautical instruments

France, Madeleine
PO Box 15555, Ft. Lauderdale, 33318; 305-584-0009. Specializing in top-quality perfume bottles: Rene Lalique, Steuben, Czechoslovakian, DeVilbiss, Baccarat, Commercials; French dore bronze, and decorative arts

Hudson, Hardy
Our Antiques Market
5453 Lake Howell Rd., Winter Park, 32792; 407-657-2100 from 11:00 a.m. to 6:00 p.m. or (home) 407-647-3454; e-mail: todiefor@mindspring.com. Specializing in majolica, American art pottery (buying one piece or entire collections); also buying Weller (garden ornaments, birds, Hudson, Sicard, Sabrinian, Glendale, or animal related), Roseville, Grueby, Newcomb, Overbeck, Kay Finch, Clewell, Tiffany, etc.

Kamm, Dorothy
PO Box 7460, Port St. Lucie, 34985-7460; 561-465-4008 or fax 561-460-9050. Specializing in American painted porcelain; author of *American Painted Porcelain: Identification & Value Guide* (Collector Books), and *Antique Trader's Comprehensive Guide to American Painted Porcelain* (Antique Trader Books); publishes *Dorothy Kamm's Porcelain Collector's Companion*, bimonthly newsletter, subscription: $28 per year

Kuritzky, Louis
4510 NW 17th Place, Gainesville, 32605; 352-377-3193. Author (Collector Books) of *Collector's Guide to Bookends*

Lawrence, Judy and Cliff
1169 Overcash Dr., Dunedin, 34698. Specializing in fountain pens and mechanical pencils

Linscott, Jacqueline C.
Line Jewels
3557 Nicklaus Dr., Titusville, 32780. Specializing in glass insulators and other telephone items; distributor of the only known set of books dealing with insulators, *North American Glass Insulators* (2 volumes), and accompanying price guide; LSASE required for information

McNerny, Kathryn
118 Creek Hollow Lane, Middleburg, 32068. Author (Collector Books) on blue and white stoneware, primitives, tools

Posner, Judy
October - May: PO Box 2194 SC, Englewood, FL 34295, fax: 941-475-2645; e-mail: judyandjef@aol.com. Specializing in Disneyana, Black memorabilia, salt and pepper shakers, souvenirs of the USA, character and advertising memorabilia, figural pottery; buy, sell, collect; informal appraisals: $5+LSASE and photo of item

Rolfes, Herbert
Yesterday's World
PO Box 398, Mt. Dora, 32756; 352-735-3947; e-mail: NY1939@aol.com. Specializing in World's Fairs and Expositions

Roush, Peggy E.
Peggy's Matching Service
PO Box 476, Ocala, 34478; 352-629-3954; e-mail: PegsMatch@worldnet.att.net. Specializing in discontinued Noritake patterns

Snyder-Haug, Diane
PO Box 815, St. Petersburg, 33731. Specializing in women's clothing, 1850-1940

Supnick, Mark
2771 Oakbrook Manor, Ft. Lauderdale, 33332; Author of *Collecting Hull Pottery's Little Red Riding Hood* ($12.95 ppd). Specializing in American pottery

Vogel, Janice and Richard
4720 S.E. Fort King St., Ocala, 34470-1501. Authors of *Victorian Trinket Boxes*

White, Douglass
Classic Interiors & Antiques
2042 N. Rio Grande Ave., Suite E, Orlando, 32804; 407-839-0004. Specializing in Fulper, Arts & Crafts furniture (photos helpful)

Whysel, Steven
7867 N.W. 11th St., Plantation, 33322; 954-382-0008. Specializing in Art Nouveau, 19th- and 20th-century art

Wieland, Robert
American Antique Prints
33 So. St. Andrews Drive, Ormond Beach, 32174; 904-672-9972. Specializing in early American prints: Currier & Ives, Kurz & Allison, and McKenny & Hall

Wise, Raphael C.
The Collector's Stop
12018 Suellen Circle, West Palm Beach, 33414; 561-793-0986. Specializing in Wedgwood Jasper Ware, Rosenthal, Moorcroft, Buffalo Deldare and Emerald Ware, Heisey, contemporary paperweights, English porcelains

Georgia

Bailey, Wayne and Gale
PO Box 173, Dacula, 30019; 770-963-5736. Specializing in Goebels (Friar Tuck)

Glenn, Walter
Geode Ltd.
3393 Peachtree Rd., Atlanta, 30326; 404-261-9346. Specializing in Frankart

Joiner, John R.
Aviation Collectors
173 Green Tree Dr., Newnan, 30265; 770-502-9565. Specializing in commercial aviation collectibles

Jones, Donald
24 Marvalingrove, Savannah, 31406; 912-354-2133. Specializing in vintage tennis collectibles; SASE with inquiries please

Illinois

Ammelounx, Andre
The Stein Auction Company
PO Box 136, Palatine, 60078; 847-991-5927 or fax 847-991-5947. Specializing in steins, catalogs available

The Barrel Antique Mall
5850 S. St. Road, I-55 Exit 90, Springfield, 62707; 217-585-1438

Brinkley, Wm. J.
Brinkley Galleries
401 S. Washington Ave., McLeansboro, 62859. Specializing in Meissen, Dresden, European porcelains, American porcelains (Cybis)

Broom, Jim
Box 65, Effingham, 62401. Specializing in opalescent pattern glassware

Danis, John
11028 Raleigh Ct., Rockford, 61115; 815-877-2410 or fax 815-877-6042; e-mail: danis6033@aol.com. Specializing in R. Lalique and Norse pottery

Davis, Jim and Margaret
Lots of Strange Things
Springfield, 217-546-4790. Specializing in glassware of the Depression years

Feldman, Arthur M.
Arthur M. Feldman Gallery
1815 St. Johns Ave., Highland Park, 60035; 847-432-8858 or fax 847-266-1199. Specializing in Judaica, fine art, and antiques

Frizzell, Doris
5687 Oakdale Dr., Springfield, 62707; 217-529-3873. Specializing in Royal Haeger and Maddux of California; co-author (Collector Books) of Royal Haeger book; SASE required when requesting information

Garmon, Lee
1529 Whittier St., Springfield, 62704; 217-789-9574. Specializing in Royal Haeger, Royal Hickman, glass animals; co-author (Collector Books) of *Glass Animals and Figural Flower Frogs of the Depression Era*

Gudgeon, Ray
Chicago, 773-935-0127. Specializing in American art pottery

Hall, Doris and Burdell
B&B Antiques
210 W. Sassafras Dr., Morton, 61550-1245. Authors of *Morton's Potteries: 99 Years* (Vols. I and II); specializing in Morton pottery, American dinnerware, early American pattern glass, historical items

Hastings, Mary Jane
310 West 1st South, Mt. Olive, 62069; phone/fax: 217-999-1222. Specializing in Chintz dinnerware

Hilst, Randy
1221 Florence #4, Pekin, 61554; 309-346-2710. Specializing in general line including fishing and hunting collectibles

Hoffmann, Pat and Don, Sr.
1291 N. Elmwood Dr., Aurora, 60506-1309; 630-859-3435; www.skognet.com/~warwick/ or e-mail: warwick@skognet.com. Authors of *Warwick, A to W*, a supplement to *Why Not Warwick?*; video regarding Warwick decals currently available

The Home Place Antiques
Durham, William; Galaway, William
615 S. State St., Belvidiere, 61008; 815-544-0577. Specializing in Tea Leaf ironstone and white ironstone

Hooks, Dee
Dee's China Shop
13050 Blackstump Rd., Percy, 62272; 618-965-3832. Specializing in R.S. Prussia, Royal Bayreuth, Haviland, other fine china

Hopp, Dennis Carl
Midcentury
Chicago, 773-935-7872. Specializing in 20th-century design, glass, pottery, metal, art

Hurney, George and Mary
Glass Connection (Mail-order only)
312 Babcock Dr., Palatine, 50067; 847-359-3839; e-mail: glasscon@star-netusa.com. Specializing in Depression glass and Paden City glass (not advising on pottery)

The Illinois Antique Center
320 S.W. Commercial St., Peoria, IL 61602

John Toomey Gallery
818 N. Blvd, Oak Park, 60301

Long, Dee
112 S. Center, Lacon, 61540. Specializing in reamers

Lubliner, Larry
Refinders mail/telephone auction
737 Barberry Rd., Highland Park, 60035; 708-831-1102 or 708-831-1160. Refinders will find your wants from 1860 to 1960

Martin, Jim
R.R. 1, 1091 215th Ave., Monmouth, 61462; 309-734-2703. Specializing in Old Sleepy Eye, Monmouth pottery, Western Stoneware

Meyer, Larry
4001 Elmwood, Stickney, 60402; 708-749-1564; e-mail: lmeyer1212@aol.com. Specializing in fire grenades and extinguishers

Miller, Larry; and Strickfaden, Dick
218 Devron Circle, E. Peoria, 61611-1605. Specializing in German and Czechoslovakian Erphila

Ochsner, Grace
Grace Ochsner Doll House
1636 E. County Rd. 2700, Niota, 62358; 217-755-4362. Specializing in piano babies, bisque German dolls

Owen, Larry and Sally
Specializing in Morten Studio dogs, etc.

Randy's Ol' Time Collectibles
Illinois Antique Center
308 S.W. Commercial, Peoria, 61602;
309-346-2710. Specializing in general line,
including hunting and fishing collectibles

Rastello, Lisa
Milkweed Antiques
5N531 Ancient Oak Lane, St.
Charles, 60175; 708-377-4612. Specializing in Depression-era collectibles

Rhoden, Joan and Charles
Memories/Rhoden's Antiques
8693 N. 1950 East Rd., Georgetown,
61846-6264; 217-662-8046. Specializing in Heisey and other Elegant glassware, general line antiques; co-authors
of *Those Wonderful Yard-Long Prints
and More*, and *More Wonderful Yard-
Long Prints, Book II*, and *Yard-Long
Prints, Book III*, illustrated value guides

Rodgers, Joanne
Stretch Glass Society
PO Box 573, Hampshire, 60140.
Membership: $18 per year; quarterly
newsletter with color photos; annual
spring convention

Schwab, Betty and Larry
The Paperweight Shoppe
2507 Newport Dr., Bloomington,
61704; 309-662-1956; e-mail:
PAPERWT1@aol.com. Specializing
in glass paperweights

Spencer, Dick
Glass and More (Shows only)
1203 N. Yale, O'Fallon, 62269; 618-632-9067. Specializing in Cambridge,
Fenton, Fostoria, Heisey, etc.

Spiess, Greg
230 E. Washington, Joliet, 60433;
815-722-5639. Specializing in Odd
Fellows lodge items

Stifter, Donna & Craig
PO Box 6514, Naperville, 60540; 630-789-5780; e-mail: cocacola@enteract.com.
Specializing in Coca-Cola, Pepsi-Cola,
Orange Crush, Dr. Pepper, Hires, and
other soda-pop brand collectibles

TV Guide Specialists
Box 20, Macomb 61455; 309-833-1809

Waite, Jim
112 N. Main St., Farmer City, 61842;
800-842-2593. Specializing in Sebastians

Wells, Rosalie J. 'Rosie'
22341 E. Wells Rd. S, Canton, 61520; 1-800-445-8745; e-mail: Rosie@RosieWells.com.
Publishes *Rosie's Weekly Collectors' Gazette*
and annual price guides for *Precious
Moments Collectibles, Hallmark Ornaments,
Merry Miniatures and Kiddie Car Classics,
Boyds Bears & Friends, The Enesco Cherished Teddies Collection, Charming Tails,*
and *Precious Moments Company's Dolls!*
Check out Rosie's Internet site:
www.RosieWells.com. Rosie has hosted
eight International Conventions for Precious Moments Collectors, hosts the semi-annual Midwest Collectibles Fest, held in
Westmont, IL, each March and October.
For hot tips and to record Voice Ads,

Rosie offers a touch-tone 900 line (1-900-740-7575). Send for a category list (86
categories, including antiques) or see our
web site! Call Rosie at 800-445-8745 for
information on limited edition collectibles.

Wilson, Jack D.
3926 N. Keeler, Chicago, 60641-2915; 773-282-9553; e-mail: jdwilson1@earthlink.net; web site:
home.earthlink.net/~jdwilson1/. Specializing in Phoenix and Consolidated
glass; buying Ruba Rombic; author of
Phoenix & Consolidated Art Glass: 1926-1980

Yester-Daze Glass
c/o Illinois Antique Center
320 S.W. Commercial St., Peoria,
61604; 309-347-1679. Specializing in
glass from the 1920s, '30s, and '40s;
Fiesta; Hall; Pie Birds; Sprinkler Bottles; and Florence figurines

---

Indiana

AAA Antique Shop
US 6 West, Nappanee, 46550; 219-773-4912. Specializing in trunks

Alexander, Charles
221 E. 34th St., Indianapolis, 46205;
317-924-9665. Specializing in American dinnerware

Boram, Clifford
Antique Stove Information Clearinghouse
Monticello; free consultation by
phone only: 219-583-6465

Crossroads Antique Mall
311 Holiday Square, Seymour, 47274;
812-522-5675. Open 7 days a week

Dilley, David
PO Box 225, Indianapolis, 46206;
765-284-7443; e-mail: glazebears@aol.com
or bearpets@aol.com. Specializing in Royal
Haeger and Royal Hickman

Edwards, Bill
620 W. 2nd, Madison, 47250. Author
(Collector Books) on carnival glass

Egelhoff, Larry
Still Bank Collectors Club of America
4175 Millersville Rd., Indianapolis,
46205; 317-846-7228. Specializing in
still banks, safe banks, antique safes

Freese, Carol and Warner
House With the Lions Antiques
On the Square; Covington, IN 47932.
General line

Fred, James A.
Antique Radio Labs
5355 So. 275W, Cutler, 46920; 765-268-2214. Specializing in radios made
from 1922 to 1950

Garrett, Jerry and Sandi
Jerry's Antiques (Shows only)
1807 W. Madison St., Kokomo, 46901;
765-457-5256. Specializing in Greentown glass, old postcards

Gilley's Antique Mall and Collectibles
1209 W. Main (US 40), Plainfield,
46168; 317-839-8779. Open daily
from 10 a.m. to 5 p.m., features booths
with over 250 dealers; outdoor summer weekend flea market

Haun, Ted
2426 N. 700 East, Kokomo, 46901;
765-628-7028. Specializing in American pottery and china, '50s items, Russel Wright designs

Highfield, James
6301-D University Commons, South
Bend, 46635; 219-272-4200. Specializing in relief-style Capo-di-Monte-style porcelain (Doccia, Ginori, and Royal Naples)

Heiss, Virginia
7777 N. Alton Ave., Indianapolis,
46268; 317-875-6797. Specializing in
Muncie, AMACO, Brandt Steele,
Marblehead, Kenton Hills

Keagy, William and June
PO Box 106, Bloomfield, 47424; 812-384-3471. Co-authors of *Those Wonderful Yard-Long Prints and More, More
Wonderful Yard-Long Prints, Book II,*
and *Yard-Long Prints, Book III*, illustrated value guides

Leslie, Beverly
Secretary/Treasurer of Uhl Collectors
Society
801 Poplar St., Boonville, 47601; 812-897-3681. Contact for newsletter and
membership information

McQuillen, Michael J. and Polly
McQuillen's Collectibles
PO Box 50022, Indianapolis, 46250-0022; 317-845-1721. Writer of column, *Political Parade*, which appears
monthly in *AntiqueWeek* other newspapers; specializing in political campaign memorabilia, advertising, sports
memorabilia; buys and sells

Old Storefront Antiques
PO Box 357, Dublin, 47335; 317-478-4809.
Specializing in country store items, tins,
primitives, pharmaceuticals, advertising,
etc.; active in mail order with catalogs available; information requires LSASE

Pruitt, Ted
3350 W. 700 N., Anderson, 46011. *St.
Clair Glass Collector's Book*, available
($15 ea) from Ted at above address

Scowden, Virgil
Williamsport, 47993; 317-762-3408
or 317-762-3178. Antiques museum,
general line, tours

Slater, Thomas D.
Slater's Americana
1325 W. 86th St., Indianapolis, 46260;
317-257-0863. Specializing in political
and sports memorabilia

Stofft, Jeanette
Marnette Antiques
Tell City, 47586; 812-547-5707. Specializing in Ohio art pottery, buy and sell; no
phone appraisals; SASE required

Swayzee Antique Mall
115 N. Washington St., Swayzee,
46986; 317-922-7903

Webb's Antique Mall
over 400 Quality Dealers
200 W. Union St., Centerville, 47330

Wright, Bill
325 Shady Dr., New Albany, 47150.
Specializing in knives: Bowie, hunting,
military, and pocketknives

Iowa

Addy, Geneva D.
PO Box 124, Winterset, 50273; 515-462-3027

Ambrose, Craig
3717 6th Ave., Apt. 244, Des Moines,
50313; 515-288-4595. Specializing in
quilts; author of *Picture Book and Price
Guide to Antique Quilts*, available from
author for $45+postage

Arnbal, Una
Woodland Antiques
242 Trail Ridge Rd., Ames, 50014;
515-292-1005. Specializing in china,
glass, Lomonosov figurines, Danish
collector plates

Beeks, Dale
PO Box 117, Mt. Vernon, 52314;
319-895-0506. Specializing in instruments of science technology and
medicine, also surveying instruments
and microscopes

Bilsland, William M., III
PO Box 2671, Cedar Rapids, 52406-2671; 319-368-0658. Specializing in
American art pottery

DeGood, Hal and Meredith
The Baggage Car
3100 Justin Dr., Suite B, Des Moines,
50322; 515-270-9080. Specializing in
Hallmark collectibles; publishers of
Hallmark newsletter

DeLozier, Loretta
1101 Polk St., Bedford, 50833; Monday -
Friday: 9:00 a.m. to 4:00 p.m., 712-523-2289 or fax 712-523-2624; e-mail: Leftonlady@AOL.com. Author (Collector
Books) of *Collector's Encyclopedia of Lefton China, Identification & Values*, Books I
and II and the *1999 Lefton Price Guide*;
specializing in Lefton China; buy, sell &
consign; fee for written appraisals; price
list available for each pattern or series

Devine, Dennis; Norman; and Joe
D & D Antique Mall
1411 3rd St., Council Bluffs, 51503;
712-323-5233 or 712-328-7305. Specializing in furniture, phonographs, collectibles, general line. Joe Devine: Royal
Copley collector

Jaarsma, Ralph
De Pelikaan Antieks
812 Washington St., c/o Red Ribbon
Antique Mall, Pella, 50219. Specializing in Dutch antiques

Picek, Louis
Main Street Antiques
110 W. Main St., Box 340, West
Branch, 52358. Specializing in folk art,
country Americana, the unusual

Westmoreland Glass Society
Jim Fisher, President
513 5th Ave., Coralville, 52241; 319-354-5011. Membership: $15 (single) or $25 (household)

Kansas

Anthony, Dorothy Malone
World of Bells Publications
2401 S. Horton, Fort Scott, 66701; 316-223-3404. Specializing in publishing and selling books on all types of small bells

Maundy International
PO Box 13028-GG, Shawnee Mission, 66282; 1-800-235-2866. Specializing in watches — antique pocket and vintage wristwatches

Old World Antiques
4436 State Line Rd., Kansas City, 66103; 913-677-4744 or fax 913-677-4879. Specializing in 18th- and 19th-century furniture, paintings, accessories, cocks, chandeliers, sconces, and much more

Rash, Jim
135 Alder Ave., Pleasantville, 08232; 609-646-4125. Specializing in advertising, cereal, and cartoon figures

Smies, David
Pops Collectibles
Box 522, 315 So. 4th, Manhattan, 66502; 913-776-1433. Specializing in coins, stamps, cards, tokens, Masonic collectibles

Snyder, Charlie and Rose
Charlie's Collectables
R.R. 4, Box 79, Independence, 67301; 316-331-6259. Specializing in cookie jars and accessories, salt and pepper shakers, pottery

Street, Patti
Currier & Ives (China) Quarterly Newsletter
PO Box 504, Riverton, 66770; 316-848-3529. Subscription: $12 per year (includes 2 free ads)

Tinsley, Rosella
105 15th St., Osawatomie, 66064; 913-755-3237. Specializing in primitives, kitchen, farm, woodenware, and miscellaneous (phone calls only, no letters please)

Kentucky

Courter, J.W.
3935 Kelley Rd., Kevil, 42053; 502-488-2116. Specializing in Aladdin lamps; author of Aladdin — The Magic Name in Lamps, Revised Edition, hardbound, 304 pages; Aladdin Electric Lamps, softbound, 229 pages; and Angle Lamps Collectors Manual & Price Guide, softbound, 48 pages

Florence, Gene
Box 7186H, Lexington, 40522. Author (Collector Books) on Depression glass, Occupied Japan, Elegant glass, kitchen glassware

Hornback, Betty
Betty's Antiques
707 Sunrise Lane, Elizabethtown, 42701. Specializing in Kentucky Derby glasses

Johnson, Wes, Sr.
3606 Glenview Ave., Glenview, 40025. Specializing in Cracker Jack: toys, point of sale, packages, etc.; Checkers Confection, Schoenhut toys, Victor Toy Oats, Universal Theatre (Chicago), old toys; please include SASE

Ritchie, Roy B.
PO Box 384, Hindman, 41822; 606-785-5796. Co-author of Standard Knife Collector's Guide and Standard Guide to Razors; specializing in razors and knives, all types of cutlery

Stewart, Ron
PO Box 151, Combs, 41729; 606-435-2412. Co-author of Standard Knife Collector's Guide and Standard Guide to Razors; specializing in razors and knives, all types of cutlery

Willis, Roy M.
Heartland of Kentucky Decanters and Steins
PO Box 428, Lebanon Jct., 40150; web site: www.ka.net/heartlandky. Huge selection of limited edition decanters and beer steins — open showroom; include large self-addressed envelope (two stamps) with correspondence; fee for appraisals; decanter price guide (listings only, no pictures, information on marketing decanters): $9.50 ppd.

Louisiana

Langford, Paris
Kollecting Kiddles
415 Dodge Ave., Jefferson, 70121; 504-733-0667 or e-mail: BBEAN415@AOL.COM. Specializing in all small vinyl dolls of the '60s and '70s; author of Liddle Kiddles Identification and Value Guide (now out of print); please include SASE when requesting information

Maine

Blake, Brenda
Box 555, York Harbor, 03911; 207-363-6566; e-mail: Eggcentric@AOL.com. Specializing in egg cups

Hathaway, John
Hathaway's Antiques
3 Mills Rd., Bryant Pond, 04219; 207-665-2124. Specializing in fruit jars; mail order a specialty

Hillman, Alma
Antiques at the Hillman's
362 E. Main St., Searsport, 04974; 207-548-6658. Co-author (Collector Books) of Collector's Encyclopedia of Old Ivory China, the Mystery Explored, Identification & Values; specializing in Old Ivory China

Rinaldi, John
Nautical Antiques and Related Items
Box 765, Dock Square, Kennebunkport, 04046; 207-967-3218. Specializing in nautical antiques, scrimshaw, naval items, marine paintings, naval items, etc.; fully illustrated catalog: $5

Zayic, Charles S.
Americana Advertising Art
PO Box 57, Ellsworth, 04605; 207-667-7342. Specializing in early magazines, early advertising art, illustrators

Maryland

Ezell, Elaine; & Newhouse, George
Cruets Cruets Cruets
PO Box 1609, Pasadena, 21123-1609; 410-551-4101 (daytime) or 410-255-6777. Specializing in cruets and glass

Humphrey, George C.
4932 Prince George Ave., Beltsville, 20705; 301-937-7899. Specializing in John Rogers groups

Katz, Jerome R.
Katz Collectibles
Antique Station, Frederick, 21702; 301-695-0888. Specializing in technological artifacts; please include SASE when requesting information

Meadows, John, Jean and Michael
Meadows House Antiques
919 Stiles St., Baltimore, 21202; 410-837-5427. Specializing in antique wicker, furniture (rustic, twig, and old hickory), quilts, and tramp art

Rudisill's Alt Print Haus
Rudisill, John and Barbara
PO Box 199, Worton, 21678; 410-778-9290. Specializing in Currier & Ives; calls for information wil be taken in return for a contribution (honor system) to the American Heart Association

Screen, Harold and Joyce
2804 Munster Rd., Baltimore, 21234; 410-661-6765; e-mail: hscreen@home.com. Specializing in soda fountain 'tools of the trade' and paper: catalogs, Soda Fountain Magazine, etc.

Weisblut, Robert
International Ivory Society
11109 Nicholas Dr., Wheaton, 20902; 301-649-4002. Specializing in ivory carvings and utilitarian objects

Welsh, Joan
7015 Partridge Pl., Hyattsville, 20782; 301-779-6181. Specializing in Chintz; author of Chintz Ceramics

Yalom, Libby
The Shoe Lady
PO Box 7146, Adelphi, 20783; 301-422-2026. Specializing in glass and china shoes; author of book

Massachusetts

Adams, Charles and Barbara
Middleboro, 02346; 508-947-7277. Specializing in Bennington (brown only)

Cooper, Ryan
205 White Rock Rd., Yarmouthport, 02675. Specializing in flags of historical significance and exceptional design

Dunbar's Gallery
Leila and Howard Dunbar
76 Haven St., Milford, 01757; 508-634-8697 or fax 508-634-8698. Specializing in advertising and toys

Ford, Frank W.
237-26 South Street; Shrewbury, 01545. Specializing in Fostoria Specialty Company glassware

Frei, Peter
PO Box 500, Brimfield, 01010; 1-800-942-8968. Specializing in sewing machines (pre-1875, non-electric only), adding machines, typewriters, and hand-powered vacuum cleaners; SASE required with correspondence

Hess, John A.
Fine Photographic Americana
PO Box 3062, Andover, 01810. Specializing in 19th-century photography

Longo, Paul J.
Paul Longo Americana
Box 5510, Magnolia, 01930; 978-525-2290. Specializing in political pins, ribbons, banners, autographs, old stocks and bonds, baseball and sports memorabilia of all types

MacLean, Dale
183 Robert Rd., Dedham, 02026; 781-326-3010 or 781-329-1303 (evenings). Specializing in Dedham and Dorchester potteries

Morin, Albert
668 Robbins Ave. #23, Dracut, 01826; 978-454-7907. Specializing in miscellaneous Akro Agate and Westite

Vigue, Norm
3 Timberwood Dr. #306, Goffstown, 03045; 603-647-9951. Buying and selling TV, western, cartoon-show collectibles, animation art and 1-sheets, radio cereal premiums, board games, and 1930s through 1950 space (including Buck Rogers, Flash Gordon, Captain Video, Tom Corbett, etc.)

Wellman, BA
PO Box 673, Westminster, 01473-0673; e-mail: BAWELLMAN@NET1PLUS.COM. Specializing in all areas of American ceramics, dinnerware, figurines, and art pottery

Michigan

Brown, Rick
Newspaper Collector's Society of America
Lansing, 517-887-1255 or info@historybuff.com. Specializing in newspapers

Culver, Bob
Night Light Club
38619 Wakefield Ct., Northville, 48167; 248-473-8575. Specializing in miniature oil lamps

Gunsaulus, Jack
Gray's Gallery
Jack's Corner Bookstore
583 W. Ann Arbor Trail, Plymouth, 48170. Specializing in porcelain, books, jewelry, glass

Haas, Norman
264 Clizbe Rd., Quincy 49802; 517-639-8537. Specializing in American art pottery

Hogan, Walter P.
520 N. State, Ann Arbor, 48104; 313-930-1913. Specializing in Kellogg Studio

Iannotti, Dan
212 W. Hickory Grove Rd., Bloomfield Hills, 48302-1127S; 248-335-5042. Specializing in modern mechanical cast-iron banks; member of The Mechanical Bank Collectors of America

Krupka, Rod
2615 Echo Lane, Ortonville, 48462; 248-627-6351. Specializing in lightning rod balls

Kurella, Elizabeth M.
The Lace Merchant
Box 222, Plainwell, 49080; 616-685-9792. Publisher of newsletter and books on lace and linens; specializing in lace and linens

Marsh, Linda K.
1229 Gould Rd., Lansing, 48917. Specializing in Degenhart glass

Nedry, Boyd W.
728 Buth Dr., Comstock Park, 49321; 616-784-1513. Specializing in traps (including mice, rat, and fly traps) and trap-related items

Nickel, Mike
A Nickel's Worth
PO Box 456, Portland, 48875; 517-647-7646. Specializing in Roseville art pottery and juvenile pieces, Weller, Rookwood, Kay Finch, Ceramic Arts Studio, Josef, and Florence figurines

Oates, Joan
685 S. Washington, Constantine, 49042; 616-435-8353; e-mail: koates@remc12.k12.mi.us. Specializing in Phoenix Bird chinaware

Rairigh, Glen
Americana Auctions
12633 Sandborn, Sunfield, 48990; 800-919-1950. Specializing in Skookum dolls and antique auctions

Ross, Michelle
PO Box 94, Berrien Center, 49102; 616-925-1604. Specializing in Van Briggle and American pottery

Webster, Marty
6943 Suncrest Drive, Saline, 48176; 313-944-1188. Specializing in California porcelain and pottery, Orientalia

Minnesota

Anderson, James
Box 120704, New Brighton, 55112; 651-484-3198. Specializing in old fishing lures and reels, also tackle catalogs, posters, calendars, Winchester items

Harrigan, John
1900 Hennepin, Minneapolis, 55403; 612-660-2794 or (in winter) 561-732-0525. Specializing in Battersea (English enamel) boxes, Moorcroft, and Toby jugs

Ketcham, Steve
Steve Ketcham Antiques (shows and mail order only)
Box 24114, Edina, 55424; 612-920-4205. Specializing in and buying early American bottles; Red Wing stoneware (no dinnerware); advertising signs, trays, trade cards, pocket mirrors, etched beer and shot glasses; please include SASE for reply

Koehn, Joanne M.
Temple's Antiques
PO Box 46237, Eden Prairie, 55344; 612-941-7641. Specializing in Victorian glass and china.

Miller, Clark
4444 Garfield Ave., Minneapolis, 55409-1847; 612-827-6062. Specializing in Anton Lang pottery, American art pottery, Scandinavian glass and pottery

Nelson, C.L.
Box 222, Spring Park, 55384; 612-473-5625. Specializing in 18th-, 19th-, and 20th-century English pottery and porcelain, among others: Gaudy Welsh, ABC plates, relief-molded jugs, Staffordshire transfer ware

Podpeskar, Doug
624 Jones St., Eveleth, 55734-1631; e-mail: thepods@northernnet.com. Specializing in Red Wing dinnerware; prefers letters with clear photos of items to be identified along with LSASE for return.

Putratz, Barb
Spring Lake Park, 612-784-0422. Specializing in Norman Rockwell

Schoneck, Steve
HG Handicraft Guild, Minneapolis
PO Box 56, Newport, 55055; 651-459-2980. Specializing in American art pottery, Arts & Crafts, HG Handicraft Guild Minneapolis

Missouri

Duncan, Pat and Ann
Box 175, Cape Fair, 65624; 417-538-2311. Specializing in Holt Howard, Lefton, Roseville, etc.

Gillespie, Steve, Publisher
Goofus Glass Gazette
400 Martin Blvd, Village of the Oaks, 64118; 888-452-5554 or fax 816-452-554; e-mail: goofus@mid-west.net. Specializing in goofus glass, curator of 'Goofus Glass Museum,' had 4,000+ piece collection of goofus glass; buy, sell & collect goofus for 30+ years; expert contributor to forums on goofus glass; contributor to web sight for goofus glass

Heuring, Jerry
28450 US Highway 61, Scott City, 63780; 573-264-3947. Specializing in Keen Kutter

International Rose O'Neill Club
Contact Karen Stewart
PO Box 668, Branson, 65616. Dues: $7 (single) or $10 (family) includes newsletter *Kewpiesta Kourier*, published quarterly

Kleinbeck, Allen
Parkside Antiques
1414 Park Court, Kansas City, 64111; 816-561-4439. Specializing in American dinnerware and glassware

Roberts, Brenda
Country Side Antiques
R.R. 2, Marshall, 65340. Specializing in Hull pottery and general line; author of *Collectors Encyclopedia of Hull Pottery, Roberts' Ultimate Encyclopedia of Hull Pottery* and *The Companion Guide to Robert's Ultimate Encyclopedia of Hull Pottery*, all with accompanying price guides; SASE required

Siegel, Brenda and Jerry
Tower Grove Antiques
3308 Meramec, St. Louis, 63118; 314-352-9020. Specializing in Ungemach pottery

Scott, John and Peggy
Scotty's Antiques
4640 S. Leroy, Springfield, 65810; 417-887-2191. Specializing in Depression-era glassware and pottery, Florence Ceramics

Tarrant, Jenny
Holly Daze Antiques
4 Gardenview, St. Peters, 63376; e-mail: JennyJOL@aol.com. Specializing in early holiday items, Halloween, Christmas, Easter, etc.; Always buying Halloween collectibles (except masks and costumes) and German holiday candy containers

Wendel, David
F.E.I., Inc.
PO Box 1187, Poplar Bluff, 63902-1187; 573-686-1926. Specializing in Fraternal Elks collectibles

Wiesehan, Doug
D & R Farm Antiques
4535 Hwy. H, St. Charles, 63301. Specializing in salesman's samples and patent models, antique toys, farm toys, metal farm signs

Williams, Don
PO Box 147, Kirksville 63501; 660-627-8009 (between 8 a.m. and 6 p.m. only). Specializing in art glass; SASE required with all correspondence

Winslow, Ralph
Box 1175, Laurie, 65038. Specializing in Dryden Pottery

Nebraska

Larsen, Robert V.
3214 19th St., Columbus, 68601. Specializing in old hatpins and hatpin holders; please include SASE when requesting information

Neely, Nancee P.
16592 Hascall, Omaha, 68130; 402-330-7033. Specializing in Fairing boxes

New Hampshire

Apakarian-Russell, Pamela
Halloween Queen Antiques
PO Box 499, Winchester, 03470. Specializing in Halloween (and other holidays) and postcards

Brenner, Larry
Brenner Antiques
1005 Chestnut St., Manchester, 03104; 603-625-8203; e-mail: elberenee@aol.com. Specializing in Royal Bayreuth

Holt, Jane
Jane's Collectibles
PO Box 115, Derry, 03038. Specializing in Annalee Mobilitee Dolls; list sometimes available

Winston, Nancy
Willow Hollow Antiques
648 1st N.H. Turnpike, Northwood, 03261; 603-942-5739. Specializing in Shaker baskets, primitives, country smalls, paper Americana, iron, and copper

New Jersey

Anderson, Suzy McLennan
Heritage Antiques & Appraisal Services
65 E. Main St., Holmdel, 07733; 908-946-8801 or fax 908-946-1036. Specializing in American furniture and decorative accessories; please include photo and SASE when requesting information; appraisals and identification are impossible to do over the phone

Bilane, John E. (Mail order only)
2065 Morris Ave., Apt. 109, Union, 07083. Specializing in antique glass cup plates

Dezso, Doug
864 Paterson Ave., Maywood, 07607-2119; 201-488-1311. Specializing in nodders (comic German), glass candy containers, Tonka; SASE required for information

Doorstop Collectors of America
Doorstopper Newsletter
Jeanie Bertoia
2413 Madison Ave., Vineland, 08630; 609-692-4092. Membership: $20 per year, includes 2 newsletters and convention; send 2-stamp SASE for sample

George, Dr. Joan M.
ABC Collector's Circle
67 Stevens Ave., Old Bridge, 08857; fax: 732-679-6102 or e-mail: drgeorge@nac.net. Specializing in educational china (particularly ABC plates and mugs)

Harran, Jim and Susan
208 Hemlock Dr., Neptune, 07753; 908-922-2825. Specializing in English and Continental porcelains with emphasis on antique cups and saucers; author of *Collectible Cups and Saucers, Identification and Values* (Collector Books); available for $20.95 ppd.

Litts, Elyce
PO Box 394, Morris Plains, 07950; 201-361-4087. Author (Collector Books) of *Collector's Encyclopedia of Geisha Girl Porcelain* (out of print; ask your reference librarian or used bookstore to secure you a copy)

Lockwood, Howard J.; Publisher
Vetri: Italian Glass News
Box 191, Fort Lee, 07024; 201-969-0373. Specializing in Italian glass of the 20th century

Meschi, Edward J.
129 Pinyard Rd., Monroeville, 08343; Phone/fax: 609-358-7293. Specializing in Durand art glass, Icart etchings, Maxfield Parrish prints, Rookwood pottery, occupational shaving mugs, oil paintings, and other fine arts; author of *Durand — The Man and His Glass*, available from author for $43 ppd.

Middleton, Dave and Anne
Pot O' Gold Antiques
PO Box 124, Allenwood, 08720; 732-528-6648. Specializing in epergnes, historical and figural Staffordshire, Flow Blue, fine glass

Patalano, Diane. I.S.A.
Appraisals, Liquidations and Auctions
PO Box 144, Saddle River, 07458. Specializing in banks, Black Americana, furniture, spatterware, various antiques and collectibles

Perzel, Robert and Nancy
Popkorn
3 Mine St. (near Main St.), PO Box 1057, Flemington, 08822; 908-782-9631. Specializing in Stangl dinnerware, birds, and artware; American pottery and dinnerware

Poster, Harry
Vintage TVs
Box 1883, S. Hackensack, 07606; days: 201-794-9606; 24-hour fax: 201-794-9553. Writes Poster's Radio and Television Price Guide; specializes in vintage televisions, transistor radios, 3-D stereo cameras

Rago, David
17 S. Main St., Lambertville, 08530; 609-397-9374. Specializing in Arts & Crafts, art pottery

Rash, Jim
135 Alder Ave., Egg Harbor Township, 08234; 609-646-4125. Specializing in advertising dolls

Rosen, Barbara
6 Shoshone Trail, Wayne, 07470. Specializing in figural bottle openers and antique dollhouses

Vines, Linda L.
Yesterday Once More
PO Box 43721, Upper Montclair, 07043; 973-748-4990; e-mail: lja@viconet.com. Specializing in Snow Babies, all holidays (Christmas, Easter, Halloween), dolls, toys, and Steiff

Visakay, Stephen
Vintage Cocktail Shakers (By appointment)
PO Box 1517, W. Caldwell, 07007-1517; e-mail: SVisakay@aol.com. Author of book and specializing in vintage cocktail shakers and bar ware.

New Mexico

Hardisty, Don
Artistic Restorations
3020 E. Majestic Ridge, Las Cruces, 88011; For information and questions: 505-522-3721, fax 505-522-7909. Specializing in Bossons, Hummels, postcards, rare coins. Don's Collectibles carries a full line of current issues and most discontinued Bossons and Hummel figurines of all marks. Postcard inventory includes over 500,000 with many original photo cards and all current issues of Legend (lot purchase offers now being accepted). When mail ordering Bossons & Hummels, you may dial toll free 800-267-7667. e-mail: donbossons@zianet.com/ or visit Don's web page: www.zianet.com/donsbossons/

Manns, William
PO Box 6459, Santa Fe, 87502; 505-995-0102; e-mail: zon@nets.com. Co-author of Painted Ponies, hardbound (226 pages), available from author for $40 ppd.; specializing in carousel art and cowboy antiques

Moyer, Patsy
Box 311, Deming, 88031; 505-546-4019 or 505-546-2525; fax 505-546-2500; e-mail: sctrading@zianet.com. Collector Books author on dolls

New York

Austin, Bruce A.
1 Hardwood Hill Rd., Pittsford, 14534; 716-387-9820 (evenings); 716-475-2879 (week days); e-mail: BAAGLL@RIT.EDU. Specializing in clocks and Arts & Crafts furnishings and accessories including medalware, pottery, and lighting

Badders, Veldon
692 Martin Rd., Hamlin, 14464; 716-964-3360. Author (Collector Books) of Collector's Guide to Inkwells, Identification & Values; specializing in inkwells

Calison, Jim
Tools of Distinction
Wallkill, 12589; 914-895-8035. Specializing in antique and collectible tools, buying, and selling

Dimitroff, Thomas P.
Dimitroff's Antiques (Appointment only)
140 E. First St., Corning, 14830; 607-962-6745. Specializing in Steuben and cut glass

Doyle, Robert A.
Absolute Auction & Realty, Inc./Pleasant Valley Auction Hall
PO Box 1739, Pleasant Valley, 12569; web site: www.auctionweb.com/aar-ny. Antique and estate auctions twice a month at Pleasant Valley Auction Hall; Free calendar of auctions available

Endter, Barbara
29 Sandalwood Dr., Rochester, 14616-1513; 716-621-1433. Specializing in Chase Brass & Copper Company

Fer-Duc Inc.
Ferrara, Joseph
433 W. 21st St. #7F, New York, 10011-2906; 212-627-5023. Specializing in American art pottery (Ohr and Rookwood), 19th- and 20th-century American paintings

Gerson, Roselyn
PO Box 40, Lynbrook, 11563; 516-593-8746. Author/collector specializing in unusual, gadgetry, figural compacts, vanity bags and purses, solid perfumes and lipsticks

Handelsman, Burton
18 Hotel Dr., White Plains, 10605; 914-428-4480 (home) and 914-761-8880 (office). Specializing in occupational shaving mugs, accessories

Herley, Patrick J.
PO Box 606, E. Setauket, Long Island, 11733; 516-928-6052; e-mail: pherley@ms.cc.sunysb.edu. Specializing in Goss china

Jordan, Ruth E.
Meridale, 13806; 607-746-2082. Specializing in cut glass, American Brilliant period

Kaonis, Keith; Publisher
Collectors Eye and Antique Doll Collector Magazines
6 Woodside Ave., Suite 300, Northport, 11768 or PO Box 344, Center Port, NY 11721-0344; 516-261-4100 or 516-361-0982 (evenings). Specializing in Schoenhut toys

Laun, H. Thomas and Patricia
Little Century
215 Paul Ave., Syracuse, 13206; 315-437-4156. Summer residence: 35109 Country Rte. 7, Cape Vincent, 13618; 315-654-3244. Specializing in firefighting collectibles. **All appraisals are free and we will respond only to those who include a self-addressed stamped envelope (photograph is requested for accuracy).**

Malitz, Lucille
Lucid Antiques
Box KH, Scarsdale, 10583; 914-636-7825. Specializing in lithophanes, kaleidoscopes, stereoscopes, medical and dental antiques

Malloy, Alex G.
Alex G. Malloy, Inc.
PO Box 38, South Salem, 10590; 203-438-0396. Specializing in ancient and medieval coins; antiquities, numismatic literature

Michel, John and Barbara
Iron Star Antiques
200 E. 78th St., 18E, New York City, 10021; 212-861-6094. Specializing in yellow ware, cast iron, tramp art, shooting gallery targets, and blue feather-edge

Rifken, Blume J.
Author of Silhouettes in America — 1790-1840 — A Collector's Guide; specializing in American antique silhouettes from 1790 to 1840

Safir, Charlotte F.
1349 Lexington Ave., 9-B, New York City, 10128-1513; 212-534-7933. Specializing in cookbooks, children's books (out-of-print only)

Schleifman, Roselle
Ed's Collectibles/The Rage
16 Vincent Rd., Spring Valley, 10977; 914-356-2121. Specializing in Duncan & Miller, Elegant glass, Depression glass

Smyth, Carole and Richard
Carole Smyth Antiques
PO Box 2068, Huntington, 11743. Authors of The Burning Passion — Antique and Collectible Pyrography, available from authors at above address for $22.95 ppd. (New York: add $1.74 state sales tax), and Neptune's Treasures, A Study & Value Guide on Antique Shell Decorated Love Tokens, Souvenirs, Whimsies; call for price

Steinbock, Nancy
Nancy Steinbock Posters
518-438-1577. Specializing in posters: travel, war, literary, advertising

Tuggle, Robert
105 W. St., New York City, 10023; 212-595-0514. Specializing in John Bennett, Anglo-Japanese china

Van Kuren, Jean and Dale
Ruth's Antiques, Inc.
PO Box 152, Clarence Center, 14032; 716-741-8001. Specializing chocolate molds, Buffalo pottery Deldare ware

Van Patten, Joan F.
Box 102, Rexford, 12148. Author (Collector Books) of books on Nippon and Noritake

North Carolina

Finegan, Mary
Marfine Antiques
PO Box 3618; Boone 28607; 828-762-3441. Specializing in Johnson Brothers dinnerware; replacement service; author of book ($14 +postage and handling)

Hughes, Kathy (Mrs. Paul)
Tudor House Galleries
1401 E. Blvd., Charlotte, 28203; 704-377-4748. Specializing in relief-molded jugs, 18th- and 19th-century English pottery and 19th-century oil paintings

Iannantuoni, Jean-Paul
4179 Brownwood Lane, Concord, 28027-4501. Specializing in Royal Doulton secondary market

Kirtley, Charles E.
PO Box 2273, Elizabeth City, 27096; 919-335-1262. Specializing in monthly auctions and bid sales dealing with World's Fair, Civil War, political, advertising, and other American collectibles

Newbound, Betty
2206 Nob Hill Dr., Sanford, 27330. Author (Collector Books) on Blue Ridge dinnerware, milk glass, wall pockets, and figural planters and vases; specializing in collectible china and glass

Sayers, R.J.
Southeastern Antiques & Appraisals
PO Box 629, Brevard, 29812. Specializing in Boy Scout collectibles, Pisgah Forest pottery, primitive American furniture; author of Guide to Scouting Collectibles, Revised 1996 Edition, available from author for $32.95 ppd.; member NEAA Appraisers

Southern Folk Pottery Collector's Society, Shop, and Museum
1828 N. Howard Mill Rd., Robbins, 27325; 910-464-3961 or fax: 910-464-2530. Specializing in historical research and documentation, education and promotion of the traditional folk potter (past and present) to a modern collecting audience

Taylor, Terry
3648 Prides Rd., East Bend, 27018. Co-author of Collector's Encyclopedia of Salt Glaze Stoneware (Collector Books); specializing in salt glaze stoneware

North Dakota

Farnsworth, Bryce
1334 14½ St. South, Fargo, 58103; 701-237-3597. Specializing in Rosemeade pottery; if writing for information, please send a picture if possible, also phone number and best time to call

Ohio

Bassett, Mark
PO Box 771233, Lakewood, 44107; 216-221-6025. Specializing in Ohio art pottery (including Roseville, Cowan, Weller, Rookwood, others), Cleveland art and craft, Art Deco, and other 20th century design movements; author of *Introducing Roseville Pottery* (1999) and *Cowan Pottery and the Cleveland School* (1997), both published by Schiffer

Batory, Mr. Dana Martin
402 E. Bucyrus St., Crestline, 44827. Specializing in antique woodworking machinery, old and new woodworking machinery catalogs; author of *Vintage Woodworking Machinery, an Illustrated Guide to Four Manufacturers*, currently available from Astragal Press, PO Box 239, Mendham, NJ 07945 for $25.45 ppd. In order to prepare a definitive history on American manufacturers of woodworking machinery, Dana is interested in acquiring by loan, gift, or photocopy, any and all documents, catalogs, manuals, photos, personal reminiscences, etc., pertaining to woodworking machinery and/or their manufacturers. Also available for $7.50 money order: 30+ page list of catalogs, owner's manuals, parts lists, company publications, etc. (updated quarterly). NO phone calls please.

Benjamin, Scott
PO Box 556, LaGrange, 44050-0556; 440-355-6608; www.oilcollectibles.com (visit website or call). Specializing in gas globes; co-author of *Gas Pump Globes* and several other related books, listing nearly 4,000 gas globes with over 1,800 photos, prices, rarity guide, histories, and reproduction information (currently available from author); also available: *Petroleum Collectibles Monthly* magazine; please inquire

Blair, Betty
Golden Apple Antiques
216 Bridge St., Jackson, 45640; 614-286-4817. Specializing in art pottery, Watt, cookie jars, chocolate molds, Beanie Babies, general line

Budin, Nicki
Curio Cabinet
679 High St., Worthington, 43085; 614-885-1986. Specializing in Royal Doulton

Business Recollections, Antiques and Collectibles
Nada Sue Knauss
1211 Potter Rd., Weston, 43569; 419-669-4735. Specializing in pottery, postcards

China Specialties, Inc.
Box 471, Valley City, 44280. Specializing in Autumn Leaf

Cimini, Joan
67183 Stein Rd., Belmont, 43718. Specializing in Imperial glass; Candlewick matching service

Cincinnati Auction Gallery
225 E. 6th St., Cincinnati, 45202; 513-381-2128. Specializing in American art pottery (especially Rookwood), American and European fine paintings, watercolors

Collectors of Findlay Glass
PO Box 256, Findlay, 45840. An organization dedicated to the study and recognition of Findlay glass; *The Melting Pot* Newsletter published quarterly; convention held annually; membership: $10 per year

Distel, Ginny
Distel's Antiques
4041 S.C.R. 22, Tiffin, 44883; 419-447-5832. Specializing in Tiffin glass

Ebner, Rita and John
Columbus, 43232. Specializing in door knockers, cast-iron bottle openers, Griswold

Forsythe, Ruth A.
Box 327, Galena, 43021. Author of *Made in Czechoslovakia*, books I and II; SASE required

Graff, Shirley
4515 Grafton Rd., Brunswick, 44212. Specializing in Pennsbury pottery

Guenin, Tom
Box 454, Chardon, 44024. Specializing in antique telephones and antique telephone restoration

Hamlin, Jack and Treva
145 Township Rd. 1088, Proctorville, 45669; 740-886-7644; e-mail: trevajo@ezwv.com. Specializing in Currier and Ives by Royal China Co. and Homer Laughlin China; buy and sell

Hoopes, Ron
PO Box 21, 43731; 740-342-1384. Specializing in Gonder

Hothem, Lar
Hothem House
Box 458, Lancaster, 43130. Specializing in books about Indians and artifacts

Kao, Fern Larking
PO Box 312, Bowling Green, 43402; 419-352-5928. Specializing in jewelry, sewing implements, ladies' accessories

Kerr, Ann
PO 437, Sidney, 45365; 937-492-6369. Author (Collector Books) of *Collector's Encyclopedia of Russel Wright Designs*; specializing in work of Wright; interested in 20th-century decorative arts

Kier, Don and Anne
2022 Marengo St., Toledo, 43614; 419-385-8211. Specializing in general glass and china, 19th-century antiques, autographs, Brownies, Royal Bayreuth

Kitchen, Lorrie
Toledo, 419-478-3815. Specializing in Depression-era glass, Hall china, Fiesta, Blue Ridge, Shawnee

Klender, James and Grace
Town & Country Antiques & Collectibles
PO Box 447, Pioneer, 43554; 419-737-2880. Specializing in pattern glass, and general line

Kline, Mr. and Mrs. Jerry and Gerry
Members of North American Torquay Society and Torquay Pottery Collectors' Society
604 Orchard View Dr., Maumee, 43537; 419-893-1226. Specializing in collecting Torquay pottery

Maggard, Deborah
P.O Box 211, Chagrin Falls, 44022; 440-247-5632; e-mail: debmaggard@worldnet.att.net. Specializing in elegant glassware, china, and Victorian art glass

Mathes, Richard
PO Box 1408, Springfield, 45501-1408; 513-324-6917. Specializing in buttonhooks

Millman, Tom and Linda
231 S. Main St., Bethel, 45106; Phone/fax: 513-734-6884 (after 9 p.m.). Specializing in perfume lamps, other antique and unique lighting

Moore, Carolyn
445 N. Prospect, Bowling Green, 43402. Specializing in primitives, yellow ware, graniteware, collecting stoneware

Murphy, James L.
1023 Neil Ave., Columbus, 43201; 614-297-0746. Specializing in Radford, Vance Avon

National Imperial Glass Collectors' Society, Inc.
PO Box 534, Bellaire 43906. Dues: $15 per year (plus $1 for each additional member in the same household); quarterly newsletter; convention every June

Pierce, David
27544 Black Rd., PO Box 248, Danville, 43014; 614-599-6394. Specializing in Glidden pottery; fee for appraisals

Rees, Debbie
Zanesville. Specializing in Watt, Roseville juvenile, and other Roseville pottery, Zanesville area pottery, cookie jars, and Steiff

Riebel, James; Krause, Terry
Pottery Peregrinators
Zanesville, 740-452-7687. James is author of *Sanford's Guide to Nicodemus*, available from the author; specializing in American art pottery, Nicodemus, and carnival glass and Millersburg glass; promoter Zanesville's Voyage through the Past, Antique Pottery and Dinnerware Show & Sale, 14th and 15th of July

Roscoe, Mike
2227 Wernert Ave., Toledo, 43613-2717; 419-244-6935. Specializing in toys, advertising, coin-operated machines, furniture, and miscellaneous

Shields, Lorne
PO Box 211, Chagrin Falls, 44022-0211; 440-247-5632. Specializing in bicycles

Trainer, Veronica
Bayhouse
Box 40443, Cleveland, 44140; 216-871-8584. Specializing in beaded and enameled mesh purses

Tucker, Dan
Toledo, 419-478-3815. Specializing in Depression-era glass, Hall china, Fiesta, Blue Ridge, Shawnee

Walter, John
The Old Tool Shop
208 Front St., Marietta, 45750; 740-373-9973; fax: 740-373-9059 or e-mail: toolmerchant@sprynet.com. Specializing in all types of antique tools; for detailed information on Stanley tools, John Walter's *Antique & Collectible Stanley Tools Guide to Identity and Value* is highly recommended, 885 pages, over 1500 crisp photos and engravings, current values, softcover: $35 ppd., hardcover: $45 ppd.; *1999 Stanley Pocket Price Guide*: $12 ppd.

Whitmyer, Margaret and Kenn
Box 30806, Gahanna, 43230. Author (Collector Books) on children's dishes; specializing in Depression-era collectibles

Wilkins, Juanita
The Bird of Paradise
Wapakoneta. Specializing in R.S. china, Old Ivory china, colored pattern glass, lamps, and jewelry

Young, Mary
Box 9244, Wright Brothers Branch, Dayton, 45409; 937-298-4838. Specializing in paper dolls; Author of several books

Oklahoma

Bess, Phyllis and Tom
14535 E. 13th St., Tulsa, 74108; 918-437-7776. Authors of *Frankoma Treasures*, and *Frankoma and Other Oklahoma Potteries*; specializing in Frankoma and Oklahoma pottery

Klein, Bob and Dondee
1002 Walnut Court, Guthrie, 73044; 405-282-6545. Specializing in Tamac pottery

Moore, Art and Shirley
4423 E. 31st St., Tulsa, 74135; 918-747-4164 or 918-744-8020. Specializing in Lu Ray Pastels, Depression glass

Scott, Roger R.
4250 S. Oswego, Tulsa, 74135; 918-742-8710 or fax 918-583-1226. Specializing in Victor and RCA Victor trademark items along with Nipper

Watson, Kitty
Kitty's Kewpie-Corner
201 Dena Dr., Guthrie, 73044; 405-282-2287. Specializing in Rose O'Neill items; Kewpies, Scootles, and other related works

Willis, Ron L.
2110 Fox Ave., Moore, 73160. Specializing in militaria

Oregon

Abrahams, Peter
1948 Mapleleaf Rd., Lake Oswego, 97034; 503-636-2988 or e-mail: telscope@europa.com. Specializing in telescopes, binoculars, microscopes. Peter studies and collects optics: telescopes, binoculars, hand magnifiers, and microscopes and especially seeks reference material on these subjects, including books, catalogs, repair manuals, and histories.

Bartsch, Henry
Antique Registers
Box 444, Rockaway, 97136; 503-355-2932. Specializing in servicing antique cash registers (by appointment)

Brown, Marcia
Sparkles
PO Box 2314, White City, 97503; 541-826-3039 or fax 541-830-5385. Co-author and host of 3 volumes: *Hidden Treasures* videos; specializing in rhinestone jewelry; please include SASE if requesting information

Coe, Debbie and Randy
Coe's Mercantile
Lafayette School House Mall #2, 748 3rd (Hwy. 99W), Lafayette, 97127. Specializing in Elegant and Depression glass, art pottery

Davis, Patricia M.
4326 NW Tam-O-Shanter Way, Portland, 97229-8738; 503-645-3084. Antique and personal property appraisals

Foland, Doug
1811 N.W. Couch #303, Portland, 97209. Author of *The Florence Collectibles, an Era of Elegance*, available at your local book store or from Schiffer publishers

Hirshman, Susan and Larry
Everyday Antiques
2011 E. Main St., Medford, 97504; Specializing in china, glassware, kitchenware

Main Antique Mall
30 N. Riverside, Medford, 97501. Quality products and services for the serious collector, dealer, or those just browsing

Medford Antique Mall
Jim & Eileen Pearson, Owners
1 West 6th St., Medford 97501

Miller, Don and Robbie
541-535-1231. Specializing in milk bottles, TV Siamese cat lamps, seltzer bottles, red cocktail shakers

Morris, Sue and Dave
PO Box 1519, Merlin, 97532. Specializing in Watt pottery and Purinton pottery; author of *Watt Pottery — An Identification and Value Guide*, and *Purinton Pottery — An Identification and Value Guide*

Morris, Thomas G.
Prize Publishers
PO Box 8307, Medford, 97504; e-mail: chalkman@cdsnet.net. Author of *The Carnival Chalk Prize*, Books I and II, pictorial price guides on carnival chalkware figures with brief histories and values for each

Ringering, David
Kay Ring Antiques
4063 Durbin Ave., S.E., Salem, 97301; 503-364-0464 or pager: 503-588-3747; e-mail: DRinge1023@aol.com. Specializing in Rowland & Marsellus and other souvenir/historical china with scenes of buildings, parks, and other tourist attractions of the 1890s-1930s. Feel free to contact David if you have any questions about Rowland and Marsellus or other souvenir china. He will be happy to answer questions about souvenir china.

Roberts, Fred and Marilyn
Bah Humbug Collectibles
890 Biddle Road #265, Medford, 97504; fax: 541-776-0641; e-mail: bahhumbug@juno.com. Specializing in Hummels

Pennsylvania

Alekna, Stan and Sally
732 Aspen Lane, Lebanon, 17042-9073; 717-228-2361 or fax 717-228-2362. Specializing in Toy Soldiers

Barker, Jim
Toastermaster Antique Appliances
PO Box 746, Allentown, 18105; 610-439-0751 or e-mail: jbar@enter.net. Specializing in early electric toasters and fans, Porcelier and Royal Rochester; unusual electric toasters always wanted

Barrett, Noel
Rosebud Antiques
PO Box 1001, Carversville, 18913; 215-297-5109. Specializing in toys

Bodine, Clarence H., Jr., Proprietor
East/West Gallery
41B Ferry St., New Hope, 18938. Specializing in antique Japanese woodblock prints, netsuke, inro, porcelains

Cerebro
PO Box 327, E. Prospect, 17317-0327; 717-252-2400 or 800-69-LABEL; fax: 717-252-3685; e-mail: Cerebro@Cerebro.com. Specializing in antique advertising labels, especially cigar box labels, cigar bands, food labels, firecracker labels

Damaska, Ron
738 9th Ave., New Brighton, 15066; 724-843-1393. Specializing in Fry cut glass, match holders; SASE required when requesting information

Garvin, Joann
PO Box 182, Beaver Falls, 15010; 412-843-3999. Specializing in Fiesta

Gottuso, Bob
Bojo
PO Box 1403, Cranberry Township, 16066-0403; phone/fax: 724-776-0621. Specializing in Beatles, Elvis, KISS, Monkees, licensed Rock 'n Roll memorabilia

Hagenbuch, James
Glass-Works Auction
102 Jefferson, East Greenville, 18041; 215-679-5849. America's leading auction company in early American bottles, glass, and barbershop memorabilia

Hain, Henry F., III
Antiques & Collectibles
2623 N. Second St., Harrisburg, 17110; 717-238-0534. Lists available of items for sale

Hartz, Ray
120 Amberwood Ct., Bethel Park, 15102; 412-833-6777; e-mail: rhartz@bellatlantic.net. Specializing in old, unusual playing cards: US and foreign, war, transformation, advertising

Hinton, Michael C.
246 W. Ashland St., Doylestown, 18901; 215-345-0892; e-mail: oldstuff@worldnet.att.net. Owns/operates Bucks County Art & Antiques Company and Chem-Clean Furniture Restoration Company; specializing in quality restorations of a wide range of art and antiques from colonial to contemporary; also owns Trading Post Antiques, 532 Durham Rd., Wrightstown, PA, 18940, a 60-dealer antiques co-op with 15,000 square feet — something for everyone in antiques and collectibles

Holland, William
William Holland Fine Arts
1554 Paoli Pike, West Chester, 19380; 610-344-9848 or fax 610-344-0651; web site: www.hollandarts.com. Specializing in Louis Icart etchings and oils, Art Nouveau and Art Deco items; author of *Louis Icart: The Complete Etchings* and *The Collectible Maxfield Parrish*

Irons, Dave
Dave Irons Antiques
223 Covered Bridge Rd., Northampton, 18067; 610-262-9335 or fax 610-262-2853; www.ironsantiques.com. Author of *Irons By Irons* and *More Irons By Irons* (both soft-cover), available from author, (both contain pictures of over 1,600 irons, current information and price ranges, collecting hints, news of trends, and information for proper care of irons); specializing in pressing irons, country furniture, primitives, quilts, accessories

Ivankovich, Michael
Michael Ivankovich Auctions, Inc.
PO Box 2458, Doylestown, 18901. Specializing in early 20th-century hand-colored photography and prints; author of *The Collector's Value Guide to Popular Early 20th Century American Prints*, (1998) $19.95; *The Collector's Guide to Wallace Nutting Pictures*, $17.95; *The Wallace Nutting Expansible Catalog*, $14.95; *The Alphabetical and Numerical Index to Wallace Nutting Pictures*, $14.95; and *The Guide to Wallace Nutting Furniture*, $14.95; also available: *Wallace Nutting General Catalog, Supreme Edition* (reprint), $13.95; *Wallace Nutting: A Great American Idea* (reprint), $13.95; and *Wallace Nutting's Windsor's: Correct Windsor Furniture* (reprint), $13.95; related books available are *The Guide to Wallace Nutting-Like Photographers of the Early 20th Century*, $13.95; and *The History of Sawyer Pictures* by Carol Begley Gray, $14.95. All these books are currently available at the above address. Shipping is $3.75 for the first item ordered and $1.50 for each additional item.

Knauer, Judy A.
National Toothpick Holder Collectors Society
1224 Spring Valley Lane, West Chester, 19380-5112; 610-431-3477. Specializing in toothpick holders and Victorian glass

The Krauses
Krause, Gail
97 W. Wheeling St., Washington, 15301; 412-228-5034. Author of book on Duncan glass

Kreider, Katherine
Kingsbury Antiques
PO Box 7957, Lancaster, 17604-7957; 717-892-3001. Author of *Valentines With Values*, available for $22.90 ppd. ($24.09 PA residents) and *One Hundred Years of Valentines*, available for $28.90 ppd. ($30.40 PA residents); No free appraisals. Stop by Booth #315 at Black Angus, in Adamstown (new section) and talk about valentines

Levi, Anita
Allegheny Mountain Antique Gallery
5151 Clear Shade Dr., Windber, 15963; 814-467-8539. Specializing in novelty clocks, advertising tins, primitives, holiday decorations, quilts, purses, Black memorabilia, linens, stoneware, Roseville, kitchenware, Art Deco

Lindsay, Ralph
PO Box 21, New Holland, 17557. Specializing in target balls; SASE required with correspondence

Lowe, James Lewis
Kate Greenaway Society
PO Box 8, Norwood, 19074; e-mail: JLewisLowe@juno.com. Specializing in Kate Greenaway

Maier, Clarence and Betty
Mail order: The Burmese Cruet
Box 432, Montgomeryville, 18936; 215-855-5388; burmesecruet@erols.com; burmesecruet.com. Specializing in Victorian art glass

Merchants Square Mall
Jim & Annetta Vitez, Managers
1901 S. 12th St., Allentown, 18103; 610-797-7743

Posner, Judy
June - September: R.D. 1 Box 273 SC, Effort 18330, fax: 717-629-0521; e-mail: judyandjef@aol.com. Specializing in Disneyana, Black memorabilia, salt and pepper shakers, souvenirs of the USA., character and advertising memorabilia, figural pottery; buy, sell, collect; informal appraisals, $5 LSASE and photo of item

Reimert, Leon
121 Highland Dr., Coatesville, 19320; 610-383-6969. Specializing in Boehm porcelain

Rosso, Philip J. and Philip Jr.
Wholesale Glass Dealers
1815 Trimble Ave., Port Vue, 15133; 412-678-7352. Specializing in Westmoreland glass

Weiser, Pastor Frederick S.
55 Kohler School Rd., New Oxford, 17350; 717-624-4106. Specializing in frakturs and other Pennsylvania German documents; SASE required when requesting information

Rhode Island

Gacher, John
The Zsolnay Store
152 Spring St., Newport, 02840; 401-841-5060; web: www.drawrm.com. Specializing in Zsolnay, Fischer, Amphora, and Austro-Hungarian art pottery

The Occupied Japan Club
c/o Florence Archambault
29 Freeborn St., Newport, 02840-1821. Publishes bimonthly newsletter, *The Upside Down World of an O.J. Collector;* SASE required when requesting information

South Carolina

Greguire, Helen
Helen's Antiques
216 Mountain View Rd, Landrum, 29356; 864-457-7340. Specializing in graniteware (any color), carnival glass lamps and shades, carnival glass lighting of all kinds; author (Collector Books) of *The Collector's Encyclopedia of Graniteware, Colors, Shapes & Values* (updated values, $28.45 ppd.); second book on graniteware now available with prices updated to 1997 (same price); also available is *Carnival in Lights,* featuring carnival glass, lamps, shades, etc. ($13.45 ppd.); and *Collector's Guide to Toasters and Accessories, Identification & Values* ($21.95 ppd.); all available from author; please include SASE when requesting information; looking for people interested in collecting toasters to form a national club

Roerig, Fred and Joyce
1501 Maple Ridge Rd., Walterboro, 29488; 843-538-2487. Specializing in cookie jars; authors of *Collector's Encyclopedia of Cookie Jars, An Illustrated Value Guide,* (three in the series), publishers of *Cookie Jarrin' with Joyce: The Cookie Jar Newsletter*

Tennessee

Chase, Mick and Lorna
Fiesta Plus
380 Hawkins Crawford Rd., Cookeville, 38501; 931-372-8333. Specializing in Fiesta, Harlequin, Riviera, Franciscan, Metlox, other American dinnerware

Foil, Richard and Sue
Serendipity Antiques at Antiques Unlimited; State St. Birstol; 540-628-8315. Authors of book on Cumbow China

Grist, Everett
PO Box 91375, Chattanooga, 37412-3955; 423-510-8052. Specializing in covered animal dishes and marbles

Hudson, Murray
Murray Hudson Antiquarian Books & Maps
109 S. Church St., Box 163, Halls, 38040; 901-836-9057 or 800-748-9946; fax: 901-836-9017. Specializing in antique maps, globes, and books with maps, atlases, explorations, travel guides, geographies, surveys, etc.

Kline, Jerry
Florence Showcase
3070 Sugarwood Dr., Kodak, 37764; 423-933-4011; fax: 423-933-4492. Specializing in Florence Ceramics of California, Rookwood pottery, Shelley English china, English chintz

Weddington, David
Predicta Sales & Service
2702 Albany Ct., Murfreesboro, 37129; 615-890-7498. Specializing in vintage Philco Predicta TVs

Texas

Babcock, Bobby
Jubilation Antiques
5108 Saddleridge Cove, Austin, 78759; 512-418-9373. Specializing in Maxfield Parrish, Black memorabilia, and brown Roseville Pine Cone

Cooper, Marilyn
8408 Lofland Dr., Houston, 77055; 713-465-7773. Specializing in figural toothbrush holders, Pez, candy containers

Dockery, Rod
4600 Kemble St., Ft. Worth, 76103; 817-536-2168. Specializing in milk glass; SASE required with correspondence

Docks, L.R. 'Les'
Shellac Shack; Discollector
Box 691035, San Antonio, 78269-1035. Author of *American Premium Record Guide;* specializing in vintage records

Fer-Duc Inc.
Joseph D. Ferrara
2814 College Plaza #5112, Dallas, 75205; 214-368-1113. Specializing in American art pottery (Ohr and Rookwood), 19th- and 20th-century paintings

Frese, Leo and Wendy
Three Rivers Collectibles
Box 551542, Dallas, 75355; 214-341-5165. Specializing in RumRill, Red Wing pottery and stoneware

Gibbs, Carl, Jr.
PO Box 131584, Houston, 77219-1584; 713-521-9661. Author of *Collector's Encyclopedia of Metlox Potteries,* autographed copies available from author for $27.95 ppd.; specializing in American ceramic dinnerware

Groves, Bonnie
402 North Ave. A, Elgin, 78621. Specializing in boudoir dolls

Malowanczyk, Abby and Wlodek
Collage-20th Century Classics
2820 N. Henderson, Dallas, 75206; phone/fax: 214-828-9888; also may be reached at 3017-B Routh St., Dallas, 75201; 214-880-0020; e-mail: txcollage@aol.com and web site: www.collageclassics.com. Specializing in architect-designed furniture and decorative arts from the modern movement

Norris, Kenn
Schoolmaster Auctions and Collectibles
PO Box 4830, 513 N. 2nd St., Sanderson, 79848; 915-345-2640. Specializing in school-related items, barbed wire, related literature, and L'il Abner (antique shop in downtown Sanderson)

Pringle, Joyce M.
Antiques and Moore
3708 W. Pioneer Pkwy., Arlington, 76013; www.Antiquesandmoore.com/glas/ or chip@antiquesandmoore.com. Specializing in Boyd, Summit, and Mosser glass

Rosen, Kenna
Rosen Estate Sales & Appraisals, Inc.
9138 Loma Vista, Dallas, 75243; 972-503-1436; e-mail: ke-rosen@swbell.net. Specializing in Bluebird china, quality estate sales

Silvermintz, Karen
6164 Ravendale Lane, Dallas, 75214; 214-826-1107. Specializing in American dinnerware

Smith, Allan
1806 Shields Dr., Sherman, 75092; 903-893-3626. Specializing in children's lunch boxes, Coca-Cola, Dr. Pepper, Pepsi Cola, RC Cola, western stars' items, character tin windup toys, and most character collectibles

Thompson, Chuck
Chuck Thompson & Associates
10802 Greencreek Dr., Suite 703, Houston, 77070. Send LSASE for free list of Chuck's tobacciana publications. His entertaining and instructive column, *Fables for Collectors,* is featured each month in *Collectors News* magazine.

Tucker, Richard and Valerie
Argyle Antiques
PO Box 262, Argyle, 76226; 940-464-3752; e-mail: lead1234@gte.net or rtucker@jw.com. Specializing in windmill weights, shooting gallery targets, figural lawn sprinklers, cast-iron advertising paperweights, and other unusual figural cast iron

Turner, Danny and Gretchen
Running Rabbit Video Auctions
PO Box 701, Waverly, 37185; 615-296-3600. Specializing in marbles

Waddell, John
2903 Stan Terrace, Mineral Wells, 76067. Specializing in buggy steps

Wilkins, James R.
Olden Year Musical Museum
Box 381951, Duncanville, 75138-1951; 972-298-5587; e-mail: 1museum@cyberramp.net. Specializing in music boxes, phonographs, grind organs, nickelodeons

Woodard, Dannie; Publisher
The Aluminist
PO Box 1345; Weatherford, 76086. Annual subscription: $20 (includes membership); second book available concerning aluminum for $24.95+shipping & handling

Utah

Anderson, Tim
Box 461, Provo, 84603. Specializing in autographs; buys single items or collections — historical, movie stars, US Presidents, sports figures, and pre-1860 correspondence. Autograph questions? Please include photocopies of your autographs if possible and enclose a SASE for guaranteed reply.

Anderson, Warren R.
America West Archives
PO Box 100, Cedar City, 84721; 435-586-9497; e-mail: awa@netutah.com. Specializing in old stock certificates and bonds, western documents and books, financial ephemera, autographs, maps, photos; author of *Owning Western History,* with 75+ photos of old documents and recommended reference guide (available for $18 (soft cover) or $28 (hardback) ppd., from author

Killmer, Jo
PO Box 1424, Provo, 84603; 801-375-1211. Specializing in silverplate patterns, also sterling, china, general line of antiques, Roseville

Spencer, Rick
Salt Lake City, 801-973-0805. Specializing in sterling and silverplate flatware, hollow ware, Shawnee, Van Telligen, salt and pepper shakers; no free appraisals

Vermont

Barry, Kit
88 High St., Brattleboro, 05301; 802-254-3634. Author of *Reflections 1* and *Reflections 2,* reference books on ephemera; specializing in advertising trade cards and ephemera in general

Virginia

Bradfield, Jeff
Jeff's Antiques
90 Main St., Dayton, 22821; 540-879-9961. Also located in Pat's Antique Mall (I-81), Exit 227, Verona, and Rolling Hills Antique Mall, I-81, Exit 247B, Harrisonburg. Specializing in candy containers, toys, postcards, sugar shakers, lamps, furniture, pottery, and advertising items

Cranor, Rosalind
PO Box 859, Blacksburg, 24063. Specializing in Elvis collectibles; author of *Elvis Collectibles* and *Best of Elvis Collectibles,* available from author for $21.70 each (ppd.)

Flanigan, Vicki
Flanigan's Antiques
PO Box 1662, Winchester, 22604. Specializing in antique dolls, hand fans, and Hawaiian dolls; please include SASE with correspondence; fee for appraisals, thank you

Friend, Terry
839 Glendale Rd., Galax, 24333; 540-236-9027 after 9:30 p.m. E.S.T.; e-mail: friend@TCIA.net. Specializing in coffee mills; SASE required

Haigh, Richard
10607 Baypines Lane, Richmond, 23233; 804-741-5770. Specializing in Locke Art, Steuben, Loetz, Fry, Italian; SASE required for reply

Lechner, Mildred and Ralph
Box 554, Mechanicsville, 23111; 804-737-3347. Author (Collector Books) on glass salt shakers; specializing in art and pattern glass salt shakers circa 1870-1940; directors of Antique and Art Glass Salt Shakers Collectors Society Club, 1991-92. **Please note: Mildred and Ralph have absolutely NO involvement or dealings concerning novelty salt shakers or their values.**

MacAllister, Dale
PO Box 46, Singers Glen, 22850. Specializing in sugar shakers and syrups

Monsen, Randall; and Baer, Rod
Monsen & Baer
Box 529, Vienna, 22183; 703-938-2129. Specializing in perfume bottles, Roseville pottery, Art Deco

Reynolds, Charles
Reynolds Toys
2836 Monroe St., Falls Church, 22042; 703-533-1322. Specializing in limited-edition mechanical and still banks, figural bottle openers

Schleyer, Jim
Box 243-E, Burke, 22015. Former editor of the newsletter, *Toy Gun Perveyors* and author of *Backyard Buckaroos — Collecting Western Toy Guns*, which contains nearly 2,500 photographs and value guide. Toy gun inquiries that include a SASE will be graciously answered.

Windsor, Grant S.
PO Box 3613, Richmond, 23235-7613; 804-320-0386. Specializing in Griswold cast-iron cookware; SASE required for inquiries. Grant currently has a reprint of Griswold Catalog S, dated November 1, 1895, 20 pages. It contains much information and illustrations of several items not seen in catalogs previously known. Information is revealed which specifically dates the 'World's Fair' griddle; currently available for $11.50 each (ppd.); for orders of 10 or more: $7.50 each (ppd.).

Washington

Frost, Donald M.
Country Estate Antiques (Appointment only)
14800 N.E. 8th St., Vancouver, 98684; 360-604-8434. Specializing in art glass and earlier 20th-century American glass

Haase, Don (Mr. Spode)
D&D Antiques
PO Box 818, Mukilteo, 98275; 425-348-7443; e-mail: mrspode@aol.com or Don@mrspode.com or home page at www.mrspode.com. Specializing in Spode-Copeland China

Jackson, Denis C., Editor
The Illustrator Collector's News
PO Box 1958, Sequim, 98382; 206-683-2559. Copy of recent sample: $3. Specializing in old magazines & illustrations such as Rose O'Neill, Maxfield Parrish, pinups, Marilyn Monroe, Norman Rockwell, etc.

Payne, Sharon A.
Antiquities & Art
9104 163rd Ave. NE, Granite Falls, 98252; 360-691-4847. Specializing in Cordey

Rothe, Linda
10020A, Main St. #422, Bellevue, 98004. Specializing in Black Americana

Weldin, Bob
Miner's Quest
W. 3015 Weile, Spokane, WA 99208; 509-327-2897. Specializing in mining antiques and collectibles (mail-order business)

Wheeler-Tanner Escapes
Tanner, Joseph and Pamela
3024 E. 35th Ave., Spokane, 99223; 509-448-8457. Specializing in handcuffs, leg shackles, balls and chains, restraints, and padlocks of all kinds (including railroad) locking and non-locking devices; also Houdini memorabilia: autographs, photos, posters, books, letters, etc.

Whitaker, Jim and Kaye
Eclectic Antiques
PO Box 475 Dept. S, Lynnwood, 98046. Specializing in Josef Originals and motion lamps; SASE required

Zeder, Audrey
1320 S.W. 10th Street #S, North Bend, 98045 (Appointment only). Specializing in British Royalty Commemorative souvenirs (mail-order catalog available); author (Wallace Homestead) of *British Royalty Commemoratives*

West Virginia

Fostoria Glass Society of America, Inc.
Box 826, Moundsville, 26041. Specializing in Fostoria glass

Wisconsin

Antique Associates Mall
220 Walnut St.; Suite #1, Spooner, 54801; 715-635-6666. Furniture, glassware & china, quilts, dolls, toys, books, pottery, primitives, lamps; open: Mon. - Sat. 10 a.m. - 5 p.m.; Sunday by chance

Apple, John
John Apple Antiques
1720 College Ave., Racine, 53403; 414-633-3086. Specializing in brass cash registers and parts

Genens, Joe
PO Box 124, Lake Geneva, 53147; 414-248-0559. Specializing in Norman Rockwell

Helley, Phil
Old Kilbourne Antiques
629 Indiana Ave., Wisconsin Dells, 53965; 608-254-8770. Specializing in premiums, German and Japanese tin toys, Cracker Jack, toothbrush holders, radio premiums, pencil sharpeners, and comic strip toys

Knapper, Mary
Phoneco, Inc.
207 E. Mill Rd., PO Box 70, Galesville, 54630; 608-582-4124. Specializing in telephones, antique to modern

Matzke, Gene
Gene's Badges & Emblems
2345 S. 28th St., Milwaukee, 53215; 414-383-8995 or fax: 414-645-8288; e-mail: badgeone@asapnet.net. Specializing in police badges, leg irons, old police photos, fire badges (old), patches, old handcuffs, and memorabilia

Rice, Ferill J.
302 Pheasant Run, Kaukauna, 54130. Specializing in Fenton art glass

Clubs, Newsletters, and Catalogs

ABC *Collectors' Circle* (16-page newsletter, published 3 times a year)
Dr. Joan M. George
67 Stevens Ave., Old Bridge, NJ 08857; e-mail: drjgeorge@nac.net or fax 732-679-6102. Specializing in ABC plates and mugs

Abingdon Pottery Collectors Club
Elaine Westover, Membership and Treasurer
210 Knox Hwy. 5, Abingdon, IL 61410; 309-462-3267. Dues $8 for single, $10 per couple; specializing in collecting and preservation of Abingdon pottery

ACME (Association of Coffee Mill Enthusiasts)
c/o Terry Friend
839 Glendale Rd., Galax, VA 24333; 540-236-9027 after 9:30 p.m. EST; e-mail: friend@TCIA.net

Akro Agate Collectors Club and *Clarksburg Crow* Newsletter
Roger Hardy
10 Bailey St., Clarksburg, WV 26301-2524; 304-624-4523 (evenings) or West End Antiques, 97 Milford St., Clarksburg, WV 26301; 304-624-7600 (weekdays). Annual membership fee: $25

The Akro Arsenal, quarterly catalog
Larry D. Wells
6301 Walnut Valley Dr., Ft. Wayne, IN 46818; 219-489-5842

Alex G. Malloy, Inc.
PO Box 38, South Salem, NY 10590; 203-438-0396. Specialized catalogs on antiquities, and ancient and medieval coins

The Aluminist
Dannie Woodard, Publisher
PO Box 1346, Weatherford, TX 76086. Subscription: $20 (includes membership)

America West Archives
Anderson, Warren
PO Box 100, Cedar City, UT 84721; 435-586-9497; e-mail: awa@netutah.com. 26-page illustrated catalogs issued 6 times a year; has both fixed-price and auction sections offering early western documents, letters, stock certificates, autographs, and other important ephemera; subscription: $15 per year

American Antique Deck Collectors
52 Plus Joker Club
Clear the Decks, newsletter
Ray Hartz, Past President
Rhonda Hawes, Membership
204 Gorham Ave., Hamden, CT 06514 ($25 in US and Canada, $35 foreign). Specializing in antique playing cards

American Bell Association, Int., Inc.
c/o The Bell Tower, PO Box 19443, Indianapolis, IN 46219. Dorothy Malone Anthony, Past President

American Hatpin Society
Virginia Woodbury, President
20 Montecillo, Rolling Hills Estates, CA 90274; 310-326-2196. Newsletter published quarterly; meetings also quarterly

Antique and Art Glass Salt Shaker Collectors' Society (AAGSSCS)
17460 Caloosa Trace Circle, Ft. Myers, FL 33912

Antique & Collectors Reproduction News
Antiques Coast to Coast
Mark Chervenka, Editor
PO Box 12130, Des Moines, IA 50312-9403; 515-274-5886 or (subscriptions only) 800-227-5531. 12 monthly issues: $32 per year in US; $41 in Canada; $59 all other foreign

Antique Advertising Association of America (AAAA)
PO Box 1121, Morton Grove, IL 60053; 708-466-0904. Publishes *Past Times* Newsletter; subscription: $35

Antique Bottle & Glass Collector Magazine
Jim Hagenbuch, Publisher
102 Jefferson St., PO Box 180, East Greenville, PA 18041. Subscription: (12 issues) $21 in US ($24 in Canada)

Antique Bowie Knife Collectors Assn.
Roger Baker, Member
Box 620417, Woodside, CA 94062

Antique Comb Collectors Club International
Antique Comb Collector Newsletter
Belva Green, Editor
90 S. Highland Ave., #1204, Tarpon Springs, FL 34689-5351; 727-942-7354; e-mail: comber@gte.net

Antique Journal
Michael F. Shores, Publisher
Jeffrey Hill, Editor/General Manager
1684 Decoto Rd., Suite #166, Union City, CA 94587; 800-791-8592

Antique Journal Northwest
Michael F. Shores, Publisher
Jeffrey Hill, Editor/General Manager
3439 North East Sandy Blvd., Suite #275, Portland, OR 97232; 888-845-3201

Antique Purses Catalog: $4
Bayhouse
PO Box 40443, Cleveland, OH 44140; 216-871-8584. Includes colored photos of beaded and enameled mesh purses

Antique Radio Classified (ARC)
PO Box 2, Carlisle, MA 01741; 978-371-0512

Antique Souvenir China Collectors
Gary Leveille, Director
5 Brook Lane, Barrington, MA 01230

Antique Stove Association
Macy Stern, Editor of *Antique Stove Association Quarterly*, 5515 Almeda Rd., Houston, TX 77004; 713-521-0934 or 713-528-1295

Antique Telephone Collectors Association
Box 94, Abilene, KS 67410; 785-263-1757. An international organization associated with the Museum of Independent Telephony

Antique Trader Weekly
Nancy Crowley, Editor
PO Box 1050, Dubuque, IA 52004-1050. Featuring news about antiques and collectibles, auctions, and events; listing over 165,000 buyers and sellers in every edition; Subscription: $37 (52 issues) per year; toll free for subscriptions only: 800-334-7165

Antique Wireless Association
Ormiston Rd., Breesport, NY 14816

Appraisers National Association
120 S. Bradford Ave., Placentia, CA 92870; 714-579-1082. Founded in 1982 by Dr. David Long, Ph.D., President of the College for Appraisers, to provide for a standardization of educational requirements for certification of its appraiser members and assure the public that A.N.A. appraisers not only have a broad range of knowledge in personal property valuation, but are held to the highest ethical and professional standards in the industry

Ashtray Collectors Directory
Chuck Thompson
10802 Greencreek Dr., Suite 703, Houston, TX 77070. Annual publication listing all known ashtray collectors with addresses and specialties, $9.95 ppd.

Association of Coffee Mill Enthusiasts
c/o John E. White, Treasurer
5941 Wilkerson Rd., Rex, GA 30273. Annual dues: $30, covers cost of quarterly newsletter and copy of membership roster

Auction Times for the West
Michael F. Shores, Publisher
Jeffrey Hill, Editor/General Manager
2329 Santa Clara Ave., Suite 207, Alamedo, CA 94501; 800-791-8592

Autograph Times
2303 N. 44th St., #225, Phoenix, AZ 85008; 602-947-3112 or fax 602-947-8363. Subscription: $15 (US) per year

Autographs of America
Tim Anderson
PO Box 461, Provo, UT 84603; 801-226-1787 (please call in the afternoon); www.AutographsofAmerica.com. Free sample catalog of hundreds of autographs for sale

Autumn Leaf
Bill Swanson, Editor
807 Roaring Springs Dr., Allen, TX 75002-2112; 972-727-5527
Gwynne Harrison, President
PO Box 1, Mira Loma, CA 91752-0001; 909-685-5434

Avon Times (National Avon collectors' newsletter)
c/o Dwight or Vera Young
PO Box 9868, Kansas City, MO 64134. Inquiries should be accompanied by LSASE

Beatlefan
PO Box 33515, Decatur, GA 30033. Subscription: $7 (US) for 6 issues or $21 (Canada and Mexico)

Black Memorabilia Illustrated Sales List ($2 and LSASE)
Judy Posner
June - September: R.D. 1, Box 273 SC, Effort, PA 18330, fax: 717-629-0521; October - May: PO Box 2194 SC, Englewood, FL 34295, fax: 941-475-2645; e-mail: judyandjef@aol.com or URL: www.judyposner.com. Buy-Sell-Collect

Bojo
PO Box 1403, Cranberry Township, PA 16066-0403. Send $3 for 38 pages of Beatles, toys, dolls, jewelry, autographs, Yellow Submarine items, etc.

Bookend Collector Club
c/o Louis Kuritzky, M.D.
4510 NW 17th Place, Gainesville, FL 32650; 352-377-3193; lkuritzky@aol.com

Bossons Briefs, quarterly newsletter
Available through membership of International Bossons Collectors Society, 1787 Morgan Valley Rd., Rockmart, GA 30153

Boyd's Art Glass Collectors Guild
PO Box 52, Hatboro, PA 19040-0052

Boyd's Crystal Art Glass
Jody & Darrell's Glass Collectibles Newsletter
PO Box 180833, Arlington, TX 76096-0833. Publishes 6 times a year; subscription includes an exclusive glass collectible produced by Boyd's Crystal Art Glass; LSASE for current subscription rates; sample copy of newsletter: $3

British Royal Commemorative Souvenirs Mail Order Catalog
Audrey Zeder
1320 SW 10th St. #S, North Bend, WA 98045

Buckeye Marble Collectors Club
209 Crocus Court, Newark, OH 43055

The Buttonhook Society
Box 287, White Marsh, MD 21162. Publishes bimonthly newsletter *The Boutonneur*, which promotes collecting of buttonhooks and shares research and information contributed by members

Candy Container Collectors of America
The Candy Gram Newsletter
Joyce L. Doyle
PO Box 426, North Reading, MA 01864-0426. Send SASE for application

Candy Containers of America
119 N. Mars, Wichita, KS 67212
Or contact: Jeff Bradfield
90 Main St., Dayton, VA 22821

The Cane Collector's Chronicle
Linda Beeman
15 2nd St. N.E., Washington, D.C. 20002; $30 for 4 issues

The Carnival Pump
International Carnival Glass Assoc., Inc.
Lee Markley
Box 306, Mentone, IN 46539. Dues: $20 per family per year in US and Canada or $25 overseas, payable each July 1st

The Carousel News & Trader
87 Parke Ave. W., Suite 206, Mansfield, OH 44902. A monthly magazine for the carousel enthusiast; subscription: $22 per year; sample: $3

The Carousel Shopper Resource Catalog
Box 47, Dept PC, Millwood, NY 10546. Only $2 (+50¢ postage); a full-color catalog featuring dealers of antique carousel art offering single figures or complete carousels, museums, restoration services, organizations, full-size reproductions, books, cards, posters, auction services, and other hard-to-find items for carousel enthusiasts

Cast Iron Marketplace
PO Box 16466, Saint Paul, MN 55116. Available to hobbyists/dealers on a monthly basis to buy/sell/trade products made by the great foundries from our industrial past; subscription: $30 per year (includes free ads up to 200 words per issue)

A Catalog Collection
Kenneth E. Schneringer
271 Sabrina Ct., Woodstock, GA 30188-4228; 770-926-9383; e-mail: trademan68@aol.com. Specializing in catalogs, promochures, view books, labels, trade cards, special paper needs

Central Florida Insulator Collectors
3557 Nicklaus Dr., Titusville, FL 32780-5356; 407-267-9170; e-mail: bluebellwt@aol.com. Dues: $10 per year for single or family membership (checks payable to Jacqueline C. Linscott); dues covers the cost of *Newsnotes*, the club's monthly newsletter, which informs members of meetings and shows, articles of interest on insulators and other collectibles. Members are invited to use free advertising of items for sale or trade. The club meets quarterly in members' homes and hosts a show each January which is open to the public. For club information send SASE to above address.

Ceramic Arts Studio Catalog Reprints
Wellman, BA
PO Box 673, Westminster, MA 01473-0673; e-mail: BAWELLMAN @NET1PLUS.COM. Also offers many other catalog reprints from dinnerware to art pottery; specializing in all areas of American ceramics, art pottery, dinnerware, and figurines

Ceramic Arts Studio Collector's Association
PO Box 46, Madison, WI 53701; 608-241-9138. Publishes newsletter, *CAS Collector*, a 22-page bimonthly; annual membership: $15; sample copy: $3; inventory record and price guide also available

Chicagoland Antique Amusements Slot Machine & Jukebox Gazette
Ken Durham, Editor
909 26 St., N.W., Suite 502, Washington, D.C. 20037; web site: www. GameRoomAntiques.com. 20-page newspaper published twice a year; subscription: 4 issues for $10; sample: $5; send SASE for free list of books

China Specialties, Inc.
Fiesta Collector's Quarterly Newsletter
PO Box 471, Valley City, OH 44280

Chintz Connection Newsletter
PO Box 222, Riverdale, MD 20738.
Dedicated to helping collectors share
information and find matchings; subscription: 4 issues per year for $25

Coin-Op Newsletter
Ken Durham, Publisher
909 26th St. N.W., Suite 502, Washington, D.C. 20037; web site:
www.GameRoomAntiques.com. Subscription: $15 per year; sample: $5;
send SASE for free list of books

The Cola Clan
Alice Fisher, Treasurer
2084 Continental Dr., N.E., Atlanta,
GA 30345

Collectors of Findlay Glass
PO Box 256, Findlay, OH 45840. An
organization dedicated to the study and
recognition of Findlay glass; newsletter
The Melting Pot, published quarterly;
annual convention; membership: $10
per year

Compact Collectors
Roselyn Gerson
PO Box 40, Lynbrook, NY 11563; 516-
593-8746 or fax 516-593-0610; e-mail:
compactlady@aol.com. Publishes *Powder
Puff* Newsletter, which contains articles
covering all aspects of compact collecting, restoration, vintage ads, patents,
history, and articles by members and
prominent guest writers; seekers and
sellers column offered free to members

Cookie Crumbs
Cookie Cutter Collectors Club
Ruth Capper, Secretary/Treasurer
1167 Teal Road S.W., Dellroy, OH
44620. Subscription $12 per year (4
issues); payable to CCCC

*Cookie Jarrin' With Joyce: The Cookie
Jar Newsletter*
1501 Maple Ridge Rd., Walterboro,
SC 29488

Cookies
Rosemary Henry
9610 Greenview Lane, Manassas, VA
20109-3320. Subscription: $12 per
year (6 issues); payable to Cookies

The Copley Courier
1639 N. Catalina St., Burbank, CA
91505

Cowan Pottery Museum Associates
For information write: CPMA,
POBox 16765, Rocky River, OH
44116 or contact Victoria Naumann
Peltz, Curatorial Associate, Cowan
Pottery Museum at Rocky River Pub-
lic Library, 1600 Hampton Rd., Rocky
River, OH 44116; 440-333-7610, ext.
214. Annual dues. $35, includes sub-
scription to biannual *Cowan Pottery
Journal* Newsletter

Cracker Jack® Collector's Assoc.
The Prize Insider Newsletter
Roberta Bowen
305 E. Minton Dr., Tempe, AZ 85282;
602-831-1402. Subscription/member-
ship: $18 per year (single) or $24
(family)

Creamers, quarterly newsletter
PO Box 11, Lake Villa, IL 60046-
0011. Subscription: $5 per year

Currier & Ives Catalog
Rudisill's Alt Print Haus
PO Box 199, Worton, MD 21678.
Please include LSASE

Currier & Ives China by Royal Newsletters
c/o Jack and Treva Hamlin for information. 145 Township Rd. 1088,
Proctorville, OH 45669; 740-886-
7644; e-mail: trevajo@ezwv.com. We
buy and sell; 2 different newsletters
and a book now available (over 100
pages); there is also a collector club

Currier & Ives (China) Quarterly
c/o Patti Street
PO Box 504, Riverton, KS 66770;
316-848-3529; e-mail: streetp@and-
merch.com. Subscription: $12 per
year (includes 2 free ads); holds annual reunion

Czechoslovakian Collectors Guild
International
PO Box 901395, Kansas City, MO
64190

The DAZE, Inc. (formerly *The Depression Glass DAZE*)
Teri Steele (Cox), Publisher
The Nation's Marketplace and Meet-
ingplace for American glass, china,
and pottery collectors, Box 57,
Otisville, MI 48463; e-mail at
dgdaze@aol.com or call 800-336-9927
for trial subscription offer

*The Dedham Pottery Collectors Society
Newsletter*
Jim Kaufman, Publisher
248 Highland St., Dedham, MA
02026; 800-283-8070

Disneyana Illustrated Sales List ($2
and LSASE)
Judy Posner
June - September: R.D. 1, Box 273
SC, Effort, PA 18330, fax: 717-629-
0521. October - May: PO Box 2194
SC, Englewood, FL 34295, fax: 941-
475-2645; e-mail: judyandjef@aol.com
or URL: www.judyposner.com. Buy-
Sell-Collect

Docks, L.R. 'Les'
Shellac Shack
Box 691035, San Antonio, TX
78269-1035. Send $2 for a 72-page
catalog of 78s that Docks wants to
buy, the prices he will pay, and shipping instructions

Doorstop Collectors of America
Doorstopper Newsletter
Jeanie Bertoia
2413 Madison Ave., Vineland, NJ
08630; 609-692-4092. Membership:
$20 per year, includes 2 newsletters
and convention; send 2-stamp SASE
for sample

*Dorothy Kamm's Porcelain Collector's
Companion*
PO Box 7460, Port St. Lucie, FL 34985-
7460; 561-465-4008 or fax 407-460-
9050. Published bimonthly,
subscription: $28 per year

Dragonware Club
c/o Suzi Hibbard
849 Vintage Ave., Fairfield, CA
94585; SRHACS@Pacbell.net.
Inquiries should be accompanied by
long SASE; all contributions welcome

Drawing Room of Newport
Gacher, John
152 Spring St., Newport, RI 02840;
401-841-5060; web: www.drawrm.
com. Book on Zsolnay available

Ed Taylor Radio Museum
245 N. Oakland Ave., Indianapolis,
IN 46201-3360; 317-638-1641

Eggcup Collector's Corner
67 Stevens Ave., Old Bridge, NJ
08857. Issued quarterly; subscriptions:
$18 per year (payable to Joan
George); sample copies: $5

The Elegance of Old Ivory Newsletter
Box 1004, Wilsonville, OR 97070

Fenton Art Glass Collectors of Amer-
ica, Inc.
PO Box 384, 702 W. 5th St.,
Williamstown, WV 26187

Fiesta Club of America
PO Box 15383, Loves Park, IL,
61132-5383; 815-964-3981

Fiesta Collector's Quarterly Newsletter
PO Box 471, Valley City, OH 44280.
Subscription: $12 per year

Figural Bottle Opener Collectors
Linda Fitzsimmons, 9697 Gwynn Park
Dr., Ellicott City, MD 21042; 410-
465-9296. Please include SASE when
requesting information

Florence Collector's Club Newsletter
Rita Bee, Editor; Beth Dunigan, Pub-
lisher; c/o Florence Collector's Club
Membership Chairman
PO Box 122, Richland, WA 99353.
Subscription: (6 issues per year) $20

Fostoria Glass Society of America, Inc.
PO Box 826, Moundsville, WV 26041

Frankoma Family Collectors Association
c/o Nancy Littrell
PO Box 32571, Oklahoma City, OK
73123-0771. Membership dues: $25
(includes quarterly newsletter); annual convention

Friar Tuck Collectors Club
Bob Furman
PO Box 262, Oswego, NY 13827.
Quarterly newsletter, annual conven-
tion; write for membership applica-
tion and information

Friends of Degenhart
c/o Degenhart Museum
PO Box 186, Cambridge, OH 43725; 740-
432-2626. Membership: $5 ($10 for family) includes *Heartbeat* Newsletter (printed
quarterly) and free admission to museum

H.C. Fry Society
PO Box 41, Beaver, PA 15009. Founded in
1983 for the sole purpose of learning about Fry
glass; Publishes *Shards*, quarterly newsletter

GAB! (Glass Animal Bulletin!)
PO Box 143, N. Liberty, IA 52317. Subscription: $16 (12 issues), ads free to subscribers

The Glass Post, monthly newsletter
PO Box 205, Oakdale, IA 52319;
phone/fax: 319-626-3216. Subscription:
$25 per year, ads free to subscribers

The Glass Menagerie, bimonthly newsletter
Susan Candelaria, Editor
5440 El Arbol, Carlsbad, CA 92008

Goofus Glass Gazette
Steve Gillespie, Publisher
400 Martin Blvd., Village of the Oaks,
MO 64118; 888-452-5554 or fax 816-
452-5554; e-mail: goofus@mid-west.net

The Gonder Collector
917 Hurl Dr.
Pittsburgh, PA 15236

Grandpa's Depot
John 'Grandpa' White
1616 17th St., Suite 267, Denver, CO
80202; 303-628-5590 or fax 303-628-
5547. Publishes catalogs on railroad-
related collectibles

Griswold & Cast Iron Cookware Association
Grant Windsor
PO Box 3613, Richmond, VA 23235;
804-320-0386. Membership: $15 (for
single) or $20 (for 2 members per
address) payable to club

Haeger Pottery Collectors of America
Lanette Clarke
5021 Toyon Way, Antioch, CA 94509;
925-776-7784. Newsletter published 6
times per year; dues: $20

*The Hagen-Renaker Collector's Club
Newsletter*
c/o Jenny Palmer
3651 Polish Line Rd., Cheboygan, MI
49721-9045

Hake's Americana & Collectibles
Specializing in character and personality collectibles along with artifacts
of popular culture for over 20 years.
To receive a catalog for their next
3,000-item mail/phone bid auction,
send $3 to: Hake's Americana; PO
Box 1444M, York, PA 17405

Hall China Collector's Club Newsletter
PO Box 360488, Cleveland, OH 44136

Head Hunters Newsletter
c/o Maddy Gordon
PO Box 83H, Scarsdale, NY 10583. Subscription: $24 yearly (quarterly issues)

Homer Laughlin Eagle
c/o Richard Racheter
1270 63rd Terrace South, St. Petersburg, FL 33705

*How to Open and Operate a Home-
Based Antiques Business; How to Rec-
ognize and Refinish Antiques for
Pleasure and Profit; and How to Start a
Home-Based Antique Business*
Jacquelyn Peake, author
Globe Pequot Press
PO Box 833, Old Saybrook, CT
06475 or any book store

Ice Screamer
c/o Duvall Sollers
PO Box 132, Monkton, MD 21111.
Published quarterly; dues: $15 per year; annual convention held in late June in Lancaster, PA

Ideal Collectors Club
c/o Judith Izen
PO Box 623, Lexington, MA 02173; e-mail: jizenres@aol.com Membership: $20 per year, includes a quarterly newsletter; subscribers get free wanted/for sale ads in each issue

The Illustrator Collector's News (TICN)
Denis C. Jackson, Editor
PO Box 1958, Sequim, WA 98382; e-mail: ticn@olypen.com. Subscription: $18 per year; $3 for sample copy of bimonthly publication; publishes price and identification guides on various illustrators and old magazines, write for further information

Indiana Historical Radio Society
245 N. Oakland Ave., Indianapolis, IN 46201-3360; 317-638-1641

International Association of Calculator Collectors, *International Calculator Collector* Newsletter
Guy Ball, Co-Editor
PO Box 345, Tustin, CA 92781-0345; e-mail: mrcalc@usa.net. Subscription: $16 per year ($20 foreign); sample copy: $3

International Club for Collectors of Hatpins and Hatpin Holders (ICC of H&HH)
Audrae Heath, Managing Editor
PO Box 1009, Bonners Ferry, ID 83805-1009. Bimonthly *Points* newsletter and *Pictorial Journal*

International Association of R.S. Prussia, Inc.
Theresa Newcomer, Secretary
PO Box 446, Mount Joy, PA 17522. Membership: $20 per household; yearly convention

International Ivory Society
Robert Weisblut, Co-Founder
11109 Nicholas Dr., Wheaton, MD 20902; 301-649-4002. $10 annual membership fee includes 4 newsletters

International Nippon Collectors Club (INCC)
c/o Yvonne Matlosz
9101 Sulkirk Dr., Raleigh, NC 27613. Publishes newsletter 6 times a year; holds annual convention

International Perfume and Scent Bottle Collectors Association
Randall B. Monsen, President
PO Box 529, Vienna, VA 22183 or fax 703-242-1357. Membership: $35 (USA) or $48 (Foreign); newsletter published quarterly

International Rose O'Neill Club
Contact Karen Stewart
PO Box 668, Branson, MO 65616. Publishes quarterly newsletter *Kewpiesta Kourier*; dues: (includes newsletter) $7 (single) or $10 (family)

International Society of Antique Scale Collectors
Bob Stein, President
300 West Adams, Suite 821, Chicago, IL 60606; 312-263-7500. Publishes *Equilibrium* Magazine; quarterly president's newsletter; annual membership directory and out-of-print scale catalogs; annual convention

Iron Talk
Jimmy Walker, Editor
PO Box 68, Waelder, TX 78959. Journal of antique pressing irons; news of prices, patents, markets, collectibles, collectors, history, reference, advice, and much more; one-year bimonthly subscription: $25 in US (Texans add $1.94 tax); $30 foreign

John F. Rinaldi
Nautical Antiques and Related Items (Appointment only)
Box 765, Dock Square, Kennebunkport, ME 04046; 207-967-3218; or fax 207-967-2918. Illustrated catalog: $5

Josef Originals Newsletter
Jim and Kaye Whitaker
PO Box 475, Dept. S, Lynnwood, WA 98046. Subscription (4 issues): $10 per year

The Lace Merchant
Elizabeth M. Kurella, Publisher
Box 222, Plainwell, MI 49080; 616-685-9792

Lang's Sporting Collectables, Inc.
14 Fishermans Lane, Raymond, ME 04071; phone/fax: 207-655-4265. Specializing in fishing tackle and related accessories

The Laughlin Eagle
Joan Jasper, Publisher
Richard Racheter, Editor
1270 63rd Terrace S., St. Petersburg, FL 33705. Subscription: $14 (4 issues) per year; sample: $4

Les Amis de Vieux Quimper (Friends of Old Quimper)
c/o Mark and Adela Meadows
PO Box 819, Carnelian Bay, CA 96140; e-mail meadows@cwo.com. SASE required for written reply

License Plate Collectors Hobby Magazine
Drew Steitz, Editor
PO Box 222, East Texas, PA 18046; phone/fax: 610-791-7979. Bimonthly publication with many photographs, classifieds, etc.; $18 per year (1st class, US); sample: $2

Line Jewels, NIA #1380
3557 Nicklaus Dr., Titusville, FL 32780

Mabel Lucie Attwell Catalogs
J. David Ehrhard
7212 Valmont St., Tujunga, CA 91042

Majolica International Society
Suite #103, 1275 First Ave., New York, NY 10021. Dues: $35 per year, entitles member to attend annual meeting and to receive the quarterly newsletter *Majolica Matters*

Marble Collectors' Society of America
Claire Block, Secretary
PO Box 222, Trumbull, CT 06611. Publishes *Marble Mania*; gathers and disseminates information to further the hobby of marbles and marble collecting; $12 adds your name to the contributor mailing list ($21 covers 2 years)

Marble Collectors Unlimited
PO Box 206, Northboro, MA 01532

Martha's Kidlit Newsletter
Martha Rasmussen, Editor and Publisher
Box 1488, Ames IA 50014; 515-292-9309; e-mail: mart515@aol.com. For children's booklovers and collectors; Subscription: $30 in US, all others: $31

Midwest Open Salt Society
c/o Ed Bowman
2411 W. 500 North, Hartford City, IN 47348. Dues: $10 ($6 for spouse)

Midwest Sad Iron Collector Club
c/o Lynette Conrad, Secretary
24 Nob Hill Dr., St. Louis, MO 63138-1458; 314-741-4171

Miniature Bottle Club of the Great Lakes
19745 Woodmont, Harper Woods, MI 48225. Dues $5 per year; 4 meetings per year

Mt. Washington Art Glass Society
PO Box 107, Hyde Park, NY 12538-1122. Publishes MWAGS *Review*, to educate, inform and provide helpful information to anyone interested in art glass; holds annual convention; subscription/membership: $30 (single) or $40 for (2 persons in 1 household)

Murray Hudson Antiquarian Books and Maps
109 S. Church St., Box 163, Halls, TN 38040; 800-748-9946 or 901-836-9057; fax: 901-836-9017. Buyer and seller of antiquarian maps (especially pocket, wall, US Civil War, and railroad maps) and books with maps (atlases, travel guides, geographies, gazetteers, explorations, land surveys, etc.), especially of Southeastern and Southwestern US prior to 1900; also world globes, map jigsaw puzzles, and gameboards prior to 1950; contact for catalog

Mystic Lights of the Aladdin Knights, bimonthly newsletter
c/o J.W. Courter
3935 Kelley Rd., Kevil, KY 40253; 502-488-2116. Information requires LSASE

National Association of Avon Collectors
c/o Connie Clark
6100 Walnut, Dept. P, Kansas City, MO 64113. Information requires LSASE

National Association Breweriana Advertising
2343 Met-To-Wee Lane, Wauwatosa, WI 53226; 414-257-0158. Membership: $20 (US), $30 (Canada) or $40 (Overseas); publishes *The Breweriana Collector* and Membership Directory; holds annual convention

National Association of Watch & Clock Collectors, Inc. (NAWCC)
514 Poplar St., Columbia, PA 17512-2130; 717-684-8261, www.nawc.org (Headquarters, Museum, Library, School). Benefits include annual subscriptions to two publications, free research, participation in national and regional meetings, and the camaraderie of 35,000 fellow collectors worldwide; call/write for information/application.

National Autumn Leaf Collectors' Club
Bill Swanson, Newsletter Editor
807 Roaring Springs Dr., Allen, TX 75002-2112; 972-727-5527 or fax 972-727-2107; e-mail:bescom@att.net or Gwynne Harrison, President
PO Box 1, Mira Loma, CA 91752-0001; 909-685-5434 or fax 909-681-1692; e-mail: morgan99@pe.net

National Blue Ridge Newsletter
Norma Lilly
144 Highland Dr., Blountville, TN 37617. Subscription: $15 per year (6 issues)

National Bobbin Heads Club
Larkins, Barry
PO Box 9297, Daytona Beach, FL 32120; 904-253-7040

National Cambridge Collectors, Inc.
PO Box 416, Cambridge, OH 43725; 740-432-4245 or fax 740-439-9223; e-mail: NCC-Crystal-Ball@compuserve.com; web site: www/Cambridgeglass.org

National Cuff Link Society
c/o Eugene R. Klompus
PO Box 5700, Vernon Hills, IL 60061; phone/fax: 847-816-0035. $30 annual dues includes subscription to *The Link*, a quarterly magazine

National Depression Glass Association
Anita Woods
PO Box 69843, Odessa, TX 79769; 915-337-1297. Publishes *News and Views*

National Graniteware Society
PO Box 10013, Cedar Rapids, IA 52410

National Greentown Glass Association
1807 W. Madison, Kokomo, IN 46901

National Imperial Glass Collectors' Society, Inc.
PO Box 534, Bellaire, OH 43906. Dues: $15 per year (+$1 for each additional member of household); quarterly newsletter; Convention every June

National Insulator Association
1315 Old Mill Path, Broadview Heights, OH 44147

National Milk Glass Collectors' Society and *Opaque News*, quarterly newsletter
c/o Helen D. Storey
46 Almond Dr., Cocoa Townes, Hershey, PA 17033. Please include SASE

National Reamer Association
c/o Debbie Gillham
47 Midline Ct., Gaithersburg, MD 20878

National Shaving Mug Collectors Association
Penelope G. Nader, President
320 S. Greenwood St., Allerton, PA 18104; 610-437-2534. To stimulate the study, collection, and preservation of shaving mugs and all related barbering items; provides quarterly newsletter, bibliography, and directory; holds 2 meetings per year; dues: $15 per year

National Shelley China Club
Rochelle Hart, Secretary/Treasurer
591 West 67th Ave., Anchorage, AK 99518-1555. Membership: $25 per year, 4 quarterly newsletters plus many other benefits and publications, 9 years old, 550 members and growing, 1999 conference in Atlanta, GA; 10th-year anniversary in 2000 — Portland, OR

National Society of Lefton Collectors
c/o Loretta DeLozier
1101 Polk St., Bedford, IA 50833; 712-523-2289 (Mon. - Fri. 9:00 a.m. - 4:00 p.m.). Quarterly newsletter, annual convention; Dues: $25 per year

National Toothpick Holder Collectors Society
Toby Shugart, Membership
PO Box 417, Safety Harbor, FL 34695-0417. Dues: $15 (single) or $20 (couple); includes 10 *Toothpick Bulletin* newsletters per year; annual convention held in August; exclusive toothpick holder annually

National Valentine Collectors Association
Evalene Pulati
PO Box 1404, Santa Ana, CA 92702; 714-547-1355. Specializing in Valentines and love tokens

NM (Nelson McCoy) Xpress
Carol Seman
8934 Brecksville Rd., Suite 406, Brecksville, OH 44141-2318

New England Society of Open Salt Collectors
Chuck Keys
21 Overbrook Lane, East Greenwich, RI 02818; Dues: $7 per year

Newspaper Collector's Society of America
Rick Brown
info@historybuff.com or 517-887-1255. Web site: www.historybuff.com, an extensive, searchable, 300,000-word reference library of American history with an emphasis on newspapers publishing speeches; interactive crossword puzzles; regular auctions of ephemera, historic documents, and newspapers; a mall with over one hundred different online catalogs of paper collectibles; and much, much more!

Night Light Club
Culver, Bob
38619 Wakefield Ct., Northville, MI 48167; 248-473-8575. Specializing in miniature oil lamps

North American Torquay Society
Jerry and Gerry Kline, Archivists
604 Orchard View Dr., Maumee, OH 43537. Quarterly newsletter sent to members; information and membership form requires #10 SASE

North American Trap Collectors' Association
c/o Tom Parr
PO Box 94, Galloway, OH 43119-0094. Dues: $15 per year; publishes bimonthly newsletter

North Dakota Pottery Collectors Society and Newsletter
c/o Sandy Short
Box 14, Beach, ND 58621. Membership $15 per year including spouse; annual convention in June; quarterly newsletters

Novelty Salt & Pepper Shakers Club
Lula Fuller
PO Box 679388, Orlando, FL 32867-7388; 407-678-1219. Publishes quarterly newsletter; holds annual convention; dues: $20 per year in US, Canada, and Mexico ($5 extra for couple)

Nutcracker Collectors' Club and Newsletter
Susan Otto, Editor
12204 Fox Run Dr., Chesterland, OH 44026. $15 for membership and quarterly newsletters ($17 foreign), free classifieds for members

The Occupied Japan Club
c/o Florence Archambault
29 Freeborn St., Newport, RI 02840-1821. Publishes *The Upside Down World of an O.J. Collector*, a bimonthly newsletter; information requires SASE

Old Sleepy Eye Collectors Club of America, Inc.
PO Box 12, Monmouth, IL 61462. Membership: $10 per year with additional $1 for spouse (if joining)

Old Stuff
Donna and Ron Miller, Publishers
2115 McDonald Lane, PO Box 1084, McMinnville, OR 97540. Published 6 times annually; copies by mail: $3.50 each; annual subscription: $18 ($32 in Canada)

On the LIGHTER Side Newsletter (bimonthly publication)
International Lighter Collectors
Judith Sanders, Editor
136 Circle Dr., Quitman, TX 75783; 903-763-2795 or fax 903-763-4953. Annual convention held in different cities in the US; subscription fees: overseas rate, US and Canada rate, and a junior and senior citizen rate; please include SASE when requesting information

Open Salt Collectors of the Atlantic Regions (O.S.C.A.R.)
Wilbur Rudisill, Treasurer
1844 York Rd., Gettysburg, PA 17325. Dues: $5 per year

Open Salt Seekers of the West, Northern California Chapter
Sara Conley
84 Margaret Dr., Walnut Creek, CA 94596. Dues: $7 per year

Open Salt Seekers of the West, Southern California Chapter
Janet Hudson
2525 E. Vassar Court, Visalia, CA 93277. Dues: $5 per year

Pacific Northwest Fenton Assoc.
PO Box 881, Tillamook, OR 97141; 503-842-4815. Newsletter subscription: $20 per year (published quarterly, includes annual piece of glass made only for subscribers)

Paper Collectors' Marketplace
PO Box 128, Scandinavia, WI 54977-0128; 715-467-2379 or fax 715-467-2243; e-mail: pcmpaper@gglbbs.com; www.tias.com/mags/pcm. Subscription: $19.95 in US (12 issues)

Paper Pile Quarterly Magazine
Ada Fitzsimmons, Editor
PO Box 337, San Anselmo, CA 94979; 415-454-5552 or fax 415-454-2947; e-mail: apaperpile@aol.com. Sales and features magazine for paper buyers & sellers since 1980; quarterly cataloged sales of paper items, large forsale and wanted sections, auction results, book reviews, quarterly price guide & show schedule; subscription: $20 per year (shipped 1st class); sample copy: $5 (returnable as credit toward subscription or advertising)

Paperweight Collectors' Association, Inc.
PO Box 1263, Beltsville, MD 20704; 410-828-5722. Membership: for 1 or 2 people at 1 US address is $25 per year; $35 for non-US addresses; sustaining membership for 1 or 2 people at 1 US address is $55 per year and includes a copy of the annual bulletin; sustaining membership for 1 or 2 people at 1 non-US address is $65 per year if the annual bulletin is sent surface ($75 for air mail); publishes 4 newsletters a year; the annual bulletin is now hardcover, the next convention will be in 2001 with unconfirmed location

Peanut Pals
Robert Walthall, President
PO Box 4465, Huntsville, AL 35815; 205-881-9198.
Associated collectors of Planters Peanuts memorabilia, bimonthly newsletter *Peanut Papers*; annual directory sent to members; annual convention and regional conventions; dues: $20 per year (+$3 for each additional household member); membership information: PO Box 652, St. Clairsville, OH, 43950; sample newsletter: $2

Pen Collectors of America
PO Box 821449, Houston, TX 77282-1449; phone/fax: 713-496-2290. Quarterly newsletter, *Pennant*; annual membership fee: $25 (Includes newsletter and access to extensive reference library)

Pen Fancier's Club
1169 Overcash Dr., Dunedin, FL 34698; 727-734-4742 or fax: 727-738-0476; e-mail: penfanc@aol.com. Publishes quarterly catalog of vintage pens and mechanical pencils, books, parts, and information; subscription: $20 per year; sample: $4

Pepsi-Cola Collectors Club Express
Bob Stoddard, Editor
PO Box 1275, Covina, CA 91723

Perrault-Rago Gallery
17 S. Main St., Lambertville, NJ 08530. Specializing in 20th-century decorative arts, particularly art pottery and decorative tiles

Petroleum Collectibles Monthly
Scott Benjamin and Wayne Henderson, Publishers
PO Box 556, LaGrange, OH 44050-0556; 440-355-6608; www.pcmpublishing.com (visit website or call). Suscription: $29.95 per year US, Canada $38.50, International $65.95, samples $4.50. Scott is our advisor for Gasoline Globes and is devoted to gas and oil collectibles.

Phoenix and Consolidated Glass Collectors' Club
Tom Jiamachello, Secretary
41 River View Drive, Essex Junction, VT 05452; 802-878-2682; e-mail: TOPofVT@aol.com. Membership: $25 (single), $35 (family) per year; please make checks payable to club

Phoenix Bird Collectors of America (PBCA)
685 S. Washington, Constantine, MI 49042; 616-435-8353. Membership: (payable to Joan Oates) $15 per year, includes *Phoenix Bird Discoveries*, published 3 times a year; also available: 1996 Updated Value Guide to be used in conjunction with Books I-IV: $6 ppd.

Pickard Collectors Club, Ltd.
Membership office: 300 E. Grove St., Bloomington, IL 61701; 309-828-5533 or fax 309-829-2266. Membership (includes newsletter): $20 a year (single) or $25 (family)

Political Collectors of Indiana Club
Michael McQuillen
PO Box 50022, Indianapolis, IN 46250-0022; 317-845-1721. Official APIC (American Political Items Collectors) Chapter comprised of over 100 collectors of presidential and local political items

Porcelain Collector's Companion
c/o Dorothy Kamm
PO Box 7460, Port St. Lucie, FL 34985-4760; 561-464-4008 or fax 561-460-9050

Porcelier Collectors Club
21 Tamarac Swamp Rd., Wellingford, CT 06492. Publishes *Porcelier Paper* Newsletter, $2.50 for sample copy which contains much information and classified ads

Pottery Today
Bimonthly publication by Paradise Publications, PO Box 221, Mayview, MO 60471. Subscription: $15 (6 issues) per year

Powder Puff Compact Collectors' Chronicle
Roselyn Gerson
PO Box 40, Lynbrook, NY 11563; 516-593-8746 or fax 516-593-0610; e-mail: compactlady@aol.com

Psalm Card Collectors
Contact Chuck Thompson, Editor of newsletter: 10802 Greencreek Dr., #703 Houston, TX 77070-5367. For all interested in holy cards, religion, literature, poetry, hobbies, and clubs; starter pack available: includes selection of 3 different size Psalm cards and more information, send name and address (2 postage stamps)

Purinton Pastimes
PO Box 9394, Arlington, VA 22219. Newsletter for Purinton pottery enthusiasts; subscription: $10 per year

R. Lalique
John Danis
11028 Raleigh Ct., Rockford, IL 61115; 815-877-2410 or fax 815-877-6042; e-mail: danis6033@aol.com

R.A. Fox Collector's Club
c/o Pat Gibson
38280 Guava Dr., Newark, CA, 94560; 510-792-0586

Ribbon Tin News Newsletter (quarterly publication)
Hobart D. Van Deusen, Editor
28 The Green, Watertown, CT 06795; 860-945-3456; e-mail: rtn.hoby@worldnet.att.net. $30 per year for 24+ color plates; for collectors of typewriters, typewriter ribbon tins, and go-withs; indexed subscribers' list and participation in occasional mail/phone auctions

Rosevilles of the Past Newsletter
Nancy Bomm, Editor
PO Box 656, Clarcona, FL 32710-0656. $19.95 per year for 6 newsletters

Rosie Wells Enterprises, Inc.
22341 E. Wells Rd. S., Canton, IL 61520; e-mail: Rosie@RosieWells.com. Write for free literature; publishes secondary market price guides for Precious Moments® collectibles, Hallmark ornaments, Merry Miniatures and Kiddie Car Classics, Boyds Bears and Friends, Cherished Teddies, Charming Tails, and Precious Moments Company's Dolls. Check out Rosies internet site www/RosieWells.com/. Rosie has hosted eight international conventions for Precious Moments Collectors and hosts the semiannual Midwest Collectibles Fest each March and October. For Hot Tips and to record voice ads, Rosie offers a touch-tone 900 line (1-900-740-7575). Send for a category list or see our web site! Call Rosie at 800-445-8745 for information on limited edition collectibles.

Salt & Pepper Illustrated Sales List ($2 and LSASE)
Judy Posner
June - September: R.D. 1, Box 273 SC, Effort, PA 18330; fax: 717-629-0521; October - May: PO Box 2194 SC, Englewood, FL 34295, fax: 941-475-2645; e-mail: judyandjef@aol.com or URL: www.judyposner.com. Buy-Sell-Collect.

Schoenhut Collectors Club
c/o Pat Girbach
1003 W. Huron St., Ann Arbor, MI 48103-4217 for membership information

Shawnee Pottery Collectors' Club
PO Box 713, New Smyrna Beach, FL 32170-0713. Monthly nation-wide newsletter; SASE (c/o Pamela Curran) required when requesting information; $3 for sample of current newsletter

Shot Glass Exchange @
PO Box 219, Western Springs, IL 60558; 708-246-1559. Primarily prepro-hibition glasses; subscription: (includes 2 semi-annual issues, available in US only) $13 per year, single copy $8.

Society of Inkwell Collectors
5136 Thomas Ave. South, Minneapolis, MN 55410; e-mail: soic@concentric.net; also available at: zwww.soic.com. Membership: $25.00 per year, includes subscription to *The Stained Finger*, a quarterly publication

Southern California Marble Club
18361-1 Strothern St., Reseda, CA 91335

Southern Folk Pottery Collectors Society Newsletter
1828 N. Howard Mill Rd., Robbins, NC 27325; 910-454-3961 or fax 910-464-2530. Specializing in historical research and documentation, education, and promotion of the traditional southern folk potter (past and present) to a modern collecting audience; membership dues include absentee auction catalogs, access to member pieces, opportunities to meet potters, participate in events, newsletter information, and more

Southern Oregon Antiques & Collectibles Club
PO Box 508, Talent, OR 97540; 541-535-1231 or fax 541-535-5109. Meets 1st Wednesday of the month; promotes 2 shows a year in Medford, OR

Stangl/Fulper Collectors Club
PO Box 538, Flemington, NJ 08822. Yearly membership: $25 (includes quarterly newsletter); annual auction in June; American pottery and dinnerware show and sale in October

Stevengraph Collectors Assn.
David L. Brown
2103-2829 Arbutus Rd., Victoria, British Columbia, Canada, V8N 5X5; 250-477-9896

Still Bank Collectors Club of America
c/o Larry Egelhoff
4175 Millersville Rd., Indianapolis, IN 46205. Membership: $35 per year

Stretch Glass Society
PO Box 573, Hampshire, IL 60140. Membership: $18. Quarterly newsletter with color photos; annual spring convention

Style: 1900 The Quarterly Journal of the Arts & Crafts Movement
David Rago
333 N. Main St., Lambertville, 08530; 609-397-4104

Surveyors Historical Society Identification Committee
D.R. Beeks
PO Box 117, Mt. Vernon, IA 52314; 391-895-0506

Susie Cooper Catalogs
J. David Ehrhard
7212 Valmont St., Tujunga, CA 91042

Swan Seekers Network
9470 Campo Rd., Suite 134, Spring Valley, CA 91977; 619-462-5517; e-mail: jimer@swanseekers.com or Web page: www.swanseekers.com. Business hours: 10:00 a.m. - 4:00 p.m. Pacific Time, Monday - Thursday; Publishes *Swan Seekers News* and *Swan Seekers Marketplace* periodicals ($28 per year US, $38 foreign); specializing in Swarovski crystal

Table Toppers
1340 West Irving Park Rd., PO Box 161, Chicago, IL 60613; 312-769-3184. Membership: $18 (single) per year, which includes *Table Topics*, a bimonthly newsletter for those interested in table-top collectibles

The Tanner Restraints Collection
3024 E. 35th, Spokane, WA 99223; 509-448-8457. 40-page catalog of magician/escape artist equipment from trick and regulation padlocks, handcuffs, leg shackles, and straight jackets to picks and pick sets; books on all of the above and much more; catalog: $3

Tarrant, Jenny
Holly Daze Antiques
4 Gardenview, St. peters, MO 63376. Send large SASE for monthly holiday lists; all illustrated photos of antique holiday items

Tea Leaf Club International
324 Powderhorn Dr., Houghton Lake, MI 48629. Publishes *Tea Leaf Readings* Newsletter; membership: $20 (single) or $25 (couple) per year

Tea Talk
Tina M. Carter, Teapot Columnist
Diana Rosen/Lucy Roman, Editors
PO Box 860, Sausalito, CA 94966; 415-331-1557

The TeaTime Gazette
Linda Ashley Leamer
PO Box 40276, St. Paul, MN 55104

THCKK
The Hardware Companies Kollector's Klub
For information contact Jerry Heuring, 28450 US HIghway 61, Scott City, MO 63780; 573-264-3947. Membership: $15 per year

Thermometer Collectors' Club of America
Richard Porter, Vice President
PO Box 944, Onset, MA 02558

Thimble Collectors International
6411 Montego Rd., Louisville, KY 40228

Three Rivers Depression Era Glass Society
Meetings held 1st Monday of each month at 6:00 p.m. at Old Country Bouffet, Heidleburg, PA
For more information call: Edith A. Putanko at John's Antiques & Edie's Glassware, Rte. 88 & Broughton Rd., Bethel Park, PA 15102; 412-831-2702

Tiffin Glass Collectors
PO Box 554, Tiffin, OH 44883. Meetings at Seneca County Museum on 2nd Tuesday of each month; Tiffin Glass Museum, 25 S. Washington, Tiffin, OH, Wednesday - Sunday from 1:00 p.m. - 5:00 p.m.

Tins 'n Signs
Box 440101, Aurora, CO 80044. Subscription: $25 per year

Tobacco Antiques and Collectibles Market
Chuck Thompson, Publisher
PO Box 11652, Houston, TX 77293. Subscription: $9.95 (12 issues); $19.95 in Canada and Mexico; all other foreign countries: $30 for 6 issues

Tops & Bottoms Club (Rene Lalique perfumes only)
c/o Madeleine France
PO Box 15555, Ft. Lauderdale, FL 33318

Toy Gun Collectors of America Newsletter
Jim 'Buzz' Buskirk, Editor & Publisher
3009 Oleander Ave., San Marcos, CA 92069; 760-599-1054. Published quarterly, covers both toy and BB guns; Dues: $12 per year

Trick or Treat Trader
PO Box 499, Winchester, NH 03470; 603-239-8875. Subscription: $15 per year for 4 quarterly issues

Twin Winton Collectors Club
www.twinwinton.com

Uhl Collectors' Society
Beverly Leslie, Secretary/Treasurer
801 Poplar St., Boonville, IN, 47601; 812-897-3681
Dave and Donna Swick, Newsletter
506 Martin St., Newton, IL 62488; 618-783-3455

Vaseline Glass Collectors, Inc.
Madolyn Courter
PO Box 125
Russellville, MO 65074; e-mail: mcourter@socketis.net

Vaseline Glass Collectors, Inc.
P.O. Box 125, Russellville, MO 65074. An organization, whose sole purpose is to unify vaseline glass collectors, newsletter *Glowing Report*, published bi-monthly; convention will be held annually; membership: $20 per year

Vaseline Glass Newsletter
Jerry Chambers
2163 Pomona Place, Fairfield, CA 94533; 707-425-6166 after 4:30 p.m. P.S.T.

Vernon Views, newsletter for Vernon Kilns collectors
PO Box 945, Scottsdale, AZ 85252. Published quarterly beginning with the spring issue, $10 per year

Vetri: Italian Glass News
Howard Lockwood, Publisher
PO Box 191, Fort Lee, NJ 07024; 201-969-0373. Quarterly newsletter about 20th-century Italian glass

Vintage Fashion & Costume Jewelry Newsletter/Club
PO Box 265, Glen Oaks, NY 11004; 718-939-3095; e-mail: VFCJ@aol.com; fax: 718-939-7988. Year's subscription (4 issues): $15 in US, $20 in Canada, $25 International; back issues available at $5 each

Vintage TVs
Harry Poster
Box 1883, S. Hackensack, 07606; Days: 201-794-9606; 24-hour fax: 201-794-9553. Specializes in vintage TVs, transister radios, 3-D stereo cameras; catalog available online: www.harryposter.com

The Wade Watch
Wade Watch Ltd.
8199 Pierson Ct., Arvada, CO 80005; 303-421-9655 or 303-424-4401; fax 303-421-0317. Year's subscription (4 issues): $8 in US; $14 International; articles and photos welcome, but if to be returned, enclose SASE

Walking Stick Notes
Marilyn Vlahos, Editor
2611 Catalpa Ave., Pascagoula, MS 39567-1806. Please write to Marilyn Vlahos at the above address for information about her publication plans

The Wallace Nutting Collector's Club
PO Box 22475, Beachwood, OH 44122. Established in 1973, holds annual conventions, usually in the northeastern portion of the country. Generally recognized national center of Wallace Nutting-like activity are Michael Ivankovich's Wallace Nutting & Wallace Nutting-Like Specialty Auctions, held 4 times each year. These auctions provide the opportunity for collectors and dealers to compete for the largest variety of Wallace Nutting and Wallace Nutting-Like pictures available anywhere. These auctions also give sellers the opportunity to place their items in front of the country's leading enthusiasts. When writing for information please include a close-up photograph which includes the picture's frame and a SASE.

Warwick China Collectors Club
Pat & Don Hoffmann, Sr.
1291 N. Elmwood Dr., Aurora, IL 60506-1309; 630-859-3435; web page: www.skognet.com/ warwick or e-mail: warwick@skognet.com

Watt's News Newsletter, for Watt pottery enthusiasts
c/o Watt Collectors Association
PO Box 1995, Iowa City, IA 52244. Subscription: $12 per year; quarterly newsletter, annual convention

The Wedgwood Society of New York
7 Palatine Ct., Syosset, NY 11791-1105. Membership: $27.50 (single) or $32.50 (family); publishes newsletter (6 times per year) and a scholarly magazine, *Ars Ceramica*, of original articles published by the Society; 6 meetings per year

Westmoreland Glass Collector's Newsletter
PO Box 143, North Liberty, IA 52317. Subscription: $16 per year; this publication is dedicated to the purpose of preserving Westmoreland Glass and its history

Westmoreland Glass Society
Jim Fisher, President
513 5th Ave., Coralville, IA 52241; 319-354-5011. Membership: $15 (single) or $25 (household)

The Whimsey Club
c/o Lon Knickerbocker
PO Box 312, Dansville, NY, 14437. *Whimsical Notions*, quarterly newsletter with colored photos; Dues: $8 per year; annual get together

The White Ironstone China Association, Inc.
PO Box 855, Fairport, NY 14450-0855. Newsletter available for: $25 (single) or $30 (2 individuals at same address)

Willow Review
PO Box 41312, Nashville, TN 37204. Send SASE for information

World's Fair Collectors' Society, Inc.
Fair News Newsletter (bimonthly publication for members)
Michael R. Pender, Editor
PO Box 20806, Sarasota, FL 34276-3806; 941-923-2590. Dues: $17 per year in US, $20 in Canada, and $30 overseas

The Zsolnay Store
152 Spring St., Newport, RI 02840; 401-841-5060; Web: www.drawrm.com. Zsolnay book available

Index

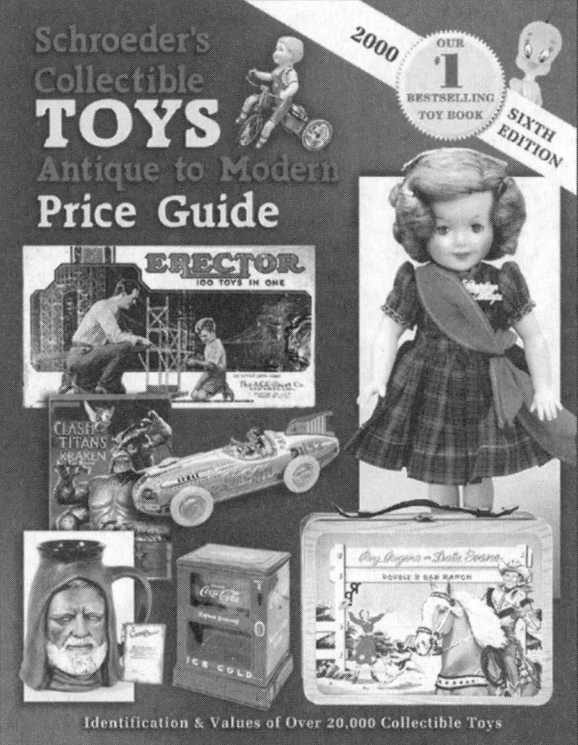